W9-AEM-597

ENCYCLOPEDIA
OF
WORLD CRIME

HOW TO USE THIS ENCYCLOPEDIA

ALPHABETICAL ORDER

Each entry name in the *Encyclopedia of World Crime* is bold-faced and listed alphabetically. Biographical entries are alphabetized by the subject's last name. Everything preceding the comma is treated as a unit when alphabetizing. Hyphens, diacritical marks, periods following initials, and spaces do not influence its alphabetization. For example, **La Pietra** follows **Lang**, and **Black Bart** follows **Black, Robert**. Names with prefixes such as **de, von**, or **le** are listed under the most common form of the name, such as **de Gaulle, Charles** and **Ribbentrop, Joachim von**. Names beginning in **Mc** or **M'** are treated as if spelled **Mac**; thus **McManus, Fred** appears before **MacMichael, Sir Harold**. Asian names, in which the family name comes first, are alphabetized by the family name, omitting the comma. Identical names are alphabetized chronologically. Monarchs commonly known by one name, such as **Elizabeth I** or **Louis XIV**, are usually listed under that name only and would precede an identically spelled surname in entry order. Entries with numbers or abbreviations in them are alphabetized as though spelled out. When an entry heading refers to an event rather than to a person, it is alphabetized according to the first key word in the commonly used title, as in **Popish Plot** or **King Ranch Murders**. When the names of two or more people head an entry, it is usually alphabetized according to the most prominent person's last name.

ENTRY HEADINGS

Appearing in boldface type at the beginning of each *Encyclopedia of World Crime* entry is the name by which that entry is most commonly known. Entries are categorized alphabetically under the name of the offender, criminal event, or the professional in the field of crime. If a crime remains unsolved, the entry is found under the victim's name, and is denoted by the abbreviation **unsolv.** in parentheses immediately preceding the crime category. Other entries appearing under the victim's name include **assassinations**; thus, information concerning the assassination of President Abraham Lincoln would be found under Lincoln and not John Wilkes Booth. The royal or political title or military rank held by the assassination victim precedes the category abbreviation. Parenthetical remarks immediately following an entry name indicate an alternate spelling, that person's original or maiden name, or the entry's alias if preceded by **AKA:**. These names also appear in boldface.

Following the name are **date(s)** relevant to that entry. The letter **b.** preceding the date signifies that only the person's date of birth is known, while the letter **d.** signifies that only the person's date of death is known. The letter **c.** (circa) signifies that the date which immediately follows is approximate. In some cases **prom.** (prominent) is used to denote the year(s) in which that entry was noteworthy. All years B.C. are designated as such.

In a number of entries the phrase **Case of** follows the date, designating that the person named was tried for the crime which follows but found Not Guilty.

The **country** designation in each entry heading refers to the country in which the crime was committed or the country in which persons in the field of crime are known professionally. The country is named as it was known at the time the crime was committed; thus, Russia is referenced prior to the Russian Revolution, while U.S.S.R. is used for crimes committed since that time. Entries where crimes are committed in more than three countries or committed on the high seas are designated as Int'l (International).

The last piece of information contained in the Entry Heading is the **crime category**, designating the crime(s) the subject was convicted of, or the professional field of crime with which the subject is associated. For persons wrongly convicted of a crime, prior to the crime category is the designation (**wrong. convict.**). If however, the subject's conviction was overturned on a legal technicality or there is some doubt as to his actual innocence, then the designation (**wrong. convict.?**) is used. In some cases a question mark may follow the crime category. This denotes that there is uncertainty as to whether the crime in question actually occurred; e.g., **mur.?**, might denote that there is some doubt as to whether a person was killed, committed suicide, or died from other causes.

A number of entries may include more than one person if the criminals or professionals worked together. When the relevant dates of a **multiple name entry** coincide, one date will follow the last person named in the entry heading.

REFERENCES

After each **Encyclopedia of World Crime** entry, the references used in compiling it are cited. The abbreviation **CBA** denotes **CrimeBooks Archives**. Other sources are cited in four categories: nonfiction, fiction, drama, and film. Nonfiction works are listed first, alphabetically by the author's last name. If two or more works by the same author are used, the second and all following citations are indicated by a blank line and are alphabetized by the first word (ignoring articles A, An, The). If a source is anonymous, this is indicated in parentheses after the title. Sources without a specific author (pamphlets, reports, tracts, trial transcripts, compilations, etc.) are listed alphabetically by the title. Plays based on a case appear after (**DRAMA**) and are listed alphabetically by author. Fictional accounts of a case appear alphabetically by author after (**FICTION**). Films based on the case appear after (**FILM**), and are listed chronologically, each title followed by the year of its U.S. release. Silent films are denoted by the letters preceding the year of release. Often alternate titles (**alt. title**) of films follow U.S. titles in parentheses.

Cross references immediately following an entry refer the reader to entries containing additional information relevant to the case, person, place, or event being consulted. Direct references are also used frequently throughout the volumes to lead the readers from a well known name (alias, victim, event) to the name under which that entry appears (**Bonney, William H., See: Billy the Kid**).

KEY TO ABBREVIATIONS USED IN THE *ENCYCLOPEDIA OF WORLD CRIME*

2d lt.	= second lieutenant
abduc.	= abduction
abor.	= abortion
accom.	= accomplices
adm.	= admiral
adult.	= adultery
Afg.	= Afghanistan
Ala.	= Alabama
Alb.	= Albania
Alg.	= Algeria
Arg.	= Argentina

Ariz.	= Arizona		forg.	= forgery
Ark.	= Arkansas		Fr.	= France
assass.	= assassination		Ga.	= Georgia
asslt.	= assault		gamb.	= gambling, gambler
asslt.&bat.	= assault and battery		gen.	= general
attempt.	= attempted		geno.	= genocide
atty. gen.	= attorney general		Ger.	= Germany
Aus.	= Australia		Gr.	= Greece
Aust.	= Austria		Guat.	= Guatemala
banish.	= banishment		harass.	= harassment
Bav.	= Bavaria		her.	= heresy
Belg.	= Belgium		hijack.	= hijacking
Ber.	= Bermuda		Hond.	= Honduras
big.	= bigamy		host.	= hostage
blk.	= blackmail		Hung.	= Hungary
Bol.	= Bolivia		Ice.	= Iceland
bomb.	= bombing		Ill.	= Illinois
boot.	= bootlegging		impris.	= imprisoned
Braz.	= Brazil		Ind.	= Indiana
brib.	= bribery		Indo.	= Indonesia
Brit.	= Britain/England including Wales		Int'l.	= International
Bul.	= Bulgaria		Ire.	= Ireland
burg.	= burglary		Isr.	= Israel
Calif.	= California		Jam.	= Jamaica
can.	= cannibalism		Jor.	= Jordan
Can.	= Canada		jur.	= jurist
cap. pun.	= capital punishment		Kan.	= Kansas
capt.	= captain		kid.	= kidnapper, kidnapping
coin.	= coining		Kor.	= Korea
col.	= colonel		Ky.	= Kentucky
Col.	= Columbia		La.	= Louisiana
Colo.	= Colorado		law enfor. off.	= law enforcement officer or official
comdr.	= commander		Leb.	= Lebanon
Conn.	= Connecticut		loot.	= looting
consp.	= conspiracy		lt.	= lieutenant
cont./ct.	= contempt of court		lt. col.	= lieutenant colonel
corr.	= corruption		lt. comdr.	= lieutenant commander
Cos.	= Costa Rica		lt. gen.	= lieutenant general
count.	= counterfeiting		lt. gov.	= lieutenant governor
cpl.	= corporal		Lux.	= Luxemburg
crim. insan.	= criminal insanity		lynch.	= lynching
crim. just.	= criminal justice		Mac.	= Macedonia
crim. law.	= criminal lawyer		maj.	= major
crim. neg.	= criminal negligence		mansl.	= manslaughter
crime preven.	= crime prevention		Mass.	= Massachusetts
crime&punish.	= crime and punishment		Md.	= Maryland
criminol.	= criminologist or criminology		med. mal.	= medical malpractice
ct. mar.	= court-martial		Mex.	= Mexico
Czech.	= Czechoslovakia		Mich.	= Michigan
Del.	= Delaware		Mid. East	= Middle East
del.	= delinquency		milit.	= military
Den.	= Denmark		milit. des.	= military desertion
det.	= detective		Minn.	= Minnesota
Dom.	= Dominican Republic		Miss.	= Mississippi
Dr.	= doctor		miss. per.	= missing persons
duel.	= dueling		Mo.	= Missouri
Ecu.	= Ecuador		mob vio.	= mob violence
El Sal.	= El Salvador		Mont.	= Montana
embez.	= embezzlement		Mor.	= Morocco
emp.	= emperor or empress		mur.	= murder, murderer
esc.	= escape		mut.	= mutiny
esp.	= espionage		mutil.	= mutilation
Eth.	= Ethiopia		N. Zea.	= New Zealand
euth.	= euthanasia		N.C.	= North Carolina
execut.	= executioner		N.D.	= North Dakota
extor.	= extortion, extortionist		N.H.	= New Hampshire
fenc.	= fencing		N.J.	= New Jersey
Fin.	= Finland		N.M.	= New Mexico
fing. ident.	= fingerprint identification		N.Y.	= New York
Fla.	= Florida		Neb.	= Nebraska

necro.	= necrophilia		toxicol.	= toxicologist
Neth.	= Netherlands		treas.	= treason
Nev.	= Nevada		Tun.	= Tunisia
Nic.	= Nicaragua		Turk.	= Turkey
Nig.	= Nigeria		U.A.E.	= United Arab Emirates
Nor.	= Norway		U.K.	= United Kingdom
obsc.	= obscenity		U.S.	= United States of America
Okla.	= Oklahoma		U.S.S.R.	= Union of Soviet Socialist Republics (after 1918)
Ore.	= Oregon			
org. crime	= organized crime		unsolv.	= unsolved
P.R.	= Puerto Rico		Urug.	= Uruguay
Pa.	= Pennsylvania		Va.	= Virginia
Pak.	= Pakistan		vandal.	= vandalism
Pan.	= Panama		Venez.	= Venezuela
Para.	= Paraguay		vice dist.	= vice district
path.	= pathologist		vict.	= victim
penal col.	= penal colonies		Viet.	= Vietnam
penol.	= penology, penologist		vigil.	= vigilantism
Per.	= Persia		Vt.	= Vermont
perj.	= perjury		W.Va.	= West Virginia
Phil.	= Philippines		Wash.	= Washington
pick.	= pickpocket		west. gunman	= western gunman
pir.	= piracy		west. lawman	= western lawman
Pol.	= Poland		west. outl.	= western outlaw
pol.	= police		wh. slav.	= white slavery
pol. mal.	= police malpractice		Wis.	= Wisconsin
polit.	= politician		Wyo.	= Wyoming
polit. corr.	= political corruption		Yug.	= Yugoslavia
poly.	= polygamy			
porn.	= pornography			
Port.	= Portugal			
pres.	= president			
pris.	= prison			
prof.	= professor			
prohib.	= prohibition			
pros.	= prostitution			
R.I.	= Rhode Island			
rack.	= racketeering			
rebel.	= rebellion			
rev.	= reverend			
rob.	= robbery			
Rom.	= Romania			
Roman.	= Roman Empire			
Rus.	= Russia (prior to 1918)			
S. Afri.	= South Africa			
S.C.	= South Carolina			
S.D.	= South Dakota			
sab.	= sabotage			
Saud.	= Saudi Arabia			
Scot.	= Scotland			
sec. firm	= security firm			
secret crim. soc.	= secret criminal societies			
secret soc.	= secret society			
Sen.	= Senegal			
sgt.	= sergeant			
Si.	= Sicily			
Sing.	= Singapore			
skyjack.	= skyjacking			
sland.	= slander			
smug.	= smuggling			
sod.	= sodomy			
Sri.	= Sri Lanka			
Sudan	= Sudan			
suic.	= suicide			
supt.	= superintendent			
Swed.	= Sweden			
Switz.	= Switzerland			
Tai.	= Taiwan			
Tan.	= Tanzania			
tax evas.	= tax evasion			
Tenn.	= Tennessee			
terr.	= terrorism, terrorist			
Thai.	= Thailand			
tort.	= torture			

TYPES OF ENTRIES

Biographical; case studies; celebrated trials; criminal secret organizations; direct references; historic and current techniques in police science; historical events and places; literary fiction based on criminals or crime events; unsolved crimes.

DICTIONARY

More than 20,000 terms used in America, U.K., and elsewhere by the underworld and law enforcement, from ancient times to the present, are listed in a dictionary (Vol. V).

TYPES OF SUPPLEMENTS

VOL. IV: Arson; Assassination; Bombing; Burglary; Capital Punishment; Computer Crime; Detectives, Notable; Drugs; Dueling; Firearms and Ballistics; Forensic Sciences, Notable Experts; Fraud; Hijacking; Identification Systems; Kidnapping; Looting; Lynching and Vigilantism; Mob Violence (Riots); Organized Crime; Police; Prisons; Robbery; Skyjacking; Terrorism; Toxicology; War Crimes and Criminals; Western Lawmen; Western Outlaws and Gunmen.

DICTIONARY (VOL. V): International Acronyms for Prominent Organizations and Operations; U.S. Correctional Systems; Landmark U.S. Crime Legislation; Landmark U.S. Federal and State Court Decisions; U.S. Correctional Systems; U.S. Crime Commissions; U.S. Federal Bureau of Investigation Offices by City.

INDEX

The index contains the following: Bibliography; Subject Index; Proper Name Index.

D

Dabner, Louis, and **Seimsen, John** (AKA: **The Gaspipe Murderers**), d.1908, U.S., rob.-mur. The San Francisco earthquake of 1906 was a devastating tragedy that not only laid ruin to a great city, but ushered in a period of unrestrained lawlessness.

In the wake of the disaster there were daily reports of robbery, assault, and looting. Between July and October, five prominent businessmen were robbed and beaten to death by two thugs who were dubbed the Gaspipe Murderers. They used a fourteen-inch-long iron bar to bash in the skulls of Japanese bank president M. Munekato and his assistant, A. Sasaki; the city coroner Dr. Leland; a shopkeeper, William Friede; and Johannes Pfitzner, the son of the chief architect under Emperor William of Germany.

Alarmed by the presence of dangerous killers that had thus far eluded detection, California's Governor Pardee offered a $1,500 reward for the killers. There were no new leads until Nov. 3, 1906, when a jewelry store belonging to Henry Behrend was robbed by three men. They got away with $75.

Behrend fought off two of his assailants, who had struck him repeatedly with the same iron bar used in the earlier Japanese bank robbery. The third man continued to struggle with the jeweler until police arrived.

The arrested man was identified as Louis Dabner, whose father was a wealthy businessman in Honolulu. He told police that his roommate, John Seimsen, had earlier passed himself off as an heir to a large plantation in Hawaii in order to marry Hulda Von Hoffen, daughter of a rich San Francisco jeweler. Seimsen was tricked into a confession by police. A third man, Harry Kearney, had escaped, but was later arrested in Washington for a second, unrelated robbery.

Dabner's father refused to believe that his son could be involved in such a heinous crime. Young Dabner had maintained his innocence, but when he was confronted by his father, he broke down and confessed to the robberies and murders he had carried out with Seimsen.

An ex-convict named James Dowdall had been wrongly convicted of murdering Dr. Leland, but he was set free when Dabner and Seimsen were charged with first-degree murder. Dabner pleaded not guilty, but was convicted and sentenced to hang along with his partner Seimsen. The judge's ruling was upheld by the Supreme Court, and the two were hanged at San Quentin in July 1908.

REF.: *CBA; Duke, Celebrated Criminal Cases of America.*

Dabney, Condy, b.1894, U.S., (wrong. convict.) mur. Leaving his wife and two children behind, Condy Dabney left his home in Coal Creek, Tenn., in January 1925, to find work as a miner in Coxton, Ky. He found work, earned his employer's confidence, and lived for a time as an inconspicuous miner.

Then in July a local girl named Roxy Baker disappeared. Within the next two months, three men and three women vanished, including 14-year-old Mary Vickery, who had been seen with Dabney. The Tennessean had given up his job in the coal mines to drive a cab, and Mary Vickery had reportedly ridden in his cab. Two months later, the remains of a young woman were found in an abandoned shaft, and Dabney was suspected as her killer.

Marie Jackson, the state's primary witness, testified that on the morning Vickery disappeared, Dabney had picked her up in his cab and tried to assault her in a clearing outside of town.

Jackson's testimony was contradicted by a second eye witness, and the girl's father could not say with certainty whether the body he identified was that of his daughter. However, Dabney was found Guilty and sentenced to life in prison. A year passed before justice intervened.

While making his rounds, policeman George Davis stopped at a hotel in Williamsburg, Ky., where he noticed the name of Mary Vickery on the guest ledger. She was, indeed, the girl thought dead. She explained that she had left Coxton on Aug. 23, 1925, to get away from her stepmother. She had ridden in Dabney's

taxi, she said, but had never met Marie Jackson. Jackson's perjured testimony was believed to have been inspired by jealousy—Dabney had spurned Jackson's advances—and a desire to claim a $500 reward. Dabney was immediately pardoned and charges were filed against Jackson for false swearing.

REF.: *CBA; Borchard, Convicting the Innocent.*

Dacey, Edwin, prom. 1947, Brit., mur. Edwin Dacey lived with his wife Iris Dacey and her parents in the town of Doncaster, England. A veteran of WWII, Dacey was training to become a miner so that he could save enough money to buy a home. However, things did not go according to plan. He drank heavily, and became violent toward his wife.

In July 1947, Iris's father had had enough of Dacey's outbursts. He ordered his son-in-law out of the house, forcing Dacey to find lodging in Edlington, six miles south of Doncaster. Early in the morning of Aug. 25, Dacey accosted his wife in the streets and seized his infant son, Alan, from her arms. Four days later, the little boy was found dead near the banks of the River Don. He had been repeatedly stabbed and hit over the head.

When confronted by the police, Dacey explained that he had given Alan to a pair of strangers who were going to take him to his own parents. He then confessed, whereupon he was convicted of murder and sentenced to die. But on the day of his execution, Dacey was stricken with a case of appendicitis. He recuperated, and was later pardoned.

REF.: *Butler, Murderers' England; CBA.*

Dacoity, prom. 1800s, India, rob. The Indian and Burmese tradition of committing robbery in groups led to a legal offense called dacoity, defined as armed robbery by five or more people. The people who engaged in such activities, usually as entire families, were called dacoits. Certain tribes in India lived a nomadic life supported by organized theft, usually preying on small villages. Dacoits attacked and rounded up villagers, raped the women, and stole all the valuables. They often burned villages to the ground. Groups of travelers were frequently prey for such groups. Usually the unlucky travelers would be killed and buried quickly in shallow graves, leaving no sign that they had ever passed that way.

The children in dacoit tribes were given a role to play in the activity as soon as they were able. The wives expected their husbands to participate and to take a leadership role. The women generally participated too. When, in the late 19th century, British troops began to control India more completely, they prevented the dacoits from moving around so freely. Special legislation enacted in 1912 provided for the movement of problem tribes to areas where they could be contained. Individuals were required to register, and more specific control of the tribes could be maintained, while other livelihoods were developed for the tribes.

In Burma, which had a similar tradition of tribal crime, the situation was compounded in the mid-1800s when the British dissolved the Burmese army. The unsettled soldiers frequently gathered in gangs to commit crimes. The problem was not solved until a native Burmese force replaced the British Army.

REF.: *Adam, The Indian Criminal; CBA; Hilton, A Popular Account of the Thugs and Dacoits, The Hereditary Gang Robbers and Garrotters of India; Mackenzie, Secret Societies; Sleeman, Reports on Budhuk, Alias Bagree, Dacoits and Other Gang Robbers by Hereditary Profession; Scott, Concise Encyclopedia of Crime and Criminals.*

Dadd, Richard, 1818-86, Brit., mur. A promising young painter who attended the prestigious Royal Academy School, Richard Dadd was the leader of a small group of young artists who called themselves "The Clique" and met every week in bohemian Soho, London. Members included artists William Powell Frith, Augustus Egg, Henry O'Neil, and John Phillip, and editor Samuel Carter Hall, of *Art Union* magazine. Dadd rapidly developed a severe persecution mania. The artist's father, Robert Dadd, said his son was only excitable, adding, "I can always manage him without difficulty." But Dadd became increasingly violent, once attempting to slice off his own birthmark.

On Aug. 26, 1843, the younger Dadd purchased a razor and a seaman's knife. Two days later, he left with his father for the Ship Inn at Cobham. At around 11 p.m., Dadd attacked and murdered his father, then fled to Dover and sailed across the Channel to Calais. In a French railway carriage, he attacked a fellow passenger and tried to cut his throat with a razor. Dadd was arrested and taken to a Montereau police station, where he confessed to killing his father. When he was transferred to the Clermont Asylum, doctors found in his pocket a list of people he intended to slay. His father's name was first. When police in London searched Dadd's studio, they found portraits of his friends Egg, Frith, and Stone, all with their throats cut. Ten months after his arrest, Dadd was returned to England. On Aug. 22, 1844, Rochester magistrates recommended that the 26-year-old artist be transferred to the Criminal Lunatic Department of the Bethlehem Hospital in London. He was never brought to trial. Later transferred to Southwark, and then Broadmoor in 1864, Dadd continued to paint canvasses, stage designs, murals, and patterns and pictures on glass, producing more than 100 works in his forty-two years of confinement. He died on Jan. 8, 1886, at the age of sixty-eight.

REF.: Altick, *Victorian Studies In Scarlet;* Butler, *Murderers' England; CBA.*

Daddano, William, Sr. (AKA: **Willie Potatoes, Dado, Blinky, Dr. Miller, William Russo**), 1912-75, U.S., org. crime. Born on the West Side of Chicago, William Daddano began his criminal career with the infamous Forty-Two Gang, headquartered in the old Maxwell Street district.

His willingness to use strong-arm tactics earned Daddano the admiration of Sam Giancana and Sam Battaglia, heirs to the Chicago crime syndicate. Willie's criminal record dated back to 1936, and included nine arrests for bank robbery, larceny, and auto theft. In 1944, he was arrested while holding up a West Side bank for three million war ration coupons. It was a mob crime, but Daddano never revealed the names of his accomplices. After WWII, he emerged as a top syndicate enforcer, participating in at least twenty murders.

Willie earned his famous nickname because of his fondness for salted shoestring potatoes, which he always carried with him. By the 1950s, he controlled syndicate gambling in Cicero, Berwyn, and the far western suburbs in DuPage County. In May 1966, he was indicted for hijacking $1 million worth of silver bullion, but was acquitted.

Investigations by an FBI task force led by Vincent Inserra led to his conviction in 1969, of conspiring to rob a Franklin Park Bank—a crime that was planned six years earlier.

Willie Daddano was sentenced to fifteen years at the federal penitentiary in Marion, Ill. He died there on Sept. 9, 1975. See: **Battaglia, Samuel; Giancana, Sam.** REF.: *CBA.*

Dafydd ap Gruffydd, d.1283, Brit., prince, treas. Last native prince of Wales. The year prior to his death he attacked an English garrison and became prince of Gwynedd from 1282-83, later being betrayed, captured, and executed. REF.: *CBA.*

Dafydd ap Llywelyn, c.1208-46, Brit., polit. corr. Imprisoned his half-brother Gruffydd in 1239 and a year later succeeded his father as prince of Gwynedd, eventually becoming prince of Wales after taking the title from King Henry III of England. REF.: *CBA.*

Dagoe, Hannah, d.1763, Brit., burg.-rob. Born in Ireland, Hannah Dagoe met Eleanor Hussey, a poor, hard-working widow, while shopping. Dagoe struck a conversation with Hussey, and learned that the widow lived alone. Dagoe began watching the house where the widow rented a modest room. Realizing that Hussey was away, she broke in and stripped the room of its valuables, including the few keepsakes left to Hussey by her husband.

Dagoe was arrested, tried at the Old Bailey, and convicted. In prison she tracked down a fellow inmate who had testified against her, stabbing and wounding him. Dagoe's fellow prisoners

were relieved on May 4, 1763, when she was loaded into a wagon for the trip to the gallows at Tyburn.

During her last ride, Dagoe refused to listen to the praying priest who accompanied her. She appeared relaxed until the wagon stopped under the great Tyburn tree from which the waiting rope dangled. Though Dagoe had been bound, she somehow managed to free herself. Suddenly, she jumped to her feet and grabbed the hangman, almost knocking him to the ground. As they struggled, she dared the executioner to hang her.

Thief Hannah Dagoe attacking her executioner.

With that, Dagoe removed articles of clothing, throwing them to the shocked crowd. When the executioner finally managed to slip the noose around her head, she cheated him out of his job. Dagoe leaped from the cart before he had a chance to give the signal and her neck broke as she reached the end of the rope. Dagoe died instantly.

REF.: Bleackley, *Hangmen of England; CBA;* Mitchell, *The Newgate Calendar;* Nash, *Look For the Woman.*

Daguebert, Achille, prom. 1920, Fr., mur. Achille Daguebert was court martialed and dishonorably discharged from the French army in 1918, for impersonating an officer.

In November 1920, while managing a garage outside Boulogne, he met two Englishmen named William Gourlay and Mr.Norman who wanted to sell their Vauxhall automobile. Daguebert agreed to buy the car for £600 and to take delivery on Nov. 30. Gourlay and Norman flipped a coin to see who would deliver the car.

Gourlay lost the toss and was driven by a chauffeur to Daguebert's shop. After drinks and lunch, the two men went to the mechanic's private office to complete the transaction. As Gourlay signed the receipt, Daguebert pulled out a Browning pistol and shot him in the back. He then told the waiting driver that Gourlay had gone to Boulogne alone. That night, Daguebert buried the body in his backyard. When police questioned him about Gourlay's disappearance, Daguebert told them that Gourlay drove off with three other Englishmen in a gray automobile.

Six months later, while Daguebert was in custody for auto theft in Calais, a local man told detectives that the prisoner had approached him months before with a proposition to murder a Paris garage owner. Detectives dug up Daguebert's yard on June 21, 1921, and found Gourlay's remains.

Daguebert was tried at the St. Omer Assizes on June 23, 1922. Despite his claims that the shooting was not premeditated and that he was drunk when it happened, he was sentenced to die on the guillotine. But French president Alexandre Millerand commuted the sentence to life imprisonment. Daguebert served twenty years in prison, and in 1941, was exiled to French Guiana, where he was ordered to remain until 1961.

REF.: *CBA;* Greenwald, *They Have Murdered In France.*

Dahlgren, John Adolphus Bernard, 1809-70, U.S., firearms designer. Designed an 11-inch gun in 1851, named the Dahlgren gun. He was an admiral in the Union navy during the Civil War. Books authored: *The System of Boat Armament in the United States Navy; Shells and Shell Guns.* REF.: *CBA.*

Dahman, John, d.1820, U.S., rob.-mur. Dahman, a riverboat worker, killed fellow immigrant Frederick Nolte while he was sleeping, stole his money and goods, and dumped his victim's body into the Ohio River near New Albany, Ind., on May 25, 1820. The next day Dahman robbed and shot to death John Jenzer and threw the body into the river. Dahman was arrested when personal items from his victims were found on his person. Dahman, who had reportedly killed nine men, broke out of jail before his trial and fled to Canada. A local sheriff tracked him down and returned him to Indiana without the benefit of extradition. After a brief trial, Dahman was hanged.

REF.: *CBA;* Kidder, *The Life and Adventures of John Dahman; The Life, Trial and Execution of John Dahman.*

Dahme, Father Hubert, 1868-1924, U.S., (unsolv.) mur. The elderly Reverend Hubert Dahme was inexplicably murdered on Main Street, Bridgeport, Conn., shortly before 8 p.m. on Feb. 4, 1924. A young man approached the priest as he stood at a corner, lighting his pipe. The man moved up behind Father Dahme, pulled a pistol, placed it at the back of the priest's head, and fired, killing the clergyman instantly. This public execution was witnessed by several persons who saw the young man flee up the street and disappear into the darkness.

A short time later a drifter named Harold Israel was arrested and identified as the killer. He was scheduled for trial and was to be prosecuted by State's Attorney Homer Cummings. The lawyer, who conducted his own investigation, was disturbed as he studied the evidence against Israel. He learned that Israel had been browbeaten by police. Forced to stay awake almost two days without nourishment and in an exhausted condition, Israel half-admitted the Dahme killing. Cummings shocked the court by later coming to Israel's defense instead of prosecuting him, demonstrating among many points of defense, that the gun found on Israel could not have been used to murder the priest. Israel was released, and the Dahme killing remains unsolved to this day. See: **Cummings, Homer Stille; Israel, Harold.**

REF.: Block, *Science vs. Crime; CBA;* Godwin, *Killers Unknown;* Kunstler, *The Case for Courage;* Nash, *Almanac of World Crime;* (FILM), *Boomerang,* 1947.

***Daily Chronicle,* The,** 1905, Brit., libel. In March 1905, Mary Davis sued the London *Daily Chronicle* for libel when they wrongly accused her of kidnapping an infant. It turned out the baby was her own. She retained attorney Marshall Hall who had often feuded with the *Daily Mail* over their reporting of cases he tried. He won an £800 judgment for his client, but was miffed when the *Daily Mail* referred to him as "Mr. M   Hall" in their account of the trial. He considered the space between the 'M' and his last name a deliberate insult.

REF.: *CBA;* Marjoribanks, *For the Defense, The Life of Sir Edward Marshall Hall.*

***Daily Express,* The,** 1924, Case of, Brit., libel. In the elections of 1924, Lady Terrington of Maidenhead won a seat in Parliament. The London *Daily Express* described her as the "Best Dressed Woman M.P." and, in an exclusive interview, predicted that she would "brighten the atmosphere at Westminster." Objecting to the paper's flippant attitude, she filed libel charges shortly before the Armistice Day celebration. The paper won acquittal when their attorney, Sir Edward Marshall Hall, contrasted the solemnity of the occasion with what he called a "trifling grievance" on the part of Lady Terrington.

REF.: *CBA;* Marjoribanks, *For the Defense, The Life of Sir Edward Marshall Hall.*

***Daily Mail,* The,** 1932, Case of, Brit., libel. An article in the London *Daily Mail* of Jan. 26, 1932, accused spiritualist medium Meurig Morris of deceiving clients. An advertisement for The *Daily Mail,* which read "Trance Medium Found Out," prompted the spiritualist to file libel charges against the newspaper and the article's author, Charles Sutton. During her testimony, Mrs. Morris lapsed into a trance-like state and spoke in a deep masculine voice. Her performance amused the gallery, but enraged Justice Henry McCardie, who ordered her removed from the courtroom. Lady Conan Doyle and Sir Oliver Lodge testified on her behalf, explaining that a medium in a trance was speaking with a voice from the great beyond. On Apr. 19, 1932, the libel suit against the *Daily Mail* was dismissed. "One wonders whether some witnesses are not in a world of illusion," said Justice McCardie, who, less than a year later, took his own life after a period of erratic behavior on the bench. See: **McCardie, Sir Henry.**

REF.: Bowker, *Behind the Bar; CBA;* Marjoribanks, *For the Defense, The Life of Sir Edward Marshall Hall.*

Dainard, William J. (AKA: **William Mahan**), and **Waley, Harmon Metz,** prom. 1930s, U.S., rob.-kidnap. William Dainard was born on a farm in Cando, N.D., in 1902. His father, Samuel Dainard, moved the family to farmlands near Vidora, Saskatchewan. When Sam Dainard died in 1914, the family struggled to maintain a small farm, but Dainard and his brothers and sister were forced to abandon it when Louise Dainard died in 1921. The 19-year-old Dainard broke into a liquor warehouse and fled to Montana before being brought to trial. There he stole a car, was caught, and following a quick trial, sent to the Montana State Penitentiary for two years. He was paroled within a year and for a while sought honest work, laboring as a coal miner in Malta, Mont.

But the work was too exhausting for Dainard. According to FBI Director J. Edgar Hoover, Dainard put aside his pick, turned to a fellow miner one day, and said: "You can work your head off if you want to. I'm through with it. There's too much easy money laying around for a fellow who's game for a crooked job." Dainard quit and went to Oakville, Wash., where, on Jan. 31, 1927, he robbed the local bank at gunpoint, fleeing with more than $5,000. He quickly spent this loot and, six months later, Dainard, gun in hand, robbed the Rathdrum State Bank in Rathdrum, Idaho, taking more than $100,000 in cash and securities.

Dainard spent lavishly on women, bought new cars, and stayed in the best hotels. But he bragged about his crooked ways and was soon arrested and identified as the lone robber of the Oakville and Rathdrum banks. He was sent to prison for twenty years for the Rathdrum job and a detainer in Washington was placed on him. Once he had served his time in Idaho, he would face another long term in Washington. At twenty-five, the tall, dark-haired, handsome Dainard boasted to his fellow prisoners that he would never serve his full term, that he would escape "anytime I please." He did plan a prison break, but the plot was revealed and Dainard was given eighteen months in solitary confinement. In 1930, he met another hardcore prisoner, Harmon Waley, a 20-year-old burglar from Tacoma, Wash., with a long criminal record.

Waley was impressed with the swaggering Dainard and thought of him as a prison "big shot." Waley, however, was glib where Dainard was tight-lipped. Waley's smooth talk finally convinced authorities that he had reformed and he was paroled within a year. Within three months, he was convicted of another robbery, but Waley persuaded the judge to give him a suspended sentence. He then promptly robbed a store and was given a sentence of from two to five years in the Washington State Prison. Waley was paroled again in September 1933, when his friend Dainard was also given an unconditional pardon from the Idaho State Prison and walked free. The Washington detainer still pending against Dainard was apparently forgotten.

Dainard and Waley did not immediately team up. Dainard first embarked on a series of robberies after which he resumed an alias and pretended to be a stove salesman. In 1934, when Dainard entered a Tacoma bank and attempted to rob it, a female teller panicked and screamed hysterically. Dainard hit her so hard with the butt of his gun that he thought he had killed her. He fled to a Spokane hotel and later learned that the teller had lived, but he resolved that bank robbery was too dangerous and that kidnapping, then being practiced widely by gangsters in the Midwest, involved less risk and returned more profit. He contacted his friend Harmon Waley. Dainard, Waley, and Waley's wife Margaret then planned to kidnap 9-year-old George Weyerhauser after reading in a local newspaper that the boy's father, J.P. Weyerhauser, had inherited a large timber fortune.

On May 24, 1935, Dainard dragged the Weyerhauser boy off a Tacoma street and drove off. A short time later, a ransom demand for the boy's return was sent to J.P. Weyerhauser, the kidnappers ordering him to deliver $200,000 to them. Meanwhile, Dainard, Waley, and Margaret Waley dragged the boy from hideout to hideout, from caves and holes in the earth throughout Idaho, then to houses in Washington. The money was finally paid and the Weyerhauser boy was released. He had been chained to trees and rocks for days, kept in dark holes, and he was finally placed in a car trunk and driven to a remote wilderness spot and released to fend for himself against the elements. Fortunately, he found a farmhouse and was soon reunited with his parents in Tacoma. Dainard and Waley each took $100,000 and fled in separate directions. They left a trail of marked bills, however, and FBI agents dogged them for months.

Dainard, realizing that agents were following the trail of the marked money, looked for Waley and his wife in Salt Lake City, but he was too late. Margaret Waley was already under arrest, apprehended after she had gone through several Salt Lake City stores spending the marked bills recklessly. Waley was cornered in his apartment, and while agents were battering down his locked door, he tried to burn tens of thousands of dollars in the marked bills in a stove, but agents stopped him before he was able to destroy all the evidence. The Waleys identified their fellow kidnapper as William Mahan, giving Dainard this alias with the thought that they were not violating the underworld code of silence.

Waley's lawyers pointed out to the court at his trial that the Weyerhauser boy had not been harmed and therefore the mandatory death penalty under the Lindbergh kidnapping law, which specified a death penalty if the victim had been killed, did not apply. It was expected that Waley would, nevertheless, receive a life sentence. On June 21, 1935, he was placed on trial in the U.S. district court in Tacoma, Wash. He pleaded guilty and the court sentenced him to forty-five years in prison, a lenient sentence according to standards of the time. Margaret Waley was tried before a jury on July 13, 1935, and was convicted. She was given a twenty-year sentence.

Dainard, the mastermind behind the Weyerhauser kidnapping, remained at large until May 7, 1936. For almost a year after Waley's capture, Dainard lived a miserable life. He was afraid to spend the ransom money and every time he did, police and FBI agents were hot on his trail. He moved about the Northwest and then the Southwest, living like a hobo, in dirty, ragged clothes, with tens of thousands of dollars sewn into the lining of his tattered coat. Finally, tired of this furtive existence, Dainard went on a money changing spree, almost racing from store to store and bank to bank in California, going from Sacramento to San Francisco and then Los Angeles, where he was almost caught by an alert bank teller. Dainard bought a broken-down 1929 car and drove to San Francisco. There, sleepless, he took a bed in a flophouse, so tired that he left his bag with the ransom money in the back seat of the unlocked car.

FBI agents traced the car and soon discovered it in the San Francisco parking lot. When Dainard approached the car the next morning, on May 7, 1936, he saw the money bag still there. He reached for it, and then heard a federal agent shout: "Hands up, Dainard! We're federal officers! Don't try to resist!" Dainard's hand instinctively dropped to his pocket, where a .45-caliber revolver rested. He then jerked his hand upward, deciding it was futile to resist the dozen FBI agents closing in on him. Dainard was tried quickly and given a sixty-year sentence, beginning at the federal penitentiary at McNeil Island. Waley had been sent to McNeil Island in 1935, but had then been transferred to Alcatraz. Dainard joined his friend Waley on the Rock the following year. Both men were released in the 1960s. One rumor had it that Waley, who had once worked for the Weyerhauser family, returned to work for the very person he had kidnapped decades earlier.

REF.: Alix, *Random Kidnapping in America, 1874-1974; CBA;* Heaney, *Inside the Walls of Alcatraz;* Hoover, *Persons in Hiding;* Johnston, *Alcatraz Island Prison;* Moorehead, *Hostages to Fortune;* Nash, *Almanac of World Crime.*

d'Albe, Dominique, d.1569, Fr., mur. In 1569, Dominique d'Albe was paid 50,000 escus to poison a French admiral during the siege of Chatellerault and Poitiers. He was later executed for the crime.

REF.: *CBA;* Thompson, *Poison and Poisoners.*

d'Albret, Jeanne, 1528-72, Fr., (unsolv.) mur. In the late sixteenth century, poisoning was in vogue among murderers from Italy to France. Thus did Jeanne d'Albret, a lineal descendent of the Gascon dynasty of Landes, founded in the eleventh century, and mother of Henry IV, King of France from 1589-1610, meet her death.

Legend has it that d'Albret met her untimely end by wearing poisoned gloves that she had retrieved from a box. The box, however, had a false bottom beneath which the assassin had placed belladonna, hyoscyamus, and opium. So Jeanne d'Albret inhaled the poisonous fumes from the box while she slept and from her gloves when awake.

REF.: *CBA;* Thompson, *Poison and Poisoners.*

Dale, George R., 1867-1936, U.S., consp. In the 1920s, George R. Dale, publisher of the Muncie (Ind.) *Post-Democrat,* became an outspoken opponent of the locally powerful Ku Klux Klan. He once had to fight off three Klansmen who tried to kidnap him. Soon after the attack, Dale was arrested on trumped-up charges of liquor possession. When he publicly blamed the Klan for his arrest, citing powerful local officials including Judge Clarence W. Dearth, the liquor charges were dropped. But Judge Dearth charged Dale with contempt of court for making the allegations, fined him $500, and sent him to jail for ninety days. Dale appealed to the Supreme Court of Indiana, which refused to hear the case because, as they put it, "the truth is no defense" against contempt charges. Dale continued the appeal process to the U.S. Supreme Court.

On Feb. 19, 1927, while Dale was still charged with contempt, he published an article in his newspaper charging that Judge Dearth packed juries with Klansmen and that Dearth and Muncie mayor John Hampton were responsible for two local murders which proper law enforcement would have prevented. On Mar. 31, Sheriff Harry B. McAuley arrested Dale on criminal libel charges and held him in lieu of $3,000 bond. But this time the Klansmen's tactics backfired, and the Indiana House of Representatives started impeachment proceedings against Judge Dearth. On July 15, 1927, Indiana governor Ed Jackson paroled Dale on the contempt charge, though Dale still had to pay the $500 fine and remain under supervision.

In 1929, George Dale was elected mayor of Muncie. Four years later, he was arrested again on liquor conspiracy charges, and this time convicted and sentenced to eighteen months. But suspected perjury at Dale's trial led Senator Van Nuys of Indiana to petition for Dale's pardon, which President Franklin D. Roosevelt granted on Dec. 14, 1933. See: **Ku Klux Klan.** REF.: *CBA.*

Dale, Sir Thomas, d.1619, U.S., polit. corr. As marshal of Virginia from 1611-16 he instituted martial law, publishing and enforcing a strict code named after himself; his years in office were termed "the five years of slavery." Dale served from 1614-16 as the colony's governor. REF.: *CBA.*

Daley, Dominic, and **Halligan, James,** d.1806, U.S., rob.-mur. Dominic Daley and James Halligan were thugs and highwaymen, preying upon lone travelers. In March 1806, they attacked several merchants, robbing them. One of their victims, Marcus Lyons, resisted and was killed near Wilbraham, Mass. Weighting the body with a large stone which they tied about the victim's neck, Daley and Halligan dumped the body in the Chicopee River. Both men fled on foot, walking to Cos Cob, Conn., 120 miles distant. They were arrested after passing bills from several banks where Lyons had done business. Some of the victims' belongings were also found on the thieves. The lawyer for Daley and Halligan had little evidence with which to defend his clients. He attempted to prove that Daley and Halligan had been accused of Lyons' murder simply because they were Irish immigrants, (strong anti-Irish sentiments were then prevalent in the U.S.). He ended his summation with: "Do not therefore believe them guilty because they are Irishmen." Both men, known thieves, were convicted and hanged.

REF.: *A Brief Account of the Murder of Marcus Lyons; CBA; Report of the Trial of Dominic Daley and James Halligan.*

Dalitz, Morris Barney (AKA: **Moe**), 1899-1989, U.S., org. crime. Morris "Moe" Dalitz organized the Cleveland Mafia with four associates in the 1920s. He emerged as one of two powerful Jewish gangsters in the U.S., ranking with Meyer Lansky in prestige and influence. Dalitz was a veteran of the Detroit Purple Gang. He moved his base to Cleveland when he began a partnership with the "four young Americans"—Al and Chuck Polizzi, and Frank and Tony Milano—and the Angersola Brothers. The alliance continued for decades as the Cleveland mob consolidated its hold over the local bootlegging rackets and then expanded into Las Vegas.

Cleveland crime boss Moe Dalitz.

Moe Dalitz's young mobsters became known as the Mayfield Road Mob. In the 1920s, they conquered the Porello brothers and the Lonardo family in the struggle for autonomy in Northeast Ohio. After the Volstead Act was repealed in 1933, Dalitz and his allies pushed the gambling business into West Virginia, Kentucky, and Indiana before deciding to pull out. The family moved to Las Vegas and bought the Desert Inn, the first step in their plan to gain a foothold on the "strip." Dalitz was the most powerful syndicate presence in Nevada until Anthony Spilotro arrived in town in the 1970s. Dalitz cultivated friendly relations with the Italian Mafiosi, but never relinquished control of his rackets.

Dalitz was an imposing figure, even in his sixties. Prize fighter Sonny Liston threatened Dalitz one night. "...You'd better kill me," Dalitz warned, "because if you don't, I'll make one telephone call and you'll be dead in twenty-four hours." The boxer left the restaurant.

In the late 1960s, when the IRS began investigating his tax records, Dalitz sold the Desert Inn to Howard Hughes. Dalitz retired to his lush California retreat and died of natural causes in Las Vegas on Sept. 6, 1989.

REF.: *CBA; Cohen, Mickey Cohen: In My Own Words; Cressey, Theft of the Nation; Demaris, The Last Mafioso; Eisenberg and Landau, Meyer Lansky; Gage, The Mafia Is Not an Equal Opportunity Employer; Gosch and Hammer, The Last Testament of Lucky Luciano; Messick, Lansky; ____, Secret File; ____ and Goldblatt, The Mobs and the Mafia; Peterson, The Mob; Reid, The Grim Reapers; Velie, Desperate Bargain: Why Jimmy Hoffa Had to Die; Zuckerman, Vengeance Is Mine.*

Dallas, George Mifflin, 1839-1917, U.S., jur. Received appointment to the Third Circuit Court of the U.S. by President William Harrison in Dec. 16, 1891, and published the *Analytical Tables of the Law of Evidence,* which was to be used with Stephen's *Digest of the Law of Evidence.* REF.: *CBA.*

Dalmas, Augustus, prom. 1844, Brit., mur. "He was mad, it

does seem," said British author Thomas Carlyle of his neighbor Augustus Dalmas, who on the night of Apr. 29, 1844, hacked his companion Sarah M'Farlane to death while they were walking across the Battersea Bridge. Sentenced to die for the murder of M'Farlane—a widow Dalmas had kept company with and who had been caring for his four children since the death of his wife—the French chemist was later declared a hopeless lunatic and committed to an asylum to live out his life.

REF.: Altick, *Victorian Studies In Scarlet; CBA.*

Dalrymple, Sir James, 1619-95, Scot., jur. Served as Scottish member of parliament in 1672 and Scottish privy councilor in 1674. He left Scotland in 1682 to avoid repression by John Graham of Claverhouse, but returned with William of Orange in 1688 becoming First Viscount of Stair in 1690. Dalrymple worked on *The Institutions of the Law of Scotland* (1681). REF.: *CBA.*

Dalrymple, Sir John, 1648-1707, Scot., treas.-mur. Placed in prison during the repression of secret religious meetings by John Graham of Claverhouse from 1682-84. He was responsible along with the king and Breadalbane for massacring the Macdonald clan of Glencoe in 1692. He was king's advocate from 1686-88, lord advocate under William III, and First Earl of Stair in 1703. REF.: *CBA.*

Dalton, Baron Hugh (Edward Hugh John Neale Dalton), 1887-1962, Brit., lawyer. Served as member of Parliament from 1924-31 and 1935-59, as Board of Trade president from 1942-45, and oversaw the nationalization of the Bank of England. REF: *CBA.*

Al Jennings, left, with J. Frank Dalton, who claimed to be Jesse James.

Dalton, J. Frank, 1847?-1951, U.S., west. outl.? As early as 1935, J. Frank Dalton of Gladewater, Texas, publicly claimed that he was the one and only Jesse Woodson James and that he had not been killed by Bob Ford in 1882, rather that a stranger was killed instead. Researchers at the time traced Dalton back to about 1886 when a man by that name was wanted for horse stealing in Limestone County, Texas. Dalton was also identified as a fake in 1935 by several old-time circus riders who insisted that he had traveled with their show shortly before 1900, playing an "old-time frontiersman." In the late 1930s, Dalton gave another interview to a disbelieving newsman in Corpus Christi, again claiming that he was the real Jesse James. He claimed that he had fought with William Quantrill the guerilla leader during the Civil War and that he had helped to set up a double who was shot to death in St. Joseph, Mo., by the Ford brothers in a scheme in which he could escape while another man's body was passed off as that of James. He offered little evidence then, or later, in 1949, when J. Frank Dalton made national headlines, thanks to promoter, Rudy Turilli.

At that time, Turilli "discovered" Dalton in Lawton, Okla., where the old man, claiming to be 100 years of age, again insisted that he was Jesse James. Turilli located a few doddering old westerners who supported the old man's claims, supposedly identifying Dalton as James, but these men hardly knew the real Jesse James. Bandit Al Jennings visited the old man at Meremac Caverns near Stanton, Mo., a small resort which was managed by Turilli, and where Turilli had brought Dalton to appear as a side-show attraction for tourists. Jennings took one look at the old man and unhesitatingly exclaimed: "It's Jesse, by God!" The identification, however, was unimpressive to experts since it was well known that Al Jennings belonged to a generation of bandits who operated long after the killing of Jesse James in 1882. Jennings, in fact, had never met Jesse James.

The most telling interview with J. Frank Dalton was conducted by Homer Croy, an expert on Jesse James. He asked Dalton to hold up an index finger, and the old man complied. Croy then announced that Dalton was the most unique human being he had ever met, pointing out that Jesse James had blown off the tip of his index finger while cleaning a pistol when riding with Quantrill; Dalton appeared to have grown a new finger. This fact and many other glaring discrepancies soon convinced most outlaw experts that J. Frank Dalton was nothing more than a colorful, colossal fraud. The old man died on Aug. 16, 1951, and was buried in Granbury, Texas. See: **James, Jesse Woodson.**

REF.: Argall, *The Truth About Jesse James*; Bartholomew, *The Biographical Album of Western Gunfighters*; Breihan, *The Complete and Authentic Life of Jesse James*; *CBA*; Drago, *Outlaws on Horseback*; Elman, *Fired in Anger*; Hall and Whitten, *Jesse James Rides Again*; Hunter and Rose, *The Album of Gunfighters*; James, *Jesse James and the Lost Cause*; Settle, *Jesse James Was His Name*; Turilli, *I Knew Jesse James*; Walker, *Jesse James*.

Dalton, Sir John, prom. 1347, Brit., kid.-mur. In medieval England, the forcible abduction of wealthy young heiresses was barely acknowledged as a crime. The kidnapper simply took what he believed was his, and then paid a small fine to the Crown for an official pardon. The family of the heiress more often than not was forced to surrender a dowry to the offender and sanction the marriage.

One such incident occurred on Good Friday, 1347, when Sir John Dalton of Northamptonshire ran off with Margery de la Beche from her estate in Beams, Wiltshire.

The young widow of the keeper of the Tower of London, de la Beche at the time was legally married to Gerard de l'Isle. This, however, did not prevent Dalton from spiriting her away, and looting the storeroom of the manor and killing several servants in the process. One of the guests in the house was Prince Lionel, son of King Edward III. When the king heard about the attack, he stated his disapproval and expressed concern for the life of his son. Nevertheless Dalton was eventually granted his pardon, and Gerard de l'Isle was without a wife. REF.: *CBA*.

Dalton, William Marion, See: **Doolin, William M.**

Dalton, Willie, 1904- , Case of, U.S., rob. Willie Dalton of Chicago once said that he "couldn't stand the sight of so much money lying around loose," so he decided to clean up the mess himself.

Dalton worked as a clerk at the Northern Trust Bank on South La Salle Street. One day in 1921, he stuffed $772,000 worth of Liberty bonds into his satchel. He cashed a $500 bond at a brokerage house on Madison Street and bought a used Ford. Dalton got only as far as west suburban Naperville before the Ford broke down. He spent the night at a hotel, and the next day boarded a southbound train to Bloomington, Ill. He realized the seriousness of his situation when he saw his picture on the front page of a newspaper another passenger was reading. There was a $26,000 reward on his head.

Dalton arrived in the little town of Heyworth in central Illinois, where he ate lunch in the diner and then played pool with the locals. Constable John Draper and his son Paul quietly arrested Dalton, whom they identified from the picture in the paper.

Willie Dalton was tried twice in 1921. Both times the jury was unable to agree on a verdict. They were not sure whether this was a calculated bank robbery, or just a schoolboy's whim. A third trial in 1924, acquitted Dalton. REF.: *CBA*.

Dalton Brothers, prom. 1890s, U.S., west. outl. The Dalton brothers and their dedicated riders comprised the last great bandit gang of the Old West, one as daring and outlandish as the James and Younger boys. For the most part they upheld the oddly chivalric codes of the West, refusing to rob women on trains and stagecoaches, shooting it out with lawmen rather than surrendering as a matter of their homespun honor, and insisting on "dying game." For all these reasons and more, the Daltons came to ruin and death in Coffeyville, Kan., in 1892. The Dalton boys, or more precisely, the four sons who became outlaws, were distant blood relatives of the notorious Younger brothers, and even more distantly related, it was claimed, to the James boys. Like the infamous James-Younger brothers, the Daltons were born in Missouri, which was aptly named in the nineteenth century the "Mother of Bandits."

Lewis Dalton was born in Kentucky and fought in the Mexican War of 1848. He moved to Missouri where he married Adeleine Younger, whose father was a cousin to the Younger brothers. This union produced fifteen children in all, most of whom grew up to be law-abiding citizens. Four sons, all born in Cass County, Mo., did not. These were Emmett (1871-1937); Grattan, called Grat, (1865-92); Robert, called Bob, (1868-92); and William Marion, called Bill, (1866-95). The boys were raised behind a saloon Lewis Dalton ran, but Dalton decided that this atmosphere was a bad influence on his sons. They moved, first to Kansas where the family struggled to maintain a small farm, and later to the Indian Territory, living near Coffeyville, Kan., which would be the scene of a bloody shootout in 1892 that would take the lives of two of his sons.

The family moved again to Oklahoma where the first of the sons, Frank Dalton, took up the gun, not as an outlaw, but on the side of the law, becoming a U.S. marshal in 1884 for Judge Isaac Parker in Fort Smith in 1884. Dalton was a courageous officer who was killed on Nov. 27, 1887, while attempting to arrest three peddlers illegally running whiskey to the Indians. Seeking vengeance, the three youngest boys, Grat, Bob, and Emmett, applied for silver stars. Grat was appointed to fill Frank Dalton's position as U.S. Marshal by Marshal John Carroll. Bob joined Grat as a posseman and was later appointed deputy marshal, and Emmett, the youngest, worked on a ranch but later became a posseman under the direction of his older brothers. The Daltons were effective lawmen, fast with their guns and fearless when running down wanted felons. They also became a law unto themselves, rustling herds of horses and selling these to willing buyers near Baxter Springs, Kan.

Judge Parker was enraged at this outlawry and revoked the Daltons' appointments, issuing warrants for their arrest. But the boys had by that time fled to Oklahoma to visit their mother who was living with their brothers, Charles and Henry, who had developed successful farms near Kingfisher. Their father, Lewis Dalton, had died in 1889 in Oklahoma. The Dalton brothers held a family meeting. Bob and Grat wanted the boys to travel to California to join another brother, Littleton, who had moved to the West Coast years earlier to farm. Bob Dalton, who was to become the aggressive leader of the Dalton Gang, suggested all the brothers go to California and "pick the trains and banks clean." Charles and Henry said no, that a bandit's life was not for them. They would stay in Oklahoma and take care of their mother. Bob and Grat would go to California. Emmett wanted to travel with Bob and Grat, but his older brothers told him he was too young and that he was to stay at home with Mrs. Dalton. Emmett pleaded his case, reminding his brothers that he had helped Bob rob a faro game in 1890. "That don't make you no train robber," snorted Grat. Emmett stayed in Oklahoma while Bob and Grat rode west to California.

Gang leader Bob Dalton and sweetheart Eugenia Moore, 1889.

Above left, Frank Dalton, a brave lawman and the only Dalton brother who remained honest.
Above right, Bill Dalton, who rode with the Doolin Gang and was later killed by lawmen while reportedly playing with his children.
Middle right, Bill Dalton shown in death.

Left, Grat Dalton and, right, Emmett Dalton, who lived until 1937.

The Condon Bank in Coffeyville, Kan., scene of the Daltons' doom.

Littleton Dalton wanted no part of robbery and told his brothers Bob and Grat that he intended to continue farming. Bill Dalton, however, joined his younger brothers and the three Daltons stopped the Southern Pacific's Train Number 17 on Feb. 6, 1891, near Alila, Calif. Wearing masks, Bob and Grat leaped into the engine's cab and forced engineer George Radcliff to bring the train to a halt. Bill Dalton, using a rifle, then began firing above the heads of the passengers to keep them crouching in their seats, while Grat and Bob forced Radcliff to accompany them to the express car. When Radcliff tried to slip away in the darkness, one of the brothers wheeled about and sent a bullet into his stomach, killing him.

More trouble awaited the brothers inside the express car. Guard Charles C. Haswell refused to unlock the express car door. Several loads of buckshot from shotguns were fired into the door, and Haswell grabbed his own shotgun and fired several times from a small hole in the door. He claimed later that he hit one of the bandits who, failing to get the door to the express car open, fled in disgust and anger. The first train robbery attempted by the Daltons had ended in utter failure. Bill and Grat were later captured while Bob Dalton managed to escape, riding back to Oklahoma. Bill Dalton was freed after a quick trial, but Grat was sentenced to twenty years. He managed to escape and he, too, rode back to the familiar landscape of Oklahoma. There Emmett joined his older brothers, now dedicated to a life of crime which Bob tried to excuse by blaming the Southern Pacific for placing rewards of $6,000 each on their heads. "They put the running irons on our hides," Bob was fond of saying. This was an old excuse, one used by the James and Younger brothers before them, but the Daltons saw themselves as heroic outcasts who had been driven to banditry by the forces of evil establishments.

At this time, the Daltons rounded up some of the toughest, meanest gunmen and thieves in the Oklahoma Territory, forming a fearsome gang that would soon make outlaw history. Members included Dick Broadwell, Charley Pierce, Bill McEhanie, Bill Doolin, George "Bitter Creek" Newcomb, and "Black Face Charley" Bryant. The gang first struck the Santa Fe's Texas Express near Wharton, Okla., in early 1891. This time when the bandits ordered the guard to open the door to the express guard, there was no resistance. The outlaws easily forced the safe inside and took more than $14,000. The robbery was without gunfire, which disturbed Black Face Charley Bryant who told the Daltons that he was looking forward to some gunplay. Bryant once stated that "I want to get killed in one hell-firing minute of smoking action." He would later get his wish. As the bandits were about to ride away from the train, Bryant halted and said, "We should go into those passenger cars and get everything those people have." Bob Dalton, with his brothers backing him up, snorted: "Those are working folks like us and we don't steal from them." With that he ordered the gang to ride away. Black Face Charley closed his mouth and rode with them in silence.

Bryant took his share of the robbery to Hennessey, Okla., where he promptly got drunk and then staggered into the street, firing his six-gun wildly into second-story windows. Marshal Ed Short arrested him and, after learning that he had apprehended the infamous Black Face Charley, put Bryant aboard a train headed for Wichita, where he would stand trial before a federal judge on charges of bank and train robbery. While Short left Bryant manacled to a steel post in the baggage car to take a smoke, the outlaw managed to free himself and grab a gun just as the lawman re-entered the car. Both men leveled their six-guns at each other and fired, emptying their guns into one another. They both fell dead.

The fate of Black Face Charley did not bother the Daltons, especially Bob Dalton, the most daring and inventive of the gang. Dalton told members of his gang that Bryant had been a fool and that if they kept their heads and followed his methodical plan of train and bank robbing, all of them would be able to "retire in about twelve months." With that thought in mind, the gang next raided a Missouri-Kansas & Texas Express outside of Lellietta,

Okla., stopping the train and quickly looting the express car on the night of Sept. 15, 1891, taking between $3,000 and $14,000, according to varying reports. None of the train passengers were molested or robbed, according to Dalton custom, and the robbery took less than fifteen minutes, with no gunfire exchanged between the Daltons and the express car guard. The gang was becoming proficient.

Aiding the bandits was Eugenia Moore, Bob Dalton's sweetheart. Unknown to other members of the gang, including Bob's own brothers, Moore acted as an undercover intelligence agent. She would inquire of various railroads which trains were the best protected, on the pretense that she intended to ship money and valuables but was fearful of robbery since so many trains were being held up. She was assured by railroad officials that her valuables would be safe on trains carrying considerable cash, payrolls, and bank shipments, since these trains would be guarded by armed express agents in the mail cars. Thusly, Eugenia Moore obtained the schedules of trains carrying considerable cash and passed this information on to her lover, Bob Dalton, who then planned and executed the robberies with lightning efficiency. To his brothers and other followers Bob Dalton seemingly possessed an uncanny ability to select just the right trains to rob.

Moore learned that a Santa Fe train would be carrying a large amount of cash. This train was stopped on July 1, 1892, near Red Rock in the Cherokee Strip at about 9 p.m. when seven bandits, their faces covered by kerchiefs, fired their six-guns and intimidated the crew and passengers. They quickly forced the door of the express car and held the guard at bay while they took $11,000 from the small safe. Within twenty minutes, the bandits had remounted their horses and ridden off into the hills, whooping and hollering triumph as they went. Flushed with this success, the Daltons struck again only two weeks later, seven or eight of its members walking into the depot at Adair, Okla., in the Cherokee Strip at 9 p.m. on Sept. 15, 1892. The gang held up the station master, looting the safe in his office. When the Missouri-Kansas & Texas train pulled into the station, the bandits were waiting for it. One outlaw jumped into the cab of the engine, holding the engineer at gunpoint, while the rest of the gang went to the express car, backing a wagon up to it.

The express guard refused to open the door to the mail car, but after the bandits fired several shots through the door and threatened to use dynamite to blow up the entire car if need be, the guard opened the door. Some of the Daltons jumped inside and quickly and took $17,000 from the safe. As they threw the money bags onto the back of the wagon, the bandits were startled by the sudden fusillade unleashed from some of the passenger cars which carried a large force of Indian police and railroad detectives. The bandits drove the wagon away as they returned shots, a withering crossfire that wounded Dr. B. Youngblood and killed Dr. W.L. Goff, who were sitting on the porch of a nearby drugstore when the gun battle erupted and had no time to take cover. Also wounded was Chief Charley LaFlore of the Territorial Police and L.L. Kinney, a railroad detective. Deputy Marshal Sid Johnson was also wounded by one of the bandits he thought he recognized as Grat Dalton. Ironically, Johnson had served with Grat and Bob Dalton when they had all been marshals in Fort Smith. Although hundreds of shots had been fired, miraculously none of the bandits were wounded, and they escaped intact with the stolen money.

The robbery at Adair caused the Daltons to be identified as the most feared gang of outlaws in the West. Their bold raids and their ability to escape capture time and again made them legends within two years of the time the gang began operating. The gang managed to evade the hundreds of lawmen searching for them. They had benefited well through their experiences as U.S. marshals, knowing the tracking techniques of their pursuers. They also had dozens of hideouts where they were safe from detection, especially the caves in which they once played in as boys along the Canadian River, and other hard-to-find areas throughout the Indian Nation. But this on-the-run life had, the Daltons knew,

Bob Dalton in death.

Grat Dalton in death.

Bill Powers in death.

Bob and Grat Dalton, dead, held by Coffeyville lawmen.

Dick Broadwell in death.

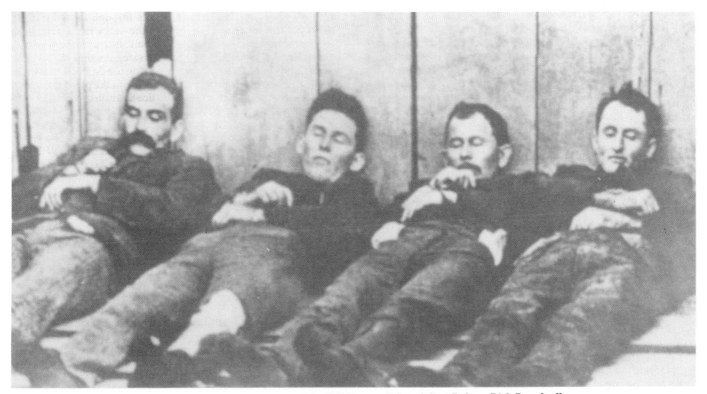

The lesson of the Coffeyville raid: four dead outlaws, left to right, Bill Powers, Bob and Grat Dalton, Dick Broadwell.

only won them the image of infamous outlaws.

To Emmett Dalton, such notoriety meant the doom of his plans to marry his childhood sweetheart, Julia Johnson. Before the Red Rock raid, Emmett Dalton had ridden to the Johnson ranch and, while his brothers stood guard, visited Julia for what he believed would be the last time. He told her that he wanted to marry her but that he had thrown in his lot with his brothers Bob and Grat and there was no turning back now. He was headed, not toward the altar, but for Boot Hill. Emmett would later write: "What had I to offer Julia, a man with a price on his head and no clear way to extricate myself from the compounding results of crime? I rode away. An outlaw has no business having a girl, no business thinking of marriage."

All that Bob Dalton was thinking about was achieving something that even the notorious James-Younger gang had failed to do—rob two banks at the same time. Jesse and Frank James, with the Younger brothers and others, had ridden into Northfield, Minn., in 1876, intending to rob two banks, but the raid proved to be disastrous when the local citizens fought them off and decimated the gang. This time, Bob Dalton vowed, it would be different. He would lead the Dalton Gang into his old hometown of Coffeyville, Kan., and there boldly rob the Condon and First National Banks. Before this raid, Bob Dalton must have had deep reservations about his surviving his own wild scheme. Only a few weeks before the bloody Coffeyville raid, he learned that his girl, Eugenia Moore, had suddenly died of cancer after only a short illness. He stared at her picture for some hours before throwing it into the campfire around which the Daltons warmed themselves. The following day the three Dalton brothers rode to Kingfisher to see their mother for what might be the last time. They sat on their horses, watching the ranch house from the cover of trees, afraid to go near the house since they rightly believed that it was being watched by possemen who were hunting the Daltons throughout the southwest.

The brothers watched their mother move past the windows of their boyhood home as they sat silent that night on horseback, all thinking back to an earlier time. Wrote Emmett later: "For a moment we saw her in the distant window, her flitting form setting the house in order for the night. None of us dared look at each other. With one accord we spurred our horses. And at the sound I saw her turn her face to the window, listening intently, as if she heard the passing hoofbeats. Such was Bob and Grat's last outspoken salute to the grand old lady who bore them." The gang that headed north toward Coffeyville and into western legend the next day included Bob, Grat, and Emmett Dalton, Dick Broadwell, Bill Powers, and Bill Doolin, the last three all experienced hardcase outlaws from Oklahoma. In the early morning of Oct. 5, 1892, when the gang was only twenty miles outside of Coffeyville, Bill Doolin's horse began to limp and he dismounted. He told Bob Dalton that he would return to a ranch they had passed a few miles back and get another horse and catch up with the gang. Dalton nodded and Bill Doolin began walking his horse back down the road. This accident was to save Doolin's life. By the time he located a horse and raced after the Daltons, he was already too late. He heard the muttering gunfire in Coffeyville and realized the raid was a failure. He turned his horse about and headed for Oklahoma.

Emmett Dalton was a reluctant member of the gang that rode into Coffeyville. He had originally argued with Bob Dalton against the raid. He pointed out that they had relatives buried in Coffeyville and that many of the townspeople were their friends. Bob Dalton had ignored this plea and went ahead with the raid. Rather than let his brothers ride into danger alone, Emmett, ever loyal, decided to go with them. As the outlaws neared Coffeyville, they slipped false beards on their faces, but when they rode down Maple Street at 9:30 a.m. the Daltons were recognized by Aleck McKenna who had known the brothers when they were boys. McKenna watched as the gang rode to an alley between Maple and Walnut streets, one that would later be called Death Alley, and tethered their horses. Then Grat Dalton, Powers, and

Broadwell walked across the street to the C.M. Condon Bank, while Bob and Emmett Dalton went into the First National Bank.

McKenna went to the window of the Condon Bank and, peering inside, saw Grat Dalton draw his six-gun and aim it at the cashier, Charles Ball. McKenna turned on his heels and raced down the middle of the street, shouting: "It's the Daltons! It's the Daltons! They're robbing the bank!" Several passersby thought McKenna had gone out of his mind, some laughed. But Cyrus Lee, who had also known the Daltons when they were youngsters, recognized Bob Dalton inside the First National Bank and took up the cry of alarm. Dozens of Coffeyville citizens raced to the hardware store and armed themselves, then ran back outside and trained their guns on the fronts of the two banks.

Inside the First National Bank, Bob and Emmett Dalton heard the cries of their names but kept about their business. Bob held two guns on Thomas G. Ayres, cashier, and W.H. Shepherd, the teller, along with three customers, J.H. Brewster, C.L. Hollingsworth, and A.W. Knott, who was a deputy sheriff. Emmett was behind the teller's cage, shoving more than $21,000 into a grain sack. Grat Dalton, Powell, and Broadwell were having less success inside the Condon Bank. Before him stood Vice President Charles T. Carpenter, bookkeeper T.C. Babb, and Charles Ball, the cashier, who was arguing with Dalton, telling him he could not open the safe.

"Open the safe and be quick about it," Grat Dalton ordered Ball.

The cashier shook his head, repeating the same line he had earlier delivered: "It's a time lock and it won't open until 9:45 a.m." Ball, of course, knew that the safe, containing $18,000, was closed but unlocked. He was stalling for time.

The oldest of the Dalton brothers leveled his gun only a few inches from Ball's head, snarling: "Open it or I'll kill you!"

Again the courageous cashier repeated his lie about the time lock. He then began to push several bags of money from behind the teller's cage, most of it in small bills and silver, about $4,000 worth, an attempt by Ball to keep the bandits from the substantial cash inside the safe.

Grat looked at the clock on the wall and saw that it was 9:42 a.m. "We'll wait," he said, a wait of three minutes would cost four of the five bandits their lives.

Bob and Emmett Dalton grabbed the grain sacks with the large bills inside the First National Bank and began heading for the door when they saw the street filling with gun-carrying citizens. Bullets began crashing through the bank windows and thudding into the walls and teller's cage. Bob Dalton stood in the open doorway for a moment, then slammed it shut. "The back way," he told Emmett. He motioned with his six-gun for Shepherd, Ayres, and Knott to go before them out the back door and into the street. Lucius M. Baldwin, a clerk who had grabbed a rifle at the first alarm, was approaching the group from the First National. Bob Dalton handed the grain sack full of money to Emmett, saying to him: "Look after the money sack. I'll do the fighting. I have to get that man." He then raised his rifle just as Baldwin was aiming his own gun. Dalton fired first, a dead shot that plowed into Baldwin's head. The clerk toppled to the dusty street, dying of the fatal wound.

By now the outlaws abandoned their hostages. Bob and Emmett Dalton were trotting toward the alley where their horses were tied. From across the street, Grat Dalton, Broadwell, and Powell were running toward the same spot. Dozens of guns barked after them, kicking up dust from the street, banging into buildings. Bootmakers George Cubine and Charles Brown, who had fixed the shoes of the boys when they were young, had taken up positions in a chemist's shop; both held rifles in their hands. Cubine took aim to fire at Bob Dalton as he ran past the shop, but the outlaw whirled about and fired a single bullet that killed him. When he fell, Brown caught the rifle dropped by Cubine; before he could fire it, another shot from the deadly accurate Bob Dalton killed him also. Almost at that second, Thomas Ayres, the cashier from the First National Bank who had raced to Isham's

Hardware Store when Bob and Emmett released him, ran to the street with a rifle, aiming at Bob Dalton. Before he could shoot, Dalton fired one shot from the hip and again his aim was true, the bullet striking Ayres in the cheek, killing him.

By the time the five bandits reached the alley and their horses, they quickly realized that they had run into a death trap. Dozens of citizens converged on the alley from both ends, letting loose a withering fire. "Get out, get out," Grat Dalton shouted to the others, but there was nowhere to go. As they struggled to lead their horses out of the alley and mount them, they were greeted by walls of deadly gunfire. Several bullets struck Powers, the first to be shot down, but he leaped up again, firing two six-guns at his tormentors. Broadwell was shot in the arm, then in the back, and fell; he, too, got up once more, firing. Bob Dalton was then shot, then Emmett. At that moment, Marshal Charles T. Connelly, who had once been the schoolteacher of both Bob and Grat, came marching down the alley, firing his six-gun at Grat Dalton. The outlaw advanced on the lawman, firing his own weapon. Dalton's bullets cut down Connelly, but as the marshal fell he sent a bullet into Grat Dalton's chest. Bob Dalton moaned in anguish as he saw Grat sink slowly against a wall and die.

Bill Powers, wounded several times, managed to get into the saddle, but just as his horse galloped out of the alley, Powers was riddled, blown from his mount. He lay dead in the street as the vigilantes stepped over his body, advancing on the other bandits. With an amazing burst of energy, Dick Broadwell leaped into the saddle of his horse. Bleeding from several wounds, Broadwell spurred his mount at a gallop down the other end of the alley, smashing through a group of citizens who pumped bullet after bullet into him. Broadwell went a short distance before falling dead from the saddle. Now only two of the outlaws were left alive and on their feet—Bob and Emmett Dalton. Livery stable owner John J. Kloehr, and the town barber, Carey Seaman, raced down the alley with shotguns in their hands. At a distance of five feet, Kloehr fired a barrel into Bob Dalton's chest, sending him to the ground with a mortal wound.

Emmett Dalton fired several rounds which drove Kloehr and Seaman to temporary cover. He threw the money sack over his saddle, crawled up on his mount and was about to make his getaway when he heard his brother Bob groan. He reached down to pull Bob Dalton up behind him on the horse, but the outlaw leader said with his last breath: "Don't mind me, boy. I'm done for. Don't surrender! Die game!" As the brothers clasped each other's hands, Kloehr jumped out from behind a doorway and fired another barrel from his shotgun, sending the load into Emmett Dalton. The last outlaw fell to the ground. For an eerie moment, all was silent. Only the heavy gunsmoke drifted from the mouth of the alley. The citizens walked slowly forward and finally one of them shouted: "They're all down!" The vigilantes were surprised to find Emmett Dalton still alive, although he had been shot twenty times. He was taken to a local doctor and given medical attention and survived. A rush of angry citizens crowded about the slain outlaws. Many cut locks of hair from the heads of Bob and Grat Dalton. Then the bodies of Broadwell, Powers, and both Dalton boys were placed on boards and propped up so that Coffeyville lawmen and citizens could pose with the corpses for photographs that later became famous in the West. Such was the inglorious end of the last great western outlaw band. Bill Dalton and Bill Doolin would, within a few years, join Bob and Grat Dalton in early death as a result of their bandit ways. Only Emmett Dalton was to outlive his criminal brothers and friends and the wild era that spawned them. Bill Dalton would later ride with the Doolin Gang and be shot to death by lawmen.

Emmett Dalton was tried for the murders of Cubine and Baldwin, even though many had witnessed Bob Dalton committing these murders. Emmett Dalton was sent to prison for life, but he proved to be a model prisoner and was released in 1907. Waiting for him was Julia Johnson. They were married and lived happily together for thirty years. Emmett Dalton would prove to be a model citizen and an implacable foe of crime, championing

law and order in his writings and lectures. He would live until 1937, but six years before that time, the last of the Dalton brothers returned to Coffeyville to visit the common grave that held the bodies of Broadwell, Powers, and his brothers Bob and Grat. He stood before this solemn plot of ground and then, as he pointed to the spot, said for the benefit of many standing next to him: "I challenge the world to produce the history of any outlaw who ever got anything out of it but that, or else be huddled in a prison cell...The biggest fool on earth is the one who thinks he can beat the law, that crime can be made to pay. It never paid and it never will and that was the one big lesson of the Coffeyville raid." See: **Doolin, William M.**

REF.: American Guide Series, *Tulsa, A Guide to the Oil Capital;* Anderson, *A Quarter Inch of Rain;* Barnard, *A Rider of the Cherokee Strip;* Bartholomew, *The Biographical Album of Western Gunfighters;* Beebe, *Hear the Train Blow;* Block, *Great Train Robberies of the West;* Boynton, *The Rediscovery of the Frontier;* Bracke, *Wheat Country;* Brady, *Recollections of a Missionary in the Great West;* Breihan, *Badmen of Frontier Days;* _____, *Outlaws of the Old West;* Bristow, *Lost on Grand River;* Canton, *Frontier Trails;* Cantonwine, *Star Forty-Six, Oklahoma;* CBA; Cheek, *The Story of the American Pioneer Family;* Chrisman, *Fifty Years on the Owl Hoot Trail;* Clark, *Then Came the Railroads;* Cox, *Luke Short and His Era;* Croy, *He Hanged Them High;* Cunningham, *Trigger Marshal;* Dalton, *Beyond the Law;* _____, *When the Daltons Rode; The Dalton Brothers and Their Astounding Career of Crime* (Anon.); *The Dalton Gang;* Day, *Gene Rhodes, Cowboy;* Debo, *The Cowman's Southwest;* _____, *Tulsa: From Creek Town to Oil Capital;* Dillon, *Wells Fargo Detective;* Doctor, *Shotguns on Sunday;* Douglas, *The History of Tulsa;* _____, *Territory Tales;* Drago, *Outlaws on Horseback;* _____, *Red River Valley;* _____, *Road Agents and Train Robbers;* Duke, *Celebrated Criminal Cases of America;* Duncan, *History of Montgomery County, Kansas;* Eisele, *A History of Noble County, Oklahoma;* Elliott, *Last Raid of the Daltons;* Elman, *Fired in Anger;* Emery, *Court of the Damned;* Fanning, *Great Crimes of the West;* Farquhar, *History of Livingston, California;* Fellows, *This Way to the Big Show;* Finger, *Foot-Loose in the West;* Fishwick, *American Heroes, Myth and Reality;* Flanagan, *Out West;* Foreman, *A History of Oklahoma;* Gard, *Frontier Justice;* Gardner, *The Old Wild West;* Gay, *History of Nowata County;* Gillis, *To Hell and Back Again;* Gish, *American Bandits;* Glasscock, *Bandits of the Southern Pacific;* _____, *Then Came Oil;* Graves, *Oklahoma Outlaws;* Greene, *America Goes to Press;* Hagen, *Indian Police and Judges;* Hall, *The Beginnings of Tulsa;* Hanes, *Bill Doolin, Outlaw;* Harkey, *Mean as Hell;* Harman, *Hell on the Border;* Harrington, *Hanging Judge;* Harrison, *Hell Holes and Hangings;* Hendricks, *The Bad Man of the West;* Holloway, *Texas Gun Lore;* Hopping, *A Sheriff-Ranger in Chuckwagon Days;* Horan, *Desperate Men;* _____, *Desperate Women;* _____, *The Great American West;* _____ and Sann, *Pictorial History of the Wild West;* Hough, *The Story of the Outlaw;* Houts, *From Gun to Gavel;* Howe, *Timberleg of the Diamond Tail;* Hunter and Rose, *The Album of Gunfighters;* Hutchens, *One Man's Montana;* Hutchinson, *The Life & Personal Writings of Eugene Manlove Rhodes;* Johnston, *My Home on the Range;* Jones, *The Experiences of a Deputy U.S. Marshal of the Indian Territory;* Kane, *100 Years Ago With the Law and the Outlaw;* King, *Main Line;* Koller, *The American Gun;* Krumrey, *Saga of Sawlog;* Lake, *Under Cover for Wells Fargo;* Lamb, *Tragedies of the Osage Hills;* Lavender, *The American Heritage History of the Great West;* Lawson, *Dalton Boys and the M.K. and T. Robbery;* _____, *The Dalton Boys in California;* Linzee, *Development of Oklahoma Territory;* McCarty, *The Enchanted West;* McKennon, *Iron Men;* Masterson, *The Katy Railroad and the Last Frontier;* Menefee, *History of Tulare and Kings Counties;* Millar, *Hail to Yesterday;* Miller, *Bill Tilghman, Marshal of the Last Frontier;* Miller, Langsdorf and Richmond, *Kansas, A Pictorial History;* Morris, *Oklahoma, Yesterday-Today-Tomorrow;* Nash, *Bloodletters and Badmen;* Newsom, *The Life and Practice of the Wild and Modern Indian;* Nix, *Oklahombres;* O'Neal, *Encyclopedia of Western Gunfighters;* Osborn, *Let Freedom Ring;* Penfield, *Western Sheriffs and Marshals;* Preece, *The Dalton Gang;* Raine, *Famous Sheriffs and Western Outlaws;* _____, *Guns of the Frontier;* Rainey, *The Cherokee Strip;* Rascoe, *Belle Starr;* Rath, *Early Ford County;* Ray, *The Dalton Brothers and Their Oklahoma Cave;* _____, *The Oklahoma Bandits;* Rennert, *Western Outlaws;* Rich, *The Heritage of Kansas;* Ridings, *The Chisholm Trail;* Rouse, *A History of Cowboy Flat;* Sabin, *Wild Men of the*

Wild West; Sanders, *The Sumner County Story;* Schlesinger, *The Rise of the City;* Shackleford, *Gunfighters of the Old West;* Shirley, *Buckskin Joe;* _____, *Heck Thomas, Frontier Marshal;* _____, *Henry Starr, Last of the Real Badmen;* _____, *Law West of Fort Smith;* _____, *Six-Gun and Silver Star;* _____, *Toughest of Them All;* Shoemaker, *Missouri Day by Day;* Small, *The Best of True West;* Small, *History of Tulare County;* Smith, *Garden of the Sun;* Sonichsen, *Outlaw Bill Mitchell Alias Baldy Russell;* Stansbery, *The Passing of the 3D Ranch;* Sterling, *Famous Western Outlaw-Sheriff Battles;* Sutton, *Hands Up!;* Tilghman, *Marshal of the Last Frontier;* _____, *Outlaw Days;* Timmons, *Twilight on the Range;* Ward, *The Dalton Gang;* Warden, *Thrilling Tales of Kansas;* Wellman, *A Dynasty of Western Outlaws;* _____, *Glory, God and Gold;* Williams, *The Dalton Brothers in Their Oklahoma Cave;* Wilson and Taylor, *Southern Pacific;* (FILM), *When the Daltons Rode,* 1940; *The Daltons Ride Again,* 1945; *The Dalton Gang,* 1949; *Return of the Badmen,* 1948; *The Daltons' Women,* 1950; *The Cimaron KId,* 1951; *Montana Belle,* 1952; *Jesse James Versus the Daltons,* 1954; *The Dalton Girls,* 1957; *The Dalton That Got Away,* 1960; *The Outlaws Is Coming,* 1965; *The Last Ride of the Dalton Gang,* 1988.

Daly, James, d.1864, U.S., west. gunman-outl. Daly was a member of the gang led by "Three-Fingered" Jack McDowell, operating outside of Aurora, Nev. Daly and McDowell ran a saloon in Aurora and were credited with many gunfights. A man named Lloyd picked a fight with Daly, shooting him in the leg. Daly slowly drew his gun and shouted as he fired: "I'll dance to your music all night." As Lloyd fired several wild shots at Daly, the gunman fired a single shot that brought Lloyd down. Vigilantes later arrested Daly, McDowell, and two others and hanged them for various crimes in February 1864 near Aurora. See: **McDowell, Jack.**

REF.: Bartholomew, *The Biographical Album of Western Gunfighters;* *CBA.*

Daly, James, and **Stevenson, Thomas,** prom. 1899, U.S., burg. For nearly three years, a pair of burglars baffled and frustrated the Chicago police. Their target was always the same: Primley's Chewing Gum factory on Wabash Avenue. Between 1896 and 1899, the building was robbed seven times. When there was nothing left to take, the thieves left an envelope, asking Mr. Primley: "Just please leave something next time or we will get even."

Police chief Joseph Kipley's investigation led finally to the arrest of the chewing gum bandits. Thanks to a tip from a small boy in the streets, James Daly and Thomas Stevenson were captured on Wabash Avenue. Two bicycles, large quantities of gum, and an umbrella were found and identified as Primley's. Daly was given an indeterminate sentence. Stevenson, still a minor, was sent to a reformatory.

REF.: *CBA;* Wooldridge, *Hands Up.*

Daly, T.F. Gilroy, b.1931- , U.S., lawyer. Served as member of the Connecticut Planning Committee on Criminal Administration, the chairman of the subcommittee on organized crime from 1967-72, Connecticut deputy attorney general from 1971-75, and as Connecticut special assistant to the attorney general from 1975-76. He received commendations from U.S. Attorney General Robert F. Kennedy, U.S. Attorney for the Southern District of New York, Robert M. Morganthau, and U.S. Commissioner of Narcotics Henry Giordano. He was appointed to the District Court of Connecticut by President Jimmy Carter in 1977. REF.: *CBA.*

Dalzeel, Alexander, c.1662-1715, Brit., pir.-treas.-mur. Born in Port Patrick, Scot., Alexander Dalzeel, like many youths of his day, went to sea at an early age. By the time he was twenty-three, he was master of a ship and had made six successful voyages.

Dalzeel drifted down to Madagascar in 1685. He was by then decidedly dishonest and he enlisted with the infamous pirate Captain Avery. An apocryphal story has it that Dalzeel captured a ship carrying the daughter of the Great Mogul. Although she was on her way to be married, Captain Avery married the woman himself. As a reward, Avery made Dalzeel a captain and gave him his own ship and crew.

Dalzeel served Avery for about a year before assuming an independent command. In the West Indies, Dalzeel's pirates could find no suitable prey. Their provisions dwindled and starvation threatened. Finally, they spotted a ship. But as Dalzeel's rather small ship closed on the prize, the pirate realized his prey was a well-armed Spanish galleon that had somehow gotten separated from the fleet.

Having committed himself to the attack, Dalzeel decided to attempt to capture the more powerful ship or die trying. Dalzeel ordered that a hole be drilled in the side of his own ship as he approached the galleon, so that his crew would have to win or drown. His pirates boarded the ship at dusk, guns and swords ready, but they met little resistance. The Spaniards had spotted the pirate ship earlier. But when the Spanish captain studied the pursuing vessel, he dismissed it as too small and decrepit to be a threat. The captain retired to his cabin to play cards and was rudely interrupted when Dalzeel burst through the door, gun in hand, ordering the captain to surrender. Those who resisted were killed; within minutes the ship belonged to the pirates. Dalzeel set sail for Jamaica with his prize.

Dalzeel was captured for the first time after attempting to capture a fleet of twelve pearl ships guarded by a Spanish man-of-war. A condition of his surrender was that Dalzeel and his men would not be forced into slavery or hard labor, a common practice at the time. They were to be released on shore. Dalzeel was soon back in Jamaica, outfitting another ship. He then set sail for Cuba. On the way, he came upon three Spanish ships on the way to Havana. The pirates were vastly outnumbered, and Dalzeel was again captured.

This time Dalzeel was to be hanged on board the ship. The night before the scheduled execution, he stabbed his guard to death and used two earthen jugs to float to shore. Within a few days, Dalzeel joined another band of pirates and persuaded these cutthroats to attack and capture the ship that had recently been his jail. Near Jamaica, a storm wrecked and sank the ship. Dalzeel, however, managed to ride out the storm in a canoe.

Some time later, Dalzeel wangled a commission as a French privateer and had considerable success taking prizes from the English and others not aligned with King Louis XIV. He was captured and taken to England where he was tried and convicted as a traitor. In 1712, he was sentenced to be drawn, then hanged and quartered. But the Earl of Mar interceded, and Dalzeel received a pardon, cheating the hangman for a second time. No sooner was this dedicated corsair free then he went back to France and to his greatest love, piracy. Dalzeel's last victim was a French ship whose crew suffered greatly at the pirate's hand. Embittered by his own imprisonment, Dalzeel took vengeance on the French sailors. He ordered their necks tied to their heels so they could not swim and then threw them overboard. Dalzeel gloated as he watched the hapless men drown. Some time later he was captured in Scotland and taken to London to be tried. He was hanged on Dec. 5, 1715.

REF.: *CBA;* Smith, *Highwaymen.*

Damaskinos (Dimitrios Papandreou), 1891-1949, Gr., consp.-treas. Exiled from 1938-41 for opposing the Metaxas regime. He later returned and acted as regent for King George II, who was in exile, from 1944-46. REF.: *CBA.*

d'Amboise, Bussy, prom. 1572, Fr., duel-mur. Bussy d'Amboise was a noted swordsman during the reign of King Henry III of France. He killed dozens of Parisian Huguenots, including one of his relatives during the bloody St. Barthelemi Massacre in 1572, which was engineered by Catherine de Medici.

The philandering d'Amboise roamed the countryside in search of women, willing to challenge anyone to a sword duel. On the Rue St. Honoré, Bussy was accosted by Louis Balbis Crillon, a famous knight who had served the king during the Wars of the Holy League. The story goes that when d'Amboise asked Crillon the time, the knight shot back, "It is the hour of thy death!" Crillon drew his sword, but the men were quickly separated, and d'Amboise lived to taste battle again.

REF.: *CBA*; Melville, *Famous Duels and Assassinations*.

Dame, Lige, b.1888, and **Decker, Earl**, prom. 1931, U.S., (wrong. convict.) mur. On a cool November night in 1931, Sheriff Manley Jackson stopped a car in Pocahontas, Ark., for a routine license-plate check. The driver pointed a .45-caliber pistol at Jackson and forced him to walk over to a gravel pit adjacent to the roadway. He shot the sheriff five times in the back before speeding off.

Lige Dame and Earl Decker of Randolph County, Ark., were taken into custody and grilled for eight hours by police in Memphis, Tenn. Dame confessed to shooting Jackson, whose father was a state senator at the time. He implicated Pocahontas police chief John Slayton and Decker, who maintained his innocence even after conviction.

Dame later repudiated his earlier confession, only to make another in the presence of the warden of the Arkansas State Penitentiary and a reporter with the Arkansas *Gazette*. A sanity test was eventually ordered for Dame.

In 1941, Decker was paroled. Dame died in prison, and Chief Slayton spent his remaining years and life savings trying to clear his good name.

The crime was forgotten until 1971, when the Pocahontas *Star-Herald* reprinted excerpts from the *Alvin Karpis Story*. The notorious 1930s bank robber vividly described the murder of a Pocahontas sheriff committed while he was driving through town in the company of Ma Barker's son Freddie Parker. Karpis claimed that it was Barker who fired the shots that killed Jackson. The Karpis autobiography was published thirty-five years after the Pocahontas murder. See: **Karpis, Alvin**. REF.: *CBA*.

Damiens, Robert Francis, See: **Louis XV**.

Damon and **Pythias**, See: **Phintias**.

Dampier, Edith, prom. 1932, Case of, Brit., mur. On a January evening in 1932, the Herefordshire police were called in with the report of a suicide at Hunter's Hall, Lea, a small village east of Ross-on-Wye, England. Benjamin Parry, thirty-one, a servant in the house, was sitting in an armchair, with a wound in his neck and a gun between his knees. According to Mrs. Edith Dampier, mistress of the house, Parry had killed himself. Famed forensic pathologist Sir Bernard Spilsbury contended that the wound could not have been self-inflicted, and ballistics expert Robert Churchill concurred. Rumors circulated of an affair between Parry and Dampier. She was charged with murder, but found unfit to stand trial and sent to an asylum.

REF.: Browne, *The Scalpel of Scotland Yard*; *CBA*; Hastings, *The Other Mr. Churchill*.

Dampier, William, 1652-1715, Brit., pir. William Dampier was already a seasoned buccaneer when he joined the pirate expedition to capture Panama City and the Spanish settlement there. In 1680, the pirates left Jamaica for Darien, Pan. Three-hundred-and-thirty-one pirates began the journey, assisted by local Indians who took them to Santa Maria, where the pirates seized two small ships in preparation for the final assault on Panama.

The Spaniards, who had been lying in wait, engaged the pirates with five heavily-armed ships in the harbor of Panama. The pirates won the battle, but could not decide what to do next. Dampier joined the faction that sailed south along the South American coast. When the pirates quarreled among themselves, Dampier joined the forty-four seamen who wanted to return to Panama and make their way to the Caribbean.

In 1683, Dampier sailed around Cape Horn and joined forces with some English and French pirates who had captured a number of rich prizes on the high seas. In the Pacific, Dampier joined Captain Swan aboard the *Cignet*, and together they sailed for the Philippines on a privateering mission for the Duke of York. Swan engaged the Spaniards in combat despite having been ordered not to by the Crown. The crew abandoned Captain Swan in the Philippines, and under the direction of Dampier, discovered the north coast of Australia. They arrived in England in 1691, where Dampier wrote a best-selling account of his adventures titled *A New Voyage Round the World*. Dampier won a commission, and sailed the *HMS Roebuck* to the South Seas. He lent his name to the Dampier Strait in Indonesia and the Dampier Archipelago off Australia.

REF.: *CBA*; Chatterton, *The Romance of Piracy*; Dofoe, *A General History of the Most Notorious Robberies and Murders of the Most Notorious Pirates, 1717-1724*; Ellms, *The Pirates' Own Book*; Gosse, *The Pirates' Who's Who*; Innes, *The Book of Pirates*; Lloyd, *William Dampier*; Mitchell, *Pirates*; Pringle, *Jolly Roger: The Story of the Great Age of Piracy*; Rankin, *The Golden Age of Piracy*; Scott, *Concise Encyclopedia of Crime and Criminals*; Williams, *Captains Outrageous: Seven Centuries of Piracy*; Woodbury, *The Great Days of Piracy*.

Dana, Francis, 1743-1811, U.S., jur. Served in Continental Congress 1776-78 and 1784-85, and signed Articles of Confederation in 1778. He later served as associate justice of the Supreme Court of Massachusetts from 1785-91 and chief justice from 1791-1806. REF.: *CBA*.

Dana, Richard Henry, 1815-82, U.S., lawyer. Wrote about maritime law in *The Seaman's Friend* in 1841. He was a prosecuting attorney from 1867-68 at the trial of Jefferson Davis. REF.: *CBA*.

Danaher, John Anthony, b.1899, U.S., jur. Served as secretary of state for Connecticut from 1933-35 and as U.S. senator from 1939-45. He was a member of the president's Commission on Internal Security and Individual Rights from 1951 and was appointed to the District of Columbia Circuit Court by President Dwight Eisenhower in 1953. REF.: *CBA*.

Danby, Benjamin, d.1832, Brit., (unsolv.) mur. In December 1832, essayist Charles Lamb was living with his wife at the residence of Edward Moon at Enfield, England, when Lamb's daughter Emma paid an unexpected visit. Lamb went to the Crown and Horseshoe Inn to buy refreshments. He later recalled that the pub was in a "cheerful blaze." A game of dominos was in progress, and Lamb was invited to join in. One of the players, a sailor named Benjamin Danby, told Lamb he had known him since he was a child, when Danby's father was Lamb's hairdresser. Lamb did not remember the man, but he did recall the old hairdresser with fondness.

Lamb soon went home, leaving Danby, Cooper, Sleath, and Johnson to their merriment. He later learned that Danby lapsed into drunkenness and squandered his money. Late that night, the thoroughly intoxicated Danby was robbed and murdered in Holt's White Lane leading out of Enfield. Appearing at the inquest the next day, Lamb said there was something peculiar about the domino players that night. He noted, "One often fancies things afterwards that did not perhaps strike one at the time. I have felt queer ever since. It has almost sickened me of the Crown and Horseshoe, and I shan't hastily go into the taproom again."

REF.: Altick, *Victorian Studies In Scarlet*; *CBA*.

Dance, George (AKA: **George the Younger**), 1741-1825, Brit., architect. Oversaw the rebuilding of Newgate Prison in 1770. REF.: *CBA*.

Dancey, Alfred, prom. 1849, Brit., mansl. On Dec. 23, 1849, friends William Braund and Henry Coggan, both nineteen, and Edward Horgan, who was slightly younger, were crossing the Bedminster Bridge when they met two 14-year-olds, Alfred Dancey and his friend, Collins. When the older boys began taunting Dancey, whom they did not know, a heated argument with verbal abuse ensued. Dancey pulled a gun from his pocket and Collins held a life preserver in front of his chest. The frightened Horgan backed off, rejoining his friends, who had already pulled back. Meeting the others near the house of Bristol magistrate Samuel Brown, Horgan told of Dancey's threat. Shortly after, Collins and Dancey came over and the arguments heated up again. Braund, who had taken the life preserver, was picking up Collins off the ground when Dancey fired at Braund and killed him. Several passersby did not interfere up to this point, presumably unaware of Dancey's weapon. Dancey fled, but was soon picked up by a van driver who had witnessed the scene. When asked about the killing, Dancey replied, "I did it in passion," adding, "I hope a doctor's been sent for." At the police station, Dancey said the pistol had gone off half-cocked. At the inquest, the charge was willful murder. Dancey was tried at Gloucester on Apr. 4, 1850, and was found Guilty of manslaughter, the reduced charges resulting in part because of his request for a surgeon. He was sentenced to ten years of transportation.

REF.: *CBA;* Wilson, *Children Who Kill.*

D'Andrea, Nicholas J., 1932-81, U.S., (unsolv.) org. crime-mur. While answering an anonymous distress call on Sept. 13, 1981, members of the Crete, Ill., Township, Fire Department made a grisly discovery. The charred remains of a man were pulled from a burning car on Fairhorn Road, east of Illinois Highway One. Dental records identified the victim as Nicholas J. D'Andrea, reputed mob figure and right-hand man to Albert (Caesar) Tocco, who ruled the south suburban operations for the Chicago crime syndicate.

D'Andrea had been beaten to death and his body stuffed in the trunk of the family's 1970 Mercedes-Benz. At the time of his death, the government was investigating his role in an organized car-theft ring and ongoing vice activities in Cook, Will, and Lake counties. D'Andrea's brother, the late Armand D'Andrea, of Joliet, Ill., was involved in mob operations.

The slaying of Nicholas D'Andrea was believed to be in retaliation for the shooting of Alfred Pilotto at the Lincolnshire Country Club in Crete. Tocco and Pilotto were former associates. When Pilotto was gunned down, officials surmised that it was the murderous Tocco who had ordered the hit. See: **Tocco, Albert Caesar.** REF.: *CBA.*

D'Andrea, Philip, d.1952, U.S., org. crime. Phil D'Andrea completed his apprenticeship in the Chicago mob as Al Capone's top bodyguard. From the very beginning his status in the organization was a lofty one. D'Andrea occupied a lavish office suite adjacent to Capone at the gang's command post: the lavish Lexington Hotel on South Michigan Avenue. Even though his brother and uncle were both Catholic priests, D'Andrea wanted no part of the religious life.

Chicago gangster Phil D'Andrea.

His loyalty was always with Al Capone. When the Chicago crime boss went to trial for income tax evasion in 1931, D'Andrea followed him into court packing a .38-caliber pistol. In his pocket court bailiffs found a courtesy card from the Illinois Police Association, and the West Park Police Association extending him "all rights and privileges." A written request from a Chicago Police officer seeking promotion to the Detective Bureau was among D'Andrea's papers. His influence extended to the highest echelons of the Chicago Police Department.

In 1943 D'Andrea was one of eight mobsters indicted by a New York Grand Jury along with Willie Bioff and George Browne in the Hollywood extortion case. Bioff and Browne turned state's evidence against the racketeers in return for reduced sentences. As a result of their testimony Phil D'Andrea was sentenced to ten years in the federal penitentiary in Atlanta. He served less than one third of his time, thanks to the friendly intervention of a Washington politician who inveigled the United States Parole Board to reduce the sentence. In addition to D'Andrea, such Chicago mob luminaries as Paul "the Waiter" Ricca, Louis "Little New York" Campagna, and Charles "Cherry Nose" Gioe were granted their freedom. In failing health, D'Andrea made his last public appearance before the Kefauver Rackets Committee in 1950. The panel took pity on the aging gangster and excused him.

REF.: *CBA;* Fried, *The Rise and Fall of the Jewish Gangster in America;* Gage, *Mafia, U.S.A.;* Kobler, *Capone;* Lait and Mortimer, *Chicago: Confidential;* McPhaul, *Johnny Torrio;* Messick, *Secret File;* ____ and Goldblatt, *The Mobs and the Mafia;* Morgan, *Prince of Crime;* Reid, *The Grim Reapers;* Smith, *Syndicate City;* Spiering, *The Man Who Got Capone.*

Dane, Nathan, 1752-1835, U.S., jur. Served in Continental Congress from 1785-87 and wrote the eight volume *General Abridgment and Digest of American Law,* in 1823 with additional volume in 1829. Harvard Law School's Dane professorship is named for him. REF.: *CBA.*

D'Angely, Eva, prom. 1905, Brit., pros. On May 1, 1905, London police arrested a Frenchwoman, Eva D'Angely, on a charge of soliciting. She spoke little English, and through a man who accompanied her, the police learned that she had been in the country only two months. The man, who identified himself as her husband, explained that he had been waiting for her before her arrest.

Because D'Angely was a newcomer to the city and in consideration of the testimony offered by her husband, the charges were dropped. The newly installed Liberal government seized upon the acquittal of D'Angely as somehow reflective of a larger, more widespread corruption that infected the police force and the court system. A Royal Commission was established to investigate D'Angely's charges, but by the time it reported its findings, she had fled the country.

The police had been hoodwinked. Well-dressed pimps often would assume an air of respectability by posing as husbands, throwing the police off the scent. In this case, D'Angely and the man succeeded in throwing the government into an uproar.

REF.: Browne, *Rise of Scotland Yard; CBA.*

D'Anglemont, Germaine (Germaine Houet), b.1891, Fr., mur. In the 1910s and 1920s Germaine D'Anglemont became the darling of Paris. Once a humble orphan, D'Anglemont rose from poverty to lead a fabled life as mistress to some of the most famous men in Europe.

Born into miserable poverty as Germaine Houet, she adopted the name D'Anglemont from a novel. After running away from an orphanage at the age of fifteen, D'Anglemont arrived in the City of Lights where she soon employed her charms to lure a Dutch millionaire, Van Horschoot, to her bed. From that day on she had countless wealthy lovers, all eager to be in her company. There was Prince Franz Josef from the royal house of Bavaria who is said to have perished from a broken heart when the mademoiselle spurned his offer of marriage, a Polish count named Wielsinski, and the Aga Khan.

Years passed, and with them a measure of the beauty that so captivated a generation of eligible men. In her later years, D'Anglemont kept company with a handsome young politician named Causeret, who served the French legal system as Chief Magistrate. By this time, D'Anglemont was a jealous, possessive lover. She hired a detective to trace Causeret's every movement. One day in 1939, after Causeret told D'Anglemont that he was to meet with an older gentleman, the detective reported that Causeret had purchased silk pajamas.

Angered by what she thought to be a betrayal of her love, D'Anglemont shot Causeret to death in her flat on the Place Beauvais. At her trial, the judge and jury took pity on the aging courtesan. She was found Guilty, but in consideration of her circumstances, a recommendation for mercy was granted. Germaine D'Anglemont received eleven months in prison amid the well-wishes of her many friends and admirers.

REF.: *CBA;* Corder, *Murder My Love.*

Daniel, Peter Vivian, 1784-1860, U.S., jur. Served as U.S. district judge in Virginia from 1836-41 and U.S. Supreme Court associate justice from 1841-60, appointed by President Martin Van Buren. As a Supreme Court justice, he voted against the majority in *Prigg v. Pennsylvania* in 1842, the case which stated that only the federal government could enact fugitive slave laws. He voted with the majority in the Dred Scott case, *Scott v. Sanford,* in 1857, the landmark case which held that all blacks came to the

U.S. as property. REF.: *CBA*.

Daniel, Robert, and West, John, d.1948, U.S., rape-mur. On July 20, 1948, a pair of dangerous convicts escaped from the Ohio State Reformatory Farm. Making their way through the Ohio countryside, they murdered Superintendent John Niebel, and his wife, then raped the couple's young daughter.

Daniel and West eluded statewide roadblocks, killing a truck driver and a motorist before being overtaken at last. John West, who was described by prison psychologists as having the intelligence of a "near moron," was gunned down in the ambush. Robert Daniels was taken back to prison and eventually executed. REF.: *CBA*.

Daniel, Vickie, 1947- , Case of, U.S., mur. District Judge Leonard Giblin of Liberty, Texas, had earned a reputation as a strong "law and order" man. So when he acquitted Vickie Daniel of murdering her husband, Price, on Oct. 30, 1981, there was a strong reaction: "We were all shocked...there's a message there; you can kill...and get away with it," Price Daniel's sister said, revealing the sentiments of many.

Vickie was working as a waitress in 1976 when she married Price Daniel, Jr., the son of former Texas governor and U.S. Senator, Price Daniel, Sr.. Price, Jr., was a lawyer and real estate tycoon. The couple had quarreled bitterly and often about their impending divorce. However, this time, Vicki feared for her safety. The 34-year-old housewife and mother seized a .22-caliber rifle and pointed it at her husband. When he refused to back away she fired a shot into the air as if to warn him. Then, when a second shot rang out, her mind went blank. "He said he was going to kill me," she told a hushed courtroom in Liberty. She continued, "I didn't want him to hit me anymore. I moved back, I don't remember anything. I closed my eyes." Despite her testimony, the sheriff's office succumbed to strong pressure from Price Daniel, Sr., and charged the widow with murder.

Fingerprints revealed in trace metal tests confirmed that Price Daniel, Jr. had, indeed, had his hands on the gun barrel before the fatal shot was fired. This evidence compelled Judge Giblin, after a five-day bench trial, to acquit Vickie Daniel of murder charges. "As you know, I'm so law and order oriented that I couldn't {sic} hardly say the words Not Guilty," Giblin said. REF.: *CBA*.

Daniels, Benjamin F., prom. 1900s, U.S., west. lawman. Daniels began as a buffalo hunter in the 1870s while a teenager and was a deputy sheriff in Arizona in the early 1880s. In 1887, Daniels was bartending at Fort McKavett, in Menard County, Texas, when John Vaden, a gunman, goaded Daniels into a duel. Both men drew their six-guns and fired almost at the same instant. Daniels' aim was true, and he killed Vaden on the spot. He was never indicted for the shooting. In 1884, Daniels tracked down William Delaney, a lethal desperado who was one of the killers responsible for the Bisbee, Ariz., Massacre. Daniels later worked as a deputy in Oklahoma under Bill Tilghman and served with Teddy Roosevelt's Rough Riders in the Spanish-American War, fight-

Lawman Ben Daniels.

ing at San Juan Hill and earning Roosevelt's praise. Roosevelt later appointed Daniels a U.S. marshal. He served in Arizona and New Mexico with distinction during the 1900s and retired with honors. See: **Bisbee, Ariz., Massacre; Delaney, William E.**

REF.: Bartholomew, *The Biographical Album of Western Gunfighters*; *CBA*; Hunter and Rose, *The Album of Gunfighters*.

Daniels, James, d.1865, U.S., mur.-lynch. In 1865, James Daniels murdered a man named Gartley in a gambling dispute. The two reached for their guns at the same time, but Daniels was faster. Gartley dropped dead to the floor, and upon hearing the news of his death, his widow suffered a fatal heart attack. The Montana Vigilance Committee did not lynch Daniels, but turned him in to authorities.

Daniels, a Californian, was convicted of second-degree murder and sentenced to three years in prison. He served only a few months before receiving a pardon. A clerical error seems to have resulted in Daniels' early release. The vigilantes vowed to correct the mistake.

After his release, Daniels swore revenge against the men he held responsible for his imprisonment. But when he slipped back into Helena, the vigilance committee seized him and hanged him without benefit of trial. REF.: *CBA*.

Daniels, May, prom. 1926-27, Fr., (unsolv.) mur. Jean Euchin, a farmer near the Commune of Wimille, a seaside resort in the Boulogne region of France, was walking across his field on Feb. 26, 1927 when he found the decomposing remains of May Daniels, a 21-year-old nurse who had been missing since October. Daniels had been been strangled, and littered around her body were a hairbrush, a bracelet, curling tongs, a perfume bottle, a hypodermic syringe, and a box that probably once contained morphia tablets. Daniels had disappeared on Oct. 6, 1926. The day before, she had spent her day off with a friend, Marcella McCarthy, also a nurse. They had taken an impromptu trip from Brighton, England, to Boulogne aboard the pleasure boat, the *Waverley*. While in France, the two women decided to take a side trip and explore the Saint Beauve Beach. Daniels apparently accompanied McCarthy on this trip as local residents reported seeing the pair together in a hotel later in the day, inquiring about lodging. The next day, Oct. 8, however, McCarthy was reported to have gone alone to the British Consulate where she requested a passport. Then, boarding the channel boat alone, she returned to England.

Dr. Charles Paul, a French pathologist, performed the autopsy and said that Daniels had been strangled by "a very strong hand," a man's hand. McCarthy said that as the two women were crossing from Brighton to Boulogne, a middle-aged man stared at them and later followed them through the streets of Boulogne. But McCarthy's statements showed several minor discrepancies. McCarthy said they had gone to the pier together, Daniels had gone to the cloakroom, and she never saw her again. McCarthy saw the boat depart, and thought that Daniels had gone alone. McCarthy contacted the British Consulate, explaining Daniels' disappearance, then wired her sister for money, and stayed in a convent for a few days until the cash came. McCarthy's dates and those of Consul G.H.B. Gilmour were different.

In April, W.J.E. Mark came forward to say he had seen a woman of Daniels' description on Oct. 10, four days after Daniels vanished. On Sept. 30, French criminal Charles Gras said he had murdered Daniels, but the ex-convict was known to be a great liar, and nothing developed from his "confession." Scotland Yard was said to be investigating a convict serving time at Parkhurst who was alleged to have a photograph of Daniels in his cell. Daniels' brother, Harold Daniels, said, "It is utter nonsense to suggest...that she committed suicide because of some secrets she wished to take to the grave." The French police questioned a man arrested in Boulogne for theft, whose wife said he had killed the young woman. This, too, went nowhere, and the slaying of Daniels remains unsolved.

REF.: *CBA*; Greenwall, *They Were Murdered In France*; Morain, *The Underworld of Paris*.

Daniels, Murl, 1924-49, and **West, John Coulter**, d.1948, U.S., mur. While incarcerated in the Mansfield Ohio Reformatory, Murl Daniels and John Coulter West swore that if they were ever free they would return to kill a guard named Harris who had treated them badly. Daniels was serving a twenty-five-year sentence for robbery, and West was in prison for stealing the tires off a truck.

When Daniels and West were paroled, they committed a series of armed robberies throughout the Midwest, and killed a tavern owner. The two then returned to Mansfield, but were unable to find Harris. They decided to get his address from John Elmer Niebel, Harris' immediate superior. Daniels and West roused Niebel one night and led him into a cornfield along with his wife and daughter. The robbers planned to tie them to a post and force Niebel to reveal the whereabouts of Harris, but they forgot to bring any rope, so they simply shot the family and drove to Cleveland.

One of the most intensive manhunts in Ohio history began. Daniels and West drove around the state, avoiding one roadblock after another. They commandeered a car and a truck and killed both drivers before they were finally tracked down. The killers climbed aboard a haulaway carrying new Studebakers. The police became suspicious when they realized the vehicle was driving back toward the plant rather than away from it. When the truck stopped, West began firing, wounding a policeman before being shot to death. After the death of his cohort, Daniels was forced to surrender. He was executed in the electric chair on Jan. 3, 1949. REF.: *CBA*.

Mrs. Daniels returning home drunk to her murderous husband.

Daniels, Thomas, prom. 1761, Brit., mur. Although Thomas Daniels was convicted of murdering his wife, it is possible that no murder took place. Daniels was a carpenter when he met Sarah Carridine, and the two decided to marry. His parents would not approve so the two agreed to live together. When his parents learned of this arrangement a quarrel ensued. Daniels, who worked for the father, was immediately fired.

Needing a job, Daniels signed on board the privateer *Britannia*. Sarah was not happy, but Daniels promised to marry her when he returned with his fortune. In Daniels' absence, Sarah took up with a friend of Daniels', John Jones. In eight months, Daniels returned from the sea. Not only had he not made his fortune but he lacked the money to pay for a marriage license. He finally raised the cash by pawning his watch; Sarah and Daniels were married. However, even after the wedding, Sarah continued her affair with Jones.

Daniels soon discovered the deception. His wife, confronted with her infidelity, promised to break off with Jones, but continued seeing her lover. Moreover, Sarah, always a heavy drinker, began to consume more and more alcohol. The marriage deteriorated rapidly.

Returning home one night, Daniels found himself locked out. He forced the door open and a violent struggle followed. According to Daniels, his wife hit him over the head with a hard object and he fell to the floor. Daniels was lying face down on

the floor, he later stated, so he did not see what happened next. He heard Sarah shout, "Oh save me, save me!" When he looked up she was gone.

Her body was later found beneath the open window. Even though there were no marks on the corpse, a surprising fact, considering the struggle described by Daniels, the husband was arrested and charged with murder. He insisted throughout the trial that his wife had thrown herself from the window, presumably thinking she had killed her husband. Daniels was nevertheless convicted and condemned to death. Because the evidence was so contrary to this verdict, Daniles was immediately pardoned by the king.

REF.: *CBA*; Mitchell, *The Newgate Calendar*.

Daniels, Thomas H. (AKA: Daniel H. Thomas), d.1819, U.S., count.-rob.-mur. Thomas H. Daniels was a practicing counterfeiter and flagrant horse thief who robbed and killed Jacob Gould in Stoneham, Mass., on Nov. 25, 1819. Daniels was apprehended a short time later and placed in Middlesex Prison where, on Dec. 13, 1819, he hanged himself with a handkerchief. Before his death, Daniels told a prison guard that with his long record of convictions he did not expect to win his trial over the Gould killing.

REF.: *CBA*; *Some Particulars of the Life of Thomas H. Daniels*.

Danilo (Danilo Petrovic Njegos), 1677-1737, Montenegro, ruler, mur. Danilo Petrovic Njegos was the first prince-bishop of Montenegro by birth. Danilo led the massacre of Mohammedans in 1702 and was almost killed by the Turks that same year. REF.: *CBA*.

Danilo I (Danilo Petrovic Njegos), 1826-60, Montenegro, ruler, assass. Danilo I discontinued the title of Prince-bishop of Montenegro in 1851 and reigned as crowned prince from 1852-60. Danilo I pursued a reform policy which was opposed by some and which ultimately may have led to his assassination. REF.: *CBA*.

Daniloff, Jeanne, b.c.1868-91, Fr., suic.-mur. Born to a Russian count attached to the court of Czar Alexander, it may have been possible for Jeanne Daniloff to live a privileged life if only her father hadn't squandered all of his money at the gambling tables of Europe. This would not be the first time that chance would let Jeanne Daniloff down.

In 1884, Daniloff met a young French lieutenant, George Weiss, whose regiment was stationed in Algiers. She became his mistress, and later, his wife. In 1889, Weiss left the military and they moved to Ain-Fezza. There, Daniloff spent all her energies raising children and attending to the needs of her husband. That is, until her husband introduced her to the hypnotic Rasputin-like engineer, Felix Roques.

Roques, who was working on the West Algerian railway, began to spend his leisure time luring Daniloff into having an affair with him. She declined his advances at first, but eventually broke down, deciding to leave the matter entirely to chance. On Nov. 13, 1889, Daniloff made the decision to become Roques' mistress by the flip of a coin.

By March 1890, Daniloff was pregnant with Roques' child and her husband had become an encumbrance to the life she preferred. On May 18, Daniloff and Roques decided on the solution: poison George Weiss with arsenic. Pushing beyond her guilt, Daniloff began, in September, to add the deadly chemical to his soup and milk.

Weiss became violently ill, but did not die. When a family friend named deGuerry intercepted a letter from Daniloff to her lover who was waiting for her in Madrid, his lingering suspicions about Daniloff's improprieties were confirmed. He turned the love letter over to police, and as a result, Felix Roques was arrested.

Having failed in an attempt to kill herself, Daniloff went to trial on May 28, 1891, at the Cour d'Assises in Oran. "I did not act of my own free will," she told the court, "I obeyed the orders given me by the man I loved: these orders were imperatively repeated in the last letters I received before my arrest."

The next day, Daniloff was found Guilty of attempted murder. But the court also determined that there were extenuating circumstances surrounding the case. Daniloff was sentenced to twenty years of penal servitude and her lover Felix Roques, who had committed suicide while in prison, was held fully responsible for his mistress' actions.

Unable to face twenty years in jail, Jeanne Daniloff ingested a packet of strychnine and, like her lover, died alone in her prison cell.

REF.: *CBA;* Irving, *Studies of French Criminals of the Nineteenth Century;* Sanders, *Murder in the Big Cities.*

Dann, Laurie Wasserman, 1957-88, U.S., suic.-mur. The question most often asked about child murderer Laurie Dann after the shooting tragedy that left an 8-year-old boy dead and five other youngsters wounded, was how could a woman with a long history of mental illness obtain a permit to carry a .357 magnum?

On the morning of May 20, 1988, Dann, a 30-year-old divorcee, drove to several area homes where she had worked as a baby sitter leaving packages of food laced with arsenic on the doorsteps. She soon arrived at the home of Padraig and Marian Rushe in Winnetka, Ill., a suburb on Chicago's fashionable North Shore. The couple had employed Dann as a baby-sitter for their two sons, aged four and six. Dann was to drive the boys to a carnival, but instead went to the Ravinia Elementary School, where she set fire to a plastic bag filled with incendiary liquid. The fire was quickly extinguished. Dann then drove to a daycare center in Highland Park and after lurking around the grounds with a gasoline can, returned to the Rushe home. She locked the two Rushe children in the basement where their mother was doing laundry, and set fire to the stairwell. But, Mrs. Rushe shattered a window to escape with her children.

Meanwhile, Dann drove to the Hubbard Woods Elementary School. She casually walked into the building carrying three handguns, slipped into the boys' rest room, and fired on 6-year-old Robert Trossman with the .357 magnum. The boy crawled into the hallway, where a teacher found him and notified the principal. By then Dann had entered the second grade classroom of Amy Moses, thirty, who had divided the children into six study groups. Brandishing the second gun, Dann ordered the teacher to line up the children at one end of the room. Moses tried to disarm Laurie Dann, whose shots hit six children. Eight-year-old Nicholas Corwin was fatally wounded. The other five youngsters, Lindsay Fisher, eight, Kathryn Miller, seven, Mark Tebourek, eight, Peter Munro, eight, and the Trossman boy were removed to area hospitals after Dann fled the building. The school was in chaos when the police arrived a few minutes later.

Dann drove her white Toyota into a tree a few blocks from the school. She abandoned the car and entered the home of Ruth Ann Andrew and her son Philip, a 20-year-old University of Illinois college student. She told them she had been raped and had shot the rapist, but now the police were after her for the killing. When Philip Andrew tried to wrest the gun from Dann, she shot him. After a harried phone call to her mother, Dann holed up in the second floor washroom while police officers from nine adjoining suburbs surrounded the house. Dann's father, Norman Wasserman, with whom she had lived following her divorce from Russell Dann, pleaded with his daughter to surrender to authorities. A police commando squad from the Northern Illinois Police Alarm System stormed the house, but Laurie Dann had already shot herself to death.

Laurie Dann attended the University of Arizona in the late 1970s, but never earned a degree. A former boyfriend remembered her as dangerous and unstable. He had received a series of threatening phone calls from Dann after the relationship ended. In 1982, she married Russell Dann, whom she met while working as a waitress at a North Shore country club. The marriage ended four years later, and while the divorce was pending, Russell Dann told police that an assailant had entered his room one night and stabbed him with an ice pick. He believed the intruder was his estranged wife, but could not be certain. The case was dropped due to insufficient evidence. Laurie Dann later accused her ex-husband of raping her and bought the first of three handguns.

Shortly after Russell Dann reported the ice pick incident, Laurie Dann's former boyfriend in Tucson, Ariz., began receiving more threatening calls and letters, which prompted an FBI investigation. Agents traced Dann to the University of Wisconsin, where she was sporadically attending classes as a "guest" student and had a reputation as a dangerous eccentric after several acquaintances reported their property vandalized. Neighbors at the student housing complex recalled that Dann had ridden the elevators up and down for no apparent reason. Dann moved back to her parents in Glencoe, where she had a police record for shoplifting and had allegedly vandalized homes where she worked as a baby-sitter. "The parents had a responsibility and a duty to act," said attorney Robert Patterson, who filed a lawsuit against the Danns on behalf of Philip Andrew. The Illinois Mental Health and Developmental Disabilities Code mandates the involuntary commitment of individuals who are deemed a threat to themselves and members of the community.

Lawsuits against the Danns accumulated. Meanwhile, the five wounded children returned to school after receiving medical and psychological treatment. A few months later, Police Chief Herbert Timm told a gathering of 280 police investigators and school officials, "If it can happen in an idyllic community like Winnetka, which really does believe it's Camelot, then it can happen anywhere." REF.: *CBA.*

Danos, Abel (AKA: **Mammouth**), d.1952, Fr., burg.-treas.-tort.-mur. Before WWII, Abel Danos was known to the French police as a crafty burglar who posed as a gas collector and meter reader. In this way, he was able to gain easy admittance to numerous houses and apartments in Paris. But it was the arrival of the occupying German army in 1940 that provided Danos with his big break.

A fat, disagreeable man, Danos began forging Gestapo identification cards, which he used with some success in extorting money and valuables from French citizens. However, Inspector Pierry Bony of the French Gestapo arrested Danos and threatened him with death unless he agreed to go to work for him.

In the next few years, Danos tortured and executed more than 100 Resistance fighters and their families. He was arrested in 1944 when France was liberated, but he managed to escape from the confines of the crowded, underguarded prison. He set himself up as a black-market profiteer, finally returning to his original occupation of hold-up man. In October 1948, he killed two Italian policemen during robberies in Milan and Genoa. There were additional murders attributed to this diabolical killer before he was taken by police in 1948. When Danos' father heard the news about the secret life his son had led, he hanged himself.

Danos served three years in a French prison before surviving members of the Resistance demanded that he face a firing squad. After some political wrangling, the request was granted. Danos was taken to Fort Valrien on Mar. 14, 1952, and executed in the same spot where so many members of the Resistance had died because of his treasonous acts during the war.

REF.: *CBA;* Goodman, *Villainy Unlimited.*

Danquah, Joseph Kwame Kyeretwi Boakye, 1895-1965, Ghana, treas. Joseph Kwame Danquah helped found the United Gold Coast Convention in 1947 and became legislator of Gold Coast assembly from 1951-54. He was placed in prison from 1961-62 and 1964-65 for opposing the dictatorial policies of President Nkrumah. REF.: *CBA.*

Danton, Georges Jacques, 1759-94, Fr., treas. Instigated the Tuileries riots in 1792. He served as revolutionary minister of justice and was elected to the National Convention. The following year he called for the death of King Louis XVI and was elected president of the Jacobin Club, which sought a strong republican government. With the rise of Maximilien Robespierre and the Reign of Terror, Danton was imprisoned and sentenced to death by the guillotine. REF.: *CBA.*

D'Aquino, Iva Toguri (AKA: Tokyo Rose), 1916- , U.S., treas. Before the bombing of Pearl Harbor plunged the U.S. into WWII, Iva Toguri lived a quiet, normal life in Los Angeles, Calif. A first-generation Japanese-American, she liked actor James Stewart and the U.C.L.A. football team. She seemed an unlikely traitor.

When the war in the Pacific began in December 1941, Toguri was visiting her sick aunt in Tokyo after being granted authorization for a six-month stay by the U.S. government. She became one of six Japanese-American women trapped behind enemy lines. In November 1943, she went on the air for the first time. To lonely sailors and GIs she became widely known as Tokyo Rose. She was actually one of seven women to play the part.

In a syrupy voice laden with sarcasm, Toguri introduced American records and spread defeatist propaganda to U.S. troops in the Pacific. She had been selected as the female voice of "Zero Hour" by Radio Tokyo on the recommendation of Major Charles Cousens, an Australian army officer captured at the battle of Corregidor. Cousens was pressured into producing radio programs by his Japanese captors. At first she read from rather bland scripts that had been written by Cousens and Wallace Ince, a U.S. army officer who was also seized at Corregidor. But soon the tone of the broadcasts became very slanted against the allied war effort.

"Hi boys...this is your old friend," she would say at the beginning of each broadcast. "I've got some swell new recordings for you just in from the States. You'd better enjoy them while you can, because tomorrow at 0600 you're hitting Saipan...and we're ready for you. So, while you're alive, let's listen to..." And so it went for nearly two years. She was arrested as a war criminal following the Japanese surrender, and was extradited back to the U.S. to stand trial.

The maven of the airwaves sat motionless as the prosecution made its opening remarks on July 5, 1949. In published interviews, Toguri claimed that her broadcasts were coached by Japanese propagandists. Whether Tokyo Rose was forced to disseminate anti-U.S. diatribes or had done so voluntarily remains a matter of conjecture.

The twelve-week trial yielded a Guilty verdict. Toguri became the sixth U.S. citizen to be convicted of treason since the close of the war. The others included Nazi propagandists Douglas Chandler and Robert Best; army deserter turned storm trooper James Monti; Mildred (Axis Sally) Gillars; and Tomoya Kawakita, who served as an interpreter in a Japanese prisoner of war camp. Toguri was sentenced to ten years in prison and assessed a $10,000 fine. She served six-and-one-half years at the Alderson Federal Reformatory in West Virginia before earning her release in 1956. On Jan. 19, 1977, President Gerald Ford officially pardoned Tokyo Rose for her war-time activities on behalf of the Japanese. At the time, she was the owner and manager of Toguri's, an Oriental gift shop on Chicago's North Side. See: **Best, Robert Henry; Gillars, Mildred; Joyce, William.** REF.: *CBA.*

D'Aragona, Giovanna (AKA: Duchess of Malfi), 1478-1513, Italy, assass. The tragic story of Giovanna D'Aragona, the Duchess of Malfi, has been retold by several generations of famous playwrights, including Lope de Vega, who first dramatized her murder in 1618. In 1623, the *Duchess of Malfi* was republished by the English playwright John Webster, and has since gone through many revivals.

The play is based on the Renaissance story of Giovanna D'Aragona, who was married when she was only twelve. Following the death of her husband in 1620, Giovanna became the Duchess of Malfi. Determined not to allow the young widow to remarry, her brothers Duke Ferdinand and the Cardinal took secret steps to break up her romance with her steward, Antonio Bologna. Giovanna secretly married the penniless steward and had a son by him. Several years passed, and the identity of the husband remained secret. The Duchess gave birth to two more children. Meanwhile, the scheming brothers hired a spy, Daniel de Bosola, to determine the identity of the father. One night, Duke Ferdinand and his confederate entered the bedchambers of Giovanna determined to pry the truth from her.

The frightened young woman accidentally divulged her husband's identity, and the cardinal excommunicated both of them. Then, at the Duke's urging, Bosola killed the Duchess. When the principal conspirators died, the rights of the surviving son were restored. REF.: *CBA.*

d'Aragona, Tullia, prom. 1540s, Ital., pros. As a result of the publication of Aretino's titillating *Dialogues,* Pope Paul III (1534-49) ordered a general crackdown against Italian vice. A number of famous courtesans, including Tullia d'Aragona, were reclassified as prostitutes and stripped of their former privileged status in society. D'Aragona was the daughter of another famous courtesan, Giula Ferrarese.
REF.: Bullough, *Illustrated History of Prostitution; CBA.*

Darbey, Maurice, prom. 1956, Brit., (unsolv.) attempt. mur. On Nov. 1, 1956, a package was delivered to the Bristol, England, home of Maurice Darbey, a veteran of Dunkirk who worked for a tobacco company. The package exploded when Darbey opened it at the breakfast table. Darbey lost one eye and sustained an injury to the other. His wife, daughter and father were also injured. The explosive was charged with gelignite, which ignited when two studs, connected by wire to a battery, were released. The only clues were the handwritten address, the Paddington-Notting-Hill London district postage mark, the posting date, Oct. 31, and a piece of metal marked "Enosis," the slogan of a Greek-Cypriot terrorist organization. Darbey had never been to Cyprus, and was not known to have enemies. It was thought that the bomb had been mailed to him by mistake, or that the name may have been planted to confuse police. The maker or makers of the bomb were never found.
REF.: *CBA;* Furneaux, *Famous Criminal Cases, Vol. 4.*

Darby, Laetitia, prom. 1810, Brit., pros. Darby was the mistress of Sixteen-string Jack, a notorious British criminal who was hanged during the reign of King George III. After her lover died, Darby took up with the Duke of York, the son of King George.
REF.: Bleackley, *Hangmen of England; CBA.*

D'Arcy, Patrick, d.1967, Ire., suic.-mur. Patrick D'Arcy was a lady-killer involved with a mother and her daughter at the same time. He murdered them both in 1967.

The battered body of 28-year-old Maria Domenech was found at the bottom of a steep cliff on the west coast of Ireland. The dark-haired young social worker from New York had joined D'Arcy at Orly Airport in Paris just two days before. They had flown to Ireland the same day, and chartered a car in Dublin to drive across the country. When they arrived at Moher two days later, D'Arcy threw her over the side and rifled her handbag of traveler's checks.

At the same time, Maria's 51-year-old mother Virginia Domenech was reported missing from her home in New York. Her body was never found, though investigators surmised that D'Arcy panicked and killed them both when he was no longer able to carry on a multiple affair. The answers to the puzzle were never supplied by the killer, who committed suicide in a Florida motel room several weeks after Maria's body was found. REF.: *CBA.*

Darcy, Thomas (Baron of Templehurst), c.1467-1537, Brit., treas. Led troops of Henry VIII in France in 1513. He broke off relations with the king over the issue of papal authority in 1529 discussed a possible European invasion of England by the forces of Holy Roman Emperor Charles V in order to restore Catholicism. He was arrested for treason, tried, and beheaded. REF.: *CBA.*

Darden, Willie Jasper, 1933-88, U.S., mur. On a rainy day in September 1973, Helen Turman was tending to her furniture store in Lakeland, Fla., when a black man entered. He examined some items on display, then left. He returned a few minutes later, and pressed a gun to Mrs. Turman's back. At that moment, her husband, James Turman, returned from feeding their two poodles. The gunman whirled around and fired a shot into the unsuspecting man's head. He then ordered Mrs. Turman to perform oral sex in the presence of her dying husband.

A 16-year-old named Phillip Arnold ran in to see what the commotion was all about. The killer fired a shot at Arnold, hitting him in the jaw. Two more bullets further wounded the teenager, who stumbled out the door calling for help. The same day, two other whites were killed in unrelated shooting incidents. Hostility was running at a fever pitch.

The next morning Willie Darden was arrested in Tampa, thirty miles away. Eyewitnesses told police that he was the man who had crashed his car into a telephone pole a little before 6:00 p.m. the night before. A detective located a .38-caliber Smith & Wesson pistol buried in a ditch about forty feet from the pole. Police were not sure at what time Mr. Turman had been shot, but estimates placed the time of the shooting between 5:15 and 6:00 p.m. It would have been difficult for Darden to drive through Lakeland and crash his car into the telephone pole at 6:00 if he had committed the murder. This puzzling factor helped keep Darden alive for fourteen years as his court-imposed death sentence went through an exhausting series of appeals.

Darden, who had a previous record of seven felony convictions for robbery and forgery, became a national celebrity. His case was publicized by Amnesty International, and a flock of show-business people, including actress Margot Kidder and rock star Peter Gabriel, filed protests with Florida prison officials and Governor Bob Martinez. A Darden defense committee was even organized in the Netherlands.

In published interviews from his jail cell in Starke, Fla., Darden accused the courts of overt racism. "It was close to election time," he said. "They needed a suspect. I was available." Darden denied carrying a gun, and produced eight witnesses who verified his whereabouts at the time of the shooting. But the positive identification given by Mrs. Turman and Arnold helped convict Darden. In March 1988, his appeals exhausted, Willie Darden died in the electric chair. REF.: *CBA*.

Dardi, Virgil David, prom. 1950s, U.S., fraud. Virgil Dardi had been a world-beating American businessman since the 1930s but he was never implicated in any wrongdoing until he encountered the super stock swindler, Lowell McAfee Birrell. Meeting Birrell at a cocktail party, Dardi was impressed with the con man's aggressive notions about business, and was even more impressed when Birrell urged him to become chairman of the board of his newly-acquired United Dye Company, a successful firm. Dardi was soon corrupted by Birrell to the point where he willingly allowed Birrell to siphon off more than $2 million of United Dye's assets and watched without objection as Birrell sold off all his stock in the gutted company.

Dardi went further, merging the crippled United Dye with the Handridge Oil Company, a firm controlled by con man Alexander Guterma and Las Vegas gamblers Irving Pasternak and Samuel Garfield. Dardi and Guterma, through a series of boiler room operations, floated and sold more stock in the merged firms, taking $5 million in profit and leaving the firm a gutted wreck. Shares that once sold for $15 per share were toppled to $1 per share. Some of the boiler room captains, irked at not being paid, informed authorities and Guterma was arrested. He informed on Dardi, who was tried, convicted, and given a seven-year prison term. Guterma was sent to prison for five years. Dardi's once well-respected career was finished, and he entered prison cursing the name of Lowell Birrell. See: **Birrell, Lowell McAfee**.

REF.: *CBA; Nash, Hustlers and Con Men*.

Darius III (Darius Codommanus, AKA: Old Persian Darayavaush), d.330 B.C., Persia, king, assass. When Alexander the Great's Greek troops moved east across Asia Minor and into Persia, they met the troops and satraps (governors) of King Darius III. The king himself was defeated at the battle of Arbela-Gaugamela, although he managed to escape into Bactria (now part of Afghanistan). There Bessus, one of Darius' satraps who had decided that Alexander was going to win, killed Darius and welcomed Alexander into his domain. REF.: *CBA*.

Dark Fountain, The, 1982, a novel by Jay Robert Nash. This work is based upon the horrific exploits of coast-to-coast strangler Earle Leonard Nelson (U.S.-Can., prom. 1926-28). REF: *CBA*. See: **Nelson, Earle Leonard**.

Darko, Alfred, 1940-   , Ger., burg. Under a nondescript suburban home outside Berlin, a storeroom contains 150 million Nazi files and documents that were seized by the Allies in 1945. The U.S. government maintains the storeroom, which is in a converted German bunker once used by the Nazis for wiretapping. A staff of curators and archivists assists researchers, the press, and criminal prosecutors who require specific information about former Nazis, but it is otherwise off-limits to the general public.

Beginning in 1983 it seemed that someone on the staff was stealing documents and selling them. The suspicions were confirmed when an employee named Alfred Darko was arrested in December 1988. Darko, a citizen of the Ivory Coast, had lived in West Germany for twenty years before his arrest.

He admitted to pilfering up to 4,000 items and selling them to private collectors for up to $3,000 per item. Darko said he was only carrying out orders from his superiors, but he steadfastly refused to reveal their identities. Among the missing items was a dossier on Klaus Barbie, the "Butcher of Lyons" who had recently been sentenced to life in prison for war crimes.

On Jan. 9, 1989, Judge Clemens Basdorf sentenced Darko to twenty-eight months in prison, admitting that there were other unnamed accomplices who probably would never be brought to trial. REF.: *CBA*.

Darlan, Jean Louis Xavier François, 1881-1942, Fr. Africa, assass. Served as French naval forces commander in chief in 1939, vice premier in 1941, and minister of defense from 1941-42 in Vichy regime, heading up all military operations. Following allied invasion of North Africa he became French African chief of state in 1942 and was assassinated on Christmas Eve. REF.: *CBA*.

Darling, Charles John (First Baron Darling of Langham, AKA: Little Darling), 1849-1936, Brit., jur. Appointed to the High Court in 1897 by Lord Chancellor, Lord Halsbury. Before retiring in 1923 he tried numerous murder cases, including the 1921 trial of Herbert Rowse Armstrong, who poisoned his wife. REF.: *CBA*.

Darling, Thomas, prom. 1596, Brit., witchcraft. In 1596, 14-year-old Thomas Darling of Burton, England, claimed to have witnessed "visions of hell" after being separated from his uncle in a forest near his home. The next day, he complained of illness, and of strange green cats and angels that tormented him. A physician stated that the boy did not suffer from any physical malady, but may have suffered from a "spell." Young Thomas lent credence to the suspicions by telling of a "little old woman...with three warts on her face" who had bewitched him after he tipped over her egg basket.

An elderly woman named Alice Gooderidge was seized and accused of being a witch. She was forced to implicate her husband and her mother, Elizabeth Wright, after the inquisitor nearly burned her feet off in front of an open fire. The case reached a swift conclusion when the exorcist, John Darrell, arrived in the village on May 27, 1596, to rid the boy of his "demons."

Darrell was in fact a trained ventriloquist who staged a "conversation" with a devil so that Tom Darling might be cured. Though he had admitted to staging the entire affair, Darling was physically coerced into admitting that he had been possessed and then cured by the exorcist. Gooderidge, who had been sentenced to twelve months in prison, died in her cell. REF.: *CBA*.

Darnand, Joseph, d.1945, Fr., war crimes. Joseph Darnand commanded the French secret militia on behalf of the Vichy Government during WWII. Patterned after the German SS, the *milice* brutally enforced the rule of Pierre Laval's collaborationist government. Darnand and 200 militiamen were captured by the British army in Italy on May 12, 1945. He was tried as a war criminal by the French government and shot by a firing squad on Oct. 10. "Long live France!" he cried, seconds before he was shot. See: **Laval, Pierre**. REF.: *CBA*.

Darnley, Lord Henry Stewart, 1545-67, Case of, Scot., (unsolv.)

mur. The relationship between Mary, Queen of Scots and Queen Elizabeth I played a major role in British crime history. In 1565, the staunchly Catholic 20-year-old Lord Henry Stewart Darnley became Mary's second husband. Although he was granted the title of king as an honor, he decided he wanted to inherit the throne of Scotland on Mary's death. There were a number of people ready to remove him from the line of succession. Darnley became jealous of Mary's trust in her secretary, David Rizzio. He and others probably conspired to kill Rizzio, who died on Mar. 9, 1566. Darnley diverted the blame to his accomplices, at least temporarily.

Soon, however, a number of conspirators, possibly including both Queen Mary and Elizabeth, became convinced that Darnley had to go. The young king was recovering from smallpox at a mansion near Edinburgh on the night of Feb. 9, 1567, when Mary came to visit him. After she left, a team of murderers entered Darnley's bedchamber and strangled him. Then they blew up the house to cover their tracks. Mary later married the Earl of Bothwell, who was suspected of having engineered Darnley's death. Mary's followers turned against her and forced her to flee to England. Eliza-

Lord Henry Stewart Darnley, murder victim.

beth kindly granted her "safety," in the form of eight years' house arrest. Elizabeth also tried to use the murder of Darnley against Mary, but the court refused to accept the "casket letters" which Mary had written as evidence of guilt. The queen finally executed Mary in 1587. After Elizabeth's death, the son of Mary and Darnley became James I, the King of England. See: **Rizzio, David.**

REF.: *CBA;* Davison, *The Casket Letters;* Johnson, *Famous Assassinations of History;* Linklater, *Fatal Fascination;* Nash, *Open Files;* Whitelaw, *Corpus Delicti.*

Darrow, Clarence Seward, 1857-1938, U.S., crim. law. Born in Kinsman, Ohio, Clarence Darrow was admitted to the bar in 1878, practicing in Chicago from 1887. He proved to be one of the most dynamic and electrifying speakers who ever addressed a jury. He was also an astute judge of character and a master of human psychology—attributes which won for him a number of spectacular cases. Long before Darrow's career ended, he had become the most celebrated criminal lawyer in the U.S. and he remains a legendary figure in the varied annals of criminal justice. Fearless and high-principled, Darrow was the champion of great liberal causes. He was one of the lawyers defending Socialist leader Eugene V. Debs in 1894 when Debs was charged with conspiracy in the Railroad Union case. Early on, Darrow became an unwavering opponent of capital punishment. In a famous speech delivered at the Cook County Jail in 1902, Darrow stated: "Hanging men in our county jails does not prevent murder. It makes murderers." It is not by accident that in the more than 100 cases where Darrow's clients were charged with murder, not one of them suffered capital punishment. It was Darrow's strenuous opposition to capital punishment that led him to befriend and champion the much-criticized John Peter Altgeld, who, as governor of Illinois in 1893, pardoned three of the labor leaders convicted in the Haymarket Riot of 1886. Impoverished and his political career ruined over the pardons, Altgeld was saved from destitution by Darrow who hired him as a member of his law firm in 1902.

Labor consumed Darrow's talents as he went to the rescue of union leaders who were decidedly the underdog in the early days of unionism. Some of these individuals were corrupt and deceitful but Darrow took them at their word and believed in their purposeful causes. Despite their personal weaknesses, he undertook their defense when it was not only unpopular to do so but often dangerous as anyone associated with certain union leaders

was considered a radical out to overthrow the government and the American way of life. At the beginning, Darrow had developed a comfortable, lucrative practice with the Chicago and Northwestern Railroad. He abandoned this uncomplicated position to defend Eugene V. Debs in 1894 after Debs was charged with a conspiracy in calling a great railroad strike that paralyzed train movements. The strike was called by Debs, who was the secretary-treasurer of the Brotherhood of Locomotive Firemen, when train magnate James J. Hill, boss of the Great Northern, imperially announced that he intended to cut the wages of railroad workers across the nation. Pullman workers had already gone on strike after receiving a twenty-five percent pay cut, and Debs ordered his union members to strike in sympathy with the Pullman employees.

The railroads west of Chicago were utterly crippled, and federal troops were called out to protect non-union workers, as well as compel union members back to work. Violent clashes between troops and workers resulted in the deaths of thirty persons, and Debs was accused of creating a conspiracy to undermine the government. Darrow, unlike labor lawyers of the past, vigorously defended his client, presenting an aggressive attack as his defense, going to the heart of the problem—the miserable conditions endured by workers and unfair wages paid union members. He was really defending the right of unions to exist. His words were stirring and staunch, and even though Debs was jailed for violating an injunction, Darrow emerged as one of labor's leading and most eloquent spokesmen, a romantic figure who was portrayed as a white knight riding to the rescue of the common man. U.S. Supreme Court Justice Willaim O. Douglas later stated that "Darrow represented both the poor and the rich. But he never, I think, represented the strong against the weak, the mighty against the masses."

Darrow continued defending unions and made headlines in 1902-03 when he represented anthracite miners on strike in Scranton, Pa. Darrow's most sensational case up to that time involved the controversial William D. "Big Bill" Haywood, leader of the violent Industrial Workers of the World (IWW), members of which were better known as Wobblies, who were locked in mortal combat with western mining bosses. On Dec. 20, 1905, Frank Steunenberg, former governor of Idaho, was killed by a bomb which went off when he opened the front gate of his home. The terrorist killer was Harry Orchard and he quickly implicated Haywood and other I.W.W. officials who were then charged with murder. Haywood's defense was led by Darrow who reduced the jury to tears in his stunning summation. Haywood was acquitted. The prolonged trial drained Darrow of his energy, and he was unnerved that he had been defending an element of labor that intrinsically believed in violence as a means of solving labor disputes. He returned to Chicago, claiming that he would no longer represent labor causes but, in 1911, he found himself once more embroiled in a controversial labor case, that of the McNamara brothers.

The great attorney was less successful in his defense of the McNamara Brothers who stood accused of blowing up the Los Angeles *Times* Building on Oct. 1, 1910, causing the death of twenty men. Darrow, for a $50,000 fee and using a defense fund of $200,000, defended the McNamaras under the presumption that they were innocent, but he soon came to believe that both men were guilty. They faced certain execution and Darrow, at the suggestion of labor writer Lincoln Steffens, pled his clients guilty to save their lives. The Brothers were given life sentences but this was not the end of Darrow's woes. Harrison Gray Otis, reactionary publisher of the *Times* had hired the Burns Detective Agency to obtain evidence during the trial not only on the McNamara Brothers but on Darrow himself and they were later able to bring charges against Darrow for bribing jurors. Darrow, who had not received his fee in the McNamara case, now had to defend himself in a vicious bribery case, hiring the flamboyant, heavy-drinking Earl Rogers to defend him. Rogers brilliantly convinced a jury that Darrow was innocent, and the case ended with a hung jury.

Darrow at 19 and his mentor, Gov. John Peter Altgeld.

Darrow at the McNamara trial, and with Lincoln Steffens, 1911.

Above, Clarence Darrow in 1903
and, right, in 1893 in Chicago.

Darrow, right, with Chicago official Fred Lundin, 1923.

Henry Demarest Lloyd, John Mitchell, and Darrow, 1903.

Richard Loeb, Darrow, and Nathan Leopold, Chicago, 1924.

Above left, Darrow at the time of the Leopold-Loeb case and, above right, pleading for the lives of his clients before Judge Caverly.

Broke, Darrow was able to return to Chicago only when an unknown benefactor provided $1,000.

The Los Angeles experience had exhausted Darrow to the point where he felt his career had really ended. His reputation had, indeed, been tarnished, but his career was far from over. His most spectacular cases awaited him in the Roaring Twenties. Up to that time, Darrow spent more and more time taking criminal cases in Chicago, successfully defending small-time criminals until underworld kingpins like gambler Mont Tennes became his clients for large fees. Darrow also demonstrated on occasions his agnostic attitudes which never varied and would come into heavy play with his confrontation with William Jennings Bryan in the 1925 Scopes trial. Typical of the great lawyer's posture here was a 1913 speech he made to a gathering of the Walt Whitman Fellowship in which he humorously stated: "Whitman was not a religious man. Few great men have been."

Always a man of issues, Darrow abandoned his pacifism in 1914 and endorsed Wilson's War policy three years later. In 1919, he condemned the Volstead Act and resulting Prohibition as laws that would only bring about more crime, even predicting in oblique terms the rise of organized crime through the enforcemt of Prohibition. He continued representing unpopular clients such as the Milwaukee anarchists of 1917, several dozen of whom had organized meetings to oppose U.S. involvement in WWI. One of them, Amedeo Lilli, harangued crowds with the inflamatory line: "We don't believe in this war...We don't believe in any government. Wilson is a pig, the American flag a rag, and this country is a jail." At one meeting, on Sept. 9, 1917, Tony Formaceo, a devout anarchist, was asked to move on by a policeman. In response, he drew a gun and was killed in the resulting gun battle. The entire group was arrested and, following a fifteen-day trial, were each given harsh sentences. Darrow appealed these sentences pointing out that the Milwaukee court had not considered the cases of each defendant separately and many of the sentences were unfair. In March 1919, Darrow argued before the state Supreme Court and succeeded in overturning nine out of the eleven convictions.

Even more controversial at this time was Darrow's defense of the newly formed Communist Labor Party, members of which, in 1919, were charged with advocating the violent overthrow of the government. Much was made of Communist involvement in a labor strike in Seattle which was apparently aimed at establishing a political stranglehold on that city, as claimed by one witness in the Chicago trial, Ole Hanson, a former mayor of Seattle. When Darrow appeared for the defendants, crowds booed and jeered him outside the courthouse. Inside the courtroom, Darrow made an impassioned speech before the jury, stating the credo of his professional career: "I shall not argue to you whether the defendants' ideas are right or wrong. I am not bound to believe them right in order to take their case, and you are not bound to believe them right in order to find them Not Guilty. I don't know whether they are right or wrong. But I do know this—I know that the humblest and the meanest man who lives, I know that the idlest and the silliest man who lives, should have his say. I know he ought to speak his mind. And I know that the Constitution is a delusion and a snare if the weakest and the humblest man in the land cannot be defended in his right to speak and his right to think as much as the greatest and the strongest in the land. I am not here to defend their opinions. I am here to defend their right to express their opinions." He made his point but he lost the case, with all twenty defendants being convicted and drawing long prison terms. Sixteen of these defendants were later pardoned by the governor of Illinois on Nov. 29, 1922, some said through Darrow's considerable political clout.

Politicians of high standing accused of low crimes also sought and got Darrow's aid, including Fred Lundin, the campaign manager for William Hale "Big Bill" Thompson, the most venal mayor in Chicago's colorful history. In 1922, Lundin was accused of misappropriating more than $1 million in school funds, awarding expensive contracts to firms which he owned. Darrow put

Lundin on the stand, knowing that his client, addicted to old-fashioned morning coats, wire-rimmed glasses, and hand-knotted bow ties would give the impression of a bumbling but well-intentioned person incapable of masterminding such grandiose fraud. Here Darrow played to the gallery in telling the jury: "If Fred Lundin or any other man in this case could be convicted on this evidence, made up of suspicions and cobwebs, then I want to retire to a cannibal island and be safe! This is an infamous conspiracy against the liberties of man." Lundin was acquitted, but one newspaper wag commented that "only with the help of God and Clarence Darrow did he escape the penitentiary."

In June 1924, Clarence Darrow, at the age of sixty-seven, assumed the most sensational criminal defense of the 1920s, that of Nathan Leopold, nineteen, and Richard Loeb, eighteen, two spoiled sons of millionaires who had ruthlessly murdered a 14-year-old boy, Robert Franks, as a warped intellectual exercise. The two egotistical murderers merely wanted to see if they could get away with committing what they thought would be the perfect crime. They kidnapped and murdered the boy on May 21-22, 1924, then tried to collect a ransom from the wealthy Franks family, even though they did not need money, this being the ruse to convince police that they were dealing with professional criminals. But through their own strutting efforts, the two youths involved themselves in the search for the Franks boy and thus implicated themselves. Both later admitted the "thrill" killing, blaming each other. Public feeling against Leopold and Loeb was at a fever pitch and their deaths were universally demanded. Darrow was hired to save their lives by their wealthy parents who promised enormous fees which he never collected.

Darrow decided that the only way to save the youthful killers was to abandon any thought of a jury trial, knowing that a jury would undoubtedly recommend the death penalty for two such cold-blooded murderers. He opted for a bench trial and pled his clients guilty, placing the burdensome life-or-death responsibility upon one man, Judge John Caverly, chief justice of the Criminal Court of Cook County. Opposite Darrow was State's Attorney Robert Emmet Crowe, a tough-minded, shrewd prosecutor who had lost to Darrow in the Lundin case in 1922. When Darrow changed the plea of Leopold and Loeb from not guilty to guilty and his clients so accepted the plea before Judge Caverly, Crowe was stunned. His whole case, prepared by a bevy of aides for weeks had been aimed at proving the youths guilty. Moreover, Darrow introduced the thought that if the young men had not come from rich families, he would have had an opportunity to plea bargain with the prosecution for life sentences but since Leopold and Loeb came from incredible wealth his clients had to face but one course, the death penalty. "If we fail in this defense," Darrow told Judge Caverly: "it will not be for lack of money but on account of money."

With great energy and passion, Darrow, throughout the lengthy trial, managed to do the impossible, implant within Judge Caverly's mind an element of sympathy for two killers who deserved no sympathy. His closing summation before the judge was prosaic and masterful. Said Darrow in part: "Your Honor will never thank me for unloading the responsibility upon you, but you know that I would have been untrue to my clients if I had not concluded to take this chance before a court, instead of submitting it to a poisoned jury in the city of Chicago...Poor little Bobbie Franks suffered very little. There is no excuse for his killing. If to hang these two boys would bring him back to life, I would say let them hang, and I believe their parents would say so, too." Darrow acknowledged the murder without reservation and took the attack against Crowe's insistence for the death penalty, creating doubt in Judge Caverly's mind over the motivations for such a demand on the part of the prosecution. Darrow portrayed Crowe's posture as one of revenge, not justice.

Darrow did not spare his clients in his lengthy addresses to the court, portraying them with an abundance of intellect but lacking in human compassion. They lacked normal human emotion and were therefore abnormal, a point Darrow had repeatedly tried to

Clockwise, from top left: Old rivals Darrow and William Jennings Bryan, 1925; Darrow arguing at the Monkey Trial; from left, Thomas and Thalia Massie, Mrs. Grace Fortescu, Sheriff Gordon Ross, seamen A.O. Jones, E.J. Lord, and Darrow at the sensational Massie murder trial in Hawaii, 1931; Darrow in, 1936 with his wife Ruby; with Judge John J. Raulston, left, with gavel raised, and his harrassed client, John T. Scopes, and others, Dayton, Tenn., 1925; Darrow being searched before entering court in Hawaii to defend Massie, 1931.

make by having psychiatrists (or "alienists" as they were then called) testify that both defendants were legally insane. "I know that they cannot feel what you feel and I feel," Darrow intoned to Judge Caverly, "that they cannot feel the moral shocks that come to men that are educated and who have not been deprived of an emotional system or emotional feelings. I know it, and every person who has studied this subject knows it well. Is Dickie Loeb to blame because out of the infinite forces that conspired to form him, the infinite forces that were at work producing him ages before he was born, that because out of these infinite combinations he was born without it? If he is, then there should be a new definition for justice."

For spellbinding hours, Darrow pled for the life of Leopold and Loeb: "The easy thing and the popular thing to do is to hang my clients. I know it. Men and women who do not think will applaud. The cruel and the thoughtless will approve...I am pleading for the future. I am pleading for a time when hatred and cruelty will not control the hearts of men, when we can learn by reason and judgment and understanding and faith that all life is worth saving and that mercy is the highest attribute of men." With such words, Darrow's critics later pointed out, the brilliant attorney had indirectly placed Judge Caverly in a position to judge himself as being a thinking, merciful man, one devoid of cruelty and revenge, one who would spare the lives of the killers to protect his self-esteem and image with future historians. The two-day pleading before Judge Caverly drained Darrow's energy to the point of near collapse. He would later write: "When I closed I had exhausted all the strength I could summon. From that day I have never gone through so protracted a strain, and I could never do it again, even if I should try."

There were times when Judge Caverly's eyes seem to well up with tears (there were never tears running down his cheeks as described by some writers). He deliberated long and hard over the case, being a fair-minded and liberally-bent judge, a posture Darrow studied well before deciding to plead his case directly to the bench. When Judge Caverly appeared on the day of his decision, his demeanor was decidedly nervous. He opened his remarks by saying that because the defendants had pled guilty they were entitled to no special consideration, a statement that sent daggers of fear through Leopold and Loeb who felt that they were about to be given death sentences. Further, Judge Caverly said that he believed both youths were no more abnormal than any other criminals. Judge Caverly then shocked the court and the nation by turning from the path of death to that of life, saying that he did not like to impose the death penalty on juveniles. He abruptly sentenced both killers to life imprisonment and ninety-nine years for kidnapping. These sentences were to run concurrently so that there would be no chance for parole. Darrow had done the impossible by saving two clients who had, by all counts, been condemned.

The reaction from the nation's press was universal condemnation of Judge Caverly's decision, but Darrow's prestige shot sky-high as a legal miracle worker. He was never to receive his full fees for saving the youths. Moreover, in his zeal to save their lives, he had made presumptuous statements that defied fact. In his remarks about how "little Bobbie Franks suffered very little," he had ignored what the coroner, the killers and most news reporters already knew, that the perverse killers had slowly strangled the boy and then mutilated his body, according to one account, by pouring acid on his genitals. The killers were distasteful to Darrow and he avoided talking at length about them for the rest of his life. Both were practicing homosexuals and when Richard Loeb was killed by another prison inmate whom Loeb tried to rape in 1936, Darrow's only response was: "Dickie Loeb is better off dead."

Darrow went on to other famous cases, including the so-called "Monkey Trial" of 1925, where a young teacher, John T. Scopes was charged with teaching the theories of Charles Darwin and his concepts of evolution in Dayton, Tenn., the "Bible Belt" of fundamentalism. Here, in a wild, almost zany legal confrontation between the agnostic Darrow and the fundamentalist champion William Jennings Bryan, the issue became one of science versus the organized religions of old. Darrow lost this, case but he eloquently demonstrated the need for educational enlightment. In 1931, Darrow was again in the nation's news by defending Navy officer Thomas Massie in a sensational murder case stemming from the rape of Massie's wife by four natives in Hawaii. This was another instance where the great criminal lawyer managed to save his clients from execution but caused the court to hand down a sentence so lenient that it produced howls of protest for decades to come. The great lawyer led the defense of the much-publicized Robert Elliott Burns, who had escaped from a Georgia Chain Gang. Darrow appeared in Trenton, N.J., to argue against the extradition of Burns, then living in New Jersey, back to Georgia's chain gang, offering petitions with hundreds of thousands of names and graphically illustrating the horrors of the medieval penal system in Georgia. So persuasive was he that Governor Moore, in an unprecedented move, refused Georgia's writ, and Burns remained free. The remainder of Darrow's life was spent in limited travel, reading and some lectures, although he was less in demand as the 1930s evaporated.

Though a much-publicized agnostic, Darrow visited mediums and even made up a list of questions with his literary friends George Jean Nathan and H.L. Mencken, that were to be asked from the dead, if there was a way the dead could answer such queries. Darrow's last days in Chicago were full of hardship and physical pain. He had lost most of his money through bad investments and he slowly lost his prize possession, his mind, to senility. He was eighty when he died on Mar. 13, 1938, and his funeral address was given by Judge William H. Holly who found that he could not do justice to the great criminal attorney with his own words so he spoke the lines that Darrow himself had intoned over the casket of John Peter Altgeld forty years earlier. In effect, Darrow had the last word, delivering by proxy his own eulogy. Though many criminal lawyers have since come upon the scene since the day of Clarence Darrow, none have equaled, in image and reputation, this greatly human and compassionate giant. See: **Altgeld, John Peter; Burns, Robert Elliott; Debs, Eugene Victor; Haywood, William; Leopold, Nathan; McNamara Brothers; Massie, Thomas; Scopes, John T.**

REF.: Adamic, *The Story of Class Violence in America;* Adams, *Age of Industrial Violence, 1910-15;* Allen, *Only Yesterday;* Andrews, *Battle for Chicago;* Ashley, *The Railroad Strike of 1894;* Bancroft, *The Chicago Strike of 1894;* Barnard, *Eagle Forgotten: The Life of John Peter Altgeld;* Beer, *Hanna;* Borah, *Haywood Trial;* Bradley, *Along the Way;* Bridges, *The God of Fundamentalism and Other Studies;* Bright, *Hizzoner Big Bill Thompson;* Brommel, *Eugene V. Debs;* Browne, *Altgeld of Illinois;* Bryan, *The Memoirs of William Jennings Bryan;* Buder, *Pullman;* Burns, *The Pullman Boycott;* Burns, *The Masked War;* Busch, *Casebook of the Curious and True;* ____, *In and Out of Court;* ____, *Prisoners at the Bar;* Cargill, *Intellectual America;* Caesar, *Incredible Detective;* Carwardine, *The Pullman Strike;* CBA; Chaplin, *Wobbly;* Clement, *Rebel America;* Cleveland, *The Government in the Chicago Strike of 1894;* Coleman, *Eugene V. Debs;* Commons, *The History of Labor in the United States;* Crandall, *The Man from Kinsman;* Culin, *A Trooper's Narrative of Service in the Anthracite Coal Strike, 1902;* Currey, *Chicago: Its History and Its Builders;* Darrow, *The Story of My Life;* David, *The History of the Haymarket Affair;* Debs, *Writings and Speeches;* De Camp, *The Great Monkey Trial;* Destler, *Henry Demarest Lloyd and the Empire of Reform;* Doty, *The Town of Pullman;* Douglas, *Go East, Young Man;* Erbstein, *The Show-Up: Stories Before the Bar;* Ford, *The Darrow Bribery Trial;* Fried, *The Rise and Fall of the Jewish Gangster in America;* Friedheim, *The Seattle General Strike;* Friedman, *The Pinkerton Labor Spy;* Gertz, *A Handful of Clients;* Ginger, *Altgeld's America;* ____, *The Bending Cross;* ____, *Six Days or Forever;* Gompers, *The McNamara Case;* ____, *Seventy Years of Life and Labor;* Grover, *Debaters and Dynamiters;* Gunn, *Wisdom of Clarence Darrow;* Gurko, *Clarence Darrow;* Haleman-Julius, *Clarence Darrow's Two Great Trials;* Hapgood, *The Spirit of Labor;* Harrison, *Stormy Years;* Harrison, *Clarence Darrow;* Harvey, *Samuel Gompers;* Haywood, *Bill Haywood's Book;* Hecht, *A Child of the Century;* Higdon, *The Crime of the Century, The Leopold* and Loeb Case; Hoffman, *The Twenties*; Holly, *A Forgotten Governor*; House, *Crimes That Shocked America*; Howe, *The Confession of a Reformer*; Husband, *The Story of the Pullman Car*; Johnson, *Carter Henry Harrison I*; Josephson, *Sidney Hillman*; Kaplan, *Lincoln Steffens*; Kasner, *Debs*; Knudten, *Criminological Controversies*; Kobler, *Capone*; Koenig, *Bryan*; Kogan, *The First Century*; ____, and Wendt, *Big Bill the Builder*; ____, *Chicago: A Pictorial History*; Kurland, *Clarence Darrow*; Leopold, *Life Plus 99 Years*; Lewis and Smith, *Chicago: The History of Its Reputation*; Lippmann, *American Inquisitors*; Lloyd, *Henry Demarest Lloyd*; Lord, *The Good Years*; Lowe, *Lost Chicago*; Lundberg, *Imperial Hearst*; Lynch, *Criminals and Politicians*; McKenna, *Borah*; Manning, *The Chicago Strike of 1894*; Messick, *Organized Crime In Chicago*; Mitchell, *Organized Labor*; Mordell, *Clarence Darrow, Eugene V. Debs and Haldeman-Julius*; Murray, *Red Scare*; Musmanno, *Verdict!*; Nash, ____, *Almanac of World Crime*; ____, *Bloodletters and Badmen*; ____, *Hustlers and Con Men*; ____, *Murder, America*; ____, *People to See*; Nathan, *The Intimate Notebooks of George Jean Nathan*; Older, *My Own Story*; Orchard, *The Confession and Autobiography of Harry Orchard*; Perlman and Taft, *History of Labor in the United States*; Perry, *A History of the Los Angeles Labor Movement, 1911-1941*; Pierce, *A History of Chicago*; Poole, *Giants Gone: Men Who Made Chicago*; Ravitz, *Clarence Darrow and the American Literary Tradition*; Reppetto, *The Blue Parade*; Reynolds, *Courtroom*; Robinson, *Bombs and Bribery*; St. Johns, *Final Verdict*; Sayer, *Clarence Darrow: Public Advocate*; Scopes, *Center of the Storm*; Scott, *The Concise Encyclopedia of Crime and Criminals*; Sellers, *Classics of the Bar*; Smith, *Syndicate City*; Spiering, *The Man Who Got Capone*; Steffens, *The Autobiography of Lincoln Steffens*; ____, *The Letters of Lincoln Steffens*; Stimson, *Rise of the Labor Movement in Los Angeles*; Stone, *Clarence Darrow for the Defense*; Stuart, *The 20 Incredible Years*; Swanberg, *Citizen Hearst*; Swing, *Forerunners of American Fascism*; Taft, *The A.F. of L. in the Time of Gompers*; Taylor, *Pioneering on Social Frontiers*; Tebbel, *The Life and Good Times of William Randolph Hearst*; Tierney, *Darrow, A Biography*; Van Slingerland, *Something Terrible Has Happened*; Wagenknecht, *Chicago*; Warne, *The Pullman Boycott of 1894*; Weinberg, *Attorney for the Damned*; ____, *Clarence Darrow, A Sentimental Rebel*; Whitehead, *Clarence Darrow—The Big Minority Man*; ____, *Clarence Darrow, Evangelist of Sane Thinking*; Whitlock, *Forty Years of It*; Williams, *William Jennings Bryan*; Winkler, *W.R. Hearst*; Wolf, *Fallen Angels*; Wood, *The Introductory Chapter to the History of the Trials of Moyer, Haywood, and Pettibone, and Harry Orchard*; *The World's Most Famous Court Trial: Tennessee Evolution Case*; Wright, *Rape in Paradise*; Yaffe, *Nothing But the Night*; Yarros, *My Eleven Years with Clarence Darrow*.

Dartmoor Prison Riot, 1932, Brit., riot. Built to house the French prisoners captured during the Napoléonic Wars, Dartmoor Prison in Devon was among the harshest, most imposing penal structures in England. Inscribed above its massive iron gate were the words *Parcere Subjectis:* "Spare the Vanquished." The meaning was quickly lost to the thousands of men who abandoned all hope in their cold, dark cells.

On Jan. 24, 1932, the prisoners revolted. At a prearranged moment, they hurled their tin plates of foul-tasting porridge at the prison guards, beginning one of the most famous prison riots in British history. Governor Stanley Roberts of Dartmoor ordered the men into the exercise yard. As they passed by a pile of stones, the inmates bolted from the ranks and began throwing the rocks at their guards.

Running wildly through the yards, the leaders of the mutiny called for a charge against the warden's office. Believing that he could reason with the men, Colonel G.D. Turner of the Home Office emerged from Governor Roberts' private chambers. He was besieged by the rioters and nearly kicked to death. A prisoner named George Thomas Donovan successfully drove off the attackers.

Meanwhile, the rioters had set fire to the governor's office and looted the guards' dining area. Unable to stop the carnage, a contingency of police from nearby Plymouth was summoned. Led by Chief Constable A.K. Wilson, the officers engaged the prisoners in a short bloody skirmish. After an hour, the men were driven back into their cells and order was restored. Amazingly, no one was killed.

An inquiry was held in Princetown on May 10, 1932. The ringleaders received additional sentences ranging from six months to twelve years. Donovan, who had put his life on the line to save Colonel Turner, was pardoned by the king. Twenty-seven other men who had assisted the guards had their sentences reduced. REF.: *CBA*.

D'Artois-de Bourbon Duel, prom. 1778, Fr., duel. The duel between the Comte d'Artois, Charles Phillipe, later Charles X, the younger brother of King Louis XVI, and the Duc de Bourbon, Louis Phillipe d'Orleans, resulted from an argument at a masked ball at the Paris Opera in 1778.

The Duchess de Bourbon, was infatuated with d'Artois. He, however, was having an affair with the Duc de Bourbon's former mistress, Madame de Carillac. At the ball, d'Artois and Carillac appeared in the same costume, and their affectionate behavior so enraged the jealous duchess that she brutally berated Carillac, causing her to leave the ballroom. D'Artois in turn struck the duchess about the face, crushing the mask she wore. The Parisian court, especially the friends of the duchess, were outraged at d'Artois' conduct. The king ordered all parties to let the matter rest. But the duchess was unappeased, and asked Queen Marie Antoinette to intervene. As the honor of her brother-in-law, d'Artois, was at stake, the queen convinced Louis to allow a duel. A mock duel was arranged to satisfy the public, and it was secretly agreed that no one would be injured. After a few half-hearted lunges, d'Artois and Bourbon reconciled their differences. For violating the laws against duelling, both men were sentenced to a week in "exile" at their respective country estates.

REF.: *CBA*; Melville, *Famous Duels and Assassinations*.

Dashwood, Francis, 1708-81, Brit., sex perversion. Francis Dashwood was the fifteenth baron of the le Despencer family and a wealthy profligate who lived only for bizarre sexual gratification. He founded the Hell Fire Club in 1755, a secret society whose members were later dubbed "The Mad Monks of Medmenham." They met in the ruins of Medmenham Abbey on summer nights to indulge in orgies, black masses, and perverted sex rituals that mocked the Catholic Church. Its members produced pornographic works and promoted political sedition. In addition to Dashwood, the group's ringleaders included George Bubb Dodington, Laurence Sterne, and John Wilkes. Two of its members were responsible for proposing the notorious Stamp Act in Parliament, which eventually led to the American Revolution.

Sir Francis Dashwood

Dashwood later became chancellor of the exchequer (1762-63) and joint postmaster general (1770-81). See: **Hell-Fire Club**.

REF.: *CBA*; Mannix, *The Hell Fire Club*.

Dashwood, Samuel, and **Silverosa, George**, prom. 1942, Brit., rob.-mur. On Apr. 30, 1942, the pawnshop of Leonard Moules, in Hackney Road, Shoreditch, England, was robbed, and Moules was knocked unconscious with the butt of a revolver. The 71-year-old man was then beaten with a blunt instrument. He died eight days later from his injuries. The only clue was a palm print inside the safe. When Detective Inspector Keen overheard a soldier in a cafe say that two men, "George and Sam," were examining a revolver, he made inquiries and soon arrested Samuel Dashwood, twenty-two, and George Silverosa, twenty-three, both former gang members with long criminal records. Silverosa confessed to robbing the shop, and Dashwood admitted hitting the old man. At the trial at the Old Bailey, both men declined to testify, probably to avoid cross-examination. Dashwood rejected the services of the appointed counsels, Serjeant Sullivan and E.W. Fordham, telling Justice Wrottesley, "I object to them saying anything in my defense." Both men were found Guilty and sentenced to death. While awaiting their fate at Pentonville Prison, Silverosa attacked two warders with a poker, seriously injuring them, just a few days before he and Dashwood were executed. REF.: *CBA*.

Dato, Joseph, See: **Adonis, Joseph.**

Dato Iradier, Eduardo, 1856-1921, Spain, premier, assass. The Spanish statesman and jurist Eduardo Dato Iradier was Spain's minister of interior (1899-1900), minister of justice (1902-03), and served as mayor of Madrid (1907) and minister of foreign affairs (1918). He became premier in 1913 and held this post until he was assassinated by an anarchist on Mar. 8, 1921. REF.: *CBA*.

Dauber, William E. (Billy) 1935-80, and **Dauber, Charlotte,** 1945-80, U.S., org. crime-(unsolv.) mur. As he left the Will County Courthouse on July 2, 1980, William (Billy) Dauber, a top mob hit man and boss of Chicago's south suburban chop-shop ring, summed up his recent activities to reporters. "I just live quietly in the country, that's all," he said. His peaceful life was nearing its end.

Dauber was one of only a handful of rural southern men to crack the inner circle of Chicago's crime syndicate. Born in the Appalachians, Dauber first came to the attention of reputed mob boss James "Jimmy the Bomber" Catuara as someone who might prove useful to the outfit. Catuara's fortes were gambling and vice in the south suburbs. Under his tutelage, Dauber became a top assassin, responsible for at least twenty murders.

Under Catuara's auspices, Dauber began muscling in on the lucrative chop-shop racket operated in Cook County by Steven Ostrowsky. Between 1969 and 1980, at least twenty men who were caught up in this dangerous and illegal business were cut down by syndicate gunmen. Counted among the dead was Jimmy the Bomber, who was shot in his red Cadillac on July 28, 1978, after Dauber had joined up with Albert Caesar Tocco, the new "muscle" in suburban chop-shop operations.

In 1973, Dauber was convicted of mail fraud and interstate transportation of a stolen car that had been used in the commission of a murder. He was released in 1976, and he immediately assumed a position as syndicate enforcer for Tocco. Those familiar with Dauber's tactics recalled how he would slip his arm around his victim's shoulder in a good-natured way. Then, in an unguarded moment, he would whip out his pistol and shoot him in the head.

On July 2, 1980, Dauber and his wife, Charlotte, received a continuation from Judge Angelo Pistilli on charges that they had hidden large quantities of cocaine and weapons in their suburban home. The couple was driving home from the courtroom when a Ford Van pulled alongside and gunmen opened fire. Dauber tried futilely to evade the gunfire. His car careened into an apple tree where it was later discovered by two farmers. The van was located a mile up the road where it had been set on fire by the unknown killers.

Officials speculated that the murders had been planned for some time. Charlotte had been complaining bitterly about the shabby treatment toward her husband by some of his former associates. In a bar a few days before the hit, her loud protests were overheard by at least one disgruntled mob figure. Charlotte's outspokenness may have prompted the mob to part with its long-standing policy of leaving the wife out of her husband's affairs.

The fact that Dauber had been flooded with federal indictments and may have been cooperating with the government was another compelling reason given for the murders. See: **Tocco, Albert Caesar.** REF.: *CBA*.

d'Aubray, Marie Madeleine Dreux, See:**Brinvilliers, Marie de.**

Daud Khan, Sardar Muhammad, 1909-78, Afg., pres., assass. Member of the royal family, he was Afghanistan prime minister from 1953-63 and leader of a coup against King Muhammed Zahir Shah in 1973. That same year he proclaimed Afghanistan a republic and named himself president. During a leftist military coup in 1978 he was assassinated. REF.: *CBA*.

Daugherty, Harry Micajah, See: **Teapot Dome Scandal.**

Daugherty, Roy (AKA: **Arkansas Tom Jones**), 1870-1924, U.S., west. outl. Roy Daugherty drifted from Missouri to Oklahoma under an assumed name when he was only fourteen. He called himself "Arkansas Tom Jones" because he claimed to have hailed from there. In the 1890s, he joined Bill Doolin's gang in holding up a number of banks in Oklahoma. On Sept. 1, 1893, Daugherty was trapped by lawmen in a hotel in Ingalls, Okla. Doolin and the others had left town, leaving Daugherty to fight off the posse from his second-floor room. When he refused to surrender, Deputy Jim Masterson emptied the hotel and threatened to blow it up with dynamite.

Daugherty was captured, tried, and convicted of manslaughter. Sentenced to a **Roy Daugherty, alias Arkansas Tom Jones.** fifty-year prison term, he was paroled in 1910, thanks to the efforts of his brothers, both ministers. For a short time he ran a restaurant in Drumright, Okla., and then drifted to Hollywood, where he hoped to make money acting in westerns. But Daugherty soon returned to bank robbery. With the law on his heels, Daugherty took refuge in the home of Red Snow in Joplin, Mo. Detectives trapped him there on Aug. 16, 1924, and killed him in a gunfight. See: **Doolin, William M.**

REF.: Bartholomew, *The Biographical Album of Western Gunfighters;* Breihan, *Badmen of Frontier Days;* _____, *Outlaws of the Old West;* CBA; Clark, *Then Came the Railroads;* Cowling, *Geography of Denton County;* Croy, *Trigger Marshal;* Cunningham, *Famous in the West;* Drago, *Outlaws on Horseback;* _____, *Road Agents and Train Robbers;* Gard, *Sam Bass;* Graves, *Oklahoma Outlaws;* Hanes, *Bill Doolin;* Harrington, *Hanging Judge;* Hendricks, *The Bad Man of the West;* Holloway, *Texas Gun Lore;* Horan, *The Wild Bunch;* Hunter and Rose, *The Album of Gunfighters;* Jones, *The Experiences of a U.S. Marshal of the Indian Territory;* McGinty, *The Old West;* McReynolds, *Thirty Years on the Frontier;* Miller, *Bill Tilghman;* Newson, *The Life and Practice of the Wild and Modern Indian;* Nix, *Oklahombres;* O'Neal, *Encyclopedia of Western Gunfighters;* Osborn, *Let Freedom Ring;* Peak, *A Ranger of Commerce;* Prather, *Come Listen to My Tale;* Raine, *Famous Sheriffs and Western Outlaws;* Raymond, *Captain Lee Hall of Texas;* Shirley, *Heck Thomas;* _____, *Six-gun and Silver Star;* _____, *Toughest of Them All;* Sutton, *Hands Up!;* Tilghman, *Outlaw Days;* Wellman, *A Dynasty of Western Outlaws;* White, *Trigger Fingers.*

D'Autremont (or DeAutremont) Brothers, prom. 1920s, U.S., rob.-mur. Roy, Ray, and Hugh D'Autremont were farm boys who made their living as lumberjacks in the thick forests near Eugene, Ore. As a child, Hugh, the oldest, had often talked of the notorious train robbers of the past, and his younger twin brothers, Roy and Ray, would join him in re-enacting the daring holdups committed by the James and Younger brothers. Such play, however, became a disastrous and bloody reality in 1923 when the three D'Autremonts decided to rob Train No. 13 of the Southern Pacific. On Oct. 11, 1923, the three brothers, dressed in overalls and carrying shotguns, their faces masked by colorful handkerchiefs, stopped Train No. 13 as it emerged from a tunnel, also numbered 13, just north of the California border outside of Siskiyou, Ore.

Engineer Sidney Bates and fireman Marvin Seng turned in the engineer's cabin to see two figures, Roy and Ray D'Autremont, crawling over the tender. Ray D'Autremont leveled a shotgun at them and barked: "Stop right now!" Bates brought the train to a grinding halt, which left the engine and tender and part of the mail car standing outside the tunnel with two baggage cars, four passenger coaches, and two sleepers inside the tunnel. Both Bates and Seng were ordered to jump down from the engine and accompany the taller of the two bandits to the mouth of the tunnel. They saw a third man, Hugh D'Autremont, run up to the mail car with a bundle that had wires dangling from it and place this on the ledge outside the door of the mail car. The third man then ran off down the tunnel. The device then blew up, flames shooting from the interior of the mail car. The entire mail car then caught fire.

Hugh D'Autremont raced up to his brothers and yelled: "We've got to get that car out of the tunnel!" He brandished a revolver in Bates' direction, ordering: "Get in that cab and move it out a bit." Bates climbed back into the cab of the engine and yanked on the throttle, but the train did not move. Hugh D'Autremont asked him why he was not moving the engine forward and the engineer shook his head, saying that it was stalled because he had brought the old locomotive to a sudden stop and caused old mechanisms in the train to break down, but he might have been stalling. "Get out of there!" Hugh ordered Bates, and the engineer once more climbed down from the cab. At that moment, brakeman Charles O. Johnson, holding a lantern, came running down the tracks through the tunnel, wanting to know why the train had stopped.

Hugh aimed his revolver at Johnson, roaring in anger: "You! Get over there and uncouple the mail car from the rest of the train. The brakeman meekly obliged but he failed to uncouple the car. The three brothers stood helplessly at the tunnel entrance watching the mail car burn and with it, they thought, a fortune in cash and jewels it was supposedly carrying. Johnson then turned and walked back to the bandits, trying to explain why he could not uncouple the car. Hugh D'Autremont was by then beside himself with rage. He lifted his revolver and fired one shot at the brakeman, the bullet struck Johnson in the head and killed him on the spot. A few seconds later, Ray and Roy D'Autremont, following Hugh's lead, turned without a comment and emptied their shotguns into Bates and Seng, killing both of them. A fourth crew member, Edwin Daugherty, a clerk who had been inside the mail car, was also dead, burned to death when the car was set afire from the bomb blast.

Train robber Hugh D'Autremont.

The would-be train robbers then fled the scene empty-handed. All their careful plans had netted them not one dime of loot and had produced four bodies, lives stupidly taken in anger. All the brothers knew that they would be hunted across the land for this senseless crime. Passengers alarmed at the sudden stop of the train now climbed from cars and groped their way along the tunnel toward the flaming mail car. A conductor appeared and ordered them back in the cars. He spotted the dead men and ran to a phone in the tunnel, calling the station at Ashland, Ore., sixteen miles away. Daniel O'Connell, chief of the Southern Pacific's railroad detectives, took another train to the area with several of his men. When he arrived a few hours later, he found the scene swarming with local police and postal detectives who had been called because the mail car had been attacked.

Search parties found the revolver Hugh D'Autremont had used, thrown away in panic. At the top of a hill where the bandits had slipped out of their overalls, one pair of overalls was found. The overalls belonged to Roy D'Autremont; they had slipped from his grasp as he raced after his brothers. These clues still left the lawmen with a blank as to the identities of the bandits. Detective O'Connell, however, knew of the many cases solved by Edward Oscar Heinrich, a private detective of sorts with amazing abilities. Heinrich was a scientist with a laboratory in Berkeley, Calif. He was called "the Edison of crime detection," and could determine from a single piece of thread the identity of a killer; a button might help him pinpoint a notorious thief. Heinrich had been called upon by many West Coast police departments to aid them in finding notorious felons, and O'Connell felt that he might be able to help solve the mystery of the Southern Pacific train robbery.

The overalls were sent to Heinrich who began to examine them under his microscope. Within days, he sent the following report back to O'Connell, "Look for a left-handed lumberjack who's worked around fir trees. The man you want is white, between twenty-one and twenty-five years of age, not over five-feet-ten-inches tall and he weighs about 165 pounds. He has medium light brown hair, fair complexion, small hands and feet, and is rather fastidious in his personal habits. Apparently, he has lived and worked in the Pacific Northwest." Heinrich added a postscript which promised more information in a matter of days. O'Connell's men scoffed at the report but the chief detective knew better. He and several of his men visited Heinrich in Berkeley some days later, and the mild-mannered Heinrich carefully explained how he had gathered his information. The size of the overalls had determined the wanted man's height and weight. Small chips of wood in one pocket determined the fact that the man was a lumberjack and since these were in a right-handed pocket, the man would be left-handed when sawing. The chips were from a tree that could only be found in the Northwest portion of the U.S. A single strand of hair caught around a button of the overalls had determined the man's hair color and complexion. Heinrich had also found some nail cuttings in another pocket and from this determined the size of the man's hands and feet and the fact that he was fastidious.

An even more important discovery had been made by Heinrich by the time O'Connell and his men arrived. The scientist had dug into the small pencil pocket of the overalls and had found, wadded up, a registered mail receipt, numbered 236-L. Postal inspectors quickly identified this as having been sent by Roy D'Autremont from Eugene, Ore., to his brother Hugh living in Lakewood, N.M. Officers rushed to Eugene and there interviewed the boys' father, Paul D'Autremont, who said he had not heard from his sons. Hugh and the twins had disappeared a day before the date of the train holdup. He did admit that his son Roy D'Autremont was left-handed, worked as lumberjack, and was "very clean in his habits," thus confirming Heinrich's description of the man.

Though authorities now had complete descriptions and photos of the wanted men, the search for the killer brothers went on for four years. More than two million flyers with pictures of the brothers on them were distributed throughout the U.S. and in several foreign countries. Rewards totalling $15,000 for the capture of the D'Autremonts were also posted. Then, in March 1927, Sergeant Thomas Reynolds of the U.S. Army, temporarily stationed at the military barracks on Alcatraz Island (later to become the celebrated federal penitentiary in the middle of San Francisco Bay) walked into the post office at the camp and glanced at circulars posted on the wall. His eye was caught by a familiar face, and he blurted: "That's Brice!" He soon informed authorities that he knew one of the men whose photo adorned the poster, Hugh D'Autremont, whom Reynolds had known as an army private named Brice when they were both stationed in the Philippines, assigned to duty with the 31st Infantry Division.

Authorities in Manila were contacted, and Hugh D'Autremont was arrested and returned to the military prison at Alcatraz. He identified himself and said he had joined the army in Chicago. D'Autremont undoubtedly thought that by enlisting he had found a place where no one would look for him. The same kind of coincidence worked in the capture of the remaining two brothers a few weeks later. Albert Cullingworth, an elderly steel worker in Steubenville, Ohio, was leafing through a crime magazine and stopped to stare at some photos in an article about a train robbery that had occurred in Oregon four years earlier. He recognized two of the men in the photos immediately as "the Goodwin twins." Cullingworth called the FBI, and both brothers were arrested by agents within days. Ray and Roy D'Autremont admitted their true identities but, like their brother Hugh, denied having had anything to do with the Oregon train killings.

Edward Oscar Heinrich was called upon to testify in the trial of Hugh D'Autremont and he again recited his amazing discoveries. The chain of circumstantial evidence indicting the D'Autremonts was so impressive that Hugh was convicted. When the twins heard this, they confessed, as did Hugh. All three brothers were given life sentences in the Oregon State Penitentiary at Salem. Hugh D'Autremont was paroled on Nov. 24, 1958. Ray D'Autremont was paroled in 1961 but Roy D'Autremont, whose overalls betrayed him to the observant eye of Edward Oscar Heinrich, remained for the rest of his life in a state asylum for the insane. See: **Heinrich, Edward Oscar.**

REF.: Block, *Great Train Robberies of the West;* _____, *Science vs. Crime;* _____, *The Wizard of Berkeley;* Boucher, *The Quality of Murder; CBA;* Cooper, *Ten Thousand Public Enemies;* Gribble, *Clues That Spelled Guilty;* _____, *Stories of Famous Detectives;* King, *Main Line: Fifty Years of Railroading with the Southern Pacific;* Lucia, *Tough Men, Tough Country;* Nash, *Bloodletters and Badmen;* _____, *Citizen Hoover;* Robinson, *Science Catches the Criminal;* Wilson and Taylor, *Southern Pacific.*

Davenant, Sir William (or **D'Avenant**), 1606-68, Brit., consp.-treas. Rumored to be the illegitimate son of William Shakespeare, he became poet laureate in 1638. As a royalist for the cause of Charles I he was arrested on a mission to Virginia for Henrietta Maria in 1650, and placed in the Tower of London from 1650-52, where he wrote *Gondibert.* John Milton helped obtain his release, but he was imprisoned once again in 1659 for his involvement in the uprising led by Sir George Booth. REF.: *CBA.*

Davenport, Barnett, d.1780, U.S., mur. Barnett Davenport was employed as a servant in the home of Caleb Mallery in Litchfield, Mass. On the night of Feb. 3, 1780, Davenport crept into Mallery's bedroom and strangled him and his wife, then murdered a grandchild sleeping nearby. He looted the Mallery house and set fire to it to hide his crimes. He was seen leaving the scene of the murders and quickly confessed after being arrested. He was tried and hanged on May 8, 1780.

REF.: *A Brief Narrative of the Life and Confession of Barnett Davenport; CBA.*

Davenport, Ira Erastus, 1839-1911, and **Davenport, William Henry Harrison,** 1841-77, U.S., fraud. Davenport and his brother William Henry Harrison Davenport were swindlers who practiced spiritual fraud, claiming to be mediums who could conjure the spirits of the dead, bring back relatives to communicate with the living. They bilked the gullible and naive American rich out of untold fortunes, using all sorts of inventive gimmicks—mirrors, sliding panels, sound and light devices—to present images of the deceased. Ira Davenport later claimed to be the world's leading sleight-of-hand expert, but he was exposed by the American magician, Harry Houdini. REF.: *CBA.*

Davenport, Lizzie, prom. 1892, U.S., pros. At the time of the Chicago World's Fair in 1892, a large black woman named Lizzie Davenport maintained a brothel in the old Custom House Levee near the Dearborn Street train station. It was a den frequented by the rougher elements of the city. The Davenport brothel was a "panel house" in which hired thugs would assault the patrons from concealed passageways or false walls during sex. The police from the nearby Harrison Street station estimated that at least $500,000 in cash, jewels, and gold had been stolen from unsuspecting patrons during the years Davenport ran her business. The police were often thwarted by "cappers," specially posted lookouts who tipped the owner about impending raids.

Davenport built a special room made from heavy oak to repel the police. It was said that a cannonball could not penetrate its thick doors. Thus, the police had to resort to more ingenious methods to close down the brothel.

Detective Clifton Wooldridge and a squad of men secured a quantity of red pepper and an auger which was used to bore through the doorway leading to the room where the prostitutes had sequestered themselves. A crude smoke bomb composed of the red pepper was lit. The fumes quickly permeated the room, and within seconds the coughing and gagging women were forced to retreat from their fort into the awaiting patrol wagon. The brothel was at last forced to close.

REF.: Asbury, *Gem of the Prairie; CBA;* Wooldridge, *Hands Up.*

David, Immanuel, prom. 1979, U.S., suic. For nearly a year, the family of Immanuel David, a self-proclaimed religious prophet, lived in the elegant International Inn in downtown Salt Lake City, Utah.

On July 31, 1978, Immanuel locked himself in a car and left the motor running, thus committing suicide. Three days later, his wife and six children plunged from their eleventh-floor terrace. Witnesses told police that the young children appeared to have been reluctant, and had to be pushed by their mother.

There was one survivor, 15-year-old Rachel David, who sustained serious internal injuries and broken bones. She maintained her vital signs but was unable to respond to external stimuli, facing a slow rehabilitation. REF.: *CBA.*

Davidson, George Maxim (AKA: **Thomas Ronald Ryman Max Davies**), b.c.1903, Brit., big.-blk. George Maxim Davidson got a job cleaning airplane engines and married in 1923. He and his wife had two children. On Sept. 3, 1932, Davidson disappeared. He began a new life, living in high style and claiming to be a doctor. He married Gwendoline (Edwards) Davies, twenty-two, in early 1937. In the summer of that year, he traveled with his new wife to Portsmouth. At a dance, they met a naval officer whom Gwendoline visited at his lodgings, where he only offered her drinks.

Davidson then sent a confession, purportedly written by the girl, to the officer, who was married and seeking future promotions. One month later, Davidson told the officer that he had initiated a divorce suit against Gwendoline, and in the suit had listed the officer as a co-respondent. Contesting the suit would cost £400, Davidson told him, but the lawyers might withdraw the suit if the expenses to date were paid. The officer then met with Davidson, the girl, and Charles Thomas Duke, forty-three, who posed as a lawyer. Davidson gave the fraudulent lawyer a check for £140 and then badgered the officer for reimbursement. The officer finally went to the police and the three impostors were arrested, tried, and convicted on charges of blackmail. Davidson was sentenced to four years of penal servitude, Edwards was given a nine-month prison term, and Duke received eighteen months in prison with hard labor. REF.: *CBA.*

Davidson, Harold Francis, 1874-1937, Brit., morals. The rector of the small parish of Stiffkey, England, the Reverend Harold Davidson was married with five children. For twenty years, the ambitious clergyman had spent six days a week in London's notorious West End, with twice-monthly mid-week trips to Paris. Davidson spent his time doing what he considered to be rescue work among young, pretty prostitutes between sixteen and eighteen. He said of himself that he was known as the Prostitutes' Padre. He talked to the women for hours about the wrongs of their ways, spending his small wages on gifts for them, especially lingerie, and occasionally taking a woman on a trip to Paris to visit fashionable night spots like the Moulin Rouge and the Follies Bergére.

In 1931, one of his London "flock," Rose Ellis, exposed her reformer of eleven years to the press. Detectives were assigned to trail the then 57-year-old Davidson. With a growing reputation as a seducer and pest, the aging man became less welcome in the world he had frequented for several years. By Mar. 29, 1932, the rector was brought before a consistory court on five charges of immoral conduct. The Bishop of Norwich pressed the charges against Davidson at the Great Hall of Church House in Westminster. Maintaining that he had done nothing wrong, Davidson believed himself to be a martyr. After a three-month trial, he was found Guilty on all charges and was "removed, deposed, and degraded" from his church position. After his appeal to the Privy Council was dismissed, Davidson spent the next five years appearing in side-shows and seaside arcades. On July 28, 1937, he was giving a performance in the lion's cage at the Skegness Amusement Park when he fell over the lioness and was mauled by the lion. Davidson died three days later. REF.: *CBA.*

Davidson, Jane, d.1861, Brit., suic.-mur. After her daughter died, Jane Davidson became infatuated with her son-in-law, William Horsley, who rented a room at the family inn in Carlisle, England.

Davidson, who was in her forties at the time, would do anything to win the young man's love and keep other, younger women at bay. She consulted a fortune teller who predicted that her husband of many years would soon die and that she would marry a much younger man. Encouraged by the good news, Davidson purchased some potions that would act as a charm to keep other girls away from her son-in-law's door while she awaited her good fortune.

She became despondent when the young man continued his flirtations, and she strangled him with a tie before ingesting a deadly quantity of arsenic. She thus committed suicide.
REF.: Butler, *Murderers' England; CBA.*

Davidson, Peter, prom. 1925, Brit., burg.-forg. Peter Davidson was a member of the Gerald Kennaway gang, notorious in England for many bank frauds and forgeries in the period between the two world wars.

Davidson led a group of postal thieves for Kennaway, who were known as kite-fishers. In order to steal from the mailboxes, Davidson would create a mold of the postman's keys. He would then duplicate each specially numbered key and rifle through the mail before the carrier arrived. He took envelopes containing bank drafts and checks to Kennaway's hideout, where duplicates were made. The forgeries were mailed to their original destinations while the real checks were deposited into the Kennaway account.

Detectives from Scotland Yard arrested Davidson, but he refused to testify against Kennaway. For his refusal to cooperate with the police, Davidson was sentenced to five years of hard labor. See: **Kennaway, Gerald.**
REF.: *CBA;* Nicholls, *Crime Within the Square Mile.*

Davidson, Thomas Joseph, b.1900, Brit., mur. Thomas Davidson, a poultry farmer in Stockley, Middlesex, England, was separated from his wife. She lived with their 8-year-old son, John Desmond, in Hanwell at the home of a Mrs. Clack.

In December 1933, Davidson went to his wife's house to pick up his son. After a brief argument with Mrs. Clack, Davidson left with Johnny. The boy was never seen again. The police were summoned, but all Davidson would say was that his son had died in the canal and a funeral was about to take place.

Six months later, Davidson confessed to murdering his son. He explained that he no longer wanted to go on living after his wife refused to come home. Taking his son's hand, Davidson jumped into the canal, but recovered on the opposite shore. His son did not survive.

Davidson said he buried the boy in a shallow grave near a garbage dump in Yiewsley, but neither he nor the police could find the body. During the trial, Davidson retracted his earlier confession, saying he had found the boy in the canal. However, the jury found him Guilty of murder. His death sentence was later commuted to life in prison.
REF.: Brock, *A Casebook of Crime; CBA;* Shew, *A Companion to Murder.*

Davidson, Thomas Whitfield, 1876-1974, U.S., jur. Received appointment to the northern district court of Texas from President Franklin D. Roosevelt in 1936 and published *The Trial of Aaron Burr and the Trial of Abe Rothschild.* REF.: *CBA.*

Davies, Evan Thomas, prom. 1941, Brit., (unsolv.) mur. On a routine patrol with his sergeant, Constable Evan Thomas Davies entered an air-raid shelter on the night of Dec. 11, 1941. The sergeant followed Davies in and saw him talking to two young men. As the sergeant entered, one of the men dropped a tommy-gun, and the other fired two shots. Both youths escaped by another exit. There was no apparent motive for the slaying. Although forensic pathologist Robert Churchill determined that the bullets had been fired from a 9-mm Steyr pattern automatic pistol, the killer was never found.
REF.: *CBA;* Hastings, *The Other Mr. Churchill.*

Davies, Gerald, 1942- , Brit., mur. A young schoolboy on his lunch break in a suburb of London discovered the body of 52-year-old Mrs. Stephenson, near a cemetery. She was found 100 yards from her home. A three-foot-long metal pipe lay across her corpse. Stephenson was the third woman in several weeks to be attacked in that area. Within twenty-four hours, 15-year-old Gerald Davies was arrested. When he was tried three months later, it was revealed that he had owed £3 to a schoolmate and had decided to rob to get the money. Carrying the metal tube and wearing gloves, he murdered Stephenson with a fatal blow to the back of her neck. Her purse contained only two bus tickets. The defense psychiatrist contended that Davies was maladjusted, but prosecution witnesses, including a psychiatrist and the principal medical officer of Brixton Prison, maintained that Davies was not abnormal. Found Guilty of capital murder, and sentenced to an indefinite detention, Davies was the first youth under sixteen to be indicted for murder in Wales or England under the 1957 Homicide Act, enacted on Mar. 21, 1957.
REF.: *CBA;* Wilson, *Children Who Kill.*

Davies, Idris, 1920- , Case of, Brit., mur. Twenty-four-year-old British naval petty officer Idris Davies came home from two and a half years' foreign service in 1944 to find his wife had taken a lover named Edwin Bob Taylor, who lived in the Hampshire village of Droxford.

Davies begged her to end the affair, and then appealed to Taylor, to no avail. Mrs. Davies said that she would stay with her husband only if he agreed to accept Taylor. For the next four weeks, Davies tried to make the best of the situation as his wife openly embraced her lover across the dinner table. On July 5, Taylor appeared at the Davies household after being ordered to stay away. He said that he had arrived to "comfort" Mrs. Davies, ill in bed. At 10:30 p.m., shots were heard. Davies notified the police that he had shot a man with a sixteen-bore shotgun. The police found Taylor dead at the foot of the stairs.

Idris Davies explained that he had suffered a blackout and could not remember what happened. A pathologist from Weybridge explained that this was possibile. Forensic expert Robert Churchill examined the murder weapon and concluded that a crack in the stock of the gun may have caused the weapon to go off in the heat of a struggle. Since Davies had no recollection of the events and there were no eyewitnesses, a jury at the Winchester Assizes acquitted him after only twenty minutes' deliberation.
REF.: *CBA;* Hastings, *The Other Mr. Churchill.*

Davies, Sir John, 1569-1626, Brit., jur. Held position of attorney general for Ireland from 1606-19. He made an attempt at establishing Protestantism in Ulster, was named speaker for the parliament in Ireland from 1613-19, and in 1926 was named lord chief justice of the British parliament, but died prior to serving.
REF.: *CBA.*

Davies, John Michael, 1933- , Brit., mur. John Davies was a member of a ferocious South London gang known as the Teddy Boys. In the summer of 1953, he was indicted for a murder that drew attention to the problem of juvenile delinquency in London. The victims were two young men who inadvertently made disparaging remarks to the gang members near the bandstand of Clapham Common.

On July 2, 17-year-old John Ernest Beckley and his friend Frederick Chandler were walking on the north side of the common when they were set upon by gang members who had taken exception to their comments. The assailants wore the traditional tight-fitting stovepipe trousers and "zoot suits." Beckley and Chandler boarded a bus and were on their way to safety when the "Teddy Boys" dragged them off at the next stop. Chandler got back on the bus, but Beckley ran in the other direction, pursued by the gang, who cornered him. "Go on, stab me! Stab me!" he cried. The murder was witnessed by seven commuters who were either on the bus or waiting on the platform. The police identified five other gang members in addition to Davies: 15-year-old Ronald Coleman; Terence Power, a 12-year-old carpenter; Allan Albert Lawson, an 18-year-old carpenter; Terence David Woodman, sixteen; and the oldest of the gang, 21-year-old John Frederick Allan. All of them were known to the police, having committed a number of petty offenses.

The murder trial of Davies and Coleman began at the Old Bailey in September 1953. The other four boys were tried on lesser charges. The question before the courts was whether Coleman knew that Davies had a knife when he ordered the attack on Beckley. The defendants entered a plea of not guilty through their attorneys, Derek Curtis-Bennett and David Weitzman. The jury was unable to agree on a verdict, and the Crown dropped its case against Coleman. The smug Davies was retried on Oct. 19, 1953. He had one stock answer for his accusers. He said that he never had a knife and never used a knife. Because of the eyewitness testimony supplied by bus passenger Mary Frayling, Davies was convicted of murder and was sentenced to die.

Murderer John Michael Davies.

The Court of Criminal Appeal and the House of Lords both turned down his request for a reprieve, but the home secretary commuted the death penalty to life imprisonment on Jan. 22, 1954.

REF.: *CBA; Furneaux, Famous Criminal Cases, Vol. 1; Jacobs, Aspects of Murder; Parker, The Plough Boy; Wilson, Encyclopedia of Murder.*

Davies, Sir **Louis Henry,** 1845-1924, Can., jur. Served as premier and attorney general of Prince Edward Island from 1876-79, was knighted in 1897, named to the Canadian Supreme Court from 1901-24, and served as chief justice from 1918-24. REF.: *CBA.*

Davies, Richard, prom. 1880s, Brit., mur. Two boys were charged with the murder of their father, reputedly a cruel man who abused his wife. The younger son was reprieved, but the older son, 18-year-old Richard Davies, was tried, convicted, and sentenced to hang. The public felt sympathy for Davies, and on the night before his scheduled execution the post office stayed open all night in case he received a last minute reprieve by telegram. Reluctantly, hangman James Berry executed the boy the next day.

REF.: *Atholl, The Reluctant Hangman; CBA.*

Daviess, Samuel, prom. 1818, Case of, U.S., mur. Samuel Daviess, who was running for the Kentucky legislature, was stopped on a Harrodsburg, Ky., street by Henry Pendleton Smith. Both men began to argue, and Smith suddenly slapped Daviess' face. Daviess drew a gun and fatally shot Smith in full view of dozens of witnesses. In September 1818, Daviess was tried for the murder of Smith but was acquitted on grounds of self-defense, a verdict stretched beyond reason by a jury made up of Daviess supporters.

REF.: *CBA; Nash, Almanac of World Crime; The Trial of Samuel Daviess.*

Davin, Guy, b.c.1906, Fr., theft-mur. As a child, Guy Davin stole increasingly large sums of money from his mother, and as a youth he snatched purses and stole cars. He was also known for his temper and decadent lifestyle. On Dec. 17, 1931, the 26-year-old Davin was seen with American gangster Richard Wall, one of Al Capone's aides. They lunched with two others at a Parisian restaurant, and later Davin took Wall for a ride in his stolen car. When they reached the St. Cucufa Woods, Davin shot Wall three times with a revolver, robbed him, and then drove the car to an isolated place where he jumped from the running board just before the car crashed into a tree. Davin confessed to the murder when arrested. He was tried, convicted, and sentenced to penal servitude for life on Devil's Island.

REF.: *CBA; Cohen, One Hundred True Crime Stories.*

Davis, Angela Yvonne, b.1944, Case of, U.S., consp.-kid.-mur. A black militant was accused of providing guns used in a courtroom escape attempt by three San Quentin inmates in which four people were killed.

In 1969, Angela Davis, twenty-five, was dismissed from her position as an acting assistant professor of philosophy at the University of California after she acknowledged that she was a member of the Communist Party. A Superior Court overruled the dismissal, but university regents refused to reappoint her, saying that several speeches she made contained "inflammatory rhetoric."

On Aug. 7, 1970, at the Marin County Civic Center in San Rafael, Calif., guns registered to Davis were smuggled into a courtroom by Jonathan Jackson, seventeen, and given to three black prisoners. They took five hostages, including Superior Court Judge Harold J. Haley, an assistant district attorney, and three women jurors. The judge, who had a gun taped to his neck, later died in the getaway van with Jackson and two of the escapees. Ruchell Magee was the only survivor of the three prisoners.

Davis was placed on the FBI's Ten Most Wanted list. On Oct. 13, 1970, she was arrested in New York City, and two months later was extradited to Marin County, Calif. Davis and Magee were named as co-defendants, but their cases were separated in July 1971, when Magee demanded that the trial be held in a federal court. In the fall of 1971 a change of venue was granted because of Davis' high profile, and she was tried on murder, kidnapping, and conspiracy charges in Santa Clara County, Calif. During the trial, Davis was accused of planning and supplying guns for the escape attempt. Prosecutors also charged that the hostages were to be used as a bargaining tool to free the Soledad brothers, three black prisoners in Marin County charged with killing a white guard. Davis was said to be in love with George Jackson, one of the Soledad brothers. She admitted that she loved Jackson, but denied involvement in the plot. On June 4, 1972, Davis was acquitted of all charges by an all-white jury.

REF.: *Becker, Hitler's Children—The Story of the Baader-Meinhof Terrorist Gang; CBA; McClellan and Avery, The Voices of Guns.*

Davis, Bruce A., b.1948, U.S., rob.-mur. Bruce Davis was arrested in December 1971 for the murder and robbery of James Earl Hammer, a Washington, D.C., businessman. He was convicted and received a five to fifteen year sentence. After that trial, he was extradited to Chicago, Ill., to stand trial for the murder of Reverend Carlo M. Barlassina, a priest from Buffalo, N.Y., who was strangled and robbed in a downtown Chicago hotel on June 29, 1971. Davis was convicted of murdering the priest and received a sentence of twenty-five to forty-five years.

He served his sentence for the Washington murder in a psychiatric ward at the Medical Center for Federal Prisoners in Springfield, Mo., from Feb. 15, 1973, to Jan. 31, 1979. He was then transferred to Menard Correctional Center in Chester, Ill., to serve his term for the Chicago murder. There, on Oct. 24, 1982, Davis murdered Joseph Cushman, fifty-two, a prison work farm foreman, with an ax, and escaped from the prison. A policeman in Smithers, W.Va., noticed Davis at a gas station, called reinforcements, and captured him a short time later on the road. Davis told West Virginia officials he had been homosexually raped as a teenager, and that he escaped from Menard after he broke his arm in an incident in which an inmate made advances toward him. Davis also confessed to about thirty murders across the U.S. and Puerto Rico during the 1960s and 1970s. An Illinois court convicted him of the murder of the foreman, and sentenced him to life imprisonment. REF.: *CBA*.

Davis, David, 1815-86, U.S., jur. Served as Illinois Circuit Court judge from 1648-62, U.S. Supreme Court associate justice from 1862-77 and as U.S. senator from 1877-83. Davis was the Senate's pro tem president from 1881-83. Stephen Douglas and Abraham Lincoln were two prominent lawyers in his Illinois Circuit Court; Lincoln eventually nominated Davis to the Supreme Court. As a Supreme Court justice he authored the majority's opinion in Ex parte Milligan, 1866, which ruled that neither Congress nor the president could declare a state of martial law unless the area in question were in open rebellion. REF.: *CBA*.

Davis, Edward, prom. 1688-92, U.S., pir. When pirates Edward Davis, Lionel Wafer, and John Hinson, surrendered to Captain Allen of the H.M.S. *Quaker* in Fall 1688, they believed they would be pardoned based on the king's proclamation of Aug. 6, 1688, which offered clemency to all reformed pirates. The three were seized by Captain Simon Rowe of the frigate H.M.S. *Dunbarton* after their surrender. The men confessed, and signed a statement, but the governor told them that they had not surrendered but had been taken by a government representative, and were not eligible for the pardon. All were held in the Jamestown, Va., jail. Davis, who was once called "the greatest and most prudent commander who ever led the forces of the buccaneers at sea," was the leader of the gang, which amassed a fortune that swayed opinion against them. The three pirates had accumulated several chests, weighing between 400 and 500 pounds, packed with gold coins of all nations, broken silver plate, and melted-down silver, valued at between £5,000 and £6,000. Included in their loot were four pairs of silk stockings, two paper books, and several pieces of "dampnifyed" ribbon. Four years after they had been incarcerated by Rowe, the pirates were brought before His Majesty's Privy Council in London, and were ordered released and pardoned. They petitioned King William III for the return of their booty, most of which was returned, with the condition that they donate £300 and one fourth of their valuables to the founding of Virginia's College of William and Mary.

REF.: Botting, *The Pirates; CBA*; Rankin, *The Golden Age of Piracy*.

Davis, Edward, d.1841, Aus., rob.-mur. Edward Davis and five other convicts escaped a chain gang in 1839 and went looting and robbing across New South Wales, Australia, for more than a year. Davis became a popular figure as the band gained notoriety. Davis and his gang captured one posse sent after them, stole the lawmen's guns and horses, and rode off laughing. After they ransacked Isabella Kelly's house, she tracked them down to reclaim her possessions, but instead fell in love with Davis. She visited the hideout so frequently the gang was forced to move.

The gang avoided bloodshed until 1840 when they killed a British man who tried to defend himself. A posse led by Edward Denny Day caught up with the outlaws in the Page River Valley. Davis and five others were hanged on Mar. 16, 1841. REF.: *CBA*.

Davis, Edward Lee, prom. 1900s, U.S., burg. Edward Lee Davis was responsible for several burglaries in an industrial area of San Jose, Calif. Police heard the sound of breaking glass from a farm machinery plant. They arrested the 19-year-old Davis when they found him parked in an alley with office equipment in his back seat. At the station, police examined his tennis shoes and found a small piece of glass, which matched the glass from the broken window at the plant. Davis pleaded guilty, was convicted, and sentenced to six months in the county jail.

REF.: Block, *Science vs. Crime; CBA*.

Davis, Edward M., prom. 1900s, U.S., law enfor. off. A Los Angeles, Calif., native who joined the Los Angeles Police Department in September 1940, Edward Davis served as chief of police there from Aug. 29, 1969, to 1978. He was also president of the International Association of Chiefs of Police. Additionally, Davis served as chairman of the Police Task Force of the National Advisory Commission on Criminal Justice Standards and Goals of the Law Enforcement Assistance Administration, (LEAA), a

group that prepared the *Report on Police*, 1973. He also directed an LEAA national committee that created the *Police Chief Executive Report*, 1975, a work that formulated standards for choosing and keeping leading law enforcement executives. REF.: *CBA*.

Davis, Eliza, c.1815-37, Brit., (unsolv.) mur. On May 9, 1837, just after 6 a.m., when the King's Arms saloon in London opened, two customers noticed a trail of blood, and followed it up the stairs. Just then, the servant boy, Matthew Hitchcock, came running downstairs exclaiming that the barmaid, 21-year-old Eliza Davis, had been slain, her throat cut. When Police Superintendent John Carter arrived on the scene, he soon turned the investigation over to Inspector Aggs and Constable Pegler. The saloon owner, Wadley, said Davis had knocked on his door at the usual time of 6 a.m., and must have been killed just after he handed her the keys. A penny, a half-empty glass of ale, and a bloody bread knife were found on the bar, and Wadley recalled an "ill-looking fellow" who had been coming in for the last week, and had once gotten angry at Davis when she refused him a drink on credit. Although Pegler and Constable Roderick searched for several days for the man Wadley described, and arrested thirteen suspects in ten weeks, the police gave up their search on July 20. Davis' killer was never found.

REF.: *CBA*; Cobb, *The First Detectives*.

Davis, George Breckenridge, 1847-1914, U.S., jur. Authored *Outlines of International Law*, 1887, *The Elements of Law ... Constitutional and Military*, 1897, and *A Treatise in the Military Law of the United States* 1898, and he was the U.S. army's judge advocate general, 1901. REF.: *CBA*.

Davis, George James (George Huntley), and **Watts, William, (Charles Williams)**, d.1830, Brit., pir. Eighteen unruly prisoners in an Australian penal colony were to be transferred by ship from Botany Bay to Macquarrie Harbor. The convicts, including George Davis and William Watts, overpowered the crew and soldiers, eventually setting them ashore on an uninhabited island. The ship of felons set sail for Japan, but they encountered hostility there. When they landed in China, British officials arrested the four survivors and sent them back to Britain to be tried for piracy. Although all four were convicted and given the death sentence, two of them were reprieved. The other two, Davis and Watts, were hanged on Dec. 17, 1830, the last men hanged for piracy at Execution Dock.

REF.: *CBA*; Thomson, *The Story of Scotland Yard*.

Davis, Gregory, 1966- , U.S., sex. asslt.-mur. On Mar. 31, 1987, Addie Reid, an 80-year-old widow, was beaten, sexually assaulted, and strangled to death in her Hattiesburg, Miss., home. When Gregory Davis, a 23-year-old minister's son who lived in Jackson, was arrested on unrelated burglary charges on Aug. 27, 1987, he told Detective Cleon Butler that he would not talk, and he asked for a lawyer. In testimony at a pretrial hearing, Davis' defense attorney, Alvin Binder, said that on Aug. 28, Davis, who had still not talked to a lawyer, confessed to the killings of Reid, 81-year-old Mary Dewitt, and 83-year-old Bertha Tanner. Like Reid, Dewitt and Tanner were beaten, sexually assaulted, and strangled. Convicted by a Hattiesburg jury in January 1988, Davis was sentenced to death for murdering Reid. After the Mississippi Supreme Court upheld his death sentence on July 26, 1989, Hinds County District Attorney Ed Peters said that Davis would not be tried for the other two slayings. The date of execution for Davis, who remains on Death Row at the State Penitentiary at Parchman, was set for Sept. 20, 1989, but additional appeals could delay the case for years. REF.: *CBA*.

Davis, Howell, d.1720, Brit., pir. Born in Milford Haven, in Pembrokeshire, Wales, Howell Davis was raised to become a seaman and became a pirate only by chance. Davis was serving as the first mate on aboard the slave ship *Cadogan*, en route from Nassau, Bahamas, to Madagascar, when it was captured by the buccaneer Edward England. The pirates murdered the captain of the *Cadogan* and attempted to force the crew to sign oaths of allegiance. When Davis refused, Captain England, impressed with his bravery, returned the ship to him, advising him to sail for Brazil, dispose of the slave cargo, and keep the profits. After England departed, Davis and the crew decided to resume their original course—toward Barbados.

On reaching port, the colonial authorities arrested Davis and accused him of piracy. When Davis was released from prison three months later, he sailed up to New Providence, Bahamas, determined to become a pirate. Davis was disappointed to find that Governor Woodes Rogers had broken up the pirate colony. Rogers agreed to make an accommodation with Davis and gave him command of the *Buck,* a cargo ship laden with a rich payload earmarked for the French and Spanish traders. With a crew of cutthroats and murderers, Davis sailed to Martinique where he drew up articles of piracy—an open declaration of war against all nations. From Coxon's Hole, Cuba, the pirate crew seized two French ships before sailing under the British flag to the Cape Verde Islands. Thus disguised, the *Buck* was welcomed into friendly ports and given the protection of the colonial powers. Davis next sailed to Gambia in western Africa, where he purported to be a Liverpool, England, trader. There he stole warehouses of gold and ivory before joining forces with two other notorious pirates of the day, Oliver La Buze and Thomas Cocklyn.

British pirate Howell Davis.

In the next few months, the *Buck* captured several English and Dutch prizes. Davis transferred his crew and cargo to a Dutch ship, the *Royal Rover.* Near the coast of Anamaboe, in western Africa, Captain Davis seized a slave ship named the *Princess* on June 5, 1719. The second mate, also from Pembrokeshire, was 36-year-old Bartholomew Roberts. The Welsh pirate took his new-found protégé along, allowing him to choose whether he wanted to become a pirate. In 1720, Davis arrived at the Prince's Island, a Portuguese settlement where he planned to capture the governor and hold him for a £40,000 ransom. To lure the governor on board, Davis offered him the chance to inspect twelve slaves offered for sale. One of the slaves escaped and warned the governor. Davis and his escort were shot and killed as they made their way toward the governor's mansion. The surviving crew

members of the *Royal Rover* nominated Bartholomew Roberts to succeed Davis.

REF.: Botting, *The Pirates; CBA;* Cabal, *Piracy and Pirates;* Defoe, *A General History of the Robberies and Murders of the Most Notorious Pirates, 1717-1724;* Ellms, *The Pirates' Own Book;* Gosse, *The Pirates' Who's Who;* Innes, *The Book of Pirates;* Lydon, *Pirates, Privateers and Profits;* Mitchell, *Pirates;* Pringle, *Jolly Roger: The Story of the Great Age of Piracy;* Williams, *Captains Outrageous: Seven Centuries of Piracy;* Woodbury, *The Great Days of Piracy.*

Davis, Jack, 1845-79, U.S., rob. Jack Davis turned up in Virginia City, Nev., in the late 1860s, and after failing at gambling, began robbing stagecoaches. In 1870, he joined John Chapman of Reno in train robbery. They pulled the first successful stickup of a train in the Far West when they held up the Central Pacific near Verdi, Nev., on Nov. 4, 1870. They split the profits, about $40,000.

Their reckless spending of the stolen money eventually led to their capture. Davis served only six years of a ten-year sentence, and then joined desperados Joel Collins and Sam Bass. They tried stagecoach robbery, but two stages simply refused to stop when ordered to do so, and a third produced only $3 and a gold watch. The Davis-Bass Gang became a laughingstock among other western outlaws.

In desperation, Davis proposed going after a train. At Big Springs, Neb., on Sept. 18, 1877, the gang removed $60,000 from a train passing through town. After splitting the take, Davis and his partners went their separate ways. He moved to New Orleans, where he wasted his share of the loot, and by 1879 was back in Nevada, robbing stagecoaches. He took a shot in the face from a scattergun fired by Eugene Blair of the Wells Fargo. Davis escaped, but no one is sure where he went. He was reported in Nicaragua as late as 1920. See: **Chapman, John T.** REF.: *CBA.*

Davis, James J. (AKA: **Puddler Jim**), and **Miller, Theodore G.,** and **Mann, Conrad Henry,** and **Western Union Telegraph Co.** prom. 1930s, Case of, U.S., fraud. Pennsylvania Senator James Davis joined the Order of the Moose in 1906 and became director general of the organization. He increased membership from 247 to 600,000, and took a special interest in the Moose orphanage at Mooseheart, Ill. His fundraising techniques, however, led to his indictment in 1932 on charges of conspiring to run interstate lotteries.

Investigators accused Davis, Theodore Miller, director of the Moose's propagation department, Conrad Mann, president of the Kansas City Chamber of Commerce, and Western Union Telegraph Co. of running a scam in which members' tickets to a charity ball included chances in a lottery. Davis reputedly pocketed about $150,000, and others skimmed money for "expenses." When Davis was tried the first time, a mistrial was declared when a juror was accused of trying to influence other jurors. Davis and Miller were acquitted at the second trial on Oct. 12, 1933. Mann and Western Union were acquitted later. REF.: *CBA.*

Davis, John, b.1876, U.S., theft. In 1922, John Davis stole a watch and $5 in Dillon County, S.C. Such a crime was then a capital offense for a black man. More than sixty years later, John Davis was still imprisoned at the maximum-security Central Correctional Institution in Columbia, S.C. In 1981, the 105-year-old prisoner was the state's only inmate with Triple-A status, which allowed him to leave whenever he wished. Davis was released Nov. 24, 1982. REF.: *CBA.*

Davis, John A., 1761-1847, U.S., jur. Held office as U.S attorney for the District of Massachusetts, 1796-1801, and was appointed to the District Court of Massachusetts by President John Adams, Feb. 8, 1801. REF.: *CBA.*

Davis, John Chandler Bancroft, 1822-1907, U.S., jur. Served as a U.S. court of claims judge, 1878-83, and a reporter for the U.S. Supreme Court, 1883-1902, where he edited volumes 108-86 of the *United States Reports.* REF.: *CBA.*

Davis, John W., b.1782, U.S., mur. In 1838, the budding community of Atlanta, Ga., had its first murder of note. John W.

Davis got into an argument with John B. Nelson, who operated Nelson's Ferry Road (now called Nelson Street). What harsh words the two men had for each other is unrecorded, but Davis did kill Nelson and then escaped into the wilds.

Governor George M. Troup offered a reward of $250 for the capture of Davis, a great sum of money in those days, which caused many an impoverished farmer to take his hunting rifle down from the mantle and begin beating the woods for the killer. The *Southern Record* published the murderer's description: "John W. Davis is between fifty and fifty-six years of age, five feet six or seven inches high, stout built, round face, swarthy complexion, dark hair, a little grey with somewhat of baldness, and a shaking of his limbs at times as if affected by palsy."

Davis was captured, but details of his trial are unavailable. He was not executed, however, but committed in 1849, as records show, to the Lunatic Asylum of DeKalb County. REF.: *CBA*.

Davis, John Warren, 1867-1945, U.S., jur. Served as U.S. district attorney for New Jersey, 1913-16, and was appointed by President Woodrow Wilson to the District Court of New Jersey, May 1916, and the 3rd Circuit Court of the U.S., 1920. REF.: *CBA*.

Davis, Julius Richard (Dixie), prom. 1930s, U.S., crim. lawyer. Julius Richard Davis was the crafty criminal attorney who represented New York mobster Dutch Schultz during the early 1930s, cleverly defending his client against charges of murder, assault, and tax evasion. Davis was more than an attorney to Schultz; he was his close friend and, some claimed, his aide in illegal operations. After Schultz's gangster execution in 1935, Davis wrote a sensational series of articles detailing his relations with Schultz. See: Schultz, Dutch.

REF.: *CBA*; Fried, *The Rise and Fall of the Jewish Gangster In America*; Gosch and Hammer, *The Last Testament of Lucky Luciano*; Messick, *Lansky*; ____, *Secret File*; ____ and Goldblatt, *The Mobs and the Mafia*; Peterson, *The Mob*; Sann, *Kill the Dutchman!*; Thompson and Raymond, *Gang Rule In New York*.

Davis, Larry Ronald, b.c.1944, U.S., big.-theft-asslt.-pris. esc.-kid.-rape-mur. Larry Davis, twenty-seven, walked into a jewelry store in Atlanta, Ga., and tried to use credit cards stolen from Susan Doty, a 25-year-old Atlanta woman who had been reported missing. The store manager identified Davis from police mug shots. Police sought Davis, who had previously been arrested for kidnapping, auto theft, concealed weapons, assault, escape, and writing bad checks. He was also under indictment for fraud and sought for armed robbery.

Some time later, Doty's checkbook was found along a highway in Georgia and, near it, her body, strangled and sexually assaulted. Still on the run with Betty Jean Smith, his wife in a bigamous marriage, Davis got as far as San Antonio, Texas. When Smith noticed Susan Doty's name on credit cards that her husband was using, she went to the police and told them where to find Davis. Davis, who said he was on morphine when he attacked Doty, confessed to murder and was convicted. He received four consecutive life terms. REF.: *CBA*.

Davis, Lolita, d.1940, U.S., suic.-mur. Eleven-year-old Chloe Davis of Los Angeles awoke on the morning of Apr. 4, 1940, to strange sounds. She found her mother, Lolita Davis, beating her two sisters, Daphne, ten, Deborah Ann, seven, and her 3-year-old brother Marquis to death with a hammer. Chloe managed to get the hammer away from her mother. When Lolita tried to set fire to Chloe's hair, it did not ignite, so she turned the flame to her own, and succeeded only in making her nightgown flare off her, leaving her naked. She then lay down on a mattress, slit her wrists with a razor blade, and told her daughter to "Hit me until I quit talking." When Chloe asked why, her mother replied that the demons were after her. The child did as she was asked, stopping occasionally to get water for her mother and, once, at her mother's urging, to finish killing her brother, who was moaning. "I always did what mother told me to do," she said. Even though the claw head came off the hammer, the girl continued "conking" her mother until she was silent. Then she

got dressed and went to a neighbor's house to telephone her father, saying he'd better come home right away.

Los Angeles authorities and psychiatrists first believed that Chloe herself killed her siblings and her mother. A police psychiatrist, Dr. Paul de River, said of Chloe, "She is cool, has no depth of feeling, has great powers of imagination for fantasy and is distinctly capable of planning and committing the murders. But so far, I believe her story more than I disbelieve it." It was not until the next day that Chloe remembered to tell the police about her mother slitting her wrists. Then she learned that her mother had, in fact, bled to death, and did not die of bludgeoning. Chloe's father, Barton Davis, said that his wife Lolita had been mentally ill and had frequently threatened suicide to escape the "demons" that pursued her. When the family doctor verified his story, Chloe was released. She was later made a ward of the state. REF.: *CBA*.

Davis, Ralph Orin, b.c.1918, U.S., mur. Ralph Davis, sixty-nine, had served in WWII and had been held prisoner by the Japanese for two-and-a-half years. In 1981, Davis moved from California to Mt. Pleasant, Iowa. His new neighbors in Iowa did not know that Davis had been acquitted of a murder charge on Jan. 16, 1980. He had been charged with the shooting of a neighbor in Bell Gardens, Calif., after a dispute in which Davis accused the neighbor's children of throwing rocks at his truck.

But Davis' new neighbors knew he was eccentric. Unemployed, he rode a motorcycle around town with his dog riding behind him in a milk crate. He reportedly shot birds in a neighbor's yard because they ate cherries from his tree. On Dec. 10, 1986, Davis stormed into a city council meeting, furious that his backed up sewer had not been fixed. He shot Mayor Edward M. King, fifty-three, and wounded Joann Sankey, thirty-nine, and Ronald Dupree, forty-four. Davis was tried and found Guilty of two counts of attempted murder and one count of first-degree murder, which carried a mandatory sentence of life imprisonment. REF.: *CBA*.

Davis, Dr. Sterling Blake, prom. 1976, U.S., consp. Sterling "Cooter" Davis, Jr. had spent twenty-three months in jail in Mexico for marijuana posession, while his father, Dr. Sterling Blake Davis, tried every means to negotiate his son's release. When all other methods failed, Davis hired a Dallas truck driver to break into the prison. Don Fielden, thirty-one, hired one back-up man and a 15-year-old Dallas boy for the carefully planned escape.

On Mar. 12, the operation began as the three slipped into Mexico just before dawn. They experienced difficulties with a customs agent, a much larger number of Mexican police and officials in the jail than expected, and bolt cutters that snapped before the bars were cut. But Fielden managed to get the keys and free young Davis, along with several others. The jail, where Davis claimed he was beaten and forced to sign a confession, held twice as many people as there were pallets to lie on, and the floors were covered with human excrement. Others claimed to have been tortured with cattle prods and electrical devices there. Three days after his escape, Davis turned himself in to U.S. federal authorities for violating parole. In the Mexican jail, he had been expecting a six-year sentence for marijuana, and had an additional four years tacked on for an attempted escape. He had bribed an assistant warden with $2,000 to let him dig his way out, but the warden had told the guards. Davis said he and another American had been "marked" and were attacked by a gang of eight prisoners, who only let them go when a guard fired a rifle between them. Dr. Sterling Davis was convicted on federal charges of conspiracy on Oct. 1, 1976 in Del Rio, Texas, and was given a five-year sentence. Fielden, pleading guilty to transporting a weapon illegally and to conspiracy, was sentenced to four years. The others involved in the prison break were given shorter sentences. REF.: *CBA*.

Davis, Thomas Cullen, 1933-   , Case of, U.S., mur. In 1977, T. Cullen Davis became the richest man ever to be tried for his life. His personal fortune was estimated to be worth $1 billion, most of it from his father, Ken "Stinky" Davis, who started a small

Texas oil business which eventually grew into a multinational conglomerate controlling eighty companies. In 1968, his father died, leaving Cullen one third of Kendavis Industries International. That year, Cullen married a twice-divorced woman named Priscilla Lee Wilborn, and built her a sprawling $6-million mansion in Fort Worth.

Mrs. Davis scandalized the society matrons of Fort Worth. Davis accused his wife of infidelity, and she later testified that he was abusive to her and to his stepdaughter, Andrea. In 1974, Priscilla filed for divorce. Cullen moved into a motel and began an affair with another woman while Priscilla stayed in the Davis mansion with her daughter. She entertained an odd assortment of lovers, including drug trafficker W.T. Rufner. She then began seeing a six-foot-nine-inch former basketball player from Texas Christian University named Stan Farr.

The divorce trial was scheduled to begin on Aug. 2, 1976, before Domestic Relations Court judge Joe Eidson. Cullen Davis seethed when he heard that Eidson granted his wife a delay. When the judge ordered him to pay a lump sum of $52,000 for home maintenance and attorneys' fees, and increase support payments from $3,500 to $5,000 a month, Davis was furious. That night, an intruder disabled the security system and entered the mansion. Farr and Davis returned home around midnight. The assailant had already killed 12-year-old Andrea and wounded Gus Gavrel, a visitor to the mansion. The gunman fired four shots at Farr, killing him instantly. He shot Priscilla in the chest, but the wound was not fatal. She struggled to a neighbor's home and pounded on the door for help.

The case against Cullen Davis seemed to be open and shut. He could not account for his movements between the time he left his office at eight and the midnight shooting. Davis was indicted for the murder of his stepdaughter Andrea. On Aug. 22, 1977, Davis came to court well prepared. He had retained as his legal counsel the legendary Houston lawyer Richard "Racehorse" Haynes, who had often boasted of his skill in selecting juries. The flamboyant Haynes had successfully defended several Houston police officers who were charged with kicking a prisoner to death. "I knew we had that case won when we seated the last bigot on the jury," he recalled later.

Haynes was equally effective during the twelve-week trial of Cullen Davis. It was one of the longest murder trials in Texas history, and probably the most sensational. On Nov. 17, 1977, the jury found the defendant Not Guilty in the shooting death of Andrea Wilborn. His new girlfriend, Karen Master, wept for joy. But he still had to answer to capital murder charges in the death of Farr, and conspiracy charges for allegedly taking out a contract on the life of Judge Eidson.

Hitman David McCrory provided FBI agents with tapes of incriminating conversations in which Cullen Davis discussed murdering Eidson to avenge the humiliation he had caused him during the divorce proceedings. McCrory said that Davis plotted the deaths of fifteen "enemies," including his wife. The FBI tape-recorded and video-taped secret meetings between the men. Davis charged that this was nothing more than an elaborate "sting" operation designed to trap him in a web of lies. As to the incriminating remarks he had made to his former employee McCrory, Davis explained that he was only trying to elicit information that might help him win a favorable divorce settlement.

With Racehorse Haynes again acting as counsel, Cullen Davis went on trial for the second time in less than two years. The trial was held in Fort Worth. On Nov. 9, 1979, the jury acquitted Davis of soliciting for murder and conspiracy to commit capital murder. After the verdict was returned, Tarrant County district attorney Tim Curry announced that the remaining murder charges would be dropped. Racehorse Haynes was said to have pocketed $3 million in legal fees for his work.

REF.: Cartwright, *Blood Will Tell: The Murder Trials of R. Cullen Davis; CBA.*

Davis, Vincent, d.1725, Brit., mur. Vincent Davis, a butcher, was well-known by his Smithfield neighbors as a vicious brute who frequently beat his wife. He stabbed her to death, and was hanged for it at Tyburn on Apr. 30, 1725. Before he was executed, he wrote letters to various people, imploring them to save his body from dissection.

REF.: *CBA;* Turner, *The Inhumanists.*

Davis, Wallace, Jr., b.1952, U.S., polit. corr. In November 1986, Chicago alderman Wallace Davis, Jr., thirty-four, was indicted on charges of extortion, fraud, and racketeering. Seven others were also indicted in Operation Incubator. His former secretary, Joanne McKinley, thirty-two, charged that when Davis drove her home on Feb. 26, 1987, he struck her with a pistol to try to elicit information about what she had told a federal grand jury the previous May. She alleged that he put the gun near her head and fired into the air. She required eight stitches for a wound. Davis was acquitted of assault charges on July 13, 1987.

On Oct. 13, Davis was convicted of extortion, racketeering, and attempted extortion. He forced his niece, Etta Harris, twenty-four, to pay kickbacks from her salary as a ward secretary in 1984 and 1985. In exchange for $3,000 from William Kasten and Charles Scala, owners of a restaurant in his ward, Davis delayed the city's demolition of their building. He also accepted a $5,000 bribe from FBI informant Michael Raymond on Dec. 18, 1985. Davis assured Raymond that Datacom Systems, Inc., a company that collected money from unpaid parking tickets, would be removed from consideration for a city contract. Davis was sentenced to a prison term of eight and a half years. REF.: *CBA.*

Davis, William (AKA: **The Golden Farmer**), c.1635-89, Brit., rob.-mur. A farmer and the father of eighteen children, William Davis supplemented his income by operating as a highwayman, robbing his countrymen for over forty-two years without ever arousing the suspicions of his neighbors.

Davis usually took the direct approach, guns blazing, as he assaulted some well-protected coach rumbling along on a lonely stretch of road. In one encounter, Davis met Sir James Day riding alone. He told Day, whom he knew to be a Justice of the Peace, that he had barely escaped being robbed by two highwaymen. Only the speed of his horse had saved him, Davis said. Day informed Davis that if he had been robbed during daylight, present laws would compel local authorities to make good his loss, if he brought suit to recover. The farmer thanked Day for the advice, then rode ahead and lay in wait for Day. When the aristocrat approached, Davis shot the judge's horse and demanded his money. Day, seeing he had no choice, quickly handed over his purse. The farmer thanked him for the money and reminded Day he had lost nothing. The county authorities would return his funds if he brought suit, Davis said, parroting the judge's own words.

After paying his landlord a large amount of rent, Davis disguised himself and followed the landlord, robbing him and taking his own money back as well as additional cash the landlord possessed. On another occasion, he spotted an old man dressed in shabby clothes. Davis knew this elderly gentleman to be well-off. He told the old man that he suspected that four highwaymen planned to rob him. Davis asked the old gentleman to hide his money for him, explaining that the highwaymen would certainly spare the old man because of his ragged appearance. The old man agreed, telling Davis that his own money was secreted in his shirt for safekeeping; he would put the farmer's money there, too. The two set off together. At a quiet spot in the road, Davis asked for his money. He then took the old man's purse.

Throughout his long career, Davis delighted in puncturing the pomposity of his victims. Such was the case with a barrister named Broughton who was staying at an inn in Uxbridge. Davis asked Broughton if he could recommend a lawyer, and the barrister volunteered himself. The farmer explained that some of his neighbors' cattle were invading and damaging his land. The barrister explained that his neighbors could be charged with *damage fesant.* Davis played upon the vanity of his next victim. The following day, riding with Broughton on the road to London, the farmer asked the barrister to give him the legal terms for certain illegal actions. The egotistical lawyer was happy to parade his legal expertise. When they came to a secluded spot, Davis asked the barrister to name the crime where one person forcibly takes money from another. "That's a robbery," Broughton replied, explaining that such a crime was punishable by death.

Davis immediately drew his pistol and announced that he was committing that very crime, enjoying the barrister's shock and outrage before riding away with his purse.

Davis' blatant contempt for the law Broughton represented brought about his own painful death. At the age of sixty-four, the highwayman, by then widely known and sought by authorities, was identified in London's Salisbury Court. A butcher attempted to stop him, and Davis shot him dead. The butcher, however, had slowed his escape and Davis was captured. He was sent to Newgate Prison, then to the gallows, executed on Dec. 20, 1689. The highwayman's body was then put on display, hanged in chains.

REF.: Butler, *Murderers' England; CBA;* Pringle, *Stand and Deliver;* Smith, *Highwaymen.*

Davison, William, c.1541-1608, Scot., (wrong. convict.) Employed as Queen Elizabeth I's Scottish secretary, 1586-87, who she falsely accused and imprisoned, 1587-89, for obtaining her signature with unnecessary haste on the death warrant of Mary, Queen of Scots. REF.: *CBA.*

Davitt, Michael, 1846-1906, Ire., smug.-rebel. An Irish nationalist, who, for attempting to smuggle guns into Ireland, served seven years of penal servitude, later being imprisoned for seditious speeches after setting up the Land League, 1879, to fight for independence and the struggle for ownership of land. He wrote *Leaves from a Prison Diary,* 1884, and joined William O'Brien in founding the United Irish League, 1898. REF.: *CBA.*

Davria, Govind Narayen (AKA: Prince of Forgers), prom. 19th Cent., India, count.-forg. Govind Davria combined his talent for forgery with counterfeiting operations and organized an extensive ring that included bank employees. He operated a lucrative business in Bombay for some time, using employees of the Bank of Bombay, including a clerk and the cashier, to pass the bad notes. Another bank clerk detected their system and blackmailed the gang. When Davria paid him off with a forged note, the clerk went to police, who arrested Davria and several others. They were tried, but acquitted on a technicality.

Police, including Bombay detective Mir Abdul Ali, continued to track Davria and finally located him in Berar. After winning the trust of Davria's associates, the detective began negotiations for a large purchase of counterfeit money. Davria was finally captured at a meeting to close the deal. He committed suicide his first night in jail by setting himself on fire.

REF.: *CBA;* Wren, *Masterstrokes of Crime Detection.*

Davys, John (John Davis), c.1550-1605, Sing., (unsolv.) mur. As a British navigator and explorer he sought the Northwest Passage, 1585, discovering Baffin Bay, 1587, a strait named for him, Davis Strait, and the Falkland Islands, 1592. He was murdered off the coast of Singapore by Japanese pirates. REF.: *CBA.*

Dawani (Muhammad ibn Jalal ad-Din Dawani), 1427-c.1503, Iran, jur. Authored commentaries on Islamic law. REF.: *CBA.*

Dawkins, Iris, c.1951-60, Brit., (unsolv.) mur. A 9-year-old girl, Iris Dawkins, was found murdered in a playground in Mayfield Park, near Southampton, on Feb. 21, 1960. Her body had been stabbed thirty-nine times. A 10-year-old boy was charged with the murder, but on July 13, 1960, Justice Pilcher directed the jury to acquit the boy on the grounds of insufficient evidence.

REF.: *CBA;* Furneaux, *Famous Criminal Cases, Vol. 6.*

Dawson, Charles, d.1916, Case of, Brit., hoax. Men working in a gravel pit near the village of Piltdown, Sussex, in 1908 found part of a skull that appeared to be human. Charles Dawson, a local antiquarian and lawyer was walking nearby and took the skull, which interested him. Other pieces soon came to hand, and in 1912, Dawson presented his "Piltdown Man" to the scientific community in London, giving it the scientific name *Eoanthropus dawsoni.* Sir Arthur Smith Woodward, head of the Geology Department at the British Museum, began an investigation of the bones. He eventually reported that Piltdown Man was the "missing link" between ape and man and must be at least half a million years old. Dawson took great pride in his discovery before he died in 1916. The physical evidence supporting Charles Darwin's theory of evolution shocked the world. Many questioned the authenticity of the find, and its implications. But as other discoveries about ancient man were made in coming years, Piltdown Man took its place in the tables of evolution.

The remains of Piltdown Man lay in the cupboards of the British Museum for forty years, until Dr. K.P. Oakley of the museum took them out in 1953 to test an idea. Oakley had discovered that fluorine water in soil was absorbed by bone at a predictable rate that could be used to determine the age of the bone. He studied the Piltdown bones, which were supposedly found in a fluorine-rich area, and discovered that the cranium was no more than 5,000 years old. Then he and Dr. J. E. Weiner, using radioactive carbon dating, showed that the jawbone was from a modern orangutan. Piltdown Man was a hoax. Charles Dawson became famous not for discovery, but for fraud.

REF.: *CBA;* MacDougall, *Hoaxes;* Nash, *Zanies.*

Dawson, Charles I., 1881-1969, U.S., jur. Held office of attorney general for Kentucky, 1920-24, and appointed to the Western District Court of Kentucky by President Calvin Coolidge, 1925. REF.: *CBA.*

Dawson, Daniel, d.c.1811, Brit., fraud. Daniel Dawson and Cecil Bishop, two seasoned racetrack bettors, planned to make their fortunes killing off two favored horses. According to their plan, they injected a deadly amount of arsenic into the horses' trough. Dandy and Pirouette, picked to win the 1811 Newmarket Spring race, died along with four other horses.

Dawson had bet heavily against the two front-runners and had tipped other people to do the same. Police caught them both and Bishop confessed. Dawson was acquitted on a technicality, but was later indicted on another charge and hanged.

REF.: *CBA;* Dilnot, *Triumphs of Detection.*

Dawson, James, c.1717-46, Brit., treas. Hanged, drawn and quartered on Kensington Green for his participation in attempting to help James II regain the throne. William Shenstone's ballad *Jemmy Dawson* deals with Dawson's betrothed dying of grief the same day as his execution.

REF.: Bleackley, *Hangmen of England; CBA.*

Dawson, John, c.1888-1934, Brit., (unsolv.) mur. John Dawson, a 46-year-old farmer in Bashall Eaves, England, had just finished an evening playing dominoes at the Edisford Bridge Hotel on Mar. 19, 1934. As he arrived at the gate of his farm, he heard a clicking noise and felt something hit his back. Thinking that perhaps someone had thrown a stone as a joke, he went inside and ate dinner.

The next morning his back felt stiff, so he asked his sister to examine it. She was appalled to find his back covered with blood, wounded just below his left shoulder. Although Dawson protested, his sister called a doctor, who directed that he be taken for treatment to a nursing home in Blackburn. Gangrene had already set in, and Dawson refused to have an operation. He died on Mar. 21, 1934, of blood poisoning. An autopsy later revealed a homemade bullet about one-half inch long. Police never found the killer.

REF.: Butler, *Murderers' England; CBA;* Hastings, *The Other Mr. Churchill.*

Dawson, Sie, c.1910-64, U.S., mur. On Apr. 14, 1960, Maggie Clayton, thirty-six, and her 2-year-old son, Roger, were found beaten to death in Gasden County, Fla. Their bodies were found by her husband, Alva Clayton, and two other men. Sie Dawson, a black man who had worked for the Claytons for ten years as a babysitter and handyman, was accused by his employer and arrested. For seven days, Dawson was denied counsel and driven continuously from jail to jail, interrogated at each stop. Dawson finally confessed after County Deputy Sheriff Robert Martin threatened to hand him over to a mob if he didn't confess.

During the trial, Dawson testified that Clayton had become angry when he smelled whiskey on his wife's breath and had beaten her to death with a hammer. However, an all-white male jury convicted Dawson of murdering the child. He received the death sentence, but was never tried for the murder of Mrs. Clayton. Two years later, the 54-year-old Dawson died in the electric chair. REF.: *CBA*.

Day, Alexander (AKA: **Marmaduke Davenport**), prom. 1723, Brit., fraud. One of England's early confidence men, Alexander Day wore elegant clothes, and employed a coach and a liveried coachman. He would arrive at one expensive shop after another, an apparently regal and rich customer. He would then order goods to be delivered to a large house, rented for a short time. Day would introduce himself as Marmaduke Davenport, claiming to be a member of a well-to-do London family. Invariably, the expensive goods were delivered on promise of a later payment.

The payments, of course, never arrived. When the shopkeepers went to collect, they would find Day gone. By then he had rented another house, bilking other shopkeepers with the same pay-later scheme. Day was arrested mistakenly in May 1723, identified as a highwayman who had been robbing the mail. He was soon discovered to be the wrong man. But suspicious officials found six fraud indictments pending against Day. He pleaded innocent, insisting that he had every intention of paying for the goods. After a long trial, Day was convicted and sentenced to serve two years in Newgate Prison. Worse for his pride, the trickster was also sent to the pillory.

REF.: *CBA*; Mitchell, *The Newgate Calendar*.

Day, Alfred, prom. 1870s, U.S., west. gunman-outl. Alfred Day was a follower of Jim Taylor during the bloody Sutton-Taylor feud in south Texas in the 1870s. He drove cattle north to the railheads in Kansas for the Taylor family and doubled as a gunman when needed. He reportedly shot Bill Sutton in the Bank Saloon at Cuero, Texas, and he was listed as a fugitive in 1876 in Gonzales County. Day survived the Sutton-Taylor feud and lived into the next century, writing a book about his experiences in the 1930s. See: **Sutton-Taylor Feud**.

Outlaw Alfred Day.

REF.: Bartholomew, *The Biographical Album of Western Gunfighters*; *CBA*.

Day, Jack, d.1961, Brit., mur. Jack Day suspected his wife of having an affair, and allegedly said he would shoot anyone he found with her. On Aug. 23, 1960, Keith Arthur visited Day's wife. Arthur was married with two children, but was said to brag about his success with other women. According to a babysitter, Day came home with a gun in his hand and, after arguing, shot Arthur. Day then hid the man's body at a farm outside of town.

Police later found an unlicensed .38-caliber revolver in the garage where Day worked as a car salesman. They also found blood, soil, fertilizer, and straw on Day's clothing and shoes. Day contended that the gun had accidentally discharged, but he was convicted of murder and executed.

REF.: *CBA*; Tullett, *Strictly Murder*.

Day, James, prom. 1936, Case of, U.S., mur. Nathan Leopold and Richard Loeb, the young Chicago students who killed Bobbie Franks as an intellectual experiment, went to Stateville prison in Joliet, Ill., where their money paid for privileged living among the convicts. They were also allowed to continue their homosexual relationship. But in 1935, Loeb became interested in another man, James Day, who was serving seven years in prison. Day did not return the interest, but Loeb continued to pursue him. On Jan. 28, 1936, Day decided to confront Loeb, and said he would meet him in the shower room. Loeb arrived with a razor,

determined to get what he wanted from Day.

Loeb forced Day to remove his clothes, which Day did, hoping he would get a chance to attack. But when Loeb tried to join him in the shower, Day kicked him in the groin. A fight began for the razor, and continued under steaming-hot water. The two grappled, first standing, then sliding around on the floor. First Loeb had the knife, then Day got it and slashed blindly, knowing, as he said in his trial, that "I would die there unless by super-human efforts I could get out from under him." When Loeb "fell mumbling," Day rinsed the blood off his body and stepped out of the shower. The bleeding Loeb lunged at him again, then ran out of the shower room.

Loeb had fifty-six slash wounds on his body. When he died a few hours later, Day was charged with murder. He pleaded not guilty and was acquitted by a jury. See: **Leopold, Nathan.**

REF.: Busch, *Prisoner at the Bar*; *CBA*; Messick, *Kidnapping*; Nash, *Bloodletters and Badmen*.

Day, Raymond (AKA: **Tom Brown**), b.c.1947, U.S., fraud. In 1978, three months after commodity options trading was declared illegal by the U.S. government, backroom brokers set up Archaray Enterprises in New York and began selling non-existent options in gold, silver, platinum, and heating oil. They defrauded close to 500 investors nationwide of more than $2 million. Raymond Day, thirty-three, the crooked company's director, was convicted of fraud and of violating the commodity option sales law, and was sentenced to four years in prison. REF.: *CBA*.

Day, William L., 1878-1936, U.S., jur. Served as U.S. attorney for the Western District of Ohio, 1908-11, and appointed to the Northern District Court of Ohio by President William Taft, May 9, 1911. REF.: *CBA*.

Day, William Rufus, 1849-1923, U.S., jur. As U.S. secretary of state for four months, 1898, he helped negotiate a peace treaty with Spain in the war over Cuba, resulting in the purchase of the Philippines for $20 million. He also served as U.S. circuit court of appeals judge, 1899-1903, at the appointment of his close personal friend, President William McKinley, and U.S. supreme court associate justice, 1903-22, at the appointment of President Theodore Roosevelt. While on the supreme court he wrote the majority opinion in *Dorr v. United States*, 1904, which held that the due process clause of the U.S. Constitution was not guaranteed to residents living in U.S. territories unless Congress specifically incorporates the territory. He authored the opinion in *Weeks v. United States*, 1914, which stated that any evidence acquired through illegal search and seizure could not be used in federal court. REF.: *CBA*.

Daybreak Boys, prom. 1850s, U.S., org. crime. The only way to gain admission to the Daybreak Boys was to kill someone in cold blood. Most of the initiates to this New York City gang were barely past the age of consent. The New York police estimated that between 1850 and 1852 the gang was personally responsible for the theft of $200,000 in property, and the murders of twenty to forty persons. On occasion the Daybreak Boys sank ships just to demonstrate to police their willingness to kill and destroy.

Many famous underworld characters of the post Civil War era got their start with this gang, including: Slobbery Jim, Sam McCarthy, Sow Madden, Bill Howlett, Nicholas Saul, and Patsy the Barber. In 1858, when the gang's activity began to escalate, the New York police initiated a crackdown. In several all-out gun battles, twelve of the Daybreak Boys were killed. A year later the gang was virtually out of existence.

REF.: Asbury, *The Gangs of New York*; *CBA*; Haskins, *Street Gangs*.

Dayton, Alston Gordon, 1857-1920, U.S., jur. Held office of prosecuting attorney for Upshur County, W. Va., 1879-84, and Barbour County, W. Va., 1884-86, and was appointed to the Northern District Court of West Virginia by President Theodore Roosevelt, Mar. 5, 1905. REF.: *CBA*.

Dayton, Jonathan, 1760-1824, Case of, U.S., treas. Jonathan Dayton, who had been a member of the Continental Congress (1787-89), later became a U.S. senator (1799-1805). He was charged with plotting with Aaron Burr to establish a separate nation within U.S. territory, but he was released without trial in 1807. See: **Burr, Aaron**. REF.: *CBA*.

Daza, Hilarión (Hilarión Grosolé), 1840-94, Bol., pres., 1876-80, assass. Served as Bolivian president, 1876-80, before revolutionary forces overthrew him and he fled into exile until 1894, being murdered by a mob upon his return. REF.: *CBA*.

Dazeley, Sarah, 1819-43, Brit., mur. Sarah Dazeley reputedly claimed she wanted to marry seven times in ten years. She married her first husband, Simeon Mead, in 1836. They had a son who, along with his father, died of an unknown illness. She married William Dazeley, twenty-three, in February 1841, and he too died a year later. A third man was nearly at the altar but apparently had a change of heart.

Dazeley received no financial gain as a result of her husbands' deaths, but an investigation was begun into the mysterious deaths. Dazeley was arrested in London and taken home to Wrestlingworth. When the bodies of her dead husbands and baby were exhumed, arsenic was discovered in the baby and her second husband. The 24-year-old Dazeley was tried, convicted, and executed for the murders.

REF.: Butler, *Murderers' England*; *CBA*.

Deacon Brodie; or, The Double Life, 1885, a play by Robert Louis Stevenson and W. E. Henley. William Brodie (Scot., 1788), who exemplified the dual personality, a respected citizen by day, a master criminal by night, was the role model for the protagonist of this less than effective drama. See: **Brodie, William**; *Strange Case of Dr. Jekyll and Mr. Hyde, The*. REF.: *CBA*.

Dead Man's Alley, prom. 1890s, U.S., rob.-mur. In Chicago in the mid 1890s, Dead Man's Alley was frequented by a gang of between 100 and 200 men, women, and children, in the neighborhood of Taylor Street, Plymouth Place, and Polk Street. The place was infamous for robberies, shoot-outs, and violent fights. Frequented by highwaymen, murderers, and thieves, Dead Man's Alley was assigned to Detective Clifton R. Wooldridge after several complaints about the gangs and the high number of incidents.

One night at roll call, Wooldridge requested fourteen men; he divided them up into squads of two, three, and four. All rode street cars and descended on Dead Man's Alley, in the center of a neighborhood known by the name of "Coon Hollow." The alley was packed with about three hundred people. They fled when they saw Wooldridge, but were captured by the policemen posted at different entrances of the alley. Wooldridge then descended on the prostitutes and thieves, taking out warrants for all the brothels, and raiding them the next day. About twelve thieves met secretly on July 4, 1895, and planned to shoot the detective that night, since the sounds of gunfire would be lost in the noise of firecrackers and other holiday explosions. A woman passing by heard the plan, and reported it to the police, who placed additional officers and plains-clothes body-guards around Wooldridge. Within two weeks, Dead Man's Alley was cleaned up.

REF.: *CBA*; Wooldridge, *Hands Up*.

Dead Man's Tree, prom. 1910-30, U.S., org. crime. The first gangland battle ground of Prohibition Chicago was the Bloody Nineteenth Ward on the near West Side. Here a growing Italian population fought for control of the emerging bootleg rackets against the tenacious Irish gangs and their embattled political leader, Alderman Johnny "de Pow" Powers. The immigrant Italians looked to Tony D'Andrea, a defrocked priest turned pimp and counterfeiter, to provide political leadership. D'Andrea had waged several spirited but unsuccessful campaigns to unseat Powers, and the feud continued to escalate.

The D'Andrea forces were backed by the Genna Brothers, Pete, Angelo, Tony, and Jim, who supplied the muscle. Alderman Powers also had the necessary firepower to wage this battle. Between 1919 and 1921, bombings and assassination characterized the day-to-day existence in the Nineteenth Ward. A poplar tree on Loomis Street in the heart of the "alky cooking" district of Little Italy served as a place where the rival factions posted the name of the next victim, hoping to scare and intimidate the

opponent into submission. Nearly thirty men who lost their lives in the Powers-D'Andrea war saw their names appear on the Dead Man's Tree before they died. One of the last was Tony D'Andrea. REF.: *CBA*.

Dead Rabbits, prom. 1840s-60s, U.S., org. crime. The Dead Rabbits was a fierce, huge gang of thugs, pickpockets, robbers, and killers who inhabited the Lower East Side of New York City from the 1840s through the 1860s, dominant in the 1850s. When openly warring with other gangs, their gruesome battle flag was a dead rabbit impaled high on a spear. Most of the Dead Rabbits were Irish and Welsh immigrants. These mobsters—the gang often numbering as many as 500—controlled most of the Five Points area, waging bloody battles with the Roach Guards and the awesome Plug-Uglies. The worst was the Dead Rabbits Riot of 1857 that involved more than 1,000 battling gangsters and lasted for days. By the end of the Civil War, the power of the Dead Rabbits waned, and gang members were either driven out of their haunts in the Five Points or were absorbed by other rising gangs. See: **Dead Rabbits Riot; Plug-Uglies; Roach Guards**.

REF.: Asbury, *The Gangs of New York*; *CBA*; Nash, *Bloodletters and Badmen*.

Dead Rabbits Riot, 1857, U.S., mob vio. The Fourth of July, 1857, was a time of high gala for many New Yorkers. But that day and the one following for many gangsters and policemen marked the end of their lives. Early in the morning of the Fourth, throngs of Dead Rabbits and Plug Uglies invaded a Bowery Boys haunt at 42 Bowery. They were met by scores of Atlantic Guards and Bowery Boys, and the battle lasted several hours, the Bowery gangs eventually driving the Rabbits and Guards back into the Five Points. In the afternoon, the gangs were at it again, this time the brickbats, clubs, and paving stones flying from Pearl and Chatham Streets to the northern end of Park Row.

The newly established Metropolitan Police tried to quell the riots but were beaten off, several officers sent to the hospital. Smugly, the Municipal Police, not yet amalgamated into the new state-run force, remained aloof, refusing to aid the Metropolitans and stating that the riots were none of their business.

The next morning saw the largest number of gangsters ever assembled in one spot at one time in America. More than 5,000 thugs belonging to all the Five Points gangs marched into the Bowery, where they were met in mortal combat by an equal number of gangsters. The Roach Guards raced into the Green Dragon, a Bowery Boys hangout, and ripped it to pieces, tearing up the floorboards, smashing the furniture, and guzzling the saloon's liquor supply to the last drop. Reeling away, the Five Pointers marched to Bayard Street, where a mighty army of Bowery thugs awaited them, the Atlantic Guards in the lead.

There was a deafening roar as the two enormous crowds clashed and the killing began. Again the police were summoned, but when they tried to force a club-wielding wedge into the immense throng, the gangs instantly united against them. Hundreds of policemen joined this greatest of all gang battles, and the lines of the combatants swayed back and forth for several hours, raging along Worth and Center Streets. At length the gangs gave way, particularly after several leaders of the Dead Rabbits were shot. The police, too, retreated, taking with them only two gang members whom they had knocked unconscious.

Seeing the police depart, the gangsters swarmed back onto Bayard and Bowery Streets. They entered the houses and drove the residents onto the street. Some of the more truculent inhabitants were thrown out windows. Dead Rabbits crawled to the tops of buildings and hurled paving stones and bricks down upon the fading police.

The insidious Isaiah Rynders, New York's political and gang boss, was seen hovering in the background of the street battle. For once, the notorious captain decided the riots were out of hand. He attempted to persuade the gang leaders to break off the action, but several turned in their traumatic anger and threatened to "knock off" his head. Rynders slipped away to the office of Police Commissioner Simeon Draper, stating that "if you don't call out the entire force to put these boys down, I'll get the military."

"Get the military," Draper said, and went to look after his wounded.

General Sandford, who had so expertly bluffed Mayor Wood into quelling the Police Riot a month earlier, arrived in the riot area with three regiments at about 9 p.m. The troops smartly took their positions, their ranks even, their weapons ready. The gangsters took one look at the guardsmen and whooped into retreat.

Although only eight men were reported killed in this free-for-all, with another 100 injured, it was commonly believed that as many as 100 gangsters had been slain in the two-day battle, for dozens of new graves appeared in the dark tenement basements of the Five Points and the Bowery. The police concluded that the gangs had dragged off their dead to bury on their own, to keep the numbers of their fallen a secret, lest the badly terrorized citizenry think them less than invincible. Awful as the Dead Rabbits Riot was, New York's most destructive week was yet to come in the form of the New York Draft Riots of 1863. It would prove to be a blood bath unequalled in the history of the city. See: **New York Draft Riots**; **Police Riot**, 1857.

REF.: Asbury, *The Gangs of New York*; *Asmodeus in New York* (Anon.); Barnard, *Forty Years the Five Points*; Barnes, *The Metropolitan Police*; Brace, *The Dangerous Classes of New York*; *CBA*; at the Five Points; Brace, *The Dangerous Classes of New York*; *CBA*; Costello, *Our Police Protectors, A History of the New York Police*; Haskins, *Street Gangs, Yesterday and Today*; Headley, *The Great Riots of New York, 1712-1872*; Kobler, *Capone*; Martin, *Secrets of the Great City*; Peterson, *The Mob*; Reppetto, *The Blue Parade*; Thrasher, *The Gang*; *The Volcano Under the City* (Anon.); Walling, *Recollections of a New York Chief of Police*.

Deák, Ferenc, 1803-76, Hung., lawyer. Served as Hungarian minister of justice, 1848, and in c.1861 was generally recognized as the country's leader. REF.: *CBA*.

Deakin, Alfred, 1856-1919, Aus., lawyer. Appointed the commonwealth of Victoria's first attorney general, 1901, and the commonwealth's prime minister, 1903-04, 1905-08, and 1909-10. REF.: *CBA*.

Dean, Cyrus B., d.1808, U.S., smug.-mur. Jonathan Ormsby and Asa Marsh were revenue agents who tried to stop a band of smugglers from taking a load of potash from Vermont to Canada. The leader of the smugglers, Cyrus Dean, killed both agents with a hunting rifle that was reportedly longer than nine feet. Dean and his men were apprehended some weeks later, and Dean was convicted of killing both Ormsby and Marsh on Aug. 23, 1808. He was condemned and hanged a few weeks later.

REF.: *CBA*; *The Trial of Cyrus B. Dean*; Whitehead, *Border Guard*.

Dean, Dan, prom. 1890s, U.S., rob. A well-organized team of boy thieves operating in downtown Chicago in the late 1890s managed to steal almost $2,000 worth of property before they were caught. Several complaints had been filed at Chicago's Harrison Street police station against a gang that preyed on a busy stretch of Wabash Avenue. Several officers were assigned to catch the criminals, but the thieves were still at large. Detective Clifton Rodman Wooldridge was riding the Wabash Avenue streetcar one evening when he noticed five or six boys get on at Twelfth Street and position themselves around a prosperous looking rider. One pushed him from behind, while another picked his pockets. Wooldridge pulled a gun and the thieves jumped off the car. He chased them to the 1300 block of South State Street where they entered a rooming house. Watching the house for two hours, Wooldridge observed a number of boys enter with bundles, take them to a front room on the third floor, leave empty handed, and return later with more packages.

Wooldridge returned to the building the next night with several police officers. In the third floor room, they discovered two boys with a patrol wagon-sized load of laundry, whiskey, tobacco goods, groceries, and other valuables. Arresting them, Wooldridge stationed a policeman at the front door, telling him to let anyone up but no one out. One by one, seven boys walked into the

detective's trap. One of the arrested youths confessed, informing Wooldridge of the whereabouts of the rest of the gang. A total of sixteen arrests were made.

Dan Dean was the captain of the gang. Their daily schedule involved stealing papers in the early morning, picking pockets near the State Street stores during the day, thieving from grocery and laundry wagons in the evening, and taking overcoats from hallways whenever possible, finishing the day's activities by lifting robes and horse blankets. Tried before Justice Bradwell in mid-December, the young criminals were fined between $10 and $75 each.

REF.: *CBA*; Wooldridge, *Hands Up*.

Dean, Dayton, prom. 1936, U.S., mur. The investigation of a murder in Detroit, Mich., uncovered the existence of the Black Legion, a group of 200,000 Michigan citizens dedicated to fighting—and sometimes murdering—blacks, Jews, Catholics, communists, and anarchists.

On May 13, 1936, the body of Charles Poole was found in a pasture on Detroit's West Side. A neighbor, Frank Shettlehelm, said he heard several shots just before midnight on May 12. A number of cigarette butts and several empty shells from a .38 revolver were found near the corpse. Ralph Hyatt, Poole's co-worker, told Inspector Navarre that he had been with Poole the night of his death, drinking with several friends, including a man named Eugene Sherman, at some West Side bars. When Sherman was brought in for questioning he told police that he had gone to Poole's home that night, and that a man came over to invite Poole to join the Timken Axle Company baseball team later that night. Poole left for the meeting, and was never seen again.

The detectives told Becky Poole her husband was dead at the hospital; she had just given birth to a daughter. Detectives Meehan and Havrill worked on the investigation, when a call came in from Poole's friend Sherman, who had just seen one of the men who had been looking for Poole the night of his death. The detectives rushed to the Fort Street location and picked up Harvey Davis, and brought him in for questioning. Davis admitted knowing Marcia Rushing, Becky Poole's sister, and her husband, Owen Rushing. Havrill interviewed the couple again, and Marcia Rushing began sobbing uncontrollably, saying, "We can't tell you! You don't know those people! They kill people that talk. They carry guns, and there are thousands and thousands of them—like the Ku Klux Klan—only bigger and more awful." Owen's brother, Lowell Rushing, was one of them. Havrill and Meehan brought Lowell to Davis, who claimed never to have seen him before. But when Meehan asked Davis, "What about your organization?," Davis fell for the trap and said, "I can't tell you." With a list of names, the detectives began to round up members, including Erwin Lee and John Bannerman, discovering blackjacks, .38 revolvers, and robes of black satin trimmed with skull and crossbones in their homes.

The most crucial suspect they turned up was Dayton Dean, who was the only one who brave enough to talk. He told the story of the Black Legionnaires, a secret "patriotic" organization of white, native-born, Protestant Americans, sworn to defending the laws, according to their interpretation of decency, especially regarding womanhood. At a meeting of the Wolverine Republican League, a pseudonym for the Black Legion, was called, at Finlander Hall the organization charged Charlie Poole with mistreating his wife. After wearing down uninitiated members who left after endless hours of speeches and business meetings, the Black Legionnaires locked the doors and swore to kill the man they said had not only beat his wife, but killed his own unborn child in the process. Several men were dispatched to find their prey, while others put together rope, ceremonial gear, and instruments to punish Poole. Facing a group of seven men with ropes and guns, Poole professed his innocence, but was shot down. Learning that Poole was actually an upright family man, Dean regretted his mistake, adding, "But I was just following orders from my superiors."

The Black Legion case remained in the press for some time as reports of vicious vigilante killings and beatings continued to grow. Dean unveiled a twisted conspiracy of a group similar to the Klan, to which he had belonged in 1922, rising to the station of captain. He joined the Black Legionnaires in 1933, attending his first meeting in a small town north of Detroit. With secret rites of "Black Knights" signing death's head agreements in blood, vowing to use extra-legal methods to preserve the white race and keep it strong, members received .38 caliber cartridges with the warning that they would be killed if they ever broke their oaths. Davis testified to a plot to take over the government which involved planting typhoid germs in milk supplies to create a national emergency during which the Black Legionnaires would seize government arsenals, power plants, and buildings. Dean explained how, as death squad leader, he had been assigned to assassinate Mayor William Voisine of Encorse, Mich. Voisine was charged by the organization for hiring blacks for civic jobs. When an attempt to bomb Voisine's home failed, the frustrated Legionnaires murdered Silas Coleman "to see what it was like," Davis explained. Coleman was picked up by Davis, who promised him that he would be taken to a contractor's to collect some back wages owed to him. Davis instead took the black man to a swamp, ordering him out of the car with the words, "Okay, nigger, start running," while a hunting party chased him through the swamps and murdered him.

At least fifty deaths were attributed to the Black Legion, including that of John Bielak, a union organizer; Paul Avery, a prison guard who was a former member of the group but had been excommunicated; and Paul Piddock, a steelworker. Dean's testimony helped convict twelve killers. He was sentenced to a term of life in prison, and the Black Legion disappeared.

REF.: *CBA*; Rodell, *Detroit Murders*.

Dean, Dovie, prom. 1954, U.S., mur. Dovie Dean, a grandmother of eight from Ohio, was arrested, tried, and convicted for murdering her husband by feeding him rat poison. Sentenced to die in the electric chair, she was executed in 1954. The press, amazed by the fact that the woman never wept during her trial, called her "the Murderess Without Tears."

REF.: *CBA*; Godwin, *Murder U.S.A.*

Dean, Laurence Michael, prom. 1964, Brit., mur. In December 1963, Lawrence Michael Dean, eighteen, brought the dead body of Susan Moon, his four-month-old daughter, to a doctor. Dean explained he had found her dead in her crib; when the examining doctor noticed bruises on the child's body, Dean said she had hit her head a few days earlier. The coroner performing the autopsy, Dr. Francis Camps, found several fractured ribs, a ruptured liver, fractured skull, and several recent bruises on the child's abdomen, jaw, and scalp. Dean said that when he had found his daughter not breathing, he gave her artificial resuscitation, probably causing the damage in the process. Incredibly, this excuse was accepted and an "open verdict" was returned by the coroner. Dean moved to Wadhurst, in Sussex, with his wife, who soon gave birth to their second child, Michael. Five weeks later, Dean brought Michael to see a doctor; the infant died in the doctor's arms. Dean claimed that after being fed, the child began whimpering and breathing laboriously.

The autopsy of Dean's second child, by coroner Dr. Keith Simpson, revealed nineteen bruises in six different parts of the body, and a ruptured liver. Dean explained that when the child began to roll off his lap, Dean tried to save him, but his "knee came up and hit him in the abdomen." His story was rejected. Both deaths were reported to the director of public prosecutions, and Dean was tried for the murders of both children on Jan. 19, 1965, at the Old Bailey. Dean's conviction for murder was the first in England for such a case. He was sentenced to death, but later reprieved and imprisoned for life.

REF.: *CBA*; Simpson, *Forty Years of Murder*.

Dean, Margie (Margie Celano), 1896-1918, U.S., rob. Margie Dean was one of the first bank robbers to use an automobile. Born in Paris, Dean emigrated to New York while still a child. She carved out a living in the slums of the city by shoplifting, and later moved to Chicago. Not long after her arrival there, Dean was arrested for stealing diamonds from a jewelry store. She was

sent to the Joliet Penitentiary, where she met Eva Lewis, who in turn introduced her to Frank "Jumbo" Lewis, head of a tough criminal gang which also included Roscoe Lancaster, Roy Sherrill, a night club lounger, and Dale Jones, one of the leaders of the mob. After her release, Dean began a romance with Jones, married him, and then joined the outlaw gang. The Lewis-Jones gang and their new recruit made good use of the automobile in their escapes. Dean's skill behind the wheel impressed Lewis, who made her the gang's getaway driver.

On Sept. 24, 1918, the gang found themselves trapped in a house on Mont Gall Avenue in Kansas City. Police had surrounded the house, forcing Lewis and his men to blast their way out. Dean and her husband managed to escape through the front door, but Lancaster fell to the floor, fatally wounded. "Jones is nuts!" he gasped. "He wants to get in the movies. I'm going now, but be sure to tell young fellows not to go this way because they all wind up like this!" The casual remark of the dying man sent the Pinkertons to Los Angeles, where they believed Dean and her husband had fled. Because of a unique perfume she was known to wear, Dean was found living in a bungalow on Sierra Madre Avenue under the name of Mrs. Forbes. She and her husband were spotted leaving their home on Nov. 24, 1918. Detectives followed the couple to a gas station in suburban Arcadia, where Jones stopped to fill the tank of their Marmon touring car. Dean recognized the unmarked police cars instantly. She pulled out a shotgun and opened fire, hitting Deputy Sheriff George Van Vliet in the face. Twelve police officers took aim on the Marmon, riddling the vehicle and its occupants with bullets. Jones and Margie Dean fell to the pavement dead.

REF.: *CBA*; Nash, *Look For the Woman*.

Dean, Dr. Sarah Ruth, prom. 1933, U.S., mur. On Aug. 8, 1933, District Attorney Arthur Jordan charged Dr. Sarah Ruth Dean, a 33-year-old eminent Greenwood, Miss., pediatrician, with killing her lover, Dr. Preston Kennedy. Dean and Kennedy had worked together for several years and had been lovers for some time; their romance began while Kennedy was still married. On July 27, 1933, they had a midnight tryst at the Kennedy Medical Building in Greenwood; Kennedy became ill after drinking what he later said was a poisoned whiskey highball that Dean gave him. On Aug. 1, he was then sent to Jackson Hospital for treatment. Five days later, Kennedy died after allegedly telling his brothers that he had been slain. Dean was arrested on murder charges, and on Feb. 3, 1934, she was tried in the Leflore County Circuit Court in Greenwood, Miss., in front of Judge S.F. Davis.

At the trial, Henry Kennedy, Preston's brother, explained that Preston had told him that Dean had poisoned his whiskey and that his drink had "a strong metallic taste—an astringent taste." Henry Kennedy contended that his brother was planning to remarry his first wife, and that Dean had previously destroyed that family. On Feb. 7, defense attorney Dick Kenman turned over 145 love letters that Dean had written to Kennedy. District Attorney Arthur Jordan handed out copies of one of the letters to members of the press, noting: "That's the last letter she sent. He never got it." The letter said: "I want to turn over something to you."

On Feb. 9, defense attorney J.J. Breland contended, in questioning Dr. Barney Kennedy, the other brother, that the dying man had been "unconscious or in a stupor" at his deathbed. There was additional controversy about the medicines that the dying doctor had been treated with at the Jackson Hospital, and no explanation as to why the autopsy had been performed after both the embalming and the burial. State chemist Dr. W.F. Hand gave his expert testimony regarding the amount of mercury found in the body of the deceased, admitting that the amount was "minute."

On Feb. 27, Dr. Sarah Ruth Dean took the stand to say that Dr. Kennedy had divorced his wife in order to marry her, had given her a diamond ring that she had worn for almost two years, and had threatened to "kill them both" when Dean broke off their engagement with the intention of marrying another man, Franklin C. Maul. She denied putting mercury in Kennedy's drink. On Mar. 3, 1934, after almost five weeks of testimony, the jury returned a verdict of Guilty. Judge Davis sentenced Dean to life at hard labor in the state penitentiary. The case was then taken to the State Supreme Court where the judgment was upheld by a tie decision. Dean then appealed to the state governor for a pardon. On July 8, 1935, Mississippi Governor Martin Sennett Conner granted Dean a full pardon, based on "the benefit of information not available to the courts either in the original trial or on appeal," and Dean was freed. REF.: *CBA.*

Deane, Silas, 1737-89, Case of, U.S., embez.-treas. Silas, a lawyer, journeyed to France during U.S. Revolution to obtain aid and supplies, 1776-78. Upon his return he was accused of embezzling by Arthur Lee, at which time he returned to France, 1780, to prove the accusation was false. Deane was then accused of being a traitor following the publication of letters he wrote to U.S. revolutionary officials while in France. The letters described the chances for a United States as bleak and urged for a reconciliation with Britain. His character was vindicated by Congress, 1842. REF.: *CBA.*

Deane-Tanner, William Cunningham, See: **Taylor, William Desmond.**

DeAngelis, Anthony (AKA: Tino), prom. 1963-64, U.S., fraud. In a colossal fraud dealing with salad oil tanks, Anthony "Tino" DeAngelis was able to bilk banks and investors out of $219 million. DeAngelis claimed to have many salad oil tanks throughout the U.S. containing vast amounts of oil. His tanks, however, had false or hollow bottoms with only a portion of the tank filled with salad oil. Suspicious officials not taken in by this ruse were bribed into giving DeAngelis phony receipts showing full tanks. The swindler then used these receipts to borrow millions of dollars which he used in an attempt to corner the cottonseed and soybean markets on the commodities exchange, thinking that once he had made his "killing," he

Salad oil swindler Tony DeAngelis.

would convert the hollow salad oil tanks to full capacity. His fake receipts, however, were scrutinized by officials who examined the tanks and discovered the truth. DeAngelis was charged with fraud in 1965, convicted, and given a twenty-year prison sentence. All but $1 million from the so-called Great Salad Oil Swindle was recovered.

REF.: *CBA;* Nash, *Hustlers and Con Men.*

DeAngelo, Pietro, b.1855, U.S., mansl. In September 1913, Pietro DeAngelo, a 58-year-old Sicilian, accused Caspar Matarello, twenty-eight, of making his daughter a loose woman. The young man tried to flee his accusor, but the enraged father fatally shot him before he could get away.

Police learned from Matarello's widow that he had left her and their two children in Brooklyn to live with a young girl. DeAngelo was arrested in Rochester, where he was staying with a relative. He was convicted of manslaughter and sentenced to five years in prison, of which he served three-and-a-half years.

REF.: *CBA;* Willemse, *Behind the Green Lights.*

Dean-Siddel, Elizabeth, and **Blaisdell, Steven,** and **Foley, Carole,** prom. 1977, Fr., drugs. Elizabeth Dean-Siddel, fifty-four, a croupier in a casino in Reno, Nev., was also the head of a group of hashish smugglers. Tried in a court in Marseilles, France, Dean-Siddel was given a six-year jail term for her part in the attempt to smuggle 1,700 pounds of hashish into France via a car ferry from Morocco. Accomplices Steven Blaisdell, twenty-three, was given a two-year term, and his mother, Carole Foley, forty-six, was sentenced to four years. REF.: *CBA.*

Dearborn, Mich., Massacre, prom. 1932, U.S., pol mal. The

effects of the Depression on the Detroit automotive industry led to a bloody confrontation between a gang of unemployed men and the local police on Mar. 7, 1932. Nearly 3,000 men marched against the hiring offices of the Ford Motor Company in Dearborn, a suburb south of Detroit. The workmen, most of them recently laid off by Ford management, demanded their jobs back, free medical care at the company hospital, a seven-hour day, and equal treatment for blacks.

The crowd formed at Oakland Boulevard shortly before 2 p.m. to begin the two-mile march. The organizers hoped that Ford officials would meet with a workers' delegation at the factory. Instead, the marchers were met by a squad of Dearborn police. The mayor of Dearborn, a cousin of Henry Ford, ordered the police to "hold the line" and to keep the marchers out of the plant. The demonstrators pushed past the police line, and fighting broke out.

The police tear gassed the marchers, who retaliated with rocks and pieces of jagged ice. The Dearborn Fire Department, positioned along Miller Road near Gate Three, shot an icy jet of water at the workers. In the resulting fray, police shot and killed four marchers and injured dozens more. On Mar. 12, the victims were buried, with 30,000 people attending the funeral, some carrying protest banners, one of which read: "Ford gave Bullets for Bread." REF.: *CBA.*

Dearnley, Albert Edward, prom. 1923, Brit., mur. On May 24, 1923, James Frederick Ellis, a drum bugler with the Leichester Regiment at Aldershot, England, disappeared. Of all of his comrades questioned, only Lance-Corporal Albert Edward Dearnley had any suggestions as to his whereabouts. Dearnley said that Ellis, his close friend, had recently suggested that they desert together and return to their hometown. On this evidence, it was presumed that Ellis had abandoned his post. Authorities in his hometown were told to watch out for Ellis.

On Sept. 26, a man gathering berries discovered Ellis' decomposing body. The corpse was bound up in a military raincoat that covered the head, with the arms wrapped around the body, the hands and feet tied behind the back, and the knees and ankles pulled together in a position that would have caused great pain. Ellis had been gagged, and had obviously suffocated quickly. Questioned a second time, Dearnley said he and Ellis had played a game of Cowboys and Indians, and that when he last saw Ellis, the soldier was trying to free himself. Dearnley also admitted that he had quarreled with Ellis over a girl, and that they often argued and made up later. Two days after his arrest, Dearnley withdrew his earlier statements, saying that he had gone for a walk with Ellis, who had suggested they take turns testing their skills using a rope as a lasso, and that he had left Ellis tied up "as a bit of punishment for his having insulted my sweetheart."

Pathologist Sir Bernard Spilsbury testified at Dearnley's trial, held before Mr. Justice Avory in November at the Winchester Assizes, with Rayner Goddard for the prosecution, and attorney R.E. Dummett for the defense. Spilsbury said that the way Ellis was trussed had almost immediately started to suffocate him, that there would be no way that he could have moved or made a sound, and that he had died within ten minutes at the most. Dearnley testified that he had no idea that Ellis would die as a result of the trussing, saying that he had intended to leave him there until early the next morning. Dearnley had later been detained, and had assumed that Ellis had worked himself free of the rope and had deserted. Evidence was given that Dearnley had told his girlfriend, "You have no need to worry any more about Ellis. He is dead, and he is not a mile from here."

Dummett asked for reduced charges of manslaughter, but the jury found Dearnley Guilty of murder, and he was condemned to die. The convicted man's appeal was denied, as was a last-minute petition for a reprieve. The evening before he was scheduled to die, when the coffin and grave had already been prepared, additional facts were brought before the House of Commons and the Home Secretary. Dearnley was retried, and Spilsbury's opinion that Ellis was masochistic and had asked to be tied up was important. Dearnley's sentence was commuted to penal servitude for life.

REF.: Browne, *The Scalpel of Scotland Yard; CBA;* Woodland, *Assize Pageant.*

Dear Old Gentleman, The, 1936, a novel by George Goodchild and Carl Eric Bechhofer Roberts was based on the Sanyford mystery (Brit., 1862). See: **Sandyford Mystery.** REF.: *CBA.*

Déat, Marcel, 1894-1955, Fr., treas. Organized and established the Rassemblement National Populaire, 1940, in collaboration with Nazis occupying France, and became the minister of work and social affairs for Pierre Laval's Vichy regime, 1944. Following the liberation of France he was condemned in absentia for treason, 1945. REF.: *CBA.*

Death Corner, prom. 1910s, U.S., org. crime. The intersection of Milton and Oak Streets in Chicago's Little Italy gained notoriety as Death Corner in the first decades of the twentieth century. The Black Handers reigned in the Italian enclave north of the Chicago River. Thirty-eight people were murdered there between January 1910 and March 1911.

Nervous shopkeepers and residents dared not go the the police. They continued to pay the Black Hand extortionists rather than risk execution on Death Corner. See: **Black Hand; Shotgun Man; White Hand Gang.** REF.: *CBA.*

Death House Mike, See: **Alex, Michael.**

Death in the Deep South, 1936, a novel by Ward Greene. The trial and lynching of the innocent Leo Frank (U.S., 1915) for the killing of 14-year-old Mary Phagan, is the basis of this work of fiction. Author Greene was a reporter on the Atlanta *Journal* at the time of the Phagan murder and he covered the Leo Frank trial and its bloody aftermath. So haunted was Greene by the murder of this guiltless man, hanged by a kill-crazy mob whipped to frenzy by racist agitators, that he became obsessed with the case and finally went to New York, locked himself in a room at the Waldorf, and wrote his novel in three weeks. A motion picture, *They Won't Forget,* was based on this novel. See: **Frank, Leo Max.** REF.: *CBA.*

Death Walks in Eastrepps, 1931, a novel by Francis Beeding. Jack the Ripper is the role model for the protagonist who slays six in London's East End. See: **Jack the Ripper.** REF.: *CBA.*

Deaver, Bascom Sine, 1882-1944, U.S., jur. Served as U.S. attorney, 1926-1928, and appointed to the Middle District of Georgia by President Calvin Coolidge, 1928. REF.: *CBA.*

Deaver, Michael K., 1938- , U.S., perj. On Mar. 18, 1987, 49-year-old Michael K. Deaver, who served as U.S. president Ronald Reagan's deputy chief of staff from 1981 until May 1985, was indicted by a federal grand jury on five counts of perjury, following a nine-month investigation. Deaver, who remained a close friend and advisor to both Reagan and his wife, Nancy Reagan, was accused of lying to the grand jury panel and to Congress about his lobbying activities. With the eighteen-page indictment, Deaver became the first person to be charged under the 1978 provisions of Ethics in Government Act allowing for the appointment of special prosecutors.

Whitney North Seymour, Jr., who served as special prosecutor in the Deaver case, charged the former White House official with lying in his answers about his company's involvement with the Canadian and South Korean governments, as well as with two private businesses, Trans World Airlines (TWA) and Smith Barney Harris Upham & Company. South Korea had paid Deaver's consulting firm $475,000 a year, and TWA and manufacturing plants in Puerto Rico each paid his firm $250,000 annually. Deaver unsuccessfully tried to block the indictment through a suit charging that the Ethics in Government Law was unconstitutional because it infringed on the executive branch's law enforcement responsibilities.

Federal District Judge Thomas Penfield Jackson presided over the seven-week trial in Washington, D.C., which began in late October 1987. Deaver's chief counsel, Herbert J. Miller, who had been attorney for President Richard M. Nixon, did not call any of the nearly 200 defense witnesses to the stand, nor did he call

his own client. Deaver's alcohol abuse was a highly publicized element in the trial, with his defense team using it as a rationale for his false statements. But Judge Jackson told the jury not to consider alcoholism to be a mitigating factor.

On Dec. 16, 1987, the jury, after twenty-seven hours of deliberation, found Deaver Guilty on three charges of lying under oath about using his influence with the White House when functioning as a highly paid lobbyist. He was found Guilty of: lying to a House subcommittee about his attempts to arrange a meeting between a South Korean trade envoy and the president, telling a federal grand jury he could not remember trying to help retain a federal tax policy that would assist Puerto Rican manufacturers, and telling the grand jury he could not remember contracts he had made for TWA. Deaver was acquitted of telling the grand jury he was not involved in selecting a Reagan administration envoy to Canada regarding acid rain, and of telling Congress he had not made contacts with several White House staff members in order to benefit his clients.

Judge Jackson sentenced Deaver on Sept. 23, 1988, to a suspended three-year jail term, and fined $100,000 for lying about his lobbying activities. Jackson also barred Deaver from lobbying the government for profit for three years, and ordered him to perform 1,500 hours of community service. Jackson said that Deaver's alcoholism "does not excuse but helps to explain" why the former deputy chief of staff lied. Deaver, who faced up to fifteen years' imprisonment, told reporters, "It was a very fair sentence, if I had been guilty." Deaver proposed fulfilling his community service obligation by counseling other alcoholics. On Feb. 2, 1989, Deaver abandoned the appeal of his conviction. explaining he wanted to "get on with my life." REF.: *CBA.*

de Balsham, Inetta, prom. 1264, Brit., harboring thieves. One of the earliest cases where a condemned person survived the hangman in England was that of Inetta de Balsham, who had been convicted and condemned for harboring thieves during the time of King Henry III. The woman had been hanged on a Monday at 9 a.m. and continued to hang until the following Thursday when she was found to be still alive. This incredible occurence was later explained when it was discovered that de Balsham's windpipe was deformed and had ossified so that the rope never cut off her ability to breathe. So impressed was King Henry with de Balsham's incredible survival that he pardoned the woman on Aug. 16, 1264.

REF.: Atholl, *Shadow of the Gallows; CBA;* Nash, *Almanac of World Crime.*

Debar, Ann O'Delia Diss (Editha Salomen, AKA: Countess Landsfeldt, Baroness Rosenthal, Vera P. Ava), prom. 1849-1901, Brit., fraud. With the reputation of one of the ten most dangerous swindlers of her time, Ann O'Delia Diss Debar preyed on wealthy people with an ersatz blend of phony spiritualism, hypnotism, and other forms of fraud.

Born Editha Salomen, Debar broke away from her father who lived in Kentucky. At twenty, she claimed to be the "Countess Landsfeldt and Baroness Rosenthal in the peerage of Bavaria," and the daughter of dancer Lola Montez and King Louis I of Bavaria. She swindled several young businessmen by using charm and guile, and she gained around £50,000. She quickly spent the money, became addicted to opium, and had a breakdown that landed her in a hospital. One day she attacked both a doctor and an attendant, and was sent to an asylum where she met young Dr. Messant and married him. Messant died a year later. Debar then turned to hypnotism for money, and rapidly built up a clientele. Marrying General Diss Debar, Editha changed her name to Ann O'Delia. She had several children, and then bilked a recently widowed New York lawyer, Luther R. Marsh.

With the 70-year-old Marsh present, Debar became seized by a trance and pretended that the spirit of his late wife was sending messages through her. Marsh suggested Debar move into his Madison Avenue home. Bringing along her husband and children, Debar set up quarters and opened a temple of spiritualism which attracted many rich people. Developing a scheme to combine her supposed connection with the spirit world and business, Debar summoned the great masters, commissioning for Marsh a painting by the spirit of Raphael, paid for in advance and delivered, still wet ten, days later. Many other great masters were called to produce works from the other side, and Debar even arranged meetings with Shakespeare and Charlemagne for her eager employer. Debar then took her scam a step further, calling up the spirit of a little girl who advised Marsh to give his property to the spiritually "advanced" Debar. She was finally stopped by the old man's relatives. Although she returned his deeds, Debar was brought to court on charges of fraud and trickery. But Debar's charisma was strong enough to convince one juror of her good intentions, and, although convicted, she was given a light sentence of six months in jail.

On her release, Debar briefly pursued a disastrous career in musical comedy then divorced her husband and took to the road, lecturing under the name Madame Vera P. Ava. She was thrown out of a Chicago lecture hall by an angry crowd that felt she offended public taste, but she continued to lecture on subjects ranging from health to politics. Resurrecting herself as the Countess Landsfeldt, Debar was arrested on swindling charges and was sent to prison for operating under false pretenses. On her release, she met a wealthy old man whom she married, fleeced, and divorced before moving to New Orleans. Marrying again, this time a man named Jackson who was a confederate in her dubious trade, she gave "Psychic Lectures" until the police ordered them out of town. She returned to Chicago, collected funds as "Sister Mary" for a fictitious orphanage, and also was ordered to leave town. Debar and Jackson soon immigrated to South Africa to set up a Theosophical University in Cape Town, then fled to England where they operated as "Theo" and "The Swami." Scotland Yard Chief Detective Inspector Kane brought evidence against them; they were tried in 1901, with Lord Carson and Sir Charles Mathews prosecuting. Jackson was sentenced to ten years' penal servitude, and Debar was given seven years.

REF.: *CBA; Dilnot, Celebrated Crimes.*

de Beauvallon, Rosamond, b.1819, Fr., perj.-duel. On Mar. 7, 1845, Rosamond de Beauvallon, twenty-six, a staff member of *Le Globe,* and Alexandre Henri Dujarier, twenty-nine, general manager of *La Presse,* quarreled over a game of baccarat at a Paris dinner party. De Beauvallon charged that Dujarier had treated him discourteously, insisting on paying the baccarat debt to him but not paying others, and he challenged Dujarier to a duel. The two men met at the Bois de Boulogne on Mar. 11.

Dujarier, an inexperienced shooter, fired the first shot. De Beauvallon, the better marksman, shot Dujarier in the face, fatally wounding him. Rumors emerged that de Beauvallon had fired his pistols before the duel, a violation of the rules. He fled to Spain, but was tried for the murder in Rouen. He was found Not Guilty, but evidence later surfaced supporting the claim that the guns had been fired on the morning of the duel.

De Beauvallon was tried and convicted of perjury. He was sentenced to eight years in prison, but was released at the start of the Revolution of 1848.

REF.: *CBA; Hall, The Bravo Mystery and Other Cases.*

de Beer, Petrus Cornelius, c.1891-1926, S. Afri., mur. Petrus De Beer, an agent of the South African Railway Administration, hired a governess and nurse to care for his four children. Soon after she arrived, she claimed that de Beer began to make unwanted advances. On Jan. 11, 1926, the family, the governess, and her sister were traveling by train from Fort Beaufort to Cookhouse, South Africa. Just before they went to sleep, de Beer got two glasses of ginger ale from the bar car and gave one to his wife and the other to the governess and her sister. The governess later said she saw her employer put some powder into one of the glasses. His wife began having convulsions, and died at 1 a.m.

Police found a bottle of strychnine in a cabinet at de Beer's home, and an autopsy revealed one-seventh of a grain of strychnine in his wife's body. Both de Beer and the governess were arrested and tried in Grahamstown. The young woman was

acquitted, but de Beer was convicted of murder and hanged in East London, South Africa, on July 30, 1926.

REF.: Bennett, *Too Late For Tears; CBA.*

Debevoise, Dickinson Richards, b.1924- , U.S., jur. Authored the "Proposed Amendments to the Federal Rules of Criminal Procedure," which appeared in the *New Jersey Law Journal,* 1975, and received appointment to the District Court of New Jersey from President Jimmy Carter, Sept. 28, 1979. REF.: *CBA.*

de Bocarmé, Count **Hippolyte,** See: **Bocarmé,** Comte **Hippolyte de.**

De Boe, William Thomas, c.1912-35, U.S., rob-rape. William De Boe, twenty-three, was convicted of robbing a Kentucky store and raping the wife of the owner. He was hanged in the Livingston County jail yard, where gawkers could clearly see the proceedings over a low fence. De Boe ranted at the crowd of 1,500 for nearly half an hour before becoming the first white man hanged in Kentucky for rape. REF.: *CBA.*

DeBoer, Frank, c.1935-77, U.S., asslt.-kid. Frank DeBoer drove a truck for the J.H. Patterson lumber company in Florence Station, Ill., until he was injured and placed on sick leave. When he returned to work in the spring of 1976, he argued with his supervisor, William Van Raalte, striking him on the head with a cane. He was fired and the Korean War veteran remained unemployed. He was placed under court supervision after pleading guilty to battery.

On the morning of Mar. 21, 1977, DeBoer's wife called police, saying that her husband had armed himself and was driving to the lumber yard. After seeing police cars, DeBoer drove to the home of his aunt and his uncle, Walter Bunnell, in Freeport, Ill. There, his aunt persuaded DeBoer to go home and offered to drive him. On their way, policeman Lyle Kuhlmeyer and Lieutenant Roland Munda pulled their car over. DeBoer shot Kuhlmeyer as he stepped out of the car. His aunt fainted, Munda offered himself as a hostage, and the two men continued to DeBoer's home in Florence Station. Once the house was surrounded by police, DeBoer called the sheriff's office and said the police had fifteen minutes to clear away from the house. Fifteen minutes later, he came out of the house firing at the officers. He died of head and chest wounds. REF.: *CBA.*

De Bono, Emilio, 1866-1944, Ital., law enfor. off.-treas. Helped in the organization of Italian fascist party, joining Benito Mussolini in the March on Rome. He also was chief of police and in command of the fascist militia. In 1943 De Bono voted against Mussolini in the Fascist Grand Council, and was then tried and executed for treason. REF.: *CBA.*

de Bourbon, Charles Louis (AKA: **Duke of Normandy** or **Karl Wilhelm Naundorff**), 1785-1845, Fr., (unsolv.) kid. During the French Revolution, King Louis XVI and Marie Antoinette were placed under house arrest with their children, including Charles Louis de Bourbon. In 1793, the king and queen were guillotined and the royal children were imprisoned in Temple Prison in Paris. In December 1794, when a member of the National Assembly checked on the 9-year-old boy, the child's arms and legs were badly swollen. The boy, a deaf mute, died six months later without being formally identified.

In 1815, when the Bourbon family was reinstated, many claimed to be the royal heir, who was thought to have been kidnapped and replaced at Temple Prison. In 1830, when the Bourbons were ousted by another revolution, a Prussian watchmaker living in London, Karl Wilhelm Naundorff, claimed to be the missing boy. Although he did not wish to rule, he wanted to claim the title. Naundorff said the king of Prussia had arranged his new identification. A former royal governess met the watchmaker and believed his story, but French officials remained unconvinced. Three attempts were made on his life, and he spent four years in London's Newgate debtor's prison.

Naundorff died in the Netherlands on Aug. 10, 1854. His autopsy revealed a scar on his upper lip, a mole on his thigh, and vaccination marks on an arm that were identical to a description of the royal heir given by his former governess. REF.: *CBA.*

de Brinon, Fernand, d.1947, Ger., war crimes. French politician Fernand de Brinon urged rapprochement with Germany after WWI. When the Nazi armies overran his country in 1940, de Brinon was appointed envoy to Germany from the collaborationist Vichy government. After the German surrender in 1945, de Brinon was arrested and charged with giving aid and comfort to the enemy.

During the trial at Fort de Montrouge outside Paris in February 1947, former premier Edouard Daladier testified that de Brinon entertained German foreign minister Joachim von Ribbentrop in his home. De Brinon said little in his own defense, but reminded the courts that he had secured pardons for 1,000 French nationals during the occupation.

The jury of the French High Court of Justice convicted de Brinon on Mar. 7, 1947, and he was executed by firing squad on Apr. 15. REF.: *CBA.*

de Brinvilliers, Marie, See: **Brinvilliers, Marie de.**

Debs, Eugene Victor, 1855-1926, U.S., treas. The son of a Terre Haute, Ind., grocer, Eugene Debs was a working man, becoming a railway laborer while in his teens. He organized the local of Brotherhood of Locomotive Firemen in 1875 and became its secretary in 1880. Debs founded and became the first president of the American Railway Union in 1893 and in the following year led a successful strike against the Great Northern Railway after James J. Hill threatened to cut his employees' wages. Debs was a fiery orator, tall and prematurely bald with deep-set eyes, a wide mouth, and a jutting chin.

Presidential candidate Debs.

George Pullman, the autocratic railway magnate, manufactured his cars in Pullman, Ill., a self-contained community named after him, where his workers rented his houses, and bought their food at his grocery stores. He arbitrarily cut his employees' wages by 25 percent. Such brutal moves even caused James J. Hill to thunder: "Any man who won't meet his men half way is a damned fool!" Debs, incensed at Pullman's treatment of his workers, called out this powerful union in support of the Pullman laborers and crippled the nation's freight and passenger service in a country-wide strike.

When rioting broke out in Pullman, President Grover Cleveland ordered troops into the area to crush the workers; and in the clash between the railway workers and the soldiers, thirty men died. Debs was ordered to end his strike and refused. He and three of his aides were indicted for violating a federal injunction to cease his strike and also for conspiring against the government. Clarence Darrow, the brilliant young lawyer from Chicago who specialized in labor cases, successfully defended Debs on the conspiracy charge, winning an acquittal, but Debs was found Guilty of violating the federal injunction and was sent to prison for six months. While Debs was in prison, his strike was crushed and his union was ended.

One of Debs' fellow convicts in the Woodstock, Ill. prison was Milwaukee socialist Victor L. Berger, who loaned Debs his copy of Karl Marx's *Das Kapital*. So impressed was Debs by Marx's theories that he immediately embraced the cause of socialism. He became the standard bearer of the Socialist Party in five presidential elections, 1900, 1904, 1908, 1912, and 1920. Debs' best showings were in his first two runs for the presidency, when he gleaned more than a million votes in each election. In 1905, Debs joined the more radical elements of labor and founded the violence-prone Industrial Workers of the World union, the IWW, better known as the Wobblies.

Debs was violently opposed to America's participation in WWI, and he looked upon the Espionage Act as a political device to silence opposition to President Woodrow Wilson's decision to enter WWI. The fire-eating Debs, however, defied the government and came out publicly against America's involvement in the war. He thundered from rostrums to deliver diatribes against "the master class" and "the junkers of Wall Street." When he was threatened with arrest for violating the Espionage Act, Debs shouted: "I would a thousand times rather be a free soul in jail than to be a sycophant and coward in the streets." In Canton, Ohio, Debs fulminated with one of his most memorable lines: "They cannot put the socialist movement in jail!" He was indicted and tried for treason in September 1818 in Cleveland.

When prosecutor F.B. Kavanagh finished his case against Debs, the socialist leader rose and congratulated him on his moving oratory and then announced that he had no defense witnesses to offer. Further, he said he would present his own summation before the jury, stating that he would not deny any subversive statements he had made in the past. His own eloquence was moving but it represented a political cause that found little or no support in the U.S., then or later. "I admit being opposed to the present form of government. I admit being opposed to the present social system. I am doing what little I can to do away with the rule of the great body of people by a relatively small class and establish in this country industrial and social democracy...You may hasten the change; you may retard it; you can do no more to prevent it than you can prevent the coming of the sunrise on the morrow," he said.

He was found Guilty, but before sentencing, Debs again took the opportunity to use the court as a final podium, saying to the judge: "Your Honor, years ago I recognized my kinship with all living things and I made up my mind that I was not one bit better than the meanest of the earth. I said then, I say now, that while there is a lower class, I am in it; while there is a criminal element, I am of it; while there is a soul in prison, I am not free." Debs was sentenced to ten years behind bars. Before he was led away, a little girl rushed to Debs carrying a dozen American Beauty roses, his favorite flower, thrusting these into his arms and then fainting. Debs carried the roses *and* the little girl to an anteroom where he waited until she was revived.

Debs appealed the verdict, writing his own brief and arguing that the Espionage Act violated freedom of speech. Justice Oliver Wendell Holmes wrote the opinion which denied Debs' appeal. Because the federal prisons were then overcrowded, Debs was imprisoned in the State Penitentiary at Moundsville, West Va., in April 1919. When he reached the gates of the prison, Debs turned to news reporters and said in his usual stentorian tone: "I enter the prison doors a flaming revolutionist—my head erect, my spirit untamed, and my soul unconquerable." He was then sixty-four years old and suffering from lumbago and other assorted ailments.

After being transferred to the federal penitentiary in Atlanta as inmate 9653, Debs was visited, in May 1920, by a delegation which informed him that the Socialist Party had once more nominated him for the presidency. Debs ran for the office while in prison, being allowed to issue a weekly bulletin. Even so, he produced 915,302 votes. As a conciliatory measure to the leftists and radicals (who had not been shipped back to Europe *en masse*), Attorney General A. Mitchell Palmer urged President Wilson to release Debs on Lincoln's birthday in 1921.

Wilson, who had an abiding hatred for Debs, curtly stated to his secretary, Jospeh P. Tumulty: "Denied. I will never consent to the pardon of this man. While the flower of American youth was pouring out its blood to vindicate the cause of civilization, this man Debs stood behind the lines, sniping, attacking and denouncing them...I know there will be a great deal of denunciation of me for refusing this pardon. They will say that I am cold-blooded and indifferent, but it will make no impression on me. This man was a traitor to his country and he will never be pardoned during my administration."

Debs, hearing of this, bitterly attacked Wilson, announcing: "It is he, not I, who needs a pardon. If I had it within my power I would give him the pardon which would set him free. Woodrow Wilson is an exile from the hearts of his people...the most pathetic figure in the world. No man in public life in American history ever retired so thoroughly discredited, so scathingly rebuked, so overwhelmingly impeached and repudiated as Woodrow Wilson."

When Warren G. Harding ran for the presidency in 1920, he promised general amnesty as part of his campaign. Attorney General Harry Daugherty, reviewing all those cases which might apply to the amnesty, interviewed Debs personally and found him to be a "harmless" sickly old man. He recommended his release to Harding and the president freed Debs on Christmas Day 1921, inviting the old socialist to the White House where Harding greeted Debs warmly, glasping his hand and saying: "I have heard so damned much about you, Mr. Debs, that I am very glad to meet you personally."

Debs then returned to Terre Haute and his wife, Kathleen Debs. He died in an Elmhurst, Ill., rest home on Oct. 20, 1926, largely forgotten as the "Saint of Socialism." See: **Darrow, Clarence Seward; Haywood, William; Pullman Strike.**

REF.: Brommel, *Eugene V. Debs;* Butterfield, *The American Past;* Carroll, *Labor and Politics; CBA;* Clement, *Rebel America;* Coleman, *Eugene V. Debs;* Commons, *History of Labor in the United States;* Crandall, *The Man from Kinsman;* Darrow, *The Story of My Life;* Debs, *Writings and Speeches;* DeLeon, *American Labor's Who's Who;* Ginger, *Eugene V. Debs, The Making of an American Radical;* Gunn, *Wisdom of Clarence Darrow;* Gurko, *Clarence Darrow;* Harrison, *Clarence Darrow;* Haynes, *Social Politics in the United States;* Hillquit, *History of Socialism in the United States;* Hughan, *American Socialism of the Present Day;* Kasner, *Debs;* Kelly, *Twentieth Century Socialism;* Kurland, *Clarence Darrow;* Laidler, *American Socialism;* ____, *History of Socialism;* Lowenthal, *The Federal Bureau of Investigation;* MacKaye, *Americanized Socialism;* Mordell, *Clarence Darrow, Eugene V. Debs and Haldeman-Julius;* Morgan, *Prince of Crime;* Powers, *Secrecy and Power;* Radosh, *Debs;* Reppetto, *The Blue Parade;* Sayer, *Clarence Darrow, Public Advocate;* Schlossberg, *The Workers and Their World;* Selvin, *Eugene Debs;* Stone, *Clarence Darrow for the Defense;* Symes and Travers, *Rebel America;* Tierney, *Darrow, A Biography;* Toledano, *J. Edgar Hoover;* Velie, *Desperate Bargain: Why Jimmy Hoffa Had to Die;* Weinberg, *Attorney for the Damned;* ____, *Clarence Darrow, A Sentimental Rebel;* Whitehead, *Clarence Darrow—The Big Minority Man;* ____, *Clarence Darrow, Evangelist of Sane Thinking.*

De Bourbon, Duc, See: **D'Artois-De Bourbon Duel.**

DeCarlo, Angelo (AKA: Gyp), 1902-73, U.S., extor.-org. crime. In a secret conversation with a mob associate recorded by the FBI, Angelo DeCarlo explained the reason for his continuing popularity in New Jersey crime circles: "All these other racket guys who get a few bucks want to become legitimate." Of the many things DeCarlo may have wanted, legitimacy was not one of them. He was the boss of Mafia "juice" operations in New Jersey for years, and ruthlessly eliminated any rival who stood in his way. During one of his many revealing conversations captured on tape by the FBI between 1961 and 1963, DeCarlo reminisced about one of his "humane" hits in which he allowed the victim to be shot through the heart...because it was a painless way to die.

As a result of the publication of these sensitive tapes, several politicians saw their careers shattered. Newark Mayor Hugh Addonizio and Hudson County political boss John J. Kenny were ruined in politics when their links to organized crime figures were made public. Entertainer Frank Sinatra was also embarrassed by the high praise accorded him by DeCarlo.

In 1970 DeCarlo was sentenced to twelve years in prison on an extortion charge stemming from the arsenic poisoning of Louis Saperstein. A year-and-a-half later, President Richard Nixon granted the New Jersey mobster a full pardon on the grounds of deteriorating health. DeCarlo's petition, claiming that he was dying of cancer, skipped the usual channels and was funneled directly through Attorney General Richard Kleindienst who approved it and gave it to White House Counsel John Dean. Nixon signed the papers, it was thought, because of Frank Sinatra's influence with Vice-President Spiro Agnew. Special Watergate Prosecutor Archibald Cox investigated the unusually speedy manner on which DeAngelo's case was handled, but found no conclusive evidence of wrongdoing.

DeCarlo died on Oct. 20, 1973, five days short of a government deadline requiring him to pay a $20,000 fine handed down at his sentencing. See: **Addonizio, Hugh J.**

REF.: *CBA;* Gage, *Mafia, U.S.A.*

Decarnelles, Suzanne, prom. 1967, Fr., mur. Paul Decarnelles, a man in his forties, married a wealthy heiress to improve his failed singing and painting careers. His wife, Suzanne Decarnelles, was a competitor in show jumping horses and a fast car aficionada. Her money could not help her husband's lack of talent, but she did buy him a garage. When Paul refused to fix her Jaguar, she took a 7.65mm automatic from his collection and murdered him on Mar. 3, 1967. Although Decarnelles claimed self defense, a ballistics expert proved that the husband had been bending down to reach a low cupboard when he was shot.

REF.: *CBA;* Heppenstall, *The Sex War and Others.*

de Castro, Iñez, c.1320-55, Port., assass. Dom Pedro, the Crown Prince of Portugal, was widowed in 1344, and left with a young son, Ferdinand. Dom Pedro soon decided to marry the Countess Iñez de Castro. But de Castro was not of high enough rank to marry Dom Pedro, and King Alfonso IV, would not consent. Dom Pedro obtained special permission from the Pope, secretly married de Castro, and had two children with her. The king's advisors urged Dom Pedro to marry again, but he consistently rejected their proposals. Advisers Diego Lopez Pacheco, Pedro Coello, and Alvaro Calvarez, told the king that, if the rumors of Dom Pedro's secret marriage to de Castro were true, his grandson Ferdinand might be endangered, and de Castro's son might succeed to the throne. While Dom Pedro denied the charge in a secret meeting with the king, he admitted to his father that de Castro was so dear to him that he would not marry anyone else.

When Dom Pedro went away on a hunting trip, he was concerned about de Castro's safety, and left her and their children at a convent in Coimbra. King Alfonso came to the convent, demanding to see her. When she threw herself at his feet, imploring mercy, he took pity on the woman and her children, and let them live. But his angry counselors persuaded the king to sanction her murder, and de Castro was slain that night. The bereaved and enraged Dom Pedro called together an army to avenge her death, and took his followers into the castles and mansions where the counsellors lived, destroying the lands and razing the castles to the ground.

King Alfonso reconciled with his son through the assistance of the Archbishop of Braga. Returning to court and promising not to take revenge on the advisers, Pedro came to power two years later, when King Alfonso died. The three murderous counsellors, Pacheco, Coello, and Gonsalvez, fled Portugal, seeking refuge in Castile. The tyrant, Pedro the Cruel, delivered them to Dom Pedro in exchange for Castilians who had taken refuge in Portugal. Coello and Gonsalvez were transported to Portugal, then tortured and executed. Pacheco escaped and fled to Aragon. King Pedro assembled his high court at Cataneda, to announce publicly his marriage to de Castro, ordering that the fact be proclaimed throughout every town, city, and village. The children he had with his late wife were declared legitimate, and Pedro ordered de Castro's vault opened. Her embalmed corpse was dressed in a royal robe and placed on a throne. A crown was placed on her head, and all the nobles of the monarchy were made to kneel and kiss the hem of her robe. De Castro's body was then placed in a metal coffin and escorted by knights and noblemen to Alcobaza, where it was placed in a royal vault. De Castro's tragic tale was celebrated by poets and novelists.

REF.: *CBA;* Johnson, *Famous Assassinations of History.*

Decatur, Stephen, 1779-1820, U.S., naval off.-pir. The pirates of North Africa, mostly Turks and Moslems who controlled Algiers, Morocco, Tripoli, and Tunis, declared open war on U.S. shipping in 1801. The Pasha of Tripoli, to extort more cash from the U.S., chopped down the flagstaff of the U.S. consulate, drawing an immediate response from President Thomas Jefferson. No longer would the U.S. continue a policy of appeasement and bribes to the North African pirates, said Jefferson, and he ordered the tiny U.S. fleet into the Mediterranean to bombard Tripoli.

The heroic U.S. naval leader Stephen Decatur.

On Oct. 31, 1803, the USS *Philadelphia,* a 36-gun American frigate commanded by Captain William Bainbridge, ran aground in Tripoli's harbor and was captured. The pirates turned the guns of the ship against the U.S. blockading fleet commanded by Captain Edward Preble. To eliminate this threat, Lieutenant Stephen Decatur, a firebrand officer, led seventy-four men into the harbor in small boats on the night of Feb. 16, 1804.

A wounded U.S. sailor saving Decatur's life while battling Tripolitan pirates.

Decatur and his men slipped aboard the *Philadelphia,* and after a wild fight with the Turkish pirates, killed all the guards on board. They then set fire to the *Philadelphia,* rendering it useless to the pirates, and escaped with only one fatality. Decatur, a fiery

patriot, repeatedly proved his courage during the Tripolitan pirate war. On another occasion, he and his men boarded a pirate ship. Decatur, wielding a cutlass and a pistol, was knocked to the deck of the enemy gunship, but before the pirate captain could cut his throat, Decatur fired a fatal shot into the pirate's throat. At that moment, with Decatur prone on the deck, another pirate ran forward and was about to decapitate Decatur with a swing of his scimitar, but a wounded American sailor jumped forward and placed his head in the way, receiving the blow and dying in place of Decatur. The American sailor was said to be either Daniel Frazier or, more likely, Reuben James, after whom several U.S. warships were later named. The Turkish pirates in Tripoli, due to the continuing U.S. blockade, sued for peace in 1805.

Decatur, in 1815, again led a punitive squadron to the Mediterranean Sea to prevent Algerian pirates raiding U.S. ships. The brilliant Decatur once again quelled the main Algerian pirate fleet off the coast of Spain and then forced Algiers, Tripoli, and Tunis to pay $81,000 for the American ships captured or destroyed by the pirate captains. He forced the North African potentates to sign treaties forbidding them to collect "tribute" or bribes from the U.S. When the Dey of Tripoli pleaded with Decatur for a small token of tribute in the form of gunpowder to save face, Decatur retorted: "If you insist upon receiving powder as tribute, you must expect to receive (cannon) balls with it!"

Following Decatur's expedition against the North African Turks and Moslems in 1815, U.S. ships went unmolested by pirates. Decatur, the hero of the hour, returned in triumph to the U.S. At a banquet in his honor at Norfolk, Va., Decatur uttered his famous toast: "Our country! In her intercourse with foreign nations may she always be in the *right,* and always successful, *right or wrong!*" Decatur was killed in a duel with naval officer James Barron on Mar. 22, 1820. See: **Decatur-Barron Duel.**

REF.: Bowers, *Jefferson and Hamilton;* Butterfield, *The American Past; CBA;* Cowburn, *The Warship in History;* Eggenberger, *A Dictionary of Battles;* Lewis, *The Romantic Decatur;* Potter, *Sea Power;* Pratt, *The Compact History of the United States Navy.*

Decatur-Barron Duel, 1820, U.S., duel.-mur. In the early 1800s, the British Royal Navy frequently boarded the vessels of other nations to search for British deserters. Such actions against American shipping eventually sparked the War of 1812. A sidelight to this greater conflict was the pistol duel between Stephen Decatur, commissioner of the U.S. Navy, and Commodore James Barron, who had been discharged for an act of cowardice.

In 1807, Sir George Berkeley, vice admiral of His Majesty's Navy, asked Decatur to return three deserters from the H.M.S. *Melampus* who had enlisted for duty aboard the U.S.S *Chesapeake.* Barron, who commanded the ship, refused to surrender the men when he found they were U.S. citizens. Berkeley ordered any ship of the Royal Navy encountering the *Chesapeake* on the high seas to detain the ship and arrest the three deserters. The Crown recalled Berkeley to England and rescinded the order. But it was too late. Captain Humphries of the H.M.S. *Leopard* moved against the *Chesapeake* after it pulled out of port on June 22, 1807.

The *Leopard* closed to within twenty yards of the *Chesapeake* before unleashing a deadly broadside that killed twenty-one American sailors and severely crippled Barron's ship. Commodore Barron surrendered, and the British seamen came aboard, arrested four deserters and returned to their ship, leaving the *Chesapeake* to limp back to Norfolk. By year's end, Barron was suspended for five years after being found Guilty of failing to clear his ship for action. One of the officers on the tribunal was Stephen Decatur, who had previously sailed with Barron on the U.S.S. *United States.*

Publicly disgraced, Barron lived in Europe for ten years. Meanwhile, Decatur became a popular naval hero after his brilliant expedition against the pirates of the Barbary Coast. Barron resented Decatur, who had lowered the flag himself in 1815 after failing to escape the British blockade of New York harbor. The two men exchanged furious letters.

Finally, Barron challenged Decatur to a duel, and Decatur

accepted on Mar. 8, 1820. They met near the present-day Anacostia River Park, midway between Washington and Baltimore, on Mar. 22, seconds at their side. The men selected their pistols and positioned themselves exactly eight paces apart. They fired their pistols at precisely the same moment. Each man was hit by his opponent's bullet, but only Decatur was seriously wounded. The man who coined the slogan, "my country...right or wrong," died an agonizing death some hours later. He was forty-one. In time, James Barron recovered from his gunshot wound. He was never prosecuted for the duel. REF.: *CBA*.

Decavalcante, Samuel Rizzo (AKA: **The Plumber**), prom. 1960s, U.S., extor.-consp.-org. crime. The release of nearly 2,300 pages of secret recordings made by the FBI between 1961 and 1965 corroborated much of Joe Valachi's earlier testimony about the inner workings of the Cosa Nostra. When the newspapers published the information in 1969, it contained records of the conversation of Samuel Rizzo Decavalcante, the indiscreet Mafia chieftain "bugged" by the FBI for four years. He ran a plumbing supply store in New Jersey and ran a sixty-man Mafia family in Princeton. The transcripts proved that the Mafia was governed by a national commission which established parameters and attempted to monitor the activities of its members.

New Jersey crime boss Sam Decavalcante.

Decavalcante was a minor figure in the Mafia hierarchy, an itermediary between commission members and the warlike Bonanno crime family. In one conversation, "Sam the Plumber" described Joe Bonanno's son Bill as a "bedbug." The younger Bonanno was being groomed to take over the family. Of even greater interest, Decavalcante followed a peculiar but rigid code of honor. He was committed to the sanctity of family life and wondered what steps could be taken to resolve domestic disputes between his son and daughter-in-law. Yet Decavalcante carried on affairs with the sister of his business partner and several other women.

After the tapes became public in 1969, Decavalcante was convicted on an extortion-conspiracy charge and sentenced to fifteen years in prison. By the 1980s, he had moved to Florida hoping to open resort casinos. But voters there defeated the legalization of gambling.

REF.: Bonnano, *A Man of Honor; CBA*; Gage, *Mafia, U.S.A.;* ____, *The Mafia Is Not an Equal Opportunity Employer*.

Decazes, Elie (Elie Decazes et de Glücksberg), 1780-1860, Fr., jur-law enfor. off. Served as the minister of police, 1815, premier of the country, 1819-20, and after being forced to resign following the assassination of Duc de Berry, he became a duke and peer of France, 1820. REF.: *CBA*.

Decembrist Plot, prom. 1825, Rus., consp. The Decembrists were a loosely amalgamated group of Russian revolutionaries who preferred the ascension of Constantine to the Russian throne, rather than his brother, Nicholas I, following the death of their father, Alexander I. Mostly members of the upper class, the group included former military officers, freemasons, and members of secret patriotic organizations. The rebellions in St. Petersburg and Chernigov were easily quelled, and Nicholas I personally participated in an investigation which brought 121 Decembrists to trial. Five leaders were executed, another thirty-one were imprisoned, while the remaining eighty-five were banished to Siberia. REF.: *CBA*.

Decken, Karl Klaus von der, 1833-65, Somalia, (unsolv.) mur. As a German explorer, he was the first European to attempt climbing Mt. Kilimanjaro, 1862, and was later killed by Somali natives. REF.: *CBA*.

Decker, Bernard Martin, b.1904- , U.S., jur. Served on the Illinois Superior Court Committee which rewrote instructions for criminal juries in the state, 1961, the Fair Trial-Free Press subcommittee of the committee on the Operation of Jury Systems, 1966-69, and was appointed to the Northern District Court of Illinois by President John Kennedy, Apr. 2, 1963. REF.: *CBA*.

de Coligny, Gaspard, See: **Coligny, Gaspard de**.

de Contreras, Fernando, prom. 1530, Alg., kid.-extort. Fernando de Contreras, a priest from Sevilla, Spain, traveled to Algiers in 1530. He negotiated with Barbarossa, a Barbary pirate, to release kidnapped children. Barbarossa stipulated that the children would be freed only if they prayed for rain to relieve the drought-stricken city. Father de Contreras led the freed children through the town and within minutes, rain fell on the parched city. REF.: *CBA*; Moorhead, *Hostages to Fortune*.

de Crespigny, Sir Claude (AKA: **Charles Maldon**), prom. 1886, Brit., executioner. In 1886, a man calling himself Charles Maldon paid executioner James Berry £10 to let him assist at the executions of the Netherby Hall murderers. Maldon was later recognized as Claude de Crespigny, a baronet and Essex magistrate known for his adventurousness. De Crespigny explained that he had participated in the executions because if he became sheriff one day, he would never ask someone to do something he himself would not be willing to do. De Crespigny may also have wanted to assist Berry because one of the condemned men was suspected of killing an Essex police inspector. REF.: Atholl, *The Reluctant Hangman; CBA*.

DeCroat, Arthur, prom. 1945, U.S., rob.-mur. Dorothy McCready, a widow, had worked as a secretary to Mrs. Frederick Fisher. When McCready failed to appear for work on May 1, 1945, her employer had her daughter call McCready's house. A man answered the phone, but hung up when asked where McCready was. Several hours later, a neighbor and a friend found McCready's bludgeoned corpse on the living room floor. Her bedroom was heavily bloodstained, with lamps knocked over, bed clothes strewn about, and peanuts scattered. District Attorney Walter Winne found no leads; McCready had no enemies, no near relatives, and an inheritance promised to charity. An expensive diamond ring was on her finger, and nothing had been taken from the house. A few nights before the murder, McReady had called Arthur DeCroat, a handyman who had worked for her for several years, and she had asked him to come over immediately. She feared an intruder and had recently bought a revolver. She was pacing the living room, and seemed to be "in some kind of trouble," DeCroat said.

Police Detective Michael Orrechio saw the peanuts thrown about the room, and surmised that McReady had known the killer. Further investigation turned up DeCroat as a suspect. Detectives raided his house for clothing and found evidence of blood stains and discovered peanuts in the pocket of his clothes. DeCroat confessed, explaining that he had been stealing from McReady. That night he had been drinking, and broke into McCready's home, hit her, took $24 from her purse, and dragged her body downstairs to the living room. DeCroat explained, "I tried to wash her face. She'd always been a good friend to me." He had answered the phone later when he returned to the house hoping to find more money.

REF.: *CBA*; Rice, *Forty-five Murderers*.

Dederich, Charles E., and **Kenton, Lance**, and **Musico, Joseph**, prom. 1978-81, U.S., (attempt.) mur. The Synanon Foundation, a privately owned and operated drug rehabilitation organization, was founded in 1958 in Santa Monica, Calif. The Synanon approach to curing drug addiction received both praise and condemnation. Newly arrived addicts were forced to go "cold turkey"—completely abstaining from drugs. The militaristic approach employed by Synanon's founder, Charles E. Dederich, was reflected in the group's mandatory close-cropped hairstyles. Patients indoctrinated into the Synanon lifestyle were required to work for the foundation as counselors in return for their room and board.

The Synanon Foundation ran into trouble in the late 1970s as it moved away from its traditional role as a national drug rehabilitation center and became a quasi-religious cult. There were numerous reports that members who attempted to leave the group were seized and detained against their will.

On Jan. 17, 1978, Kim Myers, a former Synanon member, was kidnapped and assaulted six days after the organization had filed a $77 million libel suit against *Time* Magazine. Myers' abductors held him responsible for the article which focused attention on some questionable policies such as obligatory intermarraige of Synanon members and the forced termination of marriages to persons outside the group. The lawsuit against *Time* was dismissed in February 1980. Then, on July 15, 1979, Dederich and two Synanon "Imperial Marines"—Lance Kenton and Joseph Musico—were convicted of attempted murder after placing a rattlesnake in the mailbox of Attorney Paul Morantz, who had successfully sued the organization on behalf of several of its members.

Dederich was sentenced to five years of probation and assessed a $5,000 fine. Kenton and Musico each received one-year jail sentences and three years' probation. Meanwhile, indictments were handed down against seventeen past and present members of the Synanon Foundation as a direct outgrowth of the Myers investigation. Synanon filed another libel suit, for $43 million, against the American Broadcasting Company. Former member Bernard Kolb testified that he knew of at least a dozen instances of former members physically intimidated by other Synanon members. He said that Myers had been beaten so badly that he hardly recognized him in a photograph taken after the beating.

On June 5, 1981, Marin County Judge Joseph G. Wilson dismissed charges against twelve Synanon members on grounds of insufficient evidence. Among them were Liz Missakian and Ronald Cook, two former Synanon presidents; former Synanon attorney David Gomez; Chris Haberman, an investigator for Synanon's law office; Philip Bourdette, the director of the law office; Rodney Mullen, who headed the squad for delinquents; and Theodore Dibble, Arnett Jamison, William Lundberg, Doug Muhly, and Bruce Levine. REF.: *CBA*.

de Deurwaerder, Louis, prom. 1940, Belg., mur. Louis de Deurwaerder cheated on his wife Alexandrine, first having an affair with a family friend, and then with a young typist. He met the typist in 1947, and asked his wife, a devout Catholic, for a divorce, which she refused. Shortly after, her husband became interested in pharmacopoeia, the study of drugs, and he informed his wife that he would begin giving her various poisons as experiments. She uncomplainingly took the poisons, which were given in unusually high doses, and she meticulously recorded the effects in a diary. In March 1949, he gave his wife five injections of morphine. Soon after, thunderstruck friends and neighbors urged her to leave him, but she replied, "My husband may do what he wishes with me." On Apr. 7, 1949, de Deurwaeder gave his wife, who was suffering from colic, an enema of soapy water and sublimate of mercury. He left the house and when she screamed in pain, neighbors called her father.

Alexandrine died, and her father gave police the diary. During his trial, de Deurwaerder said, "I only hoped to weaken her a little so that she would agree to a divorce or a separation." He was convicted and sentenced to death. However, at that time in Belgium, however, those condemned to death were not executed, but continued to live in solitary confinement with no legal or civil rights, even though a notice of execution was posted. REF.: *CBA;* Reynolds, *Murder 'Round the World.*

Dedmond, Roger Zane, 1940-   , U.S., (wrong convict.) mur. In early December 1967, Roger Zane Dedmond, twenty-eight, began serving an eighteen-year sentence at a Union, S.C., county prison camp for the manslaughter death of his wife. Although Dedmond persistently claimed innocence, a Union police officer testified that Dedmond had confessed to killing his wife. Ded-

mond said he could not remember where he was when his wife was slain.

In February 1968, Bill Gibbons, managing editor of the Gaffney *Ledger,* received a call from a man who said he had three stories. The caller explained how he had murdered two women. He gave Gibbons details that led police to the strangled bodies of Nancy Carol Parrish, twenty, and Nancy Christine Rinehart, fourteen. He also said that he had been involved in the killing of Lucille Dedmond. A few weeks later, the self-described "psycho killer" called Gibbons again, providing more details, saying, "I killed them with them all begging me not to do it. The only reason I'm telling you this is to get that other boy out." When Gibbons tried to convince the man to surrender, he replied, "They'll have to shoot me like the dog I am." A few hours later, 15-year-old Opel Diane Buckson was taken, screaming, from a school bus stop, and pushed into the trunk of an old black car. Two local men noticed a car parked in the woods twelve miles north of Gaffney; officers found the stabbed, strangled body of Buckson inside. Lee Roy Martin, thirty-one, the Gaffney textile mill worker who owned the car, was arrested.

Released from prison on Apr. 30, 1968, Dedmond said, "They tried to tell me I killed her. I knew in my heart I never did kill her, and I never did confess to it." Martin was tried before Judge James B. Morrison of Georgetown, S.C., and pleaded guilty to two counts of murder. He was sentenced to two consecutive terms of life imprisonment on each count. See; **Martin, Lee Roy.** REF.: *CBA.*

Deeming, Frederick Bayley (AKA: **Albert O. Williams, Albert Ward, Droven, Drewen, Baron Swanston, Lord Dun**), 1854-92, Brit.-Aus., big.-fraud-mur. Frederick Deeming was a man of enormous ego who considered himself an accomplished con man, but his schemes produced little money over a number of years and

he is best remembered as a mass murderer. His early background is sketchy, but it is known, through Deeming's later admissions, that his mother and father were confined in a mental institution and he himself had been subject to mental disturbances as a child, which earned him the youthful sobriquet of "Mad Fred." After marrying, Deeming left his wife in Birkenhead, England, and sailed to Australia, ostensibly looking for work. He found a job as a gas fitter in Sydney, but was later arrested for stealing company property and given a brief prison term. His wife joined him in Sydney and Deeming

Australian mass killer Frederick Deeming.

spent a short time at honest labor. He then filed a bankruptcy fraudulently and was arrested. After posting bail, Deeming and his wife and children fled, going to Port Adelaide, where he was living in 1888.

By that time, Deeming had resolved to earn his living as a con man. He sailed for St. Helena and en route bilked two brothers named Howe of a small sum. He moved about with his family for the next few years, living in Cape Town, Durban, Johannesburg, Port Elizabeth, and Kimberley. His frauds usually involved jewelers. Deeming would pose as a diamond mine operator and sell bogus shares in his mines. He was a fluent, if flamboyant, talker and easily convinced the more rural and gullible victims to invest heavily in his nonexistent mines. He even managed to defraud a considerable sum from the National Bank in Johannesburg. Next he mulcted a man named Grice of about £2,800 with the promise of selling him a large part of a gold mine he claimed to have in Klerksdorp. When Grice was about to meet Deeming to obtain his shares, he was informed through a confederate that Deeming was dead, having succumbed to a sudden illness.

Detectives were now on Deeming's trail and he knew it. He sent his wife and four children back to England and then, through a circuitous route, went to England himself. Detectives followed him there, and he again sailed for Australia and back again to England, using aliases. Once in England, Deeming began posing as wealthy men or members of the aristocracy. He passed a number of bad checks, bigamously married several women, and then fled to Antwerp, where he announced he was Lord Dun. He married and bilked another woman, deserting her as he had others, by suddenly leaving his hotel and paying with a bad check. Returning to England, he gave a bogus check for £285 to a jeweler in Hull for several gems. He immediately embarked for South America, posing as a millionaire and entertaining passengers with wild stories of his imagined adventures in Africa. When arriving in Montevideo, Deeming was arrested by detectives who had been tracking him half way around the world. He was returned to England where he tried unsuccessfully to escape several times.

Katie Rounsfell testifying at Deeming's trial, 1892.

On Oct. 16, 1890, Deeming was sentenced to nine months in prison for swindling the Hull jeweler. He was released on July 16, 1891, going to the Commercial Hotel in Liverpool, where he registered under the alias of Albert O. Williams. He claimed that he was an officer from an Indian regiment and that he was looking for a suitable home where his colonel would live in retirement. He specified that the house to be rented for the colonel have a concrete floor—this later proved part of his plan to murder his family. He was already having an affair with Emily Mather, although Deeming's wife came to visit him at the Commerical Hotel. Deeming later rented a cottage, Dinham Villa, at Rainhill, and moved his wife, Maria, and four children into it. He then killed all five, crushing their heads with a heavy instrument while they slept. He dug up the concrete floor in the kitchen and buried

the bodies beneath, cementing the floor over them and even hiring a few workers to complete the job.

Some weeks later Deeming brought Emily Mather to the cottage and, according to his bizarre statements later, danced a jig for her on the concrete floor above the bodies of the family he had ruthlessly slaughtered. He married the woman and, after attempting to claim damages for a picture he had sent by rail to another town and being refused, Deeming and his new wife sailed for Australia in October 1891. He was by then using the name Droven and later Drewen, and settled with his wife in Melbourne, where he rented a house on Andrew Street in Windsor. A short time later, tiring of his wife, Deeming killed her and put her body beneath a cement bedroom floor of his own creation.

Deeming filed an application at a marriage bureau in Melbourne, but he suddenly left the city on Jan. 5, 1892, believing that detectives might be looking for him. On the boat sailing for Sydney, Deeming, introducing himself as Baron Swanston, met a young woman, Katie Rounsfell (or Rounsville), and promptly proposed marriage. She accepted and they planned to wed in a short time. Once in Sydney, Deeming took a job with a gold mine at Southern Cross. He sent for Rounsfell, who was just preparing to join him, when detectives arrived to tell her that her fiancé was a mass murderer. By that time, Deeming had been arrested for the murder of Mather. A rental agent named Connor had inspected Deeming's vacated Melbourne house on Andrew Street and, while walking in the bedroom, noticed the freshly cemented floor, which had been rushed and had not dried properly. Connor kicked the lumpy cement that had cracked and a slab flipped over to reveal the face of a dead woman, eyes open, staring up at him.

The killer had been careless, leaving documents with his alias of Williams and the address in Rainhill. Australian detectives contacted police in Liverpool. The Dinham Villa cottage was inspected, and the five slain bodies of Deeming's first family were found. Deeming was tracked down through his many identities, arrested for murder at Southern Cross on Mar. 11, 1892, and taken to Melbourne where thousands of curious citizens turned out to see "the monster." One group of vengeance-seeking residents tried to grab the killer and lynch him, but he was saved by police and jailed, pending trial. While behind bars, Deeming wrote syrupy letters to Rounsfell, telling her that he was innocent and asked that she send him money. She was an heiress, and Deeming had planned to have her funds transferred to his accounts and then kill her. She sent no money.

While in prison, Deeming suffered from what appeared to be epileptic fits, but his guards and prison doctors insisted that these fits were faked by Deeming who they considered a consummate actor. His fits might have occurred because Deeming was suffering from advanced stages of syphilis. At his trial, Deeming insisted that he was insane and had been for most of his life. He told a tale of seeing his dead mother almost every day and that this hideous apparition had urged him to murder all women he met. While standing in the dock, he addressed the court, reading from a long speech he had written and one in which he insisted that he was being prosecuted for a murder that he never committed. He also claimed Emily Mather was alive, although her corpse had long been officially identified and buried. At the end of the speech, Deeming turned to the gallery of witnesses and said: "You people are the ugliest human beings I have ever seen!"

These pretended mad acts gained Frederick Deeming nothing. He was judged sane, convicted, and sentenced to death. While awaiting execution, he attempted to gain as much notoriety as possible, announcing that *he* was Jack the Ripper; this claim was, like most he had made in life, false, contradicted by the events of his life. Deeming was in jail at the time of the Ripper murders in London's West End. On May 23, 1892, Deeming was taken before a crowd of 10,000 cheering spectators and publicly hanged.

REF.: Bennett, *Murder Will Speak;* Brock, *A Casebook of Crime; CBA;* Dearden, *Some Cases of Sir Bernard Spilsbury and Others;* Dilnot, *Celebrated Crimes;* Douthwaite, *Mass Murder;* Gribble, *Famous Manhunts;* Logan, *Great Murder Mysteries;* _____, *Masters of Crime;* Marjoribanks,

For the Defense; Nash, *Almanac of World Crime;* O'Sullivan, *A Most Unique Ruffian;* Stevens, *Famous Crimes and Criminals;* Whitelaw, *Corpus Delicti;* Wilson, *Encyclopedia of Murder.*

Deering, John, 1899-1938, U.S., rob.-mur. John Deering, thirty-nine, was arrested in Hamtramck, Mich., in July 1937 as a robbery suspect. Having served a seventeen-year jail term, the ex-convict who had once shot his way to freedom was so determined not to be jailed again that he confessed to having murdered Oliver R. Meredith, Jr. in a Salt Lake City robbery in May 1937, rather than serve a fifteen-year jail sentence for the Michigan robbery.

Extradited to Utah, Deering was convicted of first-degree murder. He dispassionately maintained that he was a habitual criminal and should be killed. The judge concurred with Deering's sentiments, offering him the choice of being shot or hanged. Deering preferred to be shot, explaining that he had chosen that because "when I was a kid raising hell everyone told me I'd end up on the gallows, so I thought I'd fool them."

In November 1938, Deering was taken at dawn to the Utah prison courtyard, strapped into a chair, blindfolded, and a target was placed over his heart. At the order of Sheriff S. Grant Young, a firing squad of five deputies raised their guns and executed him. REF.: *CBA.*

DeFeo, Ronald Joseph, Jr., 1951- , U.S., mur. On Nov. 13, 1974, Deborah Cosentino was driving home from her job as a barmaid in Amityville, N.Y., at about 3:45 a.m., when she noticed that the house of the DeFeo family was blazing with light. Around 3:00 a.m., John Nementh, a teenage neighbor, had been awakened when he heard the DeFeo family's sheepdog howling. At 6:35 p.m. a call came in to the Suffolk County Police Department to report a shooting. Joey Yeswit reported that the entire DeFeo family, except for the eldest son, had been slain. Officer Kenneth Greguski of the Amityville Village Police arrived at the home to find the bodies of Ronald DeFeo, Sr., his wife, Louise DeFeo, and four of their children, Dawn, eighteen, Allison, thirteen, Mark, eleven, and John, nine. All were lying face down, shot with .35-caliber bullets. Ronald Joseph DeFeo, Jr., the only surviving member of the family, sat at the kitchen table crying and mumbling incoherently, though just after shooting the victims, he had calmly showered and then gone to visit his girlfriend, telling her "something strange" was going on at his house, and later getting a heroin fix. DeFeo told another friend at a bar that he was going to "break a window to get in" to his home. At about 6:30 p.m. DeFeo returned to the bar, shouting for help, and brought several friends back to the Ocean Street house. One of them, Yeswit, called the police. When police arrived, they found DeFeo at the kitchen table sobbing.

Detective Gaspar Randazzo was the first officer to question DeFeo, who suggested the name of an alleged Mafia hit man with a grudge against his family as the possible killer. Describing his activities the day of the killings, DeFeo explained that when he had broken into the house, all the lights were out except for one in the living room. DeFeo told homicide detective George Harrison, "I hope you find out who did it." Then, detectives discovered empty boxes for rifles in DeFeo's room. Within a short time, they were reading him his rights.

The case was tried in October 1975 before Judge Thomas M. Stark, with Gerard Sullivan, prosecuting attorney, and Bill Weber for the defense. On Nov. 19, the jury found DeFeo Guilty on six counts of second-degree murder, and he was sentenced to twenty-five years to life in prison, which he is now serving at the New York State Correctional Facility in Dannemora, N.Y. Jewelry and $200,000 that DeFeo stole from his family home, have never been recovered. A non-fiction account of the case, *High Hopes, The Amityville Murders,* published in 1981, was written by prosecutor Sullivan.

REF.: *CBA;* Fox, *Mass Murder;* Sullivan and Aronson, *High Hopes: The Amityville Murders;* (FILM), *The Amityville Horror.*

Defoe, Daniel (AKA: **Andrew Moreton**) 1660-1731, Brit., sedition. An English journalist and novelist known for championing nonconformists and dissention, Daniel Defoe wrote a severe satire against the Church, entitled *The Shortest Way with the Dissenters.* Government members were so angered by it that they advertised in the London *Gazette* for Defoe's arrest, offering a £50 reward and describing him in great detail. When Defoe learned that the printer and publisher of the pamphlet had been jailed, he turned himself in—they were then set free. Tried at the Old Bailey in July 1704, Defoe pleaded guilty, allegedly on the promise of a secret pardon. He was fined two hundred marks, and was ordered to appear in the pillory three times. Before his first time in the pillory, Defoe wrote a poem that immediately became famous; *Hymn to the Pillory* was put into type and sung by the crowd that gathered when Defoe first came before the public to supposedly be humiliated. Not only did the people sing Defoe's own hymn of dissention to him, they surrounded him with flowers, and put garlands on the pillory, saying they wished those who had put him in there were in that position, instead. As Defoe wrote later, they "expressed their affections by loud thanks and acclamations when I was taken down." Defoe spent a year in prison before the queen sent money to his wife to pay the fine and so released him.

Writer Daniel Defoe, sent to the pillory for endorsing nonconformity.

In 1706, the queen sent Defoe to Scotland as a secret agent to promote union within the government. He proved himself a skilled journalist during that time. After his discovery as a secret agent, he lived under the name Andrew Morton.

REF.: Andrews, *Old-Time Punishments; CBA.*

DeFoor, Martin, and **DeFoor, Susan,** d.1879, U.S., (unsolv.) mur. Early on July 26, 1879, Martin Walker, the young grandson of Martin and Susan DeFoor, noticed that his grandparents had not risen at their usual time. Martin found the elderly couple brutally slain, both nearly decapitated by axe blows. The Fulton County, Ga., residents were not known to have any enemies, and robbery did not appear to be the motive, as a bag containing $18 in silver was untouched, as were several other articles of value. Martin DeFoor's wallet, which contained only promissory notes, was taken along with his boots which were found about 400 feet from the house in a wooded area. An upstairs room, reachable only by ladder, showed evidence of recent occupancy, including a rumpled bed, and human excrement found in an adjacent lumber room. Sheriff William A. Wilson and his deputies concluded that the killer had hidden upstairs and waited until night to murder the DeFoors. The axe, covered with blood and ashes, was found in the fireplace, and the back door was unlatched from the inside. The DeFoors were buried together in a single grave in the Montgomery family cemetery in Bolton, Ga. REF.: *CBA.*

DeFranzio, Louis, prom. 1910, U.S., wh. slav. On Aug. 10, 1910, Louis DeFranzio, was tried in a Boston court and sentenced to nine months in the House of Correction for forcing a Canadian woman into a life of prostitution. "Sallie A." testified that she had attempted several escapes from DeFranzio's brothel, but was repeatedly forced back or prevented from leaving by DeFranzio.

REF.: *CBA;* Roe, *Great War on White Slavery.*

deFreeze, Donald, See: **Symbionese Liberation Army.**

de Gaulle, Charles, 1890-1970, Fr., pres., attempt. assass. When would-be assassins ambushed Charles de Gaulle's limousine, his only response was, "What, again?" The leader of the Free French in WWII, self-proclaimed liberator of France, and president of France from 1958-69, de Gaulle survived at least thirty-one assassination attempts during his public career. The first known attempt occurred in Dakar, Senegal, in 1944, when a man angered by the sinking of the French fleet at Mers-el-Kébir tried to shoot de Gaulle, whom he held responsible. Many French Algerians later tried to kill de Gaulle for his failure to prevent Algerian independence, but his security measures thwarted their attempts.

The attempt that came closest to succeeding occurred on Aug. 22, 1962. Gunmen attacked de Gaulle's limousine as it traveled through Petit-Clamart, a suburb of Paris. Two motorcycles preceded him and a second Citroën followed his. De Gaulle, his wife, his son-in-law, and a chauffeur were in the first car. When submachine guns opened fire on the vehicles, the well-trained drivers continued on as if nothing were happening. De Gaulle himself did not even deign to duck until after Colonel Alain de Boissieu, his son-in-law, shouted at him twice. De Gaulle leaned forward just as bullets flew past the back of his head. Colonel Bastien-Thiry was arrested a month later for the attempt. De Gaulle survived several other attempts, and died in 1970.

REF.: Bell, *Assassin; CBA;* Heppenstall, *The Sex War and Others;* (FICTION), Forsyth, *Day of the Jackal.*

De Graff, William, b.c.1856, Case of, U.S., mur. On June 9, 1911, a tug pulled three barges loaded with coal out of Port Richmond, Pa. Aboard the *Glendower* barge was Captain Charles D. Wyman, fifty-five, deck hand William Nilsen, twenty-four, cook William De Graff, fifty-five, and a donkeyman, Antonio Priskich, twenty-seven, who tended the donkey engine. That day, when Captain Wyman did not come to lunch or dinner, Priskich and De Graff checked on the captain and found him dead. Wyman was wrapped in blankets with bruises and cuts on his head. All of the crew were arrested, and De Graff was indicted for murder.

De Graff had come aboard the *Glendower* in May 1911, one month before the murder of Captain Wyman. Two witness testified that De Graff disliked the captain, but De Graff denied the allegations. Prosecutors argued that the hunchbacked cook was the only person who had access to the captain. No motive, however, was found, and the possibility of a stowaway was raised, leading to De Graff's acquittal.

REF.: *CBA;* Pearson, *Five Murders.*

DeGroot, Robert, 1951-82, U.S., suic.-mur. On Nov. 9, 1982, Robert DeGroot, thirty-one, owner of the Bobill Music Store in Waukegan, Ill., called a priest to discuss his upcoming divorce from his 27-year-old wife of two years, Anne. The priest then notified police in Park City, Ill., that he thought DeGroot might commit suicide. Police found no one at DeGroot's Park City home. According to Lake County Coroner Barbara Richardson, DeGroot had left for the home of Anne DeGroot's parents, where his estranged wife was staying with her three children: Maureen Mahar, nine, from a former marriage; Robert DeGroot, eighteen months, and Ian DeGroot, three months. When her husband arrived, brandishing a .30-caliber carbine, he told Anne's brother-in-law, Mark Boarini, that he had "better get out before he gets his." Boarini rushed from the house to notify police. About ten minutes later, DeGroot fired seven shots, killing Anne, Robert, and Maureen, and seriously wounding Ian, who was found still in his mother's arms. DeGroot then shot himself. According to Richardson, DeGroot "was under extreme depression and did not want the divorce." REF.: *CBA.*

Dehays, Jean, prom. 1949, Fr., (wrong. convict.) rob.-asslt. In December 1949, longshoreman Jean Dehays was tried at the Nantes Court, with René Floriot defending him against charges or robbery and assault. Dehays had confessed to his crime but it was speculated that police had beaten it out of him. At the trial, Dehays was on crutches with one leg in a cast; officers explained that he had fallen down the stairs at the police station. Dehays was sentenced to ten years of hard labor. Four years later, René Dutoy and Raymond Pruvot confessed to the crime Dehays had been convicted of, absolving him of the robbery. At the hearing to obtain rehabilitation at the ensuing trial, Floriot told the court, "You will never stop the police from beating up suspects."

REF.: *CBA;* Goodman, *Villainy Unlimited.*

De Hory, Elmyr, 1914-   , Spain, fraud. A Hungarian national, Elmyr de Hory was a stateless artist who allegedly sold millions of dollars worth of fakes, many of them to a Texas millionaire. De Hory, who had great contempt for art connoisseurs who "know more about fine words than fine art," developed an extremely successful mail order business in forgeries. He wrote to leading museums and galleries, offering to show his small collection of works by modern artists. He would answer a positive response by sending a photograph of whatever picture the museum was interested in, later delivering it by mail. De Hory painted each work himself. He was so proficient at imitating Pablo Picasso that he once boldly asked Picasso to authenticate one of his fakes. Picasso looked at de Hory's nude, done in his own style, and remarked, "I remember painting her. It did take rather a long time to complete, though, as I could not resist making love to her." Picasso signed the forged work. De Hory, who was in the United States plying his trade between 1949 and 1959, boasted that he could paint a portrait in just forty-five minutes, drawing a "Modigliani" in ten, and then creating a "Matisse". At the age of sixty, de Hory was taken from his island home in Ibiza, Spain, in 1974, and jailed on Majorca for four months. No formal charge was made, and he was released. American author Clifford Irving, who would later be jailed for his forged biography of wealthy eccentric Howard Hughes, wrote a book about de Hory, called *Fake.* See: **Irving, Clifford.**

REF.: *CBA;* Rose, *The World's Greatest Rip-Offs.*

Deibler, Henri, prom. 1938, Fr., execut. In 1938, Henri Deibler informed the French Ministry of Justice that he would rather go on strike than execute a female criminal. Deibler had executed more than 300 men, but not one woman. He became concerned when Josephine Mory was sentenced to death for murder. although when her sentenced was commuted to life imprisonment, Deibler was relieved and called off his strike. A similar "hangman's strike" was threatened in England when Rhoda Willis was scheduled to be hanged. Several civilians, including one woman, volunteered to carry out the sentence.

REF.: Atholl, *Shadow of the Gallows; CBA.*

Deiotarus, d.40 B.C., Galatia, consp. Crowned by Pompey king of Galatia, c.64 B.C., he was defended by Marcus Cicero, 45-44 B.C., after being accused of attempting to assassinate Julius Caesar, who was subsequently murdered, before completion of the trial, Mar. 15, 44 B.C. REF.: *CBA.*

Bank robber John De Jarnette and girlfriend Doris Lee Nelson, acting tough for the camera, 1962.

De Jarnette, John Kinchloe, 1921-   , U.S., rob. Bank robber John De Jarnette surrendered meekly to FBI agents in Hollywood, Calif., on Dec. 3, 1962. The 41-year-old drug user and hold-up man was playing monopoly with his girlfriend, Doris Lee Nelson, at the time. De Jarnette's arrest ended a massive FBI manhunt following three bank robberies in Ohio and Kentucky.

On Sept. 10, 1962, he held up the Liberty National Bank & Trust Company in Louisville. A month later De Jarnette robbed another branch of the same bank, this time for $36,000. His biggest heist—a city record at the time—took place on Oct. 22, when he robbed the Provident Branch Bank of Cincinnati, Ohio, of $37,232. In addition to bank robbery, De Jarnette was wanted in Kentucky for obtaining illegal drugs through fraud. Shortly afterward his name was added to the FBI's Ten Most Wanted List.

Extradited back to Louisville, De Jarnette pleaded guilty to robbing the two branches of the Liberty National Bank. On May 8, 1963, U.S. District Judge Henry L. Brooks sentenced De Jarnette to two twenty-five year sentences. On May 14, the same judge added a third twenty-five year sentence for the Provident Bank robbery. All three terms were to be served concurrently. In 1984, John De Jarnette was ordered released after serving twenty years of his original sentences.

Three other men who conspired with De Jarnette in the robberies were tried separately. On Jan. 18, 1963, Robert Eugene Johnson, Jr., driver of the getaway car, was sentenced to four years. Rudolph Kruse, Jr., twenty-two, pleaded guilty to robbery charges and was sentenced to prison. The third co-defendant, Robert Lee Cook, forty-one, was acquitted. REF.: *CBA*.

Dejean, Maurice, prom. 1955, U.S.S.R., adult. In 1955 Maurice Dejean arrived in the U.S.S.R. with his wife, Marie Claire Dejean, to serve as French ambassador. Aware of Dejean's inclination toward infidelity, KGB Lieutenant General Oleg Gribanov assigned Yuri Krotkov, a Russian scriptwriter who worked with the KGB, to bait Dejean and set him up for future favors to the Russian secret police. Krotkov won the ambassador's trust by charming his wife, giving her ballet tickets, and taking her out on river cruises and to fancy dinners. Eventually, Dejean joined his wife and the screenwriter.

After arranging a trip in the country for Mrs. Dejean, Krotkov arranged for an attractive interpreter, "Lydia," to spend the day showing Dejean an exhibition of paintings. Within hours, the ambassador and the interpreter had become lovers. The KGB photographed the event. To strengthen their hold on the French diplomat, the KGB sent Lydia out of town and introduced Dejean to "Larissa," another actress. They also became intimate and, in June 1958 two large men burst into their love nest, one acting the part of the angry husband, threatening Dejean with blackmail. The anxious Frenchman consulted one of Krotkov's friends—the same Gribanov who had set up the seductions in the first place. Gribanov generously reassured the errant ambassador, feeling secure that Dejean's favor to his protector could be easily pulled in at a future date.

Krotkov defected, and Dejean was eventually recalled to Paris by President Charles de Gaulle, who had him extensively interrogated by counter-espionage men. Apparently, the KGB had never claimed their repayment for the favor. De Gaulle dismissed Dejean, saying: "So, Dejean, you enjoy the company of women." REF.: *CBA*.

DeJong, prom. 1890s, Neth., theft-mur. The theory that "Bluebeard" types of criminals who woo and then rob and murder women are often handsome men is disproved by the Dutch criminal DeJong. A short man with yellow teeth and bad breath, DeJong wooed, swindled, and slayed about twenty women in Europe in the 1890s. Other unattractive criminals who romanced women and then robbed and killed them included H.H. Holmes, who had a murder castle in Chicago; French murderer, Henri Landru; and Harry Powers, who murdered several women in West Virginia. See: **Landru, Henri Desire; Powers, Harry.**
REF.: *CBA*; Hynd, *Sleuths, Slayers and Swindlers*.

De John, Nick, See: **Calamia, Leonard.**

de Kaplany, Dr. Geza (AKA: **The Acid Doctor**), 1926- , U.S., mur. In the annals of medical murderers it is difficult to find one as cruel and inhuman as the monstrous Dr. Geza de Kaplany, convicted of the torture-murder of his beautiful wife in 1963. De Kaplany was a Hungarian refugee who, in 1962, was working for a San Jose, Calif., hospital as a well-paid anesthesiologist. He was

arrogant, vain, and wholly self-centered, a man few called friend. He was attracted to a stunning model and beauty queen in the Hungarian community of San Jose and avidly pursued the 25-year-old woman, finally marrying her in August 1962. Hanja de Kaplany, however, found her new husband to be a strange and unpredictable man. After only a few days of marriage, according to later statements made by de Kaplany, the doctor found himself impotent, unable to make love to his ravishingly beautiful wife. He acted in a paranoid manner, convincing himself that all the bachelors in the apartment complex where they lived were having affairs with his wife.

A beautiful model, Mrs. Geza de Kaplany, was tortured to death by her physician husband.

He vowed to "ruin" her beauty, "to fix her."

On the morning of Aug. 28, 1962, neighbors heard loud music blaring from the de Kaplany apartment and through this, piercing screams. After repeatedly pounding on walls, windows, and the front door to the de Kaplany apartment, without getting a response, the neighbors called police. Officers arrived and banged on the front door until the music inside suddenly stopped. The door slowly opened. Grinning madly and sweating, dressed only in his underwear, his hands covered with rubber gloves, Dr. de Kaplany stood before the officers, telling them that he had been at work. The officers stepped inside and went to a nearby bedroom where they reeled back in shock. On the bed, naked, was his wife, horribly mutilated but alive. It was learned how de Kaplany had spent several days preparing to perform this "work." He had decided to "operate" on his wife, to disfigure her to the point where no other man would look at her, let alone covet her once alluring body.

De Kaplany had purchased hi-fi equipment some days earlier and installed several extra speakers in the apartment. He had also gotten a manicure so that he would not puncture the rubber gloves he would wear when handling the many bottles of sulfuric, nitric, and hydrochloric acids he brought from the hospital to his apartment and carefully arranged on the bedroom bureau while his wife slept. He then leaped upon his wife, stripping her, and tying her hands and legs to the bedposts. He then walked into the other room and turned on the hi-fi to its maximum volume. When he returned to the bedroom he held up a note for her to read, one which de Kaplany had written the night before on his own prescription forms. It read, "If you want to live—do not shout; do what I tell you or else you will die."

Then de Kaplany began making small incisions all over his wife's body, pouring various acids into the open cuts which caused the poor woman to scream in agony. The "Acid Doctor" ignored her pleas and screams as he systematically obliterated her face, slashing and cutting, savagely mutilating her genitals and breasts. After an hour of this barbarous torture, the police arrived to stop the monster. By then his wife was fatally injured with third-degree corrosive burns. She was removed by hospital attendants who, attempting to cover her body with ointments, burned their hands on her acid-coated body. The brave young woman lived for twenty-one days while her mother, unable to bear her child's cries of anguish, prayed at Hanja's bedside for her daughter to die.

Following his wife's death, de Kaplany, was jailed and charged with murder. He claimed that he had not intended to kill his wife, only spoil her good looks. He explained his horrendous torture of Hanja as being "my one-hour crack-up." The doctor went to trial for murder before Judge Raymond G. Callahan on Jan. 7,

The de Kaplanys on their wedding day; a few weeks later the barbaric de Kaplany butchered his wife.

1963, a little more than a month after his wife's death. He pled not guilty and not guilty by reason of insanity. On the witness stand de Kaplany appeared calm and composed, patiently explaining that he never intended to kill his wife, only destroy her beauty so she would not be attractive to other men, so that he believed he could have her all to himself. It was the only way he believed he could regain his peace of mind, which had been wracked with jealousy, and restore his ability to make love.

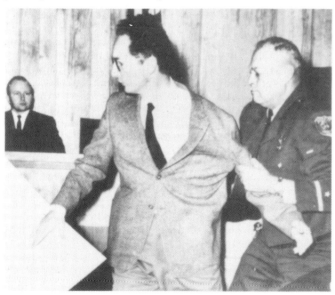

Dr. de Kaplany at his murder trial, reacting violently to exhibits of his wife's carved-up corpse.

When the prosecution displayed photos of the victim as police had found her, de Kaplany lost all composure, viewing the photos with hysterical outbursts, shouting to the court: "I am a doctor! I loved her! If I did this and I must have done this—then I am guilty!" The trial dragged on for thirty-five days, at the end of which de Kaplany was found Guilty. He was sentenced to prison for life but he was, for reasons never explained, classified as a "special interest prisoner." This was made clear to some extent when de Kaplany was prematurely released in 1975, six full months

before his first official parole date would have gone into effect. When news reporters probed the reason for this, they were told that de Kaplany was released since his expertise as a "cardiac specialist" was vital to a Taiwan missionary hospital.

This was far from reality since de Kaplany was never a heart specialist. Ray Procunier, who headed the parole board reviewing de Kaplany's case, resigned his position before he could be interviewed by news reporters, stating that he had quit his position for "personal reasons." De Kaplany by then was long gone, departed for Taiwan, to assume his unspecified medical duties, having literally been smuggled out of the country before his release and departure was made public. This was one of the most flagrant abuses of the parole system in California history, releasing a maniac to continue administering medical treatments to those unaware of the torture-murder of his wife. At last report, de Kaplany still resides in Taiwan, working and enjoying his freedom.

REF.: Anspacher, *The Acid Test; CBA;* Nash, *Almanac of World Crime;* _____, *Murder, America.*

de Kerninon, Countess **Suzanne,** prom. 1924, Fr., mur. Suzanne Fleury, a widow and professional singer, met Count le Roux de Kerninon in Algeria. They married and moved to Brest with her son, Emile Fleury. The countess, eight years older than her husband, preferred life in Paris and the Côte d'Azur to his country estate, and she forced the count to sell the estate and live near the Fleurys in Lannion.

The count then took Bernardine Nedellec, a typist, as his mistress, and when his wife discovered his indiscretion, she was furious. The countess was further angered when she found that the count planned to leave his mistress a large sum of money. He changed his will, but on Sept. 21, 1924, the countess shot her husband four times. She contended that her husband was going to shoot himself and that the gun accidentally fired when she tried to take the weapon away. However, she was convicted and sentenced to eight years in prison for her husband's death.

REF.: *CBA;* Heppenstall, *Bluebeard and After;* Morain, *Underworld of Paris.*

DeKing, Lillian, prom. 1929, Case of, U.S., mur. On March 25, 1929, six state law enforcement agents invaded the Aurora, Ill., home of Peter and Lillian DeKing. Suspecting Peter DeKing of bootlegging, one of the agents clubbed him over the head with the butt of a shotgun; when Lillian DeKing raced to her unconscious husband's side, she was killed by a blast from one of the agent's shotguns. Ella Boole, a member of the Women's Christian Temperance Union, responded when hearing of the death, "Well, she was evading the law, wasn't she?"

REF.: *CBA;* Kobler, *Ardent Spirits.*

Dekker, James, prom. 1981, Case of, U.S., pol. mal.-mur. On July 9, 1981, 22-year-old Ernest Lacy was picked up in Milwaukee, Wis., by police officers James Dekker, George Kalt, and Thomas Eliopul because he matched the description of a suspect in an attempted rape. Witnesses at a coroner's inquest said they had seen the three officers straddling Lacy while his hands were cuffed behind his back. Lacy, a mentally-disturbed black man who was afraid of police, died as the result of lack of oxygen to the brain, possibly caused by pressure on his back and a pinched nerve from his brain to his heart. He was declared dead at a hospital about an hour after the real suspect had been identified. On Oct. 15, 1981, a Milwaukee coroner's jury recommended that the three policemen be charged with reckless conduct in the death, and that Kenneth Kmiecek, the driver of the police van, and Robert Enters, his assistant, be cited for misconduct in public office. Lacy's death for a crime he did not commit set off the biggest demonstrations in Milwaukee since the 1960s civil rights marches. Police Chief Harold Brier said the jury's decision would be devastating in the "terrible impact it could have on the morale of the department." More than 100 witnesses testified at the inquest, which was televised.

Milwaukee district attorney E. Michael McCann said on Feb. 2, 1982, that the charges against the officers would be hard to prove, and decided not to appeal the dismissal of reckless homicide charges against officers Dekker and Kalt. The charges were dismissed by Judge Janine Geske. REF.: *CBA*.

De Koven, Jean, See: **Weidmann, Eugene.**

Delacourt, Rose, prom. 1800s, Fr., (unsolv.) mur. Immortalized by writer Edgar Allan Poe in his story, *Murders In The Rue Morgue,* the killing of Rose Delacourt at the end of the last century still remains unsolved. A prostitute, Delacourt lived in a one room flat at the top of a large Parisian apartment house on the Rue Montmartre. She usually returned home in the early hours of the morning, let in by the wife of the concierge. The night of her death, Delacourt came home around 2 a.m., half-joking to her landlady about having "no luck lately." The landlady told her not to get depressed, and knocked on her door ten hours later with the usual cup of chocolate. When there was no answer, she presumed Delacourt was tired and thought no more about it. But by late afternoon, she became concerned and banged on the door loudly, still getting no response. The police broke open the door and found Delacourt in bed, covered by bedclothes that seemed not to have been moved at all. She was stabbed through the heart with a blow so strong that the weapon—either a very long-bladed knife or a short sword—had completely pierced through her body and had penetrated three or four inches deep into the mattress.

The door to Delacourt's room was locked on the inside, bolted at both the top and the bottom. There was one window in the room, securely fastened on the inside, which faced out to a sheer drop of fifty or sixty feet to the pavement below. Articles of jewelry were untouched on the dressing table, and no weapon was found in the room. The landlady said that Delacourt had returned alone the night before, and that no one could have entered the building without she or her husband knowing. One of the most popular theories, later used by Poe in his story, was that a large monkey had come in and left through the chimney. But investigators found that the chimney was far too narrow to admit an ape powerful enough to kill the woman. Also, there were no traces of soot in the room. The possibility that the killer had opened and then replaced the locks by use of a powerful magnet was also proved impossible, as were theories that panels had been cut and replaced in the windowpane or the flooring. See: *Murders in the Rue Morgue;* **Poe, Edgar Allan.**

REF.: *CBA;* Stevens, *From Clue to Dock;* (FICTION) Poe, *Murders in the Rue Morgue.*

De La Hoz, Licenciada M., prom. 1920s, Mex., kid. Licenciada M. De La Hoz, considered Mexico's top lawyer, along with accomplices Antonio Casasus and Fernando Jimenez, kidnapped Don Alejandro Carrara, a well-known advisor of Mexico's elite. De La Hoz had served as Carrara's lawyer. When he went bankrupt, he kidnapped his client. A ransom note was sent to Carrara's sister, Doña Maria Carrara, asking for 250,000 pesos in gold coin, the exact amount of money that the family could raise in a short time.

A famous Mexican detective, Valente Quintana, took note of the amount of the ransom request, an amount their financial advisor would have known. When De La Hoz pulled Quintana from the case, the investigator asked for a typed release. The release was typed on the same machine as the ransom notes.

After De La Hoz was arrested, he led police to Carrara, who was unharmed. The gang was tried and convicted, and De La Hoz, who defended himself, received an eighteen-year sentence. Casasus and Jimenez were sentenced to twelve years in prison.

REF.: *CBA;* Cohen, *One Hundred True Crime Stories.*

Delaitre, Pierre-Joel, 1913-53, Brit., smug.-suic.-mur. Pierre-Joel Delaitre was a profligate youth, reared in the luxurious eighteenth-century Chateau de Mainteniac. He took horses from the tenant farmers and raced them recklessly across the country and later drove his race car at dangerous speeds through the crowded marketplace. He wasted his family fortune, then turned to smuggling, but was caught and forced to pay a substantial fine. Even his mother used to say, "Pierre is no good." On the night of his wedding, he chased his bride with a shotgun. They were divorced immediately after their honeymoon. Then forty, Delaitre met Eileen Hill, a typist from London who was vacationing on the Breton Coast. In a whirlwind romance, Delaitre took Hill to nightclubs in Paris, and she became his mistress. Returning to London, Hill dyed her hair blonde and announced her plans to marry her lover. But on her second trip to France, she returned with a black eye after running away from Delaitre while he was sleeping. Two detective agencies located Hill for Delaitre, and when he came to see her, she refused to marry him but did agree to spend one last week in his company.

Delaitre rented room 223 in the Ritz, one of the hotel's most elegant. On a March morning, the maid, receiving no response to her knock, called police to break down the door. The room was a shambles. Hill lay dead in bed, strangled, her throat slashed with a razor. Delaitre had cut his own throat, then scribbled an incoherent note before tying one end of a nine-foot rope to his neck, attaching the other to the bed, and walking backwards to strangle himself. The Ritz, appalled and anxious, destroyed the antique bed, removed the numbers from room 223, and erased the number from the hotel registry. REF.: *CBA*.

de la Mare, Gertrude, 1908- , Brit., mur. Gertrude de la Mare, a slow-witted woman who was estranged from her husband, worked as a housekeeper for the elderly Alfred Brouard. She and her 3-year-old daughter lived with the old man at his home on Guernsey, one of the Channel Islands. On Feb. 6, 1935, at 9 a.m., de la Mare told her next door neighbor, "The old man is dead. He had cut his throat." Police officers found Brouard lying in his bed, with his throat cut from left to right. A letter left for the police said there was "no blame attaching to Mrs. de la Mare," and left the funeral arrangements to the housekeeper. A will, supposedly left by Brouard, was written by a semi-literate and purported to leave everything—possessions that amounted to only around £60—to de la Mare. The attorney general, Ambrose Sherwill, contended that both documents were forgeries by de la Mare, who had murdered her employer in a "predetermined plan to make herself rich." De la Mare, when first questioned, instructed her daughter to tell the police what Brouard used to say when he saw the bread knife, which had been the murder weapon. When the child did not speak, the mother explained, "She wants to say that Mr. Brouard said, when he sharpened it, that we would be able to butcher ourselves with it."

Following the prosecutor's opening remarks, the entire court piled into cars and drove to the farmhouse where Brouard died. A policeman re-enacted the death, showing how it would have been impossible for the farmer to cut his own throat from left to right with his right hand. De la Mare's mother testified that her daughter had told her three days before the employer's demise that Brouard had committed suicide, and corroborated this premature announcement. The housekeeper had also gone to a real estate agent to inquire about buying a large house, later admitting that she had no money. The most damning evidence of all was the dress of her small child. It was flecked with bloodstains, which the prosecutor contended had gotten on the garment when the mother dressed her child right after murdering the old man. The question of de la Mare's sanity was debated by doctors. Found Guilty of murder by the jury, which brought in a divided six-to-five vote regarding her sanity, de la Mare was sentenced to die by hanging. An appeal to the king reprieved de la Mare on May 14, 1935. Weeks after her release, she left Guernsey and vanished.

REF.: *CBA;* Rowland, *Criminal Files.*

Delamare, Louis, 1922-1981, Leb., polit., assass. Louis Delamare, French ambassador to Lebanon, was a popular diplomat who shunned bulletproof cars. He was assassinated on Sept. 4, 1981, when gunmen in another car forced his chauffeured limousine off the road in what appeared to be a kidnapping attempt near the line between the Christian and Muslim sections of Beirut. Although French diplomats made no public statements, the obvious suspects were supporters of Khomeni's Islamic revolution in Iran. The Iranian government had denounced and threatened

France because it had given political asylum to Abolhassan Bani-Sadr, former president of Iran, as well as to Massoud Rajavi, the head of the Iranian urban guerilla group Mujahhedin Khaeq, who were involved in a war of assassination against the Ayatollah's regime. See: **Khomeni, Ayatollah Ruholla**. REF.: *CBA*.

de Lamotte, Comptesse (AKA: **Jeanne de St. Remy de Valois**), prom. 1785, Fr., fraud. Parisian jewelers Boehmer and Bassenge forged a fabulous necklace for King Louis XV to give to his mistress, Madame du Barry. The jewelers spent several years collecting more than 600 diamonds to create the necklace, which was worth £85,000, but the king died in 1774. Facing ruin, Boehmer finally approached the queen, Marie Antoinette, about buying the costly necklace.

The queen declined, so Boehmer went to the Comptesse de Lamotte. She was favored by the queen, and Boehmer promised her a large sum if the queen bought the necklace. The Comptesse agreed, and went to Cardinal Louis de Rohan, with whom she had been intimate before her marriage. She told him the queen was in love with him, and persuaded him to buy the necklace for her. She then told Boehmer that the queen would buy the necklace, but would not negotiate the price herself.

She set up a meeting between the cardinal and the queen—actually a heavily veiled woman—in a garden at Versailles. Several days later, the cardinal sent the necklace to the queen via the comptesse.

Amid rumors about the necklace, de Rohan was arrested on Aug. 15, 1785. He admitted sending diamonds to the queen, but was acquitted and exiled to the abbey of la Chaise-Dieu. Marie Lejay was put in prison for impersonating the queen. The Comptesse was sentenced to be whipped, branded, and imprisoned in Salpetrière. Her husband was also condemned, but he escaped with the necklace to Britain, where he sold some of the diamonds. The comptesse later escaped from prison, possibly with the aid of Marie Antoinette, and joined her husband in London.

REF.: *CBA;* Stevens, *From Clue to Dock*.

De Lancey, James, 1703-60, U.S., jur. Appointed New York Supreme Court judge, 1731-33, and the court's chief justice, 1733-60. REF.: *CBA*.

Delaney, Daniel (AKA: **Daniel Melaney, Terence Hogan, J.W. Williams**), prom. 1911-13, Brit., fraud. In August 1911, Daniel Delaney was walking through the London Zoo when he dropped a crucifix in front of a vacationing Australian schoolmaster and his companion, whom the teacher had met the day before. This ploy was commonly known in the criminal world as "Dropping The Cross." When the companion picked up the cross and called Delaney back, the con man thanked them profusely, then suggested they all go out for a drink. On the third round, Delaney began to explain in a hushed voice about an uncle from Australia who had recently died and left him a vast fortune. Delaney dropped the name of a famous lawyer who was allegedly representing him, and described how a stipulation in the legacy required him to give a certain amount of the money to underprivileged, promising young boys. He then suggested that the Australian teacher help him distribute the cash. Delaney asked the teacher to bring in his own funds, explaining that the lawyers would need proof of the teacher's status as a man of substance. The teacher eagerly withdrew several hundred pounds from a local bank, and met Delaney, who produced £100 of his own. The teacher's companion provided £250 to prove his worth. Delaney got up from the table with the money and never returned. The mysterious companion also disappeared. Police caught up with Delaney some time later.

In addition to the legacy scam, Delaney bilked funds from unsuspecting Roman Catholics by pretending to be collecting "Pearls for the Pope." The Mansion House Police Court eventually ended this con game. Around Christmas 1915, Delaney lifted about £1,967 worth of rings from London's Leeds Jewelers. The gregarious criminal was again working with a companion; both were arrested. Delaney was tried at the Assizes and sentenced to three years of penal servitude. Just prior to the Leeds robbery,

Delaney had bilked a New Zealand farmer of £1,000 with the legacy scam. Working under the name Terence Hogan, Delaney showed up in London again in 1923. Offering to serve as guide and companion to a visiting American doctor, he used the inheritance con game, asking the doctor to help him distribute his £40,000. To demonstrate his integrity and willingness to be involved the doctor came up with £400, which Delaney took. Arrested again, Delaney was tried at the Old Bailey and sentenced to three years in prison.

REF.: *CBA;* Nicholls, *Crime Within the Square Mile*.

Delaney, Denis W., prom. 1952, U.S., polit. corr. In June 1951 a rash of tax scandals surfaced in the U.S. In their wake, Boston's IRS collector, Denis W. Delaney, was suspended by President Harry S. Truman. By September 1951 a grand jury had indicted Delaney on nine counts of bribery and misconduct in office. At his trial in January 1952, Delaney was confronted by the testimony of a Boston wool merchant, Maxwell Shapiro, who explained that in April 1949 Daniel Friedman and Hugh Finnegan had come to his office and informed him that they knew he owed the government more than $140,000 in back taxes. They had come, they said, from a friend of his, Denis Delaney, and were tax experts who could help him, for a fee of about 25 percent of what he would save. Shapiro interrupted them to call Delaney privately and ask if the supposed tax experts were "all right." Delaney said they were. Shapiro paid the men $5,000. Following a visit to Washington, Friedman told Shapiro things were "under control," and collected another check for $5,000. For the next two years, no one from the IRS tried to collect taxes from Shapiro. Friedman confirmed Shapiro's testimony in court, detailing how he had sold his services as a tax expert to several Boston firms, and explaining that his success as a fixer was the result of information given to him by Delaney. The income from this business was, Friedman said, split between them.

On the stand, Delaney denied almost everything, saying he had only steered Friedman toward insurance prospects, and was being rewarded with commission checks. When his health failed, Delaney explained, the checks had come in handy, and he had scrupulously reported the $10,000 of extra income in 1949. Delaney's physician, Dr. Lewis Glazer of Chelsea's Soldier's Home, confirmed that Delaney had been ill but said that he had never billed him for any services or treatment; Delaney corroborated that he had not paid Glazer. The prosecutor pointed out that there was an $825 medical-fees deduction on Delaney's tax return; the former collector had no explanation for the discrepancy. Delaney was found Guilty and was sentenced to two weeks in prison and a $10,500 fine. He was the first internal revenue collector to be convicted in a tax scandal. REF.: *CBA*.

Delaney, Robert Augustus, prom. 1924, Brit., burg. Known to Scotland Yard as the first "cat burglar," Robert Augustus Delaney started a fashion in crime with his acrobatic leaps and soundless disappearances from London rooftops. Delaney carried a slim steel tool resembling a putty knife, which he used both for slipping window locks and opening jewel cases, and coiled four yards of black silk rope around his waist. Two men died trying to imitate his daring approach. A thief known as "Irish Mac" died impaled on spike railings, and "The Doctor" fell from a 40-foot portico in the St. James area, crawling two miles with £8,000 worth of jewels in his pocket before he died.

In 1924, Delancy stolen a total of £30,000 in five weeks from the wealthy Park-Lane district. Detective Tommy Symes and another officer mapped out the area of the crimes and waited two nights in Green Park to try to catch the burglar. On the second night, Delaney appeared, nimbly vaulting a railing and then flitting across the balcony of an elegant mansion while a dinner party was in full swing downstairs. The two officers called in the alarm, and lights flashed on in the upstairs rooms, but the cat burglar once again escaped, leaping across a nine-foot gap between buildings and soundlessly disappearing with jewels valued at about £2,000.

Measuring the balcony where Delaney had leaped, the police officers noticed a small, delicate shoe print made by rubber-soled evening shoes, which they traced back to the craftsman who had custom-made the slippers for an "R. Rad" at 52 Half-Moon Street. No such address existed, so the detectives investigated bars and lounges in the area, until about a week later, at the Range Bar they saw a well-dressed man with a silent footstep. It was Delaney, wearing his rubber-soled shoes. Trailing him by taxi, they followed him to 43 Half-Moon Street. Two days later, Delaney met with a fence to sell some of the stolen goods. The detectives, armed with this evidence, went to his home, broke into his upstairs rooms, and explained to the startled Delaney that they were "just looking for some money and jewelry." Delaney rejoindered, "I suppose it's too much to hope that you gentleman are burglars?" When £800 was found hidden in the mattress, and caches of stolen jewels in the dresser hidden behind drawers, the cat burglar was arrested, tried at the Old Bailey, convicted, and sentenced to three years of penal servitude. He spent the next twenty years in and out of jail, and died at Parkhurst Prison on Dec. 14, 1948.

REF.: *CBA;* Fabian, *Fabian of the Yard.*

Delaney, William E. (AKA: **Bill Johnson, Mormon Bill**), 1856-84, U.S., west. outl. Born in Scranton, Pa., on July 11, 1856, William E. Delaney later tended bar in Harrisburg and left that town in 1880 after being involved in a murder, moving to Arizona. He worked briefly as a miner and was later reported to have killed a man in Graham County. In 1883, Delaney killed three men in saloon shootout in Clifton, Ariz., according to one account. On Dec. 3, 1883, Delaney rode into Bisbee, Ariz., with John Heath, Daniel Kelly, and others, holding up a store and killing four persons, including a woman, and wounding a dozen more. Delaney had been one of the gang members stationed outside the store and he was clearly seen to shoot down two men and may have killed the woman.

The gang members split up with Delaney riding to Sonora, Mexico, later moving to Minos Prietas where lawman Ben Daniels tracked him down and arrested him on Jan. 5, 1884. He was returned to Tombstone, Ariz., where he and three others were convicted of the Bisbee Massacre and sentenced to hang. Delaney boasted that he did not fear the hangman, saying: "No man will stand it better than I." He insisted that he and Heath were innocent of the Bisbee killings, right up to the moment that he mounted the gallows in Tombstone on Mar. 3, 1884. See: **Bisbee, Ariz., Massacre; Daniels, Benjamin F.; Heath, John; Kelly, Daniel**.

REF.: Bakarich, *Gunsmoke;* Bartholomew, *The Biographical Album of Western Gunfighters;* Burns, *Tombstone, An Iliad of the Southwest; CBA;* Chisholm, *Brewery Gulch;* Florin, *Boot Hill;* Franke, *They Ploughed Up Hell in Old Cochise;* Ganzhorn, *I've Killed Men;* Gardner, *The Old Wild West;* Ladd, *Eight Ropes to Eternity;* McCool, *So Said the Coroner;* Marshall, *The Wham Paymaster Robbery;* Miller, *Arizona, The Last Frontier;* Myers, *The Last Chance, Tombstone's Early Years;* Nunnelley, *Boothill Grave Yard;* Raht, *The Romance of Davis Mountains and the Big Bend Country;* Raine, *Guns of the Frontier;* Ringgold, *Frontier Days in the Southwest;* Way, *Frontier Arizona.*

Delano, Columbus, 1809-96, U.S., fraud-polit. corr. As U.S. secretary of the interior, 1870-75, he was accused of fraud in handling the Bureau of Indian Affairs. He resigned after a congressional investigation found him to be negligent and incompetent in his duties, 1875. REF.: *CBA.*

De la Pommerais, Dr. Edmond, 1845-64, Fr., mur. Dr. Edmond De la Pommerais left Orléans, Fr., in 1859 to set up a private practice in Paris. He advertised himself as the "Count de la Pommerais" at the Paris gambling tables. In 1861, he married Mademoiselle Dabizy, the daughter of one of his patients and heiress to a fortune.

But the girl's mother had stipulated that the inheritance could not revert to the De la Pommerais family until her own death. She died just months later. As Madame Dabizy's physician, De la Pommerais certified the cause of death to be Asiatic cholera. The doctor was also conducting a secret affair with Séraphine de Pauw, the widow of one of his former patients. She had three small children, and faced financial problems. De la Pommerais

proposed a scheme whereby he would insure de Pauw's life for 500,000 francs. After several payments had been made, Madame de Pauw was to feign an illness. Fearing greater loss, the insurance company would offer to settle for 5,000 francs. When she signed the policy, the doctor persuaded her to name him beneficiary.

Supposedly to simulate illness Dr. De la Pommerais gave de Pauw a strong dose of digitalis, a vegetable poison. She became quite ill and soon died. The cause of death was listed as cholera, common in Paris during the summertime. The insurance company first seemed willing to pay the doctor the full 500,000, but an anonymous letter to the Paris police warned them about the possibility of murder. The body was exhumed, an autopsy performed, and poison detected.

Digitalis poisoner Dr. Edmond de la Pommerais.

The doctor was tried for the murders of both his mistress and mother-in-law, but was acquitted for the death of Madame Dabizy. De la Pommerais was found Guilty of poisoning Séraphine de Pauw, convicted mainly on the testimony of de Pauw's sister, who knew about the insurance fraud. He was sentenced to die on the guillotine. To the very last moment, he expected to be reprieved, but he went to his death in 1864.

REF.: REF.: *CBA;* Curtin, *Noted Murder Mysteries;* Ellis, *Black Fame;* Furneaux, *The Medical Murderer;* Kingston, *Dramatic Days at the Old Bailey;* Nash, *Almanac of World Crime;* Thorwald, *The Century of the Detective;* _____, *Proof of Poison;* Wilson and Pitman, *Encyclopedia of Murder.*

de Lara, Enrique, b.1891, U.S., mur. In September 1908, a wounded Santo Domingo clergyman, Father Arturo Ascencio, was found in New York City's Central Park, with a revolver nearby. He died later in the hospital, and the death was initially deemed a suicide. Captain Carey and Detective Jimenez learned that one of the priest's frequent visitors at his Upper West Side hotel was Enrique de Lara, a 17-year-old student from Santo Domingo who had recently come to New York and renewed an old acquaintance with Ascencio. The two men had taken a walk together in Central Park the day of Ascencio's death, as they often did, according to a woman who knew them both. When the officers questioned de Lara on Sept. 22, he admitted stealing a watch and $15 from the priest after shooting him because he had talked in a way that made de Lara angry. "He was about twenty paces in front of me before I could get my revolver out of my pocket. Then I fired," de Lara said. After admitting his guilt, de Lara tried to kill himself by taking morphine which he had hidden in his shoe. He pleaded guilty to second-degree murder and was sentenced to a twenty year term in a state prison. He was released twelve years later.

REF.: Carey, *Memoirs of a Murder Man; CBA.*

De La Roche, Harry, Jr., b.c.1958, U.S., mur. In 1976, Harry De La Roche, Jr. enrolled in the Citadel, a military academy in Charleston, S.C., at the urging of his father, Harry De La Roche, Sr., who wanted his son to pursue a military career. Harry Jr. disliked the college intensely. He had arguments with his company sergeant, and upperclassmen often tormented him. For Thanksgiving, the freshman returned home to Montvale, N.J.

On Nov. 28, 1976, he shot his father Harry, forty-four, his mother, Mary Jane, fifty, and his two brothers, Ronald, fifteen, and Eric, twelve. He initially claimed that his brother Ronald had committed the murders after a fight over marijuana, and that he

then killed Ronald while temporarily insane. His lawyer suggested that the "private hell" Harry suffered at military school led to the slayings. In De La Roche's confession, obtained at the time of his arrest, he said that he shot his parents as they slept and then shot his brothers in their bedroom. He was convicted of all four murders and sent to Trenton State Prison to serve a life sentence.
REF.: *CBA;* Fox, *Mass Murder;* Roesch, *Anyone's Son.*

Delay, Dallas Ray, 1940- , U.S., extor.-mur. On Jan. 17, 1973, Dallas Ray Delay entered the home of bank president Robert Kitterman in Grandin, Mo., and forced him, his wife Bertha, and their daughter Roberta at gunpoint into a wooded area. The gunman then attached a dynamite device to Kitterman's chest, told him it could be detonated at any time, and ordered him to go to his bank, get money, and bring it back to him in the woods. Kitterman did so while the bank was closed for lunch, telling an employee of the situation. Police found the Kitterman's bodies later that day, each tied by the wrists to a tree and shot once through the temple. Delay was aresed on Jan. 20, and later convicted of extortion and murder.

The U.S. Court of Appeals in 1974 reduced his sentence for murder from 320 years to 100 years. Delay will begin serving it after he completes a twenty-year term at the Missouri State Penitentiary on extortion charges.
REF.: *CBA;* Godwin, *Murder U.S.A.*

Delbos, Yvon, 1885-1956, Fr., jur. Served as the French minister of foreign affairs and of justice, 1936-38. REF.: *CBA.*

de Leeuw, Huibrecht Jacob, b.c.1895, S. Afri., embez.-mur. Huibrecht Jacob de Leeuw became the town clerk of Dewetsdorp, South Africa in 1921. During the next six years he dipped into the town funds. Mayor Pieter Johannes von Maltitz was highly suspicious, but said nothing until his term ended. On April 1, 1927, Reverend P.J. Viljoen became mayor and formed a committee including von Maltitz, Viljoen, and Reinhold Johannes Ortlepp to investigate the city finances. The 32-year-old town clerk was told of the upcoming investigation and given a week to put the books in order.

Desperate and unable to repay the money, de Leeuw decided to blow up the books and the investigators with dynamite kept at the town hall to exterminate rats. At 3:20 p.m., on Apr. 8, as the investigators examined the books, the town hall blew up. De Leeuw jumped from a window, and the three officials, their clothes on fire, rushed from the building. The former mayor died shortly after the explosion, Ortlepp died the next day, and Viljoen died on Apr. 11. De Leeuw was arrested that night at his home. During his trial, his 18-year-old clerk, Brandes, testified that he had seen de Leeuw taking the funds to pay private debts, and that he had heard investigators say they had evidence against the clerk. De Leeuw was convicted, sentenced to death, and hanged on Sept. 30, 1927.
REF.: Bennett, *Up For Murder; CBA;* Whitelaw, *Corpus Delicti.*

Delgado, José Matias, 1768-1832, Salvador, rebel. Led a brief uprising against Spanish authorities in San Salvador, 1811, and was elected the United Provinces of Central America's national constitutional assembly president, 1823. REF.: *CBA.*

Delgado Chalbaud, Carlos, 1909-50, Venez., pres., assass. Led the military coup against President Rómulo Gallegos, 1948, and was serving as president of the military junta, 1948-50, when he was assassinated. REF.: *CBA.*

Dellacroce, Aniello (AKA: Mr. Neil, Father O'Neill), 1914-85, U.S., org. crime. The literal translation of Aniello Dellacroce's name is "little lamb of the cross," an ironic contrast, according to one government law enforcement official. "He likes to peer into a victim's face, like some kind of dark angel at the moment of death." Playing the religious angle for all it was worth, this Mafia don often traveled about the country under the alias of Father O'Neill or Timothy O'Neill.

In the 1950s, Dellacroce served as a loyal soldier in Albert Anastasia's crime family. When Carlo Gambino shoved Anastasia aside in 1957, Dellacroce became an underboss and was poised for a takeover when things suddenly changed. Before Gambino

died in 1976, he designated Paul Castellano, a conservative business type, as his successor. Castellano lacked the vision and power of Dellacroce, but he had an added advantage in that he was Gambino's brother-in-law. Realizing that he was not strong enough to win a war against Dellacroce's family, he attempted to appease Dellacroce by giving him full control of the Manhattan territory.

As time passed, Dellacroce expanded the business into Atlantic City and attracted the more youthful, violence-prone members of the family. The Gambino family was said to be active in linen supply and liquor distribution to the gambling casinos. The Mafia "Young Turks" favored a policy of continued diversification into hijackings, airport cargo heists, and narcotics—which Castellano personally disdained. Out of respect for the wishes of the late Carlo Gambino, Dellacroce held the younger members, notably John Gotti, in check. The guns were turned on the "enemy," Carmine Galante, boss of the Bonanno family. The struggle for control of drug distribution along the Eastern seaboard extended from the streets of Manhattan to Canada, and continued until late in the 1970s.

Gotti finally got his chance after Dellacroce passed away from cancer on Dec. 2, 1985. Two weeks later, assassins believed to be Gotti's men shot Castellano and his heir-apparent Thomas Bilotti outside an East Side steak house. "When Dellacroce died, it left Gotti without a rabbi," observed a New York policeman.

After Aniello Dellacroce was buried, *Time* Magazine published a story naming him as a high-ranking mob informer for the FBI. The article went on to say that Dellacroce had told the FBI of Carmine Galante's imminent death and had provided details on the disappearance of Jimmy Hoffa. It is widely believed that the story was planted by the FBI to shake up other Mafia power brokers at a vulnerable time for the mob. See: **Castellano, Paul; Galante, Carmine.** REF.: *CBA.*

Delony, Lewis S., b.1857, U.S., west. lawman. The son of a Texas Ranger who fought in the Mexican and the Civil Wars, Lewis Delony left home at the age of fourteen to seek his fortunes on the road. In Clinton, he became a store clerk, an assistant postmaster, and a deputy sheriff before accepting a temporary appointment as a Texas Ranger in 1877. For the rest of his life, Delony served as a part-time law enforcement official while running several businesses in Texas.

His most notable gunfight occurred in Eagle Pass, Texas, in the spring of 1882. While riding with Spencer Adams, a young boy alerted the two rangers to the murder of a deputy sheriff in town. Adams and Delony rode into town and found the outlaw dancing in the local saloon over the bodies of the fallen lawman and a Mexican woman. Delony arrested the killer, but as he prepared to lead him away, another man lunged at him with a knife. Delony whirled around and shot the assailant in the chest. The two Texas Rangers were forced to retreat from town by a hostile crowd before arresting the sheriff's slayer. However, Delony was able to return to arrest his prisoner.
REF.: *CBA;* Delony, *Forty Years a Peace Officer;* O'Neal, *Encyclopedia of Western Gunfighters;* Sonnichsen, *I'll Die Before I'll Run.*

De Lorean, John Zachary, 1925- , Case of, U.S., fraud-rack.-drugs. The Pontiac division of General Motors (GM) rolled out the first GTO in 1963. It was a sleek mid-sized automobile with an enhanced engine and sporty lines that appealed to a generation obsessed with speed and road performance. The car was the brainchild of GM's whiz kid John Z. De Lorean, a flamboyant young engineer who single-handedly revolutionized the Detroit auto industry in the early 1960s.

John De Lorean was the son of a Detroit assembly line worker. After earning an engineering degree, De Lorean went to work for Chrysler. He returned to college at night and earned the first of two master's degrees. At twenty-seven, De Lorean took a job with the Packard Motor Car Company designing transmissions. He was promoted to director of research and development, and in a few years was thought of as the resident genius of the younger set. Hired away by GM, De Lorean was named director of advanced engineering in the Pontiac division, and given absolute freedom to design sporty new cars with appeal for the baby boom generation. The GTO and the radically redesigned Firebird were De Lorean's personal expression of this strategy.

By the end of the 1960s, John De Lorean had abandoned conservative behavior for a youthful lifestyle. His flamboyance was tolerated by GM officials only while his car designs returned a profit to the company. In 1972, after many heated arguments with his superiors, De Lorean then the head of North American truck and car manufacturing, left GM to pursue his own dreams. With beautiful 22-year-old fashion model Christina Ferrare, his third wife, De Lorean traveled between Beverly Hills, Calif., and his $7.2 million duplex in Manhattan.

In 1976, the one-time boy genius organized the De Lorean Car Company promising to deliver a sporty vehicle of "radical design" for $8,000. However, by the time his coupe was introduced, the price tag had swelled to $24,000. De Lorean received large amounts of investment money from Hollywood investors and maneuvered Great Britain into a bidding war with Puerto Rico "to sponsor the firm." After dozens of trips to London on board the Concorde, John De Lorean announced that he had accepted $110 million from the British Labor Party to build a plant in Ulster, N. Ire. By the end of 1982, he had succeeded in convincing the British to pump a total of $156 million into the shaky venture.

The first of the stainless steel sports cars began rolling off the line. A total of 10,000 vehicles were produced in Ulster, but the stiff price tag discouraged many potential buyers in the U.S. British prime minister Margaret Thatcher cautioned De Lorean that production would be ceased unless additional outside capital was found for the company. While the company's existence was in danger, De Lorean announced his intention to buy Chrysler, a plan which struck many industry observers as preposterous. When he attempted to go public with his stock, the Securities and Exchange Commission rejected his proposal. De Lorean made one last desperate attempt to raise some quick cash to save the company.

In 1982, he began secret negotiations with James Timothy Hoffman, a drug trafficker and former neighbor to the De Loreans. Hoffman agreed to help sell South American cocaine in Los Angeles. The plan was to purchase fifty-five pounds of cocaine valued at $24 million from dealers in the Caiman Islands and sell it on the open market for an approximately $120 million. The profits from the sale were to be diverted to the struggling plant in Ulster. Unbeknownst to De Lorean, Hoffman plea-bargained with the government and offered to turn informant. During a four-month FBI "sting" operation, listening devices recorded De Lorean's conversations with Hoffman and others. One such "bug" was placed in room 501 of the Los Angeles Sheraton Plaza Hotel on Oct. 19, 1982. When drug smuggler William Morgan Hetrick and his aide Stephen Arrington delivered the sample cocaine to the hotel for De Lorean's inspection, the undercover agents burst into the room and caught the auto tycoon holding a sack of cocaine.

Charged with conspiring to distribute narcotics, De Lorean was placed on trial in the U.S. District Court of Los Angeles in March 1984. His attorneys, Howard Weitzman and Donald Ré portrayed their client as a misguided maverick, "lured, lied to, and pushed into a trap set by government agents." Weitzman accused Hoffman of tricking De Lorean into a compromising situation by promising to deliver money from "bonafide investors" that would restore the auto company to financial health. Federal drug agent John M. Valestra tersely replied: "the tapes speak for themselves."

U.S. District Judge Robert Takasugi was specific in his instructions to the jury. "If you find John De Lorean committed the acts charged, but did so as a result of entrapment you must find him not guilty." The jury deliberated for twenty-nine hours over a seven-day period before arriving at a verdict. They agreed with the defense that the actions of the FBI and the DEA constituted entrapment. De Lorean was found Not Guilty on all

eight counts on Aug. 16, 1984. In September 1985, a Detroit grand jury indicted him on federal fraud and racketeering charges stemming from his alleged misappropriation of company funds. A jury later acquitted him on these charges. In August 1987, De Lorean agreed to pay $9.36 million to his various creditors in an out-of-court settlement. However, a $53 million judgment brought against him by the British firm, DSQ Property Company Ltd., was allowed to stand by U.S. District Judge Richard Suhrheinrich. REF.: *CBA*.

Delorme, Abbé **J. Adelard**, d.1942, Case of, Can., mur. On Jan. 7, 1922, Raul Delorme was found dead on a Montreal street with his hands tied, pieces of bed quilt wrapped around his head, and six bullet wounds in his skull and neck. Last seen the night before at the house he lived in with his half-brother, Abbé J. Adelard Delorme, a Roman Catholic priest, the dead man shared a considerable interest with his brother in his late father's estate. When the Abbé went to identify the body, onlookers were surprised at his apparent casual attitude. In Quebec at that time, a religious man was considered to be above suspicion and, in many ways, Delorme remained in this light throughout the subsequent two years of legal proceedings. The coroner who examined the corpse was so appalled at the idea of Delorme being a suspect that he refused to consider the possibility.

Delorme offered a $10,000 reward for the capture of his brother's killer. Continuing to seem unconcerned, the Abbé frequently pointed out that he was a priest, possibly as a way of explaining his unusual calm. Nevertheless, Delorme was held on the charge of murder following the final inquest.

The evidence against Delorme was staggering. Although the body had been discovered in the snow in the Montreal suburb of Notre Dame de Grace, also known as Snowdon Junction, the doctors who examined the corpse did not believe that he had been killed there. The boots were clean and dry and, though one bullet had penetrated his chest, it had not made a hole in his coat. The deceased had almost certainly been slain elsewhere, then carried by car to the place where it was discovered. The dead man was last seen alive at the home he shared with the Abbé. Neighbors had heard several gunshots the night of the murder. Fresh car tracks proved that the car had been in and out at a late hour, which coincided with the time the body had been moved. The car was bloodstained. The quilt wrapped around the corpse's head matched fragments found in the Delorme home. Ten nights before the killing, the Abbé had purchased a .25-caliber revolver, and a week before his brother's death he had taken out an $88,000 life insurance policy on Raul, a 24-year-old student at the time of his death. Delorme's only defense was to suggest that his brother had been killed by strangers. The two sisters of the Abbé adamantly insisted that Raul had called the house a few hours after the supposed time of his death; it turned out that they believed this because their living brother had told them it was true.

In June 1922 Delorme's defense moved that the Abbé was unfit to be tried by reason of insanity, which the judge countered, suggesting that the jury consider him as a man, not a religious official. Delorme objected to the implication that there was insanity in his family, upset at the suggestion. He remained unconcerned throughout the legal proceedings, feeling confident that, as a priest, he could not be convicted of murder. The jury accepted the plea of insanity after ten minutes of deliberation, and Delorme was committed to an asylum.

Discovering that he would not be able to administer his family's estate while he was legally insane, the Abbé insisted on being released and tried again. In June 1923, he was brought into court, this time before Sir Francis Lemeiux, Quebec's chief justice, who was called upon to preside because of the controversy surrounding the case. The trial lasted for more than a month, during which 170 witnesses were called. Because two of the six jurors stood firm for acquittal, and a unanimous conviction was required, the case was tried a third time. The final jury reversed the previous verdict, and the Abbé Delorme was freed on Oct. 30, 1924, coming into an inheritance of $250,000, with an additional $88,000 from the insurance money. Delorme died of a brain hemorrhage on Jan. 19, 1942.

REF.: *CBA;* Hastings, *The Other Mr. Churchill.*

DeLorme, Marion, 1611-50, Fr., treas. The mistress of Marquis de Henri Cinq-Mars Coffier de Ru'ze, who was executed for treason in 1642, Marion DeLorme went on to become the mistress of many nobles. Cardinal Mazarin ordered her arrest in 1650, on charges of complicity with the leaders of the Fronde uprising, but when officers arrived at her lodgings, they found this beautiful courtesan dead, supposedly a suicide. Many legends surround this mysterious woman, including one that has her escaping to London where she lived for decades under an assumed name. See: **Cinq-Mars,** Marquis **de Henri Coffier de Ru'ze.**

REF.: Belloc, *Richelieu; CBA;* (DRAMA) Hugo, *Marion Delorme;* (FICTION), de Vigny, *Cinq-Mars.*

De Los Santos, George (AKA: **Chiefie**), b.c.1945, U.S., (wrong. convict.) mur. After spending almost eight years in Trenton State Prison for the murder of a Newark, N.J., used-car dealer, an innocent man was released and exonerated.

On Oct. 15, 1975, George De Los Santos was convicted for fatally shooting Robert Thomas on Jan. 10, 1975, and for possession of drugs with intent to distribute. In 1983, theology student James McCloskey, forty-one, was researching the case when he uncovered evidence that cast doubt on the credibility of the primary witness, as well as other witnesses. De Los Santos was convicted mainly on the testimony of Richard DelliSanti, a cellmate at the Essex County Jail, who claimed he heard De Los Santos confess after his arrest. DelliSanti had previously testified for the state that he heard confessions from two other cellmates, and he was arrested at least twenty-four times after the De Los Santos trial.

On July 26, 1983, the conviction of De Los Santos, thirty-eight, was overturned by U.S. District Court Judge Frederick B. Lacey, who contended the testimony "reeks of perjury." The judge ordered De Los Santos' release and called for another trial. In October 1983, however, the prosecutors announced they would not retry De Los Santos because they were skeptical about DelliSanti's credibility. REF.: *CBA.*

Del Petrarca, Robert, 1948- , U.S., mur. On May 14, 1973, the bodies of two women were found strangled to death in the basement of a home in Montclair, N.J. Both women, 45-year-old Renee Cali and her daughter, 24-year-old Leslie Grant, wore bathing suits and were situated in a way that suggested a double suicide. But, organized crime was suspected, because Renee Cali's husband John Cali and his brother had been brought before a New Jersey State commission to testify about municipal corruption in Somerset and Middlesex counties. Both denied any knowledge of such corruption. On Aug. 4, 1973, while in custody for the attempted strangling of an 83-year-old South Orange woman, 26-year-old Robert Del Petrarca was charged with the murders of Cali and Grant. Del Petrarca, who had been a window washer for the Calis, had been paroled from the Bordertown Reformatory two months before the double slaying. He was formally indicted on Sept. 28, 1973, and brought to trial on Mar. 12, 1974, in the Essex County Superior Court of Judge Ralph L. Fusco. On Mar. 25, Petrarca was convicted of first-degree murder, and on May 16, 1974, he was sentenced to two consecutive life terms for the double murder. REF.: *CBA.*

Del Toro Cuevas, Emilio, 1876-1955, Spain, lawyer. Served as prosecuting attorney for Spain, 1898-99, and for the U.S. Superior Court of the District of Columbia, 1901. Also received appointments to the Superior Court of Puerto Rico from President William Taft, Mar. 25, 1909, and from President Warren Harding, Dec. 22, 1921. REF.: *CBA.*

Deluca, Frank (Francesco Deluca), b.1898, U.S., org. crime. Named in the famous Kefauver Report, a 1950 exposé of organized crime in America, Frank Deluca and his brother, Joe Deluca, were important ruling leaders in the Mafia. Born on Mar. 1, 1898, in Sicily, Deluca reigned as a prominent leader in the

Kansas City, Mo., branch of the Mafia, functioning in the underworld as a smuggler and narcotics dealer and distributor. With arrests for carrying concealed weapons, violating the Alien Registration Act, and murder, Deluca was listed in the files of the U.S. Narcotics, Alcohol, and Tobacco Tax Unit; the IRS; the Immigration and Naturalization Service; the Justice Department; and the Kansas City Police Department. See: **Deluca, Joseph.** REF.: *CBA.*

Deluca, Joseph (Giuseppi Deluca), b.1893, U.S., org. crime. Along with his brother, Frank Deluca, Joseph Deluca was one of the leading rulers of the Kansas City, Mo., Mafia. He was born in Sicily Mar. 17, 1893, and had criminal arrests in the U.S. dating from 1930, including several arrests for violations of federal narcotics laws. With his brother, Deluca was identified in the Kefauver Report of 1950, which exposed organized crime in the U.S. Both Delucas were engaged in drug smuggling and distribution of narcotics. See: **Deluca, Frank.** REF.: *CBA.*

DeLucia, William, 1945- , U.S., theft. On May 15, 1980, William DeLucia, thirty-five, David J. McCulley, thirty-one, and Lloyd A. Santana, thirty-one, flew from Los Angeles to Atlanta, Ga., on Eastern Airlines flight L-1011. McCulley and Santana rode in regular seats, but DeLucia traveled in the baggage compartment in a 3-by-4-by-5-foot box marked "Musical Instruments." Equipped with foam padding, an oxygen tank, food, a flashlight, and clothing, an airline spokesman said all DeLucia "had to worry about was loneliness." Authorities suspected the three California men of planning to steal registered mail, with an estimated value of $1 million, by having DeLucia switch the mail from mail pouches to personal bags. Four suitcases containing the mail were seized when the three suspects were arrested. When McCulley and Santana asked about the box of "instruments" in Atlanta, they were arrested. All three men were charged with violating stowaway and postal laws, and were convicted of mail theft. DeLucia came out of the box at Atlanta's Hartsfield International Airport when the lid came off as it was being unloaded by an airlines employee. REF.: *CBA.*

Delvain, Pierre, See: **Bousquet, Pierre.**

Demades, 380-319 B.C., Gr., polit. corr.-consp. Accepted bribes, for which his rights to be a citizen were taken from him, 323-22 B.C. He was ordered by either Cassander or Antipater to be executed for his connections with Perdiccas. REF.: *CBA.*

Demara, Ferdinand Waldo, Jr. (AKA: **The Great Imposter**), 1922- , U.S., milit. desertion-fraud. Although he never finished high school, Ferdinand Demara, also known as "The Great Imposter," forged credentials to occupy innumerable academic posts in distinguished American schools. Self-educated, Demara became an expert in several professional fields, often displaying astounding abilities, particularly in medicine and penology. He deserted the U.S. Army and Navy during WWII and joined a Catholic seminary as a novice. He forged academic documents and added a Ph.D. to his name, teaching at DePaul University for a short period. Adding more academic credits and honors to his dossier, Demara went on to teach at Gannon College in California and St. Martin's College in Washington State.

As a teacher, Demara was well-liked and highly rated as one who effectively enlightened students. He was exposed several times and quietly dismissed from the academic institutions where he fraudulently represented himself as a professor. No charges were filed since the institutions invariably wanted to avoid embarrassing publicity. He was apprehended by the U.S. Navy for desertion and was sent to prison for a short period of time. When released, he joined the Royal Canadian Navy as a physician, serving as a surgeon lieutenant during the Korean War. At one point, he operated on more than twenty men, taken aboard his destroyer, removing a bullet next to one man's heart and removing a lung from another, both men surviving. Astoundingly, Demara performed these delicate operations from knowledge he gained only from medical textbooks which he was able to commit to memory. He was mentioned in dispatches as performing gallant service and recommended for a medal. It was then that he was exposed as a fraud and cashiered from the Canadian service.

Instead of pursuing a legitimate career Demara continued his impersonations, explaining to a priest that the urge to do so was overwhelming: "It's in my blood...I love it, being able to be someone else, anyone I please." He expressed great contempt for U.S. educational systems and felt he was superior to most formally trained people, a vanity that was to lead him into one fraudulent escapade after another. Perhaps his most spectacular impersonation was that of an expert penologist. He faked credentials and was hired as a special consultant at Huntsville State Prison in Texas where, in 1955, he single-handedly prevented a prison riot by stepping among murder-bent prisoners and talking them out of killing several guards taken hostage. Again, Demara was exposed and fled. He continued his impersonations, teaching in rural Maine before dropping out of sight. It is assumed, given this man's insatiable desire to be someone else, that he is continuing his outlandish impersonations at this writing.

Imposter Ferdinand Waldo Demara as a priest.

REF.: *CBA;* Crichton, *The Great Imposter;* Hunt, *A Dictionary of Rogues;* MacDougall, *Hoaxes;* Nash, *Zanies;* (FILM), *The Great Imposter,* 1960.

Left, millionaire Sir Harry Oakes, and his son-in-law, right, Count de Marigny, accused of Oakes' murder.

deMarigny, Count Alfred Marie de Fouguereaux, prom. 1943, Case of, Bahamas, mur. The society murder in July 1943 of Sir Harry Oakes, a close personal friend of the Duke of Windsor, and the wealthiest land owner in the British Bahamas was never solved, although all the circumstantial evidence pointed to Count Alfred deMarigny, Oakes' son-in-law. The count and his wife Nancy were the darlings of the Bahamas social set. They drifted from one gala party to the next, unaffected by the war raging in Europe. "The war? I do not follow the news. Why should I?" the count said.

Oakes, a self-made American aristocrat, disapproved of his daughter's decision to marry deMarigny, a divorced Frenchman who claimed to have been born of noble stock on the island of Mauritius in the Indian Ocean. Sir Harry threatened to disown

his daughter, giving his son-in-law a possible motive for murder. After a falling out with deMarigny, Oakes threatened to send his daughter back to Bennington College in Vermont, which would have left the Count virtually penniless.

When Sir Harry was murdered at his lavish fifteen room home, evidence suggesting that deMarigny had killed his father-in-law was jumbled, and insufficient to convict. A handprint, said to be the count's, was found on a screen next to Oakes bed, but was confused with other prints found on a piece of glassware. In November 1943, deMarigny was found Not Guilty. However, according to the jury's recommendation, the count was asked to leave the island. This decision was made without the permission of the Duke of Windsor, governor of the Colony.

It was commonly believed that Oakes' real killers were Mafia hit men sent in by Meyer Lansky to do the job when Oakes refused to sanction a scheme to build casinos in Nassau. Oakes' close personal friend, Harold Christie, a business associate of Lansky, allegedly acted as liaison between the Duke of Windsor and the mobsters, but at the last minute, Oakes backed down and declared he would have nothing to do with such an arrangement. It was hypothesized that Lansky's people murdered Oakes in revenge.

REF.: Bocca, *The Life and Death of Sir Harry Oakes; CBA;* Houts, *Who Killed Sir Harry Oakes?;* Hughes, *The Complete Detective;* Hynd, *Murder, Mayhem and Mystery;* Jones, *Unsolved!;* Nash, *Open Files;* Nassau Daily Tribune, *The Murder of Sir Harry Oakes;* Purvis, *Great Unsolved Mysteries;* Symons, *A Reasonable Doubt.*

Demascio, Robert Edward, 1923- , U.S., jur. As assistant U.S. attorney in Detroit, 1954-61, he was the head of the Criminal Division. He also was appointed to the Eastern District Court of Michigan by President Richard Nixon, March 1971. REF.: *CBA.*

de Masel, Madame, prom. 1800s, Fr., (unsolv.) mur. Madame de Masel, a rich widow, was stabbed to death. When her body was discovered, three hairs were found in one hand, and police suspected they might have been from the killer. At that time, however, police had no way to analyze the hair scientifically and were unsure if the hair was human. Later, police official Francois M. Goron, who maintained that hair could be useful in solving crimes, claimed that this unsolved case was used to discredit his theory.

REF.: Block, *Science vs. Crime; CBA.*

De Mau Mau Gang, prom. 1972, U.S., org. crime-mur. On Oct. 15, 1972, the De Mau Mau Gang, a gang of dishonorably discharged Vietnam War veterans, all of them black, were charged with slaying two white families and several others. Referred to by Cook County sheriff Richard J. Elrod as "gang leaders and triggermen," Reuben Taylor, twenty-two, Donald Taylor, twenty-one, Michael Clark, twenty-one, Nathaniel Burse, twenty-three, Edward Moran, Jr., twenty-three, and Robert Wilson, eighteen, were held without bail in Chicago's Cook County Jail. Several of the accused had been expelled in the spring of that year from Malcolm X University, a West Side school, where an official described the De Mau Maus as "bitter and full of hatred." Dr. Charles G. Hurst, Jr., president of Malcolm X, said the gang members were expelled from the school after they had repeatedly intimidated teachers and beaten up students. He described them as "desperate men venting their frustration," and said that "there never seemed any motivation in their violence." According to Hurst, they were also "into drugs." Hurst considered the group neither politically, nor racially motivated, their outbursts having nothing to do "with color or race. It was just plain hatred."

The six were charged in the Aug. 4, 1972, slayings of retired insurance executive Paul Corbett, his stepdaughter, wife, and sister-in-law in their home in Barrington Hills, Ill.; in the murder of Stephen Hawtree and two members of his family in Monec, Ill.; the murder of William Richter, an army specialist, in Highland Park, Ill., and the murder of Southern Illinois University student Michael Gerchenson, who was found near West Frankfort, Ill. Ballistics tests linked all the murders.

Tried in the courtroom of Associate Judge Paul G. Caeser, four of the gang members, Clark, the two Taylor brothers, and Burse, entered the circuit court building swearing at the cameras and television crews. Everyone entering the court, including the press, was searched for concealed weapons. Angry at the cameramen who were taking his picture, and at delays, Clark shouted to a deputy sheriff, "What the hell's going on? Richard Speck didn't get as much publicity as this." Donald Taylor suggested they "sing a song for the pigs," and all four rendered a chorus of "God Bless America." Reuben Taylor asked a deputy for marijuana in payment for the singing.

On Nov. 10, all four pleaded not guilty at their arraignment before Judge Richard J. Fitzgerald in criminal court to charges of murdering the Corbett family. On June 14, 1973, Burse and Moran were found dead in the Lake County, Ill., jail where they were awaiting trial; unconfirmed reports said that they had been strangled. On Oct. 10, 1974, Clark and the Taylor brothers were found Guilty of murdering the Corbetts. Donald Taylor and Michael Clark were given 150 to 200 year jail terms, and Reuben Taylor was sentenced to 100 to 150 years. See: **Speck, Richard.** REF.: *CBA.*

DeMelker, Daisy Louisa Cowle Sproat, d.1932, S. Afri., mur. Daisy Cowle was married to William Cowle for fourteen years, and they had one son, Rhodes. In 1923, the South African nurse killed her husband with strychnine and collected £1,700 from his life insurance policy. She then married Robert Sproat. This time she waited only four years before killing him for £4000 in savings. In 1931, she married Clarence DeMelker, a famous rugby player. But her son, Rhodes Cowle, now twenty, wanted the money that he thought should have come to him from his father. Rather than give him what she had, Daisy DeMelker purchased arsenic and killed him.

The pharmacist from whom she purchased the arsenic, after hearing of young Rhodes' strange death, went to the police and reported the purchase. When arsenic was found in Rhodes' body, the bodies of Daisy's two late husbands were also exhumed and found to contain strychnine. Daisy de Melker was found Guilty of the murders by a Johannesburg court and was hanged on Dec. 30, 1932.

REF.: Bennett, *Murder Is My Business;* ____, *Genius For the Defense;* ____, *Up For Murder; CBA;* Cohen, *One Hundred True Crime Stories;* Nash, *Look For the Woman;* (FICTION), Millin, *Three Men Die.*

DeMeo, George, 1934- , U.S., consp.-smug. In 1980, police officers and customs officials seized stockpiles of weapons in Belfast, London, and Dublin. New Yorkers George DeMeo, forty-six, and his nephew, Robert Ferraro, thirty-one, were charged with conspiring to buy and transport to the Irish Republican Army, rifles and as much as one million rounds of ammunition stolen from the Marine Corps base at Camp Lejeune, N.C., and Fort Bragg, N.C., during an eight-year period. In a trial in September and early October 1980, Justice Department prosecutors called as witnesses business associates and employees of Howard Barnes Bruxton, Jr., a Wilson, N.C., gun store owner also charged with illegal arms dealings. Many of the witnesses traded their testimony for suspended or pro-rated sentences. Binford Benton, Bruxton's former partner, pleaded guilty to lesser charges and received a suspended sentence. He said Bruxton often sent rifles parcel post or by train to Yonkers, N.Y., where they were loaded into trunks of Cadillacs owned by Ferraro or DeMeo. "They were stockpiling them," Benton explained, "and then shipping them out of the country." He estimated that he had sold 1,000 guns illegally and acquired around two million rounds of ammunition from the military. On Oct. 3, after deliberating for six hours, the Raleigh, N.C., jury found all three defendants Guilty on all counts. Judge Franklin Dupree, Jr. dismissed all counts against Ferraro except one conspiracy charge, saying he "seems to have been in the unfortunate position of being among those present." On charges of conspiracy, smuggling weapons, and falsifying records, Dupree sentenced DeMeo to ten years in prison and a $20,000 fine, and gave Bruxton five years in prison and a $20,000 fine. Ferraro was

given five years and fined $5,000, but was immediately eligible for parole. REF.: *CBA.*

Demetrius I Soter, See: **Antiochus V.**

Demetz, Frédéric Auguste, 1796-1873, Fr., jur.-pris. reform. Founded the prison farm colony of Mettray, 1840, where youthful offenders were trained in worthwhile occupations. REF.: *CBA.*

Demir, Bulent, 1943-80, Case of, Turk., deputy mayor, assass. Political violence in Turkey escalated after the June 22, 1980, assassination of Deputy Mayor Bulent Demir, an official of the leftist Republican Peoples Party. His death became one of almost 1,800 deaths attributed to politics since Suleyman Demirel took over as prime minister in November 1979. He was the fifth official of his party, which opposes Demirel, killed in June.

The 36-year-old Demir, as one of several deputy mayors in Ankara, was gunned down by four men with automatic weapons outside his brother's grocery store. The assassination was part of the ongoing struggle between right and left political factions in Turkey. Prior to Demirel's rule, 1,844 people were killed for political reasons during the twenty-one months that Bulent Ecevit of the Republican Peoples Party was prime minister. REF.: *CBA.*

Demjanjuk, John (Ivan Demjanjuk), 1921- , Ger., war crimes. Only twice in the history of Israel was a man brought to trial for crimes committed during WWII. The first was Karl Adolf Eichmann, who was hanged in 1962 for being the architect of the extermination of Jews held in concentration camps by the Nazis. The second, John Demjanjuk, was tried for being one of the many men who actually performed the executions that Eichmann prescribed.

Following the war, Demjanjuk emigrated to the U.S. in 1952, moving to Cleveland, Ohio, where he was employed as an auto worker for thirty years. With the discovery in 1974 of a Nazi identification card bearing the name of Ivan Demjanjuk in U.S.S.R. archives, Israeli authorities accused Demjanjuk of being a prison camp guard known as "Ivan the Terrible." He earned the moniker from the brutal treatment dealt to those awaiting death, beating and whipping victims, even tearing flesh from some. The guard was in charge of escorting more than 850,000 Jewish prisoners to the gas chambers in 1942 and 1943 at the Treblinka death camp in Poland. Before extradition was permitted in February 1986, after a lengthy process, Demjanjuk had his U.S. citizenship taken away in 1981 for lying on his immigration application.

Demjanjuk's trial began on Feb. 16, 1987, with the prosecution, under Michael Shaked, determined to prove that the 45-year-old identity card matched the defendant. The defense, headed by Israeli attorney Yoram Sheftel, attempted to prove that the card was a Soviet forgery manufactured to humiliate anti-Soviet Ukrainians in the U.S. During the trial, one of the three judges, Dalia Dorner, interrupted the lawyer and remarked, "...if this is your line of defense, then you really have a very, very severe problem." Demjanjuk, who did not testify until August 1988, claimed that he too was a prisoner of war after his capture by the Germans—a claim no one has been able to verify or dispute.

Inconsistencies existed in the defendant's history of his war experiences. Handwriting experts failed to agree whether or not the identity card signature matched Demjanjuk's. The trial, which took place on the stage of a converted movie theater, lasted thirteen months, with the panel of three judges finding Demjanjuk Guilty on Apr. 13, 1988. He was sentenced to death, but his conviction is under appeal, Sheftel claiming that the judges in the case were biased in their verdict. The defendant's appeal was delayed by the suicide of one of his defense lawyers, Dov Eitan, who jumped from the fifteenth floor of a building on Nov. 29, 1988. REF.: *CBA.*

Demon, Henri, prom. 1951, Fr., attempt. mur. Henri Demon was a big man and a "good boss" in the small town of Phalempin, near Lille, France, where he had turned his father's small forge into a growing company that manufactured agricultural machinery. Because his father said he should be married, the 22-year-old Henri married a childhood friend, Alice, who was three years older than he. They soon had two children. Then Alice Demon, a faithful Roman Catholic, decided to withold sex rather than risk having more children. Henri made do with brothels for a time, but Alice made a horrendous scene when she thought he was involved with his secretary.

Henri established that there were sometimes prowlers around his house. On June 12, 1951, he woke Alice, saying he heard someone moving around in the garden. He went down, fired some shots, and returned, claiming that someone had indeed been there, and had fired at him but missed in the dark. He told the police about the episode the next day. Then, a month later, on the night of July 9, he was sitting up reading when he called Alice to come down because someone was in the yard. She came down, but sensing danger, turned and went upstairs. Just then Henri fired at her. His bullet struck her in the back, damaging her spinal cord and crippling her for life. Unaware that she was still alive, he used his second gun and a remote-activated mechanism to shoot himself in the arm.

But, that, of course, was not the story Demon told. His story involved intruders. But if there were intruders, police asked, why did the dog not bark, and why did Demon keep mumbling, "If they succeed in extracting the bullet from my wife, the ballistics experts will prove it did not come from *my* gun."? Ballistics experts quickly showed that the bullets came from different guns.

Henri Demon was arrested within thirty-six hours of the shooting. He readily confessed, but then recanted before his trial. When Alice learned that he was denying everything, she broke the silence she had been kept for their sons' sake and told her story. Henri was tried at the end of 1952 and promptly found Guilty. Only his wife's plea for mercy kept him from the guillotine. He was sent to prison for life. The French system, exacting civil as well as criminal penalties, fined him so much money in damages that he was forced to sell his business.

REF.: *CBA*; Goodman, *Crimes of Passion;* Heppenstall, *The Sex War and Others.*

deMora, James, See: **McGurn, Jack.**

DeMore, Louis, prom. 1934, U.S., (wrong. convict.) mur. A classic example of being in the wrong place at the wrong time—or better, saying the wrong statement at the wrong time—is seen in the case of Louis DeMore, who made the remarkably uncanny mistake of informing police that he fit the description of the man they were after.

DeMore moved to St. Louis, Mo., from Chicago in April 1934, the same day that a man attempted to rob a street car. When the attempted robbery failed, the bandit fled, only to stop running as police officer Albert R. Siko caught up with him. He stopped so suddenly that Siko ran by, and as he did the robber grabbed the patrolman's gun and fired three bullets into Siko. The only clue at the scene were the bullet shells and a gray hat. Later that night at a restaurant, police officers were discussing the case. DeMore, who was leaving the restaurant, overheard the description of the bandit and exclaimed he matched the suspect. This statement led police to arrest the out-of-towner, when it was learned that he had registered at his hotel under an assumed name, presumably because he wished to start a whole new life after leaving his wife. DeMore was identified by the streetcar driver and apparently the dying Siko, who nodded at seeing DeMore before slipping into a coma and dying the next day. The three female streetcar passengers were unsure of identification. The prisoner was held for murder, and while in jail learned, erroneously, from other prisoners that he would be executed. To escape death he quickly confessed to the crime, and was just as quickly sentenced to death by the judge.

Police arrested George Couch just ten days after arresting DeMore, and after searching the man's apartment found the gun that had killed Siko, the gun that DeMore said he had thrown in the river. Perplexed police asked DeMore how a gun thrown into the river could come into Couch's possession. DeMore then admitted he had confessed only to save his life, which was never in danger, and had hoped the real killer would eventually be caught. Couch, who had spent ten years in prison for an Indiana armed robbery, was convicted and sent back to prison where he was later killed by an inmate. DeMore was pardoned on Oct. 1, 1934 by Governor Guy Brasfield Park.

REF.: *CBA*; Radin, *The Innocents.*

de Moreno, Don Pedro Suarez (AKA: Count de Tinoco, Marquis de la d'Essa), 1901-04, Fr., big.-theft-count.-fraud. In 1883 Pedro Suarez de Moreno went to prison for stealing bed linen from the Hotel Kassam in Dalk, France. After his release, he lived with his wife, Elizabeth, and their eight children. In 1902 he was in trouble for selling counterfeit railroad tickets and was forced to flee to the U.S.

He surfaced again in France in 1902, calling himself a general. He visited families, including winegrowers Emile Lapierre and his wife, telling them that they were heirs to a $500 million fortune. At the insistence of the delighted French families, de Moreno was sent to the U.S. to recover the wealth. Over the next few years, they willingly sent him expense money.

His free ride ended when two of his victims caught up with him in the U.S. De Moreno was tried in France and sentenced to hard labor.

REF.: *CBA*; Train, *True Stories of Crime.*

Denby, Edwin, See: **Teapot Dome Scandal.**

Denby, James Jordan, 1930- , Case of, Nicaragua, smug. Private pilot James Jordan Denby was forced by Nicaraguan Sandinista gunfire to land his Cessna-172 single-engine plane on a beach about 150 miles southeast of Managua. Denby, a native of Carlinville, Ill., who owns a ranch in Costa Rica, was forced down and captured when his plane flew over Nicaraguan territory. Denby was charged with transporting guns to the right-wing Contra rebels who oppose the leftist ruling Sandinistas.

The first U.S. citizen charged with such a crime, Eugene Hasenfus parachuted from his cargo plane laden with arms that Sandinistas shot down. He was sentenced to thirty years but served only one month before release. Denby, however, was freed on Jan. 30, 1988, after spending seven weeks in custody, claiming innocence. He was absolved of any wrongdoing by a judge in Nicaragua on Feb. 8, 1988. REF.: *CBA.*

Denham, Sir John, 1559-1639, Ire., jur. Presided as lord chief justice on the king's bench in Ireland. REF.: *CBA.*

Denhardt, Henry H., 1876-1937, Case of, U.S., mur. Henry H. Denhardt was a prominent man in Kentucky. He had served as the prosecuting attorney for Bowling Green for ten years, Warren County judge for two terms, the state's lieutenant-governor from 1923 to 1927, adjutant general to Governor Ruby Laffoon, and had been appointed National Guard brigadier general. During this time he also made many enemies, most notably in 1935 when he defied a court order and led his troops into Harlan County to supervise voting in the election between his friend Laffoon and Albert B. Chandler. He was pardoned by Laffoon prior to his trial.

However, on Nov. 6, 1936, he made three mortal enemies. That night, after a long drive in Kentucky, and the eventual breakdown of the general's car, 40-year-old Verna Garr Taylor died of a bullet wound to the heart. Denhardt and Taylor had been seeing each other since June, and had talked of marriage, before her body was found lying in a ditch 200 yards from Denhardt's car. Evidence against Denhardt, who claimed it was suicide because the widow's daughters opposed the marriage, looked fairly conclusive. The .45-caliber gun that killed the woman was Denhardt's, blood was found on the coat Denhardt was wearing, and more blood was found 410 feet from where the body lay, indicating she had been carried there. Paraffin testing of Taylor's and Denhardt's hands showed he might have fired a gun but that she had not, and a witness related how Denhardt spoke of Taylor in the past tense before it was known she was dead. Nevertheless, a jury was unable to reach a decision in April 1937, returning a vote of seven to five in favor of acquittal, so a second trial for murder was ordered. It was the night before his second trial that the slain woman's brothers—Roy, Jack, and Dr. E.S. Garr, enacted their revenge upon Denhardt.

On Sept. 20, 1937, Denhardt was gunned down by the Garr brothers while returning to his Shelbyville, Ky. hotel after dinner with his lawyer Rodes E. Myers.

Depending on which version is to be believed, the brothers either acted in self-defense when the general allegedly reached for his hip, or the three attacked Denhardt who ran a zig-zag across the street toward the hotel trying to avoid being shot. Denhardt was shot seven times. The murder charge against Jack Garr was dismissed by Judge Charles C. Marshall because he had not fired a gun. Later that day, Oct. 22, 1937, Roy Garr was found Not Guilty. Kentucky Attorney General Hubert Meredith called the self-defense plea entered by defense attorney, state Senator Ralph Gelbert, ridiculous. Gelbert countered that Roy had "a right to shoot a mad dog." The case against Dr. E.S. Garr, who was in a mental institution following the murder, was dismissed in February 1938. REF.: *CBA*.

Denicke, Ernest, prom. 1906, Case of, U.S., mur. Following the 1906 earthquake that devastated San Francisco, National Guard captain Ernest Denicke came out of retirement to help police prevent looting and maintain order. Denicke saw a man carrying chickens, which the captain assumed the man had stolen. Denicke ordered a nearby sentry to tell the man to drop the chickens and move along. The soldier did this, but the man took exception to the sentry's prodding him with a bayonet—as Denicke had instructed him to do—and he fought with the soldier. After the man had disarmed the sentry, Denicke shot and killed the man. During the night the man's body was weighted down with iron and flung into the bay by Lieutenant Charles Herring. It was later learned that the chickens were not stolen and Denicke was arrested on May 24 for killing John Doe (the unknown man's body was never recovered).

At the trial on May 27, 1906, police Judge Shortall dismissed the charge after hearing the evidence. However, Denicke was again arrested for the same crime and sent before Superior Court Judge Cook by Judge Lawlor. On Nov. 28 a jury found Denicke Not Guilty.

REF.: *CBA*; Duke, *Celebrated Criminal Cases of America*.

de Nicola, Morris (AKA: Motzie), b.c.1894, U.S., wh. slav. Morris de Nicola controlled the Connecticut operations of a white slave empire that yielded yearly profits of about $2 million. For his management of the brothels, de Nicola, forty-two, was convicted on ten counts of prostitution. He was sentenced to seven years in the federal penitentiary at Lewisburg, Pa., and fined $1,000. Mary Testa, his 29-year-old wife and business partner, was convicted and sentenced to one year and one day in the women's penitentiary at Alderson, W. Va. Michael Taverner, thirty-four, of Waterbury, Conn., was tried as a partner in one of the largest brothels and sentenced to seven years in prison. Nine other syndicate members were convicted and received sentences varying from one week suspended to one year and one day imprisonment.

REF.: Bullough, *Illustrated History of Prostitution*; *CBA*; Nash, *Almanac of World Crime*.

Denison, Edward Everett, prom. 1929, Case of, U.S., smug. A large package arrived for Republican Congressman Edward Everett Denison after he had spent a winter vacation in Panama. Due to a leak spotted by a railway employee, Prohibition agents were called in to examine the trunk delivered to the Ohio legislator's office. Inside the trunk, thirty quarts of a variety of liquors were found. Denison claimed at his trial that the package had been mistakenly shipped to him. The jury acquitted him.

REF.: *CBA*; Kobler, *Ardent Spirits*.

Denke, Carl, d.1924, Ger., can.-suic.-mur. In post-WWI Germany, economic conditions left many people unemployed and starving. A famine in 1918, the year the Armistice was signed claimed thousands of lives. Carl Denke, the landlord of a public house in Münsterberg, Silesia, was unaffected by the economic turmoil all around him. In fact, Denke often provided free shelter for an army of homeless tramps who passed through the city. By

all appearances, he was a God-fearing, law-abiding man who played the organ in the local church on Sundays. Denke was also a cannibal.

Denke was accused of murdering at least thirty people between 1921 and 1924, and devouring parts of the corpses. Denke preserved some of the remains in a tub of brine, and kept a ledger of names and the dates the vagrants checked into his resort. The ghastly nature of his crimes was discovered on Dec. 21, 1924, when a coachman who lived one floor above heard pitiful cries. He rushed downstairs and found a robust young man bleeding profusely from the scalp. The man, one of Denke's boarders, had been struck with a hatchet. Before he lapsed into unconsciousness, he gasped that Denke had assaulted him from behind. Police were summoned and during a search of the premises the vats of bones and pickled flesh were discovered. Denke was taken to the jail where he used his suspenders to hang himself.

REF.: *CBA*; Nash, *Almanac of World Crime*; Wilson, *Encyclopedia of Murder*.

Denman, George, 1819-96, Brit., jur. Served as high court justice for the queen's bench division, 1881-92. REF.: *CBA*.

Denman, Thomas, 1779-1854, Brit., jur. The 1st Baron Denman, was Queen Caroline's solicitor general, 1820, maintaining the queen's innocence throughout his defense of her before the bar of the House of Lords that same year. Appointed attorney general, 1830, where he prosecuted the reform rioters, 1832, and served as lord chief justice, 1832-50, condemning Moxon, on a charge of blasphemy for publishing the complete works of Percy Bysshe Shelley, 1841. REF.: *CBA*.

Denman, William, 1872-1959, U.S., jur. Received appointment to the 9th Circuit Court of the U.S. from President Franklin Roosevelt, 1935, and served as chairman for the committee of the U.S. Judicial Conference that dealt with appeals for which the prison sentence had already been served, 1945. REF.: *CBA*.

Denney, Robert Vernon, 1916-81, U.S., law enfor. off.-jur. Acted as special agent for the FBI, 1940-41, a member of the U.S. House of Representatives, 1967-71, and was appointed to the District Court of Nebraska by President Richard Nixon, Jan. 20, 1971. REF.: *CBA*.

Dennis, Edward, d.1786, Brit., execut. Succeeding executioner Thomas Turlis in 1771, was Edward Dennis, an industrious plodder who was said to be somewhat dim-witted. Famous criminals he hanged during his fifteen-year reign included John Rann, the Reverend William Dodd, Robert Perreau and Daniel Perreau, and William Wynne Ryland. Dennis spent twelve years as executioner at Tyburn, then finished his term at Debtor's Door outside Newgate Jail.

The hangman figured as the basis for a character in Charles Dickens' novel, *Barnaby Rudge*, based on the part Dennis played in the Newgate Prison riots. As Dennis was walking home along Holborn, he joined a crowd looting a shop at New Turnstile. Authorities were informed, and he was arrested. The executioner insisted that the mob had forced him to join in, threatening to burn him; he was found Guilty and sentenced to death. Begging for mercy, Dennis pleaded, "My will was innocent, but my body was compelled." The hangman was pardoned a few days later, released "so that he could hang his fellow rioters." The first executions in front of Newgate took place on December 9, 1783, carried out by Dennis and William Brunskill, who succeeded Dennis after he died on Nov. 21, 1786. See: **Brunskill, William; Dodd, William; Perreau, Daniel; Perreau, Robert; Rann, John; Ryland, William Wynne, Turlis, Thomas.**

REF.: Atholl, *Shadow of the Gallows*; Bleackley, *Hangmen of England*; *CBA*; Laurence, *A History of Capital Punishment*; Potter, *The Art of Hanging*.

Dennis, Gerard Graham, 1920- , U.S., theft-burg. A movie depicting a jewel thief's life story garnered Gerard Dennis $10,000, which he received while in prison. Dennis spent much of his youth in and out of jail for minor offenses and housebreaking in Ontario. He was convicted fourteen times before his escape in 1943 while serving a two-year prison term. He fled to the U.S. where he became involved in crimes on a much larger scale. In Westchester County, N.Y., Dennis stole $140,150 worth of jewels and furs from several estates. On Aug. 17, 1946, he stole $15,000 from the home of Mrs. Ralph H. Kruse. During the theft of $9,000 from a home in New Rochelle on Oct. 20, 1946, he shot the owner Marshall E. Tulloch in the hand, and in a Bronxville burglary on Jan. 17, 1947, he netted $18,000 from Mrs. George B. Luhman's home. Dennis was adept at breaking into houses and knew how to cut diamonds and disguise furs to resell the stolen merchandise.

During the summer of 1947 Dennis was forced to head west to California after a botched attempt by Gloria Horowitz to sell diamonds for him in Philadelphia. While in California, Dennis stole $357,635 from homes in the Beverly Hills and Hollywood areas, before returning to Cleveland with eleven packages of diamonds to sell.

A nephew of jeweler Irwin Nussbaum, Zoltan Greenhut, recognized Dennis' face from a poster and called police, who arrested him in February 1949.

The jewel thief was returned to Weschester County to stand trial before Judge Elbert T. Gallagher for the crimes he committed. At first Dennis refused to plead guilty, but later confessed to seven burglaries. He was sentenced to eighteen years to life in prison, a sentence which was reduced to fifteen to twenty-three years by Judge James D. Hopkins on Jan. 19, 1960, for good conduct. Dennis' exploits turned profitable after his arrest. He was given $10,000 for providing the story to the 1950 movie *The Great Jewel Robber*. REF.: *CBA*.

Dennis, Richard, prom. 1804, U.S., mur. Richard Dennis was the son of a wealthy resident of Charleston, S.C. The elder Dennis and James Shaw had been carrying on a protracted feud which ended when the younger Dennis waited on a Charleston street for Shaw, and shot him to death when he turned a corner on Aug. 20, 1804. Richard Dennis, despite his father's influence, was convicted and hanged.

REF.: Carpenter, *Report of the Trial of Richard Dennis; CBA*.

Dennis Kearney Riots, prom. 1848, U.S., mob. vio. Chinese immigrants began arriving in San Francisco in February 1848. By 1852, about 8,000 Chinese had immigrated, and by 1877, white laborers, threatened by the cheap labor provided by the Chinese, began to harass and assault them. Dennis Kearney, a member of a debating club in downtown San Francisco, regularly spoke out against the right of Chinese to compete in the labor pool; soon he held meetings out of doors, often in front of the City Hall dome. His speeches stirred up hostility toward the immigrants, and later incited the Dennis Kearney Riots. In response to a number of work strikes occurring on the East Coast at that time, a mass meeting was held in San Francisco on July 23, 1877, during which orators, including Kearney, prophesied that conditions would worsen in San Francisco unless the Chinese were forced to leave. After the meeting, a gang of thugs wrecked several Chinese laundries, setting fire to one.

By the next day, a citizen's Committee of Safety was organized to lend support to the police force, which consisted of only one hundred and fifty men, insufficient for handling the situation. William T. Coleman, a former leader of a vigilante group, headed the committee of 5,000 citizens which met at Horticultural Hall on Stockton and Post Streets. On July 25, the group fought off a mob that burned a lumber yard near the mail dock, and attempted to burn the dock where the Chinese landed. Police and the safety committee held back the thugs and several men were shot and wounded. REF.: *CBA*.

Dennison, Stephen Heath, 1909-   , U.S., rob. The case of Stephen Dennison is one in which a great miscarriage of justice was committed not once *twice*. Dennison came from a broken home in Salem, N.Y. His father George beat his mother Mary so severely that she left him in 1917 and moved with Stephen to her father's small farm. Stephen was a good child but a slow learner, flunking several grades. At sixteen he was still in the seventh grade. He quit school to go to work to help his mother and elderly grandfather. While looking for work on Sept. 9, 1925,

Dennison passed a road stand which was closed. He intended to buy a hot dog and sat down to wait for the owner, Nellie Hill, to return. When she did not, the hungry youth took out a pocket knife and cut a hole in the canvas covering the stand. He reached inside and from the counter took some candy bars and cigarettes, worth a total of about $5. A passerby saw Dennison run from the stand and the youth was later arrested by A.M. Alexander, undersheriff of Salem. He was charged with burglary in the third degree.

With his nervous mother at his side, Dennison later appeared in the Salem court before Judge Erskine C. Rogers. This was his first offense and he pled not guilty. Judge Rogers appointed the boy a lawyer, Herbert Van Kirk, from Greenwich, N.Y., who talked briefly with the youth and then changed Dennison's plea to guilty. Rather than send the boy to Elmira Reformatory, Judge Rogers gave him a ten-year suspended sentence but ordered him to report once a month for a year to the Reverend Claude Winch, a Methodist minister in town. Dennison got a job and dutifully reported to the minister. He was later fired for smoking in the men's room of a machinery company. Dennison then failed to report to the minister, missing four

Stephen Dennison, age seventeen, when he entered Elmira Reformatory in New York.

appearances. He was picked up while walking along a Salem street carrying a bucket while en route to pick berries. Sheriff N. Austin Baker took him directly to see Judge Rogers, who told him that he had violated his parole.

Judge Rogers then summarily sentenced the boy to Elmira Reformatory for "an indeterminate sentence until discharged by due process of law." Judge Rogers told Dennison that he would probably be released in about thirteen months. This sentence, one rendered without compassion for a first-offender and one that left the time to be served open-ended, might as well have been a life sentence. It was later reported that Judge Rogers had been influenced by Sheriff Baker who believed, without one shred of evidence, that Dennison had been responsible for a number of petty thefts in Salem and that it was best "to get rid of the boy." Irrespective of the reason, Judge Rogers' brutal sentence of Stephen Dennison, one that taints that jurist's name to this day, doomed a good-natured boy to the horrors of savage prison life. It was another case of "turning the key and throwing it away." The "thirteen months" confinement turned into thirty-four years of frustration, mental agony, and physical pain.

Dennison entered Elmira Reformatory on Aug. 14, 1926. He was not released in thirteen months but was required, because of the ambiguously worded sentence of Judge Rogers, kept in confinement for the entire ten years Rogers had originally imposed, a ten-year sentence for stealing $5 worth of merchandise. He was later transferred to another institution at Napanoch where, after years of vicious treatment from prisoners and guards alike, Dennison, in 1936, was judged insane and sent to the cellblock for the criminally insane at Dannemora. His memory weakened, his responses slowed, and his reasoning impaired by beatings and brutalities, Dennison was sent to Dannemora and forgotten. By then his mother was dead and his impoverished brothers and sisters found no way, as had been the case in the past, to pay for a legal campaign to free him. Years later, while regaining his lucidity, Dennison wrote to his half-brother George, imploring him to "go after a lawyer. I don't know why I am being held as a slave. I don't belong in this place."

George Dennison went to George Wein, a lawyer in Glens Falls, N.Y., who turned the case over to William Vincent Canale. He investigated and soon learned that Stephen Dennison had been transferred to the mental ward of Dannemora without the benefit of a lawyer or trial, to which he was entitled, or the opportunity to produce witnesses on his own behalf or challenge witnesses testifying against him. The court's action was not related to any

Stephen Dennison at the time of his release, only fifty-one but prematurely aged by prison horrors.

of Dennison's relatives, friends, or a lawyer acting on his behalf. Worse, in 1936 Dennison had been committed to the hospital at Dannemora *after his original sentence had expired* and *without his knowledge.* This disgraceful miscarriage of justice was partly set right by attorney Canale who first battled to have Dennison set free.

On Dec. 12, 1960, he was brought to a courthouse wearing an antiquated ball-and-chain and handcuffs. Only minutes later Charles H. Lewis, assistant attorney general for N.Y., admitted that the state had wrongfully detained Dennison in 1936. Judge Robert C. Main asked Dr. Ross E. Herold, assistant superintendent of Dannemora State Hospital, if Dennison would be a danger to himself or to the community if released. Dr. Herold said no and Judge Main ordered Stephen Dennison released after thirty-four years in prison. Canale then sued the state of New York, seeking compensation for Dennison's long and illegal ordeal in the New York penal system. Although only fifty-one at the time of his release, Dennison's hair had turned completely white and he was bent and stooped from prison hardships. Before being officially released, Dennison was given two pennies taped to a piece of cardboard, all that he had in his pockets when arrested and shipped off to the reformatory in 1926.

After protracted appeals and trials, the dogged attorney Canale triumphed on Mar. 16, 1966, when the New York State Court of Claims awarded Dennison $115,000. In making the award, Judge Richard S. Heller stated that "no sum of money would be adequate to compensate the claimant for the injuries he suffered and the scars he obviously bears. In a sense, society labeled him as a sub-human, placed him in a cage with genuine sub-humans, drove him insane, and then used the insanity as an excuse for

holding him indefinitely in an institution with few, if any, facilities for genuine treatment and rehabilitation of the mentally ill."

The end of Dennison's story was as bitter as the years taken from him by the state of New York. Judge Heller's decision was reversed and the claim dismissed by a higher court. Stephen Dennison never received a dime of the $115,000 once awarded to him. Though Canale continued to seek justice for Dennison, his firm financing the cause, all appeals were denied or not even heard. Dennison was last seen alive in 1985 by his lawyer, Canale, in Glens Falls, N.Y., where Dennison had worked for some years as a janitor. Dennison's wrongful imprisonment stands as an ugly monument to an indifferent and compassionless bureaucracy. His imprisonment at the hands of Judge Erskine C. Rogers, and his continued illegal imprisonment at the hands of other New York officials after having served his original harsh sentence, stands as a great disgrace of the American judicial and penology systems.

REF.: *CBA;* Freeman and Hoffman, *The Ordeal of Stephen Dennison;* Nash, *Bloodletters and Badmen.*

Dennison, Theodore, prom. 1850s, U.S., theft. Not long after leaving the Chicago police force in the 1850s, after having served as the city's first detective, Allan Pinkerton was employed by the U.S. Post Office to solve a number of thefts of bank drafts and money orders. Nor was it long before the newly appointed Special U.S. Mail Agent had solved the crimes with the arrest of a nephew of the postmaster.

Working undercover as a mailroom clerk, Pinkerton soon observed Theodore Dennison pocketing envelopes. The clerk earlier had admitted he was dexterous enough to know when a package contained money. Pinkerton approached Dennison, tackling the man as he attempted to flee. An exhaustive search of Dennison's apartment at first produced no evidence, but then Pinkerton removed the backs of pictures on the walls. Behind the wall hangings were bank notes totaling $3,738; the highest was $1,503 deposited behind a picture of the Virgin Mary. Dennison confessed to his crimes and was sent to prison.

REF.: *CBA;* Horan, *The Pinkertons.*

Denton, Thomas, and **Jones, John**, d.1789, Brit., count. Denton was a tinkerer who had the knack of duplicating and improving on the inventions of others. He was, however, easily bored, and this led him into a life of crime and to an eventual sentence of death.

Most of Denton's mechanical refinements were quickly sold to others; he began a metal plating business, which proved to be his downfall. He met a man who made counterfeit coins, and Denton thought he could improve on the process. The coins were so expertly made that authorities examining the coins thought them genuine.

Denton was finally arrested when his counterfeiting tools were found in his possession. Denton and his accomplice, John Jones, were hanged at Newgate on July 1, 1789, along with John Ward, a burglar, and George Green a highwayman.

REF.: *CBA;* Mitchell, *The Newgate Calendar.*

D'Entragues-Caylus Duel, prom. 16th Cent., Fr., duel-mur. Rather than wait idly by while the duelists, King Henry III's favored D'Entragues and Caylus, fought one another, the seconds themselves engaged in fighting.

The seconds to D'Entragues were Riberac and Schomberg, while those for Caylus were Maugerin and Livaret. As the duel began near the Porte St. Antoine ramparts, Riberac suggested to Maugerin that the two should put an end to it. Maugerin disagreed and suggested that they should duel. Riberac was the victor but his wounds led to his death the next day. Schomberg and Livaret also began fighting when they saw Maugerin and Riberac. Here, as in the main duel, only one man died: Schomberg was killed by a wound to the chest after he cut Livaret in the cheek. D'Entragues, like Riberac, was severely cut, but managed to survive. Caylus was not as lucky; he died later claiming that his opponent had unfairly used a dagger as well as his sword. D'Entragues replied it was Caylus' own stupidity not to bring a dagger.

REF.: *CBA;* Melville, *Famous Duels and Assassinations.*

Denvile, Sir Gosselin, and **Denvile, Robert,** prom. 1310, Brit., rob.-mur. The son of a distinguished knight, Sir Gosselin Denvile and his brother Robert Denvile squandered their considerable inheritance in a few short years, and then turned to highway robbery to maintain their aristocratic lifestyle. Much admired by their fellow highwaymen, the Denviles became successful and were soon leading a band of about 150 thieves. They robbed the rich and poor alike, indifferent to royal or religious victims. They robbed cardinals, monks, and even broke into nunneries where they robbed and raped nuns. In Westmoreland, the sadistic Gosselin Denvile set a nun on fire.

On another occasion the Denviles came upon a Dominican monk, Bernard Sympson, who was traveling alone in the woods. After robbing the monk of his gold, they forced him to climb a tree and deliver a sermon. The brothers were so impressed with his words that they returned his gold and added some of their own before setting Sympson free. But the sermon did nothing to change these contradictory creatures.

Often members of this much-feared band would dress as friars to disguise their true profession. Their impersonations were so effective that even King Edward II became one of their victims. He was traveling to Norwich with an entourage of forty people when 200 friars appeared on horseback. The king and his party accepted the religious band as genuine and soon Gosselin was given an audience. When he announced his true purpose, robbery, it was too late for Edward to resist. After the king had handed over his purse, Gosselin made a great show of physically searching the king for any hidden money.

This brazen robbery led to the downfall of the Denvile gang. The outraged king placed a large dead-or-alive reward on the brothers. A smaller reward was offered for the capture of any other gang member. Within six months more than fifty of Gosselin's men were executed. But the brothers remained free and active. With what remained of their band, the Denviles invaded the palace of the Bishop of Durham. They literally stripped the place—leaving the bishop and his servants bound hand and foot, naked.

Gosselin's lust and the vengeance of a jealous husband brought about the band's ruination. Gosselin had often trysted with a married woman, a hostess of an inn on the road to Yorkshire. With rewards to goad him, the cuckolded husband of the hostess found a profitable revenge. He informed the sheriff of the outlaws' presence and was then a witness to the carnage that soon followed. Hundreds of the sheriff's men surrounded the house; more than 200 of them would not live through the night. But the brothers were soon taken, along with twenty-three members of the gang. They were brought to York and hanged en masse without the benefit of a trial.

REF.: *CBA;* Pringle, *Stand and Deliver;* Smith, *Highwaymen.*

Deo, Mrs. Josiah, d.1801, U.S., mur. Mrs. Josiah Deo, of Paltz, N.Y., was deeply religious, according to most contemporary reports, conducting prayer meetings in her home several times a day with her family. She apparently suffered for a number of years from a mental disorder which manifested itself on Sept. 6, 1801. Mrs. Deo sent several family members on errands and then murdered three of her children, cutting their throats. She then slashed her own throat and was found dying a short time later.

REF.: *CBA;* Horrid Murder and Suicide.

De Palma, William, 1938-   , U.S., (wrong. convict.) rob. In 1968 William De Palma of Whittier, Calif., was arrested and convicted of armed robbery based on forged fingerprint evidence. For the sixteen months following his sentencing, De Palma remained in McNeal Island Prison in Washington State.

When the facts of the case were revealed, De Palma was freed. On Aug. 12, 1975, he was awarded a $750,000 settlement for the time he spent in prison. It remains the highest compensation ever given to an individual for a wrongful conviction. REF.: *CBA.*

De Peyster, Abraham, 1657-1728, U.S., jur. Served on the New York Supreme Court, 1698-1702. REF.: *CBA.*

de Poulaillon, prom. 17th Cent., Case of, Fr., mur. Madame de Poulaillon wanted to get rid of her old and wealthy husband, so she consulted Marie Bosse. She brought Bosse one of her husband's shirts, which Bosse saturated in a potent solution of arsenic. She told de Poulaillon that wearing the shirt would cause extreme skin irritation and pain. The wife reputedly paid her advisor about £800 for her services.

The wife's plot was thwarted when someone warned her husband and he had her arrested. She stood trial, and although she confessed her crime, the judges were captivated by her wit and gracious manners. She was acquitted amid boisterous applause.

REF.: *CBA;* Thompson, *Poison and Poisoners.*

Deppe, Robert Edmund, and **Falkenstein, Julius,** and **Liberman, Samuel,** prom. 1953, U.S., smug. The case of a ring of smugglers that had been transferring diamonds into the U.S. from Belgium was finally cracked when it was learned from an informant in Belgium that a New York furrier was receiving the gems.

At first authorities were unable to obtain any evidence against Julius Falkenstein, the furrier, but the result of a call to Falkenstein from a Belgian airline employee led agents to the smuggler, Robert Edmund Deppe. Agents had sifted through several months' worth of outgoing calls from the Henry Hudson Hotel by Sabena Airlines employees before realizing that the pilot, Captain Deppe, was the man to tail. Deppe was observed for weeks by the U.S. Customs Service's Racket Squad, commanded by Tom Duncan, until he made a delivery to the home of Mrs. Julia Michelson. Inside the two envelopes delivered was $233,230 worth of diamonds. Michelson did not know what the envelopes contained; she was being used by the smugglers only as a drop-off point. Three days later, Samuel Liberman showed up to pick up the diamonds but was arrested by agents Abe Eisenberg and Harold Smith. Falkenstein and Deppe confessed to participating in the smuggling operation. Deppe was deported to Belgium, and Falkenstein and Liberman were sentenced to one year in prison—sentences that were suspended—and fined $2,500 each.

REF.: *CBA;* Whitehead, *Border Guard.*

Left, the beautiful Duchess de Praslin and, right, the duke, who murdered her for another woman.

de Praslin, Duke (Theobald Charles Laure Huges or **Duc de Choiseul-Praslin**), 1810-48, Fr., mur. De Praslin was the scion of a distinguished noble French family that was directly related to the line of the reigning King Louis Philippe. In 1829, at the age of nineteen, Duke de Praslin married Fanny Sebastiani, who also came from a noble line and was the niece of the Duke of Coigny. Petite and pretty, de Praslin's bride brought with her a huge dowery which enriched the dwindling de Praslin coffers. The union produced ten children and the couple seemed relatively happy, spending their days in a comfortable Paris house on the Rue St. Honoré, which belonged to the Sebastiani family. They also spent time in a gloomy, dank castle in Melun, the ancestral de Praslin estate.

The many de Praslin children needed additional supervision and, in 1841, an attractive, intelligent, and utterly desirable housekeeper and governess arrived. Her name was Henriette Deluzy-Desportes, but the de Praslin family referred to her as Mademoiselle Deluzy. The duke, by then tired of his wife, who had worn herself out in twenty years of childbirth and maintaining a staggering household, slowly attached his affections to the reliant, strong-willed governess. For six years, the duke carried on a cautious affair with Deluzy who actually became the female head of the house and the woman the de Praslin children turned to for emotional support. The duchess was all but ignored in this strange atmosphere. Finally, unable to endure the impossible situation anymore, she asked the duke to break off the affair and send Deluzy away. He refused, curtly informing his wife, "My dear, if she goes, so do I."

The de Praslin servants find the Duchess horribly murdered.

The duchess then played her last card, threatening to divorce her husband unless he gave up his mistress. Fearing the loss of his wife's considerable income, de Praslin promised that he would set matters straight and call a halt to his unfaithfull practices. He suggested that his wife take the children to the Melun estate while he made final arrangements to send Deluzy away. In July 1847, the duchess and the children went to the country, but de Praslin, instead of dismissing the voluptuous governess, rented a luxurious apartment for her on the other side of Paris and spent almost a whole month in Deluzy's bed. The duchess returned to her Paris house to find her husband absent. Fanny de Praslin went to bed with nervous apprehension. She noticed that the hinges of the door leading to her bedroom had been removed. She consoled herself that she was safe, neverthless, since the house was full of

servants and her husband's bed chambers were close by. A cord was close to the duchess' bed which, when pulled, would ring bells in the servants' quarters, summoning them.

At a little after 4 a.m., on Aug. 18, 1847, the still house was suddenly filled with the piercing shrieks of a woman, screams so loud that they could be heard in the street outside by passersby. This was followed by choking and coughing and then ominous silence. Responding to these cries inside the house were two servants, August Charpentier, de Praslin's valet, and Emma Leclerc, personal maid to the duchess. The doors to the duchess' bedroom were bolted and the entrance to her bathroom was jammed shut with a wedge. The valet found that the exit from the bedroom to the garden was also locked and he broke a panel of glass, getting inside a passageway that connected the bedrooms of the duke and duchess. The door between the bedrooms was unlocked.

Inside the dark bedroom of the duchess, the valet could smell gunsmoke and blood. He was joined by another servant and the two of them investigated the bedroom, finding Fanny de Praslin lying on the floor, her head against a sofa. Her nightgown was covered with blood and more than forty savage wounds had pierced her flesh.

Charpentier looked through the window of the bedroom and saw for a fleeting moment a tall, gaunt figure wearing a red brocaded nightgown, a vision he later described, "like a red devil!" Charpentier turned to another servant named Merville and gasped, "The duke."

"Then why doesn't he give the alarm?" asked Emma Leclerc, who stood now holding a guttering candle over the grisly scene. Examining the duchess, the servants grimaced in horror as they discovered sword cuts slashed across the small woman's breasts. Furniture was toppled everywhere and a trail of blood indicated that the duchess had run around and around the room, chased by a monster who savagely slashed at her. There was a discernable trail of blood leading from the bedroom to the door that led to that of the duke's bedroom. Suddenly, the duke strode into the room, standing before his slain wife and servants and then exclaiming in a practiced voice, "Oh, my God in Heaven! Some monster has murdered Fanny! Get a doctor!"

August Charpentier knew it was too late to call a doctor. He went into the street and stopped a policeman. Chief Inspector Pierre Allard of the Sûreté arrived a short time later. He examined the bedroom and found a pistol under a divan. He sniffed its muzzle but realized it had not been fired. The duchess' head had been crushed with a heavy instrument and Allard believed that the pistol had been the murder weapon. Allard asked the duke if he knew the owner of the pistol. "Yes," replied the duke in a rather off-handed way, "It is mine." He then said he had grabbed the pistol in his bedroom when he heard his wife's screams and had run into her bedroom, where he found her lying on the floor. When he lifted her, he said, his clothes became coated with blood. He did not want to frighten the children, he said, so he returned to his bedroom to change, then returned to the bedroom to find the servants bending over his wife's body.

Allard checked all of the duke's swords and knives and found them to be spotless and in their wall mounts. The duke sat in a chair implacably staring back at his inquisitor. Allard pointed out the trail of blood that led from the duchess' bedroom to that of the duke's. De Praslin reminded the inspector that he had already admitted lifting his wife's bleeding body and that her blood had soaked his clothes and caused the trail when he went to his room to change. Allard then pointed out that the butt of the Duke's pistol was coated with blood and that hairs obviously from his wife's head still clung to it. It was not a weapon that had been seized to ward off a murderous home invader but a murder weapon.

Moreover, Allard had noticed that the duke was limping and he asked de Praslin to explain this injury. De Praslin then became aloof, assuming an injured and offended air. He finally responded airily, "I have no further explanations to make. I am a peer of

France. I do not account for myself to police officers." With that, he dismissed Allard but the inspector decided the duke was, indeed, the murderer. He concluded that it would be dangerous to place such a distinguished personage in custody, that to do so was to risk his career, but he believed he had no choice. Armed with considerable evidence, Allard went to ministers of the king some days later and accused the duke of murdering his wife. He had obtained the diary kept by the duchess, along with her letters, all of which were filled with descriptions of her husband's infidelities with Deluzy. Here, of course, was the motive for the murder. De Praslim killed his wife so that he could be with his sensual mistress. King Louis Philippe had no choice but to sign the order for de Praslin's arrest.

The lavish de Praslin palace in Melun, France.

Inspector Allard first came under heavy criticism for arresting a nobleman. But the intrepid Allard prepared a meticulous report, in which he described how he had inspected the butt of the pistol with a magnifying glass and found the hairs affixed to it, mingled with blood. Moreover, he had taken some hairs from the murder victim's head and matched these to those on the gun. This proof, coupled with the duchess' letters and diary, convinced the king that de Praslin would have to face a trial that would certainly prove sensational and embarrassing to the crown. The king reportedly sent de Praslin a small bottle of poison and a message that he should do the honorable thing and preserve the good image of the aristocracy by committing suicide. De Praslin not only drank the poison but broke up the bottle and swallowed the small shards of glass to make sure of his demise.

There were some bizarre sequels to this murder. Before her death, the duchess had had a recurrent nightmare, one she had described to friends and servants. She had dreamed of awakening to see the Devil standing over her, dressed in a shiny bright red costume, moving ominously toward her and then retreating until disappearing into a wall. Years after the duke and duchess were dead, one of their children found a bright red brocaded balmasque costume of Mephistopheles. The duke had apparently worn this on several occasions, appearing before his wife at night in an attempt to drive her insane, a condition which would have allowed him to divorce her.

Henriette Deluzy was also arrested and jailed for three months while Allard and other officers incessantly interviewed her. She repeatedly stated that she had had nothing to do with the murder of her employer the duchess, and Allard was finally convinced of her innocence and released her. Deluzy migrated to the U.S., settling in New York, where she later became the principal of the Female Art School. She married the Reverend Henry M. Field in 1851 and moved in high literary circles, becoming one of the most distinguished women in New York, although her past, on rare occasions, emerged to haunt her. At one high-society gathering at the Century Club, a Count Goureski, familiar with the de Praslin scandal, hissed repeatedly through his false teeth at Henriette Field, "Mur-der-ess! Mur-der-ess!" The elderly count was finally asked to leave or be thrown through a window.

Nathaniel Hawthorne, who lived near the Fields, learned of

Deluzy's scarlet past and, in *The Marble Faun,* based his mysterious character Miriam on her. When Henriette Field died in 1875, her funeral was attended by all the literary and high society lights of the city and her casket was borne to its grave by such luminaries as William Cullen Bryant and Peter Cooper. The famous diarist George Templeton Strong marked her passing, writing, "Died. Mrs. Henry Field...I knew her at one time quite well and she was universally liked, being uncommonly clever and cultivated. Her plainness made it incredible that the Duke de Praslin should have been in love with her."

REF.: Brock, *A Casebook of Crime;* CBA; Dunphy and Cummings, *Remarkable Trials;* Fouquier, *Causes Célèbres;* Hugo, *Things Seen;* Kobler, *Some Like It Gory;* Loomis, *A Crime of Passion;* Pearson, *Instigation of the Devil;* Wyndham, *Crime on the Continent;* (FICTION), Field, *All This and Heaven Too;* Shearing, *The Strange Case of Lucile Clery.*

Deputy, Martin (AKA: **Depew**), b.1895, and **Werner, Walter,** 1901- , and **Mele, Charles,** c.1900, and **Browning, William Lacy,** c.1900, U.S., kid. Martin Deputy, alias Depew, thirty-seven, was sentenced to life imprisonment for helping to kidnap Nell Quinlan Donnelly, wealthy head of a clothing company, and her chauffeur on Dec. 16, 1930. He and the other kidnapers demanded a ransom of $75,000 from her husband, threatening to blind his wife with acid and to kill the chauffeur if they were not obeyed.

Walter Werner, 31-year-old auto mechanic, also was sentenced to life in prison and Charles Mele, gambler, got a thirty-five year sentence, for their roles in the crime. William Lacy Browning, a Kansas farmer, would remain in prison for twenty-five years for arranging the use of the cottage where Donnelly was held captive.

Donnelly and her chauffeur were released after thirty-five hours of being held hostage by the men. No ransom was ever paid and police believe their release came as a result of pressure from local mob members who wanted no more publicity shed on their Kansas City operations. REF.: *CBA.*

de Rais, Gilles, See: **Rais, Gilles de.**

de Rana, Patas (AKA: **El Coyote**), prom. 1890s, U.S., west. gunman-outl. Patas de Rana was a member of the Forty Thieves Gang headed by the ruthless Vincente Silva who controlled Las Vegas, N.M., in the early 1890s. He was said to have been one of Silva's most trusted lieutenants until the outlaw chieftan shot his wife and the gang turned against him, electing de Rana to shoot Silva. It was also reported that Antonio Valdez, another top Silva gunman, did the actual shooting of Silva, but both shared the $10,000 reward for this feared outlaw leader. The gang later broke up and de Rana was imprisoned for a number of years before disappearing. See: **Silva, Vincente.**

REF.: Bartholomew, *The Biographical Album of Western Gunfighters;* CBA.

Deringer, Henry, 1786-1869, U.S., firearms inventor. Invented the derringer, which is a short-barreled pistol small enough to fit in a pocket, c.1852. REF.: *CBA.*

De Rosa, Anthony, d.1752, and **De Rosa, Emanuel,** prom. 1750, Brit., rob.-mur. On a June night in 1751 William Farques was returning to his London home after dining with an uncle. He never reached his destination. His body was found about midnight lying in the road a few yards from the Barking Dog pub; it was still warm. But the trail of his murderers was not only cold, it was nonexistent. Not until the day after Christmas when Emanuel De Rosa was arrested and charged with disorderly conduct was the case finally solved. De Rosa immediately confessed to the murder and implicated two accomplices. According to his confession, De Rosa along with Anthony De Rosa, who was not a relative, and a man known only as Fullagar were out looking for someone to rob when they spotted Farques near the Barking Dog. They demanded his money, and he answered that he had none. Fullagar struck him on the head with a club weighted with iron but Farques did not fall. Anthony De Rosa drew a knife and stabbed the already stunned Farques five or six times in the chest, and he fell to the ground mortally wounded. The other two robbers searched the fallen man and found that, although the victim had lied about having no money, he was not far from the truth. The murder produced the grand sum of eleven shillings to be split among three adult men.

To receive a lenient sentence, Emanuel De Rosa invited Anthony De Rosa to visit him while he was a prisoner in Bride-well. The killer arrived at the prison with the very knife that Emanuel De Rosa claimed had been used to murder Farques. He was quickly taken into custody, proclaiming his innocence. Anthony De Rosa produced two witnesses who insisted he was not at the scene of the crime, but these suspicious characters were disbelieved. De Rosa was sentenced to death and his alibi witnesses were charged with perjury. En route to the gallows Anthony De Rosa continued to cry out his innocence. He was nevertheless hanged at Tyburn on Mar. 23, 1752.

REF.: *CBA; The Newgate Calendar.*

de Rothschild, Leopold See: **Tebbitt, William.**

de Rougemont, Louis, prom. 1898, Brit., hoax. In 1898, a man calling himself Louis de Rougemont offered a London magazine the rights to his story of thirty years as a cannibal chieftain on an island off the northern coast of Australia. The magazine's editors checked out some details with geographers who knew the region, and got the approval to print the saga.

De Rougemont claimed that he had been shipwrecked alone in the late 1860s. He spent two years on the small island where he landed, surviving on tropical fruit, turtle, and fish. His life changed, however, when an aboriginal family—man, woman, and two children—were blown to the island in a storm. The five of them built a boat that took them to the island where the woman, called Yamba, had come from. There Yamba became his wife, and he led an idyllic existence—until he learned about the cannibalism. De Rougemont described the process the islanders used to cook their meals and the relish with which they tore apart the huge roasts and devoured them. The Englishman became king of the cannibals when they saw him kill a marauding alligator, though he wryly admitted to readers that it was pure accident. The king and Yamba decided to try to reach civilization. But on the way de Rougemont fell ill and Yamba, having to decide whether to care for him or their new baby, chose to kill and eat the infant. Somehow, Yamba disappeared before he returned to London.

As de Rougemont's tales grew more fantastic, the public began to question them. Finally, a rival newspaper discovered that the storyteller was actually a Swiss butler who had researched his tales in the British Museum. The story was suspended, but de Rougemont had had his day in the sun.

REF.: *CBA;* Mehling, *Scandalous Scamps.*

Déroulède, Paul, 1846-1914, Fr., consp.-banish. Involved in certain plans of overthrowing the government, 1899 and 1900, leading to his banishment for 10 years, for which he was given amnesty, 1905, and allowed to return to France. REF.: *CBA.*

Derrick, prom. early 1600s, Brit., execut. The first hangman to be recorded in history was an Elizabethan sailor named Derrick. Condemned to die, along with twenty shipmates, for a rape, Derrick got off by volunteering to hang all of his cohorts. Apparently he did such a good job of hanging them over the side of the ship that he was appointed public executioner afterwards. Believed to have executed Guy Fawkes, along with his conspirators, after they tried to blow up Parliament. Derrick's name lives on, used today to identify a type of crane that has a horizontal beam and dangling rope, similar to the instrument which the executioner used to hang his comrades. His assistant, Gregory Brandon, was given the title of "Esquire" as a joke when, in 1616, the Garter King of Arms granted Brandon a coat of arms in order to confuse the York Herald. Long after the joke, Brandon kept the title, which was claimed by other executioners for some time afterwards. See: **Brandon, Gregory; Fawkes, Guy.**

REF.: Atholl, *Shadow of the Gallows;* Bleackley, *Hangmen of England; CBA;* Laurence, *A History of Capital Punishment;* Potter, *The Art of Hanging.*

Dershowitz, Alan, 1938- , U.S., crim. law. One of the most passionate defenders of First Amendment rights, Alan Dershowitz

has been "the lawyer of last resort" in notable cases involving pornography, murder, and civil rights. Born in 1938, Dershowitz grew up in the Boro Park section of Brooklyn and graduated *magna cum laude* from Brooklyn College in 1959. In 1962, he graduated first in his law school class at Yale, after serving as editor of the *Yale Law Review.* He turned down an immediate appointment to the faculty of Harvard Law School to become a clerk for David Bazelon, the chief judge of the U.S. Court of Appeals in Washington, D.C. A year later, Dershowitz served U.S. Supreme Court Justice Arthur Goldberg in the same capacity. In 1964, Dershowitz accepted the Harvard offer. Three years later, 28-year-old Dershowitz became the youngest tenured law professor in Harvard's history. A year later, he taught a non-credit course on the legal issues surrounding the Viet Nam War.

Dershowitz joined the American Civil Liberties Union and emerged as a highly visible advocate of civil freedoms, defending Benjamin Spock's participation in the anti-war movement, as well as several Harvard students facing expulsion for similar charges. In 1972, Dershowitz counseled William Kunstler in the appeal of the "Chicago Seven" conviction, and defended both leftist professor Bruce Franklin and reactionary William Shockley in a case testing the government's right to limit free speech for reasons of national security. In 1977, he tested the same principle in the case of Frank Snepp, a former CIA official who wrote of secrets of the Viet Nam War. In 1969, Dershowitz had successfully defended the release of a sexually explicit film, the Swedish-made *I Am Curious (Yellow),* earning a dismissal after the Supreme Court refused to hear the case. In 1976, he defended a porn star charged with conspiracy to transport an obscene film in interstate commerce.

As a criminal lawyer, Dershowitz successfully defended Sheldon Seigel, a member of the Jewish Defense League accused of bombing the office of impresario Sol Hurok. In 1974, Dershowitz traveled to the Soviet Union as a member of a defense team for fourteen Russian Jews and two others accused of skyjacking a plane to Sweden. The effort earned the early release and subsequent migration to Israel for many of the accused. Dershowitz is best known for his successful appeal in the 1982 case of Claus von Bulow. The Rhode Island socialite had been sentenced to thirty years for attempting to murder his heiress wife with a fatal injection of insulin. The case was overturned in April 1984, after Dershowitz argued that von Bulow had been the victim of an illegal search, and the withholding of notes and medical evidence by the prosecution. Dershowitz, the author of several books and articles including *The Best Defense* and *Reversal of Fortune,* concedes that most of his clients are guilty of the crimes for which they are charged. However, he considers their defense a professional obligation because it protects constitutional rights for all citizens. See: **Von Bulow, Claus.** REF.: *CBA.*

Derues, Antoine Francois (AKA: **Derues de Cyrano de Bury, Lord of Candeville, Beaupré, Ducouday**), 1744-77, Fr., mur. Antoine Francois Derues, a simple Parisian grocer and failed moneylender, murdered a woman and her son in his efforts to become a gentleman.

Although deeply in debt to numerous creditors, Derues bought the estate of Etienne Saint-Faust de Lamotte at Buisson-Souef in December 1775. Derues had passed off himself and his wife Marie Louise Nicolais, whom he married in 1772, as heirs to great fortunes. He claimed Nicolais was to inherit a small sum from the estate of the late Despeignes-Duplessis, who had been killed. He told friends that his wife's last name was Nicolai, the name of a very wealthy French family. Derues' ability to convince people of his higher position in life made it possible to dupe the de Lamottes out of their estate for 130,000 livres, a sum he could never afford. The agreement called for settling the sale in June 1776, but on Dec. 16, with the sale still not complete, Mme. de Lamotte and her son arrived in Paris to finish the business with the grocer. She soon became ill and under the care of Derues, who was poisoning her, she died—a fact he concealed from the public as part of his plan to take control of Buisson-Souef without paying for it.

Derues believed that the only way to obtain the de Lamotte estate was for it to appear as though Mme. de Lamotte had finished the sale and then run off with a former lover, taking the money he had paid her. After killing the woman on Feb. 1, 1777, he conveyed her in a large trunk to a vacant cellar, where posing as a man named M. Ducourday he buried her, claiming the body to be bottles of wine. He then killed the boy in the same manner, taking the 14-year-old to Versailles where he died Feb. 15 and was buried as the nephew of M. Beaupre, another assumed name. The grocer now could spread the story of the woman running off and he could claim the estate. Unfortunately for Derues, the story was not believed, even after he posed as the dead woman in Lyons on Mar. 7, forging her signature a second time. Derues was arrested when handwriting experts declared the documents of sale to be forgeries and his wife was arrested in April after she too failed to impersonate Mme. de Lamotte. On Apr. 18 the dead woman's body was discovered and examined, along with her son's body which was exhumed on Apr. 23, and it was proven that she and her son were murdered with a corrosive poison.

At the trial on Apr. 30, 1777, Derues was found Guilty and sentenced to death. Torturing him on May 6 by confining his legs in wood and then driving wedges into his flesh did not bring about a confession; nor did he confess later at Notre Dame, though he did profess that his wife was not a party to his wrongs. He was placed naked, except for a shirt, on the wheel at the Place de Grève, where he then had his bones broken with an iron bar before being thrown alive into a fire. Derues' ashes were then scattered by the winds and caught by the souvenir-seeking crowd. His wife was at first charged only with forgery, but was freed in February 1779 when experts agreed it was not her doing. De Lamotte, however, believed Nicolais was guilty of conspiracy in his wife's death, and saw to it that she was tried accordingly. In March 1779 she was found Guilty and sentenced to be flogged, branded with a V, (indicating *voleuse* or voluptuary) on both shoulders, and was sentenced to life in prison. Nicolais never completed the sentence—though she mysteriously gave birth to a second child in prison two months later—for the Salpetriere Prison was overrun by revolutionaries on Sept. 4, 1792, and she was murdered.

REF.: *CBA; Irving, A Book of Remarkable Criminals.*

de Sade, Marquis, See: **Sade, Donatien Alphonse Francois, comte de.**

DeSalvo, Albert Henry (AKA: **The Boston Strangler, The Green Man, The Measuring Man**), 1931-73, U.S., rob.-rape-mur. Between June 1962 and January 1964, thirteen Boston-area women were sexually assaulted and then strangled to death by a fiend the press dubbed the "Boston Strangler." This man proved to be Albert Henry DeSalvo. Born in Chelsea, Mass., in 1931, DeSalvo was one of six children. His father was a severe taskmaster who beat him and the other children over the smallest infraction. He did not spare his wife either, using his fists on the poor, overworked woman whenever he was displeased. DeSalvo's father was also criminally bent and served two prison terms for theft before his wife divorced him in 1944. Like his father, DeSalvo began stealing when in his teens, and was charged with breaking and entering several times before joining the army at age seventeen. He served in the occupation forces in Germany, where he began boxing on a U.S. army team. Small, but squat and tough, DeSalvo became the U.S. Army welterweight and, while stationed in Frankfurt, met and married a petite German girl.

Returning to the U.S. with his new wife, DeSalvo was stationed at Fort Dix, N.J., where, in January 1955, he was charged with molesting a 9-year-old girl, his first sex offense. The child's mother, fearing publicity would affect her daughter, refused to prosecute. The Army, therefore, had no case against DeSalvo and released him. He received an honorable discharge a short time later and moved back to Boston with his wife. DeSalvo worked as a handyman and he and his wife had two small children. DeSalvo's sex drive was almost overwhelming. He exhausted his

wife Irmgard, who told him to control himself. DeSalvo demanded sex from her on an almost non-stop basis. "Five or six times a day don't mean much to me," he later stated. Finally, Irmgard told her husband, "Al, you can learn by yourself to control yourself. It is just a matter of self-control."

When it came to sex, however, DeSalvo had no control. He thought about sex night and day, according to his later admissions, and he found little release. He was arrested for breaking and entering and given a suspended sentence in 1958 and a short time later he embarked on a sexual game whereby he became known to the police as "Measuring Man." DeSalvo approached young, attractive women in their apartments, telling them he represented a modeling agency and that they had been selected as possible candidates for modeling in television commercials. If chosen, they could make considerable money and would become famous, and they might even be offered a movie contract. Hundreds of young women opened their apartment doors to him after hearing this pitch and DeSalvo, clipboard and tape measure in hand, would then measure the woman's vital statistics. At these times DeSalvo would not make overt sexual approaches but he did seduce a number of these gullible females. He later claimed that many of the would-be models, however, seduced *him* and invited him back.

On Mar. 17, 1960, Cambridge, Mass., police responded to an alarm of a break-in and they chased and caught DeSalvo. He had thrown away a screwdriver which he had been using to force apartment door locks, but this was recovered. On his person was found a pair of gloves and a tailor's measuring tape. He admitted that he was the "Measuring Man" about which the police had received scores of complaints. DeSalvo received a two-year sentence for breaking and entering and was released in ten months. The police did not list him as a sexual deviant, but put him on their list of potential burglars. When DeSalvo was released from prison, he returned to his family, but he now became more aggressive, breaking into apartments and tying up and raping females. He was described by his victims as the "Green Man" since he wore green work pants and shirt. DeSalvo later bragged that he tied up and raped six women in one morning. Moreover, he ranged throughout New England, assaulting, according to police in Massachusetts and Connecticut, hundreds of women. DeSalvo put the number at more than 1,000.

In the summer of 1962, DeSalvo began to add murder to his sexual attacks, raping and strangling his victims, the first of whom was 55-year-old Anna Slesers, found in her apartment on Gainsborough Street in Boston, her body placed in a lascivious position. DeSalvo had used a cord to strangle his victim and had tied the ends in a bow beneath her chin, a technique he would continue to employ, as if it were his trademark. Within two weeks, DeSalvo attacked and killed 85-year-old Mary Mullen, a victim he later reluctantly talked about since she reminded him of his grandmother. On June 30, 1962, DeSalvo raped and strangled Helen Blake, a 65-year-old nurse. Next was Nina Nichols, a woman in her sixties. She fought her attacker, digging her nails into his arms as he strangled her from behind.

On Aug. 19, 1962, DeSalvo raped and strangled 75-year-old Ida Irga. Jane Sullivan, sixty-seven, died at DeSalvo's hands the next day. Boston police were inundated with demands to solve the rash of horrible rape-murders. Though scores of sexual deviants were arrested and questioned, DeSalvo escaped attention. DeSalvo refrained from making more attacks until Dec. 5, 1962, his wedding anniversary. He later claimed that then, as on former attacks, he became obsessed with the image of violent sex, that the top of his head "was so hot that I thought it would explode." He spotted an attractive girl entering an apartment and followed her. DeSalvo knocked on her door and employed the usual technique that invariably gained him access to an apartment, saying through the door that he was a repair man sent by the landlord to check the pipes and toilet. The girl, however, refused to let him inside. He went to another apartment and knocked on the door. Inside was 25-year-old Sophie Clark, a tall, attractive black woman. She opened the door a crack and DeSalvo per-

Top row, left to right, Albert DeSalvo, the infamous Boston Strangler, 1967; Desalvo victims Helen E. Blake and Ida Irga. Middle row, left to right, Joann Graf, Patricia Bissette, Sophie Clark, and Mary A. Sullivan. Bottom right, DeSalvo under arrest in Boston.

suaded her to open the door, saying that he was from a modeling company, using his old Measuring Man technique. As he walked inside the apartment, Clark turned her back on DeSalvo, who later reported that he was stunned by her curvacious body. He leaped on her from behind, subduing her, raping her and strangling her, leaving her as he had the others, her naked body propped upward, legs spread, the bow tied beneath the cord he had used to strangle her.

His next victim was Patricia Bissette, a 23-year-old secretary he had visited years earlier as Measuring Man. On Dec. 8, 1962, she invited him inside, gave him a cup of coffee and, when she turned her back, he placed his arm around her throat and then raped her, strangling her with her own nylons. On Feb. 16, 1963, DeSalvo gained entrance to the apartment of a woman who was home sick. He attacked her, but she fought so desperately, scratching him and biting him while screaming out for help, that DeSalvo fled. (This woman, whose identity is withheld, proved that by ignoring quiet submission to the rapist, as is often counseled, she had saved her life.) On Mar. 9, 1963, 69-year-old Mary Brown allowed DeSalvo into her apartment, thinking him a workman sent by the landlord to fix her stove.

This time DeSalvo's violence was unchecked. He had brought along a lead pipe, which he used to crush his victim's head. He raped Brown *after* killing her. He then drove a fork into her breast several times, leaving it embedded in the flesh. He also strangled her, although, by that time, she was dead. On May 6, 1963, instead of driving to work, DeSalvo drove to Cambridge, "on an impulse" he later said, and there spotted pretty Beverly Samans, a 23-year-old undergraduate living on University Road. He gained entrance to her apartment, tying her to bedposts. He then blindfolded and gagged her and then repeatedly raped her. DeSalvo used the girl's nylon stockings to strangle her. Before leaving his victim, DeSalvo got out his jackknife and began stabbing the girl. The autopsy reported twenty-two stab wounds. DeSalvo later stated, "Once I stabbed her, I couldn't stop. I kept hitting her and hitting her with that knife...She kept bleeding from the throat...I hit her and hit her and hit her..." His savage bloodlust exhausted, DeSalvo walked into the kitchen, wiped off the handle of the knife and dropped it into the sink. When found by police, this knife offered no fingerprints.

DeSalvo's eleventh victim was 58-year-old Evelyn Corbin, whom he strangled and raped on Sept. 8, 1963. When Corbin failed to make an appointment, police were summoned and they found the woman as they had the others, except that she had been manually strangled. The killer had left his trademark, a nylon with a bow, tied about her ankle. Boston police seemed helpless to catch the killer. The city was in a near panic with thousands of husbands constantly calling their wives or staying home from work to protect them against a fiend who seemed to come and go at will. Not a single person reported seeing this mass killer and police were admittedly stymied.

A special "Strangler Bureau" was set up and a dedicated detective force began running down the slimmest clues around the clock. Dozens of sex offenders, muggers, and even peeping toms were rounded up, questioned, and subsequently released. At one point, the brilliant medium, Peter Hurkos, was brought into the case. He examined a number of personal items belonging to suspects and gave an startling and somewhat accurate description of the killer, although he never pinpointed DeSalvo or any other person as the Boston Strangler. A number of good suspects were kept under surveillance, but proved innocent. On Nov. 23, 1963, a day following President John F. Kennedy's assassination in Dallas, Texas, DeSalvo struck again, gaining entrance to the apartment of Joann Graff, a 23-year-old dress designer. He raped and strangled her with her own black leotards, tying these in a bow about her neck. Following the killing, DeSalvo went home, helped his wife clean up their apartment, played with his children, watched a television news report, and then sat down to dinner. DeSalvo had watched a television report on the death of Joann Graff. He later stated, "I knew it was me who did it but why I

did it and everything else, I don't know...I wasn't excited. I didn't think about it. I sat down to dinner and didn't think about it at all."

On Jan. 4, 1964, DeSalvo struck for the last time, claiming his thirteenth victim, 19-year-old Mary Sullivan. Once inside her apartment, he flourished a knife, tied up the girl, and raped her. He then strangled her with his hands. He left her naked and, as a bizarre afterthought, inserted a broom into her and placed a card he found in the apartment between her toes which read, "Happy New Year." In Fall 1964, a young woman reported being sexually assaulted in her apartment, describing a man police identified as DeSalvo, using the same technique as DeSalvo had when labeled the Measuring Man. DeSalvo was arrested for breaking and entering, held on a $100,000 bond, and sent to the mental institution at Bridgewater. Amazingly, police never coupled DeSalvo with the crimes of the Boston Strangler. Officials later stated that DeSalvo's police rap sheet listed him only as a felon guilty of breaking and entering. Police records revealed nothing of his sexual offenses.

At Bridgewater, DeSalvo claimed that he was hearing voices and he was diagnosed by psychiatrists as "schizophrenic." On Feb. 4, 1965, he was ordered to be detained indeterminately by Judge Edward A. Pecce. Another inmate at Bridgewater, George Nassar, who had killed a garage attendant and who was himself a suspect in the Strangler killings, met DeSalvo and, after listening to him talk for some time, mostly about sex and violence, came to believe DeSalvo was the Boston Strangler. He informed his young lawyer, F. Lee Bailey, and Bailey interviewed DeSalvo, recording his conversations. DeSalvo admitted being the Strangler and even added two killings to the known murder count of thirteen. More importantly, DeSalvo related facts about the murders which the police had kept secret, the positioning of the naked bodies, the tying of bows in the strangling cords, nylons, and pantyhose, the wounds inflicted, all the sordid details that only the killer would have known.

Police were still puzzled since they had no eyewitness who could positively identify DeSalvo. Bailey was convinced that DeSalvo was the killer and said so, but officials were disinclined to officially prosecute DeSalvo as a mental patient. DeSalvo was kept in confinement and the strangulation murders stopped. Most reliable authorities considered DeSalvo the Boston Strangler, including court authorities who transferred DeSalvo to the Walpole State Prison where, in his cell, on Nov. 26, 1973, he was found dead, stabbed to death in his heart.

REF.: Boar, *The World's Most Infamous Murders;* Cartel, *Serial Mass Murder; CBA;* Fox, *Mass Murder;* Frank, *The Boston Strangler;* Godwin, *Murder U.S.A.;* Gribble, *The Dead End Killers;* Lustgarten, *The Illustrated Story of Crime;* Nash, *Murder, America;* Wilson, *Encyclopedia of Modern Murder;* (FILM), *The Strangler,* 1964; *The Boston Strangler,* 1968.

Descamps, Édouard Eugène François, 1847-1933, Belg., jur. The baron was a member of the Hague Tribunal. REF.: *CBA.*

Deschamps, Etienne, 1830-92, U.S., mur. Motivated by his lustful urges, Etienne Deschamps concocted an absurd story in order to dupe a superstitious New Orleans carpenter, Jules Deitsch, into surrendering his 12-year-old daughter, Juliette. Deschamps told Deitsch that he could locate the buried treasure of the New Orleans pirate Jean Lafitte by conjuring up his spirit through the body of a virgin girl. On Jan. 30, 1889, Juliette and her 9-year-old sister Laurence were sent to the Deschamps residence for the first of the "occult experiments."

Deschamps was born in Rennes in 1830. He was wounded at the Battle of Sevastapol during the Crimean War. In 1870, following a brief career in politics, Deschamps was exiled because of his extreme views, and traveled to Brazil and then to New Orleans where he founded a French colony.

To Deitsch, who believed in magnetic physiology—skills that the wily Deschamps claimed to possess—the story of Lafitte's pirate treasure seemed plausible enough that he was willing to lend his eldest daughter to the scheme. After months of very careful planning and seduction, the experiment went awry on Jan.

30. Deschamps had placed a chloroformed handkerchief over Juliette's face and asked her what she saw. "God, the Holy Virgin, and Jackson Square," Juliette replied. Deschamps administered more chloroform, but soon realized that he had given the girl an overdose. He sent the 9-year-old Laurence home to her father with the message that he, Deschamps, was going to die. When Deitsch arrived, he found Deschamps lying next to Juliette. He had tried unsuccessfully to kill himself with a dental instrument.

Deschamps was arraigned for murder and went on trial Apr. 29, 1889. A few days later, while in a New Orleans jail cell, Deschamps again attempted suicide. After two days he was found Guilty. An appeal was taken to the Supreme Court on the grounds that the defense did not have sufficient time to prepare its case. A second trial commenced on Mar. 28, 1890. In the interim, Deschamps became violent, unruly, and threatened that if he were ever to return to France, he would see to it that the government declare war on the U.S. for the outrage.

Deschamps was found Guilty in his second trial, and was ordered to hang. On Apr. 19, 1891, the day the execution was to be carried out, Robert H. Marr, the judge who had presided over both of the Deschamps murder trials mysteriously vanished on his way to vote in a local election. Marr was never seen again, and people began to wonder if there was any connection to Deschamps. Late that night the Lieutenant Governor sent notice that Deschamps had been given a temporary reprieve while the medical authorities debated his sanity. However, on May 12, 1892, Deschamps finally went to the gallows.

REF.: *CBA*; Tallant, *Ready To Hang*; Wilson, *Encyclopedia of Murder*.

de Scotiney, Sir **Walter**, prom. 1230, Brit., mur. The main counselor of the Earl of Gloucester was convicted along with Sir Walter de Scotiney of poisoning the Abbot of Westminster and William Gloucester, brother of the Earl, who narrowly escaped death himself.

During the meeting of Parliament convened by King Henry III at Westminster in 1230, both the Abbot of Westminster and William Gloucester died from ingesting poison, said to have been given to them at the breakfast table of Lord Edward, King Henry's eldest son. The Earl of Gloucester also was poisoned at this time but, due to his strong constitution, survived the attempted assassination. He did, however, lose all of his hair and nails and many of his teeth. The crime was believed to be the work of Sir Walter de Scotiney, Chief Councillor and administrator of the Earl of Gloucester. At the request of the Countess de L'Isle, Scotiney was arrested, apprehended in London at the end of February. Also arrested and charged was William de Bussey who, according to a chronicler of the time, had committed "villainies if related must excite horror and astonishment." William de Bussey was the principal councillor and adviser of William de Valence. Both men were brought before judges to be sent to jail and kept in chains until they were tried the following year. Scotiney was convicted, condemned, and executed.

REF.: *CBA*; Thompson, *Poison and Poisoners*.

Desgrandschamps, Charles (AKA: **Charlot les-grands-pieds, Bigfooted Charlie**), d.1947, Fr., rob.-mur. Charles Desgrandschamps was a moderately successful thief. Not only was he known for concealing a 6.35-mm automatic pistol in his hat's wire frame, but he was involved, along with Emile Buisson, in the first holdup employing a front-wheel drive car, a Citroen Traction, as a getaway vehicle. The robbery occurred on Dec. 27, 1937, when Buisson and Desgrandschamps held up two bank couriers outside the Troyes branch of the Banque de France.

In July 1947, Desgrandschamps attempted his first robbery of an expensive restaurant. Joining were Dubois, Foncard, and Vidal. Before the robbery, the four men did a great deal of drinking, and thus arrived at the Cafe des Gourmets later than they had hoped. Desgrandschamps informed the waiter, Jacques Becker, of their intent, at which Becker swung at the gangster with an iron bar, causing Desgrandschamps, to fire his gun and kill another waiter, Leveque. When the iron bar hit Desgrandschamps, he fired again, this time shooting his comrade Dubois in the kneecap, an injury

which caused him to pull the trigger on the Sten submachine gun he was holding. Dubois unfortunately had the gun pointed at his leader, emptying at least one-half of the twenty-round magazine into Desgrandschamps. Realizing things were not going well, the gangsters fled the cafe, driving off while Becker fired shots from the restaurant owner's gun after them.

Three hours later, the dying Desgrandschamps was dropped off outside the Boucicaut Hospital by his three confederates. Police later discovered that the man was the same Desgrandschamps who was sentenced to prison thirteen times and who had been sentenced to death in absentia for giving aid to the Nazis during WWII.

REF.: *CBA*; Goodman, *Villainy Unlimited*.

Desha, Isaac B., prom. 1825, U.S., mur. Isaac B. Desha was the arrogant, spoiled son of the governor of Kentucky, a thoroughly disreputable and amoral young man who impulsively insulted his elders and peers, beat slaves at a whim, and made life generally impossible for all who encountered him. A wealthy landowner, Francis Baker, who was traveling through Kentucky en route to his home in Natchez, Miss., met Desha on the road. Baker told Desha he was lost and Desha said that he knew a comfortable place to sleep for the night and in the morning, he could resume his journey with the proper guides. Baker followed Desha down a lonely road where the youth turned on him, beating him unconscious with a club, and then cutting his throat. Desha was later found with some of Baker's goods, and he was arrested and twice tried, condemned each time. Before Desha was hanged, his father intervened and pardoned him in one of the most flagrant misuses of governmental authority.

REF.: *A Statement of the Trial of Isaac B. Desha*; *CBA*; Johnson, *Famous Kentucky Tragedies and Trials*.

Deshayes, Catherine (AKA: **La Voisin**), d.1680, Fr., witchcraft-mur. The reign of King Louis XIV of France, the Sun King, was a period of great excess—in style, in food, in love, in obsession with the occult—and in murder, much of it done by poison with the assistance of the self-styled witch called La Voisin, whose real name was Catherine Deshayes. This dramatic hag of a woman probably murdered or provided the means to murder thousands of people during the 1670s in Paris, culminating in an attempt, paid for by the king's mistress, the Marquise de Montespan, to kill the king himself.

When young Catherine Deshayes's husband, Antoine Monvoisin, failed in business, Catherine developed a small business as a seer, telling people's fortunes. She earned enough to buy a cottage of her own. Her clients spread the word about her fortunes, which brought customers of higher quality to her cottage. Gradually, she developed a sideline: providing the means for murder. When people asked when their spouses would die so that they could marry someone else, La Voisin provided them the poison to ensure their partners' deaths. Aristocrats began to indulge in this practice, and La Voisin, calling herself an alchemist, became known as the prime provider of reliable poisons.

La Voisin soon added witchcraft to her repertoire. She invited aristocrats to Black Masses, held with the help of a defrocked priest. During the dramatic ceremonies, participants gave themselves to the devil. When de Montespan, the king's mistress and mother of seven of his children, began to fear the loss of her position, she too became a devotee, seeking a guarantee of fidelity on the part of the king and death to those who sought to replace her. De Montespan took part in the Black Masses, sometimes serving as the naked living altar over which infants were slain to provide warm blood to drink. La Voisin herself threw the dead babies into a fire.

La Voisin was the object of passions, too. She had a variety of lovers who satisfied her bizarre needs with public displays of sadism, beatings of her hapless husband, and orgies. She came to feel invulnerable, capable of anything, even killing the king. When the priests of St. Vincent De Paul and police lieutenant Nicolas De la Reynie began to investigate her activities, de Montespan feared they were actually working for the king, who wanted a new mistress. She decided to retaliate, and paid La Voisin 100,000 gold crowns to poison him. The witch planned to present the king with a petition written on poisoned paper.

On Mar. 5, 1679, the sorceress failed to get the paper directly into the king's own hands, so she determined to try again a week later. But one of her thousands of customers told the authorities about the plot, and De la Reynie's men broke into her home and arrested her. The witch talked freely of everything except the names of her aristocratic clients. But her daughter, Marguerite Monvoisin, readily listed them all. King Louis called a special court of justice, the Chambre Ardente, before which 442 persons appeared. Thirty-six of these were executed, none of whom were aristocrats. Twenty-six aristocrats were instead banished from the court. Well over 200 people were sent to prison. The king granted de Montespan a personal interview, during which she displayed her hysteria. Rather than endanger the royal succession by executing her, the king banished her to a distant castle.

An artist's conception of Catherine Deshayes, mass poisoner and convicted witch.

As for Catherine Deshayes, or La Voisin, she was tortured in almost every way available to her jailers, but she only laughed. The witch's tongue was cut out, and she was burned alive at the stake on Feb. 22, 1680.

REF.: *CBA;* Nash, *Look For the Woman;* Summers, *The Geography of Witchcraft;* Thompson, *Poison and Poisoners;* Wilson, *Witches;* (DRAMA), Sardou, *L'Affaire des Poisons;*

De Sigoyer, Alain de Bernardi, See: **Bernardy, Sigoyer de.**

De Silva, Charles Percival, prom. 1947-73, Brit., fraud-suic. Originally from Ceylon, with a good education and a wealthy grandfather, Charles Percival De Silva came to England in 1947. A gracious, intelligent man, he spent a quarter of a century either defrauding wealthy, gullible society people, or spending time in jail for his scams, which he referred to as "one of my little games." Operating primarily out of London's fashionable West End, De

Silva became known and respected by members of London's wealthy establishment whom he would eventually swindle out of about £3 million. In 1951, he spent his first term in jail, sentenced for attempting to swindle Selfridge's store out of more than £2,000 in nylons, a then scarce commodity. Released from jail, De Silva talked about a £200,000 plot he was involved in to supply guns for overthrowing General Francisco Franco, but a few months after these boasts the confidence man was declared bankrupt, in debt for £109,000. De Silva then found a "mug"—this was how he referred to wealthy people he could bilk—who was impressed by social connections and, getting an invitation to a party held by the prestigious Lady Dorothy Macmillan, gave her a large check for one of her favorite charities, impressing the wealthy "mug" sufficiently to get her to invest large amounts in fraudulent schemes soon after.

On another occasion De Silva met an American multimillionaire who had a penchant for young girls. Organizing a team of prostitutes, all dressed as schoolgirls, De Silva threw a party for the American, convincing him that the young ladies had been provided by the Mother Superior of a convent school; the millionaire wrote a check for £25,000 to be paid to the nonexistent Mother Superior. Jailed for six years for trying to sell £700,000 worth of fictitious trawlers from Ceylon to Sweden, De Silva was also linked with the theft of three Old Masters from Amsterdam, a heist that netted £600,000, and of trying to sell forged plates for counterfeiting £1 and 10 shilling notes. In 1973, faced with the prospect of yet another trial the following month at the Old Bailey, he booked into an elegant Euston hotel under a false name and committed suicide, overdosing on drugs.

REF.: Borrell, *Crime In Britain Today; CBA.*

Desmettre, Pierre, d.c.1875, Fr., execut. Prior to the French Revolution in the towns of Douai and Saint-Omer, the art of torture was practiced by a family deeply rooted in the profession. But after the revolution a new family tradition was begun when Pierre Desmettre took over the position of executioner from his brother, Louis Desmettre, who was summarily dismissed. During his career Desmettre always had Mass said for the person he would execute that day. He performed executions until he was forced to retire at the age of fifty-five. He reportedly went insane in his retirement.

REF.: *CBA;* Lenotre, *The Guillotine and Its Servants.*

Desmoulins, Camille (Lucie Simplice Camille Benoit; AKA: Procureur de la lanterne), 1760-94, Fr., treas. Stirred up crowds, July 12, 1789, following the dismissal of Jacques Necker the previous day, which inevitably led to the start of the French Revolution and the storming of the Bastille two days later. Along with Georges Jacques Danton, he was arrested and executed by Maximilien Robespierre after a mock trial; two weeks later his wife, Lucille Duplessis, was also guillotined. REF.: *CBA.*

Desnoyers, Guy, prom. 1956, Fr., mur. To avoid a scandal, Father Guy Desnoyers decided it would be best to kill the girl he had impregnated and her unborn child.

As the priest of the small town of Uruffe, France, in the province of Lorraine, Desnoyers was still rather young and greatly attracted to the village's young women. Such was the case of 19-year-old Régine Fay, who was noticeably pregnant in the fall of 1956. Fay decided against leaving home to have the baby or having an abortion—a decision which greatly concerned the priest, who feared the child might have features similar to his and thus tarnish his name. On Dec. 2, 1956, Desnoyers told his parishioners that he would be out of town for a few days. However, he returned two nights later to keep an appointment he had made with Fay. Desnoyers claims he attempted to absolve Fay of her sins. But upon her refusal, he killed her. The priest shot her through the back of the neck, and then proceeded with a grotesque mutilation which he declared was in keeping with his religious faith. He took a pocketknife and slit open the girl's abdomen, and then after further slashing her, Desnoyers baptized the child he had ripped from Fay and proceeded to destroy any likeness to him the baby might have had. Later that evening, Desnoyers conducted the search for the missing girl and was the leader of the party which discovered her body.

Police soon discovered that the bullet that killed Fay was of the same caliber as the 6.35-mm gun owned by Desnoyers, and with the discovery of a blood-stained handkerchief, the priest confessed. Although the prosecution sought the death penalty, the jury found him Guilty with extenuating circumstances, and the President of the Nancy Court, Judge Louis Facq, sentenced Desnoyers to life in prison.

REF.: *CBA;* Gribble, *The Deadly Professionals;* Heppenstall, *The Sex War and Others.*

de Soto, Benito, prom. 1827, Spain, pir.-rape-mur. When Benito de Soto seized a Portuguese slave ship, he renamed it the *Black Joke* and took off on a cruise that was the most notorious pirate event of that era.

Hired in 1827 to be mate on the *Defensor de Pedro,* Benito de Soto gained control of the slaver ship which was sailing from Buenos Aires, while the captain was on shore. He turned non-mutineers adrift in a small dingy, and took off with the ship which he renamed the *Black Joke.* Within a few weeks, the pirate crew captured an East Indian ship, the *Morning Star,* raped the wives and daughters of soldiers and seamen traveling home on leave, and put other passengers and officials in the hold to drown as water slowly seeped into the damaged hull. The *Black Joke* pillaged and looted several other ships in and around the Azore Islands, slaughtering many of the passengers. East Indian ships were instructed to collect at St. Helena and travel in convoy. At La Coruña, de Soto's birthplace, the pirate obtained false papers and took off for Cadiz, hoping to dispose of his spoils there. When the *Black Joke* was wrecked on rocks near Cadiz, de Soto and his crew posed as honest seamen whose captain had been drowned. The wreck was about to be sold for salvage when some drunken pirates talked too much and arrests were made. De Soto escaped to Gibraltar, where he was soon arrested, tried, and hanged.

REF.: *CBA;* Mitchell, *Pirates.*

Desouches, Thierry, c.1952-63, Fr., (unsolv.) kid.-mur. Thierry Desouches was eleven years old when he was kidnapped in May 1963. The boy's body was found in Paris, but the kidnappers and murderers were never brought to justice.

REF.: *CBA;* Heppenstall, *The Sex War and Others.*

Despard, Edward Marcus, d.1803, Brit., treas. For being the leader of a plot to assassinate King George III, Colonel Edward Marcus Despard was convicted of high treason, along with six accomplices, and sentenced to be hanged and drawn and quartered. This sentence was later changed to his being hanged and beheaded. He was executed on Feb. 21, 1803, on the roof of Horsemonger Lane Jail, also called the New Jail in the Borough.

On the day of the execution, each convicted man was placed in a cart without wheels and dragged by horses to the gallows. Despard went last and alone. Executioner William Brunskill allowed the prisoners to hang for an hour before a masked man, perhaps a surgeon, severed their heads. As each head was removed, Brunskill lifted it up for the crowd to see and called out, "This is the head of a traitor."

REF.: Bleackley, *Hangmen of England; CBA;* Laurence, *A History of Capital Punishment.*

Despenser, Hugh, 1262-1326, Brit., polit. corr.-consp. Restored as chief adviser to the king by Edward II, 1322, after he and his son had been expelled the year before. He was named Earl of Winchester by the king, 1322, captured by the baronial forces of Queen Isabella and hanged for his manipulation of the king. REF.: *CBA.*

Despenser, Hugh le, d.1265, Brit., (unsolv.) mur. Served as the last of the justiciaries of Britain, he was murdered at Evesham. REF.: *CBA.*

Despenser, Thomas, 1373-1400, Brit., consp. Implicated in the death of the Duke of Gloucester, and betrayed and beheaded for his complicity in the conspiracy against Henry IV. REF.: *CBA.*

de Sperati, Jean, prom. 1954, Fr., count. As a young collector of stamps, Jean de Sperati had been stuck with a fake stamp; enraged, he decided to show up all stamp experts as frauds, and involved himself intensively and exhaustively in becoming an expert at printing, inking, gumming, plating, and perforating stamps. By 1911, at age twenty-seven, Sperati's first fakes appeared in Berlin, heralding his forty-three year career in stamp forgery. In 1944, he was arrested for the first time, charged with trying to export capital and eventually fined 300,000 francs, the exact price of the stamps he had sent to Lisbon from France. When Sperati was able to prove that the stamps were forged, he received a suspended one-year jail sentence for fraud, and philatelists everywhere panicked. By 1954, the total number of known Sperati fakes in the world was set at 558, and growing. The fifteen million anxious dealers and stamp collectors of the world were in an uproar when the British Philatic Association (BPA), dedicated to "the protection and help of all interested in stamp collecting," stepped in. Negotiating with the 69-year old Sperati at his Aix-les-Bains home, the BPA bought him out, purchasing all of his stock, inks, dyes, proofs, and papers, for the alleged sum of $15,000. Sperati had made over 500 stamps in his career, with an estimated total value of more than $5 million. His expertise was so great that he repeatedly was called in to court trials as the only unassailable expert to determine when materials were forgeries. Sperati's stamps can probably be found in many of the finest collections in the world.

REF.: *CBA;* McGuire, *The Forgers.*

Dessalines, Jean Jacques, 1758-1806, Haiti, emperor, assass. The former slave gave aid to Toussaint L'Ouverture in the rebellion against French authority on Haiti, 1797. He was forced to surrender to the French led by Charles Leclerc, 1802, but with support of the British was able to expel the French, 1803. Dessalines established a republic and proclaimed himself Emperor Jacques I, 1804-06. He was assassinated by Henri Christophe and Alexandre Sabès Pétion.

REF.: *CBA;* (DRAMA), O'Neill, *The Emperor Jones;* (FILM), *The Emperor Jones,* 1933.

de Stamir, Victor (AKA: **Victor Stamirowski),** prom. 1918, Brit., rob.-mur. One morning in November 1917, a maid discovered Captain Tighe lying in a pool of blood in his room at Winkfield Lodge, Wimbledon Common. Tighe was taken to the hospital, where he died four days later, never regaining consciousness. Chief Inpector William Gough linked the murder weapon, a poker found near the body, and a poker left behind at the tradesman's entrance by which a criminal escaped during a robbery ten days earlier. He also found similarities between that theft and several robberies in the Streatham neighborhood. Gough talked to a jeweler who had been tricked into purchasing some of the stolen items, and got a description of the man who had sold them. The jeweler noticed the wanted man in a shop in Wardour Street, followed him, and had Victor de Stamir arrested. He had a long criminal record, which included desertion from the British army. The young Frenchman's house was searched, and two inexpensive watches and a raincoat stolen from Tighe's house were found. De Stamir claimed he had robbed the house, but that the murder had been committed by an Australian soldier who accompanied him. His story was not convincing, and de Stamir was found Guilty of killing Tighe. He was executed in February 1918 at Wandsworth Prison.

REF.: Brock, *A Casebook of Crime; CBA;* Dilnot, *Triumphs of Detection;* Kingston, *Dramatic Days at the Old Bailey.*

DeStefano, Mario Anthony, c.1915-75, U.S., org. crime-mur. Mario Anthony DeStefano was convicted of murder at the age of twenty in 1935; he was again convicted of murder in 1973. In between, DeStefano was involved in a number of illegal activities including loan sharking and vote fraud, for which he received a $1,000 fine in 1966. He also allegedly murdered his brother.

In 1935 DeStefano was sentenced to thirty years in prison for murder, for which he served fourteen years in an Illinois prison. He and his brother Sam DeStefano are credited with bringing the "juice loan" racket to Chicago, where the two would squeeze payments out of those who borrowed money. The two are also believed to have shot and killed their brother, Mike DeStefano, who was found in the trunk of a car on Chicago's West Side, Sept. 27, 1955. Although neither was ever a part of Chicago's organized crime inner circle, the brothers were allowed to operate their enterprise for a percentage of the profit. DeStefano was the pair's muscle and Sam was the brains, though he once angered the mob by using a bullhorn in court to denounce his enemies. Sam was shotgunned gangland style in his Northwest Side garage on Apr. 14, 1973.

The brothers also were accused, along with Charles Crimaldi and Anthony Spilotro, of the torture death of loan shark Leo Foreman in 1963. The trial came about in 1973, after Sam's death, and DeStefano was found Guilty and sentenced to twenty to forty years in prison. This conviction was reversed on July 9, 1975, by the Illinois Appellate Court. DeStefano died of a heart attack on Aug. 12, 1975 before the second trial. REF.: *CBA*.

Chicago Mafia mobster Sam DeStefano shouting through a bull horn at police for arresting a "sick" man.

DeStefano, Sam (AKA: **Mad Sam**), 1909-73, U.S., org. crime. When questioned about the 1955 execution of his younger brother Michael, Sam DeStefano broke into uncontrollable laughter. The interrogators repeated their questions, but DeStefano grew more raucous. His brother was a drug addict, and when Sam Giancana ordered him killed, the elder DeStefano saw to it—without remorse or apparent regret.

Sam DeStefano functioned as the Chicago mob's most efficient executioner for the better part of three decades. When Giancana needed someone eliminated, he would most often entrust the job to DeStefano, a criminal psychopath who enjoyed inflicting torture before administering death. DeStefano was responsible for the murder of Leo Foreman. Foreman was taken to the sound-proof basement of a mob associate's suburban home, were DeStefano ordered his associates to shoot him in the non-vital areas first. Emerging from an upstairs bedroom Sam chortled: "I told you I'd get you. Greed got you killed!" After Foreman was dead, his executioners tore chunks of flesh from his arms.

DeStefano's arrest record dated back to 1927, and included convictions for rape, bank robbery, assault with a deadly weapon, and possession of counterfeit sugar stamps. A veteran of Sam Giancana's "42 Gang"—composed of West Side thugs and bootleggers—DeStefano graduated to loan sharking and narcotics trafficking by the 1960s. In 1965, he was convicted of conspiracy and sentenced to prison for three to five years. On Feb. 22, 1972, DeStefano threatened the life of former mob associate and government informant Charles Crimaldi in the elevator of the

Dirksen Federal Building in Chicago. Crimaldi had been a participant in the torture-murder of Leo Foreman. For this, DeStefano was sentenced to three-and-a-half years.

DeStefano never lived to serve out his prison term. In 1973, the 64-year-old mobster was shotgunned to death in the garage of his West Side home.

REF.: *CBA*; Demaris, *Captive City*; ____, *The Last Mafioso*; Reid, *The Grim Reapers*.

d'Estrées, Gabrielle, d.1599, Fr., (unsolv.) mur. Although King Henry IV of France reportedly had fifty-six mistresses during his life, his favorite was Gabrielle d'Estrées, whom he would have married if not for her sudden death.

D'Estrées met the king when he visited her parents' castle in 1590, and though she married Nicholas d'Amervals, she became Henry's mistress in December 1592. She maintained this position for more than six years, and was to have become his wife when the king's divorce to Marguerite de Valois was complete. However, the marriage never took place. Arriving in Paris on Apr. 6, 1599, d'Estrées spent the night at the palace of an Italian named Zametti, who gave the king's mistress a bottle of perfume. On Apr. 8 she became severely ill, with violent convulsive attacks, before slipping into a coma and dying two days later. It is believed that the Grand Duke of Tuscany was responsible for her poisoning.

REF.: Bullough, *Illustrated History of Prostitution*; CBA; Thompson, *Poison and Poisoners*.

d'Etampes, Anne, Duchess, prom. 16th cent., Fr., pros. The queen of France, Eleanor of Spain, chose Anne, Duchess d'Etampes to be her husband's mistress. King Francis I, however, was not content with only one mistress, and d'Etampes had to compete with Francoise de Chateaubriant for his affections. At one point, d'Etampes requested that Francis give her the jewels he had already given Chateaubriant in order to claim her dominance. Chateaubriant willingly returned the jewels, but first melted the gems down, making them worthless. See: **Chateaubriant, Francoise de.**

REF.: Bullough, *Illustrated History of Prostitution; CBA*.

Detectives, Notable, See: Supplements, Vol. IV.

DeTell, Hugh, prom. 1867, U.S., rob. DeTell, along with 21-year-old Arizona cowboy Walter Sinclair and a German immigrant known only as Faust, went on a robbing rampage on the Carson City road in California, stopping stages in July 1867. Jame B. Hume, the top Wells Fargo detective in the state, tracked the trio down, setting a trap for the robbers at Echo Creek Bridge, a few miles south of Lake Tahoe, Calif., cutting off the bandits' retreat into Nevada. Hume and his men opened fire when the bandits rode up to the bridge and they returned fire, wounding Hume. Faust was killed in the ambush, Sinclair was captured, and DeTell escaped, only to be arrested by Hume's men near Brockliss's Bridge over the American River. Both DeTell and Sinclair were given long prison terms.

REF.: *CBA*; Dillon, *Wells Fargo Detective*.

de Thuin, Raul, prom. 1966, Mex., forg.-count. An artist who reportedly studied at the Sorbonne in Paris, Raul de Thuin operated as a stamp forger for more than thirty years, producing thousands of excellent fakes.

Originally from Belgium, de Thuin had perpetrated forgeries in France, Honduras, Belgium, and Mexico for approximately thirty to forty years. Probably trained as a master counterfeiter in Honduras, de Thuin specialized in two techniques: overprinting, or imprinting additional words on already existing stamps, and surcharges, a device by which a country alters the face value of a stamp by overprinting a new denomination. He also counterfeited complete stamps. In 1950, de Thuin began counterfeiting overprints of the Canal Zone stamps, offering a selection to James T. DeVoss, an American collector who was also a U.S. intelligence officer under General Dwight D. Eisenhower and an expert in Canal Zone stamps. DeVoss began a sixteen year campaign to put de Thuin out of business. However, in that time, de Thuin produced millions of dollars worth of stamps.

On Dec. 11, 1966, Colonel DeVoss and James H. Beal, a specialist in Mexican stamps, met with de Thuin in Merida, and were amazed to find out that he operated with primitive equipment, making presses from blocks of wood and using mostly small photoengravings produced locally. The elderly man—de Thuin was seventy-six at the time—talked freely about his operations. DeVoss and Beal concluded a contract with de Thuin, who signed a confession admitting to his counterfeiting, and agreeing to stop. Using only pen and ink, de Thuin had drawn most of the overprints with a free hand. DeVoss and Beal purchased 1,636 plates de Thuin had used in his operations, and all his original drawings, correspondence, files, and business accounts.

REF.: *CBA;* McGuire, *The Forgers.*

Detlavs, Karlis, c.1910-   , Case of, Latvia, war crimes. The U.S. Immigration and Naturalization Service accused Karlis Detlavs of committing atrocities during WWII and enacted deportation proceedings against him on Oct. 13, 1976. The government claimed that Detlavs had lied about his activities when he came to the U.S. on Dec. 20, 1950, and thus had entered the country illegally.

Detlavs denied the accusation that he had served as a soldier in the Latvian Legion from 1941 to 1944 and that he had then collaborated with the Nazis to send thousands of Jews to their deaths. He allegedly helped select Jews for execution in the Pogulanka Woods in June and July 1941, and participated in shootings of Riga Ghetto Jews in October 1941.

The retired factory worker living in Baltimore, Md., first appeared in court on Nov. 15, 1976. On Jan. 9, 1978, 72-year-old Frida Michelson claimed that on Dec. 8, 1949, Detlavs had struck her and forced her with a machine gun toward a Nazi death pit in the Rumbula forest outside Riga, Latvia. It is alleged that 30,000 Jews were murdered at the Rumbula forest on Nov. 30 and Dec. 8, 1941. Detlavs, who was represented at his trial by Ivars Berzins, had the charges against him dismissed by immigration Judge Emil Bobek on Feb. 26, 1980, because the judge was not convinced that any of the witnesses had clearly identified the defendant. REF.: *CBA.*

Detollenaere, Jean-Baptiste (AKA: Delaunay), d.1909, Fr., burg.-suic.-mur. A series of burglaries were committed by a gang known as the Antiquaries or Church Robbers, who stole a number of artifacts from churches and museums in France. The leader of this gang was Jean-Baptiste Detollenaere, who had already been sentenced to death by the Oise Court in 1905 for attacking and killing a postman named Pillon while robbing him of 400 francs at St. Just-en-Chaussée on Aug. 3, 1904. On May 25, 1908, the burglaries began at the Limoges Cathedral, and continued on Aug. 5, at the Church of St. Viance; the Church of St. Vaury on Oct. 26; the Church of the Souterraine on Mar. 25, 1909; the Church of Huriel in April; and the Museum at Gueret on Apr. 27.

After the last crime, two gang members were captured by the police at Limoges. These two informed the authorities of their leader's identity. Paris Sûreté Sub-Chief Robert Blot, accompanied by his secretary Peyrot des Gachons, Chief Inspector Dol, and inspectors Mathieu and Mugat went to Detollenaere's apartment on July 18, 1909. When the door was opened, and before Mugat could get inside, Detollenaere stuck out a revolver and shot Blot, who died later at a pharmacy. The gang leader then shot Mugat twice in the back, killing the inspector before locking the door once more. Before the police could break the door down, two more shots were fired and Detollenaere was dead.

REF.: *CBA;* Morain, *The Underworld of Paris.*

de Tourville, Count Henri, prom. 1871-84, Aust., arson-mur. When Henri de Tourville worked as a waiter at a Parisian restaurant, an Englishman who was a frequent diner thought his manners and attitude were so refined and pleasing that he hired him as a companion. Taking de Tourville along on a trip to Constantinople, Mr. Cotton disappeared forever. Within two years de Tourville had obtained the rank of barrister, with lots of ready money, and the new Count arrived at Scarborough to find a wealthy wife. He married a woman who stood to inherit £30,000

upon the death of her mother, Mrs. Ramsden. Shortly after the wedding, de Tourville visited his mother-in-law carrying with him a pair of pistols. A shot rang out and de Tourville rushed from the room, crying that Mrs. Ramsden had shot herself in the head. At the inquest, the count explained how Mrs. Ramsden had picked up one of his practice pistols and it had gone off. Much later, when de Tourville was exposed as a fraud, the body was exhumed and it was clearly revealed that Ramsden had been murdered. The Countess de Tourville gave birth to a son, to whom she had willed most of her inheritance, and soon died in her sleep. De Tourville hired a nurse for his child, insured her, and then set fire to the house they all lived in. He managed to escape, and called out for help as the fire killed the baby and the nurse.

When the insurance company decided not to pay, de Tourville was forced to look to another marriage as a source of revenue. He married a Mrs. Miller, a childless widow, on Nov. 11, 1875, at Craven Hill. His new wife had provided him a £40,000 legacy in her will in the event of her death. On a long Continental tour, the couple was accompanied by a maid, Sarah Clappinson. De Tourville and his bride went for a hike at Trafoj in Austria, near Spondinning, on July 16; the Count returned alone, explaining that his wife had fallen down a ravine and he needed a carriage to bring her home. With a police inspector and three other men, de Tourville returned to the spot. The battered body of Madame de Tourville lay at the bottom of a ravine. At the inquest, the District Judge stopped the proceedings short, declaring he was satisfied that the death was accidental. De Tourville returned to London, but the citizens of Trafoj insisted on an exhumation of the body and a Higher Court ordered the arrest and extradition of the count. On Nov. 4, 1876, de Tourville appeared at Bow Street before a magistrate, Mr. Vaughan. Cross examined by Sir Henry Poland, Clappinson denied having said to the Innsbruck Hotel keeper "of course he killed her," but the innkeeper insisted that she had said just that, and de Tourville was extradited, tried before an Austrian court, and found Guilty of murder. Convicted to twenty years imprisonment in a fortress in that country, he died in 1884, having inherited £40,000 which he was never able to spend.

REF.: *CBA;* Kingston, *Dramatic Days at the Old Bailey;* Lambton, *Thou Shalt Do No Murder;* Russell, *Best Murder Cases.*

Detroit Child Murders, 1976-77, U.S., (unsolv.) mur. Oakland County, Mich., northwest of downtown Detroit, is home to moderately affluent suburban communities, well-policed, and generally free of the multitudinous crimes that plague nearby Detroit. However, suburban Oakland County was the scene of seven child murders between Jan. 15, 1976, and Mar. 16, 1977. These unsolved crimes defied the efforts of over fifty law enforcement agencies that joined in the hunt for the killer.

On Jan. 15, 1976, 16-year-old Cynthia Cadieux became the first victim. Cynthia was killed after leaving her girlfriend's house in suburban Roseville, and her unclad, bludgeoned body was later found on a desolate stretch of

Police sketch of the killer of seven children in the Detroit area.

road. Less than a week later, 14-year-old Sheila Srock was shot to death by a home invader at her sister's Birmingham home. In August 1976, Jane Louise Allan, thirteen, was found on a public road outside Miamisburg, Ohio. The evidence suggested that she had been bound, gagged, and smothered. Although these first three murders seemed unconnected, the next four murders were clearly the work of one individual.

Mark Stebbins, a 12-year-old Ferndale youth disappeared shortly after leaving the American Legion Hall on Feb. 13, 1976. He was found dead a week later in Southfield. There was evidence of sexual molestation. Similar to the Stebbins murder, Jill Robinson, twelve, vanished shortly after walking out of a hobby shop in Royal Oak on Dec. 22, 1976. Like the Stebbins boy, Jill Robinson's body had been washed and arranged in a funeral position. The body was found near the I-75 Freeway in Troy on Dec. 26. Seven days later Kristine Mihelich of Berkley left her house to buy a magazine. Her body was found adjacent to a rural road in Franklin Village on Jan. 21, 1977. Again, the corpse had been thoroughly cleaned and arranged in the traditional funeral position.

The only eye-witness account of the killer was given to police following the disappearance of 11-year-old Timothy King on Mar. 16, 1977. According to the witnesses, a white man between twenty-five and thirty-five driving a Blue Gremlin was seen conversing with the King boy outside a local drugstore. Timothy's body was found next to a road in suburban Livonia on Mar. 23, 1977. He had been suffocated and sexually assaulted.

The killer was never heard from again. Investigators from over fifty police departments focused their search on the owners of blue Gremlins in the Detroit area, but not one suspect emerged. Birmingham police chief Jerry Tobin speculated that the murderer might have been an affluent businessman. "We think he is a white-collar-class person or a professional man—somebody who is trusted, like a doctor, a policeman, a member of the clergy." The ritualistic nature of the crimes—the fact that the bodies had all been washed and laid in the traditional funeral position—suggested to police that the killer might have been foreign-born, perhaps Middle Eastern. An informant with a Middle Eastern accent told a local psychiatrist that he could point out the murderer in one of Detroit's gay bars. However, the informant never showed up. The investigation dragged on for months with no viable clues.

REF.: *CBA;* Nash, *Open Files.*

Detroit Government Corruption Scandal, 1940s, U.S., polit. corr. Circuit Court Judge Homer Ferguson was appointed by the court to seek out and clean up any political corruption he could find in Wayne County, Mich., particularly in Detroit and suburban Hamtramck. He found gambling houses, brothels, and policy operations netting an estimated $10 million per year, run with complete cooperation from the local government and police force, who were also running their own baseball pool. Ferguson's one-man grand jury indicted 151 people on Apr. 22, 1940, including former Detroit Mayor Richard William Reading, the county prosecutor and sheriff, ten police lieutenants, six detectives, thirty-four sergeants, and thirty-seven patrolmen. He also indicted a co-manager of heavyweight boxing champion Joe Louis.

The first trial ended on Apr. 28, 1941, with prosecutor Duncan Cameron McCrea, Sheriff Thomas C. Wilcox, and twenty-one other defendants being found Guilty of participating in a graft conspiracy. Key prosecution testimony during the three-month trial was provided by former chief investigator for McCrea Harry Colburn, who pleaded guilty and then informed the state that he had given McCrea more than $100,000 in protection money collected from vice operations. McCrea and Wilcox were each sentenced to up to five years in prison and fined $2,000. Reading, mayor in 1938 and 1939, was convicted along with boxing manager and alleged syndicate policy operator John Roxborough; Detroit's numbers racket head Everett I. Watson; gambler and operator Elmer "Buff" Ryan; twelve suspended police officers, including John P. McCarthy and Arthur Ryckman; and seven numbers racket employees. On Jan. 7, 1942, Judge Earl C. Pugsley sentenced Reading—already fined $10,000 after entering a guilty plea on an earlier charge of concealing income—to four to eight years in prison, and Roxborough and Watson to two-and-one-half to five years in prison.

Further mass trials had similar results. Former County Auditor Edward H. Williams pleaded guilty to bribery and graft receipt and was sentenced Feb. 25 to five to ten years in prison. A trial

of fifty-three defendants found twenty-seven Guilty on June 6, 1942, including the former mayor's son, Richard W. Reading Jr., former Deputy Superintendent William J. Heidt, and former Chief Inspector Fred R. Clark.

Detroit Race Riot, 1943, U.S., mob vio. The U.S. entry into WWII provided blacks with the opportunity to campaign for civil rights long denied them by white society. The "Double V" campaign, initiated by numerous agencies serving the black community stressed victory at home and abroad. The logic of the campaigners was that if a man were to risk his life in the service of his country, he should not be denied basic civil rights under the law. The push for equality was magnified in Detroit where the automobile unions observed a long standing policy of preventing blacks from joining local unions. In April 1941, the black community won important concessions from the Ford Motor Company which recognized the right of the UAW to permit black members.

A white backlash followed as many blue-collar workers feared the loss of jobs, security, and housing. For the next two years, the racial climate in Detroit was tense. Complicating the volatile situation were the tirades of right-wing zealots like Father Charles Coughlan, who commanded tremendous influence over the airwaves. On June 20, 1943, whites and blacks clashed at Belle Isle, a popular municipal recreation park in the middle of the Detroit River. The disturbance was quelled by police, but in the process they incurred the wrath of the black community after they searched for weapons in automobiles and on the personal property of blacks only. A number of blacks were arrested while the whites involved in the conflict were generally left alone.

Rumors circulated through the city of various atrocities committed against both white and black women. The Roxy Theatre, in an all-white neighborhood, was the scene of renewed violence. Blacks were driven from the auditorium, and were not given adequate police protection. Soon, the trouble spread to the commercial districts along Woodward Avenue and Hastings Street where the windows of retail establishments were smashed. Police attempted to stop the looting, but in the process shot and killed a number of innocent bystanders. Members of the black community reported numerous instances of police brutality committed by white officers. On June 22, State Policeman Ted Anders fired indiscriminately into the St. Antoine Branch of the YMCA, wounding one man. The residents of the YMCA dormitory were forced to line up against the wall and be subjected to a frisk. There was no evidence of provocation nor were any weapons found. The Detroit riot claimed thirty-four lives; twenty-five of those killed were blacks.

REF.: *CBA;* Hofstadter and Wallace, *American Violence;* Lee and Humphrey, *Race Riot;* Shogan and Craig, *The Detroit Race Riot: A Study in Violence;* Sternsher, *The Negro Depression and War.*

Detroit Race Riot, 1967, U.S., mob vio. The year 1967 witnessed major civil disturbances between blacks and whites in a number of U.S. cities. The most serious of these riots occurred in Newark, N.J., and Detroit, Mich. The National Advisory Commission on Civil Disobedience concluded that: "white racism is essentially responsible for the explosive mixture which has been accumulating in our cities since the end of WWI."

By far the most devastating eruption of urban violence occurred in Detroit after the local police raided five "blind pig" saloons and gambling dens on July 23. Eighty-two black patrons were arrested and driven away in squad cars while angry residents pelted the vehicles with stones and brickbats. The next morning, a full-blown race riot had broken out as entire city blocks were looted and burned to the ground by rioters. The National Guard was called in by the mayor and governor, but the inexperienced troops were ill-prepared to deal with the situation and fired indiscriminately.

Detroit police were later assailed for their harsh tactics against suspects brought in for questioning. Of the twenty-seven individuals arrested for looting, twenty-four of them were dismissed. In all, forty-three persons were killed, 7,200 suspects were taken into custody, and millions of dollars in property was destroyed.

REF.: *CBA;* Hersey, *The Algiers Motel Incident;* Hofstadter and Wallace, *American Violence; Report of the National Advisory Commission on Civil Disorders.*

Deupree, Jim, c.1936- , U.S., fraud-forg.-theft-burg. Drinking cost Jim Deupree three marriages, caused his father to remove him from his will, and cost him his freedom.

In 1971 Deupree was convicted of writing bad checks and spent twenty-two months in prison. The Indiana man's next run-in with the law occurred in December 1975, when he broke into a Shelbyville, Ind. business while intoxicated, and stole $40 in cash and several payroll checks. He spent the cash on liquor, but was arrested the next day after a bank camera took his picture while he tried but failed to cash a payroll check with a forged signature. Deupree was convicted and returned to the Michigan City prison, but spent only fourteen months there before being transferred to a work-release program in Indianapolis. It was there that he began drinking again, and again broke the law. He stole his employer's car, but was not arrested until he had driven to Kansas, which led to his conviction for interstate transportation of a stolen vehicle. Deupree was released from prison in October 1979. REF.: *CBA.*

Deutscher, Albert, c.1920-81, Case of, U.S.-Ger., suic.-war crimes. Before WWII Albert Deutscher lived in the village of Worms, a German enclave in the Soviet Union that was overrun by the Nazis by August 1941. According to the U.S. Office of Special Investigations Deutscher belonged to the Nazi Selbstschutz (self-defense), which defended the area. The office also accused Deutscher of shooting to death hundreds of unarmed Jewish prisoners shipped by train to the region in January and February 1942. The truth of these allegations may never be known, however, for Deutscher was killed by a train on Dec. 18, 1981.

Deutscher's 36-year-old son, Alfred Deutscher, denied that his father, who immigrated to the U.S. in 1952, could have been involved in killing defenseless people. Prosecutor Allan Ryan, director of the special investigations office, said the government's case was quite strong, but because of Deutscher's death would not be pursued. Deutscher died a few hours after a federal lawsuit seeking revocation of his U.S. citizenship was filed. Albert claimed his father's death was accidental, but the Cook County, Ill., medical examiner determined Deutscher's death to have been suicide. REF.: *CBA.*

Devann, Patrick (AKA: Paddy), d.1817, Ire., mur. The leader of a secret society in Ireland, Patrick Devann convinced a number of followers that because they had taken oaths of secrecy and were bound to one another before the law it was their duty to murder anyone who stood in their way, even a former member.

The society led by Devann held many of its first meetings at Wild Goose Lodge, the home of a member named Lynch. But as the society increased in size and the meetings began interfering with Lynch's private life, he asked Devann to take his meetings elsewhere. Devann did as he was asked but not before warning Lynch of the consequences of such an act. Lynch's home and family were soon plagued by a number of attacks where Lynch was beaten and furniture was destroyed. The attacks continued for some time until Lynch decided to break his oath to the society and turn in the culprits. Two of those convicted were executed. At that, Devann sought vengeance. Gathering his society about him he encircled the Lynch home, each man carrying a spear and flame. Inside the home was stored a great deal of flax, which proved to be quite combustible when Devann gave the signal to set the Wild Goose Lodge on fire. He and his men stood around the burning building to ensure that no one was able to leave the inferno. With the flames leaping about her, Mrs. Lynch in desperation tossed her baby to the men hoping at least the child might be saved. The baby was caught on a spear and thrown back into the blaze. Thirteen people were killed in the fire.

Those who committed the atrocious crime were eventually brought to justice. Eleven murderers were hanged and gibbeted in Louth, Ire., the county where the house had stood. Devann was captured in Dublin and brought to trial on July 19, 1817. He was found Guilty and hanged for murder; his hanging took place inside the burned-out ruins of Wild Goose Lodge. He too was gibbeted with the others.

REF.: *CBA;* Forster, *Studies In Black and Red.*

Deveaux, Jean-Marie, c.1942- , Fr., (wrong. convict.) mur. The body of 7-year-old Dominique Bessard was found lying in a pool of blood in the cellar of her home on July 7, 1961. Her throat was slit nearly to the bone and her stomach slashed three or four times with a knife. Rather than face an injection with truth serum, Jean-Marie Deveaux, the 19-year-old assistant to Dominique's father, confessed to the horrible crime.

Deveaux's confession came on Sept. 1, 1961, just three days after he had feigned an attack upon himself because he believed the police suspected him of the murder. His confession, however, did not quite match the conclusions of the forensic and pathology experts. Deveaux told how he had first stabbed the girl in the stomach and then cut her throat, contrary to findings that her throat must have been cut first because she had lost so little blood from her abdomen. Deveaux, however, told police over the phone that Dominique had been murdered before it was known she had been killed. On Feb. 7, Deveaux was found Guilty of murder and sentenced to twenty years in prison by Judge Combas. Because of the efforts of his lawyer, Soulier, and his priest, Father Boyer, Deveaux spent only six years in prison—during which time he cut his wrist deep enough to sever a tendon—before the conviction was overturned.

REF.: *CBA;* Heppenstall, *The Sex War and Others.*

Devens, Charles, 1820-91, U.S., jur. Served as Massachusetts Supreme Court justice, 1873-77, as U.S. attorney general, 1877-81, and again as Massachusetts Supreme Court justice, 1881-91. REF.: *CBA.*

Deventer, Conrad Theodor van, 1857-1915, Neth., jur. Served as a member of parliament, 1905-09 and 1913-15. REF.: *CBA.*

De Vere, Pearl, prom. 1897, U.S., pros. The Old Homestead, a house of prostitution in Cripple Creek, Colo., was owned at one time by Hazel Vernon. Vernon built up her clientele by avoiding publicity and scandal, and affecting an air of refinement and decorum at the house that she cornered the market on the so-called "carriage trade," or big spenders. In 1897, Vernon sold the Old Homestead to a woman named Pearl De Vere. De Vere came from Denver, and financed her Myers Avenue brothel with help from a wealthy Denverite. De Vere lost money and, when the Denver backer stopped supplying funds, the situation became desperate. De Vere committed suicide by overdosing on morphine after she had spent a gay and apparently carefree evening at a wild party with her clients and employees. Money for her burial was raised by public subscription, and, on a January afternoon, the former madame was buried at Pisgah cemetery.

REF.: *CBA;* Drago, *Notorious Ladies of the Frontier.*

Devereux, Robert (Earl of Essex), 1566-1601, Brit., treas. Robert Devereux, the second Earl of Essex, was born in 1566, and given an upbringing considered ideal for an Elizabethan gentleman. His father died when the boy was ten, and Devereux's mother married Queen Elizabeth's favorite, the Earl of Leicester. Essex began attending court at an early age, and by his twentieth year was himself the queen's favorite. Their relationship was turublent, however. Essex objected when the queen, without his permission, imprisoned Mary, Queen of Scots in his house at Chartley. Likewise, Elizabeth was furious when, in 1590, Essex secretly married Sir Phillip Sidney's widow. But the queen forgave him, and she often interceded in disputes between Essex and another flamboyant courtier, Sir Walter Raleigh. During these years, Essex distinguished himself in military service in Holland, France, and Spain. But he met with difficulty in the Irish campaign of 1599, when he made questionable battle decisions and concluded a truce with the Earl of Tyrone against Elizabeth's wishes. He defended his actions on his return to London, but was stripped of his offices.

In 1601, urged on by Lord Mountjoy and the Earl of Southampton, his co-commander in Ireland, Essex tried to rouse the citizens of London to rebel against Elizabeth's inner circle of counselors, whom he believed had betrayed her and promised the English crown to the Spanish infanta upon her death. The rebellion failed, and Essex was arrested. Most reluctantly, Elizabeth condemned him to die.

Essex was led to the Tower on Feb. 25, 1601. He made a speech at the scaffold, asking directions on how to behave, and forgave the executioner who knelt before him and begged for his absolution. After he asked for help from God, the kneeling Earl waited for the ax to fall, saying to the executioner, "O strike, strike." His head was severed in three blows; he was knocked senseless by the first. His body and head were carried to the Tower church in a prepared coffin, and he was buried there, next to the Earl of Arundel and the Duke of Norfolk.

REF.: *CBA;* (FILM) *The Private Lives of Elizabeth and Essex*, 1939.

Devereux, Walter, c.1541-76, Ire., mur. As the 1st Earl of Essex and the 2nd Viscount of Hereford, he traitorously captured Irish leader Sir Brian MacPhelim and had him executed, 1574. He was appointed by Queen Elizabeth of England as the earl marshal of Ireland, and had hundreds of Sorley Boy's followers massacred, 1575. REF.: *CBA.*

de Vidil, Alfred Louis Pons, prom. 1861, Brit., attempt. mur. Baron Alfred Louis Pons de Vidil, fifty-five, and his son Alfred John de Vidil, twenty-three, were returning on June 28, 1861, from a long horseback ride. Baron de Vidil, low on funds for some time, had begun contemplating the £30,000 he stood to inherit if his son were to die without a will. Although both men were tired from their seventeen mile ride, the Baron continued and kept veering off toward secluded areas. Alfred had just followed the Baron to Orleans Road when he felt "a violent blow on my head," according to his later deposition, and then another. The young man dismounted, stumbled over to a couple standing nearby, and begged for protection. The riderless horses then appeared, followed by the Baron who claimed that his son had been thrown from his horse. Alfred did not contest this explanation. The couple took Alfred to the Swan Inn. The Baron followed and gave the local doctor, Mr. Clarke, the same story. When the Baron was out of the room, Alfred finally related the facts of the assault and begged no to be left alone with his father. The doctor sent an assistant with the de Vidils on their return trip to London, and Alfred was transported to the safety of his uncle's house in Duke Street, Westminster.

The Baron fled to Paris, but returned soon after, attended by two French policeman. He stood trial in England on Aug. 24, 1861, at the Central Criminal Court. Alfred de Vidil, although he had previously given a complete deposition describing his father's attack, now refused to testify against him. But an old laborer returning home had also seen the incident from about 100 yards away, and gave a detailed report. Although the worker had since died, his deposition was effective in the prosecution. Oddly, the jury found the Baron Guilty only of unlawfully wounding his son, not of attempted murder. Baron de Vidil was sentenced to a year at hard labor.

REF.: Brookes, *Murder In Fact and Fiction; CBA.*

de Villemessant, Hippolyte-Auguste Delaunay, and **Vitu, Auguste-Charles-Joseph**, prom. 1872, Fr., libel. On Feb. 9, 1872, French General Louis-Jules Trochu signed a complaint against *Le Figaro*, a popular daily newspaper in Paris, accusing publisher and owner Hippolyte-Auguste Delaunay de Villemessant and journalist Auguste-Charles-Joseph Vitu of publishing and writing articles that defamed him. On Feb. 28, he secured an indictment for seven counts of libel. The paper accused Trochu, a soldier since 1854, of resigning just before the disasterous January 1871 battle of Buzenval, after he had announced that he would never surrender. Le Figaro also charged him with carrying out the repressive decisions of General Saint-Arnaud in 1851, and with telling the empress-regent in 1870 that if she did not name him governor of Paris, he would not be responsible for the actions of his 12,000 soldiers. Trouchu also allegedly aided the revolutionaries by letting it be known that these 12,000 men were camped in Paris.

The case was clearly a political trial masquerading as a civil suit. Villemessant who founded *le Figaro* in 1854, plainly recognized the aloof, reserved Trochu as a popular target. Vitu, a conservative Bonapartist, believed that the Second Empire had been forsaken by those who should have protected it, and that this betrayal was responsible for France's conquest by Prussia in 1871. The case was heard at the Court d'assizes of the Seine in late March and early April 1872. Villemessant explained that his antagonism was toward Trochu as a man, rather than as a soldier, and that his intention was not to libel the General but to write truthful history. On April 2, the jurors left at noon, deliberated for three hours, and returned a verdict of Not Guilty on all matters of defamation, but Guilty on all matters of outrage. The outrage conviction was made based on the fact that Trochu was judged not as a private citizen but as a public figure invested with public authority. Villemessant and Vitu were each sentenced to one month in prison and fined 3,000 francs. They were also required to pay court costs. The vindicated General Trochu resigned his seat in the National Assembly on July 1, 1872, and retired from military life the following year, at the age of fifty-eight. REF.: *CBA.*

De Villiers, Jacob, 1868-1931, S. Afri., jur. Named attorney general and chief justice. REF.: *CBA.*

de Villiers, James Arthur, 1891-1929, S. Afri., (unsolv.) mur. On Aug. 9, 1929, 38-year-old James Arthur de Villiers, a Cape Town, S. Afri., cab driver, reported as usual for his evening shift. Respected and well-liked by his co-workers, he was the sole support of his wife and three small children. Waiting for his turn, de Villiers moved up to the front position at roughly 9:40 p.m. and answered the next call. "Salt River Road, near the new garage," he was overheard to say.

De Villiers drove to the railway and factory district of Salt River, some three miles from the center of Cape Town. There he saw only Reginald Louw, who neither called for a taxi nor knew of anyone who had. De Villiers returned to Salt River Road and drove toward Maitland where he picked up another fare. About 11 p.m., bus driver Stephanus Prins, drove past a figure slumped by the side of the road near a cemetery. Stopping to investigate, he found a man barely alive who had been shot through the heart. Prins drove the dying man to the Maitland Police Station but de Villiers died on the way.

De Villiers' cab was found abandoned on the Cape Town Road, its motor running. At 2:10 a.m. a policeman searched it, finding only a cartridge from a .25-caliber automatic pistol. No other evidence turned up. Vagrants, prostitutes, and cab drivers were questioned, and informers from Cape Town's underworld were out in force to try to locate the killer, but the seemingly senseless murder of James de Villiers remains a mystery.

REF.: Bennett, *Murder Is My Business;* ____, *Up For Murder; CBA.*

De Villiers, John Henry, 1842-1914, S. Afri., jur. The Baron De Villiers was the Union of South Africa's first chief justice, 1910, and the country's acting governor general, 1912 and 1914. REF.: *CBA.*

Devil Man, The, 1931, a novel by Edgar Wallace. Charles Peace, a one-man crime wave for twenty years (Brit., 1859-79), was the inspiration for this work of fiction. See: **Peace, Charles.** REF.: *CBA.*

Devil's Island, prom. 1852-1953, Fr., penal col. Between 1852 and 1947, France sent 70,000 convicts and political prisoners to a steamy archipelago off the Atlantic Coast of French Guiana known as the Iles Du Salut, or Salvation Islands. Three islands, Royal, St. Joseph, and Devil's, comprised the penal settlement that had once been a leper colony. The most infamous of the three islands was the Ile du Diable, or Devil's Island, where Captain Alfred Dreyfus was housed from 1895 until 1899 as punishment for sharing military secrets with the Germans.

Dreyfus was wrongly convicted, but languished inside a miserable wooden hut in solitary confinement. Because Devil's Island was reserved for political criminals, there were only a few prisoners there at a time. Dreyfus was the sole resident during his imprisonment, which ended on June 5, 1899, with his official exoneration. During WWI, Devil's Island was populated mostly by convicted spies and deserters. French underworld figures shipped to the colony ended up on Royal Island, which held a large penitentiary. Of the 70,000 prisoners sent to these desolate, jungle islands, fewer than 5,000 ever returned to Europe. The shark-infested waters discouraged escape by sea, and wild animals, disease, and quicksand waited inland.

A few prisoners attempted the seemingly impossible. René Belbenoit, a thief sent to Guiana in 1921, escaped from Devil's Island on four occasions, but was caught and dragged back each time. His exploits were described by novelist Blair Niles, who visited Belbenoit on several occasions. On Mar. 2, 1935, Belbenoit, weakened by malaria and starvation, escaped a fifth time. He made his way to Panama where the local newspaper sent his story over the wire services to New York. Belbenoit's tale led to worldwide condemnation of the French penal system.

Other prisoners, like Henri Charriere, also known as Papillon, slipped away from the island to join the South American underworld. Charriere recorded his exploits in book form and became a wealthy man. As a result of the pressure from the Salvation Army, the French government stopped sending its convicts to the islands in 1946. The last of the prisoners were freed in 1953, and Devil's Island soon became a tourist attraction.

REF.: Belbenoit, *Dry Guillotine*; ____, *Hell on Trial;* Carriere, *Papillon; CBA;* Karup-Nielsen, *Hell Beyond the Seas;* Lagrange, *Flag on Devil's Island;* Niles, *Condemned to Devil's Island;* (FILM), *The Dreyfus Case,* 1931; *The Life of Emile Zola,* 1937; *Devil's Island,* 1940; *Strange Cargo,* 1940; *I Was A Prisoner on Devil's Island,* 1941; *Passage to Marseille,* 1944; *We're No Angels,* 1955; *I Accuse!,* 1958; *I Escaped from Devil's Island,* 1973; *Papillon,* 1973.

Devine Securities Theft, 1935, U.S., (unsolv.) rob. Recovery of less than one-third of the securities stolen from the Wall Street firm of C.J. Devine & Co. led U.S. investigators across the Atlantic Ocean to France and Monaco, where the French Sûreté Generale uncovered an international stolen securities operation.

The securities firm was robbed of $1.5 million worth of negotiable bonds on Jan. 28, 1935. A phone call received by Manhattan police detective Henry P. Oswald led to the discovery that the bonds had crossed the Atlantic. Federal agents were called in and a woman named Marchioness Pia Ferrari Davico was questioned, which led to the questioning of imprisoned fence David Frank. Frank tipped off authorities to a possible gang in Monte Carlo. From there the Sûreté Generale learned from Prince Louis II of Monaco that the securities were in his country. The police finally seized a Czechoslovakian and a Hungarian carrying $440,000 worth of Devine securities. REF.: *CBA.*

Devitt, Edward James, b.1911, U.S., jur. Served in the U.S. House of Representatives, 1947-48, and was appointed to the District Court of Minnesota by President Dwight Eisenhower, Dec. 12, 1954. He wrote "Improvements in Federal Sentencing Procedures," in *Federal Rules Decisions,* 1959, and "How can we Effectively Minimize Unjustified Disparity in Federal Criminal Sentences," in *Federal Rules Decisions,* 1966. REF.: *CBA.*

Devlin, Henry, prom. 1880s, Scot., mur. Henry Devlin was convicted of ruthlessly murdering his wife and sentenced to be hanged. Unfortunately for Devlin, executioner James Berry miscalculated the proper drop from the scaffold at Duke Street Prison in Glasgow and the man was slowly strangled to death when his neck failed to break. See: **Berry, James.**

REF.: *CBA;* Laurence, *A History of Capital Punishment.*

Devlin, Sir **Patrick Arthur,** 1905-   , Brit., jur. Became the Duchy of Cornwall's attorney general, 1947, and appointed to the king's bench division, 1948, which made him the youngest High Court justice. He was named a Lord Justice of Appeal after leading the Commission of Inquiry into the Nyasaland disturbances, 1959, and was the judge for the cases of Leonard Jack Thomas and Renee Duffy, who were both accused of murder. REF.: *CBA.*

Devol, George, 1829-1902, U.S., gamb. George Devol was a card sharp, a cheat, and skilled player of three-card monte during the forty years he spent sailing the great paddlewheel ships that traversed the Mississippi River during the mid-nineteenth century. His partner, Canada Bill Jones, played the role of the gullible dupe, while Devol raked in $2 million by his own estimate.

In his published memoirs entitled *Forty Years a Gambler on the Mississippi,* Devol described himself as "a cabin boy in 1839; could steal cards and cheat the boys at eleven; stack a deck at fourteen...fought more rough and tumble fights than any man in America and was the most daring gambler in the world." Faro, three card monte, and rigged games of poker were his particular specialties. Victims who recognized that they were being cheated would not hesitate to pull a gun or knife. During these tense moments when his life hung in the balance, the gambler would extricate himself from the dilemma by "butting" heads with the swindled victim. Devol's cranium was the envy of the Mississippi con men. He used it many times to cold-cock adversaries, and became known as the man with the "most awesome cranium".

From time to time Devol would butt heads with circus performers for prize money. He knocked unconscious the famous Billy Carroll of Robinson's Circus, who promoted himself as "the man with the thick skull," or "the great butter." It was a title Carroll was forced to relinquish. "Gentlemen, I have found my papa at last," he said. In 1887, Devol published his memoirs and drifted into semi-retirement. After his death, the Cincinnati *Enquirer* stated that Devol had won and lost more money than any other gambling blackleg in history.

REF.: Asbury, *Sucker's Progress; CBA;* Chafetz, *Play the Devil;* Devol, *Forty Years a Gambler on the Mississippi;* Hamilton, *Men of the Underworld;* Nash, *Hustlers and Con Men.*

De Wet, Christiaan Rudolph, 1854-1922, S. Afri., treas. Led the Orange Free State as commander in chief, 1900, led Afrikaner opposition to the South African government, 1914, and was placed in prison, 1915, on a charge of treason; being released after promising to discontinue political agitation. REF.: *CBA.*

Dewey, Thomas Edmund, 1902-71, U.S., dist. atty. At a time when New York City was threatened with gangster rule, Thomas Edmund Dewey emerged from political obscurity to lead the fight against criminal lawlessness. In the process, he sent some of New York's most notorious criminals to prison. But according to Charles "Lucky" Luciano, a mob boss imprisoned by Dewey for thirty to fifty years only to be released for political reasons, the prosecutor was secretly involved with the syndicate in order to raise money to further his political aspirations.

Dewey was born in Michigan, and attended Columbia Law School, finishing in a record two years time. Dewey practiced law from 1925 until 1931 when he accepted a position to serve as chief assistant to George Medalie, U.S. Attorney for the Southern District of New York. While serving under Medalie, Dewey established his reputation as a "rackets buster" for his vigorous prosecution of gangster Irving "Waxey Gordon" Wexler, who was jailed for ten years for income tax evasion. Dewey resumed his private practice until July 1935 when Governor Herbert H. Lehman appointed him to ferret out organized crime in New York City after a grand jury expressed its abhorrence

Racket buster Thomas E. Dewey.

with District Attorney William C. Dodge, a Tammany Hall lackey who refused to prosecute gangsters. For the next eighteen months, Dewey led a spirited uphill charge against organized crime. He targeted for investigation loan sharks, brothel keepers, numbers runners, and mob bosses. He revealed, among other things, how Luciano had organized New York prostitution into a "chain store" operation. Luciano had learned from the mistakes of Al Capone and Waxey Gordon in one sense. He assiduously paid his taxes to the government. Therefore it took a concerted effort to link the acknowledged "boss of bosses" to the flourishing New York vice rackets. Dewey succeeded in bringing Luciano back to New York from his refuge in Hot Springs, Ark. In May 1936, Luciano was convicted on ninety counts of prostitution and sent to prison.

By this time, other New York gangsters demanded that something be done about the District Attorney. Dutch Schultz proposed to "hit" Dewey in October 1935, but was vetoed by Luciano and other ruling members of the Mafia commission who had a long-standing policy of non-interference with "newspaper guys, cops, or DA's." Schultz was adamant about this however, and he assigned a stakeout of Dewey's Fifth Avenue apartment. Each morning a man and a little boy would walk past Dewey's building. The boy pedaled a bicycle, and by all appearances was accompanying his father on an early morning stroll. Schultz planned to corner Dewey in his neighborhood drugstore while he called his office and shoot him with a silencer. Fearful of the political reprisals that would certainly befall the New York mobsters, they decided to execute Schultz before his plan was carried out. He was gunned down in a chop house in Newark, N.J., in the fall of 1935 by Luciano's men. Dewey did not find out about this episode until 1940.

In December 1937, Tom Dewey was elected District Attorney after he had been slated to run by the anti-Tammany reform mayor Fiorello LaGuardia. The New York *World-Telegram* gushed: "Hoodlums Start Out as Dewey Starts In." His first year in office witnessed the conviction of Tammany Hall boss James J. Hines, the district leader in Harlem who ran the $1 million per year numbers racket. The arrest and conviction of Hines was Dewey's biggest coup to date. He later sent to prison Gurrah Shapiro, Richard Whitney, the German-American Bundist Fritz Kuhn, and Louis (Lepke) Buchalter, the highest ranking mobster to go to the electric chair. It was alleged by the Hearst press that in 1944 Lepke had offered Dewey a deal. In return for his life he promised to implicate Sidney Hillman, president of the Amalgamated Clothing Workers and one of President Franklin Roosevelt's top labor advisors.

Dewey turned down Lepke's offer, knowing the full impact such revelations would have on his presidential campaign. The right-wing press canonized him for his decision not to accommodate a gangster. The Republican Convention nominated Dewey as their standard bearer in 1944, but it proved too great a task to defeat Franklin Roosevelt. Dewey was attacked by his political opponents after the war when Luciano was suddenly released. In *The Last Testament of Lucky Luciano*, the gangster charged that Dewey had been on the take all along. The price of Luciano's freedom was a $90,000 campaign contribution. These dark allegations tarnished Dewey's career. He seemed to have lost interest in the anti-crime crusade, evidenced by his unwillingness to cooperate with the Kefauver Senate Investigating Committee in 1950. The committee wanted to question Dewey about Luciano's pardon among other things, and why gambling was allowed to flourish in Saratoga, N.Y., the famous resort for the Manhattan social set. Meyer Lansky, the highest ranking Jewish gangster in the U.S., was said to have operated there with impunity.

In the 1960s, the former governor became a stockholder in Mary Carter Paints which had a stake in several gambling resorts in the Bahamas controlled by Lansky. The *Wall Street Journal* uncovered the Lansky-Mary Carter-Dewey connection and won a Pulitzer Prize. The Mary Carter casinos opened on time, prompting one critic to sum up Dewey's career in these terms: "From racketbuster to racketbacker." See: **Buchalter, Louis; Gordon, Waxey; Luciano, Charles.**

REF.: Alexander, *The Pizza Connection;* Blumenthal, *Last Days of the Sicilians;* Bonanno, *A Man of Honor;* Campbell, *The Luciano Project;* CBA; Cressey, *Theft of the Nation;* Demaris, *The Director;* Eisenberg and Landau, *Meyer Lansky;* Fried, *The Rise and Fall of the Jewish Gangster in America;* Gage, *The Mafia is not an Equal Opportunity Employer;* Gosch and Hammer, *The Last Testament of Lucky Luciano;* Hibbert, *Roots of Evil;* Katz, *Uncle Frank;* Lait and Mortimer, *Chicago: Confidential;* Levine, *Anatomy of a Gangster;* McPhaul, *Johnny Torrio;* Maas, *The Valachi Papers;* Messick, *Lansky;* ____, *Secret File;* ____, *Syndicate In the Sun;* ____ and Goldblatt, *The Mobs and the Mafia;* Nash, *Citizen Hoover;* Navasky, *Kennedy Justice;* Overstreet, *The FBI In Our Open Society;* Peterson, *The Mob;* Powers, *Secrecy and Power;* Reppetto, *The Blue Parade;* Reuter, *Disorganized Crime;* Sann, *Kill the Dutchman;* Scott, *The Concise Encyclopedia of Crime and Criminals;* Servadio, *Mafioso;* Sullivan, *The Bureau: My Thirty Years in Hoover's FBI;* Thompson and Raymond, *Gang Rule In New York;* Toledano, *J. Edgar Hoover;* Ungar, *FBI;* Walker, *Dewey: An American of this Century;* Wicker, *Investigating the FBI.*

DeWit, Paul, prom. 1980, U.S., pros.-mur. Paul DeWit, an aspiring young actor, went for dramatic coaching to Everett Clarke, an old-time Chicago radio actor whose spine-chilling voice had enlivened such programs as "The Shadow," "The Whistler," and "Chicago Theater of the Air."

Clarke taught in a building full of art studios, the Chicago Fine Arts Building. On Sept. 9, 1980, Ann Lang, an artist who worked next door to Clarke, heard among the noises and music of the building, a shout: "No, Paul! God, no, Paul!" Assuming that the shout was part of a dramatic script, Lang looked casually out her window, where she saw a young man climb out the window of Clarke's studio and go down the fire escape. That night, friends of Everett Clarke found him dead in his studio, stabbed to death with a pair of scissors.

Paul DeWit's name was in the appointment book, and he had been seen at the studio that day. During his trial for murder, his attorney, Lorna Propes, tried to get him ruled innocent by reason of insanity, claiming that he had become increasingly paranoid since his arrest for male prostitution two months earlier. But the jury found DeWit Guilty, and he was sentenced to twenty-two years in prison.

REF.: *CBA;* Nash, *Murder Among the Mighty.*

Cornelius and John De Witt, assassinated in 1672.

De Witt, Cornelius, d.1672, and **De Witt, John,** 1625-72, Neth., assass. Two brothers who served a Dutch Republic were slain by a murderous mob when the political climate shifted. The sons of a prominent citizen of the city of Dordrecht, John De Witt and Cornelius De Witt were defenders of civil rights, like their father, and worked for democratic principles throughout their careers. The talented brothers rose to high honors at early ages, with Cornelius known for his legal and military skills, and John distinguishing himself as a statesman and administrator. At twenty-five, John was elected pensionary of Dordrecht, becoming Grand Pensionary of Holland two years later, in 1652. He used his considerable political influence to oppose the House of Orange.

When John De Witt came into power, Holland was at war with England, and the Dutch admirals had suffered several devastating defeats. The Dutch military's weakened situation was compounded by De Witt's ambitious attempts to prevent France from acquiring the Spanish Netherlands. After Louis XIV had fortified France on all sides to prevent Holland from retaliating, the French king declared war on the tiny lowland country. De Witt found he had misjudged the situation; although he knew the French king was angry at the Dutch Republic's preventing his acquisition of the Spanish Netherlands, he never anticipated Louis taking the drastic action of crushing the much smaller country. As the slow, grinding war of invasion took its course, 20-year-old Prince William of Orange began to appear to the Dutch populace as a savior from the destruction brought on by De Witt's folly. As French forces pressed in on their attacks, De Witt, as head of the government, tried to negotiate better peace terms than he would if France captured all of the country. The House of Orange denounced De Witt's measures as treason, demanding that Prince William be put in power.

Two assassination attempts were made on the De Witt brothers in Summer 1672, instigated by the House of Orange. On July 2, the Prince of Orange was elected to the position of Stadtholder of Holland and Zealand for life. Not long after, Cornelius De Witt was arrested and put into prison at the Hague, where he was tortured for four days. Forced to sign a document revoking the Perpetual Edict, Cornelius De Witt added "V.C." underneath his name, explaining when asked that the letters stood for "vi coastus," Latin for "yielding to violence."

On Aug. 20, 1672, John De Witt was called to the infamous Buitenhof Prison in Hague, and told that his brother wanted to see him. The brave former pensionary complied with the summons, and was trapped by a howling mob, which yelled, "Hurrah for Orange! Death to the traitors!" The mob forced open the prison doors, dragged Cornelius from his cell, where he had been left with the sentence of perpetual banishment, and brutally murdered both men, then beat and kicked the corpses, stripped the bodies, and dragged the remains to a gibbet, and hung them by their feet. The bloodthirsty murderers also tore flesh from the dead men, selling it in the streets as souvenirs.

REF.: *CBA*; Johnson, *Famous Assassinations of History.*

De Wolf, Orrin, prom. 1845, U.S., mur. Orrin De Wolf occupied a room at the boarding house run by William Stiles in Worcester, Mass. Stiles' wife, a voluptuous and unfaithful woman, seduced De Wolf and reportedly suggested that her lover kill Stiles so they could be together. On the night of Jan. 14, 1845, De Wolf waited until Stiles was asleep and then crept into his bedroom and strangled the landlord with a silk handkerchief which Mrs. Stiles had loaned him for the deed. Although Mrs. Stiles reported her husband's death from natural causes, physicians soon discovered that he had been murdered, and De Wolf was quickly implicated by other boarders who had seen him with Mrs. Stiles. De Wolf confessed when confronted, but he did not implicate his lover, and Mrs. Stiles was never charged. De Wolf was tried and condemned, but his death sentence was later commuted to life imprisonment.

REF.: *CBA; Trial of Orrin De Wolf.*

Dharmavamsa, d.1007, Indo., jur. Ruled Eastern Java as king, 991-1007, and was a compiler of legal doctrines. REF.: *CBA.*

Dhiliyiánnis, Theódoros (Theódoros Diliyiánnis, Deligiánnis), 1826-1905, Gr., prime minister, assass. Served as prime minister of Greece, 1885-86, 1890-92 and 1895-97, but resigned from post after Greek army was defeated in war with Turkey. He was later assassinated. REF.: *CBA.*

Dhlomo, Sicelo Godfrey, c.1969-88, S. Afri., (unsolv.) mur. The killing of 18-year-old Sicelo Godfrey Dhlomo led to finger-pointing by the U.S. press and the government of South Africa, each accusing the other of causing the youth's death.

Dhlomo's body was found on Jan. 25, 1988, with a bullet lodged in his head, not far from his mother's home in Soweto, S. Afri. The black activist had given an interview to the Central Broadcasting System television network stating that he had been physically beaten while detained by police. His interview aired in a program entitled "Children of Apartheid." Police had held Dhlomo in connection with a May 1986 killing of a Soweto teacher. The

woman had a tire doused with gasoline placed about her neck and set on fire; a type of killing known as "necklacing." Dhlomo was acquitted of the murder charge.

Government officials contend that a CBS director coached Dhlomo into making the statement about his mistreatment while in custody, and that the youth had signed an affidavit to that effect just five days before his death when police questioned him concerning the interview. CBS denied the allegations. South African Law and Order Minister Adriaan Vlok added that the murder was probably committed by those who wanted Dhlomo to remain silent about the truth of his interview, stating that the South African Communist Party and African National Congress would kill even children to destroy the country. While the government maintains it had no involvement in the killing, Dhlomo's lawyer Tayob Kamdar, pointed out that he and the youth's family were officially informed of the death four hours prior to police discovery of the body. REF.: *CBA.*

Diagoras (AKA: The Atheist), c.450-400 B.C., Gr., blasphemy. Sentenced to death by the Athenians for acts of impiety, but fled to Corinth, escaping punishment. REF.: *CBA.*

Dial-A-Porn Case, 1987-88, U.S., obsc.-porn. A 12-year-old boy spent an afternoon in June 1987 listening to sexually explicit recordings over the telephone, and then two weeks later convinced a 14-year-old girl to have sex with him. The parents of both children sued the phone company, Pacific Bell, and the two companies which provided the pornographic services, for $10 million. This civil suit in turn led to stiffer regulations by the U.S. government.

In the spring of 1988, federal legislators created a law that bans all sexually obscene dial-a-porn operations, companies which offer customers the opportunity to listen to uncensored prerecorded sexual fantasies for a nominal fee, from transmitting messages which are easily accessible to anyone who can use a phone, including children. The first action taken by the Federal Communications Commission against such a firm resulted in a fine of $50,000 imposed upon Audio Enterprises, Inc., of Mill Valley, Calif., on Nov. 7, 1988. Wendy King of Audio Enterprises signed the agreement made in court which stipulates that the company will not be allowed to transmit further messages unless they are toned down, and made accessible only to those over eighteen by use of access codes, credit cards, or other devices. REF.: *CBA.*

Diamond, Jack (John T. Nolan, AKA: **John Thomas Diamond, John Hart, John Higgins, Legs**), 1897-1931, U.S., org. crime. No other gangster of the bootlegging 1920s survived more bullet wounds than Jack "Legs" Diamond, who was called the "Clay Pigeon of the Underworld." This vain, gaudy, and lethal gangster came to believe that he was invulnerable, once stating, "the bullet hasn't been made that can kill me." In that absurd belief, Legs Diamond was proved wrong. Born in the down-and-out Kensington district of Philadelphia in 1897, Diamond was delivered by a midwife. He and his brother Eddie (Edward Diamond, born in 1899) were raised in an impoverished Irish immigrant neighborhood and were practicing petty theft at an early age. How Diamond got the nickname "Legs" is in dispute. Some reports have it that this sobriquet was bestowed upon him while he was living in Philadelphia where he was known as an expert dancer. According to an underworld story, the moniker was applied to Diamond because of his ability to elude police after stealing packages from delivery trucks in Manhattan as a member of the Hudson Dusters gang.

When Diamond's mother Sara died in 1913, John Diamond, Sr., took his two sons, Jack and Eddie, to Brooklyn where they settled down and worked as a laborer. His sons grew up in the crime-ridden streets of New York, both becoming members of the Hudson Dusters, a gang of sneak thieves largely on the decline since 1916 when police smashed most of the gang's rackets. Legs Diamond was the most aggressive of the brothers and he soon rose in the ranks of the gang, coming to the attention of such gang bosses as Johnny Spanish Joseph Weyler, "Little Augie" Orgen, and Nathan "Kid Dropper" Kaplan. Beginning in 1914, Diamond ran up a staggering number of arrests for burglary, assault, and robbery, serving short stints in the New York City Reformatory. In 1918, he was drafted into the U.S. Army to serve in WWI. Diamond, however, had no intention of soldiering and went AWOL. When he was later picked up by military police, he was charged with desertion and given a five-year sentence in Leavenworth. He served a year and a day, being released in 1920. He worked briefly as a bodyguard for Arnold Rothstein, the wealthy gambler and financier to most New York racketeers. A short time later Diamond went to work for one of Rothstein's partners, Little Augie Orgen.

When Legs returned to New York, he found that Kid Dropper Kaplan was now in almost total control of Manhattan bootlegging, the Volstead Act having gone into affect only a few months earlier. Kaplan had murdered his most important rival, Johnny Spanish, on July 29, 1919, and the vast, lucrative Manhattan territory became a battleground where the underworld armies of Kaplan and Little Augie Orgen waged war, vying for control of bootlegging at the dawn of Prohibition. Diamond joined Orgen and was soon the gangleader's most trusted lieutenant. Others in Orgen's formidable gang included Charles "Lucky" Luciano, Waxey Gordon, and Louis "Lepke" Buchalter. Diamond and Gordon aided Orgen in setting up distribution for Orgen's bootleg liquor and beer, Luciano the prostitution and drug rackets, and Buchalter, through strong-arm squads headed by his enforcer, Jacob "Gurrah" Shapiro, took over the garment district and its unions for Little Augie.

Kid Dropper Kaplan, however, proved to be a constant thorn in Little Augie's side, driving his men out of rich bootleg territories and taking over speakeasies once controlled by Orgen. Little Augie went to Diamond and ordered him to eliminate Kaplan—no easy chore. Legs merely nodded and then went to a neurotic little gangster named Louis Kushner (nee Cohen) whom Diamond knew also bore a deepseated hatred for Kaplan, who had been blackmailing Kushner for the beating of a garment worker, threatening to have the worker sign a complaint against him unless Kushner continued his regular monthly payments to one of Kaplan's goons. Diamond told Kushner that he could become an important man if he shot Kaplan to death. The dimwitted Kushner agreed to shoot the gang boss at whatever location Diamond designated. Next Diamond went to Jacob Shapiro and asked him to sign a complaint against Kaplan for shooting at him in early 1920 on Essex Street in a wild gun battle where the Kaplan-Orgen factions shot it out for a number of minutes, resulting in the killing of two passersby. At first Shapiro thought Diamond had gone crazy. Gangsters do not take other gangsters to court, Shapiro reminded him. But this was part of Diamond's plan. He said to Orgen and Shapiro: "Get him into court. Once we pinpoint him, we can get to him."

Shapiro signed the complaint and Kaplan was summoned to answer assault charges in the Essex Market Court on Aug. 28, 1923. He arrived with half his gang members and a gun was found in his possession. Yelled the gang chief: "I had to carry it! Self defense! Little Augie and the Diamonds are after me! They want to kill me!" The gun was held by the court and Kaplan placed on bail. Since Shapiro had not appeared in court, the present charge was dropped and Kaplan was released. Diamond, with Kushner at his side, watched from across the street as Kaplan was escorted down the stairs of the courthouse building by police captain Cornelius Willemse. Diamond shoved Kushner forward and the youthful gangster, a gun in his pocket, walked swiftly across the street where squads of police were ushering Kaplan toward a detective squad car. Kaplan got into the car with Willemse sitting next to him. Kushner worked his way through the crowd to the back of the car, jumped onto the bumper, and, as hundreds of police and passersby gaped in shock, rapidly fired several shots through the back window of the car. One shot wounded the driver in the ear, while another blew off the straw-boater worn by Captain Willemse. Kaplan dove to the floor of the car unharmed. Kaplan's wife, Veronica Kaplan, who was on the sidewalk

nearby became hysterical, then leaped forward and held onto Kushner screaming: "Don't shoot him! Don't shoot him!" Kushner pushed her down and then smashed out the glass of the window, took careful aim, and fired a shot which struck Kaplan in the head. He looked up at Captain Willemse for a moment, a grimace on his florid face, then croaked: "They got me." The next second he was dead. Dozens of policemen, meanwhile, surrounded the killer, holding revolvers to Kushner's head. He dropped his gun and asked for a cigarette, smiling and gloating with the words: "I got him." Kushner, through Orgen's connections with Tammany politicians, received a minimum sentence. For eliminating Little Augie's most dangerous rival, Diamond received an enormous slice of Kaplan's bootleg and narcotics rackets, which led from Manhattan to Albany, N.Y.

Diamond's fortunes soared. His new riches allowed him to buy large touring cars, nightclubs, and live in resplendent apartments. He surrounded himself with tough gangsters, loyal only to him, not his boss Orgen. He also surrounded himself with gorgeous showgirls. His wife Alice, to whom he had been married since 1920, stayed at home, ever loyal to her husband, and allowed him to tend to his business, whatever it was. (Alice Diamond later stated, after her husband had been shot to death, that she had no idea he had been a gangster for a decade.) When Diamond was not overseeing his bootleg and narcotics empire, he spent most of his spare time with Marion "Kiki" Roberts, a blonde Manhattan showgirl who became his mistress. Alice Diamond knew about Kiki Roberts, but she treated her husband's mistress as if she were Legs' hobby. She pointed to her wedding ring when reporters asked her about Miss Roberts. "She may have some of my husband's attentions," she said proudly, "but I have the man."

Alice Diamond hero-worshipped her gaunt, hollow-eyed gangster spouse and adorned the walls of her home with dozens of photos of Diamond. On a large photo of Legs mounted above the fireplace mantle in the living room, Alice had written across the picture: "my hero." To Kiki Roberts, Diamond was a wealthy patron who showered jewels and furs on her, not to mention a private bank account that swelled each year from Diamond's bootleg fortunes. Diamond, however, was not true to either his wife or Kiki Roberts. He actually had several mistresses—a harem of them plucked from the chorus line of his nightclub, the Hotsy Totsy Club, located on Broadway between 54th and 55th streets. This infamous speakeasy, which Diamond owned with Hymie Cohen, was the scene of several bloody shootouts. To this club trooped the powers of the New York underworld, paying homage. These included Waxey Gordon, Owney Madden, Vannie Higgins, Larry Fay, "Big Bill" Dwyer, Charles "Lucky" Luciano, Dutch Schultz, and Louis "Lepke" Buchalter.

Buchalter, however, went to see Diamond for other reasons. He intended to take over the garment industry unions, stripping Orgen of one of the most lucrative rackets in New York. He asked for Diamond's help, but Legs refused to commit himself. On Oct. 15, 1927, Diamond met with Orgen at Little Augie's headquarters at Delancy and Norfolk streets. The two men stepped from Orgen's offices and began walking down the street. A few minutes later, a cab pulled up to the curb and, as Orgen was about to step into it, the back door swung open and a machine gunner crouched on the floor let loose a burst. Twelve bullets smashed into Orgen, and he dropped dead to the pavement. Diamond, also caught in the quick barrage, took a bullet in the leg and another in the arm. He left a trail of blood as he staggered down the street, collapsing inside a doorway as the cab and its killers roared off down Norfolk Street.

Diamond was found by police and rushed to a hospital. Some hours later, after the bullets had been removed from his body, Diamond was propped up in a hospital bed and surrounded by inquiring detectives. He snarled the code of the underworld at them: "Don't ask me nothin'! You hear me? Don't ask! And don't bring anybody here for me to identify! I won't identify them even if I know they did it!" He collapsed into unconsciousness. Legs Diamond knew Orgen's killers the minute the cab stopped.

He recognized Jacob "Gurrah" Shapiro at the wheel of the cab and the small, wiry man on the floor of the cab with the machine gun was none other than rackets boss Louis "Lepke" Buchalter. When Diamond emerged from the hospital, he sent Buchalter a message, telling him that he had no interest in the garment industry rackets. He would keep to his bootlegging and narcotics peddling.

With Orgen gone, however, Dutch Schultz felt that much of Orgen's bootlegging territory rightfully belonged to him and he moved into Manhattan from Brooklyn, his army of goons invading Diamond's territory also. Diamond had amassed quite an array of gunmen by then, lethal killers such as Charles Entratta (alias Charlie Green), A.J. Harry Klein, A. Treager, Jimmy Hart, Tony Fusco, Paul Quattrochi, Jimmy Dalton, Salvatore Arcidicio, John Herring, and John Scaccio, also known as Willie Talamo, a beer distributor for Diamond who specialized in torturing bartenders into buying Diamond's home-made brew. The battle between Diamond and Schultz waged for more than two years, with Schultz's legions getting the worst of it. Diamond's men actually controlled all the major highways in upstate New York along which bootlegged bonded whiskey was trucked from Canada. Much of Diamond's bootleg empire was secretly financed by multimillionaire rackets king Arnold Rothstein and Diamond, in turn, shared the enormous profits with his benefactor. When Rothstein was murdered in 1928, Diamond lost his bankroll and his organization began to slip. Moreover, when he tried to absorb Rothstein's rackets, the remnants of Rothstein's gang offered stiff resistance.

While battling the gunmen of Schultz, Waxey Gordon, and others, Diamond became involved in a wild gun battle himself in the middle of his Hotsy Totsy Club. William "Red" Cassidy and some other smalltime hoodlums entered the club on the night of June 13, 1929, demanding service and insulting everyone. Diamond and Charles Entratta, Legs' chief enforcer, stepped up to the group and told them to act politely. Cassidy called Diamond a "pimp," and tried to hit him. Cassidy and his friends then advanced on Diamond and Entratta, who pulled guns and began firing. Cassidy was mortally wounded and was helped downstairs by some of his friends. He was rushed to a hospital but died in the ambulance. Upstairs, his head still resting on the bar, two loaded .38-caliber revolvers stuck in his waistband, Cassidy's friend, Simon Walker, was also dead. Walker had recently been paroled from Sing Sing.

Diamond and Entratta went into hiding and when they surfaced, surrendering to police, they were quickly released from an original charge of murdering Walker and Cassidy, due to "lack of evidence," even though there had been more than two dozen witnesses. These witnesses, of course, were all contacted while Diamond and Entratta hid out, and threatened with death if they identified Legs or his enforcer as the men who did the shooting. The battle with Dutch Schultz continued to take its toll on both sides. Then Schultz's top aide, Joey Noe, talked the hot-headed Schultz into meeting with Diamond to establish a truce. Schultz balked at the idea at first, telling Noe : "I don't trust Legs. He's nuts. He gets excited and starts pulling a trigger like another guy wipes his nose." Diamond felt the same way about the Schultz, remarking: "I don't trust the Dutchman. He's a crocodile. He's sneaky. I don't trust him."

The meeting was nevertheless arranged and both gang leaders met at the Harding Hotel. Diamond told Schultz that he would relinquish the rights to the mid-town beer territory which Schultz had preempted in 1929 and that his men would stop trying to retake that territory. Diamond, however, insisted that Schultz pay him for giving up such a lucrative territory and Schultz reportedly gave Diamond $500,000 in cash on the spot. Diamond explained that his other rackets were taking up too much of his time anyway. He departed with the suitcase full of cash. Schultz and Noe then left the hotel and when on the street, two men ran from an alley and shot Noe to death. Schultz pulled his own gun and began advancing on the two rival gangsters, firing at them. The men

fled. Another Schultz aide arrived and the Dutchman roared in rage: "That damned double-crosser Diamond just shot Joey. I'm gonna kill him for this!" Finding Diamond was next to impossible, so Schultz sent killers to murder Eddie Diamond.

Eddie Diamond had been sickly for some time with lung trouble. Legs had sent him to Denver for his health and there Eddie was ambushed as he drove in his car. More than 100 .45-caliber bullets sprayed at him from machine guns held by three killers. Miraculously, Eddie Diamond survived the attack, later dying of tuberculosis in a New York sanitorium. But Diamond vowed that every one of the men who tried to kill his brother, the only person to whom he was ever loyal, would pay with their lives. The first of these was Eugene Moran, one-time bodyguard to Arnold Rothstein (and who had once posed for Arrow Shirt ads) who had gone to work for Schultz. Diamond's men caught Moran in Manhattan, shot him in the head, and took him and his car to the Newark, N.J., dump where the body and car were set afire. Frank "Blubber" Devlin and James Pietro were next; both killed and their bodies dumped in New Jersey.

The killings went on and on. Diamond's men murdered Tom "Fatty" Walsh, Moe Schubert, James Ahern, James Batto, Harry Vesey, and Antonio Oliverio, all former Rothstein men who had joined Schultz. All were gunned down, most killed by ace Diamond executioner Joe McDonald, an expert with a submachine gun. Dutch Schultz fought back, sending his gunman to New York's Hotel Monticello in October 1929. There they found Diamond with Kiki Roberts, dining in his pajamas in her suite. They smashed down the door and let loose a withering barrage of submachine gun fire that tore the place to shreds, planting five bullets in Legs Diamond. Roberts went unscratched. Again, Diamond survived. He decided a European trip would be healthier than dodging the Dutchman's bullets in New York. He traveled to England and Belgium where he reportedly established drug connections before returning to New York.

Back in New York, Diamond moved his headquarters to Acra, N.Y., living with his wife in the Aratoga Inn. One day in April 1931, Diamond stepped from the inn and gangsters from a passing car shot him to pieces, but he once more survived. Dutch Schultz started to believe that Legs Diamond was invincible, complaining to his top gunmen: "Can't anybody shoot that guy so he won't bounce back up?" In December of that year, Diamond and several men moved to Albany, N.Y., attempting to convince local bootleggers, Grover Parks and James Duncan, to work with them. Parks and Duncan refused and Diamond's men dragged them to an Albany hotel room where James Scaccio and others tortured the men, burning them with lighted cigarettes, sticking lighted matches beneath their fingernails, and searing their backs with red hot pokers. Parks and Duncan finally agreed to work with Diamond.

Both men, however, went to the police with the whole ugly story when they were released, and Diamond and Scaccio were arrested and tried in Troy, N.Y., on a kidnapping charge. Diamond barely escaped conviction but Scaccio was convicted and sent to Sing Sing for ten years. Diamond promised that he would get him out within a few months, but Diamond instantly forgot his loyal stooge. To celebrate his release, on Dec. 17, 1931, Diamond, his wife, and friends went to an Albany speakeasy, and after several hours of drinking, Diamond excused himself, saying that he had to see some "newspaper pals," and would return to his party within a half hour. He got into a cab and John Storer drove the gang leader to 21 Broeck Street where Kiki Roberts had an apartment. Diamond stayed with his mistress for three hours, then staggered back to Storer's cab, very drunk, and told him: "take me home," giving the address of 67 Dove Street, a rather shabby boarding house.

At this address, Diamond needed help unlocking the front door of the building. Storer then put the key into Diamond's pocket and the gang leader shakily climbed the stairs to a rather seedy single room, a hideout. (His wife was staying at another address. Following his usual procedure, Diamond had rented several single

Gangster brothers Jack and Eddie Diamond, 1929.

"Legs" Diamond, center, under arrest, 1931.

"Legs" Diamond's wife, Alice.

Marion "Kiki" Roberts

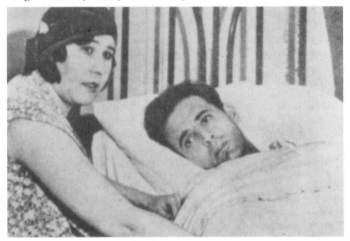

Wounded again, Diamond is consoled by wife Alice.

Diamond gunman Charles Entratta.

Jacob "Little Augie" Orgen

Diamond gunman Thomas "Fatty" Walsh.

Jack "Legs" Diamond, 1930.

The burial of Jack "Legs" Diamond, December 1931.

rooms in the city so that no one trying to kill him would be certain where to find him.) Once inside the room, Diamond collapsed on a single frame bed and fell into a deep sleep. Minutes later two men drove up to the Dove Street address, got out of a long black car, and went into the boarding house, using a key that opened the front door. They climbed the stairs and to gain entrance to Diamond's room they used another key or the key the drunken gangster may have mistakenly left in the door. They switched on a flashlight and saw Legs Diamond asleep on the bed in his underwear, oblivious to their entrance. They grabbed him, held him up, and fired three bullets almost point blank into his head. They then fled, but on the stairs, according to the housekeeper, Mrs. Laura Wood, who heard them, one of them turned and said he was going back to "finish the job...That guy ain't human and it will take a lot to get him for sure." The other man grabbed his partner and said: "Oh, hell, that's enough. C'mon!" Both men then ran down the stairs, out to the car, and sped away.

Wood called Alice Diamond immediately, as she had been instructed in case of any trouble. Then she called the police. Alice Diamond arrived first, rushing up to the open room and cradling the body of her slain husband, screaming: "My God, Jack, what have they done to you? They killed my dear Jack! Someone do something!" But there was nothing anyone could do. This time, Jack "Legs" Diamond was dead. A police doctor pronounced him dead, but police could not pry Alice Diamond away from the corpse. They fought for ten minutes to release her vise-like grasp of her hero while she screamed: "No! No! You can't have him! He's mine, he belongs to me! Let me stay with Jack!" The hysterical, sobbing Alice Diamond suddenly composed herself, so abruptly that it startled officers. Before leaving the building, she turned cooly to detectives and said: "I didn't do it."

Obviously, because of Diamond's torrid and open affair with Kiki Roberts, Alice Diamond had every reason to want her husband dead. But so did dozens of others, including Dutch Schultz, Vincent Coll, Waxey Gordon, Owney Madden and other rival gangsters. Two underworld figures, Salvatore Spitale and Irving Bitz, later emerged as the prime suspects since it was all but proven that they had given Diamond more than $200,000 to establish a drug connection during his European trip. They later learned that he had not done as planned, but spent the money on his own pleasures. These two men, it was claimed, were the killers of Legs Diamond, but proof was lacking and neither was ever charged. The killing of Jack "Legs" Diamond remains unsolved. See: **Buchalter, Louis; Coll, Vincent; Fay, Larry; Higgins, Vannie; Hudson Dusters; Kaplan, Nathan; Luciano, Charles; Madden, Owen; Orgen, Jacob; Rothstein, Arnold; Schultz, Dutch; Spanish, John.**
REF.: Addy, *The Dutch Schultz Story*; Asbury, *The Gangs of New York*; Campbell, *The Luciano Project*; Carpozi, *Bugsy*; ____, *Gangland Killers*; CBA; Clarke, *In the Reign of Rothstein*; Cook, *Mafia!*; Curzon, *Legs Diamond*; Eisenberg and Landau, *Meyer Lansky*; Feder and Joesten, *The Luciano Story*; Fried, *The Rise and Fall of the Jewish Gangster in America*; Gage, *The Mafia is Not an Equal Opportunity Employer*; Gaylord, *The Rise and Fall of Legs Diamond*; Gosch and Hammer, *The Last Testament of Lucky Luciano*; Hopkins, *Our Lawless Police*; Horan, *The Desperate Years*; Katcher, *The Big Bankroll*; Katz, *Uncle Frank*; Kobler, *Ardent Spirits*; Levine, *Anatomy of a Gangster*; Maas, *The Valachi Papers*; McClellan, *Crime Without Punishment*; Merz, *The Dry Decade*; Messick, *Lansky*; ____, *Secret File*; ____ and Goldblatt, *The Mobs and the Mafia*; Nash, *Bloodletters and Badmen*; Peterson, *The Mob*; Powers, *Secrecy and Power*; Reppetto, *The Blue Parade*; Rothstein, *Now I'll Tell*; Sann, *Kill the Dutchman*; ____, *The Lawless Decade*; Smith, *Syndicate City*; Thompson and Raymond, *Gang Rule in New York*; Walker, *The Nightclub Era*; Willemse, *Behind the Green Lights*; (FICTION), Kennedy, *Legs*; (FILM), *The Rise and Fall of Legs Diamond*, 1960; *Portrait of a Mobster*, 1961.

Diaz, Aldolfo, prom. 1926, Nic., pres., attempt. assass. A failed attempt on the life of Aldolfo Diaz, the man recognized by the U.S. as Nicaragua's president, left only a cut in his heel, while the driver of his carriage received a far worse fate in defending Diaz.

Diaz, the conservative president opposed by a liberal, Dr. Juan Sacasa, was riding alone in his carriage when the attack occurred in December 1926. Two men wielding machetes jumped in the right-hand door of the carriage; at the same moment Diaz fled the vehicle through the left-hand door, having his left heel slashed by a machete. The carriage driver then attacked the would-be assassins, who in turn easily fought him off leaving the man bleeding profusely from the vicious attack. He died later in the hospital where Diaz had driven him, after the two assailants fled at the sight of police. REF.: *CBA*.

Diaz, Anacleto, 1878-1944, Phil., jur. Served as prosecuting attorney for Ilocos Sur on the Philippine Islands, 1911-13, and was appointed to the Superior Court of the Philippine Islands by President Franklin Roosevelt, Jan. 8, 1934. REF.: *CBA*.

Diaz, Robert R., 1938- , U.S., mur. Robert R. Diaz finished nursing school at the age of forty and moved from Gary, Ind. to Apple Valley, Calif. He was arrested on Nov. 23, 1981, following the investigation into the unexplained deaths of sixty hospital patients in Los Angeles, Riverside, and San Bernadino counties in California. Officials were able to link Diaz to twelve deaths from overdoses of lidocaine. Eleven patients died between Mar. 30 and Apr. 22, 1981, at the Community Hospital of the Valley in Perris where Diaz worked, and one died at San Gorgonio Pass Memorial Hospital on Apr. 25, the one night that the temporary nurse worked there.

Diaz, who waived his right to a jury trial, appeared before Riverside Superior Court Judge John H. Barnard on Oct. 31, 1981. Deputy District Attorney Patrick F. Magers produced seventy-one witnesses, including several co-workers who stated that Diaz had predicted patients in stable conditions would soon become ill—they later died. Three syringes were also displayed in court as those used in the murders. The defense, conducted by Public Defender Michael B. Lewis and Deputy Public Defender John J. Lee, provided experts who claimed that the large amount of lidocaine in the corpses may have accumulated over time, but their testimony was far outweighed by the prosecution's case. Barnard found Diaz Guilty on Mar. 29, 1984, and on June 15 sentenced him to die in the gas chamber. See: **Harvey, Donald; Jones, Genene.** REF.: *CBA*.

Diaz de Solis, Juan, c.1470-1516, Spain, (unsolv.) mur. Succeeded Amerigo Vespucci as Spain's chief pilot, 1512, and sailed to South America and entered the estuary at Rio de la Plata, becoming one of the first European explorers to do so. He continued his voyage up the Uruguay River where he met his death during an ambush by Charrúa Indians. REF.: *CBA*.

Diaz de Vivar, Rodrigo, (AKA: El Cid, El cantar de mio Cid), c.1043-99, Spain, banish. The legendary El Cid was a national hero of Castille for his exploits on the battlefield, but due to an unauthorized raid upon Toledo, 1081, King Alfonso VI had him banished. He was called back, 1087, in order to fend off an attack by the Almoravids, and became the chief magistracy for the Muslim government in Valencia, 1094. REF.: *CBA*.

Diblanc, Marguerite, prom. 1872, Brit., mur. Madame Caroline Riel, French mistress to General Lord Lucan (who had been responsible for the notorious charge of the Light Brigade) was extremely arrogant with her servants. In 1872, when a Belgian cook, 29-year-old Marguerite Diblanc, was deemed unsatisfactory because the soup was not to Mme. Riel's taste, she was given only a week's pay along with her notice on Apr. 7. The cook argued that a month's pay was usual, but got no agreement, so she strangled Riel with a rope and hid her body in a pantry, where no one else was apt to go. Then she stole some money and jewels and quietly spent the remainder of the day going about her business. When other employees and Riel's daughter looked for Mme. Riel, Diblanc made an excuse for her absence.

That night, saying that she was just going out for the evening, Diblanc fled to France, where she stayed with friends and repaid them an old debt. Meeting another Belgian friend, she told him the whole story, which he promptly related to the police. Diblanc was extradited, tried, and found Guilty of murder. Although she was sentenced to death, her sentence was commuted to life in prison in recognition of her provocation by Mme. Riel's known temper.

REF.: Altick, *Victorian Studies in Scarlet*; Brock, *A Casebook of Crime*; CBA; Forster, *Studies In Black and Red*; Franklin, *Woman In the Case*; Kingston, *Dramatic Days at the Old Bailey*; Wilson, *Encyclopedia of Murder*.

Dicey, Albert Venn, 1835-1922, Brit., jur. Authored the following works: *Lectures Introductory to the Study of the Law of the Constitution*, 1885, which some consider to be part of the British constitution, *Digest of the Law of England with Reference to the Conflict of Laws*, 1896, and *Lectures on the Relation Between Law and Public Opinion*, 1905. REF.: CBA.

Dick, Evelyn Maclean White, 1922-   , Can., mansl. Evelyn White's first husband died in 1946. That same year she married a 39-year-old bus driver named John Dick, but she refused to allow him to live with her. Evelyn did not want her marriage to disrupt her affair with Bill Bohozuk, a steel worker she had been seeing for some time. Complicating matters further were the domestic arrangements Mrs. Dick had with her mother and father. Both parents did not care much for their new son-in-law and insisted that she live with them.

Evelyn Dick, Canadian child-killer.

On Mar. 16, 1946, John Dick's mutilated body was found by some children in a remote mountainous area near his home town of Hamilton, Ontario, Can. Under police questioning, Evelyn made three statements which implicated herself and Bohozuk in the murder. Detectives searched the Dick home and found a basket of ashes in the basement which appeared to be human remains. In addition, the body of Evelyn's infant son Peter was found in a suitcase.

Evelyn, her mother, father, and Bohozuk were charged with murder on Sept. 23, 1946. Evelyn Dick was convicted after the first trial, but was granted a re-trial under appeal. In 1947, she claimed to have been an unwilling accessory, and blamed her father for the murder. Evelyn was acquitted. The verdict was assailed in the press. Four days later she was tried for the death of her child, found Guilty of manslaughter, and sentenced to life imprisonment. Her father pleaded guilty and received a five-year sentence. Bohozuk was eventually discharged.

REF.: Campbell, *Torso*; CBA; Nash, *Look For the Woman*.

Dick, Frank, prom. 1949-69, U.S., rob-asslt. Soon after his discharge from the navy, Frank Dick was caught trying to rob a chicken coop and was given a four-month jail sentence in 1949. After being released, Dick committed mostly bungled petty crimes for about five years, and decided to become a stick-up man in 1955. Captain John Klevenhagen, who arrested Dick several times, said of the inept and violent Galveston, Texas, thief, "He isn't smart enough to be a good lunch-box burglar, but he'll damn sure hurt you if he gets the chance." After holding up the madam of a brothel he often patronized, Dick avoided arrest by punching a police officer in the stomach. He escaped again a few days later from another brothel, this time with a policeman's bullet in his leg.

Moving from Texas to Kansas City, Mo., he went back to burglary, and was caught trying to rob a well-lit store. Dick was sent to prison for a year, and returned to Texas when he was released in 1957. He was soon arrested in Houston. Out on bail, he disappeared and was rearrested in Lansing, Kan. He returned to his home state, and was sentenced to another jail term. In 1969, he was released on parole, and soon decided to rob Wolfson's, an exclusive Houston jewelry store. He put down $500 on a ring, which he went to inspect several times as he cased the establishment. To gain experience for the jewelry store robbery, Dick first held up a supermarket in September 1969, getting away with $6,000. In November, he walked into the jewelry store carrying a large sack, with a bullet still in his shoulder from the supermarket job.

Dick ordered Wolfson, his wife, and a salesman into a back room, took irons from his sack, and shackled them. After forcing Wolfson to open the safe, Dick cleaned it out and was emptying the display cases when a customer about to enter the store saw Dick with a gun and notified a nearby policewoman, who called for assistance. Police surrounded the store. Dick emerged, forcing the clerk to walk in front of him as a hostage. Police Lieutenant Michna ended up changing places with the clerk, and Dick forced him into Foley's, a large department store across the street. Then, deciding a policeman was a dangerous hostage, Dick freed him and grabbed Mrs. Elia Narvaez. Finally, as police neared, Dick panicked. He shot Detective Wyatt in the stomach, then shot Mrs. Narvaez, Officer Michna, and another policeman. Dick then collapsed, shot in the back and the legs. All of the victims survived, as did Dick, who was sentenced to three 45-year terms for shooting the policemen and another twenty-five years for wounding Mrs. Narvaez. REF.: CBA.

Dick, Jack, c.1928-74, Case of, U.S., theft-forg.-fraud-embez. In the early 1970s, Jack Dick convinced hundreds of people to invest in his Black Watch Farms cattle corporation.

Dick's misadventures began with his father's manufacturing business, which Dick allegedly bankrupted after taking over in 1957 and pocketing $250,000 of company money. When he attempted to purchase Carpenter Steel Co. in 1959, a court ordered him to never again sell securities in New York, because he failed to protect investors against loss. The Securities and Exchange Commission obtained a permanent injunction against Dick in April 1960 after he tried to use another's name to buy $290,000 worth of stock.

Then came Dick's coup de grâce, Black Watch Farms. For investors, it meant paying only twenty-five percent, rather than fifty percent, in taxes on the money they invested. For Dick, it meant not having to invest a dime of his own money, while reaping millions. Investors paid $3,500 for a cow that Black Watch Farms had purchased for only $650 or $750. By June 30, 1969, the company that began with one farm in Wappinger Falls, N.Y., had grown into more than sixty ranches in twenty states, and had revenues totalling nearly $30 million. But Dick had bailed out by that time. In July 1968 he sold the farms to the Bermec Corporation for shares that he in turn sold for $5 million. Bermec did not know that Dick had embezzled $3.2 million between 1966 and 1968 by forging cashier's checks, or that Black Watch Farms would soon be bankrupt because of poor management, a bankruptcy that would also bring down Bermec as well.

While the farms were going under in 1969, Dick's father sued him for $20 million, claiming that his son had promised him one half of his earnings because the elder Dick had once helped his son when he was broke. The suit was thrown out of court, but the criminal case against Dick for fraudulent practices as head of Black Watch Farms was just beginning. Dick died in January 1974, before the charges against him were resolved.

REF.: CBA; Moffitt, *Swindled*.

Dick, Robert Paine, 1823-98, U.S., jur. Served as U.S. district attorney for North Carolina, 1853-61, and was appointed to the Western District Court of North Carolina by President Ulysses Grant, June 7, 1872. REF.: CBA.

Dickens, Sir Henry Fielding, 1849-1933, Brit., jur. As queen's counsel, the sixth son of Charles Dickens was barrister for the defense of Kitty Byron, 1902, who had murdered her stockbroker lover outside the Lombard Street post office; and was the prosecuting barrister for both abortive trials of William Gardiner, who allegedly killed Rose Harsent. He also served as London's Common Sergeant, 1917-32. REF.: CBA.

Dickey, Orange C., 1920-   , U.S., law enfor. off. Before WWII, Sergeant Orange Dickey was employed as a campus policeman at Pennsylvania State College. When the war began, Dickey was assigned to the Criminal Investigation Division, and stationed in Naples where he learned an American criminal was living in exile—New York crime boss Vito Genovese who had fled to Italy in 1937 to escape a murder indictment. Before Benito Mussolini was deposed, Genovese was one of his most ardent supporters. In 1944 when the tide of the war had gone against the Italian fascists, the mobster had prudently switched sides. Genovese joined the staff of Charles Poletti, the former New York lieutenant-governor who was stationed in Naples as the Allied commander, and worked as an interpreter and allied informant.

Genovese became a black market operator, secreting away millions of dollars obtained through the illicit sale of medicine, foodstuffs, cigarettes, and liquor. Described as "trustworthy," and "loyal" by his superiors, Genovese roamed freely throughout Italy visiting supply depots and military bases. Genovese enjoyed the protection of the U.S. government and conducted his business with impunity. Dickey arrested Genovese in Naples, and then spent the next few months trying to find a U.S. prosecutor willing to try the case. In November 1944, the FBI replied to his inquiry, informing Dickey that a warrant would soon arrive from Brooklyn on an earlier murder charge still pending against Genovese.

In the meantime, Dickey was under pressure to release Genovese, or at least transfer him out of the military prison. He consulted with Brigadier General William O'Dwyer, who in his civilian days had successfully prosecuted Murder Inc. O'Dwyer provided little to no help. He casually informed Dickey that Genovese was of "no concern" to him. The warrant arrived in December, and Genovese attempted to bribe Dickey with an offer of a quarter-million dollars. Dickey refused.

On board the ocean liner bound for New York, Genovese said to Dickey: "Kid, you are doing me the biggest favor anyone has ever done to me. You are taking me home. You are taking me back to the U.S.A." Genovese's statement was prophetic. After they arrived in New York on Jan. 8, 1945, the government's star witness, Peter LaTempa, was murdered while in protective custody. LaTempa died from poisoning while in his cell, and the case against Genovese collapsed. The Mafia boss was freed and resumed control of his crime family.

REF.: *CBA;* Maas, *The Valachi Papers;* Peterson, *The Mob;* Reid, *Mafia.*

Dickinson, Charles, See: **Jackson-Dickinson Duel.**

Dickinson, Charles Monroe, 1842-1924, U.S., consul general. Served as the U.S. consul general to Turk., 1897-1906, obtained the release of Ellen M. Stone, who was a U.S. missionary held captive by Bulgarian outlaws, and was the consul general to the entire Near East, 1906-08. REF.: *CBA.*

Dickman, John Alexander, 1865-1910, Brit., mur. Wages clerk John Innes Nesbit regularly made the brief train trip from a bank in Newcastle back to Alnmouth, in Northumberland, carrying a leather satchel containing the money to pay his coal mine's wages. But his journey of Mar. 18, 1910, ended in death. His body was found stuffed beneath the train seat, and the satchel containing £370 was missing. In Nesbit's head were bullets of two different calibers. On the floor was a small wad of paper. Plenty of witnesses along the way had seen him with another man identified as John Dickman, a 43-year-old bookie. Even Nesbit's wife, who usually came down to the train for a brief chat as it passed through Nesbit's hometown, had seen him with Dickman. Dickman left the train at a station two miles from where Nesbit was last seen alive.

Dickman had an answer for everything the police asked, but his story did not add up, especially when it was found that he was badly in debt and that he had purchased a gun through the mail. A line-up was held, at which Percival Hall, a co-worker of Nesbit's who had seen him board the train with a man, picked out Dickman. But, it was learned later that Hall had caught a glimpse of Dickman before he was placed among eight other men. The money satchel was found down a pit near where Dickman left the train.

Dickman's trial began on July 4 at Newcastle Assizes. Mrs. Nesbit identified Dickman as the man she saw with her husband. Nine employees testified that Dickman had taken pains to learn about the wages transport method and schedule. But the defense claimed that the two kinds of bullets proved that the murder had been committed by two different people and, therefore, Dickman, never seen with anyone else, was not the murderer. However, when the ticket collector testified that Dickman had had the exact fare in one hand while his other hand was held completely out of sight (the inference being that the satchel was in it), the jury found Dickman Guilty and sentenced him to death. An appeal based on Hall's premature sighting of Dickman was turned down. Dickman was hanged on Aug. 10, 1910. Later, it was learned that Dickman had wrapped paper around the slightly smaller bullets to make them fit his gun. They did not fire very well, but the proper bullets did their job. The paper from the smaller bullets was found on the carriage floor, but not recognized.

REF.: Birmingham, *Murder Most Foul;* Bresler, *Scales of Justice;* Brookes, *Murder In Fact and Fiction;* Butler, *Murderers' England; CBA;* Goodman, *The Railway Murders;* Hasting, *The Other Mr. Churchill;* Lambton, *Thou Shalt Do No Murder;* Logan, *Guilty or Not Guilty?; Notable British Trials;* Shew, *A Companion to Murder;* Shore, *Crime and Its Detection;* Whitbread, *The Railway Policeman;* Wilson, *Encyclopedia of Murder.*

Dickson, Christopher, and **Gibson, John,** and **Weymouth, Charles,** d.c. 1713, Brit., rob. These three robbers are remembered for impersonating devils. In one of their early attempts at robbery they accosted an old man only to find that he had no valuables except for a pair of cheap glasses. The old man begged Dickson to return the spectacles, but the robber refused. John Gibson finally spoke up, telling Dickson that it was unlikely that any of them would live long enough to require the aid of eyeglasses, and that they might as well return them to the old man, which the vicious Dickson grudgingly did.

Hearing that the owner of a Berkshire inn was superstitious, these three thieves concocted a bizarre robbery scheme. The bandits killed an ox and cut off its feet. That night they stopped at the inn in Berkshire County and ate a large supper and then retired to their room, taking with them large bags filled with straw; now they stuffed the straw up the chimney and filled the bags with all the valuables in the room.

In the morning a chambermaid looked in the room and screamed at the sight of cloven feet hanging over the ends of the beds. She now believed that the men were actually devils in disguise and went to the innkeeper with this tale. The innkeeper crept up to the door and peeked through the keyhole to confirm the grisly scene. The three men later appeared in the dining room and ate a large breakfast. When they asked for their bill the innkeeper insisted that there would be no charge for their stay, so fearful was he of these would-be devils.

The thieves thanked him and quickly departed, their bags stuffed with stolen goods. When the theft was discovered the innkeeper was even more relieved, now that he knew they were robbers, not devils.

The three were finally arrested and charged with robbing three men on the Queen's Highway. They were convicted and sentenced to death and hanged at Tyburn. REF.: *CBA.*

DiCocco, Paul, Sr. (AKA: Legs), 1924-89, U.S., org. crime. Paul DiCocco was known as an organized crime associate with more than four decades of convictions on gambling charges. The bookmaker was thought to be the Capital District's major link with organized crime. With ties to several known mobsters, DiCocco was said to control racketeering operations in Montreal, along with New York mob boss Carmine Galante. He was also linked to Nicholas Robilotto, president of the Teamsters Local 294; both were charged with conspiring to underbid other construction companies. DiCocco's Schenectady, N.Y., luncheonette was often raided for gambling. In 1951, DiCocco was the central figure in a Schenectady County grand jury investigation of gambling and corruption, after he allegedly had a traffic ticket removed from city records. Although Police Chief Joseph A. Peters denied ordering the ticket removed, he resigned his post within days. In 1957, DiCocco was subpoenaed by Mayor Samuel S. Stratton, who ordered him to testify at a City Hall investigation regarding his organized crime connections. In a thirty-minute period of questioning, DiCocco invoked the Fourth and Fifth Amendments seventy-six times. A grand jury investigation in the 1970s dragged on for years; DiCocco was eventually indicted on charges of contempt and perjury.

In 1977 DiCocco pleaded guilty to obstructing governmental administration and to contempt just before a retrial was scheduled to begin; the first trial had ended in a hung jury. He was fined $1,000, placed on three year's probation, and jailed for sixty days. In November 1985, DiCocco pleaded guilty to felony charges of coercion in connection with a Massachusetts-based gambling ring's efforts to extend operations to five New York counties, including Schenectady. DiCocco's neighbor's knew him as a generous man who gave away food and cash at his luncheonette to needy people, and helped others find jobs. He was on parole at the time of his death in August 1989. See: **Galante, Carmine.** REF.: *CBA*.

Di Cristina, Giuseppe, prom. 1920s-70s, Si., org. crime. Long a Mafia don in Sicily, Giuseppe Di Cristina ruled the province of Riesi and Ravanusa, where he was responsible for ordering the murders of at least twenty men each year for six decades. A big, burly man, Di Cristina established a Mafia family that still rules the area today. This murderous Mafia don was arrested in the early 1970s and was one of the dozens of Mafia members who appeared in the Palmero show trials but was acquitted. He was later tried for ordering the murder of two men in Agrigento in 1974 but, as usual, he was acquitted.

REF.: *CBA;* Servadio, *Mafioso.*

Di Cristina, Paul (Paulo Marchese), d.1909, Si.-U.S., org. crime. Di Cristina, born and raised in Palermo, Si., was a prominent member of the Mafia in the 1890s, working with Francesco Matesi, a brigand who robbed and raped at will during the night but during the day served as a member of the city council of Palermo. Both these Mafia dons extorted money from all levels of their society but were opposed in 1900 by a family named Sienna. The pair entered the Sienna home and slaughtered seven people, then fled to the U.S. Di Cristina went to New York while Matesi went to New Orleans, where he became the Mafia don.

In New York, Di Cristina established Black Hand rackets and was involved in various murders. One of these was the slaying of Benedetto Madonia, whom he chopped up and stuffed into a pickel barrel after Madonia refused to meet Di Cristina's Black Hand demands. This killing was investigated by the intrepid Lieutenant Joseph Petrosino, a burly New York cop who headed the Italian Squad (a unit responsible for apprehending Italian and Sicilian criminals who had illegally migrated to the U.S.) When Petrosino got on Di Cristina's trail, the Mafia don left for New Orleans where he joined Matesi and helped to establish a powerful Black Hand racket there.

Matesi had changed his name to Francesco Genova, under which he owned and operated a macacroni factory in Donaldson, about seventy miles outside of New Orleans. He and Di Cristina grew wealthy through their New Orleans rackets. Anthony and Salvatore Luciano (no relation to Charles "Lucky" Luciano) were property owners who also owned a macaroni factory in Donaldson and saloons in New Orleans. They refused to pay Matesi-Genova and Di Cristina any Black Hand money and were summarily marked for murder. The Luciano brothers, however, first attempted to kill the Mafia dons, firing at them with shotguns on a New Orleans street with shotguns. They missed and Matesi-Genova and Di Cristina pursued them through the streets in a running gun battle until all were stopped by startled police officers. The Sicilians would not answer any police questions or even admit to having shot at each other.

Then Salvatore Luciano admitted that he had fired at Matesi-Genova. The Mafia don laughed and said: "The man is crazy. He didn't shoot at me. I know him well. We have always been friends. There isn't any reason why he should wish to kill me. On the contrary. He is quite crazy." The men were released, but a short time later Matesi-Genova and Di Cristina sent four killers to the home of Salvatore Luciano and these men summarily stabbed Luciano to death. Anthony Luciano responded to his brother's screams, and ran to his home with shotgun in hand; he blasted one assailant to death and wounded another while the other two fled. The wounded man was later tried for the murder of Salvatore Luciano but acquitted.

Anthony Luciano then sought out Angelo Ferrara, one of his brother's escaped murders, and killed him with a double blast from his shotgun. Police arrested Luciano as he stood over Ferrara's body. "I am satisfied," Luciano told them. "I have killed the man who slew my brother." He was acquitted in a quick trial but he was marked for death by Di Cristina and Matesi-Genova. The Mafia dons recruited a young man named Espare, recently arrived from Sicily, and sent him to kill Luciano. Espare took several months to establish a friendship with Luciano and then, while the unsuspecting Luciano was showing Espare photos of his children, the Mafia assassin pulled out a revolver and fired six bullets into Luciano's back. Espare was later apprehended and tried. Found guilty, he was hanged, the first time an Italian was hanged in New Orleans for the murder of another Italian.

Matesi-Genova was implicated in the Luciano killing, and that of a kidnapping-murder of a 6-year-old boy. He was arrested on suspicion of the child's murder and held while his criminal record in Sicily was unearthed. New Orleans police informed police in Palermo that they wished to ship Matesi-Genova back to his home country but the Sicilian police refused to accept him. Matesi-Genova was ordered to leave New Orleans and he departed, last seen in London in 1910.

Di Cristina now reigned supreme as the top Mafia don in New Orleans but he, too, ran afoul of stubborn Sicilians who refused to pay his extortion demands, chiefly the wealthy wine merchants who made up the Giacona family. Di Cristina sent four men to shoot Alfredo Giacona while he sat on his back porch of his mansion on Chartres Street. The old man was ready for them, firing two revolvers as the four youths charged him. He killed three and wounded the fourth, who was found some blocks away by police following his bloody trail.

John and Tony Barrecco then drove a wagon load of gunmen past the Giacona residence, and the gang peppered the house with bullets but injured no one. The Barrecco brothers were arrested for attempted murder, but Di Cristina spent more than $5,000 in their defense and the brothers were acquitted, raising Di Cristina's stature in New Orleans. He grew ever richer and soon began traveling between New York, New Orleans, and Palermo, Si., recruiting new Mafia members to serve him in all three cities. His American wealth and his ability to escape arrest, earned him the esteem of Mafia dons in Sicily and he was appointed as a full Mafia don and member to the Grand Council of the Mafia in Palermo. He was in Palermo when Lieutenant Joseph Petrosino, working with the Sicilian police to identify New York criminals wanted in Sicily, arrived in Palermo in 1909.

Di Cristina actually met with Petrosino, pretending to be a wealthy landowner and friend of the police, one who could help Petrosino in pinpointing wanted fugitives. The two reportedly dined together on Mar. 12, 1909, the night Petrosino was murdered on orders from Di Cristina, shot to death by several Mafiosi who gunned him down in the main square of Palermo. This murder caused an international scandal, and police pressure in Sicily became so intent on finding the killers of Petrosino that Di Cristina departed for New Orleans. Here, in the fall of 1909, Di Cristina boldly reassumed his Black Hand operations, going about the streets in his elegant buggy, stopping at stores run by Sicilians and Italians, and demanding daily extortion payments under the threat of murdering whole familes and burning down their shops.

When Di Cristina arrived at the grocery store owned by Pepitone, the grocer, who had refused to pay Black Handers in the past, decided not to banter words with the Mafia don. He stepped out of his store with a shotgun in his hands and fired two barrels into Di Cristina, killing him. Pepitone was tried and convicted of manslaughter and sent to prison for twenty years. He was pardoned within six years, but his son Michele was accidentally killed in 1919 by Mafia assassins thinking he was Di Cristina's killer. REF.: *CBA*.

Diderot, Denis (AKA: Pantophile Diderot), 1713-84, Fr., insurgent. Imprisoned for writing *Lettre sur les Aveugles,* 1749; Diderot is most famous for his collaboration with Jean Le Rond d'Alembert, the *Encyclopedie,* 1751-72, which included articles written by Jean-Jacques Rousseau, Voltaire, Baron de La Brède et de Montesquieu, Anne-Robert-Jacques Turgot, François Quesnay, Georges-Louis Buffon, and others. REF.: *CBA*.

Didius, Julianus (Didius Salvius Julianus, Marcus Didius Severus Julianus), 133-193, Roman, emperor, assass. Purchased the right to be Roman emperor at an auction of the Praetorian Guard following the death of Emperor Pertinax, 193, but was assassinated by invading Danube soldiers who favored Lucius Septimus Severus. REF.: *CBA*.

Diem, Ngo Dinh, See: **Ngo Dinh Diem.**

Diener, George Edward, prom. 1972, Case of, U.S., mur. Teenager Richie Diener was thoroughly involved in the drug culture of the early 1970s. He smoked hashish and marijuana, and at seventeen began taking the barbiturate Seconal. Tension between Richie and his father increased and reached a climax when Richie crashed his mother's car on Feb. 27, 1972. Diener sent his drugged but uninjured son home before calling police. Later, at their home in East Meadow, Long Island, an argument broke out over Richie's plans to go out for the evening after he took four more pills. Fearing for their safety, his parents retreated to the basement with an automatic pistol. Richie came down the stairs with an icepick, but returned for a steak knife before daring his father to shoot him, which Diener promptly did, killing his son with a bullet to the heart. The Nassau County grand jury did not indict Diener, a superb marksman, claiming he acted in self-defense in killing his son.

REF.: *CBA;* Godwin, *Murder, U.S.A.*

Dier, Richard A., 1914-72, U.S., jur. Served as U.S. attorney for the Department of Justice in Omaha, Neb., 1969, and was appointed to the District Court of Nebraska by President Richard Nixon, December 1971. REF.: *CBA*.

Dies, Martin, 1900-72, U.S., lawyer. Elected to the U.S. Congress, 1931-45 and 1953-59, and was House chairman for the committee investigating activities considered un-American. REF.: *CBA*.

Diesbach, Niklaus von, 1435-75, Swiss, jur. Served as chief magistrate for Bern, 1465-66 and 1474-75. REF.: *CBA*.

Dies Committee Investigation, prom. 1942-45, U.S., subversion. In 1942, Attorney General Francis Biddle reported that of the 1,100 people of the Federal payroll who were listed by Congressman Martin Dies and his Dies committee investigation as having subversive connections, the FBI found only two worth firing, and one who required discipline. With that, the Dies Investigation was discredited. The investigation had cost $495,000 as of September 1942, and the FBI investigation had cost another $100,000. Representative Dies had come to national attention in 1938, when he became chairman of a recess committee appointed to investigate un-American activities. Elected to Congress in 1931, he charged that France, Italy, Russia, England, Germany, and Japan all maintained propaganda machines in the U.S.; he introduced a bill calling for deportations. In 1944, Dies charged that the government was riddled with seditious radicals. But a newspaper that had previously supported his investigations called them "a witch hunt sure to play into Hitler's hands." Those accused of treasonous behavior by Dies included newspaper columnist Walter Winchell and chairman of the CIO Poltical Action Committee, Sidney Hillman.

Dies withdrew from politics on May 12, 1944, and his departure was expected to mean the end of the controversial House Committee of Un-American Activities, which he had chaired for six years. Although House Republicans decided on Nov. 15, 1944, to discontinue the committee, Missippi Representative John I. Rankin asked for a suprise roll-call vote which gave permanent tenure to the Un-American Activities Committee. The Committee had great power during the slanderous anti-communist campaign of Wisconsin State Senator Joseph Raymond McCarthy, from the late 1940s until 1954. See: **Biddle, Francis Bevereley; McCarthy, Joseph Raymond.** REF.: *CBA*.

Dietl, Marilyn, prom. 1978, U.S., mur. Rather than allow her 18-year-old daughter to enter a world of prostitution, Marilyn Dietl shot her to death.

Judy Dietl graduated from Colchester, Vt., High School where she was voted the prettiest girl in the class of 1977. She moved to Boston, Mass., with her friend Diane Brochu, and enrolled at Bay State Junior College. The girls lived at the nearby YWCA to save on expenses. They began dating two men who turned out to be pimps. Judy's mother learned of the situation when Brochu dropped out of school. Judy did not know she was dating a pimp, but agreed to return home with her mother in the spring of 1978. Judy eventually decided to return to her boyfriend in Boston. Her mother, convinced she would end up a prostitute, decided to stop her. On May 5, 1978, Judy and her mother went for a ride. They two got out of the car in the parking lot behind the Ohavi Zedik Synagog in Burlington, Vt., where Dietl emptied a .38-caliber revolver into her daughter's chest, arms, and legs. Dietl then had someone call the police. She was found Guilty of second-degree murder and sentenced to five to fifteen years in the Chittenden County Correctional Center. REF.: *CBA*.

Dietrich, Joseph (AKA: Sepp), b.1893, Ger., war crimes. As a military leader, Joseph "Sepp" Dietrich was second rate. His blundering at the Battle of the Bulge in 1943 cost the lives of 37,000 German soldiers. But as a devoted Nazi, Dietrich had few equals.

In 1931, he was given command of Hitler's elite SS Guard. Three years later, on June 30, 1934, Dietrich and Michael Lippert ruthlessly purged 1,000 members of Ernst Roehm's SA Storm-troopers, who were perceived to be a threat to the Führer. Dietrich organized a firing squad that disposed of six senior officers from the SA. In 1945, Dietrich was in command of a division in Belgium. In the last stages of the war, Dietrich ordered the execution of 142 U.S. soldiers captured at Malmédy. The general's cold-blooded actions in this regard resulted in his conviction at the war crimes tribunal in 1946. The Allied court sentenced Dietrich to twenty-five years in prison.

He served ten years in Landsberg Prison in Bavaria before his release was ordered on Oct. 22, 1955. Less than two years later, Dietrich and Lippert were back in court again. This time the former Nazi general had to answer to murder charges stemming from the 1934 Roehm purge. On May 14, 1957, Lippert and Dietrich were each sentenced to eighteen months in prison by a court in Bonn. The defense maintained that Dietrich's actions were consistent with normal military protocol during the time of a government crisis. The court called Dietrich's actions lawless terrorism. REF.: *CBA*.

DiFronzo, John (AKA: No Nose), 1928-   , U.S., org. crime. John DiFronzo first came to the attention of the Chicago Police in 1949 when he was caught holding up a Michigan Avenue clothing store. During the subsequent shootout, he was clipped in the nose by a police bullet, hence the famous nickname. In 1952, DiFronzo emerged as a prime suspect in the murder of Charles Gross, a shady politician from the West Side. The Gross shooting was never officially solved. A veteran of the "Three-Minute" Gang, DiFronzo made the papers again in 1964 when he was identified and arrested as one of the ringleaders of a "juice" loan racket that included former policemen Albert Sarno and Chris Cardi.

Following the imprisonment of Joseph "Doves" Aiuppa in 1986 for his role in skimming $2 million from Las Vegas casino profits,

Joseph Ferriola was chosen by Aiuppa to run mob operations in Chicago's western suburbs. But because of Ferriola's ostentatious lifestyle, which drew unwanted attention to the crime syndicate, Aiuppa named DiFronzo to take over while he remained in prison. See: **Aiuppa, Joseph; Ferriola, Joseph.** REF.: *CBA.*

Digby, Sir Everard, 1578-1606, Brit., consp. Executed for his involvement in the Gunpowder Plot of 1605. REF.: *CBA.*

Digges, Sir Dudley, 1583-1639, Brit., jur. Served in parliament, 1610, 1614, 1621, 1624-26 and 1628, and began the case calling for the impeachment of Buckingham, 1626. REF.: *CBA.*

Diggs, Charles C., Jr., prom. 1978-81, U.S., fraud-polit. corr. Charles C. Diggs, Jr., once the U.S. House of Representatives' senior black member, was convicted by a federal jury on Oct. 7, 1978, of eleven counts of mail fraud and eighteen counts of taking kickbacks from government employees. A Democrat from Detroit, Mich., he was elected to Congress thirteen times before he was found to have taken about $66,000 between 1973 and 1977 from employees' paychecks. Diggs increased the salaries of some of his employees so that he could receive the extra income. He resigned his seat the day after the U.S. Supreme Court denied his appeal on June 2, 1980. On July 24, Diggs began serving his sentence of three years in the federal prison at Maxwell Air Force Base in Alabama. He was released to a halfway house on Feb. 25, 1981, to serve the last three months. REF.: *CBA.*

Dikko, Umaru, prom. 1984, Case of, Brit., kid. Two crates marked "diplomatic property" were discovered July 6, 1984, aboard a Nigerian Airways plane bound to Lagos, Nig. from Stansted Airport, about thirty miles north of London. The crates turned out to contain four men, three of whom were heavily drugged.

Umaru Dikko, the former Nigerian Transport Minister in the government of Shehu Shagari, was found unconscious in one of the crates. He had fled Nigeria after the army seized power on Dec. 31, 1983, and imprisoned Shagari. Inside the crate with Dikko was a conscious man equipped with needles and drugs. The second crate contained two other drugged men. All three drugged men were believed to have been captured earlier in the day on the street outside Dikko's home. Dikko, known as the "most wanted man" by the Nigerian government, was rescued by British anti-terrorist police. REF.: *CBA.*

Dilke, Sir Charles, prom. 1886, Case of, Brit., adult.-perj. By not taking the witness stand and denying the charges against him, Sir Charles Dilke was found Guilty of adultery by public opinion. At a second trial to clear his name, he was branded a perjurer as well as an adulterer.

Dilke was a promising British politician in 1886 when a Mrs. Crawford confessed to her husband that she had had an affair with Dilke. On this evidence alone a trial was held. During the trial, Dilke's counsel, Sir Henry James and Sir Charles Russell, did not allow him to testify, although he could prove the allegations false. Justice Butt agreed with Dilke's lawyers, and the trial ended with a divorce decree filed against the wife and a co-respondent for adultery. Dilke then made the mistake of calling for a second trial to clear his name by claiming the court had been deceived. A second trial was held, and the evidence Crawford presented was even more damaging to Dilke's character, but her testimony also contradicted evidence displayed by Dilke. He had proven with documents and witnesses that he could not have been with the woman on the dates cited. The jury found the court was not deceived in the first trial, which gave credence to the belief that Dilke was an adulterer. But now he had perjured himself on the witness stand. Much later, the great advocate Sir Edward Marshall Hall obtained proof of Dilke's innocence from a servant girl, Fanny, said by Crawford to have shared in the affair. Fanny denied ever knowing anyone by the name of Crawford, but said police had warned her not to testify.

REF.: *CBA;* Marjoribanks, *For the Defense, The Life of Sir Edward Marshall Hall.*

Dillard, E.H. (AKA: **Dr. Baxter**), prom. 1897, U.S., forg.-fraud. E.H. Dillard also known as Dr. Baxter, was a very well spoken, stylishly dressed black man, who arrived in Chicago from the west in 1897. Convincing a Pullman car porter, A.B. Williams, that he was a very wealthy doctor, Dillard offered him a job as his secretary for $150 a month. Williams accepted, taking Dillard to his Dearborn Street boarding house, where the landlady, Ella Clark, arranged for two of the best rooms to be refurnished for the "doctor" and his secretary. Dillard took Williams to the stockyards the next day and showed the man thousands of heads of cattle which he claimed were his. Also, Dillard convinced Williams that he was expecting two checks of $1,500 and a draft from an Australian bank for $36,000. Dillard borrowed cash from both Williams and Clark, and wrote the landlady a bad check for his board. Arrested by Detective Clifton R. Wooldridge, Dillard was found to have bilked large amounts of money from many Chicagoans by pretending to be a successful stock raiser and buyer. Several people appeared to press charges, and Dillard was held to the criminal court on Sept. 16, 1897, by Justice Hall under a $3,500 bond. Arraigned before Judge Gary on Oct. 6, 1897, Dillard pretended to be insane, but this last act failed and he was found Guilty following testimony by about thirty witnesses. Dillard was sentenced to a lengthy jail term.

REF.: *CBA;* Wooldridge, *Hands Up.*

Dillard, Norman, (AKA: **Skip**), 1960- , U.S., rob. Co-captain of the DePaul University Blue Demons basketball team from 1981-82, Skip Dillard turned to robbery to support his cocaine addiction when he failed to become a professional basketball player. Dillard committed fifteen armed robberies over a seven week period, eight of them during the first nine days of September 1987.

The former guard's spree began on July 21, 1987, and ended when Dillard was arrested, after robbing his thirteenth Chicago gas station, on Sept. 9. He used a steak knife in the hold-ups, which brought him a total of $3,261, never more than $500 at a time. Andrew L. Robinson, thirty, acted as a getaway driver in three of the robberies. Dillard's final robbery was witnessed by federal Judge Francis J. O'Byrne, who later identified Dillard. He pleaded guilty to the robberies and was sentenced on Oct. 3, 1988, by Cook County Criminal Court Judge William Cousins to eleven years in prison. Co-defendant Robinson got seven years. REF.: *CBA.*

Dillen, Bob, 1951- , U.S., (wrong. convict.) rob.-rape-kid. Between July 1979 and November 1980, Bob Dillen was arrested thirteen times in Pennsylvania and Indiana, standing trial in five cases on charges of robbery, rape, and kidnapping. In each case, at least one eyewitness identified Dillen as the criminal. After a Fotomat shop in Castle Shannon, Pa., was robbed, the kidnapped clerk led police to a Venango County cabin where she had been held—police found Frank Jeziorski, twenty-eight, who confessed to all the crimes Dillen had been accused of. Police Superintendent Robert Kroner, whose investigators eventually tracked down Dillen's look-alike, said that the fact Dillen was cleared was proof that "our legal system works." But Dillen's career as a freelance photographer was destroyed, his father's $30,000 retirement fund was used for legal fees, and his wife left him. Dillen expressed bitterness toward the police, saying, "This thing about being innocent until proven guilty isn't true. Once you're there, you're it. They don't look for anyone else." Dillen's lawyer, John Murtagh, helped crack the case; after an October robbery of a Fotomat shop, he suggested that Dillen leave town; when two more were robbed on Oct. 28, Murtagh proved Dillen was hundreds of miles from the crime scenes. Three days later, Jeziorski was arrested. On July 1, 1981, Jeziorski was sentenced to thirty-five to seventy years in prison for robbery, robbery associated with theft, and kidnapping. REF.: *CBA.*

Dillinger, John Herbert (AKA: **John Hall, John Donovan, Frank Sullivan, Carl Hellman**), 1903- ? , U.S., rob. No bandit in twentieth century America so captured the public imagination and frustrated the efforts of police and federal agents as did John Herbert Dillinger, a shrewd farm boy from the flatlands of Indiana whose name is synonymous with bank robbery. The history of his notorious reputation is varied and few writers have bothered to investigate his real nature, exploits, and eventual fate, preferring to repeat the lurid newspaper tales of the day. The real story of this strange and unpredictable criminal is more astounding than the fictional profiles created about him in countless detective magazines. Delivered by a midwife on June 22, 1903, in his father's Indianapolis home, Dillinger's birth was surrounded with some mystery. His mother and father, John and Mollie Dillinger were already middle-aged at this time and Mollie Dillinger was not a well woman, dying of apoplexy in 1906 when John was only four years old.

Audrey Dillinger, his 15-year-old sister, took care of the child while his father, John Wilson Dillinger, maintained his thriving grocery store on Bloyd Street and looked after several houses he owned and rented. One claim later insisted that the closeness between Audrey and her little brother, fiercely maintained throughout Audrey's lifetime, was maternal—Audrey had really given birth to John out of wedlock, and his father was an unknown Indianapolis youth. Then considered a rigid social taboo, the elderly Mrs. Dillinger assumed responsibility for John. Photos of Audrey Dillinger and little John show a marked similarity in features, but those with young Dillinger and the elder Dillinger show decided differences in physical makeup. Audrey married Emmett Hancock in 1906 at the age of nineteen, living next door to her father in one of his houses on Cooper Street. When her mother died, Audrey, with her husband, gave up her own house and moved into her father's house to take care of little Johnny. Audrey Dillinger Hancock gave birth to seven children, beginning in 1908, but she continued to watch over John until her father remarried.

The elder Dillinger wedded Elizabeth Fields of Mooresville, Ind., in 1912. This union produced two children, Hubert, born in 1914 and Doris, born in 1916. Little John lived a normal life, playing outside his home on Cooper Street with a favorite tricycle. The elder Dillinger often took him to his grocery store where the child would sit on the seat of a horse-drawn wagon and travel the streets of Indianapolis while deliveries were made. Even after the elder Dillinger remarried, Audrey spent as much time with little John as she did with her own children. While teaching piano, Audrey tried to interest little John in the instrument but his interest and abilities were limited. He entered Public School 38 in Indianapolis and proved to be an average student—not brilliant according to his teachers—but one who was quiet and caused little or no trouble. After fourth grade, Dillinger attended Public School 55.

Though teachers and classmates later reported Dillinger to be an average student, his peers did notice that he seemed "tougher" than most of the other boys. No one was able to best him in a fight—even when he was opposed by more than one boy—although by nature, he was easygoing and did not look for trouble. One classmate remembered Dillinger, in sixth grade, going to the class bully and telling him to stop picking on smaller children or "I'll give you something to remember." He was occasionally truant from school, like the other boys and stole berries from a nearby orchard, like the other boys and went swimming in Fall Creek, like the other boys. He loved baseball and, unlike the other boys, excelled at the game, proving to be a good pitcher and a swift infielder. His aim in throwing out runners was deadly accurate. Along with the other boys, classmates later remembered, Dillinger played cops and robbers and did not care which side he was on.

In grammar school, Dillinger showed little interest in academic subjects but became intensely interested in anything mechanical, according to Elizabeth O'Mara, one of his teachers. Unlike some of the other boys in her class, she later pointed out, he never stole the small change she kept in her desk. The boy had a wry sense of humor and played subtle, harmless pranks that secretly amused O'Mara. Dillinger was a polite child, tipping his hat to teachers and adults he knew when on the street. When he received some bad grades, Dillinger signed the elder Dillinger's name to a report card and this earned him severe punishment from the elder Dillinger, a severe taskmaster who, it was claimed, locked John in a bedroom on occasions. Another report had it that little John

was, at one time, chained to a bed when he refused to obey, but this is not to be believed given the boy's usually quiet and unassuming ways. Another story, offered up by writer John Toland, reports John giving some gum to a pretty girl in his father's store and, being caught in the act, hit so hard by the elder Dillinger that the boy flew over a counter, his lip running blood. This is fiction.

While in sixth grade, Dillinger, part of a small gang of boys but not its leader, stole some coal from the Pennsylvania Railroad yards and sold it to neighbors. He and the other boys were dragged out of bed one night and taken before a local magistrate who lectured the boys about stealing and then placed them in the custody of their parents. It was reported that Dillinger was the only defiant one in the gang, staring back at the judge, arms folded, his cap pulled low over his eyes, his jaw slowly working a piece of gum. The judge ordered him to remove the gum and Dillinger took it out of his mouth and slowly stuck it on the bill of his cap while grinning at the judge who remarked: "Your mind is crippled." This, too, is a piece of Toland's fiction. Dillinger was not wearing a cap, nor was he chewing gum at this hearing. He was just as frightened as the other boys, having been dragged out of bed by a policeman who barely allowed him to put on his shirt, pants, and shoes. He did not defy the judge nor was he singled out in any way before the magistrate released the boys.

Following his graduation from grade school, Dillinger was suddenly uprooted and went with the elder Dillinger to live on a farm in Mooresville, Ind., seventeen miles south of Indianapolis. The elder Dillinger sold his store and houses and bought the farm, a lifetime ambition. He also wanted his children to grow up on a farm, rather than in the city which he felt held too many corruptive influences. John continued his education, entering high school, but he dropped out at sixteen, taking a job at a veneer mill where he was considered a good worker, one who helped out his fellow workers when needed and was called a "right guy" by his co-workers. After five months, he grew bored with this job and went to work as a runner for the Indianpolis Board of Trade, a job he held for four months. He then went to work for the Reliance Specialty Company, a machine shop where he worked, on and off, for several years. Dillinger was thought to be "honest and industrious" by his employer, James P. Burcham, but he lost interest in the work and would not appear for some months, preferring to take odd jobs and ride about on his beloved motorcycle.

More to please his stepmother than to fulfill his own ambitions, Dillinger returned to school, but he dropped out of his first semester at Mooresville High. The elder Dillinger asked that he help out on the small farm the Dillingers were then working, but John made up one excuse after another and went back to his machinist job. Said the elder Dillinger years later: "My people have been farmers for generations. I liked the land. John never did. Said it was too slow...I guess the city kind of got hold of him." In nearby Martinsville, Dillinger watched a local amateur baseball team go through its workouts and then joined the squad, proving to be an expert infielder. He was assigned the position of second base. At about the same time, he fell in love with Frances Thorton, the stepdaughter of his uncle Everett Hancock and he asked for her hand, but the uncle ended the affair when he informed Dillinger that he and his stepdaughter were too young to think of getting married. Everett Hancock did not tell his nephew that he really wanted Frances to marry a boy from Greencastle, Ind.

Dillinger, angry and feeling rejected, returned to Indianapolis where he began drinking heavily. His father was alarmed to hear neighbors tell him that they had seen Johnny patronizing whores in Indianapolis. John later went to a doctor for treatment of gonorrhea. It was then, on the night of July 21, 1923, the day before his twentieth birthday, Dillinger committed his first serious crime. He was standing outside the Friends Church in Mooresville, thinking to attend, when he saw a key in the ignition of a car belonging to Oliver P. Macy. Friends saw him get into the

John Herbert Dillinger, at the age of six months.

Audrey and John Dillinger.

Dillinger at age seven.

John with his father on the farm, 1915.

Dillinger at sixteen.

John Dillinger, left, in the U.S. Navy.

Second baseman Dillinger, standing, second from right.

Little John in the delivery wagon, 1907.

car and drive away. John Dillinger had stolen his first car. He drove the car to Indianapolis and parked it on a quiet street, then began walking about aimlessly. A policeman stopped him at midnight and he gave his real name. As the officer was calling the station house from a call box, Dillinger disappeared. Nothing came of the car theft. Macy refused to press charges and only a few people knew about the incident.

The theft made Dillinger nervous and, thinking he might be arrested for taking Macy's car, he enlisted in the U.S. Navy at an Indianapolis recruiting office, giving his real name but a fake St. Louis, Mo., address. He was sent to Great Lakes, Ill., for basic training and from there wrote a letter to Macy, insisting that he did not steal his car and that he had a girlfriend in Indianapolis who would vouch for his statements. Macy did not respond. On Oct. 4, 1923, Dillinger's basic training was completed and, as a fireman third class, he was assigned to duty on the U.S.S. *Utah,* one of the United States' great battleships which was destined to be destroyed by the Japanese at Pearl Harbor on Dec. 7, 1941. Dillinger's navy experiences would be brief and unrewarding.

No sooner was Dillinger on board the *Utah* than he went AWOL, on Oct. 28, 1923, disappearing for a full day. He was reprimanded when he returned and he went AWOL again, drawing a deck court-martial on Nov. 7, resulting in ten days' solitary confinement on bread and water which allowed a full ration of food every third day. He also lost $18 in pay. Defiant, Dillinger went AWOL again and another five days punishment was added to his sentence. He served all his time, but when the battleship anchored in Boston on Dec. 4, 1923, Dillinger left the *Utah* forever, deserting the U.S. Navy. He was posted as a deserter, and a $50 reward for his apprehension was offered, but never collected.

Dillinger did not return home until March 1924, telling his family and friends that he did not like the navy and that he had received an honorable discharge because of illness. He went back to occasional work as a machinist and that spring played baseball for the St. Martinsville team. Watching one of the games where Dillinger made some spectacular plays as a second baseman was 16-year-old Beryl Hovious. The two dated, fell in love, and were married on Apr. 12, 1924. Dillinger and his young bride lived at the Mooresville farm and at Hovious family's home in Martinsville. Dillinger was still restless and spent little time at home with his wife, going out late to poolrooms and bars in Martinsville. Often, his wife would go looking for him, tracking him down and dragging him home. In Gebhardt's poolroom, Dillinger befriended the man who would set him on the road to a criminal career, Edgar Singleton, thirty-one, married with several children. Singleton, an ex-convict who was one of the umpires for the Martinsville baseball team, had a criminal record of thefts dating back several years. It was Singleton who suggested that he and Dillinger pick up "some easy money" by robbing a Mooresville grocer, Frank Morgan. Singleton told Dillinger that Morgan took his weekly receipts home every Saturday night and it would be easy to relieve him of his money.

Both men lay waiting for Morgan on Saturday night at 10:30 on Sept. 6, 1924. As Morgan passed the Mooresville Christian Church, Singleton and Dillinger attacked him. It was never made clear which one struck Morgan with the heavy bolt wrapped in a cloth, but the grocer was hit several times and knocked to the sidewalk. He got up and Dillinger pulled a revolver from his pocket, waving it at Morgan while demanding him to turn over his money. The feisty 65-year-old Morgan, however, was not about to surrender his hard-earned money, and he boldly knocked the gun from Dillinger's hand. It went off when it struck the sidewalk and the sound echoed down the deserted Mooresville street. Morgan then began to yell for help, and both would-be robbers panicked and bolted for Singleton's car which was parked in a nearby alley. Singleton got in and drove off, leaving Dillinger, who had stopped to retrieve the gun, to flee on foot.

Sheriff John Hayworth answered Morgan's distress calls and took the injured grocer to a doctor; it took eleven stitches to seal Morgan's head wounds. Then Hayworth questioned several youths in Mooresville who told him that the most likely suspect was John Dillinger. Hayworth drove out to the Dillinger farm and took him to see Morgan. The grocer was unsure of the identity of his attackers and was surprised to see Dillinger who had often visited his store. "You wouldn't hurt me, would you, John?" he asked the 20-year-old.

"No, Mr. Morgan," Dillinger said.

Hayworth's information, however, led him to believe Dillinger was guilty and he placed John in the Martinsville jail. On Sept. 9, Dillinger was brought before the grand jury in Morgan County and indicted for attempted robbery. He was placed in jail again, pending trial, and the elder Dillinger visited him there. John broke down, admitting the robbery and the elder Dillinger urged John to tell the whole truth to the county prosecutor, Fred Steiger, which he did, on the promise of receiving a lenient sentence. Edgar Singleton was arrested on Sept. 15, 1924, after Dillinger implicated him in his confession.

It was Dillinger's misfortune (and that of the entire Midwest's as events of a decade later proved) to be tried before Judge Joseph Williams, the most severe, uncompassionate jurist in the county. With no lawyer to defend him, Dillinger pled guilty to conspiracy to commit a felony and assault with intent to rob. Judge Williams ignored the fact that Dillinger was a first offender and gave the youth the maximum sentence under the law, two concurrent sentences of two to fourteen years and ten to twenty years in prison, fining him $100 and disenfranchising him for twelve years. Prosecutor Steiger reneged on his promise of leniency, never mentioning the deal he had made with the elder Dillinger and his son. Edgar Singleton was also convicted a few weeks later, but he had the presence of mind to hire a lawyer and received a much lighter sentence, being paroled in two years.

Russell Peterson, the deputy sheriff who delivered Dillinger to the Indiana State Reformatory at Pendleton, sympathized with Dillinger and his family, telling the elder Dillinger that he did not agree with the brutal sentence handed down by Judge Williams. Said Peterson later: "He was just a kid. He got a raw deal. You just can't take ten years away from a kid's life." Dillinger quickly added six months to his sentence by trying to escape from Pendleton where he had been sent to serve his sentence. On Oct. 10, 1924, he slipped out of a work detail, returned to the cells, and hid in a large pile of excelsior inside one of the work sheds. When he was discovered missing that night, all the lights in the reformatory were turned on and Dillinger was forced from the excelsior when it was lighted by guards and it began to burn around him.

Escape was constantly on Dillinger's mind. When first being brought before A.F. Miles, warden of Pendleton, Dillinger calmly listened to Miles instruct him in the rules and regulations. Then Dillinger said: "I won't cause you any trouble except to escape."

"I've heard that kind of talk before," Miles replied.

"Yeah, well I'll go right over the administration building," Dillinger promised.

After he testified at Singleton's trial, Dillinger, escorted again by Deputy Peterson, was sitting at a soft drink stand in Indianapolis, waiting for a train to take him back to Pendleton. He suddenly kicked the table over on Peterson, sending the deputy crashing to the ground, and ran across the capital lawn, across Senate Avenue, and into a run-down tenement area. Peterson followed, gun in hand, trapping Dillinger in a blind alley. He fired his gun in the air and Dillinger quietly surrendered and was taken back to Pendleton. Here, the kind deputy agreed to tell the warden of the incident only after getting a promise that Dillinger would not be punished for trying to escape. He kept trying. In November 1924, Dillinger fashioned a homemade hacksaw and cut through the bars of his cell, slipping into a corridor. He was quickly caught and six more months were added to his sentence.

Dillinger's list of offenses grew. On Jan. 31, 1925, Dillinger was charged with being disorderly and was reprimanded. On Feb. 26, 1926, he was caught gambling and thirty days were added to his sentence. In August 1926, he was again charged with being disorderly and another thirty days were added to Dillinger's term. He grew sullen and depressed and, on Dec. 27, 1926, he started a fight and was sent to solitary confinement. He was released in a few days but started another fight on Dec. 31, and went back into solitary. Warden Miles described Dillinger at this time as troublesome, adding: "There is very little I can say in his favor." Meanwhile, the U.S. Navy, informed of Dillinger's imprisonment, dropped its fugitive warrant for him and issued him a dishonorable discharge. Also, his wife of five months, Beryl Hovious, who visited and wrote to him for a few years, slowly turned against him, writing him less, and less, and finally divorced him in 1929.

Before that time, however, Dillinger established two friendships that were to continue in his bank robbing heyday. The first was with a man who would deeply influence Dillinger's thoughts and behavior. Harry Pierpont was a well-educated, shrewd, and tough young bankrobber, who was sent to Pendleton after single-handedly robbing a Kokomo, Ind., bank. The second friendship was with Homer Van Meter, a wild young man who had also been sent to Pendleton for bank robbery. Dillinger, to earn the respect of these men, acted tough and got into trouble almost as if to show Pierpont and Van Meter that he was worthy of their admiration, that he was "tough enough" to endure solitary confinement or any other punishment authorities gave him. Pierpont and Van Meter disliked each other, however, and, after several vicious fist fights, they had to be separated in different cell blocks. Both proved so incorrigible that they were sent to the state prison at Michigan City, Ind.

In 1929, Dillinger expected a favorable response from the parole board. He had maintained a good record for several years and believed that he would be released, particularly with Indiana governor Harry Leslie sitting in on the hearing in July 1929. Dillinger had played well for the Pendleton baseball team and had heard that Governor Leslie, after watching him perform in some games, had remarked: "That kid ought to be playing major league baseball!" He appeared before Leslie, Warden Miles, and board member John Hoy. Miles reviewed his file and a brief discussion was held. Dillinger was told by Leslie: "Maybe you ought to go back for a few years." Realizing that he would not get his parole, Dillinger asked the board to grant a special request, then startled Leslie, Miles, and Hoy by asking if he could be sent to the state prison.

"Why do you want to go to Michigan City?" Governor Leslie asked him.

Dillinger remembered Leslie's interest in him as a baseball player and shrewdly replied: "Because they have a real baseball team up there."

The governor nodded and then told Miles and Hoy that such a notion might not be a bad idea, that if he got better experience playing baseball at Michigan City "it might lead to an occupation for him later." The request was granted, but Dillinger's desire to go to the state prison had nothing to do with his playing baseball. His wife had recently divorced him and his two best friends, Pierpont and Van Meter, had been sent to Michigan City. He undoubtedly felt that, if his parole was denied, he would have nothing more to live for than to get into the state prison with the top professionals in crime, especially the expert bank robbers to whom he was instinctively drawn. He had, at that moment, decided to become a professional criminal whenever he managed to get out and that when he did, it would be with the benefit of an education taught by the country's master bank robbers.

The gates of the Big House opened for John Dillinger on July 15, 1929, and he happily took his place among the prison popula-tion, renewing his friendships with Pierpont and Van Meter. Pierpont introduced Dillinger to experienced bank robbers John Hamilton, Charles Makley, Russell Lee Clark, and others who would form the core of the super bank robbing gang that would later operate under the nominal leadership of Pierpont and Dillinger. Hamilton, at thirty-four, was the most experienced of the group, having robbed banks throughout the Midwest. He was known as "Three-Fingered Jack" Hamilton, having lost the index

and middle fingers of his right hand in an accident years earlier. Intelligent and tough, Hamilton taught Dillinger the necessity of "casing" a bank—learning its assets and its security measures—be-fore robbing it. He also outlined the need to inspect the town in which the bank was located and the best escape routes from it. Special maps had to be made of the back roads going in and out of the area. Hamilton was considered one of the "tough cons" in Michigan City, but he seldom got into trouble, his worst offense occurring in 1932 when he was caught and punished for, of all things, skipping rope in the machine shop.

From Walter Dietrich, another hardcase bank robber who had been part of the gang once led by Hermann K. Lamm before being smashed in a police dragnet in 1930, Dillinger, Pierpont, and the others learned additional techniques. Dietrich, the only survivor of the gang, detailed Lamm's methods of robbing banks—intricate casing, surveillance of the bank, mapping escape routes, and the ever-important aspect of timing yourself when inside the bank, allowing for just enough time to perform the robbery before the estimated arrival of police. It had been Lamm's unswerving discipline that had allowed him to operate for a decade before mishap brought about his end. Dietrich proudly told his fellow inmates at Michigan City how Lamm would stand at the entrance of a bank with a stopwatch and, at the required moment, shout orders for gang members inside the bank to drop whatever they were doing and leave immediately, strictly adhering to his timetable. If the schedule demanded that a gang member not reach for another wad of bills when the time allotted for the robbery was up, that gang member retreated, obeying orders. Lamm, of course, was used to giving orders, having been an officer in the Prussian Army before WWI.

Charles "Fat Charley" Makley was another important member of Dillinger's coterie. At forty-four, he was long on experience as a bank robbery. Born in Ohio, Makley had been robbing banks since the early 1920s and had been sent to Michigan City after robbing a bank in Hammond, Ind. He was also a natural comic and vied with Van Meter at being the gang's clown. Russell Clark was a big, brooding man, imprisoned for bank robbery in 1927. He was the strong man of the bunch and his record at Michigan City was peppered with prison breaks, instigating riots, and several attempts to kill guards who displeased him.

Pierpont and the others groomed Dillinger well and for a purpose. All of his mentors were serving long prison terms with little hope of parole, but Dillinger was due to go before the parole board shortly and it was planned that once he was outside the walls he would perform several robberies of banks Pierpont, Makley, and Hamilton had mapped out with great detail. Dillinger would use the proceeds of these robberies to finance a mass prison break which would allow all of his closest friends to escape and join him. With that constant thought in mind, Pierpont taught Dillinger to assume the penitent posture, telling him that the authorities would be watching his every move, even reading his letters to family members to see if he had truly reformed and actually meant to go straight once he was released, knowing this would be taken into account by the parole board.

Dillinger's letters became more and more contrite. He wrote mostly to Audrey Dillinger, the closest family member, telling her how much he was looking forward to getting out of prison and helping out at the farm. To a niece, he wrote: "I know right from wrong and I intend to do right when I get out. I suppose you think that I do not try to make my time clear (without trouble) but, honey, I do try, and a lot of times when I want to start something that might get me into trouble I think of Sis (Audrey) and don't do it."

In April 1933, Indiana governor Paul McNutt received an amazing petition seeking the parole of John Dillinger from the state prison at Michigan City. There were 180 names signed to the petition which the elder Dillinger had obtained and sent on. Among those signing was grocer Frank Morgan, the very man Dillinger had attacked in 1924. Most important was the signature of Judge Williams who had rendered the harsh sentence to Dillinger, undoubtedly regretting the lengthy term he had assigned to the farm boy. Judge Williams even attached a solicitous letter which read, in part: "I have read the petition on behalf of J.H. Dillinger for clemency. I see that B.F. Morgan signs the petition. He was the party that was assaulted. I join in the recommendation for clemency petitioned for. Mr. Singleton, his partner, only received a sentence of from two-to-fourteen years and has been out of prison for about six years. As the trial judge I am entirely free to say that I think he should receive clemency as you in your judgment may see fit to grant, and trust that he may be paroled without delay to his father who will act, if appointed, as his parole officer...The father of this prisoner is getting up in years and needs the assistance of his son on the farm...I believe the prisoner has learned his lesson and that he will go straight in the future and make a useful and honorable citizen."

Governor McNutt sent the petition on to the parole board in May 1933 and here, on May 9, 1933, it was reviewed by Delos Dean, J. Tom Arbuckle, and Wayne Coy. Dean voted to parole Dillinger and Arbuckle agreed with him. Despite the petition and the positive stance of his fellow board members, Coy was disinclined to make a recommendation. Instead of voting against the parole, however, he merely abstained and the order was given to release John Herbert Dillinger, Inmate 13225, from the custody of the Michigan City, Ind., State Prison. The prison received the order on May 10, 1933, but for some reason it was not acted upon. A short time later, Elizabeth Dillinger suffered a stroke and was dying. The elder Dillinger wired the prison on May 20, asking why the parole had not been put into effect. The parole was put through two days later and Dillinger's half brother, Hubert, picked up John as he stepped through the gates and to freedom on May 22, 1933, after serving almost nine years. Both immediately drove to the Dillinger farm in Mooresville but they were too late. They saw the undertaker pulling into the yard just as they arrived. Elizabeth Dillinger had died an hour earlier.

The man that appeared at the farm that night was not the boy who had gone bewildered to prison almost nine years earlier. He had a man's rough face and a smile that seemed twisted when he smiled at all which was seldom. He was depressed over the death of his stepmother, a kindly, giving woman he felt he had disappointed. The man sitting in the Dillinger parlor that night was worldly, self-assured, and distant, so much so that Audrey Dillinger Hancock, who stayed close to him, noticed the difference. He caught her staring at him and said: "Don't worry. Everything's going to be all right."

As if to assure the family that he meant to stay out of trouble, Dillinger visited with Mrs. Gertrude M. Reinier, pastor of the Friends Church in Mooresville, having several talks with her. On Father's Day, a month later, John sat in church with the elder Dillinger and the rest of the family while Mrs. Reinier delivered a moving sermon on the Prodigal Son, directing most of her statements at John Dillinger. He was seen to weep openly during the sermon and, following the services, Dillinger went to Mrs. Reinier and said to her: "You will never know how much good that sermon has done me."

A few weeks later Dillinger embarked on a series of petty holdups in the Indianapolis area. He teamed up with a 19-year-old hoodlum named William Shaw and another thug simply called Sam. The trio robbed an all-night supermarket of a small amount and split the loot in a local tavern. Dillinger, who had told Shaw that his name was Dan Dillinger, left early, saying he had to report to his parole officer. Shaw, a vain thief, insisted that gang members wear white caps and glasses and that they would strike terror among victims once they were known as the "White Cap Gang." Dillinger was amused by these antics and went along with the disguise but soon opted for a straw boater. The man named Sam dropped out of the gang and was replaced by Paul "Lefty" Parker, supposedly an expert wheelman, claiming he could outrun any police car. After borrowing revolvers from a saloon keeper, the trio robbed a number of drugstores and supermarkets before Dillinger drove off to Kentucky in a stolen car to see friends.

Dillinger returned to Indianapolis on July 7, 1933, and met with Shaw in the home of Shaw's mother. Shaw took Dillinger to his room where Dillinger asked for a knife to cut open a briefcase he had been carrying. It was full of wadded big-numbered bills. Although he never asked, Shaw was convinced that Dillinger had robbed a bank. Dillinger had stuck up a bank in Kentucky which had been on Pierpont's list of "ripe" banks to be robbed. This list was hopelessly outdated, however, since the Depression was deepening and many of the banks on Pierpont's list had gone under or were in receivership. Dillinger, Parker, and Shaw robbed the bank of New Carlisle, Ind., of $10,500, but the gang was suddenly dissolved when Parker and Shaw were arrested by police. By then Dillinger had been joined by Harry Copeland, whom he had known at Michigan City and who had recently been paroled from the state prison. Dillinger was driving a stolen Chevrolet with Copeland in the passenger seat. In the alley behind Shaw's home, they saw a police car and officers with guns drawn. Standing in front of the officers, hands in the air, were Shaw and Parker. Dillinger immediately threw the car into reverse and backed out of the alley at high speed. Shaw saw Dillinger escape, later commenting: "He drove faster backward than some people drive forward."

On July 17, 1933, Dillinger selected another bank from Pierpont's list, driving with Copeland to tiny Daleville, Ind. The bank was a one-story, red brick building with a single teller, Margaret Good. That morning, a young man wearing a pressed blue suit and a straw boater walked casually into the bank and looked around. He then produced a gun and said: "This is a stickup, honey." He startled Good by vaulting over the five-foot wooden barrier surrounding the teller's cage and once inside, scooped up the money from the drawer. Copeland, who had parked a stolen car in front of the bank, also walked inside and stood by the door, gun drawn, lining up customers as they entered. Dillinger entered the vault and took everything of value, including a collection of antique coins and two diamond rings left there by bank president, J.M. Barnard's daughter, who had taken them off to play tennis.

After collecting about $3,500, Dillinger herded the customers and Margaret Good into the vault and shut the door, after seeing that it could be opened from inside. The 22-year-old Good opened the door a few minutes later. When police and a newspaperman arrived, she described the robbery in dramatic terms, speaking kindly of the leader, Dillinger, saying: "I think he knew I was a kid and was sorry to scare me. He didn't want to scare me any worse than he had to." This almost-sympathetic attitude toward John Dilliner would become a familiar refrain over the next year, mostly due to Dillinger's polite manner when robbing a bank and his soft-spoken promises not to injure those he was holding at gun point, an attitude that would change drastically when he later associated with the likes of Baby Face Nelson.

A few days after the Daleville robbery, Dillinger drove to Dayton, Ohio, and there called on Mary Longnaker, a married woman estranged from her husband, and the sister of James Jenkins, one of Dillinger's friends still doing time in the state prison at Michigan City. He invited Mary to go to the World's Fair in Chicago. She happily accepted on the condition that they also take her girlfriend, Mary Ann Bucholz. Dillinger drove to Chicago with the two women and registered at the Crillon Hotel where the women shared one room and Dillinger had a room to himself. Miss Bucholz became alarmed when she walked into Dillinger's room and saw a pistol on his bureau but Mary seemed to know that her new boyfriend was a man of the underworld and she delighted in showing her girlfriend his wallet which was bulging with large bills.

Mary and Dillinger attended the fair for several days and posed for photos which Dillinger asked passing policemen to snap for them, such was his offbeat sense of humor. He even took several photos himself of policemen patrolling the fair grounds. They dined in the better restaurants and went dancing in such nightclubs as the Island Queen. On their way back to Dayton, Mary asked

Dillinger at the World's Fair in Chicago, 1933, shown above left and center with girlfriend Mary Longnaker; he asked a passing policeman to take these photos.

Dillinger with girlfriend Evelyn "Billie" Frechette, 1934.

Capt. Matt Leach, Indiana State Police.

Dillinger under arrest for bank robbery, being taken to Crown Point, Ind., under heavy guard, 1934.

Tucson, Ariz., police photo of John Dillinger, 1934.

Dillinger, handcuffed, hatless, arriving in Chicago from Tucson, 1934.

J. Edgar Hoover, 1934.

Evelyn Frechette, 1934.

if they could stop at the state prison in Michigan City and visit her brother, Jenkins. Dillinger agreed. The trio stopped in Michigan City and here Dillinger bought a large basket of fruit, telling Mary to give it to her brother. He cut a small hole in the top of a banana and inserted several $50 bills into it. He then wrote a note which Mary was to read to Jenkins while talking with him through the cage in the visitor's room. This she did, the message ending with the words "sit tight." Mary also told Jenkins to "eat the banana first." Before the trio left the prison parking lot, Dillinger handed $50 to a guard and told him to "give it to Jenkins so he can have his teeth fixed." It is not known whether the guard recognized Dillinger but it is presumed that he did and said nothing. Many of the guards at the prison were corrupt and their confidence could be purchased easily.

After Dillinger returned Mary Longnaker and Mary Ann Bucholz to Dayton, he was off on another bank raid. He, Copeland, and an unidentified bandit (who may have been Glen "Big Foot" Zoll), on Aug. 4, 1933, raided the First National Bank of Montpelier, Ind. Dillinger and Copeland entered the bank and Dillinger, carrying a sugar sack turned inside out, vaulted the guard rail—an action that was fast becoming his trademark. He scooped up the cash while Copeland trained a .38-caliber revolver on the employees and customers. Dillinger took $3,900 from the counter cages and another $6,200 from a small safe in the corner. The vault was closed and Dillinger seemed to accept the word of bank president M.D. Tewksberry when he said that nothing was in the vault and that the government bonds held by the bank were stored in a Fort Wayne vault. Dillinger found a .45-caliber automatic in the safe and took it, remarking: "This is a good gun." When he was leaving the bank he patted the sack bulging with currency and coin and said: "This is a good haul."

The bandits fled in a stolen car and were seen changing license plates by farmer Albert Stoll ten miles outside of town. Although police set up roadblocks at several points on roads leading from Montpelier, the bandits escaped using rural routes that had been obviously mapped earlier. Ironically, they had just missed being slaughtered. The First National Bank at Montpelier had been the target of several other bank robbers and, in 1931, local officials had taken precautions. The office above the bank contained a corner office facing the street which was occupied by the local sheriff, mayor, and an attorney, all equipped with high-powered rifles. These three men had cut down a gang of bandits in 1931, killing one and wounding others. However, on the day Dillinger and his men struck the bank in 1933, all three men were elsewhere.

Some days later, Mary Longnaker received a letter from Dillinger in which he talked about taking her and her two daughters to South America with him, saying they could all live well and be happy in some South American country. This was a recurrent desire expressed by the bandit. Forrest Huntington, a former Pinkerton detective, was hired by the American Surety Company which had to repay the Montpelier bank loss. It was Huntington's job to find the bandit who had already been identified as Dillinger. He learned that the bank robbers had eaten lunch at Barr's restaurant only an hour before robbing the bank. Moreover, one of the bandits who had worn a Panama hat had visited an ex-convict in town three days before the robbery.

On Aug. 14, 1933, five men in a long green sedan pulled up in front of the Citizens National Bank of Bluffton, Ohio. One man stayed behind the wheel of the car, which was parked the wrong way, two men remained on the sidewalk in front of the bank as sentinels, and two more entered the bank. Inside the bank, Dillinger and Copeland, both wearing expensive suits and straw hats, pulled guns. Dillinger ordered cashier Roscoe Lingler to "stand back, this is a stickup!" He vaulted the barrier and began stuffing money into a sack. He turned and said to Oliver Locher, the bookkeeper: "You've got more money in here. Where is it?" As Locher pointed to a huge vault, the bank alarm went off. Copeland shouted to Dillinger: "They're after us! Let's go!"

Dillinger ignored Copeland and the alarm. He tugged at a locked drawer, demanding the key. At the same time the two men on the sidewalk, seeing curious crowds assembling down the street in response to the bank alarm, began to fire their guns high, bullets chunking into second-story windows and walls. Finally, Dillinger and Copeland emerged and the five men piled into the sedan and roared away. The take was meager, only $2,100. Angered, Dillinger vowed to obtain more cash quickly, telling Copeland that he needed money to finance "something big," this being the mass breakout of his friends from Michigan City State Prison. Still using Pierpont's list of banks, a "soft jug" was selected, the large Massachusetts Avenue State Bank in Indianapolis.

On Sept. 6, 1933, Dillinger, Copeland, and Hilton Crouch, a professional dirt racetrack driver, drove up to the bank and Dillinger and Copeland went into the bank. Copeland, opening a long coat, produced a submachine gun and trained it on the customers and tellers, ordering everyone to keep quiet and saying "this is a stickup." Dillinger again vaulted the guard rail and scooped up every dime he spotted, including $500 in heavy coin. Copeland kept glancing at the street as more customers entered the bank, ten in all. He herded them away from the windows. "Hurry up, will you?" he called to Dillinger. Minutes later both men left the bank and slipped into the De Soto which Crouch then drove up the street. This time the take was considerable, the largest haul yet, $24,800. Dillinger took half of this amount as the major share going to the planner and leader of the raid.

A few days later Dillinger drove alone to the state prison and crept along one of the outer walls, throwing several loaded revolvers over the wall. These weapons landed on the baseball field and were found the next morning and taken to Warden Louis Kunkel. This had been according to plan. Dillinger, a wise convict-trained criminal, reasoned that someone would have leaked information to the warden of an impending break. He also reasoned that after the revolvers were found, prison officials would believe that the delivery of the weapons constituted the intended break and would relax their guard for the real break to come. He then went to the home of Mary Kinder in Indianapolis, leaving money with her and telling her to buy clothes and food for fourteen men who would be coming to visit her soon, including her brother, Earl Northern and her sweetheart, Harry Pierpont, then both still in state prison.

In Chicago, Dillinger contacted the foreman of a thread-making company, one which supplied the state prison at Michigan City with thread for its shirt-making factory. The bandit bribed the foreman to allow him to doctor a barrel of thread inside which Dillinger placed three automatic pistols. He then marked the barrel with a small red "X," the pre-arranged signal to Pierpont and others that the barrel contained weapons. On Sept. 24, 1933, several barrels of thread were delivered to the prison. Walter Dietrich, alerted to the special shipment, spotted the barrel marked with the red "X" and placed it in a button box in the factory and alerted Pierpont, Makley, Clark, and others. By then, however, Dillinger was already back in police custody.

In September, Dillinger visited his girlfriend, Mary Longnaker, in Dayton, Ohio. Her house had been watched for weeks since Detective Forrest Huntington had learned her identity, from photos and some letters Dillinger had somehow dropped following the Montpelier robbery. Police showed the landlady, Lucille Stricker, photos of Dillinger, and she was asked to call if he visited Mary Longnaker. When Dillinger appeared on the night of Sept. 20, 1933, Stricker called Dayton detectives Russell K. Pfauhl and Charles E. Gross who rushed to the Longnaker home on West First Street, arriving at about 1:30 a.m. Carrying shotguns, the detectives kicked open the door to the Longnaker apartment and there, in the middle of the room stood Dillinger, showing Mary photos that had been taken at the World's Fair. "Stick 'em up, Johnnie," ordered Pfauhl. The photos fell from his grasp as Dillinger's hands went upward and then momentarily stopped and began to slowly drop toward his vest where a revolver was nestled in a shoulder holster. Pfaul lifted his shotgun and aimed it directly at Dillinger's head, saying in a low but firm voice: "If you do, John, I'll kill you on the spot."

Mary Longnaker tried to distract the detectives by pretending to faint, but Pfaul was having none of it. "Stop that play-acting," he said to her as she lay on the floor between Dillinger and the detectives. "Get up on your hands and knees and crawl out of the way," ordered Pfaul. "Right now!" Mary, on hands and knees, crawled out of the way and the detectives stepped forward and clamped handcuffs on Dillinger while removing his revolver from its holster. The detectives found another .38-caliber revolver stuffed between some cushions on the couch and two more in his luggage in the trunk of Dillinger's 1933 Ford Terraplane car parked outside. They also found a large supply of roofing nails in the back seat, these nails were thrown in the wake of Dillinger's car when being pursued. He would simply throw them out of the window, covering the roadway behind him and causing police car tires to be punctured into instant flats.

As the detectives took more than $2,000 in cash from Dillinger's pockets, the bandit began to relax, saying: "When you fellows came in I didn't know if you were part of another gang or not. I know uniformed police, but not plainclothesmen. I thought you were somebody else." The bandit kept up this pleasant chatter but refused to admit to any robberies. He was wanted mostly by the state of Indiana but Dillinger wanted to avoid being taken to the state prison at all costs, one which might jeopardize the prison break he had set in motion. He suddenly admitted to robbing the bank in Bluffton, Ohio, and was removed to the Lima, Ohio, Jail, an old, lightly guarded building. Dillinger correctly reasoned that his friends from Michigan City, once outside the walls, would return the favor and he was selecting the easiest jail from which they could affect his release.

On Sept. 26, after Walter Dietrich notified Pierpont that Dillinger's smuggled guns had arrived and were hidden in the shirt factory, the leader of the gang approached other members of the plot in the prison yard. The 31-year-old, blue-eyed, sandy-haired Pierpont, called "Handsome Harry" by his friends, told the group: "All right boys, if you want to go and take a chance, we will go now." G.H. Stevens, superintendent of the shirt factory, and Albert Evans, assistant warden, were taken prisoner and used as hostages as ten men made their way across the yard to the first steel gates. Here guard Frank Swanson challenged the group but Evans whispered to him: "They've got guns. Open the gate or they'll kill us." Swanson opened the gate and he, too, was taken prisoner and marched in front of the convicts.

At a second gate, guard Fred Wellnitz refused to open up and was slugged unconscious by the convicts who took his keys and opened the gate. The procession then walked solemnly into the administration building where eight clerks, including two women, were herded into a vault, along with Warden Kunkel who was not recognized by the convicts. When 72-year-old Finley Carson, one of the clerks, moved too slowly to please one of the convicts, he was shot in the stomach. Lawrence Mutch, superintendent of prison industries, was spotted and was ordered to open up the adjacent arsenal so the convicts could seize submachine guns and shotguns. Mutch refused and was beaten senseless.

Then the ten convicts, Harry Pierpont, Charles Makley, Russell Clark, John Hamilton, Walter Dietrich, Edward Shouse, Joseph Fox, Joseph Burns, Jim "Oklahoma Jack" Clark (no relation to Russell Clark), and James Jenkins, Mary Kinder's brother, rushed out of the administration building and into the parking lot where they bumped into Sheriff Charles Neel of Harrison County who had just delivered a prisoner. Burns, Fox, Dietrich, and James Clark grabbed Neel and pushed him into his own car and drove it out of the lot. Pierpont and the others ran to the street and stopped the first passing car, one driven by Herber Van Valkenberg. They forced Van Valkenberg, his wife, and 89-year-old grandmother from the car, and sped off with it.

Captain Matt Leach of the Indiana State Police, who was later to become obsessed with hunting Dillinger, organized several posses and set up roadblocks to recapture the escaped prisoners.

The car in which Dietrich, Fox, Burns, and James Clark were traveling with their hostage, Sheriff Neel, crashed into a ditch and was abandoned. This group, heading for Chicago, struck out on foot, hiding in thick underbrush and moving at night through torrential rains. Fox and Burns suggested that they tie Neel up to a tree but James "Oklahoma Jack" Clark told them that if they did that the elderly sheriff would die of exposure. Dietrich, Burns, and Fox then told Clark that he could take care of Neel. They parted company near Hobart, Ind. Clark took Neel to Gary on an interurban train and, once in Gary, the sheriff bought them both dinner. Neel gave Clark his topcoat to hide his prison denims and the bandit left his hostage. Sheriff Neel walked into a police station a short time later, shocking officials who had assumed he was dead. Three companies of armed militia were milling about the place, demanding to know which way the convicts went. The exhausted Neel gave so many vague answers to questions that searchers had no idea where to look and it was later suggested that he had purposely avoided pinpointing Clark, still in the area, in gratitude for saving his life.

Clark, however, did not get far. He reached Hammond where he took a cab to a boarding house. The taxi driver led police to him the next day. Clark was returned to the Gary police station where he was warmly greeted by Sheriff Neel who slipped him $5 before he was taken back to the state prison at Michigan City. "I might as well be dead now," Clark said en route back to prison. "I just wanted to be free a couple of years so I could get proper medical attention." He suffered from stomach ulcers and would die of them. Fox and Burns would be recaptured in a short time and Walter Dietrich, after joining up with the College Kidnapper Gang headed by handsome Jack Klutas in Chicago, would be arrested and returned to prison in January 1934.

The other six men roared toward Indianapolis and the home of Mary Kinder. Her brother James Jenkins, however, never made it home. As the car in which the six convicts raced around a curve, a door flew open and Jenkins fell out. The car started to back up to retrieve Jenkins but sounds in the nearby woods were thought to come from posses moving toward the convicts and the car suddenly sped off. Jenkins made his way alone to the outskirts of Bean Blossom, Ind. There he encountered three farmers armed with shotguns who were part of the dozens of posses looking for the escaped prisoners. With one of Dillinger's smuggled pistols in his hand, Jenkins ran up an alley after wounding one of the farmers in the shoulder, and the farmers chased after him, blasting away with their shotguns. Jenkins received a barrel load in the side of the head and he fell mortally wounded and died a few hours later. His father, the Reverend George Jenkins, arrived to identify the body and said: "I'm glad it's like this. Better like this than that he killed somebody else."

On Sept. 28, 1933, Pierpont, Russell Clark, Hamilton, Makley, and Shouse arrived at the home of Mary Kinder, remaining there to plan a bank robbery to fund the prison release of John Dillinger. Makley suggested that they rob the bank in St. Marys, Ohio, his home town, a bank he knew would yield considerable cash. Pierpont, Makley, Clark, Hamilton, and Shouse raided the First National Bank of St. Marys on Oct. 3, 1933, parking their stolen green Hudson in front of the bank. Pierpont and Makley went inside while Hamilton and Clark covered the street and Shouse stayed at the wheel of the car. Pierpont cleaned out the tellers' cages while Fat Charley Makley stood next to the door and herded customers at gunpoint to the vault as they entered the bank.

Several persons recognized Makley, including the bank's president, W.O. Smith. Makley, smiling and chewing gum, casually talked with Smith of old days in St. Marys while courteously ushering him to the vault. Smith appeared just as friendly, asking Makley innocuous questions about the health of his family, stalling, of course, to prevent the bandits from getting at the cash inside the vault. "It's on a time lock, Charley," Smith told his old friend, "and it won't open for hours." Just then the time mechanism loudly clicked off and Smith realized that his ruse had failed.

"Looks like it decided to open early today," Makley said through a wide grin. He opened the vault and motioned the customers and employees inside. He also entered and cleaned out the cash on the shelves with Pierpont while Clark stepped inside the bank to act as lookout. More than $14,000 was stuffed into a sack and as the bandits closed the vault door, Pierpont said: "If anyone steps out of this vault and cries an alarm before we leave we'll blow the side of this building out with machine gun fire!" He, Makley, and Clark stepped into the street and, joined by Hamilton, got into the Hudson which Shouse drove off at moderate speed.

Dillinger, meanwhile, awaited trial for the Bluffton, Ohio, bank robbery in a cell in the Lima, Ohio, Jail. The decrepit building was poorly guarded. Dillinger was a celebrated prisoner, having had his name in the headlines for months as newsmen chronicled his crime wave. Sheriff Jess Sarber was a kind lawman whose wife Lucy made delicious meals for Dillinger but the Sarbers thought Dillinger was just another farm boy gone wrong and attached no particular importance to him. He was placed in the small cell block at the rear of the building. In adjoining cells were Art Young, awaiting sentencing for a second-degree murder conviction, and George Miller and Claude Euclid, two prisoners who had committed minor offenses. Dillinger had told Miller that he expected his friends to "spring" him but he was uncertain when they would make their move.

Harry Pierpont made his move on the night of Oct. 12, 1933. First, he and Russell Clark visited Lima attorney Chester M. Cable, asking him to call the jail so that Dillinger's sister, who was outside in a car, could visit him. Cable thought the two men looked like "tough customers," and he said that it would take some days to arrange such a visit. When the two men left, Cable called Sheriff Sarber, who was sitting in the front office in his shirt-sleeves, reading some reports at his desk. Sarber took Cable's warning lightly, thinking that reports of Dillinger's gangster friends nothing more than "a lot of nonsense, cartoon nonsense." In the same office, Lucy Sarber sat in a nearby chair piecing a crossword puzzle together. In another chair, reading a newspaper, was Deputy Wilbur Sharp. He and Sarber were both unarmed, although Sarber's revolver was in the center drawer of his desk.

At 6:25 p.m., Pierpont and Clark boldly walked to the front of the jail and saw that it was unguarded. Across the street and down the block, at various posts assigned to them by Pierpont, stood John Hamilton, Charles Makley, Ed Shouse, and Harry Copeland, recently arrived from Indiana to help in the freeing of John Dillinger. Shouse later told lawmen when captured that there was no real plan that night, only "to free Dillinger, and stick together and help each other if we could, and, if we couldn't, make a break for it, and go for ourselves." This fierce loyalty to one of their own was a singular trait of the 1930s bank robbers, the independent bandits of the day who, thinking themselves superior to the city gangster, retained certain values and friendships even at the risk of their lives. Dillinger had earlier freed them. They were obligated to free him.

Pierpont, Makley, and Clark went up the stairs of the jail while Copeland, Shouse, and Hamilton stayed with the escape car. The three men, all well-dressed and wearing hats with wide brims pulled low over their faces, went inside and approached Sheriff Sarber who looked up from his desk. "Can I help you?" he said.

"We're officers from Michigan City," Pierpont said. "We want to talk to the prisoner John Dillinger."

Deputy Sharp kept reading his paper and Mrs. Sarber never looked up from her puzzle. Sheriff Sarber nodded and said: "I guess that will be all right. But first you will have to show me your credentials."

Pierpont's eyes narrowed as he pulled out a pistol and aimed it at Sarber's head. "Here's our credentials."

"Oh, you can't do that," Sarber said, his mouth agape and he instinctively tried to push the gun aside.

Pierpont fired two shots quickly, one striking Sarber in the hip and one ploughing into the sheriff's stomach. He fell out of his chair and onto the floor. Sharp and Lucy Sarber were frozen in shock in their chairs. Pierpont then barked: "Give us the keys to the cells." When Sarber tried to rise on his elbow, Makley dashed forward and hit him on the head with his gun butt, splitting the skull to the bone. He hit him once more.

Lucy Sarber jumped up screaming: "I'll get the keys! Don't hurt him anymore!"

Inside the cellblock, Art Young and Dillinger, who had been playing cards through the bars of their adjoining cells, suddenly sat up and Young said: "John, your gang has come for you." Dillinger slipped on his coat and stood by the cell door. He asked Young if he wanted to "come along," but Young declined the offer.

Pierpont, grinning, entered the cellblock and unlocked the door of Dillinger's cell. Both men then ran into the office, but Pierpont stuck his head back inside the door and looked down the corridor where the other prisoners were yelling to be set free. "Get back there, you bastards," shouted Pierpont. "We came for John. The rest of you can leave when we've gone."

In the office Dillinger saw Sheriff Sarber on the floor, bleeding to death, his wife holding him, sobbing. He knelt close to the sheriff, the man who had been so kind to him and said without looking at his liberators: "Did you have to do this?"

"Men," moaned Sarber to his attackers, "why did you do this to me?" He turned his head slightly to look up at his weeping wife and said: "Mother, I believe I am going to have to leave you."

Pierpont and Makley then forced Mrs. Sarber and Deputy Sharp into the cell block and locked the door. All of the gang members then left the office while Sheriff Sarber died within minutes. Outside, Dillinger climbed into the long sedan with the rest of the gang and sped away. The supergang that would terrorize the Midwest was now united. Only minutes after Sarber's body was found, dozens of motorized posses chased after the Dillinger gang but they found no trace of the gangsters. By midnight the gang reached Indianapolis and stayed with Mary Kinder. Also waiting for Dillinger was Evelyn "Billie" Frechette, a Menominee Indian girl, daughter of the chief, who had run away from the reservation in northern Wisconsin to become a hat check girl at the World's Fair. Dillinger had met her while visiting the fair with Mary Kinder and had seen her briefly before his capture at Mary Longnaker's apartment. The gang made immediate plans to arm its members and then quickly raid a number of banks.

On Oct. 14, 1933, Dillinger, Pierpont, and Makley entered the police station at Auburn, Ind., drawing guns and holding at bay police officers Henry West and Fred Kreuger. The bandits seemed to know that Chief of Police Charles Davis and Sheriff John P. Hoff would be absent at that time. Dillinger walked up to Kreuger, who had been sitting with his back to the front door of the station, eating popcorn, before he turned around to see a revolver poked into his face. Said Dillinger: "You might as well sit still. We don't want to kill anyone unless we have to. Have you got any guns." Kreuger started to reach for the gun on his hip, but Dillinger's hand went quickly to the holster and withdrew it while he remarked: "Oh, no! I'll get it." West was disarmed by Pierpont while Makley stood at the door, casually leaning against the wall, watching the street where Hamilton and Clark chatted on the sidewalk and Shouse sat at the wheel of a car.

West and Kreuger surrendered the keys to the gun cabinet and the bandits took turns carrying out weapons, including a Thompson submachine gun with several pans of ammunition, two .38-caliber revolvers, a .30-caliber Springfield rifle, a Winchester automatic rifle, a shotgun, a .45-caliber Colt automatic, a .44-caliber Smith and Wesson, a .44-caliber Spanish, and a German Luger. The gangsters also grabbed three bulletproof vests and many boxes of ammunition. The police officers were then locked in a cell. As he left, Dillinger turned to the elderly Kreuger and said: "I have heard of you for thirty years," a strange remark that was obviously intended to flatter the policeman. The gangsters then fled.

News photos of John Dillinger while he was a prisoner at Crown Point, Ind., haled as Public Enemy Number One, March 1934.

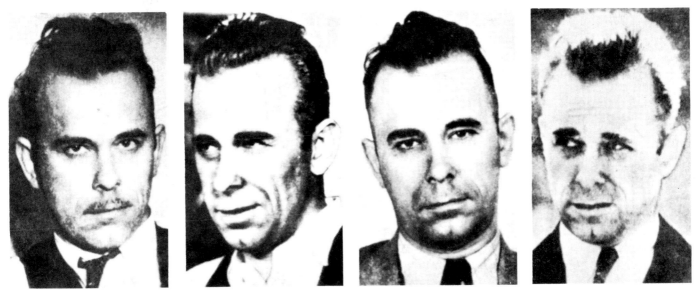

Police photos of John Dillinger at the height of his crime wave in 1933-34.

Police photos of Dillinger after his Ohio arrest, 1933.   Dillinger and Harry Pierpont; Indiana state prison photos.

Swarms of police in Indiana and Ohio were now frantically searching for what the newspapers had termed The Terror Gang. Dillinger's home in Mooresville was staked out but this only served to annoy the elder Dillinger who stated that "Johnny would not have caused all this trouble if Judge Williams had never given him such a harsh sentence" in 1924 and if the prosecutor at that time had lived up to his promise of a lenient sentence in exchange for a plea of guilty. "It was Judge Williams' fault, all of it." Ohio police also searched and then watched the homes of Harry Pierpont and Charles Makley but saw no sign of these men. Newspapers throughout the Midwest gave over their front pages to the daring bandits who could so easily defy the law, marching right into jails and police stations to free comrades and loot arsenals. On Oct. 20, 1933, the Dillinger gang did it again, this time raiding the police station at Peru, Ind.

At 11 p.m. that night, Leo "Red" Eakins, who worked as a porter at the Model Restaurant a few doors away from the Peru police station, walked into the station and was greeted by a tall, young man, fastidiously dressed in a three-piece suit and wearing a wide-brimmed hat. He held a gun in his hand. The stranger, Pierpont, grabbed Eakins by the arm and pulled him into the back room, saying: "Come back here. I want to show you something." Eakins thought it was some sort of joke until he stepped into the back room to see three police officers, Eddie Roberts, Eldon Chittun, and Ambrose Clark sitting in chairs, looks of terror on their faces as another gunman, Dillinger, held a gun on them. Said Eakins later: "I still thought they were in fun until I noticed the cops' knees shaking. Then I knew it was a holdup."

To make the policemen even more uneasy, Pierpont said without humor: "I haven't killed anybody for a week and I'd just as soon shoot one of you as not. Go ahead and get funny." The policemen remained motionless as another man appeared with a robe, spreading this out on the floor. Onto this gang members dumped two Thompson submachine guns, two sawed-off shotguns, four .38-caliber Police Specials, two 30.30 Winchester rifles, six bulletproof vests, three police badges and many boxes of ammunition. The robe was then tied about the cache of weapons and carried outside while Makley marched the officers and Eakins into the basement where they were locked up. As Deputy Robert Tillett arrived in front of the station, he saw a blue Hudson pull away from the curb and a good-looking young man wave at him.

News of the Peru raid stunned law enforcement officials in the state and elsewhere, the second raid on a police arsenal within a week. Funds were quickly collected to build special security posts, install barbed wire, and put in barred windows around all Indiana police stations. Security at the state prison in Michigan City and at the reformatory in Pendleton was beefed up, as authorities believed that the Dillinger gang was assembling enough weapons for an army of gangsters to attack these institutions in order to free the entire prison populations. The American Legion offered to put 30,000 volunteers onto Indiana highways in armed patrols to look for the bandits and the National Guard was put on active status, its officers reporting on the availability of poison gas, airplanes, and tanks in combating the Terror Gang. The U.S. Army provided local police with dozens of armored cars with heavy-caliber machine guns mounted on top.

Attorney General Homer Cummings received a message from the Indianapolis *Times* requesting FBI help for Indiana since the local and state police seemed helpless to stop or capture the Dillinger gang. J. Edgar Hoover was alerted to have his field agents cooperate with local police but there was little the Bureau could do on its own at this time. No federal laws then existed which allowed agents to pursue the Terror Gang. Bank robbery, stealing cars and transporting them across state lines, and other offenses committed by bandits of the day were only state offenses and federal authorities had no jurisdiction in such crimes. It was John Dillinger and his henchmen who would bring about the federal legislation that would allow Hoover's G-Men to act, but this would not be for some time.

When details of the Peru raid were released to the press, the public fascination with Dillinger and his gang members increased, mostly due to the inventiveness of the gangsters. It was later learned that Dillinger and Pierpont had brazenly walked into the Peru station and informed the armed policemen there that they were tourists, thinking of depositing considerable money in the local bank. They were apprehensive, they said, of risking their money in a bank that might not be able to withstand an attack of the Dillinger gang. What types of weapons did the police have, they asked, to repel such an attack. Ambrose Clark proudly took Dillinger and Pierpont to the police arsenal to display its weaponry and it was at this moment that Dillinger and Pierpont pulled guns and put the policemen under guard. Pierpont's girlfriend, Mary Kinder, later reported that she had driven along with the gang on this raid and was sitting in the back seat of the big Hudson when Pierpont, Dillinger, and others ran from the Peru station and filled the back floor of the car with guns and ammunition. "My God," she exclaimed at the time, "what are you going to do? Start a young army?"

On the morning of Oct. 23, 1933, Charles Makley appeared in the bustling town of Greencastle, Ind. He asked a town official for a permit to sell Oriental rugs, saying that he was a sailor who had obtained these rugs in the Far East. He planned, he said, to keep his deposits in the local bank and then made inquiries about its security measures. He was not issued the permit. At 2:45 p.m. that day, five men, including Makley, arrived in front of Greencastle's Central National Bank, double-parking a black Studebaker. Five men got out, one—Russell Clark—going down the street and standing near the local police station, another—John Hamilton—standing at the entranceway to the bank, acting as "the tiger" or sentinel, the other three, Dillinger, Pierpont, and Makley, going into the bank. Makley stood inside the door while Dillinger and Pierpont went to the tellers' cages. Pierpont went to a window and asked Ward Mayhall, assistant trust officer of the bank, to change a twenty-dollar bill. Mayhall told him to go to the next window and be served by Harry Wells. From beneath his long coat, Pierpont produced a submachine gun, sticking the muzzle through the window at Mayhall. "*You* change it, bub, and give me everything else you have in the drawer."

A second later Dillinger shouted to everyone in the bank: "Don't press anything or there will be a lot of dead people in here!" He vaulted the barrier, smashed a glass pane in the door leading to the tellers' cages and went inside, going from cage to cage, scooping money into a sugar sack. Makley pushed the eight customers inside the bank to a wall, lining them up and the bank's dozen employees were herded to the same wall while Makley trained a submachine gun on them. The robbery went smoothly and was obviously well-planned. It was later learned that Pierpont had once worked in Greencastle at one of the plants and knew the town well. Also, Makley, in in his early rounds of the town, had inspected the bank and had learned that the guard in a cage above the tellers' windows would be leaving that cage at about 2:30 p.m. to stoke the furnace downstairs. That is precisely what happened. The elderly guard, Leo Ratcliff, left the cage only moments before the gangsters entered the bank. They also knew that each teller's cage was equipped with an alarm button which is why Dillinger warned them not to "press anything" at the onset of the robbery.

As Dillinger forced Wells to open the vault, Pierpont surveyed the customers and employees lined up against the wall. All had their hands high in the air. Pierpont realized that these cowed victims could be seen through the bank's large open windows and he shouted to them: "Put your hands down and keep them at your sides and don't move! We're not advertising." Makley held a stopwatch in his hand and kept glancing at it and then the street and Hamilton who stood outside. One middle-aged woman started to go into the bank and then apparently changed her mind. Hamilton gently held her arm for a moment and said: "Better go inside, lady." The foreign-born woman jerked her arm away and turned on her heel, saying angrily: "I go to Penny's and you go to hell!"

Makley pressed the top of the stopwatch and then yelled out to Dillinger: "It's five minutes!" Dillinger had completed cleaning out the vault and the tellers' cages and he jumped onto a ledge, sailing in spectacular fashion over the ten-foot barrier of the teller's windows, to the public side of the bank. As he was about to leave he noticed a farmer standing in the line of customers next to the wall. The man held some bills in his hand.

"Is that your money or the bank's?" Dillinger asked the farmer.

"Mine," the farmer said.

"Keep it," Dillinger told him. "We only want the bank's." This gesture was undoubtedly made by Dillinger the farmboy remembering his youth and the farm in Mooresville and the old man who struggled to bring crops out of the flat stubborn earth of Indiana. (This gesture was later attributed to Clyde Barrow in the movie *Bonnie and Clyde* but anyone knowing the true nature of Barrow and his prostitute lover would realize that Barrow was incapable of such a beau geste, that the Texas bandit and killer would have snatched the farmer's meager savings and shot him to death for "kicks.")

Within minutes Dillinger and Pierpont had gathered $18,428 in cash and $56,300 in bonds, which the gang would later fence for 50¢ on the dollar, after paying a commission to mastermind Eddie Bentz, who had reportedly provided information on the bank and its holdings at the time, Bentz being the master bank "caser" for almost all the notorious bank robbing gangs of that era. As the gang members left the bank, Dillinger, carrying the sugar sack stuffed with the money, including $400 in halves, $200 in quarters and $18 in silver dollars, bumped into Rex Thorlton, a grocery store manager who was about to make a deposit. Thorlton, as he was entering the bank, was reaching for his bankbook and money in a back pocket and Pierpont believed he was reaching for a gun. Pierpont brought his gun butt down hard on Thorlton's head. The grocer fell, knocking Dillinger's hat off. Realizing who the bandits were, Thorlton, according to one story, apologized to "Mr. Dillinger," handing him back his hat.

The robbers got into the Studebaker and drove down to the end of the block, picking up Clark, who was still standing lookout, and then drove along dirt roads and disappeared, avoiding all roadblocks set up a short time later. They followed routes they had specially mapped which would allow them to drive for fifty miles without ever using a highway and thus evade pursuers. The Greencastle robbery was one of the best-planned and executed crimes committed by the Terror Gang, one which displayed an extraordinary amount of precaution and sophisticated planning. This, more than the awful reputation the gang had earned within a few weeks, alarmed local, state, and federal officials. They realized that they were dealing not with bungling thugs but with intelligent, crafty men who were well-armed and prepared to kill anyone who stood in their way. Much of this posture was due to the style and attitude of Harry Pierpont, the real brains of the gang.

Pierpont was also a better-than-average amateur psychologist. He proved to be the most daring of the gang and had steel nerves but he was also impulsive and knew it, so he preferred that Dillinger take the limelight during the robberies, knowing that Dillinger enjoyed showing off by vaulting the tellers' cages. When Dillinger's name began to be a household word through his exposure in the nation's press and on radio, the bandit told Pierpont that he intended to write to certain radio announcers to correct their mispronunciation of his name. The name Dillinger was Germanic and contained a hard "g." The press and public pronounced the name with a soft ending and Pierpont persuaded Dillinger to let it stand that way, telling his fellow thief that it was better that way, that his name sounded like the pistol, derringer, and was thus synonymous with a lethal weapon.

With large funds at their disposal, gang members rented expensive apartments in Chicago, which they used as a base, much to the annoyance of the Capone gang and other members of organized crime in the city, since these urban gangsters felt that independent bandits like Dillinger brought too much police attention to their area and, often enough, police raids of suspected Dillinger hideouts which snared members of organized crime in illegal gambling dens and bordellos. Members of the Dillinger gang enjoyed their stolen loot by taking their girlfriends to musical shows, nightclubs, and the better restaurants. They bought tailor-made suits and imported ties and hats. They purchased fast cars, using only stolen autos for robberies. They planned carefully each of their robberies, holding long meetings and studying their targets, buying information from such expert bank casers as Eddie Bentz.

During their meetings, only Dillinger and Pierpont talked, describing the approach to the bank, and how it was protected and how much money it would probably be holding. Hamilton, the "old pro" of the group, occasionally made remarks about techniques to be employed. Makley, Clark, Copeland, and Shouse invariably kept silent and listened as their mentors outlined their next move. None of these men were heavy drinkers. Dillinger himself was a light cigarette smoker and drank mostly beer, taking an occasional shot of whiskey. They were also in excellent physical condition after having undergone years of prison discipline.

Opposing the gang were a number of competent lawmen in several states, the most dogged being Captain Matt Leach, head of a special Dillinger force of the Indiana State Police. Leach was a rather pompous, self-serving officer who believed he could outsmart the Terror Gang. He thought to undermine the gang by publicly naming Pierpont as the gang leader, believing this would cause dissension among members and eventually cause them to split up but nothing of the kind ever happened. Leach insulted Dillinger in print at every opportunity and Dillinger, more than once, called Leach to threaten him. The captain once insisted that Dillinger had called him on the phone and said: "We'll get you! Watch your ass!" Sergeant Frank Reynolds, a member of the "Dillinger Squad" headed by Captain John Stege of the Chicago Police Department, also claimed to have received an identical call from Dillinger.

Leach, however, remained in the news as the law enforcement watchdog on Dillinger's trail. The captain had his photo taken at every opportunity, mostly in heroic poses, as he made sweeping statements about how he and his men would soon have the Dillinger gang in custody. At one point, Leach called a press conference to report that he had received in the mail an 1896 publication entitled "How To Be a Detective," which he said the taunting Dillinger had sent to him. This later proved to be untrue; the author later learned that newspaperman William L. "Tubby" Toms of the Indianapolis *News* had sent the publication to humiliate Leach for his strutting ways. Leach was forever giving newsmen profiles of Dillinger, who had, for him, become the arch criminal of the century. It was Leach's belief that Dillinger's own inflated self-confidence and "wise guy" posturing would bring about his ruination. It is true that Dillinger placed phone calls to Leach and, on one occasion, said: "This is John Dillinger. How are you, you stuttering bastard?" (In the 1973 motion picture *Dillinger,* such phone calls are shown to be made from Dillinger to Melvin Purvis, but this was pure fiction, as was most of the idiotic script for this film.)

Dillinger became a Midwest mania. Every robbery of note was attributed to him and the Terror Gang. When the Western State Bank of South Bend was robbed of $5,000 on Oct. 24, 1933, the robbery was credited to Dillinger, but the actual thieves were apprehended a short time later. Even small jobs such as the robbery of the tiny bank in Filmore, Ind., which yielded robbers only $130, and the theft of $400 from the People's Loan and Trust Company in Modoc, Ind., were at first attributed to Dillinger. Moreover, the public was fascinated with John Dillinger and his friends simply because they were robbing banks in an era when bank reputations were at an all-time low. Banks were looked upon as mean-spirited institutions that ruthlessly foreclosed on farmers and shopkeepers, that put decent families into the street, that made of a hardworking middleclass a nation of hobos and bums during the Depression. Bankers were economic despots and tyrants, unthinking, uncaring, and without compassion, hateful creatures who preyed upon the misery of misfortune of good people. Dillinger avenged these real or imagined wrongs, it was thought by many, when he raided a bank; a farmboy striking back, as it were, against a bureauratic system, rooted not in the good earth of agrarian U.S., but in the corrupt foundations of the cities where venal politicians and bankers squandered the country's wealth, gluttonously consuming the product of honest toil.

Letters by the thousands objecting to any smear of this offbeat folk hero poured into newspapers that editorialized against Dillinger and his men. One letter to an Indianapolis newspaper attacked an editorialist who had lambasted Dilliger: "This person calls Dillinger cheap. He isn't half as cheap as a crooked banker or a crooked politician because he did give the bankers a chance to fight, and they never gave the people a chance." Another said: "I am for John Dillinger. Not that I am upholding him in any of his crimes, that is, if he did any. Why should the law have wanted John Dillinger for bank robbery? He wasn't any worse than bankers and politicians who took the poor people's money."

Meanwhile, all was not well within the ranks of the Terror Gang. Ed Shouse had begun drinking heavily and his nerves seemed shattered. He was a supposed expert getaway driver yet he handled the wheels of cars so nervously as of late that gang members feared driving with him. Worse, gang members believed that Shouse might be informing lawmen of their movements. Shouse had been asking many questions concerning the day to day movements of gang members. The suspicions of Dillinger and Pierpont were correct. Shouse had turned informer. He, along with another police informant, Art McGinnis, who knew Dillinger and sometimes provided him with guns, tipped police that Dillinger was suffering from an irritating rash, and that he was taking treatment from Dr. Charles Eye, whose offices were located at 4175 W. Irving Park Blvd.

Chicago Police Department Captain John Stege ordered several men of his Dillinger Squad to stake out Dr. Eye's office, and on Nov. 15, 1933, Dillinger, indeed, showed up. He was driving his favorite car, a Hudson Terraplane, with Evelyn Frechette at his side. As he approached the physician's office, Dillinger noticed several unmarked police cars parked nearby, all of them parked the wrong way. He changed gears and roared off down the boulevard. Detectives saw the Terraplane turn about abruptly and they gave chase. In a frightening burst of speed, Dillinger quickly outdistanced all the squad cars except one occupied by Sergeant John Artery and officer Art Keller. Both cars raced along Irving Park Boulevard at 80 m.p.h., narrowly missing pedestrians, street trolleys, and parked cars. When the cars were hood to hood, Keller leaned out a window and began pumping shells from his shotgun at Dillinger.

"Hey," Evelyn Frechette said to her lover, "somebody's shooting at you." Dillinger grinned, seeming to enjoy the chase and the hazard of the shotgun bursts which exploded the glass of his car but left him uninjured. He jammed his foot down on the accelerator. The Terraplane, a powerful car, seemed to jerk in mid-flight and then surge suddenly forward. Dillinger saw a narrow sidestreet and, when almost at the corner, he spun the wheel of the car which took the corner almost on two wheels as the police squad roared past it down Irving Park. By the time Artery turned the car around and returned to the sidestreet, Dillinger had vanished. Keller threw his shotgun into the back seat in disgust and grudgingly complimented Dillinger by saying: "That bird can sure drive!"

Shouse later appeared in Mary Kinder's apartment, a meeting place for the gang and here Kinder overheard him tell Hamilton that they might do better if they robbed a few banks on their own. Kinder shouted at Shouse: "You ain't gonna do a damned thing, Ed. There ain't nobody going noplace until we all talk it over! This has always been a friendly bunch and you ain't gonna take no two or three and go rob a bank." Dillinger had no love for Shouse, believing that Shouse, when drunk on earlier occasions, had made a play for his girlfriend, Evelyn Frechette. He took a

wad of bills from his pocket and tossed this to Shouse. "There's your money. You're through. Now get your ass out!" Shouse left the gang and was later captured and jailed.

For some time gang members had been eyeing the American Bank and Trust Company in Racine, Wis. The gang moved to a hideout in Milwaukee and from there made plans to rob this bank. The resulting successful robbery was so well planned that its intricate preparations smacked of Eddie Bentz's techniques. Someone, perhaps the master bank caser himself, arrived in Racine in early November 1933, staying at the Hotel Racine, only a block from the bank. Bentz undoubtedly checked the bank's current assets by visiting the local library and reading the banking reports published by law in the local press. He then went to the bank every day at 2:30 p.m., the time that the actual bank robbery would occur, to check conditions at that time, noting the movements of guards, city police and employee activity inside the bank, along with the number of customers to be expected at that hour. Escape routes were carefully planned. He noted stoplights, traffic police, and the distance from the bank to the city limits and how much time, at normal driving speed, it would take to get out of town.

On Nov. 20, 1933, a brand new 1934 blue Buick sedan with yellow wire wheels pulled up in front of Racine's American Bank and Trust Company at Main and Fifth Streets. Harry Pierpont, looking dapper and elegant in a new custom-tailored suit, entered the bank with a roll of paper tucked under his arm. Without a word to anyone, Pierpont went to the large bay window and, unraveling a Red Cross Poster, pasted this on the window. This was designed to obstruct any view of the inside of the bank by passersby outside but Mrs. Henry Patzke, the bank's bookkeeper, merely noticed a handsome young man putting up the poster and thought he had been given permission to do so. She went back to her work. Then, in quick order, Dillinger, Makley, and Hamilton entered the bank. Makley went to the head teller, Harold Graham, who was in a cage and was busily counting coins.

"Stick 'em up," Makley ordered, poking a submachine gun at Graham.

The head teller did not look up, thinking someone was kidding him. He merely said: "Go to the next window, please."

Makley, annoyed, repeated his demand: "I *said* stick 'em up!"

Then Graham looked up and made a sudden movement which caused Makley to instinctively fire a burst from the gun. A bullet struck Graham in the arm and another in the hip, sending him crashing to the floor where he reached up and pressed an alarm button beneath the ledge of the teller's cage. The alarm did not sound inside the bank but did go off at Racine Police headquarters. Officers Cyril Boyard and Rudy Speaker got the report of the bank alarm going off but they took their time responding, driving slowly toward the bank in a circuitous route. The alarm had gone off many times in the past, mostly when a clerk or teller accidentally hit the alarm button.

Inside the bank, Dillinger, Pierpont, and Hamilton ran down the aisle behind the tellers' cages. Pierpont carried a submachine gun. Dillinger shouted: "Everybody flat on their stomachs!" L.C. Rowan, an assistant cashier, who was sitting at a front desk, hit an alarm button which caused another bell to go off in the police station and this also started a bell clanging outside the bank. Just at that moment police officers Franklin Worsley and Wilbur Hansen, answering the alarm, walked into the bank and Pierpont began to disarm them. Hansen tried to back out of the door but Clark, who was standing guard outside, shoved him back into the bank. Then Hansen appeared to go for his gun and Makley let loose a burst from his submachine gun which wounded the officer and caused the women in the bank to begin screaming.

Dillinger and Pierpont had walked Grover Weyland, the president of the bank, to the vault where Weyland took his time unlocking it, stalling until the police arrived. Pierpont jammed a submachine gun into Weyland's stomach and shouted: "Get into the vault and open it up, and you'd better not miss it. We don't like bank presidents. We'd as soon shoot you as look at you!"

Dillinger gangsters, left to right, Edward Shouse, Homer Van Meter, John Hamilton, and Harry Pierpont, bank robbers all.

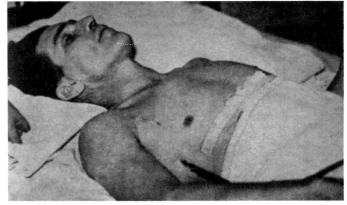

Dillinger associates "Baby Face" Nelson, left, and Tommy Carroll, who lies dying of police bullets after being trapped in a 1934 dragnet.

Dillinger gangster Charles Makley who died in the Ohio electric chair, 1934.

Bank robber Russell Clark.

Dillinger hideout: The Little Bohemia Lodge in northern Wisconsin.

Weyland finally managed to open the vault and Dillinger and Pierpont stepped inside with the bank president. Pierpont, who had fired a burst from his gun at Officers Worseley and Hansen when they first entered the bank, took time to reload his weapon, slipping another pan of ammunition onto the Thompson. As he was doing so, he pointed the gun in the direction of George Ryan, a young bank teller who was flat on the floor.

"For God's sake, mister," Ryan implored, "point that gun the other way!"

Pierpont smiled at him and said: "As long as you're a good boy, you don't have to worry."

Outside crowds were gathering in front of the bank and Clark fired several warning shots for passersby to stay away. No one seemed to understand that the bank was being robbed. Dillinger finally emerged from the vault and he leaped over the tellers' cages, shouting triumphantly: "I've got it all." He did not have it all. While hurriedly going through the drawers of the tellers' cages, Pierpont and Dillinger had overlooked more than $50,000 in cash which was wadded up and in the back of a drawer, covered with deposit receipts. The gang, however, took $27,789 before leaving the bank. When the gang emerged, police officers across the street fired, aiming high so as not to hit the crowd members in front of the bank. Clark, Makley, and Hamilton fired back, raking the buildings across the street, smashing second-storey windows. Then the gang pushed several female bank employees onto the running board of the large Buick, got inside and roared down the street, the hostages hanging on the car and preventing police from firing at it.

Following their own maps, the gang sped along dirt roads and later deposited their hostages in a lonely spot. Dillinger jocularly asked one of the females if she could cook. She replied: "After a fashion."

"Some other time," Dillinger said and the car shot forward, quickly disappearing over a rise. The gang then cut south and headed for Florida, driving to Daytona Beach where members rented several cottages. They chartered fishing boats and fished for marlin. They sat about playing cards and listening to the radio. Mary Kinder and Evelyn Frechette cooked for them. From Daytona, the gang moved west, driving to Tucson, Ariz. About the time the gang arrived in Tucson, on Jan. 15, 1934, the First National Bank of East Chicago was robbed of more than $20,000. A 43-year-old motorcycle policeman, William Patrick O'Malley, tried to stop two men when they fled the bank and he was cut in half by their machine gun fire. The robbery and murder were attributed to John Dillinger and John Hamilton, although it is improbable that either man could have participated in this robbery since both were in Arizona at the time, according to most reliable accounts. This was, however, the first and only murder ever credited to John Dillinger.

In Tucson, the gang's luck went bad. A fire broke out in the Congress Hotel where Clark and Makley were staying and they gave hundreds of dollars to firemen to carry their bags out of their rooms. A fireman lugging one of the heavy suitcases became suspicious and opened it up to discover a submachine gun and several pistols. He notified local police and both Clark and Makley were arrested without a fight. Then Dillinger, Pierpont, and their girls, Opal Long, Clark's girl friend, Mary Kinder, using the alias Bernice Thompson, and Evelyn Billie Frechctte, using the alias Anne Martin, were captured. Pierpont and Makley were quickly extradited to Ohio to stand trial for the murder of Sheriff Sarber, while Dillinger was sent back to Indiana to stand trial for the killing of Officer O'Malley. The girls were also shipped back east, charged with obstructing justice, and in Mary Kinder's case, aiding in the prison escape at Michigan City. John Hamilton was not apprehended, having left Tucson a few days earlier, ostensibly to case another bank in the Midwest.

The gangsters were placed in the Pima County Jail while their hastily hired attorney, John Van Buskirk of Los Angeles unsuccessfully fought against several writs demanding extradition to Indiana and Ohio. The first arriving to demand extradition was a large delegation from Indiana, including Captain Matt Leach, Prosecutor Robert Estill of Lake County, Ind., Sheriff Lillian Holley and her nephew, Undersheriff Carroll Holley, and Police Chief Maker of East Chicago, Ind. One in this group saw Dillinger in a cell and shouted: "He's the one who killed O'Malley," a point too sorely made in that Estill and others from Indiana knew there was considerable doubt about Dillinger actually being in East Chicago, Ind., when the motorcycle policeman was killed. (Police Chief Maker's presence in Tucson was strange in that he had no official capacity. It was later claimed that Maker was present to make sure that the O'Malley killing was, indeed, pinned on Dillinger, even though he knew that someone else had killed the policeman. Maker represented a small but widely corrupt police force, with several of its officers being in the pay of gangsters, including Sergeant Martin Zarkovich, who would later be deeply involved in Dillinger's so-called execution and permanent escape.)

Dillinger had repeatedly denied being in East Chicago on Jan. 15, 1934, and said he could prove it; so did attorney Van Buskirk. They knew that if convicted of thc O'Malley killing, it would mean a death sentence. Matt Leach, in a confidential interview with the press, all but admitted that certain politicians in Indiana planned to have "Johnny executed for the East Chicago robbery and killing, no matter what it cost." Leach beamed with triumph when he entered the lockup at the Pima County Jail. He walked straight to Dillinger's cell and stuck his hand through the bars. Dillinger lamely took it in a brief shake. As Leach walked past the cell holding Pierpont, Handsome Harry exploded: "I should have killed you when I had the chance, you dirty son-of-a-bitch! You put my mother in jail in Terre Haute, you bastard! If I ever get out of this, the first thing I going to do is kill you, you rat!"

Dillinger later told newsmen on his plane trip back to Indiana that Pierpont and he had been walking down an Indianapolis street one night some weeks earlier and discovered that Matt Leach, their pursuer, was walking directly in front of them and it was all Dillinger could do to prevent Pierpont from killing the lawman on the spot. The statement Pierpont made about his mother referred to a time when Indiana officers had arrested Mrs. Pierpont and Fred Pierpont and held them in the Terre Haute Jail for questioning for some days. Leach, however, had nothing to do with this. After officials inspected the prisoners, crowds of curious citizens clamoring for a view of the notorious Terror Gang were allowed to go into the Pima Jail lockup in small groups. By this time, Dillinger had tired of all the bravado. He snarled at a guard: "if anyone one of those bozos or besocks gets close to my cell I'll brain them." He lay on his bunk, face to the wall. Ever the clown, Makley convinced a young Texan locked up in the cell opposite to impersonate Dillinger for the crowd. The Texan happily agreed to do so, as long as he was paid by those posing with him for photos next to his cell. He earned so much money that he was able to pay off his attorney and the fine for his minor offense and was released the next day.

Fat Charley Makley, though he knew he and Pierpont were wanted for the murder of Sheriff Jess Sarber, acted as if he were being detained on a speeding charge. A newspaperman, Jack Weadcock, stood by Makley's cell and reminded him that they had known each other as youths in St. Marys, Ohio: "You once shoed horses in my father's blacksmith."

"So you're George's kid," Makley said. And then he got conspiratorial, telling Weadlock that the most dangerous man in the gang was Harry Pierpont, whom everyone in the gang called Pete. "If anything happens here, you watch out for Pete. He's a wild man." He said that Dillinger was not as tough as Pierpont but "every one of us trusts Johnny...He's got a level head and he's the smart one." Makley then lapsed into childhood memories and nostalgically remembered the hardworking members of his family. "They were honest, at least, even if never rich. But I could not take that kind of life. Look at my dad. He worked like the devil all his life and what did he get out of it? I've lived as long in forty minutes at times as my dad did in forty years." Clark, the towering giant of the gang, had been hit twice in the head with gun butts by arresting officers and his head had been opened up and had required several stitches. He wore a bloody bandage around his head and sat quietly in his cell, his eyes furtively darting back and forth, as if looking for an opportunity to escape. He refused to talk to anyone but he did make a remark to one guard, a feeble joke: "When I get out of here I'm gonna wear a football helmet. Every time we get in trouble, I get hit over the head." Of all of the gang members, only Clark could look forward to surviving a trial in that he was the only member of the gang not charged with murder.

Dillinger was by then so notorious that his capture made national headlines. An army of newsmen descended on Tucson and he was interviewed endlessly, saying nothing of importance and denying that he had anything to do with the East Chicago robbery and O'Malley's death. Newsmen accompanied him on the plane back to Chicago and Sol Davis, a photographer for the Chicago *Times* who bought all four vacant seats on the plane, took endless photos of the bandit while engaging him in chatty conversation. When the plane landed in Chicago, dozens of gun-carrying guards were on hand to surround the prisoner who was led through a phalanx of newsmen to a waiting car which would take Dillinger to the Crown Point Jail, the so-called "escape-proof jail." It appeared that the Dillinger Terror Gang was smashed, finished once and for all. A great show of force was displayed in Crown Point with newsreel photographers recording the dozens of armed vigilantes roaming the grounds and streets in front and back of the jail, while national guardsmen, state and local police paraded back and forth, thousands of men arrayed to prevent Dillinger gangsters from again releasing him. But there were few Dillinger gangsters still at large. John Hamilton had gone into hiding. Homer Van Meter, who had been released from Michigan City, Ind., was somewhere in St. Paul, Minn. All the rest, Copeland, Shouse, Makley, Clark, Pierpont, and Shaw were in custody.

Dillinger was photographed upon his arrival with Prosecutor Estill and Sheriff Holley. In an act of brazenness, Dillinger leaned his arm on Estill's shoulder and the prosecutor, exhausted by the trip, paid no attention to it. This photo, however, later proved to be disastrous for Estill, making him appear chummy with the very man he was to prosecute. The picture that would cost Estill his next election. Scores of newsmen took photos and motion pictures for the newsreels. Questions were pumped at Dillinger like bullets spitting out of a submachine gun. He was treated like a visiting movie star.

"How long does it take for you and your men to rob a bank?" one newsman asked.

"Oh, about one minute and forty seconds flat," Dillinger bragged.

"How did you get caught in Tucson?"

"Makley and Clark. They paid those firemen too much money to carry their bags down from that burning hotel. If those saps had made it only a couple of bucks, we'd still be safe and happy."

"Weren't you almost caught in Chicago by the police there?"

"Yeah, in November of last year when I was going to see a doctor on Irving Park Boulevard. That was because a stool pigeon turned me up to the police." Dillinger narrowed his eyes and looked directly into the cameras, as if hoping McGinnis would see the newsreel and hear his chilling words, knowing what to expect if Dillinger ever regained his freedom: "His name is Art McGinnis. I fed him and clothed him when he was broke but he squealed on me."

"How did you live, you, Pierpont, Clark, Makley, and the others?"

Dillinger grew nostalgic for a period of time that was only a few months in the past, almost as if he were talking about deep time, decades earlier: "Those were exciting times. We moved from house to house. Rented one, stayed a few days, and moved on when the neighborhood got too hot. But we used to go downtown (in Chicago) to the theaters whenever we wanted to."

"What's your favorite movie?"

"The Three Little Pigs."

The interview ended and Dillinger was taken to a cell on the third floor of the jail. The newsmen joined the thirty Chicago police officers and their leader, Captain John Stege, who had escorted Dillinger to the Crown Point Jail in a motorcade brimming with machine guns. The Chicago police were sitting in the jail's dining room, eating a roast beef dinner. There was a huge barrel of beer in the center of the long table at which they ate. Hoosier hospitality was in full force.

The following day, front page stories in all the newspapers reported how Crown Point had been turned into an impregnable fortress. Said one story: "The measures taken by Sheriff Holley to guard her noted prisoner makes it almost impossible to stage an attempt to rescue him and none will be tried...The jail is floodlit and in a protected corner a special police officer sits night and day with a machine gun trained on Dillinger's cell, ready to repel any attempt to liberate him."

The day after Dillinger's arrival at Crown Point, he availed himself of the one phone call to which he was entitled, calling Chicago criminal attorney, Louis Piquett. The attorney visited Dillinger the next day. The 53-year-old Piquett was a most unusual criminal lawyer with a colorful past. He had been a lead miner in Platteville, Wis., before moving to Chicago to become a bartender. He studied law at night and, without a college degree, passed the Chicago bar in 1916 at the age of twenty-six. From 1920 to 1924, he was a prosecuting attorney for the city and proved to be a spellbinder in court. He went into private practice and effectively represented a host of criminals, mostly those on Al Capone's payroll. It was Piquett who had, in spite of overwhelming evidence of guilt, saved Leo Brothers from the electric chair when defending him in 1931 on the charge of killing the corrupt Chicago *Tribune* reporter, Jake Lingle. Piquett was a close associate of the crooked politicians and gangsters who ran Chicago at this time and his contacts with the underworld were widespread.

After conferring with his client, Piquett announced that Dillinger would never go to the electric chair for killing Officer O'Malley. "We have an iron-clad alibi," boasted Piquett to the press, "which will prove that John was in Florida on Jan. 14, 1934, and could therefore not have been in East Chicago on the following day when the officer was killed." On Feb. 9, 1934, a pre-trial hearing before Judge William J. Murray proved to be explosive. Prosecutor Estill demanded that Dillinger be tried within ten days for the killing of O'Malley, but Piquett demanded more time, saying it would take at least four months to round up all the witnesses in Florida who would testify to his client's being in that state at the time of the O'Malley killing. Estill continued to insist on ten days and Piquett leaped from his seat, yelling: "That would be legal murder! There's a law against lynching in this state!"

Estill also rose and yelled back: "There's a law against murder, too!"

Judge Murray set the date of the trial for March 12, 1934. Estill was edgy about the possibility of Dillinger being freed. He asked Judge Murray to transfer the prisoner to Michigan City, Ind., for safekeeping at the state prison. Judge Murray refused to move Dillinger, saying: "a hundred men couldn't take him out of that jail." He added that he could not, under the law, transfer Dillinger, unless there was a threat of mob violence and no vigilantism threatened the prisoner. Guards around the jail had proved to be alert.

A sighteseer was stopped while driving slowly past the front of the jail. His car was searched and his identity determined him to be an innocent man. A photographer took a photo of the rear of the jail and was suddenly surrounded by six gun-toting guards, his camera confiscated. This was returned to him after his credentials were checked but the film he had exposed was kept by the jail guards. No one was trusted near the jail and guards were all too aware of the subtle ways in which the Dillinger gang operated; how its members had posed as newsmen in robbing banks, boldly interviewing bank presidents about their security systems and measures, thus learning the bank's weak points; how they had also posed as policemen and sheriffs, obtaining vital information from legitimate lawmen. Several hundred men kept an around-the-clock vigil, expecting an army of gangsters to come roaring into Crown Point at any moment to free America's most celebrated bandit.

The army of guards, however, were looking the wrong way. Dillinger's deliverance would not come from without but from within. The notorious prisoner sat in his cell most of the time whittling and chatting with other prisoners. He was permitted by Judge Murray to visit with his lawyer, Piquett, at least five or six times, in a private room with no one else present. Moreover, Evelyn Billie Frechette, out on bail, was permitted to visit Dillinger on Feb. 26, 1934. She went to the jail accompanied by Piquett, but was thoroughly searched by Sheriff Holley. Piquett was never searched. Dillinger also met briefly with the elder Dillinger, an awkward meeting where the bandit apologized for creating such notoriety for his family.

Piquett was confident that he could successfully defend his client against the murder charge, having put together an impressive list of witnesses who were willing to swear that Dillinger was in Florida at the time of the East Chicago robbery and shooting. Moreover, he had given Estill the names of three Indiana citizens who would also swear that Dillinger was not the machine gun killer of O'Malley, that they had seen the shooting and would identify another man. This information sent shock waves through the East Chicago Police Department where a case against Dillinger had been a foregone conclusion. Still, Dillinger apparently felt that no number of alibi witnesses could save him from a murder conviction the state insisted on having. He decided to escape on his own.

Dillinger had spent hours each day whittling, working with a penknife on a piece of wood he took from the top of a washboard. He fashioned an automatic pistol, according to the best reports, and then, using a razor, cut out the fine details of the gun, blackening it with boot polish so that it looked very real. At 9:15 a.m., on Mar. 3, 1934, as Dillinger and fourteen other prisoners were walking about the exercise room in the rear of the second floor of the jail. Sam Cahoon, a 64-year-old turnkey, unlocked the bullpen holding the prisoners and was about to enter, carrying buckets of hot water and soap for the prisoners morning wash-up, when Dillinger rushed to Cahoon's side as the bullpen door swung open, and jammed the wooden gun into his ribs, saying: "Get inside quick or I'll kill you." He quickly took Cahoon and two porters prisoner, placing them in a cell. He then crept down a deserted corridor and, around the corner, spotted Ernest Blunk. He forced Cahoon to call Blunk to the exercise area and when the turnkey did so, Blunk was made a prisoner, believing Dillinger was holding a ".45-caliber automatic."

Blunk was then sent to call up three more guards and Warden Lou Baker, as Dillinger, menacing him with the fake gun, hid in a nearby corridor. The guards, turnkey Cahoon, Blunk and then Warden Baker, along with thirteen prisoners were all locked into cells by the energetic Dillinger. He was joined by a prisoner, Herbert Youngblood, awaiting trial for murder. Dillinger had asked Youngblood and Harry Jelinek, awaiting trial for robbery, if they wanted to join him. Jelinek declined, but Youngblood replied: "Yes, sir, Mr. Dillinger, I believe I do." Youngblood grabbed a heavy mop handle and used this to corral prisoners with Dillinger. The wooden gun employed by Dillinger throughout this time appeared to be different to each guard he intimidated with it. To Deputy Kenneth Houk, the gun was "a .38-automatic," and Houk later insisted that it was real: "When I hear people say that he got out with a wooden gun I get so mad I could spit. You look down the barrel of one and you know the difference between a wooden gun and a good one. There's, a difference between metal and wood covered with shoe blacking."

The problem was that none of the guards stared at the gun for more than a few seconds and none of them at the time, including Houk, would have been foolish enough to challenge the gun's genuineness. All of the prisoners up to this point were unarmed and Dillinger was desperate to obtain a real gun before his ruse was discovered. Pushing Blunk in front of him, Dillinger went downstairs through a side corridor and spotted Warden Hiles who was carrying a real .45-caliber automatic. He quickly disarmed Hiles and marched him and Blunk back to the cells on the second floor. He then went back downstairs while Youngblood guarded the prisoners and walked into the empty front office.

Dillinger found two Thompson submachine guns lying on a window sill and grabbing these, returned to the second floor. He handed one of the machine guns to Youngblood and then took up a collection, getting $15 from the guards. He then produced his wooden gun and ran its barrel slowly along the bars of the cell holding the guards and Warden Baker. "I did it all with my little toy pistol, gentlemen," he told them. All but Houk would later agree that the gun Dillinger held up to them was a clever fake. Blunk later stated: "It was the best imitation of a gun I ever saw." It was later claimed that Louis Piquett, or even Evelyn Frechette had smuggled a real automatic to Dillinger during one of their jailhouse conferences, but most evidence points to the use of a wooden gun.

Again using Blunk as a shield, Dillinger and Youngblood went downstairs and through the side corridor to the open yard and crossed this to the jail garage. None of the cars inside the garage had keys in the ignition. Dillinger locked several jail employees in a laundry room, including Mrs. Mary Linton, Warden Baker's mother-in-law, who had just returned from a shopping trip, having been driven by a bailiff. Mrs. Linton took one look at the man holding the submachine gun and said: "My God! You're John Dillinger!"

Dilliner motioned to her and the bailiff to join the others in the laundry room, saying: "Right. You do as I tell you." After locking these two up, Dillinger asked Blunk where the nearest public garage was located. Blunk told him three doors down from the back of the jail garage and the three men stepped outside, Dillinger wearing Blunk's overcoat. They walked down the street in full view of patrolling guardsmen and passersby, none taking note of the trio. They then stepped into the rear of the Main Street Garage where Dillinger saw mechanic Edwin Saager leaning at work on a car, his head beneath the car's hood.

"Which car in here is the fastest?" Dillinger asked.

Saager glanced at him, thinking Dillinger to be a deputy and pointed to a black Ford V-8 with a red headlight and a siren. It was parked facing toward the garage doors. "That one," said Saager, "the Sheriff's car."

"Come on, let's go," Dillinger ordered Saager.

"I can't," replied the mechanic, still thinking he was talking to a deputy who was going out on a routine patrol. "I'm working on a car."

Dillinger hit Saager's leg with the machine gun and the mechanic straightened up and then went white. He got into the back seat of the car as ordered. Dillinger got in beside him and ordered Blunk to get behind the wheel and drive. Youngblood climbed in next to Blunk and the car rolled slowly out of the garage. Robert Volk, a postal employee who was part of the vigilante force and carried a .45-caliber automatic, was in the garage at the time and watched the whole scene, but was frozen with fear at the sight of Dillinger and did nothing.

Blunk drove slowly, but purposely went through a red light to attract the attention of police lining the street. The police, however, believing the occupants of the car to be Sheriff Holley and deputies, merely smiled and waved them on. When the V-8 reached the city limits, Dillinger ordered Blunk to drive onto the macadam road running alongside the Pennsylvania Railroad tracks. Meanwhile, Volk regained his composure and raced to a phone, calling the police department. "Dillinger's escaped!" he screamed over the phone.

"What?" said an incredulous voice at the other end. "You're nuts! You want us to lock you up?" Finally, Volk managed to

Dillinger, while a prisoner at Crown Point, leans on the shoulder of prosecutor Robert Estill.

Guards surrounded the Crown Point jail.

Sheriff Lillian Holley, left, dejected after Dillinger's escape; Dillinger, right.

Dillinger holding wooden gun.

Herbert Youngblood

The bullet-scarred facade of Little Bohemia.

convince some jail authorities that the most desperate outlaw in America was once more free. The news stunned Sheriff Lillian Holley who sank into a chair in near collapse. Some minutes later she called the state police to report the escape.

"How did it happen?" she was asked.

"It's too ridiculous for words," she replied. Later she met the press, almost in a state of shock, saying: "Dillinger took one chance in a million and all the breaks were with him and against me...How this could have happened I don't quite see." Sheriff Holley was a rare exception in 1934 America, a female sheriff. She was actually filling out the term vacated when her husband died. But she came under criticism as a female, being too soft with Dillinger and other prisoners. It was even pointed out that she had, in photos taken with Dillinger, looked at her prisoner with almost a look of admiration.

"You think your job is too big for a woman?" one reporter asked her.

"Oh, hell's fire, of course not," she replied in disgust.

Deputy Houk did show a certain amount of admiration for the desperado, saying of Dillinger: "I never heard him cuss or be abusive in any way, shape or fashion. The morning he came out, he was tough, but not the tough "killer" type. He would have killed if his life had been at stake, but as far as being a deliberate killer, I can't believe John Dillinger was that way. I'm skeptical as to whether they would ever have found him guilty of that East Chicago charge...I don't believe the man *was* there."

As posses fanned out in every direction looking for Dillinger, the bandit sat in the back seat of the V-8, telling Blunk to "take your time, take your time. Thirty miles an hour is enough. There's no hurry." The bandit chatted freely with his hostages. Youngblood said nothing, sitting like a wooden Indian next to Blunk, his submachine gun trained on the driver. Dillinger grew philosophical, saying to Blunk, an educated penologist: "You know, a prison is like a nut with a worm in it. The worm can always get out." He then directed Blunk to take many turns, following gravel roads. He then jocularly asked Blunk and Saager: "How would you like to go to Ohio and get those other guys (Pierpont and Makley) out?" His hostages did not respond. Near Peotone, Ill., the car ran into muddy roads washed out by heavy rains the night before. Dillinger ordered everyone out of the car and chains were put on the back wheels. "Take your time, boys," Dillinger said in a low voice. "What's time to me?"

After the chains were fixed on the wheels, Dillinger reached into his pocket and handed Saager $4, telling him that this money was for carfare for himself and Blunk. "I'd give you more, but I only got fifteen dollars. I'll remember you at Christmas." He got behind the wheel and told Youngblood, who was in the back seat, to lie down in the back. The V-8 slowly moved down the road, going south. Saager and Blunk stood in the middle of the road, listening to Dillinger whistle, hum and then sing a few lines from the song *I'm Heading for the Last Roundup*.

News announcing the spectacular escape held the nation in suspense and wonder. It appeared that no prison, no matter how strong, how well fortified and guarded, could hold John Dillinger. He became a living legend, his fame broader and more full of impact than that of Jesse James in the nineteenth century, because Dillinger struck with electrifying speed, using fast cars and machine guns, utilizing all the techniques and inventions of modern society to best law enforcement agencies that appeared helpless before him. Indiana attorney general Philip Lutz stated: "The nation is horrified and shocked at the escape of this notorious bank robber and I am surprised that Lake County officials let him get away."

Tough, old Captain Stege of the Chicago Police Department shook his head in amazement, saying: "How in the name of common sense could a prisoner go through six barred doors to freedom?...But I told them it would happen. I pleaded with Governor McNutt's secretary to put him in the penitentiary. Now, bright and early Monday Dillinger will rob a bank to get funds. Then, when he gets together with John Hamilton, the two of them will raid a police station some place and get guns and ammunition. Then maybe they'll come back to Chicago for another game of tag."

Stege was right. Dillinger did contact John Hamilton as soon as he drove Sheriff Holley's souped-up car across the Illinois line, making arrangements to meet not in Chicago but in St. Paul, Minn., then one of the "safe" cities for the independent bank robbers of the era, a town whose heavily bribed politicians and police looked the other way. This was the safe haven of the Barker gang and Alvin Karpis, a town filled with underworld bosses with strong political connections, such as Harry Sawyer and Boss John J. McLaughlin. But by driving the stolen Sheriff's car from Indiana to Illinos, Dillinger had violated a new federal law, illegally transporting a stolen vehicle across a state line, and this then put him under the jurisdiction of the FBI. Hoover promptly made Dillinger Public Enemy Number One and ordered his agents in all bureaus to make the Indiana outlaw their primary duty.

Dillinger soon abandoned the stolen car and separated from Youngblood, giving him a few dollars and wishing him well. Youngblood made his way to Michigan where he was later cornered and killed when he decided to shoot it out with lawmen. Dillinger, driving another stolen car, met with his attorney Piquett on a Chicago street. Piquett later reported this meeting and he claimed that he pleaded with the bandit to surrender. "I told him that it was impossible for him to defeat the law. I told him that it was my duty to advise him to surrender, and let me take him to Town Hall station. He said he would do all that later." He then met Evelyn Frechette, who had already rented a room where Dillinger stayed for a short time before going on to St. Paul. Here Dillinger met with Hamilton who gave him $1,500. Dillinger bought a new wardrobe, a new car, and rented a nice apartment for himself and Frechette in Minneapolis.

The new Dillinger gang was then formed. Homer Van Meter arrived with two new tough recruits, Eddie Green, a nerveless getaway driver, and Tommy Carroll, an ex-boxer and experienced bank robber who had looted banks in Iowa and Nebraska. Another man was needed, the gang felt, and, against Van Meter's wishes, Dillinger brought Lester Gillis into the gang. Gillis, better known as Baby Face Nelson, had worked for some Chicago gangsters such as Bugs Moran. He was a West Coast bank robber who stood five foot, four inches high, and had a streak of murderous insanity. A hot-head, Nelson's idea of bank robbing was to roar up to a bank shooting, enter shooting, and escape shooting. "Kill everybody in sight, mostly the cops, and take off," he told Dillinger. "That way, they know you mean business!"

"This rooster is nuts," Van Meter said, sneering at Nelson.

"You say that again and we'll settle it with guns," Nelson sneered back.

Dillinger stepped between the two men, saying: "We'll do it my way, Nelson, or you can look for work somewhere else." Nelson nodded and kept silent. Then Hamilton outlined plans for the gang's first robbery. On Mar. 6, 1934, driving a large green Packard which had been stolen from a St. Paul car dealer, the gang entered Sioux Falls, S.D., parking the car next to the Security National Bank and Trust Company at 10 a.m. A secretary in the bank looked out the bank window and noticed the six men in the car and joked to a clerk: "Look, there's a bunch of holdup men." The clerk placed his finger over a button that would trigger the bank alarm.

Dillinger, Hamilton, Van Meter, and Nelson entered the bank, while Carroll took the "tiger" position of lookout just outside the bank entrance, a submachine gun beneath his long winter coat. Eddie Green sat behind the wheel of the Packard, waiting. Before Dillinger could make his customary announcements, Nelson whipped out his submachine gun and screamed shrilly: "This is a holdup! Lay down on the floor!" As Hamilton, Nelson, and Van Meter trained guns on the customers and employees, Dillinger ran behind the teller's cages, to that of the head teller, Robert Dargen. He put his automatic down on the counter and began to scoop up bills, shoving these into the sugar sack he held in his other

other hand. Dargen looked at the automatic and thought for a moment of grabbing it, then decided that such a move would be suicide. Meanwhile, the clerk pressed the alarm button and a bell began to clang loudly outside the bank.

The bank robbers remained calm. Dillinger continued emptying the drawers from the tellers' cages then ordered Dargen to open the vaults at the rear of the bank. Dargen said that it was a complicated affair, that each vault required five different combinations to open them. Van Meter then proved that he was as volatile as Nelson. He ran forward and jammed the barrel of his submachine gun into Dargen's ribs, shouting: "Open it up, you son-of-a-bitch, or I'll cut you in two." Dillinger said nothing. Dargen told Van Meter if he took the gun away, he'd open the vault. When the vault was opened, Van Meter filled another sack with about $14,000 in bills. Van Meter then ordered Dargen to open the next vault, but the head teller told him that he did not have the combination and that the vault contained only non-negotiable bonds. "Get the damned bank president out here now!" yelled Van Meter.

Someone called the local police station and said there was trouble at the bank but neglected to tell the desk sergeant that the alarm was ringing. The sergeant turned to an officer and told him to "go up to the bank. Probably some drunk bothering the customers." The officer strolled up to the bank and when he entered, walking past Carroll, the ex-boxer whipped out his submachine gun and prodded the officer into the bank where Hamilton disarmed him and told him to lie on the floor. The constant clang of the alarm bell outside the bank made Nelson jittery. He began to move erratically about the foyer of the bank, screaming: "I'm going to kill the man who hit that damned alarm!" He pointed his machine gun at a teller and screamed: "I know it was you!"

"No, no," the teller said, trembling. "Look, my button here is sticking up. If I had pressed it down it would still be down."

Dillinger called from the vault area to Nelson: "Forget that! Just get the money!"

At that moment Nelson saw off-duty policeman Hale Keith get out of a car near the bank and cross the street. He had seen large crowds swelling about the bank and thought he should investigate. As he approached the bank he hitched up his belt and Nelson thought he was drawing a gun. The diminutive gangster jumped a guard railing and leaped onto the top of a desk, letting loose a burst of machine gun fire which shattered the plate glass window and cut down Keith, sending him wounded to the pavement. Nelson, his face flushed red, turned and screamed: "I got one of them! I got one of them!"

In the street Tommy Carroll, a cool-headed gunman, rounded up the entire police force of twelve officers who had arrived in small groups to learn the cause of the alarm bell. Even the embarrassed chief of police, M.W. Parsons, stood with his men against the wall of a building with his men as Carroll guarded them. A short distance away more than a thousand curious spectators milled about. The gang finally emerged carrying about $49,000. They took five female hostages and a teller, Leo Olson with them. Nelson, though there was no reason for it, stood at the bank's entrance and shot out the glass of the window in the door, then swaggered outside and ordered the women to hang onto the running boards of the big Packard. The gang members got inside and the car labored up the street. A shot fired by patrolman Harley Chrisman punctured the radiator and the car stopped. The hostages leaped off but Nelson shouted: "Get back here!" The hostages again took their positions hanging onto the car, but one girl complained, saying she could no longer hold on. Dillinger told her to get off and the car lumbered around a corner, then another.

The Packard slowly made its way out of town, loaded down with six bankrobbers and five hostages while its radiator steamed and huffed. Dillinger stopped the car several times to have roofing nails spread over the road behind them. Outside of town, the bandits stopped a motorist and switched cars, leaving the hostages to stand freezing along the muddy road. They were picked up by a sheriff's car some time later, the officers complaining that they had to stop several times to repair flat tires, one officer complaining: "Some damned fool spilled roofing nails from his truck all over the road." Taking back roads, the gang did not arrive back in Minneapolis until midnight. There, in Dillinger's apartment, the gang split up the loot. Nelson insisted on counting it so that he would not be "cheated," reminding the others that "I shot the cop, didn't I?" His petite wife Helen, a dark-featured young woman, sat some distance away, saying nothing. Van Meter objected to Nelson counting the money but Dillinger, who was recognized as the leader of this gang decided the argument, saying: "Let Lester count the money." Nelson sat down, his submachine gun on his lap, and carefully counted out six even amounts of money.

Dillinger later called Louis Piquett and told him he was sending several thousand dollars to Mary Kinder and that he and Mary should arrange to hire "the best attorneys you can get for Harry and Charley." At that time Pierpont and Makley were about to be tried for the murder of Sheriff Sarber. He then told Eddie Green to scout another bank, "one with a lot of cash. We are taking big chances and we should be getting big amounts." He told Billie Frechette that once he had accumulated enough money they would travel to South America or Mexico and live out their lives in comfort. Green returned in a few days, reporting a bank stuffed with money, the First National Bank of Mason City, Iowa, which reportedly held more than $240,000.

The gang struck the bank in Mason City on Mar. 13, 1934. This time, at Dillinger's insistence, Nelson stayed outside, near the getaway car which Eddie Green was driving. Carroll once again took the position of the "tiger," standing outside the bank entrance with a submachine gun hidden beneath his gray overcoat. Dillinger, Hamilton, and Van Meter entered the bank, but Van Meter suddenly went running about, screaming for the bank president. Willis Bagley, the president, saw Van Meter racing about the lobby and ran for his office, thinking "a crazy man was loose" inside the bank. He ran to the office and Van Meter ran after him, jamming the barrel of this gun into the door opening just as Bagley slammed it shut. Bagley leaned against the door and Van Meter yanked on the gun, freeing it. Bagley slammed the door shut and locked it, but Van Meter, who knew Bagley had the key to vault, angrily fired through the door, wounding Bagley. He then joined Hamilton and Dillinger to help clean out the tellers' cages.

Hamilton went into the vault with cashier Harry Fisher, but a door with bars slammed shut, separating Hamilton from the teller. On the shelves around Fisher, Hamilton could see more than $200,000 in neat stacks. He ordered the teller to shove the stacks of money through the bars, but Fisher purposely selected the stacks of one-dollar bills, then five-dollar bills, until Hamilton, flourishing his automatic shouted: "Just gimme the big bills!" Crowds were assembling in the street. Gas bombs fired by a guard in a cage high above the tellers' cages had filled the bank with smoke which poured out of the bank entrance. Bank alarm bells went off everywhere. Dillinger and Van Meter shouted to Hamilton that "we have to go! We're going!" Hamilton begged for more time, shouting: "It's hell to leave all that money back there!" With only $52,000 in their sacks, the bandits finally left the bank, but they were greeted by a street packed with curious citizens.

Nelson, who was standing at a nearby alley entrance, was approached by a middle-aged woman who wagged her finger at him. "Young man, do something, can't you see the bank is being robbed?" He produced a submachine gun and waved her away, saying: "Lady, you're telling me?" Down the street, Dillinger was lining up citizens, waving a submachine gun. From an upstairs window, John Shipley, an elderly policeman, fired a single shot that wounded Dillinger in the arm. Dillinger switched the submachine gun to his good hand, then his gun stuttered and its bullets raked the walls and windows of the building in which Shipley had taken cover. Shipley retreated after firing his one shot. Police did not respond to the robbery with great speed. When the alarm went off, officers believed that a motion picture company, which had been shooting a film the day earlier around the bank, was at work re-enacting a bank robbery, that all of it was make-believe. (It is quite possible that the bandits themselves had arrived a day earlier and had photographed the bank and the surrounding area, explaining that they were making a Hollywood film in order to disguise the real bank robbery the next day.)

Taking more than a dozen hostages, the robbers left in an overloaded Buick. So many hostages were clinging to the car that Dillinger asked a few women to step off the running boards. Before the car lumbered out of town, one of the female bank employees yelled: "This is where I live! Let me off!" Dillinger let the woman go. Outside town, on a paved road, Dillinger ordered Nelson to spread roofing nails behind them. The bantam-weight gangster leaped from the car and tossed nails recklessly in all directions. Dillinger leaned out a window and said to him in disgust: "You're spreading nails under our own car, Lester." A police car containing Police Chief E.J. Patton and other officers inched up the road after the Buick. Inside officers urged Patton to open fire on the escaping Buick. "We can't do that," Patton said, "or we might hit the hostages." Nelson spotted the police car and let loose a burst from his submachine gun. The police turned off the road and stopped.

Two hours later, the Buick stopped to let off the last hostages. The gang drove back to Minneapolis, Hamilton brooding all the way over how the cashier Fisher had tricked him. "I should have killed that man," he said. Both Hamilton and Dillinger had received slight wounds and were treated in St. Paul by Dr. N.G. Mortenson, the city health officer. Both went on their way to mend quickly and plan their next robbery. But FBI agents in St. Paul, who had been diligently tracking Dillinger's movements, believed he was living under the alias of Carl Hellman with Billie Frechette in a St. Paul rooming house.

Dillinger and Frechette took a trip back to Indiana and, incredible as it may seem, drove right into the yard of the Dillinger farm in Mooresville without anyone taking note. No lawmen had been posted to stake out the home of the most wanted man in the country. A family reunion was held with Audrey Dillinger and her family present. The elder Dillinger tried to persuade his son to surrender but John put him off. The family ate a large dinner, talked about old times and John posed for photos outside the house. He stood with Frechette as Audrey took snapshots and there was talk of marriage and, again, South America. In one shot, Dillinger posed with the wooden gun he had made in Crown Point in one hand and a real submachine gun in the other. Dillinger left the wooden gun with Audrey and she kept this crime relic until the day she died in 1988.

Meanwhile, the Ohio trial of Harry Pierpont and Charles Makley for the murder of Sheriff Sarber had ended in conviction, despite the testimony of Pierpont's mother that her son was eating dinner with her in their Leipsic, Ohio home on the night Sarber was killed. Mrs. Pierpont, who had coddled Harry throughout his life, hid his face with her scarf when newsmen in court tried to photograph him. Pierpont did not help his own cause on the witness stand, shouting at the prosecutor: "I'm not the kind of man you are, robbing widows and orphans. You'd probably be like me if you had the nerve!" Handsome Harry was condemned to die in the electric chair, as was Charles Makley. Russell Clark was also tried but received a life sentence. (Clark would die of cancer only a few weeks after his release from prison in 1973.) Both Pierpont and Makley were not surprised at receiving death sentences. When Pierpont returned from his sentencing, Makley, sitting in the next cell of the Lima, Ohio, Jail, asked him: "What was it, Harry?"

"Well, what would it be?" Pierpont replied.

A day later, Makley returned after being sentenced. "What did you get, Charley?" asked Pierpont.

Makley sat down on the bunk in his cell, shoved an entire pack of gum into his mouth and then replied: "I got everything." He added a moment later: "We all have to die once."

Still, authorities believed that Dillinger might try to rescue his close friends Pierpont and Makley before they were transferred to the state prison. The Lima jail was surrounded by guards, and searchlights played over every square inch of the building at night. Vigilantes, local and state police, and national guardsmen were everywhere, waiting for Dillinger to arrive. Dillinger, meanwhile, barely escaped an FBI trap on Mar. 31, 1934. Agents R.L. Nalls and R.C. Coulter had finally pinpointed his address in St. Paul. They went to the Lincoln Court Apartments and knocked on the door of Carl Hellman, the alias Dillinger was then using. Billie Frechette opened the door a crack and told the two agents that her husband, Mr. Hellman, was asleep, and that she was not dressed. She said she would wake him and put on some clothes. She closed the door and locked it, then ran to the bedroom and told Dillinger that police were in the hallway.

The agents were waiting nervously in the hall when they noticed a man walking up the stairs to the third floor where they stood. It was Homer Van Meter.

"Who are you?" Agent Coulter asked him.

Van Meter gave him a broad smile and said: "I'm a soap salesman."

Coulter looked him over closely. "Yeah, well if you are, where are your samples?"

"In my car outside," Van Meter said glibly. "Come on downstairs, fella, and I'll be glad to show them to you."

Coulter followed Van Meter down the stairs but at the landing on the second floor the bandit pulled an automatic and wheeled about, shouting at the FBI agent: "You asked for it, so I'll give it to you!"

The agent, helpless, opted for a quick retreat. He bolted straight past Van Meter, going down the stairs three at a time and through the front doors. Van Meter was about to go upstairs again but remembered the other lawman and left the building. He ran into the street where he spotted a horse-drawn delivery wagon, its driver gone. Van Meter jumped onto the seat of the wagon, put the driver's cap on his head and then whipped the horse wildly so that it leaped forward at a gallop with Van Meter making an unorthodox, clattering escape.

Agent Nalls heard the commotion downstairs and went to investigate. When Dillinger stepped into the hallway carrying a machine gun, he saw the hallway empty. He went to the front stairs and fired a burst from the gun, then retreated with Frechette down a back staircase to the rear door of the apartment building. Just as he and Frechette reached his Hudson Terraplane, Nalls appeared and fired a shot at Dillinger, wounding him in the leg. Dillinger jumped into the car, Frechette at his side, and roared away down the alley, escaping. He and Frechette went to Eddie Green's apartment and Green brought an underworld doctor to patch up Dillinger's leg. The gang then decided to leave St. Paul immediately, realizing that FBI agents had them spotted. Pat Reilly, who did odd jobs for the gang, suggested that everyone go to a resort in northern Wisconsin, a backwoods retreat where no one, including the FBI, would think to look for them. Before going to this retreat, Dillinger and Frechette made a quick "business" trip to Chicago. On Apr. 9, 1934, Dillinger and Frechette had a mysterious meeting with someone at a tavern located at 416 N. State Street. Dillinger was apprehensive and sent Billie Frechette into the tavern to await a contact person while he stood across the street. A few minutes later, three men who seemed to Dillinger to be "feds" rushed into the tavern and arrested Frechette. She was hustled out of the tavern to a waiting car and she looked at Dillinger from the car window as he sank back into the shadows of a doorway. Frechette was jailed, charged with harboring Dillinger, a fugitive.

Dillinger soon returned to St. Paul, and with Van Meter, Carroll, Hamilton and Nelson, along with three women, he traveled southeast to the Little Bohemia Lodge in Manitowish Waters, Wis. Its owner, Emil Wannatka, welcomed the visitors,

Dillinger's crooked lawyer, Louis Piquett.

Polly Hamilton Keele

Anna Sage, 1934.

Hoover, Attorney General Cummings, Purvis.

Martin Zarkovich and Anna Sage, shown together in the late 1920s, lovers and partners in prostitution.

The Biograph Theater, July 22, 1934, the night the FBI claimed to have shot and killed John Dillinger.

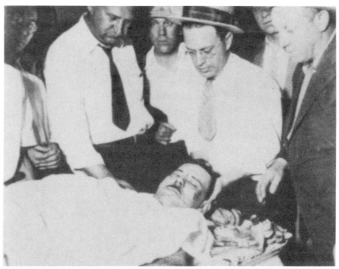

Dr. Charles D. Parker holds the head of the body in the morgue.

although he later claimed that the gang members were strangers to him and had forced their way into his lodge, which was not yet officially open. Wannatka later insisted that the gang barged in on him and his family unannounced and they were more or less prisoner-hosts to the gang, but it is likely that Wannatka, who had once owned a Chicago speakeasy and was associated with gangsters Terry Druggan and Frankie Lake, knew the gang was going to use his lodge as a hideout. The gangsters sat around drinking and playing cards. Marie Conforti, Van Meter's girl, helped to make meals with Helen Gillis and Jean Delaney Crompton Carroll, the wife of Tommy Carroll. Everybody spent a good deal of time trying to cheer up Dillinger, who was depressed and sullen over the arrest of Billie Frechette.

Melvin Purvis, the FBI agent in charge of the hunt for Dillinger in Chicago, received a tip that Dillinger and his gang were hiding out in the Little Bohemia. On the night of Apr. 22, 1934, he and other agents flew to Rhinelander, Wis., and then commandeered several cars and drove down the narrow roads surrounded by dense forests to the lodge. By then FBI agents had been armed, but their training in weaponry was limited. Purvis himself was a shoot-from-the-hip lawman, excitable, impulsive, even reckless, the very type J. Edgar Hoover wanted to weed out of the bureau. Purvis was also a man who craved the limelight and cultivated publicity. He put himself before the bureau and the only man in the FBI able to take such a position was Hoover himself. In reality, Purvis was a ruthlessly ambitious agent who may have harbored thoughts of replacing Hoover.

The FBI under Purvis' leadership in Chicago underestimated Dillinger, believing him to be a cretinous outlaw who resorted to the gun first and last. Purvis did not study Dillinger's habits and character, but followed the machine gun image of him the press had created. Agents in this era were either lawyers or accountants with little or no street experience dealing with gangsters or the independent bank robbers of the 1930s. They relied on tips from newsmen and informants passed along to them from local police departments to track federal fugitives. They learned much of their search and seizure technique, according to the author's contacts inside the Bureau, from watching Hollywood movies, and they emulated movie police grilling suspects and using the third degree.

Hoover, desperate to prove the FBI effective during the crime wave of the 1930s, made Dillinger Public Enemy Number One, mostly due to Dillinger's national publicity, which rankled Hoover. Technically, Hoover overreached himself in making Dillinger Public Enemy Number One. As a federal fugitive, Dillinger's most serious crime was crossing a state line with a stolen auto, and that offense was the only one which allowed Hoover and his agents to pursue Dillinger. It certainly was not a crime that would win Dillinger the dubious honor of being named the most sought criminal in America. Ironically, Hoover increased Dillinger's notoriety by naming him Public Enemy Number One, perhaps with the thought that once the Bureau had captured or killed Dillinger, its own status would surpass that of Dillinger or any other infamous gangster.

When Purvis led his men through the dark woods toward the Little Bohemia Lodge, he had no idea how many gang members might be inside, what their fire power might be, or the possible escape routes they might use. He merely assembled his eight heavily armed agents in front of the lodge and advanced like General Custer charging in a frontal attack into the valley of the Little Big Horn. As the agents went forward, three men emerged from the lodge, wobbly-legged, to get into a coupe parked in front of the lodge. The driver turned on the radio and Purvis ordered the men to get out of the car but got no response. (Two survivors later denied Purvis' claim that he shouted such a command to the men.) When the men in the car did not respond, Purvis and his men opened fire with submachine guns, automatics and automatic rifles, riddling the car and blowing its occupants to pieces. All three men in the car were CCC workers and one of them, Eugene Boiseneau, was killed outright, a slaying that was, immediately after the abortive raid, attributed to Dillinger.

The gunfire outside the lodge alerted Dillinger and his men to the presence of the FBI. They had been playing cards with Wannatka and they jumped up and peered through the front windows, turning off the lights. Inside the lodge were Dillinger, Hamilton, Van Meter, Carroll and their women. Baby Face Nelson and his wife Helen were sleeping in a cottage nearby. Dillinger and the others raced upstairs without a thought of fighting it out with lawmen. They had no idea that the front area of the lodge was crawling with FBI men since Purvis never identified himself or his men to the occupants of the lodge. The attackers could have been local vigilantes, national guardsmen, state troopers, or local lawmen for all the Dillinger gang knew. As Dillinger and the other men grabbed their weapons, coats, hats and cash, Purvis and his men let loose a deafening fire that raked the front of the lodge, smashed windows and destroyed china and bric-a-brac in the first floor rooms.

At that moment, Dillinger and the others slipped out a back window on the second floor, lowering themselves to a small roof and then dropping about ten feet to the ground. They ran single file to Little Star Lake behind the lodge and ran along the water's edge into the trees, going north. The only member of the gang to offer resistance was Nelson. He leaped half-dressed from his bed at the sound of gunfire, grabbed a submachine gun, and ran outside to see from a flanking position the FBI men charging the front of the lodge. Believing his associates were still inside and returning fire, he joined in, letting loose a burst from his Thompson, which drew fire from Purvis and other agents. The agents stopped their attack on the lodge and angled toward Nelson, who soon realized that he was hopelessly outnumbered. He fled into the woods, abandoning his wife.

Purvis resumed his attack on the lodge. Its occupants, the women who had accompanied the gang, and Wannatka and his family, had taken refuge in the basement. They huddled there for hours as the FBI blasted the lodge with automatic fire and tear gas bombs. Some time later, oblivious to the one-sided battle that was going on, Pat Reilly, with Patricia Cherrington at his side, drove into the long driveway leading to the parking lot in front of the lodge. The agents wheeled about and opened fire on the car after Reilly realized he was driving into a trap and threw the auto into a quick reverse. One tire was shot flat and the windows of the car were shot out, but Reilly and Cherrington remained unharmed. Back on the highway, Reilly threw the car into gear and shot ahead, weaving crazily up the road on the flat.

Dillinger, Van Meter, and Hamilton reached the home of E.J. Mitchell and there tried to start an old truck parked in the yard, but it would not turn over. They spotted a coupe parked in a neighbor's yard and took it, heading for St. Paul. Tommy Carroll, who had gotten lost in the woods, wandered into Manitowish Waters, a small town about a mile from the Little Bohemia, and stole a Packard and began driving to St. Paul. Nelson, who had gone in the opposite direction from the rest of the gang, stopped a car carrying G.W. Lang and his wife and forced the elderly couple at gunpoint to drive him out of the area. The car broke down near the home of Alvin Koerner, and Nelson raced to the house. Koerner, however, suspicious after hearing the gunfire from the nearby lodge, called police to tell an officer that a strange car had parked in his yard and a man with a gun was approaching the house. He hung up just as Nelson reached his front door.

Another car containing Emil Wannatka, his two bartenders and his brother-in-law, George LaPorte, then arrived at the Koerner house. LaPorte had driven to the lodge in response to a desperate phone call from Wannatka. When LaPorte arrived on a side road near the lodge, Wannatka and his two bartenders escaped and LaPorte drove them away while the FBI agents continued to pepper the lodge. Once in the Koerner house, Wannatka saw Nelson, his former guest, and he tried to placate the jittery gangster. Nelson told Wannatka to shut up and lined everyone in the house up against a wall. He then ordered Wannatka and Koerner outside, telling them they were his hostages. He told

Wannatka to start LaPorte's car, but Wannatka flooded the engine.

At that moment, about 11 p.m., another car drove into Koerner's lot. In it were two FBI agents Jay Newman and H. Carter Baum, along with constable Carl C. Christiansen. Newman was driving and Baum sat next to him, cradling a submachine gun in his lap. The car stopped just behind and to the right of LaPorte's car. Christiansen, who was sitting in the back seat, later remembered how "this little jack rabbit flew right out of nowhere." Nelson had leaped from the front of the LaPorte car and raced up to the FBI auto, just as Newman opened the door and was about to step out.

Nelson held a machine pistol, described later by Christiansen as "a forty-five Colt converted into a machine gun with a long clip and a pistol grip." The little gangster screamed: "I know you bastards are wearing bullet-proof vests so I'll give it to you high and low!" With that he began firing point blank into the car. First Newman fell, hit over the eye. He collapsed onto the dirt lot. Baum struggled to hold up the machine gun as he stepped out of the other door, but Nelson's bullets tore through his neck and killed him instantly. Christiansen, fumbling for his .38-caliber Smith & Wesson, jumped from the car and ran for the cover of a nearby wood pile, but he was floodlit by the headlights of Newman's idling car and Nelson shot him in the back several times, knocking him down. Christiansen crawled to Baum's side but saw that he was dead.

Newman somehow came to, and while holding his bleeding head, the courageous agent lifted his automatic and fired a wild shot in Nelson's direction. Nelson was by then berserk, screaming and cursing and firing in all directions. Wannatka ran to a snow bank and Nelson fired at him, shouting: "You traitor, you informed on us!" Wannatka was unharmed and he managed to crawl over the bank and into some woods. He got up and began running back to the Little Bohemia. Nelson then jumped into the Ford that had been driven by Newman and backed out of the yard so violently that Koerner's house was showered by gravel kicked up by the tires. Nelson roared onto the highway and raced southward. Newman staggered to his feet and went to Koerner's house. He knocked on the door, but those inside refused to let him in, thinking he was another gangster bent on havoc. Christiansen later remembered that those in the house "let us lie there for about an hour before anyone dared to come outside."

Wannatka emerged from the woods near Little Bohemia, his hands and legs bleeding from the thorny underbrush. The noise of his movements caused the agents still positioned in front of the lodge to train their guns on him. "Hands up, you! Hands up!" shouted an agent in his direction. Wannatka staggered forward, exhausted, panting, as Purvis and other agents surrounded him, guns aimed at his head. "All your men are dead at Koerner's," gasped Wannatka.

Purvis squinted at Wannatka, saying: "How do you spell your name and address?"

"What?" Wannatka said, amazed at Purvis' seeming indifference to the news that his agents had been killed. "Are you crazy? I told you that all your men have been killed at Koerner's house. Did you come here for Dillinger or for me?" Wannatka then filled a truck with hay and, after another argument with Purvis, drove back to Koerner's to retrieve the dead and wounded. The body of the 29-year-old Baum was placed on the hay and driven to a nearby mortuary. Newman and Christiansen survived their wounds.

By dawn, the battle of the Little Bohemia was over. The inside of the lodge was thick with teargas and the three mob women, Marie Conforti, Helen Gillis and Jean Carroll, staggered choking from the building, their hands in the air. All of the quarry had fled and escaped. Purvis' embarrassment was thorough, but that of his boss, J. Edgar Hoover, was increased by the fact that the director had announced at 2 a.m. Washington, D.C., time (midnight at the Little Bohemia) that the Dillinger gang was surrounded and its members had no chance of escape. Then the bad news came in that Dillinger and the others had escaped. Hoover finally got hold of Purvis and told him how disappointed he was.

There was more bad news to come. When it was discovered that the agents had wounded several innocent persons and killed Eugene Boiseneau, newspapers across the country ran banner headlines attacking Hoover and the Bureau for recklessness, some even charging manslaughter. Senator Kenneth McKellar later held hearings investigating the Little Bohemia fiasco and charged Hoover and Purvis with irresponsible acts that had caused the death of an innocent man. Several Republican senators began campaigns to have Hoover demoted or even removed from office. Instead of being portrayed as heroes, the FBI agents were held up to ridicule. Hoover, privately incensed at Purvis for being disgraced, gave orders to Purvis and other agents to get Dillinger "at all costs." So driven were Hoover and Purvis to right their wrong and to recapture public opinion that they would grasp at any straw to deliver John Herbert Dillinger. Their desperation would lead them into an even greater debacle.

The killing of innocent men by the FBI created a scandal that provided material for Will Rogers, then America's favorite humorist. Wrote Rogers: "Well, they had Dillinger surrounded and was all ready to shoot him when he come out, but another bunch of folks come out ahead, so they shot them instead. Dillinger is going to accidentally get in with some innocent bystanders some time, then he will get shot."

Some side benefits came of the Little Bohemia failure, however, in that twelve anti-crime bills in Congress which had long been delayed were finally enacted. Throughout the Midwest, the Dillinger mania caused local legislators to provide their police departments new equipment, including city-wide and state-wide radio systems, the lack of which allowed Dillinger and bandits like him to escape police dragnets and roadblocks. Indirectly, Dillinger had caused an improvement in U.S. law enforcement procedures.

The Dillinger gang was still on the run. Hours after leaving Wisconsin in the stolen car, Dillinger, Van Meter and Hamilton were about to drive across a bridge spanning the Mississippi near Hastings, Minn., about twenty miles south of St. Paul. Deputy Sheriff Norman Dieter and three other lawmen were guarding the bridge, alerted that Dillinger might try to escape along that route to St. Paul. A fast-moving Ford then came into sight and the lawmen leveled their automatic weapons in its direction. The driver, Dillinger, saw the roadblock across the bridge and spun the car about, driving away. Dieter and the others jumped into their car and gave pursuit, catching up with the Ford some miles down the road. They saw that it had Wisconsin license plates, the same as one of the cars having been stolen near the Little Bohemia shootout. Dieter fired a shot at the tires and this caused Van Meter, sitting in the back seat, to smash the back window of the Ford and thrust forth an automatic. Van Meter began shooting at the officers, who returned fire. One of the bullets fired by the officers ploughed into the back of John Hamilton before Dillinger was able to outdistance and lose the lawmen.

The car driven by the bandits was too shot up to continue and Dillinger drove it off the road twenty or so miles outside of St. Paul. He then stopped a car driven by Roy Francis. Francis, his wife and small boy were in the car and the gangster ordered them into the back seat. Dillinger, Van Meter, and Hamilton climbed into the car. The badly-wounded Hamilton said he needed something to drink and Dillinger pulled into a gas station where he bought Hamilton and the Francis boy bottles of pop. Francis and his family were left unharmed at a farmhouse down the road while the gangsters drove the new V-8 toward St. Paul. They met Reilly later that day, but Hamilton was not with them. Reilly later told police that Hamilton had died before Dillinger could find a doctor and that his body was buried in a stone quarry by Dillinger and Van Meter. Quicklime had been poured over the body to obliterate the face and fingers and thus prevent identification.

Dillinger and Van Meter reportedly returned to Chicago but Public Enemy Number One was no longer his easy-going self, telling Van Meter that he was a jinx. He had been unnerved by the harrowing escape from Little Bohemia and he vowed to "get away for keeps." Everyone around him had died or wound up in prison. He had heard that Billie Frechette had been convicted of harboring him in St. Paul and had been given an eighteen-month prison term. From May to July 1934, Dillinger's movements were in deep shadows and little activity is reported, although it was claimed that on June 30, 1934, Dillinger, Van Meter, and Nelson were joined by Charles Arthur "Pretty Boy" Floyd and that his formidable group of bank robbers raided the Merchants National Bank of South Bend, Ind., taking a mere $18,000 in cash, but it is doubtful that any of these men participated in that robbery. Floyd was elsewhere in the Midwest at the time and Nelson was in California. In June 1934 Dillinger did rob, with James Henry "Blackie" Audett and others, some banks in Iowa, Kansas, and Nebraska, according to Audett's statements to the author forty-five years later. Audett claimed that Dillinger was looking to make a "permanent escape" and that arrangements for such would be costly. This necessitated the string of bank robberies Dillinger, Audett, and other lesser known bandits committed.

It is known that Dillinger spent a good deal of time in Chicago in June and July of 1934, talking several times to Louis Piquett while making those escape arrangements, but the escape was not to South America or Europe, but an escape from the world of the living. The FBI later claimed that during June 1934, Dillinger went into deep hiding, and that a minor hoodlum, Arthur O'Leary, took Dillinger and Van Meter to the home of James Probasco in Chicago, a hideout set up by Louis Piquett. Here, according to the Bureau, Dillinger and Van Meter had plastic surgery performed on their faces and had their fingerprints burned away with acid, these operations conducted by two underworld physicians, Dr. Harold B. Cassidy and Dr. Wilhelm Loesser. Probasco, however, was not picked up until July 25, 1934, a day after a shooting at Chicago's Biograph Theater, one in which Melvin Purvis insisted John Dillinger was killed. Probasco was held incommunicado at the Bureau Headquarters in the Banker's Building and, on July 30, 1934, suddenly fell, jumped, or was pushed from a nineteen-story window in FBI offices, crashing to his bloody death in an alley below. His death was ruled a suicide.

Investigation into the shooting at the Biograph on July 22, 1934, occupied the author for a number of years in the research and writing of two previously published works, *Dillinger: Dead or Alive?* and *The Dillinger Dossier.* The mysterious, and to some degree, still baffling events occurring at that time are these: Dillinger, for all purposes of the FBI manhunt, had utterly disappeared sometime in June 1934. Law enforcement officials combed the country for him, but no trace could be found, even though dozens of men looking like Dillinger were arrested and later released. Since most of his known associates were either dead or in prison, and since he had stopped seeing his usual contacts, except for the underworld lawyer Piquett, lawmen became more frustrated with each day's search.

The author's research revealed that Dillinger was, indeed, residing in the Chicago area, but that he had, in early June, entered into a scheme that would bring about his permanent escape. He would be killed, or, more precisely, someone else would be killed in his place and he would thus be free to live out his life with the aid of considerable cash he had accumulated within the last six to nine months, more than $250,000, according to one estimate. Through Piquett, Dillinger met with Martin Zarkovich, a crooked police sergeant with the East Chicago, Ind., Police Department. For more than a decade, Zarkovich had been taking bribes and kickbacks from bootleggers and brothel owners in Lake County, Ind., and he had persuaded several of his fellow officers to also enjoy such underworld spoils. Zarkovich, since about 1920, had known a notorious bordello keeper, Anna Sage, a Romanian immigrant who ran several whorehouses in northern Indiana. The enterprising sergeant had even supplied her with runaway girls and had seen to it that her operations were pro-

tected, receiving a cut of her take. When Anna Sage was run out of northern Indiana, she set up shop in Chicago, running a bordello out of a sprawling North Side home. Zarkovich continued to supply her with girls, driving them from Indiana to Chicago, where he was still on Anna's payroll. Martin Zarkovich was a money man, a cop on the take, and, if the subtle scheme arranged by Louis Piquett worked, he would not only enjoy a large fee for his services, but collect a considerable chunk of the $20,000 reward money offered for John Dillinger, as long as *he made sure* that Dillinger was officially declared dead.

In mid-July, Zarkovich met with Anna Sage, who had a customer deeply involved with one of her girls, Polly Hamilton Keele, a slender, attractive brunette. Zarkovich studied this man from afar, watching him go in and out of Anna Sage's place. He used the name James Lawrence, but Polly Hamilton called him Jimmy. Lawrence, who told people he worked at the Board of Trade, was a minor hoodlum and pimp who actually worked on and off for Anna Sage bringing Hamilton customers. He lived on Pine Grove Avenue and was always looking for a dishonest dollar. Further investigation of his background, according to Audett, revealed that he had no known living relatives in the Midwest. He was an ideal candidate.

According to Audett, Piquett then contacted Lawrence and made a deal. He would pay this young man $30,000 to pretend to be Public Enemy Number One, John Dillinger. The crafty lawyer explained that this would take no effort at all and certainly would not be dangerous. He would simply go on with his normal activities but drop a little hint here or there. If arrested, he could easily prove he was not Dillinger. Piquett held up his hands to wiggle his fingers. Lawrence's fingerprints would prove he was not the wanted outlaw. Lawrence asked why he was being asked to do this. Piquett told him that he would be only one of several "decoys" who would be used to give the real Dillinger enough time to leave the country. Lawrence accepted his odd assignment and received a $5,000 down payment with a promise to receive additional payments each week.

Unknown to Lawrence, there were many others involved in the plot to pass Lawrence off as Dillinger, and this included Martin Zarkovich and Anna Sage. A few days later, Sage began to make remarks to Lawrence about his striking resemblance to newspaper photos of Dillinger. "A lot of people tell me that," Lawrence replied. He began to swagger a bit, even occasionally talk out of the side of his mouth in the best gangster tradition of the movies. Meanwhile, Ray McCready, a mortician who maintained a funeral home at 4506 N. Sheridan Road, sat down at his desk on July 14, 1934, and opened his ledger to a blank page to record a death that had not yet occurred. McCready entered the name of John Dillinger in his ledger, using the July 14, 1934, *twice* on the same page, though the shooting outside the Biograph Theater would not happen until July 22, 1934, six days later. From later events, it can be assumed that McCready had already been contacted by someone and told that he would be handling the body.

On July 20, Martin Zarkovich, a lynch pin in the conspiracy, appeared in the offices of Chicago Police Department Captain John Stege, who headed the Dillinger Squad. In front of Sergeant Frank Reynolds, Stege's aide, Zarkovich offered to provide information that would lead Stege and his men to Dillinger. But there was a condition, Zarkovich said, explaining that he wanted revenge for the killing of his good friend Pat O'Malley, the cop killed in the East Chicago bank robbery in January of that year. There could be no live capture of Dillinger, Zarkovich insisted. He, Martin Zarkovich, must be allowed to execute the man, once the trap that he, Zarkovich, devised, was sprung.

John Stege was an old hand at fighting criminals and one of the best cops in Chicago, an honest and upright lawman who liked to believe that, after so many years in dealing with the worst elements of society, he still maintained scruples and a sense of decency. Stege stood up and said angrily to Zarkovich: "I'd give even John Dillinger a chance to surrender." He then ordered Zarkovich out of his office, as Zarkovich knew he would, for this

Anna Sage, the "Lady in Red."

Anna Sage, deported, 1934.

Harry Pierpont on trial.

Arthur W. O'Leary

Biograph victim's death mask.

Russell Clark, under arrest.

Dr. Harold B. Cassidy and Dr. Wilhelm Loesser, the two physicians the FBI claimed altered Dillinger's fingerprints in 1934; Loesser, a parole violator, was kept incommunicado by agents until providing medically absurd testimony in 1935.

Dillinger's father, 1934.

John Dillinger, 1963?

Dillinger's story was told by his father at an Indiana theater.

meeting was a setup, a reference point to which another man, Melvin Purvis, would be directed. Purvis would naively accept the murderous motivation of Martin Zarkovich and subsequently accept the East Chicago cop's story about Dillinger as being genuine. Some hours later, Zarkovich called Melvin Purvis, who was desperate to apprehend Dillinger and, according to one report, had a deadline from his boss Hoover to do so or begin looking for another career.

Zarkovich was thoroughly familiar with the dilemma facing the trigger-happy Purvis and he also knew that the FBI chief was reckless and easily deceived. Purvis' erratic and lethal conduct at Little Bohemia had proved that to the world. He informed Purvis that he could "set up Dillinger" for him and Purvis leapt at the opportunity, arranging to meet Zarkovich the next afternoon in the lobby of the Great Northern Hotel. This was the residence of Sam Cowley, who recently had been placed in the Chicago Bureau of the FBI, a special agent with powers equal to Purvis. Purvis ran the office, but Cowley had veto power over his activities and served as Hoover's watchdog. Yet, Sam Cowley, an experienced and intelligent agent, was just as desperate as Purvis to arrest John Dillinger.

Zarkovich met with the two agents the next day and told them that he knew a brothel keeper through his official capacities, not mentioning his personal relationship with Anna Sage. Dillinger, he had learned, was patronizing one of Sage's girls and he believed he could set up Public Enemy Number One for the Bureau. He could arrange a meeting that night with Anna Sage if the agents wanted to meet her. There were a few conditions to this deal, however, Zarkovich added. One, he must be allowed revenge for the killing of his pal, Patrolman O'Malley; he must be allowed to execute John Dillinger. The agents said nothing. The second condition involved Anna Sage who was not a U.S. citizen. She had been designated by the immigration authorities as "an undesirable alien" and there were proceedings against her to deport her to Romania. Sage, for her cooperation, would want these proceedings dropped. Again the agents said nothing, but Purvis agreed to meet with Anna Sage that night.

So frantic were these agents to apprehend Dillinger that they took at face value whatever Martin Zarkovich told them and without bothering to check on this rural policeman, a man they had not met up to this moment. Neither Purvis nor Cowley ordered the customary background check on Zarkovich. If they had, they would have easily seen that they were dealing with a man whose word and reputation was suspect. They could have looked into their Bureau files to see that Zarkovich had been involved in a federal conspiracy in 1931, and local records would have revealed his ties to organized crime in northern Indiana, Anna Sage's brothel operations, and a close association to Louis Piquett, Dillinger's lawyer. Zarkovich, guessing this might be the case, gave the agents very little time to think about his proposition or his background, telling them that if they were to move on his information, it would have to be in a matter of hours.

Three decades later, Virgil Peterson, a member of the Chicago Bureau of the FBI who worked with Purvis on the Dillinger case, was asked by the author why FBI agents, particularly Purvis and Cowley, had not checked the backgrounds of Zarkovich and Sage. Peterson, indignant, responded angrily: "That has nothing to do with it! These people had information and we had to get this guy! You don't go around asking questions when you're after someone like Dillinger! And these people had information. No, they're backgrounds had nothing to do with it!" Purvis did call Captain Stege, however, and learned that Zarkovich had been to see him with the same offer concerning Dillinger, but that Stege had declined on the grounds that he would not sanction legal murder. Purvis, by then, undoubtedly felt that if he did not accept Zarkovich's proposition, some other law enforcement agency might and the FBI would be deprived of closing its most important criminal case, a cornerstone case, as events proved, upon which the reputation of the FBI and the image of the "G-Man" was later built.

The *kind* of information Zarkovich and Sage were peddling also had nothing to do with the real John Dillinger. That night, Melvin Purvis sat in a Pierce-Arrow with Martin Zarkovich, who was sitting in the back seat. The car was parked on a quiet, tree-lined north side Chicago street. Behind Purvis' car was another car with Sam Cowley in it. As planned, at 9 p.m. sharp, the thick, fast-walking figure of Anna Sage appeared. She walked past the car looking straight ahead. "She's making sure there's no trap," said the ever-dramatic Purvis to Zarkovich. Then Zarkovich put his hand out the window and signaled to Sage and she got in, sitting next to Purvis. Cowley was surprised to see Purvis suddenly drive away. This lone car later parked at the lakefront. Zarkovich remained silent in the back seat while Anna Sage told Purvis that a man named James Lawrence, who had been visiting one of her girls, Polly Hamilton, had admitted to her that he was John Dillinger (this was, of course, untrue). Lawrence had a lot of money, wore the best clothes, and had mentioned the names of many Dillinger gangsters. She said Hamilton did not know Lawrence's true identity. She could deliver this man into the hands of the FBI, Sage told Purvis, if the Bureau persuaded the immigration authorities to drop deportation proceedings against her.

The ever-impetuous Purvis wasted no time in accepting Sage's terms, leaping at the opportunity to finally catch the elusive Dillinger. As far as immigration officials were concerned, Purvis promised to set things right. "I'll call them off," he said, but Melvin Purvis had no authority to make such a promise. Moreover, he arbitrarily raised the reward for Dillinger then and there, stating that $25,000 would be paid to everyone involved in delivering Dillinger, with shares going to Zarkovich, his boss, Captain Tim O'Neill, who had helped set up the FBI meeting, Sage, and even Polly Hamilton. The reward was to be paid through the U.S. attorney general's office, but Attorney General Homer Cummings had not authorized Melvin Purvis to increase the reward. In light of later events, it is obvious that Purvis would say or do anything in order to capture Dillinger.

Purvis then drove Anna Sage back to her Halsted Street address. By driving off with Anna Sage and leaving Cowley behind and in the dark, Purvis had made the Dillinger case exclusively his since no one but Zarkovich and he could identify Anna Sage. Before he dropped her off, Purvis was told by Sage that she would be calling him some time next day, that she, Hamilton, and Lawrence-Dillinger would be going to a movie, probably the Marbro Theater, and she would phone Purvis as soon as she knew what show they would be attending. Purvis nodded agreement. After he drove off, Purvis had a little talk with Zarkovich and it was then that the FBI man undoubtedly agreed that Zarkovich, in return for setting up Lawrence-Dillinger through Sage, would be allowed to execute the man. Purvis now felt that the disgrace and blunder of the abortive Little Bohemia Lodge raid would be wiped out and that he would be redeemed in the eyes of J. Edgar Hoover and the country that thought of him as a reckless and trigger-happy lawman.

Zarkovich's real motive for killing Lawrence, of course, had nothing to do with seeking revenge for the dead policeman, O'Malley. Lawrence could only be accepted as Dillinger if he were dead, and if later identification of him proved him someone else, it would be Melvin Purvis' responsibility. Zarkovich and the men behind him, Louis Piquett, Blackie Audett, and even Dillinger himself correctly figured that when and if the FBI did realize the wrong man had been killed, Hoover and company would be disinclined to make such information public, especially after the recent fiasco at Little Bohemia. Dillinger, through his emissaries, could then make arrangements with certain federal authorities to let the matter lay and quietly make his "permanent escape," living a comfortable life under another identity. Zarkovich also knew that he would never be named as Lawrence's killer, according to his agreement with Purvis, since this was an FBI operation and Purvis would not embarrass the Bureau by admitting that he allowed a non-FBI person to kill Lawrence. (The shooter at the

Biograph was never revealed by the Bureau, who insisted that, indeed, an agent did kill Lawrence, but used the lame excuse to hide his identity by saying that they did not want to place this "agent" in jeopardy from revenge-seeking Dillinger associates. The Bureau knew such a threat did not exist since all known Dillinger gangsters were by then dead or in prison.)

The next morning, July 22, 1934, Purvis assembled about twenty FBI agents and told them to be prepared to rendezvous at a Chicago theater where they would apprehend John Dillinger. Agents were sent to the Marbro Theater where they checked the streets and the theater, detailing positions they would later take. Purvis and Cowley decided that they would let Anna Sage, Polly Hamilton, and Lawrence-Dillinger go into the theater and wait until after the movie to make their move. When Anna Sage did call the anxious Purvis, she upset his careful plans by telling him that she, Hamilton, and Lawrence-Dillinger would be going to *either* the Marbro or the Biograph that night, she wasn't certain. This presented a terrible dilemma for Purvis. Zarkovich was on hand to solve it for him. Since only Zarkovich and Purvis knew what Anna Sage looked like, he, Zarkovich, would go to the Marbro and Purvis would go to the Biograph, with agents stationed at both theaters. Whoever spotted Sage first would call the other and the forces would join.

This, too, was part of Zarkovich's (or perhaps Piquett's) subtle, crafty plan. Zarkovich knew that the trio would appear at the Biograph, which is why he suggested he go to the Marbro. In that way, Purvis and only Purvis would identify Anna Sage and thus take full responsibility. It would then be *an FBI identification,* not one made by an East Chicago policeman and the killing of Lawrence would also be the exclusive responsibility of the FBI and Agent-in-Charge, Melvin Purvis. That night the two groups of lawmen waited at the two theaters and Purvis, standing next to the Biograph on Lincoln Avenue, saw Anna Sage turn a corner at 8:30 p.m. and head toward the theater. With her was a young woman, Polly Hamilton, and a young man wearing glasses, a straw hat and no coat, only a white shirt and slacks. As they paid for their tickets and went into the theater, Purvis called Cowley and Zarkovich at the Marbro and told them to come with their men to the Biograph.

More than twenty agents were positioned outside the Biograph while Sage, Hamilton, and Lawrence watched Clark Gable, William Powell, and Myrna Loy star in *Manhattan Melodrama,* a gangster film. Purvis had assumed full responsibility for the stakeout and had made the identification of Anna Sage on his own, as well as the man he believed to be Dillinger. This identification was the most absurd aspect of the entire Biograph affair. Contrary to all FBI procedures, the man about to be shot was not identified prior to his appearance that night. In fact, so reliant on the word of Anna Sage was Melvin Purvis that whomever she showed up with that night at the Biograph, he, Melvin Purvis, would accept as John Dillinger.

Purvis was sitting in his car in front of the theater when the trio appeared. Said Purvis later: "He had passed my car before I saw him, but I had studied every available photograph of him so carefully that I recognized the back of his head immediately." There were no known photographs of *the back of John Dillinger's head,* so Purvis' identification remains all the more mystifying and ridiculous. At a little before 10:30 p.m., Purvis got out of his car and took up a position near the box office of the theater, standing a little south of this cubicle. Further south, hidden in a doorway of a closed and dark shop stood Martin Zarkovich, a .45-caliber gun in an unbuttoned holster. At 10:30 p.m., the movie ended and the crowd inside began to spill out onto the sidewalk. Anna Sage, Polly Hamilton, and Lawrence-Dillinger suddenly appeared and Purvis nervously lit a cigar, the prearranged signal to Zarkovich that the prey was heading his way, going south down Lincoln Avenue. The direction the trio took, of course, was engineered by Anna Sage, who led the way out of the theater, taking Hamilton and Lawrence, walking behind her, straight past Zarkovich, a detail worked out between Zarkovich and his good friend Sage.

She would later describe her fifteen-foot walk to the death spot and how she glanced to the side to see the tall, burly East Chicago policeman, hat pulled low on his face, lurking in the shadows of the doorway. "I saw Zarkovich," she told newsmen, just before the trio reached the alleyway.

At that point, Anna Sage dropped back, pulling Polly Hamilton with her, so that the young man took several steps forward, alone. At that point Zarkovich, a man of six-feet-four-inches, swiftly came up from behind Lawrence and violently pushed him to the ground. The young man fell forward, crashing to the cement so that his head was over the lip of the sidewalk and into the gutter of the alley. Zarkovich already had his .45 in his hand and quickly pumped two bullets into the prone figure, the bullets smashing into the man's head, one bullet emerging from beneath the right eye, the other entering the neck and embedding in the skull. The big policeman fired another shot that went wild and ricocheted off the pavement. (The autopsy later performed on the deceased meticulously describes the path of the bullets, both fired at a forty-five degree angle, proving the victim to be prone when shot.) Zarkovich then slipped his gun back into its holster and joined the milling crowds as Purvis and his men rushed forward.

Women in the crowds began to scream (two had been superficially wounded by Zarkovich's bullets and several male voices, including Zarkovich's, were heard to shout: "They got Dillinger! They got Dillinger!" A large crowd ringed the man on the sidewalk. He did not move, and a pool of blood from his head wounds swelled around his smashed straw boater and broken glasses. Some people leaned down and dipped their handkerchiefs into the blood for grim souvenirs. At this moment, James Henry "Blackie" Audett, by his own later admission to the author, left his car, which had been parked across Lincoln Avenue since early that day, and joined the crowd. "It was my job to make sure that Lawrence was dead, that Zarkovich had killed him," Audett told the author in 1979.

Purvis broke through the crowd, holding his gun, and, with his foot, rolled the body over, realizing that the man was dead. He also realized, despite his prior "identification" of Lawrence as Dillinger, that the dead man did not look like John Dillinger. Reporters had already arrived and heard Purvis blurt in surprise: "That's not Dillinger's nose." He quickly caught himself and then said: "Neat bit of plastic surgery that," thus introducing for the first time the FBI theory of Dillinger having had plastic surgery—an excuse, really, to explain away the fact that the dead man did not look like the John Dillinger of yesterday. FBI agent Alan E. Lockerman stated to the author in 1968: "Identification was made there. I believe it was made later, at the morgue. Of course, his identification was perfectly well established when he came out of the theater. Otherwise, he wouldn't have been killed."

The FBI later claimed that one of its agents had shot down Lawrence-Dillinger because "he drew a gun and fired at agents closing in on him." This was an outright lie. The man shot at the Biograph had no gun. An FBI historian later said that the man "pulled a .38 from his waistband." Another fabrication. The dead man would have had to walk down a public street, go into a theater filled with people, emerge in a dense crowd, all while wearing a .38, in plain sight, tucked into his trousers. A short time later, when Hoover was building a monument to the FBI around the apprehension of John Dillinger, FBI Headquarters in Washington, D.C., set up an FBI museum with many showcases for the public to inspect. In one was placed the so-called weapon pulled by the man at the Biograph on July 22, 1934. This weapon, a .38 Colt automatic, bore the serial number 119702 and a check of the records of Colt's Patent Fire Arms Manufacturing Company, revealed that this weapon was sold for the first time to the L.H. Kurz Company, located in Des Moines, Iowa, on Dec. 19, 1934, *five months after the death of the man the FBI insisted was John Dillinger.*

Identification of the dead man was not made at the morgue, as Agent Lockerman supposed. The body arrived without any personal identification and was accepted by Dr. Charles D. Parker, an assistant coroner's physician. A ring, a watch made in 1907 and worth very little, a wallet with unknown contents, and about $7 was taken from the body in the Chicago police wagon before the body arrived at the city morgue. Dr. Parker stayed with the body from the moment it arrived at the morgue at about 11 p.m. until the next morning, July 23, 1934, and, in his statements to the author, saw no one take fingerprints of the dead man. A fingerprint card showing altered fingerprints identified as John Dillinger's was later introduced to support identification, but this card is dated "July 22, 1934," a date on which no one took the dead man's prints; it also contains several technical errors dealing with the whorl and ridge counts of Dillinger's prints which indicates that the card was a plant later used to shore up the shaky identification of the dead man, a fingerprint identification made on a Chicago Police Department Print Card, not an official FBI card, a card that anyone like Louis Piquett could easily obtain.

Purvis later proudly displayed the dead man's artifacts on his desk for newsmen to photograph, but these were items that spoke for the innocence of the dead man, not the claimed disguise of John Dillinger. The straw hat the dead man had been wearing had had its brim smashed and bent, further proving that the man had been pushed down while wearing the hat. A bullet hole had *then* been made through the bent part of the brim, which would not have occurred had the man been upright when shot. Moreover, the glasses the man was wearing were also displayed. These were gold-rimmed octagonal prescription glasses, not the cheap dark sunglasses one would use in a disguise. Dillinger's eyesight was, of course, 20-20.

The most telling document was the autopsy performed on the slain man by Dr. J.J. Kearns, chief pathologist for the Cook County coroner. The original document disappeared almost the moment it was completed (confiscated from public records, one might assume, by Melvin Purvis or other federal authorities, once it was realized that the FBI under Purvis had again killed the wrong man, Eugene Boisineau being the first). Kearns' autopsy was meticulously conducted and could not later be challenged by the FBI or Hoover. It was performed with another doctor checking Kearns' every discovery and a medical nurse writing down what both doctors verbally described. Dozens of medical students were in attendance, watching every move made by Kearns, one of the top pathologists in America at the time. The author obtained through Kearns a copy of this autopsy in 1968, and its startling revelations include the fact that the dead man had brown eyes, and all of Dillinger's records (also obtained by the author from the files of the U.S. Navy, local and state governments in Indiana, Illinois, Arizona, and Ohio, and FBI documentation) show him to have blue or blue-gray eyes. The color of the iris does not change after death and color contact lenses were not available until four decades later.

Also, the dead man was missing Dillinger's known scars, a half-inch scar on the back of his left hand and another pronounced scar on his upper lip. Known birthmarks were missing as were two bullet wounds Dillinger was known to have received during bank robberies of recent months, one in the arm, the other in the leg. The dead man was shorter and heavier than Dillinger would have been and he possessed a top right incisor tooth which is clearly missing from the mouth of John Dillinger in motion picture footage taken of him at Crown Point, Ind., only four months earlier. The tooth in the dead man's mouth was real, not false. Kearns took out the dead man's heart and studied it, noting that it was in a severe rheumatic condition, a chronic condition that had existed since childhood. Dillinger had never had a rheumatic heart. Such a condition would have prevented Dillinger from playing baseball, joining the Navy, or performing the running and scaling feats he was seen to enact when robbing banks. The man on the slab in the morgue who Kearns examined had been executed, according to the angle of the bullets entering his body as carefully charted by the pathologist.

But the FBI announced that John Dillinger was dead and that news was welcomed by Dillinger himself, according to Blackie Audett. After seeing that Zarkovich had performed his duty and that the man on the sidewalk outside the Biograph was, indeed, dead, Audett walked across Lincoln Avenue, got into his car and drove to Aurora, Ill., and parked in front of a small rented cabin. He entered the cabin and said to the man sitting at a table, playing solitaire: "You're dead now, John." Dillinger, according to Audett, got up and shook his hand. Audett urged him to leave the Midwest but Dillinger told him he wanted to "see the folks just once more." He also wanted to make sure that the body being passed off as his own would not be disturbed.

The body was shipped from the morgue to the far north side mortuary of Ray McCready, the man who had entered Dillinger's death date in his ledger six days before the shooting at the Biograph. It was thought by the conspirators that this would be a safe place for it, out of the reach of prying newsmen. When the elder Dillinger and Audrey Dillinger Hancock arrived to pick up this body and take it back to Mooresville, Ind., for burial, they both immediately denied that it was John Dillinger but quickly overcame their shock and, prodded by a member of the conspiracy, suddenly remembered a scar on the leg which Dillinger had received when a child, a scar that did appear on the body but one that Dillinger himself never received. Following the burial of this body in Crown Hill Cemetery, Indianapolis, Dillinger arranged to have the coffin dug up and reburied, this time surrounded by tons of cement mixed with chicken wire and scrap iron. The director of the cemetery later told the author: "The only way to get that body out of there now is to blow it up and there wouldn't be enough left to put into a cookie jar."

Dillinger paid several thousand dollars to have this chore performed. The Dillinger family was nearly broke and the elder Dillinger had to borrow the $50 to cover McCready's embalming efforts. Following the reburial, Dillinger climbed into a car and was driven to the West Coast by Blackie Audett who told the author that he left Dillinger at the Indian reservation in Klamath Falls, Ore., just north of the California border and that he later married an Indian girl. "Evelyn Frechette was an Indian, a Menominee," Audett stated, "and John was partial to Indian ladies." Audett, who corresponded with Audrey Dillinger to the day of his death in 1979, claimed that up to that time, John Herbert Dillinger was still alive, living on the West Coast.

The question remained: Why would he not surface after all these years? The answer is that there is no statute of limitations on the capital offense of murder and he would still have to stand trial for the murder of Officer O'Malley. He would also have to stand trial for his part in the conspiracy to murder an innocent man, James Lawrence, the patsy who took his place and unwittingly sealed his own fate. Others knew well the existence of the conspiracy, including Harry Pierpont who, according to Audett, was informed by the prison grapevine of John's "permanent escape" before he and Makley went to the electric chair in Ohio in September 1934 for the murder of Sheriff Sarber. Pierpont was smiling as he sat in the chair and he said cryptically: "Today, I am the only man who knows the 'whos and hows' and, as my end comes very shortly, I'll take this little story with me."

Most of the Dillinger gang had been destroyed by that time. Tommy Carroll was shot to death by detectives outside Waterloo, Iowa, in the summer of 1934. Eddie Green had been shot in the back by FBI agents while trying to escape a dragnet on Apr. 3, 1934. Homer Van Meter was trapped by FBI agents on Aug. 23, 1934, and he died in a gun battle as he ran up a St. Paul alley. Baby Face Nelson, the worst of the lot, would go to his death in a blazing machine gun battle with FBI agents Sam Cowley and Herman Hollis, killing both of them, in Barrington, Ill., on Nov. 27, 1934. Russell Clark would be paroled from prison in 1970 and die a short while later of cancer. Evelyn Billie Frechette would die about the same time of cancer. So, too, would Martin Zarkovich, who received $5,000 of the federal reward money. Anna Sage, who had worn an orange skirt on the night of the Biograph shooting, one that was made to appear red beneath the bright lights of the marquee and was thus called The Lady in Red, was given $5,000 in reward money and then shipped back to Romania. Before leaving the U.S., she cursed Melvin Purvis for lying to her, and she later threatened while living in Bucharest, "to tell the real story about the Dillinger shooting." She died mysteriously a short time later, murdered, according to Audett, "to keep her mouth shut."

Melvin Purvis, the most spectacular FBI agent in the Bureau during the early 1930s, went on to greater glory, tracking down and killing Charles Arthur "Pretty Boy" Floyd in the fall of 1934. But by June of 1935, he and his boss Hoover had such harsh words that he left the Bureau. Following his resignation, all Purvis could murmur was: "I'm glad to be out of here!" He later went on the radio, peddling an inflated G-Man image and became the chief of the Post-Toasties Junior G-Man Squad. Still later Purvis tried his hand at running a radio station and other enterprises which more or less failed. On Feb. 29, 1960, Purvis called his doctor and said he was despondent over an unstated matter. He made an appointment with the physician but never appeared. Instead, he looked over his extensive weapon collection and selected the .38 Police Special he had carried on the night of the Biograph shooting. He then stepped into his backyard and blew out his brains. Purvis had reportedly received a letter a short time earlier, one from an elderly man in California who claimed to be John Dillinger.

In the early 1960s, this old man sent several letters (and snapshots of himself) from California, one to the Indianapolis *Star* and one to Emil Wannatka, Jr., son of Dillinger's host at Little Bohemia in 1934. Both letters claimed that "the wrong man" had been killed at the Biograph and contained information that only Dillinger would seem to know, one line reading: "The dead man had brown eyes and black hair." This man was never found and it is not known if he was Dillinger or not. If Dillinger were alive at this writing, he would be eighty-seven years old. See: **Audett, James Henry; Federal Bureau of Investigation; Floyd, Charles Arthur; Hoover, J. Edgar; Lamm, Herman K.; Nelson, George; Purvis, Melvin.**

REF.: Asbury, *Gem of the Prairie;* Audett, *Rap Sheet;* Bennett, *Murder Is My Business; CBA;* Clayton, *Union Station Massacre;* Cooper, *Designs in Scarlet;* _____ , *Here's to Crime;* _____ , *Ten Thousand Public Enemies;* Cromie and Pinkston, *Dillinger: A Short and Violent Life;* Davis, *Mafia Kingfish;* Demaris, *The Director;* Edge, *Run the Cat Roads;* Gish, *American Bandits;* Godwin, *Murder, U.S.A.;* Gosch and Hammer, *The Last Testament of Lucky Luciano;* Halper, *The Chicago Crime Book;* Hamilton, *Men of the Underworld;* Hibbert, *The Roots of Evil;* Hoover, *Persons in Hiding;* Karpis, *The Alvin Karpis Story;* Lait and Mortimer, *Chicago: Confidential;* Louderback, *The Bad Ones;* Lowenthal, *The Federal Bureau of Investigation;* McClellan, *Crime Without Punishment;* Messick and Goldblatt, *The Mobs and the Mafia;* Morgan, *Prince of Crime;* Nash, *Almanac of World Crime;* _____ , *Among the Missing;* _____ , *Bloodletters and Badmen;* _____ , *Citizen Hoover;* _____ , *Dillinger: Dead or Alive?;* _____ , *The Dillinger Dossier;* _____ , *Hustlers and Con Men;* _____ , *Look for the Woman;* _____ , *People to See;* Powers, *Secrecy and Power;* Purvis, *American Agent;* Reppetto, *The Blue Parade;* Robinson, *Science Catches the Criminal;* Sann, *Kill the Dutchman;* Scott, *The Concise Encyclopedia of Crime and Criminals;* Sullivan, *The Bureau: My Thirty Years in Hoover's FBI;* Thorwald, *The Century of the Detective;* Toland, *The Dillinger Days;* Toledano, *J. Edgar Hoover;* Wellman, *A Dynasty of Western Outlaws;* Whitehead, *The FBI Story;* Wicker, *Investigating the FBI;* (DRAMA), Sherwood, *The Petrified Forest;* (FICTION), Burnett, *High Sierra;* (FILM) *G-Men,* 1935; *The Petrified Forest,* 1936; *Parole Fixer,* 1939; *Persons in Hiding,* 1939; *Undercover Doctor,* 1939; *Queen of the Mob,* 1940; *High Sierra,* 1941; *Dillinger,* 1945; *Baby Face Nelson,* 1957; *FBI Story,* 1959; *Young Dillinger,* 1965; *Dillinger,* 1973; *The Lady in Red,* 1979.

Dillon, William, c.1954- , U.S., fraud. By obtaining advance copies of *Business Week* magazine, stockbroker William Dillon was able to purchase stocks recommended by the magazine's "Inside Wall Street" column before the public learned of the hot commodities and sent prices skyrocketing. Dillon paid employees at the Connecticut printing plant $30 for each issue the day before it was scheduled to hit the newsstands. It was alleged that with

this scheme, Dillon made at least $2,000 a week. When news of his activities reached executives at the brokerage firm where Dillon worked—Merrill, Lynch, Pierce, Fenner & Smith—Dillon was fired from his job at their New London, Conn., office in July 1988. He pleaded guilty to wire fraud in a Manhattan, N.Y., Federal District Court. On Apr. 11, 1989, Judge John Walker sentenced Dillon to six months in prison, 200 hours of community service, and ordered him to pay the Securities and Exchange Commission $118,000 in restitution. REF.: *CBA.*

Dilworth, Dwight, d.1916, U.S., (unsolv.) mur. On the night of Sept. 3, 1916, Dwight Dilworth was sitting in his car with a female friend in Van Cortland Park in New York City when two gunmen tried to rob him. When he refused their demands for his money, they shot him three times in the chest. Dilworth's female companion fainted when the shots were fired and was unable to see the killers.

REF.: Carey, *Memoirs of a Murder Man; CBA.*

Dimitrijevic, Dragutin (AKA: Apis, Colonel Apis), 1876-1917, Serb., assass.-terror. Founder of the Black Hand Society, Dimitrijevic was chief of Serbian military intelligence (1913-1916). Born in Belgrade (then Serbia, now the capital of Yugoslavia), Dimitrijevic graduated from the military academy in Belgrade in 1895, commissioned a lieutenant that year. He quickly associated himself with the most ardent Serbian nationalists of the army corps. He championed, as did his scheming peers, a Serbia free of foreign influence and control, and especially hated the political and economic ties to the then all-powerful Austro-Hungary empire of the severe Hapsburgs, whose tentacles curled through every corner of the Balkans.

A Draconian figure who could have easily doubled as The Black Prince in *The Prisoner of Zenda,* Dimitrijevic was shrewd and quick-witted. He lacked little charm and knew how to manipulate the hot nationalistic passions of his fellow officers with drink, song, and elaborate conspiracies. His consuming passion was not only to strengthen Serbia but to unite Austrian-dominated Bosnia with his country, then add one Balkan state after another to the Serbian colors, creating, as it were, a single and powerful Slavic state. Dimitrijevic would not see such a federation in his lifetime, though decades beyond him, Marshal Tito (Josef Broz) would head just such a country and all but venerate the memory of Dimitrijevic.

At the turn of the century, this young officer's schemes turned sharply toward terrorism when he and fellow conspirators of the Serbian officer corps decided to rid their country of its Obrenovic rulers, King Alexander I and his morganatic wife Queen Draga, believing these whimsical sovereigns would spell the destruction of Serbia. Enlisting the aid of about fifty key officers, including Queen Draga's own brother-in-law, Colonel Alexander Mashin, Dimitrijevic coolly and carefully planned the assassination of Alexander and Draga.

On the night of June 11, 1903, Dimitrijevic led a group of heavily armed officers into the Belgrade palace and, after slight resistance and much searching for the royal couple, found his victims and personally emptied his revolver into the king and queen. He then joined with his fellow assassins, almost all of whom were drunk, in hacking the corpses to pieces with their sabres and tossing the bodies from a balcony to the royal gardens below so that the naked victims could be viewed by passing citizens the next day and realize the awesome and terrible power of Captain Dimitrijevic.

This brutal, gruesome regicide earned for Dimitrijevic the fearful respect of the Serbian military and the distant gratitude of Peter I, the new king who replaced Alexander, Peter being of the exiled Karageorgevic dynasty which had long battled with the Obrenovic line for the Serbian throne. Dimitrijevic was rewarded with a position of great power where his special aptitudes for deceit, terrorism, and conspiracy could flourish; he was assigned to Serbian military intelligence and promoted to the rank of Lieutenant-Colonel. He took on the code name of Apis ("The Bee") and soon this name was known to the espionage chiefs of

Europe to represent a blood-lusting terrorist who would stop at nothing to achieve his political ends.

The odd thing about Dimitrijevic, among many strange and mysterious quirks, was that though he operated with cat-like secrecy most of the time, he confided to aides throughout his legendary career that it was he, Colonel Apis, who had plotted the assassinations of King Constantine of Greece, King Nicholas of Montenegro, King Ferdinand of Bulgaria, and even Kaiser Wilhelm of Germany. That assassination attempts had been made against these sovereigns, or aborted attempts, was known, but none of these monarchs died as a result of Apis' machinations. His aides knew this, yet their chief had engineered the deaths of Alexander and Draga and, later, Francis Ferdinand of Austria. These very real assassinations were enough to convince The Black Hand's inner circle that their chief's claims of other extravagant plots were real and that he was, indeed, Europe's master of regicide.

When, in 1908, the Austro-Hungarian empire annexed Bosnia and Herzegovina, Dimitrijevic and other Serbian nationalists began a campaign of terrorism in territories which were heavily populated by Serbs. Three years later, in early 1911, Dimitrijevic founded The Black Hand Society, a secret paramilitary organization dedicated to the preservation of Serbian nationalism and the undoing of the Bosnian-Herzegovinian annexations. As Colonel Apis, Dimitrijevic ordered the assassinations of puppet Austrian administrators in the annexed countries and even planned to kill the then all-powerful Austrian monarch, Franz Josef.

All important Austrian terrorist organizations, such as they were, fell under Dimitrijevic's domination, and sensitive military information from all parts of the Hapsburg empire flowed freely to him. He and his minions equipped and trained assassins and sent them forth to kill Austrian officials at every opportunity. In the early summer of 1911 Dimitrijevic recruited a naive young Serbian zealot, Bogdan Zerajdic, and sent him to Sarajevo, Bosnia, to murder Emperor Franz Josef, who was about to visit that city. Though Zerajdic failed to kill the Austrian monarch, the assassin later emptied his revolver into General Varesanin, an Austrian-appointed provincial governor.

Such failures left Dimitrijevic undaunted. He and his fellow Black Hand conspirators continued to recruit and train assassins by the scores and, in 1913, when Dimitrijevic was named as chief of all Serbian military intelligence, the Black Hand was able to funnel top-secret information to its Bosnian agents regarding the liquidation of pro-Austrian Serbians and Austrian leaders. It was in his powerful capacity of intelligence chief of the Serbian high command that Dimitrijevic learned, far in advance of a public announcement, that Archduke Francis Ferdinand, heir to the Austrian throne, would be visiting Sarajevo in June 1914. He immediately began elaborate plans to have the Austrian heir assassinated, interviewing many likely candidates for the chore. Included among these recruits was Gavrilo Princip and two of his friends, all fanatical Serbian nationalists. These three were only a few of those selected to kill Francis Ferdinand and Dimitrijevic thought the Princip group the least likely to achieve its ends. Nevertheless, through incredible luck and a series of even more incredible blunders on the part of authorities, Princip succeeded in murdering the archduke and his wife on June 28, 1914, an assassination that caused a series of mushrooming crises that led directly to WWI—a four-year carnage that claimed the lives of millions, all traceable to the ubiquitous Colonel Apis.

Though the world never knew the identity of the real catalyst behind the killing of Francis Ferdinand—at least not until decades later and then only in the inner circles of international intelligence—the Serbian government and the reigning monarch, Peter I (Karageorgevic), certainly had to know of Dimitrijevic's role in the assassination, though they later denied any such knowledge. To further enhance their innocence, these authorities continued to sponsor and promote the master assassin, Dimitrijevic, elevating him at the outbreak of WWI to the rank of general.

Peter I, to ameliorate his suspicion with the conniving Dimitrijevic, removed himself from the throne at the outbreak of hostilities, claiming ill health and naming his son, Alexander, as prince regent of Serbia, which had thrown its lot in with the Allies. But Serbia's fortunes disintegrated when the powerful armies of Germany, Austria-Hungary, and Bulgaria invaded its small kingdom, forcing the government and the monarchy to retreat into Albania and then Greece. With the fleeing Belgrade government went Colonel Apis and his closest aides.

At Salonika, Alexander, obviously fearing in 1916 that Germany would win the war and he would be held responsible for the Sarajevo assassination, among other offenses, called General Dimitrijevic to his headquarters, accusing him of plotting to kill his father, King Peter, and himself though the auspices of the still-active Black Hand Society. The Byzantine logic practiced here by Alexander was obliquely directed to Germany, and more or less said that Francis Ferdinand was murdered by vile assassins who just happened to be Serbians but that these dreadful creatures had nothing to do with the Karageorgevic dynasty. In fact, the men behind the Sarajevo murders also tried to destroy the Karageorgevic sovereigns. Alexander had discovered these terrorist masters lurking within his own ranks and purged them from the Serbian honor rolls.

Dimitrijevic was arrested, along with his two most trusted aides, Major Tankosic and Major Tsiganovic, both of whom had helped Apis murder Alexander and Draga thirteen years earlier. They and other Black Hand exponents were tried secretly and condemned. So secret was this trial that all public mention of it was suppressed under Alexander's direct order. For more than twenty years following this trial, it was illegal even to possess any record or document connected with the Black Hand trial. Serbian newspapers were proscribed from printing a single word about it, and teachers who uttered any references to it were subject to instant arrest.

The trial, brief as it was, ended with a conviction and condemnation for Dimitrijevic and his two aides. All three were quickly taken to a secluded spot in the shadow of Mt. Kaimakshalan in Macedonia and shot, their bodies buried in unmarked graves. This occurred in early 1917, but the exact date is lost to history; what is retained is the sinister career of one of the most devastating master assassins of the modern age. In 1953 Marshal Tito announced to the world that Dragutin Dimitrijevic, also known as Colonel Apis, was a genuine hero of Serbian history and restored his "good name" to the ranks of Yugoslavia's honored dead. See: **Alexander I (Karageorgevic); Alexander I (Obrenovic); Black Hand Society; Francis Ferdinand; Varesanin, Gen. Marijan.**

REF: Bell, *Assassin!;* Buranelli, *Spy/Counter-Spy; CBA;* Graham, *St. Vitus' Day;* Hardman, *The Rise and Fall of the Hapsburg Monarchy;* Macartney, *The Hapsburg Empire;* Rowan, *Secret Service;* Seton-Watson, *Sarajevo;* Straus, *The Desperate Act, The Assassination of Franz Ferdinand at Sarajevo;* Vucinich, *Serbia Between East and West;* Webster, *Secret Societies and Subversive Movements;* West, *Black Lamb and Gray Falcon.*

Dimitrov, Georgi Mikhailovich, 1882-1949, Case of, Bulg., consp. Aided in the organization of Bulg. Communist party, 1919, led uprising in Bulgaria, 1923, for which he was exiled, and was headed the Comintern in Berlin, 1929-33. Due to the brilliant defense he provided himself, which won him worldwide recognition, Dimitrov was acquitted of the charges brought against him for plotting the Reichstag fire, 1933. He served as the first prime minister of the Bulgarian People's Republic. See: **Reichstag Fire.** REF.: *CBA.*

Dimmick, Walter, prom. 1921, U.S., theft. On July 3, 1901, the U.S. Mint in San Francisco discovered a shortage of $30,000 in $20 Double Eagle gold pieces.

Security at the mint was tight, with seventeen guards working the day shift and twelve at night. The vaults were automatically locked during non-business hours. A lock expert determined that the time-lock mechanism for the vault which was robbed had at some point been turned off. The combination to that lock was known only to chief cashier Harold Colton, with a sealed envelope containing a back-up in the safe of superintendent Frank Leach. At least that was the standard procedure. It was also routine to change the combination whenever more than one person knew the numbers or when someone took over the position in charge of that vault. Colton had replaced Walter Dimmick, who was promoted to chief clerk. But rather than have a locksmith change the combination, Dimmick informed Colton he could do the job himself, as he had done when he took over as cashier. In this manner Dimmick learned the combination. Guards were instructed to inspect all bags, but Dimmick continually visited the mint after hours. The guards became accustomed to his visits and eventually stopped inspecting his suitcase. Dimmick removed the 1,500 gold pieces on St. Patrick's Day, 1901. He was finally found Guilty at his third trial, after two hung juries, and sentenced to five years in prison. REF.: Caesar, *Incredible Detective; CBA.*

Dimmig, John, prom. 1887, Case of, U.S., mur. Henry Benhayon, the 27-year-old half brother of poisoning victim Mrs. Bowers, was found dead of cyanide poisoning on Oct. 23, 1887. In the room where the body was found were three letters, possibly written by the Benhayon. The letters pertained to the death of his sister, allegedly at the hands of her husband Dr. J. Milton Bowers. But one of the letters contained Benhayon's apparent confession to the poisoning. No suicide note was found. As the landlady did not recognize Benhayon, suspicion fell on the man who had earlier inquired about renting that room, John Dimmig. Dimmig had married the Bowers' housekeeper, Theresa Farrell, who had already been accused of perjury during the trial of Dr. Bowers. Questions arose as to the authenticity of the letters. Dimmig was charged with murder on Nov. 12, 1887, and went to trial Feb. 20, 1888, before Superior Court Judge Murphy. The jury was twice unable to reach a verdict, and a third trial began on Dec. 10, 1888. The jury took twenty-three hours to decide that Dimmig was Not Guilty. His acquittal rested largely on the disagreement of handwriting experts about the genuineness of Benhanyon's confession. The confusion also led the district attorney to drop the case against Dr. Bowers. REF.: *CBA.*

Dimmock, Phyllis, See: **Wood, Robert William Cavers.**

Dimond, Anthony Joseph, 1881-1953, U.S., jur. Served as special U.S. attorney for the District of Columbia, 1913, and was appointed to the District Court for the Territory of Alaska by President Franklin Roosevelt, Jan. 24, 1944, and to the Territorial Court for the Territory of Alaska by President Harry Truman, Jan. 27, 1949. REF.: *CBA.*

Dimsdale, Thomas J., 1831-66, U.S., writer. In the 1860s, Thomas Dimsdale, an English professor and graduate of Oxford University, was the first person to chronicle the exploits of the famous Montana Vigilance Committee. Dimsdale supported vigilantism for its role in preserving order when no other recourse existed.

Dimsdale moved to Virginia City in the early 1860s. In 1864 he was appointed the region's first superintendent of public instruction by the territorial governor. In August he was named editor of the Montana *Post,* the first important newspaper in the territory. In the pages of the gazette, Dimsdale profiled the activities of the vigilantes and lent particular support to the individuals who hanged the murderer James Daniels, a gambler who killed another man during a dispute. When Daniels was given a light sentence and then set free by the courts, local residents were outraged.

Daniels was hanged, Dimsdale wrote, "not because he was pardoned, but because he was unfit to live in the community." In 1866 a number of his accounts of these self-appointed upholders of the law were published in the book *Vigilantes of Montana.* Shortly after its publication, Dimsdale died on Sept. 22, 1866. The book was reissued in 1953 by the University of Oklahoma Press. See: **Daniels, James; Montana Vigilantes.** REF.: *CBA.*

DiNapoli, Vincent, 1937-   , U.S., org. crime. A two-year federal undercover investigation begun in 1977 and known as Li'l

Rex (for Long Island labor, racketeering, and extortion) ended Vincent DiNapoli's lucrative drywall construction business.

DiNapoli, reputedly a leader in the organized crime family of the late Thomas Luchese, became involved with drywall construction—generally the largest subcontract for federal rehabilitation projects—in 1976, six years after a Bronx, N.Y., conviction for possession of stolen property, and the same year he was convicted for a horse race fixing conspiracy. On each conviction, DiNapoli spent less than a year in prison. Between 1977 and 1981, construction companies owned by DiNapoli earned $25.3 million on twenty-four drywall contracts with the U.S. government. The government leaves the hiring of contractors to the general contractor chosen by the Department of Housing and Urban Development.

DiNapoli was charged with running a racketeering operation to monopolize the drywall construction market in Long Island, N.Y. Among eleven other men indicted by a Brooklyn federal grand jury on Mar. 9, 1981, was New York City District Council of Carpenters' president Theodore Maritas. Both Maritas and DiNapoli were charged with racketeering, including use of non-union labor, and an attempt to extort $100,000 from housing project developer Benjamin Rosen. DiNapoli was found Guilty and sentenced to five years in prison, which he began serving on Feb. 15, 1983. REF.: *CBA.*

di Nardi, Nicolletta, prom. 1970s, Case of, Italy, kid. Public outcry over the kidnapping of 11-year-old Nicolletta di Nardi was so great that patrons of her father's jewel shop in Milan, Italy, left the shopkeeper money to help him raise the $2.4 million ransom. REF.: *CBA.*

Dingaan (or **Dingane**), prom. 1820s-30s, Natal-S. Afri., mur. A vicious Zulu chief, Dingaan gained power by murdering his half- brother around 1828. He welcomed the Boers and made a pact in 1838 with their leader, Pier Retief, then massacred the colony. Dingaan was defeated by Andries Pretorius in 1838 and was overthrown in 1840 by his brother, Umpanda, with the aid of the Boers. REF.: *CBA.*

Dinnan, James A., 1930-   , U.S., cont./ct. When a former instructor at the University of Georgia, Dr. Maija Blaubergs, brought a sexual discrimination suit against the school in 1980, Professor James A. Dinnan was sent to jail for contempt of court.

As part of the investigation into those charges, Blaubergs' attorneys wanted to poll members of a nine-person tenure committee that voted several months earlier against recommending permanent faculty status for Blaubergs. In June, six members told Judge Wilbur Owens of the Federal District Court of Georgia how they voted. But the 50-year-old Dinnan refused to reveal his decision, saying that "it was a secret ballot under a legal system." The angered judge sentenced the teacher to three months in prison on July 3, fining him $3,000.

Dinnan went to jail wearing his ceremonial robes to symbolize his belief that academic freedom was at stake. "If I have to go back to prison a second, third, or fourth time, then I will do it," he said. The United States Court of Appeals for the Fifth Circuit turned down the appeal, stating that it wanted to relay "a clear signal to would-be wrong-doers that they may not hide behind academic freedom to avoid responsibility for their actions." REF.: *CBA.*

Dinneen, Joseph F., c.1897-1964, U.S., crime writer. Joseph Dinneen probably made more money from the Boston Brink's robbery than the men who planned and executed it. As the top crime reporter for the Boston *Globe* for thirty-four years, Dinneen knew the city's underworld. His contacts included Tony Pino, the mastermind behind the 1950 Brink's heist that netted the gang $1.2 million. After winning Pino's confidence, Dinneen got the story, though he always believed that there was an inside man who helped the burglars carry out this seemingly flawless crime. Dinneen later published a book about the Brink's robbery, titled *Anatomy of a Crime,* which was made into a motion picture, later released as *Six Bridges To Cross.*

Dinneen began his journalistic career on the Boston *Record* in 1919 after three years at Suffolk Law School. He joined the *Globe* staff in 1922 and covered the travels of William Cardinal O'Connell for several years. In 1934, Dinneen made a name for himself by helping to solve a murder case in which the wrong men went to jail. The two men were later released and each given $2,500 for false imprisonment. The released men were forced to pay $1,000 each to the Boston politician responsible for winning them the restitution money. After hearing about the extortion, Dinneen reported it in the *Globe*. The politician later went to jail. REF.: *CBA*.

Dio, Johnny (John Dioguardi), 1915-79, U.S., org. crime. Labor racketeer Johnny Dio got his start as an assassin for Louis Buchalter and Jacob Shapiro in New York. In the days of Murder Inc., Dio was one of the or-ganization's most valuable soldiers. By the time he was twenty-four, Dio was a sea-soned veteran of many Mafia wars and the boss of his own criminal organization. Thom-as Dewey described him as "a young gorilla who began his career at the age of fifteen."

Dio specialized in the area of "labor relations." When Teamster boss James Hoffa moved in on the New York local, Dio supplied the neces-sary force. The McClellan Rackets Committee identified Hoffa and Dio as the two men most responsible for syndicate takeover of the lucrative trucking business in

Mafia enforcer Johnny Dio.

New York. In 1956 when journalist Victor Riesel began attacking Hoffa in print, a Mafia goon believed to be Dio threw acid in his face. After police assembled a group of witnesses, they backed down at the last minute after receiving threats from Dio's hench-men.

In 1962 Mafia informant Joseph Valachi provided the Senate committee with illuminating details about Dio's activities. Valachi owned a dress shop in the Bronx that employed non-union Puerto Rican women. "I never belonged to any union," he said. "If I got in trouble, any union organizer came around, all I had to do was call up John Dio or Tommy Dio and all my troubles were straightened out." The Dragna crime family of Los Angeles also depended on Dio. When they decided to prevent the Internation-al Ladies Garment Workers Union from driving the underpaid Mexicans workers from the non-union shops, they brought Dio in for consultation. Largely through Dio's efforts, the Dragna group secured waivers on every important stipulation in the contract. The undocumented Mexicans continued to work for low wages.

In 1973 Dio was convicted of stock fraud and was sentenced to fifteen years in prison. He died in a Pennsylvania hospital after being moved there by federal authorities. See: **Dragna, Jack; Dragna, Louis Tom.**

REF.: *CBA*; Cohen, *Mickey Cohen: In My Own Words*; Cressey, *Theft of the Nation*; Demaris, *The Last Mafioso*; Fried, *The Rise and Fall of the Jewish Gangster In America*; Gage, *Mafia, U.S.A.*; _____, *The Mafia is not an Equal Opportunity Employer*; McClellan, *Crime Without Punishment*; Messick, *Secret File*; Maas, *The Valachi Papers*; Martin, *Revolt in the Mafia*; Navasky, *Kennedy Justice*; Ottenberg, *The Federal Investigators*; Overstreet, *The FBI In Our Open Society*; Peterson, *The Mob*; Pileggi, *Wiseguy*; Reid, *The Grim Reapers*; Velie, *Desperate Bargain: Why Jimmy Hoffa Had To Die.*

Diocletian (Gaius Aurelius Valerius Diocletianus Jovius), 245-313, Roman., polit. corr. Became Roman Emperor, 284, and along with Maximian ruled the empire as the Augusti, 286, adding Galerius and Constantius Chlorus, aka the Caesers, as associate

rulers, 293; Diocletian being recognized as the leader of the four. While ruling from Egypt he tried to fix prices and wages that favored soldiers with an edict, 301, and issued another edict against Christians, 303, for which a terrible persecution was carried out for the next ten years, 303-13. He abdicated the throne in 305. REF.: *CBA*.

Diodotus II, d.c.230 B.C., Bactria, king, assass. Effected a peace with the Parthians, but was assassinated by Euthydemus, a usurper to the throne. REF.: *CBA*.

Diogenes, 412-323 B.C., Gr., kid. (vict.). The cynical Greek philosopher Diogenes, on a voyage from Athens to Aegina was captured by pirates and sold as a slave to a wealthy man from Corinth who gave him back his freedom. According to legend, Diogenes, holding a lantern, once traveled the dark streets of Athens "looking for an honest man." Another legend has Alex-ander the Great visiting this eccentric, who, often as not, lived in a tub, and when the great conqueror asked what service he might perform for Diogenes, the philosopher remarked acidly: "Stand from between me and the sun." REF.: *CBA*.

Dion, c.408-353 B.C., Syracuse, assass. Acted as the regent of nephew Dionysius the Younger, named himself master of Syracuse, 355 B.C., and was assassinated two years later. REF.: *CBA*.

D'Iorio, Ernest, prom. 1933-35, U.S., mur. On Dec. 6, 1933, the Detroit, Mich., home of Jennie Zablocki, her parents, and five siblings was found in a shambles. Jennie's body was found with a lamp cord wound tightly around her neck and tied to a door knob. Her body showed ten bloody wounds. Witnesses told police that a car believed to be her boyfriend's was parked in the driveway at the approximate time of death. Her boyfriend, Anton Cebelak, was arrested for Zablocki's murder, which he denied committing. George Moitke later informed police that it was his car, not Cebelak's, that was in the Zablocki driveway. Moitke finally told police that the killer was Ernest D'Iorio, the boyfriend of Sonia Marzek, Zablocki's best friend. D'Iorio admitted killing Zablocki because she threatened to tell Marzek that he was on parole. D'Iorio pleaded guilty to second-degree murder and was sentenced to twenty to forty years in prison by Judge Arthur J. Gordon on Jan. 11, 1935.

REF.: *CBA*; Cohen, *One Hundred True Crime Stories*.

DiPalermo, Joseph (AKA: Joey Beck), 1907- , U.S., org. crime-drugs-consp. With a criminal record dating back to 1928, Joseph DiPalermo, also known as Joey Beck, was an associate of organized crime leaders Carmine Galante, Charles Luciano, Vito Genovese, Joseph Bonanno, and Joseph Valachi. DiPalermo's many arrests included charges of violation of liquor laws, counter-feiting, homicide, and violations of Federal narcotics laws. He was one of the most notorious drug traffickers in the U.S., working with international heroin suppliers in Montreal and Italy. Along with Genovese and thirteen others, DiPalermo was convicted in 1959 in Federal Court of a $12 million dollar narcotics conspiracy. Sent to the Atlanta Penitentiary, the long-time Mafia henchman was supposedly the target of a murder ordered by Valachi in May 1962. Instead, a man who looked like DiPalermo was slain. As a result, DiPalermo became a Cosa Nostra informer. DiPalermo was said to have become involved in a large scale Manhattan drug operation following his release from jail. See: **Bonanno, Joseph; Galante, Carmine; Genovese, Vito; Luciano, Charles; Mafia, The; Valachi, Joseph.** REF.: *CBA*.

DiPasquale, Anthony Louis, c.1902- , and **Catalano, Anthony Joseph**, c.1905- , U.S., extor. Alexis C. Barbeau, the 28-year-old head of a New York manufacturing company, received a letter demanding $20,000 in $5 bills, with a warning that if he did not pay he and his mother would be courting tragedy. Barbeau ignored the letter at first, hoping the letter had been sent by a prankster. However, the next night, Oct. 2, 1938, the phone rang at Barbeau's home. Barbeau, who was single and lived with his mother, was out at the time. His mother, alone in the house, picked up the receiver to hear a snarling voice tell her: "If you don't follow instructions in the letter, it'll be just too bad for you!" Then the line went dead.

By the time her son returned later that night, Mrs. Katherine Barbeau was hysterical. Barbeau calmed her as best he could and, after seeking the advice of a close friend, he decided to call the FBI. John W. Warnes, the special agent in charge of the Buffalo, N.Y., office, was sympathetic to Barbeau's plight but, as he explained, there was nothing he could do. No federal laws had been broken. He advised Barbeau to call the Buffalo Police and told Barbeau to contact him if the situation changed, adding that there might be an opportunity for the FBI to enter the case later.

Buffalo Police detectives Bart J. O'Leary and Richard Mack read the extortion letter and then advised Barbeau to follow instructions so it would appear that he intended to give in to the demands of the extortionist. The next day, Oct. 5, the following ad appeared in the personal column of the Buffalo *Times:* "Donald, all is forgiven; come home. Mother."

After placing the ad, Barbeau was to await further instructions. He received a telegram the next night. Barbeau was told to be at the Lafayette Hotel in Buffalo on Friday evening at 7:00 p.m. The detectives helped Barbeau put together a bundle of newspaper clippings, cut to the size of U.S. currency. When finished, the bundle was the same size as $20,000 in $5 bills would be, but there was only one real bill in the package. A single $1 bill had been added, its serial number recorded, for identification purposes.

Barbeau went to the hotel as directed and found a seat in the lobby. Detectives were already stationed throughout the lobby and around the hotel. A bellboy paged Barbeau and informed him that he had a call. When he picked up the telephone receiver, a rough voice told him to leave the hotel and return at 8:00 p.m. He followed instructions and the same drill was repeated at the stipulated time. This time, however, the harsh voice told him to go to a saloon on Niagara Street and await instructions. At the bar he was paged again. After hanging up the receiver he walked out of the bar; the detectives trailed along behind. He walked the quiet street and then turned into a dark alley. At the mouth of the alley he dropped the bag and continued on. A figure walked from the shadows, picked up the bag, then started to walk away. Almost instantly he was surrounded by the police. "Hey, what's the idea?" he cried, "I ain't done nothing!"

The police took the man to headquarters for questioning and after a short while, discovered to their surprise that he was telling the truth. The suspect had been on his way home and had spotted the bag. Thinking it might be of some value, he had picked it up. It was simply a case of an innocent man being in the wrong place at the wrong time. This intervening passerby had, however, destroyed days of police work and had almost certainly tipped the extortionist to the fact that the police were now aware of his activity, if not his identity.

Barbeau went home that night dreading the next call from the extortionist. On Oct. 14, one week to the day of the botched drop, a letter arrived at Barbeau's home. This one was more brutally direct than the first; if demands were not met, Barbeau's death and that of his mother's would follow. The extortionist now knew the police were involved, but this did not frighten him; if anything the man now seemed more vicious, more desperate. The only good news was the method of delivery. The extortion letter had come through the U.S. mails—a federal violation. Barbeau called the FBI and this time they entered the case.

The FBI proved as luckless as the Buffalo Police at first. Once again a personal ad was placed. Again Barbeau was instructed to go to a Buffalo hotel, this time the Ford Hotel, where he was to register under the name of Donald Cook. Barbeau did as directed. He waited for a call but none came. Almost two hours after he had registered, the FBI checked with the front desk and discovered that Cook's name and room number had not been given to the switchboard operator, an oversight. Checking with the operator, agents discovered that a call had indeed come through. The caller had been told that no one named Donald Cook was registered. The FBI waited a while longer but no one called back. Barbeau returned home.

On Oct. 25, six days after the mixup at the Ford Hotel, he received another letter from the extortionist. He now promised that Barbeau would meet a horrible death in the very near future if he did not meet his demands. This was to be his last chance, the letter warned. He was instructed to return to the Ford Hotel at 1:00 p.m., Oct. 29. This time the call came through. Barbeau was instructed to take the 5:06 p.m. train to Erie, Pa., the next day and watch for a white flag, at which point he was to throw the money off the train. "You got that?" the crook demanded.

"Yes."

"Don't try nothin', or you'll be sorry," the man threatened before he hung up.

Barbeau followed instructions, but he never saw the white flag. The FBI had agents on the train and in cars on the two highways that ran parallel to the railroad line between Erie and Buffalo. The plan had been for the engineer to be informed as soon as the bundle was dropped, at which point he would give two long blasts on his whistle and stop the train. The agents on the train would jump off and hopefully some of those in the cars would hear the whistle and move toward the train.

Two days later, Nov. 1, the extortionist wrote again, one month to the day of the first demand. So far, the extortionist had achieved nothing but spend his own money. He had paid for phone calls, telegrams, and postage stamps, possibly even train tickets, but he had not received a dime in return. Now he ordered Barbeau to make the train trip again, this time on Saturday afternoon. Once again he was instructed to drop the bundle after seeing the white flag.

Special Agent Warnes had a new plan to capture the extortionist. Not only would he have agents on the train and on the roads paralleling the railroad, but he would put one in the sky as well. He contacted the Curtiss-Wright Corporation, and they agreed to supply one of their planes, along with their top test pilot, H. Lloyd Child, who was also a lieutenant in the U.S. Naval Reserve.

As the train pulled out of Silver Creek, which was Barbeau's home town, a white flag appeared, waving up and down on the end of a stick which was held out of a railroad work shanty. Barbeau threw the package off the train and a nearby agent signaled the engineer. The engineer stepped on a button which flashed a light on top of the train; this was a signal for the plane to swoop down. The engineer also blew two long blasts on his horn as a signal to the agents on the highway. At the same time he brought the train to a sudden stop, and the agents aboard the train jumped to the ground.

Lieutenant Childs spotted two men almost before they found the bundle of phony money. The plane followed the two men as they ran down the railroad tracks, trying to hide from this "eye in the sky," as they leaped into the underbrush. Childs radioed their position to agents on the ground, and it wasn't long before the two men nearly ran into the arms of a waiting FBI agent. The bundle was found nearby but the men denied everything. They claimed they were merely walking in the woods. Anthony Joseph Catalano, thirty-three, and Anthony Louis DiPasquale, thirty-six, were returned to Buffalo and charged with extortion and misuse of the U.S. mail. After two days of questioning, Catalano, free on bond on a charge of robbery, finally broke down and admitted his guilt. The scheme, he told the agents, had seemed like "an easy way to get a lot of money."

DiPasquale held out until the trial in December 1938, but when he saw the evidence against him he joined Catalano in pleading guilty. DiPasquale was sentenced to five years imprisonment. Catalano, because of his previous record was sentenced to twelve years in the federal penitentiary. The two had spent more than a month attempting to claim a package that contained one U.S. dollar. REF.: *CBA.*

Dipo Negoro, Pangeran (AKA: **Raden Mas Ontowirjo**), c.1785-1855, Indo., war crimes. Instigated the Java War, 1825-30, which was an anti-Dutch conflict, and for which he was convicted and exiled. REF.: *CBA.*

Dishonored Lady, 1931, a play by Margaret Ayer Barnes and Edward Sheldon, based upon the murder case of Madeleine Smith (Scot., 1857), who is called Madeleine Carey in the drama. See: **Smith, Madeleine.** REF.: *CBA*.

DiSimone, Frank (DeSimone), d.1968, U.S., org. crime. Frank DiSimone inherited the leadership of the Los Angeles crime family, one of the least prestigious Mafia territories, from Jack Dragna. Like Dragna before him, DiSimone was a less than forceful leader. In an ignominious beginning to his eleven year rule, Desimone was fingered by FBI agents at the Apalachin Conference in upper state New York.

The Chicago and New York factions of the Mafia subordinated DiSimone to the role of junior partner, or clerk. When Joseph Bonanno, the head of one of New York's most powerful crime families, attempted a power grab in the mid-1960s, DiSimone was chilled to find his name on a list of intended victims. Bonanno was anxious to eliminate any threat, real or otherwise, that stood in the way of his ambitions. Until he died of natural causes in 1968, DiSimone lived in constant fear of assassination. According to FBI informant Jimmy "the Weasel" Fratianno, DiSimone never went out at night and was scared of his own shadow. See: **Bonanno, Joseph; Dragna, Jack.**

REF.: *CBA;* Demaris, *The Last Masfioso;* Reid, *The Grim Reapers.*

Disintegrating Checks, Case of, prom. 1988, U.S., fraud. Early in 1988, personal checks deposited to several banks in Chicago and Tennessee began to disintegrate. In as little as three hours after their deposit, the chemically treated checks dissolved into tiny pieces resembling confetti or ashes. The Chicago Clearing House Association, a check processing company, began warning banks about the bogus checks after they turned up at five Chicago banks and two in Tennessee. The checks were usually for amounts between $3,000 and $5,000, and though some banks would not reveal specific information on losses, it is believed that the perpetrators got away with up to $70,000.

The problem was first detected after a man opened a savings account on Feb. 16, 1988, at the Northern Trust Bank in Chicago, with a $4,000 check drawn on another account in California, which later proved false. On Feb. 25, he withdrew the $4,000 from one of the bank's branch locations. On Mar. 2, the bank received the remains of the original check in a check carrier. The check was by then reddish brown in color and was laced with thousands of tiny holes, rendering it completely illegible. The scheme usually worked because banks often verified a depositor's account and honored the check before it was processed fully, so not even a microfilm image of the check existed for the bank to use in tracing the check writer.

Bank tellers later said that they had noticed the checks because they were burnt orange in color and had an oily feel. The checks were often written out in green ink. The chemical treatment that caused the checks to dissolve could also damage other checks or papers that came into contact with them. The Chicago Police Department conducted an investigation, but the FBI was also called in to determine whether the chemical used on the checks could be harmful to humans. Within weeks, the police crime lab had identified the chemicals, but the department refused to release the information. In one case, an employee of a large Chicago food store chain was processing checks on Mar. 4 when she noticed a check, one of two totalling $8,000, that the store was forwarding to the Northern Trust Bank for payment, beginning to "sweat and deteriorate from its borders." She tried to save the check in a check carrier, but it had already, only four hours after deposit, dissolved beyond legibility.

Within two weeks, similar cases were discovered at the National Bank of Commerce in Memphis, Tenn., and at the Munford Union Bank in Munford, Tenn., resulting in losses of about $20,000. The FBI questioned a woman in Millington, Tenn., whom they believed was connected with the scheme. She had presented a check drawn on a Chicago account to the Memphis bank for deposit. But since the bank placed a 10-day hold on the out-of-state check, it began to dissolve before the woman could withdraw the money. A Munford bank teller later said a check for $4,000 had been wet when a woman deposited it, but was told that a drink had been spilled on it. After regulatory agencies warned banks of the problem, the checks stopped appearing. No arrests were made in the case. REF.: *CBA*.

Distafano, Ralph P., d.1972, U.S., suic.-mur. In 1968 Ralph P. Distafano threatened the life of President Lyndon B. Johnson, charges were dropped when he agreeed to enter a mental institution. A few months later he was discharged and took a job as a security guard. Distafano was arrested in Savannah, Ga. in possession of a .32-caliber pistol and forty-one rounds of ammunition after he made threatening statements about President Richard M. Nixon. Again the charge was dropped. Later that year, on June 21, 1972, he entered a Cherry Hill, N.J., employment agency and fired seventy bullets from two .22-caliber rifles. Six men were killed and six others were critically wounded. He then shot himself in the head. REF.: *CBA*.

Distant Shore, The, 1935, a play by Donald Blackwell and Theodore St. John. The activities of mild murderer Dr. Hawley Harvey Crippen (Brit., 1910) form the basic elements of this production. See: **Crippen,** Dr. **Hawley Harvey.** REF.: *CBA*.

DiVarco, Joseph Vincent (AKA: **Little Caesar**), prom. 1960s-70s, U.S., org. crime. Joseph DiVarco, owner of a shirt store on Rush Street in Chicago, was a long-time member of the Chicago syndicate, and by the mid-1960s controlled many of the gambling and prostitution operations on the Near North Side, working under the direction of Ross Prio, the overall boss of Chicago's North Side. DiVarco and Jimmie "The Monk" Allegretti supervised most of the syndicate-backed nightclubs in the Rush Street area, and their B-girl operations alone were estimated to produce several million dollars each year. DiVarco, according to reliable sources, fulfilled several murder contracts during the reign of Sam Giancana. His influence waned when Giancana was murdered in 1975. See: **Giancana, Sam; Prio, Ross.**

REF.: *CBA;* Cressey, *Theft of the Nation;* Demaris, *Captive City;* Nash, *Bloodletters and Badmen;* Reid, *The Grim Reapers.*

Diver, Jenny (Mary Young, Mary Jones), 1700-40, Brit., rob. Mary Young was born in northern Ireland in 1700, and her mother soon abandoned her. Young lived for many years with a kindly woman who taught her to read, write, and sew, but she ran away to England at the age of fifteen when her foster mother refused to allow her to see a young man who wanted to marry her. Young never intended to marry the boy, but tricked him into financing her journey to London, where she met Anne Murphy, who oversaw a pack of cunning thieves.

Murphy promised Young a life of ease if she joined her gang of pickpockets who worked near St. Giles parish. They taught Young to rifle pockets, and soon she became proficient. Known to all as Jenny Diver, Mary Young's favorite technique was to pose as a pregnant woman. At one prayer meeting, she fastened artificial arms to the sides of her garments and then dipped into her neighbors' pockets with her cleverly concealed hands. When she stole watches from two women in the church pew and made her exit, one victim said, "...Her watch must have been taken either by the devil or the pregnant woman!" But the other victim asserted that Young had sat in the pew with her hands primly clasped during the entire service.

Jenny and her friends practiced the badger game and a variety of other swindles. The money she made allowed her to attend theatre and society functions with the rich and well-born. Few realized that the woman with the fine clothes and sophisticated air was the infamous Jenny Diver. The London *Evening Post* for Apr. 11, 1738, reported: "She is one of the expertest hands in town at picking pockets; she used to attend well-dressed at the Opera House, play houses, etc., and it's reckoned made as much annually by her practice as if she had the finger of the Public Money!"

Jenny retired to the countryside briefly, but was eventually arrested in London in 1733 and held in Newgate for four months, then sentenced to be transported to America. Later, back in London, she was again nabbed by the law on Apr. 4, 1738, and again transported, but she returned to her old haunts in the city.

On the road to Walbrook on Jan. 17, 1740, Young and her latest male accomplice took thirteen shillings from a woman who offered such stiff resistance that there was time for the constable to arrive and take the robbers away. Young was indicted for stealing, found Guilty, and sentenced to die on the gallows. On Mar. 18, 1740, she was taken to Tyburn in a mourning cart, accompanied by a company of heavily armed guards, and was hanged, repentant for her many past crimes. Years later, the character of Jenny Diver was celebrated by Bertolt Brecht in his *Threepenny Opera*.

REF.: *CBA;* Hunt, *A Dictionary of Rogues;* Mitchell, *The Newgate Calendar;* Nash, *Look For the Woman;* Potter, *The Art of Hanging.*

Divine, Father, See: **Baker, George.**

Dix, Dorothea Lynde, 1802-87, U.S., pris. reform. Institutional reformer Dorothea Dix addressed the Massachussetts Legislature in 1843. She condemned the brutal and indifferent attitudes toward the treatment of insane persons with such moving and eloquent terms, that she brought about immediate reform measures. These reforms were also applied, through her constant lobbying, to prisons where inhuman treatment and punishments were stopped. The modernization of hospitals and asylums came about through the efforts of this inspired woman. REF.: *CBA.*

Dix, Enoch George Wilfred, b.1892, Brit., mansl. Though neither pheasant nor head groundskeeper season, on a cold October night in 1927 near Bath, England, 35-year-old Enoch Dix shot and killed both.

The Whistling Copse gave the wind and trees a voice. It provided a home for man and beast alike, sheltering all from storms, but it could do nothing to stop poacher and killer Enoch Wilfred Dix. This particular night began like many for Dix. An avid hunter, he entered Whistling Copse just before midnight—the start of the legal hunting season—carrying a small-bore, single-barreled revolver called a .410, a quiet and collapsible poacher's pistol. But not far away, two of Lord Temple's keepers could hear its muffled shots. Headkeeper William Walker and underkeeper George Rawlings decided to investigate. They soon stumbled upon Dix hiding in the forest. An argument over illegal hunting quickly escalated into murder. Three shots sounded. One bullet went through Walker's throat and killed him instantly. The other two shots were fired by Rawlings at Dix.

It was not difficult to arrest Dix for poaching, but the police had to be tricky in deciding whether he had been shot by Rawlings and thus the man who should be charged with murder. They stripped Dix naked and found not only Rawling's shots in his flesh but numerous other pellet holes. No longer able to deny poaching, Dix told authorities that Rawlings had fired first and that his gun had gone off by mistake after he was struck.

Investigator Churchill was called in and his calculations eventually settled the bloody dispute. To determine who had fired first and from what distance, Churchill tested the guns' firing power at test patterns on whitewashed steel plates using makes and cartridges identical to those used that night. From this he estimated that the shot that hit Dix was fired at not less than fifteen yards and that the major portion of the shot was stopped by a tree before hitting him. If Dix's gun had gone off in response to his being shot, as Dix maintained, Churchill decided that he must have fired at a range of not less than fifteen yards. But the diameter of the shot spread from Dix's gun was twenty-seven to thirty inches. The autopsy on Walker proved that the gun must have been fired at less than five yards, almost point-blank range.

Presiding Justice Shearman instructed the jury to determine whether Dix shot Walker from close or far. If the jury believed Dix shot Walker at close range so he could more easily escape, then Dix must be guilty of murder.

In two and a half hours Dix was found Guilty, not of murder, but of the lesser crime of manslaughter. The jury foreman defended the decision saying jury members believed Dix did not fire the gun to kill Walker. With that, Dix, who had referred to the Whistling Copse as "the Whistling Corpse" throughout the trial, was sentenced to fifteen years' penal servitude.

REF.: *CBA;* Hastings, *The Other Mr. Churchill.*

Dixon, Fred Michael, 1951- , U.S., rob. On Jan. 4, 1979, a Purolator Security vehicle made its usual Thursday night stop at the Table Top Restaurant in Lakeport, Mich. Two of the three guards, Glenn Harper and Paul Pudnick went inside for coffee while the third, guard Fred Michael Dixon, twenty-eight, guarded the truck. When the men returned forty-five minutes later, Dixon was gone, along with $1,516,900 in unmarked bills. Left behind in the truck was a crumpled, handwritten note from Dixon saying he had taken the money, and asking his co-workers not to call the police. According to Purolator's Detroit manager, Russell Dye, Dixon had worked for the company for four years and had a spotless record. On Jan. 5, Dixon was arrested at his parent's Livonia, Mich., home after sending word through his lawyer, Angelo A. Plakas, that he wanted to surrender. Special agent for the FBI in Michigan, O. Franklin Lowie, said all of the stolen money, except for $148 used to buy suitcases to carry it, was recovered.

On May 24, 1979, Dixon was fined $1,000 and given a four year suspended sentence by Detroit Federal District Judge Julian Cook, Jr. Four years earlier, Purolator, a Detroit-based security company that operates in several states, was robbed of what was then the largest cash haul in American history when a company vault in Chicago was robbed of $4.3 million. On Oct. 20, 1974, five men were arrested in conjunction with the vault theft; they had set fire to the more than $20 million, that they left in the vault, intending to disguise the amount they had stolen. It was estimated that around $1 million of the money was never recovered. The Purolator Company was hit again in April 1979, in Waterburg, Conn., when $1.9 million was stolen in a raid during which three guards were slain. REF.: *CBA.*

Dixon, James, 1953- , U.S., (wrong. convict.) bat.-attempt. mur. James Dixon made $50,000 in 1975 without lifting a finger. He did not inherit the money or win a lottery. He simply spent the year in prison accused of a crime he did not commit.

The 24-year-old Chicagoan was jailed for 362 days for allegedly shooting Sergeant Richard Scanlon in August 1975 after Scanlon intervened in a fight between Dixon and his grandfather. Charged with attempted murder, Dixon spent nearly one year in jail after pleading guilty to the lesser charge of aggravated battery. In August 1976, state's attorney investigators were tipped by a phone caller that Scanlon had shot himself with an illegal pen gun. Soon, Dixon's plea was withdrawn and all charges stricken. Scanlon was charged with official misconduct and obstruction of justice and suspended from the police force.

Dixon's $50,000 settlement, approved by U.S. District Court Judge Julius J. Hoffman, resulted from an out-of-court decision made by attorneys for Dixon and the city corporation counsel's office. Dixon had sued several police officers for $1 million.

A similar incident occurred with Dixon earlier when he was held for three years for murder. The Illinois Appellate Court overturned that conviction saying police improperly withheld knowledge of a critical defense witness from Dixon's lawyers. See: **Hoffman, Julius J.** REF.: *CBA.*

Dixon, Margaret, d.1753, Scot., mur. Margaret Dixon, the wife of a fisherman conscripted into the navy became pregnant by a lover. The baby may have been born dead, but the authorities believed she killed it. At the time, that was a common response to the births of illegitimate children, the mothers of whom were required to sit in church three Sundays in a row and be publicly chastised. Dixon claimed that she had been unconscious when the child was born, and that it was gone when she awoke. She did not know what had happened to it. The jury in an Edinburgh court found her Guilty of murder and sentenced her to be hanged.

In 1753, Maggie Dixon was hanged and taken down from the gallows. But as her friends took her body to be buried, she revived. Within a few hours, after being bled, she was able to walk back to her own village of Musselburgh. Because the verdict of the court had been carried out, the law could not touch her.

When her husband returned from the sea, they remarried and she later had a family with him. She was thereafter known to the locals as "Half-hanged Maggie."

REF.: Atholl, *Shadow of the Gallows;* Brock, *A Casebook of Crime;* CBA; Culpin, *The Newgate Noose;* Mitchell, *The Newgate Calendar;* Nash, *Look For the Woman;* O'Donnell, *Should Women Hang?;* Potter, *The Art of Hanging.*

Djemal Pasha, Ahmed, c.1872-1922, Turk., gen., assass. Greatly influenced Turkey to ally with the Central Powers during WWI, fleeing from the country at the end of the war, 1918, later being assassinated. REF.: *CBA.*

Dmitri (Dmitry, Demetrius, Dmitri Ivanovich), 1581-91, Rus., czar, assass. As the last of the Rurik line of Russian czars, he was also the youngest son of Ivan the Terrible and was probably assassinated by the regent, Boris Godunov. REF.: *CBA.*

Dmitri I (Dmitry I, Demetrius I; AKA: False Dmitry, Pseudo-Demetrius), d.1606, Rus., czar, assass. Dmitri I is believed to have been the first pretender to the Russian monarchy. Born Yury Otrepyev and known as Gregory, in 1601, Dmitri I claimed to be the son of Ivan IV. The imposter was placed on the throne by the Russian army when Boris Godunov died in 1605. He ruled for about a year before he was killed by Vasily Shuysky. REF.: *CBA.*

Dmitri II (Dmitry II, Demetrius II; AKA: False Dmitry, Pseudo-Demetrius), d.1610, Rus., czar, assass. Dmitri II held power in Russia as a false czar for about three years, from 1607 until he was murdered in 1610. REF.: *CBA.*

Dmitri III (Dmitry III, Demetrius III; AKA: False Dmitry, Pseudo-Demetrius), d.1610, Rus., czar, assass. As the third imposter of this name to the Russian throne, he claimed to be the son of the second Dmitri imposter. Like his predecessor, he too was killed. REF.: *CBA.*

Dmitri IV (Dmitry IV, Demetrius IV; AKA: False Dmitry, Pseudo-Demetrius), d.1612, Rus., czar, assass. In 1611, Dmitri IV also claimed to be the son of Dmitri II. But in reality, he was a deacon named Sidorka. His ruse was quickly exposed and he was executed. REF.: *CBA.*

Dmitriev, Radko (Radko Dimitriev), 1859-1919, Rus., gen., assass. Commanded the 3rd Russian army, 1914-15, and was most likely killed by Bolsheviks. REF.: *CBA.*

Doane Gang (or Doan), prom. 1780s, U.S., rob. Led by Moses Doane, the Doane Gang was the most powerful criminal band of highwaymen in early Pennsylvania. The gang never numbered fewer than twenty or thirty ruthless men, and always at the core were the six Doane brothers. The gang, prominent during the 1780s, preyed on wealthy travelers, coaches, and even towns in eastern Pennsylvania, headquartering in Bucks County. Members in small groups raided into New Jersey, but the most sensational robbery committed by the Doanes, led by Moses, Levy, and Abe Doane, occurred in October 1781 when the gang rode into Newton, Pa., and took over the entire town. The bandits captured city treasurer John Hart and forced him at gunpoint to turn over more than $2,000 in gold. The Doanes rode to the city's school-house, where they gleefully counted out their shares.

The Doanes operated throughout the American Revolution and took advantage of the chaos and confusion war brought. They gave their political support, and when it suited them, their military aid to the British. As Tories, the Doanes were hated by the Revolutionists as raiders of American storehouses and treasuries. The Doanes also robbed American tax collectors, but they refused to turn over monies taken from these collectors to the British, keeping the cash for themselves and telling their British superiors that "these here are the spoils of war." The gang went to pieces after several of its leaders were captured and hanged, the first being James Fitzpatrick, who was known as "Sandy Flash." Fitzpatrick was captured in 1787 and was convicted of robbery and treason, then hanged. In the following year, Moses, Abraham, and Levy Doane were overpowered when they attempted to raid a small Pennnsylvania town and were later hanged. This triple hanging spelled the finish of the Doane Gang.

REF.: *CBA;* Nash, *Almanac of World Crime;* _____, *Bloodletters and Badmen.*

Dobbs, Hannah, c.1821-76, Brit., Case of, mur. Evidence suggested that Hannah Dobbs masterminded the murder of eccentric, wealthy Matilda Hacker, but enough doubt existed during the trial to acquit the maidservant from Bideford, England.

What came to be known as the Euston Square Mystery of 1879 first developed with the discovery of a badly decomposed body in the forgotten basement of a lodging house. From the remains and information revealed in interviews, several facts concerning the murder were uncovered.

Tight round rope grooves around the body's neck pointed conclusively to either strangulation or hanging. Suicide was ruled out because the body had been carefully concealed and a thorough attempt had been made to speed up decay with quicklime and other chemicals.

The woman was about fifty-five, made evident by graying hairs discovered with the remains. Her clothing, a silk gown, jacket, lace shawl, hood, and bonnet, indicated that the victim had intended to leave her home, was fairly wealthy and, from the style of the bonnet, had died about three years earlier.

An interview with Hannah Dobbs, the woman eventually charged with the murder and who had lived at the house and worked as its maidservant at the time of the murder, indicated that a woman had lived on the second floor for six weeks before leaving in October 1877. Dobbs said the woman was about fifty-five, and called herself Miss Huish, a name she doubted. She said the woman had a gold watch and chain which she wore only on Sundays.

With that admission Dobbs gave herself away. Detectives traced the watch and chain to a local pawnbroker who identified Hannah Dobbs as the person who pawned them. Apparently she had worn them openly while working at Euston Square until being told to get rid of them because it was not her place to wear fine jewelry. Dobbs also had been seen with a cash box known to have belonged to Hacker.

People who remembered Hacker, namely the police, explained why she called herself Huish. The woman apparently had many eccentricities, which included a fierce objection to paying her taxes. To avoid the law, she moved and changed her name often. A letter in her handwriting to one of her rent collectors proved she had been alive on Oct. 10, 1877. After that, letters sent to her were returned, ironically, to the dead letter office. On Oct. 14, a neighbor recalled hearing a scream coming from Euston Square. Hacker and Dobbs were known to be alone together in the house at this time. Severin Bastendorf and his wife, housekeepers at Euston Square, both were out.

A medical examination proved the victim was struck with a heavy instrument, then dragged downstairs, probably still alive, and strangled. Chemicals were poured over the body to accelerate decomposition.

It seemed straightforward and clear. Dobbs was with the victim at the time of death and seen with the victim's precious belongings after the death. She had motive, means, and opportunity. She was acquitted just the same.

The defense argued successfully that there was no proof that Dobbs killed Hacker. It might be likely, but was not certain. After all, another lodger and the landlady had keys and might have come in. Further, the defense argued that with the possibility of being seen so great, Dobbs would not have risked dragging the body from an upstairs room downstairs by herself. In addition, the accused remained in the house the following year, a difficult thing to do knowing that at any time she could be caught. She also would have had every opportunity to dispose of the body.

The Euston Square Mystery remains just that. Only Hacker and her assailant knew the truth.

REF.: Brock, *A Casebook of Crime;* CBA; Lambton, *Echoes of Causes Celebres.*

Dobbs, Johnny (Michael Kerrigan), d.1892, U.S., rob.-mur.

Johnny Dobbs moved from Patsy Conroy's gang of youthful river pirates and became one of the top criminals of the Victorian underworld, ranking with Abe Coakley, Red Leary, Jimmy Hope, "Banjo" Pete Emerson, and the "King of the Bank Robbers" George Leonidas Leslie.

In 1878, Johnny Dobbs masterminded one of the celebrated bank heists of the era, the $2.7 million robbery of the Manhattan Savings Institution. He participated in dozens of other bank robberies up and down the East Coast. With his earnings he opened a saloon near the Mott Street Police Station in Lower Manhattan that became the headquarters of a fencing ring which netted Dobbs $650,000. In the belief that George Leslie was informing on his gang, Dobbs had Leslie murdered.

Dobbs spent most of the 1880s in prison serving sentences on a variety of criminal charges. A week after his release from the Massachusetts State Prison in May 1892, Dobbs died in the alcoholic ward of New York's Bellevue Hospital. He died penniless and had to be buried with the money his mistress received from a pawned broach Dobbs had once given her. See: **Leslie, George Leonidas.** REF.: *CBA.*

Dobell, Charles Joseph, and **Gower, William,** prom. 19th Cent., Brit., mur. Charles Dobell, seventeen, and William Gower, eighteen, confessed to a Salvation Army officer that they were guilty of a previously unsolved murder. Executioner James Berry hanged the two teenagers in Maidstone Gaol, England.

Berry was at first untroubled by the executions of the two confessed killers, but soon after, he began having nightmares about the boys. In nineteenth century Britain, no allowance was made for youthful offenders. Capital punishment was imposed for most crimes, and boys and girls as well as men and women were routinely hanged.

REF.: Atholl, *The Reluctant Hangman; CBA.*

Dobie, Armistead Mason, 1881-1962, U.S., jur. Contributed to law reviews, including a collaboration with F.D.R. Ribble and Raymond Moley, "Criminal Justice in Virginia," 1931; and received appointment to the Western District Court of Virginia from President Franklin Roosevelt, 1939 and later that year, Dec. 16, to the 4th Circuit Court of the U.S. REF.: *CBA.*

Dobkin, Harry, c.1893-1943, Brit., mur. Three days after he married the former Rachel Dubinski in 1920, Harry Dobkin, a Russian-born laborer living in London, walked out on her. The couple's brief union produced a child nine months later. Although the courts ordered him to pay child support to Rachel, Dobkin was regularly imprisoned over a twenty-year period for failing to pay the court-ordered compensation.

In April 1941, Dobkin went to work as a fire spotter for a paper storage building behind a bombed out church in St. Oswald's Place, Kennington. On Apr. 15, he reported a fire in the vestry of the destroyed chapel. The authorities extinguished the blaze, but as such fires were common during the London Blitz, they made no effort to determine the cause. However, a team of workmen clearing debris from the area on July 17, 1942, pulled up a loose paving stone and unearthed a badly burned human skeleton.

Home Office pathologist Dr. Keith Simpson conducted an autopsy and found that someone had severed the limbs from the body in a crude attempt to disguise a murder. When the missing persons ledger was checked, it was found that 49-year-old Rachel Dobkin was reported missing by her sister just three days before the cellar fire on Apr. 12, 1941. The body was eventually identified as that of Rachel Dobkin.

Harry Dobkin immediately became the prime suspect in the investigation and was eventually arrested and charged with Rachel's murder. Dobkin's trial began at the Old Bailey on Nov. 17, 1942. The evidence of guilt was conclusive, especially after the victim's dentist took the stand and testified that the top jaw and the teeth and gums were those of Rachel Dobkin. Dobkin had strangled his wife in a dispute over maintenance payments. The fire had apparently been started in order to conceal the remains. Harry Dobkin was convicted and hanged at Wandsworth Prison on Jan. 27, 1943.

REF.: *CBA;* Firmin, *Murderers In Our Midst;* Gribble, *Clues That Spelled Guilty;* Lefebure, *Evidence For the Crown;* Shew, *A Companion to Murder;* Simpson, *Forty Years of Murder;* Wilson, *Encyclopedia of Murder.*

Docherty, "Dutch", and **Meehan, Martin,** prom. 1971, Ire., pris. esc. In late December 1971, Belfast's most notorious Irish Republican Army (IRA) leaders, Dutch Docherty and Martin Meehan, escaped from the Crumlin Road Prison in Belfast. After their absence was discovered at nightly roll call, a massive roadblock was called. Andersontown and other areas populated by Catholics burned bonfires while people danced in the streets to celebrate the leaders' escape. A two-day search of homes of hundreds of known IRA sympathizers yielded nothing. Security chiefs were convinced that Docherty and Meehan had fled to Ireland, and they called off the search. It was later discovered that the IRA members had been hiding in the prison the entire time and had climbed over the wall to freedom only after the security chiefs called off the search. See: **Irish Republican Army.**

REF.: Borrell, *Crime In Britain Today; CBA.*

Dr. Jekyll and Sister Hyde, 1971, a film directed by Roy Ward Baker. Though this picture is based on the Robert Louis Stevenson classic, it fuses Jack the Ripper's *modus operandi* of killing women and mutilating their bodies, along with other nuances peculiar to the Ripper (Brit., 1888). See: **Jack the Ripper.** REF.: *CBA.*

Dr. Moon, 1934, a novel by Catherine Meadows (published in England under the title *Henbane*). The mild British murderer, Dr. Hawley Harvey Crippen (Brit., 1910) is the basis in fact for this work of fiction. See: **Crippen, Dr. Hawley Harvey.**

Rioters forcing entry to the New York Hospital, 1788.

Doctors' Riot, 1788, U.S., mob vio. The Doctors' Riot was a demonstration of fear, superstition, and religious mania that possessed the New York citizenry-at-large in 1788. It was also the first time in America that science assumed the form of the fanatic and the shape of the sinister.

Doctors in New York were sore put in the 1780s to obtain bodies for scientific dissection. The medical profession, then blooming, was allowed only the bodies of executed murderers and other felons convicted of serious crimes, on the proviso that the families of the deceased gave their permission for disinterment and dissection. Since the general feeling was that it was sinful to desecrate the entombed by digging them up, permission was rarely given. Medical students had to be content with studying the few imported skeletons dangling from hooks in their classrooms at the New York Hospital.

A dissection craze on the part of students inexplicably began in the winter of 1787-88 and, to obtain fresh bodies upon which to operate, students and doctors alike paid professional ghouls exorbitant rates for body snatching. The students then joined in on the grave robbing, and soon an alarming number of well-planted corpses began to disappear.

Stories, whispered low in the pubs, told of how doctors had not only torn open the graves of strangers and blacks but had stolen the bodies of distinguished citizens and young women. Of the women, it was said, most of these bodies were placed on display in medical classrooms, and students performed lewd acts upon them in mock operations.

Added to these putrid fantasies was the lunatic gesture on the part of one young physician at the New York Hospital, a sadistic act that provoked a nightmare of rioting. In the spring of 1788, a group of young boys were playing near the hospital. A surgeon spied them from a window and, grinning like some madman, held up a human arm to their gaze. Some of the boys approached the window in which the doctor stood, and blinked in stupefied horror. The doctor recognized one of the lads and motioned for him to crawl up a short ladder nearby. The boy climbed up to the window and the doctor thrust the severed arm in his face, saying, "This is your mother's arm, boy!" He laughed like one insane as the terrified child ran home screaming. His mother had died a week earlier.

The boy informed his father, a burly mason, about the gruesome event and the father, knowing full well the bodysnatching stories then current, raced to the graveyard where his wife was buried. He clawed at the earth with his bare hands. Opening his wife's grave, the mason discovered his wife's body gone. He returned to his work and told his fellow masons of the theft. Incensed, scores of men picked up tools and marched to the hospital.

Raging with curses and hurling rocks through windows, the mob increased in numbers, hundreds more running up to the corner of Pearl and Broadway where the hospital was located. With one surging bound, the huge mob broke through the hospital doors on a rampage through the building, ransacking classrooms, crushing skeletons, vials, and medicines to gritty powder on the floors, overturning desks and chairs, smashing lamps. In one room, the rioters found several corpses freshly robbed from their graves and, huddled in a corner, a group of terrified medical students.

The crowd went berserk with anger, some carrying the bodies out over their heads, others in a blind rage rushing to the students and belting them with leather tongs, cracking their heads with clubs and hammers. The students were dragged bloody from the hospital and ropes were placed about the necks of several of them. The rioters intended to lynch every last one of them.

A moment before the mob began to move away from the hospital, the mayor and several respected citizens of New York arrived and stood in the way. The mayor appealed to the mob, stating that, indeed, the medical students were guilty of criminal acts but that the law should run its course; they would be locked up and tried for their grave robbing. The speech somehow pacified the mob, and the students were released to the custody of the mayor. The students were locked up and the crowd dispersed.

Instigated by a night of heavy drinking, horror-studded anecdotes about the body snatchers inflamed the rioters. The crowd again assembled the next morning in front of the hospital. Once more, the mayor and a swarm of dignitaries talked the rioters out of destroying the building. It was resolved, however, that a large delegation from the mob would thoroughly inspect not only the hospital and Columbia College for more corpses, but the homes of every physician in the city. This they did, but no bodies were found. The rioters stood about nonplused for some time. There was nothing left to do, and slowly these men began to drift away toward their homes. Then, some inspired rabble-rouser shouted: "To the jail! To the jail, where the fiends are locked up!"

Quickly reassembling, the huge mob marched to the jail and once there, began to demand that the students and physicians locked inside be released to them.

"Bring out your doctors!" chorused the mob. "Bring out your doctors!"

It was obvious that this crowd could not be placated and that they intended to lynch the students and doctors who, white-faced, cringed away from the windows of the jail. Their guards manned these openings and prepared for the first assault. A constant barrage of ripe fruit, rocks, and clubs slammed against the stout, brick building. Several clots of raging rioters charged again and again at the sturdy jail door with a battering ram but were unable to break it down.

This time the mayor called out his militia. The troops marched down the street in even ranks, but the crowd, brutalized by its own rage, refused to budge and, amazingly, the troopers did not drive out the mob before them but passed through the crowd. More shocking, the troops kept right on marching down the street and out of sight. This ineffectual performance served only to bolster the courage of the rioters, who began their attacks on the jail in earnest.

Waves of bricks and debris from the tumultuous sea of people around the building dashed against the brick jail. Many attempted to dive through the windows but were repulsed time and again by the defenders inside. Mere numbers could not overwhelm the jail, and only a handful of rioters at a time could make any thrusts at the few windows. The rioters were fighting, after all, for unnamed vengeance; the defenders were battling for their lives and those of their prisoners.

Suddenly, another group of soldiers, twelve in all, appeared at the end of the street. The pitiable band of troopers only caused jeers of derision from the crowd. What good could such a handful do, most thought, when an entire company had failed to dislodge them? The hooting rioters did not wait for the troops to approach but launched an attack themselves. The running masses swept into the soldiers. Rioters grabbed weapons away from the startled militiamen and smashed them to pieces on the street. It was during this melee that John Jay and Baron Friedrich Wilhelm von Steuben, a hero of the Revolution, were both wounded as they attempted to quell the rioters.

The twelve soldiers, their uniforms ripped to tatters, were sent scurrying down the street, thankful to escape with their lives. All that afternoon the rioters busied themselves with trying to batter down the jail door and force their way through the windows. Each time they were driven back with cracked heads, bloody faces, and broken hands.

By nightfall the defenders stood exhausted at their posts. They agreed that they could not hold back the mob much longer. One guard turned to the traumatized students and doctors and told them: "It is best you prepare to die."

Minutes later, while the rioters were lighting torches and preparing for another assault, a heavy, uniform tramp of boots could be heard approaching. Far up the street, the multitude of suddenly silenced rioters saw coming toward them a full battalion of soldiers with experienced officers leading them. Hundreds of bayonets gleamed in the moonlight, a sea of silvery spikes waving ominously forward.

The rioters had chased away troops that day without a shot, and the sight of more militia caused little fear. Confidently, the crowd held its ground even when ordered to disperse. They then unleashed a maelstrom of brickbats, rocks, and other objects at the troopers. Several soldiers were knocked down, and howls of laughter greeted their falls.

Undaunted, an officer rode up and ordered his men to form into firing ranks. Quickly, the militiamen took their position. The crowd remained unmoved, curious as they watched the troopers lift their muskets. "Ready!" shouted the officer. "Aim! Fire!" The volley smacked into the first row of rioters and tumbled scores before a hail of lead. Before the awe-struck crowd could react, the soldiers sent another volley into their midst, and dozens more fell on the ground dead, dying, or wounded.

The shock caused the rioters to break and then flee wildly down the streets toward their homes. The street in front of the jail was littered with the dead, and blood flowed along the gutters in thick streams. At least seventy had been shot, and about twenty either perished outright or died a short while later. The Doctors' Riot was over, but the plight of New York physicians continued.

Doctors were hounded from their homes for days, and there was a mass exodus of physicians from the city that lasted several weeks. Some doctors were actually driven from the city precincts by club-wielding citizens. Then the madness subsided and the physicians again took up residence in the city.

REF.: Butterfield, *The American Past; CBA;* Chaplin, *Rumor, Fear and the Madness of Crowds;* Heaps, *Riots U.S.A. 1765-1965.*

Dodd, Jeff, prom. 1946, Case of, U.S., mur. A 35-year-old black tenant farmer, Leon McAtee, was held for several days in a Holmes County, Miss., jail for allegedly stealing a saddle from Jeff Dodd, a white planter. When Dodd claimed that he needed McAtee to help harvest his corn crop, the sheriff released the farmer to Dodd. With his son and several neighbors, Dodd took McAtee to his pasture and beat him with a rope. McAtee's wife watched as her husband doubled over in a truck going down the road. His body was found floating in the bayou, about sixty miles from the scene of the murder.

Prosecutors in predominately black Holmes County tried Dodd, his son, and three other men for McAtee's slaying. District Attorney Harold Dyer, Jr. said, "The citizen of Holmes County holds a white man accountable if he commits a crime, the same as he holds a Negro accountable." After a three-hour hearing, during which it was revealed that McAtee had not stolen Dodd's saddle, the local judge released each of the defendants on a $2,000 bond, until the grand jury reconvened. In the October trial in Lexington, Miss., the judge freed two of the accused—the jury took four minutes to acquit the remainder. REF.: *CBA.*

Dodd, William, 1729-77, Brit., forg. A preacher and author, the Reverend William Dodd was an unlikely candidate for the gallows. Known as the "Macaroni Parson" for his foppish style of dress, Dodd published the popular *The Beauties of Shakespeare* in 1751. He lived well beyond his means and fell into debt, and on Feb. 4, 1777, he asked a broker named Robertson to take out a loan on bond from a young nobleman, whose signature Dodd forged. Robertson arranged the £4,200 loan, but the lender soon became suspicious. Robertson and Dodd were arrested and Dodd offered a complete restitution. The charges against Robertson were dropped, but Dodd was brought to the Old Bailey on Feb. 19, 1777, to plead to the indictment for fraud. Dodd was found Guilty, with a recommendation of mercy. On May 26, 1777, he read a moving appeal at the Old Bailey, but was sentenced to death and warned not to expect a reprieve.

Though he had led a dissipated life, he had done som charitable acts, and q massive effort to help Dodd began. Letters and editorials appeared in several newspapers, 30,000 signed a petition, and many high-ranking citizens exerted private influence. But at the Privy Council meeting of June 13, 1777, Lord Mansfield supported the king's prejudice against the flamboyant clergyman, and Dodd's execution date was set. While awaiting execution, the unhappy minister wrote another book, *Thoughts in Prison.* Though Dodd could not escape his fate, several plans were made to revive him after hanging. The executioner, Edward Dennis, was allegedly bribed to adjust the noose in a way that would allow Dodd to survive, and Dodd's body was to be taken to an undertaker's house where a distinguished doctor, William Hunter, would try to revive him. Two thousand soldiers were stationed in Hyde Park near the gallows to prevent Dodd's rescue by his friends. A huge crowd watched from Newgate to Tyburn, lining the streets ten deep, as Dodd was carried in a mourning coach to the execution place on June 27, 1777. The body was cut down at the end of an hour, and although Dennis appeared to have held Dodd's legs up to lessen the force of the rope, the street traffic caused a delay before the body could be taken to the undertaker. Dodd was dead by the time they arrived. See: **Dennis, Edward.**

REF.: Earl of Birkenhead, *Famous Trials of History;* Bleackley, *Hangmen of England; CBA;* Cooper, *Lesson of the Scaffold;* Laurence, *A History of Capital Punishment;* Potter, *The Art of Hanging.*

Dodsin, Sir Gerald, b.1884, Brit., lawyer. Provided defense for the murder trial of Wallace Benton and junior counsel in the prosecution of accused murderers Arthur Henry Bishop and Arthur James Farraday Salvage. He also authored *The Law Relating to Motor-cars* and *The Road Traffic Act, 1929.* REF.: *CBA.*

Doe, Charles, 1830-96, U.S., jur. Charles Doe was chief justice of the New Hampshire Supreme Court from 1876 until his death. He is best remembered for his accomplishments in the fields of evidence and procedure. He is credited, along with Isaac Ray, for formulating the New Hampshire Rules and he was the first judge to call for the integration of law and science in the field of criminal responsibility. REF.: *CBA.*

Doelitzsch, Fritz, b.c.1893, Egypt, mur. Fritz Doelitzsch and his accomplice, Herman Klaus, both German, risked their lives to rob wealthy Syrian merchant Max Karam in his luxurious villa on the coast near Alexandria. The two performed an expert job of breaking in but panicked when Karam fought to save his fortune. Robbery turned into murder and Doelitzsch and Klaus ran away without touching the safe.

Police were impressed with the professional way the intruders had entered the home without detection, attempted to commit their deed, and left without leaving a clue. But when the two robust Germans had one too many beers and started bragging about their dubious accomplishment, police were on them in seconds.

Katina awoke early on the morning of Jan. 15, 1923 and went about her duties as the Karam villa maid. But her daily routine took a jag when she discovered her friend and employer motionless, slumped beside his bed entangled in the mosquito net that had hung over his bed, and an overturned commode stained with blood and buckshot lying on the body.

The initial investigation seemed to indicate an inside job. An entry hole carved on a ground floor wall opened into the exact spot which would allow a person to reach in and unlock the door. Police thought it unlikely that strangers would have been able to position their entry so perfectly. Further, it appeared the assassins knew the layout of the house well.

But interviews with the widow Karam, with Katina, and other staff members, and with Karam's brother and sister-in-law who also lived in the house, cleared all as suspects. The Medico-Legal Department in Cairo eventually took over the investigation and concluded that the robbery had been committed by professional or semi-professional burglars, for the intruders had entered the home through a lower door, crossed the hall, and climbed the marble staircase to the first floor to avoid the nightwatchman. The burglars then cut the bell and telephone wires in both Karams' suites.

An autopsy on Karam revealed that the 40- or 50-year-old man was exceptionally strong and able to take care of himself. Regardless, the assassins had overcome him by striking him with an iron crowbar three or four times from the front to the back of the vertex. It appeared that Karam then jumped out of bed and became entangled in the mosquito netting. He may have shouted for help loudly enough to scare off the intruders, but only until one shot him in the back of the head. The intruders then ran off in a panic and no attempt was made to open the safe. Wounds inflicted by the crowbar and gun originated from different directions, proving conclusively that there were, indeed, two assailants in the crime.

Police were baffled until a French woman named Henriette stepped forward requesting the £2,000 reward in exchange for incriminating evidence she could provide. The killer was her lover's best friend, she said. She overheard him one night, after he drank too much, bragging about a burglary he and a cohort had committed. The names she gave were Fritz Doelitzsch and Herman Klaus. The police then found everything they needed in Doelitzsch's unkempt Alexandria room. Inside the pockets of a jacket they found wood and plaster fragments identical to fragments from Karam's house. Hairs on the collar of a suit proved to be those of Karam.

Tracked down, the pair were brought into the German Embassy in Alexandria and subjected to a strict German court trial. The evidence had Klaus and Doelitzsch down cold. The two soon confessed to being the men sought in the murder but, because German law requires determination of who actually killed the victim, both men denied firing the fatal shot. Separate recollections by Klaus and Doelitzsch each implicated the other. But Doelitzsch's story was better than his partner's for Klaus' had made the grave error of trying to pin both the crowbar and pistol attacks on Doelitzsch. Police already knew that two persons had been involved in the brutality waged against Karam. Klaus had to be lying. The attorney-general charged Klaus with murder and deemed the act premeditated because, he said, if it had not been, both men would have fled immediately after Karam woke.

The defense counsel did not lose the case for the accused. They lost it for themselves. In light of a preponderance of evidence the court departed from precedent, found both men Guilty of murder, and handed down life sentences for both.

REF.: *CBA; Jacobs, Pageant of Murder.*

German Admiral Karl Doenitz, convicted of war crimes in 1945.

Doenitz, Karl, 1891-1980, Ger., war crimes. As Grand Admiral of the Nazi Navy, Karl Doenitz was a submarine strategist who was in charge of U-boat attacks against Allied shipping during WWII. Appointed by Adolf Hitler as his successor on Apr. 30, 1945, Doenitz presided over Germany's surrender following a last unsuccessful attempt to surrender in the West and continue fighting the Russians in the East. After announcing that Doenitz was taking over, Hitler committed suicide the same day. Tried at the Nuremberg Trials that began in January 1946, Doenitz was one of five members of the German High Command and the German General Staff who were tried before the International Military Tribunal as war criminals. The primary and most controversial issue in the ten-month-long trials was the question of whether the military and naval men could be tried as criminals for conducting aggressive warfare, or whether they were merely obeying orders.

In his opening remarks, Colonel Telford Taylor, the prosecuting attorney, contended that the defendants bore responsibility for planning and executing illegal warfare and for "crimes against humanity in a general conspiracy against the peace." Taylor added that the General Staff and High Command gave full support to the Nazi leader's plans for Germany to dominate Europe. In October 1946, three of the war criminals, Hermann Göring, Joachim von Ribbentrop, and Rudolph Hess, were sentenced to death by Presiding Lord Justice Sir Geoffrey Lawrence. Doenitz was sentenced to ten years in jail. Released from the Spandau Prison in Berlin on Oct. 1, 1956, Doenitz wrote personal memoirs in which he insisted that he had no knowledge of the atrocities Hitler had committed until the war ended, and maintained that

he had only been following orders. Doenitz had been a key figure in military planning, and had "attended top-level conferences where major decisions were discussed." He died in December 1980, at the age of eighty-nine, and was buried without military honors. See: **Göring, Hermann; Hess, Rudolf; Hitler, Adolf; Lawrence, Sir Geoffrey; von Ribbentrop, Joachim.**

REF.: Borkin, *The Crime and Punishment of I.G. Farben; CBA;* Carell, *Hitler Moves East;* Congdon, *Combat, European Theater, World War II;* Cooper, *The Nuremberg Trial;* Davidson, *The Making of Adolf Hitler;* ____, *The Nuremberg Fallacy;* ____, *The Trial of the Germans;* Dollinger, *The Decline and Fall of Nazi Germany and Imperial Japan;* Fest, *Hitler;* Gilbert, *Nuremberg Diary;* ____, *Hitler Directs His War;* Hoyt, *The Sea Wolves;* International Military Tribunal, Nuremberg, *Nazi Conspiracy and Aggression;* Jarman, *The Rise and Fall of Nazi Germany;* Knieriem, *The Nuremberg Trials;* Lewis, *The Fight for the Sea;* Lochner, *The Goebbels Diaries;* Manvell and Fraenkel, *Himmler;* Martienssen, *Hitler and His Admirals;* Mendelssohn, *The Nuremberg Documents;* Morgan, *German Atrocities;* Neave, *On Trial at Nuremberg;* Orlow, *The History of the Nazi Party, 1933-1945;* Payne, *The Life and Death of Adolf Hitler;* Shirer, *End of a Berlin Diary;* ____, *The Rise and Fall of the Third Reich;* Smith, *Reaching Judgment at Nuremberg;* Speer, *Inside the Third Reich;* ____, *Spandau: The Secret Diaries;* Strawson, *Hitler and Military Commander;* Thomas, *The Murder of Rudolf Hess;* Toland, *The Last Days;* Trevor-Roper, *The Last Days of Hitler; Trial of German Major War Criminals; Trial of the Major War Criminals Before the International Military Tribunal, Nuremberg;* Vogt, *The Burden of Guilt;* Warlimont, *Inside Hitler's Headquarters, 1939-45;* Ziemke, *Battle for Berlin: End of the Third Reich.*

Doetsch, Gunter, 1926-82, U.S., suic.-mur. Gunter Doetsch, fifty-six, pleaded for help when he told friends he planned to kill himself and his two young children. Nobody took him seriously, and so, on June 29, 1982, the middle-aged executive from the fashionable Chicago suburb of Lake Forest drove his son Gunter Alexander Doetsch II, five, and daughter Catherine Doetsch, two, along a rural highway near scenic Lake Geneva, Wis., and shot them both. He immediately turned the gun on himself.

Doetsch's neighbors were incredulous. Not one had any inkling things were wrong in the Doetsch household. To them the family was a privileged group with a lovely $200,000 ranch-style home with an indoor swimming pool on a one-and-a-half-acre lot. Doetsch owned Scientificom, a firm that produces audio-visual aids for the medical industry.

But Joyce Doetsch, thirty-five, Gunter's second wife, knew the truth. The couple had been having marital problems for some time and Joyce had filed for divorce, saying her husband was of a "violent and uncertain temper who occasionally displayed his temper by striking objects within his reach and by beating his head against the wall." She was scheduled to leave for Martha's Vineyard, Mass., with the children the day after the murders. Joyce also knew of Doetsch's financial troubles. The Lake Forest National Bank had filed a lawsuit in April to foreclose on a $95,000 mortgage on the family's home.

Neighbors still could not believe it. One said, "He certainly didn't seem like anyone who was going to die." Except that he had told friends that was his plan. REF.: *CBA.*

Dogin, Henry S., c.1935- , U.S., law enfor. off. Henry S. Dogin, forty years old, replaced the previous Drug Enforcement Administration head on May 30, 1975, in response to allegations of corruption and abuse of power under John R. Bartels, Jr.'s leadership. Dogin promptly proved himself to be a superior director by earning the Attorney General's Award for Exceptional Service in December of the same year. This award, the highest honor bestowed by the Department of Justice, is given for outstanding contributions to the department's objectives and to the interests of the public. Dogin was credited with reestablishing public confidence and trust in an agency besieged by crisis and controversy.

Before becoming the DEA's acting head, Dogin served as top prosecutor in the Justice Department's criminal division. He had been assistant district attorney in New York City and an assistant counsel for the New York Harbor Waterfront Commission between 1961 and 1971 when he became an official of the Law Enforcement Assistance Administration. He served as deputy assistant attorney general in the criminal division where he supervised the department's organized crime strike forces from November 1973 until his appointment as DEA head.

President Richard M. Nixon established the DEA in July 1973, thus consolidating the functions of the Treasury Department and the old Bureau of Narcotics and Dangerous Drugs. Though Dogin was highly favored to be chosen permanent director of the DEA, he resigned as acting head to join the New York state Division of Criminal Justice Services as deputy commissioner in charge of planning. Dogin received his bachelor's degree from Cornell University and a law degree form Columbia University. He and his wife, Cynthia Dogin, have two daughters. See: **Bartels, John R., Jr.; Nixon, Richard.** REF.: *CBA.*

Doherty, Charles Joseph, 1855-1931, Can., jur. Served on the Quebec Superior Court, 1891-1906, as a member of parliament, 1908-21, and as the minister of justice, 1911-21. REF.: *CBA.*
Doherty, Daniel, See: **Molly Maguires.**
Dohrn, Bernadine Rae, c.1948- , U.S., asslt. Raised in Wisconsin, Bernadine Rae Dohrn graduated from the University of Chicago Law School in 1967. She became deeply involved in the radical 1960s organization Weather Underground and its violent "Days of Rage" anti-war demonstrations in New York City in 1969, activities that forced her to hide from authorities—and her parents—for nearly eleven years.

Once on the FBI's Ten Most Wanted list, Dohrn faced federal charges of involvement in an alleged bombing plot in Flint, Mich. Additional federal charges in connection with "Days of Rage" disorders were dropped when it was learned that the federal government had obtained its evidence through illegal telephone wiretaps. However, Dohrn still faced three state indictments, including mob action, flight to avoid prosecution, and assault in allegedly kicking a policeman in the groin and striking another with a club. The charges against Dohrn represented Class 3 felonies and carried a maximum penalty of five years in jail. After spending years with her companion William Ayers and working primarily as a Manhattan waitress, Dohrn finally decided to turn herself in in 1980, as a result of negotiations between her attorney, Michael Kennedy, and outgoing State's Attorney Bernard Carey.

Dohrn initially pleaded not guilty to her three indictments on Dec. 3, 1980, in Chicago's Cook County Criminal Court and took her opportunity before the judge to restate her support for underground work and her belief in the innocence of black and third-world political prisoners and freedom fighters. Her case was transferred to Judge Fred G. Suria, Jr., who had heard other cases involving the disorders of the late 1960s. He reduced Dohrn's bond from $300,000 to $25,000 after her attorney said she was virtually destitute.

Bernadine Dohrn, found Guilty of assault.

Dohrn thought better of her first plea and began her Jan. 13 trial with a plea of guilty to all outstanding charges against her. With that, she was fined $1,500 and placed on probation for three years. Dohrn left the courtroom insisting she and the judge had "different views of America," that she did not believe the "system" had changed, and that she was still "committed to the struggle ahead." Since her trial, Dohrn has married and had three children. She currently works as an attorney in New York. See: **Ayers, William; Kennedy, Michael; Suria, Fred G., Jr.**

REF.: *CBA;* Hacker, *Crusaders, Criminals, Crazies: Terror and Terrorism In Our Time;* Laquer, *Terrorism;* McLellan and Avery, *The Voices of Guns.*

Dokyo, d.772, Japan, treas. Organized a successful coup against Emperor Junnin, 764, and placed the former empress Koken on the throne as the empress Shotoku. He became her prime minister, 765, and archbishop, 766, and by using an oracle hoped to be named the successor to the throne, for which he was banished by the Fujiwara family upon Shotoku's death, 770. REF.: *CBA.*

Dolabella, Publius Cornelius, c.70-43 B.C., Roman., extor.-polit. corr. Gained control of the Roman consulship upon the assassination of Julius Caesar, 44 B.C., but later was proclaimed an enemy to the public for his crimes and extortions while serving Marcus Antonius. To avoid capture after his defeat at Laodicea, Dolabella had one of his soldiers kill him. REF.: *CBA.*

Dolan, James J., 1848-98, U.S., west. gunman. James Dolan immigrated to the U.S. from Ireland and served on the Union side during the Civil War, later serving in the West and being mustered out at Fort Stanton. He went to work as a clerk for L.G. Murphy in Lincoln, N.M. He became a junior partner to Murphy, who was a cattle baron at war with John Tunstall, Alexander Mc-Sween, and others, including Billy the Kid. Dolan was proficient with a six-gun, an expertise that he proved on May 1, 1877, when he shot and killed 20-year-old Heraldo Jaramillo, an employee who pulled a gun on him. Dolan insisted at his trial that Jaramillo tried to murder him on behalf of the Tunstall faction, and he was acquitted. After Murphy died, Dolan became the chief opponent of the Tunstall-McSween faction, using his considerable funds to hire an army that eventually shot down all his adversaries. Dolan was later elected to the Territorial Council and died on his large ranch, the Flying H, on the site of John Tunstall's old ranch, on Feb. 26, 1898. See: **Billy the Kid; Lincoln County War.**

Gunman James Dolan, victor in the Lincoln County War.

REF.: Bartholomew, *The Biographical Album of Western Gunfighters; CBA;* Fulton, *Maurice Garland Fulton's History of the Lincoln County War.*

Dolan, Johnny (AKA: Dandy), c.1850-76, U.S., org. crime. Dandy Johnny Dolan created several innovations as a member of the Whyos, a New York street gang active after the Civil War. Dolan is credited with inventing a copper eye gouger which, when worn on the thumb, could pluck out a victim's eyeball in one swift move. Dolan also imbedded sharp ax blades in the soles of his boots. After wrestling an opponent to the ground, he stomped on him.

The Whyos quickly adopted Dolan's weapons for use in battles with rival gangs. In 1876, James H. Noe, a brush manufacturer, caught Dolan redhanded trying to rob his factory. Dolan used his eye gouger and came away with two souvenirs, which he proudly showed to his comrades. In the attack Mr. Noe was beaten to death. The police apprehended the young tough after they identified a cane he had stolen from Mr. Noe. Johnny Dolan was tried for murder, found Guilty, and executed on Apr. 21, 1876. See: **Whyos Gang.**

REF.: Asbury, *The Gangs of New York; CBA.*

Dolden, Kenneth Stuart, c.1922-46, Brit., (unsolv.) mur. As the winter of 1946 set in, life for the victim Kenneth Stuart Dolden, twenty-four, was displaying all the promises of youth. His war service was ending, allowing him to plan his wedding and future life with Jacynth Bland, twenty-one. He had many friends and hopes for a promising career. It all ended needlessly one Saturday night at Epping Forest, a young lovers' retreat, when a stranger wrenched open the back door of the car in which Dolden and his fiancee sat. The shadowy figure, guarded by a cloth cap pulled low over his head and a handkerchief wrapped high around his face, ordered Dolden out of his car. Then, without another word, the stranger shot young Dolden—three times—at point-blank range. As silently as he had approached, the stranger from the black forest vanished into the night.

Dolden made a heroic attempt to pursue his attacker but, weakened by his wounds, fell to his knees. Bland ran through a cold, darkened wood, screaming for help. She stumbled upon a car with another young couple parked along the highway. The driver instructed Bland and his date, whom he had just met that night, to wait alongside the road while he rushed off to the forest to look for Dolden and his assailant. That man was never seen again.

Word eventually reached the police, who scoured the forest for clues. They found an unconscious Dolden but no sign of his attacker. Detectives looked not just in the forest for clues but at the dying young man as well. Once sturdy and strong, young Dolden spent his last hours passing in and out of consciousness, trying desperately to aid detectives in capturing his murderer. He told them all he knew. "Hit on head..three shots fired...no idea who he was...wearing overcoat...think he was after the car..."

It was not enough to go on. Senior detectives from Scotland Yard were called in and an intense investigation ensued. For the next several days, every friend, relative, acquaintance, and couple who frequented Epping Forest were interrogated. But after days of struggling for a breakthrough, the only thing detectives could deduce was that there was no reason Dolden should have been murdered. He had no enemies. He hadn't argued with anyone recently. No other man was after his fiancee. Detectives considered, but readily rejected, Dolden's dying supposition that the man was after his car. The assailant had made no apparent effort to take the car. As for the man whom Bland asked for help, who promised to investigate but instead disappeared, police concluded that because he had been with a woman he had just met it was likely he was either married or held a responsible position in town and did not want to become involved in anything that could become public.

Unable to establish any motive or gather vital evidence, the police were left to play a guessing game which could serve no other purpose than to stimulate their curiosities. At the inquest on Kenneth Dolden, in January 1947, a verdict of murder by a person or persons unknown was returned. Police continued among themselves to wonder aloud what may have happened that November night. It may have been a big mistake. The murderer was so sure of himself, so deliberate in his attack and killing, but perhaps he realized too late that he had taken the wrong man's life. It is still anybody's guess.

REF.: *CBA; Firmin, Murderers In Our Midst; Simpson, FForty Years of Murder.*

Dole, Sanford Ballard, 1844-1926, U.S., lawyer. Served on Hawaiian supreme court as associate justice, 1887-93, as Republic of Hawaii president, 1894-1900, and as a U.S. district court judge, 1904-15. REF.: *CBA.*

Dolet, Étienne, 1509-46, Fr., her. Charged and convicted of atheism, for which he was imprisoned, 1542, 1544 and, 1546, tortured and finally burned at the stake. REF.: *CBA.*

Dolezal, Frank, c.1886-c.1938, Case of, U.S., suic.-mur. Dolezal, fifty-two, was not bothered by the murderous life he had lived for more than four years. But having other people know about it, and pass their harsh, yet justified, judgment on him, was too much to take. The man held for the bloody murders that plagued Ohio in the 1930s took his own life at the Cuyahoga County Jail while awaiting trial.

The first sign of something wrong appeared on Jackass Hill, where two boys went exploring after school only to discover a man's naked, headless body. Police turned up a second headless corpse, and eventually, two heads. Autopsies revealed that both men had been tied and decapitated while still alive. More horrifying, the beheading was carefully and thoughtfully done with slicing cuts, one at the front of the neck, running ear to ear, the other with a sweeping single blow from the rear. Little else could be discerned. One man was identified as Edward Andressy, who had expressed fears to friends about going out alone because an angry husband had threatened him for bothering his wife.

Four months later, Frank Dolezal provided investigators with more clues. These came in the form of a dismembered human body found inside two canvas bags and a hidden basket near Kingsbury Run. Two weeks later this puzzle was complete with the discovery of the legs and the left arm of a female. Police learned her name, Florence Sawdey Polillo, but her head never was found.

The grueling tale continued when the tattooed body of a young man was chanced upon by boys playing in a field. Then, in mid-summer, the decapitated head of another naked man appeared in a West Side creek. The discovery of parts of a male body stuck under a low bridge in mid-September marked one year since the murderous hell had begun. Thus far, at least four people had lost their lives in grisly murders, and worse still, no end was in sight.

That was grimly evident when, months later, a young woman's mutilated torso was discovered on the ice and snow-covered Lake Erie. Along with summer came more beheadings. A boy, while skipping stones on the Cuyahoga River, found a skeleton wrapped in a sack. Hopes that this might offer clues to the killer's identity were soon dashed and the police continued what seemed a futile task. Decapitated "No. Nine" was found one month later in the Cuyahoga River, the body parts of a male. Identification was impossible but the victim was believed to have been in his thirties.

And so it continued in the Cleveland area for four years, body after decapitated body discovered, each atrociously murdered. The unknown killer was identified only as an inhuman monster, and a blood-drenched ghoul.

Spring 1938 turned up the body of a female, characteristically beheaded, and, a possible clue to the killer's identity. The coroner noted the severed leg cleanly and expertly cut at the knee and ankle. The murderer, however diabolical, was skilled with a knife and had the luxury of dismembering his victims at a leisurely pace. It was perhaps a step closer to apprehending the fiend. After victim "No. Ten" the police went into high alert in searching for the killer, but their efforts proved futile.

Meanwhile, victims eleven and twelve were discovered. One, a young woman, was found under a rock pile along the lake, the body dismembered, and it appeared as though the killer had attempted to sever the head but had given up. The other, also located along the lakeshore was badly decomposed and nothing remained but about forty bones and a skull wrapped in an old quilt. The baffled police and detectives, including a former special agent of the FBI, had taken on the case only to give up and lose credibility. Now a new special agent appeared on the scene suggesting the obvious, that the police look for the place where this madman did his butchering. The places to look could be narrowed down if one remembered that, first, no shrieks were heard, so the murderer probably worked in a fairly soundproof place. Next, the place would have been kept clean but not obviously so. Lastly, it must have facilities to store parts of dismembered bodies. The detectives scouted all such likely places, ice cream warehouses, factories, breweries, before they changed their strategy by centering on people versus places.

This was just the fine tuning the new agent's plan needed to work. Police descended on a bar known to have been a favorite hang-out for two of the victims. From there a house-to-house search began and they learned of a man named Frank who had an unusual interest in very large knives. After continuous, shot-in-the-dark questioning, the investigators slowly learned more about this man than they could stomach. He had once worked in a Cleveland slaughterhouse, had lived close to the two victims' favorite tavern, as well as the site where several of the bodies were found, and he owned a chef's supply of butcher knives. He was not such a tidy cleaner, however. Investigators found long-dried human blood between the tile cracks in his bathroom. His name was Frank Dolezal, and finally, after years of terror, he fell into police custody.

Riotous crowd demonstrations against this prize catch and threats from fellow jail inmates proved more than this serial killer could emotionally withstand. Before a trial was even scheduled, Dolezal made a noose and from rags he had hoarded and hanged himself.

REF.: *CBA;* Gribble, *The Dead End Killers.*

Dolgoruki, Pëtr Vladimirovich, (Pëtr Vladimirovich Dolgorukov), 1817-68, Rus., treas. Authored the book *The Truth about Russia,* 1860, for which he was exiled. REF.: *CBA.*

Dollfuss, Engelbert, 1892-1934, Aust., chancellor, assass. The illegitimate son of a laborer and a farmer's daughter, the future chancellor of Austria never grew beyond four feet, eleven inches and many incorrectly considered him a dwarf. After his mother, Josepha Dollfuss, married Leopold Schmutz of Kirnberg in Lower Austria, Engelbert Dollfuss was raised on his stepfather's farm, later entering the Episcopal seminary, graduating in 1913 and attending the University of Vienna. Dollfuss planned to study law, but he joined the Imperial Austrian Army in 1914 at the outbreak of WWI. He entered officer candidate school and served along the Alpine front, facing the Italians, from 1915 to 1918. By the time Dollfuss was mustered out of the army as a first lieutenant, the old Austro-Hungarian Empire, ruled for centuries by the Hapsburgs, had ceased to exist.

Dollfuss's rank and medals won during the war meant nothing in civilian life, since Austria had been defeated and the consensus of the public was that the old royalty, as typified by Emperor Franz Josef, the nobility surrounding the throne and the military that had energetically pursued the war, had brought the nation to social chaos and economic ruin. After working his way through college as a farm laborer, Dollfuss married in 1921, selecting a German wife. He took his doctorate in law in 1922. Always pro-German, Dollfuss joined the ultra-conservative Christian Social Party (now the Austrian People's Party) and rose through the ranks. He was appointed president of the powerful Federal Railway Board in 1930. The following year, Dollfuss was appointed minister for agriculture.

In 1932, Austria was undergoing a severe economic depression, as were most of its European neighbors, and its government, torn between reactionary rightists and revolutionary leftists, was in a state of chaos. In a particularly stormy parliamentary crisis, Dollfuss, in May 1932, was named federal chancellor (or prime minister). Dollfuss's support came from the coalition of the Heimwehr (or Heimatschutz), meaning Home Guard, and the Peasant Party. The Heimwehr was a paramilitary organization led by reactionary officers who had sought to reestablish the supremacy of the military in Austria, much like Hitler's Brown Shirt legions in Germany. The Heimwehr was headed by Major Emil Fey in Vienna and in the provinces by Prince Ernst Ruediger von Starhemberg, a descendant of an old Austrian line of nobility. Starhemberg was really a pleasure-seeking playboy who acted more like a boy scout leader with his men than a military chief. The prince considered his men a weak military force that, in his own words, acted out the part of "a kind of Praetorian Guard."

Major Fey, who proved to be the pivotal person in the plot to assassinate Dollfuss in 1934, was one of the most decorated officers in Austria, a war hero who wore the coveted Cross of Maria Theresa. Fey commanded the Vienna Heimwehr and had an abiding hatred for Marxists and all political leftists. Though the Heimwehr was a fascist organization, Fey always expressed his political ideas in vague terms, stating that he was first and foremost a soldier, a military man sworn to uphold the government. He was, like all the Heimwehr members, anti-Semitic and anti-leftist, following the same twisted ideologies as Adolf Hitler and his minions in Germany, except that the Heimwehr was careful not to offend the Catholic Church because Austria was and had been for centuries a predominately Catholic country.

Dollfuss himself, a clever power-hungry martinet, held the same beliefs as the Heimwehr and his goal was the utter destruction of all opposition, chiefly the socialists, and assumption of total

dictatorial powers. He feared Hitler and his expansionist plans for Austria on one hand and on the other the powerful Republican Defense Corps, or *schutzbund,* headed by elderly leftist General Theodor von Koerner-Sigmarigen, known simply as General Koerner. The socialists, who had gained 44 per cent of the Austrian vote in 1930, numbered in the millions and their own paramilitary forces wielded considerable power. Dollfuss sought protection against both Hitler and the Austrian socialists by forming an alliance with Italy's Benito Mussolini and going to Rome in 1933 to sign an arms pact. Mussolini promised to blunt any moves toward annexation of Austria by Germany, but he insisted that Dollfuss move against the Republican Defense Corps. Dollfuss promised to destroy this organization and Mussolini, as a show of force to Hitler, moved his best Alpine troops into the Brenner Pass.

Hitler, newly in power in Germany, was not prepared to face Mussolini's Italy or any other nation in a show of force. He nevertheless encouraged the thousands of Austrian Nazis actively to undermine Dollfuss's government. By 1933, Dollfuss became dictator of Austria, dissolving Parliament and outlawing all parties except his own. The Austrian Parliament had, in essence, destroyed itself in a bizarre session on Mar. 4, 1933. A representative left the floor to go the washroom and asked a colleague to vote for him, but the colleague marked the ballot incorrectly. The speaker of the house, Dr. Karl Renner, noting the irregularity, declared the balloting invalid and this led to a fiery debate in which Renner abruptly resigned as president of the assembly. His deputy resigned, and so did the next deputy. In the explosive debate that followed, no one officially closed the session. Under Austrian law, only the president of the assembly or one of his deputies could convoke a new assembly. Because none existed, Dollfuss seized the opportunity to abolish Parliament, stating that it could not function under the law. The Parliament had eliminated itself, he stated in a Mar. 7, 1933, declaration. He then assumed completed governmental powers. He banned all public meetings and gatherings, and began strict censorship of the press.

Dollfuss believed he had successfully choked off opposition to his regime inside Austria, but he began to feel the weight of Nazi influence. Austrian Nazis, however, lobbied for a fusion or *Anschluss,* of Germany and Austria, both German-speaking nations with common customs and traditions. This concept was not new. For decades there had been strong movements to join the two countries and now, with the Hohenzollern and Hapsburg dynasties gone following WWI, the prospect of an *Anschluss* seemed inevitable and was supported with a show of threatening force along the German border, where Hitler amassed thousands of well-equipped troops. In Munich, one of Hitler's leading Brown Shirt chiefs, Theo Habicht, was named "Inspector General for Austria," a pompous and illegal title conferred by Hitler upon a German with no credentials or legitimate office in Austria.

Habicht, a propaganda expert, began a smear campaign in which Dollfuss was portrayed as a pawn of the Jews, the Catholic Church and foreign powers. Powerful radio stations along the German border beamed this propaganda into Austria around the clock. Austrian Nazis suddenly appeared in all major Austrian cities, painting the swastika everywhere. Nazis set off bombs in churches, synagogues, and in the offices of liberal newspapers in June 1933, and many persons were killed and injured. Then the Nazis attacked Dollfuss's military police. A group of Nazis threw hand grenades into a group of officers in Vienna, killing several. Now that the Nazis were attacking his own fascist forces, Dollfuss acted, banning the Nazi Party in Austria, arresting and imprisoning almost 1,500 Nazis. Leaders such as Alfred Edward Frauenfeld, *Gauleiter* of Vienna, fled to Germany and the protection of Habicht's organization. Habicht boldly created the Austrian Legion, 15,000 strong and made up of Nazi expatriates from Austria. He armed these troops, who paraded menacingly up and down the German border, threatening invasion at any moment.

Dollfuss, unnerved, tried to contact Hitler to negotiate some sort of truce, but Hitler made himself unavailable. Dollfuss's representatives were shunted off to see Habicht in Munich or the German ambassador in Vienna, Dr. Kurt Rieth, and there the answer was always the same: *Anschluss*. Habicht, after some negotiations, brazenly demanded that before further truces could be considered, all charges against Nazis in Austria be dropped and that *he* be made vice chancellor, even though he was not an Austrian citizen. With such outlandish proposals, no hope of a settlement remained between the besieged Dollfuss and the Nazis. Dollfuss did make Major Fey vice chancellor, but this failed to appease the Nazis and so he invited Habicht to fly to Vienna and meet secretly with him in his home. Habicht was *en route* when Dollfuss called off the meeting. The chancellor had been pressured by Fey and Starhemberg to cancel the Habicht meeting as beneath the dignity of proper political protocol, as Habicht had no accredited standing to negotiate anything. When the German ambassador was notified of this decision, Habicht was already in the air and his plane was radioed personally by Hitler, who ordered the eager Habicht to return to Munich.

Then a sudden move from the left, unexpected by the Dollfuss government, brought the Heimwehr into the streets of Vienna in full and deadly force. On the night of Feb. 11, 1934, socialist leaders began shipping arms to workers in Vienna, Linz, and other cities in Austria, calling them to arms against Dollfuss' totalitarian state. The messages sent out by various *schutzbund* leaders were intercepted, and on Feb. 12, 1934, police stormed the socialist democrat headquarters in Linz, attempting to disarm workers, and were fired on by heavily armed leftist radicals led by Richard Bernaschek. Otto Bauer, Julius Deutsch, and other socialist leaders in Vienna called a general strike and seized all important government buildings in Vienna. Government troops were joined by the Heimwehr, and these two forces soon had the *schutzbund* on the defensive.

Dollfuss ordered the military to attack the huge housing areas occupied by the socialists, chiefly the Karl Marx House in Vienna, which housed several arsenals. Fey wheeled out his artillery, at the little dictator's explicit orders, and took great delight in shelling this complex. Light mountain howitzers of WWI vintage were trained on the Karl Marx House and the Goethe House, which strategically overlooked a major bridge spanning the Danube. Shelling commenced on the night of Feb. 12, 1934, and the socialists offered stiff resistance in Vienna and elsewhere, but after four days, Austria's brief civil war was over, the government and Heimwehr troops having crushed all resistance in Vienna, Linz, Steyr, and Kapefenberg. Many socialist leaders were rounded up and summarily hanged, hundreds were imprisoned. The 128 government and Heimwehr dead were buried with full military honors with Catholic Cardinal Theodor Innitzer offering elaborate services. Cardinal Innitzer made no secret of his support for fascist regimes; he would later curry favor with Hitler's Austrian puppets when the country was taken over by the Nazis. The 193 socialists killed in the fighting were buried in a mass grave without ceremonies. Most of the socialist leaders, such as Bauer and Deutsch, went into exile.

About 400 more on each side of the conflict had been wounded, and Dollfuss emerged victorious but stigmatized for having ordered artillery to fire on civilians. The world's press was quick to point out that hundreds of women and children in the Karl Marx and Goethe apartment houses were also the targets of Dollfuss's directed shells. No longer was diminutive Engelbert Dollfuss "that charming little chancellor from Austria." He was as brutal a fascist as Hitler and Mussolini. The Austrian people did not side against the tyrant, but they no longer trusted Dollfuss and the workers remained hostile to his regime. Hitler, on the other hand, was startled by the direct action taken by Dollfuss; he had underestimated the little dictator's will to act. Mussolini sent Dollfuss open letters of admiration for crushing the socialists.

Hitler's minions found it increasingly difficult to attack Dollfuss as a tool of western democracies and a supporter of socialists after his iron-fisted action against the socialists, his continued oppressions against the Jews and his establishment of a totalitarian state almost identical to that in Germany. The Nazis took new turns in their propaganda, mailing millions of letters to Austrian citizens in which Dollfuss's photo was adorned with the words: "I am a traitor to my people." The message inside each letter detailed Dollfuss's refusal to reunite Austria with Germany, a historic destiny. Meanwhile, dedicated Nazis inside Austria held secret meetings and planned Dollfuss's downfall. These included many Nazi fanatics who would later become notorious such as Ernst Kaltenbrunner, a lawyer from Linz who would become one of Heinrich Himmler's top aides and be responsible for millions dying in concentration camps. Also included in these active Austrian Nazi groups was Albin Rauter, a Heimwehr officer who would later become SS chief in the Netherlands and be shot there in 1949 as a war criminal, and Otto Globocnik, *Gauleiter* of Vienna in 1938 following the *Anschluss* and later SS chief in Lublin, Pol., who would take his own life at the end of WWII.

Joining the Nazis were right-wing Austrian politicians, the most important of whom was Dr. Anton Rintelen, Austrian ambassador to Rome, who had held several important positions in the Austrian government since 1922 and who had routinely harrassed and arrested socialists and left-wing leaders since the early 1920s. Rintelen had coveted the chancellorship of Austria, and in early 1934, contacted Habicht in Munich, thinking the Nazis were the building blocks to his political ambitions. Habicht's chief of staff, Dr. Rudolf Weydenhammer, took more than a dozen trips to Rome from Munich in the spring of 1934, to plot with Rintelen for the overthrow of Dollfuss. Rintelen's intrigues with the Nazis brought other right-wing Austrian leaders such as Dr. Walter Nagelstock, editor of the powerful *Neue Wiener Journal,* and Franz Winkler, former vice chancellor, into the Nazi camp. With the indirect help of these men, Habicht instituted a terrorist campaign in Austria in the spring of 1934, his men planting bombs in electrical and water works, train stations, and telephone exchanges. On May 19, the Nazis blew up many sections of railway track around Vienna, crippling commercial traffic. The terrorist acts were committed by the Austrian Brown Shirts or SA (*Sturmabteilung*), which made up the largest segment of Austrian Nazis, although there existed a small but fanatical SS (*Schutzstaffel*) group, SS Standarte 89, led by Fridolin Glass.

While these terrorist acts continued, Hitler traveled to Italy and cemented relations with Mussolini. *Il Duce* agreed to allow the Nazis to conduct a coup (or putsch) whereby Dollfuss would be replaced by a "neutral" Austrian leader who would call for an election, which would then be controlled by the Nazis and deliver a vote for *Anschluss,* thus fusing Austria to Germany and creating a superstate which would become Mussolini's staunchest ally. Once the Italian dictator gave Hitler the go-ahead, Dollfuss' fate was sealed. Dr. Gustav Otto Waechter, one of the leaders of the National Socialists in Austria, traveled to Germany on May 31, 1934, and explained to Gerhard Koepke, director of the Foreign Affairs Ministry, that the Austrian Nazis were ill-prepared to carry out a prolonged propaganda and terrorist campaign against Dollfuss. The bombings had only created hostility and apprehension toward the Nazis on the part of the public and the SA and SS Nazis in Austria were few in number and ill-organized. Waechter proposed that instead of a lengthy political campaign to get rid of Dollfuss, the dictator should be eliminated in one quick move.

On June 6, 1934, Hitler was briefed about Waechter's visit and statements and he called in his henchman, Theo Habicht, giving him orders to attempt a violent putsch in Austria. Habicht, in turn, contacted the underground Nazi leaders in Austria, many of these being in the police force in Vienna, including Dr. Leo Gotzman, a police chief, and Dr. Steinhaeusl, a forensic expert. Inside the chancellery itself, Habicht had planted a Nazi mole, Franz Kamba, a plainclothes policeman who occasionally guarded Dollfuss. More than 1,000 members of the Vienna police force were secret Nazis. In the army, the Nazis had high-placed men such as Lieutenant-Colonel Adolf Sinzinger, chief-of-staff for the Vienna command, and one of his aides, Major Rudolph Selinger,

Chancellor Engelbert Dollfuss.

Conspirator Anton Rintelen.

SS leader Franz Holzweber.

Assassin Otto Planetta.

Dollfuss reviewing troops.

Heimwar leader Emil Fey.

The Karl Marx Hof after bombardment, February 1934.

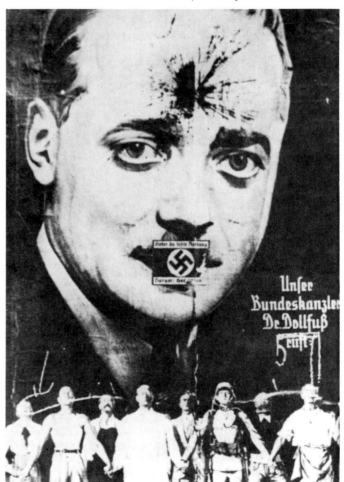
Nazi defacement of Dollfuss poster in Vienna.

acted as liaison to the secret Nazis in the Vienna police force.

Hitler, through Habicht, designated the SS Standarte 89 as the striking arm of the Nazi revolutionaries who would overthrow Dollfuss. These Austrian SS members were better educated and occupied higher social positions than the thugs of the SA. Most, like Paul Hudl and Otto Planetta, were older men who had served in the Austrian army during WWI. Hudl had been an officer in the Imperial Austrian Army while Planetta, who would become Dollfuss' personal executioner, ironically served as an enlisted man in the same regiment as his victim. The Nazi plan was in two parts, and Operation Summer Festival was the code name of the first phase. This was a military action concentrated in the capital. The entire Cabinet was to be arrested in the chancellery building—including President Wilhelm Milas and Chancellor Dollfuss—by the main force of the SS Starndarte 89, while a splinter portion of this group captured the central radio station in the Ravag Building in the heart of Vienna in order to broadcast to the nation the lie that the government had resigned and that Dr. Anton Rintelen had been named chancellor. Once this was accomplished, the second part of the Nazi plan could begin. Operation Price Shooting was a nationwide uprising to be led by Austrian Nazis throughout the country, who would seize all strategic buildings and government operations in major cities and towns and crush the Austrian army.

It was rightly concluded by the Nazis that, to have the second phase succeed, the first phase must be accomplished. If Vienna did not fall to the Nazis, the rest of the nation would resist the Nazis in force and this would mean that the well-equipped Austrian army would be able to eventually overthrow the Nazis in the provinces. The Nazis knew their forces were sizeable but still in the minority in Austria. They reasoned correctly in assuming the socialists would not lift a finger to save the Dollfuss regime and this eliminated a large part of the opposition the Nazis would have normally faced. The Heimwehr was the only serious opposing force that concerned the Austrian Nazis. Major Fey may have been contacted by the Nazis and may have secretly agreed to withhold Heimwehr support from Dollfuss at the critical moment. He had privately complained about not being rewarded properly for his services to the regime and may have thought to advance himself by secretly cooperating with the Nazi putschists. Although no clear evidence suggests this was the case, Fey's subsequent actions suggest monumental indecision on his part, if not outright collusion with the Nazis, which contributed to a state of near chaos when the attack against the government began.

The Austrian Nazis were told that they could expect no help from the German Army or even SS Germans, since this would be looked upon as a blatant act of aggression. They would, as Austrians, have to take over their own country. The SS Stardarte 89 was a pitiable force to achieve such ends, only about 150 men, supplemented by secret Nazi sympathizers in the police force, Austrian Army, and Heimwehr, if these traitors would, indeed, act. Of uncertain use was the Austrian SA or Brown shirts, an unreliable bunch of ruffians, according to most SS leaders. There was a great deal of distrust of the Austrian Brown shirts by the SS, although SA leader Hermann Reschny was kept informed of all the details of the plot. One SA chief, a man named Kirchbach, warned Austrian authorities of an impending coup and mentioned the names of Waechter, Glass, and Weydenhammer. Meanwhile, Dollfuss was alarmed when Hitler purged the SA on June 30, 1934, ordering the executions of scores of SA leaders throughout Germany, including his once-trusted aide, Ernst Roehm. He believed that Austria was next but he had no idea where the Nazis would strike. Prince Starhemberg, after a visit to Hungary, returned with warnings from the Hungarian Prime Minister, Gyula Gömbös, who told Starhemberg that Major Fey should not be trusted. Then Starhemberg took a convenient vacation to Italy.

On July 23, 1934, Dr. Anton Rintelen arrived in Vienna, moving into a suite at the luxurious Hotel Imperial. Meeting him there was Rudolf Weydenhammer, visiting Vienna in disguise, using a British passport. Other conspirators arrived and it was decided that they would have to act on July 24, 1934, the date on which the Austrian cabinet would hold its final session before the summer recess. Fridolin Glass ordered his top aide, Franz Holzweber, who wore glasses and a copycat Hitler mustache, to lead the attack on the Austrian chancellery. Hans Domes and fifteen men were to seize the central radio station in the Ravag Building. Once the Cabinet had been arrested and the radio station had broadcast the "resignations" and Rintelen's appointment, Glass was to contact the traitorous Austrian officer, Lieutenant-Colonel Sinzinger, who was expected to order his regular Austrian troops to support the Nazi conspirators.

The Nazis were set, on July 24, to truck its main contingent to the chancellery, and arrive at 5:45 p.m. to arrest the leaders of the government but they learned from Rintelen late on the night of July 23 that the meeting of the cabinet ministers was postponed until July 25. This so unnerved some of the conspirators that they had second thoughts about participating in the coup. One of these, Paul Hudl, one-time officer in the Imperial Guard, nervously met the next morning with a friend, Rudolf Wurmbrand, another former officer, and informed him of the plot. Wurmbrand, as Hudl expected, informed police. An official police report was sent to the chancellery at 4:30 p.m., but since nothing occurred on that day, as the report stated, the report was merely filed and forgotten.

The next day, July 25, 1934, the conspirators made arrangements to strike that afternoon. One of their number was Johann Dobler, a policeman in Vienna who had been a member of the Nazi party before the party was outlawed. He had been recruited for the putsch as late as July 23 by Josef Steiner, a fellow policeman who told him that a number of police officers would be joining the SS Standarte 89 once that elite group of conspirators took over the chancellery. Dobler grew jittery on the morning of July 25 and contacted several persons in the government, outlining the plot. Emil Fey received Dobler's report through two top aides and incredibly, did not act upon it immediately. He hesitated and then decided to wait and see if any more reports about a coup were received.

Meanwhile, the SS Standarte 89 assembled in a gym on Siebeusternstrasse, dozens of men arriving either in the uniform of the Austrian army or as civilians carrying bundles beneath their arms. The SS members planned to don Austrian Army uniforms and thus make an easier entrance into the chancellery. Trucks then began to arrive and the Nazis marched out of the gym and into the trucks. All of this was witnessed by a policeman, Anton Marek, who at 12:10 p.m., called the chancellery. Fey was informed and finally he took Dollfuss aside and told him that the government members were about to be attacked by the Nazis. At first Dollfuss refused to believe the report but Fey insisted that it was true. Dollfuss addressed the cabinet nervously, stating: "Fey just told me something. I don't know if there is anything behind it but perhaps it's better to interrupt our session now. Every minister should return to his own department. I shall let you gentlemen know when we can continue."

Dollfuss overruled objections and dismissed the cabinet, asking Fey, Baron Erwin Karwinsky, and General Wilhelm Zehner to remain with him. In Dollfuss' inner office, the Chancellor asked Fey to repeat what he had told him earlier in front of Karwinsky and Zehner. Fey was a man of few words and proved it, stating: "I have received a message that an attack is planned against the Ballhausplatz. A gym in the Siebeusternstrasse is supposed to have something to do with it." Fey did not mention that he had ordered one of his nearby Heimwehr regiments to march to the chancellery to protect the government. Meanwhile, the special forces of the Vienna police were concentrated about the Michaeler Platz where, a report confirmed, conspirators were gathering to assassinate Dollfuss. This left the chancellery almost unguarded. The police force, whether through its conniving Nazi members or through sheer ineptitude, was guarding the wrong place at the wrong time. There was a token unit of soldiers at the front of the chancellery, but they were not fighting troops and they had no ammunition in their guns.

Policeman Marek called the chancellery again to report that more trucks were being loaded and were leaving for the seat of government at the Ballhausplatz. He called a third time, frantically shouting over the phone: "Four more trucks have driven up in front of the building (the gym). Those men are mounting the trucks. There is no more time to lose!" Dollfuss heard this news and sent General Zehner to leave the chancellery and return with troops. Karwinsky called police headquarters, demanding special squads of "alarm police" be sent to the chancellery immediately but only a motorcycle policeman arrived, ordered to "observe events."

Oddly, Dollfuss gave no thought at this time of leaving the chancellery, perhaps believing that the guards stationed at the front of the sprawling building would be able to stop any intruders, but Fey could have told him that this handful of unarmed men would be helpless against 150 well-armed, well-trained, fanatical Nazis. The guards at the front of the baroque, cream-colored government building did not even notice the invaders when they arrived. At 12:50 p.m., a contingent of soldiers arrived, as usual, to relieve those on duty at the entrance to the chancellery, and right behind them were eight trucks loaded with the Nazi conspirators. The trucks merely drove in behind the relief troops and into the main courtyard where they climbed out of the trucks in their makeshift Austrian Army uniforms. Ten policemen guided them into the court and these men were led by Paul Hudl, who had informed on his fellow conspirators but, when nothing came of his warning to July 24, decided to go ahead with the putschists on the following day. The SS men were led by Franz Holzweber and Otto Planetta, both dressed in the uniforms of Austrian captains.

The regular troops were stripped of their useless rifles by the SS men while police officials and Fey's Heimwehr officers on duty at the entrance merely stood by, watching. The Nazis rounded up all the chancellery employees and servants and locked them in basement rooms. Dollfuss, Karwinsky, and Fey looked out the windows to the courtyard and saw the trucks arriving, believing these men to be troops sent by General Zehner. Major Karl Wrabel, Fey's top aide, then burst into Dollfuss' private office to shout: "The Nazis are in the building!" Karwinsky grabbed the Chancellor by the arm and told him of an abandoned cloak room on the third floor, saying: "Chancellor, come to the third floor. You will be safe there." At the same time, a personal servant to Dollfuss, named Hedvicek, appeared and shouted that the Chancellor would only be safe by getting to the corner room, an office next to Dollfuss' private chambers, which led down the back stairs to the Minoritenplatz where no Nazi men were stationed. Hedvicek was right but he acted too late. By the time he pulled Dollfuss into the corner room, SS men raced into the chancellor's private chambers and trapped Dollfuss while his servant fiddled with the door leading to the back staircases.

Karwinsky, Fey, and Wrabel had already been placed under arrest. Otto Planetta and others ran into the corner room and saw Dollfuss and Hedvicek. Planetta ran forward, gun in hand, aiming this at Dollfuss, who raised his hands to his face as if to protect himself. Planetta, without a word, fired twice and the Chancellor fell to the floor. He cried out for help but Planetta only sneered and then shouted: "Get up!" Planetta later claimed at his trial that he rushed into a darkened room and that he saw three shadowy figures. One of them raised his arm and he thought he was about to be fired upon and instinctively fired only one bullet, unintentionally shooting Dollfuss. Two bullets, nevertheless, struck Dollfuss at a distance of six inches, one creating a superficial wound in the neck. The other was fatal, entering his throat and spinal column and exiting beneath the right armpit.

The SS men left Dollfuss on the floor to bleed to death. SS man Viktor Stiastny leaned down and unbuttoned the Chancellor's jacket, not to give him relief but to see if reports that Dollfuss wore a bulletproof vest were true. They were not. Stiastny then took the Chancellor's wallet and handed this to Franz Holzweber, who was then marching into the room to inspect the premises. (The wallet was later found stripped of its cash by the Nazi thugs.) Forty minutes passed before the SS men asked some of the prisoners downstairs if any of them knew how to administer first aid. Rudolf Messinger and Johann Greifeneder, two policemen loyal to the government, volunteered and were taken upstairs to see that Dollfuss had been shot. It was 1:45 p.m. Dollfuss was unconscious on the floor, bleeding. Ten SS men stood about the corner room doing nothing. Planetta sat at a desk, smoking. The policemen demanded that a doctor be sent for but Hudl, in charge of the police siding with the SS men, refused to do so.

The policemen were allowed to pick up Dollfuss and place him on a couch. They were given bandages and they tried to stop the bleeding. Hudl, now nervous, stood over Dollfuss, who became conscious. Hudl told him that if he had not resisted he would not have been shot. Dollfuss seemed confused, talking in a low voice, saying that he, too, had once been a soldier. "How are my ministers?" he asked. An SS man told the Chancellor that they were alive and well. Then, perhaps thinking that he was talking to regular army officers, Dollfuss stated: "A major, a captain, and several soldiers came in and shot me."

Then an incredible political argument ensued, but perhaps it was no more incredible than the comic opera plot and assassination. One of the SS men shouted: "You are to blame for all this, bringing misery to the National Socialists of Austria."

"I have always tried to the best I could," moaned Dollfuss. "I always wanted peace."

"If that was the case," yelled another Nazi, "why didn't you make peace with Germany?"

Replied Dollfuss in a weakening voice: "Children, you simply don't understand." He then asked to see his Minister of Education, Kurt von Schuschnigg, but was told by Hudl that Schuschnigg was not in the chancellery. Hudl then pressured the dying Dollfuss to call Rintelen and have him form a new government to save Austria from chaos.

Dollfuss did not respond to this but asked the policemen trying to help him to move his arms and legs, adding: "I feel nothing. I think I am paralyzed." He asked for a doctor. Hudl refused this request. He asked for a priest. Hudl or Planetta refused.

Outside, loyal Austrian forces were closing in on the Nazis. Only fifteen minutes after the SS Standarte 89 occupied the chancellery, Fey's Heimwehr regiment arrived, along with troops from General Zehner and squads of police. They surrounded the building and began arresting everyone walking about the area, including Nazi leader Fridolin Glass, who was picked up a block away from the chancellery in the disguise of an old peddler. Another leading conspirator, Waechter, sat in a restaurant nervously eyeing the troops surrounding his co-plotters. It had been his job to enter the chancellery and negotiate the surrender of the cabinet, but eight of the eleven ministers had fled the building before the Nazis arrived. Now, there was nothing to negotiate. Dr. Rintelen and Weydenhammer sat in the Hotel Imperial, waiting for good news that did not come.

The surrounded Nazis also waited for the Nazi sympathizers with the army and police to come to their aid, but this did not happen. These traitors remained silent at their posts, realizing that the coup had already failed once the cabinet ministers and President Miklas had escaped and were safe. General Zehner was in complete control of the army and more units arrived to strengthen the cordon surrounding the chancellery. Holzweber seemed gripped by inertia, cut off from his superiors Glass and Waechter. He gave no orders and was later to say at his trial: "I had been told that there would be no bloodshed, that a new government had already been formed, and that Rintelen was present at the Ballhausplatz. Then, at the chancellery, I missed the leaders of the uprising."

President Miklas was contacted at his lakeside retreat in Velden, and here he talked by phone to Schuschnigg, making him provisional chancellor, telling him to "use all forces of the government to restore law and order. Take measures against the rebels and, above all, liberate the captive members of the government. They are to be delivered safe and sound from their captivity." More and more troops poured into the area around the chancellery, waiting for orders to storm the ornate building. Holzweber and his men closed the windows of the chancellery and drew the blinds so that the place was soon an oven as the hot July sun beat down on it. The SS men anxiously walked about the corridors smoking, asking about their reinforcements, and dripping sweat. There was a sense of doom and failure among their ranks, even though their comrades had earlier seized the radio station and announced the fall of the Dollfuss regime and the appointment of Rintelen, before they themselves were captured.

In Berlin, the man behind the coup, Adolf Hitler, was listening to a performance of *Das Rheingold* at the annual Wagner festival in Bayreuth. Two aides who were in constant phone contact with Vienna scurried in and out of Hitler's box to whisper the news of the coup to him, and their reports described a Nazi success. Hitler was so overjoyed that he could hardly contain himself, grinning and squirming in his chair. Following the performance, Hitler ordered a large dinner in a nearby restaurant and then said, "I must go across for an hour and show myself or people will think I had something to do with this."

Inside the Austrian chancellery the conspirators were growing desperate. Gun in hand, the impetuous Planetta shouted at the dying Dollfuss on the couch: "Get down to brass tacks, Chancellor. We're not interested in talk. Order Fey to stop the armed forces from any action. Rintelen should be authorized to form a new government."

Dollfuss was in a semi-conscious state and responded with the vague remark: "There should be no bloodshed. Rintelen should make peace."

"Say what you have to tell us!" screamed an SS man.

But Engelbert Dollfuss was breathing his last. A ribbon of bloody foam formed on his lips. He lapsed in and out of consciousness. Again the administering policemen requested a doctor and Holzweber and Planetta angrily refused. A priest was requested and again refused. The SS men now felt their cause was doomed and they would, at least, revenge themselves on Dollfuss by refusing him any comfort, physical or spiritual, in his last moments. They intended for the chancellor to die, this was apparent. After getting nothing of value from Dollfuss, the Nazis sat about watching him die, silently staring at the little dictator with hatred.

Dollfuss spoke his last at about 4 p.m., his thoughts incoherent as he slipped into babble: "Children, you are so good to me. Why are the others not like you? I only wanted peace. We never attacked. We only had to defend ourselves. May the Lord forgive them. Give my regards to my wife and my children." Although the chancellor died at about 4 p.m., news was not released by the Nazis of his death until about an hour later and this was leaked by the conspirators. The Nazis approached Karwinsky and asked that he negotiate with the troops outside but Karwinsky proved truculent. They went to Fey, who had apparently made a secret deal with the Nazis. He wrote in pencil on a scrap of paper: "Dr. Dollfuss has been injured and resigned from the government. He has appointed Dr. Rintelen as his successor. All armed forces are now under Fey's command." The Nazi plainclothes policeman, Kamba, was given this message and he managed to get through the lines outside and deliver the message to Police Chief Eugen Seydel, who ignored it and then had Rintelen arrested.

Fey later appeared on a balcony, Holzweber, next to him, holding a pistol to his head. Another SS man held Fey's ankles so he could not leap to the courtyard below. The Heimwehr men below shouted loyalty oaths to their commander. Fey shouted back: "Men, the persons within the chancellery are in danger but everything will be all right." Fey went back inside the building and later made several calls to other officials, insisting that Rintelen take charge of the government, but he was curtly informed that Schuschnigg was now provisional head of the government and that

he would tolerate no more defiance on the part of the SS men. They were to surrender or be wiped out to the last man. Fey was asked about Dollfuss' condition and, though he knew the Chancellor was dead, replied: "His injuries are rather serious." For such preposterous behavior, Fey's political career came to an end, but his true role in the coup attempt was kept secret so as not to undermine the new Austrian government under Schuschnigg, and to keep the Heimwehr, ever loyal to Fey, within the ranks of the government.

Of the fifteen Nazis who had shot their way into the radio station, killing several guards and forcing an announcer to broadcast the downfall of Dollfuss and the appointment of Rintelen, thirteen had been driven to the top floor of the Ravag Building and were captured after a gun battle. One SS man had been killed and another escaped. When two officers went to Rintelen's suite to arrest him at the Hotel Imperial, Rintelen shot himself but bungled the suicide, only wounding himself in the side. He was taken to a hospital where he later recovered. He would later be imprisoned, released shortly before the German *Anschluss* and becoming a German functionary, dying almost unknown and certainly unlamented in 1946.

The Nazis in the provinces rose briefly but all too late, and were crushed by the Austrian army and the Heimwehr. The fate of the SS men in the chancellery was negotiated with Schuschnigg, who agreed to allow the Nazis safe conduct to the German border if they surrendered their arms. This the Nazis did but, as they were climbing into trucks to be transported out of the country, Dollfuss' half-naked body was discovered and Schuschnigg announced that the Nazis had violated the agreement which was based on no loss of life. Now, it was revealed that they had assassinated the chancellor and for that they would have to stand trial. All were arrested and imprisoned in the police barracks at the Marokkanergasse. All were later placed on trial and vigorously prosecuted, especially after Hitler denounced the Austrian Nazis.

The German dictator soon realized that Habicht and his Austrian henchmen had failed. Hitler quickly backed away from the coup and separated himself from his Nazi followers, ordering a halt to broadcasts from Germany which urged the overthrow of the Austrian government. Hitler issued his regrets at "the cruel murder" of Dollfuss and stated that the coup was "purely an Austrian affair." Habicht was fired and sent to a menial post. Franz von Papen replaced the German ambassador to Austria with orders to reestablish "normal and friendly relations." The strutting, insidious Hitler was suddenly seized by the thought that the Western European countries might hold him accountable for the bungled coup in Vienna and place Dollfuss' murder at his door, where it rightfully belonged. He so firmly denounced the Austrian SS men that the Schuschnigg government had no qualms in prosecuting Dollfuss' killers.

In the Vienna police barracks where the Nazis were confined, a police officer identified Holzweber as having served in the Austrian army. Some of the plotters, when they heard the rumor (and it was never anything but) that every tenth SS man was to be shot, identified Holzweber as their leader. Planetta's name was offered by some of the Nazis as the man who shot Dollfuss and Planetta, thinking all the others would go free if he confessed, admitted to shooting the chancellor, but he insisted that his gun had gone off by accident and that he had only fired a single shot. (Admitting to having fired two shots, of course, would have destroyed the credibility of Planetta's claim that the shooting was accidental, there being a more deliberate period of time in firing the second shot.)

Otto Planetta thought of himself, like the Nazi thug Horst Wessel, a martyr to the National Socialist cause. He wrote a hasty note which read: "Dear Parents: Farewell! I go to save my comrades' lives. Otto." Lawyers were appointed for the defendants Holzweber and Planetta and pled both men Not Guilty. Both of the accused insisted that they had had no intention of injuring Dollfuss, and that they believed that the government had

Clockwise from above: A dead Austrian policeman is dragged away from the embattled Ravag Building during Nazi takeover; the Nazi-occupied Chancellory Building, July 25, 1934; the chancellory office, where Dollfuss was murdered; President Miklas and Kurt von Schuschnigg, the new chancellor, following Dollfuss' funeral; Dollfuss lying in state; Dollfuss, dead from Planetta's bullet.

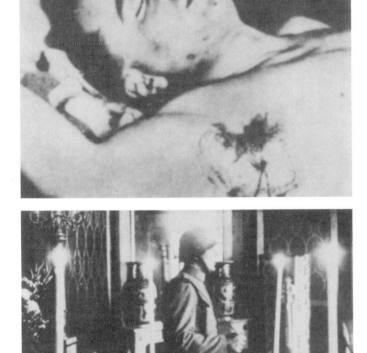

already changed hands (a typical Nazi excuse for first creating a coup and then later claiming that the coup was already a *fait accompli*). Planetta again insisted that his arm had been brushed by the excitable little Dollfuss and that he had accidentally fired only one shot. On the witness stand, he even went so far as to claim that he did not recognize Dollfuss in the darkened corner room of the chancellery and that he thought an Austrian soldier was attacking him. Hedvicek, Dollfuss' body servant, insisted otherwise, testifying that the room was brightly lighted and the blinds open when Planetta ran toward Dollfuss and shot him, and that he easily recognized the chancellor.

Both Holzweber and Planetta were convicted of armed sedition and murder. On July 31, 1934, both men were condemned to death. There would be no appeals. Three hours after they were sentenced, Holzweber and Planetta were marched into the prison courtyard and there the chief executioner, Lang, and two of his aides met them. The executioners were all dressed in black suits and they wore long black gloves. The condemned men had been accorded the privilege of receiving last rites from priests, a favor they had refused to grant Dollfuss. Holzweber was the first to hang. He was escorted up the stairs to the gallows and the rope was fixed about his neck. He sneered at the witnesses in the courtyard, lifted his head and screamed shrilly: "I die for Germany! Heil Hitler!" The three hangmen pulled on the rope and manually hanged Holzweber, jerking him upward. He slowly strangled to death, taking twelve minutes to die. Planetta followed. He, too, shouted: "Heil Hitler!" He was then yanked upward and died of slow strangulation.

These men were not heroes to their leader, Hitler. He called them inept fools and, unknown to Holzweber and Planetta, gave orders during their trials that if they should escape punishment and if they stepped foot on German soil, both were to be thrown into one of the Reich's newly created concentration camps. However, when the *Anschluss* occurred four years later, these very men, as Hitler had done with Horst Wessel, who had been killed in a 1920s street brawl, were lionized by Der Fuehrer, labeled martyrs to the Nazi cause, and streets in Vienna were named after them. Hitler used any kind of propaganda tool to further the image of his bloody reign, even dead bunglers.

Others shared the fate of Holzweber and Planetta. Hans Domes, who had led the small SS contingent in the raid on the Ravag Building, was condemned and executed for murdering several people. Also condemned and executed were four policemen who had sided with the SS Standarte 89 and one soldier. Policeman Paul Hudl, because of his distinguished military record in WWI, and because he had made a half-hearted attempt to warn authorities of the putsch, was spared and given a life sentence. All of the other Nazis were imprisoned for various lengthy terms. These men would be released in 1938 when Hitler annexed Austria into the German Reich. This was made easier by the weak-willed and indecisive Kurt von Schuschnigg, whose mealy mouthed appeasement of Hitler eroded the authority of the Austrian government and eventually saw it become a Nazi puppet state under the command of the sinister collaborators Edmund Glaise-Horstenau and Arthur Seyss-Inquart. See: **Himmler, Heinrich; Hitler, Adolf; Roehm, Ernst; Seyss-Inquart, Arthur; Wessel, Horst.**

REF.: Andics, *Der Staat, den keiner wollte;* ____, *Fuenfzig Jahre unseres Lebens;* Benedikt, *Geschichte der Republic Oesterreich;* Bornstein, *The Politics of Murder;* Brehm, *Der Boehmische Gefreite;* Brook-Shepherd, *Prelude to Infamy; CBA;* Eichstaedt, *Von Dollfuss zu Hitler;* Fest, *Hitler;* Gehl, *Austria, Germany and the Anschluss;* Gregory, *Dollfuss and His Times;* Gullick, *Austria from Hapsburg to Hitler;* Hartlieb, *Parole: Das Reich;* Heiden, *Der Fuehrer: Hitler's Rise to Power;* Henderson and Morris, *War in Our Time;* Langoth, *Kampf um Oesterreich;* Lorenz, *Der Staat wider Willen;* Maass, *Assassination in Vienna;* Nash, *Almanac of World Crime;* Neumann, *Behemoth: The Structure and Practice of National Socialism;* Paine, *The Assassin's World;* Papen, *Der Wahrheit eine Gasse;* Payne, *The Life and Death of Adolf Hitler;* Reich, *Der Freiheitskampf der Ostmark Deutschen;* Rintelen, *Erinnerungen an Oesterreichs Weg;* Ross, *Hitler and Dollfuss;* Schuschnigg, *Dreimal Oesterreich;* ____, *Im Kampf gegen Hitler;* Shirer, *The Rise and Fall of the Third Reich;* Starhemberg, *Between Hitler and Mussolini;* Winkler, *Die Diktatur in Oesterreich;* Zernatto, *Die Wahrheit ueber Oesterreich.*

Domat, Jean (Jean Daumat), 1625-96, Fr., jur. Wrote the work introducing concepts of Roman law into French jurisprudence, entitled, *Les Lois Civiles dans leur Ordre Naturel,* 1689-94. REF.: *CBA.*

Dombkiewicz, Peter, prom. 1930, U.S., rob.-attempt. mur. There is a time and place for everything. Dombkiewicz learned the hard way that a court trial on robbery charges, before a judge, jury, newspaper reporters, and more, is neither the time nor the place to suddenly brandish a scalpel and attempt to cut the throat of one's accuser.

While facing charges of stealing $9,000 from Buffalo, N.Y. jeweler David Glickstein, Peter Dombkiewicz pulled out his weapon and tried to kill the man. "That's how *I* treat squealers," he shouted. Glickstein was not seriously injured in the incident and returned to the courtroom in time to hear the jury say, "Guilty." REF.: *CBA.*

Domby, Victor, prom. 1853, Fr., mur. After committing a Lyons, Fr., murder, Victor Domby shoved his victim in a trunk "to be left till called for." He eventually directed his friend Calloux to pick up the trunk at a train station, not telling the dupe what was in it. Police first suspected Calloux of the crime, but it didn't take much time or additional evidence to find the real perpetrator.

REF.: *CBA;* Pearce, *Unsolved Murder Mysteries.*

Domela, Harry (AKA: Count So and So, Prince Lieven, Prince William of Hohenzollern, Baron Korff), 1904- , Ger., fraud. Orphaned at a young age and imprisoned for theft as a youth following WWI, things could only have gotten better for the young Russian Harry Domela. They did, in fact, when he met Baron Wolf Luderitz, sophisticated tramp and penniless aristocrat. Domela looked to the baron as a mentor who taught him the ways of aristocracy and of fraud and deception as well. Luderitz sent Domela on his way to fame and fortune as a door-to-door Potsdam cigar salesman. Introducing himself as "Count So and So" proved to be a selling point for status-conscious customers. He explained that his aristocratic family suffered from hard economic times, and customers believed him. The "count," readily accepted among the wealthy, entertained lavishly and enjoyed his new-found blue blood.

Later, Domela moved to Heidelberg where he elevated himself to the status of Prince Lieven, thus enabling him to prey on students. The Count So and So/Prince Lieven was also Baron Korff, of Erfurt, in Thuringia. But once known as a prince, it was hard to settle for mere baronet, so Domela started a convincing rumor that "the Baron is really Prince William of Hohenzollern, Prince Louis' brother." He enjoyed his attention in Thuringia and when he eventually moved to Berlin, he enjoyed royal treatment there as well.

But it was all a royal sham, and by January 1927 word was out that the Count/Prince/Baron was just an ordinary man. Domela was arrested for fraud. Awaiting trial in Cologne, Domela was surprised to learn that he had become a folk hero, the people loving him for showing what a farce royalty was. A fund was established for him in the left wing *Tagebuch* and he was eventually presented DM25,000 for his efforts. At his trial, the prosecutor had a nearly impossible time proving injury because each witness claiming to have dealt with Domela as royalty swore that he had only helped them. He was sentenced to seven months but was freed immediately because he had already served his time awaiting trial.

Domela then wrote his autobiography, sold 70,000 copies, and pocketed DM300,000. He bought a movie theater and starred in his own movie, *The False Prince.* REF.: *CBA.*

Domenico di Giovanni (AKA: Il Burchiello), 1404-49, Italy, treas. Exiled for political reasons, he was well known for his obscure humor and burlesque sonnets. REF.: *CBA.*

Dominici, Gaston, 1877-1965, Fr., mur. Elderly Gaston Dominici, the patriarch of a large French farm family living near Lurs, Provence, became the hub of one of the most sensational murder cases in modern French history. Sir Jack Drummond, a brilliant 61-year-old British biochemist, his wife Ann, forty-six, and their daughter Elizabeth, ten, were vacationing in France, driving through the Durance Valley. They decided to camp on the night of Aug. 4, 1952, and pulled their car off the road outside the town of Lurs, near a farmhouse. The Drummonds pitched a tent and began to dress for bed. Someone hiding in nearby bushes and watching them was discovered by Drummond, who berated the Peeping Tom, who, in turn, shot Drummond and his wife to death and chased the terrified Elizabeth Drummond through the tall grass and crushed her head with the butt of a carbine.

The bodies of the Drummond family were found the next morning by railway workers. Police also received a report from 33-year-old Gustave Dominici that he had also discovered the bodies on a large, sprawling farm called La Grande Terre, belonging to his father, Gaston Dominici. The deaths of the prominent Drummond and his family members made headlines in Paris, London, and New York, and Edmond Sebeille, the superintendent of police in Marseilles, personally directed the investigation. Sebeille was convinced that the killer or killers were part of the Dominici family at La Grande Terre. The family included Gaston Dominici, seventy-five, his reticent wife Marie, his son Gustave, Gustave's wife, Yvette, and their child. Another son, 49-year-old Clovis Dominici, lived on a nearby farm. Supt. Sebeille methodically conducted dozens of interviews with residents and workers in the area. One of the railway workers who had discovered the bodies told the superintendent that

Sir Jack Drummond, murder victim.

Ann Drummond, murder victim.

Elizabeth Drummond, murder victim.

Gaston Dominici, mass murderer.

Gustave Dominici had stated that Elizabeth Drummond was alive when he found her, although she was apparently dying of head wounds. Sebeille confronted Gustave Dominici, who admitted this was the case, but he was quick to say that he had nothing to do

with the murders.

Sebeille ordered Dominici's arrest for failing to come to the aid of a dying person. He was tried at Digne on Nov. 13, 1952, convicted, and sentenced to two months in prison. The sentence was appealed and Dominici was released. Sebeille, however, persisted in visiting the Dominici family, questioning members over and over throughout 1953. Finally, with Gustave and Clovis Dominici present in the farmhouse alone with the superintendent, Sebeille openly accused Gustave of murdering the Drummonds. Gustave's nerves were frayed by the prolonged police investigation and he shouted: "It was my father!" Sebeille looked at Clovis and

La Grande Terre, the Dominici farm in Provence, France.

the older brother nodded. Gustave then stated that he heard two shots at about 1 a.m. on the night of the murders and he ran to the field where he saw his father with an American carbine. He had just shot the Drummonds after being caught spying on them and had bludgeoned the little girl. Gustave, terrified that his father might turn on him, fled and returned at 5:30 to find Elizabeth Drummond in a dying condition. He left her to be found later, still fearing that his father would kill him if he knew Gustave had witnessed the murders.

The fierce old man, with a head of white hair, a droopy mustache, and dark, beady eyes, was arrested and taken to jail. He cursed his sons when he learned that they had informed on him and he later confessed to police that he had indeed slaughtered the Drummond family because Jack Drummond had accused him of gaping at his half-dressed wife and making lewd advances to her. The proud old man felt it was his right to do as he pleased on his own land, even to commit sexual assault and murder. The old man made several confessions but these were later retracted and denied when Gaston Dominici was placed on trial at the Digne Assize Court in November 1954. Before that time, Dominici accompanied police to the scene of the murders which were reenacted before him, so unnerving the hoary old killer that he tried to commit suicide by jumping off a railroad bridge.

At the end of the eleven-day trial, Gaston Dominici was found Guilty and sentenced to death. As the old man was led from the dock and back to his cell, he turned to the court and hissed: "My sons—what swine!" Dominici's death sentence was commuted to life in prison. Meanwhile more developments and revelations in the case left considerable doubt about who had killed the Drummonds. One story had it that the old man killed the adults but someone else in the Dominici family murdered the child. Another account insisted that Gaston Dominici was a senile old man who confessed out of ignorance and confusion and that his sons had done the killings. The old man was released in 1960 and returned to La Grand Terre where he lived until 1965, inside a household that held nothing but hostility and hatred.

REF.: Canning, *Fifty True Tales of Terror; CBA;* Furneaux, *Famous Criminal Cases, Vol. 2;* Greenwall, *They Were Murdered in France;* Heppenstall, *The Sex War & Others;* Laborde, *The Dominici Affair;* Lustgarten, *The Story of Crime;* Rowan, *Famous European Crimes;* Scott, *Concise Encyclopedia of Crime and Criminals;* Wilson, *Encyclopedia of Murder.*

Dominique, Robert, c.1946- , U.S., attempt. mur. Robert Dominique was sentenced to the Illinois State Penitentiary at Joliet, when he was thirty-one, after a jury found him Guilty of attempted murder and deviate sexual assault.

Illinois Criminal Court Judge Frank W. Barbaro levied the stiff sentence of 100 to 200 years in prison on Robert Dominique for atrocities he committed against a 21-year-old Loyola University student in Chicago. Dominique stabbed the co-ed eight times in an alley on Nov. 13, 1975, after she refused to have sex with him. She sustatained punctured lungs and today suffers difficulty breathing as a result of the attack.

According to the judge and Assistant State's Attorney William Hedrick the convicted man had attacked other women in the same neighborhood. One victim lost her eye in her struggle with Dominique, who was a drug addict and had once spent seven years in a New York State mental hospital. REF.: *CBA.*

Dominiquez, Orin, 1950-82, U.S., mur. Orin Dominiquez, thirty-two, and Forest Park, Ill., police officer Michael Caulfield, twenty-two, are both dead because Dominiquez was erroneously found to be mentally fit. This supposedly stable individual had been arrested more than forty times in fifteen years, serving two terms in the Joliet Correctional Center for robbery and arrested four times in the year he died, 1982.

On Sept. 30, 1982, just three weeks after Caulfield had graduated from the police academy, he and another officer brought Dominiquez in after they saw him loitering and had learned that there were outstanding traffic warrants against him. The day before, a Chicago police officer had taken Dominiquez to a mental health clinic for evaluation because family members were urging him to seek help. Clinic doctors suggested he voluntarily admit himself but said they were unable to force him to stay because he did not meet the requirements for involuntary admission.

When the police brought Dominiquez in and freed his hands for fingerprinting and booking, he grabbed Officer James Sebastian's gun and started shooting. He was shot and killed by Officer James McNally, but not until he had killed Caulfield. REF.: *CBA.*

Domitian (Titus Flavius Domitianus Augustus), 51-96 A.D., Roman., assass. The second son of Vespasian and Flavia Domitilla, Domitian was born on Oct. 24, 51 A.D. He became praetor in 70 A.D., and succeeded his brother Titus as emperor in 81 A.D. His fourteen-year reign was marked by constant military campaigns, and toward the end of his rule, he became petty and jealous of all whom he suspected of coveting his power, instituting a reign of terror (93-96 A.D.). He began ordering the arbitrary executions of innocuous persons in his court over the slightest offenses, instilling fear among nobles. Domitian possessed an intense hatred for Jews and often degraded anyone in his court whom he thought might be Jewish, once ordering a 90-year-old man to strip before the entire court to see if he was circumcised.

The emperor regularly humiliated his empress, Domitia, simply for perverse pleasure. He divorced her on a whim and then ordered her back to his "divine bed." He insisted that he was a god and his courtiers and aides had to address him as such or face instant execution. Domitian burst forth with invective about freedmen one day, saying that none could be trusted and would turn on their masters at every opportunity. He then ordered the execution of his secretary, Epaphroditus, a freedman who had reportedly helped Nero commit suicide when everyone had abandoned him. When Domitian off-handedly decreed the death of the harmless Flavius Clemens, his absent-minded cousin, Cocceius Nerva, an esteemed jurist, headed a plot to kill the tyrant, with the blessings and connivance of Empress Domitia.

On the day before his assassination, Domitian had fearful visions. He claimed to be clairvoyant and to see the future, although he also surrounded himself with many soothsayers to assure him that no harm would come to him. He was terrified of danger and pain, and kept most of his own Praetorian Guard at a distance, ordering all weapons, particularly lances, to be kept from his sight. On that day, Domitian was presented with a gift, a bowl of apples. "Serve them tomorrow," he said, "if tomorrow ever comes." He then turned, his eyes rolling in his head, and said to some courtiers: "There will be blood on the Moon as she enters Aquarius and a deed will be done for everyone to talk about." He went to bed and slept fitfully, leaping from his bed at midnight, screaming for a soothsayer who had earlier stated that lightning storms of previous days portended a change of government. Domitian ordered the soothsayer killed.

At dawn, Sept. 18, 96 A.D., Domitian scratched a pimple and a trickle of blood ran down his cheek. "I hope this is all the blood required," he said cryptically. Another soothsayer had told the emperor a short time earlier that he should fear the fifth hour of this day and Domitian repeatedly asked what time it was. At one point, a freedman told him it was the sixth hour, lying, and the emperor seemed to relax, believing his time of peril had passed. He leisurely relaxed in his bath, but was told that a courier had arrived with important news. Domitian, dripping from his bath, raced to see Stephanus, a freedman, who stood in Domitian's bedroom offering the emperor a list of names that, Stephanus insisted were part of a conspiracy to kill the emperor. The freedman wore a woolen bandage on his arm, having feigned an injury some days earlier to excuse the presence of the bandage. Hidden inside the bandage was a dagger.

Domitian read the list with obsessive interest, mumbling that he would have every person listed executed immediately. With his eyes ravenously scrolling through the list and thus diverted, Stephanus withdrew the hidden dagger and stabbed Domitian in the groin. The emperor screamed to a servant to retrieve a dagger he kept beneath the pillow of his bed but this knife had no blade. The emperor, gushing blood, hysterically leaped upon Stephanus, grabbing the blade of his dagger, cutting his hands. Domitian clawed at his assailant's eyes, while shouting for help. Stephanus kept stabbing him. Help arrived, but it was aid given to Stephanus, not the emperor. A subalturn, Clodianus, raced forward to

The Emperor Domitian, murdered by Stephanus.

stab Domitian, as did Maximus, a freedman, Satur, a head chamberlain, and one of the imperial gladiators. With seven stab wounds, Domitian rolled over, a bloody wreck, dying.

The tall, ruddy body was carried on a common litter from the palace and it was cremated by Domitian's old nurse, Phyllis, in her garden on the Latin Way. She then took the ashes to the Temple of the Flavians and here mixed them with Domitian's niece, Julia, who had died as a result of an abortion after Domitian had raped and impregnated her. The elderly Cocceius Nerva became emperor and ruled for two years.

REF.: Africa, *Rome of the Caesars;* Balsdon, *The Romans;* Carcopino, *Daily Life in Ancient Rome; CBA;* Dill, *Roman Society from Nero to Marcus Aurelius;* Gibbon, *The Decline and Fall of the Roman Empire;* Grant, *The World of Rome;* Robinson, *History of Rome;* Rostovtzeff, *The Social and Economic History of the Roman Empire;* Suetonius, *The Twelve Caesars.*

Donadieu, Alfredo-Hecktor (AKA: Enrico Sampietro), 1900- , Fr.-Mex., fraud-count.-forg. Alfredo-Hecktor Donadieu, became one of the leading counterfeiters of the early twentieth century. He was born on Feb. 17, 1900, in Marseilles, Fr., into a lower middle-class family. His father made his living recording deaths on tombstones. But Donadieu had rugged good looks, street smarts, and artistic talent. At eighteen he became an apprentices in his uncle's jewelry shop, where he discovered his talents as an engraving artist, met an important, albeit illegal, business contact, and also met his first love Maria.

Under the direction of Alberto Sampietro, Donadieu soon became an apprentice counterfeiter, engraving sentimental messages on jewelry by day and bank note details on printing plates by night. Soon he met another member of the ring, Antoinette, forty, also known as Aunt Toinon, and he began to divide his attention between Marie and Antoinette.

Eventually the quartet saw an untapped market in North Africa where they used a clothing store as a front for counterfeiting. Sampietro bought huge quantities of clothing and food paid for with homemade hundred franc notes. He then resold the merchandise at half price, making certain not to accept any hundred franc notes in payment.

Soon they found their way back to France, where Aunt Toinon, jealous of Maria, promptly told police about Donadieu's proficiency with a plate and knife. Sampietro escaped but Donadieu and Maria were seized. Maria was later freed but Donadieu received a ten-year term at Devil's Island. It was the first of several imprisonments for the engraver-gone-astray.

In prison, he formed an escape party, inviting seven men to go with him. They stole a small boat and headed for Brazil. Two drowned. The five who made it to shore discovered they were still in French Guiana. Two more died from malaria. The remaining three struggled to cross the border to Brazil, where they were promptly rearrested and taken back to the island.

Donadieu tried to escape again. This time four men ventured to Venezuela. One died of malaria but three were successful. Donadieu then started his own counterfeiting organization. With some Venezuelans, he made bank notes himself and delegated the disbursement of the bills to his employees. He managed to make a quick few thousand, but was anxious to return to Naples where his old friend Sampietro promised him a fine position. To accomplish this, Donadieu married a Venezuelan woman, fathered a son, and then used his legitimate standing in the country to obtain a passport and leave. He told his wife he had important business in Naples and would return to her in several months.

Donadieu begrudgingly took a job with the Ufficio Informazione, the Italian War Ministry's espionage bureau for the Mussolini administration, forging passports, letters, and telegrams. Though essentially apolitical, he took this new position only because he believed it would afford him the best opportunity to take revenge against his informer, Antoinette, whom he knew to be living in a Naples' slum. When he opened the door, the horrendous sight of a body and mind taken over by tertiary syphilis sickened him. "Be a friend once again and kill me," she laughed. Instead, Donadieu made arrangements to send her support money each month.

Donadieu spent the next several years jumping from one fraud scheme to the next. He won a permanent overseas assignment with the U-I, fell in with a dope-smuggling gang for a time, and convinced his new colleagues that counterfeiting had a brighter future. In 1930 he and his group relocated in Cairo, where his partners were quickly seized. He escaped with his new girlfriend, a Frenchwoman named Alice. The two sailed to Barcelona where the Spanish police were waiting for him. He hid out with a French prostitute named Louise and joined the Spanish Foreign Legion for a short time. Once back in Barcelona he sent for Louise and together they crossed the Portuguese border into Lisbon. Then they sailed to Panama. The two bought a women's clothing store which she managed until her death from malaria in 1932.

But that was not all. Donadieu got entangled with some revolutionary Venezuelans who persuaded him to work for them. About the only thing he got out of this arrangement was a new identity. His partner won two hundred Colombian pesos in a poker game with a fellow named Enrico Sampietro, who in turn handed over his Italian passport as security for the money he owed. Donadieu then won the passport from his friend and assumed that man's identity. To this day, Donadieu is Enrico

Sampietro in Mexican newspapers.

But to Amada Casas, Mexican beauty and leader of the Cristeros, the underground pro-church force against the 1936 Mexican Government, he was Donadieu, her true love. When the two met they immediately fell deeply in love. She became interested in counterfeiting and he became interested in the Cristero movement. When, in 1937, he was arrested and sentenced to ten years in the Federal District Penitentiary in Lecumberri, Casas used other Cristeros' leaders support and, within a year, had freed him. The two then entered a labor of love, Donadieu devoting his engraving skills solely to the Cristero movement. He made plates for Mexican currency and the rebels printed and distributed them. With their earnings they bought arms and maintained underground headquarters in various Mexican states.

This worked well for ten years, but, as had happened before, Donadieu was arrested, convicted, and sentenced to prison. Now forty-eight, mellowed and wiser, Donadieu took his twelve-year sentence rather well. Life at Lecumberri was not too bad. He made friends with his neighbor, Leon Trotsky's assassin Ramon Metcador del Rio, earned $8 apiece for portraits done of inmates and visitors, and was allowed intimate visits with Casas each Thursday. He showed little regret for his actions or inprisonment. All along he made the best of his situation. His plans after his scheduled release in 1960 did not, however, include counterfeiting. "That is only for young, foolish men," he said.

REF.: Bloom, *Money of Their Own; CBA.*

Donahoe, Jack (AKA: **Bold Jack**), 1806-30, Brit., rob. It did not take long for Jack Donahoe to establish himself as a criminal. Donning the suits of the gentlemen he robbed, he was dubbed "The Wild Colonial Boy."

Jack Donahoe was convicted of his first felony at age eighteen. Three years later he escaped from prison and was immediately recaptured for robbery. The two convicts arrested with him were quickly hanged but young Donahoe escaped, and with a £20 reward on his head, "Bold Jack" began a career of bushranging, winning the nickname of "The Wild Colonial Boy." His crime forte was to rob well-dressed gentlemen about his own size and swap his dusty threads for his victim's new suit.

On Sept. 1, 1830, Jack Donahoe was shot and killed by a police officer. REF.: *CBA.*

Donahue, Cornelius (AKA: **Lame Johnny**), 1850-78, U.S., west. lawman-west. outl.-lynch. "Lame Johnny," Cornelius Donahue, attended college in Philadelphia, but yearned to experience firsthand the thrills and dangers of the western frontier. He moved to Texas to become a cowboy, but his physical impairment kept him away from the big jobs. In desperation he became a horse thief.

Donahue left Texas in the mid-1870s when things got too hot for him. In Deadwood, a rough frontier town in the Dakota Territory, Donahue was hired as a deputy sheriff. He quickly demonstrated his skills with a six shooter. Later on he found a job in the mines, but someone recognized him in 1878 as a Texas horse thief. Donahue fled, and began holding up stagecoaches and stealing horses from the Pine Ridge Indian Reservation. A livestock detective named Frank Smith arrested Johnny on Indian land, and attempted to return him to Deadwood on a stage coach. On the way back to town, a masked rider pulled the coach over and waved Donahue out. It was first thought that one of his pals had come to free him, until they found the body of Lame Johnny swinging from a tree the next day. The identity of the gunman was never established, but the miners who remembered him renamed a creek in the Black Hills the "Lame Johnny." REF.: *CBA.*

Donahue, John Xavier, 1933-53, U.S., mur. Police officers lay their lives on the line even on routine patrols. State trooper Ernest J. Morse lost his life on Connecticut's Merritt Parkway in February 1953 attempting to hand out an ordinary speeding ticket.

The speeder, young, dark-haired John Donahue, was described by Dr. Harry Hemmendinger, defense psychologist at Donahue's murder trial, as a man without a conscience who would kill again if it suited his purposes. He had killed Morse the minute the officer stepped out of his car to hand the ticket.

The jury considered the evidence for little over an hour and returned a verdict of Guilty of murder in the first degree, which automatically carried the death sentence. Judge Thomas E. Troland scheduled an emotionless Donahue to die on Dec. 5, 1953. REF.: *CBA*.

Donahue, Maurice H., 1864-1928, U.S., jur. Served as prosecuting attorney for Perry County, Ohio, 1887-93, Ohio Superior Court justice, 1910-19, and appointed to the 6th Circuit Court of the U.S. by President Woodrow Wilson, Nov. 13, 1919. REF.: *CBA*.

Donald, Jeannie Ewen, b.1896, Scot., mur. In 1934, the Donalds and the Priestlys of Aberdeen, Scot., lived in close quarters in an apartment building on Urquhart Road. Alexander and Jeannie Donald did not care for the Priestly family. The disagreement between Mrs. Donald and Mrs. Priestly dated back to 1929, and the two women did not speak. Eight-year-old Helen Priestly picked up on the tension and taunted Jeannie Donald, calling her "coconut," a nickname the older woman deeply resented.

On Apr. 20, 1934, Helen's mother sent her to the store to buy a loaf of bread. Helen paid for the bread and ran off down the street, never to be seen alive again. A search for the child in the city parks, hospitals, and schools produced no trace of her. The next morning, a neighbor at 61 Urquhart Road, near the Donald residence, found a brown sack in the hallway. The sack contained the body of Helen Priestly. Since the search party had already checked the building, the murderer was thought to have left the body there the previous evening.

The body bore marks of strangulation, but not of sexual assault. A maintenance man later said that he heard two screams from inside the building. Suspicion fell on the Donalds, who had refused to join the search for the girl. Alexander Donald proved that he was at work when the child disappeared. But Jeannie Donald did not have an alibi, and blood stains were found in her kitchen cupboard. She was arrested and charged with murder. Her trial began in the High Court of the Justiciary in Edinburgh on July 16, 1934. Pathologists proved the bacteria in the girl's body were similar to those in the Donald house, and the receipt for the bread that Helen bought was found in the Donalds' fireplace.

Mrs. Donald was found Guilty of murder and was sentenced to death. Her sentence was later commuted to life imprisonment, but she served less than ten years and was released on June 26, 1944.

REF.: *CBA*; Jacobs, *Pageant of Murder*; Nash, *Look For the Woman*; *Notable British Trials*; Roughead, *Tales of the Criminous*; Shew, *A Companion to Murder*; Smith, *Mostly Murder*; Thorwald, *The Century of the Detective*; ____, *Dead Men Tell No Tales*.

Donally, James, prom. 1779, Brit., extor. When Charles Fielding the son of the Earl of Denbigh was accosted on the king's highway Jan. 18, 1779, it was Fielding who was charged with a crime. James Donally informed Fielding that if he did not give him some money he would take him to a magistrate and charge him with a very wicked deed. Fielding, rather than risk his reputation, complied, handing over half a guinea. As usual, in such cases, this led to another demand, this one coming two days later. Once again Fielding complied, this time handing Donally one entire guinea.

The error that led to Donally's downfall was mistaking Lord Fielding for his brother, Charles. Donally attempted an extortion scheme on Lord Fielding but Lord Fielding proved truculent. Fielding was accosted twice by Donally; the first time he refused to hand over money and then attempted to capture the extortionist who managed to get away. Two days later Donally tried again; this time Lord Fielding caught him. On Apr. 29, 1779, Donally was convicted and received a long prison sentence.

REF.: *CBA*; Mitchell, *The Newgate Calendar*.

Dondone, John, prom. 1932, U.S., rob.-mansl. The body of George Hultz, a 72-year-old recluse in Connecticut, was found when police dragged the lake near his cabin. His Redding district lakeside cabin had burned down, and there was evidence of bloodstains and violence in the area. Investigators believed that the killer had clubbed him to death, then burned down the house hoping to make it look as if Hultz had perished in the fire. John Dondone, a 22-year-old farmhand who had worked with Hultz, was a prime suspect. Engaged to marry, Dondone's marriage plans supposedly were thwarted by his $15 monthly salary. Tony Reggio, the brother of Dondone's fiance, told police that Dondone was really a special investigator for the state police, had amassed $8,000, and intended to purchase her a ring. The officers, suspicious, persuaded Reggio to convince Dondone to buy the sister a diamond engagement ring, after which the jeweler told them that Dondone had paid him $100 in cash for it.

James Donally, seated at left, was convicted of extortion in 1779.

When police picked him up and told him he could go to prison for impersonating a policeman, Dondone said he had shot the old man in self defense, after Hultz fired at him. Dondone then changed his story, saying that it had all been an accident. Denying the arson, and pleading guilty to manslaughter, Dondone was sentenced to twelve to fifteen years in the state prison. He was paroled and deported to Italy on Dec. 9, 1932.

REF.: *CBA*; Rice, *Forty-five Murderers*.

Donegan, Edward, prom. 1920, U.S., brib.-fraud. In 1919, Edward Donegan made his living selling logs that had washed ashore on the south Brooklyn, N.Y., waterway for firewood. By 1920, he was maintaining two homes—one for his family, and one for a mistress—and was depositing as much as $500,000 into the bank each month. Donegan made his fortune due to the New York State Prohibition Bureau precaution against fraudulent withdrawal permits. A new rule required all bonded liquor warehouses and distilleries to wire the state director for confirmation of its authenticity upon receipt of a permittee's order. By seducing a young clerk, Regina

Bootlegger Edward Donegan.

Sassone, Donegan received notice through her of all distiller's queries. While Sassone delayed the reply, Donegan would use one of two different strategies. If the permit was legitimate, he would approach the permittee, pretending to be a prohibition official, and offer to expedite the process for a fee, which he usually received. If the permit was spurious, Donegan would threaten to arrest the permittee, and then ask for $20 per case of liquor to authenticate the permit. If the proposal was accepted, Sassone would type a confirming telegram, stamp New York State Prohibition Director Charles R. O'Connor's signature, and give the missive to Donegan to send by Western Union. Donegan paid Sassone $100 per telegram. Bribing another clerk, Mary Parkins, who recruited several others, Donegan set up his headquarters at the Hotel McAplin, eventually dealing directly with bootleggers, selling them stolen or forged permits.

Intelligence Unit Chief Elmer Irey became suspicious of the extravagant parties given by Parkins at the hotel headquarters. When Agent Harold Stephenson of Washington was invited to a party, Donegan offered him $10,000 to produce a permit for withdrawing 100 barrels of whiskey. Stephenson reported the bribe to Irey. A few days later, Intelligence Unit Agent Walter P. Murphy and several other agents arrested Donegan in the hotel suite. He was carrying $45,000 in cash and a number of distiller's telegrams querying O'Connor about permits, which would have released an estimated $4 million worth of whiskey. Donegan offered bribes of $5,000, then $25,000, then called in his associate, Samuel Bein, also known as Sigmund "Beansie" Rosenfeld, who raised the bribe to an extra $2 for every case of liquor. A federal grand jury indicted Donegan, Bein, Parkins, and Sassone for conspiring to violate the Volstead Act and stealing government documents. The IRS ordered Donegan to pay more than $1.6 million plus penalties. Rosenfeld died in February 1922, missing the trial by three weeks. Parkins' charges were dropped when she turned state's witness. Sassone was aquitted when she made a full confession on the stand. Attorney William Fallon defended Donegan, who was convicted, fined $65,000, and sentenced to ten years in the Atlanta penitentiary.

REF.: *CBA; Kobler, Ardent Spirits.*

Donellan, John, d.1781, Brit., mur. Coveting the estates of Sir Theodosius Boughton, who lived at resplendent Lawford Hall in Warwickshire, England, Captain John Donellan poisoned his host with essence of laurel water in 1780. This was later uncovered at a probing inquest which led to Donellan's conviction and execution; he was hanged at Warwick in 1781.

REF.: Boughton-Leigh, *Memorials of a Warwickshire Family;* Camps, *Camps on Crime; CBA;* de la Torre, *Villainy Detected;* Glaister, *The Power of Poison;* Guttmacher, *The Mind of the Murderer;* Morley, *Leafy Warwickshire;* Roughead, *The Fatal Countess;* (FICTION), Shearing, *The Crime of Laura Sarelle;* Thompson, *Poison and Poisoners.*

Dongan, Thomas, 1634-1715, U.S., blk. When British King James II appointed Thomas Dongan the new English Governor of New York in 1683, wholesale blackmail of city fathers and merchants ensued. Dongan struck the Common Council, almost all of whom were Dutch, for $1,500 for himself and an additional $120 for his secretary. Dongan promised not to report to his superiors the illegal trading, price-fixing, and taxes conducted by the Dutch in return for this "hush money." This, of course, was outright blackmail. Dongan cavalierly explained to his superiors in England, when the matter was brought to their attention, that he was merely selling favors and privileges and that he had "granted nothing more than what they had from my predecessors." His explanation was accepted as satisfactory in that Dongan was merely continuing a practice already set down as precedent, the traditional excuse for open corruption practiced by politicians to this day.

Added to this venal attitude, Dongan, a staunch Irish Catholic, decreed in 1685 that Jews could not own shops or openly worship. Gustavus Myers succinctly summed up the dilemma of the Jew: "Excluded from regular branches of business, he had to turn scavenger in picking up old rags, or dealing in cast-off clothes, or other such out-of-the-way lines. More by way of innuendo than anything else this course was presented...as an example of 'Jewish resourcefulness.' The implication was that the Jew would descend to any means, however low, to wrest a living, and from the basest start, would use his adroitness to attain success. But the real and tragic point was characteristically ignored. Namely that the bigotry against Jews, solidified into repressive laws, left them no choice; their resort to narrow opportunities, regarded with contempt by their oppressors, was far less an example of Jewish 'resourcefulness' than it was a shameful proof of an inhumanity loading them with onerous discriminations."

Jews in New York lived in terror for the first century of that genteel British rule. It was not uncommon for gangs of rowdies to break into the homes of Jews while the owners were present and take what they pleased. None of the authorities stood in the way of these thugs—particularly Thomas Dongan, who later retired with wealth and honors.

REF.: *CBA;* Marcuse, *This Was New York!;* Myers, *Bigotry in the United States.*

Donnell, Richard, prom. 1970, U.S., mur. In October 1978, Richard Donnell was doing time in a federal prison for transporting stolen goods, when the State pressured him to testify about a homicide he had committed years earlier. With the help of Leslie Eugene Dale, a member of the Johnston Gang, Donnell had beaten and drowned dishwasher John "Jackie" Baen, after they learned that Baen would inform on Donnell and Dale. Eight years after the murder, Chester County investigators exhumed Baen's body from the Glenwood Memorial Garden Center, determined to find a cause of death other than drowning. The frightened Donnell admitted to his participation in the murder, and agreed to testify against Dale, in exchange for a reduced charge of voluntary manslaughter, and a prison sentence of not more than three years. Since he was already doing that much time, Donnell never served any additional time for murdering Baen.

REF.: *CBA;* Fox, *Mass Murder.*

Donnelly, Edward, d.1808, U.S., mur. Donnelly was an alcoholic and a wife-beater, abusing his wife so regularly that neighbors in Carlisle, Pa., grew accustomed to the shrieks from Mrs. Donnelly. On the night of Aug. 9, 1807, Donnelly returned home in a drunken stupor and began striking his wife, Catherine. He battered her mercilessly, but the poor woman's screams only brought a remark from a neighbor to a friend: "There's Ned licking his wife again." Donnelly struck Catherine so hard that he killed her. In desperation he dismembered the body and began burning it, piece by piece, taking two days to turn the remains into ashes. It was several weeks later when her jawbone and teeth were discovered in the ashes and Donnelly was then charged with the murder. He was tried in November 1807, convicted, and sentenced to death. On Feb. 4, 1808, Donnelly confessed to the murder and he was hanged at Carlisle four days later, on Feb. 8, 1808.

REF.: *CBA;* Duncan, *The Confession of Edward Donnelly; Confession of Edward Donnelly;* Nash, *Bloodletters and Badmen; A Sketch of the Trial of Edward Donnelly.*

Donnelly, James, prom. 1880, Case of, Can., mur. James Donnelly and his family were victims of a 100-year-old feud between two Irish groups, the Whiteboys terrorist society of Tipperary, and a small opposition society called the Blackfeet, with which the Donnelly's were associated. The Donnelly family murders were documented in several books, folk songs, and radio and stage plays, as well as a number of essays and other treatments. On Feb. 3, 1880, 65-year-old Biddulph Township, Ontario, farmer, James Donnelly wrote a letter to attorney Edmund Meredith, in London, Ontario, asking him to represent a vigilante committee in a suit against the Donnellys. The committee claimed the family had burned the barns of a neighbor, Pat Ryder, a month earlier. Explaining, "They are using us worse than mad dogs," Donnelly asked for Meredith's services "to attack them at once, as they will never let us alone until some of them are made an example of." Sometime between midnight and 2 a.m. on Feb. 4, about forty disguised men attacked the two Donnelly farm homes using shotguns, revolvers, spades, clubs, and pitchforks to murder James Donnelly, Sr., his wife, Johannah Donnelly, his sons,

Thomas Donnelly and John Donnelly, and his niece, Bridget Donnelly, who was raped and strangled. The bodies were soaked with coal oil and set on fire. Two surviving witnesses identified six men. The first trial in London, Ontario, resulted in a hung jury. At the second trial, the prisoners were acquitted. When a third case was brought against two other alleged conspirators, the Crown dropped the proceedings, even though a grand jury had brought in a bill against the accused. The murders, which had been carefully planned in extensive meetings, were screened by a complicated network of alibis, and were condoned by a publicity campaign by the killers and their supporters.

REF.: *CBA*; Miller, *Twenty Mortal Murders*.

Donnelly, James, prom. 1900, U.S., (wrong. convict.) mur. James Donnelly, convicted of the first-degree murder of a Chickasaw Indian in California in 1900, remained in prison, facing the death penalty, because a dying man's confession to the crime was not put in writing. The U.S. Supreme Court upheld Donnelly's conviction saying the confession presented by Joe Dick, an Indian, was inadmissible because it was neither put in writing nor presented first-hand, even though other circumstances of the murder pointed to Dick as the guilty man. The Supreme Court decision was not handed down without disagreement. Justices Oliver Wendell Holmes, Horace H. Lurton, and Charles Evans Hughes dissented.

Ironically, the rule dismissing hearsay was originally laid down to protect a defendant from unsubstantiated accusations. See: **Holmes, Oliver Wendell; Hughes, Charles Evans; Lurton, Horace H.** REF.: *CBA*.

Donnelly, Dr. James P., d.1858, U.S., mur. Dr. James Donnelly lived at the Sea View House in Navesink, N.J., where he was beginning a medical practice. He was considered a promising young physician with a bright future, but he was a habitual gambler and a poor loser. He lost $55—all the money he possessed—to Albert S. Moses on Aug. 1, 1857. After brooding over this loss, Donnelly went to Moses's room, and while Moses was asleep, tried to steal the money. Moses suddenly awakened and Donnelly stabbed him in the throat, killing him. Donnelly, seen leaving the victim's room, was arrested soon after Moses's body was discovered. He was quickly tried and convicted. Donnelly was hanged on Jan. 5, 1858.

REF.: *CBA*; Morris, *The Highland Tragedy; The Trial of James P. Donnelly*.

Donnelly, Nell Quinlan, See: **Deputy, Martin.**

Donoghue, William, 1908- , Brit., mansl. Forty-two-year-old William Donoghue's idea of fun was raising his blood-alcohol level to a life-threatening height. So, on Dec. 7, 1950, he and his drinking pal Thomas Meaney consumed enough alcohol to kill three average individuals. Drunk, they stumbled back to Donoghue's home and passed out.

Sometime before midnight, Donoghue decided he would be more comfortable in bed and staggered to his room. But Meaney was deadweight on Donoghue's bed and looked like a dummy put there by his friends as a practical joke. Donoghue, being a fun-loving sort, played along. He dragged the "dummy" to the floor and proceeded to stab it with a bayonet he used as a bread knife. Next, he dragged the body out on the landing and crawled into bed for a good night's sleep.

Donoghue arose the next morning to find a bloodied floor, Meaney's body, and the realization of what he had done.

Donoghue relayed to the court what he could remember of the night. Strangely, his story seemed believable. People who saw the two the night before described them as very drunk, but perfectly friendly with one another. The police surgeon who examined Donoghue found no wounds that suggested a struggle. An empty gin bottle stood next to the blood-stained bayonet. A neighbor testified waking near midnight to three thuds and then silence. Meaney's clothes were not torn or disordered and all blood samples taken came from him. He suffered sixteen stab wounds to the left side of his head and neck, but there were no "protective" wounds of any kind on his hands.

During Donoghue's trial at the Old Bailey in February 1951, his counsel, John Maude, described him as an inoffensive, quiet, and respectable little man. The principal medical officer helped Donoghue out further by testifying that he had, in fact, been drunk enough to actually believe he was stabbing a dummy. Donoghue was convicted of manslaughter and sentenced to three years in prison, saved from a murder conviction because he had had too much to drink.

REF.: *CBA*; Simpson, *Forty Years of Murder*.

Donohue, Alice, d.1908, U.S., (unsolv.) mur. On June 12, 1908, Daniel Donohue told authorities that his wife, Alice Donohue, was missing from their Oakland, Calif., home. He said he returned from a lodge meeting the night before to find her gone but her jewelry and money intact, and he concluded that she must have become insane and committed suicide. Donohue offered a reward for knowledge of his wife's whereabouts, but he later decided that she had left with another man and so he withdrew the offer. He then went back to his original theory of suicide.

On Aug. 28, the decayed remains of Alice Donohue were found under the floorboards in a furniture factory six blocks from her home. Daniel Donohue's display of grief was not consistent with his earlier behavior, nor were his answers to police questions. When he first reported his wife missing, he had made a point of the fact that she left her money and jewelry at home. But after the body was found, Donohue said her money, pearl earrings, gold watch, and wedding ring were missing.

A spade found alongside the body was traced to Donohue's neighbor Gustave Arkill, who joined Donohue as a prime suspect. Arkill's real name was Gustave Ahlstedt and he had been charged with the attempted murder of his first wife in 1898. He did in fact murder his second wife's lover, but was acquitted in 1902. Four years later, he was accused of stealing a land deed. Authorities noted that Donohue and Ahlstedt held long, mysterious conferences together. Donohue also tried to claim his wife's insurance money the same day he displayed overwhelming grief over her death. Investigation revealed that Donohue was not entitled to the insurance money because he had never been Alice's lawful husband. Apparently, Alice Steward had married young and left her husband without obtaining a legal divorce. Upon hearing the news, Donohue killed himself with a .38-caliber revolver.

The case against Ahlstedt was dismissed, and no one was ever charged with Alice Donohue's murder.

REF.: *CBA*; Duke, *Celebrated Criminal Cases of America*.

Donohue, John, prom. 1893, U.S., theft. On a bitterly cold November day in 1893, John Donohue risked his life and threatened his arresting officer's life over a stolen horse blanket.

Charles Day, proprietor of the Warwick Hotel, had just placed a fine cover on his horse to prevent the animal from chilling. Donohue saw the blanket, yanked it off the horse's back, and darted along an alley and across the path of Detective Clifton R. Wooldridge. Wooldridge jumped on a passing vehicle and speedily approached the man with the purposes of retrieving the blanket and arresting the petty thief. It should have been a simple arrest but turned into a chilling battle.

Donohue threatened to kill Wooldridge if he came close. A struggle followed as Donohue fought for Wooldridge's gun. Fortunately, the two were fighting just outside a building where the trial board, a group established to investigate the conduct of officers charged with brutality, happened to be meeting. All seventy-five attendants ran to the scene. With their help, the detective overpowered Donohue before either was mortally wounded.

After a night's rest in jail Donohue pleaded guilty to disorderly conduct, was fined $100, and sent to the House of Correction for six months.

REF.: *CBA*; Wooldridge, *Hands Up*.

Donohue, Thomas, prom. 1868, Case of, U.S., rob.-mur. On Oct. 17, 1868, four men burst into the offices of Alexander W. Rea, manager of a coal company outside Centralia, Pa., and demanded that he turn over the payroll. When Rea resisted, the bandits opened fire, shooting Rea six times and killing him. Thomas Donahoe, John Duff, Michael Prior, and Patrick Hestor were arrested a short time later, but only Donohue was charged with Rea's murder and tried. Evidence against Donohue was skimpy and he could not be shown to be Rea's killer. He was acquitted and the murder remained unsolved.

REF.: *CBA; The Rea Homicide.*

Donovan, Conrad (AKA: **Rotten Conrad**), c.1870-1904, and **Wade, Charles**, c.1882-1904, Brit., mur. The general criterion for conviction in a criminal case is "beyond a reasonable doubt," and that is why the jury sent Conrad Donovan, thirty-four, and his half-brother Charles Wade, twenty-two, to the gallows following the Oct. 12, 1904, murder in Stepney, England. Not until Donovan said on his way to his death that he had not meant to kill Emily Farmer could the townspeople rest assured that they had convicted the right men.

It was hard to believe, however, that Donovan and Wade had not meant to kill Farmer who was found, hands bound and face down, choked by a gag placed in her mouth. Her home had been ransacked, obviously in a robbery attempt.

An easy target, Farmer lived alone and owned a small newspaper and tobacco shop in what was deemed a bad neighborhood. When alone, she enjoyed adorning herself with fine jewelry. She had been attacked once before and luckily escaped because passing police heard her scream.

It finally took two sturdy men to take her on. The fact that they were apprehended was due to a tipoff provided by a fish curer named Rae who had seen the two men, whom he knew to be gang members, emerge from the shop the morning of the murder. Rae led detectives to men's hideout and identified them.

The testimony of a Sunday school teacher convicted the pair. The night before the murder, he had gone to see that the chapel was safely locked up and saw Wade talking to another man not far from Farmer's shop. The next morning the teacher passed the same men as they walked close to the shop. At Brixton Prison, he identified Donovan as the second man.

After three days of deliberation, jury members found both men Guilty of murder. There was little evidence, but it was enough. The two men were hanged the next day.

REF.: *CBA; Wensley, Forty Years of Scotland Yard.*

Donovan, George Thomas, b.1897, and **Taylor, Percival Leonard**, 1904- , and **Weaver, James**, 1907- , Brit., (wrong. convict.) mur. If a statement made by the murder victim before his death had been allowed in court as evidence, three men convicted of murder and sentenced to penal servitude for life likley would have been found Not Guilty.

George Donovan, thirty-one, Percival Taylor, twenty-four, and James Weaver, twenty-one, were all found Guilty of the 1928 murder of chemist Ernest Friend-Smith, found fatally wounded after being struck repeatedly by a large, soft object. His gold watch, chain, and £15 in treasury notes were taken. Court of Criminal Appeal Lord Chief Justice Heward remarked during the murder trial at his surprise that the victim did not provide a statement concerning his assailants before he died, for he had lingered for one month following the attack. But Friend-Smith had provided a statement, not deemed important enough to be read in court.

The three accused men were subsequently found Guilty based only on circumstantial evidence. Tacky green and white fluff was found sticking to the victim's pants, and a car eventually traced back to Donovan, Taylor, and Weaver had worn upholstery and frayed floor mats in the same color. A barmaid at the St. James' Hotel believed she saw the three accused and a man fitting Friend-Smith's description and said they all left together. Further, a Hastings woman said Donovan had told her he was in trouble with the police for hitting an old man in the jaw and would leave Brighton as soon as possible.

The jury concluded that Donovan, Taylor, and Weaver must be guilty and Justice Avory handed down a harsh condemnation. The decision made to convict the three unfortunates was based

on circumstantial evidence which at the time was all the evidence the jury thought existed.

Twenty-seven years after the trial, after Donovan had died and Weaver and Taylor had been released from prison, William Teeling, conservative Member of Parliament for the pavilion division of Brighton, revealed that Sir Ernley Blackwell had been shown a statement made by Friend-Smith before his death concerning his assailants. Blackwell showed that statement to his counselors and asked them what they would have done if they had known about it at the time. The overwhelming, tragic response was that they would not have found the men guilty. Yet Major Lloyd George, home secretary, maintained he did not consider the statement admissible in court because it was not done in the form of a proper dying declaration.

REF.: *CBA; O'Donnell, The Trials of Mr. Justice Avory; Shew, A Second Companion to Murder.*

Donovan, James J., prom. 1942-46, Case of, U.S., polit. corr. In 1942, while James J. Donovan was mayor of Bayonne, N.J., the county prosecutor raided nightclubs and taverns there, arresting more than forty people. Eleven black people were held, without being charged, for five months in the county jail, with bail set at $5,000. Not long after the raids began, Donovan was charged by a grand jury for misconduct in office. The black citizens had been picked up as supposed material witnesses, and had been intimidated into signing prepared statements. During their months in jail, they were not allowed to see attorneys or their families. When brought forward to testify at a hearing in early November, several said they were merely standing and watching the raid when they were arrested. They were returned to jail after the hearing, and within a week a federal judge gave them another hearing. Indicted for misconduct on June 30, 1942, were Donovan, former Police Chief Cornelius J. O'Neill, and former Deputy Mayor Daniel J. Sweeney. The three Bayonne officials fought for four years against the indictments. At a March 1946 trial, all three were acquitted on grounds of insufficient evidence. The extended delay between the indictment and the trial was the result of an appeal made to the state supreme court by their lawyer, former Judge John Warren, who had asked for a review to test the validity of the indictment. REF.: *CBA.*

Donovan, Raymond J., 1931- , Case of, U.S., fraud. An eight-month trial in 1986-87 monopolized the lives of 58-year-old Raymond Donovan, who resigned as U.S. labor secretary in light of criminal allegations against him, and seven other defendants, prosecuting and defending attorneys, twelve jurors, including one who suffered an emotional breakdown during the trial, and the families of everyone involved. But in the end the eight men charged with fraud and grand larceny were found innocent of all charges. It took the jury less than ten hours and one vote per defendant to come to its decision of Not Guilty.

Accusations against Donovan began after his nomination for labor secretary in 1980 by President Ronald Reagan. Though the charges against him did not involve his role in Reagan's administration, he felt compelled to resign in 1985 after he was ordered to stand trial. The charges, put forth by Bronx District Attorney Mario Merola, centered on Donovan, five executives of the Schiavone Construction Co. of Secaucus, N.J., and New York Senator Joseph L. Galiber, democrat of the Bronx, and William P. Masselli, Galiber's partner in the now-defunct Jopel Contracting and Trucking Corporation of Bronx, N.Y. The eight men and two companies were accused of plotting to swindle the New York City Transit Authority of $7.4 million on a subway construction project in the late 1970s and early 1980s.

Jury Forewoman Rosa Milligan said the charges were politically motivated and should never have been filed. There was no evidence to back the charges, juror Caesar Brown said.

"It's a cruel thing they did to me," Donovan lamented as he left the court a free and innocent man. See: **Merola, Mario; Reagan, Ronald**. REF.: *CBA.*

Donovan, William Joseph (AKA: **Wild Bill Donovan**), 1883-1959, U.S., lawyer. Named assistant to the U.S. attorney general

1925-29, head of the Office of Strategic Services, 1942-45, major general, 1944, and ambassador to Thailand, 1953-54. REF.: *CBA.*

Doody, William (AKA: Baby Face, Wee Willie), 1902-55, U.S., mur. William Doody looked like the neighborhood boy who delivers papers and mows lawns, but he was the kind of man who would pump a bullet through someone's head to get a wallet. "Baby Face" Doody, twenty-seven, terrorized Chicago, murdering two men in cold blood; but he paid for it with his life.

Doody was wanted dead or alive after killing the guard and tyrannizing passengers during the 1929 holdup of an Illinois Central train. He killed Chief of Police Charles Levy of Berwyn, Ill., and robbed a Cicero, Ill., post office of $18,000, wounding a U.S. postal inspector. Eventually, police closed in on him. Twenty or more sharpshooting policemen brandishing shotguns and revolvers surrounded his West Side Chicago apartment, watching and waiting on the roof and on flights of rickety stairs leading up to a rear apartment. Once there, they cut the screen door, crept into a room, and confronted him. Doody was putting his socks on when they entered and he just sat there, looking sheepish. He surrendered easily, said he was relieved the chase was over, and blamed his problems on bad company.

Despite his boyish charm, Doody was readily convicted of Levy's murder and sentenced to death. Appeals continued for twenty-five years, but on Sept. 29, 1955, the baby-faced killer died in Stateville Prison, Joliet, Ill. REF.: *CBA.*

Doo Lew (AKA: Frank Lew, Lew Wah, Lew Gar), prom. 1900, U.S., drugs. Seventeen-year-old Truls Halvorsen learned quickly that a mistake does not have to be final. Fortunately, this young Norwegian sailor decided to assist authorities in apprehending Doo Lew, U.S.-Hong Kong contact for one of the world's largest drug rings of the 1950s, after his initial involvement with them.

Halversen worked aboard Norway's *Fernhill,* earning a mere pittance, unable to afford the fine suits Chinese tailors sold to seamen. One such tailor, sensing the boy's impoverished position and youthful innocence, pegged Halvorsen as perfect for the opium-smuggling business. The Chinese offered the Norwegian $1,350 to smuggle ten bags of opium, each weighing about one pound, from the ship now anchored at Hong Kong, past customs to the vessel's ultimate destination of San Francisco. The money promised represented more than two years' pay for the boy, and he believed opium was nothing more than something smoked in ornate pipes in distant and darkened Oriental hideaways. He agreed to do it.

The ship set sail the next morning with Halvorsen, the San Francisco delivery address, half a coupon to match up with another half carried by the drug receiver, and ten bags of opium tied to his waist. But Halvorsen had one more thing with him the smugglers had not counted on: a conscience. With plenty of time to think during the long voyage to Suez, Halvorsen had desperate second thoughts. Unable to stand the illegality of the scheme, he contacted his pastor, John Henriksen, confessed his wrong, described the deal in detail, and asked if there would be any way to right his wrong.

The minister and FBI agents worked together in devising a plan for Halvorsen to help trap the drug dealers. The pressure mounted when, upon arriving in San Francisco, he learned his extra baggage had a street value of $3 million. But along with his conscience, Halvorsen had keen intelligence and an overwhelming desire to make amends. Together he and an undercover agent, posing as a fellow seaman, met Lew and his men in a prearranged hotel room. Halvorsen carried out the deal. With the exchange of money the agent drew his gun, whirled Lew around, handcuffed his hands behind his back, and, in doing so, wiped out one of the largest narcotics rings in the world. Lew was sentenced to four years in prison and Halvorsen was awarded $1,000.

REF.: *CBA;* Whitehead, *Border Guard.*

Dooley, Alvin, prom. 20th Cent., U.S., mansl. Alvin Dooley built a powerful police career upon ground too shaky to sustain it. When the first winds of challenge blew, the life he had

struggled to erect came down in one insane minute, leaving one man dead, one wounded, and Dooley guilty of manslaughter.

Dooley's premature birth in New York in the early 1900s was an omen of things to come. Fighting his frail beginnings, Dooley worked overtime to compensate for what he had been. What he became was a successful, popular Long Island policeman eventually elected president of the Police Benevolent Association, building funds to aid police widows and children with donations of $100 to $12,000. Later, he became secretary-treasurer of the association's parent group, The Police Conference of Nassau County. He was proud of his accomplishments and happy with his life.

But then came Dooley's one fear in life: that politics would worm its way into the police force and he would lose everything. In 1937 Louis F. Edwards, a hard-driven, domineering man, was elected mayor of Long Beach. Within two years, Edwards had altered the New York villa to his liking and had his eye on Dooley's PBA. Using corrupt power, he persuaded the members to vote for Detective James Horan as the group's new president. Despite initial resistance enough men were bullied by Edward's threats to get Horan elected, ousting Dooley.

Dooley was enraged. On Nov. 15, 1939, he confronted Edwards and Horan at Edwards' home. With five shots, he killed Edwards and critically wounded Horan.

At Dooley's Jan. 22, 1940, trial before Judge Cortland A. Johnson, his attorney, Samuel Leibowitz, struggled to convince an angry jury what he knew to be true. The man before them had been insane at the time he committed the act and, in fact, Edwards had been driving the man crazy for months. Day by day, public sentiment, which had made Edwards out to be a folk hero and Dooley as despicable, shifted. People began to sympathize with the man whose fears of losing it all were realized. The jury rejected charges against him of first-degree murder and found him Guilty of first-degree manslaughter. The ex-policeman was spared a death sentence, but he would spend the next ten to thirty years behind bars. See: **Leibowitz, Samuel S.**

REF.: *CBA;* Russell, *Best Murder Cases.*

Dooley, Rafer (AKA: Barefoot Dooley), prom. 1900, U.S., rob. Rafer Dooley, born and reared in rural Tennessee, wanted to make something more of his life than his backwoods parents had made of theirs. With an eighth grade education and a strong work ethic, he left the hills for St. Louis and later Chicago, taking odd jobs until he found his niche, as so many during Prohibition had, in the liquor hijacking business. Crime pays, he maintained. "If the venture succeeds, like when me and my constituents were distributing liquor on the North Side (of Chicago), it pays fine, very fine indeed," he said.

Early on Dooley worked for Dinty Colfax, who headed a liquor delivery group later called the "Egan Rats." Dooley relayed messages for his boss and ran whiskey across the border from Mexico to California. Conscientious, competitive, and lucky, his efforts paid off when, at eighteen, he relocated to Chicago.

Dooley rubbed elbows with Al Capone, Fred "Killer" Burke, and Gus Winkler. Because he had proven himself a hard and talented worker, the Irish North Side mob, under the leadership of Dion O'Bannion, made him responsible for whiskey distribution, but only in a five-block Chicago area. Dooley was hurt, and once or twice his life was threatened, but with a reputation for having the most vicious left hook in Chicago, he always came out all right.

He was virtually unconquerable by even the harsh California police. Arrested several times, Dooley was only convicted once, on a return trip to California in 1927, for robbing the cash box at a rodeo. After he had served his one-year sentence, Dooley reentered society with renewed conviction to work harder at what he did best. See: **Burke, Fred R.; Capone, Alphonse; O'Bannion, Charles Dion; Winkler, Gus.**

REF.: *CBA;* Kobler, *Ardent Spirits.*

Doolin, William M., 1858-96, U.S., west. outl. Bill Doolin, the son of an Arkansas farmer, rode into the Indian Territory (later Oklahoma) in 1881, working as a cowboy at the H-X Bar ranch, where the Dalton Brothers occasionally worked. Doolin was a taciturn, tough cowboy who was quick with his gun, and he left the ranch after being involved in a shooting in Coffeyville, Kan., in 1891. Two lawmen had tried to break up a beer party, and when they began pouring the brew on the floor, several cowboys, including Doolin, pulled their six-guns and fatally shot the two deputies. Doolin fled, joining the Daltons. Doolin participated in several train and bank robberies with the gang, but he escaped being killed with most of the Daltons on Oct. 5, 1892, when the gang raided two banks in Coffeyville.

Doolin missed the Coffeyville raid when his horse ostensibly pulled up lame and he told Bob Dalton that he would go to a nearby ranch to find another mount and join the gang later. By the time Doolin arrived at the Coffeyville city limits, the Daltons had died in a hail of bullets fired by irate citizens. Another story has it that Doolin quit the gang just before the Coffeyville debacle after arguing with Bob Dalton over how the spoils from the raid would be divided.

Oklahoma outlaw Bill Doolin, dead.

In 1893, Doolin married a preacher's daughter and then organized one of the most notorious outlaw bands in Oklahoma history, Doolin's "Oklahombres." The gang included Bill Dalton, last of the outlaw brothers; Dan Clifton, better known as Dynamite Dick; George "Bitter Creek" Newcomb; George "Red Buck" Weightman; Tulsa Jack Blake; Charley Pierce; Bob Grounds; Little Dick West; Roy Daugherty, also known as Arkansas Tom Jones; Alf Sohn; Little Bill Raidler; and Ole Yantis. For three years this gang raided banks, trains, and stagecoaches at will, headquartering in the wide open town of Ingalls, Okla.

On May 30, 1893, Doolin and three of his gang robbed a train near Cimarron, Kan. As they were fleeing, a large posse led by the noted lawman Chris Madsen cut off the band and a wild gunfight ensued in which Doolin was shot in the right foot. The outlaws escaped under the cover of darkness. After a number of robberies, a small army of lawmen slipped unnoticed into the outlaw town of Ingalls on Sept. 1, 1893. Inside the Ransom and Murray saloon, Doolin, Dalton, Clifton, Weightman, Newcomb, and Blake were drinking heavily. Roy Daugherty went to his room on the second floor of the City Hotel. As the gang members sat down to a poker game, Newcomb stepped into the street to check the horses. Dick Speed, one of the deputies who had taken cover across from the saloon, impulsively fired a shot at Newcomb and the battle of Ingalls commenced. Newcomb gave the alarm and then escaped by riding out of town in a hail of bullets. Meanwhile, the outlaws inside the saloon and Daugherty from his room fired their weapons from windows at the posse members.

As Deputy Speed raced down the street, one of the gang members shot him dead. Errant bullets killed Del Simmons, a boy watching the fight, and struck another citizen in the chest. The guns fell silent for some minutes and one of the deputies called out to Doolin, asking him and his men to surrender. "You go to hell!" Doolin shouted back and the fighting again erupted. Doolin and his men then dashed to the livery stable, mounted their horses, and fired wildly at the lawmen who shot at them as they rode in the same direction as Newcomb. Bill Dalton was trapped behind a fence and lost his horse. Deputy Lafe Shadley ran forward to kill Dalton with a shotgun but Dalton whirled about and shot Shadley dead. Then Doolin reappeared, racing down the street on his horse, riding to the spot where Dalton stood. He pulled Dalton up on the back of his horse and the two raced out of town.

The gang continued their raids, the largest haul being about $40,000, taken from an East Texas bank, but their days were numbered as more and more lawmen took to their trail. The greatest lawmen of the day, Chris Madsen, Bill Tilghman, and Heck Thomas, formed posses and chased the Doolins through five states, never giving gang members a moment's peace. Doolin was considered a fair-minded man and he reportedly saved Tilghman's life one night by stopping the gang's arch killer, Red Buck Weightman, from shooting Tilghman from ambush. Tilghman's posse was close on the heels of the Doolins one morning. Doolin and his men had just eaten a large breakfast at a farmhouse. As the gang leader stepped outside, he saw Tilghman and his men riding down a distant hill toward the farm. The hospitable farmer thought that the Doolins were part of a posse. Doolin told him that "the other boys coming along now" would be hungry and would want breakfast, too, and that they would pay for all the meals. Tilghman and his men arrived, ate a hearty meal, and were then told by the farmer that "the other boys" had told them Tilghman would pay for the meals. The lawman reluctantly dug into his pocket and paid the farmer for the food his own men and the outlaws had eaten.

In Southwest City, Mo., on May 20, 1895, the Doolin gang raided a local bank, but J.C. Seaborn, the state auditor, seized a gun and tried to stop the bandits. He was dead and Doolin seriously wounded in the head when the outlaws rode from the town. A few weeks later, near Dover, Okla., the gang was camped near the Cimarron River when lawmen suddenly swooped down on them. Tulsa Jack Blake, on guard, warned the gang and traded shots with the posse. Blake was shot and died of his wounds as Doolin and the others escaped. By this time, there was little left of the Doolin gang. Most of its members had ridden off to their own bloody fates. Doolin's own end was also drawing near. He was in Eureka Springs, Okla., when Bill Tilghman tracked him to a bathhouse where the two men fought with fists until the powerful Tilghman knocked Doolin cold and arrested him. Tilghman brought his notorious prisoner to Gutherie, Okla., to stand trial for train and bank robbery. Thousands lined the streets of the town to catch a glimpse of the outlaw. Doolin was cheered as he was taken to jail. He vowed he would never go to prison, and some weeks later he engineered a mass jail break in which he and thrity-seven other prisoners escaped.

Riding to Mexico, Doolin hid out at the ranch of writer Eugene Manlove Rhodes, but he pined for his family and was determined to have his wife and child with him. He rode back to his family, who were then living in Lawson, Okla. On the night of Aug. 25, 1896, Doolin was approaching his father-in-law's farmhouse, where his wife and child were staying. Lawmen led by Heck Thomas, however, had learned of Doolin's presence in the area and were waiting in ambush. Doolin appeared on foot, leading his horse, carrying a rifle, whistling as he walked in the bright moonlit night. Suddenly Thomas shouted from behind some bushes, calling to the outlaw to surrender. Doolin raised his rifle which was shot out of his hand by several shots fired by posse. Doolin then drew his six-gun and fired twice before a blast from a shotgun fired by Deputy Bill Dunn and rifle bullets fired by Thomas cut him to pieces. The outlaw's body was later displayed, naked from the waist up, to show the many holes made by shotgun pellets. See: **Blake, John; Clifton, Daniel; Dalton Brothers; Daugherty, Roy; Madsen, Christian; Newcomb, George; Pierce, Charles; Raidler, William; Thomas, Henry Andrew; Tilghman, William Matthew, Jr.; Weightman, George; West, Richard.**

REF.: American Guide Series, Tulsa, A Guide to the Oil Capital; Bartholomew, The Biographical Album of Western Gunfighters; Botkin, A Treasury of Western Folklore; Breihan, Badmen of Frontier Days; ___, Great Lawmen of the West; Bristow, Lost on Grand River; Bryant, Great American Guns and Frontier Fighters; Canton, Frontier Trails; CBA; Chilton, The Book of the West; Chrisman, Lost Trails of the Cimarron; Clark, Then Came the Railroads; Croy, Trigger Marshal; Dalton, Beyond the Law; ___, When the Daltons Rode; Day, Gene Rhodes, Cowboy; Debo, Tulsa: From Creek Town to Oil Capital; Douglas, The History of

Tulsa, Oklahoma; ____, *Territory Tales;* Drago, *Outlaws on Horseback;* ____, *Red River Valley;* ____, *Road Agents and Train Robbers;* Eisele, *A History of Noble County, Oklahoma;* Elman, *Fired in Anger;* Foreman, *A History of Oklahoma;* Gard, *Frontier Justice;* Gardner, *The Old Wild West;* Glasscock, *Then Came Oil;* Graves, *Oklahoma Outlaws;* Hanes, *Bill Doolin;* Harrington, *Hanging Judge;* Harrison, *Hell Holes and Hangings;* Hendricks, *The Bad Man of the West;* Hertzog, *A Directory of New Mexico Desperadoes;* Holloway, *Texas Gun Lore;* Horan, *Desperate Women;* ____, *The Great American West;* ____ and Sann, *Pictorial History of the Wild West;* Howard, *This is the West;* Howe, *Timberleg of the Diamond Tail;* Hunter and Rose, *The Album of Gunfighters;* Hutchinson, *The Life and Personal Writings of Eugene Manlove Rhodes;* Johnson, *Famous Lawmen of the Old West;* Jones, *Fiddlefooted;* Jones, *The Experiences of a Deputy U.S. Marshal of the Indian Territory;* Krumrey, *Saga of Sawlog;* Lamb, *Tragedies of the Osage Hills;* Lake, *Under Cover for Wells Fargo;* Linzee, *Development of the Oklahoma Territory;* McReynolds, *Thirty Years on the Frontier;* Masterson, *Famous Gunfighters of the Western Frontier;* Miller, *Bill Tilghman, Marshal of the Last Frontier;* Monaghan, *The Book of the American West;* Mootz, *Blazing Frontier;* Morris, *Oklahoma, Yesterday, Today, Tomorrow;* Nash, *Bloodletters and Badmen;* Newsom, *The Life and Practice of the Wild and Modern Indian;* Nix, *Oklahombres; Oklahoma, The Beautiful Land;* O'Neal, *Encyclopedia of Western Gunfighters;* O'Neal, *They Die But Once;* Osborn, *Let Freedom Ring;* Penfield, *Western Sheriffs and Marshals;* Preece, *The Dalton Gang;* Raine, *Famous Sheriffs and Western Outlaws;* ____, *Forty-Five Caliber Law;* ____, *Guns of the Frontier;* Rainey, *The Cherokee Strip;* Ray, *The Oklahoma Bandits;* Rayburn, *The Eureka Springs Story;* Rouse, *A History of Cowboy Flat;* Sabin, *Wild Men of the Wild West;* Schmitt and Brown, *The Settler's West;* Scott, *Such Outlaws as Jesse James;* Shirley, *Buckskin and Spurs;* ____, *Heck Thomas, Frontier Marshal;* ____, *Six-Gun and Silver Star;* ____, *Toughest of Them All;* Sonnichsen, *Outlaw Bill Mitchell;* ____, *Tularosa;* Stansbery, *The Passing of the 3D Ranch;* Sterling, *Famous Western Outlaw-Sheriff Battles;* Sutton, *Hands Up!;* Tilghman, *Marshal of the Last Frontier;* ____, *Outlaw Days;* Wellman, *A Dynasty of Western Outlaws;* Younger, *True Facts of the Lives of America's Most Notorious Outlaws;* (FILM), *Return of the Badmen,* 1948; *The Doolins of Oklahoma,* 1949; *Cattle Annie and Little Britches,* 1981.

Dooling, John Francis, Jr., 1908-81, U.S., jur. Received appointment to the Eastern District Court of New York from President John Kennedy, Sept. 22, 1961, and was a member of New York City bar association's special committee on penology. REF.: *CBA.*

Dooling, Maurice Timothy, 1860-1924, U.S., jur. Served as district attorney for San Benito County, Calif., 1892-96, and was appointed to the Northern District Court of California by President Woodrow Wilson, May 18, 1913. REF.: *CBA.*

Dorbell, Tom, c.1669-1714, Brit., rob.-rape-mur. Dorbell was an apprentice glove maker in Blandford when he ran away to London and, following in the footsteps of countless others, fell in with hardcore thieves. By the time he was seventeen, he had become a highwayman. His first attempt at highway robbery should have made him yearn for the glove shop in Blandford. He stopped a Welshman on the road and threatened to shoot him if he did not turn over all his money.

The Welshman explained that he had no money of his own, only some belonging to his employer which he could not surrender, even at the threat of death. Dorbell put his pistol to the Welshman's head and swore he would shoot if the money was not immediately turned over. The Welshman thought for a moment and then handed the money over. Before Dorbell could ride off with the loot, the Welshman asked for a favor. Would the young thief mind putting a bullet hole through his jacket so his boss would think he had put up a fight before giving up the money? Dorbell agreed; it seemed like a reasonable request. Had he not recently quit an apprenticeship? Dorbell knew the severity of certain employers.

The Welshman hung his coat on the branch of a tree and Dorbell fired once. The Welshman admired his shooting and asked Dorbell to fire again. This scene was repeated until Dorbell replied that he would like to add yet another hole to the jacket, but he had run out of bullets. At this moment, the Welshman drew his own pistol, which had been hidden, and demanded the return of the money. Dorbell meekly turned it over and watched as the Welshman retrieved his jacket, a trophy of his cunning maneuver, and rode away with a wave and a smile. Dorbell learned his lesson and he also acquired some cunning of his own. For the next five years he operated as a successful highwayman and then he walked into a Winchester courtroom and confessed to another man's crime. The guilty man was the son of a wealthy squire. Dorbell had been hired by the squire to somehow free his son, who had been charged with highway robbery. Dorbell sat with the other spectators and listened as the damning evidence was put forward. The jury returned a verdict of Guilty, but before the judge could pass sentence, Dorbell started to chant, "Oh, what a sad thing it is to shed innocent blood! Oh, what a sad thing it is to shed innocent blood!" When he would not quiet down, he was taken into custody and brought before the very same judge who asked him to explain himself. Dorbell explained he was guilty of the crimes for which the young man had been convicted, and that he found it impossible to stand by and watch an innocent man be executed for crimes he had not committed. After hearing this, the judge ordered the guilty man acquitted. Dorbell was then taken to the Winchester jail to await trial on the charges.

When the trial date arrived, Dorbell shocked the courtroom by pleading not guilty. After some deliberation, the judge realized he had no choice but to release Dorbell. Certainly, there were no witnesses who would dare testify against the daring young highwayman. They had testified against the other man and to have changed their testimony would have caused them to be charged with perjury. Two young highwaymen were now free, one escaping justice, and the other making a mockery of it. Dorbell was also that much richer, by the payment he had received for his act of trickery. The money did not last long and once again Dorbell was back on the highway plying his trade.

One day he attacked the Duke of Norfork's coach on the Salisbury plains. The Duke and his servants refused to "stand and deliver" and in the gunfight that followed, Dorbell's horse was shot out from under him. He was captured and brought to Salisbury where he was tried, convicted, and sentenced to death.

But the wily highwayman had plans to cheat the hangman. He had long ago learned that there was one set of laws for the rich and the well-connected and another set for everyone else. He found a well-established lawyer, offering to pay him fifty guineas if he could secure a pardon. The lawyer rode to London and, through his influential contacts, returned with a pardon in hand. The lawyer rode his horse mercilessly to arrive just as Dorbell was being led to the gallows. Legend has it that as soon as he handed the reprieve to the sheriff, his horse dropped dead.

This close call so frightened Dorbell that he actually led an honest life for the next seven years, employed as a servant of a wealthy woman in London. Dorbell, however, had not wholly converted to a life of honesty. As proof of this, he did not bother to pay the lawyer who had arranged the pardon and saved his life. The lawyer lived to regret ever obtaining the pardon and the wealthy woman lived to regret ever hiring Dorbell; her niece was to die before she learned her lesson.

The employer thought she was doing her niece a favor when she talked her brother Nevil Thompson into sending his daughter from Bristol to London so the niece could receive a better education. The girl was sixteen. Dorbell delivered the message and was to be the niece's escort on the trip back to London. On the trip to London, Dorbell suddenly knocked the girl to the floor of the coach; he tied her and raped her, even though she fainted before he finished. Dorbell then stole the large sum of money she carried and any other valuables he could find and cut a hole through the back of the coach, slipping out undetected by the coachman.

Two hours later the coach reached an inn, at which time the girl was discovered. The niece was bruised and bloodied; after she told her story several of the townsmen immediately mounted and went after Dorbell. The girl survived only one day, dying a few moments after her mother arrived at her bedside. Dorbell was captured two days later and taken to Newgate Prison in London, then transferred to Newgate Prison in Bristol where he was convicted and sentenced to death. He was hanged on St. Michael's Hill on Mar. 23, 1714. His body was then cut down and hanged in chains.

REF.: *CBA; Smith, Highwaymen.*

Dorfman, Allen M., 1923-83, U.S., (unsolv.) assass. To this day no one knows for certain who gunned down convicted labor racketeer and insurance multimillionaire Allen Dorfman. The 60-year-old husband, father of three, who was a good friend and business associate to Mafia giants like Anthony Spilotro and labor leaders like Jimmy Hoffa, president of the Teamsters, had just finished dining at T.J. Peppercorn's restaurant in the Lincolnwood, Ill., Hyatt Hotel on Jan. 20, 1983, when he was killed by a volley of bullets.

Approximately one month earlier, Dorfman had been convicted, along with Teamsters president Roy Lee Williams and three other men, of attempting to bribe U.S. Senator Howard Cannon, Democrat from Nevada, to hold off a trucking deregulation bill. Dorfman faced a stiff prison sentence for this and other indiscretions. He would also be tried in federal court on charges that he blew up the Lake Forest, Ill., home belonging to the late Robert Kendler, a real-estate developer, after Kendler refused to buy out Dorfman's 50-percent share in a real-estate endeavor the two had planned. Furthermore, Dorfman awaited the outcome of an indictment returned a week earlier. Before the fatal shooting, he had attempted to raid the funds of a labor union located in San Francisco.

Two days prior to his assassination, Dorfman had won back control of Amalgamated Insurance Agency Services, Inc., and three other businesses he owned, when a federal judge dismissed a court-appointed receiver who had been overseeing Dorfman's estate since his conviction in December.

Amalgamated was a corporate front behind which Dorfman's $9-million-plus estate was routed. The walls of this gilded empire had begun crumbling under their own weight several months before Dorfman's untimely death because of his conviction and building charges. Key players speculating over the identity of the man's assailant said Dorfman had become vulnerable to pressure from the government and was deemed dangerous to Mafia operations.

Names most often connected with the Dorfman murder included Teamsters president Williams and mobster Joseph "The Clown" Lombardo, convicted along with Dorfman for attempting to bribe Cannon. Alva Johnson, convicted car thief who spent twenty-three years in prison and then served as a government informer, said Marshall Caifano, a supposed member of the Chicago Mafia, told him Lombardo was the guilty man.

Dorfman led a double life—one the esteemed, elegant businessman, the other the shady participant in mob activities. A former high school gym teacher, he first became involved in the insurance business in 1949, when he formed the Union Insurance Agency. Early in 1950, the firm won part of a Teamsters health and welfare insurance contract, and it is likely that this is when Allen Dorfman first began his dealings with the mob. He and his wife owned an opulent $750,000 home in Deerfield, Ill., a $350,000 summer home in Southern California, and a 167-acre lodge and horse-breeding farm in Eagle River, Wis. In 1977, he was chosen the Little City Foundation's Man of the Year. Dorfman befriended many businessmen and politicians, including Mayor Michael Bilandic. Unluckily for him, however, he associated with a rougher crowd as well. See: **Caifano, Marshall Joseph; Hoffa, James Riddle; Lombardo, Joseph; Spilotro, Anthony; Williams, Roy Lee.**

REF.: *CBA;* Davis, *Mafia Kingfish;* Demaris, *The Last Mafioso;* Fried, *The Rise and Fall of the Jewish Gangster in America;* Morgan, *Prince of Crime;* Navasky, *Kennedy Justice;* Peterson, *The Mob;* Reid, *The Grim Reapers;* Velie, *Desperate Bargain: Why Jimmy Hoffa Had to Die;* Zucker-

man, *Vengeance Is Mine.*

Dorion, Sir **Antoine Aimé,** 1816-91, Can., jur. Held position as minister of justice, 1873-74, and was chief justice for the court of the queen's bench in Quebec, 1874-91. REF.: *CBA.*

Dorislaus, Isaac, 1595-1649, Brit., jur., assass. Participated in the Bishop's War, 1640, and in the army of Essex, 1642, he was the acting judge advocate. He also sat on the admiralty court, 1648, and was assassinated the following year. REF.: *CBA.*

Dormoy, René Marx, 1889-1941, Fr., assass. Socialist minister of the interior during France's Popular Front Days, René Marx Dormoy made lasting enemies with his outspoken remarks against popular groups of the day, including Communists and pro-Nazis. He publicly condemned Marshal Henri Pétain while in the Chamber of Deputies following France's fall in WWII, and, working for a return of democracy, was interned. Just months before his death, the 52-year-old former minister was released and placed under constant police surveillance at Montelimar in the Rhone Valley.

The police must have lifted their guard for the split second it took someone to plant a clockwork bomb under Dormoy's bed, killing him instantly when the device detonated as he slept. The explosive was the work of one of his enemies. The big question lies in which one. REF.: *CBA.*

Dorotheus, prom. 6th Cent., Syria, jur. At the request of Emperor Justinian he collaborated on legal doctrines; the Digest, 533, with Tribonian and Theophilus, an introduction to the Digest, known as the Institutes, 533, and the second edition of the Codex, 534. REF.: *CBA.*

Dorr, Thomas Wilson, 1805-54, U.S., consp. Instigated Dorr's Rebellion in Rhode Island, and organized the People's party, submitting a more liberal state constitution, 1841, which the electorate passed almost unanimously, but which government officials declared illegal. He was elected governor by the People's party, 1842, which resulted in a second government for the state. Dorr was convicted and sentenced to life imprisonment in 1844, but granted amnesty the following year. REF.: *CBA.*

Dorrego, Manuel, 1787-1828, Arg., pres., assass. Acted as provisional governor of Buenos Aires on return from exile in U.S., 1820, won election as governor of Buenos Aires, 1827, and as provisional president was captured and assassinated by rebels who favored General Juan Lavalle. REF.: *CBA.*

Dorsey, Charles (AKA: **Moore, Thorne**), prom. 1879, U.S., rob.-mur. Charles Dorsey's neighbors in Union City, Ind., were so fond of him they did not care if he had robbed a stagecoach and killed one of its passengers. Now he was a prosperous wood merchant and they liked him. Despite threats of mob violence, a detective apprehended the villain and saw that justice was done.

On Sept. 1, 1879, John Patterson, alias John Collins, and cohort Charles Dorsey held up the Eureka stage. Only banker William Cummings of Moore's Flat, Calif., put up a struggle to save a gold bar then worth $6,700. He lost his life at the hands of Dorsey.

The robbers finished their job, rode off, and later split the proceeds. Patterson furthered his criminal career in St. Louis, where the law caught up with him and he was hanged. Dorsey used his share of the gold bar to start a legitimate wood business in Indiana. But the truth caught up with him as well. Under protest from the townspeople, Detective Lees had Dorsey tried. He was convicted and sentenced to life at San Quentin Prison. It is believed that he would have gotten a death sentence if his clever attorney had not referred to Dorsey's brilliant war record for the benefit of jurors who had been soldiers themselves. Dorsey escaped from prison in 1887 but was recaptured in 1890.

REF.: *CBA; Duke, Celebrated Criminal Cases in America.*

Dorsey, Richard, and **Lietke, Andrew** (AKA: Andy Ryan), prom. 1910, U.S., wh. slav. On Jan. 5, 1910, Richard Dorsey and Andrew Lietke were finally arrested for a crime they had been committing for years. These two were in the business of tricking rural girls and women into the city under the pretense of their becoming store employees. Once they had the unsuspecting, unsophisticated ladies away from home, they would sell them to prostitution rings for a hefty profit. It took several years, but someone finally discovered their operation. The two were tried and convicted. For destroying the lives of innocent girls, Dorsey and Lietke were sentenced to six months in the House of Correction and a fine of $300 each.

REF.: *CBA*; Roe, *Great War On White Slavery.*

DOSAAF, 1965, U.S.S.R., embez. In 1965, crooked Soviet businessmen organized a design operation called DOSAAF, or the Voluntary Society for Aid to the Soviet Armed Forces, that covered an embezzlement scam.

By the time the jig was up, the group had completed experimental operations under twenty-eight research contracts dealing with underwater apparatus and underwater research. Their activities were out in the open, but their bookkeeping was kept well hidden, because, for a least some DOSAAF affiliates, that is how they made their money. Instead of starting an organization bank account, the director opened several savings accounts in his own name. Contracts were signed for work that had nothing to with underwater exploration or research and many were embezzling. Those who did were prosecuted.

REF.: *CBA*; Chalidze, *Criminal Russia.*

Dos Santo, Francisco (AKA: Francisco Son), d.1806, U.S., mur. A sailor serving on board a U.S. merchant vessel, Francisco Dos Santo was a shifty seaman with an unsavory past, having committed several burglaries and robberies. He proved near mutinous to his captain, Archibald Graham. When the ship docked in New York harbor, the captain was visited by his daughter and Dos Santo made some suggestive remarks to her which Captain Graham overheard. Enraged, Graham knocked Dos Santo down and threatened to have him jailed if he ever again came near him, his daughter, or his ship. For two days, Dos Santo trailed Captain Graham in his travels around New York and finally, while hiding in an alley, attacked Graham from behind, stabbing him to death. Dos Santo was recognized as he fled and was quickly arrested and tried on a charge of murder in New York on Jan. 9, 1806, being found Guilty. He was sentenced to death and hanged on Mar. 28, 1806.

REF.: *CBA*; *A Full and Particular account of the Trial of Francisco Dos Santo; The Trial of Francisco Son.*

Doss, Nannie (AKA: Arsenic Annie), 1905-65, U.S., mur. Nannie Doss of Tulsa, Okla., murdered eleven people because, she said, "I was searching for the perfect mate, the real romance of life," which left everyone wondering why it was necessary for her to do away with her mother, two sisters, and the nephew of one of her deceased husbands. The crimes of Nannie Doss came to the attention of the police in October 1954 when Dr. N.Z. Schwelbein decided to conduct an autopsy on Mrs. Doss' fifth husband, Samuel. Dr. Schwelbein had been the first to examine Mr. Doss after he was admitted to the local hospital. The stomach pains Doss complained of seemed highly suspicious to Schwelbein. "Whatever he had might kill somebody else," Nannie said. "It's best to find out."

Nannie Doss with husband Samuel.

The results of the autopsy startled even the most trained medical observers. There was enough arsenic in Samuel Doss to kill twenty strong men. The police took Nannie Doss into custody. She expressed bewilderment. Samuel had eaten his stewed prunes and there was certainly no arsenic to be found there. The police were relentless. Before the Miranda Supreme Court decision, a suspect could be questioned for hours without an attorney present. It was known as the third degree, and for

the next several days Mrs. Doss sat under the hot light. Police asked her about her fourth husband, Richard Morton, who had perished under similar circumstances. "I never heard of any Richard Morton," she demurred. The police pressed further. "What? You don't remember your previous husband?" "Oh, that Richard Morton!" Suddenly it was all clear to her. "Yes, I was married to him."

Finally, Doss broke down and told an incredible story. She had poisoned four of her five husbands, and two infant children. Her first husband survived, but two of their three children died at an early age. The symptoms were always the same: horrible stomach pain followed by sudden death. Nannie gave husband [Arlie Lanning], rat poison for breakfast one morning. Mystified investigators went tracking through graveyards in search of other victims. By the time the bodies of the victims had been exhumed

Nannie Doss at her trial in Tulsa, Okla., with daughter Melvina and grandchildren.

the death toll stood at eleven. Large quantities of arsenic were found in the remains. At least four of the victims had perished in great pain. At her trial, Nannie Doss ticked off the names of the victims and circumstances of the murders. She said that she had collected small insurance premiums on each of her husbands, but financial gain was never the real motive. Nannie Doss had ended the lives of her husbands, she explained, because they were "dullards."

Marriage was unlike anything Doss had read about in *True Romance*, her favorite publication. Convicted of murder, Mrs. Doss was sent to prison for life. She died there of leukemia in 1965. Copies of romance magazines were found strewn about her cell.

REF.: *CBA*; Holmes, *Serial Murder;* Nash, *Look For the Woman;* ____, *Murder, America.*

Dossena, Alceo, prom. 1927, U.S.-Italy, forg. The 700-year-old *Madonna and Child* wooden sculpture owned by the Cleveland Museum of Art, had certainly survived well the thirteeen centuries since its construction. But when the museum randomly decided to check its authenticity, their tests found that the religious icon was held together with modern nails and was only seven years old.

The museum had purchased the statue from the Italian art gallery of Fasoli & Palesi whose representatives had guaranteed that the work was authentic. But after an investigation, Italian artist Alceo Dossena admitted to carving the piece and selling it, among others to Fasoli & Palesi, as an imitation, not as an authentic discovery. Dosseno quickly became somewhat of a local folk hero, and enjoyed a booming business as it became fashionable to own a Dossena "fake masterpiece." Trendy Italians were filling their homes with his affordable copies of more famous works. Dossena was cleared of all charges while the gallery of Fasoli & Palesi went out of business.

REF.: *CBA; Wade, Great Hoaxes and Famous Imposters.*

Dostler, Anton, d.1945, Ger., war crimes. One down, many to go. General Anton Dostler was the first Nazi general to be executed for war crimes. Dostler, who had ordered the execution of fifteen American soldier-prisoners of war, was executed himself, in December 1945, by a U.S. firing squad in Aversa, Italy. Dostler's defense, that he was following Adolf Hitler's orders, did not get him far. To shoot uniformed men without a trial violates the international code of war. See: **Hitler, Adolf.** REF.: *CBA.*

Dost Mohammad Khan, 1793-1863, Afg., rebel. Participated in rebellion against Mahmud Shah, 1818-26, and gained control of the throne, 1826, beginning the Barakzai dynasty. He was captured by the British, 1840, but regained throne, 1843, when British troops were driven out of Kabul. REF.: *CBA.*

Dostoevsky, Fëdor Mikhailovich, 1821-81, Rus., treas. The great Russian novelist, Fëdor Mikhailovich Dostoevsky, was born in Moscow and served in the army from 1841 to 1844, resigning his officer's commission to write. He became deeply involved in radical political causes, although he was never overtly linked to anarchists dedicated to murdering the czar and overthrowing the government. He became involved with an intellectual group headed by Mikhailm Vasilyevich Petrashevsky which was little more than a literary circle meeting to discuss the novels of French socialists. This group, along with Doestoevsky, was arrested by czarist police on April 23, 1849, and charged with running an illegal printing press and printing treasonous propaganda.

All of the group's members were imprisoned and kept behind bars for eight months. Then, Dostoevsky and the others were suddenly pulled from the cells and taken to a prison yard where an execution squad stood before them, ready to shoot them to death. At the last minute, with the execution squad aiming its weapons at the terrified group of intellectuals, an officer appeared and stopped the execution, telling the so-called conspirators that their actual punishment had been prison sentences in Siberia. Dostoevsky never forget this horrifying experience and would use the scene in his novel, *The Idiot.*

Dostoevsky was sentenced to serve four years hard labor at the prison in Omsk, after which he was to serve an obligatory four years in the army. The author's prison years brought him into contact with the lower classes, an experience no other Russian writer of high birth had undergone, and one that gave him a vast wealth of knowledge concerning the Russian people, as well as deep insights into the Russian character which permeated his later novels. Dostoevsky's prison experiences produced a direct work, *The House of the Dead,* which, though gloomy and shocking, has brilliant passages which were supposedly inspired by the New Testament, the only book the author was permitted to read while serving his sentence in Omsk.

REF.: *CBA; Mochulsky, Dostoevsky.*

Doto, Joseph, See: **Adonis, Joseph.**

Dotson, Clint, d.1904, and **Fleming, Jim**, d.1902, U.S., mur. Prison bars and family ties could not keep vicious Clint Dotson, born and bred in Montana, from killing again.

Dotson already was serving a life sentence for murdering prospector Gene Cullinane. He had plenty of quiet time in prison to devise a way to get himself absolved of all charges in that murder. He summoned a good friend, Jim Fleming, and offered him a share of $50,000 he had made in a Union Pacific robbery if Fleming would kill Dotson's father, staging the scene to make it look as though Oliver Dotson had killed himself in remorse for being the one truly guilty in the Cullinane murder. The plan almost worked.

But clever undersheriff John Robinson did some fancy questioning and was able to get Fleming to admit that he had killed old man Dotson and staged the scene to look like suicide.

The two men were sentenced to death. Fleming was hanged on Sept. 6, 1902, and Dotson in April 1904. REF.: *CBA.*

Dotson, Gary, c. 1957- , U.S., (wrong. convict.) rape. In 1977, a 16-year-old suburban Chicago high school girl, Cathleen Crowell, panicked after having sex with her boyfriend. Afraid that she might be pregnant, Crowell made up a story about being abducted and raped, a crime she claimed occurred on July 9, 1977. She identified Gary Dotson as her attacker. Dotson was convicted of the assault in May 1979 and was sentenced to twenty-five to fifty years in prison. Six years later, in March 1985, Crowell, now Cathleen Crowell Webb, a mother, married and living in New Hampshire, recanted the story of her rape. She explained that she was a reborn Christian and could no longer tolerate her guilt over falsely identifying Dotson. National attention focused on the case, and after serving six years, Dotson was released from jail on Apr. 4, 1985, on a $100,000 bond. A week later, he was back in prison, after Cook County Circuit Court Judge Richard Samuels ruled that Webb's testimony was false. On May 1, Dotson was released on a $100,000 bond set by the Illinois Supreme Court, and he agreed to take a lie detector test. Results indicated that he told the truth when he said he did not rape Webb, and that he had never seen the girl before she accused him. A three-day televised hearing by Governor James Thompson reexamined evidence in the case. Thompson concluded that Dotson had raped Webb, but he commuted Dotson's sentence to the six years already served, refusing to pardon him.

During the next two years, Dotson was involved in a number of run-ins with the law. He was charged with drunken driving and assault against his wife and a tavern worker; his parole was revoked. On Jan. 21, 1987, Dotson was sentenced to a year of court supervision, and ordered to continue treatment for alcoholism. He was fined $500 for driving while drunk in March 1987. Continuing to seek a new trial to clear his name, Dotson was frustrated twice when judges ruled that Webb's recantation was not believable. In August 1987, Dotson was arrested and jailed again, accused of hitting his wife during a fight. Although his spouse dropped the charges, his parole was revoked by the Illinois Prisoner Review Board. He was returned to jail, then released on Dec. 24, 1987, on "a last chance order," signed by the governor. Two days later, Dotson was charged with disorderly conduct and battery in a Calumet City bar. Within five weeks, those charges were dropped.

In 1988, new genetics tests by a California scientist indicated that Dotson could not have been responsible for a semen stain that was the state's key physical evidence in the original trial. He was paroled again after serving six months for violating his "last chance" release, and on Aug. 14, 1989, the rape charge against him was dropped. Webb's lawyer, John McLario, spoke for his client, Cathy Webb, saying, "We're pleased that Gary has truly been proved innocent of these crimes." Dotson told reporters he believes that being once convicted of rape is a "stigma" that he will carry with him for years. An admitted alcoholic, he said he would return for alcohol abuse treatment for another month or more. REF.: *CBA.*

Doty, Sile, 1800-76, U.S., theft. Doty ventured to America in the early nineteenth century because he believed the New World offered him greater opportunities to use his intelligence and skills to become successful. By his own accounts, Doty was accomplished. He also was a wicked thief.

Sile Doty did his best to improve robbery technology. His specialty was breaking and entering, especially into jewelry stores and hotels, which he entered with delicate tools he devised himself. His burglary kit included "the best set of keys in the nation," a pair of thin pliers that could be inserted in any keyhole to turn the key, and an ample supply of putty for taking impressions of keys.

Skillful and sly, he once made handcuffs for a not-too-bright sheriff, keeping a key for himself and passing out duplicates to all of his friends. A few months later the sheriff approached Doty complaining that a "lock-picking" scoundrel had escaped from him with the handcuffs. Good-natured Sile made him a new pair.

Also a good businessman, Doty rose to the top ranks of thieves and eventually organized a vast crime ring which encompassed New England and most of the young Midwest.

He bragged that crime did pay, but even he had professional setbacks, spending at least twenty years of his life, on and off, in the Jackson Penitentiary in Michigan. At age seventy-two Doty at last changed his mind. "Crime no longer pays," he said.

REF.: *CBA;* Hamilton, *Men of the Underworld.*

Doty Affair, 1926, Syria, milit. des. Young Bennet J. Doty of Memphis, Tenn., apparently did not know what he was doing when, in the early 1920s, he left his southern home and gave up his U.S. citizenship to join the French Foreign Legion. When he discovered that traipsing through mosquito-infested African jungles was not for him, he set himself up for execution.

Doty abandoned the French lines in southern Syria where the Legion was campaigning against the Druse tribesmen, deserting his post before armed rebels.

A Damascus court-martial tried Doty for desertion. In an attempt to make an example of him, the Foreign Legion planned to give him the most extreme punishment allowed for his crimes: death.

While there was no legal pull in the U.S. to save Doty's life, there was just enough emotional pull. Doty's father persuaded Tennessee Senators Tyson and McKellar to ask the State Department in Washington to save his son's life. The department, in turn, instructed Ambassador Herrick to intercede with French Premier Aristide Briand. The Premier negotiated with War Minster Painlevé, who contacted Damascus just in time and Doty's life was spared. Instead, he was sentenced to eight years at hard labor and spent those years building roads in Africa, very much relieved. REF.: *CBA.*

Douat, Vital (AKA: **Roberti, Bernardi, Signor Rubini**), prom. 1865, Fr.-Brit.-Neth., fraud. The criminal always returns to the scene of the crime. In the case of Vital Douat, the place was Europe and the crime fraud. It took Scotland Yard detective Druscovich and European police two tries and two crimes, but they finally nabbed the man and sentenced him to penal servitude. Douat's wife and accomplice disappeared when her husband committed his first crime and never was heard from again.

The Douats' Bordeaux, France, wine business looked prosperous in the mid-nineteenth century. The couple lived well in their villa on the outskirts of town, entertained lavishly and often, but all the while they were going further into debt. People thought it strange that such a keen business tycoon would have forgotten to insure his life for the sake of his wife, but excused his error in judgment when the middle-aged Douat took out a large policy from a Paris insurance company.

People began to understand things better when Douat declared bankruptcy and, ostensibly to create a new life for himself, moved to London. By then, Bordeaux friends suspected that Douat had plenty of money stashed away which he had forgotten to mention to authorities when declaring bankruptcy.

Suddenly, Douat died. Something about the composed way his wife demanded her insurance money tipped officials off that something was amiss. Her manner, coupled with the coincidences of the life insurance, the suspicious bankruptcy, the flight, and death, were too extraordinary. Scotland Yard detective Druscovich jumped on the case.

He learned of a landlord who earlier had had a tenant named Bernardi, a fat, jovial Frenchman, who left suddenly when a strange man no one had ever seen before died. Bernardi threw the man an elaborate funeral and disappeared. Then Druscovich met a French waiter who had briefly met fellow Frenchman Bernardi. The two shared conversation, jokes, wine, and one practical joke. The waiter told how Bernardi had gotten him to write a mock death certificate, as a joke for Bernardi's friend,

Douat, which he was to send to him with a letter saying that now he understood his silence since he was dead.

Next, Druscovich interviewed those in charge of planning the funeral for Bernardi's friend and learned that a M. Douat had been buried nearby. No one had seen the deceased placed in the coffin because friend Bernardi had insisted on doing that job himself. Druscovich knew that the next place he had to go was the cemetery and into the coffin.

He found just what he was looking for: nothing. The mystery was solved. Douat had clearly staged his own funeral so his wife could collect the insurance money. But by now the man had gone to the U.S. and his wife was nowhere to be found. There was nothing the British authorities could do but wait.

Patience paid off. Trusting Douat, who had found business poor in the New World, had returned to Europe, this time to live and work (and swindle) in Holland. Not only did he come back, but he tried the same swindle again when he staged a fire in his new shipping business to collect insurance money. He was promptly found Guilty of this crime by the Dutch, at which point the French said they would like their chance with him. He was found Guilty of fraud there, too, and sentenced to penal servitude on Devil's Island.

REF.: *CBA;* Cobb, *Critical Years at the Yard;* Dilnot, *Triumphs of Detection.*

Double Indemnity, 1943, a novella by James M. Cain. Though the manner of murder and the occupations of the killers are different, the husband slayers are strongly tied to real-life murderers Judd Gray and Ruth Snyder (U.S., 1927). (Published in Great Britain as *Three of a Kind.*) A motion picture of the same name was also produced (1944). See: **Snyder, Ruth May.** REF.: *CBA.*

Double S Murder, See: **Morrison, Steinie.**

Doudet, Célestine, b.1817, Case of, Fr., mur. Queen Victoria praised highly and found governess work for a young Frenchwoman later charged with murdering two children in her care. Despite the fact that three young British girls, the girls' aunt, uncle, and father, a physician, and several witnesses all told the same gruesome story of the torture and subsequent death of children at the hands of Célestine Doudet, twenty-seven, the jury found her Not Guilty of the charges against her.

Dr. Marsden, a widower and father of five girls, sought a governess for his brood and was highly impressed with Doudet, especially since the Queen herself had given her such a lofty recommendation. But Doudet began her strange treatment of the girls virtually the day she went to work. First, she informed their father that the children harbored horrible vices including lying, cheating, and stealing. Foolishly, the father accepted her words at face value and instructed the young woman to deal with the children strictly.

The doctor remarried, and Doudet, who had convinced him she was indispensable, revealed plans to move to Paris and begin a boarding school for young ladies. Marsden implored the woman to take his girls with her, for which he would pay highly. Once in Paris, however, Doudet did not open a boarding school but something like a torture chamber. According to information that would seep through later, Doudet was physically and mentally destroying the girls she was being paid to care for and educate. She would later be charged with striking the girls, starving them, locking them in closets for days at a time, tying them to the floor and the foot of her bed, and kicking them. A doctor would testify that her actions contributed to the deaths of two of Marsden's daughters.

Despite an overwhelming amount of evidence supporting the claims of Doudet's bestial actions, she was found, in 1855, Not Guilty of contributing to the death of young Mary Ann Marsden.

The outraged Marsden family and friends made sure the case was not closed there. Soon, Doudet faced charges of having beaten the three surviving Marsden girls. The case was tried in Paris on Mar. 9, 1855, and Doudet was found Guilty and sentenced to two years' imprisonment. Her appeal backfired. Eventually she was condemned to five years' imprisonment and forced to pay the costs of both trials.

REF.: *CBA;* Hartman, *Victorian Murderesses;* Williamson, *Annals of Crime.*

Dougal, Samuel Herbert (AKA: Sidney Domville), 1846-1903, Brit., forg.-mur. Samuel Dougal, a military man, joined the Royal Engineers at the age of twenty and was assigned to Chatham. In 1869, after three years in the service, he married Miss Griffiths. In 1873, after having children by several mistresses, Dougal went with his regiment to Halifax, Nova Scotia, where he was promoted to sergeant and given spacious living quarters in the Military Lumber Yard apartment block.

In 1885, after he was promoted to quartermaster sergeant, Dougal's wife became sick and died. The army sent Dougal back to Enbland to recover from his grief. When he returned to Canada, Dougal had brought with him a new wife, who brought with her a lavish dowry. Then, within weeks, the second wife died. No one seems to have questioned Dougal, who soon married the daughter of a local farmer and took her with him to England when his regiment was transferred. After she bore him a child, Dougal sent the woman back to her father in Canada.

Eventually, Samuel Dougal retired from the military with a small pension. While serving with the Royal Military Hospital in Dublin, Dougal committed several forgeries. He passed two bogus checks in the names of Lord Wolseley and Captain Viscount Frankfort. He served one year in prison for these crimes and was released in January 1897.

In September 1898, Dougal met Camille Cecile Holland in a rooming house in Ladbroke Grove. She was a few years older than Dougal, but he was captivated by her and her £7,000 income and determined to make her his wife. The couple married, rented a home in Parkmore Hassocks, Sussex, and then moved to Saffron Walden in Essex. On Apr. 27, 1899, they moved again, into an elegantly appointed cottage which they called Coldham Farm. Dougal hired a series of housemaids and had affairs with all of them, which angered his wife.

Mrs. Dougal told her husband to get out. The current maid and lover voluntarily left and Mrs. Dougal soon consented to travel with her husband on a shopping trip. Dougal shot her with a handgun while they were traveling in their buggy and left her body in a drainage ditch. He then claimed her savings accounts, deeds, and stock shares by forging her signature on transfer papers. He said his wife had left him. For the next four years Dougal lived a life of ease. On Mar. 19, 1903, Dougal was arrested by the Essex Police after a bank teller detected a forgery on a banknote he tried to cash. Police searched his farm and found the decomposed remains of a woman in the drainage ditch. A pathologist's inquiry showed that the victim had been shot through the head. Clothing established that the corpse was Mrs. Dougal's.

On June 22, 1903, Samuel Dougal went on trial at the Chelmsford Assizes. He was found Guilty of murder and hanged.

REF.: Altick, *Victorian Studies In Scarlet;* Arthur, *All the Sinners;* Brock, *A Casebook of Crime;* Butler, *Murderers' England; CBA;* Dilnot, *The Real Detective;* _____, *Triumphs of Detection;* Hastings, *The Other Mr. Churchill;* Kingston, *Law-Breakers;* Lambton, *Thou Shalt Do No Murder;* Laurence, *A History of Capital Punishment;* Nicholls, *Crime Within the Square Mile; Notable British Trials;* Pearson, *More Studies In Murder;* Shew, *A Companion to Murder;* Shore, *Crime and Its Detection;* Wilson, *Encyclopedia of Murder;* Wood, *Survivors' Tales of Famous Crimes;* (DRAMA), Corwin, *The Moat Farm Murder.*

Doughty, Jack (AKA: Charley Cooper), prom. 1920, Can., theft. Canadian authorities wasted at lot of manpower in 1920 in convicting and sentencing Jack Doughty to seven years at Kingston Penitentiary for stealing $105,000 in Victory Bonds. In the end, a dupe named Bill Richardson, who had earned a detective's badge and pistol through a correspondence school course, found Doughty and earned a $15,000 reward. Even with this, the greater mystery was never solved.

For months detectives, police, and fortune hunters after the reward searched for Doughty, who had stolen a large sum of money out of millionaire Ambrose J. Small's safe-deposit vault and disappeared just days after the newly rich Small had vanished. Police wanted Doughty for stealing the money, but more than that, they wanted to question him about Small's disappearance.

After months of effort, Doughty, now living under the name of Charley Cooper, was finally located in small Oregon City, Ore. He admitted the theft and said he had promised to retrieve the money and return it when detectives arrived in Toronto. But he had no clue as to where Small was and had no idea the police were searching for him. Small had not been hiding from the law out West. He had had marital difficulties and needed to get away, Doughty said.

Nobody knows what Small's excuse would have been.

REF.: *CBA;* Miller, *Twenty Mortal Murders.*

Douglas, Alfred, 1923, Brit., libel. Lord Alfred Douglas claimed in his *Plain English* newspaper that Winston Churchill in 1923 conspired with Sir Ernest Cassel to publish a fraudulent report of the Battle of Jutland, for the purpose of creating a panic on the neutral stock exchanges to sell German stocks at a high price and buy British stocks at a lowered value. Churchill denied the charges. The jury, instructed that truth is a defense against libel, said Douglas had indeed criminally libeled Churchill. Justice Avery sentenced the publisher to six months in jail and permanently bound to the court for good behavior against the threat of another six months in jail. REF.: *CBA.*

Douglas, David, d.1440, Scot., executed. Beheaded, along with his brother, William, the 6th Earl of Douglas, after a mock trial conducted by James II of Scotland. REF.: *CBA.*

Douglas-Mahun Duel, 1712, Scot., duel-mur. James Douglas, the 4th Duke of Hamilton and Duke of Brandon was slain by Charles Mahun. The event is told of in William Thackeray's *Henry Esmond.* REF.: *CBA.*

Douglas, James (Fourth Earl of Morton), c.1516-81, Scot., treas. During the middle of the sixteenth century, James Douglas witnessed an execution at the Halifax gibbet, and was so impressed with the lethal machine that he ordered a model of it made. When he returned to Scotland in 1565, the machine had not been used for a considerable time, earning it the name of "The Maiden."

Morton was a suspect in the poisoning murder of the Earl of Atholl, Treasurer of the Kingdom, who died at a reconciliation feast given by Douglas, his rival. After considerable controversy and examinations by several doctors, it was declared that the Earl of Atholl died of natural causes, and no charges were brought against Douglas. Known for his cruelty and greed, Douglas eventually fell out of favor through court politics, and was executed by the same "Maiden" machine he had commissioned, on June 2, 1581. On the scaffold, he denied poisoning the Earl of Atholl. For twelve months after Douglas' death, in High Street, Edinburgh, his head was left up on a pinnacle on the nearby tollbooth. REF.: *CBA.*

Douglas, Janet, d.1537, Case of, Brit., witchcraft-attempt. mur. Maybe the Castle Glamis would not be the perfect place to take the family during a trip to the British Isles. Past guests tell stories that seem strange but are really quite frightening when measured against sixteenth century events that took place on the ghostly premises.

One Glamis guest, brave enough to step forward, told of being suddenly awakened to the vision of a pale face with large, mourning eyes looking into the room from across the courtyard. Its disappearance was followed by shocking screams. Looking out the window, the guest saw an old woman carrying a small bundle come up from a doorway and hurry across the yard. That same night, a different guest was awakened to loud hammering that continued for hours.

The next morning the frightened guests learned that there was no earthly explanation for what they had experienced. But, as one guest learned later, on that date in 1537 scaffolding had been erected for the execution of Janet Douglas, widow of the Sixth

Earl of Glamis and convicted witch. Douglas had also been convicted of attempting to poison King James V, a crime for which she was eventually found Not Guilty.

REF.: *CBA; Furneaux, True Mysteries.*

Douglas, Jean (AKA: **Lady Glamis**), d.1536, Scot., mur. In 1536, Jean Douglas, Lady Glamis of Scotland and granddaughter of "Bell-the-Cat," was tried and convicted of murdering her husband and for having conspired to murder King James V. For her traitorous crimes, Douglas was burned to death.

REF.: *CBA; Thompson, Poison and Poisoners.*

Douglas, John, 1721-1807, Brit., writer. Exposed William Laudner's forgeries in a work defending John Milton, which he authored, 1750. REF.: *CBA.*

Douglas, Richard, d.1858, and **Douglas, Philip**, prom. 1858, Brit., fraud. Richard Douglas' adoption of the title "Sir Richard Douglas of Orpington House, Kent" was his first lie. From there he went on to defraud the innocent all over England. Probably his greatest professional achievement was when as a "baronet," posing as a messenger, he overheard a jewelry store conversation between the proprietor and wealthy Lady Chesterfield. It seemed the lady needed a collection of valuable stones reset. They were said to be worth £20,000. That afternoon the store manager was to pick up the stones at Lady Chesterfield's estate. Douglas rushed to the nearest post office and obtained the lady's address with ease. He went to the estate and convinced Lady Chesterfield's secretary that he was the store manager due to pick up the stones. Within a week, Douglas made £9,000 from the jewels.

Following an unfortunate courtship with a wealthy London widow, Douglas not only lost the woman's hand in marriage but also her fortunes. Down and out, he tried one final scheme. He called on a benevolent and wealthy clergyman he had heard of in the guise of an elderly priest who had fallen on hard times. Douglas set the stage by moving to the poor side of town, and there waited for the priest.

But instead, Inspector Allen arrived with a warrant for the "baronet's" arrest. Trapped, Douglas and his son were tried and sentenced to imprisonment. Douglas died in 1858.

REF.: *CBA; Kingston, Remarkable Rogues.*

Douglas, Sawney, c.1611-64, Brit., rob. Sawney was born in Scotland, where he took part in the rebellion against England which began in 1641. He later bragged that he massacred twenty-nine men, women and children before English rule was restored in 1660. Sawney Douglas moved to England where he took up the dubious trade of highway robbery to punish those who had defeated his cause, or so he rationalized.

On one occasion, Douglas, with no pistol or horse, befriended a servant on horseback. When the opportunity presented itself, he used a branch from a tree to knock the man off the horse and then, as the servant lay helpless, he struck him again and again until the servant was unconscious. At this point, Douglas relieved him of his two pistols and whatever money he could find and rode away on the victim's horse.

Douglas' next victim was Mayor Thurston of Thornbury whom he robbed near Maidenhead Thicket. Next was the Duchess of Albemarle, the wife of General Monk whom he robbed of considerable money and jewels. After converting the jewels to cash, Douglas purchased fine clothes and presented himself as a gentleman in Westminster where he rented a room from a man named Knowles. The landlord's daughter was attractive and of marrying age. Sawney attempted to win the girl's heart, along with her portion of her father's estate, the dowry that would be hers upon marriage. The girl, however, rebuffed Sawney who nevertheless continued his advances. One evening the girl fell asleep while the two were talking; while she slept Sawney removed a necklace of thirty-two pearls from her neck, cutting the string into tiny pieces and swallowing the pearls.

When the girl awoke, she searched for her pearls. Sawney claimed he had no idea what had become of them. When the girl became accusatory, Douglas suggested that the girl search him. Just as the young woman was reaching into Douglas' pocket, the young man she had been seeing walked into the room. Then he turned on his heel, believing the girl was about to make love to Douglas. The girl explained how her necklace had vanished. When the girl's boyfriend heard her story, he and his friends placed Douglas in a sack and held him out the window two stories above the street, threatening to drop him if he did not produce the pearls. At first Douglas promised to return the pearls if given some time, but the men were relentless in their demands and Douglas told them the truth. The men did not wait for nature to take its course. They forced a foul liquid down his throat, and eventually Douglas disgorged. Thirty-two pearls were recovered. Douglas was then evicted from his lodgings.

Douglas soon returned to highway robbery. After a few successful years of looting hapless travelers, he attempted to rob the Earl of Sandwich, who shot Douglas' horse out from under him. The highwayman was imprisoned at Newgate, convicted and sentenced to death. He was hanged at Tyburn on Sept. 10, 1664.

REF.: *CBA; Smith, Highwaymen.*

Douglas, Stephen Arnold (AKA: **Little Giant**), 1813-61, U.S., jur. Served on the Illinois Supreme Court, 1841, in the U.S. House of Representatives, 1843-47, and as a U.S. senator, 1847-61. He was defeated by James Buchanan as Democratic nominee for president, 1856, and by Abraham Lincoln in the general election for presidency, 1860. REF.: *CBA.*

Douglas, Sir William (AKA: **Knight of Liddesdale**), c.1300-53, Scot., mur.-assass. Murdered the lieutenant of Edward de Bailol, 1337, thus siding with David II of Scotland. He himself was murdered by his own kinsman, William, First Earl of Douglas, while on a hunting trip. REF.: *CBA.*

Douglas, William, c.1327-84, Scot., mur. Became First Earl of Douglas after killing Sir William Douglas, 1353, broke his allegiance with David II, 1363, due to the king's misuse of money raised for his ransom, but was later reconciled, and served as justiciar for southern Scotland, 1371. REF.: *CBA.*

Douglas, William, c.1423-40, Scot., executed. The Sixth Earl of Douglas and Third Duke of Touraine was beheaded along with his brother David Douglas following a farcical trial by James II of Scotland. REF.: *CBA.*

Douglas, William, c.1425-52, Scot., earl, assass. The Eighth Earl of Douglas was attacked and murdered by James II of Scotland and his followers for not severing his association with the Earl of Crawford. REF.: *CBA.*

Douglas, William O(rville), 1898-1980, U.S., jur. Served as Columbia and Yale universities' professor of law, 1927-34, and U.S. Supreme Court associate justice, 1939-75, becoming the youngest ever to sit on the nation's high bench and eventually having the longest tenure of any justice. President Franklin Roosevelt appointed him for his liberal values and throughout his career as a supreme court justice he almost invariably upheld civil and individual rights over the rights of government. Three times during his appointment attempts were made to impeach him, in 1953, 1966 and 1970. The first time was over his granting a stay of execution to atomic spies, Ethel and Julis Rosenberg, the second time over his alleged immoral character, his fourth marriage being to a 23-year-old, and the last time over his relations with the Albert Parvin Foundation, which received funds from gambling operations; but none of these attempts had much support. During the liberal Earl Warren court of the 1960s, he and justice Hugo Black formed the nucleus of opinions that overturned earlier court decisions he had so strongly opposed in more conservative courts.

In *Mapp v. Ohio*, 1961, Douglas and the court declared that states, like the federal government, could not use illegally obtained evidence. *Gideon v. Wainwright*, 1963, saw all state criminal defendants charged with committing serious crimes afforded the right to an attorney, a measure the justice had long sought. Individual rights were again trumpeted by Douglas in *Miranda v. Arizona*, 1966, where the court ruled that a criminal suspect must be read and advised of his rights by the police; rights which include the right to remain silent and have counsel present during interrogation. Continuing his belief in the individual's rights, he was the sole dissenter in *Terry v. Ohio*, 1968, which held that police have the right to detain and frisk someone for weapons if the police feel such an action is necessary for their safety or others present.

When Warren Burger became chief justice in 1969, Douglas once again assumed the role of dissenter in a conservative supreme court. Cases such as *U.S. v. White*, 1971, and *Adams v. Williams*, 1972, saw his dissent over decisions that allowed electronic surveillance and warrantless searches.

Douglas concurred with the majority however, in *New York Times v. U.S.*, 1971, which held that the press had the right to publish government documents, namely the Pentagon Papers, as long as those documents posed no threat to the country's security. Douglas again concurred with the majority in abolishing the death penalty, *Papachristou v. City of Jacksonville*, 1972, and in allowing a woman to decide whether or not to have an abortion, *Roe v. Wade*, 1973. REF.: *CBA*.

Douglass, Robert, d.1825, U.S., count.-mur. Robert Douglass was one of the most daring counterfeiters in western New York. Douglass was also a heavy-drinking bully who had been arrested several times for assault.

During one such bout of drinking, Douglass became involved in a violent argument with Samuel H. Ives in Troopsburgh, N.Y., that ended with Douglass stabbing Ives to death in front of several witnesses. His trial on Mar. 21, 1825, on charges of murder, was a speedy affair, and he was convicted, sentenced to death, and hanged at Bath on Apr. 29, 1825.
REF.: *CBA; The Trial of Robert Douglass.*

Doumer, Paul, c.1857-1932, Fr., pres., assass. French president-elect Doumer noted on Wednesday, May 13, 1931, how strange and delightful it was that the number thirteen, far from being unlucky for him, had arisen as significant during his long political life. He had just been elected the thirteenth president of France on the thirteenth day of May in the year whose last two digits, if reversed, made thirteen. When he served as governor of Indo-China, he reached Saigon on the thirteenth day of the month and Hanoi on the thirteenth day of the following month. "And certainly no unlucky happening followed either of those two thirteens!" he rejoiced.

Exactly one year following his observation of the omen, on Friday, the thirteenth of May, 1932, President Paul Doumer was assassinated. Doumer, who lost four of his five sons in WWI, was sponsoring a book sale held by French war veterans at Paris' Rothschild Foundation and had just returned an autographed book when a tall, husky Russian, Dr. Paul Gorgulov lunged forward spraying bullets from his Colt pistol. Caught in a crush of 500 spectators, Doumer slumped slowly to his knees, blood gushing from the mortal head wound and spoke his final words, "*Est-ce possible?*" (Is it possible?).

At the trial in the summer of 1932, Gorgulov had his turn to speak. "I did not shoot Paul Doumer! I shot the president of the Republic of France! France, listen to me! When I came to France, I saw people living in security and plenty and I thought of millions of Russian peasants groveling out their lives in starvation and misery. My crime is a protest in the name of the enslaved Russian people..."

Apparently Gorgulov was unaware that in France the president did not direct the policies of the country.

After twenty-nine minutes of jury deliberation, Dr. Gorgulov was pronounced Guilty. One month after that he was pronounced dead, by the guillotine. Before he died, Gorgulov saluted the jury on making a fine decision and proclaimed, "Vive la France! Vive la Russia! I love you unto death."

Doumer was the second French president to be assassinated. President Marie François Sadi Carnot, stabbed to death by an Italian anarchist at Lyons on June 24, 1894, was the first. See: **Carnot, Marie François Sadi.**
REF.: *CBA*; Heppenstall, *Bluebeard and After.*

Dove, Frank, and **Dove, Fred**, and **Williams, George**, prom. 1920s, U.S., (wrong. convict.) mur. On Aug. 5, 1922, Cyrus Jones, a mailman who drove a taxicab on the side, was shot on the highway a mile and a half from his hometown of Swansboro, N.C. According to Jones, the men who attacked him included "Collins, Williams, and Doves."

Arrested for the murder were Willie Hardison, George Williams, and brothers Frank and Fred Dove. At their trial, prosecutors proved to the jury that the Collins that the dying mailman had referred to was actually Willie Hardison. And with the aid of Hardison's testimony—later to be discovered perjured—the jury convicted all four men for Jones' murder and all were senteced to death.

But on the morning of his scheduled execution, Hardison admitted that he alone had murdered Jones and the other three were innocent. He explained that he had perjured his testimony because he was afraid of being lynched, and as soon as he was out of Raleigh, where the lynching threats originated, and when he no longer had a motive or hope of clearing himself or of getting his sentence reduced, he admitted everything. Hardison was electrocuted, but the debate over who killed Jones continued.

In August 1925, Williams and the Doves petitioned North Carolina governor Cameron Morrison for a full pardon, stressing the fact that they were convicted solely on Hardison's purjured testimony. The governor also received letters requesting executive clemency for the three imprisoned men from Mr. Powers, the attorney who had prosecuted the men in the first place, and H.E. Stacy, who had assisted Powers. More than 400 people signed and sent a petition demanding the pardon, including leading citizens of Onslow County, four original jurors, the Swansboro postmaster, an ex-sheriff, the current sheriff, and the clerk of the Superior Court. Even trial Judge E. H. Cranmer pleaded with the governor, saying, "After thought, reflection, and prayer, I recommend, my dear Governor, that you pardon George Williams, Frank Dove and Fred Dove." Cranmer then commuted the men's sentences to life in prison.

Three more years passed before justice was done. On Mar. 1, 1928, Governor McLean granted a pardon. Frank and Fred Dove and George Williams were released after serving six years for a crime they had not committed. REF.: *CBA*.

Dove, William, 1826-56, Brit., mur. Possibly the first sign that William Dove, thirty, was different was when, as a child, he poured alcohol on his bedroom curtains and set them on fire. Or maybe it was when he cut himself with knives so he could write his name in blood. The last sign of Dove's derangement was when he pumped his wife's body full of deadly strychnine.. For this, he was indicted on murder charges on Mar. 1, 1856, and was executed in York.

Dove was best described by a schoolmaster who knew him well as "a dull boy, and a bad boy" and did not improve with age. Dove was expelled from school because of dangerous antics he played on classmates and because teachers deemed him mentally inept. Following this, Dove's optimistic father had the boy learn farming. This, too, was to no avail. The younger Dove's antics continued, simply transferred from classmates to farm animals. He was caught on several occasions putting vitriol on the tails of cows and into the horse trough, burning half-grown kittens, and setting fire to the shrubs. His father gave him a few more years to come around. During this time he was seen lying on the ground and crying for no apparent reason, complaining about noises in his house and reaping his corn about two months before it was ready. Somehow during all of this, he got married.

Then he focused his pranks on his wife, once threatening her with a pistol. The honeymoon wore off, leaving Dove and his wife bitterly fighting, occupying separate beds, and rarely meeting. They tried but were unable to get a divorce. Dove's only way out was murder.

According to testimony provided at Dove's murder trial, the man began purchasing strychnine, ostensibly to kill pesky cats and rats in his home, from his physician's pupil. He learned about the poison from the good doctor when an acquaintance died from an apparent poisoning. Dove was impressed with the revelation that this deadly poison could not always be detected during an autopsy. Time after time the surgeon's student gave Dove the poison. Soon Dove learned where it was kept and he started helping himself. But all this time, Dove wasn't killing household pests. For more than a week, his wife lay sick in bed, rallying a little only to worsen the next day. On Mar. 1, 1865, she died. Before she died, however, Mrs. Dove warned her good friend Elizabeth Fisher, that her body should be examined in the event of her death.

The examination revealed more than enough strychnine to kill Mrs. Dove. People did not have to look long or hard to figure out who was behind the sick woman's lethal feedings. Between the outright purchases of strychnine and the premature concerns over a coroner's finding, all hands pointed to Dove, who was convicted of killing his wife. In passing down the verdict, however, the jury recommended the court show mercy toward Dove on the grounds of his limited mental capacities. Nevertheless he was executed.

REF.: Browne, *Trials For Murder by Poisoning; CBA.*

Dover, Thomas, 1660-1742, Int'l., pir. Thomas Dover was second in command of the pirating expedition, headed by Woodes Rogers, which harassed Spanish ships off the South American Pacific coast. The English pirates took Alexander Selkirk from the island where he had lived alone for two years; Selkirk's adventure would be the inspiration for author Daniel Defoe's novel, *Robinson Crusoe.* When, in 1709, the pirates invaded Guayaquil, Peru, they celebrated their victory by bedding down in a church where plague victims had recently been buried. One hundred eighty of the men returning to the ship showed signs of infection. Dover ordered the ship's surgeon to take 100 ounces of blood from each man and dose them with sulphuric acid. Only eight of the crew members died. When he returned to England, Dover set up a medical practice, and was known as "Dr. Quicksilver" because of his belief in the effectiveness of mercury as a treatment for venereal diseases. The one-time pirate originated "Dover's Powder," a combination of ipecacuanha, opium, and sulphate of potash, that has remained popular.

REF.: *CBA;* Hunt, *A Dictionary of Rogues.*

Dow, Leslie (Les), d.1896, U.S., law enfor. off. Lawman Les Dow was born in Texas, but became deputy sheriff of Chaves County in New Mexico after giving up his hotel and saloon business. He later became a cattle inspector and range detective for the Texas and New Mexico Sanitary Association. His career in law enforcement also included a stop in Eddy County, N.M., where he served as sheriff and deputy U.S. marshal.

Dow was involved in a number of gunfights on the New Mexico and Arizona frontier, including the famous 1896 shootout in the San Simon Valley with Black Jack Christian and his gang. Dow and his posse of seven lawmen fired on the gang as they prepared to break camp. Christian and two other outlaws escaped. In April 1896, Dow was shot down in Carlsbad, N.M., while scanning a pile of letters in the postal station. The gunman was an old adversary named Dave Kemp, who fled from the building before Dow could get off a shot.

REF.: Bartholomew, *The Biographical Album of Western Gunfighters; CBA;* Gibson, *Colonel Albert Jennings Fountain;* Harkey, *Mean As Hell;* O'Neal, *Encyclopedia of Western Gunfighters;* Sonnichsen, *Tularosa.*

Dow, Neal (AKA: Father of the Maine Law), 1804-97, U.S., law enfor. off. As mayor of Portland, Me., 1851, he drafted a prohibition law which was passed and led to cleaning up of liquor traf-ficking in the area. He ran as the Prohibition party candidate for U.S. president, 1880. REF.: *CBA.*

Dowd, John F., prom. 1930s, U.S., polit. corr. Boston politicians who were so slipshod as to be sent to jail during Mayor James Curley's corrupt administration (as well as convicted felons) found a real home in the Suffolk County Jail, run by its genial host, Sheriff John F. Dowd. Sheriff Dowd began his career in Curley's Roxbury Tammany Ward as one of Curley's battery of public speakers. Though he failed to graduate grammar school, Dowd was appointed Curley's Director of Americanization in 1921.

From there he rose to the mayor's secretarial staff.

Heading up Curley's much-vaunted Christmas Fund, Dowd appropriated untold thousands of dollars for his own purse. In 1938, the short, overweight, dark-haired Dowd, a livid scar from his battle experiences in WWI angling across his cheek, ran for the office of high sheriff. This was the plum he had been seeking all along and, once in office, his pockets were soon brimming with illegal payoffs, bribes, and kickbacks. He took over a jail housing an average of 275 prisoners and having 200 permanent employees, all of the latter courtesy of Curley's massive patronage system.

From his first day at the job, Dowd informed every employee that the only way a worker at the jail could have job security was to purchase it directly from him. He had set a scale of kickbacks before he ever took the post. The twenty-six scrubwomen in the jail were ordered to pay him $250 a year to retain their $18-a-week jobs. One elderly chorewoman begged to keep her job without paying; she had an invalid son to support. Dowd fired her. Guards were charged between $500 and $2,500 by the parsimonious sheriff to keep their jobs; deputy sheriffs had to pay $2,500 to $5,000. Johnnie Dowd overlooked no details.

The extra fees paid to deputy sheriffs serving writs and legal processes were split each month from a common pool. Dowd appropriated $500 each month from the pool for his own pocket. Only days after he occupied the sheriff's office, Dowd tallied up his additional sources of income and was suddenly dejected. His job extortion and pool raiding revenue was unsatisfactory, so he appealed to the Boston City Council, where he had once been president, for a $2,000 salary increase. His request promptly denied, the sheriff looked about for other immediate sources of income. He increased his levies against his employees who, in desperation, turned about frantically to mortgage homes, sell cars, and gut their savings accounts.

Those who failed to pay their monthly kickbacks were fired, and new employees stepped forward with money in hand. One of Dowd's jailers, despondent over his dismissal, committed suicide. The sheriff was not without feeling. He ordered his employees to purchase out of their own funds a special floral wreath, which was sent to the funeral home in his name.

The Depression caused hundreds of jobless persons to apply at the jail for jobs (many, of course, used their positions to establish rackets of their own). Even when Dowd had no jobs to offer these clamoring position-hunters, he took their money as down payments against future kickbacks they would owe once they were hired. The sheriff, however, had no intention of employing them.

More personal revenue for Dowd was provided by his prisoners. The jail he operated became known in underworld circles as "hospitality hotel", where all manner of comforts were available to convicted felons as long as they had the money to pay for them. Dowd reserved for his top-paying guests ping-pong tables, radios, books, and a solarium with deck chairs. Meals were catered to prisoners from Boston's best restaurants. High-rolling inmates, such as former state representative Robert Dinsmore, who had been jailed for complicity, and others were allowed to avail themselves of Dowd's well-stocked cocktail bar at almost any hour of the day.

Incongruous as it appears, the Reverend William M. Forgrave, once the superintendent of the Anti-Saloon League of Massachusetts and a resident in Dowd's institution following a conviction of larceny, was the jail's booking agent for numbers, pool, and racetrack betting. The Reverend busied himself by making his daily rounds of the cells and collecting the various wagers he had booked the day before.

Dowd was solicitous of his guests, visiting them in their cells, the doors of which were always kept open. He inquired after their health and the quality of the food served to them, and wondered if there was anything else he might do to make their stay more pleasant. Most were allowed to use the jail's phone at will and at any hour of the day or night.

Lavish champagne parties were held in cell blocks housing the more prosperous prisoners, and women were allowed to visit privately at all hours. On many occasions, Dowd drank and partied with his charges. He spent most of his time berating and humiliating the guards in front of the prisoners, calling them "screws" and "stool pigeons".

In the words of one journalist: "Guards and prison officials became the servants and errand boys of the prisoners, who ordered guards about, had them rustle up drinks, mail letters or make telephone calls, and rewarded them with insults. Prisoners had access to arms and ammunition, but none had any intention of making a break for freedom. This was a comfortable and painless way of paying their so-called debt to society. The guards, however, came to be afraid for their lives."

Those jail workers most obedient to special prisoners were allowed the privilege of waiting on Dowd himself, shining his shoes, polishing his car, mixing his drinks, and slavishly serving him elegant, catered meals. Discharged prisoners, notorious criminals, and infamous gamblers were allowed to visit with prisoners almost anytime on the proviso that Dowd received his fees. Prisoners, too, for the right price, were permitted to come and go as they pleased. Several of Dowd's topflight clients were driven by limousine on sunny days to golf courses, where they were observed playing the links.

Preposterous but verified is the story of one prisoner who asked Dowd if he could attend the funeral of a deceased politician in a distant city. "Sure," Dowd said through his cigar, "but you gotta pay the guard's expenses." This meant that Dowd would send along a guard to chaperon the prisoner, not to assure the inmate's return, but to provide him with another excuse to add a "service fee."

The prisoner did leave the jail in company with a guard. They did not return as expected by nine o'clock that night. At dawn, the visitor's bell at the front gate clanged loudly, and jail officers threw open the door to see the prisoner supporting his guard, who had passed out in his arms, dead drunk. "I been trying to get this guy to come back since four o'clock yesterday afternoon," the inmate explained, "but, no, he wouldn't come. He wanted to go nightclubbing."

Such was Dowd's concept of running a jail. His credo held out for better than two years and then someone talked about conditions at the jail to a civic-minded Reuben Lurie, an auditor for the superior court. Lurie went to the Boston Bar Association and a full-scale investigation was launched. Dowd was not a tarrying man. With more than $100,000 in cash from his ill-gotten gatherings, he fled to New York. Days later, he was picked up wandering down 77th Street in a daze. In his pocket he had $6,000 in big bills and a gold sheriff's badge, which he attempted to swallow when officers tried to take it away from him.

Boston reporters later discovered him confined in Bellevue Hospital. Doctors told the newsmen that the sheriff had developed a common disease. His fun-loving, nonstop drinking in the Suffolk County Jail had taken its toll. John F. Dowd was an incurable, terminal alcoholic. See: **Curley, James Michael.** REF.: *CBA*.

Dowdall, James, prom. 1906, U.S., rob. Three months after an earthquake devastated San Francisco, Calif., in April 1906, the city was still a shambles. A wave of looting and other crimes swept the city for several months, while the police force was reduced to one-fifth its original size.

James Dowdall was charged with mugging Coroner Leland on July 10, 1906. Dowdall and an accomplice ambushed the doctor and stole over $100 and personal belongings from him at gunpoint. Dowdall, later identified by his victim, was convicted and sentenced to fifty years in prison.

REF.: *CBA*; Duke, *Celebrated Criminal Cases of America*.

Dowdall, Michael Douglas, 1940- , Brit., mansl. On Christmas Eve 1958, the mutilated body of Veronica Murray was found in her Kilburn apartment. Murray, a prostitute, had been beaten severely with a 6 lb. dumbbell, which lay bloodied beside her bed. Her attacker had burnt a series of circular marks into her skin after she died. The marks led police on a year-long hunt that ended in the capture of a 19-year-old psychopath.

In November 1959 following a string of attacks on women throughout London, a Fulham woman was found nearly dead in her apartment. She had been strangled with a silk stocking, and her body showed the same marks found on the corpse of Veronica Murray. The victim survived, and told police her attacker was a young male who chain-smoked and drank heavily. She said she met him the night before while celebrating her birthday, and when she refused to have sex with him he attacked her and mutilated her with a cigarette lighter, which she described.

The lighter had a unique shape, and when a photograph appeared in the newspaper, it was quickly traced to a Welsh Guardsman named Michael Dowdall. Dowdall's fellow guardsmen frequently called him a sissy. He had tried to change his image by boasting of his sexual prowess in London during weekend leave.

After his arrest, Dowdall confessed to the attempted murder of the Fulham woman, the murder of the prostitute in Kilburn, an attack on a 65-year-old woman near Sloane Square, and several burglaries and robberies during the past year. Dowdall gave a detailed account of the Murray murder and told police that he became violent and forgetful when he drank, and that he drank almost every weekend.

When questioned about his motives, he told officers he committed the crimes "because my army mates think I'm queer and I have tried to show them they're wrong."

Dowdall was charged with murder and tried at the Old Bailey. The jury found him Guilty of manslaughter on the grounds of "diminished responsibility." He was sentenced to an indeterminate term in prison.

REF.: *CBA*; Furneaux, *Famous Criminal Cases, Vol. 6*; Jackson, *Occupied With Crime*; Traini, *Murder For Sex*.

Dowe, Anne, prom. 1560, Brit., slander. In 1560 a charge that Lord Robert murdered his wife scandalized the Royal Family.

With the ruling class already in an uproar, Anne Dowe of Brentwood openly explained a possible motive for the murder. She said that Lord Robert and the Queen had long been involved in an affair, and that the Queen had borne a son from the relationship. Her accusation so shocked the Queen that she imprisoned Dowe for her slander.

REF.: *CBA*; Williamson, *Historical Whodunits*.

Downey, John, prom. 1900s, Brit., suic. John Downey was an amateur photographer, and enjoyed taking pictures of women clothed in underwear brandishing firearms. For one such photo, he enlisted Lyndsey Riggs to act as model in a macabre scene simulating his own death. He dressed Riggs in underwear and a nightgown and had her point a gun at him as he lay at her feet. Downey planned to take the photograph as Riggs pulled the trigger, firing a blank at his prone body.

But Downey had put real bullets in the chamber, and when Riggs fired the revolver she unknowingly killed him. Downey left a suicide note absolving the girl of the crime, and he had recorded his death on film.

REF.: *CBA*; Moore, *Wolves, Widows, and Orphans*.

Downing, William, prom. 1890s, U.S., west. lawman-west. outl. William Downing served as a deputy under Burt Alvord and reportedly organized the posse that searched for Alvord after he turned outlaw and robbed a train near Cochise, Ariz., on Sept. 9, 1899. Out of deference to his old boss, it was said, Downing allowed Alvord to escape. Downing later went into the lumber business and then started down the outlaw path himself. One report has it that Downing, an enigmatic person, killed more than thirty men. Another claimed that Down-

Outlaw Bill Downing.

ing was the mysterious Frank Jackson, the only gang member who escaped the disastrous Round Rock robbery of 1878 when Sam Bass was killed. Even Downing's death is a mystery. He was reported killed in 1900 in Wilcox, Ariz., by Deputy Billy Speed. Another report has it that Downing was killed in 1908 when officers arrived to arrest him on a wife-beating charge. According to another account, Downing lived into the 1920s. See: **Alvord, Burton; Bass, Samuel.**

REF.: Bakarich, *Gunsmoke*; Bartholomew, *The Biographical Album of Western Gunfighters*; *CBA*; Chisholm, *Brewery Gulch*; Chrisman, *Fifty Years on the Owl Hoot Trail*; Gard, *Sam Bass*; Hunter, *Cap Mossman*; Hunter and Rose, *The Album of Gunfighters*; Lesure, *Adventures in Arizona*; Liggett, *My Seventy-Five Years Along the Mexican Border*; McCool, *So Said the Coroner*; O'Neal, *Encyclopedia of Western Gunfighters*; Penfield, *Dig Here!*; Ringgold, *Frontier Days in the Southwest*; Rynning, *Gun Notches*; Schultz, *Southwestern Town*; Shirley, *Buckskin and Spurs*; Sonnichsen, *Billy King's Tombstone*; Thorp, *Story of the Southwestern Cowboy*; Walters, *Tombstone's Yesterdays*; Way, *Frontier Arizona*; Webb, *Texas Rangers*.

Downs, Elizabeth Diane, 1956- , U.S., asslt.-mur. In 1983 a brutal attack on a divorced mother and her three children shocked the town of Springfield, Ore. Elizabeth Diane Downs told police that an unidentified "shaggy haired man" flagged down her car outside Springfield and shot dead her 7-year-old daughter Cheryl, then critically wounded 3-year-old Danny and 8-year-old Christie, and shot Downs in the arm before he fled.

In February 1984 Downs was arrested and charged with murder in the death of daughter Cheryl and the attempted murder of her two other children.

Downs, a 27-year-old divorcée, is believed to have attacked her children because they stood between her and her new boyfriend, who insisted he did not want children.

Downs maintained her innocence during a lengthy trial. When a tape recording of the song *Hungry Like the Wolf* by Duran Duran, which had been playing during the attack, was played in court, Downs was seen tapping her foot and singing along with the song.

Downs was convicted of murder, two counts of attempted murder, and two counts of first-degree assault. She was sentenced to five concurrent terms, including life plus five years minimum for murder with a firearm, two terms of thirty years each for attempted murder, and two terms of twenty years for assault. In closing, presiding Judge Gregory Foote told Downs: "The Court hopes the defendant will never again be free. I've come as close to that as possible." The leading prosecutor in the case, Lane County Assistant District Attorney Fred Hugi, adopted Downs' two surviving children.

Three years later, in July 1987, Downs escaped from the prison in Salem, Ore., where she had been confined since July 1984. She was recaptured ten days later at a nearby house she was sharing with 36-year-old Wayne Seifer, estranged husband of a fellow inmate.

Downs was later transferred to a New Jersey penitentiary. She has written a 318-page book chronicling her struggle to clear herself. Over 50,000 copies of *Diane Downs: Best Kept Secrets* were printed by May of 1989.

REF.: *CBA*; Rule, *Small Sacrifices*.

Dowry Murders, prom. 1980s, India, mur. The tradition of dowries was established thousands of years ago in India. As the practice became increasingly corrupt during the 1960s, the marriage incentive was outlawed. But it still flourishes today, as shown by the alarming increase in "kitchen accidents" in India over the past decade. Marriage has become a means of acquiring material wealth, and wives have become a disposable commodity to be eliminated as seen fit.

During the 1980s, husbands have been murdering their wives in increasingly large numbers after first extorting as many valuables from their in-laws as possible. Once the in-laws stop providing additional dowry items, the wives are disposed of in what has become known as a "kitchen accident." Most of the

"kitchen accidents" reported since 1980 are murders in which a husband ties his wife to a kitchen chair and sets her afire. The husband is then free to remarry and receive yet another dowry.

A typical dowry could include video recorders, stereos, refrigerators, automobiles, motorcycles, and money.

Newly-formed women's rights organizations have been tracking the "kitchen accidents" since 999 deaths were reported in 1985. That number rose to 1,319 in 1986 and to 1,786 in 1987. The Ahmedabad Women's Action Group in the state of Gujarat claims that the numbers are much higher since most domestic quarrels in India go unreported. Research conducted by the organization has shown that more than 1,000 women are executed annually in Gujarat alone. REF.: *CBA*.

Dowse, Margaret (AKA: **Margaret Trinder**), 1932- , and **Trinder, Stanley**, prom. 1956-60, Brit., theft-forg. Margaret Dowse committed a series of robberies between 1956 and 1960, successfully evading police until her lover was apprehended while betting on the horses.

Dowse's robbery spree began in 1956 when she stole £5 from a savings account by forging the signature of the depositor. She and boyfriend Stanley Trinder then developed a scheme to rob grocers, butchers, and other shopkeepers as they traveled from town to town.

Upon reaching a new city, Dowse and Trinder searched the local newspapers for shopkeepers seeking help. Dowse applied for the position, and once she had the job, gained the trust of her employer. She would later steal daily deposits or the weekly payroll. The couple would then skip town, constantly moving from city to city. At the time of their capture, Dowse and Trinder had stolen more than £12,000 and were wanted in forty-one cities throughout England.

Their downfall came in 1960, when Trinder was recognized from a photo in a police newspaper by two off-duty police officers at the racetrack. He later led police to the home he shared with Dowse.

Dowse was convicted on five counts of larceny, forgery, and falsification of documents. She and Trinder were each sentenced to five years in prison.

REF.: *CBA*; Jackson, *Occupied With Crime*.

Doxsee, Tom, prom. 1949, U.S., mansl. In March 1949 eight members of the Kappa Kappa Kappa fraternity at Dartmouth College marched into Massachusetts Hall to teach know-it-all ex-soldier Ray Cirotta a lesson in humility.

They stormed into his dormitory room, where he was studying. The leader of the Tri-Kaps, Tom Doxsee, grabbed Cirotta by the lapels and was the first to punch him in the stomach. After beating him repeatedly and ransacking his room, the fraternity boys left Cirotta bleeding on the floor. Cirotta made it to the bathroom and cleaned the blood off his face, but was later rushed to the hospital where he died of a cerebral hemorrhage.

Tom Doxsee was charged with manslaughter, and he and the other Tri-Kappas involved in the beating were suspended by Dartmouth administrators. Doxsee appeared in court in June, where he changed his plea from not guilty to no contest. The judge gave Doxsee a $500 fine and a sentence of one to two years, which he later suspended. Doxsee left the courtroom disappointed, believing the sentence too harsh. REF.: *CBA*.

Doyle, Sir **Arthur Conan**, 1859-1930, Brit., det. crime writer. Born in Edinburgh, Scot., on May 22, 1859, Arthur Conan Doyle was the second child of Charles and Mary Doyle. He demonstrated a talent for writing when at the age of six he wrote a story about a Bengal tiger and illustrated the little notebook he had filled. He was educated in Edinburgh, and while studying in the medical college he, like so many others, including Robert Louis Stevenson, came under the academic spell of Dr. Joseph Bell, a teaching surgeon whose powers of observation and deductive reasoning suggested to Doyle the image of the wholly new master detective who would later become the immortal Sherlock Holmes.

Before his encounter with the incisive Bell, Doyle, an avid reader in his teens, devoured the works of Edgar Allan Poe. The

Left, Doyle as a student and, right, his mentor Dr. Bell.

Doyle at work on a Holmes story, circa 1889.

Sidney Paget's illustration of Watson and the great Sherlock.

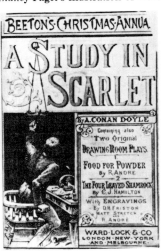

Left, the first Holmes story, and right, Doyle in old age.

Arthur Conan Doyle, at the height of his career in 1901.

stories remained a main source of literary inspiration throughout Doyle's lifetime. Doyle was fascinated with stories such as *The Gold Bug* and *The Murders in the Rue Morgue.* He was also fascinated with Poe's analytical French detective, Auguste Dupin, whose intellectual powers were superior to those of most men and who analyzed events, character traits, and objects with a steel-trap mind that could easily determine important clues leading to the criminal. Dupin, the first truly great literary detective, was later to become the role model for Sherlock Holmes.

Following his graduation, Doyle began his medical practice in Plymouth in the south of England and later moved to Southsea. In 1885, while attending a young man stricken with cerebral meningitis, Doyle met and fell in love with the youth's sister, 27-year-old Louise Hawkins. They married on Aug. 6, 1885. Also in that year, Doyle began toying with the idea of creating an invincible private detective and he started writing a story about a character he named Sherriford Hope. Doyle later changed the character to Sherlock Holmes, using the name of American jurist and physician Oliver Wendell Holmes, whom Doyle admired. The original character, Hope, lived at 221B Baker Street, London, with his friend, Ormond Sacker. This character would later become the indomitable Boswell to Holmes, Dr. John H. Watson, whose role model was Doyle's friend, Major Alfred Wood.

The brilliant Holmes and his loyal Watson made their first appearance in *A Study in Scarlet,* which appeared in *Chamber's Journal* on Mar. 8, 1886. It was in this story that Doyle showed his seemingly unbeatable detective with a deep, dark fault that made him more human: Sherlock Holmes was addicted to cocaine. Doyle drew from his own father, Charles Doyle, who was epileptic and compelled to take drugs. Doyle's second Holmes story, *The Sign of Four,* was inspired by the works of Wilkie Collins, particularly *The Moonstone.* The evil genius who proved to be Holmes' most ardent and inventive foe, Professor James Moriarty, was certainly based on the American master criminal Adam Worth—bank robber, stealer of priceless paintings from art galleries in London, and the mastermind of a criminal network that stretched from New York to London to Paris.

Worth, who began his astounding criminal career in the late 1860s, was called by American detective Allan Pinkerton "the Napoleon of crime." In Doyle's tale, *The Final Problem,* he has Holmes describe this sinister genius to Dr. Watson in terms that outline the character of Adam Worth: "He is the Napoleon of crime, Watson. He is the organizer of half that is evil and nearly all that is undetected in this great city. He is a genius, a philosopher, an abstract thinker. He has a brain of the first order. He sits motionless, like a spider in the centre of its web, but that web has a thousand radiations, and he knows well every quiver of each of them. He does little himself. He only plans. But his agents are numerous and splendidly organized....This was the organization I deduced, Watson, and which I devoted my whole energy to exposing and breaking up."

The physical makeup of Worth, a tall, sallow-faced, stoop-shouldered man, was described by Doyle with unerring accuracy in Holmes' chilling conversation with Watson: "He is extremely tall and thin, his forehead domes out in a white curve, and his two eyes are deeply sunken in his head. He is clean-shaven, pale, and ascetic-looking, retaining something of the professor in his features. His shoulders are rounded from much study, and his face protrudes forward, and is forever slowly oscillating from side to side in a curiously reptilian fashion." Though Moriarty's physical description and *modus operandi* are based on Worth, some of his exploits are certainly drawn from England's own master criminal, Jonathan Wild, who headed a vast underworld network and was known as the "Prince of Robbers." Wild was executed in 1725 as a receiver of stolen goods.

Doyle's stories about Sherlock Holmes caught the imagination of the public in 1888, the year that Jack the Ripper terrorized London. The London police seemed helpless before the vicious killer who stalked women in the city's West End, slaughtering prostitutes at will in the White Chapel area. The London police demonstrated a frustrating and alarming ineptitude in their attempt to catch this madman, and the public sought the comfort of a detective who could best any villain, apprehend any criminal, no matter how clever or dangerous. This man, although he was cut from the fabric of Doyle's fiction, was none other than Sherlock Holmes. If the bungling London police would fail, Holmes would not. If the constables on the foggy streets of the great city could not locate and bring Jack to justice, Holmes would at least triumph over evil in the pages of the *Strand* magazine. Indirectly, Jack the Ripper helped establish the popularity of Doyle's greatest character. It is interesting to note that many aspects of the Ripper's crimes can be found in the Holmes stories. Doyle himself was intrigued by the slashing killer and came to believe that the murderer, by virtue of the manner in which he expertly carved up his victims, was a midwife with surgical skills.

The success of Doyle's stories concerning his unforgettable detective came slowly, but within a few years, the Sherlock Holmes tales were sold widely. Each new story sold so well that Doyle devoted his career to writing, although he looked upon his greatest creation, Holmes, as someone not really worthy of his efforts. Doyle did not consider his detective fiction "serious writing," but it made him rich and world famous. Doyle wished to be considered a writer on subjects held in greater intellectual esteem. After serving as a physician in the Boer War in 1900, Doyle wrote *The War in South Africa: Its Causes and Conduct.* The book, which was critical of the British strategy in the war, was an enormous success, selling more than 300,000 copies in less than two months. Because of his humanitarian service in the war, Doyle was knighted in 1902.

Having ignored his wife and his personal life in his exhaustive production of Holmes stories, Doyle decided to kill off Holmes in *The Final Problem.* Holmes and his mortal enemy, Moriarty, fight to the finish and, together both fall, ostensibly to their deaths, into the Reichenbach Falls, a "dreadful cauldron of swirling water and seething foam." Doyle's enormous reading public reacted with as much concern and dismay as if Holmes had been a living, breathing person. Thousands of letters poured into the offices of Doyle's publishers, all begging the author to revive the great detective. Doyle, however, adamantly refused to resurrect Holmes. The author did not, as suggested by numerous writers, grow to hate and resent his creation, but he was certainly tired of creating puzzles for Holmes to solve, and of a character for whom he had constantly to create new personality traits that would amaze readers.

To a friend Doyle wrote: "I have had such an overdose of him that I feel towards him as I do towards *pâté de foie gras,* of which I once ate too much so that the name of it gives me a sickly feeling to this day." Doyle's publishers and public, however, hounded him constantly, and Doyle finally brought Holmes again to life in October 1903 in *The Empty House.* When the story went on sale, the bookstores and stalls in London were mobbed by thousands of purchasers who literally fought for copies.

Doyle himself was a better-than-average amateur sleuth, who was identified by Dr. Joseph Bell, his mentor, as the real role model for Holmes, but Bell apparently wished to deny that Holmes was a version of himself. Doyle nevertheless became obsessed with a murder in Glasgow, Scot. On Dec. 21, 1908, 83-year-old Marion Gilchrist was found murdered in her flat. Shortly before, witnesses saw a well-dressed young man leaving the flat. He was later identified as Oscar Slater, who was tried, found Guilty, and condemned to death. Doyle believed that Slater had been wrongly identified and sought to prove his theory. He battled with Scottish officials for years, finally winning a new trial for Slater in 1928, in which he was found innocent. Slater was released, later writing to Doyle to call him the "breaker of my shackles." In another case, that of George Edalji, who had been imprisoned for killing animals in the Midlands, Doyle proved Edalji's innocence and effected his release.

In the last decade of his life, Doyle became consumed with

spiritualism, immersing himself in occult studies and seances. He visited countless mediums and became obsessed with contacting spirits in the "Beyond," even stating to his wife, Jean Leckie Doyle (whom he had married in 1907, a year after the death of his first wife, Louise) that he would send her a message from the spiritual world after his own death. He ignored his publisher's pleas for more tales about Sherlock Holmes and spent a great deal of time giving lectures on spiritualism. His audiences were polite but unenthusiastic. They wanted the great Sherlock, not ghostly apparitions. Doyle died on July 7, 1930. Some days later, Mrs. Doyle admitted that her husband had, indeed, sent her a message from the "Beyond." Asked what that message was, Mrs. Doyle smiled and said: "Oh, it is beautiful and sweet—but private." See: **Edalji, George; Jack the Ripper; Slater, Oscar; Wild, Jonathan; Worth, Adam.**

REF.: Adams, *Edwardian Portraits;* Blakeney, *Sherlock Holmes, Fact or Fiction?;* Bullard and Collins, *Who's Who in Sherlock Holmes;* Carr, *The Life of Sir Arthur Conan Doyle; CBA;* Christopher, *Houdini, The Untold Story;* Doyle, *The True Conan Doyle;* Eames, *Sleuths, Inc.;* Ernst, *Houdini and Conan Doyle;* Hall, *The Late Mr. Sherlock Holmes and Other Literary Studies;* Harrison, *In the Footsteps of Sherlock Holmes;* ____, *The London of Sherlock Holmes;* ____, *The World of Sherlock Holmes;* Harwick, *The Sherlock Holmes Companion;* Higham, *The Adventures of Conan Doyle;* Hoehling, *The Real Sherlock Holmes;* Holroyd, *Baker Street Byways;* Joyce, *Edinburgh, The Golden Age;* Klinefelter, *Sherlock Holmes in Portrait and Profile;* Lamond, *Arthur Conan Doyle;* Nash, *Almanac of World Crime;* ____, *Open Files;* ____, *Zanies;* Nordon, *Conan Doyle;* Pointer, *The Public Life of Sherlock Holmes;* Roberts, *Holmes and Watson;* Rosenburg, *Naked is the Best Disguise; Sir Arthur Conan Doyle Centenary, 1859-1959;* Smith, *Baker Street and Beyond;* Smith, *The Incunabular Sherlock Holmes;* ____, *Profile by Gaslight;* Starrett, *The Private Life of Sherlock Holmes.*

Doyle, James, prom. 1925, Case of, Brit., mur. As James Doyle and his fiancee sat privately in the Doncaster cricket grounds, a spot frequented by lovers, on the evening of Dec. 16, 1924, they were startled by a noise from the opposite side of the boundary wall surrounding the cricket field. In the dark, Doyle drew his knife and rose to investigate. When he reached the wall, he saw that two men, Albert Needham and Wilfred Thrussle, were spying on the lovers in the cricket field. Doyle and Needham fought until Needham fell to the ground, stabbed twice in the abdomen.

Doyle appeared in court on Mar. 25, 1925, on charges of murder. Defense attorney Sir Edward Marshall Hall maintained that Doyle killed Needham in self-defense, since both peeping toms were larger men who threatened his safety. Thrussle testified that they meant no harm, and that going to the cricket grounds to watch couples had become a hobby for him and Needham. The jury empathized with Doyle and found him Not Guilty.

REF.: Bowker, *Behind the Bar; CBA;* Marjoribanks, *For the Defense, The Life of Sir Edward Marshall Hall;* Shew, *A Second Companion to Murder.*

Doyle, James Edward, 1915- , U.S., jur. Served as attorney for the U.S. Department of Justice's Criminal Division, 1940-41, assistant U.S. attorney for the Western District of Wisconsin, 1946-48, and was appointed to the Western District Court of Wisconsin by President Lyndon Johnson, Apr. 29, 1965. REF.: *CBA.*

Doyle, Martin, d.1861, Brit., attempt. mur. The Criminal Law Consolidation Acts came too late for Martin Doyle, who was the last man hanged for attempted murder in England.

Doyle was executed on Aug. 27, 1861, two months before the new laws effectively outlawing execution for crimes other than treason or willful murder went into effect on Nov. 1.

REF.: Andrews, *Old-Time Punishments; CBA;* Potter, *The Art of Hanging.*

Doze, Grace, d.1927, U.S., (unsolv.) mur. In Buffalo, N.Y., more than 200 people viewed a body before it was identified as that of Grace Doze. The 30-year-old woman had been beaten, strangled, and then thrown into Ellicott Creek. Her body was found four days after she left home on May 17, 1927. Although there were reports that she and her husband frequently quarreled and that she had threatened to leave him, the police found no

reason to hold him. The murder was never solved. Grace Doze's son, Clifford, who was only three at the time his mother was killed, had been told that his mother simply disappeared. It was not until fifty years later, when he read newspapers commemorating the day Charles Lindbergh arrived in France after flying across the Atlantic, that Doze learned the truth.

REF.: *CBA;* Nash, *Open Files.*

Dozier, James L., See: **Savasta, Antonio.**

Dózsa, György, d.1514, Hung., rebel. György Dózsa organized the peasants of Hungary into an army and effectively fought off invading Turks, but he kept his force intact in an attempt to eliminate the aristocracy. His rabble forces were defeated at Timisoara and Dózsa was captured. His form of execution was undoubtedly one of the most bizarre and painful on record: he was grilled alive over a glowing throne of red-hot iron. REF.: *CBA.*

Drabing, Michael Edward, 1955- , U.S., mur. Three members of the Schneider family were out for the evening in nearby Lincoln, Ill. Only 17-year-old Terri Schneider was home with her 19-year-old boyfriend Jeffrey Richardson, at 11 p.m. on Aug. 19, 1976, when the doorbell rang. Terri opened the door and found 21-year-old Michael Drabing, a Lincoln housepainter, standing on the porch. Running through Drabing's head were thoughts of Charles Manson, and in his hand was a hunting knife.

Drabing burst into the house and forced Schneider and Richardson into a bedroom, where he bound their hands and feet. He then hid in the house to await the arrival of the rest of the Schneider family.

Shortly afterwards, 44-year-old hog farmer Lloyd Schneider, his 45-year-old wife Phyllis, and another daughter, 16-year-old Cheryl, arrived home. They entered the house and found the two teenagers tied up in the bedroom. They slammed the bedroom door in the intruder's face as they raced to free Terri and Jeffrey, but Drabing knocked the door off its hinges. Richardson and Cheryl Schneider jumped out the window as Drabing burst into the room and ran to where Lloyd and Phyllis were working to free Terri. He began stabbing the three of them with his hunting knife. Outside, Cheryl ran to a neighbor's house to call for help and Jeffrey hailed a passing car on a nearby highway.

By the time police arrived at the home, Drabing was gone. He left behind the mutilated bodies of Phyllis Schneider, Lloyd Schneider, and their daughter Terri.

Drabing was arrested the following day at Abraham Lincoln Hospital where he sought treatment for cuts on his leg. He recounted his story in great detail to local police. Charged with three counts of murder, Drabing was scheduled for trial three months later.

The bench trial lasted eight days in December, during which time Drabing's defense attorney, Walter Kasten, attempted to portray Drabing as a schizophrenic and psychotic who should not be held accountable for his actions. But Drabing himself said, "I know exactly what I was doing at the time of the murders, and it was right... Nothing could stop me from murdering them."

Drabing testified that the triple murder was sparked by the book *Helter Skelter* and its television adaptation chronicling the activities of Charles Manson and his "family" of murderers in California. Drabing, like the Manson family, believed that the mass murder of the nation's rich citizens would start a revolt that would end in the overthrow of the capitalist society.

Drabing was beginning with the Schneider family. He provided a long list of targets, including the governor of Illinois.

On Dec. 16, 1976, more than 250 people crammed the courtroom to hear Judge James D. Heiple's verdict. The irreverent Drabing, who had twice fallen asleep during the proceedings, rocked slowly in his chair as Heiple explained that Drabing's own testimony had convinced him that he was mentally stable on the night of the murders. After Heiple read his verdict of Guilty and adjourned the trial, those in attendance applauded. The unremorseful Drabing said only that he regretted that Cheryl Schneider and Jeffrey Richardson had escaped.

Heiple sentenced Drabing to three concurrent terms of 75 to 100 years on Jan. 21, 1977. See: **Manson, Charles.**

REF.: *CBA; Holmes, Serial Murder.*

Drachman, Louis, d.1913, Fr., mur. Background concerning Louis Drachman is sketchy, but it is known that he was born and raised in rural Provence and later moved to Marseilles where he was arrested in 1911 for burglaries and sexual attacks on prostitutes along the city's docks. He was judged insane and confined to a local asylum, from which he escaped in late 1912. Using the alias Nordeau, Drachman went to work as a janitor for several Marseilles boarding houses. On the night of July 18, 1913, Drachman waylaid a priest, Father Josef Marochel, who had been visiting the sick in one of his buildings, and killed him. Donning the priest's cassock, Drachman went to a small church, St. Michel of the Angels, and boldly took a position in a confessional. When Pierre Wrangel went into the confessional, Drachman reached through the screen and strangled Wrangel to death. Then Drachman burst from the confessional, screaming "Vengeance is the Lord's." He ran from the church, and when police found Wrangel's body, a chase ensued which led to a wharf where Drachman ran into the water and drowned.

REF.: Alois, *The Homicidal Maniac, Ten Studies; CBA.*

7 Draco (Dracon), prom. 7th Cent. B.C., Gr., jur. Drafted the first law codes for Athens, c.621 B.C., which led to the coining of the term draconian, for death was prescribed for almost all crimes.
REF.: *CBA.*

Draga, Queen, See: **Alexander I (Obrenovic).**

Dragna, Jack, 1891-1957, U.S., org. crime. Born in Corleone, Sicily, the home of many U.S. mobsters, Jack Dragna headed the "Mickey Mouse Mafia" of California for about a dozen years in the 1940s and 1950s. Dragna never gained control of the Southern California and Las Vegas rackets, which were always run from New York or Chicago. His bumbling and his failure to eliminate powerful eastern rivals earned the "Mickey Mouse Mafia" its title.

Dragna's family emigrated to the U.S. in 1898, but they returned to Sicily in 1908. Dragna came to Los Angeles in 1914, and was convicted of extortion a year later. He

California Mafia-syndicate boss Jack Dragna, 1946.

served a three-year sentence in San Quentin, the only prison term of his career, despite numerous arrests on a variety of charges. He was chosen to lead the Southern California mob by his East Coast overseers because he was considered the best of a bad lot. The Dragna gangsters were successful at petty extortion, but could not gain a foothold in the Las Vegas casinos.

When the eastern mobs looked west for a new home for the racing wire, Benjamin "Bugsy" Siegel was put in charge by Charles "Lucky" Luciano, who ordered Dragna not to interfere. Siegel set up the Las Vegas casino business, leaving Dragna out. Then the Chicago crime family sent their emissaries to Hollywood to muscle in on the movie industry. There was little Dragna could do, having failed in his many attempts to assassinate Siegel's top lieutenant in California, Mickey Cohen. Meyer Lansky decided to push aside Siegel.

Siegel was murdered by top Lansky triggerman Frankie Carbo, but it was made to look as if Dragna's people had carried out the execution. With Siegel out of the way, there was speculation that the Dragna crime family would gain autonomy in Las Vegas. Lansky offered to let Dragna buy into the Flamingo for $125,000, but neither Dragna nor his associates in Los Angeles could raise the money.

Jack Dragna died in 1957, succeeded by family members Frank

DeSimone, Nick Licata, and Dominic Brooklier. In 1974, Jack's nephew, Louis Tom Dragna, was dubbed the "Reluctant Prince" for turning down a chance to run the L.A. rackets. Instead he struck a deal in 1975 with New York's Gambino family to share the Western territories. The realignment was further complicated by the arrival of Chicago gangster Anthony Spilotro and Brooklyn-born Mike Rizzitello, who came to stake their own claims. Jimmy Fratianno became the West Coast point man, with Rizzitello as his top lieutenant. See: **Cohen, Mickey; DiSimone, Frank; Dragna, Louis Tom; Fratianno, Jimmy "the Weasel"; Siegel, Benjamin.**

REF.: Bonnano, *A Man of Honor; CBA;* Cohen, *Mickey Cohen: In My Own Words;* Davis, *Mafia Kingfish;* Demaris, *The Last Mafioso;* Eisenberg and Landau, *Meyer Lansky;* Fried, *The Rise and Fall of the Jewish Gangster In America;* Gosch and Hammer, *The Last Testament of Lucky Luciano;* McClellan, *Crime Without Punishment;* Messick, *Lansky;* Peterson, *The Mob;* Reid, *The Grim Reapers;* Smith, *Syndicate City;* Zuckerman, *Vengeance Is Mine.*

Dragna, Louis Tom (AKA: **The Reluctant Prince**), 1920- , U.S., org. crime. Dragna's influence in West Coast crime circles was more illusory than real. His timidity in carrying out acts of violence against rivals was told by Mafia informant Jimmy "the Weasel" Fratianno. Fratianno recalled the time when Dragna was sitting in conference with another killer of note, Frank "Bomp" Bompensiero, when "Russian" Louie Strauss walked in. In seconds' time, Fratianno garroted Strauss from behind. When Dragna expressed his admiration for the quick, calculating way "the Weasel" had eliminated an enemy, Fratianno replied that "he ought to try killing someone himself sometime."

It was unlikely that Louis Tom Dragna would resort to violence if there was someone else to do it for him. Louis was the nephew of Jack Dragna, once described as the "Al Capone of the West." His own father had served as *consigliere* of the family until Jack's death in 1957. At the time, Louis was active in the dressmaking business. He learned his trade from Johnny Dio, a veteran labor union infiltrator from New York who had muscled in on the garment district on behalf of Jimmy Hoffa. Dio flew in from New York to teach his young protegé how to "protect" his company, Roberta Manufacturing, from union organizers. Roberta Manufacturing eventually earned $10 million a year, thanks in part to Dio.

Louie Dragna temporarily took over the reins of the Los Angeles crime family when Dominic Brooklier was sent to prison. Because Dragna, referred to as the "Reluctant Prince," lacked the gumption to rule the West Coast rackets with any degree of authority, Brooklier named Fratianno a co-leader. Named as one of eleven "undesirables" by the Nevada gaming commission in 1960, Louie Dragna was banned from the casinos. In 1975, he agreed to an arrangement with the Carlo Gambino crime family of New York to "carve up" the Las Vegas territory. How much of this actually came back to Dragna is a mystery, for the Chicago and New York families had subordinated the California faction.

In 1980 Dragna and four associates—Jack LoCicero,

California crime boss Louis Tom Dragna.

Sam Sciortino, Dominic Brooklier, and Mike Rizzitello—were convicted of conspiracy and extortion charges when the Organized Crime Strike Force revealed their role in shaking down the lucrative pornography industry. U.S. District Judge Terry J. Hatter, Jr. imposed a light sentence on Dragna, taking note of the fact that he had only one prior conviction. The judge described Dragna as "genteel," saying that he had been drawn into the family business out of a sense of misguided loyalty. The Bureau of Prisons rejected Hatter's recommendation that Dragna be confined to a minimum security prison and ordered that he be sent to a more secure facility.

Hatter then tossed out the original sentence and ordered that Dragna spend one year in a community treatment center and be fined $50,000. Dragna was allowed to spend his days working at Roberta Manufacturing with the stipulation that he return to the treatment center at night. See: **Dio, Johnny.**

REF.: *CBA*; Davis, *Mafia Kingfish*; Demaris, *The Last Mafioso*; Nash, *Bloodletters and Badmen*; Peterson, *The Mob*; Reid, *The Grim Reapers*; Toledano, *J. Edgar Hoover*; Zuckerman, *Vengeance Is Mine.*

The **Dragna family** of California, left to right, Louis, Tom, Frank, Guilermo, Adamo, and Paul Dragna.

Dragna Family, prom. 1930s-80s, U.S., org. crime. The Dragna Family, headed by patriarch Jack Dragna, established a Mafia-syndicate crime organization in Los Angeles during the early 1930s, which was preempted by Benjamin "Bugsy" Siegel, who arrived later in the decade to take over all organized crime rackets in the area on behalf of the national syndicate. The Dragna family grudgingly cooperated with Siegel, sharing much of their operations with him and the national crime cartel under the implied threat of death, but Dragna members conspired to have Siegel and certain members of his cartel killed in 1947. The family regained control of the rackets following Siegel's death. See: **Dragna, Jack; Dragna, Louis Tom.** REF.: *CBA.*

Drago, Luis Maria, 1859-1921, Arg., jur. Served as the minister of foreign affairs, 1902-03, and authored the Drago doctrine, 1902, which held that a European power could not use a public debt as an excuse to exercise territorial occupation or armed intervention in Latin America. REF.: *CBA.*

Dragoti, Stan, 1933- , Ger., drugs. "I will never be on drugs again," said American film director Stan Dragoti as he left a German courtroom after receiving a suspended sentence and a $54,350 fine for attempting to smuggle cocaine through Frankfurt International Airport. Dragoti was arrested on May 13, 1979, when he tried to smuggle 22 grams of cocaine in a bathing suit while en route to the Cannes Film Festival in France.

Dragoti stood before Judge Harold Illmer and confessed that he had been using cocaine for nine months, beginning in September 1978, when he learned that his wife, model Cheryl Tiegs, was involved in an affair. Dragoti, whose movie *Love At First Bite* was up for an award at the Cannes festival, maintained that his life had taken such a downturn that he abused cocaine as a mental crutch.

Following the 8-hour trial, Judge Illmer told the courtroom that he felt Dragoti was not a criminal, and that overwhelming pressure had led to his involvement with cocaine. REF.: *CBA.*

Drake, Charles Daniel, 1811-92, U.S., jur. Represented Missouri in the U.S. Senate, 1867-70, and served as U.S. court of claims chief justice, 1870-85. REF.: *CBA.*

Drake, Sir Francis, c.1545-96, Int'l., pir. The naval heroics of English admiral Sir Francis Drake amounted to little more than piracy. When the Spanish demanded of Queen Elizabeth I that Drake be executed for attacking their ships, the Queen might have acquiesced in order to assure peace, but the Spanish also demanded a return of £1.5 million in treasure that Drake had stolen during his around-the-world voyage. When the Queen knighted Drake on board his corsair the *Golden Hind*, the Spanish were outraged and began preparing for war.

Francis Drake was born in Devonshire, and apprenticed to sea as a pirate by his cousin Sir John Hawkins. In 1567, Drake stood at the helm of the *Judith* during an expedition to the Gulf of Mexico. He earned a reputation as a fearless, if not cunning, seaman during three expeditions to the New World. In 1572, he was commissioned a privateer by the Queen and was the first Englishman to see the Pacific Ocean. During the voyage Drake sacked the town of Nombre de Dios, and played havoc with Spanish shipping in the region.

He returned to England to prepare for his eventual trip around the world, a journey of piracy licensed by the Queen. Drake embarked in December 1577, saling through the Cape Verde Islands and past Brazil. Continuing past the Straits of Magellan and up the coast of Chile, Drake seized as many Spanish ships as he could, amassing a fortune of plundered cargo in the hold of his ship. He sailed across the Pacific, through the Indian Ocean, and around the Cape of Good Hope. By this time the Spanish ministers demanded that "El Draque" hang for his peacetime

Sir Francis Drake, holding spear, bareheaded, and his privateers, surrounded by hostile natives.

piracies. Drake returned to Plymouth in September 1850. Elizabeth carefully weighed Drake's service to her against the irate demands of the Spanish. After six months, she went to Deptford and knighted him. In subsequent privateering missions, Sir Francis

Drake sailed with the blessings of the throne, although the Spanish refused to consider him as anything more than a common pirate.

REF.: Andrews, *Elizabethan Privateering: English Privateering During the Spanish War, 1585-1603;* Cabal, *Piracy and Pirates;* CBA; Chatterton, *The Romance of Piracy;* Ellms, *The Pirates' Own Book;* Gosse, *The Pirates' Who's Who;* Innes, *The Book of Pirates;* Lloyd, *Sir Francis Drake;* Lydon, *Pirates, Privateers and Profits;* Mitchell, *Pirates;* Pringle, *The Story of the Great Age of Piracy;* Rankin, *The Golden Age of Piracy;* Scott, *Concise Encyclcopedia of Crime and Criminals;* Williams, *Captains Outrageous: Seven Centuries of Piracy.*

Drake, Leroy (AKA: Pious Leroy), b.1897, U.S., mur. Leroy Drake had lived with his Uncle Henry and Aunt Nell Steinhauer for most of his life. The couple raised Drake in the traditions of the church, and he was a model nephew. The couple became depressed after Drake's sudden theft of an automobile. According to Drake, they were unable to understand his motives and blamed themselves for his actions.

In order to ease their suffering, Drake poisoned them with sodium cyanide-laced coffee. He dragged their bodies into their car and drove it into Los Angeles harbor. "I had caused my uncle and aunt so much heartache," said Drake, "that I decided I'd done wrong to them and I thought giving them poison was the best way to right that wrong and save them from further hurt."

Drake was apprehended one week later when a bank clerk noticed a check drawn on the Steinhauer account bore a forgery of Henry Steinhauer's signature. Police investigated and found that Drake had gone on a spending spree after murdering the couple. He had purchased a new sportscar for himself and had showered his girlfriend with gifts.

Drake was charged with the murders of the couple. Jurors did not accept his rationale for the killings. Drake was convicted of murder and sentenced to life in prison.

REF.: CBA; Kobler, *Some Like It Gory.*

Drake, Philip (AKA: Felipe Drax), prom. 1800s, U.S., pir. An American, Philip Drake changed his name to Don Felipe Drax, pretending to be a Brazilian after the English slave trade ended. His book, *Revelations of a Slave Trader,* published in 1860, stated that he had shipped more than 70,000 slaves in a five year period. He claimed that "business is getting better every year." Drake held up to 2,000 blacks on an island he owned in the Gulf of Mexico, keeping them there to sell to dealers in Rio de Janeiro, Havana, and New York. In 1862, the U.S. finally enforced an 1808 law that defined the importation of slaves as an illegal act of piracy.

REF.: CBA; Mitchell, *Pirates.*

Drake, Thomas Jefferson, 1797-1875, U.S., jur. Served as prosecuting attorney for Oakland County, Mich., 1827-30 and 1850-52, and received appointments to the Territorial Court for the Territory of Utah from President Abraham Lincoln, Jan. 27, 1862, and President Andrew Johnson, Jan. 19, 1866. REF.: CBA.

Drake Swindle, 1590s-present, Int'l., fraud. The Drake Swindle is one of the oldest and most widely practiced frauds. It began with the death of the British buccaneer, Sir Francis Drake, who had looted billions of dollars of gold and gems for the coffers of Queen Elizabeth I. From the moment of Drake's death, on Jan. 28, 1596, countless sharpers and con men practiced a fantastic fraud in his name, growing richer than the so-called Drake heirs ever hoped to be. The scheme was a simple one wherein the tale was told that Drake and Queen Elizabeth had an illegitimate son who was denied the rightful fortune his father left to him—billions which the British government was holding, and from which interest accumulating. Almost anyone and everyone named Drake, the con men insisted, were entitled to a share of Sir Francis' fortune and, as soon as energetic and dedicated lawyers legally pried loose this staggering fortune, all the Drake heirs would be enormously rich.

The heirs were contacted and asked to contribute to the considerable legal fees it would take in freeing the fortune through the courts. Tens of thousands of gullible suckers over the centuries willingly gave their funds, some their life savings, to unscrupulous confidence tricksters in this crusty scam. Not until the emergence of Oscar Merrill Hartzell, a shrewd Wisconsin farm boy, however, did the Drake Swindle go into high gear, being operated on an international scale that would have stunned the imaginative Drake himself with its magnitude. See: **Hartzell, Oscar Merrill.**

REF.: CBA; Nash, *Hustlers and Con Men.*

Draper, Shang, prom. 1870s-80s, U.S., org. crime. During the 1870s, Shang Draper's New York gang perfected the badger game. Draper employed thirty women in his saloon on Sixth Avenue to entice drunken men to join them for an escapade at a nearby hotel on Prince Street. There, the victim would be assaulted and robbed by one of Draper's confederates, hidden in a secret panel cut from the wall. The Draper gang was finally broken up by New York Police Captain John H. McCullagh, but Draper continued to operate his saloon until 1883.

In later years, Draper emerged as a prime suspect in the robbery of the Manhattan Savings Institute and other crimes.

REF.: Asbury, *The Gangs of New York;* CBA; Peterson, *The Mob.*

Draper, William, c.1920-53, U.S., rape-mur. Draper was convicted in 1950 for the brutal rape-murder of a 73-year-old Rochester, N.Y., woman, Jennie O'Keefe, mother of John O'Keefe, a Rochester Police officer. Her brutally beaten body was found in the early morning on July 17, 1949, near a road in Greece, N.Y.

The break in the case came that same evening when two girls walking along a road a few miles away found a girdle traced to the victim. They also found a wallet belonging to William Draper, twenty-nine, a Rochester laborer. He was quickly arrested. Draper denied involvement until he was led to the morgue and shown the victim's body. His confession soon followed.

The sex killer told detectives that he had met the lonely woman at a bar and grill and that the two went for a ride. He made advances which the woman refused. Then, according to the confession, he beat her with his fists and dragged her from the car where the attack continued. The woman finally lost consciousness and, after a time, Draper dragged her back into the car. A few hours later, when he realized that O'Keefe was dead, he stopped alongside the road outside of Greece and once again dragged the woman from the car.

After his first conviction in 1950, the jury recommended leniency and the judge sentenced Draper to life imprisonment. He appealed the conviction to state and federal courts and it was finally overturned. A new trial was ordered but this time the jury made no recommendation for mercy. On Apr. 27, 1952, Judge Daniel J. O'Mara sentenced Draper to die in the electric chair.

On July 23, 1953, after eating the final bowl of ice cream he had requested, Draper was led to the electric chair at Sing Sing Prison. At 11:04 p.m. he became Sing Sing's 570th person to be executed. REF.: CBA.

Draw, Derrick, prom. 1971, U.S., mur. Detroit police stumbled on the frozen body of 16-year-old Gary Frandle in a downtown alley. The youth had been beaten, stabbed, and his ears had been amputated.

Frandle had disappeared the previous day after telephoning his mother to explain that he was on his way home from his girlfriend's house and would be hitchhiking back to suburban Warren, Mich. When Frandle had not arrived by 11 p.m., his mother notified authorities.

Police searched for Frandle. One witness saw him climb into a 1966 Plymouth driven by two black men near the intersection of Twelve Mile and Van Dyke roads. With the description of the driver, 21-year-old rookie police officer William Tullock led police to the home of Derrick Draw, an employee of General Motors Tech Center. Tullock had once worked with Draw at General Motors. Draw denied all knowledge of the crime until his Plymouth was discovered to contain evidence implicating him in the boy's death.

Lionel M. Alexander, Draw's 19-year-old companion and fellow General Motors employee, told police that he and Draw had picked up Frandle as they drove home from work. He explained that Draw beat the boy in the back seat of the car and, disregarding Alexander's pleas that he stop, stabbed Frandle and sliced off his ears in response to instructions from a United Urban League speaker known only as Enoch. Alexander told authorities that Enoch, speaking at a gathering of black ghetto residents, said, "To prove yourself as a black warrior, bring in the ear of a dead white man."

The man called Enoch denied that he made any such statement. He soon resigned from the Urban League to avoid further embarrassing the organization.

On the testimony of Alexander, Draw was convicted of second-degree murder and sentenced to life at Michigan's Jackson State prison. REF.: *CBA*.

Drayton, John, 1766-1822, U.S., jur. Employed as warden for the city of Charleston, S.C., 1788, served two terms as governor of the state, 1801-03 and 1809-10, and was appointed by President James Madison to the District Court of South Carolina, May 4, 1812. REF.: *CBA*.

Drayton, William, 1732-90, U.S., jur. Served as first judge for South Carolina District Court, 1789-90. REF.: *CBA*.

Drayton, William Henry, 1742-79, U.S., jur. Named South Carolina's chief justice, 1776, and a member of the Continental Congress, 1778-79. REF.: *CBA*.

Dreamer, Robert, 1898-1937, U.S., mur. Bloodhounds were used on Dec. 30, 1927, in an attempt to track down the brutal murderer of Thelma Young, seventeen. The murder occurred the night before, in Washington, Pa. Police later complained that thousands of curiosity seekers gathering at the murder site obliterated the killer's scent.

For the next eight years, that trail remained cold. The murderer not only escaped detection, but as later revealed, he passed the victim's house twice each day, on his way to and from work, often greeting members of her family.

The long-sought break in the case came when two young women were attacked, in separate episodes, near the scene of Thelma's murder. Both women managed to free themselves from the attacker. The attacker had fired three shots at one of the women as she fled. It was the other woman, however, who proved dangerous to the attacker. She recognized the man as neighborhood resident Robert Dreamer, a 38-year-old railroad worker. He was quickly arrested for the two bungled attacks. Officer Clark Miller, one of the arresting officers, pointed out the similarities between the recent attacks and the murder of Thelma Young more than eight years before. At first, Dreamer denied any knowledge of the Young murder.

He was arrested on Jan. 21, 1936. Eight officers from the state, county, and Washington Police operated around the clock in questioning the suspect, a non-stop interrogation that went on for five days. On the fifth day, he was shown a button found near Thelma's body. "Did you ever see this before?" one of the officers asked.

"Yes," the suspect admitted, "It's off of a raincoat I used to have."

"When did you lose it?"

"I guess the night of the murder."

"What murder?" one of the officers asked.

"The night Thelma was killed," Dreamer answered. Then he calmly confessed to killing Thelma Young, the sister of one of his best friends and a schoolmate of the woman who was now his wife.

Dreamer's wife, the former Mary Caldwell was also questioned by police. When asked if her husband had ever mentioned killing Thelma, Mary Dreamer replied, "Only once. We were out one night with another girl, and he quarrelled with her. He grabbed her by the throat, half in fun. 'I'll fix you like I did Thelma,' he told her." Dreamer's wife said her husband had been joking. When asked later if she would stand by her husband, she answered, "No. If he did what they say he confessed, then he had better stay right where he is now."

Clyde Young, one of Thelma Young's brothers (there were fifteen children in the Young family), and a boyhood friend of

Dreamer's said, "Of course, none of us ever suspected him. But I often wondered why, right after the killing, he quit going around with me."

"Who would have thought that a neighbor had killed our girl?" said Iva Young, the mother of the murdered girl.

Dreamer was convicted of the murder and sentenced to death. He was also a suspect in the brutal murder of Elizabeth Louden, sixteen, who was found beaten to death near her home in Walker Mills, three days before Dreamer's arrest on Jan. 21, 1936. Dreamer never confessed to the crime, but Walker Mills police put together a strong circumstantial case against him. He worked in a railroad yard only two miles away, fit the description of the man that Elizabeth had told friends was following her, and had admitted to police that he had attacked young girls for over ten years. Although he was never tried for this second murder, the Louden murder case was closed on Feb. 1, 1937, one half hour after Dreamer was executed. Robert Elliott, the executioner at Sing Sing who some called the loneliest man in the world, pulled the switch at the Pennsylvania state prison in Rockview that sent Robert Dreamer to his death. Elliott, who traveled between prisons in New York, New Jersey, and Pennsylvania, plying his grim trade, had executed nearly a thousand men. REF.: *CBA*.

Dreesman, Robert, 1948-88, U.S., suic.-mur. On New Year's Day, 1988, in Algona, Iowa, Robert Dreesman, a 40-year-old with a history of mental illness, shot six relatives to death with a rifle before taking his own life. As the family was seated around his parents dining room table, Dreesman entered the room and shot 79-year-old John Dreesman, his father; 74-year-old Agnes Dreesman, his mother; 48-year-old Marilyn Chuang, his sister visiting from Hawaii; and her three children, 12-year-old Jason, 11-year-old Jennifer, and 8-year-old Joshua. Dreesman shot each person in the head and chest before taking his own life with a rifle blast to the head. Friends speculated that Dreesman committed the murders because of the attention his parents focused on his nephews and niece. REF.: *CBA*.

Dreher, Dr. **Thomas**, 1875-1929, and **Le Boeuf, Ada**, d.1929, and **Beadle, James**, prom. 1929, U.S., mur. Ada Le Boeuf, a resident of the Louisiana bayou country, began seeing Dr. Thomas Dreher about her headaches in December 1926. In the next few months, Dr. Dreher visited the Le Boeuf residence frequently. Ada Le Boeuf's husband, Jim Le Boeuf, preoccupied with sport fishing in the swampy bayous in and around Lake Palourde, paid no particular attention to the visits.

Le Boeuf was oblivious to the local gossip about a possible affair between his wife and Dreher. One evening, however, when Le Boeuf failed to return his boat on time, James Beadle, the boat's owner, made the comment, "Just because you are careless with your property, you can't be free with mine!" Pressed by Le Boeuf for his meaning, Beadle told him the gossip. Although Le Boeuf confronted his wife about the affair, Ada claimed that the sole purpose of Dr. Dreher's visits had been to bring her headache medicine.

On July 1, 1927, the Le Boeufs set out across Lake Palourde to visit relatives. They left for home at midnight. Five days later Jim Le Boeuf's body was fished out of the water. There were bullet holes in the head and evidence that the corpse had been weighted down with heavy irons. When questioned about her husband's murder, Ada Le Boeuf claimed he had been seeing another woman. Although Dr. Dreher admitted conspiring to murder Le Boeuf, he accused James Beadle of firing the shots.

Beadle likewise admitted to a part in the murder but claimed Dreher had actually shot Le Boeuf. When Ada Le Boeuf, Dreher and Beadle came up for trial the next year, all three were convicted of first-degree murder. Despite the fact that no woman had ever been executed in Louisiana, Ada Le Boeuf was sentenced to hang alongside Dr. Dreher. Amidst protest, Governor Huey Long decided that this case should break precedent, saying that a reprieve would be a "mockery against decency and order." The couple were hanged together on Feb. 1, 1929.

REF.: *CBA*; Furneaux, *The Medical Murderer*; Nash, *Almanac of*

World Crime; Whitelaw, *Corpus Delicti;* Wilson, *Encyclopedia of Murder.*

Drew, Charles, c.1715-40, Brit., mur. Charles Drew, the son of a wealthy lawyer, had been keeping company with Elizabeth Boyer. When she asked him if he ever intended to propose marriage, he told her to be patient, explaining, "it will be worse for us both if I do it now, for my father will certainly disinherit me."

"I wish somebody would shoot the old dog," Elizabeth Boyer replied. Boyer's wish was soon to come true. Feb. 1, 1740, Drew's father was found in his home, dead of a gunshot wound.

Charles Drew was immediately suspected of committing the murder; he moved to London as the investigation continued, offering a large reward to anyone who gave information leading to the conviction of the murderer. This offer led to the arrest of a smuggler named Humphreys who had been seen in young Drew's company. The offer of a reward, meant to clear Drew's name, did just the opposite. Investigators learned from the smuggler that he and Drew had gone to the victim's house on the night of Jan. 31, 1740. Drew had promised the smuggler considerable money for murdering his father, supplied Humphreys with a pistol that had been loaned to Drew by none other than Elizabeth Boyer, who reportedly planned the murder. Charles Drew hid nearby as Humphreys walked to the door of the house. But at the last minute, the smuggler decided he could not do the deed. Drew sprang from the darkness, took the pistol in his own hand, and knocked on the door. When his father opened it, Drew shot him dead.

Drew was arrested and jailed at Newgate. He tried to buy his way out of prison, promising a jailor half of his ill-gotten fortune if he would help him escape. The jailor appeared interested but informed the warden instead. Drew was moved to the condemned cell and guarded day and night. He was convicted after a protracted trial and was hanged on Apr. 9, 1740. The execution of Drew was attended by the largest crowd ever assembled to witness a hanging. Elizabeth Boyer was never brought to trial.

REF.: Armitage, *Bow Street Runners; CBA;* Mitchell, *The Newgate Calendar.*

Drew, Daniel, 1797-1879, U.S., fraud. A tall, lean, narrow-eyed illiterate, Daniel Drew, with typical pioneer spirit, learned and practiced fraud with the alacrity of an aggressive opportunist. He began as a drover, and horse trader who, in 1815, made enough money from a cattle scheme to put his other spectacular frauds into action. In that year, Drew drove a large herd of cattle to the New York pens of Henry Astor, the brother of John Jacob Astor. He was a strange-looking cattleman, wearing a giant floppy hat, baggy pants, prodding his cattle onward with an umbrella while riding a mule. He thus appeared before Henry Astor, who looked over Drew's livestock and exclaimed: "Drew, that's the finest-looking herd of cattle I've ever seen!" He paid

Pioneer con man Daniel Drew.

Drew top dollar, but three days later, Astor was amazed to see that this herd had turned into the worst-loooking animals on four hooves, all of them sickly and so thin that their ribs almost poked through the flesh. Drew had simply driven his herd without water for three days, mixing salt in the cattle's food and allowing them to drink just before delivery, causing the animals to look fat and weigh in at almost twice the normal weight.

With his shady profits from Astor, Drew bought a broken-down ferry line which consisted of an ancient paddle-wheeler,

Water Witch, an old tub that leaked from every board and joint and was wholly unseaworthy. Yet, with a coat of paint and Drew's elaborate plans to build more ships, he convinced Commodore Cornelius Vanderbilt that he would soon outstrip Vanderbilt's lucrative steamship services. Vanderbilt, enormously rich, paid a huge sum to Drew, buying out the line, only to discover that he had bought nothing more than a hulk and some rotting docks. Drew would go on victimizing Vanderbilt for millions of dollars, especially in his enormous stock fraud during the so-called "Erie War," in which his junior partners, James "Big Jim" Fisk and Jay Gould, attempted to take over the Erie Railroad, in which Vanderbilt held considerable stock. Drew employed the same mulcting method on Vanderbilt as he had on Henry Astor, except that he watered stock instead of cattle.

Drew, Fisk, and Gould made it appear that they were going to start buying up all the Erie stock, which caused the greedy Vanderbilt to make such huge purchases of the stock that he believed he had cornered all the stock Erie possessed. But new Erie stock kept appearing on the floor of the then-unregulated stock exchange in New York. Drew, through his henchmen Fisk and Gould, was simply printing up more and more shares and selling these worthless certificates to Vanderbilt. The stock soared to a bloated value of $57 million, until the fraud was discovered when a broker smeared the ink on an Erie certificate with the slight pressure of his thumb and then fainted dead away under the shock. Erie stock plummeted, but by then Drew, Fisk, and Gould had bilked as much as $10 million from the gullible Vanderbilt.

From 1873 to 1876, shrewd, old stock-watering Drew found himself trapped in one exchange panic after another until he was reduced to the status of near-pauper, having only $500 left of his millions. When he filed for bankruptcy, Drew listed his possessions as "seal-skin coat, watch and chain, bibles and hymn books." Though he died impoverished, Drew is oddly remembered today as a religious benefactor. In 1852, while still flush, Drew had endowed several religious groups with on-going funds that allowed the razing of the Old Brewery, a vile charnal house in New York City, where countless murders had been committed and vice ran rampant. In 1866, Drew established Drew Theological Seminary in Madison, N.J., leaving that institution with permanent funds so that his name would be forever associated with it. Drew's aim, of course, was to establish a good and worthy name to shield his fraudulent activities from public view but never embracing the teachings of the institutions he founded. He died a mean old schemer, having finally learned to read in his old age but giving this up after having perused only one book, *Pilgrim's Progress.* See: **Fisk, James, Jr.; Gould, Jay.**

REF.: Butterfield, *The American Past; CBA;* Fuller, *Jubilee Jim;* Josephson, *The Robber Barons;* Lane, *Commodore Vanderbilt;* Moore, *Wolves, Widows, and Orphans;* Nash, *Hustlers and Con Men;* O'Connor, *The Astors.*

Drew, Joseph, d.1808, U.S., mur. Ebenezer Parker, a deputy sheriff, appeared at a Cape Elizabeth, Me., shop to arrest one of Joseph Drew's co-workers on a felony charge, but Drew interfered when Parker ordered him out of the way. Drew, a powerful man, struck Parker so hard that he killed him. Drew was hanged before a large crowd in Portland, Me., on July 21, 1808.

REF.: *CBA; The Life and Confession of Joseph Drew.*

Drew, Pearl, 1900- , U.S., mansl. Pearl Drew forced her 7-year-old daughter to testify that Pearl's father murdered her unemployed husband. Marvin Drew was shot to death in the bedroom of his Ashland, Miss., home in July 1929 while he slept with his daughter Dorothy Louise.

Pearl Drew's father, known as "Pop" Gunter, was charged with the murder and convicted primarily on the false testimony of his granddaughter Dorothy Louise. Gunter was sentenced to twenty-five years in prison, but was released in November 1929 by Mississippi Governor Theodore Gilmore Bilbo. Pearl confessed that she killed her husband because of his excessive drinking and womanizing. In a second trial, she pleaded guilty to the charge of manslaughter. REF.: *CBA.*

Drey, Frederick, See: **Mors, Frederick.**

Dreyfus, Alfred, 1859-1935, Fr., (wrong. convict.) treas. Alfred Dreyfus was born in Mulhouse, Alsace, the son of a wealthy textile manufacturer. When Germany annexed Alsace in 1870, following the Franco-Prussian War, the Dreyfus family, preferring to remain French, moved to Paris. Two older brothers, Jacques and Mathieu, remained behind to continue operating the lucrative family business. Always patriotically French and dreaming of becoming a soldier, Dreyfus entered the École Polytechnique, where he was an excellent student, becoming an artillery expert and graduating with the rank of second lieutenant. He was posted to the Fourteenth Regiment of Artillery in 1880. A dedicated officer, Dreyfus was promoted to first lieutenant. He married Lucie Hadomard in 1889, and the union produced two children. An esteemed officer, a loving husband and doting father, Dreyfus supplemented his military income with a considerable private income from his family business and he lived well.

After his promotion to captain, Dreyfus was nominated to the staff college, L'École Supérieure de Guerre, and finished the challenging two-year course with honors, ranking third in his class. The only bad mark on his record came from an anti-Semitic general who complained that he was concerned with having a Jew on the General Staff. This biased opinion was ignored, and Dreyfus was appointed to the General Staff on Jan. 1, 1893, as a probationer (*stagiare*). For more than a year, Dreyfus was a model officer. At this time, top officers in the French General Staff became increasingly alarmed at the leakage of top secret information.

The wrongly convicted Capt. Alfred Dreyfus.

Details about military fortifications and newly developed military weapons were finding their way into German hands.

The military attaché at the German embassy in Paris, Lieutenant-Colonel Max von Schwartzkoppen, was apparently receiving this information. Some time in September 1894, Major Hubert Henry of the Statistical Section of the French Intelligence Bureau brought a memorandum, or *bordereau,* to his superiors, and claimed that this document, unsigned, written in French, and torn into four pieces, had been recovered from Schwartzkoppen's office in the German embassy by a maid named Bastian who was really a French spy. She had plucked the *bordereau* from the wastebasket next to the German attaché's desk and secreted it out of the German embassy in Paris and into Henry's hands.

French officers studied the *bordereau* and concluded that it contained specifications on artillery emplacements and other vital data, and that it had been written by a General Staff officer expert in the use of artillery. Suspicions soon focused upon Captain Alfred Dreyfus. Officers who disliked Dreyfus because he was Jewish, or because he was humorless and rather distant, or because he did not socialize with the officer corps and remained close only to his family and a few friends, came forward to denounce him as the traitor. Moreover, so-called handwriting experts concluded that the *bordereau* had, indeed, been written by Dreyfus, even though Dreyfus' handwriting and that of the *bordereau* author were completely dissimilar. The handwriting experts claimed that there was a reason for this: Dreyfus, knowing he was writing a document that could prove his treason, disguised his handwriting.

On Oct. 15, 1894, Dreyfus was arrested, imprisoned, and charged with high treason, the order signed by General Auguste Mercier. Dreyfus' court-martial occurred from Dec. 19 to 22, 1894. The entire proceedings constituted a kangaroo court where Dreyfus' guilt had been predetermined by a group of anti-Semitic officers headed by General Mercier. The infamous Major Henry testified that "a person of integrity" whom he would not name had told him that Dreyfus was a traitor. Contrary to all French law, the defense was denied knowledge of any of the so-called "evidence" against the accused, and Dreyfus was convicted out of hand. In this instance, Major Mercier du Paty de Clam handed the president of the court a sealed envelope in which the so-called "evidence" against Dreyfus was contained. Dreyfus, following his conviction, was sentenced to life imprisonment in "a fortified place," and was to be publicly humiliated.

The anti-Semitic press, which was widespread and rabid, had whipped up such race hatred against Dreyfus that thousands gathered in public places and before government buildings to display their anger at the fact that Dreyfus was not to be executed. Screams for his blood and head echoed throughout the streets of Paris for weeks. On Jan. 5, 1895, the day of Dreyfus' official degradation, he stood, emaciated, in a military courtyard while General Darras raised his sword and a sergeant of giant proportions stepped up to the convicted man. General Darras announced: "Dreyfus, you are unworthy to wear the uniform. In the name of the French people we deprive you of your rank."

"I am innocent!" Dreyfus suddenly shouted. "I swear that I am innocent! Long live France!"

The towering sergeant tore from Dreyfus' uniform the gold braid epaulets, stripes, medals, and decorations, broke his sword and tossed it to the ground. The stripes from the kepi hat were torn away, the numbers from the high collar, the buttons from his coat.

"In the name of my wife and children, I swear that I am innocent!" shouted Dreyfus. "I swear it! Long live France! You are degrading an innocent man!"

Huge crowds assembled behind an open iron fence and screamed over and over "Death to the traitor! Kill him! Execute him!" Dreyfus was marched, stripped of all rank and honors, around the square in front of the troops. He stopped briefly before a corps of newspapermen and said: "You will say to the whole of France that I am innocent." Dreyfus, his shoulders bent, was then put into a police van. On Jan. 17, 1895, the cashiered Dreyfus was sent to Devil's Island, once a leper colony off the coast of French Guiana, where France's most hellish penal colony was located. Here Dreyfus lived in isolation. His guards were ordered not to speak to him and he was denied visitors. His mail was heavily censored and he was, for all purposes, forgotten.

Only Dreyfus' family and closest friends continued to believe in his innocence, along with a single, courageous French officer, Lieutenant-Colonel Georges Picquart, who, troubled by the whole affair, conducted his own investigation and finally uncovered the real author of the *bordereau,* Major Ferdinand Walsin-Esterhazy. Picquart went to the General Staff and revealed that Major Henry had recognized the handwriting of the *bordereau* as that of his close friend Esterhazy and sought to save him by putting the blame on the innocent Dreyfus. Picquart pointed out that French military secrets had continued to flow to the Germans through Esterhazy long after Dreyfus had been sent to Devil's Island. Picquart had obtained documents of Esterhazy's in August 1896, whose writing and that of the *bordereau* proved identical. Picquart's superiors, General R.C.F. de Boisdeffre, chief of staff; General Jean Baptiste-Billot, war minister; and General Charles-Arthur Gonse, deputy chief of staff, refused to accept Picquart's evidence and ordered him to cease his investigation. He replied that the French army and government had to reverse the decision concerning Dreyfus before others discovered his innocence and the fact that the General Staff had protected Esterhazy, the real traitor. Esterhazy was silenced and sent out of the country on useless missions while his assistant, the insidious Major Henry, continued to create more forgeries to undue Picquart's revelations.

Left, the infamous *bordereau,* **and right, a sample of Dreyfus' handwriting.**

Mathieu Dreyfus, however, continued to fight for his brother's exoneration, and he soon learned of Picqaurt's discoveries and publicly denounced Esterhazy.

The French high command had no choice but to order a court-martial of Esterhazy on Jan. 10 and 11, 1898. The hearing was short and conclusive, clearing Esterhazy of all charges, a flagrant cover-up that caused one of the leading journalists of the day, Émile Zola, to denounce publicly the military caste system that protected its own corrupt members and the government that backed it. In one of the momentous publishing events in any century, on Jan. 13, 1898, Zola published his celebrated article *J'Accuse,* addressed to the president of the French Republic, on the front page of the powerful *L'Aurore.* The fearless Zola, risking criminal charges and imprisonment, accused the government and several generals of criminally covering up the deeds of Esterhazy to save their own reputations, of illegally railroading the innocent Dreyfus, and of compounding their offenses through forgeries, lies, and the destruction of evidence. Zola's masterful attack was called "a moment in the conscience of mankind" by the great French author, Anatole France.

There was no immediate triumph. Zola was convicted of libel, his name was struck from the ranks of the Legion of Honor, and he went to live in exile in England for a year. But France's greatest writers and journalists soon sided with Zola—Jean Jaurès, Léon Blum, Anatole France, Georges Clemenceau—and the press finally created enough pressure to have Dreyfus brought back from Devil's Island and retried. Major Henry by then had cut his own throat, realizing that he was about to be revealed as the culprit who had protected the traitor Esterhazy. Dreyfus was tried again at Rennes from Aug. 7 to Sept. 9, 1899. More than 300 journalists from all over the world attended, and thousands choked the streets around the courthouse.

The rigid, unyielding French high command, however, refused to admit its error and, on the part of certain officers, its outright fraud in convicting Dreyfus in 1894. Dreyfus was again found Guilty, "with extenuating circumstances," a verdict which shocked a world that now had come to believe in Dreyfus' innocence.

French president Emile Loubet, however, issued a decree which pardoned Dreyfus. The cashiered captain was not appeased. His insistence on full vindication led to a long legal campaign which finally, in 1906, saw the French Court of Appeal quash the Rennes verdict, and pronounce Dreyfus completely innocent of the crime he had been charged with twelve years earlier. He was restored to the French Army and given the rank of major. Dreyfus was awarded the Cross of the Cavalier of the Legion of Honor. He served honorably and with distinction during WWI, and was promoted to lieutenant-colonel and named an officer of the Legion of Honor. After a long illness, Dreyfus died in 1935. The victimized Dreyfus had the final triumph of outliving his nemesis by one year. Esterhazy, when finally exposed at the turn of the century, fled France and lived in England where he later confessed his guilt. He died in shame and without friends in 1934.

REF.: Bourdrel, *Historie des juifs en France; CBA;* Chapman, *The Dreyfus Case;* Dreyfus, *L'Affaire telle que je l'ai vécue;* Dreyfus, *Capitaine Alfred Dreyfus;* Halasz, *Captain Dreyfus;* Herzog, *From Dreyfus to Petain;* Hoffman, *More Than a Trial;* Hubert, *The Dreyfus Affair and the French Novel;* Johnson, *France and the Dreyfus Affair;* Kedward, *The Dreyfus Affair;* Larkin, *Church and State After the Dreyfus Affair;* Lewis, *Prisoners of Honor: The Dreyfus Affair;* McGrady, *Crime Scientists;* Reinach, *Historie de l'affaire Dreyfus;* Scott, *The Concise Encyclopedia of Crime and Criminals;* Snyder, *The Dreyfus Affair;* _____ and Morris, *A Treasury of Great Reporting;* Stevens, *The Tragedy of Dreyfus;* Thomas, *L'Affaire sans Dreyfus;* Thorwald, *The Century of the Detective;* Tuchman, *The Proud Tower;* (FILM), *The Dreyfus Case* (Brit.), 1931; *The Life of Emile Zola,* 1937; *The Dreyfus Case* (Ger.), 1940; *I Accuse!,* 1958; *Dreyfus ou l'intolérable vérité,* 1974.

Drinan, John Albert, 1848-1931, Fr., (unsolv.) mur. John Albert Drinan, a deaf 83-year-old, lived the last three weeks of his life in a Nice boarding house until his mysterious death in 1931.

Drinan was found lying dead among shards of broken glass at the bottom of a stairwell on Jan. 6. It was presumed that he had tripped while coming downstairs to refill his glass pitcher with water. A coroner's report discovered that he had sustained a skull injury, resulting in a cerebral hemorrhage that caused his death.

No one suspected that Drinan had amassed an estate valued in excess of £200,000. His will left his estate, totalling £230,000, to the Poor Boxes of the London Police Court. Authorities quickly investigated his finances. They found several documents forged with Drinan's signature authorizing the transfer of more than £100,000 to the account of one of his acquaintances, Joseph Haiat. Haiat fled to Egypt after completing the transactions, where it is believed he faked his own death to evade capture. With Haiat gone, police had only one suspect in the forgery case: Cecil James Beale, the former British Vice-Consul in France who witnessed the transfers. Beale, who had verified the signature on the documents as truly Drinan's, was charged with approving the forgeries, and sentenced to fifteen months in prison.

Haiat was never captured, but it is believed that he and an accomplice, a middle-aged, French-speaking woman, could have helped police solve Drinan's murder. His death remains unsolved.

REF.: *CBA; Greenwall, They Were Murdered In France.*

Driscoll, Danny, c.1860-88, U.S., org. crime. Danny Driscoll and his partner, Dan Lyons, commanded a tough New York street gang in the 1880s known as the Whyos. They were the last of the deadly assault gangs of Manhattan, which had included at various times the Dead Rabbits, the Bowery Boys, and the Five Points. The New York police did not waste an opportunity to drag Driscoll to the gallows, even if the charges against him warranted less than hanging.

In 1887, Driscoll was involved in a gun battle with John McCarthy, a member of the Five Points, over the favors of prostitute Breezy Garrity, who stood by to see which of the two ruffians would prevail. A stray bullet from Driscol's gun struck Garrity and killed her. The police arrested him and the prosecution pushed for the death penalty. Driscoll was a prime suspect in several other murders, and the Whyos were infamous. He was hanged at the Tombs on Jan. 23, 1888. See: **Lyons, Danny; Whyos Gang.**

REF.: Asbury, *The Gangs of New York; CBA.*

Driscoll, Daniel, d.1928, **Rowlands, Edward**, d.1928, **Rowlands, John**, prom. 1927, and **Price, William Joseph**, prom. 1927, Brit., mur. Welsh rugby player and welterweight boxer David Lewis died in the hospital on Oct. 4, 1927, after his throat had been sliced with his own knife during a drunken brawl with four other men outside a Cardiff pub on Sept. 30.

In November 1927 Daniel Driscoll, Edward Rowlands, John Rowlands, and William Joseph Price were charged with the murder. Lewis, a prominent athlete, had been seen drinking in the pub with the four men before the fight. The men had all been close friends until the evening of Sept. 30 when they quarreled over drinks and brawled outside the pub.

During their trial, the four defendants maintained that they had no intention of harming Lewis, and that his death was purely accidental. They told of the drunken argument in which Lewis drew the knife. John Rowlands said he forced the weapon from his grasp and later used it in self-defense.

But the jury believed the prosecution, that Driscoll held Lewis by the arms as the Rowland brothers slashed his throat. Driscoll and the Rowlandses were found Guilty of murder, though Price was acquitted of all charges. Following the trial, John Rowlands was declared insane and remanded to the Broadmoor Asylum. Edward Rowlands and Daniel Driscoll were hanged on Jan. 27, 1928, at Cardiff Prison.

REF.: Asbury, *The Gangs of New York; CBA;* Shew, *A Second Companion to Murder.*

Driver, Samuel Marion, 1892-1958, U.S., jur. Served as prosecuting attorney for Douglas County, Wash., 1922-23, and Chelan County, Wash., 1935-37. He also was U.S. attorney for the Eastern District of Washington, 1937-40, was appointed to the Eastern District Court of Washington by President Harry Truman, Apr. 13, 1946, and was a member of the Committee on Administration of the Criminal Law, 1956-58. REF.: *CBA.*

Drogo de Hauteville, d.1051, Fr., count, 1046-51, assass. The Norman successor to his brother Guillaume Iron Arm as the Count of Apulia, 1046, was the victim of an anti-Norman conspiracy. REF.: *CBA.*

Dropsie, Moses Aaron, 1821-1905, U.S., lawyer. Bequeathed his estate for the founding of the Dropsie College for Hebrew and Cognate Learning, which opened in 1909 and is now known as Dropsie University. REF.: *CBA.*

Drossner, Charles Jean (AKA: **Jose de Braganca, Jose Brancanza, Jose Carlos Brazanca, Douglas Compbelle, Douglas Campbell, Daniel Chester, Vincente Montoya**), prom. 1918-32, U.S., forg. Between 1918 and 1932, Charles Jean Drossner used eight different identities in forgeries and other crimes throughout Europe and North America. As of 1932, Drossner was wanted in scores of cities in Europe.

Drossner's criminal career began after his expulsion from France in 1918 for writing a bad check in Paris. Four years later, he was arrested in Bayonne, and sentenced to six months in prison and fined 4000 francs for writing another bad check and for disobeying the original expulsion order. Drossner appeared in Rome two years later, where he served seven months for swindling in 1924.

Back in France, Drossner again tried his hand at forgery and was again caught. He was convicted in 1932, but, facing a life sentence as a repeat offender, he eluded authorities and fled the country. He turned up in Wisconsin later that year, where he was once again arrested for forgery, and imprisoned at Wisconsin State Penitentiary in Waupin, Wis.

REF.: *CBA;* Robinson, *Science Catches the Criminal.*

Drouet, Jean-Baptiste, 1763-1824, Fr., consp. As a French revolutionary, he identified Louis XVI at Sainte-Menehould, as the king tried leaving the country, which resulted in the king's capture at Varennes, 1791. He also served on the National Convention, 1792, in the Council of Five Hundred, 1795, and was involved in the Babeuf conspiracy, for which he was imprisoned but escaped. See: **Babeuf, François Emile.** REF.: *CBA.*

Drouet, Jean-Baptiste, 1765-1844, Fr., exile. As a general for Napoleon I, the Comte d'Erlon made himself noteworthy at the battles of Jena, 1806, Friedland, 1807 and Waterloo, 1815; being exiled under a death sentence, 1815-30, after the fall of Napoleon. The sentence revoked, he became the governor general of Algeria, 1834-35, and installed as marshal of France, 1843. REF.: *CBA.*

Drown, Ruth, prom. 1952-65, U.S., fraud-theft. A Southern California utilities employee, Ruth Drown emerged as a healer in 1929, using radio as a diagnostic aid. After briefly attending an osteopathy school and a chiropractic college in Los Angeles, she became a licensed chiropractor in California. Organizing Drown Laboratories, Inc., the doctor rigidly believed her own theories, and developed them for thirty-five years. According to every investigation into her practices, they were entirely without merit. Drown appealed to the American Medical Association for the first time in 1934 for an investigation of her basic invention, the Homo-Vibra Ray machine. Angered but undaunted when the AMA returned a negative report, Drown continued to sell her product throughout the U.S., branching out to England and Western Europe by 1940, and founding the School of Radio Therapy in 1941. Drown claimed that the Homo-Vibra Ray could diagnose and treat disease by remote control, photographing the tissues and bones of patients through elusive "vibrations," picked up from a blood sample taken through the ear. By the late 1940s, after a Chicago *Tribune* article ridiculed Drown's teachings, the doctor demonstrated her machine before a University of Chicago board. Earlier, she had been charged in Los Angeles for violating interstate commerce and misbranding in the sale of one of the Homo-Vibra Rays. The university investigation was a disaster for Drown, who continued to defend her machines. According to the University of Chicago board, the photographs were "simple fog patterns produced by exposure of the film to white light before it has been adequately fixed." With the AMA branding her a fraud, Drown faced the California charges which arose after Wilson Ellis, an Evanston, Ill., businessman, purchased a Homo-

Vibra Ray for his sick wife. In 1951, Drown was tried, convicted on a misdemeanor charge, and fined $1,000.

Drawing up a complaint for a $5 million damage suit, the angered charlatan charged ten medical groups, including the AMA, and the U.S. Pharmacopoeial Convention, an organization chartered by the U.S. Congress, along with 154 medical corporations. Her complaint, which called for the dissolution of the AMA, maintained that she was prosecuted to create a monopoly for the defendants in violation of anti-trust laws. It was thrown out. For another thirteen years, Drown continued to ply her trade. When two California agents for the L.A. District Attorney's office and the California Bureau of Food and Drug Inspection posed as clients in 1963, Drown diagnosed blood samples, supposedly taken from their children—the samples had been taken from a turkey, a sheep, and a hog. Charged with two counts of grand theft and two counts of attempted grand theft, Drown's trial was scheduled for early April 1965. Three weeks before her case came to court, on Feb. 12, 1965, Drown died of heart disease. Investigators found she had had a stroke fourteen months earlier and had been under the care of a legitimate doctor since that time.

REF.: *CBA;* Young, *The Medical Messiahs.*

Chicago gangster Vincent "The Schemer" Drucci, before and after a police arrest, 1927.

Drucci, Vincent (AKA: **The Schemer**), 1895-1927, U.S., org. crime. Chicago-born Vincent Drucci became a street criminal at an early age, robbing pushcarts and stealing coins from pay phones. As a youth, he joined the safecracking gang led by Charles Dion O'Bannion, which also included Earl "Hymie" Weiss and George "Bugs" Moran. The gang would later dominate, through the 1920s, the lucrative and affluent bootleg territory of the Forty-second and Forty-third wards. Drucci was deadly, with wild ideas of killing all rival gangsters in Chicago, which earned him the nickname "The Schemer." Al Capone thought Drucci was the deadliest of his North Side opponents, and The Schemer lived up to his lethal reputation time and again. Drucci's willingness to draw his guns and wade into the ranks of rival gangsters caused newsmen to dub him "The Shootin' Fool."

Though Sicilian himself, Drucci sided with the predominantly Irish mobsters in the O'Bannion ranks, and he had a special hatred for Sicilian gangsters, particularly those in the Genna Brothers' mob of the Near West Side. Drucci was credited by Chicago police with killing a dozen men, including Genna mobsters Giuseppe "The Cavalier" Nerone on July 8, 1925, and Samuel "Samoots" Amatuna, on Nov. 11, 1925. Drucci emulated the exaggerated manners of his boss, O'Bannion, careful to observe gangster protocol. After he and Jim Doherty murdered Amatuna, Drucci sent a huge floral piece to his victim's funeral, purchased, of course, at a discount from the florist shop owned by the O'Bannions.

In 1926, when the battle for bootlegging territory in Chicago was at its zenith, Capone ordered Drucci, Weiss, and Moran killed,

but these elusive foes were not so easily eliminated. Louis Barko, one of Capone's top executioners, led a Capone contingent on Aug. 10, 1926, in tracking Drucci and Weiss to the Standard Oil Building on Michigan Avenue, and there, in full view of thousands of passersby, opened fire. Drucci and Weiss pulled their guns and the battle raged for several minutes as the crouching and dodging Drucci and Weiss darted behind parked cars to exchange fire with the Capone men. Citizens threw themselves to the pavement or ran wildly down the sidewalk or the street; cars jerked to tire-screeching halts as the gunfight continued, bullets shattering plate glass windows of stores and chipping large hunks of concrete from the sides of stately buildings. Weiss made a slow retreat from his assailants, but Drucci, in typical fashion, *advanced* on his would-be killers, his deadly fire driving Barko and three others back into their car. They continued firing at Drucci from the windows of the car and Drucci stood in the middle of sidewalk, firing back, dancing madly about to avoid the bullets that thudded and whanged at his feet. He laughed hysterically as if it were a game.

A police car arrived, its siren crying out, and Barko and the other Caponites fled in their car. On the cement lay James Cardan, a passerby wounded in the leg, who was, miraculously, the only person hit in the battle where more than thirty shots had been fired. Drucci was still looking for battle, however, and, as Barko's car roared away, The Schemer ran to the street and jumped on the running board of a passing auto, waving his revolver in the face of the startled driver and shouting: "Follow that goddamned car!" Policemen from the arriving squad car ran up to the slow-moving car and dragged Drucci off the running board.

The gangster merely shrugged when officers asked him what had happened. "It wasn't no gang fight," he said. "A stickup, that's all. They wanted my roll." Policemen searched the gangster and found a roll of bills that added up to $13,500. Drucci would not explain why he was carrying such a sizeable sum. Detectives later concluded that Drucci was on his way to see political fixer and boss of the Twentieth ward, Morris Eller, whose offices were in the Standard Oil Building. Barko and his men, police believed, interrupted Drucci and Weiss as they were about to meet with Eller and make their monthly payoff to him for political and police protection. Barko, who was identified by witnesses as the leader of the attack, was later found and brought before Drucci at detective headquarters. "I never seen that guy before in my life," said Drucci.

Amazingly, on Aug. 15, 1926, only five days after the wild shootout, Capone gunmen once again tried to shoot Drucci and Weiss on the same spot. The North Siders retaliated on Sept. 20, 1926, when twelve carloads of O'Bannion gangsters, led by Weiss, Drucci, and Moran, drove slowly past Capone's headquarters, the Hawthorn Inn in Cicero, and riddled the place. Louis Barko was the only gangster wounded. Drucci was one of those brought before Barko, and he repeated Drucci's line

CPD Detective Danny Healy, right, showing Chief of Detectives William Shoemaker the gun Drucci tried to take from him.

from weeks earlier: "I never seen that guy before."

In the following year, Drucci worked hard for the election of William Hale "Big Bill" Thompson, the corrupt mayor who worked hand-in-glove with Chicago gangsters. Drucci planned to kidnap one of Thompson's political foes, Dorsey R. Crowe, alderman for the Forty-second Ward, and hold him until after the election so he could do little damage to Thompson's campaign. The Schemer arrived at Crowe's offices on Apr. 4, 1927, with two henchmen, Albert Single and Henry Finkelstein. They beat up Crowe's secretary and wrecked the office when they learned that Crowe was not there. Police were called, and the three thugs were arrested and thrown into a squad car. Drucci was particularly insulting, snarling: "I don't know nothin', coppers!" when Detective Danny Healy questioned him.

Healy was one of the finest and toughest detectives on the Chicago force, an utterly fearless officer who had, only a few months earlier, encountered three bandits on Armitage Avenue and single-handedly shot it out with them, killing one and wounding the other two. Drucci knew Healy well and hated him. The Schemer knew that Healy had an abiding hatred for Chicago gangsters and went out of his way to provoke them, such as the time he bumped into South Side gang boss Polack Joe Saltis, a beefy giant who tried to toss Healy in the gutter and wound up being beaten senseless by the young detective. In the ride to the Criminal Courts Building, Drucci told Healy that he would never serve an hour in jail and that his lawyer would have him out with a writ of *habeas corpus*. At that moment, Maurice Green, the lawyer for the O'Bannion mob, was waiting at Criminal Courts with just such a document.

Healy told Drucci: "Shut up and sit back."
"Nobody talks that way to me," Drucci snarled.
Healy held his gun on the savage Drucci and again ordered him to keep quiet.
Drucci shouted: "I'll fix you for this, you kid copper! I'll get you if I have to sit on your doorstep, you s.o.b.!"
"Shut your mouth!" Healy roared back.
"You take your gun off me," Drucci said menacingly, leaning forward, "or I'll kick hell out of you!"
Drucci suddenly lunged at Healy, knocking the gun sideways, smashing his fist against the detective's jaw, screaming: "I'll take you and your tool (gun)! I'll fix you!"
Healy, desperate to protect himself, shifted the gun from one hand to the other and then fired four bullets into Drucci, who was swinging on him. The 31-year-old Drucci fell to the floor, yelling: "Damn you, kid copper! Now see what you did, you bastard!" Just as the squad car pulled up to the Criminal Courts Building, Vincent "The Schemer" Drucci died. Green was told that his "client" had arrived and was shown Drucci's bullet-ridden corpse.

Green stormed into the office of William "Old Shoes" Shoemaker, chief of detectives, demanding that Healy be arrested for murdering his client. "I don't know anything about anyone being murdered," Shoemaker told him. "I know that Drucci was killed while trying to take a gun away from an officer. We're having a medal made for Healy."

Drucci was buried in typical gangland fashion. He was given a lavish funeral in Sbarbaro's Funeral Home, where he lay in state while scores of gangster friends solemnly visited his $10,000 silver casket. More than $30,000 in flowers adorned the funeral rooms. The largest floral arrangement was from the last of the North Side gang leaders, George "Bugs" Moran, a silken banner across a large broken wheel of white and purple flowers reading: "Our Pal." Cecilia Drucci, a blonde flapper, accompanied her husband's corpse to Mount Carmel Cemetery and, as she was leaving, she turned to the gathered newsmen and said: "A policeman murdered him but we sure gave him a grand sendoff." See: **Capone, Alphonse; Moran, George; O'Bannion, Charles Dion; Weiss, Earl.**

REF.: Asbury, *Gem of the Prairie;* Bennett, *Chicago Gangland;* Boettiger, *Jake Lingle;* Burns, *The One-Way Ride; CBA;* Ellis, *The Social History of the Machine Gun;* Enright, *Al Capone on the Spot;* Farr, *Chicago;* Hellmer, *The Gun That Made the Twenties Roar;* Kobler, *Ardent Spirits;* ____, *Capone;* Landesco, *Organized Crime in Chicago;* Lewis and Smith, *Chicago: The History of Its Reputation;* Lyle, *The Dry and Lawless Years;* McPhaul, *Johnny Torrio;* Murray, *The Legacy of Al Capone;* Nash, *Bloodletters and Badmen;* ____, *People to See;* Pasley, *Al Capone;* ____,

Muscling In; Peterson, *The Mob;* Smith, *Syndicate City;* Sullivan, *Chicago Surrenders;* ____, *Rattling the Cup on Chicago Crime;* Wendt and Kogan, *Lords of the Levee.*

Drug Enforcement Agency (DEA), 1968- , U.S., law enfor. agen. Before 1920, responsibility for enforcing laws against the distribution and consumption of illegal narcotics belonged to the Treasury Department's Internal Revenue Service (IRS). In 1927, the task of drug enforcement was transferred to the Prohibition Unit of the IRS, which was primarily concerned with tracking down and arresting violators of the Volstead Act.

Recognizing the growing threat posed by the drug trade in the U.S., in 1930 the government created a wholly independent agency: the Bureau of Narcotics, which was linked to the Treasury Department. Under the leadership of Harry J. Anslinger, who served as commissioner from 1930 until 1962, the bureau expanded its operations, and developed the first real blueprint of the worldwide network of drug manufacturers and distributors. Since 1962, there have been seven DEA administrators: Henry L. Giordano, 1962-68; John E. Ingersoll, 1968-73; John R. Bartels, Jr., 1973-75; Henry Dogin, 1975-76; Peter Bensinger, 1976-81; Francis Mullen, 1981-85; John C. Lawn, 1985-present. In 1968, a sister agency, the Bureau of Drug Abuse Control, Food and Drug Administration, was formed as a division of the Department of Health, Education, and Welfare. These two regulatory agencies were merged in 1968, to form the Bureau of Narcotics and Dangerous Drugs. In 1973, this along with the U.S. Customs Service (Drug Investigations), the Office of National Narcotics Intelligence, Office of Drug Abuse Law Enforcement, and Narcotics Advance Research Management Team, formed present DEA.

The modern-day Drug Enforcement Agency enforces Titles II and III of the Comprehensive Drug Abuse Prevention and Control Act, passed by the Congress in 1970. In 1982, the U.S. attorney general gave the FBI jurisdictional power to conduct its own drug investigations. This change in organizational structure now provides the FBI director with supervisory power over the enforcement of anti-drug statutes. See: **Anslinger, Harry Jacob; Lawn, John C.**

REF.: Blumenthal, *Last Days of the Sicilians; CBA.*

Gangster clowns of Chicago, left, Frankie Lake, and, right, Terry Druggan.

Druggan-Lake Gang (AKA: The Valley Gang), prom. 1920s, U.S., org. crime. The Chicago-based gang headed by Terry Druggan and Frankie Lake, two trigger-happy bootleggers who controlled a sprawling territory between Cicero and Chicago's Little Italy, acted as a satellite to the Torrio-Capone mob. Both Druggan and Lake, as young teenagers, joined the old Valley Gang then captained by such killers and robbers as Paddy "The Bear" Ryan, Walter "Runty" Quinlan, and Heinrich "Big Heinie" Miller. When the boys grew to maturity, they took over the Valley Gang, and, in the early 1920s, the mob was known by the names of its leaders. Druggan was the nominal leader, a dwarf-like character who lisped when excited, especially when he was shooting down a gangster opponent or hijacking a truck loaded with liquor. He wore expensive fedoras and tailor-made tight-fitting suits, as did his junior partner, the oafish Frankie Lake, an ex-fireman who aped his boss in every manner. Both men wore horn-rimmed glasses, which gave them the appearance of mild-mannered businessmen, but this was offset by their wildly dancing eyes, looking maniacal when they confronted enemies in gang battles.

Like the North Side gangsters who followed the hot-headed Charles Dion O'Bannion, both Druggan and Lake were devout Catholics, despite the many murders they committed and assorted crimes they delighted in performing. Once, when hijacking a truckload of beer from some Jewish gangsters, Druggan waved his pistol in the faces of his cowed captives, pointing to a nearby church, and shouted: "Hats off, you Jews, when you're passing the house of God, or I'll shoot them off!"

Druggan and Lake both became millionaires during Prohibition, and they were the typical flashy gangsters portrayed in the films. They were driven about in expensive limousines by liveried chauffeurs, and Druggan's apartment boasted solid gold doorknobs. The toilet seat in his huge bathroom was silver plated and bore Druggan's initials. He had a butler and several maids, converted from the underworld. Druggan and Lake owned a private train car, but they used it only once, after its windows were shot out by rival gangsters as it rolled through Gary, Ind. The fortune accumulated by the two thugs came from their arrangement with Joseph Stenson, who gave them 50 percent of five huge breweries at the dawn of Prohibition so that he could continue to operate.

Capone, by 1925, was taking more than 40 percent of the profits from these breweries, but he provided Druggan and Lake with an army of gunmen to protect their territory, gangsters under the command of Danny Stanton. These underworld terrorists included William "Gunner" McPadden, Hughey "Stubby" McGovern, Raymond Cassidy, and Frank "Dutch" Carpenter. All of these men died by the mid-1920s, killed in the beer wars, mostly in the brewery-rich Druggan-Lake territory. But where rival gangsters could not reach this pair of lunatic bootleggers, the law did, jailing both men in 1924 for refusing to cease operating their breweries. The imprisonment did not impede for a moment the continued affairs of Terry Druggan and Frankie Lake. The minute the pair went behind bars in the Cook County Jail, they called aside corrupt Sheriff Peter Hoffman and gave him $20,000 in cash. "This cash is for the usual considerations and conveniences," Druggan told Hoffman. A few minutes later, Morris Eller, the oily political boss of the Twentieth ward, arrived at the jail and told Hoffman to "treat the boys right. You know, make life a little easy for them."

Life for Druggan and Lake changed very little during their brief stay at the jail. They were seldom in their cells or even in the jail. A reporter appeared one day to interview the pair and was told by a secretary: "Mr. Druggan and Mr. Lake are out right now...an appointment downtown. They'll return after dinner." Once the story broke, Hoffman was convicted of malfeasance, fined $2,500, and sentenced to thirty days in his own jail. Said the miffed Hoffman as he was placed in a cell by one of his own deputies: "I don't know what the fuss is all about—I was only accomodatin' the boys." Both gangsters met the same fate as their boss, Al Capone. They were convicted of income tax evasion in 1932 and sent to Leavenworth. When they were released, they discovered that their territory and their henchmen had been absorbed by rival gangs. They became functionaries of the Capone gang and both died in relative obscurity in the 1950s. See: **Capone, Alphonse; Hoffman, Peter; Torrio, John.**

REF.: Asbury, *Gem of the Prairie;* Bennett, *Chicago Gangland;* Boettiger, *Jake Lingle;* CBA; Dedmon, *Fabulous Chicago;* Demaris, *Captive City;* Ellis, *The Social History of the Machine Gun;* Enright, *Al Capone on the Spot;* Helmer, *The Gun That Made the Twenties Roar;* Kobler, *Capone;* Landesco, *Organized Crime In Chicago;* Lewis and Smith, *Chicago: The History of Its Reputation;* Lyle, *The Dry and Lawless Years;* McPhaul, *Deadlines and Monkeyshines;* ____, *Johnny Torrio;* Murray, *The Legacy of Al Capone;* Nash, *Bloodletters and Badmen;* ____, *People to See;* Pasley, *Al Capone;* ____, *Muscling In;* Smith, *Syndicate City;* Sullivan,

Chicago Surrenders; ____, *Rattling the Cup on Chicago Crime;* Wendt and Kogan, *Lords of the Levee.*

Drugs, See: **Supplements,** Vol. IV.

Drumm, Maire, 1920-76, Ire., vice pres., assass. Maire Drumm, former vice-president of the national Sinn Féin party, which supported liberating the Irish Republic from British control, was gunned down by an unknown assassin as she recovered from cataract surgery in Belfast's Mater Hospital.

The 56-year-old Drumm had championed the cause of the revolutionary Irish Republic Army (IRA) and had been arrested many times for her vocal support of the movement.

On the evening of Oct. 28, 1976, two gunmen hid for several hours inside the Mater Hospital, waiting for a chance to execute Drumm. As she stood in her hospital ward, a young man dressed in hospital clothes shot her three times in the chest. Drumm was rushed to surgery, where she died ten minutes later. The suspects were never found, and no one ever took credit for the assassination of Drumm.

REF.: Bell, *Assassin;* CBA; Demaris, *Brothers In Blood: The International Terrorist Network;* Dobson and Payne, *The Terrorists—Their Weapons, Leaders and Tactics;* Schreiber, *The Ultimate Weapon—Terrorists and World Order.*

Drummond, Margaret, d.1497, Scot., (unsolv.) mur. Margaret Drummond and her two sisters were found poisoned in 1497. Drummond had long been the mistress of King James IV, and it is believed that Scottish nobles conspired to kill her to induce James IV to marry.

REF.: CBA; Thompson, *Poison and Poisoners.*

Drummond, William, c.1617-88, Scot., tort. Served in the Scottish parliament, 1669-74, 1681-82 and 1685-86, became 1st Viscount of Strathallan, 1686, and is popularly believed to be the one who brought the thumbscrew from Russia as a means of torture. REF.: CBA.

Drummond, William Wormer, d.1888, U.S., jur. Appointed to the Territorial Court for the Territory of Utah by President Franklin Pierce, Jan. 10, 1855. REF.: CBA.

Drury, William, 1902-50, U.S., pol. mal.-(unsolv.) mur. In 1946 when detective William Drury of the Chicago Police was hot on the trail of the murderer of gangster James M. Ragen, he was suddenly dismissed from the force. Two of the three witnesses for the case that Drury and Captain Thomas Connelly had worked on claimed the two officers had coerced them into testifying before the grand jury. When Drury and Connelly themselves refused to testify before the grand jury, they were suspended, and charged with conspiracy to bring about false indictments of murder against the witnesses.

Drury and Connelly were discharged in October 1947, and a gruelling court battle to win back their jobs ended when the Supreme Court refused to hear their case. The dismissal stood, becoming the first time a policeman was fired for refusing to testify to his conduct in a case.

Out of a job, Drury wrote a series of articles for a Miami newspaper about the influx of Chicago gangsters to South Florida. He opened a detective agency in Chicago, and advertised his services to anyone interested in crushing the careers of Chicago gangsters. He also told Police Captain Daniel A. "Tubbo" Gilbert's opponent for Cook County sheriff that he had evidence connecting Gilbert to organized crime. The opponent won the election.

Drury was apparently troublesome enough to earn a death warrant from the underworld. At 6:45 on the evening of Sept. 26, 1950, he was shot to death by two men while he backed his Cadillac into his garage. His killers were never identified.

REF.: CBA; Harrison, *Criminal Calendar II.*

Druse, Roxana, and **Druse, Mary,** prom. 1889, U.S., mur. The Druse family of rural Little Falls, N.Y., usually kept to themselves, although those who knew him liked farmer John Druse. Roxana Druse, his wife, was another matter. She was mean and insulting, and let everyone know that she resented being a farmer's wife. In November 1889, Roxana, horrified by the thought that her considerably older husband was soon going to be totally dependent on her, decided to kill him. As he walked by her one evening, she struck him on the head with an ax. As her slightly feeble-minded daughter, Mary, watched, she cut off his head and then dismembered the body so that the parts would fit into a big boiler hanging inside the fireplace. She had heard somewhere that cooked meat would not smell when burned, unlike fresh flesh, so she boiled the parts before cutting them up smaller and burning them in the fireplace. Unfortunately, her information was incorrect, and the smoke from the burning flesh was black and miasmic.

When friends looking for John learned that he had not gone to visit relatives, as Roxana first claimed, they cornered his son, John Druse, Jr.. Although he had not known about the murder when it happened, he had since learned that his mother and sister were murderers, and he told the whole story. Roxana Druse promptly confessed everything but would not disclose the location of her husband's head. The two women were tried and found Guilty. Mary was sentenced to life in prison. Roxana Druse was sentenced to death and hanged.

REF.: *CBA*; Nash, *Murder, America*; ____, *Look For the Woman*.

Drusilla, Livia, prom. c.15-38 A.D., Roman., mur. Livia Drusilla was the third wife of the Emperor Augustus, who was the great-nephew of Julius Caesar and the ruler of Rome from 27 B.C. to 14 A.D. The early Augustan age was marked by a flowering of the arts and scientific achievement. But by the time of Augustus' death, in 14 A.D., Rome was a city of debauchery and excess.

Assassination, especially by female poisoners, was prevalent in Rome then. The most notorious of these killers was Livia Drusilla, who wanted her son Tiberius, by her former husband Tiberius Claudius Nero, to succeed Augustus on the throne. Standing in the way were Marcellus, husband of Augustus' daughter Julia, and Julia's two sons. To assure the succession of Tiberius, Livia Drusilla poisoned Augustus' son-in-law and grandsons. Tiberius ascended the throne after Augustus' death in 14 A.D., which was also thought to have been caused by Livia Drusilla.

REF.: *CBA*; Johnson, *Famous Assassinations of History*.

Drusus, d.33, Roman., noble, assass. The son of Vipsania Agrippina and Germanicus Caesar, he was placed in prison by Emperor Tiberius and killed by forced starvation, due to the emperor's jealousy of Drusus' popularity with the people. REF.: *CBA*.

Drusus, Marcus Livius, d.91 B.C., Roman, tribune, assass. As tribune, 91 B.C., he sought return of judicial functions to the senate, establishment of colonies, citizenship for Italians, and reduced grain prices; all of which were passed but later abolished by the senate. He was assassinated as the Social War or civil war began. REF.: *CBA*.

Drusus Caesar (AKA: **Drusus Junior**), c.15 B.C.-23 A.D., Roman., consul, assass. Became Illyricum governor, 17, and joined his father Emperor Tiberius as consul, 21, before being poisoned by his wife Livilla and her lover, Lucius Aelius Sejanus, likely at the bidding of Tiberius. REF.: *CBA*.

Dryden, John, 1631-1700, Brit., (unsolv.) asslt. John Dryden, the English poet and playwright, became Britain's Poet Laureate after an education at Trinity College, Cambridge. Dryden's distinguished career was marred by a six-year feud which led to violence in 1679.

In 1673, Dryden dedicated a play to John Wilmot, the Earl of Rochester. But Wilmot aligned with rivals of Dryden, and when *Essay on Satire,* supposedly written by Mulgrave but attributed to Dryden, was published in 1679, it contained an attack on Wilmot. When the essay was widely circulated four years later, Wilmot wrote a letter to a friend, which included a threat to harm Dryden. On Dec. 18, 1679, Dryden was badly beaten while returning from a favorite coffee-house. It was alleged that Wilmot was behind the attack, but nothing could be proved, despite a £50 reward. REF.: *CBA*.

Drysdale, Alexander, d.1855, U.S., rob.-mur. In 1855, 25-year-old George Gordon was a hard-working teller at the bank in Atkinson, Miss., of which his uncle was vice president. So conscientious was he that he often returned to the bank in the evenings to provide services for customers unable to visit the bank during regular business hours. When the bank failed to open on time one morning, Gordon's uncle went to investigate and found Gordon murdered, his head bashed in and a $100 bill in his hand. Under his bloody body was a sheet of paper bearing a series of figures. Police discovered remnants of burned clothing in the bank fireplace, and it was determined that $128,000 in cash was missing. Alexander Bannister, the bank president, called in detective Allan Pinkerton, whose agency, though only five years old, was already famous.

Pinkerton identified several people who might have been at the bank the evening of the murder. By examining bank records he linked the figures on the sheet found under Gordon's body to the account of Alexander Drysdale, the county clerk. Drysdale was also found to be left-handed, a detail which corresponded to the coroner's description of the murderer. Pinkerton returned to Chicago, but secretly sent to Atkinson his agents Timothy Webster, Kate Warne, and a young man named Green. Webster pretended to be in the market for a plantation, and investigated the property next to Drysdale's. Warne also claimed to be looking for a home, and Green took a job in a shop where locals often gathered to gossip.

The investigation produced little until Webster discovered that Green bore a striking resemblance to the murdered Gordon and that Drysdale was a very superstitious man. Webster arranged for Drysdale to take him on a tour of the adjacent plantation. As the two inspected the property, Green, dressed as Gordon and bloodied, emerged twice from behind trees, causing Drysdale a noticeable shock. Then Warne faked an accident near the Drysdale plantation and was taken there to recover. She spread a red liquid around Drysdale's floors at night, and Green, as Gordon's ghost, continued appearing around the house. By this time Drysdale, sleepless and extremely nervous, was beginning to fail physically and his doctor ordered him to bed. Webster had noticed that Drysdale was particularly sensitive to two spots in the area, one under a boulder in the local creek and another on his plantation. Webster investigated, and found $23,000 in coins under the boulder and $105,000 in currency on the plantation.

Though the evidence against Drysdale was mounting, Pinkerton knew that he would need more than circumstantial evidence to convict him. Pinkerton returned to Atkinson and helped serve an arrest warrant on Drysdale, who fainted. When Drysdale recovered, he agreed to defend himself before the bank board, but Green, playing Gordon's ghost, appeared there too and Drysdale again fainted. Upon his second recovery, Drysdale was confronted with the evidence against him and confessed that he had gone to the bank seeking a loan to finance his heavy debts, but had instead murdered Gordon and stolen the money. Drysdale then went to the bathroom, where he killed himself with a shot to the head from a pistol he had hidden on his person. REF.: *CBA*.

Duane, James, 1733-97, U.S., jur. Served on the Continental Congress, 1774-84, as mayor of New York City, 1784-89, and after appointment by President George Washington, as judge of the U.S. District Court for New York, 1789-94. REF.: *CBA*.

Duane, William, 1760-1835, Case of, U.S., consp. Criticized Indian authorities, for which he was deported from India to Britain, but returned to his home in the U.S., 1795, eventually becoming sole editor of the *Aurora,* 1798-1822. Accused, but acquitted, of inciting a riot, 1799, later being indicted by the Sedition Law, 1799; a charge which Thomas Jefferson dismissed upon Jefferson's election to president. REF.: *CBA*.

Duane, William John, 1780-1865, U.S., polit. corr. Removed from his position as U.S. secretary of the treasury, 1833, when he refused to withdraw government deposits from the U.S. Bank prior to a session of Congress. REF.: *CBA*.

Duarte, Juan Pablo, 1813-76, Dom., consp.-rebel. Considered the father of the Dominican Republic's independence, he founded La Trinitaria, 1838, a secret society that sought independence from

Haitian rule. At the failure of rebellion, 1843, he was exiled, returning the following year when independence was declared, but again sent into exile by his rival, Pedro Santana. REF.: *CBA*.

Du Barry, Marie Jeanne Bécu, c.1746-93, Fr., comtesse, assass. The Comtesse du Barry was the mistress of Chevalier Jean du Barry, 1764-68, and of King Louis XV, 1768, before marrying Comte Guillaume du Barry. With the assistance of the Duc d'Aiguillon she ruled the king and his court, 1769-74, retiring upon the king's death. The Revolutionary Tribunal condemned her to death, which was carried out by the guillotine.

REF.: Bullough, *Illustrated History of Prostitution; CBA*.

Dubois, Frank, and **Donaldson, Archibald**, and **Dunne, Edward**, and **Moore, George**, and **Nelson, Harry**, and **Sheehan, John J.**, prom. 1901, U.S., gamb.-fraud. Twenty-five men from a Chicago gambling operation were charged with twelve different counts each—a total of 300 charges.

A classified ad in a Chicago paper on June 2, 1901, read: "WANTED—A party with $1,000; will handle his own money. Will bear investigation." A Chicago man named Seabrook answered the ad, and was told of a plan that guaranteed a good return on his investment.

The promoter, known as "Mr. Kane," told Seabrook that a man who worked at the racetracks on the East Coast would withhold the results of horse races until he had told Mr. Kane the winners, giving Mr. Kane (and anyone else he let in on the scheme) time to place heavy bets on horses that had already won.

Seabrook went did to the police with his information. Detective Wooldridge took charge of the case, and instructed Seabrook to continue with the plan as if he suspected nothing.

Seabrook kept his appointment at the poolroom, where he was to place bets totaling $1,000. When he arrived, he found several other men preparing to do the same. The poolroom was apparently receiving results from every racetrack in the country.

Detective Wooldridge and seven other detectives waited until a race was about to begin, then entered the poolroom shouting "Stop a minute! Put $5,000 on Sidney Lucas." The gamblers tried to escape, but all exits had been blocked. Police arrested everyone on the premises. An investigation of the poolroom showed that the telegraph wires supposedly carrying the race results were not connected. The entire operation was fraudulent.

In all, twenty-five men were arrested and charged with crimes from fraud to vagrancy and illegal gambling. The trial was held on July 13, and among those found guilty were the four leaders of the swindle, Archibald Donaldson, John J. Sheehan, George Moore, and Harry Nelson, who were fined $100 each.

REF.: *CBA*; Wooldridge, *Hands Up*.

Dubrock, Melvin, 1934- , U.S., polit corr. In 1986, Melvin Dubrock took a gift from the wrong person. His mistake brought to a sudden halt a thirty-one-year career that had culminated in a job as assistant deputy commissioner of Streets and Sanitation Department in Chicago, Ill.

In exchange for helping a New York collection company win city contracts, Dubrock accepted $4,600 in cash and airline tickets from Michael Raymond, an undercover FBI agent involved in Operation Incubator.

Dubrock was fired when he refused to cooperate with the investigation. He pleaded guilty, and U.S. District Judge Ilana D. Rovner sentenced him to ninety days in jail, relinquishment of the bribe to the government, a $1,000 fine, and five years' probation with 500 hours of community service. REF.: *CBA*.

Dubuisson, Pauline, 1929- , Fr., mur. During the German occupation of France, Pauline Dubuisson openly conducted an affair with 55-year-old Colonel Von Domnick, who commanded the German Hospital in Dunkirk. Only sixteen at the time, her indiscretions doomed her after the liberation. Like many other Frenchwomen who had consorted with Nazis, Dubuisson was publicly humiliated in the square of Dunkirk by having her head shaved.

In 1946, she took up the study of medicine at Lille University, where she met and fell in love with Félix Bailly, also a student.

During her two-year affair with him, she had many lovers, and recorded their names and sexual preferences on a secret list. In 1949, Bailly moved to Paris and planned to marry Monique Lombard. For eighteen months, Félix Bailly heard nothing from Dubuisson.

Pauline suddenly appeared in Paris in March 1951 to try to win back Bailly's affections. On Mar. 10, Dubuisson purchased a .25-caliber handgun, explaining to the registrar that she needed it for self-protection. She left her rooming house on Mar. 15 after leaving a note for the landlady stating that she intended to shoot first herself, then Bailly. The astute landlady sent wires with this information to Bailly and his parents. When Bailly heard about this, he acquired several bodyguards, but Dubuisson slipped past the sentries and shot Bailly in his apartment. His body was found a short time later by a friend. Dubuisson was lying unconscious nearby. She had tried to asphyxiate herself with gas.

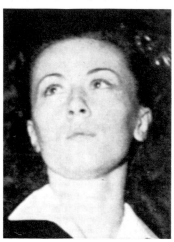

French killer Pauline Dubuisson.

She recovered from her suicide attempt to stand trial at the Assizes of the Seine on Nov. 18, 1953. Pauline's diffidence earned her the nickname "Mask of Pride." Bailly had cast her out, she explained, and life no longer meant anything. Pauline Dubuisson was found Guilty of murder and was sentenced to life imprisonment.

REF.: *CBA*; Goodman, *Crime of Passion*; Gribble, *Adventures In Murder*; Heppenstall, *The Sex War and Others*; Nash, *Open Files*; Rowan, *Famous European Crimes*; Wilson, *Encyclopedia of Murder*.

Duca, Jon, d.1933, Rom., prime minister, assass. Romanian prime minister Jon Duca opposed the rise of powerful fascist organizations in his country and was particularly forceful in combating the Iron Guards led by Cornelius Codreanu. No longer able to tolerate the violent outbursts from the Guardists, Duca, in early December 1933, outlawed the appearance of its uniformed brigades in any public areas. Codreanu, in turn, ordered Duca's execution. The prime minister, while alighting from a train in a Carpathian station on Dec. 30, 1933, was approached by five Iron Guards who all produced guns and promptly shot Duca to death. See: **Codreanu, Cornelius Zelea; Stelescu, Michael**. REF.: *CBA*.

Duchateau, Daniel, 1937-78, Fr., kid. Daniel Duchateau in 1978 helped Alain Caillol mastermind the kidnapping of Belgian millionaire Baron Edouard-Jean Empain from his Paris apartment. The ransom was $8.6 million, but the caper ended disastrously for the kidnappers when Paris police set up a phony ransom drop on a highway outside the city. Five members of Caillol's gang, including Duchateau, were ambushed when they attempted to pick up their loot.

Three of the kidnappers escaped. Caillol was arrested and taken into custody, but Duchateau was killed The haggard baron was released and returned to his family. See: **Caillol, Alain**. REF.: *CBA*.

Du Chatelard, prom. 16th Cent., Scot., consp. A French nobleman and lover of Mary, Queen of Scots, Du Chatelard came to Scotland from the Court of Valois in France and quickly won the favor of the new queen. But the young poet-musician lacked discretion.

He was caught one night hiding behind the curtains in the queen's bedroom, and was expelled from the palace. He soon won back the queen's affection, and was discovered once again hiding in her chambers, this time under her bed. He was tried for conspiracy against the queen's life, found Guilty, and sentenced to hang.

The queen could have pardoned him, but chose not to, and Du Chatelard was hanged at Holyrood Palace, directly in front of the windows of the queen's living quarters. His final words, directed to Mary as she stood watching, were: "Farewell, thou who art so beautiful and so cruel, who killest me, and whom I cannot cease to love!"

REF.: *CBA*; Johnson, *Famous Assassinations in History.*

Duchowski, Charles, and **Schader, Charles,** and **Staleski, Walter,** and **Rizo, Gregorio,** and **Torrez, Robert,** and **Roa, Bernardo,** prom. 1926-27, pris. esc.-mur. In May 1926, seven convicts at the Stateville Penitentiary in Joliet, Ill., attempted a prison escape with a crowbar and several pairs of scissors. When Deputy Warden Peter N. Klein resisted them, Charles Duchowski broke his skull with a crowbar, and the others—Charles Schader, Walter Staleski, James Price, Gregorio Rizo, Robert Torrez, and Bernardo Roa, stabbed Klein with scissors. The convicts planned to spring Nathan F. Leopold, Jr., the "thrill killer," who was also incarcerated at Joliet, but were unable to release him from solitary confinement. Threatening him with scissors, they forced Captain John Kelley to lead them out of the grounds, and drove away in Klein's car. A posse recaptured five of them that night, and Duchowski was found weeks later on the Mexican border. Price was never found. Their trial began in October 1926, in Joliet. On Dec. 21, they were convicted of Klein's murder and were sentenced to death on the gallows by Judge F.A. Hill.

On Mar. 12, 1927, the condemned men attempted another break, with guard Edward F. Gibbons helping them in their escape. The Mexican criminals played guitars and harmonicas and sang to cover the sound of bars being sawed. Another sawed while pretending to be praying before a religious altar. The key to the Americans' cells was locked in the jail safe, so the Mexicans took off alone, forcing Deputy Sheriff John Krincich to drive them to nearby Indiana Harbor, Ind. There they smashed the car, kept Krincich with them, and forced a taxi driver to chauffeur them. In a chase, Sergeant John Klaske and two of his men forced the taxi to the curb. The Mexicans opened fire, wounding policemen Leo Grant and William Forst. Grant died later. Cab driver John Marciniak was also wounded. All of the convicts surrendered, except Roa, who escaped. In June, Schader, Rizzo, Staleski, and Duchowski again attempted to break out of jail. Rizzo was shot and killed in the attempt. Sheriff Markgraf was taken hostage but escaped unharmed. Three of the convicts surrendered, and Schader and Rizzo briefly escaped again in the confusion. Jailer Leo Land and policeman E.A. O'Neill shot and killed Rizzo.

On July 15, 1927, Duchowski, Torrez, and Staleski were hanged at Will County Jail in Joliet as a crowd of about 500 watched. Mrs. Klein, widow of the slain warden, had asked permission to spring the trap that sent the convicts to their death, but her request was refused. REF.: *CBA*.

Duck, Aug Tai, d.1886, U.S., rape-suic.-mur. Captain and Mrs. J. C. Wickersham lived on a secluded ranch twelve miles outside Cloverdale, Calif., with their Chinese servant, Aug Tai Duck. There were many American Indians in the area, some of whom were friends with the Wickershams. When they called on the ranch, it was customary for them to stand in the distance and yell for the owner until they were acknowledged and invited to approach. This is what a few Indians did when they neared the Wickersham ranch on the morning of Jan. 21, 1886. But after repeated calling there was no answer. A neighbor was brought to the home to find out what the problem was.

Captain Wickersham and his wife had been murdered. The captain was found sitting in front of his untouched dinner, with shotgun blasts to his head and chest. Mrs. Wickersham was found on her bed, bound, beaten, raped, and shot in the chest. Aug Tai Duck was nowhere to be found. Due to heavy rains, the police were not able to investigate until Jan. 22. They found the servant's apron soaked in blood, an empty shotgun, and four used cartridges. That afternoon, Aug Tai Duck was charged with the murders.

The servant, in fact, had been gone since he committed the crimes on Jan. 18. He had run to Cloverdale and confessed to his uncle, Ah Kum. Ah Kum recommended that he return to China immediately. Duck left for San Francisco to catch a ship. Fearing that he would be considered an accomplice, the uncle went to San Francisco himself and told police of his nephew's plans. They tried to get to the steamer *Rio de Janeiro* before it set sail, but the boat left with Aug Tai Duck aboard.

U.S. authorities instructed the Japanese to apprehend the criminal when the ship anchored at Yokohama. They did so, but then sent him to British authorities in Hong Kong to await extradition. On Mar. 29, 1886, in prison in Hong Kong, Aug Tai Duck hanged himself in his cell with the silk sash he used as a belt.

REF.: *CBA*; Duke, *Celebrated Criminal Cases of America.*

Dudley, Ambrose, c.1528-90, Case of, Brit., consp. Supported the claim of his sister-in-law Lady Jane Grey, 1554, for which he was pardoned, became Earl of Warwick, 1561, and participated in Mary Queen of Scots' trial, 1586. REF.: *CBA.*

Dudley, Edmund, c.1462-1510, Brit., treas. Advised Henry VIII, c.1485-1509, but upon the king's accession to the throne was convicted of treason, 1509, earlier having been acquitted of the charge of embezzlement, 1509. During his imprisonment in the Tower of London, he wrote a political allegory, *The Tree of Commonwealth,* and was then beheaded for his crime. REF.: *CBA.*

Dudley, Guildford, d.1554, Brit., consp. Married Lady Jane Grey, 1553, as part of his father's, John Dudley's, plot to alter the succession of the British crown to fall upon Lady Jane at the death of King Edward VI. He was beheaded along with his wife. REF.: *CBA.*

Dudley, John, 1502-53, Brit., consp.-mur. Became Viscount Lisle, 1542, the Earl of Warwick, 1546 and the Duke of Northumberland, 1551. He had Somerset, the Earl of Worcester, executed, 1552, and had his fourth son, Guildford Dudley, marry Lady Jane Grey, in an attempt to alter the succession of the British throne, after having King Edward VI sign his agreement to such a transaction. Dudley was executed for his resistance to the succession of Queen Mary. REF.: *CBA.*

Dudley, Joseph, 1647-1720, U.S., jur. Served as judge in the general court of Massachusetts, 1673-76, and superior court chief justice, 1686-89, for Sir Edmund Andros' government. At the collapse of the Andros administration, 1689, he was imprisoned and sent to Britain where he was acquitted of the conspiracy charge. Elected as governor of Massachusetts, 1702-15. REF.: *CBA.*

Dudley, Richard, c.1635-81, Brit., rob.-mur. This infamous highwayman was born into a wealthy family, but his profligate father lost the estate and Richard's only real inheritance was a captain's commission received from King Charles II as payment for his father's service to the crown. Dudley soon left the military for the life of a highwayman, selecting only victims who were rich and titled.

He was arrested after robbing the Duke of Monmouth, convicted and sentenced to a prison ship. Soon after being released he returned to his old habits. One of his victims was John Wilmot, the Earl of Rochester, who chided Dudley for his actions.

"I don't think I commit any sin in robbing a person of quality," Dudley told the Earl "because I keep generally pretty close to the text 'Feed the hungry and send the rich away empty.'" And, in fact, this was Dudley's style. When he took a large sum from any wealthy traveler, he made a point of sharing some of his loot with poor peasants who came to think of him as a Robin Hood.

One day, between London and Tunbridge, he came upon the keeper of Newgate Prison, Captain Richardson. Ironically, Richardson had once been Dudley's warden. When he ordered Richardson to hand over his valuables, the jailor refused, reminding Dudley that he could make his life miserable should the highwayman ever return to Newgate again, which, given his current pursuits, was likely.

Dudley responded, "I expect no favor from the hands of a jailor, who comes of the race of those angels that fell with Lucifer from Heaven, whither you'll never return again. Of all your bunches of keys not one hath wards to open that door; for a jailor's soul stands not upon those two pillars that support Heaven, Justice, and Mercy; it rather sits upon those two footstools of Hell, Wrong, and Cruelty. So make no more words about your purse, for have it I will, or else your life." Richardson dutifully turned over all Dudley demanded.

After robbing General Monk, Dudley fled the country, returning after two years and taking up his old trade. He robbed a Justice of the Peace on the road between Horsham and Midhurst, tying the man to a donkey he had found grazing in a nearby field. "I'll make one justice of the peace carry another," he told the man before riding away.

Dudley later attempted to rob the Duke of Lauderdale as he was riding near Hounslow Heath, but he was caught and jailed at Newgate. Whether Richardson had his revenge is not recorded, but the law of England did. Richard Dudley, highwayman and wag, was hanged at Tyburn, on Feb. 22, 1681, at age forty-six.

REF.: *CBA*; Pringle, *Stand and Deliver*; Smith, *Highwaymen*.

Dudley, Robert, See: **Robsart, Amy.**

Dudley, Thomas, b.1853, and **Stephens, Edwin,** b.1848, Brit., can.-mur. The *Mignonette* withstood two days of storms in early July 1884, but on the third straight day of rain, the thirty-one-ton yacht could stand the buffeting no longer. Hundreds of miles west of Africa and twenty degrees south of the equator, it sunk quickly. The four-man crew only had time to grab two one-pound tins of turnips and set their dinghy afloat. It would be almost a month before three survivors were rescued, and they would have quite a story to tell about the fate of the fourth man, the 17-year-old cabin boy, Richard Parker.

Captain Thomas Dudley, thirty-one, First Mate Edwin Stephens, thirty-six, Seaman Edmund Brooks, thirty-nine, and the young Parker set sail from Southampton, Eng., on May 19, 1884, bound for Sydney, Aus. Their first stop was to be the Cape of Good Hope, S. Afri., but they were hit by the storm on July 5. They had no water in the dinghy, but were able to collect some from the occasional storms that passed over. On July 10, they killed a small turtle, their sole nourishment for eight days.

Parker, who had not been feeling well, drank sea water on July 23, which severely worsened his condition. On July 25, Dudley and Stephens discussed killing the dying boy. Stephens refused to participate in the killing. Captain Dudley told Parker what he was doing just before driving a knife into his throat.

When the German-registered *Montezuma* picked up the dinghy on July 30, it was clear that the three men who survived had done so by eating their cabin boy's corpse. They made no attempt to hide it, and Dudley made a full confession in his account of their days adrift. On Sept. 8, he and Stephens were arraigned on murder charges.

The trial occurred on Nov. 6, 1884, at the Cornwall Winter Assizes, and later was passed up to the Royal Courts of Justice. There, the five senior judges of the Queen's Bench Division found Dudley and Stephens Guilty and sentenced them to death. The sentence was later commuted to six months' imprisonment without hard labor.

REF.: Brock, *A Casebook of Crime*; *CBA*; Wilson, *Encyclopedia of Murder*.

Duel in the Sun, 1944, a novel by Niven Busch. The daring lady stagecoach robber, Pearl Hart (U.S., 1899), is undoubtedly the basis in fact for Busch's heroine, Pearl Chavez. A motion picture of the same name was also produced (1946). See: **Hart, Pearl.** REF.: *CBA*.

Duell, William, b.1724, Brit., rob.-rape-mur. William Duell raped Sarah Griffin, robbed her, then murdered her in a barn in Acton. But he is remembered as one of the most famous survivors of a hanging in British criminal history.

Duell was hanged at Tyburn on Nov. 24, 1740, along with four other criminals. His body was removed to Surgeon's Hall, where an attendant began preparing for dissection and analysis. Suddenly, the attendant noticed that Duell was breathing. A surgeon was called, and after some crude forms of resuscitation were employed, Duell was able to sit up and drink some wine. He was returned to prison at Newgate, where he fully recovered from his brush with death within four days.

It was illegal to attempt execution a second time, so on Feb. 14, 1741, Duell was exiled from Britain.

REF.: Atholl, *Shadow of the Gallows*; Bleackley, *Hangmen of England*; *CBA*; Culpin, *The Newgate Noose*; Mencken, *By the Neck*; Nash, *Almanac of World Crime*; Potter, *The Art of Hanging*; Turner, *The Inhumanists*.

Duelling, See: **Supplements,** Vol. IV.

Duer, John, 1782-1858, U.S., jur. Appointed New York City Superior Court judge, 1849-57, and chief justice, 1857. REF.: *CBA*.

Duer, William, 1747-99, U.S., polit. corr. Served in the Continental Congress, 1777-79, and as assistant U.S. secretary of the treasury to Alexander Hamilton, 1789. As assistant secretary he was sued by the government for financial peculiarities, and he was imprisoned for debt, which led to a financial panic, 1792. Duer died in prison. REF.: *CBA*.

Duer, William Alexander, 1780-1858, U.S., jur. Served as New York Supreme Court justice, 1822-29, and as Columbia College president, 1829-42. REF.: *CBA*.

Duff, Edmund, and **Sydney, Vera,** and **Sydney, Violet,** prom. 1928-29, Brit., (unsolv.) mur. In a close family in South Croydon, Edmund Duff and his sister-in-law, Vera Sidney, and his mother-in-law, Mrs. Violet Sidney, were poisoned to death. On Apr. 26, 1928, Edmund returned home and told his wife, Grace Duff, that he felt sick. After finishing a meal and a beer, the 59-year-old man grew increasingly ill, and died the next night. Dr. Robert Brönte, a pathologist, determined that Duff died of natural causes. Ten months later, Vera Sidney began suffering unexplained illnesses and became violently ill after eating soup prepared by the housekeeper, Mrs. Noakes, who also got sick. After eating lunch with a neighbor, Mrs. Greenwell, Sidney became worse. Greenwell recovered after six days, but Sidney died soon after, on Feb. 15, 1929. Dr. Binning, the family physician, said that Sidney had died of gastric influenza. On Mar. 4, 1929, Violet's son, Thomas Sidney, visited her to discuss Vera Sidney's will. The next day, Sidney's married daughter, the widowed Grace Duff, visited her mother. Violet Sidney complained of a bitter taste in her medicine and later told her daughter, "I have had some poison." She died that night.

On Mar. 22, the bodies of Violet and Vera were exhumed, and Sir Bernard Spilsbury found traces of arsenic in both. Two months later Duff's body was exhumed. Arsenic was discovered in every tissue tested. Mrs. Sidney's estate, worth £11,000, was divided equally among the surviving children. A prolonged inquest took place, with Grace Duff and Thomas Sidney as the two key witnesses. The arsenious oxide found in the bodies had been kept in quantities as a garden weed killer. The jury brought in an open verdict of murder against persons unknown. By September 1929, the police officially concluded work on the case, and the three South Croydon poisonings remain unsolved. See: **Blandy, Mary; Cotton, Mary Ann Robson Mowbray; DeMelker, Daisy Louisa Cowle Sproat; Jegado, Helene; LaFarge, Marie; Smith, Madeleine.**

REF.: *CBA*; Symons, *A Reasonable Doubt*.

Duffield, Austin Christopher, prom. 1927, Gibraltar, mur. Lieutenant Duffield's motive for murdering his regimental commander, Colonel Fitzgerald, was the supposed ineptitude of his superior. "It is better that one man should die," he explained during his trial, "than that the whole regiment should be ruined." His only regret, he said, was that he did not have an extra bullet with which to kill himself after killing the colonel.

Lieutenant Duffield refused to plead insanity, insisting that he was fully aware of his actions. He was found Guilty of murder and sentenced to death. His sentence was later reduced to life imprisonment, which he served at Parkhurst Prison and Maidstone, in England.

REF.: Brock, *A Casebook of Crime; CBA.*

Duff-Smith, Markham, 1945-   , and **Janecka, Allen Wayne**, prom. 1979, U.S., mur.   When the Houston, Texas, medical examiner's office finished the investigation of the deaths of Diana Wanstrath, thirty-six, John Wanstrath, thirty-five, and their son, 14-month-old Kevin Wanstrath, the ruling was that on July 6, 1979, Mrs. Wanstrath had shot her husband and son and then herself.

Detective Johnny Bonds found it strange that a gun was never found at the scene. Though the case was closed, Bonds did not stop his investigation.

The Wanstraths left a large inheritance, so the search focused on family heirs. The family was gathered and told that they would be subjected to polygraph tests. Markham Duff-Smith, a 34-year-old investor and the adopted brother of Mrs. Wanstrath, brought his attorney with him to the test, which he failed.

Detective Bonds discovered that Duff-Smith's mother, Trudy Zabolio, had also died under suspicious circumstances. Her case had been ruled a suicide by strangulation. Bonds believed that both cases were murders, but he needed proof.

An anonymous caller told him that Duff-Smith had arranged his mother's death through a middleman who hired a hit man. The middleman was identified only as a "realtor and coin collector." Interviews with Duff-Smith's business associates turned up one coin collector: Walter Waldhauser, Jr. Detective Bonds dug through Duff-Smith's trash and found correspondence from Allen Wayne Janecka, a prison inmate.

Janecka confessed to the murders of Zabolio and the Wanstraths. Waldhauser had hired Janecka, but he agreed to testify against Duff-Smith in exchange for exoneration from charges. Both Duff-Smith and Janecka were found Guilty of murder in April 1981 and sentenced to death. REF.: *CBA.*

Duffy, Sir Charles Gavan, 1816-1903, Ire., treas. Founded an Irish nationalist organization, the Nation, 1842, along with T.O. Davis and John Blake Dillon. He was imprisoned, 1848-49, on the charge of treason for nationalist agitation and involvement in insurrections. Duffy moved to Australia, 1856, where he served as a member of the Victoria House of Assembly, 1856-80, and prime minister, 1871-72. REF.: *CBA.*

Duffy, Clinton T., 1898-1982, U.S., law enfor. off. The son of a prison guard for California's San Quentin Prison, Clinton T. Duffy was born Aug. 24, 1898. Raised and schooled in the city of San Quentin, he began work at the prison as a clerk. In the late 1930s, riots and hunger strikes were common at San Quentin. The unrest resulted in the removal of the warden and entire prison board in 1940. At age forty-two, Mr. Duffy became the youngest warden of a major prison when he was contracted as the "temporary" warden for thirty days. He immediately put into effect reforms he had envisioned during his years of service. His focus was was rehabilitation rather than punishment, a novel idea at the time.

He eliminated corporal punishment in favor of discipline based on witholding of inmate privileges. He organized a newspaper and radio station, fully staffed by inmates, and allowed model prisoners to attend night school off the prison grounds. Critics thought he had gone too far, but there was never an escape attempt. Within a year Warden Duffy could walk anywhere in San Quentin Prison without fear of harm.

An avid opponent of the death penalty, Mr. Duffy wrote *88 Men and 2 Women*, a book which detailed his argument against capital punishment. "I hated the death penalty in my youth," he wrote, "and after thirty-two years of correctional experience, I abhor it even more today.... 'Who are the people of any state to say that a person, no matter how horrible his crime, deserves to die?"

Mr. Duffy died Oct. 11, 1982, after a long illness, in Walnut Creek, Calif. His contribution to modern penology changed the focus of discipline from retribution to reform. REF.: *CBA.*

Duffy, Sir Frank Gavan, 1852-1936, Aus., jur. Appointed Australian high court justice, 1913-31, and Commonwealth of Australia chief justice, 1931-34. REF.: *CBA.*

Duffy, Kevin Thomas, b.1933, U.S., jur. Served as U.S. attorney and assistant chief of the Southern District of New York, 1958-61, and was appointed to the Southern District Court of New York by President Richard Nixon, 1972. REF.: *CBA.*

Duffy, Renee, 1928-   , Brit., mur. Renee Duffy asked of the courts an extended definition of self-defense. She had been severely and repeatedly beaten by her husband, George Duffy, to whom she had been married for a year and with whom she had a son. Her mother saw the results of these beatings, and on several occasions threw Mr. Duffy out of the house until he pleaded to come back.

Mrs. Duffy, nineteen, never complained. She told others that the numerous bruises, black eyes, and scratches were accidental. She told no one of her 23-year-old husband's cruelty.

Finally, on Dec. 7, 1948, her submissiveness turned to fury. After another beating, she decided to leave her husband. As she prepared to go, he attacked her again, but she pushed him away and ran to the kitchen to find a hammer with which to defend herself. He told her she could not take the baby. She remembered only that she hit her husband twice with the hammer.

From the looks of the bedroom where Mr. Duffy's unconscious body was discovered, she hit him more than twice. The police found Mrs. Duffy and her child at her sister's home. She was charged with attempted murder on Dec. 8, and when Mr. Duffy died later that day, the charge was changed to murder.

The trial began in March 1949 at the Manchester Assizes. Justice Devlin, in a summation later called classic by higher courts, explained to the jury that the husband's history of violence could not be considered, except in relation to its contribution to his murder. "What matters is whether this girl had time to say, 'Whatever I have suffered, whatever I have endured, I know that: Thou shalt not kill.'"

The jury, consisting of ten men and two women, took an hour-and-a-half to come to a verdict of Guilty, with a strong recommendation for mercy. Justice Devlin sentenced Rene Duffy to death. On Apr. 4, her appeal was heard and denied, but a few hours later the governor of Strangeways Prison notified her that she had been given a reprieve.

REF.: *CBA*; Harrison, *Criminal Calendar;* Shew, *A Second Companion to Murder.*

Dugan, Eva, 1878-1930, U.S., mur. The first woman to be executed in the state of Arizona, Eva Dugan was convicted of the murder of the Tucson rancher for whom she worked. She murdered him in hopes of inheriting his property, but fled in his car soon after she had buried his body. After serving a one-year sentence in New York for stealing the car, she was charged with the murder.

Cheerful to the end, Mrs. Dugan faced the hangman on Feb. 21, 1930. She shook the warden's hand, kissed each of the prison guards she had grown close to during her stay

Mrs. Eva Dugan, first woman hanged in Arizona.

at the State Prison in Florence, Ariz., and ascended the steps to the gallows. REF.: *CBA.*

Dugdale, Richard Louis, 1841-83, U.S., penol. Became a member of the New York Prison Association executive committee, 1868, and in an association report, authored, *The Jukes, a Study in Crime, Pauperism, Disease, and Heredity*, 1875. The report was published again, 1877, along with *Further Studies of Criminals.* REF.: *CBA.*

Dugger, Thomas E. (AKA: **The Ape Man**), c.1905-36, U.S., kid. In May 1935, Dugger, a Los Angeles gardener, was convicted on charges of assaulting, robbing, and kidnapping three California women. He had been dubbed "The Ape Man" for his huge, stooped shoulders and his misshapen hands. Dugger had brutalized his victims, one of whom lost an eye when the kidnapper attacked her. On May 2, 1936, Dugger wolfed down a large breakfast in his cell at San Quentin before walking wordlessly up the steps to the gallows. Dugger became the first man executed under California's new kidnapping law which was enacted in the wake of the Lindbergh kidnapping. REF.: *CBA*.

Duguit, Leon, 1859-1928, Fr., jur. Held professorship at Bordeaux, 1886-1928, and authored a number of legal works, including, *Traité de droit constitutionnel*, 1921-25, and *Le Pragmatisme juridique, 1924.* REF.: *CBA*.

Dujarier, Alexandre Henri, See: **de Beauvallon, Rosamond.**

Duke's Restaurant, prom. 1940s-50s, U.S., org. crime. The unofficial headquarters of La Cosa Nostra during the 1940s and 1950s was a restaurant near the Palisades Amusement Park in Cliffside, N.J. The restaurant, known as Duke's, was said to serve good food and, of greater interest to the Internal Revenue Service, Manhattan District Attorney Frank Hogan, and a number of other law enforcement officials, host clandestine meetings in the back room. Behind a sliding panel in the dining area was a secret anteroom where top Mafia bosses conducted their "affairs of the table." Every Tuesday, the top crime leaders from New York and New Jersey met to discuss business issues, sometimes with the leaders of the other crime families from across the U.S.

The Mafia national commission, composed of the "Big Six," could gather there, and be reasonably sure of avoiding interference by the police. For years, unmarked surveillance cars from the offices of the New York DA and other investigating agencies would be told to "move on" by Cliffside Park Police thought to be on the take from Joe Adonis. The Big Six included Jake Guzik and Tony Accardo from Chicago; Frank Costello of New York; Longy Zwillman, boss of New Jersey, and a powerhouse in state politics; and Meyer Lansky, whose influence spanned the U.S.

During the Senate's Kefauver hearings of 1950-51, tough guy Tony Bender was asked about the significance of Duke's. He pleaded the Fifth Amendment. Willie Moretti likened it to Lindy's on Broadway, as the place to see and be seen. However, when Adonis was deported in 1953, Duke's ceased to be the favorite syndicate clubhouse in the New York region. REF.: *CBA*.

Dulcino of Novara, d.1308, Italy, consp. Burned at the stake for being the leader of the Apostolic Brothers. REF.: *CBA*.

Dulin, William, prom. 1933, U.S., (wrong. convict.) mur. When former boxer Mickey Erno and his friend Socks Brewer sold a diamond ring, they split the profits. But William Dulin and Fred Hayes had also been in on the deal. When Dulin and Hayes discovered the deception, they were understandably upset. And when Mickey Erno's body was found under a bridge in Long Beach, Calif., on Jan. 17, 1933, with a bullet in the head, Dulin and Hayes were indicted for his murder.

Mayme Proctor, a close friend of Hayes, testified at the trial in April 1933 that Hayes had told her in detail how the crime had been committed. He had said that nobody could "double-cross him and get away with it," she told the court. Proctor's testimony seemed quite damaging, until the defense proved that she had been threatened by police with a jail term if she did not testify.

The case against Hayes was still strong, but evidence of Dulin's involvement was sketchy at best. Near the end of the trial, Hayes accepted full responsibility for the murder. But both men were found Guilty and sentenced to life imprisonment. Dulin's conviction was appealed, but not overturned. Finally, in 1936, at the request of a number of officials, including Dulin's trial judge, California Governor Merriam pardoned Dulin. REF.: *CBA*.

Dulles, John Foster, 1888-1959, U.S., lawyer. Aided in drafting the U.N. Charter, 1944-45, negotiated peace with Japan, 1949-51, and served as U.S. secretary of state, 1953-59. Dulles is known as the most powerful secretary of state in history. REF.: *CBA*.

Dumas, René François, 1757-94, Fr., pres., assass. Served as the Revolutionary Tribunal president during the Reign of Terror,

for which he was guillotined along with Maximilien Robespierre. REF.: *CBA*.

Dumini, Amerigo, and **Poveromo, Ameleo**, and **Viola, Giuseppe**, prom. 1924, Italy, mur. Born in St. Louis, Mo., Amerigo Dumini became a noted Italian gangster and politician. He served in both world wars, surviving wounds that should have been fatal. In 1924, he organized the murder of Italian official Giacomo Matteotti, for which many people blamed Benito Mussolini. Mussolini actually tried Dumini and four accomplices for the murder, but the trial was mainly for show. Dumini received an exceedingly light sentence of two months.

But in 1947, a new Italian government tried Dumini again. This time, he said he and and his cohorts had driven along the Tiber until they found Matteotti, then brutally beat him and loaded him in the car. He died from injuries sustained in the attack and was buried in a shallow grave in nearby woods.

Dumini was sentenced to life imprisonment, but the sentence was immediately reduced to thirty years. Poveromo and Viola, two accomplices still at large, were sentenced in absentia to life imprisonment. REF.: *CBA*.

Dumollard, Martin, and **Dumollard, Marie**, prom. 1862, Fr., mur. A French farmer near Montluel hired serving girls to help in his house. But they frequently just walked away, it seemed, requiring him to find replacements. Martin Dumollard often went to an employment agency in Lyons to hire new help, and sometimes he just approached young girls himself, asking if they would like jobs. Although the body of one of the maids was found in the woods in 1855, the case was left open and nothing more was said. Six years later, however, young Marie Pichon of Lyons was approached about a serving position by an easily described man. When they did not go directly to the big house he said he represented, she became cautious and was ready to run when he pulled out a rope and tried to put it around her throat.

The authorities investigated and discovered at the Dumollard farm at least ten fairly new corpses of young women, along with piles of clothing. Marie Dumollard, unable to keep silent, confessed that her husband killed the girls, and she kept or sold the clothing as she chose. Some bodies were tossed into the nearby Rhone River, others were buried. In January 1862, the couple were tried at Bourg while mobs of angry townspeople tried to lynch them. They were both found Guilty. Martin was sentenced to be guillotined. Marie, as his accomplice, was sent to hard labor in prison for twenty years.

REF.: Bierstadt, *Curious Trials and Criminal Cases*; Brock, *A Casebook of Crime*; *CBA*; Forster, *Studies In Black and Red*; Heppenstall, *Bluebeard and After*; Lambton, *Thou Shalt Do No Murder*; Nash, *Look For the Woman*; Whitelaw, *Corpus Delicti*; Wilson, *Encyclopedia of Murder*.

Dumont, Emma, See: **Madame Moustache.**

Dun, Thomas, prom. 1100, Brit., rob.-mur. Dun was famous for his many disguises. One day he would be a beggar, the next day a soldier, the day after that, a gentleman or a merchant. If he saw something he wanted, he would take it by guile or by cold-blooded murder. One day Dun came upon a wagon filled with corn, being pulled by five horses on the road to Bedford. Without warning, Dun charged the wagon, stabbing the driver to death. He pulled the poor man off the road and buried him in a shallow grave before driving the wagon to Bedford where, presenting it as his own, he sold not only the load of corn but the wagon and the horses.

Dun usually worked the road between St. Albans and Towcester with a band of highwaymen. He was also known to rob houses when the road traffic was slight. One day, along with some companions, Dun knocked on the door of a wealthy knight's house and presented himself as a fellow gentleman. Dun and his entourage were led to the knight where the pretense continued. Then Dun put a dagger to the knight's breast and he was told that if he did not deliver 1000 marks he would die. The money was paid.

During this period the sheriff was hotly pursuing Dun. The manhunt, however, did not worry the highwayman; in fact, he used the manhunt as a ruse to continue his thievery. One night he and a band of men presented themselves at a castle, claiming to be sheriff's men and demanding to search the castle for Dun. When a search of all the rooms turned up nothing, Dun announced that Dun must be hiding in the trunks where the valuables were kept. When these treasure chests were opened he and his men looted whatever could be carried back to the woods.

Dun robbed successfully for over twenty years, terrorizing the countryside before he was finally found by the sheriff's men in an inn near Dunstable. He waited until they were upon him, then jumped to his feet, stabbed two of the men to death, and escaped on horseback. More than 150 townspeople followed with a strange assortment of weapons—household utensils, farming implements. When Dun came to the river he stripped and, holding a knife with his teeth, jumped into the water. Swimming furiously, Dun discovered that there was no safe place to go ashore. Every time he tried to leave the river, the townspeople were waiting. Finally exhausted, he staggered ashore where a group of angry citizens knocked him unconscious. Dun was locked in Bedford Jail while a stage for his execution was erected. The notorious highwayman did not receive a trial; two executioners were used because of Dun's enormous strength. He escaped from their grasp nine times before he was finally pinned down. Dun was then slowly dismembered alive while a huge hooting crowd looked on.

REF.: *CBA*; Pringle, *Stand and Deliver*; Smith, *Highwaymen*.

Dun, Timothy, and **Chapman, Jack**, and **Rag, Isaac**, and **Thurland, Tom**, and **White, Will**, prom. 1716, Brit., rob.-mur. Returning from the Sadler's Wells Theater on Mar. 31, 1716, the elderly Mrs. Knap was attacked by five thugs, robbed, and killed. Jonathan Wild, who controlled Britain's underworld, turned in the murderers himself to prove that no crime could be committed without his approval.

Within two weeks, Wild had rounded up the five. Will White was the first, followed shortly by Jack Chapman and Isaac Rag. Tom Thurland was found in Smithfield. But Timothy Dun managed to stay at large for a while longer.

While three of the men were hanged—Rag turned King's evidence—Wild searched for the last man. Since Dun was a criminal and would need money soon, he knew he would not have to wait long. Eventually, Dun's wife came looking for Wild, who had one of his men follow her home to Dun's hiding place. Dun was chased down, handed over to the police, and also hanged for murder.

REF.: *CBA*; Postgate, *Murder, Piracy and Treason*.

Dunbar, Reuben A., 1829-51, U.S., mur. A resident of Albany, N.Y., Reuben Dunbar lived with the wealthy Lester family as an adopted son. After the widowed Mr. Lester died, the 21-year-old Dunbar tried to become the sole inheritor of the Lester estate by murdering his stepbrothers, Stephen V. Lester, eight, and David L. Lester, ten, on Sept. 28, 1850. He clubbed little Stephen to death and hanged David from a tree. Dunbar then put in a claim for the property. Dunbar said that the Lester boys had run away, but skeptical authorities searched the Lester property and soon unearthed the bodies of the two legal heirs and charged Dunbar with murder. Dunbar was tried in November 1850 and convicted, later confessing to the double slaying before he was hanged on Jan. 31, 1851, in the courtyard of the Albany Jail.

REF.: *CBA*; Cuyler, *Trial of Reuben Dunbar for the Murder of Stephen V. Lester and David L. Lester*; *A Full and Truthful Confession of Reuben A. Dunbar*; Hammond, *The Closing Argument in the Case of the People vs. Reuben Dunbar*; *Life and Awful Confession of Reuben Dunbar!*; *The Most Foul and Unparalleled Murder in the Annals of Crime, Life and Confession of Reuben A. Dunbar*; Nash, *Bloodletters and Badmen*.

Dunbar, Ronald Patrick, prom. 1957, Brit., rob.-mansl. The insanity plea was given a thorough examination in the case of Ronald Dunbar, who murdered Mrs. Selina Mewes, eighty-two, in Newcastle, Eng., on Mar. 5, 1957.

Mrs. Mewes was almost totally deaf and lived alone. It was rumored that she kept large amounts of cash in her home. On Apr. 30, five days before her murder, someone broke into her house and stole £78. She was found dead in her bed by a constable on Mar. 6, her head badly beaten, her home a shambles.

Later that day, Dunbar entered the Newcastle C.I.D. station and said, "I am admitting to the murder on Scotswood Road this morning." Dunbar once lived in one of the houses Mrs. Mewes owned, and had occasionally obtained small loans from her. He claimed he was responsible for the Apr. 30 robbery as well. He told the police that he had been ransacking the apartment in search of money when she awoke. He struck her with a bottle, removed a few ten-shilling notes from under her pillow, and fled. The next morning, when his wife told him that Mrs. Mewes was dead, he told her he had done it. Mrs. Dunbar convinced him to give himself up, telling him that the police would eventually catch him anyway.

Dunbar's trial was held at Newcastle Assizes in May 1957, with Geoffrey Veale prosecuting and P. Stanley Price defending. Justice Ashworth presided. Dunbar pleaded not guilty.

Veale told the court that earlier on the evening of the murder, Dunbar told Alexander Curry, a friend with whom he had been drinking, "words to the effect that if he heard the next day about a place where a back wall was climbed and there was a dog, it was not him that had done it." (Mrs. Mewes owned a small dog.) "This is not a case of sudden loss of temper," Veale told the jury, "not a case of a man provoked. It is a case of a burglar committing his crime and battering to death the witness that he thinks has recognized him."

As to the insanity defense, both sides presented experts. The defense tried to show that Dunbar was an "inadequate psychopath." The prosecution's witness, the resident physician at Durham Prison, where Dunbar was held, said that although Durham showed signs of emotional instability he was not psychopathic.

Price, in closing the defense's case, stated, "The truth was that there was no thought at all in the man's mind. Does that sound to you like a man behaving like a dangerous child? I think it is a very striking description and a very apt one."

The jury, consisting of eight men and four women, found Dunbar Guilty of murder. He was sentenced to death—the first death penalty in British legal history. The charge, however, was reduced to manslaughter by the Court of Criminal Appeal, which accepted Dunbar's defense of "diminished responsibility," and Dunbar was spared capital punishment.

REF.: *CBA*; Furneaux, *Famous Criminal Cases, Vol. 5*.

Duncan I, d.1040, Scot., king, assass. After succeeding his maternal grandfather, Duncan ruled as king of Scotland from 1034 until he was opposed by Maelbaethe, or Macbeth, who murdered him. Shakespeare's drama *Macbeth* is based upon this political assassination. REF.: *CBA*.

Duncan II, d.1094, Scot., king, assass. Held captive in Normandy, later securing the aid of Normans and English to force his uncle, Donaldbane from the Scottish throne, 1093. Not long after, Duncan was assassinated by followers of Donaldbane. REF.: *CBA*.

Duncan, Elizabeth, c.1904-62, and **Baldonado, Augustine**, c.1934-62, and **Moya, Luis, Jr.**, c.1937-62, U.S., mur. "There is nothing good that can be said about Elizabeth Duncan," said her own attorney. When seen in court, the respectable-looking middle-aged woman had a lifetime behind her of getting what she wanted: a new husband while still married to an old one; a new house when she did not have the money for a mortgage payment, let alone the down payment; and an annulment of her son's marriage, acquired by having another man pretend to be her son. When she went on trial in Santa Barbara, Calif., for engineering the murder of her son's wife, a college friend of her son, Stephen Gillis, who was also one of her many husbands, said, "She had a tremendous spell on everybody that she came in contact with, and no matter what lie she told, no matter how fantastic, it was believable."

The investigation of "Mother Duncan" revealed an amazingly chaotic life. Born Hazel Sinclara Nigh in Kansas City in 1904 (or 1906, or 1913, or possibly 1900), she first married, at fourteen, a man named Dewey Tessier. She had three children, but sent them to an orphanage. In the following years, she married at least eleven, and possibly as many as twenty men. Only rarely was she actually free to do so, but that did not bother her. Many of the marriages were annulled on the basis of nonconsummation, although she sometimes managed to blackmail her husbands into support payments. She ran beauty shops, cafés, massage parlors (was arrested for prostitution), and a real estate business.

Perhaps because she never kept a husband, she was fiercely determined to hang on to her son, Frank, whom she had by Frank Low in 1928. She later changed Frank's last name to Duncan, because that particular husband had a better credit rating than most of her husbands. Frank managed to set through college and obtain his law degree. His mother delighted in attending his court cases and cheering her son on, always careful to identify herself as the attorney's mother. There is some evidence that they had an incestuous relationship. Gradually Mrs. Duncan became obsessed with the idea that one day her son would marry and leave her.

In November 1957, Frank and his mother quarreled about buying a beauty parlor, and the son ordered his mother out of his apartment. She responded by taking sleeping pills, ostensibly to commit suicide. In the hospital, one of her nurses was Olga Kupcyzk, a 29-year-old Canadian. Olga and Frank fell in love, and his mother began the maneuverings that would end in murder. Olga became pregnant, and as she and Frank talked of marriage, Elizabeth Duncan began harassing her over the phone, even threatening to kill her. Duncan began discussing murder with best friend, Mrs. Emma Short. Frank and Olga married secretly, but Frank went home to his mother on the wedding night so she would not suspect it. But his mother found out, and intensified her campaign against her daughter-in-law.

She started by inserting a notice in the paper, signed by Frank, saying that he would not be responsible for any debts except those of his mother. She and Emma Short planned to kidnap Frank and convince him to divorce his wife. But Frank did not act as anticipated and the plot failed. Next, she posed as Olga and hired an ex-convict, Ralph Winterstein, to pose as her son and get an annulment. Winterstein was later convicted of perjury. The harassment proved ineffective, so Elizabeth Duncan began to search for a hired killer.

Working with Mrs. Short's help, Duncan found Luis Moya, Jr., a 21-year-old parolee, and his friend, Gus Baldonado, twenty-six. They agreed on a price of $6,000 for the murder of the seven-months-pregnant Olga Duncan. Elizabeth Duncan did not have that kind of money, but she managed to keep the killers interested with a cash "advance" of a couple hundred. On Nov. 17, 1958, they knocked on Olga's apartment door and told her that her drunk husband was in the car. She went to the car and, once there, they knocked her out and drove off. When they reached a culvert in the mountains south of Santa Barbara, they strangled her (having to "take turns" to finish the job, Moya later testified) and buried her body.

As Olga's friends and husband were searching for her, Moya and Baldonado were demanding their $6,000 from Elizabeth Duncan. She put them off again and again. Then, when she was questioned by the police about her relationship with Olga, Duncan, hoping to scare the killers into leaving town, told the police that she was being blackmailed by two Mexicans and described Moya and Baldonado. The police found and arrested Moya, but Duncan refused to identify him. Emma Short, however, told them the whole story. Baldonado, under arrest, finally told where the body of Mrs. Duncan's daughter-in-law could be found.

Elizabeth Duncan, Luis Moya, and Gus Baldonado went to trial in Mar. 1959, and all three were found Guilty of murder and sentenced to death. The jury left it to Judge Charles F. Black-stock to determine whether Duncan should be sent to a mental hospital, but he rejected that option. The trio were executed in the gas chamber at San Quentin on the same day, Aug. 8, 1962.

REF.: *CBA*; McComas, *The Graveside Companion*; Wyden, *The Hired Killers.*

Duncan, J.C., prom. 1870s, U.S., embez. J.C. Duncan, president of Duncan's Bank in San Francisco, disappeared along with over $1.2 million in account funds on Oct. 8, 1877. Following a tip, Captain of Detectives I.W. Lees tried, but failed to capture Duncan on a schooner at Hathaway's Wharf. The fugitive had not, in fact, sailed away, and Lees found him on Feb. 24, 1878, at his wife's apartment, hiding inside a bureau. Duncan was released after four trials resulted in hung juries, and reportedly died three years later.
REF.: *CBA*; Duke, *Celebrated Criminal Cases of America.*

Duncan, Sir Patrick, 1870-1943, S. Afri., lawyer. Held position in South African parliament, 1910-20 and 1921-36, and as the Union of South Africa's governor general, 1937-43. REF.: *CBA.*

Duncan, Robert Morton, 1927-   , U.S., jur. Served as trial attorney for the attorney general of Ohio, 1957-59, city prosecutor for Columbus, Ohio, 1960-63, chief counsel to the attorney general of Ohio, 1963-66, and was appointed to the Southern District Court of Ohio by President Richard Nixon, May 1, 1974. REF.: *CBA.*

Duncan's Saloon, prom. 1890s-1910s, U.S., pick. Bob Duncan gave up his unofficial title as the "King of the Pickpockets" in 1896 in order to open a Chicago saloon and eatery that could serve as a home away from home for other members of his profession. In the next few years, Duncan's on State Street became the headquarters for at least twenty pickpocket gangs. Because Bob Duncan "had it in right" with the Chicago Police, the thieves could expect to be left alone. Sometimes a police officer or two known to be on the take would loiter in a gang's territory to provide intended victims with a false sense of security.

Wandering tramps used Duncan's as a mail drop and often squandered their savings at the bar. One of the most famous hoboes of the day, Wyoming Slivers, spent his $10,000 inheritance there in six months of drinking with twenty of his cronies. Ten of the tramps died from delirium tremens. Slivers, meanwhile, lost an ear and three fingers in one of the famous brawls at Duncan's. The conduct of many of his patrons eventually led to the revocation of Bob Duncan's saloon license. REF.: *CBA.*

Dundas, Robert (AKA: **Lord Arniston the Elder**), 1685-1753, Scot., jur. Served as Scotland's solicitor general, 1717-20, the country's lord advocate, 1720, and as a member of parliament, 1722-37. He also reintroduced not guilty or guilty as possible verdicts a jury could choose from. REF.: *CBA.*

Dundas, Robert (AKA: **Lord Arniston the Younger**), 1713-87, Scot., jur. Held the positions of Scottish solicitor general, 1742-46, and lord advocate, 1754. In the Douglas peerage case, Dundas voted against Archibald (Stewart) Douglas, 1767. REF.: *CBA.*

Dunford, Peter Anthony, c.1946- , Brit., mur. Peter Anthony Dunford was saved from the gallows fifteen days before his scheduled execution after the House of Commons voted in December 1864 to end the use of hanging as a form of capital punishment. Dunford had been convicted of murdering a fellow inmate at the Wakefield Jail. REF.: *CBA.*

Dungee, George, and **Coleman, Wayne,** and **Isaacs, Carl,** and **Isaacs, Billy,** prom. 1970s, U.S., rape-mur. Six members of a farming family in Seminole County, Ga., were shot in the head, one by one as they returned to their brother's home on May 14, 1973. A daughter-in-law, Mary Alday, was assaulted, repeatedly raped, and sodomized before being shot. Her body was found lying near a green Chevrolet in a patch of woods a distance from the trailer where the bodies of her husband, Jerry Alday, father-in-law, and three brothers-in-law were found. Police linked the car to Richard Miller, a college student who was also murdered. They determined that the car had been stolen by Wayne Coleman, Carl Isaacs, and George Dungee, all three of whom had recently escaped from a minimum-security correction center in Maryland.

Billy Isaacs, the 15-year-old brother of Isaacs and a relative of Coleman, became a state's witness. He testified that he picked the others up following their escape, and drove them to Georgia. The three were burglarizing the Aldays' trailer when they returned home with their relatives. As they entered the trailer, they were killed by Carl Isaacs, Coleman, and Dungee. Dungee, whose jail term for failing to pay child support would have ended a month before he escaped, fatally shot Mary Alday two times in the back. Wayne Coleman, who had been serving time for robbery, explained the day this way: "I'd like to kill about a thousand more people. That's why I need to get out of here, so I can do something to ease this hate that's in me. When I kill, I feel a release." Coleman, Dungee, and Carl Isaacs were sentenced to die. Billy Isaacs was sentenced to 100 years imprisonment.

REF.: *CBA*; Godwin, *Murder U.S.A.*

Dunham, James C., b.1864, U.S., mur. James C. Dunham, husband and father of a one-month-old infant, murdered six people, including his wife and in-laws near San Jose, Calif., then virtually disappeared.

U.S. mass murderer James Dunham, who vanished in 1896.

On May 26, 1896, for no apparent reason, Dunham shot his wife and her mother, Mrs. McGlincy to death, attacked servants Robert Briscol and Minnie Schessler with a hatchet, then fatally shot Colonel McGlincy and his stepson, James Wells, as the two men returned home. Dunham then searched for George Schaible, a family employee, who escaped by hiding in the stables. Dunham spent that night at Smith's Creek Hotel, but was never seen again. His abandoned horse was recovered in Indian Gulch four days after the crime, and a $2,200 reward was posted. William Hatfield from Sherman, Texas, was wrongly identified as the killer, but was charged due to a legal technicality on Oct. 23, 1908. Hatfield was immediately exonerated.

REF.: *CBA*; Duke, *Celebrated Criminal Cases of America*; Horan, *The Pinkertons*.

Dunkins, Horace Franklin, Jr., prom. 1980s, U.S., rape-mur. The U.S. Circuit Court of Appeals in Atlanta refused to halt the execution of Horace Franklin Dunkins, Jr., rejecting defense claims that Dunkins was mentally retarded. Dunkins was one of two men charged with the 1980 rape and murder of Lynn McCurry, twenty-six, a Warrior, Ala., mother of four who was found tied to a tree with surgical tape outside her home. McCurry had been raped and stabbed sixty-six times while her four children slept inside the house. The other suspect, Frank M. Harris, seventeen at the time of the slaying, pleaded guilty to murder and was given a life sentence. Dunkins was convicted of murder and executed at the Altmore, Ala., penitentiary on July 15, 1989, after appeals of his case were rejected. REF.: *CBA*.

Western outlaw "Three-Fingered" Jack Dunlap.

Dunlap, Jack (Dunlop; AKA: Three-Fingered Jack), prom. 1890s, U.S., west. outl. Jack Dunlap was an Arizona bank and train robber active in the 1890s. Following his release from custody in 1895, he joined Black Jack Christian's gang, and later the Burt Alvord-Billy Stiles mob, which held up trains.

In Fairbank, Ariz., on Feb. 15, 1900, Dunlap and his cohorts, including Louis Owens and Owens' brother George, Bravo Juan Yoas, and Bob Brown tried to stick up an approaching train. They fired on the express messenger, Jeff Milton, but managed only to clip him in the arm. Milton recovered his wits and fired some buckshot into Dunlap's side. Badly wounded, the outlaw was rescued by his companions and removed to safety.

REF.: Bartholomew, *The Biographical Album of Western Gunfighters*; *CBA*; Haley, *Jeff Milton*; O'Neal, *Encyclopedia of Western Gunfighters*.

Dunlap, Leon A., 1911-45, and **Riggs, David**, 1922- , Case of, U.S., boot.-mur. The bad reputation of a murder victim led to the acquittal of his killer. Frank Hogan, nicknamed "Rumpty Rattles", was found shot to death in the doorway of a Chinese resturant in Charleston, S.C., on Oct. 25, 1927. His former business partner, Leon A. Dunlap, was charged with the murder, based on the fact that he had been seen searching for Hogan only hours before the shooting. Although he had served in the police force, the victim was a man of questionable integrity. He was deemed "absolutely unworthy of belief" by Congressman J.D. Post and his colleagues during a special hearing regarding the controversial election of Richard S. Whaley to Congress in 1913, and disliked by his family because of his bad temper and penchant for extramarital affairs.

On Oct. 24, two other bootleggers met with Hogan, David Riggs, his son-in-law, and Dunlap to tell them that the cost of whisky would be increased 50 cents a gallon. Things apparently did not go well between Hogan and the others, because after the meeting, Dunlap and Riggs were seen purchasing a $55 shotgun and buckshot, and then waiting for Hogan to enter the Peking Chop Suey Resturant where his girlfriend worked. According to trial witnesses—some of them policemen—Dunlap was also overheard advising Hogan to get his gun.

During the trial, Dunlap argued that he had killed in self-defense. Hogan's bullet wounds did indicate that his right hand had been raised, but later, Dunlap admitted he shot Hogan from a second story window. There was so much evidence incriminating Dunlop that his lawyer, A. Russell McGowan, formulated his defense around the ill-feelings the Hogan family continued to harbor toward their relative even after his death and the wishes of the accused to be home with their families for Christmas. On Dec. 24, both men were found Not Guilty. Dunlap was freed but later jailed for bootlegging. He was also later sentenced to five years imprisonment and fined $2,000 for violating internal revenue laws regarding liquor in January 1936.

REF.: *CBA*; Rodell, *Charleston Murders*.

Dunlevy, John, prom. 1924, U.S., kid. From age fifteen to seventeen, Elsie Dunlevy of Manchester, Iowa, was a sexual prisoner. Her family sent her to live with her uncle, John Dunlevy, in Chicago. He held her prisoner in his apartment on Broadway. The family in Iowa assumed that she was missing somewhere between Iowa and Chicago. It was almost two years before Elsie could think of a way to smuggle out a letter. An aunt informed the authorities, and Dunlevy was promptly arrested. He was tried and sent to prison.

REF.: *CBA*; Nash, *Among the Missing*.

Dunlop, James, 1793-1872, U.S., jur. Served as criminal court judge for the District of Columbia, 1845, appointed to the District of Columbia Circuit Court by President James Polk, Dec. 23, 1845, and appointed to District of Columbia Circuit Court by President Franklin Pierce, Dec. 3, 1855. REF.: *CBA*.

Dunlop, John Colin, 1785-1842. Scot., law enfor. off. Employed as the sheriff of Renfrewshire, 1816-42. REF.: *CBA*.

Dunn, Beverly Wyly, 1860-1936, U.S., bomb. Graduated from West Point, 1883, organized the Bureau of Explosives for the American Railway Association, and worked there after leaving the army, 1911. He invented the high explosive, dunnite or explosive D., and investigated the Black Tom explosion in Jersey City, N.J., 1916. REF.: *CBA*.

Dunn, Bill, d.1896, U.S., west. gunman. Bill Dunn and his four brothers Bee, Dal, Calvin, and George most often operated as bounty hunters. But the Dunn brothers were better known as the proprietors of a road ranch outside Ingalls, Okla., where passing travelers were waylaid after being put up for the night. On May 2, 1895, two desperados known as Charley Pierce and Bitter Creek Newcomb arrived at the Dunn ranch to spend the night. As they stabled their horses, Bill and one of his brothers ambushed them outside the barn to collect the $5,000 bounty on Newcomb in Guthrie. A year later, on Aug. 28, 1896, the outlaw leader Bill Doolin was killed much the same way. Dunn and his posse surrounded the family's farm in Lawson, Okla., and waited for the fugitive to appear at the door. When he showed himself, Dunn demanded his surrender.

Doolin refused and was shotgunned to death. Later that year, the people of the county grew angry over Dunn's tactics. On Nov. 6, Dunn answered his critics by blaming Deputy Sheriff Frank Canton for the brutal way in which Newcomb and Pierce had been killed. In the streets of Pawnee, Canton confronted Dunn. Dunn drew first, but Deputy Canton fired a .45-caliber slug into Dunn's forehead, killing him instantly.

REF.: Canton, *Frontier Trails; CBA;* Croy, *Trigger Marshal;* O'Neal, *Encyclopedia of Western Gunfighters;* Shirley, *Six-gun and Silver Star.*

Dunn, Jack, 1945-86, U.S., bat. Dunn, a Vietnam War veteran who had flashbacks and was on prescription medication for anxiety blackouts had been drinking up to two liters of vodka a day when he shot his wife of three years, paralyzing her for life.

Jack Dunn married Penny Dunn in Chicago, Ill., on May 12, 1983, formalizing a relationship that had been filled with violence and abuse. During their eight years together, neighbors had often called the police, and Dunn was arrested several times on charges of disorderly conduct. Friends and relatives of Penny Dunn had become accustomed to having the battered woman seek refuge with them; yet she consistently refused to call the police. Often, their fights were over Dunn's girlfriend in Indiana. Dunn, who had been a combat engineer in Vietnam, experienced flashbacks, used quantities of drugs, and more than once had overdosed on heroin.

On the evening of Nov. 12, 1986, Dunn and his wife were arguing about a phone bill that listed several calls to Indiana, when the 41-year-old Dunn began to wave a gun above his wife's head. He fired a bullet that tore through her cheek and lodged in her collarbone. Dunn quickly called police, saying, "I just shot my wife right in the face." He then carried Penny Dunn to the bathroom and placed her on her knees, her head hanging over the tub to prevent her from choking on her own blood. By the time paramedics arrived she had lost enough oxygen to cause permanent neurological damage. In a coma for thirty-one days, Penny Dunn sustained disabilities that resulted in a condition called intention myoclonus. She can only wave her limbs when she tries to move, and, as a result, she will probably be hospitalized for the rest of her life.

Dunn's two-day, non-jury trial was heard before Cook County Circuit Court Judge Donald E. Joyce. The defense argued that Dunn's efforts to save his wife's life by hanging her over the bathtub proved that he did not intend to kill her. Apparently convinced of this, Joyce ruled to reduce Dunn's charges to unlawful use of a weapon and aggravated battery. Prosecutors contended that Dunn's 1980 conviction for burglary qualified him for a jail term of up to ten years (the reduced charges carried a maximum sentence of five years). Dunn was sentenced to five years at the Vandalia Correctional Center, with parole eligibility in two-and-a-half years. REF.: *CBA.*

Dunn, John M. (AKA: **Cockeye**), 1911-49, and **Sheridan, Andrew** (AKA: **Squint**), 1900-49, and **Gentile, Daniel** (AKA: **Danny Brooks**), 1907- , U.S., mur. When Andrew Hintz was fatally shot in the doorway of his New York City apartment by three men on Jan. 8, 1947, it was clearly the outcome of rivalry struggles on the city's crime-ridden waterfront. Hintz was in charge of hiring longshoremen on Pier 51 on the Hudson River, a position eagerly sought by others wanting to receive kickbacks from grateful employees. He lived for three weeks after the shooting, and was able to identify the gunman, John M. Dunn, from his hospital bed. Dunn had served time for extortion and had been arrested nine times since 1926. He worked for the American Federation of Labor, as did Hintz. Andrew Sheridan, another AFL worker and an accomplice to the crime, was apprehended by the FBI in Hollywood, Fla., on Mar. 17. Daniel Gentile, the second accomplice, turned himself in to the district attorney's office thirteen days later. Both men worked for Dunn.

In January 1948 all three were convicted of murder and sent to Sing Sing to await the electric chair. Gentile's sentence was commuted to life imprisonment on July 6, 1949, because he was unarmed at the time of the slaying and had cooperated with District Attorney Frank S. Hogan's investigation into waterfront crime. Dunn and Gentile were electrocuted the next day. REF.: *CBA.*

Dunnigan, John, prom. 1900s, Case of, U.S., mur. On Aug. 30, 1906, Officer James S. Cook of the San Francisco police was fatally shot three times in the stomach by one of four men he had seen removing cable from outside the Home Telephone Company. The four men were arrested, including John Dunnigan, based on a description Officer Cook gave before he died on Sept. 5, at the age of thirty-two. The charge against Dunnigan was dropped due to lack of evidence.

REF.: *CBA;* Duke, *Celebrated Criminal Cases of America.*

Dunnigan, Madeline Green, 1923- , U.S., embez. Oscar H. Gropper, owner of the Gropper Leather Goods Corporation, jumped out his apartment window on Feb. 20, 1945, after learning that his bookkeeper-cashier had embezzled more than $26,000. Madeline Green Dunnigan, who was called "Lady Robin Hood" by New York newspapers, pleaded guilty, and was sentenced to two to four years in prison by Judge George L. Donnellan. Dunnigan stole the funds by fixing the corporation's books to reflect non-existent salary raises, and by entering a friend's name on the payroll. She used the money to pay her parents' medical bills and to buy expensive gifts for her friends; expenditures that her husband's shipyard worker income could not afford. REF.: *CBA.*

Dunsdon Brothers, prom. 18th Cent., Brit., rob.-mur. These highwaymen commonly robbed victims traveling from London to Cheltenham and burglarized country homes at night. They were finally prosecuted, one week after the oldest brother killed a man during a quarrel at their headquarters, the Capp's Lodge Inn. After being convicted, the Dunsdons were executed, and their bodies hung on display on an oak tree near the doorway of the Capp's Lodge.

REF.: *CBA;* Stevens, *From Clue to Dock.*

Dunstan, c.910-88, Brit., witchcraft. Charged with practicing black magic, for which he was thrown out of the court of King Athelstan, named abbot of Glastonbury by King Edmund, c.943, branded an outlaw and exiled to Flanders by King Eadwig, 955-57. He was brought back by King Edgar, and appointed the bishops of Worcester and London, 959, and the archbishop of Canterbury, 961; Dunstan was later canonized. REF.: *CBA.*

Dunstance, Norman Jackson (AKA: **Norman Cameron**), prom. 1960s, Brit., fraud. A former pilot of the Royal Air Force defrauded wine consumers and newspapers of more than £547,996, after purchasing the Coronet Wine Company of London under the name Norman Cameron. After acquiring the company, Dunstance instantly changed its policies, allowing no more credit, demanding cash in advance, and requiring a minimum purchase of a dozen bottles. Dunstance advertised the company in many British newspapers, and, by the end of 1968, when he disappeared to Paris, had some 15,487 customers. When Dunstance left, the company was £547,996 in debt, holding £219,500 in assets. He lived extravagantly, vacationed in the Bahamas, and on one occasion, bought £112,000 in diamonds in New York City. He may have been able to elude capture entirely if he had only stayed away from England. But in 1973, he was apprehended by a customs official at Heathrow Airport for carrying £500, violating the £300 limit. In the process, he was identified by some of his victims. Dunstance was convicted of fraud, and, in September 1973, began a six-year prison term. Every creditor who was defrauded by Dunstance received 21 pence.

REF.: Borrell, *Crime In Britain Today; CBA.*

Dunster, Henry, c.1609-59, U.S., her. Named Harvard College's first president, 1640-54, who after being forced to resign was tried and convicted for holding views that opposed those of the church concerning infant baptism, 1655. REF.: *CBA.*

Duny, Amy See: **Cullender, Rose.**

Dupin, André Marie Jean Jacques, 1783-1865, Fr., lawyer. Handled the defense of Marshall Michel Ney, 1815, served as Chamber of Deputies president, 1832-40, and Legislative Assembly president, 1849-51. See: **Ney, Michel.** REF.: *CBA.*

Duplantier, Adrian Guy, 1929- , U.S., jur. Co-authored the *Louisiana Criminal Procedure Formulary,* 1970, and was appointed to the Eastern District Court of Louisiana by President Jimmy Carter, May 26, 1978. REF.: *CBA.*

du Plessis, Andries Stephanus, 1916-37, S. Afri., rob.-mur. The profession of illicit gold buying—known as "I.G.B."—was a violent one. Black market gold was the chief motive for two sets of slayings in South Africa in the 1930s.

Spiros Paizes, thirty-one, and Pericles Paxinos were proprietor and employee, respectively, of the Waldorf Cafe in Brakpan, twenty-five miles from Johannesburg. The morning of Oct. 29, 1936, they were found dead in a ditch off Jubilee Road outside Brakpan. Their bodies had been set afire to prevent identification, but police were able to identify them. Paizes had been shot in the head, and Paxinos had been killed with a heavy blow to the skull.

A friend of the two Greeks admitted that their cafe was a front for illicit gold buying, and that Paizes had said a deal was closing on the evening of Oct. 28. He and Paxinos left in a car with five other men around midnight. A witness heard shots around 1 a.m. on Jubilee Road, and others reported seeing a car with several people at about 12:40 a.m. near where the bodies were found.

On Nov. 2, in nearby Sandspruit, the Samuel Berman family sat down to dinner with an employee at Berman's gas station, Barney Liebowitz. A man wearing a mask and helmet entered the home and ordered Liebowitz to stand up. As he did, the intruder shot him four times with a revolver. Berman was shot in the head as he fled the gunman. The gunman found Essie Liebowitz in her bedroom with her baby and shot her. She died moments later. The intruder then raided Berman's safe, stealing foreign and domestic money, documents, and jewelry. He drove home to Strubenvale, where police waited to arrest him for the murders of Paizes and Paxinos.

Andries Stephanus du Plessis was a cocky 20-year-old. A fan of detective magazines and books, he believed that he could pull off clever, undetectable crimes. If the murders were any indication, he was not the adept criminal he believed himself to be. At his trial, which began Mar. 15, 1937, overwhelming evidence linked him to the crimes. In his car, police found partially washed-out bloodstains and the helmet used in the Sandspruit killings. A glove found at Berman's store matched one he was wearing when arrested. The keys to Berman's store and safe were found on du Plessis' person, and a gas station attendant identified him as the man who bought a two-gallon can of gas the night the Greeks were killed and burned.

There was also clear evidence that du Plessis did not act alone, but he never implicated accomplices. He did, however, charge three innocent men as his partners, and claimed that he was actually the unwilling companion of the gang. But prosecutor A. V. Dickinson discredited his story. The final blow to du Plessis came when the man he identified as the trigger-man took the stand and proved conclusively that he was nowhere near the scenes of the murders when they occurred.

On Mar. 31, 1937, Justice B. Tindall, with Magistrates C. Currie and C.A. Backeberg concurring, rendered his verdict on du Plessis: Guilty of all five murders. Du Plessis was sentenced to hang.

When all his appeals failed, du Plessis attempted suicide by cutting his wrists with a smuggled razor blade. He was saved, however, and finally hanged on June 17, 1937.

REF.: Bennett, *Genius For the Defense;* ____, *Too Late For Tears; CBA.*

Du Ponceau, Pierre Étienne (or **Duponceau**, AKA: **Peter Stephen**), 1760-1844, U.S., lawyer. Authored numerous legal and historical works. REF.: *CBA.*

Dupont de l'Eure, Jacques Charles, 1767-1855, Fr., lawyer. Served in the Council of Five Hundred, 1795, the Chamber of Deputies, 1814, as the minister of justice, 1830, and as provisional government president, 1848. REF.: *CBA.*

Dupont-Fournier Duel, prom. 1800s, Fr., duel. A 19-year-old duel ended with the winner refusing to shoot his opponent. M. Dupont and M. Fournier's feud began when Dupont was assigned by General Moreau to keep Fournier out of a party. Since Fournier had recently killed a youth named Blumm in a duel, the general feared that Blumm's friends would attack Fournier at the ball. A sword fight ensued, and though Fournier was seriously wounded, he vowed to meet Dupont again. A month later, they dueled again and Dupont was gravely injured. After the third duel, in which neither man was seriously hurt, they made a pact to duel every time they met. The two jousted many times, always starting with proper handshakes. They became generals, and, in 1813, met unexpectedly in Switzerland, where Dupont explained that they needed to end their battle—one way or another—because he was planning to marry. They agreed to meet in a wood at Neuilly and to duel with pistols—Fournier's specialty. Dupont tricked Fournier into shooting his jacket and hat, then declined to fire when it was his turn.

REF.: *CBA;* Melville, *Famous Duels and Assassinations.*

Dupont, Norma (AKA: **The Maid**), and **Vox, Archie** (AKA: **George Bryder, The Mouse**), prom. 1900s, Brit.-U.S., burg. A romantic partnership culled more than £33,000 in money, jewels, and other valuables. The pair's crimes, which were staged in the U.S., England, France, and Argentina, usually followed the same pattern. Dupont would take jobs as a maid, then let Vox steal from safes in the homes where she worked. In 1911 they stole more than £15,000 in gems and money from a Washington woman who had brought Dupont back from London to be her maid. They later robbed a home near Paris of £7,000.

Dupont was arrested in 1913 by Detective Woodhall of Scotland Yard, for taking £1800 cash from a safe from a Devon woman's safe, but the charge was dropped for lack of evidence. The pair returned to Paris, where they reportedly stole gems and uncut diamonds valued at £20,000 and continued to rob safes throughout several countries. They were finally captured in the U.S.; Dupont was sentenced to three years in prison, Vox five. Vox eventually left Dupont for another woman, after stealing her money from bank accounts in New York. She died in Paris at the age of thirty-six.

REF.: *CBA;* Woodhall, *Secrets of Scotland Yard.*

Duport, Adrien-Jean-François, 1759-98, Fr., jur. Created a new judicial system for the National Assembly, fled from France following the fall of the monarchy, 1792, and returned after Reign of Terror ended, 1794; only to flee to Switzerland after a coup d'état, 1797. REF.: *CBA.*

Dupre, George, prom. 1953, Can., hoax. A Sunday school teacher and Boy Scout leader who intrigued audiences with his lectures about how he spied while posing as a mental defective in a Normandy village was proven a complete fraud.

George Dupre of Calgary, Alberta, told fascinating stories of his adventures in France as a spy who posed as a mental defective. *The Man Who Wouldn't Talk,* a book telling Dupre's story, was written by Quentin Reynolds, published in 1953, and condensed in *Reader's Digest.* The hoax was exposed when a former Royal Canadian Air Force officer showed photographs of Dupre in Canada that proved he had been there during the time he claimed to have been tortured in France.

REF.: *CBA; MacDougall, Hoaxes.*

Dupree, Lewis 17X, prom. 1970s, Case of, U.S., mur. Lewis Dupree and other reputed members of the so-called Black Liberation Army in New York, a highly militant revolutionary organization in the early 1970s, were accused of being in a Harlem mosque on Apr. 14, 1972, when New York Police Department officers Philip Cardillo and Vito Navarra investigated a disturbance. Cardillo and Navarra entered the Harlem Mosque at 102 West 116th Street, the 10-13 signal telling them to go to the second floor of the building which served as headquarters for the Black Muslims, officially called The Nation of Islam. It had been erected in 1966 on the same site where another mosque had burned down following the murder of Malcolm X.

As soon as the officers entered the building, they were surrounded by dozens of Black Muslims who began to punch and kick them. It was obvious the policemen had been set up as victims in a planned act of violence, a show of force that was to serve as an object lesson to governmental authority. Knocked to the floor, repeatedly hit and kicked, both officers were at the mercy of screaming, stomping Muslims. Navarra, his face bloodied, managed to fight his way to the mosque door where a wedge of policemen tried to work past the Muslims surrounding them, the officers having responded to the now full-scale riot. As Navarra managed to clear the door, it was slammed and locked behind him. Cardillo and another officer, patrolman Ivan Negron, who had arrived after Cardillo and Navarra were still prone inside the mosque. Surrounding them, kicking and punching them, were scores of yelling Muslims, all of whom were trying to get at the officers' holstered guns. Negron held on to his, but the unconscious Cardillo had his weapon taken.

Officers looking through the mosque windows could see Negron curl his body into a protective ball, protecting his gun. Cardillo, however, was unconscious and his gun was ripped from its holster. One towering Muslim stood over the inert Cardillo lifting him "like a pail of water" and dropping him to the floor, kicking him in the face. This man, who was later identified by officers and a Muslim informant named Foster 2X Thomas, then knelt down and put Cardillo's gun to the officer's head and fired point blank, killing him. This hulking killer was later identified as Lewis 17X Dupree. When the officers outside broke the windows of the mosque and began firing into the ceiling, the Muslims scattered, running pell-mell for the exits. Negron got to his feet and began firing at one man who held a gun, but he was so exhausted from the beating he had taken that his aim was poor and the fleeing Muslim escaped unharmed. When police finally forced the front doors open and rushed inside, officer Cardillo was already dead.

Dupree was tried twice for killing Cardillo, and in both instances several witnesses positively identified him as the murderer. Yet he managed to go free following his second trial in January 1977. The second trial, held in the state supreme court in Manhattan with Judge Aloysius J. Melia presiding, was notable in that a jury of eight whites, three blacks, and one Hispanic could not reach an agreement, despite the seemingly overwhelming evidence against Dupree. One of the jurors was quoted as saying: "The majority felt in our gut that this man did it, but we could not find him guilty on the evidence." The questionable evidence was the testimony of eyewitness Foster 2X Thomas, the turnabout Muslim, because his statements were in conflict with those of police officers and according to one juror: "it was impossible for the eyewitness to have seen everything in such detail" while the riot was ensuing.

Controversy surrounded the case. It was later charged that the court allowed a good deal of interference from political bosses, including Mayor John V. Lindsay. To pacify the Black Muslims, it was said, Lindsay and others exerted influence so that no conclusion could be reached logically. These charges were never supported in fact, despite the concerted efforts of the New York City Patrolmen's Benevolent Association, which claimed that "high-ranking police personnel and political figures interfered with governmental administration to the extent that prime suspects of this vicious crime were permitted to walk away from the scene and escape possible detection and apprehension." See: **Black Liberation Army.**

REF.: *CBA; Grosso and Devaney, Murder at the Harlem Mosque.*

Dupuy, Charles-Alexandre, 1851-1923, Fr., attempt. assass. French politician Charles-Alexandre Dupuy was born in 1851 and was first elected to the Chamber of Deputies in 1885, representing Haute-Loire. A moderate republican, Dupuy served as minister of education, and on Dec. 5, 1893, was elected president of the Chamber. It was only four days later, on Dec. 9, that anarchist Auguste Vaillant threw a homemade bomb in the Chamber in an attempt to assassinate Dupuy. The bomb missed its target, but the explosion did wound several spectators. Dupuy is supposed to have said calmly after the blast, "The debate continues, gentlemen," and won political points for his poise under pressure.

Dupuy became premier in 1894, and it was under his government that Captain Alfred Dreyfus was charged with treason, wrongly convicted, and condemned. Questions about Dupuy's handling of the Dreyfus Affair would haunt him for the rest of his political life. He resigned as premier in 1899 and served as the senator from Haute-Loire until his death in 1923. See: **Casimir-Périer; Dreyfus, Alfred; Vaillant, Auguste.** REF.: *CBA.*

Durand, Earl, 1913-39, U.S., mur. The son of a respected rancher, Earl Durand had admired backwoods heroes since his earliest childhood and modeled himself after the character of Daniel Boone. Jailed for shooting game out of season, Durand, according to his father, "went nearly crazy thinking about having to give up his outdoor life," and killed two officers as he made his escape. Another three men would die before Durand himself was slain.

Durand was well known around Powell, Wyo., where he grew up. An inveterate woodsman, he left school after the eighth grade to hunt and camp in the Beartooth Mountains east of Yellowstone National Park. Sleeping in shelters and caves which he called "forts," Durand grew a beard to his chest and hair to his shoulders. In mid-March 1939, when game wardens came to arrest the 26-year-old woodsman for killing an elk out of season, they found him eating raw meat from a cow he had recently killed, also illegally. Sentenced to six months in jail for shooting the elk, and facing a possible additional ten years for slaughtering the cow, Durand was held in the Cody County jail. According to a later statement by his rancher father, he seemed "to have gone insane." He took the keys from Deputy Sheriff Noah Riley and then forced him to drive to the Durand ranch. When Under-Sheriff D.M. Baker and Marshal Charles E. Lewis followed, Durand killed them with three shots from his gun. He then clubbed Riley unconscious, and forced his father to give him provisions before heading for the mountains, where he was soon followed by a posse of eighty Montana and Wyoming law officers, headed by Sheriff Frank Blackburn.

About thirty miles northwest of Cody, near Clark's Fork Canyon, in a fortress of boulders and timber, Durand lay in wait for his pursuers. The letter Durand left for Blackburn bore the return address of "Undertaker's Office, Powell, Wyo.," and said: "Of course I know I am done for and when you kill me I suggest you have my head mounted and hang it up in the courthouse for the sake of law and order." It was signed, "Your beloved enemy, Earl Durand." After the posse had circled Durand's hideout, riflemen Orville Linabary and Arthur Argento started directly toward him. He killed them both with shots to the abdomen. That night, Durand looted the corpses, smashing their rifles, and taking boots from one body and bootlaces from the other. Making a false trail, Durand escaped his fortress and, while the posse searched for him with bloodhounds, Durand held up a car on the road. He soon went striding into Powell's First National Bank with a rifle and a six-shooter, where he grabbed $3,000 in cash and started shooting randomly through the bank's walls and windows while Bank President Bob Nelson, three employees, and five customers looked on. Telling his terrified captives, "They'll plug me anyway," Durand fired forty or fifty shots, then tied Nelson and employees Maurice Knutson and John Gawthorp together at the wrists with twine, and pushed them in front of him into the street.

Although no one was visible on the streets, bullets began whizzing around Durand and he began shooting. Gawthorp was hit, and fell to the pavement, dead. Otis Gillette, owner of a nearby gas station, loaded his rifle and handed it to a 17-year-old school boy, Tipton Cox, who, like many local boys, knew and admired Durand. Cox fired at his hero, then watched him crumple to the ground. After crawling back into the bank, Durand put a gun to his temple and fired. The bank president shot the dead man one additional time through the head. REF.: *CBA*.

Durand, Guillaume (Gulielmus Durandus, Durantis, Duranti, AKA: Duranti the Elder), c.1230-96, Fr., jur. Served as canon law professor at Bologna, drafted statutes set forth at the Council of Lyons by Pope Gregory X, 1274, and authored *Speculum indiciale*, 1271-76. REF.: *CBA*.

Durant, Jack, and **Nash, Kathleen**, and **Watson, David**, prom. 1945, U.S., rob.-smug. Three American armed forces officers stationed at a castle in Germany just after World War II made a clumsy and destructive attempt to smuggle over $1.5 million worth of stolen jewels that they found hidden in the basement of the old castle.

In November 1945, WAC Captain Kathleen Nash was stationed at the Kronberg Castle at Wiesbaden near Germany. Home of Prince Wolfgang and the Countess of Hesse, granddaughter of Queen Victoria of Britain, the castle had been requisitioned as a recreation center for members of the U.S. Armed Forces, and Nash was serving as hostess. One day Mess Sergeant Roy Carlton told Nash that an elderly janitor had said that during the war, the Countess had secretly hidden a package in the basement of the house. Investigating, Nash had the janitor dig up the concrete in the basement. They found a lead box containing several packages of jewelry worth at least $1.5 million, including priceless treasures crafted by Europe's most famous artisans. Nash, her boyfriend, Air Force Colonel Jack Durant, and Nash's friend, Major David Watson, decided to steal the jewels. They pried them loose from their settings, and melted down the finely wrought gold into a length of gold wire; destroying the delicate and irreplaceable work. Durant then persuaded a former secretary who thought it was costume jewelry, to carry several pieces with her back to the U.S. Nash gave her share of the spoils to Watson, who mailed it to the U.S. in care of her sister, Mrs. Eileen Lonergan.

Arriving back in the U.S. on Mar. 12, 1946, Durant sold several of the diamonds, and used one to make a down payment on a car. Through an unsuspecting friend in Chicago, Dr. Reuben Mark, Durant made a connection with a buyer, Mr. Horowitz, who appraised 102 of the diamonds and offered $125 a carat. Durant required that the deal be made in cash. Meantime, in Germany, the Countess had discovered the theft and reported it to army authorities. Federal agents were assigned to the case, and the Army's criminal investigation division and customs agents talked to the janitor, who put them on Durant's trail. Dr. Mark contacted Durant and, on Apr. 19, 1946, Durant appeared for questioning in Chicago, maintaining his innocence and insisting he had purchased the jewels from a German civilian for 3,000 marks and an Elgin watch. After the Customs agents said they would hold the diamonds pending further investigation, Durant and Nash drove to his brother's house in Falls Church, Va., where they buried an ink bottle containing fifty diamonds and two large emeralds, along with an eight ounce roll of gold wire, near his house. A month later, on May 18, the couple buried another bottle nearby; it contained amethysts and more diamonds.

The War Department cancelled the remainder of Nash's and Durant's leaves, ordering them back on duty. They got married in the brief interim before returning to duty. In early June, Customs and Army agents began questioning the newlyweds in Chicago. Durant confessed, taking full responsibility and clearing

his brother of any participation. Agents dug up the buried treasure in Virginia and, after Durant made several unmonitored calls to mysterious connections, more, though not all of the jewels, were recovered. Kathleen Nash Durant also retrieved those that had been mailed to her sister in Wisconsin, releasing them with the code word "cemetery." The Durants were each sentenced by a military court martial to fifteen years in prison. Major Watson was given a three-year sentence for his part in the conspiracy.

REF.: *CBA*; Whitehead, *Border Guard*.

Durant, Henry Fowle (Henry Welles Smith), 1822-81, U.S., lawyer. Gave up practicing law when his son died, conducting revival meetings in New Hampshire and Massachusetts, 1864-75, and founded Wellesley College, 1870. REF.: *CBA*.

Durgan, Bridget, 1843-67, U.S., mur. A servant in the home of Dr. Coriell of New Market, N.J., Bridget Durgan resented Mrs. Ellen Coriell, and she grumbled and made insulting remarks whenever Mrs. Coriell gave her an order. The 24-year-old maid, who was excessively ugly according to most reports, also envied Mrs. Coriell's beauty, as she revealed in her conversations with friends and neighbors. In the spring of 1867, Durgan's mercurial temper flared up repeatedly at Mrs. Coriell until she was ordered to leave the Coriell house immediately and seek employment elsewhere. The maid exploded, grabbed a butcher knife in the kitchen, and plunged it into Mrs. Coriell's breast, killing her. Durgan was quickly apprehended, tried, and hanged.

REF.: Brendan, *Life, Crimes, and Confession of Bridget Durgan; CBA; The Life and Confession of Bridget Durgan;* Nash, *Look For the Woman*.

Durkheim, Emile, 1858-1917, Fr., criminol. Criminologist Emile Durkheim, who taught at Bordeaux (1887-1902) and at the University of Paris (1902-17), devoted himself to the study of anti-social behavior. He believed that crime was a normal part of social interaction, and that criminality was a "normal" aspect of society rather than one of a pathological nature. Without crime, Durkheim stated, there would be no evolution in law. Durkheim stated that anti-social behavior developed when an environment created a lack of individual identity, thus giving rise to the criminal personality. REF.: *CBA*.

Durnan, Robert J., prom. 1987, U.S., law enfor. off. Fighting the war against drugs on his Delaware turf, state trooper Robert J. Durnan discourages dealers and pushers by stopping suspicious-looking cars.

Working the fifteen-mile strip between the Delaware Memorial Bridge and the Maryland border, Durnan believes his success in arresting drug offenders and dealers is the result of the many stops he makes, creating "more chances of finding contraband." From 1986-87, his dedication resulted in more than twelve major arrests, with cocaine worth more than $5 million confiscated. Dealers who had previously used the route are apparently switching to other forms of transportation or other routes. REF.: *CBA*.

Durrant, William Henry Theodore (Theo), 1874-98, U.S., mur. On the surface, William Henry Theodore Durrant, called Theo by his friends, was a mild-mannered, pleasant youth who was the soul of propriety, a much respected church worker, and a bright medical student who promised to have a distiguished career as a doctor. He was also, on the other side of his personality, a sexual pervert and homicidal maniac. Durrant attended Cooper Medical College in San Francisco at 22nd and Bartlett streets, and was a member in good standing at the Emanuel Baptist Church, where he was also an assistant Sunday school teacher. Durrant earned money from the church as an usher at Sunday services, and was the secretary to the church's youth group, Christian Endeavor. He often worked about the church, fixing pews, plastering cracks in walls, and sealing leaky pipes.

The true nature of Theo Durrant emerged quite suddenly in spring of 1895. An attractive young parishioner was invited to inspect the church library one Sunday after services. He escorted her into the library and asked if she would wait a few minutes while he attended to something important. The young woman agreed and Durrant left the library, but returned a short time la-

William Henry Theodore Durrant and his victim, Minnie Williams.

Scene of murders: the Emanuel Baptist Church in San Francisco.

Left, Durrant dragging Blanche Lamont's body to the belfry; right, the discovery of Minnie Williams' corpse.

The powerful hands of Theo Durrant, used to murder two women.

Durrant receiving flowers from female admirers at his trial.

Durrant's parents dining while their son lies in a coffin.

ter, grinning and stark naked, and advanced on the girl. She let out a scream and then picked up her long skirts and raced from the library. No formal charges were made, but rumors of Durrant's eccentric behavior were whispered throughout the congregation. When the tale reached the ears of the church elders, it was dismissed as "idle gossip." Moreover, Durrant, as everyone knew, had just met and was enamored with high school senior Blanche Lamont, who had plans to become a teacher.

Lamont and Durrant were seen stepping off a streetcar on Apr. 3, 1895, at about 4 p.m., and they strolled into the church. Theo took the girl into the church library where he quickly shed his clothes. This brought a scream from Blanche Lamont. Unlike her predecessor, she did not run from the library but stood still in shock. As she continued to scream, Durrant's grin vanished. He angrily raced to the girl and placed his powerful hands about her throat, choking the life out of her. She fell limp into his arms and he carried her into an anteroom, where he dressed. He then dragged the body slowly up the stairs to the belfry.

At one point Durrant had to climb a ladder, and as he did so, he dragged the body of his victim after him by her long, luxurious hair. Once in the belfry, Durrant sexually assaulted the corpse and then placed a wooden block beneath its head, as if it were a makeshift pillow. He then climbed down the ladder and entered the church, where an organist noticed his disheveled appearance. "I was fixing a gas jet and I inhaled some fumes by mistake," Durrant said in explanation. He then walked calmly from the church.

When Blanche did not return home that night, her relatives notified police and officers arrived at Durrant's door the next day, telling him that the girl had last been seen alive in his company. Durrant glibly told officers that he had no idea where the girl might be. He added that there were a lot of gangs wandering about San Francisco, always looking for young girls to press into their white slavery rackets. Perhaps, Durrant theorized for police, Blanche was seized by these "vile beasts," dragged off, and sold to a brothel in a distant city. This notion was not as absurd then as it would appear today. San Francisco was still a wild city, especially in the area known as the Barbary Coast, where such shanghaiing of young girls actually went on. Police said they would investigate Durrant's idea, and the young churchman became a popular figure, particularly with young, naive girls who thrilled to Durrant's tales of women in distress.

One of these young women was Minnie Williams, a petite, 21-year-old parishioner who met Durrant many times in the library, where the two had sexual relations. Even though Williams was a willing sex partner, Durrant, moved by the dark forces within him, still felt compelled to kill her. While making love to her, Durrant, as he later stated in his detailed confession, suddenly tore away a part of the woman's dress and jammed it down her throat with such force that she suffocated to death. He then withdrew a long knife and slashed the woman's throat, wrists, and face. He took an hour to mutilate other parts of the body. Then, squatting in his victim's blood, he suddenly threw himself upon the corpse for another period of prolonged sex. Though Durrant never explained why he had killed Williams, police later came to believe that Durrant absentmindedly admitted killing Blanche Lamont to Minnie and she threatened to tell police unless he married her.

Durrant made little effort to hide Williams' body, placing it in the library closet. The next morning, a group of women entering the library discovered the horrific scene. The walls and floor of the library were blotched with Minnie Williams' blood. Some fainted at the gory sight while others went screaming for the police. A patrolman ran into the church from the street and quickly found Minnie's body in the closet. Detectives were called, and one of them, following "a hunch," climbed the stairs and ladder to the belfry and there found the body of Blanche Lamont, describing the corpse later as "white like a piece of marble."

Detectives then returned to Durrant's lodgings and found the youth asleep. He calmly denied having anything to do with the

two bodies in the church. But a search of his room soon revealed Minnie Williams' purse, which Durrant had hidden in one of his suitcases. Durrant's spectacular trial followed. He sat in court smiling and waving to scores of young women who thought him "handsome in a dark sort of way." These women wrote him mash notes and presented him with flowers every day of the trial. More than 100 witnesses testified at the trial, but the most damning were those who insisted that they had seen Durrant with the two victims shortly before their disappearances and deaths. He was found Guilty and condemned to death, but Durrant's lawyers stalled the hangman through several appeals.

The youthful killer finally mounted the scaffold to be hanged on Jan. 7, 1898. The hangman came forward, about to drop the noose about Durrant's neck. The condemned man said: "Don't put that rope on, my boy, until I talk." He was given no chance to talk, however, and was promptly sent through the trap.

Durrant's parents watched him die, a strange pair who sat smiling in the courtyard as their son dangled from the end of the rope. "They seemed proud of the whole thing," the prison warden later stated. The Durrants went to the warden's office to claim their son's body later. It was resting in a wooden coffin. As a gesture of courtesy, the warden asked the Durrants if they were hungry. Yes, they answered, they had had nothing to eat all day. The warden ordered them some dinner and, in the presence of their son's body, the Durrants sat down at a table, greedily eating roast beef and boiled potatoes.

The open coffin next to them showed their son's horribly distorted features, blackened face, bulging eyes, a swollen tongue protruding from his mouth that the condemned had almost severed with his teeth at the moment of death. Mrs. Durrant glanced a few times to the face of her murderous child and showed no emotion, merely turned back to her husband and said: "Papa, I'd like some more of that roast beef."

REF.: *CBA;* Charteris, *My Favorite True Mystery;* Churchill, *The Pictorial History of American Crime;* Dunbar, *Blood in the Parlor;* Kobler, *Some Like It Gory;* Leach, *The Crime of the Century, or The Mystery of Emanuel Baptist Church;* Logan, *Great Murder Mysteries;* Mencken, *By the Neck;* Nash, *Bloodletters and Badmen;* Peixotto, *Report of the Trial of William Henry Theodore Durrant;* Rodell, *San Francisco Murders;* Scott, *The Concise Encyclopedia of Crime and Criminals;* Symons, *A Pictorial History of Crime;* Taussig, *Letter F, or Startling Revelations in the Durrant Case;* Whitelaw, *Corpus Delicti.*

Duryée, Abram, 1815-90, U.S., law enfor. off. Served in Civil War as brigadier general, 1861, and as brevet major general, 1865, and later as New York City police commissioner, 1873. REF.: *CBA.*

Dusseldorf Monster, See: Kurten, Peter.

Dustin, Hannah (or Duston, Hannah Emerson), 1657-c.1736, U.S., kid. Kidnapped by Indians, 1697; she safely escaped by killing and scalping ten of her captors while they slept. REF.: *CBA.*

Dutartre, Peter, d.1724, U.S., mur. Christian George, a religious fanatic and cult leader from Europe, arrived in Charleston, S.C., and quickly assembled a group of followers who came under his spell. The group moved to a barricaded fortress in the Orange quarter of South Carolina. Charleston residents were shocked at the news that the commune in the Orange quarter had abandoned all civilized customs and its members were practicing free love. Word came that George was sleeping with all the wives of his followers, including the attractive Judith Dutartre, wife of Peter Dutartre. The Dutartres were George's most devoted followers, and Dutartre naively ordered his wife to sleep with George when the leader demanded it. When Judith Dutartre became pregnant, Charleston's religious leaders became enraged. Justice Symmons branded the Dutartre offspring "the Devil's child," and led a large group to the commune, where he demanded the cultists surrender to his authorities. Barricaded, the cultists defied Symmons, and when he approached the log fortress, Dutartre grabbed a musket and fired a shot that killed Symmons. A stronger police force then arrived and stormed the barricades, arresting Dutartre, Peter Rombert, and Christian George. All were tried in Charleston on Sept. 29 and 30, 1724. They were convicted and hanged a short time later.

REF.: *CBA; Garden, A Brief Account of the Deluded Dutartres; Nash, Bloodletters and Badmen.*

Dutch Henry (Henry Borne), d.1930, U.S., west. outl. Henry Borne, a German immigrant called Dutch Henry, became known for horse thievery. After arriving in the U.S., he joined the Seventh Cavalry, but quit in the late 1860s. Shortly afterward, Borne was arrested at Fort Smith, Ark., for absconding with twenty government mules. He was sentenced to prison, but escaped just three months later and became a full-time horse thief, an avocation he pursued until the automobile replaced the horse. Dutch Henry sometimes had over 300 men on his payroll who were prepared to steal any herd, no matter how large.

It was said that the crafty Dutchman once sold a sheriff his own recently stolen horse, and "Dutch Henry" came to mean a stolen horse. In 1878, Bat Masterson arrested Henry, but he escaped punishment. The state of Arkansas finally succeeded in putting Dutch Henry away after they connected him with the Fort Smith robbery years earlier. He spent the next twenty years behind bars, and emerged from prison to discover that there was no longer a market for horse thieves. Hollywood borrowed his legendary name for many scripts featuring western badmen. REF.: *CBA.*

Dutch Mob, prom. 1860s, U.S., org. crime. East of the Bowery, from Houston Street to Fifth Avenue in New York, a gang of pickpockets called the Dutch Mob operated for over a decade. The gang numbered 300 in its heyday, and its rulers, Little Freddie, Sheeney Mike, and Johnny Irving, became so notorious that the press dubbed the neighborhood "pickpocket's paradise."

The Dutch Mob relied on a number of ruses. They staged street fights to attract a crowd, then picked the pockets of the spectators. Or a member of the Dutch Mob would pick a fight with someone, and a confederate would appear to "rescue" the victim. While he expressed his thanks, his pockets would be deftly picked.

The district was cleaned up in 1877 by Captain Anthony J. Allaire. Flying squads of police were sent in to beat and slug anyone remotely resembling a pickpocket. The Dutch Mob faded after 1877, and its leader, Johnny Irving, took up bank robbery. REF.: *CBA.*

Dutch West India Company, 1620s-50s, Neth., brib.-embez.-extor. Peter Minuit arrived on board the *Sea-mew* on May 4, 1626, as the official representative of the Dutch West India Company, which proved to be a notoriously corrupt organization which flagrantly practiced bribery and slavery. To secure the Dutch foothold in the New World, he went about the task of purchasing Manhattan. All Indians were alike to Minuit, so he approached the first chief he encountered with an offer to buy the island. In his ignorance, he selected Seyseys, chief of the small tribe called the Canarsees. The real owners of the island, or the tribe that occupied the greater land area of Manhattan, were the Weckquaesgeeks. Minuit did not even know this tribe existed, and did his business strictly with Seyseys, paying him and his tribe members about sixty guilders worth of trade goods (the equivalent of about $2,000 today). Seyseys ceded the land to the Dutch in a formal meeting and departed with his people.

The transaction was a fuzzy affair for the Indians. Seyseys attached little importance to the sale, especially of land occupied by another tribe. In the words of one historian, "Seyseys wasn't quite sure what it meant to sell land—the land was, after all, Mother Earth to the Indians, and they felt you could no more sell it outright than you could sell the sky..."

The victimized Weckquaesgeeks were ignored, and when the Dutch settlers pushed across their lands they shot down any natives who protested. Those Indians who provided the Dutch with rich pelts of fur were given rum and trinkets. These early settlers, unlike the original founders of Plymouth and Jamestown, strictly sought plunder. An early historian aptly branded them "the despoiled and intimidated subjects of a venal ring. Under the company's mercantile charter its officers were able to elude the penalty for extortion and tyranny..."

Each Dutch trading party on Manhattan at the time was headed by a foreman or master, who was called the *baas*—the name bastardized over the years to "boss." The first political-business leader in American to be labeled "boss" was "Boss" Walton who, in 1764, headed up the powerful Walton House in Franklin Square.

Where the Puritan fathers of New England deigned not to soil their images with slave-owning (but were not above pocketing the price of Massachusetts Indians sold into slavery), the Dutch on Manhattan were using African blacks as slaves as early as 1628. In a letter written on Aug. 11 of that year, Dominie Jonas Michaelius wrote, "from the Island of Manhatas in New Netherland" to "the honorable, learned and pious Mr. Adrian Smotius" in Amsterdam: "It has pleased the Lord, seven weeks after we arrived in this country, to take from me my good partner, who as been to me for more than sixteen years a virtuous, faithful, and in every respect amiable yoke-fellow...I find myself by the loss of my good and helping partner very much hindered and distressed—for my two little daughters are yet small; maidservants are not to be had, at least none whom they advise me to take; and the Angola slaves are thievish, lazy and useless trash."

The Dutch Charter of Liberties and Exemptions of 1629 states that "The Company will use their endeavors to supply the colonists with as many blacks as they conveniently can, on the conditions hereafter to be made...In like manner the Incorporated West India Company shall allot to each Patroon twelve Black men and women, out of the prizes in which Negroes shall be found, for the advancement of the Colonies in New Netherland." The first wheeling-dealing boss of the budding Dutch colony was a spurious fellow named Cornelius Van Tienhoven. The Indians were confused and cheated on a wide scale by this rascal, who not only fluently spoke several Indian dialects but dressed like the natives, pretending in spirit to be one of them. Like Simon Girty a century-and-a-half after him, Tienhoven disarmed the naive natives by seeming to adopt their ways. One indignant report about him, circa 1633, stated: "He has run about like an Indian with little covering and a patch before him."

So successful was this malevolent actor that the Dutch West India Company appointed him koopman, or bookkeeper, of their Manhattan domain. In this capacity, Tienhoven, who controlled public works funds, exacted the first known bribes in that area.

In 1638 Tienhoven was named secretary to the colony by the newly appointed director-general, William Kieft, who had often been accused of embezzlement. At his secretary's suggestion, Kieft laid a tax on the corn of all tribes in the Manhattan territory, and when they refused to pay, Tienhoven led punitive expeditions against them. His worst slaughter was done against the Raritans south of Staten Island in 1640, when Tienhoven and seventy other men all but annihilated the tribe.

Three years later, word came from the Weckquaesgeeks that they were being hunted down by their fierce enemies, the Mohawks. They begged the Dutch for protection, and Kieft promised them sanctuary at a camp called Pavonia (later the site of the Erie ferry) and at Corlear's Hook (later the site of the Grand Street ferry). Knowing the whereabouts of the last remnants of Manhattan's native dwellers, Kieft, Tienhoven, and "an old freebooter" named Captain Maryn Andriensen conspired to completely wipe out the tribe.

On the nights of Feb. 25 and 26, two heavily armed Dutch parties raided both camps and killed the Weckquaesgeeks to the last child. They cut off their heads and returned to the New Netherland fort with these gory trophies. Women and children in the Dutch settlement, following the return of their men, amused themselves by kicking the heads of the Indians up and down New Amsterdam's streets. Even Tienhoven's 70-year-old mother-in-law enthusiastically joined in the grim fun, booting the head of one Indian so hard, that brains splattered upon her shoes and dress.

When the Mohawks found the headless bodies of their enemies, they were led to think that these atrocities had been committed by other Indians, which is what the Dutch intended them to believe. War, nevertheless, ensued between the Dutch and the neighboring tribes (who, as a rule, did not decapitate their fallen enemies). The battles were in favor of the Dutch, who possessed the only firearms on the island.

Director-general Kieft, a man not known for mercy, yielded in 1644 to petitions signed by many of the 400-odd residents of the Dutch settlement (where eighteen languages were spoken), requesting that Angola slaves who had worked for the Company for "a number of years" have their liberty. Those included were too enfeebled to work more anyway, so Kieft's magnanimous proclamation of freedom was only a deathbed comfort. He made sure to state in his public announcement that "all their children already born or yet to be born shall be obliged to serve the company as slaves."

Even when Peter Stuyvesant began his paternal rule of New Amsterdam in 1647, the right to traffic in slaves was not questioned. In that year, the Dutch Board of Audit reported that the colonists in New Netherland should be allowed to "export their produce even to Brazil in their own vessels...and to trade it off there and carry back slaves in return."

Stuyvesant, a crusty, testy tyrant, stomped around New Amsterdam with a peculiar wooden leg (he had had his right leg shot off by Portuguese soldiers in a battle on the tropic isle of Cape Martin in 1644). The wooden peg affixed to his stump brandished silver bands, which gave rise to the nickname "Old Silver Nails." (Stuyvesant's farm, or *bouwerie,* would later become the site of Manhattan's roaring Bowery.)

The peg-legged Dutch leader considered the colonists under his command nothing more than "boobies, rascals, bearskinners, villains, scoundrels and thieves." Shortly after he took over the director-general post, Stuyvesant was shocked to learn that "one full fourth part of the city of New Amsterdam have become bawdy houses for the sale of ardent spirits, of tobacco and beer." He instituted the first Sunday closing in America, but inventive saloon owners created side-door openings to dodge this blue law, a device perpetuated to the present century. (The first two New Amsterdam taverns, opened in 1642, were the City Tavern, later called City Hall, and Philip Geraedy's Tavern.)

Heavy fines were levied against innkeepers who flagrantly broke the law, but members of the early police force, called rattle-watchers (it was their job to rattle the doors of the pubs to make sure they were locked), took fees from owners without reporting them. This police extortion occurred as early as 1658.

Peg-leg Stuyvesant saw no evil in slave-trading. He received one-fourth, along with his council, of the $6-a-head tax that the Dutch West India Company levied on the sale of each black auctioned off in New Netherland. The director-general even bought a huge lot of slaves for his private use. These slaves were to work his considerable estate, he pointed out, and were intended "not for lucre." In 1664, the year Stuyvesant surrendered control of New Amsterdam to a British flotilla, he had no qualms in selling off scores of slaves to obtain monies for the feeding of his garrison. At that besieged period, Stuyvesant welcomed the slave ship *Gideon* with a "God be praised!" when that ship managed to slip into the harbor. He was sorely disappointed when he discovered only 300 starved slaves chained in her holds, remarking that they were "a very poor assortment."

The English were not beneath trafficking in slaves either and, in fact, convinced the Dutch in 1651 to sell them slaves for their incipient settlements at nearby Gravesend and Flushing. One petition from the English there to the powerful Dutch in New Amsterdam complained that the settlers were "too much fatigued from work," and that they needed "servant men," chiefly blacks, "at whatever price you will order." Old World morality no longer applied, the formal request stated; slavery was an expediency "for we are as a young tree or little sprout now, for the first time shooting forth to the world, which, if watered and nursed by your

honors' liberality and attention, may hereafter grow up a blooming Republic." They got their slaves.

The first official slave ship, the *White Horse,* arrived at the Dutch colony in 1655, but the slaves dragged from its holds were infected with dysentery and other diseases. Still, many brought as much as $125 a head, a princely amount for those days. One girl being taken to the home of her new Dutch master collapsed. "She is only drunk," the slaver in charge told the new owner. "Have no fear, she is of sound heart." The girl was dead before she arrived at the owner's plantation.

REF.: Booth, *History of the City of New York; CBA;* Flick, *The History of the State of New York;* Locke, *Birth of America ("The Dutch Colonial Failure in New York");* Marcuse, *This Was New York!;* Stone, *History of New York City;* Thatcher, *Indian Biography* (2 Vols.); Wertenbaker, *The First Americans;* ____, *The Founding American Civilization: The Middle Colonies.*

Du Tilb, Arnold, prom. 16th Cent., Fr., fraud. In one of the most astonishing cases of fraud ever recorded, Arnold du Tilb successfully masqueraded as Martin Guerre, the head of a household in Rieux, in the province of Languedoc, France, completely fooling Guerre's wife, family and close friends for three years before his true identity was finally revealed in a long legal battle.

Du Tilb noticed how often he was mistaken for Guerre in public. Guerre was not a responsible husband and after he had deserted his wife and son for a number of years, du Tilb put his plan into action. He spent a great deal of time acquainting himself with every facet of Guerre's life. When he felt comfortable playing his role, he approached Mrs. Guerre and introduced himself as the prodigal husband. She believed the man was her husband after he asked for a pair of pants and told her precisely where they could be found.

For three years, the ruse was kept alive. Guerre's wife even had two more children by du Tilb. But a stranger passing through town told of a Martin Guerre in a distant province who had lost a leg in the battle of St. Quinten, and who spoke of a family in Languedoc. The traveler's report encouraged the suspicions of Guerre's uncle. Du Tilb was finally taken into custody and a trial was prepared.

The impostor gave a magnificent performance. He described Biscay, Guerre's birthplace, and gave the names, ages, and occupations of friends and relations there. He spoke of his wedding and the guests who attended. He even revealed intimate details of his relationship with his wife, which convinced many of his authenticity.

But a shoemaker testified that the shoes he made for Guerre were size twelve and the prisoner barely fit a size nine. Guerre was a great fan of wrestling and the man on trial knew nothing of the sport. Guerre's dialect was characterized as Biscayan, a mixture of Spanish, French, and Gascon patois. Du Tilb's accent was quite different. Du Tilb's defense answered with testimony by Guerre's four sisters, a number of his friends from Biscay, and his wife, who all swore that the man before them was really Guerre.

After weighing the evidence on both sides, the court decided against du Tilb. He appealed to the Parliament of Toulouse, which postponed a further decision until the other man claiming to be Martin Guerre was located. The real Guerre was eventually brought back to his hometown and a second trial began.

Du Tilb, of course, denied having any knowledge of this "impostor." But on seeing the man with the peg leg, Guerre's four sisters and wife ran to him, sobbing that they now saw their mistake, and that du Tilb was the impostor.

Du Tilb was finally found Guilty. He was ordered first to make a public apology at Artigues, and then to be hanged in front of the Guerre home, after which his body would be burned. Before the sentence was carried out, Arnold du Tilb made a full confession.

REF.: *CBA;* Forster, *Studies in Black and Red.*

Du Toit, Petrus Hendrik, 1910- , Case of, S. Afri., mur. Considering the length of the "Siege of Sidney Street," it is surprising that more people were not killed. In New Rush (later known as Kimberley), S. Afri., Christoffel Johannes Botha Viljoen was about to be dismissed from the police force for a number of violations of conduct. On Apr. 25, 1932, the night before Viljoen was to be fired, he met Petrus Hendrik Du Toit, twenty-one, another relatively new constable. Viljoen talked Du Toit into calling in sick for work and accompanying him to the movies. During the evening, Viljoen said of the superior responsible for his discharge, Sergeant Jan Abraham Smit, "I told him he could default me, but he will have to stand the consequences..."

After the movies, Viljoen spent most of the night writing a long, incoherent letter to his family, indicating that a fatal conclusion of some kind was imminent.

Du Toit was supposed to report to the police barracks on the morning of Apr. 26, but Viljoen headed him off at home. Against his better judgment, Du Toit accompanied Viljoen to a bar. After a number of drinks, they finally found their way to the back door of the barracks. Viljoen said he was planning to shoot everybody he could. He told Du Toit that if he did not help, he would shoot him as well. Du Toit, quite drunk, did not take the threat seriously.

Shortly after 11 a.m., they entered the barracks. Viljoen immediately grabbed a rifle, but Constable E. A. Boshoff, believing Viljoen suicidal, wrested the weapon from him. Du Toit, angry that Viljoen had caused him to be so irresponsible, skirmished with Viljoen, but was quickly detained, calling his friend a "damned traitor." Soon after, Du Toit found Viljoen's pistol in his side. "Now, I'll show you who the damn traitor is," Viljoen sneered.

Holding Du Toit at gunpoint, Viljoen disarmed the constables near him. He ordered Du Toit to load a rifle and a revolver, and to collect all the other guns in the barracks. As this order was carried out, Mounted Constable J. P. C. Van Zyl, unaware of the danger, strolled in. Viljoen brandished a revolver, but Van Zyl pushed it aside, laughing "We're all friends here," and walked on. Viljoen threatened him again, and Van Zyl finally realized he was in danger. He lunged at Viljoen and tried unsuccessfully to disarm him. He told Viljoen he was breaking the regulations. "I take no more notice of regulations," Viljoen barked. "You will still see blood flow."

Viljoen went looking for Sergeant Smit but could not find him. He then ordered Du Toit to begin firing out a window into the barracks yard. Amazingly, the mild-mannered Du Toit did as he was told. "Shoot whatever you see, and make sure that you get Jan Abraham Smit if he shows himself," Viljoen instructed as he took up his position at a window facing the busy Transvaal Road. "Don't miss the officers, either."

At any time during the course of this incident, Du Toit could have turned his gun on Viljoen. But the meek officer testified later that he was simply too frightened to challenge the crazed man. He claimed that he never intended to hit anyone with his shots, and that he verbally warned everyone he could to take cover before firing in their direction.

The two men continued firing for an hour. Douglas Matyalana, a laborer, was wounded and died three days later. A man walking with Matyalana, Elias Bolai, was shot twice in the back while fleeing. Although Du Toit swore that he never aimed his gun at anyone, one of his bullets apparently struck Thomas Edward Drude, a diamond digger, in the upper jaw.

Constable Van Zyl, watching helplessly, decided to try once more to stop Viljoen. Again, he was unsuccessful, and again Viljoen threatened to shoot him dead if he interfered further.

Finally, Du Toit was hit in the head by a bullet from Constable Petrus Grobbelaar's revolver. He called to Viljoen, then fell unconscious. Believing Du Toit dead, Viljoen turned a gun on himself and, with one shot to his head ended his life and the siege on Sidney Street.

Du Toit's wound was superficial, and on May 13, 1932, he was charged with aiding and abetting murder. The trial opened on

Aug. 8, with Mr. Justice C. Botha presiding. Du Toit's defense was an "absence of common purpose" and "compulsion." On Aug. 10, the jury found him Not Guilty. After a stern warning from the judge about the effects of liquor on one's rational faculties, Du Toit was set free. A private investigation resulted in his dismissal from New Rush's police force.
REF.: Bennett, *Up For Murder; CBA.*

Dutra, Eurico Gaspar, 1885-1974, Braz., rebel. As minister of war, 1936-45, he was the leader of a coup that overthrew President Vargas, 1945, and made him president of Brazil, 1946-51. REF.: *CBA.*

Dutreuil de Rhins, Jules Léon, 1846-94, Tibet, mur. (vict.) As French explorer of the regions of Chinese Turkistan and Tibet, 1891-94, he was killed by eastern Tibet natives. REF.: *CBA.*

Dutthagamani (or **Dutugümunu**), d.77 B.C., Ceylon, rebel. As the king of Ceylon, 101-77 B.C., he led Buddhist Sinhalese in an uprising against Indian Tamil Hindus; building the Brazen Palace at Anuradhapura, on the site of a battle victory. REF.: *CBA.*

Dutton, Stephen (AKA: **Steve the Swindler**), prom. 1941, U.S., fraud. Arrested at the age of ninety-seven for stealing a three-ton paper machine, Stephen Dutton bellowed a challenge at the courtroom, "I'm as good a man as I was fifty years ago. Hit me on the chest!"

Arrested in early April 1941, Dutton had been in his day a fast man with money, preferring always to use other people's money. Glib and silver-tongued, he was ranked with con men like Perrin Sumner and men like Grand Central Pete and Paper Collar Joe. Having served three terms in Sing Sing, with this most recent offense, the nonagenarian ran the risk, under New York's Baume's law, which made a fourth conviction automatically punishable by life imprisonment, of being jailed for the rest of his days. Apparently unconcerned, Dutton pleaded not guilty, and blithely explained to Magistrate Nicholas Pinto how he had been passing through his old neighborhood when he happened by a building and remembered a three ton paper cutter that belonged to him from years ago. Breaking in, he dismantled the 6,000 pound machine and carted it by horse to sell to a junk man. The sturdily built Dutton, who had never worn glasses and had acute hearing, stomped around the courtroom rambling on in a loud voice, telling tales about his life, including stories of meetings with President Abraham Lincoln when Dutton served in the Pennsylvania 71st Infantry in 1861.

In mid-April, Magistrate Pinto sighed, and dismissed the charge of theft, advising Dutton to "try to behave from now on." REF.: *CBA.*

French-born British highwayman Claude Duval viewing the hanging bodies of two thieves, a fate that befell him in 1670.

Duval, Claude (or **Du Vall**), 1643-70, Brit., rob. Highwayman Claude Duval was born to a miller and a tailor's daughter in Domfront, Normandy. Duval's parents raised him in the Roman Catholic faith, earnestly hoping that he would find a worthwhile trade. When, at the age of fourteen, he was forced to leave home because his parents could no longer provide for him, Duval headed for Paris where he made the acquaintance of many Royalists exiled by the Protector Oliver Cromwell. One such gentleman, the Duke of Richmond, brought him to England in 1660 when Charles II was restored to the throne.

With Charles' restoration to the throne, the English peerage emerged from hiding. Once again the lavish carriages travelled the highways carrying opulently dressed nobility. And, once again, highwaymen who had lost their living under Cromwell began to flourish. Duval joined their ranks shortly after arriving in London.

Soon, the Frenchman became the toast of society as he robbed the fine coaches with grace and style. Duval's daring and provocative manner appealed to his victims even as their pockets were being picked. Outside of Hounslow Heath one day, Duval and his gang stopped a carriage. A female occupant was playing a small wind instrument known as a flageolet. It so happened that Duval, who also played the instrument, was carring one in his pouch. Duval requested the honor of a dance with the lady.

The party alighted from the coach and the dance commenced. All agreed that Duval danced the "courante" well. Afterward the highwayman said to the knight: "Sir, you have forgot to pay for the music." "No I have not," he replied. He pulled out £100 and handed it to Duval who tipped his hat. "Sir, you are liberal and shall have no cause to repent your being so; this liberality of yours shall excuse you the other £300."

Duval, who boasted of his romantic prowess, had his amorous affairs recounted in Dr. William Page's *Memoirs of Duval*. Although a rogue, Duval was not without his admirers. When Duval was arrested at the Hole-in-the-Wall public house on Chandos Street, he was sent to Newgate. King Charles II, and a score of highborn women who knew him intimately tried to intercede on his behalf. However, Duval was found Guilty of robbery and hanged at Tyburn on Jan. 21, 1670. An appropriate inscription was etched on his tombstone. "Here lies Duval: Reader, if male thou art, Look to thy purse; if female to thy heart!"

REF.: *CBA*; Gollomb, *Master Highwaymen*; Hibbert, *Highwaymen*; Pringle, *Stand and Deliver*; Scott, *The Concise Encyclopedia of Crime and Criminals*; Smith, *Highwaymen*.

Duval, Jean, prom. 1608, Can., consp.-attempt. rob.-attempt. mur. A locksmith from France, and a man known for his violence, Jean Duval came to the New World in 1606, with a group of other settlers. Duval first display his hostile behavior around the Cape Cod area, when he and four other men ignored the order of their leader, Jean de Biencourt de Poutrincourt, to return to the ship in order to avoid a conflict with the Indians. Of the five men, four were killed, while Duval escaped the ambush, returning to Port Royal with the ship. In July 1608 Duval was with famous French explorer Samuel de Champlain when Champlain raised the French fleur-de-lis over the new city of Quebec. Duval conspired with four companions to murder Champlain, and all others who resisted the rebels' attack, then strip the fort of valuables, taking Champlain's ship to sail to the Basques first and then on to Europe. One of the fellow conspirators, Antoine Natel, confessed the plot to a friend. Champlain planned a party for the plotters, disarming them after they were drunk. They were tried by the entire population of the fort, in the first court to be convened in New France. The prisoners confessed, and Duval was revealed as the leader of the scheme. The jury, officers and sailors on the colony's ship, found Duval Guilty and voted for death. The three other conspirators were given suspended death sentences and were sent back to France in irons. Natel was pardoned. Duval was partially strangled first, then his body was hanged upon a gibbet before he died. The corpse was cut down, beheaded, then stuck up on a pike "in the highest place in the fort" to serve as a warning to would-be conspirators.

REF.: *CBA*; Miller, *Twenty Mortal Murders*.

Duval, William Pope, 1784-1854, U.S., jur.-law enfor. off. Served in the U.S. House of Representatives, 1813-15, appointed to the Territorial Court for the Eastern Territory of Florida by President James Monroe, May 18, 1821, governor for the Territory of Florida, 1822-34, and federal law agent for Florida, 1841. REF.: *CBA*.

Duvalier, François (AKA: **Papa Doc Duvalier**), 1907-71, Haiti, polit. corr.-tort.-mur. For fifteen years, François Duvalier ruled Haiti by means of a vicious secret police force and exploitation of the native voodoo religion. Known to all as "Papa Doc," Duvalier was elected president in 1957. A trained doctor, he had worked on a U.S. medical aid program before turning to politics. The black peasants, who represented about 95 percent of Haiti's population, were thrilled to have a leader who described himself as a medicine man and a skilled witch doctor with roots in the black magic religion of voodoo. Duvalier promised to share these powers with his followers and claimed to use witchcraft and black magic to

"Papa Doc" Duvalier, mass murderer.

summon the devil. Duvalier also vowed that the millions of dollars of American aid, the main income of Haiti, would be used to raise the living standards in a country with 90 percent illiteracy, an average life span of thirty-five years, and an average personal income of £1 per week. A few years after he was elected, it became obvious that Duvalier intended to share his power with no one. Diverting most of the American aid into his own private bank accounts, he led a secluded existence in his mansion. Duvalier declared himself president for life in 1964, and ordered the army to kill his political opponents, whose corpses were strung up on Port-au-Prince lamp posts with voodoo symbols engraved in their flesh. Duvalier explained that the dissenters had been destroyed by the forces of "Baron Samedi," the avenging spirit of witchcraft, a voodoo demon whose soul had been raised from the dead to do the bidding of the devil.

The populace became even more terrified by the brutal Tonton Macoutes, a 10,000-member secret police force which murdered hundreds of army officers who threatened to rebel against Duvalier. Looting the countryside and stealing from the starving peasants, the Tonton Macoutes always murdered their victims in voodoo rituals. When U.S. president John F. Kennedy announced that American aid to Haiti would cease as long as Duvalier was in control, Papa Doc said that he had put a curse on the president. When Kennedy was assassinated six weeks later, the Haitians were convinced that Papa Doc's voodoo was the cause. Duvalier was soon literally bleeding his people dry, rounding up thousands of Haitian citizens daily and giving them a week's wages for a litre of blood, which he then sold to America for transfusions at £12 a litre. Dying of heart disease and diabetes in 1971, Duvalier altered the nation's constitution to allow his 19-year-old son, playboy Jean-Claude Duvalier, known as "Baby Doc", to become president for life.

"Baby Doc" Duvalier continued in power, enriching himself and his extravagant wife, Michèle, while Haiti's decline continued until it was by far the poorest nation in the Western Hemisphere. Unrest and open rebellion finally drove Jean-Claude Duvalier from power, and he and his family fled the country on Feb. 14, 1986. They landed in the ski resort of Grenoble, Fr., where they began to live on the estimated $400 million they had stolen from their country. See: **Kennedy, John F.** REF.: *CBA*.

Duvall, Gabriel, 1752-1844, U.S., jur. Served in the U.S House of Representatives, 1794-96, as chief justice for the general court of Maryland, 1796-1802, and on the U.S. Supreme Court as an associate justice, 1811-35, following the nomination of President James Madison. As a supreme court justice he held a dissenting opinion in *Mima Queen and Child v. Hepburn*, 1813, where he argued that hearsay should be admissable in determining a slave's free status. Duvall authored the court's opinion in *Le Grand v. Damall*, 1829, holding that a slave was entitled to freedom if his master leaves him property upon the master's death. REF.: *CBA*.

Duvall, John L., prom. 1927, U.S., brib. In September 1927, Indianapolis mayor John L. Duvall was charged in a legal proceeding by prosecuting attorney William H. Remy, and found Guilty in a Marion County Criminal Court of accepting bribes. Fined $1,000, Duvall was given a thirty-day jail sentence and ordered disenfranchised until Nov. 2, 1929. Duvall had been accused of accepting a $14,500 payment from William H. Armitage, a politician and gambler, in return for naming three city officials. Duvall was said to have later removed this privilege from Armitage when he realized it conflicted with earlier promises he made to the Ku Klux Klan for certain considerations. Those defending Duvall accused Armitage's brother, James Duvall, of perjury against Duvall, who was known to be a Klan sympathizer. Prosecutors of the Indiana mayor said he practiced corrupt behavior in office and got caught "trying to play both ends against the middle." REF.: *CBA*.

Duvall, William Potts, prom. 1869, U.S., mur. A self-styled faith healer who traveled extensively lost four wives under mysterious circumstances, and was finally brought to trial for the murder of the fourth.

Living in Janesville, Wis., in 1869, William Potts Duvall, forty-five, had been married six months, and living in Wisconsin only six weeks when his pregnant wife, Elizabeth Moore, suddenly died, on Apr. 29. Despite giving several different reasons for her untimely demise, Duvall was suspected of murder by Janesville constable J.W. Plato. Duvall contended that when he was awakened by his wife's groaning, he summoned the landlady, Phebe Wintermute but by the time she reached Moore's room, the recent bride was dead. A local doctor, Henry Palmer was called in. Duvall told him his wife had died of apoplexy. Later, Duvall explained to the undertaker that Moore had passed on as a result of "a fit," and still later he related to newspaperman Daniel Wilcox that she had succumbed to epilepsy. Two additional reasons he gave for his wife's death were "a blind spell" and "mercurial rheumatism of the heart." Plato, investigating the death, felt unconvinced by Duvall's excessive and boisterous grieving. At the inquest, Duvall once again contradicted his earlier diagnoses, referring to her bad health and odd habits, like getting up in the middle of the night to satisfy her "thirst for wine." When Duvall disagreed with Dr. Palmer's opinion of "tetanic spasms" as the cause of death, a second doctor, Dr. J.B. Whiting, was called in and a post mortem was conducted.

Mrs. Duvall's stomach was removed at the post mortem, ordered by Justice Hudson, and it was discovered that she was very healthy, five months pregnant, and had probably died of strychnine poisoning. The stomach was sealed in a jar and sent to Chicago Medical College expert, Professor F. Mahla, for further examination. Duvall was arrested the next day and charged with the murder of his wife. Mahla's report confirmed the presence of strychnine in the deceased's stomach, and Duvall was indicted by the Grand Jury of Rock County for poisoning his wife. Protesting that there was a conspiracy of doctors against him, Duvall demanded a change of venue and was transferred from Janesville to Elkhorn in Walworth County.

The trial began in March 1870, when he was brought before Judge Lyon. H.A. Patterson, district attorney of Rock County, and John R. Bennett, representing the State of Wisconsin, handled the prosecution. William R. Ebbets and George R. Peck represented the defense. A key witness for the prosecution was Lewis Smith, who had known the Duvalls in Hastings, Minn., and had overheard Duvall, who was affectionate towards his wife in public, threatening her with murder when they quarrelled privately. As the prosecution reviewed Duvall's past, it was revealed that all three of his previous wives had died abruptly and under suspicious circumstances. A letter Duvall attempted to smuggle out of prison

to his four children was offered as further evidence against him. Duvall's letter contained detailed instructions of what testimony and information the children should give regarding the deaths of Duvall's four wives, advising them to "be diligent and prepared, talk it over much." Although the faith healer's children sincerely believed in their father's innocence, the jury did not; on Mar. 10, he was found Guilty of first-degree murder. In October the Wisconsin Supreme Court ruled that Duvall's indictment was valid, and on Oct. 22, Judge Lyon sentenced Duvall to life imprisonment at Waupun Prison. REF.: *CBA*.

Du Vergier de Hauranne, Jean (AKA: Saint Cyran), 1581-1643, Fr., consp. Regarded as the co-founder of Jansenism, he joined Cornelis Otto Jansen in criticizing contemporary Roman Catholicism, for which Cardinal Armand-Jean du Richelieu had him arrested and placed in prison, 1638-42. REF.: *CBA*.

Dwe, San, prom. 1928, Brit., mur. Because he was removed from his job of caring for the elephants at the London Zoo, San Dwe murdered his co-worker.

In 1927 San Dwe came from Burma to the Zoological Society in London to be in charge of a white elephant, which was returned to Burma within the year because it could not adjust to the climate. Dwe stayed on to look after two zoo elephants that gave children rides when his co-worker, Mohammad Sayed Ali, returned to Calcutta. On Ali's return to London in June 1928, Dwe was relegated to more menial jobs, giving up both his post and the extra pay to Ali. The two men shared rooms above the zoo's tapir house. On Aug. 24, 1928, two policemen heard groans as they passed by. Investigating, they found Dwe scantily dressed, hysterical, and with an injured foot. In the rooms above the tapir house they found the body of Ali, brutally murdered. In broken English, Dwe explained that four men had broken into the tapir house and killed Ali, and that they had managed to escape. The murder weapons, a sledge hammer and pick axe, were found on the premises.

Dwe was tried at the Old Bailey in November before Justice Swift. Curtis Bennett, for the defense, brought no evidence, asserting that the prosecution had not proven its case. The jury found Dwe Guilty, discounting his story of intruders as a fabrication. The death sentence Dwe received was later commuted to life imprisonment. In 1932, a special board released Dwe and sent him back to Burma.

REF.: Bixley, *The Guilty and the Innocent*; Browne, *The Scalpel of Scotland Yard*; Browne and Tullett, *Bernard Spilsbury: His Life and Cases*; CBA; Fay, *The Life of Mr. Justice Swift*; Shew, *A Second Companion to Murder*.

Dwight, Theodore William, 1822-92, U.S., law prof. Employed as Columbia Law School municipal law professor, 1858-91. REF.: *CBA*.

Dwight, Walton, prom. 1878, Case of, U.S., fraud. A Civil War colonel with a distinguished military career married well, went bankrupt, and seemingly died under suspicious circumstances, at the age of forty-one.

Born in 1837, Walton Dwight attained the rank of Colonel during the American Civil War, then retired when he was severely wounded at Gettysburg. Marrying the wealthy Miss Deusenberry, this tall, physically imposing, robust man bought timber lands in Canada, became a lumber dealer, operated a mine in Pennsylvania, was a landlord in Chicago, and built a grand hotel in Binghamton, N.Y., before becoming mayor of that city around 1871. But soon after he finished his term as mayor his financial operations failed. Having spent all his fortune, Dwight then spent his wife's, accumulating a deficit of $400,000. On Nov. 15, 1878, Dwight apparently died of gastric fever. During the last six months of his life, Dwight had applied to every insurance company in the U.S. but one, which he may have merely overlooked, purchasing life insurance coverage that totaled between $390,000 and $420,000. He then began to take great risks with his health like swimming the Susquehanna River in chilly weather, and taking large doses of morphia and gelsemium. On the final day of his life, in a room in a Binghamton hotel, he saw friends, signed legal papers, and had the beard and long hair he had worn for years shaved off. The only person present at his death was a man named Mr. Hull, previously suspected of shady dealings.

Many insurance companies contested payment on Dwight's life insurance policies. With a test case by the Germania Company, their main contention was that the body they had seen for inspection had been strangled, the bedposts of the bed proving to be adequate for hanging. But there was also doubt that the body produced was that of Col. Dwight. Dwight's will suspiciously stipulated a number of public bequests, including $5,000 for the coroner who was to view his corpse, and $10,000 for the surrogate who was to administer his will. Two of the insurance companies, including Equitable of New York, paid their $50,000 policies in full. The litigation dragged on for years, with various theories abounding: that another body had been substituted for Dwight's; that he had slipped out the back door; that Dwight had simulated death with the gelsemium, a drug capable of producing a state of suspended animation. At the trial, Dr. John Swinburne, one time mayor of Albany, testified that the body he saw at the autopsy was not Col. Dwight's. The insurance companies eventually paid Dwight's estate the comparatively small sum of $2,000 per policy. But many never accepted the Colonel's death, and imagined him living the free and easy life somewhere under a new identity.

REF.: *CBA*; Pearson, *More Studies In Murder*.

Dworecki, Reverend Walter (AKA: **Iron Mike**), c.1891-1940, and **Schewchuk, Peter**, 1918- , U.S., mur. On the night of Aug. 7, 1939, when Reverend Dworecki of Camden, N.J., reported his 18-year-old daughter missing to the local police, he, in fact, knew where the girl was. Not until the next day was the body of Wanda Dworecki found, beaten and strangled, lying in some weeds near a cemetery on the outskirts of town. The pastor of the Polish Baptist church appeared shocked by the grisly death, as did his parishioners. Three weeks later, the parishioners were shocked again, as was the nation, when the minister was arrested and charged with first-degree murder. Dworecki was accused of hiring a local youth to kill his own daughter in a murder-for-profit scheme.

Dworecki had promised to pay Peter Schewchuk, 21-year-old carnival roustabout, $100 for killing the girl; he arranged his own daughter's date with death by instructing her to meet the youth, a former boarder in the minister's home, on a Camden street corner. Schewchuk met the girl on the evening of Aug. 7, bought her a soft drink, and then took her to a secluded lover's lane, where he strangled and beat Wanda Dworecki to death.

This was the second time the minister had paid to have his daughter killed. In April that same year, he had paid two local youths, Alexander Franklin and John Popolo, $50 but they had botched the job. They abducted Wanda, beat and choked her, and then had thrown the unconscious girl from their speeding car on a rural road twenty-five miles outside of Camden. But Wanda had survived. Her avaricious father, who had once been charged with arson-for-profit, continued with his scheme until finding the money-hungry Schewchuk to perform the murder for a mere $100. His daughter was insured for $5,000 with a double-indemnity clause making the girl's death by accident or murder worth $6,000 to Dworecki, who would never see a dime of the money.

In August, the minister hired Schewchuk, but, learning a lesson from his previous murder attempt, only gave the youth a 50¢ advance on his $100 fee. It was all the money Schewchuk would ever receive for his role in the killing, and 10 cents of that money he'd spent on the soda which was Wanda Dworecki's last drink, leaving the killer a profit of 40¢ for the killing.

Schewchuk surrendered on Aug. 26, 1939, describing the entire scheme to police; the minister's arrest soon followed. The two were arraigned on Aug. 29, and both attempted to plead guilty. But Judge Gene Mariano refused to accept the plea, which, under New Jersey law, would have made them ineligible for the death penalty, and ordered a plea of not guilty instead.

On Oct. 5, 1939, a jury of seven men and five women returned a verdict of Guilty against Dworecki. Judge Clifford A. Baldwin

instructed the defendant to stand and approach the bench. "You have been convicted by a jury of your peers and must be sentenced to death in the electric chair," the judge intoned and then asked the minister if he had anything to say.

"Well, I'm not guilty of that," Dworecki stammered.

"May God have mercy on your soul," the judge said.

On Mar. 28, 1940, after spending an hour in prayer with prison chaplain Reverend John B. Oman, Dworecki walked to the death chamber of the New Jersey State Prison at Trenton and was strapped into the electric chair a few minutes after 8 p.m. The two ministers prayed together before the electric current shot through Dworecki's body. On May 2, 1940, Peter Schewchuk was sentenced to life imprisonment by Judge Baldwin. REF.: *CBA*.

Dwyer, Paul Nathaniel, See: Carroll, Francis M.

Dwyer, R. Budd, 1940-87, U.S., polit. corr-suic. Convicted of bribery, R. Budd Dwyer, Pennsylvania state treasurer, called a press conference in Harrisburg, the state capital. After thirty minutes of protesting his innocence and accusing the judge who tried him of imposing "medieval sentences," Dwyer pulled a revolver from a manila envelope, put the barrel in his mouth, and shot himself in front of a large audience of reporters and television cameras.

In December 1986 State Treasurer Dwyer, and Robert B. Asher, former state Republican chairman, had been found Guilty of eleven Federal charges which stemmed from the Pennsylvania Treasury Department's decision of 1984, to award a contract of $4.6 million to a California computer company without taking other bids. Two officials from the computer company testified that they had obtained the contract by offering a $300,000 payoff to Dwyer. According to their testimony, Asher had found out about the money and ordered it to be diverted to the Republican State Committee. The convictions, which were made in the Williamsport, Pa., Federal District Court, were the result of an extensive investigation that could have strongly shifted the local balance of power from the Republicans to the Democrats.

Dwyer would have been sentenced on Jan. 23, in Williamsburg, faced up to fifty-five years in prison, and would, according to the ruling of State Attorney General Leroy S. Zimmerman, have been automatically removed from office. At his last news conference, Dwyer talked about thirty minutes, then called three aides to his side. He handed a sealed envelope to each. One contained an organ-donor card, in another were detailed funeral instructions, and in the last was a letter to Governor Casey. Sweating profusely, Dwyer then pulled a revolver from a manila envelope, warning people to stay away. One reporter cried out, "Budd—don't do it!" as others ran for cover. Dwyer put the barrel of the gun into his mouth and pulled the trigger. He was pronounced dead at 11:31 a.m., one-half hour later.

Dwyer's letter to Governor Casey expressed confidence that Casey "will be the great Governor that Pennsylvania needs at this time," and recommended that his wife of twenty-three years succeed him in the office of Treasurer. A reporter for The Philadelphia *Inquirer*, Fred Cusick, stated, "I should have run and grabbed him when he pulled out the envelope. I knew that was it." REF.: *CBA*.

Dwyer, William Vincent (AKA: **Big Bill**), prom. 1922-26, U.S., brib. The men who dispersed the available liquor during Prohibition made a lot of money and controlled a lot of people. A leading bootlegger in New York was "Big Bill" Dwyer. Starting as a stevedore on the docks, he was hired by a friend, George Shevlin, when Prohibition started, as manager of the trucks, garages, and other equipment needed to keep illegal liquor flowing into the city. Dwyer built garages in which entire trucks and their heavy loads could disappear and never be found unless one knew how to open secret doors. By the time he broke away from Shevlin, Dwyer had organized a supply system that reached from the vineyards and breweries of Europe to the warehouses of Manhattan.

Unlike some of the other smugglers of the era, Dwyer brought those who wanted a piece of the action into business with him instead of disposing of them. He bought immunity from city hall through James J. Hines of Tammany Hall. He also controlled a number of Coast Guard boats and their crews. Once his shipments reached land, their safety was guaranteed by the large number of policemen on his payroll.

Millionaire bootlegger "Big Bill" Dwyer.

The bribing of coastguardsmen took Dwyer to jail in 1926, when an undercover investigation for the federal Prohibition Bureau found enough evidence to send him away for two years. With time off for good behavior, he was out in thirteen months. Dwyer gradually became respectable as the owner of casinos, racetracks, a football team, and two ice hockey teams. He and his wife and five children lived in luxury at Belle Harbor, Long Island.

REF.: *CBA;* Eisenberg and Landau, *Meyer Lansky;* Katz, *Uncle Frank;* Kobler, *Ardent Spirits;* Levine, *Anatomy of a Gangster;* Lynch, *Criminals and Politicians;* McPhaul, *Johnny Torrio;* Messick, *Secret File;* Peterson, *The Mob;* Sann, *Kill the Dutchman;* Thompson and Raymond, *Gang Rule in New York.*

Dye, Troy, and **Anderson, Edward,** and **Lawton, John,** prom. 1878, U.S., consp.-mur. On Aug. 1, 1878, two men came down the Sacramento River on a boat and asked a Chinese man where they could find the residence of Aaron M. Tullis, a hard-working older man who had amassed a fortune of around $100,000. About 6:30 p.m., neighbors across the river heard three shots fired at the Tullis residence. The next morning, Tullis was found murdered with one bullet wound in the neck and one in the small of his back. Valuables were not removed from the body, and Tullis was not known to have any enemies.

As soon as the death was announced, Public Administrator Troy Dye, new at his post, applied to administrate the estate, but was denied that role when a friend of Tullis' objected and appointed a brother of the deceased instead. In their investigation of the case, Sheriff Drew and Deputy Harrison discovered a piece of lumber with numbers marked on it at the scene of the crime. A salesman at a Clarkville, Calif., lumberyard said he had sold the materials to Edward Anderson who had said he wanted to build a boat. Anderson knew Dye—he had worked for him in a butcher business. Dye admitted that the boat Anderson referred to had been built at his home. On Aug. 1, Dye was arrested. He broke down two days later and confessed to District Attorney G.A. Blanchard, admitting that he had become involved in a conspiracy with Anderson and Tom Lawton, to murder people in order to collect cash percentages from the estates he administered. The three men had carefully planned to murder Tullis, with Dye providing two pistols.

Faced with Dye's detailed confession, Anderson, who had boasted to Dye of committing two other murders as well, admitted his guilt. Lawton escaped before Dye made his confession, and was never captured. Although Dye claimed never before to have participated in a crime, it was found that a saloon he ran was a gathering place for thieves, and that a man named George Lawrence and another young man had recently disappeared from the premises after turning over their properties. Lawton, Anderson, and Dye were indicted for murder on Oct. 29, 1878. Dye was tried on Jan. 7, 1879, in the Sixth District Court, with attorney Creed Haymond entering a guilty plea for his client. On Jan. 10, a jury found Dye Guilty with a death penalty attached to the judgment. The next day, Anderson's case was tried. He was also found Guilty and sentenced to die by hanging. Though they appealed to the Supreme Court, the decision was sustained, and both men were executed on May 29, 1879.

REF.: *CBA;* Duke, *Celebrated Criminal Cases of America.*

Dyer, Albert, prom. 1937, U.S., necro.-mur. Albert Dyer had worked for a year as a traffic guard at a school in Inglewood, Calif. During that time, he got to know the children who crossed his corner. When three little girls whom he knew from the school—Jeanette Stephens, eight, Melba Everett, nine, and Madeline Everett, seven—disappeared while on a picnic, the 32-year-old man had his wife start a scrapbook of the newspaper coverage. The couple had lost two babies of their own, so they felt particularly involved. Dyer also helped in the massive search that was conducted after the girls failed to come home from the park on June 26, 1937. Two days after the picnic, their bodies were found in a deep gully in the hills near Inglewood. Both girls had been strangled with rope and then their bodies raped.

The police worked through suspect after suspect, as angry mobs milled outside city hall. Finally, they came to Albert Dyer, who readily confessed. He said that he had met the girls in the park and told them where they could catch rabbits. They followed him into the hills, where he killed them. Dyer had to be held in Los Angeles to keep the Inglewood citizens from lynching him. Tried and found Guilty, Albert Dyer was hanged at San Quentin on Sept. 16, 1938. REF.: *CBA.*

Dyer, Amelia Elizabeth, 1839-96, Brit., mur. Amelia Dyer worked as a babysitter in her home for ten years before moving to Reading. There she advertised her services, using references that included work with the Salvation Army.

Soon after Dyer's arrival in town, bodies of infants began to be found in a canal, all with ribbons around their necks. Dyer readily admitted that she had pocketed the fees and killed the babies. Brought to trial, Amelia Dyer was found sane and Guilty. She was hanged at Newgate on June 10, 1896.

REF.: Butler, *Murderers' England;* CBA; Kingston, *Dramatic Days at the Old Bailey;* Nash, *Look For the Woman;* O'Donnell, *Should Women Hang?;* Whitelaw, *Corpus Delicti.*

Dyer, David Patterson, 1838-1924, U.S., jur. Served as the prosecuting attorney for the 3rd Circuit, 1860, as U.S. attorney, 1875, as U.S. attorney for the Eastern District of Missouri, 1902-07, and was appointed justice for the Eastern District Court of Missouri by President Theodore Roosevelt, Apr. 1, 1907. REF.: *CBA.*

Dyer, Eliphalet, 1721-1807, U.S., jur. Judge of the Connecticut Superior Court, 1766-93, and chief justice, 1789-93. REF.: *CBA.*

Dyer, Ernest, prom. 1920-22, Brit., forg.-suic.-mur. Soon after the end of WWI, two former army officers decided to go into business together. Eric Tombe, twenty-five, and Ernest Dyer, twenty-seven, started a motor business, but the venture failed twice. In 1920, the partners agreed to purchase a stud farm and racing stable in Kenley at Surrey, known as The Welcomes, with Tombe providing most of the capital. Dyer, his wife, and three children, moved into a farmhouse at the Welcomes. In April 1921, the farmhouse burned down, and Dyer's insurance claim was rejected. He had insured the property, which cost £3,000, for four times that amount. Dyer, who was profligate, borrowed money from Tombe and then forged his partner's name on some checks, resulting in an angry quarrel. In April 1922, the two men had planned to meet a party of friends in Paris, but Tombe never showed up, and Dyer explained his absence by showing a telegram that said Tombe had been called abroad. Soon after, a letter from Tombe arrived at his bank, giving instructions to transfer £1,350 to his Paris bank, and empowering Dyer to draw upon it. In July of that same year, another letter from the absent partner gave Dyer free reign over the London account as well. Tombe's concerned father, Reverend Tombe had been searching for his son, and went to the bank, where he was shown the letter as reassurance, but declared it to be a forgery. Within two months, Tombe's entire £2,570 had been withdrawn.

Dyer began using Tombe's name to pass bad checks. Three months later, a man named Fitzsimmons had placed an ad for men to contact him regarding excellent employment opportunities, requiring only a cash deposit. On Nov. 16, 1922, a detective came to the Bar Hotel in Scarborough to see Fitzsimmons, who was actually Dyer. As Dyer grabbed for his pocket, he and the detective struggled, and Dyer fatally wounded himself. In his room were Tombe's suitcase, passport, and 180 checks with Tombe's signature written in pencil. Ten months after Dyer's death, Tombe's father went to Scotland Yard. Superintendent Francis Carlin and a few men found the corpse of Tombe just as his mother had seen it in her nightmares, at the bottom of a well at the Welcomes, covered with debris. He had been killed by a shotgun blast at close range.

REF.: Brock, *A Casebook of Crime; CBA;* Gribble, *Murders Most Strange;* Speer, *The Secret History of Great Crimes.*

Dyer, Sir James, 1512-82, Brit., jur. Served as member of parliament, 1547 and 1553, as common pleas judge, 1556, chief judge, 1559-82, and the first jurist that compiled the reports from law cases, covering the years 1513-82, to use as precedents for future cases, 1585. REF.: *CBA.*

Dyer, Mary, d.1660, U.S., her. Mary Dyer arrived in America from England in 1636 with her husband William, and they settled in Boston. In 1650, Mary returned to England and underwent a transformation: she converted to the Quaker faith. Returning to the colonies, she tried to spread the Quaker gospel among New Englanders, who made her an outcast for it.

She was imprisoned in Boston and later banished from Massachusetts. In 1657, she was run out of the New Haven, Conn., settlement. The Massachusetts legislature passed a law making it a capital crime for anyone who had been banished to return to the colony. Dyer challenged this law and was promptly imprisoned and sentenced to death. Through the efforts of her son, she was released. In May 1660, she challenged this law a second time, almost daring the local governor. She was arrested again, but this time the death sentence was carried out. Mary Dyer became a martyr of the Quaker movement when she was hanged on the Boston Common on June 1, 1660. REF.: *CBA.*

Dyer, Reginald Edward Harry, 1864-1927, India, geno. Born in the Punjab, General Reginald Dyer was the essence of British colonialism, a stern, unbending martinet who considered the Indians in his jurisdiction "sub-human." Dyer was in command of the Punjab during the rise of Gandhi and the non-violent movement to rid India of its British masters. Dyer banned all gatherings, and when he heard that a large group of Indians were assembling on a square in Amritsar on Apr. 13, 1919, he ordered out his troops. Dyer led a detachment into the square, and without warning, ordered his troops to open fire on the helpless natives. More than 400 Indians were slain and hundreds more were wounded. This massacre caused Dyer to undergo an official investigation in October 1919. Dyer, stiff and refusing to explain his actions, was severely censured and was forced to resign from the service in March 1920. His actions, perhaps more than any single act, galvanized the Indian people to unite under Mahatma Gandhi in ousting the British from India through non-violent campaigns. REF.: *CBA.*

Dymoke, Sir Thomas, c.1428-71, Brit., consp. Beheaded by Edward IV for participating in a Lancastrian uprising, 1469, that sought to place Henry VI on the British throne. REF.: *CBA.*

Dympna (Dimpna), prom. 7th Cent., Belg., mur. (vict.). While attempting to flee the incestuous designs of her father, this Irish princess was killed by him at Gheel, thus making her a Christian martyr and saint. REF.: *CBA.*

Dyon, William, and **Dyon, John**, prom. 1828, Brit., mur. When two men were hanged for murder, an acquaintance wanted to buy the ropes they swung from.

William Dyon and John Dyon were hanged together for murder in 1828 at York. A friend of the murdered men did not attend the execution, but went later by coach to York intending to buy the ropes that hanged them. Although he was willing to pay a good price for the instruments of death, which he intended to use as bell ropes, upon reaching the castle where they were hanged, he was informed that there were orders prohibiting the sale of hanging ropes.

REF.: Atholl, *Shadow of the Gallows; CBA.*

Dyveke (Duiveke, AKA: Little Dove), c.1491-1517, Den., (unsolv.) mur. Christian II of Denmark's mistress, who suddenly died, probably by poison. REF.: *CBA.*

Dzerzhinski, Feliks Edmundovich, 1877-1926, Rus., rebel. Sent to Siberia for causing political agitation, 1897, but escaped, 1899, and was once again banished, 1905-12, for taking part in the Russian revolution of 1905. He was imprisoned again, 1912-17, but set free following the revolution of 1917, organized and made leader of Cheka, later known as OGPU, 1917-21, which was the secret police of the U.S.S.R. REF.: *CBA.*

E

Eadric Streona (Edric), d.1017, Mercia, mur.-assass. Alderman of Mercia from 1007-17. He married the daughter of Aethelred II in 1009, allowed the Danes to plunder Wessex in order to spare Mercia, wreaked havoc on St. David's during his invasion of Wales in 1011, and instigated the slaying of the Danish thanes Sigeferth and Morcar in 1015. He joined the forces of Canute the Great, king of Denmark, to conquer Wessex and Mercia in 1015, deserting his wife's brother, Edmund II Ironside, in the process. Later Eadric rejoined Edmund, but only long enough to desert him, leaving Edmund to be defeated by Canute at the battle of Assandun, or Ashingdon in Essex. Eadric's treachery may have led to Edmund's death in 1016. Canute reinstated Eadric in his earldom, but had him assassinated because he could not be trusted. REF.: *CBA.*

Aviator Amelia Earhart, third from right, in New Guinea, 1937, moments before takeoff on her last flight.

Earhart, Amelia Mary, 1898-1937, U.S., aviator, mur.? One of the first American female pilots of note, Amelia Earhart was the first woman to cross the Atlantic Ocean in an airplane when flying from Newfoundland to Wales in 1928. In 1932, Earhart became the first woman to fly the Atlantic in a solo flight. She was also the first pilot to fly solo from Hawaii to the mainland in 1935, flying to Oakland Calif.'s Bay Farm Airport in eighteen hours and fifteen minutes. Earhart was a brilliant determined aviation pioneer who had been enamored of flying since she saw her first plane take wing in a 1908 Des Moines, Iowa air show. Born in Atchinson, Kan., on July 24, 1898, Earhart came from a well-to-do family. She greatly admired her grandfather, a wealthy Kansas judge, and often dreamt that she would some day become a member of the U.S. Supreme Court. Her father, Edwin Stanton Earhart, settled claims for the railroads and drank heavily, causing him to lose many jobs.

The Earhart family drifted about the Midwest, little Amelia often living with her grandfather in a stately home where she spent most of her time in the huge library, poring over the works of Sir Walter Scott and Charles Dickens. She attended six schools before graduating from Hyde Park (Ill.) High School in 1916. The following year, she worked for the Red Cross in Toronto, Ontario, aiding soldiers wounded in WWI. It was then that she met several fighter pilots and became obsessed with flying. She enrolled at Columbia College in New York in 1919, intending to study medicine, but she abandoned this ambition after visiting her father in California that year. He took her to an air show where she met the spectacular barnstorming pilot Frank Hawks, an expert at aerial stunts. Hawks took Earhart for a ride and she vowed from that moment to become a professional pilot.

From then on, Earhart devoted herself to flying, learning to pilot rickety biplane relics from WWI, although she continued her studies at Columbia until dropping out in 1925, later saying: "I lacked the patience. I wanted to be doing something, not preparing for it." For three more years, Earhart devoted herself to flying and learning the infant techniques of aviation. In 1928, a socialite group, headed by Mrs. Frederick Guest, whose husband had served in the British Air Ministry under Lloyd George, purchased from explorer Commander Richard E. Bird a tri-motored Fokker airplane named *Friendship.* It was the aim of Mrs. Guest and her friends to have a woman pilot fly this plane across the Atlantic. George Palmer Putnam II of the Putnam publishing empire, part of Mrs. Guest's circle, found Earhart in Boston and selected her for the mission. Putnam dubbed her "Lady Lindy," because of her sharply defined features, which gave her a slight resemblance to the great aviation pioneer, Charles A. Lindbergh, the pilot who had made history by flying the Atlantic solo for the first time in 1927.

Earhart flew the *Friendship* from Newfoundland to Wales on June 17, 1928, landing at Bury Port, Wales, twenty hours and forty minutes later. Actually, the hard-living, alcoholic Wilmer L. Stultz had flown the plane, despite the fact that he insisted upon downing a fifth a day and that he had almost drowned himself by getting blind drunk and falling off a pier just before the flight. Earhart, however, was toasted as the copilot and the first woman to fly the Atlantic. She wrote a book about her flight (as Lindbergh had done) while staying at the Putnam estate, the work later dedicated to Mrs. Dorothy Putnam, the publisher's wife. Putnam was utterly captivated by the driving Earhart, who habitually wore man's clothes and was seldom out of her leather flying jacket. He divorced his wife in 1931 and married Earhart on Feb. 8, 1931, after she had refused six times to marry him. At Earhart's insistence, the marriage was an open one. Earhart, through Putnam's money and connections, was promoted into one of America's star pilots, although she did set many startling records on her own.

The Putnam marriage was, at Earhart's insistence, an open one. During her marriage, the pilot had many reported affairs. Her paramours included Eugene Vidal, the father of author Gore Vidal, her navigator Fred Noonan, and daredevil pilot Paul Mantz, who was later killed while flying the rebuilt plane used in the film, *Flight of the Phoenix.* Putnam devoted his life to promoting Earhart, ignoring her infidelities and selling his wife's image through a line of *Friendship* luggage and mannish clothes for women, especially women's leather jackets featuring buttons shaped like airplane rivets. Earhart, meanwhile, became a star in her own right, flying from Harbor Grace, Newfoundland, to Londonderry, Ire., in fourteen hours and fifty-six minutes on May 20, 1932, becoming the first woman to fly the Atlantic solo. She went on to establish many more records and, in 1937, she announced that she would fly around the world in the most powerful plane of that day, one purchased for her by Putnam for $50,000. This plane was a Lockheed twin-engined, 10-passenger, 10-E Electra, which was stripped to add large gas tanks to give it a 4,500-mile range. Earhart called it "my flying laboratory" after installing a modern navigation area and packing it with the most sophisticated instruments of the day.

Much has been written of Earhart's around-the-world jaunt—one that would bring about her premature death. It was later claimed that Earhart had been secretly contacted by high-ranking U.S. officials, perhaps even President Franklin Delano Roosevelt himself—whom she knew on a social basis, having dined at the White House and taken Eleanor Roosevelt for a moonlight flight. According to this account, which has some factual support, Earhart was told that the Japanese were fortifying certain islands in the Far East. Her around-the-world flight was to be a secret spy mission, and that Earhart's real job was to photograph landing fields and military installations newly established by the Japanese in their insidious plans to invade the Pacific islands. The flight ensued with much publicity and by the time Earhart reached New Guinea, the world was watching her progress. She and Fred Noonan, her navigator, took off in the Electra on July 2, 1937, flying from Lae, New Guinea, and ostensibly heading for tiny Howland Island, where ships were stationed to monitor her progress. Howland, however, was located near Saipan, an island where there had been a great deal of activity by the Japanese military.

Some hours later radio monitors picked up some frantic messages from Earhart, who had been flying through storms. She reported "overcast" skies and seemed to be confused, not receiving messages beamed to her from the Coast Guard cutter *Itasca,* stationed with other ships near Howland Island. Her last message, at 3:45 p.m. on July 2, indicated that she and Noonan were battling headwinds and that they had somehow lost their bearings. This message was planned, according to later accounts, an excuse that would allow Earhart to abandon her scheduled course and fly over the Japanese islands where she and Noonan could photograph important military installations. When Earhart's plane failed to appear at Howland, a great search of the area was conducted and this search by American warships and planes, it was later stated, was also part of the scheme to investigate Japanese activities. Earhart would pretend to get lost, land at a secret base, and then U.S. forces would use her disappearance as an excuse to search the area and examine Japanese installations. Earhart would later be conveniently located after the spy mission had been accomplished.

The search, however, failed to turn up Earhart, Noonan or the missing Electra. Earhart's disappearance made headlines around the world and she became, like Judge Joseph Crater, one of the most celebrated missing persons. Reports later insisted, and there was some evidence of this, that the plane had crashed on an atoll near Saipan and she was taken prisoner by Japanese troops, Noonan having been killed in the crash. Earhart was reportedly seen by prisoners later kept in Japanese concentration camps. She was reportedly moved from camp to camp, the Japanese militarists thinking to exchange her as an important hostage should the tide of war turn against them. She was, however, murdered by her captors in the early 1940s, while trying to escape, according to one account, and her body secretly buried on Saipan. Bones found on this island following WWII were claimed to be hers. Parts of the Electra were also identified after having been found on Saipan. Another story followed this account but went even further, claiming that Amelia Earhart, world celebrity, had survived all these harrowing experiences and had returned to the U.S. after WWII, using an alias and living as a housewife in New Jersey, a tale as improbable as the adventurous pilot's improbable life.

REF.: Barker, *Great Mysteries of the Air;* Briand, *Daughter of the Sky; CBA;* Churchill, *They Never Came Back;* Earhart, *Last Flight;* Goerner, *The Search for Amelia Earhart;* Klass and Gervais, *Amelia Earhart;* Nash, *Among the Missing;* Putnam, *Soaring Wings.*

Earhart, Bill, d.1896, U.S., west. gunman. Bill Earhart, an itinerant cowboy, was born in Jack County, Texas, and moved to New Mexico in 1883 with two friends, Jim and Clay Cooper. In 1888 Earhart became embroiled in a dispute with cattleman John Good, an influential rival of the Cooper brothers whose ranch Earhart worked on. The altercation sparked a bitter range war in 1888 between the Coopers and the Goods. In August John Good's son was allegedly killed by five men, including Earhart, near Las Cruces, N.M. There was a lengthy shootout but the only fatalities were two horses. Peace was eventually restored to the region, and Earhart drifted back into Texas, where he was killed in a saloon brawl in Pecos in Fall 1896.

REF.: *CBA;* Sonnichsen, *Tularosa.*

Earle, Willie, 1922-47, U.S., lynch. An example of Southern white "lynch law" occurred in South Carolina in 1947 when a black man was dragged from his cell and murdered by an angry mob. Willie Earle was being held in the Pickens County Jail for questioning in conjunction with the stabbing death of a Liberty,

S.C., taxi driver. A large mob of armed Greenville residents, many of them taxi drivers, descended on the jail demanding that Earle be turned over to them. The jailer complied.

First, Earle was taken to the Saluda Dam where members of the mob questioned him. Following the questioning, Earle was driven to Bramlett Road in rural Greenville County where he was stabbed, clubbed, and shot to death. In their subsequent investigation, the FBI identified twenty-eight persons in the lynch mob, of which no fewer than twenty-six confessed to taking part in the Earle murder. Despite Governor Strom Thurmond's promises that justice would be done, all twenty-six defendants were acquitted. REF.: *CBA.*

Earls, John, 1802-36, U.S., mur. Born in Williamsport, Va., John Earls was a fisherman rarely satisfied with his catch. Shortly after Earls divorced his first wife to marry Catharine Earls, he fell in love with Maria Moritz. To ensure that Moritz would stay with him, Earls began to plot his wife's murder. On two separate occasions, he laced Catharine's food with small doses of arsenic. Although she became violently ill, she recovered both times.

In October 1835, Earls put arsenic into some chocolate that his mother was preparing for Catharine. When his wife became ill, Earls then put arsenic into the tea that his mother and daughter brought to relieve Catharine.

When his wife died, Earls denied any guilt. During the trial, the defense attacked the credibility of the medical examiners and said that Catharine had committed suicide. When the jury found him Guilty, Earls confessed, explaining that his desire for Moritz had driven him to poison Catharine. Earls was hanged on May 24, 1836, at the age of thirty-four. REF.: *CBA.*

Earp, Wyatt Berry Stapp, 1848-1929, U.S., west. lawman. No other American lawman of the Old West inspired more legends than the soft-spoken, nerveless Wyatt Earp. Unlike most of his peers, Earp survived countless gun battles and physical encounters with outlaws because of his extraordinary patience and resolute manner. He was not a fast-draw artist. While gunslingers pulled their weapons and wildly shot away at him, Earp would coolly draw his own weapon and, while bullets whizzed and thudded about him, take careful aim and fire. His aim was generally true, as was his purpose as a lawman in a half-dozen western towns where the rule of the day was robbery and murder.

The Earp family, of Scottish origin, dated back to pre-Revolutionary Virginia. Earp's parents, Nicholas and Virginia Earp, settled in Hartford, Ky., and here produced seven children: James, 1841; Virgil, 1843; Martha, 1845; Wyatt, 1848; Morgan, 1851; Warren, 1855; and Adelia, 1861. Wyatt, named after his father's commander during the Mexican-American War, Colonel Wyatt Berry Stapp, also had a half-brother, Newton, born in 1840 to his father and his first wife. The Earps moved to Iowa and here established a large farm. The Earp boys learned early to respect the law. Their father, according to Wyatt's later recollection, had a "regard for the land (that) was equaled by his respect for the law and his detestation for the lawless elements so prevalent in the West. I heard him say many times that while the law might not be entirely just, it generally expressed the will of the decent folks who were trying to build up the county, and that until someone could offer a better safeguard for a man's rights, enforcement of the law was the duty of every man who asked for its protection in any way."

The older sons, Newton, James, and Virgil Earp, served in the Union army during the Civil War. James was so severely wounded that he returned home, permanently disabled, but this did not prevent him from later serving as a lawman in several western towns. Wyatt attempted to enlist at age fifteen but his father caught him and returned him to the family farm. The family then moved to California and, en route, to protect against marauding Indians, Nicholas Earp gave Wyatt his first weapon, "a cumbersome weapon," Earp recalled later, a combination rifle and shotgun. He later acquired a six-gun and practiced shooting every day, becoming a deadly marksman. He left California, going East in the mid-1860s where he worked as a buffalo hunter for the railroads and the U.S. Cavalry, a railroad worker, and sometimes a scout for wagon trains, as his father had been.

According to his own recollection, Earp met James Butler "Wild Bill" Hickok in Kansas City in 1871, along with the legendary gunmen, scouts, and western legends of their own day. These included Jack Gallagher, Jack Martin, Billy Dixon, Billy Ogg, and Jim Hanrahan. "The names may not mean much to another century," Earp recalled in the 1920s, "but in my younger days, each was a noted man." It was Hickok who convinced Earp to become a buffalo hunter, pointing out that he had made thousands of dollars at hunting these beasts to provide food for U.S. troops. "Bill Hickok was regarded as the deadliest pistol shot alive," Earp would later recall, "as well as a man of great courage. The truth of certain stories of Bill's achievements may have been open to debate but he had earned the respect paid to him."

Earp was a rare exception among his fellow frontiersmen. He did not drink, never cursed, and enjoyed only one vice—gambling, chiefly poker. Earp, during the early 1870s, operated mule and wagon trains and this job took him to Ellsworth, Kan., in August 1873. It was here that the Earp legend began. Ellsworth was the railhead where huge herds of cattle, driven from Texas, were shipped east to the slaughterhouses of Chicago. The town was wild with drunken cowboys spending their pay, shooting up the town, and creating havoc. Two of these were Billy and Ben Thompson, lethal gunmen who would rather resort to gunplay than talk out an argument. On Aug. 15, 1873, both Thompsons were drunk and had started several arguments with two gamblers, John Sterling and Jack Morco, the latter also a local policeman. The Thompsons exchanged shots with Sterling and Morco, who had charged into a saloon, guns blazing at the Thompsons. Ben Thompson fired several shots and drove them off, but Billy Thompson, a homicidal maniac and a hopeless alcoholic, inexplicably turned his gun on Sheriff Chauncey B. Whitney, a friend of the Thompsons who had been drinking with them at the bar. Billy let loose both barrels from his shotgun, killing Whitney on the spot. Ben Thompson turned about in shock and shouted at his brother: "My God, Billy! You've shot your best friend." Ben Thompson then ushered his drunken brother outside, put him on a horse, and sent him out of town.

Across the street, Wyatt Earp watched these events without interfering. He saw Ellsworth mayor James Miller enter the saloon and demand that Thompson surrender his guns. Thompson refused and Miller stepped outside, going to Marshal J.W. Norton and his deputies Ed Crawford and Charlie Brown, who stood petrified at the Pacific Depot down the street, refusing to go after Thompson. Miller, swearing in frustration at his immobile police force, passed Earp who reportedly said to him: "It's none of my business but if it was me I'd get me a gun and arrest Ben Thompson or kill him." Miller then went to Norton, tore the badge from his shirt, and walked back to Earp, saying: "I'll make it your business. Here's your badge. Go into Beebe's (hardware store) and get some guns and arrest Ben Thompson." Earp nodded, went to the store and strapped on two used .45-caliber six-guns and then went after Thompson, who had stepped into the street. Thompson, who knew Earp, asked what he wanted. Earp told him to throw down his shotgun.

"What are you going to do with me?" Thompson asked him.

"Kill you or take you to jail," Earp replied.

Thompson threw down his shotgun and Earp marched him to jail. He was later fined $25 for disturbing the peace and released. A murder warrant was sworn out for his brother Billy. This, at least, was the story told by many who supported the Earp legend. The great lawman's detractors, however, insisted that Earp never faced down Thompson. There is documentary evidence, however, that proves Earp was present in Ellsworth on Aug. 15, 1873, and Mayor Miller's documents indicate that he not only deputized Earp to disarm and arrest Thompson but that he later offered him the job of town marshal at $125 a month. Earp declined, handing Miller back his badge, and told him that he intended to go into the cattle business with his brothers. He left Ellsworth to meet his brothers in Wichita, but waiting for him was another call to keep law and order. The tall, strong, slender Earp rode into Wichita in 1874 and here he would face an army of gunmen, all looking to establish a reputation by killing lawmen.

Mayor Jim Hope encountered Earp on the streets of Wichita and made him a deputy marshal, serving under the town marshal. Hope had heard of Earp's arrest of the lethal Ben Thompson in Ellsworth and wanted this fearless man on the local police force. Legend and fact mixed freely concerning Earp's exploits in Wichita. There were stories recounting how Earp cowed the gunslinging Manning brothers, Gyp, Joe, and Jim, and how he squared off against the towering brute, George Peshaur, knocking him unconscious after a ten-minute slug match (Earp was a better-than-average boxer). Ben Thompson arrived in Wichita, but whenever he saw deputy marshal Earp, he crossed the street and sulked in shadows. When cattle baron Abel Head "Shanghai" Pierce arrived in Wichita at the head of a huge herd, his wild, reckless cowboys threatened to wreck the town. Pierce led his men up and down the main streets as they fired their pistols in the air, creating mayhem—a practice then called "hurrahing the town." Earp stopped this by walking calmly up to Pierce and yanking the cattleman from his horse, clubbing him alongside the head, and dragging him to a cell while his stupefied men stood paralyzed in shock.

Most of Earp's duties consisted of tax collecting, a chore he found distasteful, and rounding up drunken cowboys, many of whom were gunmen who looked for combat with lawmen, eager to carve more notches on their guns. One such cowboy, W.W. Compton, was wanted for horse stealing. Earp identified Compton as he emerged from a saloon one night and collared him. Compton shouted that his name was "Jones," but Earp ignored this plea. He dragged the wanted man to a lamppost and looked him over. "You're Compton all right and you're under arrest," Earp told him. Compton squirmed from the lawman's grasp and dashed away, crossing the street and cutting through a back yard, Earp in pursuit. The lawman ordered Compton to halt and when he continued running, Earp fired a single shot that struck the horse thief in the buttocks. Compton pitched forward over a clothesline, bringing down womens' undergarments which had been drying there. Earp picked up the cursing Compton and dragged him to jail while he was still adorned with fluttering nighties.

William Smith, the other deputy marshal in Wichita, decided to run for the office of marshal, that position then held by Michael Meager, who was Earp's friend and favored him. One night in 1876, Smith made insulting remarks about his boss Meager while drinking in a Wichita saloon. Earp ordered him to keep quiet, "or step outside." Smith, drunk, made the mistake of going into the street where Earp beat him senseless in a rather one-way brawl. Smith filed a complaint against his fellow deputy Earp. The town council, to save face, ordered Earp removed from the police force and fined him $30. Earp, disgusted at being punished for defending the honor of his employer, left Wichita, his brother Morgan at his side, and rode to Dodge City, then called the Queen of the Cow Towns, the wildest, most dangerous town in Kansas.

Located near Fort Dodge, the railroads made Dodge City the railhead for all cattle shipping. The vast herds of the southwest were driven to this town, and with them came a mushrooming community, where cash was plentiful and saloons and bawdy houses flourished. Gamblers, prostitutes, gunmen, and thieves of all stripes flowed into Dodge which was soon dubbed "the Gomorrah of the Plains." Mayor George M. Hoover had heard of Earp's no-nonsense reputation and sent for him. When Earp arrived he was quickly made a deputy marshal. His job was to police the lawless red light district, and to arrest drunks and gunmen. He invariably kept his six-gun holstered and used his fists to corral unruly citizens, but he did draw his weapon when outnumbered on several occasions, not to fire it but to use the butt as a club. He received $250 each month in salary and $2.50

An early photo of Wyatt Earp, 1879.

Morgan Earp, 1881.

"Big Nose" Kate Fisher

Left, Wyatt Earp in 1881, and, right, in old age.

Wyatt Earp's close friend, John H. "Doc" Holliday.

Left, James Earp, and, right, Virgil Earp, 1881.

Wyatt Earp, 1880, and his second wife, Celia Blaylock.

per arrest. Earp earned every dollar.

Earp's prowess with a gun was proven on enough occasions to cause the Dodge City *Times* to warn gunslingers not to draw their guns on Earp "unless you got the drop and meant to burn powder without any preliminary talk." Earp, as chief deputy, established what came to be known as the Deadline, prohibiting the carrying of guns north of the railroad tracks, the "civilized" part of Dodge with its better shops, a school, and a church.   Any gunman stepping into this area wearing his six-gun was quickly arrested by Earp and his deputies, Morgan Earp, William Barclay "Bat" Masterson, and Jim Masterson. By the fall of 1876, Earp wearied of his knuckle-breaking chores. He turned in his badge and, accompanied by Morgan Earp, the lawman set out for the Black Hills outside of Deadwood, S.D., where gold had been found. He returned to Dodge City on May 7, 1877, after James H. "Dog" Kelley, Dodge City's new mayor, wired him, asking him to help with the Texas cowboys who were shooting up the town. Kelly made Earp assistant city marshal.

Only days after pinning another star on his chest, a group of drunken cowboys rode up to the marshal and pulled their guns, taunting him. At that moment, John Henry Holliday, a young dentist from Georgia who had rented an office on the second floor of the Dodge House, leaned out a window with a shotgun, which he trained on the cowboys as he shouted down to them: "The marshal has his gun put away! Put yours away!" The cowboys nervously looked up to see the shotgun aimed at them and then holstered their weapons, all except the ringleader. Earp reached up and pulled this man from his saddle, knocking the gun out of his hand, and hitting him so hard he knocked him senseless. Before dragging the man off to jail, Earp looked up at Holliday and waved. The lawman and the deadly dentist were close friends ever after. Holliday would go on backing Earp's play, risking his life time and again for Wyatt Earp, especially on that fateful day when he walked with Wyatt, Morgan, and Virgil Earp down to O.K. Corral in Tombstone in 1881 to face the roaring guns of the Clanton-McLowery gang.

Bat Masterson was then sheriff of Ford County, a position he was elected to after his good friend Wyatt Earp encouraged him to run for the office. On many occasions, Masterson and Earp would confront a half-dozen drunken cowboys and subdue them with their pistol butts rather than shoot them. Only flying bullets compelled Earp to draw his weapon. So incensed were certain cattle barons at Earp's manhandling of their cowboys that they posted a $1,000 reward to anyone who would kill Wyatt Earp. A few misguided gunmen tried to collect, one of these being George R. Hoyt.

One night while Earp stood outside the Comique Theater in front of the plaza, listening to the packed crowd inside applaud comedian Eddie Foy, Hoyt rode wildly through the streets, six-gun in hand. He spied Earp and wheeled his horse about, racing across the plaza and, while his horse reared and bucked, fired shot after shot at the marshal. He emptied his gun at Earp, his wild shots missing. Earp coolly withdrew his weapon and fired three times. His first two shots missed the gunman, who was being tossed about by his skittish horse, but the third shot ploughed into Hoyt's forehead. The gunman toppled from his horse, mortally wounded. Hoyt died of his wound a month later.

Earp had to deal with all kinds of killers. James W. "Spike" Kennedy was a hot-headed Texas gunman whose family had showered wealth and favor upon him. Kennedy fell in love with the lovely Dora Hand, who was also known in Dodge City as Fannie Keenan. Dora had been raised in a proper Boston family, had studied voice, and reportedly begun a promising opera career before some unknown tragedy caused her to move West. She had sung in a dozen western hellholes, like Hays and Abilene, and in Dodge City she sang for the raucous, drunken cowboys in saloons and bawdy houses. Mayor James H. Kelley, called Dog, because he once handled General Custer's hounds, made Dora a star by featuring her at his saloon-theater, the Alhambra. Here Kennedy met her and attempted a clumsy seduction. Kelley grabbed the

young Texan and threw him out of his place. Kennedy swore revenge and, early one October morning before dawn, rode into Dodge City and fired two bullets through the front door of Kelley's two-room frame shack. The mayor was not there at the time, but Dora Hand was asleep in the back room and one of the bullets slammed through a wall and killed her.

Kennedy then rode wildly out of town, hooting, and firing his weapon. Earp found the dead woman a short time later and then organized one of the most spectacular posses on record, one that included Bat Masterson, Charles Bassett, and William Tilghman, all famous lawmen of their day. For more than a hundred miles, the four lawmen, Earp in the lead, raced across the prairie after Kennedy. The lawmen brought along extra horses and rode them in relays, whereas Kennedy simply rode his poor mount to death. It collapsed near Meade City. The Texan was kind enough to send a bullet into the stricken animal, but this loud report echoed across the plains and brought the lawmen in hot pursuit. They raced up to Kennedy who took cover behind the body of his dead horse, and fired at them. Masterson, an expert shot, fired a single shot from his rifle. This struck Kennedy's arm, shattering it so that he could not fire his six-gun. Earp and the others closed in as Kennedy shouted: "You s.o.b.'s, I'll get even with you for this!"

As the lawmen rode back to Dodge City, Earp turned in the saddle and told Kennedy: "Your shot killed Dora Hand, not Kelley."

The tough cowboy began to weep and then sobbed: "I wish you had killed me."

In Dodge City, Kennedy was taken to a doctor who removed four inches of bone from his shot-up arm. He was then tried for the murder of Dora Hand but freed for "lack of evidence." Kennedy rode back to Texas where his wealthy parents took him in. He was not heard from again. There were other wild men to tame and Earp stayed in Dodge until 1879, keeping the peace. His pay was meager and the gratitude of citizens was even thinner. In 1879, Earp received a letter from the owners of the Oriental Saloon in Tombstone, Ariz., asking him to come to that town with his brothers to protect the lavish emporium from the gunmen and thugs employed by rival saloon owners. Earp was offered a partnership in the Oriental, which would guarantee him a fortune, more than $1,000 a month. Scarred and worn out with keeping the peace in a half-dozen towns, Earp and his brothers Morgan, Virgil, and James, agreed to the deal and left for Tombstone in 1879. The ever-loyal Doc Holliday also packed up his guns, his cards, and his Bowie knife, and rode along with the Earps.

Tombstone was then the last of the wide-open hellholes. The town teamed with rustlers, thieves, gunmen, gamblers, and whores— the worst flotsam of the West. The community had been founded by wandering prospector Edward Schieffelin. He told a friend that he would find gold or silver in the shadows of the Dragoon Mountains in southeastern Arizona. The friend replied: "All you'll ever find is your tombstone." Schieffelin did strike a bountiful vein of silver, which caused a stampede to the area. Miners quickly dug through silver veins yielding more than $30 million, and the strike then evaporated. What was left was a ramshackle community peopled by the worst dregs of society, a town Schieffelin had whimsically named Tombstone, after the fate his friend had predicted for him.

When Wyatt Earp, his brothers, and Holliday arrived in Tombstone, Pima County sheriff Charles Shibell made Earp a deputy. As a deputy county sheriff, Earp worked with town marshal Fred White but he found Cochise County sheriff John H. Behan siding with the local gunmen. Behan, Earp quickly learned, supported and received money from the most notorious cattle thieves and rustlers in the West, the burgeoning Clanton-McLowery gang, which was headed by Newman H. Clanton, or Old Man Clanton, as he was called. Behan and his crooked deputies looked the other way while the Clantons looted cattle and horses and held up stagecoaches, parceling out some of their spoils to the corrupt sheriff. Clanton's sons, Joseph Isaac (known as Ike), Peter, Finneas "Finn" Clanton, and Billy Clanton, were hard-

Outlaws Newman H. Clanton and his son, Isaac Clanton.

The O.K. Corral, Tombstone, Ariz., mid-1880s.

Outlaws Frank and Tom McLowery, Clanton allies.

The Earps and Clantons battle in the O.K. Corral.

The robbery of the Tombstone stage by Clanton outlaws, 1881.

Pete Spence, killed by Wyatt Earp.

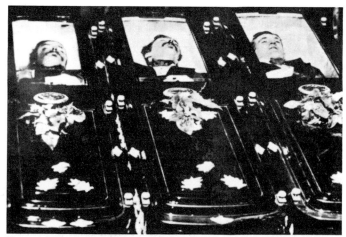

Tom and Frank McLowery and Billy Clanton, in their coffins, 1881.

Sheriff John Behan.

John Clum, Earp ally.

riding cowboys who learned at an early age the art of rustling from their criminally-bent father. Frank and Tom McLowery (or McLaury) worked a small ranch next to the Clanton spread and also worked the Clanton herds, which were mostly stolen and which the McLowerys had helped to thieve from Mexican ranches south of the border.

In addition to the quick guns of the Clantons and McLowerys, lawmen had to contend with an army of fast-draw artists such as Curly Bill Brocius (William B. Graham), Johnny Ringo (Ringgold), Pony Deal, Pete Spence, Frank Patterson, Billy Claiborne, and Frank Stilwell. All of these men, especially Brocius and Ringo, were dour-faced, alcoholic killers, and would shoot a man for staring at them. Stilwell was a sneaky murderer who ran livery stables in the towns of Charleston and Bisbee. He had shot a Mexican cook to death some years earlier simply because the man served him tea instead of coffee. He reportedly killed an elderly miner and took his claim, which Spence used to obtain the livery stables.

It was Brocius who first ran headlong into Wyatt Earp. On an October night in 1880, accompanied by Billy Clanton, Frank and Tom McLowery, Pony Deal, and Brocius rode up and down Allen Street firing their weapons recklessly and harassing anyone foolish enough to walk the rickety slatboard sidewalks. Sheriff White stopped the cowboys at Sixth and Allen streets, and Brocius began to draw his holstered weapon. White reached out and grappled with the gunman, grabbing Brocius' gun, which went off. The bullet struck White in groin and he fell to the dusty street. Just then Earp appeared, ran to Brocius and, pulling his six-gun, brought it down with such force on Brocius' head that he knocked the gunslinger unconscious.

White was rushed to a doctor's office and there magnanimously told witnesses that he had been shot by his own carelessness. He then died. Earp, meanwhile, had confronted the other gunmen, telling them that he would kill any one of them that reached for a weapon. He ordered them out of town and they meekly complied as Earp dragged the unconscious Brocius to jail. Brocius, thanks to White's dying statement, was later released. He would later be shot in the mouth on May 25, 1881, by lawman William Breakenridge, and then hang up his guns, moving to Texas to live out his life in obscurity. Earp, however, later claimed that he tracked down Brocius and killed him.

Meanwhile, Doc Holliday, who busied himself in gambling and gunfights, confronted Sheriff Behan one day in the Oriental when Behan accused Holliday of manipulating a faro game. The deadly dentist challenged Behan, who quickly retreated when Holliday taunted him in front of a jeering crowd. From then on, Behan hated both Earp and Holliday, who later stated that Behan "would spend money to have me killed." But the men who wanted the Earps and Holliday dead were the Clantons. Earp had warned the leader of the gang, Ike Clanton, that he would no longer tolerate the gang's lawless ways in Tombstone. He also ordered Clanton to run his stolen herds of cattle back into Mexico. Then, in March 1881, the Kinnear & Co. stagecoach leaving Tombstone was robbed and driver Bud Philpot was killed by the holdup men. So, too, was passenger Peter Roerig, who was riding atop the stage when the holdup gang began firing at it. The stagecoach, driven by guard Bob Paul, who had answered the bandits with gunfire, managed to elude the thieves and reach Benson.

Earp put together a posse of his brothers Morgan and Virgil Earp, "Buckskin Frank" Leslie, Bat Masterson, and others and began tracking the bandits. The lawmen managed to corner a small-time thief, Luther King, who confessed that he had held the horses of the bandits in their abortive attempt to stop the stagecoach. He named the thieves as Harry Head, Jim Crane, and Bill Leonard, all friends of the Clantons. Earp turned King over to Behan, who was part of the posse and the sheriff returned to Tombstone with the prisoner while Earp and the others sought the other bandits. They failed to track down the killers and rode into Tombstone to discover that King had escaped from Behan's jail. He simply walked out an unlocked back door, according to

most reports, while the crooked Behan looked the other way. When Earp accused Behan of letting King escape, the sheriff then claimed that Doc Holliday, Earp's friend, had tried to rob the stage.

Holliday laughed this charge off, pointing out that Behan hated him for earlier embarrassing the sheriff in front of half of the town. The gun-toting dentist then pointed out that he would have gotten the bullion on the stage by simply shooting the horses, if he had been present which, he insisted, he had not. Earp then concocted a plan to catch the real criminals. He went to Ike Clanton and asked him to bring Head, Crane, and Leonard to a rendezvous. If Clanton cooperated, Earp said, Clanton would receive the sizeable reward then offered for the killer of Philpot and Roerig. He, Earp, would be credited with the arrest and would surely be swept into the office of Pima County Sheriff in the next election. At least, that is the story the insidious Ike Clanton later told to embarrass Wyatt Earp.

Further confusion was created by Big Nose Kate Fisher, also known as Elder. Drunk some time later, she slobbered to Behan a story about how her estranged lover Doc Holliday had indeed held up the stage and shot Philpot and Roerig. Behan swore out an arrest for Holliday the next day, but Earp and friends put up a $5,000 bail. When Big Nose Kate sobered up the next day, she admitted lying about Holliday. He was released and Big Nose Kate left Tombstone and the arms of Doc Holliday forever.

The Bisbee stage was then held up on Sept. 8, 1881, and lawmen interviewed the passengers, who said that one of the masked holdup men had grabbed the $2,500 in gold bullion and then said to the other bandits: "Have we got all the sugar?" Earp, Billy Breakenridge, and others were shocked to hear this statement which they knew was a favorite phrase of Frank Stilwell, who was Sheriff Johnny Behan's chief deputy. Boot marks at the scene of the robbery were matched to Stilwell's boots. He and Pete Spence, Stilwell's livery stable partner, were arrested in Bisbee and returned to stand trial in Tombstone. Both men, of course, were close associates of Ike Clanton, who was incensed that his friends were jailed. He began a smear campaign against Wyatt Earp, saying to anyone who would listen: "Wyatt Earp is telling lies about me in town."

Then one of Clanton's riders, Billy Claiborne, who liked to be called "Billy the Kid," a drunk, braggart, and killer-from-ambush, was arrested and charged with a murder and placed in the Charleston jail. Ike Clanton and others led a raid that freed Claiborne and at the time the gang leader boasted that if the Earps ever dared to jail one of his men in Tombstone, the same thing would happen, a brag that made its way back to Wyatt Earp. All of Tombstone knew that the simmering feud between the Clantons and Earps would break into open warfare. This was looked upon as a family against family confrontation by those who favored the Clantons which removed the myriad illegal acts of the Clantons from the consideration they deserved. The Earp faction was headed by law-and-order citizens such as Mayor John Clum, who had appointed Virgil Earp city marshal in June 1881. Clum and his vigilance committee wholly backed the Earps and were considered the "good citizens" of Tombstone. They were hopelessly outnumbered by the outlaws and gunmen.

The feud boiled over on Oct. 25, 1881, just after midnight. Several gunmen, including Ike Clanton and Doc Holliday, had gathered for a predawn snack in the lunchroom of the Alhambra. Holliday was absolutely fearless, some said mentally unbalanced. He had a long record of bloody gunfights in Denver, Dodge City, and other cattle towns where his fast gun was legendary. "He had a mean disposition and an ungovernable temper," according to his friend Bat Masterson, "and under the influence of liquor was a most dangerous man...among men who did not fear him (he) was very much disliked." The small-framed Holliday, armed with a six-gun despite the ordinance against carrying firearms (a law few in Tombstone obeyed), approached Clanton and said: "Ike, you threaten the Earps again and you'll have to face me, you and your rotten gang." Clanton sneered and swore at Holliday. "You s.o.b.

The deadly gunfighter Ben Thompson, who was disarmed by Wyatt Earp in Ellsworth, Kan., shown circa 1875.

William Smith, with whom Earp had a bloody fistfight in Wichita, Kan., shown at right in 1875.

The legendary lawman, William Barclay "Bat" Masterson and Dodge City, Kan., circa 1879.

Drunken killer Billy Thompson and Tombstone, Ariz., at the time of the Earp-Clanton feud, 1881.

of a cowboy!" Holliday roared back. "Go get your gun and go to work."

"The Earps are going to get plenty of fight from us," Clanton said to Holliday.

Just then Morgan Earp entered the room, heard the remark, and told Clanton: "Go heel yourself! You can have all the fight you want right now."

Clanton spread back the bottom of his coat to show that he was not armed. In a quavering voice he said: "Don't shoot me in the back, will you, Morg?" He then turned and walked out of the lunchroom but he returned a half hour later, still unarmed, going to the gambling hall of the Alhambra and boldly sitting down to a poker game with, of all people, Morgan Earp. But also sitting at the table was the venal Johnny Behan, Clanton's sponsor, along with Tom McLowery, Clanton ally. The game broke up some hours later, and Clanton was about the leave the Alhambra. Doc Holliday appeared and again berated Clanton. Jim Flynn, a city policeman, appeared and broke up the argument. It was about 7 a.m., Oct. 26, 1881.

Two hours later Ike Clanton saw city marshal Virgil Earp in the middle of the street and walked up to him, a sneer on his face. The loud-mouthed Clanton said: "If you were one of them threatening me last night, you can have your fight." The gang leader then turned about and sauntered away. Virgil Earp thought he was still half drunk. About noon Morgan and Virgil Earp, patrolling the streets, saw Ike Clanton and approached him, seeing that he carried a gun in his belt, hidden behind his coat. They ordered him to turn in his gun and he refused. Virgil Earp pulled his six-gun and, with a lightning move, banged it against Clanton's head. Clanton, half conscious, was then dragged by the Earps into court where Judge Wallace fined the gunman $25 for carrying a concealed weapon.

Just as the cowed Clanton was about to be released, Tom McLowery ran into the court room, screaming oaths at the Earps. Wyatt Earp was on hand and he slammed his six-gun against McLowery's head. He then dragged the unconscious McLowery to the street and threw him into the mud. Clanton then helped McLowery to his feet and, both swearing at the three Earp brothers, they went down the street, vowing revenge. A half hour went by before a town drunk appeared before the three Earps and told them: "There are some men want to see you fellows down at the O.K. Corral."

Wyatt Earp stepped forward and asked: "Who are these men?"

"The McLowery brothers, the Clantons, and Bill Claiborne."

The somber lawman turned to his brothers Virgil and Morgan and said: "Let's go." The three tall Earps checked their six-guns. They began their historic walk to the O.K. Corral wearing long black coats, black, broad-rimmed hats, shiny boots, and starched white shirts with string ties. Before they had gone half a block, Doc Holliday suddenly appeared. He was carrying a shotgun. Wyatt Earp nodded in his direction and the loyal gunman joined the Earps, all four men striding confidently down Fremont Street. The residents of Tombstone watched them go by, resolute and knowing what waited for them at the narrow, small corral which squatted between two adobe buildings down the street.

Someone on the sidewalk standing close to Doc Holliday as he passed by, said to the determined dentist: "Let them have it."

"All right," was Holliday's only reply.

Johnny Behan, who was sitting in a barber shop getting a shave, saw the Earps marching down the street. He jumped out of the chair and ran into the street, the barber's sheet still tucked about his neck, lather on his face. Behan was close to the O.K. Corral at Fourth and Fremont streets and he was soon joined by Frank McLowery. The two conferred and then McLowery walked quickly back to the O.K. Corral where he joined his brother Tom, Ike and Billy Clanton, and Billy Claiborne. Behan turned and went up the street where he approached Virgil Earp, having a brief conversation with him. Behan later claimed that he told Earp that it was his duty to disarm the men at the O.K. Corral, not to bring a gunfight to them, a lie. Behan actually tried to

arrest the Earps but Wyatt brushed him aside, saying: "We won't be arrested today by you, Behan."

They continued on their way, with Behan standing in the middle of the street looking after them. A few minutes later the four men turned about and faced the entrance of the little corral where the five rustlers stood waiting. Virgil Earp was the ranking lawman and he spoke for the Earps: "You men are under arrest. Throw up your hands!"

Frank McLowery and Billy Clanton reached for the six-guns on their hips. Virgil Earp shouted: "Hold it, I don't mean that. I've come to disarm you!" Behan later insisted that Tom McLowery claimed he was not armed and that Billy Clanton shouted to the lawmen and Holliday: "Don't shoot me. I don't want to fight." According to best reports, these were typical Behan fabrications. All of the outlaws were armed, not only with six-guns but with rifles, either in their hands or in scabbards on their nearby horses and within reach.

The two groups stood motionless for some moments. Then, almost at the same second, Billy Clanton and Wyatt Earp drew their guns. Then Frank McLowery drew his six-gun and both he and Billy Clanton fired at Wyatt at the same time, their shots going wild. Wyatt fired once, his bullet striking Frank McLowery in the stomach. At that second, the boastful coward, Ike Clanton, leaped forward, running to Wyatt Earp and whining as he grabbed the lawman's sleeve: "Don't shoot me! Don't kill me! I'm not fighting!"

"The fighting has now commenced," Earp shouted at him. "Go to fighting or get away!"

Ike Clanton left his brother and Billy and his friends by dashing across the street and disappearing down an alley while the gunfight went on. "Throw up your hands!" said Virgil Earp but the outlaws were now firing rapidly at the Earps. Frank McLowery, the first to receive a mortal wound, staggered through the smoke of the banging six-guns and moved slowly across the street, gun still in hand. He pitched forward and fell on the wooden sidewalk but he managed to get off another shot which whizzed past Wyatt Earp. Billy Claiborne fired several shots at Virgil Earp and then fled in the direction Ike Clanton had taken, running into the street, firing as he ran, racing into the nearby photographic studio owned by C.S. Fly, where he hid from the lawmen.

Tom McLowery, six-gun blazing, stepped toward the entrance of the corral. He fired a shot at Morgan Earp and two at Doc Holliday which ripped through Holliday's coat. Holliday aimed his shotgun and fired both barrels into McLowery, blasting him to death. As he fell, the second McLowery brother to die, he squeezed off a round that ploughed into Morgan Earp's shoulder. Billy Clanton, age nineteen, had received a wound in his right hand from a shot fired either by Morgan or Virgil Earp, but the tough little gunman shifted his six-gun to the left hand and fired several bullets, one of which struck Virgil Earp in the leg and sent him to the ground. He then followed Billie Claiborne's escape route, running down the street toward Fly's photographic gallery. As he ran, he fired at the Earps, one of his bullets creasing Holliday's back. The Earps fired back at him and he was hit another three times. He fell in front of the gallery.

Everyone was now down. Only Wyatt Earp stood alone, unharmed, as the smoke from gun battle drifted down the street, offering a clear view of the carnage. Earp turned and followed Billy Clanton, standing over him. The mortally wounded gunman looked up at Earp, cursing him and saying: "God, God, won't someone give me some more cartridges for a last shot?" He then sank back and died. The historic gunfight at the O.K. Corral was over and within days became western legend. It had lasted no more than two or three minutes and from thirty to fifty shots had been fired by both factions. Two lawmen, Virgil and Morgan Earp, were seriously wounded, and Doc Holliday was slightly injured. Three dead outlaws lay in the street: Tom and Frank McLowery and Billy Clanton. Stories and whole books would be written about this most famous of Western gun battles and more than a half-dozen motion pictures would record the event. Few such incidents in the history of the Old West were marked with such passionate lore. And, because of this standup, high noon fight, the memory of Wyatt Earp would be forever linked to the image of raw courage and dedication to duty.

Wyatt Earp walked back to his stricken brothers and he and the slightly wounded Holliday lifted Morgan and Virgil Earp to their feet and helped them back up the street to a doctor's office. While Virgil and Morgan were recuperating, Virgil Earp was discharged as city marshal and Wyatt Earp and Doc Holliday were arrested on charges of murder, on warrants sworn out by the cowardly Ike Clanton and his sneaky sidekick, Sheriff Behan. Justice of the peace Wells Spicer heard the case and quickly dismissed the charges against Earp and Holliday. This was not the end of the Clantons, however.

Ike Clanton organized other outlaws who would shoot down the Earps from ambush in the coming months. Virgil Earp, who had recovered from his wounds, was entering the Oriental Saloon on the night of Nov. 28, 1881. Several shots were fired at him from the shadows and a bullet entered his back. He was crippled for the rest of his life. Morgan Earp was next. On the night of Mar. 17, 1882, four Clanton henchmen, Pete Spence, Frank Stilwell, Hank Swilling, and Florentino "Indian Charlie" Cruz, slipped behind a stack of kegs in Hatch's Saloon and when Morgan Earp entered and began to play pool, the four gunmen opened up and shot Earp in the back, killing him.

Wyatt Earp, joined by Holliday, put the body of Morgan Earp on a westbound train. They, along with the crippled Virgil Earp and James Earp, who had been permanently crippled in the Civil War and did not serve as a lawman, traveled west toward California. But Wyatt and Holliday got off the train at Tucson, Ariz. There they were met by Warren Earp, who had rounded up Texas Jack Vermillion, Turkey Creek Jack Johnson, and Sherman McMasters, three specially appointed lawmen. This posse then went in search of the killers who had shot down Morgan and Virgil Earp. Wyatt had received word that Clanton gunmen would be waiting at Tucson to ambush the surviving Earp family members in the train yards.

Wyatt and the other posse members searched the yards and, according to Wyatt's later statements, they saw four figures crouching behind some flatcars. Wyatt approached them and one of them, Pete Spence, bolted, running on top of a flatcar and then turning to fire on Earp. Wyatt fired a single bullet from his six-gun which smashed into Spence's heart, killing him. When he turned, now cradling a shotgun, Earp saw Frank Stilwell step from the shadows. He had reserved his anger for Stilwell who was the one who had led the ambush of Morgan Earp. Outlaw and lawmen stood only a foot or so apart and, in Earp's own words, "Stilwell caught the barrel of my Wells Fargo gun with both hands. I forced the gun down until the muzzle of the right barrel was just underneath Stilwell's heart. He found his voice: 'Morg!' he said, and then a second time, 'Morg!' I've often wondered what made him say that...I let him have it. The muzzle of one barrel was just underneath the heart. He got the second before he hit the ground."

With his brother Warren, Doc Holliday, Vermillion, Johnson, and McMasters at his side, Wyatt Earp tracked down each and every one of Clanton's hired killers. According to his own later statements, Earp found Florentino "Indian Charlie" Cruz outside of Tombstone. Wyatt told the gunman to count to three and both men then drew. Cruz fell with a bullet in his heart. Wyatt raced after Curly Bill Brocius, both men riding their mounts to death on a harrowing plains chase which ended at Iron Springs. Here Brocius advanced on Earp as the intrepid lawman stoically marched toward his prey, both firing as they moved. Brocius fell, shot to death, as Earp pumped one bullet after another into him. In the shadows of the Whetstone Mountains, Earp tracked down and killed Johnny Ringo.

The Clanton family had been reduced to N.H. "Old Man" Clanton, Ike, and Finn. N.H. Clanton was shot to death in July 1881 while he was on a rustling raid. Finn, a non-violent member of the clan, lived out a calm life, dying at the turn of the century. Ike Clanton, while Earp and his men sought out the killers of Morgan Earp, fled to Mexico and hid under an assumed name. When Earp gave up the search for him, he returned to the Tombstone area, but he took up his old rustling ways and was shot to death in 1887 by lawmen.

Doc Holliday, Earp's good and loyal friend, lived only a few more years after the historic O.K. Corral gunfight. Wracked with consumption, he was taken to a sanitorium near Glenwood Springs, Colo., by Wyatt Earp and here the deadly dentist died, his Bowie knife still tied about his neck, his six-gun at his side, and his shotgun on the bed with him. Wyatt Earp outlived them all. His life was nomadic for several decades. The great lawman had married for the first time in 1870, but his wife died a few months following the wedding. Earp's second wife, Celia "Mattie" Blaylock, who had accompanied him to Tombstone, separated from the lawman after his Tombstone days and tragically wound up living in the seedy gold and silver towns as a prostitute, committing suicide in Pinal, Ariz., on July 3, 1888.

Earp finally moved to his family home at Colston, Calif., marrying again, to Josie Earp in 1882 while in San Francisco. He returned to Tombstone briefly and then wandered about the West through the gold camps of Idaho and Colorado, but his reputation was too much with him. He traveled to Alaska during the gold rush at the turn of the century. Earlier he was a referee of notable boxing matches. (His most notable fight was the championship battle between Bob Fitzsimmons and Tom Sharkey in 1896.) Earp raised thoroughbred horses in San Diego in the 1890s. He and his wife prospected throughout Nevada and briefly owned and operated a Tonopah saloon. They finally settled in Los Angeles. Only a few months before his death in 1929, Earp told his story to Stuart Lake.

He died at the age of eighty on Jan. 13, 1929, in the arms of his wife, Josie. Wyatt Earp's last words to his biographer were: "The greatest consolation I have in growing old is the hope that after I'm gone they'll grant me the peaceful obscurity I haven't been able to get in life." Some claimed he had stretched the truth, but if he had, it mattered little. The facts of his astounding, spectacular life needed no embellishment. He remains, in fact and fiction, the greatest U.S. lawman of the Old West, and the considerable efforts on the part of certain revisionist historians have failed to change that image. Wyatt Earp lived and the great deeds of his day happened in a West where the legend of the hero cannot perish. See: **Bassett, Charles; Brocius, William; Claiborne, William; Clanton-McLowery Gang; Holliday, John H.; Masterson, William Barclay; Ringo, John.**

REF.: Argall, *Outlawry and Justice in Old Arizona;* Axford, *Around Western Campfires;* Bakarich, *Empty Saddles;* Bartholomew, *Wyatt Earp, 1848-1880, The Untold Story;* _____, *Wyatt Earp, 1879-1882, The Man and the Myth;* Bechdolt, *When the West Was Young;* Beebe, *The American West;* Benedict, *The Roundup;* Bishop, *Old Mexico and Her Lost Provinces;* Blythe, *A Pictorial Souvenir;* Boyer, *The Suppressed Murder of Wyatt Earp;* Breakenridge, *Helldorado;* Breihan, *Great Lawmen of the West;* Brent, *Great Western Heroes;* Briggs, *Arizona and New Mexico, 1882;* Brophy, *Arizona Sketch Book;* Brown, *Reminiscences of Senator William M. Stewart, of Nevada;* Burns, *Tombstone;* Carr, *The West is Still Wild;* Carter, *The Old Sergeant's Story;* Casey, *The Black Hills and Their Incredible Characters;* CBA; Chafetz, *Play the Devil;* Chilton, *The Book of the West;* Chisholm, *Brewery Gulch;* Chrisman, *Fifty Years on the Owl Hoot Trail;* _____, *The Ladder of the Rivers;* _____, *Lost Trails of the Cimarron;* Clark, *The Came the Railroads;* Clum, *Apache Agent;* _____, *It All Happened in Tombstone;* Coolidge, *Fighting Men of the West;* Corle, *Desert Country;* Cox, *Luke Short and His Era;* Cunningham, *Triggernometry;* Cushman, *The Great North Trail;* De Veny, *The Establishment of Law and Order on Western Plains;* Dobie, *Cow People;* Drago, *Great American Cattle Trails;* _____, *Outlaws on Horseback;* _____, *Red River Valley;* _____, *Wild, Woolly & Wicked;* Dunlop, *Doctors of the American Frontier;* Durham, *The Negro Cowboys;* Dykstra, *The Cattle Towns;* Eaton, *Bucky O'Neill of Arizona;* Elman, *Fired in Anger;* Erwin, *The Southwest of John H. Slaughter;* Farber, *Texans With Guns;* Fast, *The Last Frontier;* Fisher and Holmes, *Gold*

Rushes and Mining Camps; Florin, *Ghost Town Album;* Forrest, *Arizona's Dark and Bloody Ground;* Franke, *They Plowed Up Hell in Old Cochise;* Frantz, *The Arizona Cowboy;* French, *Railroadman;* Ganzhorn, *I've Killed Men;* Gard, *Frontier Justice;* Gardner, *The Old Wild West;* Glasscock, *Gold in Them Hills;* Godwin, *Murder U.S.A.;* Greever, *The Bonanza West;* Gregory, *True Wild West Stories;* Haley, *Jeff Milton, A Good Man with a Gun;* Hall-Quest, *Wyatt Earp, Marshal of the Old West;* Hamlin, *Hamlin's Tombstone Picture Gallery;* Hammond, *The Autobiography of John Hays Hammond;* Hart, *Old Forts of the Southwest;* Hart, *My Life East and West;* Haskell, *City of the Future;* Hendricks, *The Bad Man of the West;* Hening, *George Curry;* Hogan, *The Life and Death of Clay Allison;* Hollon, *The Southwest, Old and New;* Holloway, *Texas Gun Lore;* Hopper, *Famous Texas Landmarks;* Horan, *Across the Cimarron;* ____, *Desperate Men;* ____, *The Great American West;* ____ and Sann, *Pictorial History of the Wild West;* Hunter, *The Story of Lottie Deno;* Hunter and Rose, *The Album of Gunfighters;* Hutchinson, *The Life & Personal Writings of Eugene Manlove Rhodes;* ____, *A Notebook of the Old West;* Jaastad, *Man of the West;* Jahns, *The Frontier World of Doc Holliday;* Jameson, *Heroes by the Dozen;* Jelinek, *Ellsworth, Kansas, 1867-1947;* ____, *Ninety Years of Ellsworth;* Johnson, *Famous Lawmen of the Old West;* Johnston, *The Last Roundup;* Kane, *100 Years Ago with the Law and the Outlaw;* Keithley, *Bucky O'Neill;* Kelly, *The Sky Was Their Roof;* Kemp, *Cow Dust and Saddle Leather;* King, *Mavericks;* ____, *Wranglin' the Past;* Knight, *Wild Bill Hickok;* Koller, *The Fireside Book of Guns;* ____, *The American Gun;* Lake, *Under Cover for Wells Fargo;* Lake, *Wyatt Earp, Frontier Marshal;* Lamar, *The Far Southwest;* Lesure, *Adventures in Arizona;* Lockwood, *Pioneer Days in Arizona;* Ludlum, *Great Shooting Stories;* Lyon, *The Wild, Wild West;* McCarty, *The Enchanted West;* McCarty, *The Gunfighters;* McClintock, *Arizona;* McCool, *So Said the Coroner;* McCready, *Railroads in Days of Steam;* Marshall, *Swinging Doors;* Martin, *The Earps of Tombstone;* ____, *Tombstone's Epitaph;* Masterson, *Famous Gunfighters of the Western Frontier;* Metz, *John Selman;* Michelson, *Mankillers at Close Range;* Miller, *Bill Tilghman, Marshal of the Last Frontier;* Miller, *Arizona, The Last Frontier;* ____, *The Arizona Story;* Miller, *Kansas Frontier Police Officers;* ____, *Some Widely Publicized Western Police Officers;* ____ and Langsdorf and Richmond, *Kansas, A Pictorial History;* ____ and Snell, *Great Gunfighters of the Kansas Cowtowns;* ____, *Why the West Was Wild;* Monaghan, *The Great Rascal;* Moody, *Stagecoach West;* Morgan, *Shooting Sheriffs of the Wild West;* Myers, *Doc Holliday;* ____, *The Last Chance;* Nash, *Bloodletters and Badmen;* North, *The Saga of the Cowboy;* O'Connor, *Bat Masterson;* ____, *Pat Garrett;* Olsson, *Welcome to Tombstone;* O'Neal, *Encyclopedia of Western Gunfighters;* Orman, *A Room for the Night;* Paine, *Texas Ben Thompson;* Parker, *Gold in the Black Hills;* Parkhill, *The Wildest of the West;* Parrish, *The Great Plains;* Parsons, *The Private Journal of George Whitwell Parsons;* Patch, *Reminiscences of Fort Huachuca;* Pence, *The Ghost Towns of Wyoming;* Penfield, *Western Sheriffs and Marshals;* Plenn, *Texas Hellion, The True Story of Ben Thompson;* Preece, *Lone Star Man;* Quiett, *Pay Dirt;* Raine, *Famous Sheriffs and Western Outlaws;* ____, *Guns of the Frontier;* ____, *Riders West;* Rascoe, *Belle Starr;* Rath, *Early Ford County;* Rickards, *Buckskin Frank Leslie;* ____, *Mysterious Dave Mathers;* Ringgold, *Frontier Days in the Southwest;* Robinson, *The Story of Arizona;* Rosa, *The Gunfighter, Man or Myth?;* ____, *They Called Him Wild Bill;* Ruth, *Great Days in the West;* Ryan, *A Skeptic Dude in Arizona;* Sanders, *The Sumner County Story;* Santee, *Lost Pony Tracks;* Schmedding, *Cowboy and Indian Trader;* Schmitt, *Fighting Editors;* Shirley, *Pawnee Bill;* Sims, *Gun-Toters I Have Known;* Sloan, *History of Arizona;* Small, *The Best of True West;* Snell, *Painted Ladies of the Cowtown Frontier;* Sonnichsen, *Billy King's Tombstone;* Stanley, *Clay Allison;* ____, *Dave Rudabaugh;* ____, *Fort Bascom;* ____, *Jim Courtright;* Steckmesser, *The Western Hero in History and Legend;* Sterling, *Famous Western Outlaw-Sheriff Battles;* Streeter, *The Kaw;* ____, *Tragedies of a Kansas Cow Town;* Taylor, *Colorado, South of the Border;* Thompson, *Bat Masterson, The Dodge City Years;* Tilghman, *Marshal of the Last Frontier;* ____, *Spotlight: Bat Masterson and Wyatt Earp;* Toledano, *J. Edgar Hoover;* Train, *On the Trail of the Bad Men;* Turner, *Avery Turner;* Upshur, *As I Recall Them;* Vestal, *Queen of Cowtowns;* ____, *Short Grass Country;* ____, *Wagons West;* Wallace, *Gunnison County;* ____, *History With the Hide Off;* Walters, *Tombstone's Yesterdays;* Ward, *Bits of Silver;* Waters, *The Colorado;* ____, *The Story of Mrs. Virgil Earp;* Waters, *A Gallery of Western Badmen;* Watson, *A Century of Gunmen;* Way, *The Tombstone Story;* Wellman, *The Blazing Southwest;* ____, *Glory, God and Gold;* ____, *The Trampling Herd;* White, *Bat Masterson;* White, *The Autobiography of a Durable Sinner;* ____, *My Texas 'Tis of Thee;* ____, *Texas, An Informal Biography;* Whittemore, *One-Way Ticket to Kansas;* Wilson, *Treasure Express;* Wilson, *Out of the West;* Wister, *Owen Wister Out West;* Wright, *Dodge City;* Wyllys, *Arizona;* (FICTION) Henry, *Who Rides With Wyatt;* (FILM), *Law and Order,* 1931; *Frontier Marshal,* 1932; *Frontier Marshal,* 1935; *In Early Arizona,* 1938; *Dodge City,* 1939; *Frontier Marshal,* 1939; *Law and Order,* 1942; *Tombstone, The Town Too Tough to Die,* 1942; *My Darling Clementine,* 1946; *Winchester 73,* 1950; *Masterson of Kansas,* 1954; *Wichita,* 1955; *Gunfight at the O.K. Corral,* 1957; *Cheyenne Autumn,* 1964; *The Outlaws Is Coming,* 1965; *Hour of the Gun,* 1967; *Doc,* 1970.

Earp Brothers, prom. 1870s-1880s, U.S., law enfor. off. Born and raised in the Midwest by a hard-working farming father, the Earp brothers, Morgan, Virgil, Warren, and Wyatt, all became law enforcement officers. Morgan, the most easy going of the brothers, served as a marshal in Butte, Mont., and was later sheriff of Ford County, Kan., before joining his brothers Virgil and Wyatt in Tombstone, Ariz., in 1880. He and Virgil and Wyatt Earp, and John H. "Doc" Holliday faced the Clanton-McLowery clan in the 1881 battle of the O.K. Corral. Morgan Earp was killed on Mar. 18, 1882 while playing billiards with Bob Hatch in Campbell and Hatch's Billiard Parlor in Tombstone. Several armed men, members of the Clanton-McLowery gang, shot Morgan Earp through an open back door of the billiard parlor and then fled. Bullets penetrated his spinal column and stomach. Wyatt Earp was watching the game at the time and rushed to the alleyway but found the killers had fled.

Morgan Earp was taken to a couch in an adjoining card room and there, while his brothers Wyatt, Virgil, Warren, and James stood by with the Earp wives, he died in less than an hour. Three doctors tried desperately to save Earp but his wounds were fatal. When several men tried to remove him to a doctor's office, Morgan cried out: "Stop, I can't stand it! This is the last game of pool I'll ever play." He whispered a few words into Wyatt's ear and then died. Wyatt Earp and others avenged the murder of Morgan Earp by tracking down and killing the murderers of Morgan Earp.

Virgil Earp served in the Union Army during the Civil War, along with his older brothers James and Newton. After the war, Virgil drove a stagecoach out of Council Bluffs, Iowa, and was, with his brothers Morgan, James, and Wyatt, later involved in a wild two-hour street brawl with five other men in Lamar, Mo., where Wyatt was a peace officer. He later served on the Dodge City police force and moved to Arizona in 1876, prospecting and farming. He briefly served as a deputy and helped to track down two outlaws, killing one in a gun battle. He arrived in Tombstone to serve as marshal in June 1881.

The following October, Virgil, along with his brothers Morgan and Wyatt, and Doc Holliday, shot it out with the Clanton-McLowery outlaws at the O.K. Corral. Following this battle, Clanton gunmen, on the night of Dec. 28, 1881, shot Virgil Earp from ambush as he left Tombstone's Oriental Saloon. The gunmen fired shotguns from the shadows, wounding Virgil, who was rushed to a doctor's office where buckshot had peppered his left side and arm, along with his back. His wife Allie appeared and Virgil told her: "Never mind, I've still got one arm left to hug you with."

Wyatt Earp arrived and, just before Virgil was given gas in preparation of an operation, he said to his brother: "Wyatt, when they get me under, don't let them take my arm off. If I have to be buried I want both arms on me." He survived and kept his arm but was a cripple for life. Virgil Earp was taken to the family homestead in Colton, Calif., where he recovered from his wounds. He later prospected with his wife and, still later, was elected city marshal of Colton. He then returned to prospecting with his wife Allie and died of pneumonia in Goldfield, Nev., in 1905.

Warren Earp, the youngest of the Earps who served as lawmen, joined his brothers Morgan, Virgil, and Wyatt in Tombstone in

1880. He was made a deputy by his brother Virgil, then marshal, but he was absent from Tombstone when his brothers Virgil, Morgan, and Wyatt shot it out with the Clanton-McLowery outlaws. Warren Earp later joined Wyatt in tracking down the killers of Morgan Earp. Warren Earp later prospected and served as a stage driver in Globe, Ariz. He moved to Wilcox, Ariz., and there, in 1900, got into a drunken fight with a cowboy named Johnny Boyet. Boyet shot and killed Warren, who was unarmed at the time. Boyet was acquitted on grounds of self-defense, the jury believing that even an Earp without a gun was more dangerous than an opponent with a blazing six-gun in his hand. See: **Clanton-McLowery Gang; Earp, Wyatt Berry Stapp; Holliday, John H.; O.K. Corral.** REF.: *CBA.*

Earth to Ashes, 1939, a novel by Alan Brock. Two murder cases figure prominently in this work of fiction, the author obviously drawing upon the so-called "Blazing Car Murder" committed by Alfred Rouse (Brit. 1930) and the strange, unsolved murder of Evelyn Foster (Brit. 1931). See: **Foster, Evelyn; Rouse, Alfred Arthur.**

Earullo, Fred, 1946- , U.S., pol. mal.-mansl. Three Chicago policemen were arrested after Richard Ramey, fifty-one years old, died of massive internal and external injuries from a beating after he was arrested for smoking on a Chicago transit train. On July 6, 1980, Ramey, a former mental patient, was allegedly kicked, beaten, and punched while handcuffed in the Jackson Park transit station by Chicago police officers Fred Earullo, thirty-two; Fred Christiano, thirty-five; and Louis Klisz, thirty-four. An autopsy showed Ramey had fifteen broken bones. On Dec. 15, 1981, Christiano was acquitted of murder charges. Eight witnesses testified that they watched as the officers beat Ramey. One police officer testified that he had responded to a "battery in progress" call and had seen Ramey walking under his own power, handcuffed, and offering no resistance. When the officers and the arrested man reached another station less than a mile away Ramey had to be carried and was not wearing shoes. Assistant state's attorney Frank DeBoni said both Earullo and Klisz were "exceptionally brutal and heinous," and that both had beaten and kicked the handcuffed man. On Dec. 23, after an eleven-day trial, Earullo and Klisz were convicted of involuntary manslaughter and official misconduct. Defense attorney Samuel S. Banks said he would appeal the case. On Feb. 3, 1982, Earullo, a ten-year veteran of the force, was given a two-and-a-half year prison sentence. Judge Cieslik said Earullo played a "nominal" role in the crime, moving witnesses away from the scene, explaining, "This is police business." Klisz, a twelve-year veteran of the force, whose actions the judge said bordered on "sadistic," was sentenced to an eight-year jail term. REF.: *CBA.*

East, Winifred, 1901-29, Brit., (unsolv.) mur. On the evening of Mar. 13, 1929, Winifred East caught the 7:42 train out of Barnehurst, England, but she never made it home to Essex. The decapitated body of the 28-year-old woman was found along the railroad tracks the following morning. The passengers and employees that rode the train could give British police little information. A window in East's compartment had been broken, but there were no witnesses. An autopsy ruled out sexual assault, but confirmed that East had been struck several times in the small of her back. The victim's empty purse was found along the tracks, which led officials to believe robbery was the motive for the murder. The case remains unsolved.

REF.: *CBA;* Whitbread, *The Railway Policemen.*

Eastman, Edward (Edward Osterman, AKA: Monk, Joseph Marvin, Joseph Morris, Edward Delaney, William Delaney), 1873-1920, U.S., org. crime. A brutal, cretinous thug who never hesitated to hit a person, any person, who displeased him, Edward Eastman was one of the first powerhouse crime bosses in New York City. He was a thorough product of the streets, with little formal education, yet he was clever and inventive. Eastman also possessed an instinctive ability to serve the right masters, these being the powerful bosses that ran Tammany, New York's ruling political club. His wealth and influence stemmed from Tammany's supreme authority and it was Tammany that nurtured and supported this most feared of gangster killers.

Eastman was born in the Williamsburg section of Brooklyn. His father, an upstanding grocer, set up his son in a small pet shop next to the grocery when Eastman was about twenty. Although the youth had a deep fondness for cats and birds, he had no business aptitude, or at least expressed an utter disinterest in the lifestyle of a shopkeeper. He departed for Manhattan where he assumed the name of Edward Eastman and quickly got a job as the top bouncer in a hellhole called the New Irving Hall. By this time Eastman had been in so many fights that his face had come to resemble a much-scarred basketball. One contemporary writer described him at this time, about 1893, as having "a bullet-shaped head...a broken nose and a pair of cauliflower ears. He had heavily veined, sagging jowls, and a short bull neck, plentifully scarred with battle marks, as were his cheeks." Eastman always appeared as if needing a haircut and he wore a derby hat several sizes too small that perched awkwardly atop his lion's head. Police of the day claimed that Eastman affected his small hat and tight-fitting checkered suits to accent his bulky body and make himself appear more formidable than his actual five-foot-five-inch frame.

That Eastman was fearsome there was no doubt. At the New Irving and other bars where he kept the peace as a bouncer, Eastman strutted about with a large club, a pistol on his hip, and brass knuckles on both hands. He took great pride in beating up unruly customers and his club, after about nine months of use, bore forty-nine notches. These carved gashes supposedly represented victims of Eastman's rage, knockouts all, but some claimed they represented deaths of those who got in the gangster's way. Eastman proved himself a tidy man in some respects. After counting up the forty-nine notches, the thug looked over to the bar to see a small, quiet man sitting unobtrusively, hunched over a beer. Eastman marched up to this unsuspecting tippler and without warning or provocation

Edward "Monk" Eastman, New York gangster.

brought his club down on the stranger's head, smashing the man unconscious to the floor. When asked why he attacked this obviously innocent creature, Eastman, pulling out a knife and gouging out another notch on his club, replied: "I just wanted to make it an even fifty."

While working in the dives of Corlear's Hook and later at Silver Dollar Smith's (a famous drinking spa where the floor was inlaid with silver dollars), Eastman encountered several low-echelon Tammany politicians who saw potential use for this uncompromising thug. He was taken into the Tenth Ward clubhouse as a member and told to organize a gang of arm-breakers who would assure elections in Tammany's favor. Eastman went about his job with vigor and by the mid-1890s, he was commanding more than 1,200 of the most vicious gangsters, controlling the Lower East Side of Manhattan with such absolute authority that police never interfered with his rackets and patrolmen stepped into the gutter to let the peacock-strutting Eastman pass by. Rival gangsters had fearfully noted Eastman's monkey-like face and had christened him Monk, a name that stayed with the thug for the rest of his volatile days.

Eastman made his home two floors above a laundry near Broome and Chrystie streets. His meals were cooked by a bevy of young prostitutes who also worked the streets for him, turning back 90 percent of their profits to Eastman. These unhappy ladies were regularly beat up by Eastman and one of them had the audacity to complain to the police who arrested the gang boss. Eastman merely laughed at the arresting officer, saying: "It ain't nothin', officer. Rosie here ain't as dainty as she could be." He pointed to the complaining woman at the officer's side, telling the policeman that he had escorted the woman to a restaurant where she had made a "pig of herself. I tol' her not to wipe her nose wit da tablecloth. Manners is important! Anyway, I only give her a little poke, just enough to put a shanty on her glimmer. But I always takes off me knucks first."

As a gang boss, Eastman paid his hundreds of thugs well, giving them 30 percent of the take from all robberies they committed in his territory. These apprentice hoodlums were mostly Jewish and represented the last great Jewish gang in New York. Among their ever-increasing numbers was Arnold Rothstein, later to become America's most notorious racket-banker, sports event fixer, and high-rolling gambler. Others who aped Eastman with his brash manners, clipped speech and willingness to fight included Max "Kid Twist" Zwerbach, Big Jack Zelig, and a host of other thugs who would make infamous names for themselves at the turn of the century.

Those who worked for Eastman began as teenagers, learning the art of pickpocketing, then graduating to petty thievery and finally armed robbery. The larger boys Eastman selected for his goon squads, which would swoop down on strikebreakers or union men, whomever the bosses paid them to hospitalize. So many men were sent to Bellevue as a result of Eastman's beatings and those administered by his men that the recovery ward was dubbed Eastman Pavilion. But it was at election time when Eastman and his armies of goons took their bloody bows, delivering the entire Lower East Side of New York into Tammany's greedy hands with gruesome regularity. "He was the best man they ever had at the polls," one Manhattan detective later grudgingly remarked about Eastman.

Strong-arm work returned good pay for those days, so much so that Eastman printed up a list of prices for clients. Services provided by his thugs included: "Ear chawed off, $15; Leg or arm broke, $19; Shot in leg, $25; Stab, $25; Doing the big job (murder), $100 and up." By the time Eastman issued this brutal wish-list in 1898, he had already established gangster tradition by going fully armed, being the first New York gang boss to carry a pistol at all times, along with his customary blackjacks, brass knuckles, and club. Eastman would look over each day's assignment sheets and select a blackjacking or beating assignment for himself, commenting: "I likes to beat up a guy every now and then. It keeps me hand in."

"The boss will stand for anything but murder," one of Eastman's goons told a reporter at the turn of the century, unless, of course, the killing was approved by Eastman himself. Monk's prestige grew to such impressive proportions that he acted as a crime broker, licensing gamblers, bordello owners, and thieves so that they could operate in his domain for a daily price. Eastman himself had murdered more than fifty men, it was reported, and his wholesale killings soon spread outside his territory which, by 1900, caused him to confront the powerful Five Points Gang under the command of Paul A. Kelly (Paolo Vaccarelli). Tammany, as usual, played a double hand by encouraging Kelly, a much more refined gangster who used his muscle prudently, to edge into Eastman's rackets. Moreover, Tammany began to support Kelly by giving his operations police protection and this encouraged the police to begin pressuring Eastman.

Kelly himself ordered Eastman killed in early 1901 and his Five Pointers, numbering more than 1,000 gun-carrying gangsters, put out a red alert for the gang boss. Eastman himself made their search easy when he boldly sauntered into Five Points territory, the Bowery, one night armed with only his trusty brass knuckles and a slingshot. As he approached Chatham Square a half dozen Five Pointers jumped him. Eastman fought like a lion, knocking down three of his attackers but a fourth pulled a gun and fired two bullets into Eastman's stomach before fleeing with the others.

Eastman closed the gaping wound with his fingers and staggered to Gouverneur Hospital, where doctors did not expect him to live. Yet he slowly recovered, refusing to name his assailants to the police, upholding the criminal code of silence, merely stating that, "I'll take care of dem myself." When released from the hospital two weeks later, Eastman conferred with several of his top prostitutes, one of whom lured Eastman's attacker into his domain, where the gang boss was waiting. The man's corpse was found in the gutter the next morning, his skull crushed and every major bone in his body broken.

Police began to make raids into Eastman's territory, closing up his once tightly protected crap games, brothels and gambling dens. In July 1903 Eastman and others were interrupted while beating a coachman who refused to turn over his receipts. News reporters miraculously appeared on the scene as the cuffs were put on the gang boss and he was quoted as shouting to a sergeant: "You're arresting me, huh? Say, you want to look where you're goin'! I cut some ice in this town! I made half the big politicians of New York!" This quote made Eastman a household name and caused Tammany to get a good case of the jitters. Though Eastman was cleared of the assault charges, defended by Thomas Grady, a state senator and Tammany man, the gang boss had now proven himself to be dangerous to the political machine that supported him and Tammany bosses gave Kelly the green light to eliminate Eastman's operations. In August 1903, a group of Five Pointers were en route to Rivington Street to disrupt one of Eastman's heavily protected crap games when a half dozen Eastman thugs encountered them near the Allen Street arch of the Second Avenue elevated train. Both groups opened fire, beginning the worst gang battle in New York history.

Two policemen tried to quell the potshooting gangsters who had taken refuge behind the pillars of the elevated, but they were sent running with bullet holes through their uniforms when both gangs opened fire on them. A Five Pointer was shot to death but Kelly's men did not retreat. They sent a runner for reinforcements, as did the Eastmen goons. Gangsters from both camps came on the run to the battle scene until there were several hundred men firing at each other in a pitched battle. The gang bosses, Eastman and Kelly, also arrived at the scene. The gunfight went on for more than two hours, and by midnight could be heard blocks away. Police were reluctant to interfere but finally officers in flying squads were sent to the area. By that time the Five Pointers had had enough since more and more Eastmen gangsters were streaming into the area. The Five Pointers retreated, leaving two dead and five wounded. Eastman counted one of his own men dead and two wounded. He was arrested as he was leaving the area but was discharged a half hour later after telling a magistrate, "I heard dis gunfire and was curious to see what it was about. I was walkin' by when the cop puts the cuffs on me."

The pitched gun battle caused Tammany to take direct action. Big Tim Sullivan, who had been Eastman's protector for a decade, ordered Manhattan sheriff Tom Foley to arrange a truce between Eastman and Kelly. The gangsters met, their gunmen armed to the teeth and surrounding them, in Eastman's hangout, The Palm, a restaurant close to his Chrystie Street dwelling. Foley sat between the two men and told them that the gang warfare must stop, that their gangs were to stay in their own territories and cease the violence or Tammany would not be responsible for their political safety. The gang bosses agreed to a truce but some weeks later it was violated when an Eastman thug named Hurst arrogantly marched into a Bowery dive and started an argument with a Kelly lieutenant named Ford about whose boss was more famous. Hurst was jumped by several Five Pointers and his nose was broken and his ear was chewed off. He was sent running from the district. When Eastman heard the news he demanded that Kelly turn Ford over to him for punishment or "I will wipe youse guys off the face of de earth!"

Kelly only snorted his contempt for his hulking adversary and refused to turn Ford over. Eastman, fearful of losing Tammany support, then proposed that Kelly, a one-time boxer, meet him in the ring to settle the matter. Kelly agreed and the two gang bosses, surrounded by hundreds of their men, pistols at the ready, got into the ring in the back of a Bronx saloon, selecting this neutral spot to keep the truce from being violated in their own territories. For two hours the gang bosses knocked each other about, Eastman landing powerful overhand rights, Kelly, the more scientific boxer, jabbing the heavyset gang boss. The men fought to a draw, exhausted at the end of this marathon battle, collapsing against each other. The fight solved nothing. The Eastmans and Five Pointers were once more battling and even Tom Foley's second warning meant nothing, especially to Edward Monk Eastman. Tammany's increasing problems with the unruly and uncontrollable Eastman were conveniently solved by Eastman himself on Feb. 2, 1904.

Accompanied by one of his top thugs, Chris Wallace, Eastman went on a vengeance trip out of his territory, all the way to Sixth Avenue and Forty-second Street, to blackjack a man who had mistreated one of his more expensive prostitutes. On the way the pair spotted a tipsy well-dressed young man staggering down the street. Behind him walked a roughly-dressed character Eastman thought was a mugger. The gang boss was never one to overlook easy plunder. He and Wallace decided to steal the victim away from the mugger. They pulled guns and jabbed them into the face of the startled young man, grabbing him by the lapels of his evening coat and demanding his wallet. To the utter surprise of the gangsters, the man whom they had seen trailing the young man was no mugger at all but a Pinkerton detective who had been assigned to watch the wayward scion of a wealthy family as he made his nocturnal vice jaunt.

The Pinkerton detective drew his own gun and fired at Eastman and Wallace, who immediately decided that flight was the best policy in a territory where they had no influence. Eastman and Wallace ran down the street, the Pinkerton in pursuit, firing as he chased the thugs. Wallace escaped unharmed but the lumbering Eastman turned a blind corner and his luck ran out; he slammed right into a burly policeman who instinctively brought down his billy club on the gang leader's bullet-like head, knocking him unconscious. Eastman was dragged by the feet to a paddy wagon and taken to the Thirtieth Street Police Station, where he was charged with highway robbery and felonious assault. The gang boss laughed uproariously, telling officers that he would be released within an hour after his friends heard about the arrest. His appeals to Tammany, however, fell on deaf ears this time. Big Tim Sullivan had no more use for the strong-arm thug who compulsively committed low-life street crimes and failed to run his gang as an efficient and controlled organization working only for Tammany's good.

Eastman frantically sent messenger after messenger to see Sullivan and Foley but their response was silence. The gang boss was tried and convicted, given a ten-year sentence in Sing Sing, and sent away to serve his time. This was the end of Edward Monk Eastman as a gang overlord, leaving Paul Kelly the top man of organized crime in New York. Kelly was approached by news reporters and feigned grief over Eastman's incarceration, saying: "Monk was a soft, easy-going fellow but he had a gang of cowards behind him—second story men, yeggs, flat robbers, and moll buzzers. But he was a game fellow. He fought everyone's battles. I'd give ten thousand dollars to see him out of prison." Tammany, on the other hand, would not pay a red cent to see its own homegrown brute released from prison. Eastman stayed behind the big walls wearing striped prison garb for five years, until his release in June 1909, when he reentered an underworld that knew him only as a legend from a distant past. His loyal chief lieutenant, Kid Twist Zwerbach, had been killed in rival gang wars in 1908 and his gang had mostly disbanded.

The once-feared gang boss was an anachronism when he emerged from prison. He moved back to his old neighborhood but was ignored by the gangland bosses and by Tammany. Kelly was still running almost all illegal operations in Manhattan, his power and influence spread far beyond Five Points. New men like Johnny Torrio and Al Capone, who worked for Kelly, exercised a new brand of underworld ethics. They used the gun, not fists or clubs as did Eastman, preferring to shoot a victim to death rather than merely cripple a rival and thus eliminate him forever. Eastman was allowed to establish some penny-ante gambling and prostitution rings to survive. He was arrested and jailed several times for opium smoking, robbery, and running whores. His name was not prominently mentioned again until he promptly enlisted at the outbreak of hostilities between the U.S. and Germany in 1917. When Eastman stripped for a medical examination, the doctors gasped at the number of scars on his body from old knife and bullet wounds received in innumerable gang battles. Asked if he had been in any previous wars, Monk Eastman replied laconically: "Oh, a lot of little wars around New York."

War proved to be Eastman's meat. He served with distinction on the Western Front, earning several medals for valor. Eastman miraculously survived several frontal attacks and was responsible for wiping out a number of machine gun nests. Upon his return, the gangster was hailed by the press as a hero, which moved Governor Al Smith, on May 3, 1919, to sign an executive order restoring the one-time gangland boss to full American citizenship. But Eastman had no intention of reforming and was soon busy trying to organize a new gang in his old stomping grounds, attempting to establish himself as a successful bootlegger at the dawn of Prohibition. But the new breed would not tolerate the aging gangster's intrusion into their lucrative rackets. Eastman was marked for death and his body was found on Dec. 26, 1920, in front of the Bluebird Cafe. He had been shot five times and his corpse dumped in front of the restaurant where he had conducted his small bootlegging operation.

Somehow Monk Eastman's past sins were forgotten and the press hailed the fallen gangster as a war hero who deserved a full military funeral with honors, which he got. Police delved deeply into his last active days and turned up a Prohibition Enforcement Agent named Jerry Bohan with whom Eastman had been collaborating in a bootlegging enterprise. In December 1921, Bohan confessed to killing Eastman in a quarrel at the Bluebird Cafe over a tip to a waiter but, of course, this was the killer's lame excuse. The real reason, as authorities pointed out later, was that Eastman had been cutting into bootlegging territory and was ordered killed for his interloping. Bohan made a deal with the prosecution and pleaded guilty to manslaughter in the first degree. He received a three-to-ten-year sentence and was paroled in 1923. Thus ended in ignominious silence the saga of Monk Eastman, New York's first great gangster of the modern era. See: **Kelly, Paul; Sullivan, Timothy; Tammany Hall; Zelig, Jack; Zwerbach, Maxwell.**

REF.: Asbury, *The Gangs of New York; CBA;* Clarke, *In the Reign of Rothstein;* Fried, *The Rise and Fall of the Jewish Gangster in America;* Haskins, *Street Gangs;* Katcher, *The Big Bankroll, the Life and Times of Arnold Rothstein;* Levine, *The Anatomy of a Gangster;* Lewis, *The Apaches of New York;* McPhaul, *Johnny Torrio;* Messick and Goldblatt, *The Mobs and the Mafia;* Nash, *Bloodletters and Badmen;* Peterson, *The Mob;* Reppetto, *The Blue Parade;* Rowan, *The Pinkertons;* Thompson and Raymond, *Gang Rule in New York;* Willemse, *Behind the Green Lights.*

Eastman, Robert (AKA: **Lame Bob Roberts**), prom. 1908, U.S., Case of, suic.-mur. After bilking investors out of thousands of dollars, former New York broker Robert Eastman deserted his family and purchased twenty-two acres of land in Maryland. Living under the name Roberts, Eastman became good friends with his neighbors, Colonel Charles A. Thompson and his wife. Eastman became even better acquainted with the Thompson's adopted, married daughter, Edith May Woodill. On a visit to the Thompson's farm in June 1909, Edith informed her parents she was going to spend a few days in Baltimore. Mrs. Woodill never made it into the city on June 19; Eastman met her and they spent the day together.

Two days later, the Thompsons became concerned about their daughter, but Eastman told them not to worry. Three days later, the bloated, nude body of a young woman was discovered in a creek on Eastman's property. Her skull had been crushed and the corpse was badly swollen, but officials were able to identify Edith Woodill through dental records. A search for Eastman ensued, but he committed suicide before he could be captured. Despite a letter to his wife in which he detailed a bizarre party that resulted in another man murdering Woodill, authorities determined that Eastman had acted alone.

REF.: *CBA;* Duke, *Celebrated Criminal Cases of America.*

Easton, Lord, See: **Parke, Ernest.**

Easton, Rufus, 1774-1834, U.S., jur. Served as U.S. attorney, Missouri attorney general from 1821-26, and received appointment from President Thomas Jefferson to the Louisiana Territorial Court in 1805. REF: *CBA.*

East St. Louis Race Riot, 1917, U.S., mob vio. In the first quarter of the twentieth century, competition for jobs in the industrial sector of East St. Louis, Ill., sparked a savage race riot—one in which police aided white rioters. When, in April 1917, union employees at an aluminum plant in East St. Louis called a strike, the company responded by bringing in non-union workers, many of them blacks, The next month the strike was broken, and the union vanquished. Angry workers blamed the black strikebreakers for their defeat.

In May and June there were scattered incidents of rioting and acts of violence perpetrated against individual blacks. The worst of the violence, however, began on July 1 when a group of armed whites drove through black neighborhoods, randomly firing into homes. When the whites made a second run through the district, the blacks fired back. The police arrived in an unmarked Ford, a car similar to the one driven by the white gunmen. In what was most likely a case of mistaken identity, two policemen were shot by blacks. As the news of the shootings spread through town, a large-scale riot erupted in which street cars were stopped and black passengers were assaulted, clubbed, and shot.

After most of the fighting had been quelled, a group of 100 armed blacks barricaded themselves behind a fort. The group surrendered their arms when the local militia offered them safe passage out of town. The official accounts recorded forty-eight dead—thirty-nine black, and nine white. Unofficial estimates placed the number of black deaths at 100. The destruction of property was also widespread. Over 300 buildings were gutted, The charges against those policemen who aided the white gunmen were dropped in return for an agreement that three among them (to be chosen by drawing lots) plead guilty to charges of rioting. The rest paid fines totalling only $150. REF.: *CBA.*

Eastwood, John Francis, 1887-1952, Brit., jur. As defense lawyer he secured the acquittal of Theodosios Petrou in 1933, who was charged with killing a fellow native of Cyprus, Dr. Angelos Zemenides, despite testimony given by ballistics expert Robert Churchill which proved the murder weapon was owned by Petrou. He also provided defense for the murder trials of Arthur James Mahoney, Sidney George Paul, and Henry Sidney Smith. Eastwood also held a post in Parliament from 1931-40, served as king's counsel, and as a London magistrate from 1940-52. REF.: *CBA.*

Eaton, Helen Spence, 1912-34, U.S., pris. esc.-mur. On July 11, 1934, Helen Eaton, twenty-two, escaped from the Arkansas state prison farm for women for the fourth and final time. She was on a work detail at a farm near Jacksonville, Ark., when she asked permission to return to the prison to take some medicine. When she did not return the prison was searched. In Eaton's locker, prison officials found a note stating: "I'll never be taken alive." It was also discovered that Eaton had stolen a pistol before making her escape. Authorities knew they faced a dangerous chore in recapturing Eaton, who was known as "the toughest woman in Arkansas."

Eaton had been serving a term for the murder of Jack Worls whom she shot to death in a DeWitt, Ark., courtroom in 1930. Worls had been standing trial for the murder of Eaton's father, Cicero Spence, a riverman. The jury was about to begin deliberations when Eaton, who decided Worls would be found not guilty,

rose from her front row seat and executed Worls herself. She was sentenced to five years but the state supreme court later reduced her sentence to two years. She was paroled in 1933, moved to Little Rock, Ark., and worked as a waitress, but her conscience was bothering her. Soon after her 1933 release Eaton went to Little Rock Police and confessed to the murder of Jim Bohots, a restaurant operator Eaton had worked for in DeWitt while her conviction for the previous murder was under appeal. According to Eaton, Bohots had made unwelcome advances towards her. In July 1933, she was sentenced to ten years for the second murder.

Eaton had been an incorrigible prisoner, escaping from the prison three times earlier. She had been returned each time, twice tracked down by bloodhounds. A few hours after her final escape she accosted a farmer's wife in a farm house seven miles northeast of the prison. Eaton demanded that the woman drive her out of the area. Instead, the wife ran into the fields where her husband was working. Eaton fled into the woods, and the farmer called the police. An hour and a half later, she was spotted by police and, as her note had warned, she elected to shoot it out. Helen Eaton died in a hail of bullets, the toughest girl in Arkansas to the very end. REF.: *CBA.*

Eaton, Nathaniel, c.1609-74, U.S., fraud. As Harvard College's first appointed head from 1638-39, he was dismissed from his position for financial irregularities, incurring a fine and excommunication from the Anglican Church. He fled to Virginia and eventually to England, where he later died in a prison for debtors. REF.: *CBA.*

Ebbo of Reims (Ebo), c.775-851, Ger., polit. corr.-consp. Archbishop of Reims from 816-35. He opposed his benefactor, Louis I, by supporting Louis' son Lothiar I, in deposing his father as the Holy Roman Emperor in 833. Louis I was restored to the throne in 834, whereupon, Ebbo was stripped of his title and placed in prison in 835. Lothiar I illicitly reinstated Ebbo as archbishop from 840-41, though later Charles II the Bald had him banished. He escaped to Rome and was named archbishop of Hildesheim by Louis the German in 846. REF.: *CBA.*

Ebel, Johann Wilhelm, 1784-1861, Case of, Ger., her. Accused of sectarianism and immorality for creating the Mucker society, a theosophic and mystic group that was dissolved in 1839. Ebel suffered through a six year trial between 1835-41, before being exonerated of the charges. He was nevertheless dismissed as the Königsberg pastor, a position he had held since 1816, on a charge of neglect. REF.: *CBA.*

Eberhardt, Fred O., prom. 1930, Case of, U.S., consp. As publisher of the Tallahassee *Florida State News,* Fred O. Eberhardt was an outspoken critic of Florida Governor Doyle E. Carlton. When Eberhardt was arrested by Jacksonville Sheriff W. B. Cahoon in August 1930 and charged with conspiracy to kill the governor, he was dumbfounded. The publisher claimed that his arrest was a political plot and that authorities had harassed him for a year. For his part, Carlton said he was not shocked people were trying to unseat him.

Cahoon refused to reveal any details surrounding the investigation, hinting only that Eberhardt was trying to gain control of the gambling and liquor industries on the East Coast. In September 1930, Judge J.C. Madison dismissed conspiracy charges against Eberhardt, citing the state's lack of evidence. REF.: *CBA.*

Ebermayer, Ludwig, 1858-1933, Ger., jur. Played an important role in the reformation of penal laws in Germany. REF.: *CBA.*

Ebner, Esther, d.1829, Brit., mur. For the crime of starving her young apprentice to death, Esther Ebner was hanged in 1829. REF.: *CBA;* O'Donnell, *Should Women Hang?*

Eboli, Ana de Mendoza de, 1540-92, Spain, consp. Mistress of King Philip II of Spain involved in court intrigues which were revealed by the secret agents of Don John of Austria. She was banished by the Spanish court. REF.: *CBA.*

Eboli, Thomas (AKA: Tommy Ryan), prom. 1950s-60s, U.S., org. crime. New York gangster Thomas Eboli had been a professional prizefighter and later became a strong-arm man in

Vito Genovese's Mafia family, taking over the family when Genovese was sent to prison in 1959. Credited with either personally murdering or ordering the deaths of at least twenty men, Eboli was killed in 1972 in one of the Mafia wars in New York.

REF.: Bonanno, *A Man of Honor;* CBA; Cressey, *Theft of the Nation;* Davis, *Mafia Kingfish;* Gage, *Mafia, U.S.A.;* Gosch and Hammer, *The Last Testament of Lucky Luciano;* Katz, *Uncle Frank;* Maas, *The Valachi Papers;* Martin, *Revolt in the Mafia;* Peterson, *The Mob;* Reid, *The Grim Reapers;* Zuckerman, *Vengeance is Mine.*

Echeverria, Esteban, 1809-51, Arg., her. Banished from Argentina by the dictator, Juan Manuel de Rosas for introducing European romantics' literary ideas into Spanish America. REF.: *CBA.*

Ecker, Lewis C., II, 1943- , Case of, U.S., rape-mur. On the night of May 22, 1967, Judith K. Robeson, twenty-five, an aide to Senator Frank Carlson of Kansas planned to attend a lecture on sailing to be held near her Washington, D.C., apartment. Robeson worked as a research assistant for Senator Carlson, but she also spent many hours working as an amateur artist and on her hobby, sailing. Her father, Mark Robeson, of Mission Hills, Kan., would later tell reporters "there were not enough hours in the day for her to get everything done." The young man who was to attend the lecture with Robeson became alarmed when she failed to show at the hall. Friends called her the next day and, getting no answer, they contacted authorities. Anthony Armenta, manager of the building where Robeson lived, found Robeson dead in the living room of her sixth floor apartment. Her naked body showed signs of being beaten, and an autopsy later revealed that Robeson had been sexually assaulted.

On May 28, 1967, Lewis C. Ecker II, the 24-year-old son of a prominent Washington physician, was arrested and charged with first-degree murder. Ecker, a bakery truck driver who had served three years in the U.S. Army, had once lived in the building where Robeson had been murdered. Several neighbors reported hearing screams on the night of the murder, but none of them called the police. There was no sign of forced entry. Police, however, received a tip from an unnamed visitor to Robeson's apartment building who reported seeing a man leaving her apartment only a short time before her body was discovered. A description of this young man was given to police and a composite sketch drawn and quickly published in the local paper. Ecker, the next day, stopped at a service station and began a conversation with some youths who were washing their car windows.

"Have you heard anything about that girl who was killed?" he asked them. They told him no, nothing more than what the papers had reported. After the young men spotted twelve moldy loaves of bread in the trunk of his white 1966 Falcon, Ecker explained that he worked as a delivery man for a baker. Ecker's car seemed unusual to the youths in that it had three rear-view mirrors on it and it had been painted completely white, even the chrome had been painted white. When Ecker drove off, the two youths looked at the composite of the killer that appeared in a newspaper one of them had just purchased. "That's the guy," one said, and he flagged down a police car. (The moldy bread in Ecker's car explained his absence from his delivery schedule. He had missed some deliveries and had put the bread in his trunk, deliveries that should have been made at the time Judith Robeson was being murdered.)

The identification by the two youths, along with other information which Washington Police refused to disclose, caused Ecker to be arrested and charged with Robeson's murder. The court took note that Ecker had had a record of mental illness dating back to the time he was three years old. There was no doubt in the minds of many that Ecker had sexually assaulted and murdered Robeson.

Ecker pleaded not guilty and after a trial before U.S. District Judge John Lewis Smith, Jr. he was found Not Guilty by reason of insanity. The court ordered that Ecker be committed to the psychiatric ward at St. Elizabeth's Hospital in Washington, D.C.

Doctors there diagnosed Ecker as having a "sociopathic personality disorder, sexual deviation with organic component." Ecker was described by St. Elizabeth staff members as a sadist. "He's one of the sickest people we've ever had in this hospital," one staff member said. Ecker spent the first four years in a maximum-security ward and was then transferred to a minimum-security unit and given extensive privileges.

In September 1978, it was discovered that the patient had rented a one-bedroom apartment in Washington, with money he received in Social Security disability benefits, and that he frequently met his girlfriend, a former security guard at St. Elizabeth's, at the apartment. The hospital was preparing to ask Judge Smith for Ecker's unconditional release when this scandal exploded. It was also charged that the patient had been allowed to keep a stack of pornographic material in his hospital room. After the love nest was discovered, Ecker's privileges were revoked. As of this writing, more than twenty-two years after Judith Robeson's brutal slaying, he is still confined at St. Elizabeth's. REF.: *CBA.*

Eckles, Delena R., 1806-88, U.S., jur. Prosecuting attorney for Monroe and Clay counties, Ind., from 1838-41, and appointed by President James Buchanan to the territorial court of Utah in 1858. He presided over the Sixth Judicial Circuit Court of Indiana from 1864-70, was professor of law at Indiana University from 1872-73, and was a special judge for the Sixth Circuit Court of Indiana in 1880. REF.: *CBA.*

Ecklund, Edward, 1883-1933, U.S., (unsolv.) mur. With construction of the new House Office Building in Washington, D.C., almost completed in January 1933, paymasters Edward Ecklund and Harry Stumm were crossing the street from the old building to pay a crew of painters. The two men were stopped by a pair of men, who demanded the $2,000 they were carrying. When Ecklund, fifty, and Stumm, forty-eight, resisted the robbery attempt, they were shot and the gunmen jumped in a taxi. Ecklund was killed instantly and Stumm was taken to a hospital with a bullet lodged near his heart, the payroll still stuffed in his pocket. REF.: *CBA.*

Edalji, George, b.1876, Brit., maiming of animals (wrong. convict.) A Persian living in the small mining village of Great Wyrley, Staffordshire, Eng., George Edalji was the son of a vicar, the Reverend Shapurji Edalji. In 1888, obscene messages and insults about the Edaljis were scrawled on the sides of village buildings. A dim-witted servant girl was arrested on libel charges but released for lack of evidence. She left the village but the messages continued. Trademen in the area then began receiving orders for goods, ostensibly ordered by the Edaljis, but when deliveries were made it was discovered that the Edaljis neither ordered the goods nor had the money to pay for them.

In 1892, the chief constable for the village, G.R. Anson, found a key to the front door of the local grammar school and accused George Edalji of stealing it. The 16-year-old boy denied it but the hard-headed Anson insisted that George Edalji was guilty, despite the fact that he had found the key on the front doorstep of the Edalji home, an unlikely place for Edalji to hide the key. Moreover, Anson accused George Edalji of writing obscene letters to his own parents. The racial hate campaign on the part of the letter-writer continued. Then, on Aug. 17, 1903, the village was shocked to learn that a rash of animal maimings had occurred. A pit pony had been gutted and cattle in the area had been slaughtered with a sharp instrument.

Local police immediately accused George Edalji of the heinous crimes. Police stated that Edalji's coat was examined and animal bloodstains had been found on it. His razor bore the hairs of the horse that had been slain and horsehairs on Edalji's coat also matched those of the slain horse. The accused man's boots, police insisted, were caked with mud from the area where the cattle and horse had been slain and mutilated. Edalji, by then a struggling solicitor, was arrested, convicted, and sentenced to seven years at hard labor. After serving three years, Edalji was released. In 1906, in an effort to clear his name, Edalji wrote a series of articles for a small newspaper, *The Umpire.* One of its readers was Arthur Conan Doyle, creator of Sherlock Holmes.

Doyle read Edalji's articles and sent for the young man. Upon meeting Edalji, Doyle observed that he was myopic and wore thick glasses. Doyle took the young man to an eye specialist who told the famous author that, in his opinion, Edalji was nearly blind. Doyle concluded that Edalji could not have managed to traverse the bushy terrain of Great Wyrley on the night of the animal maimings and killings and that the frail youth certainly could not have wielded a razor in the dark. Armed with a letter from Scotland Yard which gave him authority to investigate the case, Doyle visited the constabulary at Great Wyrley where, to the consternation of the local police, he examined the so-called evidence which had convicted Edalji.

The razor supposedly used to kill and maim the animals was examined by an expert who claimed that the hairs on it came from the elder Edalji. The hairs on George's coat were, indeed, horsehairs, but Doyle learned from tight-lipped officers that this coat had been mixed with blankets used by the slain horse *before* it was introduced as evidence. The horsehairs came from the blanket, not the slain horse. Moreover, the blood on the coat was from uncooked meat Edalji had been carrying about on the night of the animal slayings. Doyle inspected the area where the maimings took place, taking samples of the loam and having another expert compare it with that on Edalji's old boots, which were still held in evidence. The mud on the boots was completely dissimilar to that of the area where the animals had been maimed.

Then Doyle obtained several of the obscene letters written about and to the Edalji's. He had a top handwriting expert compare them to Edalji's writing. The expert stated that George Edalji had not written the obscene letters. Doyle then examined the backgrounds of some of Edalji's classmates and discovered one unbalanced youth who had had the habit of slashing pillows and writing obscenities on walls. The youth later became a sailor. The anonymous letter writer of years earlier had talked about going to sea. Doyle came to believe that this youth, Royden Sharp, who had been a classmate of Edalji's, developed a deep-seated hatred for foreigners, especially Persians, and that it had been Sharp who conducted the smear campaign. He may also have been the slayer of the animals, but Doyle learned that another youth, Harry Green, had confessed to the animal slayings and maimings but the police had suppressed his confession and arranged to have him move to South Africa. Certain members of the local constabulary obviously framed evidence against Edalji out of racial prejudice and hatred.

Doyle assembled his evidence and presented it to the Gladstone Commission of the Home Office, which studied his findings and then cleared Edalji of the animal maiming, but commission members insisted that Edalji had written several anonymous obscene letters to his own parents, despite the findings of the handwriting experts. Enraged, Doyle wrote a series of thundering articles for the London *Daily Telegraph* which convinced the public that George Edalji was not only innocent but had been wrongly convicted on framed evidence. The Persian solicitor was never fully cleared, but the intense controversy surrounding his case caused the establishment of the Court of Criminal Appeal. Doyle emerged from this investigative interlude with the image of an author who possessed many of the skills demonstrated by his immortal Sherlock Holmes, especially his deductive reasoning and keen sense of observation. Like Holmes, Doyle was a champion of the underdog and this was never more in evidence than in the Oscar Slater case of 1908, a genuine murder mystery that immersed Doyle in a prolonged campaign to vindicate a wrongly convicted man. See: **Doyle, Arthur Conan; Slater, Oscar.**

REF.: *CBA;* Cobb, *Trials and Errors;* Hall, *Sherlock Holmes and His Creator;* Higham, *The Adventures of Conan Doyle;* Nordon, *Conan Doyle;* Stevens, *From Clue to Dock.*

Edde, Raymond, 1914- , Leb., (attempt.) assass. For Raymond Edde, a prominent Christian leader in Lebanon, 1976 was a long year. The 62-year-old man, who lived in pro-Muslim West Beirut, survived three attempts on his life, but suffered leg wounds in each of the shooting incidents. Edde had been criticized for refusing to support militant Christians during the Civil War and had spoken out against Syrian involvement during the Lebanese crisis. REF.: *CBA.*

Eddowes, Catherine, See: **Jack the Ripper.**

Edel, Frederick W. (AKA: **The Man With Five Hundred Names**), prom. 1928, U.S., mur. The door to Emeline Harrington's New York apartment was open for five days before a neighbor discovered her body on the bathroom floor. The 39-year-old actress had been beaten to death and robbed.

Less than one month later, in January 1928, Connecticut police were alerted to a suspicious guest who left a New Haven hotel without paying his bill. The man's room contained a suitcase filled with bills made out to Mrs. Harrington and letters addressed to Frederick W. Edel. The police were familiar with Edel because he had been acquitted of murder in 1925 and was currently in violation of parole.

In March 1928, a postal **Murderer Frederick Edel.** clerk in Hopkins, Minn., recognized Edel from a wanted poster when the suspect tried to buy a money order. As the clerk moved to alert police, Edel ran out of the post office but was captured a mile away. He was returned to New York and charged with the murder of Emeline Harrington. Edel confessed that he had used more than 500 aliases, but refused to admit that he killed Harrington. Edel was convicted of murder and sentenced to death in 1928. Less than two years later, New York Governor Franklin D. Roosevelt commuted Edel's sentence to life in prison. New evidence was uncovered following the original trial, which prompted several of the jurors who convicted Edel to inform the governor that the new information created a reasonable doubt in their minds. While Roosevelt said he did not believe the evidence proved Edel innocent, it did warrant a reduced sentence.

REF.: Carey, *Memoirs of a Murder Man; CBA;* Wilson, *Encyclopedia of Murder.*

Edelmann, Johann Christian, 1698-1767, Ger., her. Persecuted for being a freethinker, his works were burned publicly in Frankfurt and Hamburg. After hiding in Altona for a year, Holy Roman Emperor Frederick III allowed Edelmann to return in 1749, under the condition that he not publish his writings. REF.: *CBA.*

Edelson, Mitchell, Jr., 1930- , U.S., perj. In May 1974, former Cook County Assistant state's attorney Mitchell Edelson, Jr. told a federal grand jury that he knew nothing about a crime syndicate plot to fence stolen stocks and bonds. In April 1977, U.S. District Court Judge Frank J. McGarr sentenced Edelson to one year in prison for lying to the grand jury in 1974. During the two-week bench trial, Edelson's attorney argued that his client had been entrapped by federal investigators. While Edelson was never implicated directly in the stolen securities scam, McGarr ruled that he was knowledgeable of the fencing operation and, therefore, Guilty. REF.: *CBA.*

Edelstein, David Norton, 1910- , U.S., jur. Attorney for the U.S. Department of Justice, assistant attorney general, and appointed by President Harry S. Truman to the Southern District Court of New York in 1951. REF.: *CBA.*

Edgar, Jimmy L., 1959- , and **Edgar, Johnny**, 1955- , and **Hayes, Ralph Eugene**, 1957- , Case of, U.S., mur. Four days after police discovered the body of a 19-year-old black man, Michael A. Donald, hanging from a tree on a residential street in Mobile, Ala., three white men were arrested. Ralph Eugene

Hayes, Johnny Edgar, and Jimmy Edgar were charged with first-degree murder after police found the dead man's identification near the Edgar brothers' apartment. Hayes was living across the street from the murder site at the time of his arrest.

On June 6, 1981, a federal grand jury in Mobile released the Edgar brothers and Hayes from all criminal charges after determining that the prosecution's case was based on perjured testimony. REF.: *CBA*.

Edgar the Peaceful (Eadgar), 944-75, Brit., reform.-law enfor. Became king of Mercia and Northumbria in 957, succeeded his brother, Eadwig the Fair, and formed a united England upon Edwig's death in 959. He recalled Saint Dunstan from exile, naming him chief adviser and archbishop of Canterbury in 961. He finally received the belated crown of all England in 973, tried improving the judicial system, and organized a navy to defend the island from pirates. REF.: *CBA*.

Edgerton, Alonzo Jay, 1827-96, U.S., jur. Prosecuting attorney for Dodge County, Minn., and U.S. senator representing Minnesota in 1881, before receiving appointment from President Chester A. Arthur to the Dakota Territorial Court in 1881. REF.: *CBA*.

Edgerton, Henry White, 1888-1970, U.S., jur. Special assistant to the U.S. attorney general from 1934-35, and appointed by President Franklin D. Roosevelt to the District of Columbia Circuit Court in 1938. REF.: *CBA*.

Edgerton, Sidney, 1818-1900, U.S., jur. Served as prosecuting attorney for Summit County, Ohio, from 1852-56, and in the U.S. House of Representatives from 1859-63. His term as representative for Ohio ended with his appointment by President Abraham Lincoln to the territorial court of Idaho in 1863. He later governed the Territory of Montana from 1864-66. REF.: *CBA*.

Edghill, Carlos Antonio, b.1953, U.S., mur. When New York State Supreme Court Justice Hyman Barshay sentenced Carlos Antonio Edghill to two concurrent twenty-year prison terms for shooting two police officers, he said his hands were tied by a recent court ruling outlawing the death penalty. Officer Robert W. Mandel was killed and officer Peter J. Christ wounded when Edghill shot the policemen during a narcotics investigation in Brooklyn on Apr. 19, 1977. Edghill, an illegal alien from Panama, had been released from jail on a gun charge, less than eight hours before the shooting incident.

Police Commissioner Michael J. Codd called for Edghill to be executed and accused the courts of leniency in releasing the prisoner on $500 bail. Edghill confessed to the shootings and was given the maximum allowable sentence by Barshay in March 1978. REF.: *CBA*.

Edinburgh Mock Battle Death, 1942, Scot., mansl. In a mock battle during the summer of 1942, in Edinburgh, Scot., a detachment of the Home Guard and an attacking force of Regular soldiers were fighting with blank ammunition when one of the Home Guard men collapsed. He had been seriously wounded by a rifle bullet and died soon after. A post-mortem examination revealed that the bullet was fired at close range. Edinburgh Central Intelligence Department officers established where the shot had been fired from, and found a live shell cartridge case among the blank empty cartridges and identified the killer by fingerprints on the cartridge. The soldier who killed the Home Guard man had no grudge against the other soldier, but felt it was a good idea to add realism to the maneuvers by shooting an occasional live cartridge. Examined by a psychiatrist, he was found to have a diminished sense of responsibility due to his mental condition, and was tried by military authorities on the charge of firing ball ammunition without authority. Found guilty, he was sentenced to twenty-eight days detention, after which he was transferred to a branch where he would not be required to bear arms.

REF.: *CBA*; Smith, *Mostly Murder*.

Edmonds, Edmund, prom. 1872, Case of, Brit., mur. Edmund Edmonds, the solicitor for Newent, Gloucestershire, England, lived with his wife Ann and their three sons. When his brother

died, Edmonds took in seven nephews and nieces. One niece, Jeanette, often quarreled with her adopted father. By her adolescence, Jeanette had attracted the attention of the family physician, Matthew Bass-Smith, a middle-aged father of four.

In 1860, Ann Edmonds' younger sister Mary, known as Aunt Polly, came to live in the household. Edmonds was enchanted by his 28-year-old sister-in-law, particularly after his wife's health began to fail. Dr. Bass-Smith attended Mrs. Edmonds, almost on a daily basis. In 1866, when Jeanette Edmonds was seventeen, Bass-Smith tried to seduce her. He succeeded a year later, soon after Ann Edmonds' death on Feb. 24, 1867, from what was believed to be apoplexy. But actually, Edmund had quarreled bitterly with his wife that night about his affairs, and had struck her over the head. The doctor believed that with Ann out of the way Jeanette would give in to him, so Bass-Smith attributed the death to natural causes. The rest of the family members went along with the cover-up to avoid a scandal. Aunt Polly offered servant Ann Bradd a bribe to keep quiet, then took her sister's place in Edmund Edmonds' bed. In 1869 she had a miscarriage.

Meanwhile, 50-year-old Dr. Bass-Smith began his own affair with 18-year-old Jeanette, which continued for the next four years without Edmund Edmonds suspecting. On Oct. 8, 1871, Edmonds intercepted a letter from Jeanette to her lover and ordered her out of the house. Jeanette turned to the doctor, who took her to London, but he could not afford to maintain her in the city. Jeanette then asked Reverend Keene of Newent for help, and he placed her in the Home For Fallen Women at Hammersmith. When her uncle refused to allow her to fetch her personal belongings, Jeanette confessed all to the vicar and accused Edmund of murder.

Dr. Bass-Smith tried to intervene, and when Edmonds refused to back down, threatened to make such a noise that "the dead would rise from their graves." Edmunds tried to have Bass-Smith struck from the medical register for unprofessional conduct, but the doctor told the Gloucester coroner that he wished to revoke Ann Edmonds' death certificate because he suspected foul play. Her remains were exhumed and an examination was conducted on Feb. 14, 1872. Jeanette said she had witnessed her uncle's assault on his wife but had remained silent out of fear. She also admitted her relationship with Bass-Smith.

On Feb. 19, 1872, Edmonds was charged with murder. Because of sensational publicity, Edmonds petitioned the court for a change of venue from the Gloucestershire Assizes to the Old Bailey in London. It was there that the trial began on May 8, 1872. The prosecution had no hard evidence. The coroner found no sign of injury to the skull. Because of the badly decomposed state of the body it was difficult to determine how Ann Edmonds died. Aunt Polly refuted Jeanette's testimony about the quarrel the night of the murder. Defense attorney Huddleston assailed Jeanette's credibility and character. The jury, after fifteen minutes of deliberation returned a verdict of Not Guilty, and Edmund Edmonds walked out a free man.

REF.: *CBA*; Franklin, *Woman In the Case*.

Edmondson, Mary, d.1759, Brit., mur. Although Mary Edmondson was convicted and executed for the death of her aunt more than 200 years ago, there are still doubts about her guilt and the actual circumstances of the aunt's murder. Edmondson was a farm girl from Leeds who went to live with her aunt, a widow named Walker, in the town of Rotherhithe. One night, neighbors heard the girl cry out "Help! Murder! They have killed my aunt!" When the neighbors rushed into the house they found Mrs. Walker lying on the floor near a table with her throat cut. Mary then told neighbors that four men had entered through the back door and, before making off with some of the valuables in the house, one had grabbed Mrs. Walker and slit her throat, and another, a tall man dressed in black, warned Edmondson that if she spoke one word, she would soon follow her aunt to the grave.

The neighbors thought Edmondson's story implausible; there were no signs of a struggle and it did not appear that anyone had ransacked the place. A later inspection turned up many of the articles Mary claimed stolen. These items were found hidden in the outhouse. The girl also had a cut on her arm which she insisted had occurred when one of the men hit her with the door as they made their escape. Edmondson was tried and convicted at Kingston, but she continued to proclaim her innocence until the very end. Moments before she was executed, on Apr. 2, 1759, she told the crowd gathered to witness her death, "It is now too late to trifle either with God or man. I solemnly declare that I am innocent of the crime laid to my charge. I am very easy in my mind, as I suffer with as much pleasure as if I was going to sleep. I freely forgive my prosecutors, and earnestly beg your prayers for my departing soul."

REF.: *CBA;* Mitchell, *The Newgate Calendar.*

Edmund (Eadmund, AKA: The Martyr), c.841-70, Brit., king, assass. King of East Anglia from 855-870 succeeding his father King Alkmund. He was defeated at the battle of Hoxne in 870 by invading Danes, who tortured and beheaded him for his refusal to renounce Christianity. Edmund was eventually canonized by the Catholic Church. REF.: *CBA.*

Edmund I (Eadmund I, AKA: The Deed-doer; The Magnificent), c.922-46, Brit., king, assass. Succeeded his half-brother Athelstan to the throne of England in 939. He agreed to a truce with the king of Northumbria, Olaf Sihtricson, that protected the five Danish boroughs from Northumbrian invasion, but broke it in 944, driving King Olaf out of Northumbria, entrusting the conquered land to Malcolm I of Scotland in 945. Edmund was stabbed to death by an exiled thief at Pucklechurch. REF.: *CBA.*

Edmunds, Christiana, b.1828, Brit., mur. Christiana Edmunds was a lonely, unmarried, middle-aged woman when she met and fell for a Brighton physician, Dr. Beard, ignoring the fact that he was married. She wrote to him regularly, called him to her home when she was not ill, and accosted him in the street. Finally the doctor told her she must leave him alone. Edmunds decided to change Dr. Beard's marital status.

She obtained some strychnine and added it to some chocolates that she sent to Mrs. Beard. The doctor's wife took one small taste, rejected the gift, and told her husband. When he accused Edmunds of trying to poison his wife, she tried to prove to him that the chocolates had been poisoned when she bought them. She had a boy buy chocolates at a confectioners in town, added strychnine, and then had a different child return them for exchange. Weeks later, a 4-year-old boy, Sidney Barker, died. The police located Christiana Edmunds through the poison record book at the pharmacist where she had bought the strychnine, though she made an attempt to obtain the book and destroy the page listing her signature as "Mrs. Woods."

Edmunds was tried for murder. During the trial, she tried to blame her actions on her pregnancy by Dr. Beard, but a medical examination showed that claim to be false. She was found Guilty and sentenced to hang, but later her sentence was commuted to life in an asylum. She died at Broadmoor in 1896.

REF.: Bowen-Rowlands, *Seventy-two Years at the Bar;* Butler, *Murderers' England; CBA;* Gribble, *Such Women Are Deadly;* Gross, *Masterpieces of Murder;* Kingston, *A Gallery of Rogues; ____, Law-Breakers;* Kobler, *Some Like It Gory;* Marjoribanks, *For the Defense, The Life of Sir Edward Marshall Hall;* Nash, *Look For the Woman;* Pearce, *Unsolved Murder Mysteries;* Stevens, *From Clue to Dock;* Williamson, *Annals of Crime.*

Edmunds, George Franklin, 1828-1919, U.S., lawyer. Served as U.S. senator representing Vermont from 1866-91, where he was considered to be an authority on constitutional law. While serving in the Senate he chaired the judiciary committee from 1872-79 and 1881-91, and was responsible for the passage of the Edmunds Act, a law prohibiting polygamous marriages in U.S. territories in 1882. He wrote most of the Sherman Antitrust Act in 1890. REF.: *CBA.*

Edmunds, William Charles, 1935- , Brit., mur. Blanche Mary Matthews, who lived with six cats in Monmouthshire, England, was so fearful of being burglarized that she had the downstairs windows of her house sealed shut. On Nov. 19, 1955,

the spinster's worst nightmare was realized; an intruder broke a window and attacked the 70-year-old woman. Matthews suffered nine broken ribs, numerous cuts and bruises, and a wound to the throat. A neighbor, Alice Knight, called the police, but when Constable Norman Ellis arrived, Matthews lay barely breathing on her bloodstained bed. She died in a hospital two days later.

During his rounds earlier on the evening of the murder, Ellis had encountered a blood-spattered William Charles Edmunds, who told the officer he had been in a fight. The policeman had let Edmunds go at the time of the incident, but visited the 21-year-old laborer when the murder was discovered. Officials discovered Edmunds' bloodstained clothing in his apartment, and found two rings that had been stolen from Matthews. Edmunds was charged with murder and he subsequently confessed, but tried to prove he was insane at the time. Despite testimony from family and friends that he was mentally unstable, the jury wasted little time in returning a murder conviction. Because of a recent ruling in the House of Commons, Edmunds was spared the death penalty.

REF.: *CBA;* Furneaux, *Famous Criminal Cases, Vol. 3.*

Edmundson, Calvin Jerome, 1962- , U.S., burg.-rob.-rape. From 1984 to 1988, Prince George's County, Md., was plagued by a serial rapist. The first two rapes occurred in December 1984 in the suburbs of Washington D.C., the second coming a few minutes after midnight on Christmas Day. For the next three years the attacks continued, all following a similar pattern. Most of the victims were grabbed from behind as they got out of their cars near their homes. Although most of the attacks occurred after nightfall, a few took place during daylight hours. The women were threatened with either a knife or a tool. By February 1988, the rapist had reached a frenzied state, with eight reported rapes or rape attempts that month, all linked to the same man. The police were sure that other attacks were going unreported. On two occasions that month, the rapist struck twice on the same day. The final two attacks, both unsuccessful, came within two hours of each other on Feb. 25, in Fort Washington. A little more than an hour after the last attack, Calvin Edmundson, a 26-year-old ex-con who had twice pleaded guilty to robbing and assaulting women, was arrested while getting into a stolen car in Fort Washington. Edmundson, according to police, soon confessed to the rapes and signed a ten-page confession. But he later recanted and pleaded not guilty, claiming that he had been coerced into signing the statement after being threatened by police. "All I know is I was in the wrong place at the wrong time," said Edmundson, a Sunday School teacher who was married and had two daughters.

In November 1988, Edmundson was found Guilty of the attempted rape of a 20-year-old woman on Sept. 25, 1986. Assistant State's Attorney Deborah Johnston said at least four more trials were scheduled. "The state is very pleased with the verdict," Johnston said, "but we have a long way to go with Mr. Edmundson. We will continue to try him until such time as he gets an appropriate sentence."

As of Apr. 18, 1989, with more trials to come, Edmundson had been convicted of three rapes, one attempted rape, and on burglary and robbery charges. He had been sentenced to four life terms and two twenty-year terms, the sentences running consecutively. REF.: *CBA.*

Edward (AKA: Saint Edward; The Martyr), c.963-978, Brit., king, assass. Edward was the son of King Edgar, who ruled England between 959 and 975, and supported the monastic orders in the political conflicts within the church.

King Edgar died in 975, and Edward succeeded him. Reaction against the old king's policies led to conflicts, but Edward was not prominent in them. In 978, while visiting his brother Ethelred at Corfe Castle, the young monarch was ambushed by a group of soldiers and killed. The earliest account of the murder was written in the year 1000 in the *Life of St. Oswald,* by a monk. Two soldiers on horseback approached the king on a public road and one of the men offered him the traditional "kiss of peace," while the other seized his arm and violently pulled him in the opposite direction. The first soldier then drew a dagger and stabbed the king. The horse bolted and Edward fell to the ground dead.

A few days later, Ethelred, whom historians believe instigated the attack to gain the throne, succeeded his brother as king. Several years latter, Edward was canonized and a shrine was built to him at Shaftesbury in the south of England. The spot was a place of pilgrimage until King Henry VIII dissolved the monastic orders in the sixteenth century. The shrine's artifacts disappeared until British archeologist J. Wilson Claridge discovered Edward's leaden casket on Jan. 2, 1931. It was only twenty-one inches long and eleven inches wide. The bones in it had been carefully arranged and were well preserved. Dr. Thomas E.A. Stowell, of the Royal College of Surgeons conducted a forensic investigation and deduced that the bones were of a man who died between his seventeenth and twenty-first year. Stowell also reported that the left forearm had been twisted inward, confirming the account in the *Life of St. Oswald*. REF.: *CBA*.

Edward (Earl of Warwick), 1475-99, Brit., (wrong. convict.) consp. Imprisoned in the Tower of London by Henry VII in 1485. He was falsely accused of conspiracy for which he was executed along with Perkin Warbeck, who had attempted to escape his tower imprisonment. REF.: *CBA*.

Edward II, 1284-1327, Brit., king, assass. Edward II, of the house of Anjou or Plantagenet, was the profligate son of Edward I, known as Longshanks, who died while leading a campaign to crush the Scottish legions of Robert Bruce. Edward II lamely pursued the subjugation of Scotland, his father's obsessive ambition, and was ultimately defeated at Bannockburn by Robert Bruce. His wife, Isabella, daughter of Philip the Fair, King of France, whom he married in 1308, treated Edward with contempt, after his many infidelities. A cabal of nobles backing Isabella and her French lover, Roger de Mortimer, forced Edward II to abdicate in 1327. He was held prisoner in Berkeley Castle where he was tortured and then murdered.

REF.: *CBA; Bingham, The Life and Times of Edward II; Hutchinson, Edward II: The Pliant King.*

Edward V, 1470-1483, Brit., king, assass. Son of Edward IV, Edward V and his younger brother, the Duke of York, were taken from the home of their maternal uncle, Earl Rivers, by their paternal uncle, the Duke of Gloucester, at Northampton, following the death of Edward IV. Gloucester, a scheming usurper with an utterly villainous nature, threw the young boys into the Tower of London and held them prisoner while he coerced an assembly of lords and commons to depose Edward V. Gloucester then cruelly ordered both boys smothered to death. He assumed the throne of England as Richard III, but was called Richard Crookback because of his lameness. See: **Richard III**.

REF.: *CBA;* (DRAMA) Shakespeare, *Richard III.*

Edward VII, 1841-1910, Brit., king, (attempt.) assass. In April 1900, the future King Edward VII was still the Prince of Wales. Europe was in an uproar of protest over Britain's actions in the Boer War in South Africa, which many saw as an unwarranted exercise of British power over a small, helpless people. The English at large, and the royal family in particular, were the targets of vicious attacks in the continental press. It was against this backdrop that Edward set out with his princess by train to visit Denmark. While the train was stopped in the Gare du Nord in Brussels, Bel., on Apr. 4, a 15-year-old boy named Sipido approached and fired two shots at the royal couple, but no one was injured. Sipido and three alleged accomplices were arrested and tried; the other three were acquitted, but Sipido was convicted. Consideration was given to the political circumstances and he was ordered held under government supervision until the age of twenty-one, but he soon escaped to France. REF.: *CBA*.

Edward VIII, 1894-1972, Brit., king, (attempt.) assass. On the morning of July 16, 1936, King Edward VIII was scheduled to review British troops in Hyde Park. At the time, Scotland Yard was searching for Jerome Bannigan, a club-footed Scot who preferred to be known as George Andrew McMahon. Police

wanted to question McMahon, who operated an herb shop in Notting Hill, about a threatening letter he had written to Home Secretary Sir John Simon, complaining of persecution by British police. McMahon said he had been roughed up by police during a previous arrest, and his life had been irreparably damaged ever since the incident. The 34-year-old herbalist begged Simon to investigate.

Shortly after noon, as the hoofs of horses and the heels of soldiers mixed with the marching band, King Edward rode down the street greeting the thousands of people who had assembled. As the king passed the Wellington Arch, McMahon stepped through the crowd with a loaded revolver. Part-time police officer Anthony Gordon Dick saw the armed man lurching toward the king and knocked McMahon's loaded gun into the street. Seconds later, police arrested McMahon, who was charged with presenting a revolver near the king.

McMahon, who fancied himself a social reformer, was known by neighbors as a friendless crackpot with an explosive temper. As McMahon's trial began, he claimed that he never intended to shoot the king, but that his protest was strictly symbolic. Next, he told the court that he intended to commit suicide in front of the king to call attention to his plight. Finally, McMahon told a story of being offered £150 by some foreign spies to kill the king, claiming that he had tossed the pistol in the street to protect the king and save himself. The jury took only ten minutes to find McMahon Guilty. He was sentenced to only one year of hard labor, and McMahon begged the judge to put him in prison as long as he could to protect him from the foreign terrorist organization that had employed him.

REF.: *CBA; Paine, The Assassins' World.*

Edward of Norwich (Edward Plantagenet), c.1373-1415, Brit., kid. Named by Richard II as the fleet's admiral from 1391-98. He was given the dukedom of Albemarle in 1398, succeeded his father, Edmund of Langley, to become the Second Duke of York in 1402, and was placed in prison briefly for his role in Henry IV's kidnapping of Edmund de Mortimer and his brother in 1405. He was killed during a battle at Agincourt. REF.: *CBA*.

Edwards, Daniel J., 1957-   , and **Rish, Nancy D.**, 1962-   , U.S., kid.-mur. For the second time in two nights, Stephen Small received a call from an alleged officer of the Kankakee, Ill., police force. On the evening of Sept. 1, 1987, Small ignored a request from the "police" to come down to his office and identify what had been taken in a burglary. The next night, the caller said the Frank Lloyd Wright-designed home that Small and his wife Nancy had been working to restore had been burglarized. He had spent a great deal of time trying to return the former restaurant to its original condition since the sale of the family's communications company in December 1986. Small went to investigate the matter at 12:30 a.m.

Before Small could climb into his wife's 1987 Mercedes, two men grabbed him and threw him into a van. Three hours later, the kidnappers called Small's wife and asked for $1 million ransom. Small, the great-grandson of Len Small, governor of Illinois from 1921 to 1929, got on the phone and told his wife to "call our attorney." The phrase was a pre-arranged signal between Small and his wife to call the FBI. The 40-year-old father of three had been concerned about possible kidnapping since the $60 million sale of Mid America Media Group.

At around 3 p.m. on Wednesday, a woman called Mrs. Small to make arrangements for the money drop, but Nancy's request to speak to her husband was denied.

Three hours later, Jean Alice Small, Stephen's aunt and publisher of the Kankakee *Daily Journal,* received a call from the kidnappers and was berated for involving the police. She was warned that every member of the Small family would be killed if they did not cooperate. Small was in a box with only a forty-eight-hour supply of air and inside the box were two car batteries, a gallon jug of water, a few candy bars, and a thin plastic tube. He had been handcuffed, but the chain had been cut before the box was placed three feet underground and covered over with dirt.

At midnight, Small's wife was told by one of the kidnappers that she would receive final instructions for the ransom delivery on Thursday. Police searched for a white van that was missing its front bumper and closely watched Nancy Rish, a cleaning lady, who had been observed leaving the area where one of the ransom calls had been made. The kidnappers failed to contact the Small family on Thursday, and on Friday morning police searched the Bourbonnais townhouse where Rish lived with her boyfriend, Daniel Edwards, an unemployed ex-drug dealer. When questioned by police, the couple finally admitted to the kidnapping. A police plane spotted Small's Mercedes about five miles southeast of Kankakee. With Edwards' help, Small's body was discovered in a praying position in the plywood coffin near the car. An autopsy revealed that Small had died from suffocation shortly after he was buried alive.

During Edwards' trial in May 1988, it was revealed he had sent a threatening letter to the Smalls while he was in jail. In less than an hour, the 31-year-old Edwards was found Guilty and sentenced to death for Small's kidnapping and murder. In a separate trial, the 26-year-old Rish maintained her innocence, but Kankakee County Judge John Michela disagreed and sentenced her to life in prison without parole plus thirty years for her role in the failed kidnapping plot. REF.: *CBA.*

Edwards, Darrell A., 1962- , and **Lohbauer, John**, 1961- , and **Vallejo, Daniel**, 1961- , U.S., bat.-burg.-mur. Ed Worrell had just finished his shift as a member of the Texarkana, Ark., police force, and was getting a ride home from two on-duty officers at 1 a.m. on Feb. 3, 1977. During the ride the on-duty officers, Paul Howell and James Clark, responded to a burglary call at a local discount store. Only minutes after the three officers stepped from the squad car, both Worrell and Clark were shot in the back with a high-powered rifle. Howell managed to radio for help and the three teenaged gunmen—Darrell Edwards, fifteen, John Lohbauer, fifteen, and Daniel Vallejo, sixteen—were apprehended. Worrell died less than an hour after he was shot.

The youths, runaways from Elgin, Ill., were allegedly on their way to Mexico and had just arrived in Texarkana. The trio was charged with burglary, first-degree battery, and murder in the shootings. In August, Lohbauer pleaded guilty to first-degree murder and was sentenced to life in prison. During a separate trial, Vallejo and Edwards both pleaded guilty and were given forty-year prison terms on the murder charges and twenty years on the other two charges. REF.: *CBA.*

Edwards, Edgar (AKA: Edwin Owen), d.1903, Brit., mur. In 1902, Edgar Edwards, recently released from prison, told an acquaintance he intended to buy a grocer's shop and hire someone to run it for him. Edwards hired a man named Goodwin to run the shop. He also asked Goodwin to obtain a heavy sash-weight for the door. On Dec. 1, 1902, Edwards arrived at the shop in Camberwell, England, while owner William John Darby was talking to a customer. In the next hour, Edwards, using the sash-weight, killed Darby, his wife, and their small daughter in the living quarters over the shop. He pawned Darby's gold watch and chain, then returned to the shop in time to meet Goodwin and his wife. Two days later, Edwards rented a house in Leyton, and on Dec. 5 began to move in furniture from the Darby apartment.

On Dec. 10, Edwards instructed Goodwin to close the shop as he was going to sell it. He dug a very deep hole in the back garden of the Leyton house on Dec. 16 and buried six sacks containing the cut-up bodies of the Darby family. A neighbor saw him digging the hole but not burying the sacks.

On Dec. 23, Victoria Park grocer John Garland met Edwards at his Leyton home to discuss arrangements for selling his business. When Edwards went after the elderly Garland with a new sash-weight, Garland broke a glass in the front door and screamed for help. Edwards was arrested for the attack. During their investigation, police found business stationery in the Leyton house with the name of William Darby of Camberwell, whom police knew to be missing. When the neighbor saw the police at the Leyton house, he told them about Edwards digging a hole, and

the bodies were found. The murder weapon was found in the empty, blood-stained second-floor apartment above the Camberwell shop.

Edwards was arrested for murder and was tried before Justice Wright. Although he refused to plead, the jury found Edwards Guilty and he was hanged within a few weeks.

REF.: *CBA;* Dearden, *Aspects of Murder;* Ellis, *Prisoner at the Bar;* Felstead, *Sir Richard Muir;* Jacobs, *Pageant of Murder;* Logan, *Masters of Crime;* Shew, *A Second Companion to Murder;* Taylor's *Principles and Practice of Medical Jurisprudence.*

Edwards, George Clifton, Jr., 1914 - , U.S., jur.-law enfor. off. Held position on the Advisory Council of Judges for the National Council on Crime and Delinquency from 1953-75, served on the Supreme Court of Michigan from 1956-61, as police commissioner for Detroit from 1962-63, and was appointed by President Lyndon B. Johnson to the Sixth Circuit Court of the U.S., in 1963. For the U.S. Judicial Conference, he chaired the committee on Administration of Criminal Law from 1965-71, and sat on the Advisory Committee on Criminal Rules from 1965-71. He was a member of the National Commission on Reform of Federal Criminal Laws from 1967-71, and received the Judiciary Award from the Association of Federal Investigators in 1971. He published a number of legal works, including the following: *The Law of Criminal Correction,* with Rosensweig, Rubin and Weihofen; *The Police on the Urban Frontier;* and a biography of his father, *Pioneer-at-Law.* He also authored numerous articles and essays, including: "Why Justice Cooley Left the Bench: A Missing Page of Legal History," *Wayne Law Review;* "Due Process of Law in Criminal Cases," *Journal of Criminal Law, Criminology and Police Science;* "Interrogation of Criminal Defendants - Some Views on *Miranda v. Arizona,*" *Fordham Law Review;* "Commentary on Judicial Ethics," *Fordham Law Review;* "Symposium - Prisoners' Rights," a foreword to "Penitentiaries Produce No Penitents," *Journal of Criminal Law, Criminology and Police Science;* "Commentary: Murder and Gun Control," *American Journal of Psychiatry;* and "Exorcising the Devil of Appellate Court Delay," *American Bar Association Journal.* REF.: *CBA.*

Edwards, Herbert H., prom. 1880s, U.S., fraud. In the 1880s a Cleveland, Ohio, doctor, Herbert H. Edwards, claimed to be descended from Robert Edwards. The ancestor assumed by Dr. Edwards was alleged to have owned, in 1770, sixty-five acres of Manhattan Island, including the site of the Woolworth Building. The Cleveland doctor founded the Edward Heirs Association, continued by his son, with the intention of recovering the family's property, which he said had fallen out of their hands through legal trickery.

REF.: *CBA;* MacDougall, *Hoaxes;* Nash, *Hustlers and Con Men.*

Edwards, John, prom. 19th Cent., Brit., consp. When John Edwards fell in love with a well-to-do widow, Mrs. Canning, he masterminded a plan for the two to be married and still retain the money she received annually from the estate of her late husband. Widows who remarried were cut off from their husband's wealth in nineteenth century England. Edwards, who was blind, arranged for the marriage under an assumed name and then hired two men to torture Mr. Gee, a lawyer who handled Mr. Canning's estate. Gee was lured to a house in Whitechapel and forced to sign over Canning's entire estate by a man who claimed to be Mrs. Canning's brother.

The lawyer escaped and the three men were soon arrested. During the trial it was revealed that Mrs. Canning was married to Edwards, and that he had conceived the plot. Edwards was convicted of conspiracy charges.

REF.: *CBA;* Kingston, *Dramatic Days at the Old Bailey.*

Edwards, Joseph Sinnott (AKA: Jose Sinnott, Joseph Wickham), 1964- , U.S., mur. A native of Chicago, Joseph Edwards is wanted by the FBI for the murder of his adoptive parents. The victims were shot at close range with a .9-mm. handgun. Edwards has been missing since the murders in the early 1980s. At this writing, Edwards is still at large. REF.: *CBA.*

Edwards, Louis F., d.1939, U.S., polit., assass. In 1937, Louis

Edwards, the owner of a paint business, defeated incumbent Long Beach, N.Y., Mayor Charles Gold in a hotly contested election, and promised to turn the small town into a first-class resort. Edwards proceeded with his plans to change the town's image. He also ordered a police booth to be built across from his home and asked the police chief for round-the-clock protection. When Edwards cut the city's motorcycle force from four to two men, Officer Alvin Dooley was reassigned to patrol a deserted stretch of beach. Dooley, a longtime head of the Long Beach Police Benevolent Association and veteran cop, was unhappy about the switch.

Soon after the new mayor was elected, a woman filed a grievance with the mayor, charging that Dooley had been rude to her. Although the woman later dropped the complaint, Edwards still conducted a hearing. Dooley was found innocent of any wrongdoing, but the incident marked the first smudge on his record in twelve years of police work. Dooley's despair was compounded when he learned that Edwards was working behind the scenes to have him removed as president of the Benevolent Association. Under the threat of dismissal, the mayor had leaned on many of Dooley's colleagues to elect Detective James Horan as association president. Horan was the mayor's chauffeur and bodyguard.

When Dooley lost the November 1939 election by three votes, his world started to crumble. The credibility that he had built up as a police officer and member of the community was awash in the rage he felt for the mayor. He started drinking and neglecting his family. On the morning of Nov. 15, Dooley confronted Edwards and Horan in front of the mayor's house. The policeman fired five shots, killing Edwards and seriously wounding Horan. Dooley, who had been drinking, allegedly told neighbors: "I hope they both die."

Arrested and charged with first-degree murder, Dooley's attorney Samuel S. Liebowitz set about trying to prove his client was insane at the time of the crime. District Attorney Edward Neary sought the death penalty for Dooley. As the trial began on Jan. 22, 1940, Neary attempted to establish the late mayor as a saint, while Liebowitz depicted Dooley as a tormented man who was being victimized by a power-mad official. The defendant's parents and son testified that Dooley had been devastated by losing the election. The jury deliberated eleven hours before returning a Guilty verdict on the reduced charge of first-degree manslaughter. Dooley had been spared the death the penalty, but was sentenced by Judge Cortland A. Johnson to ten to twenty years for manslaughter, plus five to ten years for being armed with a dangerous weapon.

REF.: *CBA; Russell, Best Murder Cases.*

Edwards, Mack Ray, 1918-70, U.S., suic.-kid.-mur. When Mack Ray Edwards turned himself in to Los Angeles police on Mar. 6, 1970, he handed over a loaded pistol and told authorities where they could find three girls he had kidnapped. After police recovered the unharmed girls, Edwards described six murders he had committed in a seventeen-year span, and asked to die. Edwards told officials that he was confessing to the crimes because his sense of guilt kept him from eating or sleeping.

Edwards admitted to sexually molesting and killing Stella Darlene Nolan, an 8-year-old girl whose body was recovered seventeen years after her 1953 death. He confessed to shooting Gary Rochet, a 16-year-old boy from Granada Hills in 1968, and murdering 13-year-old Donald Allen Todd six months later. While no bodies were discovered, the construction worker also confessed to the murders of Don Baker, Brenda Howell, and Roger Madison. The 11-year-old Howell was the younger sister of Edwards' wife.

For years Edwards worked as a heavy-equipment operator, and lived quietly with his wife and two children outside San Fernando, Calif. At the same time, he carried on a double life in which he molested and murdered children. Edwards admitted abducting and molesting Nolan, and told authorities he strangled the girl and threw her off a bridge. He said he then went home, but returned to the scene later and to find the girl dazed but alive. Edwards said he stabbed the child to death and buried her at a construction site where he was working.

When his trial began, Edwards told Judge L. Thaxton Hanson that there was no need to tie up the courts because he was guilty and deserved to die. During his trial, Edwards twice attempted suicide, and reprimanded his court-appointed lawyer when the attorney argued against the death penalty. In his haste to die, Edwards requested that he be moved ahead of the 100 men who were awaiting execution.

Edwards was convicted on three counts of murder and sentenced to die. Not content to wait for the judicial system to administer justice, Edwards hanged himself with a television cord in his cell at San Quentin Prison on Oct. 30, 1971. REF.: *CBA.*

Edwards, Matthew, prom. 1947, Brit., mansl. In September 1947, a shopkeeper's wife was wheeling her nine-month-old daughter in a stroller. Leaving the baby outside, she went to serve some customers, and returned to find the stroller and the infant gone. A rapid search of the North England coastal town revealed the upside-down stroller in a pit filled with water; the baby had drowned. A policeman questioned 9-year-old Matthew Edwards, who said that he had taken the stroller. "There was a baby in the pram and I threw it in the water. I just wanted to do it." At the trial he was allowed to plead guilty to manslaughter instead of murder, and was ordered to be detained for a maximum of five years.

REF.: *CBA; Wilson, Children Who Kill.*

Edwards, Ninian, 1775-1833, U.S., jur. Served on the Kentucky Court of Appeals as chief justice in 1807, as governor for the territory of Illinois from 1809-18, as a U.S. senator representing Illinois from 1818-24, and as governor of Illinois from 1826-30. REF.: *CBA.*

Edwards, Paul, and **Shaw, Jill,** prom. 1975, U.S., mur. Paul Edwards and his wife Clover managed an apartment complex in Stone Mountain, a popular vacation resort in Georgia. Jill Shaw was a tall, muscular brunette who was staying with the couple in 1974 until Mrs. Edwards discovered the woman was also sleeping with her husband. Even after Shaw left the resort, the affair continued. The lovers then devised a plot in which they planned to kill Mrs. Edwards and live happily ever after.

On Jan. 30, 1975, Edwards gave Shaw his revolver. Early the next morning as he sought to establish an alibi by talking to a teller at a local bank, Shaw drove to Edwards' apartment, seemingly to talk with his wife. During the conversation, Shaw shot Edward's wife in the face twice, killing her almost instantly. As pre-arranged, Paul returned home to find his wife dead and called for an ambulance. When police arrived, Edwards claimed robbery as the motive, but authorities abandoned that theory when they found $50 in the victim's purse.

Meanwhile, Shaw waited for Edwards at an Atlanta airport. She had left a message for him with a security guard and said that it was for someone whose wife had been shot in the face. The lovers were soon arrested and charged with murder. Edwards and Shaw were sentenced to life in prison for killing Mrs. Edwards.

REF.: *CBA; Godwin, Murder U.S.A.*

Edwards, Robert Allan, 1913-35, U.S., mur. Two days before Edwards planned to elope with Freda McKechnie, police discovered the young woman's body in Harvey's Lake, outside of Wilkes-Barre, Pa. She had been clubbed over the head and drowned on July 30, 1934. When first questioned by the police, Edwards admitted that he had been with his pregnant girlfriend on the evening of the murder, but said he had dropped her off and gone home. When told police found tire tracks that matched his car in the sand at the beach, Edwards concocted a story about McKechnie fainting. He said he clubbed her over the head so people would think McKechnie had bumped her head. Edwards' third story was a confession, in which he admitted smashing McKechnie over the head with a blackjack and leaving her in the lake.

On trial for first-degree murder, the prosecution introduced evidence that linked Edwards romantically with an East Aurora, N.Y., woman and said he killed McKechnie because he wanted to marry Margaret Crain. The 21-year-old man took the stand in his own defense and said he was innocent. While he admitted his attraction to Crain, he told the jury he planned to marry McKechnie. Following eight hours of deliberation, Edwards was convicted of murder and sentenced to death. He died in the electric chair on May 6, 1935.

REF.: *CBA*; Kilgallen, *Murder One;* Whitelaw, *Corpus Delicti.*

Edwards, Vernon David, Jr., b.1937, U.S., mur. When Edwards turned himself into police in Decatur, Ga. in July 1972, and confessed to two Florida slayings, he said his conscience had finally caught up with him. Thirteen years earlier, after getting drunk and being spurned by an older woman at an office party, Edwards stopped at a cottage on the Miami block where he lived. Edwards admitted that he had watched 55-year-old Ethel Ione Little undress a number of times, but his intent that evening was to rob the spinster so he could continue his drinking binge.

Little's landlord found his tenant early on the afternoon of Dec. 15, 1959. She was naked and her body had been tied to the four bedposts. The killer had sliced off Little's left breast in addition to stabbing, strangling, and sexually assaulting the woman. Despite the efforts of Miami Detective Mike Gonzalez the Little slaying had remained unsolved for thirteen years.

Edwards also confessed to the 1961 murder of cocktail waitress Johanna Block. The 33-year-old victim was stabbed repeatedly with a pair of scissors, strangled, and beaten about the face. Mary Alice Bratt, who had known Block quite well, aided police in the initial investigation, but the case remained unsolved until 1972, when Mary Alice Edwards convinced her guilt-ridden husband Vernon to turn himself in to police. Dade County Court Judge Paul Baker accepted Edwards' guilty plea and sentenced the house painter to life imprisonment.

REF.: *CBA;* Henderson, *The Super Sleuths.*

Edwardson, Derrick, 1926-   , Brit., mur. Five days after the disappearance of 4-year-old Edwina Taylor, British police discovered the girl's body in the basement of a house on Aubyn's Road in Upper Norwood. Taylor's skull had been fractured and she had been strangled. Police directed their attention towards Derrick Edwardson, the building's ground-floor tenant, who had a lengthy criminal record, including an arrest for the assault of a 5-year-old.

The police found a note in Edwardson's locker at work; he admitted killing the girl, but said he had not raped her. He would turn himself in, he wrote, because "I cannot get the smell of her decaying body out of my system." On Sept. 9, 1957, Edwardson surrendered to police. He pleaded guilty to charges of murder and was sentenced to life in prison.

REF.: *CBA;* Wilson, *Encyclopedia of Murder.*

Eftimoff, Simeon, d.1933, Bul., assass. Simeon Eftimoff, a Macedonian journalist and leader of the militant Mikhailoffist faction, was assassinated in January 1933 outside the Royal Palace in Sofia, Bul. The two gunmen, Christo Trojanoff and Ivan Petroff, also Macedonians, wore hunting clothes and had dogs with them. Armed with shotguns and bombs, they fired on Eftimoff and his entourage. The sixty shots in the courtyard brought Czar Boris III, the despotic ruler of Bulgaria, to the windows, in time to see the dogs and hunters run off.

Eftimoff was fatally shot and eight other people were injured during the shooting. Petroff was arrested on the spot, and Trojanoff was wounded. He was removed to the Alexander Hospital, where two sentries stood guard outside his room. Late one night, sister Catherine Konstantinoff strode past the guards and shot Trojanoff through the head with a pistol she had hidden in her dress. "As a good Macedonian," she said, "I could not hesitate." REF.: *CBA.*

Egan, Frank J., and **Tinnin, Albert,** and **Doran, Verne,** prom. 1932, U.S., mur. Frank J. Egan was a well-known, well-liked public defender in San Francisco during the 1930s. In trying to maintain a classy, generous image, he went severely into debt.

Looking around for a way to solve his problems, his glance fell on Mrs. Jessie Scott Hughes, an elderly client who had made him her executor and heir. When the police had previously warned her that Egan had fantasized about her death, the woman had scoffed and insisted that he was like her own son.

Egan's chauffeur and another man were both "in debt" to Egan because of his assistance in getting and keeping them out of prison. When he asked for their help, they did not feel they could say no. On Aug. 29, 1932, Egan and Dr. Housman went to the fights and made sure they were seen there. That night, Albert Tinnin and Verne Doran drove Egan's car into Mrs. Hughes' garage. When Mrs. Hughes came out to chat for a few minutes, Tinnin knocked her unconscious and placed her on the floor and Doran ran her over with the car. Then they drove out to a highway, and dumped her body as if it had been struck by a hit-and-run driver.

Captain of Inspectors Charles W. Dullea who had eavesdropped on Dr. Housman's office and heard Egan wishing Mrs. Hughes dead, located the car that neighbors had seen at the old woman's garage and found gray hairs on it that matched hers. He also, just on the chance that it might pay off, had Tinnin and Doran brought in. They readily told the whole story and Egan was brought in, his carefully contrived alibi useless. All three were tried and found Guilty of murder. Each man was sentenced to life in prison.

REF.: Block, *Wizard of Berkeley;* CBA; Cohen, *One Hundred True Crime Stories;* McComas, *The Graveside Companion.*

Egan, John, prom. 1931, Brit., burg. John Egan made criminal history in England when he became the first man ever convicted on the basis of palm prints. He was arrested and charged with three counts of breaking and entering and one count of attempting to break into a London shop in 1931. While Scotland Yard had been using a fingerprint system for identifying criminals for a number of years, Egan's trial at Old Bailey marked the first time palm-prints had been allowed as evidence in a British court.

The defendant pleaded guilty to the four charges and confessed to several more burglaries. Egan was sentenced to fourteen months in prison.

REF.: *CBA;* Cherrill, *Cherrill of the Yard.*

Egan's Rats, prom. 1920s-30s, U.S., org. crime. Around the turn of the century, Jellyroll Egan organized a gang called the "Rats" to supply strong-arm muscle to businessmen trying to prevent unionization in St. Louis, Mo. The beginning of WWI essentially eliminated the need for the gang's services. However, when Prohibition began, the Rats were resurrected by Dinty Colbeck, Egan's successor. Under Colbeck's guidance, the Rats moved into more lucrative ventures, such as bootlegging.

By the mid-1920s, Colbeck enjoyed a measure of political influence in the city. His gang was responsible for a number of jewelry thefts, mostly carried out by Red Rudensky, one of the best safecrackers in the business. Colbeck also occasionally supplied hired killers. It is commonly believed that Fred Burke and several other members of Egan's Rats were responsible for Chicago's St. Valentine's Day Massacre in 1929. Another Rat of note, Leo Vincent Brothers, was arrested and convicted for the murder of Chicago *Tribune* reporter Jake Lingle in June 1930. Brothers. whose actual guilt remains in doubt, went to prison.

Following the repeal of Prohibition, Egan's Rats declined. When Colbeck was murdered in the late 1930s, the last of the gang members moved into new criminal enterprises. See: **Burke, Fred R.**

REF.: *CBA;* Cohen, *Mickey Cohen: In My Own Words;* Kobler, *Capone;* McPhaul, *Johnny Torrio;* Nash, *Bloodletters and Badmen;* Peterson, *The Mob;* Thompson and Raymond, *Gang Rule in New York;* Thrasher, *The Gang.*

Egdell, George, and **Richardson, Charles,** prom. 1879, Brit., burg. For nine years, Richardson and Egdell lived on time borrowed from Michael Brannagan and Peter Murphy. In February 1879, two burglars broke into an Edlingham rectory and wounded the rector, M.H.G. Buckle, and his daughter. Although

Buckle and his daughter survived the shootings, the nature of the crime was so contemptible that a great deal of pressure was put on Police Superintendent Harkes to apprehend the assailants. Shortly thereafter two poachers, Brannagan and Murphy, were arrested and charged with burglary and attempted murder.

While the trial was filled with contradictory evidence, Justice Manisty seemed to have found the defendants guilt a foregone conclusion. Despite pleas from Brannagan and Murphy that they were innocent, Manisty sentenced the men to twenty years in prison. It was years later, and only through the determination of Mr. Perry, the Vicar of St. Paul's, Alnwick, that the truth of the matter was revealed. A parishioner told Perry that Egdell had been out the evening of the burglary, and that Egdell's wife asked a number of people to cover for him. Egdell finally confessed his part in the crime to the clergyman, adding that he feared retribution from his partner Richardson.

Egdell and Richardson were finally arrested and tried on charges of burglary only. Judge Baron Pollock sentenced Egdell and Richardson to five years in prison and ordered the release of Brannagan and Murphy. The wrongly convicted men were each given £800. A subsequent police investigation revealed the authorities had conspired to imprison Brannagan and Murphy. Three policemen were brought to trial on conspiracy charges, but acquitted when the judge declared they had only followed orders from Harkes, who had died prior to the 1888 trial.

REF.: Brock, *A Casebook of Crime*; CBA; Ellis, *Black Fame*.

Eghise, Mauricio, prom. 1936, Mex., drugs. Mauricio Eghise, the son-in-law of the chief of police in Mexico City, figured prominently in a drug smuggling operation that worked between the Mexican capital and Shanghai in the 1930s. Al Scharff, a U.S. customs agent, was assigned to destroy the ring that had been importing heroin from China and shipping it to Paris, Buenos Aires, and Istanbul. With the help of Mexican authorities, Scharff was able to take a series of cables from Shanghai and track down the smugglers.

Eghise tried to slit his throat in jail, but survived the suicide attempt and was deported to Turkey.

REF.: CBA; Roark, *Coin of Contraband*.

Egmont (or **Egmond**), Count **Lamoraal van** (AKA: **Graaf van Egmont**), 1522-68, and **Montmorency, Filips van** (AKA: **Count Hoorn, Graaf van Hoorn** (or **Hoorne**), c.1524-1568, Belg., treas. As Prince of Gavre, Count Lamoraal van Egmont negotiated the marriage of Mary Tudor of England with Philip II of Spain in 1554, and he fought with distinction for Spain in the war against France from 1557-59. In 1561, Count Egmont and Filips van Montmorency, better known as Count Hoorn, along with Dutch ruler William of Orange, spoke out against the religious persecution of Protestants in Belgium and the Netherlands as decreed by King Philip II. While Egmont and Hoorn refused to join William of Orange in his demands for religious freedoms and the establishment of guaranteed rights for the Spanish provinces, they continued to oppose the king's establishment of a domineering and inflexible brand of Catholicism.

Counts Hoorn and Egmont were outspoken in their opposition, but they were badly outnumbered in Brussels. On a mission to Madrid, Egmont was berated by the king after the Count pleaded with him to relax his strict provincial laws. Philip eventually grew weary of the many complaints he was receiving from Belgium, and dispatched the Duke of Alba to the province in an attempt to restore order in the name of the Catholic church.

The Duke, backed by a large army made up of Spanish and Italian soldiers, stormed into northwestern Europe to quell the uprising. The soldiers quickly secured the provinces and established the Council of Troubles, consisting exclusively of Spaniards and later known as the "Council of Blood." After finding it impossible to organize resistance to the Duke's massive army, William of Orange fled to Germany and urged Counts Egmont and Hoorn to follow.

Executions of "traitors" and "heretics" by the newly-established Council of Blood were so widespread that gallows were erected in almost every town. Counts Egmont and Hoorn were denounced by the council in 1567 and brought up on charges of treason. Tried before the council, Egmont and Hoorn were convicted and sentenced to death. In 1568, Egmont and Hoorn were beheaded along with eighteen other noblemen at the public square in Brussels. Their executions sparked the rebellion the freed the Netherlands from Spanish rule.

REF.: CBA; Johnson, *Famous Assassinations of History*.

Egyptian Dragons, prom. 1957, U.S., mur. Looking for a cool spot on a stifling New York City night in July 1957, 14-year-old Michael Farmer and 16-year-old Roger McShane thought the pool at High Bridge Park in Washington Heights might be the answer. At the same time, eighteen armed members of a Manhattan street gang called the Egyptian Dragons were headed towards the park to confront The Jesters, a rival gang. When the Jesters failed to show for the rumble, the Dragons remained in the mood for mayhem. Farmer and McShane were preparing to enter the pool when they were attacked by the Dragons. The handicapped Farmer was beaten and stabbed to death, and McShane was seriously injured with knife wounds in his back and stomach. Police arrested eighteen suspects in the case, and seven gang members went on trial for murder in February 1958. The other eleven boys, all juveniles, were sentenced to the state reformatory for their part in the slaying.

Assistant District Attorney Robert R. Reynolds alleged that Dragon leaders Louis Alvarez, seventeen, and Charles "Big Man" Horton, eighteen, had led the attack. The prosecution charged that Farmer had been beaten, kicked, and punched prior to being stabbed. The trial took ten weeks, engaged twenty-seven defense lawyers, and cost the state nearly $250,000. After a day of deliberation, the jury convicted Alvarez and Horton on charges of second-degree murder on Apr. 15, and the pair were sentenced to twenty years to life in prison. Leroy "Magician" Birch, nineteen, and Leoncio "Jello" DeLeon, seventeen, were convicted of second-degree manslaughter and sentenced to five to fifteen years. Three gang members, Richard Hills, seventeen, George Melendez, sixteen, and John McCarthy, fifteen, were acquitted of all charges.

REF.: CBA; Hibbert, *The Roots of Evil*; Wilson, *Children Who Kill*.

Egyptian Well Murder Case, prom. 1900s, Egypt, mur. When Egyptian authorities discovered a skeleton in a dry well, the collection of bones had been wedged between the walls of the well and folded over for more than six months, officials said. After finding a hole in the top of the skull, police assumed the wound had resulted from a head-first fall into the well. Before closing the case, the skeleton was transported to an expert in forensic ballistics. The doctor determined the approximate vital statistics of the corpse, but in piecing the puzzle together he came across evidence which failed to support the accidental death theory.

The hole in the skull was caused by a bullet wound, the expert said, and there was nothing in the well that would have caused the body to contort into the position in which it was discovered. Experts also found a homemade bullet in the breast bone, surmising that the victim had possibly been lying down when shot. Some decayed pieces of cloth sacking led the forensics experts to the conclusion that the body had been stuffed into a sack and dropped down the well, thus its awkward position in the well. Eventually, the murder victim was identified and authorities traced the crime to a former co-worker who confessed to the killing.

REF.: CBA; Smith, *Mostly Murder*.

Ehrlich, Eugen, 1862-1922, Aust., jur. Instructed law students at Czernowitz in Vienna from 1899-1914, wrote *Grundlegung der Soziologie des Rechts*, and was recognized as founder of legal sociology. REF.: CBA.

Ehrlich, Jacob (Jake), 1900-71, U.S., crim. lawyer. Born on Oct. 15, 1900, on a plantation outside of Washington, D.C., Ehrlich lived an adventuresome life before he became one of America's foremost criminal attorneys. He ran away from home at age sixteen and joined the Maryland Militia, serving in the punitive expedition against Pancho Villa in Mexico under the command of Gen. John Pershing. He returned to the U.S. to study law at Georgetown University, but after two semesters he reenlisted for duty in WWI. Ehrlich was sent to France as a lieutenant and saw considerable action.

Following the war, Ehrlich bummed his way west on freight trains to San Francisco in 1920, and there held all manner of jobs—delivering groceries, working for the railroads, washing dishes, and fighting professionally as a lightweight boxer. He delivered subpoenas and went to school nights, studying law. He passed the California bar on Mar. 7, 1922. Thus began a remarkable legal career with Ehrlich specializing in criminal cases. In thirty years of practice, Ehrlich defended fifty-six persons charged with murder and did not lose one of them to the executioner.

Ehrlich was involved with many spectacular cases, including the defense of theatrical mogul Alexander Pantages who stood trial for rape in 1931 (with Los Angeles attorney Jerry Geisler); San Francisco madam Dolly Fine, who was charged with keeping a bawdy house; fan dancer Sally Rand, facing a morals charge; drummer Gene Krupa, charged with drug abuse; blues singer Billie Holliday, also charged with drug abuse; husband slayer Laverne Borelli; gangster Waxey Gordon; and forger and crook Alfred Leonard Cline, suspected of multiple murder. His advice to all clients was always the same:

Criminal lawyer Jake Ehrlich.

"Never plead guilty." He became so famous that whenever someone in San Francisco got in trouble they immediately called out: "Get Jake."

In all his cases, Ehrlich presented a dapper appearance with starched collars and cuffs, and neatly pressed pinstripe suits. He exuded confidence and was one of the most convincing speakers to ever address a jury. Judges delighted in hearing Ehrlich's cases since they knew to expect the unexpected. He not only became rich representing clients charged with criminal offenses but he, on many occasions, worked for nothing to defend those he believed were wrongly accused.

One day, while entering vagrancy court on another matter, Ehrlich noticed a sandy-haired teenager, lips quivering in fear as she waited to be charged with vagrancy. He talked briefly with the 16-year-old girl, and learned she was a runaway from Montana where both her parents had recently died. She had been found in the company of two sailors whom, she insisted, had given her shelter in their room for the night. Ehrlich then announced to the court that he was defending the girl, pleading her not guilty to vagrancy charges.

The great criminal attorney waved away objections from the prosecution and then delivered the kind of eloquence expected from Jake Ehrlich in any case, great or small: "From my own experience—which the court will agree has been extensive in these matters—I tell you that the city and county of San Francisco is preparing to make a prostitute of this frightened little girl. Put her through the humiliating police procedure, throw her in with those you have convicted of the oldest profession, and you can make of her, too, a woman of the streets. She should be returned to her home."

Replied the emotionless judge: "There are no funds for sending her home, Mr. Ehrlich."

"There are now," said Jake Ehrlich and he reached into his own wallet and withdrew enough money for the girl's trip home, plus an allowance for some new clothes and money to keep her off the streets of Billings, Mont., until she could find a job. The court released the girl. Like most great men, Ehrlich was sentimental, and like all noble men, he sprang to the defense of the helpless

and the hopeless, often without pay and often without thanks.

But he did hear from the Montana girl again. She wrote to Ehrlich six years later, simply sending her letter "To Lawyer Jake—San Francisco," a letter that was delivered to the then famous attorney. The girl told him that she was married to a rancher and had just given birth to a son. "His name is Jacob, for you," she wrote. "I didn't learn your last name but if it hadn't been for you I would not be here—and neither would he." Throughout his colorful life, Jake Ehrlich treasured that letter beyond all fees, all awards, all recognition. See: **Borelli, Laverne; Cline, Alfred Leonard; Holliday, Billie; Krupa, Gene; Pantages, Alexander; Rand, Sally.**

REF.: *CBA;* Ehrlich, *A Life in My Hands;* Noble and Averbuch, *Never Plead Guilty;* Reppetto, *The Blue Parade.*

Eichhorn, Karl Friedrich, 1781-1854, Ger., jur. Established historical school of German law. REF.: *CBA.*

Eichmann, Karl Adolf (AKA: Adolf Barth, Ricardo Klement), 1906-62, Ger., war crimes. Karl Adolf Eichmann joined the emerging Nazi Party in 1932. Like Adolf Hitler, Eichmann grew up in Austria. He was forced to drop out of college after WWI when his father lost his factory job in Linz. The humiliation of German defeat in the war disillusioned Eichmann, as it had so many other youths during that period. His adherence to National Socialism—still an outlaw movement in Austria in 1932—led to Eichmann's dismissal from his job. When the police tried to arrest him, the 26-year-old Eichmann escaped across the German border and became a member of the SS Austrian Legion preparing for the coming attack on Austria. In the coming years Eichmann rose in the Nazi hierarchy and impressed his superiors with his knowledge of Jewish history and customs. In 1938, just as Hitler was taking control of Austria, Eichmann, on a flight to Austria with Reinhardt Heydrich and Heinrich Himmler, was made responsible for rounding up Austrian Jews. He was named leader of the SS bureau IV A 4 B of the Gestapo Internal Affairs, dealing with Jewish religion. The fate of all Jews in Nazi occupied territories rested on him.

After Poland fell, Eichmann proposed sending 4 million Jews to live in Madagascar under a Nazi ruler. But following the 1941 German invasion of Russia, such "soft-hearted" plans were rejected outright. Eichmann's SS Einsatzgruppen followed the crack Panzer divisions across the Soviet Union, machine gunning Jews along the way. Even Himmler was horrified by the carnage. He ordered Eichmann to devise

Adolf Eichmann at his trial in Israel.

more "humane" executions. Eichmann chose Cyclon B gas and ordered the construction of specially designed gas chambers. The gas, first tested on Russian prisoners of war, was adopted for use in all the concentration camps. Crematories capable of incinerating 9,000 prisoners a day were built at the same time.

Even when the Allied armies began to close in, Eichmann refused to stop the killing. Himmler suggested using the surviving Jews as bargaining chips and ordered Eichmann to end the slaughter. "No one will walk out of Auschwitz!" Eichmann shot back. "There is only one way they will leave—through the smokestacks!" With Russians advancing toward Budapest, Eichmann fled and told his SS associates that he was going to commit suicide. Instead, he donned the uniform of a Luftwaffe corporal and used the alias Adolf Barth and surrendered to U.S.

troops. Eichmann then escaped the internment camp and made his way back to northern Germany. He lived as a lumberjack for the next three years before he used the Nazi underground network to secure passage through Switzerland to Rome, Italy. Pretending to be an anti-Communist refugee, Eichmann traveled as "Ricardo Klement" under a forged passport. The Vatican's relief department gave him Italian Red Cross documents, and he traveled to Argentina, where dictator Juan Perón, a graduate of the German officers school in Potsdam, provided safe haven for fugitive Nazis.

Eichmann reached Buenos Aires in 1950. He found work as a surveyor for the German-American engineering firm Capri. He traveled in South America frequently in the next few years, arriving in Bolivia, Paraguay, and Brazil. Eichmann's wife Veronika and the children stayed in Europe and told authorities that Eichmann was dead. In 1947, Veronika had tried to have him declared legally dead, but Simon Wiesenthal, a civil engineer and survivor of a concentration camp, was dubious. Jewish leaders stepped up their efforts to find Eichmann.

Left, Adolf Eichmann at twenty-five and, right, in 1940 as a member of Himmler's SS.

Left, Eichmann in 1952 while living in Argentina as Ricardo Klement, and, right, in 1960 as a prisoner in Israel.

Manos Diamant, a Polish Jew active in the underground during the war, planted a woman as a domestic in Mrs. Eichmann's rented house in Bad Aussee, in central Austria. She tried to learn Eichmann's whereabouts, but could not even find a photograph. Diamant sought out Eichmann's former mistress, who showed him a photograph from which Wiesenthal identified Eichmann. In 1952, Veronika Eichmann and her children went to Argentina by boat and enjoyed the full protection of the government for the next six years.

In 1959, Israeli agents found out that prominent former Nazi Dr. Johannes von Leer was traveling to South America and they believed he would lead them to Eichmann. In Buenos Aires, von Leer contacted Ricardo Klement, whom the Israeli government determined through fingerprints to be Eichmann. Their legal claims on Eichmann were shaky since his crimes occurred before the state of Israel existed. But the Israelis decided they must take Eichmann anyway.

For the celebration of Argentina's 150th anniversary of freedom from Spanish rule, Israel decided to send "reinforcements" along with the usual diplomatic crew. On May 11, 1960, Eichmann was abducted in Buenos Aires by occupants in a black sedan. The occupants jumped out of the car, grabbed Eichmann, and took him to a secluded villa outside the city where he was held incommunicado for the next nine days. Eichmann agreed to accompany the agents back Tel Aviv to be tried. On May 20, an El Al jet left Buenos Aries with Eichmann on board. Argentina's president, Arturo Frondizi, issued a formal protest to Israel. But President David Ben-Gurion of Israel asked for Argentina's indulgence, citing the "profound motivation and supreme moral justification of this act."

Eichmann's trial began in April 1961 at Jerusalem's Beit Haam (House of the People). For four months, survivors of the Holocaust came forward to relate chilling eye-witness accounts of Nazi atrocities. Eichmann sat impassively behind a bulletproof glass and plastic cage constructed to shield him from assassination and to keep his friends from slipping him a vial of poison.

On Dec. 15, 1961, the court sentenced Eichmann to hang. In his final statement, he said, "I am not the monster I am made out to be. This mass slaughter is solely the responsibility of political leaders. My guilt lies in my allegiance to the colors and the service." Eichmann was executed on May 31, 1962, at the Ramle Prison in Israel.

REF.: *CBA;* Henderson, *The Super Sleuths;* Messick, *Kidnapping;* Sparrow, *The Great Abductors;* Wilson, *Encyclopedia of Murder;* (FILM), *Operation Eichmann,* 1961.

Eichorn, Hermann von, 1848-1918, Ger., field marshal, assass. Hermann von Eichorn, a Prussian career officer, led the 10th German Army against Russia during WWI, and later the Eichorn military group in Kurland and later the Kiev group. He commanded the occupation forces in the Ukraine. On Aug 1, 1918, Eichorn and his aide, Captain von Dressler, were shot to death in Kiev by B. Danskio, a fanatical sailor who had been assigned to assassinate Eichorn by the leaders of the Left Social Revolutionary group at the Kronstadt Naval Base.

REF.: *CBA;* Fischer, *The Life of Lenin;* Ulam, *The Bolsheviks.*

Eichstätt Witch Trials, prom. 1615, Ger., witchcraft. From 1603 to 1630, the Bishop of Eichstätt, Johann Christoph, led a witch hunt in which 113 women and nine men were burned and more than 150 others were convicted of witchcraft in Germany. By 1627, Christoph came under pressure from the townspeople for confiscating the property of convicted witches. In an effort to prove his crusade was strictly religious and not personal, the bishop, after twenty-four years, stopped seizing estates.

The trials often consisted of victims being arrested on the basis of circumstantial or insubstantial evidence, and then being tortured into admitting they were witches. The defendants were not allowed any legal representation, there was no testimony from witnesses, and the victims were allowed to see a priest only after being sentenced. Anna Käser was charged with attending a sabbat, a meeting of witches, in 1629. The charges came out of forced confessions of previous trial victims. After hours of brutal torture, Käser confessed to being a witch. She was beheaded and burned at Neuberg.

REF.: *CBA;* Robbins, *The Encyclopedia of Witchcraft and Demonology;* Zwetsloot, *Friedrich Spee.*

Eike von Repgow (Eyke, Eiko, Ecco, Ebko, Heiko, Repgau, Repegouw, Repkow), prom. 13th Cent., Ger., jur. Authored the beginnings of German legal writings with a treatise on Saxon law written in Latin, called *Sachsenspiegel,* and possibly wrote *Sächsische Weltchronik,* which was not published till much later in 1877. REF.: *CBA.*

Prohibition agents extraordinaire, left, Moe Smith, and, right, the indefatigable Izzy Einstein, seizing an illegal still in Manhattan, 1923.

Einstein, Isidore (Izzy), 1880-1938, **and Smith, Moe,** 1887-1960, prom. 1920s, U.S., law enfor. Izzy Einstein and Moe Smith were the clown princes of Prohibition, dry agents who enforced the Volstead Act with a vengeance but whose unorthodox and colorful style captured the imagination of the country. Einstein was the leader of this two-man crusade against booze and speakeasies. A former salesman and a postal clerk at the dawn of Prohibition, Einstein, at age forty, applied for the job of a federal Prohibition agent and was teamed up with Moe Smith. Einstein spoke several languages, played the harmonica, trombone, and violin, and was married with four children. He stood five foot five inches and weighed 225 pounds, a roly-poly, jolly cutup who was street smart and had an uncanny acting ability. He had a knack for impersonation and understood people better than most amateur psychologists.

Einstein was brash and bold, and after going on the federal payroll at $2,500 a year, he was immediately assigned to inspect a suspected speakeasy in Brooklyn. He went directly to the place and pounded on the door. The door slot slid back and a grim face stared back at him. "Who are you and what do you want?" Einstein was asked.

"I'm Izzy Einstein and I want a drink."

"Who sent you?"

"My boss sent me. I'm a Prohibition agent. I just got appointed."

The man on the other side of the peephole exploded with laughter. He threw open the door and ushered Einstein into the speakeasy, belly laughing and slapping Einstein on the back. "Come on in, pal," he said. "That's the best gag I've heard all year." He turned to a well-dressed man and said: "Hey, boss, get a load of this guy. Says he's a Prohibition agent and he wants a drink! You got a badge, too, pal?"

"Here it is," Einstein said and produced his badge. This caused the doorman and the owner, along with the bartenders, to erupt into gales of laughter. Einstein was given a drink on the house and quickly downed it, realizing at that instant that he had destroyed the evidence. He tried to grab the bottle but the bartender snatched it up, quickly understanding that Einstein was, indeed, what he said he was. After this first failure, Einstein

rigged up a flat bottle which he hid under his coat, fastened to his belt. Einstein attached to it a funnel and a rubber tube which went into the flat bottle. Izzy would then enter a speakeasy, order a drink, take a sip and, while the bartender was making change, pour the rest of the liquor into the funnel, thus obtaining the evidence to convict the speakeasy operators. "I'd have died if it hadn't been for that little funnel and bottle," Einstein later stated. "And most of the stuff I got in those places was terrible."

Later, when the tubby agent was famous, he entered a speakeasy to see his own portrait above the bar, black crepe draped about the frame, a sign beneath reading: "This man is poison." He was told that he was unknown and had to leave the bar. "Why, don't you know me," he said. "I'm Izzy Epstein, the famous Prohibition agent."

The bouncer pointed to the portrait and said: "Get the name right, buddy, the bum's name is Einstein!"

"Don't you think I know my own name. It's Epstein!"

After some argument, Izzy proposed they settle matters by betting drinks that his name was Epstein and that he was the celebrated agent. The bet was made and Einstein seized the bottle, arresting all inside the speakeasy. In early 1920, after only a few weeks as a Prohibition agent, Einstein recruited his good friend Moe Smith into the Prohibition service. Smith, who operated a small cigar store, was taller than Einstein but almost as pot-bellied, weighing in at 235 pounds. The pair looked like Tweedle Dum and Tweedle Dee, but they were most effective at their jobs. Nothing was too spectacular for these characters. In 1922, they pretended to be fruit peddlers and entered a livery stable to find a fresh horse, saying theirs had been stolen from their cart which was dismantled outside at the curb. Once inside, following a tip, Einstein and Smith found a secret passageway that led to a basement which proved to be a winery. Einstein and Smith arrested everyone in the livery.

Izzy was the virtuoso of the pair and was invariably the one who gained entrance to the speakeasy. He posed as a long-haired violinist, actually playing his instrument once inside a speakeasy as a signal for Moe to break inside with other agents. Einstein also posed as a Polish count, a beauty contest judge and, when invading the sedate Assembly, a swanky speakeasy where New York jurists met to imbibe, Einstein announced himself as a magistrate. He arrested the indignant jurists and the owners. On another occasion, he and Smith, wearing torn football uniforms and helmets, banged on the door of a sportsmen's speakeasy and shouted: "Let us in! We won the game and we want to celebrate!" They were admitted and promptly made their arrests.

No scheme to trap bootleggers was too bizarre for the enterprising Einstein and Smith. On one occasion they slaved away as gravediggers in a cemetery across from an infamous roadhouse. The operator of the speakeasy took pity on them and offered to sell them "a couple of pints at cut rate prices." They accepted, took a few swigs and then arrested their startled benefactor. The largest haul the dynamic pair made was at a Bronx garage where they confiscated 2,000 cases of bottled whiskey and 365 barrels of whiskey and brandy. Some days later, the pair swooped down Broadway, making wholesale arrests of the owners of the most famous booze parlors in New York, including Shanley's, Jack's, the Ted Lewis Club, Reisenweber's, and the Beaux Arts. The tuxedoed and evening-gowned patrons, however, were allowed to pay their checks before being escorted outside. Einstein was a considerate agent. He always allowed the speakeasy owners operating restaurants to collect their checks "so they wouldn't get stuck with the food bills."

Einstein also proved to be exceptionally courageous. He and Smith, who were so successful that they were sent on special missions to raid speakeasies in Chicago, Detroit and other cities, encountered gangsters in their adventures, and on several occasions Einstein came close to being shot. One time he arrested a speakeasy owner in Chicago and the man pulled a pistol from behind the bar. The gun jammed when the gangster pulled the trigger. "I grabbed his arm and he and I had a fierce fight all over the bar," Izzy later remembered, "but I finally got the pistol. I don't mind telling you that I was afraid, particularly when I found that the gun was loaded." In Detroit, a bartender jammed a gun into Einstein's ample paunch when he was told he was under arrest. Izzy calmly pushed the gun aside and without blinking an eye said: "Put that up, son. Murdering me won't help your family."

Einstein struck throughout the country with lightning speed. He got off a train in Atlanta and within twenty minutes arrested a confectionery shop owner for selling booze. After being in Cleveland for a half hour he single-handedly raided the most popular speakeasy in town. He didn't have to leave the railroad stations in St. Louis and Chicago to make his arrests, getting off the trains and locating small speakeasies in the depots. The spectacular Einstein and Smith became so famous that stories of their humorous feats filled newspapers and magazines coast to coast, publicity that irked their superiors, who felt that some of the limelight should have been theirs. Both men were fired on Nov. 13, 1925, "for the good of the service," according to one terse

Left, Izzy taking inventory of captured booze, and, right, Izzy (inside bootlegger's cache) with partner Moe.

Left, Izzy disguised as a peddler, and, right, Izzy dressed as a Texas rancher.

statement by their federal bosses. One superior carped that "the service must be dignified. Izzy and Moe belong to the vaudeville stage." They opened up a small insurance company and became quite successful. Smith lived to the age of seventy-three, dying in 1960. The inimitable Izzy Einstein died on Feb. 17, 1938. All four of his sons had become successful lawyers.

REF.: Allen, *Only Yesterday*; Asbury, *The Great Illusion*; Barrett, *The Jazz Age*; *CBA*; Botkin, *Sidewalks of America*; Kobler, *Ardent Spirits*; Leighton, *The Aspirin Age, 1919-1941*; Levine, *Anatomy of a Gangster*; Merz, *The Dry Decade*; Nash, *Almanac of World Crime*; Pickering, *The Early Days of Prohibition*; Reeves, *Ol' Rum River*; Sann, *The Lawless Decade*; Sinclair, *Prohibition: The Era of Excess*; Walker, *The Night Club Era*.

Eisele, Garnett Thomas, 1923 - , U.S., jur. Served as assistant U.S. attorney from 1953-56, and received appointment from President Richard M. Nixon to the Eastern District Court of Arkansas in 1970. REF.: *CBA*.

Eisele, Joseph, d.1824, U.S., rob.-mur. A notorious highwayman, Joseph Eisele operated around Parkersburg, W.Va., where, in the space of a few years, he robbed and murdered three men. He was in the act of robbing another and was about to kill his victim when he was interrupted by travelers on a lonely road and was quickly apprehended. Eisele was convicted of murder and hanged at Parkersburg in 1824.

REF.: *CBA*; Smith, *The Gambler's Fate*.

Eisemann-Schier, Ruth, See: **Krist, Gary Steven.**

Eisen, Maxie, prom. 1920s, U.S., org. crime. Eisen was allied with Charles Dion O'Bannion in Chicago during the early 1920s, helping O'Bannion to infiltrate several unions. He then controlled these for O'Bannion and, after his murder in 1924, for the Saltis-McErlane gang. Maxie Eisen later became a political fixer who survived the Chicago gang wars of the 1920s by working for the Capone gang.

REF.: *CBA*; Fried, *The Rise and Fall of the Jewish Gangster in America*; Gage, *The Mafia Is Not an Equal Opportunity Employer*; Kobler, *Capone*, Landesco, *Organized Crime in Chicago*.

Eisner, Kurt, 1867-1919, Ger., Socialist leader, assass. A respected Jewish journalist and scholar, Kurt Eisner was also a leading German socialist who, on Nov. 7, 1918, announced the overthrow of the German monarchy in Münich, Bavaria, and the formation of a republic. The diminutive Eisner, with a long, gray beard and wearing a floppy black hat, led a few hundred scantily armed socialists and Communists to the government buildings in Munich and took control without firing a single shot. Eisner became the first president of the Bavarian republic. He championed separatism and denounced plans of the German army and other right-wing elements to reestablish the federal government. In February 1919, after he had admitted Germany's guilt in creating WWI, Eisner was shot to death in Münich by Count Anton Arco-Valley, a right-wing army lieutenant.

REF.: *CBA*; Clark, *The Fall of The German Republic*; Greenberger, *Red Rising in Bavaria*; Gumbel, *Vier Jahre politischer Mord*; Hecht, *A Child of the Century*; Hillmayr, *Roter und weisser Terror in Bayern*; Mitchell, *Revolution in Bavaria, 1918-1919*; Payne, *The Life and Death of Lenin*; Shirer, *The Rise and Fall of the Third Reich*.

Ejercito Revolucionario del Pueblo, See: **ERP.**

Ekai, Paul Wakwaro, prom. 1980, Kenya, mur. Joy Adamson arrived in Kenya in 1937. The wealthy daughter of a prominent Austrian family, in 1960 her account of her years spent training an orphaned lion cub named Elsa was published as *Born Free*. It became a best seller and drew worldwide attention to the wildlife preservation activities of Adamson and her husband George, a former game warden.

Joy Adamson lived in a remote game reserve 170 miles north of Nairobi. Each evening before the sun went down, she took a walk around the perimeter of the Shaba Game Reserve. On the night of Jan. 3, 1980, she did not return and a search party led by Pieter Mawson went out to look for her. Not far from the camp, they found Adamson with multiple stab wounds. There was evidence that she had been clawed by a wild animal, but a physician in Isiolo determined that the attacker was human. Death was caused by a simi, a double-edged knife used by the natives. The president of Kenya ordered an immediate inquiry. Three suspects were arrested, including Paul Wakwaro Ekai, a herdsman who had once worked for Adamson. Local magistrate Toweet Arap Aswani charged Ekai with murder on July 12, 1980, after two and a half months of hearings.

Ekai, who claimed that he was eighteen, though published reports had him as old as twenty-three, was found Guilty of murder on Aug. 28, 1981, and was ordered detained at the president's pleasure. He narrowly escaped Kenya's mandatory death penalty after convincing the courts that he was not yet eighteen at the time he committed the murder. Ekai may have killed Adamson because of a personality conflict with his former employer. According to Joy Adamson's former secretary, Kathy Porter, the famed naturalist had retreated into a world of her own, and had little patience with her employees.

REF.: *CBA*; Wilson, *Encyclopedia of Modern Murder.*

Ekisler, Zarch Avedis Hatchadour, prom. 1925, Brit., (unsolv.) asslt.-rob. A blow to the head with a fire poker can do strange things to one's memory. When British police found Zarch Avedis Hatchadour Ekisler, an Armenian merchant, he was unconscious. His office had been looted and his personal belongings were missing. He was taken to the hospital in critical condition. While awaiting treatment, an unconscious Ekisler began to mumble "Rod, Rod."

The Armenian recovered from his wounds and when told about the incident, gave police the complete name of his friend Rod. In hopes of solving the case, authorities brought the two men together, but Ekisler told police that Rod was not the perpetrator. The merchant never could recall who had attacked him, and the case went unsolved.

REF.: *CBA*; Nicholls, *Crime Within the Square Mile.*

Elagabulus (Varius Avitus Bassianus, Marcus Aurelius Antonnus), 204-222, Roman., emperor, assass. A great nephew of Roman emperor Septimius Severus, Elagabulus was born in Syria to a family of hereditary high priests of Baal, which were called Elah-Gabal. He became emperor in 218 after the fall of Macrinus and after his mother, Julia Soemias, presented him to the court as the illegitimate son of emperor Caracalla. A ruthless despot, Elagabulus executed most of Rome's best and heroic generals out of envy. He then imposed the religion of Baal on the Roman people and inflicted harsh punishments on all who displeased him.

He was notorious for his homosexual debaucheries and kidnaping and raping of young men. When the populace appeared on the verge of revolution, Elagabulus, at the urging of his grandmother, Julia Maesa, adopted his young cousin, Alexander of Alexianus, naming him son and heir, this young man promising to be a moderate replacement for the tyrant Elagabulus. When Elagabulus threatened to disinherit Alexander, members of the Praetorian Guard, on Mar. 11, 222, hacked the despot to pieces, along with his mother, throwing the bodies into the Tiber. REF.: *CBA.*

Elah (Ela), d.c.876 B.C., Israel, king, assass. King of Israel from 887-886 B.C. He was murdered by his servant Zimri in Tirzah the year after he succeeded his father Baasha to the throne. REF.: *CBA.*

Elazar, Sasson Shalom (AKA: Nissien), d.1910, Brit., suic.-(attempt.) mur. In March 1910, Sasson Shalom Elazar inexplicably shot his brother Louis following a brief meeting in the London offices of Sassoon & Company, where Louis was employed. Sasson, a Turkish Jew living in Britain, was arrested and Louis, with six gunshot wounds, lingered near death in Guy's Hospital. Miraculously, Louis recovered, but neither he nor his brother could offer any clues to the attack. In April, while awaiting trial for attempted murder, Elazar hanged himself from a metal vent with a silk handkerchief.

REF.: *CBA*; Nicholls, *Crime Within the Square Mile.*

Elbert, John, b.1920, and **Ferdinand, Phil**, prom. 1942, and **Humphrey, Josephine**, b.1924, U.S., mur. The cantankerous Giovanni Leonidas lived in a shack just outside of Beverly Hills and eked out a living selling goat's milk. Leonidas had few friends, but most of the people in the Sigismundo Valley had heard rumors that the hermit kept a stash of gold in his tiny house.

On Sept. 6, 1942, John Elbert and Paul Ferdinand, with Josephine Humphrey as a lookout, rented a car and went to Leonidas' shack. After forcing their way into the house, Elbert and Ferdinand tied up the old man and tried to get him to reveal the whereabouts of the gold. Torturing him, the pair burned the soles of the old man's feet with matches, but Leonidas refused to talk. When police found the goat-herder he was barely alive.

Before his death, Leonidas told authorities, "They wanted my gold...they could not make me tell."

After two weeks of investigating the case, police discovered that a car was seen in front of Leonidas' house on the day of the murder and had been rented by Elbert. He and Ferdinand were soon arrested and charged with murder. Humphrey was arrested later and served as chief prosecution witness against Elbert and Ferdinand, who were found Guilty and sentenced to life imprisonment. Humphrey pleaded guilty to the charge of manslaughter and was given a ten-year suspended sentence. Fortune-hunters scoured Leonidas' hillside home for months following the murder, but no gold was ever discovered.

REF.: *CBA*; Cohen, *One Hundred True Crime Stories.*

Elbrick, Charles Burke, prom. 1969, Braz., kid. (vict.). In September 1969, American ambassador Charles Burke Elbrick was kidnapped in Rio de Janiero by a group of Brazilians. In return for Elbrick's freedom, the kidnappers demanded the release of fifteen comrades whom they believed had been jailed unfairly. The exchange was made and attention was called to the brutal tactics of the Brazilian police. At the same time, the incident triggered a rash of political kidnapings.

REF.: *CBA*; Moorehead, *Hostages to Fortune.*

Elby, William (AKA: Dun), c.1675-1707, Brit., burg.-rob.-mur. Elby began his life of crime as a water-pad on the Thames River, slipping down the river in a boat in the dead of night and stealing from unoccupied boats or from people sleeping aboard boats. He soon turned to housebreaking where he worked with several notorious criminals including Peter Bennet and Samuel Shotland both of whom were later hanged at Tyburn. Shotland pulled his shoes off and threw them into the crowd of spectators gathered for his execution on Dec. 30, 1702. "My father and mother often told me that I should die with my shoes on," he told the waiting crowd, "but you may all see that now I have made them both liars."

That same day, another of Elby's accomplices, John Goffe, was also hanged at Tyburn. Elby had seen many of his friends and business associates die by the hangman's noose, but he had not changed his ways. On June 6, 1707, James Hackett, who had committed many burglaries with Elby, went to his death at Tyburn. Toothless Tom, another old associate was hanged on Mar. 22, 1703. John Estrick was hanged on Mar. 10, 1702. William Stanley was hanged on Jan. 26, 1703. Elby spent many short terms in Newgate Prison, and there he met many others who would soon be hanged. He joined them on Sept. 13, 1707, when he was hanged for the murder of Nicholas Hatifield, a servant of James Barry.

REF.: *CBA*; Smith, *Highwaymen.*

Elder, Ronald, prom. 1943, U.S., mur. Ronald Elder was in love with June Reinman. Although the girl was a few years older than he was, she was pretty and popular with most of the boys in Pendleton, Ore., in 1943. After nursing his crush on Reinman for a considerable length of time, Elder decided to confront her. One afternoon in October he met the 16-year-old girl in a field as she was out hunting rabbits. Elder offered to teach her how to shoot fish, and the girl let him carry her gun. When Elder told her that he loved her, Reinman failed to take the youngster seriously. Elder was enraged and shot the girl as she walked away from him. He smashed her in the head with the gun butt and tossed the gun in the creek.

Several hours later, Elder joined in the search for Reinman, whose body was later discovered by her father. Although he was questioned about the murder, Elder was not suspected during the initial investigation. It was only after a number of leads fizzled that police again questioned Reinman's friends. Elder was taken to the scene of the crime and asked to recall what had happened the afternoon he and Reinman were together. After being presented with incriminating evidence, Elder confessed to the killing and was sentenced to life in prison.

REF.: *CBA*; Rice, *Forty-five Murderers.*

Elder, Thomas Edwin, b.1882, Case of, U.S., asslt. In August

1937, Thomas Edwin Elder, the retired Dean of Mount Hermon School in Northfield, Mass., was tried for assault. The school's retired cashier, Stephen Allen Norton, said that he was leaving his garage on the night of May 25, 1937, when Elder, who wore a long coat, appeared in the doorway, pointed a gun at him, and said, "Norton, I want to talk to you." Norton ducked into his house and called the Greenfield police, who picked Elder up the next morning at his Alton, N.H., poultry farm. Elder said he had spent the night with his wife at the Eagle Hotel in Keene, N.H., thirty miles from Greenfield, and that he did not own a long coat. At the trial, District Attorney David Keedy called a local gas station owner to the stand, who testified that he had seen Elder wearing a long coat. A chambermaid at the Eagle Hotel said that Elder's half of the bed had not been slept in. Also called to the stand was Dr. Henry Franklin Cutler, predecessor of Headmaster Elliot Speer, another Mount Hermon leader who had been slain with a shotgun in an unsolved murder in 1934. Elder, who had been questioned in conjunction with the Speer case, had retired to the poultry farm not long after the inquest following Speer's slaying. Cutler testified that Norton and Elder were on such bad terms that Norton bored a hole in Elder's office wall to spy on him and his secretary; they were, Norton reported to Cutler, having an affair. After six hours of deliberation, the jury acquitted Elder of the charges of assault with intent to frighten, and assault with intent to murder. See: **Speer, Elliot.** REF.: *CBA*.

el Dnawy, Abd el-Kadir, and **Abdullah, Sameer Mohammed,** and **Badran, Ibrahim,** prom. 1972, Ger., terr.-mur. When he answered a 4:30 a.m. knock on the door, Moshe Weinberg, the wrestling coach for Israel's Olympic team, was greeted by a group of armed Arab terrorists. Dressed in athletic clothes with their weapons stuffed in tennis bags, the guerillas, or fedayeen, had scaled the fence that surrounded the Olympic housing compound and converged on the apartment complex which housed twenty-six Israelis. Weinberg, dressed only in his underwear, caught a glimpse of a gun as he opened the door and yelled for sleeping members of the Israeli team to flee the Munich apartment. As he fought to keep out the seven men, Weinberg was cut down by machine gun fire. Weight lifter Josef Romano was also killed as the terrorist group pushed its way into the second floor apartment.

While the rest of Munich slept on the morning of Sept. 5, 1972, the Black September Organization made its way systematically through six apartments and rounded up nine hostages; nine athletes managed to escape the terrorist purge due to Weinberg's warning cries. The hostages were bound together in three groups and thrown onto a bed. The gunmen, identifying themselves as Palestinians, tossed a handwritten poster out a window, threatening to kill the hostages if hundreds of jailed Arabs were not released by Israel. Munich police quickly surrounded the three-story Building Thirty-One as Weinberg's body was dragged out of the building and retrieved by German paramedics. While officials negotiated with the Group, the games of the Twentieth Olympiad continued only a few blocks away. The Germans were stalled by Israeli officials, who refused to give in to the terrorist demands and a noon deadline came and went. The Arabs then upped their demands to include safe passage out of the country and threatened to kill two athletes every half hour until their demands were satisfied.

German Chancellor Willy Brandt's offer of an unlimited ransom was rejected by the Arabs. German officials then offered themselves as hostages, but the terrorists steadfastly clung to their demands. Brandt asked Egypt's President Anwar Sadat to intervene, but the chancellor was ignored. In front of the Israeli Parliament, Prime Minister Golda Meir reiterated that Israel would not give in to the terrorist dictates. Hans Dietrich Genscher, the interior minister of Germany, headed the negotiating team and managed to persuade the Black Septembrists to extend their deadline to 4 p.m. Genscher insisted upon visiting the hostages and found the nine men alive with their arms bound behind their backs. Olympic officials finally suspended the games at 4 p.m.

By 9 p.m., German officials decided it would be too dangerous to try to overtake the Palestinians in the Olympic Village and they set up an ambush at nearby Fürstenfeldbruck Air Base. After convincing the terrorists their demands would be met, German security officials cleared an underground passageway in the village. Shortly after 10 p.m., the Arabs moved their bound and blindfolded prisoners along the corridor to a waiting bus. Twenty people, including three German officials, were then bussed to where three helicopters waited. The Germans climbed into one helicopter and the Israelis and their captors piled in to the other two helicopters for the fifteen-minute trip to the base.

When the helicopters touched down on the runway next to a Lufthansa jet, the Palestinians ordered the pilots to stand in front of their crafts while they inspected the airliner 170 yards away. Nearly 500 German soldiers were stationed around the base along with countless German and Israeli intelligence officers. As the two Arabs returned to the helicopters with an Israeli captive, the firing began. Technicians at the West German airport had rigged the base lights to go out and for flares to illuminate the area in which the helicopters were parked.

The five other terrorists jumped from helicopters and began trading gunfire with the German sharpshooters. By the time the shooting had ceased after midnight, the nine hostages had either been shot or died during a grenade explosion. Four terrorists were gunned down in the ambush, but Abd el Kadir el Dnawy, Ibrahim Badran, and Sameer Mohammed Abdullah were captured by the Germans. The three had been wounded and were charged with first-degree murder by officials. A German police officer was also killed and a helicopter pilot seriously wounded in the gun battle.

The members of Israel's Olympic team who died at Fürstfeldenbruck were: David Berger, a weight lifter, an American who had emigrated to Israel; Mark Slavin, a wrestler, a Russian immigrant; Zeev Friedman, a weight lifter; Eliezer Halfin, a wrestler; Kehat Schorr, a shooting coach; Amitzur Shapira, coach of the women's track team; Andre Spitzer, a fencing coach; and Yacov Springer and Yosef Gutfreund, security personnel.

The Olympics were resumed after a memorial service for the slain Israelis. On Sept. 8, ten Arab guerilla bases were attacked by Israel's Air Force in retaliation for the Munich massacre.

REF.: Becker, *Hitler's Children—The Story of the Baader-Meinhof Terrorist Gang; CBA*; Clutterbuck, *Guerrillas and Terrorists*; Demaris, *Brothers In Blood: The International Terrorist Network*; Dobson and Payne, *Counterattack—The West's Battle Against the Terrorists*; _____, *The Terrorists—Their Weapons, Leaders and Tactics*; Hacker, *Crusaders, Criminals, Crazies—Terror and Terrorism In Our Time*; Laquer, *Terrorism*; Liston, *Terrorism*; O'Ballance, *Language of Violence—The Blood Politics of Terrorism*; Paine, *The Assassins' World*; Schreiber, *The Ultimate Weapon—Terrorists and World Order.*

Eldon, John Scott, 1751-1838, Brit., jur. Served as member of Parliament from 1783-99, British solicitor general from 1788-93, and attorney general from 1793-99, where he handled the prosecution of Horne Tooke, who was acquitted of treason. He became baron in 1799, court of common pleas chief justice from 1799-1801, British lord chancellor from 1801-06 and 1807-27, and was named First Earl of Eldon in 1821. See: **Tooke, Horne.** REF.: *CBA*.

Eldredge, James E., d.1859, U.S., mur. Engaged to Sarah Jane Gould, James Eldredge, a native of Louisville, N.Y., suddenly panicked when he learned that his fiancée was pregnant. When she was ill, he brought her a homemade remedy which he claimed would cure her ailment, a mixture of arsenic and Dr. Rogers' Syrup of Liverwort & Tar. Before Gould died in horrible agony, she talked to doctors about Eldredge's homemade remedy and the bottle was examined and the poison detected. Eldredge was convicted of murder and was given a life sentence. He died in the Canton, N.Y., jail of consumption on Mar. 23, 1859.

REF.: *CBA; Statement of James E. Eldredge; The Trial for Murder of James E. Eldredge.*

Election Riot, Philadelphia 1834, U.S., mob vio. President

Andrew Jackson's veto of a congressional bill rechartering the Bank of the United States precipitated a financial crisis and further ill will between the two principal political parties of the nation, the Whigs and the Democrats. In April 1834 Jackson supporters clashed with prominent Whigs in the streets of New York over the banking issue. The most violent confrontation occurred in Philadelphia on Oct. 14, 1834, when a band of riotous Jacksonians assaulted the Whig headquarters in Moyamensing Township on election night.

The more numerous Jackson forces tore away campaign handbills, smashed lanterns, and struck peaceable Whig voters. The Whigs rallied their forces and attacked the Jackson encampment near the District Hall, where they cut down the hickory pole—the symbol of Andrew Jackson and the Democracy. The indignant Jackson people reformed near Southwark for yet a final assault on Whig headquarters. They destroyed the Liberty Pole, ransacked the Whig tavern, and set fire to a block of buildings. When the riot had ended, one man was dead, fifteen to twenty injured, and $5,000 worth of property destroyed.

REF.: Bowers, *Party Battles of the Jackson Period; CBA;* Hofstadter and Wallace, *American Violence;* James, *The Life of Andrew Jackson.*

Election Riots, Baltimore, 1856-59, U.S., mob vio. The Native American Movement, or "Know Nothings," wielded tremendous political power in a number of U.S. cities during the 1850s. Baltimore, Md., in particular, was the sight of election day violence when gangs of armed thugs sought to prevent immigrant Irish and other foreign-born citizens from voting. Dozens of these nativist gangs existed in Baltimore: the Rough Skins, Rip Raps, Plug Uglies, and Blood Tubs. The Blood Tubs received their nickname from their practice of dunking Irish victims in a vat of animal blood before chasing them down the street.

When the Democratic political clubs or Irish immigrants responded to the threats posed by these young hooligans, violence was inevitable. There were three election day riots in 1856, and additional outbreaks of violence in 1857, 1858, and 1859. The riot on Oct. 7, 1856, was particularly violent, as members of a volunteer fire company joined forces with the Rip Raps to terrorize the Twelfth Ward voting polls. After being repelled by Democratic sympathizers, the Rip Raps retreated to the fire house where they armed themselves with muskets and small firearms. They fired on voters from their vantage point in the market house, killing several persons, and wounding dozens of others. In the Eighth Ward the Democrats held the polling place, repelling the Rip Raps with their guns. The violence at the polls prevented immigrants and native-born voters alike from casting their votes. When the fighting ended, five persons had been killed, and forty-five more wounded.

The election riots continued in Baltimore for the next four years, until 1859, when the State Legislature invalidated a highly suspect Know-Nothing victory, reorganized the city police force, and initiated a number of reforms designed to put a stop to election day violence. By 1860 the Know-Nothing movement was declining, not only in Baltimore, but throughout the U.S. REF.: *CBA.*

Election Riots, Philadelphia 1742, U.S., mob vio. One of the earliest election day riots in U.S. history occurred in Philadelphia on Oct. 1, 1742 over the question of authorizing the militia to engage the Indians on the frontier in combat. Philadelphia's Quakers opposed any plan sanctioning violence. Their opponents, the Proprietary Party, composed of rugged Scotch-Irish frontiersmen, was eager to expand westward. The elections in Philadelphia brought the differences of these two groups into sharp focus.

For a long time the German Quakers controlled the polling place in the Court House simply by guarding the stairs. Voters climbed the staircase from the street in an orderly manner, cast their vote, and exited on the other side. In October 1742 the Proprietary Party recruited a number of burly sailors from the Port of Philadelphia. Armed with truncheons and other crude weapons, the seventy sailors descended on the Court House, assaulted the

election magistrates, and cleared the stairway by force. The local constabulary succeeded in driving the invaders off after a furious rock-throwing battle. Once order was restored, the Quakers resumed control of the election. REF.: *CBA.*

Elfvin, John Thomas, 1917 - , U.S., jur. Assistant U.S. attorney from 1955-58, justice on the New York Supreme Court in 1969, U.S. attorney from 1972-75, and appointed by President Gerald R. Ford, to the Western District Court of New York in 1974. REF.: *CBA.*

Elianor, Dame, prom. 1441, Brit., witchcraft. Dame Elianor, Roger Bolinbrooke, and Thomas Southwell were arrested and charged with trying to harm King Henry VI in 1441. Elianor was taken into custody while walking down a London street without the customary hood women wore in fifteenth-century England. A popular rumor at the time was that Elianor had conspired with Margery Gudermaine, who was known as the witch of Rye, in concocting an evil potion. Supposedly, Elianor had seduced the Duke of Gloucester with her sorcerous concoction, causing the Duke to marry her. For her alleged crimes against the king, Elianor was sentenced to be hanged at Tyburn, but Henry VI was more forgiving to the conspirators, granting them a last-second reprieve.

REF.: *CBA;* O'Donnell, *Should Women Hang?*

Elio, Francisco Javier, 1767-1822, Spain, governor, assass. Led force that recaptured Montevideo from the British in 1807. He was named viceroy of Buenos Aires in 1810, and governor of Valencia and Murcia in 1813, but was removed from office in 1822, by liberal revolutionaries who had him executed. REF.: *CBA.*

Eliot, Sir John, 1592-1632, Brit., polit. corr. Member of Parliament in 1614 and from 1624-29. He sought the impeachment of George Villiers, the First Duke of Buckingham, for his conduct in war, especially for the failure at the battle of Cadiz in 1625, but Charles I dissolved Parliament before impeachment proceedings could take place. Eliot's refusal to pay the government for a forced loan led to his imprisonment from 1627-28. He tried to abolish the king's right to taxation through resolutions in the House of Commons, forcibly holding control of the House as resolutions were passed prior to the dissolution of Parliament by Charles I in 1629. For his actions, he was fined £2,000 and placed in the Tower of London from 1629-32, where he died. REF.: *CBA.*

Elisabeth de France (Elisabeth Philippine Marie Hélène), 1764-94, Fr., assass. Attempted to escape from France with her brother King Louis XVI. They were captured by revolutionaries and guillotined. REF.: *CBA.*

Elizabeth, 1837-98, empress of Aust., Switz., assass. Popular with her people because of her philanthropy, beauty, and charm, Elizabeth, empress of Austria from 1854 to 1898, was accompanied by the Countess Sztaray, the Baron von Berzeviczy, and six servants, when she traveled to Geneva, Switz., to see an old friend, the Baroness Julia Rothschild, at Schloss Pregny. Traveling incognita as the "Countess of Hohenembs," the empress took rooms on Sept. 9, 1898, at the Hotel Beau Rivage, objecting when the head of police, M. Vireux, assigned several of his officers to be on duty near the hotel. Insisting that they be withdrawn, the empress said, "Nobody could want to injure me." After shopping on the morning of Sept. 10, and having had a light lunch, she decided to walk to the steamer dock with the countess, a lady-in-waiting, and a footman. Her special request that there be no guards or police on duty was honored. The boulevard was almost empty when a young man rose from a bench, stared at them, and struck the empress with his fist. The assailant ran away, followed by a cab driver. Elizabeth told Countess Sztaray, "I can manage to walk on board if you will be good enough to give me your arm." Just after she crossed the gangway, the empress fell to the deck. She was carried to a cabin and placed on a sofa where Captain Roux suggested that she be taken ashore. Knowing how Elizabeth disliked inordinate attention, Sztaray asked Roux to continue the voyage, and the ship cast off, but soon turned back when it was discovered that the empress was bleeding. She was carried back to the Beau Rivage by crew members, but when Dr. Golay came a few minutes later, the empress was dead.

The medical examination revealed that the blow had been struck with enough force that it penetrated Elizabeth's rib, piercing her lungs and heart. The fleeing assassin, Luigi Lucheni, was apprehended by a policeman at the Place des Alpes. The weapon, a triangular file, was discovered the morning after the murder, in a garden near the scene of the crime. Lucheni, the illegitimate son of a priest, had been imprisoned for theft in his youth, and for breach of discipline while serving in the Italian army. Rejected by a former officer, Prince d'Arragona, who he had once worked for after his military service, Lucheni swore he would be "avenged on society," and became involved with many anarchist groups that were all over Europe at that time. Boasting about his crime, and singing and dancing in his cell, Lucheni wrote long letters to a Neapolitan journal, saying he was fully responsible for the assassination, and claiming himself "an Anarchist by conviction." Doctors declared him sane and responsible, saying he was "merely vicious." Tried on Nov. 10, 1898, exactly two months after the murder, Lucheni was brought before a tribunal at the Salle d'Assizes of the Palais de Justice at Geneva. Prosecuting was M. Navazza, and the emperor of Austria was represented by Baron Giskra; the tribunal consisted of M. Bourgy, as president, with Racine and Schutzle serving as assessors. Completely unrepentant, Lucheni declared, "If the chance offered, I should commit my action again." Found Guilty of premeditated murder, he was sentenced to penal servitude for life. Twelve years later, in 1910, Lucheni hanged himself from the barred window of his cell at Evêché Prison.

REF.: Bell, *Assassin; CBA;* Wyndham, *Crime on the Continent.*

Elizabeth I, 1533-1603, Brit., queen, (attempt.) assass. The only daughter of King Henry VIII and Anne Boleyn, Elizabeth I, the Tudor Queen, began a forty-five year reign in 1558 which was characterized by royal intrigues against her imprisoned Catholic rival Mary, Queen of Scots, and by an adventurous foreign policy aimed at forging strong alliances with other Protestant nations. During her rule, Elizabeth incurred the wrath of the Spanish government over the privateering antics of Sir Francis Drake and others. Despite strife with Spain, England became the foremost world power during the Elizabethan era, and its navy became the most formidable in the world.

Queen Elizabeth lived in almost constant terror of assassination. Tasters sampled all of her food. Each glove and handkerchief was sanitized before she touched them. The precautions were not unjustified. One of the queen's own physicians was arrested for his involvement in a poison plot in 1593. The would-be assassin, Roderigo Lopus, a Portuguese Jew, arrived in England in 1559. A decade later Lopus became a Fellow of the College of Physicians. In time he ingratiated himself with members of the Royal household, and in 1586 was appointed to the queen's personal staff. Lopus became a trusted advisor of the Earl of Essex who attempted to recruit him as a spy against King Philip of Spain. Lopus rejected this offer but attached himself to several Portuguese political exiles including Stephen Ferrera de Gama, who had been exiled for conspiring against Philip. De Gama continued his intrigues in England, drawing Lopus into a scheme to poison Elizabeth and the Spanish king.

For his role in the plot, Lopus was to be paid 50,000 crowns. In 1593, an incriminating letter sent to de Gama was intercepted and Elizabeth ordered him arrested. Although no other letters were found, an investigation led by the Earl of Essex discovered that de Gama was a Spanish spy. Lopus was arrested and brought before Lord treasurer Sir Robert Cecil. After much deliberation, Lopus was sent to the Tower of London in January 1594. His trial commenced at the Guildhall on Feb. 28, 1594. Sir Edward Coke prosecuted the case, and showed that Lopus had been working for Antonio Perez, who secretly aspired to the Spanish throne. Lopus was convicted and was hanged at Tyburn on June 7, 1594.

REF.: *CBA;* Thompson, *Poison and Poisoners;* Williamson, *Historical*

Whodunits; (FILM), *Mary of Scotland,* 1936; *The Virgin Queen,* 1955; *Richard III,* 1956; *The Story of Mankind,* 1957; *Mary, Queen of Scots;* 1971.

Elizabeth II, 1926- , Brit., queen, (attempt.) assass. On June 13, 1981, 17-year-old Marcus Sarjeant of Capel le Ferne fired a cap pistol at Britain's Queen Elizabeth II, reigning queen since 1953, during the annual trooping of the colors ceremony. The unemployed youth pleaded guilty to willfully firing a gun at the queen with intent to harm, a crime under the 1842 Treason Act.

Sarjeant was preoccupied by political assassination. A police investigation revealed that his room was covered with news clippings about the subject. "I have little doubt that if you had been able to obtain a real gun, or live ammunition or your father's gun, you would have tried to murder her majesty," said Chief Justice Lord Lane, who sentenced Sarjeant to five years in prison. Although the queen's horse was frightened by the incident, she was unhurt. REF.: *CBA.*

Ellero, Pietro, b.1833, Italy, criminol. Ellero was a noted criminologist and was active in Italian politics. REF.: *CBA.*

Ellery, William, 1727-1820, U.S., jur. Signed the Declaration of Independence in 1776, served as a member of the Continental Congress from 1776-81 and 1783-85, and was named Rhode Island's chief justice in 1785. REF.: *CBA.*

Elliot, Sir Gilbert (Lord Minto), 1651-1718, Scot., consp. Took part in Archibald Campbell, the Ninth Earl of Argyll's, unsuccessful invasion of the western Highlands in 1685, for which he was condemned, but later pardoned. He became First Baronet of Minto in 1700, and served as justice for the court of session in 1705. REF.: *CBA.*

Elliot, Sir Gilbert (Second Baronet of Minto), 1693-1766, Scot., jur. Son of Lord Minto, Elliot was a member of Parliament from 1722-26, and chief justiciary from 1733-66. He narrowly escaped death during an uprising wherein Charles Edward seized the Scottish throne in 1745. REF.: *CBA.*

Elliot, William, prom. 1960, Brit., (unsolv.) mur. At 3:30 a.m. on June 13, 1960, a bloodstained sports car was found crashed into a lamp post in Park Road, Chesterfield, England. Its owner, William Elliot, a 61-year-old estate clerk, was found dead nine hours later on a deserted moorland road about fourteen miles away. Police said that William Atkinson had been attacked one week earlier in Boythorpe Road, which runs parallel to Park Road. The two men were friends, and looked so much alike they could be doubles. Both frequented the same bar, a public house called the "Spread Eagle" in Chesterfield. Atkinson had apparently been attacked by someone who mistook him for Elliot. Atkinson told police his assailant was about twenty-five years old, six feet tall, and had a distinctive accent. Police questioned Michael Copeland, a 21-year-old Royal Corps of Signals soldier on leave from Germany, who was suspected of stabbing and killing another man, for which he was jailed for twenty-eight days. On Mar. 29, 1961, a 48-year-old research chemist, George Gerald Stobbs, was found beaten to death just a few yards from where Elliot's corpse had been found. The bloodstained car of the second victim was left fourteen miles away on the same road where Elliot's vehicle had been, and clues led police again to the Spread Eagle pub, where the landlord told of hearing a customer say, "You haven't heard the last of Clod Hall Lane," referring to the road near where both bodies were found.

On July 3 another killing was reported. Arthur Jenkinson, a 63-year-old single man, was found gassed in his apartment in Chesterfield; the day before, police had asked him to identify a photograph. The coroner gave a verdict of suicide, saying he believed Jenkinson was worried about something. Two other Chesterfield residents, John Mart, sixty-six, and Albert Waddoups, forty-six, were found gassed also; both had been questioned in connection with Stobbs' murder. On Oct. 1, 1961, Michael Copeland stated in a *News of the World* article that he had been attacked in Chesterfield by hoodlums and his clothes had gotten bloodstained as a result, denying involvement in the deaths. According to Copeland, the police believed the murderer of Elliot and Stobbs had a vendetta against homosexual men. Copeland said police suspected him because he frequented the same bars as the victims. The murders remain unsolved.

REF.: *CBA; Furneaux, Famous Criminal Cases, Vol. 7.*

Elliott, Alfred, 1944- , U.S., fraud-rack. For seventeen years, Alfred Elliott worked for the law firm of Schiff, Hardin & Waite. The firm handled numerous corporate merger transactions and securities work, and the attorney was privy to much information. Elliott was charged with racketeering, tax violations, and federal wire and securities fraud.

As part of an agreement with the U.S. Securities and Exchange Commission in December 1986, Elliott was forced to relinquish $500,000 in profits and fines to the U.S. REF.: *CBA.*

Elliott, George, 1860-1916, Brit., jur. Handled the defense in a number of famous murder trials, including the case of George Chapman, whom many consider to be Jack the Ripper, and that of Arthur Devereux. He unsuccessfully defended Samuel Herbert Dougal, who was hanged in 1903 for killing Camille Cecil Holland in 1899. He defended Horace George Rayner (Cecil Whiteley), who shot William Whiteley dead and then fired a bullet into his own head in 1907, which he survived. The death sentence was subsequently reduced to twenty years by Home Secretary Elliot Pierron. He became a justice in 1909. REF.: *CBA.*

Elliott, James Douglas, 1859-1933, U.S., jur. Served as state's attorney for Bon Homme County, S.D., in 1887-91, U.S. attorney for South Dakota, and was appointed by President William H. Taft to the District Court of South Dakota in 1911. REF.: *CBA.*

Elliott, Joe (AKA: **Little Joe**), prom. 1870-80, U.S.-Turk., forg.-rob. Joe Eliott was a counterfeit artist to whom no currency was foreign. He operated in the U.S. and in Turkey, creating and passing forged documents. After escaping from a Turkish prison, where he had been housed after being found Guilty of counterfeiting, Eliott returned to the U.S. and fell in love with actress Kate Castleton. He pursued the theater queen for months, bombarding her with flowers, expensive dinners, and jewelry he had stolen. The couple eventually married, but it was not long before someone told the former Miss Castleton how her new husband made his living. When she confronted Eliott, he admitted guilt and promised to go straight. After a year of relative calm, Eliott was arrested in New York on charges of attempting to forge a $64,000 check. Castleton stuck with her husband while he served his prison sentence, but one year later the couple were divorced.

Eliott talked his wife into a second marriage, but it was short-lived as the convict could not abandon his criminal lifestyle. The couple were divorced a second time and Eliott went on to commit a number of robberies and pull off a number of counterfeiting scams in Europe.

REF.: *Barton, True Exploits of Famous Detectives; CBA.*

Elliott, Joe, prom. 1890s, U.S., west. gunman. Joe Elliott was a range detective, stock inspector, and hired gun for the powerful Cattle Grower's Association of Wyoming. He earned his reputation as a gunman during the Johnson County War of the 1890s. On Apr. 9, 1892, after nearly a year of skirmishes between the Cattle Grower's Association and the small ranchers, Elliott and fifty men ambushed Nate Champion, leader of the small ranchers of Johnson County at the KC ranch. After surrounding the ranch; Elliott and his men shot Champion and Nick Ray, Champion's partner. The methods employed by Elliott and his men in the attack provoked considerable agitation and resulted in Elliott being banished from Wyoming. Although he threatened to return one day to kill his enemies, he was never seen in Wyoming again, and the Johnson County War faded into history. See: **Champion, Nathan D.**

REF.: *CBA; Horan, The Pinkertons; Mercer, Banditti of the Plains; O'Neal, Encyclopedia of Western Gunfighters; Smith, War on the Powder River.*

Elliott, John M., 1820-79, U.S., jur., assass. As Judge John M. Elliott approached the Capitol Hotel in Frankfort, Ky., on Mar. 26, 1879, Thomas Buford stopped him and asked if he wanted to go snipe hunting. When Elliott declined, Buford asked him to go out for a drink, and then shot the judge.

Buford's vendetta against Elliott dated back nearly a year to when the judge upheld a lower-court ruling that took his sister's farm from her. Elliott swore he would get even with the men who took his sister's land, and who he believed caused her death by doing so.

Mary F. Buford had bought 400 acres and she was sued for loans held by Jane Guthrie, who asked that the property be sold for the outstanding debt. A court decision ordered the land sold and Mary Buford lost the land and the $20,000 she had already paid. Buford appealed her case, and Judge Elliott upheld the previous ruling. By the time Elliott heard the case, Mary had died and Thomas Buford had been appointed administrator of her estate. At Buford's murder trial, he was acquitted on the grounds that he was insane at the time of his crime.

REF.: *CBA; Johnson, Famous Kentucky Tragedies and Trials.*

Elliott, Robert G., 1873-1938, U.S., execut. Elliott was the official executioner for the state of New York and also electrocuted condemned prisoners in New Jersey and Pennsylvania. He electrocuted 387 persons before retiring. Included among these were Ruth Snyder, Judd Gray, and Bruno Richard Hauptmann, notorious murderers. Elliott, though deadly proficient in his job, announced before his retirement that "the happiest day I'll ever experience will be the day that capital punishment is wiped from the statute books, leaving me a man without a job."

REF.: *CBA; Elliott, Agent of Death.*

Ellis, Blaine, 1920-52, U.S., mur. When Blaine Ellis went to visit his boss, George Mensinger, at midnight during the first week of April 1952, he shot and killed the rancher with a shotgun. Ellis then gunned down Mensinger's wife as she tried to call for help, wounding the baby held in her arms. A neighbor, Clifford McDonnell, tried to stop Ellis as he drove off the Mensinger property, but Ellis shot him in the neck. While trying to make his way out of Merriman, Neb., Ellis' car stalled and another of Mensinger's neighbors, Deo Gardner, pulled up to offer help. Ellis shot Gardner, then drove off down the dark, deserted farm road.

In the morning, Ellis arrived at the farm of Andy Andersen and decided to hide out in the rancher's barn. While more than 100 men surrounded the barn, Ellis set the structure on fire and retreated to a tool shed. After several hundred rounds of ammunition were pumped into the shed, Ellis called for the ranchers to come and get him. When the wounded murderer was dragged into Andersen's yard and asked why he killed Mensinger, he said: "He bawled me out a few times. I don't know. Just the meanness in me. I've been a bad boy." The killer died in an airplane en route to a hospital. REF.: *CBA.*

Ellis, Charles, prom. 1935, U.S., mur. Charles Ellis, a butcher, and Frank Cohen, a druggist, operated businesses across the street from each other in the Jamaica section of New York City. The two men were good friends going in opposite directions. Ellis had exhausted his credit with wholesalers and was being pressured by his landlord for rent money. Cohen's pharmacy business was prospering. He and his wife had a 6-month-old baby and Cohen was known throughout the community for his generosity. One of the chief beneficiaries of the druggist's kindness was Ellis.

It was just past noon on May 24, 1935, when police found Cohen's body slumped behind his store counter. His skull had been smashed and the cash drawer had been emptied. As police scoured the neighborhood for witnesses, Ellis was in and out of the pharmacy offering suggestions and trying to assist police in their investigation. Authorities located a young girl who said she was in the drug store the morning of the murder, but never saw Cohen. She did see, however, a man wearing a white apron leave the store. As evidence pointed toward Ellis, police discovered he had paid off an overdue loan the night of the murder and placed, and paid for, a large order with a meat distributor.

Ellis soon confessed to the murder of his friend. He said that Cohen had caught him going through the cash drawer and so he bashed the druggist over the head with a pestle. After being judged "sane" by psychiatrists, Ellis pleaded guilty to second-degree murder and on Feb. 25, 1936, was sentenced to twenty-five years to life imprisonment.

REF.: *CBA;* Radin, *Twelve Against the Law.*

Ellis, John, 1874-1932, Brit., execut.-suic. "Socially it is a sad business being a hangman." That comment was made by John Ellis, the High Hangman (chief executioner) of England, before he committed suicide. Ellis had started out his working career as a hairdresser, a trade he learned from his father. Dissatisfied, he went into training to be a hangman and started in 1901. He helped hang Sir Roger Casement, George Smith, Crippen, and Edith Thompson. He moved around from prison to prison as required, sometimes having to be in three places on three consecutive days. Although he was required to hang two other women during his service, the execution of Edith Thompson often was used as an example of why women should not be hanged. She apparently fell, unconscious, and had to be carried to the gallows, though some reports said that she had been given a shot of morphine, which had knocked her out, instead of the liquor that men usually were given.

After seven years as assistant executioner and sixteen years as chief executioner, Ellis retired in 1923, after having conducted over two hundred hangings. Soon afterwards, he tried to commit suicide by shooting himself, but he only succeeded in injuring his neck. Blaming the attempt on having taken a drink, he promised the judge not to do it again. In 1932, after nine years of retirement on a farm, breeding chickens and whippets, he cut his throat and died. His wife, son, and others who knew him said that he had never been right after hanging Edith Thompson.

REF.: Atholl, *Shadow of the Gallows; CBA;* Duff, *A New Handbook on Hanging;* Laurence, *A History of Capital Punishment;* O'Donnell, *Should Women Hang?;* Potter, *The Art of Hanging.*

Ellis, Ruth (Ruth Neilson), 1926-55, Brit., mur. In 1944, when Ruth Ellis of Manchester, England, was seventeen, she took up with an American flyer who was soon killed. Shortly after his death, she gave birth to a child. In 1950, she married George Ellis, a dentist, but was divorced within a year. Three years later she got a job at London's Carrolls Club, where she met the love of her life, sports car driver David Blakely.

In 1954, Ruth Ellis met a friend of Blakely's named Desmond Edward Cussen and became infatuated with him. For nearly a year she saw both men. Blakely at first accepted the situation, but there were frequent quarrels between him and Ellis which often resulted in violence. Blakely began seeing younger women, and Ruth retaliated

Ruth Ellis, hanged in 1955.

by drawing closer to Cussen, which angered Blakely. On Christmas Eve 1954, Blakely caught Ellis and Cussen together in Cussen's apartment. During the argument that followed, Ellis swore she would never see Blakely again.

But the tortuous relationship continued for a few more months until Blakely announced, on Apr. 6, 1955, that he was going to Hampstead, a suburb of London, to see a mechanic about a race car. Suspecting him of meeting someone else, Ellis went to his apartment and knocked. There was no answer, but Ellis would later swear she heard a woman's laughter through the door. The next day she saw Blakely and a woman together. "I had a peculiar idea that I wanted to kill him," she admitted. Ellis took a taxi to the Magdala Pub in Hampstead on the evening of Apr. 10. As she left the cab, Blakely emerged from the pub with his friend Bertram Clive Gunnell, a car salesman.

Blakely darted to the other side of the car in an apparent attempt to hide. Ellis produced a pistol and shot him. Staring at Gunnell, she coolly said, "Now call the police." At the station Ruth freely confessed her guilt. Her trial began at the Old Bailey on June 20, 1955. Christmas Humphreys, representing the Crown, asked Ellis directly, "When you fired that revolver at close range into the body of David Blakely, what did you intend to do?" Without a moment's hesitation, she replied, "It was obvious that when I shot him I intended to kill him." A jury of ten men and two women deliberated for fourteen minutes before returning a verdict of Guilty. Justice Havers passed the death sentence. Ruth Ellis was to hang on July 13, 1955, at the Holloway Women's Prison in North London.

In the days before the execution, opponents of capital punishment collected some 50,000 signatures on appeals for clemency to the Home Office, but all were turned down. She was the last woman hanged in England.

REF.: *CBA; Celebrated Trials;* Furneaux, *Famous Criminal Cases, vol. 3;* ____, *They Died By the Gun;* Godwin, *Murder U.S.A.;* Hancock, *Ruth Ellis;* Heppenstall, *The Sex War and Others;* Hibbert, *The Roots of Evil;* Marks and Van Den Bergh, *Ruth Ellis: A Case of Diminished Responsibility;* Nash, *Look For the Woman;* O'Donnell, *Should Women Hang?;* Potter, *The Art of Hanging;* Sanders, *Murder Behind the Bright Lights;* Webb, *Line-up for Crime;* Wilson, *Encyclopedia of Murder;* ____, *Murderess;* (FILM), *Dance With A Stranger,* 1985.

Ellis, Thomas, prom. 1886, U.S., pol. mal. Thomas Ellis was appointed to the San Francisco Police Department in 1886 after helping a police captain make an arrest. Ellis was later promoted to sergeant and put in charge of Chinatown, an area rife with gambling. In 1904, the police infiltrated the Chinese gambling ring and Ellis was charged with neglect of duty for failing to curb the illegal activity. Ellis confessed that he had been bribed to permit the gambling, was found Guilty on Feb. 15, 1905, and dismissed from the police force.

REF.: *CBA;* Duke, *Celebrated Criminal Cases of America.*

Ellsome, Charles, b.1889, Brit., mur. It took a jury less than one hour to convict Charles Ellsome of murdering his girlfriend, Rose Render, on Aug. 21, 1911. The couple had quarrelled in the street, witnesses testified, and Ellsome stabbed Render. The 22-year-old laborer denied that he killed Rose despite evidence that he had purchased a knife the day before the murder.

When Ellsome's case went to the court of appeals, his murder conviction was overturned on the grounds that Judge Avory had misdirected the jury. Ellsome was the first convicted murderer to be freed under Britain's appeal system, and the court could not retry him.

REF.: Bechhofer, *Sir Travers Humphreys;* Browne, *Sir Travers Humphreys;* Butler, *Murderers' England; CBA;* Jackson, *Mr. Justice Avory;* O'Donnell, *The Trials of Mr. Justice Avory;* ____, *Cavalcade of Justice;* Shew, *A Second Companion to Murder.*

Ellsworth, James, d.1924, U.S., fraud-mur. James Ellsworth, a native of Bangor, Maine, worked as a claims adjuster for the small Lattimore Insurance Company. He busied himself at night arranging accidents and then paying off insured customers who split the insurance money with him. When Lewis Lattimore discovered Ellsworth's scheme, he confronted his errant adjuster on Sept. 14, 1924. Ellsworth suddenly went berserk and shot his employer three times in the chest, mortally wounding him. Lattimore staggered to his desk as he was being shot, grabbed a gun in a desk drawer and returned fire, getting off one shot which slammed into Ellsworth's forehead, killing him. The bodies of both men were found in Lattimore's office a short time later, along with a memo by Lattimore outlining his suspicions of Ellsworth's crooked ways. REF.: *CBA.*

Ellsworth, Oliver, 1745-1807, U.S., jur. Represented Connecticut in the Continental Congress from 1777-84, and served as justice for Connecticut Superior Court from 1785-89. As a delegate to the Constitutional Convention, he resolved the representational debate between states with Connecticut Compromise, which established a senate and house of representatives in 1787. He is also credited with naming the newly formed country the United States. He was one of Connecticut's first two senators from 1789-96, chairing the committee responsible for organization of the federal judiciary, and co-authoring the Judiciary Act of 1789. Upon the resignation of John Jay, Ellsworth was appointed by President George Washington as the U.S. Supreme Court's second chief justice from 1796-1800. While serving as chief justice, he defined the procedures by which a case for review could be brought before the Supreme Court in *Wiscart v. Dauchy* in 1796. Ellsworth's ruling stated that cases brought before the nation's highest court by a writ of error "removes nothing for re-examination but the law," while those on appeal, such as the above case, renders "the facts as well as the law to review and retrial." REF.: *CBA*.

Ellsworth, William Wolcott, 1791-1868, U.S., jur. Governor of Connecticut from 1838-42, and associate justice on the Connecticut Supreme Court from 1847-61. REF.: *CBA*.

Ellul, Philip Louis, 1927- , Brit., mur. Philip Louis Ellul and fellow gangster Tommy "Scarface" Smithson were feuding in London's West End in 1956. One year earlier, Smithson, a part-time casino croupier, had disfigured the face of his ex-boss, George Caruana, in an extortion attempt. At the same time Smithson demanded money from Caruana, Ellul, a Maltese hoodlum, was also threatened with the same kind of facial rearrangement.

On June 25, 1956, Smithson and Ellul met in Caruana's Carlton Vale gaming house. Smithson was waiting for Caruana's return with club hostess Marlene Mary Bates when Ellul and two other men, George Spampinato, twenty-two, and Joseph Zammit, twenty-six, arrived. As soon as he saw Ellul, Smithson jumped up and asked him if he remembered the incident at the club. The two men started to scuffle, and Ellul shot Smithson in the arm and left the room. Ellul returned moments later to check on Smithson's condition, but when he entered the room, Smithson lunged at him with a pair of scissors. Ellul fired as Smithson advanced, hitting him in the neck. Smithson died from gunshot wounds sustained in the incident, and Ellul was arrested on a charge of murder.

The 29-year-old Ellul confessed to shooting Smithson, but said he did it in self-defense. He told authorities that Smithson had threatened to run him out of town, and would not listen to reason when he returned to Bates' room on the night of the killing. In less than two hours, Ellul was found Guilty of murder. Mr. Justice Ashworth recommended mercy as Ellul had been provoked. His death sentence was later commuted to life in prison.

REF.: *CBA*; Furneaux, *Famous Criminal Cases, Vol. 4*; Wilson, *Encyclopedia of Murder*.

Elmore, Belle, See: **Crippen, Dr. Hawley Harvey**.

Elphinstone, Arthur, 1688-1746, Scot., consp. Joined Charles Edward in uprising that led to Charles' being crowned king of Scotland in 1745. He was later taken captive at Culloden Moor and beheaded. REF.: *CBA*.

El Rukn Gang, The, c.1960-present, U.S., org. crime. Born out of the racial violence of the 1960s, the El Rukn Gang's reign of terror has continued for more than twenty years. The undisputed leader of the El Rukns, Jeff Fort, united a number of Chicago street gangs in the mid-1960s, including his own Blackstone Rangers, under the name of the Black P Stone Nation. The gangs operated under the guise of spreading religion and helping the black community, but over the years, they were involved in drug sales, extortion, murder, racketeering, bribery, and weapons and explosives trading.

Fort dominated the criminal network with the help of the gang's "Main 21," a group of generals who were assigned to oversee specific areas of the organization. In 1972, a number of gang members, including Fort, were convicted of swindling the U.S. government out of close to $1 million in a job-training scam. After serving five and one half years in prison, Fort was released from the Leavenworth, Kan., Federal Correctional Institution in 1976 and changed the name of the gang to the El Rukns. The

new name was to coincide with the group's new-found religious beliefs, Fort said. The group operated out of the former Oakland Theater, on South Drexel Boulevard. Through a wide range of illegal activities, the El Rukn gang built up large real estate holdings and expanded its base of operation to many midwestern cities, including, Milwaukee, Wis., and Columbus, Ohio.

In 1982, with the joint cooperation of the Chicago Police Department, FBI, U.S. Attorney's Office, U.S. Drug Enforcement Administration, Cook County State's Attorney's Office and U.S. Treasury Department's Bureau of Alcohol, Tobacco and Firearms, officials began a four-year investigation of the El Rukns. Under the moniker of the Organized Crime Drug Enforcement Task Force, officials made more than fifty drug purchases from gang members. They recorded thousands of hours of conversations between imprisoned leader Fort and gang members in Chicago while Fort was serving a drug-related sentence in Bastrop, Texas. The police were also able to crack the group's bizarre telephone code which was integral to their narcotics and weapons distribution network. During the investigation, some twenty people, including a number of current or former high-ranking gang officials testified before a federal grand jury in 1986.

In an October 1987 trial, former high-ranking gang member Tramell Davis testified against the street gang and described a bizarre plot to secure $2.5 million from Libyan leader Muammar Gaddafi in exchange for acts of terrorism in the U.S. Davis told authorities that the group made a videotape for Gaddafi, which featured gang members pretending to be city leaders from around the country, pledging allegiance to Gaddafi. The prosecution played hours of tapes in the courtroom which Davis helped to translate. At the end of November, Fort was sentenced to 260 years in prison for his part in the Libyan conspiracy plot.

Davis and Anthony Sumner were two of the first high-ranking gang members to testify against the organization. In 1988, Davis' testimony led to the July arrest of Noah Robinson, the half-brother of then presidential candidate Jesse Jackson. Robinson was accused of planning the murder of Janice Denice Rosemond, who had testified against the El Rukns before a Chicago grand jury. In September, gang leader Eugene "Bull" Hairston was gunned down just two blocks from El Rukn headquarters. Police were unable to establish a motive, but Hairston's narcotics traffic involvement on the South Side may have been a possibility. Hairston's status with the gang was in question at the time of his slaying. One month later, Fort and three other gang members were convicted of the 1981 slaying of rival gang leader Willie "Dollar Bill" Bibbs.

The situation continued to worsen for the El Rukns as three gang members were convicted in Rockford, Ill., of charges of trying to intimidate a witness. In November 1988, Chicago police and federal agents searched the El Rukn headquarters and found drugs, weapons, and cash and made several arrests. The El Rukns also faced federal charges for delinquent taxes. See: **Fort, Jeff; Morgan, Derrick; Robinson, Noah**. REF.: *CBA*.

Elsas, Ferdi, prom. 1988, Neth., kid.-mur. On Sept. 9, 1987, Dutch grocery tycoon Gerrit-Jan Heijn, fifty-six, was kidnapped from his villa in Bloemendaal, an exclusive Haarlem suburb. Lengthy and unsuccessful negotiations followed between the kidnappers and the Heijn family through advertisements in national newspapers. On Oct. 14, relatives demanded proof that Heijn was all right, and received in the mail what appeared to be the little finger of the tycoon's left hand. According to police spokeswoman Anne Geelof, the finger had been severed the day Heijn was abducted, which was also the day he was killed. In the longest-running kidnapping case in Dutch history, the Heijn family paid a $4.5 million ransom in diamonds and cash. A 250-guilder note from that money was found by an Amsterdam bank employee, and the bill was traced to Ferdi Elsas, a 45-year-old, unemployed architect. Most of the ransom money was found in Elsas' Landsmeer home and under the carpet in his car. Charged with murder, extortion, and kidnapping, Elsas confessed. He was arrested with his wife and their three children. Heijn's body was found buried in a forest in the eastern Netherlands on Apr. 6, after police arrested the five suspects in the case. In July 1988, Elsas was sentenced to twenty years in jail for the abduction and murder of Heijn. REF.: *CBA*.

Elsom, Eleanor, d.1722, Brit., mur. Tried and convicted for the murder of her husband in 1722, Eleanor Elsom was sentenced to be burned to death. She was brought to the stake in Lincoln, England, dressed in a tar-covered cloth with a tarred bonnet placed upon her head. Elsom's arms and legs were also covered with tar and she was placed on top of a tar barrel. She was bound to the stake by three ropes, which the executioner tightened, and then the barrel was pulled out from under her feet. Elsom's lifeless body smoldered for more than thirty minutes before the blaze was extinguished.

REF.: *CBA*; Andrews, *Old-Time Punishments*.

Elton, Charles, prom. 1900-04, U.S., law enfor. off. Among the many ordinances and innovations Charles Elton sought during his four-year reign over the Los Angeles Police Department was an upgrade of the communication system. If the equipment wasn't going to work properly and assist the department it should be disassembled, he said. As Chief of Police, Elton also advocated the hiring of an additional police matron, an expense allowance for officers who rode bicycles, and city permits for everyone who sold newspapers or shined shoes. REF.: *CBA*.

Elton Case, The, 1921, a play by William Devereaux. Bridge expert Joseph Elwell, who was found mysteriously shot in the head (U.S., 1920) and whose killer was never found, was the basis in fact for this drama. See: **Elwell, Joseph P.** REF.: *CBA*.

Elwell, Joseph Browne, 1875-1920, U.S., (unsolv.) mur. Millionaire bridge expert and ladies' man extraordinaire, Joseph Elwell was killed by persons unknown on the morning of June 11, 1920. His violent death is considered by criminal historians to be one of the classic murder mysteries of this century. Nothing in Elwell's early life remotely suggested the inexplicable fate he would later meet. Born in Cranford, N.J., to middle-class parents, Elwell attended public schools and proved to be a good student, alert and enterprising. He moved to Brooklyn in 1900 at age twenty-five, seeking work. He found it in a hardware store where he was soon the most productive salesmen.

Charming, polite, and dapper, Elwell was given a sales job at $60 a month, plus commissions; he traveled from store to store with his line of hardware goods, always on the lookout for new business. To develop contacts, Elwell joined several social clubs in Brooklyn, including the Irving Republican Club, where the consuming passion of members was bridge whist. Elwell had always been good with cards, having a remarkable memory which allowed him to recall every card played in a game. He soon became so adept at bridge that he earned more money from the game than from his job.

At the suggestion of club members, he began teaching bridge whist to socially prominent people, collecting sizeable fees that soon allowed

Joseph Elwell, whose 1920 murder remains a nagging mystery.

him to quit his sales job and earn a handsome living at cards. As Elwell's reputation grew as the foremost bridge expert of his day, his social position improved vastly. He was soon invited into the dens and parlors of New York's rich and famous, as a teacher of bridge, the game of the social elite, and as a celebrity. In this heady circle Elwell met Helen Derby, former wife of a successful lawyer, whom he married in 1904. The couple had a son, Richard,

a year later and settled down in Manhattan.

Elwell began to write books on bridge, with his wife's considerable help, and these soon headed the best-seller lists. His *Elwell on Bridge* would become one of the most widely-read books in America, returning huge royalties to his coffers, which were already burgeoning. It is estimated that as early as 1908 Elwell was earning $20,000 each year from his card tutoring. He invested wisely in real estate and the stock market and his fortunes bloomed; Elwell was soon banking tens of thousands of dollars. Acting on tips from his social contacts who assiduously worked the Market, Elwell accumulated huge fortunes in cotton futures.

The card expert purchased a handsome three-story brownstone at 244 W. 70th St. and hired a staff of servants. Traveling with the smart set, Elwell soon found it necessary to buy expensive vacation homes in Palm Beach, Fla., Saratoga Springs, and Long Island. As he prospered, Elwell began to have affairs with other women, from chorus girls to social sirens, even other men's wives. His wife found this new lifestyle insufferable and the couple separated in 1916, with Elwell paying $200 a month for all of Helen's expenses, plus paying handsomely for his son's private schooling. He found the arrangement satisfying, for it permitted him to live the life of the playboy, and soon his female friendships expanded into a regular harem.

Elwell's Manhattan home.

More than fifty women (some reports later gave the number as high as seventy), became close friends of Elwell. He carefully wrote down their phone numbers and addresses in his little black book, later found by police, along with pertinent information about their sexual abilities and deficiencies. Into another ledger, he meticulously entered amounts of money he paid to these women, either as loans or as "gifts." He never paid in cash, always by check, and these canceled checks he kept in a black metal box next to the name and address book and the ledger, tucked neatly into a top drawer of his desk, all of which was hidden randomly by a few magazines, so that he could quickly access these items for additional entries to be made.

Because of the heavy female traffic in and out of his townhouse, Elwell made sure that his three house servants lived elsewhere. They included William H. Barnes, the valet and part-time secretary (he would later claim he was Elwell's business manager), Edward Rhodes, the chauffeur, and housekeeper Marie Larsen. But even the seemingly inexhaustible Elwell had to slow down, and by early summer of 1920 he became nervous about the many women in his life. He found them at his front door, on his stoop, and ringing his phone off the hook. Mrs. Larsen, a loyal, silent type, was kept busy collecting female underclothes in her employer's bedroom and even throughout the other rooms of the townhouse.

In late May 1920, Elwell ordered the locks changed on the front doors of his house but Mrs. Larsen thought this move was prompted less by the bevy of women in her employer's life than by the break-in a year earlier, when three thieves broke the basement window in the rear. They looted the place, only to be arrested by detectives while in the house, called there by an alert neighbor who had seen the burglars enter. (These men were serving prison sentences when Elwell was murdered a year later.)

For several years, in addition to his other pursuits, Elwell had taken a keen interest in horse racing and had invested in a small stable in Covington, Ky., The Beach Racing Stable, which he owned jointly with turf man William H. Pendleton. Moreover, he spent thousands of dollars to buy two great stallions with another sportsman, Phil Chinn, a track celebrity. By the spring of 1920, horse racing fascinated Elwell as much as bridge and he found himself spending more and more time at the track and making plans to enlarge his stable, hiring Lloyd Gentry, a noted trainer, to get his horses in shape to enter significant races that year.

In early June 1920, Elwell began seeing Viola Kraus, a pretty brunette who had filed for divorce from Victor von Schlegell, a top executive at the United States Rubber Company. Von Schlegell had been a famous football player for Yale in 1898 and he and his estranged wife moved in the same social circle as Elwell. Viola Kraus was the sister of Mrs. Walter Lewisohn, business tycoon and Broadway celebrity. Lewisohn managed several stock portfolios of Elwell's and it was through him that the bridge expert met and became enamored of Viola. All of these ultra-polite high society people came together on the night of June 10, 1920, although not intentionally.

That evening Elwell accompanied Viola and the Lewisohns to the Ritz-Carlton Hotel, attending a 7:30 dinner. As they were retrieving their coats, the foursome turned to see Victor von Schlegell with Emily (Elly) Hope Anderson, a beautiful young singer from Minneapolis who was studying in New York. Oddly, Miss Anderson had been a friend of Elwell's. The parties exchanged cordial greetings and then broke into ironic chuckles. Viola Kraus had just that day been granted a divorce from von Schlegell. A few hours later the Elwell party was seated at the New Amsterdam Roof to view the "Midnight Frolics" and they were joined by a South American journalist and *bon vivant,* Octavio Figueroa.

Elwell looked to a nearby table, pointed to its occupants, and his party broke into laughter. Seated next to them was von Schlegell and Miss Anderson. Von Schlegell grinned and said: "I can't keep away from Vi even if the judge said today that we needn't be together again." Von Schlegell and Miss Anderson left early but the Elwell party stayed until closing time, leaving the New Amsterdam at 2 a.m. Elwell and Viola had some cross words, or so Viola later told police, and he therefore refused to get into the taxi carrying the Lewisohns and Viola, saying that he would get another cab. The Lewisohns later claimed that Elwell merely said the cab was too crowded and that he would talk to them the next day.

The bridge expert walked to Seventh Avenue where he hailed a cab driven by Edgar Walters, who drove to a newsstand where Elwell purchased a copy of the *Morning Telegraph,* and then took the bridge expert to his home on West 70th Street. Elwell gave him a thirty-five cent tip, walked across the street, and went up the three stairs to the front doors of his house, entering at exactly 2:30 a.m., according to Walters who wrote down his fare at that time.

Elwell, alone in his townhouse, or that is what has always been presumed, did not go directly to bed that night, but was busy on the phone. Viola Kraus later claimed that she called him about 3 a.m. to patch up the mild argument they had had.

The chair in which Elwell was found dead.

The bridge expert apparently made several calls himself that night, one, according to telephone company records, made to William H. Pendleton, Elwell's racetrack partner, at Far Rockaway 1841. Pendleton later testified that his phone, which was next to his bed,

never rang that morning and his maid, who had an extension of the same number in her room, also stated that the Pendleton phone never rang that morning. At 6:09 another long distance call, to an unknown party in Garden City, Long Island, was made, ostensibly by Elwell. Obviously, Elwell was disturbed about something, as he decided to stay up all night making phone calls, and yet this is not supported by the fact that he was found mortally wounded a few hours later, dressed only in his pajamas, his feet bare.

It was already daylight when milkman Henry Otter, a driver for the Sheffield Dairy Company, walked up the stairs of Elwell's house, leaving a quart of milk in the small vestibule, finding the two outer doors open. Otter logged the delivery at precisely 6:15 a.m. At 7:10 a.m., Charles S. Torey, the mailman, arrived with a number of letters. He went into the vestibule, dropped the letters on the tile floor, then twice rang the buzzer which was outside the main door leading into the house. This was the mailman's usual signal that he had delivered the mail.

Mrs. Marie Larsen, the housekeeper, appeared at the front door at 8:10 a.m. She unlocked the main door inside the vestibule—only she and Elwell had keys to this door since the locks had been recently changed—and entered the house, carrying the bottle of milk. As she walked down the hall toward the kitchen to prepare Elwell's breakfast, Mrs. Larsen thought she smelled smoke. She later described the smell as "powder smoke." She passed the open doors leading to the living room and saw Elwell sitting in the large plush-upholstered chair next to a card table.

At first Mrs. Larsen thought she was staring at a stranger. The man was completely bald and he was toothless. She had never before seen her employer without his toupee or his false teeth. Before her, slumped in the chair, his chin upon his chest, was Joseph Elwell. He was wearing his pajamas, the top unbuttoned, revealing a chest of gray hair and a flabby belly. His feet were bare. In the middle of his forehead, directly between the eyes, was a hole from which blood was flowing. But the man was still alive, breathing heavily, according to Mrs. Larsen. She dropped the milk bottle and ran outside to the street.

Seeing milkman Otter in the street collecting empty bottles, Mrs. Larsen called to him: "Call an ambulance, quick! Mr. Elwell has been shot!"

Replied Otter: "I'm not a policeman, I don't know how to call an ambulance. Run up to the corner and tell the cop about it."

Mrs. Larsen raced off to blurt her discovery to a traffic cop who, in turn, accompanied her back to the Elwell house. He too noted that the man was still breathing and tried to use the phone on a small table next to the chair in which the wounded Elwell slumped. It was not working, so the officer went next door where he called police headquarters, asking that an ambulance be sent immediately. The call was registered at exactly 8:31 a.m. The ambulance arrived within minutes and it raced off with its dying cargo to a nearby hospital. Elwell was pronounced dead two hours later, without regaining consciousness.

Before the ambulance drivers took Elwell out of his chair, Mrs. Larsen and the traffic cop noticed that a letter from the horse trainer, Lloyd Gentry, had been opened and was resting in the dying man's lap. Another letter, one from Elwell's son, then sixteen and writing from his boarding school, lay unopened on the floor with five other pieces of mail, all advertisements. By the time homicide detectives arrived, they were presented with a murder without a body to examine, as it had already been removed. They were deprived of viewing the exact position of Elwell's body, how he was sitting, the positions of his legs and arms—all important aspects of their subsequent investigation.

From the first moment the police entered the picture, this case became a cause célèbre. As soon as it was learned that Joseph Elwell had been shot, the top brass appeared, including District Attorney Edward Swann, Captain Arthur Carey, later a deputy inspector in charge of the Homicide Bureau, and Inspector John Cray, of the Detective Division, one of New York's best sleuths. Following close at hand was the city's noted medical examiner,

Charles S. Norris. As an army of police filed into the Elwell home a host of reporters followed, gathering in the street and demanding answers the police could never provide, as it turned out.

At first Norris thought the man had committed suicide and Carey agreed with him. Then a spent bullet was found on the table next to the chair where Elwell had sat. On the wall behind the chair was a mark which police soon realized had been caused by the bullet fired into Elwell's head. The bullet, a .45-caliber steel jacket, had gone through the victim's head, struck the wall behind him at an upward angle, ricocheted off the wall and bounced onto the table. The empty cartridge shell was found at Elwell's bare feet before he was removed from the house. The cartridge and bullet had been made in 1917 by the U.S. Cartridge Company for the army. The gun from which they had been fired was a heavy .45-caliber automatic, strictly government issue, a gun that was never found.

Marie Larsen, the Elwell housekeeper.

Norris' examination of the body convinced authorities that murder had been committed. Elwell had powder burns on his face and Norris concluded that the gun firing the fatal bullet was held not closer than three and not farther than four feet from his head. Moreover, the exit wound was higher by an inch than the entry wound, causing the police to believe that the killer fired the weapon from a sitting or crouching position. This was supported by the mark on the wall behind Elwell's chair which was above the spot where his head rested in the stuffed chair.

On the mantle across the living room, police found a cigarette stub, not the brand smoked by the victim, but without telltale lipstick marks. Though the entire house was dusted, no fingerprints were found, other than Mrs. Larsen's and that of the victim. The phone standing on the table next to the victim's chair was out of order and police reported that this had "been tampered with." Mrs. Larsen reported that the phone had not been working for two days and yet this phone, the only one in the house, had been used by Elwell throughout the night to make long distance calls, according to the phone company, and Elwell had received a call from Kraus, according to Viola Kraus, only hours before he had been murdered.

The time of death was fixed by Norris, the medical examiner, at forty-five minutes before Mrs. Larsen found the dying man, or at 7:25 a.m. Captain Carey theorized that Elwell had heard the postman's ring and had gone downstairs immediately in his pajamas. Eager to read the letter from his horse trainer, Gentry, he sat down in his chair, opened the letter, and was shot only twenty minutes later. Carey later claimed that a burglar could have entered the house after Elwell opened the heavy inner door to get his mail, and left the door ajar. The man, however, would have had to inexplicably spend twenty minutes in the hallway before entering the living room to kill Elwell, and then leave the premises within forty-five minutes. There was no way to exit or enter the place, except by the front door which was closed and locked when Mrs. Larsen arrived at 8:10 a.m. Still, this would have been enough time to gather considerable valuables. But a thorough examination of the house revealed that nothing had been taken. On the third floor, the location of Elwell's sumptuous bedroom, the dead man's jewelry and other valuables were present. There was $400 in his tuxedo pants pocket, draped neatly over a chair. All of his clothes were as he had left them and no drawers had been opened, no closets or other rooms entered.

None of the dozens of people in the street between 7 a.m. and the time Mrs. Larsen arrived saw anyone leave the Elwell house.

A painter had been working next door from 7 a.m. on, until he saw Mrs. Larsen run from the house and he insisted he saw no one else leave the building. A burglar was ruled out in that nothing had been taken and it was unlikely that even the most novice intruder would think to enter a house in broad daylight, risking quick detection. Since bars were on the basement windows and the back door was heavily bolted, no one could have entered except by the front door. It was thought that perhaps someone had been in the house with Elwell all along, perhaps a female companion, but there was no trace of another person having spent the night either in the guest bedroom or in Elwell's adjoining bedroom. Detectives took pains to notice that only Elwell had slept in the bed, and on top of the bedspread in his pajamas, it having been a hot night. The pillow on the other side of the bed had no indentation.

That Elwell knew his killer was not ruled out. The man allowed his killer to get very close to him, but whether that killer was male or female was never determined. Yet the victim's vanity was such that everyone who knew him realized he would never have allowed any acquaintance, let alone a lover, to see him without his toupee and teeth. No woman, including his wife or his housekeeper, had ever viewed Joseph Elwell without a toupee and his expensive false teeth. Police later found the toupee, which had been neatly put away by its owner before going to bed. His teeth were still soaking in a glass in the bathroom. There had been no house guest; Joseph Elwell had spent his last night on earth all alone. A heavy weapon such as the .45 used to kill Elwell was eliminated a weapon a female would have used. Too

Left, Emily Anderson, one of the last people to see Elwell alive, and, right, Helen Elwell, long-suffering wife of the murdered man.

heavy, too much of a jolt when firing, Captain Carey said, adding that it was not the kind of automatic a lady would use. Still, the police, once they discovered Elwell's list of lady friends, began to consider each a likely suspect, interviewing every one of them. They did not rule out family members, although these had been well taken care of by the wealthy Elwell. He had purchased a fine home for his parents, and his brother and two sisters, who, along with his much-ignored wife, had concrete alibis for the night. Mrs. Elwell even admitted that she was about to file for a divorce at her husband's insistence. She stood little to gain by Elwell's death, knowing he had not made provisions for her in his will.

Police investigated every one of Elwell's business and social associates, even traveling to Saratoga, Palm Springs, and Kentucky to look into his far-flung business ventures. They scoured racetracks all over the East Coast, following up leads that only led to ignorant racetrack touts. What perplexed the police even more was the obvious fact that Elwell had no dedicated enemies. He owed money to no one, was apparently generous with money, and no one begrudged him his lifestyle, not even his abandoned wife. At first, Viola Kraus became a suspect of sorts, since she called Elwell's house an hour after he had died in the hospital. A detective answered the phone and asked her to come over. She did, confused and upset as she pushed her way through a mob of reporters at the door. She had no idea that Elwell was dead, she said, and had arrived to retrieve a pink kimono left nights earlier. This was given to her by housekeeper Larsen, who had hidden it from the police to prevent Viola from being compromised—which she was anyway. (If Mrs. Larsen could hide a kimono before investigators arrived, some sleuths later speculated, she could certainly have hidden the murder weapon, but no motive for doing so could be established.)

Others were quickly compromised. When police insinuated that von Schlegell had a motive for killing Elwell because the bridge expert had taken up with his ex-wife, the businessman said he had no interest in what Viola did with her life. He then produced Miss Anderson, who testified that she was having breakfast in von Schlegell's apartment at the very time someone was blowing a hole into the bridge expert's head. Viola Kraus produced the Lewisohns who insisted that she had slept in their apartment on the morning of the murder and did not leave their apartment until almost noon on that day.

Still, the police doggedly kept after anyone associated with the dead man, running down Elwell's lover list. There was the wealthy divorcee, Mrs. Josephine E. Wilmerding, whom the press dubbed "the woman in white" and who provided a concrete alibi. (Viola Kraus was labeled "the woman in pink" because her kimono was of a pink hue.) Bridge pupil Mrs. Schuyler L. Parsons had an unshakable alibi. So did Countess Sonia Szinswaska of Poland and Princess Dalla Patra Hassan el Kammel. On and on the investigation dragged. For years the police interviewed the most casual Elwell acquaintances, following every slim clue. At one point, they grilled Mrs. Larsen's husband mercilessly because he had served in the army and may have, at one time or another, fired a .45-caliber automatic. Police spent months looking for a disheveled soldier who had been seen talking to Elwell days before he was shot but this man was never found. The murder weapon, along with the killer, was never found. The Elwell family did not suffer. Elwell's mother, Mrs. Jennie A. Elwell, died in February 1927 and left more than $125,000 to her surviving son and two daughters, most of this being money Joseph had given her. Elwell's wife struggled to save her murdered husband's estate for her son and was, for the most part, successful. Wronged woman that she was, Mrs. Elwell even had a decent marker erected over her philandering spouse's grave in a Ridgewood, N.J., cemetery. After the burial ceremony, Mrs. Elwell was badgered by reporters for any kind of statement. She refused, however, to make one as she walked solemnly from the scene. But before getting into a car, the woman turned and said matter-of-factly: "Mr. Elwell was a piker all his life—and a chaser of women."

REF.: Carey, *Memoirs of a Murder Man; CBA;* Churchill, *The Pictorial History of American Crime;* Crouse, *Murder Won't Out;* Gross, *Masterpieces of Murder;* Jones, *Unsolved;* Lebrun, *It's Time to Tell;* Nash, *Almanac of World Crime;* ____, *Open Files;* Pearson, *More Studies in Murder;* Purvis, *Great Unsolved Mysteries;* Sann, *The Lawless Decade;* Sutherland, *Ten Real Murder Mysteries Never Solved;* Wilson, *Encyclopedia of Murder;* Willemse, *Behind the Green Lights;* Woollcott, *Long, Long Ago;* (DRAMA), Devereux, *The Elton Case;* (FICTION), Van Dine, *The Benson Murder Case;* (FILM), *The Benson Murder Case,* 1930.

Elwell, Robert, prom. 1950, U.S., mur. Before he reached the age of ten, Robert Elwell had already had his first sexual encounter. He later had intercourse with his two sisters and was present on a number of occasions when his father threatened to have sexual relations with his sisters. At eleven, Elwell fell down a set of stairs and suffered a head injury. The fall marked a tragic turning point in Elwell's life. He resumed wetting the bed, could not adjust to school, and began to suffer epileptic fits.

After a year and a half in the U.S. Marines, Elwell was discharged for medical reasons. He had suffered numerous blackouts and required extensive medical observation. What the Marines characterized in Elwell as an "immature personality" turned into ugly, aggressive behavior after his discharge. He was accused of assaulting two girls. In May 1950, Elwell killed his aunt, Mrs. Tully, in her Melrose, Mass., home. When questioned

by the police, he first denied any knowledge of the crime, and then told a tale in which two men had murdered his aunt and forced him to drive them to Portland, Maine, with the body in the trunk.

Upon further questioning, Elwell admitted to killing his aunt and dumping her brutalized body in a ditch in Maine. At a preliminary hearing, Elwell wanted to plead guilty, but because of his mental instability a formal plea of not guilty was entered. On trial for murder, Elwell's attorneys pleaded their client guilty but insane. The defense argued that Elwell's history of epilepsy and troubled childhood combined to form an uncontrollable personality. Elwell said that he recalled striking his aunt, but his next memory of the evening was buying gasoline in Maine. A jury found Elwell Guilty and he was sentenced to death. His sentence was later reduced to life in prison.

REF.: *CBA;* Neustatter, *The Mind of the Murderer.*

Ely, Walter Raleigh, Jr., 1913 - , U.S. jur. Assistant attorney general for Texas in 1939, special counsel for the U.S. Senate in 1955, and was appointed by President Lyndon B. Johnson to the ninth circuit court of the U.S., in 1964. REF.: *CBA.*

Embezzlement, See: Fraud, Supplements Vol. IV.

Emerald Hunters Slayings, Case of, prom. 1987, Col., mur. Despite attempts by the Colombian government to control the emerald mining business, the search for the precious green gems remains a veritable free-for-all. In 1987, the government exported more than $40 million worth of emeralds, which did not include what the independent prospectors, or *guaqueros,* and smugglers were able to move out of the South American country. Nearly 90 percent of the world's emerald supply comes from Colombia.

As the sun rose to meet the peaks of the Boyacá mountains of central Colombia one summer morning in 1987, the prospectors were already hard at work. The *guaqueros* were looking for emeralds, sifting through silt that had been washed downhill from a mountainside mining site. As the men worked, twenty-five uniformed, armed men approached the prospectors. The gunmen, disguised as soldiers, forced eleven miners and *guaqueros* to lie down in the mud, where they were then executed. When Colombian soldiers came to investigate the slayings, none of the witnesses would talk about the execution. REF.: *CBA.*

Emerson, William D., prom. 1898, Case of, Brit., mur. The Wesley Stock Company, a touring group of actors, was performing *The Candidate* on Apr. 1, 1898, at the London Music Hall. Billed as a "satire on Canadian politics," the play was not popular and had not been reviewed, so the Friday night audience of three hundred was especially welcome to the cast. The lead actor, William D. Emerson, was concerned, however, about two weeks of overdue wages, especially since his actress wife, Laura Emerson, had just lost a purse with all their money, and they had a young daughter to support. The unpopular and incompetent stage manager, James Tuttle, had often withheld wages, so Emerson and the other actors told the stage hands to hold the 8:30 curtain and told Tuttle that unless wages were paid, they would not perform. Tuttle gave $8.00, one week's wages, but Emerson demanded the second weeks' pay as well. At 8:45, the audience was growing impatient, calling out for the show to start. When Emerson continued to refuse to perform, the 250 pound Tuttle charged on stage and hit Emerson in the face. The thespian responded by pulling out a gun and shooting the stage manager, who crashed to the floor. When the curtain was raised and one of the actors stepped forward to ask for a doctor in the house, the audience greeted the remark with peals of laughter, believing the question to be a joke. Soon the audience understood what happened and sent for Dr. F.P. Drake, who pronounced Tuttle dead. Police officer Robert Egleton arrested Emerson.

Public sympathy in London was with Emerson, who was an officer in the U.S. Naval Reserve. At the coroner's inquest, which drew a large crowd, the verdict was favorable to Emerson; it was decided that Emerson shot in self defense. While Emerson was in custody, a campaign was launched for defense funds and for the support of his wife and child. At the trial, the defense claimed the actor had the .32-caliber revolver to assist the prop people with offstage sound effects of gunfire and firecrackers. Emerson was found Not Guilty of murder, and left the packed courtroom to the sound of cheers and applause.

REF.: *CBA;* Miller, *Twenty Mortal Murders.*

Left, **Leonard Emery,** and, right, **James Powers,** wrongly convicted.

Emery, Leonard Richard, 1926-   , and **Powers, James Edmunds,** 1931-   , and **Thompson, Arthur Joseph,** 1928-   , Brit., (wrong. convict) attempt. mur. On the night of Oct. 16, 1953, Police-Constable Cecil Pye was nearly beaten to death when he tried to investigate some suspicious activity on Marlow High Street. As he ran to a telephone booth to get help, Pye was chased by two men with golf clubs. From across the street in her third-floor apartment, Mrs. M. Brown watched as the two assailants battered the officer. A few days after the incident, two men, James Edmunds Powers and Arthur Joseph Thompson, who had been questioned the morning of the attempted murder, were arrested. One month later Leonard Richard Emery was arrested. The trio was charged with causing grievous bodily harm to a police officer. Pye survived the attack, but took thirty-seven stitches in the head.

Throughout the trial, which began on Jan. 25, 1954, the three men maintained their innocence. They had spent the evening in question drinking tea at a friend's house, they said. During the trial Mrs. Brown identified Emery as one of Pye's attackers and the officer said that Thompson and Emery were both responsible for the attack. The defense argued that there was no evidence to link the three men to the crime, but the jury found the trio Guilty. Emery, a baker and ex-convict, was sentenced to ten years in prison. Thompson, a molder, was sentenced to seven years, and Powers, a truck driver, was sentenced to four years for the attack and an additional year for protecting the other two men.

It was only because of the untiring work of Thompson's employer Lewis Williams and Thompson's brother-in-law Leslie Mitchell that justice was finally served in this case. The two men spent countless hours tracking down leads and finally getting the case reopened. In November 1955, two prisoners Geoffrey Joseph, thirty-eight, and William Purdy, thirty-three, confessed to the attack on Pye. After corroborating the stories, Emery, Thompson and Powers were pardoned and released from prison. Each was given a small stipend for the time they spent in prison.

REF.: *CBA;* Furneaux, *Famous Criminal Cases, Vol. 3.*

Emery, Muriel Gertrude, See: **Rowley, Reginald Walter.**

Emery, Ronald, 1961-   , U.S., theft-rape-mur. When Carolyn A. Culler failed to keep a dinner date with her boyfriend Ross Johnson, he drove to her Arlington Heights, Ill., apartment. On the night of Feb. 9, 1979, Johnson found the 20-year-old woman's naked body—she had been strangled to death. Culler's limbs had been bound with an electrical cord, and a pillow was placed over her face. Her car and a small amount of money were taken, but left at the scene was a note with Ronald Emery's name and telephone number. The 17-year-old California native was arrested less than two weeks later during a dramatic chase that involved Des Plaines police officers David Wysopol and Wayne Adams. Police found Culler's car about a block from Emery's Mount Prospect apartment.

Culler had apparently met Emery while hitchhiking during the first week of February. A couple of days later, he showed up at her apartment to buy "thai sticks," a potent form of marijuana. Emery admitted raping Culler after she refused his sexual advances. He was charged with murder, rape, and grand theft. In September 1970, Emery was convicted of all three charges by Associate Judge Edward Fiala and sentenced to seventy-three years in prison. REF.: *CBA.*

Emin Mehmed (Eduard Schnitzer, Emin Effendi), 1840-92, Zaire, pasha, assass. Appointed governor of an equatorial province of the Ottoman Empire in 1878, but was forced to flee in 1883, during the Mahdi revolt. In 1887 he was named pasha by the Egyptian government. He was rescued from exile by H.M. Stanley in 1888, only to be imprisoned and deposed upon his return to his government. Released from prison in 1889, he was unable to regain his position and returned to exploring. He founded Bukoba station for the German East Africa Company in 1890. He was murdered near Stanley Falls, Zaire by Arabs. REF.: *CBA.*

Emlay, Cyrus, 1766-1801, U.S., mur. A black servant in the home of Humphrey Wall, Cyrus Emlay planned to murder his master and loot his home in Chesterfield, N.J., before fleeing. He hacked Wall to death with an ax while Wall was asleep and then stole all the valuables in the house before setting fire to it. Neighbors quickly responded to the blaze and found Wall's body. Moreover, Emlay was seen fleeing from the scene of the crime, his arms loaded down with silverware and silks. At his trial, on May 28, 1801, Emlay said that he was an alcoholic and was in a drunken stupor when he committed the murder, but this did not save him from the gallows. He was hanged on June 12, 1801.

REF.: *CBA; A Short Account of the Trial of Cyrus Emlay.*

Emma Mine, prom. 1860s-70s, U.S., fraud. In 1868, when silver was discovered in Utah's Little Cottonwood Canyon, New York mining speculator James E. Lyon organized the Emma Silver Mining Co. and offered shares to the public. When Lyon brought Senator William M. Stewart of Nevada into the arrangement, the two men decided to sell stock in the Emma Mine to English investors for a $25,000 consulting fee. Yale Professor Benjamin Silliman, Jr. provided a favorable report on the mine's ore deposits. Next, an English board of directors was organized, including three members of Parliament and the U.S. minister to the Court of St. James. Baron Albert Grant was paid £170,000 to float the stocks, but it paled in comparison to the £600,000 income the directors were to have received.

The Emma Silver Mining Company's stock climbed quickly from £20 to £50 per share. The first sign of trouble occurred when a competing firm, the Illinois Tunnel Company announced that the claim had not been recorded properly. The English firm was accused of mining ore from the claim in order to pay shareholder dividends. Next, it was learned that the owner of Illinois Tunnel, Trevor W. Park, also had served on the board of directors and had reaped a handsome profit from that affiliation. In 1872 Emma Mining announced that its ore deposits were depleted. The original investors escaped financial injury, but the other shareholders all lost their money. Although Park continued speculating in silver for the next several years, and was thought to have made some money at it, the Emma Mine fraud successfully discouraged independent investment in Utah for some time to come. REF.: *CBA*.

Emmeloth, David, 1956-78, U.S., mur. It was a despondent David Emmeloth who returned from a fishing trip in Kankakee, Ill., on the evening of July 28, 1978. As he and a friend were driving home, Emmeloth was reminded of how he and his deceased father used to fish nearby. The two fishermen had been drinking much of the day and Emmeloth's partner was forced to stop the car twice as his distraught passenger attempted to jump from the moving vehicle. When Emmeloth finally returned to his Blue Island home, on Chicago's far South Side, he told his mother, "I feel like I've got the devil in me and it's got to come out."

Marge Emmeloth was scared by her son's behavior and ran across the street to enlist the aid of Timothy Gee and his stepbrother David Gee, two of her son's longtime friends. As the Gee brothers tried to calm Emmeloth, he grabbed a knife and inflicted a superficial wound on his mother's throat. Mrs. Emmeloth and her 14-year-old son fled the house. At the same time, David Emmeloth grabbed a 12-gauge shotgun from his upstairs bedroom and returned to kill the Gee brothers.

When police arrived, Emmeloth walked out the front door clothed in a bathrobe carrying the shotgun. The officers ordered him to drop the gun, but Emmeloth just smiled and walked towards the squad car. By the time a backup unit arrived, Emmeloth was seated in the patrol car. Once again, the police told him to surrender the shotgun, but Emmeloth fired and wounded one of the officers. The Blue Island police then opened fire on Emmeloth. The murderer tumbled out of the car with nine bullets in him. REF.: *CBA*.

Emmet, Robert, 1778-1803, Ire., treas. Robert Emmet, whose father was a respected physician and lord-lieutenant of Ireland, entered Trinity College in October 1793, but objected to the administration's attitudes toward political dissidents, especially the outlawed United Irishmen, to which his older brother Thomas belonged.

In 1798, Emmet withdrew from the university to join the United Irishmen who sought expulsion of the British from Ireland. Emmet went to France in 1802 and urged his exiled countrymen to back a French invasion of Ireland. Though his friends thought the idea impractical, Emmet returned to Dublin in October 1802 to whip up support for an open insurrection. But he had made his plans known to an Englishman named Lawrence who told the authorities. The insurgents distributed a stockpile of weapons in July 1803, and Emmet planned to lead an attack against the Dublin castle, known as Pigeon House. But treachery within his own ranks, general incompetence, and a lack of direction doomed the effort from the start. The revolution came to little more than a street brawl.

Discouraged, Emmet hid in the Wicklow Mountains. Major H.C. Sirr seized Emmet on Aug. 25 and returned him to Dublin where he was placed on trial, convicted of treason, and hanged on Sept. 20, 1803. REF.: *CBA*.

Emmet, Thomas Addis, 1764-1827, Ire., rebel. Like his brother, Robert Emmet, he was an Irish nationalist, who as a director of the United Irishmen in 1797, was placed in a Scottish prison from 1798-1802, following the revolt of Lord Edward Fitzgerald in 1798. Released on the promise that he would remove himself from the British Empire, he practiced law in New York from 1804-27, and opposed Daniel Webster before the U.S. Supreme Court in the case of *Gibbons v. Ogden* in 1824. REF.: *CBA*.

Emmett-Dunne, Frederick, c.1923- , Ger., mur. Sergeant-Major Frederick Emmett-Dunne of the Royal Electrical and Mechanical Engineers became infatuated with the German-born wife of fellow soldier Reginald Watters toward the end of 1952. The two men were stationed in Duisburg, Ger., at the time. Emmett-Dunne lived in the Fourth Infantry barracks, and Watters lived with his wife Mia near the grounds of the technical training school. He was a popular, easy-going man apparently unaware of his wife's relationship with Emmett-Dunne.

In the early morning hours of Dec. 1, 1953, Sergeant Watters was found hanging from the banister of Block Two in the Glamorgan Barracks, apparently a suicide. Later that day, Emmett-Dunne issued a statement saying that he had driven Watters back to quarters at 7 p.m. the night before. No one else had seen Watters until he was found the next morning. Dr. Alan Womack conducted the post-mortem, and concluded that death was the result of shock brought on by strangulation. Womack, young and inexperienced, concluded that Watters' death was a suicide.

Murderer Frederick Emmett-Dunne.

The matter was forgotten until June 3, 1954, when Mia Watters hastily married Emmett-Dunne in England, fueling old rumors. A former army special investigator communicated his growing suspicions to Scotland Yard, which prompted a re-opening of the case. Watters' remains were exhumed in February 1955 and given to pathologist Dr. Francis Camps, who startled the press by announcing "that this man never died from hanging, but that he died as a result of a severe blow across the front of the throat." It was the kind of blow that a military man trained in self-defense might inflict during intense hand-to-hand combat. Frederick Emmett-Dunne, now living quietly with his wife in Taunton, Somerset, was charged with murder on Apr. 15, 1955. His trial began in Düsseldorf on June 27. The prosecution was led by Mervyn Griffith-Jones. The defendant was represented by Derek Curtis-Bennett, who claimed that Emmett-Dunne killed Watters in self-defense, and staged the suicide because of a growing fear that he would be drummed out of the service.

Emmett-Dunne said he met Watters outside the barracks. The young sergeant accused Emmett-Dunne of carrying on with his wife while he had been away on an army exercise in Cologne two months earlier. Emmett-Dunne said Watters produced a pistol, and that in an effort to disarm him, he struck him a glancing blow to the throat. He had not meant to kill Watters, only to disable him. On July 7, the jury retired and after an hour and a half, they returned with a Guilty verdict. Sergeant-Major Emmett-Dunne was to die on the gallows. The verdict was confirmed on July 19, with one amendment. Emmett-Dunne was spared the death penalty in light of an accord signed in Bonn on May 26, 1952, by the British government, which outlawed capital punishment on federal lands by military authorities. The sentence was commuted to life imprisonment. The convicted murderer served ten years and was then released.

REF.: Camps, *The Investigation of Murder*; *CBA*; Furneaux, *Famous Criminal Cases, vol. 3;* Heppenstall, *The Sex War and Others;* Jackson, *The Crime Doctors;* _____, *Francis Camps;* Rowland, *More Criminal Files;* Wilkinson, *Behind the Face of Crime;* Wilson, *Encyclopedia of Murder*.

Empain, Baron, 1937- , Case of, Fr., kid. The wealthy Belgian native was abducted close to his flat in Paris on Jan. 23, 1978. In the event of his kidnapping, Baron Empain had warned his wife not to give in to any ransom demands. It was not until Empain's wife received the little finger of her husband's left hand that she called the police. For sixty-three days, Empain was held captive as officials and the kidnappers negotiated for his release. The ransom demands were reduced from $20 million to $8 million and a drop site was arranged. During the alleged payoff, French police killed one kidnapper, captured Alain Caillol, and three others escaped.

Under French law in 1978, the crimes of kidnapping and murder were punishable by death. The police pressured Caillol, the son of a wealthy manufacturer, to lead them to Empain. If the kidnapping victim were to die, officials said, Caillol would be guillotined. The leader of the kidnapping ring phoned his accomplices and told them to release Empain or risk having their heads chopped off. On Mar. 26, Baron Empain was freed and police subsequently captured the rest of the kidnappers.

REF.: *CBA; Clutterbuck, Kidnap and Ransom.*

Empecinado, El (Juan Martin Diaz), 1775-1825, Spain, rebel. Commanded guerilla troops during the Peninsular War against France from 1808-14. As a constitutionalist in the 1820 revolution, he was taken captive and gibbeted in an iron cage in 1823. While resisting execution he was stabbed to death. REF.: *CBA.*

Empson, Sir Richard, d.1510, Brit., treas. House of Commons speaker in 1491. While serving as Henry VII's tax collector, he was beheaded with his cohort, Edmund Dudley, after being found Guilty of treason. See: **Dudley, Edmund.** REF.: *CBA.*

Emspak, Julius, prom. 1951, U.S., cont./ct. In 1949 Julius Emspak was brought before a House Un-American Activities subcommittee. Emspak, the secretary-treasurer of the Electrical Workers Union, said the committee had no right to "go into...my beliefs and my associations..." and referred to the committee as a "Kangaroo Court," berating the members as "corrupt," and calling its questions, a "beautiful frame to hang people." He was charged with contempt for refusing to answer questions. He claimed that by his accusations of the House Committee he asserted his constitutional rights against incriminating himself. In March 1951, a federal judge in Washington ruled that Emspak had not properly claimed his constitutional rights, and fined him $500 for contempt of Congress and gave him a six-month jail sentence. REF.: *CBA.*

Ender, Otto, 1875-1960, Aust., jur. Chancellor of Austria from 1930-31, and minister of the Engelbert Dollfuss government from 1933-34, where he oversaw the writing of a new federal constitution. Nazi officials imprisoned him from 1938-45. REF.: *CBA.*

Endor, Witch of, Biblical, witchcraft. In the Old Testament, King Saul was worried about the impending attack of the Philistines. Through the Witch of Endor, Saul wanted to contact his dead predecessor, Samuel. Although the art of black magic was forbidden, Saul turned to the necromancer for help. At the séance, Saul was convinced that he heard the voice of Samuel, while others were sure it was little more than a trick of ventriloquism perpetrated by the Witch of Endor.

REF.: *CBA; Robbins, The Encyclopedia of Witchcraft and Demonology; Wilson, Witches.*

Endrigkeit, Christiane Gabriele, 1961- , and **Ahmed Nawaf Mansour Hazi**, 1950- , Case of, Ger., terr.-mur. In April 1987, an explosion demolished a West Berlin discotheque, killing two U.S. soldiers, a Turkish woman, and injuring more than 200 people. With an accusatory finger leveled at the Libyan government for the bombing of the La Belle disco, President Ronald Reagan ordered U.S. planes to attack Libya.

In January 1988, West German police arrested the 27-year-old Christiane Gabriele Endrigkeit on suspicion of planting the bomb at the popular hangout for U.S. servicemen. Police alleged that Endrigkeit and Ahmed Nawaf Mansour Hazi, who was already serving a fourteen-year prison sentence on a bombing charge, had conspired to destroy the disco. The case came to trial in December 1988, but West German officials abandoned the prosecution proceedings for lack of evidence. REF.: *CBA.*

Engel, Sigmund (AKA: Eugene Gordon, Carl Arthur Laemmle, Jr., Paul Marshall, H. Paul Moore), b.c.1874, U.S., fraud-big. When asked why he had committed bigamy 200 times, the smooth-talking Sigmund Engel replied, "...womenania...Surely they can't punish me for enjoying lovely women...I go for the fifty-seven varieties," he told journalists.

Sigmund Engel was the acknowledged master of the matrimonial con. He practiced it with amazing success across two continents and a half-dozen nations. Engel married at least 200 women, taking them for $6 million by his own estimate. He lived in Europe in the early years of the twentieth century. He first married in Vienna and continued on a dizzying pace through the capitals of Europe in search of widows with $5,000 or more. His name first appeared on police rap sheets in the U.S. in 1917. By the time of his final arrest in 1949, Engel had been arrested twenty-two times and had served four prison sentences. It was estimated that he had married at least forty women in the U.S. before 1927. With a glib line and persuasive charm, Engel would meet his intended victims in some public place and say, "Why, you look just like my wife! I mean my former wife, God bless her, she's dead these last four years." Within minutes the charmer would convince the woman to have lunch with him.

At various times Engel passed himself off as Carl Arthur Laemmle, Jr., of Universal Studios. Engel would suggest to the woman that they have lunch together, as he looked at his watch and muttered under his breath that he would shortly be placing an important phone call to Hollywood. Engel would remark on his companion's fine appearance and ask her to appear in his next film. Few were able to resist. On other occasions, he was an oil baron, Lord Beaverbrook, Howard Hughes's attorney H. Paul Moore, or a shipping magnate. He always flashed a big bankroll to convince his target that he was a man of means. Courtship and then marriage inevitably followed, after which he usually succeeded in convincing the bride to sign over her savings account to him to "avoid problems later." With the victim's money in hand, Engel would depart, with the explanation that he was off to purchase some new luggage. Of course he never returned.

By 1949, Engel had earned a vast, illegal fortune, and one reason for his success was that he never stayed too long in one town. His violation of this principle proved his undoing. In Chicago in June 1949, he met Reseda Corrigan, a 39-year-old widow had just left a singing lesson. A whirlwind courtship followed during which Engel took Corrigan and her daughters to Milwaukee to see a grave he falsely claimed to be his mother's. Placing flowers next to the tombstone, he said: "Mother, this is the little girl I am going to marry."

The wedding was set for June 7, but the day before the event Engel vanished. He sent his fiancée and her daughters to a beauty parlor and left them. A week later, Corrigan received a phone call. Engel asked her to take the first train out of Chicago and meet him in New York's Grand Central Station. Corrigan went, but Engel was not there. Broke, she lived in the station for eight days, sleeping in the washrooms and on public benches. When she returned home, Corrigan filed a complaint with the Chicago Police Department and a picture of Engel was published in a newspaper shortly afterward.

By this time, Engel had moved on to his next victim, 59-year-old Genevieve C. Parrot, a widow with six sons. She had met Engel at the Palm Grove Inn, but knew him only as "Paul Marshall," a rich banker who lived at the Blackstone Hotel downtown. But Parrot had seen the picture of Engel in the paper. Alarmed, she asked her sister-in-law Marianne Hagen, a Chicago policewoman, for advice, and was told to play along with Engel. After agreeing to marry Marshall, Parrot asked him to purchase some new luggage for their honeymoon. Engel agreed, and went downtown on the afternoon of June 24, 1949, to the Charles Wilt luggage store on Michigan Avenue, unaware that the sales clerks and customers were actually police.

As Engel tried to leave the store with his luggage, he was nabbed by police officers and taken to the Town Hall station. The 73-year-old swindler quickly became a cause célèbre. A piano was provided for his amusement, and police personally escorted him

Left, mass bigamist Sigmund Engel with wife Pauline Langton; middle, another Engel wife, Florence Barrett; right, another Engel wife, Annette Kubiak.

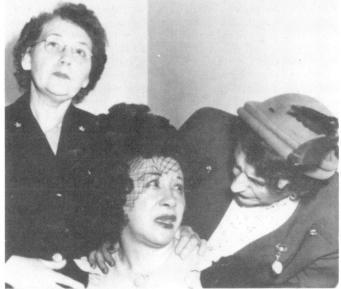

Left, Engel wife Irene Grimes; middle, wife Reseda Corrigan (center); right Engel, calmly awaiting trial in his cell, reading the Bible.

Left, bigamist Engel in a court packed with wives, and, right, swinging at his lawyer, J. Edward Jones, for losing his case.

to dinner. Within the next few weeks, a number of Engel's former wives and swindled girlfriends came forward to tell their stories. They were present when the trial finally opened before Judge George M. Fisher in October 1949.

Reseda Corrigan gave the court an amusing inside look at Engel's "technique." "I first met him on South Michigan Avenue, just after I'd left a singing lesson, and he came up and grabbed me by both hands. He said 'It's amazing, amazing, amazing. You look so much like my dead wife I would have thought she had walked out of her grave.'" The widow blushed, and then went on with her story. "I said, 'Unhand me, you villain'...But he was so gentlemanly, so refined...He told me he liked petite women and I am only five feet one inch." The bigamist was freed on bail after the first day of hearings. One woman pushed her way toward Engel for an autograph. He smiled and signed the book: "Sigmund S. Engel, Lover of 1001 Women." Defense attorney J. Edward Jones threw up his hands in frustration. "I'm trying to prove you're not that!" he said.

Some of the most damaging testimony was provided by Annette Kubiak of South Bend, Ind., who met Engel in October 1948 in front of the Oliver Hotel. He introduced himself as H. Paul Moore, a rich California attorney, and a week later they were married in Michigan City. Returning to South Bend, Engel threw a lavish party at a posh country club. At her husband's urging, Kubiak sold her home, valued at $22,000 for only $12,500. The buyer's $5,000 earnest money wound up in Engel's pocket. Kubiak never saw it again. The couple traveled to Chicago, where they checked into the Stevens Hotel before Engel fled. When these facts came to light at the trial, defense attorneys objected that a wife could not testify against her husband. Judge Fisher eventually decided Engel's legal wife was 64-year-old Corrine Perry of Los Angeles, who surrendered her entire life savings of $2,673 to the con man who called himself "Eugene Gordon." In the face of all the evidence, Engel still had some admirers. Pauline Langton of New York City said that she forgave the scoundrel for stealing $50,000 in jewelry and abandoning her. During the trial, Langton moved in with Engel at his Chicago hotel. The state's attorney objected to this arrangement, and issued an order banning Engel from living with Langton. As the couple left the courtroom arm in arm, Engel smiled at reporters and said: "But you can take it from me—she's the only lady in the lot." Engel's jocular attitude slowly began to change as more women appeared on the stand and repeated essentially the same story. "It's like playing the same record over and over, the way they say I made love to them," he said. "...I wouldn't be seen dead in the hotel with them," he shouted. "They are all gold diggers who tried to get my money...I'll show the state. I'll rip hell out of their case."

But after eight days of deliberation, the jury returned a Guilty verdict, and on Nov. 9, Engel was sentenced to prison for two to ten years. Reporters pushed for interviews. Engel explained, somewhat modestly, that he had been inspired by the king of the conmen, Joseph "Yellow Kid" Weil. Weil, who was living in Chicago, bristled. He called a press conference where he denounced Engel. "There isn't a day that someone doesn't abscond with a woman's money. Preying on the love of a woman for money is one of the most despicable ways of making a livelihood I ever heard of," Weil said.

Before he entered the prison compound, Engel gave reporters some advice about conning women. Among his points:
1. Always look for the widows. Less complications.
2. Establish your own background as one of wealth and culture.
3. Make friends with the entire family.
4. Send a woman frequent bouquets. Roses, never orchids.
5. Don't ask for money. Make her suggest lending it to you.
6. Be attentive at all times.
7. Be gentle and ardent.
8. Always be a perfect gentleman. Subordinate sex.
REF.: *CBA;* Nash, *Hustlers and Con Men.*

Engelbert I, c.1185-1225, Ger., assass. Archbishop of Cologne from 1216-1225, he attempted to improve living conditions by restoring law and order. His cousin, Count Frederick of Isenbury, instigated his assassination, which led to Engelbert's martyrdom and canonization. REF.: *CBA.*

Engelbrekt Engelbrektsson, c.1390-1436, Swed., rebel. Led rebellion of peasants and miners from Bergslagen area against Erik of Pomerania in 1434, which resulted in a national revolt. After a truce in 1435, honoring the constitutional rights of Sweden, he renewed the rebellion in 1436, as Erik's repression continued. Engelbrekt captured Stockholm the same year, before being killed by a rival revolutionary. REF.: *CBA.*

Engelstein, Joseph, and **Brust, Julius,** and **Stolerman, James Bernard**, prom. 1923, Brit., arson-fraud. The owner of a furniture company, Joseph Engelstein made a fortune shortly after WWI. As he found himself getting accustomed to living a life of luxury, the bottom fell fell out of the furniture market, and his company suffered. The Polish immigrant staged a burglary at his mansion on the outskirts of London and collected £2,000 from his insurance company. Next came a fire at Engelstein's furniture factory. He told insurance investigators that an employee had dropped a lighted cigarette and touched off the blaze. Engelstein collected another £1,200 for the factory fire. The arson-for-profit scheme was so successful that Engelstein and his partner, Julius Brust, were offering their services throughout London.

In May 1923, there was a powerful explosion at Stolerman Brothers, Ltd., a cabinet-making company on Columbia Road. Three men were seen leaving the building and a search was initiated for Engelstein and Brust. When police found James Bernard Stolerman, he was nursing burns on his head and hands. He told authorities that the injuries had been incurred when the water heater exploded in his bathroom. When Engelstein was finally questioned a few weeks later, he told police he'd burned himself while attempting to shove burning waste shavings back into a grate. Little did Engelstein know police had him under surveillance since the night of the fire and were aware he'd been hospitalized for injuries suffered in the explosion. The three men were arrested on charges of arson and conspiracy to defraud an insurance company.

Four months after the premature explosion had ended their arson adventures, all three were convicted. Engelstein received a six-year sentence, Stolerman received five years, and Brust received a four-year sentence.

REF.: *CBA;* Wensley, *Forty Years of Scotland Yard;* Woodhall, *Secrets of Scotland Yard.*

England, Edward, prom. 1719-22, Brit., pir. The Irish buccaneer Edward England was once described by the author Daniel Defoe as "having a great deal of good nature...courageous, not over-avaricious, humane, but too often over-ruled." England's unfortunate victims probably regarded him somewhat differently. In one instance, England lashed an enemy captain to a pole and ordered his crew members to throw broken glass at the man. Finally, England ordered that he be shot through the head.

The pirate captain began his career at sea, sailing out of Jamaica as first mate on a sloop, but was pressed into pirate duty when his ship was seized by Captain Winter and taken toward New Providence. There, England voluntarily became a pirate captain. With a crew, the captain sailed out of New Providence to plunder the shipping lanes off the coast of Africa. In the spring of 1719, England and his men seized ten vessels belonging to the British government. On the way to the West Indies, England continued to wreak havoc on British and Portuguese shipping. At various native settlements along the way, the pirate crew dropped anchor and engaged in debauchery before setting the towns on fire and killing peasants.

In August 1720, the pirate captain sailed his vessel, the *Fancy,* to Johanna Island near Madagascar. There, England and a fellow pirate captain, John Taylor, encountered the *Cassandra* and the *Greenwich,* commanded by James Macrae and Richard Kirby. When Macrae spied the two pirate ships descending on his port bow, he implored Captain Kirby of the *Greenwich* to come to his aid. Instead, Kirby withdrew from the bay to observe the ensuing battle from a safe distance. Macrae and his crew withstood a merciless bombardment from the pirate ships, but at night, the crew of the *Cassandra* sailed away from their ship in a long boat. Captain England's men stormed the ship and took £75,000 from the cargo hold.

Irish pirate Edward England.

After ten days, Captain Macrae returned to the harbor to bargain for the return of his ship and its cargo. England and Taylor argued bitterly over what they should do with Macrae. Taylor, and many of the men believed they should put him to death, but England was inclined to show mercy. Macrae was soon freed. The pirates exchanged the badly crippled *Fancy* for the *Cassandra*. With the remaining crew, Macrae managed to reach India and was promoted by the East India Company for heroism under fire. England, for showing weakness, was deposed by Captain Taylor and forced to sail in a long boat to Madagascar where he died in poverty.

REF.: Botting, *The Pirates; CBA;* Chatterton, *The Romance of Piracy;* Defoe, *A General History of the Robberies and Murders of the Most Notorious Pirates, 1717-1724;* Ellms, *The Pirates' Own Book;* Gosse, *The Pirates' Who's Who;* Innes, *The Book of Pirates;* Mitchell, *Pirates;* Pringle, *Jolly Roger: The Story of the Great Age of Piracy;* Rankin, *The Golden Age of Piracy;* Williams, *Captains Outrageous: Seven Centuries of Piracy;* Woodbury, *The Great Age of Piracy.*

England, John, 1786-1842, Aus., pris. reform. Instigated the reformation of prisoner transportation from Britain to Australia and convinced the British government to allow Anglican clergy to work in penal colonies of Australia. Known as the founder of Australian Catholicism, he became bishop of Charleston, S.C., in 1820. REF.: *CBA.*

Englefield, Sir **Francis,** c.1520-96, Brit., her. Knighted in 1547 when Edward VI came to the throne, he opposed establishing the Protestant religion in England. Upon the accession of Mary Tudor, he became privy councillor in 1553. He served as a member of Parliament from 1553-58, where he closely advised Mary I on the persecution of Protestants. He fled to Europe when Elizabeth I became queen of England in 1558, and sought Spain's intervention on behalf of Catholic exiles. REF.: *CBA.*

Engleman, Dr. **Glennon E.,** 1927- , U.S., mur. Glennon E. Engleman, a dentist from south St. Louis, Mo., who would sometimes treat people for free, was a killer who murdered for money and power. Respected in a blue-collar community of St. Louis, Glennon encouraged women to marry future victims, and

take out insurance on their new spouses' lives. After killing them, Engleman and the wives would share the profits. The murders of seven people were linked to Engleman; over twenty-two years, he was alleged to have killed five men and two women. The first death, on Dec. 17, 1958, was the shooting of James Bullock near the Art Museum in Forest Park. Bullock had been married for six months to Engleman's former wife, Ruth Ball Engleman Bullock, who collected $64,500 in life insurance when her husband died. She later invested $15,000 in a dragstrip, in which Engleman was both director and shareholder. Although police interviewed Engleman and Bullock, there was not enough evidence for a case against them. The widow later remarried.

The next death connected to Engleman was that of Eric Frey, a partner with the dentist in the dragstrip operation. Frey was the victim of a dynamite explosion at the dragstrip on Sept. 26, 1963. Engleman was the first person to reach Frey, and pronounced him dead. Based on the dentist's statement, the Franklin County coroner ruled the death an accident. Frey's widow, Saundra Frey, was a niece by marriage to Engleman, and gained $37,000 in insurance benefits when her husband died. She later invested $16,000 in the dragstrip. At one of Engleman's trials years later two witnesses said that Engleman had bragged about murdering his partner. Peter Halm was shot in the back with a rifle in a wooded area near Pacific, Mo., on Sept. 5, 1976. He was lured there by his wife, Carmen Miranda Halm. Mrs. Halm had known Engleman since childhood and had once worked for him as a dental assistant. She would later testify that her marriage had been planned by Engleman so that Halm could be killed for insurance money. Carmen Miranda Halm shared her $60,000 in life insurance benefits with her brother, Nicholas Miranda. She was granted immunity when she testified against her former employer. The prosecutor in the Halm case, Gorden Ankney, remarked on the peculiar "hold" Engleman had over Miranda. Ankney said, "I'll never forget the sadness of Carmen Halm. She wasn't a killer, but he got her involved through manipulation."

The next three murders, to which Engleman would later confess, were those of the Guswelle family. On Nov. 3. 1977, Arthur Guswelle and his wife, Vernita Guswelle, were slain on their farm outside Edwardsville. Their son, Ron Guswelle, was murdered on Mar. 31, 1979, in his garage; his body was later dumped in East St. Louis. The killings were alleged to be a conspiracy between Barbara Guswelle, who was married to Ron, and Engleman, who she had met in 1960 when they lived in the same St. Louis apartment building. Guswelle stood to inherit more than $500,000 from the combined insurance of the Guswelles and her husband. Guswelle was cleared of charges of murdering her in-laws but was convicted in April 1985 of murdering her husband. She was sentenced to fifty years in jail.

The car bombing murder of Sophie Marie Barrera on Jan. 14, 1980, was different from the previous killings in that there was no conspiracy involving insurance benefits. Barrera, who ran a dental lab, was suing Engleman for $14,500 in unpaid bills. After this slaying, Ruth Bullock began to fear that Engleman would destroy her if she became angry. She went to the police, and agreed to be wired, taping conversations that helped convict Engleman. On June 19, 1985, Engleman pleaded guilty to three counts of murder, for slaying Barrera and the Guswelle couple. All three killings were committed in Madison County. He was sentenced to two fifty-year jail terms. Richard B. Dempsey, Engleman's former defense attorney, described his client: "I think probably his desire to control individuals was his driving force—to make all the little dummies walk in line and sing at the same time."

REF.: Bakos, *Appointment For Murder, The Story of the Killing Dentist; CBA.*

Engles, George, prom. 1870-88, Fr.-Spain, forg. An expert forger, George Engles' biggest swindles were perpetrated in Europe. The American would often enlist the aid of another person to try to pass off his forgeries. One day in Paris, Engles found himself in a desperate situation. He had stolen checks from a Spaniard in Madrid and attempted to cash one at a French bank. Just as the clerk was ready to hand the money to Engles, he began to speak to the con man in fluent Spanish. Engles knew very little Spanish, but managed to pull off the scam by pretending to be deaf and dumb.

The artist himself got conned in Paris a few years later by Marie, a French girl he had been dating. Engles had the girl keep more than £1,000 for him as the heat from French police intensified. The girl told Engles that she and her mother were being investigated by police and the forger told her to burn the notes she had been holding for him. To escape authorities, Engles returned to the U.S. for a short while. When he returned to France, Engles discovered that Marie and her husband had purchased an expensive restaurant in Paris.

REF.: *CBA;* Kingston, *Dramatic Days at the Old Bailey.*

English, Charles Carmen (Charles Inglese, AKA: Chuckie English), 1914- , U.S., org. crime. Until Sam Giancana was gunned down in his suburban Chicago home in 1975, Charles "Chuckie" English enjoyed a position of importance in the local chapter of the Cosa Nostra. Described as "one of the family" by Giancana's daughter Antoinette, this "kindly uncle" functioned as one of Giancana's closest advisors and top enforcers. In an effort to elude government surveillance, English and Giancana conducted virtually every major conference on the fairways—often trailed by FBI agents. Once when Giancana had enough of this, he sent English to deliver a terse message: "If Bobby Kennedy wants to talk to me I'll be glad to talk to him and he knows who to go through." (Frank Sinatra was the implied intermediary between the Kennedy administration and the Chicago mob boss.)

English's criminal record dates back to 1933 and includes arrests for extortion, robbery, loan sharking, counterfeiting phonograph record trademarks, and hijacking. During the McClellan Committee Hearings, English pleaded the Fifth Amendment no fewer than fifty-six times. For many years he exerted influence over the politicians controlling the West Side's Twenty-ninth Ward, and was the syndicate point man in Arizona when Giancana decided to extend his sphere of influence. The "legitimate" business English was most often identified with was Lormar Distributing, a phonograph record firm.

After Giancana was shot to death by unknown killers—English had eaten dinner with him earlier that same evening—the jukebox and record kingpin fell from grace. Allegedly English had refused to cooperate with Giancana's killers, and was banished to Florida in punishment. In Florida, English made a living working as a common street bookie. English returned to Chicago in the early 1980s, this time to serve as a foot soldier under Joseph "Joey the Clown" Lombardo. See: **Giancana, Sam.**

REF.: *CBA;* Davis, *Mafia Kingfish;* Demaris, *Captive City;* Nash, *Bloodletters and Badmen.*

English, George Washington, b.1866, U.S., polit. corr. In 1917, President Woodrow Wilson appointed George Washington English as Federal Judge for the Eastern District of Illinois. Less than ten years later, English became the tenth federal judge to be impeached by the House of Representatives. By a vote of 306 to 62, English was ousted on charges of "tyrannical, coarse, indecent manner and abuse of power" as well as "conspiracy in management of bankruptcy cases for the profit of himself, friends, and relatives."

English and a local judge, Charles B. Thomas, were involved in a scam in which English funneled most bankruptcy proceedings to Thomas. In return for the lucrative cases, Thomas would then deposit money controlled by the court into a bank in which he and English were stockholders. English also managed to get his son a job at the bank, where the younger English received commission on the deposits in addition to his salary. Acting on a tip, reporters from the St. Louis *Post-Dispatch* broke the story and a federal investigation was begun in 1925. REF.: *CBA.*

Englisis, Nicholas, and **Englisis, Anthony,** and **Feinberg, Saul,** and **Brown, Nathaniel,** and **Mansberg, Marvin,** prom. 1946-53, U.S., gamb.-brib.-rack. When the University of Kentucky hired a new football coach in 1946, Nicholas Englisis lost his athletic scholarship and left school. Two years later, the former high school star from Brooklyn was back on the Lexington campus trying to convince some Wildcats basketball players to shave a few points in return for cash payments. Englisis managed to secure the services of two of Kentucky's top players. Nathaniel Brown followed the team during the season, dispensing cash and directing the duo on how to beat the bookmaking odds.

In 1950, the gamblers hooked up with members of Bradley University's basketball team. As the payoffs became more substantial, New York bookmakers became aware of the group's link to Bradley and wanted in on the action. A man named Mr. Klukofsky originally bankrolled the betting ring, but gave way to Jack West and Joseph Benintende. Englisis and company were pushed into the background. By 1951, a federal investigation had caught up with the five men who had initiated the gambling ring. Two years later, Nicholas Englisis and Saul Feinberg were sentenced to indeterminate sentences, while Anthony Englisis and Brown were ordered to serve six-month sentences. Marvin Mansberg was sentenced to nine months in prison. West and Benintende were also sentenced to multiple-year prison terms for their part in the point-rigging scheme.

REF.: *CBA;* Danforth, *The D.A.'s Man.*

Enkhardt, Max, 1910-1979, Aus., mur. On the afternoon of Nov. 3, 1969, Enkhardt, fifty-nine, kissed his sleeping wife Anna Enkhardt and then shot her dead. In 1970, in Melbourne's Criminal Court, Enkhardt pleaded not guilty, claiming the death was a mercy killing. "My wife was badly mangled in a car accident in 1968," he told the court. "She was very ill. She needed my help...My wife was convinced she had incurable cancer. In 1968 she was in great pain and losing weight...In 1969 we got behind in our rent and my wife was getting sicker and sicker.

"I felt helpless. I worked at many things but they offered no success. I was marked for failure. I drank sometimes but I could not control my drinking. We talked a lot. The weekend before she died I picked her up, carried her to the bathroom and put her on the scales. She weighed six stone (eighty-four pounds). She was very ill. She had some sort of convulsive fit. I thought she was going to die on the Monday night. She was certain she had cancer." On Monday morning the real estate agent called to tell Max they would have to vacate the house that same day. "I couldn't tell her."

When the doctor arrived, Enkhardt went to get a bottle of brandy. When he returned he gave his wife some medicine. "She was very ill...she said it was the end. I drank the rest of the brandy. I couldn't stand it. I went outside and got the pistol which had been in a trunk since we were married. I kissed her before I shot and she didn't show any response to my kiss. I loved her. I only did it for her. Believe me. I didn't come here to grovel for anything. She was my love...my only love for thirty-five years...she didn't nag me, she loved me. I couldn't bear to see her suffer."

Enkhardt testified that he then tried to kill himself but the gun jammed. The dead woman's sister testified that she had gone to visit Anna Enkhardt at 4 p.m. on the day of the killing. "I leaned over to talk to her and could see the blood all over her. I shouted out several times but could get no answer. I called outside a few times. Suddenly Max approached from the garage. I said, 'What have you done to Anna?' and he said, 'Nothing.'

"I went into the kitchen and he followed and I said again. 'What have you done to Anna' and he replied, 'I killed her'." According to the sister, Max had never mentioned trying to kill himself.

An all-male jury found Enkhardt Guilty of murder and Justice McInerney sentenced him to death. The sentence was later commuted to twenty years and in August 1978, after serving almost nine years Enkhardt, who had been a model prisoner, was released. He said he felt like a man out of place and time. "I have got no one, no family, nothing,...where do I go?"

Enkhardt continued to insist upon his innocence. "All that's left to say is, my conscience is clear. I can face my maker. He knows." A few months later in September 1979, after a year of freedom, he was hit by a car in Elsternwick. He had better luck than his wife who had lingered on in pain for sixteen months after being hit by a car. Enkhardt died soon afterwards. REF.: *CBA*.

Enricht, Louis, b.1846, U.S., fraud-theft. In 1916, Long Island inventor Louis Enricht convinced a skeptical press and even Henry Ford that converting water into engine fuel was possible. Before Enricht's scheme was debunked, President Woodrow Wilson promised U.S. consumers penny-a-gallon fuel.

Enricht summoned the press to his Farmingdale, Long Island, residence on Apr. 11, 1916, to demonstrate his gasless flivver. He asked reporters to examine his engine and see that the gas tank was devoid of fuel. Enricht produced a white china pitcher filled with water into which he poured a vial of greenish liquid, and deposited the mixture in the tank. After a few wheezing sputters, the automobile kicked into gear and everyone went for a ride. The reporters were apparently satisfied that Enricht had achieved the seemingly impossible. Publisher William E. Haskell of the Chicago *Herald* visited Enricht, and satisfied with the truth of Enricht's claims, returned to Chicago to announce the coming "automotive revolution."

Henry Ford also examined the car and arrived at a similar conclusion. He gave Enricht a $10,000 check for exclusive rights to the invention. Enricht was not content to deal with Ford alone and began negotiations with Hiram P. Maxim, son of the inventor of the rapid-fire Maxim gun who offered Enricht a $100,000 down payment for the formula to the cheap gasoline substitute.

Railroad tycoon Benjamin Yoakum was the next to take an interest in the project. He promised President Wilson that Enricht, with whom he had formed a partnership known as the National Motor Power Company, would deliver the secret formula to him. When Enricht began stalling, Yoakum hired Pinkerton agents to follow him. In 1917 Yoakum accused Enricht of consorting with Franz von Papen, German military attaché in Washington. Yoakum charged that the meeting took place on a German submarine moored off Baltimore Harbor on Aug. 3, 1916, and accused Enricht of giving his formula to the Germans. Police confiscated Enricht's safe deposit box, but found only twenty liberty bonds.

The government lost interest in the matter until Enricht announced in 1920 that he could manufacture 460 gallons of gasoline from one ton of peat. The Patent Office ridiculed the claim, saying it was contrary to all known laws of chemistry. Enricht organized a new company, and managed to bring in $40,000 of new investments. A year later, he was indicted for grand larceny. On Feb. 28, 1923, Justice Lewis J. Smith of Nassau County sentenced Enricht to a three to seven year term in Sing Sing after the inventor failed to return the money to his investors. In April 1924, Enricht was released from prison. He died a short time later without divulging his secret. It was believed that acetone and liquid acetylene mixed with water caused the car to move. However, the mixture is much more expensive than ordinary gasoline and corrodes the engine after prolonged use.

REF.: *CBA;* Mehling, *Scandalous Scamps;* Nash, *Hustlers and Con Men.*

Enright, Maurice (AKA: Mossie, Mossy), d.1920, U.S., org. crime. Enright was a pioneer labor racketeer who used a small army of thugs to strong-arm his way into many influential and wealthy unions from the early 1900s. He was a power in Chicago, aiding Big Jim Colosimo in his rise to supreme underworld boss by providing political protection, along with associates John "Bathhouse John" Coughlin and Michael "Hinky-Dink" Kenna, aldermanic bosses of Chicago's red light district, the First Ward. Maurice Enright was murdered in 1920, the same year in which his crime boss, Colosimo, was killed by Al Capone. See: **Capone, Alphonse; Colosimo, James.**

REF.: *CBA;* Demaris, *Captive City;* Kobler, *Capone;* Landesco, *Organized Crime in Chicago;* Thrasher, *The Gang.*

Enright, Richard, prom. 1920s, U.S., law enfor. off. Enright

was an outspoken NYPD lieutenant who became critical of his Harvard-trained superior, Arthur Woods, police commissioner from 1914-17. Enright was all cop and insisted that the only persons eligible for high rank in the NYPD were policemen with experience, not criminologists. He succeeded Woods and reigned as commissioner for eight years, 1918-25. Enright's yearly reports, unlike the brief statistical reports of his predecessors, invariably ran hundreds of pages and were full of his fulminations against political enemies, a self-glorifying document that pronounced him the "only expert on crime in New York."

NYPD Commissioner Richard Enright.

Enright, however, was a powerful and eloquent speaker and he assumed the leadership of an international association of chiefs of police, which did much to streamline police procedures throughout the U.S. Much to Enright's credit, a national system of crimiminal identification records came into existence, and in 1930, these records were transferred to the FBI and became the heart of its identification system.

REF.: *CBA;* Reppetto, *The Blue Parade.*

Enright, William Benner, 1925 - , U.S., jur. William Benner Enright served as deputy district attorney for San Diego, Calif., from 1951-54, chaired the committee on Criminal Law and Procedure of the State Bar of California from 1965-66, and served on the Judicial Process Task Force's Council on Criminal Justice in 1970. Enright was a member of both the advisory board of the joint legislative committee on Criminal Justice for Revision of the Penal Code and the California Bar's Special Committee on Criminal Justice. He was appointed justice of the court of the Southern District of California by President Richard M. Nixon in 1972. He has published various legal articles, including: "California's Aggravated Kidnapping Statute — A Need for Revision," *San Diego Law Review;* "The Much Maligned Criminal Lawyer," *California State Bar Journal.* He also appeared in a film for the San Diego County Bar Association, *A Model Criminal Trial.* REF.: *CBA.*

Entebbe, Raid on, prom. 1976, Uganda, terr.-host. On June 27, 1976, an Air France jet flying from Tel Aviv to Paris with 244 passengers and twelve crew members was skyjacked after refueling in Athens. A man and a woman, each holding a pistol and a hand grenade, commandeered the aircraft along with two others. The man, 27-year-old West German Wilfried Böse, who had adopted the name Achmed el-Kibesi, a Palestinian martyr slain in the Gaza guerrilla wars, claimed that he was taking the plane in the name of the PLO, the Guevara Group, and the Gaza Brigade. The woman, flying under the name of Mrs. Ortega, was believed to be either West German anarchist Gabriella Teidman Kreiger or Turkish terrorist Barin Acturk. The couple and two Arabs boarded the plane during the Athens stopover. The plane was diverted to Benghazi, Libya, where it was refueled, a pregnant woman was released, and the passenger passports were collected. Six hours later, the plane departed for Entebbe Airport in Uganda, where it would sit on the runway for the next six days.

Soldiers quickly surrounded the skyjacked plane, and Ugandan president Idi Amin appeared. Through an intercom, Böse explained that the skyjacking was in retaliation for France's supplying Israel with sophisticated weaponry. The plane doors opened, and the skyjackers left to a warm reception on the ground. After talks with Amin ended, the plane taxied to a warehouse building and the passengers were allowed to disembark. But they were quickly reminded that they were still hostages, not only of the terrorists, but of the government of Idi Amin.

On June 29, Israel refused to negotiate with the terrorists, who had demanded the release of fifty-three prisoners, including forty held in Israel, by midday on July 1. Later that day, the Israeli hostages were segregated from the others. The following day, forty-seven non-Israeli women and children were released. The July 1 deadline was extended until July 4. On July 2, the Israeli hostages collectively wrote a letter, thanking Amin for his hospitality and imploring their government to bargain for their release.

In mid-afternoon on July 3, 1976, three Hercules aircraft left Israel, following normal flight paths as they approached Entebbe. Seven hours later, one of the craft glided to the runway, while another identified the landed craft as one containing the demanded prisoners. But it really contained Israeli troops, and when it came to a stop, the other two planes landed and three jeeps filled with commandoes headed for the terminal. The Ugandan troops responded with gunfire, killing Lieutenant Colonel Yehonatan Netanyahu, one of the Israeli command leaders, who would be their only casualty. The hostages were freed and all of the skyjackers were killed in a furious exchange. Three hostages died as a result of errant bullets. The rest were herded onto the waiting planes, and in less than an hour were on their way to freedom in Israel.

REF.: Becker, *Hitler's Children—The Story of the Baader-Meinhof Terrorist Gang*; *CBA*; Clutterbuck, *Guerrillas and Terrorists*; Demaris, *Brothers In Blood: The International Terrorist Network*; Dobson and Payne, *Counterattack—The West's Battle Against the Terrorists*; ____, *The Terrorists—Their Weapons, Leaders and Tactics*; Hacker, *Crusaders, Criminals, Crazies: Terror and Terrorism In Our Time*; Hastings, *Hero of Entebbe*; Laquer, *Terrorism*; Liston, *Terrorism*; O'Ballance, *Language of Violence—The Blood Politics of Terrorism*; Ofer, *Operation Thunderbolt: The Entebbe Raid*; Schreiber, *The Ultimate Weapon—Terrorists and World Order*; Stevenson, *Ninety Minutes at Entebbe*; (FILM), *Operation Thunderbolt*, 1978.

Entratta, Charles (AKA: **Charlie Green**), d.1931, U.S., org. crime. A New York thug and thief, Charles Entratta had a string of arrests for robbery and assault before teaming up with Jack "Legs" Diamond in the mid-1920s. He was Diamond's partner in one of Legs' more profitable speakeasies, the Hotsy Totsy Club, where, in 1929, Diamond and Entratta shot it out with rival gangsters, killing Simon Walker and William "Red" Cassidy. Though more than fifty people witnessed the shootings, no one could be found to testify against Diamond and Entratta. Three of the club's waiters, according to one report, were killed by Entratta, which silenced all other potential witnesses.

Entratta was Diamond's chief enforcer and managed several bottling plants and distribution of bootleg liquor to all of Diamond's speakeasies. He also practiced a sideline specialty in kidnapping wealthy stockbrokers and holding them for considerable ransom. Entratta was working in the office of his Brooklyn bottling plant when three gunmen rushed into his office in 1931 and shot him to pieces. Entratta's death heralded the fall of Diamond's underworld empire. See: **Diamond, Jack.**

REF.: *CBA*; Levine, *Anatomy of a Gangster*.

Enver Pasa (Enver Bey), c.1881-1922, Turk., rebel-assass. Leader of the Young Turks who forced Sultan Abdul-Hamid in 1908, to reinstate the constitution of 1876, following the uprising at Macedonia. He headed the assassination of minister of war Nazim Pasa during negotiations after the Balkan war in 1913, deposed grand vizier Kiamil Pasa, and compelled the sultan to place Young Turks in government positions, dismissing all officials not adhering to Young Turk policy. Upon the death of Young Turk grand vizier Mahmud Sevket in 1913, he proclaimed himself minister of war in 1914, becoming ruler over all Turkey with Cemal Pasa and Talât Bey, and siding with Germany in WWI. At the end of WWI he fled from Turkey, later trying to organize a resistance to Soviet authority over Turks in Central Asia, which led to his death in battle. REF.: *CBA*.

Enzinas, Francisco de (Encinas, AKA: Dryander), c.1520-c.52, Spain, her. Dedicated his New Testament Spanish translation in 1542 to Emperor Charles V, who then turned him over to the Spanish Inquisition, by whom he was imprisoned. He escaped and fled to Wittenberg where he wrote of his captivity. REF.: *CBA*.

Enzio (Enzo, Henry), c.1225-72, Sardinia, treas. Married Sardinian heiress Adelasia in 1238, proclaimed himself king of Sardinia in 1243, though he never wielded any authority. He was defeated by the Bologneseo and held captive from 1249-72. REF.: *CBA*.

Epes, William Dandridge, d.1849, U.S., mur. Francis Adolphus Muir sold William Epes some property in Dinwiddie County, Va., but when Epes failed to pay off the mortgage, Muir told Epes that he would foreclose and move Epes off the land. Epes asked Muir to meet him at his farm, and when the landowner appeared Epes shot him and hid his body. To cover Muir's absence, Epes wrote a number of letters, ostensibly in Muir's hand, which stated that Muir was traveling about the country on business. Epes then pawned Muir's watch, which was identified by a relative, and police soon arrested the farmer. He was convicted and hanged.

REF.: Brunet, *Trial of William Dandridge Epes*; *CBA*.

E.P.L.F., See: **Eritrean People's Liberation Front.**

Eppolito, Jimmy, 1946-80, U.S., (unsolv.) mur. Jimmy Eppolito lived a dual existence. He worked for Carlo Gambino, the head of one of New York's leading crime families, and he also assisted a children's charitable organization that was a favorite of President James E. Carter. In 1979, Eppolito had a picture taken with the president's wife Rosalynn and proudly displayed the photograph for family and friends.

In March 1980, Eppolito and his 64-year-old father were murdered as they waited in a car. The crime bosses had ordered a hit on the younger Eppolito, because they believed he was attracting too much attention to himself. The case remains unsolved. REF.: *CBA*.

Epremesnil, Jean-Jacques Duval d', 1746-94, Fr., jur., assass. Sought the establishment of a constitutional monarchy during the French Revolution, and fought against royal interference with the authority of the Parliament of Paris in 1788. He served as member of the States-General in 1789 and in the National Assembly in 1791, where he protested introduction of a new constitution. He was guillotined along with his wife, Francoise Augustine, at the orders of the Revolutionary Tribunal. REF.: *CBA*.

Epstein, Albert, and **Warren, Benjamin**, prom. 1971, U.S., arson-mur. Albert Epstein, owner of a five-story brick apartment building in New York City, wanted to collect a large insurance settlement. He engaged former tenant and arsonist Benjamin Warren to torch the building, and Warren recruited three young men to help him. When the fire started, Warren locked his three accomplices in a storage closet where they died in the blaze. Epstein was sentenced to ten years and Warren to twenty.

REF.: *CBA*; Nash, *Almanac of World Crime*.

Epstein, Joseph (AKA: Joey Ep), 1901-76, U.S., gamb. Chicago-based Joseph Epstein was one of the biggest bookies in the U.S. during the 1930s and 1940s. He operated offices at Madison and Clark streets in Chicago, and he would cover wagers that bookies throughout the U.S. could not handle. He soon became a multimillionaire and acted the part of a cultured gentleman. He read voraciously and possessed an enormous library, considering himself a Talmudic scholar. He was certainly the most intellectual bookie in America. Epstein prided himself in his honesty and had the reputation of always paying his losses and keeping his word. He was mild-mannered and extremely courteous.

The gambler, heavily protected through police and political payoffs, was a regular visitor to the better nightclubs in Chicago, always having a ringside table reserved for himself whether he was in attendance or not. He encountered a beautiful 17-year-old girl named Virginia Hill, a barefoot runaway from Alabama, and spent a fortune on her, turning her into a lady. First, he arranged a job for her as a manicurist in the swanky Sherman House. Next, Epstein groomed her for more lucrative work, training and using her as a bag woman for his national payoffs. Hill traveled the country, carrying huge amounts of cash which were payoffs on wagers or splits to Epstein's organized crime connections. Although he worked directly with bookmaking operations controlled by the crime syndicate, Epstein's own operations were free of control by the national crime cartel. He did, however, pay the cartel duty on all his declared earnings.

Virginia Hill enjoyed immense riches as Epstein's mistress. The doting gambler showered her with furs, jewels, and cash, maintained apartments for her in Chicago and New York, and even bought her an expensive Beverly Hills home. Then Hill met slick New York gangster Benjamin "Bugsy" Siegel and dropped Epstein, becoming Siegel's mistress. Their tempestuous relationship ended when Siegel was shot to death in Hill's sumptuous Beverly Hills home in 1947. Epstein went on supporting Hill for years, until she moved to Europe and married a ski instructor.

Epstein retired from his gambling operations in the late 1950s and enjoyed his illegal millions, remaining in Chicago. He was a robust man who walked several miles a day through the Chicago Loop. A non-smoker, he took pains to lecture total strangers on the dangers of smoking cigarettes. Epstein died of a heart attack on Oct. 18, 1976.

REF.: *CBA;* Eisenberg and Landau, *Meyer Lansky;* Katz, *Uncle Frank;* Lait and Mortimer, *Chicago Confidential;* Messick, *Lansky;* ____, *Secret File.*

Epton, George Cyril, b.1907, Brit., mur. When police finally found Winifred Virginia Mulholland, the 26-year-old woman had been dead for three days. Mulholland's body was discovered under a balcony in Brixton. After determining that her death was not an accident, police questioned George Cyril Epton, who lived in an apartment above where the body was discovered. The 41-year-old engineer said he did not know the woman. On the following day, Epton was charged with murder. Police had discovered blood stains and what they believed to be the murder weapons in Epton's apartment.

After pleading not guilty, Epton proceeded to tell the courtroom how he met Mulholland at Piccadilly and invited her home to supper. After they had supper, Epton accused the woman of stealing money from him. He said Mulholland denied taking £9 and he struck her, sending her headfirst into the fireplace mantelpiece. Epton said he saw his money by her feet as she lay unconscious and proceeded to beat her about the face with one of her shoes. For three days he left the corpse lying beside his bed, and then dumped her body over the balcony. Epton was found Guilty of murder and sentenced to life in prison.

REF.: *CBA;* Harrison, *Criminal Calendar.*

Erbstein, Charles, 1876-1927, U.S., lawyer. During the first two decades of the twentieth century, Charles Erbstein was one of the more visible defense attorneys in Chicago. Three times his overly impassioned defense brought an indictment for misconduct, which he fought successfully each time. Erbstein lived lavishly in an Astor Street home, motoring to his suburban estate in one of his two Rolls Royces.

Erbstein was born in Cleveland in 1876, but moved to the west side of Chicago as a youngster. Apathetic about school, he drifted through various jobs until he became a copy boy at a newspaper. The exposure to the police beat led him to begin night courses at the Chicago Kent College of Law. Graduating in 1897, Erbstein struggled in

Criminal lawyer Charles Erbstein.

his practice until 1905, Erbstein won a new trial and subsequent acquittal for James "Jocko" Briggs, a man scheduled to be hanged. In 1910, Erbstein served his first of three stints as both defense counsel and defendant when he was cited for misconduct in the bribery trial of Lee O'Neal, accused of paying legislators to elect William Lorimer as a U.S. senator. Erbstein was acquitted after mounting a phony campaign for the office of state's attorney against the incumbent John Wayman, who was attempting to prosecute him.

In 1911, Erbstein was acquitted a second time on charges that he had conspired against state's attorney Wayman. In 1916 and 1917, while defending three police officials, he was involved in an incident with Assistant State's Attorney John Beckwith, which led to the two slapping each other in the face. Ebstein retired from criminal law in 1919, never having lost one of his more than 100 murder clients to the death penalty. Erbstein practiced civil law until his death at age fifty-one on May 27, 1927. On his death bed, Erbstein, the man who had been raised Jewish but converted to Catholicism, whispered to family members attending him, "Get the priest. I'm goin' west."

REF.: *CBA;* Hecht, *A Child of the Century;* Kobler, *Capone;* Messick and Goldblatt, *The Mobs and the Mafia.*

Erdman, Frank, prom. 1910, Case of, U.S., attempt. mur. When one of Omaha's most prominent politicians phoned police to report a suspicious-looking suitcase on his porch, authorities discovered a crudely constructed bomb inside the bag. Only hours later, Frank Erdman was arrested and charged with attempted murder on May 22, 1910. Erdman, a small-time hood, had recently argued with the politician, who was connected to gambling operations in the Nebraska town. John O. Yeiser, a lawyer, was doubtful whether someone who really wanted to a kill another man would do such a sloppy job. Reports said the suitcase contained a visible white string that stretched to a porch railing.

Yeiser visited Erdman in jail and offered to defend him, free of charge. The prisoner said it was no use. Even though he did not plant the bomb, Erdman said, he did not have an alibi and admitted to hating the politician. On trial, the prosecution had nine witnesses testify that Erdman was in the vicinity of the politician's house on the day of the murder. Two young girls testified they saw the suspect at around 2:15 p.m. The reason they were so sure of the time was that it followed their religious confirmation, of which they happened to have a picture.

To counter the evidence, Yeiser secured an astronomer from Creighton University, who testified that by the angle of the sun's shadow, the photo was taken at 3:20 p.m. Ultimately, the State Supreme Court released Erdman. For several years after the incident, investigators took photos at the church on May 22 at 3:20 p.m., and found that the sun's shadow matched the original picture. REF.: *CBA.*

Erickson, Frank, prom. 1930s-50s, U.S., org. crime. Frank Erickson worked for New York gambler and fixer Arnold Rothstein, and when Rothstein was murdered in 1928, Erickson reportedly took over what was left of Rothstein's then-crumbling crime rackets. He later served as an ally to crime syndicate directors Meyer Lansky, Frank Costello, and Joseph Adonis. Aligned with Lansky and Costello, Erickson helped to develop the syndicate-operated gambling casinos in Havana, Cuba, under the regime of Fulgencio Batista and later operated the widespread syndicate gambling

Gambler Frank Erickson.

interests in New Jersey, Florida, and in Las Vegas, Nev.

REF.: *CBA;* Eisenberg and Landau, *Meyer Lansky;* Fried, *The Rise and Fall of the Jewish Gangster in America;* Gosch and Hammer, *The Last Testament of Lucky Luciano;* Katz, *Uncle Frank;* Kobler, *Capone;* McPhaul, *Johnny Torrio;* Messick, *Lansky;* Peterson, *The Mob;* Reid, *The Grim Reapers;* Smith, *Syndicate City;* Thompson and Raymond, *Gang Rule*

Erickson, Lewis, prom. 1890s-1910s, U.S., fraud. Lewis Erickson, of Medina Township, Wis., fooled antique collectors with fake prehistoric stone implements. Erickson said he learned the art of making antiques by accident when he bit off a piece of an arrowhead made of flint to entertain himself while he was sick at home. Using steel pincers, he managed to form a reasonably sharp apex, eventually producing implements that were bought by experienced archaeologists, who paid large sums for the fake antiques. According to the Wisconsin State Historical Society director, Charles E. Brown, the fraud was discovered by some prospective customers when, in the maker-of-antiquity's absence, his father showed them into Erickson's workshop. Professor Albert Ernest Jenks, of the University of Minnesota, wrote an exposé of Erickson in 1900, titled *A Remarkable Counterfeiter.* Ten years later, Erickson himself came to director Brown's office and asked for a copy of the book. With the author's consent, the subject had the book reprinted two years later to distribute among his friends. REF.: *CBA;* MacDougall, *Hoaxes.*

Erik IV (or **Eric IV,** AKA: **Ploughpenny**), 1216-50, Den., king, assass. Succeeded his father Waldemar II to the Danish throne, where he ruled from 1241-50. Throughout his reign he faced civil war, and was murdered by his brother Abel, who was later killed during the attack of Frisians in 1252. REF.: *CBA.*

Erik Blódox (or **Eric Bloodaxe,** AKA: **Bloody Axe**), d.954, Nor., mur. King of Norway from 930-35, upon abdication of his father, Harald I Fairhair, securing his claim to the throne by murdering seven of his eight brothers. His cruel reign ended when his half-brother Haakon I defeated him. He fled to England, where he ruled Northumbria before dying in battle. REF.: *CBA.*

Eritrean People's Liberation Front, prom. 1987, Eth., terr. In 1985, nearly one million Ethiopians died as the result of a famine in the North African country. Two years later, the country faced a similar horror. The summer had been marked by flooding and long dry spells, and grain prices had more than doubled due to hoarding.

In late fall of 1987, a lengthy convoy of trucks filled with grain for the starving Ethiopians was making its way through the mountainous region of the Eritrea Province. Despite the vehicles clearly displaying United Nations flags, the drivers were ambushed by a group of guerrillas. Using guns, grenades, and gasoline, the rebel forces killed one truck driver, torched twenty-three trucks, and obliterated more than 400 tons of grain. The Eritrean People's Liberation Front claimed responsibility for the attack and said that the trucks were loaded with "bullets, bombs, and fuel oil." The EPLF warned the U.N. that any future shipments would have to be cleared by the group. REF.: *CBA;* O'Ballance, *Language of Violence—The Blood Politics of Terrorism.*

Erlach, Charles Louis d' (**Karl Ludwig d'Erlach**), 1746-98, Switz., assass. Bernese army general in chief who was defeated during a French invasion at Fraubrunnen and killed by his own forces. REF.: *CBA.*

Erlach, Jérôme d' (**Hieronymous d'Erlach**), 1667-1748, Switz., law enfor. off. Served as Bern's chief magistrate from 1721-47. REF.: *CBA.*

Erler, Robert John, prom. 1968, U.S., pris. esc.-mur. Robert Erler, a Vietnam veteran who joined the Hollywood, Fla., police department, almost had psychic powers in perceiving where, under a respectable facade, crime might be taking place. He was known for finding stolen cars that had not yet been listed as stolen, and seeing an apparently deserted house and knowing that it was occupied by crooks on the run.

All that changed on Aug. 12, 1968, when Erler, walking along the beach at night, found a woman and her daughter sleeping on the sand. He told Mrs. Dorothy Clark and her 12-year-old daughter Merilyn Clark to go along to his trailer to sleep, that his wife and son were there. But he and his wife were divorced, and no one was there but Erler. He raped Mrs. Clark, then took Merilyn outside and shot her five times, killing her. He then shot Mrs. Clark five times, but the older woman survived. Erler called his police station and said he had killed two people but did not identify himself. Instead, he appealed for them to stop him and hung up. He reported for duty the next morning and, of course, had no trouble leading his colleagues to the body of the girl and Mrs. Clark.

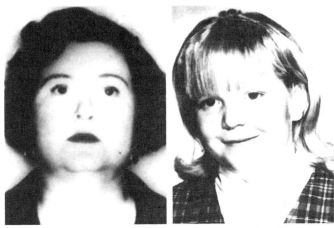

Left, Mrs. Dorothy Clark and daughter Merilyn, murdered by Erler.

Before Mrs. Clark could recover, Erler resigned from the force, citing as his reason that his mother was dying of cancer in Arizona. However, Erler's phone call to the police had been recorded, and when Mrs. Clark recovered, she and the police were able to identify him. Erler allowed himself to be returned to Florida to stand trial where he was found Guilty and sentenced to ninety-nine years in prison plus six months at hard labor. After four years in the penitentiary, he was transferred to a minimum-security prison. He later escaped through an alligator-filled moat. Erler was eventually apprehended in Mississippi—an escapade in which he had been captured, then broke free, and finally stopped by gunshot blasts.

Killer cop Robert Erler.

REF.: *CBA;* Nash, *Murder, America.*

Ernst, Karl, d.1934, Ger., assass. Ernst was a thug who was raised from the criminal dregs of Berlin. He had been a bellhop in a Berlin hotel, pimping whores to guests, and he later became a bouncer in a notorious homosexual cafe in Berlin when he was recruited personally by Ernst Roehm, head of Hitler's SA (Brown Shirts). Ernst rose through the SA ranks by beating up political opponents, and was eventually named as head of the SA in Berlin by Roehm. In June 1934, Ernst's name was added to the murder list created by Heinrich Himmler, Hermann Goering, and Josef Goebbels, under Hitler's supervision, which included all those political opponents and truculent leaders within the Nazi Party ranks that Hitler wanted eliminated. Chief among these was his long-time associate, Roehm. All of Roehm's SA leaders were to be assassinated, including Ernst, one of the few who was not part of Roehm's homosexual coterie.

On June 30, 1934, during this purge, later known as the Night of the Long Knives, Ernst was labeled a criminal by SS chief Heinrich Himmler. Goebbels announced that day that Roehm and his SA were trying to wrest political control from Hitler, then the newly appointed chancellor of Germany, and the SA leaders would be "exterminated as enemies of the state." Ernst, at that time, was being driven to Bremen with his new bride, and planned to leave by ship for an extended honeymoon in the Canaries. His car was stopped by SS gunmen, and his armed chauffeur and bodyguard, thinking the SS were members of a right-wing takeover of the government, went for their guns and were shot to death.

Ernst was dragged from his car and handcuffed, then taken to the cadet school at Lichterfeld in Berlin where he and 150 other top SA men were placed in a coal cellar. The men were then dragged out in groups, lined up against a wall, and shot to death without the benefit of trial. Ernst was dragged out and placed against the wall, believing until the moment of his death that his revered leader, Adolf Hitler, had himself been killed in a political coup. He raised his handcuffed hands and shouted: "Heil Hitler!" just moments before bullets tore into his body, killing him. Ernst died believing that he and the Nazi Party had gone down to glorious defeat when it was Hitler himself who had

SA leader Karl Ernst, assassinated by his fellow Nazis in 1934.

arbitrarily signed his death warrant. An even more bizarre story has it that when the SS arrested Ernst he thought it was all a crude wedding joke and was laughing and displaying his handcuffs at the last moment of his life to the very SS men who shot him.

REF.: *CBA; Fest, Hitler;* Heiden, *Der Fuehrer;* Henderson and Morris, *War In Our Time;* Höhne, *The Order of the Death's Head: The Story of Hitler's SS;* Shirer, *The Rise and Fall of the Third Reich.*

ERP (AKA: **People's Revolutionary Army**), prom. 1970s, Arg., kid. With the political unrest in Argentina in the early 1970s, many dissident factions jockeyed for control of the government. Several guerrilla groups, including The People's Revolutionary Army, or ERP, and the Fuerzas Armadas Revolucionarias (FAR), were working against the country's militaristic government. The ERP was famous for stealing from the rich and giving to the poor. They stopped trucks in the street and commandeered their wares for the country's impoverished citizens. They also intimidated foreign companies into donating money and supplies to the poor.

In 1972, the guerrillas entered a new era of extortion when they began kidnaping foreign businessmen for outrageous ransoms. Within a three-year period, more than 150 businessmen were kidnapped in Argentina. While many victims were returned unharmed, the companies often had to battle police on how to resolve the kidnapings. Argentinian authorities wanted to discourage the abductions and encouraged companies not to meet the ransom demands. Meanwhile, companies were fortifying their Argentinian operations or moving out of the country altogether.

In 1975, the Argentina Anti-Communist Alliance, a paramilitary organization backed by Isabella Perón, circulated a death list and then went about enforcing the document. One year later, General Jorge Videla toppled the Perón government and installed a junta, which imprisoned thousands of people and murdered hundreds more, including many guerrillas, over the next few years.

REF.: *CBA;* Dobson and Payne, *The Terrorists—Their Weapons, Leaders and Tactics;* Laquer, *Terrorism;* Moorehead, *Hostages to Fortune;* Schreiber, *The Ultimate Weapon—Terrorists and World Order.*

Erpenstein, John, d.1852, U.S., mur. An immigrant from Germany, John Erpenstein settled in New Jersey and took up with another immigrant, Dora Muller. Erpenstein, however, was a married man, and when his wife and three children arrived from Germany, he decided to get rid of Mrs. Erpenstein. He fed her a bread-and-butter sandwich liberally sprinkled with arsenic. Physicians called to the side of the dying woman detected the poison and Erpenstein was charged with murder. He was convicted and executed in Newark, N.J., on Mar. 30, 1852.

REF.: *CBA;* Tolstoy, *The Night of the Long Knives;* (FILM), *The*

Damned, 1970.

Erroll, Lord, See: **Broughton,** Sir **Henry John Delves.**

Erskine, Thomas (First Baron Erskine of Restormel), 1750-1823, Brit., lawyer. Successfully defended the cases of Captain Baillie of Greenwich Hospital in 1778, Admiral Lord Keppel in 1779, and the case of Lord George Gordon in 1781, where the doctrine of constructive treason was destroyed. He was a member of Parliament from 1783-84 and 1790-1806, attorney general for the Prince of Wales from 1783-92, and aided in passage of Charles Fox's Libel Act in 1792, which gave juries complete power in a libel suit. He was unsuccessful in the trial of Thomas Paine for treason in 1792, but secured the acquittal of Horne Tooke, accused of high treason in 1794. In the defense of James Hadfield, who was accused of shooting at George III in 1800, he was able to prove him Not Guilty by establishing the plea of insanity, thus attacking the current theory of criminal responsibility. During the end of his career, he fought for the emancipation of slaves and provided Queen Caroline with defense in his last speech before the House of Lords in 1820. REF.: *CBA.*

Erskine of Carnock, John, 1695-1768, Scot., jur. Professor at Edinburgh from 1737-65 who authored *Principles of the Law of Scotland* and *Institutes of the Law of Scotland.* REF.: *CBA.*

Erwin, Richard Cannon, 1923 - , U.S., jur. Became a member of the North Carolina Penal Study Commission in 1968, and presided over the North Carolina Court of Appeals from 1978-80, before receiving appointment from President Jimmy Carter to the Middle District Court of North Carolina in 1980. REF.: *CBA.*

Erzberger, Matthias, 1875-1921, Ger., polit., assass. A leader of the left-leaning Center Party of Germany, Matthias Erzberger opposed Germany's entry into WWI, and he helped to further peace proposals in the Reichstag in 1917. Erzberger assumed many governmental posts following WWI and was intensely hated by right-wing and reactionary groups for accepting the Versailles treaty. He headed the Wurttemberg Center Party in the Reichstag in 1920. On Aug. 26, 1921, while Erzberger and another member of the Reichstag were strolling outside a Black Forest resort, two ex-officers of the fanatical right-wing Nation-

German political leader Matthias Erzberger, assassinated in 1921.

al Organization Consul rushed up to Erzberger and emptied their pistols, killing the German political leader on the spot.

REF.: *CBA;* Clark, *The Fall of the German Republic;* Epstein, *Matthias Erzberger and the Dilemma of German Democracy;* Laquer, *Terrorism;* Shirer, *The Rise and Fall of the Third Reich;* Vogt, *The Burden of Guilt.*

Escalante, Ramon, prom. 1920s, U.S., drug smug. Ramon Escalante, a Wisconsin produce dealer, was arrested and charged with smuggling drugs from Mexico into the U.S. Escalante had devised a plan wherein burros were trained to cross the Rio Grande River at night in search of premium feed. Packets of marijuana were attached to the animals in Mexico, and retrieved after they had crossed to the United States. With a number of cattle crossings in the area authorities would not be suspicious of a pack of burros. The drugs were then transported to Escalante's Allengrove, Wis., home and distributed in Chicago and New York.

U.S. customs agents were already searching for a drug smuggling ring when they came across the body of a young Mexican, who had been beaten to death northwest of Brownsville, Texas. Al Scharff led three other agents on horseback into the thick terrain that covered the U.S.-Mexico border. The agents discovered a small house which contained feed for racehorses, but no people. As they camped overnight, the men were awakened by a thundering herd of burros. When Scharff managed to corral one of the burros, he discovered that its pack contained a stash of marijuana. The agents followed the animals to the house they had found earlier in the day. In the morning two men came to pick up the marijuana. After agents had killed one of the smugglers, the survivor, El Nango, agreed to help authorities nab the ringleader. Escalante was arrested just outside of Allengrove.

REF.: *CBA*; Roark, *The Coin of Contraband*.

Eschbach, Jesse Ernest, 1920 - , U.S., jur. Jesse Ernest Eschbach was appointed to the Northern District Court of Indiana in 1962 by President John F. Kennedy. In 1976, Eschbach became a member of the Federal Criminal Jury Instruction Committee of the Seventh Circuit in 1976. REF.: *CBA*.

Escobar Gaviria, Pablo, 1949- , Col., drugs-org. crime. In the late 1970s, Jorge Luis Ochoa Vásquez, Carlos Lehder Rivas, and Pablo Escobar Gaviria, a new generation of Colombian narcotics traffickers came to power in Medellin. They monopolized production of cocaine, and were the first to "mass market" it in North America, controlling every phase of the operation from manufacturing, to distribution, to political payoffs.

Escobar Gaviria, who became one of the richest men in the world, was born into modest circumstances in the village of Rionegro, seventeen miles outside Medellin. In 1976, police arrested him for possession of thirty-nine pounds of cocaine, but the arresting officer was soon killed, and nine judges refused to hear the case after receiving death threats. The official records disappeared from the courthouse, and Escobar Gaviria never went to trial. With his worth estimated at $2 billion, he bought vast tracts of land in Colombia, including a lavish estate near the Magdalena River that included a private zoo. But Escobar Gaviria also built low-cost housing and a hospital, earning him favorable press and the devotion of the poor of Medellin. In 1982, he was elected to the Colombian Congress as an alternate representative from Antioquia, giving him immunity from arrest.

By 1982, Fabio Ochoa Restrepo had formed a cartel to squeeze out independents and contain losses from drug seizures by the Colombian or U.S. governments. Escobar Gaviria's people controlled U.S. distribution, laboratories, transportation, and aircraft; Ochoa Vásquez provided "muscle" and bribes to officials. By 1984, the Medellin cartel controlled roughly 80 percent of the cocaine in the country. The cartel brought coca paste from Bolivia and Peru to secret laboratories in Colombia, Nicaragua, and Panama, then shipped the final product to warehouses in the Bahamas, Mexico, the Caicos, and Turks Islands.

Under U.S. pressure—and following the assassination of Colombian minister of justice Rodrigo Lara Bonilla on Apr. 30, 1984, possibly at the instigation of Escobar Gaviria—President Belisario Betancur Cuartas of Colombia agreed to extradite all drug traffickers to the U.S. for trial. In 1984, he authorized aerial spraying of marijuana fields, with the support of the Colombian judicial system and a number of newspapers. The cartel fought back. Between 1985 and 1987, drug gangsters assassinated fifteen judges, including Supreme Court Justice Hernando Baquero Borda, killed on July 31, 1986, after negotiating an extradition treaty with the U.S. On Aug. 13, Ochoa Vásquez was released from prison.

Colombian drug king Pablo Escobar Gaviria.

On Nov. 18, 1986, indictments against Escobar Gaviria and nine other men were announced in Miami on charges including racketeering and smuggling at least sixty tons of cocaine into the U.S. Several counts in the indictment stemmed from information provided by Barry Seal, a cartel pilot who turned DEA informant in 1984 and was found out and killed in 1986. On Feb. 18, 1987, the Supreme Court of Colombia, fearful for their lives, declared they would not rule on the extradition of citizens to the U.S. The warrant for Escobar Gaviria's arrest was cancelled and the charges dismissed. See: **Lehder Rivas, Carlos; Ochoa Vásquez, Jorge Luis**.

REF.: *CBA*; Shannon, *Desperados*.

The hanging of bandit Rafael Escobar in Jackson, Calif.

Escobar, Rafael, prom. 1850s, U.S., west. outl. Rafael Escobar was a bandit who plagued southern California in the early 1850s, robbing stagecoaches and stores almost at will. He reportedly shot and killed a number of people who resisted his robberies. He was tracked down and taken to Jackson, Calif., but he was hanged by the local vigilance committee before reaching trial.

REF.: Bartholomew, *The Biographical Album of Western Gunfighters*; *CBA*.

Escobedo, Daniel, 1939- , U.S., child abuse-mur. Charged with the 1960 slaying of his brother-in-law, Daniel Escobedo's murder conviction was overturned four years later by the U.S. Supreme Court in a landmark case. In handing down the 5-4 decision, the court ruled that the Sixth Amendment right to legal counsel was ineffectual if suspected criminals were provided with lawyers only after police had been able to interrogate them. They ruled that Escobedo's confession had been obtained illegally and the 26-year-old Chicagoan was released from prison.

Escobedo claimed the Chicago police would not leave him alone upon his release. He was constantly being harassed by patrol cars, and in April 1965, he was charged with selling drugs to an undercover officer. Although he was acquitted of the drug charges, Escobedo was arrested several times over the next two years. In 1967, he was convicted on a federal narcotics charge and served seven years in prison. Upon his release, Escobedo, a high school dropout, had trouble finding and holding on to a job.

In a 1984 New York Times article, Escobedo said, "In the beginning, the case was the best thing that could have happened, not just for my freedom but lot [sic] of others in the same predicament. But since then until now, it has done nothing but cause me a lot of aggravation and grief."

In October 1984, Escobedo was found Guilty of two counts of taking indecent liberties with his 12-year-old stepdaughter and sentenced to twelve years in prison. REF.: *CBA*.

Eskridge, Joseph, prom. 1870, Case of, U.S., mur. On the morning of Dec. 4, 1870, Howard Brantley was shot to death as he dozed in front of a fire in a Mississippi train station. As officials removed the body from the Shuqualak, Miss., depot, they discovered a note from Brantley's wife asking him to meet her at the station. When officials finally tracked down Minerva Brantley, she was in Macon, Ga., and showed little emotion when informed that her husband had been murdered. A passenger who rode the train with Mrs. Brantley told police that she asked for her husband when the train stopped in Shuqualak, but continued on to Macon when she did not receive an answer.

While Minerva Brantley was uncooperative with the authorities, the police learned of a stranger who had been in Shuqualak the night before the murder. When police finally caught up with the mystery man, Joseph Eskridge, in Alabama, he denied any knowledge of the crime. But a routine investigation turned up the fact that Mrs. Brantley and Eskridge were the subject of many rumors in their hometown of Selma, Ala., and that the pair had insured the life of Mr. Brantley for $20,000. It was also learned that Brantley and Eskridge had spent some nights together in Livingstone, Miss., and had purchased a double-barrelled shotgun. The couple was arrested and charged with murder, but Minerva was released on $1,000 bond. Only days later she helped Eskridge escape from prison. The gunman was arrested again and finally tried for murder. He was found Guilty and sentenced to die, but Eskridge was pardoned; some believe he bribed the lieutenant-governor in the governor's absence. Mrs. Brantley was never recaptured and charges against her were dropped.

REF.: *CBA; Dilnot, Triumphs of Detection.*

Esparragoza Moreno, Juan José (AKA: El Azul), prom. 1985, Mex., drugs.-org. crime. Known as "El Azul" because his skin was so dark it looked almost blue, drug trafficker Juan José Esparragoza Moreno was one of the dozen or so men working under Ernesto Fonseca Carrillo, Rafael Cáro Quintero, and Miguel Angel Félix Gallardo of the Guadalajara drug cartel. The Mexican gangster was one of three partners, Fonseca Carrillo and Cáro Quintero included, who turned 220 acres of desert in the state of San Luis Potosi into a marijuana field, under the watchful, approving eyes of the Federales. The tract of land, seven miles from the nearest paved road, was made known to the U.S. DEA in May 1982, by an informant of agent Enrique Camarena. After an aerial reconnaissance by the DEA, the plantation was raided and 200 tons of sinsemilla marijuana was recovered. No drug traffickers were apprehended, due, as it was learned later, to a Mexican federal judicial police officer's warning of the impending raid. See: **Cáro Quintero, Rafael; Fonseca Carrillo, Ernesto.**

REF.: *CBA; Shannon, Desperados.*

Esparza, Rebecca, 1961- , and **Esparza, Richard,** 1961-88, U.S., (unsolv.) kid.-mur. In what they thought would be an easy auto theft, two men jumped into a parked van with its engine running on the west side of Chicago in March 1988. In the back of the van were the owners Rebecca and Richard Esparza, who had just left a wedding reception for Richard's mother. The assailants shot 27-year-old Richard in the head and drove Rebecca south to 134th Street and the Calumet Expressway. Despite repeated pleas for her life, the kidnappers shot Mrs. Esparza in the head and left her for dead on a secluded forest preserve road.

It was not until eight months later that police finally got some information about the attackers. After months in the hospital, Rebecca Esparza finally recovered, but couldn't remember any details of the evening she and her husband were kidnapped. It was only after being hypnotized by Dr. Kenneth LeFebvre, that Esparaza was able to give a description of the assailants. The killers remain at large. REF.: *CBA.*

Espinosa, Gaspar de, c.1484-1537, Pan., jur. Took part in the Pedro Arias de Avila Pedrarias expedition in 1514. He was named chief justice of Panama, where he presided over the sedition trial of Vasco Nuñez de Balboa and condemned him to death in 1517 upon the order of Pedrarias, the governor of Panama. REF.: *CBA.*

Espinosa Brothers, prom. 1860s, U.S., west. outl. In 1861, three Mexican citizens, Julian, Felipe, and Victorio Espinosa entered the U.S. reputedly to avenge the deaths of six relatives who had perished during the Mexican-American War, by killing 100 "gringos." The Espinosas travelled to Colorado, where, in the next two years they killed twenty-six U.S. citizens. Most of the Espinosas' victims were also robbed, often immediately after being paid—a fact which casts some doubt on their professed motive of revenge.

When the trio's leader, Felipe Espinosa, offered to stop the killings in return for a land grant of 5,000 acres, Colorado officials responded by posting a reward of $2,500 for Felipe—dead or alive. When the killing continued, local vigilante groups were organized, and tried to catch the Espinosas, but often ended up hanging the wrong person. Finally, Victorio Espinosa was caught in the Fairplay-California gulch and lynched. Felipe remained at large and continued killing.

In desperation, the U.S. Army hired Tom Tobin, a renowned U.S. scout, to bring in the two remaining Espinosas. Eschewing a fifteen-man backup, Tobin, riding alone, caught up with the two renegades at Indian Creek and killed them before they could fire a shot. Tobin cut off their heads and returned to Fort Garland to claim his reward money. Because of a cash shortage Tobin received only $1,500 and a quantity of buckskins. The heads of the Espinosas became a ghoulish but popular local attraction. As late as 1955, Kit Carson III was exhibiting them in sideshows. When local experts denounced them as fakes, Carson, grandson of Tom Tobin, said that he had always insisted the real skulls were buried behind Fort Garland. REF.: *CBA.*

Esposito, Anthony, 1906-42, and **Esposito, William,** 1912-42, U.S., rob.-mur. What started as a payroll robbery on Jan. 14, 1941, ended with two people dead, one of them a New York City policeman killed by a "corpse" in the midday rush just off Fifth Avenue. The Esposito Brothers, armed with pistols, boarded an elevator behind Alfred Klausman, fifty-five, who was returning to the linen firm where he was office manager. Klausman had just picked up the firm's $649 payroll at a nearby bank. Between the second and third floors, the brothers placed a gun to the elevator operator's head and ordered him to stop the car and face the door. The elevator operator did as he was told; he then heard Klausman cry, "No! No! No!" A shot rang out and the office manager slumped to the floor, dead, a gunshot wound in the head. The brothers ordered the operator to take the elevator to the street level where they then ran into a department store. The operator summoned police and the chase was on. The brothers ran out of the store and jumped into a cab waiting on Madison Avenue, but the street was jammed with traffic. They threatened to kill the driver if he did not move the taxi, but traffic was at a standstill. The Espositos jumped out of the cab. The cabdriver ran up to police officer Edward Maher, fifty-two, who was directing traffic on the corner, yelling "Stick-up!" and pointing to the fleeing brothers.

Maher, a twenty-eight-year police department veteran who was scheduled to retire in less than a month, gave chase as the killers headed towards Fifth Avenue. The street was jammed with pedestrians, but Maher managed to get a clear shot at one of the killers. He fired twice and William Esposito fell face down on the 35th Street sidewalk. His brother continued running, turning onto Fifth Ave. He ran into a dime store. A crowd gathered around the fallen brother; the man appeared dead. Maher grabbed Esposito by his overcoat and started to turn him over. "Back up, please," he warned the crowd. "Someone's liable to get hurt." As the corpse rolled over a .38-caliber revolver appeared in its hand. The gun barked twice and Maher fell to the sidewalk, dead. A Brooklyn cabdriver, Leonard Weisberg, jumped on Esposito, and tried to take the weapon from the killer. Esposito fired again. Weisberg fell to the sidewalk, a bullet in his throat. Esposito discarded the empty revolver and reached into an overcoat pocket for still another gun. Angry spectators, seeing their chance, finally overpowered the killer.

Meanwhile, Anthony Esposito raced into the basement of the Woolworth's store on Fifth Avenue, pocketing his weapons. He calmly walked up the stairs with shoppers, police, however, had trailed him. Six police officers met Esposito at the top of the stairs. After a brief struggle, the second Esposito brother was taken into custody.

The Espositos were both arrested, hospitalized, and then indicted on charges of first-degree murder. The hero cabdriver, Leonard Weisberg, was also hospitalized and eventually recovered. He was promised a cab of his own as a reward for his heroism.

For slain police officer Edward Maher, Jan. 14 had always been his unlucky day. On that date twenty-one years earlier, 1921, his wife had died and he was left alone to raise his 5-month-old son, Edward Jr. Other bad luck had also befallen the officer on that same date and he began to refer to it as his "jinx day."

A more traditional bad luck day awaited the murderous Esposito brothers. On Mar. 13, 1942—Friday the 13th—the brothers paid for the two lives they had taken by losing their own in the electric chair at Sing Sing. REF.: *CBA*.

Esposito, Giuseppe, prom. 1879-81, Italy-U.S., blk.-extor.-kid.-org. crime. A prominent member of a Sicilian gang headed by Leoni in the 1870s, Giuseppe Esposito headed to the U.S. following a crackdown on crime by the Italian government. Esposito was involved in the 1880 kidnapping of a British clergymen in which the Leoni gang received £5,000 ransom after they chopped off the ears of the victim. In the same year Esposito fled to New Orleans. The gangster bought a boat, which he named *Leoni,* and dredged the gulf for oysters. After months of relative calm, Esposito picked up where his Italian trail of terror had ended. Esposito pushed out the local Mafia boss, Tony Labruzzo, with his Black Hand gang. The gang offered protection to local merchants in exchange for money. Soon Esposito had acquired a fleet of boats and his organization was controlling the lucrative dock area of the city.

In 1881, Esposito's chief rival Labruzzo told authorities that Esposito was in New Orleans, and the Italian government hired two New York police detectives to capture him. At the same time, David Hennessy was appointed police chief of New Orleans and one of his first promises to the public was to arrest and deport Esposito. Hennessy and fellow officers arrested the gang leader and put him on a boat bound for New York. Italian Army officers met Esposito's boat and returned him to Italy, where he was convicted of extortion and sentenced to life in prison.

REF.: Asbury, *The French Quarter; CBA*.

Esposito, Joseph (AKA: **Diamond Joe, Dimey**), 1872-1928, U.S., org. crime. Diamond Joe Esposito, born in Accera, Italy, on Mar. 28, 1872, migrated to the U.S. at age twenty-three. He took day labor jobs, first in Boston and later in Brooklyn, before moving on to Chicago where he opened a bakery in the Nineteenth Ward (now the Twenty-Fifth) in 1905. Esposito worked several rackets on the side and was always heavily armed. In addition to running his bakery, Esposito also worked as a hod-carrier and organized a work force into a union, of which he became treasurer. Esposito exercised considerable power in his new role and became quite wealthy. He also organized the Circolo Accera Club, which consisted of fellow immigrants from the village near Naples which had been Esposito's birthplace. As president of this club, Esposito financed several small businesses and took a large portion of each enterprise. To further ingratiate himself, Esposito paid for the fares of scores of his fellow Italians when they migrated from the Old World.

"Diamond Joe" Esposito.

In the summer of 1908, Esposito began dating a woman who was also seeing a barber, Mack Geaquenta. One day in August 1908, Esposito sat down in one of Geaquenta's barber chairs and, while getting a shave, got into an argument with his rival. Suddenly, his face coated with lather, Esposito leaped out of the chair, pulled a gun, and shot the enraged Geaquenta in the mouth as the barber advanced on him. Geaquenta fell dead. Esposito's lawyers stalled his murder trial for almost nine months, and by the time he appeared in court, all the witnesses to the shooting had either disappeared or lost their memories. Esposito was released. This killing solidified his position in the Italian community as a local don. So powerful and rich was Esposito that he was able to command silence from the witnesses. Esposito flaunted his riches after that, his pedestrian mind symbolizing power in the form of diamonds. He ordered a $50,000 belt buckle studded with diamonds which spelled out his name. His cuff links and shirt studs were made of diamonds. He ambled down the street like some portly Italian Santa Claus, glistening like a Christmas tree, dispensing money to the poor.

Like the man he most admired—James "Big Jim" Colosimo, who was fast becoming the crime boss of Chicago—Esposito organized his own gang of strong-armed men to enforce his edicts in the Nineteenth Ward. After Colosimo built his sumptuous Colosimo's Cafe, Esposito typically aped Big Jim by opening his own restaurant, the posh Bella Napoli at 850 South Halsted Street. To this restaurant flocked local Italian hoodlums, including a vicious killer named Cuono Coletta, who got drunk at a party in the Bella Napoli and began shooting at random strangers. One of Coletta's bullets struck the hand of Sam Esposito, Diamond Joe's brother, blowing away a fingertip. Then one of Esposito's bodyguards leaped up and shot Coletta in the head, killing him. The slaying was not investigated.

So famous did Esposito become that out-of-town crime bosses like New York's Frankie Yale often visited him, seeking advice on racket operations. Chicago political leaders also conferred with Diamond Joe, currying his favor in delivering the Nineteenth Ward vote which he wholly controlled by 1913. In that year, Esposito invited the entire ward to his wedding reception after marrying 16-year-old Carmela Marchese. (He was then forty-one.) The affair was enormous, lasting three days and costing Diamond Joe $65,000. He paid $40,000 for the wine alone, but this kind of lavish display of wealth was in keeping with the image and style Esposito wished to project.

By 1920, at the advent of Prohibition, Esposito was elected Republican committeeman for the Nineteenth Ward and gave a wild celebration party at which his enforcer, Tony "Mops" Volpe, one of Chicago's fiercest killers, beat up several uninvited guests. Volpe was made a deputy sheriff a short time later through Esposito's political influence. This allowed Volpe to protect Diamond Joe's extensive alky-cooking empire, which spread throughout Melrose Park, Chicago Heights, and many Chicago districts. Thousands of Italian immigrants, under the threat of being exposed as illegal aliens and facing deportation, were virtual prisoners of Esposito and his henchmen, and were forced to operate alky-cooking operations wherein they produced cheap liquor, wine, and beer in enormous quantities. This was then distributed under the noses of Prohibition agents throughout the city, gleaning millions for Diamond Joe and his associates.

Feeble efforts were made to suppress Diamond Joe's alky-cooking empire, but for the most part local law enforcement officials and federal agents were ineffective in closing down his operations. The Bella Napoli was raided in 1923 for serving wine and padlocked for a year, while Esposito was fined a mere $1,000. He laughingly paid the fine and happily went about his million-dollar business. Diamond Joe's coffers were enriched even more when he began supplying all the sugar for the Genna Brothers' stills. Esposito also installed hundreds of giant stills in his own ward, producing great amounts of near-poisonous liquor.

When the Genna Brothers went to war with Al Capone, Esposito sided with Scarface but immediately suffered the consequences. John Tucillo, an Esposito brother-in-law and top liquor distributor and enforcer who worked for Esposito and Ralph Sheldon, a Capone ally, was machine-gunned to death and his body dumped on Sheldon's doorstep. Phillip Leonatti, another Esposito brother-in-law, was the next to be gunned down by the Gennas. Leonatti was not a gangster but had been selected as a victim as a message from the terrible Gennas to quit Capone's legions.

Esposito remained loyal to Scarface, but after the destruction of the Gennas, Diamond Joe and Capone fell out, and on the morning of Mar. 21, 1928, Esposito received a phone call from one of Scarface's lieutenants, Frank Nitti, according to one report, and was told to "get out of town or get killed." Capone by then reigned supreme in Chicago and all of Esposito's old underworld allies, Colosimo, Johnny Torrio, and the Genna Brothers, were either murdered or had left the Chicago rackets. But Diamond Joe proved truculent and resisted such suggestions. His top bodyguards, Ralph and Joe Varchetti, urged him to retire, go to his remote farm near Cedar Lake, Ill., and raise chickens.

"I can't go now," Diamond Joe told them, explaining that his son was sick with scarlet fever. "Besides," he added with finality, "I promised Senator Deneen that I would run for ward committeeman." Senator Charles S. Deneen, ostensibly a reform politician, had long been a backer of Esposito. Diamond Joe later that day told his aides that the call was probably "some slug trying to scare me out of town so he can grab my operations. I'm not that dumb!" That night, while walking down Oakley Boulevard toward his home, the heavyset Diamond Joe froze in his tracks as he heard a shot ring out. He was accompanied by the Varchetti brothers who flanked him on either side. "I thought it was a blowout," Ralph Varchetti later told police. Then there was silence and the trio continued to walk down the street. Then, from ambush, a hailstorm of bullets pierced the silence and Diamond Joe, hit with fifty-eight bullets, toppled dead to the cement.

The murderous fusillade had been unleashed from a large touring car that had slowly overtaken the trio of gangsters. Said Ralph Varchetti later: "Then there were more shots and Joe says 'Oh, my God!' and I knew he was hit. I dropped to the sidewalk and lay flat, with my face in the dirt. The shots came in bursts of fire from an automobile...When the firing stopped a second, I looked up and they fired again. I dropped flat, and this time waited until they were gone. I got near Dimey and tried to wake him. He was gone."

Only a few doors down the street, sitting in front of an open window of their home, were Carmela Esposito and her three children, waiting for Diamond Joe. Hearing the gunfire, the 31-year-old Carmela ran down the street and threw herself on the body of her slain husband, screaming: "Oh, is it you, Giuseppe?" The unharmed, helpless Varchetti brothers stood over her and their dead boss, holding guns, pointing them uselessly down the dark street where the murder car had vanished. Sobbed Carmela: "He was so good to the Italian people and this is what he got for it! I'll kill! I'll kill them for this!" But there would be no vendetta for Carmela Esposito. The widow was left to raise three small children who grew up never knowing their father's killers. Since all the bullets dug out of the body were garlic-tipped, police speculated that the murder had been the handiwork of Capone's top killers, Albert Anselmi and John Scalise, who made a practice of tipping their bullets in garlic—in the mistaken belief that if the wound was not mortal the garlic would poison their intended victims to death. However, these Capone gunmen were never questioned and the killers of Diamond Joe Esposito remained anonymous. See: **Anselmi, Albert; Capone, Alphonse; Colosimo, James; Genna Brothers; Torrio, John; Yale, Frank.**

REF.: Asbury, *Gem of the Prairie;* Burns, *The One-Way Ride;* Demaris, *Captive City;* Kobler, *Capone;* Landesco, *Organized Crime in Chicago;* McPhaul, *Johnny Torrio;* Morgan, *Prince of Crime;* Nash, *Bloodletters and Badmen;* Pasley, *Al Capone;* ____, *Muscling In;* Sullivan, ____, *Rattling the Cup on Chicago Crime;* Willemse, *Behind the Green Lights.*

Espoz y Mina, Francisco, 1781-1836, Spain, consp. Fought against the French in Navarre employing guerilla warfare from 1808-14, and lived in exile from 1814-20, following the failed attempt to overthrow Ferdinand VII. He was exiled again after defeat at Catalonia when he led the Liberal army against the French to restore Ferdinand's power in 1823. He returned in 1834 to lead the Spanish army against the Carlists. REF.: *CBA.*

Espronceda y Delgado, José de (AKA: the Spanish Byron), 1808-42, Spain, rebel. José de Espronceda y Delgado spent most of his life in exile, especially in Paris, London, and Lisbon, for his involvement with revolutionary efforts beginning in 1822. He became a leading advocate for Spanish Romanticism. REF.: *CBA.*

Essad, Pasa, c.1863-1920, Turk., king, assass. Joined the Turkish revolutionary movement in 1908, headed defense of Scutari from 1912-13, but surrendered the city to the attacking Montenegrins. He aided Prince William of Wied in gaining the Albanian throne in 1914 and became minister of war and the interior, but was removed from the country when his designs upon the throne were discovered. After WWI, during which he led the Albanian delegation in Paris, he was proclaimed king of Albania by the so-called National Assembly, but never sat on the throne. In 1920 he was assassinated in Paris by an Albanian. REF.: *CBA.*

Essex, Mark James Robert, 1949-73, U.S., mur. Mark James Robert Essex, a black man, grew up with religious parents in the small town of Emporia, Kan. Joining the Navy in 1969, he encountered discrimination and developed an intense hatred for whites. After receiving a general discharge after two years of service for "character and behavior disorders," he became involved in militant black politics. When he returned home from the service, he could not hold down a job because, a former friend explained, "he couldn't stand taking orders from white people. After spending time in New York with black radicals and becoming increasingly bitter and militantly opposed to white society, Essex, twenty-three, moved to New Orleans. He lived in four apartments during his five months in the city, making few friends. Just before Christmas he wrote to his mother, declaring that "the white man is my enemy," and "I will fight to gain my manhood or die trying." He gave away a few prized possessions to friends, and completed his plans for a sniper attack.

On Jan. 7, 1973, Essex, armed with a .44-caliber rifle and several thousand rounds of ammunition, positioned himself in a concrete bunker on the roof of a seventeen-floor Howard Johnson's Motor Lodge, about five blocks from New Orleans' French Quarter. He began firing from the motor lodge at about 10:15 a.m., after setting fires in several empty rooms to draw out people to shoot. By the time he finished his twelve-hour, guerrilla warfare rampage, nine persons would be killed and nine more wounded. Essex fired on guests as they fled from their rooms after the fire alarm was sounded. Five people killed were hotel guests, four were policemen; one of them was Deputy Police Chief Louis Sirgo. Hundreds of policemen surrounded the hotel, as a crowd of thousands watched. Firemen used their trucks for protection against the sniper as they attempted to fight the hotel fire. Police sharpshooters fired hundreds of bullets into the concrete bunker. At night, with a borrowed Marine helicopter, police moved in on Essex, killing him with about thirty red tracer bullets. A newsman who observed the scene from the building next door said the officers in the helicopter fired at the dead body for three or four minutes. The .44-caliber Magnum rifle, smashed into four pieces from the bullets shot into it, was the only weapon found on the roof, lying near Essex's corpse. Ballistics tests confirmed that the rifle was the same weapon used in the New Year's Eve 1972, attack on New Orleans police, in which a 19-year-old cadet was killed.

REF.: *CBA;* Hernon, *A Terrible Thunder;* Holmes, *Serial Murder.*

Estabo, Tranquellano, prom. 1890s, U.S., west. gunman. Within a few months in 1895 this notorious Mexican outlaw was involved in three gunfights. Near Phoenix, N.M., Tranquellano Estabo and some friends got into a fight with Walter Paddleford and some other men. Three of the Mexicans were killed in the shootout, but Estabo escaped unhurt. A few months later, after mortally wounding a man during a card game in a Phoenix saloon, Estabo went into the street and began shooting his pistols. When ordered to stop by Sheriff Dee Harkey and his assistant Cicero Stewart, Estabo replied with gunfire. When Estabo jumped on his horse and tried to escape, Harkey gave chase. Three miles out of town. Estabo was forced to surrender. The frightened gunman was returned to town where he was nearly killed by Stewart. Estabo's life was spared and he was put in jail to await trial.

REF.: *CBA;* Harkey, *Mean As Hell;* O'Neal, *Encyclopedia of Western Gunfighters.*

Estee, Morris March, 1833-1903, U.S., jur. District attorney for Eldorado County, Calif., from 1864-66, and appointed by President William McKinley to the District Court for the territory of Hawaii in 1900. REF.: *CBA.*

Esterhazy, Marie Charles Ferdinand, See: **Dreyfus, Alfred.**

Estes, Billie Sol, 1925- , U.S., fraud. The crooked machinations of Billie Sol Estes were performed in the garb of a checked suit, ten-gallon hat, and ornate cowboy boots coated with fertilizer. Estes was the first, but certainly not the last, of the "good old boys" from Texas who managed to build a multimillion-dollar fortune based upon the gullibility of finance firms, government allotments, and high-level contacts within the federal government.

Before he was thirty, Estes, the son of a country preacher from Clyde, Texas, was named by the U.S. Junior Chamber of Commerce as one of America's ten outstanding young men of the year. In accepting his award, Estes told one and all that the reason for his success was good living. He did not drink, smoke, or dance and generally lived the good life, following the dictates of the Lord.

Super con man Billie Sol Estes under arrest.

But the dictates Estes truly followed were his own inner voices of deceit and greed. He had, in the late 1950s, acquired thousands of acres of land in and about Pecos, Texas, calling himself a cotton farmer. He *appeared* to be as rich as the oil barons of his native state. He shared his wealth, spending freely, giving lavish gifts to local bigwigs, and contributing mightily to the political campaigns of those who might someday overlook the rough corners of his landed empire. This included Senator Ralph Yarborough and Congressman J.T. Rutherford, who represented the Pecos area.

When John F. Kennedy became president, Estes, who thought of himself as a pioneer, moved in on the New Frontier. He purchased $6,000 worth of tickets, at $100 a ticket, to the presidential birthday party celebrating the New Frontier in 1962 and made a beeline for Washington. His aim, really, was not the office of the presidency but the Department of Agriculture, which, through clever manipulation of crop allotments and a few gifts to officials, he had managed to con into naming him as a board member to the National Cotton Advisory Committee, although he had little or no cotton.

What Estes did have was a monopoly on grain storage. He had bought up a great number of grain storage elevators during the mid-1950s on credit, of course, when he realized that the government paid handsomely for grain storage. For three years alone, 1959-1961, he collected $8 million in storage payments from the federal government for storing more than fifty million bushels of grain. This lucrative enterprise did not appease the entrepreneur's greed, however, and he hit upon a scheme to further enrich himself, knowing that government subsidies in cotton were ridiculously high.

The government had set high prices for cotton allotments, but these allotments applied to only long-established cotton acreage.

Estes' Texas land, however, was mostly barren of cotton; he had never grown the crop and was therefore not entitled to allotments. The Texas promoter decided that he would merely go out and buy land that did have allotments for cotton crops. This proved to be somewhat difficult, but Estes solved the problem or, to nervous government inspectors, appeared to have solved it. He and his agents roamed through Georgia, Alabama, Oklahoma, and Texas, locating farmers who were about to lose their lands to the government.

The proposition was simple. Estes found more than 3,000 acres that had existing allotments, and went to the farmers about to lose this land. Under a special proviso, the government would allow the transferring of allotments by farmers who bought new land. They could transfer the cotton crop allotment to new tracts of land from old acreage having the existing allotment. Billie Sol said that he would sell them *his* land so that the allotments could be transferred to that acreage. Through his financial contact, he would arrange for mortgages to be taken out for them so that they could ostensibly acquire his property, but they would have to agree to default on the mortgage payments so that the Estes land would revert to its original owner, Billie Sol, who would then have his original land *and* the federal allotments transferred to it. Of course, the Texas boy wonder paid the farmers under the table for their trouble.

The scheme worked well. Even though certain government officials in the Department of Agriculture going over these deals found them suspicious and wrote unflattering reports about Estes' methods—reports that were filed in the offices of Under-Secretary Murphy's minions—the under-secretary steadfastly approved of the allotments to Estes, saying that Billie Sol was an upstanding citizen who was greatly helping the economy to flourish.

While the allotment scheme was flowering, Estes embarked on a new adventure in economic swindling, a strange and bizarre scheme dealing with simple fertilizer. Anhydrous ammonia, a liquid fertilizer which was easily applied to crops and proved to increase crop production almost overnight, was much in demand by farmers throughout Texas. Estes, knowing this, approached hundreds of farmers and offered to sell them the fertilizer at between $40 and $60 a ton, which was $50 less per ton than the going retail rate. They leaped at his purchase price which was, of course, designed to corner the anhydrous ammonia market. He would lose great sums, but in the end he would reap new fortunes when complete control of the product was his. He made up the losses through the income generated by his grain storage business.

There was one big problem—the fertilizer had to be stored in expensively manufactured tanks. Billie Sol sold these tanks through a labyrinthine mortgage system to farmers and businessmen in West Texas, assuring them that he would take full responsibility for any problems with the tanks. The profits from such an investment, Billie Sol demonstrated on paper, would be enormous. Thousands of mortgages were taken out for the tanks, and Estes took these to finance companies who bought them at a discount.

Billie Sol's bank accounts swelled. He was the king of the grain storage business, reaped fortunes on cotton crop allotments, and had moved into the fertilizer business so successfully that he appeared to have gotten complete control of the market. Though there were murmurs about his odd techniques by bureaucrats in far-off Washington, Texas authorities greeted the success of their native son with backslapping pride.

Doubts about Billie Sol did form in the minds of some local Pecos businessmen, who went to Oscar Griffin, the young editor of the tiny Pecos *Independent & Enterprise.* The newspaper editor listened to the suspicions cast upon Billie Sol's methods and was astounded to learn that he had, within months, cornered the anhydrous ammonia market.

Griffin began a tedious investigation into Estes' fertilizer scheme, a probe that would later earn him the Pulitzer Prize. His research provided eye-popping figures. The Texas wonder boy had sold, through a series of involved mortgage arrangements, more than 33,000 storage tanks, which were listed as being located throughout West Texas. The editor, after consulting with fertilizer experts, quickly learned that such a vast number of tanks could not possibly dot the broad stretches of land around Pecos.

The large financial institutions in New York and Los Angeles which had arranged for millions of dollars in mortgages for the 33,000 storage tanks were contacted, but representatives of these institutions were cautious. Billie Sol was a V.I.P. client with powerful friends in Washington, D.C. His business involved vast amounts of money, and they did not intend to annoy the Texas genius. Investigators were sent out to make polite inquiries about the storage tanks.

Initially, investigators thought the whole procedure was senselessly repetitive. They had already checked a number of Billie Sol's storage tanks, and had checked the serial numbers on the tanks built by the Superior Manufacturing Company of Amarillo, Texas.

Dutifully, the investigators went about their work, going first to Billie Sol's office where the affable tycoon went over lists of storage tanks and their locations and corresponding serial numbers. The investigators then drove to the sites, checked the serial numbers, and reported back to the home offices that everything was in order. One investigator, however, Frank Cain, a lawyer for the Pacific Finance Company in Los Angeles which had invested heavily in buying up the storage tank mortgages, did not go to Estes' office first.

The lawyer, working out of Dallas, went to Pecos, Texas, unannounced and conducted a private investigation. He could not locate a single storage tank bearing the firm's corresponding serial numbers. Next, he went to Amarillo and inspected the premises of the Superior Manufacturing Company, which constructed the tanks. He learned that two of Billie Sol's close friends operated this firm. Moreover, he quickly realized that this company could not have produced 33,000 storage tanks with its limited facilities. As it turned out, the firm had not manufactured more than a few hundred tanks.

What the Amarillo firm had produced was thousands of plates with serial numbers on them—more than 33,000, in fact. Normally, such plates were welded onto a tank, but those used by Estes were interchangeable, and could be slipped into brackets so that the switching of plates was a simple matter. And this is exactly what Billie Sol had been doing. Whenever an investigator appeared, he would direct him to the location of a storage tank but send ahead of the investigator a crew of men who would switch the serial number plates so that they corresponded to those on the investigator's list. The system was so streamlined that Billie Sol would supervise the operation via short-wave radios installed in his office and in the jeeps being driven by his plate-switching crews.

When the finance companies learned, to their great dismay, that they had been gulled in one of the oldest Peter-to-Paul scams, a full-scale state inquiry ensued. Those involved in Estes' storage tank scheme began to talk. J.S. Wheeler, who operated a Pecos fertilizing company, told Texas officials that he saw through the Estes scheme early on and confronted Billie Sol, who merely laughed and told him that the finance firms were easily hoodwinked. "They'll never catch up with you," Estes had chuckled. "These people are stupid."

It was all a clever game to Estes, who then went on to tell Wheeler how ranchers had employed the same technique in falsifying assets when getting huge loans on their ranches. They would merely put up their cattle as collateral, then drive the banker around and around on their vast tracts of land so that he could get a general count of the livestock available. The easily fooled banker would really be counting the same cattle over and over again but from a different vantage point on the same ranch. "It's the same thing with the tanks," said Billie Sol reassuringly. "We'll starve them to death looking for equipment."

Cain's investigation proved out-and-out fraud; it was the end of the Texas Tycoon. Following the storage tank revelations, the federal government inspected the allotments given Estes for his cotton lands. It was learned that Under-Secretary Murphy and other officials had visited Estes in Texas and had been taken to swanky stores, such as Neiman-Marcus, where expensive wardrobes and other items were bestowed upon them. Murphy and the others were asked to resign their posts, which they did. The cotton allotments were revoked.

Estes himself blithely faced prosecution, perhaps never believing until it was too late that he would actually be convicted for his schemes. His attitude did not change, even when Frank Cain first confronted him with the truth and told him: "You realize that you are subject to criminal penalties?"

At that moment, Estes shrugged and lamely admitted that the millions he had scammed through the storage tank scheme was "penitentiary money." Billie Sol's unshakable belief in his own immunity seemed, at first, to be justified. Although a Texas court convicted him of fraud and sentenced him to eight years in prison, the U.S. Supreme Court overturned this ruling and sentence, stating that Estes' trial had been televised and, because of the press coverage, Billie Sol had been denied due process of law.

Jubilant in this decision, Estes made plans to go back to his bilking operations, but was shocked to find himself again on trial, this time for mail fraud. A U.S. District Court found him Guilty and he received a fifteen-year sentence. The Supreme Court did not overturn this conviction, and the swaggering Estes went to prison, his crazy dreams of empire shattering with the clank of his cell door.

Yet, today in West Texas, the sharper is still held in high regard by some residents who thought the Estes schemes as merely shrewd business mores. Of course, these admirers lost no money in Billie Sol's $22 million storage tank scam. Said one during the trial of the Texas wonder boy: "Hell, the man was only trying to make a living!"

Estes served six years on the mail fraud conviction, entering prison in 1965 and emerging in 1971. Promising to stick to the straight and narrow, Estes took a job as a truck dispatcher for a petroleum firm in Abilene, Texas, and regularly reported to his parole officer. He pointed out to his parole officer that he had learned his lesson and that nothing was then beneath him, including manual labor, where he "even washed trucks and fixed flats." To make a few extra dollars, Estes explained, he worked as a straw boss on his brother's cattle ranch.

But the habitual criminal in Billie Sol Estes was hard at work on yet another swindle. This time, Estes' scheme involved the purchasing and leasing of nonexistent steam-cleaning machines used to wash equipment in the oil fields. Knowing the hustler's old techniques of claiming equipment that did not exist, officials inspected the Estes operation and quickly proved fraud. This time, Estes was allowed to plead guilty to one charge only, tax evasion. He went back to prison in 1979 to serve a five-year term. Estes was released in 1983, and again he claimed that he would follow only the honest path and that his name would never again be involved with crime.

Yet the world heard from the hustler once more in the following year, when he came forward to clear up an old murder as a favor to a U.S. Marshal, Clint Peoples. Before entering prison in 1979, Estes had promised Peoples that he would solve the death of Henry Marshall, who was found shot and poisoned on his small West Texas ranch in 1961, and whose death had been originally labelled a suicide. Estes, in 1984, went before a grand jury and claimed that Marshall had gotten on to his cotton swindles and, as an official of the Department of Agriculture, was about to expose Estes' far-flung operations.

The hustler then met with Lyndon Baines Johnson, who was linked to Estes' cotton swindles along with some Johnson aides, according to Estes. Following a meeting where Johnson concluded that Marshall would ruin them all, Estes claimed, the newly inaugurated vice president ordered Malcolm Wallace, a family friend (who had once been convicted of killing a man), to execute

the troublesome Marshall, which he did. Most authorities utterly dismissed this Estes tale, although the grand jury Estes addressed on the matter, along with a judge hearing the old case, ordered that the Marshall death be changed in the records from a suicide to a homicide. A short time later, Billie Sol Estes was charged with sexually assaulting his housekeeper. He was then sixty. See: **Marshall, Henry.**
REF.: *CBA*; Davis, *Mafia Kingfish*; Nash, *Hustlers and Con Men*; Toledano, *J. Edgar Hoover*; Wade, *Great Hoaxes and Famous Imposters.*

Estes, Cornell Avery, 1962- , Case of, U.S., mur. In 1979, 16-year-old Cornell Avery Estes was convicted of murdering Donna M. Turner and sentenced to twenty years in prison. Less than one year later, Estes was freed when another man confessed to murdering Turner. In March 1984, the Maryland Board of Public Works awarded Estes $16,500 in damages to compensate for the time he had been erroneously confined. But the announcement of Estes' cash award was tempered by the fact he was serving a three-year prison term for breaking and entering. REF.: *CBA.*

Estes, Joe Ewing, 1903 - , U.S., jur. Appointed by President Dwight D. Eisenhower to the Northern District Court of Texas in 1955, and served on the Advisory Committee on Rules of Evidence in 1965. REF.: *CBA.*

Estes, William Lee, 1870-1930, U.S., jur. Appointed by President Woodrow Wilson to the Eastern District Court of Texas in 1920, and published *Law Enforcement and the Courts* in 1929. REF.: *CBA.*

Estrada, Pedro Luis (AKA: **Pablo Estrada, Pete Estrada, Pedro Epstrade, Moe**), 1963- , U.S., mur. A former professional boxer, Pedro Luis Estrada did not confine his violence to the ring. In his spare time, Estrada served as protection for drug dealers in New York City. The FBI is currently searching for Estrada in connection with three drug-related murders. At this writing, Estrada is still at large. REF.: *CBA.*

Estrada Palma, Tomás, 1835-1908, Cuba, rebel. Fought in the Cuban revolution from 1868-78, and acted as the provisional government's president from 1875-77. While in exile in Honduras and the U.S., from 1878-1902, he became leader of the movement for independence in 1895, succeeding José Marti y Pérez. He was Cuba's first president from 1902-06, and was re-elected in 1906. He resigned, however, in 1906 after being charged with election fraud. REF.: *CBA.*

Ethelbert (Aethelberht or **Aegelbriht** or **Albert**), d.794, East Anglia, king, assass. Beheaded at the orders of Offa, the Mercian king. He was later revered as the patron saint of the cathedral at Hereford. REF.: *CBA.*

Ethelred (Aethelred II, AKA: **the Unready**), c.968-1016, Brit., king. King of England from 978-1016, following the assassination of his half-brother, Edward the Martyr. He avoided invading forces led by Olaf Tryggvesson of Norway and Sweyn I of Denmark in 994, by paying them off, and enacted laws concerning military and police codes. In 1002 he ordered the massacre of Danish settlers, and was again forced to buy peace from consequent renewed Danish invasions in 1006 and 1011. In 1013 as Danish King Sweyn I ascended to the British throne, Ethelred fled to Normandy. He later return to expel Canute in 1014. REF.: *CBA.*

Eto, Ken (AKA: **Tokyo Joe, Joe Montana**), 1921- , U.S., org. crime. On Jan. 18, 1983, facing a possible ten-year prison sentence for gambling and racketeering, mob boss Ken Eto was in need of money. His major asset was a shuttered Lyons' restaurant called Marilou's. Eto, the highest-ranking Asian in the Chicago crime family, was a major figure in the city's multimillion-dollar gambling racket. The Korean had established *bolita*, a game in which a bettor wagers that the number he chooses will be the winner, as a solid source of income for the syndicate. Shortly after he was convicted, North Side gambling lieutenant Joseph DiVarco told Eto to meet Jasper Campise and John Gattuso, a Cook County deputy Sheriff, in the restaurant's parking lot, where he would be introduced to a potential buyer. Accompanied by his accountant, Eto drove to the designated meeting site only to be told by

Campise and Gattuso that he was late and the buyer had already left.

On the morning of Feb. 10, 1983, Eto met with DiVarco and another mob boss, Joseph Arnold. Once again, Eto was instructed to meet up with Campise and Gattuso that evening and the three friends would rendezvous at a West Side restaurant with North Side gambling boss Vincent Solano. Eto drove to the designated dinner site with Campise seated beside him and Gattuso in the back seat. After pulling the car into the parking lot at the Montclare Theater, 7129 W. Grand Ave., and shutting off the engine, Gattuso put a .22-caliber pistol to Eto's head and fired three shots. Eto slumped down in the front seat of the car as Campise and Gattuso fled the scene.

Miraculously, the gun shots had only grazed Eto's head and by playing dead he managed to convince the gunmen their mission had been accomplished. The 63-year-old Eto staggered into a nearby pharmacy, where police and an ambulance were notified. While being treated for superficial wounds, Eto stated that he wanted to talk to the FBI. The Korean's acting ability had turned a mob-ordered hit into a bungled assassination attempt. Eto told authorities he would not talk without being placed under protective custody. When the FBI agreed to shelter Eto and his wife, he told them Solano had ordered the hit to prevent him from testifying against the mob. Campise and Gattuso were arrested the next day and charged with attempted murder.

Upon surviving the attempt on his life, Eto told the FBI he was no longer obligated to the people he had worked for over the past thirty years. In exchange for protection, Eto began to reveal the secrets of the crime syndicate's gambling operations. In March, both Campise and Gattuso made bail, but their freedom was short-lived. Four months later, the bodies of the two mobsters were found in the trunk of Campise's car in a Naperville condominium complex. Gattuso and Campise had been stabbed to death and Gattuso had also been strangled, apparently for their failure to carry out the hit on Eto. In August 1983, Eto was sentenced to thirty months probation for operating a gambling ring.

In 1985, Eto testified in front of the President's Commission on Organized Crime. Wearing a hood to protect his "new identity," Eto testified in front of his former boss that Solano had ordered him killed. Eto also provided lengthy testimony on the inner workings of Chicago's crime syndicate. See: **Solano, Vincent.** REF.: *CBA.*

Eto Shimpei, 1835-74, Japan, consp. Helped bring about imperial restoration in 1868, and influenced the transfer of new government to Tokyo from Kyoto. His Korean invasion plans were rejected, leading to his resignation from the cabinet in 1873. He organized Aikoku Koto, a dissident group which sought parliamentary government, and led an uprising in his native Saga region in 1874, for which he was executed. REF.: *CBA.*

Ettelson, Leonard B., and **Gleason, John S., Jr.,** prom. 1976-77, U.S., fraud. Two wealthy members of Chicago's banking elite were caught in an extensive case of fraud. Leonard B. Ettelson, a conservative and wealthy man, headed a prestigious law firm, owned an exclusive California resort, La Quinta, and served as a hospital trustee and on the board of a college. John S. Gleason Jr., a businessman and banker, was president of the Mercantile Bank of Chicago and politically connected. Together, the two men, who had been friends since the late 1950s, amassed more than $32 million in debt. They were considered to be partners who used their insider connections to arrange easy loans for each other, side stepping government and bank rules. Around fifty-six banks and a large number of private citizens were bilked in the fraud.

Their fortunes continued to grow until the recession of 1973, when Gleason's earnings from agricultural property fell at the same time that loans became harder to get. Ettelson, who had been borrowing heavily for years, began to lose money on La Quinta and other properties and holdings. From 1973 to February 1975, Gleason converted about $528,700 of the Mercantile Bank's money for his own use, resigning from that bank on Feb. 1, 1976, and filing for bankruptcy three weeks later. Ettelson began taking out short-term loans from banks, professional acquaintances, and friends to pay off old loans. Confronted by his law partners for looting the estate of a deceased friend who had made Ettelson trustee for somewhere between $1 to 1.9 million, Ettelson resigned from the law firm he had been in charge of for forty years. A former chief federal judge in Chicago, William J. Campbell, and his wife, Marie Campbell, filed suit against Ettelson, charging him with stealing $250,000 worth of securities owned by Mrs. Campbell. Ettelson admitted that he had sold the securities of his oldest friend's wife in order to pay off other debts.

On Dec. 9, 1976, Ettelson's maid found him dead in his bathroom; the death certificate listed "heart disease" as the cause. Drovers Bank, formerly owned by Ettelson, held court judgements that totalled $2,322,931 on defaulted loans to companies Ettelson had controlled. The Mercantile Bank, owned by Gleason, said Ettelson owed the bank $740,000 on a personal loan, as well as $19.4 million on loans he had guaranteed, mostly to his own companies. Ettelson also owed a $2.3 million mortgage on the La Quinta resort. Gleason pleaded guilty in June 1977 to misapplying more than $500,000 in funds while serving as chairman of the board at the Mercantile National Bank. He accepted a three-year plus one-day prison term handed down to him by U.S. District Court Judge Alfred Y. Kirkland. REF.: *CBA*.

Eugenikos, Markos, c.1392-1445, Gr., her. Markos Eugenikos led anti-union sentiment after refusing to sign a decree of union between Greek and Roman factions of the Catholic churches in 1439, and was subsequently imprisoned from 1440-42. Eugenikos was cannonized as a saint of the Orthodox church in 1734. REF.: *CBA*.

Eulenburg, Botho Wend August zu (Graf zu Eulenberg), 1831-1912, Prussia, polit. Served as Prussian House of Representatives member from 1863-70, and minister of interior in 1878, during which time he conceived the Social Democrat law and sought administrative reforms. As Prussian prime minister in 1892, he opposed his predecessor Leo von Caprivi, over the controversial amendment of the criminal code and was subsequently dismissed along with Caprivi in 1894. REF.: *CBA*.

Eulenburg und Hertefeld, Philipp Friedrich Karl Alexander Botho zu (Fürst zu Eulenburg und Hertefeld), 1847-1921, Case of, Ger., homosexuality. Adviser and friend of William II, he served in Vienna as German ambassador from 1894-1902, and became a prince in 1900. While a member of the House of Lords, he was charged with homosexuality, after being implicated in the unproven revelations of Maximillian Harden in 1906. REF.: *CBA*.

Eunus, prom. Second Cent. B.C., Roman., rebel. Eunus proclaimed himself King Antiochus after leading a slave revolt in 135 B.C., which seized the city of Enna, Sicily. Lucius Calpurnius Piso and Publius Rupilius suppressed the revolt in 132-31 B.C. REF.: *CBA*.

Europol, prom. 1960-70, Italy, sec. firm. The private Italian security firm Europol was launched in 1962 by a group of right-wing extremists. Political unrest and a number of kidnapings sparked the growth of security firms in the 1960s. The Europol guards were most often ex-servicemen and police officers trained in the martial arts. Europol was among the first Italian firms to employ women as bodyguards. Private security firms became so popular in Italy that the guards outnumbered police in some cities. REF.: *CBA*; Moorehead, *Hostages to Fortune*.

Eusebius of Dorylaeum, d.c.452, Gr., clergy. Denounced the heretic Nestorius and called for his condemnation in 431. He was appointed bishop of Dorylaeum in 448. After he denounced the heresy of his friend Eutyches, he was deposed and placed in prison. He escaped to Rome and there was restored by the Council of Chalcedon in 451. REF.: *CBA*.

Eustace the Monk, d.1217, Fr.-Brit., pir. After renouncing his loyalty to God, Eustace the Monk was available to the highest bidder. The itinerant Flemish clergyman first plundered French

ships for the British, but soon turned to robbing British ships. Eustace fled England in 1212 and found work with the French government. Five years later, he led an ill-fated attack on Britain. The ex-monk's ship was ambushed in the Straits of Dover. The

Eustace the monk and pirate, terror of the Middle Ages, being beheaded in battle.

British blinded the French sailors by throwing lime on the ship, and then fired a volley of arrows. Eustace was captured by British soldiers and beheaded at sea.

REF.: Botting, *The Pirates*; *CBA*.

Eustachy, Dr. Lauren, prom. 1884, Fr., attempt. mur. Dr. Lauren Eustachy was a highly respected physician in the small French town of Pertuis. Early in the 1880s, a young doctor, Dr. Tournatoire, arrived and soon began taking Eustachy's patients. He also bested Eustachy in a town council election. Eustachy called Tournatoire a thief, a coward, and a drunkard. The slanders resulted in a libel suit which Eustachy lost. Several weeks after the verdict, Eustachy sent a box of poisoned thrushes to the Tournatoire residence. They were served at the midday meal, and the wife and the cook suffered horrible cramps and hallucinations, but both recovered.

Tournatoire chemically analyzed the thrushes and discovered that they contained atropine, derived from the poisonous belladonna plant. Eustachy was also known to have recently won a quantity of the expensive thrushes during a local lottery. Eustachy was charged with attempted murder, the trial began in 1884, and Eustachy claimed the poisoning was a practical joke. The court disagreed, sentencing him to eight years in prison.

REF.: *CBA*; Furneaux, *The Medical Murderer*; Nash, *Almanac of World Crime*; Wilson, *Encyclopedia of Murder*.

Euthydemus, See: **Diodotus II**.

Eutropius, d.c.399, Roman., consp.-mur. Orchestrated the marriage of Eudoxia and Emperor Arcadius in 395, and became the Eastern empire's most powerful person after the murder of rival Flavius Rufinus. In 399, he was the first eunuch to ever become a consul. The same year, he was overthrown by Gainas, and was exiled to Cyprus where he eventually was beheaded. REF.: *CBA*.

Evangelista Slayings, 1929, U.S., (unsolv.) mur. Benjamino Evangelista arrived in the U.S. from Italy at the turn of the century and settled in Philadelphia, where he worked as a section hand on a railroad. There he met Aurelius Angelino, who shared with Evangelista a fanatical belief in occult mysticism. In 1919, Angelino murdered two of his children. He was sent to an asylum, escaped in 1923, and was never seen again. Evangelista moved his family to Detroit and wrote an unpublished tome called the *Oldest History of the World, Discovered By Occult Science in Detroit Michigan* and opened a "temple" in the basement of his home. A large, "seeing eye" hung from the ceiling, and the local Italian immigrants believed Evangelista had curative powers. Faith healer and mystic Evangelista became a wealthy, powerful man.

On July 2, 1929, an unknown killer slaughtered Evangelista and his entire family. The bodies were found the next day, all six decapitated. Sixty police officers were assigned to the case. Only one fingerprint taken from the scene of the crime, and no suspects were found. Italian Umberto Tecchio, suspected as a Black Hand

Extortionist and previously exonerated in a murder case, was one suspect. He had been making mortgage payments to the Evangelistas and had visited their home the night of the murder. For lack of evidence, Tecchio was dismissed as a suspect. He died a natural death in 1934. Several weeks after Tecchio's death, his widow told police that Evangelista had been killed with two machetes used during the ritualistic ceremonies. The machetes had been kept by her late husband. Newsboy Frank Constanzo told police that he had seen Tecchio standing on the Evangelista's front porch the night of the murders. The murders of the Evangelista family were never officially solved, though Tecchio and murderer Angelino remained prime suspects. The thumbprint found at the scene of the murder was left-handed, as was Angelino. REF.: *CBA; Nash, Open Files.*

Evans, Charles (AKA: **Daniel Evans**), d.1875, U.S., mur. Horse thief Charles Evans was arrested and bound over for trial in April 1875 on suspicion of murdering an 18-year-old boy named Seabolt in the Oklahoma Indian Territory. Seabolt's body was found minus his boots and his cash. The law soon caught up with Evans, at which time he was riding on the dead man's horse. Despite contrary evidence, Evans insisted that he had recently purchased the animal. Although Evans was found Not Guilty, the judge, who was resigning, neglected to sign the proper papers to free Evans. As a result, Evans was held for another trial with a new magistrate.

In June Evans appeared in court only to discover that the trial judge was Isaac C. Parker, later known as the "Hanging Judge." Although Parker would have been justified in releasing Evans, he ordered that a new trial proceed. Evans was confident of an acquittal until Seabolt's father pointed to the boots that Danny Evans was wearing and identified them as having once belonged to his son. With that, Judge Parker sentenced Evans to hang. See: **Parker, Judge Isaac**. REF.: *CBA.*

Evans, Chester, 1945- , U.S., mur. Chester Evans, a member of Chicago's Black P. Stone Nation gang, was convicted of murdering two men in 1973 and sentenced to thirty to ninety years in prison. Throughout the trial, Evans maintained his innocence. He spent the evening of Nov. 29, 1969, in Milwaukee with friends, Evans said, and was nowhere near the 1000 block of East 46th Street in Chicago, where the shootings took place. He was convicted solely on the testimony of 16-year-old Robert Lee Johnson, who saw the murders from across the alley. After being interrogated by Chicago police for eleven days, Johnson signed a statement naming Evans as the murderer. Johnson also implicated Lawrence Griffin in the shootings.

In prison, Evans studied painting and religion. In 1978, he was credited with saving a female prison guard from almost certain death during a prison riot. Despite the help of his godfather, the Reverend George Clements, an influential leader in Chicago, Evans' 1981 request for parole was denied. REF.: *CBA.*

Evans, Christopher (AKA: **Bill Powers**), 1847-1917, U.S., west. outl. Born in Vermont, Christopher Evans moved as a child to Canada and served in the Union Army during the Civil War. Following the war, Evans served as a scout for the U.S. Cavalry and reportedly worked as a guide to Major Marcus Reno of the 7th Cavalry. Evans later claimed that he was at the Battle of the Little Big Horn and survived with the remnants of Reno's command. He later moved to California with his brother Tom, and after years prospecting and working as a miner, bought a quarter section of "railroad land" in Tulare County. Nearby was a mine owned and operated by George and John Sontag. When the Sontags turned to train and bank robbery, Evans joined them.

The Sontags and Evans robbed throughout California, and one report had it that they robbed a train at Kasota Junction, Minn., in 1892. The trio robbed a train in California earlier, according to one account, and Grat Dalton was wrongly convicted of this raid. In January 1892, a posse tracked down Evans and the Sontags in a San Joaquin Valley barn. Following a fierce battle, George Sontag was captured but Evans and John Sontag escaped.

Lawmen continued to pursue Evans and Sontag and finally cornered them on Sept. 13, 1893, at Sampson's Flat, Calif. In an eight-hour battle, two deputies and John Sontag were killed. Evans was wounded many times by detective Frank Burke. He was dragged unconscious to jail. On Dec. 13, 1893, Evans was convicted of murder and robbery, but he escaped jail with the help of Ed Morrel, a fellow prisoner. He and Morrel were recaptured after being wounded near Slick Rock, Calif., and Evans was sent to prison for life, entering Folsom Prison in February 1894. Released in May 1911 at age sixty-four, Evans moved to Oregon to homestead and died on Feb. 9, 1917. See: **Sontag Brothers**.

California bandit Chris Sontag.

REF.: Bartholomew, *The Biographical Album of Western Gunfighters;* Block, *Great Train Robberies of the West;* Burt, *American Murder Ballads; CBA;* Conger, *Texas Rangers;* Dillon, *Wells Fargo Detective;* Dixey, *The Collis Express Robbers;* Doctor, *Shotguns on Sunday;* Duke, *Celebrated Criminal Cases in America;* Glasscock, *Bandits of the Southern Pacific;* Haley, *Jeff Milton;* Holbrook, *The Story of the American Railroads;* Horan and Swiggett, *The Pinkerton Story;* _____ and Sann, *Pictorial History of the Wild West;* Hunter and Rose, *The Album of Gunfighters;* King, *Main Line;* Koller, *The American Gun;* Lewis, *High Sierra Country;* Maxwell, *Evans and Sontag;* Morrel, *The Twenty-fifth Man;* O'Neal, *Encyclopedia of Western Gunfighters;* Preece, *The Dalton Gang;* Smith, *Garden of the Sun;* _____, *Prodigal Sons: The Adventures of Christopher Evans and John Sontag;* Sutton, *A Life Worth Living;* Torchiana, *California Gringos;* Vandor, *History of Fresno County;* Warner, *A Pardoned Lifer;* White, *Lead and Likker;* Wilson and Taylor, *Southern Pacific.*

Evans, David, prom. 1700s, Brit., mur. After being tried and convicted of murdering his girlfriend, David Evans stood on the gallows at Carmarthen, England with a rope around his neck. As the hangman released the trap door, the rope broke sending Evans, unhurt, to the ground below the scaffold.

Since the apparatus had accidentally failied, the crowd that had assembled to watch him die, began chanting for officials to let the convicted murderer go free. Evans said they had tried to hang him once and failed, therefore they had no power to try again. The prisoner was caught when he tried to escape and returned to the scaffold, whereupon the hangman successfully completed his appointed duty.

REF.: *CBA;* Laurence, *A History of Capital Punishment.*

Evans, Evan, 1679-1708, and **Evans, William**, 1685-1708, Brit., rob. Evans' father was an innkeeper in South Wales where Evans met some men calling themselves "gentlemen of the road." Evans was well-educated, serving an apprentice to a lawyer when he chose the other side of the law instead. He became a highway robber following in the footsteps of his father's customers.

Not long after the young man was arrested, placed under guard, tied to his horse and was on his way to the jail at Shrewsbury. He spotted a pheasant sitting peacefully on a tree and attempted a ruse by telling his guard how successful he had once been at bagging such game. Then he asked if he might borrow the guard's gun for a shot at the pheasant. The naive guard agreed, and he was soon staring down the barrel of his own gun.

Evans escaped and made his way to London where, because of his education, he was able to secure employment as a clerk to Sir Edmund Andrews, the governor of Guernsey. He held the job for more than three years but then returned to his former career. His younger brother, William Evans, joined him. The brothers attached lofty codes to their illegal profession. When they uttered the traditional command of "stand and deliver," they expected their victims to observe the proper protocol and comply without hesitation. One couple they stopped affronted the Evans duo by refusing to turn over their valuables. They were stripped naked and left tied to a tree for their breach of the rules regarding highway robbery.

The brothers robbed a member of Parliament in Bagshot Heath, and a bricklayer near Kilburn Warren. One day in Surrey, they met a group of constables leading thirty prisoners. When questioned, the constables explained that the men were being taken to the garrison at Portsmouth to be inducted into the King's service. The constables admitted that they would be paid ten shillings for every man delivered. The brothers ambushed the constables later that day, robbed them and released the prisoners, cheating them of their bounty.

Evan and Will Evans were captured in 1708 and hanged at Hertford. Evan was twenty-nine, his brother twenty-three.

REF.: *CBA*; Smith, *Highwaymen*.

Evans, Franklin B. (AKA: The Northwood Murderer), prom. 1872, U.S., mur. A drifter by nature and a third-rate con man by trade, Franklin B. Evans was living with Sylvester Day, his brother-in-law, in 1872. Day's 13-year-old granddaughter Georgianna Lovering also lived with her mother in the Strafford, N.H., home. Evans had set up a number of snares for pigeons and partridges on the property and his granddaughter often accompanied him to check the traps.

On the evening of Oct. 24, 1872, Evans asked the young girl to check the snares the following morning because he had to work. When his granddaughter failed to return home, Day began searching for the girl in the woods. The search party found some of Georgianna's possessions, but could not find her. Evans was arrested after it was learned that he had never gone to work on the morning of the Oct. 25 and that witnesses saw him in the vicinity of where the girl was last seen.

Murderer Franklin B. Evans.

After protesting that he was innocent, Evans, under the influence of alcohol, finally told police where they could find Georgianna's body. The girl had been strangled, mutilated with a knife, and raped by her great uncle, who told officers that he had set the traps not for birds, but for Georgianne. During his trial, the defense attorney P. Webster Locke attempted to portray his client as insane. A parade of physicians and relatives testified that Evans was mentally unbalanced. Locke also said police had used improper techniques to solicit a confession from Evans. After a three-day trial, the jury deliberated less than fifteen minutes before pronouncing Evans Guilty of first-degree murder. The Northwood Murderer was sentenced to death. REF.: *CBA*.

Evans, Haydn Evan, prom. 1947, Brit., mur. When the battered corpse of Rachel Allan, a 76-year-old washerwoman, was found outside her house in Hillside Terrace on Oct. 12, 1947, police had no clues as to her killer other than that she had spent the evening at the Butcher Arms public house. The key to her front door was still in her hand, and walls and doors nearby were bloodstained from the vicious assault.

Glamorgan County police notified Scotland Yard, and Detective chief superintendent John Capstick was put in charge of the investigation. Asking local police constable Stephen Henton to supply a list of any possible murder suspects, Henton submitted a list that included the name Haydn Evan Evans. Evans had been seen at the pub earlier that night wearing a brown suit and had

quarreled with Allan when she teased him about his new clothes. Questioned in the home he shared with his parents and sister, the 22-year-old coal miner said he had been at the Butchers Arms the Saturday night of the slaying, but was wearing a blue suit and did not own a brown one.

Taken to the police station for further questioning, Evans confessed to killing Allan, but still denied owning a brown suit. Capstick returned to Evans' home, and asked the mother to check her son's room once more for the missing suit. While she was out of the room, Capstick pulled up the upholstery on the couch where she had been sitting and discovered the blood-stained clothing. More traces of blood and fragments of skin tissue and bone were found on Evans' socks and trouser cuff. Tried in the Cardiff Assizes Court before Justice Byrne, Evans was found Guilty of murder and was executed on Feb. 3, 1948.

REF.: *CBA*; Heppenstall, *The Sex War and Others*; Wilson, *Encyclopedia of Murder*.

Evans, Henry, d.1828, U.S., mur. A farmer living in Watertown, N.Y., Henry Evans rented land from Joshua Rogers but when he failed to make the scheduled rent payment, Rogers obtained an eviction notice and served it on Evans who refused to comply. Rogers, accompanied by Henry Diamond, returned to the farm to forcibly remove Evans from the property. Upon their arrival, Evans went berserk, he attacked both men with an ax and bludgeoned them to death. He was arrested a short time later, convicted, and on Aug. 22, 1828, executed at Watertown.

REF.: *CBA*; *Trial and Dying Confession of Henry Evans*.

Evans, Jesse, b.1853, U.S., west. outl. Jesse Evans arrived in Lampasas County, Texas, when he was a young man. He worked for a short time as a cowboy before drifting into New Mexico in 1872 to work on John Chisum's ranch. A few years later he became an outlaw, primarily engaged in cattle rustling and armed robbery. He rode the range with Billy the Kid, Frank Baker, and Tom Hill. When the Lincoln County War broke out Evans sided with the Dolan-Riley faction. The first violence in the protracted range war occurred when rancher John Tunstall was murdered on Feb. 18, 1878. As part of a posse formed by Sheriff William Brady, Evans, Hill, and other Dolan-Riley supporters confronted Tunstall on his ranch. Finding him helpless and on foot, they shot and killed him.

With a price on his head, Evans fled to Southwest Texas where he resumed his cattle rustling activities. On July 3, 1880 near Presidio, Evans shot and killed Texas Ranger George Bingham near Cibola Creek. Ranger Tom Carson shot John Gross through the head, and the remaining members of the gang were forced to surrender. Jesse Evans was sentenced to ten years in prison but managed to escape from a work detail in May 1882 and was never heard from again. See: **Lincoln County War**.

REF.: Bartholomew, *Jesse Evans*; _____, *Kill or Be Killed*; Bechdolt, *Tales of the Old Timers*; Breihan, *Badmen of Frontier Days*; _____, *Outlaws of the Old West*; Brent, *The Complete and Factual Life of Billy the Kid*; Burns, *The Saga of Billy the Kid*; *CBA*; Coe, *Frontier Fighter*; _____, *Ranch on the Ruidoso*; Collison, *Life in the Saddle*; Coolidge, *Fighting Men of the West*; Cunningham, *Famous in the West*; _____, *Triggernometry*; Erwin, *The Southwest of John H. Slaughter*; Fergusson, *Murder and Mystery in New Mexico*; Fulton, *Maurice Garland Fulton's History of the Lincoln County War*; Garrett, *The Authentic Life of Billy the Kid*; Haley, *Jeff Milton*; Hamlin, *The True Story of Billy the Kid*; Hendricks, *The Bad Man of the West*; Hertzog, *A Directory of New Mexico Desperadoes*; Holloway, *Texas Gun Lore*; Hough, *The Story of the Outlaw*; Hoyt, *A Frontier Doctor*; Hunt, *The Tragic Days of Billy the Kid*; Keleher, *Violence in Lincoln County*; King, *Pioneer Western Empire Builders*; _____, *Wranglin' the Past*; Klasner, *My Girlhood Among Outlaws*; Madison, *The Big Bend Country of Texas*; Metz, *John Selman*; Moore, *The West*; Mullin, *A Chronology of the Lincoln County War*; Nolan, *The Life and Death of John Henry Tunstall*; North, *The Saga of the Cowboy*; Nye, *Pistols for Hire*; O'Neal, *Encyclopedia of Western Gunfighters*; Otero, *The Real Billy the Kid*; Raht, *The Romance of Davis Mountains and the Big Bend Country*; Raine, *Famous Sheriffs and Western Outlaws*; Rennert, *Western Outlaws*; Scobee, *Fort Davis, Texas*; Small, *History of Tulare County*; Sonnichsen, *I'll Die Before I'll Run*; Sterling, *The Autobiography of Tom Sterling;* Stover, *Son-of-a-Gun Stew;* Webb, *The Texas Rangers.*

Evans, John, prom. 1722, Brit., pir. Evans, a seaman from Wales, found himself out of work in Jamaica in 1722, and, along with a few other displaced sailors, decided to become a pirate.

They rowed out of Port Royal in a small canoe. For a short time they used this tiny vessel to paddle about the island, housebreaking at night. Tiring of such petty crime, Evans and the others seized an unprotected sloop at anchor. Evans announced himself captain, and those crew members who had been on board accepted his authority. After taking the ship, Evans and his men went ashore to celebrate at a tavern. As darkness fell, they prepared to return to the ship. The tavern keeper invited them to come back again. They did, returning in the middle of the night and rousing the man from his sleep as they looted his inn. Evans and his men then began a serious life of piracy on the high seas. They christened the sloop *Scowerer,* and mounted four guns on her rails. Their first victim was a Spanish sloop which they attacked near the island of Hispaniola, overwhelming the crew and taking considerable spoils. Next, Evans came upon the ship *Dove,* sailing from New England to Jamaica under the command of Captain Diamond. The pirates captured the ship off the coast of Puerto Rico, going away with rich plunder, as well as several seamen who joined their crew.

On Jan. 11, 1723, the *Scowerer* overtook the *Lucretia and Katherine* under Captain Mills near the island of Disseada and kidnapped the first mate. A few days later, the pirates captured a Dutch sloop near the island of Ruby, sailing this ship as their own. The pirates sailed for the Grand Caiman Islands when mutiny erupted. A seaman challenged Evans to a duel following an argument. Evans agreed to fight the man once ashore. As the sloop neared land the seaman suddenly refused to go ashore. Evans then took out his cane and started to beat the man. The seaman pulled a pistol from his shirt and shot the captain through the head. The crew planned to slowly torture the seaman to death, but before they could decide on a method two of the crew members lost patience and shot the man dead.

There was now only one person aboard who was a competent navigator, the mate who had been kidnapped from the *Lucretia and Katherine,* but he refused to navigate. The pirates, thirty strong, then went ashore at the Caiman Islands with £9,000 between them, vanishing. The kidnapped mate and a cabin boy who had stayed aboard sailed the ship into Port Royal, Jam., to report their adventures and the last days of Captain John Evans.

REF.: *CBA; Gosse, History of the Pirates.*

Evans, Larry Dean, 1950- , and **Ward, Homer Lee,** 1956- , and **Kelly, Dewer R.,** 1934- , and **McCray, Michael J.,** 1956- , and **Snell, William,** 1931- , and **Cundiff, Thomas,** 1959- , U.S., consp. Six correctional officers from the Stateville, Ill., penitentiary were convicted of attacking and beating three prison inmates in a shower room on Jan. 1, 1979. The assault was carried out shortly after the guards had left a New Year's Eve party.

Lieutenant Larry Evans ordered five of his fellow guards to take three convicts, Lee Arthur Smith, Walter Lee Sims, and Robert R. Stamps, from the prison's "B" House to the shower area. There the prisoners were kicked and pummeled with fists, handcuffs, and boots. The assault was motivated by racial hatred and a desire for revenge. Smith, a convicted robber, had been transferred from the minimum-security facility in Downstate Logan after beating up a guard.

Although the six guards were charged with aggravated battery, the Will County State's Attorney decided not to prosecute for lack of evidence. However, they were dismissed from their jobs a short time afterward. On Feb. 7, 1979, attorneys for the three inmates filed a $14 million damage suit against the six. There were no further developments until Jan. 31, 1980, when a federal grand jury indicted the six guards for conspiracy and violation of civil rights. Defendant Thomas Cundiff pleaded guilty to reduced charges and agreed to testify against the other five guards. He told the

court that Evans, who conceived the idea, was motivated by a desire to avenge an earlier incident in which a Stateville guard had been assaulted by the three prisoners.

On Dec. 30, 1981, a federal district court jury in Illinois found the remaining five men Guilty. On Feb. 20, 1981, the five former prison guards were sentenced. Evans received a five-year sentence, Ward and Kelly were each sentenced to four years in prison, while McCray was sentenced to three years, and Snell to two years. Thomas Cundiff, who had testified against the other five, had been sentenced earlier to two years' probation. REF.: *CBA*.

Evans, Mary, 1957- , U.S., lawyer, pris. esc. Prior to accepting a job as a public defender in London, Ky., Mary Evans wanted to handle one last case for Tennessee attorney James A. H. Bell. She wanted to help defend convict William T. Kirk on murder charges. Assigned to assist Bell and research the case, Evans began to spend an inordinate amount of time at Brushy Mountain State Penitentiary in Clinton, Tenn. The 36-year-old Kirk was serving a sixty-five-year sentence for armed robbery and was scheduled to go on trial, along with six other white inmates, for killing two black inmates. Evans arranged for Kirk, accompanied by three prison guards, to visit the office of a prison-appointed psychologist, Gary Salk, in March 1983. The doctor was to interview Kirk and do some testing on the convict.

During the course of the Mar. 31 interview, Evans and Kirk spent a great deal of time conferring in Salk's outer office. Only moments after Kirk left to have a cigarette, the convicted felon overtook the three guards with a gun provided by Evans. Kirk marched the men into the doctor's office, where he and Evans disarmed the guards, and bound and gagged the four men. For more than four months, the fugitive couple evaded police. Evans and Kirk spent most of their time in Florida motels and at the dog tracks until they were arrested in August 1983.

In a plea-bargain agreement, Evans pleaded guilty to helping her client escape from prison, in exchange for the prosecutor's recommendation that she undergo psychiatric treatment and receive a suspended sentence. Psychiatrists testified during the trial that Evans had a history of instability, including one suicide attempt. In a controversial end to the case, Judge James Scott sentenced the attorney to three years in prison. Kirk was sentenced to forty additional years in prison on charges of escape and armed robbery; he had taken $25 from Salk. REF.: *CBA*.

Evans, Michael, 1958- , and **Terry, Paul,** 1959- , U.S., kid.-rape-mur. For the kidnapping, rape, and murder of 9-year-old Lisa Cabassa, teenagers Michael Evans and Paul Terry were tried twice after the initial conviction was thrown out of court. On the night of Jan. 15, 1976, Cabassa disappeared on her way to a friend's house. Police found the girl's body the following day in an alley on the South Side of Chicago. The authorities had no solid leads in the case until Judith Januszewski finally told police she had seen Evans take the girl from the corner of 86th Street and Saginaw Avenue.

During the June 1976 trial, Januszewski repeated her story and also identified Terry as the second assailant. On the basis of her testimony, a jury found the two men Guilty of murder, deviate sexual assault, aggravated kidnapping, and taking indecent liberties with a child. Criminal Court Judge Earl Strayhorn rescinded the Guilty verdict upon learning the prosecutors had withheld information from the defense attorney. The case was thrown out because the state's attorney's office failed to disclose they had given Januszewski $1,250 for moving expenses after she claimed to have been threatened by Evans' friends. A jury found the two youths Guilty a second time in April 1977. REF.: *CBA*.

Evans, Orinda Dale, 1943 - , U.S., jur. Counsel for the Atlanta Crime Commission from 1970-71, and was appointed by President James E. Carter to the Northern District Court of Georgia in 1979. REF.: *CBA*.

Evans, Rees W., 1835-53, U.S., mur. Only eighteen, Rees Evans ordered a suit of clothes from clothier Louis Reese of Wilkes-Barre, Pa. He used this ruse to entice the clothier to meet him in a lonely spot, ostensibly to pay for the suit of clothes, where he planned to rob and kill Reese. When the clothier appeared in a buggy near an open field, Evans jumped from behind a tree with a gun in his hand, shooting Reese in the head and stealing his money and belongings. The clothier's gold watch was found on Evans a few days later and he was quickly tried and convicted. The youth confessed his crime but asked that the confession not be published until after his hanging. Rev. B.B. Emory, the local minister to whom Evans confessed, refused to abide by this agreement, saying that immediate publication of the confession would show that Evans was wholly repentant and was willing to stand before a large crowd to die as an admitted murderer. The confession was published and was sold briskly by hawkers hired by Emory who moved through the throng gathered at the site of Evans' execution in 1953.

REF.: *CBA;* Emory, *Life, Trial and Confession of Rees W. Evans.*

Evans, Timothy John, See: **Christie, John Reginald.**

Evans, Walter E., and **Ledbetter, Miles H.,** prom. 1929, U.S., (wrong convict.) pol. mal. While investigating the theft of two diamond rings, Los Angeles police officers Walter E. Evans and Miles H. Ledbetter happened to visit the home of convicted felon Harry D. McDonald in July 1928. More than one year later, McDonald was arrested on charges of receiving stolen property. In the course of his confession to the district attorney, McDonald implicated more than fifty police officers, including Evans and Ledbetter, in a bribery scandal.

The officers were brought to trial in October 1929. Based on the testimony of McDonald, his wife, and their maid, Evans and Ledbetter were found Guilty of taking bribes. On July 2, 1930, the policemen began serving prison terms in San Quentin. A police probe into the case continued after the men were incarcerated. It ultimately revealed the prosecution witnesses had perjured themselves, and that the officers were completely innocent. On Jan. 5, 1931, California Governor C. C. Young pardoned Evans and Ledbetter and awarded them stipends of $4,533 and $3,313, respectively. REF.: *CBA.*

Evans, Walter Howard, 1870-1959, U.S., jur. Walter Howard Evans served as district attorney for the state of Oregon from 1912-21. In 1931, Evans was appointed by President Herbert Hoover to the U.S. Customs Court and was named an honorary life member of the Oregon State District Attorney's Association. REF.: *CBA.*

Evarts, William Maxwell, 1818-1901, U.S., lawyer. William Maxwell Evarts was the chief counsel who secured the acquittal of President Andrew Johnson during impeachment proceedings in 1868. Evarts served as U.S. attorney general from 1868-69, and later as U.S. secretary of state from 1877-81. In 1884, Evans was elected U.S. senator representing New York and served from 1885-91. REF.: *CBA.*

Evatt, Herbert Vere, 1894-1965, Aus., jur. Counsel to the king in 1929, federal high court justice from 1930-40, member of Parliament from 1940-60, minister of external affairs and attorney general from 1941-49, and New South Wales chief justice from 1960-62. REF.: *CBA.*

Everett, John, d.1729, Brit., rob. Everett, a well-educated apprentice salesman, ran away and joined the army. A successful soldier, he was discharged with the rank of sergeant, and went to London where he became an officer for Whitechapel Court. Everett held that post for seven years before being discharged for freeing some prisoners who did not pay their debts. He was also sued for the amount of the debts, and being unable to pay, lost his rank and was compelled to rejoin the army as a form of punishment. It was there that Everett met Richard Bird who suggested that they take up the lucrative career of highway robbery. Everett quickly agreed.

At first, the two were successful at this illegal trade. However, after a few years Everett was arrested, convicted, and sentenced to three years in New Prison at Clerkenwell. Because of his past experience in the army, he became a prison trusty and after his term expired, stayed at the prison as a full-fledged turnkey. But

after the warden died, Everett was dismissed by the new warden.

Everett returned to his old trade on the highway, but then married a wealthy widow and retired. Bird then reappeared and talked him into committing one last robbery for old-time's sake. The pair had obviously lost their technique and were arrested in Essex. Everett turned state's evidence against his old friend and Bird was convicted and hanged.

British highwaymen Everett and Bird holding up the Hounslow Heath stage.

After Everett was released, he slipped back into old ways. After robbing a woman named Ellis near Islington, he was arrested, convicted, and sentenced to death. Everett was hanged at Tyburn on Feb. 20, 1729.

REF.: *CBA;* Mitchell, *The Newgate Calendar.*

Everett Massacre, prom. 1916, U.S., mob vio. The radical Industrial Workers of the World (IWW), which encompassed the tenets of both Communism and industrial unionism was particularly strong in the Pacific Northwest and in the mining camps of Nevada. Business owners were fiercely opposed to the IWW, known as the Wobblies, and usually organized against them. When the radicals tried to hold street demonstrations, local officials turned them away.

The Wobblies countered by organizing "Free Speech" fights, in which they deliberately got themselves arrested in order to overcrowd the jails and force an accommodation. This tactic was used frequently in California during the early 1900s, and in Washington several years later. In August 1916, the conflict shifted to Everett, Wash., where a number of Wobbly agitators were put on boats and sent back to Seattle after attempting to intervene in a shingle weaver's strike. When they attempted to rent a launch to return to Everett, business leaders and members of the Commercial Club had them deported.

Several months later they again tried to return. On Oct. 30 their boat was met by heavily armed deputies who beat them back with the butts of their guns and heavy wooden clubs. Dismayed by the recurring violence, the citizens of Everett organized a protest meeting which the Wobblies said they would also attend. On Nov. 5, 260 wobblies chartered the steamer *Verona* for the return trip to Everett.

At the docks of Everett the boat was greeted by Sheriff McRae and his men, who refused to let the IWW organizers land. As the Wobblies lowered the *Verona*'s gang plank, the men on shore began shooting. The IWW men fired back. In the ten-minute gun battle that followed, seven men were killed and many more injured. The shooting ended when the boats engineer backed the vessel out of the harbor. REF.: *CBA.*

Evergreen Park Mail Robbery, See: **Cleaver, Charles.**

Everitt, Frank (AKA: The Duke), 1890-1946, Brit., unsolv. mur. Within two weeks in 1946, the bodies of cab driver Frank

Everitt and Reuben Martirosoff were found in London. Both victims had been shot in the head. Everitt's body was found stuffed into a small National Fire Service shelter. Martirosoff's body was found in his car in Notting Hill, not far from where Everitt's abandoned cab was found two weeks earlier. Both men had been in the driver's seat when they were shot from behind.

Police arrested Marian Grondkowski and Henry Malinowski for the murder of Martirosoff. The two men accused each other of pulling the trigger and were both convicted of murder. During questioning, Malinowski accused Grondkowski of murdering Everitt. But officials concluded that .32-caliber handgun they recovered from Grondkowski's house could not have killed Everitt, and the murder remains unsolved.

REF.: *CBA;* Jackson, *Occupied With Crime;* Simpson, *Forty Years of Murder.*

Everleigh Sisters, prom. 1900-10s, U.S., pros. The celebrated Ada and Minna Everleigh, two beauteous, bountiful sisters from the south, ran the most opulent and famous bordello in America for more than a decade. When they retired, the Everleighs took millions of dollars with them and they reappeared with new identities, accepted in high social strata as ladies of leisure and culture. Born in Kentucky, Ada (1876-1960) and Minna (1878-1948) were raised as southern belles, given every comfort and high education by their lawyer father. Their given name, according to one report, was Lester (although this was contested by other accounts). Both married while in their twenties, but when these marriages failed and their father died—leaving them about $35,000—the sisters joined an acting troupe in the mid-1890s. The show folded in Omaha and the Everleighs, realizing that that town was enjoying a boom, thanks to the Trans-Mississippi Exposition, startlingly decided to open a boardinghouse. "We were looking for a nice town in which to invest our money," Minna later stated.

When the girls realized that almost all the other boarding-houses in town were really bawdy houses, they recruited some beautiful permanent guests and converted their place to a bordello. Recalled Ada later: "We had already made our investment in the boardinghouse and it was simply a matter of doing the right thing with it." The girls protected their good southern name by inventing the name Everleigh, a name created from the manner in which their grandmother had signed her letters to them when they were small girls: "Everly Yours." The Omaha bordello flourished, thanks to the good taste of the Everleighs. Each room was richly appointed and the talk of the town was the $15,000 gold-plated piano which sat in the front parlor. The sisters themselves worked in their own brothel, offering their services to special customers. They retired early to the status of madams, believing their talents were best applied as managers. When the exposition ended in 1899, the Everleighs, after doubling their money, traveled throughout the U.S., looking for a good location where they could establish an elegant brothel.

When the sisters arrived in Chicago they found that the most lavishly decorated sex spa, one opened some years earlier by Lizzie Allen, who had since gone on to her reward, was available. The Everleighs gave $70,000 to the owner, Christopher Columbus Crabb, and received a lifetime lease on the place. The place was really two adjoining three-story buildings at 2131-33 South Dearborn Street. They redecorated the place, turning it into the most luxurious bordello in the U.S. The brothel featured several tastefully decorated restaurants where famous men from the social and business world came to dine. The parlors were decorated with huge, expensive paintings and tapestries. There was a waterfall in one room and orchestras in large halls offering night-long music. The girls who worked for the Everleighs were severely screened by the sisters, whose criteria was rigid.

Ada Everleigh proudly gave an interview to a newspaperman in which she said: "I talk to each applicant myself. She must have worked somewhere else before coming here. We don't like amateurs. Inexperienced girls and young widows are too prone to accept offers of marriage and leave. To get in, a girl must have a good face and figure, must be in perfect health and must

understand what it is to act like a lady. If she is addicted to drugs or drink, we don't want her." Hundreds of women were turned away by the sisters and hundreds more placed their names on waiting lists at the Everleigh Club. Only the most beautiful, intelligent, and graceful women worked for the Everleighs, who conducted regular courses in etiquette and insisted that their girls continue to read the books in the heavily-stocked library, kept in a huge room at the club. The Everleighs chose the wardrobes for their girls and spent lavishly on them, avoiding the gaudy and gauche. Nothing garish or crude was allowed. An Everleigh girl was allowed to show an ankle or a bit of bosom, but the flaunting of flesh was strictly prohibited.

Cleanliness was strictly enforced. All the girls received three baths a day from black maids and the hair of each girl was styled each day. Beauticians serviced the girls exclusively, as did manicurists who gave daily manicures and pedicures to all the girls. In the evening, the girls were adorned in the most stunning, expensive gowns ever seen in a brothel. They wore real gems, diamond and ruby necklaces, emerald brooches, pearls, sapphires, many of the rare stones loaned each evening to them from the Everleigh collection. These jewels were estimated to be worth several million dollars. The girls split their income with the madams and their average income was between $500 and $1,500 a week. Many of the girls accumulated great fortunes and some retired from the Everleigh Club as millionaires. Most married millionaires.

Almost from the day the Everleigh Club opened on Feb. 1, 1900, the place became the most celebrated whorehouse in the U.S. Customers arriving at the Club were astounded at the opulence that surrounded them in large salons named the Turkish Room, the Japanese Room, and the Persian Room. The carpets, gilt-edged mirrors, the imported statuary, velvet and plush covered furniture stunned and edified the wealthiest of customers, which included the barons of business, the tycoons of industry, U.S. bluebloods, and multimillionaires such as John "Bet-A-Million" Gates and foreign royalty such as Crown Prince Henry of Prussia. Hovering behind the operation were the two venal politicians, John "Bathhouse John" Coughlin and Michael "Hinky Dink" Kenna. These two clownish alderman controlled the First Ward which housed the Levee and they collected a share of the take from all vice operations. The money they took from the Everleigh Club made them wealthy.

The bagman collecting from the Everleighs, sponsored by Coughlin and Kenna, was James "Big Jim" Colosimo, later the crime boss of Chicago. He offered special protection to the Everleighs and personally handled any maverick detective from another district who demanded a payoff or a politician who insisted upon a slice of the take. Colosimo delighted in spending hours inside the huge kitchen in the Club, one that featured several chefs who prepared gourmet meals each night for the Club's several restaurants. Colosimo would make his own spaghetti in the kitchen and regale the sisters with his underworld tales. He was on hand almost at a moment's notice if any guest ever caused a disturbance, although the sisters had several bouncers of their own. Such conduct was rare on the part of visitors, but the Club did have occasional outbursts of violence. A butler shot his employer on the front steps of the Club one night. When police arrived, the butler stood over his victim, saying to the wounded man: "You can afford the Everleigh Club but you can't afford to pay my salary, sir?"

Across the street from the Everleigh Club sat the low-class seraglio operated by the vicious madam, Victoria Shaw. One night, the son of a railroad magnate was killed in Shaw's place and the body was smuggled into the Everleigh Club. Madam Shaw intended to have the sisters charged with the murder but the Everleighs were too smart for her. They were tipped to the scheme and had the body taken back to Victoria Shaw's brothel where police found it under the madam's bed the next morning. On another occasion, the son of a department store tycoon was reportedly killed by one of the Everleigh girls, and, according to

Left, Minna Everleigh and, right, Ada Everleigh.

Minna Everleigh, shown as a "working madam" in Omaha.

A cameo of Ada Everleigh as an Omaha, Neb., madam, 1898.

Ada Everleigh, center, with cowboy at her gilded bar in Omaha.

The Music Room in the Everleigh Club in Chicago.

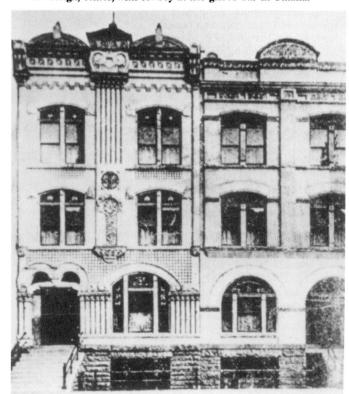

The Everleigh Club, Chicago, on South Dearborn Street.

the tale, his body was smuggled to the family mansion where it was "discovered," the death attributed to a gun which had gone off by accident while he cleaned it.

Prices at the Everleigh Club were, for that day, astronomical, $500 and up, depending upon the services sought. Customers could pay in cash or could make out checks to "cash" and these would be endorsed by the Utopia Novelty Company to save clients any embarrassment. Each room occupied by an Everleigh girl was sumptuously decorated and above each huge, custom-built bed was a large mirror affixed to the ceiling, one of Ada's ideas. There was also a bowl full of firecrackers next to each bed, Minna's idea, which the girls lit and exploded to heighten the ecstasy of their guests. Gambling rooms were also available and here the sisters offered roulette, poker, craps, and other games.

For more than a decade, the sisters were the toast of the red light district, but then several religious reformers such as Gipsey Smith invaded the Levee, leading torchlight parades and loudly denouncing the whorehouses and gambling dens. Public pressure mounted and soon the politicians were confronted by angry citizens' groups demanding that the red light district be closed down, especially the world-famous Everleigh Club. The politicians resisted for some years but finally, on Oct. 11, 1911, Mayor Carter Harrison, bowing to public pressure, ordered the Everleigh Club closed. The sisters shrugged, gave huge bonuses to their girls and sold many of their decorations. They then packed their best statuary, tapestries, paintings, and the gold-plated piano and moved to New York where, under an assumed name, they moved into a mansion.

Unknown in New York, the ladies became the toast of the literary world and they held regular poetry readings each week, which drew high-society friends to their side. They were accepted into the highest social strata of the city and went about as grande dames of literature, sponsoring young writers and worthy musicians as much-respected patrons of the arts. Minna lived to the age of seventy-one, dying on Sept. 16, 1948. On her deathbed she stated to a newspaperman, an old friend: "We never hurt anybody, did we? We never robbed widows and we made no false representations, did we? Any crimes they attributed to us were the outcries of jealousy. We tried to get along honestly. Our business was unholy but everybody accepted it. What of it?"

Her body was placed into an expensive coffin and her sister Ada shipped it to Roanoke, Va., to be buried in the family plot. Ada joined her, dying at eighty-four, on Jan. 3, 1960. She was buried next to Minna beneath a marker named "Lester."

REF.: Asbury, *Gem of the Prairie*; Beebe and Clegg, *The American West*; Bullough, *Illustrated History of Prostitution*; CBA; Demaris, *Captive City*; Kobler, *Capone*; Lait and Mortimer, *Chicago Confidential*; Landesco, *Organized Crime in Chicago*; McPhaul, *Johnny Torrio*; Nash, *Bloodletters and Badmen*; ____, *Look for the Woman*; ____, *People to See*; Smith, *Syndicate City*; Wasburn, *Come Into My Parlor*; Wendt and Kogan, *Bet A Million!*; ____, *Big Bill of Chicago*; ____, *Lords of the Levee*.

Evers, Medgar, 1926-63, U.S., (unsolv.) mur. Medgar Evers once said that he was not afraid to die to advance the cause of civil rights in the south. "It might do some good. If I die, it will be in a good cause. I've been fighting for America just as much as the soldiers in Vietnam."

Evers rose from abject rural poverty to become the only full-time NAACP field representative in Mississippi. Educated at Alcorn A.&M., Evers saw action in WWII before returning to his home state to take part in the fledgling civil rights movement. In Jackson, shortly before his death, Medgar Evers coordinated a massive civil rights rally that drew some of the biggest names in black show business. A few weeks later someone threw a Molotov cocktail into the driveway of his home in Jackson.

Shortly after midnight on June 13, 1963, Evers pulled into the driveway of his home with a load of T-shirts stamped "Jim Crow Must Go." They were to be handed out to a group of civil rights demonstrators the next day. Lurking in the bushes was 42-year-old Byron De La Beckwith, an ex-Marine and white supremacist who had been distributing anti-integration pamphlets in Jackson.

Known to his friends in the Ku Klux Klan as "DE-lay," Beckwith took aim at Evers with a high-powered rifle.

A bullet struck Evers in the back, killing him instantly. The Springfield rifle, complete with a telescopic sight on the barrel, was found in a honeysuckle patch 100 yards from the Evers home. The shooting galvanized public opinion against the segregationists. Even Governor Ross Barnett, a long-time opponent of integration, conceded that it was a "dastardly act." A $21,000 reward was offered for the killer. The FBI assisted in the case, and Beckwith was arrested on June 22 and charged with the murder of Evers. A latent fingerprint found on the sight of the .30-caliber rifle by Captain Ralph Hargrove of the Jackson police identification bureau put the FBI on Beckwith's trail.

The accused killer went on trial for the first time on July 8, 1963. Members of the White Citizen's Legal Fund offered to pay his expenses, moved by "the awesome spectacle of one man standing alone against the preponderant power, authority, wealth and ingenuity of the Federal Government." Tried by an all-white male jury in Jackson, Beckwith expected a favorable outcome. On Feb. 7, 1964, Judge Leon Hendrick declared a mistrial in the case after the jury reported that it was unable to return a verdict. After eleven hours of deliberation and twenty ballots, the vote stood at seven to five in favor of acquittal. The five votes for conviction came as a surprise to many court observers. Apparently they were not swayed by the testimony of two police officers who claimed to have seen Beckwith in his home town of Greenwood, ninety-five miles from Jackson, on the night of the shooting.

Beckwith went on trial a second time, but another mistrial was declared by Judge Hendrick on Apr. 17. Governor Barnett and leaders of the white supremacist movement showed up in court to shake Beckwith's hand and wish him good luck. "Such actions were sufficient to warrant a mistrial," the judge added.

Under Mississippi law a defendant could be tried an unlimited number of times for the same crime, but in this case Beckwith was freed on a $10,000 bail. He returned to his old job of selling fertilizer to the Delta farmers, and continued his efforts on behalf of the segregationists.

In 1973, Beckwith was arrested again after he was caught planting a bomb near the home of Adolph Botnick, regional director of the Anti-Defamation League of B'nai B'rith in New Orleans. On Jan. 19, the smiling southern Klansman was unanimously acquitted by a racially mixed jury.

REF.: *CBA*; Toledano, *J. Edgar Hoover*.

Every, Henry (AKA: John Avery, Long Ben), b.c.1665, Brit., pir. A legendary character, British pirate Henry Every, known to his cutthroat crews as "Long Ben," was born near Plymouth about 1665 (some reports have him born as early as 1653), and went to sea early. In the early 1690s, Every served under the pirate, Captain "Red Hand" Nichols. By 1693, Every captained a slave ship along Africa's Guinea coast. In the spring of 1694, Every truly launched his career as a pirate. He began as first mate aboard the 46-gun ship, *Charles II*, which left Bristol, commissioned by the Spanish government as a privateer, assigned to stop French smugglers from raiding Spanish colonies in the Caribbean. Every and many of his followers undoubtedly signed on board this ship with the secret plan of taking over the vessel and conducting a pirate expedition in the Indian Ocean.

Captain Gibson of the *Charles II* was a confirmed alcoholic and, while the ship was in port, he took more than his share of punch and fell into a stupor in his cabin. Every and his men quietly secured the hatches, weighed anchor, and set sail. Hours later, when Gibson was rocked to revival by the heavy swells of the Atlantic, Every appeared in his cabin and told him that he had taken over the ship. "I am bound to Madagascar with a design of making my own fortune, and that of all the brave fellows joined with me." Every gave Gibson the choice of either joining him and the mutineers intent on piracy or leaving the ship in an open boat. Gibson and five or six others chose to leave the ship and were set adrift in a small boat, left to make their way to shore, which they did.

Every renamed the ship the *Fancy* and sailed to Madagascar flying his newly designed pirate flag, four silver chevrons on a red background. Once in the Eastern seas, Every and his men attacked vessels of all nations, looting and plundering at will. Every ordered the heavy upper masts of the *Fancy* stripped so that the ship's speed was increased. He could now outrun any pursuer. The *Fancy* made the island of Johanna its home port and when a heavily-armed French ship made the mistake of sailing into the harbor one day, the *Fancy* quickly attacked it and overwhelmed the crew, who turned out to be pirates. The French ship was loaded with plunder taken in the Red Sea from Moors and this loot enriched the crew of the *Fancy*. Moreover, Every's numbers swelled when forty Frenchmen from the captured ship joined his piratical band.

So bold did Every become that he wrote a letter, or a pirate's manifesto, so to speak, and left this with a native chief at Johanna, asking that it be delivered to the captain of the first British ship to enter the port after the *Fancy* had departed. This curious document, blending English patriotism and roaring pirate bravado, declared:

To All English Commanders:
    Let this satisfy that I was riding here at this instant in the ship *Fancy*, man of war, formerly the *Charles II* of the Spanish expedition who departed from La Caruña 7th May 1694, being then and now a ship of forty-six guns, 150 men and bound to seek our fortunes. I have never as yet wronged any English or Dutch, or ever intend whilst I am commander. Wherefore, as I commonly speak with all ships I desire whoever comes to the perusal of this to take this signal, that if you or any whom you may inform are desirous to know what we are at a distance, then make your ancient (ship's flag) up in a ball or bundle and hoist him at the mizen peak, the mizen being furled. I shall answer with the same, and never molest you, for my men are hungry, stout and resolute, and should they exceed my desire I cannot help myself. As yet an Englishman's friend.

                              At Johanna, 18th February 1695
                              Henry Every

    (He inserted a postscript) Here is 160 odd French armed men at Mohilla who waits for opportunity of getting any ship, take care of yourselves.

An English East Indian sailed into the harbor at Johanna a short time later and was handed this remarkable document but instead of earning appreciation from the British, at the promise of being left unharmed, Every's bold declaration branded him a hunted pirate by the British and all nations. He would forever be pursued as a felon and became one of the few British pirates never granted amnesty. The *Fancy*, meanwhile, sailed into the Red Sea where it was met by four other pirate ships from the U.S. colonies. In August 1695 Every was elected commander of this powerful fleet.

At first Every's pirate fleet had little luck in running down its prey, the treasure ships of the Great Mogul. One fleet of twenty-five ships slipped past the pirate vessels in the night but, at dawn, Every spied two ships coming into view. The huge *Gang-i-Sawai*, one of the largest vessels on the sea at the time, was so enormous and powerful that the Indian commanders believed her to be unbeatable in battle. This ship carried 200 battle-seasoned sailors, 600 musketeers and 600 passengers. It had sixty-two guns and towered over anything on the oceans. Its lone escort, the smaller *Fatah Mohamed*, was also a powerful warship. Every thought nothing of sailing after these two ships in the *Fancy*, intent upon capturing and destroying them both.

The *Fatah Mohamed* purposely lagged behind the behemoth *Gang-i-Sawai* to do battle with Every but after the *Fancy* drew alongside the *Fatah Mohamed*, letting loose a broadside that ripped into the side of the Indian ship, the *Fatah Mohamed* quickly surrendered. It carried more than £50,000 in gold and silver and this treasure was quickly taken aboard the *Fancy*. Most of the Indian crew were slain before Every pushed off in pursuit of the lumbering *Gang-i-Sawai*. This ship was returning from Mecca after a pilgrimage and carried many high-ranking Indian officials, as well as relatives of the Great Mogul. The *Gang-i-Sawai* was considered by Indian historian Khafi Khan to be the greatest ship ever built. It carried more than 500,000 pieces of gold and silver which were to be delivered to the coffers of the Great Mogul at the Indian port of Surat. Eight days before it reached that destination, the fast-moving *Fancy* overtook the giant *Gang-i-Sawai*. Though the Indian ship could easily outgun Every's ship and its musketeers outnumbered the pirates five to one, its commander was a coward and, at when he first glimpsed the *Fancy*, he fled below decks, hiding with twenty young women, concubines of the Great Mogul. He ordered the women to don turbans so that they might be mistaken for men and he dressed himself as a slave.

British pirate Henry Every, the bold Long Ben of the Caribbean.

Above decks, misfortune quickly overtook the *Gang-i-Sawai* when its first salvo aimed at the *Fancy* resulted in one of its own guns blowing up and killing five or six of its crewmen. Fires broke out, causing panic among the crew and musketeers who saw it as an omen of disaster. Then Every's best gunners fired a shot which blew away the main mast of the Indian vessel, causing it to lose control. The ship maneuvered about wildly and the *Fancy* circled it like a wolf stalking an injured stag. Then Every ordered the *Fancy* to come alongside the great Indian ship and when grappling hooks pulled the two ships together, the pirates literally had to climb upward to board the towering *Gang-i-Sawai*. The pirates, goaded by the lure of the fabulous riches, eagerly battled the phalanxes of musketeers, driving them overboard and killing them in large groups.

Every lost about twenty men but more than 300 of the Indians were slain. The loot was taken aboard the *Fancy* and the women on board were raped. Most of the prisoners were tortured by the pirates into disclosing where their valuables were hidden and then left to die. Following the barbaric slaughter, Every and his men selected the most attractive women on board and took these hapless females with them when the *Fancy* sailed away, leaving the burning hulk to sink. The *Gang-i-Sawai* did not go to the bottom, however, but managed to stay afloat and later limp into port with its few surviving crewmen who told the tale of Every's bestial attack.

The plunder from the Indian ships made the pirates rich. Every took two full shares and then spread the loot throughout his five-ship fleet. Each pirate received about £1,000 and younger seamen, ages sixteen to eighteen, received £500. Boys in the pirate crews under the age of sixteen were given £100 and set ashore to set themselves up in "honest apprenticeship." Many of Every's crew members retired then and there, leaving the ship on the tropical island of Réunion where they quit piracy and became gentleman planters. So depleted was Every's crew that he took on ninety African slaves and converted them to seamen before setting sail for the Bahamas. The pirates anchored in St. Thomas some weeks later.

Every and his men were welcomed by the Bahamian governor, Nicholas Trott, whom the pirates had bribed with more than £7,000 in gold and great quantities of ivory and other precious goods. Trott gave Every and his top aides a formal dinner in the Governor's mansion and then saw them off when they set sail for Jamaica. Here Every and his men sent a request for pardon to Governor William Beeston, offering him £24,000 for the official favor. Beeston, an honest man, refused and Every sailed back to St. Thomas where the pirates gave the *Fancy* to Governor Trott for his protection. The men got drunk and allowed the ship to be driven ashore during a gale. It was a total wreck, only its guns salvaged from the storm. The pirates disbanded, many going to the U.S. colonies where some were later imprisoned.

Every, who changed his name to Benjamin Bridgeman, and a few of his top men bought sloops and sailed for England, the least likely hideout since they were all posted there as wanted felons. The sloops arrived in various Irish and English ports, but the pirates soon drew attention to themselves by swaggering about the towns and spending their stolen riches like rajahs. One man, John Dann, was caught in Rochester, near London, wearing a coat lined with gold sovereigns and weighing more than twenty pounds. The pirates stupidly displayed rare gems and paid greatly inflated prices for horses, thus drawing attention to themselves. Twenty-four of them were captured and six were hanged. The rest were sent to penal service in the U.S. colonies. The only pirate to escape was the bold Every. He landed his sloop near Dunfanaghy, about thirty miles northwest of Londonderry in County Donegal, Ire.

The fate of Every was never learned. Some of his men claimed he went to Dublin or Scotland, or to Exeter, near his birthplace, Plymouth. Daniel Defoe gave one account twenty years later that the shrewd Every, living under the name of Bridgeman, settled down in the town of Bideford, in Devon where he tried to negotiate the sale of a sack of diamonds with greedy merchants. The merchants gave him a small down payment against the gems, promising the balance after they had been sold. However, they gave Every only a pittance each week so that he was finally reduced to begging and died a pauper with hardly enough money to buy a cheap coffin. Another version has it that Every lived high for many years and died in bed, the squire of a large Irish estate.

Every's looting of the *Gang-i-Sawai* became legendary and inspired thousands of British seamen to become pirates. In India, the Great Mogul's advisers turned on the British East India Company, accusing it of engineering the piratical attack on their greatest ship. Dozens of British officers were thrown into prison and many died of torture and malnutrition. One was even stoned to death. The East India Company lost millions in trade because of Every's actions and it took years before the Company earned back the good grace of the Indian leaders.

REF.: Bradlee, *Piracy in the West Indies and Its Suppression*; Brooke, *Book of Pirates*; Burney, *The History of the Buccaneers of America*; Cabal, *Piracy and Pirates*; Chatterton, *The Romance of Piracy*; *CBA*; Cochran, *Freebooters of the Red Sea*; Course, *Pirates of the Eastern Seas*; Craton, *A History of the Bahamas*; Defoe, *A General History of the Robberies and Murders of the Most Notorious Pirates, 1717-1724*; Drury, *Madagascar*; Ellms, *The Pirates' Own Book*; Fisher, *Barbary Legend*; Gascoigne, *The Great Moghuls*; Gosse, *The History of Piracy*; Grey, *Pirates of the Eastern Seas*; Haring, *The Buccaneers of the West Indies in the Seventeenth Century*; Innes, *The Book of Pirates*; Mitchell, *Pirates*; Parry, *A Short History of the West Indies*; Pringle, *Jolly Roger: The Story of the Great Age of Piracy*; Rankin, *The Golden Age of Piracy*; Scott, *Concise Encyclopedia of Crime and Criminals*; Smith, *Highwaymen*; Snelgrave, *A New Account of Some Parts of Guinea and the Slave Trade*; Williams, *Captains Outrageous: Seven Centuries of Piracy*; Woodbury, *The Great Days of Piracy in the West Indies*.

Ewart, Hamilton Glover, 1849-1918, U.S., jur. Represented North Carolina in the U.S. House of Representatives from 1889-91, served as criminal court justice for Henderson County, N.C., from 1895-96, as circuit court judge for North Carolina from 1897-98, and was appointed by President William McKinley to the Western District Court of North Carolina in 1899. REF.: *CBA*.

Ewart, William, 1798-1869, Brit., reformer. Member of Parliament between 1828-37 and 1839-68. He helped abolish the hanging of prisoners from chains in 1834, put an end to the death penalty for cattle rustling and similar crimes in 1837, and sought the repeal of capital punishment. REF.: *CBA*.

Ewart-Biggs, Christopher, d.1976, Case of, Ire., assass. Rarely had the Irish Republican Army (IRA) targeted British diplomatic officials or individual soldiers for assassination before 1976. Their campaigns of terror were directed mostly against commercial sites: pubs, retail outlets, buses, and factories. That is why the murders of Christopher Ewart-Biggs and Judith Cooke, secretary to Brian Cubbon, the Permanent Under-Secretary of the Northern Ireland Office, came as such a shock on July 21, 1976.

Ewart-Biggs was the newly-appointed British ambassador. He was a man of dignified composure who had an impressive military record in the OAS during the Algerian crisis. His presence in Ireland indicated to the IRA factions that London wanted a diplomat who was concerned more with political matters than just hosting social receptions.

On the morning of the July 21, Ewart-Biggs, Cubbon, Cooke, and the chauffeur Brian O'Driscoll left the state house on Glencairn and turned onto the Murphystown Road accompanied by an escort car from the Irish Special Branch. As the Jaguar passed over a culvert that had been filled with lethal gelignite, two men who had been seen carrying FN rifles in the countryside ignited a charge which sent the vehicle flying into the air. Cooke was killed instantly. Ewart-Biggs sustained a broken neck and a smashed sternum. He died before the police could arrive on the scene. Cubbon and O'Driscoll escaped with minor injuries.

The murders prompted an angry response from British officials, and an outpouring of sympathy from the Dublin government and the six Protestant counties. The IRA assassins were never found.

REF.: Bell, *Assassin*; *CBA*; Dobson and Payne, *The Terrorists—Their Weapons, Leaders and Tactics*.

Exner, Judith Campbell (Judith Eileen Katherine Immoor), 1934- , U.S., org. crime. From the very beginning Judith Exner, formerly Judith Campbell, flew in fast company. Born and raised in Pacific Palisades, Calif., the woman who was to become the mistress of both a U.S. President and the leader of the Chicago-organized crime family, was thrust into the limelight at an early age.

At the age of sixteen, Judith attended a Hollywood party where she was introduced to her first husband, William Campbell. She married the young actor two years later, and began running around with the Hollywood set that included at various times Charlton Heston, Eddie Fisher, and Debbie Reynolds. The Campbells were divorced in 1958. After a brief fling with Frank Sinatra, which Exner called off because she feared his erratic and often violent behavior, she met Senator John F. Kennedy at the Sands Hotel in Las Vegas. This was on Feb. 7, 1960, a month before the New Hampshire primary.

According to Campbell, they began a torrid love affair which spilled over into the first two years of his presidency. A week after her first clandestine rendezvous with Kennedy at the Plaza Hotel in New York, Exner was introduced to the second great love of her life—Chicago mobster Sam Giancana. Their first meeting took place at the Fontainebleau Hotel in Miami Beach, the second week of March 1960. Sinatra acted as a go-between. "I didn't know then that Sam was the Chicago Godfather," Exner recalled. "But I did know he was important to Frank because of the way Sinatra acted around him, bowing and scraping and being so deferential."

It was not long afterward that Exner was recruited to be the "liaison" between Giancana and Kennedy. In her published memoirs Exner alleges that Kennedy and the Chicago "Godfather" first met before the crucial West Virginia primary. Giancana purportedly was asked to influence a favorable outcome for the Democrats. "I think I may need his help in the campaign," Kennedy said over the phone one day.

The meeting took place on Apr. 12, 1960, at the Miami Beach hotel. Kennedy was obviously very pleased with the outcome, and promised Exner that he would leave his wife Jackie Kennedy if he failed to secure the Democratic nomination in July. With these reassuring words from the handsome young candidate, Exner absolved herself of any guilt and plunged headlong into an affair.

With Giancana silently pulling the strings of the state's corrupt political machine, Kennedy easily won the West Virginia primary, garnering 61 percent of the vote. As a token of good faith, the mobster helped deliver Chicago's key "river wards" into the Kennedy column in the November election. Political observers generally conceded that "Momo" Giancana's efforts in Chicago was the critical factor in Kennedy's narrow victory over Richard Nixon.

After the disastrous Bay of Pigs operation in April 1961, Exner was pressed into courier duty once more. Kennedy phoned her a few days after the botched invasion attempt and requested that she fly immediately to Las Vegas to pick up a secret envelope from mobster Johnny Roselli, a high-ranking member of the Dragna crime family of Los Angeles. The envelope was delivered to Giancana in Chicago, and another meeting between the president and the Mafia boss was scheduled, this time at the Ambassador East Hotel on April 28.

Exner waited in the bathroom while Kennedy and Giancana discussed important matters—presumably a covert CIA-Mafia plot to assassinate Cuban dictator Fidel Castro. The plot was code named Operation Mongoose. The Cosa Nostra was vitally interested in Castro's demise in order to restore lucrative gambling operations to Havana. The poison pens, exploding cigars, and contaminated suits, however, failed to reach their intended target. Operation Mongoose was a failure as much as the Bay of Pigs had been.

There were several more hastily arranged deliveries between Giancana's people and the president. White House telephone logs revealed at least seventy phone calls between the president's office and Exner over an eighteen-month period. According to Kennedy's personal secretary Evelyn Lincoln, an FBI memorandum crossed her desk linking Exner to the mob. "At that very moment when I saw that, I stopped receiving her calls," Lincoln said in 1975.

Their relationship continued into 1962 when things began to cool off. Attorney General Robert Kennedy targeted top Mafia leaders for investigation, and federal agents began dogging the tracks of Exner who resented the intrusions into her privacy. The president reassured her that there was nothing to be alarmed about. "Don't worry," he said. "They won't do anything to you. And don't worry about Sam. You know he works for us."

Kennedy attributed the harassment to FBI Director J.Edgar Hoover. "It's just part of Hoover's vendetta against me," he told Exner. On Mar. 22, 1962, Hoover warned Kennedy about the potential damage to his public image that he might endure if he continued his dealings with Exner who had been linked to the mob. By mid-summer the affair was over. Relations between

Exner and Kennedy had become strained. She turned to Giancana for solace, and soon found herself in a second affair. "I didn't know he was a murderer," she recalled. "I wouldn't have believed it." When Giancana proposed marriage Exner called the whole thing off.

The Kennedy-Giancana-Exner affair was buried with the president in 1963. Giancana was murdered in his suburban Chicago home in 1975, and Roselli's body was found floating in an oil drum off the cost of Florida. It quickly became old news in the Washington rumor mill until a Senate investigating committee began probing Kennedy's links to organized crime in December 1975. Exner's name was leaked to the Washington *Post*, as someone that Kennedy had enjoyed a close personal relationship with. The report showed that the "president's friend was also a close friend of John Roselli and Sam Giancana and saw them both during this same period."

Exner convened a press conference where she heatedly denied any "conspiratorial ties" to these men. Her relationship with Kennedy and Giancana was of a personal nature, she said. Years later Exner, now married to her second husband Dan Exner, decided to speak out about the scandalous affair with Kennedy. She explained that the doctors had pronounced her terminal after removing one of her lungs in 1988. Her intention was to "put her life in order" so that she could die in peace. See: **Giancana, Sam; Hoover, J. Edgar; Roselli, John.**

REF.: *CBA;* Morgan, *Prince of Crime.*

Eyler, Larry W., 1953- , U.S., mur. Convicted mass-murderer Larry Eyler first emerged as a suspect on Sept. 30, 1983, when an Indiana state trooper driving south along I-65 noticed two men climbing out of a roadside ditch. One of the men, later identified as Larry Eyler, was carrying a bag that contained sections of rope. The second man told the police officer that his name was Darrell Hayward, and that he had been offered $100 to engage in roadside sex with Eyler.

A quick search of the police records revealed that Eyler, originally from Indianapolis, was a suspect in a series of Indiana sex murders. After spending the next twelve hours in custody, Eyler was released by the Indiana police. When he returned to his Chicago apartment on Oct. 3, detectives from Lake County, Ill., were waiting for him. Eyler was suspected in the Aug. 31 murder of 28-year-old Ralph Calise, whose remains were found in suburban Lake Forest.

Eyler was released a second time, but was placed under police surveillance. The police had reason to believe that Eyler was the man responsible for the deaths of at least twenty young men in four states. The 30-year-old house painter lived in Chicago during the week, but commuted to his other residence in Terre Haute, Ind., on weekends.

Indignant over what he called police harassment, Eyler filed a lawsuit against Lake County and the Indiana State Police. While the case was being prepared by his attorneys, Eyler was arrested on Oct. 30 and charged with the murder of Calise, based on evidence found in the back of his truck. A piece of rope which Eyler used to tie his victims up was located in the cab.

However, the judge declared that the evidence had been obtained illegally, and Eyler was ordered released. Free to kill again, the house painter from Indiana wasted little time. On Aug. 21, 1984, the body of Daniel Bridges was found in a garbage dumpster on Chicago's North Side. Eyler pleaded not guilty to charges of aggravated kidnapping, armed violence, unlawful restraint, and murder. Held without bond in the Cook County Jail, Larry Eyler was convicted and sentenced to die by Judge Joseph Urso on Oct. 3, 1986. "You are an evil person," the judge said. "You truly deserve to die for your acts."

The case was air-tight after Assistant State's Attorneys Richard Stock and Mark Rakoczy brought into court several men who testified to having been handcuffed and beaten by the defendant. Frustrated in their earlier attempts to bring the felon to justice, police and the families of the twenty victims who were slain between 1982 and 1984 were at last satisfied that justice had been

Michel Eyraud   **Gabrielle Bompard**   **Toussaint-Augustin Gouffé**

served. "One of the most dangerous people that ever stepped in this building is now behind bars for good," Rakoczy said. REF.: *CBA.*

Eyman, David L., 1961-76, U.S., unsolv. mur. The smoldering body of 15-year-old David L. Eyman was found in the early morning hours of Aug. 14, 1974, on the County Line Road north of Cass County in an isolated rural area of Kansas City, Kan. The teenage boy had been bound with half-inch thick rope, his body doused with gasoline and set on fire. The Metropolitan Major Case Squad made an intensive nine-day search for the killer, mobilizing twenty-five officers, before turning it over to four Kansas City detectives, among them Vernon D. Wilson. Eyman had been hanging out at a pool hall the night of the slaying, then went to his girlfriend's house, smoking two marijuana cigarettes on the way. After spending around four hours at her house, he called home for a ride, but was refused. He told his girlfriend he would walk or hitchhike the 1.9 miles home, leaving her house at 12:45 a.m.

Several police officers believe that Eyman's killer is a former law enforcement officer in the area who briefly assisted in the investigation of the murder. The suspect was involved in several suspicious incidents while serving as an officer in law enforcement agencies and fire departments, including shoot-outs with criminals who always managed to escape before other officers arrived on the scene and multiple incidents of violence. This man was also suspected of setting fires and then reporting them. According to a colleague, "He found more fires in five years than all the other officers in the metropolitan area." Agreeing to take a lie detector test in conjunction with Eyman's murder, the suspect was found to be lying when he denied that he had tied the boy up, set him on fire, and killed him. A detective who had served with the man believed the suspect was about to admit guilt when he was confronted with circumstantial evidence. The suspect quit his law enforcement job and moved from the area soon after the questioning. The question of who murdered Eyman remains unsolved. REF.: *CBA.*

Eyraud, Michel, d.1891, and **Bompard, Gabrielle**, Fr., mur. An army deserter and operator of many illegal businesses, the middle-aged Michel Eyraud, though married, took up with a larcenous prostitute, Gabrielle Bompard. The pair operated a badger game in which Bompard lured well-to-do men to her Paris apartment. Eyraud would burst in during their lovemaking, pretending to be Bompard's outraged husband, and demand payment from the compromised man. Their scheme worked well for some time, but Eyraud grew impatient to make his fortune.

After Bompard brought home a wealthy solicitor, Toussaint-Augustin Gouffé, and Eyraud learned that his lover's patron kept large sums of money in his office, he resolved to murder the solicitor and steal the funds. On the night of July 27, 1888, Bompard brought Gouffé to her rooms on Rue Trouson-Ducoudry and enticed him to her couch. As the solicitor was making love to her, Bompard tied the thick cord of her dressing gown around his neck. At this prearranged signal, Eyraud stepped from behind a curtain and, using a series of pulleys and ropes he had erected earlier for this gruesome chore, suddenly yanked the startled victim upward toward the ceiling. The solicitor struggled wildly in mid-air, but within a few minutes, strangled to death. Eyraud waited until he was sure his victim was dead before slowly lowering him to the floor. After rifling his victim's pockets and finding the keys to Gouffé's office, Eyraud went home to his wife and went to bed. His prostitute lover went to sleep while Gouffé's body stiffened on the floor next to her. Eyraud arrived the next morning and Bompard helped him stuff the rigid corpse into a trunk.

Taking the key to Gouffé's office, Eyraud let himself inside and began searching for the 14,000 francs the foolish solicitor had shown to Bompard some days earlier. Eyraud tore the place apart, but failed to find the money which, ironically, was in plain sight in a small cardboard box on top of Gouffé's desk. Eyraud panicked when he heard a watchman in the hall of the office building and fled through a window. He rushed back to Bompard's apartment and there, in a state of manic frenzy, made love to his murderous accomplice on the floor next to the trunk holding the body of their victim. (Bompard later told this tale matter-of-factly but, for propriety's sake, insisted that Eyraud had forced her into sex.)

The next day the killers rented a carriage the next day and loaded the trunk into it. They drove to Millery, near Lyon, placed the body in a wood and dumped the trunk on the bank of the Rhone River. The pair then went to Marseilles and then to London where they took a boat to New York. Once there, fearing detection, Eyraud and Bompard traveled to Canada. A year later, the corpse of the victim was discovered, but it was so badly decomposed that identification seemed impossible. Yet Francois Goron, chief of the Sûreté, a dogged detective of remarkable skills, found a partly legible label on the trunk. He studied this label under a microscope and made out a Paris address which pinpointed the place of the trunk's origin. Then an equally brilliant forensic scientist, Professor Alexandre Lacassagne, examined the decomposed body and compared its vital statistics with those of known missing persons. He discovered that the victim's hair was auburn. Lacassagne learned that an ankle of the dead man was tubercular and certain bone malformations led him to believe that the dead man had walked with a limp. This fit the condition of the missing Gouffé.

Gabrielle Bompard under arrest, being measured by Alphonse Bertillon.

Gouffé's brother-in-law, who had failed to identify the corpse earlier, agreed that Gouffé had indeed limped and had had a bad ankle. He told police that his widowed brother-in-law was a ladies' man and that he had seen Gouffé in the company of a man and woman two days before his disappearance. The brother-in-law, after studying police photos of known criminals, picked out mug shots of Eyraud and Bompard and police began searching for the pair. Photos of the killers were widely circulated in Europe and the U.S. The murderous pair, however, had traveled to western Canada. From Vancouver, they went to San Francisco and here Bompard met a gullible young American who fell desperately in love with her. Bompard told him that her travelling companion intended to kill her to cover up a terrible crime he had committed in her presence in Paris. She ran away with the American and Eyraud followed them, hunting them from city to city.

Bompard returned to Paris, however, and there she told her American lover that she **The trunk in which Gouffé's body was** was involved in a murder. A few days later, believing that she had **hidden.** been identified, Bompard turned herself into the police. She admitted knowing Gouffé and luring him to her apartment, but she placed all the blame for the solicitor's murder on Eyraud, saying that the thug had planned to kill her client without her knowledge. Eyraud read Bompard's story in the newspapers and then wrote Goron at the Sûreté, filling twenty pages to say that Bompard was framing him and that he had nothing to do with the Gouffé murder. The letter was traced to Havana, Cuba, where Eyraud was arrested and returned to Paris. He and Bompard were officially charged with the Gouffé murder and were placed on trial in December 1890.

Each of the accused blamed the other for the Gouffé's murder. At the end of five days, the jury returned a verdict of Guilty against Eyraud. He was sentenced to death. Bompard, on the other hand, pleaded her femininity which counted heavily with French juries. She, too, was found Guilty, but received only a twenty-year sentence at hard labor. Eyraud considered the sentences unfair, telling newsmen before his execution: "It was *her* idea, not mine. Why should I forfeit my life alone? Why not the woman, too?" He was guillotined on Feb. 3, 1891. Bompard was released years later and wrote her lurid memoirs.

REF.: Brock, *A Casebook of Crime; CBA;* Gribble, *Famous Feats of Detection and Deduction;* ____, *Strange Crimes of Passion;* Irving, *A Book of Remarkable Criminals;* Jackson, *The Portable Murder Book;* Kobler, *Some Like It Gory;* Lambton, *Thou Shalt Do No Murder;* Liston, *Great Detectives;* Logan, *Wilful Murder;* Morland, *Hangman's Clutch;* Nash, *Look for the Woman;* Pearce, *Unsolved Murder Mysteries;* Rowland, *More Criminal Files;* Symons, *A Pictorial History of Crime;* Thorwald, *The Century of the Detective;* ____, *Dead Men Tell Tales;* Tyler, *Gallows Parade;* Whitelaw, *Corpus Delicti;* Wilson, *Encyclopedia of Crime.*

Ezaki Katsuhisa, 1942- , Case of, Japan, kid.-extor. Japanese confectionery king Ezaki Katsuhisa, forty-two, was bathing outside his Kobe home on Mar. 18, 1984, when he was kidnapped by three men. The kidnappers demanded $4.3 million in cash or 220 pounds of gold bullion for the release of Ezaki, the president of Ezaki Glico, a company with annual sales of more than $500 million. Three days after the abduction, Ezaki escaped.

In the wake of the kidnapping, two suspicious fires broke out at Glico plants in April. An anonymous caller intimated that $1.3 million could end the assault on the Glico industry. Police arrested a man who had been kidnapped, allegedly to pick up the payoff, but the Osaka man couldn't lead police to the kidnappers.

In May, letters were sent to Japanese news organizations claiming that cyanide had been placed in packages of Glico candy. While authorities failed to find any evidence of tainted candy, supermarkets and shop owners pulled the candy off their shelves. For six weeks, Glico's production came to a standstill. The company laid off more than 1,000 employees and Ezaki estimated Glico's losses at $130 million. The Osaka police received a number of derogatory letters from the criminals, but failed to apprehend the perpetrators. REF.: *CBA.*

F

Fabiano, Sandra, 1946- , Case of, U.S., child abuse. In the spring of 1987, Sandra Fabiano operated the Mother Goose Pre-School in Palos Hills, a southwest suburb of Chicago. Fabiano enjoyed her work, and was herself the mother of two grown children. Then her own personal nightmare began.

On May 3, 1987, a 3-year-old girl was taken to Christ Hospital in Oak Lawn; her mother complained that her daughter had been sexually molested. Dr. Kathryn Mueller conducted a physical examination and submitted a report which concluded that the girl's hymenal opening measured twelve millimeters, or three times the normal size for a child her age. The hospital notified the Palos Hills Police Station, and within two days there were other unconfirmed reports of young children who were molested by a female staff member at the pre-school. Police Chief Daniel Hurley turned the case over to the Mass Molestation Task Force, a group of investigators working out of the Illinois state's attorney's office.

Over 120 pre-schoolers who had attended Fabiano's center were interviewed at the police station. Eight other children accused the 41-year-old proprietor of making improper advances toward them, but inexplicably no audio or video recordings were made by Assistant State's Attorney Diane Romza at the time of the interviews. "They wrote down what the kids told them," said Catherine Ryan, defense attorney for Fabiano, "and a lot of it conflicted even from what one would say from interview to interview." Romza's "bullying" tactics in the interview room were a concern to at least one father. "The specific question that really rattled me," said Jeffrey Hiskitt, "was 'we want to ask you again about the incident that took place with you and the other girls and Sandy. I want to make sure you're telling the truth this time.' To me that was coercive. It implied she was not telling the truth before." The Hiskitt girl told investigators that nothing improper had transpired.

Eight days after the 3-year-old victim was first examined by Dr. Mueller, doctors took a second look and discovered no sign whatsoever of an enlarged hymen. Medical experts testified at the trial that it was impossible for a 12-millimeter opening to disappear that fast. The conflicting medical evidence was puzzling, but there were additional doubts raised in the minds of Cook County jurors who learned that the little girl's mother was a heavy cocaine abuser.

Fabiano was charged with fifteen counts of child abuse against four different youngsters. However, she stood trial on three counts of sexual molestation against only one girl. Her well-publicized trial began on Mar. 18, 1989, before Cook County Circuit Court Associate Judge Frank Meekins. Defense Attorney Stephen Komie told the nine-man, three-woman jury that the real issue was not Fabiano, but the credibility of the 24-year-old mother who was "bingeing on cocaine just weeks before the trial." The woman had checked into a hospital detoxification center on Feb. 24.

After two weeks of lurid and contradictory testimony, Fabiano was acquitted on Mar. 30. The remaining charges against her were dropped on May 25 after prosecution attorneys decided against subjecting the children to the ordeal of a second trial.

For Fabiano, the long and painful ordeal would continue. Though she was acquitted, the Department of Children and Family Services revoked her day-care license on Apr. 17, 1989. Even more painful was the scorn and rejection heaped on her by residents and neighbors of the south suburban community. One young mother walked up to Fabiano on the street and muttered under her breath: "I hope they burn you." "I hesitated," Fabiano recalled, "and I turned around and I walked away from her." And so, too, did she walk away from the child-care business. At present Fabiano plans to return to college to earn a degree in business administration. REF.: *CBA*.

Fabre d'Églantine (Philippe François Nazaire Fabre), 1750-94, Fr., treas. Member of the National convention in 1792, he was closely tied to revolutionary leaders Georges Jacques Danton and Camille Desmoulins. Maximilien Robespierre accused him of being lenient with those opposed to revolution, for which he was guillotined in Paris along with Danton and Desmoulins in 1794. REF.: *CBA*.

Fabrizi, Nicola, 1804-85, Italy, consp. Aided in leading Milanese rebellion against Austria in 1831, tried to lead uprising in Savoy in 1834, established a secret Italian legion at Malta, and helped instigate revolutions in Sicily in 1848 and 1860. He served as minister of war in 1860, and chief of staff in war with Austria from 1866-67, for Giuseppe Garibaldi. REF.: *CBA*.

Jake "The Barber" Factor, at the time of his faked kidnapping in 1933.

Factor, John (Jake, Jacob, AKA: Jake the Barber, Norman D. Spencer, Harry Wise, J. Gest), 1894-1984, Brit.-U.S., fraud. John Factor was born in poverty in London in 1894. At an early age, he moved to the U.S. with his family, settling in Chicago. Here, in an immigrant ghetto on the West Side, he learned well the art of sneak-thievery and petty racketeering. By the time he was in his teens, Factor was inventing schemes to swindle others. To keep himself in walkabout money, Factor became a barber, first in a West Side shop, and later graduating to a posh salon at the Morrison Hotel in downtown Chicago. Here Factor met high-rolling confidence men, and he soon joined forces with several swindlers specializing in postal con games. He was indicted for mail fraud in 1925, but escaped a prison sentence.

Through his contacts, Factor met Al Capone, crime boss of

Chicago during the 1920s, and through Capone, many other racketeers, including Jack "Legs" Diamond of New York. In 1930, Factor convinced Diamond, then cash-heavy from his bootlegging and other rackets, to invest in a wild scheme whereby Factor would swindle hundreds of thousands of British investors. Reportedly armed with $500,000 of Diamond's money, Factor and several confederates left for London. There he established himself in a luxury suite in Grosvenor Square, using various aliases, such as Harry Wise and J. Gest. With him was his right-hand man, Arthur Jack Klein.

Factor in 1943 when he was convicted of mail fraud.

Factor then pumped a fortune into establishing the Broad Street Press, which published a number of financial publications, including *The City News, The Stock Exchange Observer, The Financial Observer,* and *Finance.* These publications came into being, written and edited by Factor's stock-swindling henchmen, for the sole purpose of promoting useless stock. Factor had undoubtedly studied the career of British swindler Horatio William Bottomley, who had successfully bilked enormous sums from British investors in the previous two decades, promoting useless stock through his financial publications.

After buying millions of ten-shilling shares in Vulcan Copper Mines and Rhodesia Border Mines at bargain basement prices, Factor peddled these worthless stock certificates through two dozen specially-trained salesmen with Klein overseeing their door-to-door pitches. Factor ingratiated himself with the Prince of Wales and other British dignitaries, while his photo appeared in newspapers with these leading social figures. He was accepted as a brilliant U.S. financier, who was bringing financial prosperity to the small British investor, through his development of companies reported to be laden with priceless copper and diamonds. The reports, of course, came from Factor's own financial newspapers, which were given away free to millions of readers, and which urged readers to buy the useless Vulcan and Rhodesia stocks.

Factor and his minions gleaned more than an estimated $5 million from gullible British investors before fleeing England just a few steps ahead of Scotland Yard. Yet Klein and several other so-called directors of the Broad Street Press and the empty copper and diamond companies were arrested and tried in 1931. These included Herbert John Spellen, Frederick Newbery, and the firm's solicitor, Barnett Leon Elman. All of them, including Klein, received long prison terms. Factor, however, had slipped through the Scotland Yard net and was already back in the U.S.

Jack "Legs" Diamond expected to receive several million dollars in return for his investment in the scheme, but suddenly learned that Factor intended to renege on his bargain. Diamond threatened to have Factor killed, but Diamond himself was murdered. His killing, still unsolved, is attributed to any one of Diamond's many underworld rivals, from Dutch Schultz to Charles "Lucky" Luciano. Some reports have it that Factor arranged for the Diamond murder.

The British government pressed U.S. authorities to extradite Factor to England to stand trial for his swindles, but authorities in Chicago, where Factor had heavily bribed officials and also used his influence with Al Capone, informed the British that Factor had "committed no crimes in Illinois" that would affect British laws. The British continued to press extradition demands through U.S. officials, battling through the U.S. court system against Factor's highly-paid attorneys. In 1933, just when it appeared that Factor was about to lose his battle, Factor was reportedly kidnapped by a bootlegging gang headed by Roger "The Terrible" Touhy and held for a large ransom, which was later paid, and Factor was released. "I was treated like a dog," Factor claimed and he was held as a witness against the Touhy gang. His son, Jerome Factor, was also kidnapped a short time later, reportedly by the same gang, and Factor claimed that he paid $50,000 for his son's safe return. Strangely enough, the car in which Jerome Factor had been kidnapped was later identified as belonging to Al Capone, Factor's close friend.

The Touhy kidnapping of Factor and his son, of course, were hoaxes, cleverly devised to prevent Factor from being extradited to England to stand trial and certain conviction for the gigantic swindle there. Since he had to testify against Touhy and his men, Factor was held in jail as a material witness and put in a cell to "protect him from gangland reprisals." This was also nonsense, since Touhy's so-called gang was nothing more than a small group of entrepreneurial bootleggers who had never been involved in kidnapping. The gang did, however, control a very lucrative territory Al Capone and his henchman, Murray "The Camel" Humphreys, coveted. By framing Touhy for the faked Factor kidnapping, which Capone arranged with Humphreys' connivance, Factor could use Touhy as an excuse to fend off his extradition and Capone and Humphreys could take over Touhy's Far North Side bootlegging operations.

Factor and his attorneys knew full well a U.S. law which stated that if a person held to be extradited is not removed within sixty days of his arrest, he could be released under a writ of *habeas corpus* and thereby evade extradition. That was exactly what happened. Factor stayed in jail, ostensibly in "protective custody" so that he could testify against the Touhy gang, and this period of time exceeded the sixty days. During this period, Factor identified Touhy and others as his kidnappers, and these men, convicted on Factor's lies (according to Touhy and many others) were sent to prison for life. Factor's lawyers then appeared and informed authorities that their client had been held in jail over the sixty-day limit and was therefore, according to the U.S. Statute of Limitations, ineligible for extradition. He was released and left Chicago immediately, going to Los Angeles where he began investing his millions in real estate.

In 1943, Factor was back in the news when he and ten others were convicted in a mail fraud in which the ring had manipulated liquor warehouse receipts. Factor was sentenced to serve six years in the federal prison at Sandstone, Minn. He entered Sandstone in August 1943 and was released in February 1948. Factor returned to Los Angeles and continued his mysterious real estate investments. Moreover, he began to pump considerable sums into newly-built Las Vegas casinos, including 65 percent interest in the Stardust Hotel and Casino. Factor continued to give heavy donations to the campaigns of politicians at the local, state, and federal level. He contributed $20,000 to the election of John Kennedy, and $5,000 to that of Richard Nixon in 1959 before the presidential elections.

In that same year, Roger Touhy, who had been sent to prison for life for kidnapping Factor in 1933, was released from prison in Illinois. The judge who released him announced that the Factor kidnapping had been "a hoax." Touhy had written a best-selling book, *The Stolen Years,* in which he pilloried Factor and Murray "The Camel" Humphreys for framing him and his men. Only twenty-three days after his parole, Touhy was killed on the porch of his sister's home in Chicago by shotgun blasts, a killing undoubtedly urged by Factor and most certainly carried out by Humphreys' gunmen.

So controversial was this slaying that federal authorities moved to have Factor deported back to his native England, using as their case Factor's 1943 conviction and other shady practices, along with the Touhy killing, including parole violations. Formal deportation proceedings against Factor began in December 1962, but President Kennedy, on Christmas Eve of that year, granted Factor a full pardon. Three years later, in 1965, Murray "The Camel" Humphreys was charged by the federal government with stock manipulation, wherein he had made $42,000 in an overnight stock transaction which had been arranged by Factor.

Factor admitted helping Humphreys make this money on an inside deal, saying that he was merely returning a favor, that Humphreys had arranged to have his son returned to him after the 1933 kidnapping. In truth, according to reliable sources, Factor was repaying Humphreys for killing Roger Touhy, who had exposed his faked 1933 kidnapping. Humphreys could certainly have helped in getting Jerome Factor released in 1933, since it was Humphreys who arranged for that faked kidnapping.

Meanwhile, Factor piled up his millions in California through real estate investments, which were aided mightily by local politicians and other influential residents. He kept his ties to the presidency, or attempted to do so. In 1968, Factor paid more than $350,000 in contributions and loans to Hubert H. Humphrey in his unsuccessful bid for the presidency. He went on making charitable contributions almost to the day of his death on Jan. 22, 1984.

Factor once handed out $20 bills to more than 1,000 blacks in Fayette, Miss., calling a press conference and announcing to newsmen: "I know what it is to be poor and hungry and to be discriminated against." He later contributed $1 million to establish a youth center in Watts, a depressed black area of Los Angeles. At the same time, Factor contributed $6,000 to the election campaign coffers of Los Angeles district attorney Joseph A. Busch. This inventive swindler, once described by the Los Angeles *Times* as a "prominent Democratic philanthropist," died peacefully in bed and was buried in the Hollywood Cemetery, his remains laid to rest alongside stellar actors and actresses he had wined and dined in life. See: **Capone, Alphonse; Diamond, Jack; Humphreys, Murray; Touhy, Roger.**

REF.: *CBA;* Nicholls, *Crime Within the Square Mile;* Touhy, *The Stolen Years.*

Fagan, Michael, 1949-   , Case of, Brit., theft. A peculiar incident that sent the staff of Buckingham Palace and the staid members of Parliament into a furious uproar occurred in the wee hours of the morning on July 9, 1982. In a scandalous breach of palace security, an unemployed decorator from London's North End slipped undetected into Queen Elizabeth II's private bed chamber while she slept.

Barefoot, and clad in a pair of blue-jeans and a T-shirt, Michael Fagan sat down six feet from the royal bed and chatted amicably with the queen for ten minutes before being discovered by a chambermaid.

The next day, the lurid London press seized on the story. Fagan was arrested 200 yards from the queen's bedroom. The next day, Scotland Yard detectives announced that the prowler was the same man who had been arrested on June 7 for stealing a bottle of wine from the queen's cellar. Brought before the courts on July 19, Fagan laughed and waved to his wife and children. He explained to the jury that palace security was not good, and that he wanted to call attention to it.

Fagan was not charged with the intrusion, and was cleared of stealing the bottle of wine. He remained in the custody of a maximum security hospital in Liverpool where he remained until Jan. 20, 1983. REF.: *CBA.*

Fagard, Edmond, and **Gense, Gérard,** and **Dubois, Aline,** prom. 1954, Fr., rob. In the French town of La Bassée, Sergeant Edmond Fagard of the local *gendarmes* was regarded as somewhat of a despot. Theater-goers would recall with amusement his habit of hiding behind the drapes in movie houses in order to apprehend patrons who lit up a cigarette. Smoking in public theaters was prohibited under French law.

Fagard, by all accounts an incorruptible policeman, had one lamentable weakness. His beautiful 28-year-old mistress, Aline Dubois, demanded that he maintain her in the style she was accustomed to as the wife of a career soldier who was serving in French Indo-China. Dubois had another love interest: a habitual criminal named Gérard Gense, who suggested that Fagard should help them in the commission of a robbery if he truly wanted to

hold on to his mistress. He proposed that the three of them hold up the postal clerk at the Las Bassée station. Fagard went along with the plan against his better judgment.

On Dec. 3, 1954, Gense bludgeoned the aging postman, Guillaume Blondel, over the head while Fagard tossed the mail bag into the car driven by Dubois. The same night, Gense took a train to Paris with his share of the loot. He spent it wildly, and enjoyed a riotous time at the postal department's expense. In just twenty-four hours, Gense had dropped about 10 million francs which caused the Parisian police to take notice. When he was questioned about the suspicious origins of this money, he confessed to the crime and implicated Fagard and Dubois.

The gendarme, who was about to depart for Algeria and a new assignment, was arrested and tried along with his young lover. On Mar. 10, 1957, the three robbers were found Guilty. Fagard and Gense were sentenced to twenty years at hard labor. Dubois received five years of solitary confinement.

REF.: *CBA;* Goodman, *Villainy Unlimited.*

Fahmy, Marie-Marguérite (Marguérite Laurient, AKA: Princess), b.1891, Case of, Brit., mur. Frenchwoman Marguérite Laurient began her affair with Prince Ali Kamel Fahmy Bey in May 1922 in Paris, following her divorce from her first husband. The 23-year-old Prince Ali, attached to the French legation in Cairo, was extravagant and had a sadistic bent. It was rumored in Egypt that Ali was homosexual. Prince Ali was captivated by Laurient, an elegant brunette divorcee ten years his senior, and took her back to Cairo where he suggested they live together. When she balked, the prince proposed marriage, and Laurient accepted, but with conditions. A contract was drawn up that

Marie Fahmy, husband slayer, 1923.

permitted her to wear western-style clothing and to divorce the prince at any time. In return she would convert to the Muslim faith, thereby ensuring Ali's inheritance. But when the religious ceremony took place, Fahmy ordered the divorce clause removed, allowing him to take three wives if he pleased.

Marguérite found Fahmy to be an abusive husband. He frequently beat her and assigned a houseboy to follow her throughout her day, even as she undressed. The couple traveled to London on July 10, 1923, and registered at the elegant Savoy Hotel. That night they quarreled bitterly about an operation Marguérite was scheduled to undergo. Prince Ali wanted it performed in London, but Marguérite insisted on traveling to Paris to have it done.

Prince Ali Fahmy, the victim.

While they ate supper in the hotel dining room, the band leader strolled by the table to take requests. "I don't want music. My husband has threatened to kill me tonight!" Marguérite said. The couple retired to their suite at 1:30 a.m. A luggage porter passing their door a short time later saw Fahmy burst from the room in agitation, his face scratched. "Look at what she has done!" he said. But the porter only reminded him to keep quiet. Seconds later three shots rang out. The porter rushed to the room to find the prince lying dead.

The lurid trial of Marguérite Fahmy opened in London's Central Criminal Court on Sept. 10, 1923. Representing the defendant were two of Britain's most able lawyers, Sir Edward Marshall Hall and Sir Henry Curtis-Bennett. Hall's defense was brilliant if unorthodox. He portrayed the prince as a stalking brute whose entourage had made Marguérite's life miserable, and who, on the night in question, tried to kill her. Fearing for her life she wrestled the gun away from him and then pulled the trigger of the Browning .32-caliber pistol. In a chilling recreation, Hall took the actual murder weapon and demonstrated the shooting for the benefit of the jury. For an instant he pointed the weapon at the jury, acting out the role of Prince Ali who had advanced on his wife in a threatening manner. The hushed courtroom watched Hall drop the gun to the floor. The lawyer later insisted that part was an accident, but it had a powerful effect on the jury, which returned a verdict of Not Guilty after only an hour's deliberation.

REF.: Ashton-Wolfe, *The Underworld*; Bowker, *Behind the Bar*; Burt, *Commander Burt of Scotland Yard*; CBA; Fay, *The Life of Mr. Justice Swift*; Furneaux, *They Died by the Gun*; Gribble, *Strange Crimes of Passion*; Hastings, *The Other Mr. Churchill*; Henry, *Detective-Inspector Henry's Famous Cases*; Marjoribanks, *For the Defense, The Life of Sir Edward Marshall Hall*; O'Donnell, *Cavalcade of Justice*; Shew, *A Companion to Murder*; Thomson, *The Story of Scotland Yard*; Warner-Hooke and Thomas, *Marshall Hall*.

Fahy, William, prom. 1924, U.S., rob. One of the most daring train robberies of the twentieth century was staged on June 12, 1924, near the little town of Rondout, Ill., just another whistle-stop on the Chicago, Milwaukee, and St. Paul line.

Outside of town, train number fifty-seven was grounded to a halt when a gun-toting stowaway thrust the barrel of a rifle into the neck of the fireman. Four men, whose faces were disguised by army gas masks, scurried from a parked car nearby. They fired a bullet into the glass window in the mail car where eighteen clerks were sorting mail. The men were forced to vacate the car when a gas bomb thrown by one of the robbers landed in their midst. The robbers escaped with sixty-four mail bags later valued at $3 million. It was a puzzling case that required an expert criminal investigator. It was the kind of case that was tailor-made for William Fahy, one of the shrewdest postal inspectors on the line.

A problem arose when one of Fahy's men received a phone tip that the mastermind of the mail heist was Fahy himself. The woman who tipped the police was brought before Rush Simmons, the chief of postal inspectors. She explained that her husband had been sent to prison by Fahy for a crime he never committed. During his period of incarceration, she flirted with Fahy who, by this time, had fallen madly in love with her. In a moment of passion he carelessly admitted to planning the Rondout train robbery. Inspector Fahy was arrested and jailed for his role in the crime. REF.: CBA.

Fair, Laura D., 1837-1919, Case of, U.S., mur. Born in a small Mississippi town in 1837, Laura Fair became a widow at the age of seventeen when her first husband died of cholera. She entered a convent in Mobile to forget about life, but Fair was not the kind to remain in one place for long. She married a rabble-rouser named Thomas Grayson, but eventually divorced him and moved to San Francisco with her mother.

Her third husband, Colonel William D. Fair committed suicide with a Colt revolver, leaving behind $300 in property and an infant child named Lillias Lorraine. Desperately in need of cash, she moved to Sacramento to open a rooming house, but this ended in a complete financial disaster. Laura became an actress, appearing at the Metropolitan Theater in San Francisco in *The Marble Heart* and *School For Scandal*. The reviews were favorable, but Laura was not interested in show business. She set out

for Virginia City, Nev., to strike her claim on the Comstock Lode.

By pawning a diamond ring left to her by the colonel, Fair had enough money to open a small hotel called the Tahoe House. It was here in September 1863 that she met Alexander Parker Crittenden, a prominent corporate lawyer and the father of seven children. In 1849, Crittenden was elected to the first general assembly convened in California.

When he first met Laura Fair at her rooming house, he was struck by her beauty. In order to gain her trust, Crittenden claimed that he was a widower. The charade continued until Fair confronted him with the truth. Crittenden explained that he was trapped in a loveless marriage and would try to get a divorce. But the affair continued for the next seven years.

Crittenden's dalliance with Laura Fair scandalized San Francisco society. He was roundly criticized for appearing in public one day with his wife on one arm and his mistress on the other. Each time Laura threatened to leave him, his tearful pleas and false promises always brought her back.

First, she broke off the affair, which by now had grown monotonous, in order to marry Jesse Snyder, a lodger at the Tahoe House. Crittenden refused to let the matter end. He forced the couple to separate and was gleeful when Fair caught her husband in bed with a local trollop. A divorce was granted on Oct. 5, 1870. Fair made it clear to Crittenden that the affair could not resume until he made some accommodations with his wife. But in the next four weeks she met with him in his private rooms where they dined and romanced together.

On Nov. 3, Laura waited as Crittenden greeted his wife as she stepped off the *El Capitan*, after the vessel had moored at the Oakland wharf. She boarded the boat and crept up on the couple as they sat together on a nearby park bench. She pulled the trigger of her five-shooter and fired on her lover. The Harbor Police, accompanied by young Parker Crittenden, arrested Laura in a nearby saloon. Two days later Crittenden died, and Fair was charged with murder.

Fair's trial lasted twenty-six days at the Fifteenth District Court. A Guilty verdict was returned on Apr. 26, 1871, and Fair was sentenced to die on June 3 by Judge Samuel Dwinelle. It was the first time the state of California had ever sentenced a woman to death. Before the appointed hour of execution, a stay was granted, and in February 1872, a higher court overturned Laura's conviction on the extraordinary grounds that the closing arguments to the jury had been made in the wrong order and that the prosecution had allowed witnesses to attack the defendant's character. Fair was granted a new trial.

In September 1872, she appeared before Judge Reardon. This second trial ended with a Not Guilty verdict. The press was outraged by what one newspaper described as "a cold blooded apology for crime." For several days afterward James Crittenden followed her around town, threatening physical harm. But Fair was a resourceful woman, a tough survivor in an age that frowned upon moral indiscretions in women.

She outlived the judge and the prosecution team, drifting into obscurity in a quiet residential area of San Francisco. Her daughter Lillias Lorraine died in 1913 after failing in her attempts to become an actress on Broadway. The cause of death was listed as starvation. Laura was found dead in her tiny room above a San Francisco store in October 1919. The caterwauling of her hungry felines prompted neighbors to call the police.

REF.: CBA; Duke, *Celebrated Criminal Cases of America*; Fair, *Wolves in the Fold*; McComas, *The Graveside Companion*; *Official Report of the Trial of Laura D. Fair*; Paine, *The Assassin's World*; Rodell, *San Francisco Murders*; Seagle, *Acquitted of Murder*; (FICTION), Twain, *The Gilded Age*.

Fairbanks, Jason, 1780-1801, U.S., mur. Elizabeth Fales was the only woman who had ever paid any attention to Jason Fairbanks, who was plagued with chronic ailments and a deformed right arm, so he took it badly when her parents refused to consider his marrying their daughter or refused even his entering their house in Dedham, Mass. Fales had been kind to Fairbanks, but never intended him to take her attention for anything more than friendship. Fairbanks, however, took it as much more, even forging her signature on a false certificate to announce their marriage.

On May 18, 1801, Fairbanks met Fales in the shrub-enclosed pasture next to the Fales house. She wanted to make him understand that she would never marry him, while he intended to persuade her to let him publish the marriage announcement. Instead, Fairbanks staggered from the pasture, blood pouring from a self-inflicted wound, and dropped a blood-covered knife. Fales' father found his daughter in the pasture dying of massive knife wounds and the torn-up certificate strewn about.

In August 1801, Fairbanks was found Guilty of murder. His many supporters, however, convinced of his innocence, helped him escape from jail, and one of them, a man named Dukeham, rode with him toward Canada. M. P. Holt, a member of the posse in pursuit of Fairbanks and the $1000 reward, found him in an inn in Whitehall, Vt., and forcibly held him until help arrived. On Sept. 10, 1801, Fairbanks was hanged in Dedham.

REF.: *Biography of Mr. Jason Fairbanks and Miss Eliza Fales; CBA; A Correct and Concise Account of the Interesting Trial of Jason Fairbanks, for the Barbarous and Cruel Murder of Elizabeth Fales; A Deed of Horror!, Trial of Jason Fairbanks;* Fairbanks, *The Solemn Declaration of the Late Unfortunate Jason Fairbanks; A Mournful Tragedy;* Nash, *Bloodletters and Badmen;* ___, *Murder, America; Report of the Trial of Jason Fairbanks.*

Fairchild, Thomas Edward, 1912 - , U.S., jur. Justice of Wisconsin Supreme Court from 1936-38, attorney general for Wisconsin from 1949-61, U.S. attorney from 1951-52, and committee member of the Milwaukee Community Welfare Council in 1954, which was designed to evaluate revision of the state Children's Code, pertaining to proceedings in juvenile court. In 1965, he authored the article, "Post Conviction Rights and Remedies in Wisconsin," *Wisconsin Law Review.* President Lyndon Johnson appointed him to the Seventh Circuit Court of the U.S. in 1966, and he served as a member of the U.S. Judicial Conference's committee on Probation Systems from 1968-72. REF.: *CBA.*

Fairlie, Walter, d.1920, Brit., suic.-mur. Walter Fairlie had been married for four years when he murdered his wife while on a leisurely stroll through London one fine spring day in 1920. Eyewitnesses later recalled how nice they looked together, walking arm-in-arm.

The events leading up to the tragedy began in 1916 when Fairlie returned home to England after being cashiered out of the army. He met Gertrude Lilian shortly afterward, and married the Welsh girl against the wishes of her parents. There was one child from the marriage, but this did not discourage Fairlie from cavorting with other women. In December 1919, Gertrude Fairlie obtained a legal separation from her husband and cut off his generous allowance.

Angry and depressed by this turn of events, Fairlie confronted his wife outside her place of employment in April 1920, during the lunch hour. As they walked down the street, Fairlie pulled out a pistol and shot his wife and then himself before anyone could intervene. The three-year-old child had become an orphan.

REF.: *CBA;* Nicholls, *Crime Within the Square Mile.*

Fairris, Hurbie Franklin, Jr., 1933-56, U.S., mur. When Hurbie Fairris, Jr. was sent to the electric chair in January 1956 for murdering Detective Bennie Cravatt during a robbery, he was continuing an old family tradition.

The Oklahoma boy had an interesting, but sordid past. When he was 16-months-old his uncle Ray Hamilton was electrocuted in Texas for killing a prison guard. Hamilton was an early associate of Clyde Barrow and Bonnie Parker. Another uncle, Iwana Fairris was serving a life sentence for various crimes. His mother, separated from Hurbie's father when her son was a tyke, had shot and killed two husbands. The first shooting was ruled committed in self-defense, but when Mrs. Fairris shot her third husband, she drew a five-year prison sentence.

Fairris had a girlfriend named Peggy Ann Fry who was serving time in a West Virginia prison for transporting a stolen car across state lines, and his brother Bethel Fairris was in jail for burglary. It had come as no surprise that Hurbie Fairris, Jr. had resorted to a life of crime. His stint on death row at the Oklahoma State Prison was "longer than I've ever stayed in one place before," he explained. He had no final words for the executioner other than to say "let's get on with it." REF.: *CBA.*

Faisal (Faisal Bin Abdulaziz), 1905-75, Saud., king, assass. The Saud Dynasty established political autonomy in the Arabian Peninsula early in the twentieth century under the leadership of Ibn Saud. His son Faisal learned politics first hand, and while still in his teens led an army of 45,000 Bedouins into battle against his father's enemies. Faisal's military successes earned him rapid promotions, and in the 1920s he won important victories in Jidda, Mecca, and Medina, forcing Sharif Hussein to withdraw his forces from the region. As a result, Ibn Saud was able to establish the boundaries of the modern-day Saudi Arabia in 1932. For the next thirty-two years Faisal served as his father's

King Faisal of Saudi Arabia, assassinated in 1975.

foreign minister. After Ibn Saud's death, custom mandated that Faisal's elder brother Saud assume the throne, but he proved a weak leader and squandered his country's oil money to finance luxuries for himself and his many wives.

In 1964, the Royal Council deposed Saud and sent him into exile in Greece, and Faisal succeeded him. He followed a cautious, pro-western philosophy and his eleven year reign is best remembered for the 1973 Arab oil embargo against the West. Faisal's anti-Israeli policies and the enormous wealth oil brought to his kingdom made him the most powerful leader in the Arab world. On the morning of Mar. 25, 1975, King Faisal was preparing to meet a special Kuwaiti delegation at the Ri'Assa Palace. A young man suddenly stepped from the crowd to speak with the Kuwaiti oil minister, whom he recognized from college days. As the ministers entered the reception room, the stranger followed close behind. As

Prince Faisal Bin Musaed, the king's nephew and assassin.

King Faisal lowered his head to accept the customary kiss of greeting from the oil minister, the uninvited guest drew a revolver and fired three shots at Faisal, two of them hitting Faisal. "My brother is avenged!" the assassin screamed. The killer was arrested on the spot and identified as Prince Faisal Bin Musaed Bin Abdulaziz, the 27-year-old nephew of the king, who had studied in the U.S. at San Francisco State College. The prince had been arrested in 1969, with actress Christine Surma, for peddling LSD and hashish. Through the intervention of the Saudi embassy, they were released after pleading no contest.

In 1974 the prince returned to Saudi Arabia and accepted a position as instructor at Riyadh University. His was considered an unstable personality, and his politics were not agreeable to the family. He had visited certain radical factions in East Germany and had participated in an aborted 1969 plot within the military. But the real motive for the king's assassination was the 1966 murder of Prince Faisal's brother Khalid, who was killed by Saudi police during a demonstration against the Riyadh television station. Religious fundamentalists believed that Koranic law barred the projection of human images on TV. Faisal had tried unsuccessfully to persuade his uncle the king to execute the policemen responsible for the shooting. After the assassination, the prince was declared legally sane, and was beheaded with a gold-hilted sword. His head was placed on a wooden stake for public display.

REF.: *CBA;* Demaris, *Brothers In Blood: The International Terrorist Network;* Nash, *Almanac of World Crime;* O'Ballance, *The Language of Violence—The Blood Politics of Violence.*

Faisal II, 1935-58, Iraq, king, assass. King of Iraq since the age of three when his father died, Faisal II was not crowned until 1953. In his majority, he favored strong ties with the West. Pro-Arab factions in his army felt otherwise, however, and on July 17, 1958, General Abdul Karin Qassim led a coup d'état in Baghdad by taking over the city's communications. After a two-hour battle, the rebels took the palace, promising the king and his family safe passage out of the country. Instead, the entire royal family was murdered outright by machine gun. A mob then tore Prime Minister Nuri-el-Said's body in half and the deputy premier's body into pieces. The Qassim regime, power mad from the start, ended with the overthrow of Qassim and his execution in 1963.

REF.: *CBA;* Nash, *Almanac of World Crime;* O'Ballance, *The Language of Violence—The Blood Politics of Terrorism;* Sparrow, *The Great Assassins.*

Faithfull, Starr (Starr Wyman), 1906-31, U.S., (unsolv.) mur. On June 8, 1931, a wandering beachcomber named Daniel Moriarity, making his rounds on a Long Island, N.Y., beach made a gruesome discovery. Washed up on the sand was the body of a beautiful woman with long hair. Moriarity pulled the body away from the water line and summoned the police. A check of the missing person's files turned up the oddly poetic name Starr Faithfull, a 25-year-old woman, whose disappearance had been reported three days earlier by her step-father Stanley, a retired manufacturing chemist.

An autopsy showed that Starr had died from drowning. But the police weren't sure if it was murder or suicide. District Attorney Elvin Edwards was convinced she had met with foul play. There were visible lacerations on the upper arms—probably inflicted by someone with a powerful grasp. The evidence of rape was inconclusive and medical examiners debated the point for two days. Edwards, however, was certain that the girl had been criminally assaulted and was anxious to establish hard evidence to back up his belief. A check of the woman's background revealed that she was the daughter of Frank W. Wyman, divorced from Starr's mother in the early 1920s. Mrs. Wyman was a Bostonian of high social standing. She had lived with her two daughters, Starr and Tucker, at Faithfull's home in Greenwich Village. Before the Depression the girls had vacationed in Europe. The junket abroad only served to whet Starr's appetite for more of the good life. But the family suffered some financial reversals putting further trips out of reach.

Unable to join the privileged globe trotters, Starr lived vicariously in their world by crashing the last-night parties on ocean liners, slipping off the ship minutes ahead of the final call. While pursuing her own peculiar fantasy, Starr made the acquaintance of Dr. George Jameson-Carr, ship surgeon aboard the *Franconia,* he a serious-minded intellectual, well versed in the arts and literature. Starr fell hopelessly in love with the doctor, but soon came to understand that not only did he not share her rapture, but he found her advances annoying. When Jameson-Carr asked her to leave his quarters, Faithfull stumbled out of the room in a drunken stupor and disappeared into the crowd.

Unbeknownst to the doctor, she remained on board, forcing the captain to summon a tug boat to pick her up as the ship headed down river toward the open sea.

On June 4, the date of her disappearance, Starr was observed wandering the docks where the *Mauritania* and *Ile de France* were about to set sail. After leaving home that morning, Starr went to a Manhattan department store where she wrote a brief farewell note to Jameson-Carr, sent to England via the *Olympic.* "Hello Bill, Old Thing: It's all up with me now. This is something I am going to put through. The only thing that bothers me about it—the only thing I dread—is being outwitted and prevented from doing this which is the only possible thing for me to do. If one wants to bet away with murder one has to jolly well keep one's wits about one."

There was speculation that Starr had stowed away on board and then committed suicide from the deck of one of the great liners as it left the port of New York. Edwards was still insisting that she had been murdered, when new revelations about her past hit the papers. A year earlier Starr had been found in a hotel room with a man identified as Joseph Collins, thought to be a male prostitute. Hearing her cries for help, hotel guests alerted the police. When they entered her room they found her naked and bleeding. Starr was taken to Bellvue Hospital where she spent the night screaming for her parents to come and get her. "I was drinking gin as far as I know...I don't remember...I suppose somebody knocked me around a bit," she said. The police dismissed Collins, even though there was little doubt he had beaten Starr. Police found a diary which she called her "Mem Book," which alluded to a man she was conducting an affair with, identified only as "A.J.P." The entries mentioned continuing sexual torment. "Spent night A.J.P. Providence. Oh Horror, Horror, Horror!!" Stanley Faithfull provided additional details to the press, revealing that Starr had been seduced at the age of eleven by an elderly Boston financier whom he called "X." Following up on this, the press linked "X" to "A.J.P.," coming up with the name of Andrew J. Peters, former U.S. Congressman and one-time mayor of Boston.

As a young girl, Starr had played with the mayor's children. Mrs. Faithfull was distantly related. A large sum of money, estimated to be between $20,000 and $80,000 had been paid to the Faithfulls as a "settlement," for damages done to Starr. The former mayor had allegedly enticed the young girl into his home, drugged her, and raped her. Peters issued denials of wrongdoing. District Attorney Edwards then announced that he had positively identified the killers who had taken Starr to Long Beach, drugged her, and drowned her. He claimed that one of the killers was a prominent New York politician and promised to arrest both of them within thirty-six hours. However, when pressed for further details, Edwards retreated and a follow-up statement was never issued and no suspects were taken into custody.

Suicide seemed to be the only plausible theory. Dr. Jameson-Carr returned from England and revealed the existence of three suicide letters sent by Starr between May 30 and June 4. "I am going now," she wrote to Jameson-Carr in care of the liner *Berengaria* on May 30, "to end my worthless disorderly bore of an existence before I ruin anyone else's life as well." She described in melodramatic detail what she imagined to be the perfect death experience. "I am going to drink slowly, keeping aware every second. Also I am going to enjoy my last cigarettes. I won't worry because men flirt with me in the streets—I shall encourage them—I don't care who they are." The ship's doctor was in Belgium when he received word of her death. He rushed back to New York to try to clear up the mystery. Stanley Faithfull declared the letters were forgeries. After careful analysis, a battery of handwriting experts declared the letters were genuine. Those familiar with the case concurred that Starr Faithfull killed herself over an unrequited love. Her sister Tucker recalled an occasion in London when Starr attempted suicide by taking twenty-four grains of allonal, but was revived by physicians.

Starr Faithfull, the beautiful flapper, in evening gown and at the beach, in a retouched tabloid photo; Starr's head was superimposed on a model's body.

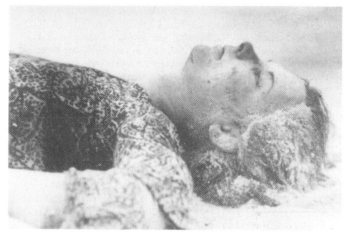

There was sand in Starr's lungs; she had been suffocated.

Detectives examine the body of Starr Faithfull, June 8, 1931.   Left, ether addict Starr and, right, Stanley Faithfull.

Morris Markey, a journalist for the *New Yorker* Magazine was not convinced by this logic. In 1948, he offered the more titillating theory that Starr had been murdered on the very same night she planned to kill herself. The unknown assailant was someone she had picked up in town. Her scribbled letter to Jameson-Carr on June 4 had, after all, promised that she would encourage any man who came her way. The killer, Markey surmised, grew frustrated by her teasing games. "And then I think she teased this unknown man beyond endurance...he mauled her...then he was frightened...and decided that he would never tell of it," Markey wrote. The assailant dragged Starr Faithfull to the water and held her head under until she was dead. The first autopsy performed on Starr showed the presence of two grains of Veronal, not enough to induce death. There was enough food in her system to suggest that she had eaten a final meal before meeting her death. The second autopsy, ordered by D.A. Edwards found that while she was probably not raped, Starr Faithfull had recently engaged in sexual intercourse. The presence of bruises on the corpse suggested that the love-making had turned violent. After drowning her, the killer retraced his steps in the shallow waters in order to avoid leaving incriminating footprints.

REF.: *CBA; Crouse, Murder Won't Out; Franklin, Woman In the Case; Goodman, Posts-Mortem: The Correspondence of Murder; Jones, Unsolved; Leighton, The Aspirin Age, 1919-1941; Nash, Open Files; Purvis, Great Unsolved Mysteries; Wilson, Encyclopedia of Murder.*

Fakhr al-Din II, c.1572-1635, Leb., ruler, assass. Considered the father of modern Lebanon, he defeated Christian Maronite ruler Yusuf Sayfa in 1607 and united the Maronite and Druze mountain districts under his rule. The Ottomans later exiled him from 1614-18. By 1631 he had obtained most of Syria and Palestine. The Ottomans defeated him in 1633, captured him in 1634, and executed him. REF.: *CBA.*

Fakkak, The, prom. 10th Cent., Spain, kid. The Fakkak was an organization of middle men formed in the tenth century to serve as intermediaries for Muslim families whose members were abducted by rival Christian factions. The Fakkak negotiated the ransom demand and helped to secure the release of the victims after formal contracts had been signed with the families. REF.: *CBA.*

Falieri, Marino (Falerio, Falier), c.1278-1355, Italy, consp. Led the Venetian army during the siege of Zara in 1346. He was elected chief magistrate of Venice in 1354, and was executed in 1355, after he was found Guilty of conspiracy to murder Venetian patricians in order to install himself as prince. REF.: *CBA.*

Falkirk Cat Burglar Case, prom. 1937, Scot., burg. Sometimes a thief or a killer can be found by the clothing he wears. In 1937, a man was arrested in Scotland on Nov. 28 after he was caught breaking and entering into a store. His method of entry and the fact that he wore no shoes at the time of arrest was markedly similar to two other burglaries in the district that had occurred several months earlier.

The three pairs of shoes found outside the buildings were sent to the criminal research laboratory where they were analyzed for common features. Footwear will leave the manufacturer in the same condition, but will attain a distinct identity of its own after prolonged use by the purchaser. Uneven patterns of wear, the depth of lace impressions in the upper, and the outline of the person's foot will reveal much about the physical comportment of the individual. In this case, the police learned that the cat burglar suffered from a deformed left leg and foot. The suspect was convicted and sentenced to prison based on the analysis of his shoes, which matched that of a cripple.

REF.: *CBA; Smith, Mostly Murder.*

Fall, Albert Bacon, 1861-1944, U.S., polit. corr. Kentucky-born Albert Fall moved to the New Mexico territory for his health and there taught school, herded cattle, and then became a mining prospector and oil wildcatter. He had little luck but his friend, Edward L. Doheny, a wealthy lawyer, became a millionaire oil man. Fall then entered politics and in 1921 became one of New

Mexico's two senators. Through his friendship with then-President Warren G. Harding, Fall was named Secretary of Interior. Fall quickly fell prey to graft since his New Mexico properties were heavily mortgaged and he was badly in need of money. In secret, Fall leased federal lands in Teapot Dome, Wyo., and in Elk Hills, Calif., to his close friend Doheny, head of the Pan American Oil Co., and to Harry Sinclair, owner of Mammoth Oil Co. The oilmen lavished riches upon Fall, with Doheny delivering $100,000 in cash in a little black bag to Fall. Sinclair then delivered $260,000 to Fall in Liberty Bonds.

The secret leasing deals were exposed when other oil men complained that the oil lands were turned over to Doheny and Sinclair without competitive bidding. Fall was charged with taking bribes and he, Doheny, and Sinclair underwent a number of trials. Doheny treated the court battles as petty annoyances, saying that he had given Fall $100,000 because he was "an old friend," and that the payoff was "a mere bagatelle," which caused a nationwide uproar. The ailing Fall was finally convicted, fined $100,000, and given a year in jail. He claimed poverty and the fine was dropped. Because of his ill health, Fall was allowed to serve his time in the sunny New Mexico State Penitentiary. When he was released, Fall was a broken man, living out the rest of his life as an impoverished invalid, dying in 1944 in El Paso, Texas. See: **Teapot Dome Scandal.**

REF.: Adams, *Incredible Era; CBA;* Chapple, *The Life and Times of Warren G. Harding;* Daugherty, *The Inside Story of the Harding Tragedy;* Mee, *The Ohio Gang;* Messick, *Secret File;* _____ and Goldblatt, *The Mobs and the Mafia;* Nash, *Citizen Hoover;* Noggle, *Teapot Dome: Oil and Politics in the 1920s;* Overstreet, *The FBI In Our Modern Society;* Powers, *Secrecy and Power;* Reid, *The Grim Reapers;* Russell, *The Shadow of Blooming Grove;* Sinclair, *The Available Man;* Sullivan, *Our Times.*

Falleni, Eugene (AKA: **Harry Leo Crawford, Jean Ford**), 1876-1938, Aus., mur. Born in Florence, Italy, Eugene Falleni, whose real name might have been "Eugenie" Falleni, since she was a girl, moved with her parents to New Zealand at an early age. She was a strong, compactly built young woman who yearned to be a man. At the age of sixteen she passed herself off as a cabin boy and signed on with a Norwegian barque engaged in commercial trading along the Pacific rim.

Falleni worked hard and acquired enough of the masculine affectations to fool her shipmates. An Italian named Martello was the only one to see through her ruse. A relationship developed between them, and by the time the vessel moored in New South Wales in 1899, Falleni was pregnant. The child she bore was named Josephine, but seeing no easy way out of her predicament, Falleni continued to pass herself off as a man to secure higher wages and better employment.

Josephine was placed in the care of an Italian couple named De Anglis who resided at Double Bay. Falleni identified herself as Harry Crawford, and paid the De Anglises a small stipend to care for Josephine. At the same time she began to court a widowed cook and housemaid, Annie Birkett, who worked for a prominent physician, Dr. Clarke. Birkett was easily deceived, and quickly fell under the influence of Crawford. She pooled her life savings and bought a small candy store in Balmain, a suburb outside Sydney, Aus. Birkett's teenaged son Harry tried to dissuade his mother from foolishly marrying Crawford.

Nevertheless, this is just what Annie Birkett did in 1914, and for the next three years they lived together as "man and wife." When Mrs. De Anglis died a year later, Josephine came to live with the Crawfords. She kept her rightful mother's dark secret from Harry, but the widow Birkett finally understood what had taken place. Falleni-Crawford decided to kill Birkett, lest she reveal her true identity and foil her ambitions and future plans. On Sept. 28, 1917, while the two were picnicking near Chatswood, Falleni bludgeoned Birkett to death and then incinerated the body under a heap of logs. The crime had been cleverly disguised, and it wasn't until two years later, in 1919, that Crawford was arrested and charged with murder. Harry Birkett had gone to live with his aunt during this time, and Falleni found herself a second "wife."

Convinced that his mother had been murdered by Falleni, Harry and his aunt went to the police. An examination of dental charts established it was the body of Annie Birkett. Confronted by the police with an arrest warrant and the probability of confinement in the men's section of the prison, there was little else to do but confess to her identity. Crawford admitted that she was a woman and was forced to appear in female clothing on Oct. 5, 1920, for the first time since her daughter was born.

She was found Guilty and given the death sentence, which was commuted to life imprisonment. Falleni-Crawford remained at the Long Bay jail for ten years, before earning her release in February 1931. Following her discharge from custody, she assumed a woman's identity. Under the name of Jean Ford, she opened a lodging house in Paddington, which she maintained until 1938 when the place was sold. Several months later, on Oct. 6, 1938, Falleni was struck by a car and killed instantly.

REF.: *CBA; Gurr and Cox, Famous Australian Crimes.*

Falling, Christine, 1963- , Case of, U.S., mur. Abandoned at the age of three, Christine Falling was shuttled among various Florida orphanages and relatives who did not want her. At the age of fourteen she dropped out of high school to marry her boyfriend. The marriage lasted six weeks. A 1979 court record called attention to the complete absence of parental supervision, and the probability that Falling was likely to run away.

The troubled young woman eventually went to live with another boyfriend, Robert Johnson, in his trailer camped outside Perry, a rural farming community in the Florida pan-handle. Falling earned her living as a baby-sitter, looking after the young children of Blountstown and its surrounding communities. On Feb. 22, 1980, 2-year-old Cassidy Marie Johnson died from what physicians diagnosed as encephalitis. She was under Falling's care at the time of her sudden and mysterious death.

A year later, in February 1981, Falling's nephew, 4-year-old Jeffrey Davis, failed to awake from his nap. Just three days later the boy's cousin, Joseph Spring, of Lakeland, also died in his bed. Both children were being supervised by Falling, but the doctors concluded that death was as a result of myocarditis, an infection of the heart. Falling checked into a local hospital shortly afterward complaining of a stomach illness. Her condition was diagnosed as a viral infection of the digestive tract—a strain which had been found in the Spring boy's blood.

Then in July 1982 there was another infant death reported in Perry, due east of Blountstown. Eight-month old Jennifer Daniels, half sister of Joseph Spring, died in Falling's arms while she and the infant's mother were shopping. On July 3, 10-week-old Travis DeWayne Coleman was found dead in the trailer that Falling shared with Johnson. Like the other four deaths, this one was also listed as due to "natural causes." In this case, the Coleman boy had suffered from what examining physicians described as infant death syndrome.

Falling told reporters that she was a "confused victim of grim coincidence." Dr. Robert Gunn of the state Department of Health looked at it another way. "I know of no lethal virus that would kill children in that manner," he said. "There's some kind of coincidence or connection, but I don't think it's a medical one."

Three weeks after the death of Travis Coleman, Falling was arrested and charged with first-degree murder. Held without bond, the young woman entered a plea of not guilty before Circuit Judge W.L. Bailey on Aug. 27. She changed her plea on Dec. 3, to avoid a jury trial and the likelihood of a death sentence. In return, the state agreed to drop murder charges stemming from the deaths of two Lakeland boys, and an elderly man from Perry in January 1982. Falling was sentenced to life imprisonment, with parole eligibility in twenty-five years.

Commenting on the outcome of the bench trial, Defense Attorney Baya Harrison III noted that her client faced six potential death sentences. "The bottom line is, the state made us an offer that we could not refuse," she said. REF.: *CBA.*

Fallon, Mickey, and **McDonald, Eddie,** prom. 1934, U.S., mur. Before dawn the morning of Mar. 3, 1934, Joe Arbona was gunned down in his car on New York's fashionable upper West Side at 183rd and Riverside Drive. The hysterical screams of his fiancée Lillian Dawson awakened residents to the tragedy. When police arrived, Arbona was dead. A gun shot had torn away most of his jaw.

Three men and one woman held them up at gunpoint, Dawson explained, but she was unable to provide a positive identification.

Three weeks passed before the New York police could identify the killers. Officers alerted Assistant District Attorney P.F. Marro that a missing girl had returned home after living it up in Manhattan in the company of her boyfriends. Detective John Bunschrow questioned a waitress at the restaurant where the girl once worked. She could not remember their last names, but provided enough salient facts so that Bunschrow felt compelled to write a full report to his superior, Lieutenant Thomas Neilson. He, in turn, notified Lieutenant James Donnelly.

Marro and Donnelly entered the case, and extracted the first names of the other girl's boyfriends: Harry, Eddie, and Mickey. The waitress was driven around the vicinity of 125th Street and the Hudson River where one of the young men had recently bragged about holding up a shopkeeper. The store owner said that he had been robbed of a .45-caliber Colt revolver, which was the same weapon that had killed Arbona.

Confronted with this evidence, the ex-witness confessed to the police. She identified Mickey Fallon as the trigger man the night of the murder, and Eddie McDonald as the one who supplied the car. According to her, the selection of Arbona as their victim was purely haphazard. A third man, Harry Hood, moved into the front seat with the girl to act as decoys in case a police car drove by.

The four were indicted on charges of second-degree murder on Mar. 22, 1934. McDonald received thirty years to life at Sing Sing Penitentiary, and Fallon was sentenced to thirty-five years to life. Harry Hood was acquitted in a jury trial, and the ex-waitress who was in it for a good time was dismissed after a motion was filed by Assistant District Attorney Marro.

REF.: *CBA; Cohen, One Hundred True Crime Stories.*

Fallon, William Joseph, 1886-1927, U.S., crim. lawyer. Fallon was known as "The Great Mouthpiece" and was one of the most flamboyant and successful criminal attorneys in New York during the 1920s. He defended more than 100 people on charges of murder, and more than half of these were acquitted, with the rest receiving minor prison sentences. Fallon's methods were decidedly shady and he reportedly bribed jurors, paying the person half the bribe money before the trial and promising the other half after the verdict; the second was payment never made. Some claim he also bribed police officers and detectives, as well as expert witnesses, but many of these statements stemmed from his defeated adversaries.

The tactic employed most effectively in court by Fallon was his lengthy hammering and emotion-charged address- es, invariably directed to one juror he had selected in ad- vance of each trial. Fallon

The flamboyant criminal lawyer, William J. Fallon, in court, 1920.

would research the background of a juror, and by the time trial convened he would know that juror's background, political makeup, racial and sexual inclinations, and thereby know exactly what arguments would appeal to that person. An incredible amount of Fallon's cases ended with a hung jury, eleven-to-one, and this made him suspect. Fallon's explanation was that it was the one juror that he would concentrate on who would be the holdout and that hung juries had nothing to do with tampering.

Fallon's clients ranged from whorehouse madams to big-time gangsters. He represented with equal aplomb and for considerable fees pimps, panderers, gamblers, bootleggers, and swindlers. He not only gave legal counsel to Arnold Rothstein, the underworld boss of New York, but according to one account, he even supervised many of Rothstein's rackets. His most colorful client, Nicky Arnstein, matched his own flamboyance. Arnstein stood accused of masterminding an enormous Wall Street bond robbery in 1919 and got off with a minimum sentence, thanks to Fallon's masterful courtroom antics.

In 1924, Fallon was charged with bribing a juror and brought to trial. This all came about because of a political battle between William Randolph Hearst and New York political boss, "Big Tom" Foley. Hearst, a newspaper magnate who owned twenty-two daily newspapers at the time, had been politically blocked from seeking high office in New York by Foley and others. When Hearst learned that Foley had taken money from stock bucket-shop operators Fuller and McGee, he ordered a phalanx of his New York reporters on the *American* to expose his political opponent. Foley, however, survived the bad publicity. In the course of the Hearst-ordered newspaper investigations, Fallon came under heavy scrutiny as the lawyer for Fuller and McGee.

Hearst's newspaper henchmen persuaded one of Fallon's aides, Ernest Eidlitz, to inform on his boss. Eidlitz insisted that Fallon had bribed a juror named Charles Rendigs, the lone juror who had held out for an acquittal for Fuller and McGee who had been on trial for fraud. Rendigs admitted being bribed and was sent to prison. Fallon was indicted, but he vanished from sight. Hearst's news hounds found him days later hiding in the apartment of his mistress. He was placed on trial ten days later, but Hearst's crusade against Fallon blew up in his face. Fallon's attorneys, when questioning potential jurors, repeatedly asked the same unnerving two questions: "Are you familiar with William Randolph Hearst? Are you familiar with Marion Davies?" This was the first time that the long-kept secret affair between the married Hearst and the movie actress was made public.

It got worse for Hearst as Fallon's trial progressed. Fallon took the stand in his own defense and there embarrassed the powerful Hearst before the world. He claimed that Hearst was persecuting him because Eidlitz, whom Fallon claimed had recanted his bribery charges against him, had told Hearst newsmen that Fallon possessed the birth certificates of two illegitimate children born to Hearst and an actress and that Hearst had told his newspaper editors: "We must destroy Fallon at any cost!" With this the courtroom exploded, and the prosecution moved to have the shrewd, fabricating lawyer's remarks stricken from the court record, but it was too late. Fallon's statements were now a matter of public record which newspapers competing with the Hearst press were all too happy to print.

Of course, Fallon had created the whole story, but he was so convincing that the jury promptly acquitted him and he exited the courtroom to thunderous applause from the spectators. The Great Mouthpiece had triumphed through an incredible, bold fiction. The Broadway lawyer reveled in his notoriety and went on acting the playboy, but his excessive drinking finally took its toll. Fallon appeared in court on a minor matter concerning baseball manager John McGraw in Spring 1927. As he began to address the court, Fallon suddenly collapsed. He was taken to his wife's apartment at the Hotel Oxford and there, on Apr. 29, 1927, he died of a gastric hemorrhage and heart attack.

REF.: *CBA*; Fowler, *The Great Mouthpiece: The Life Story of William J. Fallon;* Hynd, *Murder, Mayhem and Mystery;* Katz, *Uncle Frank;* Lait and Mortimer, *Chicago: Confidential;* Logan, *Against the Evidence;* Messick, *Secret File;* _____ and Goldblatt, *The Mobs and the Mafia;* Peterson, *The Mob;* Reppetto, *The Blue Parade;* Swanberg, *Citizen Hearst;* Thompson and Raymond, *Gang Rule in New York;* (FICTION), Wilstach, *Under Cover Man;* (FILM), *State's Attorney,* 1932; *Criminal Lawyer,* 1937.

Fall River Legend, 1948, a ballet choreographed by Agnes DeMille, music by Morton Gould. This work is based upon the celebrated Borden case (U.S., 1892). So popular was this work that for many years it was regularly performed by the American Ballet Theatre group. See: **Borden, Lizzie.** REF.: *CBA*.

FALN (Fuerzas Armadas de Liberación Nacional, AKA: The Armed Forces of National Liberation), prom. 1974-84, U.S., bomb.-terr. Between 1974 and 1977, forty-nine bombs exploded in various federal and state offices in New York City, Chicago, Newark, and Washington, D.C., by a Puerto Rican terrorist group calling itself the Fuerzas Armadas de Liberación Nacional, popularly known as the FALN.

By 1980 the organization had claimed responsibility for 120 dynamite bombings that claimed five lives and resulted in $3.5 million in property losses. The campaign of terror drew attention to the plight of Andres Figueroa Cordero and three accomplices who shot up the House of Representatives in 1954. Cordero, who was in poor health, was serving an eighty-one year prison sentence. The FALN demanded his immediate release, and the political independence of Puerto Rico from the U.S.

The first bomb was exploded on Aug. 31, 1974, at the Lincoln Center in New York. No one was injured in this blast, but it wasn't long before the FALN bombers claimed their first victims. On Jan. 24, 1975, four bystanders were killed when an explosion ripped through the chic Fraunces Tavern in New York City.

Police and FBI agents were at first stymied in their attempts to identify the members of this group. Because little was known about the FALN it was impossible to assess its numerical strength or the amount of weapons it had in its possession.

On Nov. 3, 1976, there was a major breakthrough in the investigation when Chicago Police discovered a bomb factory on Haddon Avenue, on the city's near Northwest Side. Fourteen cases of dynamite sticks, which had been stolen from a construction site in Littleton, Colo., were seized at the home of Carlos Alberto Torres, the first suspected FALN terrorist identified by police.

Torres was connected with the National Commission on Hispanic Affairs for the Protestant Episcopal Church. The commission was organized in 1970 to promote self-help and awareness among members of the Hispanic community. A grand jury in New York subpoenaed records of the Episcopal Church to determine if there was a conclusive link to the FALN.

Travel records covering the years 1971 to 1976 showed that Commission members traveled regularly between Puerto Rico and the U.S. In March 1977, Maria Cueto, executive director of the Protestant Episcopal Church, and her secretary Raisa Nemiken were ordered to jail by Federal District Judge Marvin Frankel after both women refused to testify before the grand jury. Earlier, a specially trained police dog had sniffed out traces of dynamite in Cueto's Manhattan apartment.

By the mid-1980s, a clearer picture of the FALN had emerged, and a number of its top leaders were placed behind bars or were facing criminal indictments.

On Feb. 18, 1981, ten FALN members from Chicago were sentenced to prison from fifty-five to ninety-year prison sentences for their role in at least twenty-eight bombings from 1975 to 1979. Torres, who was identified as the ringleader of the group received seventy years. A target list of 100 potential bombing sites selected by FALN operatives had been seized by FBI agents at Torres' apartment in Jersey City shortly before he was arrested in Evanston, Ill. Potential victims were notified, and advised to beef up security. "Puerto Rico belongs to the Puerto Rican people," Torres told reporters. "We have nothing to lose except the American noose around our necks."

Judge Thomas R. McMillan noted that none of the defendants

showed remorse. "I'm convinced you're going to continue (terrorist activities) as long as you live. If there was a death penalty, I'd impose the death penalty on you without any hesitation."

The campaign of terror continued, as Torres and other jailed leaders said it would. On Dec. 31, 1982, four bombs exploded at government offices in Manhattan. Three police officers were seriously injured in the New Year's Eve blast. A communique received from an anonymous tipster, named fugitive FALN leader William Morales as the individual responsible for this latest outrage. The man who called the New York *Post* said that Morales had entered the U.S. for the second time in eighteen months to coordinate a united effort with the Black Liberation Army and the radical Weather Underground to "wage war" against government installations. This claim was discounted by the FBI, which had no evidence to link the various underground extremist movements.

In recent years the FALN has kept a low profile, though it is impossible to predict if and when the group will perpetrate a new wave of terrorist attacks. See: **Weather Underground Organization.**

REF.: *CBA;* Dobson and Payne, *The Terrorists—Their Weapons, Leaders and Tactics;* Laquer, *Terrorism;* Liston, *Terrorism;* Sloan, *Simulating Terrorism.*

Falsen, Christian Magnus, 1782-1830, Nor., jur. Led party that sought independence from Swedish rule. He wrote the greater part of the Norwegian constitution, served as attorney general for the kingdom in 1822, and was the president of Norway's Supreme Court in 1827. REF.: *CBA.*

Familiars, prom. 16-17th Cent., Brit., witchcraft. In the historic lexicon of witchcraft, the familiar was a demonic spirit manifested in the body of a small domestic animal, often a cat. According to Reginald Scot, who first described them in his book *Discovery of Witchcraft,* published in 1584, the Devil, upon making his covenant with a witch, awards her with a "low-ranking demon in the shape of a small domestic animal" who will offer advice and counsel.

The published confession of Ursula Kempe, in *A True and Just Record* of the St. Osyth Witch Trials of 1582, described how the familiar assisted the witch in the practice of the black arts. They carried out the evil deeds against the enemies of the witch, and as a reward were permitted to suck blood from her left thigh.

In 1647 Matthew Hopkins, in his *Discovery of Witches,* lent credence to these superstitions when he claimed to have observed familiars at work in the cell of accused witch Elizabeth Clark. Hopkins was denounced as a fraud and a charlatan by members of the British clergy, but his testimony had so whipped up the people of Essex, that seven women were executed as witches.

Accounts of the demonic familiar are found exclusively in British and Scottish folklore.

REF.: Bishop, *Executions; CBA;* Seth, *Witches and Their Craft;* Wilson, *Witches.*

Fan Chung-Yen, 989-1052, China, law enfor. off. Implemented a reform plan that abolished corruption, created a solid local militia system, and equalized land ownership, as Emperor Jen Tsung's chief minister from 1043-52. REF.: *CBA.*

Fantle, Ernest, 1904- , Brit., mansl. Ernest Fantle, who worked as a travel agency courier, married his wife Sylvia in 1942. During the war, thirty-eight of his family members in Czechoslovakia were killed by the Nazis. He lived in his native land after the war, but moved to England when the communist government threatened to kidnap his wife and child. He served as a commissioned officer in the Royal Air Force until his retirement in 1954.

Three years later, Sylvia took up with Horace Lindsay, a wealthy dress manufacturer from Piccadilly. In May 1958, Sylvia told her husband that she had been unfaithful, and wanted out of the marriage. In despair, Fantle purchased a Swiss service revolver and a box of shells from a gun dealer in Interlaken. He returned to London where he phoned Lindsay at his office. There was an urgent matter to discuss, he said, and a meeting was arranged at Lindsay's flat for the morning of July 19.

At the appointed hour the two men greeted each other cordially. In a white smoking jacket, Lindsay assumed an air of distant superiority. He promised to look after Fantle's child, but there was no hope of a reconciliation with Sylvia. In desperation, the grieved husband produced the service revolver and shot Lindsay four times in the face and chest. The murder had taken place exactly twenty-four hours after the Fantles celebrated their wedding anniversary.

Fantle was charged with murder, but the court reduced the crime to one of manslaughter based on what the judge viewed as "serious provocation." Justice Salmon sentenced Fantle to three years imprisonment. Had the trial occurred just two years earlier it is likely that the defendant would have received the death penalty. The Homicide Act of 1957 no longer made it necessary for the defense to prove that the killer had acted in self-defense, or because of a certainty that his life was in danger.

REF.: *CBA;* Furneaux, *Famous Criminal Cases, vol. 6.*

FAR (Fuerzas Armadas Revolucionarias), prom. 1968-70, Guat., kid.-mur. The FAR, a Guatemalan-based terrorist group, has used kidnapping and extortion as the means to further its radical political goals. Several prominent U.S. and European diplomats have suffered death at the hands of FAR operatives.

In 1968 U.S. Ambassador Gordon Mein was machine-gunned while attempting to escape from his abductors. The FAR issued a statement the next day explaining that the kidnapping was planned in order to facilitate the release of Camilo Sanchez, one of the revolutionary leaders detained in a Guatemalan jail.

Two years later, in March 1970, West German Ambassador Count Karl von Spreti was kidnapped and held for $700,000 ransom. When the Guatemalan government refused to negotiate with terrorists, his bullet-riddled body was found in a peasant's hut. The German diplomats were immediately recalled.

REF.: *CBA;* Laquer, *Terrorism;* Moorehead, *Hostages to Fortune.*

Fard, Wallace D. (AKA: **F. Mohammed Ali, Walli Farrad, Professor Ford, Farrad Mohammed, Wallace Fard Muhammad),** c.1877-c.1934, U.S., miss. per. Founded the Nation of Islam or Black Muslim movement in 1930. His followers considered him to be Allah incarnate. He disappeared in 1934, and was never heard from again. REF.: *CBA.*

Farese, Thomas R., 1943- , U.S., forg.-theft-extor. Before 1974, Thomas Farese was just another career criminal. He was a down-and-out loser who had been sentenced to prison for a number of crimes committed from Massachusetts to Los Angeles. His last stretch in a federal detention center resulted from the sale of a stolen painting to an FBI agent. Following his release from the prison camp at Eglin Air Force Base in Florida on June 21, 1974, Farese's life began to change. The penniless ex-con became a millionaire businessman and movie mogul in three short years. The FBI, wondering how this was possible, began an investigation.

In November 1975, Farese purchased three tanker ships for $438,000 from money tucked away in a bank account in the Cayman Islands. The account was listed under the name of Consolidated Shipping, a shadowy holding company belonging to Farese. In March 1976, Farese purchased a Fort Lauderdale restaurant-night club called The Bridge for $840,000, which he then leased back to his brother Angelo Farese who secured the necessary liquor license. Farese branched out into motion pictures the next year when his film company, Olympic Productions, underwrote *Hollywood Man,* a low budget thriller which starred veteran character actor William Smith. Farese cast his brothers Angelo and Jude Farese in the movie, which was sold to Intercontinental Releasing Corp. of Beverly Hills.

Farese enjoyed his new life as resort owner and shipping magnate. He spent much of his time at his opulent beach-front home in Fort Lauderdale while puzzled government agents speculated on the source of his new-found wealth. It was widely known that during his incarceration at Eglin, Farese made the acquaintance of Nicholas "Jiggs" Forlano, a co-partner of Charles

(Ruby) Stein, who operated the largest loan-shark ring in Manhattan. In 1965 a state commission reported that Stein and Forlano had $5 million in outstanding loans on the streets of New York. Stein later went to jail in 1973 after being convicted of interstate gambling in New York City. He served less than one year.

When Forlano suffered a heart attack at the Aqueduct Race Track in 1977, the details of any secret business transactions with Farese died with him. Dominic Gambardella of New Haven, Conn., was another racketeer who was tied in with Farese. Gambardella, convicted on Jan. 7, 1972, for operating a stolen credit card ring, later owned 20 percent of The Bridge. Many questions remain about Farese's ties to organized crime. Until the answers are supplied, Farese will remain a man of enduring mystery. Said one prominent Florida banker who attempted to investigate his creditor's background: "It's like the guy was born a couple of years ago." REF.: *CBA*.

Faria, Albert, and **Simmons, William**, and **Chadwick, William**, prom. 1930s, U.S., mur. On a rainy day in East Orange, N.J., two sullen strangers entered the HI-Hat Lunchroom. When the counterman emerged they ordered him to open the cash drawer.

At that moment, Patrolman Thomas Ennis, a WWI veteran, entered the diner. The gunmen shot him in the stomach and fled. With the cooperation of the Newark Police Department, the killers of the East Orange policeman were quickly identified and captured. Playing a hunch, Lieutenant Joseph Cocozza investigated the Hi-Hat employees. He learned that an ex-convict named William Chadwick had recently been employed at the Newark branch.

His accomplice Albert Faria was seized at a hospital in Hoboken where he was being treated for a gunshot wound. Faria was a notorious stick-up man who had been arrested six years earlier. In the office of Joseph Linarducci, captain of the Essex County homicide squad, a third man, William Simmons, confessed to the crime and identified Chadwick as the "finger man" of the operation. He picked the time and the place based on the layout of the lunchroom. Faria and Chadwick broke down and admitted their roles in the robbery. The three men were quickly brought to trial. Faria and Simmons, who had carried out the robbery, were held responsible for the death of the police officer. They were sentenced to death. Chadwick received fifteen years in prison.

REF.: *CBA*; Cohen, *One Hundred True Crime Stories*.

Farinacci, Prospero, 1544-1618, Italy, jur. Served as Pope Paul V's procurator general, and authored *Praxis et Theorica Criminalis* in 1616, which greatly influenced penology in countries under Roman authority until the reforms of Cesare Beccaria. REF.: *CBA*.

Faris, Charles Breckenridge, 1864-1938, U.S., jur. Prosecuting attorney for Pemiscot County, Mo., from 1893-99, served as circuit judge for the Twenty-eighth Judicial District of the Circuit Court of Missouri from 1910-12, and as justice for Division Two of the Missouri Supreme Court from 1912-19. He received appointment from President Woodrow Wilson to the Eastern District Court of Missouri in 1919, and from President Franklin D. Roosevelt to the Eighth Circuit Court of the U.S. REF.: *CBA*.

Farley, E.E., prom. 1899, U.S., fraud. Bucket shops and fake investment companies were the bane of Chicago's financial district in the 1890s. Under the shadow of the Board of Trade building on LaSalle Street hundreds of these otherwise respectable-looking business establishments bilked investors out of thousands of dollars.

In October 1899, Detective Clifton Wooldridge closed down a number of these places on Adams Street, including the Turf Investment Company owned and operated by E.E. Farley. A full staff of stenographers and clerks gave the appearance of a busy, well-run office that was there to serve the serious investor. Farley was arrested and charged with running a confidence game, and his literature and equipment were seized.

REF.: *CBA*; Wooldridge, *Hands Up*.

Farley, George, b.c.1881, U.S., mur. On Feb. 17, 1938, T. Dwight Crittenden, a 60-year-old Hollywood character actor who had joined the Los Angeles Marshall's office in 1926, went to a rundown section of the city to perform an eviction as a follow-up to a twenty-four hour notice served the day before. The tenant, George Farley, a 57-year-old laborer, had not paid his $7.50-a-month rent since May 1937. Crittenden and his helper Leon W. Romer, also age sixty, stood on the front porch along with a caged, warbling canary. Suddenly a rifle blast rang out and tore into Romer's chest, killing him instantly. The canary continued to sing as Crittenden dropped, killed by a gunshot wound in the head.

Farley's wife ran out of the house and the police, called by neighbors, quickly surrounded and ordered the killer to surrender. Another shot rang out, then Farley appeared briefly in the front doorway, the rifle in his hands. "Here I is. Come an' get me!" he shouted. Police opened fire and Farley was hit in the thigh as he ducked back into the house.

For the next hour the gun battle raged, the police pumping bullets and tear gas into the house and Farley returning fire from his .40-.82 caliber rifle. All the while, the caged canary on the front porch continued to sing, a bizarre counterpoint to the chorus of gunfire and shouts. After almost an hour, the return fire ceased and a squad of police carefully entered the house. They found Farley face down in a rear room. He had been shot five times—in the arm, chest, and thighs. He was placed under arrest and removed to a nearby hospital. The double murder had occurred over $67.50 in back rent. REF.:*CBA*.

Farley, John, 1943- , U.S., mur. A 26-year-old paper hanger from Brooklyn, John Farley was accused of raping and murdering Margaret Burke, forty-nine, in an alley after following her out of a Queens, N.Y., bar on Aug. 21, 1968. Because Farley had an extra set of Y chromosomes, his defense attorney, Marvin Kornberg, contended that his client had characteristics of a "supermale," and was predisposed to violence as a result. Based on research done in European prisons, a theory developed that a disproportionate number of criminals convicted of violent crimes possessed the extra Y chromosome. The prisoners found to have the extra chromosome were also tall and mentally dull and had facial acne. During the trial in the Queens Supreme Court, Justice Peter T. Farrell dismissed the original rape charge against the six-foot-three-inch, 240-pound defendant. Lawyer Kornberg asked the jury to find Farley not guilty by reason of insanity, but on Apr. 30, 1969, after ten hours of deliberation, the jury found the defendant Guilty of first-degree murder. On July 10, 1969, Farley was sentenced to a prison term of twenty-five years to life. REF.: *CBA*.

Farmer, Daniel Davis, d.1822, U.S., mur. Daniel Davis Farmer dallied with widow Anna Ayer in Goffstown, N.H., but when, on Apr. 4, 1821, she informed him that she was pregnant with his child, he went crazy, grabbed a club, and beat his lover to death. Farmer then tried to burn the widow's house down around her body, but was discovered. Tried and convicted, Farmer was hanged at Amherst, N.H., on Jan. 3, 1822. Farmer wrote and published his own confession to make money for his relatives and provide some last-minute luxuries for himself before his execution.

REF.: *CBA*; Farmer, *The Life and Confessions of Daniel Davis Farmer*; Rogers and Chase, *Trial of Daniel Davis Farmer*; Smith, *Mostly Murder*.

Farmer, Jack, 1952- , and **Farmer, Mike**, prom. 1988, and **Farmer, Pamela**, 1961- , and **Fucaloro, Anthony**, prom. 1988, and **Byrski, Martin**, prom. 1988, and **McNab, Kevin**, prom. 1988, and **Villapando, James**, prom. 1988, U.S., drug smug.-consp.-mur. Jack Farmer and his wife Pamela Farmer, a former paralegal in Chicago, were the leaders of a multi-million-dollar cocaine ring known as the Little Mafia which terrorized Near West Side residents with home invasions, extortion, and murder, to finance their lucrative drug operations.

Described by government attorneys as a "cruelly and calculating manipulative man," Farmer personally executed two of his customers who were delinquent in their payments. In 1978, he shot 22-year-old Robert Hertogs through the head while the pair were driving down a Chicago street. A government informant described in detail the gruesome murder of Al (Maniac) Norris, and how Farmer bragged about paying off his lawyers and a Chicago judge to fix the case. Kent Fisher observed the execution-style murder of Norris from a railroad overpass near Peoria Street on May 12, 1982. The victim pleaded for his life and promised to make his payments, but Farmer forced Norris against the wall and shot him in the back of his head. Fisher notified police and identified Farmer as the man who shot Norris.

Farmer was indicted for murder and put on trial in August 1982, but Judge Maurice Pompey dismissed the charges because of the state's lack of evidence. The drug trafficker had paved the way for a dismissal by greasing his lawyer Dean Wolfson with a $45,000 bribe to give Judge Pompey. Wolfson was later sent to jail on charges stemming from the Operation Greylord investigation of judicial corruption in Cook County, Ill.

The Farmers and thirteen members of the Little Mafia were indicted on Apr. 14, 1986, for running a cocaine ring. Jack Farmer escaped while on a court-authorized furlough from the Metropolitan Correctional Center on Apr. 10, 1987. Defense Attorney Alan Blumenthal was going over some pre-trial issues with his client when Farmer tried to strangle him with a neck-tie.

Farmer changed into street clothes and disappeared out of the building and into his wife's car. They drove to Florida and lived undercover for more than a year before being arrested by FBI agents in Lantana on June 1, 1988. A grocery store clerk tipped off local FBI agents after recognizing Farmer on a telecast of *America's Most Wanted,* a syndicated television program. He was operating under the alias of Robert J. Niewiadomski and had been on the Most Wanted list for only three days before his capture.

Extradited to Chicago, Farmer, his wife, and seven others connected with the Little Mafia were tried in November 1988 for racketeering, conspiracy, and drug trafficking. On Feb. 28, 1989, Judge James F. Holderman of the U.S. District Court meted out a forty-year prison sentence against Farmer. Pamela received twenty-five years. Farmer blamed media distortion for his conviction.

On Mar. 8, Holderman sentenced Kevin McNab and Martin Byrski to fifteen years each for their role in the drug conspiracy. Mike Farmer received fifteen years, while James Villapando received twelve. Anthony Fucaloro, convicted on lesser charges, was given two years on Mar. 16. See: **Greylord Judicial Investigation.** REF.: *CBA.*

Farnham, Eliza Woodson (Eliza Woodson Burhans), 1815-64, U.S., penal reform. As Sing Sing prison's matron of the women's division from 1844-48, she initiated a number of reforms. REF.: *CBA.*

Farouk I (Faruq al-Awwal), 1920-65, Egypt, fraud. King Farouk nearly bankrupted Egypt with his many frauds and acts of duplicity. He was so corrupt and incompetent that the leaders of the western powers, in Cairo in 1943 for a wartime summit, ignored him, despite his position as the official host. The son of Fuad I, Farouk succeeded him in 1936. Before he was deposed by Gamal Abdel Nasser in 1952, the king squandered at least $600 million from the nation's treasury on personal pleasures. Oranges were a staple crop of Egypt, most of them raised on Farouk's own lands. To eliminate competition from Palestine, Farouk imposed a heavy import tariff on oranges, but the public outcry was so great that the king kept the tariff in effect only one year.

King Farouk enjoyed the Cairo night life and ordered the best establishments to reserve the best spot for him at all times. In matters of diplomacy Farouk was an outright extortionist. A visiting U.S. businessman once passed around an expensive jeweled cigarette lighter for Farouk's entourage to admire. After the king examined the piece, he slipped it into his coat pocket. "That is

my wife's wedding present to me," the man protested, "I can't possibly let it go." Farouk reminded the airline executive that he was also after precious Egyptian air space. He could have the lighter back, or the air rights, but not both. After considering the matter, the executive allowed the king to keep the lighter. Farouk suggested that he submit the cost of the lighter on his expense account, which the man later did.

The dissolute King Farouk of Egypt.

The deposed Shah of Iran was another of Farouk's unwitting victims. When Shah Riza Khan Pahlavi died in exile in South Africa, the body was shipped back to Teheran via Cairo. Farouk displayed the magnificent casket containing the body of the Shah for several days, but when the shah's casket was shipped back to Teheran, the jewel-encrusted sword and the medals which were to accompany the shipment were missing. King Farouk said that his government was doing everything in its power to apprehend the thief. The treasures were located only in 1952, after Farouk had been toppled, and by order of President Nasser, returned to Iran. When Nasser's revolution finally came, Farouk was prepared. He sailed from Alexandria in grand style, taking with him 400 trunks crammed with expensive souvenirs.

REF.: *CBA;* Demaris, *Brothers In Blood: The International Terrorist Network;* Moore, *Wolves, Widows and Orphans.*

Farr, John William, 1920- , U.S., rob. John Farr remains wanted by the FBI for a series of bank robberies. He had previously been convicted for larceny of an automobile, burglary, and theft. Small in stature with blue eyes and gray hair, Farr might seem more like someone's grandfather than a notorious bank robber. He is a heavy smoker who suffers from the ravages of emphysema, and has been known to accept work as a movie projectionist. At this writing, Jack Farr is still at large. REF.: *CBA.*

Farran, Rex Francis, prom. 1948, Brit., (unsolv.) mur. Although Captain Roy Farran was acquitted for the murder of a young Jewish boy named Alexander Rubowitz, he could not leave Palestine behind him when he returned home to England. Threats followed him, including one note that read, "We will follow you to the end of the world." Farran was in Scotland on vacation when a package arrived for him at his parents' home in Wolverhampton, England. His younger brother, Rex, unable to restrain his curiosity, opened the package which contained an oversized edition of Shakespeare. He lifted the cover and was blown up by a bomb planted inside. Twenty-five-year-old Rex Farran died two days later. Although authorities were certain that the Palestinian retribution had missed its mark, they could do nothing to bring specific individuals to justice.

REF.: *CBA;* Nash, *Open Files;* Shew, *A Second Companion to Murder.*

Farrell, Edgar Joseph Raymond (AKA: **Raymond Cyril White**), 1897-1939, Case of, Aus., suic.-mur. In northeast Victoria, the town of Corryong was disturbed by the mysterious deaths of two sisters. Some time before these incidents, two employees at a dairy farm near Corryong took a strong and immediate dislike to each other. The older of the two suspected his enemy, Raymond Cyril White, of trying to take his job. One evening he spat out his meal of stew and tea, saying it was inedible and bitter-tasting. Dogs who ate it were dead by morning. White had disappeared. A government forensic scientist, Charles Anthony Taylor, discovered that the animals had died of strychnine poisoning, and determined that the coarse-grained poison had probably come from India. A tin with a Madras, India, label was found in the bush. White was found and questioned but released for lack of evidence.

White moved on to Walaw and applied for work at the Pines, a farmstead run by two sisters, Elizabeth Brennan, forty-two, and Joanna Brennan, thirty-five. White soon asked the younger sister to marry him, but was refused. He then asked Elizabeth to wed, and was accepted. Joanna took a short vacation, then returned and made out a will, leaving her property and share of the farm to her sister. On Apr. 25, 1928, White and Joanna went off to shoot ducks by the creek in celebration of a holiday. Joanna was killed when, according to her sister, "a gun went off and hit her." Her testimony was oddly impersonal, as was that of her fiancé, who spoke repeatedly of "the deceased." Joanna's death was ruled an accident, and White and Elizabeth married.

Eleven years later, a fire damaged their farmhouse and they collected a hefty insurance payment of almost £1,500. Rumors of arson dredged up old suspicions regarding Joanna's death. On Feb. 19, 1939, White and Brennan were out driving when their car plunged over a culvert. White escaped, and tried to fight the intense flames as the car burned. When his wife was found dead, he had only a vague recollection of the tragedy. Constable Orr wondered why White had let the car burn so long before getting help, and the coroner wondered why the body had been left to burn until it was completely destroyed. Detective Fred Delmonico began an investigation. He learned that White was a discharged soldier who had served in Africa. Dr. Crawford Mollison, government pathologist, then discovered that White was really Edgar Joseph Raymond Farrell, a deserter, and that he had shot his wife to death before engineering the burning to hide all evidence. A small unmelted nugget of gold—probably a wedding ring—and the murder weapon—a .22-caliber revolver found at the bottom of a dam—proved to be Farrell's undoing. He disappeared before he could be charged with his wife's murder, and was found dead near a memorial to dead soldiers near Albury. He had shot himself, leaving a note that said he could not live without his wife. He also left behind a broken fuel pipe, definite evidence that he had engineered her death. REF.: *CBA.*

Farrell, Stephen, and **Reed, Bjorn,** prom. 1920s, U.S., rob. Lawrence Corrado was home with his wife the day the Metropolitan Finance Company of New York was robbed. The owner of the business, Frank Burgert, was shot and killed by two gunmen who fled down the back stairs and into an awaiting car. The crime was witnessed by five female employees who were in the office at the time. The license plate was easily traced, and the owner was arrested along with his friend Corrado. Both men were identified in a police lineup, and booked for the murder of Burgert. Corrado was imprisoned at Tombs, a massive stone prison with thick walls.

Mrs. Corrado knew her husband was innocent, but she needed an alibi, or someone to verify her story. While visiting her husband at the prison she met the brother of the other accused

man who owned the car. He seemed to sympathize with her plight, and passed along some information. "I was in the holdup," he said. "And your husband and my brother were not with me."

This information was told to her attorney Vincent Impelliteri, who would one day become the mayor of New York City, and Charles Breitel, the Assistant District Attorney at the time. Detective William Devine was slowly convinced that Mrs. Corrado was telling the truth. A tape machine was installed in her apartment, and the conversation with the alleged driver of the car was recorded for the detectives to hear. The man identified an Irishman named Stephen Farrell and a Swede, Bjorn Reed as the real robbers.

Both men worked at the Westchester Auto Wrecking Company. They were placed in a second police lineup and picked out without hesitation by the four women who admitted to making a grievous mistake the first time around. Corrado was subsequently cleared, and Farrell and Reed both received long prison terms.

REF.: *CBA;* Danforth, *The D.A.'s Man.*

Farrell, William Patrick, b.c.1930- , U.S., rape-mur. On Saturday night, Feb. 5, 1955, Ann Yarrow, a 23-year-old student at New York University's graduate school, placed a long-distance phone call to her father, Don Yarrow, in Ventura, Calif. Yarrow was not home. Ann, who was staying at a girlfriend's East 4th Street apartment while the friend was out of town, left a message asking her father to call when he returned. When Don Yarrow returned home, he placed a 3 a.m. call to his daughter. The phone range repeatedly, rousing a neighbor from sleep, but Ann Yarrow never answered it.

On Sunday morning Ann's girlfriend, Herta Payson, returned from her trip. She climbed the six flights of stairs to her top floor apartment and put the key in the lock. The door gave easily. She walked into the bedroom and turned in horror at the carnage that greeted her. Ann Yarrow's body lay on a mattress on the floor. She was nude except for a tan sweater which had been pulled over her neck. She had been raped, strangled, stabbed thirty-seven times, and then her corpse had been mutilated.

The police questioned Miss Yarrow's friends and colleagues, including a married man who worked with the slain girl at the Center for Human Relations Studies, a division of New York University. They also interviewed the married man's wife but neither was charged. A few days after the murder, Angelo (Mike) Morelli was arrested with suspicious bruises on his face and held for the murder, but he never was brought to trial.

On the morning of Mar. 1, 1955, William Farrell, a 25-year-old Brooklyn furniture repairman, forced his way into the apartment of his father-in-law, Charles Yessler, and began to attack the man, chasing him from the apartment which was a block from the apartment where Ann Yarrow had been slain less than a month before. As Yessler ran to a nearby police station, Farrell began to attack his sister-in-law, Irene Miller.

When police arrived, Farrell fled the house and a foot chase followed. He threw a bread knife at one of the officers and a warning shot was fired in return. He finally was caught in a cemetery between First and Second Avenues. Under questioning Farrell, who had twice been hospitalized in a mental ward at Bellevue Hospital, admitted the Yarrow murder. Moments later he recanted the confession, but soon admitted the murder again. Police finally put together this story: On the night of the murder, Farrell had spotted Ann Yarrow walking in Greenwich Village. He followed her to her apartment and later knocked on the door. Yarrow opened the door and, not recognizing Farrell, tried to close the door again. Farrell forced his way inside. After leaving the apartment, Farrell threw the murder weapon into a sewer on Second Avenue. Following Farrell's directions, police recovered the knife. At first, Farrell identified it as his own, but a while later he changed his mind and said he had never seen the knife before. Farrell was found insane and committed to an asylum. All charges against Angelo Morelli were dropped. REF.: *CBA.*

Farrett, Jane, prom. 1671, Brit., crime&punish. Jane Farrett, the widow of a Selby, England, shoemaker was sentenced to be "ducked" in the community pond three times after being found Guilty of breaching His Majesty's peace on Oct. 5, 1671. Farrett's incessant scolding was called "a great annoyance and disturbance of her neighbors."

REF.: Andrews, *Old-Time Punishments; CBA*.

Farrington, Hilary, d.1870, and **Farrington, Levi**, d.1871, U.S., rob. A set of identical twins born in Mississippi, Hilary and Levi Farrington rode with William Quantrill during his bloody forays into Lawrence, Kan., and Centralia, Mo., during the Civil War. When the war ended they returned home to take up robbery. In 1870, the Farringtons, assisted by William Barton and Bill Taylor, pulled off a daring train robbery outside Union City, Tenn. The gang stole more than $20,000 from the express car and disappeared into the countryside.

The capture of outlaw Levi Farrington (gun raised) in 1871.

The Southern Express Company brought detective William Pinkerton and his men into the case. They found Hilary Farrington in a deserted farmhouse in Verona, Mo., and captured him after a shootout. Pinkerton took the prisoner to the steamboat *Illinois*, for a boat ride down the Mississippi to jail. While trying to escape, Farrington grabbed a revolver from one of the guards but lost his balance and was knocked overboard. The paddle wheel on the stern crushed him to death.

Levi Farrington was tracked down a year later in Farmington, Ill. He was taken to the Obion County Jail in Union City, where a vigilante band broke in on him one night and shot him to death.

REF.: *CBA;* Horan, *The Pinkertons;* Nash, *Bloodletters and Badmen;* Rowan, *The Pinkertons.*

Farrow, Thomas, b.c.1863, and **Crotch, Walter**, b.1877, and **Hart, Frederick Duncan Tabrum**, b.1877, Brit., fraud. In the early years of the twentieth century, Thomas Farrow made a sport of lambasting the "Big Five" of the British banking world for what he considered licensed usury. Farrow outlined his beliefs in a controversial book titled *In the Moneylenders' Clutches: Shylock at the Bar, Land Banks for England,* and *Banks for the People.* He argued for the creation of a People's Bank to end the suffering of the poor people and the crime of usury. Unfortunately for the people who regarded him as a popular hero and champion of the underdog, Farrow and his associates turned out to be the real shylocks in one of the largest bank frauds of the time.

The bank was incorporated in 1907 with a working capital of £1 million. Farrow's partner in the venture was Walter Crotch, a distinguished Dickens scholar and non-fiction author. Farrow's customers never knew that the bank had never been formally recognized. The Institute of Bankers refused to sanction the enterprise and its checks could only be cleared through cash.

Farrow's was little more than a savings club, and the losses on its balance sheet were cleverly disguised by the auditor, Frederick Hart. In 1920, the bank received a tender offer from the New York investment firm of Norton, Read & Co. Farrow's asking price was £500,000 plus an additional £100,000 for Crotch and himself. In August, an independent auditor from the Read Company made a shocking discovery. The balance sheets which had reported a six-and-a-quarter percent dividend were false. Farrows was in the red £2.8 million, despite claimed assets of more than £4.6 million. Just before Christmas 1920, the bank suspended payments to its customers and closed for good.

Farrow, Crotch, and Hart were indicted and for issuing false financial reports. Their Christmas holiday was spent in Brixton Prison, a hard fall for these once shining stars of the financial district. A naive faith that in time religion would somehow come to their rescue to bail out the company had proven to be an illusion. Guided by this faith, Farrow and Crotch had juggled their books to reflect a false profit.

In June 1921, all three were found Guilty of fraud. Farrow and Crotch were sentenced to hard labor for four years each, and the bookkeeper Hart received twelve months of hard labor.

REF.: *CBA;* Nicholls, *Crime Within the Square Mile.*

Farwell, Hartwell, prom. 1922, U.S., mansl. The charred remains of Theophil Hosten were found in a flaming haystack three miles outside of Portage, Wis., on Jan. 12, 1922, by three local men attempting to put out the fire before it destroyed their property. Hosten was identified by a padlock found in his pocket. The padlock opened the doors of a garage in nearby Dane County. When last seen the night before, Hosten was making his way to the home of his fiancée, Alice Farwell, who lived on a farm she owned jointly with her brother Hartwell Farwell.

District Attorney T.G. Lewis and Sheriff William McCormick suspected Hartwell. There was bad blood between the men ever since Alice began seeing Hosten. Hartwell was a jealous, possessive brother who was not anxious to see someone like Hosten lay claim to the family farm. Tire tracks leading away from the hay stack identically matched Hart Farwell's automobile, which resulted in his arrest the day after the murder.

In the Dane County Jail in Madison, Farwell confessed to killing Hosten on Jan. 10, 1922, using a .32-caliber pistol. He shot Hosten down in self-defense, Farwell claimed. The Hosten had picked up a stick and had threatened him. Afterward the body had been moved to several locations before it was left in the hay pile in Columbia County.

In court the long history of the Farwell-Hosten feud was recounted. Each man had threatened the other with violence from time to time. But Farwell's contention that he acted in self-defense earned him a reduced charge of second-degree manslaughter. He was sentenced to seven years in prison, the maximum sentence. When he was discharged from Waupun Penitentiary he found that Alice had married Harry G. Phillips. He did not care much for him either, and began a brand new feud.

REF.: *CBA;* Derleth, *Wisconsin Murders.*

Fashion Plates, The, See: **Hudson Dusters.**

Fasi, Frank F., 1920- , Case of, U.S., polit. corr.-brib. Frank Fasi was a powerful three-term mayor of Honolulu, who was indicted on two counts of bribery, Mar. 21, 1977, after he allegedly conspired with his campaign manager Harry C.C. Chung to receive $500,000 in kickbacks from real-estate developer Hal Hansen.

In return for the money that was pumped into his campaign war chest, Mayor Fasi promised to select Hansen's firm, Oceanside Properties, Inc., as the contractor in a future urban renewal project targeted for downtown Honolulu. The company was awarded the contract for the $50 million Kukui Plaza on Feb. 5, 1971.

The case was brought to trial in December 1977, but the bribery charges were dropped by Circuit Court Judge Toshimi

Sodetani when Hansen, the state's key witness, refused to testify about alleged payoffs. Hansen refused to cooperate because he feared that his testimony would be used against him in a separate, but pending federal case charging the developer with mail and wire fraud.

Fasi blamed his troubles on Governor George Ariyoshi, whom he accused of blocking his gubernatorial bid. In 1978 the mayor ran for the office of governor but lost to his old adversary. REF.: *CBA.*

Fasoli, Alfredo, and **Pallesi,** prom. 1928, Italy, fraud. Alceo Dossena was perhaps the greatest of the twentieth century master art forgers. The little Italian stonecutter replicated perfect masterpieces from his studio deep in the heart of Rome. Using ancient marble dug out of the Greek ruins, he created what appeared to be genuine fifteenth century tomb pieces, Grecian goddesses, and marble fonts. At first he created his sculptures as a hobby, not believing that anyone would pay much for a copy.

An antique dealer named Alfredo Fasoli had an eye for beauty, and offered to peddle the stonecutter's work to interested parties on the international market. A Roman art dealer bought what he believed to be a centuries-old masterpiece for a handsome price. Fasoli and his accomplice Pallesi pocketed most of the money, giving Dossena only a taste. The two art dealers put him on a permanent retainer and within the next few years, Dossena's imitations were sold to the New York Metropolitan Museum of Art, the Cleveland Museum, and a score of private art investors including William Randolph Hearst and Helen Clay Frick. The museums and wealthy collectors had easily been duped. Dossena had purportedly invented a chemical process that gave his work the look and feel of a priceless antiquity.

Not until Dossena blew the whistle on his confederates in 1928 was the fraud exposed. Representatives of the Frick estate visited Italy to investigate the collection they were about to buy. At the same time Dossena was shocked and angry to learn that his work was being misrepresented and passed off as ancient masterpieces.

Dossena filed a $66,000 lawsuit against Fasoli and Pallesi. The artist was cleared of all wrongdoing by the government, and continued his work until his death seven years later. On Mar. 9, 1933, an auction of "genuine" Alceo Dossena's was held in the grand ballroom of the Plaza Hotel in New York. Thirty-nine pieces were auctioned for $9,125. Each purchaser was given a certificate from the Italian government certifying the work as a "genuine fake."

REF.: *CBA;* MacDougall, *Hoaxes.*

Fatah, Al, See: **Arafat, Yasir.**

Fauchet, Claude, 1744-93, Fr., rebel. Member of the Legislative Assembly in 1791, and the National Convention in 1792. He was later appointed the constitutional bishop of Calvados. He joined the Girondist movement in 1792, and was executed along with the movement's leaders in 1793. REF.: *CBA.*

Faulds, Henry, 1843-1930, criminol. Henry Faulds was an early pioneer in fingerprint science. After obtaining his medical degree in England, Faulds spent his later years trying to convince Scotland Yard that fingerprints left at the scene of a crime could be identified as easily as those taken from the prisoner at the station house. Faulds' interest in fingerprinting dated to 1880, when he published a letter on the subject in *Nature.* Between 1886 and 1888, Faulds offered to demonstrate his findings to Scotland Yard, but they were not interested. Law

Criminologist Henry Faulds, early-day fingerprint pioneer.

enforcement agencies of the period relied on the Bertillon system of body measurements to classify prisoners. Others, notably Sir Edward Henry, Juan Vucetich of Argentina, and Sir Francis Galton made the breakthroughs at the turn of the century that brought fingerprinting into wide use. See: **Bertillon, Alphonse; Faurot, Joseph Arthur.**

REF.: *CBA;* Faulds, *Guide to Finger Print Identification;* Scott, *The Concise Encyclopedia of Crime and Criminals;* Wilton, *Fingerprints: History, Law and Romance.*

Faulkner, Richard, 1792-1807, Brit., mur. For the youthful British murderer Richard Faulkner, the march to the hangman's noose was an unpleasant side-trip into terror.

Faulkner was only fifteen when he murdered George Burnham, the son of a widow. Mrs. Burnham had greatly offended Faulkner by accidentally throwing garbage on his head. When Faulkner encountered her son George one day, he smashed the boy over the head with a wooden plank and then strung him up from the beam of a nearby barn in retaliation.

Faulkner was an unrepentant murderer who repeatedly defied the judge and the court of the Wisbech Assizes with angry emotional outbursts. He was sentenced to die on July 10, 1807, but in the last few days of his life Faulkner refused to give penance for his crime and became so unruly that his jailers were forced to invent a little ruse to trick him into docility. They located a 12-year-old boy who strongly resembled his victim. He was dressed in Burnham's clothes and was told to walk by the cell. He was so convincing that Faulkner turned to jelly; he truly believed that he had seen a ghost who had come to warn him about the afterlife. Faulkner became quiet and repentant right up to the moment he was hanged on July 13, 1807.

REF.: Atholl, *Shadow of the Gallows; CBA;* Wilson, *Children Who Kill.*

Fauntleroy, Henry, 1784-1824, Brit., forg. Though they might commit serious crimes, gentlemen were not often hanged in the England of old. So the public was convinced that banker Henry Fauntleroy, scheduled to be executed for forgery, would somehow evade the hangman. Fauntleroy, virtually raised in his father's bank, took control of it as a very young man, only to discover that it was nearly insolvent. Rather than let it fold, however, he began to cover its accounts by gambling, forging deposits, using one account to cover another, and similar forays into illegality. He was so successful at maintaining the illusion of prosperity that he lived the illusion, too. He kept mistresses, bought multiple houses, and enjoyed travel and high living. The house of cards collapsed in 1824, however, when an estate held by the Bank of England, for which Fauntleroy was an executor, was found to have been wiped clean. He had taken the proceeds from the sale of stocks and bonds and had transferred them to his own bank. He was eventually found to have embezzled at least £500,000 of other people's money.

Tried amid much fanfare, Fauntleroy was found Guilty and sentenced to hang. The public opposed the death penalty for such a crime, however, and tried to obtain a commutation from King George IV. But the Bank of England, determined to use Fauntleroy as an example for other would-be embezzlers, brought pressure to bear, and on Nov. 30, 1824, the forger was hanged. A crowd of nearly 100,000, most of whom believed they would witness some sort of last-minute reprieve or even an abduction of the convicted man by his friends, gathered to watch. Fauntleroy was hanged as scheduled, but many continued to believe that he was later resuscitated and was alive and well on the continent.

REF.: Bleackley, *Hangmen of England;* Browne, *The Rise of Scotland Yard; CBA;* Cooper, *Lesson of the Scaffold.*

Faure, Felix François, 1841-99, Fr., pres., (unsolv.) assass. The weak and ineffectual Felix François Faure was the seventh president of the Third Republic from 1895 until the time of his death. His term was marked by his steadfast refusal to reopen the Alfred Dreyfus case, and on-going turmoil with Britain in the Sudan.

Faure maintained a comely, vivacious mistress named Marguerite Steinheil who joined him in his bedroom at the Elysée Palace each afternoon between pressing matters of state. Marguerite would occasionally administer an aphrodisiac and it may have been one too many doses of her love potion that finally did him in on Feb. 16, 1899. Whether Faure died with Marguerite at his side was never established. Years later Steinheil would argue that she was only visiting the president in order to assist him in the writing of a French political history. As a token of his appreciation, Faure had presented her with an exquisite pearl necklace in a gold box, which can be seen in published photos appearing in Steinheil's 1912 autobiography, *My Memoirs.*

Though she was never implicated in the death of President Faure, she was later accused of killing her mother and husband in Paris on the night of May 30, 1908. She was acquitted of these crimes based on a skillful defense presented by her attorney, and the lingering suspicions that her husband, the painter, was a homosexual. Steinheil lived to the age of eighty-five. After her death in 1954, the long-suppressed allegations of her sexual trysts with the French president and others began to leak out. See: **Steinheil, Jeanne-Marguerite.**

REF.: Brophy, *The Meaning of Murder; CBA.*

Faurot, Joseph Arthur, 1872-1942, U.S., law enfor. off. A member of the New York Police Department, Faurot is credited with instituting the use of fingerprinting in New York. He attended the 1904 Louisiana Purchase Exposition in St. Louis and there witnessed a demonstration of fingerprinting by Scotland Yard experts. British police had by then adopted this method of identification over the then-popular Bertillon system. The St. Louis Police Department was so impressed by the demonstration that this force became the first in the U.S. to adopt the use of fingerprinting.

Faurot returned to New York and attempted to persuade his superiors to adopt the same system. Police Commissioner William McAdoo, however, sent Faurot to England to study the new fingerprinting identification system at Scotland Yard. When he returned, he was able to identify several known criminals through fingerprinting. Faurot also solved a number of murder cases through fingerprints. His successes led the NYPD to adopt fingerprinting as the chief method of criminal identification in 1911. Faurot continued to be its leading exponent until his retirement in 1930. He is acknowledged as the founder of fingerprint identification in the U.S. See: **Bertillon, Alphonse; Faulds, Henry.** REF.: *CBA.*

Faust, Reinhold, b.1843, U.S., bomb. For twenty-one years Reinhold Faust harbored a terrible secret. If he told it to the Chicago police, or officials from the National Deposit Company, with whom he had done business those many years, he might be returned to the Joliet Penitentiary.

His troubles began on Nov. 16, 1917, when he attended the opera *Dinorah* at the Auditorium Theatre. Midway through the first act Faust left his seat and headed toward the lobby. There was a burst of flame from a luminous object and the blood-curdling scream of a woman. It was a bomb, but before it could be exploded Fireman Michael Corrigan pulled out the wick. The next week Banker James Forgan received an extortion letter demanding $100,000 or possible death from a bomb explosion. Faust was arrested by the police for sending a threatening letter, but he was not charged with planting the bomb at the Auditorium Theatre.

While being led to jail, Faust threw away the key to a safety deposit box where he had stashed four black-powder gas pipe bombs. He left to serve fourteen months in Joliet for bothering Forgan, but was forced to continue paying the rental fee on the safety box for the next twenty-one years.

Faust was in a bind. He could not get at the bombs because he did not have a key. He also could not ask the safety deposit company to open it for him. Faust continued to pay his $10-a-month rental fee until the company moved in the early winter months of 1939.

In March Faust was reunited with his gas-pipe bombs in the courtroom of Judge Matthew Hartigan. In consideration of his advanced age, Judge Hartigan cleared Faust of his past crimes. Said the aging bomber: "I was fanatic enough to do that thing. I wanted only to scare people. I am just a peaceable old man now." REF.: *CBA.*

Fausta (Flavia Maximiana Fausta), 289-326, Roman., empress, assass. Daughter of Maximianus Herculius, she married Constantine the Great in 307, and gave birth to emperors Constantine II, Constantius II, and Constans. She is rumored to have convinced Constantine to execute Crispus, his eldest son by another marriage. It is believed that Constantine had Fausta suffocated in a heated bath when the accusations she made against Crispus were proven false. REF.: *CBA.*

Faustina (Annia Galeria Faustina), prom. c.125-75., Roman., pros. Annia Galeria Faustina was a prominent courtesan of Rome who continued to entertain her clients long after her marriage to an attorney. She would only engage in sexual acts with men who were willing to meet her exorbitant prices.

REF.: Bullough, *Illustrated History of Prostitution; CBA.*

Faversham Witches, prom. 1645, Brit., witchcraft. Joan Williford, Joan Cariden, and Jane Holt were executed for witchcraft in Faversham, Kent, on Sept. 29, 1645. Their deaths were mandated by the Inquisitors after Williford was forced to "confess" to having entered into a covenant with the Devil twenty years earlier. Holt, Elizabeth Harris, and Joan Argoll were named as three other witches in a case typical of the witchcraft persecutions of seventeenth century England. Although accurate court records do not exist from that time, popularly published chapbooks detailing the confessions served to fan the hysteria that spilled over into the early years of the next century.

REF.: *CBA; The Examination, Confession, Trial and Execution of Joan Williford;* Robbins, *The Encyclopedia of Witchcraft and Demonology.*

Favor, Arsenio, 1948-   , Case of, U.S., mur. No one was really sure if Dr. Arsenio Favor harbored criminal intent against his wife Nenita at the time of her death on Feb. 8, 1977. The jury that acquitted him in the second of two murder trials had a mass of circumstantial evidence, that was not convincing in and of itself. There was little else for them to do but acquit the Filipino doctor. Still, there were lingering, unresolved questions. How could Nenita Favor have died so suddenly?

Dr. Favor arrived in the U.S. in 1973. He was joined by his wife a year later. The couple settled in Fort Lee, N.J., but continued to live as citizens of the Philippines. Dr. Favor joined the staff of the Harlem Hospital as a surgical resident, and was known to have suffered through an unhappy marriage.

A week before her death, Nenita was operated on for the removal of a benign tumor. On Feb. 8, Favor brought her back to the hospital when a surgical wound became inflamed. She was admitted to the surgical ward for some post-operative treatment, but died under mysterious circumstances the next night. The New York Medical Examiner's Office investigated the matter, but was unable to determine a logical cause of death, or the presence of a deadly chemical substance in the tissue.

A neighbor later reported finding a half-empty vial of sucostrin, a muscle relaxant, in Dr. Favor's medicine cabinet. The drug is typically used in surgery and is administered in small quantities. Sucostrin can paralyze the respiratory muscles and bring on instant death if used carelessly. Of greater concern to medical examiners investigating Dr. Favor, was the fact that sucostrin contains choline which was also found in the body. A lethal dose of the drug would be all but impossible to trace in the autopsy.

It was up to District Attorney Robert Morgenthau to supply a motive for murder, which wasn't difficult given Dr. Favor's past marital problems. The physician was linked to Dorca Jordan, a woman Favor had been seeing for some time before his wife's death. Once Nenita was out of the way, Dr. Favor planned to move back to the Philippines with her.

The Filipino doctor was twice tried for murder. The first trial ended in a hung jury on June 10, 1978, when the jury reported to the judge that they were hopelessly deadlocked after twenty-five hours of deliberation. On May 5, 1979, Favor was acquitted in the Supreme Court of Manhattan, when the jury found the evidence in the case unsubstantial to merit the return of a Guilty verdict. REF.: *CBA*.

Favras, Marquis de (Thomas de Mahy), 1744-90, Fr., treas. Royalist at the outset of the French Revolution, he planned the royal family's unsuccessful escape from Paris in 1789. He was later taken captive and hanged. REF.: *CBA*.

Favre, Jules (Gabriel Claude Jules), 1809-80, Fr., lawyer. Garnered fame with defense of Felice Orsini, who had failed in an attempt to assassinate Napoleon III in 1858. He led the opposition to the Second Empire from 1863-68, and aided in the negotiations of the Treaty of Frankfurt, which brought the Franco-Prussian War to an end. He also served in the Senate from 1876-80. REF.: *CBA*.

Fawkes, Guy (AKA: Guido Fawkes, John Johnson), 1570-1606, Brit., treas. Guy Fawkes was the well-educated son of a court official in York, England. He had been raised as a Protestant, but when his father died, his mother remarried and Fawkes took the religion of his stepfather, a Catholic. Fawkes became a fervent Catholic and, at the age of twenty-three, sold off his considerable land holdings and traveled to Flanders where he fought with the Spanish army. Fawkes' religious dedication soon brought him to the attention of Thomas Winter, who belonged to a fanatical Catholic group intent upon overthrowing the Protestant government of England, which had enacted punitive and cruel laws against the Catholic minority of the country.

Fawkes was taken into the group, which was headed by Robert Catesby, son of a wealthy squire, and Sir Everard Digby. Fawkes became the chief organizer of what later became known as the infamous Gunpowder Plot. Using the alias John Johnson, Fawkes rented a house close to the Parliament building, posing as a servant to another conspirator, Thomas Percy. The conspirators met in this house and began tunneling under the House of Lords on Dec. 11, 1604. They abandoned the tunnel two months later, when only halfway through a nine-foot-thick wall they found a passageway into the basement of the Parliament building. Here the conspirators planted thirty-six barrels of gunpowder which they covered with iron bars and rocks so that when the powder exploded, it would rip the entire building to pieces and kill all within, including all the Protestant members of Parliament and King James I.

Guy Fawkes, fourth from right, with fellow conspirators of the Gunpowder Plot.

On the night of Nov. 4-5, 1605, Fawkes prepared to explode the gunpowder but one of his fellow conspirators, William Parker, Lord Monteagle, gave the plot away. Parker had converted to Catholicism when marrying. He had joined the plotters but then reverted to his old faith of Protestantism. Parker then felt it was his duty to turn in his fellow conspirators and reported the plot to Robert Cecil, secretary of state. His reward was a pension of £700 a year. Sir Thomas Knyvet, a magistrate, led a group of men into the vaults beneath the Parliament building and arrested Fawkes just as he was to ignite the gunpowder.

Fawkes was taken to the Tower of London where he refused to answer Cecil's questions. James I ordered Fawkes tortured and, after repeated punishments, he broke his silence on the rack. Fawkes signed a confession, gave his real name and the names of the rest of the conspirators. He was tried and convicted of treason on Jan. 27, 1606. Catesby and Percy were hunted down and killed in a gunfight. On Jan. 31, 1606, Fawkes, Winter, Robert Keyes, Ambrose Rokewood, and four others were hanged, beheaded, and drawn and quartered. Fawkes, a handsome man with a rich auburn beard, showed courage to the last, refusing to denounce his belief in Catholicism. Guy Fawkes Day in England is celebrated on Nov. 5, wherein Fawkes is burned in effigy. See: **Gunpowder Plot.** REF.: *CBA*.

Fay, Floyd (AKA: Buzz), 1952- , U.S., (wrong. convict.) mur. A carpenter was wrongly convicted of murdering a store owner, and spent two-and-a-half years in prison before his name was cleared.

On the evening of Mar. 28, 1978, a masked man armed with a sawed-off shotgun walked into Andy's Carry-Out in Perrysburg, Ohio, where Fred Ery, twenty-six, was working behind the counter. Ery called the man an obscene name, and the gunman shot him in the neck and fled. Before dying four hours later, Ery said, "It looked like Buzz, but it couldn't have been." On Mar. 29 Floyd "Buzz" Fay, twenty-six, of Toledo, Ohio, was arrested. Based on Ery's identification and the misinterpreted results of two lie detector tests, Fay was convicted of aggravated murder on Aug. 11, 1978. His conviction was upheld in the Ohio Court of Appeals on July 5, 1979.

Imprisoned at the London Correctional Institute in London, Ohio, Fay was represented by public defender Adrian Cimerman, twenty-eight. Following tips implicating three teenagers, Cimerman located the driver of the getaway car, who was serving in the U.S. Army in West Germany. The youth confessed in exchange for immunity, and incriminated Cliff Markland, nineteen, and William Quinn, nineteen. They were charged with the murder, and on Oct. 30, 1980, Fay was released and all charges were dropped on Nov. 17, 1980. He returned to his job building bridges and crusaded against lie detector tests. REF.: *CBA*.

Fay, Joseph S., d.1972, and **Bove, James V.**, 1902-56, U.S., consp.-rack.-extor. In 1918 Joseph S. Fay joined the union in Newark, and soon was elected delegate of the New Jersey Local 825 of the Operating Engineers Union. He was then elected business agent "for life" of the Local, representing men who ran hoists, engines, steam shovels, and derricks. By the time he was named vice president of the international union, he wielded enormous power, and was demanding kickbacks from contractors.

In 1942, Fay and James Bove, also an international vice-president, were in charge of union labor for the Delaware Aqueduct Water Supply construction project. They threatened the contractors with a strike unless extortion money was paid. After a police investigation, the two were indicted in May 1943 for conspiring to extort $703,000 from the contractors. On Mar. 15, 1945, they were convicted of extortion, and on Apr. 5 they were each sentenced to eight-and-one-half to fifteen years and fined $500. Bove was also sentenced to ten to twenty years on grand larceny and forgery charges.

Fay still exercised power from Sing Sing prison. Politicians and labor leaders visited him frequently until Governor Thomas E. Dewey ordered the visits stopped and Fay transferred to Clinton Prison. He was paroled on Feb. 8, 1958, and died Aug. 10, 1972. The 54-year-old Bove died in Attica State Prison on June 27, 1956.

REF.: *CBA*; Danforth, *The D.A.'s Man*.

Fay, Larry, 1888-1932, U.S., org. crime. Larry Fay, the dapper, wealthy bootlegger of Broadway, had ambition to go beyond his gangster status, reaching into show business and even high society. He grew wealthy in the New York rackets and was killed over a petty pay raise. Fay began as a product of Manhattan's streets as a member of the Gophers. His mentors were racketeers and killers Owney Madden, "Big Frenchy" DeMange, and William P. "Big Bill" Duffy. He branched out on his own at the dawn of Prohibition, becoming a rum-runner. In 1920, Fay was driving a cab and took a fare to Montreal, Canada. There he discovered that he could buy a case of bonded Canadian whiskey for as little as $10 and loaded several cases in his cab. He drove this back to New York, hidden beneath a hollow area between the back seat and trunk of his cab. His profit was considerable.

Fay began taking regular trips to Canada in his cab, always returning with more liquor. He was stopped occasionally and fined for carrying the illegal substance. By 1922, Fay had built up a nest egg of more than $500,000 from his taxicab rum-running but, unlike other early-day bootleggers such as "Big Bill" Dwyer and George Remus, he stopped while he was ahead, using his funds to buy dozens of cabs and going into other rackets. A flashy dresser, Fay designed his own cabs, making them as stylish as himself. All of his taxis were loaded with nickel trimming; he installed lights for the first time on top of the cabs and even affixed lights to the sides of the cabs. All had musical horns whose mellifluous tone served as advertisements for his company and made the Fay cabs easily identifiable.

New York gangster Larry Fay, the role model for *The Great Gatsby*, shown at a police station, 1925.

Those who drove Fay's cabs were recruited for their brawn. When competing cab drivers tried to cut off Fay's cabs from fares or dominate a cabstand, the Fay men waded, fists flying, into rival taxi drivers. Moreover, Fay employed an army of strong-arm men who monitored the important cabstands along Broadway in Manhattan. If a Fay driver was faced with too many opposing drivers, Fay's thugs stepped in and settled the matter. The man in charge of these wide-ranging goon squads was Owney Madden, who had been one of the leaders of the Gopher Gang, Fay's alma mater.

Madden had been sent to Sing Sing for murder. When he was released in 1923, his old follower Fay gave him the job of goon squad leader in his taxi empire, a position that helped Madden reestablish himself in the underworld and a favor which Madden would never forget. He would repay Fay by backing the Broadway gangster in many new nightclubs, speakeasies, and rackets. Moreover, Fay arranged to end the long-standing feud between Madden and Big Frenchy DeMange, who had been one of the leaders of the fierce Hudson Dusters gang, rivals to Madden's Gophers. Madden and DeMange became close friends and merged their rackets, forming one of the most powerful criminal combines in New York during the 1920s. DeMange was given to investing in Broadway shows and favored ownership of nightclubs. Fay was influenced by the showboating DeMange and began to open a number of posh speakeasies himself, hiring expensive entertainers.

One of Fay's most profitable rackets was his control of milk deliveries throughout New York. Through carefully built-up contacts with New York politicians in Tammany Hall, Fay was able to muscle into the milk business. He organized all the milkmen and controlled this union with a tight fist, Madden's thugs beating up any milkman who proved reluctant in kicking back part of his dues to Fay's henchmen. He also levied a duty on each can of milk coming from every dairy in the area. Fay reaped millions through this racket, which was supported by corrupt political boss James J. Hines, a Tammany powerhouse who dispensed racket support to those who made regular payoffs to him and his political hacks and police officials on the pad.

With his fortune goading him to higher aspirations, Fay purchased a huge estate in Great Neck, N.Y., and gave immense, lavish parties at his mansion, inviting the wealthy and the socially elite who knew him vaguely as a high-society bootlegger. Fay's parties were thick with Broadway talent, and he always employed full, tuxedoed orchestras. Social leaders mixed with gangsters and molls, while armies of servants served seemingly endless trays of gourmet food. Buffet tables stretched across Fay's enormous dining room and were repeated throughout the four-tier patio.

Author F. Scott Fitzgerald, who then lived near Fay's sprawling mansion, attended several parties and studied the long-faced gangster. Fay seemed disinterested at his own fetes, strolling in his elegantly tailored suit through a phalanx of strangers who did not know him; trailing behind Fay were always a number of silent, dark-complexioned men, his bodyguards, careful to make sure that everyone observed proper conduct and no one annoyed the boss. Fitzgerald would use Fay as his role model for the gangster classic, *The Great Gatsby*. Fay, of course, lacked all of the fictional Gatsby's physical attractiveness, charm, and charisma. He was tough and culture-hungry, looking for recognition as a legitimate businessman.

To that end Fay opened nightclub after nightclub, taking in a raucous, hard-drinking, brassy blonde, Mary Louise Cecilia Guinan. Everyone knew her as "Texas Guinan," nicknamed after the state of her birth. She had been a silent film star, later a singer, but when she teamed up with Fay she became his star attraction, a bold and quick-witted hostess who greeted every customer with the same salutation: "Hello, sucker!" She was the star of the El Fey Club, which was padlocked many times for serving liquor during the Roaring Twenties but always managed to open up again, often at a new location. Going through its doors were the most celebrated people in New York, including newspaper columnists Walter Winchell and Mark Hellinger. Hellinger would later tell Fay's story on film in *The Roaring Twenties*, with James Cagney essaying the role of the bootlegging Fay.

As the riches poured into Fay's coffers, he traveled to Europe, thinking of opening clubs in Paris and London.

Fay's speakeasy partner, Texas Guinan.

He thought better of the idea and returned to the U.S. with dozens of trunks loaded with tailor-made Bond Street clothes. He was a clothes horse, one who owned several dozen suits of the finest quality. Hundreds of silk shirts filled a large dressing room in Fay's mansion, and scores of shoes lined the racks of his closets. His hats were made by a special hatmaker and his six-car garage was occupied by a Marmon, a Pierce-Arrow, a Cadillac, and assorted sports cars.

Fay's fortunes went into sharp reverse in the early 1930s. His clubs began to close and his milk racket collapsed when union members revolted and threw out the racketeers. Fay opened one last club, the Casa Blanca, but it was a pale imitation of the nightspots Texas Guinan had made famous years earlier. The club was cheaply furnished and the entertainment consisted of a stand-up comedian and some overweight chorus girls. Fay wandered about his mansion, now empty of glamorous guests, and he spent most of his days worrying how he would meet his weekly payroll. He disbanded most of his gang members and cut employee salaries. One of these hapless employees, Edward

The lovely Evelyn Crowell, who became Mrs. Larry Fay.

Maloney, a man with a wife and four children, told Fay that he could not survive on a half salary. Fay merely shrugged. Maloney got drunk, and, on the night of Jan. 1, 1932, staggered into Fay's office, pulled out a gun, and shot his gangster employer four times, killing him. Maloney was sent to Sing Sing Prison for eight to sixteen years. Fay went to a cemetery with few mourners to accompany him. At his graveside stood a beautiful blonde, the former Evelyn Crowell, who had become Mrs. Larry Fay only a few years earlier. She told newsmen at the funeral services that she knew nothing of her husband's underworld activities. To her, Larry Fay was a businessman and loving husband. None of Fay's Broadway friends or his political associates appeared to see him lowered into the earth. The press gave the death of this once-powerful bootlegger little play. It was an ignominious end for the colorful gangster, who was celebrated in movies and high fiction.

REF.: *CBA*; Churchill, *The Year the World Went Mad*; Fried, *The Rise and Fall of the Jewish Gangster in America*; Horan, *The Desperate Years*; Katz, *Uncle Frank*; Kobler, *Ardent Spirits*; Levine, *Anatomy of a Gangster*; Lynch, *Criminals and Politicians*; Messick, *Lansky*; ____, *Secret File*; Nash, *Almanac of World Crime*; ____, *Zanies*; Peterson, *The Mob*; Sann, *Kill the Dutchman*; ____, *The Lawless Decade*; Thompson and Raymond, *Gang Rule in New York*; Walker, *The Night Club Era*; (FICTION), Fitzgerald, *The Great Gatsby*; (FILM), *The Great Gatsby*, 1926; *The Roaring Twenties*, 1939; *The Great Gatsby*, 1949, *The Great Gatsby*, 1974.

Fay, Peter Thorp, 1929 - , U.S., jur. Appointed by President Richard Nixon to the Southern District Court of Florida in 1970, has served on the Judicial Conference committee designed to implement provisions of the criminal justice act since 1975, and was appointed by President Jimmy Carter to the Fifth Circuit Court in 1981, which has since been redesignated as the Eleventh Circuit. REF.: *CBA*.

Faysom, David, 1959- , U.S., mur. On Oct. 6, 1981, David Faysom, twenty-two, befriended 13-year-old Nicole Lee, who had run away from her home in Chicago. He bought her a meal and persuaded her to work for him as a prostitute. Nicole was reluctant and pretended to be sick to avoid appointments that Faysom arranged, according to Karen Brandon, eighteen, who formerly worked for Faysom. On Oct. 9, the pimp drove Lee and Brandon into an alley and ordered Lee to take off her clothes. He scolded her for not making enough money. He then told her to "Show me your heart," and shot her with a handgun. When she promised to make more money, he shot her again.

In January 1983, Faysom was convicted of murder, pandering,

armed violence, and unlawful restraint. On Feb. 16, Judge R. Eugene Pincham sentenced him to life in prison with no chance for parole. The judge later commuted the sentence to seventy years in prison. Brandon, who was originally charged with murder, pleaded guilty to concealing a homicide and was sentenced to a thirty-month probation. REF.: *CBA*.

Fazekas, Suzanne, d.1929, Hung., mur. The women of Nagyrev, Hung., an isolated village southeast of Budapest, while their husbands were away during WWI, took lovers from among the prisoners of war in nearby camps. After several years of such promiscuity, the war ended and the husbands returned. But domesticity no longer satisfied the women of Nagyrev, and with the help of local midwife Suzanne Fazekas, they began poisoning their husbands. Once the murders had begun, anyone considered inconvenient was in danger. Fazekas sold arsenic to the women, which she obtained by boiling the flypaper she purchased in bulk. Officials later learned that, for several years, Nagyrev and a neighboring village bought more flypaper than the rest of Hungary combined.

The first murder occurred as early as 1911, the beginning of a spree that lasted nearly twenty years and involved perhaps fifty women. Returning husbands, relatives who owned land, mothers-in-law, even recalcitrant children—few were exempt from Fazekas' poison. Added to the ease of perpetration was the fact that the

Hungarian mass murderer Suzanne Fazekas.

official who approved death certificates was Fazekas' cousin, so when outsiders noted the region's high death rate, a routine check of the death certificates showed nothing amiss. Further, the village of Nagyrev and its neighbor, Tiszakurt, were so isolated that no one paid much attention—until 1929, when two potential victims of Mrs. Ladislaus Szabo claimed that she had tried to poison them. Once she was arrested, she implicated another woman, Mrs. Bukenoveski, who confessed to having obtained arsenic from Fazekas five years earlier to kill her mother. The mother's body was exhumed and found to contain arsenic.

Fazekas was arrested, held only briefly when she refused to talk, and then released—free to run from house to house in Nagyrev, letting the women know what was happening, and telling the police whom to arrest. When they came for Fazekas again, she admitted them to her house, drank her own poison and died before their eyes. Thirty-eight women were arrested, chief among them Susanna Olah, the "White Witch of Nagyrev," who also sold arsenic and was believed to possess the power to protect the women from the law. Each woman had her own victims and reasons: Rosalie Sebestyen's husband bored her, Maria Szendi was tired of her husband always having "his own way"; Maria Varga could no longer put up with her husband, who had returned from the war blind—she preferred her young lover, but after five years disposed of him and his grandfather; Mrs. Kardos had an invalid son who was a burden to her—she found it easy to kill him because she had already eliminated a lover and her husband; Juliane Lipka killed, not for love but for real estate—in seven to eight years she disposed of seven relatives, gradually becoming the richest woman in the region.

Eventually, twenty-six women were tried for murder. Eight were sentenced to death and seven to life in prison. The rest received varying prison terms. Three of the women committed suicide. The bodies of those hanged were displayed as a warning to others.

REF.: *CBA;* Glaister, *The Power of Poison;* Nash, *Look For the Woman.*

Fazy, Jean Jacob (James Fazy), 1794-1878, Switz., lawyer. Placed in prison and fined for his radical republican beliefs. He led the opposition favoring a democratic constitution in 1841, and led the government of Geneva from 1846-53 and 1855-61. Prior to being deposed in 1862, he helped write the 1848 constitution and completely modernized the city. Upon his return to Geneva in 1871, from self-imposed exile in Paris, he became a professor of international law. REF.: *CBA.*

Fearn, Donald, 1919-42, U.S., tort.-rape-mur. Donald Fearn, twenty-three, lived in Pueblo, Colo., with his wife and child. He was fascinated by the torture and mutilation rituals of the Penitentes, formerly a sect of the Pueblo indians, and wanted to participate in a similar ritual. On Apr. 22, 1942, while his wife gave birth to another child, Fearn kidnapped Alice Porter, seventeen, and drove her to an old adobe church once used by the Penitentes. He laid her on a bloodstained altar, bound her naked body with red-hot wires, and tortured her through the night. He then raped the nearly dead girl, killed her by hitting her on the head with a hammer, and threw her body in a well. As he drove away, Fearn's car got stuck in mud and a farmer helped him out.

Later, when the girl's body was found, the farmer remembered helping Fearn, whose fingerprints were found on an awl. To protect him from lynch mobs, Fearn was tried in Canon City, Colo., where he was convicted. He went to the gas chamber on Oct. 22, 1942. REF.: *CBA.*

Featley, Daniel (Daniel Fairclough), 1582-1645, Brit., her. Incarcerated for criticizing Calvinist teaching and for his royalist sympathies in 1643. REF.: *CBA.*

Fedayeen, c.1948-   , kid.-terr.-bomb.-mur. The Fedayeen, which means "those who sacrifice themselves," are Palestinian guerrillas fighting to destroy Israel. Organized after the 1948 Arab-Israeli conflict, the terrorists, well-trained, financed, and armed, base themselves primarily in Jordan and Lebanon. Never organized into one unit, the Fedayeen are members of groups such as the Palestinian Liberation Organization (PLO), Al Fatah, and the Popular Front for the Liberation of Palestine (PFLP).

The Fedayeen grabbed world attention several times with dramatic attacks. In February 1970, they blew up forty-seven people flying Swissair from Israel to Zurich.

On May 30, 1972, three Japanese terrorists flew from Paris to Lydda Airport in Tel Aviv. After collecting their baggage, they took automatic guns from their suitcases and mowed down all bystanders. The terrorists, members of the Rengo Sekigun or United Red Army, fighting for international revolution, murdered twenty-eight people and wounded seventy-five. Kozo Okamoto, twenty-four, was the only surviving assassin. Two hours after the attack, Ghassan Kanafani, 36-year-old top planner for the PFLP, gave the organization credit for the slayings. One month later Kanafani was killed in retaliation by dynamite rigged to his sports car. Okamoto was tried, convicted, and sentenced to life in prison.

The Black September Organization, also supported by Fedayeen members, was responsible for assassinating Jordan's prime minister Wasfi Tal. On Sept. 5, 1972, Fedayeen zealots struck again, this time in Munich at the Olympic Games. Eight Arabs climbed a fence at 4 a.m. and entered a building where Israeli athletes and coaches were staying. The Arabs shot two Israelis and took nine hostages, hoping to negotiate the release of Arabs confined in Israel. Israel refused to negotiate. After arranging a plane for the terrorists and their hostages, German authorities trapped them at the airport. Five guerrillas died in the ensuing gunfire and all nine Israelis were killed by surviving gunmen Ibrahim Badran, Abd el Kadir el Dnawy, and Mohammed Abdullah. The Israeli victims were coaches Kehat Schorr, Amitzur Shapira, Andre Spitzer, and Moshe Weinberg, referees Yosef Gutfreund and Yacov Springer, and athletes David Berger, Zeev Friedman, Eliezer Halfin, Josef Romano, and Mark Slavin. The terrorists were held until Oct. 29, 1972, when two other Black September members hijacked a Lufthansa plane and demanded their release. The plane, originating in Lebanon, picked up the three in Yugoslavia and then flew to Tripoli, Libya, where the crew and passengers were released.

REF.: Becker, *Hitler's Children—The Story of the Baader-Meinhof Terrorist Gang; CBA;* Cluttterbuck, *Guerrillas and Terrorists;* Demaris, *Brothers In Blood: The International Terrorist Network;* Dobson and Payne, *Counterattack—The West's Battle Against the Terrorists;* ____, *The Terrorists—Their Weapons, Leaders and Tactics;* Hacker, *Crusaders, Criminals, Crazies: Terror and Terrorism In Our Time;* Laquer, *Terrorism;* Liston, *Terrorism;* O'Ballance, *The Language of Violence—The Blood Politics of Terrorism;* Schreiber, *The Ultimate Weapon—Terrorists and World Order;* Sloan, *Simulating Terrorism.*

Federal Bureau of Investigation (FBI), 1907-present, U.S., law enfor. agency. The origins of the Federal Bureau of Investigation, popularly known as the FBI, date back to Mar. 3, 1871, when Congress provided $50,000 for the then 9-month-old Department of Justice, specifying that this amount was for the "detection and prosecution of crime." At that time the Department of Justice had but one agent for such detection and prosecution. By 1894, the Department of Justice had on staff a special agent, later called a general agent, who supervised other "examiners" and investigated violations of the Indian Intercourse Act. Another special examiner investigated the treatment of federal prisoners and seven other examiners investigated the conduct of court officials. This scanty investigative force was responsible for reviewing "official acts, records and accounts," and investigated important cases throughout the country for U.S. attorneys.

In 1906, the Treasury Department loaned thirty-two agents to the Department of Justice, but such practices were cancelled in a bill by Congress on May 27, 1908. Encouraged by President Theodore Roosevelt, Attorney General Charles J. Bonaparte, on July 26, 1980, issued an order which created a permanent investigative force answerable only to the attorney general. This consisted of nine former Secret Service agents, thirteen "peonage investigators," and twelve examiners concerned with banking, bankruptcy, antitrust, naturalization, and land fraud. Not until Mar. 16, 1909, was this force given a name. On that date, Attorney General George W. Wickersham issued an order in which he christened the new force the "Bureau of Investigation." At the same time the title of the Chief Examiner was changed to "Chief of the Bureau of Investigation." First of these chiefs was Stanley W. Finch, who was really the first director of the Bureau.

U.S. attorneys, marshals, clerks of U.S. courts, and U.S. commissioners fell within the scrutiny of the Bureau, and its agents busied themselves with examining the records and documents produced by these federal employees, the accent of their investigations being financial. Not until 1910, with the passage of the White Slave Traffic Act, did Bureau agents launch into full-scale criminal investigations. In 1917, with America's entry into WWI, the Espionage, Selective Service, and Sabotage Acts were passed and this caused increased activity in the Bureau as they ran down spies, saboteurs, and draft dodgers. The National Motor Vehicle Theft Act was passed in October 1919 and this further increased the Bureau's burdens, its agents having to chase down thieves stealing autos and driving them across state lines.

The Bureau's leadership changed often during these embryonic times. Finch was replaced on Apr. 30, 1912, by Alexander Bruce Bielaski. William Allen was acting director in February 1919 before William J. Flynn became director in July 1919. He was succeeded by the noted private detective William J. Burns on Aug. 22, 1921. A day after Burns resigned, on May 10, 1924, J. (John) Edgar Hoover was appointed as the Bureau's director by Attorney General Harlan Fiske Stone. Hoover was to occupy this powerful position until his death in 1972, a reign of forty-eight years.

By the time Hoover took over the directorship of the Bureau, the organization had grown considerably. The original number

FBI headquarters on Pennsylvania Avenue in Washington, D.C., built at a cost of $126 million and named after the Bureau's most durable director, J. Edgar Hoover.

of thirty-two agents had expanded to 346 and these investigators were supported by 294 non-investigative employees who served as clerks, forensic experts, and administrative personnel. Nine Bureau field offices were established in 1920 and these offices, directed by a field superintendent, were answerable to the main headquarters in Washington, D.C. The field superintendents were renamed special agents in charge.

During the Harding Administration, William J. Burns had his hands full with investigating widespread political corruption. The Teapot Dome Scandal, which reached into the White House, was only one of the problems facing the indefatigable Burns. His agents were also battling political radicals who spread terrorism and, in the Deep South, the rise of the Ku Klux Klan brought about civil rights violations which were investigated by Bureau agents. There was corruption inside the Bureau with devious agents, such as Gaston B. Means, who acted as a bagman or liaison between Harding Administration employees and corrupt businessmen who were busy stealing government lands and funds.

Hoover, young and inexperienced, was nevertheless honest. He loathed Means and other agents of his ilk and only accepted the Stone appointment as director if he were allowed to clean the Bureau's house. He was given these broad powers and Hoover busily went about weeding unreliable and dishonest Bureau members out of the 444 Special Agents, along with thoroughly screening the remaining 200 non-agent employees. Hoover abolished the seniority rule of promotion and instituted appraisals based on performance of employees.

Hoover had joined the Bureau in 1917 and, at the height of the Red Scare in 1919, became special assistant to the attorney general, A. Mitchell Palmer. It was Hoover who prepared the legal briefs that allowed Mitchell to act against the lunatic radicals who began exploding bombs in Washington, D.C., and New York in 1919, and it was Hoover who urged Mitchell to order the Red Raids, a nationwide arrest sweep of all suspected anarchists, socialists, Bolsheviks, and other far left radicals.

After Hoover's takeover of the Bureau, strict new rules were instituted. Recruited agents had to be between the ages of twenty-five and thirty-five, and had to have a law or an accounting degree. Hoover regularly toured the field offices and imposed tight regulations on conduct and procedure. He and his specially picked aides established laboratory and identification divisions for the Bureau. A manual of rules and regulations was written and issued to all agents. New agents had to undergo rigorous training. The name "Bureau of Investigation" was changed to the "United States Bureau of Investigation" on July 1, 1932. The Bureau also assumed jurisdiction of U.S. kidnaping and extortion cases at this time. On July 1, 1935, Congress officially renamed the "United States Bureau of Investigation" the "Federal Bureau of Investigation," the name it now bears.

From 1924 to 1934 the Bureau maintained between 581 to 842 employees but the organization did not come into the media limelight or catch the public eye until the early 1930s when it actively fought a bloody war with a host of infamous kidnapers and bank robbers. These included the Barker Brothers, Charles Arthur "Pretty Boy" Floyd, George "Baby Face" Nelson, John Dillinger, George "Machine Gun" Kelly, and Alvin Karpis. It was in this era that FBI men were given the name "G-Men," largely due to Hoover's fertile imagination. Hoover was publicity-conscious and spent considerable effort promoting the image of the FBI as a crime-busting organization, eventually overcoming the public's infatuation with the bank robbers and kidnapers of the early 1930s.

FBI agents were greatly hampered in making serious arrests since they were not allowed to carry arms. Following the ruthless gangster slaying of an unarmed FBI agent and other law enforcement officers in the notorious Kansas City Massacre of 1933, federal legislation was passed, which allowed agents to make arrests, to bear arms and use them. Up to this time, FBI agents could not make independent arrests, but had to get the approval of local law enforcement agencies to do so and this was always a joint arrest arrangement. Local law enforcement officials also had to approve of the use of firearms by agents on specific cases up to this time.

Once agents were allowed to carry and use guns, they were

trained in the use of all types of automatic weapons, including submachine guns, and effectively employed these weapons in subduing the gangs of the 1930s. Although Hoover and his men triumphed over the independent kidnapers and bank robbers of the 1930s, the Bureau, as critics later pointed out, did not aggressively investigate and dismantle the operations of the national crime cartel or syndicate which came into existence as early as 1929.

The Bureau's authority was strengthened in May and June 1934 with the passage of a series of anti-crime bills enacted by Congress. This legislation allowed the Bureau to investigate cases involving stolen property, racketeering, bank robbery, and flight to avoid prosecution. The Bureau increased its work force considerably during the 1930s in combating the national crime wave. In the late 1930s, with the rise of fascism in Europe and in the U.S., particularly the development of the German-American Bunds, which swore allegiance to Hitler's Third Reich, the FBI became highly active in ferreting out spies and saboteurs. Throughout WWII, the Bureau worked with the Army and Navy in combating espionage and sabotage, thus becoming an intelligence agency as well as a law enforcement force. Later federal legislation clearly authorized the FBI to continue its intelligence-gathering operations inside the U.S., but this sometimes brought the Bureau into conflict with the Central Intelligence Agency, the CIA, which was and is responsible for intelligence operations outside the U.S.

During WWII, more than 13,000 people were employed by the Bureau. Following the war, the FBI roster was reduced to about 10,000 employees. Hoover's authority within the FBI was supreme, although his close friend, Clyde Tolson, who had been Hoover's aide since 1936, became associate director in 1947. The late 1940s and 1950s saw the Bureau concentrate on Soviet espionage in the heyday of the Cold War. The Bureau did solve many spectacular cases during the 1950s, including the mass bombing committed by Jack Gilbert Graham, the Brink's robbery, and the kidnapings of Bobby Greenlease and Peter Wienberger. In 1950, the Bureau instituted its "Ten Most Wanted Fugitives" list which continues to this day in an enlarged form.

In the 1960s, the Bureau dealt with civil rights violations and a new crime plague—skyjackings. Radical left wing groups advocating extreme violence—bombings, riots, mayhem, robbery, and even murder—also plagued the U.S. in the 1960s. The FBI doggedly pursued and successfully arrested members of the Weather Underground, Black Panther Party, and other anarchist groups. With the passage of the Organized Crime Control Act of 1970, the FBI became more active in investigating the activities of the crime syndicate, although Director Hoover had maintained for years that no such organization ever existed.

On May 2, 1972, Hoover's long, hard-fisted reign of the FBI came to an end when he died in his Washington, D.C., home. He was succeeded on May 3, 1972, by L. Patrick Gray III who instituted many changes inside the Bureau, including a new FBI Academy at the U.S. Marine Corps base in Quantico, Va. At this time, the Bureau was confronted with investigating the tangled web of the Watergate Scandal and, in this era of change, the Bureau appointed its first female agents. On Apr. 27, 1973, Gray was succeeded by William Ruckelshaus and he was, in turn, replaced by Clarence M. Kelley, a career law enforcement official, who became the director of the FBI on July 9, 1973.

On Feb. 23, 1978, William H. Webster replaced Kelley and John Otto replaced Webster as acting director on May 26, 1987. On Nov. 2, 1987, William Steele Sessions became director of the FBI and he remains in this position as of this writing. Sessions has had a distinguished career as a Department of Justice attorney, heading the Government Operations Section of the Criminal Division. He was later a federal judge before becoming Director of the FBI in 1987.

The Bureau presently functions as the chief federal agency investigating most serious federal crimes as well as maintaining an enormous clearing house of statistical information. More than 50 million fingerprints are on file in the FBI, the largest such repository in the world. These are cross-checked against criminals arrested at the state and local level to verify identification. Moreover, the Bureau maintains non-criminal files on more than 100 million Americans. In 1932, the FBI began a forensic science laboratory specializing in blood analysis, ballistics, and other criminological studies, placing this at the service of all local and state police departments.

The Bureau's National Police Academy, established in 1935, which is staffed by FBI personnel and local and state police officials, offers a twelve-week course in FBI training and graduates return to state and city departments to train others in police procedures. Since the Hoover-dominated era, the Bureau has earned considerable respect throughout the U.S. among the law enforcement community, as well as the general public, as the chief law enforcement agency in the U.S., one with high integrity which produces consistent, excellent investigative results. See: **Alcatraz; Barker Brothers; Bentz, Edward; Bielaski, Alexander Bruce; Black Panthers, The; Burns, William J.; Dillinger, John; Finch, Stanley W.; Floyd, Charles Arthur; Flynn, William J.; Graham, Jack Gilbert; Gray, L. Patrick; Hall, Carl Austin; Hoover, J. Edgar; Karpis, Alvin; Kelley, Clarence M.; Kelly, George; Kennedy, John F.; Kennedy, Robert F.; Nelson, George; Otto, John; Palmer, A. Mitchell; Purvis, Melvin; Red Raids; Ruckelshaus, William D.; Seadlund, John Henry; Sessions, William Steele; Stone, Harlan Fiske; Watergate; Weather Underground Organization; Webster, William H.**

REF.: Alexander, *The Pizza Connection;* Blumenthal, *Last Days of the Sicilians;* Campbell, *The Luciano Project; CBA;* Cohen, *Mickey Cohen: In My Own Words;* Cooper, *Ten Thousand Public Enemies;* Cressey, *Theft of the Nation;* Davis, *Mafia Kingfish;* Demaris, *The Director;* Eisenberg and Landau, *Meyer Lansky;* Fox, *Mass Murder;* Fried, *The Rise and Fall of the Jewish Gangster in America;* Gage, *Mafia U.S.A.;* ____, *The Mafia Is Not an Equal Opportunity Employer;* Gosch and Hammer, *The Last Testament of Lucky Luciano;* Katz, *Uncle Frank;* Kirby and Renner, *Mafia Enforcer;* Lait and Mortimer, *Chicago: Confidential;* McClellan, *Crime Papers;* Martin, *Revolt in the Mafia;* Messick, *Secret File;* ____, *Syndicate in the Sun;* ____ and Goldblatt, *The Mobs and the Mafia;* Nash, *Bloodletters and Badmen;* ____, *Citizen Hoover;* ____, *The Dillinger Dossier;* ____, *Hustlers and Con Men;* Navasky, *Kennedy Justice;* Ottenberg, *The Federal Investigators;* Overstreet, *The FBI in Our Open Society;* Pileggi, *Wiseguy;* Powers, *Secrecy and Power;* Reid, *The Grim Reapers;* Reppetto, *The Blue Parade;* Reuter, *Disorganized Crime;* Sann, *Kill the Dutchman;* Scott, *The Concise Encyclopedia of Crime and Criminals;* Shannon, *Desperados;* Sullivan, *The Bureau: My Thirty Years in Hoover's FBI;* Toledano, *J. Edgar Hoover;* Tully, *Inside the FBI;* Ungar, *FBI;* Velie, *Desperate Bargain: Why Jimmy Hoffa Had to Die;* Whitehead, *The FBI Story;* Wicker, *Investigating the FBI;* Zuckerman, *Vengeance Is Mine;* (FILM), *G-Men,* 1935; *Let 'Em Have It,* 1935; *Show Them No Mercy,* 1935; *Federal Bullets,* 1937; *Confessions of a Nazi Spy,* 1939; *Persons in Hiding,* 1939; *Parole Fixer,* 1940; *Queen of the Mob,* 1940; *Dillinger,* 1945; *The House on 92nd Street,* 1945; *The Street With No Name,* 1948; *FBI Girl,* 1951; *Walk East on Beacon,* 1952; *Baby Face Nelson,* 1957; *The FBI Story,* 1959; *Pretty Boy Floyd,* 1960; *FBI Code 98,* 1964; *Young Dillinger,* 1965; *Bloody Mama,* 1970; *Dillinger,* 1973; *The Private Files of J. Edgar Hoover,* 1978.

Federicci Family, See: **Ruiz, Henri.**

Fein, Benjamin (AKA: **Dopey Benny**), b.1889, U.S., org. crime. Born into the poverty of the Lower East Side of New York, Benjamin Fein was an undersized, poorly educated youth who began as a street thief and pickpocket. His peers nicknamed him "Dopey Benny" because his heavy eyelids made him appear moronic. Fein was, however, a shrewd and cunning youth with great organizational skills. He headed a gang of armed robbers by 1905 and by 1910 had served several terms in Elmira Reformatory, the most serious being a three-and-a-half-year term for armed robbery. He joined the gang led by Big Jack Zelig and concentrated on strong-arm rackets with unions and manufacturers, especially in the burgeoning garment industry.

Fein and his goon squads would rent themselves out to either union forces or company owners, usually the former, and would beat up those opposing union organization in a given firm. He would also represent the owners and beat up union leaders, charging from $10 to $600, depending upon the type of injuries desired on the part of his client. During this period of labor unrest, Fein averaged $20,000 a year as a strong-arm man. He paid his men $7.50 an hour, high wages in that era. At times, Fein joined forces with Joseph "Joe the Greaser" Rosenzweig and his mobsters, but, often as not, Fein and his men were battling Rosenzweig's men when both gangs represented opposite sides of a union squabble.

Smaller gangs of union sluggers joined forces in 1913 and tried to wipe out the Fein and Rosenzweig mobs in order to take over their lucrative strong-arm rackets. A pitched battle of more than fifty gangsters took place at Grand and Forsyth streets. Though hundreds of shots were fired, only a few of the gangsters were wounded. Fein was arrested for assault in late 1914 and he patiently awaited trial, expecting his political friends to arrange his release. When none appeared to help him, Fein struck a deal with District Attorney Charles Perkins and made a full confession of his labor strong-arming. Eleven gangsters and twenty-one union officials were indicted because of Fein's revelations but none were brought to trial.

New York gangster and labor racketeer "Dopey Benny" Fein, 1910.

Fein was arrested for the murder of Frederick Strauss, a court clerk who had been killed in a 1914 gangster shootout as he was passing the scene of the gun battle near St. Mark's Place. Witnesses failed to identify Fein as the gunman who took Strauss' life and Fein was released. He was rearrested in 1917 for labor slugging and again released. Fein, by then, had lost most of his sluggers in gang wars. Rosenzweig had been sent to Sing Sing on a manslaughter charge in 1915 and Fein was left without gangster or union allies. He decided to abandon the rackets and, using his considerable savings, he became a garment manufacturer. He was so successful that he retired about ten years later and disappeared from public record.

REF.: Asbury, *The Gangs of New York;* Carey, *Memoirs of a Murder Man;* CBA; Haskins, *Street Gangs;* Levine, *Anatomy of a Gangster;* Peterson, *The Mob;* Thompson and Raymond, *Gang Rule in New York;* Willemse, *Behind the Green Lights.*

Fein, Mark, prom. 1963-64, U.S., mur. Wealthy, up-and-coming New York businessman Mark Fein settled a $7,200 bet by murdering the bookie instead of paying him. "We had words and I shot him," Fein said of the murder of Rubin Markowitz on Oct. 10, 1963. And that was how Fein put it when he called his girlfriend, prostitute Carmela Lazarus, also known as Gloria Foster, Gloria Kendall, and by at least thirty other aliases. He asked her help in disposing of the body. When she came to his Manhattan apartment, Fein had already acquired a large trunk in Spanish Harlem and deposited Rudy's body in it.

Gloria called in a couple of male friends who carried the heavy trunk down to a rented station wagon. Leaving Fein behind, they drove to the Harlem River and pushed the trunk into the water. When the trunk was found, the police discovered a list of Rudy's "clients" on his body. The name "Gloria Kendall" was on the list. When the police located Lazarus, she promptly told what had happened. Fein was arrested and tried. Although his

defense attorney tried to get the jury to seriously question whether a prostitute with thirty aliases could be relied on to tell the truth, Mark Fein was found Guilty and sentenced to thirty years to life in prison.

REF.: *CBA;* Reuben, *The Mark Fein Case.*

Feinberg, Wilfred, 1920- , U.S., jur. Appointed to the Southern District Court of New York by President John F. Kennedy in 1961, and by President Lyndon B. Johnson to the Second Circuit Court of the U.S., in 1966. He published the article "Expediting Review of Felony Convictions" in the *American Bar Association Journal* in 1973. REF.: *CBA.*

Feldman, Joseph, 1917- , U.S., theft. On Sept. 19, 1975, fire investigators checked the Greenwich Village apartment of Joseph Feldman after a fire in another part of the building. They discovered more than 15,000 books from the New York Public Library, valued at about $125,000, crammed into the apartment with only a two-foot path through the four rooms. Twenty workers moved the books back to the library in seven truckloads.

Feldman, a 58-year-old lawyer, was arrested and charged with criminal possession of stolen property. He pleaded guilty and was sentenced in May 1976 to five years probation with psychiatric care. He explained that he had taken the books over the previous ten years because, "I like to read." REF.: *CBA.*

Feldman, Richard L., 1926- , and **Martenson, Richard,** 1946- , and **Goldstein, Michael,** 1942- , U.S., fraud-rack. Three men were indicted on Dec. 18, 1981, on charges of mail and wire fraud and racketeering. Their scheme, based in Miami, Fla., cheated about 1,100 investors of more than $4.5 million. The investigation was directed by U.S. Assistant District Attorneys Joseph N. Hosteny and Ludwig E. Kolman.

Richard Feldman, fifty-five, of Palm City, Fla., Richard Martenson, thirty-five, of Excelsior, Minn., and Michael Goldstein, thirty-nine, of Plantation, Fla., were charged with selling fraudulent metal futures contracts in gold, silver, platinum, and other precious metals through First Guarantee Metals Company. Between July 1979 and January 1980, they sold contracts worth about $11 million, but some investors received a return on their share. The crooks used some of the money to pay commissions, salaries, and operating costs, and put the rest into bank accounts.

Feldman, the company's owner, and Martenson, a supervisor and salesman, were convicted on Dec. 6, 1982, of thirteen counts of wire and mail fraud and one count of racketeering. Goldstein, the general counsel, pleaded guilty to one count of commodities fraud. Feldman and Martenson were sentenced to twelve years in prison, and fined $38,000 each. REF.: *CBA.*

Félix Gallardo, Miguel Angel (AKA: **El Padrino**), 1946- , Mex., drugs-org. crime. Miguel Angel Félix Gallardo, a Sinaloa (Mex.) State Police officer in the 1970s, helped Rafael Cáro Quintero and Ernesto Fonseca Carrillo rise to preeminence in the Guadalajara drug trade. After serving as a police officer, Félix Gallardo was employed as a bodyguard to Governor Leopoldo Sánchez Celis. He came to know powerful politicians and influential socialites in Sinaloa who enabled his drug empire to flourish. Félix Gallardo used his connections to benefit Cáro Quintero and Fonseca Carrillo, earning him the sobriquet of "El Padrino," as

Miguel Angel Félix Gallardo, Mexican drug king.

godfather of the Guadalajara drug cartel. Félix Gallardo revolutionized the drug industry of Mexico after realizing that the future lay in cocaine, not marijuana or heroin. Refined cocaine arriving from the laboratories of Colombia was nearly impossible to detect. While, marijuana crops were easily detected, even from the air.

Félix Gallardo joined forces with Honduran chemist Juan Ramón Matta Ballesteros, and together the two helped establish Mexico as the "pipeline" to the U.S., making Félix Gallardo the most powerful cocaine trafficker in the Western Hemisphere and his drug cartel virtually unstoppable. Félix Gallardo laundered some of his money through the Bank of America in San Diego. Cocaine profits from the West Coast were taken by truck to Guadalajara, and wired back to the Bank of America. Félix Gallardo's money handler, Tomás Valles Corral, withdrew the money in sums of $40,000 to $50,000, which was then sent on to the suppliers in Colombia. The canceled checks gave the DEA its first clue of the scope of the operation.

The arrests of Cáro Quintero and Fonseca Carrillo in connection with the murder of DEA agent Enrique Camarena barely affected Félix Gallardo's empire. Rather, he expanded his operations to include distribution centers in Europe and possibly Tegucigalpa, Hond., where his old partner, Matta Ballesteros, lived. Félix Gallardo was thought to have contacted Pablo Gaviria Escobar of Colombia prior to Félix Gallardo's arrest on Apr. 8, 1989, in Culiacán, Mex. Described as the "number one narcotics trafficker in Mexico" by Attorney General Enrique Alvarez del Castillo, Félix Gallardo was charged with drug trafficking and bribery. See: **Cáro Quintero, Rafael; Escobar Gaviria, Pablo; Fonseca Carrillo, Ernesto; Matta Ballesteros, Juan Ramón.**

REF.: *CBA;* Shannon, *Desperados.*

Fellows, Dick (Richard Perkins, AKA: Richard Kirtland), prom. 1870s-80s, U.S., west. outl. Stagecoach robber Dick Fellows had to ride horseback to carry out his crimes, but the California badman was no equestrian, as he proved in his miserable attempt to rob a Wells Fargo Stage bound for Caliente, Calif. Fellows had been released from San Quentin in 1874 after serving nearly four years for robbery and assault when Governor Newton Booth was duped into believing that he had become a Christian in jail. Fellows hired a horse from a livery man before setting out to rob the stage on Dec, 4, 1875. Since holdups were common, the Wells Fargo Company assigned four guards disguised as passengers to ride on the stage to guard three boxes of gold. Fellows had not count-

California bandit Dick Fellows.

ed on a balky horse when he set out. Just out of town the animal reared and threw the robber to the ground. Fellows became unconscious. The horse went back to the stable, leaving its rider on the ground. When he returned to town a short time later, Fellows decided to rob the northbound stage instead.

Fellows stopped the Bakersfield stage at gunpoint and ordered the driver to give him the strongbox. Then, to everyone's surprise, he began whistling "The Arkansas Traveler." "A most creditable performance," wrote the San Francisco *Chronicle* later. The second horse proved more cooperative, but he had forgotten to bring his tools. Once he was safely away from the stagecoach, he was hindered by the darkness and could not find a suitable stone to open the box, so he picked it up and walked back to his horse. The animal suddenly ran away, leaving Fellows. He set off on foot, carrying the heavy box over his shoulder. In the darkness he stumbled down an eighteen-foot embankment, landed in Tunnel Number Five of the Southern Pacific Railroad, and broke his left leg. Fellows dragged himself to the tent of a Chinese laborer where he took an axe. He then opened the box and took out $1,800, made a pair of crutches for himself, and made his way

to the Fountain Ranch. There he stole a horse and rode to an abandoned hut where he was eventually arrested by company detectives. The *Chronicle* commented on the affair, reporting, "When it is considered that the stage was robbed by a man with a broken leg and with a little single-barreled pistol, it becomes ludicrous."

On June 8, 1876, Fellows was sentenced to eight years in prison. By the next morning, Fellows had escaped through a hole tunneled in the floor and made his way to the Kern River where he took a horse. But Fellows was captured, and this time, he was sent straight to San Quentin where he was given a job in the prison library. He was freed in May 1881, and sought legitimate employment with the Santa Cruz *Daily Echo.* He offered his services as a Spanish teacher, but soon reverted to armed robbery. On July 19, he held up the San Luis Obispo-Soledad stage, but his take was only $10. Close to the Russian River, Fellows robbed the Mills-Point Arena coach, but the box contained only a letter in Chinese. Between July 1881 and January 1882, Fellows robbed three stage coaches around San Luis Obispo. With Wells Fargo agents pursuing him, Fellows was captured in a cabin outside Los Gatos. They jailed him in San Jose on Feb. 4, 1882, and some 700 spectators came to gaze upon the wily bandit. Then Fellows was taken to San Francisco and sentenced to life at Folsom State Prison. Fellows had barely arrived when he made his third escape from prison. Several blocks away, Fellows grabbed the reins of a horse and tried to ride away, but the horse threw him to the ground and he was taken into custody again.

REF.: Block, *Great Stagecoach Robbers of the West; CBA;* Dillon, *Wells Fargo Detective;* Jackson, *Bad Company;* ____, *Tintypes in Gold;* Wilson, *Treasure Express.*

Felton, John, See: **Villiers, George, Duke of Buckingham.**

Fenayrou, Gabrielle, b.1850, and **Fenayrou, Marin,** d.1882, Fr., mur. Gabrielle Gibon married Marin Fenayrou in order to save her father's pharmacy in Paris. Marin, a druggist, did what was expected of him at first, working hard to keep the store going. But then he tired of it and turned to gambling and heavy drinking. Gabrielle Fenayrou, who had not wanted to marry the unattractive Marin, spent most of her eight-year marriage in an affair with 21-year-old Louis Aubert, whom she met when he was her husband's assistant. But when Aubert wanted to break off the affair, Gabrielle told her husband what had been going on and encouraged him to kill the man who had cuckolded him. He obliged, stabbing and smashing the skull of Aubert, then dumping the body into the Seine on May 28, 1882.

Gabrielle confessed to both her part and her husband's in the murder. Marin was sentenced to be guillotined. Gabrielle was sentenced to life in prison, though she was pardoned in 1903.

REF.: *CBA;* Hartman, *Victorian Murderesses;* Irving, *A Book of Remarkable Criminals;* Morain, *Underworld of Paris;* Nash, *Look For the Woman;* Whitelaw, *Corpus Delicti.*

Fenger, Christian, 1840-1902, U.S., path. Chief pathologist for Cook County Hospital in Illinois from 1878-93, and professor of surgery for Northwestern University in 1893, and for Rush Medical College in 1899. REF.: *CBA.*

Fenians, prom. 1858-80, Ire.-Brit.-U.S., rebel. Following the United Irishmen movement, the radical Fenians emerged in the early 1860s. Named for the "fiann," "féinne," or "Fiana Éireann," a fearsome band of third-century Irish warriors who owed allegiance to Finn MacCumhaill, the Fenians were committed to terrorism to win independence for Ireland.

By 1848, Ireland was experiencing economic depression. For several years, potato crops failed, and nearly one million people emigrated. Those who remained saw the repeal of the Corn Laws in 1846 and the British Free Trade policy as further efforts to bring Ireland to its knees. In 1848, a small band of Irish rebels attempted an insurrection, but the government deported the top leaders. Michael Doheny, James Stephens, and John O'Mahoney escaped to the U.S., where they organized the Fenian Brotherhood (or Irish Republican Brotherhood) in 1858, a secret society whose

Fenians attacking a police van in Manchester, England, in 1867 to free two of their leaders, Col. Kelley and Capt. Deasey.

American Fenians invading Canada in 1866, led by William Roberts.

goal was the overthrow of British rule in Ireland. The members of the Brotherhood were organized into cells of ten. Many of the members did not even know who their associates were as they swore fealty to a revolutionary ideal. The initiate would repeat, "I, ____, do solemnly swear, in the presence of Almighty God, that I will do my utmost, at any risk, while life lasts, to make Ireland an independent democratic Republic; that I will yield implicit obedience, in all things not contrary to the law of God, to the commands of my superior officers; and that I shall preserve inviolable secrecy regarding all the transactions of this secret society that may be confided to me."

By the end of the Civil War, the U.S. Fenians were so entrenched in local government that most chapters became open about their activities. In 1863, they held a convention in Chicago where they declared their intentions to found an Irish Republic, a goal they believed would best be realized by invading Canada and founding a Canadian Republic. Three raids against Canada were staged in the next few years. In 1867, they tried to seize the arsenal of Chester Castle in England as a step in the long-anticipated Irish rebellion. However, the revolt was quickly and effectively crushed. By the 1880s, the once-secret society was infiltrated with British spies and informers. Their eventual successors, the Clan-na-Gael, were no more successful. They set off explosions at the Tower of London, the House of Commons, and the London Bridge, but the terrorist acts caused little damage. In turn, the Clan-na-Gael became the Irish Nationalist Party (Sinn Fein) in 1905. See: **Cronin, Patrick; Irish Republican Army.**

REF.: *CBA;* Cobb, *Critical Years at the Yard;* Desmond, *The Drama of Sinn Fein;* Griffiths, *Mysteries of the Police and Crime;* Henry, *The Evolution of Sinn Fein;* Jackson, *Occupied With Crime;* Macardle, *The Irish Republic;* Mackenzie, *Secret Societies;* Pinkerton, *Murder in All Ages;* Pollard, *The Secret Societies of Ireland.*

Fenn, William P., prom. 1860s, U.S., law enfor. off. William P. Fenn served as the Chief of Police of St. Louis, Mo., from Oct. 22, 1866, until his dismissal by the Board of Police Commissioners on June 30, 1868. Fenn initiated the mounted patrol and, in 1868, was instrumental in establishing the School of Instruction, the oldest formal program for training law enforcement recruits in the U.S. REF.: *CBA.*

Fennick, Rachel (AKA: **Red Rae, Ginger Rae**), 1907-48, Brit., (unsolv.) mur. On Sept. 26, 1948, Scotland Yard police broke into the apartment of Rachel Fennick, a 41-year-old prostitute who lived in the Soho section of London. They found her dead, with multiple stab wounds to her chest and back, probably inflicted by a stiletto, The weapon, however, was never found. The killer of Ginger Rae, as she was known because of her auburn hair, was never found. Another prostitute, Helen Freedman, was fatally stabbed a month earlier in the same section of London, but that case, too, remains unsolved.

REF.: *CBA;* Harrison, *Criminal Calendar;* Shew, *A Second Companion to Murder.*

Fenning, Elizabeth, 1794-1815, Brit., (wrong. convict.) attempt. mur. In 1815, Elizabeth Fenning, twenty-one, was hired as a cook in the household of Robert Turner. After several weeks with the family, she made yeast dumplings for dinner one night, and they were eaten by Turner, his wife, his father, Elizabeth, and an apprentice named Thomas King. Within a few minutes of eating the dish, they all suffered extreme pain and vomiting.

The next morning, suspecting arsenic poisoning, Turner examined the bowl in which the dumplings had been mixed. He discovered a white powder, which he gave to a surgeon, Mr. Marshall, who identified it as arsenic. Turner also found that a packet of arsenic for killing mice was missing from a drawer in his office. When the leftover flour and yeast used to make the dumplings were checked, they contained no arsenic. Elizabeth was arrested for the poisoning.

She swore her innocence and virtually no evidence existed, but she was tried in April 1815, convicted, and sentenced to death. Though the public supported her and several people tried to get the sentence commuted, Fenning, clothed in white, was hanged at Newgate on July 26, 1815. Years later, in 1834, Robert Turner confessed before he died that he, not Fenning, put arsenic in the dumplings.

REF.: Birmingham, *Murder Most Foul;* Bleackley, *Hangmen of England;* Brock, *A Casebook of Crime; CBA;* Laurence, *A History of Capital Punishment;* O'Donnell, *Should Women Hang?;* Potter, *The Art of Hanging;* Stevens, *From Clue to Dock;* Thompson, *Poisons and Poisoners.*

Fenton, James, d.1908, U.S., (unsolv.) mur. Police officer James Fenton was walking his beat in West Oakland, Calif., on the afternoon of Jan. 4, 1908, when he noticed a suspicious man carrying a suitcase. He asked the man where he was headed. "To San Francisco," the man answered. When Fenton asked to examine the contents of the suitcase, the stranger pulled a hand gun and shot Fenton. The wounded police officer wrestled with the criminal until a barber, Mr. Shields, ran out of his shop, grabbed Fenton's revolver, and shot the assailant. Fenton died on the spot and the killer, whose identity was never established, died shortly after.

When the suitcase was opened, police discovered $3,000 worth of stamps which had been stolen from the post office in Campbell, Calif., on Jan. 2, 1908.

REF.: *CBA;* Duke, *Celebrated Criminal Cases of America.*

Fentress, Albert, 1941- , U.S., can.-mur. On Aug. 18, 1979, Albert Fentress, thirty-nine, a history teacher at Poughkeepsie Middle School in New York, wrote two scripts concerning murder and sexual mutilation. Two days later, he invited Paul Masters, eighteen, into his house for a drink. Fentress then assaulted, mutilated, and shot the boy. Afterward, he cut the body into pieces, and cooked and ate them. Fentress, who had no previous record, was committed to a mental institution indefinitely. REF.: *CBA.*

Fenwick, John, See: **William III.**

Ferber, Neil, 1947- , U.S., (wrong. convict.) mur. On May 27, 1981, two men rushed into a south Philadelphia, Pa., restaurant, and started shooting. They murdered organized crime figure Chelsais (Steve) Bouras, fifty, and his companion, Janette Curro, fifty-four, who were among a party of seven. Mobster Raymond Martorano was also at the table.

In June 1981, police arrested Neil Ferber, a 39-year-old resident of northeast Philadelphia, in connection with the slayings. His cellmate, Jerry Jordan, claimed that Ferber had confessed while awaiting trial. Ferber was convicted of murder, primarily because of his cellmate's testimony. He was sentenced to execution in the electric chair.

The condemned man then hired lawyer Dennis Cogan, who proved that Jordan was not a credible witness. Jordan reversed his position, said he did not think Ferber was the killer, and failed a lie detector test on Dec. 26, 1985. A test before the trial yielded similar results, but was not shown to the defense. Based on this new evidence, Ferber was released Dec. 31, 1985. The prosecution declined to retry Ferber, and all charges against him were dropped. REF.: *CBA.*

Ferdinand (AKA: Infante of Portugal, The Constant Prince), 1402-43, Port., treas. Son of King John I and younger brother of King Edward of Portugal and Henry the Navigator. As the grand master of the Order of Aviz, he greatly encouraged the failed campaign against Tangier in 1437, whereupon he agreed to sacrifice himself as a hostage. His death came after suffering cruel tortures in his lengthy captivity, for which the Catholic Church beatified him in 1470. REF.: *CBA.*

Ferdinand I (Don Fernando), c.1379-1416, Spain, polit. corr. Second son of John I of Castile, he served as co-regent from 1406-16, for his nephew King John II of Castile. Through bribes and the aid of the antipope Benedict XII and St. Vincent Ferrer, he was able to secure the throne of Aragon. His reign from 1412-16, marked the end of a lengthy domination of Aragon by Catalan rule. REF.: *CBA.*

Ferdinand II (AKA: King Bomba), 1810-59, Two Sicilies, polit. corr. Succeeded his father Francis I in 1830, as king of the Two Sicilies, and although he promised reforms, he instituted authoritarian policies, political persecutions, cruel repressions, and a servile attitude toward Austria. During his reign there were numerous revolts and conspiracies, notably in 1837, 1841, 1844, 1847, and 1848. The last revolt led to heavy bombardment of the Sicilian cities between 1848-49, giving rise to his nickname. REF.: *CBA.*

Ferdinand of Portugal (Ferrand), 1186-1233, Port., impris. Son of Sancho I of Portugal, he held the title Count of Flanders and Hainaut from 1211-33. He participated in the anti-French confederation under the command of King John of England and Holy Roman Emperor Otto IV. At the Battle of Bouvines in 1214, he was defeated and placed in a Paris prison until around 1227. REF.: *CBA.*

Ferguson, Bessie (AKA: Mrs. J.J. Loren, Mrs. Sidney D'Asquith), d.1925, U.S., (unsolv.) mur. Twelve-year-old Roger Thomas of Contra Costa County, Calif., was tracking through the marshy swampland across the bay from San Francisco on Aug. 24, 1925, when he discovered a bundle wrapped in newspaper. Inside, he found a human ear, some blonde hair, and a piece of scalp. The boy and his father telephoned Constable George Conlon and told him to come right away to the swamp. "Looks like murder," Conlon said. Reinforcements were brought and the search party fanned across the rugged terrain until they came across a small cabin owned by Mrs. Graham. A bloodstained hatchet was found, which convinced authorities they had found the murder weapon. But chemical analysis showed that the blood on the hatchet did not come from a human.

The next day, Aug. 25, Deputy sheriff J.W. Smiley reviewed the missing persons file. He found the names of two women, one of whom, Mrs. J.J. Loren, had been reported missing by her brothers Robert and William Ferguson, who lived in Oakland. They said that their sister, a nurse, had left home on Aug. 19 to meet Sheriff Frank Barnet of Alameda County, a close friend. But Barnet denied knowing about such a meeting, and the police determined that Loren, whose maiden name was Bessie Ferguson, had registered in the Antlers Hotel in San Francisco that night. While the police tracked Ferguson's movements, the swamp yielded more bone fragments. An upper and lower jaw were taken to three San Francisco area dentists who had treated Loren. Then the sheriff learned that her name was not Loren, but Mrs. Sidney d'Asquith. A few days later, a brown coat and matching shoes that Bessie Ferguson had been seen wearing at the Antlers Hotel were pulled from the swamp. "It's my daughter's! I know the man, but he didn't do it!" screamed Ferguson's mother. "He sent her to a doctor and they poisoned her. Find the doctors! Oh my daughter!"

Implicated in the case were Dr. J. Loren Pease, an Oakland dentist, Dr. Joseph Moyer, and Gordon Rowe, an accountant. Ferguson had been forced to work for Rowe as a stenographer by her drunken husband, Sidney d'Asquith, whom she divorced in 1918. Each of the men was involved with Ferguson at some time. A stack of letters indicated that Ferguson was blackmailing them. Each was led to believe that she was pregnant with his child. Her mother maintained that Ferguson had never had any children. A set of baby clothes found in the swamp led police to believe that one of Ferguson's boyfriends had murdered her to escape blackmail. If insurance fraud was the motive, only her mother would have gained from Ferguson's two policies. The remains were sealed in a keg and stored in the basement of the Alameda County courthouse to await a final solution to the mystery, which was never reached.

REF.: Block, *The Wizard of Berkeley;* Boucher, *The Quality of Murder; CBA;* McComas, *The Graveside Companion;* (FICTION) Mavity, *The Tule Marsh Murder.*

Ferguson, Champ, d.1865, U.S., rob.-war crimes-mur. During the Civil War, Champ Ferguson led a small group of men supporting a Southern army under Colonel Claiborne in May 1862. These guerrillas were supposed to attack enemy supply lines, but Ferguson's group, like most of the other guerrilla bands, became robbers and murderers. Ferguson operated mostly in Tennessee and Kentucky, and was said to have murdered more than twenty-two people, including Lieutenant Smith, who was slain as he lay injured in a hospital.

Many of the guerrillas surrendered under the Amnesty Proclamation after the war. When Ferguson did not turn himself in, he was outlawed. He was captured on May 24, 1865, near Alexandria, Tenn., and tried before a U.S. military court. He was convicted and sentenced to death on Sept. 30, and was hanged on Oct. 20, 1865.

REF.: *CBA;* Mencken, *By the Neck.*

Ferguson, David, c.1745-71, Brit., mur. The life of a sailor has never been an easy one, but aboard the *Betsey* commanded by Captain David Ferguson, this hard life could often be rewarded with a cruel death. On a trip from the crown colony of Virginia to the island of Antigua in the late 1660s, four of Ferguson's crew died. When he returned to Virginia he was charged with murder in one of the deaths, but was acquitted. In 1770, he was again charged with murder, this time for the death of his 13-year-old cabin boy, who the captain reprimanded for coming on deck while wearing only one stocking.

At a trial at the Old Bailey on Dec. 17, 1770, witnesses testified that Ferguson, who frequently beat the boy, had knocked him down after the lad had come topside wearing only one stocking. He then kicked the boy as he lay on the snow-covered deck. The weather was brutally cold, but the captain kept the boy on deck for an hour. After this punishment, the boy was once again knocked down by Ferguson, who then continued kicking the boy. The next day the cabin boy was found dead in the hold of the ship.

The captain defended himself by saying the weather was bad and several of the crew had to be disciplined to force them to work. Ferguson claimed that on the trip back to England, the ship was wrecked on the coast of Sussex. Major Watson and Captain Lilly, who were passengers, testified that it was only the conduct of Captain Ferguson that saved them during this time. However, the jury found Ferguson Guilty and on Jan. 5, 1771, he was hanged at Newgate Prison. After being cut down, his body was hanged in chains on the shore of the Thames River as a warning to other sea captains who thought to replace authority with murder.

REF.: *CBA;* Mitchell, *The Newgate Calendar.*

Ferguson, Fenner, 1814-59, U.S., jur. Prosecuting attorney for Calhoun County, Mich., and was appointed by President Franklin Pierce to the Northeast Territorial Court in 1854. REF.: *CBA.*

Ferguson, Frank, and **Hance, James,** and **Irwin, J.A.,** prom.

1889, Case of, U.S., med. mal. Mind reader Sir Washington Irving Bishop, a medium prone to cataleptic episodes, dazzled his audiences during a European tour. When he returned to New York in 1889, however, the city's most prominent theatrical club publicly declared him a fraud.

On May 12, 1889, Bishop visited the club, hoping to prove himself the greatest mind reader in the world. Three doctors were present that evening: Frank Ferguson, a brain surgeon, James Hance, and J.A. Irwin. As the guests lingered over liqueurs, the mind reader suffered a convulsion and fell over. The doctors tried to revive him, but finally pronounced him dead and took the body to a funeral home. There, they performed an autopsy of sorts, removing the heart and brain. They carried out the procedure in secret because, at the time, performing an unauthorized autopsy was a misdemeanor punishable by a $500 fine or one year in prison.

After Bishop's mother found his disfigured body, an inquest was held. Though Bishop's doctor testified that catalepsy is not usually fatal, that Bishop usually recovered in six to twelve hours, and that he was probably conscious at the funeral parlor, the doctors were charged only with violating sanitation laws. The coroner reprimanded the doctors and they were cleared of charges.

REF.: *CBA;* Kobler, *Some Like It Gory.*

Ferguson, James Edward, 1871-1944, U.S., polit. corr. Elected governor of Texas from 1915, but faced impeachment within two years and was dismissed from office in 1917. REF.: *CBA.*

Ferguson, Paul Robert, and **Ferguson, Thomas Scott,** prom. 1968, U.S., mur. The Ferguson brothers were just two in a long line of homosexual boyfriends that actor Ramon Novarro, the "Latin Lover," invited to party at his home in Hollywood. The famed sultry-looking star of the silent screen who made women swoon had stopped making movies in the 1930s. He had built up his fortune in the real estate business and was still living very well thirty years later. On the night of Oct. 30, 1968, he invited 22-year-old Paul Ferguson and 17-year-old Tom Ferguson to his home. The brothers had heard a rumor that Novarro

Silent film star Ramon Novarro, murdered in 1968.

kept at least $5,000 in cash in his house, and they began demanding to know where it was. While Paul tortured and beat Novarro so he would tell where the money was hidden, Tom looked around the house, tearing hundreds of valuable paintings from the walls, shredding couches, ripping out drawers. He took time out to telephone a friend in Chicago, Brenda Lee Metcalf, and they talked for almost an hour, while Metcalf heard Novarro's screams in the background. Eventually they found only the money that Novarro had in his pockets, but when they left the mansion, the great screen actor was dead, suffocated by a sexual device.

The next day, Novarro's secretary, Edward J. Weber, found the destruction and the dead body. The police, carrying out their regular routine, checked Novarro's long-distance telephone calls for the previous month and located Brenda Lee Metcalf. She told about the call she had received from the Fergusons, old friends who had lived in Chicago until Paul went to Hollywood and Tom ran away from home to join him.

Paul tried to place the blame for the gruesome murder on Tom. At first Tom believed his older brother when he said that Tom, as a juvenile, would only get six months in jail. But Julius Libow of the Juvenile Court said that Tom would be tried as an adult, and at the trial in August 1969, each brother tried to convince the court that the other had committed the murder.

District Attorney James Ideman held that Paul had committed the crime. "It was...done cruelly by a man who has no respect for himself or others...who has no remorse, no compassion, no

Two hustling killer brothers, Tom, left, and Paul Ferguson, right, at their trial with lawyers.

regrets...and who got his brother to perjure himself," Ideman said. Both men were found Guilty of murder and sentenced by Superior Court Judge Mark Brandler to life in prison, with a recommendation that they never be paroled.

REF.: *CBA;* Nash, *Murder Among the Mighty.*

Ferguson, Richard (AKA: **Galloping Dick**), prom. 1770-1800, Brit., rob. Born in Hertfordshire, the son of a valet, Richard Ferguson worked as a stable boy and was promoted for his good work. But his taste for debauchery kept him from keeping any job for long. Ferguson spent his £57 inheritance quickly, and fell in love with a woman who was the mistress of Lewis Jeremiah Abbershaw, a highwayman. When Abbershaw held up Ferguson's employer, the two men met, and Ferguson realized that he wanted to be a robber also. Managing a few thefts himself, Ferguson was encouraged by Abbershaw to keep his regular employment, explaining that he could obtain useful information on the activities and wealth of his employers that would help him to rob more effectively. Betrayed by an informer, Abbershaw was arrested in 1795. He killed one Bow Street Runner and wounded another, and was hanged in August 1795. Ferguson continued his criminal pursuits for another five years, until he too was hanged, in 1800. See: **Abbershaw, Lewis Jeremiah.** REF.: *CBA.*

Ferguson, Robert, d.1714, Scot., consp.-treas. Participated in the plot to assassinate Charles II in 1683, known as the Rye House Plot, and involved in the conspiracy to kill William III in 1696. He was charged with treason and placed in Newgate Prison in 1704, but posted bail and never faced the charge. See: **Rye House Plot.** REF.: *CBA.*

Ferguson, Walter, c.1894-1939, U.S., mur. Walter Ferguson's tirades frequently disturbed his neighbors in a Manhattan tenement. Only Elizabeth Schneider, fifty-five, a midget and his upstairs neighbor, could calm him. In July 1939, the 45-year-old Ferguson started raving again, and when Schneider went down to quiet him, he grabbed her and pulled her into his room. Insurance collector Sam Fox saw the incident and ran for a police officer. When they returned, Ferguson yelled, "Nobody can come in here but Jesus Christ!"

The two men forced open Ferguson's door and found him standing naked over the bathtub, holding the midget under water. The policeman grappled with Ferguson, but the maniac managed to drown Schneider. Fox then called three more policemen to the scene, where Ferguson fended them off with a table and chairs until he suddenly died of a heart attack. REF.: *CBA.*

Fernandez, Manuel (AKA: **Richard C. Jackson**), d.1835, U.S., pir.-mur. Manuel Fernandez pretended to be a captain of a merchant vessel but he and his cutthroat crew made voyages on the Atlantic Ocean for only one purpose, to attack other vessels and loot them. They were pirates down to the last man. One of

Fernandez' crew members, John Roberts, seduced Fernandez' wife and when the pirate discovered the secret liaison, he challenged Roberts to a duel. Roberts refused so Fernandez shot and killed the interloper. Fernandez was tried for murder and was found Guilty; he was hanged at Bellevue Prison on Nov. 13, 1835.

REF.: *CBA; The Life and Adventures of Manuel Fernandez.*

Fernandez, Manuel, d.1873, U.S., mur. Manuel Fernandez was the first man to be legally hanged in the Arizona Territory. In December 1872, Fernandez stabbed a shopkeeper to death in Yuma, Ariz. A Mexican man usually would have been quickly lynched, but Fernandez was duly tried. Yet, he received the same sentence he would have received through vigilante justice. He was executed on May 3, 1873. REF.: *CBA.*

Fernandez, Raymond Martinez, See: **Beck, Martha Julie.**

Fernandez Alonso, Severo, 1849-1925, Bol., jur. Bolivia's first vice president, and served as president from 1896-99. He left office after civil war erupted as a result of his plan to change the nation's capital to Sucre. He eventually became a supreme court justice and the National Congress president in 1921. REF.: *CBA.*

Fernandez-Badillo, Juan B., 1912 - , P.R., jur. Assistant attorney general for the Puerto Rican Department of Justice from 1947-52, and acting attorney general from 1952-53. He was attorney general for Puerto Rico from 1957-58, and solicitor general from 1959-67, before receiving appointment from President Lyndon Johnson to the District Court of Puerto Rico in 1967. REF.: *CBA.*

Fernandez de Córdoba, Francisco, c.1475-c.1526, Spain, consp. Accompanied Pedro Arias Dávila on expedition to Panama in 1514, and was ordered by Arias to seize Nicaragua in 1522. He established León and Granada in 1523, and forswore his allegiance to Arias, for which he was executed. REF.: *CBA.*

Ferrandini, Cypriano, and **Luckett, Mr.,** and **Howard, Mr.,** prom. 1861, U.S., consp. Detective Allan Pinkerton uncovered a plot to assassinate president-elect Abraham Lincoln as he passed through Baltimore on the way to his inauguration.

Early in 1861, Pinkerton met with Samuel Morse Felton, the president of the Philadelphia, Wilmington & Baltimore Railroad. Felton was concerned about Southern conspirators in Maryland, and Pinkerton agreed to investigate the situation in Baltimore. There, he and his detectives became friendly with Mr. Luckett, a secessionist, Cypriano Ferrandini, an Italian revolutionary working as a barber, and Mr. Howard, a young gentleman loyal to the South. They learned that Ferrandini would head a band that planned to assassinate Lincoln in Baltimore.

Pinkerton and Felton notified Lincoln and his close friend Norman Buel Judd. The president-elect agreed to travel to Harrisburg, Pa., on Feb. 22, 1861, and then board a sleeper train which would pass through Baltimore in the night and arrive in the capital the next morning. Lincoln arrived in Washington unharmed at 6:00 a.m. When his wife rode by train through Baltimore, mobs pressed against the car and shouted obscenities at her.

Controversy surrounded the plot later, including questions as to whether it had ever existed. In 1867, one historian credited John A. Kennedy, chief of detectives in New York City, with the discovery of the plot. In 1872, Ward H. Lamon, Lincoln's former associate who was present when Lincoln boarded the sleeper, claimed the plot was a fraud, concocted by Pinkerton for his own glory. In 1895, however, he acknowledged that Lincoln's life was in danger during the inaugural trip. Lamon may have been offended because he had accidentally been given a copy of Pinkerton's record book, in which he referred to Lamon as "a brainless, egotistical fool."

REF.: *CBA;* Horan, *The Pinkertons.*

Ferrar, Robert, d.1555, Brit., her. Bishop at St. David's from 1548-54. He became a martyr of the Reformation after being executed by Mary I for heresy. REF.: *CBA.*

Ferrara, Florence, 1913- , U.S., mur. On Nov. 28, 1942, a woman under a strange delusion went to Missouri Baptist Hospital in St. Louis. She calmly walked into the office of Dr. Marion Klinefelter, a nationally-known bone surgeon. She greeted the physician by saying, "Well, Mister Mad Man, how are you?" The women pulled a gun from her coat and shot the doctor in the head. As Klinefelter slumped in his chair, the woman shouted, "Now, Mister Wilder, you're exposed." She then fled.

The 69-year-old physician, known to colleagues as a "poor man's doctor" because of the volume of work he did without fees, died before reaching the emergency room.

An hour later, the police arrested 29-year-old Florence Ferrara in the parking lot where she left her automobile. She confessed to the killing and gave this unusual account: "Dr. Klinefelter is not the man I shot. The man shot is named Meldrum Wilder and he is the one who killed Dr. Klinefelter in 1904. He has been posing as Dr. Klinefelter ever since and has been chloroforming and crippling people for years. In 1936, I had an infected finger and he treated me for that, but he didn't get me and he's been trying to get me ever since. So last summer I went over to East St. Louis and bought a pistol for my own protection, and this morning I decided to go out and see him face to face.

"I said, 'Mister Wilder, here I am,' and he grabbed the telephone. He wanted to get somebody to use ether on me, so I shot him in self-defense. He had been having me followed, watched, and the men who were following me were trying to place a cloth filled with chloroform on my face so they could take me to the doctor and he could break my bones."

After being evaluated by psychiatrists, Ferrara was diagnosed as insane and was institutionalized for life. REF.: *CBA*.

Ferrarese, Giula, prom. 1500s, Italy, pros. Giula Ferrarese was a well-known courtesan. During the reign of Pope Paul III, from 1534-49, he instituted a system under which courtesans were reclassified as prostitutes. Ferrarese's daughter, Tullia d'Aragona, lost her high social position when her mother was declared a prostitute. A puritanical movement gained such momentum that, in 1566, Pope Pius V ordered all prostitutes to leave Rome, but the directive caused such confusion that they were allowed to stay.
REF.: Bullough, *Illustrated History of Prostitution; CBA*.

Ferre, Charles Théophile, 1845-71, Fr., law enfor. off. Prefect of police for Paris in 1871, believed to have directed the execution of clerical hostages when the release of Louis-Auguste Blanqui was not obtained by Louis-Adolphe Thiers. Later that year he was apprehended and shot. REF.: *CBA*.

Ferrer, Jaime, 1917-87, Phil., (unsolv.) assass. A Filipino cabinet minister and his driver were gunned down by three armed men on Aug. 2, 1987. Chauffeur Zosimo Calderon was driving Jaime Ferrer, the 70-year-old secretary of local government under President Corazon Aquino, home from church in a Manila suburb. Three young men, two armed with handguns and one with a submachine gun, fired on Ferrer and his driver. Ferrer was killed on the spot, and Calderon was fatally injured. Ferrer was the first cabinet member assassinated since Aquino became president in February 1986.

In 1984 Ferrer, a member of the anti-Marcos Filipino Democratic Party, won a parliamentary seat. In November 1986, Ferrer, known as a staunch rightist, was appointed to the cabinet. In this position, he supported the establishment of unarmed right-wing vigilante groups in villages as protection against Communist insurgents. He also fired supposedly leftist government agents, and discharged officials who did not campaign for Aquino in the May 1987 elections. The Manila-based urban guerilla unit of the Communist New People's Army revealed that Ferrer had been targeted for assassination. Agents of Ferdinand Marcos were also suspected. REF.: *CBA*.

Ferrer Guardia, Francisco, 1859-1909, Spain, consp. Found innocent in 1907, of complicity charges in the attempt on the lives of King Alfonso XIII and Queen Victoria of Spain. Upon news of a rebellion in Barcelona, he was arrested, tried, convicted on charges of complicity, and executed in 1909. His trial resulted in the downfall of the Maura y Montaner ministry and vehement animosity abroad toward Spain and the Catholic Church. REF.: *CBA*.

Ferrers, Katherine (AKA: **Lady Katherine Fanshawe, The Wicked Lady**), d.1660, Brit., (unsolv.) mur. In 1660, near the village of Markyate, the body of Katherine Ferrers, also known as Lady Katherine Fanshawe, was found. She had been shot and was dressed in men's clothing. The heiress to the fortune of her famous family, Ferrers was married when she was twelve years old to Thomas Fanshawe, who was sixteen; his relatives soon acquired control of Ferrers' property. By the time she was eighteen, Lady Fanshawe was living with only a few servants in an old house. She became involved with a farmer and highwayman, Ralph Chaplin, and after Chaplin was executed, Ferrers began to dress like a man and terrorized the area, killing and injuring harmless people without robbing them. She became known as "The Wicked Lady" and was the subject of two British films by that name, in 1946 and 1983. Although the actual cause of Ferrers' death was never solved, she was suspected of having been shot when she attacked a wagon as it crossed Normansland Common near Wheathampstead.
REF.: Butler, *Murderers' England; CBA*.

Lawrence Ferrers shooting his steward, John Johnson, 1760.

Ferrers, Lawrence Shirley (Fourth Earl Ferrers), 1720-60, Brit., mur. Lawrence Ferrers was a descendent of the Plantagenet family, but his wealth and social standing could not disguise his disagreeable temperament. In 1752, Ferrers married the daughter of Sir William Meridith. He treated his wife cruelly until she petitioned Parliament for a legal separation, which she was granted in 1758, along with money to be paid by Ferrers.

Once, armed with a gun, Ferrers threatened his servant and ordered him to kill Ferrers' brother. While Ferrers' wife distracted him, the servant fled and told Ferrers' brother what had happened. The brother and his wife left the estate immediately. Not so lucky was a man named John Johnson, who was named by the courts to act as the receiver of the rents on behalf of Ferrers' estranged wife. Johnson had first refused to accept the task, but Ferrers persuaded him to do so.

The relationship between the two men quickly soured. Ferrers suspected Johnson and the trustees of cheating him out of a contract for some coal mines. The charge was unfounded, but Ferrers resolved to kill Johnson. Ferrers was living in the village of Stanton-Harold in Leicestershire, and Johnson was his tenant. On Jan. 18, 1760, Johnson arrived at Ferrers' door as ordered. Ferrers produced a written "confession" of Johnson's imagined villainy and ordered him to sign it. When Johnson refused, Ferrers ordered him to drop to his knees. He shot Johnson in the chest, then summoned a surgeon to attend to his wounds.

By the time the surgeon arrived, Ferrers had consumed a large quantity of port wine. He told the doctor, "Now I have spared

The well-attended execution of Lawrence Ferrers, at Tyburn in 1760.

his life, I desire you would do what you can for him." Johnson died the next morning. Ferrers, however, locked himself in his house and refused to surrender to the authorities. Meanwhile, a mob gathered outside his home. A collier named Curtis finally helped take Ferrers into custody and accompanied him to the jail. A verdict of willful murder was returned and Ferrers was bound over for trial, arriving in London on Feb. 14. After two months' confinement in the Tower of London, Ferrers was brought before the House of Lords on Apr. 16. There was no question about his guilt, so the issue of his sanity occupied much of the deliberations. Ferrers defended himself, claiming that he had not been in his right mind when the shooting took place, but his arguments failed to persuade the courts. A verdict of Guilty was returned and on May 5, Ferrers was taken to Tyburn to be executed. After hanging, the body was removed to Surgeon's Hall for dissection and public display, according to the sentence of the courts.

Ferrers in death on public exhibit, London, 1760.

REF.: Atholl, *Shadow of the Gallows*; Bleackley, *Hangmen of England*; Brock, *A Casebook of Crime*; Brookes, *Murder In Fact and Fiction*; CBA; Culpin, *The Newgate Noose*; Hibbert, *Roots of Evil*; Lambton, *Echoes of Causes Celebres*; Mencken, *By the Neck*; Mitchell, *The Newgate Calendar*; Potter, *The Art of Hanging*; Turner, *The Inhumanists*; Wilson, *Encyclopedia of Murder*.

Ferri, Enrico, 1856-1928, Italy-Fr., criminol. A protégé of Cesare Lombroso, Enrico Ferri was born in Mantua, Italy. He attended the University of Bologna, studying statistics and its application to criminology. He continued his studies in Paris and later contributed sweeping analyses of French crime. His beliefs were centered around environment, race, physical makeup of criminals, climate, geographical locations, age, sex, organic and psychological conditions, all of this going toward the development of the criminal personality. Ferri detailed his criminological theories in *The Theory of Imputability and the Denial of Free Will*. Ferri later returned to Italy and, in 1921, at the request of dictator Benito Mussolini, put together a new penal code which was named the Ferri Project or the Ferri Draft.

REF.: *CBA*; Hibbert, *The Roots of Evil*.

Ferriola, Joseph (AKA: **Joe Nicol, Joe Nagall, The Spooner, Mr. Clean**), 1927-89, U.S., rack.-org. crime. Known as Mr. Clean because he once ran dry-cleaning businesses in Chicago, the flashy Joseph Ferriola rose to head the Chicago mob.

Ferriola, who grew up on Chicago's Near West Side, reportedly got his start in organized crime collecting juice, the money paid back on loans carrying exorbitant interest rates. Early in his mob career, he served as the enforcer for Sam Giancana, a notorious Chicago mobster. He also ran the syndicate's gambling business in Lake, McHenry, and northern Cook Counties in Illinois. In 1970, he and four others were convicted of conspiring to operate an interstate gambling operation. Ferriola was sentenced to five years in prison, along with Jackie Cerone, but he only served about three years.

During the 1970s and 1980s, Ferriola again worked as Chicago's chief enforcer. Beginning in the early 1980s, power in the Chicago mob began to shift because chief Tony Accardo was ill and semi-retired. At that point, Ferriola controlled most of the day-to-day operations, and vied for power with Joseph Aiuppa. Ferriola assumed the top position in 1985, after Accardo retired and Aiuppa was convicted for pocketing untaxed casino profits. However, the mob was displeased with Ferriola's extravagance. He bought an expensive home in Oak Brook, dined in elegant restaurants, and wore expensive clothes. Ferriola reportedly left the position three years later, possibly at the urging of mobsters under him. He died in a hospital in Houston, Texas on Mar. 11, 1989, at age sixty-one, apparently from heart disease. See: **Accardo, Tony; Aiuppa, Joseph; Giancana, Sam.** REF.: *CBA*.

Ferrucci, Francesco (Ferruccio), 1489-1530, Italy, treas. Sought restoration of the Medici family. While attempting to defend Florence from Emperor Charles V and Pope Clement VII, he was vanquished and executed at Gavinana. REF.: *CBA*.

Ferry, William F., b.1909, U.S., miss. per. Everyday, William F. Perry, a 26-year-old Pelham Manor, N.Y., man visited his deceased wife's grave at the Gates of Heaven cemetery at Valhalla to place fresh flowers on her grave. His blue sedan was familiar to workers at the cemetery, and they saw him as usual on Feb. 5, 1935, as he put a single flower on his wife's grave, and then drove out of the cemetery gates. This was the last that was ever seen of Perry, or of his car. Although the nearby Hudson River was dragged and patrolled, neither the man nor the vehicle ever surfaced.

REF.: *CBA*; Livingston, *The Murdered and the Missing*.

Fersen, Hans Axel, 1755-1810, Swed., assass. Fersen lived at the palace of Versailles and was on intimate terms with Marie Antoinette. Disguised as a coachman, he attempted to secure the royal family's escape from France, before they were overtaken at Varennes in 1791. He was proclaimed Earl Marshal of Sweden in 1801, and advised King Gustav II in the war with France in 1805, before being killed in an uprising. REF.: *CBA*.

Fesch, Jacques, d.1957, Fr., rob.-mur. A banker's son wanted money from his father to buy a boat, but the father refused his request. On Feb. 25, 1954, the son, Jacques Fesch, robbed a Paris shop that sold money and coins of more than 300,000 old francs. The store owner, Alexander Silberstein chased Fesch, who pulled a gun on a printer who got in his way during the escape. Police joined the chase, and Fesch shot and killed one officer. He then ducked into a subway station, where a bank clerk slammed a gate in his face. Fesch was arrested and spent three years in jail before his trial in the spring of 1957 in Paris. He was convicted, sentenced to death, and executed on Oct. 1.

REF.: *CBA*; Heppenstall, *The Sex War and Others*.

Feuerbach, Paul Johann Anselm von, 1775-1833, Ger., jur. Specialized in penal reform and criminology, authoring the work *Lehrbuch des Gemeinen in Deutschland Gültigen Peinlichen Rechts* in 1801. He entered the service of the Ministry of Justice in

Munich in 1805. He introduced criminal law theory dealing with psychological coercion or intimidation, obtained the abolishment of torture in 1806, and sought strict conformity in the application of penal laws by judges, with attention to exemplary instead of vindictive punishment. He drafted Bavaria's penal code which took effect in 1813, and was named the first president of the Appellate Court of Ansbach's first president from 1817-33. REF.: *CBA.*

Fewell, Stanford Ellis, prom. 1952, U.S., (wrong. convict.) mur. In 1949, the 9-year-old cousin of Stanford Fewell was sexually assaulted and murdered in a town near Birmingham, Ala. That same day, Fewell visited his mother and four other people at the Fewell farmhouse, thirty miles from the scene of the murder.

Three years later, in 1952, two girls accused Fewell of making sexual advances toward them. Police in Jefferson County, Ala., remembered the 1949 slaying, and, certain they had the killer, questioned Fewell for fourteen days, denying him access to counsel. On the fifteenth day, when they threatened to arrest his mother for collusion in the crime, Fewell confessed because he was worried that his sick mother would be jailed. After police posed suggestive questions, Fewell easily gave a statement with all the correct details of the murder. He was tried, convicted, and sentenced to thirty years in prison. On appeal, the conviction was upheld.

Skeptical of the ruling, Clancy Lake, the former city editor of the Birmingham *News,* and Fred J. Bodeker, a private detective in Birmingham, reexamined the evidence. They found that the conviction was based solely on the questionable confession, and they produced four witnesses who corroborated Fewell's alibi. The Alabama Parole Board freed Fewell, who left Kirby Prison in Montgomery, Ala., on May 4, 1959, seven years after the erroneous conviction.

REF.: *CBA;* Raab, *Justice In The Back Room.*

Fian, John (AKA: John Cunningham), d.1591, Scot., witchcraft-treas. After being tortured by her employer, a servant girl accused several people, including teacher Dr. John Fian, of an intricate witchcraft conspiracy to kill King James VI. Seventy people were incriminated during the famous trials of the North Berwick Witches in 1590. Fian, singled out as the leader, was charged with witchcraft and high treason on Dec. 26, 1590. He was accused of conspiring with the devil to wreck a ship on which the king had voyaged, of worshiping the devil, bearing the devil's mark, robbing graves, and experiencing "ecstasies and trances."

When Fian refused to confess to any of the charges, he was subjected to thrawing, a procedure in which his head was bound with rope and the rope pulled in different directions. Then he was put in the "boots," a vise used to crush the legs. After being tortured with pins, Fian confessed to all of the charges, but he later retracted the confession. He then suffered more torture, including another session with the vise, but he maintained his innocence. The king's council and James VI personally condemned him to death. Fian was strangled and burned in the Castle Hill of Edinburgh at the end of January 1591.

REF.: *CBA;* Hughes, *Witchcraft;* Linton, *Witch Stories; News from Scotland, Declaring the Damnable Life of Dr. Fian, A Notable Sorcerer;* Pitcairn, *Criminal Trials in Scotland, from A.D. 1488 to 1624;* Robbins, *The Encyclopedia of Witchcraft and Demonology;* Seth, *Witches and Their Craft;* Sinclair, *Satan's Invisible World Discovered;* Summers, *Geography of Witchcraft;* Webster, *Collection of Rare and Curious Tracts on Witchcraft and Second Sight;* Wilson, *Witches.*

Fibiger, Johannes, 1867-1928, Den., pathologist. Recipient of the 1926 Nobel Prize for physiology and medicine. REF.: *CBA.*

Ficker, Julius von, 1826-1902, Ger., jur. Authored *Forschungen zur Reichs und Rechtsgeschichte Italiens,* a four-volume work dealing with Italian law from 1868-74. REF.: *CBA.*

Fidelity Investment Association, prom. 1938, Case of, U.S., fraud. On Dec. 19, 1938, a receivership petition was filed against Fidelity Investment Association, a national investment loan company headquartered in Wheeling, W.Va. The Securities and Exchange Commission (SEC) accused the company of not maintaining required reserves against $276 million in outstanding certificates, of diverting investors' money to company directors and officers, and of acquiring funds and property by making fraudulent statements. Additionally, nine Pennsylvania contract holders accused Fidelity of handling accounts "recklessly, carelessly, and wrongfully."

On Jan. 31, 1939, Federal Judge William E. Baker dismissed the petition after examining a report showing the company was solvent. REF.: *CBA.*

Fiedler, Paulette, 1949-   , U.S., mur. Paulette Fiedler, a 38-year-old employee of the Illinois Department of Children and Family Services, shot and killed her supervisor, Dale Rowell, thirty-nine, as he sat at his desk in the Lombard, Ill., office. Another worker, Robert Heft, thirty-nine, heard the shot and when he went to check, Fiedler shot him as well.

Prior to the killing, the state had tried to discharge Fiedler, but a psychiatrist determined that she was fit to work. Fiedler's sex discrimination suit against her union was dismissed on the morning of the crime. She had also filed several complaints accusing her supervisor and others of treating her unfairly.

When Fiedler's trial began, she first claimed she was mentally unfit and pleaded guilty by reason of insanity. However, in September 1988, a jury found her competent to stand trial. She was convicted in November of murder and attempted murder. Fiedler was sentenced on Dec. 1, 1988, to life in prison. REF.: *CBA.*

Fiehler, Karl, b.1895, Ger., consp. Member of the Sturmabteilung, he participated in an attempted coup d'état in 1923, resulting in his arrest and imprisonment for over a year. Later he became a leader of the Sturmabteilung and the National Socialist party's deputy chief. REF.: *CBA.*

Field, Albert S., b.c.1805, U.S., mansl. On the evening of Sept. 20, 1825, Jonathan Gray, eighteen, Daniel Woodward, and John Battey were standing near the shop of Rhode Island shoemaker Albert Field when they spied a peach tree in a garden owned by Field's father. They decided to steal some peaches. A neighbor, Philip Horsewell, stopped in the shop to tell Field that two boys were taking peaches from the tree. Field grabbed his gun, went outside, and fired to scare the boys, thinking he had aimed high. Field and Horsewell went to see if they could find a hat or coat to identify the culprits. Instead, they discovered Gray, wounded. He died about two hours later.

Field was tried for murder, and convicted on a charge of involuntary manslaughter. He was sentenced to one year and nine months in prison and fined $900.

REF.: *CBA; Report of the Trial of Albert S. Field.*

Field, David Dudley, Jr., 1805-94, U.S., lawyer. Instigated the adoption of the Field Code of Civil Procedure in 1848, in New York and in a number of other states. He drew up New York's penal codes in 1865, and he contributed to the *Draft Outline of an International Code* in 1872, which was an attempt at formulating codification of international law. REF.: *CBA.*

Field, Frederick Herbert Charles, 1899-1936, Brit., mur. The body of prostitute Norah Upchurch, twenty, was found inside an abandoned London shop on Oct. 2, 1931. The discovery was made by a sign fitter and his assistant, Frederick Field. Field told police that the day before he had given the shop keys to a man he thought was a prospective buyer of the property. The man, Field explained to coroner Ingleby Oddie, had prominent gold fillings in his teeth. Coroner Oddie brought the suspect before the jury at the inquest, and as he had no gold fillings, an open verdict was returned. After nearly two years, on July 25, 1933, Field informed the editor of the *Daily Sketch* that he murdered Upchurch. Field recounted in detail how he had brought the girl into the shop and then strangled her. He claimed he emptied her handbag of money and dropped it into a ditch at Rose Hill, Sutton. Field repeated the story to police and was arraigned on a charge of willful murder. At his trial at the Old Bailey in September, Field retracted his confession, saying that it was his intent all along to clear his name. His confession contained so many factual errors that it was impossible to link Field conclusively with the murder. Justice Rigby Philip Swift directed the jury to return a verdict of Not Guilty. Field apparently wanted publicity and the reward money offered by the newspaper.

Killer Frederick Field.   **Upchurch, murder victim, 1931.**

Following Field's acquittal, he joined the Royal Air Force, but soon deserted his squadron. He avoided the law until Apr. 4, 1936, when middle-aged Beatrice Vilna Sutton was found suffocated in her apartment at Elmhurst Mansions, Clapham. That same night, Field advised a girlfriend to look for an interesting item in the newspapers. The girl's mother grew suspicious and notified police, who booked Field on suspicion. At the station, he confessed to killing Sutton, but again gave incorrect details. Before Justice Charles, Field repudiated his earlier statements. When asked how he had been able to describe accurately the victim's injuries, Field claimed it was supposition. After fifteen minutes of deliberation, the jury convicted Field, and on June 30, 1936, Field was hanged.

REF.: Archer, *Killers in the Clear*; Bixley, *The Guilty and the Innocent*; Brock, *A Casebook of Crime*; Browne and Tullett, *The Scalpel of Scotland Yard*; *CBA*; Firmin, *Murderers In Our Midst*; Jackson, *Occupied With Crime*; Oddie, *Inquest*; O'Donnell, *The Old Bailey and Its Trials*; Shew, *A Companion to Murder*; Symons, *A Reasonable Doubt*; Wild, *Crimes and Causes of 1933*; Wilson, *Encyclopedia of Murder*.

Field, Frederick Vanderbilt, 1905- , U.S., cont./ct. Tried before a federal judge in a Washington, D.C., court in March 1951, Frederick Vanderbilt Field was charged with contempt of Congress for refusing to answer thirty-two questions regarding his activities as a long-time supporter and underwriter of the Communist Party in the U.S. Field refused to answer the queries on the grounds that his answers would incriminate himself. He was acquitted of contempt charges in March. In July 1951, a Manhattan federal district court called in the 46-year-old Vanderbilt to testify regarding the disappearance of four men who were leaders in the U.S. Communist Party. Field, who was secretary of the Civil Rights Congress bail fund, which had put up about $450,000 for the Communists in the preceding three years, was a registered foreign agent and a lobbyist for communist China. He said he knew nothing about the four fugitives, Gus Hall, Henry Winston, Robert Thompson, and Gilbert Green, and refused to answer Judge Ryan's demands for the names of the people who had put up the bail money. Field continued to insist his answers might be self-incriminating. Ryan found Field Guilty of contempt of court, and sentenced him to jail for ninety days, or until he agreed to talk. The chairman of the bail fund, author Dashiell Hammett, was also found Guilty of contempt, and was given a six-month jail sentence. REF.: *CBA*.

Field, George Morton, prom. 1915, U.S., mur. A dynamite blast powerful enough to level a church and kill an intended victim, failed to destroy a single sheet of paper, which implicated George Morton Field. Field, in 1915, was the wealthiest man and the religious leader in rural Mustoch, Kan., where he often delivered vitriolic sermons from the pulpit.

Field also had a girlfriend, Gertie Day, a church choir member, who was more than twenty years his junior. When Gertie Day informed him she was pregnant, he agreed to pay her $2,000 to leave the area, but soon worried of possible blackmail. He planted a dynamite bomb beneath the church, and when Gertie Day arrived to pick up the money, she was killed in an explosion which leveled the church. However, the paper the dynamite was wrapped in, a sermon soon to be delivered by George Field, was found untouched in the rubble. Clerks in Kansas City confirmed that Field had purchased the dynamite and he was arrested by Sheriff James R. Carter. Field was convicted of the murder of Gertie Day and sentenced to life imprisonment. He died while incarcerated, in 1926. REF.: *CBA*.

Field, Jack Alfred, 1901-21, and **Gray, William Thomas**, 1892-1921, Brit., mur. William Gray, born in South Africa, sailed to England during WWI where he married an Eastbourne girl who supported him while he kept company with Jack Field. Field was well-known to the police as a petty hoodlum, and after leaving the Navy in April 1920, wandered aimlessly about Eastbourne. On Aug. 19, 1920, the two men met typist Irene Violet Munro, seventeen, and the trio was observed by William Putland and Frederick Wells, who followed them through town. Munro and her companions walked toward the Crumbles, a two-mile stretch of wasteland outside Seaside, Eastbourne. Putland and Wells followed the party just to the outskirts of Pevensey. The next day, a 13-year-old boy picnicking at the Crumbles stumbled upon Munro's battered body. Wells identified Field and Gray on Aug. 24, as Munro's companions, and police learned that the suspects had tried to enlist in the military within an hour of Munro's disappearance. They were charged with murder and brought to trial at the Lewes Assizes on Dec. 13, 1920. The prosecution contended that Munro had refused them sex, and Field and Gray had knocked her to the ground, then hit her with a heavy stone. The jury found them Guilty, appeals were dismissed, and the two were hanged at Wandsworth Prison on Feb. 4, 1921. Before they died, each accused the other of the murder.

REF.: Adamson, *A Man of Quality*; Bowker, *Behind the Bar*; Brock, *A Casebook of Crime*; Browne and Tullett, *The Scalpel of Scotland Yard*; Butler, *Murderers' England*; *CBA*; Cutherbert, *Science and the Detection of Crime*; Duke, *The Stroke of Murder*; Goodman, *Posts-Mortem: The Correspondence of Murder*; Jackson, *Mr. Justice Avory*; Knowles, *Court of Drama*; Lang, *Mr. Justice Avory*; Marjoribanks, *For the Defense, The Life of Sir Edward Marshall Hall*; *Notable British Trials*; Shew, *A Second Companion to Murder*; Speer, *The Secret History of Great Crimes*; Warner-Hooke, *Marshall Hall*; Wilson, *Encyclopedia of Murder*.

Field, Richard Stockton, 1803-70, U.S., jur. Attorney general for the state of New Jersey from 1838-41, professor of law for Princeton University from 1847-55, U.S. senator from 1862-63, and appointed by President Abraham Lincoln to the District Court of New Jersey in 1863. REF.: *CBA*.

Field, Stephen Johnson, 1816-99, U.S., jur. Brother of David Dudley Field, Jr., he served as justice on the California Supreme Court from 1857-63, and as chief justice from 1859-63, before being appointed by President Abraham Lincoln to a newly created seat on the U.S. Supreme Court in 1863. As a supreme court justice he influenced the development of constitutional law, hearing cases that called into question the Fourteenth Amendment. In the *In re Neagle* case in 1889, which was personally linked to the justice, the court ruled that federal officials could not be held criminally responsible for their actions if said actions occurred while performing their official duties. REF.: *CBA*.

Field, William (AKA: Green), d.1773, Brit., rob. William Field's erratic work habits as a livery servant usually led to unemployment, and so, like many discharged footmen, he became a highway robber. In one six-month period, he was known to have stolen more than £700.

On one occasion when Field attempted to rob Colonel Luttrell, the colonel pulled a pistol and shot at the highwayman. Field pulled his own pistol, but it would not fire and he was forced to flee empty-handed.

Field was caught and escaped the gallows by being sentenced to a term of seven years in America. After he was sold into slavery, he managed to escape to New York. Field made his way back to London where he teamed up with a notorious highwayman known as Hawke. The two committed many robberies, often four or five in a night.

British highwayman William Field, arms folded, being sold as a slave in America.

Field began to play the role of a gentleman and he soon married. He continued his nightly work with Hawke without his wife's knowledge. Field and Hawke were eventually caught and taken to the jail at Tothill Fields. Hawke made good an escape, but Fields was brought to trial, convicted and sentenced to death. He was executed at Kennington Common on Sept. 1, 1773.

REF.: *CBA;* Mitchell, *The Newgate Calendar.*

Fielden, Don, 1945-　, Mex., pris. esc. In February 1976, Dr. Sterling Black Davis of Dallas hired truck driver Don Fielden to free his son from a Mexican jail. Fielden, a former marine sergeant, began planning a breakout to free Sterling Black "Cooter" Davis, Jr., twenty-nine, who had been arrested in May 1974 for transporting 80 kilos of marijuana.

Fielden traveled three times to the jail in Piedras Negras, a town just across the U.S.-Mexican border, to study the layout. Back in Dallas, Davis paid him $5,000, and Fielden located a backup man and a 15-year-old accomplice. On Mar. 12, the three drove across the border to the jail in the early morning. While the teenager stayed in the car, the other two rounded up the jail officials. Davis tried to cut through the cell bars with bolt cutters, but the tool broke. He then found the jailer's keys and freed about twenty-six men and women. The three men who engineered the breakout, along with Davis, drove back across the border to Eagle Pass, Texas, where Davis called his father. The younger Davis surrendered to U.S. officials three days later for parole violations. In 1972, he had been convicted for possession of 350 kilos of marijuana. REF.: *CBA.*

Fielding, Charles, prom. 1924, U.S., mur. Lottie Freeman of Cumberland County, Maine, first married William Sanborn. He disappeared in the summer of 1910, leaving his wife alone on the farm with three children. Next, two farmhands disappeared. In 1915, Freeman married Alphonse Cote and had one more child. But in November 1924, Cote, too, vanished. Freeman had

plotted his death with Charles Fielding, a plumber married to her half-sister. Fielding shot Cote in the back and he, Freeman, and her second son, Ralph, buried the body in the field.

When Freeman reported the disappearance of her second husband, saying he had taken money from her purse and Ralph's bank account, Deputy Sheriff Norton became suspicious and checked her history. He and two other officials visited her farm where they talked with Freeman, her son, and Fielding, and also discovered a pile of ashes. When the three were brought in for questioning, Ralph confessed, as did Fielding, who was infatuated with Freeman. But Freeman admitted nothing. Charges against Freeman's son were eventually dropped, and Freeman died before Fielding's trial. Fielding was convicted of murder and sentenced to life in prison. He was later transferred to a state hospital for the insane.

REF.: *CBA;* Rice, *Forty-five Murderers.*

Fielding, Sir Henry, 1707-54, Brit., law enfor. off. Sir Henry Fielding had two careers. He was a renowned novelist and playwright, author of such classics as *Tom Jones, Jonathan Wild, Joseph Andrews,* and *Tom Thumb.* Called to the Bar on June 20, 1740, Fielding also became justice of the peace in Westminster and Middlesex in 1748. The position was unpaid, though it was understood that Fielding could earn £1,000 for himself through the "usual perquisites." His predecessor, Colonel Thomas De Veil, had easily cleared that amount, but Fielding disagreed. "How he did this is to me a secret," he said. Through hard work and honesty, Fielding earned £300, most of which usually ended up in the hands of his clerk.

Fielding's decision to establish a police force came during a deadly crime wave that paralyzed the city. A riot in the Strand district of London on July 1, 1749, caused serious property damage and injuries. Order was finally restored, but only after a military detail had been dispatched to the riot zone. Afterward, Fielding selected a handful of "thief takers" from among eighty unpaid parish constables in Westminster and turned them into the famous Bow Street Runners. They were first known to Londoners as "Mr. Fielding's People," and the Runners evolved into an efficient urban police agency.

Fielding convinced the government to pay him a regular salary drawn from the Secret Service Fund, but he failed to get them to allocate a regular police budget. He remained at Bow Street for five years, devoting all of his energy to crime fighting. In 1751, he published *An Inquiry Into the Causes of the Late Increase in Robbers.* Fielding theorized that the motivation for crime is not for necessities, but a desire to acquire luxuries.

Henry Fielding, pioneer police official.

Fielding made good use of the London press to publish police reports. He founded a criminal records office and laid the groundwork for the formation of the modern Metropolitan Police, organized by Robert Peel in the nineteenth century. Fielding died in 1754, and his work at Bow Street was taken over by his half-brother John. See: **Bow Street Runners; Fielding, Sir John.**

REF.: *CBA;* Dudden, *Henry Fielding, His Life, Work and Times;* Fielding, *An Enquiry into the Causes of the Late Increase in Robbers;* Hibbert, *Highwaymen;* Pringle, *Stand and Deliver;* Scott, *The Concise Encyclopedia of Crime and Criminals.*

Fielding, Sir John (AKA: **The Blind Beak**), d.1780, Brit., law enfor. off. Blind from birth, Sir John Fielding worked as an assistant magistrate to his half brother, Henry, at the Bow Street Magistrate's Court in London. Upon Henry's death in 1753, John took over the duties. Gangs of highwaymen continued to prey on

British travelers, and the Duke of Newcastle demanded a plan of action. Fielding created a plan for the Bow Street court to operate around the clock with two "runners" on duty at all times. When an alarm sounded, the runners would ride to the scene of the crime immediately. The Fieldings asked the Crown for a stipend to pay informants. Parliament approved the measure, estimated to cost £600 a year, but appropriated only £200 per year. By the time Henry died, violence had significantly decreased, and the exploits of the Bow Street Runners were widely publicized in the *Public Advertiser.*

John Fielding, magistrate at Bow Street Court.

In 1755, John Fielding published a *Plan For Preventing Robberies within Twenty Miles of London,* the first of several works on crime prevention. Fielding also requested a Light Horse regiment, a group of private citizens paid by the government, to be posted near the public turnpikes. First, eight men were hired, and by the end of 1763, ten men were assigned to the Horse Guard. After clearing the roads around London, Fielding proposed that the Guard be made permanent, but the government refused, and the Horse Guard disappeared until 1805 when it became a London fixture. Fielding was knighted in 1761, and died at Brompton Place on Sept. 5, 1780. See: **Fielding, Sir Henry.**

REF.: *CBA;* Hibbert, *Highwaymen;* Pringle, *Stand and Deliver.*

Fields, Vina, prom. 1890s, U.S., pros. Vina Fields operated the largest brothel in Chicago during the 1890s, employing at least forty prostitutes during normal trade, and as many as eighty for special occasions, such as the World's Fair of 1893. Fields, a black woman, employed black prostitutes for an exclusively white clientele. For fifteen years, beginning in 1885, she operated one of the safest and most amiable houses on Custom House Place. Neither drunkenness, nor overt solicitation from the girls was allowed. The girls were paid better, and they were expected to behave with decorum, facing fines and menial duties for rule infractions. Fields secluded her daughter in a convent school and performed charitable duties in the neighborhood by providing hundreds of free meals to needy, unemployed people. Even the anti-vice force had to admit that Vina Fields did have a "heart of gold." REF.: *CBA.*

Fieschi, Giuseppe Maria (Joseph Marie Fieschi), 1790-1836, Fr., consp.-terr. Attempted assassination of the French King Louis Philippe in 1835, resulting in the death of eighteen people. His execution, as well as his accomplices', took place in Paris.

REF.: *CBA;* Heppenstall, *French Crime in the Romantic Age.*

Fiesco, Giovanni Luigi (Fieschi, Gian Luigi, Comte di Lavogna), 1522-47, Italy, consp. With Francis I of France, Pope Paul III, and Pier Luigi Farnese, the Duke of Parma, he conspired to overthrow the Doge of Genoa, Andria Doria and his appointed successor, nephew Gianettino Doria. REF.: *CBA.*

Fife, Henry, d.1857, U.S., mur. Charlotte Jones was the niece of George Wilson and Elizabeth M'Masters, an elderly brother and sister who lived together in Elizabeth Township, Pa., and possessed considerable wealth. McKeesport shoemaker Henry Fife, who was Jones' paramour, learned that the elderly brother and sister had saved a substantial amount of cash and had hidden this in their home. He, Jones, and an accomplice, Monroe Stewart, went to the home of Wilson and M'Masters one night and there attacked the man and woman who were both in their seventies. They stabbed Wilson to death and crushed the skull of his sister with clubs, then looted an iron chest where the victims

kept their money. Some of these bills were later identified and all three killers were arrested. They were convicted and hanged, including Stewart, who was the first to confess, implicating Fife and Jones in a futile hope of evading the gallows.

REF.: *CBA; Lifes and Confessions of Henry Fife and Charlotte Jones.*

Figg, Elizabeth, c.1938-59, Brit., (unsolv.) mur. Elizabeth Figg, twenty-one, of Archway, North London, was apparently driven by car to Barnes. On June 17, 1959, her strangled and assaulted body was found close to a lovers' lane by the Thames. Police never found her murderer.

REF.: *CBA;* Furneaux, *Famous Criminal Cases, vol. 6.*

Figner, Vera Nikolaevna, 1852-1942, Rus., consp. One of the many conspirators in the plot to assassinate Russian czar Alexander II in 1881, Vera Figner was imprisoned in Shlisselburg fortress for twenty years. Upon her release in 1904, she was sent into exile in Archangel, held under house arrest, and was freed during the Revolution of 1917. Figner later published *The Prisoners of Shlisselburg, After Shlisselburg,* and *Memoirs of a Revolutionary.* See: **Alexander II.** REF.: *CBA.*

Figueras-Chiques, Jose-Maria, 1851-1910, P.R., jur. Prosecuting attorney in 1897, and criminal court justice for Mayaguez, P.R., from 1897-98. He was appointed by President William McKinley to the Supreme Court of Puerto Rico in 1900. REF.: *CBA.*

Figulus, Publius Nigidius, prom. 1st Cent. B.C., Roman., consp. Backed Marcus Cicero in the Catilinarian conspiracy, and supported Pompey during civil war. He died in exile following banishment. REF.: *CBA.*

Filangieri, Gaetano, 1752-88, Italy, jur. Authored the work *Scienza della Legislazione* from 1780-85. REF.: *CBA.*

Filewood, James (AKA: **Vilet),** c.1691-1718, Brit., rob. James Filewood left his family's poultry business to become a thief. He began his criminal endeavors by picking expensive handkerchiefs, then moved on to stealing money and watches. Because it was one of the best places to ply his trade, he never missed church on Sunday.

When Filewood was arrested and tried at Oxford, he was given a legal exemption that was typically made available to clerics. Instead of being hanged, the defendant was first required to prove he could read, then was burned on the hand and set free. Though Filewood was illiterate, he passed the test with the help of a student who whispered words into his ear. "O Lord," read the student. "O Lord," repeated Filewood, whose thumb was covering the rest of the line. "Take away thy thumb," said the student. "O Lord," continued Filewood, "take away thy thumb."

The judge was so amused by this display of literacy that he granted Filewood the exemption. But the thief's luck was not always as fortunate. On another occasion he was charged with stealing an alarm watch but was discharged because the watch could not be located. As he walked from the bench, the alarm suddenly sounded from his pocket, and Filewood was quickly sentenced to Newgate.

Filewood's last arrest was for picking the pocket of Mrs. Francis Baldock. He was tried and convicted at Old Bailey and sentenced to death. On Oct. 31, 1718, he took his final trip up the Holborn River to Tyburn where he was hanged.

REF.: *CBA;* Smith, *Highwaymen.*

Fillis, George Frederick, prom. 1932, Brit., fraud-arson. A beach photographer and his partner nearly succeeded in their scheme to collect insurance for a fire they set in their loft and work space. But as they went to call the fire department to report the "accident," they ran into police.

George Frederick Fillis, sixty-three, and Tom John Lonnen, forty-one, were photographers at the resort beach area of Bournemouth, England, and made a sketchy living during the months of good weather. Strapped for funds in a lean off-season, Fillis took out an insurance policy on his stock in October 1932 for £1,675, adding another £300 of insurance on his fittings and fixtures. Three weeks later, at ten minutes before midnight, the photography studio and dark room were on fire. Walking outside to see if there were any witnesses, the unlucky partners saw two policemen; one watched Lonnen rushing to a nearby telephone. Seven minutes later the fire brigade arrived and doused the conflagration in twenty minutes.

Fillis and Lonnen contended that they had been heating the kettle on a gas ring when some methylated spirits had been dropped by Fillis. But it was discovered that there were two fires in the studio, one on the ground floor where the gas ring was, and the other in the loft, where a trap door was tightly shut. The studio reeked of paraffin, and empty oil drums were found on the premises. During the five-day trial, both men insisted that the fire was an accident, alleging that it must have traveled to the loft area by way of celluloid negatives drying upstairs. The jury found them Guilty of arson, conspiracy, and false pretenses. Fillis, who had served a four-year term of hard labor thirty years earlier, was sentenced to four years again. Lonnen was sent to jail for eighteen months.

REF.: *CBA;* Woodland, *Assize Pageant.*

Fillon, Anna (AKA: The President), prom. 18th Cent., Fr., pros. Anna Fillon, one of the madams known as "bordel mothers" in the early eighteenth century, bore such a strong resemblance to Presidente Fillon of Alençon that she was mistaken for the president when she was visiting Paris, and was known from that time on as "The President." In her later life, Fillon married a count and became socially acceptable.

REF.: Bullough, *Illustrated History of Prostitution; CBA.*

Financier, The, 1912, a novel by Theodore Dreiser. The corrupt traction tycoon and convicted thief, Charles Yerkes, Jr., was the role model for this work of fiction. See: **Yerkes, Charles, Jr.** REF.: *CBA.*

Finch, Heneage (First Earl of Nottingham), 1621-82, Brit., jur. Authority on municipal law, he served as solicitor general in 1660, and as attorney general in 1670. He became Baron Finch and lord chancellor in 1674, and was declared the earl in 1681. REF.: *CBA.*

Finch, Sir John (Baron of Fordwich), 1584-1660, Brit., polit. corr. King's counsel in 1626, speaker of the House of Commons from 1628-29, became the Court of Common Pleas chief justice in 1634. His treatment of William Prynne and John Langton was considered brutal—Prynne lost his ears in the pillory, was sentenced to life in prison, and had his cheeks branded with an S and an L for seditious libel. He found Charles I's policy of garnering money from ships constitutional in the trial of John Hampden in 1637. He served as lord keeper in 1640, until his impeachment that same year by the Long Parliament. REF.: *CBA.*

Finch, Dr. Raymond Bernard, b.1918, and **Tregoff, Carole,** prom. 1959-71, U.S., consp.-mur. Dr. Raymond Finch, a prominent physician in Los Angeles, divorced his first wife, Francis, to marry another woman, Barbara, who divorced her husband so that he could marry Francis. Barbara Finch was shocked when she discovered that the man she had gotten divorced to marry was a wife-beater. In the spring of 1959, she was convinced that he was trying to kill her and she told her lawyer.

In the meantime, Raymond Finch's new mistress, Carole Tregoff, left her job as his secretary and moved to Las Vegas. Finch met her there whenever possible, and it was there, the prosecution held, that they planned to murder his wife. On July 18, 1959, the pair went to Finch's home in West Covina, Calif., and waited for Barbara to return home in the evening. When she saw them waiting,

Dr. Bernard Finch, convicted wife-slayer.

Barbara drew a gun, threatening to shoot them unless they left. She was shot in the back, the sound drawing the maid, who saw Dr. Finch standing over his wife. She called police and the two conspirators were arrested.

The police found on the lawn of the house an attaché case that they called a "do-it-yourself murder kit." It included, among other items, a gun, a butcher knife, and two hypodermic needles. They also located John Patrick Cody, whom Finch had hired to follow his wife and whom Carole had tried to hire to kill Mrs. Finch. The jury was brought to tears by Dr. Finch's testimony of how his dying wife had taken the blame on herself for their problems and, saying that she loved him, had died. That jury was not able to reach a verdict. Neither was a second jury. It was only on the third try that the prosecution was able to obtain a

Finch's mistress Carole Tregoff, convicted with her lover of killing Barbara Finch in 1959.

verdict of Guilty against the pair. They were both sentenced to prison for life. Carole Tregoff was released in 1971.

REF.: Ambler, *The Ability to Kill; CBA;* Corder, *Murder My Love;* Godwin, *Murder U.S.A.;* Kilgallen, *Murder One;* Nash, *Almanac of World Crime;* ____, *Bloodletters and Badmen;* Wolf, *Fallen Angels;* Wyden, *The Hired Killers.*

Finch, Stanley Wellington, b.1872, U.S., law enfor. off. When the Bureau of Investigation was opened on Mar. 16, 1909, Stanley W. Finch became its first chief. An editor, publisher and lawyer, Finch was born in Monticello, N.Y., and graduated from Baker University in Kansas and Corcoran Scientific School in Washington, D.C., attending business colleges in Albany, N.Y., and Washington, D.C. He graduated from the National University Law School in the nation's capital in 1909. Finch married Laura Lillian Dyer on Dec. 14, 1899, and had three children, Harold Wellington, Lillian Dorothy Wellington, and Norma Gwendolyn Wellington. He began service in the Department of Justice in 1893, and served as a clerk,

Stanley Finch, first chief of the Bureau of Investigation, precursor of today's FBI.

chief bookkeeper, special examiner, and then chief examiner of the U.S. Courts. As chief of the Bureau of Investigation from 1909-13, Finch worked as commissioner for the suppression of white-slave traffic.

Finch was president of the General Novelty Manufacturing Co. from 1914-15, and served as secretary of the General Welfare League in New York for from 1917-19. He was the editor of *World's Welfare Magazine* in 1918, and then of *The World's News* in the following year. He also served as a special assistant to the U.S. Attorney General from 1922-25, and founded the Finch Corporation in 1927. REF.: *CBA.*

Finch-Hatton - Wellesley Duel, 1828, Brit., duel. After he published a letter that defamed the character of Arthur Wellesley, First Duke of Wellington, George William Finch-Hatton was challenged by him to a duel.

Finch-Hatton, Tenth Earl of Winchelsea, was an ardent champion of Protestantism in the House of Lords, and had been active in an October 1828 protest meeting at Penenden Heath, railing against Catholic emancipation and pledging to resist such a move to the death. Politically hostile towards the Duke of Wellington, Lord Winchelsea sent a letter to the *Standard* newspaper in which he assailed the duke's character. When Wellington reacted by writing a letter demanding an apology, Winchelsea refused, and a duel was arranged.

With Sir Henry Hardinge attending Wellington as a second, and the Earl of Falmouth standing by for Winchelsea, it was discovered at the appointed time that Wellington did not have duelling pistols; they had to be borrowed from Hume, the attending physician. After receiving Wellington's fire, Finch-Hatton fired his pistol into the air. Finch-Hatton's second then produced a written explanation which Wellington refused to accept until the word "apology" was added to it. The men separated with as much cold hostility as when they had met. See: **Wellesley, Arthur.**

REF.: *CBA; Melville, Famous Duels and Assassinations.*

Fine, David S., and **Armstrong, Karleton,** prom. 1970, U.S., bomb.-mur. In 1970, during the Vietnam war protests that raged around many of the nation's campuses, the Army Mathematics Research Center at the University of Wisconsin-Madison was bombed; three of the four men responsible were captured.

The bomb exploded outside Sterling Hall in the early morning hours of Aug. 24, 1970. Robert Fassnacht, thirty-three, a physics researcher, was killed in the blast; three other people were injured. Charged in connection with the explosion were Karleton Armstrong, twenty-three; his brother Dwight Allan Armstrong, twenty-one; Leo Burt, twenty-five; and David S. Fine, twenty-one. The bombing was the last and biggest of those that occurred on the strife-torn Madison campus.

In 1972, Karleton Armstrong was captured in Toronto, convicted in Madison, Wis., and sentenced to a ten-year prison term for his part in the explosion. U.S. District Court Judge James Doyle ruled that Armstrong's sentence would run concurrently with a twenty-three-year term he was serving for second-degree murder and arson for the same bombing.

On June 8, 1976, Fine pleaded guilty to reduced state charges of third-degree murder; earlier that day he had pleaded guilty and been convicted on federal charges of unlawful flight to avoid prosecution and conspiracy. Fine's guilty pleas followed negotiations between defense attorneys and prosecutors.

Federal charges of possessing and using an unregistered device to commit a felony, and an additional charge of unlawful flight were dropped in exchange for Fine's guilty pleas. Fine, who had been arrested in San Rafael, Calif., in 1976, was sentenced to a seven-year prison term, and was paroled on Jan. 11, 1979, because "he had held a job" and had "no conflict with the law" during his five years as a fugitive.

Dwight Armstrong, who had been captured in Toronto on Apr. 10, 1977, just two miles from where his brother had been arrested in 1972, was charged with murder and arson. He pleaded no contest on May 6 to a state charge of second-degree murder. The defendant told the court the bombing was a "well-intended act" to protest the war in Vietnam. On June 8, 1977, Dwight Armstrong was sentenced by Judge William Sachtjen to seven years in a state prison; he had driven the getaway car after the bombing.

Karleton Armstrong was freed from the Fox Lake, Wis., Correctional Institute, where he had served eight years of his sentence, on Feb. 1, 1980. At a 1978 news conference prior to his release, Armstrong said he was sorry that someone was killed in the explosion, and sorry that negative public response to the event crippled the anti-war movement in the U.S., but said that if the bombing had left only physical destruction of the Army Mathematics Research Center, he would not have been sorry. REF.: *CBA.*

Fine, Herman, prom. 1975. U.S., drugs. A former philosophy teacher at New York's Hunter College, Herman Fine used his organizational and business acumen in an attempt to smuggle $2 million worth of hashish.

In August 1975, the *Hermit,* a fifty-four-foot yacht owned by 25-year-old Lady Rose Yorke, left from Marabella on Spain's southern coast to sail for Morocco, where a ton of hashish was loaded on board. With its $2 million cargo safely installed, the *Hermit* left for a three-week journey across the Atlantic, anchoring at a spot about twenty-five miles off eastern Long Island. According to U.S. States Attorney David A. DePetris, on Sept. 1, a twenty-three-foot motor boat pulled up to the yacht and two members of the *Hermit,* the leader of the smugglers' group, and Marysia Pryzybyl, a young British woman, transferred to the other boat. The yacht then traveled on to Mystic, Conn., where Robert Purvor and Pamela Goodchild joined them. Drug Enforcement Administration and Customs Service agents, who had been tipped off by an informer, were waiting in Mystic. Four members of the drug-smuggling team were arraigned in Mystic: Daniel David Caton, Philip de Baer, Sherwood Michele, and Dr. Christopher Troy.

Pleading guilty in a Brooklyn federal court to reduced charges of possession and intent to distribute illegal drugs were Fine, Goodchild, Michele, Pryzybyl, Caton, Purvor, Troy, and Richard Bergenstein. Fine was sentenced in October 1976 to three years in federal prison and a $20,000 fine by Judge Jack B. Weinstein in Brooklyn. Lady Yorke, daughter of the Earl of Hardwicke, was tried in London and given a two-year suspended sentence and a $170 fine. Lady Yorke's defense attorney said that the convent-educated woman had met Fine when she was seventeen and was studying at a computer school where he taught, and had been so under his influence that she could not terminate their relationship. REF.: *CBA.*

Fine, Louis (AKA: **Henry Miller**) prom. 1932, U.S., mur. When the owner of a boarding house noticed an unpleasant odor coming from a new tenant's room, he called police to investigate. Inside a double trunk they found the strangled corpse of an elderly woman.

Julius Hoffman, proprietor of the Philadelphia rooming house, was pleased to receive three weeks of rent in advance from his new boarder, Henry Miller. But on Mar. 7, 1932, Hoffman called the Atlantic County, N.J., police to report a repulsive smell in Miller's room, and Police Captain Frank J. Harrold discovered the body of a white-haired woman in the double trunk.

Hoffman explained that Miller, about forty years old, had the peculiarity of always wearing a dark felt hat pulled down over his face. The trunk, Harrold found out, had been delivered at night by two local truckers, and was sent from Atlantic City at 4:00 p.m. on Mar. 4 via the Pennsylvania Railroad. Investigating leads on elderly women in the vicinity who had been listed as missing, police discovered that Mamie Schaff, a wealthy widow, recently had disappeared. According to her maid, who positively identified the body, one of Schaff's boarders, Louis Fine, had left town the day after his landlady, leaving a note asking the maid to keep his room clean until he returned, and telling her to let Mrs. Schaff know he would be back. In Fine's possessions police found a locked strongbox; inside were several letters, one of them addressed to "H. Miller" in Atlantic City, N.J.

Waiting for Fine's return, police hid in his room and surprised him on the night of Mar. 7. Accused of murder by Harrold, Fine claimed he knew nothing and had just returned from a business trip to New York City. Fine also had a heart attack, though only a mild one, and was taken to an Atlantic City hospital. Assured by doctors that Fine was not seriously ill, police brought Hoffman in as the first witness; he positively identified Fine as the man he had known as Henry Miller, as did several other witnesses. Police had found Mrs. Schaff's will, naming Fine as her beneficiary, and when it was learned he was also wanted in New York for murdering an older woman, he was indicted.

While in prison awaiting trial, Fine continued to deny his guilt, but was overheard by guard Harold Johnson as he exclaimed, "The old fool! I wanted her to give me some money. It was the only way I could get it." On June 6 Fine's trial began, and on June 10 the jury deliberated for two hours to return a verdict of Guilty of first-degree murder, with no recommendation of leniency. Fine was sentenced to die in the electric chair, the first time in thirty years that the death penalty had been imposed in an Atlantic County courtroom.

REF.: *CBA*; Cohen, *One Hundred True Crime Stories*.

Fingerprinting, See: **Identification Systems,** Supplements, Vol. IV.

Fink, Isadore, prom. 1930, U.S., (unsolv.) mur. Isadore Fink was a slight, frightened man who had immigrated to Harlem, N.Y., after WWI. Working sixteen hours a day as a laundry helper for ten years, Fink had saved almost $1,000 to buy a laundry of his own. An isolated, solitary man, Fink lived in a tenement house. Fearful of the world, Fink had a strong iron bolt which he put on the door between an elderly woman's two rooms and his store. The few acquaintances and neighbors Fink talked to knew that he was beset by the anxiety that someone would rob his one-room shop and home; every window and entrance was protected by strong bars. One February night Fink delivered a package of laundry, then returned home and locked himself in at about 10:10 p.m.

A few minutes later the old woman who lived behind Fink heard three shots in the store, and called the police. Both the front door and the door between the rooms of the old woman were bolted, so the policeman asked a child to slip through the transom into the room and open the door. At the back of the store lay Fink's still-warm corpse, with two wounds in the head and one in the hand. No gun was found, and the coroner explained to police that Fink had been murdered, as the bullets were fired in a way that excluded the possibility of suicide. For twenty-four hours police combed the room for signs of a revolver, secret panels, or trap doors. Experts searched for fingerprints and found only Fink's. After a month of frustration, the case was closed; Fink's death remains a mystery. Author Ben Hecht wrote a story about Fink called *The Mystery of the Fabulous Laundryman*.

REF.: Boucher, *The Pocket Book of True Crime Stories*; *CBA*; (FICTION), Hecht, *Actor's Blood*..

Fink, Mike, c.1770-1823, U.S., (unsolv.) mur. Accomplished marksman and Indian scout, he was referred to as "King of the Keelboatmen" on the Mississippi and Ohio rivers. He was a member of the William Ashley and Andrew Henry fur trapping expedition to the upper Missouri River region in 1822, and was later shot to death. REF.: *CBA*.

Finlay, Edwin, 1934-52, Brit., suic.-mur. Edwin Finlay, whose childhood was spent in the shadow of the massive bombings of England during WWII, grew up to become a killer at the age of eighteen.

Finlay was eight years old in 1942, at the height of the bomb attacks on England. He later became a bank clerk at a Glasgow bank and, at age eighteen, successfully stole £900 from the institution where he worked. Although he was under no suspicion, Finlay decided to purchase three revolvers "in case of trouble." On July 18, 1952, when two plain-clothes policemen came to question the clerk, he shot them both, wounding one and murdering Police Constable John MacLeod, then turned the gun on himself, committing suicide.

Curiously, the six boys with whom Finlay had gone through childhood wartime experiences all met unhappy ends: two were hanged, one was killed in a battle with police officers, one was sentenced to life in prison, and one was jailed.

REF.: *CBA*; Cobb, *Murdered On Duty*.

Finlay, Robert Bannatyne (First Viscount Finlay), 1842-1929, Brit., jur. Served as queen's counsel in 1882, as solicitor general from 1895-1900, as attorney general from 1900-06, and as lord chancellor from 1916-18. In 1921, he was one of the first judges to sit on the Permanent Court of International Justice at The Hague. REF.: *CBA*.

Finlay, William (Baron Finlay), 1875-1945, Brit., jur. Sat on the King's Bench Division of the High Court from 1924-38, presiding over the indictment proceedings of Norman Thorne and Arthur Charles Mortimer, and the Dartmoor mutiny trial at Princetown in 1932, involving thirty-one prisoners. He succeeded his father, Robert Finlay, as the Second Viscount Finlay of Nairn in 1929, and was appointed a lord justice of appeal in 1938. REF.: *CBA*.

Finley, Ruth, prom. 1978-81, U.S., crim. insan. The mysterious harassment of a middle-aged couple in Kansas continued for three years, until an astute Wichita police chief realized that the "Poet" who had emotionally abused and even physically assaulted and abducted Ruth Finley was herself.

On Nov. 6, 1978, a conservative, respectable Wichita, Kan., couple, Ed Finley and his wife Ruth Finley, came to police headquarters to report that someone was frightening Ruth with letters and phone calls containing ugly, disturbing rhymes. In the three years and $370,000 that police spent trying to track down the taunter, the so-called "Poet" wreaked havoc on the lives of the Finleys, eventually escalating the harassment to include others. On Nov. 21, 1978, Finley told police his wife had been abducted from downtown and driven around for four hours before she managed to escape. Ruth Finley was kept under heavy surveillance for five weeks; then the watch was suspended. The letters continued until August 1979, when Finley was admitted to St. Joseph Medical Center with three knife wounds, including one which had nearly fatally punctured her kidney. She explained that she had been attacked in a parking lot.

The letters were sent to Dr. Murray S. Miron, a consultant in psycholinguistics, who had been a prominent expert in the Son of Sam case. Miron declared the poet to be "severely psychotic, schizophrenic, wily, pathological, paranoid, and a loner with a deep feeling of persecution." In the year following Miron's assessment, the Poet's antagonism escalated. A knife wrapped in newspaper and addressed to Mrs. Finley was found near her office at the phone company; calls were made to the Health Department to inform them that Ruth was spreading venereal disease; and another was made to the mortuary to say Finley was interested in information about plots. Urine, eggs, feces, and an unlit Molotov cocktail were left on the Finley porch. Their Christmas wreath was burned, and the Poet left a fragment of his trademark red bandana each time.

By late summer of 1981, letters were being sent by the Poet to other people, including Sharon LaMunyon, wife of Wichita Police Chief Richard LaMunyon, who then became involved in the case. He began to notice odd details, like the fact that the only footprints ever found at the scene were Ruth Finley's. He also realized that when police cameras were switched to the backyard, activities of the Poet moved to the front yard, and vice versa. LaMunyon ordered a secret twenty-four-hour surveillance of the Finley house. On Sept. 17, 1981, a police helicopter watched the couple drive to a mailbox; two of the five letters posted by Ruth Finley were from the Poet.

Ed Finely was given a polygraph exam on Oct. 1, and was cleared of any involvement with the harassment. After Detective Mike Hill had questioned Ruth for more than an hour, he asked if she needed help. She broke down and said "yes," later recalling, "I wasn't sure I was guilty. But I did know something was very wrong with me."

In November 1981 Finley went into psychotherapy with Dr. Andrew Pickens, and slowly came to understand that the Poet she had created was a response to being repeatedly raped and abused by a neighbor when she was three years old. She had never told anyone about the rapes, and had later found refuge in poetry. According to Pickens, Finley's reaction was a common response to trauma, called a dissociative reaction, in which the conscious mind splits and one group of mental activities begins to function as a separate unit, almost as if it were another person. In 1978, when Finley was threatened by her husband's ill health, and additionally frightened by a serial killer in Wichita who bound, tortured, and strangled his victims, her childhood trauma was reactivated and her psychological defense mechanism clicked in to place, creating the Poet as her repressed emotions and subconscious fears were triggered.

After five years of therapy, Finley, whose marriage and work both survived her ordeal, wanted to tell her story to the community, hoping it might help others. Accompanied by Pickens, she went on local television in 1989. Of the response mail that poured in, nearly all of it was supportive and sympathetic. See: **Berkowitz, David.** REF.: *CBA.*

Finney, Warren Wesley, prom. 1933, U.S., forg.-fraud-embez. In August 1933 a scandal erupted in Emporia, Kan., when a national bank examiner had questions about bonds held by the National Bank of Topeka, Kan. The U.S. District Attorney routinely made a request of State Treasurer Tom Boyd, asking to check the bonds against those held in the Kansas state vaults. To his surprise, Boyd refused. Obtaining permission from Governor Alfred M. Landon, the district attorney got access to the vaults and, within less than an hour, discovered $329,000 in forged bonds.

Warren Wesley Finney and his son, Ronald Finney became the primary suspects. The elder Finney owned Emporia's Fidelity State & Savings Bank, Farmers State Bank of Neosho Falls, and, through his wife, the Eureka Bank of Eureka. His son Ronald, a gregarious man known for his lavish spending, had bought bonds for Hinsdale County, Colo., attempting to turn an old mining settlement into a vacation resort; he was charged with conspiring with Hinsdale officials to buy up the bonds at thirty cents each and refunding them at their full dollar price. As a bond broker, the younger Finney had also had double sets of false bonds printed for school districts and municipalities, signed with forged signatures by his employee, Leland Caldwell. One set of the bonds had been deposited with State Treasurer Boyd, who later admitted allowing Finney to take away $150,000 of the bonds he had left with the state. More than $1 million in bond forgeries eventually surfaced.

By December 1933, Warren Finney's banks were closed and Boyd had been fired from his post as state treasurer. Warren Finney was convicted of embezzling $63,000 from his Emporia Fidelity State & Savings Bank. He was denied a new trial and was sentenced to three to fifty years in prison on twelve indictments, giving him a total term of thirty-six to 600 years in prison.

Appealing the case, Finney was then hit with several additional indictments from a federal grand jury in Topeka. The one-time leading citizen was charged with sending raised checks through the mail, using the mails to defraud, sending false telephone company statements by mail, and misapplying $146,000 from a national bank. Also indicted were his employee Caldwell; Boyd; Carl W. McKeen, president of the National Bank of Topeka; and C.L. Cooke, president of Topeka's Prudential Investment Co.

Ronald Finney pleaded guilty before Judge P.H. Heinz on Dec. 28, 1933, and was sentenced to hard labor in the state penitentiary for thirty-one to 635 years. He was released after serving eleven years, and moved with his wife to Florida, where he became involved in the advertising business. He died on Oct. 1, 1961, at the age of sixty-four. REF.: *CBA.*

Fioravanti, Alfredo, prom. 1918, U.S., fraud. In 1918, the Metropolitan Museum of Art in New York City paid $40,000 for the seven-foot statue of an Etruscan warrior, believing the piece to have been buried since pre-Roman times. Missing from the figure was one arm and the thumb from the other hand. In 1960 Alfredo Fioravanti confessed to museum officials that he had made the statue along with five other men. As proof, Fioravanti produced the missing thumb, which fit the figure perfectly. REF.: *CBA.*

Fiore, Pasquale, 1837-1914, Italy, jur. Authored international law treatises. REF.: *CBA.*

Fiorentino, Claudio, prom. 1987, Italy, (unsolv.) kid. Claudio Fiorentino was released from jail in early October 1985, along with his two brothers. The Fiorentinos had been charged with illegally exporting foreign currency from their jewelry empire; $17 million worth of funds were thought to have been exported. The news of the fortune attracted the attention of many Sicilian kidnappers and, on Oct. 10, 1985, Claudio Fiorentino fell prey to them. For the next twenty-two months, the jewelry heir was kept blindfolded and chained in an underground hideout near Palermo, where he was nearly starved. Police believe that, during the two years in which Fiorentino's family paid installments to save his life, the jeweler was sold by one gang to another, eventually winding up in the clutches of the Sicilian Mafia. After his family had made the final payment, Fiorentino was tossed out of a car on a country road on Aug. 14, 1987. The wraith-like man staggered into a roadside hotel where the owner, Vincenzo Ajello, mistook him for a drug addict. According to Ajello, "He looked like an old man. His beard was down to his navel and he barely managed to stay on his feet." REF.: *CBA.*

Fiorenza, John, 1913- , U.S., rape-mur. When upholsterer Theodore Kruger and his assistant, John Fiorenza, came to deliver a love seat they had repaired on a rush order to a Beekman Place apartment on New York City's fashionable East Side on Apr. 10, 1936, they got no response. They found the apartment door open, and left the love seat with a bill on the cushion. Kruger then noticed the bathroom door ajar, and saw a woman's legs at an odd angle. Thirty-four-year-old Nancy Evans Titterton, a married writer, lay dead in the bathtub, raped, and then strangled with pieces of her own clothing, which had been ripped. Fiorenza then called police.

Homicide officers found no trace of any struggle in the Tittertons' apartment, indicating that Titterton knew her killer and had let him in. A dent on the bedspread showed the outline of a man's footprint, and traces of mud were also found there. Besides Kruger and Fiorenza's palm and fingerprints, the only other clues were a cord, about thirteen inches long, found underneath the body. Chief Medical Examiner Dr. Thomas A. Gonzales noticed chafing on Titterton's wrist, and noted that her hands had been bound together. The time of death was set at 10:30 a.m.

Titterton's husband, a television executive who was at work when his wife was killed, was cleared of any connection with the death. Neighbors in the building proffered many leads with descriptions of sneak thieves and suspicious callers, and a delivery boy and a janitor were kept under surveillance after questioning by the police. Finally, an animal hair was discovered in the mud found on the bedspread—the type of hair used as a stuffing in furniture. Numerous detectives visited Kruger's store on Second Avenue to talk with Fiorenza. One detective snipped samples off several large coils of cord, while another talked with Kruger, who mentioned Fiorenza's chronic tardiness, and reiterated the fact that his assistant had been late the morning of the murder. Fiorenza, he explained, was on probation for stealing a car, and had reported to his probation officer that morning, telephoning his employer from court, and returning around noon. Later that same day, a piece of the cord was found to match that found in the bathtub, and police remembered that the courts had been closed on Apr. 10, Good Friday. Brought in for questioning, Fiorenza, who had four prior arrests, confessed he had lied about being in court; after several hours, he admitted to raping Titterton, whom he had talked with the day before the murder, and with whom he had become obsessed. Found Guilty of first-degree murder, he died in the electric chair at Sing Sing Prison.

REF.: *CBA*; Hynd, *Murder, Mayhem and Mystery*; Radin, *Crimes of Passion.*

First National Bank of Chicago, 1977, U.S., (unsolv.) rob. Employees of the First National Bank of Chicago learned on Oct. 11, 1977, that $1 million in currency had vanished just before the Columbus Day weekend. At first it was believed that a bank employee had made a clerical error, but then officials determined the money had been taken from a cart. The thief could easily have concealed the money in his clothing.

An employee related to a Chicago mobster emerged as the only suspect. The employee would not take a lie detector test and was eventually fired. However, police did not have enough evidence linking the suspect to the theft, and charges were never filed. In May 1981, twenty-three of the stolen $100 bills were found in Savannah, Ga. The bills apparently had been buried underground. The money was thought to have been used in a cocaine payoff.

REF.: *CBA; Nash, Open Files.*

First National City Bank of New York, prom. 1967-68, U.S., fraud. In August 1967 the Everything Charge Credit Card was sent through the mails to customers of the First National City Bank of New York. Good for purchases of up to $400, the credit card stipulated that, for purchases of over $40, merchants were to check with the issuing bank and make sure that the card was being properly used, and had not been stolen or otherwise fraudulently obtained. In the fall of 1967, the cards were used by a group of people to make purchases and get cash credits. Card holder's names were forged, and purchases were made and then either fenced or returned for cash refunds. It is not known how the cards were obtained. No fictitious names were used, and no attempts were made to imitate signatures of the actual card holders.

On June 14, 1968, multiple-count indictments were brought against eleven people; the charges included grand and petty larceny, criminal possession of stolen goods, and second-degree forgery. It was estimated that the eleven people charged had defrauded the bank of $100,000. Also indicted on charges of second-degree criminal facilitation were five store owners who had made out multiple sales slips to keep purchases below the $40 maximum, in order to sell large quantities of merchandise.

The Everything Credit Card scandal was the third major credit card fraud ring cracked by the Bronx County District Attorney's office. District Attorney Burton Roberts commented that credit card ring cases put a large investigatory and paperwork burden on the department. In the First National City case, the eleven indictments produced more than 1700 separate counts.

REF.: *CBA; McGuire, The Forgers.*

Fischart, Johann (AKA: **Mentzer** or **Mainzer**), 1546-90, Ger., jur. Advocate before the Supreme Court at Speyer from 1580-83, and as magistrate at Forbach in 1583. REF.: *CBA.*

Fischer, Karl, 1918- , Aust., (unsolv.) kid. An avid anti-Fascist, Karl Fischer survived a concentration camp only to be kidnapped later in his native Austria. Fischer was condemned by the Austrian regime of Schuschnigg for his anti-Fascist activities and his membership in a banned anti-Stalin group of Communists, and was sentenced to five years of hard labor. When a general amnesty was called in 1938, Fischer fled to France as a political refugee. The Vichy authorities in 1943 turned Fischer over to the Nazis, and he was held in the Buchenwald concentration camp until it was liberated by the Americans. Fischer's mother had also been sentenced by the Nazis to five years in prison for her anti-Fascist propaganda activities.

On his release from Buchenwald, Fischer returned to his mother's Austrian home, and found work in the American Zone of Linz. A woman friend, Vera Kerschbaumer, warned him that the Communist party was watching him. Kerschbaumer, the daughter of the editor of the local Communist paper, and a member of the party herself, said that the secretary-general of the Communist Party in Upper Austria, Haider, had suggested that she report Fischer. Another Communist party member warned Fischer that he should break off his relationship with Kerschbaumer. On Jan. 22, 1947, Fischer accompanied Kerschbaumer to her home in the Russian zone of Austria, and vanished after he dropped her off.

Although Fischer's disappearance was reported to the Socialist deputies, the mayor of Linz, the Austrian delegate to the United Nations Organization in London, Dr. Koref, the State Secretary, Mantler, and the Socialist Minister of the Interior, no apparent action to find him was made. The Communist paper reported Fischer's "puzzling disappearance," and asked that information be reported to the police. Fischer was believed to have been taken to a Russian concentration camp.

REF.: *CBA; Dewar, Assassins at Large.*

Fischhof, Adolf, 1816-93, Aust., rebel. One of the leaders in the Viennese revolution in 1848. The same year he was elected president of the Executive Committee of Security, but in 1849 on suppression of revolution he was briefly imprisoned. REF.: *CBA.*

Fish, Hamilton Albert Howard (AKA: **Robert Hayden, Frank Howard, John W. Pell, Thomas A. Sprague**), 1870-1936, U.S., can.-mur. Raised in a Washington, D.C., orphanage, Albert Fish blamed his later heinous crimes on his years in the orphanage where sadistic cruelty was inflicted upon children. "Misery leads to crime," Fish later stated. "I saw so many boys whipped it ruined my mind." Fish later claimed to have molested more than 400 children in a span of twenty years. He was a sneaky child killer who, according to a psychiatrist examining him before his execution, "lived a life of unparalleled perversity. There was no known perversion that he did not practice and practice frequently."

Fish married in 1898 and the union produced three children. For many years he lived a normal life, working hard as a house decorator and painter. But Fish's mind seemed to snap in 1917 when his wife ran away with a half-witted lover, John Straube. Fish had taken his children to a movie and, upon returning home, he found the place stripped of the furniture and his wife gone.

The brazen Mrs. Fish returned with Straube in tow some time later, asking to stay with Fish. He told her she could return to the family but Straube had to depart. Mrs. Fish ordered her bumbling lover to leave but Fish later found Straube hiding in the attic of the Fish house. Mrs. Fish smuggled him into the attic during the night. Straube stayed in the attic for weeks while Mrs. Fish smuggled him food and visited him nocturnally for sexual bouts. When Fish discovered Straube in the attic he ordered his wife and her dim-witted lover from the house.

The family never saw Mrs. Fish again. Fish himself began to act strangely a short time later. He took his family to a small cottage in Westchester County, N.Y., and there practiced bizarre rites, climbing to the top of a hill at night and baying at the moon: "I am Christ! I am Christ!" He made meals that consisted of raw meat, serving this to his children and saying: "That's the way I like my meat and you'll have to eat it that way, too." He ran around at night naked and howled at the moon, antics that later earned him the press sobriquet, "The Moon Maniac."

Fish took to beating himself and then encouraged his own children and their friends to paddle his bare buttocks until his flesh bled. Fish made a paddle studded with inch-and-a-half nails. His perplexed son, Albert Fish, Jr., discovered this device and asked his father why he had constructed such an instrument. "I use them on myself," Fish blurted to the boy. "I get certain feelings over me. When I do, I've got to torture myself." He burned himself with white hot pokers, needles, and irons. For many years he collected articles on cannibalism and became obsessed with flesh-eating, carrying these rare journalistic writings with him until the clippings yellowed and finally crumbled to dust.

Fish was involved in several postal swindles and spent three months in jail for practicing a confidence game in the mails. He was then examined by psychiatrists but released as a "harmless" old man suffering from a "severe guilt conscience." Fish was later examined at Bellevue Asylum in New York but was again released as a non-violent masochist. He was known by authorities to practice self-flagellation, burning of his own flesh, coprophilia, and other self-punishing acts such as inserting small needles beneath his flesh.

An avid reader of the lovelorn columns, Fish answered scores of ads from lonely widows. Forty-six of these letters were later recovered and submitted as evidence at Fish's murder trial but the

Albert Fish, murderer and cannibal, who, according to psychiatrists, "lived a life of unparalleled perversity. There was no known perversion he did not practice and practice often."

Mrs. Budd and her children; Grace Budd stands at right; she went away with Fish on June 3, 1928, and never returned.

Fish's murder retreat, Wisteria Cottage in White Plains, N.Y., where the cannibal killed and dismembered little Grace Budd.

Police and newsmen crowding about the burial site of Grace Budd's remains outside of Fish's blood-stained Wisteria Cottage, 1934.

Albert Fish, under arrest, after signing his horrific confession in which he admitted to decades of murder and cannibalism.

Fish examining his confession in preparation for a trial he expected to lose; he spent his time reveling in his terrible past.

Albert Fish, second from left, handcuffed to another prisoner, entering Sing Sing Prison; he looked forward to his execution.

prosecution refused to read from them, so filled with vile obscenities were they. Fish informed these lonely women that he was not at all interested in marriage. He merely wanted them to paddle and punish him. He got no offers. It is not certain when Albert Fish embarked on murder as a way of satisfying his dark inner longings. He later confessed to murdering a man in Wilmington, Del., in 1910. He also said he murdered and mutilated a boy in New York in 1919 and that same year he murdered another boy on a houseboat in the Georgetown area of Washington, D.C.

By the late 1920s, Fish avidly sought children to attack and, by his own later admission, he molested and murdered 4-year-old William Gaffney on Feb. 11, 1927. On Mar. 3, 1928, Fish abducted and murdered 12-year-old Grace Budd, the crime for which he paid with his life in Sing Sing's electric chair. Using the name Frank Howard, the killer ingratiated himself to the Budd family. After several visits to the Budds in Manhattan, Fish convinced the naive Budd family members that he was a kindly old gentleman who merely dropped by to see their children. Fish brought them presents and when he suggested that he take 12-year-old Grace to a children's party, Mrs. Budd allowed Fish to take the girl. It was the last time the Budds saw Grace alive.

The trusting Grace Budd left her home with Fish on June 3, 1928, taking a train with him to White Plains, N.Y. Between them on the seat was a box in which Fish kept what he later described as his "instruments of hell." The box contained a butcher knife, a cleaver, and a saw. The old man and Grace got off the train but Grace quickly went back aboard and then returned with the box which Fish had forgotten. The pair walked the long distance to the Fish cottage where Fish took all his clothes off. The girl screamed: "I'll tell Mama!" Fish jumped forward and strangled Grace. He then decapitated her and sawed her body in half. In a later confession, so grisly and gruesome in detail that it caused listeners to retch, Fish happily recounted how he carved up the girl's body and made a stew out of it which he lived on for several days.

The Budds reported their daughter's disappearance but continued to believe that Grace had somehow survived and was alive. Then, in 1934, for inexplicable reasons, Fish sat down and wrote a letter to the Budds, telling them that he had murdered their daughter. He took great pains to point out that he had not sexually molested her before killing her. It was about this time that Fish, walking down a street in Fort Richmond, Long Island, spotted 5-year-old France McDonel playing outside his home. He picked up the boy and carried him away, taking him to Wisteria Cottage in White Plains where he strangled the boy.

By then detectives had traced the letter Fish had sent to the Budd family and they found the old man shortly after he had killed the McDonel boy. One puzzled detective asked Fish why he had risked revealing himself by writing the letter. The killer became defensive. He told detectives that he had kept track of police activity on "the case in the papers. If they had accused someone else I would have come forward. My best days are over." Fish was brought before the Budds and they identified him as the Frank Howard who took their daughter away with him. The area around Fish's Wisteria Cottage was dug up and Grace Budd's remains were found.

Placed on trial, Fish's attorneys pled the cannibal killer not guilty by reason of insanity but the prosecution provided a small army of psychiatrists who testified that he was sane. After a prolonged trial, Fish was found Guilty and sentenced to death. Fish was sent to Sing Sing, handcuffed to another killer named Stone. Ironically, both Fish and Stone had had forefathers who had fought in the American Revolution. While awaiting execution, Fish delightedly told newsmen and prison officials that he was ecstatic at the prospect of being electrocuted in Sing Sing's electric chair. "What a thrill that will be if I have to die in the electric chair," Fish said with a broad smile. "It will be the supreme thrill. The only one I haven't tried."

On Jan. 16, 1936, Fish walked without help into Sing Sing's

execution room and sat down almost eagerly in the electric chair. He helped the executioner affix the electrodes on his legs. The enthusiasm Fish displayed toward his own painful death shocked the reporters who were present to witness his execution. Fish, the oldest prisoner ever to be electrocuted in Sing Sing, smiled happily as the electrodes were applied to his head. When the switch was pulled, a massive jolt of 3,000 volts coursed through Fish's body. A blue cloud of smoke rose from the top of the old man's head as he let out a guttural laugh. He did not die. Thanks to the hundreds of tiny needles he had inserted in his body over the years, the metal in the old man's abused body actually short-circuited the electric chair. Another prolonged charge of electricity had to be sent through his body before Albert Fish was pronounced dead.

The cannibal's last statement had been given to one of his defense attorneys only an hour before Albert Fish encountered his "supreme thrill." Reporters begged the attorney to release the statement but the lawyer grimly shook his head, saying: "I shall never show it to anyone. It was the most filthy string of obscenities that I have ever read."

REF.: Angelella, *Trail of Blood;* Boar, *The World's Most Infamous Murders;* Browne, *The Rise of Scotland Yard; CBA;* Dickson, *Murder By Numbers;* Fox, *Mass Murder;* Grierson, *Murder by the Numbers;* Heimer, *The Cannibal;* Livingston, *The Murdered and the Missing;* Masters, *Perverse Crimes in History;* _____ and Lea, *Sex Crimes In History;* Nash, *Almanac of World Crime;* _____, *Bloodletters and Badmen;* Playfair, *Crime In Our Century;* Scott, *Concise Encyclopedia of Crime and Criminals;* Wertham, *The Show of Violence;* Wilson, *Encyclopedia of Murder.*

Fisher, Bishop, prom. 1535, Brit., treas. When a popular clergyman was executed for treason, his head was posted on a pole, but the attempt to frighten his followers backfired.

Executed in June 1535 for treason, Bishop Fisher was beheaded, and after his body was buried, his head, which had been parboiled, was set up on a pole and placed high on London Bridge as a warning. But, in the fourteen days that it stood on the bridge, the head did not decay despite the weather being extremely hot. According to the official report, it "grew daily fresher and fresher, so that in his lifetime he never looked so well; for his cheeks being beautified with a comely red, the face looked as though it had beholded [sic] the people passing by, and would have spoken to them."

Many people took this as a miracle, and a sign that the heavenly powers were pleased to receive the beloved bishop. So many came to see the head that traffic was completely blocked, and at the end of fourteen days, the executioner was ordered to go at night and toss the head into the Thames River.

REF.: *CBA;* Bishop, *Executions.*

Fisher, Dennis, prom. 1975, U.S., mur. When a young, healthy farmer suddenly and inexplicably disappeared, his wife and a farmhand came under suspicion, and soon confessed to murder.

In Delaware County, Iowa, the sheriff's office received a missing person's report from 19-year-old Myra Miller, mother of three, telling how she and her husband, Howard Miller, had an argument two weeks earlier, after which he had gone to Dubuque, driven there by the Millers' farmhand Dennis Fisher.

The sheriff found no reason for the prosperous farmer to have left the home which he valued and cherished. Nor had the farmer contacted any of his Dubuque relatives.

In the next two months, Fisher and Myra Miller auctioned off most of the farm machinery and cattle. Arrested on Apr. 23, they were discovered to be in the process of moving to a new home in West Plains, Mo. According to police, both admitted their guilt the night they were arrested, with Fisher admitting that he shot his employer when Miller threatened to kill his wife because of her liaison with the farmhand. Digging up the dirt floor of the calf shed at the Miller farm, police found the corpse with bullet holes in the right shoulder and the head. Fisher was sentenced to life in prison with the help of Myra Miller's testimony against him, while the widow, originally charged with murder, was allowed

to plead guilty to reduced charges of conspiracy to obstruct justice, in exchange for her evidence against Fisher.
REF.: *CBA; Godwin, Murder U.S.A.*

Fisher, Frederick Charles, 1875- , Phil., jur. Appointed by President Woodrow Wilson to the Supreme Court of the Philippine Islands in 1917, and wrote the article, "Some Peculiarities of Philippine Criminal Procedure," *Virginia Law Review* in 1932. REF.: *CBA.*

Fisher, George Purnell, 1817-99, U.S., jur. Served as Delaware attorney general from 1855-60, U.S. attorney from 1870-75, and was appointed by President Abraham Lincoln to the District Court of the District of Columbia in 1863. REF.: *CBA.*

Fisher, John (AKA: John of Rochester), 1459-1535, Brit., her. Appointed the bishop of Rochester in 1504, and imprisoned in the Tower of London by Henry VIII when he refused to recognize the king's marriage to Anne Boleyn in 1534. In 1535, he was named archbishop by Pope Paul III. He rejected the Act of Supremacy, which declared the king the supreme head of the church, and was consequently beheaded at the behest of Henry VIII. REF.: *CBA.*

Fisher, John King (AKA: King Fisher), 1854-84, U.S., west. law enfor. off.-gunman. John King Fisher was born in Collin County, Texas. His mother died when he was five and his father, a cattleman who established several ranches throughout Texas, left the boy on his own. At the age of fifteen, Fisher stole a horse and, following his arrest, he escaped, hiding out on one of his father's ranches. At sixteen, he broke into a house in Goliad, Texas, was caught and was sentenced to the state penitentiary for a year, though he served only four months. Upon his release, Fisher became an honest cowboy and learned how to break wild horses and drive cattle. He learned how to use a six-gun and he became a crack shot and a quick draw. He later bought a ranch which he called the Pendencia near

Texas gunman turned peace officer, John King Fisher.

Eagle Pass, Texas. There he placed a sign at a crossroad which read: "This is King Fisher's road. Take the other one!"

During the 1870s, Fisher took up rustling and he also became a shrewd gambler. He was quick to anger and quicker to draw his gun. He claimed in 1878 that he had killed seven men, mostly in gambling arguments, and he was not including "several Mexicans." He was a colorful dresser who favored fringed shirts, red sashes, and bells on his spurs. Anyone ridiculing his apparel, inevitably faced his guns. The most persistent legend about Fisher was his killing of four Mexican *vaqueros* in a cattle pen on his own ranch. These men arrived at Fisher's place to buy cattle but appeared as though they were about to steal his herd.

When they refused to leave his ranch, Fisher suddenly brought down a branding iron on the skull of one, crushing it. He outdrew a second Mexican and killed him with a single shot through the head. Then he spun around and shot the other two men as they, too, were drawing their weapons, killing both *vaqueros*. These four deaths were never verified, except in tall tales about King Fisher which abounded throughout Texas during his lifetime and after. He was arrested several times for rustling and murder in 1875 but the charges were later dropped.

In 1876, Fisher married and sired four daughters. His new domestic life did not temper his outlaw impulses. He went on rustling and was arrested many times for murder, although the charges were invariably dropped for lack of evidence. In most of these instances, Fisher simply threatened witnesses with death if they dared to testify against him. Fisher was not the best of drinking companions. While in a bar in Zavala County, Texas, on Dec. 25, 1876, a cowboy named William Donovan refused to buy Fisher a drink, and the gunman fired three bullets into Donovan, killing him. In 1877, Fisher was arrested by Texas Ranger Lee Hall and charged with murder. Fisher however, was expertly defended in court by Major T.T. Teel and was found Not Guilty.

Fisher began to reform in the late 1870s, so much so, that instead of shooting another gunman in an argument he thought better of it and tried to reholster his six-gun. He was drunk at the time and his gun went off accidentally and Fisher shot himself in the leg. He was tried for another murder but was cleared of this charge. By 1881, Fisher became a champion of law and order and he was sworn in as a deputy sheriff in Uvalde County. For a short time he served as acting sheriff. In 1883, while acting sheriff of Uvalde County, Fisher rode out to the ranch owned by Tom and Jim Hannehan. The brothers were suspected of having robbed a stagecoach. When Fisher confronted them, both brothers went for their guns. The lightning-fast Fisher shot Tom Hannehan dead and wounded his brother who surrendered and turned over the money stolen from the stage.

Early in 1884, Fisher announced that he was a candidate for sheriff in the upcoming election. He went to Austin, Texas, on official business and there met an old friend, the fierce gunfighter Ben Thompson who gave Fisher an autographed photo of himself. After visiting several Austin bars together, Thompson decided to accompany Fisher to San Antonio which was along the route Fisher was taking when returning to Uvalde. Once in San Antonio, both men caroused through the saloons and talked boisterously of their gunslinging pasts. Thompson began to abuse a black porter in one saloon and Fisher warned him to stop this. Both men were theater-goers and they attended a play at the Turner Hall Opera House on the night of Mar. 11, 1884.

When the pair left the Opera House at 10:30 p.m., they decided to attend the Vaudeville Variety Theater, an inappropriate selection in that Thompson had been in this gambling hall two weeks earlier and had killed its proprietor, Jack Harris. Thompson and Fisher had several drinks at the bar there, then went upstairs to the theater to watch the show. They sat in a large box, drinking heavily and were shortly joined by Joe Foster and Billy Simms, former partners of the deceased Jack Harris. Bouncer Jacob Coy then joined the group in the box. Thompson made several critical remarks about Harris and when Foster objected, Thompson jerked his six-gun from its holster and jammed it into Foster's mouth, playfully cocking the weapon.

Coy leaped forward and grabbed Thompson's weapon. Fisher stood and took several steps backward in the box, saying he was leaving "before trouble started." Thompson then joined him but before the two men could leave the box, Coy, Foster, and Simms

Gunman Ben Thompson, killed with Fisher in a San Antonio theater.

pulled their weapons and blasted the two men. They were aided by three armed men lurking in the shadows of the next box, gambler Canada Bill (no relation to famous Canada Bill Jones), Harry Tremaine, a performer at the theater and close friend of the slain Jack Harris, and a bartender named McLaughlin. These men had aimed shotguns and rifles into the box and had stationed themselves as part of the planned ambush of Ben Thompson.

Fisher and Thompson were riddled with bullets, Fisher struck thirteen times in the head and chest and killed on the spot. Thompson was struck with nine bullets and also collapsed dead in the box. As he fell, the still deadly Ben Thompson managed to get off several shots. Coy received a minor wound and Foster was struck in the leg, the bullet striking an artery. Foster's leg had to be amputated and he died a few days later from shock and loss of blood. Despite his attempt to reform and work on the side of the law, John King Fisher's past embraced him at the end and brought about his bloody, premature death at the age of thirty. See: **Thompson, Ben.**

REF.: American Guide Series, *Texas, A Guide to the Lone Star State;* Asbury, *Sucker's Progress;* Barkley, *History of Travis County and Austin;* Breihan, *Badmen of Frontier Days;* ____, *Great Gunfighters of the West;* ____, *Outlaws of the Old West;* Bushick, *Glamorous Days;* Casey, *The Texas Border and Some Borderliners; CBA;* Chapel, *Guns of the Old West;* Cook, *Fifty Years on the Old Frontier;* Corner, *San Antonio de Bexar;* Cunningham, *Triggernometry;* Curtis, *Fabulous San Antonio;* Dobie, *A Vacquero of the Brush Country;* Durham, *Taming of the Neuces Strip;* Fenley, *Grandad and I;* Fisher, *Texas Heritage of the Fishers and the Clarks;* ____, and Dykes, *King Fisher: His Life and Times;* Foster-Harris, *The Look of the Old West;* Hendricks, *The Bad Man of the West;* Holloway, *Texas Gun Lore;* Hough, *The Story of the Outlaw;* House, *City of Flaming Adventure;* ____, *Cowtown Columnist;* Hudson, *Andy Adams;* Hunter and Rose, *The Album of Gunfighters;* Huson, *Refugio;* James, *Frontier and Pioneer Recollections of Early Days in San Antonio;* Jennings, *A Texas Ranger;* Knight, *Wild Bill Hickok;* Koenigberg, *King News;* Leakey, *The West That Was;* McCarty, *The Gunfighters;* McGiffin, *Ten Tall Texans;* Marshall, *Swinging Doors;* Masterson, *Famous Gunfighters of the Western Frontier;* Michelson, *Mankillers at Close Range;* Miller, *Footloose Fiddler;* North, *The Saga of the Cowboy;* O'Neal, *They Die But Once;* Penfield, *Western Sheriffs and Marshals;* Peyton, *San Antonio: City in the Sun;* Plenn, *Texas Hellion: The True Story of Ben Thompson;* Raine, *Famous Sheriffs and Western Outlaws;* ____, *Guns of the Frontier;* Ramsdell, *San Antonio;* Raymond, *Captain Lee Hall of Texas;* Rifkin, *King Fisher's Roads;* Ripley, *They Died With Their Boots On;* Roberts, *Springs from Parched Ground;* Rosa, *The Gunfighter: Man or Myth?;* Sabin, *Wild Men of the Wild West;* Siringo, *Riata and Spurs;* Strauss, *Levi's Roundup of Western Sheriffs;* Streeter, *Prairie Trails and Cow Towns;* Waters, *A Gallery of Western Badmen;* White, *Lead and Likker;* White, *Texas;* Young, *Life and Exploits of S. Glenn Young.*

Fisher, Joseph Jefferson, 1910- , U.S., jur. District attorney for San Augustine County, Texas, from 1939-46, and the county's District Court judge from 1957-59, before President Dwight D. Eisenhower appointed him to the Eastern District Court of Texas in 1959. REF.: *CBA.*

Fisher, Julius, c.1914-46, U.S., mur. Catherine Cooper Reardon, 37-year-old librarian at the Washington, D.C., Cathedral, went home for lunch on Mar. 1, 1944. She shared a small three-room apartment with her invalid widowed mother. After lunch Catherine returned to work. When she had not returned home by nine that night, a friend reported her missing to the police.

The following morning the Washington police received an anonymous call. "A young woman has been murdered at the Washington Cathedral," a male voice said, "You fellows had better get busy." At the same time John Bayliss, the curator of the library, and Helen Abbey Young, an archivist, had just reported to work. They noticed bloodstains on the basement floor and began a search of the library. In the attic they found Catherine Reardon's coat, gloves, hat, and purse. In the sub-basement they found Reardon's battered body. Only moments after the anonymous call the police were notified of the murder.

The victim had been beaten on the head and neck. Her clothes were bunched around her head and her panties were missing. At first police believed the woman had been sexually assaulted. Within the hour, the police had a suspect in the case. He was Julius Fisher, thirty-two, a workman at the library. In his home they found bloodstained clothes. Fisher, who was in a restaurant when police arrived, pulled a .32-caliber revolver but was quickly subdued by detectives E.E. Scott and Richard Felber. Fisher confessed that he killed Reardon when she complained about his work. The murder weapon was a piece of firewood. The killer had not raped the woman but removed her panties to "sop up the blood." The autopsy confirmed this.

On Dec. 20, 1946, Fisher went to the electric chair at the District of Columbia Jail. That same day two other men were executed in the same jail for the murder of women. Joseph Dunbar Medley was executed for the murder of Nancy Boyer, and William Copeland was executed for the murder of his sister-in-law. REF.: *CBA.*

Fisher, Kitty, prom. 18th Cent., Brit., pros. A high-class and vivacious prostitute, Kitty Fisher was known for her whimsical behavior, once deciding for a period of time only to have customers who were members of the House of Lords.

In London in the eighteenth century, Fisher was noted for her great beauty and her business sense, adding to a successful career as a prostitute. She was known for her wit, judgment, and elegance, and she charged 100 guineas a night for her services. Among her large and prosperous clientele, Fisher counted the king's brother, the Duke of York, who one time left £50 on her dressing table in the morning. Fisher was so offended that she decreed that he should never be allowed in her room again, and showed how disdainful she was of his gift by putting it between two slices of bread and butter and eating it for breakfast. Demanding extravagant, and sometimes impossible, gifts from her lovers, Fisher enjoyed eating strawberries in winter, and reveled in other unusual and excessive behavior.

REF.: *CBA;* Henriques, *Prostitution.*

Fisher, Lavinia, prom. 1819, U.S., rob.-mur. When covered wagons transported goods through South Carolina during the days of the early nineteenth century, an enterprising couple became highway robbers, along with their gang, at the Six Mile House.

Lavinia Fisher and her husband, John Fisher, were notorious in Charleston, S.C., for some time before they were arrested. They threatened the wealthy wagon trade and were suspected of murdering travelers as well as robbing them on the highway and at crooked roadside inns in corrupt gambling games. The Fishers were the target of a cavalcade on Feb. 18, 1819. Their head-quarters, the Six Mile House, was off the highway in the upper part of South Carolina, near the strategic point where the roads forked towards Georgia. Gang members included William Hayward, a criminal with a long police record; Joseph Roberts; and John Andrews. When the cavalcade arrived, the inhabitants of the infamous gang left, returning the next day. David Ross, who had been left to guard the house, was beaten, choked, and pummeled by the tall and attractive Lavinia until he managed to escape. The Amazon-like woman was rumored to have poisoned travelers' food and then to have slid their bodies down a trap door into the cellar.

The gang was finally arrested after John Peoples swore an affidavit against them, saying he had been watering his horse near their home when nine or ten people, including Lavinia, came out to beat and rob him. Judge Charles Jones Colcock issued a warrant, and Colonel Nathaniel Green Cleary, along with several deputies armed with muskets, bayonets, and a keg of powder, arrested the group, burning the house to the ground.

The prisoners were taken to jail on Magazine Street; within a few days, James Sterritt and John Smith were also arrested in conjunction with the highway robberies. When Coroner Jervis Henry Stevens found two skeletons near the Six Mile House, Hayward, Roberts, and the Fishers were held without bail, and brought before Judge Elihu Hall Bay on Mar. 23 for a hearing. Soon after the hearing, another criminal was added to the group. René Jacobs was taken into custody; he had recently robbed the house of Philip Walker, about ten miles from the Six Mile homestead, and made a full confession of his involvement with the gang.

The case was brought to trial on May 27, with attorney John

Davis Heath for the defense, and Robert Y. Hayne, who would later become famous for debating Daniel Webster in the Senate in 1830, for the prosecution. The gang was found Guilty of highway robbery. On June 2, John and Lavinia Fisher were brought before Judge Charles Jones Colcock. He accepted Heath's motion for a new trial to be held in January 1820. On Sept. 13, John Fisher and Roberts escaped from jail, taking Lavinia with them; all were recaptured within a few days, and then kept under heavy guard. At the Constitutional Court hearing in January Judge Colcock rejected the Fishers' plea for a new trial, and they were condemned to hang. Before a huge crowd, at about 1:00 p.m. on Feb. 18, 1820, the statuesque couple, arm in arm, entered the hangman's coach to be carried to their deaths. They embraced at the scaffold, and were hanged together. Hayward, later convicted of highway robbery, was hanged in early August, and Roberts, who had pleaded guilty to assault, was fined $1,000 and given a one-year jail term.

REF.: *CBA; Rodell, Charleston Murders.*

Fisher, Margaret, prom. 1722, Brit., pros.-rob. Margaret Fisher, a prostitute, was accused of robbing Daniel McDonald after inviting him to her room for a drink. At her trial at the Old Bailey in 1722, she claimed that she was the one invited, and that no robbery had taken place. She was found Guilty of theft and sentenced to death. But she then informed the court that she was pregnant. A jury of matrons examined Fisher, and found this to be the only truth she presented in court. She was pardoned.

REF.: *CBA; Mitchell, The Newgate Calendar; Nash, Look For the Woman.*

Fisher, William, 1911- , U.S., (wrong. convict.) mur. Wrongly convicted of first-degree manslaughter, William Fisher spent eleven years in prison, and another forty years trying to clear his name and get compensation for his unjust sentence.

In 1933, Fisher was at Belden's, a Harlem speakeasy and dance hall, when a brawl broke out. In the foray, he was gashed in the leg, hit in the head, and carried out the back door before two men were killed by gunshots; one of them was Fisher's acquaintance. Assistant District Attorney Miles O'Brien linked Fisher with the gun that the prosecutor said had been the murder weapon, and Fisher was convicted of manslaughter and sentenced to fifteen to thirty years. Fisher made good use of his time at Sing Sing Prison and the Comstock Correctional Facility, studying law, filing his own appeals, and finding new evidence in his case. In 1944, after eleven years in prison, Fisher was paroled.

At legal proceedings in 1936 and in 1958, it was established that O'Brien knew there was no connection between Fisher and the gun, and that he had suppressed evidence, including ballistics findings and police testimony, which proved Fisher was innocent. Years later, the wrongly convicted man explained O'Brien's behavior: "He was a highly ambitious person who wanted to become a judge. And, in the process, he was willing to send someone like me—a working stiff with no funds, no connections, and no knowledge of legal matters—to prison." O'Brien never achieved his desire to become a judge.

Fisher, who married and fathered two children, spent most of his working years driving moving vans and coal trucks before retiring in 1976. Six bills before the New York State Legislature requesting permission to sue the state for his wrongful incarceration were vetoed by Governors Nelson Rockefeller, Hugh Carey, and Mario Cuomo. In 1983, the 72-year-old man told a reporter, "I'm not the type to walk away. When you pick a fight with me there's got to be a winner or a loser."

In 1984, the state waived its immunity in a bill signed by Governor Cuomo. In 1986, the courts awarded Fisher $750,000 for his imprisonment. REF.: *CBA.*

Fisk, James, Jr. (AKA: Jubilee Jim, Prince Erie, Big Jim) 1835-72, U.S., fraud. Jim Fisk was a towering, broad-chested, and jovial confidence man, the most spectacular swindler of his era. He was known as Jubilee Jim because of his expansive and expensive style of living. He was also called Prince Erie because of his wild manipulation of the Erie Railroad Stock which caused a Wall Street panic that became legendary. Many times a millionaire before his murder by Edward "Ned" Stokes in 1872, Fisk began dirt poor and without a formal education. Yet his native intelligence and shrewd judgment was to benefit him time and again in his confrontations with America's super rich. He bested the greediest of America's tycoons and became the supreme robber baron of his day through nerve and an acute sense of the ridiculous.

Fisk was born in Pownal, Vt., on Sept. 12, 1835. He was a strapping youth at the age of fourteen and he left his homestead to travel with Van Amburgh's circus, working first as a roustabout, then a barker. He stayed with the circus for eight years. At age fifteen he married circus performer Lucy Moore. He then returned to Pownal to work in his father's peddling business. Fisk was so effective a salesman that he had soon built up the business to make it an attractive purchase by Marsh & Co., a large Boston firm. He went to work for this firm as a salesman but when the Civil War began Fisk went to Washington, D.C., and obtained huge contracts for blankets to be used by the Union Army, though his supplies did not exist. He then purchased blankets at cut rates from depressed mills and made his first fortune. Fisk was not above bribing Union Army officials to obtain more Army contracts for such supplies and his coffers filled again.

Following the war, Fisk became a hated carpetbagger, traveling through the South using his war spoils to buy up enormous amounts of confiscated cotton at bargain prices. He then moved to New York, entered the brokerage business and peddled cotton at high rates, gleaning enormous profits. He befriended at this time another entrepreneur, Jay Gould, and together this pair set out to outwit the financial giants of the U.S. Fisk and Gould, in 1867, joined forces with the crafty and unscrupulous Daniel Drew who had made his fortune years earlier by watering livestock (purposely withholding water from cattle, then letting them drink their fill until they achieved a bloated weight at point of sale).

Drew had swindled his arch business enemy, Commodore Cornelius Vanderbilt, years earlier by selling him a steamship line without steamships. Vanderbilt, as greedy as Drew, owned the lucrative New York Central Railroad and cast covetous eyes on Drew's Erie line. Drew made Fisk and Gould directors of the Erie Railroad. Fisk planted newspaper reports that Erie stock was about to be purchased in large amounts by a secret consortium and this prompted Vanderbilt to begin buying up Erie stock, attempting to take control of the railroad. In that era, little or no regulations governed stock sales so that when Vanderbilt began buying huge blocks of Erie stock, Fisk and Gould simply printed more certificates and flooded the market. Once valued at about $20 million, Erie soared to an inflated value of $57 million.

Vanderbilt bought and bought and still could not corner Erie. Said Fisk to Gould as they stood next to their printing operations where Erie stock was being created: "If this printing press don't break down, I'll be damned if I don't give the old hog (Vanderbilt) all he wants of Erie!" Vanderbilt finally uncovered the watered stock swindle when one of his buyers received new Erie stock certificates and the ink smeared on his fingerprints, causing him to collapse in shock. Fisk, Gould, and Drew, with more than $6 million stuffed in carpetbags, escaped ahead of Vanderbilt's detectives by fleeing to New Jersey on the ferry.

The robber barons took refuge in Jersey City, fortifying a hotel called Taylor's Castle and surrounding the place with more than 100 thugs imported from New York. Vanderbilt's own army of strong-arm men arrived to retrieve the commodore's millions but they were beaten off, Fisk himself leading his men in a head-bashing attack. Fisk gave interviews to New York reporters from his New Jersey bastion, boldly admitting that he had bested Vanderbilt by floating Erie stock, and saying that he and Gould were nothing more than two enterprising young men who were trying to expand their business interests. Gould, tight-lipped, refused to meet with the press. He spent days in his room at Tay-

Left, "Big Jim" Fisk and, right, his paramour Josie Mansfield.

The NYC brownstone Fisk bought for Josie.

Big Jim dining with friends during his heyday.

Fisk's lavish office in New York.

Commodore Fisk, on board his yacht, toasting President Grant.

The gold corner panic, 1869.

Gould escaping process servers.

Erie investors prying open Gould's office doors, 1872.

Stokes waiting to kill Fisk.

Edward "Ned" Stokes, shooting Big Jim to death in 1872.

Jubilee Jim Fisk in his coffin.

lor's Castle, writing down schemes in which to swindle Vanderbilt out of more millions. Drew told Fisk and Gould that he was disgusted with both of them and resented being an exile in New Jersey. Then Gould, at Fisk's urging, stuffed $1 million into a carpetbag and left in the middle of the night, secretly traveling to Albany, N.Y., the state's capital.

The next day Helen Josephine "Josie" Mansfield, a ravishing and successful actress who had become Fisk's mistress, arrived to keep Fisk company in Jersey City. Fisk showered Mansfield with jewels and furs and invited the press to interview her. Newsmen wrote columns about her "buxom beauty" and "dazzling white skin." Meanwhile, Gould met quietly in Albany with William Marcy Tweed, the most corrupt state senator in the legislature. Tweed would later take over New York's political power base, Tammany Hall and become the country's leading grafter. Gould simply bought the state legislature through Tweed, paying some senators as much as $70,000 and others only $5,000. They voted approval of all existing Erie stock, even legitimatizing another huge block of stock still in the hands of Drew, Fisk, and Gould. Vanderbilt was thusly deprived of legal action in the gigantic Erie swindle.

Vanderbilt nevertheless continued to file lawsuits but dropped the involved legal actions when Fisk, Gould, and Drew agreed to return $4.5 million of his stolen money. The robber barons agreed, keeping almost $3 million more they had taken from Vanderbilt. The commodore was willing to split the difference, figuring that he was recouping money he might never see again. With their profits, the ambitious Fisk and Gould made bold plans to corner the gold market in 1869. Gould first bribed Abel R. Corbin, brother-in-law of President U.S. Grant, to spy in the White House and learn whether or not the Grant Administration intended to keep a lid on releasing gold reserves. When Corbin informed Gould that no gold would be released into the open market for some time, Fisk and Gould began buying up the $15 million in gold then in the marketplace.

To disguise their identities, Fisk and Gould employed purchasing agents to sign gold purchases for them. To keep Grant from knowing of his move, Fisk invited the president on board his resplendent yacht, *The Providence,* and there wined and dined the liquor-loving Grant. Fisk was in his element, elegantly attired in his admiral's uniform and hosting an enormous seaboard fête. Fisk questioned the president about administration plans to release gold in the future but the crafty Grant, suspecting Fisk's intentions, merely puffed on his cigar and gulped down whiskey while engaging Fisk in innocuous and uninformative conversation.

Meanwhile agents for Fisk and Gould bought gold in a frenzy, driving the price up from 133 to 165. When gold reached this peak, Fisk and Gould sold out there enormous holdings and reaped about $10 million each. The sell-off caused a panic which culminated on "Black Friday," Sept. 24, 1869. Thousands of investors were ruined and dozens committed suicide or went insane. Fisk and Gould went on to plan more grand schemes. One of these was the acquisition of a productive oil refinery owned by Edward S. "Ned" Stokes. Fisk and Stokes became fast friends and Fisk introduced Stokes to his mistress, Josie Mansfield. Stokes, who was born in Philadelphia on Apr. 27, 1841, and came from an aristocratic Pennsylvania family, was immediately attracted to Mansfield and the two began to meet secretly.

Fisk began to spend lavishly on Mansfield and himself. He bought Pike's Grand Opera House at Eighth Avenue and 23rd Street, moving into sumptuous offices in this building. He bought a brownstone for Mansfield nearby and he gave lavish parties regularly. Fisk added more mistresses to his roster, at least a dozen, driving around in his huge carriage with no fewer than six beautiful women. He wore a new suit of clothes each day and he glittered with diamonds. He backed musicals in the Opera House and spent most of his time selecting seductive females to appear in his shows, adding these women to his list of mistresses, all of which soon alienated Josie Mansfield and drove her into the arms of Ned Stokes.

Fisk by then had bought stock in Stokes' oil refinery. When Fisk heard that Stokes was secretly visiting Mansfield, he exploded, swearing out a warrant for Stokes' arrest, claiming that his business partner had embezzled $50,000 from their joint ventures. Stokes was jailed overnight on Jan. 4, 1871, until he could arrange bail. The next day Stokes sued Fisk for slander. Then Fisk, to punish Mansfield for going over to Stokes, charged Mansfield and Stokes with blackmailing him. Josie Mansfield sued her former lover for libel. Stokes was brought to trial first on Jan. 6, 1872, where he was humiliated by Fisk's lawyers.

After the first day of the trial, Stokes returned to his hotel and pocketed a four-chamber Colt revolver. He then dined with Josie Mansfield that night and learned from her that Fisk would be entertaining out-of-town guests at the Broadway Central Hotel. Stokes went to the hotel and waited in an upstairs hallway, gun in hand, for Fisk to appear. Late that night Fisk arrived and began to climb the grand staircase to his suite of rooms when Stokes appeared at the top of the stairs. He took slow and careful aim at the man he hated. "I've got you at last!" Stokes shouted down to the portly Fisk.

Fisk looked frantically at some hotel employees standing helplessly nearby, crying out: "For God's sake, will no one help me?"

Stokes fired two bullets, one striking Fisk in the arm, the other ploughing into Fisk's ample stomach, a mortal wound. Fisk fell onto the stairs while Stokes ran out a back exit of the hotel. Jubilee Jim, with the help of some bellboys, stood up and, despite his bleeding wounds, climbed the long stairs to his rooms. He died at 10:45 a.m. the following day. As he lay bleeding to death, Fisk asked Mansfield to visit him. Her answer was to pack the jewels and furs he had given her and flee the city. Mrs. Lucy Fisk, however, loyal to the end, did arrive to kiss her husband goodbye. A few minutes later Fisk died and his wife told reporters through sobs: "He was a good boy." Fisk lingered long enough in Room 213 to identify Stokes as the man who shot him. Inspector Thomas Byrnes brought Stokes before the dying Fisk and Fisk nodded and then said: "He is the man who shot me."

Stokes was promptly arrested and put on trial. He insisted that he encountered his former business partner by accident, that he had been at the Broadway Central to meet friends and that when he saw Fisk coming up the stairs, Fisk reached for a revolver and he shot Fisk in self defense. This was, of course, a brazen lie, but his lawyers managed to confuse the jury to the point where they could not agree. Stokes was tried twice more and, at the conclusion of the third trial, was found Guilty and sentenced to six years in Sing Sing. Josie Mansfield, who had testified for him, saw him off at the train station in Manhattan, kissing him goodbye and promising to wait for Stokes.

A few days later Mansfield hired a theatrical manager who booked a European tour for her. Mansfield left for Paris and began giving lectures about her spectacular love life with Jubilee Jim Fisk and Ned Stokes. She never returned to the arms of Stokes but remained in Paris where she grew rich. She lived to the age of eighty, dying in 1931, unmarried and alone in a small Left Bank studio. At the end, she reached for two photographs, one of Stokes and one of Fisk.

Stokes emerged from prison and used up his considerable fortune in poor investments. He then became manager of the prestigious Hoffman House, one of New York's most resplendent hotels. Stokes acquired some interest in the hotel and again grew rich. He died in his Fifth Avenue mansion in 1901, also unmarried. Next to his bed on a table was the very Colt revolver he had used to murder Fisk, his rival in business and love.

REF.: Adams, *Chapters of Erie;* Bowers, *The Tragic Era;* Butterfield, *The American Past; CBA;* Churchill, *The Pictorial History of American Crime;* Clews, *Fifty Years in Wall Street;* Croffut, *The Vanderbilts and the Story of Their Fortune;* Duke, *Celebrated Criminal Cases of America;* Fuller, *Jubilee Jim: The Life of Colonel James Fisk, Jr.;* Hacker, *The United States*

Since 1865; Halstead, *Life of Jay Gould: How He Made His Fortune;* Hendrick, *The Age of Big Business;* Hunt, *A Dictionary of Rogues;* Jones, *The Life of James Fisk, Jr.;* Josephson, *The Robber Barons;* Lane, *Commodore Vanderbilt;* Lewis, *Nation-Famous New York Murders;* Marcuse, *This Was New York!;* Medbery, *Men and Mysteries of Wall Street;* Moody, *The Railroad Builders;* Morgan, *Prince of Crime;* Myers, *History of the Great American Fortunes;* Nash, *Bloodletters and Badmen;* ____, *Hustlers and Con Men;* ____, *Murder Among the Mighty;* Northrop, *The Life and Achievements of Jay Gould;* Peterson, *The Mob;* Seitz, *The Dreadful Decade;* Smith, *Commodore Vanderbilt: An Epic of American Achievement;* Thompson and Raymond, *Gang Rule in New York;* Van Metre, *Economic History of the United States;* Warshow, *Jay Gould: The Story of a Fortune;* White, *The Book of Daniel Drew;* (FILM), *The Toast of New York,* 1937.

Fitts, Oliver, c.1771-1816, U.S., jur.   Attorney general for North Carolina from 1808-10, before being appointed by President James Madison to the Mississippi Territorial Court in 1810. REF.: *CBA.*

Fitz, Alfred, b.1846, Brit., mur.   Most murders of children by other children are called "motiveless murders," and the majority of them occur in slums.   Such was the case of Alfred Fitz.   In 1855, the 9-year-old was found Guilty of manslaughter.   A Liverpool boy, Fitz had become angry with a playmate, James Fleeson, and hit him with a brick.   With another boy, Fitz threw Fleeson into the canal where Fleeson drowned.   On Aug. 22, both Fitz and his accomplice were tried in Liverpool Crown Court and sentenced to twelve-month terms in the Liverpool Jail.

REF.: *CBA;* Wilson, *Children Who Kill.*

Fitzalan, Edmund (Second Earl of Arundel), 1285-1326, Scot., consp.   Captured by Queen Isabella and Roger de Mortimer and executed for allying with King Edward II of England, Isabella's estranged husband. REF.: *CBA.*

Fitzalan, Henry (Twelfth Earl of Arundel) c.1511-80, Scot., consp.   Opposed the bid of Lady Jane Grey for the British Crown, favoring Mary Tudor and her sister Elizabeth, as rightful heirs. A leading noble among Catholics, he was twice suspected of involvement in Catholic plots against Elizabeth I, for which he was imprisoned. REF.: *CBA.*

Fitzalan, Richard (Fourth Earl of Arundel, Earl of Surrey), 1346-97, Scot., consp.   Opposed King Richard II in conspiracy with the faction to seize the throne led by Thomas of Woodstock, the Duke of Gloucester.   In consequence, he was imprisoned and beheaded. REF.: *CBA.*

Fitzgerald, Charles J., b.1886, U.S., mur.   Charles Fitzgerald had a criminal record dating back to 1908 when he was convicted of burglary and was sent to prison for three years.   He was released in 1910 but was convicted the following year of murdering a deputy sheriff in Montana and given a 100-year sentence. Fitzgerald served thirteen years in the Montana State Prison.   He was released in 1924 and moved to California.   In 1926, Fitzgerald, sitting in a parked car in San Gabriel, Calif., was approached by two policemen, officers Elmer H. Griffin and R.D. Bence.   The officers found liquor hidden in the car occupied by Fitzgerald and some of his friends and arrested the men for violating the Volstead Act, prohibition then being in effect.   Suddenly, someone in the car fired a weapon and Griffin fell dead and Bence lay seriously wounded on the street.

Fitzgerald was charged with murdering Griffin, although he denied ever firing the weapon.   He later claimed that his lawyer suggested he plead guilty and that the Los Angeles district attorney promised that he would receive no more than a 10-year sentence.   He was sent to Folsom Prison for life in 1926.   Fitzgerald was placed in a 7-by-9-foot cell.   He saw the stars at night only once in forty-five years, in 1927 when he was removed to a schoolhouse during a prison riot.   Fitzgerald was denied parole thirty-nine times before being released from Folsom in 1971 at age eighty-five.   He was California's oldest inmate, having served the longest prison sentence at Folsom. REF.: *CBA.*

Fitzgerald, Gerald (Fourteenth Earl of Desmond), c.1538-83, Ire., assass.   Opposed the Tenth Earl of Ormonde, and was imprisoned in London for his clan's misdeeds from 1562-64.   Later he was captured in battle and placed in the Tower of London from 1567-73.   He continued to fight in Munster upon his return to Ireland in 1573, and was proclaimed an outlaw and traitor for rebelling against Queen Elizabeth from 1579-80, and ravaging the town of Youghal between 1579-80.   With Sir William Pelham and the Earl of Ormonde's success in battle, he was driven into hiding.   His pursuers finally caught up with him in the Kerry Mountains where he was captured and killed at Glanaginty. REF.: *CBA.*

Fitzgerald, Mamie, prom. 1896, U.S., rob.   In December 1896, George Smith met a young woman, Mamie Fitzgerald, on State Street in downtown Chicago and began flirting with her. Taken with his companion, Smith asked for permission to visit her, and they were soon ensconced in a corner saloon, sharing a bottle of wine.   After most of the liquid was gone, Fitzgerald became very affectionate, placed her head on Smith's chest, and neatly bit off the diamond stud on his shirt bosom, then reiterated her permission for Smith to call on her.   As Smith stood up, he felt the screw from his shirt slide down his pants leg and realized he had been robbed, but Fitzgerald was already gone.

Complaining to a nearby policeman, Smith watched out for his sharp-toothed companion, and spotted her several weeks later at a State Street bar.   Smith obtained a warrant from the Harrison Street Station, and Detective Clifton Rodman Wooldridge arrested Fitzgerald at the Boston Saloon.   Held on a $500 bond, she was indicted and arraigned before Judge Gibbons, and found Guilty of larceny.   Her motion for a new trial was granted, and a few weeks later Fitzgerald so effectively acted the part of a repentant, reformed thief that Gibbons allowed her to go free, requiring only that she return in two weeks with proof of gainful, legitimate employment, and that she report on probation monthly for one year.

REF.: *CBA;* Wooldridge, *Hands Up.*

Fitzgerald, Thomas Richard, 1880-1919, U.S., mur.   On July 22, 1919, 6-year-old Janet "Dollie" Wilkinson failed to come home for dinner.   Around midnight, her parents, who operated a grocery store on Chicago's Rush Street, around the corner from their Superior Street home, reported to police that she was missing. They mentioned to police a neighbor, Thomas Fitzgerald, who worked as an elevator operator in a Rush Street hotel, as a possible suspect because he had shown unusual interest in the little girl.   Police brought Fitzgerald to the station for questioning, beginning a six day interrogation that newspapers dubbed "the fourth degree."

Fitzgerald, whom police described as "a moron," admitted during questioning that he knew the Wilkinson girl, but denied any knowledge of her whereabouts.   One of his fellow employees, however, told police that he had seen the girl sitting on Fitzgerald's lap in the basement of the hotel only a week before.

Given this, police and reporters grilled the suspect for more than eight hours, during which time he was not allowed to use his eyeglasses.   At one point a reporter dressed as a priest entered the room, and the police left the two alone.   "As a priest of the church it is my duty to visit my brethren in distress," the reporter said.

"Yes, Father," Fitzgerald answered.

"I want you to tell me the truth.   If the girl is alive, tell me where she is and I'll have her sent back, so they will never know you had her..."

"But..."

"Now wait, my friend, if she is dead I'll have the body located and..."

"If I knew I'd tell you, Father.   I know you are bound by the vows of the church not to repeat what I tell you in confession, but I don't know.   I really don't.   So help me God, I don't."

Sometime later another reporter came in and posed as a relative of the dead girl.   "If you loved your mother, tell us the truth," he pleaded with Fitzgerald.   "The girl's mother is nearly dead from grief and suspense. She cannot live another eight hours unless she knows where Janet's body is. Tell us! Tell us! Tell us!"

Fitzgerald was unmoved by the plea: "Why, if I knew I'd tell you."

Through hours and hours of relentless questioning, Fitzgerald continued to deny his guilt. "I wish to sleep," he told his interrogators. "Please let me alone."

But he wasn't allowed to sleep. The police and reporters worked in shifts; a few would slip away for breakfast or a catnap as another crew took their place. Their prisoner was forced to stay awake. When his head would nod, somebody would slap him lightly until he was fully awake. "Tell us the truth," they would demand.

At last, Fitzgerald looked up, "Send down Mr. Howe," he said quietly.

A few minutes later Lieutenant Howe was at his cell. "You have been the only friend I have had. I wouldn't tell anyone else. But I think I'll tell you. I'm afraid you'll think me a horrible man," Fitzgerald said.

"No, I won't," the police officer said. "What I'll think is what I have thought all the way through this case: that you have a diseased brain. Tell me the truth, my man."

"I did it," Fitzgerald said with his head bowed, "I killed her."

"How did you do it?"

"Just the way you have described it twenty-five times, Mr. Howe. Just as you told me. Every time you described the killing in detail I shivered."

"I know you did, Fitzgerald, I saw you tremble."

"It was just the way you pictured it, even to the taking of Dollie's body down to the coal pile...I'll show you the spot. I want you to stick by me and be a friend. I need friends. And say, Mr. Howe, you won't hang me now, will you? I've confessed, haven't I? They won't string me up if I'm crazy, will they? Tell me, Mr. Howe."

"I don't know," Howe said.

"I didn't mean to kill her," Fitzgerald explained later. "When I married fourteen years ago I found I was not fit for marriage. I lured Janet into the apartment with candy. While I held her in my arms she screamed, and in my excitement I choked her. She was unconscious. I hurried down to the basement with her and covered her with coal." When police examined the body they found cuts on her head and broken teeth. It was later determined that the girl was probably still alive when Fitzgerald buried her in the coal.

Assistant Cook County State's Attorney James C. O'Brien was assigned to the case. O'Brien was known in the argot of the underworld as a "rope man" for the many death sentences his prosecutions had achieved. He was also known as "Red Necktie" O'Brien for the color of the tie he was known to wear to sentencing hearings, to remind the judge and jury of the victim's blood. In the Fitzgerald case he was successful again. On Oct. 17, 1919, Thomas Richard Fitzgerald was hanged for the murder of Janet Wilkinson. REF.: *CBA*.

Fitzgerald, William Francis, 1846-1903, U.S., jur. District attorney for the Eleventh Judicial District of Mississippi from 1878-84, and was appointed to the Arizona Territorial Court by President Chester Arthur in 1884. He also served as associate justice for the California Supreme Court in 1893-94, attorney general for California from 1895-99, and justice for the Superior Court of California from 1899-1903. REF.: *CBA*.

Fitzgibbon, John (First Earl of Clare), 1749-1802, Ire., jur., duel. Attorney general in 1783 issued repressive policies and took severe steps against the Whiteboy raids in 1785, becoming the first native of Ireland to be the lord chancellor from 1789-1802, whereupon he urged passage of the Act of Union in 1800. REF.: *CBA*.

Fitzherbert, Sir Anthony, 1470-1538, Brit., jur. Authored *La Grande Abridgement* in 1514, a work attempting to systematize the entire body of law. He served as Common Pleas Court justice in 1522, agreed to sign impeachment articles against Wolsey in 1529, and sat on the courts that condemned Saint John Fisher and Sir Thomas More in 1535. REF.: *CBA*.

FitzOsbert, William, prom. 1196, Brit., treas. Executed for the crime of sedition, William FitzOsbert had the dubious distinction of being the first man to be hanged at Tyburn, the most well-known execution site in the world.

In 1196, William FitzOsbert was hanged at London for committing treason. An account of his death was written by Ralph of Diceto, who described "...his hands bound behind him, his feet tied with long cords, is drawn by means of a horse through the midst of the city to the gallows near Tyburn." Along the banks of London's Tyburn River grew many elm trees from which criminals were hanged. The gallows, in those days, was often known as The Elms, including gallows at locations other than Tyburn, such as the Smithfield Elms. In 1220, King Henry III ordered the sheriff of Middlesex to have two gibbets erected where the gallows was formerly raised, at The Elms.

REF.: *CBA*; Laurence, *A History of Capital Punishment*.

Fitzpatrick, Sir Charles, 1851-1942, Can., jur. Served as Canada's chief justice, as deputy governor general from 1906-18, and as lieutenant governor for Quebec from 1918-23. REF.: *CBA*.

Fitzpatrick, Edward, prom. 1743, U.S., mur. Edward Fitzpatrick was a convicted felon who was imprisoned in the Boston jail. While behind bars, the illiterate Fitzpatrick asked one of the guards to read to him from the Bible. The jailer selected passages about murder and the eternal flames awaiting killers. So frightened did Fitzpatrick become after listening to these fire and brimstone tales, that he promptly confessed to the murder of Daniel Campbell of Rutland, Mass., on Mar. 8, 1743. He went on to tell authorities that he buried Campbell's body and then stole from the victim's house some muslin lace, a snuff box, and a pair of shoes with silver buckles. Fitzpatrick was given an additional prison sentence for the crime.

REF.: *CBA*; *The Examination and Confession of Edward Fitzpatrick*.

Fitzpatrick, James (AKA: The Sandy Flash), d.1787, U.S., rob. James Fitzpatrick, an Irishman, settled in eastern Pennsylvania, and became a member of the Doane gang of highwaymen. In the early 1780s he formed his own gang, robbing wealthy landowners in Delaware and Chester counties. Fitzpatrick, although nondescript enough to go unrecognized in public places, became known as the "Sandy Flash." He often bought rounds of drinks for the members of the posses pursuing him. In 1785, a reward of £200 was offered for his capture. He eluded his pursuers until late 1786, when he was cornered by a posse and taken prisoner in Chester, Pa. In January 1787, Fitzpatrick was hanged in the Old Chester Jail. REF.: *CBA*.

Fitzpatrick, Richie, 1880-1905, U.S., org. crime. Richie Fitzpatrick, an Irishman, became a leading gunman in a largely Jewish gang headed by Monk Eastman. To gain the confidence of an Eastman foe, Fitzpatrick devised a cunning ruse which was later used by the Corleone brothers in *The Godfather*. Allowing himself to be searched, then telling the dive owner he would not follow Eastman's orders to assassinate him, Fitzpatrick went to the bathroom, returned with his planted gun, and fatally shot the dive owner. In 1904, after Eastman was arrested, Fitzpatrick became involved in a power struggle with Kid Twist, and the gang began to split. In early 1905, at a peace conference in New York's Chrystie Street, Fitzpatrick was shot to death before the talks began by Kid Twist, who was also recognized for his cunning. See: Kelly, Paul; Zwerbach, Maxwell. REF.: *CBA*.

Fitzsimmons, Richard, prom. 1977, Case of, U.S., embez. The son of former Teamsters President Frank E. Fitzsimmons was accused by a federal grand jury of embezzling funds from the union to pay for personal insurance policies, but was acquitted of the charges.

On Feb. 4, 1977, Richard Fitzsimmons was indicted for embezzling $5,000 in severance pay funds from the union's pension fund to buy close to $1 million of life insurance for himself, a lawyer, a business agent, and about twenty-one other members of Teamster Local 299. Also charged with embezzlement and conspiracy was Anthony Sciarotta, a Pontiac, Mich., business agent for the Teamsters. Accused of covering up the activities of Sciarotta and Fitzsimmons by assisting in back dating loan documents was attorney Stuart Sinai.

The Detroit chapter of the International Brotherhood of Teamsters was once headed by James R. "Jimmy" Hoffa, who disappeared on July 30, 1975. It had been a power base for both Hoffa and the elder Fitzsimmons. According to U.S. States Attorney Philip Van Dam, the indictments were part of an eighteen-month investigation by the Justice Department into similar pension plans. Fitzsimmons, Sciotta, and Sinai all pleaded not guilty to the charges on Feb. 8, 1977. On Apr. 28, 1978, a Detroit jury returned verdicts of Not Guilty for all three men. See: **Hoffa, James Riddle**. REF.: *CBA*.

Fitzthedmar, Arnold, 1201-c.1275, Brit., criminol. Compiled a chronological record of London's sheriffs and mayors from 1188-1274, and was considered the best available source on politics and institutions in London during that time period. REF.: *CBA*.

Fitzurse, Reginald, See: **Becket, Thomas**.

A New York policeman uncovering a den of thieves in the Five Points, 1825.

Five Points, prom. 1820s-1900, U.S., vice district. New York City's first significant vice district was the Five Points, the original spawning place of the old-time gangs, in the heart of the Sixth Ward. This tenement-jammed area spread from Broadway to Canal Street, from the Bowery to Park Row. At its vortex was the dreaded Five Points which came together at a wide intersection of Orange, Mulberry, Anthony, Little Water, and Cross streets. From 1820 to the end of the century, this area was America's throbbing heart of crime.

British author Charles Dickens, no stranger to poverty and the vice surrounding it in England, was appalled in 1842 when he was conducted by police through the miserable area. He recorded the vision in his *American Notes:* "Let us go on again...plunge into the Five Points. This is the place: these narrow ways, diverging to the right and left, and reeking everywhere with dirt and filth. Such lives as are led here, bear the same fruits here as elsewhere. The coarse and bloated faces at the doors have counterparts at home, and all the world over. Debauchery has made the very houses prematurely old. See how the rotten beams are tumbling down, and how the patched and broken windows seem to scowl

The teeming Five Points, 1829.

dimly, like eyes that have been hurt in drunken frays. Many of those pigs live here. Do they ever wonder why there masters walk upright in lieu of going on all-fours and why they talk instead of grunting?

"What place is this, to which the squalid street conducts us? A kind of square of leprous houses, some of which are attainable only by crazy wooden stairs without. What lies beyond this tottering flight of steps, that creak beneath our tread?—a miserable room, light by one dim candle, and destitute of all comfort, save that which may be hidden in a wretched bed. Beside it, sits a man: his elbows on his knees: his forehead hidden in his hands. 'What ails this man?' asks the foremost officer. 'Fever,' he sullenly replies without looking up. Conceive the fancies of a feverish brain in such a place as this!

"Mount up these other stairs with no less caution (there are traps and pitfalls here, for those who are not so well escorted as ourselves) into the housetop where the bare beams and rafters meet overhead, and calm night looks down through the crevices in the roof. Open the door of one of these cramped hutches full of sleeping Negroes. Pah! They have a charcoal fire within; there is a smell of singing clothes or flesh, so close they gather round the brazier, and vapors issue forth that blind and suffocate. From every corner as you glance about you in these dark retreats, some figure crawls half-awakened, as if the judgment hour were near at hand, and every obscene grave were giving up its dead. Where dogs would howl to lie, women, and men, and boys slink off to sleep, forcing the dislodged rats to move away in quest of better lodgings.

"Here too are lancs and alleys, paved with mud knee-deep, underground chambers, where they dance and game; the walls bedecked with rough designs of ships, and forts, and flags, and American Eagles out of number; ruined houses opened to the street, whence, through wide gaps in the walls, other ruins loom upon the eye, as though the world of vice and misery had nothing else to show: hideous tenements which take their name from robbery and murder: all that is loathsome, drooping, and decayed is here."

Grocery stores in the Five Points during this time sold vegetables but doubled as backroom saloons where the cheapest kind of rotgut was sold, and thugs and criminals of all stripes gathered to plan their next robberies. The vegetables decayed on the street but business in the backrooms boomed. One of these filthy dens, operated by Rosanna Peers, became the hub for the first fierce mob of the Five Points, the Forty Thieves gang headed up by

Edward Coleman, a towering thug.

Coleman and his cronies planned all their robberies and raids, as well as their battles with other gangs competing for the spoils of the district, in Rosanna's back room. The den also served as a school for young children—apprentice hooligans—who were taught the ways of pickpockets, sneak thieves, and street battlers whom they greatly admired, having no other heroes except the

The Five Points, 1851.

adult criminals around them. This junior group was dubbed the Forty Little Thieves and, in addition to bringing all their stolen loot to their tutoring Fagins, these wayward children provided a system of watchmen who detailed the movements of the police.

Other grocery stores fronting for drinking dens produced equally deadly gangs such as the Roach Guards, Plug Uglies, Dead Rabbits, the Chichesters, and the Shirt Tail Gang. Of this brawling lot, the Plug Uglies and the Dead Rabbits were the most lethal. The Plug Uglies were all behemoth Irishmen who stomped through the neighborhood. They wore hobnailed boots with which to crush the skulls of opponents. They carried enormous clubs, knives, pistols, and often axes stained with the blood of previous victims. High plug hats filled with leather and wool were the trademarks worn by gang members, and these were worn low to the eyes to give an even more sinister appearance.

The Five Points, 1859.

The Dead Rabbits were a splinter gang of the original Roach Guards, organized by a disgruntled Roach Guardsman named Shang Allen. His two lieutenants, Tommy Hadden and Kit Burns, would become millionaires after investing the spoils from their gang activities into enormous Fourth Ward gambling and drinking dens. Each of the Five Points gangs that roamed the shadowy streets about Paradise Square had distinguished marks or insignias such as the hats worn by the Plug Uglies. The Shirt Tails, a vicious gang of panel thieves, wore their shirts outside of their trousers like the Chinese. The sartorial Roach Guards wore red

pantaloons with blue stripes down the sides.

The Dead Rabbits represented the most unique collection of thugs in New York during the heyday of the repulsive Five Points. Also known as the Black Birds, the Dead Rabbits wore a lurid red stripe down the sides of their trousers. Their gang leader always walked about with a dead rabbit impaled upon a large spike. Members of this gang were peacock proud of their status, for, in the criminal argot of the day, the word "rabbit" meant a fierce hooligan and a "dead rabbit" was the most fierce hooligan.

Although the Five Points gangs fought to the death against each other, they often merged as common allies in pitched battles with the gangs of the Bowery and the Fourth Ward. It was not uncommon in the 1820s and 1830s to see the Roach Guards and Dead Rabbits murdering each other in gang fights one day and the next day see both gangs united in a battling brotherhood as they tore into the ranks of gangs from other districts.

All these terrible gangs faded by the late 1880s, and were replaced by crafty gang leaders such as Paul Kelly, and, later, Johnny Torrio and Frankie Yale. By the time Kelly and Torrio took charge of the New York underworld in this area, all the surviving gangs of the Five Points came under common leadership, a super gang known as the Five Points Gang. The most notorious graduate of the Five Points Gang was Al Capone. See: **Capone, Alphonse; Dead Rabbits; Kelly, Paul; Plug-Uglies; Roach Guards; Shirt Tails Gang; Torrio, John; Yale, Frank.**

REF.: Asbury, *The Gangs of New York; CBA;* Dickens, *American Notes;* Fried, *The Rise and Fall of the Jewish Gangster In America;* Gage, *Mafia, U.S.A;* Haskins, *Street Gangs;* Kobler, *Capone;* Landesco, *Organized Crime In Chicago;* Levine, *Anatomy of a Gangster;* McPhaul, *Johnny Torrio;* Nash, *Bloodletters and Badmen;* Peterson, *The Mob;* Spiering, *The Man Who Got Capone;* Thompson and Raymond, *Gang Rule In New York.*

Five Points Gang, prom. 1900-19, U.S., org. crime. New York City's Five Points Gang served as a prep school for crime during the early twentieth century, graduating such luminaries as Al Capone, Charles "Lucky" Luciano, Johnny Torrio, and Frankie Yale. Headed by Paul Kelly, a former bantamweight prizefighter born Paolo Antonini Vaccarelli, the 1,500 member gang provided guns and muscle for businessmen. The gang's activity diminished by 1915, as the rackets dwindled before Prohibition. See: **Kelly, Paul.**

REF.: Asbury, *The Gangs of New York; CBA;* Fried, *The Rise and Fall of the Jewish Gangster In America;* Gage, *Mafia, U.S.A;* Haskins, *Street Gangs;* Kobler, *Capone;* Landesco, *Organized Crime In Chicago;* Levine, *Anatomy of a Gangster;* McPhaul, *Johnny Torrio;* Nash, *Bloodletters and Badmen;* Peterson, *The Mob;* Spiering, *The Man Who Got Capone;* Thompson and Raymond, *Gang Rule In New York.*

Five to Five, 1934, a novel by D. Erskine Muir. The infamous Slater case (Scot., 1908) is the background for this novel. See: **Slater, Oscar.**

Flaccus, Lucius Valerius, d.c.86 B.C., Roman., assass. Served as consul in 100 B.C., censor in 96 B.C., and again as consul following the death of Gaius Marius in 86 B.C. He opposed Lucius Sulla whose rivalry with Marius had led to civil war, but aided in the war against Mithradates VI, before his lieutenant Flavius Fimbria killed him. REF.: *CBA.*

Flaccus, Marcus, d.121 B.C., Roman., assass. Roman consul in 125 B.C., who supported extending citizenship to Latins. For this he was killed by rioting mobs at the same time the movement's leader, Gaius Sempronius Gracchus, committed suicide. REF.: *CBA.*

Flack, William, prom. 1853, Brit., mur. A fired handyman with a grudge against an elderly housekeeper took revenge by brutally slaying his former employer.

The Rectory of Bacton, north of Stowmark, England, was, in 1853, an isolated building, protected by a moat, nearly a mile away from the church it served. Living there were Reverend Barker, and Maria Steggles, both octogenarians, and two servants, a young girl and an outdoor laborer, 18-year-old William Flack.

On May 8, the Reverend Barker and the serving girl went to church, leaving Steggles to prepare the Sunday dinner. Returning, they discovered the housekeeper viciously murdered, her throat slashed and with a severe blow to her head. The prime suspect was Flack, who had recently been fired after he had been overheard saying he planned to "steal some of the old parson's mouldy sovereigns." Flack had also been caught gathering eggs from Barker's henhouse, and was known to resent Steggles.

Before his arrest, but after the killing, Flack was heard saying that he had intended to murder the elderly woman, but "she's dead now so it's all right." Accused, Flack tried to implicate another man, who had an unassailable alibi. After he was convicted, Flack confessed, saying he had always helped with ringing the bells before Sunday service and that right after he assisted with this service, he went to the rectory to murder Steggles.

REF.: Butler, *Murderers' England; CBA.*

Flade, Dr. Dietrich, prom. 1581-89, Ger., witchcraft. A prominent political leader in the country districts of Treves in Germany, Dr. Dietrich Flade was an obstacle to the rampant witchcraft accusations and trials, and soon became one of the scourge's most eminent victims.

From a prominent family, and later marrying into even greater wealth and social position, Flade was selected by the Prince-Archbishop of Treves to suppress the heretics in that area, beginning with the Protestants, then evolving into the banishment of the Jews, and eventually focusing on the wholesale murder of the "witches." For twenty years Flade was in charge of the secular courts, becoming Vice-Governor of Treves in 1580, and Rector of the University in 1586.

A learned and loyal leader, Flade became an obstruction to the witchcraft trials when he questioned the practice, though not the theory, and delayed prosecutions. The persecution intensified, with popular support for the prosecutors of witchcraft by frightened citizens who were stymied by a series of natural calamities (including bad weather, and plagues of grasshoppers, snails, and mice), which had destroyed harvests for nearly twenty years. The newly elected Governor, Johan Zandt von Merll set up a case to remove Flade, hoping to make him a scapegoat, by accusing him of plotting against the Archbishop, and bringing in a number of witnesses to swear against him. A boy claimed he had heard Flade at a black magic sabbath boasting how he had administered an almost fatal dose of poison to the Archbishop, and an accused woman, "Maria the old Meieress," in exchange for the promise that she would be strangled before she was burned, shouted repeatedly that Dr. Flade was a witch. Following Maria's naming, several other accused witches began calling Flade a sorcerer.

On Apr. 15, 1588, Zandt produced Marethe of Euren to swear that Flade had urged the destruction of crops at a sabbath, calling up a plague of hailstorms and snails, and, by July 4, 1588, Peter Ormsdorf, a notary who had discovered he could make a good living from torturing people to obtain testimony, brought extensive evidence against Flade. On Oct. 3, 1588, Flade tried to flee and was caught; his efforts to save himself were considered an admission of guilt.

The formal trial opened on Aug. 17, 1589; after being tortured, Flade confessed to such crimes as throwing dirt clods into the air in the name of the Devil; the clods were supposedly then transformed into crop-destroying slugs. On Sept. 18, 1589, the once eminent Dr. Flade was executed, burned at the stake after being "mercifully and Christianly strangled."

REF.: Burr, *Selections from His Writings; CBA;* Carpenter, *Dietrich Flade;* Robbins, *The Encyclopedia of Witchcraft and Demonology;* Wilson, *Witches.*

Flanagan, Sean Patrick, 1961-89, U.S., mur. In 1987 in Las Vegas, Sean Patrick Flanagan, twenty-six, met James Lewandowski, a 45-year-old chef who bought the younger man clothes and rented a room for him. Not long after accepting Lewandowski's assistance, Flanagan strangled and then dismembered the older man, leaving body parts in plastic bags in a trash bin near the motel

where he stayed. Four days after murdering Lewandowski, Flanagan took a ride with pianist Albert Duggins, fifty-nine, before he killed him. Arrested for jaywalking in Orange County, Calif. soon after Duggin's murder, Flanagan voluntarily returned to Las Vegas to show police the vacant lot where he had left Duggins' corpse.

Refusing to seek appeals of his death penalty, Flanagan explained, "Every man who has committed a crime of murder knows deep down inside he should die for taking another man's life." The confessed killer gave a seven-page statement in which he said he hated his homosexuality, and thought he might have been motivated to kill other homosexual men with "the thought that I would be doing some good for our society."

Before his death by lethal injection on June 23, 1989, Flanagan told Deputy County District Attorney Dan Seaton, "You are a just man." Strapped to a gurney at the Nevada State Prison in preparation for the execution, Flanagan lifted his head to tell Seaton, "I love you." Since the 1976 U.S. Supreme Court ruling allowing states to resume using the death penalty, Flanagan was the fourth person to be executed in Nevada, and the 114th person to be put to death nationally. REF.: *CBA.*

Flandrau, Charles Eugene, 1828-1903, U.S., jur. District attorney for Nicollet County, in the territory of Minnesota. He was appointed by President James Buchanan to the Minnesota Territorial Court in 1857, and served as justice for the Minnesota Supreme Court from 1858-64. REF.: *CBA.*

Flannery, Thomas Aquinas, 1918 - , U.S., jur. Assistant U.S. attorney from 1950-52 and U.S. attorney from 1969-71, prior to his appointment by President Richard Nixon to the District Court for the District of Columbia in 1971. REF.: *CBA.*

Flatt, George W., d.1880, U.S., law enfor. off. In 1879, George Flatt was a lawman in Caldwell, Kan., with the reputation for having killed men before. He also operated an elegant saloon with William Horseman.

On July 7, 1879, in Caldwell, Flatt was involved in a shootout after two men, George Wood and Jake Adams, began firing pistols while drinking at the Occidental Saloon. Constable W.C. Kelly and Deputy John Wilson, accompanied by Flatt and W.H. Kiser, entered the saloon. During the ensuing shootout Flatt killed the two outlaws, while Kiser was grazed in the temple and Wilson was wounded in the wrist.

On Oct. 29, 1879, Flatt, by now the marshal, and his deputy, Red Bill Jones, sought to arrest John Dean for being drunk and disorderly. As Flatt approached Dean, the latter turned and fired. When the shots missed their mark, Dean escaped on horseback. On June 19, 1880, Flatt himself became drunk and raucous and began to have trouble with Frank Hunt. Flatt was persuaded to leave for home, but insisted instead on stopping at Louis Segerman's restaurant. As he approached the restaurant, he was fatally shot at the base of the skull, his spinal cord severed. While his killers were never brought to justice, Frank Hunt and William Horseman were widely suspected.

REF.: *CBA;* Drago, *Wild, Woolly and Wicked;* Miller and Snell, *Great Gunfighters of the Kansas Cowtowns.*

Flaum, Joel Martin, 1936- , U.S., jur. Director of the Police Legal Advisory Program, assistant attorney general for Illinois from 1969-70, commissioner for the Illinois Law Enforcement Commission from 1970-72, member of the Chicago Bar Association's committee on criminal law, and was appointed by President Gerald Ford to the District Court of Illinois in 1974. He served on several committees of the Chicago and American Bar Associations, including the committee to draft indigent criminal legislation. REF.: *CBA.*

Flavell, Joseph Edward, 1902- , Brit., mur. A slow-witted crane driver, 24-year-old Joseph Edward Flavell was violently jealous of his half-brother, James Thomas Bayliss, an intelligent and promising 14-year-old art student. In March 1926, at the home they shared in Dudley, Flavell killed the sleeping Bayliss with an ax. Flavell confessed to Birmingham police, explaining his sibling had not felt any pain because, "I did it while he was asleep." At the trail at the Worchester Assizes, he was defended by attorney Marshall Hall. Evidence showed that there was a history of Bright's disease and epilepsy in Flavell's family, and some of his relatives had been confined to or had died in asylums. It was also determined that Flavell, who was known as "the village idiot," had a history of cruelty to animals. Hall's plea for a guilty but insane verdict was rejected. Flavell was found Guilty of murder, and Justice Avory sentenced him to death. On appeal, the sentence was commuted to penal servitude for life.

REF.: Bowker, *Behind the Bar; CBA;* Marjoribanks, *For the Defense, The Life of Sir Edward Marshall Hall;* Shew, *A Second Companion to Murder.*

Flavian, c.390-449, Turk., assass. As bishop of Constantinople from 447-49, he condemned the heretic Eutyches, which led to his excommunication in 449, by the Council of Ephesus. He was killed by his theological opponents. In 451, the Council of Chalcedon canonized him as a martyr. REF.: *CBA.*

Flavius, Gnaeus, prom. 4th Cent. B.C., Roman., jur. Responsible for public introduction of *Jus Flavianum* in 304 B.C., a work on the technical rules of legal processes. REF.: *CBA.*

Bank robber Jake Fleagle and the lone fingerprint that led to his capture.

Fleagle Gang (Jake Fleagle), prom. 1920s, U.S., rob. Of four brothers, Jake and Ralph Fleagle turned bad early in their youths. During the 1920s, they led a fierce and clever band of bank robbers. Born in Iowa, the Fleagles moved with their parents to Kansas, but left the farm in 1910 for San Francisco. Jake, whose full name was William Harrison Fleagle, and Ralph Emerson Fleagle took jobs as streetcar conductors. Jake, who was known as Wolf to his friends, was an inveterate gambler and he soon quit streetcar work, traveling up and down the Sacramento Valley following floating crap games. He was the younger of the two and the energetic, inventive leader of what later came to be known as the Fleagle gang.

Jake Fleagle drifted into Oklahoma, and needing cash to feed his gambling habit, performed a crude holdup. He was quickly apprehended and convicted of second-degree robbery, and given a year and a day in the state prison at McAlester. Here he met a host of experienced robbers, and when he was released he resolved to become a robber, but his system was unique. He had learned in prison how most bandits were caught because they stayed together in bands and one member of a gang invariably led to the identification and capture of the next. Jake sent for his brother Ralph and explained that they were going into the robbery business but that they would never use the same men twice. Moreover, the brothers would rob gamblers and thieves like themselves.

Recruiting a band of robbers, the brothers traveled back to California's Sacramento Valley. Using a few new assistants on each raid and wearing masks, they would barge into a crap game where thousands of dollars were changing hands, scoop up the money at gunpoint and depart. They paid their assistants each $1,000 and kept the rest, as much as $25,000 from some of the bigger games. The brothers then returned home, depositing large amounts of cash in local Kansas banks. Their mother told neighbors how proud she was of her two boys now that they had gone into the stock business. Jake and Ralph also let it be known that they were cattle buyers as well as stock investors.

The huge deposits from the once impoverished farm boys drew suspicion on the part of some bankers. Jake had a habit over the years of depositing and later withdrawing great amounts of cash, explaining that he required the cash to make horse and cattle purchases. In 1927, Jake lost more than $50,000 in a Pueblo, Colo., gambling house and withdrew this amount from a small Kansas bank which held some of his deposits. The withdrawal caused a run on the bank that ultimately ruined it. The brothers, after a decade of robbing crap games, bordellos, and gambling dens, switched for reasons of safety to bank and train robbing. They had not been identified as the robbers of these crap games but their methods were known and they feared personal identification by members of organized crime.

They traveled far in their search for stolen wealth, robbing banks and trains in California, Oregon, Washington, and Montana. After each robbery they would pay off their associates, disband their gang, and return to Kansas to make more heavy cash deposits. No one ever thought to link recent robberies with the Fleagle deposits. To hide their activities and to have a headquarters from which to launch new strikes, Jake and Ralph bought a remote ranch, claiming they were raising horses on its sprawling acres. They intentionally selected an area which was accessible only through a maze of rutted roads.

A granary on the property was converted into a large garage which could house several cars and trucks. The Fleagles had workmen rebuild one side of the granary so that an entire side of the building could be raised by automatic pulleys to admit the vehicles. The ranch house was an arsenal brimming with submachine guns, automatics, even grenades, all stolen by others from federal warehouses and bought by Fleagle agents so that the purchases could not be traced.

Jake and Ralph, by then in their middle age, Ralph gone gray-haired and Jake with a lined face from years of dissipation, decided that they would commit a few more big bank robberies and then retire. One bank the Fleagles had cased, the First National Bank of Lamar, Colo., promised enormous returns. According to Jake's research, this bank would yield more than $200,000. The Fleagles then recruited two new assistants, George Johnson Abshier, a one-time bootlegger from Grand Junction, Colo., and Howard Royston of San Andreas, Calif. Jake Fleagle had committed some robberies with Royston several years earlier.

Several times the gang started for Lamar but turned back because of the superstitious Fleagles. A black cat had crossed their path, a yellow dog had run next to their car, a cloud had covered the sun just as they approached the town. Finally, on May 23, 1928, the four men drove into Lamar and parked in front of the bank. Just as they were getting out of the car, Ralph shook his head in premonition, saying: "The date is all wrong. You know what day it is? Twenty-three skidoo!"

"Aww, nobody's thought of twenty-three skidoo in years," said Jake Fleagle.

Abshier said, cradling a rifle in his arms: "If we're going to get caught, we'll get caught. All this superstition has nothing to do with it."

The four men adjusted masks over their faces and entered the bank. Abshier and Royston herded employees and customers against the wall while the Fleagles, holding large grain sacks, ran behind the cashiers' cages and scooped up bundles of cash. They were lucky in finding the vault open and they cleaned it out, taking about $218,000. The four men then began to back out of the bank.

Just as the bandits reached the door, A.N. Parish, the elderly bank president, dove for a desk drawer and withdrew an ancient .45-caliber revolver. It had not been used in fifteen years, but it was loaded. Parish aimed the weapon at Royston and fired. The bullet struck the bandit in the jaw, smashing it to pieces. The bandits fired back. A hail of bullets struck Parish, killing him on his feet. His son, J.N. Parish, ran forward to grab his father as he fell. The son took the old weapon from his father's hand but before he could aim it at the bandits, he, too, was shot to death.

The bandits then ordered Everett Kessinger, assistant cashier, and E.A. Lungren, a bank teller, to accompany them. They were forced to stand on the running boards of the car, which prevented a local sheriff pursuing the bandits from firing at them. Ralph Fleagle made sure of this by firing a rifle bullet into the radiator of the sheriff's car. Lungren was freed, but the gang held Kessinger hostage as they proceeded into western Kansas. Royston was in great pain from his wound and his friend Abshier wanted to stop and find a doctor to treat the wounded bandit. Jake Fleagle insisted they drive on to the ranch, where they would take care of Royston.

When the bandits reached the Fleagle ranch, Kessinger was tied up. At Abshier's insistence, Jake and Ralph Fleagle drove into Dighton, Kan., and asked Dr. W.W. Wineiger to return with them to their ranch to attend to "a ranch hand who had his foot crushed by a tractor." The physician agreed and drove his own car to the ranch, following a car driven by Ralph Fleagle. Jake Fleagle sat next to Dr. Wineiger, a man he did not know. He lowered the window of the car, which was stuck. Fleagle had to press the glass with his hand to force the window down.

When Dr. Wineiger arrived at the ranch, he quickly realized that Royston had been shot. He objected to treating the wound, but the Fleagles ordered him at gunpoint to treat their fellow bank robber. After Dr. Wineiger treated Royston's wounds, his hands were tied behind his back and he was driven in his car to a remote canyon. One of the bandits shot him in the back with a load of buckshot, killing him, then kicked his body into a gully. His car was pushed into the gully after him.

To set authorities on the wrong track in case they found the body, Ralph Fleagle wrote a note and left it with the body. It read: "Sweet revenge from Enterprise. Oh, you murderers, ye doctors!" The doctor's body was found a short time later and it was first thought that a relative of a one-time patient who had died under Dr. Wineiger's care had taken revenge. Kessinger's body, also bound and blindfolded, was found in a shack near Liberal, Kan. He had been shotgunned to death in the same manner as doctor Wineiger.

Meanwhile, the Fleagles fled to St. Paul, Minn., taking their mother with them on an extended "vacation" from their exhaustive "cattle buying." Abshier followed the Fleagle car with the wounded Royston, giving him morphine stolen from the murdered Dr. Wineiger. Bonds taken from the Lamar robbery were carried by the Fleagles to St. Paul where, through the gang's underworld connections, they would be fenced. In St. Paul, an underworld doctor treated Royston's wound.

Meanwhile, investigators did not connect the murder of Dr. Wineiger with the Lamar robbery, although they did bring in a fingerprint expert, R.S. Terwilliger, who dusted the doctor's car. He was able to find only a single fingerprint, that of Jake Fleagle, made when the bandit had forced the window open on the night he lured the physician to his ranch. This print was sent to the Identification Unit of the FBI in Washington, D.C., but there was little hope that it could be matched to any known criminal.

Four known bandits were rounded up: Floyd Jarrett and Whitey Walker, Oklahoma bandits Alfred Oliver, an ex-convict, and Charles C. Clinton, a preacher who hated doctors because his wife had died during an operation while Clinton was in prison. These four men were taken to Lamar, and all were identified as the bank robbers, despite the fact that the real bandits had all worn masks. The four men were nevertheless charged with murder and bank

robbery and were about to stand trial when the FBI fingerprint lab reported that the fingerprint found on the window of Dr. Wineiger's car matched that of a man who had been a prisoner in the Oklahoma Penitentiary in 1916, convict number 6591, Jake Fleagle.

Ralph Fleagle was tracked down and arrested, in Illinois. Royston was later found in California and arrested, and then Abshier was caught in Colorado. Jake Fleagle was the last of the gang to be tracked down. He was located at a chicken farm in Branson, Mo. Fleagle went for his guns and was shot to death. His brother Ralph, Abshier, and Royston were all later hanged at the Colorado State Penitentiary in Cañon City, Colo. The four other suspects were released, thanks to a single fingerprint identified by the FBI Identification Unit. The Fleagle case is a classic fingerprint identification in the U.S.

REF.: *CBA*; Cooper, *Ten Thousand Public Enemies*; Edge, *Run the Cat Roads*; Gish, *American Bandits*; Wellman, *A Dynasty of Western Outlaws*; Whitehead, *The FBI Story*.

Flechter, Victor, prom. 1885-95, U.S., (wrong. convict.) burg. When an elderly German musician's prized Stradivarius violin was stolen, he became so despondent that he lost the will to live. After the musician's death, a dealer in musical instruments was wrongly convicted of stealing the violin and lived with the expense, shame, and guilt of the conviction for eight years.

In 1885 Jean Bott and his wife, Matilda Bott, emigrated from Germany to the United States, settling in New York City so the elderly man, a former orchestra leader in Saxe Meiningen, could give lessons and continue to play his beloved "Duke of Cambridge" Stradivarius violin. With a meager income, Bott unhappily decided to put his violin up for sale, and, through Victor S. Flechter, a dealer and friend, offered the Stradivarius to Nicolini, husband of the famous opera singer, Adelina Patti. But when Nicolini offered Bott a certified check, the financially inexperienced musician insisted on cash, and Nicolini, believing himself insulted, tore up the check and cancelled the deal. Flechter, angry at losing his commission, was later presumed to have stolen the violin in revenge.

On Mar. 31, 1894, not long after the Nicolini incident, Bott returned home to find he had an unknown caller in his absence, and the Stradivarius was gone. A sad and fruitless search ensued, with Flechter giving Mrs. Bott a letter suggesting she offer a $500 reward for the instrument's return; she did, with no result. The grieving woman went to the District Attorney, visiting the Criminal Courts building, and a detective named Colonel Allen became interested in the case, as did his friend, Harry P. Durden, and another detective, Mr. Baird. Sadly, on Apr. 28, 1895, the heartbroken Bott, whose violin had been like a child to him, died at the Botts' Hoboken, N.J., boarding house.

Matilda Bott wrote to Flechter, saying she was thinking of going back to Germany. Two days later Flechter wrote to a Central Office man, offering a genuine Stradivarius. Allen saw the letter and immediately suspected the dealer. On May 28, Mrs. Bott received a letter signed "Cave Dweller," telling her that the violin "taken from your house some time ago will be returned if you are willing to abide by agreements that will be made between you and I later on." Mrs. Bott believed the letter to be written in Flechter's hand. On June 23, Durden and Baird came to Flechter's and were shown a Stradivarius by the office clerk. Returning three days later, Flechter himself showed it to them, explaining it had come from a retired merchant named Rossman, and was offered for $5,000. Asking to be allowed to take the violin to a rear room to show to a friend, Durden brought it to Mrs. Bott, who identified it as her late husband's most prized possession. Flechter was arrested immediately; on Aug. 28 an indictment against him accused the dealer of receiving stolen goods. The jury trial lasted for three weeks, with Arthur W. Palmer for the defense and James W. Osborne for the prosecution. Widely covered in the press, the case involved the testimony of a number of violin makers, including John J. Eller, and the testimony of several handwriting experts who believed that Flechter had written the "Cave Dweller" letter to Mrs. Bott. Flechter denied any guilt, asserting that his brother-in-law, John D. Abraham, was the author of an earlier letter to Matilda Bott that was used to connect him to the "Cave Dweller" missive. Abraham helped write the earlier note. The key witness for the defense, John J. Eller, claimed that the Stradivarius was his own instrument which had been stolen by a music teacher, who later sold it to Flechter.

Flechter was found Guilty and sentenced on May 22 to a twelve-month prison term; after serving three weeks in the Tombs, he obtained a certificate of reasonable doubt and was released on bail until his conviction could be reviewed on appeal. Disgraced, his reputation destroyed, and his business ruined, after several years Flechter was given another hearing of his case at the Appellate Division of the Supreme Court; his conviction was sustained. Again he paid the $5,000 bail and was free pending yet another appeal to the State Supreme Court. On Aug. 17, 1900, Flechter found the "Duke of Cambridge" Stradivarius. In the possession of a family named Springer in Brooklyn, it was initially discovered by a violin maker, Joseph Farr, who had once worked for Flechter and had testified on his behalf at the trial. An investigation by the District Attorney's office and the detective bureau uncovered the fact that the violin had been pawned at the shop of Benjamin Fox within an hour of its theft from the Botts' home, for the sum of $4. It lay exposed on a shelf until a tailor named James Dooly bought it for $20 in December 1895; he later sold it to the Springers for $30. On July 7, 1902, the elderly Matilda Bott positively identified her late husband's violin, and Flechter was finally proved innocent. REF.: *CBA*.

Flegenheimer (or Fleggenheimer or Fliegenheimer), Arthur, See: **Schultz, Dutch.**

Fleming, Erin, 1941- , Case of, U.S., fraud. The Bank of America, as executor of the estate of the comedian and actor Groucho Marx, sued Erin Fleming, asking that she return $428,000 in cash and gifts which the bank claimed she had acquired from the elderly performer by using intimidation and bullying. Marx died in 1977. The bank demanded $500,000 in punitive damages, and claimed that Fleming had obtained the gifts, salary, commissions, and expense payments through "connivance, control, direction, wheedling, intimidation, extortion, tormenting, threats, inveiglement, deceit, duress, menace, and manipulation," while she worked as Marx's personal manager and companion at a $1,000-a-week salary. While the prosecution, headed by J. Brin Schulman, portrayed Fleming, a former actress, as a vulture who preyed on vulnerable old men, defense attorneys David Sabih and Melvin Belli, and many Hollywood celebrities who testified painted Fleming as a loving and compassionate companion who brought joy to Groucho's final years and prolonged his life by resurrecting his career.

Included among the seventy-seven witnesses who testified were actors Bud Cort, Sally Kellerman, George Burns, Carroll O'Connor, and George Fenneman, the announcer for Marx's popular 1950s television show, "You Bet Your Life," and politician Tom Hayden. Many had seen Marx and Fleming at parties at Groucho's home, and testified that Marx was in control of himself, and that the relationship was positive. Members of Marx's family, including children and ex-wives, were divided in their opinions of Fleming's actions and intentions towards her employer and close friend. According to one, Fleming called Marx "Dad," and Groucho promised on his deathbed to return to Fleming as her baby. Fleming herself spoke from the stand to say that Marx was a strong-willed person who surrounded himself with attractive young nurses because his three insurance policies paid for it, and who loved her so much that he wanted her to have everything, "even the Empire State Building." She also said she loved him. Fleming often disrupted proceedings during her own testimony. Sabih told newspaper reporters at one point that she had threatened to kill herself if the jury ruled against her. In the final

moments of the defense arguments, lawyer Sabih showed videotapes of Marx himself. During an interview with an English journalist the comedian said of Fleming, "She means so much to me. She stimulated me into working again." Fleming was heard off camera asking, "Am I using you to benefit myself?" Marx responded, "No. I'm using you to benefit me." In another tape played earlier at the trial, Marx thanked Fleming in a speech at the 1974 Oscar telecast, saying she "makes my life worth living and...understands all my jokes."

On March 30, 1983, the jury awarded about $470,000 to the Bank of America. The nine men and three women on the jury had all said they were Marx fans, as had the attorneys for the defense and the prosecution, who all presented themselves as champions of the comedian. Responding to the verdict, Belli said, "We're not going to pay a dime," asserting that Fleming was not liable for damages because she was not found guilty of fraud. On May 16, 1983, Judge Jacqueline Weiss overruled the jury's decision, reducing the damages judgment by half, leaving a $221,843 compensatory damage award. There was speculation that that amount would not cover the bank's legal costs for the five-year lawsuit. On May 20 the Bank of America agreed to waive the $250,000 in punitive damages rather than risk the possibility of a retrial of the case. REF.: *CBA*.

Fleming, Ian Lancaster, 1908-64, Brit., writer. Authored espionage novels featuring British secret service agent James Bond (007), as the central character. His novels include: *Casino Royale, From Russia with Love, Dr. No, Goldfinger,* and *Thunderball.* REF.: *CBA*.

Fleming, Jim, prom. 1899-1902, U.S., mur. On Aug. 5, 1899, Montana prospector Gene Cullinane was found dead in his cabin. Arrested for his murder were Clint Dotson, who was sentenced to life in prison, and his accomplices, Oliver Benson and Ellis Persinger, who were sentenced to ten years for robbery. In September 1901, prospector Oliver Dotson, Clint Dotson's father, was found dead in his cabin. His death, however, appeared to have been suicide; a shotgun was rigged up on an elaborate frame with a string to pull the trigger. Next to the elder Dotson's body lay a note in which he—Oliver Dotson—claimed to have murdered Cullinane. Sheriff Robinson, who had arrested Benson and Persinger in 1899, paid them a visit in prison. Both had witnessed the slaying and neither had any doubts about the younger Dotson being the murderer. Robinson then learned that Jim Fleming, Dotson's closest friend, had recently been released from prison. Robinson disguised himself as a bum, found Fleming, and slowly gained his confidence, eventually learning that Dotson had stashed $50,000 from a Union Pacific railroad robbery on the outside, and that he had offered part of it to Fleming if Fleming would murder his father. First, however, Fleming had to convince the elder Dotson to write the note that would get him out of jail. Fleming visited Oliver Dotson, got him drunk enough to write the note as a "joke," and then shot him through the heart, rigging up the shotgun to make it look like suicide. On Sept. 8, 1902, Fleming was hanged for the murder. Clint Dotson remained in prison. REF.: *CBA*.

Fleming, Mary Alice, See: **Livingston, Mary Alice Almont.**

Fleming, Patrick, d.1650, Ire., rob.-mur. When he was about thirteen, Fleming became a servant to a countess, but he did not last long at his trade. After being fired from his first position, he left his second job voluntarily, taking £200 of his employer's money. He left Ulster and headed to Dublin where he became a successful housebreaker. Fleming also took to the highway where he would demand a tribute from travelers passing over *his* road. In one morning he is said to have robbed more than 100 travelers in an area known as Hangman's Wood.

One day, Fleming assaulted the coach of Lady Baltimore and robbed her of £100 and whatever jewelry he could find. He then kidnapped her 4-year-old son and held him until he received a £300 ransom. He took £1000 from the Archbishop of Tuam. He was jailed in Cork, after committing a £200 robbery, but he cheated the hangman for a time by escaping, crawling up the chimney of the jail and fleeing into the countryside.

Fleming enjoyed two years of freedom which he used to murder eight people, including two women and a 14-year-old boy. He also cut off the nose, lips, and ears of Sir Donagh O'Bryan, who put up a fight when Fleming robbed him. After these atrocities, a £100 reward was offered for the bandit, dead or alive. He was turned in by the keeper of an inn where he regularly stayed, and fourteen members of his gang were captured when the sheriff and a small army surrounded them. Fleming and his men were hanged en masse in Dublin on Apr. 24, 1650. After Fleming was cut down, his body was hanged in chains on a road leading into the city and left there to rot as a warning to other would-be highwaymen.

REF.: *CBA;* Hibbert, *Highwaymen;* Smith, *Highwaymen.*

Fletcher, John, and **Arindell, William,** prom. 1825, Brit., rob.-kid. At a British trial of two sailors charged with felony on the high seas, a judge ruled that the testimony of a black slave must be admitted, regardless of his social status.

The case of John Fletcher and William Arindell, two free black men charged with robbing a slave named Branch Hull, taking his clothes and other possessions, and then throwing him overboard, was tried on July 19, 1825, in the Court of Admiralty Sessions in England. When Hull, who had survived, stepped forward to give his testimony, the defense attorney immediately objected to any evidence being accepted from a slave. The judge ruled that, although there was precedence for rejection of testimony by slaves, the objection was no longer valid. In the early days of slavery, he explained, "slaves were savages from the coasts of Africa," and, as such, "incompetent as witnesses." Through the "progress of Christianity and consequently of civilization," according to the judge, slaves must no longer be considered barbarians, and if their testimony was impartial and clear, it must be considered as legitimate and important as any other. The judge concluded: "It is the character of the witness, and the character of the evidence, that must prevail." On the strength of Hull's evidence, Fletcher and Arindell were convicted and hanged.

REF.: *CBA;* Poynter, *Forgotten Crimes.*

Fletcher, Joshua, and **Barber, William Henry,** prom. 1839, Brit., consp.-fraud-forg. William Barber went into business as a solicitor on Lombard Street, London, in 1836. Business was slow until he met Joshua Fletcher, an elderly doctor from Camberwell, whom he persuaded to direct some legal business his way. In time the surgeon became his most important client.

In 1839, Fletcher seized upon a money-making scheme involving unclaimed stock dividends held in trust by the Bank of England. The bank held back payment of dividends on government stock when they learned of an owner's death, holding the money in reserve until the rightful heir came forward, which did not always happen.

Barber, until then a solicitor of good repute, became Fletcher's agent in these transactions. If the rightful owner of the stocks could not be found, Fletcher found someone to impersonate the heir. It became a lucrative swindle for him, and he paid the usual fees to Barber and his partner, Bircham. Then the name of Anne Slack of Hertfordshire came to his attention. She owned stock valued at £3,500, which had passed to a man named Hulme, who had recently died. Fletcher tried to claim it by enlisting a Mrs. Saunders to pose as Jane Slack, the claimant.

The scheme was detected. Barber and Fletcher were found Guilty and transported for life. Saunders received two years imprisonment. Barber claimed that he had been paid only his usual fees for the transactions and that he knew nothing of Fletcher's swindles. In 1848, nine years after his imprisonment, this was indeed proved to be the case and Barber was pardoned.

REF.: *CBA;* Cobb, *Trials and Errors;* Stevens, *From Clue to Dock.*

Fletcher, Simon, 1606-59, Brit., rob. Simon Fletcher was the son of a baker and for four years he followed in his father's trade, but then he ran away from this apprenticeship and became the most infamous cutpurse of the day. In those times purses were worn by men and women, hanging from a girdle, and a cutpurse would ply his trade, like the more modern pickpocket, in a crowded marketplace or some similar place he could slip through the crowd, cut the purse of his victim, and carry it away.

Legend has it that one day Fletcher was crossing the London Bridge where a large crowd of people were listening to a singer. Searching for a victim, he came upon a country bumpkin, intent on the music, whose scrotum had slipped from his pants. Fletcher, mistaking it for a purse, used his knife and then walked away with it in his hand.

Because of his fame and dexterity, Fletcher was soon elected captain of all thieves. His job was to test novice thieves at their various trades and assign tasks of thievery which were most suited to their skills. Once a week, the thieves would come together and Fletcher would be given a progress report on the week's thievery. He would then assign jobs for the coming week. For this he received twenty-five percent of the take.

Fletcher enjoyed a long career as a criminal Fagin and fence, but he was eventually exposed and was hanged at Tyburn in 1659 at the age of fifty-three.

REF.: *CBA;* Smith, *Highwaymen.*

Flexner, Simon, 1863-1946, U.S., pathologist. Professor at the University of Pennsylvania from 1899-1903, director of laboratories at the Rockefeller Institute of Medical Research from 1903-35, and director of the institute from 1920-35. REF.: *CBA.*

Flinn, Charles J. (AKA: **Charles Mortimer**), prom. 1862-73, U.S., asslt.-pris.esc.-rob.-mur. A remorseless and inveterate criminal, Charles J. Flinn began thieving, and ended up committing murder. His last regret as he mounted the scaffold to die was that he could not get his hands on the woman who had given evidence against him.

Born in New Hampshire in 1834, Flinn moved to Sacramento, Calif., in 1861 and, once honest and industrious, became entrenched in criminal activity. Starting out with petty offenses, he was sent to prison in San Francisco in 1862 for robbing Conrad Phiester of $800; in 1864, Flinn again went to jail for chloroforming and then robbing Charles L. Wiggins of money and jewelry worth about $1,500. Pretending to be repentant, Flinn offered to take Special Officer Rose to Santa Clara County to show him where he had buried Wiggin's property, and took the officer's gun and savagely beat him with it, leaving him for dead.

In 1865 a prisoner brought in to San Francisco to serve a seven-year prison term for robbery proved to be Flinn; Rose recognized his assailant and was restrained by fellow officers from shooting him. Freed in 1872, Flinn became involved with a dance hall woman, Carrie Spencer. In May 1872, Caroline Prenel was strangled and another man had been indicted for the crime when Spencer confessed that Flinn had been the killer, proving her claim by producing some of the dead woman's jewelry that Flinn had given to her. Another murder, that of a Sacramento saloon keeper Mary Shaw-Gibson, who had her throat cut and had been robbed of $500, was linked to Flinn by a clump of reddish-brown hair found clutched in the murdered woman's hands. The hair matched Flinn's beard, which he had shaved off hours after the slaying. Spencer, who had been staying with Flinn, was taken into custody, and dresses belonging to Shaw-Gibson were found in his room.

At the trial, which began on Mar. 12, 1873, Spencer testified that Flinn had returned on the morning of the murder with clothes, jewelry, and about $300, explaining that he had taken it from Shaw-Gibson and had "croaked the old woman so that she could not squeal." Spencer also testified that she had visited her lover at his cell and he had handed her several sheets of paper with information, telling her to memorize it and testify accordingly or he would cut her throat. The jury deliberated thirty-five minutes before finding the accused Guilty on Mar. 15; he was sentenced to die on May 16.

One month before Flinn's hanging a masked man came to the

jail, and was shot by Deputy Sheriff Manuel Cross when he realized the man was holding a gun on him. The fatally wounded visitor ran to Flinn's cell door before dropping dead, and was identified by the condemned man as his 23-year-old brother. At the undertaking parlor, Flinn cut off a lock of his deceased sibling's hair and took it back to his cell, trying to feign insanity by believing the hair was his brother, talking to it and watching it day and night. On May 15, 1873, Flinn was hanged in the county jail.

REF.: *CBA;* Duke, *Celebrated Criminal Cases of America.*

Flint, Motley H., and **Lewis, S.C.,** and **Berman, Jacob Bennett,** and **MacKay, Henry,** and **Rosenberg, Edward,** and **Getzoff, Ben,** prom. 1927, U.S., consp.-forg.-embez.-fraud-brib. Los Angeles was a boom town in the early 1920s, with fortunes to be made in oil, real estate, and silent movies. One of the many immigrants who came west was Courtney Chaucey Julian, a Texas man with no money who struck it rich in June 1922 with land that gushed oil in Santa Fe Springs. A glib and effective pitchman, he soon established Julian Enterprises, which he later dubbed "Julian Pete's," attracting investors and building an empire largely on the money he was given by others to handle anticipated fortunes from new "gushers" that never materialized. Julian lived in the fast lane until 1924.

Stock hustler Motley Flint.

When no more oil profits sprang up after his initial strike, he decided to turn his shaky business over to two smooth operators from the midwest, S.C. Lewis and Jacob Bennett Berman. Borrowing $10 million from Los Angeles banks, the slick hustlers bilked tens of thousands of dollars from leading business men in the Los Angeles financial community. One of these executives, Motley H. Flint, the Boston brother of California Senator Frank Flint, brought in a stock pool of $1 million from the city's wealthy elite, making impossible but attractive promises. Initially, "Julian Pete's" investors got returns, but, within a short time, five million shares of worthless stock had been created. On May 27, 1927, the house of cards collapsed, with more than 40,000 investors left hanging. Flint, like a few other insiders who were well informed, got out with his money.

A federal grand jury summoned Flint to testify in June 1927. With Lewis, Berman, and several others, Flint was indicted on charges of conspiracy to violate securities laws and to obtain money under false pretenses, violating state usury laws, embezzlement, and swindling. District Attorney Asa Keyes, responsible for the prosecution, abdicated his duties, leaving the complicated affair to subordinates whose ineffectual work confused jurors so badly that all of the men indicted were acquitted, to the rage and disbelief of the 40,000 highly dissatisfied investors. Presiding Judge William Doran was appalled and told reporters that he felt Keyes had been exceedingly lax.

Facing fourteen-year jail terms for several counts, Lewis and Berman hired Edward Rosenberg to find a "fixer," Ben Getzoff, an associate of Keyes. Rosenberg made a deal through Getzoff to give $27,500 to Keyes and a lesser amount to Chief Deputy District Attorney Harold Davis as a bribe to leave the indicted men alone. Milton Pike, an anxious tailor, delivered the money, but the fearful Pike had kept a detailed diary, which was discovered and published in the newspapers; it described Berman and Rosenberg's roles in the secret testimony before the grand jury. Davis and Keyes were convicted and sentenced to terms of one-to-fourteen years in San Quentin. After nineteen months of his term, Keyes was pardoned by Governor James Rolph. Lewis

and Berman could no longer be tried in the Julian case, but were convicted of stock fraud in another company and received seven-year sentences.

Flint was indicted five more times by the grand jury; four indictments were dropped, and the fifth, a conspiracy to violate the California corporate securities act, was planned to go to trial in July 1930. Testifying in a related case on July 14, Flint completed his statements, and was shot and killed by a disgruntled man who had lost his life savings of $35,000 after investing in bank stocks on Flint's advice. Two-thirds of Flint's $750,000 estate was left to charitable organizations for "poor children, the aged in want, and young men and women in need of help to start them well in life."

REF.: *CBA;* Wolf, *Fallen Angels.*

Flittner, Anton, 1931-   , Ger., mur. Microscopic traces of fibers clutched in the palm and fingernails of Maria Floskey, who was murdered on Sept. 11, 1963, were large enough to convince detectives that the killer was Anton Flittner.

Floskey was nearly dead when Helene Rüth found her lying in the woods near a northern Bavaria lake known as the Kahler See. She was dead minutes before a doctor arrived. Before the State Criminal Office was called in on Sept. 14 to handle the investigation—local detectives had prematurely determined that the elderly woman had died of natural causes—the crime scene had been nearly cleared of clues. The woman had been strangled to death, a scarf tied about her neck, though the scarf was not the murder weapon. Investigation of the murder fell under the command of Detective Inspector Degen, who soon learned that a bicyclist had been in the area around the approximate time of the murder. It was also learned that Flittner, a machinist, was known to have been traveling in the area at the time. Flittner, who was convicted Mar. 20, 1963, for molesting his young stepdaughter and sentenced to two months imprisonment, was immediately suspected because the crime was probably sexually motivated. He denied the crime, but allowed Degen to examine several articles of clothing to compare fibers taken from the crime scene and the dead woman's hand.

Examination of the fibers was conducted by Dr. Röhm, who used the Frei-Sulzer micro-trace examination system. It was not until Nov. 6, 1963, that Röhm clearly matched Flittner's clothing to fibers from Floskey's fingernails, palm, mushroom basket, and the fir tree at the scene which on a mere whim Degen had decided to sample. Meanwhile, the detective continued to build his case against the suspect who contended his innocence.

Degen asked an elderly man, Otto Hock, who had seen the bicyclist, to return to the spot where he was the day of the murder to see if anyone who rode by matched the man he saw. Degen then had Detective Sergeant Rudingsdorfer accompany Flittner on Oct. 26 on a ride through the woods. After Flittner rode by, in this makeshift lineup, Hock identified him as the man he saw. Flittner was soon arrested, and on Nov. 11, 1963, he confessed to the murder of Floskey. The following May, a jury in Aschaffenburg found him Guilty and he was sentenced to life in prison. REF.: *CBA.*

Flobert, Louis, 1819-94, Fr., firearms. Manufactured and produced guns, especially lightweight breech-loading guns, including the rifle bearing his name. REF.: *CBA.*

Flood, Floyd, prom. 1924, U.S., (wrong. convict.) rob. Arrested in St. Louis, Mo., without a charge against him, Floyd Flood soon found himself on trial for a bank robbery in Freeburg, Ill., on Aug. 23, 1924. Flood, however, had not visited Illinois in more than a year.

The First National Bank in Freeburg was held up by six men; two remained in the getaway car, while four entered the bank with revolvers and forced bank president Russell E. Hamill to retrieve money from the vault while cashier Susie Wolf and bookkeepers Minnie Holst and Emma Wolf looked on. More than $10,000 was stolen, but some of the money was new and easily traceable. Police arrested James Breene and Ralph Southard in Jonesboro,

Ark., and Flood was taken into custody in St. Louis. Flood's arresting officer stated the man was picked up for being a "bad egg," though Flood had no criminal history. Flood countered that he was arrested because his girlfriend had refused to date the arresting officer. No reason was ever given. The police dressed Flood up like one of the bank robbers and while the Wolfs were watching ordered him to say "stick 'em up." After that he was taken to Illinois to stand trial.

At St. Clair County Circuit Court before Judge George A. Crow, all three were tried from Dec. 2 to Dec. 5, 1924. Prosecutor Hilmar C. Lindauer had no problem convicting Breene and Southard, but the bank president and several witnesses who identified the first two defendants could not positively identify Flood. In his defense, attorney Joseph B. McGlynn clearly proved that Flood had indeed been in St. Louis at the time of the robbery, with testimony from several witnesses. The jury ignored the evidence supporting Flood and found him Guilty along with Breene and Southard. All three were sentenced to ten years to life in prison on Dec. 18, 1924.

A glimmer of hope came for Flood when Breene and Southard confessed to the crime and to never having met Flood before. With the arrest in Ohio of two more bank robbers, who named the real members of the gang, McGlynn felt his chances for freeing Flood were much better. Along with Breene and Southard, the bandits were Benjamin Ingram, John Lyons, Brice McConnell, and Arthur Richardson. Flood, however, remained in prison for more than a year because the Bankers Association opposed his pardon while members of the gang were at large. The last two robbers were finally caught and convicted, and Flood was pardoned and released on Jan. 21, 1926.

REF.: Borchard, *Convicting The Innocent; CBA.*

Floquet, Charles Thomas, 1828-96, Fr., her.-duel-polit. corr. Imprisoned in Paris briefly for expressing radical sentiments concerning the reconciliation of the Versailles government and revolutionary leaders in 1871. He was named prefect of the Seine in 1882, and Chamber of Deputies president from 1885-88. As an opponent of Boulangism, he dueled with and wounded Georges Boulanger in 1888. He was again elected the Chamber of Deputies president from 1889-93, but lost re-election to another term following his implication in the Panama scandal from 1892-93. REF.: *CBA.*

Flor, Roger di (de Flor), 1280-1307, Byzantium, Caesar, assass. Commanded the Catalan Grand Company against the Turks while serving Emperor Andronicus II of Byzantium. He married a daughter in the imperial family upon his arrival in Constantinople in 1303, proclaimed himself Caesar in 1306, and was assassinated the following year at the orders of the emperor. REF.: *CBA.*

Flores, Eduardo, prom. 1948, U.S., drugs. In May 1948, a group of drug smugglers attempted to transport 116 pounds of marijuana from Nueva Laredo, Mex., to Houston, Texas. Outside Galveston, Texas, however, customs officials easily arrested the smugglers, who pulled over when they heard the siren of the vehicle in pursuit. The smugglers did not try fleeing from the authorities because the vehicle used to chase them was an ambulance.

Eduardo Flores, fearing capture, decided to have his shipment picked up in Galveston rather than Houston; an astute assumption since customs agent Al Scharff had already been informed of the upcoming shipment by Juan Garcia, who crossed the Mexican-U.S. border with the marijuana. Scharff waited inside the Broadway Funeral Parlor down the street from where Garcia awaited instructions from Flores. Two men were sent by Flores to see that no problems had occurred in the smuggling operation. After the two left with sixteen pounds of marijuana, Scharff, two police officers, and Joe Megna, the owner of the funeral home, gave chase in Megna's ambulance. Megna forced the car off the road and the men were arrested. Flores then sent a boy to pick up the rest of the shipment. The boy, who did not know what he was picking up, agreed to set a trap for Flores when apprehended

by authorities. Scharff had the boy convince Flores his car had broken down and it was safe for him to pick up the marijuana himself. Once again the ambulance gave chase and pulled over the truck with Flores, the boy, and the marijuana. Flores was sent to prison for his drug smuggling and Scharff allowed the boy to disappear.

REF.: *CBA;* Roark, *Coin of Contraband.*

Flores, Juan, 1835-57, U.S., west. outl. Juan Flores was a cattle rustler and horse thief who became famous after he was sentenced to San Quentin in 1856. He escaped with other prisoners from the seemingly impregnable prison by stealing a provision ship tied to the prison wharf. A grand plan to sail to Australia dissipated quickly, and the gang landed on the shore south of the prison. Flores, with a newly recruited gang of 50 marauders terrorized the area, looting small towns, robbing stagecoaches, and pillaging mining camps from a hideout in the hills above San Juan Capistrano. The gang kidnapped travelers, holding them for ransom, including a German settler who was shot to death in a public square after refusing to pay.

In January 1857, Sheriff James R. Barton organized a posse to apprehend the gang of thugs. However, Flores was formidable, and only three lawmen returned. Sheriff Barton was slain by gang member Andres Fontes. A larger Mexican-American posse led by Don Andres Pico was organized, which disrupted the gang and killed several members. But Flores and Fontes escaped. On Feb. 1, 1857, Flores was apprehended by a third posse led by Doc Gentry. He escaped from a ranch house, but was caught two days later and brought to Los Angeles. On Feb. 14, Flores was sentenced to be hanged, and the sentence was carried out immediately. Fontes escaped to Mexico, where he died in a gunfight shortly thereafter.

REF.: Armor, *History of Orange County, California; CBA.*

Flores, Venancio, 1809-68, Urug., pres., rebel.-assass. Led the Colorados after civil war from 1842-51, in rebellion against the government. He was elected president at his own bidding from 1854-55, but was ousted and fled to Argentina. At the backing of Argentina and Brazil he returned in 1864, claimed the provisional presidency in 1865, and won the presidential election in 1866. Four days after resigning from office, he was assassinated. REF.: *CBA.*

Florey, Howard Walter (Baron Florey), 1898-1968, Brit., pathologist. Received the 1945 Nobel Prize for medicine along with Sir Alexander Fleming and Ernst B. Chain. REF.: *CBA.*

Flour Riots, 1837, U.S., mob viol. Thousands of starving poor assembled outside of New York's City Hall on Feb. 10, 1837, to protest the price of flour. Flour prices had risen to the then-inflationary rate of $12 per barrel and threatened to go as high as $20 a barrel, thanks to a shortage of flour in storage throughout New York. The wheat crop had mostly failed the previous year and certain merchants in the area were accused of hoarding supplies, to drive up the price.

After receiving no satisfaction from city hall authorities, the mobs moved on the huge wheat and flour storage buildings of Eli Hart & Co., on Washington Street. Here watchmen were quickly overwhelmed by the raging mobs and the place was destroyed, the contents of 1,000 barrels of wheat and an almost equal number of flour ruined.

Scores of police and several companies of national guardsmen were called in to quell the rioters, and several rioters were killed and dozens more wounded when the police and guardsmen opened fire after the rioters refused to leave. The rioters then roared on to the large flour store of S.H. Herrick & Co., wrecking it before they were driven off by the badly mauled police and troopers. At least twenty were killed in these senseless riots, which did nothing to bring down the price of flour. REF.: *CBA.*

Flourens, Gustave-Paul, 1838-71, Fr., rebel. Participated in the Cretan rebellion against Turks from 1866-68, and served as a member of the Commune of Paris in 1871. He was killed in a skirmish at Chatou by a French police officer. REF.: *CBA.*

Flournoy, John Jacobus (AKA: **Deaf Flournoy**), prom. 19th Cent., U.S., big. John Jacobus Flournoy may possibly have been one of the most eccentric men of his time. He always wore a rubber raincoat even in hot Georgia summers, and though wealthy enough to afford the best horses, he rode a donkey. Flournoy's often incoherent speech was a result of his deafness, but it did not prevent him from running for state legislator a number of times in the 1830s and with a number of different political platforms, including the Temperance movement (although he frequently drank heavily), sending slaves back to Africa, and phrenology. In the first election he entered, he received ten votes, and in the next election fifteen. A third election won him twenty-five votes of 2,500. During the late 1850s, Flournoy attempted to gain an ambassadorship from President James Buchanan. He sought accreditation for Mormons in Utah, which may have led to his interest in a polygamous life.

Flournoy wrote a book which advocated what he termed trigamy, or three wives for every male. The reformer even made an attempt at testing this type of relationship when he married a 13-year-old girl while his wife was out of town, falling short of adding a third wife.

REF.: *CBA;* Furnas, *The Late Demon Rum.*

Flower, Margaret, and **Flower, Philippa,** d.1618, Brit., witchcraft. Sisters Margaret Flower and Philippa Flower confessed to destroying by witchcraft the eldest son of their former employer, Francis, the Earl of Rutland, who had fired the two.

In her confession, Philippa told how she had stolen the right-hand glove of Lord Henry Rosse and given it to her mother, alleged witch Joan Flower. Her mother stroked an evil cat named Rutterkin with the glove, placed the glove in boiling water, pricked it several times, buried the glove, and spoke an oath against Rosse. The girls were tried before judges Sir Edward Bromley and Sir Henry Hobart in Lincoln and executed in March 1618. REF.: *CBA.*

***Flowery Land* Mutiny,** 1863, Brit., mur. A 900-ton merchant vessel known as the *Flowery Land* set sail from London on July 28, 1863, destined for Singapore. The ship never reached its destination; the crew, made up of several nationalities, mutinied on Sept. 10.

Captain John Smith felt that an iron hand was needed to keep the mixed crew in line. He flogged three or four Spaniards, a Turk named Watto, and tied a Greek named Carlos to the bulwark, all within three weeks from setting sail. Shortly after midnight, several crew members enacted a mutiny. The first mate, Karswell, was the first officer to die as the mutineers beat him severely about the face before throwing the dying man overboard. Captain Smith, hearing the commotion, rushed from his cabin only to be stabbed to death. His brother suffered a similar fate. Taffir, the second mate and the only officer left alive, was spared, though brutally beaten, because his navigational skills were needed to reach land. In retaliation for not joining the mutiny, the mutineers mutilated one of the Chinese crew members and drowned the remainder. When in sight of the Brazilian coast, the ship was scuttled by the Norwegian carpenter Finn, who was not a party to the mutiny. Landing near the mouth of the River Plate, the Spaniards convinced Brazilian officials that they were ship-wrecked; neither Taffir nor Finn were able to communicate what had really happened. Taffir finally managed to find someone who spoke English, and the eight mutineers were arrested and returned to England.

The murder trial began on Feb. 3, 1864, at the Old Bailey. Carlos was acquitted of the charge, while Watto and six Spaniards were found Guilty and sentenced to death. The sentences of the two youngest Spaniards were commuted to hard labor for life. Executioner William Calcraft performed the last mass public hanging in England when all five men were hanged outside Newgate Prison on Feb. 22, 1864.

REF.: Brock, *A Casebook of Crime; CBA;* Thomson, *The Story of Scotland Yard.*

Floyd, Charles Arthur (AKA: **Pretty Boy, Jack Hamilton,** Frank Mitchell, Pretty Boy Smith), 1907-34, U.S., rob.-mur. To the dirt-poor farmers of Oklahoma, Charles Arthur "Pretty Boy" Floyd was a legendary hero. Newsmen in the state dubbed him "The Robin Hood of the Cookson Hills," the hills being a wild, almost uncharted area where Floyd often sought refuge from the posses hunting him. He was in reality a ruthless bankrobber and killer—although he was wrongly named as one of those machine gunners responsible for the Kansas City Massacre in 1933. Floyd was, like John Dillinger and many other bank robbers of his era, a farm boy who daydreamed through his youth with the fierce and ancient images of Jesse James and the Younger Brothers flashing before him.

Born and raised in Akins, Okla., in the heart of the Cookson Hills, Floyd worked on his father's farm. At the age of twenty, he married 16-year-old Wilma Hargrove and their son, Jack Dempsey Floyd, was born in 1922. While in his early twenties, Floyd demonstrated no criminal tendencies. On Saturday nights, he would appear with friends in towns like Sallisaw and Siloam Springs. Sometimes he would drive to Fort Smith, Ark., and there get drunk on his favorite brew, Choctaw Beer. His addiction to this beer earned him the nickname Chock. The winds and erosion that later created the dust bowl were at work in Oklahoma during the early 1920s and farmers, including the Floyds, consistently lost acreage to the weather until there was little topsoil left to farm. Money dwindled until Oklahoma farmers began to migrate in droves to California and other points. Others went to the cities to find work. Charles Arthur Floyd turned to robbery.

His wife pregnant, Floyd at first tried to find work as a harvest laborer, but he tired of the day-to-day existence and of dragging Wilma through hobo camps. In 1925, he bought a used pistol and rode the rails to St. Louis., where he robbed a small payroll service and then fled back to Oklahoma with his wife. Floyd was identified as the robber, and police arrested him after finding some of the payroll money on his farm. He was convicted and sent to the Missouri State Penitentiary in Jefferson City for five years. Jeff City, as the prison was called, was one of the most backward penal institutions in the U.S. There the lash was used to whip recalcitrant prisoners. Other old-fashioned punishments practiced at Jeff City included the sweatbox, ball and chain, and ice baths. Such treatment made hardened criminals of novice thieves. The penitentiary helped to forge Charles Arthur Floyd as a later Public Enemy, as it did many others.

Paroled in 1929, Floyd returned to his native state just in time to discover that Jim Mills had shot his father to death. The ancestors of Mills and Floyd had lived in Kentucky, where the two families had carried on a bloody feud for generations. That feud boiled over again in Oklahoma when Mills and Floyd's father battled over a small piece of land. Charles Floyd attended Mills' trial in Sallisaw and watched wordlessly as Mills was freed on grounds of self-defense. Floyd followed Mills into the Cookson Hills and Mills was never seen again. To avoid arrest on suspicion of the Mills disappearance, Floyd fled to Kansas City, Kan., seeking and getting protection from Johnny Lazia, crime overlord of the Pendergast Machine. He hid out in one of Lazia's whore-houses operated by Ann Chambers. When Chambers looked over the handsome Floyd, she remarked: "I want you all to myself, Pretty Boy." The nickname, which Floyd hated, stuck to him forever.

While in Kansas City, Floyd reunited with Red Lovett, who had served time with him in Jefferson City. Floyd and Lovett made up a list of banks in northern Ohio—where Floyd had relatives—and planned to rob these "jugs." They recruited Tom Bradley and Jack Atkins and roared off toward Ohio. From late 1929 through early 1930, this gang, living in an Akron bungalow, robbed a number of small town banks without mishap. But on Mar. 11, 1930, the gang went to pieces after robbing the bank in Sylvania. Roaring out of town, the gangsters traveled at high speeds, and drew the attention of a motorcycle cop, Harlan F. Manes, who gave chase. Bradley smashed the rear window of the car and fired a submachine gun, spraying the highway with bullets which smashed into Manes. The motorcycle soared off the highway and Manes fell dead on the pavement, his body riddled.

Atkins was at the wheel of the getaway car and he panicked. The car swerved off the road and crashed into a telephone pole. When the police arrived, they found Atkins, Bradley, and Floyd pinned inside the overturned car. Lovett was nowhere to be seen. The bank robbers were pried loose and thrown into cells. All three men were tried for murder. Bradley was condemned for killing Officer Manes and later went to the electric chair. Atkins was given a life sentence. Floyd was found innocent of Manes' death, but he received a 15-year sentence in the Ohio State Penitentiary for the Sylvania bank robbery. He was placed in the custody of several deputies and put aboard a train bound for the state prison in Columbus, on May 25, 1930. Floyd, who had vowed that he would never return to prison after his experience in Jefferson City, waited until the deputies fell asleep in their seats. He was not handcuffed and, sitting next to the window, he simply grabbed a suitcase, broke out the glass, dove out, and landed on the embankment as the train roared away.

Running across the open fields, Floyd found a car, jumped the wires to start the ignition and drove to Toledo, where underworld contacts hid him. He met another desperate bank robber, Bill "The Killer" Miller, and the pair embarked on a series of bank robberies throughout Michigan. Fat with bank loot, the two then returned to Kansas City, staying in the bordello operated by Sadie Ash on Holmes Street. There Floyd took up with one of the inmates, Beulah Baird, while Miller consorted with Rose Ash. Both these working girls had their own men, William and Wallace Ash, sons of the proprietor.

When Floyd and Miller went off with the women to a Kansas City speakeasy on Linwood Boulevard on the night of Mar. 23, 1931, three detectives entered the private room Floyd had rented in the speakeasy, ostensibly carrying out a Prohibition raid. Floyd had his back turned to the plainclothes policemen when they entered. As one kneeled to frisk him, he whirled about with two .45-caliber automatics in his hands, firing. He shot down all three detectives. He and Miller fled with the girls. Floyd reasoned that the Ash brothers had set him up with a police trap, and both brothers were found shot to death on Mar. 25, 1931, their bodies dumped along a highway outside Kansas City. Sadie Ash went to the police, but by then Floyd and Miller had left town with the girls.

Floyd and Miller, in May and June 1931, robbed the Mount Zion Trust Company of $4,000 in Mount Zion, Ky.; the Elliston, Ky., bank of $2,700; and the Whitehouse, Ohio, bank of $3,600. On Apr. 9, 1931, Floyd and Miller, along with the two girls, drove into Bowling Green, Ohio. Local police officers checked the license plates on their car and realized that the auto was stolen. Police Chief Galliher and officer Ralph Castner approached Miller and the girls as they were about to enter a store, ordering him to halt. Just then, Floyd, across the street, saw the two officers and drew his two automatics. He shouted to Miller: "Duck, Bill!" He began firing at the two offices. Miller dove for the cement, as did the girls. One of Floyd's bullets ripped into Castner, killing him.

Chief Galliher jumped behind a parked car and traded shots with Floyd. When Miller got up and tried to race across the street to join Floyd, Galliher shot at him, the bullet struck the bandit in the head. Miller fell to the street dead. Floyd stood brazenly in the street, his legs spread apart, his guns blazing. Beulah Baird, hysterical, reached for the fallen Miller's gun and aimed it at Galliher. The police chief shot her in the head. Floyd then abandoned the girls, raced to the gang's car and drove away. When he reached Toledo, he was hidden by the Peter Licavoli mob.

Sadie Ash was interviewed after the Bowling Green shootout and she asked reporters: "Did they get Pretty Boy?" Newsmen seized upon this name and soon the nation was aware of a new super bandit, "Pretty Boy" Floyd. Meanwhile Floyd, tired of paying exorbitant fees to Licavoli for his miserable one-room

hideout, left Toledo and returned to Kansas City, where he moved into a second-floor partitioned room above the Lusco-Noto Flower Shop at 1039 Independence Avenue—a Lazia hideout. Inside this airless, sunless room, Floyd spent his days and nights, paying $100 a night for the protection. The building housing Floyd was made up of a series of partitioned rooms which local bootleggers used to store contraband liquor.

On the night of July 21, 1931, federal Prohibition agents raided the building, chopping through partitions on the second floor with axes. Inside one small dark room filled with the stench of liquor, they found a burly man with his head on a table, a bottle of cheap booze next to him. Flashlights played upon the man, who raised his head slowly, saying: "What are you fellows looking for, whiskey?"

Agent Curtis C. Burks took a closer look at the man and then blurted to other agents: "Hey, you know who this is? It's Pretty Boy—"

At that moment, Agent Glenn Havens shouted to Burks: "He's got a gun!"

Floyd jumped from the table with two guns, .45-caliber automatics, both blazing away at the agents. Burks fell dead to the floor under Floyd's withering gunfire. Floyd then dashed through the crowd of startled agents and raced down the stairs as they fired wildly at him. Upon reaching the street, he ran down the block. Floyd turned as he ran and exchanged shots with the pursuing agents. A bystander, E.J. Wilson, was caught in the crossfire and fell dead with a bullet in his brain.

Crime boss Lazia was incensed when he heard that Floyd had killed a federal agent on mob property. He ordered Floyd to leave Kansas City or be turned in to local police. Floyd drove to Oklahoma, hiding out in the Cookson Hills. Then, alone, he robbed one-horse banks in Muskogee and Cherokee counties, entering these small banks with a submachine gun and quickly scooping up the cash. He took the time to obtain the first mortgages on shops and farms which were not recorded and tore these up or burned them, thus earning the down-home respect of local inhabitants who looked upon him as a hero.

In October 1931, George Birdwell, a 40-year-old traveling preacher who had "lost the callin'" sought out Floyd in the Cookson Hills. Explaining that he had lost his job in the oil fields near Earlsboro and that he had to support a hungry family, he begged the bandit to take him in as a fellow bank robber. Floyd taught Birdwell how to shoot automatics and submachine guns, and then the two men went on a bank robbing spree that set records for the Southwest. They robbed banks at Morris, Maud, Earlsboro, Shamrock, Konowa, and Talequah. Floyd had long dreamed of doing what the Dalton Brothers had failed to do in 1892 in Coffeyville, Kan., robbing two banks at one time. This he successfully did with Birdwell on Dec. 12, 1931, robbing the banks of Paden and Castle in Oklahoma.

Their method was simple and consistent. Floyd and Birdwell would steal a car a few hours before a robbery, then roar into a small town unprotected by lawmen. They would enter the bank, unmasked, Floyd standing at the door with a submachine gun in his hand while Birdwell ran behind the tellers' cages and grabbed the cash. They would then take two hostages and have them stand on either side of the car on the running boards as they roared out of town, setting their hostages free once out of town.

State officials, at the urging of irate bankers, issued machine guns to all local lawmen, along with tear gas and riot guns. Lieutenant Gov. Robert Burns then posted a $1,000 reward for Floyd's capture, this being added to a bank pool reward of $5,000 for the apprehension of the notorious bandit. Some days later, Floyd sent a postcard to Burns from Altus, Okla. The bandit was indignant at being portrayed as a killer and a man who robbed the poor. His postcard read: "You either withdraw that one thousand at once or suffer the consequences. No kidding. I have robbed no one but moneyed men. Floyd." Handwriting experts confirmed that the signature was Floyd's, and Burns, incensed at the threat, went on the radio, fulminating: "This is a desperate case. Floyd has terrorized the entire east-central section of Oklahoma with his outlawry. Already six killings and ten robberies have been charged to him. He must be stopped!"

Burns encouraged residents who knew Floyd's whereabouts to turn him in, but native Oklahomans, especially the hill people in the Cookson Hills, looked upon Floyd as a folk hero. John Steinbeck, in *The Grapes of Wrath,* his saga of the Okies of that era, has his character Pa Joad comment: "When Floyd was loose and goin' wild, law said we got to give him up—and nobody give him up. Sometimes a fella got to sift the law." Meanwhile, Floyd was living in Tulsa under the alias Jack Hamilton. He and Birdwell were discovered sitting in a Ford coupe on Admiral Street on Feb. 7, 1932, but when officers Wade Foor and Wilbur Wilson ordered them from the car, a burst of machine gun fire was the response. Wilson fell wounded to the street as the car roared away. Foor later claimed that he pumped five bullets into Floyd's back but the bullets bounced harmlessly off him. Floyd was obviously wearing a bullet-proof vest.

The car was found on a side street the next day, and it was traced by a tag on a recently recharged battery to Jack Hamilton, who lived at 513 Young Street. Police placed the neat frame house under surveillance and spotted a woman coming and going with a 7-year-old boy. It was Floyd's wife and their son Jack. On Feb. 11, 1932, twenty police officers and two armored cars pulled up in front of the house. Moments later, two figures darted from the back door of the house, submachine guns in their hands, the guns spitting red bursts of rapid fire. The two men, Floyd and Birdwell, leaped into a car parked in an alley and raced off as police let loose a barrage that failed to strike the car or the bandits.

Mrs. Floyd and her son were taken to police headquarters, where Wilma Floyd told officers: "I don't know anything about where Charlie hides. And I don't know anything about his plans. All I know is you'll never catch him. He can outsmart every copper in Oklahoma and the federal agents, too. I know it!" Special State Investigator Erv A. Kelly told Wilma Floyd that it was his job to catch her husband and he would do it or die in the process. Mrs. Floyd was released and immediately left Tulsa with her son, going to Bixby, Okla., sixteen miles south of Tulsa, to stay on her father's farm.

Kelly and his men followed her and staked out the farm, watching for Floyd to appear. Days and nights went by but the bandit failed to appear. Kelly knew Floyd was a family man and would show up sooner or later. He maintained the stakeout, and on the night of Apr. 7, 1932, while Kelly's men were away from the stakeout getting hot coffee, a car approached the farm with its headlights off. Kelly ran to the middle of the road, aiming a submachine gun at the car. It roared toward him and a hail of bullets spat from the window, five bullets crashing into Kelly's skull, killing him. Two deputies arrived to fire at the car but it had turned around and vanished in the dark. Floyd had killed again.

Birdwell's father died the following month and lawmen hid in the mortuary where the body lay in state, believing that Birdwell would arrive to pay his last respects. The plainclothes police were suddenly surprised by a heavyset man holding a submachine gun who had entered the mortuary through a back door. It was Floyd. He held the gun on the detectives while Birdwell entered the funeral parlor, knelt at his father's bier to say a few prayers, and then both men departed in a hail of bullets. In June 1932, officers received a tip that Floyd and Birdwell were holed up at the farm of A.W. Nichols, located twelve miles from Ada, Okla. Pontotoc County Sheriff L.E. Franklin led a posse of fifty men to the spot to see Floyd and Birdwell leap into a green sedan, which they drove up a muddy hill and then across open fields while the posse fired more than 100 shots at them. Franklin later claimed that bullets bounced off both men without harming them. He insisted that Floyd and Birdwell were wearing bullet-proof vests and steel plates over their arms and steel caps beneath their hats.

More than 500 state police and national guardsmen now joined local officers in their pursuit of Floyd and Birdwell, who were heading toward the Cookson Hills in eastern Oklahoma. The robbers slipped past roadblocks and entered the Hills where posses lost track of them near Bowlegs. The hill people refused to cooperate with police, telling them nothing. The Cookson Hills once again swallowed their favorite bandit, shielding him from harm. The police, after weeks of fruitless searching, gave up the chase. Floyd stayed in the Hills until October 1932, when he and Birdwell were joined by Aussie Elliott. A one-time shortstop for a semi-professional baseball team, Elliott had robbed several safes and had been sent to the Oklahoma State Penitentiary in 1930. He had escaped and, looking for work, immediately sought out Floyd.

Floyd, Elliott and Birdwell, on Nov. 1, 1932, drove into Sallisaw, Okla. Floyd, cradling a submachine gun, leisurely got out of a car and walked down the middle of the street of the small town. Residents recognized him and waved to him, one farmer calling out: "Howdy, Chock! What you all doin' in town?"

"Going down to rob the bank," Floyd said with a wide grin.

"Give 'em hell, Chock!" shouted another farmer who sat on a bench in front of a hardware store.

Aussie Elliott stayed behind the wheel of the car while Floyd and Birdwell sauntered into the bank. Floyd knew all of the employees and said to Robert Riggs, the bank cashier: "Howdy, Bob." He pointed to Birdwell with the muzzle of his submachine gun, saying: "This man here will tell you what we want."

Birdwell shoved Riggs behind the counter, telling him: "Everything, starting with the big bills. Just put it all in this here bag." Riggs did as he was told and he was then ushered outside to the waiting getaway car. He was told to stand on the running board as the car slowly pulled out of town. Crowds of curious residents gathered about the car as it inched forward. Floyd leaned from a window, smiling and waving his submachine gun. "That's right, folks," he announced. "It's a holdup all right."

Some miles from town, Riggs was told to get off the running board and Floyd said to him: "Goodbye, Bob, take care of yourself." The car headed off down State Highway 64, toward Fort Smith, Ark. A newsman later wrote that the Salisaw robbery was "like the hometown performance of a great actor who has made good on Broadway." The robbery netted the thieves $2,350, small money for the risk they were taking. The robbers improved on this on Nov. 7, 1932, when they walked into the American State Bank in Henryetta, Okla., and took away $11,252, the largest bank haul of Floyd's long career.

On that day, Mrs. Floyd went into a Tulsa hospital with acute appendicitis. The day following the Henryetta robbery, she was moved into a private room and received expensive around-the-clock care, the money undoubtedly provided by her bank-robbing husband. Meanwhile, Oklahoma governor William "Alfalfa Bill" Murray, enraged by the latest robberies committed by Floyd, announced to the press: "We would have had Floyd and Birdwell long ago if sheriffs and other officials in the hill country were not protecting them. Floyd has lots of friends in the Cherokee Hills. He has sent me word twice through relatives that if I would save him from the electric chair, he would come in and surrender. I sent word back to him that I would not do it."

The Oklahoma Banker's Association increased rewards for the bandits and its secretary, Eugene P. Gumm, stated: "Floyd has been the luckiest bandit who ever lived. Do not be surprised if you read, almost any day now, that Floyd and Birdwell have been slain." Charles Burns, a top police official added: "This fellow Floyd is shrewd and slippery as an eel. In a general way, we know where he is all the time. He never leaves the Hill country except for a robbery."

Birdwell, meanwhile, had become a hopeless drunk. Floyd warned him that he would refuse to work with him if he did not cease his heavy drinking, but the strain of being a fugitive caused Birdwell to go on drinking. Floyd refused to go along with Birdwell on a bank robbery in Boley, Okla., an all-black commun-

"Pretty Boy" Floyd, 1929.

Adam Richetti, 1934.

Charles Arthur Floyd, 1932.

Floyd in happy days with his son and wife.

The outlaw with his son, Jack Dempsey Floyd.

Floyd with a friend, and, right, wife Wilma.

"Pretty Boy" Floyd, dead, October 1934.

ity. Birdwell, with C.C. Patterson, a Kiowa Indian, and Charles Glass, a black who served as the getaway driver, drove into Boley on Nov. 23, 1932, at the height of the duck-hunting season. The three men entered the Farmer's and Mechanics Bank and ordered its president to open the vault. He hit the alarm button instead and Birdwell shot him dead. The town, then crowded with armed hunters who were also members of the Vigilance Committee, rushed to the bank and unleashed a withering fusillade which killed Birdwell and Glass. Patterson was crippled for life and sent to prison. The Banker's Association bestowed $1,000 on the men who shot down the bandits.

Floyd, however, was nowhere to be found. He was reported robbing banks in Maine and in California, and America waited for its premier bandit to strike next. It was later claimed, ridiculous or not, that the ever-loyal Floyd attended Birdwell's funeral, walking past dozens of armed lawmen without being identified, dressed as a woman. Such outlandish tales were typical of the type of journalism inspired by Pretty Boy Floyd. On Nov. 30, 1932, the Citizen's State Bank in Tupelo, Miss., was robbed of $50,000, and Floyd was identified as the ringleader of the bankrobbing gang by no less than twenty witnesses. Floyd wrote to newspapers denying that he had committed the robbery. He invariably objected to robberies he did not commit but kept silent about those he did enact. On one occasion, Floyd wrote to a columnist: "Thanks for compliments and the pictures of me in your paper. I'll be gone when you get this. Jesse James was no punk himself. I am not as bad as they say I am. They just wouldn't let me alone after I got out. Floyd."

Floyd stayed in the Cookson Hills until spring of 1933, and then, in Boliver, Mo., met a small-time thief named Adam "Eddie" Richetti. Floyd took Richetti under his wing and taught him the tricks of his grim trade. In April 1933, the pair held up a dance in Wewoka, Okla., taking only a few hundred dollars. The two then embarked on a series of bank robberies in Missouri, Oklahoma, and Arkansas. On June 16, 1933, Floyd and Richetti appeared in a garage in Boliver, Mo., to pick up a car being repaired by Richetti's brother, Joe, who owned the garage. The pair ran into Sheriff Jack Killingsworth, who was making inquiries about Floyd and Richetti. The outlaws disarmed the sheriff and took the fastest car in the garage.

They abandoned the car some time later, flagging down another auto driven by Walter L. Griffith, a real estate broker from Clinton, Mo. Richetti and Floyd, with Sheriff Killingsworth in tow, forced Griffith to drive them toward Kansas City while posses scoured the countryside for them. Planes were thrown into the search and Floyd ordered Griffith to park his car in a wooded area until the air search ceased. The bandit sat in the back seat holding a submachine gun. He calmly told his life story to his hostages, saying that the most cherished thing in his life was his son Jackie. "I don't lie to myself," he confided to his hostages. "Some day I'm going to go down full of lead."

Floyd and Richetti let their hostages go a short time later and continued on to Kansas City. It was here, on the morning of June 17, 1933, at Union Station, that three to four gangsters attacked a group of FBI agents and local lawmen who were delivering outlaw Frank Nash to Leavenworth in an apparent attempt to free Nash from federal custody. Opening up with submachine guns, the attacking gangsters killed one FBI agent, three local lawmen, and Nash himself, as he sat behind the wheel of a car wearing a cheap wig. The killers fled the bloody scene which became known as the Kansas City Massacre. One of the killers, Vernon C. Miller, a lawman turned gangster, was definitely identified as one of the slayers, but the identities of the others were in doubt then and remain so today, despite the FBI's long-delayed identification of Floyd and Richetti as the other killers. That Floyd and Richetti were in the area prior to the killing was established, but eyewitnesses had to be coaxed into identifying photos of the two men after the shooting.

One eyewitness to the killing was James Henry "Blackie" Audett, who was "invited" to watch the liberation of Nash by Mary McElroy, daughter of Kansas City's City Manager, Henry McElroy. She had learned of the planned attack through Kansas City crime boss Johnny Lazia and she took Audett, a Lazia associate, to Union Station that morning. They sat in a parked car and watched the entire one-sided battle. Audett, later paroled to the custody of the author, reported in 1979 that the real killers were Miller and two brothers, Maurice and Homer Denning, Lazia killers, and that "Floyd and Richetti were never there." Given the fact that Lazia had told Floyd a year earlier to stay out of Kansas City for causing too much "heat" to descend upon his rackets, it was unlikely that Lazia would entrust the freeing of Nash to a man who could too easily be identified.

It was later discovered that certain people inside the Kansas City Police Department had had knowledge of the impending attack, and all the planning and procedures of the killers pointed to the fact that this attack was an organized crime operation under Lazia's direction. Miller botched the job and was identified. He was later found murdered in Detroit at the hands of the Purple Mob, which was associated with Lazia in the then-loosely-knit national crime cartel. This killing eliminated one tie to Lazia. Since Floyd and Richetti were identified as the other killers, an identification which Lazia encouraged, his other hand-picked killers, the Denning brothers, were never sought or linked to Lazia. Floyd and Richetti were convenient "patsies," though both men, to the moment of their deaths, denied ever participating in the Kansas City Massacre.

When the press announced that Floyd and Richetti had performed the massacre with Miller, Floyd adamantly sent a postcard from Springfield, Mo., to Thomas J. Higgins, Kansas City's chief of detectives. It read:

Dear Sirs:
I—Charles Floyd—want it made known that I did not participate in the massacre of officers at Kansas City.
Charles Floyd

The handwriting was examined by experts and pronounced genuine. Floyd and Richetti were now the most wanted outlaws in America for a crime they apparently did not commit. They went to Cleveland, then Akron, Ohio, but underworld hideouts were denied to them. Then they returned to the Cookson Hills, but even this traditional hideout was no longer safe. Other wanted criminals like Wilbur Underhill, Ford Bradshaw, Edward Newton Clanton, Bob Brady, Jim Clark and finally, the Barrow gang, had fled into the Cookson Hills. Clyde Barrow, Bonnie Parker, and other members of the murderous Barrow gang drove into the Cookson Hills just ahead of posses hunting for them. This gang was particularly repulsive to Floyd. He considered them "killer punks who turn on their own like rattlesnakes." He sent word out to the hill people not to aid the Barrows. A super-posse of more than 1,000 men combed the Hills in February 1934, driving dozens of outlaws from this sanctuary. Floyd and Richetti managed to slip past roadblocks, and they headed to Toledo where the Licavoli mob offered them a hideout at high prices. To pay for this protection, Floyd and Richetti robbed banks in Anderson, Ind., Centralia, Ill., and Fort Dodge, Iowa. They then held up a string of banks in Booth, Holland, and Winameg, Ohio.

On June 30, 1934, the Merchants National Bank of South Bend, Ind., was robbed of $24,000, and Floyd was identified as one of the bandits, along with John Dillinger, George "Baby Face" Nelson, and Homer Van Meter. The outlaws shot up the street when leaving the bank and several bank employees and bystanders were wounded. On Oct. 19, 1934, Floyd and Richetti, down to their last pennies, robbed the tiny bank of Tiltonsville, Ohio, of $500. They raced northward in their stolen car to a wooded area outside of Wellsville, Ohio. The next day, a farmer called Wellsville police chief J.H. Fultz to tell him that two men were camping near his farm and that they appeared to be armed. Fultz and two deputies drove to the area and saw two men sitting on blankets, eating.

The two were Floyd and Richetti and, as soon as they spotted the lawmen, they jumped to their feet and drew automatics, firing rapidly at the officers, who returned their fire. Floyd and Richetti ran into the woods with the lawmen hot after them. A running gunfight ensued. Floyd, very fast on his feet, outdistanced Richetti, who paused, panting, next to an outhouse. Fultz fired a shot that splintered the wooden frame of the structure just above Richetti's head and the bandit threw down his gun and raised his arms in surrender. He was taken to Wellsville. Found in his pocket was $98, which Richetti insisted he had recently won in a crap game in Melina, Ohio. Richetti admitted his identity butbut would not say if his companion was the notorious Pretty Boy Floyd. Fultz wired Melvin Purvis, special agent in charge of the Chicago FBI office, that Richetti was in custody and that the much-wanted federal fugitive, Floyd, was probably hiding in the woods near Wellsville. Purvis flew to East Liverpool, Ohio, with a group of heavily armed agents.

Purvis set up his field headquarters in the Travelers Hotel in East Liverpool and Richetti was brought to him. He interrogated the bandit for hours, but Richetti would not talk about his friend Charles Arthur Floyd. Purvis arrested Richetti for the Kansas City Massacre and placed him in federal custody, although Richetti angrily denied having anything to do with the mass slayings in Kansas City. Richetti would go on denying having any part of the Kansas City Massacre. He denied the charge at his trial for that crime on June 10, 1935, and he denied the crime on Oct. 7, 1938, when he was dragged screaming to the gas chamber in the Missouri State Penitentiary, the first man so executed in that state.

After Richetti was taken away to a jail cell in East Liverpool, Purvis and his men organized huge posses that began searching the area around East Liverpool and Wellsville. Hundreds of heavily armed men now combed the woods and meadows for Floyd, who was now on foot, without a coat and carrying a single .45-caliber automatic. He had very little money and he kept off the main highways, walking down mostly country lanes. He occasionally crept to a highway to see if he could spot an old car or truck he might flag down for a ride.

Floyd appeared at a farmhouse near East Liverpool on Oct. 21, 1934. He bought a sandwich from the farm woman there, paying her $1. He asked if she had a car and she said no. Then he asked for directions to Youngstown and then headed north along a highway. The woman, who had heard radio reports of Floyd being hunted in the area, called Constable Clyde O. Birch who then called Purvis. FBI agents and local lawmen began searching the area, their dragnet tightening on Floyd. The outlaw hitched a ride from a youth on Highway 7, giving him $10 to take him to Youngstown, but the car ran out of gas near Clarkson, and Floyd took to the woods again.

Just after dawn, on Oct. 22, 1934, Floyd appeared at the farm house of Mrs. Ellen Conkle. He was exhausted, dirty, and hungry. He begged to buy a meal. The farm woman felt sorry for the stranger and made him breakfast, refusing to take any money. As Floyd was eating, he noticed through the kitchen window an old car parked in the back yard. He asked who owned the car.

"It belongs to my brother," Mrs. Conkle told him.

"Do you think he will drive me to Youngstown?" Floyd asked her.

Stewart Dyke, the brother, then entered the kitchen and told Floyd that "I got my chores to do, but I'll take you as far as Clarkson."

Both men got into the car, Floyd in the back seat. Dyke began to drive down a back lane which led to the highway. Two cars pulled into the lane in front of Dyke. Floyd's face went ashen. "Drive behind that corn crib," he ordered Dyke, waving a .45-caliber automatic. Dyke pulled the car behind the crib and Floyd jumped out, hiding behind the crib for a moment. He then stood up and sprinted across a meadow.

Melvin Purvis and his agents, along with East Liverpool policemen, jumped from the cars and raced after the gangster. Floyd cut across a cornfield that had been harvested, its rows of stubs sticking up only a few inches. There was no place to hide as he raced across open ground. The lawmen ran after him, firing submachine guns, shotguns, and automatics. Floyd was an easy target and a bullet ripped into him. He fell to one knee, his back still turned to the pursuing lawmen who kept up a searing fusillade. Floyd fell forward on his face. He rolled over on his back, then rolled over again, face to the earth. Floyd then found the energy to come to his knees, but another bullet struck him in the back and he flopped forward.

Melvin Purvis, agent Herman Hollis, and Chester C. Smith, an East Liverpool policemen, were the first lawmen to reach the stricken Floyd. Purvis waved the other lawmen back as he knelt to question Pretty Boy. He snapped handcuffs on Floyd so that his hands were pinioned behind his back and then turned Floyd onto his side. The bandit stared up at him. "Are you Pretty Boy Floyd?" Purvis asked. This was an odd question, in that the agents had opened fire on Floyd without being sure of his identity and without Floyd firing a weapon at them, although he was certainly seen to be running with the .45 at his side.

Floyd rasped back to Purvis: "I am Charles Arthur Floyd." Blood was seeping from a shoulder wound and running from a bullet hole in Floyd's leg. He was not mortally wounded, according to Officer Smith.

Purvis then asked: "Did you have anything to do with the Kansas City Massacre?" The FBI man seemed desperate for an answer here, according to officer Smith, as if to establish a reason for shooting Floyd down.

To this question Floyd answered in a firm, louder voice: "I didn't do it! I wasn't in on that." Then he asked: "What happened to Eddie?"

"He's in jail," snapped Purvis. Again the FBI agent repeated his question: "Were you at the Union Station in Kansas City last summer? Were you one of the machine gunners?"

"Hell no!" Floyd shouted. "I wouldn't tell you sons of bitches anything!" Propped up on one elbow, Floyd then said to Purvis: "You got me twice."

Purvis was dogged: "Were you at the Union Station?"

"Go to hell!" Floyd shouted.

Disgusted, Special Agent Melvin Purvis stood up. According to Officer Chester Smith, standing next to him (and who did not relate this information until 1974), Purvis then grimly turned to agent Herman Hollis and commanded: "Shoot him!"

Hollis, who would be killed by Baby Face Nelson the following month, did not hesitate, according to Smith. He aimed his automatic at Floyd, who was looking up at him, and fired twice. One bullet slammed into Floyd's stomach, the second into the bandit's chest, going into his heart and killing Floyd on the spot. Of course, this was cold-blooded murder, but Officer Smith insisted that these were the true facts in the shooting of Pretty Boy Floyd.

This ruthless slaying at Purvis' orders is not so surprising when reviewing this agent's conduct in the Dillinger case. He had allowed an East Chicago, Indiana cop, Martin Zarkovich, to shoot down a man at the Biograph Theater in Chicago three months earlier to the day, then claimed the dead man was the much-wanted John Dillinger. Purvis' idea of combating the bandits of the early 1930s was to shoot first and last and answer questions later, if ever.

Floyd's body was taken to the East Liverpool morgue and there agents and morgue attendants posed happily with the corpse as newspaper photographers recorded Pretty Boy's ignoble end. About $100 was found in Floyd's pockets, along with a pocket watch his father had given him. On the inside lid of the watch, reporters later claimed, ten scratches were found, notches the newsmen said, for the ten men Floyd had killed. The body was then shipped to Kansas City where Floyd's mother claimed it. Before returning to Oklahoma with the remains, Mrs. Floyd told newsmen: "There's something very strange about my son's death." When asked what she meant by that remark, Mrs. Floyd replied that she thought it peculiar that her son was quoted as talking to

Melvin Purvis for some time before he died in the Ohio cornfield. How could he have had such a conversation, she wondered, with a bullet through his heart, as the autopsy showed.

Floyd's funeral in his home town of Akins was a repulsive circus. Ghoulish souvenir hunters tried to pry the nails from Floyd's coffin and Floyd's younger brother, who later served as Sequoyah County sheriff, knocked a man down who was trying to chisel a piece of wood from the coffin. Mrs. Floyd banned all cameras from the funeral. When she spotted a man in a tree close to the burial site, she walked to the tree, grabbed the news photographer by the leg and yanked him to the ground. More than 10,000 people flocked to the cemetery where Floyd was buried and the legend of Pretty Boy began in earnest. He would continue in memory to be a local folk hero, killer or not. He would be considered a Robin Hood, bank robber or not.

Ma Joad, the eternal Okie mother in Steinbeck's classic novel, *The Grapes of Wrath,* summed up the attitude of the rural folks who honored Floyd the bandit:

"I knowed Purty Boy Floyd...I knowed his Ma. They was good folks. He was full of hell, sure, like a good boy oughta be....He done a little bad thing an' they hurt 'im, caught 'im and hurt 'im so he was mad, an' the next bad thing he done was mad, an' they hurt 'im again. An' purty soon he was mean-mad.

"They shot at 'im like a varmint, an' he shot back, an' then they run 'im like a coyote, an' him a-snappin' an' a-snarlin', mean as a lobo. An' he was mad. He wasn't no boy or no man no more, he was jus' a walkin' chunk a mean-mad. But the folks that knowed 'im didn't hurt 'im. He wasn't mad at them. Finally, they run 'im down and killed 'im. No matter how they say it in the paper how he was bad—that's how it was."

See: **Barrow, Clyde; Dillinger, John; Federal Bureau of Investigation; Hoover, J. Edgar; Kansas City Massacre; Lazia, John; Licavoli, Peter; Miller, Verne; Nash, Frank; Nelson, George; Pendergast Machine; Purple Mob; Purvis, Melvin.**
REF.: Audett, *Rap Sheet;* Boar, *The World's Most Infamous Murders; CBA;* Clayton, *Union Station Massacre;* Cooper, *Ten Thousand Public Enemies;* Demaris, *The Director;* Dorsett, *The Pendergast Machine;* Edge, *Run the Cat Roads;* Gish, *American Bandits;* Godwin, *Murder U.S.A.;* Hoover, *Persons in Hiding;* Hynd, *The Giant Killers;* Louderback, *The Bad Ones;* McClellan, *Crime Without Punishment;* Messick, *Secret File;* Nash, *Bloodletters and Badmen;* ____, *Citizen Hoover;* ____, *The Dillinger Dossier;* Powers, *Secrecy and Power;* Purvis, *American Agent;* Reddig, *Tom's Town;* Reppetto, *The Blue Parade;* Sanders, *Murder in the Big Cities;* Sann, *Kill the Dutchman;* Toland, *The Dillinger Days;* Toledano, *J. Edgar Hoover;* Ungar, *FBI;* Wellman, *A Dynasty of Outlaws;* Whitehead, *The FBI Story;* Wicker, *Investigating the FBI;* Wilson, *Encyclopedia of Murder;* (FICTION), Steinbeck, *The Grapes of Wrath;* (FILM), *The FBI Story,* 1959; *Pretty Boy Floyd,* 1960; *A Bullet for Pretty Boy,* 1970; *Dillinger,* 1973.

Floyd, Edward, prom. 1621, Brit., libel. Edward Floyd was sentenced to a number of odd punishments in 1621 for slandering King James I's son-in-law, the Elector of Palatine, and his wife. He was ordered not to give evidence in court, not to bear arms, to ride with a horse backwards, to be flogged, to have his ears nailed, to be pilloried, to pay a fine of £5,000, and to be imprisoned for life at Newgate Prison. After following his sentencing, a debate arose concerning the corporal punishments, and since Floyd was a gentleman, the majority decided that the man would not have his ears nailed, but would still be whipped. He then was placed in the pillory for two hours and had his forehead branded. REF.: *CBA.*

Flüe, Niklaus von (AKA: Bruder Klaus), 1417-87, Switz., jur. Elected coucillor and judge for upper Unterwalden in 1448. He intervened in a dispute between Swiss states, leading to the Stans agreement in 1481, and consequently became a folk hero. REF.: *CBA.*

Fly, William, d.1726, U.S., pir.-mur. William Fly was a pirate whose ship had been sunk in the Atlantic. Along with two of his men, Henry Greenville and Samuel Cole, he signed on board the *Elizabeth* as a common seaman. After the small merchant vessel was under sail from Boston to Jamaica in May 1726, Fly and his men attacked and killed Captain John Green and his loyal mate, throwing their bodies into the sea. Fly changed the name of the ship to *Fame's Revenge* and began preying on other small merchant vessels. The pirates captured and sank several ships, killing crews and passengers. One passenger, a man named Atkinson, was spared because of his navigational abilities. He was pressed into service as a navigator. Other seamen were forced to work and Atkinson later led these sailors in a mutiny which recaptured the *Elizabeth,* which then sailed back to Boston. Here Fly, Greenville, and Cole were convicted and hanged before a large crowd on July 10, 1726.
REF.: *CBA;* Colman, *It is a Fearful Thing to Fall into the Hands of the Living God, A Sermon Preached to Some Miserable Pirates;* Rankin, *The Golden Age of Piracy.*

Flynn, William James, 1867-1928, U.S., law enfor. off. Born in New York on Nov. 18, 1867, Flynn was educated in public schools. In 1897, he was appointed to the Secret Service, rising to the rank of Chief in 1912. Flynn accepted this position only on the condition that he could remain in the New York office of the Secret Service where he had spent fifteen years as an agent and then agent-in-charge, instead of moving to service headquarters in Washington, D.C. Surprisingly, this arrangement was accepted and Flynn spent most of his tenure as the Secret Service chief in New York where he devoted a great deal of time establishing and running his own private detective agency. Though unusual, this private enterprise was not considered to com-

William J. Flynn, chief of the Bureau of Investigation, 1919-1921.

pete with Flynn's obligations to the Secret Service.

Flynn remained as chief until 1917, although he took an eight-month leave of absence in 1910-11 to reorganize his New York-based detective agency. Occasionally he commuted to Washington, D.C., to supervise matters of the Secret Service but, for the most part, he delegated operational duties of the Service to subordinates. In December 1917, Flynn quit the Secret Service, this being at the height of America's involvement in WWI, to devote his full energies to his detective agency. Flynn's act was severely criticized as unpatriotic in the press at the time.

During the summer of 1919, left-wing radicals, which included anarchists, Communists, and Bolsehviks, began a nation-wide campaign in the U.S. to disrupt government operations. Several bombs were set off and some persons were killed. This "Red Scare," much publicized in the press at the time, moved U.S. Attorney General A. Mitchell Palmer to appoint Flynn as chief of the Department of Justice's Bureau of Investigation on July 1, 1919. Thought to be a more aggressive person than his predecessor, Flynn replaced acting Bureau chief, William E. Allen.

It was Flynn's specific duty to root out radicals and anarchists and he worked closely with a 24-year-old lawyer, J. Edgar Hoover, who had been appointed by Palmer to head the Bureau's General Investigations Division, a legal branch which prepared all briefs used in the much-criticized Red Raids occurring in December 1919. These raids brought about the arrest of 249 persons, including celebrated anarchists Emma Goldman and Alexander Berkman, who were deported to Russia on board the U.S. Army transport, *Buford*, which had been labelled "The Red Ark" by the press.

Though Flynn was responsible for giving the orders for these wholesale arrests, he received his directions from Palmer who, in turn, relied upon the youthful Hoover to provide him with the legal briefs to obtain arrest warrants. These briefs were later criticized as ambiguous and thinly researched but they nevertheless proved effective. Hoover, who became Bureau chief in 1924, built his career on these Red Raids and throughout his long career with the FBI made left-wing activities in the U.S. the chief concern of the Bureau.

Under Flynn's leadership, the Bureau, with the help of local law enforcement agencies, continued the Red Raids, which reached their peak on Jan. 2, 1920, when more than 4,000 persons throughout the country were arrested, mostly on questionable warrants or with no warrants at all. Most of those arrested were aliens and they were held for deportation while non-aliens were hailed into court to be prosecuted under anarcho-syndicalism laws. Few were convicted and most were released within months. These raids came under such heavy fire from the press that Flynn was forever stigmatized for overreaching his authority, as was Palmer, even though Hoover was the guiding force in this instance.

Flynn resigned his post as head of the Bureau on Aug. 22, 1921, and was replaced, not by Hoover, as the young lawyer might have expected, but by William J. Burns, another private detective with his own far-flung detective agency. Flynn retired to his comfortable estate at Larchmont, N.Y., where he worked as the editor and publisher of *Flynn's Weekly*. He died on Oct. 18, 1928.

REF.: Asbury, *The Gangs of New York*; CBA; Dorman, *The Secret Service Story*; Nash, *Citizen Hoover*; Powers, *Secrecy and Power*; Reppetto, *The Blue Parade*; Toledano, *J. Edgar Hoover*; Ungar, *FBI*.

Flynt, Larry C., 1943- , U.S., obsc.-org. crime. At the age of fourteen Larry C. Flynt dropped out of school and ran away from home. Seven years later he declared bankruptcy. At thirty-three, after creating a four-page newsletter that he distributed at his eight Hustler Club bars in Columbus, Ohio, Flynt produced the first copy of *Hustler* magazine in July 1974. Two years later *Hustler* sold 2 million copies, third in sales for pornographic magazines, behind *Playboy* and *Penthouse*. Although the magazine, which he describes as "tasteless, but what the people want," made Flynt a millionaire, its grossly explicit photos and content offended a number of people.

Flynt's first battle with the courts over the publication of *Hustler* was his longest. The trial for violating obscenity standards in Hamilton County (Cincinnati), Ohio, began in 1976 and did not end until 1985. After five weeks, the jury took four days to convict Flynt of the crime, and with engaging in organized crime on Feb. 8, 1977 (An Ohio statute states organized crime to be any illegal activity in which five or more persons conspire to commit). Before pronouncement of his sentence, Flynt taunted Judge William J. Morrissey, saying, "This court has not made an intelligent decision during the entire proceedings and I don't expect one now. I don't want mercy. As Gary Gilmore said, 'Let's do it.'" Gilmore had been recently executed for murder and spoke the same last words before he was shot to death. Flynt was sentenced to from seven to twenty-five years in prison and fined $10,000 for the organized crime charge, and sentenced to six months imprisonment and fined $1,000 for pandering obscenity. The sentences were concurrent. A finding of Not Guilty was returned for Flynt's co-defendants: his wife and executive editor, Althea Leasure, his brother and business manager, Jimmy R. Flynt, and magazine vice president, Al Van Schaik. Although Hamilton County prosecutor Simon Leis, Jr. was satisfied with the verdict and sentence, Flynt's fight to publish *Hustler*, led by lawyer Herald Price Fahringer, was just beginning.

On Feb. 14, 1977, Flynt was released on a bail of $55,000 while awaiting appeal. He remarked, "I will continue to fight. Many in the country will say I'm doing it in the name of pornography, but I will continue to fight in the name of freedom." Flynt's conviction spawned debate over First Amendment rights and who was to define obscenity. Less than a week after his release, on Feb. 20, Flynt's supporters ran a full page advertisement in the New York *Times*. The ad read in three-inch type: "LARRY FLYNT: AMERICAN DISSIDENT," and was signed by such prominent persons as Woody Allen, Judith Crist, Hugh Hefner, Norman Mailer, Harold Robbins, and Gore Vidal. As the debate continued, a second similar case was underway in Cleveland, Ohio.

The Cleveland obscenity charge filed on July 14, 1976, was dismissed ten months later by Judge Salvatore R. Calandra, then the case was sent back for retrial by the 8th District Court of Appeals, a decision upheld by the Ohio Supreme Court and finally the U.S. Supreme Court on May 18, 1981. Prosecutors at that time decided against pursuing the case, which had been appealed by Flynt on grounds his magazine had been singled out. Meanwhile in the Cincinnati case, the organized crime charge was dismissed on Apr. 4, 1979, by the First Ohio District Court of Appeals, which then returned the obscenity case for a retrial. On Dec. 2, 1985, the case finally ended when Hamilton County common pleas judge Robert Kraft dismissed the charge after Flynt's lawyers paid $6,392 in litigation fees and agreed not to file suit for false arrest.

During yet another obscenity trial in March 1978 in Lawrenceville, Ga., Flynt was wounded by an unknown sniper. He was returning from a lunchtime recess when the sniper fired two bullets into his abdomen. The shooting left Flynt paralyzed from the thighs down, and wounded his lawyer, Gene Reeves. Although the judge declared a mistrial, Flynt was soon in court again. Another Georgia trial cost Flynt $27,500 when an Atlanta judge ordered the publisher to pay the fine or face eleven one-year sentences following his Mar. 28, 1979, conviction for obscenity violations. Flynt then entered the jurisdiction of civil law, when a *Hustler* ad parody aroused the ire of Moral Majority leader Rev. Jerry Falwell.

The controversial ad ran in a 1983 issue of *Hustler* and depicted a drunken Falwell discussing his first sexual encounter with his mother in an outhouse, a take-off on the Campari Liqueur ads featuring entertainers talking about their first drink. Falwell sued Flynt for $45 million, claiming the ad was an invasion of privacy, libelous, and caused emotional distress. In 1984, a federal judge threw out the invasion of privacy charge, as Falwell was a well-known figure; the jury threw out the libel charge, since no reasonable person would view the ad—which was clearly marked "ad parody"—as the truth, but awarded the reverend $200,000 for emotional distress. This decision, although upheld by a federal appellate court in August 1986, was unanimously overturned by the Supreme Court on Feb. 24, 1988, with Chief Justice William Rehnquist writing the decision.

Allegations against Flynt continued even after this decision. The Los Angeles County sheriff's department reported that the publisher had offered Mitchell L. Werbell $1 million in 1983 to kill *Playboy* publisher Hugh Hefner, *Penthouse* publisher Bob Guccione, entertainer Frank Sinatra, and publisher Walter Annenberg. Werbell, however, died of a heart attack in December 1983, and other than a cancelled check that a Flynt agent stopped payment on immediately, there was no evidence of the transaction. REF.: *CBA*.

Foat, Virginia Eleanor (Virginia Galluzzo), 1942- , Case of, U.S., mur. In 1983, for the second time in her life, Virginia Eleanor Foat, was accused by her second of four husbands, John Sidote, of murdering a man for money. As in the first case, the only evidence against Foat was her husband's testimony and confession; though this time Sidote did not refuse to testify against Foot, the president of the California chapter of the National Organization for Women.

Foat and Sidote were living in New York when they met in 1964, and agreed to travel to Florida with a friend, 19-year-old Wasyl Bozydaj. Their plans were changed when Sidote was arrested for illegal possession of a gun. The three traveled instead to New Orleans, La., in October 1964. Neither the couple nor Bozydaj earned much money, and according to Sidote, he and

Foat agreed to rob someone. Foat allegedly seduced a 62-year-old man from Buenos Aires, Arg., Moises Chayo, convincing him to take a ride with her. Sidote hid in the back seat, and when Foat had driven to a secluded spot, Sidote attacked the man but was unable to subdue him. Foat then grabbed a tire iron from the trunk and struck the man over the head. Chayo was found dead in a ditch two to three weeks later, robbed of $1,400.

The confession by Sidote was denied by Foat, as was her involvement in the killing of Donald Fitting on Dec. 19, 1965, near Lake Tahoe, Nev. Following a similar scenario to the Louisiana killing, Foat allegedly seduced Fitting into going for a drive, but this time, Sidote was in the back seat intoxicated, when he claimed she shot Fitting. Sidote was arrested in Ulster County, N.Y., on Jan. 29, 1977, when authorities first learned of his and Foat's possible participation in the two 1965 killings. After his arrest Sidote confessed to the crimes, and named Foat as the perpetrator in each.

The trial for Fitting's murder was held in Minden, Nev. Sidote had already spent more than a year in prison for an involuntary manslaughter conviction for shooting to death an unruly customer at the bar he and his wife owned with another couple on Aug. 25, 1967. He struck a deal with Douglas County Prosecutor Steve McMorris to reduce the charge of murder to manslaughter if he testified against Foat. McMorris agreed, and Sidote was charged with manslaughter and robbery. On the stand Sidote reneged on his part of the bargain, and Foat was released from custody in September 1977 because the prosecution had only her husband's word as evidence. Sidote, however, did testify against Foat at the Louisiana trial for the murder of Chayo.

Although there was considerable dispute as to why the warrant for the arrest of Foat and Sidote had remained unserved since its issuance in 1977—Nevada officials claimed that they notified Louisiana officials of the defendants' whereabouts, while Louisiana authorities claimed this was not the case—the trial finally took place in 1983. Robert Glass and John Reed defended Foat, who claimed that Sidote was seeking revenge against her. Assistant District Attorney Tom Porteous argued that if the man had wanted revenge he would have testified at the 1977 trial rather than say nothing about her involvement in the Fitting murder. Sidote was given immunity for his testimony. On Nov. 16, 1983, Foat was found Not Guilty by a jury before District Court Judge Robert Burns. REF.: *CBA*.

Foata, Ange, prom. 1934, Fr., attempt. mur. Ange Foata and Jean-Paul Stefani, known as the Corsican Captain, were the muscle employed by the Carbone-Spirito mafia in France. Stefani ran the drug smuggling operation until he turned to prostitution in Paris and allowed Foata to handle business. When Stefani learned that Foata was enriching himself with a large percentage of the profits, he removed Foata from his position. The fired man swore he would seek vengeance. On Dec. 22, 1934, rather than permit this oath to come true, Stefani allegedly went to the Rat Mort bar and opened fire with his Lüger in an attempt on Foata's life. Foata survived the attack unscathed, but 7-year-old François, Foata's illegitimate son, was shot to death, making his desire to kill Stefani even stronger.

Two hours after the boy's death, the bullet-ridden body of Stefani's brother, Etienne Stefani, was found by police. Stefani was arrested for the murder of François and placed on trial in 1936. Stefani was found Not Guilty because not one of the witnesses testified as to the killer's identity. This verdict enraged Foata, who ambushed Stefani and his bodyguard, Dominique Paoleschi, at the cemetery where Stefani's wife, who died while Stefani spent twenty months in custody, was buried. Foata failed to kill Stefani with his rifle, but wounded Paoleschi. For attempted murder, Foata received seven years of hard labor.

REF.: *CBA*; Goodman, *Villainy Unlimited*.

Fogelman, Clay, prom. 1932, U.S., boot.-theft-mur. Will Carter, the owner of a gas station in Rockingham County, N.C., was shot to death on Apr. 30, 1932, by two gunmen, one of whom was seen by the man's wife when she rushed to his side after the shots were

fired. Nothing was stolen from the station; the only motive police could discover was that Carter had turned in a number of Prohibition violators. Escaped felon Clay Fogelman was identified by Mrs. Carter from a photo as one of the killers. Fogelman, who had been sent to a federal prison on Apr. 9, 1929, for auto theft and violation of prohibition laws, was serving a sentence of six-and-one-half years when he and Jimmy Napier escaped from a prison camp on Nov. 1, 1931.

As the search for Fogelman continued, another murder in Rockingham County took place. Police officers were asked to investigate a light inside the public school. One of the officers, James A. Robertson, spotted two men and flashed a light on them. They shot the officer dead, just as Carter had been killed: with six bullets, three from a .32-caliber revolver and three from a .38-caliber revolver. An informant later verified suspicions that Fogelman was the killer, and added that Napier was his accomplice. Two weeks later the men eluded police who had surrounded their hideout, and were not seen again until a daring escape in June.

Fogelman and Napier were spotted along the banks of the Ohio River in Kentucky. Napier escaped easily, but Fogelman needed a little more prodding. After putting up his arms as if to surrender to police, who then lowered their guns, he dove into the river and swam away. His escape was fairly short-lived; on July 13, 1932, he was taken captive in Englewood, Ohio, while Napier managed to escape once again. Napier was eventually killed in August by a posse when he resisted arrest. On Sept. 10, 1932, Fogelman was found Guilty of the first-degree murder of Will Carter. He was sentenced to death in the electric chair.

REF.: *CBA*; Cohen, *One Hundred True Crime Stories*.

Fogg Art Museum Coin Robbery, prom. 1973, U.S., rob. Harvard University's Fogg Art Museum houses a number of ancient artifacts, Oriental figures, and Renaissance and colonial American works of art. On Dec. 2, 1973, 5,650 Greek and Roman coins from the seventh century B.C. to the fourth century A.D. were stolen.

A carefully executed plan was used by the armed gunmen. Earlier in the day, a package had been delivered to the museum to be picked up by a Mr. Ryan. After the museum was closed and only one watchman was present, a man claiming to be Ryan returned to pick up the package. Once inside, he pulled a revolver on the guard, Charles Pierson, and then let two others in. The robbers tied up Pierson and then stole about 3,000 coins from display cases, and robbed a 300-pound safe containing another 2,650 Greek coins, predominantly silver. Museum officials valued the coins to be worth at least $2 million. Investigators, including the FBI, which was called in due to the crime's magnitude, finally caught up with the thieves on Nov. 5, 1974, when three men and two women were arrested in Providence, R.I. Approximately forty percent of the coins were recovered; another 854 coins were recovered in Montreal, Can., three days later when three others were apprehended.

Four people involved in the robbery were found Guilty on Nov. 23, 1976, and sentenced on Nov. 24 by Superior Court Judge Herbert Travis. Carl R. Dixon, thirty-one, and Louis R. Mathis, forty-five, were sentenced to twenty to thirty years in prison; Anthony B. Vaglica, fifty-two, was sentenced to fifteen to twenty years; and Maria T. Magna, twenty-three, was sentenced to five years probation for her part as an accessory.

REF.: *CBA*; Nash, *Almanac of World Crime*.

Foley, James Thomas, 1910- , U.S., jur. Appointed to the Northern District Court of New York by President Harry Truman in 1949, and appointed to the Second Circuit Sentencing Committee in 1973. REF.: *CBA*.

Foley, Roger D., 1917- , U.S., jur. District attorney for Clark County, Nev., from 1951-55, attorney general for Nevada from 1959-62, and appointed by President John F. Kennedy to the District Court of Nevada in 1962. REF.: *CBA*.

Foley, Roger Thomas, 1886-1974, U.S., jur. District attorney for Goldfield, Nev., from 1916-24, district attorney for Las Vegas from 1935-38, district judge for Nevada from 1939-41, and appointed by President Franklin D. Roosevelt to the District Court of Nevada in 1945. REF.: *CBA*.

Folk, Carl, d.1953, U.S., tort.-rape. In 1953, middle-aged Carl Folk trapped Raymond and Betty Allen in their own trailer. Folk tied up Raymond Allen, then spent an entire night raping and torturing Betty, until finally she died. Folk had been so involved in assaulting Betty that he did not realize Raymond had freed himself. As Folk prepared to douse the trailer with gasoline, planning to burn it with the Allens and their baby inside, Raymond Allen opened the door and shot Folk fatally in the stomach. REF.: *CBA*.

Folk, Joseph W., 1869-1923, U.S., lawyer. Anxious for political power, St. Louis Democrats at the turn of the century persuaded lawyer Joseph W. Folk to run for circuit attorney, in part because he had no desire to get involved in public life. St. Louis' Republican mayor was corrupt, Folk's backers explained to their candidate. What the city needed was an upright, honest circuit attorney to straighten things out. What the Democrats wanted, however, was for Folk to pressure Mayor Ziegenhein and his cohorts to give them a greater share of the spoils. Folk was elected and began his tenure by investigating charges that both sides had tried to fix the election. Democratic party leaders explained that he was only supposed to prosecute the other side, but Folk said he intended to weed out graft wherever it existed. He prosecuted Republicans and Democrats alike, making sure the guilty were sent to jail.

Two months later, after Folk's initial foray into government corruption, he investigated a million-dollar scandal involving the city's railroad system. By bribing and promising payoffs, a businessman had persuaded the St. Louis assembly to grant him right of way privileges and to smooth the way for a merger on his terms. By the time he got his franchise, he'd paid out about $300,000 in bribes. But then he sold the railroad system to an Eastern syndicate and began to renege on his financial promises. The angry politicians leaked the story to the press. They said that certain local bank accounts contained money intended for bribes. Folk read the article, and visited the certain local banks. Encountering bank managers who told him that the safety deposit boxes were private, and that it was illegal to allow unauthorized access, Folk threatened to charge them with obstruction of justice. The deposit boxes were opened, and Folk started issuing indictments. Despite anonymous threats on his life, vicious letters, and investigations by private detectives who tried to find evidence of any wrongdoing to hold against the circuit attorney, Folk held firm, ignoring as well the entreaties of respectable citizens who wished to hush up the scandal. With the help of several defendants who turned state's evidence in exchange for immunity, the bribery-crazed millionaire businessman was sentenced to three years' hard labor; several of his cohorts received two-year sentences, and others fled, forfeiting bail. Ten years of political corruption in St. Louis was uncovered by the indefatigable Folk. REF.: *CBA*.

Folkes, Robert E. Lee, 1922-45, U.S., mur. One of the most gruesome train murders on record occurred at the height of WWII when U.S. railroads were packed with servicemen. Some were transferring between bases, others going home on their final leave before shipping overseas, still others were returning to their duty stations. Ensign Richard F. James was traveling south from Seattle, Wash., with a contingent of other Navy personnel being transferred to a new base in California. The ensign's wife of four months, Martha James, twenty-one, from Virginia, was traveling with her husband aboard the Southern Pacific's *Oregonian*. When the train reached Portland, Ore. on Jan. 23, 1943, the newlyweds were separated. Mrs. James lost her reservation to some California-bound servicemen. Twenty-five minutes later, she boarded the next southbound train the Southern Pacific Railroad's *West Coast Limited,* making its 1800 mile run between Seattle and Los Angeles. Mrs. James was assigned the lower sleeping compartment in berth number 13.

At 4 a.m., as the train neared Tangent, Ore., halfway between Salem and Eugene, a woman's piercing scream broke the stillness of the sleeping car. "My God, he's killing me!" the voiced cried out. Private Harold R. Wilson, twenty-two, of the U.S. Marines, was jerked from a sound sleep. After a moment of fumbling, he snapped back the curtain on the upper compartment of berth 13 and looked into the darkened aisle, still half-asleep. A dark man was moving rapidly down the aisle toward the rear of the train. Wilson later described the man as being about 5'10", with a heavy build, smooth-shaven, with curly hair combed straight back and wearing a brown pin-striped suit. He thought the man was black, but he was not sure. As other faces peaked out from behind slightly parted curtains, the body of Martha James slipped almost silently from the lower berth into the aisle.

The nightgown-clad woman was covered with blood, her throat slashed. Wilson looked toward the end of the car, but the dark figure had disappeared. He jumped from the berth and headed toward the back of the train, but a quick search proved fruitless. On his way back to the murder car he stopped in the galley of the dining car where he found a black cook at work, wearing a white uniform. He asked the man if he had seen anyone run by and the man said no. Told that a murder had been committed in one of the sleeping cars, the man grinned and asked Wilson if he had been drinking. When Wilson returned to the sleeping car, the body of Martha James still lay in the aisle, but someone had draped a sheet over her.

Police boarded the train when it pulled into Eugene, Ore. Crew members told them that a man fitting the description supplied by Wilson had been aboard the train but could no longer be found. A trail of blood spots led from the murder berth all the way to the back of the train. The door leading to the small observation platform of the last car was open. Police believed that the man could have leaped from the train soon after the murder. Sheriff Herbert Shelton found footprints in the Tangent railroad yard and surmised that the man could have leaped off the southbound train and boarded one heading north. Police and posses of private citizens searched for the killer in the area but found nothing.

On board the train, police searched the victim's possessions, which seemed intact, and this included over $100 in cash. Robbery was ruled out as the motive. The body was removed at Eugene, but police stayed aboard the train, questioning passengers and crew, as it made its way toward California.

When the *Limited* reached Los Angeles on Jan. 25, Robert E. Lee Folkes, twenty, the black cook that Private Wilson had found in the train's galley, shortly after the murder, was arrested. According to police, he first denied but then confessed to the murder. He then recanted the confession saying he did not commit the crime but he knew who did. Police had originally suspected Folkes after finding he had a police record for, among other charges, assaulting a woman and attempting to rip rings off her fingers, and for attempting to break into a house where three women lived.

After a second confession, police put together this story of the murder: On the night of the killing Folkes had attended a booze party with other members of the dining crew and had consumed a great deal of liquor. During the party some of the crew had discussed the various attractive women aboard the train, and the striking blond in berth 13 had been prominently mentioned. After the party, Folkes put an overcoat over his white uniform and entered the Pullman sleeping car. He opened the curtain on Martha James' berth and slipped next to the woman. As he was closing the curtain, the woman suddenly awakened. "She wanted to know who I was and told me to get out," Folkes told police. He placed a knife to her chin. "I told her to keep still. She hollered and tried to throw me out. So I cut her."

Folkes, who later recanted both confessions, was convicted and on Apr. 26, 1943, Judge L.G. Lewelling sentenced him to the Oregon gas chamber. Almost two years of appeals followed. On Jan. 4, 1945, Oregon Governor Earl Snell refused to commute the death sentence and told reporters: "I have before me evidence, information, and confessions that convince me beyond a doubt of Folkes' guilt. He was tried in the circuit court, appealed to the state supreme court and then to the U.S. Supreme Court. Other appeals for habeas corpus writs were filed in the state supreme court, U.S. District Court, and the Marion County Circuit Court. In view of all circumstances, I do not see how I could possibly interfere."

The next day, Jan. 5, 1945, Folkes proclaimed his innocence for the last time, then said: "So long, everybody." With a smile on his face, he walked into the gas chamber in the state prison at Salem, Ore., without a blindfold. About 100 witnesses watched as the poison pellets were dropped at 9:07 a.m. Six minutes later, Folkes was pronounced dead.

REF.: *CBA;* de River, *The Sexual Criminal.*

Follmer, Frederick Voris, 1885-1971, U.S., jur. Attorney for the U.S. from 1935-46, and was appointed by President Harry S. Truman as a roving justice to the Eastern, Middle, and Western district courts of Pennsylvania in 1946. REF.: *CBA.*

Folsom Prison Riot, 1927, U.S., riot. On Nov. 24, 1927, a riot broke out in one of the buildings housing 1,200 prisoners in the California State Prison at Folsom during a Thanksgiving Day movie presentation.

The riot began when seven or eight inmates overpowered guard Ray Singleton, forcing their way into the adjoining prison hospital. Singleton refused to call another guard and have the main door opened, for which the prisoners armed with daggers and home-made knives stabbed him to death. One of the convicts, Tony Brown, had a gun. Prisoners then ordered guard Charles Gorhanson to comply with their request. Gorhanson signaled the switchboard operator that something was wrong by holding the buzzer longer than usual, at which time the main door was locked tight. Undaunted, the inmates marched Gorhanson to another door, taking guard Walter Neil captive along the way. Neil and Gorhanson managed to escape when the prisoners allowed the two to go through the door first, which Neil quickly shut from the other side. An alarm was sounded, which caused elderly gate-keeper Charles Gilles to die of heart failure, and the prison was shut down.

Warden Court Smith telephoned California Governor Clement Calhoun Young requesting he send troops, artillery, and explosives. The inmates refused to surrender even after Smith threatened flooding the building and drowning them. Snipers soon had the prisoners, who returned the fire with the one gun they had, pinned down within the walls, and by nightfall a doctor was badly needed.

Inside the prison, Singleton and eight others lay dead, four others were dying, and thirty-one prisoners were wounded, one of whom died while a doctor amputated his leg. The following morning, before a planned assault by tanks and 700 troopers, the prisoners agreed to surrender as long as no discipline would be meted out to those not involved in leading the riot. Smith agreed and the riot was over. Six men were charged with murder, including Brown. REF.: *CBA.*

Fong Ching (AKA: **Little Pete**), b.1864, U.S., brib.-org. crime. Fong Ching, born in Kow Kong, China, arrived in San Francisco when he was ten. The industrious youth soon learned English and eventually established his own business, F.C. Peters & Co. He also ran several gambling dens, and garnering more power, he founded the Gi Sin Seer, a tong, or organized crime group. Challenging his control, a rival group was established and they set out to murder Fong. One of their members accosted Fong's body guard, Lee Chuck, but Lee shot his opponent, murdering him. Fleeing the scene, Lee fired his gun at a police officer, J.B. Martin, who was chasing him, but Lee was captured and arrested.

Just after Lee was arrested, Fong tried to bribe Martin, offering the officer $400 to perjure his testimony. Instead, Martin arrested Fong. After the bodyguard's trial, in which he was sentenced to fifty years in prison, Fong stood trial three times. The jury disagreed in the first two trials and during the third trial, jury

members reported attempts to bribe them. Fong was finally found Guilty on Aug. 24, 1887, and was sentenced to five years in Folsom Prison. REF.: *CBA.*

Fonseca Carrillo, Ernesto (AKA: **Don Neto**), 1931- , Mex., drugs-org. crime. One of the oldest members of the Mexican drug cartel, Ernesto Fonseca Carrillo served as a senior adviser to his hot-headed young associate Rafael Cáro Quintero. Fonseca had warned Cáro Quintero of the perils involved if he should decide to kill American DEA agent Enrique Camarena. He said that the best course of action would be to "scare" Camarena, not kill him. The gang abducted Camarena on Feb. 7, 1985. By his own testimony Fonseca admitted taking part in the crime. He did not, however, confess to killing Camarena, nor did he sanction it. Once Fonseca found out what Cáro Quintero had done he slapped him in the face. "You are a pig!" he bellowed. "You don't have a brain....Camarena is an agent of the U.S. Idiot! You made the baby, now you live with it!"

Nicknamed "Don Neto" or "Sir Goodprice," Fonseca was smuggling cocaine into Ecuador as early as 1973. Nine years later he was reputed to be one of the largest wholesale traffickers of cocaine in Mexico. His ship-ments were reaching Tijuana, Los Angeles, and San Diego. DEA informants would later say that Fonseca was the bankroll behind the cultivation and distribution of marijuana and heroin, working in concert with Miguel Félix Gallardo and Cáro Quintero.

Mexican drug lord Ernesto Fonseca Carillo.

In December 1982, customs officials in San Diego indicted Fonseca and his henchmen after a highly sophisticated money laundering scheme was detected. Large amounts of cash were being smuggled between Rancho Santa Fe, Calif., and Fonseca's base of operations in Mexico. However, Fonseca fled the region on Jan. 28, 1983, just before customs agents were to install a wiretap on his phone. He remained a fugitive until Apr. 7, 1985, when quite by chance, the Mexican army ran into him in the vacation resort of Puerto Vallarta. By this time Fonseca was wanted in conjunction with the Camarena murder. The drug king was quietly arrested after soldiers had cordoned off his villa. In his possession they found a gold-plated, diamond-encrusted .45-caliber pistol. It was identical to the weapon that Cáro Quintero carried.

Fonseca was indicted for murder by a federal grand jury in Los Angeles on Jan. 6, 1988. There was talk of extraditing him to the U.S. to stand trial, but he remained in the custody of the Mexican officials. Fonseca occupied a cell in the same Mexico City prison where Cáro Quintero was being held. See: **Camarena, Enrique; Cáro Quintero, Rafael.**

REF.: *CBA;* Shannon, *Desperados.*

Fontaine, Françoise, prom. 1591, Case of, Fr., witchcraft. Unlike most women tried for witchcraft in the late sixteenth and early seventeenth centuries, Françoise Fontaine was freed by the court without being tortured except for pricking. Not only was her punishment less severe, but no other woman was accused of bewitching her. Fontaine suffered from convulsions and ex-perienced sexual fantasies.

In April 1591, Fontaine claimed that a spirit had come down the chimney of her home in Louviers, Fr., and molested her and another girl. She was imprisoned when poltergeist-like distur-bances began to occur. Other prisoners complained that Fontaine had brought strange happenings to jail, and she was tried as a witch.

At her trial, which began on Aug. 17, 1591, two priests at-tempted an exorcism, and on Sept. 2 she was stripped. Her body was completely shaved to remove any hiding places that devils might have used to allow her to be pricked more readily before a crowd of 1,200 in Notre Dame cathedral.

During her trial Fontaine fell prostrate in the form of a crucifix, among other convulsive spells, and startled the court with her vivid depictions of her sexual encounters with the devil, which she said she thoroughly enjoyed. The court let Fontaine go free.

REF.: *CBA*; Robbins, *The Encyclopedia of Witchcraft and Demonology*; Seth, *Witches and Their Craft*.

Fontaine, Peter De la, prom. 1750, Brit. big.-(wrong. convict.) forg. Captain Peter De la Fontaine, a dashing French officer, was tried in Paris for running off with a rich man's daughter, but acquitted after the girl testified that it was her own idea. His mortal wounding of a fellow officer in a duel forced him to flee the continent. After stops in a Turkish jail and the port of Amsterdam, and a five-year sojourn in Surinam, he arrived in London.

There De la Fontaine, who had acquired a sizeable fortune, met a swindler named Zannier, who claimed he was under a criminal charge and needed bond money. Convinced that Zannier owned an estate in Ireland, De la Fontaine put up the £300 bond. He never saw the money again. To add to his trouble, he married two women at the same time and was eventually arrested for bigamy. While De la Fontaine awaited trial at Newgate Prison, Zannier visited him, once again claiming friendship. The captain was so enraged that he beat the swindler with a broomstick until he was subdued by warders. Zannier, in vengeance, charged De la Fontaine with forgery.

The swindler supplied false evidence to convict the Frenchman. Even though one witness testified that the forged signature appeared to be that of Zannier, De la Fontaine was convicted and sentenced to death. He was spared, but exiled to the colony of Virginia. In 1752, De la Fontaine boarded a ship full of other convicts, and later went on to establish one of the First Families of Virginia.

REF.: *CBA*; Mitchell, *The Newgate Calendar*.

Fontan, Louis Marie, 1801-39, Fr., rebel. Sentenced to five years in prison from 1829, for writing an attack on Charles X, *Le Mouton Enragé*, but was freed during the Revolution of 1830. REF.: *CBA*.

Fonte-Joyeuse, Guy, prom. 1937, U.S., consp.-smug. Smugglers will often try to fool authorities by disguising contraband or concealing it in secret compartments of luggage. Guy Fonte-Joyeuse, the vice president and New York branch manager of the Marcel Rochas, Inc. fashion house, used the company's models to bring valuable dresses to the United States from France.

The smuggling incident, which led to Fonte-Joyeuse's arrest, began on Sept. 2, 1937, with the arrival in New York City of newly hired model and saleswoman, Countess Kyra Kapnist. Among the luggage that arrived with the countess on board the *SS Champlain* were two large trunks and a hat box, which a Rochas company official had given Kapnist to deliver to Fonte-Joyeuse upon her arrival. Fonte-Joyeuse met the countess and after bribing a baggage inspector—as it was later learned—left the pier with seventy original dresses and hats worth about $40,000.

An investigation was started by U.S. Customs officials when it was discovered that Kapnist had declared no taxable imports. This information, along with information provided by a customs agent working undercover in the fashion firm, was enough to arrest Fonte-Joyeuse.

At the fashion house, customs agents found 104 original French dresses, worth approximately $60,000. Fonte-Joyeuse was found Guilty of smuggling and of conspiracy, sentenced to one year and one day in prison, and fined $1,000. After serving six months he was paroled and then deported to France. REF.: *CBA*; Whitehead, *Border Guard*.

Foote, Henry Leander, d.1850, U.S., rape-mur. Henry Foote was under the spell of the attractive Emily H. Cooper of New Haven, Conn., but she rebuffed every advance he made to her. Foote got drunk one night and went to the young woman's house. He managed to slip some drugs into her tea and, when she was

unconscious, raped her. He then paced nervously about for some time, wondering what his victim might do when she revived. He panicked and grabbed a butcher knife, slitting Cooper's throat. Foote got drunk a few days later and babbled the murder to a friend. He was arrested, tried, found Guilty, and hanged on Oct. 2, 1850, along with James McCaffrey, who had killed another woman, Ann Smith, under similar circumstances.

REF.: *CBA*; Goodwin, *Death Cell Scenes or Notes; A Sketch of the Life and Adventures of Henry Leander Foote*; Lambton, *Echoes of Causes Celebres*.

Foote, John Anderson, 1848-1922, Brit., lawyer. King's counsel who prosecuted accused murderer Mrs. Flora Haskell, and provided defense for accused murderers, William Walter Burton and Georges Codère. REF.: *CBA*.

Fooy, Sam, 1844-75, U.S., rob.-mur. Sam Fooy, a half-breed Indian in Oklahoma Territory, went on a week-long frenzy of violence and destruction in 1875 that ended only when he tried to get $500 in savings from a school teacher and murdered her when he failed. Fooy was tried in the court of Judge Isaac Parker in Fort Smith, Ark., and was found Guilty. He was hanged on Sept. 3, 1875—at peace with God, he told a reporter shortly before he died, because he had dreamed that Jesus was waiting to receive him.

REF.: *CBA*; Nash, *Bloodletters and Badmen*.

Forbes, Charles, See: **Teapot Dome**.

Forbes, Douglas, c.1942- , U.S., (wrong. convict.) rape. A string of rapes in Tennessee led two victims to point out Douglas Forbes as the man who had assaulted them. Forbes, a postman from Elizabethton, Tenn., was playing volleyball at the Veterans Administration Hospital where he was being treated for stress when he was identified in 1973.

After the women picked out the man who taught Sunday school at the church where he was deacon, Forbes, a father of six, was arrested.

During his trial the rapes continued, but prosecutor Louis May was so sure that Forbes was the rapist he vowed to Forbes' family "that if they could prove he was innocent, I would fight to free him." The court agreed, and in 1975 Forbes was sentenced to sixty years in prison, but the prosecutor kept his word.

While in prison Forbes was attacked by another inmate in 1978 and almost killed by a sharpened broom handle that was jammed into his throat. On Sept. 9, 1980, the end of Forbes' time in prison was in sight when police arrested Jerry Williams in Johnson City, less than ten miles from Elizabethton. Williams confessed to a number of rapes, including the two Forbes was accused of committing. May then convinced Tennessee Governor Lamarr Alexander to pardon the wrongly convicted man and Forbes was released from prison on Nov. 25, 1980. REF.: *CBA*.

Forbes, Duncan, 1685-1747, Scot., jur. Lord advocate in 1725, and lord president for the Court of Sessions in 1737. He supported the British government in the suppression of the Jacobites from 1745-46, but lost favor with Britain for attempting to lessen the punishment of rebels. REF.: *CBA*.

Forbes, Josiah, prom. 1716, U.S., pir. After being shipwrecked on Cape Hatteras, Captain Josiah Forbes, who had once commanded the *John and Mary*, made a grave mistake by boasting of his exploits as a pirate when he and three of his crew arrived in Virginia. Forbes' tales of how he had driven the Spanish from manning their shore batteries led to his, and his companions, arrest for piracy in June 1716.

REF.: *CBA*; Rankin, *The Golden Age of Piracy*

Forbes, Robert Duncan (AKA: **Burnell Cleveland Fuller**), and **Harrison, Charles**, and **Isaacs, Charles**, prom. 1911, Brit., fraud. The executives of Duncan Forbes & Company of London in 1911 lived up to the company's reputation of being a great insurance company. The insurance that Robert Duncan Forbes, Charles Harrison, and Charles Isaacs provided, however, was insurance that the three men would themselves get rich at the expense of others.

Forbes, Harrison, and Isaacs offered clients interest at incredibly high rates, knowing this would induce others to invest. When they received further investments, the money could be used to pay off past investors. At one point the three men had garnered £80,000 from their swindles, but their schemes finally came to an end. The three were tried at the Old Bailey before Judge Lumley Smith for conspiracy to defraud. Eleven days later, following a failed attempt at a postponement which prosecutor Dickie Muir shot down, all were found Guilty. Forbes and Harrison each received five years of hard labor and Harrison was deported for being an alien. Forbes had been sentenced in 1901 to two consecutive terms of three years' penal servitude for fraud pertaining to a cab company. Harrison received a sentence of four years of hard labor in 1901 for false pretenses.

REF.: *CBA;* Nicholls, *Crime Within the Square Mile.*

Forbes, Vernon Day, 1905- , U.S., jur. State's attorney for North Dakota from 1940-50, and was appointed by President Dwight Eisenhower to the Alaska Territorial Court in 1954. REF.: *CBA.*

Force, Julia, prom. 1893, U.S., mur. On Feb. 25, 1893, Julia Force, a member of one of the city's most prominent families, along with being extremely unbalanced, became annoyed at her sister Minnie's humming. She walked calmly up to Minnie as she was doing some needlework and shot her dead. She then climbed the stairs to the room of her other sister, Florence, an invalid, and killed her, too. Julia apparently harbored the thought that her sisters and mother were her lifelong enemies. After murdering her two younger sisters, Julia quietly walked to the Pryor Street police station and asked to be arrested. She was sent to the state insane asylum for life.

REF.: *CBA;* Nash, *Look For the Woman.*

Ford, Arthur Kendrick, 1910- , Brit., mansl. An office manager at a wholesale chemists firm in Euston Road, London, Arthur Kendrick Ford, forty-four, was flirting with Betty Margaret Grant, twenty-seven. On Apr. 26, 1954, between 10 a.m. and 10:15 a.m., Ford visited Mr. Lushington, a chemist at the company, to ask if he had any cantharidin, sometimes called "Spanish fly," because he had a neighbor who was breeding rabbits. He thought the drug, supposedly an aphrodisiac, was commonly fed to rabbits. Lushington explained that cantharidin was "a number one poison." Ford said, "I had better not have it," and soon left.

Not long after lunch that same day, at about 2:30 p.m., Ford came back into the office with some chocolate-covered coconut ice. He did not pass the bag of sweets around, but offered it individually to some of the twenty-two women and four men working in the office, handing a piece to Grant with his fingers, and giving a few pieces to some other girls. About an hour after eating the treat June Florence Malins, twenty-one, had stomach pain. Later, Grant felt similar pain, and Ford complained of a headache. All three were to be taken to a hospital; Ford recovered, but both women soon died. Detective Superintendent Jamieson discovered that Grant and Malins had died from poisoning from cantharides. Ford confessed that he had given the drug to Grant and taken it himself, hoping it would stimulate her desire for him. He had accidentally given Malins a lethal dose.

Ford's trial for the murder of Grant and Malins took place at the Old Bailey in June, before Judge Goddard. Prosecuting attorney John Claxton explained that cantharidin was a violent irritant that causes blisters if handled, and said that the condition of both corpses indicated that the women had eaten not less than one or two grains; the "safe" dose was a maximum of about one-hundredth of a grain. Ford pleaded guilty of manslaughter and was sentenced to five years in prison.

REF.: *CBA;* Furneaux, *Famous Criminal Cases, vol. 2;* Rowland, *Poisoner in the Dock.*

Ford, Emma, prom. 1890s-1900s, U.S., rob. Even being behind bars did not stop Emma Ford from stealing. Ford's prolific criminal career began in her hometown of Nashville, Tenn. Still very young, she and her sister, Pearl Smith, were put on a train and told not to return. The two traveled to St. Louis, Mo., and oon wound up in prison serving one-year terms at the Jefferson City penitentiary for robbery. Chicago was the sisters' next stop, and soon after they arrived each was again imprisoned one year for robbery; Ford in the Chicago jail, and Smith at the prison in Joliet. After this sentence, the sisters traveled to Denver, Colo., where their attempt to rob a rancher led to the man's death. Ford and Smith were found Guilty of murder and sentenced to be hanged. A new trial was granted and because of a legal technicality the sisters were freed, but had to escape an angry crowd which did not like the court's decision. They fled back to Chicago.

In 1892 Ford teamed up with Alice Kelly, and the two robbed Perry James, a porter who later accompanied Detective Clifton R. Wooldridge in arresting the women. Kelly was found Guilty and sentenced on Mar. 19, 1892, by Judge Frank Baker to two years in prison, but Ford put up a stiff resistance. She eluded Wooldridge by ducking into the building she lived in, and with the help of her sister, though herself reputed to be as strong as two men, fought off the detective. Wooldridge managed to stick his foot in the door of their apartment, and Ford was about to hit him over the head with a metal pipe when he shoved his gun in her face. She gave up. While out on bail awaiting her trial, Ford robbed Frank Adams, C. Reid, and Charles Smith, and was again arrested by Wooldridge after resisting him with a knife. On Apr. 25, 1892, Ford was found Guilty in the robbery of James and sentenced by Baker to five years in prison. The next day she was tried, along with Smith, for the other robberies, and received an additional five years, taking all the blame for the crimes and not implicating her sister.

At the penitentiary, Ford did not give up her penchant for stealing. She stole the watch of guard F.H. Burmeister, and jailer Morris, both times returning the stolen articles. Released from prison, Ford continued her criminal vocation, stealing $42 from W.S. Duncan in Boston, Mass., on Mar. 27, 1899. After a series of aborted trials, Ford pleaded Guilty and was sentenced to one year in the Chicago jail by Judge Brentano. Ford was freed in September 1900, but was arrested again in December for robbery. In her three months of freedom, Ford admitted to stealing more than $400. She was found Guilty and sentenced by Judge Smith on Jan. 2, 1901, to one year in prison.

REF.: *CBA;* Wooldridge, *Hands Up.*

Ford, Francis Joseph William, 1882-1975, U.S., jur. U.S. attorney for the District of Massachusetts from 1933-38, published "The Grand Jury," for the *Law Society Journal* in 1938, and was appointed by President Franklin D. Roosevelt to the District Court of Massachusetts in 1938. REF.: *CBA.*

Ford, Francis Xavier, 1892-1952, China, assass. Appointed bishop of Mei-hsien in 1935, as U.S. missionary. He was killed by the Chinese Communist government for not renouncing Christianity. REF.: *CBA.*

Ford, Gerald Rudolph, Jr. (Leslie Lynch King, Jr.), 1913- , U.S., pres., assass. attempt. Born in Omaha, Neb., on July 14, 1913, Gerald R. Ford's divorced mother moved to Grand Rapids, Mich., and remarried Gerald Ford, Sr., who adopted the child and gave him his name. Ford was educated at the University of Michigan and became a football star. Following service in WWII, Ford ran as a Republican for the House of Representatives, and in 1948, was elected congressman from Michigan. Characterized as conservative, he was an early supporter of Richard M. Nixon.

Lynette "Squeaky" Fromme, who attempted to assassinate President Gerald Ford in 1975.

Upon the resignation of Vice President Spiro T. Agnew, Ford was named the fortieth vice president by President Nixon to fill Agnew's position on Oct. 12, 1973, the first vice president to take office in the middle of an administration. Upon Richard Nixon's resignation from the presidency, Ford became the thirty-eighth U.S. president (1974-77). His administration was marked by two assassination attempts, the first on Sept. 5, 1975, when Lynette Alice "Squeaky" Fromme, a follower of mass-killer Charles Manson, tried to shoot Ford at a political rally in Sacramento, Calif.

Her .45-caliber automatic misfired. Fromme was quickly arrested and tried. She was convicted and sent to prison for life. On Sept. 22, 1975, Sara Jane Moore, a political malcontent and mentally disturbed person, fired several aimless shots at Ford while he was outside a San Francisco hotel. Fast-acting Secret Service agents shoved Ford out of the line of fire. Moore had fired aimlessly and gave incoherent reasons as to why she had attempted to kill the president. She was convicted in a quick trial and sent to prison for life. See: **Agnew, Spiro; Nixon, Richard.**

REF.: *CBA;* Ford, *A Time to Heal;* Nash, *Jay Robert Nash's Crime Chronology.*

Ford, James (AKA: **Subway Slasher**), c.1956-   , U.S., rob.-mur. Passengers riding the Chicago Transit Authority's subway trains were terrorized by a man who robbed people on train station platforms at knifepoint in 1979. The "Subway Slasher," as James Ford came to be known, would often slash his victims about the face and neck during his robberies. One victim, 64-year-old Joseph Ardell, received more than just a slashing on Oct. 24, 1979. Ford nearly severed Ardell's neck while the man waited for the train home from work at the Dearborn Avenue and Monroe Street subway station. Ardell bled to death, but police arrested the killer early the next morning when he quarreled with another passenger on the train he was riding.

Following Ford's arrest, he was charged with seven more subway robberies, four in which he slashed the victims. At Ford's trial, three slashing victims identified Ford as their assailant. In his defense, Randolph Stone argued that Ford was intoxicated and criminally insane at the time of the murder. The prosecution, conducted by Nicholas J. Falkis and Brian Telander, contended that Ford had a criminal record; in 1977 he was convicted of a subway robbery—and therefore should be sentenced to death.

Ford was found Guilty of armed robbery and murder on June 10, 1981, and sentenced to life in prison without possibility of parole on July 6, 1981, by Criminal Court Judge William Cousins. Cousins ruled out the death penalty because he felt there was "mitigating" evidence that the defendant was under the influence of alcohol when he killed Ardell. REF.: *CBA.*

Ford, Lord Grey of Werke, prom. 1682, Case of, Brit., kid. The amorous affair of Ford, Lord Grey of Werke and his wife's younger sister, Lady Henrietta Berkeley, who was not yet eighteen, came to a scandalous conclusion with the trial on Nov. 23, 1682, of the lord and four of his alleged confederates for the young lady's abduction. A conclusion at the trial, however, was never officially reached, as the startling discovery made known to the court abruptly ended the case.

For four years Ford and Henrietta had had intimate relations, unknown to her family or the lord's wife, until Henrietta's mother found a letter the girl was writing to her lover. It was agreed by all parties concerned that the relationship would come to an end. The relationship, however, did not end. George, Earl of Berkeley alleged that his daughter was abducted by Ford, with the assistance of Robert Charnock, Anne Charnock, David Jones, Francis Jones, and Rebecca Jones. Ford and the others were tried on an information brought forward by Attorney General Sir Robert Sawyer before the King's Bench Bar consisting of Chief Justice Sir Francis Pemberton, and puisne judges Sir William Dolben, Sir Thomas Jones, and Sir Thomas Raymond.

The case against the defendants, prosecuted by Sergeant Sir George Jeffries, was based entirely upon testimony provided by members of the Berkeley family and those employed by the family, with key testimony given by Henrietta herself; testimony which nullified any reason to prosecute. Henrietta explained to the court that she had not been kidnapped or even seduced by

Ford into leaving her home, but had run away of her own accord. The jury was then instructed to determine the verdict, but immediately after their departure, it was learned that Henrietta had already married a Mr. Turner, and since she truly had no desire to return to her parents' home, the justices decided that there was no reason to await a verdict. A private verdict was reached that found all defendants except Rebecca Jones Guilty. At the following term the attorney general entered *noli prosequi* and the matter was dismissed. REF.: *CBA.*

Ford, Priscilla, c.1928-   , U.S., attempt. mur.-mur. Six people were killed and twenty-three injured when Priscilla Ford drove her car along a crowded sidewalk in downtown Reno, Nev., on Thanksgiving Day, 1980.

Ford's trial began on Oct. 6, 1981, where District Attorney Cal Dunlap argued that the killings stemmed from revenge aimed toward Reno, whose welfare officials took the woman's 11-year-old daughter from her in 1972. Ford's attorney, Lew Carnahan, entered a plea of insanity, despite the fact that Ford believed herself to be perfectly sane.

During the five-month trial—the longest murder trial on record in Nevada—the defendant and her attorney often argued, especially when Ford decided in late February to testify despite the arduous objections of Carnahan. On the witness stand, Ford claimed she was the incarnation of Jesus Christ, unable to commit sin, and that the killings were just an accident. She was convicted of six counts of murder and twenty-three counts of attempted murder on Mar. 19, 1982. The jury took five days before sentencing Ford to death on Apr. 28, 1982. She was the first woman sentenced to die in Nevada's gas chamber. REF.: *CBA.*

Robert Ford, posing with the gun he used to kill Jesse James, 1882.

Ford, Robert, 1861-92, U.S. west. outl.-mur. Robert Ford's name became synonymous with the word traitor at the very moment he squeezed the trigger of the six-gun that shot and killed America's most celebrated western bandit, Jesse James. Bob Ford and his older brother Charles were farm boys who lived in Ray County, Mo. By 1879, they had been recruited into the notorious gang headed by James, and were reportedly involved in several train and bank robberies led by James. Ford was a hanger-on and did odd jobs for the gang, as well as accompany James and the others on raids, invariably as the one who held the horses. He enjoyed consorting with outlaws and often made his home and that of other Ford family members available to gang members who were being sought by lawmen.

In January 1882, Wood Hite and Dick Liddell, members of the James gang on the run from the law, took refuge in the home of Martha Bolton, Bob Ford's widowed sister. At breakfast, Hite and Liddell fell to arguing while Ford sat quietly sipping his coffee. Suddenly the outlaws swore at each other and drew their guns. Hite fired four rapid shots at Liddell, one of his bullets striking Liddell's right thigh. As he was falling to the floor, Liddell shot a bullet into Hite's arm. As the two men blasted at each other, Bob Ford drew his own gun and, being Liddell's close friend, fired a single bullet at Hite, striking him in the head. Hite collapsed to the floor and died a few minutes later. Ford wrapped Hite's body in a blanket and carried it outside, slipping it over the back of a mule. He then led the animal into the woods and, about a mile from his sister's house, buried Hite's corpse in a shallow, unmarked grave.

Charles Ford, terrified that Frank James was hunting him for the killing of his brother Jesse, committed suicide in 1884.

Word of this shooting caused authorities to arrest Ford, but he was not prosecuted when he informed detectives that he had access to the much-wanted Jesse James. Missouri governor Thomas T. Crittenden met secretly with Ford and told him that if he killed the notorious outlaw, he would receive a full pardon for the Hite murder as well as the killing of James, and also receive a large reward. Ford agreed to perform the deed. Bob Ford then went to his brother Charlie and told him to have Jesse swear him in as a full-fledged member of the gang. James, though he had told several people that he did not trust the Ford brothers, especially Bob, accepted the Fords as gang members. The brothers visited the James home in St. Joseph, Mo., on the morning of Apr. 3, 1882.

Bob and Charlie went to the barn to tend the horses and then entered the house. Jesse had just sent his two children outside to play. Mrs. Zeralda James was in the kitchen, and James entered the parlor where the Ford boys were sitting. Jesse outlined his plans for another robbery. He complained of the heat and took off his coat. Then he removed his two guns and wrapped the holsters about the arm of a chair. He noticed a picture hanging crooked on the wall and stood on a chair to adjust it. As he did so, Charlie nodded at Bob, and the brothers pulled their six-guns. Jesse heard the hammers cock on their pistols

Outlaw Jesse James, shot by "the dirty little coward" in 1882.

and started to turn. As he did, Bob Ford fired a bullet into the back of his head. Jesse James toppled to the floor, dead.

Mrs. James ran into the room and Bob Ford, backing toward the front door with his brother Charlie, told her: "The gun went off accidentally."

Kneeling to cradle the bloody head of her husband, Zee James, sobbing, replied: "Yes, I guess it did."

Bob and Charlie Ford then ran from the James home, Bob shouting down the street: "I killed him! I shot Jesse James! I shot Jesse James!" A few minutes later the brothers arrived at the telegraph office and sent a wire to Governor Crittenden, claiming the reward. The wire read: "I have killed Jesse James. St. Joseph. Bob Ford." Though Ford was charged with murdering Wood Hite *and* Jesse James, Governor Crittenden pardoned him while he stood trial for the Hite murder. Ford and his brother were given large rewards and returned to the home of their parents in Richmond, Mo. Residents, however, found the traitorous killing of Jesse James so distasteful that they made life unbearable for the Fords. Charlie Ford fled Richmond when he heard that Jesse's brother, Frank James, was searching for the brothers to kill them in revenge for Jesse's death. So terrified was Charlie Ford that he kept running from town to town for two years, changing his name several times. He finally committed suicide in 1884.

Capitalizing on his betrayal of Jesse James, Bob Ford took to the stage, appearing in an act entitled *Outlaws of Missouri*. Night after night, Ford stood before the footlights chanting out that last fateful morning of Jesse James. He carefully avoided describing how he shot down America's legendary bandit *in the back*. Still, he was greeted with catcalls, jeers, hoots, and challenges shouted from the audience: "Traitor! Step outside and get what's coming to you! Frank James is looking for you, Judas!" Even his fellow troupers found Ford repulsive, all except a young chorus girl, Nellie Waterson, who fell in love with the good-looking young killer. They were married and left Missouri.

Ford took a job with P.T. Barnum's freak show and traveled through the East to again tell disgusted audiences how he shot

Ford's tent saloon, second structure from left, in Creede, Colo., where Ford was killed in 1892.

down the man who trusted him. To the Easterner, indoctrinated with the legend of Jesse James through dime novels, countless pamphlets, stories, and newspaper columns which incorrectly portrayed James as a heroic figure, Bob Ford was a loathsome creature who had committed a foul murder. He had killed a man he feared so much that he had shot him in the back rather than risk facing him in a fair gunfight. He was again greeted by angry audiences who chanted the words of a song then popular: "The dirty little coward who shot Mr. Howard (the alias James was using when killed), and laid poor Jesse in his grave!" Ford's response to the negative audience reaction was to drink heavily and squander his considerable earnings in gambling.

Dick Liddell, Ford's old outlaw friend, later joined Ford in establishing a saloon in Las Vegas, N.M., but the operation failed, chiefly because of lack of customers. Those who did enter the place kept picking fights with Ford and Liddell, calling them traitors and murderers. The Las Vegas saloon soon closed and Ford moved on to Creede, Colo., where a silver boom had begun.

N.C. Creede, an old prospector, had discovered two rich silver veins, and armies of prospectors moved into the area when hearing the news, the boom town mushrooming overnight and being named Creede. When Ford arrived, there were few buildings, and he simply put up a large tent saloon and quickly prospered, charging exorbitant prices for his beer and whiskey. He dressed as a dandy in brocaded vests, long tailcoats, and a diamond stickpin. He made so much money that he soon bought his wife Nellie a diamond brooch and other expensive jewels.

In 1892, Ford took a business trip to Pueblo, N.M., and there had to share a room with another man in a crowded hotel. The other guest was Ed O. Kelly, a man with a shady past. Ford and Kelly nodded and then had a drink together before bedding down for the night. When Ford awoke, he discovered a diamond ring missing and he angrily accused Kelly of stealing it. The two men parted with angry words, with Kelly still denying he took the ring. Kelly later heard that Ford was telling everyone in Creede that he had stolen his diamond ring. After brooding about this, Kelly went to Creede on June 8, 1892, and stormed into Ford's tent saloon. He demanded that Ford retract his statements about the diamond ring theft, but Ford refused, and, with the help of a bartender, threw Kelly out of his saloon.

Kelly obtained a shotgun and returned to the saloon, almost running toward the bar where Ford stood talking to some customers. As Ford turned to face Kelly, the shotgun roared, both barrels of buckshot tearing into Ford. One pellet drove Ford's collar button through his throat, killing him. Kelly was arrested and tried for murder. He was convicted and given a 20-year sentence in the Colorado Penitentiary. Nellie Ford returned her husband's body to Richmond, Mo., where it was buried in the Ford family plot. *See:* **James, Jesse Woodson; Kelly, Ed O.**

REF.: Altrochhi, *Traces of Folklore and Furrow;* Alverez, *The James Boys of Missouri;* American Guide Series, *Colorado, A Guide to the Highest State;* ____, *Missouri, A Guide to the "Show Me" State;* Appleman, *Charlie Siringo, Cowboy Detective;* Asbury, *Sucker's Progress;* Bancroft, *Outlaws;* Barker, *Missouri Lawyer;* Beattie, *Brother, Here's A Man;* Beebe, *The American West;* Bennett, *Boom Town Boy in Old Creede, Colorado;* Benton, *Cow by the Tail;* Black, *You Can't Win;* Botkin, *Treasury of American Folklore;* Bradley, *Lives of Frank and Jesse James;* Breihan, *The Complete and Authentic Life of Jesse James;* ____, *The Day Jesse James Was Killed;* ____, *The Man Who Shot Jesse James;* Briggs, *Arizona and New Mexico, 1882;* Buel, *Border Outlaws;* Callon, *Las Vegas, New Mexico;* Casey, *The Texas Border and Some Borderliners; CBA;* Collier, *The Reign of Soapy Smith;* Conrad, *Encyclopedia of the History of Missouri;* Cooper, *High Country;* Crittenden, *The Crittenden Memoirs;* Croy, *Jesse James Was My Neighbor;* Cummins, *The Story of Jim Cummins;* Dacus, *Life and Adventures of Frank and Jesse James;* Dale, *Adventures of the Younger Brothers;* Dalton, *Beyond the Law;* Davis, *The West from a Car Window;* DeMilt, *Story of an Old Town;* Dibble, *Strenuous Americans;* Dobie, *Coronado's Children;* Drago, *Outlaws on Horseback;* Elman, *Fired in Anger;* Fellows and Freeman, *This Way to the Big Show;* Finger, *The Distant Prize;* Fisher and Holmes, *Gold Rushes and Mining Camps of the Early American West;* Fishwick, *American Heroes, Myth and Reality;* Fletcher, *The Wayward Horseman;* Florin, *Ghost Town Album;* Garwood, *Crossroads of America;* Ginty, *Missouri Legend;* Gish, *American Bandits;* Goodwin, *Nat Goodwin's Book;* Gordon, *Jesse James and His Band of Outlaws;* Haley, *Jeff Milton;* Hall, *The Two Lives of Baby Doe;* Hendricks, *The Bad Man of the West;* Hertzog, *A Directory of New Mexico Desperadoes;* Holcomb, *History of Marion County;* Holloway, *Texas Gun Lore;* Hoole, *The James Boys Rode South;* Horan, *Desperate Men;* ____, *Pictorial History of the Wild West;* ____, *The Pinkertons;* Hunt, *To Colorado's Restless Ghosts;* Hunter and Rose, *The Album of Gunfighters;* Jackson, *Bank and Train Robbers;* James, *James Boys;* James, *Jesse James, My Father;* Kane, *100 Years Ago with the Law and the Outlaw;* La Font, *Rugged Life in the Rockies;* Lemley, *The Old West;* Lewis and Smith, *Oscar Wilde Discovers America;* Look, *Unforgettable Characters of Western Colorado;* Lord, *Frontier Dust;* Love, *The Rise and Fall of Jesse James;* McRill, *And Satan Came Also;* Mazzulla and Mazzulla, *Brass Checks and Red Lights;* Metz, *John Selman;* Morse, *Cavalcade of Rails;* Mumey, *Creede: History of a Colorado Mining Town;* Murbarger, *Sovereigns of the*

Sage; Nash, *Bloodletters and Badmen;* O'Connor, *Bat Masterson;* O'Neal, *Encyclopedia of Western Gunfighters;* Otero, *My Life on the Frontier;* Parkhill, *The Wildest of the West;* Pinkerton, *Train Robberies;* Raine, *Guns of the Frontier;* Rascoe, *Belle Starr;* Ray, *The James Boys and Bob Ford;* Rennert, *Western Outlaws;* Robertson, *Soapy Smith;* Rosa, *The Gunfighter: Man or Myth?;* Russell, *Behind These Ozark Hills;* Seeley, *Pioneer Days in the Arkansas Valley;* Settle, *Jesse James was His Name;* Shackelford, *Gunfighters of the Old West;* Shoemaker, *Missouri Day By Day;* Stanley, *Desperadoes of New Mexico;* ____, *Raton Chronicle;* Sutton, *Hands Up!;* Thorndike, *Lives and Exploits of the Jameses;* Triplett, *The Life, Times and Treacherous Death of Jesse James;* Turner, *Dirty Little Coward of Fauquier County;* Vestal, *The Missouri;* Walker, *Jesse James;* Wallace, *Gunnison County;* Waller, *Last of the Great Western Train Robbers;* Ward, *Bits of Silver;* Warman, *Frontier Stories;* Wellman, *A Dynasty of Western Outlaws;* Winther, *The Transportation Frontier;* Yost, *The Call of the Range;* Younger, *True Facts of the Lives of America's Most Notorious Outlaws;* (FILM), *Jesse James,* 1939; *Badman's Territory,* 1946; *I Shot Jesse James,* 1949; *The Great Missouri Raid,* 1952; *The Great Jesse James Raid,* 1953; *Kansas Raiders,* 1953; *The True Story of Jesse James,* 1956; *The Long Riders,* 1980; *Last Days of Frank and Jesse James,* 1989.

Forel, Auguste Henri, 1848-1931, Switz., forensic. Noted for his work in forensic psychiatry and hypnotism. REF.: *CBA.*

Foreman, James L., 1927 - , U.S., jur. State's attorney for Massac County, Ill., from 1960-64, and was appointed by President Richard Nixon to the Eastern District Court of Illinois in 1972. REF.: *CBA.*

Foreman, Percy, 1902-88, U.S., crim. lawyer. One of the most successful criminal attorneys in the U.S., Percy Foreman was a dynamic and eloquent speaker who was highly esteemed by his peers, an uncommon appreciation. In appearance, the Houston-based lawyer was, at first, a disappointment to juries. He was a hulking six-foot-four-inches tall, weighing more than 250 pounds with a massive head criss-crossed with creases and wrinkles, not unlike the baggy suits he wore. Foreman's unkempt appearance, however, was misleading, for his sense of the dramatic and his timing were acute and effective, some said outlandish.

Criminal lawyer Percy Foreman.

On one occasion, Foreman was defending a woman who had murdered her cattle-baron husband for beating her repeatedly with a whip. When Foreman addressed the jury he held a bullwhip in his hands and incessantly cracked this to make each one of his points. The jury acquitted his client. This verdict was typical for clients defended by Foreman who reportedly lost less than five percent of the more than 2,000 criminal cases he represented. One of his most brilliant defenses was that of the sexy blonde Candace "Candy" Mossler, who was accused of murdering her husband, Jacques Mossler, on June 30, 1964, in his lavish Key Biscayne, Fla., home. Also accused of the murder was Candy's nephew, Melvin Lane Powers, age twenty-four.

Both Mossler and Powers were represented brilliantly by Foreman, who overcame charges of incest as well as murder by showing the victim in the worst light possible, a man who picked up strangers, bragging about his wealth to them and inviting, as it were, his own demise. He kept Candy Mossler and Powers off the witness stand and let the jury decide on the evidence. The result was a stunning victory which, more than any other, established Foreman as one of the U.S.'s leading defense attorneys. Foreman's fee for this case was in excess of $200,000, but Candy Mossler could well afford it, since she inherited Mossler's millions.

As Foreman's reputation shot upward, so did his fees. Foreman became one of the most expensive criminal attorneys in the land, and he was notorious for overbilling rich clients. If Foreman believed in a case, however, he was known to represent clients who had little or no money. He was known to accept any kind of strange fees and once collected several elephants from a client as payment. On another occasion, he took as his fee a piano, and from another client, a pool table.

Foreman's greatest abilities lay in his shrewd selection of jury members and, during the trial, his manipulation of juries who found him utterly captivating. He was a showman first and last, but he knew the law well and employed it with creative zeal. One spectator entering a courtroom where Foreman was about to begin trying a case summed up the public's attitude toward this spectacular attorney: "I don't care whose [sic] on trial. Foreman is on stage and that's the whole show." Foreman died on Aug. 25, 1988. See: **Mossler, Candace.**

REF.: *CBA;* Dorman, *King of the Courtroom: Percy Foreman for the Defense;* Holmes, *The Candy Mossler Murder Case;* Messick, *Secret File;* Nash, *Murder Among the Mighty;* Tully, *Inside the FBI.*

Forensic Ballistics, See: **Identification Systems, Ballistics,** Supplements, Vol. IV.

Forensic Medicine, See: Supplements, Vol. IV.

Forensic Serology, See: Serology, Supplements, Vol. IV.

Forman, Phillip, 1895-1978, U.S., jur. U.S. attorney for the District of New Jersey from 1928-32, was appointed by President Herbert Hoover to the District Court of New Jersey in 1932, and by President Dwight Eisenhower to the Third Circuit Court of the U.S., in 1959. REF.: *CBA.*

Formby Gang, prom. early 1900s, U.S., org. crime. Chicago's history with organized crime may seem to have its antecedents in the 1920 gangster era, but the era of street gangs predate Al Capone by two decades. In the century's first years, the city's most violent gang was the Formby Gang, led by three teenagers, 16-year-old David Kelly, 17-year-old Bill Dulfer, and 18-year-old Jimmy Formby. The three young thugs organized hundreds of robberies and burglaries, and later branched out into murder. In 1904, Formby murdered a street car conductor, and Dulfer murdered two men during a saloon robbery. The gang dissolved after both of the ringleaders were convicted of the murders and received long prison sentences. REF.: *CBA.*

Formi, Jose, d.1853, U.S., mur. Jose Formi had the distinction of being the only legally sanctioned hanging death in the U.S. between 1849 and 1856, though the country experienced more than 1,000 murders. Formi had murdered José Rodriguez on Dec. 10, 1852, and was hanged July 20, 1853 on Russian Hill. REF.: *CBA.*

Formis, Rudolf, d.1935, Czech., (unsolv.) mur. A former member of the Nazi Party, Rudolf Formis fled to Czechoslovakia for asylum, and built a clandestine radio transmitting facility in the village of Stechovice, one hundred miles from Prague. Broadcasting from the Hotel Zahori at Stechovice, Formis denounced the Nazis, warning Germans and Czechs against the regime and making dire and accurate predictions about the course German national socialism would take.

In January 1935, three German tourists, Hand Mueller, Gert Schubert, and Edith Karlebach, arrived at the Hotel Zahori in an expensive Mercedes. After dinner one evening, Mueller complained of a headache and returned to his rooms, while Karlebach and Formis had a few more drinks, then also retired to the room. A waiter heard several shots fifteen minutes later, and rushed to the room. He was stopped by Mueller who told him to keep his mouth shut or he would be murdered. Fleeing to the cellar, the waiter came out some time later to find that the German tourists were gone and Formis had been slain.

The killers crossed into Germany that night, leaving their car behind. Early the next morning, another German picked up the Mercedes. Czech authorities made inquiries, but no trace of the three "tourists" or of the car, were found. Formis' execution was buried in a file drawer, and diplomatic relations between the countries remained cordial until the Third Reich entirely took over Czechoslovakia.

REF.: Bornstein, *The Politics of Murder; CBA;* Paine, *The Assassins.*

Forrest, Elliot, 1924- , Fr., rob.-consp.-pir. At the end of WWII, a shortage of tobacco in Europe resulted in a new smuggling trade, that of "Les Blondes"—American cigarettes which were known as "blondes" because of the light color of their tobacco. By 1952, Tangiers was at its heyday as the major center for smuggling and contraband. Hearing of the trade there, a former U.S. Navy officer who had been decorated several times in WWII, Elliot Forrest, bought a new boat and traveled there to share in the profits, bringing with him letters of credit from several American racketeers who were interested in bankrolling new ventures. After smuggling for a while, Forrest visited Marseilles in the summer of 1952, and met with Antoine Paolini, a cigarette smuggler, about becoming involved in piracy.

When cigarette loads were ordered from Tangiers, to be paid with cash on delivery at arranged pick up spots, pirates would send their own armed vessels and seize the cargos. Paolini had perfected this operation, and hired a Corsican gunman, Dominique Muzziotti, to handle the night piracies. Muzziotti was not comfortable on the sea, however, so when word of a major shipment came through, Paolini contacted Forrest. The three conferred in Marseilles, and Forrest planned to waylay the ship, *Combinatie,* as it came in with a twenty-seven-ton shipment of American cigarettes, with a wholesale value in France of £250,000, on Oct. 4. With a torpedo boat, *Esme,* Forrest and his pirate crew picked up the *Combinatie* just north of the Isle of Riou, wounded the captain, and transferred the cargo to the *Esme* before blowing out the controls of the other vessel with a hand grenade. Forrest stayed with his ship and cargo, returning to Marseilles with Muzziotti to get his share. But the *Combinatie* crew had repaired the damage quickly, and reported the assault and robbery to Marseilles police.

Forrest went to a deserted farmhouse near Cavaillon to hide out, pretending to be a mute and deaf American writer in order not to betray himself by his accent. Within a few months Muzziotti made an anonymous call to the Marseilles police, and Forrest was arrested in January 1953. The betrayal of Forrest precipitated a violent gangster vendetta in southern France, with two Corsican clans murdering each other; Muzziotti and Paolini, along with his bodyguards, were among the many victims. Forrest, held in the Les Baumettes Prison, was unaware of the slaughter taking place in his honor. By the time he came to court in the Aix Assizes on Feb. 3, 1956, only fifteen of the original thirty-eight accused were present. Fifteen had been slain in the vendetta, and eight had fled to avoid justice.

Forrest and the others remained charged with conspiracy, receiving stolen property, robbery, infringement of customs regulations, and piracy. After a week the Court ruled that there had been no piracy, but Forrest and the gang were found Guilty of the other counts. Forrest was given a three-year sentence, and fined £3,000,000. When he appealed to the Aix Court of Appeals, the court decided that robbery on the high seas had been committed, and added another three to five years to the former navy captain's sentence. The ban on American cigarettes was later lifted, and the French government gained control of the profitable monopoly.

REF.: *CBA;* Goodman, *Villainy Unlimited;* Heppenstall, *The Sex War and Others;* Wilkinson, *Behind the Face of Crime.*

Forstein, Dorothy, prom. 1950, U.S., (unsolv.) kid. On Jan. 25, 1945, Dorothy Forstein returned home from an afternoon of shopping. As she entered, an intruder from inside attacked her, leaving her seriously injured and perpetually afraid. Nothing was taken from the house, and the doors had been thoroughly locked before she returned.

Five years later, on Oct. 18, 1950, her husband, Jules Forstein, went to a political function, leaving Dorothy and her children home alone. When he returned around midnight, he found his two youngest children clutching each other in fear. They exclaimed tearfully, "Mommy's gone!" The front door had been locked. No strange fingerprints were found. Nine-year-old Marcy

Forstein said she heard sounds in the night and that she got up and peered through the crack in her mother's bedroom door. Her mother was lying face-down on the rug, and a man wearing a brown cap and jacket heaved the woman over his shoulder. Coming from the bedroom, he saw Marcy and said, "Go back to sleep, little one, your mommy has been sick, but she will be all right now." There has been no trace of the woman since that time.

REF.: *CBA*; Nash, *Among the Missing*.

Forster, George, See: **Foster, George.**

Forster, Thomas, c.1675-1738, Brit., rebel. Member of Parliament from 1708-16, who helped John Erskine, the Sixth Earl of Mar, lead the Jacobite uprising in 1715, proclaiming James Edwards, the Old Pretender, as King James III of England at Greenrig, Northumberland, in 1715. As general for the Jacobites, he surrendered later that same year. REF.: *CBA*.

Forster, W.E., prom. 1882, Ire., (unsolv.) attempt. mur. In 1882 an unsuccessful attempt was made on the life of Ireland's chief secretary, the Right Honorable W.E. Forster, when he received a package in the mail containing dynamite. The explosive was rigged to detonate upon opening of the package, but the bomb was defused by Chief Inspector of Explosives Colonel Majendie and no one was hurt. Scotland Yard placed the device in its "Black Museum" for future study.

REF.: *CBA*; Stevens, *From Clue to Dock*.

Forsyth, Alexander John, 1769-1843, Scot., firearms. Designed the firearm percussion lock between 1805-07, for which the British government provided him with a pension, after he had turned down an offer of £20,000 from Napoleon I for the invention. REF.: *CBA*.

Forsyth, Francis Robert George, and **Harris, Norman James**, and **Darby, Christopher Louis**, and **Lutt, Terrence**, prom. 1960, Brit., mur. Four broke young men prowled the streets late at night on June 25, 1960, and met up with 23-year-old Alan Jee who had taken a shortcut down an alley. Francis Forsyth, Norman Harris, Christopher Darby, and Terrence Lutt found him alone and vulnerable. Lutt, only seventeen, knocked Jee down, then the others tried to take his money. When Jee tried to fight off his attackers, 18-year-old Forsyth kicked him in the head with his pointed Italian shoes. The shoes still showed traces of blood when he was arrested.

Alan Jee died two days later. When 23-year-old Harris bragged about the killing in public, the police found the foursome. Forsyth admitted the crime in his mother's presence, saying, "I'm sorry, Mum, but I did it, and that is all there is to it." The four were tried for murder. Lutt, as a juvenile, was sent to reform school. Darby, a 23-year-old coalman who did not, according to all four, play a role in beating Jee, was sentenced to life in prison. Forsyth and Harris were hanged on Nov. 10, 1960.

REF.: Bresler, *Reprieve*; *CBA*; Furneaux, *Famous Criminal Cases, vol. 7*; Jackson, *Occupied With Crime*; Wilson, *Encyclopedia of Murder*.

Fort, Jeff (AKA: **Chief Prince Malik**), c.1947-   , U.S., bat.-fraud-drugs-consp.-rack.-mur. Growing up in Woodlawn on Chicago's South Side, Jeff Fort became involved in gangs at an early age, and though somewhat scrawny, managed to become the leader of the Blackstone Rangers, later known as the Black P Stone Nation, a gang referred to as America's most dangerous street gang in 1968. Fort was so influential among gang members and the community at large that whatever he said or asked was carried out—even murder.

By the time Fort became a nationally known figure, he had already been arrested for armed robbery and various assaults. When Fort was convicted in 1972 of defrauding the U.S. government of $1 million—by convincing the Office of Economic Opportunity to fund a phony work program for keeping underprivileged youths out of gangs—he had already been behind bars since 1970 for fleeing on a bail bond following a conviction for aggravated battery. He was paroled in 1976, and soon joined the Moorish Science Temple of America in Milwaukee, Wis., taking on the name of Chief Prince Malik. In 1978, Fort returned to Chicago and once again changed the name of his gang, this time to El Rukn. The gang became a more invincible force than ever before, controlling the illegal drug industry on the city's south side.

On Oct. 9, 1981, Fort was arrested for possession of a firearm and concealment of a fugitive, and therefore was not among the twenty-six people arrested during "Operation Top Brass" conducted by federal and local law enforcement agencies on Oct. 13. The raid was planned to arrest seventy-one persons for their involvement in heroin distribution, especially the trafficking of Talwin and pyrabenzamine, or Ts and Blues, which when combined produce effects similar to heroin. Fort, however, was convicted in 1983 of conspiring to sell cocaine, for which he was sentenced to thirteen years in a federal prison. He was serving this sentence in Texas when he was tried for federal racketeering and conspiracy charges, stemming from his agreement with Libya to commit terrorist acts. In November 1987 Fort was found Guilty, largely on the testimony of former El Rukn general Trammel Davis, who informed the court that the government of Libya had offered the El Rukn leader $2.5 million to sabotage U.S. airplanes. Fort was sentenced to eighty years in prison. For his participation with prosecutors, Davis, a co-conspirator, was given only two years in prison. Davis also testified at Fort's next trial.

With the help of former El Rukns Earl Hawkins, Anthony Sumner, and Davis, prosecutors were able to charge the El Rukn gang with the shooting death of rival gang leader Willie "Dollar Bill" Bibbs on June 15, 1981, and to keep Fort in prison presumably for life. Tried along with Fort in 1988 were: William Doyle, thirty-four, Ray Ferguson, thirty-five, Derrick Kees, thirty-one, and Derrick Porter, thirty-nine. Fred Giles, another defendant, was a fugitive. Security at the Cook County Criminal Court building was extremely tight; a metal detector was placed at the building and courtroom entrances, an armed guard in the elevator escorted all visitors to the fourth floor where the trial took place, a barricade from floor to ceiling constructed of wood and topped with barbed wire was erected outside the courtroom, and a wall of bulletproof glass separated court proceedings from the gallery. The security also included numerous guards and searches of all entering the courtroom, measures which Fort's lawyer, Thomas Peters, claimed intimidated jurors. Defense lawyers also charged that the state's key witnesses were only trying to get lighter sentences.

Hawkins was a convicted murderer sentenced to death, Sumner had been convicted of drug trafficking only after plea bargaining for the reduced sentence by informing on Hawkins, and Davis already informed on Fort. They were referred to as an "unholy trinity." Special prosecutor Randy Rueckert and Assistant State's Attorney Jack Hynes convinced jurors that Fort ordered the killing of Bibbs because Bibbs' gang, the Titanic Stones, owed him money for selling drugs on El Rukn turf, and for using the word "stone" in the gang name. All five defendants were found Guilty on Oct. 18, 1988. On Nov. 14, 1988, Judge Michael P. Toomin sentenced Fort to seventy-five years in prison to be served following the time served on his previous conviction in the terrorist conspiracy. Ferguson was sentenced to life in prison without parole, because of an earlier murder conviction. Doyle and Kees, who pulled the trigger prematurely, foiling Fort's plans to murder a large number of Titanic Stones, received fifty-five years in prison. Porter, who conferred with Fort about the killing and later left the gang in 1983, received forty-five years in prison. See: **El Rukn Gang, The**. REF.: *CBA*.

Fortas, Abe, 1910-82, U.S., jur. On July 29, 1965, Abe Fortas became the ninety-fifth person to assume the role of Associate Justice of the Supreme Court, culminating a lifetime of service in the private and governmental sectors. Born on June 19, 1910, in Memphis, Tenn., Fortas earned a bachelor's degree from Southwestern College in Memphis, before attending law school at Yale, where he served as editor-in-chief of the *Yale Law Journal* before his graduation in 1933. Immediately after graduation, he was appointed as an assistant professor of law under the tutelage of William O. Douglas, then a Yale professor. Simultaneous with his teachings, he took a part-time assignment in Franklin Roosevelt's New Deal Agriculture Department before following Douglas to the Security and Exchange Commission in 1937. In 1938, Fortas became assistant director of the SEC public utilities division, moving over to the Public Works Administration in 1939, and then becoming Under Secretary to Harold Ickes three years later.

After serving briefly in WWII, Fortas was appointed in 1945 by President Harry Truman to advise the U.S. delegation during the formation of the United Nations. In 1946 he retired from government service to found the Washington law firm of Arnold, Fortas & Porter, which became renowned for championing Civil Rights causes. He defended Owen Lattimore before a Senate subcommittee on the charge of perjury while denying Communist involvement in 1954. That same year, he widened the criminal insanity rule through his defense of Monte Durham, a convicted burglar. In 1962, before the Supreme Court, Fortas earned a unanimous ruling that states must assure legal counsel to the defendant in the defense of indigent Florida prisoner Clarence Earl Gideon.

Fortas served as Lyndon Johnson's counsel in 1948, when his name was removed from the ballot after narrowly winning a primary in his first race for Senator. The case was tried before the Supreme Court and launched Fortas as a national figure. Due to this case, Johnson and Fortas became close associates and remained so through their respective careers. With President John F. Kennedy's assassination on Nov. 22, 1963, Johnson appointed Fortas his emergency liaison as he hastily assumed the presidency. Fortas assisted Jacqueline Kennedy with funeral arrangements and also handled many of the inevitable political firings. While with Johnson, he helped in the formation of the Warren Commission, represented Bobby Baker in a civil suit, and advised Johnson when a top aid, Walter Jenkins was arrested on a morals charge. In July 1965, Arthur J. Goldberg resigned from the Supreme Court and Johnson offered the seat to Fortas. Initially rejecting the offer, Fortas accepted a week later, and after confirmation hearings, was installed on Oct. 4, 1965. He served more than three years, until involvement with Louis Wolfson, a financier under federal investigation, forced his resignation in 1969, at which time Fortas retired to private life. He died on Apr. 5, 1982.

REF.: *CBA*; Demaris, *The Director*; Gage, *The Mafia Is Not an Equal Opportunity Employer*; Messick, *Lansky*; _____, *Secret File*; Navasky, *Kennedy Justice*; Sullivan, *The Bureau: My Thirty Years in Hoover's FBI*; Ungar, *FBI*.

Fortescu, Grace, See: **Massie, Thomas.**

Fortescue, Sir John, c.1394-c.1476, Brit., jur., consp. Lord chief justice for the King's Bench from 1442-61, before losing all civil rights by order of King Edward IV for his support of deposed King Henry VI. In 1471, he was captured at the battle of Tewkesbury, but received pardon upon his recognizing Edward as the rightful king of England. He is considered one of the first constitutional lawyers in England. He authored *De Laudibus Legum Angliae*. REF.: *CBA*.

Fortis, Edmund, d.1794, U.S., rape-mur. Edmund Fortis was a runaway black slave who reached Vassalborough, Maine, managing to avoid the many posses and bounty hunters looking for him. While in hiding, Fortis spotted Pamela Tilton. He leaped in ambush, dragged her into some nearby woods, raped her, and then slit her throat. When Tilton's body was found, a wild hunt for the killer took place, with all the residents of the town searching for Fortis. He was found, quickly tried, condemned, and hanged on Sept. 25, 1794, at Dresden. Before his execution, Fortis made a lengthy confession in which he stated that his life had been devoted to "taking things not my own and lying with women."

REF.: *CBA; The Last Words and Dying Speech of Edmund Fortis.*

Fortmeyer, Julia E. (AKA: **The Baby Burner**), prom. 1870s, U.S., abor.-mansl. Known throughout St. Louis as "The Baby Burner," Mrs. Julia Fortmeyer was a practicing abortionist, as infamous in her time as New York's Madame Restell. Both women conducted illegal abortions for high profits, but without the benefit of surgical skill and proper medical care. In 1875, Mrs. Fortmeyer was charged with murdering Sarah Beehler's infant daughter. Police raided Mrs. Fortmeyer's premises and found two bodies of recently born children. The large stove in Fortmeyer's residence was loaded with human bones. Mrs. Fortmeyer was arrested and convicted of manslaughter. She was sent to prison for five years.

REF.: *CBA; Life, Crimes and Confession of Mrs. Julia Fortmeyer.*

Fortner, Clifford, 1944- , U.S., mur. When 12-year-old Lorna Lax left her parents' home near San Francisco on Nov. 14, 1959, she left a note stating she was "mad at the world" and would return the next morning. Her parents were not alarmed, explaining later that Lorna was "an unfortunate child, physically retarded and emotionally troubled." When she had not returned by Monday morning, they grew concerned.

That afternoon Norman Fortner, thirteen, found Lorna's body in a wooded area about two hundred yards from her home. Fortner told how Lax had often used the thicket as a "sex club," charging "initiation fees" of thirty-five cents to a dollar to local boys. Visitors to the sex club were questioned. Clifford Fortner, fifteen, told police he had gone to the thicket with Lorna early that night. Eventually, Fortner admitted that he had had sex with Lorna and then "something came over him." He first battered her head with a torch, then strangled her with a rope from a swing nearby, and finally stabbed her in the stomach several times. Fortner was sentenced to detention for an indefinite period of time.

REF.: *CBA*; Wilson, *Children Who Kill*; Wilson, *Encyclopedia of Murder*.

Fort Pillow Massacre, 1864, U.S., mur. In April 1864, Fort Pillow, Tenn., was under heavy attack by troops under the command of Confederate general Nathan Bedford Forrest. This Confederate leader was a spectacular and unpredictable individual. He had enlisted in the Confederate Army in 1861, and by December 1863 he had risen to the rank of major general. A cavalry leader, Forrest was the first such to employ his wild riders as infantry, dismounting his troops at unexpected moments to have them charge breastworks, shielding themselves with the bodies of their horses. His colorful quotes doted the news columns of the era. According to legend, Forrest was once asked how he achieved his amazing victories and the unschooled general replied: "I get there firstest with the mostest." When the Union commander at Fort Pillow refused to surrender, Forrest issued a demand for surrender that indicated he would show no quarter. What followed was undoubtedly the most savage massacre during the American Civil War. The reluctance of the Union commander to run up the white flag was predicated on the fact that many of his troops were blacks who had once been slaves. This infuriated Forrest and his officers since most of them had, before the war, owned vast plantations with hundreds of slaves. These very slaves now opposed them with weapons in hand, a thought too horrible to bear.

On Apr. 12, 1864, Forrest, who had repeatedly demanded the surrender of the fort, sent a chilling ultimatum to the Union commander: "Should my demand be refused, I cannot be responsible for the fate of your command." This message was interpreted by both sides as a No Quarter policy and, after the Confederates stormed and took the position, many in their ranks began shouting "No quarter! No quarter!" Of the 262 black soldiers of the Union garrison, only fifty-eight were taken prisoner. Not all the Confederate troops participated in the slaughter of the blacks, and many attempted to stop their comrades from shooting and bayoneting the defenseless prisoners, and this included—when he learned of the massacre—General Forrest himself. But the fury of murderous bloodlust was upon most of those troops in the first two waves that had assaulted and taken the fort. These men had been jeered and insulted by black troops on the fort's parapet during a truce period, goaded, as it were, into a frenzy of revenge, according to one report.

The fact remained, however, that the normally chivalrous Confederate troops, in this instance, unleashed a savage slaughter on the black soldiers. One Confederate sergeant, writing a letter home a week after the attack, stated how "the poor, deluded Negroes would run up to our men, fall upon their knees and with uplifted hands scream for mercy, but were ordered to their feet and then shot down." Thus, 204 black soldiers were murdered and the Fort Pillow Massacre, as it was termed in the North, became *the* atrocity of the American Civil War. Later, a subcommittee of the Joint Committee on the Conduct of War, following extensive interviews with survivors, concluded that the Confederates had conducted an "indiscriminate slaughter" of not only blacks but white soldiers, along with women and children, and that barracks and homes had been set afire, wounded men had been roasted in their beds, and that Confederate burial squads had "buried some of the living with the dead." Most of this report was fabrication, intentional Union propaganda to feed the wrath of Union troops, but the brutal slaughter of the 204 black soldiers was an undeniable fact which would forever taint the otherwise honorable image of the Confederate military.

Confederate troops massacring black Union soldiers at Fort Pillow in 1864.

Much of the responsibility for this massacre could be placed upon the uneducated and unorthodox Forrest, a fearless (some said mad) leader whose demand of surrender gave free rein to his embattled troops. Union general William T. Sherman stated once: "Forrest is the very devil!" Sherman vowed that he would track Forrest "to the death, if it cost 10,000 lives and break the Treasury. There will never be peace in Tennessee until Forrest is dead." The colorful, ruthless Forrest would not only survive the Civil War but would, in 1867, two years after the terrible conflict had ended, form one of America's most feared secret societies, the Ku Klux Klan. See: **Ku Klux Klan.**

REF.: Catton, *Picture History of the Civil War; CBA;* Foote, *The Civil War* (Vol 3); Werstein, *1861-1865: The Adventure of the Civil War.*

Fortsas Catalogue Hoax, prom. 1840, Belg., hoax. All the leading bibliophiles in Western Europe responded to the Fortsas Catalogue, advertising on Aug. 10, 1840, the sale of the private library of the late Jean Nepomucene-Auguste Pichauld, Count de Fortsas. The sixteen-page pamphlet, printed at Mons, announced the auction of the eccentric count's books, explaining how he had refused to own a book of which any other copy was known to exist. The director of the Belgian Royal Library, Baron de Reiffenberg, was given a special appropriation to make purchases. On the evening before the scheduled auction, the Brussels newspapers carried a notice that the sale had been cancelled because the entire Fortsas collection had been bought out by the people of Binche out of their deep regard for the original collector. Irate visitors did not easily accept local authorities denials

that any books had been purchased, and were livid because no one had ever heard of Fortsas or of the notary, M. Moulon, at whose address the auction was to have taken place. Sixteen years after the catalogue of the Count Fortsas had been printed, it was revealed that the hoaxer was Renier Chalon, an author and an antiquarian, who had mingled with the avid book lovers the day of the non-event. At a New York sale in the 1930s, a copy of the catalogue was purchased as a curiosity for $40.

REF.: *CBA;* MacDougall, *Hoaxes.*

Forty Little Thieves, prom. 1850s-60s, U.S., org. crime. The gang of Forty Little Thieves was an auxiliary branch of organized crime in New York in the mid-19th century. Composed of street children between the ages of eight and thirteen, the gang committed several crimes such as looting, burglary, and maybe murder, as well as acting as lookouts for adult criminals. The total number of the gang remained undetermined, but they were headed by a young orphan girl, Wild Maggie Carson. Maggie was saved from a life of crime when as a 13-year-old, she was sheltered by the Reverend L.M. Pease, who taught her domestic skills. Eventually she was adopted by a loving family and later had a successful marriage.

REF.: Asbury, *The Gangs of New York; CBA;* Kobler, *Capone.*

Forty Thieves, 1820s-50s, U.S., org. crime. Forty Thieves, a name later used by Tammany Hall politicians and a Harlem organized crime ring, was first used by a gang of Lower East Side Irish in New York in the early 1820s. The gang was headed by Edward Coleman, who assigned various muggings and holdups on a quota system from a speakeasy on Center Street. If gang members were not achieving a certain level of criminal commerce, they were quickly replaced by more eager criminals. The gang flourished because of internal competition until 1850, when it dissolved after members, eschewing the rigid quota system, joined other gangs or started their own.

REF.: Asbury, *The Gangs of New York; CBA;* Haskins, *Street Gangs;* Kobler, *Capone;* Nash, *Bloodletters and Badmen;* Peterson, *The Mob.*

Forty Thieves, prom. 1930s, U.S., org. crime. Forty Thieves was a black crime organization which operated parallel to the Mafia in the late 1930s in Harlem. From headquarters at 140th Street and Seventh Avenue, the gang ran the numbers rackets and an extortion ring, shaking down black businessmen for protection. They allegedly battled white Mafiosi, led first by "Dutch" Schultz and later by Mike Coppola, for control of the numbers rackets and claimed that they did not make subsequent payoffs to the mob. However, it is unlikely that the Italian empire would allow the business to flourish with passive indifference, especially after Schultz used a campaign of muggings, blindings, and murder to wrest the Harlem numbers rackets from independents. The mob also had help from police allies to bring down on the Forty Thieves.

REF.: Asbury, *The Gangs of New York; CBA;* Haskins, *Street Gangs;* Kobler, *Capone;* Nash, *Bloodletters and Badmen;* Peterson, *The Mob.*

Forty-Two Gang, 1920s-40s, U.S., org. crime. Many of Chicago's more notorious gangsters, including Mafia chieftain Sam Giancana, served their apprenticeship in the Forty-Two Gang. Started in 1925 with twenty-four members, the gang exaggerated their size and called themselves forty-two, two more thieves than Ali Baba. The gang later grew until they were actually forty-two members. Originating in the "Little Italy" neighborhood on Chicago's West Side, it became the wildest of the street gangs. The delinquents did anything for money, from robbing stores to stripping cars and attacking immigrant peddlers, then spent it frivolously in speakeasies run by the mob.

The gang paid a price for its violent existence. Within six years, thirty of the forty-two were killed, maimed, or serving time for their criminal activity. A number were confined in the boy's reformatory at St. Charles, Ill. In 1928, the head of the institution, Major William J. Butler, received a call demanding the release of gang members and threatening machine gun violence. The major did not acquiesce, and the state militia was assigned to guard the school. Newspapers editorialized that perhaps the gang members should be treated more like hardened criminals than wayward boys. The gang dissipated as the surviving members were integrated into the Chicago mob.

REF.: *CBA;* Landesco, *Organized Crime In Chicago;* Thrasher, *The Gang.*

For Us in the Dark, 1937, a novel by Naomi Royde-Smith. Browning's *The Ring and the Book* serves as the inspiration for this work which, in turn, drew its so-called facts from the Franceschini wife murder (Italy, 1697), a classic homicide. See: **Franceschini,** Count **Guido.** REF.: *CBA.*

Forwood, Stephen (AKA: **Southey, Ernest**), prom. 1865, Brit., mur. On his return to Ramsgate from living in London under the name of Ernest Southey, Stephen Forwood discovered that the wife and two children he had deserted had moved away. The next day, Aug. 11, 1865, Forwood went to the home of William Ellis, where they were staying. He wore a false beard and mustache, and green glasses. Despite this guise, Forwood's wife recognized her husband and asked him why he had run off. He yelled that he had lost £1,172 he had been saving, and then pulled out a gun and shot his wife and daughter. Before reloading the gun, which he had fired five times, Forwood removed his disguise which gave passersby time to see him. As Forbes was led away he laid his hand on his daughter's head and burst into tears, but showed no emotion during his trial. The court dismissed the plea of insanity and Forwood was executed.

REF.: Butler, *Murderers' England;* CBA.

Foscari, Giacopo, prom. 1450s, Italy, polit corr.-consp.-treas. Banished for receiving bribes intended to influence his father, Francesco Foscari, Doge of Venice, in distribution of state offices in 1445. He was banished again for implication in a political assassination in 1450, and banished a third time in 1456, for treason due to allegedly corresponding with enemies of the Venetian state. REF.: *CBA.*

Fosdick, Raymond Blaine, b.1883, U.S., lawyer. Special representative in France for the U.S. War Department from 1918-19, and undersecretary general for the League of Nations from 1919-20. He authored *European Police Systems* in 1915, and *American Police Systems* in 1920.

REF.: *CBA;* Logan, *Against the Evidence;* Peterson, *The Mob;* Reppetto, *The Blue Parade.*

Foster, Cassius Gaius, 1837-99, U.S., jur. Appointed by President Ulysses Grant to the District Court of Kansas in 1874. He published "The Pardoning Power: Its Use and Abuse," *Kansas Bar Association Reports* in 1898. REF.: *CBA.*

Foster, Cuthbert Pearson, prom. 1602, Brit., her. In 1602, Cuthbert Pearson Foster, who lived in the parish of St. Nicholas, Durham, was tried at the Ecclesiastical Court. Foster was charged with "playing at nine-holes upon the Sabbath day in time of divine service," and was given a one-time-only punishment of having to stand in the parish church during service clad in nothing but a white sheet.

REF.: Andrews, *Old-Time Punishments;* CBA.

Foster, Evelyn, d.1931, Brit., (unsolv.) rape-mur. Evelyn Foster, the 29-year-old owner of a car rental business, had made a run on Jan. 6, 1931, from her garage at Otterburn, near Newcastle, to take a customer to Birdhopecraig. As she was preparing to return, she was stopped by a man at a small way-station. He hired her to drive him to a town twenty-four miles away where he hoped to catch the bus he had supposedly missed. On the way, they stopped at Otterburn, where Evelyn spoke with her mother and the man supposedly checked at the pub to find a cheaper ride. Foster told her mother that the man was "very respectable and gentlemanly," adding that he was a bit of a dandy.

Foster picked up the man again and they drove on toward Ponteland, his destination. But just after they passed through a quiet village, the man demanded that she turn around and go back. He punched her in the eye and pushed her into the corner, taking over the wheel himself. He stopped the car at an isolated spot on the moors known locally as Wolf's Nick. He hit her again so that she tumbled into the back seat where he then raped her.

Before she could get her bearings, he tossed some sort of liquid—gasoline or acid—on the car and then set it afire. Evelyn passed out briefly, but regained consciousness and found the interior of the car on fire. She managed to escape the vehicle and lie in the cold grass when the car exploded. Two passing men saw the flames, found Evelyn, and took her home. In the brief hours before she died she told what had happened to her.

Unfortunately, the local police were ineffective; the constable arrived hours later, and no attempt was made to hunt for the murderer Foster had described. The next day, Captain Fullarton James, the Northumberland's Chief Constable, took over the case and soon decided that Evelyn Foster had made up the story, burning her car for the insurance, although she already had about $25,000 in the bank. The police gave up looking for the murderer.

Two years later, on Sept. 5, 1933, Ernest Brown, a 31-year-old farm employee who was having an affair with his boss's wife, shot his employer to death, then placed the body in a garaged car and set it on fire. The firemen put out the flames before the body had been burned, and the gunshot wound was found. Brown was convicted of murder and hanged the following February. As the murderer approached the gallows, the chaplain thought he said either "Otterburn" or "ought to burn." If it was Otterburn, possibly he was confessing to the unsolved Otterburn murder case. Brown matched the description that Evelyn Foster gave of her murderer.

REF.: Adam, *Murder Most Mysterious;* Butler, *Murderers' England; CBA;* Goodman, *The Burning of Evelyn Foster;* Gribble, *They Got Away With Murder;* Nash, *Open Files;* Shew, *A Second Companion to Murder;* Symons, *A Reasonable Doubt;* (FICTION), Brock, *Earth to Ashes.*

Foster, George (**Forster**), d.1803, Brit., mur. After he had been convicted of murdering his wife and child, George Foster was executed on Jan. 18, 1803, at the Old Bailey. While he was being hanged, several of his friends pulled his legs violently, to insure a speedier death for the condemned man. After he was taken down, Foster's body was delivered to a Professor Aldini for dissection. In the Newgate Calendar of those times, there is a description of Aldini's application of electrical currents to the dead body, in an experiment then referred to as the "Galvanic process." When the first jolt of current surged through the corpse, the jaws began to quiver, and other facial muscles contorted horribly, with one eye popping open. With the next current, "the right hand was raised and clenched, and the legs and thighs were set in motion." So terrifying was this sight that a Mr. Pass, who had attended the proceedings in an official capacity, died of fright soon after returning home. Several of the bystanders believed that the corpse was on the verge of being restored to life.

REF.: Atholl, *Shadow of the Gallows;* Brock, *A Casebook of Crime; CBA;* Parry, *Some Famous Medical Trials;* Turner, *The Inhumanists.*

Foster, James, c.1918- , U.S., (wrong.convict.) mur. James Foster spent two years on death row for a murder he did not commit. Foster, thirty-eight, a Gainesville, Ga., house painter, had lived a reckless, lawless life. He had served eighteen months for the armed robbery of a convenience store. He had had affairs with other women from the time he got married, and drove without benefit of a driver's license. When prominent Jefferson citizen Charles Drake, fifty-seven, was brutally murdered on June 19, 1956, Mrs. Drake swore to the jury that Foster was the guilty man.

Foster's was the first trial presided over by Judge Julian Bennett. Foster clutched the Bible as he presented his alibi in persuasive detail. He repeated Mrs. Drake's description of her husband's assailant and then removed his shirt to show the jury he wasn't the large, muscular man who overcame Drake. He led the courtroom in an emotional prayer, after which the jury promptly declared him Guilty. Foster cried as he was sentenced to death.

Foster's case went to the Georgia Supreme Court, which affirmed the conviction. The U.S. Supreme Court refused to review the case. When it looked as though nothing more could be done, the head of the South Carolina Law Enforcement Division, J. Preston Strom, stepped in. A year after Foster's conviction, Strom learned from an ex-convict, since deceased, that Foster was innocent. This lead turned up the real killer, Charles Paul (Rocky) Rothschild, an ex-cop from Cairo, Ill. Rothschild had borrowed William Patterson's car and, with A.D. Allen, a bootlegger, robbed and killed the wealthy Drake. When Rothschild returned Patterson's car, he told him about the killing. Patterson was later arrested and convicted for a Spartanburg, S.C., robbery, and told police Rothschild's secret. On Aug. 14, 1958, Allen and Rothschild were found Guilty and sentenced to life. Foster was finally freed. See: **Rothschild, Charles Paul (Rocky); Strom, J. Preston.**

REF.: Bedau, *The Death Penalty In America*; CBA.

Foster, Nathan, 1759-1819, U.S., mur. Foster had a foul disposition and constantly abused his even-tempered wife Eleanor throughout their long marriage, which produced several children. He began having an affair with 23-year-old Polly Mosier, who lived next to the Masonville, N.Y., farm occupied by the Foster family. Mosier, a married woman, agreed to have sex with the elderly Foster in exchange for a cow. She continued her adulterous conduct with Foster in exchange for other farm animals Foster bestowed upon her. Foster then decided to murder his wife, and visited Wight's pharmacy. While buying arsenic from Wight, Foster stupidly inquired of the pharmacist if he knew a good woman he might marry. Wight knew Foster well, and that his wife was still alive, and was therefore shocked by this question.

A short time later Eleanor Foster died a painful death. Dr. Pliny Smith, who attended her, suspected poison and examined the contents of his patient's stomach. He found arsenic. Nathan Foster was arrested and placed on trial for murdering his wife. Dr. Smith testified that he had discovered arsenic in the body of the deceased, and this was supported by Dr. Nathan Boynton, who helped perform the autopsy. Defense attorneys insisted that Mrs. Foster had died of cholera-morbus, but the jury was unconvinced and convicted Foster after a fifteen-minute deliberation. He was condemned and hanged on Aug. 6, 1819.

REF.: CBA; *Report of the Trial of Nathan Foster*.

Foster, Rufus Edward, 1871-1942, U.S., jur. U.S. attorney from 1907-09, was appointed by President Theodore Roosevelt to the District Court of Louisiana in 1909, and by President Calvin Coolidge to the Fifth Circuit Court of the U.S., in 1925. REF.: CBA.

Foster, William, d.1873, U.S., mur. William Foster was a habitual alcoholic and was given to fits of violence when under the influence. A huge man, Foster staggered onto a New York trolley car one night while on one of his periodic binges. The car was crowded, and when Avery D. Putnam refused to give up his seat to Foster, the drunkard hit him so hard that he crushed his skull, killing him on the spot. Foster was convicted and hanged, despite his lawyer's plea that his client was under the influence of "hard spirits."

REF.: CBA; Remault, *The Car Hook Tragedy*.

Foster, William, 1886-1914, S. Afri., rob.-suic.-mur. William Foster, South Africa's most notorious gangster, started with a youth's big plans to seek his fortune in German South West Africa and ended being sought by the police for murder.

Foster was only nineteen when he first landed in jail. Exploring the desert one day, he met two men driving a pack of donkeys. He joined them, only to discover upon his and their arrests that the donkeys were stolen. The men claimed they found the donkeys wandering in the desert. Foster's indignation with his false accusation kept him in jail when his companions were allowed to go free. When Foster was released from prison, he became a heavy drinker and minor criminal.

A poorly-timed robbery earned Foster twelve years of hard labor. While awaiting trial, he married his girlfriend Peggy. Foster quickly escaped from prison, robbed a bank, and killed two clerks. Police chased Foster until September 1914, when they trapped him and two companions in a cave in Kensington Ridge. One committed suicide and one turned himself in. Only Foster

remained. Foster's parents, sisters, wife, and baby daughter were sent in to persuade him to come out. All returned except Foster and his wife, who killed themselves in the cave. REF.: CBA.

Fouché, Joseph (Duke of O'trante), 1763-1820, Fr., law enfor. off. Born into wealth in Nantes, France, Joseph Fouché studied for the priesthood but abandoned his clerical pursuits, becoming a professor of philosophy. He

was from childhood passionless and restrained, possessing an incredible patience. Fouché was cunning and crafty which suited his position as minister of police under Napoleon I. He affixed his fortunes with Bonaparte early in the "Little Corporal's" career and rose to one of the most powerful positions in France, serving three terms as police minister, 1799-1802, 1804-10, and 1815.

Using an army of police spies, Fouché kept extensive files on France's underworld, as well as monitored the middle class and the nobility for

Joseph Fouché, France's Minister of Police.

any signs of rebellion against Napoleon's dictatorial regime. Fouché spent lavishly for his information and he bribed any and all who would provide him with information which he considered of a security nature. This even included huge bribes he paid to Josephine, Napoleon's consort, to obtain the innermost secrets of Bonaparte's palace.

When Napoleon learned of Fouché's involved intrigues, he removed him from his office at the Police Prefecture but found, after a couple of years, that he could not operate without this watchdog and restored Fouché to his position in 1804. By then Fouché had established through his enormous wealth his own private police force. He employed agents everywhere in France and in all the major capitals of Europe. His chain of information on the political and military workings of foreign powers enabled Napoleon to successfully invade and conquer many countries. Napoleon became so dependent upon Fouché that he turned almost all important matters of state over to this policeman, with the oft-repeated refrain: "Send it to Fouché. It is his business!"

Fouché became the most powerful man in France after Napoleon. Fouché could not restrain his love for intrigue, however, and not only countermanded Napoleon's orders myriad times but began to meddle in affairs of state which brought about his second dismissal. He attempted to secretly bring about a separate peace with England during its prolonged war with Bonaparte and when Napoleon learned of Fouché's latest intrigues and plottings, he removed the policeman from office.

Following his defeat at Waterloo in 1815, Napoleon raced back to Paris to find Fouché waiting for him with only one piece of advice: Abdicate. Napoleon bowed to Fouché's suggestion and turned over the government to this Machiavellian policeman. Fouché hastily assembled a government and made peace with the allies. He was removed from office in 1816 and ordered into exile. Fouché moved into a comfortable villa in Trieste and died there in 1820.

REF.: Brice, *Le secret de Napoléon*; CBA; Couchoud, *Voix de Napoléon*; Goldsmith, *Procès de Buonaparte*; Griffiths, *Mysteries of the Police and Crime*; Hegemann, *Napoleon*; Hunt, *A Dictionary of Rogues*; Kemble, *Napoleon Immortal*; Ludwig, *Napoleon*; Martineau, *Napoleon's St. Helena*; Scott, *Life of Napoleon*; Sieburg, *Napoléon*; Thomson, *Napoleon Bonaparte: His Rise and Fall*.

Foulke, William Dudley, 1848-1935, U.S., lawyer. Served on the U.S. Civil Service Commission from 1901-03, and as the president of the National Civil Service Reform League from 1923-24. REF.: CBA.

Foulkes, Robert, d.1679, Brit., mur. The Reverend Robert Foulkes was a minister in Salop County when he was appointed executor of the large estate of a young girl whom he then seduced. When the girl became pregnant, Foulkes moved her to London, to hide her condition from the town and his wife and family. When the child was born, Foulkes murdered the infant. He was convicted at the Old Bailey on Jan. 16, 1679, and sentenced to death. Foulkes wrote a letter to a fellow minister soon after receiving the death sentence, a self-righteous missive in which he confessed to the crime but blamed it on his young victim, who was no more than fourteen at the time of the seduction.

Wrote the clergyman: "The Devil had prepared for me a sad companion and partner in my debaucheries; she was easily tempted by me, and proved afterwards a constant temptation to me, and has been the great occasion of this dismal conclusion of our wretched course of life. Open your eyes therefore, and not only look, but contemplate upon these dreadful and tragic instances, oh, adulterers and adulteresses, and be not ensnared with a whore's charms." Later in the same letter the minister went on to tell his colleague and posterity that, despite the girl's denial at the trial, she had also taken a hand in the infant's murder.

Foulkes went to the gallows at Tyburn on Jan. 31, 1679. Once again, he could not resist preaching and once again he called his victim a prostitute: "I am come hither to satisfy the law of Man, and acknowledge the justice of that sentence. And oh! that all you may fear and tremble at God's holy and righteous judgments, which have overtaken me; and that they may make you take warning to avoid the snares of a whorish woman, and to keep the marriage bed undefiled..."

Then, having done all in his power to further destroy the life of the young he had victimized, the condemned clergyman fell silent and the hangman's noose was slipped around his neck. Reverend Foulkes then dropped through the trap to embrace eternal infamy. REF.: *CBA*; Smith, *Highwaymen*.

Foullon, Joseph François, 1717-89, Fr., assass. Commanded the French army in the Seven Years' War from 1756-63, and attempted to hide from the riotous mobs after the fall of the Bastille in 1789, but was captured and hanged from a lamppost. REF.: *CBA*.

Foulques (Fulk), c.840-900, Fr., assass. Archbishop of Reims in 883, he crowned Charles III king of France in 893, in opposition to Count Eudes of Paris. At the death of Eudes in 898, Charles was finally recognized as king and Foulques was named chancellor of France. By the order of Count Baldwin of Flanders, he was assassinated. REF.: *CBA*.

Fountain, Albert Jennings, 1838-96, U.S., west. gunman.-(unsolv.) mur. Born in 1838 in New York City, Albert Jennings Fountain traveled the world before ending up in California in the 1850s. In 1859 he began the first of many careers as a reporter for the *Sacramento Union* covering Latin America. He fought in the Civil War as a soldier in the First California Infantry Volunteers, later moving to New Mexico, where he married 14-year-old Mariana Pérez, with whom he eventually had twelve children. Fountain organized a militia to fight Indians and was wounded in 1865. The family moved to El Paso where he first became a deputy collector of customs, then county surveyor, and attorney. Fountain also fought in the Mexican War as colonel to Benito Juárez. In 1868, Fountain was elected to the Texas Senate, and was named Senate President. Later he was made a brigadier general of the Texas State Police.

On Dec. 7, 1870, Fountain and Judge Gaylord Judd Clarke were accosted in El Paso by a lawyer, B.F. Williams. Fountain, unarmed, was hit three times by Williams, but was able to stagger home. Returning with a shotgun, Fountain wounded Williams, who was fatally shot by police captain A.H. French. Although he had not provoked the assault, Fountain's public career faltered. Five years later he moved his family back to New Mexico, where he served as an assistant U.S. attorney and a state representative. He returned to his Indian wars, using his Mexican friends as allies.

In March 1883, Fountain and his son Albert were returning by train from El Paso with three fugitives. One of the three, Doroteo Sáenz attempted to escape as the train slowed in Canutillo, Texas. The alert Fountain followed the fugitive, and killed him before he could escape into the high brush.

Fountain began a bitter struggle with Albert B. Fall in the late 1880s. The feud escalated until Jan. 31, 1896, when Fountain and his 9-year-old son Henry were killed in White Sands, N.M., while returning home to Mesilla. Fountain, by that time a territorial judge, had been involved in a grand jury investigation involving alleged cattle rustling. Three men, James Gililland, Oliver Lee, and William McNew were charged with the murders, but were later acquitted. Many prominent individuals including Albert Fall were suspected, but nobody was ever convicted of the double murder. Jim "Deacon" Miller, a hired gunman, was credited with the Fountain murders. See: **Miller, Jim.**

REF.: American Guide Series, *New Mexico: A Guide to the Colorful State;* Bechdolt, *Tales of the Old Timers;* Breihan, *Great Gunfighters of the West;* ____, *Great Lawmen of the West;* Bronson, *Red Blooded;* Burns, *The Saga of Billy the Kid;* Casey, *The Texas Border and Some Borderliners;* *CBA;* Charles, *More Tales of Tularosa;* Cunningham, *Triggernometry;* Donovan, *Skill in Trials;* Fergusson, *Murder and Mystery in New Mexico;* Garrett, *The Authentic Life of Billy the Kid;* Gibson, *The Life and Death of Col. Albert Jennings Fountain;* Hamilton, *The Young Pioneer;* Harkey, *Mean As Hell;* Hening, *George Curry;* Hertzog, *A Directory of New Mexico Desperadoes;* Hunt, *The Tragic Days of Billy the Kid;* Hutchinson, *Another Verdict for Oliver Lee;* Jenkinson, *Ghost Towns of New Mexico;* Keleher, *The Fabulous Frontier;* ____, *Violence in Lincoln County;* La Farge, *Santa Fe;* Metz, *Pat Garrett;* O'Connor, *Pat Garrett;* Otero, *My Life on the Frontier;* Siringo, *History of Billy the Kid;* ____, *Riata and Spurs;* Sonnichson, *Outlaw;* ____, *Tularosa;* Stanley, *The Duke City;* ____, *The Kingston;* ____, *No More Tears for Black Jack.*

Fouquet, Nicolas (Foucquet), 1615-80, Fr., embez. Named finance superintendent in 1653. He was arrested and convicted for embezzling funds in 1661, following a trial that lasted nearly four years, and was sentenced to life imprisonment. He is considered by some to be the "Man in the Iron Mask". REF.: *CBA*.

Fouquier-Tinville, Antoine Quentin, 1746-95, Fr., lawyer. Prosecuted for the Revolutionary Tribunal from 1793-94. He professed to have tried more than 2,400 persons as counterrevolutionaries, including: his relative Camille Desmoulins, Marie Antoinette, and members of the Girondists and Hébertists, before he himself was guillotined in 1795. REF.: *CBA*.

Four Deuces, prom. 1920s, U.S., org. crime. The Four Deuces was a "one-stop" vice center run by the Capone mob on South Wabash Avenue in Chicago in the prohibition 1920s. The four story structure housed a saloon on the first floor, gambling dens on the second and third, and an opulent bordello on the fourth. To rid himself of local competition, Capone's men dragged a murder victim's body from the Four Deuces and burned it in the furnace of the neighboring Frolics Club. After police were notified that the Frolics Club's basement was being used as a crematorium, the establishment was quickly put out of business.

REF.: Asbury, *Gem of the Prairie;* *CBA;* Demaris, *Captive City;* Kobler, *Capone;* Landesco, *Organized Crime In Chicago;* McPhaul, *Johnny Torrio;* Morgan, *Prince of Crime.*

Fournier, M., See: **Dupont-Fournier Duel.**

Fournier, Télesphore, 1824-96, Can., jur. Served on the Canadian Supreme Court from 1875-96. REF.: *CBA*.

Fowler, "Bunny" (AKA: The Terror of Notting Dale), and **Milsom, Albert**, prom. c.1910, Brit., burg.-mur. It was a makeshift lantern wick that gave away robber and murderer "Bunny" Fowler and his professional burglar friend Albert Milsom. The two carefully planned their break-in at Muswell Hill Lodge in Notting Dale, England, home of the wealthy old Mr. Smith. Milsom agreed only to a robbery, but Fowler knew murder was likely.

Creaking boards and shuffling sounds awakened Mr. Smith. Milsom ran from the house as Fowler beat Smith to death.

Detectives found a child's toy lantern in Smith's house, with a wick made of dress cloth. After the murder, Albert Miller, Milsom's nephew, saw his lost lantern on a store shelf. He wanted it back and described the wick to the shopkeeper to prove the lantern was his. This information, combined with the disappearance of Fowler and Milsom, led police to the fugitives. They had joined a small traveling show, where Fowler worked as the "strong man." He and Milsom were convicted for the murder and hanged.

REF.: *CBA*; Stevens, *From Clue to Dock*.

Fowler, George E., and **Leatherberry, J.C.**, prom. 1943, Brit., mur. Two American soldiers stationed in Colchester, England, during WWII were charged and convicted of murder.

An abandoned taxi was discovered with its lights still on at 11:30 a.m. on Dec. 8, 1943, between Birch and Colchester. There was evidence of a struggle inside the car, including a bloodstained raincoat and a blue jacket with a sleeve inside out, identified as that of driver Claude Hailstone. Hailstone was last heard from the previous night between 11 and 11:10, when he told his landlady he would not be stopping for dinner because he had a job. Hailstone's body was later discovered lying in the bushes, scratched and bruised. He had been struck repeatedly and killed by strangulation. Blood from Hailstone's coat was of the rare AB type.

A raincoat found along the road was traced to Captain J.J. Weber of the 18th Canadian General Hospital, Colchester, who led police to Private George Fowler. Apparently Weber and Fowler had met and had drinks together. When Weber left the room, Fowler grabbed the overcoat and ran out.

Fowler denied any knowledge of Weber or the December killing, but a search of his belongings turned up a sergeant's tunic with type AB bloodstains, and a Dec. 6 pawn ticket for a Rolex Victory watch, which Weber had already told police was in the overcoat pocket. Fowler testified that he found the pawn ticket on Dec. 3 or 4, but the watch was not pawned until Dec. 6. Fowler frequently changed his testimony, and contradicted concrete evidence. He fit Weber's description of the man who took his coat. Fowler tried to absolve himself by implicating Private J.C. Leatherbury. According to Fowler, the two men had been riding in Hailstone's cab, Leatherberry with the expressed purpose of robbing the driver. Fowler said that when the cab stopped in Colchester, he got out and Leatherberry attacked Hailstone. By the time Fowler climbed back in the cab, Leatherberry had killed the driver.

Leatherberry's story was entirely different. He said he and Fowler weren't together the night of the murder. But a search of his belongings revealed a bloodstained shirt, pants, and vest.

Investigators found human blood under the nail of the third finger on Fowler's left hand and under all of Leatherberry's nails. The woman Leatherberry had claimed to be with on the night of Dec. 7 swore she wasn't with him then.

Both men were convicted of murder. Fowler was sentenced to life imprisonment with forfeiture of all civil rights, and dishonorably discharged. Leatherberry was sentenced to death by hanging. Just prior to his execution at Shepton Mallet, he confessed to his role in the crime, but said Fowler had actually killed Hailstone. REF.: *CBA*.

Fowler, Henry, See: **Milsom, Albert**.

Fox, Charles James, 1749-1806, Brit., consp. Appointed lord of admiralty from 1770-72, and lord of treasury from 1772-74, but was removed for his independence by King George III, who became Fox's political nemesis. Against objections of the king, he was named foreign secretary in Rockingham's ministry in 1782, but was eventually pressured into resigning, only to be reappointed, very briefly the following year. Again he was removed from office by the king until 1806. In the All-the-Talents Administration of William Grenville in 1806, he was once again appointed foreign secretary, where he revealed a plot to assassinate Napoleon I during peace negotiations with France. REF.: *CBA*.

Fox, George, 1624-91, Brit., her. Founded the Quakers, a sect

protesting Presbyterianism, and for this was persecuted and imprisoned throughout his life. REF.: *CBA*.

Fox, Henry Richard Vassall (Third Baron Holland), 1773-1840, Brit., crim. just. Served in the House of Lords, and held lord privy seal in William Grenville's All-the-Talents Administration from 1806-07. He strove to lessen the severity of the code with the introduction of a bill in Parliament seeking to abolish capital punishment for theft in 1809. REF.: *CBA*.

Fox, Isaac Garrett, c.1895-1948, U.S., rob.-suic. Isaac Garrett Fox was desperate to avoid a prison term. He had already served eight years, from 1931-39. Alone in his San Francisco hotel room, three weeks behind in his rent and unemployed, he decided to rob his second bank. He went in the South Berkeley branch of the Bank of America and came out with $8,155 in cash.

His poorly planned getaway landed him on a dead-end street. His only possible escape route was through an open field on foot. He'd have made it if not for Buggs, a bulldog that chased him across the field. At the other side Fox found an angry dog owner and a policeman. Fox jerked out his gun and stuffed it into his mouth. The gun didn't go off, but his false teeth fell out. The policeman took him in.

At Oakland's Northern Police Station, while under FBI questioning, Fox yanked the agent's gun from its open holster, put it under his chin and fired. REF.: *CBA*.

Fox, John, c.1835-56, U.S., mur. The defending attorney in the case of John Fox, twenty-one, charged with the first-degree murder of John Henry, eighteen, fought for appeal claiming a verdict was ruled against his client because nobody in town respected him. The lawyer argued no motive for murder had been established, and that Fox's conviction was based on circumstantial evidence. But the jury had already made up its collective mind; Fox had killed, and now, he too must die.

The after-Christmas blues in 1855 turned black for New Jersey residents when the body of 18-year-old Henry was discovered frozen in the snowy wood off New Brunswick's main track. His bruised body was found on Dec. 30 by Francis Heward. The young man's throat had been cut, and he now lay over the frozen stream. A gash stained his dress shirt, and a bloodied pistol handle lay just yards away. The whole horrible scene was far enough from the road and in thick enough woods to be hidden from passersby. Fox, a long-time friend of the victim, was taken into custody the following morning, and the trial that ensued turned up strong testimony against the man.

Dr. Morrogh testified that the violent contusions found on the deceased's body would have caused him to die within minutes, and that he probably had been dead for three days. Dr. Henry Baldwin, noting how the throat was sliced, said the assailant could not have helped but bloody his own hands in the process.

Henry and Fox, whom townspeople regarded as friends, had last been seen on the morning of Dec. 27. That was the last time anyone recalled having seen Henry, but more than six key witnesses swore to having seen Fox that day, near the New Jersey Railroad Company where he worked. He showed off his severely wounded and bloody hand, claiming he had fallen off a train car. He was visibly drunk and shaken, and the knee patches of his pants were black with mud. Occasionally he showed off a large roll of bills, and a gold watch and chain later identified as having belonged to Henry.

Joseph Jefferies, who also worked at the railroad depot, said he believed Fox stole a box containing valuables from the depot when he was working there in the middle of December. Among the items stolen were a large sum of money and a set of keys, both of which were found on Fox's person. Found on Henry's dead body was a lead pencil, also from the depot's box.

No one witnessed the violent deed, but after piecing together the events of late December, the jury was certain it had a clear picture. It found Fox Guilty of first-degree murder, and presiding Judge Vredenbergh handed down a death sentence. Fox, twenty-one, was hanged on July 25, 1856, between 10 a.m. and 3 p.m.—about the same time Fox had killed Henry.

REF.: *CBA; Trial of John Fox for the Murder of John Henry.*

Fox, Margaret, 1833-93, U.S., fraud. Proclaimed herself as a spiritualist medium, and toured Europe and the U.S., with her sisters, Catherine and Leah Fox, as assistants. Her success led to investigation into the phenomena of spiritualism. She finally confessed to being an imposter in 1888, only to later retract her statement. REF.: *CBA.*

Fox, Mary (AKA: **Lady Mary Primrose, Lady Olive Stanhope, Lady Cynthia Lambert, Lady Beryl Mackenzie, Lady Helen Venables**), prom. 1900s, Brit., fraud. As a young girl, Mary Fox loved to wander the Devonshire estate where she lived. It was a sad day for her when she learned that the property belonged not to her parents, but to their employer, and that she was a workman's daughter. She wished to be a lady of wealth, and despite the odds, and in opposition to the law, she followed her dreams. From Europe to North and South America, Fox convinced the wealthy elite that she was one of them. She was the fiancée of at least five young, rich men until routine investigations by the men's parents revealed her origins.

Fox pulled off her biggest fraud in London, playing Lady Helen Venables, director of a "society" matrimonial agency. She gathered women like herself for the purpose of uniting marriage and blackmail. She extracted £8,000 from one elderly man who was separated from his wife and had gone through one of the agency's bogus ceremonies. She might have gotten more if he hadn't died of a heart attack when he found out how he'd been tricked.

Fox was living the life of a lady in a Paris hotel when a gentleman came calling. Hearing the manager announce that the lady had not yet risen, the gentleman identified himself as Chief-Inspector John Sexton, New Scotland Yard. He was sent up to the woman's room and there found the body of Mary Fox, who had died in her sleep. She was buried in a pauper's grave in Paris.

REF.: *CBA; Ellis, Black Fame.*

Fox, Richard Kyle, 1846-1922, U.S., law enfor. Began publishing the *National Police Gazette* in 1877, which stressed crime and sex, becoming that era's most sensationalistic periodical. REF.: *CBA.*

Fox, Sidney Harry, 1899-1930, Brit., theft-fraud-blk.-mur. Sidney Fox was a devoted son, until his greed and ambition got the best of him. On Apr. 21, 1930, 63-year-old Rosaline Fox made a will that bequeathed all her worldly goods to her son Sidney Fox, her partner in crime. On May 1, Fox took out a life insurance policy on his mother and asked the agent a series of disturbing questions. "Would this policy cover the case of drowning? Would it apply supposing a person was poisoned, let us say, by food at a restaurant?" Six months later his mother was dead.

British murderer Sidney Harry Fox.

The Foxes were an unlikely pair. Sidney was the youngest of four children, and he was his mother's favorite. Through the 1920s, the matron and her son traveled the south coast of England, running up hotel bills which were never paid and perpetrating a series of frauds and blackmail schemes. Sidney was homosexual, but he had an affair with a married woman named Mrs. Morse at Southsea. Fox insured Morse's life for £6000 before attempting to asphyxiate her with gas as she slept. Mrs. Morse awoke in time, but discovered her collection of jewels missing. Fox went to prison in 1928 again. In 1918 he had been sentenced to three months at hard labor for defrauding a Brighton tradesman.

When Fox was freed in March 1929, he rejoined his mother. They moved about the country, visiting the best hotels of London, Canterbury, and Folkestone before ending up in Margate on Oct. 16. They rented a room at the Hotel Metropole, despite having only a few shillings between them. Sidney went to London to attend to some insurance business, and on Oct. 23 rejoined his mother at the hotel after advising the desk clerk that they would be checking out that night. That night Fox ordered half a bottle of port wine and retired for the evening. At around 11:40 p.m. Sidney burst into the hallway and called out that there was a fire in the rooms. Samuel Hopkins, who was staying in an adjacent suite, fought through the dense smoke and found Mrs. Fox. Attempts to revive her with artificial respiration failed, and Dr. Robert Nichol recorded the cause of her death as "misadventure." Sidney Fox was grief-stricken.

The next day he sufficiently recovered his composure and left the hotel without paying the bill. On Oct. 29, Rosaline Fox was buried and her son went to Norwich to file the claim on his mother's life. He was arrested there on Nov. 2 for attempting to obtain credit unlawfully. Scotland Yard had taken an interest in the case, and a post mortem examination on Mrs. Fox was ordered for Nov. 9. Sir Bernard Spilsbury, the eminent pathologist, reported that he could not find a trace of carbon monoxide in her blood, or deposits in the lungs. Death, he said, was brought on by strangulation.

Fox denied it, but was bound over for trial at the Lewes Assizes on Mar. 12, 1930. Representing the defense was J.D. Cassels, one of Britain's most capable lawyers. Sir Henry Curtis-Bennett and Sir William Jowett prosecuted the case for the Crown. They were able to prove that the defendant had advertised himself as the grandson of Sir John Leslie, and had directed his correspondence to the Royal Automobile Club, of which he was not a member. Hotel employees were similarly deceived. Through Fox's intervention, his mother had been moved into an adjoining room with a gas fire. Staff members were solicitous of the "gentlemanly" Fox who fretted over his mother's health.

The attorney general testified that the fire had been started under a chair. This accounted for the section of unburned carpet which stood between the chair and the fireplace. The only fire that could have burned so was one in which gasoline was used.

Spilsbury's post mortem report came under attack from Professor Sydney Smith and his colleague, Dr. Brontë, who stated that there was no evidence of a bruise on the larynx of the victim. Spilsbury replied that it was there when he exhumed the body. Smith then suggested that it was merely a patch of discoloration brought on by decomposition. The jury was inclined to believe Spilsbury. They returned a verdict of Guilty and Fox was sentenced to death. He was hanged at Maidstone Prison in Kent on Apr. 8, 1930.

REF.: Adamson, *The Great Detective;* Brophy, *The Meaning of Murder;* Browne and Tullett, *The Scalpel of Scotland Yard;* Butler, *Murderers' England; CBA;* Crocker, *Far From the Humdrum;* Cuthbert, *Science and the Detection of Crime;* Dearden, *Some Cases of Sir Bernard Spilsbury and Others;* Firmin, *Murderers In Our Midst;* Gribble, *When Killers Err;* Grice, *Great Cases of Sir Henry Curtis Bennett KC;* Hambrook, *Hambrook of the Yard;* Hoskins, *The Sound of Murder;* Jowitt, *Some Were Spies;* Knowles, *Court of Drama;* Leach, *On Top of the Underworld;* McClure, *Killers; Notable British Trials;* Randall, *The Famous Cases of Sir Bernard Spilsbury;* Shew, *A Companion to Murder;* Shore, *Crime and Its Detection;* Smith, *Mostly Murder;* Townsend, *Black Cap: Murder Will Out;* Whitelaw, *Corpus Delicti;* Wilson, *Encyclopedia of Murder;* Woodhall, *Secrets of Scotland Yard;* (DRAMA), Williams, *Night Must Fall;* (FILM), *Night Must Fall,* 1937; *Night Must Fall,* 1964.

Fox, William, d.1883, U.S., rob.-mur. Fox attempted to rob J.W. Howard in Nevada, Mo., shooting his victim to death in the process. He was quickly tried, convicted, and condemned to death. Before his execution on Dec. 28, 1883, Fox unsuccessfully tried to commit a bizarre suicide. He kept borrowing matches from guards for a pipe he did not smoke. After collecting the tops of the matches and finally swallowing a handful of these, he hoped to die of sulfuric poison. It did not work and William Fox went to the gallows as scheduled.

REF.: *CBA; Life and History Together with the Details of the Trial of Bill Fox.*

Fox-Davies, Arthur Charles, 1871-1928, Brit., lawyer. As king's counsel he provided the defense for the murder trial of Alexander Campbell Mason. REF.: *CBA.*

Foxen, James (AKA: **Mr. Foxton**), prom. 1818-29, Brit., execut. James Foxen was London's public hangman from 1818 until his death in 1829.

Foxen considered his work more an art than a trade. "I never like to be meddled with," he said, "because I always study the subjects which come under my hands, and according as they are tall or short, heavy or light, I accommodate them with the fall. No man in England has had so much experience as me, or knows how to do his duty better."

Foxen was known to have pointed to recent corpses looking for compliments on the fine job he had done. He executed several celebrated criminals, including banker Henry Fauntleroy, hanged in the Old Bailey on Nov. 30, 1824, for grand scale forgery. The hanging was especially exciting for the people because the condemned had been a gentleman of standing.

After Foxen's death at age sixty-one, William Calcraft became London's public executioner. Calcraft had served as Foxen's favorite apprentice in the flogging business, and diligently studied Foxen's technique. REF.: *CBA.*

Fra Angelo, d.1806, Italy, rob. Fra Angelo was a bandit leader who led a fierce group of robbers and operated under the direction of Cardinal Ruffo in his undeclared war with the Parthenopean Republic. Fra Angelo offered his services and those of his men to the highest bidder. The English employed Fra Angelo in 1806 to raid the French in Naples. In one of these raids, Fra Angelo was captured. He was hanged as a brigand on Nov. 10, 1806. He is celebrated in Auber's opera, *Fra Diavolo.* REF.: *CBA.*

Fraccari, Filiberto, 1935- , Italy, kid. vict. The family of kidnap victim Filiberto Fraccari, 40-year-old Italian gold dealer, bargained the kidnappers down from $3 million to $600,000 for the return of their beloved.

Fraccari was kidnapped while returning to his home in Verona on Christmas Eve 1975 by three men brandishing submachine guns. They originally demanded $3 million for Fraccari's return. The family offered $200,000 and the parties, after ten days of negotiations, agreed on $600,000, to be left in two suitcases inside a telephone booth. Authorities believed that the kidnappers were unnerved by the arrest of another kidnapping gang and thus expedited a settlement.

REF.: *CBA; Clutterbuck, Kidnap and Ransom.*

Frad, Willie T., b.1881, U.S., fraud. Willie T. Frad had been arrested twice in his native U.S. before the start of WWI. He spent two terms in Leavenworth Prison for mail fraud and conspiracy before he decided to become a confidence man. Between 1931-41, Frad made close to fifty transatlantic and Caribbean trips to bilk card players, showing a marked preference for stealing from financiers and highly placed captains of industry. An amateur actor usually would set up the "customer," and Frad would move in, pretending to be a very wealthy man, and making casual remarks about his inherited funds or his family business. Frad presented himself as being retired and satisfying a long-term ambition to wander Europe, visiting art galleries. The fastidious card shark concentrated on the same type of stuffy aristocrats he posed as. Keeping stakes conservatively low until the last night of the gaming, Frad would then raise the ante and go in for the financial kill. Most of his customers paid without a murmur. In a decade, the sharper was said to have made about $1 million. After New York City Intelligence Unit Agent Hugh McQuillan discovered that Frad had never bothered to pay income taxes, the card player was captured and brought up on charges. On Apr. 23, 1943, the 62-year-old Frad was sentenced to a ten-year prison term by Federal Judge William Bondy.

REF.: *CBA; Hynd, The Giant Killers.*

Fraden, Harlow, b.c.1930, and **Wepman, Dennis,** b.c.1929, U.S., mur. Harlow Fraden had always been an awkward misfit from his Bronx, N.Y., upbringing onward. His mother's treatment of him alternated between abuse and overindulgence. In the morning, she would tell him he was a sissy whom nobody would ever befriend, and in the evening he slept by an air conditioner while his parents sweltered in the next room. His mother protected him from a fire marshal after he set fire to the apartment one night. His father remained passive.

Fraden's mother had been nagging him to use his chemistry degree from New York University to get a job "like other boys." When Fraden immersed himself in poetry instead, she called him a fairy and eventually kicked him out of the house. With a generous allowance from his parents and the financial help of roommate Dennis Wepman, Fraden was managing. But when he still failed to get a job, the allowance was cut off and real problems in the Fraden family began. Aware that he would get $96,000 in insurance at his parents' death, Fraden and Wepman made plans.

In August 1953 Harlow told his parents he had finally found an appropriate job, and the family gathered for a celebration. The son poured three glasses of champagne, but added cyanide to his mother's and father's drinks. After one toast, the two were on the floor. Shortly thereafter, they were dead. Fraden staged it to look like a suicide, but followed the funeral with a series of extravagant purchases and a string of parties. Detectives became suspicious. Fraden and Wepman had a falling out, and in the end Wepman confessed everything.

Fraden was committed to the Matteawan State Hospital for the criminally insane. Wepman was diagnosed as being mentally ill, but not insane, and was sentenced to twenty years to life in Sing Sing. REF.: *CBA.*

Frampton, Walter, 1871-1939, Brit., lawyer. Assisted E.F. Lever in the defense of Frederick Guy Browne for the murder of Police Constable Gutteridge in 1927, and aided Sir Patrick Hastings in the successful defense of Elvira Barney, accused of murdering her boyfriend in 1932. REF.: *CBA.*

Franc, Max Bernard, 1930- , U.S., mur. On Aug. 25, 1987, a California rancher found a human head and torso alongside a rural highway twenty miles north of Fresno. The head was that of a teenage boy who had dyed black hair which was cut in the current punk fashion, according to the Madeira County coroner. The boy had been shot in the head and had been dead about two days.

Two days later, more body parts were found wrapped in a sheet alongside a guardrail on the Golden State Freeway near Valencia in north Los Angeles County. "Both the torso in Fresno and the body parts in Valencia were mutilated with the same type of instrument, like a chainsaw," reported Sergeant John Andrews of the Los Angeles County sheriff's office. "The way the remains were hacked, it appears to be the work of the same person." At the same time a Los Angeles equipment rental company had reported to local police that one of their chainsaws had been returned with what appeared to be blood and skin tissue on it. On Aug. 29, 1987, Los Angeles police arrested the renter, a California State University professor, Max Bernard Franc, fifty-seven, at his weekend apartment in West Hollywood, and charged him with the murder of the boy whose identity had not yet been discovered.

The arrest shocked the Cal State campus at Fresno where Franc, who was single, had taught political science since 1969. "I find it rather incredible that he has been accused of this," said David Provost, who had once been Franc's department head. "He's a very low-key kind of individual....He was one who was always seeking compromise when faculty disputes arose. He was...a very gentle type of individual."

In another statement, a professor reported that "I saw him about ten days ago on campus. He had finished his summer school course and was upbeat, friendly, chatty. He looked as positive and as constructive as I had seen him in years. Nothing seemed amiss....None of this fits the psychology of the person I know....He's not the kind to blow up. He's more the kind who tries to avoid a sticky situation."

But police investigating the man, who was known as a conservative professor in Fresno, found that Franc lived a double life. In West Hollywood, they had learned that he was a known homosexual voyeur who paid young men to allow themselves to be photographed in sexual poses. A search of his house in Fresno uncovered a large collection of homosexual pornography as well as the ongoing construction of what police believed was intended to be a soundproof room. In Franc's desk at the university, police found a handgun which later, through ballistics analysis, was identified as the murder weapon.

The victim was identified as Tracy Leroy Nute, eighteen, who had followed countless others when he had run away from his Kansas City home in hope of becoming a Hollywood actor. Instead, Nute ended up on the streets of West Hollywood where he supported himself by working as a homosexual prostitute.

The youth had visited the Gay and Lesbian Community Services Center shortly before his murder, reported Youth Services director Gabe Kruks. "He came in on a Saturday, tired of it all. He was seventeen and he wanted help....Underneath Nute's tough street punk image was a sweet kid, but confused. He had not been happy in Kansas City, but he was not happy here." Kruks said he had seen many runaways drift into a life of prostitution. "He was like a kid in a candy store, very naive. He was prostituting for survival, both material and emotional. He needed love and a little security." Instead Nute found Max Bernard Franc, death, and mutilation.

Franc refused to confess to the killing. He told police he had rented the chainsaw to cut up a dead dog that he had hit with his car. Later he admitted that the chainsaw had been used to dismember Nute's body, but he blamed the killing on an acquaintance named Terry Adams. But Adams was never found and, according to Deputy District Attorney Sterling E. Norris, who prosecuted Franc in front of Judge John H. Reid, "Adams is a figment of the defendant's imagination." On June 28, 1988, a jury in Los Angeles Superior Court found Franc guilty of first-degree murder. On July 29, 1988, Judge Reid sentenced Franc to twenty-five years to life in prison, the maximum allowed by California law, which will leave Franc eligible for parole in 2005 at the age of seventy-five. The judge then told the defendant, "You're two different people," and he urged Franc to use his education to help prepare his fellow inmates for life on the outside. REF.: *CBA*.

Francasal Fraud, 1953, Brit., fraud. At the Spa Selling Plate horse race at Bath on 2 p.m., July 16, 1953, an unknown horse which had never run before in Britain won against ten-to-one odds. Francasal's unexpected victory was marred by the fact that the "blower," a telephone link cable system, from Bath to London, had gone out of commission for the first time ever about a half hour before the race. The capital's major bookmakers had been prevented from changing any bets. After the race, it was discovered that the phone cables had been severed with a blow torch. An investigation revealed the biggest betting conspiracy in the history of British horse racing, involving a plan to cheat bookmakers out of £60,000. On July 20, detectives traced the winning horse to stables in Reading, Berkshire. Francasal was found next to another French horse, Santa Amaro, an almost perfect double, and the horse which had won the race four days earlier. Within a short time, investigators turned up the five men behind the conspiracy, arresting Henry George Kately, Lieutenant-Colonel Victor Robert Colquhoun Dill, Gomer Charles, Maurice Williams, and William Rook. On Jan. 12, 1954, all stood trial at the Old Bailey for conspiracy to defraud. The defense claimed that the two horses had been switched accidentally, and there was no evidence to link the defendants with the cutting of the cable lines. A first jury failed to reach an agreement, but the second brought in a verdict of Guilty for all but Rook, who had only purchased the horse after the race and was acquitted. Kately was

given a three year jail term, Williams and Charles pulled two years each, and Dill was sentenced to nine months.

REF.: *CBA; Greeno, War on the Underworld.*

Franceschini, Count Guido, 1658-98, Italy, mur. Born into the Italian nobility, of an old Aretine family, Guido Franceschini developed no particular ambitions throughout a pampered youth and by the time he was thirty-seven, he had accomplished little more than having spent most of the family fortune. Looking about for a suitable young lady to marry with a handsome dowry, family retainers soon presented Franceschini with a pretty thirteen-year-old, Francesca Camilla Vittoria Angela Pompilia, the child of wealthy Pietro and Violante Comparini.

Their properly arranged marriage took place on Sept. 6, 1893, but it was not, according to most reliable reports, consummated. The count and his child bride lived with the Comparini family at Arezzo, but quarrels between Franceschini and his in-laws caused the Comparinis to move to Rome. So intense was their hatred for the abusive count that the Comparinis suddenly announced that Pompilia was not their child after all; the family filed a suit against Franceschini that claimed that since Pompilia was not their child, the dowry must be returned.

The suit dragged through the courts while Franceschini grew more embittered, claiming that he had been defrauded. By 1696 the count's life was further complicated by the arrival in Arezzo of a 24-year-old nobleman, Giuseppe Maria Caponsacchi, a subdeacon in the local church where Pompilia attended mass. She was then about sixteen and attracted to the healthy, handsome youth. Caponsacchi began seeing the girl while the count watched from a distance. His jealousy aroused, Franceschini accused his wife of having an affair with Caponsacchi, and according to later reports, threatened to kill her and her lover.

On the night of Apr. 29, 1697, Pompilia and Caponsacchi fled Franceschini's Arezzo estate in an open cart, heading for Rome. They stopped at an inn fifteen miles outside of the city, in the village of Castelnuovo. In the morning they were greeted by an incensed Franceschini, who had them arrested. Authorities ordered Pompilia to be confined in the monastery of Scalette. Caponsacchi was found guilty of taking a married woman from her home, seducing her, and having carnal knowledge of her. He was banished for three years from Rome and ordered not to leave Civita Vecchia.

Pompilia, it was soon realized, was pregnant and she was ordered to return to the Comparini home where she was under house arrest until other convictions against her, including theft of jewelry and other valuables from the aggrieved count, were resolved in appeal. She gave birth to Caponsacchi's child on Dec. 18, 1697. Count Franceschini exploded when he heard that this dubious offspring might be passed off as his own and the subsequently, his estates might be lost to another man's progeny.

Franceschini hired four assassins and traveled to the Comparini home where, with the four killers matching him knife thrust for knife thrust, he killed his in-laws and mortally wounded the unhappy Pompilia, who died on Jan. 6, 1698. The killers were tracked down, and following torture that brought their confessions, Count Franceschini and the four hired killers were condemned. Guido Franceschini stalled the executioner, however, claiming to be a member of the clergy and appealing to the Pope to commute his death sentence. The Pope, however, refused to grant clemency, and on Feb. 22, 1698, Count Guido Franceschini was beheaded and the four hired killers were hanged.

Browning's great poem, *The Ring and the Book,* was wholly inspired by this love-and-death triangle but exercising literary license, he changed certain facts. He repeatedly claims that Caponsacchi was a priest and this was never a fact. The poet also states that Franceschini was nine years older than his real age of thirty-seven when he first met Pompilia, undoubtedly to present an old lecher, insensitive to Pompilia's needs and to accentuate the youthful compatibility of Pompilia and Caponsacchi. Browning also stated that the count and his killers were tried under ecclesiastical law but this, too, is in error. Franceschini and the others were tried under civil law. Moreover, the trial was held before Marco Antonio Venturini, the vice-governor of Rome, not before Thomati, as Browning's version claimed. Browning's source of information on this case was a series of pamphlets compiled as *The Old Yellow Book*. This information clearly shows the facts which Browning obviously chose to ignore in presenting a great romantic tragedy in his epic poem, thoroughly misrepresenting the actual history of his subject matter, and, sadly, misleading historians and criminologists concerned with this classic criminal case.

REF.: *CBA;* Gest, *The Old Yellow Book;* (DRAMA), Goodrich, *Caponsacchi;* (FICTION), Royde-Smith, *For Us in the Dark;* (POETRY), Browning, *The Ring and the Book.*

Francey, Henriette, b.1858, Case of, Fr., mur. Henriette Francey had been married to Paul Francey for seven years. It was in no way a perfect match. They had little in common. He was nine years her senior and was away on business more than he was home. It was during one of these business trips in 1884 that Henriette murdered Hippolyte Bazard. She initially claimed she shot him in her home because he was trying to rape her. She displayed no regret and, in fact, said she felt that in killing him she had lived up to her duty by keeping herself pure for her husband and small son.

But then it was the prosecution's turn, and Francey was not prepared for the testimony of her nosy neighbor Jules Dupaquet. He convinced the court that from his window across the street from the Franceys' home, he had seen evidence that Francey was having an affair with the local priest, Jules Hernest. Further, Dupaquet believed that Bazard knew of the liaison and was threatening to blackmail Francey if she didn't give in. Francey's maid testified that the morning after the incident, she found the room in disarray. The clock had obviously been bumped and as a result had stopped at a quarter to two in the morning. But Francey said Bazard had tried to rape her immediately upon entering the house, an hour and a half earlier. Next, the maid recalled extinguishing the lamp in the parlor before going to bed. Francey told the court that the light was on, and that was the only reason she had agreed to admit Bazard.

The mood in the courtroom shifted several times during the trial. At first, everyone believed the attempted rape story and considered Francey a heroine. The tables turned after Dupaquet and the maid testified. But revelations about her husband caused the jury to pity Francey. The couple shared nothing but the home, and then only on occasion. Francey was, in fact, driven to her affair with the priest, a man described by all as "sweet and inoffensive." The fact that Francey was compelled to commit murder to escape sexual blackmail demonstrated how desperate she was to preserve her reputation, since being virtuous in the world's eyes was the only distinction available to a bourgeois wife. If this did not excuse what she did, it at least explained it to the jury.

Francey was acquitted of all charges and sent home.

REF.: *CBA;* Hartmann, *Victorian Murderesses.*

Francia, José Gaspar Rodriguez, 1766-1840, Para., mur. For centuries Paraguay had been ruled by the Jesuits. But at the beginning of the nineteenth century, it became a divided country, and was suddenly vulnerable to tyranny. José Gaspar Francia eased into the role of dictator so insidiously that few knew what had happened until he was already absolute ruler. He first got himself elected to the junta, the parliament of Paraguay. He eagerly entertained influential visitors with food and drink, and sold them on the idea that Paraguay needed a strongman. When the time came to elect a First Consul, Francia delayed the voting until he was sure he would win.

In 1814, he asked parliament to make him dictator for a one-year "experimental period." That one year became twenty-six years of Francia's experiments in terror and bloodshed.

Francia demanded that all wealthy men contribute to the national treasury. Most protested, claiming they lacked ready cash. For their opposition, they were arrested, and killed, and their properties confiscated.

Francia also imposed his prejudice by forbidding marriage of the Spanish nobility to anyone but blacks and mulattoes.

When Francia died in 1840, the exhausted populace returned to democracy, which in time proved too feeble to withstand the next absolute ruler, Carlos Lopez. See: **Lopez, Carlos.** REF.: *CBA.*

Francis II, 1544-60, Case of, Fr., mur. The first husband of Mary Queen of Scots, Francis II was a sickly and weak-minded ruler who was rumored to have been poisoned, in part because there had been conspiracies against him by nobles. The military surgeon, Ambrôise Paré, was thought to have caused Francis' death, and Mary herself was another suspect. In the 1920s, an investigation into the case revealed that Francis, who was born with a nose and mouth obstruction that was probably adenoidal, actually died from chronic suppurative inflammation of the ear.

REF.: *CBA;* Thompson, *Poison and Poisoners.*

Francis, Catherine Florence (AKA: **Cecilie Douglas Francis**), b.1857, Brit., perj. In late June 1914, Catherine Florence Francis, fifty-seven, was charged with perjury at the Guildhall Police Court in London. The woman had become friendly with a man whom she alleged had promised to marry her. She had told him her name was Cecilie Douglas Francis, and said she was a widow. He denied promising to marry her and she brought suit against him for breach of promise. During the proceedings, the man who supposedly wronged Francis alleged that she actually was a married woman whose husband lived in South Wales and practiced as a surgeon. Francis swore out an affidavit denying that she had been married as long ago as 1879—she had also falsely given her age as sixteen years younger—and that her maiden name was not Catherine Florence Fowle. Investigators found Francis' doctor alive and well, and learned that she had received a voluntary allowance, which he paid her regularly, after she had brought her suit against the man she said had broken his promise to her. At the Old Bailey, Catherine Francis was prosecuted by Sir Richard Muir, and pleaded guilty. She was sentenced by Justice Avory to six months in the Holloway prison for women.

REF.: *CBA;* Nicholls, *Crime Within the Square Mile.*

Francis, Charles Julius (AKA: **Duc de Nevers**), b.1860, U.S., fraud-perj. By the time authorities in the U.S. and England caught up with him, Charles Julius Francis had become the Duc de Nevers, honors graduate of the National Polytechnic School, lieutenant of engineers, knight of the Legion of Honor, mechanical engineering graduate of the Zurich Polytechnic University, captain of engineers, electrical engineering graduate of the Montefiore University, officer of that academy and Major of engineers for France. His name was said to have been embroidered on the flag of the Regiment of Engineers by special order of the Senate and Chamber of Representatives. He was made lieutenant colonel of engineers and proposed as commander of the Legion of Honor on the same day. In the United States, he was reportedly an honorary member of the Commission on Railroads, Canals, and Harbors, honorary member of the Commission on Bridges and Highways, and corresponding member of the Academy of Sciences, just to name a few. All these accomplishments were fictitious.

Francis eventually tripped himself up in 1903 in London. He fraudulently obtained an automobile under the pretense that he was Charles, Duc de Nevers, son of Oscar, Prince de Nevers, for which he received a sentence of eighteen months of penal servitude. In Chicago, he was arrested for not paying a hotel bill. In New York, he posted bail for a young man picked up for speeding, swearing he owned a certain house which would back the bond. Francis didn't own the land, as the authorities soon discovered. The duke was convicted of perjury and fraud and was sentenced to five years' hard labor at the state prison.

REF.: *CBA;* Train, *True Stories of Crime.*

Francis, Connie, c.1939- , U.S., rape vict. The $2.65 million awarded to singer Connie Francis, thirty-six, following her 1974 rape did not make up for what she lost as a result of the incident.

By 1977, her soundness of mind, her husband, and her career were gone. Just prior to the rape, she had lost her third child through miscarriage, and was trying to forget her problems by continuing her prosperous singing career. Her first engagement after a nine-year hiatus was at Westbury on Long Island, N.Y. Four days into the engagement, she was raped.

Francis sued the owner of the Howard Johnson's motel where the rape occurred, for failing to provide her a secure room. She charged that the locks were defective, lighting was inadequate, and no security personnel were on duty the night of the attack. She originally sought $5 million.

On Nov. 8, she was awakened in her motel room by a man threatening her with a knife. Francis testified before a U.S. District Court jury in New York that the man covered her face with a towel, tore off her nightgown, tied her up, and raped her.

Five years after the traumatic incident, Francis was still visibly upset as she called on Congress to help victims of crime. "The rights of victims of violent crime should be at least equal in importance to the rights of the criminals who commit those acts," she told the Senate Judiciary Committee. REF.: *CBA*.

Francis, John, See: **Victoria**.

Francis, Sir Philip, 1740-1818, Brit., duel. As one of four councillors for the governor general of India from 1774-81, he accused Warren Hastings of official corruption, which led to a duel wherein he was wounded in 1779. He served as a member of Parliament from 1784-96 and 1802-07, and helped impeach Hastings in 1787. REF.: *CBA*.

Francis, Willie, 1947, U.S., mur. May 3, 1946, was the first time Louisiana strapped convicted murderer Willie Francis in the electric chair. He recalled, "They begun to strap me in the chair, and everything begun to look dazey...It was like the white folks watching was in a big swing, and they'd swing away and back and then right up close. When they put the black bag over my head, I was all locked up...with loud thinkin'."

But somehow, the electric chair was not going to kill Francis. The current failed and, for the time at least, young Francis was spared.

He came back with a story that had never been told. For the first time, people could hear what it's like to be executed. According to Francis, "It's plumb miserable."

In May 1947, after a series of attempted appeals and pleas to the State Pardon Board, Francis was sent back to the chair. His lawyer was confident he could manage another stay, but Francis said he was ready to go. Francis sat down in the same electric chair he had sat in one year earlier. This time the current didn't fail. REF.: *CBA*.

Francisco, Cornelius Henry, d.1837, U.S., mur. Cornelius and Mariah Francisco, natives of Erie, Pa., had been married less than a month when Mrs. Francisco was found dead. Physicians soon determined that she had been poisoned to death with laudanum and Francisco was charged with her murder. He confessed the killing, saying that he and his wife had formed a suicide pact because they did not want their love to grow old; however, he lost his nerve after administering the drug to his wife. He was hanged.

REF.: *CBA; Trial, with the Life and Confession of Cornelius Henry Francisco.*

Francisco, Sancho, 1948-76, Mex., drugs-mur. Sancho Francisco, born in Moreles, was one of the leading drug pushers in northern Mexico during the early 1970s, peddling heroin and cocaine through a network of newspaper boys, operating in small communities in the Baja Peninsula. In early 1976, several other drug pushers attempted to move in on Francisco's operations, trying to recruit his newspaper boys to their own networks. Francisco reportedly killed at least twelve of these pushers from April through June 1976, before he was slain on June 23, 1976, in San Vicente by unknown assassins. One report had it that the large amounts of blood found near Francisco's body were from a wild knife fight, in which, surrounded by enemies, he drew their blood before shooting himself in the head. REF.: *CBA*.

Francis Ferdinand (Francis Ferdinand von Österreich-Este) 1863-1914, archduke of Aust., assass. Son of Archduke Charles Louis and nephew of the mighty Emperor Francis Joseph of the ancient Habsburg dynasty of Austria, Francis Ferdinand was the heir apparent of the sprawling Austro-Hungarian empire. This dual monarchy, ruled with the clenched fist of Francis Joseph for decades, was made up of nations and people of many tongues and cultures. In addition to the Austrian people, the empire spread through Hungary and included all the southern Slavs. Among these mixed nationalities were the Serbs and Croats in Bosnia and Herzegovina, southern Slavic provinces controlled by Austria.

By 1914, Bosnia was a hotbed of radicals and would-be assassins led mostly by a Serbian secret organization known as the Black Hand Society or the *Ukendinjenje ili Smrt*, headed by a dedicated Serbian nationalist, Colonel Dragutin Dimitrijevic, chief of intelligence of the Serbian general staff. Dimitrijevic, known by his underground code name, Colonel Apis, had had a hand in the assassinations and attempted assassinations of many European monarchs. Colonel Apis had been responsible for leading the slaughterhouse assassination of King Alexander (Obrenovic) of Serbia and his wife Queen Draga in 1903. He had long been planning to rid Serbia of Austrian control through the assassination of Archduke Francis Ferdinand.

Francis Ferdinand von Österreich-Este typified the unyielding, unbending autocrat. He was the elegant, imperial prince of the House of Habsburg, who came in line for the Austrian throne in 1896. His uncle, the stern Emperor Francis Joseph had ruled the old empire since 1848. He had no son and his brother Maximilian von Habsburg had become embroiled in a crazy imperialistic scheme of Napoleon III, in which Maximilian was persuaded to take over Mexico with French military support, an ill-starred plan that ended when Maximilian was executed by troops under the command of the Mexican liberator, Benito Juarez.

Francis Joseph did have a son later, Crown Prince Rudolf who developed a secret love affair with Baroness Marie Vetsera and who, knowing Francis Joseph would never approve of the marriage, killed his lover and himself in 1889 at the royal hunting lodge in Mayerling. The house of Habsburg's royal line continued to extinguish itself. Next in line for Francis Joseph's throne was the Archduke Charles Louis, a Jesuit-trained religious zealot who traveled to Jerusalem and there insisted upon drinking Jordan water, against the advice of his aides. He promptly died of typhoid, and his son, Francis Ferdinand became the heir apparent.

As a child, the archduke was trained by tutors in the concepts of ruling by Divine Right and he was highly influenced at an early age by military instructors. At the age of fourteen, he was commissioned a lieutenant in the Austrian army. At the age of twenty-eight, Francis Ferdinand was a major-general. He toured the world and later wrote a book about his travels. He was a hunter and prided himself in shooting a thousand stags by the age of thirty-three, five thousand by the age of forty-six.

In 1900, the archduke fell in love with Countess Sophie Chotek von Chotkova, the daughter of an obscure Czech noble. Sophie was a lady in waiting to Princess Isabella, cousin of Francis Ferdinand. She was not a suitable wife for the archduke, the emperor told his nephew, and he forbade the marriage. The headstrong Francis Ferdinand defied the emperor, insisting that he be allowed to marry the woman he loved. Francis Joseph finally relented, but only on the condition that the archduke would be the last of his line to inherit the Austrian monarchy. Francis Ferdinand was forced to renounce the right of his children to inherit the throne. His children, and there would be three children produced in the marriage, had no rank, nor did his wife. Sophie would be a morganatic spouse.

The noble house of Habsburg shunned and mistreated this poor woman. She was snubbed and humiliated through royal court procedures. Sophie could not sit in any royal carriage with her husband, nor could she sit in a royal box where the archduke sat. At royal balls and other official court events, she could not accompany her husband in any procession but had to walk at the

Archduke Francis Ferdinand of Austria.

Francis Ferdinand and wife Sophie at Sarajevo.

The open car in which the Archduke died, 1914.

Assassin Gavrilo Princip, at right, held by guards, moments after the killing of Francis Ferdinand.

end, discreetly behind the last princess of Habsburg blood. This treatment of his wife embittered Francis Ferdinand. His disposition had already turned sour after he contracted pulmonary tuberculosis while in his twenties. At that time, his death was predicted, but he survived, only to be subject to violent fits of temper. Some court officials whispered that the archduke had gone insane because of this crippling disease, but no such condition existed.

In addition to being a pronounced religious bigot and a virulent anti-Semite, Francis Ferdinand disliked and denounced the Serbians, considering them part of a hostile Magyar race bent on the destruction of the Habsburgs. Where the Serbian nationalists sought to unify all of the southern Slavic provinces in a large national Slavic state, Francis Ferdinand, as well as his iron-willed uncle, the Emperor Francis Joseph, were bent on subduing these unruly provinces. (Except that Austria would some day have to conquer Serbia and bring this hostile country dragging and screaming into the Habsburg fold, if need be.)

At first, Francis Ferdinand displayed a liberal bent toward the Serbo-Croatian movement for Slavic unification. He spoke about the possibility of allowing these countries and the southern Slavic provinces under Austrian domination to have the kind of autonomous governments as Hungary, separate from direct Austrian control, but still dominated by the Habsburgs. But as the Serbians grew more hostile and defiant to Austria and spread their nationalistic views to Austrian Slavic states, Francis Ferdinand grew more and more reactionary. The Serbs grew in power after 1912-13, when, after two bloody but brief Balkan wars, the Turks were driven from the area. Bosnia became the center of anti-Austrian movements. The chief revolutionary at that time was Luka Jucic. One of his proteges was Gavrilo Princip, a youth with ardent beliefs in Slavic nationalism. It was this idealistic youth and other naive revolutionaries, who with three bullets, would bring an end to the Habsburg dynasty and hurl Europe into cataclysmic war.

During 1913 Austrian officials, police and military units brutally suppressed all political gatherings in Croatia and Herzgovina. In Bosnia, nationalists were sought in the street and thrown into cells without official charges. This incensed the most zealous in their ranks and a group of them planned to kill Archduke Francis Ferdinand when he arrived in Sarajevo, Bosnia, after overseeing maneuvers of the Austrian army. The Archduke looked forward to appearing in Sarajevo on June 28, 1914, because it would give him a chance to have his wife appear as his equal, riding with him in an open car at his side. She held the official title of Duchess of Hohenberg but once she appeared with the archduke, she would be recognized as royalty.

Waiting for him in Sarajevo would be a number of eager assassins. This Bosnian capital had been the scene of an earlier attempt on the life of Francis Joseph himself. On June 3, 1911, the emperor visited Sarajevo and standing among the cheering spectators was Bogdan Zerajdic, the 23-year-old son of a Serbian peasant. He had borrowed a revolver from a fellow student who had, in turn, obtained the weapon from the insidious Colonel Apis, chief of the Black Hand Society. Zerajdic hid behind a pillar as the carriage carrying the ancient emperor drove past. Unseen, he aimed the revolver, but inexplicably did not fire. Cursing himself for his inability to murder the old emperor, Zerajdic attempted to redeem himself in his own revolutionary eyes by barging into the offices of General Marijan Varesanin, the Habsburg governor of two provinces. Zerajdic shot Varesanin five times before shouting: "I leave my revenge to Serbdom!" He then sent his final bullet into his head, killing himself on the spot. General Varesanin survived his wounds and his would-be assassin, Zarajdic was dumped into an unmarked grave.

There were many such radical youths in Bosnia at this time, including Gavrilo Princip who had been born in West Bosnia on the farm of his peasant father on June 13, 1884. The parish priest entered the correct birthdate in the parish register, but made the mistake of entering the birthdate as July 13, 1884, in the civil

register, an error that was to save the boy's life years later. It was Austrian law that prevented a criminal being condemned for a crime he committed when under the age of twenty. When Princip shot and killed Archduke Francis Ferdinand his age was checked and the incorrect date written down by the parish priest indicated he was under the age of twenty by only a few weeks. He was, of course, 20-years-old, but Princip, knowing the law, said nothing, and was spared instant execution.

Princip grew up as a shepherd boy, working on his father's land but his mother, a strong-willed woman, insisted he receive proper schooling and he attended school over his father's objections in Grahovo. Although he received good grades, Princip was known to be irritable and sensitive to any kind of insult, real or imagined. He was quick to resort to violence and picked fights, especially with older boys. He did not like farm life and resented his father, a gentle and caring man, who insisted that he put aside thoughts of a higher education and remain to till the land. Jovo Princip, Gavrillo's older brother a successful Sarajevo merchant, thought first to send Gavrillo to the military school in Sarajevo as a cadet. But friends persuaded the brother not to send "a Serbian boy to a Habsburg school so he could later oppress his own people." Instead, Gavrillo attended the merchant's school to become a businessman and trader.

The youth boarded in the home of Danilo Ilic, by then a dedicated revolutionary. After three years of studying and working on his father's farm, Gavrillo Princip had been indoctrinated with the severe political philosophy of Serbian nationalism. He had confused ideas of how to go about bringing all southern Slavs into one nation, but he offered himself as a willing tool to men like Colonel Apis, the underground leaders of the Black Hand Society, and the planners of terrorism and assassination. Princip associated only with other youths who dreamed of performing heroic acts that would liberate Bosnia from the Austrian yoke, although in all their endless political fulminations, the boys never organized a plan of action.

In 1912, Princip tried to enlist in the Serbian army to fight the Turks but was rejected as too small and weak, a rebuff that further embittered him. He neglected his studies and was expelled from school. Princip traveled to Belgrade and lived a hand-to-mouth existence, begging food, sleeping in doorways, avoiding work, and devoting his waking hours to the reading and discussion of anarchism and revolution. The boy continued his studies in the Belgrade high school, using money sent to him by his generous brother Jovo Princip. He shared a tiny room with Nedeljko Cabrinovic, the 19-year-old son of a cafe owner. They shared fanatical beliefs and they spent hours planning how to assassinate Archduke Francis Ferdinand in Vienna. Then friends sent Princip a newspaper clipping from Sarajevo, one which reported that the Archduke would be visiting that city. Princip and Cabrinovic then actively sought more help and recruited one of Princip's boyhood friends, Trifko Grabez.

The three youths began to visit revolutionaries, asking for weapons to murder Francis Ferdinand, boldly telling their plans to anyone who cared to listen. They heard that Milan Ciganovic, a hero in the Serbian-Turkish war of 1912, had returned from the battlefields with weapons. They asked to borrow weapons from him to murder the archduke. He told them that he had none but that he might know of someone who could supply such weapons. Ciganovic then went to the notorious Colonel Apis who listened to Ciganovic's description of the three budding assassins. At first he dismissed the idea of using these youths, but Apis was a realist. He had tried many times to arrange the assassination of the Archduke and the Austrian emperor himself. It was Apis who had sent Bogdan Zerajdic in 1911 to Sarajevo to kill Francis Joseph, an abortive mission.

Whether the infamous Colonel Apis met with Princip and his friends is not known, but his attitude was simply to try anything or anyone who might be successful in injuring the Habsburg monarchy. He gave Ciganovic four Browning revolvers and ammunition, six bombs and some cyanide containers that they must swallow, Ciganovic told them, if they thought they might be captured. Apis, of course, did not really believe that the youths would ever get anywhere near the Archduke. The proof of this was that the cyanide containers held no cyanide, only a harmless watery substance. If Apis and his sophisticated assassins in the Black Hand Society really believed Princip and his conspirators had a chance to kill Francis Ferdinand, the cyanide containers would have contained the authentic poison. They would have wanted the boys to have committed suicide so as not to lead them through interrogation back to the source of their weapons, the Black Hand Society and the scheming Colonel Apis.

After Apis gave Ciganovic the weapons, one account has it, an aide turned to the head of the Serbian Secret Service and asked him why he was entrusting such an important mission to a group of untrained boys. Replied Apis: "They are novices, certainly, but there is an outside chance that they just might blunder into a success. We might as well give them a try at it as any other." No one was more surprised than catalyst Apris, to learn a short time later that Princip, a nonentity, had achieved what every assassin in Bosnia had waited a lifetime to do, murder the heir to the Habsburg throne.

Princip, Cabrinovic, and Grabez spent the next week practicing with their Browning revolvers, target shooting in the Kosutujak Park in Belgrade, which was empty at dusk. The three boys practiced shooting while standing still and then as they ran past their targets so that they felt they were reasonably good marksmen within a short span of time. They then planned to leave for Bosnia, but they had no money to travel to Sarajevo. Princip pawned his winter coat but this brought only a few dinars, enough for a few days' food. Again, the boys went to Ciganovic and he, in turn, went to Colonel Apis. The spy master reluctantly went into the treasury of the Black Hand Society and withdrew traveling funds for the would be assassins. Then, to make sure that the youths carried out their mission, he assigned two of his aides to guide the three revolutionaries across the border. One of these aides, Tankosic, actually escorted the boys all the way to Sarajevo to make sure that they used the Black Hand funds properly.

The day fixed for the arrival in Sarajevo of Archduke Francis Ferdinand could not have been more inappropriate. June 28 was the anniversary of the battle of Kossovo Poyle, fought and lost by Serbia in 1389. This Serbian defeat later led to the establishment of fierce Serbian nationalism, and a national holiday to victorious Bosnia, who then represented the monarchy that controlled the Austrian province. Serbians in Bosnia celebrated this day as the Feast of St. Vitus, which symbolized the Serbian triumph over the Turkish empire. All Bosnian nationalists aligned with Serbia on this day since Serbia had since broken with Austria and it was that country which represented the promise of Slavic unity.

When Princip, Cabrinovic, and Grabez arrived in Sarajevo, they were taken in by Princip's old schoolmate, Ilic, who hid the weapons and bombs beneath Princip's bed. Ilic, who had sent the newspaper clipping reporting the archduke's arrival to Princip in Belgrade, now took active command of the assassination. The 24-year-old Illic brought three more conspirators into the plot, Mohammed Mehmedbasic, a Moslem who had been tortured by associates of Leon Trotsky in France and who had, in 1913, thought to assassinate General Oskar Potoriek, military governor of Bosnia. He had been given guns and bombs by Trotsky's friends in France but, on the way to Potoriek's headquarters, Mehmedbasic grew faint-hearted and dropped the weapons and bombs out of the carriage in which he was traveling. He would now make up for that lack of character, he said. He would join Ilic, Princip and the others. Illic then enlisted two school boys, Cvetko Popovic, a member of a right-wing Bosnian nationalist group, and Vasco Cubrilovic, a 17-year-old student looking for heroic action. Ilic thought that if Princip, Cabrinovic, and Grabez failed in their attempt on the archduke's life, he would use the other three to complete the task.

Ilic himself was a confused youth full of contradictions. He delivered hortative political speeches to his six conspirators each

night in Princip's room, urging them to remain loyal to their cause. Ilic was then racked with doubt and took the weapons and bombs in a box to a train station. He placed the box on a seat, hoping authorities would find them and then took a train from Sarajevo, going more than 100 miles until his nerve returned. It brought him back to the station the next day where the box had remained unmolested, the station cat sleeping on top of it. He took the weapons and bombs back to his home and placed them once more beneath Princip's bed. Ilic then received a message from Colonel Apis, who expressed serious doubts about the feasibility of the assassination plan. Ilic panicked and tried to persuade Princip and the others to abandon the murder scheme. Princip, however, was unswerving.

Princip and his friends were amateurs, none with criminal records and all temperate in their lifestyles. Princip, who took a job to pay his way at this time, later stated: "I went around with chaps who liked to drink, but this was only so as to arouse no suspicion. They were people incapable of a great idea." To Princip, most of his peers were uninformed dolts who thought to do nothing better with their lives than while away the hours in pubs, drinking, singing, wrenching. He, Gavrillo Princip, would have to save their futures by ridding Bosnia of Austrian rule.

The object of his hatred, Archduke Francis Ferdinand, and his wife, Sophie, arrived at Ildize Spa on June 25, 1914, each traveling separately for safety, to the exclusive resort which was located a few miles south of Sarajevo. General Potiorek was on hand to welcome them and to conduct them the following day to review elite Austrian troops who were on maneuvers in the area. The couple would be celebrating their fourteenth wedding anniversary on the day they entered Sarajevo. Francis Ferdinand was counseled that there might be trouble, that an assassination plot had been rumored. He at first dismissed this as a standard hazard without grounds, but he later asked his wife not to accompany him in the parade through Sarajevo, telling her that he feared for her safety. Sophie told the archduke that if he were in danger, she insisted on being at his side to share his fate.

The route the royal couple was to take was along Sarajevo's Appel Quay, their large limousine traversing this roadway twice, first to the town hall to enjoy a formal reception at the town hall, then to motor about Sarajevo on a brief sight-seeing tour, then to the governor's Palace for lunch. This would be followed by brief visits to the museum, the mosque and army headquarters. This route was well publicized and Ilic stationed his six assassins along a 300-yard area along the Appel Quay which ran alongside the River Miljacka. Just as the archduke and his wife were boarding a train to take them into Sarajevo on the morning of June 28, 1914, Illic positioned his men, first Mehmedbasic armed with a bomb at the Cumuria Bridge. Then Vasco Cubrilovic, who had a bomb and a Browning revolver, was stationed, then Cabrinovic armed with a grenade, then himself and Popovic with Browning revolvers, then Princip with a Browning revolver, was stationed near the Lateimer Bridge and then Grabez. The last of the conspirators was positioned at the end of the quay with a bomb. They were ready. There was a pronounced absence of troops in Sarajevo that day. Francis Ferdinand had ordered his crack divisions to stay out of the city to avoid intimidating the population. He was to be escorted only by a small elite guard.

The archduke's train arrived in Sarajevo to the blare of a welcoming band. Six long touring cars awaited Francis Ferdinand and his entourage. The Habsburgs looked plump and elegant in their fine attire, the archduke in his full general's uniform and a hat with green plumes. Sophie wore a white silk dress with a red sash, a huge picture hat and a cape with ermine tails. She carried a parasol to fend off the hot June sun. The Habsburgs sat in the back seat of the second car as the caravan moved off slowly down the street, heading for the Appel Quay. The streets were festively decorated with the Austrian flag and the Bosnian colors of red and yellow. Small portraits of the archduke adorned lampposts, and the crowds seemed receptive to the royal guests, many waving and some cheering as the archduke and Sophie passed them.

As the caravan proceeded past the Cumuria Bridge, the first conspirator, Mohammed Mehmedbasic, fumbled with the bomb he was to throw, but as in the past with his plans to murder General Potiorek, he quickly lost his resolve. Mehmedbasic froze, later claiming that it was impossible to hurl his bomb since a policeman was standing right next to him in the crowd. Cubrilovic also froze. He later said he could not bring himself to shoot at the archduke or throw his bomb with the Duchess Sophie in the car, saying that he was not a "butcherer of women." But Cabrinovic did not freeze. He spotted the archduke's green plumed hat and used it as his target. (One story had it that the assassin actually asked a policeman which car held the archduke and the officer obligingly pointed out the correct car.) Cabrinovic knocked the pin out of his grenade by tapping it against a lamppost and then hurled the grenade, aiming at the green plumes on the hat of the archduke. The grenade struck the back of the folded hood behind Francis Ferdinand. Some accounts say that he saw the grenade as it was about to strike the car and, to protect his wife, raised his arm, deflecting the grenade, which then rolled in front of the car following the royal limousine and exploded.

The third car was damaged and splinters flew in all directions, injuring several spectators as well as a number of the entourage in the car, including Count Boos-Waldeck, Colonel Erik von Merizzi, and Countess Lanjus, Sophie's lady-in-waiting. The archduke said nothing, not wanting to frighten his wife as his car and the lead car sped up and then almost came to a dead stop when the chauffeurs realized what had happened. Sophie's cheek had been bruised by a small flying splinter, but it had not broken the flesh and she did not complain of any pain. Cabrinovic, the bomb thrower, suddenly dove into the River Miljacka, but the water was shallow and he could not drown himself. Security men ran down the embankment after him and he quickly mouthed the cyanide container Apis had given the assassins. It failed to do anything but burn the roof of his mouth. He was vomiting up its contents when security men grabbed him.

"Who are you?" one of the plainclothes detectives asked Cabrinovic.

He smiled grimly and then said proudly: "A Serbian hero!" He was hustled off to a jail cell.

By then the first car of the archduke's caravan had leaped forward, speeding toward the town hall. Most people in the crowds along the Appel Quay were unaware of the grenade's explosion since the cheering had increased and the roar of the crowd had muffled the explosion's noise. The first car, containing the chief of police and Mayor Fehim Effendi Curcic, who were oblivious to the explosion, raced on to the town hall to conduct official welcoming ceremonies. The second car, containing the archduke, was halted by Francis Ferdinand, who sent an aide back to the third car to determine the damages. When he was told that no one had been killed, he ordered his chauffeur to drive on "at all speed" to the town hall.

As the first, and then the second car, gathered speed, Ilic and Popovic were taken by surprise as the cars sped past them, and they did nothing. Neither did Princip nor Grabez. Princip was dazed by the lightning events, first believing that the archduke had been killed by Cabrinovic's grenade. When he realized that the attempt had failed, he stood for a moment at the Appel Quay, then crossed the embankment to Francis Joseph Street. He sat down at a small table at an outdoor cafe and ordered a cup of coffee. Inside his coat pocket still rested his unused Browning revolver.

Meanwhile, the royal couple went on to the town hall. There, unaware of what had happened, Mayor Curcic began to address the dignitaries assembled before the apparently unruffled archduke and Duchess Sophie. Francis Ferdinand grabbed his arm and said: "Mr. Mayor, what is the good of your speeches? One comes here for a visit and is received with bombs. Mr. Mayor, what do you say? It is outrageous! All right, now you may speak."

Mayor Curcic had no idea what the Archduke was talking about and a ridiculous wide smile clung to his pudgy face. He thought the archduke was joking, but was confused. Sophie whispered to her husband that she was all right and that the ceremonies should continue. The archduke was fearful, but he put on a good face and stepped to a podium following the mayor's speech to state: "I assure you of my unchanged regard and favor." He then sent Emperor Francis Joseph a wire which briefly reported the bomb-throwing incident, but he reported that he and his wife were unhurt.

The reception followed, where Sophie graciously received and chatted with the wives of Muslim notables while the archduke chatted with Bosnian dignitaries, appearing unconcerned. He then took General Potiorek aside and grimly joked about expecting "more bullets later." He asked whether he thought there might be a second attack against him. Potiorek told him that such an attempt was unlikely, that the man who had thrown the bomb was under arrest and appeared to have no confederates. The archduke then remarked: "Hang him as quickly as possible or Vienna will give him a decoration," meaning that his political opponents in Vienna would applaud the attack. Potiorek urged the archduke, for the sake or the royal image, to put on a staunch face and continue the program. Francis Ferdinand, however, insisted that he put off the regular schedule and that he motor to the military hospital where he could visit his military aides who had been wounded.

The Archduke told Sophie that he did not want her to accompany him on the rest of his tour but the duchess adamantly replied: "No, I must go with you." The royal cortege got back into the cars. Their route to the military hospital, according to the archduke's own instructions, was to follow the Appel Quay, which had now been cleared of spectators so that the cars could move rapidly to their destination. Again, the mayor's car would lead the way, followed by the archduke's car. Sitting next to the driver of the car carrying Francis Ferdinand and Sophie was the arch-duke's top aide, Count Ferdinand Harrach. He turned in his seat and said to General Potiorek, who sat in the back facing the royal couple: "Has not your Excellency arranged for a military guard to protect his imperial highness?"

Indignant at this question, General Potiorek swiveled about and snapped: "Do you think Sarajevo is full of assassins, Count Harrach?"

Harrach was not to be put off. He expressed genuine fears for the safety of the royal couple and he offered to stand on the left running board of the car to shield the couple from any further attacks. He began to swing open the car door and take this position when Francis Ferdinand motioned him back into his seat, saying: "Don't make a fool of yourself."

The motorcade drove off, and just beyond the town hall, at the Imperial Bridge, passed Grabez, who saw the archduke's car heading into crowds that were still gathering along the Appel Quay. He thought for a moment of throwing his bomb, but was afraid he might kill innocent spectators who were now surrounding the cars of the motorcade and slowing them down. Grabez ran home to his room to hide. At the corner of the Appel Quay and Francis Joseph Street, the chauffeur of the royal couple's car suddenly turned onto Francis Joseph Street, the route that had already been cancelled. General Potiorek shouted: "What's this? We've taken the wrong way!" The driver hit the brakes and tried to turn about but the crowds behind the car were swelling and causing the driver to bring the car to a crawl. It was idling for some moments right in front of Moritz Schiller's cafe and delicatessen, where Gavrillo Princip was sitting, sipping his coffee. He was only five feet from his targets, the royal couple.

"I recognized the heir apparent," Princip stated within an hour of the assassination. "But as I saw that a lady was sitting next to him, I reflected for a moment whether I should shoot or not. At the same moment I was filled with a peculiar feeling and I aimed at the heir apparent from the pavement—which was made easier because the car was proceeding slower at the moment. Where I aimed I do not know. But I know that I aimed at the heir apparent. I believe I fired twice, perhaps more, because I was so

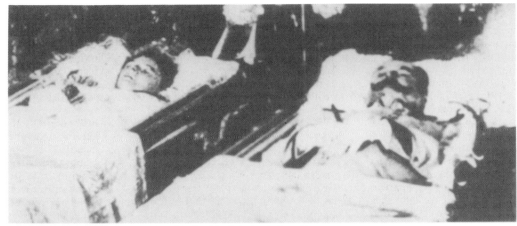

Francis Ferdinand, right, and his wife, Sophie, left, in their coffins.

Assassin Gavrilo Princip.

The Archduke and his family.

Left to right, Cabrinovic, Ciganovic, and Princip.

Some of those imprisoned for the Sarajevo assassination of Francis Ferdinand, June 28, 1914.

excited. Whether I hit the victims or not, I cannot tell, because instantly people started to hit me."

At the moment the car idled in front of the cafe, Princip stood up like an automaton and advanced on the unprotected car while drawing his Browning revolver from his pocket. He aimed without obstruction at the archduke. Just as Princip raised his weapon to fire, a policeman spotted the assassin and rushed at him, but an unemployed actor named Pusara leaped forward and shoved the policeman away, allowing Princip to get off his shots. He fired three shots, which made small popping sounds as if the gun contained blanks. The policeman regained his balance and dove for Princip, who was turning to flee. At that moment, another man, Ferdinand Behr, voluntarily stepped forward and punched the policeman in the stomach, allowing Princip to escape momentarily. He did not run, however, but stood as if in a stupor next to the car, which began to inch away from him. Princip raised the revolver again, perhaps to shoot himself, it was not clear. At that moment, another man, named Velic, knocked the revolver from Princip's hands and the assassin was then pummeled, punched, and kicked by spectators who swarmed in on him. Policemen and military officers wedged through the milling, scuffling crowd and, grabbing Princip, hustled him to safety.

Inside the royal car, General Potiorek stared puzzled at the royal couple, who stared straight ahead. Both had been shot and, apparently trying to hide their wounds from each other, said nothing for some moments as the car picked up speed. Princip's first shot had smashed through the car door and had entered Sophie's abdomen. The second shot, fired at a higher level, ploughed into the high military collar worn by the archduke, cutting the jugular vein and lodging in his spine. Suddenly, blood shot from the archduke's mouth in jets, splattering the uniform of General Potiorek, who sat dumbfounded by the scene.

"For God's sake," Sophie cried, "what has happened to you?" She sank sideways, slipping to her knees in the car, her head sliding across the archduke's chest and into his lap.

Francis Ferdinand cradled her head and cried out: "Sophie dear, Sophie dear, don't die! Stay alive for our children!" But by then the Duchess Sophie was dead in his arms. The archduke himself began to sag forward, blood now jetting from his neck wound. General Potiorek and Count Harrach, who had climbed into the back seat area, held the archduke.

"Are you suffering, your highness?" asked Hassach.

"It is nothing, it is nothing, it is nothing," he said, and then died.

The royal couple arrived dead at the hospital at 11 a.m. An hour later, Princip was taken before an examining magistrate, Dr. Leo Pfeffer. Wrote Pfeffer later: "It was difficult to imagine that so frail-looking an individual should have committed so serious a deed. Even his clear, blue eyes, burning and piercing but serene, had nothing cruel or criminal in their expression. They spoke of innate intelligence, of steady and harmonious energy. When I told him that I was the investigating judge and asked if he had strength to speak, he answered my questions with perfect clearness and in a voice which grew steadily stronger and more assured."

Princip was informed that he had killed the archduke and his wife, and was formally charged with murder. "I acknowledge it and do not complain but I am sorry that I have killed the Duchess of Hohenberg, for I had no intention of killing her." He then began to talk openly, the very thing that Colonel Apis and his Serbian henchmen of the Black Society had feared. Princip stated: "I aimed specifically at the archduke because he...is an enemy of the Slavs in general but especially of the Serbs."

By identifying his loyalties, Princip had given cause to open war between Austria and Serbia. At his trial a short time later, Princip became even more specific in detailing his motives, expressing a philosophy which could have been written in the Belgrade offices of Colonel Apis. Said Princip: "I do not feel like a criminal because I put away the one who was doing evil. Austria as it is represents evil for our people and therefore should not exist...The

political union of the Yugoslavs was always before my eyes, and that was my basic idea. Therefore it was necessary in the first place to free the Yugoslavs...from Austria. This...moved me to carry out the assassination of the heir apparent, for I considered him as very dangerous for Yugoslavia."

The trials of twenty-five Serbians were held between Oct. 12-27, 1914. Ilic was arrested and tortured, confessing everything he knew, including his contact with the Serbian Black Hand Society. The link between the assassins and Serbia was firmly established and the Austrian government soon moved to declare war on Serbia. Ilic and two others were executed. Princip, who was thought to be under the legal age for execution, was given twenty years in prison. Cabrinovic and Grabez were also sentenced to twenty years. Cubrilovic received sixteen years in prison and Popovic was sentenced to thirteen years. Cabrinovic and Grabez died of malnutrition and tuberculosis in prison by 1916, while the world war they helped to create raged on. Princip also contracted tuberculosis and the disease rotted one of his arms so badly that it had to be amputated. He lingered, half-starved, in a windowless cell, until he died on Apr. 28, 1918. Authorities entered his cell to find him curled in a tight ball on his hard bunk. On the wall Princip had scrawled the following lines:

> Our ghosts will walk through Vienna
> And roam through the palace
> Frightening the lords.

Decades earlier, the German leader Otto von Bismarck had stated that a world war would erupt some day because of "some damn foolish thing in the Balkans." This was the killing of Archduke Francis Ferdinand and his wife Sophie at Sarajevo. One month to the day of the double assassination, Austria declared war on Serbia and Austrian planes bombed Belgrade the following day. Russia declared war on Austria, then Germany joined with Austria, then England, France, and other countries formed ranks, mobilized their armies and pitched headlong into the bloodiest conflict of the twentieth century to that date. It would end in 1918, months after the death of Gavrillo Princip. The Austro-Hungarian Empire had ceased to exist by then. Princip's dream, that of a united Slavic state, came into existence with the formation of Yugoslavia. The assassin is considered a national hero of that country and a major boulevard in Belgrade is named after him.

Archduke Francis Ferdinand was buried with full military honors in Vienna with his crest and military insignias, all the regalia of rank and royalty surrounding his ornate coffin. His wife Sophie remained, in death, a pariah to the throne. Her coffin, plainer than her husband's, was placed at a lower level on the funeral bier to signify that she had no station even in death. On her coffin was placed a pair of white gloves and a black fan, symbols of a lady-in-waiting. The arch planner of these deaths, Colonel Apis, would himself be executed by his own Serbian masters in 1917, after Serbia's fortunes had soured and he was blamed for bringing ruination upon his country by arming a group of schoolboys to kill an archduke. See: **Alexander I (Obrenovic); Black Hand Society; Dimitrijevic, Dragutin.**

REF.: Baerlein, *The Birth of Yugoslavia;* Bell, *Assassin!;* Bornstein, *The Politics of Murder;* Buraneli, *Spy/Counter-Spy;* Byrnes, *Yugoslavia; CBA;* Dedijer, *The Road to Sarajevo;* Edwards, *A Wayfarer in Yugoslavia;* Gordon, *The Austrian Empire;* Harrison, *The Soul of Yugoslavia;* Hurwood, *Society and the Assassin;* Hyams, *Killing No Murder;* Jelavich, *The Balkans;* Kann, *The Multinational Empire;* Laffan, *The Serbs, Guardians of the Gates;* Laquer and Mosse, *Nineteen-Fourteen: The Coming of the First World War;* Macartney, *The Habsburg Empire, 1790-1918;* May, *The Passing of the Hapsburg Monarchy;* Melville, *Famous Duels and Assassinations;* Nash, *Almanac of World Crime;* Paine, *The Assassin's World;* Pearl, *The Dangerous Assassins;* Rowan and Deindorfer, *Secret Service: 33 Centuries of Espionage;* Seton-Watson, *Sarajevo;* ____, *The Southern Slav Question and the Hapsburg Empire;* Steed, *The Hapsburg Monarchy;* Stoyan, *World Without End;* Strauss, *The Desperate Act: The Assassination of Franz Ferdinand at Sarajevo;* Sugar, *The Industrialization of Bosnia-Herzgovina;* Tapié, *The Rise and Fall of the Habsburg Empire;* Temperley, *History of Serbia;* Terraine, *The Great War, 1914-1918;* Tschuppik, *The Reign of the Emperor Franz Josef;* Tuchman, *The Guns of August;* ____, *The Proud Tower;* Vucinich, *Serbia Between East and West;* Waring, *Serbia;* West, *Black Lamb and Grey Falcon: A Journey Through Yugoslavia;* Williams, *Heyday for Assassins;* Wolff, *The Balkans in Our Time;* Zeman, *The Break-up of the Habsburg Empire;* (FICTION), Graham, *St. Vitus' Day.*

Frank, Hans, 1900-46, Ger., war crimes. A lawyer, the overweight Hans Frank joined the Nazi Party in 1927 upon graduation from law school and became a Hitler toady and the legal brains behind the party. Though he was intellectually involved with literature and music, these were only superficial interests. Frank hungered for power as did his fellow Nazis and was rewarded by Adolf Hitler in 1933 for his fanatical devotion to the cause when Hitler took power in Germany. He was made minister of justice in Bavaria and then president of the Academy of Law and the German Bar Association. On Oct. 12, 1939, Frank was made governor general of Poland and supervised a ruthless regime which carried out endless and unspeakable atrocities, particularly the mass murder of Jews.

German war criminal Hans Frank, hanged in 1946.

Frank wrote thirty-eight volumes of diaries which were later turned over to the Allies during his Nuremberg trial. In these self-condemning documents, Frank brazenly made such statements as "The Poles shall be the slaves of the German Reich." He was assigned the task of eliminating the intellectual class of Poland and thereby rendering the country leaderless. From his all-revealing diaries, there is no doubt that Frank relished his ugly chore. It was later estimated that he personally selected 3,500 Polish intellectuals for arrest and execution in concentration camps.

Though Frank insisted at his trial that the SS and the Gestapo were responsible for the mass extermination of millions of Jews and that he had no control over these organizations, his public statements during the time of his regime in Poland had been well recorded and indicated his support and participation in these mass murders. On Oct. 7, 1940, Frank addressed an assembly of Nazi Party chiefs in Poland, stating: "I could not eliminate all lice and Jews in only one year. But in the course of time, and if you help me, this end will be attained." In Krakow the following year, he closed a cabinet meeting with the words: "As far as the Jews are concerned, I want to tell you quite frankly that they must be done away with in one way or another...Gentlemen, I must ask you to rid yourselves of all feeling of pity. We must annihilate the Jews."

At his trial in Nuremberg, Frank was alternately repentant for his crimes and filled with self-justification. His defense followed the same as the others. He was merely following orders and was not responsible for issuing the orders of persecution and mass murder. His actions indicated otherwise and he was sentenced to death. Frank was hanged on Oct. 16, 1946, in a large death chamber where a scaffold had been erected to accommodate ten Nazi chiefs who had been sentenced to death.

As Frank entered the barn-like chamber, a little smile played on his lips. He had, during his confinement, converted to Catholicism and was now full of atonement. He stood on the scaffold and said in a small voice: "I am thankful for the kind treatment during my captivity and I ask God to accept me with mercy." Frank was the only Nazi to be executed who expressed any kind of humanity. A black hood was then placed over his head and he was then sent through the trap. See: **Himmler,**

Heinrich; Hitler, Adolf.

REF.: *CBA;* Davidson, *The Making of Adolf Hitler;* Fest, *Hitler;* Gilbert, *Nuremberg Diary;* Heiden, *Der Fuehrer;* Höhne, *The Order of the Death's Head;* Neave, *On Trial at Nuremberg;* Orlow, *The History of the Nazi Party;* Payne, *The Life and Death of Adolf Hitler;* Schoenbaum, *Hitler's Social Revolution;* Shirer, *The Rise and Fall of the Third Reich;* Smith, *Reaching Judgment at Nuremberg;* Snyder and Morris, *A Treasury of Great Reporting;* Speer, *Inside the Third Reich;* ____, *Spandau: The Secret Diaries;* Vogt, *The Burden of Guilt.*

Frank, Harry, 1910, U.S., wh. slav. In 1910, young Martha was in love, and overjoyed when her sweetheart, Harry Frank, said he wanted to marry her. But as it turned out, what Frank said and what he did were two entirely different things.

Promising marriage, Frank whisked Martha away, but he did not take her on a honeymoon. He placed her in his brothel in Gary, Ind., and forced her to become a prostitute, all the time writing letters home to her sister saying all was fine. When the woman became pregnant, Frank took her back to a brothel in Chicago to be looked after by the madam. When the madam threatened to take the woman home, he grabbed Martha and placed her in a West Side Chicago bordello. There he repeatedly whipped and beat her.

Through the efforts of the brothel madame, Martha's sister, detectives, and the superintendent of police, the woman was finally found and brought home. Frank was convicted of white slavery. REF.: *CBA;* Roe, *The Great War on White Slavery.*

Frank, J.H.W., prom. 1837, Case of, U.S., mur. J.H.W. Frank was an editor for the Wabash *Mercury* in Indianapolis. He made a bet with John Woods regarding a local election. After the election, the two men fell to arguing and Wood supposedly made an aggressive move toward Frank, who stabbed Wood to death. R.A. Lockwood, a celebrated criminal lawyer of that day, successfully defended Frank in a much-publicized trial, proving self-defense. Frank was acquitted.

REF.: *CBA; Speech of R.A. Lockwood, Esq., Delivered in Defense of J.H.W. Frank.*

Frank, Jerome New, b.1889, U.S., lawyer. Authored the book *Law and the Modern Mind* in 1930. REF.: *CBA.*

Frank, Karl Hermann, d.1946, Ger., war crimes. Former Sudeten German leader in the pre WWII Czech Parliament, and later Nazi protector once said, "In the whole Czech nation, there is not a person who would not hate me or be my enemy." He was hanged in May, 1946, before 3,000 of his countrymen and women.

Among the spectators who cheered to see war criminal Karl Frank executed were seven widows from a village once called Lidice. Frank was largely responsible for the destruction of that village during the Nazi reign, and it was for this and his other heinous crimes that Frank had paid with his life. Other charges against this gray, gaunt man were treason, the murder of 300,000 Czechs and propagation of Nazism. REF.: *CBA.*

Frank, Leo Max, 1884-1915, U.S., (wrong. convict.) mur. The Leo Frank case is one of the most sensational miscarriages of justice in the history of American jurisprudence. Frank was railroaded for a murder he did not commit. Born in Cuero, Texas, in 1884, Frank was an infant when his family moved to Brooklyn, N.Y. He was a quiet, studious youth with weak eyesight that caused him to wear thick-lensed glasses. Frank attended Cornell University, and following his graduation with a degree in mechanical engineering, he became a draftsman with the B.F. Sturtevant Company of Hyde Park, Mass. Six months later he returned to Brooklyn to work as an engineer for the National Meter Company.

Frank's uncle, Moses Frank, was the majority stock holder in the National Pencil Company, organized by New York and Atlanta businessmen for several hundred thousand dollars in 1907 (now Scripto). It was housed in a four-story, run-down brick building located on Forsyth Street in Atlanta. Moses Frank offered the job of superintendent of this new factory to his nephew Leo, who readily accepted. Leo Frank spent eight months in Germany learning about the pencil-making equipment which he would have to test and retest while supervising the Atlanta company's operations. In 1907, Frank moved to Atlanta and took charge.

In 1911, Frank met and married Lucile Selig, whose father was a wealthy manufacturer of detergents and disinfectants. Both the Frank and Selig families were distinguished, cultured, and well-educated members of Atlanta's Jewish community. Frank, though nervous and shy in public, was an articulate and often eloquent writer who was thought of as an intellectual. He was also a workaholic, slaving over company paperwork in the evenings at home and on weekends. He worked long office hours during the week and was constantly trying to improve the quality of lead in the pencils his firm sold. At twenty-nine, he was considered by his employers to be one of the most promising businessmen in Atlanta. To honor this brilliant young businessman, the Jewish community elected Frank president of the B'nai B'rith association. There was never a suggestion of impropriety in anything Leo Frank did.

In spring of 1914, the firm, because it had run out of brass to bind the pencils, had temporarily laid off nine teenaged girls who worked the assembly line, including little Mary Phagan, who lived fourteen miles from Atlanta in Marietta. She was a week from turning fourteen. She arrived at the pencil factory a little after noon on Saturday, Apr. 26, 1914, to collect her back pay. Entering Frank's office, she asked for her pay and Frank handed her an envelope containing $1.20, one day's pay. She asked if the new shipment of brass had arrived and Frank told her that it had not. The girl left his office and Frank settled down to more paperwork at his desk. He later said that a few minutes later he heard a thumping sound but he attributed this to workmen who were replacing rotten planking on the fourth floor of the building. As he worked on a financial report, Mary Phagan was being sexually attacked and strangled to death in another part of the factory.

At 1 p.m., Frank went to the fourth floor and found the two workmen, Harry Denham and J. Arthur White. Mrs. White was also present. She had brought her husband his lunch. Frank said he was going home for lunch and told the workmen he would return at 3 p.m. He left the building, accompanied by Mrs. White. Before she stepped out of the front door, Mrs. White saw a large black man sitting on a box beneath the stairway near the front door. He was Jim Conley, the building janitor. Mrs. White stepped outside with Frank, and Frank locked the front door. He then went home, arriving at 1:20 p.m., according to the maid who served him a light lunch. He took a catnap and then went to watch the parade on Peachtree Street celebrating Confederate Memorial Day. At 3 p.m., Frank returned to the factory, went to his office, and worked until 6 p.m.

As Frank was leaving the factory, his night watchman Newt Lee was about to lock the front door after him when John M. Gantt approached the superintendent. Frank leaped backward, expecting trouble. He had fired Gantt a week earlier because his payroll was one dollar short. Gantt explained that he only wanted to retrieve two pairs of shoes he had left in his locker. Frank permitted him to go inside the building, accompanied by the watchman, Lee, and get the shoes. Both men reappeared within minutes, Gantt holding his shoes. Lee locked the factory door from the inside and Gantt sauntered off while Frank went to Jacob's Pharmacy where he bought his wife a box of candy. He then went to the home of his in-laws, the Seligs, where he was to meet his wife and have dinner.

Frank's encounter with the heavy-drinking Gantt had unnerved him. He called the factory three times that night until he finally got watchman Lee on the phone at 7 p.m. He asked Lee: "Is everything all right?" Lee assured him that there was no trouble at the factory. Undoubtedly, Frank thought that Gantt might return and cause problems, which is why he called, but that call was later used against him in his murder trial. The prosecution claimed the call by Frank was to see if the body of his victim had been discovered.

At 3:30 a.m., Lee, who had traversed the entire building fifteen times during his watch, went to the basement to go to the "colored toilet." He flashed his lantern to a corner where it appeared

someone had piled some rags. When he approached the pile, he suddenly froze. There was the body of Mary Phagan, her long blonde hair matted with blood. A cord used to tie pencils into bundles was tied around her neck so tightly that it had penetrated the flesh. Her tongue protruded black from her mouth and her open eyes had dust on them. Her clothes were torn and she had apparently been sexually molested.

Terrified, Lee first tried to reach Frank at home but there was no answer. Then he called police, sobbing out his report. He knew that he would be the first to be suspected of violating and murdering this innocent white girl. After getting Lee's report at Atlanta police headquarters, Sergeant L.S. Dobbs dispatched Detectives W.W. Rogers, John Black, and J.S. Starnes to the pencil factory to investigate. The three detectives went to the police car in front of the station to find newsman Britt Craig of the Atlanta *Constitution* sleeping off a drunk in the back seat. They took him along on the call and thus provided Craig with the greatest story of his career.

They arrived at the factory in fifteen minutes, and a quaking Newt Lee guided the officers to the basement, shining his lantern on the remains of Mary Phagan. "Great Jesus in the morning!" gasped Starnes. "It's a white woman!" The detectives discovered that part of the head and face had been covered by a makeshift bandage torn from Mary Phagan's petticoat, as if the killer had clumsily tried to conceal the method of his murder. One of the victim's eyes had been blackened as if she had been hit while putting up a fierce struggle. A small gold bracelet on her left wrist had cut into her as if a powerful grasp had forced it inward on the flesh.

Newsman Craig knelt next to the body to retrieve two scraps of paper with notes scribbled on them. The first read: "he said he wood love me and land down play like night witch did it but that long tall black negro did buy his slef." The second note read: "mam, that negro hire doun here did this i went to make water and he push me doun that hole a long tall negro black that hoo it was long sleam tall negro i wright while play with me."

Craig looked up at Newt Lee, a tall, slim black who was so nervous that he almost collapsed and had to be supported by one of the detectives. "Symbolic retribution," Craig said. "Girl, murdered in pencil factory, identifies her killer."

The detectives directed the beams of their flashlights onto the quivering face of Newt Lee who screamed: "It looks like he's trying to put it off on me!" Handcuffs were produced and Newt Lee was arrested on "suspicion." He was taken to jail and locked in a cell.

At 7 a.m., these same detectives arrived at Frank's home to ask him if he knew a Mary Phagan. He could not remember her name. Starnes told him that she had gone to his office to collect her pay the previous day. Frank, half-dressed, said he only knew the girls through their payroll numbers. "I would have to check."

"We'll give you a chance to check," Starnes told him. "That little girl was murdered in your factory yesterday."

Mrs. Frank asked her husband what the police wanted, calling to him as he stood with the detectives at the front door of his house. Replied Frank: "A little girl is dead." He was asked to identify the girl and Frank asked if he could finish dressing and have his breakfast.

Starnes almost shouted at him: "We have a damn murder on our hands and you want breakfast. We're going now. Come on!"

Frank accompanied the officers. He was easily bullied by these detectives, being a nervous man who avoided confrontations at all costs. The detectives had no right, of course, to order him about. They had no warrant for his arrest. This was simply a ploy. They had already identified the body of Mary Phagan hours earlier when one of the girls who worked with her identified the body. Moreover, they knew that Mary had gone to collect her pay from Frank, and they knew what time she had entered the factory. Yet Frank went to the Bloomfield Mortuary and told detectives, after viewing the body: "That's the girl I paid off yesterday." He was then taken to the factory and shown the spot in the basement where the girl was found.

"Do you have any idea who did it?" Frank asked the detectives.

"We've arrested Newt Lee," he was told by Newport Lanford, chief of detectives.

"I'm going to have to tell the owners about this," Frank said, and asked if he could go. Lanford told him he could leave but that they would talk to Frank that afternoon. Later that day Lanford grilled Frank about his movements on Saturday, the day of the murder, asking him to repeat over and over again exactly where he was in the factory when Mary Phagan arrived, and when he left the building. On Monday, detectives brought Frank to headquarters for more questioning, telling him that "Newt Lee has been saying things." Newt Lee had said nothing. He had repeatedly and without changing his story told how he found the body. He never implicated his employer, Frank.

Chief Lanford, who obviously disliked Frank, kept the young man waiting outside his office and then suddenly threw open his office door and stuck out his hand, flicking it contemptuously at Frank, almost shouting: "Come here!" Frank meekly obeyed and Lanford began to grill him about timecards at his factory. Just then, a voice boomed outside Lanford's office, that of attorney Luther Z. Rosser, one of the best criminal lawyers in Atlanta: "That man is my client and I am going into that room! Keep me out and I will get a writ of *habeas corpus!*"

Lanford threw open the door and said: "I didn't know this man had a lawyer. What's he need a lawyer for?"

Rosser ignored the bullying Lanford and turned to Frank, saying: "You make no statement unless I am present." Police Chief John Beavers then appeared in Lanford's office and Rosser told both Beavers and Lanford that the police were acting in a ridiculous fashion, that the Phagan girl obviously fought with her attacker and that if Frank was the killer he would be marked with scratches and bruises. Frank then took off his coat, tie, shirt and undershirt. "Not a mark on him," Rosser said.

Frank volunteered: "This is the suit I wore Saturday. If I had killed her my clothes would be covered with blood."

Lanford said that Frank could have changed his shirt and underwear and Frank said all his clothes were at home and he invited the police to inspect them. The police were fishing, of course, not sure who murdered Mary Phagan. They inspected Frank's clothing. Other detectives smeared what appeared to be blood on one of Newt Lee's shirts found in his shack and confronted the terrified watchman with it. He sobbed that he had not worn the shirt in a year. A city chemist examined the shirt and reported that the stain was not blood at all and had been applied by hand. Meanwhile, detectives sorted through all of Frank's clothes, clean and dirty, taking inventory. They found nothing stained.

Frank was by then composed and ready to go back to work. "I've got to get to the factory," he told his wife after the detectives left his house. "This whole episode has really broken down our production schedules." When Frank arrived at the factory, he discovered that all the women had been sent home. They had become hysterical when one of the factory machinists, R.P. Barrett, a self-styled detective, insisted that he found on his lathe five tiny bloodspots and strands of blonde hair. Mary Phagan had been murdered on the second floor, the same floor where Frank's office was located.

Then police brought Frank in for more questioning and he was asked if he wanted to talk to Newt Lee. He agreed to do this and was brought before Lee, who was handcuffed to a chair. "Newt, you'd better tell them everything you know," Frank said to his watchman.

Lee's face was coated with tears. He sobbed: "Look at me, Mr. Frank. Handcuffed, handcuffed all the time."

Replied Frank: "Well, they've got me, too."

"Before God, I don't know anything," Lee cried.

"If you do," warned Frank, "you'd better tell them or we will both go to hell."

Meanwhile, 20,000 people attended the funeral of Mary Phagan.

The Atlanta press had seen to that. The *Constitution*, the *Journal*, and the *Georgian* vied with each other daily in printing anything sensational about the case. They retold the story of Mary's tragic murder every day in spectacular fashion and gruesome detail. The *Georgian*, a Hearst paper, whipped its readers into a frenzy of vengeance-seeking with such headlines as "Body Dragged By Cord After Terrific Fight," and "Grandfather Vows Vengeance." Its narrative passages offered horror-filled descriptions: "In the room where Mary Phagan was attacked and paid out her young life to the brutality of her assailant, across the floor where her limp form was dragged, down the stairs and down through the trap door into the dirty basement where her body was found."

Other suspects were arrested. John M. Gantt was placed in a cell until his alibis were checked and he was, in the eyes of the police, proven innocent. Gordon Bailey, the black elevator operator in the pencil factory, was also arrested and then released, terrified because of the stigma placed upon him. Frank himself was finally arrested on Apr. 29, 1913, the very day that Mary Phagan was buried in Marietta. A short time later, Frank was charged with murder and scheduled for trial. Newt Lee was kept in a cell, awaiting a separate trial, one that never arrived; he would be freed the day Leo Frank was convicted.

The prosecution was headed by Hugh Mason Dorsey, an underhanded, politically ambitious solicitor general for Fulton County. He hired Pinkerton detective Harry Scott, a detective previously hired by Frank himself, to find out the facts in the case. Scott visited Frank in his jail cell and cleverly pretended to be still working for him. He told Frank that he had to be absolutely sure that he was in his second-floor offices until 1 p.m. The prosecution had the statements from physicians examining the body of Mary Phagan, which fixed the time of death *before* 1 p.m. Frank confirmed to Scott that he, indeed, did not leave the factory until 1 p.m. Next, the police took statements from all the factory workers, which caused janitor Jim Conley to come under police scrutiny.

On May 1, 1913, a factory employee reported Conley washing a stain off his shirt in the factory. Police arrested him minutes later, claiming that he was washing Mary Phagan's blood off his shirt. Conley denied it, saying that he was only preparing to appear before police to make a statement and that he did not "want to go around all those white people in a dirty shirt." He was asked to write down a few lines on a piece of paper so police could compare his handwriting with the two notes left at the murder site. Conley laughed and told detectives: "Boss, I can't write." He added that he could not read either. Conley, of course, could not have written the notes, or at least that is what he wanted the police to believe.

Conley was nevertheless locked up until police could check his claim about being drunk in a saloon on the day of the murder. Mary Pirk, a factory employee, had already accused Conley of murdering Mary Phagan when Pirk appeared before a grand jury on Apr. 28, 1913. Her claim was supported by another factory worker, Mrs. E.M. Carson, who informed the grand jury that she had told Conley before his arrest that he was lucky that he was not in jail and that she also told him that she knew Leo Frank was innocent. Mrs. Carson stated that Conley admitted to her that Frank had nothing to do with the crime.

When Frank heard about Conley's claim that he could not write, he told police: "But I know he can write. I have received notes from him asking me to lend him money. In the drawer in my safe, you will find the card of a jeweler from whom Conley bought a watch on the installment plan and you will find Conley's signed receipt. He can write." Meanwhile, Frank occupied Cell Number 2 in the Atlanta Jail Tower. He had a bunk which hung suspended from the wall by chains, a bare table and chair and a slop bucket. He wore the business suit which he had on when arrested but his wife made sure that he had changes of shirts and underwear. She also made sure that Frank received home-cooked meals each day. He ate in silence and refused to make any statements to Dorsey, who persisted in trying to hammer a confession out of him.

Frank never spoke to his guards and only briefly to his own defense attorneys. On a rare occasion, he said to one of his attorneys, Leonard Haas: "Do you really think they can pin this crime on an innocent man?" Most of Frank's concerns seemed to be centered on the pencil factory and whether the publicity about the Phagan murder had hurt its business. He avidly read the daily newspapers concerned with his own case.

Atlanta police by then were pressured every day by the newspapers to solve the city's "crime of the century." Lanford and Beavers, with the help of the conniving Dorsey, then fabricated a ridiculous story, compelling a local whorehouse madam, Mrs. Nina Formby (or Faby or Fomby, she gave many names), to sign a statement that Frank had been one of her most regular customers, that he craved sex insatiably and that on the day of the murder he desperately tried to get Mrs. Formby to give him a room at her place so he could bring Mary Phagan to the house where she could be revived. When incredulous newsmen asked Lanford why Frank would want to carry a dead girl through the streets of Atlanta in broad daylight with parades going on and the streets swelled with people, Lanford lamely replied: "He didn't know the girl was dead then."

The police, particularly the detectives investigating the Phagan case, pressured and threatened many persons to testify against Frank. One of these was Minola McKnight, the black cook who worked for the Franks. She was threatened by police into making statements against Frank which impugned his honesty and portrayed him as an adulterous husband. McKnight's husband, at that time, was being kept in jail on trumped-up charges, literally as a hostage to her testimony. Yet Mrs. McKnight eventually took the stand to defend Frank, repudiating a damaging affidavit forced from her earlier by the police, knowing full well what was in store for her because she had decided to tell the truth, despite the consequences.

Behind Dorsey's actions and those of the police was Georgia's powerhouse political leader, Tom Watson, an old time populist leader whose hatred for Jews exceeded even his intense hatred for blacks and Catholics. Watson was the "gray eminence" in this tragedy, a southern Cardinal Richelieu, pulling the legal strings from which Frank helplessly dangled. His racist newspaper, *The Jeffersonian,* constantly hammered away at Frank, libeling him regularly as a "lascivious sodomite," a pervert, and a child-killer throughout his long trial.

Watson, by this time, was well aware that many people had pinpointed Conley as the real killer and that Conley had told his own defense lawyer that he had attacked and killed the Phagan girl. But Watson was after bigger game. His attitude and that of his many followers was best summed up in a statement attributed to Watson: "Hell, boys, we can lynch a nigger any time in Georgia, but when do we get the chance to hang a Yankee Jew?" More than any other, this vicious anti-Semite was responsible for the legal persecution and subsequent lynching of Leo Frank.

It was now obvious to police that Jim Conley was becoming an embarrassment to them. They found the notes he had written to Frank in the safe at the pencil factory. Detectives went to Conley's cell and he admitted that he could write. "White folks," the big black man smirked, "I'm a liar." He said that he had lied because he knew they would say that he had written the notes. He went on to say that he was nowhere near the factory on the day of the murder. Detectives ordered Conley to duplicate the wording on the notes found at Mary Phagan's side. He did so and even the untrained detectives admitted that Conley's handwriting and that on the notes were almost identical. On May 24, 1913, Conley called a detective to his cell and said: "I did write those notes. This is the truth. I wrote those notes because Mr. Frank asked me to."

Beavers and Lanford seized on this absurd story to establish evidence against Frank. They had their orders from both Dorsey and the political bigwigs representing Tom Watson. They coaxed Conley into signing a confession, careful to point out to Conley the exact time Frank reportedly ordered Conley to write the notes, at about ten minutes before one, knowing that Frank had witnesses who would testify that he had left the factory by 1 p.m. Conley said that Frank ordered him to write the notes and also to carry Mary Phagan's body from the second floor to the basement, that Frank intended to pin the killing on Newt Lee, the "tall lean black man."

Conley said that Frank had threatened to place the murder on him if he did not do as he was told. Of course, Conley, the real killer, had written the notes, not at Frank's command, but for the exact reason he claimed Frank had told him to the write the notes: Conley murdered the girl and then wrote the notes to pin the crime on Newt Lee, never believing for a minute at that time that he could get away with blaming a white man for his crime.

Dorsey would use Conley as the state's leading witness against Frank. The solicitor general seized on Conley's claim, without exposing his knowledge that Conley had himself committed the crime, which Dorsey learned from witnesses and from Conley's own lawyer. He relentlessly built a fake case against Frank, suborning witnesses and fabricating evidence with the collusion of the police. Behind Dorsey and the police was Tom Watson, directing events from his mansion at Hickory Hill, sending out hundreds of rural anti-Semites who marched around the Atlanta courthouse during Frank's trial, and on occasion into the courthouse, shouting racial slurs and obscenities, demanding during the trial that Frank be hanged and that legal proceedings against "this damned pervert" were just a waste of time and money. They terrorized the jurors with signals such as running their fingers across their throats as if they were razors, indicating that they would kill any juror who did not vote guilty.

The nation's press covered the entire shameful farce, and for the most part, condemned the state of Georgia's tactics. Tens of thousands rallied to Frank's support. A large defense fund was gathered from Jews and non-Jews alike, and the B'nai B'rith came into its own, chiefly with the help of donors to Frank's defense fund, people who were shocked at the medieval treatment Frank was receiving. But in Georgia, the lunatic fringe, at Watson's direction, had taken control. During Frank's long trial, Dorsey and his assistants ignored proper procedures, brushed aside established facts and the trial record itself, and terrorized witnesses and created a nightmare image of Frank as a sex fiend.

Frank's attorneys were hampered and hamstrung at every turn. The trial judge, Leonard Strickland Roan, invariably agreed with the high-handed Dorsey on every point of law. Roan tolerated outrageous behavior on the part of Dorsey. Frank, all the while, sat impassive and without emotional reaction to the horrendous accusations made by Dorsey. He refused to be provoked and was dubbed by the press "The Silent Man of the Tower." He told his wife and few friends that he would measure his statements lest he bring down the wrath of the anti-Semites upon his fellow Jews in Atlanta. In so doing, he limited, even injured, his own defense. He was a man who believed he was living in a civilized society where justice would triumph; he clung to this idea and was eventually murdered for it.

Throughout the trial, Rosser and Haas attempted to conduct their own investigation of the murder, hiring the foremost detective in the U.S., William J. Burns, head of the Burns Detective Agency. He and his assistants were denied information. They were prevented by the police from interviewing key witnesses and were themselves charged with criminal activities. Burns, while checking some court records, was almost lynched by a group of Tom Watson's rabid supporters. One of these Watson advocates was an Atlanta hardware salesman, William J. Simmons, who sat through Frank's trial hooting for conviction.

Simmons later sat in a movie theater to see W.D. Griffith's *Birth of a Nation,* gripping the armrests of his seat in excitement as he witnessed scenes in that movie which showed the long-dormant nineteenth century Ku Klux Klan in action. The film, coupled with Simmons' obsessive hate for Frank, caused him to

Leo Max Frank and his wife Lucille, at the time Frank became president of Atlanta's B'nai B'rith in 1912.

Mary Phagan, the murdered 13-year-old girl.

Tom Watson, Populist leader of Georgia, a rabid racist who whipped up hatred against Frank.

The courageous governor of Georgia, John Slaton.

The reserved Leo Frank at his trial, his wife seated behind him.

Residents of Marietta, Ga., gathered about the hanging body of Leo Frank, lynched in 1915.

lead what he called the Knights of Mary Phagan up Stone Mountain one night in 1915 and torch a huge cross that had been erected there, re-establishing the dreaded Ku Klux Klan.

Conley appeared as a witness against Frank and testified in court that Frank had molested and killed the Phagan girl. With some clever acting that convinced many in the court that he was nothing more than an uneducated Negro, Conley appeared nervous and claimed that he carried the girl's body to the basement and wrote the notes under Frank's orders, saying that he had acted out of fear that Frank, a white man, would arrange to have him charged with the murder unless he did as he was told. Despite a spirited attack, Frank's lawyers were unable to shake Conley from this stance which was, of course, a lie which he used as a shield against admitting his own guilt in the case. Further, Conley brazenly told unsupported lies about Frank bringing whores to his office to have sex, that he, Conley, had seen Frank having sex with women in his office and other areas of the factory, and that Frank had tried to seduce the factory girls in his employ.

Frank's defense counsel was later attacked for mishandling his case. Reuben Arnold, who headed the defense along with Rosser and Haas, was joined by four more attorneys hired by the Franks and Seligs. They and the defendant were all well-dressed, and the Frank and Selig family members sitting nearby were in fashionable, expensive attire. The witnesses against Frank were dressed in simple clothes. Conley, who was the star witness against Frank, wore clothes that were almost rags, attire dictated by the shrewd Dorsey. Frank's natural reticence was interpreted as a sign of guilt, although he did take the stand in his own defense, offering a brilliant lengthy statement in the fourth week of his trial.

Frank told the jury: "I know nothing about the death of little Mary Phagan. I had no part in causing her death nor do I know how she came to her death after she took her money and left my office. I never even saw Conley in the factory or anywhere else on Apr. 26, 1913....The statement of Conley is a tissue of lies from first to last....Conley's statement as to his coming up and helping me to dispose of the body, or that I had anything to do with her or with him that day, is a monstrous lie. The story as to women coming into the factory with me for immoral purposes is a base lie and the few occasions that he (Conley) claims to have seen me in indecent positions with women is a lie so vile that I have no language with which to fitly denounce it....

"Gentlemen, some newspaper men have called me 'The Silent Man in the Tower,' and I have kept my silence and my counsel advisedly, until the proper time and place. The time is now; the place is here, and I have told you the truth, the whole truth." With that Leo Frank left the witness stand. He had impressed the court and moved the jury with his sincere, direct statements but he was battling for a life, his own, which had already been claimed by Tom Watson and his racist fanatics. He was found Guilty.

Before Judge Roan sentenced Frank, he was visited by William Smith, the court-appointed lawyer for Jim Conley. Smith told Roan that his client had admitted not once but many times that he had attacked and murdered Mary Phagan. Judge Roan as much as told Smith that such statements were "inadmissable" in the Frank case since they violated client-attorney confidences. He went on to sentence Frank to death. Frank's lawyers filed an appeal with the U.S. Supreme Court, which denied the appeal, with Justices Charles Evans Hughes and Oliver Wendell Holmes writing strong dissenting opinions. Stated Holmes in part: "Mob law does not become due process of law by securing the assent of a terrorized jury. We are not speaking of mere disorder or mere irregularities in procedure, but of a case where the processes of justice are actually subverted...." Judge Roan had considerable reservations about his own actions. He died a short time later, but before his death he wrote a letter to Georgia governor John M. Slaton, an honest and courageous man. Judge Roan expressed his reservations about Frank's guilt to Governor Slaton.

The governor had by then come to his own conclusion that Frank was innocent and that he had been railroaded by Dorsey,

the police and Tom Watson. Reporters had gone to Slaton with their doubts about Frank's guilt, one of these being a young newsman working for the Atlanta *Journal*, Harold Ross, later founder of *The New Yorker*. Slaton conducted his own investigation through trusted state police investigators and he learned that Frank was innocent and that Jim Conley was the real murderer. Only twenty days before he was to leave office in 1915, Slaton commuted Frank's death sentence to life imprisonment, believing that the true facts of the case would later emerge in a calmer atmosphere and Frank would be exonerated and freed. This was an heroic move on Slaton's part as he knew that Tom Watson and his brutish hordes would react violently.

On the day of Slaton's commutation, Atlanta police also feared violence and urged all Jews in the city to close their shops and stay indoors, or even leave Atlanta. Thousands of Jews left Atlanta by car and train. Hundreds of Jewish children were boarded on trains by their parents while scores of Watson's sneering supporters shouted threats. The reaction to the commutation was like a time bomb going off. Thousands of Watson's followers and the even more rabid members of Simmons' Knights of Mary Phagan (later changed to the Knights of the Ku Klux Klan), heavily armed, stormed onto the grounds of the governor's mansion, some of them barging into the mansion and screaming "Where is that Jew-loving son-of-a-bitch?" Slaton, by that time, had fled the mansion with his family and gone into hiding.

A regiment of horse-mounted national guardsmen wielding swords went into action and for two days the troops battled howling, blood thirsty mobs bent on killing Governor Slaton or any Jews they could find on the streets of Atlanta. There were even cries for the life of Slaton's wife, "a notorious liberal." Slaton escaped the state with his family and remained in exile for years. He had been warned by Watson and his minions, several state officials, not to return to Georgia where he "would be killed." John Slaton knew this would be his political fate when he commuted Frank's death sentence, but this brave man accepted the consequences rather than "let an innocent man be murdered."

Tom Watson then began to lobby for mob action and the lynching of Leo Frank who had been placed in Milledgeville Prison Farm following Slaton's last minute reprieve. There, a berserk inmate, William Green, crept up on Frank's bunk in an open prison barracks and slit his throat as he slept. Frank survived thanks to the quick action of another prisoner, a doctor, who was able to close the wound and stop the bleeding. Twenty-five stitches were used to close up the ugly wound. Watson thought Frank might prove his innocence while he lived so he urged his readers to take the law into their own hands. Green was one of these. When Green failed, Watson called on the Knights of Mary Phagan, led by the racist Simmons, to avenge the death of the murdered girl. It was also Watson who stated in his newspaper that he saw "the invisible power" of these "knights" bringing justice in the Frank case, thus providing Simmons with another title which Simmons quickly reshaped into "The Invisible Empire of the Ku Klux Klan."

Watson then published an article which, in any other state, would have caused his arrest for inciting to riot and murder. In this article, Watson declared: "The next Jew who does what Frank did is going to get exactly what we give to Negro rapists." He had pronounced Leo Frank's death sentence. Simmons and his Knights of Mary Phagan responded quickly to this order, spreading their "invisible power" over Georgia on the night of Aug. 16, 1915. They cut the telephone wires to Milledgeville Prison Farm, then, from Marietta, packed eight cars full of "knights" and drove to the institution.

The first to see the headlights of the cars approaching the prison was trustee J.W. Turner. He rushed up to a guard on duty and shouted: "They are coming for Frank! Get him out the back way!" The guard said nothing, turning away. Turner and another trustee named Bruce, then went to the warden's office, but guards there ignored their warning about invaders coming for Frank and ordered them to return to their barracks. The lynch mob, about twenty-five men, broke through the front gates of the prison farm without opposition from guards. Only three of them were masked. They split into four parties, as if practicing a drill, and began their search for Frank.

One group stormed into the home of Warden Smith and snapped handcuffs on him. A man poked a rifle into Smith's face and shouted: "We have come for Leo Frank. You will find him tomorrow on Mary Phagan's grave. You can come with us, if you want."

"Damned if I go any place with you," Smith shouted back.

Smith was held prisoner as the rest of the prison guards were rounded up and handcuffed. None made any attempt to resist the invaders. Another group, its leaders knowing exactly where Frank was located, ran to a barracks and raced to the second floor. They searched the bunks of sleeping men and found Frank, a large bandage still on his neck covering Green's vicious knife wound. The invaders had been informed of this bandage and used it to identify the man they were seeking. Frank was grabbed by his hair, arms, and legs and yanked from his bed. As he moaned in pain, the invaders handcuffed him and then half-carried him out of the barracks to a waiting car.

Warden Smith had difficulty contacting police in Augusta, since the phone wires had been cut. It took him a half hour to convince state officials and police that Frank had not been rescued by a group of his Jewish friends, but had been dragged from the prison by a lynch mob headed for Marietta. By the time state police began to pursue the mob, the lynch mob had an hour's head start. Sheriffs from several towns in a fifty mile radius put together car posses, the first time autos were used for such purpose in Georgia, and the lawmen began a desperate search for Frank and his abductors. William Frey, an ex-sheriff, was driving down the Roswell Road near Marietta at about 7 a.m. when the caravan of "knights" passed him. He later stated that he thought he saw Frank sitting between two men in the back seat of one of the cars. Frey kept driving in the opposite direction.

A short time later the caravan came to a stop on the Roswell Road next to a giant oak tree outside of Marietta. About thirty men jumped out of the cars, some masked, but most were not. Surveyors working along a nearby railroad track that dawn began to walk toward the group but men in the lynch mob waved them off with pistols. A farmer, Chandler, was driving a team in a nearby field and witnessed Frank being pulled from one of the cars.

Frank was placed beneath the oak tree and a heavy rope was put about his neck. He wore only a nightshirt. His hands were handcuffed and someone knelt to place handcuffs about his feet. Chandler, standing close behind some bushes in terror, heard the following conversation: "Mr. Frank, we are going to do what the law said to do—hang you by the neck until you are dead. Do you want to say anything before you die?" (This was said by the ringleader who was identified as a former Marietta police officer.)

Frank stood coolly staring back at his self-appointed executioners. He said nothing for some moments and then he replied: "No."

Then the ringleader asked a question which belied the purpose of the lynch mob: "We want to know if you are guilty or innocent of the murder of Mary Phagan."

Frank refused to dignify the question of a lynch mob leader. Instead, he calmly held up his handcuffed hands, elevating a finger bearing his wedding ring. He said in a firm voice: "I think more of my wife and my mother than I do of my own life. Would you return my wedding ring?"

A member of the lynch mob slipped the ring from Frank's finger. The ring was later returned to Mrs. Frank through a reporter who said he was handed the ring by a man on an Atlanta street before running off. Members of the lynch mob then placed Frank on a small battered table, tied the end of the rope to a branch of the oak tree, and kicked the table out from beneath him. Frank jerked downward, his body convulsing as he strangled to death. The mob stood silent, watching him die. When his body was at last lifeless, swaying gently from the rope. The mob's

members walked casually back to their cars and drove away.

Farmer Chandler ran into Marietta where a ceremony honoring the slain Mary Phagan was just beginning in the town square. "They got him! They got him!" Chandler shouted to the crowd. First hundreds, then thousands, followed Chandler pell-mell on foot, in carriages, in cars, to the site of the lynching. There the throngs stood to view Frank's pathetic, swaying body. An amateur photographer took two photos showing scores of gaping men, women, and children standing beneath the hanging corpse. These photos were displayed for fifteen years in the windows of small Georgia shops and on postcards sold for a nickel in rural drugstores.

The rage felt by U.S. citizens across the land over the lynching was universally expressed by the press, even in Georgia, but it solved nothing. The members of the lynch mob were never arrested, although most of their identities were well known. On hearing the news, ex-Governor Slaton wept openly. Thomas E. Watson, who had released the forces of human malice, ignorance, and prejudice gave a gloating interview with the press on the front porch of his mansion at Hickory Hill, one in which he commended Frank's killers for meting out "Georgia justice."

Then Watson stepped inside his mansion to meet with Hugh Dorsey, telling his obedient prosecutor: "Hugh, my boy, for what you did for the great state of Georgia, I'm going to send you to the United States Congress. Congressman Dorsey—how do you like the sound of that?" Dorsey loved the sound of it. He served two terms as a member of Congress from Georgia. Then he returned to Boss Watson and told him that he wanted to be a U.S. senator. Watson turned him down, saying that he, Tom Watson, intended to run for that office. He did, beating Dorsey badly, and winning the post. Watson became a U.S. senator from Georgia in 1920. When he died of bronchial asthma on Sept. 26, 1922, none of his fellow U.S. senators sent condolences.

Many years later, troubled with an uneasy conscience, Hugh Dorsey insisted from his deathbed: "Frank was guilty! Guilty! I have the files to prove it!" No such files existed. William Simmons, who had worked so well for Dorsey and Watson, went on to establish his "Invisible Empire" of the Ku Klux Klan, bringing hundreds of thousands to its hooded ranks, a secret and evil organization of hate and prejudice that would dominate southern politics for the next five decades. Following WWI, John Slaton did return to Georgia where he devoted his life to his private law practice. He died in 1955. Two years later the Georgia legislature honored this heroic man by establishing the John Marshall Slaton Memorial, referring to him as "The Incomparable Georgian." Green, the man who slit Frank's throat, was pardoned ten years later by Governor Eugene Talmadge and died a few years later, a sick, old man.

The real murderer of Mary Phagan, Jim Conley, was convicted of being an accessory after the fact to the killing and was sent to a chain gang to serve a year and day. In 1919, Conley was convicted of instigating a riot that caused the death of one man and he was sent to prison for fourteen years. After his release, Conley continued to live in Atlanta where he died in 1962 at age seventy-six. He had confessed to killing Mary Phagan only to his lawyer, William Smith, to his common-law wife at the time of the murder, Annie Maude Carter, and, later, to a fellow convict. Those confessions were pointed out to authorities in Georgia at the time of Frank's trial, but no one acted upon them.

The site of Frank's lynching became a KKK shrine where members of the hooded empire met at night with blazing crosses to celebrate their ugly triumph. The old oak tree was finally cut down and the site now lies buried beneath four lanes of Interstate Highway 75. Frank himself summed up the entire, incredible miscarriage of justice involving a man who came to be identified as America's Alfred Dreyfus. Before being sentenced to death, Leo Frank stood before Judge Roan and said in a calm voice: "The issues at the bar were lost. The poison of unspeakable things took their place."

In the spring of 1982, Alonzo Mann, who had been a 14-year-old black office boy working in the pencil factory, made a statement in which he insisted that, on the day of Mary Phagan's murder, he saw Jim Conley carrying the unconscious body of Mary Phagan from the second floor to the basement of the factory. Frank did not accompany Conley at the time and was not even in the building. Conley told him at the time: "If you ever mention this, I'll kill you!" Mann returned home and told his mother who cautioned him not to say anything about Conley. Mann, at age eighty-five, came forward, saying that he had tried to tell his story many times and as early as 1953 when Conley was still alive but that southern newsmen dismissed his story.

Mann persisted, taking a lie detector test, which he passed, and signing detailed affidavits. "I know deep down in my heart what I saw," said Mann in 1983, "and that Frank did not do this." Because of Mann's statements, the Georgia Pardon Board weighed the new evidence and considered giving Frank a posthumous pardon. "I pray to God that they will give Leo M. Frank a pardon," Mann said at the time. "It would be the Christian thing to do. He did not commit that crime." On Dec. 22, 1983, Georgia's State Board of Pardons and Paroles denied the posthumous pardon.

Board chairman Mobley Howell stated: "After an exhaustive review and many hours of deliberation, it is impossible to decide conclusively the guilt or innocence of Leo M. Frank. There are too many inconsistencies in the accounts of what happened." Jewish organizations, however, continued to petition the Board and, in 1986, the Board reversed itself and granted Frank a pardon, based on the state's "failure to protect the person of Leo Frank and thereby preserve his opportunity for continued legal appeal on his conviction, and in recognition of the state's failure to bring his killer to justice, and as an effort to heal old wounds." Seventy-three years after his legal persecution and lynching, Leo Max Frank had received justice in Georgia.

REF.: Alexander, *Some Facts About the Murder Notes in the Phagan Case*; Arnett, *The Populist Movement in Georgia*; Brewton, *The Life of Thomas E. Watson*; Buck, *The Agrarian Crusade*; Burt, *American Murder Ballads*; Busch, *Guilty or Not Guilty?*; Caesar, *Incredible Detective*; Carter, *The Angry Scar*; CBA; Chalmers, *Hooded Americanism*; Churchill, *The Pictorial History of American Crime*; CBA; Connolly, *The Truth About the Frank Case*; Dinnerstein, *The Leo Frank Case*; Faulkner, *Politics, Reform and Expansion*; Golden, *A Little Girl is Dead*; Gunther, *Taken at the Flood*; Henson, *Confessions of a Criminal Lawyer*; Hicks, *The Populist Revolt*; Higham, *Strangers in the Land*; Lawson, *American State Trials, Vol X*; Logan, *Against the Evidence*; Pfeffer, *This Honorable Court*; Powell, *I Can Go Home Again*; Randel, *The Ku Klux Klan: A Century of Infamy*; Reppetto, *The Blue Parade*; Roberts, *The Story of Mass Hysteria*; Rochester, *The Populist Movement in the United States*; Samuels, *Night Fell on Georgia*; Sutherland, *Ten Real Murder Mysteries Never Solved*; Van Paasen, *To Number Our Days*; Woodward, *Tom Watson, Agrarian Rebel*; (FICTION), Greene, *Death in the Deep South*; (FILM), *They Won't Forget*, 1937.

Frank, Reinhard von, 1860-1934, Ger., jur. Legal writer and jurist viewed as an expert on criminal law. REF.: *CBA*.

Frank, Theodore, 1936- , U.S., child abuse-mur. Although a 53-year-old California man has apparently undergone a "religious reawakening" since being imprisoned for the 1978 torture murder of a 2-year-old Ventura County girl, and though his attorney, Willard P. Wiksell, has described him as a "bright, articulate and sensitive person," Orange County Superior Judge John Ryan has ordered that Frank die in the state gas chamber.

Theodore Frank abducted little Amy Sue Seitz from her aunt's home in Ventura County on Mar. 14, 1978. Her body was found two days later in a remote part of the San Fernando Valley, twenty-six miles from her aunt's house.

The condemned man was born in St. Louis in 1936 and has spent most of his adult life in mental hospitals and prisons for molesting children in Illinois, Missouri, Arizona and California. He revealed in a personal journal that he molested as many as 150 children since the 1950s. REF.: *CBA*.

Frankel, Marvin E., 1920- , U.S., jur. Appointed by President Lyndon Johnson to the Southern District Court of New York in 1965. REF.: *CBA*.

Frankfurter, Felix, 1882-1965, U.S., jur. Professor at Harvard Law School from 1914-39, he championed a number of unpopular cases, including the defense of Nicola Sacco and Bartolomeo Vanzetti, Italian immigrants convicted of murder during the armed robbery of a shoe factory payroll in 1921. Although the two were electrocuted, his support of their appeal greatly influenced his desire to combat prejudice. He wrote *The Case of Sacco and Vanzetti* in 1927.

With James M. Landis, he co-authored *The Business of the Supreme Court* in 1927, and wrote *Mr. Justice Holmes and the Supreme Court* in 1938. He was appointed to the U.S. Supreme Court by President Franklin D. Roosevelt as associate justice in 1939. As a supreme court justice he was an advocate of judicial restraint. He wrote the majority opinion in *Wolf v. Colorado* in 1949, holding that the federal ruling prohibiting use of evidence procured from an illegal search and seizure did not apply to state laws. In *Rochin v. California* in 1952, he authored the majority's opinion which reversed a conviction based on evidence obtained from pumping a suspect's stomach.

He dissented in *Irvine v. California* in 1954, which was based partly on the decision in the Rochin case. The court held that there must be physical coercion involved in order for the evidence to be invalid, whereas, Frankfurter disagreed, stating that the majority misunderstood his earlier decision by placing undue emphasis on the physical aspect of obtaining evidence and not enough on the offensiveness of the intrusion. The Irvine case dealt with planting eavesdropping devices in a residence after breaking into the suspect's home. It is believed that Frankfurter played a key role in the court returning a unanimous decision in the unconstitutionality of public school segregation in *Brown v. Board of Education* in 1955. His decision in *Mallory v. U.S.* in 1957, dealt with the inadmissibility in federal courts of a confession obtained from a defendant during an unnecessary delay between the time of arrest and arraignment.

Writing for the majority in *Bartkus v. Illinois* in 1959, Frankfurter concluded that a defendant's due process of law was not denied by a state that tried him a second time for a crime he had already been acquitted of in a federal court. Dissenting in *Mapp v. Ohio* in 1961, Frankfurter saw his earlier decision in Wolf overruled as the court found that any evidence obtained in violation of a defendant's due process rights afforded by the Fourth Amendment could not be used in a state court. Near the end of his career he wrote the autobiographical *Felix Frankfurter Reminisces* in 1960.

REF.: *CBA*; Logan, *Against the Evidence*; Lowenthal, *The Federal Bureau of Investigation*; Navasky, *Kennedy Justice*; Powers, *Secrecy and Power*; Toledano, *J. Edgar Hoover*; Ungar, *FBI*.

Franklin, Connie, 1929, Case of, U.S., mur. In 1929, the state of Arkansas charged that four "hill barons" had burned Connie Franklin alive, and they brought charred bone fragments into the courtroom as proof. A key witness for the defense claimed that he was Connie Franklin. Tiller Ruminer, Franklin's girlfriend, said, no, he was not, and the men charged with murder, Herman Greenway, Joe White, Hubert Hester, and Bill Younger, said they did not know what anyone was talking about.

According to Ruminer, whose testimony led to the indictment of the four Arkansas men, she and Franklin were going to be married one night when they were attacked by four men. Franklin was dragged toward a camp fire and killed while she was dragged in the bushes and raped. Later, the men confronted Ruminer, told her they killed Franklin, and warned her not to tell. A deaf-mute witness used sign language to support Ruminer's story.

But it wasn't enough to convict. The jury acquitted the four men of murder. REF.: *CBA*.

Franklin, James, and **Weston, Richard**, and **Somerset**, Lord (**Earl of Essex**), and **Essex**, Lady (Countess), and **Elwes**, Sir **Gervis**, prom. 1615, Brit., mur. Four people joined forces in England, in 1615, to murder Sir Thomas Overbury, 34-year-old poet, essayist, and a man who was just trying to be a good friend.

Overbury's friend, Lord Rochester, had fallen in love with the Countess Essex, despite Overbury's numerous warnings of the woman's dubious virtue and sincerity. Dreading continued interference from Overbury, the countess staged a series of traps to stun Sir Thomas. The last trap was set for death.

The countess gathered her closest, most powerful and fiendish friends and together the five, Dr. James Franklin, Richard Weston, Sir Gervis Elwes, the Earl of Essex, and the lady herself poisoned the unsuspecting man. He never stood a chance against the medical expertise of Dr. Franklin and his assistant Weston. It was not until a year after Overbury had died, that anyone suspected anything. But when the suspicions were taken to court, the entire plot was disclosed.

Weston, a man supposedly dedicated to saving lives, had accepted heavy bribes from the countess to kill, instead. Weston poisoned the unsuspecting man with a compound of arsenic, sublimate of mercury, and white arsenic in his food, while Overbury, by the countess' orders, was imprisoned in the Tower. To ensure death, he and Franklin then administered an enema containing mercury sublimate. Sir Thomas soon died.

The defendants were tried separately. At the last minute, Weston changed his "reference to God" plea to a plea of not guilty. He was subsequently found Guilty and hanged.

Franklin was charged with providing the countess with ample supplies of poison. He swore he did not know what the poisons were being used for, but confessed to the crime nonetheless, and he, too, was found Guilty and hanged. The "brains" behind the plot, Lady Essex, was spared this ultimate punishment. She was found Guilty of murder and sentenced to death, but the sentence was not carried out. She was imprisoned in the Tower for five years and released under the agreement that she remain at a country house, never venturing beyond three miles. In 1624 she was pardoned, and in 1632 she died of natural causes. The earl was also found Guilty and he received the same light sentence as his wife.

The trials that implicated Weston and Franklin represent the first in which any type of physician was tried for a murder related to his occupation. In the seventeenth century, the time of this trial, there were no established standards distinguishing a physician from a layman. Further, it would not be until the following century that chemical tests would be devised to detect common mineral poisons.

REF.: *CBA; Parry, Some Famous Medical Trials.*

Franklin, Joseph Paul (James Clayton Vaughan, Jr.), 1950- , U.S., terr.-mur. Joseph Paul Franklin of Mobile, Ala., carried out a series of racially motivated sniper attacks from 1977 to 1980. Franklin shot and killed ten people in five states, and was a prime suspect in at least three other shootings, including that of Vernon Jordan, president of the National Urban League, who, on May 29, 1980, was shot in the back as he returned to his motel room in Fort Wayne, Ind. (In 1982 Franklin was acquitted of wounding Jordan.) He also remains a suspect in the Mar. 6, 1978, shooting of magazine publisher Larry Flynt. Flynt, whose adult magazine *Hustler* became a target of right-wing religious fundamentalist groups, was paralyzed from the waist down by a shot to the abdomen.

Franklin's father, James Vaughan, Sr., was a WWII veteran who was unable to hold a job and was jailed on numerous occasions for public drunkenness. Vaughan was away from the house much of the time, returning briefly to torment his family emotionally and physically. In 1965, he divorced Helen Rau Vaughan, who then moved her children into low-income housing in the Oakdale section of Mobile. Franklin (his real name was James Vaughan, Jr.) was a quiet loner fascinated by organized religion. His sister said that he looked up and visited every church in the Mobile area. By his senior year of high school, the boy had abandoned religion for the American Nazi movement.

Franklin dropped out of high school to devote his energies to the right-wing hate groups. He directed his aggression particularly toward biracial couples. "If he saw a black man and white woman together, he would tell them right out what he thought of them and it was never nice," his sister Carolyn recalled. In 1968 Franklin married his high school sweetheart Bobbie Louise Dorman, age sixteen. Four months later they were divorced. Franklin moved to Arlington, Va., in 1970 to offer his services to the Nazis. On Sept. 18, he stood in front of the White House passing out leaflets denouncing the state visit of Israeli prime minister Golda Meir.

On Oct. 25, 1972, Franklin was arrested and jailed for carrying a concealed weapon in Fairfax County, Va. Four years later, Franklin, who had recently joined the Ku Klux Klan, sprayed Mace in the faces of a black man and a white woman in a Washington, D.C., suburb. He was arrested on Sept. 8, 1976, but was released on bond. When he failed to show up for a December hearing, a warrant was issued for his arrest. After a March 1977 arrest for carrying a concealed weapon, Franklin traveled extensively through the South and the Midwest for the next two years, using eighteen different aliases. On July 29, 1977, he bombed a synagogue in Chattanooga, Tenn., and four days later in Rockville, Md., set off explosives at the home of a Jewish-American lobbyist.

On Aug. 7, 1977, in Madison, Wis., a sniper shot 23-year-old Alphonse Manning, Jr. and his white girlfriend Toni Schwenn in the parking lot of a shopping mall. In his 1984 confession, Franklin told police that he had intended to kill former judge Archie Simonson of Dane County after reading about a case involving two black men who assaulted a white woman. Franklin objected to the "lenient" sentence the judge doled out. When the plan went awry, Franklin said, he killed Manning and Schwenn. While posing as a plumber in 1979, he married Anita Carden, age sixteen. He dyed his hair and changed his cars frequently, always managing to remain one step ahead of the law.

Joseph Franklin was linked to the shooting deaths of Jesse Eugene Taylor and Marian Vira Bressette, an interracial couple gunned down outside a supermarket in Oklahoma City, Okla., on Oct. 21, 1979. The charges against Franklin in this instance were dropped for lack of evidence. In two separate shootings on Jan. 12 and Jan. 14, 1980, two young black men, Lawrence Reese and Leo Watkins, were killed in Indianapolis. Franklin was charged with firing on the men as they stood near a window in a residential complex. Police officials had too little evidence against Franklin to sustain a conviction.

In Cincinnati, two black teenagers were shot dead near a railroad overpass on June 8, 1980. Franklin's presence in the city was confirmed by a newspaper ad he had placed in the Cincinnati *Enquirer* offering to sell a .30-06 Remington rifle, the same type used in the shooting attack on Vernon Jordan a week earlier. Franklin was picked up in Florence, Ky., and taken to the police interrogation room, but he managed to slip away from his captors. Franklin drove his 1975 Camaro west to Salt Lake City, Utah. On Aug. 20, he took his rifle to Liberty Park where he shot David Martin, twenty, and Ted Fields, eighteen, who had been jogging with two white women. Eyewitnesses reported seeing a brown Camaro drive away from the murder scene minutes later. Police matched the tire tread marks to those taken in Florence, Ky., several weeks earlier. Before he left the city, Franklin hired a prostitute to pose nude for him, surrounded by his personal arsenal of pistols and rifles.

The FBI traced Franklin's movements to Lakeland, Fla., where he was arrested outside a local blood bank on Oct. 28, 1980. He denied his identity, and had attempted to scrape off his tattoos when police picked him up. Franklin was extradited to Salt Lake City where he faced federal and state charges for killing the Liberty Park joggers, and for violating their civil rights. U.S. Assistant Attorney Steven Snarr asked for the mandatory sentence, as he assailed Franklin for having "accomplished the very evil the Civil Rights Act is designed to address." "Do you have any more lies to tell?" the defendant screamed back. Franklin was convicted and sentenced to four life terms at the Marion, Ill., facility by

Federal District Judge Bruce Jenkins in March 1981.

The case of the Madison, Wis., couple murdered in 1977 went before Judge William D. Byrne in February 1986. The Dane County Circuit judge sentenced Franklin to two consecutive life terms on Feb. 14. "The defendant's history of violence, terror, and murder prompts this court to do all it can so that he will never kill again," Byrne said. But under current law, Franklin could be eligible for parole in October 1990. REF.: *CBA*.

Franklin, Timothy, 1971, Brit., mur. In 1971, Timothy Franklin smashed in his lover's face, wrapped a rope around her throat, and when she was finally dead, buried her six feet under the wind shelter in his flower garden in an effort to give her a Christian burial.

Franklin, a 43-year-old business consultant from North Otterington, England, met sophisticated Tina Strauss while on a business trip in Jamaica. They soon fell in love and moved in together back in England. But the whirlwind affair was over as quickly as it began. She was tired of life in the small village and he grew weary of her constant complaints and vicious temper; one more threat by her to move back to Jamaica proved more than he could stand. The final domestic battle left Strauss mangled beyond recognition.

Franklin attempted to cover up his vicious crime by burying the woman in his garden. He told friends she had left him for another man, and once flew to Jamaica to send back telegrams in her name to her mother and lawyer saying all was fine on her splendid vacation to Jamaica.

Eventually rumors concerning Strauss' real fate reached Scotland Yard Detective Arthur Harrison. Harrison contacted Franklin for questioning and knew immediately from his sweaty glance that Franklin had committed murder. All the evidence he needed to convict the killer was the date on Franklin's passport and corresponding dates on the telegrams Strauss supposedly sent from Jamaica.

In a tearful hearing, Franklin swore he killed his beloved out of self-defense. He was "devoted to her, loved her, cared for her and cherished her." But he had been overpowered by her and was fearfully forced to crush her skull, nose, cheek bone, jaw, and voice box. The jury found him Guilty, and he was sentenced to life in prison at York Assizes. REF.: *CBA*.

Franklin, William, prom. 1644, U.S., mur. William Franklin, who lived on the outskirts of Boston in the mid-seventeenth century, employed a young, sickly, and rebellious apprentice named Nathaniel Sewell. Franklin pledged he was only trying to reform the boy when he strung him up in a filthy old chimney. Sewell did not reform, but he did die. Franklin was tried, convicted, and executed for the murder. Among the trial's spectators were several incensed apprentice masters who could not believe the court would find a man Guilty for simply trying to discipline his apprentice.

REF.: *CBA*; Rodell, *Boston Murders*.

Franklyn, Rudolph, prom. 1932, Brit., rob. Rudolph Franklyn became proficient with firearms as a soldier in WWI, and he later became a member of the British-staffed Palestine Police, rising to the rank of corporal. He became a tough, seasoned trooper, tall and muscular, his face lined by the hot Mediterranean sun and wind. He was mustered out of the service in 1932. In September of that year, Franklyn entered a prestigious jewelry store on Oxford Street in London and held a gun on three clerks, ordering them into a back room and then looting the store of a fortune in gold cases and gems. This was the first time a daylight robbery had been committed by a thief armed with a gun in the area.

Within minutes, Franklyn left the jewelry store with his pockets bulging with loot. Since he had no criminal record, tracing him through descriptions given by the robbed jewelers was next to impossible. Franklyn had been seen, however, by a beggar who told investigating officers that a man stepped from the jewelry shop just after the time of the robbery and he asked him for a handout. The beggar said the tall man swore at him in Arabic, and that he wore apparel made of "raincoat cloth," which detec-

tives correctly assumed was tropical garb.

Next police checked several pawn shops and one owner told investigating officers that someone had tried to sell a gold cigarette case in a nearby pub. The pub owner reported that the gold case was had a relief of the world on its lid and that the man trying to sell it had been with the Palestine Police and that he had just returned from the Middle East and bore a suntan. Detectives then checked all men discharged from the Palestine Police in recent months and among those reported was Rudolph Franklyn. Detectives then learned that the Palestine Police had sent on Franklyn's final pay through the postal system, and officers found at the Parliament Street Post Office a receipt for the check Franklyn received which gave his address at Gloucester Road, N.W.

Inspector Robert Fabian, later superintendent of Scotland Yard, along with Detective Alfred Wyatt, boldly went to an address on Gloucester Road. The officers had the landlord knock on Franklyn's door and prepared for the worst, expecting the armed gunman to try to shoot his way to freedom. This type of criminal was unusual for the British police then and even today, where firearms are the exception with even the most ruthless of criminals. Roused from his sleep, Franklyn threw open the door to his room while Fabian and Wyatt stood on either side of the door. Franklyn, half asleep, did not expect police and was unarmed. The detectives grabbed him on either side and, after some scuffling with the tall, powerfully built man, Franklyn was put under arrest. Beneath his pillow, the detective found his automatic pistol affixed with a silencer.

Franklyn was found Guilty of armed robbery. After his conviction, the proud robber said to the court: "The ancient Britons plundered when they were poor and hungry. It's a matter of nature. What else can a man do? You can't beg in the streets if you have pride!"

Judge Sir Ernest Wild replied: "The savagery of our ancestors is no excuse for savage conduct today. Theft is not an alternative to starvation. A man too proud to beg should be too proud to steal." He then sentenced Franklyn to three years at hard labor and, as was the custom of that day in England, added that Franklyn was to receive a whipping, twenty strokes of the birch, to soften his criminal pride.

REF.: *CBA*; Fabian, *Fabian of the Yard*.

Franks, Robert (Bobby), See: Leopold, Nathan.

Franse, Steven, 1895-1953, U.S., org. crime. Steven Franse became associated with New York mobsters Lucky Luciano and Vito Genovese during the days of Prohibition. He was Genovese's most trusted ally when Genovese was forced to flee to Italy in the late 1930s. Franse guarded the things the mobster valued highly: a fortune in a vault at a Manhattan bank, and his wife, Anna, whose previous husband Genovese had killed in order to marry her. When Genovese fled to Italy prior to WWII, Anna took on other lovers. When Genovese returned after the war, Anna was no longer in love with him. A divorce hearing would have likely revealed many of the mobster's secrets. Genovese, however, was too smitten to blame her and vented his rage instead on the man paid to shelter her. In 1953, while in the kitchen of mobster Joe Valachi's restaurant, Franse was grabbed from behind and beaten by Pat Pagano and Fiore Siano. While barely alive, he was slowly strangled with a chain. REF.: *CBA*.

Frantizius, Peter von, d.1968, U.S., org. crime. Although Peter von Frantizius sold many weapons for legitimate purposes while president and general manager of Sports, Inc., a Chicago firearms dealer, he was better known as the "Armorer of Gangland." He supplied the mob with firearms from the days of Al Capone. Many a gangland murder was made possible by a von Frantizius machine gun, including that of Brooklyn mobster Frankie Yale in 1928. Von Frantizius was never prosecuted for his business dealings, and when asked why he sold six machine guns to the mob, he replied that he was told they were for the Mexican government, which was trying to quell a revolution. He prospered for over forty years, until his death in 1968, by supplying the Chicago mob's inexhaustible demands for firepower.

REF.: *CBA*; Demaris, *Captive City*; Kobler, *Capone*.

Franz, Johann Karl, prom. 1861, Case of, Brit., mur. On June 9, 1861, the parish clerk's wife from Kingswood, England, intended to spend the night alone, but in the middle of the night, she was dragged out of bed, tied with a cord, gagged, and perhaps inadvertently killed. The only clue was a wallet that contained a certificate of employment in the name of Johann Karl Franz and a letter from a popular opera star written in German—just enough evidence to implicate the wrong man.

Scotland Yard Inspector Whicher, eager to break a long string of professional failures, jumped on the case and put an all-points bulletin out on Franz.

It was not long before Franz, an impoverished German, was brought in and charged with murder. He tried to tell the police how he had come to England with two other Germans, one named Adolphe Krohn, and how they had fought with him, taking his wallet. His certificate of employment was in the wallet and without that he could not get work. When Franz heard of the murder and an outcry for a person by his name, he at first denied his identity. This heightened the authorities' suspicion.

The opera star arrived just in time. She had never heard of Franz, the man now being held for murder; she had written the letter to Adolphe Krohn.

There was insufficient evidence to accuse Franz, let alone convict him of murder. He was acquitted, Whicher was reprimanded for another failure, and the hunt for the real murderers remained unsolved.

REF.: Brock, *A Casebook of Crime*; *CBA*; Cobb, *Critical Years at the Yard*.

Franzese, Joseph, 1977, U.S., fraud. Joseph and Jerry Franzese made the mistake of believing everyone was as crooked as they were. That mistake, along with undercover work by Peter Trott, a witness to the fraud scheme, may have saved New York stockbrokerage Dean Witter & Company $2.5 million.

The 1977 plot centered around Dean Witter ex-employee Joseph Franzese, relative of John "Sonny" Franzese, reputed Mafia member, and Joseph's cousin Jerry. The two men planned to defraud Dean Witter of large sums of money. Trott became involved with the plan when, working as a salesman for the printing company Holiday Press, he acquired a contract to print a magazine for Imar Publications. When Imar failed to pay its $47,000 bill, Trott confronted Jerry Franzese, an executive of the company. Franzese told Trott he was involved in criminal activities that could be lucrative for Trott if he wanted in. The Franzeses explained in detail the plot involving Dean Witter and Trott said he'd go along. Franzese then directed Trott to cash a fraudulent check for $284 from Dean Witter to a fictitious account. Trott did this, but not without going to the police with his story first. The two men were promptly arrested and charged with fraud.

Trott (not his real name) requested compensation from the brokerage for exposing the scheme, but was flatly denied anything. He has since taken up a lawsuit, requesting $1 million in damages resulting from his relocation as a "federally protected witness." REF.: *CBA*.

Franzese, Michael, 1953- , U.S., org. crime. The Mafia man described by U. S. Justice Department heads as "the catch of the decade" may be set free in a hopeful exchange for even bigger fish.

Young, clever, and influential mob master Michael Franzese and the Justice Department may be able to meet on common ground. The payoff for the Justice Department would be indictments for a series of Mafia murders and the mob's invasion of the entertainment industry. Franzese, thirty-six, in return would be given his freedom.

The top second-generation leader of New York's Colombo family already has helped indict sports agents Norby Walters and Lloyd Bloom, who allegedly used mob money and threats of violence to obtain bargaining rights for forty-four college athletes.

The two allegedly threatened Chicago Bears wide receiver Ron Morris into signing a second agreement with them.

Franzese is regarded as one of the top money earners in the Mafia. At this writing, he is in prison after pleading guilty in 1986 to planning to cheat the government out of $1 billion in gasoline excise taxes.

Franzese is expected to cooperate with authorities. If he does not, he has an estimated seventy years left in prison. Franzese's father, John "Sonny" Franzese, once head enforcer for the Colombo family, has been in prison for more than eleven years for bank robbery. See: **Walters, Norby**. REF.: *CBA*.

Fraser, Alfred, and **Lewis, Howard Henry**, prom. 1955, Brit., rob. On Feb. 5, 1955, thieves broke into the Martin's Bank on St. James Street, Mayfair, pickaxing their way through the basement of the building next door which was being renovated. At 4 a.m., they blasted the safe open with gelignite, firing the detonators from outside the bank. About £20,353 was stolen, along with around £166 in foreign currency. On Mar. 11, three men were charged with breaking and entering; they were Alfred Fraser, forty-three, Howard Henry Lewis, twenty-nine, and Percy Horne, forty. Prosecuting attorney Christmas Humphreys contended that someone had obviously arranged to be left in the renovated building next to the bank after workman left and the building was locked up. When arrested, Lewis and Fraser both had traces of glass and dust fragments on their clothes and property, which matched that blasted out during the bank explosion. Lewis also had bills that were traced directly to those stolen in the robbery. All three men pleaded not guilty. The Central Criminal Court Jury was unable to decide Horne's guilt or innocence in receiving stolen bills, and they were discharged from giving a verdict on those counts. The presiding Common Serjeant, Sir Anthony Hawke, directed the jury to find Horne Not Guilty on the breaking and entering and stealing charges, of which Fraser and Lewis were later convicted. Fraser was sentenced to ten years' preventive detention and Lewis was given a seven-year jail term. See: **Martin's Bank Robbery**. REF.: *CBA*.

Fraser, Simon, c.1667-1747, Scot., polit corr.-consp. Simon Fraser failed in an attempt to kidnap his 9-year-old cousin and heiress to the Lovat Barony, and was outlawed for forcibly marrying the child's mother. He succeeded his father as the Twelfth Baron of Lovat in 1699, and fled to France after Queen Anne's accession to the throne. Secretly returning, he organized the Queensbury plot, claiming he would expose Jacobite plans, but fled once again when his double-crossing was discovered. He sided with the government upon his clan's invitation to return so that he could receive the estates of his cousin who had taken part in the rebellion of 1715. He was pardoned and obtained complete control of the Lovat estates in 1716. Following the battle at Culloden he was taken captive, impeached, and beheaded.

REF.: *CBA*; Lambton, *Echoes of Causes Celebres*.

Fraser, Simon, b.1878, Case of, Scot., mur. Simon Fraser suffered from somnambulism, a sleeping disorder in which the victim is unaware of his actions while "sleepwalking." On Apr. 9, 1878, the 27-year-old Glasgow man murdered his infant son during his dream state. Early the next morning, Fraser tearfully admitted his crime the next morning to his neighbor, Mrs. Janet McEwen. "He was wringing his hands and seemed to be in great distress of mind," the woman said. Following him back to the cottage, Mrs. McEwen found the body of 18-month-old Simon lying on the floor. He had been thrown against the wall.

Fraser was tormented by hideous nightmares. He told McEwen and Dr. Alexander Jamieson, the attending physician, that in his dreams he imagined a wild beast rampaging through the house. When "the beast" leaped into bed with him, he smashed it against the wall. An indictment of murder was returned, and Fraser was locked in a cell to await trial. His case was heard in the High Court of the Justiciary in Edinburgh on July 15. Witnesses came forward to testify to Fraser's good character. It was soon clear that the accused was not a cold-blooded killer, but had suffered from somnambulism for much of his life. Fraser's wife recalled that her husband had grabbed her legs one night as he dreamed that flames were about to engulf their room. He had tried to drag her to safety. Simon Fraser, Sr., the defendant's father, testified that his son had a kindly nature. "But ever since he was a little one there has been a dullness and stupidness about him," he said. To cure his sleeping problems, Mrs. Elspeth Fraser, his step-mother, placed tubs of water alongside Fraser's bed so that the cold water would wake him up. It did not always work.

Medical experts offered the opinion that the defendant could not be held responsible for his actions while in the dream state. The jury agreed and acquitted the prisoner. Lord Justice-Clerk Moncrieff accepted the verdict and directed that Fraser be released with one condition. Simon Fraser returned to his home on Lime Street and was free by day, but at night he was locked into his room from the outside while his wife kept the only key.

REF.: *CBA*; Lambton, *Echoes of Causes Celebres.*

Fratianno, Jimmy "The Weasel" (AKA: Adalena Fratianno), 1913- , U.S., org. crime. Jimmy "The Weasel" Fratianno, once a street punk in Cleveland's Little Italy, became one of the mob's most feared assassins before turning into the most candid informant since Joe Valachi. Nicknamed "the Weasel" for his slight build and ability to elude the police, he more than compensated for his physical shortcomings by his ability with a gun. Fratianno was credited with at least eleven gangland killings, nine of which he admitted. In 1947, he was ritualistically initiated into the Mafia family in Los Angeles and gradually rose to become its head. In 1954, he was sentenced to prison. When he was released six years later, he went into the trucking business and earned close to $1.4 million. Sentenced again to prison, Fratianno was released in 1970 when he began working as an informant for the FBI.

In 1977, word of his complicity leaked to the underworld. To avoid detection during the scrutiny Fratianno had brought on them, Mafia leaders were forced to spend millions altering their operations. During the next ten years, Fratianno fingered such underworld figures as Dominic Brooklier, Carmine "Junior" Persico, and Frank "Funzi" Tieri. His testimony led to the investigation of the Teamsters Pension Fund, overseen by Allen Dorfman in Chicago, and the skimming of Las Vegas casino profits by mobsters in Chicago, Milwaukee, and Kansas City. Fratianno implicated Frank Sinatra in a 1976 benefit concert scheme which netted the New York families $400,000.

On May 19, 1987, Fratianno testified that the president of the International Brotherhood of Teamsters, Jackie Presser, had admitted to having ties with Cleveland Mafia boss James Licavoli. Presser was on trial for racketeering charges stemming from alleged involvement with the Genovese family. In August 1987, the Justice Department decided Fratianno had exhausted his usefulness to the government. Fratianno, who had been instrumental in the convictions of thirty mobsters, including six Mafia bosses, was less than eager to be set free as it was common knowledge that a $250,000 contract awaited the first gunman who succeeded in killing him. Also, although Fratianno was earning adequate royalties from his two biographies, including the 1981 best-seller, *The Last Mafioso,* written with Ovid Demaris, he had grown complacent being supported by the Justice Department, which had spent over $1 million to support his lifestyle.

REF.: Bonanno, *A Man of Honor*; *CBA*; Davis, *Kingfish*; Demaris, *The Last Mafioso*; Eisenberg and Landau, *Meyer Lansky*; Reid, *The Grim Reapers*; Zuckerman, *Vengeance Is Mine.*

Fratson, George, b.c.1899, Brit., mur. Despite two attempts at appeal, widespread public doubt of his guilt, and the outright confession by another man, George Fratson remained incarcerated for murder.

Fratson, thirty, was originally sentenced to die at Manchester Assizes, England, on July 9, 1929, for the murder of George Armstrong, 65-year-old manager of a men's clothing store. Armstrong was in the habit of entertaining young men in his shop after hours. One night he entertained the wrong man, and the next day, May 4, 1929, his body was found on the floor, badly beaten. Fratson was found in a brothel in Preston and immediate-

ly arrested. Taken aback, he made fifteen different statements to the police. The first fourteen were contradictory, inconclusive, and incoherent. The fifteenth statement was a confession. At his trial he recanted his confession, claiming he was despondent and wanted to die. However, Fratson was sentenced to die.

After the sentencing, Fratson's attorney revealed a key fact that the jury had not heard. Fratson was granted a new trial so the jury could learn of a cardboard collar-box that had been found in Armstrong's shop after the murder. It was stained with blood and marked by a fingerprint that matched neither the victim nor the accused. The new testimony was enough to cast doubt about Fratson's involvement, but not enough to acquit him of the murder.

On Aug. 9, Fratson was reprieved and given still another chance at the Court of Criminal Appeal. He sat before five King's Bench judges, instead of the usual three, and all evidence was methodically re-examined. Fratson's conviction was held up and he was again given a life sentence. Years later, Fratson went insane and had to be admitted to Broadmoor Criminal Lunatic Asylum (now Broadmoor Institution).

Later still, a man named Walter Prince was found Guilty of murdering a young woman named Harriet Shaw. Faced with the death penalty, he confessed to also having killed George Armstrong. This confession carried little weight, however, when Prince was found to be insane. He was committed to Broadmoor, where both men lived out the remainder of their lives.

REF.: Brock, *A Casebook of Crime*; *CBA*; O'Donnell, *Cavalcade of Justice*; Shew, *A Second Companion to Murder.*

Fratto, Frank (AKA: **One Ear Frankie, Half-ear, Frank Farrell, Frank Frappo**), 1915- , U.S., theft-mob vio. The FBI knew him as #2890731. To the Chicago Police Department he was #E45775, and to the Illinois Bureau of Identification he was #2592250. Friends called him Frank Fratto, Frank Farrell, "Half-ear," and "One Ear Frankie," because of his severely deformed right ear.

Fratto began creating his police record in 1941 when he was arrested for attempted murder. He was arrested more than ten times for illegal acts, including escape and theft. He was convicted in 1951 on federal charges of interstate theft of whiskey, and was a prime suspect in the 1957 murder of Willard Bates and the 1963 murder of Alderman Benjamin Lewis.

A syndicate terrorist on the north side of Chicago, Fratto was involved in six different businesses including an aluminum siding and storm window firm, a savings association, and a disposal service. His brother Rudolph Fratto was known as the "garbage king" of the Rush Street saloon strip.

Fratto died of natural causes. REF.: *CBA*.

Fraud, See: Supplements, Vol. IV.

Fraunces Tavern Explosion, 1975, U.S., (unsolv.) mur. The site where Revolutionary War officers gathered more than 200 years earlier became the focal point for a modern-day revolutionary group which bombed the Fraunces Tavern Annex in Manhattan, N.Y., on Jan. 24, 1975.

Four innocent people eating their lunches were murdered and countless others severely injured when thousands of razor-sharp window glass fibers sprayed onto passersby and Tavern patrons dining inside. Most of the injured were Wall Street workers on their lunch break. One man was decapitated and others suffered broken bones and critical cuts in the explosion.

The Armed Forces of National Liberation (FALN), a group seeking the independence of Puerto Rico from the United States, claimed responsibility for the bombing. It demanded the release of Puerto Rican prisoners, and said that the bombing was in retaliation for the murder of supporters of the Puerto Rican independence movement by the CIA. The FALN previously claimed responsibility for the October 1974 bombing of several Manhattan buildings and the December 1974 booby-trapped bomb that blew up in the face of a rookie policeman. Ironically, few, if any, of the people killed or maimed in the explosions had any control over U.S. involvement with Puerto Rico or had even heard of FALN and its political ambitions.

REF.: *CBA; Fox, Mass Murder.*

Frazer, George A. (AKA: **Bud**), 1864-96, U.S., west. lawman. Texas sheriff Bud Frazer had more trouble with his deputy, Jim Miller, than with criminals. Born in 1864, the son of a judge, Frazer became a Texas Ranger in 1880. In 1990, he was elected sheriff of Reeves County. He fired Deputy Miller for stealing a pair of mules from a Mexican prisoner whom Miller had shot to death, allegedly for resisting arrest. Miller was charged, and though subsequently released, he fostered ill will which would surround the two men for the following six years. Miller opposed Frazer for the office of sheriff in 1892 and was defeated, but managed to be appointed city marshall of Pecos.

On Apr. 12, 1894, Frazer shot Miller in the right arm in front of a Pecos hotel. Miller returned the fire, but succeeded only in wounding an innocent bystander. Frazer then shot Miller repeatedly in the chest and left him for dead. Miller, however, survived. In November 1894, Frazer lost his bid for reelection and left

Western lawman Bud Frazer.

Texas to operate a stable in New Mexico. Returning to Pecos on Dec. 26, 1894 to complete his move, Frazer encountered Miller for the second time, and shot him in the arm and leg. This time, Frazer was arrested for attempted murder, and jailed. He was acquitted in May 1896. He completed the move to New Mexico, but, on Sept. 14, 1896, returned to Toyah, Texas, to visit his mother and sister, where he once again encountered Miller. This time, Miller shot first, killing Frazer with a shotgun blast to the face. See: **Miller, Jim.**

REF.: Bartholomew, *The Biographical Album of Western Gunmen; CBA; Leftwich, Tracks Along the Pecos; Shirley, Shotgun for Hire.*

Frazer, William Clark, 1776-1838, U.S., jur. District attorney for York County, Penn., and was appointed by President Andrew Jackson to the Wisconsin Territorial Court in 1836. REF.: *CBA.*

Frazier, Jessie, 1910, U.S., wh. slav. Jessie Frazier feigned friendship to trick young girls into a life of prostitution. One of her young victims, Hilda, came to Chicago from Denmark in 1910. She welcomed the hospitality extended to her by Frazier. Indeed, she believed she had found her new best friend. Things only got better. Frazier introduced the pretty youth to another friend, Harry Jocker, whom Frazier said was a theatrical agent looking for one more chorus girl that he could make rich and famous. Jocker spoke with Hilda, looked her over, and decided immediately that she would be great for the job. The job, however, was in a brothel.

Thinking she was bound for stardom, Hilda enthusiastically followed Jocker into the West Side Chicago brothel. She was kept there and forced to work as a prostitute until she was finally rescued by Detectives Bowler and Cullett. On Dec. 29, 1910, Judge Isadore Himes of the Des Plaines Street Court, tried Jocker for pandering. He was found Guilty and given the maximum sentence. Frazier was found Guilty of contributing to child delinquency and fined $100.

REF.: *CBA; Roe, The Great War on White Slavery.*

Frazier, John Linley, 1946- , U.S., arson-mur. The coastal village of Santa Cruz, about forty miles south of San Francisco, Calif., was the setting for a reenactment of the 1969 Manson

killings. On Oct. 19, 1970, the home of wealthy eye surgeon Dr. Victor Ohta went up in flames. After firemen brought the blaze under control, they found the bodies of Ohta, his wife, Virginia, their two children, Taggart, eleven, and Derrick, twelve, and the doctor's secretary, Dorothy Cadwallader. A note attached to the family's Rolls Royce read, "Halloween 1970. Today WWIII will begin, as brought to you by the people of the Free Universe. From this day forward, anyone and/or company of persons who misuses the natural environment or destroys same will suffer the penalty of death by the people of the Free Universe. I and my comrades from this day forth will fight until death or freedom against anyone who does not support natural life on this planet. Materialism must die or mankind will stop." The note was signed "Knight of Wands—Knight of Pentacles—Knight of Cups—Knight of Swords."

The ritualistic nature of the murders indicated that a cultist familiar with tarot cards was responsible. The groups of hippies camped in the adjacent woods suggested another Manson cult. Police came to suspect 24-year-old John Linley Frazier, a local car mechanic who experimented with hallucinogenic drugs. Frazier was separated from his wife and lived near a hippie commune in Felton. He was known to be a militant ecologist and tarot card practitioner. He had a criminal record at the time of his arrest, and had been seen driving Virginia Ohta's station wagon the day after the murders. Frazier refused to confirm or deny his guilt, but his fingerprints were found on the Rolls Royce. He was ruled legally sane, tried, and convicted on five counts of murder. Frazier was

Mass murderer John Linley Frazier, left.

sentenced to die in San Quentin's gas chamber, but California abolished the death penalty in 1971, automatically commuting his sentence to life imprisonment.

REF.: *CBA; Fox, Mass Murder; Godwin, Murder U.S.A.; Wilson, Encyclopedia of Modern Murder.*

Frear, Walter Francis, 1863-1948, U.S., jur. Second associate justice on the First Circuit Court for the kingdom of Hawaii in 1893, first supreme court associate justice for the Republic of Hawaii from 1893-98, and appointed chief justice by President William McKinley to the Supreme Court for the Territory of Hawaii from 1900-07. REF.: *CBA.*

Freccia, Carmela Emily, 1916- , **Frank Freccia,** 1911- , **Joseph A. Mastocciolo** (AKA: **Joe Masto**), prom. 1964, and **Frank A. Doeberl,** prom. 1964, U.S., fraud. Clyde A. Banks did most of his living after his death in 1964—on paper, at least. He was newly married to Carmela Emily Freccia, worked as manager of the Meadowbrook Realty Company in Greenwich, Conn., had recently purchased a school bus, a pickup truck, a jeep with a snowplow, three Chevrolets, and five Cadillacs, and had borrowed $73,999.96 from eleven banks in Connecticut and adjacent Westchester County in New York. Unfortunately for the banks, Clyde Banks was dead.

Records from the Veteran's Hospital at West Haven proved Banks was receiving treatments for Hodgkins Disease at the same time that he was supposedly borrowing money for his shopping sprees. Things started getting clearer when Emily Freccia presented Alexander Kish, senior vice president of the Connecticut National Bank, with the death certificate of her husband and asked for his life insurance money. Kish remembered Banks, his wife, and her brother Frank Freccia from the previous month when they took out a $5,000 loan to add a new branch to their realty company, which Banks was to manage. While they were there, "Mrs. Banks" took out an insurance policy for the loan on her husband's life. Because that is not an unusual request, Kish thought little of it at the time. But later, when he saw that Bank's death certificate listed "Hodgkin's Disease" as the cause of death, he became suspicious. He wondered if Banks had been terminally ill, why he had looked so healthy just one month ago, why he was planning to run a realty company when he was so ill, and what the odds were that he would take out such a loan and die before even one of the thirty-six payments were due?

Postal inspectors Robert DeLong and Frank McAvoy learned that the deceased's "wife" had not planned or attended the funeral—had not even sent him flowers. A closer look into the widow's background turned up countless arrests for motor theft, forgery, and usury. The inspectors looked into Banks' background and found that during the time he was hospitalized, he had supposedly been making major purchases in several stores. The plot was soon uncovered.

Banks became acquainted with Freccia when he borrowed money from her on one occasion. When Freccia learned from his ex-wife that Banks was very sick and would die soon, she decided to benefit. With the help of her cronies Joseph A. Mastociolo and Frank Doeberl, she and her brother Frank Freccia defrauded Connecticut and New York banks by applying for loans in Banks' name. By the time Banks died, they had borrowed so much that their total interest charges—which they paid with additional money borrowed in his name—were about $3,000. To get even more money, Freccia and Doeberl were married as "Mr. and Mrs. Banks." Freccia did not realize that the Veterans' Administration would not grant funds to last-minute wives and she received nothing for this act.

For the bogus loans and impersonation, both Freccia and her brother Frank received mail fraud convictions. Frank was given a four-year term and a fine of $15,000 and Emily was given a five-year term and a fine of $25,000. The judge who sentenced them said their acts were the most ruthless he had ever known.

REF.: *CBA*; Kahn, *Fraud*.

Frederick IX, 1899-1972, Den., rebel. Led resistance against the occupation of Denmark by Nazi forces, for which he was placed in prison from 1943-45, along with his father King Christian X, whom he succeeded to the Danish throne from 1947-72. REF.: *CBA*.

Frederick, Johnny, and **Keaton, David Roby,** prom. 1970, U.S., (wrong. convict.) rob.-mur. On the evening of Sept. 18, 1970, Sheriff's Deputy Thomas Revels was gunned down during the robbery of a Quincy, Fla., grocery store. After the shooting, four black youths fled the store in a single car. Five young local men, including Johnny Frederick and David Roby Keaton were arrested and charged with the robbery-murder.

Frederick, Keaton, and the three others, known as the "Quincy Five," were identified by five eyewitnesses and confessed to lie detector operator Joe Townsend in Tallahassee, Fla. One of the defendants was acquitted, one was found incompetent to stand trial, and charges were dropped against another. Frederick was sentenced to life and Keaton received the death penalty. One year later, defense attorneys representing Frederick and Keaton learned that three Jacksonville men had been arrested for the crime and two of them had confessed.

The Florida Supreme Court retried and cleared Frederick and Keaton. Both were released, following revelations that Townsend coerced false confessions from them while conducting polygraph tests, and threatened them with the death penalty if they didn't change their stories. REF.: *CBA*.

Fredericks, William M., prom. 1890-95, U.S., rob.-mur. In 1890, William M. Fredericks arrived in California and worked briefly as a barber in Shasta County before robbing a stagecoach in Mariposa County. Sentenced to three years in Folsom Prison, Fredericks there met and became friendly with convicts Frank Williams and Anthony Dalton. Soon after his discharge, Fred-

ericks gathered weapons for a prison break, headed by the leader of the Sontag and Evans gang, George Evans. In the attempted jail break, on June 27, 1893, three prisoners were killed and several more wounded. A few days after this unsuccessful attempt, Fredericks shot and wounded a Gold Run brakeman, J.T. Bruce, and then shot and killed Nevada County Sheriff Pasco at Grass Valley, because he mistakenly thought that Pasco wanted to arrest him. On the night of Mar. 14, 1894, Fredericks robbed Martin Smith in San Francisco's Golden Gate Park. Taking $150 and a gold watch and chain from the young man, Fredericks hit him on the head with the butt of a pistol and fired at the wounded man as he fled, hitting him in the wrist. Nine days later, Fredericks drew a revolver at around noon in the San Francisco Savings Union Bank at Market and Fell Streets, demanding that cashier William A. Herrick turn over the money. As Herrick reached for a pistol, Fredericks shot him dead. Another clerk fired, missing the robber, but shattering a pane of glass that splintered into Fredericks' eye, causing permanent damage.

William Fredericks, murderer and robber.

Fredericks was pursued and captured by police officer W.J. Shields. Smith, seeing the criminal's picture in the paper, came forward on Mar. 24, to identify him as his assailant. Fredericks made a full confession to Detective John Seymour, and was convicted of murdering Herrick. He was hanged at San Quentin on July 26, 1895.

REF.: *CBA*; Duke, *Celebrated Criminal Cases of America*.

Fredericq, Paul, 1850-1920, Belg., rebel. Attempted to bolster the morale of Belgians during WWI. For this he was deported from Belgium by the German government. REF.: *CBA*.

Free, James, 1954- , U.S., mur. Bonnie Serpico and Lori Summer were working in a suburban Chicago data processing office in the early morning of Apr. 24, 1978, when Army specialist 4th class James Free burst into the office and threatened to rape them. Free tied Summer to a chair and forced Serpico to undress. When she tried to escape, Free shot her dead. He then shot Summer in the leg as she pleaded for her life. The following day, Free was captured after a standoff with police in Dubuque, Iowa, where he fled to his parents' apartment.

Free, twenty-four, was tried and convicted in an Illinois court in 1979. He pleaded innocent, claiming he was under the influence of alcohol, marijuana, and PCP, and therefore not responsible for his actions. Lori Summer, who survived the attack, was the main witness for the prosecution. Free was sentenced to death, and his lawyers appealed to the state Supreme Court. In 1983, the court denied Free's appeal. REF.: *CBA*.

Freed, Emerich B., 1897-1955, U.S., jur. Prosecuting attorney for Cuyahoga County, Ohio from 1932-33, U.S. attorney for the Northern District of Ohio in 1933, and was appointed by President Franklin D. Roosevelt to the Northern District Court of Ohio in 1941. REF.: *CBA*.

Freedman, Helen (AKA: Russian Dora), prom. 1900s, Brit., (unsolv.) mur. The murder of 59-year-old prostitute Helen Freedman remains unsolved, but Scotland Yard authorities believe it was linked to organized crime.

Freedman was found beaten, stabbed, and bludgeoned to death in her Long Acre apartment. Next to her body lay the knife used in the stabbing, and investigators found a length of electrical wire tied around her neck. The electrical cord may have been the calling card of an underworld vice organization which had been "protecting" Freedman while she worked on the streets of London.

REF.: *CBA*; Harrison, *Criminal Calendar*.

Freedman, Maurice, 1896-1932, Brit., mur. An ex-policeman, Maurice Freedman, thirty-six, professed to be in love with Annete Friedson. Although he was already married, Freedman courted the young woman and constantly promoted the idea that his wife was going to divorce him. Finally, the dissatisfied Friedson decided to end the relationship and told her brother of her decision. On Jan. 26, 1932, just after this decision, Friedson went to her job in London. At about 9:30 a.m., she was found with her throat cut on the stairwell leading up to her office. Freedman was arrested the next morning as he went out for coffee with a friend. Three days after his arrest, a passenger on a bus discovered a blood-spattered safety razor behind the cushion of his seat, and took it to the Snow Street Police station. The bus' conductor remembered picking up Freedman at about 10:50 a.m. the morning of the killing. Freedman was tried at the Old Bailey before Justice Hawke on Mar. 8, with prosecutor Sir Percival Clarke bringing out that the unusual blood type found on the razor matched Friedson's own. Freedman claimed that he had gone to see the woman to change her mind about leaving him, and had brought an old fashioned straight razor along to frighten her into believing he was going to kill himself if she did not change her mind. After pleading his case with her on the stairs, he had taken the razor out and laid it against his throat, they had struggled, and she had been accidentally slashed. The safety razor blade, which was obviously the murder weapon, and which the accused said he had never seen before, would not have been able to deliver a fatal cut or cuts under those circumstances. Freedman was found Guilty of murder and was executed at Pentonville Prison on May 4, 1932.

REF.: *CBA*; Nicholls, *Crime Within the Square Mile*; Shew, *A Second Companion to Murder*.

Freedom Riders, prom. 1961, Case of, U.S., bomb.-mob vio. A New York city activist group known as the Congress of Racial Equality (CORE) organized several interracial bus trips to the heart of the deep south in the 1960s as a protest of the region's racially-motivated violence. Many of the trips ended in devastation.

The first group of Freedom Riders left Washington, D.C., in May 1961 aboard two buses. They traveled through many southern towns with only slight interference until they got to Alabama. "I could tell the difference when we crossed the state line into Alabama," said 18-year-old Charles Person, a passenger on one of the buses. "The atmosphere was tense."

As the first of the two buses arrived in Anniston, Ala., it was overtaken by a line of cars that had followed the Freedom Riders across the state line. A passenger in one of the cars heaved a homemade bomb into the bus through a window. It exploded inside, burning passengers and shooting fire the length of the bus. With flames billowing from the broken windows, the bus was forced off the road, where the mob waited to beat the passengers as they fled the bus.

As the first bus burned, the second rolled into Anniston. When it stopped, eight white men boarded and began beating passengers in their seats. News of the attacks spread quickly and supporters from nearby Birmingham arrived in Anniston to rescue the Freedom Riders.

On arriving at the Birmingham bus terminal, the Freedom Riders were again attacked by a mob. Whites bludgeoned the passengers with blackjacks and pipes for several minutes as the Birmingham police failed to respond. Birmingham Police Commissioner Eugene "Bull" Conner, told the press: "Our people of Birmingham are a peaceful people, and we never have any trouble here unless some people come into our city looking for trouble."

The Freedom Riders continued their nonviolent protests in Montgomery, Ala., where whites attempted to shoot protesters and ignited the clothing of one black man and watched him burn. Alabama Governor John Patterson said, "I cannot guarantee the protection for this bunch of rabble-rousers." In Jackson, Miss., more than 164 Freedom Riders were jailed for "breach of the peace." Many paid fines and were released, while others were held in the maximum security cells at Parchman State Penitentiary.

At the height of the racial unrest, U.S. Attorney General Robert Kennedy ordered 400 deputy marshals and treasury agents to patrol the streets of Alabama. And President John F. Kennedy declared war on the rioters and southern politicians, stating, "I hope that state and local officials in Alabama will meet their responsibilities. The U.S. government intends to meet its." REF.: *CBA*.

Freeland, Judson, and **Freeland, Belle**, prom. 1893, U.S., count. Judson and Belle Freeland were apprehended for counterfeiting in Chicago, Ill., during the city's celebrated World's Fair in 1893. The couple had passed counterfeit bills from West Virginia to Minnesota and were tried in a Chicago court on Nov. 20, 1893.

Both were found Guilty and sentenced to three years in the state penitentiary in Chester, Ill. The pregnant Belle was released from prison in September and returned to the couple's home in Virginia. Two years later, she was again arrested for passing fake bills. REF.: *CBA*.

Freeman, Arthur Vectis (AKA: **Frank Power**), prom. 1926, Brit., hoax. To promote a forthcoming movie about the life of British soldier Lord Horatio Herbert Kitchener, Arthur Vectis Freeman, using the name Frank Power, announced that Kitchener's corpse had been discovered in Norway. Rumors about the missing soldier had circulated for years. According to one theory, the *Hampshire*, which he had boarded for a secret mission in Russia when the vessel struck a mine and sank, was about to be scrapped. Thus, the British government was responsible for Kitchener's death. In a London *Referee* article of Aug. 8, 1926, Freeman said the body would be shipped to England from its burial place at a Norwegian cemetery. Governments of both countries became intensely interested in the story, with the Norwegian officials assuring the British authorities that no grave had been opened, nor had any corpse been removed. Newsreel reporters were on hand when the coffin was loaded onto a boat bound for London, and British police brushed Freeman aside when it arrived in England on August 14, 1926. The coffin opened in front of authorities was empty. Freeman insisted that it had been robbed. The hoax failed miserably, and few people went to see the movie.

REF.: *CBA*; MacDougall, *Hoaxes*.

Freeman, Charles F., prom. 1879, Case of, U.S., mur. On the evening of May 1, 1879, a unusual electrical storm hit Sandwich, Mass. Charles F. Freeman of Pocasset took it as a sign, and explained to his wife that the time had come to sacrifice their youngest daughter to God. Several weeks before, God had spoken to Freeman and told him that He would require one of his daughters as a sacrifice. On May 1, God told him which one.

As his wife prayed in another room that God would stop him, Freeman plunged a knife into 3-year-old Edith's side, piercing her heart and causing instant death.

The next evening, Freeman invited members of his Adventist congregation to his home to hear a sermon. He told his fellow churchgoers that he had sacrificed Edith, just as God had commanded. The next day police arrested Freeman and his wife for the murder of their 3-year-old daughter.

While in jail, Freeman said that God had again spoken to him and told him to get ready for the second coming of Christ on May 21. Freeman explained that no one would recognize him when he arrived. May 21 came and went uneventfully.

The Freemans were brought to court on Dec. 5, 1883. Charges were dropped against Mrs. Freeman, and her husband was found Not Guilty by reason of insanity and sentenced to life in the Danvers Insane Asylum. Less than four years later, Charles Freeman was certified sane and released from the hospital.

REF.: *CBA*; Potter, Nutter, and Stiles, *A History of the Pocasset Tragedy With the Three Sermons Preached In New Bedford*.

Freeman, Jeannace, 1940- , and **Jackson, Gertrude**, 1928- , U.S., mur. Jeannace Freeman and Gertrude Jackson took

Jackson's two children for a walk in Oregon's Peter Skene Ogden Park. Freeman and Jackson had been lovers ever since Jackson's husband left her and the children. Freeman, who dominated Jackson, had been raped at the age of four by her male baby-sitter.

In the park, Freeman stripped the 6-year-old boy and strangled him to death. Once he was dead, Freeman castrated the boy with a knife and threw his body over a cliff. Jackson then joined her in the murder of the girl. The women tossed her into the canyon to land near her brother.

Murderess Jeannace Freeman.

The naked bodies of the two children were discovered by a park visitor who told rangers she had seen two children's dolls lying at the bottom of Crooked River Canyon. Rangers identified the children as those of Gertrude Jackson, who had left her Eugene, Ore., home two days earlier with Freeman.

The two women were captured in Oakland, Calif., after a description of their car led investigators to a used car lot where Jackson had sold the automobile. They were arrested at their home and charged with the murders. Jackson immediately confessed to the crimes and explained that Freeman was the dominant partner in their relationship and had engineered the children's deaths.

Both were convicted of murder and sentenced to death. The sentences were commuted to life in 1964. REF.: *CBA*.

Freeman, John Gilbert, 1930- , U.S., mur. Described as "a danger to society," John Gilbert Freeman was to be released from the Arizona State Mental Hospital in 1975 after four years of confinement. A 1971 diagnosis of mental incompetence to kept Freeman from standing trial for the murder of seven people. By 1975, it was technically illegal to indict him.

The Arizona prosecutor's office was outraged, and a legal battle ensued between the state's attorney and defense counselors. The state supreme court reviewed Freeman's case, and ruled that he could indeed be indicted because the 1971 diagnosis prevented the state from indicting within the specified 120 days. In early 1975, Freeman stood trial for the murder of seven people in Phoenix on the evening of Sept. 3, 1971.

In May 1970, Freeman's wife, complaining of her husband's behavior, left their Phoenix home with their two children. Freeman searched for a way to explain his wife's actions. A former co-worker had recently told him of his extramarital affair. Freeman became obsessed with the idea that the unfaithful man had seduced his wife and caused the abrupt end of his marriage. He flew to destinations around the country looking for the adulterous couple. He frequently visited Novella Bentley, his former friend's wife, and questioned her about her estranged husband's activities. Bentley was never able to give him any information.

On the night of Sept. 3, 1971, Freeman purchased two .38-caliber revolvers and ammunition before visiting Novella Bentley. When Freeman arrived, Bentley was entertaining relatives in her Phoenix home. Freeman burst into the house and shot Bentley, her daughter, and her daughter's husband. Four children slept through the attack in a back bedroom. Freeman reloaded the guns, and shot each of the children in the head. Police apprehended him as he walked from the house. Shortly thereafter he was found insane and transferred to a mental hospital.

In 1975, the jury found Freeman Guilty and the judge sentenced him to seven consecutive life terms. Following sentencing, Freeman was ordered back into treatment at the mental facility that had previously certified him sane.

REF.: *CBA*; Godwin, *Murder U.S.A.*

Freeman, Ralph McKenzie, 1902- , U.S., jur. Prosecuting attorney of Genesee County, Mich., from 1931-32, and received appointment from President Dwight Eisenhower to the Eastern District Court of Michigan in 1954. REF.: *CBA*.

Freeman, Richard Austin, 1862-1943, Brit., writer. Authored a number of detective novels, including: *The Red Thumb*, in 1907, *Dr. Thorndyke's Case Book* in 1923, *Pontifex, Son and Thorndyke* in 1931, *The Penrose Mystery* in 1936, and *Mr. Polton Explains* in 1940. REF.: *CBA*.

Freeman, Samuel, d.1805, U.S., mur. Samuel Freeman, of Ashford, Conn., hired Hannah Simons to keep house for him, and she became his mistress. Freeman abused the girl and finally beat her to death. He admitted the killing and was hanged at Windham, Conn., on Nov. 6, 1805.

REF.: *CBA*; Welch, *The Gospel to Be Preached to All Men, in A Sermon Delivered in Windham at the Execution of Samuel Freeman*.

Freeman, William, 1824-47, Case of, U.S., mur. Born in Auburn, N.Y., William Freeman, a black with Indian and French blood, belonged to a family that exhibited a deep strain of insanity. His brother and sister were certified insane and Freeman's father died of brain disease. Freeman grew up without schooling, living a carefree life in Auburn's small black community. He was falsely convicted of stealing horses in 1840 and given a five-year term in Auburn Prison. Embittered over his wrongful conviction, Freeman was sullen and disobedient. Guards responded to Freeman's refractory behavior by brutalizing him. He was repeatedly flogged, and once, a guard struck Freeman on the head so hard with a board that his skull was permanently damaged and he was deafened in one ear.

Before he was released in September 1845, prison officials realized that Freeman was demented. When he was finally set free, he wandered about Auburn babbling to himself about "gettin' my pay." He came to believe that wealthy, popular John G. Van Nest, who owned a farm three miles south of Auburn, had something to do with his imprisonment. On Mar. 12, 1846, Freeman appeared at the Van Nest home, demanding his "pay." Van Nest ordered him from the premises, but Freeman produced two knives and stabbed Van Nest to death, then killed his wife and two small children. He was caught the following day and jailed, charged with mass murder. The prisoner, considered "a fiend" and "a monster," caused great excitement in the community. The pastor of the church Van Nest attended mounted the pulpit and demanded Freeman's life. Only a strong guard around the city jail prevented a mob from dragging the prisoner outside and lynching him.

Freeman's fate was predetermined in the minds of everyone except William Henry Seward, former governor of New York and later Abraham Lincoln's secretary of state. He undertook Freeman's defense, entering a plea of insanity for him on July 21-23, 1846. The court determined the prisoner could tell right from wrong, and the obviously biased Judge Bowen Whiting ruled that Freeman was sane. When Freeman was put on the witness stand by Seward and he made a poor showing, sounding confused and, at times, acting like an imbecile. Seward, in his summation, expressed shock that the state would try "a maniac as a malefactor." He made an impassioned speech which ended with an exhortation to jury members to judge his client as they would a white man, saying "he is still your brother, and mine—Hold him to be a man." But the effort was useless since Judge Whiting, in his highly prejudicial instructions to the jury, pressured its members into a verdict of Guilty.

On July 24, Judge Whiting sentenced Freeman to death, but Seward appealed the verdict and sentence. The Supreme Court ruled that Judge Whiting had made serious errors in his court conduct and dismissed the verdict, ordering a new trial. Seward visited his client in jail to find him critically ill, and in the final stages of consumption. Freeman died in his Auburn Jail cell before his next trial on Aug. 21, 1847. For Seward, the defense of Freeman and that of Henry Wyatt, another black charged with murder, proved to be a political feather in his cap. His law business boomed and he became celebrated nationwide as a champion of the oppressed. He was also vilified by racists and even threatened with violence. Seward's defense of Freeman, nevertheless, was a legal landmark for the insane charged with serious crimes who, up to that time, had received little or no consideration in U.S. courts.

REF.: *CBA*; Hall, *The Trial of William Freeman for the Murder of John G. Van Nest;* Van Deusen, *William Henry Seward.*

Freeway Phantom Murders, 1971-72, U.S., mur. On Apr. 25, 1971, Carole Spinks, thirteen, disappeared while running a quick errand to a store near her home in the southeast section of Washington, D.C. Her abductor kept her alive for more than a day, fed her, and then strangled her. The killer then placed her fully clothed body on the shoulder of I-295, a busy interstate highway. After the body was discovered, the police found little evidence; a murder pattern was to continue for the next sixteen months.

The bodies of seven young black girls were found dumped, usually along busy roads. But, after investigation, it was always learned that the victims had been killed in some unknown location, with little or no physical clues left at the scene by the killer. The next victim was Angela Denise Barnes, fourteen, who was found shot to death on July 14, 1971. She was soon followed by Darlenia Denise Johnson, sixteen, who was found strangled on July 19, 1971. Next was Brenda Fay Crockett, ten, who was found strangled on July 28, 1971, followed by Nenomoshia Yates, twelve, strangled on Oct. 2, 1971, Brenda Denise Woodard, eighteen, stabbed to death Nov. 16, 1971. Then, for almost a year, the killer was inactive. On Sept. 6, 1972, however, Diane Williams, seventeen, was found strangled. Most of the victims had been raped.

Though the girls ranged in age from ten to eighteen, they shared certain physical characteristics. Snapshots of the victims show slim, smiling, tall, vibrant girls. "The older girls looked younger and the younger ones looked older," said Captain Robert M. Boyd, head of Washington's homicide squad. "They looked between fourteen and sixteen." Five of the girls came from the same southeast neighborhood near St. Elizabeth's Hospital for the mentally ill which includes maximum security facilities for the criminally insane. Two of the bodies were found just yards from the hospital fence. Most of the residents of the neighborhood were poor and lived in small, shabby apartments; fifty percent of Washington's public housing was concentrated in the area. "Five of the cases are logically tied together." Boyd said, "Same operation. Picked up off the street, dropped on major thoroughfares...there's just too much similarity to ignore. You pretty well have to say that's the work of one man."

Four of the girls had the middle name Denise, a name they shared with the daughter of Sergeant Louis B. Richardson the detective who headed the investigation. "At the first one we had no pattern and we weren't looking for a freak or a maniac," Richardson said. "With the second one we saw what was happening and we added as much investigative power as we could." At the peak of the killings, more than seventy detectives were working on the case, but by March 1974 they had gotten nowhere.

The strangest twist in the case came when a note was discovered along with the body of Brenda Woodard in November 1971. Washington police have never disclosed the contents of the note, except to say that it contained one sentence of explanation and another of defiance. It was signed "Freeway Phantom," the name that newspapers had given the killer. The shock came when FBI handwriting experts reported that the note had been written by the victim herself and that the steady handwriting showed no signs of fear or tension. Police advanced two different theories: one was that the freeway phantom had, in fact, killed the girl. The other was that the girl was stabbed to death by a friend who had first conned the girl into writing the note, in an attempt to throw

police off the trail. There was one word in the note that led the police to believe that a lawyer might have been responsible for the contents, but that theory never led to an arrest.

Another theory was that the killer was a police officer. This, many people felt, would explain why the girls so readily got into the killer's car, especially those girls who were abducted after the series of killings had received wide publicity. These girls had been repeatedly warned about strangers. But some of those same girls had been taught to treat police officers as their friends. "You bring up your children to stop if a policeman calls because this is right," the mother of Carole Spinks said.

Two other signs pointed to someone familiar with police work as the killer: The bodies had been dumped in four different police jurisdictions, possibly to confuse the investigation, and hardly any physical evidence had been found on or near the girls, possibly by a killer who knew how important evidence was in solving a murder where the victim and killer were strangers. "We have investigated some policemen," Captain Boyd later told newsmen, "because we thought there might be a tie-in." But that investigation turned up nothing. Wherever the police turned they found another brick wall. They requested help from the public; someone must have seen something. How could seven young girls be abducted, killed, and their bodies dumped on busy highways, without a single witness, asked officers. The police received over 5,000 phone calls on one killing alone, but all these tips came to nothing.

In 1974, two and a half years after the killings began and more than a year after they ended, a police detective who worked on the case concluded: "We're no closer to solving them now then we were the day after they happened....The only way we're going to catch him now is if he does it again. And we don't want any more children killed."

The police were swift to answer charges that the killing would have been solved years earlier if the victims had been white. Detective Richardson says, "I'm black and I'm from the ghetto and in this city a homicide is a homicide. A body is a body whether it's a banker or a junkie; they get the same attention." Captain Boyd, head of Washington's homicide squad, agreed. "Nothing could be further from the truth than to say we don't care about black cases." He pointed to statistics that showed (in 1972) his men solving 90.6 percent of the black homicides and 90.9 percent of the white homicides in the Washington area. In 1973, Boyd's figures showed the police solved 92.4 percent of black homicides but only 78.1 percent of white homicides. Boyd attributed the black community's distorted view of homicide investigations to the local news media which spent little time reporting black crime.

In March 1974, after the Washington *Post* published a series of articles recapping the Freeway Phantom case, police finally received a long awaited tip. On Mar. 29 and 30, Maryland State Police arrested Edward Leon Sellman, thirty, and Tommie Bernard Simmons, twenty-six, and charged them with the murder of Angela Denise Barnes, who was fourteen years old when she was abducted and shot to death on July 14, 1971. The two men had both been first-year Washington Police officers, but both had resigned from the force before completing their probationary periods, Simmons in February 1971 and Sellman in March 1971. The Freeway Phantom killings began in April 1971.

But as soon as it appeared that the Freeway Phantom case was solved, police began to back off from that assumption. Barnes, police said, was the only victim who had been shot. She had not been raped, and her body was dumped more than ten miles outside of Washington in Waldorf, Md., the only victim found outside of the Washington metropolitan area.

Sellman and Simmons were tried and convicted for the murder of Angela Barnes, and both were sentenced to life in prison. Eighteen years after the Freeway Phantom murders first took place, the Barnes killing was the only case that had been officially solved. See: **Sellman, Edward Leon.** REF.: *CBA.*

Freeway Strangler, The, See: **Bonin, William.**

Freidgood, Dr. Charles E., 1918- , U.S., mur. Dr. Charles

Freidgood arrived at his fashionable Kensington home on Long Island, N.Y., on the afternoon of June 18, 1975, to find a group of neighbors, police, and medical technicians. They informed him that his wife was dead. Dr. Freidgood immediately reached into his briefcase, removed a certificate of death, entered the cause of death as a stroke, and authorized it with his signature. It seemed to those at the scene that the doctor had been too prepared.

His actions were considered unusual not only by the New York Medical Society, but also by the local police. They began an investigation of Mrs. Friedgood's death and requested an autopsy. Coroner George E. Hudok, Jr. found bruises on the body, suggesting a struggle before death, and dated her death between the hours of midnight and 2:00 a.m. earlier that morning. A second autopsy revealed that she had received five Demerol injections, and police secured a warrant to search the Freidgood home.

The day after his wife's death, Friedgood was turned away from New York's Chase Manhattan bank when he attempted to obtain access to his wife's safe deposit box. Undaunted, he returned four days later with a set of documents containing Sophie Freidgood's forged signature. The documents passed inspection and he took more than $600,000 in bonds, securities, jewelry, and cash from the vault. The next day he sold $50,000 in securities to the brokerage firm of E.F. Hutton.

On June 25, officers arrested Friedgood at New York's Kennedy International Airport where he had boarded a jet bound for London. They followed him to the airport after discovering love letters and a photograph of a nude woman in his dead wife's safe deposit box. They suspected him of murdering Sophie for exposing his affair. He was attempting to flee to Denmark to join his former nurse and current lover Harriet Boell Larsen. Freidgood carried no luggage other than a briefcase filled with his wife's securities, valued at over $569,000.

Friedgood was charged with murder and brought to trial on Oct. 8, 1976, before Judge Richard C. Delin. Introducing primarily circumstantial evidence and the testimony of five of the six Freidgood children, Assistant Nassau County District Attorney Stephen P. Scaring won a conviction.

On Jan. 26, 1977, Judge Delin gave Freidgood the maximum sentence, twenty-five years to life, calling his crime a "cold, calculated, and deliberate act of murder." REF.: *CBA*.

Freidland, David, 1938- , U.S., extor. Former New Jersey State Senator David Freidland was convicted of extortion in 1985 and sentenced to seven years in prison. Soon afterwards, he was reported drowned in a scuba diving accident in the Caribbean near the Bahamas, although his death was never substantiated.

After leading police on a twenty-seven-month chase, Freidland turned up alive in 1988 on the island of Male off the coast of India. He was taken into custody and extradited to the U.S. where, in January 1988, he began serving his 1985 sentence. REF.: *CBA*.

Freihoff, William (AKA: Dr. William H. Wilson), d.1908, U.S., (unsolv.) mur. William Freihoff died at his dinner table on the evening of June 26, 1908, after drinking from a glass of cyanide-laced ale. His killer later proclaimed in a letter to police, "Let those that live by poison die by poison."

Freihoff was a resident of Philadelphia, Penn., where neighbors knew him as Dr. William Wilson. It was never known whether Freihoff was an actual physician. It was reported that he had taken classes at the New York College of Physicians and Surgeons but that he never obtained a degree. Freihoff was an abortionist during a time when the operation was illegal. His killer was the grieving husband of a patient who died from the procedure.

To kill Freihoff, the man engineered a fake marketing campaign in which participants were to test a new ale brewed by the well-known Schemm Brewing Company. The killer had a false document explaining the test printed on Schemm letterhead. He mailed the letter to Freihoff and had the cyanide-laced sample delivered the following day. Freihoff was dead less than an hour after he drank the ale.

Several days after Freihoff's death, the coroner conducting the investigation received an anonymous letter from a man who confessed to the crime. The killer explained in detail the method he used to kill the man known to him as Dr. Wilson. He provided information in the letter that only the killer could have known, including several details unknown at the time the letter was mailed. The killer explained in the letter that his wife had died after Freihoff had conducted an abortion on her.

The killer showed no remorse for the crime, and told police that he had left Pennsylvania and that they would never capture him. Authorities never found the man. REF.: *CBA*.

Freisler, Roland, 1893-1945, Ger., jur. Roland Freisler served in the German army during WWI, and was captured. He was sent to a Russian prison camp but was liberated during the Russian Revolution of 1917. He became an ardent Bolshevik and returned to Germany with the idea of bringing Communism to that country. When Adolf Hitler began his rise to power in the early 1920s, Freisler, then a lawyer, eagerly quit the Communist Party and, in 1924, joined the Nazi Party, embracing the most fanatical ideas advocated by Hitler. Freisler was one of the drafters of the Nuremberg Laws which proscribed Jews in Germany. He was a radical exponent of exterminating the Jews and any of those who opposed Hitler, and he brought utter terrorism to the German high courts over which he later presided as the chief judge.

Nazi jurist Roland Freisler.

Freisler had studied the courtroom tactics of Andrei Vishinsky, the chief prosecutor during the Moscow trials of the mid-1930s, in which the Old Bolsheviks, under Stalin's orders, were convicted of imaginary crimes in mock trials. Freisler admired Vishinsky's blatant disregard for existing laws in the Moscow trials and he emulated that style when quickly railroading Hitler's enemies in court. He was vicious, obscene, and utterly irrational in his trials and sentencing. He ridiculed defendants and allowed no proper legal representation, especially to those who stood accused of attempting to assassinate Hitler in 1944 and were summarily judged and sentenced to death by Freisler.

It was Freisler's habit to insult and degrade all brought before him before he quickly sent defendants to the gallows or worse. In the case of the conspirators who tried to kill Hitler, Freisler took pains to see that Hitler's execution orders were carried out, that all of the defendants, from field marshals to cooks, died painfully by being impaled on meat hooks and tortured before being garroted to death. Freisler was truly a bestial example of Hitler's one-sided court system during the Third Reich.

Fabian von Schlabrendorff, one of those who had plotted to kill Hitler, was brought before Freisler in the People's Court on Feb. 3, 1945. Freisler began to shriek at the accused, going into one of his mouth-foaming diatribes, when a bomb from an American plane flying overhead crashed into the courthouse and blew Roland Freisler to pieces. See: **Hitler, Adolf.**

REF.: *CBA; Fest, Hitler;* Heiden, *Der Fuehrer;* Manvell and Fraenkel, *The Men Who Tried to Kill Hitler;* Orlow, *The History of the Nazi Party;* Payne, *The Life and Death of Adolf Hitler;* Schoenbaum, *Hitler's Social Revolution;* Shirer, *The Rise and Fall of the Third Reich;* von Schlabrendorff, *The Secret War Against Hitler.*

Frelinghuysen, Frederick Theodore, 1817-85, U.S., lawyer. Attorney general for New Jersey from 1861-66, U.S. senator from 1866-69 and 1871-77, and U.S. secretary of state from 1881-85. REF.: *CBA*.

French, Fulton, and **Eversole, Joseph (AKA: Old Joe),** prom.

1800s, U.S., feud. In Perry County, Ky., not long before the turn of the century, Joseph Eversole was the main merchant in Hazard, the county seat of Perry. When Fulton French moved in to start a rival shop, the prosperous Eversole welcomed him, helping set him up in business financially and politically. The two were good friends for about ten years, and then Eversole, who was known locally as Old Joe, became jealous of French's success. Local residents took sides in the quarrel and, when Tom Gayhart, of the French camp, was killed on the river while rolling logs, it was declared by his friends that he had been murdered by the Eversoles, although there was no evidence to support this.

Fulton French had left town not long after Gayhart's death, and a rough, zealous evangelical preacher, the Reverend Bill Gambrill, became the leader of the French contingent, extolling his followers to ambush the Eversoles and murder them. Gambrill was soon killed. Tom Smith, known as "Bad Tom," replaced Gambrill as the Frenches' leader, but Smith and his wife were eventually hanged for a murder that had nothing to do with the feud. (For a few dollars, they murdered their family doctor while he was staying in their house.) Then, Joe Eversole, who had not participated in any of the killings, was ambushed and slain by an unknown attacker. Not long after these events, the feuding ground to a halt and the battle between the Eversoles and the Frenches died of its own accord. REF.: *CBA*.

French, Sir George Arthur, 1841-1921, Can., law enfor. off. Formed the North West Mounted Police, now known as the Royal Canadian Mounted Police, in 1873, and acted as its first commissioner from 1873-76. He established law and order in western Canada by leading an expedition from Dufferin, Manitoba, to the edge of the Rocky Mountains in 1874. REF.: *CBA*

French, Harry, 1907- , U.S., mur. "Tonight about 6:30 Harry French shot Claude L. McCracken, editor of the Modoc *Mail,* with an automatic pistol. Condition of McCracken serious," was the message received by wire services on the evening of Mar. 25, 1937. The story was sent by McCracken as he died in his Alturas, Calif., office after being shot five times by French, the son of a rival newspaper publisher.

McCracken, forty-six, editor and publisher of the Modoc County *Daily Mail* and Associated Press correspondent, was eating dinner at his home with two newspaper employees when the drunken French burst into the house and shot him five times. French was the son of R.A. and G.P. French who had been involved in a professional rivalry since McCracken began publishing the Modoc *Mail* three years earlier.

The resentment started in 1934 when McCracken moved to Alturas and began printing his daily Modoc *Mail* in direct competition to the French family's established weekly, the *Plaindealer & Modoc County Times*. For years, the two publishers had playfully insulted each other often printing practical jokes and insinuations about the other in their respective newspapers. The Frenches' response to a McCracken letter ridiculing the *Plaindealer* was to print a falsified story on the McCrackens' arrest for narcotics. McCracken then ran several stories in the Modoc *Mail* listing individuals named French who had been arrested for various crimes. On the day of his death, the Modoc *Mail* ran a story about a Montana man named French who was hanged for stealing horses.

Upon surrendering to police, immediately after the shooting, Harry French confessed and said, "I have stood all of the insults my family can stand." He was convicted by an Alturas court on July 2. REF.: *CBA*.

French, Jim, prom. 1878, U.S., west. gunman. Jim French, a New Mexico cowboy, was one of the primary participants in the Lincoln County War of 1878. On Mar. 9, 1878, French was a member of a posse of regulators who apprehended accused murderers Frank Baker and Billy Morton. The prisoners escaped briefly, but were soon killed by the posse. Less than a month later, on Apr. 1, French turned to the other side of the law and joined four outlaws including Billy the Kid in killing Sheriff William Brady and Deputy George Hindman. French was

wounded by John Long as the ambushers fled.

In mid-July 1878, French was involved in the final shootout of the regional war, defending the store of Alexander McSween. On July 19, the store was set afire and almost totally burned. French was able to escape, and after surveying the fate of his comrades, decided to retire from the turbulence of New Mexico, and live a more obscure existence.

Gunman Jim French.

REF.: Bartholomew, *The Biographical Album of Western Gunfighters*; ____, *Jesse Evans*; Breihan, *Badmen of Frontier Days*; Brent, *The Complete and Factual Life of Billy the Kid*; Bristow, *Lost on Grand River*; Burns, *The Saga of Billy the Kid*; Casey, *The Texas Border and Some Borderliners*; CBA; Coe, *Frontier Fighter*; Coe, *Ranch on the Ruidoso*; Cunningham, *Triggernometry*; Drago, *Outlaws on Horseback*; Fulton, *Maurice Garland Fulton's History of the Lincoln County War*; ____, *Roswell in Its Early Years*; Garrett, *The Authentic Life of Billy the Kid*; Hamlin, *The True Story of Billy the Kid*; Hendricks, *The Bad Man of the West*; Hertzog, *A Directory of New Mexico Desperadoes*; Hicks, *Belle Starr and Her Pearl*; Holloway, *Texas Gun Lore*; Hough, *The Story of the Outlaw*; Hunt, *The Tragic Days of Billy the Kid*; Jenkinson, *Ghost Towns of New Mexico*; Keleher, *Violence in Lincoln County*; King, *Pioneer Western Empire Builders*; Martin, *Border Boss*; Metz, *John Selman*; Moore, *The West*; Nolan, *The Life and Death of John Henry Tunstall*; O'Connor, *Pat Garrett*; Otero, *The Real Billy the Kid*; Raine, *Famous Sheriffs and Western Outlaws*; Rascoe, *Belle Starr*; Rennert, *Western Outlaws*; Rogers, *The Lusty Texans of Dallas*; Scott, *Belle Starr in Velvet*; Shirley, *Henry Starr*; ____, *Law West of Fort Smith*; Siringo, *Riata and Spurs*; Stanley, *Desperadoes of New Mexico*; Stansbery, *The Passing of the 3D Ranch*; Wellman, *A Dynasty of Western Outlaws*; ____, *Wellman*; White, *Lead and Likker*; ____, *Trigger Fingers*.

French, Jim, prom. 1890s, U.S., arson. Jim French was the leader of an arson gang that operated in St. Louis, Mo., during the 1890s. French and his gang were stopped by private detective Michael Burns who, while undercover, infiltrated the gang and exposed their activities to a grand jury investigating the rash of fires. French stood trial in January 1894, and, primarily from information supplied by Burns, was sentenced to ten years in prison.

REF.: Caesar, *Incredible Detective*; CBA.

French Riviera Gang Wars, prom. 1970-89, Fr., org. crime-mur. On the French Riviera in 1970, more than one hundred people died in a wave of shootings which began with the jailing of crime leader "Mimi" Guerini for his part in a gangland murder. In 1977, Jacques "Tomcat" Imbert, proprietor of a nightclub in the small Riviera resort town of Cassis was shot after a clash with a gang who had assumed control of the Marseilles end of the "French Connection" drug ring. Imbert survived that attack, but was paralyzed and lost one eye. One month later each of his attackers was tracked down and shot to death.

The battle for control of this lucrative area erupted again in October 1978 when nine people were gunned down in a Marseilles bar. Although five of the victims were known criminals, the other four were apparently innocent customers, probably shot to ensure their silence. Police working closely with the FBI believed the killings to be linked to the Mafia. Profit was the obvious motive for the violence, with an estimated £70 million a year collected in the early 1980s from drugs, casino rackets, prostitution, and extortion. REF.: *CBA*.

Freneau, Philip Morin (AKA: **Poet of the American Revolution**), 1752-1832, U.S., rebel. Employed his own sailing vessel to attack and plunder British ships during the Revolutionary War. He was taken prisoner, and placed on a British prison ship until an exchange was arranged in 1780. He penned his experience in verse, entitled, *The British Prison-Ship, a Poem in Four Cantoes,* in 1781. REF.: *CBA.*

Frerichs, Friedrich Theodor von, 1819-85, Ger., path. Served as director of the University of Berlin's Charité Hospital from 1859-85, and was a founder of experimental pathology. REF.: *CBA.*

Frey, Willi, 1924-47, Ger., war crimes. Willi Frey was one of forty-eight Nazis executed at Germany's Landsberg Prison for the murder of 700,000 people at the Mauthausen concentration camp. Frey served as a secret service officer at the camp, where inmates were used in scientific experiments, buried alive, fed to ravenous dogs, and thrown into revolving cement mixers.

Frey walked to the gallows in June 1947. One of the last things he said while standing at the gallows was, "I am dying like Jesus on the cross...without fault." REF.: *CBA.*

Frick, Henry Clay, See: **Berkman, Alexander.**

Frick, Wilhelm, 1877-1946, Ger., war crimes. A bureaucrat for the Weimar Republic, Wilhelm Frick was one of the first German government officials to openly back Adolf Hitler. He supported Hitler during the early 1920s and was one who urged a lenient sentence for Hitler's abortive Beer Hall Putsch of 1923 in Munich. Throughout the 1920s—after Hitler was released from prison—it was Frick who provided funds for his presses and the organization of the Brown Shirt legions. When Hitler became chancellor, he immediately rewarded Frick by naming him minister of the interior. In this capacity, from 1933 on, Frick helped establish the dreaded state police forces of the SS and the Gestapo, created concentration camps, and suppressed Christian churches and political opposition.

Nazi war criminal Wilhelm Frick.

Though Frick helped to plan the invasion of Poland by providing logistical government services, he was removed from his office in 1943 and replaced by Heinrich Himmler, who became minister of the interior. Frick was sent to Prague where he became the "protector" of Bohemia and Moravia. Here he drafted more laws that suppressed the Czech people and was ostensibly responsible for the diabolical operations of the SS in that area. Following WWII, Frick was placed on trial as a war criminal at Nuremberg, where he was judged Guilty of establishing the Nazi conspiracy, particularly in the mid-1930s when he set up laws and regulations that allowed Himmler's SS to persecute and murder countless Jews, Christians, and political opponents of Nazi Germany.

Frick's lawyers did not put him on the witness stand, knowing the old man was still an ardent Nazi and would quickly, through his fanatical belief in Hitler's Reich, prejudice the court. He was nevertheless found Guilty and sentenced to hang with ten other Nazi leaders. On Oct. 16, 1946, Frick entered the execution chamber, the sixth Nazi chief to die by hanging. His wrists were handcuffed and the 69-year-old bureaucrat had to be supported as he shakily made his way up the steps of the scaffold. Before a black hood was placed about his head, Frick cried out: "Long live eternal Germany!" He was then sent through the trap and to his death. See: **Himmler, Heinrich; Hitler, Adolf.**

REF.: *CBA;* Davidson, *The Making of Adolf Hitler;* Fest, *Hitler;* Gilbert, *Nuremberg Diary;* Heiden, *Der Fuehrer;* Höhne, *The Order of the Death's Head: The Story of Hitler's SS;* Neave, *On Trial at Nuremberg;* Orlow, *The History of the Nazi Party;* Payne, *The Life and Death of Adolf Hitler;* Schoenbaum, *Hitler's Social Revolution;* Shirer, *The Rise and Fall of the Third Reich;* Smith, *Reaching Judgment at Nuremberg;* Snyder and Morris, *A Treasury of Great Reporting;* Speer, *Inside the Third Reich;*

_____, *Spandau: The Secret Diaries.*

Friday Market, 1938, a novel by Catherine Meadows. This work of fiction is based upon wife-killer Major Herbert Armstrong (Brit., 1921). See: **Armstrong, Herbert Rowse.** REF.: *CBA.*

Friend, Wilbert Felix, 1910-   , U.S., mur. On the early morning of Sept. 1, 1936, a woman out for an oceanside walk in La Jolla, Calif. found the badly beaten body of Ruth Muir, forty-eight, a YWCA executive secretary, near a bluff overlooking the Pacific Ocean. Following his examination, Dr. F.E. Toomey, the San Diego County coroner's surgeon reported that the woman had apparently been beaten with a club and raped the night before. San Diego Police concluded that the killer crept up behind the vacationing woman as she sat on a bench in the moonlight enjoying the ocean breeze.

Police Chief George Sears ordered a roundup of all persons arrested on morals charges in recent years and by evening more than twenty suspects had been questioned. Two of them, E. Carl Eckdohl, forty-one, and Leon Russell were held for further investigation. Eckdohl had been arrested at his hotel just as he was packing to leave town. Police also issued an all-points-bulletin for a bright yellow roadster which had been driven back and forth in front of Muir's cottage on the night she was killed. The roadster was never found and neither Eckdohl or Russell was ever charged with the murder. Unknown to police at the time, detectives had actually interviewed the murderer in their initial roundup of suspects. Not until May 1955, almost nineteen years after the murder was the case finally solved.

At that time, Wilbert Friend, forty-four, an unemployed gardener, went to place flowers on his mother's grave over the Memorial Day weekend. In the fit of remorse that followed, he called the San Diego *Union* and told a reporter that he had killed Ruth Muir. Friend had been a 25-year-old caddie at the La Jolla Country Club at the time of the murder. Friend admitted that robbery had been his original motive but when he discovered that the Muir woman had no money, he dragged her into the weeds and raped and killed her.

The killer's remorse evaporated by the time Friend came to trial in August 1955; he pleaded not guilty. After examining the details of Friend's confession a jury found him Guilty of murder and on Aug. 17, Superior Court Judge John A. Hewicker sentenced him to death. The verdict was upheld on appeal, but the California Supreme Court ordered a new sentencing trial. On June 20, 1957, Friend was once again sentenced to die. As the verdict was read, Friend bolted for the back door of the San Diego courtroom. He was tackled by two deputies who dragged him back to the defense table.

There was confusion as to how Friend would be executed. California's gas chamber law had gone into effect in 1937, a year after the murder, and a provision of that law was that murderers condemned before that date should be hanged. But in August 1958, twenty-two years after the murder, a judge ruled that because Friend had been sentenced to die, the execution could take place in the pea-green gas chamber at San Quentin Prison. Execution was then scheduled for Oct. 10, 1958. On Oct. 8, Governor Goodwin J. Knight commuted the sentence to life in prison. Friend was paroled on Sept. 23, 1974. On Oct. 23, 1978, he was released from parole and, at the age of sixty-eight, Wilbert Friend once again became a free man. REF.: *CBA.*

Fries, John, c.1750-1818, Case of, U.S., treas. Led armed insurrection of Pennsylvania Germans against tax assessors over the imposition of a federal property tax levied to support the anticipated war with France in 1799. To quell the resistance, President John Adams ordered federal troops into the area. Fries was arrested, tried, and condemned for treason. However, in 1800, he was pardoned by the president. REF.: *CBA.*

Frink, John B., prom. 1840s-60s, Case of, U.S., gamb. John B. Frink was the first policy king of New York City, operating more than 400 policy shops throughout the city. These shops operated around the clock. So successful were Frink's operations that each storefront boldly displayed piles of gold and silver coin in the windows, along with gold nuggets recently taken from California gold fields, all as a lure to those addicted to betting policy numbers. The power behind Frink was super gambler Reuben Parsons, who made millions in banking Faro operations and later lost it all in Wall Street speculations.

In 1870, new legislation outlawed the policy shops and every policy shop in New York was raided and closed up, most of these being Frink's operations. Frink was arrested and taken to court, where he argued that his account books had to be returned to him so he could mount a legal case in his own defense. The magistrate foolishly agreed and Frink and his books departed. The books were returned later and were considerably altered to prove that Frink had gone out of business in compliance with the new law. Nothing could be done to convict Frink and he was released. He vanished from the scene, taking with him the millions he had gleaned in his policy operations.

REF.: Asbury, *Sucker's Progress; CBA;* Chafetz, *Play the Devil.*

Frisco Sue, b.1853, U.S., west. outl. In 1876, 23-year-old Frisco Sue, a beautiful San Francisco prostitute and dance hall girl became discontented and decided to earn a living in the more lucrative career of violent crime. She moved to Nevada, where she took Sims Talbot, a small-time highwayman, as a partner. Their first stagecoach robbery netted them less than they had hoped, so they regrouped and waited for the stagecoach's return trip. This time the stage was filled with security guards. Talbot was shot and killed, and Frisco Sue was arrested and sentenced to prison for three years. Upon release, she returned to San Francisco, married a millionaire, and forever abandoned her career in crime. REF.: *CBA.*

Fristoe, Leonard T., b.1892, U.S., mur. In 1920, Leonard T. Fristoe was sentenced to life for the murder of two deputy sheriffs, but he escaped from prison after serving only three years of his term. Forty-six years later, in 1969, he was captured in Compton, Calif., after authorities received a tip from his son.

REF.: Boar, *The World's Most Infamous Murders; CBA.*

Frith, John, 1503-33, Brit., her. Assisted William Tyndale with his translation of the New Testament, and was compelled to leave England in order to escape religious persecution from 1528-32. He returned from abroad in 1532, was placed in prison for heresy, and burned at the stake in 1533. REF.: *CBA.*

Frith, Mary, See: Cutpurse, Moll.

Fritzsche, Hans, prom. 1940s, Ger., war crimes. During the reign of Adolf Hitler's Third Reich, Hans Fritzsche espoused Hitler's Nazi propaganda as radio spokesman. In February 1947, the Nuremberg International Military Tribunal sentenced Fritzsche to nine years in a prison camp for "political crimes against the German people." As part of the sentence, all of Fritzsche's civil freedoms and property were taken from him. REF.: *CBA.*

Frome, Mrs. Weston G., 1892-1938, and **Frome, Nancy**, 1915-38, U.S., (unsolv.) mur. In March 1938, Nancy Frome, twenty-three, of Berkeley, Calif., planned to make a cross-country railroad trip to visit her sister, Mrs. Benjamin McMakin, who lived on Parris Island, S.C. The day before she was to leave on the trip, Nancy's mother, Mrs. Weston G. Frome, expressed concern for the girl's safety. A long, solitary railroad trip across the entire country could be dangerous. The two decided to make the trip together in the family sedan. While crossing the New Mexico desert the car developed engine problems. The women barely made it into El Paso, Texas, on Mar. 25, 1938. The travelers had to wait several days before a garage could start repairs. The women took advantage of the breakdown by making several trips across the Rio Grande River to Juarez, Mexico to shop for bargain items. On Mar. 30 they picked up the car and headed east toward Dallas. They were never seen alive again.

The next day the Frome car, with the key in the ignition, was found abandoned on the Old Spanish Trail near Balmorhea, Texas. Then began a futile four-day search involving a U.S. Coast Guard plane and hundreds of civilian volunteers. Jim Milam, a truck driver from El Paso, Texas, remembered seeing the women's car and a second automobile, the day of the disappearance. Both

cars had been in the foothills of the Davis Mountains, 125 miles east of El Paso. The setting was desolate West Texas Gothic, purple mountains ringing an area of red dirt and tangled sagebrush, an area populated mostly by coyotes just miles from the Rio Grande River. According to Milam, the Frome sedan and a blue coupe had passed him Wednesday afternoon a few miles east of Van Horn. Then, strangely enough, both cars later passed him again, heading in the opposite direction.

When police went to the area they found tire tracks showing that the women's sedan had swerved off the road and had been driven through the brush for over 250 yards before being brought back to the pavement. Fifty yards further along the highway, the tracks once again went into the brush. A half mile from the highway they found the partially nude bodies of the two women face down in the red earth. Dr. W.W. Waite conducted an autopsy, and later reported that neither of the women had been raped. "Both women had been made the victims of what must have been horrible torture," the doctor said. "They had been beaten, tortured, and shot. The knuckles of the girl's hands were burned and her right hand was seared to the bone by flame or embers from a burning cigar or cigarette. Someone had jumped on the girl until her diaphragm had been ruptured." The mother and daughter had both been beaten about the face and head, and both had been shot through the left temple. When found, one of Nancy Frome's hands clutched a pack of matches, the other gripped a man's handkerchief. Her fingers and toes were dug into the red dirt. In addition to the dirt under Nancy's fingernails, blood and skin were found. She had put up a fight to stay alive.

El Paso County District Attorney Roy Jackson reconstructed the murder, believing that the murderers were either invited or forced their way into the Frome car and took over the steering wheel. When it passed truck driver Jim Milam, he thought he saw a man and a woman along with the Frome women. Other witnesses led police to believe that two men and two women were involved in the murders. "It would appear that the women struggled desperately with the driver, who later took them out of the car and shot them to death," Jackson later told reporters. Such a struggle would explain the zigzagging of the car between the brush and the road.

When Weston G. Frome, the husband and father of the dead women and a powder company executive, was told of the apparent struggle put up by Nancy Frome he said: "She would. She was the gamest little thing in the world."

A motive for the murders was never clearly established. Although $90 cash and some valuables were missing, most of the women's jewelry was found on their bodies. The theory that the daughter had been tortured to make her reveal the whereabouts of hidden money or valuables would not explain why most of the jewelry was ignored. Some police officers thought the Frome auto had been mistaken for one used by drug runners. This theory was supported by the fact that the vehicle's spare tire, often used as a hiding place by dope smugglers, had been cut open and the inner tube removed.

Evidence technicians determined that the women had been killed with a .32-caliber revolver, probably one manufactured in Spain, but the weapon was never found. All the women's luggage was missing and the car had been wiped clean of fingerprints. A $10,000 reward was offered for evidence leading to the killers, but no one ever claimed it.

Ten years after the murder, two men and two women were arrested by a West Texas Sheriff acting on an informant's tip and charged with the murders but, after extensive investigation by the Texas Rangers, the four were released. Every word of their alibi had turned out to be true. On another occasion, an apparently airtight case was built against another suspect until it was discovered that the man had been in prison at the time of the Frome murders.

By 1953, fifteen years after the murder, thousands of suspects had been questioned by the Texas Rangers and other law enforcement officials, and the records of the investigation took up three large drawers of a filing cabinet. All of the records of the case are still marked unsolved. REF.: *CBA*.

Fromentin, Eligius, d.1822, U.S., jur. U.S. senator from Louisiana from 1813-19. He served as criminal court judge in New Orleans in 1821, prior to receiving an appointment from President James Monroe to the Florida Territorial Court in 1821. REF: *CBA*.

Fromme, Lynette Alice (Squeaky), See: **Ford, Gerald Rudolph**.

Fronde Uprising, prom. 1650s, Fr., riot. The Fronde was the name of two civil wars: one in France, lasting from 1648-52; and the other in Spain, lasting from 1653-59. Beginning in 1648, the followers of Cardinal Mazarin—successor to Cardinal Richelieu—were pelted with stones by a Paris mob. In August, Mazarin ordered the arrests of the parliamentary leaders, but having no army, he was forced to release the prisoners and flee Paris two months later. Condé Conti and Longueville were arrested on Jan. 14, 1650, and released fifteen months later.

In February 1652, the Frondeurs were aided by Archduke Leopold William of Spain, who captured fortresses in northern France, and in October recaptured Paris, forcing Mazarin to flee and allowing the king to return. The Fronde shifted to Spain in 1653, with Condé aligning with the King of Spain and fighting several border battles against French forces. The conflict ended with the signing of the Pyrenees Peace Treaty on Nov. 5, 1659. REF.: *CBA*.

Front de Liberation du Quebec (FLQ), prom. 1970s, Can., terr.-kid.-mur. In late 1970, Quebec was kept on the edge of its seat as a dangerous chess game was played between the provincial government, and separatists of the Front de Liberation du Quebec. On Oct. 5, 1970, James Richard Cross, the British trade commissioner to Canada, was abducted from his Quebec home by four armed gunmen. In their ransom communiqué, the FLQ's major demands included the immediate release of twenty-three compatriots, payment of $500,000 in gold, and assured escape to Cuba or Algeria. The provincial government of Quebec refused these orders on Oct. 8, but offered to read the FLQ manifesto over television airwaves.

This did not suit the FLQ. In their next and supposedly final demand, they called for the prisoners to be released by 6:00 p.m. on Oct. 10, or Cross would be killed. The government countered with an offer of free passage in exchange for Cross' freedom. This was also not acceptable to the terrorists. But instead of murdering Cross, they kidnapped another government official: Pierre Laporte, Quebec's minister of labor. Laporte, said the FLQ, would be killed at 10:00 p.m. if all demands were not met.

Stalling for time, the government issued a statement at 9:55 p.m. that they needed proof the victims would be recovered alive. They asked, as a measure of good faith, that one man from each of the two cells of the FLQ involved in the kidnappings surrender. But the FLQ only gave "a solemn pledge to the people of Quebec" that they would honor their word and release the hostages.

The FLQ began to rouse the support of students from the University of Quebec. The government called out troops on Oct. 15, to protect its officials and public buildings. Thus secured, it made what it called its final offer to the kidnappers: if they freed Laporte and Cross, five FLQ prisoners of the government would be emancipated, and all concerned could leave the country.

During the next two days, the government issued the first peacetime declaration of a state of "apprehended insurrection," which allowed the government to take any action required to ensure national security. It condemned the FLQ, and arrested more than 250 people suspected of FLQ connections. Finally, there was a new offer from the government: the prisoners would be handed over to the Cuban consulate and the kidnappers would leave the country; upon their arrival in Cuba, Laporte and Cross would be set free by the Cuban officials. But the FLQ's patience had been tried one too many times. On Oct. 18, Laporte's body was found; he had been strangled to death.

The tension then eased to a stalemate while the government quietly went about locating Cross and his abductors. On Nov. 6,

Bernard Lortie, nineteen, was arrested in connection with the crime. On Dec. 2, the police surrounded a Montreal house where Cross was being held. Sensing the end of their ordeal, the kidnappers finally decided to give their prisoner up for free passage to Cuba. Cross was set free, and three FLQ members and four relatives were flown to safety, courtesy of the Royal Canadian Mounted Police.

The government intensely questioned Lortie until he came up with the names of three accomplices: Francis Simard, Paul Rose, and Paul's brother, Jacques. They were apprehended on Dec. 28, charged with the kidnappings, and were later found "criminally responsible" for Laporte's murder at a coroner's inquest.

During a series of trials throughout 1971, Paul Rose was found Guilty of Laporte's murder and kidnapping, for which he received two concurrent life sentences. Simard received one life sentence for his involvement in the murder, and Lortie was given twenty years for participation in the kidnapping. Jacques Rose was acquitted of all charges.

The kidnappers who escaped to Cuba were last known to be safe in France, since the French government was honoring the "safe passage" agreement the FLQ had negotiated with Quebec. REF.: *CBA*.

Frost, George William, prom. 1900s, Brit., fraud. A successful swindler at the turn of the century, George William Frost had pulled in over £13,000 in a major swindle before being arrested in 1908 and sentenced to four years in prison. Previously, Frost had served two other terms of three years each for similar convictions of fraud.

REF.: *CBA*; Nicholls, *Crime Within the Square Mile*.

Frost, John, 1784-1877, and **Jones, William Lloyd**, prom. 1839, and **Williams, Zephaniah**, prom. 1839, Brit., treas. A draper and tailor, John Frost led the failed Chartist revolt at Newport, Monmouth, in November 1839, in an attempt to force the British government to grant male suffrage, improved working conditions, and equitable payment to the lower classes.

Frost played a major role in getting the Reform Bill of 1832 passed into law—a bill that was supposed to enfranchise the working classes. His notoriety earned him the elected post of mayor of Newport in 1836, a position he held until 1837, when he realized that the Reform Bill had helped the middle class substantially, but had done nothing for the lower classes.

When the Chartists' petition for better conditions was rejected by the House of Commons in July 1839, and plans for a general strike fell apart, Frost, along with Zephaniah Williams, a local innkeeper, and William Lloyd Jones, a watchmaker, began to organize troops consisting mainly of miners, the most impoverished workers. The tension mounted until November, when the hostile group, split into three divisions, began a march on Newport, an effort that was to show the government through physical force the strength of the Chartists.

The revolt was a total fiasco. Ambushed by soldiers when they arrived in the Newport square, Frost's men were trapped. When the panic had subsided, more than ten miners had been killed and more than fifty wounded. Williams and Jones, whose battalions had yet to arrive in Newport, had time to retreat.

Frost, Williams, and Jones were eventually caught and put on trial for high treason. They were defended by Sir Frederick Pollock, a meticulous attorney who stretched every point made in the trial into a major legal issue, causing the trial to drag on for days. In the end, the leaders of the revolt were all found Guilty, but the jury was moved to recommend mercy. This advice went unheeded by the judges, who sentenced the men to death on Jan. 8, 1840. The sentence was eventually commuted to transportation to Australia.

After sixteen years in Van Diemens Land, John Frost was granted a full pardon and he returned to England for the remainder of his life.

REF.: *CBA*; Postgate, *Murder, Piracy and Treason*.

Frost, Samuel, d.1793, U.S., mur. Samuel Frost, a native of Princeton, Mass., was mentally deficient and suffered fits of violence. In 1783 he killed his father with a spike but was acquitted. While working with Capt. Elisha Allen, with whom he lived, Frost suddenly became incensed over some imagined wrong, grabbed a hoe and began beating Allen on the head, killing him. Though certifiably insane, Frost was nevertheless tried and convicted of Allen's murder. He was hanged on Oct. 31, 1793.

REF.: *CBA; The Confession and Dying Words of Samuel Frost.*

Fry, Sir Edward, 1827-1918, Brit., jur. Justice for the Court of Appeal from 1883-92, and sat on the Hague Tribunal in 1900. He was noted for his arbitration of international legal proceedings, including: the Pious Fund Case between Mexico and the U.S., between 1902-03, and the Casablanca incident between France and Germany between 1908-09. REF.: *CBA.*

Fry, Elizabeth (Elizabeth Gurney), 1780-1845, Brit., pris. reform. A Quaker minister who was interested in prison reform, Elizabeth Fry also founded an order of nursing sisters. In 1813, Fry visited the notorious Newgate Jail, and found more than three hundred women and children living in filth and wearing rags. In near bestial conditions, marriages took place at the jail; one couple produced ten children within the prison confines before the convicted criminal died. Many of the Newgate inmates were kept in chains constantly. In the terrible Press Yard, heavy weights were pushed down on prisoners until they either confessed or died.

REF.: *CBA;* Nicholls, *Crime Within the Square Mile.*

Fry, John, 1907- , U.S., (wrong. convict.) mansl. On the night of Aug. 1, 1958, John Fry drank himself into oblivion. He knew the hangover would wear off eventually, but another side-effect would end up getting him in a lot of trouble: he could not remember what happened on that night.

It also happened to be the night that Fry's common-law wife, 47-year-old Elvira May, was found brutally beaten and strangled in a bathtub in a San Francisco rooming house. Fry, fifty-one, had a history of beating the woman, and when he was found in another rooming house nearby, he was apprehended as the prime suspect in the killing. The traces of blood on the sheets of his bed and his previous assault arrests did not help his case.

Under interrogation, Fry admitted that his heavy drinking prohibited him from remembering anything about the night his wife was murdered. He was eventually charged with murder, but on advice from his state-appointed counsel, pleaded guilty to manslaughter. He was convicted and handed an indeterminate sentence of one to ten years at San Quentin Penitentiary in California.

That was the end of John Fry's story, until June 4, 1959. On that day, Richard T. Cooper, an unemployed janitor, strolled into a San Francisco police station and admitted to strangling Erlean Mosley, a hotel maid. He told them he was turning himself in because he was afraid he was going to do it again. After all, he told them, he had strangled someone else the previous August.

Before long, the district attorney's office and the police found that Cooper was telling the truth. After Fry, who had insisted he was innocent ever since his conviction, consented to a lie detector test, it was decided that he was also telling the truth. On June 16, Governor Edmund G. Brown granted a pardon, and Fry walked free and penniless, except for the $40 standard pay given to every freed convict, and $1.15 for bus fare.

Fry sued the state of California for $5,000 compensation, and was finally granted a sum of $3,000 in 1960. REF.: *CBA.*

Fryatt, Charles Algernon, 1872-1916, Brit., sab. As captain of the merchant vessel *Brussels* in 1916, he was taken captive by Germans, who charged him with attempting to smash into a German submarine. He was found Guilty, sentenced to death, and shot as a French soldier. REF.: *CBA.*

Fuchs, Bernard, and Tannenbaum, Gershon, prom. 1965, U.S., fraud. In 1965, a bank teller at the Central Home Trust Company of Elizabeth, N.J., became wary when two men applied to open an account for nearby "Marlowe University" located in Mount Holly. Familiar with the neighborhood, the teller had never heard of the school, and managed to stall both men. The Postal Inspection Service began investigating the incident when it was discovered that the university operated through the mail. The next time the men came in to the bank, both were arrested by postal inspectors. They were carrying $6,000 and it was discovered that they had taken in about $200,000 from students who were granted Bachelor's or Master's degree, for $400, and PhDs, for only $500. Bernard Fuchs, twenty-two, and Gershon Tannenbaum, twenty-three, both Orthodox rabbis from Brooklyn, had advertised Marlowe University in educational journals distributed internationally. The Marlowe University plan was "equivalent to the usual resident university course except that the student can finish it in only a few months." A fictitious faculty and staff list was included to complete the fraud, with both of the rabbis standing in to write responses for any of the staff members who received correspondence. Students applying for admission were instructed to send $100. When their thesis was approved, the remainder of the tuition was submitted, and the student became a graduate. No actual degrees were sent out, and the students would not hear from the university again. Almost all theses were accepted. Both Fuchs and Tannenbaum pleaded guilty, then withdrew their guilty pleas, and then pleaded guilty again to charges of mail fraud. In a Brooklyn Federal Court on Oct. 6, 1972, they were given suspended sentences and fined $250 each by Judge George Rosling, who placed them both on one year's probation, ordering them to repay the $2,000 they had collected. According to assistant U.S. attorney Emmanuel A. Moore, the additional collected proceeds had been returned earlier.

REF.: *CBA;* Kahn, *Fraud.*

Fuchs, Ernst, 1859-1929, Ger., jur. Legal expert famed for his role in German jurisprudence. REF.: *CBA.*

Fugate, Caril Ann, See: **Starkweather, Charles.**

Fugmann, Michael, 1884-1937, U.S., mur. During the Easter season in 1936, in the midst of labor strife in the coal-mining region near Wilkes-Barre, Pa., six men received what appeared to be gift boxes of cigars. On Good Friday, Tom Maloney, a former anthracite coal miner's union leader who had recently defected to the United Mine Workers of America and his 4-year-old son were blown up by a bomb when he opened his box. Shortly thereafter, 70-year-old Mike Gallagher became the victim of a second bomb. Luther Kniffen, a former county sheriff, received a similar parcel, but escaped injury when he inadvertently opened the bottom of the box and saw the deadly contents. Police broadcast warnings and the remaining cigar boxes were returned undetonated.

Michael Fugmann, a fervent opponent of the United Mine Workers, was apprehended and charged in the bombing attacks. Arthur Koehler, who was instrumental in tying Bruno Richard Hauptmann to the murder of Charles Lindbergh, Jr. through the physical evidence of wooden fragments from a ladder rung, was brought to Wilkes-Barre. Koehler determined that the wood used in the bombs matched wood found in the home of Fugmann. Fugmann was subsequently convicted of the murders and executed in the electric chair in June 1937, REF.: *CBA.*

Fujiwara Sumitomo, d.941, Japan, pir. Government official who was directed by the Japanese court to put an end to piracy on the Inland Sea. He turned pirate leader himself, and soon gained control of the area, before he was defeated by the Japanese government. REF.: *CBA.*

Fukunaga, Myles Yutaka, 1909-29, U.S., kid.-mur. On Sept. 18, 1928, 10-year-old Gill Jamieson, the son of a bank vice-president, was abducted from a Honolulu school. Hours later, his father Frederick W. Jamieson received a ransom note at his office demanding $10,000 for his son's return. The elder Jamieson complied, delivering $4,000 to the presumed kidnapper at a crowded band concert. When the boy was not returned, a massive search effort ensued. Twenty thousand children were released from their schools to aid the police, military, and civilian volunteers in their search for the youngster. Jamieson's bank, the Hawaiian Trust Company, offered a $5,000 reward for any information, and Sheriff Patrick Gleason offered an additional $1,000 reward. However, the boy was already dead.

The police arrested 19-year-old Myles Yutaka Fukunaga for murder. At his arraignment on Sept. 24, 1928, he pleaded guilty to a murder charge, but Circuit Court Judge Alva E. Steadman refused the plea for first-degree murder. At his trial, Fukunaga stated that he had patterned the crime after the recent kidnapping of Bobby Franks by Leopold and Loeb. He wanted the money to enable his parents to travel to Japan. Fukunaga was found Guilty for his already confessed crime and was executed in 1929. REF.: *CBA*.

Fulkerson, Samuel Cole, b.1891, U.S., fraud. In a thirteen-year career of mail fraud, Samuel Cole Fulkerson made millions of dollars with three fictitious organizations. With a network of hundreds of salesmen and at least a thousand medical practitioners, Fulkerson happily shared his profits with chiropractors, osteopaths, and medical doctors. An Iowan, Fulkerson began selling vitamins in 1940, founding a low-key food supplements and vitamin company that was doing a moderate business when, in 1949, Fulkerson went to California and had a serious car accident. Recuperating in Los Angeles, he became involved with John A. Restifo, who ran a pathology laboratory with an assistant, Robert B. Holmes. Fulkerson had an idea to set up a business that analyzed urine samples of healthy people and came up with dire reports, warning of "impaired body chemistry" and "hormonal imbalances" for which expensive and customized vitamins were prescribed as the cure. Carl R. Nelson, an osteopath, analyzed the urinalysis reports for Nutritional Research Associates, recommending vitamins according to deficiencies. The vitamins would be transmitted through practitioners, who would get half of the retail price on each bottle sold, and half of the thirty dollar charge for the analysis and dosage prescription as well. Advertising extensively in chiropractic and osteopathic journals, Fulkerson hired a pulp western writer to pen his copy—Restifo—who probably never went to college at all and was alternately referred to as an M.D. and a Ph.D.

By 1958, the Internal Revenue Service had discovered that Restifo had underestimated five years of income, and stated that he had not accounted for $207,909.49 from 1952-57. Indicted for tax evasion, Restifo fled to Mexico. Fulkerson and Holmes shifted operations to Flagstaff, Ariz. When the F.D.A. questioned Fulkerson, he told them that about 2,700 practitioners had referred patients to him; many chiropractors were by then paying fees of $175 to attend Fulkerson's seminars. A CBS producer, Jay L. McMullen, decided to expose mail order medicine scams, and wrote to Fulkerson's Nutritional Research Associates in Cedar Rapids, Iowa, without specifying his business. McMullen asked a New York City Department of Health physician to make up a "sample" which consisted of distilled water, food coloring, iodine, and a dash of urea. Although there were no hormones in the brew, Fulkerson's operation found fourteen of them, and sent a typical analysis letter, warning of "low normal range." McMullen's findings were televised by Walter Cronkite in late June 1965, and precipitated an investigation headed by Charles Miller, of the Postal Inspection Service. Fulkerson, Holmes, and Nelson were convicted of mail fraud and the operation was ended.
REF.: *CBA; Kahn, Fraud.*

Fullam, Augusta Fairfield, 1876-1914, India, mur. While stationed with her husband Edward in Agra, India, Augusta Fairfield Fullam began a love affair with Dr. Henry Lovell William Clark, a Eurasian assigned to the Indian Subordinate Medical Service. The couple met at a military ball in 1911. Clark told Fullam that he found his wife and four children no longer desirable, and Fullam responded by saying that she had had about enough of her husband, an accounts examiner. Fullam and Clark began to see each other regularly and started a correspondence that was to be their undoing. Clark wrote several notes to his wife, one of which read: "I am fed up with your low disgusting ways, for I am quite sure you don't care a damn what becomes of me. With fond love and kisses to self and the rest at home, I remain, Your affectionate husband, H.L. Clark."

By the autumn of 1911, both marriages had deteriorated badly.

Mrs. Fullam resolved to murder her husband, and enlisted Dr. Clark, whose medical skills helped him select a suitable poison. It was decided that sprinkling arsenic in Edward's soup would simulate heatstroke. But after Augusta applied inordinate quantities of the poison to the food with no visible effect, Clark injected Fullam with a powerful dose of an alkaloid poison known as gelsemine. Fullam died on Oct. 19, 1911, from what Clark recorded as "heatstroke."

On Nov. 17, 1912, four Indians with swords crept into Mrs. Clark's bedroom and slashed her to ribbons. The killers took the sum of 100 rupees, or about $5 per man. When questioned by police about his movements on the night of the murder, Clark said he was dining with Mrs. Fullam. Investigators searched her residence and found a large tin box under the bed. An officer who attempted to pry the lid open was sharply reprimanded by the murderess. "That's Dr. Clark's dispatch box—you dare not touch it!" Inside the box was a stack of carefully preserved letters. The correspondence told of the unfolding murder plot, and it proved to be enough evidence to convict the pair before the judges of the high court in Allahabad. Clark was executed on Mar. 26, 1913, after his lover turned king's evidence.

Augusta Fullam bore Clark's baby in prison. A year later, on May 29, 1914, she died in prison from what doctors diagnosed as heatstroke.
REF.: *CBA; Duke, The Stroke of Murder; Goodman, Posts-Mortem: The Correspondence of Murder; Gross, Masterpieces of Murder; Gribble, Such Women Are Deadly; Laurence, Extraordinary Crimes; Nash, Look For the Woman; Pearson, Memories of A KC's Clerk; Sanders, Murders in the Big Cities; Walsh, The Agra Double Murder.*

Fulle, Floyd, prom. 1970s, U.S., polit. corr. Floyd Fulle was serving as Cook County board commissioner in Chicago in 1975, when he was convicted of extortion, tax fraud, and perjury during an investigation by District Attorney (later Governor) James Thompson. Fulle was caught accepting thousands of dollars in bribes in exchange for special treatment in regards to zoning laws. After repeated appeals, he finally began serving his five-year sentence at the federal prison in Sandstone, Minn., on Jan. 28, 1977.

Five months after Fulle entered prison, the Supreme Court refused to overturn the conviction. Fulle's lawyers had attempted to show that Republican Fulle was the victim of Thompson's attempts to prove himself an impartial prosecutor capable of indicting members of both political parties. Thompson, also a Republican, had convicted several officials during his investigation, the majority of them Democrats. REF.: *CBA.*

Fuller, Melville Weston, 1833-1910, U.S., jur. Provided the much-publicized defense of the Reverend Charles E. Cheney from the Christ Church of Chicago, who was charged with canonical disobedience. He was appointed by President Grover Cleveland as chief justice of the U.S. Supreme Court in 1888, without having any prior judicial service or holding of federal office. As chief justice he authored over 800 majority opinions including the court's first test of the Sherman Antitrust Act in *U.S. v. E.C. Knight Co.* in 1895, and the income tax case of that same year, *Pollock v. Farmers' Loan and Trust Co.* He also served on the Permanent Court of Arbitration at The Hague from 1900-1910. REF.: *CBA.*

Fuller, Nora (AKA: Eleanor Maude Parline), 1886-1902, U.S., (unsolv.) mur. The murder of 15-year-old Nora Fuller, if it had happened only four years later, may have been a fairly easy crime to solve. By 1906, San Francisco and the rest of the U.S. had finally begun learning the technique of fingerprint investigation. Without this knowledge in 1902, the San Francisco Police Department had no way of expanding on the little evidence they had as to their prime suspect.

Eleanor Maude (Nora) Parline was born in China, the daughter of a steamboat engineer who deserted his family when she was four. Shortly thereafter, Mrs. Parline took her children and moved to San Francisco, where she married W. W. Fuller. Nora adopted this last name as her own, even though this marriage also failed.

The family had a tough time making ends meet, so in 1902, at the age of fifteen, Nora dropped out of school and looked for employment.

Her plan was to become an actress. She wrote a letter to an agency, modestly telling them of her "fairly good soprano voice." She never had the chance to test her voice on stage because she ended up answering a different employment advertisement that appeared in the San Francisco *Chronicle* on Jan. 8. It stated quite simply: "WANTED—Young white girl to take care of baby; good home and good wages." Her query received a reply on Jan. 11, which instructed her to meet a Mr. John Bennett at a restaurant on Geary St., at either 1 p.m. or 6 p.m. that day.

Nora chose the later time, and her mother sent her off with a list of groceries she was to bring home with her after the meeting with Mr. Bennett. She had been gone an hour when the Fullers' telephone rang. Nora's 12-year-old brother answered, and a voice on the other end that sounded like Nora told him that she was at Mr. Bennett's home, 1500 Geary St., and that he wanted her to start work immediately. The message was relayed to Mrs. Fuller, who told her son to tell her daughter to come home now—she could start work the following Monday. Nora told her brother she would come home and hung up. It was the last anyone heard from Nora Fuller.

Besides the fact that Nora's killer has never been found, another mystery remains: Mrs. Fuller waited five days before reporting to the police that her daughter was missing. If she had gone to 1500 Geary St. to find out why her daughter had not returned, the investigation could have started much sooner and the trail would not have been as cold. The address happened to be a vacant lot.

The San Francisco newspapers devoted much of their column space to the girl's disappearance on Jan. 16, but there was no sign of Nora for more than three weeks. Then on Feb. 8, as a real estate inspector walked through an empty residence at 2211 Sutter St. to assure its readiness for future tenants, he came across a room in which the shades had been drawn. He noticed a nude female figure lying on a bed, and in his embarrassment closed the door and tried knocking. When there was no response to his repeated knocks, he fetched a policeman. Upon entering and raising the shade, the officer found that the girl on the bed had been dead for some time, her body brutally beaten.

Mrs. Fuller confirmed that the body was her missing daughter. A coroner's report showed that she had been strangled, probably within a day of her disappearance. The house was subjected to a thorough search—thorough, at least, by police standards at the time. In fact, any number of clues may have been passed over, due to the fact that no one in the San Francisco force was using fingerprint or microscope techniques to aid in the search. An empty whiskey bottle found on the scene, which was probably covered with tell-tale prints, was disposed of early in the investigation. The search proved futile; no food had been eaten on the premises, no application had ever been made for gas or water, no fires had been built in the fireplace, and not a shred of clothing (other than Nora's) or paper could be found. Mrs. Fuller studied the wallpaper in vain for a note written or scratched by her daughter. Even the contents of Nora's purse were useless in uncovering more information. The postal card that had John Bennett's handwritten instructions, which Nora had carried when she left to meet him, had been removed from her purse.

A check with the restaurant where Nora's fateful rendezvous occurred was of some help. Witnesses said that a mustached man who stood five feet, nine inches tall, weighed about 165 pounds, and was known to the waiters as "Tenderloin," had told the cashier that a girl would soon arrive looking for him. "Tenderloin," who earned his nickname because he only ate the tenderloin portion of the porterhouse steaks he often ordered, then waited for about a half-hour before he left, paced up and down the sidewalk in front of the restaurant, and then left. The man's meeting with the girl was never witnessed by anyone.

Police found that 2211 Sutter St. had been rented to a man who called himself C. B. Hawkins, who claimed he was new in town and could give no references. The realtor discerned by the stranger's dress that he was a respectable businessman, and accepted one month's rent in cash from Mr. Hawkins. The realtor's description of Mr. Hawkins was identical to the waiters' description of "Tenderloin."

A number of people involved with providing the meager furnishings of the apartment also helped investigators. C. B. Hawkins had purchased a bed, an old chair, a second-hand mattress, two pillows, and two blankets from two furniture establishments. Some of the furniture, at Mr. Hawkins' mysterious request, had been delivered at night. The salesmen who had waited on Mr. Hawkins gave descriptions that matched the previous descriptions. One delivery boy also gave a similar description. The other delivery boy, who had the unfortunate task of delivering the merchandise at night, could not get a look at his customer. The house had no electricity, and the man who answered the door asked that the items be placed in the hallway.

Only one more lead was to come to the police. On Jan. 16, the same day that the papers first covered Nora's disappearance, an article appeared on the disappearance of one "Charles B. Hadley," a clerk for the San Francisco *Examiner* who had fallen short with his accounts. Detectives, interested that the initials were the same as their "C. B. Hawkins," decided to investigate. Hadley was no longer at the address on file, but his live-in girlfriend, Ollie Blasier, was. After much questioning, Blasier made a statement to the police that told of Hadley deserting her the night of the first newspaper articles discussing Nora's disappearance. "It is well known," her deposition went on, "that Hadley is partial to porterhouse steaks and that he eats only the tenderloin...I confess that I suspect he committed this murder."

Hadley was clean-shaven, but it did not take long to find where he had purchased numerous false mustaches. A photo of Hadley with a mustache drawn in was shown to witnesses describing Bennett and Hawkins, and they almost unanimously confirmed that this was the man they had seen. In 1900, it was discovered, Hadley had raped a 15-year-old girl, though for some reason the police had no record of an arrest or conviction for the crime. Investigators finally uncovered the fact that the man who had gone under the names John Bennett, C. B. Hawkins, and Charles B. Hadley was in fact Charles Start, wanted for an 1889 embezzlement charge in Minneapolis, Minn.

Despite thousands of circulars offering a reward for the whereabouts of Start, he was never found. In an attempt to preserve the public standing of the San Francisco police, a police captain later came to an unfounded conclusion: "Many believe that he (Start) committed suicide."

REF.: *CBA;* Duke, *Celebrated Criminal Cases of America;* Rodell, *San Francisco Murders.*

Fulton, Charles Britton, 1910- , U.S., jur. Received appointment from President John F. Kennedy to the Southern District Court of Florida in 1963. As a member of the Judicial Council of Florida, he participated in drafting the Public Defender Act in 1963. He wrote the article "How to Conduct a Criminal Trial" in 1973. REF.: *CBA.*

Fulton, Sir Eustace Cecil, 1880-1954, Brit., lawyer. Appointed to the Old Bailey as a junior prosecuting counsel during WWI, became a senior prosecuting counsel in 1932, and was appointed the Chairman of the County of London Sessions in 1936. Among the murder trials he prosecuted were: Thomas Joseph Davidson, Alfred Arthur Kopsch, Madame Fahmy, Theodosis Petrou, and both trials of Frederick Field. REF.: *CBA.*

Fulton, Katie, prom. late 19th Cent., U.S., duel-asslt. Katie Fulton was a prominent madame in the Denver underworld. She faced another madame in a duel in an attempt to end a rivalry for the affections of a gentleman named Cort Thomson. The women paced, a count of three was given, and they turned and fired. The rival's bullet hit a nearby tree trunk, but Katie's bullet struck Thomson's neck.

Thomson received only a superficial wound and was treated

at Denver General Hospital. Witnesses to the duel were evenly divided over whether Fulton was simply a bad aim, or was looking for a more permanent solution to the feud.

REF.: *CBA*; Drago, *Notorious Ladies of the Frontier*.

Funk, Walther, 1890-1960, Ger., war crimes. Dr. Walther Funk joined the Nazi Party in 1931 as an informal representative for a small group of industrialists and soon established a Nazi-dominated financial news service. By 1933, Adolf Hitler appointed him Minister of Economics. Funk toured middle European countries in 1938, arranging economic co-operation on terms favorable to Germany, and specialized in barter arrangements, but later claimed his office was eventually stripped of its authority. When he was tried, along with twenty-one other war criminals at Nuremberg in 1946, Funk said that he was "a man who stood at many doors but who wasn't always asked in." He admitted that his ef-

Nazi war criminal Walther Funk.

forts helped to gain many of the raw materials needed by the Nazis to wage war. President of the Reichsbank, Hitler's press chief and economic adviser, Funk also claimed that while he was president of the Nazi bank he was unaware that gold teeth and dental bridges removed from concentration camp victims were deposited in the bank vaults at the Elite Guard's request. Sentenced to life imprisonment at Nuremberg, Funk was discharged from Berlin's Spandau Prison on May 16, 1957, because of his weak physical condition and his age. He died in Bonn, Germany, on June 2, 1960. See: **Hitler, Adolf**; **Nuremberg Trials**.

REF.: *CBA*; Fest, *Hitler*; Gilbert, *Nuremberg Diary*; Heiden, *Der Fuehrer*; Höhne, *The Order of the Death's Head: The Story of Hitler's SS*; Neave, *On Trial at Nuremberg*; Orlow, *The History of the Nazi Party*; Payne, *The Life and Death of Adolf Hitler*; Schoenbaum, *Hitler's Social Revolution*; Shirer, *The Rise and Fall of the Third Reich*; Smith, *Reaching Judgment at Nuremberg*; Speer, *Inside the Third Reich*; _____, *Spandau: The Secret Diaries*.

Funston, John, d.1825, U.S., mur. John Funston, of Coshocton, Ohio, long held a grievance against post boy William Cartmill (or Cartmell), apparently because Cartmill dropped his mail in the mud on one occasion. Waiting in ambush, Funston shot and killed Cartmill on Sept. 9, 1825, but he was seen standing over the body and was later picked out of a police lineup by eyewitnesses. Funston was convicted and hanged at New Philadelphia, Ohio, on Dec. 30, 1825.

REF.: *CBA*; *The Trial and Confession of John Funston*.

Furguson, Arthur, d.1938, Brit.-U.S., fraud. If a well-executed, seemingly impossible swindle is a gauge of intelligence, then Arthur Furguson was nothing short of a genius. His ability to deliver a flawless sales pitch, refined through extensive training as an actor, enabled him to sell or lease historical landmarks on two continents.

The Scot began unintentionally training for his future frauds by touring with repertory theater companies in Northern England and Scotland. In one of the productions he played an American who gets bilked by a smooth con man. The role served as a sort of research and inspiration for a series of ruses Furguson carried out in the mid-1920s.

Furguson's first victim was an unsuspecting tourist from Iowa who, while strolling around Trafalgar Square, engaged him in conversation. Furguson, who was intently scrutinizing Nelson's Column in the center of the square, eventually offered the lamentable information that he was stuck with the task of organizing the dismantling and sale of the famous statue. It seems,

Furguson explained, that Britain needed to take this action to keep from defaulting on war loans to the U.S.

It is not difficult to imagine how tickled the tourist must have been when he found out there was still time to make a bid, or how accommodating this "ministry official" was in moving his offer in front of the other bids. It must have also been tragic when the demolition company, with whom the American was to arrange the disassembly, scoffed at the thought of touching the landmark, and the American realized he had been duped out of £6,000.

Furguson's ruse was so believable that Buckingham Palace and Big Ben were "sold" in much the same manner. The deals closed with down payments of £2,000 and £1,000 respectively. Furguson must have decided that if tourists were going to be so gullible, he might as well travel to them, rather than wait for them to come to him. Late in 1925, he landed in the United States.

Even in their own country, Americans seemed to be easily hoodwinked. Within a few weeks of his arrival, Furguson had leased the White House to a Texan at a marked-down price of $100,000. From there he moved on to New York and set up his next prestigious transaction: the Statue of Liberty. But this was the deal where he finally slipped up.

After pulling in an Australian tourist with a story about the need to dismantle Lady Liberty so that the Hudson Bay could be widened, he allowed his victim to take a photo of him in front of the merchandise. When one of the Australian's bankers was told why his client needed to raise $100,000, he suggested that some checking up was in order before the deal was finalized. The query finally brought the photo into the hands of authorities, who were watching out for Furguson. One of the world's greatest traveling salesmen finally had his license revoked.

Furguson served a five-year sentence and moved to California upon release, where he lived—presumably off some of his ill-gotten earnings—until his death in 1938. REF.: *CBA*.

Furnace, Samuel James, 1890-1933, Brit., suic.-mur. Samuel Furnace, a builder who served in the Black and Tans Regiment during the Irish uprising of 1921, tried to fake his death to hide a murder. On the night of Jan. 3, 1933, in a dilapidated wooden shed in Kentish Town, he murdered his friend, Walter Spatchett, from whom he had borrowed £60. Furnace had rented the building, allegedly for business purposes, and it was destroyed by a fire of mysterious origin. Firemen pulled from smoldering rubble a man at first believed to be Furnace. The victim apparently left a suicide note that read, "Goodbye to all. No work. No money. Sam J. Furnace." It was

Murderer Samuel Furnace.

known that Furnace was only £90 in debt. He was happily married and had a child, which made Coroner Bentley Purchase doubly suspicious. After examining the body, he concluded that the deceased had been shot in the back of the head, and had not died in the fire. The teeth were those of a much younger man than Furnace. Purchase's conclusions were confirmed by the discovery of an overcoat found hanging in the shed. It contained a passbook listing the name of the rent collector, Spatchett. Police surmised that Furnace murdered Spatchett for the money he was carrying, and then tried to make it look like suicide.

An intensive manhunt involved nearly every law enforcement agency in Britain. On Jan. 14, Furnace wrote a letter to his brother-in-law, Charles Tuckfield, revealing his whereabouts in Southend. Tuckfield gave the letter to the police, who arrested Furnace. He told police he had shot Spatchett by accident, and not knowing what do, he decided to burn the body beyond recognition and then fake his own death. He threw the murder weapon into Regent's Canal. In his cell, Furnace consumed hydrochloric acid and died at St. Pancras Hospital the next day. The coroner's jury found Furnace Guilty of murder.

REF.: Browne and Tullett, *The Scalpel of Scotland Yard; CBA;* Cornish, *Cornish of the "Yard";* Cuthbert, *Science and the Detection of Crime;* Firmin, *Crime Man; ____, Murderers In Our Midst;* Glaister, *The Power of Poison;* Gribble, *Famous Manhunts;* Hoskins, *They Almost Escaped;* Jacobs, *Aspects of Murder;* Shew, *A Companion to Murder;* Whitelaw, *Corpus Delicti;* Wild, *Crimes and Cases of 1933;* Wilson, *Encyclopedia of Murder.*

Furnald, Amos, prom. 1825, U.S., mansl. Amos Furnald and his wife, residents of Dover, Del., were mean-spirited parents who horribly abused their 5-year-old child, Alfred Furnald. They withheld food from the child until the boy died of starvation. Both parents were arrested but only Amos Furnald was tried and convicted of manslaughter and sentenced to five years in prison.

REF.: *CBA;* Ela, *Trial of Amos Furnald.*

Furey, Joseph, prom. 1910s-20s, U.S., fraud. The envelope switch, whereby a large sum of money is taken from a "sucker" in return for a worthless collection of newspaper clips or confetti, is an ancient con game practiced by generations of swindlers. Few of them, however, could match the skill of Joseph Furey, whose earnings from a lifetime of fraud made him a wealthy man.

Furey was a former partner of William Elmer Mead of "magic-wallet" fame. The Mead gang operated out of the Southwest, preying on wealthy businessmen in the Fort Worth area. Furey employed such noted tricksters as Charles Gerber, W.B. Spencer, E.J. Ward, and Reno Hamlin. In 1920, they selected wealthy Texas cattleman J. Frank Norfleet as their next "pigeon." Posing as a financier, Furey dropped his wallet on the ground near Norfleet. The cattleman returned the wallet to Furey, who rewarded Norfleet's honesty with a $100 bill. The Texan politely refused the gratuity, and Furey insisted upon investing the $100 in a smart stock tip on Norfleet's behalf. The next day, Furey handed $3,000 to the surprised cattleman, but told him that if he so desired, he could return the next day and invest more. The following day Norfleet received the happy news that he had earned $200,000, known in swindler's parlance as the "hurrah."

After being shown the money, the next step of the con was the "convincer." Norfleet was told that he would have to put up $20,000 as a hedge against any losses the "investment" group might sustain if the deal simply collapsed. The gullible Texan handed over the cash and the gang was prepared to decamp with its earnings when a Fort Worth law officer who was tied in with the con gang insisted that Norfleet could easily be swindled again. Norfleet was then informed that his earnings had doubled almost overnight. An additional $25,000 was required as earnest money, a sum that Norfleet was all too eager to hand over. He removed the last of his savings from the bank and turned it over to Furey and his associates. In return, Norfleet was left with an envelope of newspaper clippings while the con men scattered to the four winds.

Norfleet, incensed by his losses, went public, which started one of the greatest individual manhunts in history. "I'll get them, too, even if it takes the rest of my life," Norfleet vowed. Charles Gerber and E.J. Ward were picked up in San Francisco based on information supplied by a victim who had read about the Norfleet con in the papers. Norfleet traveled to San Bernardino to identify them. It took four years and every last penny of Norfleet's money, but he apprehended Furey in Jacksonville, Fla., on a warrant issued by the governor. Furey offered the ex-sheriff a $20,000 bribe to let him go. "Not a chance," Norfleet said. "Why have you never reformed, an intelligent man like you, a man who could have been something in the legitimate world?" Thinking about it, the con man explained that he was attracted by the excitement. Furey was deposited in a Texas jail, but the quest did not end there. Norfleet went to Denver to track the biggest fish of them all: Adolph W. Duff, better known as Kid Duffy. In the next few years the vigilante lawman rounded up 500 sharpers and con men and returned many to justice, before returning to his ranch.

REF.: *CBA;* Nash, *Hustlers and Con Men.*

Fury, 1935, a film by German director Fritz Lang. Thomas Thurmond, who was hanged with his fellow kidnapper and killer, John Holmes, by an enormous lynch mob in San Jose, Calif., (U.S., 1933) was the role model for Spencer Tracy's victimized character in this picture. Newsreels of the lynch mob in action were studied by Lang and he duplicated the actions of the thousands of citizens who dragged Thurmond and Holmes from the San Jose jail. Even the jail was precisely reproduced for the film. See: **Thurmond, Thomas Harold.** REF.: *CBA.*

Fury, Bridget (Delia Swift), 1837-72, U.S., mur. Born in Cincinnati in 1837, Delia Swift became a criminal in her early teens, later moving to New Orleans to form a female gang with Mary Jane "Bricktop" Jackson. Swift earned the moniker Bridget Fury for the impassioned pace at which she lived her life. As a 21-year-old in 1858, she was convicted for murder and sentenced to life imprisonment. Bridget was released through a general amnesty in 1862, and returned to her violent ways. A few years later she opened a brothel, where, in 1869, she was accused of robbing a customer of over $700. After serving several months in prison, she returned to find the brothel run by others. Although only in her early thirties, the pace and tumult of her life had left her in a wretched condition. She drank away her final years, and died in 1872. REF.: *CBA.*

Fusco, Joseph Charles (AKA: Joe Long, Joe Carey, Joseph Sayth, Joe Thompson, E.J. Thompson), 1902-76, U.S., org. crime. Joseph Charles Fusco began his life with the underworld apprenticing as a beer runner for Al Capone's mob. He made his mark as one of the major bootleggers of the Prohibition. The Chicago Crime Commission proclaimed him Public Enemy No. 29 in 1930. In 1931, he was indicted with Capone on 5,000 prohibition law violations. At different times during his crime career, he was also arrested for receiving stolen property, conspiracy, and assault with a deadly weapon. Despite the vast number of charges, he was never convicted.

After the end of Prohibition, Fusco left organized crime and became one of the leaders of the legitimate liquor and beer industry. He died in Chicago on Dec. 5, 1976. REF.: *CBA.*

Fyler, Alfred, prom. 1850s, U.S., mur. At first, Ruth Fyler's death seemed a simple case of murder to hide the identity of two robbers. Alfred Fyler explained at a coroner's inquest that he had left his wife in bed on the night of Feb. 22, 1854, to investigate some unusual sounds in their home in Syracuse, N.Y. He was startled by two strangers, and fled to a neighbor's home to get help. As he ran, he heard his wife scream. Mary Cummins, the Fylers' servant and the only adult other than the Fylers on the premises, corroborated Fyler's story, saying that she heard Mrs. Fyler call out for her husband just before a pistol was fired.

Mrs. Fyler had been shot in the head and stabbed numerous times, but it was the deep slash in her throat that had probably killed her instantly. There were signs that she had had quite a struggle with her attacker.

At the first coroner's inquest, Fyler was very emotional about his loss. It seemed clear that, although no one else had been implicated in the crime, Fyler certainly played no part in this heinous act. The jury had no reason to believe otherwise until Henry Fyler, the couple's 6-year-old son, took the stand. He told the jury that he had watched his mother's murder, and that the man responsible looked like his father. Mrs. Fyler had not called out, "Alfred," as the servant-girl had testified. She had yelled,

Wife-killer Alfred Fyler.

"Don't, Alfred," the command being directed to her husband as he wielded the knife that killed her. This testimony provided reason enough for a second and more meticulous inquest, after which there was sufficient evidence to arrest Alfred Fyler on suspicion of murder and Mary Cummins as an accessory.

Upon her apprehension, Cummins decided to amend her version of what happened: she thought that Fyler was the murderer, though she had no real proof. She had not said so earlier because she feared for her own life at the hands of Fyler.

Fyler's trial began on Feb. 19, 1855. A number of witnesses testified to his mental instability, and to the fact that in the past he had attempted at least once to take his own life. Cummins also offered that Fyler had attempted to poison his wife's coffee shortly before her murder. The jury, after a deliberation of five-and-a-half hours, announced a verdict of Guilty to the densely packed Onandaga County Courthouse, ending one of the most sensational and brutal murder cases in the region's history.

In May 1855, the trial judge accepted testimony from three doctors as to the extent that Fyler could be held responsible for his actions. The doctors unanimously declared him insane, and Fyler was sent to the State Lunatic Asylum in Utica, N.Y.

REF.: *CBA; A Complete History of the Murder of Mrs. Ruth Fyler.*

Fyodor II (Borisovitch, Fedor II), 1589-1605, Rus., czar, assass. Temporarily succeeded his father Boris Godunov to the Russian throne in 1605, only to be assassinated by the Russian aristocracy, known as *boyars*. REF.: *CBA.*

Fyodorova, Zoya, 1912-81, U.S.S.R., (unsolv.), mur. Over the weekend of Dec. 11-13, 1981, Victoria Fyodorova was informed by family friends that her mother, Zoya Fyodorova, had died on Dec. 11. Both women were actresses, and had received international attention in 1975 when Victoria came to New York from the Soviet Union to meet her American father, Jackson R. Tate, for the first time. During WWII Tate, an admiral, had been attached to the U.S. Embassy in Moscow, where he had met Zoya, a popular film star, and had an affair with her. At the end of the war the Russians ordered Tate to leave the country, apparently because they disapproved of the affair. Frederick Pouy, married to the younger actress, announced on December 15 that he and his wife had learned that her mother had been murdered. A cousin and close friend of the family in Moscow phoned to tell that they saw a death certificate in the city morgue. According to Pouy, the actress "was shot once in the back of the head." The case remains unsolved. REF.: *CBA.*

G

Gabaldon, Armigiro, prom. 1976, Case of, Venez., kid.-mur. While on assignment in Caracas, Venez., William Niehous, vice president of the Owens-Illinois Company, was kidnapped by anti-government insurgents on Feb. 27, 1976. The group, calling itself the Commando Armigiro Gabaldon, was thought to be a splinter faction of the Bandero Roja.

In return for the release of Niehous, they demanded a ransom of $1.25 million, and an editorial placed in several prominent newspapers in London, Paris, New York, and Venezuela denouncing the policies of the Venezuelan government. Owens-Illinois complied with both of the kidnappers' demands. The publishing of the anti-government manifesto prompted the Venezuelan government to nationalize the assets of Owens-Illinois' Venezuelan subsidiary. Niehous was never returned, and is presumed dead. REF.: *CBA; Clutterbuck, Kidnap and Ransom.*

Gabaldon, Isaac, d.1939, Spain, assass. Placed in charge of the Spanish Civil Guard, responsible for rooting out suspected Loyalists and traitors of the Franco government, Major Isaac Gabaldon emerged as a powerful figure in the new order. Major Gabaldon ruthlessly tracked down resistance fighters and then turned them over to the military tribunals where justice was swift.

Justice of another kind was meted out by vengeful Republican insurgents early in August 1939, when the major's car was ambushed near the Alcalá de Henares. Gabaldon, his teenage daughter, and their chauffeur were killed by seven hitchhikers who had flagged them down by the side of the road. The bodies were tossed into a ditch where they were found several hours later. In retaliation, the seven murderers and 100 neighborhood residents were rounded up in Madrid and accused of belonging to "The Clan of Class Vengeance with Blood," a Marxist organization opposed to Generalissimo Francisco Franco.

In the first wave of executions, fifty-three persons were shot and seven garrotted from behind. REF.: *CBA.*

Gabinius, Aulus, d.47 B.C., Roman., consp. Conspired with Clodius to overthrow Cicero in 58 B.C., and served under Julius Caesar from 49-47 B.C. REF.: *CBA.*

Gabor, George Robert (AKA: **G.E. von Krupp, Jr., Taft Thew, Jr.**), prom. 1935, U.S., fraud. George Gabor victimized the unsuspecting on both sides of the Atlantic during the Depression with a variety of aliases and clever disguises that earned him invitations to elegant receptions and affairs of state. Among the prominent citizens of the day who fell for his glib line and debonair comportment were Henry Ford, Harvey Firestone, Thomas Edison, and Myron T. Herrick.

Gabor, who was born in Hungary, came to the U.S. and posed as the visiting heir to the great Krupp armaments fortune. He was invited to tea with Edison in West Orange, N.J. He greeted Ford in Detroit, and was shown the Akron rubber plants belonging to Henry Firestone. Gabor found time in between to mingle with the attractive young debutantes listed on the social register.

He was arrested as an imposter after passing bad checks in Albuquerque, N.M., in 1926. Gabor returned to the U.S. two years later bearing a letter of introduction from Ambassador Myron Herrick. He was arrested a second time for posing as a solicitor general, a crime that carried with it an eighteen-month sentence at McNeill Island and deportation back to Hungary. In London he made the acquaintance of Ambassador Alanson Houghton, passing himself off as the esteemed Taft Thew, Jr. In this new role, Gabor found himself railside at the polo matches.

Gabor journeyed to Paris, where he prevailed upon Herrick to pay for a first-class ticket to Halifax aboard the *Lapland.* The letter of introduction read: "The bearer is an American citizen in whom I am interested in."

By this time the U.S. government was also interested. In 1935, Gabor was sentenced to Leavenworth penitentiary after being caught posing as an attaché of the U.S. embassy in Tokyo. He was released on June 23, 1936, and deported back to Hungary. REF.: *CBA.*

Gaboriau, Emile, 1835-73, Fr., writer. Author famous for detective novels featuring policemen "Monsieur Lecoq" and "Père Tabaret". His works include: *L'Affaire LeRouge, Monsieur Lecoq,* and *La Vie Infernale.* REF.: *CBA.*

Gabriel, Peter, prom. 1880s, U.S., west. lawman. A long-time lawman in Arizona, Gabriel had chased bandits through Pima County, Ariz., from 1883 when he was the sheriff of the county. He fired one of his deputies, Joe Phy, for disorderly and drunken conduct and later arrested him in Casa Grande for assault. The two men feuded throughout an election for sheriff in 1888 which Gabriel won. On May 3, 1888, in Florence, Ariz., Phy called Gabriel to the street from a saloon where both men had been drinking. The two men went for their six-shooters and, in a wild gun battle in which eleven shots were exchanged, Gabriel shot Phy several times. Gabriel was wounded in the groin and in the chest near the heart. The Sheriff walked away from the fallen Phy and staggered into the O.K. Stable where he collapsed. Phy died four hours later but Gabriel survived to stand trial and be exonerated for the shooting on grounds of self-defense. REF.: *CBA.*

Gabriel's Plot, 1800, U.S., consp. Thomas Prosser, a wealthy blacksmith who dwelled in a mansion off Brook Road near Richmond, Va., never dreamed that his personal body slave, a highly intelligent Haitian named Gabriel (1776-1800), was making feverish plans in late August 1800 to slit his throat. The restless Gabriel planned much more than that. As "General" Gabriel, he had organized in secret about 1,000 blacks in Richmond who were to rise at his command and slay every white man in the town of 5,735 persons.

Each slave foreman was to kill his master and ride his master's horse as a captain, leading scores of other blacks into the city, where the women and spoils would be theirs. Gabriel had told his followers that he intended to make Mrs. David Meade Randolph his queen once the city had been taken, because she was an excellent cook. (Mrs. Randolph, a white woman, had written a famous book on cooking which Gabriel had read.)

Solomon, Gabriel's brother, had for months secretly used Prosser's smithy to forge hundreds of double-edged swords from scythes stolen from plantations. With these, hundreds of blacks armed themselves and met seven miles north of the city on the stormy night of Aug. 30, 1800. The massacre plan was detailed by Gabriel to more than 1,000 followers. After they took the city, he explained, they would fortify it against the armies of whites sure to march against them. They would recruit blacks from all over the southland and lead sorties against other white-controlled cities throughout the state, until Virginia was wholly in their hands.

Leaders were then solemnly asked if they would kill their masters, take their masters' horses, and lead the other blacks into the planned massacre (all Frenchmen, Quakers, Methodists, and poor, old, white women who held no slaves were to be spared). One black leader named Will agreed to kill his master, but he was rejected by Gabriel as being too short; the revolt required large black men to inspire the other slaves. Gabriel badgered a behemoth slave named Albert into becoming a captain, but the slave refused to kill his master, a Mr. Young, who had "raised" him and been kind to him all his life. If someone else would kill Young, Albert said, he would lead.

Gabriel then explained that a black man named John, who worked at the penitentiary, would, with the help of other slave workers there, kill the guards and seize the arms stored in the prison armory. Another slave named Jupitor, Gabriel pointed out, would meet a contingent of the black revolutionaries at the capitol and lead them through a secret door to the armory. Using the weapons there, the blacks would next move against the governor's mansion, kill the governor, carry off his wife and daughters, and proceed to massacre most of Richmond's white population.

With his army in high spirits, Gabriel began to march on Richmond. A violent storm came up, however, and great winds and rain held up the dedicated procession. They gathered at the

Brook Bridge and waited for the storm to let up. While there, Gabriel ordered every slave to promise to live or die with the revolt. Two slaves devoted to their white masters, Tom and Pharaoh, who had been fishing in the river and had taken refuge against the storm beneath the bridge, were terrified as they heard Gabriel pronounce death for almost every white in Richmond and death for every black who refused to join the insurrectionists.

Both men quickly swam the river and, shivering and chattering, raced to the homes of Moseby and Philip Sheppard, blurting out the plot to their masters. Pharaoh reported that Gabriel had yelled to his rabid followers: "Here are our hands and hearts; we will wade to our knees in blood sooner than fail in the attempt!"

The storm prevented the onslaught of the slave revolt that night, Gabriel postponing his march until Sunday. This delay allowed the white militia to gather; there were only a handful of policemen then on duty in Richmond. The whites marched out to meet the advancing column of blacks the following day. When the slaves spotted the bayonet-thrusting white soldiers coming at them, they scattered and ran yelling across the fields, tossing their makeshift swords into the mud. Gabriel, Solomon, and the other leaders escaped but were captured, Gabriel being taken off a schooner in Norfolk Harbor a few days later. After their confessions, Gabriel, Solomon, and several others, were hanged in full view of the entire slave population in and about Richmond, the blacks driven to the scaffold to witness what happened to slaves who plotted revolt.

This single incident caused Richmonders to establish a strong police force with night watchmen patrolling the streets and crying out, much to the edification of the nerve-jangled inhabitants: "Oyez, oyez, twelve o'clock and all's well."

But all was not well for the blacks. Richmond's courts were viciously punitive whenever it came to judging blacks for misconduct. The Hustings Court docket for 1825 reveals the following penalties: a slave was given twenty lashes for stealing three dollars; another black stole three blankets to keep his family warm and was given fifteen lashes; another stole four dollars and received twenty-five lashes; another took a calico dress and got fifteen lashes; another filched a pair of boots and received thirty-nine lashes.

The conditions in which the slaves lived were abysmal. Those who worked in the elegant Richmond homes were crammed into shanties or old buildings by the dozens. The lots around these buildings by the early 1830s were heaped with offal, garbage, and filth of horses which, no doubt, led to the terrible cholera epidemic of 1832 which took the lives of 356 blacks. Only ninety-seven whites perished, and these were from the poor class.

By 1857, the whites of Richmond's ruling class, fearful of another slave uprising as they were stirred by the blistering oratory of abolitionists, and remembering with shudders the aborted Gabriel plot of 1800 and the bloody insurrection led by Nat Turner in 1831, instituted rigid regulations for blacks in and about the city.

Blacks could never walk abroad at night without special passes, or, in most instances, had to be accompanied by their masters. Blacks were restricted from riding in carriages and visiting public parks, and were prohibited from entering graveyards (whites believed that blacks, out of hate for their masters, would dig up and defile the Caucasian corpses). "Whether free or not," the new laws insisted, blacks could not congregate in groups above five and were absolutely prohibited from smoking in public, carrying canes, swearing, buying weapons, and drinking "ardent spirits." See: **Turner, Nat.**

REF.: Aptheker, *American Negro Slave Revolts;* _____, *Negro Slave Revolts in the United States, 1526--1860;* Ballagh, *A History of Slavery in Virginia;* Bell, *Old Free State;* Burke, *The History of Virginia;* Carroll, *Slave Insurrections in the United States;* CBA; Channing, *A History of the United States;* Cobb, *An Inquiry into the Law of Negro Slavery;* Coffin, *An Account of Some of the Principal Slave Insurrections;* Cooke, *Virginia, A History of Her People;* Cotterill, *The Old South;* Cromwell, *The Negro in American History;* Dodd, *The Cotton Kingdom, A Chronicle of the Old South;* Drewry,
Slave Insurrections in Virginia; Eckenrode, *The Revolution in Virginia;* Fiske, *Old Virginia and Her Neighbors;* Freeman, *R.E. Lee;* Guild, *Black Laws of Virginia;* Halasz, *The Rattling Chains: Slave Unrest and Revolt in the Antebellum South;* Higginson, *Travelers and Outlaws Episodes in American History;* Hildreth, *The History of the United States of America;* Howison, *A History of Virginia;* James, *A History of Negro Revolt;* Mumford, *Virginia's Attitude Toward Slavery and Succession;* Nearing, *Black America;* Robert, *The Tobacco Kingdom Plantation;* Russell, *The Free Negro in Virginia;* Stanard, *Richmond, Its People and Its Story;* Washington, *The Story of the Negro;* Williams, *History of the Negro Race in America from 1619 to 1880;* Wilson, *History of the Rise and Fall of the Slave Power in America;* (FICTION), Bontemps, *Black Thunder.*

Gaca, Barbara, 1948-55, U.S., (unsolv.) mur. Despite one of the most exhaustive police investigations in Detroit's history, no one has ever been suspected, arrested, or tried for the brutal rape and murder of 7-year-old Barbara Gaca.

On the morning of Thursday, Mar. 24, 1955, Barbara kissed her mother goodbye and set off down the sidewalk, rosary, pencil case, and notebook in tow, for the six-block walk to Assumption Grotto School. Eight days later, Rufus Zamora, a Grand Trunk Western railroad worker, found her body in a rural Oakland County dump site southwest of the town of Pontiac. While walking down the tracks, Zamora had spied a curious bundle lying in a pile of rusting tin, spoiled food, and crumpled beer cans. He opened the fold of the grimy army blanket to find Barbara's body, still clothed in the dress, undershirt, shoes, and socks she had been wearing when she left home eight days earlier. Nearby lay her outer clothing, scattered among her rosary and school supplies, her red and blue bandana now stained with blood and her snowsuit sliced to pieces by a knife.

Concluding that Barbara had died by strangulation on the day she disappeared, pathologist Dr. Richard E. Olsen noted that her killer later disposed of the body only after first bludgeoning, raping, and stabbing the corpse fifteen times with a small knife.

Although Barbara Gaca's body had been found, the only physical evidence left at the dump site was a set of fresh automobile tire tracks. Hoping for a lead, however small, police made plaster casts of the tracks. But nothing came of it. The brutal killer of this seven-year-old girl has never been found. REF.: CBA.

Gacha, José Gonzalo Rodriguez, See: **Rodriguez Gacha, José Gonzalo.**

Gacy, John Wayne, Jr., 1942- , U.S., mur. John Wayne Gacy had a long record of homosexual abuse, sodomy and other acts of perversion. In 1968, at the age of twenty-six, while he was married and operating a fast food operation in Waterloo, Iowa, Gacy lured a youth into a back room after closing time and handcuffed him. He tried to pay the youth to perform oral sex on him and when this was refused, Gacy attempted to sodomize the youth. The youth escaped and reported Gacy. Before going to trial, Gacy paid some thugs to terrorize the youth into not testifying against him but this only strengthened the youth's resolve and he did testify. Gacy drew a ten-year sentence but, because his past indicated no serious crime and because

Mass killer John Wayne Gacy.

he proved to be a model prisoner, he was released in eighteen months.

Moving to Chicago in 1971, Gacy went into the construction business and soon developed his own contracting company. He also continued his sexual abuses. In the year he arrived in Chicago, Gacy picked up a teenage boy and attempted to force the youth to have sex with him. He was arrested but was released when the boy failed to appear in court to testify against him. A young man later insisted that Gacy, in 1977, had held a gun on him in his Norwood Park home when he arrived to apply for work as a construction worker. Gacy attempted to force the man to have sex with him. He flourished the gun and snarled through full lips: "I killed a guy before." The construction worker did not believe Gacy, thinking he was only acting out a fantasy and nothing came of the incident. Gacy, however, had, indeed, killed several persons by this time but not until years later would the secret of this vile mass murderer be revealed.

With each sexual offense and murder that went unpunished, Gacy became more bold, daring to abduct boys from the street and force them to participate in unspeakable sexual perversions while holding them captive in his modest Norwood Park home. He then murdered them and buried their bodies. In 1977 Gacy was arrested and charged with sexually abusing a youth at gunpoint. Gacy admitted to the sexual attack and brutality but said the youth was a willing participant and was blackmailing him. He was released with a warning.

By 1978, Gacy was operating with abandon. He earned considerable money from his contracting business and he was a small but important precinct captain for the Democratic Party in Norwood Park Township's 21st Precinct. He felt that he was insulated against detection. He would drive about in his sleek, black Oldsmobile, cruising near notorious homosexual hangouts in Chicago, such as "Bughouse Square" across from the Newberry Library, and, particularly, along North Broadway in the New Town section. On March 21, 1978, Gacy picked up 27-year-old Chicagoan Jeffrey Rignall on North Broadway in New Town.

Gacy, by then grown fat with a triple chin and bulging eyes, suggested that Rignall join him in the car to smoke some marijuana and take a drive. Rignall accepted. Gacy pulled the car over to a curb and suddenly whirled about, forcing a chloroform-soaked rag over Rignall's face. Rignall passed out and vaguely remembered later traveling at high speed and then seeing an expressway exit. He awoke in the basement of Gacy's home, his body naked and pressed into a pillory-like rack which held his arms and head. Gacy, a powerful, heavyset man, was also naked, his fat, hairy belly sticking out obscenely. Gacy showed Rignall various whips, and instruments of torture, along with a number of strange-looking sexual devices, explaining lasciviously how he intended to use these implements on his victim, Rignall.

The assaults and torture went on for hours. Gacy periodically applied the chloroform and waited sadistically until his victim regained consciousness to renew his attacks. He bragged that he was a policeman, and said to his terrorized victim: "I'd just as soon shoot you as look at you." The sexual attacks became so acutely painful that Rignall wanted to die, he later said. He begged Gacy to release him, saying he would leave town and say nothing about the incident. Rignall finally blacked out with another dose of chloroform and woke up later beneath a statue in Chicago's Lincoln Park. He was fully clothed and his wallet and money were in his pockets, although his driver's license was missing. He discovered that he was bleeding from the rectum and medical tests showed that his liver had been permanently damaged by the heavy doses of chloroform that had been administered by Gacy. Rignall's face had been burned by the chloroform.

Going to the police with his story, Rignall was told that there was little hope of locating his attacker since he had no name, address or license number for the man's car. Rignall was determined to bring to justice the hulking sadist who had attacked him. He rented a car and drove the route he vaguely remembered while being abducted. He sat at the expressway exit he remembered clearly, patiently waiting in his car for hours, watching for the big black Oldsmobile. Finally, his perseverance was rewarded. The car turned off the expressway and passed Rignall's parked car. He wrote down the license number, then followed the car. It turned into a driveway at 8213 West Summerdale Avenue in

Norwood Park, an unincorporated area bordering on Des Plaines.

Having worked for a law firm which dealt with real estate, Rignall was able to check real estate records and unearth the name of his attacker: John Wayne Gacy, Jr. He went to police with this information, having performed some excellent amateur detective work. The Chicago police took his information and then told Rignall that Gacy had served time in Iowa for sodomy. Rignall had difficulty in getting the Chicago Police Department to act but finally managed to have a warrant for Gacy's arrest issued. He met CPD officers at Gacy's home, only to be told that since the subject lived in Norwood Park, he was beyond the jurisdiction of the Chicago Police. Rignall, through his attorney, finally had Gacy arrested on a misdemeanor charge of battery on July 15, 1978, but police refused to charge Gacy with a felony, despite the protests from Rignall and his attorney, Fred Richman. Some time later, Gacy agreed to settle $3,000 on Rignall for the medical bills incurred from this sexual attack.

Gacy dressed as a clown for one of his children's parties.

Everything seemed to be closing in on John Wayne Gacy in 1978. He mentioned to his neighbors that he was running out space in his home where he lived alone after his wife had left him. Gacy spoke of adding more floors to his house which perplexed residents in the area. One told him that if he needed more space it was easier to sell his home and buy a new and larger house. He agreed and made plans to sell his Norwood Park house.

At 11:30 p.m. on Dec. 11, 1978, Mrs. Elizabeth Piest appeared in the Des Plaines Police Department, asking them to check on her son Robert, age fifteen, who had been missing since 9:05 that night. She and her son had been in the Nisson Pharmacy in Des Plaines at that time. Robert, who had been looking for a job for the following summer, told his mother that he had to see a "contractor" who lived nearby. "I'll be right back," he told her but he did not return. Mrs. Piest talked to the druggist who told her that her son might be seeing John Wayne Gacy, a contractor who had given the druggist an estimate for remodeling the drugstore.

Mrs. Piest and her husband Harold, her son Ken, and daughter Kerry had searched for Robert but could find no trace of him. Des Plaines Police Captain Joseph Kozenczak heard Mrs. Piest's story and believed her son had met with foul play, especially since he had left her in the pharmacy with the words "I'll be right back," and he knew he was to accompany her home to celebrate her birthday that night. Nothing in Robert Piest's background suggested he might be a runaway. Kozenczak asked Des Plaines youth officer Ron Adams to follow up. Adams interviewed the pharmacist, Phil Terf, and again talked with the Piest family members. The following morning, Adams called the contractor, Gacy, a definite suspect at that time.

Gacy picked up the phone on Dec. 12, 1978, at 9:30 a.m. He was terse with Adams, telling him: "I don't talk to any kids. I can't help you. I don't know anything about it." Gacy had already murdered the Piest boy and the body was lying in Gacy's bedroom as he made his denials to Adam on the phone. The Des Plaines police, however, were dogged. They checked Gacy's background and found his conviction for sodomy in Iowa. Kozenczak and several officers visited Gacy that night and questioned him further. Gacy admitted nothing, merely staring back at the officers as they described the Piest boy. He then mumbled something about talking "to one of the boys about some shelves" that were discarded in the remodeling of the Nisson Pharmacy. "I don't remember who it was."

Rosalyn Carter shaking hands with Gacy, thanking him for his work with the Democratic Party.

Kozensczak asked Gacy to go to the police station and make an official statement about the Piest boy. Gacy then received a call from a relative about an uncle who had just died. He stretched out his long distance phone conversation but the policemen remained in his home. After hanging up the phone Gacy started to get his coat. Two more officers then burst through the door and Gacy suddenly became obstinate, saying loudly: "Hey, I got a lot of important work to do. I can't be going down to the police station. I know this kid is missing but that's not important to me."

"Well, it's important to the parents," Kozenczak replied, angrily impatient. Yet, without evidence, he realized he was powerless to make a formal arrest, and left after giving Gacy his card and asking him to come to the station and make a voluntary statement. Police now put Gacy under close surveillance. On one occasion, Gacy, realizing he was being watched, jumped into his car and roared off at high speed, losing his pursuers. Meanwhile, Gacy managed to remove the body of the Piest boy from his home. He put the corpse into his trunk and then drove to the Des Plaines River at Interstate Highway 55, and dumping the body into the swirling waters. This undoubtedly unnerved the mass killer since, upon his return trip home, his car inexplicably went out of control and wound up in a ditch, requiring a tow.

In the afternoon of Dec. 13, 1978, Gacy appeared at the Des Plaines police station. His clothes were disheveled and his trousers and shoes were coated with mud. His glassy-eyed appearance caused one officer on duty to describe Gacy as "spaced

out on some kind of drug." He asked for Kozenczak but the police captain was not in at the time. Gacy left. Later, Assistant State's Attorney Terry Sullivan helped Kozenczak obtain a search warrant for Gacy's house from Judge Marvin Peters, a considerable feat because such warrants were nearly impossible to obtain without substantial evidence.

The police searched Gacy's home but found little. Kozenczak spotted a receipt from the Nisson pharmacy and took it along. As it turned out, this was the most important piece of evidence in the case. The receipt was made out to the Piest boy, indicating Gacy had had contact with the boy, possibly inside Gacy's house. The killer later admitted that he had emptied his victim's pockets, thrown the receipt into a garbage can, and forgotten about it.

The police returned to the Gacy residence to take up a round-the-clock surveillance. Gacy watched the police sitting outside of his home for days. On Dec. 19, 1978, he boldly invited two of the officers into his house to have breakfast with him. As they sat down to eat, the policemen noticed a peculiar smell. Gacy explained that he had unplugged his sump pump. The resulting water flowing beneath the building had softened the dirt of the crawl space and disturbed the twenty-nine bodies Gacy had buried there over the years.

Another warrant was quickly obtained and the bodies were dug out of the crawl space. Four more bodies found in nearby rivers over the next four months, including that of the Piest boy, were linked to Gacy. The victims ranged from a 9-year-old boy to grown men such as John Butkovich, reportedly murdered by Gacy as early as 1976. Others included Greg Godzik, John Szyc, Billy Carrol, Randall Reffett, Samuel Stapleton, Michael Bonnin, Rich Johnston and Piest, the last victim of the thirty-four sexually abused and murdered by Gacy. The mass killer was tried in 1980 and sentenced to life imprisonment.

REF.: Boar, *The World's Most Infamous Murders; CBA;* Fox, *Mass Murder;* Linedecker, *The Man Who Killed Boys;* Nash, *Almanac of World Crime;* ____, *Murder, America;* Rignall, *Twenty-nine Below;* Sullivan, *Killer Clown;* Wilson, *Encyclopedia of Modern Murder.*

British thief William Gadesby in the act of robbing a store.

Gadesby, William, 1763-91, Brit., rob. Bragging that crime consumed him and was the driving force in his life, William Gadesby went to the gallows for his thievery at the age of twenty-eight. One of Scotland's most notorious thieves, Gadesby's life of crime began with the theft of a wallet from a stationer's shop. With this first success, his thirst for danger and excitement grew. Petty theft soon escalated to fraud and crimes of violence—whatever it took to acquire the property of others.

On Feb. 20, 1791, awaiting execution at the Edinburgh gallows, Gadesby, in a flamboyant white and black suit, confessed to crimes that innocent men had earlier been executed for before falling through the floor of the gallows to his death.

REF.: *CBA;* Mitchell, *The Newgate Calendar.*

Gagarin, Matvei Petrovich, d.1721, Rus., treas. Hanged in St. Petersburg because Peter the Great believed he wanted to establish Siberian independence from Russia. REF.: *CBA.*

Gagliano, Joseph (AKA: **Pip the Blind**), c.1903- , and **Loiacano, Angelo** (AKA: **Puggy**), c.1912- , and **Lucente, Anthony** (AKA: **Andy**), c.1916- , U.S., drugs. A major drug smuggler on the East Coast during the 1940s, Joseph Gagliano smuggled opium by car from Mexico to California, and then by train to his Harlem, N.Y., headquarters. In Harlem, the opium was changed first into morphine and then into heroin. As a rule, Gagliano conducted business one-on-one in back rooms, but in late 1946 he made an exception for a combat veteran with a wounded foot and met with him in a car. On Dec. 11 and 12, 1946, Gagliano closed the deal, selling the veteran—an undercover agent—five oun-

Chicago gangster Joseph Gagliano.

ces of heroin for $1,575 while a government witness watched from a baggage compartment, and a camera crew in a nearby truck filmed the deal. On Feb. 20, 1947, Gagliano, forty-three, and his confederates, 35-year old Angelo Loiacano and 31-year-old Anthony Lucente, were all convicted on charges of selling narcotics, and on Apr. 8, each man was sentenced to five-to-ten years in prison. On Apr. 11, however, before Gagliano was to begin serving his term at Sing Sing, he committed suicide by hanging himself in the Bronx County Jail. REF.: *CBA.*

Gagliano, Joseph (AKA: **Joey G., Jack Gailo, Joe Gay**), 1914-71, U.S., boot.-drugs-rob.-org. crime. Joseph Gagliano was an active member of the Chicago mob for nearly thirty years. His long criminal career dated back to 1926, and included arrests for kidnapping and armed robbery. Gagliano served as a top trigger-man and loan shark for Joey Glimco and Charles "Chucky" English in the lucrative jukebox racket, for which he collected a 90-cent monthly rental from 492 distributors using 6,975 syndicate machines. "Joey G.," as he was known to underworld associates, enjoyed considerable influence on the West Side, especially in the twenty-eighth, thirtieth, and thirty-seventh wards where John "Jackie" Cerone once ruled as Mafia overlord. See: **Cerone, John Phillip.** REF.: *CBA.*

Gagne, George, and **Wallace, Rose,** prom. 1899, Case of, U.S., fraud. George Gagne was known to the police officers of the Harrison Street Lockup in Chicago as a man with a shady past. He was a bail bondsman who frequented the South Loop vice district known as the Levee. Gagne was an experienced, clever swindler, but was clearly overmatched when he made the acquaintance of pretty Rose Wallace, a young ingenue who deceived him into thinking that she was a woman of considerable fortune back home in Indiana.

Gagne, who thought he recognized a good thing when he saw it, courted the girl and then proposed marriage in order to lay claim to her property in Evansville. Wallace convinced Gagne she was a woman of her word after he consulted with the attorney who was said to be the custodian of her property. Rose's mother, it was explained, married a wealthy California miner named Thomas Wallace, who left a $130,000 estate behind after he had died. Another $50,000 left to her by Mrs. Mary Milburn was to become Rose's after she passed her eighteenth birthday.

A hastily arranged marriage ceremony was performed in City Hall just before Gagne made his arrangements to embark for Evansville with his new wife. Before they were to board the train, Wallace slipped away to a small room she maintained at the Newport Hotel. She disguised herself as a young girl in a short

frock. Rose slipped off to the Dearborn Train Station where she pretended to be a lost little girl. Taking sympathy on the child, the police took her to the station where she gave the name of Gertrude Wallace.

Meanwhile, Gagne reported his wife missing and notified the police about the matter. After three days he was arrested on suspicion. Clifton Wooldridge of the Chicago Police Department detected some chicanery, and upon further investigation he exposed Wallace for what she really was. She defended her actions by accusing her new husband of brutality. He agreed to an uncontested divorce, and admitted that the whole affair had set him back $900. No charges against the pair were brought, though upon further investigation the story about the inheritance in Evansville, Ind., was proven to be pure fabrication. Detective Wooldridge even suspected that Wallace and Gagne had concocted the fraud together based on some dubious financial transactions that he discovered. Whatever the case, there was no real evidence of a crime. The whole affair seemed to be little more than an elaborate, pointless hoax.

Wallace went to work for the proprietor of a dime museum as a side show freak. Several years earlier she had traveled with circuses throughout the Midwest.

REF.: *CBA;* Wooldridge, *Hands Up.*

Gahagan, Usher, d.1749, Brit., fraud. Born in Ireland to honest, hard-working parents, Usher Gahagan squandered his advantages to seek his place among the counterfeiters and coin droppers of London. The particular crime he was arrested and hanged for on Feb. 20, 1749, involved the filing down of guineas in order to sell the gold dust to prospective buyers. There was much sympathy for the young Irishman. While in jail he wrote sentimental poetry that caught the fancy of all who read his verse. However, he was shown no mercy by the courts.

REF.: Bleackley, *Hangmen of England; CBA.*

Gaillard, Pierre Francois, See: **Lancenaire, Pierre Francois.**

Gaimar V (or **Guaimar; Prince of Salerno**), c.1011-52, Italy, assass. Inherited the throne from his mother in 1027. Allied with Normans, he gained control of Apulia and Calabria, but was stripped of his possessions by Emperor Henry III in 1047. After claiming some land in Campania, he was killed in 1052. REF.: *CBA.*

Gainesville Eight, prom. 1970s, Case of, U.S., consp. A former serviceman who had a history of mental illness, William W. Lemmer, accused several veterans of a bizarre plot, resulting in the trial of the Gainesville Eight. At the August 1973 trial in Gainesville, Fla., Lemmer, a former paratrooper, testified that seven members of the Vietnam Veterans Against the War and a supporter held a meeting at the apartment of Scott Camil on May 27, 1972. Lemmer claimed that the group planned an assault on the 1972 Republican National Convention in Miami Beach, using crossbows, slingshots, automatic weapons, and homemade firebombs in the attack. Lemmer, who had told a Congressional subcommittee that the Army had offered to give him a psychiatric discharge, claimed that the conspirators planned to walk among peaceful demonstrations and shoot policeman with high-powered slingshots to provoke the officers to retaliate.

Lemmer also claimed that the veterans planned to destroy buildings and police cars in the city of Miami in an attempt to draw the police away from the beach and then they were going to shoot transformers on power poles to disable power to the convention. Veering from charges in the indictment, Lemmer also accused Camil, the alleged ringleader, of training political assassination squads armed with guns obtained by trading drugs. The farce ended on Aug. 31, 1973, when all of the defendants were acquitted. They included Camil, Donald Perdue, Peter P. Mahoney, Stanley K. Michelson, Alton C. Foss, William J. Patterson, John W. Kniffin, and John K. Briggs. All except Briggs were members of the veterans group. REF.: *CBA.*

Gainus, d.400, Roman., consp.-rebel. Conspired with Stilicho in the murder of Roman politician Rufinus in 395. His revolt attempt in 399 was quashed by the Huns. Upon the defeat of his army, he was murdered. REF.: *CBA*.

Gaitan, Jorge Eliécer, 1902-48, Col., assass. Served as mayor of Bogota, Col., from 1936-40. His campaign for the presidency six years later split liberal voting factions, allowing conservatives to win the election. He was assassinated in 1948. REF.: *CBA*.

Gaither, Ernie (Little Gaither the Money Waster and Woman Chaser), prom. 1947, U.S., rob.-mur. A stickup man at age sixteen, a murderer at twenty-three, Ernie Gaither had some time to reflect on his misspent youth while locked behind the walls of Cook County Jail.

Gaither wanted to be a prize fighter, but joined up instead with a gang of outlaws who terrorized Chicago's South Side. "It was eight of us," Gaither recalled. "The names is Earl Parks who was known as Smiley because he would kill you with a smile on his face. The others: Herbert Liggins, known as Hop-a-long because he was crippled; Charles Jones, known as Pretty Boy because he was a nice-looking guy. Charles Hill was known as Colorado Kid. William Lee was known as Wild Bill. Clyde Bradford was known as Blue because he was so dark. Percy Bellmar was known as the Wheeler because he was a good driver."

Gaither went to prison for the first time in 1940 when he was implicated in a murder, but was released six years later. In 1947, he was convicted of murdering a second man in a holdup. His letter to posterity, written in the privacy of a jail cell, so moved Cook County Assistant Public Defender Frank Sain and Governor Dwight Green that they issued a stay of execution. "Any fool can put a gun in his hand and do wrong," Gaither said in his letter. "But it takes a man with guts to get a job and work for what he wants." REF.: *CBA*.

Gaius (Caius), prom. 2nd Cent., Roman., jur. Wrote the Institutes of Gaius around 161, covering the principles of Roman law. The Institutes of Justinian were based on his work. REF.: *CBA*.

Gajah Mada, d.1364, Java, law enfor. off. Recaptured the crown for King Jayanagara in 1319, as head of the royal body-guard. He was named prime minister of the Majapahit empire in 1331. He unified Indonesian islands with conquests of Bali in 1343, and Sunda in 1351. REF.: *CBA*.

Galante, Carmine (Camillo Galante, AKA: the Cigar, Lillo), 1910-79, U.S., extor.-drugs-asslt.-org. crime-mur.-assass. Carmine Galante, the godfather of the New York mob following the death of Carlo Gambino in 1976, viewed the world as corrupt. The Mafia, on the other hand, championed loyalty and fair play. This twisted logic was consistent with the diagnosis of prison psychiatrists who described Galante as a psychopath who was fond of gamesmanship. "He's a mass of contradictions," said ex-assistant U.S. attorney William Tendy, who prosecuted the mobster in 1962 and sent him to jail. "If he was walking with one person, you'd learn not to join him as a third," recalled a former intimate of Galante. "He'd pick a fight with the third person and force the second to become his ally."

New York mobster Carmine Galante, 1930.

Galante was the son of a fisherman who immigrated to the U.S. from Castellammare de Golfo, in Sicily. As a youth he commanded a vicious street gang on the Lower East Side of New York and he began killing people at age eleven. He drifted into Mafia circles sometime in the 1920s, and became a top triggerman by the time he was twenty. In 1930, Galante and several henchmen attempted and failed to rob a truck in the Williamsburg section of Brooklyn, N.Y., when police officer Joseph Meenahan

spotted four men preparing to hold up a truck driver. Galante shot at the officer and wounded him in the leg. A 6-year-old girl passing by also was clipped by a stray bullet. Neither were killed but Galante was sent to prison for twelve-and-a-half years.

Paroled in 1939, the gangster soon emerged as one of Vito Genovese's top assassins. When Genovese fled to Italy in 1935 to avoid murder charges, Galante remained behind to take care of family business. On Jan. 11, 1943, Carlo Tresca, the anti-fascist editor of *Il Martèllo* (The Hammer), was gunned down in Manhattan. Galante's car was found nearby and, though never indicted for this crime, Genovese was suspected of having ordered the hit to please dictator Benito Mussolini, friend and benefactor of the crime boss.

Carmine Galante, dying, cigar in mouth, 1979.

The Tresca murder established Galante's reputation in New York. In the next few years he defected to the crime family of Joseph Bonanno, first as a chauffeur and then as an underboss in the organization in the 1950s. Though Galante was loyal to Joseph Bonanno, he defied his boss and established a drug-smuggling network in the early 1950s, a racket launched in Fall 1954 when he and Montreal crime boss Frank Petrula flew to Italy to meet with the exiled Charles "Lucky" Luciano. Together the three organized the lucrative French Connection which converted Turkish opium into heroin in Marseilles drug factories, and eventually smuggled the finished product into Canada and the U.S.

In 1958 a federal grand jury in New York returned an indictment against twenty-four mobsters involved in drug trafficking, including Galante and Genovese. The testimony of an informant, Nelson Cantellops, helped send Galante to prison for twenty years in 1962 following two lengthy trials, legal procedures that began in 1960.

Paroled from the Atlanta Penitentiary on Nov. 23, 1974, he returned to his operation headquarters to consolidate power and drive out Hispanic and black gangs who were challenging the Mafia in drug trafficking. To his old enemies within the Cosa Nostra, Carmine Galante sent a message—forty-eight hours after his release from prison, mobster Frank Costello's tomb was blown up.

The gangster had formulated his strategy while behind bars. With Bonanno already deposed by the ruling commission, he would assume control of the family and the entire U.S. Mafia. In 1978, eight top-ranking Genovese gangsters were assassinated. Pasquale "Paddy Mac" Macchiarole, a top lieutenant in the Genovese organization (now run by Funzi Tieri) was gunned down in the spring. A week later his 33-year-old son, John, was shot down. Galante brazenly warned the heads of the other crime families to fall in behind him or face the consequences. "Who among you is going to stand up to me?" was his message.

At an alleged secret meeting in Boca Raton, Fla., Santo Trafficante, Jerry Catena, Frank Tieri, and Paul Castellano reportedly reached an agreement. The troublesome Galante had to go. On July 12, 1979, the 69-year-old Galante stopped in Joe and Mary's Restaurant in the Bushwick part of Brooklyn to have lunch and to say goodbye to his cousin, Giuseppe Turano, who was leaving for a vacation in Italy. Turano owned the restaurant. Galante was seated in an outdoor patio with his bodyguard, Leonardo "Nina" Coppolla, and two 28-year-old Mafia associates, Caesar Bonventre and Baldo Amato, when an assassination squad burst onto the patio and began firing machine guns. Galante collapsed surrounded by tomato plants and grapevines, his ever-present cigar clenched between his teeth; Turano and Coppolla were also shot dead.

"I used to say the rest of them were copper, but he was pure steel," said Lieutenant Remo Franceschini, New York's intelligence chief for organized crime. "When he spoke, he made others shudder." See: **Bonanno, Joseph; Costello, Frank; Gambino, Carlo; Genovese, Vito.**

REF.: Alexander, *The Pizza Connection*; Blumenthal, *The Last Days of the Sicilians*; CBA; Davis, *Mafia Kingfish*; Demaris, *The Last Mafioso*; Gage, *Mafia, U.S.A.*; ____, *The Mafia is not an Equal Opportunity Employer*; Gosch and Hammer, *The Last Testament of Lucky Luciano*; Kirby and Renner, *Mafia Enforcer*; Martin, *Revolt in the Mafia*; Nash, *Almanac of World Crime*; ____, *Bloodletters and Badmen*; Peterson, *The Mob*; Reid, *The Grim Reapers*; Reuter, *Disorganized Crime*; Servadio, *Mafioso*; Velie, *Desperate Bargain: Why Jimmy Hoffa Had to Die*; Zuckerman, *Vengeance Is Mine*.

Galapagos Murders, 1934, Ecu., (unsolv.) mur. Five-hundred miles west of Ecuador lies the secluded, tropical island of Charles, one of the Galapagos Islands. Adventurers such as Theodore Roosevelt, William Beebe, and actor John Barrymore had visited the area. Except for the infrequent celebrity visits, however, the Galapagos were sparsely populated.

In 1932 three Europeans landed on Charles Island for vacation. They included the Baroness Eloise Bosquet de Wagner Wehrborn, of Vienna, her lover Alfred Rudolph Lorenz, whose German passport listed a Paris residence, and Robert Philippson, a mutual friend. To their surprise they found that the island was already inhabited by fellow Germans Dr. Karl Ritter, a dentist who had left his wife, and Dore Koervin. Arthur Wittmer, his wife Margaret Walbrol, and a Norwegian sailor also lived on the island.

The baroness was frequently observed on walks toting a pearl-handed revolver—her favorite pastime was maiming animals and nursing them back to health. When visiting U.S. celebrities arrived, the baroness and her fellow travelers were gracious, but one shipwrecked couple from Chile were put out to sea in an open boat.

The baroness soon lost interest in her frail, sickly lover and decided to take up with Robert Philippson. Lorenz argued bitterly with her before deciding to move out of the hut. He went to live with the Wittmers but he moved back in with the baroness a few months later.

In March 1934, the Wittmers heard a loud argument in the baroness' hut. Investigating, they were told by a frazzled Lorenz that the baroness and Philippson had sailed away on a U.S. yacht to another South Seas location. Now he, too, would try to leave. Lorenz posted a plea on a barrel that fronted the ocean asking to be picked up by any ship passing by. Someone—possibly the baroness—saw the note and picked him up. Lorenz never made it back to civilization alive.

In November 1934, a tuna fishing boat, the *Santa Amaro*, moored off Marchena Island, in the northern part of the Galapagos, where skipper Manuel Rodriguez had spotted a small skiff on the rocks. Several yards away were the badly decomposed remains of two people. A passport lying near one body indicated

it was Alfred Lorenz. The other person's identity remains a mystery. Meanwhile, the baroness had disappeared and one could only guess that Lorenz may have killed her and then died after a nautical mishap. REF.: *CBA*.

Galaup, Jean-Francois de (Comte de La Pérouse), 1741-c.1788, Fr., assass. Renowned navigator who explored much of the Pacific Ocean. He was murdered in the Santa Cruz Islands, northeast of Australia in 1788. REF.: *CBA*.

Galba, Servius Sulpicius, 3 B.C.-69 A.D., Roman., emp., assass. Served under several Roman emperors from 39-68 A.D., as governor of Africa, Germany, Aquitania, and Spain. He joined fellow Roman governor Julius Vindex in trying to remove Nero from power. The revolt attempt was unsuccessful, but inspired similar attempts throughout the empire. He was named emperor in 68 A.D., following Nero's suicide, but was murdered by soldiers six months later. REF.: *CBA*.

Galbaio, Giovanni (Doge of Venice), d.c.803, Italy, consp.-mur. Chief administrator of Venice, Italy from 787-803. He conspired to murder Grado, the leader of the pro-Frankish political party. He was forced out of his position by a Frankish uprising led by Obelerius in 803. REF.: *CBA*.

Galbraith, James, d.1944, Brit., mur. While on shore leave in the vicinity of the Salford Docks, Chief Steward James Galbraith of the Merchant Navy met up with James William Percey, a radio officer from the vessel *Pacific Shipper*. Percey was intoxicated and in a convivial mood. He proposed that they should return to his boat for a riotous drinking party in his private chambers. The man made the mistake of letting on that he had £60 stashed in his bunk.

The steward was summoned and he brought six bottles of beer to the room, but did not linger when Percey invited him in for a quick drink. That was the last anyone saw of the drunken seaman until Apr. 8, 1944, when a dark stain that resembled blood was detected by a sailor in the berth immediately below Percey's cabin. The locked door to the radio officer's cabin was broken down and Percey's blood-soaked body was found crumpled on the floor. All that was left was four shillings.

Through fingerprints Galbraith was identified as the killer. He was tried at the Manchester Assizes and hanged on July 26.

REF.: *CBA*; Shew, *A Second Companion to Murder*.

Galea Brothers, prom. 1952, Gibraltar, smug.-org. crime. In 1952 an elaborate smuggling operation that conveyed drugs, tobacco, coffee, and other contraband into the countries of the Mediterranean region was uncovered by the British civil authorities when the *Combinatie* was seized by a gang of pirates off of Corsica. The master of the ship was bound and gagged and the smugglers used his boat for the next twelve days to move its load of cigarettes valued at £35,700 to a cove.

The vessels used to convey the goods were former British Royal Navy vessels: minesweepers, Harbor Defense Launches, and MTBs. They were small, but relatively fast and efficient crafts. To avoid harassment by the coastal authorities, the smuggling gangs from Gibraltar, Italy, and other nations would secure a British craft of this type and fly the red ensign, which guaranteed safe passage, and the protection of Her Majesty's Government on the high seas. An operation of this scope could only survive and prosper with the cooperation of higher-ranking officials.

The crews that manned these ships were invariably Spanish, Moorish, German, and Latvian. They were employed by various gangster combines like two brothers, Manuel Galea and Andrea Galea, who were headquartered in Gibraltar.

The deeper conspiracy was eventually detected, resulting in the conviction of Mrs. Florence Mary Doris Houillon, a respected British woman who owned the *Arran Mail*, a vessel that was used in the coastal smuggling operation.

In March 1954, Mrs. Houillon was sentenced to seven months imprisonment by a court in Tangier, and fined £50. The British vessel *Cottesmore* was assessed a stiff £130,000 fine by a Spanish court on smuggling charges. It was one of the ships that had been purchased for the exclusive use of the Galea brothers by a mysterious Mr. "X" of the British government.

REF.: *CBA;* Webb, *Deadline for Crime.*

Galenti, Cora, b.1898, U.S., fraud. During the 1950s and early 1960s, Cora Galenti, the eldest daughter of a Brooklyn liquor importer, claimed to have captured the secrets of eternal youth through her own special "Method of Facial Rejuvenation," which she peddled at her salon on Sunset Boulevard in Los Angeles. The treatment, which took only forty-five minutes to administer, but three weeks for the actual "effect" to take hold, was composed of carbolic acid (phenol), which if used to excess results in permanent damage to the kidneys and bladder. While none of Galenti's patients actually died from the treatment, one woman committed suicide after the substance had disfigured her face and made her unemployable.

Galenti was married at least six times. In the 1930s she arrived in Hollywood, where she worked as a wardrobe designer for a brief time. While traversing the back lots of Hollywood, Cora became interested in face peeling, following in the footsteps of Antoinette LaGasse, who established a dubious reputation by practicing this racket on star-struck ingenues and aging femme fatales. Galenti became one of her best customers before striking out on her own.

In the 1930s Cora was sued by at least twelve angry and dissatisfied women who were awarded judgments totaling $186,000, which was probably never paid. When LaGasse died, Cora inherited the formula and opened her shop on Sunset Boulevard. In 1950 she was arrested for the first time for practicing medicine without a license. For this she received a suspended sentence.

Cora advertised her magical "Parisian Method" in various Hollywood trade journals, claiming that she possessed the secret of the stars, one that had been lovingly handed down through generations of Galenti women. In 1965 she took this one step further by boasting that half of Hollywood's most glittering personalities had already undergone skin rejuvenation. *Confidential* magazine, the notorious scandal sheet of the mid-1950s, endorsed Galenti in an unabashed self-serving piece that was later translated into Chinese. Many women who read *Confidential* religiously saved their money so that they too might be able to afford the $1,800 fee she charged.

On Jan. 11, 1962, Galenti was charged in a six-count indictment for mail fraud. The U.S. Attorney in Las Vegas had completed an exhaustive investigation into her unsubstantiated claims of skin rejuvenation, concluding that not only had she swindled the public, but the treatment was a medical hazard. Nine months later a Guilty verdict was returned, and Galenti was sentenced to five years in prison and assessed a $2,000 fine.

While out on bond, she fled to Mexico City on Aug. 21, 1963, under the name Cora Smith. She quickly found an obliging man to marry, and being the new wife of a Mexican national, was granted citizenship. Galenti was soon back in business and up to her old tricks. In 1965 she renamed her business "Clinicas Galenti," and began sending out new flyers to her customers in the States from her base of operations in Tijuana.

REF.: *CBA;* Kahn, *Fraud.*

Galentine, Dr. Jay F., b.1844, U.S., mur. Jay Galentine was a veteran of the Civil War and a well respected dentist practicing in Cleveland at the time he shot and killed fellow physician Dr. William Jones. The murder was shocking, especially by 1870 standards. It involved adultery, intrigue, and the kind of scandalous behavior that members of the professional classes simply did not engage in.

Dr. Galentine freely admitted to pulling the trigger in his office on Pearl Street the night of Oct. 8. He told his story to Frank Hurd, the downstairs druggist who was sweeping his sidewalk at the time. Galentine said that he had killed Dr. Jones, who had attempted to steal his wife Mary away.

Galentine said he had not caught him in the act, but that Jones had owned up. The alleged seduction occurred while the doctor was on business in Boston, several months prior to the shooting. When Mary refused his advances, Dr. Jones forcibly entered her bedroom one night and raped her. On the way out of her bedroom, he took with him a key which he used as a kind of blackmail. Afraid that her husband would become violent, she kept the intimate details of what had transpired on the hot July night to herself.

Dr. Galentine became a popular hero in the days leading up to the trial. The Cleveland *Plain Dealer* and a competing paper, the *Leader,* vied for all the latest information about the Jones-Galentine case, each accusing the other of journalistic treachery in the reporting of the day's events and the selection of woodcut drawings. The trial began on Jan. 13, 1871. There was a great deal of mud-slinging on both sides, as the defense accused Dr. Galentine of secretly plotting to abandon his wife all along. There were frequent marital quarrels, it was reported, and Galentine's penchant for wiling away his spare time in the billiard parlor was a grave concern to Mary.

On Jan. 31, the jury returned a verdict of Guilty on a reduced charge of manslaughter. Dr. Galentine jumped up and embraced his lawyer when he was spared the death penalty. Three days later Judge S. Burke sentenced him to ten years of hard labor at the Ohio penitentiary, coupled with a $1,100 fine. After he served his sentence the doctor moved back to Cleveland, where he opened a new dental office. Mary agreed to a divorce, and in time Galentine remarried.

REF.: *CBA; The Jones-Galentine Tragedy: Embodying a Full Report of the Trial;* Rodell, *Cleveland Murders.*

Galiffi, Agata (AKA: *Flor de la Maffia*), 1915- , Arg., org. crime. Born in Italy, Agata Galiffi moved to Buenos Aires, Arg., at an early age. Her father was Juan Galiffi, a notorious gangster who was chased out of the country by the police. Arriving in Argentina's largest city, the elder Galiffi resumed his former occupation. He sent his young daughter to a highly respected school to attain refinement. Instead Agata pursued a criminal career like her father. When Juan was deported, Agata assumed command of his criminal gang, which was engaged in blackmail, kidnapping, robbery, and extortion.

In the city of Rosario, Agata Galiffi became known as somewhat of a racing buff. Her gang fixed the outcome of the horse races and muscled in on the lucrative bookmaking operations. Things went well until May 1944 when the Argentine police arrested her in the company of gang hit man Arturo Placeres, while they were racing through the streets of Rosario in their gleaming Packard automobile. When Placares refused to turn his gun on the police as Agata demanded, he was labeled a coward and she slapped him. The courts sentenced her to seven years in prison. "I am a victim of destiny!" she cried. REF.: *CBA.*

Galifi, Nicola, 1936- , and **MacDonald, Lynda Anne** (AKA: **Anna Von Bjorn**), prom. 1974, and **Fiumara, Agostino,** 1929- , and **Vinci, Michele,** 1939- , and **DiPasquale, Diego,** 1953- , and **Distefano, Luigi,** 1919- , and **Luciano, Dominic,** 1939- Can., drugs-org. crime. Posing as a corrupt official from the International Teamster's Union, agent Sam Roberts, of the Drug Enforcement Agency (DEA) helped destroy an international drug cartel based in Canada. In June 1974, the drug traffickers were poised to dump the first twenty kilograms of cocaine in the U.S.

Roberts received his tip from a Chicago businessman who attended a swank party in Toronto hosted by a former model named Lynda Anne MacDonald. Over drinks he had learned of their plan to establish a heroin and cocaine market in the city, and they wondered if he could put them in touch with a high roller willing to buy what they had to sell.

A meeting was arranged between Roberts, who posed as a corrupt union officer, and Lynda MacDonald who introduced herself as the Countess Anna Von Bjorn at a cocktail lounge near Chicago's O'Hare Airport. Roberts flashed a thick wad of bills and explained that he was ready to do business. Several months passed while the Countess investigated his "references." In September 1974, the deal was set to go down, only now the stakes had been raised. It was pure, unadulterated heroin they were talking about, not cocaine. Michele Vinci and Agostino Fiumara demanded and received further references from Agent Roberts. He supplied them with the name of a mob informant in New York. Meanwhile, Roberts checked out *their* references. It turned out that the Canadians were being backed by Carlo Gambino and his brother Paulo in New York.

The investigation continued for the next year. In October 1975, Countess Anna was arrested by the Royal Canadian Mounted Police after she peddled $20,000 worth of cocaine to Roberts. Inexplicably, she did not blow the DEA man's cover, perhaps fearing for her own life if she did.

A second agent named Jack Mann continued to deal with the drug pushers. He flew to Italy in 1977 to complete a $240,000 sale with money put up by the CIA. The Italian connection, however, refused to make the deal with him in either Rome or Milan. Back in Chicago, the Canadians, who were reasonably satisfied that their clients were legitimate, began to ship unlimited quantities of "ceramic" products into town.

Dominic Luciano arrived with the stuff on June 8, 1977, in his van. The DEA men completed the purchase and then trailed him back to Canada where he delivered the money to his uncle Agostino. Several weeks later Luciano was captured in Buffalo, N.Y., which set in motion the final wave of arrests.

The leader of the gang was Nicola Galifi, forty-four, who was the one checking agent Roberts' references. The courts sentenced him to eight years in prison. The other members of the ring received varying prison terms: MacDonald, four years; Luciano nine; Fiumara twelve; Luigi Distefano three years for his role in discussing methods of heroin delivery; and Diego DiPasquale, four years. See: **Gambino, Carlo.** REF.: *CBA.*

Galindez, Dr. Jesus de, c.1904-c.56, Case of, U.S.-Dom., (unsolv.) kid.-mur. In 1956 Generalissimo Rafael Leonidas Trujillo, the strong-arm ruler of the Dominican Republic, attempted to silence one of his harshest critics. Trujillo, whose right-wing junta enslaved the people of his nation for a dozen years in the 1940s and 1950s, ultimately failed to suppress the truth which came out shortly after his assassination in 1961.

Trujillo's enemy was Dr. Jesus de Galindez, a Spanish academic who had fled the persecutions of the Franco regime in 1939. An staunch anti-fascist, Galindez settled in the Dominican Republic where he became a legal advisor to the National Department of Labor, serving for

Dr. Jesus de Galindez

a time as secretary of the Dominican Minimum Wage Committee. He was fired by Trujillo's government after siding with striking peasants in the sugar industry. In about 1946 Galindez fled the Dominican Republic to teach political science at Columbia University in New York, where he worked on an exposé of the oppressive regime which he titled *The Era of Trujillo,* a first-hand account of the torture and murder of political dissidents under Trujillo.

Before the book was completed, on Oct. 2, 1952, Andres Resquena, publisher of an anti-Trujillo newspaper and a friend of Galindez, was shot dead in the lobby of his Manhattan apartment. Believing his life in peril, Galindez wrote a secret memorandum saying Trujillo had probably ordered his death. On Mar. 12, 1956, Galindez had just finished his evening classes and was driven to the subway entrance at 57th Street and Seventh Avenue by his student, Evelyn Lang, when Dominican agents seized him. A blinding snowstorm made it impossible for anyone to see the abduction.

Five days later his disappearance was reported. By this time he was in the Dominican Republic facing Trujillo. "Your life now is as worthless as an empty page in that book you are writing!" the dictator said. Trujillo's guards sprayed him with machine gun bullets. He was buried in an unmarked grave.

Meanwhile, unconfirmed reports drifted back to New York that Galindez had gone to Spain to lead an insurrection against Franco. Others suggested that he had been murdered for the $1 million in aid he had raised for the Basque government in exile. Those monies, however, soon were accounted for.

The true circumstances began to surface on Dec. 4, 1956, when a 23-year-old U.S. pilot, Gerald Lester Murphy, disappeared in Ciudad Trujillo. William Pfeiffer, ambassador to the Dominican Republic, learned that Murphy had been telling about secret flights he had flown on behalf of the Trujillo regime. The discovery of his car at the edge of a cliff suggested foul play.

Probing further, the FBI learned that Murphy had chartered a twin-engine Beechcraft D-18 for $800 on Mar. 5. Using the name "John Kane," Murphy said he was going to fly a businessman to Miami later that week. On the morning of Mar. 12, the well-equipped plane flew from Newark, N.J., to Amityville, Long Island, where Murphy awaited his passenger. An ambulance pulled up to the gate and a stretcher was loaded into the plane, the "passenger" tied down.

Murphy re-fueled the plane in West Palm Beach, Fla., before continuing on to the Dominican Republic. He received a sizeable amount of money and a pilot's job with Compañia Dominicana de Aviación as payment. But he could not keep quiet. Murphy told a girlfriend, Celia "Sally" Caire, about the mission. Dictator Trujillo paid $562,855 to have lawyers, press agents, and former New York State Supreme Court justice William H. Munson to write "*Report and Opinion in the Matter of Galindez.*"

In 1964, Charles O. Parker interviewed an ex-warden of the Dominican prison near Ciudad Trujillo. The man confessed that Galindez had been kidnapped, drugged, and flown to the dictator's estate for assassination. Murphy and a nurse, Ana Gloria Vieira, who had drugged Galindez, were both assassinated the same year. Vieira was beaten to death in August 1956 and pushed off a cliff in a burning car. On Dec. 1, 1956, Murphy was arrested trying to leave the country and was killed. Galindez' book, published posthumously, became popular in South America and the Caribbean.

REF.: *CBA;* Nash, *Among the Missing;* (FICTION), Chaber, *The Gallows Garden;* Marlowe, *Murder Is My Dish.*

Galindo, Broulio, and **Hernandez, José,** and **Mendival, Salvador,** and **Rivera, Faustino,** prom. 1922, U.S., (wrong. convict.) rob. While on their way through the San Gabriel Valley en route to Los Angeles where they were to pick oranges, four young Mexicans driving a rented Ford were stopped on the highway and charged with robbery. It was Apr. 5, 1922.

An hour earlier, the First National Bank of Arcadia, Calif., was robbed of $9,000 in currency, silver, bonds, and American Express Traveler's Checks. The bandits made a clean getaway until the Chevrolet they were driving plunged into a ravine. A farmer named Virgil Barlow who lived south of Arcadia saw the speeding car careen off the road and went to investigate. The disabled car had continued on for three-quarters of a mile before the bank robbers abandoned it near a bridge crossing the San Gabriel River. The police later surmised that the men had switched cars.

The four Mexicans were charged with the holdup after a cache of revolvers was found inside the Ford. They were used for rabbit shooting, they said. Several of the bank tellers and customers mistakenly picked out Galindo and Hernandez as the bank robbers. Based on this testimony, all three were convicted of armed robbery on Nov. 6. Salvador Mendival received a term in San Quentin of one to ten years. Broulio Galindo and José Hernandez were taken to Folsom Prison where they began serving sentences of one year to life.

Just as the bars slammed shut behind them, a man identified only as Jack Thomas requested an interview with the Deputy District Attorney. He told them that the Mexicans were innocent and that the real robbers were Frank Sullivan, W.F. McMahon, Tom Gray, and Eddie Burns.

The four new suspects were arrested in Los Angeles on an unrelated charge. It took nearly two years to assemble a case against them, while all the time the Mexicans languished in prison. Finally, on May 2, 1924, Mendival received a pardon. Hernandez was released on May 26, and Galindo four months later. The fourth member of the party, Faustino Rivera, died in jail. None received any compensation from the state for their time spent in jail.

REF.: Borchard, *Convicting the Innocent*; CBA.

Gall, Franz Joseph, 1758-1828, Ger., criminol. A physician, Gall was the founder of phrenology, a doctrine which attributed discernible physical characteristics to criminal types. Gall, who also pioneered theories which ascribed cerebral functions to various areas of the brain, did not coin the term phrenology. He was the first, however, to develop the theories upon which phrenology is based, particularly in his attempt to establish a definite relationship between mental faculties and the physical shape of the human skull. In 1791, Gall first published works which laid the foundation for phrenology. Though criticized in many academic circles as advancing an imperfect science, Gall persisted through the remainder of his life to uphold his belief that criminals could be determined through physical characteristics. REF.: *CBA*.

Gallagher, Eddie, c.1948- , Ire., kid. Dutch industrialist Dr. Tiede Herrema, manager of the Ferenko steel plant in Limerick, Ire., was driving to work on Oct. 3, 1975, when a man dressed as a police officer flagged him down. Eddie Gallagher, twenty-eight, asked for Herrema's name, then abducted him at gunpoint. Herrema was held in a deserted farmhouse for a week, transferred to another house for a week, and then taken to yet another in Monasterevin. With Gallagher were Marian Coyle, twenty-one, and three or four other accomplices. The Irish Republican Army (IRA) denied responsibility for the abduction. In fact, they had earlier accused Gallagher of keeping $160,000 from bank robberies committed for the IRA.

Gallagher first demanded the release of IRA prisoners Dr. Rose Dugdale, Kevin Mallon, and Jim Hyland, who were being held by the Republic of Ireland. Hyland was said to have been Coyle's lover, and Dugdale had had a child by Gallagher. The kidnappers threatened to murder Herrema if the prisoners were not released within forty-eight hours. The Irish government refused the demand, and appointed Father O'Mahoney as a mediator. O'Mahoney contacted the abductors through an intermediary on Oct. 8. For the first five days, Herrema was given no food and was kept blindfolded with his ears plugged. On Oct. 15, the government received a recording of Herrema in which he said that the abductors had threatened to cut off his foot and mail it to the government as evidence that he was alive. By Oct. 20, police discovered the car Gallagher had used, and arrested two men as accomplices. While the Monasterevin house was searched, Gallagher and Coyle hid in the attic. On Oct. 21, officers surrounded the house, trapping the abductors with Herrema in an upstairs bedroom. During the eighteen-day siege that followed, police kept Gallagher and Coyle awake with constant noise and floodlights trained on their window. After four days without food, the kidnappers accepted rations and a chamber pot. Periodically they forced Herrema to stand near the window at gunpoint, his feet tied, and shout to the police to stay away. Police bugged the room and installed surveillance cameras.

On Nov. 7, Gallagher, exhausted and suffering severe stomach pains, agreed to release Herrema and surrender. Just before giving up Herrema, Gallagher handed him a bullet from his gun as a souvenir. Coyle, however, in the entire eighteen days with Herrema, never spoke to him. Tried in Dublin, Gallagher was sentenced to a twenty-year jail term. Coyle was given fifteen years, and accomplices John Vincent Walshe and Brian McGowan were given eight years each. Gallagher responded to his sentence by calling for a campaign of violence against targets in England.

REF.: *CBA*; Clutterbuck, *Kidnap and Ransom*.

Gallagher, Eugene, 1934- , U.S., law enfor. off. Gallagher served as the chief of police in Indianapolis from Jan. 8, 1976, until Jan. 6, 1981; his Civil Service rank of captain was established prior to his retirement from the force the following May.

Chief Gallagher's twenty-one-year career on the force began Feb. 16, 1960, when he was appointed probationary patrolman. He attained regular status a year later after successfully finishing his year of probation. In December 1964, he received a department commendation as a result of his work in tracking down John Gibson, Perkins Cole, Julius Mack, and Ronald Utley after they robbed and assaulted four persons.

On Sept. 13, 1966, Gallagher was advanced to sergeant, a position he held until Apr. 4, 1968, when he was promoted to technical acting lieutenant. On June 28, 1972, he made the grade of technical captain, which paved the way for his eventual promotion to chief of police in 1976. REF.: *CBA*.

Gallagher, Jack (Three-Fingered Jack), d.1864, U.S., west. outl. Gallagher was a member of the feared Henry Plummer gang of Montana, a gunslinger who killed an estimated six men before he was hanged in Virginia City, Mont. on Jan. 13, 1864 (some accounts state Jan. 14). Plummer had already been killed by vigilantes and Gallagher and other Plummer gang members had sworn vengeance. This notorious band of train and stagecoach bandits, the vigilantes knew, would show no mercy. The vigilantes decided to act first. They rounded up Jack Gallagher, George "Clubfoot" Lane, Frank Parrish, Boone Helm, and Hayes Lyons. "Three Fingered Jack" was the fiercest of the lot. He had been Plummer's top aide and was quick on the draw. The vigilantes found him asleep in the gambling room of the Arbor Restaurant.

While Gallagher yelled oaths at the vigilantes, he was dragged outside and to the place of execution, in front of an unfinished log building at Van Buren and Wallace streets. He wore a fancy cavalryman's coat trimmed with beaver and he continued to swear at his executioners as he was lined up with the other members of the Plummer gang. All five were placed upon boxes, and ropes tied to a crossbeam were then placed about their necks.

Boone Helm thought it all a great, grim joke. He made several remarks about Gallagher's resplendent cavalry coat and then shouted to Gallagher: "Jack, give me that coat! You never gave me anything!"

Gallagher snorted: "Damned sight of use you'd have for it." He then spied someone he knew standing in the window of the Virginia Hotel across the street and shouted: "Hey, old fellow, I'm going to Heaven! I'll be there in time to open the gate for you!"

Somehow, Gallagher managed to free one hand from the ropes binding both arms behind his back and produced a small knife which he used in a vain attempt to slit his own throat. A vigilante wrestled the knife from Gallagher's hand. His arms were again tied. He asked for a drink of whiskey before he was hanged. This was brought and poured down his throat so that he was coughing when asked to make his last statement. Choking, Gallagher said: "I hope forked lightning will strike every one of you bastards dead!" Then, defiantly, he leaped off the box on which he had been placed, hanging himself and depriving the vigilantes of performing the execution. Following Gallagher to eternity were Helm, Lane, Parrish, and Lyons.

Boone Helm, the joker among the condemned outlaws, clowned and bluffed his courage out to the last. He looked up to see Gallagher in his death throes and shouted: "Kick away, old fellow, I'll be in hell with you in a minute!" Then he said to the vigilantes about to kick the box from beneath his feet: "Every man for his principles. Hurrah for Jeff Davis! (Jefferson Davis, the President of the southern Confederacy)! Let her rip!" A vigilante knocked the box out from beneath him and Helm dangled in death from the rope.

Several thousand spectators witnessed this mass vigilante execution and one of them approached the chief hangman, John X. Beidler, a leading vigilante.

"When you put that rope around Gallagher's neck," asked the

spectator of Beidler, "didn't you feel for him?"

"Yes," Beidler dryly replied, "I felt for his left ear."

REF.: American Guide Series, *Montana, A State Guide Book;* Anderson, *The Pioneer Life of George W. Goodhart;* Ankeny, *The West as I Knew It;* Barrows, *The United States of Yesterday and Tomorrow;* Bartholomew, *Henry Plummer, Montana Outlaw Boss;* Birney, *Vigilantes;* Blankenship, *And Then There Were Men;* Breihan, *Badmen of Frontier Days;* Bruffey, *Eighty-one Years in the West;* Burlingame, *The Montana Frontier;* Burrows, *Vigilante; CBA;* Clampitt, *Echoes from the Rocky Mountains;* Clark, *Bonneville County in the Making;* Connolly, *The Devil Learns to Vote;* Dimsdale, *The Vigilantes of Montana;* Fisher and Holmes, *Gold Rushes and Mining Camps of the Early American West;* Fogarty, *The Story of Montana;* Gard, *Frontier Justice;* Gardner, *The Old Wild West;* Glasscock, *The War of the Copper Kings;* Hamilton, *From Wilderness to Statehood;* Hendricks, *The Bad Man of the West;* Holloway, *Texas Gun Lore;* Hough, *The Story of the Outlaw;* Howard, *Northwest Trail Blazers;* Hutchens, *One Man's Montana;* Johnson, *Famous Lawmen of the Old West;* Judson, *Montana;* Kennedy, *Cowboys and Cattlemen;* Langford, *Vigilante Days and Ways;* Lavender, *Land of Giants;* Lesson, *History of Montana;* Mencken, *By the Neck;* Nunis, *The Golden Frontier;* Ovitt, *Golden Treasure;* Raine, *Guns of the Frontier;* Salisbury, *He Rolled the Covered Wagons;* Sanders, *A History of Montana;* _____, *X. Beidler, Vigilante;* Stout, *Montana;* Thane, *High Border Country;* _____, *The Majestic Peaks;* Thomas, *Wild Life in the Rocky Mountains;* Warner, *Montana Territory;* Winther, *The Great Northwest;* Wolle, *The Bonanza Trail;* _____, *Montana Pay Dirt.*

Gallant, Barney, prom. 1919, U.S., boot. It never occurred to Barney Gallant that he should stop selling intoxicants at his popular Greenwich Village Inn. His patrons, notably the esteemed literati Theodore Dreiser, Eugene O'Neill, and Edna St. Vincent Millay, were no doubt among the first to sign a petition demanding his release after the New York police arrested him on charges of violating the Volstead Act.

When he was arraigned on Oct. 30, 1919, for selling liquor at fifty cents a shot, Gallant became one of the first New Yorkers arrested under the recently enacted Prohibition law. Public pressure resulted in a reduced sentence of thirty days in the lock-up for this literary bon vivant. In 1921 Barney opened his famous Club Gallant on West Third Street. It became a stylish speakeasy and popular hangout during the wild and woolly 1920s, serving its customers Scotch at $16 a quart, and $25 champagne.

REF.: *CBA;* Kobler, *Ardent Spirits.*

Gallardo, Miguel Angel Félix, See: **Félix Gallardo, Miguel Angel.**

Gallardo Parra, José Luis (AKA: **El Güero**), prom. 1985, Mex., drugs-org. crime. A top-ranking lieutenant of the Ernesto Fonseca Carrillo drug cartel, José Luis Gallardo Parra allegedly led the five man team who abducted DEA agent Enrique Camarena outside the U.S. consulate in Guadalajara, Mex., on Feb. 7, 1985. According to the confession made by Fonseca Carrillo gunman Samuel "El Samy" Ramirez Razo—who along with Gallardo Parra, another gunman, and two Jalisco State police officers, Geraldo Torres Lepe and Victor Manuel López Razón, kidnapped Camarena—the four men led by Gallardo Parra forced the U.S. agent into a late-model Volkswagen Atlantic and drove him to a home where Rafael Cáro Quintero was waiting. After evading DEA officials for months, Gallardo Parra was arrested in March 1987 by the Federales, but a court order prevented the DEA from interviewing him. See: **Camarena, Enrique.**

REF.: *CBA;* Shannon, *Desperados.*

Gallatin Street, prom. 1840-80, U.S., vice district. Gallatin Street was the center of New Orleans vice between 1840 and 1880. Only two blocks long, between Barracks and Ursuline avenues, it teemed with brothels, dance halls, and boarding houses occupied by the slickest con men, rowdies, and prostitutes. The district took a perverse pride in the fact that it did not contain a single legal enterprise. A crooked police force guarded the prosperity of the district, patrolling by daylight and conveniently disappearing at night. By 1858, the street was controlled by the Live Oak Boys, a gang of thugs founded by Red Bill Wilson. The

gang collected protection money from every Gallatin Street establishment, but destroyed their customers' businesses anyway if a rival offered a larger bounty. Despite the mayhem created by Wilson and his gang, virtually every business on Gallatin Street flourished. REF.: *CBA.*

Gallego, Gerald, 1947- , U.S., kid.-mur. With the help of his wife Charlene, Gerald Gallego abducted two teenage girls named Stacey Redican and Karen Chipman Twiggs from a suburban Sacramento shopping center in April 1980. He raped and battered the two 17-year-olds to death in the back of his van while wife Charlene sped toward the Nevada state line. Their remains were found in the desert nearly a year later.

The heinous nature of the crime so angered Nevada residents, that they contributed $25,000 in private donations to defray the legal expenses of the prosecution. The murder trial of the Gallegos was held in Lovelock, Nev. The state built its case around the testimony of Charlene Gallego who had since left her husband. Murder of this kind was nothing new for Gerald. The state of California had already convicted him for the murder of Mary Beth Sowers and Craig Miller, two students from Sacramento State University who were shot to death in November 1980.

On June 8, 1984, the Nevada jury returned a Guilty verdict after four hours of deliberation. Four days later he was sentenced to death for the murders and to two life terms without possible parole for the kidnappings. REF.: *CBA.*

Galley, Edmund, See: **Turpin, Dick.**

Gallo, Samuel, prom. 1927, Case of, U.S., mur. Joseph Fantasia was known in the Italian North End of Boston as a dangerous man. He ran the numbers racket, and would surely kill anyone who got in his way. On June 11, the police at Station One received word that someone had shot the Italian outside a barber shop on Prince Street in the heart of the North End. Detectives Mark Madden and Bob Mooney answered the call and found the deceased lying face down in the gutter, with a pattern of bullet holes piercing his back. Throngs of spectators had to be pushed back and a .32-caliber handgun was found nearby.

A witness to the crime who was identified as Lewis Smith pointed out Gangi Cero as the gunman. Cero was an Italian immigrant employed by Sam Gallo, a small-time peddler who allegedly trafficked stolen garments among the North Enders. Gallo had picked him off the street when he was ragged, hungry, and penniless in order to give him a job.

Based on Smith's sworn statement that he had watched Cero run pell-mell down Hanover Street, the detectives arrested the suspect and took him to Station One for questioning. It was believed that Cero had been hired by someone to kill the Black Hander. When Gallo was brought in to relate his side of the story police noticed a fresh knife wound on his face. "Flying glass did it," he said "one of those things." The detectives nodded and filed the information away in the back of their heads.

Gangi Cero was indicted for first-degree murder in the Suffolk County Superior Court. The trial commenced in November 1927 before Judge Louis Sherbourne Cox, and the esteemed defense counsel William R. Scharton represented Cero. It turned out that Gallo had paid his rather expensive fees out of a deeper concern and because of their long friendship. But not even Scharton could save his client from conviction. A Guilty verdict was returned on Nov. 17, 1927, carrying with it the mandatory death penalty.

While the appeals process ran its course, a startling development occurred that jarred the prosecution and paved the way for a second trial. On Sept. 17, 1928, Lewis Smith told the District Attorney that he had given perjured evidence in return for $2,500 put up by Gallo and Cero's brother Genero. Why then had Gallo gone to such great lengths to provide his employee with the best legal defense possible if it was just a frame-up?

They were tried and found Guilty of perjury and sentenced to two years at the Charles Street Jail. Gallo was reunited behind bars with Cero who coldly greeted him with a knife. No one understood why he would want to stab Gallo. The mystery had deepened, but Madden continued to press ahead with the investigation. He located Fantasia's girlfriend Philomena Romano, believing she might be able to unlock some closed doors. It was learned that the dark-haired Italian woman was Gallo's former sweetheart, and had turned "tricks" for him while working as a prostitute in Providence, R.I. She corroborated Cero's earlier testimony that it was Gallo who pulled a gun on Fantasia June 11, 1927. The facial wound was inflicted by Romano one afternoon, after she took exception to his jealous badgering. As he wiped away the blood, he turned to Fantasia and said, "This is all your doing! You'll be riding a hearse soon."

Romano told her story to Detective Madden after some hesitation. She claimed to have been with Fantasia the day he left the barber shop and encountered the gunman. She agreed to tell her side of the story in court. Meanwhile, Governor Fuller of Massachusetts granted Cero a stay of execution.

Gallo was indicted for murder on Jan. 8, 1930. His trial began on Feb. 18, and it quickly developed into a battle of wits between the two accused men. Each man emphatically denied killing Fantasia, but Gallo was the one who had a compelling motive. He was found Guilty on June 5 and sentenced to the electric chair. Gangi Cero was freed, and immediately returned home to Italy.

Gallo carried his appeals all the way to the Supreme Judicial Court of Massachusetts before being granted a new trial in the Court of Appeals. The issue of his guilt or innocence hinged on the failure of the police to connect him with the murder weapon and the absence of incriminating fingerprints. On appeal he was acquitted by a jury. Afterward Gallo was deported as an undesirable and everyone still wanted know the answer to the riddle: Who killed Joe Fantasia?   REF.: *CBA*.

Left to right, Joey Gallo, unidentified friend, Larry Gallo.

Gallo Brothers (Joseph Gallo, Albert Gallo, Lawrence Gallo), prom. 1940s-70s, U.S., org. crime. In the 1970s New York columnist Jimmy Breslin lampooned the Gallo-Profaci war, which had claimed a number of high-ranking Mafiosi, by publishing a highly satirical book: *The Gang That Couldn't Shoot Straight*. Later made into a movie and premiering in New York, it did not amuse "Crazy" Joe Gallo. Nor did it amuse his hulking bodyguard Peter "Pete the Greek" Diapoulas, who panned the film. "The whole thing was funny. The Profaci war was just a bunch of laughs. Well, Breslin should have spent one night with us and found out what it would feel like if some Profaci clipped him in the ass."

Joe Gallo befriended actor Jerry Orbach who in the film played the fictional Kid Sally Palumbo, a character patterned after the Brooklyn Mafia leader. Orbach discovered to his great surprise that Gallo was a cultured man who enjoyed conversing about the great writers of the Twentieth Century such as Ernest Hemingway, Franz Kafka, and Albert Camus. Gallo's rivals in the New York underworld, however, viewed him in different terms.

The Gallo Brothers, "Crazy" Joey, Albert ("Kid Blast"), and Lawrence, were soldiers in the Brooklyn family of Joseph Profaci. In 1957 Carlo Gambino assigned Profaci the task of assassinating

Albert Anastasia. Profaci in turn, selected the three Gallo brothers to carry out the hit. On the morning of Oct. 25, 1957, Anastasia was relaxing in the barbershop of the Park Sheraton Hotel, with a hot towel draped over his face. Two gunmen burst into the shop, aimed their guns at the crime boss, and fired. Anastasia fell to the floor, hit with five bullets. Following his death, the truculent Gallo demanded a fair share of the Brooklyn action for his family. He was not content with just running his vending machine rackets. There were bigger fish to fry.

A shooting war was declared by Crazy Joe when Profaci, an olive oil distributor by his own admission, refused to accommodate the "Young Turk" faction. With such syndicate musclemen as Joseph Musumeci and Frank "Punchy" Iliano backing him, the Gallos and the Profacis shot it out in the streets of Brooklyn in a war that was to last more than a decade. After Profaci died of natural causes in 1962, Joseph Colombo, Sr. assumed control of the family. When he refused to allow the brothers autonomy in Brooklyn, the war was renewed. On June 28, 1971, Colombo was severely wounded during Italian Unity Day festivities in Columbus Square. Available evidence suggested that Joey Gallo had hired Jerome A. Johnson, a black hit man, to do the job.

Crazy Joe Gallo, arrogant New York gangster.

While serving a sentence for extortion in the 1960s, Joe had cultivated the friendship of a number of black criminals. He understood the changing urban environment and realized that sooner or later the Mafia would be forced into a position of relinquishing control of inner-city drug trafficking and loansharking. Gallo became good friends with Leroy "Nicky" Barnes, whom he personally groomed to take over the Harlem rackets. A number of other black gunmen found employment in the Gallo family following their release from prison.

Umberto's Clam House in New York's "Little Italy," site of Joey Gallo's murder in 1972.

When Colombo was murdered, mob watchers logically assumed Gallo was responsible, given his friendship with the black underworld. That same year, 1971, Joey emerged from prison with a new outlook on life. He was not the same thug who had appeared before Senator Robert Kennedy in 1959, offering the observance that Kennedy's office rug "would be nice for a crap game." Now Joey Gallo was versed in the works of Jean-Paul Sartre and the German writer Hermann Hesse. After befriending Jerry Orbach, Gallo began to move in different circles. He was introduced to a number of uptown celebrities and show people and seemed to enjoy his new-found status.

On Apr. 7, 1972, Gallo celebrated his forty-third birthday with the Orbachs, comedian David Steinberg, and columnist Earl Wilson at the Copacabana nightclub. They celebrated long into the night until Gallo, Pete the Greek, Gallo's wife, and his sister decided to adjourn to Umberto's Clam House in the Chinatown-Little Italy neighborhoods for a light repast. Gallo, his back to the door, did not notice a lone gunman enter the restaurant.

Larry Gallo, center, after learning of his brother Joe's death in Umberto's Clam House.

Armed with a .38-caliber handgun, the assassin opened up on Joey, who scrambled for the door, but the gunman kept firing. Joey Gallo died in his own blood outside the restaurant. Control of the gang reverted to the last surviving brother, Albert Gallo, who extracted his revenge before the shooting ultimately stopped. At least twenty-seven more people were killed, many of them innocent bystanders. Joey's sister would later say of him, "He was a good man, a kind man. He's changed his image, that's why they did this to him." See: **Colombo, Joseph, Sr.; Profaci, Joseph.**

REF.: Aronson, *The Killing of Joey Gallo;* Blumenthal, *The Last Days of the Sicilians;* Bonanno, *A Man of Honor; CBA;* Cressey, *Theft of the Nation;* Davis, *Mafia Kingfish;* Demaris, *The Last Mafioso;* Gage, *Mafia, U.S.A.;* ____, *The Mafia is not an Equal Opportunity Employer;* Godwin, *Murder U.S.A.;* Gosch and Hammer, *The Last Testament of Lucky Luciano;* Katz, *Uncle Frank;* Maas, *The Valachi Papers;* Martin, *Revolt in the Mafia;* Messick and Goldblatt, *The Mobs and the Mafia;* Nash, *Bloodletters and Badmen;* Navasky, *Kennedy Justice;* Peterson, *The Mob;* Pileggi, *Wiseguy;* Reid, *The Grim Reapers;* Reuter, *Disorganized Crime;* Servadio, *Mafioso;* Zuckerman, *Vengeance Is Mine.*

Gallogly, Richard Gray, 1910- , U.S., mur. In 1928, Richard Gallogly brought disgrace on the name of Richard Gray, the patriarch of the Atlanta *Journal* newspaper. The 18-year-old student at Oglethorpe University drove the get-away car after a friend murdered a drug-store cashier in Atlanta for the "thrill of it." Gallogly and his partner in crime, George "Junie" Harsh of Milwaukee, were eventually sentenced to life in prison. Gallogly's influential grandmother, Mrs. Richard Gray, tried to wheedle a pardon out of three successive Georgia governors, to no avail.

In October 1939, after serving nearly ten years, the convicted man was granted a third parole hearing before Governor E.D. Rivers. It ended when the board learned that Vera Hunt, Gallogly's wife, had confessed to two counts of shoplifting.

The request for parole was dropped, and the unhappy party set out by car to return to the Tattnall State Prison. Outside Summit, Ga., Gallogly suddenly produced a gun and ordered the car to stop. He and his new bride backed away from the car to embark on a belated honeymoon. "I think this is the most foolish thing you ever did," his mother said.

A few days later, Gallogly surrendered to police in Dallas, Texas. He fought extradition to Georgia for six months, but was finally returned to prison there in March 1940 to continue serving his life term. His wife Vera remained in Texas, charged with shoplifting. On Jan. 13, 1941, the years of effort by Gallogly's family finally paid off. Governor Rivers, on his last day in office, pardoned both Gallogly and Harsh, but only after the Atlanta *Journal* published affidavits on its front page declaring that no money changed hands in the matter. REF.: *CBA.*

Galloping Dick, See: Ferguson, Richard.

Gallo-Profaci War, 1960s-70s, U.S., org. crime. "Crazy Joe" Gallo and his brothers, Larry and Albert, were top enforcers for New York Mafia don Joseph Profaci. A bloody Mafia war broke out when the brothers demanded a share of the lucrative Brooklyn rackets they maintained for Profaci and were refused. The Gallo-Profaci factions battled throughout the late 1960s and 1970s, with many casualties. The war finally ended with the death of gang-leader Joey Gallo, who was executed in an Italian restaurant in 1972. See: **Gallo Brothers; Profaci, Joseph.** REF.: *CBA.*

Galloway, Joseph, c.1729-1803, U.S., lawyer. Opposed colonial independence from England. He served in the Pennsylvania colonial legislature from 1756-75, and the Continental Congress from 1774-75. REF.: *CBA.*

Galloway, Robert, 1932-83, U.S., suic.-mur. Robert Galloway was considered a gentle man and a loving father. He was also successful: he was president of one of the ten largest remodeling firms in the country. But for no known reason, he shot and killed his family on Nov. 19, 1983. The police received a frantic call from the daughter at 4:13 a.m. "My father shot me in the neck," she said. There was a sharp sound of bullets, and then the phone crashed to the floor. When the police arrived on the scene everyone, including the family dog, was dead.

REF.: *CBA;* Fox, *Mass Murder.*

Gallows Garden, The, 1958, a novel by M.E. Chaber (pseudonym for Kendell Foster Crossen). The Galindez case inspired this work of fiction. See: **Galindez, Dr. Jesus de.** REF.: *CBA.*

Gallus, Caesar (Flavius Claudius Constantius), c.325-354, Roman., polit. corr. Appointed caesar of Rome's eastern provinces by his cousin Constantius II and married Constantius' sister in 351. He executed many people in quashing revolutions in Isauria and Palestine. He was recalled to Rome by Constantius in 354 and executed. REF.: *CBA.*

Gallus, Gaius Vibius Trebonianus, c.205-253, Roman., emp., assass. Fought under Roman Emperor Decius in drive against Goths in 251. When Decius was killed by Goths and the army defeated in Thrace, Gallus was elected emperor, but two years later he was killed by his own soldiers. REF.: *CBA.*

Gallus Mag, prom. 1850s-70s, U.S., rob. Gallus Mag, so called for wearing galluses, or suspenders, to keep her skirt up, ran the Hole-In-The-Wall Saloon with One-Armed Charley Monell from the late 1850s until 1871 on the East Side waterfront of New York. Acts of perverse violence occurred in the saloon, many committed by Gallus Mag herself, who had a curious habit of chewing off her victims' ears and saving them in a bottle of alcohol behind the bar. She became known as Queen of the Waterfront, using her six-foot frame and the pistol hidden in her skirt to maintain order or disorder, depending on her whim. Once, in a fight for supremacy over the waterfront with female rival Sadie the Goat, Mag hit Sadie over the head with a mallet and chewed off her ear. Sadie moved to the West Side, leading the pirates who pillaged the wharves of the Hudson River. Sadie eventually returned to the East Side and admitted Mag's dominance. The two made their peace, and Gallus Mag magnanimously gave Sadie back her ear from the jar behind the bar.

REF.: Asbury, *The Gangs of New York; CBA.*

Galswintha, c.540-68, Neustria, assass. Married Chilperic I, the king of Neustria, in 567. Chilperic's mistress, Fredegund, and soon-to-be second wife, had Galswintha murdered in 568. The murder touched off a 40-year war between Neustria and Austrasia, whose queen was Galswintha's sister, Brunhilde. REF.: *CBA.*

Galton, Francis, 1822-1911, Brit., criminol. A cousin of Charles Darwin, Francis Galton was a physician by profession, but he never practiced medicine. Instead, he devoted his considerable energies to the study of statistics and anthropology. Galton, who entered British civil service, applied statistics to what he termed "the human faculty," as detailed in his work, *Enquiries into Human Faculty,* published in 1883. Galton was influenced by Cesare Lombroso, who believed there was a hereditary link to criminals and that criminals could be determined through certain physical characteristics—an early version of the now-discarded science phrenology. Galton, using Lombroso's theories as well as his own, founded the science of eugenics.

Galton developed composite photography in which he attempted to show patterns of the physical makeup of criminals that could be traced to diseases. He became interested in anthropometric photography developed by Alphonse Bertillon and visited Bertillon in Paris where he studied the French criminologist's techniques.

British criminologist Sir Francis Galton.

In 1892, Galton advanced the science of fingerprinting through his exhaustive work, *Finger Prints.* It was Galton who advanced the first statistical evidence proving that fingerprints were unique, and could, therefore, be used as a system of identification. The criminologist calculated that the chances of two fingerprints being identical were 64 billion to one. Galton never created a fingerprint identification system but Sir Edward Henry, one of his most ardent followers, developed Galton's statistical applications into a practical method of search in using fingerprints as identification. See: **Henry, Edward; Lombroso, Cesare.**

REF.: *CBA; Galton, Enquiries into Human Faculty; Scott, The Concise Encyclopedia of Crime and Criminals;* Thorwald, *The Century of the Detective.*

Galvao, Henrique, b.1896, and **de Souto, Jorge,** prom. 1961, and **Velo, Jose,** prom. 1961, Port., hijack. In a case of modern-day piracy, the 20,906-ton *Santa Maria,* the pride of the Portuguese Merchant Marine, was seized south of Puerto Rico on Jan. 22, 1961, by a renegade band of Portuguese freedom fighters calling themselves the Liberation Junta.

With 588 passengers and a crew of 350 on board, the *Santa Maria* had set sail from Lisbon on Jan. 9 for a leisurely cruise through the South Atlantic and Caribbean. After a stop at Curaçao on Jan. 21, the ship lifted anchor and steamed toward Port Everglades, Fla.

As the *Santa Maria* sailed onto the open sea near the French West Indies, twenty-four uninvited guests went to work. Shortly before midnight the third officer, Joao José Costa, was shot down by several unknown assailants as he completed his tour of duty on the bridge. Captain Mario Maia was notified of what transpired. Before he could react to what he believed to be nothing more than a berserk passenger, he was startled by an unfamiliar voice from the bridge telephone. "This is Captain Galvao, who in the name of General Humberto Delgado has taken over your ship by assault. You must not attempt any kind of resistance. It will be violently suppressed. Surrender will bring you benefits."

Galvao was a former Portuguese army officer and political dissident. He spent thirteen years in Portuguese jails for his opposition to the regime of Dr. Antonio Salazar. His seizure of the cruise ship was designed to draw attention to the plutocracy that abounded in his homeland. The one-man rule of Salazar precluded peaceful demonstrations, open dissent, and labor union agitation.

In less than forty-five minutes the ship was in the hands of the rebels. The passengers were assured they would not be hurt as the ship made its way for port or ports unknown. After six days most everyone knew that the intended destination was Brazil. Galvao was known to be on intimate terms with the new president, Janio da Silva Quadros.

The *Santa Maria* wandered about the ocean for twelve days. By this time the passengers were growing restless. The air-conditioning had ceased working and the food supply was almost spent. Further complicating Galvao's plans was the presence of the U.S.S. *Damato,* which was anxious about the fate of the forty-two Americans on board. Rear Admiral Allen Smith was permitted to board the *Santa Maria* to discuss the release of the captives, but declined to receive them on the high seas, which was considered too risky a maneuver.

Galvao steered the ship within the three-mile limit of Brazil on Feb. 1. The Brazilian government demanded that the ship unload its passengers before providing fuel and provisions. The next day the restive, hungry passengers demanded that the ship pull into port. A brief skirmish followed in which one man fell through a plate-glass window. There was little else to do, so Captain Galvao reluctantly dropped his anchor at Recife and allowed Brazilian tugboats to ferry his passengers to shore. Only the third mate had been killed during the twelve-day ordeal. On Feb. 5, the ship was again placed under the control of Captain Maia, who promptly headed for home. When asked about their experiences aboard the *Santa Maria,* a number of the first-class travelers said they considered it kind of an adventure, and bore no grudge toward Galvao or his conspirators.

On Feb. 10, 1962, Captain Galvao and thirty-two other co-conspirators were tried and convicted in absentia by the Lisbon courts. The captain was sentenced to twenty-two years in prison, and the other men received varying prison terms ranging from fifteen to eighteen years. However, none of the ship's hijackers went to jail. Like Galvao, they received political asylum in Brazil. This was not to be the case for dissident political leader Humberto Delgado, who was sent to prison for twenty years.

There was much worldwide sympathy for the exiled Portuguese leader. In December 1963, he was granted a visa to address the United Nations General Assembly about the plight of millions of Portuguese suffering under the oppressive regime. The U.S. refused a direct request from the Salazar government to extradite Galvao to Madrid. REF.: *CBA.*

Galvez, José (Marqués de la Sonora), 1729-87, Spain, jur. Visitador general of Mexico from 1765-71, where he established a new tax system and set up defense outposts. He organized the initial exploration of California in 1769. He returned to Spain where he was named Marqués in 1772, and became Minister of the Indies in 1776. REF.: *CBA.*

Galvin, Tom, prom. 19th Cent., Ire., execut. One of the most famous hangmen of Ireland was the notable Tom Galvin, who enjoyed displaying the implements of his craft at his home. Galvin would shield his face with a black hood, and place an enormous wooden bowl on his back to catch the loose stones and pebbles that poured on him at the moment of the drop. When an infrequent reprieve would be granted a condemned criminal, Galvin would always complain that he "was taking the bread out of the mouth of a poor old man."

REF.: *CBA;* Laurence, *A History of Capital Punishment.*

Gambetta, Léon-Michel, 1838-82, Fr., lawyer. Headed opposition to Napoleon III in 1860s. He escaped by balloon from Prussia's attack on Paris during the Franco-Prussian war in 1870, and formed a provisional government. Following defeat in war, he returned to serve as premier of France from 1881-82. REF.: *CBA.*

Gambi, Vincent, d.1819, U.S., pir. In the early nineteenth century, Vincent Gambi was a captain in the pirate army of the legendary Jean Lafitte, who pillaged ships in the Gulf of Mexico off the coast of Louisiana from a base in Barataria Bay. Gambi, who had murdered dozens with a broadax, considered himself a more genuine pirate than the businesslike Lafitte, and disagreed with his superior over the looting of American ships. By 1814, the U.S. Navy had driven the pirates from their base, but the pirates allied themselves with General Andrew Jackson against the British in the Battle of New Orleans in the War of 1812, and were granted a full pardon and the rights of American citizens. Gambi, with his insatiable thirst for violence, was an enthusiastic participant in the battle, killing more of the enemy than any other pirate. In 1816, Lafitte moved his forces to Galveston, Texas, and Gambi headed his own army for the next three years. But in 1819, after a quarrel over the division of loot, his followers killed him with his own ax as he slept. REF.: *CBA*.

Gambino, Carlo (AKA: **Don Carlo, Carlo Gambrino, Carlo Gambrieno**), 1902-76, U.S., org. crime. When he died on Oct. 15, 1976, law enforcement agencies across the U.S. were unanimous in the opinion that Carlo Gambino, an unassuming gangster, ruled the most powerful Mafia crime family in the U.S. Disdaining the publicity surrounding such mobsters as Joey Colombo, Gambino preferred to mingle among his own people—the Sicilian immigrants of New York—and buy fruit from the corner stands in the old neighborhood. As the top boss of Manhattan, he attempted to steer the families away from drug trafficking, believing that narcotics convictions would invite unwanted infiltration of the federal government. In this sense, Gambino was the prototype for Vito Corleone in Mario Puzo's novel *The Godfather*.

Gambino was born in Palermo, Italy, on Aug. 24, 1902. At nineteen he stowed away aboard the *S.S. Vincenzo Florida*, arriving in Newport, Va., on Dec. 23, 1921. In Brooklyn, Gambino began working for a small trucking company owned by his uncle, then joined the emerging Mafia in the 1920s as a soldier for Joseph "Joe the Boss" Masseria. After Masseria was killed on Apr. 15, 1931, Gambino switched allegiance to Salvatore Maranzano, the newly crowned Mafia "don" of New York. The arrangement lasted only until the "Young Turks" of the outfit disposed of Maranzano in September 1931. In the reorganized Mafia hierarchy, Gambino and his brothers-in-

Mafia boss Carlo Gambino, 1935.

law, Paul and Peter Castellano, became soldiers in the family under Philip and Vincent Mangano. In 1951 Gambino became an underboss in the Albert Anastasia organization after the Manganos were murdered, allegedly at the direction of Anastasia.

In 1957 the ruthless Anastasia was gunned down in a Manhattan barbershop, which afforded Gambino his first chance to head up his own crime family. FBI informant Joseph Valachi named Gambino as the instigator of this assassination. "Without Vito (Genovese) backing him, Carlo never would have went for it," Valachi said. Gambino's ascension to the status of family boss was opposed by Aniello Dellacroce, whose allegiance was to Anastasia. Gambino sent him a message by eliminating Armand Rava, an associate of Dellacroce, and then asked his rival to a meeting. Offered the position of underboss, Dellacroce prudently accepted.

In the next few years, Gambino expanded the family's influence. He made peace with Meyer Lansky in the syndicate's nationwide gambling operations, and plotted with Lansky and others to send Genovese to prison. Gambino influenced policy making with the heads of the other four New York families, especially after 1969 when Vito Genovese died in prison. The Gambino operation was extended and his control of the tough waterfront unions was nearly absolute. In 1970 he gave longshoremen the day off in observance of the first "Italian Unity Day," an event sponsored in part by Joseph Colombo. The next year, when the publicity-seeking

Colombo defied a direct order to lay low, Gambino kept the men at their jobs. Colombo was shot and killed by Jerome Johnson during the celebration.

During his career in the rackets, Gambino was arrested sixteen times and convicted six times, but he only went to jail once. In 1937, after he was convicted on tax evasion charges in connection

Mafia don Carlo Gambino, right, under arrest, 1973, a rare occurrence.

with running a million-gallon still in Philadelphia, he spent twenty-two months in prison. His poor health helped him avert legal trouble after he was indicted in 1970 on charges of conspiracy to hijack a vehicle transporting $3 million. He never stood trial. Federal immigration authorities had attempted to deport him in 1967, and the U.S. Supreme Court upheld the order in 1970 on the grounds that Gambino had entered the country illegally. Coincidentally, he suffered a heart attack, permanently delaying the deportation order. In later years he continued to suffer from heart ailments, and gradually receded into the background.

According to an inmate at the Ohio Penitentiary, Gambino had some dealings with the CIA and FBI. In 1968 agents reportedly offered him $1 million during a secret meeting at a motel in Apalachin, N.Y., to assassinate the Reverend Martin Luther King, Jr. Gambino allegedly refused. Speaking on behalf of the twenty-six families in the national syndicate, he stated that no mobster would accept such an assignment.

Before he died of a heart attack in 1976, the aging Mafia kingpin bypassed Aniello Dellacroce to name a family member, his brother-in-law Paul Castellano to serve as successor. See: **Castellano, Paul; Colombo, Joseph, Sr.; Dellacroce, Aniello.**

REF.: Alexander, *The Pizza Connection;* Blumenthal, *The Last Days of the Sicilians;* Bonanno, *A Man of Honor;* Cressey, *Theft of the Nation;* Davis, *Mafia Kingfish;* Demaris, *The Last Mafioso;* Eisenberg and Landau, *Meyer Lansky;* Gage, *Mafia, U.S.A.;* _____, *The Mafia is not an Equal Opportunity Employer;* Godwin, *Murder U.S.A.;* Gosch and Hammer, *The Last Testament of Lucky Luciano;* Katz, *Uncle Frank;* Kirby and Renner, *Mafia Enforcer;* McClellan, *Crime Without Punishment;* Maas, *The Valachi Papers;* Martin, *Revolt in the Mafia;* Meskil, *Don Carlo,* Nash, *Bloodletters and Badmen;* Peterson, *The Mob;* Pileggi, *Wiseguy;* Reid, *The Grim Reapers;* Reuter, *Disorganized Crime;* Servadio, *Mafioso;* Sondern, *Brotherhood of Evil: The Mafia;* Velie, *Desperate Bargain: Why Jimmy Hoffa Had to Die;* Zuckerman, *Vengeance Is Mine;* (FILM), *The Godfather.* 1972.

Gambrill, Henry, d.1859, U.S., org. crime-mur. Baltimore's first mass execution provided dark delight to the morbidly curious throngs flocking to the scaffold. Three of the four men scheduled to hang on Apr. 8, 1859, were members of the city's gangs which had, in the early 1850s, grown to sizes that often overwhelmed police. The gangs battled the police with paving stones and clubs when rioting, but Henry Gambrill changed all that on the night of Sept. 22, 1858. Six policemen had been called by a Mrs. Green to her home at the intersection of Pennsylvania Avenue and Biddle Street. Several rioting gangsters were arrested, and Gambrill tried to rescue some of his friends by charging into the thin police rank swinging a club. He was repulsed.

Pulling a pistol from his pocket, Gambrill walked a few paces away and then calmly turned and aimed his weapon at police officer Benton. The gangster's single shot hit the policeman in the neck and killed him on the spot. Seized and held for trial, Gambrill was definitely identified as Benton's killer by Officer Robert M. Rigdon, the principal witness. Two of Gambrill's gangster friends, Peter Corrie and Marian Cropp, were overheard to swear that they would kill Rigdon for his damning testimony. They made good their vow on Nov. 5, 1858, shooting the policeman to death as he stood with his wife in a bedroom.

Policemen in the neighborhood heard the shots and raced to Rigdon's home. They found Corrie running from the scene and arrested him. Hours later Corrie disclosed Cropp's involvement in the killing and he too was picked up. After speedy convictions, Gambrill, Corrie, and Cropp were sentenced to the gallows. The fourth man to die with them was not a gangster but a common murderer, John S. Stephens, alias Cyphus, who killed a man named King over the attentions of a whore.

Four hanged at once was a novelty for Baltimore, and the city put on a spectacular show for the thousands of visitors who traveled by special excursion trains from Washington, New York, Hanover, and Philadelphia. Marshal Herring marched his entire police force of 400 men up to jail on the brisk morning of Apr. 8 and surrounded the walls. The crowds began to arrive minutes later. About 500 distinguished Baltimoreans were given special seats inside the yard. Tens of thousands outside the walls climbed the surrounding hills and rooftops. The giant scaffold, designed to handle all four condemned men at the same time, was built in such a way that it rose several feet above the north wall of the prison so as to afford the spectators a clear view.

Baltimore gangster Henry Gambrill, executed with henchmen, 1859.

At 11 a.m., the four prisoners were led from their cells. Gambrill had been given a cloak by the sheriff, who threw it over his shoulders, saying: "Henry, this is to keep you from the air." Gambrill shot back a squinty look and snapped: "It don't make much difference how cold the air is now. I will be out of the air soon." He was the first to mount the huge scaffold, and once on the gallows he seemed to grow suddenly calm, smiling at the silent multitude that stretched before him.

Cropp, Corrie, and Cyphus lined up beside him. Several ministers talked the doomed men through their prayers. Gambrill then, still acting out his part as leader of the gang, stepped almost to the edge of the gallows and, in a clear voice that echoed out to the throng, said: "Fellow citizens, knowing that I am about to die, that I stand on the brink of eternity, I declare to you that I am innocent of the murder of Officer Benton or of having anything to do with it. When this trap falls from under me, it will launch an innocent man into eternity. I have nothing more to say. Goodbye." Gambrill stepped backward into his position under the waiting rope.

The sheriff then asked Cropp if he had anything to say,

encouraging him with a smile and hand gestures, as if requesting him to edify the crowd with a bit of verbal entertainment. Cropp complied as he gingerly stepped forward and began to sing a hymn entitled, "Hail, Ye Sighing Sons of Sorrow." Several times he turned his head slightly and encouraged Corrie and Cyphus to join him. They did, but with trembling, faltering voices. The trio sang:

> Former friends, I now must leave you,
> All my earthly hopes are o'er,
> But in Heaven I hope to meet you,
> There to meet to part no more.
>
> Cease this mourning, trembling, sighing,
> Death shall burst this sullen gloom,
> Then my spirit, fluttering, flying,
> Shall be borne beyond the tomb.

Following the song, Corrie refused to address the crowd. His whole body seemed convulsive. Tears streamed down his face. "Wipe them away," he choked to a guard, since he was incapable of doing so, his hands, like the others, tied so tightly behind his back that the ropes cut the flesh.

Cyphus, too, had his last words. The killer fairly jumped forward and shouted: "Gentlemen, here's another innocent man going to be hung. I am innocent of murder; they took me up, gave me another name and now they are going to hang me; but I am willing to die and I want you all to say that I go away perfectly happy."

The sheriff and his deputies, the formalities finally finished, stepped forward and meticulously placed the ropes around the heads of the condemned. White caps were then placed over the heads of the prisoners and a ripple of applause from the spectators on the nearby hillsides could be heard in the jail-yard. A minister on the scaffold passed down the line of rope-encircled men and held for a moment at each man's face, a soggy, camphorated handkerchief to dull the senses. As the minister made these final stops, each man said through his white hood a muttered, but audible, "Good-bye."

A newspaper of the day then described how "the rope which held the support was untied, and the sheriff, descending the long flight of stairs, pressed his foot upon the trigger of the drop. There was an instant of dreadful expectation—a momentary pause—the drop fell, and the souls of the four struggling beings winged their flight into eternity."

None of the prisoners died with broken necks; all strangled to death. Cropp was seen to die hard, almost doubling himself up twice in his death throes. Authorities allowed the bodies to hang for forty-five minutes while the elated thousands of spectators consumed the lunches and beer they had brought along for the occasion. When the bodies were partly let down, doctors determined that all the men were dead except Cyphus, whose heart was still faintly beating.

"Give them another five minutes with the rope," one doctor ordered the sheriff, and the bodies were hauled upward again to the cheers of the spectators. When the four convicted men were finally cut loose, officials agreed that the affair had been a highly successful one, that justice had been publicly demonstrated. At the last minute, a drunk inside the jail yard "ruined the proceedings" by loudly demanding the ears and noses of the deceased as souvenirs. This disorderly character was "chased by the police, and in his efforts to escape he knocked down several women, whose terrified screams alarmed everybody, and in trying to get away several persons were seriously injured."

The drunk's demand for gory souvenirs sparked requests from several wealthy citizens sitting near the gallows, who asked for pieces of the ropes used in the executions to keep as mementoes. Angrily, the sheriff gathered up the ropes and stamped toward the door of the jail, jerking his head once and spitting over his shoulder: "Don't you people have any feelings?" REF.: *CBA*.

Game, Sir Philip Woolcott, 1876-1961, Brit., law enfor. off.

Vice Marshal Sir Philip Woolcott Game was a career military officer in the Royal Air Force, serving with distinction in South Africa, India, and Italy before retiring to private life in 1929. Six years later he was appointed commissioner of the Metropolitan Police, a position he held from 1935-45. REF.: *CBA*.

Gamelin, Maurice Gustave, 1872-1958, Fr., treas. Served as inspector general of the French army and as vice president of the Higher Council of War from 1935-40. When the Germans occupied France during WWII, he was relieved of his command. He was convicted of treason at the Riom trial in 1940, and was transferred to a German prison three years later. REF.: *CBA*.

Gamson, Benny (AKA: **Benny The Meatball**), d.1946, U.S., org. crime. Benny Gamson was, in the popular lexicon of the 1940s, a "gonof," or petty thief. Short, squat, and unattractive, Benny was arrested six times in Los Angeles on suspicion of robbery. He usually beat the rap. But then Los Angeles mayor Fletcher Bowron cracked down on corrupt policemen. People like Benny were forced to keep a low profile. Also, in 1944, Mickey Cohen began consolidating his criminal empire. Benny Gamson, who had beat Cohen senseless one night with a lead pipe, became the odd man out. Fearing reprisals, he teamed up with Chicago trigger-man George Levinson.

One night in August 1945, there was a knock on the door of their Hollywood apartment. Levinson opened it, but before he could speak, gunmen pumped three bullets into his body. Benny the Meatball fled out the back calling for help, but was shot down by the mobsters, who sped away in a black automobile which was never identified. See: **Cohen, Mickey**. REF.: *CBA*.

Gandhi, Indira, 1918-84, India, prime minister, assass. Like her father Jawaharlal Nehru, Mrs. Indira Gandhi believed that India's best interests were served by a policy of non-alignment with the super powers. For sixteen years Mrs. Gandhi ruled her nation according to this principle of strict neutrality. But within her own nation, bitter political factionalism among ethnic groups threatened the fragile democracy forged by Mahatma Gandhi and maintained by the Nehru family through thirty-seven years.

In 1948, Mahatma Gandhi was gunned down by a Hindu extremist opposed to the partition of India and Pakistan. Gandhi's inability to placate the radical groups within his nation resulted in his death. Mrs. Gandhi (no relation to the father of the Indian independence movement) suffered a similar fate at the hands of the Sikhs, a religious minority comprising roughly two percent of India's population. Beginning in 1982, the Sikh community, concentrated for the most part in Punjab near the Pakistani border, pushed for a free and independent state, which they planned to call Khalistan, or "land of the pure." Fearing an attack by neighboring Pakistan, which had provided covert aid to the militant Sikhs, Gandhi took harsh measures to suppress what had become an armed revolt.

In June 1984 she ordered the Indian army into Punjab to put down an uprising which threatened to expand into a greater armed conflict. To flush out the leaders of the rebellion, soldiers entered the Golden Temple of Amritsar, a sacred Sikh shrine that had been converted into a paramilitary fortress. More than 600 Sikhs were killed, including 37-year-old leader Jarnail Singh Bhindranwale. The Sikhs considered Mrs. Gandhi's actions a moral and civil outrage. Vowing revenge, a team of assassins organized inside Punjab, but they were arrested by Indian parliamentary forces. The money, guns, and clearance papers found in their possession were allegedly provided by the Pakistani intelligence service, though the Pakistanis denied the charge.

The Sikhs struck with vengeance a few days later, on Oct. 31, 1984. Gandhi was leaving her private compound at Safdarjang Road in New Delhi to meet British actor Peter Ustinov to film a television documentary when the shots rang out.

Two of her uniformed security guards standing at attention along the path had suddenly broken ranks to shoot at Gandhi. From point blank range Beant Singh, twenty-one, fired three shots from a.38-caliber revolver. As Gandhi slumped to the ground the other uniformed guard, Satwant Singh, pumped thirty

rounds from a Sten automatic weapon into her. The two Sikhs surrendered to police and were led to the guardhouse. Beant Singh, who was a favorite of Gandhi during the five months he had been assigned to the detail, attempted to seize a gun from one of the other guards and was shot dead. Satwant Singh was wounded when he reached for a knife concealed in his turban.

Gandhi's death plunged India into deep turmoil. Confrontations between angry Hindus and separatist Sikhs resulted in wide scale arson, looting, and murder. The funeral procession through the streets of New Delhi was a quiet, somber affair. Many residents chose to remain at home because they feared violence along the parade route. Gandhi's 40-year-old son, Rajiv, assumed control of the government and urged moderation, but his pleas were largely ignored.

The government opened an investigation into the murder, and concluded that Gandhi's death was part of a larger conspiracy to undermine the Indian government. On Jan. 5, 1989, Satwant Singh and Kehar Singh, a former government worker who plotted the assassination, were hanged at Tihar Central Jail in New Delhi after their pleas for clemency were denied by the Indian Supreme Court. A third conspirator, Balbir Singh, had been convicted in 1986, but was ordered released by the Supreme Court four months before the executions were scheduled to take place.

The deaths of the two Sikhs resulted in a new wave of violence in Punjab. Four Hindus from the village of Bhujiawali were hanged in retaliation on Jan. 11. Thirty-six other people were killed in the outbreak.

Meanwhile the Indian government pressed on with its investigation of the assassination. On Apr. 7, 1989, four more conspirators were identified and charged with the murder of Indira Gandhi. Former police official Simranjit Singh Mann was quoted as saying that the easiest and most efficient way to kill her was to infiltrate the vast security network. Mann is the leader of the Akali Dal party, a militant political faction within the Sikh movement. The two triggermen were selected by a second Sikh extremist, Atinder Pal Singh of the Khalistan Liberation Army operating in Punjab. Indian police arrested two Bombay college teachers, Dilip Singh and Jagmohan Singh Tony, as co-conspirators. Their cases are still pending.

In assessing the murder of Gandhi, the commission pointed to the lax and inefficient Indian internal security division, which prevented the removal of the policeman who eventually committed the murder. A larger conspiracy involving highly placed government officials was implied in an official report released on Mar. 27, 1989. "Top officials took things for granted and allowed the matters to drift," explained Justice M.P. Thakkar, head of the investigating commission. "Officials were apathetic, shirked responsibility, and indulged in red-tapism." See: **Gandhi, Mohandas Karamchand**. REF.: *CBA*.

Gandhi, Mohandas Karamchand (Mahatma), 1869-1948, India, leader, assass. More than any other Indian leader, Mohandas Gandhi, called Mahatma by his devoted friends and followers, was responsible for ridding India of British rule through a consistent and painful policy of nonviolent rebellion. Gandhi was India's greatest political, social, and religious leader, a man of simple tastes but burning idealism, one who led by saintly example. His political achievements were enormous, his teachings inspired. Born on Oct. 2, 1869, in Porbandar, India, Gandhi came from a family of well-to-do merchants, members of the Banya, the trading class. His parents practiced Hindu and were members of the Vaishnava sect, advocates of Jainism. They hated the taking of human life and refrained from eating meat, fowl, or fish.

The British rule of India was exercised at the high levels of government, the courts, the military, and commerce involving only the largest trading firms. Gandhi's caste actually controlled the commerce of the country at large and it grew wealthy. At an early age Gandhi displayed an agile mind and an excellent memory. He learned English and spoke it fluently, graduating at the top of his class in India before being sent to London in 1888, at age nineteen, to study law. He wore Bond Street clothes and tried to adapt to British society. He entered a dancing school but gave this up as he could not follow rhythm. He tried to learn the violin but abandoned these studies, realizing he had no musical aptitude. He avoided attending law school dinners since he would be offered roast beef and be expected to drink wine, which his religion forbade. A lonely, little Indian boy ignored by his fellow students, Gandhi at this time spent much time in prayer and reflection. His lifelong habit of long meditation was honed in England as an emotional and intellectual refuge.

After receiving his law degree in 1891, Gandhi returned to India to practice law, opening offices in Bombay. He found that he knew little of Muslim or Hindu law and proved to be inept as a trial lawyer. His first case, defending a client's property rights, was a shambles. The introverted Gandhi could not bring himself to cross-examine witnesses. He later remembered: "I stood up, but my heart sank into my boots. My head was reeling and I felt that the whole court was doing likewise. I could think of no questions to ask!" He lost the case and returned his client's fee. Gandhi accepted no more trial work but confined his legal work to the drafting of wills and contracts. He failed to earn a living in Bombay as a lawyer and was an equal failure in Rajkot where his family had resettled. He looked about for new opportunities and saw one in South Africa where thousands of Indians had migrated to find work.

Gandhi accepted an assignment in South Africa at the time, representing Indian clients there in a dispute about trading rights. He worked against oppressive racial laws and still managed to win his suit. During the Boer War, demonstrating his early nonviolent bent, he organized an Indian stretcher-bearer service. Gandhi adopted the credo of *Satyagraha,* the lifestyle of nonviolence, at an early age and never swayed from this philosophical posture. Gandhi spent twenty years in South Africa battling for the rights of Indians there.

He was jailed on several occasions but he amazed his warders by his prosaic acceptance of incarceration. He passively resisted all compromise though he was a model prisoner. In the end, Gandhi achieved the near-impossible in South Africa. Through his legal efforts and social leadership, he managed to have the unjust taxes against coolies and Indians repealed. Indian marriages in South Africa were made legal and recognized under the law, thanks to his indefatigable efforts. By the time he left South Africa in 1914, Gandhi had brought about government recognition of Indians and Indian status was raised to a legal peer level in that country.

Accompanying Gandhi was his wife, Kasturbai, to whom he had been betrothed at the age of thirteen as was then the Indian custom. She was an illiterate girl and Gandhi taught her how to read and schooled her in many intellectual pursuits then denied Indian women. She bore him four children. Kasturbai joined him in South Africa in 1896, and she remained loyal to him throughout her life, despite the suffering and privation Gandhi's nonviolent crusades brought about.

After a brief sojourn to England, where Gandhi again organized an Indian stretcher corps to serve with British troops during WWI, illness forced him to return to India. He and his family set up a crude commune known as an ashram at Ahmadabad in Gujarat. They lived in a simple hut roofed by dried ferns taken from the surrounding jungle. Abstinence became the lifestyle, with Gandhi and his growing followers eating only vegetables and upholding a strict diet. Walking was a daily exercise practiced as religiously as meditation. Modern machinery was shunned. Home spun dhoti served as the only apparel of the family.

Gandhi had already established his pacifist movement to oust the British, and many of his followers were among the masses who gathered at the square, Jalianwalla Bagh in Amritsa, on Apr. 13, 1919. On that day, British General Reginald Dyer led his troops to the square and ordered the Indians to disperse. When the crowds did not break up, Dyer ruthlessly ordered his men to open fire. More than 400 Indians were slain and hundreds more injured. This genocidal massacre moved Gandhi to tour India, urging all Indians to boycott the British. He persuaded hundreds of Indian government officials to give up positions and titles bestowed upon them by the British. He urged Indian parents to keep their children from British-sponsored schools and, most effective of all, he campaigned against Indians paying any kind of tax to the British government in India.

Followers of Gandhi wore the *khaddar* or the famous "Gandhi cap." They were nonviolent and passively resisted cooperation with the British. Through this policy, Gandhi believed, he would force the British to quit India and allow the country its long-sought home rule. The result, however, was a stiffening of British resolve to hang on in India. When British rule tightened, Indians, on the other hand, resorted to violence, despite Gandhi's insistence of a nonviolent posture. In 1921, when the Prince of Wales visited Bombay, riots ensued in which fifty persons were killed. In the following year, mobs in the united provinces attacked a police barracks and set fire to the buildings, and the occupants were burned to death.

In 1924 the British decided to rid themselves of the pesky Gandhi and he was arrested, along with many of his followers, including Pandit Jawaharlal Nehru. While in confinement Gandhi began one of his historic fasts, threatening to fast himself to death until the British relented and granted home rule. This situation was to be repeated again and again, with Gandhi imprisoned and going into prolonged fasting, and the British releasing him before he could seriously injure himself in a program of self-starvation. At the beginning of WWII, Gandhi gave limited support to the British and condemned the fascist powers, but some time later he urged anti-British demonstrations that were interpreted as obstruction of the British war effort and Gandhi was once again jailed. He again went on a prolonged fast which was halted with his release in 1944.

At that time, Gandhi ostensibly retired from active political life, being replaced by his hand-picked protege, Nehru. Yet, in the following year, India was thrown into a nation-wide bloodbath when Lord Louis Mountbatten, the last British viceroy of India, thought to settle the age-old conflict between the Muslim and Indian factions in India by partitioning these two opposing religious sects in 1947, sending all Muslims into Pakistan and keeping all Hindus in India. This decision caused incredible turmoil in India and forced more than four million refugees to clog the roads of the country for more than a year. Riots, arson, murders, and widespread violence ensued.

Though independence came to India in 1946, the Hindu-Muslim conflict continued to rage. Gandhi came out of retirement to quell the nationwide strife. He toured Bengal on foot, preaching his nonviolent philosophy and attempting to bring peace between Muslim and Hindu leaders. Hindus dominated India and had for centuries. Among their countless numbers was a Hindu fanatic, Nathuram Godse, 37-year-old editor of a right-wing newspaper and an ardent member of Mahasabha, a violent Hindu organization that opposed everything Muslim. Godse blamed Gandhi more than anyone else for the partition of India and felt that this act had injured the Hindus. He resolved to assassinate Gandhi, a Hindu, whom he believed had betrayed his own religion. Godse put together a group to help him in his assassination plans and these included his younger brother Gopal, Narayan Apte, Mandanlal Pahwa, Vishnu Karkare, Pahwa Shankar Kistayya and Digambar Badge. The group located weapons and bombs.

On Jan. 20, 1948, the group made its first attempt on the life of Gandhi. Pahwa set off a guncotton explosive that went off in the middle of an open-air meeting Gandhi was conducting in the gardens of the Birla House in Delhi. No one was killed and only a few persons were slightly injured. The meeting went on undisturbed after Pahwa was seized by police. It was later claimed that Pahwa gave the names of all the conspirators to the police but that these officers did nothing to stop the continued attempts on Gandhi's life. Ten days later, on Jan. 30, 1948, Gandhi, despite warnings that there would be a second attempt on his life that day,

Gandhi as a young lawyer and in old age.

Nehru, Gandhi's successor, and Gandhi.

Gandhi mediating between Sikhs and Muslims.

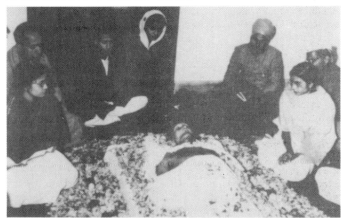

Gandhi's body lying in state in New Delhi.

The funeral of Gandhi in New Delhi.

Gandhi's killers on trial.

Assassins Nathuram Godse and Narayan Apte.

resolutely called for another meeting in the gardens of the Birla House.

Gandhi, who was weak from recent fasting, walked into the gardens shakily, supported by two grandnieces. He chatted freely with those around him, smiling and seemingly at peace. Hundreds of followers gathered about him, parting to make a path for him through the crowd. At that moment, Nathuram Godse walked quickly to Gandhi. He wore a Gandhi cap which supposedly indicated that he was a supporter of the Mahatma. He bowed in the fashion of a mendicant and then pulled a gun and fired three shots, firing almost point-blank. The bullets felled the great Gandhi. As he fell, Gandhi cried out: "Hai, Rama! Hai, Rama!" ("Oh, God! Oh, God!") The 78-year-old Indian leader died a few moments later.

The massive funeral of Gandhi that followed in Delhi was one of the most spectacular to ever occur in India. Hundreds of thousands attended the services as Gandhi's bier was pulled through flower-strewn streets. The corpse was then burned on a huge funeral pyre. By then, Godse was under arrest and awaiting trial as were the other conspirators. The assassin freely admitted killing Gandhi, proclaiming to the world that he considered his actions that of a patriot who had rid India of a Hindu betrayer who had brought misery and death to the Hindus. Godse submitted a 92-page statement to the court in which he assumed full responsibility for the assassination, stating that he alone bore the burden of guilt. The court decided otherwise, convicting all seven of the conspirators. Nathuram Godse and Narayan Apte were sentenced to death, the others to life imprisonment.

After appeals were denied, Godse and Apte were escorted to the gallows on Nov. 15, 1949. Both men stood on the scaffold and chanted: "India united!" They were then sent through the trap doors. Apte died instantly, his neck broken. Godse strangled to death, struggling for almost fifteen minutes before he succumbed. It was reported that the executioner had purposely prepared the rope incorrectly so that Godse would meet a slow death. Nathuram Godse believed that he would be remembered as an Indian hero and that his memory would live in the history of his troubled country. Just the opposite occurred. His name is never mentioned in India. The saint-like Gandhi, of course, remains as one of India's immortal humans.

REF.: Alexander, *The Indian Ferment;* Ambedkar, *Ranade, Gandhi and Jinnah;* Andrews, *Mahatma Gandhi's Ideas;* ____, *Mahatma Gandhi: His Own Story;* ____, *Mahatma Gandhi At Work;* Bell, *Assassin;* Bernays, *Naked Fakir;* Bevan, *Indian Nationalism;* Bolitho, *Jinnah;* Bose, *Studies in Gandhism;* ____, *Selections from Gandhi;* ____, *My Days With Gandhi;* Bose, *The Indian Struggle;* Campbell-Johnson, *Mission With Mountbatten;* Catlin, *In the Path of Mahatma; CBA;* Chakravarty, *Mahatma Gandhi and the Modern World;* Chintamani, *Indian Politics Since the Mutiny;* Coupland, *The Constitutional Problem in India;* Cummings, *Political India, 1832-1932;* Dantwalala, *Gandhism Reconsidered;* Das, *The Science of the Self;* Datta, *The Philosophy of Mahatma Gandhi;* Desai, *Gandhi in Indian Villages;* ____, *With Gandhi in Ceylon;* ____, *The Gita According to Gandhi;* ____, *A Righteous Struggle;* Deshpande, *Gandhiana;* Dhawan, *The Political Philosophy of Mahatma Gandhi;* Diwakar, *Satyagraha—Its Techniques and History;* ____, *Glimpses of Gandhi;* Doke, *M.K. Gandhi;* Duncan, *Selected Writings of Mahatma Gandhi;* Eaton, *Gandhi, Fighter Without A Sword;* Eliot, *Hinduism and Buddhism: An Historical Sketch;* Elwyn and Winslow, *The Dawn of Indian Freedom;* Fischer, *The Life of Mahatma Gandhi;* Gandhi, *Bapu's Letters to Mira; Basic Education;* ____, *Christian Missions;* ____, *Community Unity; Constructive Programme;* ____, *Delhi Diary;* ____, *Diet and Diet Reform;* ____, *Economics of Khadi;* ____, *Ethical Religion;* ____, *For Pacifists;* ____, *From Yiravda Mandir;* ____, *Gandhi's Correspondence With the Government, 1942-44;* ____, *A Guide to Health;* ____, *Hind Swaraj, or Indian Home Rule;* ____, *Indian Opinion;* ____, *Jail Experiences;* ____, *My Early Life;* ____, *My Soul's Agony;* ____, *Non-Violence in Peace and War;* ____, *Rebuilding Our Villages;* ____, *Rowlatt Bills and Satyagraha;* ____, *Sarvodaya;* ____, *Satyagraha;* ____, *Satyagraha Ashram's History;* ____, *Satyagraha in South Africa;* ____, *Self-restraint, Self-indulgence;* ____, *Songs from Prison;* ____, *Speeches and Writings;* ____, *The Story of My Experiments With Truth;* ____, *To a Gandhian Capitalist;* ____, *To Ashram Sisters; To the Students;* ____, *Towards New Education;* ____, *Towards Non-Violent Socialism;* ____, *Unto the Last;* ____, *Women and Social Injustice;* ____, *Young India;* George, *Gandhi's Challenge to Christianity;* Government of India, *Congress Responsibility for the Disturbances;* ____, *Gandhian Outlook and Techniques;* ____, *Homage to Gandhi;* Gregg, *A Disciple for Non-violence;* Heath, *Gandhi;* Holmes, *The Christ of Today;* ____, *My Gandhi;* Hoyland, *Indian Crisis;* Jones, *Gandhi Lives;* Kalikar, *Stray Glimpses of the Bapu;* Kirpalani, *Tagore, Gandhi and Nehru;* Lajpat, *Ideals of Non-Cooperation;* ____, *Unhappy India;* Lester, *Entertaining Gandhi;* Majumdar, *An Advanced History of India;* Masani, *Dadabhai;* Mashruwala, *Gandhi and Marx;* Mirabehn, *Gleanings;* ____, *Bapu's Letters to Mira;* Montagu, *An Indian Diary;* Mouland, *A Short History of India;* Mukerjee, *Indian Struggle for Freedom;* Muzumdar, *Gandhi Triumphant!;* Nag, *Tolstoy and Gandhi;* Nair, *Gandhi and Anarchy;* Nanda, *Mahatma Gandhi: A Biography;* Nash, *Almanac of World Crime;* Nehru, *An Autobiography;* ____, *The Discovery of India;* ____, *Eighteen Months in India;* ____, *Mahatma Gandhi;* ____, *The Unity of India;* Patel, *Life and Times of Vitalbhai;* Patel, *Letters to Sardar Patel;* Prabhu, *India of My Dreams;* ____, *The Mind of Mahatma Gandhi;* ____, *Mahatma Gandhi and Birhar;* Prasad, *Autobiography;* ____, *Gandhiji in Camparan;* ____, *India Divided;* Pyarelai, *The Epic Fast;* ____, *Gandhian Techniques;* ____, *Mahatma Gandhi: The Last Phase;* ____, *A Nation-Builder at Work; A Pilgrimage for Peace;* Radhakrishnan, *Mahatma Gandhi;* ____, *Indian Philosophy;* Ramachandran, *A Sheaf of Gandhi Anecdotes;* Raman, *What Does Gandhi Want?;* Rao, *Gandhian Institutions of Wardha;* Ravoof, *Meet Mr. Jinnah;* Rolland, *Mahatma Gandhi;* Sen, *Voiceless India;* Shahani, *Mr. Gandhi;* Sheean, *Mahatma Gandhi;* Shirer, *Gandhi: A Memoir;* Shridharani, *War Without Violence;* ____, *The Mahatma and the World;* Shukla, *Incidents of Gandhiji's Life;* Singh, *Nehru: The Rising Star of India;* Sittaramaya, *History of the Indian National Congress;* Smith, *The Oxford Student's History of India;* Smith, *Modern Islam in India;* Sparrow, *The Great Assassins;* Tagore, *Mahatmaji and the Depressed Humanity;* ____, *Sadhana;* Templewood, *Nine Troubled Years;* Tendulkar, *Mahatma;* ____, *Gandhiji: His Life and Work;* Tuker, *While Memory Serves;* United Nations Educational, Scientific and Cultural Organization, *All Men Are Brothers: Life and Thoughts of Mahatma Gandhi;* Walker, *Sword of Gold;* ____, *The Wisdom of Gandhi;* Wallbank, *A Short History of India and Pakistan;* Woolacott, *India on Trial: A Study of Present Conditions;* (FILM), *Nine Hours to Rama,* 1963; *Gandhi,* 1982.

Gandillon, Antoinette, and **Gandillon, Georges,** and **Gandillon, Perrenette,** and **Gandillon, Pierre,** prom. 1598, Fr., lycanthropy-witchcraft. Four members of a French family, a brother, two sisters, and a son were condemned as werewolves and charged with practicing witchcraft in 1598. A wolf attacked the sister of a Naizan teenager, Benoit Bidel, and as Bidel struggled with the wolf, he later said, he saw that the front paws were human hands. Because Perrenette Gandillon was in the area of the attack, she was murdered by furious peasants. Another sibling, Pierre Gandillon, was charged with witchcraft, lycanthropy, murder, cannibalization of men and animals, and making hail. Pierre Gandillon confessed after being tortured. His son, Georges Gandillon, admitted to becoming a werewolf and slaughtering two goats. Another sister, Antoinette Gandillon, was charged with becoming a werewolf, attending the sabbat, and creating hail. Pierre, Georges, and Antoinette were found Guilty of the charges and burned to death. REF.: *CBA.*

Gandolfe, Jeanne, d.1967, Fr., (unsolv.) rape-mur. In Var, Fr., 12-year-old Jeanne Gandolfe was found lying dead in underbrush not far from her parents' farm on Oct. 27, 1967. The girl had been raped and strangled. The girl's father and four brothers, local bandits, vowed revenge, but the murder went unsolved.

REF.: *CBA;* Heppenstall, *The Sex War and Others*

Ganey, James Cullen, 1899-1972, U.S., jur. Nominated to serve in the Eastern District Court of Pennsylvania by President Franklin D. Roosevelt in 1940, and nominated to the Third Circuit Court by President John F. Kennedy. REF.: *CBA.*

Gangy, Paul W., 1897-1938, U.S., mur. Gangy had a shady background as a political fixer and racetrack tout before he set up a small private detective agency in New York City in 1936. He specialized in divorce cases, sleuthing out the sex habits of spouses under his investigation. Sometime in early 1938, Gangy agreed to represent Michael Doellen, a retired small equipment manufacturer who lived outside of Syracuse, N.Y. Doellen, then eighty-one, had married a sultry brunette, Lola Banes, who was then thirty-one, but she was often absent from the Doellen country estate and her husband came to believe that she was having an affair in New York City. He hired Gangy to follow his wife and learn whether she was seeing another man.

For months the detective spent his days and nights tracking Lola Doellen every time she arrived in New York City. She stayed in the Park Avenue apartment Doellen kept in the city for occasional visits, but she seldom slept there. Gangy learned that Mrs. Doellen was seeing Alfredo Servano, a handsome small-time racketeer. He also learned that Mrs. Doellen and Servano were planning to somehow force the elderly Doellen into signing over his considerable accounts to Mrs. Doellen, who had once worked as a stripper in a Greenwich Village nightclub owned by Servano.

Gangy, who kept a record of his every move in an office diary, then decided *he* would blackmail Mrs. Doellen and Servano and he confronted them with his evidence. Servano admitted only to having an affair with Mrs. Doellen and defied Gangy to expose him. He then quarreled with Mrs. Doellen and reportedly quit the affair. Mrs. Doellen then offered her charms to detective Gangy who accepted with alacrity. Within a month, Gangy had agreed to Mrs. Doellen's plan to murder her husband. She would inherit approximately $2 million, and she promised to split this with the unscrupulous sleuth, or, at least, that is what Gangy reported in his diary.

On the night of Oct. 4, 1938, Gangy, pretending to be a prowler, drove to the Doellen country estate and broke into the manufacturer's mansion. He crept upstairs and, following Mrs. Doellen's diagram of the house, entered a darkened bedroom. He went to the bed and, grabbing a pillow, smothered the person sleeping there. Gangy then fled downstairs and rifled the study, to make it appear that a housebreaker had killed Doellen. Just as he was leaving the building, however, John Francken, the caretaker, appeared and fired both barrels of a shotgun into Gangy, killing him instantly. When police arrived they discovered the body of a woman suffocated in her bed. This was the real Mrs. Doellen, a woman of seventy-three. Michael Doellen was not on the premises, having taken a business trip to Boston.

Police in New York later uncovered Gangy's diary and were perplexed about its contents, realizing that the young woman Gangy had been following was not the real Mrs. Doellen, according to the detective's own statements. When Michael Doellen returned home the next day, detectives interrogated him but he denied ever having hired Gangy. It was speculated by investigators that Doellen may have set up the detective with a decoy to simply arrange the murder of his own wife. None of this could be proven. The woman known as Lola Banes was never located, nor was her lover Servano. Michael Doellen sold his property near Syracuse and moved first to New York City, then took an around-the-world cruise. He was reportedly accompanied by an attractive young nurse who sailed with him to Java where the retired old millionaire bought a villa and a small plantation. Doellen reportedly died sometime in 1942 when the Japanese invaded Java. REF.: *CBA*.

Gant, W.C. (AKA: **Mr. Shoot**), prom. 1923, Case of, U.S., mur. Posing as a circuit-riding parson, W.C. Gant of the Anti-Saloon League flushed out moonshiners and bootleggers throughout Tennessee during the 1920s. The self-appointed liquor vigilante frequently entrapped his victims into revealing the location of their stills.

In 1923 he went to Jefferson County, where, posing as a field hand, he heard about a large still operated by farmer Anderson Green and two brothers, Claude and Sam Bailey. Gant agreed to act as their agent, and to locate wealthy buyers in Knoxville. His first consignment was to arrive on Sept. 29.

Gant met the moonshiners at the appointed time and place and promptly ordered them to surrender, though he had no legal arresting powers. Hiding in the bushes was the only authorized law enforcement officer privy to the meeting: Agent Hill of the Prohibition Department. Ignoring Gant's command, Anderson Green turned his back and started to walk away. W.C. Gant took aim and shot him in the back. Green died three days later.

Gant was acquitted of murder when the Prohibition Bureau and the Anti-Saloon League convinced the courts in Knox County that it was Agent Hill who fired the fatal shot, not the Reverend Mr. Gant.

REF.: *CBA*; Kobler, *Ardent Spirits*.

Garabedian, David, 1961- , U.S., mur. Defense attorneys for 22-year-old David Garabedian of Dunstable, Mass., claimed that the chemical organo-phosphates found in most common garden pesticides drove their client to murder. The jury rejected this argument, but not before a psychiatrist and chemist provided expert testimony that the pesticides had affected Garabedian's mind.

The accused gardener was working at the home of Eileen Muldoon, a 34-year-old secretary, on the afternoon of Mar. 29, 1983. When the woman objected to Garabedian urinating on her lawn, he became enraged and applied a stranglehold to her neck. Then he pelted her with stones until she was dead.

Defense Attorney Robert Mardirosian argued before a Middlesex jury that his client was a "peaceful, good, hardworking boy" until the dangerous pesticides altered his thought processes in March 1983.

The jury doubted his contention and convicted Garabedian of first-degree murder on Feb. 7, 1984. He was sentenced to life imprisonment without parole. REF.: *CBA*.

Garand, John Cantius, 1888-1974, U.S., firearms. Invented a light machine gun and subsequently joined the U.S. Bureau of Standards in Washington, D.C., in 1917. He also developed the semi-automatic Garand rifle that was renamed the M-1 and adopted as the standard U.S. Army shoulder weapon in 1936. REF.: *CBA*.

Garat, Dominique Joseph, 1749-1833, Fr., lawyer. Served as French minister of justice in 1792, and as minister of the interior in 1793. He participated in the Council of Ancients and the Council of Five Hundred. He was named count by Napoleon in 1808. REF.: *CBA*.

Garcia, Amado, See: **Trujillo, Rafael**.

Garcia, Inez, prom. 1974, U.S., mur. Inez Garcia, a Cuban-Puerto Rican woman barely fluent in English, was brutally raped in a back alley of Soledad, Calif., on Mar. 19, 1974. Her assailant was 17-year-old Louis Castillo. A large, oafish bully named Jiminez kept a sharp look-out for police.

Normally a soft-spoken woman, Inez returned to her home and loaded a .22-caliber rifle, which she then turned on Jiminez. After dropping Jiminez in the street with a single shot, the gun jammed and Castillo escaped.

Despite having been a patient of a local mental hospital, Inez was arraigned on a murder charge. She was defended by the well-known attorney Charles Garry, who sought an acquittal on a diminished capacity plea. Complicating the proceedings were various radical feminist groups, who interrupted the deliberations with catcalls, inflammatory signs, and insults which may have adversely influenced the jury. Inez Garcia was convicted of second-degree murder. One of the jurors later expressed the opinion that a "rapist is not trying to kill her. He's just trying to give her a good time." With this sentiment prevailing, a conviction was virtually inevitable.

A court of appeals later overturned the conviction. But Louis Castillo was never charged or tried for rape.

REF.: *CBA*; Godwin, *Murder U.S.A.*

Garcia, Iñiguez, c.1836-98. Cuba, rebel. Leader in Cuban revolt against Spain in Ten Years' War from 1868-78, and leader of Cuban military and diplomatic efforts in Spanish-American War. REF.: *CBA*.

Garcia, Joe, Jr., 1967- , U.S., mur. Pointing to Joe Garcia's checkered driving record, Guy Chipparoni of the Illinois Secretary of State's office told reporters: "This guy had no business being on the road." Garcia, a 21-year-old Chicago resident, was driving the city's South Side on a revoked license on Aug. 23, 1988, when he crashed into a bus and ran up the sidewalk, striking two sisters.

Ester Estrada, twenty-nine, and her sister Sandra were standing near the corner of Ashland and Archer Avenues when they were hit by Garcia's vehicle, which was traveling over eighty miles an hour. The driver, under the influence of alcohol, had sideswiped a Chicago Transit bus and ran a stop sign before striking the two sisters. Ester Estrada was killed, and her sister seriously injured.

Garcia abandoned his car and fled on foot. Police arrested him eight blocks away. He was charged with reckless homicide and driving under the influence. Twice in the previous two years, Garcia's license had been suspended: once for failing to carry insurance, and a second time for leaving the scene of an accident.

On Jan. 30, 1989, Joe Garcia was sentenced to four-and-a-half years in prison after pleading guilty in the Cook County Criminal Court. He admitted to the judge that he had consumed a dozen cans of beer and had smoked marijuana before embarking on his fatal ride. REF.: *CBA*.

Garcia, Joseph, d.1878, Brit., arson-mur. To the villagers of Llangibby, Wales, Joseph Garcia seemed a likely candidate to commit murder. Less than twenty-four hours before William Watkins, his wife Elizabeth, and their three children were murdered in their home, Garcia had been released from Usk jail.

It was July 16, 1878. Garcia, a seaman in the Spanish navy before his arrest for burglary, lingered in Llangibby. He was seen drinking in a public tavern before settling in for the night alongside the steps adjoining the Watkins farm.

The next morning a farm boy discovered the bodies of Mr. and Mrs. Watkins on the garden path. The murderer had set the house on fire. The children were found stabbed to death inside. The local gossip implicated Garcia, a suspicious looking foreigner.

Patrolman P.C. Toize of the Newport Borough police force arrested him on suspicion the next day. The clothes he wore were later identified as having belonged to Watkins. Garcia was provided with an interpreter, but even then he refused to say how or why he came to possess the dead man's clothes.

Garcia was tried at the Gloucester Assizes. He pleaded not guilty to murder, but the judge expressed the opinion that all the evidence pointed to him as the murderer. It took the jury only six minutes to convict him. Joseph Garcia was hanged on Nov. 18, 1878, amid uproarious cheering for Marwood the executioner.

REF.: Bleackley, *Hangmen of England*; Brock, *A Casebook of Crime*; *CBA*; Logan, *Masters of Crime*.

Garcia, Luis, 1957-87, and **Llaguna, Roger**, 1952-1980, U.S., rob.-kid.-rape-mur. On the evening of Jan. 7, 1980, at Gina's Food Mart on Chicago's near northwest side, William Pagan, the owner of the small inner-city grocery store in a predominantly Hispanic neighborhood, was chatting with several long-time customers when two suspicious-looking men entered.

Suddenly, one of them brandished a gun and demanded the money in the cash register. The gunmen, later identified as Luis Garcia and Roger Llaguna, had long criminal records. Garcia was arrested as a non-juvenile offender in 1972 when he was only seventeen. He was charged with possession of marijuana in the first of sixteen drug-related arrests. Roger Llaguna first went to prison in 1977 for armed robbery.

Pagan and his wife Aida surrendered the cash without a struggle. Garcia then shot and killed Aida Pagan while Llaguna murdered her husband and Juan Jiminez, a customer. The killers fled the store and drove away in their gray and green sedan.

A half-hour later, the pair struck again at the Lincoln Tavern, less than a mile away. Garcia and Llaguna ordered beer and chips from bartender Dorothy Oszkandy. After finishing their drinks, they announced a holdup. Like the Pagans, Mrs. Oszkandy put up no resistance. She handed over $125, but was shot in the stomach. The wound was not fatal. In the back apartment adjacent to the tavern, 23-year-old Christine Mroz was studying for her classes at the Loop College. When Mroz attempted to flee she was shot in the chest and face. Garcia and Llaguna seized a 10-year-old girl and retreated to a nearby basement where they sexually assaulted her.

They dragged the girl from the house and drove down North Avenue. By this time, eyewitnesses had provided police with a description of the car. The killers were overtaken in a high-speed chase through the congested streets of the northwest side. Garcia was captured and Llaguna was shot after being cornered in an alley. The young girl survived the ordeal, and appeared as a prosecution witness when the case went to trial in July 1980.

Luis Garcia was indicted on four counts of murder and linked to three other fatal shootings dating back to 1979. Two of the killings took place in tavern holdups on the northwest side. On Aug. 4, 1980, the jury returned a verdict of Guilty after deliberating only eighty minutes. Garcia smirked when Judge James Bailey read the verdict. He was sentenced to death, a sentence later upheld by the state supreme court on Nov. 16, 1982.

While awaiting execution, Luis Garcia died in his cell at the Pontiac Correctional Center on Nov. 5, 1987. The cause of death was listed as an "idiosyncratic reaction to cocaine." Prison officials believed that friends or relatives smuggled the drug to him during a visit a day or two before. REF.: *CBA*.

Garcia, Manuel (AKA: **Three-Fingered Jack**), d.1853, U.S., west. outl. One of the most fierce bandits in California history, Manuel "Three-Fingered Jack" Garcia is almost as legendary in the annals of western outlaws as is his bandit chieftain, Joaquin Murieta. For years before he began following Murieta, Garcia had been robbing stagecoaches and travelers along the wild California roads, and lawmen had been searching for him. When he joined Murieta, this brigand proved to be the most bloodthirsty of Murieta's terror band.

On one occasion, after Murieta's band had roared into a mountain mining area and rounded up all the Chinese miners, Garcia reportedly hanged dozens of these hapless laborers by their queues and then, wielding a razor-sharp hunting knife, casually marched along the line of dangling victims and slit each throat with a single slash. He was later quoted as boasting of this mass slaughter, reveling to his chieftain: "Ah, Murieta, this has been a great day! How my knife lapped up their blood!" This, of course, was part and parcel of the kind of lurid dime novel narratives employed when describing the awful deeds of the mythical Murieta in the 1850s.

Murieta's band had so terrorized the residents of northern California that the governor appointed a former Texan, Harry Love, to head a special force of twenty California rangers whose specific purpose it was, no matter the cost or time it took, to hunt down Murieta and his men and bring them to justice. Captain Love and his men, who were as fierce and lethal as their prey, doggedly tracked down a band of Mexican outlaws identified as the Murieta gang, coming upon these men west of Tulare Lake near Panoche Pass on July 23, 1853.

The Mexicans were squatting about a fire and eating dinner when Love's rangers appeared, surrounding them and approaching cautiously, guns at the ready. The rangers began to ask harsh and pointed questions which the Mexicans naturally resented and said so. A handsome young Mexican stood up and walked a few paces toward the rangers, announcing that he was the leader of the band, and if the rangers wanted to ask questions they must direct them to him. The young man's actions seemed to be a signal to the other Mexicans who suddenly reached for their six-guns.

A wild gunfight erupted which saw the Mexican leader fall mortally wounded. A fierce-looking Mexican who tried to come to his rescue was shot several times and he dashed for the band's horses tethered nearby, but a withering cross fire from the rangers cut him off. He stumbled off into the thick woods, running along a trail, the rangers in pursuit. The Mexican, two guns in his hand, fired his weapons as he ran until his six-guns were empty. He then whirled, threw a hunting knife at the ranger closest to him, and fell dead of his wounds. This man was identified as Manuel "Three Fingered Jack" Garcia. The youthful leader of the band was identified as the celebrated Joaquin Murieta.

Determined that their feats be recognized and rewards given, the rangers cut off Murieta's head and placed this in a jar of alcohol so it could be preserved and returned to Mariposa as proof of the rangers' triumph. Garcia's head was too badly shot up to preserve, but his right hand, which had been mutilated years earlier in an accident, a well-known fact, was cut off and preserved so that identification was certain. The corpses of the dead Mexican bandits were left to rot in the thick forest. Several other Mexicans had escaped in the wild melee but two of the band were captured alive and put on horses, their hands tied behind their backs. The rangers headed for Mariposa.

Both Mexicans refused to admit that the dead leader of their band had been the famed Murieta. They remained silent and spoke only briefly to each other in Spanish, saying they held no hope of surviving the mobs waiting for them in Mariposa. When the rangers crossed a deep river, one of the Mexicans leaped from his horse and dove into the waters and quickly drowned. The other was delivered to the jail in Mariposa, but before he could be brought to trial a mob broke into the small frame building, dragged him out, and lynched him. The head of Murieta and the hand of the savage Garcia were put on display and drew great crowds of curious settlers who had heard of Murieta and Garcia only through wild rumor and tales that approached fable, both of these bandits being part of California folklore long before their reported demise. See: **Murieta, Joaquin.**

REF.: Belle, *Life and Adventures of the Celebrated Bandit Joaquin Murieta;* Bingham, *In Tamal Land;* Block, *Great Stagecoach Robberies of the West;* Bonsal, *Edward Fitzgerald Beale;* Buckbee, *The Saga of Old Tuolumne;* Cain, *The Story of Bodie;* Caruthers, *Loafing Along Death Valley Trails; CBA;* Fisher and Holmes, *Gold Rushes and Mining Camps;* Horan, *The Authentic Wild West;* Jackson, *Anybody's Gold;* ____, *Bad Company;* Keating, *Gold Mines of Hard Luck;* Klette, *The Crimson Trail of Joaquin Murieta;* Lydston, *Panama and the Sierras;* McLeod, *Pigtails and Gold Dust;* Marshall, *Swinging Doors;* Murphy, *The People of the Pueblo;* Nash, *Bloodletters and Badmen;* Newmark, *Jottings in Southern California History;* Prendergast, *Forgotten Pioneers;* Rogers, *Soldiers of the Overland;* Sabin, *Wild Men of the Wild West;* Secrest, *Joaquin;* Walker, *San Francisco's Literary Frontier;* Waters, *Street Tracks to Santa Fe;* Williams, *The Adventures of a Seventeen-Year-Old Lad;* Wilson, *Treasure Express;* Wood, *Calaveras;* ____, *Murphys, Queen of the Sierra.*

Garcia and Castillano dismembering their victim, Peter Lagoardette.

Garcia, Manuel Philip, and **Castillano, Jose Demas,** d.1821, U.S., mur. Garcia, Castillano, and Peter Lagoardette lived together in a deserted house in Norfolk, Va. All three were highwaymen. Lagoardette began courting a local girl in which the other two men were interested and the three quarreled violently over her. On Mar. 20, 1821, Manuel Philip Garcia and Jose Demas Castillano killed Lagoardette, then panicked. To hide their murder, they decapitated the body, along with the hands and feet, burning these in the fireplace and then fleeing. The head and other remains were found a short time later, along with clothes bearing laundry marks with the initials of Garcia and the victim. These laundry marks were traced to a local laundry and the killers were identified in the first such use of laundry marks. Garcia and Castillano were tracked down and brought to trial. After a quick conviction, both men were hanged at Portsmouth, Va., on June 1, 1821.

REF.: *An Account of the Apprehension, Trial, Conviction, and Condemnation of Manuel Philip Garcia and Jose Demas Garcia Castillano; CBA.*

Garcia, Menocal Mario, 1866-1941, Cuba, polit. corr. Fought for independence from Spain from 1895-98. He served as president of Cuba from 1913-21. His tenure was marred by corruption, repression of the people, and a number of revolts. REF.: *CBA.*

Garcia, Moreno Gabriel, 1821-75, Ecu., pres., assass. President of Ecuador from 1861-65 and 1869-75, known for consolidating the government, improving the economy, and signing a pact with the pope establishing Roman Catholicism as the chief religion. He was assassinated in 1875. REF.: *CBA.*

Garcia, Percy, 1961- , and **Bridges, Dean,** 1962- , Case of, U.S., drugs. James Hiroms of Wells County, Texas, thought his little secret was safe. Then he quarreled with his son Dean Bridges at the race track in Columbus.

Someone had buried a half-million dollars in cash at his south Texas ranch and Hiroms knew about it. Where the money came from was never adequately explained, at least by Hiroms. Since Wells County was a crossroads of the Mexican drug traffic, investigators suspected it was smuggler's loot, left there several years before. "I saw the money buried there a long, long time ago and that's all I'm going to say about that," young Bridges told police.

Bridges and his friend Percy Garcia dug up the money and decided to run away to Chicago. With $483,202.67 in small bills tucked into their suitcase, the two boys took a bus from Corpus Christi to Dallas on Jan. 31, 1977. When they arrived, they approached a stranger and offered him $8,000 to purchase a brand new Ford Thunderbird for them. The man bought the car, pocketed a $2,000 "finder's fee" for his efforts, and then disappeared.

Unsure of their directions, Bridges and Garcia ended up in Waco, 120 miles south of Dallas. Deciding they would try to reach Chicago the next day, they headed for a motel. On the way, a Waco policeman pulled them over for running a red light. The money, a handgun, and a small bag of marijuana were found inside the car.

Garcia and Bridges were returned home while investigators tried to figure out who had buried the treasure. James Hiroms, a 36-year-old sheet metal worker denied it was his money, but refused to comment on why it was buried on his property. He was jailed for contempt after refusing to answer a grand jury's questions.

Hiroms prudently refused to claim the cash and was later released. On Nov. 28, 1977, Federal District Judge Jack Roberts in Austin ordered that the money be invested in two interest-bearing accounts until the rightful owner could be found. A number of people eventually came forward to claim the money, including officials from the IRS and the state of Texas. REF.: *CBA.*

Garcia Lorca, Federico, 1898-1936, Spain, rebel. Noted poet and dramatist gunned down without trial by rebel Nationalists at the start of the Spanish Civil War. REF.: *CBA.*

Gardelle, Theodore, d.1761, Brit., mur. A successful Swiss-born painter, Theodore Gardelle in 1760 rented rooms in London's Leicester Fields from a woman named Mrs. King. In deference to his landlady, he drew her portrait, which she immediately insisted be framed and displayed. Gardelle, however, was insulted by this. He took it as a criticism of the work.

On the morning of Thursday, Feb. 19, Gardelle sent the maid off on an errand, agreeing to answer the front door should anyone call on Mrs. King. As he crept past King's bedroom doorway in search of a book, she heard his footsteps and opened her door. Standing before the painter, she was reminded of her portrait and again asked Gardelle about framing it. Gardelle, again insulted, called her impertinent, which so enraged her she struck him in the chest.

To keep from being hit again, Gardelle pushed Mrs. King. Tripping on an area rug, she fell hard against the bedpost. Gardelle ran to comfort her, but she screamed at him, saying she fully intended to tell the authorities he had tried to harm her. Gardelle then grabbed an ivory comb. Pointing the sharp-ended handle toward her, he blocked the doorway, threatening her to come no closer. She tried to push past him, so he stabbed her in the throat.

Overcome with fear, Gardelle explained to the maid that Mrs. King had been called away unexpectedly. When she pressed with too many questions he fired her and then proceeded to dismember the body of Mrs. King and hide it in pieces

British murderer Theodore Gardelle.

throughout the house—the sink, attic, and fireplace.

After days of answering to visitors about Mrs. King's leave-taking, Gardelle began to wear down. Finding inconsistencies in Gardelle's story, Thomas Pelsey, Mrs. King's suitor's servant, suspected foul play. He went to the police, who searched the house and found many of the body parts.

Once accused, Gardelle confessed, explaining he had only reacted in fear to Mrs. King's threats to expose him. Further, he had contrived and committed the cover-up under duress, under the weight of unbearable guilt for killing her. On Apr. 4, 1761, Gardelle was executed before an indignant crowd of Leicester Fields residents. Afterwards, his body was hung in chains on Hounslow Heath.

REF.: Bleackley, *Hangmen of England; CBA;* Mitchell, *The Newgate Calendar;* Pearce, *Unsolved Murder Mysteries;* Potter, *The Art of Hanging;* Wilson, *Encyclopedia of Murder.*

Australian bandit Frank Gardiner, being captured at Apis Creek.

Gardiner, Frank, b.1830, Aus., rob. For years, Frank Gardiner roamed the dusty backwoods of Australia stealing horses and robbing passing travelers. In 1849, Gardiner was sentenced to five

years in prison for stealing thirty-two horses, but he managed to escape five weeks later. He was put away a second time for horse thievery in 1854, and this time he served out his complete sentence at the Cockatoo Island penitentiary. When he was released, Gardiner tried to reform. But he quickly became bored with the straight life and went back to the highway to seek his fortune.

On June 15, 1862, Gardiner pulled off his greatest robbery. He ambushed a mail coach carrying £12,000 worth of gold dust from the Australian digging fields to the Bank of Sydney.

Gardiner matched wits with Sir Frederick Pottinger, Inspector of Police of New South Wales, in the ensuing chase, and became a folk hero for outwitting the police chief. But in 1864, the police caught the wily highwayman in Queensland after his mistress Kitty Brown revealed their whereabouts to her sister.

Gardiner was tried and convicted for an assault against two peace officers in 1854. Kitty Brown, meanwhile, fled to New Zealand and committed suicide. Then, in a controversial decision that helped topple the government, Frank Gardiner was granted his freedom in 1864. He moved to San Francisco, where he opened a barroom. Some years later, Gardiner was killed in a saloon brawl. REF.: *CBA.*

Gardiner, Stephen, c.1483-1555, Brit., polit. corr.-consp. Chancellor of Cambridge University. He helped Henry VIII win a divorce from Catherine of Aragon, and served as his secretary up to 1534. He became very powerful after the fall of Cardinal Wolsey, but was imprisoned during the reign of Edward VI in the Tower of London. REF.: *CBA.*

Gardiner, William, b.c.1868, Case of, Brit., mur. On the morning of June 1, 1902, the body of 23-year-old Rose Harsent was found by her father in the kitchen of Deacon Crisp's home, where she was employed as a maid. Harsent's throat had been cut from ear to ear. There were also slashes on her chest. An attempt had been made to set her corpse on fire with kerosene, but only the flesh on her legs and her nightgown had been charred. Next to the body lay a pharmacist's medicine bottle with a label indicating that it was meant for "Mrs. Gardiner's chdn (children)." The constable of Peasenhall, England, had heard the gossip connecting William Gardiner, the village carpenter and church elder, with Harsent, who sang in the choir at his chapel. It was rumored that Gardiner was the father of her as yet unborn child.

On the morning on June 1, James Morriss, a gamekeeper, had seen distinct footprints between Gardiner's cottage and the main house. It had rained the night before, so the footprints in the mud were fresh. Gardiner, thirty-three, owned boots with soles that matched the tracks described. A letter, apparently from Gardiner, was found among Harsent's things, setting up an assignation for midnight on May 31. Gardiner was arrested and tried for murder.

Gardiner's wife testified that she and her husband visited a neighbor on the night in question. The neighbor's testimony matched. Mrs. Gardiner also claimed that she had given the medicine bottle to Harsent when she needed some camphorated oil. Gardiner denied the handwriting on the note, denied the late visit to Crisp's house, and denied the murder. The jury, impressed by his confident, devout manner, was unable to reach a unanimous verdict. One person held out in his favor, though the others thought him guilty. Gardiner went to a second trial. Again the jury was unable to reach a verdict. This time one person held out against him while the remainder thought him innocent. The authorities decided not to pursue a third trial, and Gardiner was released.

REF.: Adam, *Murder By Persons Unknown;* Blackham, *Sir Ernest Wild, KC;* Brock, *A Casebook of Crime; CBA;* Lambton, *Echoes of Causes Celebres;* Logan, *Dramas of the Dock; Notable British Trials;* Rowland, *The Peasenhall Mystery;* Shew, *A Second Companion to Murder;* Smith-Hughes, *Eight Studies In Justice;* Villiers, *Riddles of Crime;* Wilson, *Encyclopedia of Murder.*

Gardner, Archibald K., 1867-1962, U.S., jur. State's attorney for South Dakota from 1901-05. In 1929, he was nominated to the Eighth Circuit Court by President Calvin Coolidge. He received the Marshall McKusick Award from the law school at the University of South Dakota, honoring outstanding contribution to legal ethics. REF.: *CBA*.

Gardner, Erle Stanley, 1889-1970, U.S., lawyer-detective fiction writer. Born in Malden, Mass., Gardner moved to California and practiced law in Ventura, Calif., from 1911 to 1938. In 1948, he established the Court of Last Resort, an organization founded to aid persons thought to be unjustly imprisoned. He wrote more than 100 detective and mystery books of fiction, the most popular concerned with protagonist Perry Mason, a lawyer-detective who never seemed to lose a case. Notable Mason novels included *The Case of the Velvet Claws*, 1933, and *The Case of the Amorous Aunt*, 1963. He also wrote about a district attorney he named Doug Selby, in such works as *The D.A. Calls It Murder*, 1937, and *The D.A. Goes to Trial*, 1940. Gardner also wrote under many pseudonyms, the most popular being A.A. Fair, featuring detective Bertha Cool and legal aide Donald Lam. Gardner was one of the most prolific and popular detective writers in the U.S., rivaling the venerable Agatha Christie in sales. REF.: *CBA*.

Gardner, Margery, See: **Heath, Neville George Clevely**.

Gardner, Roy, 1884-1940, U.S., rob. A lone-wolf bandit who had an abiding love of the marvelous and the limelight, Roy Gardner, was as well-known in his time as Jesse James, John Dillinger, or Willie "The Actor" Sutton. He robbed trains singlehandedly and with alacrity and was one of the most sensational escape artists in prison history, a Houdini at escapes which caused him to be listed, rightly so, as Public Enemy Number One. Inventive and imaginative, he craved adventure and, to his everlasting misjudgment, thought he could find the most exhilarating experiences in crime. Although Gardner once wrote on a prison report concerning his family that his "home influences were excellent," he refuted this claim years later, admitting to a prison psychiatrist that his parents quarreled constantly and that his mother browbeat his father and favored his sister, reserving a malicious and mean attitude toward him. Gardner hated his mother, he confessed, a hatred so intense that it caused him pain to think of her even when he reached middle-age.

Missouri-born and raised, Gardner was a problem child, brilliant in school when he attended, but rebelling against authority of all kinds. In 1902 he was placed in the State Reformatory at Booneville, Mo., after being sentenced to a two-year term for burglary. He attempted several escapes but these failed. When he did manage to escape, he thought it over and then voluntarily returned to the institution. He was asked why he had come back and replied with a shrug: "I had nowhere else to go." When released in 1904, Gardner hit the rails until he reached Denver, Colo. Impoverished, he refused to look for work, concluding that there were easier ways to make money. He walked into a Denver jewelry store and asked to see some rings. When a tray was brought, he grabbed it and raced into the street, eluding pursuers. He went into hiding and days later pawned the rings in various towns as he made his way west to San Francisco. There he wandered into a gym and, because of his splendid physique, was asked to spar some rounds with local fighters. He did, knocking out several and becoming a boxer, using the name Young Fitzsimmons. He was good enough to briefly become a sparring partner of heavyweight champion Jim Jeffries.

Tiring of the ring, Gardner, using an alias, impulsively enlisted in the U.S. Army but bristled at the regimen and also lost heavily in card games. He was caught cheating and, fearing reprisals, deserted. Next, according to his own later admissions, he wandered about the Southwest, working as a horseshoer and later as a miner in New Mexico, Colorado, Arizona and Cannaneo, Mex. He was accused of smuggling arms to revolutionaries opposing the dictator, Porfirio Diaz, in 1909. He was sentenced to death by firing squad but overpowered his guards in a small jail and escaped, fleeing to the U.S.

Returning to San Francisco, Gardner tried his old jewelry store

trick by entering Glindemann's Jewelry Store on Market Street on Dec. 20, 1910, and asking to see a tray of diamond rings. He looked them over carefully, but instead of grabbing the tray and running, as he had in the past, he told the clerk he had to think over his choice and would return later. He entered the store again just before closing time and was shown the tray of twenty-three diamond rings and then grabbed the tray, running out the door into another store and out a side exit onto Ellis Street and then on to Powell Street. The crowds were dense, filled with last-minute Christmas shoppers, exactly what Gardner had been waiting for, the crowds being too thick for pursuers to catch him. But he had not thought he would bump into a policeman in his haste. Patrolman Fella arrested him with the tray of diamonds in his hands. Convicted, Gardner was sentenced to five years in prison by Judge Lawlor who stated that Gardner's "offense in this case presents elements of great boldness and some ingenuity. The act itself would tend to indicate that there had been extensive deliberation."

Gardner entered San Quentin on Feb. 16, 1911, and became a model prisoner. He obeyed orders, followed the rules, and spent a great deal of time studying electricity. He showed no signs of wanting to escape and, when a bread riot broke out, he attempted to quell the breakout but was severely stabbed by some of the prisoners. Gardner was paroled on Sept. 16, 1913, being released two-and-a-half years early for good behavior. Prison officials were so impressed with his conduct that they arranged a job for him in a copper mine in Kennett, Calif. Gardner worked hard and later changed jobs, being employed in an iron works. His parole officer usually gave him good reports but added that Gardner was headstrong and had a hard time taking orders. When his parole period was completed, he got a job in the shipyards where he made good money and, during WWI, he made four-minute speeches to fellow workers during bond-selling campaigns. Eloquent and very patriotic, he sold a good deal of bonds.

Why Roy Gardner reentered crime after this period remains a mystery. By his own later admissions, he traveled to the Midwest where he recruited two experienced robbers and these three men, following Gardner's orders, stopped a passenger train outside of Centerville, Iowa, robbing its mail car of $54,000. Gardner took his share of the loot, one half, and went to Mexico where he gambled away everything within a week. Returning to California and settling in San Diego, he noticed that a mail messenger in the San Diego Post Office was registering a shipment of currency. He followed the messenger to the back of the building and got into the truck as it pulled away. He produced a revolver and held up the driver, fleeing with the sack of cash which contained $75,000. Gardner buried the loot but, making the mistake of getting drunk with an ex-convict with whom he had served time, he confided where he had buried the money and the ex-convict turned him in. This time Gardner was given a twenty-five-year sentence. Since the mail robbery was a federal offense, he was ordered to McNeil Island.

Several prisoners were being taken to the island in Washington by train, guarded by U.S. Marshals. Gardner managed to overpower one guard in a passageway, taking away his gun. He ordered fellow prisoners to use the guard's key to unlock his handcuffs and leg irons. Then he chained the guard and several others to pipes in the men's washroom. As the train entered the station at Portland, Ore., Gardner calmly stepped down to the platform and walked into the darkness. He went to British Columbia where he committed several holdups and then returned to California where, in Roseville, on May 20, 1921, he robbed a postal clerk of a sack of registered mail containing $55,000 in cash. A short time later Gardner committed another mail robbery which netted him $175,000. Oddly, the robber remained in the area where he had committed his crimes and was identified. He was arrested in Roseville on May 23, 1921, as he sat in a poker game. As the cuffs were put around his wrists, Gardner quipped: "I was losing anyway. Let's go. I have nothing better to do."

Pleading guilty, Gardner was given another twenty-five-year

term in prison and once again was headed for McNeil Island. This time two experienced deputies were assigned to watch his every move on the train going north to Washington. Gardner was manacled and on his leg he wore an Oregon Boot, a heavy steel device that weighed about twenty pounds and prevented the wearer from moving about easily. As the train pulled out of Portland, Gardner asked to go to the washroom. He hobbled to the room, accompanied by a guard. Once inside, he leaned over the basin and then suddenly whirled about with a gun in his hand. It was later claimed that Gardner had strapped a small pistol to his chest but this was unlikely in that he was thoroughly searched several times before and during the train trip north. More likely is the claim that a confederate strapped the pistol under the wash basin when the train idled in Portland and Gardner, working a prearranged plan, knew just when to go to the washroom to retrieve it. With the weapon held on the guard, Gardner unlocked his manacles and the Oregon Boot. Another guard entered the washroom to check on Gardner and was disarmed, handcuffed with his associate to a standpipe. Gardner then robbed the officers and when the train slowed near Castle Rock, Wash., he slipped off the train and made good his escape.

Gardner's second sensational escape made headlines but his freedom was short-lived. Five days later he was recognized in a small Washington town by an elderly constable who easily put him under arrest. This time he was delivered to McNeil Island Penitentiary. "I don't intend to stay here long," Gardner told the warden. Such boasts were commonplace and Gardner was ignored. He seemed to adjust to prison life quickly and was seen to enjoy a baseball game being played on Labor Day, Sept. 5, 1921, on the prison field. When a player hit a long ball, Gardner and two other prisoners suddenly bolted from the stands, racing across the field toward the wired fence enclosure. Guards in the towers opened fire on the trio, killing one and wounding another, but Gardner hurled himself over the fence, got to the water, jumped in, and swam to the mainland. This time authorities were genuinely alarmed at his ability to escape and he was hunted as Public Enemy Number One. His photo appeared in newspapers across the Pacific states and as far east as Chicago.

To exploit his own publicity, Gardner began mailing long letters to the San Francisco *Bulletin* which described his colorful crime career, embellished by the author to place him in the most sympathetic light. The fugitive mailed these letters from many different post offices as he kept on the move so that he could not be traced through his frequent mailings. Gardner now enjoyed taking chances and reveled in reading about himself. He began taking greater chances and on Nov. 15, 1921, he boldly entered mail car of a train about to pull out of Phoenix, Ariz. There he found mail clerk Herman Inderlied and he pointed a gun at him, ordering him to turn over the mail sacks containing cash. This was Gardner's usual procedure and clerks invariably did as he ordered. But Inderlied was not the usual mail clerk. Instead of meekly obeying Gardner's commands, he swung at the robber and knocked him to the floor of the car, then jumped on him and held him down until his shouts brought help. Gardner was taken to jail but he never forgot the clerk. Years later he recalled, "I entered a mail car at Phoenix, Ariz., with intentions to rob. The mail clerk refused to submit to robbery, and, although unarmed, he attacked me and I was forced to either surrender to him or shoot him. That mail clerk was a one-hundred percent man and I was a cheap crook. The result was inevitable."

The result saw Gardner receive another stiff sentence. He was sent to Leavenworth where he became one of the most incorrigible prisoners on record. He began to complain that an old injury to his skull had caused a small bone chip to press on his brain and this caused his criminal conduct. He insisted that surgeons perform a brain operation to rehabilitate him. X-rays revealed no such bone chip or pressure on Gardner's brain and the doctors refused to operate. Gardner exploded and refused to obey any orders. He went on a hunger strike, saying he would commit suicide. Newspapers still gave him play but they finally tired of

his antics and he became old news. He spent his first few years in Leavenworth either in solitary confinement or in isolation quarters. He was ultimately transferred to the federal penitentiary in Atlanta, Ga. In 1925, Gardner tried to tunnel under a wall but was discovered. On July 10, 1928, he and four other prisoners, using a homemade ladder, tried to climb over one of the prison's walls after obtaining two pistols and overpowering three guards. When they realized the ladder would not reach to the top of the wall and all other escape routes were blocked to them, the inmates surrendered. Again, Gardner tried hunger strikes and suicide threats. He was so impossible that he was sent west with the first shipment of federal prisoners to Alcatraz, arriving at the Rock on Sept. 4, 1934, handcuffed to another prisoner named Al Capone.

Gardner's prisoner number at Alcatraz was 110 AZ, a number he would wear for almost four years. He was a changed man, however, when he entered Warden Johnston's office. He was a gray-haired, 50-year-old, worn-out thief who apparently realized that all of his bad conduct added up to nothing more than extended prison sentences. "I'm one man who wanted to come to Alcatraz," he told Johnston. "I have had enough trouble...when I give my word you can depend on me." He then promised to follow all regulations and become a model prisoner, which he did. Gardner's conduct was so impressive that he was transferred to Leavenworth in 1936 and released from that penitentiary in 1938. He returned to San Francisco where he wrote his life story in serial form for the San Francisco *Bulletin*.

Still seeking the limelight, Gardner went on a lecture tour and later appeared in a sideshow at the Pan American Pacific Exposition in 1939, under the title of "Crime Doesn't Pay." He spoke dramatically about his long and sensational career in crime and the many escapes that had made him infamous but he was careful to instruct audiences that none of publicity he received was worth the wasted life he had created in return. Accompanying his talks, Gardner showed a series of photos of famous criminals and prisons. The competition for audiences between the exhibits caused Gardner's show to be cancelled and he found it difficult to obtain work thereafter. Despondent, he decided to go out with a flourish. On Jan. 10, 1940, he devised a spectacular suicide in his San Francisco hotel room. He placed a sign on the door which read: "Do not open this door—Poison Gas—Call Police!" Then Roy Gardner, reformed bandit, lay down on his bed, and dropped two cyanide pellets into a glass filled with acid which caused deadly fumes to fill the room. He placed a towel over his face and breathed deeply. The maid, discovering the sign a short time later, called police who found Gardner in his own gas chamber. Detectives found his bags neatly packed with all his clothes and belongings and on top of this was a fifty-cent tip for the maid. There was little evidence of the hundreds of thousands of dollars Roy Gardner had stolen. In his pocket was found his entire fortune—$3.69. He did not forget his most devoted friends at the end, leaving a note addressed to San Francisco newspaper reporters which read: "I am checking out because I am old and tired and don't care to continue the struggle. Please let me down as light as possible." See: **Alcatraz**.

REF.: *CBA*; Cohen, *One Hundred True Crime Stories*; Gollomb, *Master Highwaymen*; Heaney, *Inside the Walls of Alcatraz*; Johnston, *Alcatraz Island Prison*.

Garesio, Gian Battista, and **Garesio, Antonio**, prom. 1910, Italy, rob.-mur. Gian Garesio and his brother Antonio Garesio committed a series of highway robberies and murders near Turin, Italy. They were caught when detective Cavaliere Domenico Cappa learned that one of the brothers had spoken openly of their activities at a tavern.

Antonio was arrested first, convicted, and imprisoned on another charge. After Gian was arrested, they were both convicted for the robbery and murder of a cart driver. Antonio was given life in prison, and Gian was executed. REF.: *CBA*.

Garfield, James Abram, 1831-81, U.S., pres., assass. The twentieth President of the United States, James A. Garfield was born near Orange, Ohio. He became a teacher and was later master of Hiram College. He left this position at the outbreak of the Civil War and organized a contingent of volunteers to fight for the Union cause in 1861, becoming a major general in 1863. Garfield distinguished himself in the battles of Shiloh and Chickamauga. During the war, Garfield ran for Congress and was elected to the House of Representatives (1863-80). In 1876, he became Republican leader of the House and was in opposition to President U.S. Grant. In 1880, Garfield was a compromise candidate for the presidency, selected by James G. Blaine and John Sherman to replace Grant who was running for a third term.

Garfield took office amidst loud claims that he was nothing more than a machine politician dedicated to massive patronage systems wherein political cronies and hacks of the Republican Party were rewarded with cushy administration positions. One of those insisting on just such a job was a weird, vainglorious creature named Charles Julius Guiteau. Born in Illinois in 1844, Guiteau was a self-taught lawyer who married a 16-year-old girl while a young man but he later abandoned her when she failed to provide income for a lofty lifestyle Guiteau insisted he deserved. He practiced in the small-claims courts of Illinois and later New York, keeping most of the settlements as fees. Degrees in law were arbitrary things in Guiteau's day. Any charlatan could put up a shingle and claim to be a lawyer and Guiteau was one of these.

A political malcontent, Guiteau used the small-claims courts to shriek out his views of American politics and life in general. Judges dreaded his appearance and he was more than once held in contempt of court. On one occasion he had to be dragged away screaming invectives after launching into a political tirade, ignoring the case he was to plead. Guiteau himself was taken to small-claims courts repeatedly for failure to pay his rent and other bills. He was constantly being sued by creditors he claimed were persecuting him for his political views.

A man who had little real purpose in life, Guiteau drifted in and out of professional pursuits. At one time he was an evangelist, joining the Oneida Community and remained a member of the sect from 1861 through 1865, espousing a sort of religious communism. In the 1870s, Guiteau embraced Moody-Sankey revivalism and took to lecturing on the Second Coming, but, as with the Oneida movement, he soon became bored and disinterested with this religious group. Guiteau later became an insurance salesmen. He tried his hand at publishing and this failed, too.

Guiteau was forever running up expensive hotel bills and then finding some pretext to leave the hotel in a huff, refusing to pay the bill because the place "was overrun with bedbugs," or other trumped-up reasons which he believed allowed him to ignore his obligations. He moved to Washington where he contracted syphilis after patronizing prostitutes. This may have developed into paresis of the brain—a common side-effect of the illness—and caused his already-confused mind to become even more addled.

In 1880, Garfield went to work as a political errand boy on behalf of Rascoe Conkling, who was attempting to nominate Grant once more for the presidency. Halfway through the campaign, Guiteau switched his allegiance to Garfield. He followed Garfield from city to city, living hand-to-mouth. He wrote an erratic, almost incomprehensible speech, titled *Garfield Against Hancock,* and personally delivered this to Garfield at the Fifth Avenue Hotel in New York City at a Republican gathering. Guiteau insisted that Garfield employ the speech in his upcoming debate with General W.S. Hancock, the Democratic candidate. Garfield never used the speech and may never have read it. Guiteau was just another leaflet-passer among thousands. Guiteau, however, believed that he alone was swaying the American public in Garfield's favor. He made impromptu speeches on Garfield's behalf on New York and Washington street corners. He shrieked, screamed, and ranted his almost incomprehensible political beliefs. Most believed him to be deranged and ignored him. When Garfield was elected, Guiteau told everyone who would listen that "the General is in the White House because of me." He traveled to Washington and boldly sent a message to President Garfield,

asking that he be named ambassador to Austria. He then changed his mind and demanded that he be named head of the U.S. Paris consulate.

Hearing nothing from Garfield, Guiteau brazenly appeared at the White House in early March 1881 and walked right into the president's office, giving Garfield another copy of his *Garfield Against Hancock* speech. On the first page Guiteau had written: "Paris consulship." He nodded, explaining to the perplexed Garfield that he was a candidate for the Paris post, and left the presidential office. When he failed to hear any word from the president, Guiteau went to the State Department and reiterated his demands concerning the consulship. He was rebuffed by clerks but returned the next day and confronted Secretary of State James G. Blaine, demanding that Blaine urge the president to quickly appoint him to the Paris post. Blaine had never met Guiteau before and thought he was talking to some escaped lunatic. He nodded patiently, then walked away.

Guiteau grew anxious and, on Mar. 8, 1881, sent a note to Garfield which read: "I presume my appointment will be promptly confirmed. There is nothing against me. I claim to be a gentleman and a Christian." He appeared at the White House the next day. This time he was prevented by a secretary from entering Garfield's office. He sat in an anteroom, using White House stationery to send notes to Garfield and Blaine, demanding his appointment. A clerk approached him and told him that he was not to use White House stationery for his personal use. "Do you know who I am?" Guiteau said indignantly. "I am one of the men who made Garfield president!" He was asked to leave the White House and was barred from entering the building some days later, branded a nuisance.

Access to the president in that era was an easy thing. Even though President Abraham Lincoln had been assassinated sixteen years earlier because of lax security, there were no guards in and about the White House during Garfield's day. Security was maintained by a few unarmed male clerks. Anyone wanting to harm the president could freely enter the White House and attack the chief executive. Guiteau was not taken seriously as a real threat to the president's safety. He was just another political hack who served as an annoyance, a pest who was finally put in his place by Secretary Blaine. In May 1881, Guiteau once more confronted Blaine at the State Department building, repeating his demands for his Paris appointment. Blaine exploded, pushing the darkly bearded, hollow-eyed, diminutive Guiteau away and saying: "Never speak to me about the Paris Embassy as long as you live!"

Incensed, Guiteau returned to his small room at the Riggs House hotel in Washington to brood. On the night of May 18, 1881, he lay in bed, deciding that the best solution to his problem was to kill Garfield. He later stated: "An impression came over my mind like a flash that if the president was out of the way, this whole thing would be solved and everything would go well." First, he thought to give the president one more chance at life, deciding that Blaine, not Garfield, be removed. Guiteau wrote a letter to the president on May 22, 1880, enclosing a copy of a recently published letter from a Blaine critic to a local newspaper. Wrote Guiteau:

Private

General Garfield:
I have been trying to be your friend. I don't know whether you appreciate it or not, but I am moved to call your attention to the remarkable letter from Mr. Blaine which I have just noticed.

According to Mr. Farwell, of Chicago, Blaine is a "vindictive politician" and "an evil genius" and you will "have no peace till you get rid of him."

This letter shows Mr. Blaine is a wicked man, and you ought to demand his *immediate* resignation; otherwise you and the Republican Party will come to grief. I will see you in the morning, if I can, and talk with you.

Very respectfully,
Charles Guiteau

When Guiteau got no response from Garfield and he was once again refused admission to the White House, he resolved to kill the president. He later stated, believing himself to be inspired by God: "At the end of two weeks, my mind was thoroughly fixed as to the necessity of the president's removal and the divinity of the inspiration. I never had the slightest doubt as to the divinity of the inspiration from the first of June (1881). This was the day my mind became thoroughly fixed as to the necessity for his removal."

Borrowing fifteen dollars from a cousin who lived in Washington, Guiteau purchased a California Bulldozer .44-caliber revolver, along with a box of cartridges. He practiced his marksmanship by shooting at trees lined along the Potomac River during the evening when no one was about. Then he began to stalk the president, who walked about Washington unescorted by guards. He was able to track Garfield since the local press naively printed the president's daily schedule.

When Guiteau learned that Garfield would be attending the National City Christian Church on June 12, 1881, he appeared there and followed Garfield and Mrs. Garfield into the church. He stood behind Garfield with the revolver in his pocket but was disinclined to shoot Garfield in the church since he feared hitting Mrs. Garfield, whom Guiteau later referred to as "that dear soul." He followed Garfield and his wife to the Baltimore and Potomac train depot in Washington on June 18, 1881. The Garfields were leaving by train to journey to their retreat in Long Branch, N.J. Again he could not bring himself to fire at Garfield because his wife was present.

On the night of July 1, 1881, Garfield left the White House and walked alone along the Washington streets, going to Blaine's home. Guiteau was there behind him, walking in the dark, slipping in and out of the shadows. He resolved to murder Garfield as he left Blaine's home but Blaine came out with Garfield and walked back to the White House with the president. Guiteau was only twenty or so paces behind the pair, listening to them talk and joke. He again decided not to kill Garfield.

The next day, July 2, 1881, Garfield planned to leave Washington on an extended tour, one on which his wife and children would accompany him. Guiteau read about Garfield's departure and went to the Baltimore and Potomac depot, this time determined to kill the president. At 9:20 a.m., Garfield arrived at the depot in a carriage with Blaine. The rest of the members of the presidential entourage were already sitting in their train seats or strolling along the platform waiting for Garfield. The president, more than six feet tall, broad-shouldered, a silk top hat perched on his massive head, entered the station and all eyes were glued on his handsome, bearded face. Guiteau was on hand, having arrived at the station twenty minutes earlier.

The assassin had arisen at 5 a.m. that morning, eaten breakfast, and then had penned Garfield's obituary for the press, stating:

The President's death was a sad necessity, but it will unite the Republican party and save the Republic. Life is a fleeting dream, and it matters little when one goes. A human life is of small value. During the war thousands of brave boys went down without a tear. I presume the President was a Christian and that he will be happier in Paradise than here.

It will be no worse for Mrs. Garfield, dear soul, to part with her husband this way than by natural death. He is liable to go at any time, any way.

I had no ill-will toward the President. His death was a political necessity. I am a lawyer, theologian and politician. I am a Stalwart of the Stalwarts. I was with General Grant and the rest of our men in New York during the canvass (the 1880 election).

I have some papers for the press which I shall leave with Byron Andrews and his co-journalists, at 1420 N.Y. Ave., where all the reporters can see them. I am going to the jail. Charles Guiteau.

Guiteau also wrote a letter that morning to General William T. Sherman, commander in chief of the U.S. Army. It read: "I have just shot the President. I shot him several times as I wished him to go as easily as possible. His death was a political necessity. I am a lawyer, theologian and politician. I am a Stalwart of the Stalwarts. I was with General Grant and the rest of our men in New York during the canvass. I am going to jail. Please order out your troops and take possession of the jail at once. Charles Guiteau."

Guiteau leisurely dressed, put his revolver in his pocket along with the two letters to the press and to General Sherman and some of his own political and religious writings, and left the Riggs House without paying his bill. He went to Lafayette Park and sat on a bench for an hour, enjoying the mild sunny morning, and then went to the depot by cab. He hired a carriage to wait for him, telling the cabman he would be driving him to the local jail shortly. Guiteau had thought to shoot the president, jump into the carriage to escape the vengeance of the mob, and have himself delivered in style to the jail unharmed.

At the depot, Guiteau went to the ladies' waiting room through which, he knew, the president would walk to get into the main station before boarding his train. He walked about nervously, peering occasionally out the window—a small man with a pointed beard in a black suit, and with beady eyes darting about. Policeman Patrick Kearney thought him suspicious and kept an eye on him, as did Mrs. L. White, the ladies' attendant, but their attention was soon directed to the entrance where, at about 9:15 a.m., the president's carriage arrived. Garfield, with Blaine at his side, entered the ladies' waiting room of the depot and the president walked past Guiteau to ask Policeman Kearney what time the train would be leaving. Kearney saluted and told Garfield that the train would depart in about ten minutes.

The president and Blaine began to walk across the ladies waiting room to the main waiting area. Blaine walked in front of the president. Guiteau turned and walked after them, about ten feet away. He jerked out his revolver from a right hip pocket and extended his arm level, carefully aiming and then firing. The bullet struck the president in the back. Garfield turned to look at the assassin, a surprised look on his face. He appeared as if he did not realize he had been shot. Four seconds later, Guiteau moved sideways and fired another shot which went wild. The president, then feeling the delayed pain of the first bullet, threw up his hands with a cry, and fell to the floor, crushing his silk top hat.

Secretary of State Blaine wheeled about, shouting: "My God, he's been murdered! What's the meaning of this?"

Policeman Kearney had had his back turned to Guiteau when the assassin fired Kearney's first shot and Kearney's first thought at hearing the noise was that a small boy playing outside the depot had exploded a firecracker in honor of the president. He turned to see Guiteau fire the second shot. Guiteau then dashed in front of the officer, heading for the Sixth Street exit, and the waiting cab that would take him to jail. Kearney lunged for him, grabbing the squirming little man, yelling: "In God's name, what did you shoot the president for?"

The assassin slipped through Kearney's grasp and dashed out the exit, but a station employee grabbed him and held him until Kearney caught up to Guiteau and took a firm hold of his arms. Guiteau fought wildly to free himself from the burly policeman's hold, but he could not escape. He held up a letter, shouting: "Here! Take this to General Sherman. It explains everything!" Two men helped Kearney subdue Guiteau who stopped struggling. Said the assassin: "It's all right. Keep quiet. I wish to go to jail. Arthur (Chester A. Arthur, the vice president) is now President of the United States. I am a Stalwart of the Stalwarts." Kearney led him off to the jail as Guiteau babbled on in his false authority: "You stick to me, officer. Have me put in a third-story front at the jail. General Sherman is coming down to take charge. Arthur and all these men are my friends. I'll have you made chief of police!"

President James A. Garfield and Charles Julius Guiteau.

After hiding in the Baltimore and Potomac train station on July 1, 1881, Guiteau spotted President Garfield and Secretary of State James G. Blaine; he then rushed forward and shot Garfield in the back. Blaine is at right.

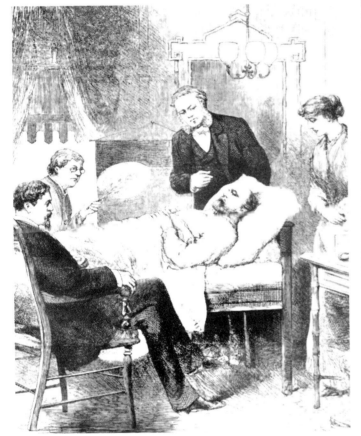

Garfield died from Guiteau's bullets two months later.

Guiteau captured and, right, admiring himself in his cell.

The hanging of Charles Julius Guiteau on June 30, 1882.

"What does he mean?" one of the men accompanying Kearney asked the policeman.

"The man's a lunatic," grunted Kearney as he dragged Guiteau along. "That's what he means."

Inside the station, Blaine knelt at Garfield's side, saying: "My poor president." Garfield was conscious but in great pain. Mrs. White, the station attendant, sat on the floor, holding Garfield's head in her lap. Dr. Smith Townsend, the district health officer, appeared on the run, dashing into the station only four minutes after the shooting, brought there by officers. He ordered police to move the crowds surrounding the president outside. Next Townsend gave Garfield spirits of ammonia and some brandy and he seemed to revive somewhat. There was very little blood in evidence from his wound. A mattress was brought and Garfield was placed on this.

The presidential entourage, when hearing the news, poured back into the station, making the place even more crowded. Police had to clear the spectators, friends, and cabinet members away from Garfield so he could breathe. Mrs. Garfield was not present. She was in New York, planning to meet her husband later. Garfield complained of a "prickly" feeling in his right leg and foot. The president's son Harry, age sixteen, ran from the train when he heard the news and knelt at his father's side, weeping and wringing his hands. "Did you see who shot my father?" he asked Mrs. White, who was still cradling Garfield's head.

"Yes," she replied, "and he has been caught."

"Somebody will pay for this!" the boy cried out.

The president was removed to private offices in the station where Dr. Townsend examined his wound, probing the bullet hole in the president's back with his finger, this in an age when sterilization was unknown. Noting there was little blood, Townsend felt that Garfield might be hemorrhaging internally, but he said reassuringly to the president: "I don't believe the wound is serious."

Garfield, weak and pale, unable to lift his arms now, smiled weakly and said: "Thank you, doctor, but I am a dead man."

A few minutes later a swarm of physicians came into the office and then a squad of hospital attendants placed Garfield on a stretcher and carried him to an ambulance outside. A large escort of mounted police clattered along with the rolling ambulance as it made its way toward the White House. Thousands ran to Pennsylvania Avenue when hearing the news to see the ambulance. Guards ran ahead of the president's stretcher into the White House, looking frantically about, believing that another assassin might be lurking inside. All of this precaution, of course, was much too late. Garfield was taken upstairs and put to bed. His physicians gave him a shot of morphine and did little else. Mrs. Garfield arrived later, rushed to Washington by special train. She remained at her husband's bedside and he seemed to rally when she appeared.

Troops were alerted and squads of heavily armed soldiers patrolled the White House grounds. Other troops were moved into the city in the initial belief that the shooting was part of a conspiracy to overthrow the government. By that time, the assassin, Guiteau, was cowering in a cell in the Washington Prison. Troops guarded this building against the crowds of angry citizens who gathered outside, many demanding that Guiteau be lynched. The letters Guiteau had written were examined by officials who were baffled at their contents. General Sherman denied ever having heard of Guiteau.

On July 3, 1881, doctors finally examined Garfield thoroughly, discovering that the bullet had entered between the tenth and eleventh ribs. It had passed on the right of his spinal column, puncturing the lower right lobe of the liver and lodged in the front of the abdomen where an aneurism or sac had been created. The aneurism had allowed the blood to continue circulating and had prolonged Garfield's life. Any attempt to remove the bullet, physicians concluded, would prove fatal. No operation was planned. General Grant wired the White House that if nihilists

were behind this shooting, the culprits should be executed immediately.

Officials also examined Guiteau, asking him if he had accomplices. "Not a living soul," he replied with a strange smile, seemingly proud that he had carried out his deed alone. "I have contemplated this thing for the last two weeks." His brother, John Guiteau, was located and he coldly informed authorities that Charles was insane and that he expected that Charles would end up in a lunatic asylum. This was echoed by Guiteau's brother-in-law, who claimed that Guiteau had once tried to kill his own sister and that he had been examined by a number of physicians over the years and had been declared insane.

Meanwhile, President Garfield's condition worsened a little each day, but he clung to life until Sept. 19, 1881, when, after complaining of pain in his heart, he died at 10:35 p.m. In Washington, the hatred for Guiteau had mounted as each day's newspapers reported the Garfield's gradual decline. Every day abuse was heaped upon the madman in print until thousands of citizens and soldiers openly demanded that he be executed without trial. The assassin's life was prolonged thanks to Garfield's valiant struggle to survive the lethal bullet. Weeks before the president died, soldiers guarding the prison decided that Guiteau should be shot before trial. Several drew lots and it fell to a trooper named Mason to shoot the assassin as soon as he looked from his cell window into the courtroom. When Mason saw Guiteau at the window, he fired a rifle but the bullet missed its mark, smashing into the wall next to the window.

Guiteau was found cringing in his cell, screaming to warders: "What do these men mean? Do they want to murder me?" He was moved to another cell with a window that looked into a transom and was less accessible than the first. Following Garfield's death, Guiteau was scheduled for trial which opened on Nov. 14, 1881. Guiteau pleaded not guilty on the grounds of insanity that had been brought about by "divine power." The prosecution established a good case of premeditated murder. Prison officials testified that Guiteau had appeared at the Washington Prison weeks before the shooting to inspect the premises and that he had pronounced that it was "an excellent jail." Prosecution witnesses included many doctors who said that Guiteau was sane and was feigning insanity. Other witnesses stated that the assassin talked about "divine inspiration" in killing Garfield only *after* he had shot the president so that he could use this as an excuse for insanity. Guiteau himself claimed that he was temporarily insane for a month, but that he had regained his senses.

Guiteau's conduct in court was anything but sane. He ranted and raved about politics and life in general, suddenly erupting with invective and vituperation. He jumped up repeatedly to label prosecution witnesses "dirty liars." Several times he ran in front of the prosecution table to point his finger at the prosecutor and scream that he was "a low-livered whelp," and "an old hog!" After the holiday season, Guiteau again appeared in court and, unsolicited, jumped up to state to the presiding judge: "I had a very happy holiday!"

Defense lawyers underwent constant abuse from their client who interrupted their pleadings, summarily firing them almost every day and then rehiring them minutes later. He insisted upon making his own summation to the jury after his lengthy trial. He frothed at the mouth as he spat out the words: "God told me to kill!" He then blamed the president's doctors for murdering Garfield. Then he shrieked: "Let your verdict be that it was the Deity's act, not mine!"

The jury returned a verdict of Guilty and recommended the death penalty. Guiteau again jumped up and wagged his finger in the direction of the jury box, yelling: "You are all low, consummate jackasses!" He was removed to his cell. He hid beneath his blankets for days, terrified of nightmares. He then penned his memoirs, which officials later described as "gibberish." On the morning of June 30, 1882, Guiteau had regained his composure. He relished the idea of being the center of attention on his day of hanging. He polished his shoes, trimmed his beard, and ate a large meal. While forking great mouthfuls of food during his last meal, Guiteau carried on an argument with God, rebuking and correcting the Deity. He was then led from his cell to the scaffold in the courtyard of Washington Prison.

On the scaffold, Guiteau cried and whimpered. He then held up his hand as the hangman approached, asking for some time to read something he had written for the occasion. The indulgent officials permitted him to withdraw a large sheaf of papers from his coat. Guiteau announced that he was about to read his "masterpiece," a long poem which he had entitled "I am Going to the Lordy." He read the poem, the rope was placed about his neck, and he was sent through the trap door to his death. Thousands had gathered outside the jail at the hour of Guiteau's execution and when they heard that he was dead, a great cheer rang out.

REF.: Alexander, *The Life and Trial of Guiteau, The Assassin; Assassination of President Garfield;* Alger, *From Canal Boy to President, or The Boyhood and Manhood of James A. Garfield; The Assassin's Doom; The Attempted Assassination of President Garfield;* Bell, *Assassin!; CBA;* Caldwell, *James A. Garfield, Party Chieftain;* Cassity, *The Quality of Murder;* Churchill, *A Pictorial History of American Crime; The Crime Avenged, or Guiteau on the Gallows;* Donovan, *The Assassins of American Presidents;* Duke, *Celebrated Criminal Cases in America;* Dunmire, *The Married Life of Charles Julius Guiteau; The Great Guiteau Trial;* Griffiths, *Mysteries of the Police and Crime;* Guiteau, *Autobiography; Guiteau's Confession; Guiteau's Crime; Guiteau Trial;* Hyams, *Killing No Murder;* Lester, *Crime of Passion; Life and Assassination of President Garfield;* Lustgarten, *Story of Crime;* Melville, *Famous Duels and Assassinations;* Mencken, *By the Neck;* Nash, *Almanac of World Crime;* ____, *Bloodletters and Badmen;* Ogilvie, *History of the Attempted Assassination of James A. Garfield;* Paine, *The Assassin's World;* Pearl, *The Dangerous Assassins;* Ridpath, *Life and Trial of Guiteau;* Rosenberg, *The Trial of the Assassin Guiteau;* Russell, *Blaine of Maine, His Life and Times;* Smith, *The Life and Letters of James Abram Garfield;* Williams, *Heyday for Assassins.*

Garland, Augustus Hill, 1832-99, U.S., lawyer. Served in the lower house of the Confederate Provisional Congress from 1861-64, and in the Provisional Senate from 1864-65. In 1867, he was elected U.S. senator, but was forbidden to take his seat. He was governor of Arkansas from 1874-76, U.S. senator from 1877-85, and was appointed U.S. attorney general from 1885-89. REF.: *CBA.*

Garland, Wallace Graydon (AKA: The Wizard), c.1903- , and **Mason, Arnold Caverly,** c.1906- , U.S., consp.-fraud. Wallace Garland, a 1925 graduate of Yale, held the patent on an automatic traffic signal and its manufacture. He created the Automatic Signal Corporation in 1927. However, he also set up other overlapping firms that fraudulently increased the value of the device. Between 1932 and 1935, salesmen peddled stock from one of the companies, the Public Service Holding Corporation. Yale Professor Irving Fisher, an economist, was suckered into the swindle, investing $300,000 of his own money and, along with others, losing a total of $3 to $5 million.

On Mar. 18, 1937, Garland, along with Arnold Caverly Mason, a 1928 Yale graduate, Walter M. Barr, David Dubrin, Harold Klein, Harry Klein, Arthur Elliott Myers, Louis Fraino, George Henriques, Russell Van Wyck Stuart, William C. Toomey, Joseph Winfield, Harvey W. Sieg, and David Weinstein were found Guilty on forty-three counts of conspiracy and mail fraud. On Mar. 25, Garland was sentenced to two years in prison. On May 6, Arnold Mason received a suspended sentence and was put on probation for one day. The others each received sentences ranging from one year and one day to three-and-a-half years in prison. Federal Judge John C. Knox said Garland was "an enthusiast" who was "less worldly wise than the other defendants." REF.: *CBA.*

Garlick, Edward Donald, 1937- , Brit., mur. Edward Garlick and his first wife made a suicide pact and she died from gas poisoning. Garlick was tried for her murder and acquitted.

Sometime later, on Oct. 11, 1962, he spotted 16-year-old Carol Ann White standing by a telephone booth. When he talked with the girl, she kidded him about his lack of sexual experience. The two went for a walk in a nearby field in West Drayton, near the London Airport, where he sexually molested and stabbed the girl. The next evening, Garlick, his second wife, two children, and their dog were walking to his mother's home. During their walk, the dog ran into the field where White's body lay. Garlick ran after the dog and "accidentally" stumbled over her body. He reported to police, but after questioning, Garlick confessed and led police to where he had buried the knife used in the attack.

Garlick was convicted of murder and sentenced to life in prison in February 1963.

REF.: Butler, *Murderers' England; CBA;* McKnight, *The Murder Squad.*

Garner, Stanley, prom. 1902, and **Answera, Louis (AKA: Vander),** prom. 1906, Brit., fraud. Using the trading name of Ashurst Meadows, & Co., a Belgian confidence man, Louis Answera, teamed up with Stanley Garner to bilk hundreds of British investors through a cleverly arranged stock fraud.

Answera secured a list of investors from legitimate brokerage houses and told them about an offer to buy into a corporate estate whose shares were being wholesaled to the public at bargain prices. Once the money was received from the investor, a share certificate would be issued bearing the suspicious name of Ashurst Meadows, & Company, which upon further investigation, was found to be nonexistent. The swindlers had long criminal records dating back to 1893. Garner was a former Liverpool solicitor who was convicted in 1894 for forgery and misappropriation of funds. He had served eight years of penal servitude before his arrest for the Ashurst fraud.

Captured and charged with fraud, Garner was sentenced to five years in prison, while Answera received a one-year prison term. Later, Answera was deported to Belgium. REF.: *CBA.*

Garner, Vance, and **Johnson, Will,** and **Hunter, Jack,** and **Richardson, Bunk,** prom. 1905., U.S., mur. One evening in the spring of 1905, Sarah Jane Smith, a white widow who lived near Gadsden, Ala., attended a show in Gadsden with her two sons. Unable to find them later, she started home alone and was attacked along the road less than a mile from the town. She reportedly called for help and when Vance Garner heard her cries, he investigated and found a man standing over her body. Garner said he was told to leave. Later he was held along with Will Johnson, Jack Hunter, and Bunk Richardson on murder charges in the Gadsden jail. Outside, a mob gathered and screamed for vengeance. Only the arrival of military reinforcements prevented a lynching.

Garner, Johnson, and Hunter were convicted of murder charges and given the death penalty. On Dec. 29, 1905, as Garner and Hunter stood at the scaffold, Hunter said he was guilty and the others were innocent. Hunter and Garner, nevertheless, were hanged, and Johnson was given a temporary reprieve. Meanwhile, Richardson, who had testified against the others, was held in Gadsden to await a hearing by a grand jury. When the locals learned of Johnson's reprieve, they were furious. On Feb. 11, 1906, twenty-five armed and masked men broke into the jail and took him three blocks away to the Nashville and Louisville bridge, where they lynched him. REF.: *CBA.*

Garnier, Gilles, prom. 1573, Fr., witchcraft-can.-mur. In 1573, in the area around Dôle, Fr., residents were terrified by reports of a werewolf. Several children had been assaulted and, in September 1573, the local government issued a warning and a declaration that anyone who killed the werewolf would not be punished.

On Aug. 24, 1573, a 12-year-old boy was murdered in a pear orchard, and in October a 10-year-old girl was killed in a vineyard. The attacks continued. On Nov. 9, 1573, a girl was assaulted in a meadow, and on Nov. 15, a 10-year-old boy was strangled and his leg torn off. In all the cases, some of the children's flesh had been eaten. Gilles Garnier, a peasant hermit who lived in a hut near Armanges with his wife, was arrested and charged with the murders. He confessed to all of the crimes and to changing himself into a werewolf. He was tried on charges of lycanthropy, the practice of becoming a werewolf through magic or witchcraft, and convicted. On Jan. 18, 1574, he was burned alive at Dôle.

REF.: *CBA;* Masters, *Perverse Crimes In History;* Robbins, *Encyclopedia of Witchcraft;* Wilson, *Witches.*

Garrecht, Francis Arthur, 1870-1948, U.S., jur. Democratic minority leader of the House of Representatives in Washington state from 1911-13. He was nominated to the Ninth Circuit Court by President Franklin D. Roosevelt in 1933. REF.: *CBA.*

Garret, Katherine, d.1738, U.S., mur. An Indian girl, Katherine Garret worked as a servant in Saybrook, Conn. She became pregnant by a local resident, who abandoned her. She killed her new-born child and tried to hide the body but was discovered. Garret was convicted of murder and executed at Saybrook on May 3, 1738.

REF.: Adams, *A Sermon Preached on the Occasion of the Execution of Katherine Garret; CBA.*

Garret, Thomas, 1689-1718, Brit., rob. Forced into thievery because of his gambling, Thomas Garret was ultimately brought down by one of his own victims.

Born in Suffolk amid wealth, education, and ambition, Garret did not turn to gambling until he was well on his way down the straight and narrow. After an apprenticeship to a Suffolk hardware dealer, his father financed the son's own hardware business. Garret then married and had a son. And then he started gambling.

Soon enough, Garret had lost his savings, his marriage, and his business. Thievery was a logical next step, so he left Suffolk for the streets of London and the life of a highwayman. Ambushing lone riders at night, Garret stole money and jewelry—anything of value to support his gambling habit.

One night at a rural inn, the innkeeper gave Garret and his partner a tip. He told them he was keeping a large purse in his safe for one of his lodgers. Would they like to be introduced? Not one to turn down an easy mark, Garret went along with the game. The next morning the three men left the inn together for London. A few miles into the trip, the highwaymen drew their guns and demanded the purse, thanked their victim, and rode off. Realizing he had been the victim of a conspiracy, the man rode back to the inn.

Tricking the innkeeper with a manufactured story—he said the two men had helped him on the road when his horse went lame and he wanted to thank them—he got the highwaymen's names and addresses.

Back in London, he paid Garret a visit. All he wanted, the man explained, was the £100 Garret had borrowed from him the night before. Fearing exposure, Garret obliged him. So, too, did his partner when the man went to him for another £100.

In London's pubs and whorehouses, Garret heard the story of the two highwaymen who were taken by their own victim. Fearing that his name would be mentioned or that it already had been, his guilty conscience began to get the best of him, and he began making mistakes, one of which led to his capture in the act of stealing money, jewelry, and a silver plate from a home in Kent.

His life of thievery bought him the gallows on Mar. 14, 1718. REF.: *CBA;* Smith, *Highwaymen.*

Garrett, Joao Baptista da Silva Leitao de Almeida, 1799-1854, Port., rebel. Participated in the 1820 liberal revolution, and fled to Great Britain and France during the war years from 1823-32. He founded the Portuguese national theatre. REF.: *CBA.*

Garrett, Patrick Floyd (Pat), 1850-1908, U.S., law enfor. off. Raised in Louisiana, Patrick Garrett was one of six children. His parents died shortly after the Civil War and, at eighteen, in 1869, Garrett went west to seek his fortune. He worked as a cattle driver in the Texas Panhandle and later became a buffalo hunter. While working in Texas, Garrett killed his first man. Near Fort Griffin, Texas, in November 1876, Garrett got into an argument with Joseph Briscoe, a burly Irish skinner. Garrett made a derogatory remark about Briscoe washing his clothes in a stream and both men got into a wild fistfight. Briscoe was a short, squat

man and Garrett was six-foot-four-inches tall. He easily bested the mule skinner but Briscoe grabbed an ax and raced toward Garrett who, in turn, lifted his rifle and fired into Briscoe's chest. The mule skinner died a few minutes later with Garrett standing over him, tears running down his ruddy cheeks.

New Mexico lawmen, standing: W.S. Mabry, Frank James, C.B. Vivian, Ike P. Ryland; sitting: Jim East, Jim McMasters, and Pat Garrett, 1884.

The plains-hardened Garrett, who had become an expert with a gun, arrived in Sumner, N.M., driving cattle. Here he got a job tending bar and later opened a small cafe. He married in 1879, but his teenage bride died of illness and Garrett married again. While tending bar and running his restaurant, Garrett also spent a considerable amount of time gambling, and at the tables he met most of the young cowboys who later became gunslingers involved in the infamous and bloody Lincoln County War. One of these was Billy the Kid. The two became so close that they were known as Big Casino and Little Casino, nicknamed after their sizes and because they were constantly playing casino poker.

When the Lincoln County war erupted between warring cattle barons, Billy the Kid and his friends shot and killed several gunmen who had murdered John Tunstall, the Kid's former employer and mentor. In 1880, Garrett was elected county sheriff with specific instructions to halt the bloody war and, most importantly, bring Billy the Kid, his former friend, to justice. So Garrett and his deputies set out after the Kid's gang and, in early December 1880, Garrett and others encountered Tom O'Folliard on the trail in Lincoln County, N.M. O'Folliard was riding to join the Kid at the time, and once he spotted the posse, he fired his Winchester several times in a running gunfight with the pursuing lawmen before outdistancing them.

Garrett, in December 1880, had just delivered some prisoners to Puerto de Luna, N.M., when he encountered a boisterous Mariano Leiva in a store. Leiva saw Garrett, by then a noted lawmen, and began stomping about the store, snarling: "No gringo can arrest *me!*" He then went to the street and shouted for all to hear, particularly the patient, tight-lipped Garrett: "By God, even that damned Pat Garrett can't take me!"

Garrett stepped onto the porch of the store, faced his antagonist, and pushed him into the street. Leiva went for his gun, firing a single bullet that went wild. Garrett drew his six-gun and snapped off two shots, one missing Leiva, the other ploughing into Leiva's left shoulder, smashing the blade. The would-be gunman was thrown over a saddle and led to jail. He was later fined $80 for attempting to murder Garrett.

In an effort to capture Billy the Kid and his gang, Garrett and a number of lawmen moved into the post hospital at Fort Sumner. One of the Kid's riders, Charlie Bowdre, had a wife who lived at the post, and Garrett was expecting that Bowdre and the others would soon ride into Fort Sumner to visit the woman. He was correct. On the evening of Dec. 19, 1880, Billy the Kid, accompanied by Charlie Bowdre, Tom O'Folliard, Billy Wilson, Tom Pickett, and Dave Rudabaugh, rode into the post. Garrett, Lon Chambers, and others stepped onto the porch of the hospital and saw O'Folliard and Picket riding ahead of the Kid and the other rest of the riders.

"Halt!" shouted Garrett and at that moment O'Folliard drew his six-gun and began blazing away at the lawmen. Garrett and Chambers fired back simultaneously and a bullet stuck O'Folliard in the chest. He and Picket, along with the Kid and the others behind him, turned their horses about and galloped away. Picket was wounded and Rudabaugh's horse later died from a wound. But the gang escaped, riding pell-mell from the post, except for O'Folliard, who suddenly wheeled his horse about and trotted back to face the lawmen. O'Folliard shouted: "Don't shoot, Garrett! I'm killed!"

Barney Mason, one of the deputies, aimed his six-gun at the wounded O'Folliard, saying: "Take your medicine, boy."

Garrett stopped him from shooting and ordered O'Folliard: "Throw up your hands! Surrender!"

"I can't raise my arms," O'Folliard said weakly as he rode slowly forward. He then fell from his horse into the arms of the lawmen, who took him to the hospital where he was put on a couch and doctors told him he had a fatal wound. A bizarre scene then ensued with Garrett and his deputies sitting at a nearby table, playing poker, while talking to the dying O'Folliard, asking him to name the members of the gang.

"Tom," Garrett told him, "your time is short." He then asked for the names of the gang members.

Replied O'Folliard: "The sooner the better. I will be out of pain." He then moaned out the names of his fellow outlaws: The Kid, Wilson, Rudabaugh, Pickett and Bowdre. O'Folliard also gave Garrett the locations of the Kid's hideouts. About half an hour later he died. O'Folliard would later be buried in a common grave with Bowdre and Billy the Kid.

Four days later, on Dec. 23, 1880, with the knowledge of the identities of the gang and their hideout, Garrett led a large posse to a rock house at Stinking Springs, N.M. The lawmen surrounded the crumbling rock house and Garrett gave orders that when the Kid stepped from this structure in the morning, he was to be shot immediately. By this time, Garrett knew that Billy the Kid was lethal and that asking him to surrender was a futile gesture. The next morning Charlie Bowdre, who was about the same size as the Kid, stepped from the rock house. From a distance, he appeared to be the Kid and Garrett raised his rifle, a signal which caused the posse to open a withering fire. Bowdre was hit twice in the chest and sent reeling back through the door of the rock house. Someone inside the house slammed the door shut and gunfire began to pour from its windows.

Then Billy Wilson could be heard to call out to Garrett that Bowdre was dying and that he wanted to step outside. Garrett shouted back that Bowdre should step from the rock house with his hands up. Suddenly, Bowdre was shoved outside by the vicious Billy the Kid, who screamed to his friend: "Kill some of the sons-of-bitches before you die, Charlie!" Bowdre, clutching his chest and bleeding heavily, could only stagger forward blindly. He fell into Garrett's arms. The lawman put the dying outlaw on his own bedroll where Bowdre murmured: "I wish—I wish—I wish." He then died.

The Kid and his men then tried to pull some of their horses tied up outside to the doorway of the house, but Garrett shot and killed one horse and the outlaws abandoned this attempt. Gunfire was exchanged periodically between the outlaws and the posse until Garrett shouted: "How are you doing, Kid?"

The Kid replied: "Pretty well, but we have no wood to get breakfast."

Shouted Garrett to his former friend: "Come out and get some. Be a little sociable."

There was no reply. Garrett stared at Bowdre's corpse and told other lawmen that he felt bad about the youth's death. Then he told his men to make several fires and begin cooking bacon and other food. This was done and the thick odor of the food being made wafted to the rock house. A white handkerchief on a stick

Billy the Kid, shot by Pat Garrett in 1881.

was then waved from a window and Rudabaugh stepped outside to ask for food. Garrett, after some discussion, told Rudabaugh that if he and the others surrendered, they would be well fed and go unharmed. The Kid and the others slowly stepped from the rock house and surrendered. The Kid was taken to Lincoln and locked up, but he later shot his way to freedom, killing two of Garrett's best deputies while Garrett was away on official business.

Garrett now set out to get the Kid, accompanied by Tip McKinney and Frank Poe. They rode into Fort Sumner on July 14, 1881, following a tip that the Kid was hiding with friends at the post.

Several accounts had it that when entering the crowded old fort, Garrett and the Kid actually passed each other, but neither recognized the other. That night, Garrett approached Pete Maxwell, a friend of the Kid's, asking if the Kid was in the vicinity. He entered Maxwell's house and went into the bedroom, sitting on the bed and questioning Maxwell. The room was unlighted and the door opened. The Kid stood there, framed in the light from the hallway. He had just left his sweetheart and had come to Maxwell to ask for the key to the meat locker so he could prepare a steak.

The Kid was in his stocking feet and wore no hat. He had a butcher knife in his hand in preparation of cutting the steak. A six-gun was jammed into his waistband. Maxwell, cowering on the bed, whispered to Garrett in the darkness: "That's him."

Billy stood squinting into the dark room, unable to see its occupants but knowing someone was there after hearing Maxwell speak to Garrett in hushed tones. Said the Kid: "Quien esta? Quien esta?" ("Who's there? Who's there?") He pulled out his six-gun and stepped into the room. Garrett fired a single shot which slammed into the Kid's chest. Then Garrett dove to the floor, expecting the Kid's six-gun to spit. The lawmen fired another shot as he leaped, but the bullet went wild. Maxwell ran from the room and Garrett followed him. The Kid lay on the floor, silent forever. His body was removed a short time later and he was buried the next day in the common grave holding Charlie Bowdre and Tom O'Folliard.

Lawman Pat Garrett, on white horse, bringing in Billy the Kid.

The killing of Billy the Kid brought Garrett fame and criticism. He was lauded for ridding Lincoln County of its most ferocious murderer, a youth who claimed to have killed twenty-one men. But the manner in which Garrett shot his quarry caused him severe criticism, especially from the supporters of Billy the Kid and those who never knew the vicious killer and had romanticized his bloody actions. In truth, he was a cheap, illiterate, back-stabbing slayer who shot from ambush and killed seemingly without cause. To those who idolized his legend, the Kid was the victim of a traitorous friend. Garrett claimed the reward for the Kid and even had to hire a lawyer to obtain this cash. The Republican Party refused to renominate him for sheriff and Garrett went into ranching, establishing operations near Fort Stanton in 1884.

Later, working for a special branch of the Texas Rangers, Garrett chased outlaws along the Texas-New Mexico border. He later supervised operations for other ranchers, established another ranch near Roswell that failed, and then tried to launch an irrigation scheme in the Pecos Valley that did not work. In 1890 Garrett ran for the office of sheriff in Chaves County, but was rejected by voters, a defeat that left him embittered. He moved to Uvalde, Texas, and set up a horse ranch. There he befriended

a political powerhouse named John Nance "Cactus Jack" Garner, later vice president in the Franklin D. Roosevelt administrations (1933-41). Garrett was elected a county commissioner in 1894, with Garner's help.

In 1896, Garrett was called back to the six-gun when Judge Albert J. Fountain and his young son disappeared and were presumed to be mysteriously murdered in White Sands, N.M.

Sheriff Pat Garrett, 1898.

Garrett became sheriff of Dona Ana County with the specific assignment of tracking down the killer of the Fountains. These murders reportedly stemmed from a dispute over a huge cattle empire and were apparently carried out by Jim "Deacon" Miller. Although Garrett suspected Miller, an independent gunman for hire and killer of dozens of persons, he could prove nothing. The Fountain case remained unsolved.

While still sheriff of Dona Ana County, Garrett and four other deputies rode out to a ranch near Wildy Well on July 13, 1898, to arrest Oliver Lee and James Gilliland, who stood accused of murder. The Lee ranch, which was about thirty miles south of Alamogordo, was well-guarded and, as the lawmen approached, a ranch hand gave the alarm. The posse members, advancing on the house, were blasted by heavy gunfire from Lee and Gilliland after Garrett had ordered the pair to surrender. Garrett received a slight wound in the side and his deputy, Kent Kearney, was mortally wounded. So intense was the gunfire from the well-barricaded Lee and Gilliland that the lawmen were forced to retreat in disgrace. Both men later surrendered, but they were acquitted after a widely publicized trial.

This disgrace, coupled with his failure to find the killer of the Fountains, caused Garrett to lose his job as sheriff of Dona Ana County. He later opened a livery stable in Las Cruces, N.M., then moved to El Paso, Texas, where he was made a customs inspector through special appointment of President Theodore Roosevelt, again with the help of John Nance Garner. He refused another appointment in 1905 and began ranching again near Las Cruces. Pressed for cash, Garrett began leasing some of his best acreage. Some of this land was leased by Wayne Brazil (or Brazel) for cattle. When Brazil moved herds of goats onto the land, Garrett said that he had violated their agreement and threatened to shoot Brazil unless he removed the goats. This led to a bitter feud.

On Feb. 29, 1908, Garrett met with Jim "Deacon" Miller and Carl Adamson, who claimed that they would lease the land Brazil had been leasing. This was an apparent ruse. Miller, the suspected killer of the Fountains twelve years earlier, had apparently been brought in to murder the stubborn Garrett. Garrett, Adamson, and Brazil then rode together to inspect the land in question. Miller rode a circuitous route and lay in ambush about four miles outside of Las Cruces. When Garrett stopped his buggy to relieve himself, a bullet suddenly smashed through the back of his head and exited above the right eye. He spun around and another bullet tore into his stomach. The lawmen fell to the earth, dead. Brazil later reported that he and Garrett had quarreled and both had drawn their six-guns and Brazil had killed the lawman. Miller, however, was the real killer. Neither Brazil nor Miller were ever tried for the murder. See: **Billy the Kid; Lincoln County War; Miller, James B.**

REF.: Alldredge, *Cowboys and Coyotes;* Argall, *Outlawry and Justice* in Old Arizona; Bancroft, *Works of Hubert Howe Bancroft, Vol. XVII*; Benton, *Cow by the Tail*; Blacker, *The Old West in Fact*; Boylan, *The Old Lincoln County Courthouse*; Boynton, *The Rediscovery of the Frontier*; Breihan, *Great Lawmen of the West*; Brent, *Great Western Heroes*; Brent, *The Complete and Factual Life of Billy the Kid*; Brothers, *Billy the Kid*; _____, *A Pecos Pioneer*; Brown, *Trail Driving Days*; Buffum, *Smith of Bear City*; Burns, *The Saga of Billy the Kid*; Callon, *Las Vegas, New Mexico*; Casey, *The Texas Border and Some Borderliners*; *CBA*; Charles, *More Tales of Tularosa*; Chilton, *The Book of the West*; Chisholm, *Brewery Gulch*; Coe, *Frontier Fighter*; Coleman, *From Mustanger to Lawyer*; Coolidge, *Fighting Men of the West*; Crawford, *The West of the Texas Kid*; Cunningham, *Famous in the West*; _____, *Triggernometry*; Dils, *Horny Toad Man*; Dobie, *Cow People*; _____, *Guide to Life and Literature in the Southwest*; Drago, *Red River Valley*; Eaton, *Pistol Pete*; Erwin, *The Southwest of John H. Slaughter*; Evans, *Adventures of the Great Crime-Busters*; Evans, *Long John Dunn of Taos*; Fable, *Billy the Kid*; Farber, *Texans With Guns*; Furgusson, *Murder & Mystery in New Mexico*; _____, *Our Southwest*; Fitzpatrick, *This is New Mexico*; Frantz, *The American Cowboy*; Fridge, *History of the Chisum War*; Fulton, *Maurice Garland Fulton's History of the Lincoln County War*; _____, *Roswell in Its Early Years*; Gann, *Tread of the Longhorns*; Gard, *Frontier Justice*; _____, *The Great Buffalo Hunt*; Garrett, *The Authentic Life of Billy the Kid*; Gaylord, *Handgunner's Guide*; Gibson, *The Life and Death of Col. Albert Jennings Fountain*; Greer, *Grand Prairie*; Gregg, *Drums of Yesterday*; Gregory, *True Wild West Stories*; Grey, *Seeking A Fortune in America*; Griggs, *History of Mesilla Valley*; Guyer, *Pioneer Life in West Texas*; Hadfield, *Picturesque Rogues*; Haley, *George W. Littlefield*; Hall, *History of the State of Colorado*; Hamilton, *The Young Pioneer*; Hamlin, *The True Story of Billy the Kid*; Hamner, *Short Grass and Longhorns*; Harkey, *Mean As Hell*; Hendricks, *The Bad Man of the West*; Hendron, *The Story of Billy the Kid*; Hening, *George Curry*; Hertzog, *Old Town Albuquerque*; Hill, *Stories of the Railroad*; Holloway, *Texas Gun Lore*; Hopper, *Famous Texas Landmarks*; Horan, *The Great American West*; _____ and Sann, *Pictorial History of the Wild West*; Horn, *New Mexico's Troubled Years*; Hough, *The Story of the Cowboy*; House, *Old Field Fury*; Howe, *Timberleg of the Diamond Tail*; Hunt, *The Tragic Days of Billy the Kid*; Hunter, *The Trail Drivers of Texas*; Hunter and Rose, *The Album of Gun-Fighters*; Hutchinson, *Another Verdict for Oliver Lee*; Hyde, *Billy the Kid*; Jenkinson, *Ghost Towns of New Mexico*; Johnson, *Famous Lawmen of the Old West*; Keleher, *The Fabulous Frontier*; _____, *Violence in Lincoln County*; Kelly, *The Sky was Their Roof*; Kemp, *Cow Dust and Saddle Leather*; Kent, *Reminiscences of Outdoor Life*; King, *Mavericks*; _____, *Pioneer Western Empire Builders*; _____, *Wranglin' the Past*; Knight, *Wild Bill Hickok*; Koller, *The American Gun*; La Farge, *Santa Fe*; Lake, *Wyatt Earp*; _____, *The Far Southwest*; Lathrop, *Tales of Western Kansas*; Lewis, *The True Life of Billy the Kid*; Lewis, *It Takes All Kinds*; Lingle and Linford, *The Pecos River Commission of New Mexico and Texas*; Looney, *Haunted Highways*; Lord, *Frontier Dust*; Love, *The Life and Career of Nat Love*; McCarty, *The Enchanted West*; McCarty, *The Gunfighters*; McGeeney, *Down at Stein's Pass*; McKennon, *Iron Men*; Mangan, *Bordertown*; Martin, *Border Boss*; Masterson, *The Tenderfoot's Turn*; Metz, *Dallas Stoudenmire*; _____, *John Selman*; Miller, *Ranch Life in Southern Kansas and the Indian Territory*; Monagham, *The Book of the American West*; Moore, *The West*; Morgan, *Shooting Sheriffs of the Wild West*; Nahm, *Las Vegas and Uncle Joe*; Neal, *Captive Mountain Waters*; Nicholl, *Observations of a Ranch Woman*; Nolan, *The Life and Death of John Henry Tunstall*; North, *The Saga of the Cowboy*; Nye, *Pistols for Hire*; O'Connor, *Pat Garrett*; O'Neal, *Encyclopedia of Western Gunfighters*; O'Neal, *They Die But Once*; Otero, *My Life on the Frontier*; Peavy, *Charles A. Siringo*; Peck, *Southwest Roundup*; Penfield, *Western Sheriffs and Marshals*; Poe, *The Death of Billy the Kid*; Preece, *Lone Star Man*; Price, *Death Comes to Billy the Kid*; Raine, *Famous Sheriffs and Western Outlaws*; _____, *Forty-five Caliber Law*; _____, and Barnes, *Cattle*; Rath, *The Rath Trail*; Rennert, *Western Outlaws*; Rhodes, *The Hired Man on Horseback*; Rhodes, *The Rhodes Reader*; _____ and Mullin, *Whiskey Jim and a Kid Named Billy*; Rittenhouse, *The Man Who Owned Too Much*; Rockwell, *The New Frontier*; Rosa, *The Gunfighter: Man or Myth?*; Ruth, *Great Days of the West*; Sabin, *Wild Men of the Wild West*; Sandoz, *The Cattlemen*; Scanland, *The Life of Pat F. Garrett*; Schaefer, *Heroes Without Glory*; Shackleford, *Gun-fighters of the Old West*; Shipman, *Letters, Past and Present*; Shirley, *Shotgun for Hire*; _____, *Toughest of Them All*; Shumard,

The Ballad and History of Billy the Kid; Siringo, *History of Billy the Kid*; _____, *Riata and Spurs*; _____, *The Texas Cowboy*; Sonnichsen, *Alias Billy the Kid*; _____, *Ten Texas Feuds*; _____, *Tularosa*; Stanley, *Antonchico*; _____, *Dave Rudabaugh, Border Ruffian*; _____, *Desperadoes of New Mexico*; _____, *Fort Stanton*; _____, *The Private War of Ike Stockton*; _____, *The White Oaks*; Steckmesser, *The Western Hero in History and Legend*; Sterling, *Famous Western Outlaw-Sheriff Battles*; Stone, *Twenty-four Years a Cowboy and Ranchman in Southern Texas and Old Mexico*; Sutton, *Hands Up!*; Thorp, *Story of the Southwestern Cowboy*; Timmons, *Twilight on the Range*; Turner, *These High Plains*; Waller, *Last of the Great Western Train Robbers*; Wallis, *Cattle Kings of the Staked Plains*; Walters, *Tombstone's Yesterdays*; Waltrip, *Cowboys and Cattlemen*; Waters, *A Gallery of Western Bad Men*; Watson, *A Century of Gunmen*; Wellman, *The Trampling Herd*; West, *Billy the Kid*; White, *The Autobiography of A Durable Sinner*; White, *Lead and Likker*; _____, *Trigger Fingers*; Williams, *Pioneer Surveyor, Frontier Lawyer*; Wilson, *Out of the West*; Wooten, *Women Tell the Story of the Southwest*; (FILM), *Billy the Kid*, 1930; *Billy the Kid*, 1941; *The Outlaw*, 1943; *I Shot Billy the Kid*, 1950; *Last of the Desperadoes*, 1956; *The Left-Handed Gun*, 1958; *The Man Who Killed Billy the Kid*, 1967; *A Few Bullets More*, 1968; *Chisum*, 1970; *Dirty Little Billy*, 1972; *Pat Garrett and Billy the Kid*, 1973.

Garris, John (Gareis, Hans J.K.), 1913-49, U.S., (unsolv.) mur. Opera singer John Garris, a native of Frankfurt-am-Main, Ger., appeared in concert performances in Germany as a pianist, conductor, and accompanist. In 1941, he traveled to the U.S. with Lutz Uhlfelder, his coach. He also changed his name from Hans J.K. Gareis to John Garris.

On Apr. 20, 1949, the opera's last night in Atlanta, 36-year-old Garris checked out of his hotel room about 6 p.m., attended the opera as a spectator, and at about 11 p.m. checked his baggage on a train. He was sighted around 3:30 a.m. on the train, about the same time a warehouse guard heard a shot near an alley. Garris was not seen again until a man found his body about 7:30 a.m. He was lying in an alley, shot through his left side.

The murder was a mystery to police. The singer was not robbed and, according to his coach, Garris was a "modest, quiet person with a very sweet disposition who had no enemies." Police theorized that he might have interrupted a burglary. Later on the day of the murder, a paroled convict was arrested in Clinton, S.C., as the main suspect in the case. After a high-speed chase, Grover (Tojo) Pulley, forty-four, was stopped by police, who found burglary tools and a gun that fired bullets similar to the one that killed the opera performer. The parolee also said he had been in Atlanta the evening of Apr. 20 and early morning of Apr. 21. Although Pulley was convicted and sentenced to ten years in South Carolina for possession of burglary tools, ballistics evidence did not indicate that the bullet that killed Garris was fired from Pulley's gun. Pulley's alibi was also substantiated by several credible witnesses. REF.: *CBA*.

Garrison, Donald Graham (or Donald Luther Garrison, AKA: Cool Hand Luke), 1916- , U.S., rob. Expert safecracker Donald Garrison, who stole between $4 and $5 million, was imprisoned a total of thirty-two years since 1932. He was first arrested as a 17-year-old when police stopped him near Tampa, Fla., for not having proper license plates. After spending six months in prison, he was again arrested in Indiana for transporting stolen chickens. He was released on Nov. 22, 1941, on a technicality—to charge a suspect with a crime, he had to be arrested within 200 feet of the scene of the crime and Garrison had traveled thirty-five miles before he was stopped.

Garrison, the subject of the 1967 film *Cool Hand Luke*, first changed his name to "Luke" while living in his native Salem, Ind. "I just liked the name," he said. "I was the only Don in Salem, Ind., and I always felt like a sissy with that name." Garrison acquired the second part of his colorful moniker, "Cool Hand," because of his reputation as an expert safecracker. He had gained experience by working for the Mosler Safe Company.

Garrison's third stay in jail was the one on which the movie, starring Paul Newman, was based. The safecracker was imprisoned in a Leesburg, Fla., prison where he worked in a chain gang before escaping. He also escaped from the Ohio State penitentiary in 1945, and estimated that he committed another 1,000 crimes while free. His unchecked activity came to a halt in 1951 when he was arrested in Palatka, Fla., for passing on a curve. He was sent back to Ohio to spend two more years in prison.

The dauntless Garrison was well-known at the Leesburg prison and he later made a name for himself at the Cummins Farm State Prison in Arkansas from 1955-62. There, he helped bring abuse of inmates to light, a practice which was investigated and became the basis for a book and the 1980 movie *Brubaker,* starring Robert Redford. Garrison later said he thought Cummins was the toughest prison he had ever served in because, "...that's where they separate the men from the boys. Life ain't worth a nickel there."

In the late 1970s, Garrison was again arrested for possession of federal money orders worth $227,000. He was convicted and sentenced to four years in prison. He was freed on a mandatory release from the Federal Correctional Institute in Lexington, Ky., on Sept. 2, 1980, and in the spring of 1981, the 65-year-old Garrison was living in a Jacksonville, Fla., half-way house.

REF.: *CBA; Pearce, Cool Hand Luke.*

Garrity, Wendell Arthur, Jr., 1920- , U.S., jur. Nominated to the District Court of Massachusetts by President Lyndon B. Johnson in 1966. He participated in the U.S. Judicial Conference's standing committee on the administration of criminal law from 1969-75. In 1975, he wrote "The Rule of Law Is Not Self-sustaining" for the American Bar Association's *Bar Leader.* REF.: *CBA.*

Garrow, Robert, 1940-78, U.S., pris. esc.-mur. In 1973, the body of 18-year-old Philip Domblewski of Schenectady, N.Y., was discovered tied to a tree in the Adirondack Mountains with a knife in his chest. When Robert Garrow was apprehended for the murder eleven days later, he was shot and his injuries caused a partial paralysis. During his trial a year later, Garrow confessed to seven rapes and to the murders of two more, 22-year-old Daniel Porter of Concord, Mass., and 21-year-old Susan Petz of Skokie, Ill. He also admitted strangling 16-year-old Alicia Hauck of Syracuse, N.Y. He was convicted for the Domblewski murder and sentenced to twenty-five years to life imprisonment.

In September 1978, Garrow was serving his time in Fishkill Correctional Facility in Beacon, N.Y., in a building for disabled and elderly prisoners. There, he was confined to a wheelchair, but the 38-year-old managed to escape the medium-security facility. He was located several days later on Sept. 11. Guards saw him lying near an interstate highway and ordered him to stay where he was. Garrow ignored the command, shooting at the guards and wounding 25-year-old Dominic Arena in the leg. Guards then shot and killed the escapee. REF.: *CBA.*

Garside, William, and **Moseley, Joseph,** prom. 1834, Brit., mur. About 1831, William Garside and Joseph Mosely were working as cotton-spinners at Hyde in Cheshire. After an argument about wages with their employer Mr. Ashton, they shot Ashton's son. They were arrested three years later when an acquaintance informed on them. They were convicted, and hanged on Nov. 25, 1834.

REF.: Bleackley, *Hangmen of England; CBA.*

Garsson, Murray, 1890-1957, and **Garsson, Henry M.,** b.1894, and **May, Andrew Jackson,** 1875-1959, U.S., consp.-brib. Brothers Murray Garsson and Henry Garsson masterminded a scheme to win munitions contracts from the U.S. government during WWII by enlisting the help of a powerful congressman, Andrew Jackson May. In 1941, Henry, who worked for a trustworthy company, used some of the firm's letterhead to write to the U.S. War Department. He proposed that a business he owned, Erie Basin Metal Products, Inc., a company that did not really exist, manufacture 4.2-inch mortar shells. The government placed an order and the brothers formed a partnership with two Chicago factory owners, Allen B. Gellman and Joseph Weiss, to produce the shells. Gradually, the government awarded the Garssons more contracts, paying them $78 million by the end of the war.

The Garssons and May were indicted on Jan. 23, 1947, when suspicions were aroused because of the brothers' close ties to May, who had served as chairman of the House Military Affairs Committee. The 71-year-old congressman was suspected of accepting bribes in return for securing government contracts for the Garssons. The three were brought to trial, where the Garsson brothers were accused of paying $53,634.07 in bribes to May, and they all faced conspiracy and bribery charges. On July 3, 1947, all three were convicted. On July 5, each received a sentence of eight months to two years in prison. No fines were levied because, explained Judge Henry A. Schweinhaut, "there has been no showing that any one of them have any substance—financial means that is." After appeals were denied, all three began serving time in December 1949. After nine months, 75-year-old May was paroled on Sept. 18, 1950, from the Federal Correctional Institute in Ashland, Ky. The Garssons were paroled in 1951, after about a year and a half in the Federal Penitentiary in Danbury, Conn. REF.: *CBA.*

Gartside, John Edward, c.1923-c.47, Brit., mur. On about May 20, 1947, a well-to-do 44-year-old and his wife were shot after apparently startling a burglar. Percy Baker, a representative for a shoe manufacturing firm, and his wife, Alice, lived in a secluded area of the Pennine Mountains. Their naked bodies were found buried not far from their home.

On May 22, John Edward Gartside, claiming to be Percy Baker, contracted with a furniture dealer in Yorkshire to sell a load of furniture for £300. While the dealer was at the Bakers' house loading the furniture, one of the Bakers' friends dropped by to visit. The dealer told her the Bakers' were separating and selling the furniture. Suspicious, the friend went to the police. Police discovered that eight of the Bakers' suitcases had been delivered to a store rented by Gartside.

After questioning, he finally admitted that he had buried the bodies and showed police where they were located. Gartside maintained that the Bakers were having a fight when he arrived, that Baker accused his wife of seeing another man, and that she grabbed a poker. Gartside said Baker shot his wife and then, when he struggled with Baker for the gun, it accidentally fired, hitting Baker. Gartside said he then shot the dying Baker twice more to end his pain. When Gartside went to trial at the Leeds Assizes in July, however, the jury did not believe his tale, which was not substantiated by the evidence. He was convicted on murder charges and hanged.

REF.: *CBA; Harrison, Criminal Calendar;* Shew, *A Companion to Murder.*

Garvan, Francis Patrick, 1875-1937, U.S., lawyer. Named alien property custodian in 1919. His purchase of some 4500 German patents in that capacity was upheld by the U.S. Supreme Court seven years later. He was appointed U.S. assistant attorney general in 1920. REF.: *CBA.*

Garvey, Marcus Aurelius, 1887-1940, U.S., fraud. Marcus Garvey preyed upon his fellow blacks, promising that he would lead all seven million Negroes in the U.S. in the early 1920s back to Africa where he would set up an independent state that provided everyone a life of ease. This would, of course, cost money, and Garvey charged all those who wished to accompany him to the promised land—some place he called the African Republic—a country that did not exist. Garvey, who had immigrated to the U.S. from England in 1914, settling in New York's Harlem, was well educated and took advantage of illiterate, gullible blacks in one swindle after another. His migratory swindle, however, gleaned him millions.

He appointed himself president of the African Republic and also bestowed upon himself many other titles, such as "admiral." Donned in extravagant uniforms, Garvey was chauffeured about in limousines and lived the high life, staying in expensive hotels and supporting several mistresses. All of this was funded by his tens of thousands of followers who poured money into Garvey's coffers, believing that he was buying up large ocean liners so all American blacks would have decent transportation to the new land. Garvey called his mythical steamship company the Black

Star Line, and he sold stock in this bogus firm, taking in millions of dollars, issuing certificates, but never buying a ship.

So powerful and well-known did this bold hustler become that he was invited to speak before the League of Nations. Garvey, bedecked in his shimmering admiral's uniform, fulminated before the world's leaders for more than an hour, lecturing them on the need for the Black Republic. Just where this country was to be located remained a mystery to his listeners and to Garvey himself.

Con man Marcus Garvey who defrauded his fellow blacks of millions.

In 1922, the U.S. postal authorities put together a solid case of fraud against Garvey and, in the following year, he was convicted of mail fraud and subsequently sent to the federal penitentiary in Atlanta to serve five years. Garvey's hollow companies collapsed while he was in prison, causing more than 100,000 blacks to lose everything they had invested. Upon Garvey's release, the con man was deported to his native Jamaica where he lived out a life of comfort, enjoying the several million dollars he had smuggled out of the country just before his arrest.

REF.: *CBA*; Nash, *Hustlers and Con Men*.

Garvey, Mike, and **Lesher, Harvey**, and **Rohan, Phil**, prom. 1927, U.S., (wrong. convict.) mur. On Nov. 1, 1927, the owner of a drug store in Los Angeles, Mr. Miles, was found lying on the floor of his shop, his head bleeding. An autopsy later revealed that he could have died from a blow to the head or from falling. When police arrived, the druggist's father said his son was bound with wire, and money was missing from the cash register.

During the investigation, police talked with 10-year-old Eddie Yates, who said he saw three men enter the store and later come out with a bag. The child identified Mike Garvey, Harvey Lesher, and Phil Rohan in police lineups and the three were questioned. Additionally, Howard C. Walton, a bootlegger, told police that the three men had been drinking at his house and that a drunken Lesher had asked, "Why did I kill him?"

The three suspects were indicted on murder and robbery charges on Dec. 20, 1927. During the trial, which began Jan. 9, 1928, they protested their innocence, saying that all three of them had been at Lesher's home, more than three miles from the scene of the crime. Their relatives and friends corroborated their alibi. However, they were convicted on Feb. 11, 1928, and sentenced to life in prison at San Quentin Penitentiary.

They began serving their sentences, and then two defense attorneys, William T. Kendrick and William T. Kendrick, Jr., took the case, pressing for a more thorough investigation. A grand jury determined that Eddie Yates had not arrived at the drug store until the ambulance showed up, and that his identification was

mere fancy. Walton, the bootlegger, retracted his testimony, saying that he wanted Garvey and Lesher arrested because he thought they were going to threaten his bootlegging business. The grand jury also found evidence that the druggist may not have been bound, and that money might not have been stolen. In all probability, the druggist fainted and fell, hitting his head. On June 20, 1930, after spending nearly two-and-a-half years behind bars, all three of the convicted men were granted full pardons by Governor C.C. Young. Rohan received $1,692 in restitution, but Garvey and Lesher were not compensated because the California Board of Control claimed that they had been engaged in criminal activities previous to their arrest. REF.: *CBA*.

Garvie, Mervyn, c.1907- , Aus., rape-mur. In 1946 Mervyn Garvie, a transient, lived in a wooden hut at Sandon Point, not far from Sydney, Australia. He stopped at a house one day asking for water, and said he was going to try to get work at a coal mine in the neighborhood.

Some time later, on Aug. 28, a couple drove to Sandon Point, a secluded spot for young lovers. Garvie approached the car, and when he looked through the windshield, Cecil Kelly opened the car door and asked him what he wanted. Garvie hit Kelly on the head with a steel bar, then attacked Kelly's fiancée. The girl, a model, had gotten out of the car before Garvie hit her with the bar, knocking her unconscious. He then raped her before dragging her back inside the car where he raped her five more times during the night. The next morning he put Kelly's body back in the car, soaked the car with gas, set it on fire, and then rolled the car in the direction of a cliff. The girl, whom Garvie thought was dead, was able to roll out of the fiery car. She reported the crime to the police and they located Garvie, who was working at the coal mine. He was tried, convicted, and sentenced to life in prison. While he was serving his sentence, he was killed by another inmate. REF.: *CBA*.

Garvie, Sheila, See: **Tevendale, Brian**.

Garvin, Edward Louis, 1877-1960, U.S., jur. Appointed to the Eastern District Court of New York by President Woodrow Wilson in 1918, and served as a justice on the New York State Supreme Court from 1941-60. He was the trustee for the National Probation Association. REF.: *CBA*.

Garwood, Robert R., c.1946- , U.S., sex asslt.-milit. des. Stationed in Vietnam with only two weeks of service left, 19-year-old Robert Garwood, a jeep driver, was captured by the Vietnamese near Da Nang in September 1965. Fourteen years later, Garwood contacted a Finnish businessman in Hanoi, saying that he wanted to return to the U.S. He arrived in the U.S. in March 1979, amid an outcry from prisoner of war survivors who alleged that Garwood had turned into a "white Vietnamese" during his years in the prison camp. Garwood, a native of Adams, Ind., was accused of violating the Code of Military Conduct and charged with desertion and collaboration with the enemy—the first soldier serving in Vietnam to face such charges. A five-man military jury, all Marine Corps officers and Vietnam veterans, tried 34-year-old Garwood, a Marine Pfc. Although his lawyer contended that Garwood went insane and became a "white Vietnamese" as a result of torture and deprivation during his imprisonment, the jury convicted Garwood on Feb. 5, 1981, of assaulting a fellow prisoner, serving as an armed guard at the prison camp, interrogating POW's, indoctrinating POW's and urging them to join the enemy, acting as an interpreter during political indoctrination meetings for the POW's, and informing on his fellow POW's. In early February, the court reduced his rank to private, dishonorably discharged him from service, and revoked all military pay from the date of conviction.

Later that month, on Feb. 23, Garwood was indicted on charges of sexual misconduct involving a child. On Aug. 7, 1980, Garwood allegedly took a 7-year-old Onslow County, N.C., girl to buy an ice cream cone. He was charged with first-degree sex offense, attempted rape, attempted first-degree sex offense, and taking indecent liberties with a child. During his trial, Garwood's lawyer argued that Garwood had been on his way to an appointment at the time of the alleged incident. On May 16, 1981, Garwood was acquitted of all charges. REF.: *CBA*.

Gary, Carlton, 1952- , U.S., rob.-asslt.-rape-mur. In the fall and winter of 1977 and 1978, the elderly female population of Columbus, Ga., was terrorized by the stocking strangler—the as yet unidentified Carlton Gary. Although Columbus was once a plantation town, and thus no stranger to crime, the level of brutality in the serial murders was more befitting nearby Atlanta. Ferne Jackson, the first victim, was found bludgeoned, raped, and strangled with one of her own stockings on Sept. 16, 1977. Little more than a week later, on Sept. 24, 70-year-old Jean Dimenstein was found in the same condition just four blocks from Jackson's home. The next victims were 89-year-old Florence Scheible, 69-year-old Martha Thurmond, and 74-year-old Kathleen Woodruff—all of whom were murdered before the year's end. The murders continued on Feb. 12 with the death of 78-year-old Mildred Borom. On Feb. 15, the county coroner announced that hair fibers found at the scenes of the crimes identified the killer as a black male. As a result, racial tensions flared; the Ku Klux Klan had threatened reprisals against the black community if the murders continued.

In 1970, 18-year-old Carlton Gary was without a home. He had spent most of his adolescence alone or in transit between relatives in Georgia, Florida, and Virginia. Rejected by his father and abandoned by his mother in favor of lovers, the highly gifted Carlton, suffering from congenital disorders, was growing up to become one of the most brutal serial killers in U.S. history. His confession in July 1970 to the murder of Nellie Farmer in Albany, N.Y., revealed the beginning of a murder and violence spree that would not end until 1983.

Having committed his first crime in 1968, Gary had an established criminal record by his twenty-first birthday. By 1973 he had been charged with robbery, assault, breaking-and-entering, and arson. Serving five years in prison for his part in the Albany robbery/rape/murder of Farmer, he was paroled in 1975 to continue on the path of destruction that often found him in and out of jail. In 1977 he escaped from a New York prison and fled home to Columbus, Ga., setting up housekeeping with a female sheriff's deputy one month before the first Columbus strangling occurred. During the winter of 1977-78, Gary and the police officer lived happily together while the brutal strangling spree ravaged the community.

In April 1978, Gary left Columbus and was convicted the following year for a series of robberies in Columbus and in South Carolina. In 1983, six years after the Columbus "Stocking Strangler" murders had ended, Gertrude Miller, who had been attacked by Gary four days before the first stocking strangling, made a positive identification that led to Gary's being convicted of murdering Florence Scheible, Martha Thurmond, and Kathleen Woodruff.

Gary never received a sentence for the 1970 murder of Nellie Farmer in Albany, a murder that was a prelude to things to come. The Farmer case remains unsolved and is considered open. In August 1986, Gary was sentenced to die and today sits on death row in Jackson, Ga. Court appeals are expected to continue for several years before he reaches the electric chair. REF.: *CBA*.

Gary, Elbert Henry, 1846-1927, U.S., lawyer. Chicago attorney who served as DuPage County judge from 1882-90. After entering the steel business in 1898, he guided the United States Steel Corporation from 1903-27. Gary, Ind., was named after him. REF.: *CBA*.

Gary (Ind.) Police Department, prom. 1979-81, U.S., pol. mal. Charles Boone, who served as Gary police chief from 1973-79, faced income tax evasion charges in which he was accused of not paying taxes on $20,000 of police money that he was said to have misappropriated for his personal use. He stood trial twice, but both ended in hung juries and the charges were dropped. During the second trial, he said he had been framed by dishonest Gary officers, including former Acting Police Chief Virgil Motley and Symeon Colquitt, former head of the narcotics unit. Boone

denounced them, saying the officers had sold confiscated firearms and drugs for profit; his charges led to a two-year investigation that began in 1979.

Investigators found evidence that Gary officers might have been involved in a high school prostitution ring, murder, selling or trading guns, and selling drugs. In 1981, a grand jury criticized the department for lax record keeping, but cleared Motley and Colquitt. Although the grand jury found no evidence of organized corrupt actions, it said the two officers had acted with gross negligence. Eleven others, including seven police officers, were indicted on gun and drug charges, and the grand jury made several recommendations. They suggested establishing evidence-keeping procedures, eliminating the narcotics squad, creating a clear chain of command, and raising pay to increase morale. REF.: *CBA*.

Garza, Catarino, 1856-97, U.S.-Mex., rebel. Born in Spain in 1856, Catarino Garza immigrated to Mexico and, in the 1880s, moved to Texas. He was well-educated and a glib speaker who could quote classic works. He was also fast with a gun and reportedly had several gun fights before he began publishing the Spanish newspaper, *El Correo*, in San Antonio. He was arrested for libel but was acquitted.

Garza announced his opposition to the dictatorship of Porfirio Diaz, president of Mexico, in 1891. He put together an armed force of more than 300 Mexicans and Mexican-Americans and led raids into Mexico and the U.S. He was charged with violation of international laws and a price was placed on his head by both U.S. and Mexican

Gunman and revolutionary Catarino Garza.

authorities. Garza later went to Cuba where he attempted to combat the oppressive regime of General Weyler. He was killed by Spanish troops in 1897, although some reports have him being killed in a revolution he led in Nicaragua.

REF.: Bartholomew, *The Biographical Album of Western Gunfighters*; *CBA*; Hunter and Rose, *The Album of Gunfighters*.

Garza, Isuaro, prom. 1900s, U.S., drugs. Police suspected Isuaro Garza of delivering to Chicago marijuana that had been smuggled across the Rio Grandeo. After staking out Garza's home in Kenosha, Wis., U.S. customs agents from Laredo, Texas, searched a visitor to the house. After finding on the man a package that contained marijuana, the officials obtained a warrant to search Garza's house. Secreted in his attic and closets, they found 720 one-pound parcels of marijuana, worth $720,000 in retail value. At the time, the seizure was the largest ever in the U.S. Garza was convicted and sentenced to five years in prison.

REF.: *CBA*; Whitehead, *Border Guard*.

Gasca, Pedro de la, 1485-1567, Spain, jur. President of Peruvian Court of Justice from 1547-50; defeated the rebellion by Quito governor Gonzalo Pizarro in 1548. REF.: *CBA*.

Gascoigne, Sir William, c.1350-1419, Brit., jur. Acted as chief justice of the King's Bench in 1400. According to Shakespearean legend, he imprisoned the future King Henry V after Prince Hal hit him for disciplining a friend. REF.: *CBA*.

Gash, Stanton, c.1949- , U.S., wrongful death. On Apr. 5, 1981, eleven-year-old Kathy Kohm disappeared while jogging in the subdivision where she lived in Christmas Lake Village, Ind. Her body was found on June 11, 1981, about a mile from her home. She had been shot once in the head and her body was partially buried under some brush. A former fire fighter, 31-year-old Stanton Gash was suspect in the case. On Apr. 5, his car had been mired in mud on a logging trail about 100 yards from where the child's body was discovered, and it was pulled from the mire that same day. Although police did not have enough evidence to charge Gash with murder, they charged him with wrongful death in a civil suit. Gash was found liable and fined $5,000 in damages. REF.: *CBA*.

Gas House Gang, prom. 1890s-1900s, U.S., org. crime. There have been many "gas house gangs" throughout the U.S. in the last 150 years but the most notorious operated in New York City for approximately two decades, centering activities in and around East 35th Street, its members to be found along Third Avenue from 11th to 18th Streets. This gang concentrated on extortion from local businesses, robbery, and the operation lowlife brothels. The gang's specialty was robbery and its expert footpads could be counted on to commit between thirty and forty armed holdups each night in its fiercely protected territory. Its members were absorbed into Paul Kelly's sprawling Manhattan gang empire by 1910. See: **Kelly, Paul**.

REF.: Asbury, *The Gangs of New York; CBA;* Fried, *The Rise and Fall of the Jewish Gangster in America;* Haskins, *Street Gangs;* Lewis, *The Apaches of New York*.

Gaskins, Donald Henry (AKA: **Pee Wee**), prom. 1970s, U.S., mur. Described by South Carolina law enforcement officials as the "meanest man in America," Donald "Pee Wee" Gaskins was remembered in different terms by his bemused neighbors in Prospect, a town of 500 located in rural South Carolina. Local residents chuckled at the mention of his name. As his nickname, Pee Wee, suggested, Gaskins was "comic," five-foot-three-inches tall with a foul temper. There was nothing amusing about Gaskins, however, especially after the police began digging up bodies in his own "personal graveyard."

Prior to the disappearance of a Florence County teenager in October 1975, Pee Wee drove around town in a hearse. No one paid much attention when he said he had started a graveyard in the woods in back of a wheat field near his home. Then police began investigating and found human bones buried a few feet below the surface. Gaskins had murdered at least nine people. The victims were locals who had angered him for one reason or another. Johnny Sellers, for example, was shot in the back because he owed some friends of Gaskins a small sum of money. Jesse Judy, who was with Sellers, was also killed.

Gaskins confessed to the murders of the nine people, including Avery Leroy Howard, Dennis Bellamy, Doreen Dempsey, and her child. Placed on trial for the stabbing death of 45-year-old farmer Silas Barnwell Yates, he was sentenced to life in prison on Apr. 27, 1977, by Circuit Court Judge Dan F. Laney, and began serving his sentence at the Central Correctional Institute in Columbia, S.C.

But not even criminals were safe from Gaskins. Convicted murderer Rudolph Tyner occupied a cell a few yards away. Tyner was serving time for the murder of an elderly couple. The stepson of the victims was not satisfied with the court-imposed sentence, however, and decided to have Tyner murdered in prison with the help of Gaskins who would be paid $400. After failing to poison Tyner, Gaskins obtained a plastic explosive known as C-4. From cell 19, he ran a wire through the air vent, telling Tyner he was installing a cell-to-cell phone system. The explosive, attached to Tyner's coffee cup, went off the instant he picked up the "phone," and killed him instantly.

"He is a back-stabbing, baby killing, mangy cur," said Jim Anders, who prosecuted Gaskins for murder the second time around. "If he were out he would kill again." Gaskins was sentenced to die in South Carolina's electric chair. At present he remains an inmate on Death Row. REF.: *CBA*.

Gasoline Trust, prom. 1935-36, U.S., consp. In April 1936, a federal grand jury began investigating the activities of eighteen major oil companies, five subsidiaries, fifty-seven company officials, and three oil trade journals. They were charged with violating the Sherman Anti-Trust Act. Charles E. Arnott, vice president of Socony-Vacuum Oil Co., was considered to have been the principal in a price-fixing plan that raised prices in Wisconsin, Illinois, Indiana, Iowa, Kansas, Michigan, Minnesota, Missouri, North Dakota, and South Dakota. The companies were accused of running two buying pools to purchase gas from small, independent refiners at artificially high prices, and then entering into long-term contracts with middlemen, selling them gas at prices determined by average prices published in *Platt's Oilgram* and the Chicago *Journal of Commerce*. They were also accused of buying extra gas.

During the trial, which began on Oct. 4, 1937, and was held in Madison, Wis., the companies argued that they were following price-fixing and stabilizing practices outlined by the New Deal and the National Recovery Administration (NRA). Prosecutors contended that the price-fixing began before the NRA, continuing after the NRA was pronounced unconstitutional, and that the companies had no authority from the U.S. government under NRA regulations. On Jan. 22, 1938, sixteen companies and thirty individuals were convicted on charges of criminal conspiracy to inflate and fix prices in 1935 and 1936. Charges against the three trade publications were dismissed.

Another twenty-two oil companies were to be tried on Sept. 26, 1938, but fourteen companies and eleven company officials pleaded *nolo contendere* in May, agreeing to pay maximum fines and court costs to avoid the cost and publicity of a trial. On June 2, 1938, thirteen firms (one merged with another) and the eleven executives were each fined $15,000 for a total of $360,000, and they divided the $25,000 in court costs. Nine other oil companies and eight administrators were still scheduled to stand trial on Sept. 26.

On July 19, 1938, the convictions were upheld for only twelve companies and five people who were originally found Guilty on Jan. 22. Each business was fined $5,000, and each individual $1,000. New trials were ordered for three firms and fifteen executives; the charges against the others were dismissed. On Mar. 11, 1939, charges were dropped against five people who were to be retried. In addition, the government dismissed charges against some of those who had never been brought to trial. On Nov. 22, 1939, the U.S. Supreme Court upheld the decision of Judge Patrick T. Stone, who presided over all the proceedings, to overturn convictions in July 1938.

After pleading *nolo contendere,* three firms and three people were fined a total of $45,000 on Dec. 12, 1940, by Judge Walter C. Lindley for their involvement in the conspiracy. Although two companies were left who were to be tried on Jan. 20, 1941, the last defendant, John W. Warner, sales manager of the Tidewater Oil Company, was fined $15,000.

From the first trial, the twelve who were eventually ordered to pay fines on July 19 included Socony-Vacuum Oil Company, Wadhams Oil Company, Pure Oil Company, Sinclair Refining Company, Shell Petroleum Corporation, Skelly Oil Company, Continental Oil Company, Mid-Continent Petroleum Corporation, Empire Oil and Refining Company, Phillips Petroleum Company, Globe Oil and Refining Company of Illinois, and Globe Oil and Refining Company of Oklahoma.

The thirteen companies who were to stand trial on Sept. 26, but pleaded *nolo contendere* and were directed to pay fines on June 2, included Socony-Vacuum Oil Company, Wadhams Oil Company, Standard Oil Company of Indiana, and Cities Service Company, as well as companies that had merged and were dropped as defendants, including Empire Oil and Refining Company, Continental Oil Company, Pure Oil Company, Shell Petroleum Corporation, Sinclair Refining Company, Mid-Continent Petroleum Corporation, Phillips Petroleum Company, Ohio Oil Company, and Skelly Oil Company.

The companies who were to go to court on Jan. 20, 1940, but opted to plead *nolo contendere* and were fined on Dec. 12, included Globe Oil and Refining Company of Illinois, Gulf Refining Company, and National Refining Company of Cleveland. REF.: *CBA*.

Gasperoni, Antonio, prom. 1814-24, Italy, rob. The village of Sonnino's reputation as a lawless and dangerous place was so pronounced that authorities at one point considered either eliminating or deporting the entire population. Bandit Antonio Gasperoni began his life as a simple and peaceful cowherd but, as a young man, fell in love with a country woman named Maria who was engaged to a violent man named Claudio. Attacked by the knife-brandishing lover, Gasperoni was able to wrest the knife from his assailant and killed him instead. Following this slaying, Gasperoni gathered together a substantial gang of outlaws and managed them with great skill. In traditional fashion, the gang lived by kidnapping wealthy people and ecclesiastics and political figures, surviving from the ransom money they extorted. As a way of convincing hesitant relatives and others of their serious intentions, the band would sometimes send an ear or hand of the victim by messenger to the family. (This technique was used again many years later in the grisly kidnapping of J. Paul Getty, III in 1973.) Remorseless about killing anyone, wealthy or poor, who got in his way, Gasperoni was generous towards the peasants who, some of them unwillingly, helped him in his battle against the law. His exploitation of rich merchants and landowners made him popular among Italy's many poor and oppressed.

With no qualms about killing, Gasperoni was nonetheless uncomfortable about the fact that he slept with his mistress without the sanction of marriage, and was in this way caught when he and his gang members were told to disarm before entering the church where he was married to his lover. As they exited from the ceremony, they were arrested by armed soldiers who waited for them; they had been betrayed by the priest. Imprisoned for life in the Civita Castellana dungeons in Rome, Gasperoni had become so well known that he was constantly visited by tourists and travelers, and was consequently given a luxurious cell where he told stories of his exploits, charging his listeners a substantial fee. See: **Getty, John Paul III.** REF.: *CBA*.

Gasre (Iran) Prison Escape, 1979, Iran, pris. esc. On Feb. 11, 1979, the Iranian government of Prime Minister Shapour Bakhtiar fell to Ayatollah Ruhollah Khomeini. According to reports, jails, prisons, and police stations that held Khomeini rebels throughout the country were stormed by armed revolutionaries when the exiled Khomeini returned to Iran. Confined in Gasre prison were two employees of Electronic Data Systems, Inc. (EDS), a computer company. According to the wealthy president of EDS, H. Ross Perot, he effected their release on Feb. 11 by paying revolutionaries to incite a mob to break into the prison, and by financing a U.S. commando team which paid the rebels and escorted the employees out of Iran.

In November 1978, the two 39-year-old EDS employees, William Gaylord and Paul Chiapparoni, were not allowed to leave Iran and were arrested Dec. 28. The 48-year-old EDS president said he first wanted to pay $12.75 million in ransom for their release, but could not because the Iranian banking system had collapsed. He then put together a commando team headed by 60-year-old Arthur (Bull) Simons, a retired Green Beret colonel who had previously led an unsuccessful mission to rescue U.S. prisoners of war near Hanoi, Vietnam. The EDS commando team consisted of fifteen members, thirteen of them EDS employees, primarily men who had formerly served in the military and had combat experience. After two weeks of training, Perot said, part of the team was flown to Iran where they met the two freed employees at a hotel ten miles from the prison. The commandos and the two freed employees then took connecting flights to Dallas, where several hundred coworkers and family members met them on Feb. 18, 1979.

Although Dallas hailed Perot as a hero, with a sign proclaiming, "Way to go, Ross Perot," U.S. State Department officials disagreed with Perot's account of the affair. Perot claimed that the two employees were held because Iran wanted to ensure that EDS would return to set up computer systems for national health care and social security records that Iran had agreed to buy under a $41-million contract. State Department officials said that the two were imprisoned because the Shah was investigating possible fraud internally and in dealings with U.S. companies. Perot also said he gave the command to start the operation on the night of Feb.

11, but news reports said the mob attacked the prison early on the morning of Feb. 11. Additionally, Perot said the two prisoners escaped amid gunfire, but news reports said that most of the Gasre prison guards set down their guns and walked away from the prison. In late February, EDS filed a $23-million breach of contract complaint, charging that Iran owed more than $5 million in back payments. REF.: *CBA*.

Gaston, William, 1778-1844, U.S., jur. U.S. representative from 1813-17, and later served on the North Carolina Supreme Court from 1833-44. REF.: *CBA*.

Gates, Daryl F., 1926-   , U.S., law enfor. off. Serving as chief of the Los Angeles Police Department for more than ten years, Daryl F. Gates innovated the first program ever used in the United States to teach children in schools how to resist peer pressure to experiment with narcotics.

Born in Glendale, Calif., in 1926, Gates graduated from the University of Southern California and became a rookie on the Los Angeles Police Force on Sept. 16, 1949, spending the next several years rising in the ranks until he was made chief of police in 1978. The forty-ninth officer to serve as police chief since the department's beginnings in 1869, Gates was responsible for policing the 1984 summer Olympic Games in L.A., which concluded without incident. Serving on many professional and educational associations, Gates was president of the L.A. County Peace Officers' Association, and advisor and author for the National Advisory Commission on Civil Disorder, as well as consultant and chairman for the International Association of Chiefs of Police.

Gates introduced the first program, DARE, to bring police officers into public schools in order to teach children how to resist peer pressure to use drugs; the DARE program is now used throughout the country. He also initiated the first SWAT (Strategic Weapons and Tactical Units) team; the L.A. SWAT team became an international model. Gates is a recognized authority on civil disorders, terrorism, and applications of air support. REF.: *CBA*.

Gates, Rick L., 1955-   , U.S., mansl. On Jan. 4, 1987, the Conrail locomotive driven by engineer Rick L. Gates collided with an Amtrak passenger train near Baltimore. Sixteen people died and more than 175 were injured. Admitting that he was high on marijuana at the time, and had ignored warnings that might have prevented the disaster, Gates pleaded guilty in February 1988 to a single count of manslaughter. Tried and convicted, he was sentenced to a five-year jail term in Towson, Md. REF.: *CBA*.

Gatley, Clement Carpenter, 1881-1936, Brit., jur. Wrote *The Law and Practice of Libel and Slander in a Civil Action* in 1924. REF.: *CBA*.

Gatlin, Alma Petty, prom. 1928, Case of, U.S., mur. A North Carolina father, Smith T. Petty, reputedly was a heavy drinker and a wife-beater. In 1927, Petty, of Reidsville, was murdered by a family member. The children later said their mother had killed their father in self-defense before she lapsed into a coma and died. Then in May 1927, after a Baptist minister, the Reverend Thomas F. Pardue, preached about repentance, Alma Petty Gatlin, one of the surviving Petty children, confessed to the clergyman that she had murdered her father with an ax and put his body in a trunk in their cellar. The preacher then went to police. Petty's body was discovered and the daughter was put on trial in Wentworth in February 1928. During the trial, Gatlin's siblings argued that their mother had killed their father, and Gatlin's lawyer questioned the propriety of a confidential confession being used as evidence in court. The jury acquitted Gatlin. REF.: *CBA*.

Gatti, Salvatore, and **Sberna, Charles**, prom. 1937, U.S., rob.-mur. During a parade in New York on Sept. 23, 1937, three robbers walked into the Rudisch Refining Company, a Manhattan firm which kept stores of gold and platinum. The armed intruders, Salvatore Gatti, Charles Sberna, and one other accomplice entered the office and tied up owner Louis Rudisch and four other employees. Meanwhile, the owner's father-in-law, Max Statz, escaped and found a policeman, John H. Wilson, who immediately rushed to the building. The officer was shot in the head, abdomen, and heart by all three criminals. The injured officer dropped his gun on the floor, and one of the robbers accidentally overturned a container of hot wax, spilling some on Wilson's gun. When the robber who had upset the wax tried to pick up the officer's gun, he instantly dropped it, and then the three criminals escaped. Wilson died that afternoon. On Sept. 24, a doctor treated Gatti for a burn on his left hand.

On Oct. 6, 1937, Gatti and Sberna were arrested and charged with murder. Gatti had previously been convicted of robbery and recently finished serving five years in Sing Sing. Sberna had an extensive police record, including sodomy and rape. Gatti was defended by Samuel Leibowitz after his mother and sister pleaded with the lawyer to take the case. The women said that Gatti had been with them on the morning of the murder and that he had burned his hand while making candy. However, when Leibowitz heard rumors that the prosecutor had Wilson's gun with Gatti's fingerprint, he confronted Gatti. Gatti still proclaimed his innocence, so Leibowitz agreed to continue on the case after Gatti signed a document releasing the lawyer from the case if Gatti's fingerprint appeared on the gun. The prosecutor delayed letting Leibowitz see the gun, and after the trial began the court refused to release the attorney from the case. During the trial, Gatti said Sberna was not guilty and he confessed to being at the scene of the crime. Gatti and Sberna were both convicted, sentenced to death, and executed in the electric chair. Gatti was the only one of Leibowitz's clients ever to be executed during his twenty-one year practice. Leibowitz's part in the case was debated for years by legal professionals. REF.: *CBA.*

Gauchet, Georges, 1905- , Fr., rob.-mur. In the fashionable Montmartre section of Paris, Georges Gauchet spent his entire inheritance from his well-to-do father, and his mother soon tired of financing her errant son. In 1930, when he was twenty-five years old, Gauchet attempted to set himself up by living off women, some of whom were prostitutes, but the scarcity of tourist business that summer did not support his plan, and by fall he was penniless. One early evening in November, he went to a jewelry store on the Avenue Mozart, in Auteuil, close to where his father had once owned a pastry shop. Attacking the owner with a wrench, Gauchet forced him into the back of the shop and bashed him with a mallet, finally murdering him with a revolver. Filling his pockets with watches and other jewelry, Gauchet returned to Montmartre by taxi, and hawked the stolen goods in bars, rather than taking them to a regular fence. An informer turned Gauchet in, and he was sent to jail at the Santé prison.

REF.: *CBA;* Heppenstall, *Bluebeard and After.*

Gault, Julian, prom. 1901, Brit.-Fr., rob.-mur. During a visit to London, the Marquis of Anglesey brought a case filled with about £150,000 worth of jewelry with him, as was his custom. He was accompanied by a French valet, Julian Gault, and stayed at the Walsingham House Hotel. During the stay, Gault talked with a French girl who was actually a jewel thief. He fell in love with her and she persuaded him to steal his employer's gems. On Sept. 10, 1901, while Anglesey went to a theater, Gault stole about £30,000 in jewelry, joined the girl outside the hotel, and went with her to a Chelsea apartment. Saying that she was leaving to make arrangements to get rid of the loot, the girl fled with her real lover. Several days later, Gault attempted to cross the Channel at Dover and was arrested. He was tried, convicted for his part in the theft, and sentenced to five years in prison. The French woman and her paramour fled to Brazil. After persistent, investigation, the jewels were recovered in Paris and returned to the Marquis.

REF.: *CBA;* Dilnot, *Great Detectives and Their Methods.*

Gaunt, Elizabeth, prom. 1685, Brit., treas. Taking pity on James Burton when he was being hunted for his participation in the Rye House plot, an alleged scheme to assassinate King Charles II and his brother James II, Elizabeth Gaunt sheltered the fugitive in her home until she was able to arrange an escape for him to Holland. Two years later, Burton returned to England to take part in the Monmouth rebellion against James II; when this political intrigue failed, Burton again took refuge at Gaunt's home. When Burton was caught, Elizabeth was charged with high treason.

The indictment was brought against her with the complicity of the man she had protected, who turned King's evidence against her and was granted a pardon to do so. The despicable Burton not only swore against Gaunt, but even arranged for his daughter and wife to give false evidence to support his mendacious story. Sentenced to be burned at the stake, Gaunt made a last speech, saying, "I did but relieve an unworthy, poor distressed family and lo I must dye for it," adding that her blood "will be found at the door of the furious judge" and "at the door of the unrighteous Jury who found me guilty on the oath of an outlawed man."

Gaunt's spirit and bravery provoked compassion and respect. William Penn, a famous Quaker who was at the execution, described how "She laid the straw about her for burning speedily, and behaved in such a manner, that all the spectators melted in tears." In Thomas B. Macaulay's history of England, he writes of his revulsion at the unjust sentence she suffered and of the "terrible day" when Gaunt was killed. She was the last woman executed in England for a political offense.

REF.: *CBA;* O'Donnell, *Should Women Hang?*

Gauntlett, Roger A., 1943- , U.S., child abuse. Roger A. Gauntlett was forty-one when he pleaded no contest to one count of first-degree criminal assault of his stepdaughter on July 12, 1984. The case was tried in Kalamazoo, Mich., and was assigned a third judge, Robert L. Borsos, after it was disclosed in 1983 that the judge who originally heard the case, John E. Fitzgerald, planned to permit Gauntlett to avoid prison by putting up $2 million for a rape counseling center. Along with a second circuit court judge, Fitzgerald disqualified himself from the case.

On Jan. 30, 1984, Borsos ordered Gauntlett to undergo five years of treatment with Depo-Provera, a drug which diminishes sexual aggressiveness by suppressing testosterone, the male hormone. Used voluntarily on an experimental basis by sex offenders for the last fifteen years, Depo-Provera is approved in the U.S. for use in certain types of cancer treatments. Although banned for use as a contraceptive in the U.S. by the Food and Drug Administration, Depo-Provera is used for contraception in other countries. Side effects of the drug include itching, loss of scalp hair, fatigue, nervousness, backache, and weight gain. Judge Borsos ordered Gauntlett's treatment to begin thirty days from the date of sentencing, and also ordered the convicted man to pay $25,000 in court costs. REF.: *CBA.*

Gauthe, Gilbert, c.1945- , U.S., porn. Reverend Gilbert Gauthe ministered to two parishes until his conduct with young boys was questioned. When Reverend Gerard Frey, Bishop of the Lafayette Diocese, challenged Gauthe in 1974, Gauthe confessed that he had engaged in "imprudent touches" with a young man, but that he would not take improper liberties again. In 1975, Bishop Frey made Gauthe the chaplain of the diocesan Boy Scouts. After parents lodged more complaints against Gauthe, the priest was transferred in 1977 to a third parish, St. John's Church in Henry, La., located near the Gulf of Mexico in a region that was largely Catholic. He served both Henry and Esther, communities populated by oil field workers and farmers.

Accusations against Gauthe again surfaced, and he was dismissed from his post in June 1983 and sent to a Catholic-run psychiatric hospital in Connecticut. When the first charges in Henry were made, the community was fiercely split, some believing that the church should not be criticized publicly. During Gauthe's trial in 1985, he was charged with thirty-four counts of molestation. Lawyers for the parents of the abused children claimed the priest mistreated as many as seventy children. Pleading guilty by reason of insanity, Gauthe admitted that he participated in oral sex and sodomy with girls and boys, including some altar boys. He said he frequently photographed the incidents, which took place in a confessional, the rectory, his van, and at a camp.

After a charge of aggravated rape was dropped, the 40-year-old Gauthe pleaded guilty to eleven counts each of child pornography, contributing to the delinquency of a minor, and crimes against nature. On Oct. 14, 1985, he was sentenced to twenty years at hard labor with the stipulation of no parole. The church acknowledged liability in the case and paid substantial sums in settlements, including $1 million to an 11-year-old boy in 1986, and $1.55 million to a former altar boy. REF.: *CBA*.

Gaveston, Piers (Earl of Cornwall), c.1284-1312, Brit., assass. Foster brother of British King Edward II, who appointed him Earl of Cornwall in 1307. He was named regent of the kingdom in 1308, while Edward went to France to marry the daughter of Philip IV. He was banished three times for insolent behavior and extravagant spending by British barons. He secretly returned to Britain in 1311, and was pardoned by Edward. He was kidnapped by the Earl of Warwick in 1312, and executed. REF.: *CBA*.

Gaviria, Pablo Escobar, See: **Escobar Gaviria, Pablo.**

Gay, Jean-Baptiste-Sylvère (Vicomte de Martignac), 1778-1832, Fr., lawyer. Appointed attorney general of Limoges in 1819, served in the Chamber of Deputies from 1821-32, and named counselor of state in 1822. From 1828-29, as minister of the interior, he attempted to reconcile the government with the people, but was removed by the king for favoring the reformist movement. REF.: *CBA*.

Gay, Marvin Pentz, Sr., c.1913-   , U.S., mansl. A family argument led to the killing of 44-year-old singer Marvin Gaye by his father. The singer, who had added an "e" to his name, hit the top of the record charts often during the 1960s and early 1970s. His seventeen Top 10 hits included: "I Heard It Through the Grapevine," "Got to Give It Up," and "Let's Get It On." However, Gaye apparently did not feel that his father appreciated his success. An attorney and friend of Gaye's, Curtis Shaw, claimed that Gaye wanted to show his father how successful he had become.

With pressures between father and son still unresolved, the younger Gaye moved into his parents' home in early 1984 because he was concerned about his mother's health. On Apr. 1, 1984, Marvin Gay, Sr., seventy, became angry because he could not locate a letter from an insurance company. Upstairs, in a second-floor bedroom of the home, his 69-year-old wife, Alberta, was talking with their son. The father, a retired minister, began shouting at his wife, telling her to help him look for the letter. The son objected, telling him, "You can't talk to my mother that way." The argument escalated, and when the father went upstairs to the room, Gaye shoved him, forcing him out. The father went downstairs where he picked up a handgun, returned upstairs and shot his son, who fell against a wall. The father stepped toward his injured son and shot him a second time. At an arraignment in September 1984, the 71-year-old Gay pleaded no contest to voluntary manslaughter. On Nov. 2, 1984, he was placed on probation for five years by Judge Gordon Ringer, who explained a prison sentence would nearly be a death sentence for the elderly man. REF.: *CBA*.

Gaydon, Jonathan (AKA: Charles Wilson), prom. 1857-79, Brit., mur. Murdering an elderly woman when he was a youth, Jonathan Gaydon escaped, joined the army, and deserted, finally turning himself in to the police twenty-two years after he had committed the crime.

On June 21, 1857, Gaydon was hiding in Chingford in the house of his father's friend, Mr. Small, planning to burglarize the place, when Small's sister, Mary White found him. Gaydon murdered the woman and escaped. When the body was discovered, Gaydon was the immediate suspect, and a reward was offered for his arrest, but was never claimed. Gaydon wandered around England until hunger forced him to join the army, where he served for six years under the name Charles Wilson. Deserting and becoming a wanderer again, Gaydon went to a Horsham police officer in the fall of 1879 and turned himself in, explaining that he had murdered White twenty-two years earlier. Prosecuted by Harry Poland, Gaydon was defended by Justice Avory, and was first sentenced to death, but later reprieved. REF.: *CBA*.

Gayles, Joseph (AKA: Socco the Bracer), 1844-73, U.S., org.

crime. Joseph Gayles, known as Socco the Bracer was the main enforcer for the Patsy Conroy gang which dominated the East River wharves in New York in the 1860s and 1870s. Gayles prowled the area armed with guns and knives, and was alleged to have murdered more than twenty men. A man of vicious temperament, he once drowned a man for not taking enough loot in a successful raid. On the night of May 29, 1873, Gayles and two cohorts, Bum Mahoney and Billy Woods, tried to ransack the cargo ship *Margaret*. But they woke the crew, who forced them off the ship and back into their boat. Police fired on them as they neared the shore. Gayles was shot in the chest, and suddenly became added weight for his two colleagues, who were trying to out-row their pursuers. As they were deciding whether to keep him or toss him overboard, Gayles died. He was quickly disposed of, and his corpse floated ashore four days later near Stanton Street.

REF.: Asbury, *The Gangs of New York; CBA*.

New York mayor William J. Gaynor, center, bleeding from an assassin's bullet, 1910; when the city editor of the New York *World* received this photo, he exclaimed: "What a wonderful photo! Blood all over him!"

Gaynor, William J., prom. 1910, U.S., attempt. assass. On Aug. 9, 1910, William J. Gaynor, New York's popular and progressive mayor of seven months, was preparing to leave for a tour of Europe and had boarded the steamer *Kaiser Wilhelm der Grosse* when a discharged city dock worker opened fire, hitting Gaynor in the back of the neck and wounding Street Cleaning Commissioner William Edwards.

Leaving for Europe on the North German Lloyd Line, Gaynor was on the upper deck at a Hoboken, N.J., pier at 8:45 a.m. when James J. Gallagher, a city dock man who had been discharged for insolence and neglect of duty, approached Gaynor and his group and fired three times. One shot went astray, one grazed Edwards, and the other ripped through the back of Gaynor's neck. A private ambulance rushed Gaynor to St. Mary's Hospital, and Gallagher was arrested immediately.

Gallagher, who had written angry letters to Gaynor and other city department heads after being dismissed, claimed his grievance against Gaynor was that he had refused to reinstate him, taking away, according to Gallagher, his "bread and butter." Gallagher told a reporter, "I intended to kill Mayor Gaynor and I failed in the attempt, that is all." He eagerly informed the press that his favorite authors were Dickens and Shakespeare, and that he had seen the latter's plays performed by the greatest actors of the day. According to reporters, the middle-aged Gallagher had no family or friends.

Gallagher was arraigned on Nov. 30, 1910, before Common Pleas Court Judge John A. Blair in Jersey City, for carrying concealed weapons and for shooting Edwards. He protested vigorously, saying, "I didn't shoot Edwards. I shot Mayor Gaynor. Why didn't they arraign me for that?" His lawyer, Alexander Simpson, told him to keep quiet. Gallagher was tried for shooting Edwards as a precaution since, in the event that Gaynor died from his wound, Gallagher might not legally have been liable to be tried for the other indictments. The three charges were assault with intent to kill Gaynor, assault with intent to kill Edwards, and carrying concealed weapons. Gallagher pleaded not guilty. The trial, at the Court of Oyer and Terminer of Hudson County, was swift, with several alienists, (the term of the times for what is now called psychiatrist), including Dr. John Reilly, testifying that Gallagher was sane and fit to stand trial. Simpson defended his client by urging the jury to dismiss the case, since there was no evidence that Gallagher had intended to murder Edwards.

Justice Swayze, who tried the case along with Justices Carey and Blair, refused to rule that there had been no intent to kill Edwards. After forty minutes of deliberation, the jury returned a verdict of Guilty, and Justice Swayze sentenced Gallagher to twelve years of hard labor, ordering him to pay the court costs of $1,000.

Gallagher had served two years and one month of his time when, on Jan. 16, 1912, Trenton, N.J. doctors George N.J. Sommer and Paul J. Cort declared that the convicted man was in the last stages of paresis, a disease of the brain caused by syphilis of the central nervous system. Gallagher was ordered by Judge Gnichtel to be transferred from the New Jersey State Prison to the State Hospital for the Insane. He was said to be suffering from hallucinations that caused him to believe attempts to murder him were being made; his condition had deteriorated to the point where he was annoying prison officials.

REF.: Asbury, *The Gangs of New York; CBA;* Logan, *Against the Evidence;* Peterson, *The Mob;* Thomas, *The Mayor Who Mastered New York: The Life and Opinions of William J. Gaynor.*

Gbrurek, Tillie, b.1865, U.S., mur. An unattractive woman, Tillie Gbrurek, decided that a matchmaker was the surest means of finding a husband. Her marriage broker found John Mitkiewitz, who married Gbrurek because she was known to be a great cook. Gbrurek kept her job in a dark, dreary factory; her lazy, unemployed husband took her money for beer. In 1911, Gbrurek, finally fed up with Mitkiewitz after twenty-six years, punched her husband, knocked him out, and forced him to go to work.

Gbrurek soon gained a reputation in her neighborhood as a fortune teller. First she predicted the death of a dog—"ancient powers" told her it would happen. The dog died within one week, as predicted. Later, she accurately predicted her husband's death. Using the proceeds from his life insurance policy, she visited the marriage broker again. This time, the matchmaker produced John Ruskowski, a railway employee. Some months later, Gbrurek predicted his death, and he too died.

Joseph Guszkowski married Gbrurek in 1914 and died soon after. She spent four years with Frank Kupczyk before he died in 1920. An additional death occurred when neighbor Rose Chudzinski died after questioning Gbrurek about the likelihood of so many natural deaths. In October 1921, the Chicago police, hearing rumors about Gbrurek, called upon Anton Klimek, Gbrurek's latest husband, who was sick in bed. Gbrurek was urging him to get better by eating her stew. The police took him to the hospital and had his stomach pumped. The contents were laden with arsenic. Gbrurek was tried for the murders of her three previous husbands. She was found Guilty and sentenced to life in prison.

REF.: *CBA;* Hynd, *Murder, Mayhem and Mystery;* Kobler, *Some Like It Gory;* Nash, *Murder, America.*

Gearish, Anthony (Anthony Gery), 1693-1713, Brit., rob. Born in Newbury, Berkshire, Anthony Gearish began his criminal career when he served as an apprentice charlatan. He eventually fled from his con-artist teacher for the high seas, where he served on board several warships before returning to London as a burglar. Here he committed over thirty felonies, including breaking-and-entering and highway robbery.

In February 1711, Gearish was convicted of robbing Anne Noel as she traveled by coach on a London highway. Gearish received a reprieve and was freed on his own recognizance. He quickly returned to thievery and was sentenced in 1714 to Newgate Prison for stealing silver valued at 45 shillings. For the crime, Gearish was condemned to death and executed at Tyburn gallows.

REF.: *CBA;* Smith, *Highwaymen.*

Geary, Charles Russell, 1892-1935, U.S., suic.-mur. Charles Russell Geary had driven from Pennsylvania to Newark, N.J., on Sept. 18, 1935, to participate in final arrangements for Kathryn Le Van's burial, who had died three weeks earlier while visiting relatives in Easton, Pa. Her husband, Orlando Le Van, fifty-five, employed by the Pennsylvania Railroad, wanted his wife buried in a grave already occupied by Geary's mother, who had died fourteen years earlier. Geary vehemently opposed the disinterment of his mother's body necessary for this burial. The relatives, including Benjamin Le Van, forty, an unemployed brother of the widower, and John S. Geary, forty-one, a nephew who worked for an interior decorating firm, had stopped at a local beer garden to continue their discussion, and were apparently, according to witnesses, on good terms at that time, until a heated discussion of the burial site arrangements ensued.

At around 12:30 a.m., Newark Police Captain Thomas Rowe received a call at headquarters; a man informed him, "I've just murdered three men and I am going to kill myself." The man gave his address and then hung up. Police crashed through the door at the South Twentieth Street address to find the lights on in the apartment, and the bodies of John Geary and the two Le Vans sprawled on the kitchen floor, two shot in the back and one through the abdomen. In the living room was the body of Charles Geary, shot through the heart with a shotgun that lay close to the corpse. The kitchen chairs were overturned, and on the table were several bank books, indicating a discussion of finances that preceded the slaughter. Further investigation into the case indicated that Geary was angry that his aunt, Kathryn Le Van, had left him out of her will. REF.: *CBA.*

Gebbia, Leonardo, c.1890-1909, U.S., kid.-mur. Six people from the Italian section of New Orleans were tried for the kidnap and murder of 7-year-old Walter Lamana in 1907. The trials, punishment and public uproar were influential in destroying the power of the Black Hand—the turn-of-the-century Mafia—in New Orleans. Walter was abducted on June 8 from where he was playing outside his father's undertaking parlor. His father, Peter Lamana, received a ransom note demanding $6,000. When the boy was not returned, the Italian population hunted for him. Several Italians were arrested but released for lack of evidence. Then it was learned that two youths had seen Walter with a man named Tony Costa. Another boy had seen Walter being pushed into a black curtained wagon. Another had seen Ignazio Campisciano, a farmer, riding by in such a wagon. The authorities went to Campisciano's farm. There, under the threat of being lynched, the farmer revealed that Walter, being fussy in captivity, had been strangled and struck with a hatchet. Campisciano told where the boy's body was.

In the avid anti-Italian atmosphere that was building in New Orleans, a number of Italians were sought and arrested. Some had to be released, but six finally went to trial. The first trial started on July 15, 1907, for the first four defendants: Tony Costa, who actually had kidnapped the child; Frank Gendusa, who probably wrote the ransom note; and Ignazio Campisciano and his wife. The four were tried while angry mobs, determined to lynch the defendants, surged outside the courtroom. The defendants were found Guilty, but not sentenced to be executed, a fact that sent the mobs into renewed fury. The trial of 19-year-old Leonardo Gebbia and his sister Nicolina Gebbia was delayed until November, so that public fury would have a chance to die down. The two were found Guilty. Leonardo, who had probably not actively participated in the abduction at all, was sentenced to death. His sister, whose role consisted of learning about the kidnapping the day after it occurred and not telling the authorities, was sentenced to life in prison. Leonardo Gebbia was hanged on July 16, 1909.

REF.: *CBA;* Tallant, *Ready To Hang;* Wilson, *Encyclopedia of Murder.*

Gecht, Robin, c.1954- , and **Kokoraleis, Andrew C.,** c.1963- , and **Kokoraleis, Thomas,** c.1960- , and **Spreitzer, Edward,** 1961- , U.S., asslt.-kid.-rape-attempt. mur.-mur. Implicated in as many as seventeen murders, several Chicago-area cult members kidnapped unaccompanied women, and mutilated, sexually assaulted, and killed them. The ringleader was Robin Gecht, a Chicago carpenter and electrician. As a teenager Gecht had been accused of molesting his sister. He was arrested in 1980 on a charge of contributing to the sexual delinquency of a 14-year-old girl. Gecht, who at one time did construction work for John Wayne Gacy, a convicted mass murderer, hired teenager Andrew Kokoraleis to work for him. Gecht apparently found loners and people in need of jobs whom he was able to manipulate, such as Edward Spreitzer, whom he met in a doughnut shop. Thomas Kokoraleis, Andrew's brother, also joined the group, and performed cult rituals involving animal and human sacrifice and cannibalism. Police later discovered an altar in the attic of Gecht's Chicago home that had six crosses painted on the attic walls.

The young men's attacks may have begun as early as 1978, and police found evidence linking them to the killings of seven women and one man. On May 23, 1981, Linda Sutton, a 28-year-old Chicago woman, vanished. Her body was found in suburban Villa Park. On May 15, 1982, Lorraine Borrowski, a 21-year-old Elmhurst secretary, was abducted as she arrived at the office. Her body was found on Oct. 10 in brush at the Clarendon Hills Cemetery near Darien. On May 29, 1982, Shui Mak, a 30-year-old factory and restaurant worker, was attacked on her way home from Streamwood to Lombard. Her body was discovered on Sept. 30 in a field in South Barrington. On June 13, 1982, Angel York, nineteen, was picked up by a man driving a van. He handcuffed her and ordered her to cut her breast. After she made a small gash, her attacker took the knife and slashed open a larger wound. Afterward, the assailant pushed York out of the van on the north side of Chicago.

The attacks continued as Sandra Delaware, an 18-year-old with a record of prostitution, was found in Chicago on Aug. 28, strangled and stabbed. On Sept. 8, Rose Beck Davis, a Broadview housewife, was discovered strangled and beaten, left on Chicago's Gold Coast. On Oct. 6, Rafael Tirado, twenty-eight, was shot to death from a car. That same day, an 18-year-old prostitute was attacked. She had entered a van with a young man who had flashed a gun and a knife and handcuffed her hands and feet. The woman was raped and forced to swallow pills that apparently caused her to black out. Her attacker mutilated her breasts and then left the woman for dead next to railroad tracks. She survived the attack and described the van in detail. On Oct. 20, the van was spotted and 21-year-old Spreitzer and 28-year-old Gecht were questioned. After the wounded prostitute identified Gecht in an informal lineup at the hospital, he was arrested and charged with rape, deviate sexual assault, armed robbery, aggravated battery, and attempted murder. Five days later, Gecht was free on bail, but when another woman said she had been attacked, Gecht was arrested again on Nov. 5. His associates, Spreitzer and 19-year-old Andrew Kokoraleis, were charged with murder. On Nov. 12, 22-year-old Thomas Kokoraleis was also arrested and charged with kidnapping Lorraine Borrowski.

All four men were convicted. Gecht was convicted on charges in connection with the attack on the surviving prostitute, including attempted murder, armed violence, aggravated kidnapping, rape, deviate sexual assault, and aggravated battery. During the sentencing, officials also displayed evidence concerning the assault on Angel York. Gecht was sentenced to 120 years in prison. Andrew Kokoraleis was convicted on charges of murdering Davis and Borowski. He was sentenced to death. His brother, Thomas, was found Guilty of murdering Borowski, but the conviction was overturned on a technicality. In a plea bargain before his second trial, Kokoraleis pleaded guilty to killing Borowski; charges in connection with the Sutton killing were dropped, and on July 16, he was sentenced to seventy years' imprisonment. Spreitzer was convicted of the murders of Sutton, Borowski, Mak, Davis, Delaware, and Tirado. He was subsequently sentenced to death. REF.: *CBA.*

Gee, Dorothy (Chang Hor-gee, AKA: Dolly), 1897-1978, U.S., embez. Before her 1964 conviction on charges of bank embezzlement, Chang Hor-gee (whose Americanized name was Dorothy "Dolly" Gee), was one of the most respected business figures in San Francisco's Chinatown. She was regarded as a shrewd executive who had gained control of the Bank of America's Chinatown branch. It was later estimated that she had embezzled $300,000 over fifty years.

The eldest of nine children, Gee was the daughter of Charlie Gee, who had immigrated to San Francisco in 1901. Gee opened a shoe store in Chinatown where he saved thousands of dollars sent to him by relatives overseas who dreamed of coming to the U.S. In 1906, an earthquake destroyed the shoe store and forced Charlie Gee to move his business across the Bay into Oakland. Overcoming his prejudice against the Chinese, Charlie Gee convinced executives of the French-American Bank to allow him to deposit $1 million. He was given a job at the bank and hundreds of Chinese, unable to deal with the bank directly, gave him their money and he deposited the money at the bank in his account.

Only Gee could understand the calculations entered into his logbook in Chinese characters. With the workload becoming too much to handle, Gee brought his daughter into the business in 1914 and she recruited new depositors. By 1919, in control of nearly $2 million in accounts, Charlie Gee sailed to Hong Kong where he opened the China Specie Bank, with branches in Canton and Shanghai. Returning to the U.S., he convinced many of his countrymen to allow him to deposit their money in his foreign banks.

In 1923, Charlie Gee's empire crumbled when the Hong Kong branch in China failed, a fact he did not know for three weeks since news traveled by steamship. During the interim, Gee sent an additional $80,000 in client money to the failed bank—money that was permanently lost. To avoid embarrassment, Charlie Gee began altering the books. He set up a fake account in San Francisco and embezzled money over a period of time to allay suspicions. In 1927 the Bank of America absorbed the Chinatown Bank and two years later Dorothy Gee became its manager. Only then did she discover her father's crimes. "We talked all night," Dorothy Gee said. "The question for me was whether I would betray my father. But I couldn't go down and betray him. And once I made that decision I just stuck with him for more than thirty years."

Under her inspired leadership the Bank of America branch flourished. She lived ostentatiously, gambling at clubs and consuming large amounts of Scotch which scandalized the traditionalists in the Chinese-American community. In 1962, six years after her father died, she remodeled the bank to resemble a Chinese pagoda, and during the dedication ceremonies she became a U.S. citizen.

Ready to retire in 1963, Dolly decided to confess. She told Bank of America president Rudolph Peterson the startling news of her fifty-year deception. On Christmas Eve, FBI agents arrested her. She was sentenced to five years at Terminal Island, but her sentence was later reduced to sixteen months. Following her brief incarceration Gee returned to Chinatown to live until her death in 1978.

Speculation continued long after her death about her hidden wealth. Some alleged that the Gees used the embezzled funds to finance a smuggling operation that brought Chinese immigrants into the U.S. Others maintained that the money was spent at the gaming tables in Las Vegas. REF.: *CBA*; Nash, *Look For the Woman*.

Geer, Louis Gerhard de, 1818-96, Swed., penal reform. Prime minister of Sweden from 1876-80, who reformed the country's penal code and upheld religious rights. REF.: *CBA*.

Gehr, Herbert, prom. 1950, Case of, U.S., mur. In July 1950, Andrea Gehr, desperately wanting a divorce from her philandering husband, snuck toward an unlit summer cottage in Long Island, accompanied by three private detectives. Herbert Gehr, her television-director husband, was inside with Dorothea Matthews. As the raiding group attempted to open the screen door, a .22-caliber rifle was fired from inside the dark house. Hit between the eyes, Andrea Gehr fell, killed instantly, and the detectives ran away. Matthews also fled, jumping out of a rear window in the cottage.

The case was brought to trial in Carmel, N.Y., in January 1951, with Herbert Gehr charged with second-degree murder, which carries a sentence of life imprisonment. Gehr claimed he had thought that burglars were breaking into the house, and said he had called out, "Who's there?" before he fired. Matthews, who was herself involved in a bitter divorce case and had recently led a raid of her own husband's apartment, contended she was only a governess to the Gehr children.

After almost two-and-a-half hours of deliberation, the jury found Gehr Not Guilty. According to one juror, the state divorce law was the real criminal in the case: "Mrs. Andrea Gehr was a martyr to this antiquated law which places evidence-gathering in the hands of professional snoopers, and in this case led to a dreadful tragedy." REF.: *CBA*.

Geidel, Paul, b.1894, U.S., mur. In 1911, Paul Geidel, a 17-year-old porter in a New York City hotel, was convicted for the murder of a hotel guest and sentenced to twenty years to life in Clinton Prison. He was released from the Fishkill Correctional Facility in May 1980, after sixty-eight years and seven months of confinement. The 85-year-old, believed to have served more time than anyone in history in a U.S. prison, was sent to a nursing home for his remaining days.
REF.: *CBA*; Cohen, *One Hundred True Crime Stories*.

Geiler von Kaysersberg, Johann, 1445-1510, Ger., witchcraft. The collected Lenten sermons of an extremely popular cathedral preacher were published in 1517, and they showed clearly how the concept of witchcraft was spread from the ecclesiastes to the common people.

Johann von Kayserberg Geiler, a doctor of theology at Basel and Frieburg, had a style and spirit that made him a celebrated preacher in Strasbourg. His Lenten sermons from 1508 were copied by Friar Johann Pauli and published in 1517 under the title, *The Ants*. Many of his sermons were about witchcraft, including information about how werewolves could have been devils acting as wolves, and how evil deeds were done, with God's permission, by the Devil, not actually by a witch. The learned Geiler explained, as an example, how it was the power of the Devil, not the witch's ointment of incantation, that caused a broomstick to fly through the air.

The first book published on witchcraft in German, Geiler's book gave credence and support to many theories about witchcraft, and was quoted by Luther in his own sermons in 1518 in Wittenberg. Another set of published sermons by Matin Plantsch, published in Latin in 1507, had also examined the idea of witchcraft. REF.: *CBA*.

Gein, Edward, 1906-84, U.S., can.-mur. One of the most horrendous killer-cannibals in U.S. history was Edward Gein, a strange little man who lived in a remote farmhouse in central Wisconsin and was the grisly role model for Alfred Hitchcock's horror movie *Psycho*. Gein and his brother Henry had been dominated at an early age by a strong-willed mother who did her utmost to warn her sons against the wiles and ways of scheming women. When Mrs. Gein died of a stroke, the 160-acre family farm outside of Plainfield, Wis., was left to her two sons. Henry Gein died in a forest fire and Ed was left alone.

Gein's mind began to take strange twists. He sealed off his mother's bedroom and the parlor and confined himself to a bedroom and the kitchen on the main floor of the farmhouse. He never used the five small rooms upstairs. He got books and periodicals dealing with human anatomy and studied these for hours when not performing his chores. There was little work to do on the farm anyway since Gein lived off the considerable funds he received through the federal soil-conservation program. Gein picked up extra cash doing odd jobs for neighboring farmers and residents in tiny Plainfield, population 700.

Then Gein began secretly digging up corpses in remote graveyards. He paid a cretinous farmer named Gus to help him, explaining to this dim-witted fellow that he needed the bodies for his "experiments." Through later confessions, Ed Gein revealed that at this time he wanted to study the female organs of bodies since he had recently read about the sex change made by Christine Jorgensen and had long harbored the secret desire to be a woman. The bodies Gein and Gus dug up were taken to a shed behind Gein's farmhouse and stored there. Gus never knew what Gein did with these corpses, or so he later said, though he probably did not care to ask.

Wisconsin cannibal-murderer Ed Gein.

Gein periodically removed the bodies from the shed and studied them for hours, then dissected them. These crude operations led to wild aberrant behavior where Gein would skin the corpses and wear the skins about as though they were shawls or scarves. He fondled female organs for hours and later admitted that wearing and caressing these gruesome human remains gave him inexplicable thrills. The little farmer butchered his cadavers with care, keeping several of his victim's heads, sex organs, livers, hearts, and intestines, and discarding the parts that held no interest for him.

When Gus was removed to a retirement home, Gein decided that it was too laborious to dig up bodies alone. It was easier, he concluded, to murder women and bring their bodies to his farmhouse for more "experiments." His first victim was 51-year-old Mary Hogan, operator of a Pine Grove, Wis., saloon. One winter night in 1954, Gein waited until all of Hogan's patrons left the remote bar. Then he walked calmly inside. Mary Hogan recognized him and told him she was closing. Gein said nothing as he walked around the bar to Hogan's side. He took a .22-

caliber pistol from his pocket, placed this close to Hogan's head, and fired a single bullet into her skull, killing her. He then dragged her body from the bar to a sled he had placed outdoors. It took the diminutive Gein several hours to drag the corpse back to his farm, his way made more difficult by a blinding snowstorm.

Gein's next known victim was Bernice Worden, who operated a hardware store in Plainfield. In November 1957 he began frequenting this store more than usual. He hung about talking to Mrs. Worden and her son, Frank Worden, who was the town's deputy sheriff. When Worden told Gein he would be going hunting on Saturday, Gein realized that Mrs. Worden would be left alone in the store. He arrived at the store and found the middle-aged woman alone. Gein went to a gun rack and took a.22-caliber rifle from the wall. He inserted a single bullet into the chamber, one he had brought with him, then turned on the startled woman and fired a shot which struck her in the head, killing her. Gein locked the front door of the store, dragged Mrs. Worden's corpse out the back, and took it to his farmhouse. He carried along the store cash register which contained $41. Both Mary Hogan and Mrs. Worden resembled, to some extent, Ed Gein's long-departed mother.

When Frank Worden returned home he had to break into the store. He found his mother and the cash register missing, and he spotted a small pool of blood on the floor behind the counter. A sales slip, half written out in his mother's handwriting, was on the counter. It was for antifreeze. Worden remembered that Gein said he would be stopping by the store to buy this item. Worden told the sheriff that Ed Gein was probably behind his mother's disappearance. The sheriff drove to Gein's farmhouse but Worden went to a West Plainfield store where he knew Gein was probably visiting friends. He found the meek little farmer just finishing dinner.

Worden confronted Gein concerning his mother's disappearance. "I didn't have anything to do with it," Gein replied in an even voice. Worden nevertheless placed Gein in custody, taking him to the local jail. The sheriff returned from the Gein farm a short time later, in shock and for some time unable to describe what he had seen there. Then he began to make a verbal inventory of the gruesome "trophies" he had found: Four human noses in a cup on the kitchen table, bracelets made of human skin, a crude tom-tom made from a coffee can with human skin stretched over the top and bottom, a pair of human lips on a string which hung from a window sill. Bracing four chairs were strips of human skin and two human shin bones propped up a table. Skin from female bodies had been made into a crude vest, leggings, and purse handles.

On the walls the sheriff had found nine death masks, the skinned faces or skulls of women. There were ten heads from female corpses, all sawed off just above the eyebrows. One skull had been made into a soup bowl. The refrigerator contained human organs, all frozen. In a pan on the stove lay human heart. The basement looked like a slaughterhouse, with pieces of human bodies hung from hooks along the walls and the floor coated with dried human gore. From what the sheriff was able to determine, the remains found in Gein's horror house were of about fifteen women.

Gein did not deny anything. He admitted his ghoulish grave robbing and the two murders of Mary Hogan and Mrs. Worden. There might have been more but he could not remember. He also talked freely about eating the dead flesh of the bodies taken from graves and those he had killed. He even talked about how he adorned himself in the crude garments made of skin and how, if the mood suited him, he would dance naked around his kitchen and bedroom, playing fitfully with his gruesome trophies. Gein talked matter-of-factly about these nightmares, as if such conduct were normal. He had been at such devilish work for a number of years and had grown used to his abnormal practices.

What did bother Gein was that he stood accused of robbing the Worden cash register. "I'm no robber," Ed Gein said indignantly as he was led away to a cell. "I took the money and the

cash register because I wanted to see how it worked." Ed Gein was sentenced to life in prison for the Worden murder. He applied for parole many times over the years but was consistently denied freedom. He died in the psychiatric ward at Mendota on July 26, 1984, of respiratory failure.

Ed Gein, seated at right, at his 1974 parole hearing; parole was denied.

The Gein farmhouse had died many years earlier. It became the symbol of everything horrible and disgusting. Local youths broke its windows and hurled rocks and snowballs at it whenever passing the place. One night several residents went to the farm and reportedly set it afire in an attempt to blot out the sinister presence of this evil place. It remained for years a blackened, gutted ruin. The remains of Edward Gein, the monstrous Wisconsin cannibal, went beneath the earth without the possibility of being disturbed, as Gein had disturbed others. He was buried secretly in an unmarked plot in a Plainfield cemetery, right next to the woman whom he loved and feared most, his mother.

REF.: Boucher, *The Quality of Murder;* CBA; Fox, *Mass Murder;* Gollmar, *Edward Gein: America's Most Bizarre Murderer;* Haines, *Bothersome Bodies;* Masters, *Perverse Crimes in History;* Nash, *Bloodletters and Badmen;* Schecter, *Deviant;* (FICTION), Bloch, *Psycho;* (FILM) *Psycho,* 1960; *Deranged,* 1974; *Texas Chainsaw Massacre,* 1974; *Psycho II,* 1983; *Landscape Suicide,* 1986; *Psycho III,* 1986; *The Texas Chainsaw Massacre Part 2,* 1986.

Gelardi, Agostino, and **Silvestri, Aguazio,** and **Azari, Giovanni,** d.1885, U.S., mur. An Italian who peddled fruit in Chicago paid for his three old boyhood friends to come to the U.S. Later, they murdered him. The three—Gelardi, Silvestri, and Azari—came to Chicago and lived at the expense of their benevolent friend, Filippo Caruso, while he helped them find jobs. But his benevolence was not enough; they wanted his money. On Apr. 30, 1885, Caruso came to see them, and they jokingly decided to shave each other. On Caruso's turn, they shaved him, wrapped him in towels, and strangled him. They found $300 hidden on him. The three men packed their Caruso's body in a large trunk and shipped it by train to Pittsburgh.

Filippo's brother, Francesco Caruso, went to the police, who had just learned that the Pittsburgh police had found a trunk at containing a body. Francesco identified the body as that of his brother. A baggage man in Chicago described the man who had sent the trunk in such detail that Inspector Thomas Byrnes of New York was able to identify him as Gelardi, a known thief in New York. Gelardi was arrested and returned to Chicago, where he and the other two men immediately began to blame the others. The three men were tried in July, found Guilty, and hanged.

REF.: CBA; Nash, *Murder, America.*

Gelfand, Michel, 1902-53, Case of, Fr., mur. Relocating to Paris from his native Latvia at the age of twenty-two, Michel Gelfand was a hosier whose world consisted mainly of nightclubs and luxury bars. Living the proverbial life of wine, woman, and song, Gelfand contracted tuberculosis and spent some time in a country clinic. He then returned to Paris, nearing age forty, to fall in love with Edith Tarbouriech, a woman who lived by her sexual favors, and had had her head shaved for consorting with occupying soldiers during the war. Gelfand supported Tarbouriech, who was about ten years his junior. She was consistently unfaithful to him. Novelist Joseph Kessel, a close friend of Gelfand's, said Gelfand often would tell him that the affair would end badly, explaining: "I'll have to kill myself, there's no other way out!"

Then Gelfand fell into a platonic affair with a woman of good reputation who was married and from a well-known French family. Tarbouriech became aware of the romance and began to blackmail her lover, extorting money, accusing him of deceiving her with another woman, and eventually demanding a fur coat and other items of clothing in order to leave Gelfand alone. With his platonic lover out of town, and no money to silence his vengeful mistress, Gelfand, on Aug. 26, 1951, went to Tarbouriech's hotel and shot her with a 6.35-mm automatic pistol, then turned the gun on himself. He missed his heart and, ten days later, left the hospital for the Santé prison.

Gelfand's first words to Examining Magistrate Chapar were that he had committed murder to save a woman's reputation, and that he would never tell her name. The trial began at the Seine Assizes on Nov. 12, 1953, with Marcepoil and Raphael as attorneys for the defense, and the advocate general for the prosecution. After a brief trial, Gelfand was found Guilty only of manslaughter, and given a two-year jail sentence. Because he had already been in jail for two years waiting to be tried, he was released immediately. Returning on his first night of freedom to the bars and nightclubs of the Champs Elysees, he was offered a job by a London firm to represent a new hosiery business in Paris. Fifteen days later he had a heart attack. He died that same night, never regaining consciousness. REF.: *CBA;* Goodman, *Crime of Passion;* Heppenstall, *The Sex War and Others.*

Genet, Jean, 1910-86, Fr., writer. Jean Genet, a petty thief, male prostitute, and pickpocket in Barcelona and Antwerp, became one of the foremost literary figures and playwrights of the second half of the Twentieth Century.

The outcast-turned-novelist was the illegitimate son of Gabrielle Genet. Abandoned by his mother, Jean was placed into reform school at the age of ten for theft. Between 1930-39, he carved out a meager living in Spain and Belgium hustling lonely women and committing various crimes. While in prison for burglary, Genet began work on his first novel, the critically acclaimed *Notre-Dame des Fleurs* (Our Lady of Flowers) 1944, which captured the essence of Montmarte, a section of Paris inhabited by the denizens of the French underworld. The *Journal du Voleur* (Thief's Journal) 1949, was an autobiographical account of the years Genet spent tramping and thieving through Europe.

After gaining literary success with the publication of two more novels, *Pompes Funèbres* (Funeral Rites) 1947, and *Querelle de Brest,* also in 1947, Genet began to express his inner self in the world of the theater. Deeply influenced by the existential philosophy of Jean-Paul Sartre, Genet explored the themes of crime and punishment, notably in his production of *Les Bonnes* (The Maids) 1947, inspired by the murders of Genevieve Lancelin and her mother by two disgruntled housemaids. The celebrated trial took place in Le Mans, scene of the Feb. 2, 1933, murders in which sisters Christine and Léa Papin stabbed and bludgeoned their overbearing, demanding employers on a darkened stairway. The two women were convicted and sentenced to hard labor. The case fascinated Genet, who followed up *Les Bonnes* with similar fare, including *Haute Surveillance* (Deathwatch) in 1949, and *Le Balcon* (The Balcony) in 1956. The violent, anarchistic nature of his work led critics to categorize Genet as the foremost proponent of the "Theater of the Absurd." See: **Papin, Christine** and **Papin, Léa.** REF.: *CBA.*

Genghis Khan (Temuchin or **Temujin),** 1162-1227, Mongolia,

kid.-mur. Mongol ruler Genghis Kahn murdered an estimated 20 million people between 1206 and his death in 1227. That means that one-tenth of the world's population was butchered by this savage ruler whose barbarity knew no limits. Still no less fearsome in death, when Khan died of natural causes it was ordered that if anyone gazed upon his coffin the next coffin would be theirs.

Genghis Khan—the name means "Universal Ruler"—was the son of a Mongol tribal chief named Yesukai. Orphaned at thirteen, the young Khan murdered his brother after quarreling over a fish. In Spring 1206, at age thirty-three, Khan established his rule over all the Mongol tribes and, in 1211, began the legendary conquest of imperial China, burning and pillaging every city and hamlet that stood in his way. Three years after his invasion, the Mongol hordes controlled the entire country north of the Yellow River and Khan forced the Kin Tartars to deliver to him 500 young men and women, and 3,000 livestock as the price of peace.

To the west lay the kingdom of the Khwarizms, a vast territory between the Ganges and the Tigris rivers, covering present-day Iran and India. At first Khan promised Shah Mohammed peace and favorable trade agreements. However, the shah lessened his chances of an agreement by murdering a caravan of 100 Mongol traders near the border town of Otrar. More envoys were sent by Khan, and they, too, were murdered, which doomed the shah and the people of his region. Between 1218-22, Genghis Khan's armies swept through Khwarizm, killing 400,000 enemy troops. The governor of Otrar was executed, with molten metal poured into his eyes and ears. In Bukhara, the defeated inhabitants were ordered outside the walls of the city and forced to watch while the women were raped. At Samarkand in May 1220, the Mongols defeated a garrison of 50,000 defenders, most of them murdered for refusing to surrender their town. In Termez every dead body was torn open by Khan's men after they found out that one old woman had swallowed her pearls to hide her valuables from the invaders. Genghis Khan took no prisoners, and would often stack the severed heads of his victims into bloody pyramids.

The atrocities continued to mount as Khan inched ever closer to the mainland of Europe. After slaughtering every man in the village of Urgenj, the women and children were abducted and forced into slavery. The carnage was shocking, and Shah Mohammed proved to be no match for the relentless Mongols. Forced into exile, he died of pleurisy in a village on the Caspian Sea. When pursuing the shah's heir, Jelaleddin, Khan cut a wide path through Afghanistan, killing thousands of innocent civilians along the way. Lahore, Melikpur, and Peshawar were conquered and a six-month siege at Herat ended in victory for the Mongol tribes. Genghis Khan carved out an empire that stretched from the China Sea to the Persian Gulf. Some of the world's largest armies proved helpless before him. In the end, only illness and old age defeated him. Khan died in August 1227, at age sixty, after naming his son Ogotai as his heir and successor. Ogotai proved to be equal to his father's legacy, as he consolidated his grip on China and extended the Mongol domain into Korea. REF.: *CBA.*

Genna Brothers, prom. 1920s, U.S., org. crime. Of all the murderous gangsters of Chicago during the Prohibition era, the Genna Brothers were the most ruthless and lethal. Life meant nothing to these bootlegging killers. They thrived on murder and terror. The six terrible Genna brothers were all born in Marsala, Sicily. They immigrated to the U.S. in 1910, their father taking a job as a railroad section hand in Chicago. The boys' mother died while they were small and they grew up wild in Chicago's Little Italy where extortion and blackmail were rampantly practiced by scores of Black Handers. Stabbings, shootings, and bombings were usual. Crime and death lurked everywhere.

America to the Gennas was a land of criminal opportunity. They had been sponsored by Diamond Joe Esposito, one of the early-day Chicago crime bosses of the West Side, and, after their father died while they were in their teens, the boys grew up with the crooked, corrupt Esposito as a father image. He encouraged them to make their way in the New World with gun and stiletto.

The "Terrible Genna" brothers dine *en famille,* 1923; the Chicago gangster brothers are, from left to right, Sam, Angelo, Peter, Antonio (the brains, in dark glasses), and Jim; Mike Genna is not present.

All six brothers were small, stocky, and swarthy, with thick black hair. After years of surviving street battles, the Gennas smiled with oily ease and practiced murder with alacrity. Sam, Angelo, and Mike Genna launched their criminal careers as early as 1912, practicing Black Hand extortion on their fellow Sicilians. Jim Genna at this time operated a brothel and his brothers Antonio and Peter worked as pimps for this operation.

In 1919 the brothers began to establish a vast alky-cooking empire in Little Italy, in preparation of making their own liquor at the dawn of Prohibition. Initially, they agreed to deliver all their cheaply produced (and often lethal) booze to the powerful criminal cartel run by Johnny Torrio and Al Capone which controlled the South and West sides of Chicago. Within a year, the Gennas decided to establish their own string of saloons and peddle their own liquor and beer, carving out a large and lucrative area in the Near West Side which became the exclusive domain of the Gennas. They sought political protection from the reigning political boss of their area, Nineteenth Ward Alderman John Powers (known as Johnny De Pow), but Powers wavered, not wishing to offend Capone and others to whom he had sworn allegiance.

The Gennas then backed their own candidate for alderman, Tony D'Andrea, and busily went about killing politicians who supported Powers in the election year of 1921. The first of these was Paul A. Labriola. Angelo Genna, aptly called "Bloody Angelo," had tried to persuade Labriola to join forces with his man D'Andrea but he had been rebuffed, told that he was no more than "a greedy little punk" by the high-handed Labriola who was a bailiff in the Municipal Court. On Mar. 8, 1921, Angelo Genna, accompanied by three of his goons, Samuzzo "Samoots" Amatuna, Frank "Don Chick" Gambino, and Johnny "Two-Gun" Guardino, waited for Labriola at the corner of Congress and Halsted Streets. When they spotted the bailiff about to cross the street the four advanced on him, revolvers drawn. In broad daylight, with scores of horrified pedestrians watching, Genna and his men let loose with a withering volley of gunfire, filling their victim with lead.

Labriola fell to the pavement, twitching from a half dozen wounds. Genna snorted: "He ain't done yet." He casually walked to the wounded Labriola and straddled his fallen body, aiming his revolver at Labriola's head. He fired three times and most of the bailiff's head vanished. "C'mon," Genna said to his men. "He's done." He took a toothpick which had been clenched between his teeth and dropped this contemptuously onto the corpse and then sauntered away. The men got into a long, black Lincoln sedan and drove slowly away. Angelo Genna had killed another man in Little Italy but this surprised no one. By then the Gennas were all millionaire gangsters, the most powerful force in the area

and they operated at whim. Whatever they chose to do, they did, and without interference from the law. The dozen witnesses to the Labriola killing never testified against the killers. To do so, they knew, would mean instant death.

The daylight murder of Paul Labriola was not performed in the usual Genna style. These killers preferred to kill from dark ambush. Angelo Genna's hatred of Labriola had caused him to abandon his usual pattern of murder. But this killing also set an example, he felt, for any who might think of opposing the Genna clan. Many of the Genna victims were slain by a group of willing killers who worked in the gang, particularly the assassins Albert Anselmi and John Scalise, who tipped their bullets with garlic in the mistaken belief that if their victims did not receive a mortal wound the garlic would cause gangrene and bring about eventual death. These two would later institute the "handshake murder," the method wherein one of the two killers would shake hands with an intended victim, in the pretense of a friendly greeting to catch the victim off guard, while the other pumped bullets into him. This was the way in which Anselmi and Scalise, with the help of Frankie Yale, murdered the North Side crime boss Charles Dion O'Bannion, in 1924.

Other equally feared killers in the Genna ranks included Orazio "The Scourge" Tropea and Guiseppe "The Cavalier" Nerone, both cold-blooded assassins. Tropea ran a sub-gang of vicious juveniles, all Sicilian youths, who acted as runners and delivery boys for the Genna alky operations which consisted of thousands of tiny apartments in the crowded tenement area. In these apartments whole families spent round-the-clock hours operating stills and producing rotgut Genna booze. Tropea believed himself to be a sorcerer, that he could merely look at someone and bring them bad luck, and the superstitious residents of Little Italy believed this was true, convinced that Tropea possessed "the evil eye." Tropea's gang consisted of such fearsome youths as Ecola "The Eagle" Baldelli, Fony Finalli, Felipe Gnolfo, and Vito Bascone. They walked about Little Italy day and night with revolvers sticking from their pockets and waistbands and, often as not, carrying shotguns. No policeman ever dared to stop them. In fact, there was a noticeable absence of patrolmen in Little Italy. Those assigned to beats in this area seldom left home. They were on the Genna payroll which amounted to $200,000 a month just for police payoffs.

Thousands depended upon the Gennas for their livelihood. Day laborers gave up their jobs to stay home and operate gurgling stills at $15 a day. The Gennas produced a gallon of cheap booze for 40¢ a gallon and they sold this to the Torrio-Capone combine for $2 a gallon. Saloons paid $6 a gallon and customers by the tens of thousands happily lapped up this awful concoction which caused several deaths each year and dozens of drinkers to go blind. The Gennas nevertheless thought of themselves as generous souls. They put together a slush fund to cover the burial costs of alky-cookers who were killed when defective stills blew up.

The Gennas also thought of themselves as businessmen who knew enough to appreciate high culture. They purchased twelve front-row season tickets to the opera each year, and reserved the finest restaurants for their family get-togethers, their favorite dining spot being the Pompeian Room of the Congress Hotel. Antonio Genna lived at the Congress in a $100-a-day suite with his blonde mistress, Gladys Bagwell, daughter of a Baptist minister in Chester, Ill., who had run away to Chicago in 1920 to sing in one of Torrio's dives. This is where "Gentleman Tony" Genna met her. The gangster gave Gladys jewels and furs and treated her like royalty. Gladys was often interviewed by the press, claiming she knew nothing of her "fiancé's" occupation.

By 1925, the Gennas had survived a dozen wild gang wars, especially with the fierce North Side gang led by O'Bannion. After O'Bannion's murder in late 1924, the Gennas began to expand their rackets. Moreover, Angelo Genna became the head of the fraternal Sicilian order, *Unione Siciliane,* which controlled all Sicilian rackets. Angelo, recently married to Lucille Spingola, daughter of politician Henry Spingola, moved with his bride into a luxurious suite at the Belmont Hotel, an injudicious location for Genna in that this was in the heart of the territory controlled by the O'Bannion gang. On May 25, 1925, Angelo Genna left his wife at the Belmont. He carried $25,000 in cash and was en route to make a down payment for a house which he expected to occupy with his wife in a few weeks. The hotel doorman brought Genna's $6,000 roadster to the hotel entrance and the gang chieftain drove off.

A long sedan followed. Inside this car sat George "Bugs" Moran, Vincent "The Schemer" Drucci, and Earl "Hymie" Weiss, who was the leader of the North Side gang now that O'Bannion was dead. At the wheel of this car was another gunman, Frank Gusenberg. These men knew that the Genna killers Anselmi and Scalise had murdered their beloved boss, O'Bannion, as a favor to Al Capone, who wanted his arch rival, O'Bannion, out of the way. Now they thought to take vengeance. By the time Angelo Genna reached Ogden and Hudson streets, he spotted the car following him and stepped on the accelerator. His roadster shot forward and Genna took the corner at Hudson with such speed that the car skidded almost on two wheels, swerved across the

"Bloody Angelo" Genna, 1925, the year he was shot to death.

street, and smashed into a lamppost, pinning the dazed Genna behind the wheel. The following car inched by the helpless roadster, windows down, Drucci, Moran, and Weiss leaning from them with shotguns, revolvers, and a submachine gun. Hundreds of bullets smacked into Genna's car and riveted his body as Bloody Angelo tried to retrieve a revolver and fire back. It was useless. He was dead in seconds, his body torn to pieces.

The next to go was Mike "The Devil" Genna. He identified the body of his slain brother in the morgue and, without leaving the building, went to a phone. He was overhead talking in Italian to Albert Anselmi, ordering him to go out immediately and kill Drucci, Moran, and Weiss. Anselmi cooed his obedience and promised quick reprisals. Anselmi and his companion Scalise, however, had another murder to perform, that of Mike Genna himself. Al Capone had learned that the Gennas had planned to have him murdered and he had secretly hired Anselmi and Scalise away from the Genna ranks, promising them fortunes if they would kill off the surviving brothers. On June 13, 1925, both

killers accompanied Mike Genna in a search for the North Side gangsters who had slain Angelo Genna. This, of course, was a pretext to get Mike Genna alone somewhere and kill him, according to Capone's orders. Ironically, the Chicago police did their work for them. A squad car with four officers inside spotted the Genna car and gave chase, believing the occupants to be armed. The police car turned on its gong but the Genna car increased in speed, going along Western Avenue. Genna was at the wheel and, when a truck suddenly swung out from an alleyway, the gang chief yanked the wheel to avoid hitting it. His car leaped across a curb and hit a pole. Genna, Anselmi, and Scalise all grabbed shotguns and jumped from the car.

The squad car arrived a minute later and a gun battle erupted. One officer was killed instantly and two others wounded by the gangster barrage but Patrolman William Sweeney returned fire and drove off Anselmi and Scalise, who ran down the street and hid for some time in a clothing store. Sweeney followed the retreating Genna who fired at him. Sweeney fired back, the bullet striking Genna in the leg. The gang chief dove through a basement window but Sweeney cornered him in the basement and took him prisoner. Mike Genna's wound proved fatal. The bullet had severed an artery. When an ambulance arrived, Genna was placed moaning on a stretcher. The vicious hoodlum kicked upward with his good leg, smashing an attendant in the jaw and knocking him unconscious. "Take that, you s.o.b.!" he roared and these proved to be his last words. He bled to death within of two hours before doctors could operate on him, never knowing that his trusted lieutenants Anselmi and Scalise had accompanied him that day to kill him.

These two killers were found a short time later trying to flee the area on a streetcar. They would later undergo several trials but escape punishment for the killing of policeman Charles Walsh through Capone's political influence and jury-fixing lawyers. Anselmi and Scalise would later try to murder Capone himself and paid for the effort with their lives. Capone persisted in his efforts to eliminate the remaining Gennas, giving orders to his myriad henchmen to kill Antonio Genna on sight. Tony Genna was the real brains behind the Genna mob, a crafty, cunning killer. But he was terrified now that his two brothers, Angelo and Mike, the toughest of the lot, had been killed, both murders occurring within a few weeks. Tony Genna knew he was next and told his brothers Sam, Jim, and Peter that he could not meet with them. He stayed inside his Congress Hotel suite, guns everywhere and ready, while he sent his mistress Gladys out to shop for his needs.

Tony Genna received a phone call from his top enforcer, Guiseppe "The Cavalier" Nerone (also known as Joe Spavia and Tony Spano). Nerone informed his boss that Capone had been behind the killing of his brother Mike. Tony was overheard by Gladys Bagwell to tell Nerone: "I've got to get out of town." Tony told Nerone that his brothers were also leaving town.

"No," Nerone told him. "First we must make plans. I build up the gang. We take Capone. Then you and the boys can come back. We must meet and talk first."

Tony Genna agreed to meet with Nerone. On July 8, 1925, Tony drove to Curtis and Grand Avenue to keep a rendezvous with Nerone. He spotted his lieutenant standing in the doorway of Cutillas' grocery, a Genna front for an alky operation. Genna parked his car and then stuck his head out of the car window, checking the street, looking through dark glasses for any ambushing gangsters. Confident that he was safe, Tony Genna got out of the car and walked up to Nerone who smiled and put out his hand. Tony took it and a moment later two men ran from another doorway and shot Genna several times in the back. (These two men were later reported to have been Anselmi and Scalise, who were out on bail while the murder of Officer Walsh was still pending against them.) Nerone and the two men dashed to a waiting car and drove off. Nerone, too, had been hired away from the Gennas by Capone, and had agreed to betray his one-time boss, rather than face Capone guns.

The killers of Tony Genna had been careless. Their victim was still alive when police found him on the sidewalk. He was rushed to County Hospital and joined by Gladys Bagwell. She wept great tears and her black mascara ran down her full cheeks. She sat at her lover's bedside, police officials standing behind her. Asked Gladys: "Who shot you, Tony?"

Genna's dying words came with a final hiss: "The Cavalier."

Police thought Genna had said "Cavallaro" and they made an exhaustive and futile search for this nonexistent killer. When detectives finally realized that Genna had uttered the nickname of his favorite killer, Nerone, the gangster was dead. Nerone had been machine-gunned to death as he sat in a barber's chair, getting a shave. His killers were Vincent Drucci and others. Capone then sent out orders that all the Genna henchmen who refused to join him be killed. A systematic slaughter ensued. Henry Spingola, who was managing the affairs of the Gennas, was shot to death on Jan. 10, 1926. His killer was Orazio "The Scourge" Tropea, and others. Tropea, too, had gone over to Capone. But Tropea, like Nerone, paid for his treachery. He was murdered on Feb. 15, 1926, shot to death as he strolled along Halsted Street. His killers were the last loyal Genna killers.

Capone had given *his* top enforcer, Frank Nitti, explicit orders to "wipe out that nest of Genna snakes, no matter if it takes forever!" Nitti sent squads of men out to look for Genna gunmen. Bascone was located in suburban Stickney and he was taken for a ride. In a remote spot, Bascone got on his knees and put his hands together in prayer, begging for his life. Capone killers shot away his hands and then sent a bullet into his brain. The same day, Jan. 24, 1926, Anselmi and Scalise trapped the fierce Ecola "The Eagle" Baldelli who made a fight of it. He wounded several men accompanying Anselmi and Scalise and this so enraged these killers that when Baldelli ran out of ammunition and was taken alive, the two assassins hacked him to pieces and scattered his remains on a North Chicago garbage dump. Tony Finalli was entering his apartment on Mar. 7, 1926, when several shotgun blasts brought an end to his life. Felipe Gnolfo was on the run for almost three years before Capone gunmen tracked him down and killed him in 1930.

The power of the Gennas was smashed. This was evident at the time of Tony Genna's funeral. When Angelo Genna was buried, he went to

Pete Genna, who fled to Italy following the murder of his three brothers.

his grave in a $10,000 bronze casket, with more than $25,000 in flowers bedecking his grave site. Almost all of Little Italy turned out to witness his funeral procession, tuxedoed gunmen walking solemnly in front of the hearse that carried the body of Bloody Angelo, revolvers bulging in inside their coats. Yet when Tony Genna was buried two months later, his coffin was of cheap wood and no flowers were sent. Gladys Bagwell did not even bother to accompany the casket to the cemetery. Police and news reporters followed Tony Genna to the grave but not a mourner appeared at the site, fearful that Capone guns might be trained upon them.

By then Jim, Peter and Sam Genna had fled Chicago. Jim Genna returned to Marsala, Sicily. Here he stole jewels from a religious statue in church and was given a two-year prison sentence. (Some claimed Jim Genna did this on purpose so that he could use the prison as a haven from the far-reaching hench-

man of Al Capone.) Sam Genna and Peter Genna hid out in the hills of southern Sicily. Years later these three brothers would quietly return to Chicago, divorcing themselves from any rackets, to run a successful importing firm which offered olive oil and cheese. They would all die in obscurity.

The lavish gangster funeral of Angelo Genna in Chicago, 1925; the tuxedoed gangsters preceding the hearse all wore guns.

A police sergeant accompanied the body of Tony Genna to its resting place in Chicago's Mount Carmel Cemetery in 1926. He noted that the Genna grave was only a few feet away from that of Charles Dion O'Bannion. Both O'Bannion and Genna had been mortal enemies in life and in death they lay almost side by side. The police sergeant turned to a reporter to state: "When Judgment Day comes and those graves are open, there'll be hell to pay in this cemetery!" See: **Amatuna, Samuel Samuzzo; Anselmi, Albert; Capone, Alphonse; Drucci, Vincent; Moran, George; O'Bannion, Charles Dion; Torrio, John; Unione Siciliane; Weiss, Earl; Yale, Frank.**

REF.: Asbury, *Gem of the Prairie; CBA;* Kobler, *Capone;* Landesco, *Organized Crime in Chicago;* McPhaul, *Johnny Torrio;* Messick and Goldblatt, *The Mobs and the Mafia;* Morgan, *Prince of Crime;* Nash, *Bloodletters and Badmen;* Smith, *Syndicate City;* Thompson and Raymond, *Gang Rule in New York.*

Genovese, Catherine (Kitty), See: **Moseley, Winston.**

Genovese, Michael, c.1907- , U.S., org. crime. After Umberto "Albert" Anastasia, head of Murder, Inc., was slain in a barbershop on Oct. 25, 1957, Michael Genovese was called in for police questioning on Nov. 26. That same month, he allegedly attended a "crime convention" in Apalachin, N.Y. His activities were under scrutiny in early 1959 when the Senate rackets committee was investigating allegations of violence and union picketing used by New York coin machine operators. In December 1964, Michael Genovese was implicated in the loan sharking rackets by a witness before a New York state investigations committee. During the various inquiries, Michael Genovese had acquired control of a company that unwrapped, rewrapped, packed, stamped, and inspected frozen meat. His brother, Vito Genovese, had first gained a controlling interest in Erb Strapping Company in 1955, but reputedly transferred his shares to Michael Genovese after being sentenced to prison. The firm's profits skyrocketed and by 1969, the company had almost a monopoly on the meat inspection business. The largest New Jersey pier and warehouse complex, Harborside Terminal, apparently stipulated that any businesses using their services to import meat had to hire Erb for the repacking and inspection. The Waterfront Commission of New York was already investigating allegations of Mafia penetration into the banana and meat industries when they revoked Erb's temporary stevedore license and denied a permanent license on May 12, 1971. The Waterfront Commission cited ties to the Genovese family, although by this time, Michael Genovese had sold his controlling interest back to the original owners. The commission also accused the company of negotiating a special contract with a longshoremen's union and of bribery. The decision was affirmed by the Appellate Division in Manhattan in early 1972. REF.: *CBA*.

Genovese, Vito (Don Vitone), 1897-1969, Italy-U.S., org. crime. One of the most feared of twentieth-century U.S. Mafia bosses, Vito Genovese proved time and again that he could betray his friends, assassinate business associates, and outwit, for the most part, his most cunning underworld rivals in his murderous climb to become the boss of bosses. He began inauspiciously enough, born of poor parents in Risigliano, Italy, near Naples on Nov. 21, 1897. He immigrated to the U.S., arriving on May 23, 1913, on board the S.S. *Taormina*. He lived in the Italian section of New York City's Lower East Side and immediately fell in with several gangs. Genovese preyed on small store owners and pushcart peddlers, selling them protection (against himself, of course), stealing, and extorting. In 1917, he met a thief who was as cunning and crafty as himself, Charles "Lucky" Luciano.

Luciano was seemingly smarter than Genovese, or Genovese let Luciano think so. He became Luciano's lieutenant and together both young men took up armed robbery and burglary. While going to meet Luciano one day in 1917, before committing a planned armed robbery, Genovese was stopped by a suspicious patrolman who frisked him and found a loaded revolver in his coat. He was arrested and given sixty days in the workhouse for carrying a concealed weapon. Genovese blamed Luciano for this first of arrests, believing either that Luciano had informed on him so that he himself could avoid an impending arrest for fencing stolen goods, or because Luciano did nothing to get Genovese out of the workhouse, even though he promised his lieutenant to get him a lawyer and pay all fines if he should get into trouble. At the time, Luciano visited Genovese in the workhouse and pleaded poverty. Genovese served every day of his sentence.

Upon his release, however, Genovese went back to work for Luciano. He was arrested in 1918, again for carrying a concealed weapon. This time he paid a $250 fine. He and Luciano were by then thriving with their small-time rackets, as lieutenants of gang boss Jacob "Little Augie" Orgen. At first, Luciano and Genovese, along with Joe Adonis, Albert Anastasia, and others concentrated on establishing a number of cheap brothels in Brooklyn and later Manhattan. Luciano and Genovese were active in bootlegging during the Prohibition era but they found flesh peddling and, by the early 1920s, narcotics, were more lucrative. Dope peddling at that time was frowned upon even by the mob bosses. It was considered "unclean," and

Mafia gangster Vito Genovese, 1935.

it was associated almost exclusively with the black underworld.

As Luciano and Genovese branched out, they found more important gangsters controlling large territories in Manhattan, the most lucrative area for rackets. These included bootleggers Big Bill Dwyer, Owney Madden, Larry Fay, Jack "Legs" Diamond, Dutch Schultz, and Nathan "Kid Dropper" Kaplan. Overseeing most of these gangs as the crime overlord of the early 1920s was the millionaire gambler and rackets czar, Arnold Rothstein. It was Rothstein who was interested in expanding the narcotics racket in New York and thus financed the smuggling of drugs into New York through Little Augie Orgen. In turn, Orgen turned over the drug traffic to his lieutenants, Luciano and Genovese. Meanwhile, the Italian crime bosses of the day, Joseph "Joe the Boss" Masseria, and Salvatore Maranzano, continued their old-fashioned rackets.

Luciano and Genovese became the chief suppliers of heroin in New York, becoming wealthy, but still operating under the commands of Orgen and Rothstein. In 1925, however, they switched their allegiance and major association to Masseria, expanding Masseria's bootlegging operations. By then Luciano and Genovese had allied themselves with many non-Italian gangs and gangsters, particularly the Bug & Meyer mob, headed by the shrewd Meyer Lansky, a friend of Luciano's since boyhood, and Benjamin "Bugsy" Siegel, Lansky's strong-arm but quick-witted protégé. Other non-Italian gangsters such as Louis "Lepke" Buchalter and his dim-witted enforcer, Jacob "Gurrah" Shapiro, became Luciano-Genovese allies.

Genovese in Italy, 1945, before being returned to the U.S. to face murder charges.

Masseria meant little to Luciano and Genovese. He was, in their terminology, an old-fashioned "Mustache Pete," a crime boss who archaically clung to ancient rackets such as Black Handing. He nevertheless commanded the loyalty of most Italian gangsters in New York. Genovese, at this time, used Masseria's Old World connections to establish a front for his rackets, a trading company which imported olive oil and other food products from Italy and Sicily. This company, of course, was used to smuggle hard drugs into the U.S. from the Middle East. Luciano and, in particular, Genovese, kept low profiles in this era. Genovese was a family man. He had married for the first time in 1924, but his wife died in 1929.

Genovese married again in 1932, wedding Anna Petillo Vernotico, a union that produced a daughter, Nancy, and a son, Philip. (He would divorce Anna in 1950.) Genovese spotted the attractive Anna at a social gathering in early 1932. She was married at the time to Gerard Vernotico. Two weeks after Genovese met Anna, her husband was found murdered on Mar. 16, 1932, strangled to death atop a Manhattan building. Next to Vernotico's body was that of Antonio Lonzo, who had also been shot to death. Lonzo had accidentally come upon the killers of Vernotico while they were strangling their victim to death and he was eliminated as a witness. The killers, identified years later by Joseph Valachi, were Peter Mione and Michael Barrese. Both were killed on Genovese's orders so that no witnesses could ever link him with the murders.

Genovese was not a nightclubbing gangster. He went home to his family at night and stayed there, planning his future in the rackets each night for long hours before going to bed. He kept a revolver beneath his pillow, one under the bed and another in the pocket of a coat that always hung on a nearby chair. His apartment, and later all the houses he occupied, were rigged with special alarm systems so that Genovese would know instantly if anyone had entered the premises. On several occasions, these home-made alarm systems, a series of bells, tin cans hooked to ropes, chimes stretched across windows, went off and Genovese would leap from his bed, grabbing his revolvers, ready to fight to the death.

During the 1920s, Genovese used his weapons often, being arrested a dozen times for assault, robbery, and murder. He reportedly killed at least six men between 1920 and 1930. In 1930, as the Depression deepened over the land, the Mafia went to war with itself in what was later described as the Castellammarese War. This internecine Mafia battle came about when the ambitious Mafia chief Salvatore Maranzano, who was from Castellammare, Sicily, decided that only Mafia members from that area, chiefly himself, were entitled to run the rackets in New York. He declared war on his arch rival, Joe the Boss Masseria. The Mafia at that time was an organization of Italians and Sicilians, although the Mafia had originally been an exclusive Sicilian criminal organization. By the mid-1920s, the Camorra, the Italian counterpart of the Mafia, had lost its influence and its forces, especially in the U.S., and had joined the Mafia in one large but rather disjointed organization. Maranzano was a purist and intended to purge the Mafia of all non-Sicilians.

Maranzano's gunmen clashed with Masseria's thugs throughout 1930-31. Dozens of gangsters were shot and stabbed to death in this ruthless war where no quarter was given. Luciano realized that such a war was futile and only slowed down the development of his dream, a crime cartel that would actually run all the rackets in the U.S. Without Masseria's approval, Luciano went to Maranzano, suing for peace. The old man insisted that there would be no peace until Masseria was dead. Luciano then decided that he would rid himself of *both* Masseria and Maranzano. Once the "Mustache Petes" were killed off, the national syndicate of crime could come into being. Luciano promised Maranzano that Joe Masseria would come to a quick end. He ordered his trustworthy Vito Genovese to lead a select "international" group of killers, Italians and non-Italians, who would execute Masseria.

Genovese in a New York Court, 1946, being acquitted of murder, listening to Judge Samuel Leibowitz chastise him.

On the night of Apr. 15, 1931, Luciano dined with his boss Masseria at Scarpato's Restaurant in Coney Island, a stronghold of Masseria. He got up after finishing his meal and went to the washroom. Masseria was left at the table alone in a restaurant that was suddenly and strangely empty of other customers. Into Scarpato's marched Genovese, two revolvers in his suit pockets. Following him were Joe Adonis, Albert Anastasia, and Benjamin "Bugsy" Siegel. The four gangsters calmly walked up to Masseria and emptied their guns into him. Masseria fell forward on the table dead. The killers walked from the restaurant without interference. Police later found Luciano waiting for them. He explained that he was in the washroom at the time of the killing.

Maranzano was initially delighted at this murder. He called off the war and declared himself boss of bosses. Maranzano did not trust Luciano and Genovese, however. He told one of his men, Joseph Valachi, who was later to become the most cele-

brated informer of the Mafia-Cosa Nostra, that "I can't get along with those two guys. We got to get rid of them before we can control anything." Maranzano did not act fast enough. Thomas Lucchese, an on-and-off ally of both Maranzano and Luciano, warned Luciano and Genovese of Maranazo's plan to eliminate them. Luciano and Genovese put together their own "hit" squad, sending four men dressed as policemen to Maranzano's Manhattan offices on Sept. 10, 1931. (This use of fake policemen had worked well two years earlier when Al Capone's killers gained entrance to a Chicago garage to line up seven men of the George "Bugs" Moran gang and machine gun them to death in what was later known as the St. Valentine's Day Massacre.) These men included Red Levine, a member

Thomas Eboli, underboss of the Genovese Mafia family in New York.

of the Bug & Meyer mob, Bugsy Siegel, Albert Anastasia, and Lucchese, who proved his loyalty to the new regime by helping kill his former boss, Maranzano. Lucchese would be rewarded by being given the leadership of one of New York's five Mafia families, a position he would retain for decades. With Maranzano out of the way, Luciano and Genovese moved to establish the national crime syndicate. Genovese did not agree with Luciano's plans to include non-Italians on the board. He was particularly opposed to Lansky and Buchalter. He also disliked the idea of Anastasia, Adonis, and gambler and political fixer Frank Costello, sitting on the board. But Luciano had his way.

Meanwhile, Genovese and his rackets flourished. He earned from between $200,000 and $500,000 each year while working under the direction of Luciano. While Luciano directly supervised his prostitution empire, which was being expanded from coast to coast, Genovese concentrated on drug smuggling and peddling. One of Genovese's side rackets was fleecing wealthy Italian businessmen in his crooked card games. In September 1934, Genovese took $160,000 from a rich Italian in the back room of a small restaurant owned by one of his henchmen, Ferdinand "The Shadow" Boccia. When Boccia learned of the staggering amount Genovese won in a game that Boccia had helped rig, he demanded $35,000 of the take. Genovese squinted his eyes in subtle shock at his lieutenant's blatant demand and said that he would consider cutting in Boccia on his spoils.

His answer came on Sept. 9, 1934 in the form of five killers—Peter Defeo, George Smurra, Gus Frasca, Mike Mirandi, and Ernest "The Hawk" Rupolo—who shot Boccia to death. Willie Gallo, a member of Mirandi's troop, learned of the Boccia killing and Genovese ordered Gallo murdered. The chore fell to Rupolo who was a friend of Gallo's. He and Gallo attended a movie a few nights later. When they emerged Rupolo pulled a gun and put it to his friend's head, pulling the trigger. Nothing happened.

Gallo turned in surprise and said: "What the hell is this?"

"A joke," said Rupolo. He fumbled about with the weapon, taking out the bullets. Then he held it up to the incredulous Gallo, saying: "Look, the gun isn't loaded." When the pair returned to Gallo's apartment, Rupolo went to the washroom and examined the gun. He oiled the firing pin, reloaded the weapon, then walked into the parlor where he fired a bullet into Gallo. Rupolo's aim, however, was bad and the intended murder victim lived to identify his assailant. Rupolo was sent to prison for twenty years. After brooding about his imprisonment and the fact that Genovese had not lived up to his word in getting adequate legal assistance for him, Rupolo, accompanied by another prisoner, Peter LaTempa, went to prison officials and began talking about Genovese and his involvement in the Boccia murder.

New York's racket-busting district attorney, Thomas E. Dewey, who would later be responsible for exposing Murder, Inc. and the existence of the national crime cartel, began looking into the Boccia killing. Genovese did not wait to be arrested. He fled the country, returning to Naples where he had long ago purchased a comfortable villa. Genovese had prepared just for such an emergency. He had taken many trips to Italy over the years, carrying huge amounts of money which he secreted in Italian and Swiss banks. When he departed the U.S. in 1937, Genovese had more than $2 million waiting to keep him in royal comfort. He left the U.S. with several expensive cars shipped ahead of him, and a retinue of servants.

Once in Italy, however, Genovese became active in the Mafia-Camorra and was soon heading up Italy's drug traffic operations. He ingratiated himself to Italian dictator Benito Mussolini through Mussolini's foreign minister and son-in-law, Count Galeazzo Ciano and became Ciano's personal drug supplier, providing Ciano with cocaine and heroin. Though Mussolini had publicly declared war on the Mafia and his secret police energetically battled this crime federation in Italy and Sicily, Mussolini allowed Genovese to operate freely in Naples, knowing full well he was a Mafia chieftain. Ciano vouched for Genovese, who contributed large amounts of money to Mussolini's personal bank accounts. He also contributed $250,000 to establish a majestic monument to Mussolini at fascist headquarters in Nola, Italy. Meanwhile, Genovese established a distribution system of drugs that trailed from the Middle East, through Italy and Sicily and then to the U.S. where his minions and those of Luciano began to expand drug trafficking in the U.S.

Genovese was reported killed during WWII, apparently bombed to death by Allied planes while dining on the veranda of his villa. Yet, when U.S. forces occupied Naples, Genovese came forward, offering his services as an interpreter. He did more than that. Genovese informed upon every black marketeer in Naples. After these people were arrested and imprisoned, Genovese was honored by the military. He smiled, took the

Joe Valachi, whose testimony helped send Genovese to prison.

accolades and then took over the black market operations of those he had betrayed. Genovese was exposed by a sleuthing CID agent, Orange Dickey, who identified Genovese as a wanted felon in the U.S., the same Genovese who had fled in 1937 to avoid being charged with the murder of Ferdinand Boccia.

Dickey personally arrested Genovese and escorted him back to New York where the arch killer was to stand trial for the Boccia murder. The two men testifying against him, Peter La Tempa and Ernest "The Hawk" Rupolo, however, were to be eliminated. From a jail cell, Genovese ordered the death of La Tempa, who was in a Brooklyn jail in protective custody. La Tempa suffered from gallstones and took pain pills regularly. He was given several tablets on Jan. 15, 1945, and, after taking a few, fell to the floor of his cell, writhing in pain. He died a short time later of massive poisoning. Just who gave La Tempa the poisoned pills was never determined, but authorities were convinced that Genovese was behind the murder. This left only Rupolo to testify against Genovese and, as Genovese well knew, this would not be enough to convict the killer. Under New York law, the corroboration of a second witness was required for conviction. A jury was forced to acquit Genovese.

Judge Samuel Leibowitz, once a brilliant criminal trial lawyer, had Genovese brought before him on June 11, 1946, and said to

the smug gang chief: "I cannot speak for the jury, but I believe if there were even a shred of corroborating evidence you would have been condemned to the electric chair. By devious means, among which were the terrorizing of witnesses, kidnapping them, yes, even murdering those who would give evidence against you, you have thwarted justice time and again." Leibowitz then dismissed Genovese who turned silently away from the bench, a smug smile playing about his lips. He felt immune from the law.

Days later Genovese met with his old lieutenants from the 1930s, Mike Mirandi and Anthony Strollo, alias Tony Bender. He ordered them to build up the narcotics rackets throughout New York and told them that "bit by bit" he would take over the city. Luciano by then had been deported to Italy and no longer exercised control of the crime cartel he had helped to create. Genovese was welcomed back to the syndicate board, but he knew he had enemies there and he systematically eliminated his opposition. He caused the execution of New Jersey Mafia boss, Willie Moretti in 1951, the murder of Costello ally Steven Franse in 1953, and that of the fierce Albert Anastasia in 1957. He then had one of his minions at-

Don Vito Genovese, en route to the federal penitentiary in Atlanta where he would die.

tempt to kill Frank Costello, who was aligned with Meyer Lansky. Genovese wanted Lanksy's lucrative gambling rackets in Havana, Cuba, but these were protected by Costello. On May 2, 1957, a Genovese goon, Vincent "The Chin" Gigante, fired several shots at Costello, wounding him in the head. Costello retired a short time later.

In 1957, it was Genovese who called the notorious Apalachin Meeting where more than 100 top Mafia-syndicate leaders met to acknowledge him as the boss of bosses, as well as to streamline the syndicate's rackets. The meeting was interrupted by the arrival of local police, causing the gangsters, Genovese included, to run like frightened children across meadows and through thick woods. For several years, Genovese dominated the five Mafia families in New York. Yet, in 1959, this most powerful of Mafia leaders was exposed by several of his own men, including the notorious informer, Joseph Valachi.

The government built a strong drug trafficking case against him and Genovese was convicted and sent to the Federal Penitentiary in Atlanta to serve fifteen years. Genovese still wielded vast power and he used it to settle old scores. In 1964, while a prisoner in Atlanta, the vengeance-seeking Genovese sent his gunmen to kill Ernest "The Hawk" Rupolo. The informer was unearthed and tortured before he was killed and his body dumped into New York's Jamaica Bay. Genovese also ordered the death of Joe Valachi but Valachi outlived the man he sent to prison. Vito Genovese died in his cell in Atlanta in 1969. See: **Adonis, Joseph; Anastasia, Albert; Buchalter, Louis; Costello, Frank; Dewey, Thomas E.; Diamond, Jack; Dwyer, William Vincent; Fay, Larry; Kaplan, Nathan; Lansky, Meyer; Leibowitz, Samuel; Luciano, Charles; Madden, Owney; Maranzano, Salvatore; Masseria, Joseph; Moretti, Willie; Mussolini, Benito; Orgen, Jacob; Rothstein, Arnold; Schultz, Dutch; Siegel, Benjamin; Valachi, Joseph.**

REF.: Alexander, *The Pizza Connection;* Blumenthal, *Last Days of the Sicilians;* Bonanno, *A Man of Honor;* Campbell, *The Luciano Project;* CBA; Cohen, *Mickey Cohen: In My Own Words;* Cressey, *Theft of the Nation;* Davis, *Mafia Kingfish;* Demaris, *The Last Mafioso;* Eisenberg and Landau, *Meyer Lansky;* Frasca, *King of Crime;* Fried, *The Rise and Fall of the Jewish Gangster in America;* Gage, *Mafia U.S.A.;* ____, *The Mafia is not an Equal Opportunity Employer;* Godwin, *Murder U.S.A.;* Gosch and

Hammer, *The Last Testament of Lucky Luciano;* Katz, *Uncle Frank;* Kobler, *Capone;* McClellan, *Crime Without Punishment;* Maas, *The Valachi Papers;* Martin, *Revolt in the Mafia;* Messick, *Lansky;* ____, *Secret File;* ____ and Goldblatt, *The Mobs and the Mafia;* Nash, *Bloodletters and Badmen;* ____, *Citizen Hoover;* ____, *Hustlers and Con Men;* Overstreet, *The FBI in Our Open Society;* Peterson, *The Mob;* Pileggi, *Wiseguy;* Reid, *The Grim Reapers;* Reuter, *Disorganized Crime;* Sann, *Kill the Dutchman;* Servadio, *Mafioso;* Smith, *Syndicate City;* Sondern, *Brotherhood of Evil: The Mafia;* Thompson and Raymond, *Gang Rule in New York;* Wicker, *Investigating the FBI;* Zuckerman, *Vengeance Is Mine.*

Gensonné, Armand, 1758-93, Fr., rebel. Led the Girondists, a moderate Republican French reform group, in an unsuccessful overthrow attempt. In 1793, he was guillotined along with other revolutionaries. REF.: *CBA.*

Gentili, Alberico (Albericus Gentilis), 1552-1608, Brit., her. Sent to London in 1580, after being branded a heretic because of Protestant beliefs. He taught civil law at Oxford University. His work in separating secular law from the Catholic doctrine established him as the originator of the science of international law. REF.: *CBA.*

Gentleman from Chicago, The, 1974, a novel by John Cashman. Thomas Neill Cream (Brit., 1891-92) is the central character in this first person narration of murder and he is dismissed as a possible candidate for Jack the Ripper (Brit., 1888), the author pointing out that Cream was in an Illinois prison at the time of the killings. See: **Cream, Thomas Neill.** REF.: *CBA.*

Gentlemen's Riot, prom. 1835, U.S., mob vio. In Boston, on Oct. 21, 1835, George Thompson, an English abolitionist, was scheduled to speak before the Boston Female Anti-Slavery Society. But Thompson fled the city before the speech when he learned that a crowd numbering about 3,000 planned to tar and feather him for his views. When the mob of socially prominent gentlemen learned of their victim's defection, they turned on William Lloyd Garrison, an anti-slavery newspaper publisher. Garrison was bound with rope and taken away, but police rescued him and protected him for the night in the city jail. No one was ever convicted for the Gentlemen's Riot. REF.: *CBA.*

Gentry, Charles, prom. 1936, U.S., mur. In early October 1936, Charles Gentry was tried by a jury of twelve black men. Before testimony in the case began Gentry's white attorney had unsuccessfully pleaded for dismissal of the charge because members of the grand jury that had voted his client's indictment had been all white. In the trial before the jury, all sawmill workers, an hour and five minutes of deliberation resulted in Gentry being found Guilty of killing Jasper Evans. Gentry was sentenced to five years in prison, though the state had asked for the death penalty. REF.: *CBA.*

Gentry, Clarence (AKA: Phil), prom. 1909-10, U.S., wh. slav. Clarence Gentry was a pimp in Chicago's South Side Levee, a stretch of "badlands" extending from 18th Street on the north to 22nd Street on the south. Within the boundaries of this two-mile vice district stood a collection of panel houses, disreputable saloons, and bordellos. Despite the determined efforts of various civic groups like the Committee of Fifteen, the vice lords of the Levee operated with impunity for nearly fifteen years. Many tales were told of girls abducted at train stations or in small towns by an army of "ropers" and "cadets" sent in by such Levee henchmen as Maurice Van Bever and Harry Cusick, (brother of Jake Guzik), bookkeeper for the Al Capone syndicate.

One young abducted woman was Mildred Clark, who met Clarence Gentry of Chicago on July 15, 1909. Clark, as she was later known in Chicago, had been with friends in Nashville, Tenn. Gentry was skilled in the art of seduction, and had a successful career in white-slave trafficking. Four days after their first meeting Gentry proposed marriage. The smitten young woman accepted. She had just turned seventeen and was eager to settle down. On July 24, they eloped to Chicago, taking a day coach out of Nashville. "Well, you know, when we got on the train, we talked about coming here to Chicago and renting a small house," she later said. "That is what he said. We would rent a small house but then he said there were no small houses to rent, they were all flats, and then he talked about how happy we would be and about his marrying me."

They arrived in Chicago the next morning. Gentry took Mildred to South Armour Avenue by street car and led her through the door into what she believed was a residential hotel. He left her alone in a room, only to return later that day with a woman known only as Maud—the madame of the house. "Clarence, if you don't mean to marry me, won't you give me enough money to get home?" Clark asked. He laughed and later drugged her. Nine or ten hours later she awoke to find that her street clothes had been replaced with a short, immodest dress, and realized she was an inmate of a brothel.

Gentry and the other members of the white-slave ring kept her locked in the room for weeks. They instructed her on what to tell the police, who occasionally dropped by the Levee brothels to interview the inmates. Clark was ordered to tell them that she was twenty-two and there of her own free will. When she attempted to write a letter home she was beaten and threatened. Clarence had shown her the severed finger of a woman. "Well, that's what happens to girls who snitch on us," he said.

Clark remained in the brothel until October 1909, when evangelist Gypsy Smith led a religious march through the streets of the Levee. The procession wound its way up and down Dearborn, Armour, and 22nd streets. Clark threw open the window of her room and called for help. "For God's sake come and get me!" A reporter, hearing her frantic pleas for help, rushed into the house and led her to freedom. Detectives assigned to the office of Clifford Roe, who had waged a campaign against the Levee pimps, quickly arrested Gentry. Clark told her story in court, despite receiving death threats. After the trial ended, she was returned to her parents' home in Nashville. On Jan. 28, 1910, Gentry was sentenced to six months in prison and fined $300 for pandering.

REF.: *CBA;* Lindberg, *Chicago Ragtime: Another Look at Chicago, 1880-1920;* Roe, *The Great War on White Slavery.*

Gény, Francois, 1861-1959, Fr., jur. Professor of civil law at the University of Nancy in 1901, and dean of the law faculty from 1919-25. He is the father of free scientific research movement in law. REF.: *CBA.*

George III (George William Frederick), 1738-1820, Brit., King, 1760-1820, attempt. assass. Colonel Edward Marcus Despard was a career soldier in His Majesty's army. The youngest of six sons born to an Irish family, Despard joined the military when he was only fifteen. His gallantry in the field was rewarded with an appointment to serve as governor of the royal province of Yucatan in what is now Mexico. The appointment was sanctioned and approved by King George III—the man Despard would one day attempt to kill.

Governor Despard ruled his colonial settlement with a firm will and iron resolve. Many people in Yucatan bitterly resented the autocratic governor. Complaints about his conduct toward the men under his command filtered back to England and Despard was ordered to return home in 1790. Though no formal charges were brought against him, Despard was so thoroughly disgraced that his brilliant prospects for a career came to an end. Bitter over this unjust turn of events, he began persuading other malcontents to rise up against the government. He was arrested for seditious actions and imprisoned in a cramped, airless cell at Coldbath Fields, Clerkenwell, from April 1798 until 1801. By the time the prisoner was at last freed, his determination to lead an insurrection was cemented.

Despard combed the back alleys of London and the seamy grog shops where he made the acquaintance of former soldiers whose anger barely surpassed his own. He forced these men to enter into a pact aimed at overthrowing the monarchial government. One man who signed this document was a 25-year-old foot soldier named Thomas Windsor who in actuality was a government spy.

The conspirators, who met at the Oakley Arms tavern in Lambeth, began to speak of killing the king on Nov. 16, 1802. It was not the first time someone had conspired against the king. On Aug. 2, 1786, a deranged woman named Margaret Nicholson approached the king's coach outside the palace of St. James to present a petition. George III paused to give the woman a moment of his time. She produced a dagger and lunged forward, but her aim was bad. Nicholson, fifty-nine, only succeeded in tearing her dress before guards led her away. She was adjudged to be hopelessly insane and was committed to the Bethlehem Hospital where she died on May 28, 1826.

The wild plot cooked up by Despard was to commence the last week of November 1802, when he and his men planned to seize the Great Gun on public display behind the British Admiralty. All Despard had to do was make sure that the two sentries on duty next to the cannon were his own men. At the opportune moment, the secret army then would fire four rounds at the King's coach as it passed through the park.

The fateful meeting at the Oakley Arms was the last the conspirators would hold. Before the plan reached its conclusion, a team of constables headed by John Stafford, clerk of the Magistrates of Union Hall, burst in the room. "There were about thirty persons in the room when I entered," Stafford told the court later. "They appeared to be all, except for Colonel Despard, of low orders of people and were very meanly dressed."

Thirteen men, including Despard, went on trial before Lord Chief Justice Edward Ellenborough in London, Feb. 7, 1803. Appearing as a favorable witness for Despard was Lord Horatio Nelson, British naval hero, who recalled the time they had served together on board the *Hinchinbrooke*. Nelson spoke of Despard's patriotism and love of country, but it was not enough to sway the prosecution. On Feb. 10, Despard and six of his co-conspirators were found Guilty and ordered to hang. The sentence was duly carried out eleven days later near the Surrey County Jail in Newington. After a brief, impassioned speech in which Despard proclaimed his desire had been to bring liberty and justice to the British people, he was hanged. Afterward, his head was severed. "This is the head of a traitor—Edward Marcus Despard!" the executioner said, holding the grisly object aloft to the crowd.
REF.: *CBA.*

George, Annie, prom. 1898, Case of, U.S., mur. When she was rejected by her fickle lover, who happened to be the brother-in-law of President William McKinley, Annie George shot him down on the steps of his new paramour's home.

In Canton, Ohio, the Saxton family was an important and influential clan with three children: Ida Saxton, who would later marry the President; Mrs. M.C. Barber; and George Saxton, a womanizer who was accepted into society despite his taste for seduction. In 1891, George Saxton met Mrs. Annie George, wooed her, and convinced her to divorce her carpenter husband. George went to South Dakota in order to obtain a divorce decree in six months on the grounds of "willful absence." By the time she returned, Saxton was on intimate terms with another woman, the widowed Eva Althouse. With no money and her reputation ruined, George reminded Saxton that he had promised to marry her. He refused.

Coming upon Saxton and his new conquest riding a tandem bicycle, George forced Saxton to go home with her at pistol point. On Oct. 7, 1898, Saxton was visiting Althouse's home and was on the porch with a bottle of wine and roses when a woman dressed in black fired four shots, fatally wounding him. After her arrest, George refused to talk without a lawyer present. A physician, Dr. Maria Pontius, examined the accused woman and testified that she found powder burns on her thumb, and burrs and needles in her clothing that matched plants growing near Althouse's residence. Still, George had the sympathy of the town, which had for almost nine years judged her to be the victim of Saxton's bad behavior.

Althouse left town, and no efforts were made to extradite her. The murder weapon, a revolver, was found near Althouse's house, but even this evidence did not convict George. Neither did the testimony of a neighbor, Mary Finley, to whom George had said

of her faithless lover that she would "shoot him so full of lead he will stand stiff." Acquitted by the jury, George was carried off from the courtroom to a hotel banquet given in her honor, and was swamped with offers to give lectures and perform at theatrical entertainments.
REF.: *Canton's Great Tragedy; CBA;* Kobler, *Some Like It Gory.*

George, Frederick Douglas (AKA: **Harold S. Gibson, Robert Thomas**), prom. 1951-54, U.S., forg. Beginning his criminal career in Louisville, Ky., George Frederick Douglas began twenty-six months of forgery in December 1951 in Albuquerque, N.M. Using the alias Robert Thomas, he deposited several checks to an account in that name, then cashed checks for $50 at two different banks before leaving town. Throughout his career as a forger, George never tried to cash fraudulent checks; he deposited them to accounts, going to banks at lunch hours or closing times when business volume was high. Hitting as many as three or four banks in a fifteen-minute period, George cashed small checks, usually for $50, netting up to $500 a day. He attempted to disguise his handwriting as additional protection against getting caught and, as his confidence increased, raised the amounts of the checks to $150.

Traveling by plane, George was able to be in several different parts of the country in one day, and followed no recognizable pattern in his direction, often backtracking or jumping to an entirely different part of the country. On Jan. 28, 1954, he arrived in Galveston, Texas, cashed several checks at a number of banks within an hour, and left town. An FBI agent who happened to be at the Galveston Police Department when reports of the forgeries reached the department recognized George's technique and was able to track him down; George was arrested as he got off the plane in San Antonio. Returning to Louisville to face trial on a federal grand jury indictment, George pleaded guilty in federal court on Apr. 9, 1954, to six counts of check forgery. He received sentences totaling a twelve-year prison term.
REF.: *CBA;* McGuire, *The Forgers.*

George, Walter, prom. 1974, U.S., asslt. In Los Angeles in the summer of 1974, James Van Pelt, a popular member of the police force, was seriously wounded by a suspected car thief who shot Van Pelt in the abdomen as he tried to stop him. The officer, who hovered between life and death for several days, was completely unable to recall his assailant. A commanding officer suggested using hypnosis to jog Van Pelt's memory, and Dr. Martin Reiser, psychologist and hypnotist for the L.A. force, was brought in. Reiser, who had taught at Pennsylvania State University, had developed the technique of "televised enactment," in which he would ask his subjects to imagine they were looking at a television screen that was playing a documentary rendition of the event in question. In a trance, Van Pelt was informed by Reiser that he would "be able to tell us exactly what the man with the gun looked like." Speaking slowly, in clipped words, Van Pelt began to describe the assailant as a heavy man wearing denim, with a strange expression on his face, like a smile or a sneer, and continued to characterize his gait, complexion, and physique. The hypnotic technique had unlocked the policeman's subconscious mind, making available to him details that he could not consciously remember.

On the strength of this description, the manhunt was renewed and, four months later, a patrolman spotted a bar patron who matched Van Pelt's description. Walter George was taken in for questioning, and charged with assault with intent to kill that same day. Found Guilty by a jury, George was sentenced to twenty-two years in prison.

First to use hypnosis in crime detection, Israel frequently uses the technique to help victims recall their assailants. In 1973, a crowded commuter bus had just left the Haifa station when a bomb exploded, tearing the vehicle apart and wounding several people. A second incident occurred soon after, when a bus on the same route was found to be carrying a bomb. The bus drivers on both vehicles were unable to remember any suspicious-looking riders until Dr. Maurice Kleinhaus hypnotized one of the men.

From a deep trance, the driver recalled a passenger with unusually sweaty hands, who had waited with a friend in an Arab area; the friend had not boarded the bus, but continued to wait in the road. A police artist sketched while the driver continued his description and, within two weeks of an intensive search, two suspects were arrested.

Although there was no direct evidence against them, the hypnotic rendition of their appearances was invaluable in bringing charges against them. One suspect was tried and convicted and given a twenty-year jail term. The other escaped, later sneaking back to Israel; with two other terrorists, he murdered a family in an apartment house before being killed by police in a gun battle. REF.: *CBA*.

George of Cappadocia, d.361, Gr., assass. Devout Arian who clashed with staunch Greek Orthodox St. Athanasius in 357. He replaced Athanasius as bishop of Alexandria and ruled with a vengeful hand. He was slain by an Alexandrian mob in 361. REF.: *CBA*.

Georgia Prison Camp Massacre, 1947, U.S., prison brutality. When armed guards in a Georgia prison camp fired on convicts from a road gang, eight prisoners were slain. Sometime later, the warden and four guards claimed the convicts had wielded iron bars when the shooting started; the surviving prisoners said they held no bars.

In mid-July 1947, prison trucks pulled up to the State Highway Camp in Georgia's coastal plain, and twenty-seven black convicts were taken out and herded in front of one of the barracks buildings. Orders were shouted and Warden W.G. Worthy moved towards the men, then fired his .38-caliber revolver. The prisoners dived under buildings and ran for cover as a volley of shots were fired. Within a minute, it was over and five men lay dead on the ground, with another three fatally wounded. A survivor said, "They mowed them down like wheat."

Worthy said the trouble began when the convicts refused to work on the highway, and that he had meant only to punish the leaders of the strike, insisting that he had not fired until one of the prisoners grabbed for his gun. According to Willie Bell, one of the convicts who said he had been the focus of the warden's rage, he had responded to Worthy's demand that he step away from the group. Worthy repeatedly shouted at him, then fired; as Bell dropped with a leg wound, the guards fired on the group. A special Glynn County grand jury was set up to investigate the incident and decided that Worthy and the guards were justified in their attack. In early October 1947, a Savannah federal grand jury indicted the warden and the guards for depriving the men of their lives without due process of law.

By Nov. 4, the federal grand jury in Brunswick, Ga., deliberated for only eight minutes before bringing in the judgment that the eight black men had not been killed by Worthy and his guards without cause. Evidence lasted six days, during which Worthy explained that a mass escape had necessitated the shooting. Survivors of the massacre said there had been no escape attempt, and Bell testified that Worthy had told him, "I'm going to kill you." In announcing the judgment that freed Worthy, along with Guy McNabb, Remer Bazemore, W.C. Lawler, and H.L. Holmes, Judge Frank M. Carlett warned the packed courtroom against making any outcry; the verdict was received without demonstration. REF.: *CBA*.

Georgia State Prison Escape, 1980, U.S., pris. esc. On July 28, 1980, inmates Troy Leon Gregg, David A. Jarrell, Johnnie L. Johnson, and Timothy W. McCorquodale escaped from the Georgia State Prison at Reidsville. Gregg, Jarrell, and McCorquodale were serving life terms for murder, while Johnson was on death row for murder, rape, and kidnapping. The prisoners used hacksaws to saw through more than a dozen rusting metal bars, and fashioned guard uniforms from prison pajamas. Suspected of having inside help, they telephoned Albany *Herald* reporter Charles Postell upon their escape. Postell then alerted authorities. Two days later, the convicts were found near Charlotte, N.C. Jarrell, Johnson, and McCorquodale were cornered in a home on

Lake Wylie and recaptured after a six-hour stalemate when police tossed tear gas containers through the windows. The owner of the house, William Flamont, was arrested and charged with harboring fugitives. The body of the fourth convict, Troy Leon Gregg, was pulled from a lake twelve miles away. He had died from blows to the head and neck.

On Aug. 27, 1980, Charles Postell and his wife were indicted by a Tattnall County grand jury and charged with helping the four convicts escape by sending them the hacksaw blades the previous month. Postell, who had conducted frequent interviews in the prison, was alleged to have purchased the blades in Baxley, Ga., and given them to an aunt of McCorquodale, who in turn mailed them to her nephew. On Nov. 13, 1980, all charges against Charles and Judi Postell were dropped. However, the previous week, Roy Lee Franklin, forty-three, of Douglasville, Ga., was arrested and charged with attempting to extort $15,000 from Postell.

A death row inmate, Carl Isaacs, was expected to be the major prosecution witness against the Postells. Franklin's son was also on death row, and the three conspired to take advantage of the Postells' plight by extorting the money in exchange for favorable testimony. On Nov. 24, Franklin pleaded guilty to the charge in the Macon, Ga., courtroom of Federal District Judge Wilbur Owens. He was sentenced on Feb. 27, 1981, to two years. REF.: *CBA*.

Geraghty, Christopher James, and **Jenkins, Charles Harry**, and **Rolt, Terence**, prom. 1947, Brit., rob.-mur. Christopher James Geraghty, twenty-one, had twice escaped from Borstal Prison when in 1947 he joined several other hardened young criminals in South London. Geraghty, who said of the prison system in Borstal that "the idea of going straight is laughed at," explained that he learned to be vicious and take pride in terrifying others while serving time. At lunch-time on Apr. 29, 1947, Geraghty, along with Charles Harry Jenkins, who had two previous convictions for assaulting police officers, and Terence Rolt, robbed a jewelry store off Tottenham Court, on Charlotte Street. The three beat two old men and fired at one of them. When assistants chased the thieves out, the robbers' stolen car was hemmed in by a truck which had backed out in front of it during the robbery attempt. The thieves attempted to flee, and a passing motorcyclist, Alec de Antiquis, bravely decided to stop them, and used his cycle to block their path. Geraghty shot de Antiquis through the head. Another passerby, George Grimshaw, also tried to stop the young criminals, and was severely beaten and kicked by them.

Police superintendent Robert Fabian was put in charge of the case. He had little to go on—two revolver bullets from different weapons, contradictory descriptions of the criminals, and no fingerprints or other clues in the abandoned get away car. Fabian and his investigators were able to get information from a cab driver which led them to an abandoned office. There they found a hat and gloves, and a raincoat with a tailor's mark that led them to the Jenkins family home. Harry Jenkins refused to talk, but Geraghty betrayed Rolt. Then, Rolt gave the details of the robbery and murder to the police when he was captured. When two revolvers were found in the mud of the Thames River at Wapping, charges of murder were brought against the criminals on May 19. Tried at the Old Bailey in July, Geraghty and Jenkins, who both had carried guns during the crime, were sentenced to die. Rolt, because of his age, was given a lighter sentence of detainment for not less than five years. On Sept. 19, 1947, Harry Jenkins and Geraghty were hanged at Pentonville Prison. Jenkins was twenty-three, and Geraghty, twenty. Their victim, Alec de Antiquis, who was a naval hero, was posthumously awarded a medal for bravery a year later.

REF.: Browne and Tullett, *The Scalpel of Scotland Yard*; *CBA*; Fabian, *Fabian of the Yard*; Jacobs, *Aspects of Murder*; Simpson, *Forty Years of Murder*.

Gerard, Alfred Robert, c.1925- , and **Callaghan, Jeremiah**, c.1925- , and **Foreman, Frederick**, c.1933- , and **Everett, Ronald James**, c.1931- , Case of, Brit., mur. An east London car dealer and reputed gangster, Thomas Albert "Ginger" Marks, was with a friend, George Evans, during the early hours of Jan. 3, 1965. Evans said they were walking along a street in east London when four men pulled up in a car. Evans said that Marks was called over to the car door, then they were three flashes and the sound of gunshots. Evans said he was fired at, and he hid under a parked van. He saw a car drive by with the legs of a man hanging out a rear passenger door. Police investigating the crime found a bullet in a wall, Marks' glasses and hat, and blood stains. The body was never found. Ten years later, on Jan. 9, 1975, three men were arrested and charged with the murder and a fourth man was also held on murder charges. Ronald James Everett, a 44-year-old driver, was acquitted of charges on Oct. 24, 1975. Several days later, on Oct. 30, the other three men, Alfred Robert Gerard, a 50-year-old salesman, Jeremiah Callaghan, a 50-year-old bookmaker, and 42-year-old Frederick Foreman, were also acquitted. REF.: *CBA*.

Gérard, Balthazar, See: **William I (William of Orange).**

Gerena, Victor Manuel, 1958-   , U.S., rob. Wanted in connection with the armed robbery of about $7 million from a West Hartford, Conn., security company, Victor Manuel Gerena is of medium to stocky build with a dark complexion and green eyes. Of Puerto Rican descent, he has worked as a machinist and a security guard, and usually wears a light mustache. In the robbery Gerena bound and handcuffed two hostages before injecting them with an unknown substance to disable them. He is presumed to be armed with a .38-caliber Smith and Wesson revolver and is considered dangerous. A reward of $4,000 has been offered for the money stolen by Gerena, with another $100,000 for any information leading to the fugitive's arrest. Gerena is believed to be extravagant with money, and may have grown a beard to disguise himself. REF.: *CBA*.

Gerghuta, Ion, prom. 1929, Rom., suic.-mur. At the end of June 1929, Ion Gerghuta, a farmer who was careful with his money, returned from the town of Kronstadt, Romania, to his village of Palmagayu. Spreading the money he had just earned from his crop sales on the kitchen table, Gerghuta gloated over his good fortune, then went to get a drink. When he returned, his tidy 6-year-old son had cleaned the dirty scraps of paper from the table, neatly sweeping them together and burning them in the fireplace. As the flames with cinders of bills shot up, Gerghuta saw what his son had done and killed him. Hearing her child's agonized screams, Gerghuta's wife, who had been bathing their 1-year-old, rushed to help him. The baby drowned in the bath water, and Gerghuta's grief-crazed wife ran from the house and drowned herself in the farm's pond. Gerghuta, seeing all this, took a revolver and killed himself. REF.: *CBA*.

Gerk, Joseph A., 1874-1957, U.S., law enfor. off. Working as a jeweler prior to serving on the police force, Joseph A. Gerk began his law enforcement career when he was appointed to the St. Louis police force on Aug. 21, 1899. He served as captain of the newly created traffic squad. In 1903, Gerk prevented a mob of 500 to 600 people from lynching a motorman. As chief of the force, from Apr. 9, 1925, until Oct. 1, 1934, Gerk installed the country's first "Show-Up Room," a room where suspects were brought before victims and others to be identified. Gerk served as the President of the International Association of Chiefs of Police, and served on the committee on uniform crime records. Gerk was also the president of the Association of Missouri Chiefs of Police. REF.: *CBA*.

German-Indian Conspiracy, prom. 1915, Ger.-India-Brit.-U.S., treas. During WWI, most Indians were willing to fight the Allied cause with Britain. Some, however, used the turmoil to advance the cause of India's independence. Germany aided this group in the hope of diverting some of Britain's energies from pursuing the war. A leader of the move for independence was 30-year-old Har Dayal, who published a newspaper in Berkeley, Calif. After being arrested for anarchy and released in 1914, he fled to Berlin, where he and Chempakaraman Pillai, who had started the International Pro-Indian Committee in Switzerland,

were hired by the Germans to conduct a campaign against the British.

In 1915, another Indian named Chattopadhya developed a plan uniting partisans in several countries to assassinate Allied leaders, such as Lord Kitchener of Great Britain, M. Poincaré of France, and the king of Italy. The plot fell apart when Scotland Yard learned of it and placed some of the conspirators in England in internment.

India sent a police official, Mr. Nathan, to Britain to stop the conspiracy. He was sent from London to Berkeley, Calif., to encourage the local police to arrest the Indian leaders still working there. Two Indian leaders were arrested and went to trial. During the trial, one, thinking the other had told all their secrets, shot his co-worker dead in the courtroom. A deputy sheriff stationed in the courtroom then shot the man with the gun, killing him.

At the end of WWI, many Indians saw that these special efforts were useful after all. The mere fact that India had continued to function efficiently with most of the "British Raj" off fighting the war showed that the British were not necessary, and a nationalist movement grew rapidly. REF.: *CBA*.

Germano, Andro, prom. 1931, U.S., riot.-suic.-mur. In 1931, Michigan had no death penalty. The Marquette Prison, near Lake Superior, held some of the state's most hardened criminals, with few of them having any hope of an early release, and many others imprisoned with life sentences without parole. In late August 1931 one of the convicts, kidnapper Edward Wiles, whispered to the prison doctor, "If I die in this hole my pals will wreck the place." Wiles did die soon after.

In early September, with the regular jail doctor away and Dr. Alfred W. Hombogen substituting, Andro Germano, serving thirty to fifty years for wounding a policeman, came into the infirmary with two pals, Leo Duver, a robber in for life, and Charles Roseburg, serving twenty to forty years for robbery. Germano claimed to be sick, and when Hornbogen approached to examine him, the convict pulled out a pistol and fired it into the doctor's heart, killing him. Two aides ran forward and were shot and killed by the prisoners. One died. Running out into the rotunda, the convicts shot down a guard and fired at the warden and his deputy. Alarms sounded and the trio of prisoners grabbed a turnkey and took his keys, heading for the main gate, but turning away as guards rushed at them. They rushed into a factory building, and kept guards and thirty other prisoners as hostages, holed up in the third floor of the building.

Volleys of shots from machine guns and rifles rang out for two hours as the convicts and the guards fired at each other. Ammunition ran low, so they made one of the guards write the warden a note demanding a car to transport them from the prison and threatening to blow up the building if he did not comply. The response was a tear gas bomb, followed by two more. When Germano said, "I guess she's all up, boys," Roseburg turned his gun on himself. Germano shot Roseburg in the head with a second bullet, then shot himself. Duver pumped another bullet into Germano before putting his gun into his own mouth and firing. Two more shots rang out from a cell block later that day, and guards discovered Frank Hohfer, a friend of the three dead convicts, had also committed suicide. REF.: *CBA*.

German Princess, The, See: **Moders, Mary.**

Gerrard, Thomas, 1687-1711, Brit., rob. A classic English burglar, Thomas Gerrard committed many crimes during his twenty-four years and was among the ranks of those eighteenth-century English lawbreakers executed for their actions.

Although not always successful, Gerrard's bungled attempts never failed to amuse. Once, having stolen a serving bowl he thought was silver and worth £60, he fled from the scene—an inn near Grantham—on foot, forgetting his horse, which he had earlier stolen in London. Later, finding the bowl almost worthless, he tossed it into a river and then remembered the horse, which at £30 was not so worthless. Angered by his loss, Gerrard returned to the inn one month later and burned it to the ground.

After many crimes far more successful than the latter, Gerrard would be undone by his penchant for alcohol, which gave him the courage he might not have had were he sober. On Aug. 10, 1710, with the help of Tobias Tanner, Gerrard broke into a private residence. Together they stole eight dozen pairs of socks, an eight-pound weight of thread, and 25 shillings. Another criminal, however, informed on them and they were taken into custody. Tanner was acquitted for lack of evidence, but Gerrard made a full confession and was duly executed at Tyburn on Aug. 24, 1711.

REF.: *CBA*; Smith, *Highwaymen*.

Gerry, Elbridge Thomas, 1837-1927, U.S., lawyer. Attorney for the Society for Prevention of Cruelty to Animals from 1870. He helped establish the New York branch of the society and served as president from 1879-1901. He initiated the movement to substitute the electric chair for hanging, as a more humane death for criminals, and was also active in obtaining better treatment for the insane. REF.: *CBA*.

Gerson, Robert, prom. 1974, U.S., mur. Robert Gerson, twenty-three, of New Jersey, resented his mother for getting him out of messes he had created for himself. So she could feed him Christmas dinner at home, Mrs. Gerson bailed her son out of jail on Christmas Eve. He had tried to rob a Chinese restaurant, but a Chinese waiter had karate-chopped him down. While she was preparing the turkey, Mrs. Gerson asked her son to turn down the television. Responding by screaming, "You're always ordering me around!" Gerson jumped on her and tried to strangle her with a child's jump rope. Unable to murder the woman, Gerson was assisted by his paramour, Lorraine, who stabbed Mrs. Gerson several times with a kitchen knife.

Though Gerson had an extensive hit list of people he called "useless" and whom he had intended to slay after killing his mother, he ran away with Lorraine and spent his mother's money until the nefarious couple were caught. Found Guilty of murder, Gerson was sentenced to fifteen years in prison. In exchange for her testimony against her former lover, Lorraine received a much shorter sentence.

REF.: *CBA*; Godwin, *Murder U.S.A.*

Gertz, Elmer, c.1907- , U.S., lawyer. Elmer Gertz was one of the foremost criminal attorneys in the U.S., representing a wide spectrum of clients including novelist Henry Miller, Dallas nightclub owner Jack Ruby, who shot presidential assassin Lee Harvey Oswald in 1963, and Nathan Leopold, Jr., the celebrated "thrill-seeking" killer of the 1920s. Oddly enough, one of Gertz's most famous cases was one in which he was directly involved.

In 1969 free-lance writer Alan Stang published an eighteen-page article in *American Opinion Magazine*, the journal of the John Birch Society, in which the author accused Gertz of conspiring to frame Chicago police officer Richard Nuccio for the killing of 19-year-old Ronald Nelson. Stang said the liberal-thinking Gertz belonged to the National Lawyer's Guild, which, according to the writer, "probably did more than any other outfit to plan the Communist attack on the Chicago police during the 1968 Democratic Convention." Stang referred to Gertz as a "Leninist" and a "Communist fronter." Nuccio was convicted in August 1968.

Gertz, a lecturer at the John Marshall Law School in Chicago responded by filing a libel suit against the author. He asked for $500,000 in compensatory damages and $1 million in punitive damages against Robert Welch Ltd., the publishers of the magazine. The case reached the Supreme Court in 1974, establishing a precedent affecting libel laws. The justices ruled that a private citizen who had become well-known quickly did not have to show actual malice to collect damages. For public figures, however, the requirement was left standing. Gertz vs. Welch dragged on for twelve years before finally being resolved on Apr. 22, 1981. The jury awarded Gertz $400,000 in damages. REF.: *CBA*.

Gesell, Gerhard A., 1910- , U.S., jur. Congressional committee member who investigated the Japanese attack on Pearl Harbor between 1945-46. In 1967, President Lyndon B. Johnson nominated him to the District Court of Washington, D.C. He was a member of the Advisory Committee on Criminal Rules from 1969-76. REF.: *CBA*.

Gessler (Gryssler or **Grissler)**, d.c.1307, Switz., assass. The struggle to free Switzerland from the oppressive rule of the Austrians is best told in the account of William Tell, whose story first appeared in a nine-stanza ballad in the mid-Fifteenth Century. Later, Frederick Schiller made him the main character of his nationalistic novel, *William Tell*.

The story begins in the district of the three Forest Cantons: Uri, Unterwalden, and Schwyz, in the Swiss Confederation. The governor, whose name was Gessler (or Gryssler) attempted to enforce the iron-fisted rule of Albrecht the First, who had deprived the Swiss cantons of their basic right to self-determination. Gessler was a petty, vindictive tyrant who put a long pole in the city market and placed a hat at the top, which symbolized the Duke of Austria—Albrecht. Every citizen passing by the pole was obligated to show proper respect to Albrecht and to Gessler's authority by removing their own hats.

One day in 1307, William Tell and his young son passed by the pole and deliberately ignored the governor's order. Tell was arrested and taken before Gessler, who considered him a dangerous agitator. He was the son-in-law of Walter Fuerst, one of the ringleaders of the so-called Ruetli conspiracy aimed at toppling Albrecht's regime on New Year's Day 1308. Gessler, eager to test Tell's reputation as a skilled archer, decreed that he should shoot an apple off the head of his young son from a distance of thirty paces. The order was carried out, and the boy escaped unharmed. But Gessler noticed that Tell had removed two arrows from his quiver. "If I had missed my aim and hit my boy," Tell said, "the second arrow was for you and, by God Almighty, it would not have gone astray!"

Gessler, the despotic Austrian ruler of Switzerland, assassinated by William Tell.

Gessler was furious. He ordered that Tell be taken to the castle at Küssnacht and confined in an underground dungeon. To reach the fortified domain of the governor, the prisoner had to be taken across an inland lake. As fate would have it, the small boat was caught up in a vicious storm and William Tell was freed from his chains and asked to guide the boat to safety. He maneuvered the craft close to the craggy shoreline and then, seizing his crossbow, leapt to safety on the rocks. Luckily for Gessler, he, too, managed to reach the shore. The governor located a horse and proceeded toward the castle fortress with his party trailing close behind. Off the main road, William Tell was lying in ambush. He took aim with the crossbow he had retrieved from the boat, and Gessler toppled from his mount, having been pierced through the heart with an arrow.

The assassination of the despotic governor was the opening shot of a general uprising that freed Switzerland from the domination of Austria. As the years passed, the story of William Tell and the apple became folklore. Scholars remained divided in their opinions as to the authenticity of the sequence of events leading up to the murder of Gessler. Nevertheless the Gesslers were prominent during this period, and Tell became a national hero for dispatching the tyrant.

REF.: *CBA*; Johnson, *Famous Assassinations of History*.

Gestapo, 1933-45, Ger. sec. pol. The Gestapo came into existence on April 26, 1933, when Hermann Goering established this secret police force in Prussia to replace Department IA, the old Prussian political police. Goering originally intended to designate this organization the Secret Police Office, in German, the Geheimes Polizei Amt, or GPA, but this was too similar to the GPU of the Soviet Union. Then a postal employee, making up a franking stamp for the new German secret police force, suggested that Goering call the new organization the Geheime Staatspolizei, the Secret State Police, or Gestapo in abbreviated form. Goering liked the sound of it; he thought the name intimidating. Gestapo became the official name within months and soon it was feared by everyone in Germany and eventually the world.

The most fearful thing about the Gestapo was that it was an organization that, by law, could operate wholly above the law. At first Goering used the Gestapo as his personal terror weapon, deploying this force of sadistic thugs to enforce his own edicts, meting out beatings, torture and murder. Gestapo members were originally the scum of German society, ex-police officers from city police forces who had been dismissed for brutality and other crimes, or military officers who had been dismissed from the army for misconduct.

In April 1934, Goering appointed Heinrich Himmler as deputy chief of the Prussian Secret Police. The Gestapo came under his command and it was expanded as a police arm of the S.S., Himmler's own creation. With pressure from the sadistic Himmler, the Prussian Supreme Court, in 1935, ruled that the Gestapo's orders and actions were not subject to judicial control. This became official on Feb. 10, 1936, when the Gestapo, by Nazi government decree, was placed above all the laws of the land. No court could interfere with this secret police organization in any manner. Dr. Werner Best, a top Gestapo official and one of Himmler's right-hand henchmen, stated: "As long as the police carries out the will of the leadership (Adolf Hitler), it is acting legally."

Legality, however, was a misnomer when it came to the Gestapo. Its agents did as they pleased—arrested and imprisoned whomever they chose and for whatever reason, merely stating that a suspect had been placed in the status of Schutzhaft or "protective custody," a catchall for any charge the Gestapo cared to later invent. Civil liberties by then had been suspended under the notorious Nazi Law of Feb. 28, 1933 and the Gestapo operated at will by this edict.

The Gestapo served as Himmler's secret police, but it also functioned as an arm of the S.S. in that it made arrests and detained persons before the S.S. determined the fate of a person. It was the S.S. that sent persons to the scores of concentration camps which the S.S. also maintained and where millions of hapless persons were summarily executed. The Gestapo, like its equally evil parent, the S.S., and its leader, Himmler, collapsed with the fall of the Third Reich in 1945. See: **Goering, Hermann; Himmler, Heinrich.**

REF.: Bullock, *A Study in Tyranny; CBA;* Crankshaw, *The Gestapo;* Davidson, *The Making of Adolf Hitler;* Delarue, *Histoire de la Gestapo;* Fest, *Hitler;* Görlitz and Quint, *Adolf Hitler: Eine Biographie;* Heiber, *Adolf Hitler: Eine Biographie;* Heiden, *Der Fuehrer;* Höhne, *The Order of the Death's Head;* Manvell and Fraenkel, *Heinrich Himmler;* Payne, *The Life and Death of Adolf Hitler;* Shirer, *The Rise and Fall of the Third Reich.*

Geta, Publius Septimius, 189-212, Roman., emp., assass. Second son of Septimius Severus, he was named augustus of Rome in 209. Following his father's death in 211, he shared the Roman emperorship for two years with his brother Caracalla. In a power struggle in 212, he was murdered by Caracalla. REF.: *CBA.*

Geter, Lennell, c.1957- , U.S., (wrong. convict.) rob. On Aug. 23, 1982, a Kentucky Fried Chicken restaurant was robbed in Balch Springs, Texas, a Dallas suburb. Within days, 24-year-old Lenell Geter, a black man, was arrested and charged with the robbery because an elderly white woman became suspicious when she noticed that Geter often went to a park after work. During his trial, five eyewitnesses identified him, although seven co-workers testified that Geter had been at work fifty miles away in Greenville. On the basis of the eyewitness identification, Geter was convicted and sentenced to a life prison term. Afterward, two more fellow workers gave depositions stating that Geter was at his desk during the robbery. Geter's story gained national

attention as the television program *60 Minutes,* covered the story, and his friends, family, and the NAACP fought his case. His lawyers claimed that the conviction stemmed from racism. After serving sixteen months in prison, an appeals court granted Geter a new trial and he was freed on Dec. 14, 1983. On Mar. 21, 1984, prosecutors announced that they were dropping charges against Geter. Afterward, Geter established the Geter Justice For All Foundation, an organization that distributes the names of civil rights agencies and lawyers to defendants. Geter's case also became the basis for a television movie, *Guilty of Innocence: The Lennell Geter Story.* REF.: *CBA.*

Getter, Charles, d.1833, U.S., mur. A Pennsylvania woman, Margaret Lawall, became pregnant and confronted Charles Getter saying he was the father. On Jan. 19, 1833, Getter was charged with fornication and bastardy, and he was faced with jail or marriage. Getter chose marriage and the couple were married that day. Getter actually liked another woman, Molly Hummer, and he spent time with her on his wedding day. During the following weeks, he reportedly said that he wanted to get rid of his wife. On Feb. 27, 1833, Getter choked and strangled his wife and left her body behind a stone wall by a lane. Getter was tried in Summer 1833, found Guilty, and executed on Oct. 4.

REF.: *CBA; Trial of Charles Getter, For the Murder of His Wife.*

Gettings, William, 1691-1713, Brit., rob. One among many thieves who flourished in eighteenth-century England, William Gettings and his peers roamed the English countryside robbing unsuspecting travelers, swindling innocent stooges, burglarizing homes and shoplifting from businesses.

On Sept. 25, 1713, the 22-year-old Gettings was executed at Tyburn for a lifetime of crime. At the time of his death, his crimes rivaled those of his more seasoned counterparts. A thief in the purest sense, Gettings would burglarize anyone, steal anything, and was not opposed to stealing from family members, nor to betraying the trust of close friends to pillage their belongings.

During one daylight burglary, Gettings entered a private residence and disassembled an entire bed, mattress, and frame, carrying it down to the second floor while the owners were home. He even got the master of the house to help him by convincing him that he had been hired to deliver the bed to the man's address. When the homeowner refused delivery of the furniture, he and his son actually helped Gettings carry it into the street.

Gettings' short life and long career ended on a Friday in September at the end of a rope. Although Gettings had lived and robbed alone, he did not die alone. Other notorious thieves executed at Tyburn that day included George Hollingsby, Thomas Turner, John Joyner, John Heath, Sarah Clifford, and Jane Wells. All were formally charged, tried, found Guilty, and punished for their thievery.

REF.: *CBA;* Smith, *Highwaymen.*

Gettler, Dr. **Alexander Oscar**, 1883-1968, U.S., toxicol. Though not a licensed physician, Dr. Alexander Gettler spent the better part of his career applying the skills of medicine to criminal investigations. Gettler, a chemist, served as the city toxicologist for New York from 1918 until his retirement in 1959. It has been said that Dr. Gettler single-handedly sent more criminals to the electric chair through scientific analysis than any detective using conventional police methods.

One sensational murder case Gettler resolved in the later stages of his career concerned a Puerto Rican sailor named Anibal Almodovar, accused of murdering his wife Louise in Manhattan's Central Park in November 1942. The suspect told police he had been dancing with a girlfriend at the time of the murder and had not set foot in the park for at least three years. Gettler proved that Almodovar was lying. The toxicologist scoured the ravine where the body was found, extracting soil samples, pieces of grass, and dried weeds. Next, he examined the trousers the accused wore that night. The dust particles, weed fragments, and blades of grass were compared through spectrographic analysis with the foliage in the ravine. The botanist Gettler brought into the case concluded that the samples were an identical match. Almodovar was tried and convicted.

Gettler examined at least 40,000 corpses during his career, and devised the accepted formula to determine whether a victim had died while inebriated. He deduced that twenty-five hundredths of alcohol per volume, found in the spinal fluid constituted legal intoxication.

Perhaps the best piece of research he performed during his career involved steam distillation of volatile liquids like benzine, chloroform, and ether—substances that evaporate quickly. Gettler established the presence of benzine in the tissue of two vagrants found dead in the basement of a Brooklyn apartment house. By steam-distilling the tissues, he recovered the volatile organic liquid and was able to establish a motive. The men, who had been paid $100 apiece by the owner to torch the tenement, had been overcome by toxic fumes from a barrel of benzine before they could ignite the torch. The owner, who desired to cash in his insurance policy, was arrested in Canada.

Gettler produced similar results with drowning victims by examining blood in both sides of the heart. "Years ago," he explained, "medical examiners and chemists only guessed when they gave drowning as a cause of death. I wanted to find out some positive way of telling and finally evolved a way precise and beyond contradiction."

Dr. Gettler gave evidence at many notable criminal trials, including the Snyder-Gray case of the 1920s, and established the cause of death for Jeanne Eagels, the famous actress whose body was destroyed in quicklime. He examined the contents of the stomach and determined that the woman had died of a drug and alcohol overdose. See: **Almodovar, Anibal; Snyder, Ruth May.**

REF.: *CBA;* Kobler, *Some Like It Gory;* Scott, *The Concise Encyclopedia of Crime and Criminals.*

J. Paul Getty III, kidnap victim, after being ransomed for $2.9 million in 1973.

Getty, J. Paul III, 1956- , Italy, kid. The grandson of the richest man in the world once confessed to a girlfriend that the only way to raise money to support his Bohemian lifestyle was to fake his own kidnapping. The offhanded remark was made by J. Paul Getty III, to a 24-year-old West German woman named Martine Zacher. Getty's words took on new significance when he mysteriously disappeared in the early morning hours of June 10, 1973, while on his way to purchase a newspaper and a comic book.

Getty, the grandson of the famous American oil-billionaire, was known as the "golden hippie" for his gypsy lifestyle in Rome's Trastevere and Piazza Navona sections. His mother, the former actress Gail Harris, at first refused to cooperate with Italian police, fearing recriminations at the hands of the gang, who demanded a ransom payment of $17 million for the safe return of her son. Speaking from London, the boy's grandfather announced that he would not pay the extortion, adding that it would only encourage

kidnappers. "If I pay one penny now, I'll have fourteen kidnapped grandchildren," he said. Four months passed. Getty's abductors then cut off his ear and sent it to the family on Oct. 21 to demonstrate that this was not a hoax.

The grandfather was forced to negotiate. He dispatched Fletcher Chase, his 54-year-old business associate, to Rome with 52,000 banknotes of lire, ($2.9 million in U.S. currency) each one carefully microfilmed by Italian police. Following the kidnappers' instructions, Chase drove a rented car southward past Naples.

Giuseppe Lamanna, knife-wielding kidnapper of Getty, under arrest, 1976.

Outside the village of Lagonegro, a Citroen automobile pulled up alongside. The occupants of the car rolled down the windows and began pelting Chase's vehicle with small pebbles as a sign to pull over. While the ransom money was being passed a third car pulled off to the side of the road. A man and a woman pretending to be tourists eyeballed the kidnappers and drove back to Rome to provide an accurate description to police. Getty was then released, after five months of imprisonment.

Eight members of the Calabrian Mafia were identified. Getty was released in December 1973 as Italian police stepped up efforts to bring the gang into custody. In early January 1974, the police closed in on the tiny village of Cicala located in the mountainous regions of Calabria in the southern tip of Italy. In a daring predawn raid, they seized Antonio Mancuso, thirty-five; Domenico Barbino, a 26-year-old hospital orderly who knew Getty from the hippie community in Rome; Vincenzo Mammoliti, forty-three; Gioia Tauro, Saverio Mammoliti; Giuseppe Lamanna; Antonio Femia; and Girolamo "Momo" Piromalli, fifty-eight, the top-ranking Mafia boss in Calabria. A 137-page indictment filed by Lagonegro District Attorney Maurizio Rossi dismissed any lingering suspicions that Getty staged his own abduction. The ransom money was to be used to finance a drug-running operation.

On July 29, 1976, Lamanna was sentenced to sixteen years in prison after being identified as the knife-wielding assailant who cut off Getty's ear. Antonio Marcuso, the only other defendant to go to jail, received eight years. The seven remaining defendants were acquitted for lack of evidence.

REF.: *CBA;* Clutterbuck, *Kidnap and Ransom;* Nash, *Almanac of World Crime;* ____, *Open Files.*

Gewin, Walter Pettus, 1908-81, U.S., jur. Prosecuting attorney of Hale County, Ala., from 1942-51. He was nominated to the Fifth Circuit Court by President John F. Kennedy in 1961. REF.: *CBA.*

Ghadiali, Dinshah Pestanji Framji, b.1873, U.S., fraud-rape. The Bombay-born Dinshah Ghadiali migrated to the U.S. in 1911 and practiced all kinds of medical fraud, particularly through crackpot machines he claimed would cure all kinds of illnesses. During WWI, Ghadiali volunteered in the New York Police Reserve Air Force. He refused any payment, but he did confer upon himself the title of colonel, one which he retained and used to indicate a position of distinction and achievement he never attained.

In 1920, Ghadiali invented what he called a Spectro-Chrome machine that, he claimed, could cure any disease or ailment, including gonorrhea, diabetes, and even nymphomania. He insisted, however, that his machine would only work on those who refrained from eating meat, from drinking tea, coffee, or alcohol, and from smoking or chewing tobacco. All patients that bathed in the bright colored lights of the Spectro-Chrome machine were warned that if they did not sleep with their heads pointing north each night, no amount of Ghadiali's medical application would work.

Ghadiali grew rich and then went on the lecture circuit. By 1925, Ghadiali, through his Spectro-Chrome therapy, was heralded as a miracle worker by the naive and the gullible. He traveled in limousines and stayed at the finest hotels. Ghadiali was accompanied for a time by a teenager whom he identified as his secretary. When Ghadiali reached Seattle in his nationwide tour, the girl suddenly appeared in a police station, swearing out a warrant for her employer's arrest, insisting that he had raped her. Since Ghadiali had transported the girl across state lines for immoral purposes, a violation of the Mann Act, he was quickly convicted and sent to the federal penitentiary at Atlanta for five years.

In prison, Ghadiali wrote his so-called memoirs, *Railroading A Citizen,* which he later published in two volumes. Ghadiali stated in his book that the teenager who had sent him to prison had lied, that it was the girl who had raped *him.* He also said that a huge conspiracy had been formed by the Ku Klux Klan, Henry Ford, blacks, Catholics, and the Department of Justice to wreck his successful medical practice and send him to prison. Upon release, Ghadiali set up shop in New Jersey, establishing an "institute," to which more than 10,000 persons flocked to take his quack cures at $90-a-year memberships. He charged $250 for those wishing to study at the institute.

Ghadiali's operations were finally closed down when several people died while baking beneath the turning, rotating, colored lights of his Spectro-Chrome machines. One patient, a diabetic, was ordered by Ghadiali to stop using insulin, and according to his son, promptly died. Ghadiali was fined $20,000 and ordered to leave the state. The quack refused to cease his illegal operations and started up his cures in one state after another until he vanished in the 1950s.

REF.: *CBA; Gardner, Fads and Fallacies;* Nash, *Zanies.*

Gheorghiu-Dej, Gheorghe, 1901-65, Rom., consp. Imprisoned from 1933-44 for participating in the Grivita railway strike. In 1944, he became secretary general of the Communist party and led the ouster of anti-Communist Romanian Premier Nicolae Radescu. He helped Russians establish the Communist government after WWII, and served as prime minister from 1952-55. His work as president of the State Council helped Romania establish a degree of independence from the Soviets. REF.: *CBA.*

Gherardesca, Ugolino della (Ugolino da Pisa), d.1288, Italy, sab. Imprisoned in 1274 for conspiring to take command of Pisa. He escaped and joined Florentine and Luccan Guelphs in a renewed drive against Pisa, regaining land in 1276. He was accused of sabotaging the Pisan war effort against Genoa in 1284. After being named captain general of Pisa in 1285, he was ousted in a conspiracy headed by Ruggiero Ubaldini, the archbishop of Pisa. In July 1288, he was imprisoned with two sons and two grandsons at the Tower of Gualandi, now known as the Torre di Fame, where they died of starvation. REF.: *CBA.*

Gholston, Kenneth, 1957- , U.S., rob.-rape. Nine men were charged with the gang rape of a 16-year-old girl and with the robbery and beating of her two male companions. The ringleader was sentenced to 228 years in prison.

A 16-year-old girl, whose identity was withheld, was traveling home around midnight on Dec. 28, 1980, on a northbound Chicago Rapid Transit train when one of her two male companions became ill. Getting off at the Thorndale station the three were approached by a group of nine men, eight of them teenagers. While some of them beat and robbed her friends, taking $30 and a pair of gloves, the others gang-raped the 16-year-old, first on top of the train platform, then underneath it. The girl, who contracted genital herpes as a result of the assault, said she could hear the rapists demanding their turn throughout the attack.

Of the six defendants tried by jury in the courtroom of Judge Earl E. Strayhorn in mid-November 1981, five were charged with participating in the sexual attack, and the sixth was charged with assaulting the girl's companions. Eight of the defendants were arrested as they rode southward on the train. Charged in the gang rape were three brothers: Kenneth Gholston, twenty-four; Danny Gholston, seventeen; and Anthony Gholston, eighteen; along with brothers David King, seventeen; and Darryl King, eighteen; and David Love, seventeen.

Love dragged the girl underneath the platform after the others had raped her; he then raped her and punched her in the face before getting back on the tracks. During the trial, the six defendants frequently laughed and made incredulous faces at their families.

Charges included deviant sexual assault, robbery, rape, conspiracy to commit robbery, aggravated battery, and taking indecent liberties with a child. Anthony Gholston claimed he had "dozed off" far from the scene of their attack, and had only hit the girl's companions after he bumped into them. Both Gholston and Dennis King, eighteen, denied raping the victim. Kenneth Gholston, the leader of the attack, had been paroled from prison just forty-eight days before the assault. It was the third time he had committed a felony while on parole or probation from another felony, according to William O'Connor who, along with lawyer Fran Norek, served as prosecuting attorney.

A heroin addict and an alcoholic since the eighth grade, Gholston had left two drug-abuse centers because he was "bored." Gholston's lawyer, Clyde Lemons, corroborated O'Connor's statements, but asked for leniency for his client because he was "the product of a cold and unconcerned society." On Dec. 28, 1981, Judge Strayhorn sentenced Kenneth Gholston to 228 years in prison, saying: "I feel you are a danger to society and should never again be permitted to walk the streets." Gholston, who will not be eligible for parole for 114 years, snarled obscenities at Strayhorn as the judge attempted to inform him of his right to appeal. Also sentenced were Danny Gholston, convicted of all charges and given fifty years in prison; Darryl King, who pleaded guilty to all charges, to twenty years in prison; Jerry Cummings, seventeen, to seven years in prison on charges of aggravated battery, conspiracy, and robbery; Anthony Hart, eighteen, to five years on a guilty plea to aggravated battery and robbery; Joseph Thurmond, eighteen, to five years on a guilty plea to robbery and aggravated battery.

On Dec. 31, 1981, Judge Strayhorn announced sentences for David Love, Dennis King, and Anthony Gholston, handing down jail terms of ninety-five, thirty, and twenty-five years, respectively. Attorney Norek, in asking for a severe sentence for Love, reminded Strayhorn that it was Love who had picked up the girl and thrown her on the tracks, punching her, and leaving her in the snow. During the sentencing, Strayhorn said that Love, while awaiting sentencing, had raped a male inmate in the Cook County Jail.

Asked for her reaction to the sentences the girl said, "They deserve it. That's as bluntly as I can put it. They deserve it." In a later interview, she spoke of how she was haunted by the assault, sometimes taunted by her schoolmates, or relived the experience in nightmares. "When I look at what happened, I don't think of just what happened to me. I not only think of my sadness, but I think of the sorrow they have caused to their families. As they were sentenced, I could feel their mothers crying behind me." REF.: *CBA.*

Giancana, Sam (Gilormo Giangono, Momo Salvatore Giangano; AKA: Momo, Sam Mooney), 1908-75, U.S., org. crime. Sam Giancana graduated from Chicago's old "42 Gang" to take his place in the Chicago chapter of La Cosa Nostra—the most violent, kill-crazy crime family in the U.S. In the 1920s, Giancana earned his stripes as a "wheelman" for the Al Capone mob. There was no job too dangerous for this young up-and-comer from the old West Side. Later, he served as a part-time chauffeur for

Tony Accardo and Paul "the Waiter" Ricca, mob luminaries who succeeded Capone and Frank Nitti in the 1940s.

When Selective Service officials interviewed Giancana for potential overseas duty in WWII, they asked him his profession. The canny mobster replied, "Me? I steal." The draft board declared Giancana a 4-H, a "constitutional psychopath" and sent him home. "They thought I was crazy," he said years later. "But I wasn't crazy. I was telling the truth." With more than seventy arrests dating from 1925, Giancana was in no position to lie. In the late 1930s, he was sentenced to a term in the prison at Terre Haute, Ind., for running an illegal moonshine still. While serving his time, Giancana met Edward "Teenan" Jones, a South Side policy boss who convinced him of the potential in the inner-city gambling rackets. When he got out, Giancana oversaw the mob takeover of South Side gambling. One by one, the black policy bosses who refused to submit to the Mafia were assassinated.

Chicago gangster Sam "Momo" Giancana.

But it was the "graying" of the Chicago mob that had more to do with Giancana's post-war rise than his skill as a statesman. Jake Guzik, Sam "Golf Bag" Hunt, Phil D'Andrea, and Louis Campagna were relics of the Prohibition era. Their retirement paved the way for the "Youngbloods" to advance into the hierarchy. Accardo and Ricca promoted Giancana to "manager of operations" in the mid-1950s. By 1957 he was considered the head of the Chicago family, a position he held until 1966, when

the government intensified its efforts against him. Chicago had experienced seventy-nine mob murders during Giancana's nine-year rule, while the next eight years saw only twenty-four killings, a reflection of Giancana's "shoot first, ask questions later" philosophy.

Giancana had little use for the old world traditions, imported from Sicily by mobsters like Carlo Gambino. Sam "Mooney" Giancana was Chicago-born and bred. Whoever produced income for the outfit earned his respect. The lucky rivals who were deposed with minimal bloodshed were left to ponder their fate. Others, like William "Action" Jackson, a Chicago juice collector, were dangled from a meat hook and tortured with cattle prods. During the administration of President John F. Kennedy, Giancana reportedly joined a CIA plot to assassinate Cuban dictator Fidel Castro. A Giancana girlfriend, Judith Campbell Exner, allegedly served as a courier between the Kennedy White House, mobster Johnny Roselli, and Giancana's residence in the Chicago suburb of Oak Park.

The botched attempt on Castro only brought more unwanted attention to Giancana. His opulent lifestyle, his celebrated affair with singer Phyllis McGuire, whom he entertained lavishly at Lake Tahoe's Cal-Neva Lodge and at his estate in Mexico, made Giancana a minor celebrity and a popular subject for newspaper gossip columnists. In 1960, he became extremely upset with McGuire when she began dating comedian Dan Rowan. As a favor to the mobster, his contacts in the CIA allegedly hired a Miami detective to conduct undercover surveillance on Rowan. Mob associate Chuckie English asked an FBI agent, who had been keeping watch on him back in Chicago, "Why don't you guys stop all this? We're all a part of the same team." The government began probing deeper into Giancana's affairs. In 1965, he was sent to jail for a year for refusing to cooperate with a federal grand jury investigating organized crime. When released in 1966, he went into self-imposed exile in Peru, Beirut, Puerto Rico, and Mexico. He traveled luxuriously, chartering the best yachts, private aircraft, and limousines. At his side was his bodyguard and confidante Richard Cain, a former Chicago policeman turned mobster.

The FBI continued to hound Giancana, even after he went into semi-retirement at his villa in Cuernavaca, Mexico. In July 1974, the Mexican government hustled him out of the villa. He was taken to the airport and flown to San Antonio, where the FBI was waiting. Returned to Chicago on the red-eye, Giancana was brought before a federal grand jury investigating syndicate gambling operations and Cain's December 1973 murder. The Chicago mob grew apprehensive over Giancana's answers to tough questions about how he had invested their money in Latin America. According to government informants, Giancana demanded that his associates take whatever steps were necessary to get the Justice Department off his back and call in certain "IOUs" from friendly congressmen. "Seven out of ten times when we hit a guy, we're wrong," the estranged syndicate boss had allegedly said. "But the other three times we hit, we make up for it." The mob chieftains in Chicago decided to eliminate Giancana before he became an embarrassment.

On June 19, 1975, just two days after returning from successful gall bladder surgery in Houston, Sam Giancana was shot seven times at close range as he stood at a stove cooking a plate of sausages and escarole in the basement of his Oak Park bungalow. The assassin was believed to be someone in the mob Giancana knew and trusted. Subpoenas were issued for several Chicago crime figures who had attended Giancana's welcome home party, including Charles "Chuckie" English, and Dominick "Butch" Blasi, longtime bodyguard. No one was ever arrested for the murder of Giancana. It was one of more than a thousand unsolved mob murders recorded by the Chicago Crime Commission since 1919. The mob's decision to shun Sam Giancana's funeral was their way of showing disrespect. See: **Accardo, Anthony Joseph; Cain, Richard B.; Capone, Alphonse; Exner, Judith Campbell; Ricca, Paul.**

REF.: Bonanno, *A Man of Honor; CBA;* Cressey, *Theft of the Nation;* Davis, *Mafia Kingfish;* Demaris, *Captive City;* ____, *The Last Mafioso;* Fried, *The Rise and Fall of the Jewish Gangster in America;* Gage, *Mafia, U.S.A.;* ____, *The Mafia is not an Equal Opportunity Employer;* Giancana, *Mafia Princess;* Godwin, *Murder U.S.A.;* Gosch and Hammer, *The Last Testament of Lucky Luciano;* Kobler, *Capone;* Lait and Mortimer, *Chicago: Confidential;* McClellan, *Crime Without Punishment;* Maas, *The Valachi Papers;* Martin, *Revolt in the Mafia;* Messick, *Secret File;* ____, *Syndicate in the Sun;* Morgan, *Prince of Crime;* Nash, *Bloodletters and Badmen;* ____, *Citizen Hoover;* ____, *Open Files;* Overstreet, *The FBI In Our Open Society;* Powers, *Secrecy and Power;* Reid, *The Grim Reapers;* Servadio, *Mafioso;* Smith, *Syndicate City;* Ungar, *FBI;* Zuckerman, *Vengeance Is Mine.*

Giannini, Eugenio, 1910-52, U.S., org. crime. Gene Giannini, thought to be a loyal soldier in Vito Genovese's Mafia army, was actually an informer for the Federal Bureau of Narcotics. While informing on top Mafiosi, Giannini was able to double-cross the bureau and continue to deal drugs. In the early 1950s, he presented a counterfeiting scheme to Charles "Lucky" Luciano, who was in exile in Italy. But Luciano suspected something was amiss and rejected the proposition. Meanwhile, Giannini was arrested with Dominick "The Gap" Petrelli for a minor matter, and sought to extricate himself with a letter to the Narcotics Bureau in Rome, reminding them of his assistance. But the letter never reached Rome. Instead, the contents were relayed to Luciano, who informed Genovese, who allegedly assigned the Mafia "hit" contract on Giannini to gunman Joseph Valachi. Three of Valachi's associates carried out the assignment on Sept. 20, 1952. A short time later, Petrelli was also killed. Valachi himself later became an informant against the mob, and it was revealed that Petrelli was a third informant. It is possible that Valachi silenced Giannini to cover his own identity. REF.: *CBA.*

Giannola, Vito, prom. 1920s, U.S., org. crime. Sicilian-born Vito Giannola became a Mafia executioner at an early age and fled Palermo, Sicily in 1915, following a murder. He migrated to the U.S., where he settled in the large Italian-Sicilian community in St. Louis. Here he became the head of the Mafia and, during the 1920s, leader of a fierce bootlegging gang called the "Green Ones", a sobriquet from Sicily, meaning Mafia gangsters from farming communities. Giannola and his brother John were later credited with the deaths of at least twenty-five persons during the 1920s when the Green Ones battled another St. Louis bootlegging gang, the Cuckoos, over territorial rights. Giannola died peacefully in his bed three decades later. See: **Cuckoos Gang; Green Ones, The.**
REF.: *CBA;* Reid, *Mafia.*

Gianola, Leonard (AKA: Needles), 1910- , U.S., theft-extor. With a record dating back to 1932, Leonard Gianola has been arrested several times on charges of theft and is known as a labor racketeer on Chicago's West Side.

Gianola was sentenced in 1932 to six months in jail for malicious mischief, with six months probation. He was once charged with vagrancy and fined $60, and was convicted in 1935 by the Chicago Police Department on federal charges of theft from Interstate Commerce, spending three years in the U.S. Penitentiary in Leavenworth, Kan. He was on the payroll of Local 46, Laundry, Cleaning and Dye House Workers International Union, and was active in narcotics. REF.: *CBA.*

Gibbons, Abigail (Abigail Hopper), 1801-93, U.S., penal reform. Daughter of U.S. abolitionist Isaac Tatem Hopper who married James Sloan Gibbons in 1833. She served as president of the Women's Prison Association, and co-developed the Isaac T. Hopper home for ex-convicts. REF.: *CBA.*

Gibbons, John Joseph, 1924- , U.S., jur. Published many articles and essays, including "To Head off the Next Violent Summer" (1967) and "White Racism and Black Power" (1968), in *New Jersey State Bar Journal.* He was nominated to the Third Circuit Court by President Richard Nixon in 1969. REF.: *CBA.*

Gibbs, Charles, d.1831, U.S., pir.-mur. Born in Rhode Island, Charles Gibbs went to sea at an early age. During the War of 1812 he served on various privateers, compiling an enviable record. When the conflict ended, Gibbs enlisted on board an Argentinian privateer that raided up and down the Caribbean. By 1821, he had turned pirate and had become the scourge of the U.S. Navy, which sent the *Enterprise* to the Gulf of Mexico to find him. Under the direction of Lieutenant Commander Lawrence Kearney, the navy seized four of Gibbs' vessels, but Gibbs slipped away.

He roamed the oceans for another ten years, killing some 400 men by his own estimate. It was said that he once personally chopped off the arms and legs of a rival captain, and had set fire to a merchant ship with the entire crew on board. On Nov. 1, 1830, Gibbs, now serving on board the *Vineyard,* participated in his final mutiny. With the cook, Thomas G. Wansley, Gibbs murdered the captain, William Thornby, and the first mate, William Roberts. Both men were thrown overboard off Cape Hatteras as the ship sailed toward Philadelphia. The mutineers scuttled the ship near Long Island and headed inland when crew members talked to authorities. Gibbs and Wansley were captured and hanged on Ellis Island on Apr. 22, 1831.

REF.: Botting, *The Pirates; CBA; Confession of Charles Gibbs the Pirate; Confessions and Executions of the Pirates; Correct Account of the Trial & Sentence of Thos. Wansley & Charles Gibbs; Execution of the Pirates;* Hopson, *The Confession of the Terrible Pirate, Charles Gibbs; Last Dying Words and Confession of Charles Gibbs; Lives and Trial of Gibbs and Wansley;* Mitchell, *Pirates; Mutiny and Murder; Trial and Sentence of Thomas J. Wansley;* Nash, *Almanac of World Crime;* ____, *Bloodletters and Badmen.*

Gibbs, Edward Lester, 1925- , U.S., mur. In the early afternoon of Jan. 10, 1950, Marian Louise Baker, a secretary in the treasurer's office of the Franklin and Marshall College in Lancaster, Pa., went to make a daily bank deposit for the school and never returned. A search for the missing woman proved fruitless.

On Jan. 14, Mrs. Frances Harnish visited her summer cottage at Mill Creek and discovered Baker's body in a hole under the house that had been made for a water heater, covered with sheets of corrugated metal. The fresh footprint of a man was visible in soft dirt near the excavation. Lancaster police commissioner Fred McCarney arrived on the scene, accompanied by detectives Captain Kirchner and Frank Matt, along with state trooper Captain Frank Gleason and several plainclothes sergeants. Dr. Charles Stahr, deputy coroner, examined the body and determined that the cause of death had been several shattering blows to the skull. Baker's rings and purse were missing, and there was no indication of sexual assault. Her wristwatch had been smashed, the time stopped at 2:36, indicating that, if this was the actual time of death, Baker had probably been slain by someone she knew, possibly a student from the college. Two carpenters who had been working near the Harnish cottage corroborated this theory when they said they had heard-high pitched screams at about 2:30 p.m., and presumed it was a child being spanked.

Intensive questioning of hundreds of people, many of them students or workers at the college who had been absent when Baker was murdered, began, headed by Captain Kirchner. On Jan. 17, the son of a local undertaker told the police that a college senior had asked him questions about how long it took a body to decompose. The queries were made just after Baker's death by Edward Lester Gibbs.

Gibbs, a 25-year-old married student attending school on a GI Bill, was a popular, well-liked student of good social and academic standing. With the increasingly tense atmosphere created by the murder investigation at the school, police kept Gibbs under careful observation, and waited until the next day to call him in to Dean Breidenstine's office for questioning. After a brief exchange with the dean, the shaken Gibbs left, only to rush over to the college president's office and announce, "I'm the man you're looking for. I did this terrible thing. I have brought disgrace on the college." Gibbs then began to cry, asking why the police had questioned everyone else and left him to "sweat it out." He confessed he had given Baker a ride in the early afternoon, parked the car at a scenic view, and had a sudden impulse to strangle the woman. He had grabbed her, she struggled, and he then choked her some more, pulled a lug wrench from his car trunk, and bludgeoned her to death. After signing his confession Gibbs told District Attorney Ranck, "I'm an intelligent man. I didn't think you'd catch me."

Tried in mid-March 1950, a jury found Gibbs Guilty of first-degree murder and recommended death after deliberating for almost five hours. After a state Supreme Court turned down his appeal for a new trial, Gibbs was electrocuted in April 1951.

REF.: *CBA*; Radin, *Headline Crimes of the Year*; Wilson, *Encyclopedia of Murder*.

Gibbs, Janie Lou, prom. 1967-76, U.S., mur. Young "Granny" Gibbs—she was only thirty-four when she became a grandmother—poisoned her eldest son and worked as a Sunday School teacher that same day. By that time, she had already killed four family members over a two-year period, each time contributing a tithe from the insurance money to her church. Janie Lou Gibbs began by killing her husband and insisted that no autopsy be performed. Three sons died over a period of some months, and Gibbs again refused autopsies. She was not able to quell suspicions when her grandson died, apparently in the same way.

When the infant and his father were found to have died from poison, other family members were exhumed and all were found to have been poisoned with arsenic. Gibbs was arrested on Dec. 24, 1967. She admitted guilt, but because of her questionable sanity, the state of Georgia took more than eight years to find Janie Lou Gibbs ready to stand trial. She was found Guilty of all five murders and sentenced to five life sentences. See: **Blandy, Mary; Cotton, Mary Ann Robson Mowbray; DeMelker, Daisy Louisa; Jegado, Helene; LaFarge, Marie; Smith, Madeleine**.

REF.: *CBA*; Godwin, *Murder U.S.A.*; Holmes, *Serial Murder*.

Giberson, Ivy, prom. 1922, U.S., mur. At around 3 a.m. on Aug. 13, 1922, two railroad workers in Lakehurst, N.J., heard a woman's screams coming from an apartment. Rushing over and trying to get in, they heard a woman begging for help, and broke in the door, finding Ivy Giberson bound hand and foot with a napkin gag clinging to her chin. In the bedroom lay the body of William Giberson, the middle-aged owner of a taxi company: he had a bullet through the base of his skull.

Ivy Giberson explained to local police that she had been awakened at a few minutes after 3 a.m. and come into the kitchen, finding two men. One had bound and gagged her while the other went into the bedroom and shot her husband when he woke up. The robbers got away with $700 in cash, which Mr. Giberson had recently withdrawn to buy a new cab.

Called in to investigate the case was Burlington County, N.J., Chief of Detectives, Ellis Parker, whose promising career would later be shattered by his involvement in the infamous Hauptmann-Lindbergh kidnapping case. At the Gibersons' apartment, Parker asked the widow to tell him again what had happened. In recalling the robbers' exact words, Ivy Giberson explained how they had not started talking until after they had shot her husband, when the man who was tying her up in the kitchen shouted to his partner in the bedroom, "Why the hell did you shoot him?" and the thief in the bedroom replied, "I had to; he was waking up." Parker then accused Giberson of murdering her husband, basing his deduction on the fact that no robber would have made such remarks. There would be no way a robber could have seen what occurred in the bedroom shooting, and would have gone to investigate the possibility that Giberson had his own gun and had shot their accomplice. Additional evidence, including the murder weapon and the facts that Giberson was interested in another man, and had purchased a widow's outfit more than a week before the murder, was brought in and Ivy Giberson confessed. She was tried and convicted, and sentenced to twenty years in the State penitentiary at Trenton. See: **Hauptmann, Bruno Richard**.

REF.: *CBA*; Cohen, *One Hundred True Crime Stories*.

Gibert, Pedro, prom. 1832, U.S., pir. On Sept. 20, 1832, the American ship *Mexican*, bound for Rio de Janeiro from Salem, Mass., carrying $20,000 in silver, was captured by a pirate schoo-

ner, the *Panda*. Captain Pedro Gibert's response to the question of what should be done with the crew was to suggest killing them.

While they looted the brig, the pirates locked the ship members in the forecastle, later slashing the sails and rigging, filling the galley with burnable materials, and setting it on fire just before they sailed away. About an hour later, the inhabitants of the *Mexican* broke free and doused the fire, letting enough smoke continue to billow to fool the departing pirates, and safely returning to Salem about six weeks later.

Gibert was captured in 1834 by the British in Africa and extradited to Boston for his trial and hanging.

REF.: Botting, *The Pirates*; *CBA*.

Gibons, Jacqueline, c.1962- , and **St. Pierre, Robert**, c.1963- , and **Wilson, Barry Alan**, c.1959- , U.S., mur. Jacqueline Gibons was an adopted child with a history of stealing, truancy, and lying. She once reportedly attacked other children with a pair of scissors. As a teenager, the girl was admitted to hospitals for emotionally disturbed children and to group care homes. Her parents, Benjamin and Sybil Gibons, made the girl seek counseling, and placed her on restrictive diets for her obesity. When she was charged with writing bad checks, her parents signed over custody to the state. Gibons returned to her adoptive parents permanently after dropping out of college.

On July 27, 1982, someone smashed Jacqueline Gibons' bedroom window and stole a pair of gold earrings. Her mother called police, though Jacqueline later reported that her boyfriend, Barry Alan Wilson, had been looking through her window and fell through the pane. Mr. and Mrs. Gibons were considering filing a complaint against Wilson, but their daughter objected. On July 29, 19-year-old ex-convict Robert St. Pierre was with the 20-year-old Gibons and her 23-year-old boyfriend at her parents' Skokie, Ill., home. Gibons' 62-year-old father was bludgeoned to death with a claw hammer in the kitchen. Gibons then picked her 60-year-old mother up at a train station and returned home, where Mrs. Gibons met a similar fate. Gibons, St. Pierre, and Wilson concealed the bodies in plastic bags in the trunk of the family car. They drove to Albuquerque, New Mexico and dumped the corpses on a side road.

Wilson was arrested in Phoenix, Ariz., on Aug. 4, 1982. Earlier, Gibons and St. Pierre had been arrested, and both had accused Wilson of committing the actual murders. At the trial of the three, however, Gibons claimed St. Pierre was the murderer. The prosecution argued that Wilson had killed Mr. and Mrs. Gibons because of the possibility they would file a complaint against him. Each attorney tried to blame the other's client. Gibons, who stood to inherit her parents' estate, was also accused. The defense argued that St. Pierre, after getting drunk, was persuaded to kill the couple. On Oct. 11, 1983, all three were convicted of murder. Gibons and her boyfriend Wilson waived their right to allow the jury to determine sentencing, and were sentenced to life in prison by Judge Leonard Grazian on Nov. 4. St. Pierre chose to have the jury decide his fate and was sentenced to death. REF.: *CBA*.

Gibson, Benjamin F., 1931- , U.S., jur. Attorney general for the State of Michigan from 1961-63. He was nominated to the Western District Court of Michigan by President James E. Carter in 1979, and was chairman of the Law Enforcement and Crime Committee of Region Six. REF.: *CBA*.

Gibson, Edward (First Baron Ashbourne), 1837-1913, Ire., jur. Member of Irish Parliament from 1875-85, and attorney general from 1877-80. He was named lord chancellor of Ireland in 1885, 1886-92, and 1895-1906. REF.: *CBA*.

Gibson, Eileen (Gay), See: **Camb, James**.

Gibson, Lindsey, prom. 1891, Case of, U.S., mur. Gibson, a native of St. Paul, Madison County, Ark., was a rarity, a southerner who had served in the Union Army. After the war, he was branded by his neighbors as a traitor and was shunned and insulted. One of Gibson's most severe antagonists was William Prater who was murdered in 1867. Gibson was labeled the killer but was not indicted until ten years later, which must be a record delay in U.S. jurisprudence. Even more amazingly, Gibson was not arrested for the killing until 1889, twenty-two years after Prater's death. He was not tried until 1891 and then was acquitted. The Gibson case is one of the most unusual on record relative to its incredible delays of due process.

REF.: *CBA; The Great Murder Trial of Lindsey Gibson in Western Arkansas.*

Gibson, Violet Albina, prom. 1926, Italy, attempt. assass. In April 1926, the year after Benito Mussolini openly instituted a Fascist dictatorship in Italy, an Irish woman, Violet Albina Gibson, tried to assassinate him. Mussolini had just left the capitol and was making his way toward a waiting car when Gibson emerged from the crowd and fired at him. Although she aimed for Mussolini's head, the bullet only grazed the tip of his nose.

A policeman grabbed the 50-year-old Gibson and disarmed her. The crowd began pulling at her and might have killed her had not Mussolini himself called out for order, reportedly saying, "Let nothing be done which will bring reproach to our beloved Italy...I do not want reprisals...." Gibson, who was the sister of the Irish peer William Gibson, the second Baron Ashbourne, was whisked off to jail. Members of her family wrote profuse apologies to Mussolini and explained that Gibson had been considered mentally unbalanced for years and had spent six months in a mental institution in England in 1923.

While the Italian government decided what to do with Gibson, she was held in a cell in Rome where she was guarded by nuns. Her account at an English bank in Rome was frozen. Her brother traveled from Dublin to Rome, where he retained Deputy Enrico Ferri, known as the Italian Clarence Darrow, to defend his sister. Some nine months after the incident, in May 1927, Gibson was allowed to leave Italy for England. A special tribunal had ruled that no further action would be taken against her due to her mental condition. Italian police escorted Gibson and her four nurses to the border. At no point did Gibson reveal her motive for the shooting. REF.: *CBA.*

Giddings, Daniel, b.c.1843, Case of, U.S., mur. Daniel Giddings, married with three children, bought a small farm in the area of Massieville, Ohio. A friend, Benjamin Wiltshire, visited the family at their home and made advances towards Giddings' wife, who soon decided to visit her parents. She packed some of her belongings and asked her husband to take her to the railroad station. When Giddings took her into town, she told him to leave her at the home of a family, telling him she could take care of the rest of the arrangements and Giddings returned home. However, during the next week, his wife remained in town and had an affair with Wiltshire. Giddings, who had a reputation as a kind, peaceful person, apparently returned to town several times, vowing to murder Wiltshire, but stopping himself because of his children. In July 1882, Giddings filed a petition for divorce, charging his wife with adultery, and a copy of the petition and a summons were served to his wife. He also sent her a personal letter. After receiving the documents, Giddings' wife begged him to take her back, threatening to commit suicide if he refused. He agreed, and after she returned, she told Giddings that Wiltshire had threatened to kill him. On Aug. 3, 1882, Giddings borrowed a pistol from a neighbor for protection, and the next day he and his wife retrieved her belongings. On Aug. 5, Giddings went into town to visit a real estate agent to list his farm before stopping into a saloon at about 2 p.m., unaware that Wiltshire was already inside. The two men drank together and then went to another saloon. Then they walked down a street and over to a cornfield where Giddings asked Wiltshire to leave his wife alone. Wiltshire apparently reached into a hip pocket, for a gun, and said that he had as much of a right to her as Giddings did, and that he would take her away or kill Giddings. Giddings then drew his gun and shot twice, killing Wiltshire. Giddings ran from the scene, and that evening he returned the borrowed gun to his neighbor. Giddings was arrested, tried, and acquitted of the murder.

REF.: *CBA; Trial of Daniel Giddings for Shooting Benjamin Wiltshire, August 5, 1882 near Chillicothe, Ohio.*

Gierbolini, Gilberto, 1926- , U.S., jur. Nominated to the District Court of Puerto Rico by President James E. Carter in 1980. He chaired the Committee on Criminal Procedure of the Judicial Conference for the Superior Court. REF.: *CBA.*

Giesler, Jerry (Harold Lee Giesler), 1886-1961, U.S., lawyer. To a generation of Hollywood film stars with legal problems, the cry was "Get me Giesler!" There was no finer defense attorney in Southern California during the motion picture studios' heyday than Jerry Giesler, a paunchy, bald Iowan. His client list included Charley Chaplin, Errol Flynn, Marilyn Monroe, Barbara Hutton, Shelley Winters, and Alexander Pantages, only a few of the Hollywood luminaries who emerged legal victors through Giesler's efforts.

Giesler was born into modest surroundings, far from the tinsel of Hollywood. His father was a banker in the small town of Wilton Junction, Iowa. As a boy, Harold Lee Giesler (pronounced "geeseler"—he was sensitive about his name) was a voracious reader. At sixteen, Giesler attended the Morgan Park Military Academy in Chicago, and later planned to attend the University of Michigan. However, a problem with his eyesight forced Giesler to abandon college temporarily. In 1905, he moved to Los Angeles where he accepted a job driving a lumber wagon. It was grueling work that paid him $2 a day. Each morning at four, he left his apartment to make deliveries, traveling the unpaved roads of Los Angeles. At the time, newspapers were filled with stories of legal battles faced by the International Workers of the World (I.W.W.). Giesler read about the brilliant courtroom tactics of Clarence Darrow, who secured an acquittal for William Haywood, accused of killing Idaho governor Frank Steunenberg. "His victory filled me with a desire to practice criminal law," Giesler wrote later in his autobiography. "The battling and tension which Mr. Darrow faced appealed to me. They still do."

Criminal lawyer Jerry Giesler, assuming the position of the body of a murder victim in court to make a point.

Inspired by Darrow and another noted defense attorney, Earl Rogers, Giesler enrolled in the University of Southern California Law School. He funded his education by starting up a bill collection agency with two fellow students. One person he pursued for payments was none other than criminal attorney Earl Rogers. At first, Rogers refused to speak to Giesler, but Giesler's persistence as a bill collector was finally rewarded with a job in Rogers' law firm. Rogers took Giesler under his wing, giving him the nickname Jerry, and making Giesler a junior partner in the firm after he completed law school. Giesler also had the opportunity to work for Clarence Darrow as attorney of record. The aging Darrow was accused of bribing two jurors to win an acquittal for the McNamara Brothers, on trial for dynamiting the Los Angeles *Times* Building in 1911. It was a riveting moment in Giesler's life. "After the trial I was walking down Broadway with Mr. Darrow when he said, 'Come in here Jerry,' and led me into a tailor shop and bought me an overcoat. That's the only fee I received for working in his two trials, but the photograph I have of myself standing between Mr. Darrow and Mr. Rogers is worth far more to me than any fee."

The turning point in Giesler's career occurred in 1931, following his blistering cross-examination of 17-year-old Eunice Pringle. Pringle, a Hollywood ingenue, accused movie mogul Alexander Pantages of statutory rape. Giesler's client, the "Great God Pan," as Pringle labeled him, was convicted in the first of two trials. However, Giesler was made head of the legal team that won acquittal for Pantages in the second trial after proving that the young woman was hired—allegedly by Joseph Kennedy—to embarrass his rival. After Pringle wore a child's dress in court, Giesler asked the judge to instruct her to wear to court the same outfit she wore on the night of the "rape." The provocative crimson gown cast her in an altogether different light, and helped earn Pantages a reprieve.

Divorce and murder cases were Jerry Giesler's specialties. In nearly fifty years before the bar, he never lost a client to the electric chair. Seventy accused murderers were successfully defended by Giesler, including 14-year-old Cheryl Crane, who stabbed gangster Johnny Stompanato on Apr. 4, 1958, to defend her mother, Lana Turner, from possible physical harm. Her action was judged a justifiable homicide. Giesler brought Lana Turner to the witness stand, and walked her through the nightmare.

For years Giesler represented stars facing career-threatening scandals. In 1942, two teen-age girls, Peggy La Rue Satterlee and Betty Hansen, filed complaints with the district attorney, charging Hollywood matinee idol Errol Flynn with statutory rape. Satterlee, a dark-haired girl of sixteen, claimed that Flynn had seduced her aboard his yacht *Sirocco* as it sailed by Catalina Island. At one point, Flynn brought her below deck to his stateroom where they gazed at the moon through a porthole. There, she claimed, the actor had ravished her. Giesler subsequently proved that it was impossible to observe the moon from that precise location. Hansen was a stage-struck farm girl from Lincoln, Neb., who met Flynn at a party in Bel Air, Calif. She accused him of improper advances in his second floor bedroom. Hansen's motive for bringing these charges, as Giesler demonstrated, was her desire to escape Juvenile Hall where she had been held on various morals charges. The Flynn case ended in an acquittal on Feb. 6, 1943.

Despite his unassuming appearance, and high, whining voice, Giesler was an intimidating courtroom presence who knew how to sway a jury. When he defended stripper Lilli St. Cyr on a charge of indecent exposure, Giesler himself appeared in court wearing the same diaphanous towel that offended the morals squad the night of the performance. The jurors, reduced to hysterical laughter at the sight of the half-naked lawyer, acquitted St. Cyr.

Giesler's exhortations on behalf of Hollywood producer Walter Wanger and actor Robert Mitchum were not as successful. In a moment of jealous rage, Wanger fired a .38-caliber slug into a man wooing his wife, actress Joan Bennett. Giesler had Wanger plead temporary insanity, and described the crime, saying, "For a brief moment, through the violet haze of early evening, Wanger saw things in a bluish flash." Wanger and Bennett both received light sentences.

Mitchum's case was one Giesler's great disappointments. The actor was convicted on a narcotics violation after attending a party in Laurel Canyon in the late 1940s. Giesler was convinced that Mitchum had been framed by his enemies. "The place had been bugged; a microphone had been planted on the wall," Giesler recounted. "But the most peculiar thing about the whole affair was that the press had the story before the cops crashed in. To put it mildly, I call that having a super nose for news." Mitchum received sixty days in prison. "My handling of the Mitchum and Wanger cases saved the motion picture industry much grief," Giesler told his biographer, Pete Martin. "But they didn't appreciate it then. They don't appreciate it now. It has always been the industry's weakness that it can only see an inch before its nose."

Not all of his clients were Hollywood celebrities. On Feb. 5, 1942, Giesler won an acquittal for gangster Benjamin "Bugsy" Siegel, accused of killing Harry "Big Greenie" Greenberg, formerly of Murder, Inc. Siegel was arrested by Los Angeles Police after New York mobster Allie Tannenbaum fingered him as the assassin. Giesler exposed Tannenbaum as a liar after he identified Siegel's Buick as the "crash car" used to stop police pursuit. Giesler convinced the court that Siegel would not have left his car at a murder scene. Siegel was helped by a California law requiring that testimony from a self-confessed participant in a crime must be corroborated by independent evidence. Siegel was freed by Superior Court Justice A.A. Scott.

Giesler commanded steep legal fees. Charley Chaplin paid the attorney $100,000 as the price of acquittal for violations of the Mann Act, a federal law prohibiting taking a woman across state lines for immoral purposes. In 1942, Chaplin had allegedly transported his "protegé," red-haired actress Joan Berry, to New York. Giesler overcame tremendous pre-trial publicity, and helped free Chaplin of the charge. Giesler did not defend Chaplin on the paternity charge that later drove the comedian from Hollywood permanently.

In Fall 1961, while preparing the defense for Carole Tregoff, accused of plotting the murder of her lover's wife, Mrs. Bernard Finch, Giesler suffered a severe heart attack. The case was turned over to Grant Cooper. Giesler never recovered. He died on Dec. 31, 1961, at his Beverly Hills home. See: **Cooper, Grant; Crane, Cheryl; Darrow, Clarence; Oesterreich, Walburga; Pantages, Alexander; Rogers, Earl; Siegel, Benjamin.**

REF.: *CBA;* Cohen, *Mickey Cohen: In My Own Words;* Giesler and Martin, *The Jerry Giesler Story.*

Giffard, Hardinge Stanley (First Earl of Halsbury), 1823-1921, Brit., jur. Served as solicitor general and lord chancellor from 1875-1905. In 1911, he opposed the Parliament Act in the House of Lords, and headed the preparations for the *Laws of England* digest from 1905-16. REF.: *CBA.*

Giffard, Miles, 1926-53, Brit., mur. Miles Giffard, twenty-seven, angry at his father for trying to break up his romance, killed him and his mother. Giffard beat his parents over their heads with an iron bar and dumped them off the cliff on which their house was perched in Cornwall, England, into the sea below.

As a boy, Giffard had been unwilling to learn and expelled from school. He indulged in petty theft, and, finally, lived off his parents. Moving to London in August 1952, Giffard met Gabriel Vallance, nineteen, and fell in love. The following November, needing a fresh supply of clothing, he returned to his parents' home. His father denounced his lifestyle and forbade him to return to London, cutting off his allowance. On the maid's evening out,

Miles Giffard, who killed his mother and father.

Giffard killed his parents, and then drove his father's car back to London. Arriving the next morning, Nov. 8, he promptly sold some of his mother's jewelry, and then cleaned up at Vallance's apartment. That evening he took his girlfriend and her mother to the movies, telling Vallance what he had done when they were alone. She thought he was joking. As he dropped her off late that evening, the police were waiting, as his parents's bodies had been found. Giffard was arrested for car theft, and the next day he confessed to the murders.

At the Bodmin Assizes in February, the defense, led by John Maude, attempted to demonstrate that Giffard was insane, based on a psychiatrist's warning to his parents that Giffard was unstable. In addition, Giffard claimed to have been regularly locked in a dark closet by a cruel nursemaid, but the jury was not moved. Miles Giffard was found Guilty and hanged on Feb. 24, 1953.

REF.: Bresler, *Reprieve;* Butler, *Murderers' England; CBA;* Furneaux, *Famous Criminal Cases, Vol. 1;* Hibbert, *The Roots of Evil;* Jacobs, *Aspects of Murder;* Neustatter, *The Mind of the Murderer;* Wilson, *Encyclopedia of Murder.*

Gifford, Adam, 1820-87, Scot., jur. Established the Gifford lectureship in natural theology with his £80,000 endowment. REF.: *CBA*

Gigante, Vincent (AKA: The Chin), c.1926- , U.S., org. crime. Vincent "The Chin" Gigante failed in his May 2, 1957, assassination attempt on New York crime boss Frank Costello, and was still involved in crime thirty years later. Gigante was aligned with Vito Genovese in the 1950s mob wars over the turf of the deposed Charles "Lucky" Luciano. Costello refused to identify his assailant, but Gigante was named by a doorman, who quickly forgot the identity in a courtroom. Eventually, Costello agreed to retire in return for a share of the mob income, and he even remained cordial with Gigante. But Costello conspired with Albert Anastasia to entrap Genovese on a narcotics charge on the condition that Gigante also be caught in the web. In 1959, Genovese was sent to prison for fifteen years, while Gi-

New York gangster Vincent "The Chin" Gigante, 1959; he presently heads a Mafia family.

gante drew a seven-year term. After his release, Gigante was formally acquitted of the attack on Costello eleven years before. He rose to a high rank in the crime family of Frank Tieri, and even higher after the 1987 conviction of Fat Tony Salerno. But there were rumors of mental illness and frequent regressions to childhood. Gigante has been heard mumbling incoherently while walking the streets of Little Italy in his bathrobe.

REF.: *CBA;* Demaris, *The Last Mafioso;* Eisenberg and Landau, *Meyer Lansky;* Gage, *Mafia, U.S.A.;* Gosch and Hammer, *The Last Testament of Lucky Luciano;* Katz, *Uncle Frank;* Maas, *The Valachi Papers;* Martin, *Revolt In the Mafia;* Peterson, *The Mob;* Reid, *The Grim Reapers;* Zuckerman, *Vengeance Is Mine.*

Gil, Constantino Orin, See: **Orton Gil, Constantino.**

Gilbert, Linda, 1847-95, U.S., penal reform. Founded the Prisoner's Aid Society in 1876, and the Gilbert Library, to furnish books for prison libraries. REF.: *CBA.*

Gilbert, Mark L., prom. 1920s, U.S., consp.-smug. Captain Mark L. Gilbert, a British citizen, commanded the *Taboga,* a rum-running ship. In June 1924, the ship was captured off the coast of New England with a small quantity of alcohol on board. Later, the ship's name was changed to the *Homestead,* and again was used to smuggle liquor. On Feb. 6, 1925, after a struggle, the ship was captured by U.S. officials. In the U.S., Gilbert was convicted on Mar. 4, 1927, on a charge of involvement in a conspiracy to smuggle liquor in connection with transporting several hundred barrels of liquor from the U.S. to Cadiz, Spain. The captain was sentenced to one year and one day at the Atlanta Penitentiary. Earlier, in 1926, Gilbert had faced a charge of conspiracy to use the mails to support stock sales of companies established by C.W. Morse. That charge was dropped. REF.: *CBA.*

Gilbert, William Schwenck, 1836-1911, Brit., Case of, libel. Famous for his comic opera collaborations with Sir Arthur Sullivan, the sensitive William Schwenck Gilbert once sued a theatrical journal for libel. Internationally famous for his theat-

rical rhyming, he once wrote a play called *The Fortune Hunter* which was refused by several London theatres before it was finally performed at Birmingham and Edinburgh. During its production, Gilbert gave an interview to a Scottish newspaper, and was quoted as having called Sidney Grundy, a renowned playwright, "a mere adapter." Gilbert was also said to have compared the English stage very unfavorably with the French, and to have doomed poetic drama to failure, explaining that no English actor could possibly make a thirty-line speech interesting. Following the publication of this interview, the theatrical world of London was enraged. Sir Henry Irving, slurred as one of the famous and, according to Gilbert, incompetent English actors, made a speech against him, and the *Era,* a theatrical journal, accused Gilbert of conceit and ingratitude toward the people who had helped him make his fortune and his reputation, saying, "His good nature has become obscured by the abnormal protuberance of self-esteem."

Suing for libel, Gilbert was represented by attorneys Lawrence Walton and Marshall Hall, with a lawyer named Carson representing the defendants. Carson, with the not-difficult task of showing that Gilbert was extremely sensitive to criticism, pleaded that the *Era* article was an equitable comment on a matter of public interest. Gilbert denied that he had ever offered a play to Irving and been refused; the famed actor made an appearance to say that he had. During Carson's closing speech, Gilbert again lost his temper and walked out of the courtroom. Although the judge, Justice Day, summed up in favor of *Era,* after deliberating for two-and-a-half hours a hung jury returned to tell Day they could not decide between the two sides, and the case was ended.

REF.: *CBA;* Marjoribanks, *For the Defense, The Life of Sir Edward Marshall Hall.*

Gilbert, William Wayne, c.1950- , and **Kinslow, Jimmy,** c.1960- , and **Gallegos, David, Jr.,** c.1954- , and **Romero, Michael,** c.1958- , and **Schmidt, Michael,** c.1963- , and **Davis, Robert Earl,** and **Torres, Hector Herman,** prom. 1987, U.S., pris. esc. On July 4, 1987, convicted murderer William Wayne Gilbert led six others in a prison break from the Penitentiary of New Mexico at Santa Fe, but all were recaptured within the month. Armed with a gun smuggled in by a guard, 37-year-old Gilbert was mopping floors at about 9 p.m., when he pointed the gun at a guard and handcuffed him to a rail. Hiding behind an ice machine, Gilbert ordered the guard to ask another guard, 22-year-old Todd Wilson, to open the door of the control center of the prison. As the door opened, the convict rushed in, shot Wilson in the shoulder, and handcuffed him. Then, opening cell doors, he freed six other prisoners and they escaped through a door in the control center up to the roof and over a barbed wire fence by using a pole. They were unobserved because the prison did not keep a night guard on duty due to budget limitations. The escapees included Gilbert, a death-row inmate convicted of killing an Albuquerque couple, Kenn and Noel Johnson, as well as his wife, Carol, and 24-year-old Barbara McMullan. His sentence had been commuted to life by Governor Toney Anaya in November 1986. Jimmy Kinslow, twenty-seven, was serving three life terms for the murder of a 38-year-old Chapparel, N.M., mother and her two daughters. Robert Earl Davis, a former police officer, had been convicted of assault, burglary, and escape. David Gallegos, Jr., 33-years-old, was serving 110 years in prison for ten armed robberies and arson, and the other three escapees were Hector Herman Torres, 24-year-old Michael Schmidt, and 29-year-old Michael Romero, an armed robber and arsonist. After the prison break, Kinslow and Romero held a brother and sister hostage for about an hour and then Romero was captured after they left the house. The rest of the fugitives were rounded up and the last three, Gilbert, Kinslow, and Gallegos, were arrested in Garden Grove, Calif. Wilson, the injured guard, recovered from his injuries. REF.: *CBA.*

Gilchrist, Marion, See: **Slater, Oscar.**

Gilchrist, Robert Budd, 1796-1856, U.S., jur. Appointed U.S. district attorney for South Carolina in 1831. He was nominated to the District Court of South Carolina by President Martin Van

Buren in 1840. REF.: *CBA*.

Gildea, Augustus, 1854-1935, U.S., west. lawman. Born in DeWitt County, Texas, Augustus Gildea served as a lawman in Texas and New Mexico. In 1878, he was John Selman's deputy in New Mexico. Earlier, Gildea had traveled to Tennessee where, from 1871-72, he was a leader of the Ku Klux Klan, organized by one-time Confederate General Nathan Bedford Forrest, ostensibly to combat carpetbaggers and lawless blacks overrunning the South following the Civil War.

Working for John Chisum in Arizona, Gildea served as a "rustler scout," hunting down rustlers raiding Chisum's huge herds of cattle. He was later a member of the Texas Rangers, according to his own statements, and was a deputy sheriff in Arizona from 1881 to 1889.

REF.: Bartholomew, *The Biographical Album of Western Gunfighters*; *CBA*.

Gilded Age, The, 1873, a novel by Mark Twain. The unbalanced San Francisco belle, Laura Fair, who shot her long-time lover to death on a ferry boat (U.S., 1870) is the role model for the heroine Laura Hawkins in this work of fiction. Also profiled is the corrupt New York political boss, William Marcy Tweed (U.S., 1873) as William M. Weed. See: **Fair, Laura D.**; **Tweed, William Marcy**. REF.: *CBA*.

Giles, James, 1941- , and **Giles, John**, 1939- , and **Johnson, Joseph, Jr.**, 1938- , U.S., (wrong. convict.) rape. James Giles, his brother John Giles, and Joseph Johnson, Jr., went fishing and swimming in Towson, Md., on the night of July 20, 1961. In the early hours of the next day, a 16-year-old white girl was found by police engaged in sexual relations with one of the black men on the banks of the Patuxent River. All three were arrested and charged with rape, based on the testimony of the girl's date, Stewart Lee Foster, who claimed the three had smashed his car's windows and taken twenty-five cents and the girl. It was later learned she had a record of promiscuity and was herself on probation.

The Giles brothers were convicted in December 1961 and sentenced to death by Montgomery Circuit Court Judge James H. Pugh, Jr. Johnson was convicted and sentenced to death in 1962. Rancor immediately arose among a number of citizens, notably Germantown scientist Harold Knapp, who took on the task of righting the wrong he felt had been done to the defendants. Knapp discovered that Montgomery State's Attorney Leonard T. Kardy had withheld vital evidence from the defense, evidence which would have backed up the defendants' claim that the girl had willingly consented to sexual intercourse. Kardy had suppressed the girl's criminal record and the fact that she was highly promiscuous—she apparently informed the younger Giles that she had had sexual relations with sixteen or seventeen men that week. The citizens supporting the defendants convinced Governor J. Millard Tawes to commute on Oct. 24, 1963, the death sentence to life in prison, while the lawyer they had retained, Joseph Forer, sought their release.

In November 1964, Judge Walter H. Moorman ruled that a new trial should be conducted because suppression of evidence had interfered with carrying out due process of the law. Kardy appealed and on July 13, 1965, the Maryland Court of Appeals overruled Moorman's decision. But the fight was not over. Forer appealed to the U.S. Supreme Court, and the court reviewed the case in March 1966. The case was then remanded by the Supreme Court to the appellate court in February 1967. Once again the case came before Moorman, this time sent by the Court of Appeals for another post-conviction hearing.

At the hearing on May 15, 1967, Moorman ordered a retrial, which the new state's attorney, William A. Linthicum, agreed was needed. On Oct. 30, 1967, the charge against the Giles brothers were dismissed by Baltimore County Judge W. Albert Menchine, when the state's two witnesses to the alleged rape failed to appear at the trial. A full pardon was issued for Johnson by Governor Spiro T. Agnew in 1968. REF.: *CBA*.

Giles, James Tyrone, 1943- , U.S., jur. Served as advisor to the Crime Prevention Association in 1978. He was nominated by President James E. Carter to the Eastern District Court of Pennsylvania in 1979. REF.: *CBA*.

Gill, Sir **Charles Frederick**, 1851-1923, Brit., lawyer. Counsel to the Irish Treasury from 1889-99. He was counsel for the state in the murder trials of Herbert John Bennett and Samuel Herbert Dougal. REF.: *CBA*.

Gillan's Saloon Case, 1891, U.S., gamb. By looking through a skylight on the roof of the building where Gillan's Saloon in Chicago was located, Detective Clifton R. Wooldridge was able to observe the illegal gambling operation on the second floor. Wooldridge reported the findings of his surveillance to Chief of Police F.H. Marsh the following morning, and the gambling house was soon out of business.

REF.: *CBA*; Wooldridge, *Hands Up*.

Gillars, Mildred Elizabeth (AKA: **Axis Sally**), 1900- , U.S., treas. U.S. troops in North Africa and Italy during WWII were treated to the siren-like voice of Mildred Gillars, better known to soldiers as "Axis Sally," who broadcasted propaganda over German radio. The soldiers generally found Gillars more entertaining than distressing, though her shows were meant to hurt morale. The U.S. government, however, did not find her broadcasts amusing, and three years after the war was over, in August 1948, the Justice Department had her extradited to Washington, D.C., to stand trial for treason.

Gillars had aspired to be an actress, but in 1927 her role in a publicity stunt for a movie dealing with unwed mothers, where she feigned suicide on a bridge in Philadelphia won not applause but an arrest. In Paris she was an artist's model in 1928, and in 1933 in Algiers she worked as an assistant dressmaker. She then moved to Germany where she taught English.

Not long after her move, she began working for German radio and soon entered into an intimate relationship with Max Otto Koischwitz, a Foreign Office radio official. Koischwitz, who Gillars testified was her "destiny," promoted her as Axis Sally and wrote the scripts she read to U.S. soldiers. The messages she delivered included reminders of wives and girlfriends back home. Other messages reported believed military secrets or depicted the horrors and hopelessness of war, especially the May 1944 broadcast entitled, "Vision of Invasion," which the jury ultimately convicted her for recording.

Gillars' seven-week trial began in January 1949 at Washington's Federal District Court before Judge Edward M. Curran. Gillars was defended by James J. Laughlin. She testified that she loved the U.S. and only read the scripts for money and her love for Koischwitz. After deliberating for fourteen hours, and disregarding seven of the eight counts, the jury found her Guilty for the "Vision" broadcast, aired one month before the Allied invasion of France, depicting the ghastly deaths that awaited any attempt to attack Adolf Hitler's Europe.

Curran sentenced Gillars on Mar. 25, 1949, to ten to thirty years in prison and fined her $10,000. Unlike other traitors Robert Henry Best and Douglas Chandler, Gillars was not sentenced to life in prison because she had not written her own material. She served twelve years, more than eleven at the Federal Reformatory for Women in Alderson, W. Va., where she was sent in August 1950. She was paroled on July 10, 1961. REF.: *CBA*.

Gillaspie, Sue, c.1939- , and **Gillaspie, Kimberly**, c.1964- , U.S., consp. A 42-year-old woman, Sue Gillaspie, and her 17-year-old daughter, Kimberly Gillaspie, had a surprise for their estranged husband and father, Kenneth Gillaspie. Unfortunately for the two, their plan to kill the man to collect on insurance was foiled by investigators who had a surprise of their own.

Gillaspie and Kimberly met with Joseph McQuaid, whom they thought was a professional hit man, at a motel in Alsip, Ill., about killing Kimberly's father. Neither mother nor daughter realized that the entire thirty-six minute conversation was secretly videotaped by Illinois Division of Criminal Investigations technical expert Kerry Galloway, who had already supervised the video surveillance of five other murder-for-hire plots in 1982. McQuaid was not a professional killer but an undercover agent.

Both defendants, who were from Hazel Crest, Ill., pleaded guilty to the charge of conspiracy and solicitation at their April 1982 trial. They each were sentenced to three years in prison. REF.: *CBA*.

Gillett, Frederick Huntington, 1851-1935, U.S., lawyer. Served as U.S. representative from Massachusetts from 1893-1925, as speaker of the house from 1919-25, and in the U.S. Senate from 1925-31. REF.: *CBA*.

Gillett, James Buchanan, 1856-1937, U.S., west. lawman. In 1875, after two years as a cowboy, 19-year-old James Gillett enlisted in the Texas Rangers. He spent the next six and a half years fighting Indians and hunting fugitives, and was involved in two gunfights. In January 1877, Gillett and five colleagues sought to apprehend Dick Dublin, who had worked with Gillett in his pre-Ranger days. They found Dublin at a ranch in Menard County, Texas, but the fugitive disappeared into a ravine when he saw the lawmen approaching. Gillett followed, and fatally shot Dublin when the fugitive refused to surrender. A year later, in February 1878, Gillett, in a party led by Lieutenant N.O. Reynolds, was escorting five prisoners to Austin for trial. Again, while in Menard County, the lawman spotted fugitive Starke Reynolds. Reynolds tried to flee, but Gillett apprehended him after a mile-and-a-half chase. On Dec. 26,

Lawman James B. Gillett.

1881, Gillett retired from the Rangers to become a railroad guard, and later became the city marshall in El Paso, Texas. In 1885, he retired to a 30,000-acre cattle ranch near Marfa, Texas, where he lived until his death in 1937. See: **Gilliland, Fine**.

REF.: Bartholomew, *The Biographical Album of Western Gunfighters*; Blacker, *The Old West in Fact*; Bruce, *Banister was There*; Casey, *The Texas Border and Some Borderliners*; *CBA*; Cunningham, *Famous in the West*; ____, *Triggernometry*; Dils, *Horny Toad Man*; Gillett, *Six Years With the Texas Rangers*; Hendricks, *The Bad Man of the West*; Holloway, *Texas Gun Lore*; Hunter and Rose, *The Album of Gunfighters*; Kemp, *Cow Dust and Saddle Leather*; King, *Pioneer Western Empire Builders*; Lackey, *Stories of the Texas Rangers*; McGiffin, *Ten Tall Texans*; Mangan, *Bordertown*; Martin, *Border Boss*; Metz, *Dallas Stoudenmire*; O'Connor, *Pat Garrett*; Raht, *The Romance of Davis Mountains and the Big Bend Country*; Raine, *Forty-five Caliber Law*; ____, *Guns of the Frontier*; Rosa, *The Gunfighter, Man or Myth?*; Scobee, *Fort Davis, Texas*; ____, *Old Fort Davis*; ____, *The Steer-Branded Murder*; Webb, *The Texas Rangers*; White, *Texas: An Informal Biography*; ____, *Trigger Fingers*; Williams, *Pioneer Surveyor, Frontier Lawyer*; Wilson, *Out of the West*.

Gillette, Chester (AKA: **Carl Graham**), 1884-1908, U.S., mur. In 1906, in upstate New York, 22-year-old factory foreman Chester Gillette murdered his pregnant girlfriend, who stood in the way of his social ambitions. Novelist Theodore Dreiser sat through much of the ensuing trial, recording the testimony of the witnesses. The material he gathered formed the basis of *An American Tragedy*, published in 1925.

As a boy, Chester had helped his parents preach for the Salvation Army in seamy red-light districts. At fourteen, Gillette was orphaned, and he began traveling the country, taking odd jobs. He worked for a time as a railroad brakeman, but this job did not interest him. Remembering that he had a prosperous uncle in Courtland, N.Y., Gillette wrote him a letter asking for a job in his skirt factory. The uncle agreed, but told Gillette he would have to start on the bottom.

Chester Gillette accepted the offer in 1904, and soon proved worthy of his uncle's confidence. He advanced to the position of shop foreman, and soon entered local society. During one of the numerous parties and balls he attended, Gillette met a beautiful young socialite and fell in love with her. The handsome young businessman was readily accepted as a social equal by the younger members of Courtland society, and there was talk of marriage.

But Gillette harbored a secret. While working at the factory, he began seeing Grace "Billie" Brown, a farm girl who had come to Courtland to work as a $6-a-week secretary. Just as Gillette's prospects were improving, Grace Brown announced that she was pregnant with his child. Gillette sent her back to her father's farm with the assurance that he would make things right. When Gillette failed to come for her, Brown wrote him a series of letters, each more desperate than the last. She threatened to expose him to his uncle. In July 1906, Gillette asked his uncle for some time off and traveled by train to Utica, N.Y., where he met Brown. They spent the night in a rented cottage before going on to Herkimer County in the Adirondacks. Billie naively believed that he had at last come to her rescue.

Murderer Chester Gillette, who sold this photo of himself to buy catered meals while in prison.

Gillette took her to Tupper Lake, where they rented a room at a resort lodge, but the area was too crowded with vacationers for what he had in mind. They pushed on to Big Moose Lake and the Glenmore Hotel, where they rented separate rooms. The next morning, July 11, Gillette hired a wooden rowboat, packed a suitcase with a picnic lunch, and rowed out into the lake with Brown around noon.

That night, Gillette was seen walking through the woods carrying his suitcase. His clothes were dripping wet. At 9 p.m., he registered at the Arrowhead Inn on Eagle Bay, then walked down to the beach and sat by a bonfire. He joined a group of tourists in a round of songs before returning to the cabin. "Has there been a drowning reported at Big Moose Lake?" he asked the clerk, who said there had not. The battered body of Grace Brown surfaced later that day. The coroner ruled that she had been murdered, not accidentally drowned. Suspicion fell on Gillette, who was traveling under the name of Carl Graham.

The police quickly caught up with Gillette, who was wearing a jaunty straw boater and seemed to be in an ebullient mood. When questioned about his connection with the deceased, Gillette became

Gillette's victim, Grace "Billie" Brown.

nervous and his replies were evasive. The murder weapon was soon found buried in the sand along the shore of Big Moose Lake. Gillette had apparently used a tennis racket to knock Brown into the water. At his trial, he claimed that Brown had attempted suicide by throwing herself into the lake. He then changed his story and said that the boat had accidentally capsized, and that

Brown had struck her head against the hull and lost consciousness. "But can you swim?" the prosecutor demanded. "Yes," Gillette answered. "And yet you made no effort to save her?" the prosecutor continued. For twenty-two days, the prosecution and defense sparred back and forth. A hundred witnesses gave testimony, and a rowboat was brought into court so the defendant could re-enact the crime. Meanwhile, Gillette sold autographed pictures of himself for $5 a piece. He decorated his cells with newspaper photos of various women. The evangelist's son had become quite a celebrity.

The Glenmore Hotel on Big Moose Lake, N.Y., where Grace Brown stayed with Gillette before he killed her.

On Dec. 4, 1906, the jury found Gillette Guilty of murder. The judge sentenced him to die in the electric chair at Auburn Prison, but to the very last Gillette continued to deny his guilt. He marched into the death house on Mar. 30, 1908, after the last of his appeals had been exhausted. Years later, when Dreiser was researching *An American Tragedy,* he rented a boat at Moose Lake and rowed to the very spot where Gillette had killed Grace Brown.

REF.: *CBA;* Cohen, *One Hundred True Crime Stories;* Corder, *Murder My Love;* Nash, *Bloodletters and Badmen;* Wilson, *Encyclopedia of Murder;* (DRAMA), Kearney, *An American Tragedy;* Piscator and Goldschmidt, *The Case of Clyde Griffiths;* (FICTION), Dreiser, *An American Tragedy;* (FILM), *An American Tragedy,* 1931; *A Place in the Sun,* 1951..

Gilligan, Amy, See: **Archer-Gilligan, Amy.**

Gilliland, Fine, d.1891, U.S., west. gunman. Fine Gilliland worked as a cowboy for the Dubois and Wentworth ranch near Hovey in Brewster County. He was also known to be deadly with a six-shooter and was involved in many gunfights. Gilliland was sent to the Leoncita water holes to round up strays when he encountered another cowboy, Henry Harrison Powe, who had lost an arm while serving in the Confederate Army during the Civil War.

The two men, who both worked for the same ranch, had been feuding for some time and fell to arguing about how a steer should be branded. Gilliland, who was armed, told Powe to "get some iron." Powe borrowed a six-shooter from Manning Clements who was standing nearby and then both Gilliland and Powe faced each other and drew. Gilliland was faster and shot Powe through the head. He then turned about and branded the steer in question.

Gilliland was marked as a murderer, despite his protests that he shot Powe in self-defense. Before he could be arrested, Gilliland mounted a fast horse and headed for the Glass Mountains. Texas Ranger Captain Jim Gillett headed a posse including noted lawmen Thalis Cook and Jim Putnam which overtook Gilliland. When the lawmen ordered him to surrender, Gilliland charged. The outlaw shot Putnam in the knee but the posse's bullets cut him to pieces. His body was returned to Brewster County for burial. His fellow cowboys were so incensed that they

retrieved the steer over which Gilliland and Powe had argued and branded it with large letters to read: "Murder" and the date of Gilliland's death. This steer wandered throughout the county for some years as a western curiosity.

REF.: Bartholomew, *The Biographical Album of Western Gunfighters; CBA;* Scobee, *Steer-Branded Murder.*

Gillis, Lester Johnson, See: **Nelson, George.**

Gilman, Ephraim, prom. 1863, U.S., mur. In love with an attractive young girl in Fryeburg, Maine, Ephraim Gilman was blocked from marriage by the girl's mother, Mrs. Harriet B. Swan. Mrs. Swan thought Gilman was a lowlife and not worthy of her daughter's hand and told him so, ordering him not to see her daughter again. Gilman exploded and strangled Mrs. Swan, then fled. He was apprehended and convicted in a speedy trial. Sent to prison for life, Gilman spent forty-three years in confinement before his parole in 1906.

REF.: *CBA; Report of the Case of Ephraim Gilman.*

Gilmore, Gary, 1940-77, U.S., mur. The execution of Gary Gilmore on the morning of Jan. 17, 1977, for the murder of a Utah gas station attendant and a motel clerk, was the first execution in the U.S. in ten years. The case became a national *cause célèbre* and was treated at monumental length by Norman Mailer in his *Executioner's Song,* which was later made into a television movie.

On July 19, 1976, only three months after his release from an eleven-year prison term for armed robbery, Gilmore killed 24-year-old service station attendant Max Jensen in Orem, Utah. The following night, in the same vicinity, he murdered 25-year-old Bennie Bushnell, a motel manager. Both victims were young married men with children, as well as students at Brigham Young

The chair in which killer Gary Gilmore was shot to death.

University. They were murdered in cold blood with gunshots to the head after being ordered to lie down. Gilmore had been distraught over the breakup with his girlfriend, Nicole Baker, the mother of two, who had already been married three times. Baker had co-sponsored Gilmore's parole, and after the two murders, it was her testimony which led to his conviction.

In October 1976, Gilmore was convicted of the slaying of Bushnell, but on Nov. 8, the Utah Supreme Court stayed his execution. Gilmore had spent eighteen of his thirty-seven years behind bars. He refused to fight the execution order, even encouraging it, demanding a death by firing squad. He garnered further attention by attempting suicide twice, and underwent a twenty-five day hunger strike during his two-and-a-half-month death watch. He refused aid from the American Civil Liberties

Union, and waived his right to appeal to the U.S. Supreme Court. At the end he had to resist the efforts of a federal judge who had granted a stay of execution at the insistence of a group of lawyers.

Shortly after 8 a.m. on Jan. 17, 1977, Gilmore was strapped into a wooden chair in front of an embankment of mattresses, plywood, and sandbags, and blinded by a hood. In his last words, Gilmore implored, "Let's do it." Five marksmen, standing thirty feet away, fired at a target placed over Gilmore's heart. Four guns contained bullets, and the fifth a blank, so that the unidentified sharpshooters would not know who fired the fatal shot. All four bullets hit the mark, and within two minutes Gilmore was dead.

REF.: *CBA;* Godwin, *Murder U.S.A.;* Wilson, *Encyclopedia of Murder.*

Gilmore, Horace Weldon, 1918-   , U.S., jur. Authored numerous scholarly articles in various legal journals. In 1980, he was nominated by President Jimmy Carter to the eastern district court of Michigan. REF.: *CBA.*

Gilmour, Christina (Cochran), 1818-1905, Case of, Scot., mur. For a number of years John Anderson had been courting Christina Cochran, but the two never married or became engaged because Anderson was not well off. In 1842, John Gilmour arrived and soon began to court Cochran as well, and after a short period convinced her to marry him on Nov. 27, 1842. This decision of Gilmour's, who allegedly told Christina he would kill himself if she refused, proved to be fatal.

Just one month after the two were married and settled in their home at Town of Inchinnan, Scot., on Dec. 29, Gilmour became violently ill, vomiting profusely. Three days before, Christina had asked a local boy to buy arsenic for her so she could poison rats.

During his illness, it was learned later, a second purchase of arsenic occurred on Jan. 7, 1843. This time, Christina bought the poison from a Renfrew shop owned by Alexander Wylie, using the name of "Miss Robertson," a sale which was witnessed by James Smith. As the sickness progressed, a farmhand noticed a packet of poison and called in a doctor—the Gilmours were against medical practitioners and did not believe one was needed—who did not detect the poison. Another doctor, Dr. Robert McKechnie, was called in. He asked Christina to preserve samples of her husband's vomit, which she failed to do. Gilmour's condition did not improve, and on Jan. 11 he died, having been married a mere six weeks, and without ever consummating the marriage.

Christina returned to her parents' home in March 1843, and talk of poisoning soon spread. She demanded that Gilmour's body be exhumed and an autopsy performed. Her father, Alexander Cochran, not wishing his daughter to be subjected to a scandal, had her whisked away against her wishes to Liverpool, and finally to New York. On Apr. 22, 1843, Gilmour's body was exhumed, and an examination revealed that he had died of arsenic poisoning. Police Superintendent George McKay caught a steamer to New York, arrived on June 2, and obtained a warrant for Christina's arrest. She arrived in New York on June 21, having crossed the ocean in a slow-moving sailing ship. After a lengthy extradition process she was returned to Scotland, leaving on Aug. 16. Less than a month later, on Sept. 14, Christina confessed to buying the arsenic, but claimed she bought it so she could commit suicide and end her unhappy marriage.

Christina's trial for murder commenced on Jan. 12, 1844, at Edinburgh, Scot., before Judges Lord Moncreiff, Lord Wood, and Lord Justice-Clerk Hope. Lord Advocate Duncan McNeill headed the prosecution, which was fairly solid against the defendant. Her defense was provided by Thomas Maitland and Alexander McNeill. Maitland conceded that arsenic had caused death, but argued death had not resulted from repeated doses, as the prosecution contended. He added that Gilmour's death could have been an accident or even suicide, but that there was no evidence proving Christina had administered the poison. The jury agreed and returned a verdict of Not Proven. See: **Blandy, Mary; Cotton, Mary Ann Robson Mowbray; DeMelker, Daisy Louisa; Jegado, Helene; LaFarge, Marie; Smith, Madeleine.**

REF.: *CBA;* Roughead, *Famous Crimes;* Wilson, *Not Proven.*

Gioe, Charles (AKA: Cherry Nose), d.1954, U.S. org. crime. Charles "Cherry Nose" Gioe, Chicago gangster, rose through the ranks of the reconstructed Capone gang during the 1930s when Frank "The Enforcer" Nitti and Paul "The Waiter" Ricca were the overlords of the Chicago crime cartel. By the late 1930s, Gioe, who specialized in extortion and blackmail, had risen to a top lieutenant's position in the Chicago mob. It was Gioe, along with Paul Ricca and Louis "Little New York" Campagna who financially backed Willie Bioff and George Browne in their West Coast rackets, particularly the massive extortion ring operated by Bioff and Browne. Hollywood moguls made huge payoffs to this ring to keep their films running in theaters where mob-controlled projectionists worked.

Bioff and Browne were exposed and began to inform on their mob associates, naming Ricca, Campagna and Gioe as their sponsors. For this betrayal, Bioff was later murdered on orders from this triumvirate. But the testimony of Bioff and Browne was enough to convict Gioe, Ricca and Campagna of extortion in 1943 and all three men drew ten-year prison sentences.

Chicago gangster Charles "Cherry Nose" Gioe at his parole hearing in 1947.

Through political connections, Gioe and the others wangled paroles in 1947. These paroles were angrily denounced by crime-fighting U.S. Senator Estes Kefauver as "a shocking misuse of parole powers."

Upon their release, Ricca, Campagna and Gioe, in that order, became the top syndicate bosses in Chicago. Other mobsters, such as Anthony "Big Tuna" Accardo and Sam "Momo" Giancana were, however, planning to take over this crime cartel and, during the 1950s, Accardo emerged as the top Mafia-syndicate boss of the city, a position he holds at this writing. Campagna died in his bed and Ricca became chairman of the board. Gioe, however, a younger man, sought to remain in power and was shot to death in 1954, reportedly by Giancana, who was then making his slow bid for Accardo's position, one that he later assumed and relinquished only through violent death. See: **Accardo, Anthony; Bioff, Willie; Campagna, Louis; Giancana, Sam; Ricca, Paul.**

REF.: *CBA;* Demaris, *Captive City;* ____, *The Last Mafioso;* Fried, *The Rise and Fall of the Jewish Gangster in America;* Gage, *Mafia, U.S.A.;* Kobler, *Capone;* Lait and Mortimer, *Chicago Confidential;* Maclean, *The Mafia;* Morgan, *Prince of Crime;* Nash, *Bloodletters and Badmen;* ____, *Citizen Hoover;* Peterson, *The Mob;* Reid, *The Grim Reapers;* Smith, *Syndicate City;* Velie, *Desperate Bargain: Why Jimmy Hoffa Had to Die.*

Giordano, Gregorio, d.1914, U.S., mur. On Aug. 12, 1913, the body of a young woman was found in the woods of Inwood Park in Manhattan. The woman's throat had been slit, her skull fractured, and her chest repeatedly stabbed. A brown-handled, seven-inch-long knife, and a shoemaker's iron last, both heavily bloodstained, were found near the body. Identification of the woman was not possible, and the body was placed on display at the morgue to be viewed by those who might recognize her.

Giordano, as killers often do, returned to see his victim, and though he claimed that the woman was his wife, Salvatrice Giordano, he immediately retracted the statement. Acting Captain William Herlihy was curious as to how Giordano could have confused the body with his wife's, who he claimed was twenty pounds lighter than the deceased and had black hair and not brown. Giordano said his wife had been missing since Aug. 11, but had not reported this to authorities. Herlihy asked neighbors about the Giordano's, and from them learned that Giordano told people his wife had gone to the country and that her description matched that of the body and not the picture Giordano had painted. The captain arrested the suspicious character and upon searching his bedroom discovered a blood-stained shirt and a pair of pants, another shoemaker's last, and a picture of Salvatrice, who seemed to resemble the dead woman. Giordano soon pleaded guilty, and gave as the motive his fear that his wife was going to leave him. A jury in the Court of General Sessions took thirty-five minutes to find Giordano Guilty before Judge Forster on Oct. 23, 1913. He was executed in the electric chair at Sing Sing Prison in April 1914.

REF.: *CBA;* Cohen, *One Hundred True Crime Stories.*

Giordano, Henry L., 1914- , U.S., law enfor. off. With a degree in pharmacy from the University of California in 1934, Henry L. Giordano left his private practice in 1941 to enter the service of the Federal Bureau of Narcotics. From 1943 to 1946, in the U.S. Coast Guard's Intelligence Division, Giordano distinguished himself as an agent and diplomat.

Giordano was named the bureau's District Supervisor for Minneapolis in 1950, and for Kansas City, Mo., where he transferred in 1954. He served the House of Representatives Ways and Means Subcommittee on Narcotics as Chief Investigator from October 1955 through April 1956. On July 29, 1956, Giordano became Field Supervisor for the Bureau of Narcotics, and on Sept. 1, 1956, he was appointed Assistant Deputy Commissioner in the Washington, D.C., office. Exactly one year later, Giordano was promoted to Assistant to the Commissioner, and further promoted to Deputy Commissioner of Narcotics on Nov. 3, 1958. On Aug. 17, 1962, Giordano was named the bureau's Commissioner of Narcotics.

As a narcotics expert, Giordano served as U.S. delegate to the United Nations Commission on Narcotic Drugs for the fourteenth session (held from April to May 1959), the eighteenth session (from April to May 1963), and subsequent annual sessions in Geneva, Switz. He also served as an alternate U.S. representative in New York from January to March 1961 for the U.N. Conference concerning the adoption of a single convention on narcotics. Giordano was knighted on Mar. 19, 1968, by Italian Ambassador Egidio Ortona, who presented Giordano with Italy's Order of Merit in recognition of his cooperative effort with the Italian government in curtailing drug traffic, an effort that resulted in the conviction of thirty-two people. He also was given the Exceptional Service Award by U.S. Treasury Secretary Henry H. Fowler, whose department oversees the Bureau of Narcotics, on Apr. 3, 1968. REF.: *CBA.*

Giovanni (Duke of Gandia), d.1497, Italy, assass. The younger brother of Cesare Borgia, who had served as the Bishop of Pampeluna and the Cardinal of Valenza, Giovanni, the Duke of Gandia, was murdered in 1497. His body, which had been stabbed ten times with a dagger, was found in the Tiber River. Sforza, the Count of Pesaro, was suspected of committing the assassination.

REF.: *CBA;* Thompson, *Poison and Poisoners.*

Girard, Henri, 1875-1921, Fr., mur. After being cashiered out of the French Hussars in 1897, Henri Girard, a petty swindler and amateur scientist, turned to crime. But even the many financial swindles he perpetrated between 1897 and 1910 did not provide him with a comfortable lifestyle, nor did they keep him out of the clutches of the law. In 1909, Girard's bogus insurance company, Crédit Général de France, was fined 1,000 francs for deceptive practices. However, in the process he met Louis Pernotte, who seemed willing to go along with Girard's schemes.

Pernotte, an insurance broker, gave Girard power of attorney. Then Girard insured Pernotte's life for 316,000 francs, which evidently didn't strike Pernotte as unusual. Meanwhile, Girard began to experiment with poison in his Paris laboratory. He realized that it was nearly impossible to come up with an untraceable poison, so he prepared a typhoid germ culture, which he planned to test on Pernotte. In August 1912, Girard poured a vial of deadly bacilli into a pitcher of water on Pernotte's dining table.

Shortly afterward, the Pernotte family left for Royan where they became ill.

They returned to Paris, but Pernotte did not recover. Shortly before Pernotte's death on Dec. 1, Girard administered an injection of camphorated chamomile. "Notice, madame," he said to Mrs. Pernotte, "that it is quite definitely your own syringe. You observe that I have nothing in my hands." It was a curious remark, but was quickly forgotten when Pernotte expired from what the family doctor diagnosed as embolism resulting from typhus. Upon Pernotte's death, Girard informed the widow that her husband had owed him 200,000 francs.

Frenchman Henri Girard, the "experimental" murderer.

Pleased with the results of this first "experiment," Girard insured the life of Mimiche Duroux and then fed him the poisonous germs. For the next three days, Girard wrote in a journal detailing the progress of the disease. However, Duroux was strong and healthy, and he did not die. Girard had to select another victim, with the help of one of his many mistresses, Jeanne Droubin. Together they chose a widow named Madame Monin, and then took out a policy on her life with the Phénix Insurance Company. Fifteen minutes after ingesting one of Girard's mushrooms in the Metro station, Madame Monin died. The insurance company began an investigation which culminated in Girard's arrest on Aug. 21, 1918. He was taken to the Fresnes Prison, where he told the guards, "Yes, I have always been unhappy, no one has ever tried to understand me. I will always be misunderstood—abnormal, as I have been called—and for all that I am good, with a very warm heart." Before the case could go to trial, Girard swallowed a germ culture and died in his cell in May 1921.

REF.: *CBA;* Heppenstall, *Bluebeard and After;* Kershaw, *Murder in France;* Thompson, *Poison and Poisoners;* Tyler, *Gallows Parade;* Wilson, *Encyclopedia of Murder.*

Girard, William S., 1935- , Japan, mansl. The shot fired by Army Specialist Third Class William S. Girard on Jan. 30, 1957, may not have eclipsed the American Revolution's "shot heard around the world," but the political reverberations were heard loudly throughout the U.S. and Japan.

A "status-of-forces" agreement between the U.S. and its allies states that military personnel are subject to local law only when the U.S. citizen commits an offense while on duty or not in the line of duty. Therefore, when Girard aimlessly fired a spent cartridge from his grenade launcher at a group of five Japanese scavengers, who were looking for pieces of scrap at the U.S. Army's Somagahara rifle range, and killed 46-year-old Naka Sakai when the projectile struck her in the back, a debate began over whether the soldier was on duty or not. The Japanese government contended that since the shot was fired during a rest period from target practice, Girard was off duty and, thus, should be tried in a Japanese court. Reluctantly, Rear Admiral Miles H. Hubbard agreed, but U.S. Secretary of Defense Charles E. Wilson did not, stating that Girard should be tried by a military court. In June 1957, this decision was reversed when Wilson, along with Secretary of State John Foster Dulles, ruled that the private's shot was not authorized, and should be tried outside a military court. This joint statement enraged a great number of Americans, and it was not until the U.S. Supreme Court ruled in July that Girard should stand trial in a Japanese court that proceedings began.

The case against Girard was held in the Maebashi District Court before Judge Yuzo Kawachi and lasted eighty-six days.

Kawachi even took his courtroom to the hill where the crime occurred, and in the midst of a rainstorm learned from private Victor Nickel, who was near Girard when the shot was fired, that the soldier had meant no harm. A prosecution witness claimed that Girard had shouted a warning first, a claim that Girard himself denied. At the end of November 1957, Kawachi found Girard Guilty, and after chiding both the scavengers and the defendant for foolishness, sentenced him to a suspended sentence of three years in prison, and a fine of $20 to pay for the expenses of witnesses. REF.: *CBA*.

Girardi, James A., c.1938-77, U.S., suic.-mur. Rather than solve his unemployment problems by finding another job, 38-year-old James A. Girardi decided to use a shotgun. During the first week of May 1977, the unemployed construction worker shot and killed his four sleeping children, and then turned the gun on himself. His brother Alfred Girardi found the bodies of the children—Albert, ten; Bonnie, fifteen; Thomas, fifteen; and Cindy, sixteen—all lying in their beds of Girardi's Briarcliff Manor, N.Y., home.

REF.: *CBA; Fox, Mass Murder*.

Giri, Laxman, c.1911-80, India, (unsolv.) mur. Swami Laxman Giri was alleged to have used candy to entice children under the age of six to desolate areas to slit their throats in a sacrificial ritual that would bring his followers immortality. He was arrested on Mar. 1, 1980, but the 68-year-old man died at the Victoria Hospital in Bangalore, India, about 800 miles south of New Delhi, on Mar. 5, 1980, before he could be tried. REF.: *CBA*.

Giriat, Victorine, and **Ladermann, César**, and **Bassot, Henri**, prom. 1902, Fr., rob.-mur. Eugenie Fougère of Paris was glad when an old friend from her earlier days, Victorine Giriat, appeared on her doorstep. In need of a companion, Fougère was able to hire Giriat for a reasonable fee. Fougère, her maid, and Giriat moved to Aix-les-Bains for the social season of 1902. Giriat's lover, Henri Bassot, a small-time hood and professional comedian, was avidly interested in Fougère, especially where she kept her many jewels. Giriat talked freely and was soon encouraging him to help himself. On the night of Sept. 21, Ladermann, a tailor from Lyons, entered Fougère's villa by a window that Giriat had left open when she and Fougère left for the evening. He killed the maid by strangling her and then waited for the other two women to return home. At about 1 a.m., the tired women entered the house and were met by Ladermann, who strangled Fougère and tied up Giriat so that she would look like a victim. Fougère's hairdresser found them the next morning. The jewelry was gone.

The police followed Giriat for several weeks and then took her in for questioning. She quickly confessed to participating but placed the blame on Bassot for planning the crime and on Ladermann for not following orders. When approached by police, Ladermann killed himself. In his room was a letter taking the blame for the killings and exonerating Bassot from complicity. He said that Giriat had planned the robbery. Bassot and Giriat were tried for robbery and murder, found Guilty, and sentenced to life in prison.

REF.: *CBA; Morain, Underworld of Paris; Nash, Look For the Woman*.

Girier, René (AKA: **René-la-Canne, Walking-Stick René**), 1920- , Fr., burg. René Girier had a taste for expensive clothes, an extravagant lifestyle, and an endless number of women. The criminal who was known for wearing a carnation in his buttonhole and carrying a cane was cunning in his avoidance of justice, but a forsaken mistress gave him away.

Following his first conviction where he admitted to burglarizing the Van Cleef & Arpels jeweller's in Deauville, Fr., of 100 million francs—Girier managed to convince the court that he was insane, and was imprisoned at the Villejuif Asylum. There he met "Madman" Mimile Buisson, who arranged their escape with the help of his brother, Jean-Baptiste Buisson, on Sept. 3, 1947. Girier was not free for long. Commissaire Charles Chenevier of the Sûreté, following the advice of a former mistress of Girier, apprehended the escaped prisoner after finding him in the arms of a woman in a Montfermeil hotel. The prisoner was placed in the Santé prison until his transfer was arranged by his lawyer, Francine "Zaza" Zaradel.

On the trip from the Santé prison to the Fresnes prison, Girier managed to undo his handcuffs—he had previously placed matches in the locks to prevent them from locking—and sawed a hole in the floor of the police van with a hacksaw he had concealed in his pants. He escaped at a traffic light, with another convict, whose leg was run over by the departing van. Zaradel denied any involvement in the escape, but shot herself in a bar a few days later. The shot was not fatal.

As before, Girier's freedom was short-lived. Again, a former lover notified Chenevier and the fashionable criminal was arrested. This time he was sentenced to twenty years of hard labor. After pronouncement of his sentence Girier was allowed to speak; the speech he gave lasted one-and-one-half days. Princess Charlotte of Monaco was so impressed with his speech on criminality, justice, and law, that she sought for and obtained his parole from prison after only six years. Girier gave up crime, settling in Reims, Fr., where he opened a bookstore, which he purchased for 10 million francs.

REF.: *CBA; Goodman, Villainy Unlimited*.

Giron, Francisco Hernandez, See: **Hernandez Giron, Francisco**.

Girty, Simon, 1741-1818, U.S., treas. Simon Girty was one of the most notorious renegades and sadistic killers in early U.S. history. He originally served in Washington's army, but he turned traitor and joined the British in 1778. Girty led British and Indian expeditions against dozens of American communities along the western and northern frontiers where helpless women and children were massacred by Indians. Girty remained at battle with American troops long after the Revolution was over, finally fleeing to Canada in 1796 to avoid capture. REF.: *CBA*.

Giubelli, Alfa Ricciotti, c.1933- , Italy, mur. As the Allied forces marched north through Italy in 1944, Communist leader Aurelio Bussi was fighting for the resistance in the town of Crevacuore, about fifty miles from Turin. He reportedly had eighty residents of the town executed, and personally killed a man and his 16-year-old daughter. He made a fatal mistake in July 1944 when he failed to kill the 10-year-old daughter of the woman he wished to seduce.

Bussi had tried in vain to win the love of 32-year-old Margherita Ricciotti, whose husband was fighting in the war. After she refused him a final time, he dragged her by the hair to the cemetery and had her shot to death while her daughter Alfa listened. A few weeks later a cemetery wall bore a message written by the girl: "Butcher, remember, one day I will kill you."

Two years later, the hatred had not subsided, as Alfa wrote in a poem: "I must live to kill the one who killed her. I must live for vengeance." She married at sixteen.

Bussi, in the meantime, had been elected mayor of Crevacuore, and decorated for his valor during the war, by the time he again met Alfa Ricciotti Giubelli in 1956. She fired six shots from her husband's 7.65-millimeter pistol into Bussi, killing him outside his home, and then surrendered.

In March 1957 Giubelli stood trial for Bussi's murder. Thousands of Italians took up her cause, and the six-man jury found her Not Guilty of premeditated murder, but Guilty of voluntary homicide, which with its lighter sentence would allow her parole in just over one year. REF.: *CBA*.

Giuliano, Salvatore (Turiddu), 1922-50, Si., rob.-mur. One of the most romanticized modern bandits of the Old World, Salvatore Giuliano was born on Nov. 16, 1922, the fourth child of Salvatore and Maria Giuliano. The elder Giuliano had worked in the U.S., in New York, Texas, and California and saved enough money to return to his native village of Montelepre, outside of Palermo, Sicily, and buy a small farm. Young Salvatore, a bright boy with a vivid imagination, attended school until the age of thirteen, when he dropped out and went into the fields to help his father raise crops. After that he transported olive oil, worked as a telephone repairman, and worked on road construction.

The bandit Giuliano, right, with his cousin Pisciotta.

Sicilian bandit Salvatore Giuliano, 1945.

Giuliano on his father's farm.

Bandit's mother, Maria Giuliano.

Pisciotta, Giuliano's killer.

Don Calogero Vizinni, Mafia boss.

Giuliano's U.S.-Sicily map.

Pisciotta under arrest.

Giuliano's body in a Palermo square, 1950.

During WWII, Giuliano returned to the transporting of olive oil. He also began to trade in the black market. He went armed since the hills about Montelepre were crawling with bandits.

On Sept. 2, 1943, Giuliano was returning home with two sacks of black market grain when two *carabinieri* (state policemen) stopped him near Quattro Molini to inspect his cargo. Giuliano pulled his pistol and shot one of the officers dead. He fled into a cane field, a bullet smacking into his side. Wounded, he managed to escape to his home. His family sent him to a doctor in Palermo and there the bullet was removed from his side. When the authorities began searching for him, Giuliano fled to the hills around Montelepre where he found scores of homeless men, army deserters, smugglers, black marketeers, murderers and bandits, the flotsam of war.

A born leader, Giuliano organized these directionless men into a guerilla force of more than fifty men. He trained them to shoot so that they killed with their first shot, hitting the chest or head. He marched them in formations around the mountaintops, as he had watched soldiers drilling when he was a boy. Then he led them in raids into villages and towns where stores were robbed and wealthy landowners were kidnapped and held for ransom.

Giuliano established headquarters in some caves high in the Sagana Mountains towering above Montelepre. These were bald, low mountains which the police would normally have secured but Giuliano and his band knew every inch of the terrain and when *carabinieri* did comb the hills for the bandits, they were invariably met with deadly machinegun fire which raked their ranks and took a great toll of lives.

As time went on, a number of legends about Giuliano were created by his romantic notion of himself. He learned that a postal official was stealing letters containing money that was sent from poor Sicilian families to their relatives in the U.S. Giuliano shot the postal employee and sent the money on to the correct recipients. He marked the letters "Divine Providence." He also shared his spoils with the tenant farmers and poor of the countryside, sending these people money and food. He became their "protector" and "benefactor."

On one occasion, Giuliano invaded the villa of the Duchess of Pratameno. When she found him in her palatial rooms, she thought he was the son of a duke, so polished were his manners. Not until he politely asked for her jewelry, did she realize that Giuliano was a common bandit. He left her wedding ring and kissed her hand, and, as he was about to depart, asked for the loan of a book she was reading, *In Dubious Battle* by John Steinbeck. He later returned the book with a thank you note, telling her that Steinbeck was his favorite author. Such gallantry and charm quickly made Giuliano into a local folk hero.

Giuliano's greatest ambition was to see Sicily annexed by the U.S. He wrote letters to President Harry Truman in which he urged Truman to make Sicily the forty-ninth state. He even drew a map showing how Sicily would be appear as an American state. Though he sided with the peasants, in the end Giuliano's support came from the landed gentry and the Mafia. He received his money and supplies from rightist groups who convinced the altruistic Giuliano that the peasants were being controlled by evil communists. On May 1, 1947, Giuliano and his men ambushed a peasant parade near Portellella della Ginestra, his men firing machine guns into the crowd. Eleven innocent people were killed, including a woman and three children.

The bandit's image was forever tarnished after this slaughter, although his authority in the mountains and countryside was more widespread and accepted than that of the police and government. Grown vain and pompous, the youthful bandit began issuing decrees and regulations, threatening to punish by death all who disobeyed. From 1947 through 1949, Giuliano was the most powerful force in Sicily but the government resolved to put an end to him. More than 300 police and national guardsmen invaded the mountains where Giuliano and his men had their retreat. Their main cave was located and a terrific battle ensued. Grenades and cannon shells were hurled into the cave but when the smoke cleared, police found no one. The bandits had fled through a rear crevice in the rocks.

In late 1949, Giuliano's kidnappings and terror raids increased drastically. On Aug. 14, 1949, seven policemen were killed and twenty more seriously wounded when Giuliano's men exploded mines under a police barracks outside of Palermo. With thousands of police and military troops looking for him, the defiant Giuliano dressed in his best clothes and drove right into Palermo, dining in the best restaurants for two days and leaving notes under his plates with large tips. One note read: "This is to show that Giuliano, the Champion of Sicily, can still come into Palermo whenever he likes." He wrote letters to the press in which he compared himself to Mussolini and Napoleon Bonaparte.

The government of Sicily finally made an all-out effort to get rid of Giuliano, but this time they only sent one man to kill him, 26-year-old Gaspare Pisciotta, Giuliano's former chief lieutenant and cousin. Pisciotta had been captured earlier and, rather than face prison or execution, he agreed to be a police spy and then to kill Giuliano on the promise that he would receive a large reward and a full pardon for past crimes. Apparently, the planned killing of Giuliano was done with the collusion and approval of Don Calogero Vizinni, Mafia overlord of Sicily, who had first backed the bandit and then condemned Giuliano when he realized he could not control him. Pisciotta found his way to Giuliano's hideout and, while the 27-year-old bandit slept, he shot him in the head, killing him. The body was then taken to Palermo and dumped in a square. A gun was placed next to the body as if Giuliano had been shot while resisting arrest. The authorities claimed, when the body was found and photographed, that Captain Antonio Perenze, of the *carabinieri,* had killed the fierce Giuliano.

Then, reneging on its promise, the government put Pisciotta on trial, along with a dozen other Giuliano lieutenants. Pisciotta, in the dock, thundered in court: "It was *I* who killed Giuliano, under a personal agreement with the Minister of Interior, Mario Scelba!" This bombshell created havoc in court and denials and charges flew in all directions. Maria Giuliano, then sixty, settled the arguments by informing the press that, indeed, the treacherous Pisciotta had murdered her beloved son while he slept. She took the witness stand in 1951 and shouted: "Pisciotta and Giuliano were blood brothers and wrote their names with drops of each other's blood. Pisciotta became a traitor, worse than Cain. His heart was always bad and Turridu's was open and generous. My son Turridu often had to tie Pisciotta to a tree and beat him to teach him manners."

Pisciotta was not released, nor given any reward. He and eleven other Giuliano bandits were sent to prison for life. On Feb. 9, 1954, Pisciotta sat in his spartan cell in Palermo's Ucciardone Prison and sipped his coffee. He suddenly screamed, fell on the floor and his body bowed in horrible agony. He died within minutes. Officials stated that Pisciotta died of a sudden heart attack but the truth was finally made known. Pisciotta had died of a massive dose of strychnine. Another Giuliano aide, Angelo Russo, also died of poisoning in prison.

The vast fortune Giuliano had accumulated through his kidnappings and robberies was never uncovered. This was estimated to be as high as £2 million, but was more likely about £500,000. This amount, it was suspected, went mostly to his family and friends, along with the bandits who served him loyally. But today, Giuliano's treasure is still sought throughout the Sagana Mountains by the poor of Sicily, and little boys who dream of fortune, fame and adventure.

REF.: Barbagallo, *Randazzo, 17 Giugno 1945: Anatomia di una strage;* Barone, *Una vita per Giuliano;* Blok, *The Mafia of a Sicilian Village, 1860-1960;* Campbell, *The Luciano Project;* CBA; Centorrino, *Economia e classi sociali in Sicilia;* Chandler, *King of the Mountain: The Life and Death of Giuliano the Bandit;* Clark, *Modern Italy, 1871-1982;* D'Alessandro, *Brigantaggio e mafia in Sicilia;* Dolci, *The Man Who Plays Alone;* Ellwood, *Italy, 1943-1945;* Ferraotti, *Rapporto sulla mafia;* Finley, Mack Smith and Duggan, *A History of Sicily;* Grasso, *Girolamo Li Causi e la sua azione politica per la Sicilia;* Gurr, *Why Men Rebel;* Hess, *Mafia*

and Mafiosi; Mack Smith, *A History of Sicily: Modern Sicily after 1713;*
____, *Italy: A Modern History;* Mannino, *Mitra e poltrone;* Maxwell,
Bandit; Miller, *The United States and Italy, 1940-1950;* Molfese, *Storia del brigantaggio dopo l'Unita;* Moorehead, *Hostages to Fortune;* Nicolosi, *La leggenda di Giuliano;* Pantaleone, *Mafia e politica;* Peterson, *The Mob;* Presidenza della Regione Siciliana, *Le elezioni in Sicilia, 1946-1956;* Renda, *Movimento di massa e democrazia nella Siclia del dopo-guerra;* Romano, *Storia dei Fasci Siciliani;* Rowan, *Famous European Crimes;* Sabetti, *Political Authority in a Sicilian Village;* Samenow, *Inside the Criminal Mind;* Sansone, *Sei anni di banditismo in Sicilia;* Schneider, *Culture and Political Economy in Western Sicily;* Servadio, *Mafioso;* Spanò, *Faccia a faccia con la mafia;* Stern, *No Innocence Abroad;* (FICTION), Nash, *The Mafia Diaries;* Puzo, *The Sicilian;* (FILM), *Salvatore Giuliano,* 1966; *The Sicilian,* 1987.

Glabe, Karen, 1942-   , U.S., mur. Karen Glabe considered divorcing her husband, Kenneth Glabe, to marry pharmacist Mitchell Link of Arlington Heights, Ill. Instead, she and Link hired an ex-policeman, Preston Haig, to kill Kenneth Glabe for a fee of $5,000. Haig stabbed Glabe to death on June 21, 1971. The crime remained on the unsolved list for eight years. Then, in May 1979, Haig and his wife, living in Roswell, N.M., had an argument, and his wife told police that he was a murderer.

Haig agreed to testify against the Links, who went on trial in July 1980. They were both found Guilty of murder, and Circuit Court judge Robert K. McQueen sentenced them each to thirty-five years to forty-five years in prison.

REF.: *CBA;* Nash, *Look For the Woman.*

Gladden, George, prom. 1870s, U.S., west. gunman. A friend of gunmen Johnny Ringo and Scott Cooley, Gladden recruited both these men and others for a Texas feud that was known as the Hoodoo War, which occurred in Mason County, Texas, in 1875. In September, Gladden and one of the Beard Brothers were involved in a fierce gunfight with dozens of gunmen from Mason County. Beard was killed and Gladden was wounded nine times. Dan Hoerster, who had a wild fistfight with Gladden earlier and represented the Mason County cattlemen, was found murdered and the killing was attributed to Gladden and Ringo. Both outlaws were captured on Nov. 7, 1876, after Ringo and Gladden had killed another range enemy, Pete Bader. They were jailed, but Ringo escaped and rode to Arizona where he would later confront the Earp Brothers as a member of the Clanton-McLowery outlaw band. Gladden, however, was sentenced to ninety-nine years. He was pardoned some time later and vanished.

REF.: Bartholomew, *The Biographical Album of Western Outlaws;* *CBA.*

Gladstone, Henry Neville, prom. 1927, and **Gladstone, Herbert John,** 1854-1930, Case of, Brit., libel. The two sons of British statesman William Ewart Gladstone fought a long and bitter legal battle to clear their father's name of charges of sexual impropriety. In 1925, writer and essayist Captain Peter Wright published a book titled *Portraits and Criticisms,* in which he accused the late William Gladstone of philandering with a variety of women. It was difficult to challenge the author's assertions in public, so Henry Neville Gladstone and Herbert John Gladstone decided to libel Wright publicly with the hope that he would sue them in a court of law. Then, with the facts of the case before the public, the Gladstones could discredit the writer and force a retraction.

The brothers wrote two highly inflammatory letters, one to Peter Wright in which they called him a liar, a coward, and a fool, and another to Wilson Taylor, secretary of the Bath Club, to which all three men belonged. The letter to Taylor asked if the fact that the charges against Gladstone were written on private club stationery concerned him. It did, of course, and he immediately expelled Wright. The Gladstones crossed the first hurdle when Wright filed suit in July 1926 for wrongful expulsion. "I wrote what I did on the authority of Lord Milner; to use Milner's own phrase, 'Mr. Gladstone was governed by his seraglio'," Wright retorted. Wright was temporarily vindicated at the hearing, and was awarded £125 for breach of contract and damage to his reputation. Not content with this, however, he filed a general libel

suit against the Gladstone brothers in January 1927.

On the witness stand, Wright recalled hearing as a boy from John Halsam that the beautiful actress Lily Langtry had been Gladstone's mistress. From Dr. Greatorex, Wright had heard that Gladstone solicited women on the street. In 1913, Wright said, a man named Cecil Gladstone was identified to him as the bastard son of the famous parliamentarian. When asked by defense counsel Norman Birkett if he considered himself a serious journalist, Wright replied, "I try not to be dull."

Wright's accusations proved to be based on gossip, Justice Horace Edmond Avory rebuked the plaintiff before the jury retired on Feb. 3, 1927. After three hours of deliberation, they found in favor of the defendants. "The jury are of unanimous opinion that the evidence which has been placed before us has completely vindicated the high moral character of the late Mr. W.E. Gladstone," they said. After the trial, Wright sent the London *Daily Mail* a letter expressing his regret over the offending passages of his book, and offered to remove it in future editions.

REF.: Bowker, *Behind the Bar; CBA.*

Glanton, John J., d.1850, U.S., mur. Sentenced to prison in Tennessee for murder, John Glanton escaped in 1845 and became a soldier in the Mexican War. In 1848, with a band of vagrants from the Texas-Mexico border towns, he founded a gang of scalp hunters who slaughtered over 1,000 Apaches and earned more than $100,000 for it. They were paid $100 for a male's scalp, $50 for a female's, and $25 for a child's. However, authorities on both sides of the border became outraged when Glanton began killing dark-complected Mexicans and Americans. The gang fled to California when a $75,000 reward was posted on them. Glanton found Yuma Indians extorting whites for a safe crossing of the Colorado River, and expected to earn vast sums for the massacre of the tribe. However, on Apr. 23, 1850, after he had killed a number of Yumas, the tribe turned on Glanton and killed him and all but three of his men in a bloody battle. The leaders of a local army detachment were thrilled that the Indians had eliminated Glanton and his marauders, and a year later named Fort Yuma in the tribe's honor. REF.: *CBA.*

Glanville, Ranulf de (Glanvil), d.1190, Brit., jur. Justiciar of Britain from 1180-89, and adviser to King Henry II. REF.: *CBA.*

Glaser, Julius, 1831-85, Aust., jur. Minister of justice in 1871. He became general procurator to the Austrian court of annulment in Vienna in 1879. REF.: *CBA.*

Glass, Charles, c.1950-   , Leb., host. The kidnapping of American Charles Glass on June 17, 1987, on a coastal road less than a mile from the Beirut International Airport in Lebanon, eventually led to better diplomatic relations between the U.S. and Syria.

Glass, thirty-six, had worked with the American Broadcasting Company television network as a reporter, and was best known for his coverage of the dramatic hijacking of Trans World Airlines Flight 847 in 1985. He was in Beirut—against U.S. advisement to all of its citizens to leave that country, because of eight previous kidnappings of Americans—writing a book on the region when the abduction occurred. At least fourteen gunmen kidnapped Glass, 40-year-old Ali Osseiran, the son of Lebanese Minister of Defense Adel Osseiran, and his bodyguard, just 350 yards from a Syrian checkpoint. The kidnapping was the first in Beirut since 7,500 Syrian troops entered the capital on Feb. 22. Within two weeks after the abduction, Osseiran and his bodyguard were released amid pressure from Syrian officials and West Beirut Shiite leaders; both men were Shiites. Glass remained in captivity until August, during which time the all-too-common "confession" was released, where Glass read a prepared text stating he was a CIA agent. His freedom was the result of an escape, but it is likely that pressure from Syrian President Hafez Assad caused Glass' Hezbullah (an Iranian-backed terrorist group) captors to allow his escape.

The U.S. saw the "freeing" of Glass as a sign that diplomatic ties with Syria should be renewed, especially because Syria is the number-one ally of Iran. REF.: *CBA.*

Glass, Jimmie, d.c.1915, U.S., (unsolv.) mur. When Jimmie Glass was four years old, his father Charles Glass became ill and needed a long rest in the country. The family left their home in Jersey City, N.J., and traveled to Greeley, Pa., on May 11, 1915. That was the last day anyone saw Jimmie alive.

After breakfast, Jimmie went exploring in the nearby fields, and by evening the entire town was searching for the boy. His disappearance soon led people to believe that Jimmie had been kidnapped. One ransom note was received, asking that $5,000 be placed in a milk bottle; but no one picked up the well-guarded but phony ransom money, and this idea was soon given up. Wild imaginations soon turned toward the idea that gypsies had run off with Jimmie, a notion that Jersey City public safety director John Bentley, and police captain Rooney, followed. A carnival was in town the day of Jimmie's disappearance, but when authorities located the carnival, the sought-after gypsies were no longer a part of the show. In the Summer of 1942, a lead in the case came in the form of a telegram from Puerto Rico.

The message, from a youth named Ismael Calderon, informed Bentley that gypsies and a boy fitting Jimmie's description were on the island. Calderon added that the gypsies—Miguel Costello, Nicolas Cruze, and Rose Cruze—were sought by police. This too turned out to be false; when the gypsies were finally caught in Cuba, Jimmie was not with them. Other leads continued to pour in, including an egg discovered in a Jersey City grocery store with the inscription, "Help. James Glass held captive in Richmond, Va." The most hopeful lead occurred in Norman, Okla., when a boy was found in a shoe store. Glass and his wife traveled to see the child and at first thought their prayers had been answered; the boy even answered to Jimmie Glass' name after prompting from an enthusiastic storekeeper, but he was not Jimmie.

Jimmie's parents, however, finally found their long-lost son. In December 1923, while hunting rabbits near Greeley, Otto Winckler discovered a skull and a pair of children's shoes with little foot bones inside. These remains were identified as Jimmie's, though there were still skeptics. There were also those who doubted whether Jimmie had merely run off, and then lain down from exhaustion and died, or drowned in the swampy land. Rooney believed that the boy was probably murdered and his body placed there much later, noting that the distance was too great for the boy to have covered, and that the ground had been thoroughly searched in 1915 when Jimmie disappeared.

REF.: *CBA; Smith, Mysteries of the Missing.*

Glass, Jimmy, c.1961-87, U.S., mur. On June 12, 1987, 25-year-old Jimmy Glass became the third person in five days sent to the electric chair in Louisiana, following a period of twenty-eight months without an execution in the state.

Preceding Glass were murderers Benjamin Berry, on June 7, and Alvin Moore, Jr., on June 9. Glass was convicted in the shooting deaths of a rural Louisiana couple. His accomplice, 35-year-old Jimmy Wingo, followed Glass to the chair just five days later. The last words Glass spoke were, "I'd just as soon be fishing."

All four men had appealed their sentences because it was claimed that the death penalty was meted out disproportionately to those who killed white people. The U.S. Supreme Court denied the appeal in April 1987. REF.: *CBA.*

Glatman, Harvey Murray (AKA: **Johnny Glynn, George Williams**), 1928-59, U.S., rob.-rape-mur. Born in 1928 in Denver, Colo., Harvey Glatman was a quiet child and was quite attached to his mother. The first indication of Glatman's pathology occurred when Harvey was twelve. When his parents noticed red welts on his neck Harvey confessed that he had put a noose around his neck, and tortured himself to achieve sexual satisfaction. A psychiatrist assured Glatman's parents that he would outgrow this habit. At seventeen, Glatman had developed an unorthodox way of meeting girls: he would snatch their purses, run ahead of them laughing, and then throw the purses back to them.

In 1945, in Boulder, Colo., Glatman accosted a teenaged girl with a toy gun. When he told her to take off her clothes, the girl screamed and Glatman ran away. He was arrested, but while free on bond fled to New York. In New York City, Glatman was arrested for robbery and sentenced to five years in Sing Sing. He received psychiatric care while in prison and was released in 1951.

Sex killer Harvey Murray Glatman.

Glatman moved to Los Angeles, and with his mother's help, trained as a television repairman and opened a repair shop. He also became an avid amateur photographer. On Aug. 1, 1957, Glatman, posing as a free-lance photographer, induced 19-year-old Judy Ann Dull to pose for him. At his apartment, Glatman told her that the assignment was for the cover of a detective magazine and required that he bind and gag her. Dull went along with his requests. Once she was bound and gagged, Glatman pulled a gun on her and raped her repeatedly. After photographing her in the apartment, he drove her 125 miles east of Los Angeles to the town of Indio. There he photographed her again before strangling her and burying her body in a shallow grave. Hitchhikers discovered her remains five months later.

Glatman's next victim was Shirley Ann Bridgeford, a 30-year-old divorcee whom Glatman met at a lonely hearts club in Los Angeles. Using the name George Williams, Glatman asked Bridgeford out on a date. Glatman drove her out into the desert, tied her up, raped her, and then photographed her before strangling her with a rope. He covered her body with branches and left it beneath a cactus.

On July 23, 1958, Glatman selected his next victim, 24-year-old Ruth Rita Mercado. She had placed an ad in a Los Angeles paper for modeling assignments. At Mercado's apartment, Glatman pulled a gun on her and raped her. As with his other victims, he took Mercado to the desert where he spent most of the next day with her, raping her periodically. After photographing Mercado in the desert, Glatman strangled her.

Judy Ann Dull, photographed by Glatman before he raped and killed her.

Glatman next approached 20-year-old French model Joanne Arena. Arena, however, became suspicious when Glatman began telling her about the assignment, and she refused to go with him. Glatman made his next and last attempt on 28-year-old Lorraine Vigil. Vigil agreed to accompany Glatman in his car to a studio he claimed he worked from in Anaheim. However, when Glatman passed the Anaheim exit, Vigil became alarmed and asked Glatman to let her out. He stopped at the side of the road where he pulled a gun on her and tried to tie her wrists. Vigil struggled with Glatman and managed to open the car door behind him. The two fell out onto the pavement where a passing policeman spotted them.

Glatman was arrested, and during a search of his apartment police found the photographs of his victims and articles of their clothing and personal belongings which Glatman had taken as souvenirs. Friends of three of the victims identified Glatman in a police lineup and he finally confessed to the rapes and murders. He was convicted three days later, after he pleaded guilty at his trial and asked for the death penalty. He was granted his wish and died in the gas chamber at San Quentin on Aug. 18, 1959.

REF.: *CBA*; Nash, *Bloodletters and Badmen*; Wolf, *Fallen Angels*.

Glaze, Billy (AKA: **Jesse Sitting Crow**), 1944- , U.S., fraud-mur. A serial killer in Minneapolis, Minn., committed three murders over a nine-month period in 1986 and 1987. All of the victims were severely beaten and sexually assaulted. Each woman had also recently moved to the city, was unemployed, was known to drink heavily, frequented the same bars, and was an American Indian. Their heritage is what led police to the killer, Billy Glaze.

The first victim was 19-year-old Kathleen Kay Bullman, who like future victims had been a teenage mother, and like the last victim had worked as a prostitute. Her partially clothed body was found near abandoned railroad tracks on July 27, 1986; a three-foot pipe used to smash her face lay across her throat. Bullman had been strangled to death. Angeline Whitebird-Sweet, twenty-six, was the second victim. Her severely beaten, naked body was discovered in a park near the American Indian Center on Apr. 12, 1987; the tree branch used to molest her lay nearby. She died of asphyxiation from the murderer stomping on her chest. The killer's final victim was 21-year-old Angela Green, whose nude body was found near railroad tracks on Apr. 29, 1987, her head crushed by a stone. Glaze was often seen in the same bars as the women. It was in these bars that suspicion first fell on Glaze.

A lifelong drifter, Glaze often erroneously boasted of being an Indian, Jesse Sitting Crow. He also ranted that all Indian women should be sexually molested and killed. Because of these ravings, a cook at the Band Box, Rae Flugge, called police on May 4, 1987, to inform them that Glaze might be the man they sought. At that time Glaze was in New Mexico, he was arrested on May 24 in Albuquerque. The case against Glaze continued to grow while he was in jail. Glaze wrote a note to a fellow inmate, Gary Branchaud, in which he confessed to the three killings; a witness to the first murder finally came forward. A grand jury indicted Glaze in June. Before his trial for murder, Glaze was found Guilty and sentenced to two years for Social Security fraud. He was also charged with swindling $3,000 in welfare checks from Lois Morrison, with whom he had lived.

At Glaze's 1989 murder trial in Hennepin County District Court before Judge Jonathan Lebedoff, the defense, led by Michael Colich and Pete Cahill, attempted to show that there was no evidence linking their client to the murders. Colich noted that the only "witness" was a 48-year-old transient named Leroy Hamblin, who could not possibly have seen Glaze in the dark after spending four hours smoking marijuana and drinking. He tried to demonstrate that the confession was merely another of Glaze's boasts, which deputy sheriff Kim Swirtz, who waited until January 1989 to come forward with his alleged confession to her, admitted was possible. Colich also pointed out that the ring Glaze gave to Morrison was not the same ring Green had been wearing; and that a medical expert testified that blood from the scene of one killing matched neither the victim nor Glaze.

Despite strong defense arguments, Assistant County Attorneys Pete Connors and Judith Hawley produced seventy-five witnesses and 120 exhibits against Glaze, while the defense could muster only four witnesses on behalf of the defendant. On Feb. 10, 1989, after thirty-five hours of deliberation, the jury found Glaze Guilty on three counts of first-degree murder—and three counts of second-degree murder—for committing intentional murder without premeditation. Lebedoff sentenced Glaze to three consecutive terms of life in prison. REF.: *CBA*.

Gleason, William E., b.1837, U.S., jur. Nominated by President Abraham Lincoln to the Dakota Territorial Court in 1865. REF.: *CBA*.

Glenn, Elias, 1769-1846, U.S., jur. U.S. district attorney in Washington, D.C., from 1812-24. In 1824, President James Monroe nominated him to the District Court of Maryland. REF.: *CBA*.

Glenn, Herschel, c.1958- , U.S., rape-mur. A Streamwood, Ill., couple attended a friend's party in Elgin and left about 1:30 a.m. on May 8, 1982. James H. Wright, eighteen, and his date, 20-year-old Lillian L. Final, drove in Wright's truck to Lord's Park. An off-duty Elgin police officer, 24-year-old Herschel Glenn, apparently approached the truck, flashed a light, and showed the couple his police identification. Then, kidnapping the couple, he shot the young man three times in the head and four times in the arm, raped the woman, and shot her three times in the head, once in her right thigh, and once in her abdomen. Glenn left the bodies on the outskirts of Elgin, about a mile apart.

Two brothers saw the officer standing next to his car, which had its headlights on, and then they saw him drag what appeared to be a body into the woods. The witnesses wrote down the car's license plate number, returned later to find the body at 4 a.m., and called the Kane County sheriff's office. Glenn's billfold was found ten feet from Wright's body and police traced the license number to Glenn. Elgin police watched Glenn's house before he left for work and he was arrested when he arrived for work at 7 a.m. About 9:30 a.m., a farmer found Final's body. Police also recovered bloodstained clothing and a .38-caliber gun from Glenn's apartment. The blood matched the couple's blood types and the bullets used in the killing had been fired from Glenn's gun. Glenn was tried and convicted on May 11, 1983, of murdering Wright and was sentenced to seventy years in prison. The former patrolman was later convicted of the rape and murder of Final and on July 20, 1987, he received a life term.

The case also raised questions about the quality of candidates accepted by the Elgin police force. The two families of the victims filed civil suits charging that between 1974 and 1980, Elgin employed fifteen new officers, including Glenn, who had been evaluated as high security risks. Glenn had also been ranked as far below average, and he had told the polygraph tester that he had shoplifted as a teenager, used marijuana about six months prior to the test, and bribed a Chicago policeman. Facing the lawsuits, the City of Elgin agreed to pay a $1.5 million settlement, which was to be divided between the two families. REF.: *CBA*.

Glenn, John, 1795-1853, U.S., jur. U.S. district attorney in Washington, D.C., who was nominated to the District Court of Maryland by President Millard Fillmore in 1852. REF.: *CBA*.

Glick, Allen, c.1941- , U.S., org. crime. Once accused of being a Mafia front man, former Las Vegas casino owner Allen Glick turned Mafia informant and provided testimony that sent five high-ranking organized crime figures and the Teamsters Union president to prison.

Glick purchased the Stardust Casino and Hotel in August 1974, with the help of a $62.7 million loan from the Teamsters Union pension fund. He obtained the fund with the help of Frank Peter Balistrieri, head of organized crime in Milwaukee. At the time, Glick claims he did not know he would be beholden to the mob, but in early 1975, Glick found out that Kansas City, Mo., mob boss Nick Civella had helped convince Roy Lee Williams—then a pension fund trustee, and later union president—to approve the loan. For the five years that Glick owned the Stardust, he never controlled the operations.

In 1977, a mob leader from Chicago who controlled the casino, Frank Rosenthal, told Glick to leave the operations to him and stay away from the casino; even threatening to buy out Glick for $10 million. It was alleged that Chicago's organized crime head in Las Vegas, Anthony Spilotro, conducted the hiring and firing of employees in 1978. A year later Glick was forced to sell the Stardust—though at a profit of $70 million—but not before he was asked another favor by the mob and the Teamsters; a favor that would be the beginning of his courtroom testimony against his one-time benefactors.

On Jan. 30, 1979, Glick was persuaded to drop his bid for Las

Vegas property near the home of Nevada Senator Howard Cannon, which Cannon was looking to buy, so that the Teamsters could bribe Cannon to stop federal deregulation of the trucking industry. Glick withdrew his bid, but Cannon never accepted the bribe.

The trial for this bribery conspiracy took place in 1982 with Glick as the key government witness. His testimony brought about the convictions of Williams and Joseph Lombardo, a ranking figure in organized crime. It was Glick's testimony that again convicted Lombardo and four others in a major government crackdown on organized crime.

In January 1982, Kansas City's federal Organized Crime Strike Force head, David Helfrey, convinced Glick to testify against several mob figures. The trial began in July 1984, and Glick's testimony corroborated evidence from FBI wiretaps that demonstrated how organized crime leaders in Chicago, Cleveland, Kansas City, and Milwaukee had covertly run Glick's hotel and skimmed $2 million in profits from 1974 to 1979.

Before the trial's completion, Kansas City mobster Carl DeLuna and Milwaukee mob boss Balistrieri pleaded guilty to the conspiracy, and on Jan. 6, 1986, a directed verdict of acquittal was ordered for John Balistrieri and Joseph Balistrieri, for lack of evidence. On Jan. 21, 1986, a verdict of Guilty was returned against Chicago mob leaders Joseph Aiuppa, John Cerone, Angelo Pietra, and Lombardo, and Cleveland mob figure Milton Rockman. REF.: *CBA*.

Glueck, Sol Sheldon, 1896-1980, and **Glueck, Eleanor Touroff**, 1898-1972, U.S., criminol. Sol Sheldon Glueck and his wife, Eleanor Touroff Glueck, who were married in 1922, joined the faculty at Harvard University in 1925 where they studied juvenile delinquents, criminals, recidivism, and rehabilitation. Together they compiled detailed case histories of criminals and delinquents in an attempt to explain why people committed crime, and to provide possible remedies.

The Gluecks discovered that the punishments given by judges did not always work in preventing crime. In fact, in their 1940 work, *Juvenile Delinquents Grown Up*, the authors found that only one-tenth of the 1,000 boys studied from Boston's Judge Baker Guidance Center were reformed, and that four out of five returned to crime within five years. This group did, however, commit fewer crimes as it became older, which the Gluecks attributed to a maturing factor—generally taking longer in juvenile delinquents than well-behaved children. According to the Gluecks, the most likely to respond to reform would be a boy whose parents were Jewish immigrants from Lithuania, Poland, or Russia, and who was well behaved until he turned thirteen; while the least likely to reform would be a boy whose parents were U.S.-born citizens of mixed religious backgrounds, and who defied authority prior to his ninth birthday. Remedies for reform prescribed by the Gluecks included using a tribunal, rather than one judge to determine the proper punishment. Further, they recommended providing a psychologist or psychiatrist, joined by an educator or sociologist. This tribunal could then monitor the progress of the individual offender.

Among the many books the two co-authored are: *Five Hundred Criminal Careers* (1930), *Five Hundred Delinquent Women* (1934), *One Thousand Juvenile Delinquents* (1934), *Later Criminal Careers* (1937), *After Conduct of Discharged Offenders* (1945), *Unraveling Juvenile Delinquency* (1950), and *Predicting Delinquency and Crime* (1959). REF.: *CBA*.

Gluskoter, Rochelle, 1940-46, U.S., (unsolv.) kid.-mur. "That's her clothing. That's my baby's clothing!" cried Miriam Gluskoter at the sight of the saddle oxfords, the red print dress, and white tweed double-breasted coat—now tattered, torn, and mildewed after lying in a ravine for seventeen months. Her baby was 6-year-old Rochelle Gluskoter, kidnapped and murdered by a man who was never found. On an afternoon in Los Angeles in 1946, Rochelle was playing in a friend's yard two blocks from home when a black convertible drove up. The man behind the wheel called to Rochelle, and whatever he said convinced her to climb up onto the front seat next to him. Jennie Schaub, Rochelle's friend's mother, happened to be standing at a window and saw the car pull away, but did not realize until it was too late that she was very likely the last person to see Rochelle alive and that she had seen her murderer.

Mobilizing a search that would be one of the largest in Southern California history, the Los Angeles Sheriff's Department enlisted the aid of mounted police, neighbors, and Boy Scouts to search Rochelle's Los Angeles neighborhood, nearby eucalyptus groves, and throughout surrounding L.A. County. The effort was an exercise in futility, however, for Rochelle's body already lay decaying in an Orange County ravine.

In the weeks that followed, police grilled the city's more infamous sex offenders and child molesters. Several suspects were held for questioning, but no concrete leads turned up until Benito Cabrerra, while hunting for small game, stumbled upon the skeleton of a small child in a ditch along Santiago Boulevard in rural Orange County.

Orange County police immediately notified their counterparts in Los Angeles and the girl's parents were summoned to identify the body. Delicatessen owners Miriam and Abe Gluskoter, accompanied by Inspector J. Gordon Bowers, the officer who had led the investigation nearly two years before, identified the remnants of clothing found on the skeleton as those worn by Rochelle on the day she climbed into the black car with the mysterious man.

The only thing missing was a gold ring embossed with the letter R—a symbol of the Gluskoters' last hope that their daughter's murderer would be brought to justice. Rochelle's ring remains missing, however, along with the finger she wore it on. Both hands were severed from the body. The L.A. Sheriff's Department has never charged anyone with Rochelle's murder, and the case of her mysterious kidnapping and death remains open. REF.: *CBA*.

Glycerius, b.c.1400s, Roman., emp., consp.-mur. Western Roman emperor from 473-74, who was unrecognized by eastern emperor Leo I. After surrendering to Julius Nepos in 474, he became bishop of Salona. In 480, he helped plan the assassination of Nepos. REF.: *CBA*.

Gneist, Rudolf von, 1816-95, Ger., jur. Professor at Berlin in 1844, a member of Prussian legislature from 1858-93, and in the German Reichstag from 1868-84. He served as a judge in the Prussian Supreme Court and as a member of the Prussian Privy Council in 1875. REF.: *CBA*.

Gobel, Jean Baptiste Joseph, 1727-94, Fr., consp. Appointed archbishop of Paris in 1791. After backing Jacques-Rene Hébert in successful overthrow of Girondists in 1792, he was guillotined by the Committee of Public Safety along with other Hébertists in 1794. REF.: *CBA*.

Goblet, René, 1828-1905, Fr., lawyer. Minister of the interior from 1879-80, minister of public instruction from 1885-86, and premier of France from 1886-87. He appointed reactionary General George Boulanger as minister of war. REF.: *CBA*.

Goddard, Rayner (Baron Goddard of Albourne), 1877-1971, Brit., jur. Counsel to the king from 1923, judge in the High Court of the King's Bench division from 1932-8, and lord justice of appeal from 1938-44, the year he was appointed a life peer. He served as the lord of appeal in Ordinary from 1944-46, and as lord chief justice from 1946-58. He displayed support for citizens who had been exploited by big business or victimized by judicial errors. He opposed probation for criminals and often criticized modern penology. He presided over the notable murder trials of William Teasdale and Nurse Waddingham. REF.: *CBA*.

Godefroy, Jacques (Gothofredus), 1587-1652, Fr., jur. Taught at Geneva in 1619, and edited *Codex Theodosianus*. REF.: *CBA*.

Godelmann, Johann Georg, prom. 1591, Ger., witchcraft. While a Rostock (Ger.) University professor of law in 1591, Johann Georg Godelmann wrote the work entitled *De Magis, Veneficis et Lamiis*, or *Sorcerers, Poisoners, and Witches*. In his book, though highly enlightened for that period, he argued that most people executed for witchcraft were simply deluded old women. He also accepted the belief in the devil's power, that witches truly existed, and that there existed a pact among the devil and witches. Godelmann further defended his theory that trials of witches should have consistent rules, stating it would be better for many witches to escape punishment, rather than to wrongly condemn one innocent person. REF.: *CBA*.

Godfrey, Edmund Berry, 1621-78, Brit., (unsolv.) mur. Sir Edmund Berry Godfrey, one of London's most respected magistrates, left his home on the evening of Oct. 12, 1678. His body was found six days later in a ditch near Primrose Hill, London. It quickly became evident that Godfrey's murder had not been motivated by robbery, as money and jewelry were found on his body. Furthermore, it appeared that Godfrey had been murdered elsewhere and his body brought to the location where it was discovered. His chest bore a deep stab wound and was covered with bruises. Rope burns were found on his neck, which was broken.

Sir Edmund Berry Godfrey, whose murder was never solved.

Godfrey's reputation for diligence and courage was enhanced by his refusal to join the mass exodus from London in 1665 to escape the plague. Godfrey stayed and reminded his colleagues that they too were obliged to continue their work. When a notorious felon dared officials to enter a hospital full of highly contagious plague victims to arrest him, Godfrey boldly accepted the challenge, and was later knighted for his courage.

Early in 1678, Godfrey received the formal complaint of Titus Oates, whose allegations regarding seditious activity by Catholics came to be known as the Popish Plot. Oates claimed that highly placed people in King Charles' court planned to overthrow the government and restore Catholicism as the state religion. Oates, unaware of King Charles' conversion to Catholicism, also argued that the plotters intended to murder the king.

Godfrey, believing that the plot had been invented by Lord Shaftesbury, an influential and strongly anti-Catholic member of Parliament, did nothing about Oates' statement, and refused to swear out warrants for those he named. When Godfrey's body was discovered, however, Oates used the murder to stir the public into a frenzy, claiming that Godfrey had been murdered by Catholics to prevent him acting on Oates' deposition.

Because of Godfrey's refusal to pursue Oates' charges and also because of the manner in which Oates later exploited Godfrey's death, it was suspected that the inventors of the Popish Plot were responsible for Godfrey's murder. Another theory states that Godfrey was murdered by Lord Pembroke, whom he had convicted of manslaughter for stomping a man to death only a few months before. None of the theories about Godfrey's death were ever proved, and the murder remains unsolved.

REF.: Earl of Birkenhead, *Famous Trials of History*; Boucher, *The Pocket Book of True Crime Stories*; *CBA*; Nash, *Almanac of World Crime*; _____, *Open Files*; Williamson, *Historical Whodunits*; (FICTION), Robinson, *Whitefriars, or, The Days of King Charles the Second*.

Godfrey, Elizabeth, 1772-1807, Brit., mur. Convicted of stabbing to death Richard Prince with a pocketknife, 34-year-old Elizabeth Godfrey was sentenced to be hanged in February 1807. Although she caused the death of just one person while alive, her death on the scaffold inadvertently resulted in the death of forty others.

To be hanged along with Godfrey were Owen Haggerty and John Holloway, who had been convicted of murdering John Cole Steel. This mass hanging produced a number of curious on-

lookers, estimated to be more than 40,000, outside Newgate Prison in London. Spectators were so eager to have a better look at the hanging or hear any last words that many were trampled or crushed.

Meanwhile on the scaffold, executioner William Brunskill failed to give Godfrey a quick death. The woman, wearing a long-sleeved white dress and cap, kicked and struggled for a half hour after release of the trap door. By the time the crowd had dispersed, forty people were dead and hundreds injured. Public executions continued in England until 1868.

REF.: *CBA*; Potter, *The Art of Hanging*.

Godfrey, Samuel E., prom. 1818, U.S., mur. Godfrey was an inmate at the Vermont State Prison. He harbored a deep resentment against Warden Thomas Hewlet who had ordered punishments for Godfrey when he broke several prison regulations. Godfrey waylaid the warden while he was making his rounds one day and killed him, then meekly surrendered to guards. Godfrey was tried and convicted of this murder and executed at Woodstock Green, Vt., on Feb. 13, 1818. Although it was freezing that day and a snowstorm swirled about the site of the execution, more than 10,000 people turned out to witness Godfrey's hanging.

REF.: *CBA*; *A Sketch of the Life of Samuel E. Godfrey*.

Godfrey of Bouillon, prom. 1097, Middle East, mur. In the name of Christianity and heeding the entreaties of Pope Urban II, who claimed that Turks were persecuting Christians, Godfrey of Bouillon led an expedition to the Middle East. His forces held Antioch, at siege for seven months in 1097, and upon surrender of the city, murdered every Turk there. Godfrey then journeyed to Jerusalem, where he employed gigantic siege towers to overcome the walls of the city. The death and destruction he brought to Jerusalem included the burning of synagogues where countless Jews seeking sanctuary were burned alive. It is believed that in just one week, Godfrey had 70,000 people put to death. REF.: *CBA*.

Godomer, See: **Chlodomer**.

Godunov, Boris Fëdorovich, c.1551-1605, Rus., assass. Chief member of the regency under the rule of Czar Fyodor I, from 1584-98. In 1591, he defeated the Crimean Tartars, in 1595 regained territory in Sweden, and recolonized Siberia. When Fyodor died in 1598, he was elected czar. Under his reign he attempted to reform the legal system. He was killed in a struggle with the false Dmitri and boyars. REF.: *CBA*.

Godse, Nathuram, See: **Gandhi, Mohandas Karamchand**.

Gods of the Lightning, 1928, play by Maxwell Anderson. This work is almost a political polemic based upon the sensational Sacco-Vanzetti robbery-murder case (U.S.,1920-1927). Anderson later used the same case as background for his play, *Winterset*. See: **Sacco, Nicola**. REF.: *CBA*.

Goebbels, Paul Joseph, 1897-1945, Ger., suic.-mur. As Minister of Propaganda and Natural Enlightenment for the Nazi Party, 1933-45, Joseph Goebbels was one of the most powerful men in Adolf Hitler's Third Reich. As such, he controlled all media, the fine arts, and shaped the sterile culture of Nazi Germany. He also suppressed free speech and a free press in Germany, supporting all of Hitler's genocidal policies regarding the extermination of the Jews. Moreover, in 1934, Goebbels was one of the architects of the wholesale slaughter of Hitler's Brown Shirts leaders. At that time he avidly helped to prepare murder lists with Hermann Goering and Heinrich Himmler, selecting hundreds of his personal enemies for summary execution, ostensibly claiming these victims to be enemies of the state. Though Goebbels was dead by the end of WWII, he was universally branded as a mass murderer, along with his evil mentor, Adolf Hitler.

Born on Oct. 29, 1897, in Rheydt, a thriving textile center in the Rhineland, Goebbels was raised a Catholic by his religiously strict parents, Fritz and Maria Goebbels. A bright child, Goebbels attended Catholic grade and high schools before winning a scholarship from the Albert Magnus Society, a Catholic organization. This enabled him to attend several colleges. In fact, Goebbels attended the universities of Berlin, Bonn, Freiberg, Cologne, Munich, Frankfurt, and Wuerzburg, where he studied philosophy, literature, history, art, Latin, and Greek. He proved equally brilliant in his college studies and went on to earn a Ph.D. from the University of Heidelberg in 1921. His goal was to be a successful author but Goebbel's work failed to impress publishers and play producers.

Goebbels produced a novel, *Michael,* an autobiographical work, and two verse plays, *The Wanderer,* about Jesus Christ, and *The Lonesome Guest.* All of this work was rejected time and again by publishers and producers which left Goebbels embittered. Coupled to his professional failure was the young man's deep resentment at having a crippled left leg. He was not, as portrayed by Hollywood during WWII, born with a club foot. At the age of seven, Goebbels contracted osteomyelitis. This inflammation of the bone marrow caused doctors to operate on his left thigh which proved a failure and left the boy with a left leg permanently shorter than the right. The left leg never fully developed and remained slightly withered throughout his life, causing Goebbels to walk with a noticeable limp.

In June 1922, Goebbels, whose political philosophy at the time was decidedly radical, walked into the Circus Krone in Munich and was electrified by a dynamic, ranting speaker, Adolf Hitler, one of the leaders of the National Socialist Party, or the Nazi Party. He embraced all of Hitler's radical right-wing beliefs that all foreigners were inferior, Germans superior, that Germany had been betrayed by its own leaders with the humiliating Versailles Treaty which had stripped Germany of its industry, its military might, and its right to make war. Goebbels wrote a letter to Hitler, one that gushed adulation: "Like a rising star you appeared before our wondering eyes, you performed miracles to clear our minds and, in a world of skepticism and desperation, gave us faith." Hitler took Goebbels into the fold and the two were, more or less, inseparable until their joint suicides twenty-three years later in a Germany they had brought to devastation.

Initially, Hitler designated Goebbels as his representative in northern Germany, chiefly in Berlin but in the mid-1920s, Goebbels came under the sway of Gregor Strasser, one of the original founders of the Nazi Party, who, however, opposed many of Hitler's plans and beliefs. Hitler won Goebbels back to the fold and made him Gauleiter of Berlin in 1926. From that moment on, Goebbels rubber-stamped Hitler's every move with glowing, slavish approval. Like his leader, Goebbels was a shrieking, hortatory speaker, and Hitler used him to rabble-rouse his audiences on many occasions. Goebbels would harangue the most zealous of Nazi gatherings with his racial rantings for sometimes as long as three to four hours before Hitler took the stage to end

Nazi Minister of Propaganda Paul Joseph Goebbels, who murdered his children and committed suicide before capture.

the sweaty, hate-filled performance, leaving himself, Goebbels, and the audience drenched and exhausted.

When Hitler became Chancellor of Germany in 1933, he appointed Goebbels his Minister of Propaganda. The diminutive Goebbels reveled in the job. He suppressed all freedom of speech. He closed down all the presses, except those advancing the warped Nazi credos of supremacy and racial hatred, and he ordered the burning of all books that did not reflect Nazi Germany's new profile. Books by the hundreds of thousands were taken from public and private libraries and thrown into huge bonfires while Nazi youths danced madly about. All films that expressed democratic thought were banned by Goebbels. All art

that did not correspond to Nazi culture was either destroyed or boxed up and stored away. Goebbels became the czar of publishing, of film making, of the fine arts, of the newspaper and radio world in Germany. His voice and his voice only spoke in the name of Hitler.

A wild womanizer all his life, Goebbels used his position to lure the most attractive women in Germany to his side, promising them jobs in the state-run motion picture industry or with the state-controlled press and radio. His mistresses lived in hotel suites throughout Berlin and before going home to his wife, Magda, and his children, Goebbels, whose craving for sex was notorious and insatiable, would visit these women for a quick tryst. In 1934, a year after Goebbels took office as Minister of Propaganda, Hitler gave secret orders for a blood purge of his strong-arm legions, the Brown Shirts (S.A.), including the execution of top S.A. leaders, Ernst Roehm, Karl Ernst, and others.

Goebbels sat down in Berlin with Himmler and Goering and made up a murder list, using Hitler's directives as an excuse to have all their enemies killed. This wholesale slaughter of the Brown Shirts, an organization Hitler had used throughout the 1920s and early 1930s to intimidate and threaten the government, occurred on June 30, 1934. The bloodbath was euphemistically termed "The Night of the Long Knives," since it brought about mass murder of hundreds of men Hitler no longer needed or wanted, perverts of all stripes, murderers and thieves, who had paraded about the landscape of Germany in brown shirts, Sam Browne belts, and jackboots, causing terrified citizens to do their bidding.

Throughout the late 1930s, Goebbels advanced Hitler's rabid racial theories on the radio and in the German press. Though he held no authority in the secret police organizations that busily exterminated millions of Jews, Goebbels established the emotional and intellectual climate in Germany where such oppression was acceptable. He encouraged xenophobic hatreds and promoted a war of aggression. Whenever Hitler required an avalanche of publicity to bolster his sagging fortunes as the war turned against him, he relied more and more on Goebbels who continued to fill the German media with lies and deceits. As the Allies closed in on the fast-dwindling Third Reich and Hitler retreated to his Berlin bunker, Goebbels went with his family into the bunker with his lunatic leader. With Russian troops battling with ragged German troops only blocks away from the bunker, on June 30, 1945, Hitler and his mistress Eva Braun committed suicide.

The next day, Goebbels ordered a Nazi physician to inject his six children with poison. The children lay in their bunks, thinking they were being given a sedative to make them sleep. They died within minutes. Then Goebbels ordered Guenther Schwaegermann, a German officer in the bunker, to obtain some gasoline, telling him: "Everything is lost. I shall die together with my wife and family. You will burn our bodies." He did not tell Schwaegermann that he had already murdered his six children. Goebbels then stepped outside the bunker with his wife Magda and turned their backs to two SS officers who, according to Goebbels' order, shot them both twice in the head. Their bodies were then burned but the nervous SS troops, eager to escape the bunker area which was then being bombarded, made a bad job of it. When the Russians overran the area a short time later, they easily identified the charred remains of the former Minister of Propaganda. See: **Ernst, Karl; Goering, Hermann; Himmler, Heinrich; Hitler, Adolf; Roehm, Ernst.**

REF.: *CBA;* Davidson, *The Making of Adolf Hitler;* Dollinger, *The Decline and Fall of Nazi Germany and Imperial Japan;* Fest, *Hitler;* Heiden, *Der Fuehrer;* Lochner, *The Goebbels Diaries;* Orlow, *The History of the Nazi Party;* Payne, *The Life and Death of Adolf Hitler;* Schoenbaum, *Hitler's Social Revolution;* Shirer, *The Rise and Fall of the Third Reich;* Speer, *Infiltration;* ____, *Inside the Third Reich;* ____, *Spandau: The Secret Diaries;* Vogt, *The Burden of Guilt;* Walther, *Der Führer;* (FILM), *Grand Illusion,* 1938; *Confessions of A Nazi Spy,* 1939; *Foreign Correspondent,* 1940; *Enemy of Women,* 1944; *The Hitler Gang,* 1944; *Kolberg,* 1945; *Hitler,* 1962; *Hitler: The Last Ten Days,* 1973; *Our Hitler,* 1977.

Goebel, Julius, b.1892, U.S., lawyer. Taught law and legal history at Columbia University beginning in 1931. REF.: *CBA*.

Goebel, Otto E., and **Flautt, Elizabeth**, and **Flautt, Irene**, prom. 1932-33, U.S., fraud. Otto E. Goebel, along with his sisters-in-law, Elizabeth Flautt and Irene Flautt, and six salesmen, convinced 400 Catholic priests and 6,000 others to invest $3 million in his National Diversified movie company for the proposed production of a movie entitled *Mary, The Virgin*. The company never produced the film and went bankrupt in 1930. Two years later, the longest criminal court case ever tried in the U.S. took place.

On Dec. 12, 1932, the trial of all nine defendants for mail fraud began. Over the next 109 days, federal prosecutor Jacob J. Rosenblum produced sixty-eight witnesses, while the defense produced thirty, including Goebel who was on the stand from Mar. 30 to May 18, 1933. After 15,000 pages of testimony had been given, 941 pieces of evidence had been displayed, and an alternate juror had died three months into the seven-month trial, federal Judge John Munro Woolsey turned the case over to the jury. In July 1933, all nine defendants were found Guilty on all charges after a day's deliberation. Goebel was sentenced to five years in prison and fined $41,000, Elizabeth was sentenced to one year and one day in prison, Irene was sentenced to four years and fined $41,000, and the remaining six received sentences of two to four years in prison, and the same fine as Goebel and Irene. REF.: *CBA*.

Goebel, William, prom. 1890-1900, Case of, U.S., mur.-assass. vict. William Goebel of Covington, Ky., had been a state senator since 1886. His personal life became inextricably involved with his political life—first he killed a man because of politics, then he was assassinated for the same reason. He was regarded as a reformer who fought against extending the powers of big business when they harmed citizens. John L. Sanford, the chief executive officer of the Farmers and Drovers National Bank of Covington, was an important influence in Kenton County, which was plagued by bitter political fighting for many years. But the fight between Sanford and Goebel became personal when Goebel opposed some banking regulations that Sanford favored. Sanford then worked successfully to oppose Goebel's election to appellate judge, a position Goebel coveted. In April 1895, Goebel bought the local newspaper, the *Ledger*, but the change in ownership was not made public. Almost immediately an article appeared claiming that Sanford's support of Joe Blackburn in the upcoming U.S. Senatorial election was based on Blackburn's brother, the governor of the state, pardoning a Sanford relative for forgery and embezzlement before he had even been tried.

On Apr. 11, Goebel, walking with W.J. Hendricks, the attorney general of Kentucky after a meeting at the courthouse, was spotted by Sanford. Keeping his right hand in his pocket, Sanford shook hands with Hendricks and then said to Goebel, "I understand that you assume the authorship of that article." When Goebel replied, "I do," the two men simultaneously pulled pistols from their pockets and fired. Goebel's bullet hit Sanford in the forehead, killing him. Sanford's bullet ended up between Goebel's body and clothing but did no damage.

A hearing was held five days later, at which a number a witnesses said they thought that Sanford fired first. Another politician also testified that he had earlier heard Sanford threaten to kill Goebel. The grand jury refused to indict Goebel for murder.

In the election of November 1899, Goebel was, by the first count, defeated for the governorship of Kentucky by William S. Taylor by 2,383 votes. On Jan. 2, 1900, Goebel and supporters challenged the results on eight different counts, all of which implied that the Republicans had stolen the election by rigging the votes.

Caleb Powers, the newly-elected Republican secretary of state, rounded up hundreds of angry mountain people and had them march on Frankfort in protest. Rumors flew that they were there to shoot someone. Everyone who had a gun started carrying it. On Jan. 30, as Goebel was walking toward the State House, he was shot through the chest, apparently from the direction of the window of Caleb Powers' office. Taylor called out the militia, which was waiting close by, to break up the angry crowds. Within hours, the Democrat-controlled state election board declared that Goebel had won the election after all. The Republicans tried to take the matter to the U.S. Supreme Court, but the Court refused to act.

The dying William Goebel was sworn in as governor of Kentucky on Feb. 3, just hours before he died. J.C.W. Beckham, who had been elected lieutenant governor, immediately became governor. One of his first acts was to establish an investigative board to find out who shot Goebel. Over the coming months, twenty men were arrested, though only five were ultimately tried: Caleb Powers, Berry and James Howard, Garnett Ripley, and Henry Youtsey. Ripley went to trial first and was acquitted, as was Berry Howard. Youtsey was found Guilty and sentenced to prison for life, although he spent much of the next seven years appearing as a witness at other men's trials.

The trial of Powers began on July 9, 1900, before a "special" jury of twelve Democrats who had voted for Goebel. One witness quoted Powers as saying, "If we can't get (Goebel) killed, I will kill him myself if necessary." Henry Youtsey had been seen actually trying out the angle of view from Powers' window. Judge Cantrill summed up in a way that left the jury little doubt that he was out to get Powers. Caleb Powers was found Guilty and sentenced to life in prison. James Howard was also found Guilty, but the two of them appealed the decisions and an identical Democrat-laden jury was chosen for the October 1901 retrial. Many prosecution witnesses were less positive than they had been before. In fact, two of them frankly admitted that the prosecutor had paid them for their testimony. But Powers was again found Guilty. The verdict was appealed again.

A third trial began on Apr. 7, 1903, with James Howard as the defendant. This time, the prosecution had new witnesses, including Youtsey, who turned state's evidence and claimed he had let Howard into Powers' office and heard the shot seconds later. Howard was again found Guilty. Powers' third trial the following August took place before a new judge, also a Goebel Democrat. Youtsey was encouraged to testify that he turned state's evidence because he had been tortured in prison and forced to change his testimony. But the Democratic jury again found the man Guilty, this time changing the penalty to death. The appeals court quashed this verdict, too, and a fourth trial was demanded.

In December 1907, the Republicans controlled the state, and a different atmosphere prevailed at Powers' trial. This time, Youtsey was indicated to be the killer. The jury was unable to reach a verdict and a fifth trial was called for. But Powers and Howard chose to ask Republican Governor Augustus E. Willson for a pardon, which he granted, placing the blame for the whole conspiracy on Youtsey.

REF.: *CBA*; Duke, *Celebrated Criminal Cases of America*; Johnson, *Famous Kentucky Tragedies and Trials*.

Goehner Kidnapping, See: **Tillman, Emil**.

Goerdeler, Carl-Friedrich, 1884-1945, Ger., consp. Mayor of Konigsberg from 1922-30, and mayor of Leipzig from 1930-37. He held post as commissioner for price control from 1931-32, and from 1934-35. After being deposed from the Leipzig post, he joined the Nazi resistance movement and was arrested in 1944, for conspiring to assassinate Adolf Hitler. He was executed by the Gestapo in 1945. REF.: *CBA*.

Goering (or **Göring**), **Hermann Wilhelm**, 1893-1946, Ger., suic.-mur. Obese, a morphine addict, and sexually perverse, Hermann Goering was the second most influential leader in Nazi Germany under Adolf Hitler. To those who did not know his real personality and character, Reich Marshal Goering, during the early years of the Third Reich, appeared to be an affable, considerate human being who seemed to blunt the atrocious behavior of his leader, Hitler. In truth, he was, from the beginning, as vicious an anti-Semite as Hitler and his blood-thirstiness equalled his mentor's avaricious appetite for conquest and mass murder. He was the highest ranking Nazi to sit in the dock at Nuremberg in 1946 to be judged a war criminal, and yet, in keeping with Goering's cunning and cowardly nature, he managed, at the last moment, to cheat the hangman.

Born on Jan. 12, 1893, in Rosenheim, Ger., in the heart of Bavaria, Goering was the son of a diplomat who served as consul-general in Haiti. He was raised in foster homes and boarding houses as a child. Ironically, one of these homes, in Austria, was that of a Jewish friend of the family. Here Goering was treated with kindness and understanding. He later re-paid this family by persecuting them and placing several family members in a concentration camp. Goering's father arranged for his son to be trained for the military at an early age and he entered the officers' school in Licherfeld, outside of Berlin, at an early age. Goering would later pick this place for mass executions of purged storm troopers he once led in street brawls during the 1920s.

Nazi Reich Marshal Hermann Goering.

Goering liked to tell the story of his beginnings as the "child of the regiments," but, as a youth, he suffered from deep depression and resentment when he was left to the barracks while his peers, for the most part landed Prussians, attended family balls and banquets where they were introduced to Emperor Wilhelm II, the kaiser. When WWI began, Goering served in the trenches of the Western Front as an infantry officer. He convinced a friend, a pilot, to teach him how to fly, and then wangled a position with the celebrated Flying Circus, commanded by the equally famous Red Baron, Manfred von Richthofen.

Goering distinguished himself by shooting down many Allied planes and winning Germany's highest air medal, the *Pour le Mérite,* the much coveted Blue Max. When von Richthofen was killed, it was Goering who became the commander of the squadron and, following the end of WWI, Goering emerged as one of Germany's greatest living war heroes. He had been coddled as a pilot, since the aviators of WWI were considered the darlings of the military. They practiced a weird code of ethics, burying the enemy pilots crashing behind their lines with full military honors, delivering the personal effects of enemy pilots after their deaths by flying low over enemy airfields and dropping these belongings, and by giving lavish parties for captured enemy pilots. Through four years of war Goering lived on champagne, caviar, and utter fear. He conquered his fear by injecting himself with morphine every day he flew into the sky to fight for Germany, an addiction he never fully conquered.

Following the war, Goering soon found himself close to bankrupt. To pay his bills, he became a transport pilot in Denmark and Sweden. In 1921, an old friend, Count Eric von Rosen, met him in Stockholm and convinced Goering to fly him home to Rockelstadt in a small plane which landed on a frozen pond in front of Rosen's castle. Goering was invited to stay with his Swedish host who turned out to be ardently pro-German. Rosen was an admirer of a new German politician named Adolf Hitler. Two flags adorned with swastikas, the symbol of the Nazi Party, hung in Rosen's huge dining hall. Rosen's wife introduced Goering to her sister, the beautiful blonde Karin von Kantzow, née Baroness Fock, who was estranged from her husband and living with the Rosens. Goering and the Baroness fell in love and she soon divorced her husband and married Goering. The Baroness was epileptic and had an 8-year-old son. She was also enormously wealthy.

Goering moved with his new family to Munich and here he half-heartedly returned to university studies, devoting a few hours each week to the study of economics. He was more interested in politics, chiefly that of the Nazi Party. The Rosens had introduced Goering to the right-wing dogma of the Nazis and this rigid, radical thought appealed to the militarist Goering. He met Hitler in 1921 and became his close associate almost immediately. Hitler realized that Goering was an important contact to high society, the officer corps, and, most importantly, money to finance his infant political party. A year later, in 1922, Goering was made head of the storm troopers, also known as the Brown Shirts (S.A.).

The brutish thugs of the S.A. were encouraged by Goering to attack any political enemies of the Nazi Party on the streets. Brown Shirts under Goering's leadership slugged and hospitalized Social Democrats, Catholics, Communists, and reserved their most vile wrath for the Jews. They forced Jews to wash cobblestones on their hands and knees, wear obscene signs around their necks, and subject themselves to the most repulsive ridicule. Goering and his goons smashed the windows of Jewish shops in all the major cities of Germany and rode about the streets screaming at startled Germans to boycott all Jewish businessmen.

Meanwhile, Goering furthered his career with Hitler by loaning his leader millions of German marks. As Depression-torn Germany sank into economic oblivion, Goering continued to support Hitler, giving him billions, and then trillions of marks to survive and keep his party functioning. When Hitler came to power in Germany in 1933, he made Goering head of the newly-born Luftwaffe, the German Air Force, as well as making him Reich Marshal. Other than Hitler, there was no more important and powerful man in Germany than Hermann Goering. He was, however, like the rest of Hitler's political retinue, nothing more than a willing stooge to Hitler and his barbaric policies. When political opposition in the German Parliament, the Reischstag, seemed to overwhelm the Nazis in the early 1930s, it was Goering who solved the problem by torching the Reischstag Building and then blaming this Nazi arson on the Communists so that he and other ranking Nazis could carry out a murderous purge of the Communists.

Hermann Goering, on trial as a war criminal in Nuremberg, 1946.

Goering was also a willing participant in the 1934 purging of the S.A. which Hitler decided to eliminate after he had no more use for this army of thieves, perverts and killers. Goering, along with Himmler and Goebbels, spent hours on the night of June 29-30, 1934, making up murder lists of thousands of political and personal enemies. These wholesale executions were carried out by Himmler's dreaded secret police, the Gestapo, and the SS. As the Third Reich broadened its dictatorship, Goering enthusiastically endorsed and carried out Hitler's orders to exterminate the Jews and political opponents. He also helped to plan the invasions of Poland and France, personally directing his Luftwaffe. He later directed the Luftwaffe to bring the blitzkrieg to England, ordering his Air Force to bomb London mercilessly in 1940-41.

Following the failure of the Luftwaffe to destroy the Royal Air Corps and bring the stubborn British to their knees, Goering lost face with Hitler and his fellow Nazis. He delegated his authority to subordinates and spent the remaining war years retreating into pleasure at his country estate of Karinhall, named after the Baroness who had died. Goering had remarried in 1935, wedding film actress Emmy Sonnemann in a lavish state ceremony in 1935, with Hitler as his best man. The Reich Marshal seldom spent time with his second wife, preferring the company of cheap whores. He soon contracted syphilis and warded off this dread disease by massive doses of morphine. Goering consumed enormous meals each day, his already corpulent body ballooning to obesity. Hitler ignored Goering in these last years, refusing to hear any criticism of his one-time financial sponsor. Meanwhile, Goering traveled about occupied France and other countries under the Nazi yoke in his private rail car, collecting priceless art treasures. He was no real critic of painting, however, as evidenced by his purchase of what he thought to be genuine Vermeers. These paintings had been created by the master art forger, Hans van Meegeren.

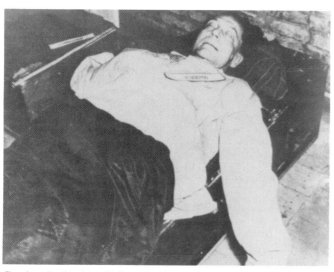

Goering, dead in his cell; he took poison only hours before his scheduled execution.

As the war came to a close, Goering fled Berlin, going to his native Bavaria where he pompously announced to Hitler, who was then barricaded in his Berlin bunker, that he, Goering, was prepared to take over the leadership of the Third Reich. Hitler had his SS troops arrest Goering but he managed to survive until he was arrested by Allied troops. Put on trial at Nuremberg as an arch war criminal, Goering used the trials as a podium to make long-winded speeches about the glories and greatness of the Third Reich. He did not, as did the other defendants, blame Hitler for his crimes, but freely admitted giving his own orders, claiming that he was a soldier doing his duty, not a criminal persecuting innocent millions. The tribunal soon proved otherwise, and Goering was found Guilty and sentenced to death.

Yet Hermann Goering, who had acted so pompously at his trial, defiant in the dock while he attempted to justify the genocidal regime of Adolf Hitler, managed to avoid the gallows from which ten other Nazi defendants were hanged on Oct. 16, 1946. Only a few minutes before he was to be taken from his cell in Nuremberg, Goering swallowed a vial of cyanide of potassium which killed him in seconds. No one was able to determine how Goering obtained the poison but it was believed that a friend smuggled it to him. It was even suggested years later that a sympathetic American officer gave the one-time WWI hero an honorable way out, allowing him, for the sake of past wartime triumphs, to take his own life rather than die ignobly on the gallows. See: **Goebbels, Paul Joseph; Himmler, Heinrich; Hitler, Adolf; Roehm, Ernst; van Meegeren, Hans.**

REF.: *CBA;* Davidson, *The Making of Adolf Hitler;* Dollinger, *The Decline and Fall of Nazi Germany and Imperial Japan;* Faber, *The Luftwaffe;* Fest, *Hitler;* Gilbert, *Nuremberg Diary;* Heiden, *Der Fuehrer;* Neave, *On Trial at Nuremberg;* Orlow, *The History of the Nazi Party;* Payne, *The Life and Death of Adolf Hitler;* Schoenbaum, *Hitler's Social Revolution;* Scott, *The Concise Encyclopedia of Crime and Criminals;* Shirer, *The Rise and Fall of the Third Reich;* Smith, *Reaching Judgment at Nuremberg;* Snyder and Morris, *A Treasury of Great Reporting;* Speer, *Infiltration;* ____, *Inside the Third Reich;* ____, *Spandau: The Secret Diaries;* Walther, *Der Führer;* (FILM), *Hitler—Dead or Alive,* 1942; *Enemy of Women,* 1944; *The Hitler Gang,* 1944; *The Magic Face,* 1951; *Night Ambush,* 1958; *Hitler,* 1962; *Battle of Britain,* 1969; *Hitler, The Last Ten Days,* 1973; *Our Hitler,* 1977.

Goes, Damiao De (Góis), c.1502-74, Port., her. Diplomat in Flanders, Poland, Denmark, and Sweden. He was an archivist who was accused of Lutheranism by the Inquisition in 1571, and imprisoned in a Batalha monastery. REF.: *CBA.*

Goethe, Robert, c.1917-   , U.S., rob.-mur. The brutal and mysterious murder of 40-year-old Dr. Silber C. Peacock on Jan. 2, 1936, in Chicago was made more fantastic than the callous robbery killing it was by the many scandalous red herrings that were fed to the police. After a night out with his wife, Ruth Pearce Peacock, and his daughter, Peacock retired for the evening, but left shortly past 10 p.m. following a telephone message purporting to be from a sick patient. Mrs. Peacock called State's Attorney Thomas J. Courtney, a friend of her husband, the next morning when her husband failed to return.

The only information available on the missing pediatrician was the note he had scribbled while on the phone: "G. Smale, 6438 North Whipple Street." This message produced the first of many bizarre leads. At that address there was no G. Smale, but a G.W. Smale lived at a similar address on the city's South Side. Peacock's body was discovered on the night of Jan. 3, in the back of his car three blocks from the address he had scribbled.

The body was in a kneeling position. A .45-caliber revolver slug had been shot through his head; the top of his head was cut seven times, presumably with his own scalpel; his skull had been crushed by numerous blows, and his left hand was smashed in the car door.

The case was handled by Detective Chief John L. Sullivan, who was soon flooded with possible scenarios. Robbery was suspected, but not likely because only $20 and two vials of drugs had been taken, leaving behind jewelry and more money. The pilfered vials implied a narcotics connection, strengthened by the rumor that Peacock was involved in a U.S. Bureau of Narcotics investigation, or that he was a drug dealer himself. A key was discovered by Deputy Coroner Edward Edlestein, which refueled the love tryst theory, but was put to rest when the key was found to fit the apartment of Edlestein's in-laws. The love affair theory did not end there, however, when it was learned that another doctor had accused Peacock of having an affair with his wife—an affair the man's wife denied. Remarkably, the crime itself proved far simpler to solve, and far less sensational than the newspapers made it out to be.

A series of robberies following the same method as the Peacock murder—a doctor was called around 10 p.m. to visit a sick patient at a lonely address, attacked, and robbed—began on Jan. 16, 1936. That night Dr. Joseph Soldinger had his car and $37 stolen; on Jan. 21, Dr. A.L. Abrahams was robbed of $56; on Feb. 14, Dr. L.A. Garness had $6 stolen, and an attempt was made on the brother of Police Captain Harry O'Connell, Dr. John P. O'Connell. Acting on a hunch, O'Connell had three area youths, believed to be armed robbers, arrested. During the questioning of Robert Goethe, eighteen (son of "crime school" operator Rose Kasallis), Durland Nash, eighteen, and 19-year-old Emil Reck, also known as "Emil the Terrible," the three managed to inform on one another and implicate a fourth confederate, 17-year-old Michael Livingston, who drove their getaway car the night of the murder. The fatal shot into Peacock's head was fired by Goethe, who later slashed the dead man's head, while Reck was attributed with senselessly beating the already dead doctor over the head. Goethe, Nash, and Reck were each sentenced to 199 years in prison, plus consecutive terms of one year to life in prison for four counts of robbery. Livingston was sentenced to thirty years in prison.

REF.: *CBA*; Hapler, *The Chicago Crime Book*; Rodell, *Chicago Murders*.

Goettel, Gerard Louis, 1928-   , U.S., jur. Served on the attorney general's Special Group on Organized Crime from 1958-59. Among his writings are "Why The Crime Syndicate Can't Be Stopped" for *Harper's* magazine in 1960, and various articles on law and organized crime for the *Columbia Encyclopedia* in 1961. In 1976, President Gerald R. Ford nominated him to the Southern District Court of New York. REF.: *CBA*.

Goetz, Bernhard Hugo, 1948-   , Case of, U.S., vigil.-asslt.-attempt. mur. On Dec. 22, 1984, Bernhard Hugo Goetz, a white electronics engineer, was riding a Manhattan subway train. As usual, he carried an unlicensed gun to protect himself; he was involved in two previous muggings and a beating by three black men in 1981. Troy Canty approached and asked him for $5. Goetz, who later confessed that he was threatened by the question though no threat was made by Canty, pulled his .38-caliber revolver, just as he had done on another day when a youth had asked for money. During the earlier occasion, Goetz admitted on videotape he hadn't shot the panhandler but commented, "He deserved to die." On Dec. 22, however, Goetz did not restrain his trigger finger. He fired the gun four more times, wounding Barry Allen, James Ramseur, and Darrell Cabey. All four were nineteen; all were black.

Nine days later, Goetz turned himself in to police in Concord, N.H., and made a videotaped confession; he later made a similar confession to New York detectives. In the confession Goetz claimed that the four had surrounded him, were hassling him for money, and that he feared he was going to be robbed. Witnesses and the victims denied this. Goetz added that "my intention was to murder, to hurt them, to make them suffer as much as possible." He also said, "Look, if I had had more bullets, I would have shot 'em all again and again...I was gonna gouge one of the guys' eyes out with my keys afterwards."

Ironically, during this same confession Goetz described himself as neither a hero or villain, but said, "What you have here is nothing more than a vicious rat. That's all it is. It's not Clint Eastwood." While on the second tape he remarked, "I know violence now from both sides. It's the worst thing in your life when you're on the losing side, and when you're on the winning side it makes you sick."

The trial of Goetz for attempted murder, assault, reckless endangerment, and illegal possession of a gun began in late April 1987 before New York State Supreme Court Justice Stephen G. Crane. During proceedings, the jury—comprising nine whites, two blacks, and a Hispanic—was shown the taped confessions and heard eyewitness accounts of what occurred, but they only heard complete testimony from one victim.

As to who started the controversial confrontation, however, witnesses disagreed. It was stated that Goetz had been itching for a showdown by sitting down among a group of rowdy youths; while others claimed that the youths had been running up and down the train aisles causing trouble. Witnesses generally agreed that only Canty approached Goetz, while all testified that at least one of the alleged attackers, Cabey, remained seated. One witness, Andrea Reid, testified that Ramseur was also seated when shot. Ramseur corroborated this statement.

Ramseur testified that he and Cabey were seated when Goetz opened fire, and that the two tried to flee before they were shot, accounting for the fact that Goetz shot two of his "assailants" in the back. But Ramseur was far from being an unimpeachable witness.

Since the shooting Ramseur had been convicted in April 1986 of raping, sodomizing, and robbing a black teenager on a rooftop at gunpoint. He was already serving an eight to twenty-five year prison term when he took the stand.

Ramseur also proved to be a boon for the defense rather than the prosecution with his continual aggressive outbursts, including a shouting match with the defense counsel and Crane. His testimony was cut short by his refusal to answer questions on two separate occasions. On May 5, 1987, he was cited once for contempt of court and on May 20 he was cited five times, for which Ramseur was sentenced to six months in prison by Crane.

Ramseur did manage to testify that Canty had started the Goetz incident; Canty admitted it earlier in the trial. Canty claimed that he had approached Goetz and asked for money, but unlike Ramseur's version, had not hassled the gunman. Like Ramseur, Canty had a criminal record of theft and was currently in a mandatory drug rehabilitation program. It was in fact the criminal records of the victims that defense lawyer Barry I. Slotnik attacked and worked to his advantage in claiming that Goetz was really the victim. Slotnik, in his opening statement, told prosecuting Assistant District Attorney Gregory L. Waples that "we might as well switch tables, because I'm going to prosecute those four, and you're going to see that those four were committing a robbery..." Waples disagreed, pointing out why one of the victims was not to give testimony.

The shooting of Cabey, who all agreed was seated during the alleged attack, resulted in his being left brain-damaged and permanently paralyzed from the waist down. Waples argued that Goetz did not act, as Slotnik claimed, in the heat of the moment, not bothering to pause between shots, but that Goetz did indeed, carefully and with calculated coolness, commit the attempted murders, as evidenced by his own taped confessions.

At one point in the confession Goetz stated that he walked up to one of his victims, Cabey, and said, "You don't look so bad, here's another," before firing his last bullet. Later, one juror, Diane Serpe, claimed that she and other jurors discounted this statement by Goetz, because it was unlikely he really said it. Serpe said, "He was so agitated ... He just wasn't being rational." The fourth victim in the shooting, Allen, did not testify but pleaded the Fifth Amendment, since the four had confessed they were on their way to rob video game machines at the time of the shooting. Two of the victims were carrying screwdrivers—the only weapons the four possessed—when shot by Goetz.

The jury began its deliberations on June 12, 1987, after seven weeks of testimony and evidence. Crane instructed the jury how to decide the gunman's fate. He stressed that Goetz should be found innocent if they had any doubt that under similar circumstances a reasonable person would not react in the same manner. Under New York law, a person has the right to defend himself with deadly force if he believes he is about to be robbed. Despite Goetz's taped confession of his desire to murder all four victims, the jury found him Not Guilty of attempted murder, assault, and reckless endangerment, but found him Guilty of illegal possession of a handgun. The decision did not end the debate, but only fueled it.

Many people saw the verdict as an endorsement for vigilantism or a racist decree that whites could shoot blacks. The jury explained that race did not enter into their decision. Benjamin L. Hooks, NAACP executive director, termed the outcome "a terrible and grave miscarriage of justice." Remarking on the jury's verdict, New York City Mayor Ed Koch stated, "Some will take this as a signal that vigilantes are acceptable, but we will not permit that."

The case itself spawned a number of books dealing with the racial and legal ramifications, as well as the psychological aspects of Goetz himself—Lillian Rubin authored *Quiet Rage: Bernie Goetz in a Time of Madness*, published in 1986. An eighty-eight minute videocassette of Goetz's confessions, entitled *The Confessions of Bernhard Goetz*, sold for $39.95 at the end of 1987. Eventually, New York State Crime Victim's Compensation Board, which had ruled in January 1987 that Canty could not receive state aid, ruled Apr. 22, 1988, that any profits Goetz made from the sale of his story could not be kept by him. This decision was made in reference to the 1979 law which prohibited David Berkowitz from profiting from his "Son of Sam" murder spree.

Goetz was sentenced for the illegal weapon charge on Oct. 19, 1987, to six months in jail, fined $5,000, instructed to perform 200 hours of community service, placed on probation for five years, and required to seek psychiatric counseling. At the request of Slotnik, this sentence was overturned by the New York Supreme Court Appellate Division, which noted that the state's gun-control law mandates at least one year in prison—a sentence that would ironically allow Goetz to be paroled sooner than the shorter six-month term which required a ninety-day minimum sentence as opposed to sixty days.

As Goetz awaited an appeal of his conviction, he told a New York gun club that the judge "should have sentenced me to a testimonial dinner and a ticker-tape parade." His appeal was denied by the New York Court of Appeals on Nov. 22, 1988, and the case was sent back to Crane for resentencing. Before Crane passed sentence on Goetz for a final time, the now famous gunman said, "I do feel this case is really more about the deterioration of society than it is about me. Society needs to be protected from criminals." For his lack of remorse Crane sentenced the criminal to one year in prison and fined him $5,000 on Jan. 13, 1989.

Goetz was placed in protective custody at the Rikers Island jail immediately following the resentencing trial. The U.S. Supreme Court refused to hear Goetz's appeal on Feb. 27, 1989. His attempt to serve less time in prison by asking for the longer one-year sentence failed on Mar. 3, 1989, when the New York State Parole Board denied his request for early release. This denial automatically denied Goetz parole for at least six more months. REF.: *CBA*.

Goetz, Fred (AKA: **Shotgun Ziegler, J. George Zeigler**), d.1934, U.S., rob.-org. crime. Fred Goetz, born and raised in Chicago, graduated from college with a degree in engineering and served in WWI as a flier. About a year after he jumped bail in 1925 on the charge of raping a 7-year-old girl, Goetz turned up working as a gunman for Al Capone. He was reputedly one of the gunmen in the St. Valentine's Day Massacre of 1929. Goetz left the ranks of organized crime some time in 1930 and became an independent bootlegger, working in Kansas City, Mo. with Vern Miller and he later graduated to bank robbery, joining Harvey Bailey and the Holden-Keating mob.

Through these men, Goetz met the Barkers and he participated in several bank robberies with Freddie and Dock Barker and Alvin Karpis. When the Barkers kidnapped millionaire Edward G. Bremer in 1933, holding him for $200,000 ransom, it wa Goetz who acted as the go-between and it was Goetz who collected the ransom money and released Bremer. Goetz began to talk too much, according to later statements of Karpis and Ma Barker and her son Freddie believed he might accidentally betray the gang. Goetz received a phone call on March 20, 1934 to meet an unknown party at a Cicero, Ill. restaurant.

When he left the restaurant, four men in a car pulling close to the curb leaned out of windows with shotguns and blasted Goetz to death. Goetz, it was later speculated, was murdered by either the Barkers for talking too much, by Capone gunmen who believed he might reveal the identities of the St. Valentine's Day Massacre, or by members of the George "Bugs" Moran gang, seeking vengeance for the massacre. Some days later, Ma Barker persuaded Goetz's grieving widow, Irene Goetz, to turn ove the $200,000 Bremer ransom money she was holding. See: **Bailey, Harvey; Barker Brothers; Capone, Alphonse; Holden, Thomas; Miller, Vernon C.; St. Valentine's Day Massacre**.

REF.: *CBA*; Gish, *American Bandits*; Kobler, *Capone*; Messick, *Kidnapping*; Nash, *Bloodletters and Badmen*; Toland, *The Dillinger Days*.

Goff, John W., 1848-1924, U.S., jur. John W. Goff began his political career in 1894 when he was elected recorder of the New York County Democratic party. As recorder, Goff served as a judge for the criminal division for the Court of Sessions. In 1907, he was appointed justice of the state Supreme Court, where he presided over the trials of Maria Barberi and police lieutenant Charles Becker, who was charged with the murder of gambler Herman Rosenthal on the night before Rosenthal was to appear in court to testify about police protection of illegal operations. The trial was marred by Goff's browbeating of defense counsel and lack of judicial integrity. His actions led the Court of Appeals to reverse Becker's conviction—Becker was found Guilty at a second trial—and severely censure Goff, thus, tainting the remainder of his career. See: **Barberi, Maria; Becker, Charles**.

REF.: *CBA*; Fried, *The Rise and Fall of the Jewish Gangster In America*; Logan, *Against the Evidence*; Peterson, *The Mob*; Reppetto, *The Blue Parade*; Scott, *The Concise Encyclopedia of Crime and Criminals*.

Goff, Nathan, 1843-1920, U.S., jur. U.S. attorney from 1868-81, member of the West Virginia House of Representatives from 1867-68, and U.S. congressman from 1883-89. He was nominated to the Fourth Circuit Court of West Virginia by President Benjamin Harrison in 1891. REF.: *CBA*.

Goffe, William (Gough), c.1605-79, Brit., jur. Served on the panel of judges at the trial where Charles I was sentenced to death in 1649. He served as major general under Commander-in-chief Oliver Cromwell until 1655. During the Restoration of Charles II, he fled to America, and spent many years in hiding. REF.: *CBA*.

Gohl, Billy, d.1928, U.S., mur. In 1903, Billy Gohl was assigned to Aberdeen, Wash., as a delegate of the Sailors' Union of the Pacific to handle payrolls, mail, and the storage of valuables. His office was built on stilts at the edge of the Wishkah River near Gray's Harbor, and had a trap door which led directly to the water. Gohl began murdering sailors who had entrusted him with their valuables. He would shoot the victim in the head as he sat across from him at his desk, methodically check the corpse for identification, and dispose of the body through the trap door. Forty-one bodies were taken from the water during a three-year period. Gohl was finally apprehended when he mistakenly thought an engraved watch found on one of his victims bore the name of the man and left it on the body, afraid that keeping it would incriminate him. The name was actually that of the watchmaker, who identified the seaman, who was traced to Gohl's office. In 1913, Gohl was convicted of two murders and sentenced to life imprisonment. The state of Washington had repealed the death penalty only one year before his trial, and lawmakers used his case to argue for restoring capital punishment, which they accomplished in 1914. In 1928, Gohl died in prison. REF.: *CBA*.

Goins Brothers, prom. 1931-32, Case of, U.S., mur. Blaine Goins and Eb Goins were cousins who lived in Kentucky near the Tennessee border where Blaine operated a moonshine business and Eb owned the local store. One day, Eb's son, Blount Goins drove four of Blaine's grandchildren to Tennessee. On the retrun trip, they were involved in an automobile accident that killed two of the children. Blaine blamed Blount for the children's deaths and an intense hatred developed between Blaine and Eb. Their disagreements culminated in the shooting deaths of both Blount and Eb on July 13, 1931. It was quickly alleged that Blaine and his sons had shot the two men. Blaine's sons were tried for the double murder, but were found Not Guilty.

REF.: *CBA*; Montell, *Killings*.

Gold Accumulator Swindle, 1897, U.S., fraud. New Englanders gave more than $400,000 to two con men in 1897 believing that their invention could mine gold from ocean water. Englishman Charles E. Fisher and Prescott Ford Jernegan, a Baptist minister from Connecticut, demonstrated their "gold accumulator" to residents of Lubec, Maine. The machine was lowered into the water, and when retrieved the following day, it was covered with flakes of gold. Fisher, a skilled diver, had planted the gold on the device during the night. After witnessing the invention, investors flocked to buy shares in the Electrolytic Marine Salts Co., driving the initial $1 price of the 350,000 shares to nearly $50. Fisher and Jernegan were given $200,000 for their services by a grateful board of directors. But when Fisher sold his shares and moved to Boston, the accumulator stopped accumulating. Jernegan also left

Lubec, allegedly to search for Fisher, but he was later arrested in France. Because he had been legally awarded $200,000 for his invention by the board of directors, Jernegan could not be held. Upon his release, he traveled to the U.S. and returned $175,000 of the money. he died in the Philippines in 1942. Fisher was never found, rumor has it that he was killed by South Sea native's after being caught with the chieftain's wife. REF.: *CBA*.

Goldberg, Arthur J., 1908- , U.S., jur. Became the general counsel of the Congress of Industrial Organizations and the United Steel Workers of America in 1948. He helped draft the merger agreement between the American Federation of Labor and the Congress of Industrial Organizations, forming the AFL-CIO. He also helped write a code of ethics for the organization. Working to reform labor rules, he assisted Senator John F. Kennedy in writing legislation that forced public disclosure of union finances. Kennedy nominated him as U.S. secretary of labor in 1960.

He was appointed associate justice of the U.S. Supreme Court by President Kennedy in 1962. In *Gideon v. Wainwright* in 1963, he favored states providing counsel to indigent defendants. In *Draper v. Washington* in 1963, he ruled that a state must answer an indigent convict's request for a free trial transcript as a means to an appeal. In *Murphy v. Waterfront Commission of New York Harbor* in 1964, he wrote the unanimous decision prohibiting federal and state courts from prosecuting a person with testimony he gave under grant of immunity in another jurisdiction. In *Escobedo v. Illinois* in 1964, he ruled that prosecutors cannot use statements made by a defendant who is deprived of his right to counsel or is not informed of his right to remain silent. In a majority decision in *Kennedy v. Mendoza-Martinez* in 1963, he overturned a federal statute revoking the citizenship of an American who left the country to avoid the draft, as a violation of due process. In *Cox v. Louisiana* in 1965, he agreed with the majority that states could keep demonstrators a certain distance from court houses.

He resigned his justiceship in 1965, to become ambassador to the United Nations, after President Lyndon B. Johnson promised him direct influence in ending the Vietnam War. After many attempts to negotiate with the North Vietnamese government, he resigned his post in 1968. He authored *AFL-CIO: Labor United* in 1956, *Defenses of Freedom* in 1966, and *Equal Justice: The Warren Era of the Supreme Court* in 1972. REF.: *CBA*.

Goldblum, Stanley, c.1926- , U.S., forg.-fraud. In 1960, the Equity Funding Corporation of America was founded in Los Angeles. By 1973 the company, under the auspices of Stanley Goldblum, reported the previous year's earnings at $22.6 million, revenues of $152.6 million, assets near $750 million, and a net worth of $143.4 million. Unfortunately for stockholders and policy holders in the funding and insurance company, the net worth of the company was actually less than zero.

Goldblum and four others, including Michael Riordan—who died in a mud slide in 1969—began the corporation. Goldblum and Riordan soon gained complete control of the business, which at that time was perfectly legitimate. Shortly after Equity Funding went public with its shares of stock, the fraud began. Near the end of 1964, Goldblum asked treasurer Jerome Evans to post as income commissions that had not, and never would be, received. Trusting his boss, Evans complied. This was the beginning of many illegal transactions performed by obliging employees. Evans left in 1969, just after a 1968 audit showed that $7.6 million of a claimed $36 million was owed to Equity Funding by its customers. Goldblum hired Samuel Lowell as controller—later promoting him to executive vice president of finance and operations—and the fraud really took off. There was even an attempt in 1970 to defraud the pope, with a purchase of a Rome spaghetti factory owned almost entirely by the Church, but it failed, as did most of the company's foreign ventures. The acquisition of U.S. corporations, especially the Presidential Life Insurance Company of Illinois in 1967, proved to be quite lucrative.

General counsel to the insurance company, Fred Levin, soon became enmeshed with Equity Funding, becoming an executive vice president with the parent company, and president of the renamed Equity Funding Life Insurance Company (EFLIC). Levin became Goldblum's new right-hand man. Business was booming. In 1964, 100,000 shares of stock were offered at $6 each, while in 1969, 5.2 million shares sold at $80 a share. But this was all imaginary, and more money was needed to keep the company—and the fraud—alive.

In 1963, Equity Funding made an agreement with the Pennsylvania Life Company wherein Penn Life allowed only Equity Funding to sell its life insurance and mutual fund shares together. In exchange Equity Funding would, with two exceptions, sell only insurance underwritten by Penn Life. To escape this agreement, Equity Funding agreed to resell insurance sold by EFLIC to Penn Life from 1968 to 1970. This new endeavor proved profitable, but would soon run itself dry. To prevent this, EFLIC began to sell worthless insurance to its employees, then phony insurance to real people, and finally phony insurance to non-existent people.

The final stage in Equity Funding began after stocks plummeted to $12 a share in 1970, but within a year 19,000 policies worth $828 million were written in the midst of a recession. Auditors, who did not take part in the fraud, were shown files of phony people, at first forged by company executives, and later mass-produced. Alan Green, a computer programmer, under the guidance of conspirator and chief actuary Art Lewis, was one of many assigned to "create" people. As the number of phony people grew, it was decided to "murder" them and collect on their insurance policies from the companies to which their insurance had been resold. Goldblum opted for genocide in early 1973 to the tune of $10 million worth of phony deaths, but was persuaded by his underlings to settle for $3 million. At that point the company began to collapse, and it was decided to make an attempt to legally save it by firing unnecessary employees, one of whom was Ronald Secrist. This turned out to be a mistake.

Secrist informed authorities of the fraud, and in March 1973 state insurance examiners in California and Illinois performed a surprise audit. Securities analyst Ray Dirks spread the rumor to the Securities and Exchange Commission and *The Wall Street Journal*, and Equity Funding stock dropped. The company was seized by California officials on Mar. 30, 1973. On Apr. 1, Goldblum, Levin, and Lowell were thrown out of the building by the company's board, and a week later the remaining principal conspirators were fired. Twenty employees were charged in the scandal; eighteen pleaded guilty, including Goldblum, who at first held out, but admitted his guilt in October 1974, just after his trial had begun and Evans had testified against him. All were sentenced in the spring of 1975. Goldblum was given eight years in prison, though U.S. Attorney William Keller had asked for twenty; Levin and Lowell received five years; EFLIC treasurer Lloyd Edens and lawyer Jim Banks received three years; Lawrence Grey Collins and Michael Sultan received two years; Green, given a two years' suspended sentence, served three months and was placed on probation for three years; public relations director Gary Beckerman received a two-year suspended sentence and probation; Evans was given a one-year suspended sentence and probation. Two outside auditors were sentenced to three months in jail, two years' suspended sentence, four years' probation, and told to donate 2,000 hours of work to charity.

REF.: *CBA*; Moffitt, *Swindled: Classic Business Frauds of the Seventies*.

Goldenberg, Jack (Abraham), c.1901-24, Brit., mur. On Apr. 3, 1924, 28-year-old William Hall, the manager of a small bank near Bordon Camp, England, was shot to death at close range in the neck and head from a .455-caliber Webley revolver—a third bullet missed the victim and struck a window. The robber-turned-murderer, escaped with more than £500 in bank notes and silver. Suspicion fell on soldiers at the camp and an officer's gun was reported missing after the murder. Private Abraham Goldenberg, twenty-two, of the East Lancashire Regiment, informed police that prior to the shooting he had seen two men outside the bank in a car—an allegation that proved to be fatal for Goldenberg.

Goldenberg boasted to the local press that "my evidence will be very important, and that it will be through me that the murderer or murderers will eventually be arrested." The soldier was correct; his evidence did convict the murderer. A sergeant-major at Bordon Camp discovered a parcel containing £500 in stolen bank notes that Goldenberg had hidden on Apr. 8, 1924, in the rafters of a latrine roof. Goldenberg, on whose person was found an additional £37 which he claimed was his own, confessed to the killing after he was arrested, but before his trial retracted the statement and told of how another man had pulled the trigger, and that he was only an accomplice. Nevertheless, the crime was still murder—the other man was never found, or ever likely existed—and Goldenberg was tried before Justice Bailhache at the June 1924 Winchester Assizes. His defense noted that the young Jewish man had been disowned by his family when he told them of his plans to marry a Christian girl, and was in need of money, hence the robbery. Neither jury nor judge found this reason for murder—nor was his plea of insanity accepted—and Goldenberg was found Guilty and hanged. Ironically, Goldenberg asked the judge after pronouncement of his sentence, "Can I be assured that the thirty-seven pounds found upon me will be declared to be my property?"

REF.: *CBA*; Hastings, *The Other Mr. Churchill*; Hoskins, *They Almost Escaped*; Wood, *Shades of the Prison House.*

Goldenberg, Mark, prom. 1900, Brit., burg. A number of London burglaries in 1900 baffled police because apparently no breaking and entry took place during the crimes. In several cases the victims' dogs had been poisoned to prevent unwanted barking during the burglary, and in one case a set of keys and a police whistle were stolen and not returned—evidence which led to the burglar's arrest.

Detective Leeson believed that the culprit was entering the buildings through upper floor windows. Following up on this hunch, Leeson discovered a button on the windowsill of a burgled house, which he traced to a local tailor's shop and soon was on the trail of the man who had lost the button, namely, Mark Goldenberg.

Leeson followed Goldenberg to his apartment, where the missing keys and whistle were found, and a button was noticed to be missing from the vest Goldenberg wore. Goldenberg did not say anything until after the prosecution had presented its case at the North London Sessions before Judge Loveland. He then remarked that he could not be the burglar because his vest was not missing a button, which he promptly displayed to the jury, noting that he had been imprisoned since his arrest. The jury found the defendant Not Guilty and he was freed—but not for long.

Apparently Goldenberg had an accomplice in crime, a seamstress named Bessie, who would see to it that dogs were properly taken care of—she had killed seven in this manner—and procure any keys if necessary. She confessed her participation, including her giving Goldenberg the button that freed him. Bessie also helped police to bring the burglar to justice for another crime—after he had tried to sell her into white slavery. Goldenberg was arrested in Liverpool, and this time found Guilty.

REF.: *CBA*; Leeson, *Lost London.*

Goldenson, Alexander, c.1866-88, U.S., mur. At nineteen, Alexander Goldenson lived with his parents in San Francisco and was greatly admired by his 13-year-old neighbor Mamie Kelly, who on Nov. 9, 1886, wrote Goldenson a letter complaining of his indifference toward her. Two days later he met the girl on her way home from school and talked with her for a short time before pulling out a revolver and fatally shooting her in the head, just above the right eye.

Goldenson quickly turned himself in to the police; after his transfer to the city jail, the news of Kelly's murder just as quickly spread throughout San Francisco. He was transferred to the Broadway jail, and later that night thousands had gathered outside to lynch the youth. Police were able to break up the crowd before a lynching could take place, and Goldenson was found Guilty and

sentenced to be hanged on Apr. 14, 1887. He appealed to the Supreme Court, but the lower court's decision was upheld, and Goldenson was executed on Sept. 14, 1888.

REF.: *CBA*; Duke, *Celebrated Criminal Cases of America.*

Goldman, Emma, 1869-1940, U.S., riot-treas. For thirty years Emma Goldman fought to affect change within the existing social structures of the U.S. She was called a "Red," a subversive, and an anarchist for her advocacy of free love, feminism, and social equality for the masses. Very often Goldman went to jail for her convictions, rooted as they were in Marxist ideology. "Her name was enough in those days to produce a shudder," recalled Margaret Anderson, a literary radical in her own right.

Goldman hardly resembled the stereotypical nineteenth century anarchist. Although she might have been mistaken for a midwestern school teacher, any real similarity to mainstream America soon ended. Emma Goldman was born in the province of Kaunas, in what is now Soviet Lithuania. Her parents were Orthodox Jews who raised her within narrow religious confines. From her earliest years, Emma was deeply troubled by the injustices around her. The forced conscription of young men into the Czarist army, and the callous manner in which the imperial soldiers treated the peasants shaped her early thinking. At the age of seven Emma's family moved to Königsberg, where she was educated in the German school system. Later, a business opportunity brought the Goldmans back to Russia, this time to St. Petersburg. Abraham Goldman, brutally repressive in every way, discouraged his daughter from intellectual pursuit. He believed that Emma's lot in life was to marry, "prepare gefüllte fish, cut noodles fine, and give the man plenty of children."

In March 1881, Czar Alexander II was assassinated by the terrorist organization Narodnaya Volya (the People's Will), an event that outraged Emma's conservative mother but struck a sympathetic chord in the mind of the impressionable 12-year-old girl. With her revolutionary fervor kindled, Goldman left Russia in the company of her sister Lena in 1885, arriving in New York on Dec. 29.

Goldman scuttled in Rochester, N.Y., where she worked in a clothing factory, earning two-and-a-half dollars a week. It was tedious and exhausting work. The stifling atmosphere of Rochester and a short, unhappy marriage to a conventional Russian Jew compounded her sense of dismay. Events in Chicago however, held her interest. The Haymarket Riot of May 4, 1886, drew sharp attention to the plight of working men across the U.S. who were agitating for the eight-hour work day. The long hours Emma had spent toiling in Garson's factory in Rochester were illustrative of the larger struggle of the common man. Emma and her sister began attending socialist meetings in Rochester.

In August 1889, leaving behind her husband, sisters, and father (who had come to Rochester several years earlier), Emma returned to New York City to join forces with the supporters of Pyotr Kropotkin, a proponent of "anarchist communism." During the 1890s the Lower East Side was a hotbed of socialist and anarchist thinking. Goldman easily blended into the cultural mainstream, contributing her own unique perspective on women's issues and free love to the ideology of the movement. The writings of Havelock Ellis and Edward Carpenter, which called for "free expression" and liberation from the dogma of sex for the sake of child rearing, profoundly influenced her thinking during this period. In 1892 she met Alexander Berkman, then a typesetter on Johann Most's anarchist journal *Die Freiheit*.

Berkman was a zealous young revolutionary committed to the violent overthrow of the system, be it capitalism, monarchy, or dictatorship. Soon after they met, Goldman and Berkman became lovers. Their stormy relationship endured long after Berkman was sent off to prison for the attempted murder of Pennsylvania industrialist Henry Clay Frick on July 23, 1892. On Aug. 30, 1893, Emma Goldman was arrested for the first time after leading a mass rally in Union Square on behalf of striking employees who belonged to the Jewish Clothing Workers Union. Goldman exhorted her followers to ignore the politicians and the labor leaders and urged them to take to the streets, "where the rich dwell, before the palaces of your dominators...and make them trouble." Charged with inciting to riot, she was thrown into a dank cell in the Tombs. While there, Emma granted an exclusive two-hour interview to Nellie Bly, the whirlwind reporter from the New York *World*. The next day her story, and the views of Johann Most and Justus Schwab appeared on the front page. Emma Goldman emerged as an eloquent spokesman for the left-wing movements in the U.S. almost by default. Her trial began on Oct. 4. It was one of the supreme ironies of history that Goldman's lawyer was none other than A. Oakey Hall, former mayor of New York City, and a one-time henchman of William Marcy "Boss" Tweed. Hall's tactic was to expose the corrupt New York Police, and in this regard he probably did no favor for his client: Goldman was convicted and sentenced to serve one year on Blackwell's Island Penitentiary.

Goldman served ten months of her sentence, emerging triumphantly on Aug. 17, 1894, to deliver a triumphant speech to 2,800 friends and supporters. "If the representatives of your government intend to prosecute women for talking, they will have to begin with their mothers, wives, sisters, and sweethearts, for they will never stop women from talking," she said. In the next year Goldman traveled abroad, delivering lectures in London, Edinburgh, Vienna, and Glasgow. Returning to the U.S. in 1896, she embarked on a cross-country mission, carrying only a suitcase of books and two diplomas. It was the first time a recognized anarchist had ever gone on the nationwide lecture circuit. "The secret of her power," according to one of her peers, "lies in the fact that she is the very embodiment of the doctrine she preaches. Every fibre of her being is electric by the spirit to which her lips give utterance."

On Sept. 6, 1901, one of Goldman's disciples fired a fatal shot into President William McKinley, while he greeted a line of well-wishers at the Pan American Exposition in Buffalo. The assassin, Leon Czolgosz, allegedly told reporters that after hearing Goldman speak he was resolved to "do something heroic for the cause." Police from across the country immediately issued warrants for Goldman's arrest, believing that she was behind an anarchist conspiracy to murder the president. On Sept. 10, she was arrested in Chicago. From her prison cell she issued a statement disavowing any connection with Czolgosz. "Anarchism did not teach men to do the act for which Czolgosz is under arrest. We work against the system and education is our watchword," she said. Goldman was detained until Sept. 24. Mayor Carter Harrison of Chicago expressed the belief that she was not personally involved in the assassination, which was borne out by the failure of the police in Buffalo to secure any evidence against her. Following her release from custody, Goldman attempted to stir up support for Czolgosz but found few supporters even among her own people. Emma was visibly angry over what she perceived to be a sell-out of Leon Czolgosz, and increasingly withdrew from the more conventional members of the movement. She returned to New York to work as "Miss. E.G. Smith" in the tenement hospitals.

She did not remain out of the fray for long, however. In 1906, with Berkman about to be released from prison, Emma founded *Mother Earth*, the news organ of the anarchist movement. The publication invigorated the movement, which had stagnated in the years following the McKinley assassination. It became a forum of ideas for such gifted writers as Floyd Dell, Robert Minor, and Maxwell Bodenheim.

The outbreak of war in Europe compelled Goldman and Berkman to organize the No-Conscription League, to encourage draft evaders and conscientious objectors to oppose "all wars by capitalist governments." The League lasted only six weeks before a New York federal marshal arrested Goldman on June 15, 1917, for obstructing the draft laws. She was sentenced to two years in prison and assessed a $10,000 fine by Judge Julius Mayer, who noted: "This is not a question of free speech, for free speech does not mean license." Goldman was sentenced to the Missouri State Prison. Berkman, her comrade until the end, was ordered to the

Atlanta Penitentiary. There they remained for the next twenty months.

Following their release from custody, the government took steps to send back the "anarchist undesirables" following passage of a Congressional bill in October 1918 that authorized the deportation of those individuals advocating revolution or sabotage. Speaking before J.Edgar Hoover and a panel of immigration officials Goldman argued that the real aim of the Anti-Anarchist Law was to suppress labor dissent in the coal fields. "A reign of terror has been established in the strike region," she said. "American Cossacks, known as the State Constabulary ride over men women and children; deputies of the Department of Justice break into striker's homes..."

In October 1919, 400,000 coal miners commenced a work stoppage which crippled the nation's heavy industries and threatened to bring the economy to a halt. The men had walked out in defiance of Attorney General A. Mitchell Palmer's injunction. Believing that the anarchist leaders were somehow behind it all, federal agents from coast to coast raided the offices of the I.W.W. and other leftist organizations. Those who failed to establish citizenship risked deportation, and the Palmer Raids succeeded in casting a wide net across the country. On Dec. 12, 1919, the Supreme Court upheld the deportation proceedings filed against Berkman. Goldman, who was in the midst of her appeals decided that she, too, would go to Russia if that was the case. "Rather than give our enemies a chance to defeat me," she said "I have decided to tell them to go to hell." Goldman, Berkman, and forty-five other radicals departed from Ellis Island aboard the *S.S. Buford* on Dec. 21. Except for a brief three-month visit back to the U.S., Goldman spent her remaining days exiled in Soviet Russia, and Europe. To Emma's surprise and ultimate sorrow, her native land had not become the socialist utopia she had imagined. In 1923, she authored a book on the subject titled *My Disillusionment in Russia*. See: **Berkman, Alexander; Hoover, J. Edgar; McKinley, William; Palmer, A. Mitchell; Red Raids**.

REF.: *CBA;* Nash, *Citizen Hoover;* Reppetto, *The Blue Parade;* Toledano, *J. Edgar Hoover;* Whitehead, *The FBI Story;* Wicker, *Investigating the FBI*.

Goldsborough, Fitzhugh Coyle, 1880-1911, U.S., suic.-mur. Fitzhugh Goldsborough was born into a wealthy family and had two interests in life: reading popular sentimental novels and doting on his socially ambitious sister. If Goldsborough ever heard his father chastise his sister for some slight offense, Fitzhugh would rush to her defense, threatening his father with physical harm if he so much as laid a hand on the girl.

In 1911, a novel by David Graham Phillips, *The Fashionable Adventures of Joshua Craig,* captured Goldsborough's overactive imagination. The story concerned a selfish, egocentric young woman of the leisure class, a character with whom Goldsborough and his sister both believed to be the sister, though they had no reason to believe that Phillips knew her.

Deranged killer Fitzhugh Goldsborough.

Phillips was a rising star in the New York literary world. Born in Indiana, he had attended Princeton before becoming a reporter for the New York *World*. Phillips once said that, given the choice, he would "rather be a reporter than president." He attained success with such best-sellers as *The Great God Success,* and was in the process of working on another book, *Susan Lenox: Her Fall and Rise,* when he encountered Goldsborough in Gramercy Park in New York on Jan. 23, 1911.

Phillips had stepped out of his apartment to mail a new short story to the *Saturday Evening Post* when Goldsborough approached him. The withered, poorly-dressed young Goldsborough could have been mistaken for a tramp, and Phillips reached into his pocket for a few pennies to give to Goldsborough. "Here you go!" Goldsborough shouted as he drew a pistol from his vest pocket. He fired several shots at close range into Phillips, killing the young writer. Seconds later, Goldsborough turned the gun on himself. "Here I go!" he shouted and fired. He died in the hospital a few days later.

The police learned the motive for the murder when Goldsborough's parents came forward to explain their son's

David Graham Phillips, murder victim.

peculiar obsession with *The Fashionable Adventures of Joshua Craig.*

REF.: *CBA;* Nash, *Bloodletters and Badmen.*

Goldsborough, Robert, prom. 1830-41, Case of, Brit., mur. Robert Goldsborough was penniless and without any food to feed his two starving children when William Huntley stopped at his home in Yarm, England, on July 30, 1830. He was his way to the U.S. after inheriting some money from his father's estate. According to Goldsborough, the usually stingy Huntley gladly offered the impoverished man some of his small fortune, a little more than £85. Goldsborough claimed that Huntley spent the night and that the next morning the two left together; Huntley on his way to the seaport of Whitby, and Goldsborough, with gun in hand, to hunt rabbits. Huntley was not seen alive again.

The disappearance of Huntley made many people suspicious of Goldsborough, since he had suddenly become quite wealthy. When asked what happened to Huntley, Goldsborough told three disparate versions: that he had joined Huntley on the road to Whitby until they reached Stokesley; that Huntley had decided to journey to Liverpool, in the opposite direction; and that Huntley had given up his plans to live in the U.S. and headed to Billsdale to visit friends, though friends there never saw Huntley. Suspicion grew stronger when Goldsborough was found burning clothes, though they could not be identified as Huntley's.

Before Goldsborough left Yarm to live in Barnsley—where he would openly wear the gold watch and chain owned by Huntley, which he stated was a gift—he told one of the searchers, who was combing the area looking for the believed-murdered man, that he should look in Stokesley Beck. In 1830, searchers found no trace of Huntley, but a skull with his jutting tooth was later uncovered.

Huntley's skeleton was discovered on a river bank at Stokesley Beck in June 1841, where workers were rerouting the water for a farmer named Nellist. With the discovery of a body, police arrested Goldsborough, based on the suspicions fostered eleven years earlier. To build up the rather weak case, a reward of £100 was offered for information. Induced by the sizeable figure, Thomas Groundy came forward and confessed that he had helped dispose of Huntley's body. He made the confession on the condition he would not hang. The confession, in which Goldsborough had confessed to Groundy, was more than likely a complete fabrication. Oddly enough Groundy, whom police had kept in custody, was found the next morning hanging in his cell. No reason was given for the suicide; whether it was guilt at sending another to death for £100, or for having committed the crime himself, or another reason. Without the confession of Groundy, the case against Goldsborough was weak.

Judge Baron Rolf, who presided at Goldsborough's trial at the York Assizes, pointed out that medical testimony had been given

that the skeleton may not have been Huntley's, and that the defendant had never hidden the fact that his new wealth had come from Huntley. The jury agreed and found Goldsborough Not Guilty.

REF.: *CBA;* Pearce, *Unsolved Murder Mysteries;* Villiers, *Riddles of Crime.*

Goldsborough, Thomas Alan, 1877-1951, U.S., jur. State's attorney of Maryland from 1904-08, and served in the U.S. House of Representatives from 1921-41. In 1939, he was nominated to the District Court of Washington, D.C. by President Franklin D. Roosevelt. REF.: *CBA.*

Oklahoma bandit-killer Crawford "Cherokee Bill" Goldsby.

Goldsby, Crawford (AKA: **Cherokee Bill**), 1876-96, U.S., west. outl. Born at Fort Concho, Texas, on Feb. 8, 1876, Crawford Goldsby was of mixed blood, being part white, Hispanic, and black, and was rejected by all races. The boy was not only a social pariah but was homeless at age seven when his parents separated. An old black woman, Amanda Foster, undertook to raise Goldsby at Fort Gibson, but she could do little with the wild boy. At age twelve, Goldsby reached an extraordinary size and he often challenged grown men. One of these was a brother-in-law who ordered him to feed some hogs. The boy grabbed a gun and shot the man to death. He was not prosecuted since he was underage.

As a teenager, the tall, heavyset Goldsby took to petty thievery. He got into fights regularly and, when he could not settle an argument with his fists, he went for his six-gun, having become an expert shot by the age of fifteen. Goldsby attended a dance at Fort Gibson in 1894 and here he fell to arguing with a burly black man, Jake Lewis, over a women. The two began a slugfest where Goldsby got the worst of it. Knocked down, the youth drew his gun and fired a shot that wounded Lewis. Goldsby then fled. Lawmen pursued him on a charge of assault with intent to kill.

At age eighteen, Goldsby fell in with the worst outlaws of the Indian nation in the Oklahoma Territory, William and James Cook. Goldsby, who was dubbed "Cherokee Bill" by Bill Cook, was with the Cook brothers when a posse cornered the three men near Tahlequah, Okla., in June 1894. Lawmen had a warrant for the arrest of Jim Cook on a charge of larceny, but when they moved forward to arrest Cook, all three youths went for their guns. The outlaws drove back the posse and then mounted their horses, riding wildly away from their camp near Fourteen Mile Creek. Goldsby, seeing one of the lawmen gaining on him, turned in the saddle and fired a single shot which struck Deputy Sequoyah Houston, who fell dead from his horse.

Goldsby rode to the home of his sister, Maud Brown, and remained here, hiding from the law. Her husband, George Brown, a vicious drunkard, took a whip to Maud one day for not responding fast enough to his orders. While he was beating the woman, Goldsby walked up behind him and shot him to death. He then rejoined the Cook brothers and others and this infamous band began robbing trains, banks, and stores throughout Oklahoma. In the summer of 1894, Goldsby appeared alone at the train depot in Nowata. He held up the station agent, Richard Richards, who went for a gun. Goldsby shot him to death, then leisurely stepped to the station platform and waited for the next train. When it pulled in, Goldsby banged on the door of the express car with the butt of his six-gun, ordering those inside to "open up and give me the money." The door flew open and conductor Sam Collins ordered Goldsby to depart. Goldsby shot Collins in the face, killing him. When a brakeman came running down the platform, Goldsby shot and wounded the man. He then mounted his horse and galloped off.

In 1894, Goldsby and others entered the Shufeldt & Son general store at Lenapah, Okla., and held up the owners. Ernest Melton, a curious resident, stuck his head in the door and the lightning-fast Goldsby pumped a single bullet into his head, killing him. For this killing, committed before a number of witnesses, Judge Isaac Parker of Fort Smith, Ark., announced a reward of $1,300 for Goldsby, dead or alive. This was the murder for which Goldsby would pay with his life. Capturing the wily Goldsby, however, was another thing. Deputy Marshal W.C. Smith then learned that Goldsby was infatuated with a Cherokee girl, Maggie Glass, a cousin of Isaac "Ike" Rogers, who had been a deputy for Smith on several occasions when posses were needed. Smith arranged to lure Goldsby to Rogers' remote farmhouse to meet his cousin Maggie.

Goldsby appeared on the night of Jan. 29, 1895, and when he fell asleep, Rogers and a neighbor, Clinton Scales, jumped the powerful Goldsby, pinning him to the couch on which he slept, and then bound him and dragged him to a buggy. The outlaw was delivered to Fort Smith to await trial for murder. On Feb. 26, 1895, Goldsby was tried for the murder of Melton by jury before Judge Parker. He was found Guilty. His mother and sister wept in court at the news, but Goldsby, confident that he would never see the hangman, turned to them and snapped: "What's the matter with you two? I ain't dead yet."

Judge Parker sentenced the smirking killer to death on Apr. 13, 1895, but Goldsby seemed unconcerned about his fate. He returned to a holding cell in the jail where he promptly sat down to play cards with Bill Cook, by then a prisoner, and others. Goldsby joked about the sentence, bragging that no one would ever put a noose around his neck. His date of execution had been set for June 25, 1895, but his crafty lawyer, J. Warren Reed, managed to file several appeals that extended the death date.

Sherman Vann, a Negro trusty at the jail, smuggled a six-gun to Goldsby for an undisclosed price and the outlaw hid this in a hole in the wall of his cell. He knocked out a brick, broke it so that only its front half remained, and put the gun behind this. On July 26, 1895, while his lawyer was still delaying his execution

through a barrage of appeals, Goldsby pointed his six-gun at armed guard Lawrence Keating, a father of four, and shouted through the bars of his cell: "Throw up your hands and give me that pistol damned quick!"

Keating reached for his gun, but not to hand it to the outlaw. He began to level it at Goldsby, when the outlaw fired a bullet into his stomach. Keating wheeled about and staggered down the corridor as Goldsby sent another bullet into his back. The guard fell dead in the main office. Goldsby was tried for this murder, convicted, and sentenced to death. Again his lawyers filed numerous appeals and the death sentence, originally fixed for Dec. 2, 1895, was put off. The U.S. Supreme Court upheld the verdict in the Keating murder, and the Goldsby's execution date was set for Mar. 17, 1896. No avenue of escape was left for Goldsby except a direct appeal to the president. This was rejected.

On Mar. 17, St. Patrick's Day, Goldsby, still arrogant, was led from his cell. He tried to convince his mother, sister, and Amanda Foster, the old Negro woman who had raised him, that he was unconcerned about his gruesome fate. He sang ditties and whistled as he walked gingerly outside to the courtyard of the Fort Smith jail. Goldsby took one look at the scaffold and said: "This is about as good a day to die as any." The murderous outlaw stood on the gallows with a rope around his neck when he was asked if he had any final words. Defiant to the last, Goldsby snarled: "No! I came here to die, not make a speech." A minute later his large body shot through the trap. His mother took the body to Fort Gibson and buried it. See: **Cook, William Tuttle.**

REF.: American Guide Series, *Tulsa, A Guide to the Oil Capital;* Bartholomew, *The Biographical Album of Western Gunfighters;* Botkin, *A Treasury of Western Folklore;* Breihan, *Great Gunfighters of the West;* Bristow, *Lost on Grand River;* _____, *Tales of Old Fort Gibson;* Canton, *Frontier Trails; CBA;* Collins, *Warpath and Cattle Trail;* Croy, *He Hanged Them High;* Dalton, *Under the Black Flag;* Douglas, *The History of Tulsa, Oklahoma;* Drago, *Outlaws on Horseback;* _____, *Red River Valley;* Draper, *A Cub Reporter in the Old Indian Territory;* Elman, *Fired in Anger;* Emery, *Court of the Damned;* Gard, *Frontier Justice;* Gay, *History of Nowata County;* Glasscock, *Then Came Oil;* Harman, *Cherokee Bill, Oklahoma Outlaw;* _____, *Hell on the Border;* Harrington, *Hanging Judge;* Harrison, *Hell Holes and Hangings;* Hendricks, *The Bad Man of the West;* Horan, *The Great American West;* _____ and Sann, *A Pictorial History of the Wild West;* Hunter and Rose, *The Album of Gunfighters;* Lawson, *The Indian Outlaw;* Lemley, *The Old West;* McKennon, *Iron Men;* Munsell, *Flying Sparks;* Nash, *Bloodletters and Badmen;* Rea, *Boone County and Its People;* Sabin, *Wild Men of the Wild West;* Shirley, *Henry Starr: Last of the Real Bad Men;* _____, *Law West of Fort Smith;* _____, *Toughest of Them All;* Stansbery, *The Passing of the 3D Ranch;* Sutton, *Hands Up!;* Watson, *A Century of Gunmen;* Wellman, *A Dynasty of Western Outlaws;* Younger, *True Facts of the Lives of America's Most Notorious Outlaws.*

Goldstein, Stuart, prom. 1970-74, U.S., mur. Stuart Goldstein intended to open up a wife-swapping commune for wealthy Chicagoans in Cody, Wyo. But he did not have enough money to purchase the dude ranch he and his 21-year-old bride had spent two weeks at in 1970. However, he did have a wealthy uncle in California whose death would bring him a large inheritance; Goldstein thus decided that murder would supply him with the necessary funds for his commune. The Chicago native was not sure he could kill his uncle, so he bought a .22-caliber automatic gun and headed to Las Vegas with the intention of committing a "practice" killing.

In Las Vegas, Goldstein and his wife met 31-year-old waitress Allyce "Jebbie" Deeter at Caesar's Palace. The two convinced the divorced mother of three to take them gambling when she finished work. Deeter was last seen alive stepping into the Goldsteins' rented Cadillac sedan on Oct. 19, 1970. The abandoned car was discovered by police on a desert road with blood stains on the front seat and floor, bullet holes in the door, and .22-caliber cartridges. A month later, Goldstein came forward voluntarily, and confessed under interrogation. His confession claimed that Deeter's death was a practice run, and was committed after he dropped his wife off at the hotel and was driving the waitress home. A lie-detector test later indicated that Goldstein's wife knew nothing of the murder. Goldstein also told police where to find the woman's body, which he had stripped to look like the victim of a sex crime. This confession was claimed by Goldstein's lawyer to be inadmissible in court because police had failed to advise the defendant of his rights. The Nevada Supreme Court overruled this motion and Goldstein was tried.

At the trial, Goldstein pleaded not guilty by reason of insanity—a psychiatrist testified that Goldstein was a man who "kills people without remorse"—but later changed his plea to guilty and was sentenced in 1974 to life in prison. Goldstein made a second confession while in prison, when he told another inmate that he had murdered Valerie Percy, the daughter of Illinois senator Charles Percy; but his admission was only one of many leads the Chicago police investigated.

REF.: *CBA;* Wilson, *Encyclopedia of Modern Murder.*

Goldstone, Charles Joseph, b.1898, and **Leavey, James Joseph,** b.1899, and **Jones, Wilfred Algernon,** 1912- , and **Morrell, George,** b.1896, and **Homer, John Arthur,** b.1882, and **Grigsby, Stanley Thomas,** b.1881, and **Levenson, Alfred Percival,** 1909- , and **Cottlieb, Nathan,** 1916- , and **Bailey, Albert Edward,** 1909- , and **Golding, Anthony,** 1900- , and **Mass, Cecil Wallace,** 1910- , and **Beach, Charles Richard,** 1903- , and **Paul, William,** 1900- , and **Wilson, Irving,** 1905- , and **Varley, Joseph,** 1913- , and **Cunningham, Alice,** 1901- , Brit., fraud. During the early 1900s, a large ring of swindlers operated in England, France, Switzerland, and Ireland. Members of the gang approached businessmen, offered to sell them an advertisement in phony or nonexistent directories for a small amount of money, and then induced them to sign an order form. The form was altered to a larger amount and months later, an agent would come to collect the fake debt. Then the agent told the businessman he could write, "cancel further issues" on a form and sign his name. In signing, however, the victim was actually imprinting another order form hidden underneath. The cheats would then show up again later to collect the second "debt."

The scam was discovered and nineteen people were indicted. A specially constructed dock was added to Winchester to accommodate the number of prisoners. The trial before Justice Lawrence began on Apr. 3, 1940, and concluded on May 15. The defendants were charged with conspiracy to defraud and all were convicted. Charles Joseph Goldstone, forty-two, James Joseph Leavey, forty-one, and Wilfred Algernon Jones, twenty-eight, were each sentenced to three years in prison and an eighteen-month term, to be served concurrently. Alfred Percival Levenson, thirty-one, and William Paul, forty, were each given a one-year term and a two-year prison term, to be served concurrently. Charles Richard Beach, thirty-seven, and Joseph Varley, twenty-seven, and Alice Cunningham, thirty-nine, each received a one-year sentence and an eighteen-month term, to be served concurrently. George Morrell, forty-four, John Arthur Homer, fifty-eight, Cecil Wallace Mass, thirty, and Irving Wilson, thirty-five, were each sentenced to one year in prison. Nathan Cottlieb, twenty-four, and Albert Edward Bailey, thirty-one, were sentenced to nine months in prison. Stanley Thomas Grigsby, fifty-nine, and Anthony Golding, forty, both received a six-month sentence. The gang earned £10,308 in the scam.

REF.: *CBA;* Woodland, *Assize Pageant.*

Golkowski, Johann (AKA: **Raschad Hussein Golkowski, Johann Leonhard**), prom. 1958, Turk., mur. Johann Golkowski met Gerhard Moritz on Mar. 5, 1958, at a Turkish border checkpoint where officials were denying Moritz, a known black market car dealer, entry into Iran. Golkowski offered to interpret the argument and even persuaded Moritz to drive with him toward Istanbul, where the phony physician was sure he could obtain a visa for his fellow German in Ankara. The two were unable to procure a visa in the country's capital and journeyed on to Istanbul. There they checked into the Yayla Palas hotel on Mar. 10. Three days later Golkowski purchased an Italian Beretta

automatic gun from a pawnshop. The next day he used it on Moritz, whose body was discovered with a bullet in his skull, several knife wounds, and a badly beaten face. That same day Golkowski returned the gun he had allegedly bought for a friend, laughingly explaining that "my friend didn't like the gun." Leaving Istanbul, Golkowski drove Moritz's car to the Mediterranean town of Mersin, where he abandoned the vehicle. The police, meanwhile, were piecing together the mystery.

Beside the corpse, found off a dusty road two hours from Istanbul, was a key to a German car with the initials G.M. imprinted on it. The initials soon led police to the hotel registry at the Yayla Palas, which further led to the pawnbroker's shop—as no murder weapon was found at the scene, a search of shops was conducted—and finally a broadcast of the killer's identity. Golkowski read of the search in a newspaper at a railway station in Adana, and decided to return to Istanbul until he could escape. He arrived in the city on Mar. 18, and had the misfortune of checking into a hotel where the clerk recognized him as the wanted man and called police. Confronted with the evidence against him, Golkowski admitted the murder, and how he had placed the body in the trunk of the car and dumped it near Gebze. He claimed that the crime was committed in self-defense when Moritz attacked him—a futile claim considering that he had purchased the gun well in advance. The court in Istanbul found Golkowski Guilty in October 1959, and sentenced him to twenty-four years in prison.

REF.: *CBA;* Whitehead, *Journey Into Crime.*

Gollancz, Sir **Victor,** 1893-1967, Brit., reform. Publisher and writer who headed humanitarian efforts to rescue Jews from Nazi Germany, feed survivors in post-war Germany, abolish capital punishment, promote nuclear disarmament, and free Arab refugees from Palestine. REF.: *CBA.*

Goluneff, Paul, b.c.1899, Bul., mur. Bad teeth and a half-eaten apple led police in Bulgaria to apprehend the murderer of 41-year-old Elena Milanoff, who was killed on Oct. 5, 1936, while taking the forty-five minute train ride from Vakarel to Sofia.

In the second-class compartment beside Milanoff's dead body, which had been stabbed in the heart, police found a shattered goldfish bowl and a dead goldfish. A half-eaten apple was discovered under a seat in third class. The apple indicated that whoever ate it only used the left side of his mouth. The eater had obviously rinsed his mouth with silver nitrate, a common solution for bad gums, as traces of the chemical were found on the fruit. Police soon learned that Milanoff's bungalow in Vakarel was in great disorder, and that an empty bottle, which had once contained silver nitrate, was found in the garden there. Commissar Kilko Dubesseneff, who was in charge of the case, became suspicious of the fiance of Milanoff's daughter, 37-year-old Paul Goluneff, who had identified the body when the daughter, 23-year-old Steffy Milanoff, had refused. Dubesseneff learned from Goluneff's dentist that the man had a prescription for silver nitrate, and when the commissar confronted Goluneff with this information, he confessed to the crime.

Goluneff admitted that he had had past relations with Milanoff, and that she had objected to his marriage to her daughter. He had left behind the bottle of nitrate after a failed attempt to persuade Milanoff against informing Steffy of the love the two once shared. He claimed he had to kill Milanoff because "she threatened to tell Steffy the truth rather than see me marry her." At the trial in February 1937, Goluneff was sentenced to life in prison.

REF.: *CBA;* Cohen, *One Hundred True Crime Stories.*

Gómez, Roberto Suárez, Sr., See: **Suárez Gómez, Roberto, Sr.**

Gondorf Brothers, prom. 1900s-10s, U.S., fraud. Fred and Charley Gondorf were super con men who operated throughout the U.S. in the late 1890s through the 1900s. For a period of fifteen years, these two sharping brothers, headquartered in New York City, operated a string of big store games that became so celebrated that they were called the "Gondorf Games." Fred and

Charley were expert poker players, and often established a small but swanky gambling den peopled with what appeared to be high society patrons. Dressed in tuxedos, the Gondorfs would arrive with a wealthy sucker and sit down to play poker with a count or an oil baron—all ringers impersonating famous people. In the course of a rigged game, they would fleece the mark for a small fortune. In 1899, the brothers swindled a rich St. Louis pawnbroker out of $200,000 in a big store poker game.

Confidence kings Fred and Charley Gondorf.

The brothers also specialized in the wire, a con game where a posh but phony betting parlor was established, replete with hustling patrons and employees, who seemed overworked in having to handle the heavy betting that went on in the parlor. A sucker was brought into this realistic gambling den, believing that the Gondorfs had a system whereby they could intercept racing results before the wire services flashed the winners to the bookie joints throughout the country. The sucker, thinking the fix was in, would bet enormous sums on what he thought was a sure winner. Adding to the sucker's confidence, the Gondorfs would bet even greater sums on the same horse.

When the true winner was announced, the Gordorfs would shout that they had been betrayed by their "inside man," and demand their money back. Of course, they were refused refunds, along with their mark who believed that he *and* his gambling friends, the Gondorfs, had been taken and would thus not suspect his hosts of victimizing him. By 1917, the Gondorfs' luck ran out and both brothers drew long prison terms in Sing Sing for fraud. When they were released, they were too old for the kind of energetic confidence games they had so long practiced. They retired and died in obscurity but relative comfort, using the spoils from their innumerable con games.

REF.: Asbury, *Gem of the Prairie; CBA*; Nash, *Hustlers and Con Men*; (FILM), *The Sting*, 1973.

Gontaut, Charles (Duc de Biron), 1562-1602, Fr., consp.-treas. Son of Armand de Gontaut, commander-in-chief under Henry IV. Gontaut was named marshall of France in 1594, and became Duke of Biron in 1598. After conspiring with Spain and then Savoy against Henry IV, he was beheaded for the crime of treason. REF.: *CBA*.

Gonzaga, Tomaz Antônio (AKA: Dirceú), 1744-1807, Braz., consp. Portuguese poet who served as a jurist at Villa Rica (Ouro Preto), Minas Geraes in Brazil. He was nominated to serve on the Supreme Court of Bahia. In 1792, he was exiled to Mozambique amidst allegations of conspiracy against the government he was serving. REF.: *CBA*.

Gonzales, Edward E., c.1941-   , U.S., rape. Three young couples thought they would enjoy a warm August night in 1970, never realizing the horror in store for them when a gang of drunk youths left one dead and another emotionally scarred by a brutal gang rape. Certainly the gang members themselves did not go out that evening with the intention of destroying young lives, especially their own.

Mike Montez, fifteen, and his girlfriend walked together through a lovely San Antonio park, enjoying the little summer vacation they had left. When they saw six drunken youths near

a concession stand, Mike made the foolhardy mistake of yelling an insult their way. The six surrounded him in an instant. He broke away from the angered group but made it only as far as a nearby park before the group caught him. He was stabbed and beaten.

Meanwhile, a 17-year-old college freshmen from New York City and her beau Donald Hilliard, twenty, sat alongside a park lake on their way home from a college dance. The gang members asked for cigarettes but made it clear that what they really wanted was the girl. Two youths grabbed Hilliard while the others repeatedly raped the girl. Hours later, the couple stumbled into a police station.

Montez' body was dragged from the lake the next morning. Shortly after that police received their first lead from an anonymous caller and staked out a gas station where two of the suspected youths usually hung out. One drove up to the station, and then, on seeing a policeman, sped away. David H. Valdez, twenty-two, was easily apprehended and his confession led the law to Edward E. Gonzales and Alberto M. Perez. Another prime suspect, 20-year-old Arturo Guerra, had been arrested and convicted of a different crime and was already serving a prison sentence.

Months later the rest of the gang of six were tried and found Guilty. Perez was judged insane and sent to an asylum while Gonzales was convicted of rape. Although charged with the murder of Mike Montez, Gonzales never stood trial for it. REF.: *CBA*.

Gonzales, Frank, c.1937-64, Case of, U.S., suic.-mur. Frank Gonzales, twenty-seven, wanted to die but not alone. He boarded Pacific Air Lines Flight 773 out of Reno, Nev., shot the pilot and copilot, and, in doing so, brought down forty-three innocent lives with him.

Gonzales, who had been troubled by marital and financial problems for months, told friends and his family he planned to kill himself. He referred to his impending death on a daily basis before the fact on May 7, 1964. The night before his flight he purchased a .357 Smith & Wesson Magnum revolver. The next morning he bought $105,000 worth of insurance at the airport and boarded a plane for San Francisco. While in flight Gonzales shot the flight crew in their backs. The last words the imperiled pilot Ernest Clark, fifty-two, and copilot Ray Andress, thirty-one, spoke were, "Skipper's shot. We've been shot. Trying to help." Then a United Air Lines pilot reported seeing "...a black cloud of smoke coming up through the undercast. Looks like oil or gasoline fire." The plane crashed into a hill near San Ramon, Calif. No one on board survived. REF.: *CBA*.

Gonzales, Dr. Thomas A., 1878-1956, U.S., path. Dr. Thomas A. Gonzales, although not a police officer, was one of New York City's finest detectives. Between 1937 and 1954, Gonzales, a forensic pathologist, served as New York's chief medical examiner, developing a detective's instinct and relish for solving a case. He developed a knack for analysis, and often disagreed with the initial diagnosis. His greatest pleasure came from freeing an innocent defendant faced with seemingly incontrovertible evidence. Gonzales would determine that a man apparently murdered had died of a heart attack, or that a woman apparently strangled had died of gas inhalation. He inherited his position from Dr. Charles Norris, who founded the medical examiner's office in 1918. Gonzales developed many theories of forensic detection, all contained in the seminal work, *Legal Medicine and Toxicology*, which he co-authored. He died in 1956, two years after his retirement.

REF.: *CBA*; Robinson, *Science Catches the Criminal*.

Gonzalez, Jose Alejandro, Jr., 1931-   , U.S., jur. Lieutenant in the U.S. Army from 1952-54. In 1962, he wrote "Insanity - The Law's Misunderstood Word" for the *Broward County Bar Journal* in 1962. From 1964-78, he was prosecutor for the State Circuit Court in Fort Lauderdale, Fla. He was nominated to the Southern District Court of Florida by President James E. Carter in 1978. REF.: *CBA*.

Gonzalez, T.A., prom. 1930s, Mex., criminol. The process by which an investigator can determine if a shooting victim died by his own hand or was murdered was pioneered in the 1930s by Mexican criminologist T.A. Gonzalez. The nitrate test, as it came to be known, involves the application of melted paraffin to the trigger finger. The cast made is then reinforced with a thin layer of cotton which is covered by hot wax. After the mold has hardened, it is removed and tested for the presence of nitrates, black specks which are always produced by the powder combustion of a fired gun. A chemical reagent composed of diphenylamine and sulfuric acid is then applied. After twenty minutes, any nitrate present will appear on the cast.

The first practical application of the nitrate test was by the Scientific Crime Detection Laboratory in Chicago in the late 1930s.

REF.: *CBA; Robinson, Science Catches the Criminal.*

Gonzalez Valenzuela, Delfina, 1909- , and **Gonzalez Valenzuela, Maria de Jesús,** 1924- , Mex., wh. slav.-mur. In January 1964, three women went to the police station in Léon, Mex., with information about their missing teenaged daughters. According to a young woman who claimed to have escaped from a brothel, their daughters were among a number of young women forced into prostitution at a nearby ranch. When police raided the ranch, they found nineteen young women apparently being held prisoner in what the local newspapers described as "a concentration camp for white slaves." In the ranch house, which was outfitted with tiny cells and myriad torture devices, the police arrested the leaders of the white slave operation, 55-year-old Delfina Gonzalez Valenzuela and her 40-year-old sister, Maria de Jesús Gonzalez Valenzuela.

Investigation revealed that the Gonzalez sisters had begun the white slave operation in 1954. Most of the 2,000 young women who had passed through the operation in ten years, ranging in age from fourteen to twenty-five, were attracted by advertisements promising respectable employment as maids. If the sisters found a girl acceptably attractive, a brothel employee raped her and then took her to a training brothel in the rural town of San Francisco del Rincón.

After training, most of the young women were sold to other brothels for between forty and eighty dollars. Those the Gonzalez sisters kept for work in their own brothel were subjected to various tortures. If the girls were recalcitrant, they were beaten, thrown into freezing baths, or forced to kneel for hours holding heavy bricks. For particularly uncooperative girls, the *cama real,* or royal bed, was employed. The "bed" was a narrow board encased in barbed wire on which the girl was forced to recline. The slightest movement caused cuts. The girls were often left on the bed for days at a time.

The Gonzalez sisters apparently had little patience with resistance. If a girl became sick, which happened frequently on the meager diet of tortillas and beans, she was taken to the ranch near Léon, and starved or tortured to death. If a girl became pregnant and did not get an abortion in time, she was killed. Police found that the brothel graveyard contained as many as fifty bodies.

Brought to trial in San Francisco del Rincón, the Gonzalez sisters adamantly denied any wrongdoing, saying that the girls whose bodies had been found had died "maybe because the food didn't agree with them." The court found the two sisters Guilty of first-degree murder, white slavery, and other crimes, and sentenced them each to forty years in prison, the maximum under Mexican law.

REF.: *CBA; Wilson, Encyclopedia of Modern Murder.*

Gooch, Arthur, d.1936, U.S., kid. Arthur Gooch was the first person to be hanged under the so-called "Lindbergh Law," which made it a capital offense to carry an abducted person across a state line if the victim is at all injured in the proceedings. But the Gooch case was different than the expected ransom-type kidnapping. On Nov. 26, 1934, Gooch and an accomplice, Ambrose Nix, both escaped convicts, were stopped by two police

officers in Paradise, Texas, for routine questioning. Gooch and Nix fought the police, injuring one, who fell through a glass showcase. The two convicts grabbed the policemen, forced them into the police car, and carried them across the Texas line into Oklahoma, where they released them. FBI agents in the area cornered Gooch and Nix in a gun battle in which Nix was killed and Gooch was captured.

When Gooch was first indicted, the indictment was worded so that the death penalty could not be exacted. He had to be re-indicted in Muskogee, Okla., where he was convicted and sentenced to death. Appeals ultimately took the case to the U.S. Supreme Court, which upheld the conviction, saying that kidnapping to avoid arrest came within the meaning of the word "ransom." When President Franklin D. Roosevelt declined to intervene, Arthur Gooch was hanged on June 19, 1936, at McAlester, Okla.

REF.: Alix, *Ransom Kidnapping In America; CBA;* Mencken, *By the Neck.*

Good, Daniel, d.1842, Brit., mur. Daniel Good was the coachman for a retired West Indian merchant. His wife, thirteen years older and known as Old Molly Good, saw him only once in a while. His 11-year-old son lived with Good and his mistress, Jane Jones, who was known as his wife. Good had met another woman, Susan Butcher, who wanted to marry him. Although it would be bigamy, the 46-year-old man agreed, then decided to murder Jones.

On Apr. 6, 1842, Daniel Good went to the tailor in Wandsworth, who let him take a pair of trousers on credit. As Good was leaving the store, he was seen grabbing another pair of trousers and hiding them under his cloak. A policeman sent by the merchant found Good in the stables and demanded to search the premises. Good ran off, locking the policeman in the stables. He found the foul-smelling torso of a woman, Jane Jones, underneath hay bales in the corner. Burned remains of her head and limbs were found in another room.

Good disappeared for two weeks while many citizens of the area panicked, and newspapers wrote editorials criticizing the police. He showed up briefly at Old Molly Good's home, taking, with her permission, some of her possessions and pawning them for getaway money. After two weeks he was located working as a bricklayer in Tonbridge, where he was recognized by a laborer who had known him as a coachman. Arrested, tried, and found Guilty, Good was promptly hanged.

In the two-week-long chase of Daniel Good, nine different divisions of the Metropolitan Police were involved, with no specific one in charge. What one group would initiate, another would cancel. With pressure from the public and the police themselves, the British Home Secretary was forced to let the police form a criminal investigation branch consisting of two inspectors and six sergeants to replace the old Bow Street Runners who had all retired or died. See: **Scotland Yard.**

REF.: Altick, *Victorian Studies in Scarlet; CBA;* Cobb, *The First Detectives;* Jackson, *Occupied With Crime;* Logan, *Masters of Crime; _____, Rope, Knife and Chair;* Pearce, *Unsolved Murder Mysteries;* Thomson, *The Story of Scotland Yard;* Wilson, *Encyclopedia of Murder.*

Good, John, prom. 1877-88, U.S., west. gunman. John Good, a large, intimidating cattle rancher in the Texas hill country, became involved in a gunfight in Blanco City on June 10, 1877. A man named Robinson accused him of being a horse thief, but Robinson's revolver got tangled in his clothing as he attempted to shoot Good. The rancher killed Robinson with four shots. Good had also been present when Ed Crawford killed Cad Pierce in Newton, Texas, and after the shootout with Robinson, Good sold his ranch and opened a hotel in Coleman, Texas. He quickly wore out his welcome and continued to move, first in 1880, to a ranch in Colorado City, and later to another ranch near La Luz, N.M. He began a relationship with Bronco Sue Yonker, a tryst which led to his second gunfight. Yonker had killed a man in 1884.

In 1885, Good's wife and children arrived in La Luz and Yonker began a relationship with a man named Charley Dawson. On Dec. 8, 1885, Good killed Dawson after a quarrel over the affections of Yonker. This time he remained in the area, building a large adobe ranch house, and accumulating a great deal of money. But his temper resurfaced in 1888 when he had a bitter argument with George McDonald. After McDonald was killed, his friends retaliated by killing Good's son, Walter. The decomposed body of Walter Good was found in the White Sands Desert. Good set out with a five-man posse to avenge his son's death and found McDonald's friends near Las Cruces. After a fierce battle, Good and his party were forced to retreat, after which he sold his ranch and moved to Arizona. He was last known to be working in Oklahoma for hourly wages.

REF.: Bartholomew, *Wyatt Earp, the Untold Story; CBA;* O'Neal, *Encyclopedia of Western Gunfighters;* Sonnichsen, *Tularosa.*

Good, Millard (AKA: **Delbert Shamblin**), c.1916- , Case of, U.S., rob.-pris. esc. Millard Good disappeared from the West Virginia Penitentiary and his twenty-year sentence in 1954 and reappeared nineteen years later in Governor Arch A. Moore Jr.'s office. In between, Delbert Shamblin worked as a farmhand on a spread just outside of Columbus, Ohio.

Millard Good and Delbert Shamblin were one and the same. As a 35-year-old, Good was arrested in West Virginia for armed robbery and maintains his innocence now as he did then, explaining that the judge and his grandfather had a falling out years before the trial, "and I paid for it."

Good spent three years and several months as a trusty of the prison before he walked away. With two hamburgers and a few green apples, he made his way from West Virginia to Ohio until he met a farmer who needed help. Good stayed on for nineteen years, unaware that his family lived just 100 miles to the west. To pay all of the legal expenses incurred following Good's trial, his wife had sold her home and she and her boys went to live with her parents.

It was the Reverend Carl Dodrill who eventually helped Good find his way back home to his wife, sons, and now daughters-in-law and grandchildren. The reverend, tipped off to Shamblin's identity by a mutual friend, called Shamblin in to St. John's United Methodist Church in Spencer, Ohio, and encouraged him to reveal his true identity. The minister then acted as a mediator between Good and the governor. With the promise of probation and the possibility of a pardon, Good reclaimed his true name. REF.: *CBA.*

Goodale, Robert, d.1885, Brit., mur. The English at Norwich Gaol in 1885 had work to do in perfecting the gallows. This fact was gruesomely evident following Robert Goodale's November execution. When Berry the executioner pulled the gallows' lever and the condemned man dropped through the trap door, the rope swung violently and underneath it lay Goodale separated, body and head.

Goodale, once a fruit farmer, had been convicted of striking and killing his wife Bathsheba with an iron bar and then throwing her body down a forty-foot well. Regardless of how he was executed, his death was certainly quicker and less painful than his victim's.

REF.: Atholl, *The Reluctant Hangman;* ____, *Shadow of the Gallows;* Bishop, *Executions; CBA.*

Goodbye, Miss Lizzie Borden, 1946, a play by Lillian De La Torre. This work, based on the Borden case (U.S., 1892), was published in the book, *Murder, Plain and Fanciful.* See: **Borden, Lizzie.** REF.: *CBA.*

Goode, Arthur Frederick, III, c.1954-84, U.S., mur. The man who said his last request would be to have sexual intercourse with a "sexy little boy" died in the electric chair in Florida State Prison on Apr. 5, 1984. Goode apologized to his parents, expressed remorse for what he had done, and then was killed. He was thirty years old.

Arthur Frederick Goode III met 9-year-old Jason VerDow of Fort Myers, Fla., on Mar. 5, 1976, while the boy waited for his school bus. Goode persuaded the boy to come with him, saying

he needed help in finding something in a nearby wooded area. "I told him he was going to die and described how I would kill him," Goode said. I asked him if he had any last words, and he said, 'I love you,' and then I strangled him." Cape Coral police questioned Goode twice concerning the incident and let him go. A week later Goode abducted 10-year-old Billy Arthes, and took him to Washington, D.C., where Goode raped and strangled 11-year-old Kenny Dawson.

A Maryland woman saw Billy and Goode and, recognizing the boy's face from a television announcement "Missing-believed kidnapped," alerted police. It took her three calls to three different police departments around her area before she found an officer who had heard of Goode and was willing to do something about it.

Police apprehended Goode and a jury tried him. He pleaded not guilty by reason of insanity, but the Maryland court gave him life imprisonment for killing Ken Dawson. Goode later was extradited to Florida and tried, convicted, and executed for killing Jason VerDow.

Goode had seemed to look upon his slayings almost with pride since his arrest, taunting the victims' parents with graphic descriptions of their sons' deaths, conducting his own defense for the Florida killing, and harassing his parents. But a new side of Goode was shown on the evening of his execution. Visibly shaking and verbally remorseful, Goode was led, almost dragged, to the electric throne, knowing now the terror he had inflicted on others. REF.: *CBA.*

Goode, Washington, d.1849, U.S., mur. Washington Goode was a young seaman who made Boston his home. He got drunk one night and stabbed fellow seaman Thomas Harding to death in a quarrel over who was the better seaman, an argument so trivial that even the court hearing the case expressed amazement and shock at the killing. Goode was convicted and hanged in Boston on May 24, 1849.

REF.: *CBA; Trial and Execution of Washington Goode.*

Goodere, Samuel, 1687-1741, and **Mahoney**, and **White, Charles**, d.1741, Brit., kid.-mur. Everyone had always preferred Sir John Dinelly Goodere to his brother, Captain Samuel Goodere. Forever the blessed child of fortune, Sir John was coddled by his mother, spoiled by his father, and loved by the family's friends and neighbors. His younger brother Samuel, on the contrary, was a problem child, and while his brother grew up to become a baronet, destined to inherit the family fortune, Samuel became a loud, obnoxious drunkard, spendthrift, and lecher. The brothers always hated each other but by 1740 their relationship had deteriorated to the point where Sir John decided to disinherit Samuel. When Samuel found out that the ever-competitive brother decided he would kill Sir John.

Samuel arranged to meet his brother in Bristol on the pretence of making amends. The siblings and each of their bodyguards met and seemed to be having a great time until Captain Goodere's hired hand, Mahoney, jumped Sir John and hauled him off to the prison quarters of Samuel's ship, the *Ruby.* Once there, Samuel directed Mahoney and Charles White to strangle his brother. When that vicious deed had been performed, Samuel tried to convince the crew that he had taken the drastic measures because his brother had gone insane. The only person the crew thought had gone insane, however, was Captain Goodere. His own men overpowered and arrested him.

Finally a baronet at age fifty-four (he inherited his brother's title), Samuel and cohorts Mahoney and White were brought before the court, convicted of their crimes, and hanged on Apr. 15, 1741.

REF.: Birmingham, *Murder Most Foul; CBA;* Sparrow, *The Great Abductors.*

Gooding, Florence, d.c.1960, Brit., (unsolv.) mur. A widow living in Oxted was generous to personal and organized charities, which made people in town believe that she kept large amounts of money in her home. A burglar broke into her house through a window, encountered Gooding, and beat her on the head. She died two days later. The only clue police found was a fingerprint smudge on one window. Despite the check of several thousand fingerprints of people in the area, a match was not made and the murder remains unsolved.

REF.: *CBA; Furneaux, Famous Criminal Cases, vol. 6.*

Gooding, Rose Emma, c.1891- , Brit., (wrong. convict.) libel. In May 1920, 30-year-old Edith Emily Swan, a well-bred woman from Littlehampton, England, said Rose Emma Gooding, twenty-nine, her next door neighbor and a woman of a lower class, had sent her obscene written material. Gooding denied it. The court said she had and sent her to prison twice. Not until Inspector Nicholls of Scotland Yard investigated was it discovered that Gooding had been wrongly accused, a victim of Britain's rigid class system.

According to Swan, Gooding had abused and threatened her and had pushed the obscene writings under her door. But Nicholls realized that the paper in Gooding's house in no way resembled the paper on which the obscenities were written. Further, writing found in Swan's house was similar to that of the notes, and the notes continued arriving even with Gooding in prison. The inspector pointed out that Gooding could not possibly have written the notes, and he wanted to know why no attorney or investigator had bothered to notice this in one of the woman's two previous trials.

Gooding was released from prison and given £250 in compensation.

REF.: *CBA; Humphreys, Criminal Days.*

Goodloe, William Cassius, 1841-89, and **Swope, A.M.,** 1844-89, U.S., mur. Family members and close friends were devastated when Goodloe, forty-eight, and Swope, forty-five, killed each other on Nov. 9, 1889, but they were certainly not surprised. To the rest of Lexington, Ky., the two deaths appeared to be a senseless tragedy.

The two men accidentally met in the hallway of the post office on Friday afternoon, each picking up his mail. When they saw each other Goodloe said, "You obstruct the way," to which Swope responded, "You spoke to me. You insulted me." With that, Goodloe drew a large dirk knife from his pocket at the same time Swope pulled a Smith & Wesson .38-caliber revolver. They entered into a short and bloody battle from which neither emerged alive. Swope died instantly and Goodloe died forty-eight hours later. To the casual observer, there seemed to be no rhyme nor reason behind the killings, but actually, the hatred between the two made killing their only way out.

Both were born in Lincoln County, Ky. Swope was more intelligent, but Goodloe was descended from a more prestigious family. They both had political aspirations that included leadership of the Republican party in Kentucky, and they sabotaged each other's efforts in hopes of securing their similar goal. And both were stubborn.

Swope and Goodloe came close to dueling once before, but friends prevented that and, they thought, cooled their animosity toward one another. Instead, Goodloe and Swope had made a silent agreement to duel again, should they ever meet. That is why both were armed and ready to fight on the day they met at the post office.

REF.: *CBA; Johnson, Famous Kentucky Tragedies and Trials.*

Goodmacher, Marks, c.1863-1920, Brit., mur. Fellow Jews of murderer Marks Goodmacher in Whitechapel, England, believed that if the man and his daughter had only sought reconciliation on the Day of Atonement as ancient custom prescribes, the two would not have died.

Instead, 57-year-old Goodmacher and his daughter Fanny Zeitoun had been quarreling so furiously that Zeitoun and her husband had moved out of the home they shared with Goodmacher. On Sept. 23, 1920, the young woman was found lying on her bed with her throat cut. At her side lay her father, also with a sliced throat. Goodmacher recovered only to be put on trial for the murder of his daughter. He was found Guilty and on Dec. 30, 1920, hanged at Pentonville Prison.

REF.: *CBA; Shew, A Second Companion to Murder.*

Goodman, John, d.1874, U.S., mur. Goodman, a resident of Sugar Creek, Ohio, got into an argument with John Hayward on Apr. 8, 1874, and killed him. Thinking that the victim's wife, Susan Hayward, had seen the murder, Goodman killed her also. He tried to sink the bodies in a stream, but the water was too shallow and the corpses floated to the surface. John Goodman, who was known to have been quarreling with Hayward, was confronted and confessed to the double murder. He was convicted and hanged on Dec. 30, 1874.

REF.: *CBA; The Sugar Creek Tragedy.*

Goodpasture, Ernest William, 1886-1960, U.S., path. Professor at Harvard University from 1915-22, and at Vanderbilt University from 1924-55. Through the use of fertile chicken eggs, he helped develop vaccines for a number of viruses and rickettsia. REF.: *CBA.*

Goodwin, Alfred Theodore, 1923- , U.S., jur. Wrote "Constitutional Law - Freedom of The Press - Punishment for Contempt" for the *Oregon Law Review* in 1950, and "Fair trial and Free Press," a chapter in *The Prosecutor's Sourcebook* in 1969. He co-authored "Witnesses," a chapter in the Oregon State Bar's *Trial Book* with John Luvaas in 1957 and 1967. He served on the Circuit Court of the state of Oregon from 1955-60, and on the state Supreme Court from 1960-69. President Richard M. Nixon nominated Goodwin to the Ninth Circuit Court of Oregon in 1969. He was also a member of the Committee on Proposed Federal Rules of Criminal Procedure from 1970-71. REF.: *CBA.*

Goodwin, Henry K., prom. 1885, U.S., mur. Henry K. Goodwin was an inventor who was also paranoid. He believed that everyone he dealt with was attempting to steal his ideas. Goodwin visited Albert D. Swan in his Lawrence, Mass., office and the two discussed Goodwin's telephone inventions. Suddenly, Goodwin stood up and accused Swan of trying to steal his patents. A struggle ensued and Goodwin killed Swan, then fled the office. He was quickly apprehended, convicted of second-degree murder, and sent to prison for life.

REF.: *CBA; The Official Report of the Trial of Henry K. Goodwin; Commonwealth v. Henry K. Goodwin.*

Goodwin, Jack (AKA: **Plump**), prom. 1700s, Brit., rob. A career criminal first arrested at eleven for pickpocketing, Jack Goodwin made a short living from crime until his execution before his twentieth birthday.

A notorious prankster, Goodwin executed senseless crimes just for the sake of adventure. He and his friends once stole the rear wheels from a royal carriage while the coachman slept. With another accomplice, Goodwin bilked money from pedestrians by having his friend pose as a blind man. Desiring authenticity, however, Goodwin dripped wax onto his friend's eyelids to glue them shut and make sure he could not see during their ruse. The two thieves collected over £4, enough money to pay for their way to London, but within ten miles of the city, Goodwin double-crossed his accomplice by pushing him into a deep stream and fleeing with all the money.

At eighteen, Goodwin was arrested for pickpocketing and sentenced to Newgate Prison. He was condemned to death and afterwards received the second of two reprieves from the court. Neither curtailed his illegal activities, however, and he was eventually arrested for robbery and executed at Tyburn with two of his peers—Arthur Chambers and Dick Morris.

REF.: *CBA; Smith, Highwaymen.*

Goodwin, James, d.1874, Brit., mur. Death by hanging was anything but quick and painless for hanging victim James Goodwin, who took five minutes to die. Goodwin, convicted of murdering his wife, died in agony on May 25, 1874, in Newgate Prison, England. After falling through the trap door, his breast heaved convulsively and he raised his tied hands repeatedly to his throat in a vain attempt at relief during those horrible dying minutes.

REF.: *CBA; Potter, The Art of Hanging.*

Goodwin, Joyce, c.1947- , Brit., mansl. Fourteen-year-old

Joyce Goodwin, an epileptic, held the family terrier as she chatted with her 16-year-old brother and her father in their home in a town on the south coast of England. Her brother off-handedly remarked that she was not treating the dog well and then went upstairs to get the other family dog, perhaps to protect it from her. While he fetched the dog, an outraged Joyce was getting a weapon—her brother's .410 shotgun. When the boy returned, she shot him in the chest.

Found Guilty of manslaughter on the grounds of diminished responsibility, she was sent to an institution for handicapped persons.

REF.: *CBA;* Wilson, *Children Who Kill.*

Goodwin, Marvin Clyde, 1960- , U.S., mur. Marvin Goodwin, twenty-nine, last seen in New Orleans, La., is currently being sought in connection with a slaying in which the victim was abducted, robbed, and then killed. It's likely he is armed with a .38 caliber handgun. Goodwin is black, five feet, eight inches tall, and has black hair and brown eyes. He may be trying to hide out by working as an automobile mechanic or gas station attendant under an assumed name. He should be considered very dangerous. REF.: *CBA.*

Goodwin, Paul, 1916- , U.S., (wrong. convict.) mur. A Seminole, Okla., police officer, Chris Whitson, was shot to death in 1936. Paul Goodwin, twenty, and Horace "Buster" Lindsey were arrested and charged with the murder. Goodwin was denied access to counsel for seventy-nine days. During the trial, the prosecution presented a statement from Lindsey accusing Goodwin of shooting the officer, but did not tell the jury that Lindsey, before blaming Goodwin, had twice confessed to the shooting. Additionally, the prosecution suppressed testimony by a witness who heard Goodwin say, "Don't do that, Buster, don't do that," when the officer was shot.

Lindsey was sentenced to life in prison and on Oct. 17, 1936, Goodwin also received a life sentence. On July 7, 1961, Goodwin was paroled, but in 1962, he was convicted of armed robbery in Kingfisher County and he received another five-year term. Then on Mar. 6, 1969, a federal district court ordered Goodwin's release on the grounds of the suppressed testimony, prejudicial pretrial publicity, and denial of legal counsel in the first trial. Goodwin was released from the penitentiary at McAlester, Okla., on Mar. 7, 1969. REF.: *CBA.*

Goodwin, Solomon, d.1772, U.S., mur. Solomon Goodwin went canoeing with his close friend, David Wilson. The two began to argue and suddenly Goodwin seized an oar and struck Wilson, who was knocked from the canoe and drowned. This was seen by a number of witnesses who later testified against Goodwin. He was convicted of murder, although his case today would have been considered manslaughter at best, since no premeditation was in evidence.

Goodwin was executed at Falmouth, Mass., on Nov. 12, 1772. As he stood on the scaffold before a large crowd, Goodwin was subjected to a fifteen-minute religious harangue by Reverend Ephraim Clark, who opened his chastising remarks with: "There you stand, a condemned malefactor, filled with all the horrors of a shameful and painful death! Oh, sad state, indeed! But your present distress, however great, is nothing compared with the horror that your poor soul will be filled with instantly as it leaves your body!"

REF.: *CBA;* Clark, *Sovereign Grace Displayed in the Conversion and Salvation of a Penitent Sinner.*

Goolde, Maria Vere, 1877-1908, and **Goolde, Vere**, d.1908, Fr., mur. Maria Girodan, a young Frenchwoman of intemperate ways, married Vere Goolde and then squandered his small inheritance. The alcoholic Irishman was her third husband, and she took him to the gambling tables of Monte Carlo where they lost their money in games of chance. Marie approached a wealthy Swedish widow named Emma Erika Levin for an advance of £40, which the Gooldes never intended to pay back. When Levin asked for her money, Maria bludgeoned her to death with a poker. The frenzied couple then carved up the body and stuffed the remains

into their trunk.

The Gooldes sailed for Marseilles on the Monte Carlo Express on Aug. 5, 1907, taking their gruesome cargo with them. When they reached their destination, Maria instructed the shipping clerk to send the trunk on to Charing Cross, England. However, alarmed by the presence of blood and an overpowering odor, the young man, Monsieur Pons, contacted the couple at the Hôtel du Louvre. Maria assured Pons that the trunk contained poultry that they wished to ship home.

Pons was not satisfied with this explanation. He contacted the railway police, and upon opening the trunk, they discovered the body. The victim was identified, and a concierge at the Villa Menesimy in Monte Carlo found the murder weapon. The Gooldes were returned to Monte Carlo to stand trial. There it was learned that Maria's first two husbands had died under mysterious circumstances. The couple was sentenced to life imprisonment at the French penal colony at Cayenne, French Guiana, where Maria died of typhoid fever in July 1908. Vere survived the penal colony another year, and then committed suicide in September 1909.

REF.: *CBA;* Dilnot, *Rogues' March;* Gribble, *Adventures In Murder;* Kingston, *Remarkable Rogues;* Kingston, *Trunk Crimes, Past and Present;* Nash, *Look For the Woman;* Russell, *Guilty or Not Guilty?;* Sanders, *Murder Behind the Bright Lights;* Whitelaw, *Corpus Delicti;* (FICTION), Lowndes, *The Chink in the Armour.*

Goozee, Albert, prom. 1956, Brit., mur. When Goozee murdered a woman in June 1956 because of her possessiveness and the woman's 14-year-old daughter because he desired her, the court found him Guilty of murder and sentenced him to life in prison.

Albert Goozee was Mr. and Mrs. Leakey's tenant in a Parkstone lodge when he and the landlady became involved. Together with her 14-year-old daughter Norma Leakey, they formed a ménage à trois.

During a camping trip in Bignell Wood near Cadnam, about four miles west of Southampton, Goozee was found on the road suffering from a knife wound. In the wood, beside campsite preparations lay the bodies of Mrs. Leakey and her daughter. Though Goozee insisted that all three had gone mad and began attacking each other at random, authorities soon deduced that the woman and girl had been attacked first by Mrs. Leakey's former tenant and lover, who then had inflicted the knife wound on himself to make things look better. A letter found in Goozee's car told the whole grisly tale. "...Mrs. Leakey still comes after me so I have come to the only possible way out before I go after another young girl."

REF.: Butler, *Murderers' England;* CBA.

Gophers, 1890s-1910s, U.S., org. crime. Hell's Kitchen in Manhattan was controlled by the powerful Gophers gang, an area that ran from Fourteenth to Forty-Second Street and from Seventh to Eleventh Avenues. Members of this awesome gang usually met in the cellars and basements of deserted buildings, and thus the name of the gang was born.

More than 500 street-hardened gangsters paid allegiance to the Gophers, a formidable force that even Monk Eastman and his minions avoided. There was never a clear-cut leader of the Gophers, a gang that seemed to be ruled by an underworld committee which included Marty Brennan, Stumpy Malarkey, and Newburg Gallegher. Its chieftains usually met to plan robberies and count the loot from its tightly controlled bordellos and cheap gambling dens at their headquarters, Battle Row. This was a saloon operated by Mallet Murphy, who was named for the type of weapon he invariably employed when dealing with truculent customers or invading members from gangs other than those controlled by the Gophers.

Murphy, in lieu of a bludgeon or a bungstarter, wielded a heavy wooden mallet to send his victims to the floor of his saloon or propel them rocket-like through the swinging doors and into the street. Hell's Kitchen was undoubtedly the most dangerous place for a stranger to visit in New York. Hoodlums of every stripe loitered by the dozens along every block waiting for victims to mug and rob. One of the most energetic of these was a Gopher named Happy Jack Mulraney. His sobriquet stemmed from the fact that the muscles of his face had been injured in childhood street fighting so that they were partially paralyzed, causing Mulraney to wear a crooked smile, happy on one side and dour on the other. This gangster was extremely sensitive about his deformity and his superiors played upon it every time the Gophers planned a raid into rival territory, telling Mulraney that some gangster had made sarcastic remarks about his looks. This sent Mulraney into a frenzy and, while in such a state, he was unleashed upon the most hard-bitten of the Gopher enemies to wreak death and destruction.

Oddly, the murder for which Mulraney was permanently sent to prison involved no rival gangster but one of his best friends. Paddy the Priest, owner of a Tenth Avenue saloon, was tippling beers one evening with Mulraney when his curiosity overcame him; the saloon-keeper asked the gangster why he only smiled on one side of his face. With that, Mulraney exploded, pulled a gun, and sent a bullet into his friend's forehead, killing him. Mulraney then sat down again across from the dead Paddy, who was sprawled over the table. He casually lifted his mug of beer and gulped it down, seeming to wait for the police who had been summoned. Before officers yanked him away, Mulraney addressed the body of his fallen friend, saying: "I ain't smilin' on either side of me face!"

The most notorious Gopher member was One-Lung Curran. (He would eventually die of his physical deficiency.) A muscle-bound character, Curran took a fancy to police uniforms and began to attack any officer foolish enough to enter Hell's Kitchen alone on patrol. (These were rare rookies who invariably wandered into the deadly area; police usually patrolled the area in groups and while riding armed wagons—and then only sporadically. Curran would knock the officer senseless, then strip him of his long, blue coat. He took these coats to his mistresses and ordered them to cut it to his own size and make certain alterations he specified. One-Lung possessed dozens of these coats, which his harlot paramours had made into garish uniforms of Curran's own peculiar designs. The gang chieftain wore these proudly when prancing about his fiefdom. This weird sartorial attire became the rage with the Gophers so that all the gang members had to possess their own self-designed uniforms. Police for months were suddenly attacked and stripped of their tunics so that groggy officers in their undershirts, staggering into the precinct station at Forty-Seventh Street, became a common sight.

A generation of gangsters grew up following Curran and other Gopher leaders into ferocious underworld battles and criminal professions, which gang instructors were all too pleased to impart to children at age six and seven. The gang fostered many sub-gangs for juveniles, including the Baby Gophers, who were taught how to steal and fight in the street by their elders. Satellite gangs like the Parlor Mob, the Gorillas, and the Rhodes Gang all operated under the direction of the Gophers, but their members never made an illegal move of importance without Curran and other Gopher leaders giving their approval.

A female contingent of the Gophers was led by a roaring tough vixen named Battle Annie, whose gang was aptly called the Lady Gophers. They met in Murphy's Battle Row saloon and officially called themselves The Battle Row Ladies's Social and Athletic Club. A huge woman, Battle Annie could muster a force of several hundred women, who served as reserves to the Gophers in pitched battles with invading gangs. For almost a decade, Battle Annie and her club-wielding followers hired themselves out as strikebreakers or union pickets during several violent union disputes.

With the passing of One-Lung Curran and the imprisonment of most of the other leaders, the Gophers declined in power shortly before WWI. The Gophers did produce several gang members who went on to establish themselves with other gangs, including the sinister Goo Goo Knox who helped form the lethal Hudson Dusters; James "Biff" Ellison, who joined crime boss Paul Kelly and later tried to unseat him; and a slender British immigrant boy who later became known as Owney "The Killer" Madden, a future New York crime czar of the bootleg era. See: **Hudson Dusters; Kelly, Paul; Madden, Owen.**

REF.: Asbury, *The Gangs of New York;* CBA; Godwin, *Murder U.S.A.;* Haskins, *Street Gangs, Yesterday and Today;* Katz, *Uncle Frank;* Kobler, *Capone;* Levine, *Anatomy of a Gangster;* Lewis, *The Apaches of New York;* Messick and Goldblatt, *The Mobs and the Mafia;* Nash, *Bloodletters and Badmen;* Peterson, *The Mob;* Poston, *The Gang and the Establishment;* Reppetto, *The Blue Parade;* Riis, *How the Other Half Lives;* Stokes, *The Iconography of Manhattan;* Thompson and Raymond, *Gang Rule in New York;* Thrasher, *The Gang.*

Gordel, Dominic, d.1631, Fr., witchcraft. Virtually the only thing a person accused of witchcraft in the 1600s could look forward to was death. In essence, a person charged with sorcery had one of two options. He could admit his guilt and be burned to death, or he could maintain his innocence, go through excruciating torture, and then be burned to death. French priest Gordel chose the latter.

Dominic Gordel was charged with engaging in sorcery, attending satanic gatherings, and committing acts of deviltry. Those testifying against him included four children and persons already convicted as witches. Authorities asked him if the accusations were valid, a fatal question with no way out. Gorbel answered no. His subsequent torture ran from painful thumbscrews on his hands to excruciating vise grips and stretchings, to the eventual, intolerable, fatal burning. His defense ranged from, "Jesus, Maria. I do not even know what a sabbat is," to "I am dying! I am broken! Father everlasting, help me! I deliver myself into the hands of the good angels."

Gordel's cries went unheeded as torture and interrogation intensified. The priest who first begged to be believed later begged to die. "I cannot take any more!" he cried. All the while he maintained his innocence and for it eventually gained his final desire of death.

In the end, the man was taken to the Tower of La Joliette near a fire with a guard where he was most likely given his final request. REF.: *CBA.*

Gordianus, Marcus Antonios III (Gordianus Pius), 225-244, Roman., emp., assass. Grandson of Roman Emperor Gordianus I, and son of Gordianus II, whose death in battle precipitated the suicide of Gordianus I. He was named roman emperor in 238, by the Praetorian Guard after the death of his father and Gordianus I. His father-in-law, Timesitheus, helped Gordianus build up the Roman army and defeat the Goths, conquer Antioch, and win several battles against the Shapur-directed Persian forces. He was murdered by his own troops who wanted Timesitheus' successor, Philip the Arabian, to lead them against Persia. REF.: *CBA.*

Gordon, Annie, d.1926, Fr., (unsolv.) mur. The prime police suspect in the murder of Annie Gordon could not possibly have been the culprit. True, Casimir Salacheck, a Pole, had been a member of a gang of bandits, and was employed at the boarding-house opposite the villa where Englishwoman Gordon was murdered and had "vanished" the day of the murder, July 21, 1926. Though he was seen drinking heavily in a local tavern the night of the murder, evidence also showed that he slept that night in Lyons, two hundred miles away.

No police followed up on Salacheck nor was any further investigation undertaken into other possible leads in the Annie Gordon murder. All the police knew days after the murder is all they now know or will ever know. The middle-aged woman's body was found in bed, with eyeglasses on and an open book beside her to appear as though she had died of natural causes. Police at first said she had expired naturally. A doctor refused to sign her death certificate, though, saying she had suffocated, and police were forced into their half-hearted investigation.

The police thought about possible suspects, followed one shortly, and then gave up. Investigators termed it the "Juan-les-

Pins Murder" because it took place in the French estate of the same name. Investigators today look back on the episode in disgust and it is considered to be one of the most botched murder probings ever.

REF.: *CBA; Greenwall, They Were Murdered in France.*

Gordon, Clara, c.1921, U.S., mur. Gordon, fifty-four, murdered 30-year-old Sharon Reid in 1975 by stabbing her more than 200 times, but, said Chicago Circuit Court Judge Kenneth Wendt, "She is not guilty of any crime." The woman was released with no conviction or criminal record.

Wendt found Clara Gordon innocent of an act she undoubtedly committed because psychiatrists testified that she was insane. Psychiatrists also warned that Gordon could be very dangerous to society if she drank even a slight amount of an alcoholic beverage; but, they pointed out, though she was an alcoholic, she was not psychotic.

Wendt reluctantly made his announcement less than two years after the crime, saying he would commit her if only he had jurisdiction over the case. Frustrated, he called for a change in Illinois' mental health code giving a judge or jury the power to decide whether individuals like Gordon should be freed. REF.: *CBA.*

Gordon, Eugene Andrew, 1917-   , U.S., jur. Nominated to the District Court of North Carolina by President Lyndon B. Johnson in 1964. He joined the Advisory Committee on Crime Rules in 1976. REF.: *CBA.*

Gordon, George (First Viscount Aboyne), b.1649, Scot., treas. Eldest son of George Gordon, who became the First Marquis and the Sixth Earl of Huntley. He refused the National Covenant which persecuted Episcopalians. He allied himself with the king during the civil war, and participated in the 1645 attack of Aberdeen. Two years later, he was refused a pardon by the Scottish Parliament and was eventually beheaded for his treason. REF.: *CBA.*

Gordon, George, 1751-93, Scot., libel. Son of the Third Duke of Gordon, he was promoted to lieutenant in the navy in 1772, and served in Parliament from 1774-81. In 1778, he organized Protestant groups seeking the repeal of an act that lessened repression of Roman Catholics, leading 50,000 people in a march on the houses of Parliament, inciting the Gordon, or No-Popery Riots of 1780, in which angry mobs forced open prisons, destroyed Roman Catholic chapels, and attacked the Bank of England. He was acquitted of treason due to the skillful defense presented by Thomas Erskine, but in 1786, he was excommunicated, and converted to Judaism. The following year, he was convicted of libeling Marie Antoinette, and spent the rest of his life in prison at Newgate. REF.: *CBA.*

Gordon, Harry W. (Wilhelm Johannsen), 1905-41, U.S., mur. "It got so I couldn't get the sight (of dead bodies) out of my mind. Ever since, I'd get blue flashes when I'd been drinking, and would have to kill." Thus did Harry W. Gordon explain why he murdered Florence Johannsen in 1933, Betty Lena Coffin in 1935, and Irene McCarthy in 1940. It had all started with his job as a janitor at New York's Mount Sinai Hospital morgue, where he saw all those dead bodies.

On the evening of Oct. 19, 1933, Wilhelm Johannsen showed up on the doorstep of his estranged wife, Florence, wanting to talk. He had been drinking, and she knew it, but she let him in. This talk, like most, turned into an argument, and then became violent. Florence heaved a flower pot at Wilhelm, so Wilhelm strangled Florence with his hands. Then, laying her body across the bed, he mutilated her with a boning knife, imitating what he'd seen at Mount Sinai's morgue.

Johannsen fled to Brooklyn, changed his name to Harry W. Gordon, and met Lydia, who would eventually become his second wife. Harry and Lydia were married in New York but soon after moved to southern California. Lydia opened a flower shop in Long Beach and Harry became a merchant seaman. Although he worked out of the docks at Los Angeles, his work often took him out of town for several days at a time. One such trip took him to San Francisco.

On the evening of Apr. 5, 1935, a man and a woman checked into a hotel on San Francisco's waterfront as Mr. and Mrs. H. Meyers. The next morning, Mrs. Meyers, later identified as Betty Lena Coffin, was found dead in the hotel room. Coffin, whose long police record included arrests for narcotics and prostitution, was discovered nude, having been severely beaten, strangled, and mutilated with a razor.

On Mar. 10, 1936, Jerome von Braun Selz, being held in connection with the stabbing murder of another woman, was linked to the Coffin murder. The hotel night clerk had identified him as the man who had checked in with Coffin.

In 1940, Gordon lost his job as a seaman. Unable to find work on the Los Angeles docks, he drove north to San Francisco in June of that year, hoping for better luck. On June 25, 1940, the body of Irene McCarthy was found in a Fourth Street hotel. Having met Gordon on the evening before in a waterfront bar, she checked into a hotel with him as Mr. and Mrs. J. Wilkins of Los Angeles. The next morning, a hotel maid found McCarthy's nude body wedged between the bed and the wall. McCarthy had been slashed with a sharp weapon and strangled with a belt, still tied around her neck.

Unable to find work in San Francisco, Gordon returned home to Long Beach. On July 8, three weeks after the McCarthy murder, Gordon was apprehended and held on suspicion of killing the woman. His wife, Lydia, shocked at the charges, refused to believe them. The next day, however, Gordon confessed to the McCarthy murder and to the murder of his first wife, Florence Gordon, seven years earlier. Twenty-four hours later, having been extradited to San Francisco, Gordon revealed yet anohter crime, confessing to yet a third murder—that of Betty Lena Coffin in 1935.

Three months later, Gordon stood before Superior Court Judge Alfred Fritz and explained that he knew he was a menace to society and that he did not care what happened to him. "I've killed three women, and I'd probably do it again unless they get me out of the way," he said. On Oct. 16, 1940, Gordon received two death sentences for the murders of Coffin and McCarthy, and Fritz scheduled him for a date with the San Quentin gas chamber on Dec. 20. The day the decision was handed down, Lydia Gordon decided not to support her husband any longer. She filed for divorce.

After more than a year of appeals, and a plea for a stay of execution based on religious beliefs, Gordon was executed at San Quentin. The cyanide gas took only ten minutes to work, and at 10:11 a.m. on Sept. 4, 1941, Gordon was pronounced dead. REF.: *CBA.*

Gordon, Iain Hay, 1932-   , Ire., mur. In the village of White Abbey outside Belfast, N. Ire., in the late evening hours of Nov. 12, 1952, Patricia Curran, a 19-year-old student at Queen's University and the daughter of a prominent local judge, was stabbed thirty-seven times and left for dead in a wooded glade on the outskirts of town. Her brother, Desmond Curran, found her later that night after he became worried and went out to search for her.

Patricia died a short time later. Chief Superintendent John Capstick of Scotland Yard was called into the case by the Royal Ulster Constabulary. Capstick concluded from the careful arrangement of Patricia's clothes near the body that she had known her assailant. Two months passed before the arrest of 21-year-old aircraftsman Iain Hay Gordon, which followed extensive questioning of the military personnel stationed at the R.A.F. camp at Edenmore. Gordon's black eye first aroused Capstick's suspicions. The soldier explained that the injury resulted from a "playful scrap" in the barracks. Desmond Curran, who had frequently received Gordon at his home, told of the airman's strange obsession with violent crime and of his amazement that Curran's murderer had inflicted so many knife wounds when only four were needed.

The police interrogated Gordon at length. They were not satisfied with his alibi or his far-fetched stories. Finally, after three days of questioning, Gordon broke down and confessed to killing Curran in a fit of passion. He explained that he had met her at the bus stop the night of the murder and wished to walk her home. As they approached the girl's home, he suddenly grabbed her and began showering heated kisses on her. Afterward, he stabbed her with a service knife which he then threw in the sea. The wood-handled knife was found during a search of the beach on Jan. 8.

Right, murderer Iain Hay Gordon.

Gordon was tried at the Belfast Assize Court on Mar. 2, 1953. He pleaded guilty but insane to the charge of murder. Dr. Arthur Lewis, a London psychiatrist, theorized that Gordon was suffering from schizophrenia and hypoglycemia, and said that the defendant probably did not know he was doing wrong. On Mar. 7, the jury found Gordon Guilty, but also insane.

REF.: Capstick, *Given in Evidence;* CBA; Firth, *A Scientist Turns to Crime;* Furneaux, *Famous Criminal Cases, vol. 1;* Scott, *Scotland Yard;* Wilson, *Encyclopedia of Murder.*

Gordon, James, b.c.1836, U.S., mur. German immigrant John Gantz was killed for being in the wrong place at the wrong time. The wrong place was the western territory of the U.S., where Denver, Colo., now stands, and the time was 1860. James Gordon, too, was a victim of circumstance. Growing up in the West, with the closest thing to law five hundred miles away across the desert, made men wild. There were no sheriffs, no judges, and no courts. However, when Gordon murdered the youthful Gantz on July 18, 1860, there was just enough law in town to try and convict him of willful murder. Hanging from a scaffold on the breezy bank of Cherry Creek, Colo., Gordon became a somber notice that law had pushed its way to the western frontier.

Gordon had a fine childhood. His father had been a farmer on a ranch a few miles north of Denver. The family got along well. There was no reason for Gordon to choose a life of crime other than the fact that crime was rampant and often left unpunished.

He worshipped Charles Harrison, the ablest, meanest, and most dangerous man in fledgling Denver, his two claims to fame being that he never killed without warning and he never missed a shot. On July 12, 1860, just one week before Gordon murdered Gantz, Harrison killed a black man because he dared to enter his tavern. No arrest was made. Inspired, young Gordon got drunk, pulled out a pistol, and terrorized his hometown. In the end, an innocent German immigrant, a stranger to Gordon, was dead. According to one witness, the only words the man ever spoke to his assailant were, "For God's sake, don't kill me."

Gordon did a good job of evading the police. But the arm of the law, now long enough to stretch west, caught up to him as he made his way to Texas. Authorities protected him from enraged lynch mobs as they brought him back to stand trial in Cherry Creek. He survived the trip, but was not so fortunate with his trial. On Oct. 2, the jury found him Guilty of murder and on Oct. 6, he was hanged.

REF.: CBA; Rodell, *Denver Murders.*

Gordon, John, and **Gordon, William,** prom. 1844, U.S., mur. Amasa Sprague, one of the richest men in Rhode Island, dictated policy in the town of Providence. His brother was a U.S. senator from the state, and Sprague more or less decreed his own laws. He was rabidly anti-Irish, and when he heard that a newly-arrived Irish immigrant named Gordon had applied for a liquor license, he blocked the request. After the license was denied, two of Gordon's brothers, John and William Gordon, waited for Sprague one night and beat him to death. Both John and William were identified as the attackers and convicted of the murder. William Gordon was sent to prison while John Gordon was hanged on Feb. 14, 1845, despite protests from the Irish community that the Gordons had been convicted by a jury bought with Sprague money.

REF.: CBA; Larned, *A Full Report of the Trial of John Gordon and William Gordon, Charged with the Murder of Amasa Sprague; Synopsis of the Trial of John & Wm. Gordon.*

Gordon, John Williams, c.1931-   , Case of, Brit., mur. Evidence suggested that Gordon, twenty-four, murdered George Ford McNeill on July 12, 1955. However, evidence also implicated a man named Robert Matthews in the killing of McNeill. Still other facts pointed to someone called John Wallace Palmer as the culprit. McNeill was known to have homosexual tendencies and this was deemed instrumental in determining a possible motive for the crime. Using this and other facts gathered, enough proof built up against Gordon to have the Glasgow, Scot., free-lance writer convicted of the murder, enough contradictory support to have his sentence reprieved, and enough doubt raised in everyone's mind to keep all of England guessing "who done it" for decades.

Before sending the seven-man-and-eight-woman jury off to make its decision, the judge implored each member to consider all the facts carefully.

The facts were these. The only fingerprints found in the dead man's apartment were those of McNeill and Gordon, but that did not prove that no other person had been in the house. True, the first person to know about the killing was McNeill, and his actions in light of this knowledge invited suspicion. He said he had come home and seen the dead man and panicked. In panicking, he hid the body, saying he feared accusation, and then he left the country. In one day he went to London, then to Newhaven, up to Southampton, and across the Channel to Le Havre and Paris. The next day, he skipped to Germany, returned to Paris, then went to Belgium, Italy, and back again to France. There, Gordon said, he attempted to join the French Foreign Legion at Marseilles but was rejected because he was not French. Next, he traveled to Barcelona and from there to Madrid and Seville and back to Barcelona where he ended up in prison because he had run out of money.

During Gordon's trial two other suspects were brought before the court. Matthews, an inmate of a mental hospital, confessed to the murder. But his statement contradicted information the police knew to be true about the case. For example. Matthews said he killed McNeill on July 11, but police knew McNeill was alive on July 12. Further, police described Matthews' manner as anxious to say anything that would help get Gordon off.

A third suspect was Palmer, who had been to see McNeill on July 12, the day he was killed. Palmer had a serious criminal record including the charge of murdering a girl. In that case, he had been found insane and committed to Perth and then discharged in 1952. He swore he played no part in McNeill's murder, but it was revealed that McNeill was insisting that Palmer reveal his past history of emotional instability to his new fianceé. Possibly Palmer killed McNeill for fear that McNeill would disclose what Palmer was afraid to.

Sir John Cameron pointed out for the defense that Gordon made no attempt to adopt a pseudonym and that there was as much circumstantial evidence against Matthews as against Gordon. Cameron further hinted at another individual involved in the crime, a Mr. 'X.' "He remains a mystery," Cameron said. "He has not been traced. In spite of all the inquiries he has not come forward. He is clearly not Gordon. It seems to me that the circumstance of his silence is something that is much more suspicious in itself than Gordon's decamping and movements after death."

"There are too many tormenting questions," Sir John told the jury, "too many circumstances unknown and perhaps unknowable."

The jury was far from convinced. After fifty-eight minutes of deliberation, it passed a verdict of Guilty but only by majority decision. Gordon was reprieved because of the element of doubt. There was much doubt raised in his case and all agreed that he was convicted solely on his "guilty behavior" following the murder.

REF.: *CBA;* Furneaux, *Famous Criminal Cases, vol. 2.*

Gordon, Judah Leib (Judah Leib Asher, AKA: **Leon Gordon**), 1830-92, Lithuania, consp. Author and poet who was imprisoned in 1879 on trumped-up charges of conspiracy. From 1879-88, he co-edited *Ha-melitz,* a Hebraic publication, and became a prominent writer during the Haskalah, the Hebrew Enlightenment. REF.: *CBA.*

Gordon, Lauden, and **Gordon, Lockhart,** prom. 1804, Case of, Brit., kid. The brothers Lauden and Lockhart Gordon had grown up at their mother's school in Kensington. There they became acquainted with a little girl who grew up to become an heiress known as Mrs. Lee. When the brothers came back into her life, Mrs. Lee was living alone in her own substantial establishment in London. Lockhart had become a clergyman, but Lauden, who had lived for some years in the Caribbean, was in debt. Meeting Mrs. Lee again, Lauden began to court her and called frequently at her house. She later claimed that she tried to discourage him, yet she always made appointments to see him.

On Jan. 15, 1804, both men came to dinner at Mrs. Lee's house. At 7 p.m., a coach pulled up and the men hustled the woman into it, commanding it to drive to Uxbridge. There they got another chaise to Tetsworth and went into an inn. The postboys on the coaches were certain that Mrs. Lee was laughing and enjoying the trip. Mrs. Lee swore in court that she had been taken against her will, though she did admit that she let Lauden come into her room at the inn, but only because she feared for her life if she did not let him in. They spent the night together at the inn, then returned to London, where Mrs. Lee charged the two men with abduction.

The judge stopped the trial soon after this point was made, acquitting Lauden and Lockhart Gordon of kidnapping charges. The Reverend Lockhart Gordon was sent on his way, but Lauden was kept in jail for debt.

REF.: Bierstadt, *Curious Trials and Criminal Cases; CBA.*

Gordon, Lon, d.1894, U.S., west. outl. Lon Gordon was a member of the ferocious Bill Cook gang, which looted and terrorized its way through the Indian territory in Oklahoma during the early 1890s. After the Cook gang struck the Chandler Bank in Oklahoma, the Creek Light Horse Police Force, made up of Indians from the Cherokee Strip, tracked the Cook gang across

the territory and finally cornered Gordon and Henry Munson near Supulpa. The outlaws chose to shoot it out with the Indian police and both were killed in the battle on Aug. 2, 1894. REF.: *CBA.*

Gordon, Nathaniel, 1832-62, U.S., kid.-pir.-mur. The importation of African slaves into the U.S. was outlawed in 1808 and was declared to be an act of piracy in 1820. Anyone who captured black Africans for the purpose of impressing them into slavery was to be sentenced to death. The only man executed for violation of the slave bill was Capt. Nathaniel Gordon of Portland, Me., who was hanged in New York City on Feb. 22, 1862.

The hanging of slaver Nathaniel Gordon, 1862.

From the time he was a small boy, Gordon had been a sailor. He started out as a cabin boy, but through hard work and determination became the skipper of his own ship. On Apr. 17, 1860, Gordon's ship, the *Erie,* sailed from Havana, Cuba, stocked with beef, bread, pork, and rice. After thirty days at sea, the crew of the *Erie* began to suspect that their captain was planning to exchange the provisions for the slaves. They summoned Gordon to a meeting, but he rebuked the men and ordered them back to work. The *Erie* reached the mouth of the Congo River on the west coast of Africa in July 1860. On Aug. 7, the ship dropped anchor and took on board 897 Africans, who were quartered in a narrow passageway between the decks. Gordon quickly set sail for Cuba. However, the captain of the *Michigan,* a man-of-war, learned of the intrigue and gave chase.

The *Michigan* seized the *Erie* and its crew searched the cargo hold, where they found that eighteen slaves had died of suffocation and many others were barely alive. The *Michigan*'s captain placed the captain and crew of the *Erie* under arrest, took the slaves to Monrovia, and freed them. Gordon's two controversial trials in New York showed that he had tried to assuage several of his men by offering them a dollar for each slave brought on board. On Nov. 8, 1861, Captain Gordon was found Guilty. A higher court denied his appeal and scheduled his execution for Feb. 22, 1862.

Two days before Gordon was to hang, his wife and mother traveled to Washington where they hoped to see President Abraham Lincoln. The president's son Willie died the same day, however, so the women never got to plead their case. The night before the execution, Gordon tried to kill himself by ingesting strychnine, evidently smuggled to him in a package of cigars. Gordon became ill, but did not die. After a doctor declared him out of danger, the captain was hanged.

REF.: *CBA;* Duke, *Celebrated Criminal Cases of America;* Mencken, *By the Neck;* Mitchell, *Pirates.*

Gordon, Peyton, 1870-1946, U.S., jur. Served in the Judge

Advocate General Corps of the U.S. Army for a year and a half, earning the rank as major. In 1901, he became U.S. Attorney in Washington, D.C., was nominated to the Superior Court of Washington, D.C., by President Calvin Coolidge in 1928. REF.: *CBA*.

Gordon, Vivian (Benita Franklin Bishoff), See: **Greenberg, Sam,** and **Stein, Harry.**

Gordon, Walter A., b.1894, U.S., jur. Policeman in Berkeley after earning law degree from the University of California at Berkeley from 1919-30. He was nominated to the District Court of the Virgin Islands by President Dwight D.Eisenhower in 1958. He was a member of the National and California Parole and Probation Associations and the American Prison Association. REF.: *CBA*.

Gordon, Waxey (Irving Wexler), 1889-1952, U.S., org. crime. Gordon was born and raised in New York's Lower East Side and was a sneak thief and pickpocket at an early age. He became so adept at picking pockets that he earned the name Waxey; his peers claimed that he used wax on his fingers to ease wallets from pockets. In the 1910s, Gordon worked for the Dopey Benny Fein gang, helping to organize labor sluggers who broke up picketing strikers. Gambling and rackets czar Arnold Rothstein noticed Gordon and hired him away from Fein, using him as a rumrunner during the early days of Prohibition. Gordon was so successful that he soon controlled almost all rumrunning along the New York and New Jersey coastlines, smuggling into the U.S. enormous amounts of Canadian-bonded whiskey.

One-time big-shot gangster Waxey Gordon, under arrest, 1951.

Wealth poured into Gordon's coffers, a staggering $2 million a year, and Gordon proceeded to live like royalty. He had the best hotel suites in Manhattan, a lavish mansion in New Jersey, and another in Philadelphia. He bought breweries and distilleries, and owned scores of speakeasies in New York and New Jersey. Gordon became the epitome of the showy gangster of the 1920s. He traveled about in limousines, and there were always tall, statuesque chorus girls at his side. When Arnold Rothstein was mysteriously murdered in 1928, Gordon's protection began to vanish, and he made uneasy alliances with a new breed of gangsters who were then establishing a national crime cartel—Meyer Lansky, Louis Buchalter, and Charles "Lucky" Luciano.

Lansky and Gordon did not get along well, as each suspected the other of invading his bootlegging and gambling territories. Several deaths were attributed to an undeclared war between both gang chiefs. Luciano and Lansky finally arranged to have Gordon taken out of the picture in 1933. Thomas E. Dewey, the racket-busting New York district attorney, was given information which proved that Gordon had not paid income taxes for ten years, a period of time in which Waxey had gleaned more than an estimated $5 million. Lansky and Luciano were the reported suppliers of this sensitive information. The government built a strong case against Gordon and he was sent to federal prison for ten years.

When released, Gordon was a man without a place. His old gang was gone and so was his fortune and political influence. He joked to newsmen: "Waxey Gordon is dead. Meet Irving Wexler, salesman." But Gordon did not reform. He operated a few small gambling dens in New Jersey, and then tried to get rich quick by peddling narcotics. In 1951, he was arrested for selling a packet of heroin to an undercover narcotics agent. The aging gangster

begged the agent to take all his cash, his rings, and his watch and let him go. When the agent refused, Gordon begged the agent to shoot him, rather than arrest him for "peddling junk." This kind of arrest was repugnant to the once-mighty bootlegger who had backed Broadway shows and had financed the careers of many young acting hopefuls who later became film stars. Gordon was nevertheless tried and convicted. He was sent to Alcatraz for twenty-five years and died there on June 24, 1952. See: **Fein, Benjamin; Lansky, Meyer; Luciano, Charles; Rothstein, Arnold.**

REF.: Campbell, *The Luciano Project; CBA;* Eisenberg and Landau, *Meyer Lansky;* Fried, *The Rise and Fall of the Jewish Gangster in America;* Gage, *The Mafia is not an Equal Opportunity Employer;* Gosch and Hammer, *The Last Testament of Lucky Luciano;* Hynd, *The Giant Killers;* Katz, *Uncle Frank;* Lait and Mortimer, *Chicago: Confidential;* Levine, *Anatomy of a Gangster;* McPhaul, *Johnny Torrio;* Messick, *Lansky; ____, Secret File; ____, Syndicate in the Sun; ____* and Goldblatt, *The Mobs and the Mafia;* Nash, *Zanies;* Ottenberg, *The Federal Investigators;* Peterson, *The Mob;* Reppetto, *The Blue Parade;* Sann, *Kill the Dutchman;* Smith, *Syndicate City;* Thompson and Raymond, *Gang Rule in New York.*

Gordon, William (Sixth Viscount Kenmure), d.1716, Scot., treas. Commanded troops in southern Scotland during the uprising of 1715. He was seized at Preston by John Gordon and beheaded. REF.: *CBA*.

Gordon, William, prom. 1733, Brit., rob. William Gordon was found Guilty of robbery and sentenced to hang on the Newgate gallows in 1733. He obtained an unusual stay of execution from Dr. Chovet, a surgical researcher interested in windpipes.

Until 1733, Chovet conducted all his experimental windpipe surgery on dogs, but William Gordon's imminent death provided an opportunity to conduct his windpipe experiment on a human guinea pig. His examinations of windpipes made him feel capable of being able to perform an operation on Gordon that would allow him to survive his scheduled hanging. The results sent Gordon to a longer, more gruesome death than even the executioner had in mind.

Chovet approached Gordon confident that he could surgically open his windpipe in such a way prior to Gordon's hanging to allow him to survive his experience on the Newgate gallows. During a visit, ostensibly to bid Gordon farewell, Chovet made an incision in Gordon's windpipe that allowed the man to continue breathing even after his mouth and nostrils were stopped. The next day, Gordon marched confidently off to the gallows.

Gordon was hanged, along with others, on schedule. But unlike the others, Gordon did not die on schedule. After he had hung for forty-five minutes, he was cut down and rushed to a house in Edgware Road, near Tyburn, where Chovet was waiting. The surgeon performed his operation, but Gordon merely opened his mouth, groaned, and died. REF.: *CBA*.

Gordon-Baille, Mary Ann, b.1857, Brit., fraud. Mary Ann Gordon-Baille accumulated her wealth through a fraud that worked well for her in most of the major cities of Europe. Starting with Dundee, Scot., she leased beautiful homes, then furnished them lavishly, always putting off payment. She sold the goods to a fence as quickly as she could, took the money, and moved on to another city. More personal swindling became a part of her program, too. In 1885 in London, she took an elderly peer for more than £18,000.

Gordon-Baille returned to Scotland where she gathered contributions to resettle the indigent crofters of the poor Highland farms to Australia. She bought land in Australia with the contributions. She and her new husband, Richard Percival Bodeley Frost, took the contributions and moved to Australia, where they lived in comfort for several years. Soon after returning to England, she was arrested for passing bad checks, after which she was sent to prison for five years while Frost was sentenced to only eighteen months. When she was released, the grand days were over, and Mary Ann Gordon-Baille Frost lived out her final years on petty swindles and brief terms in jail.

REF.: *CBA;* Nash, *Look For the Woman.*

Gordon-Gordon (AKA: Lord Glencairn), d.1872, U.S., fraud.

Few nineteenth-century con men matched the Englishman Gordon-Gordon (his real name remains a mystery) for pluck and sheer gall. A first-rate swindler, he was so adept that he dared take on the biggest name in American finance, robber baron Jay Gould.

Gordon first appeared in Edinburgh in the winter of 1868 posing as the wealthy nobleman Lord Glencairn, and visited the salon of Marshall and Son, one of the city's fashionable jewelers. He selected several precious jewels and paid for them by check. When the transaction cleared the bank, his credit in the city was established. His next and all following jewel purchases were paid for by credit. By the spring of 1869, when the bills came due, the merchants realized that they were out £25,000. But by then Gordon had vanished, along with his foppish secretary.

Mrs. Gordon-Baille, confidence woman.

When next seen, Gordon was selling the local gentry in Minneapolis, Minn., on a wild scheme to buy vast tracts of land in the wilderness and build gleaming new cities for the displaced residents of Scotland. As fantastic as the proposal appeared, the locals believed it, especially after Lord Gordon deposited $40,000 in cash in a local bank. The coming land boom would make Minnesota a financial Mecca, he predicted. The residents lavished Gordon with all the luxuries then available in the Northwest.

The real target of Gordon's swindle was not the small-time businessmen of Minneapolis, but New York City railroad tycoon Jay Gould. The Minnesota adventure was merely an elaborate screen to attract publicity. With great fanfare, the soft-spoken cultured con man arrived in Manhattan in February 1872 with forged letters of introduction to Gould and other tycoons. His coming was reported in the local gazettes, and he made a close ally of the editor of the New York *Tribune,* Horace Greeley.

At their first meeting in the Metropolitan Hotel, Gordon told Greeley of his plan to buy up millions of shares of Erie Railroad stock and drive out Gould once and for all. The plan was music to the ears of Greeley, who aspired to the White House and for whom Gould was a major obstacle. "I've heard he's an impossible rascal," Gordon said. Yes, that much was true, the editor conceded. "That simply won't do, will it, Mr. Greeley?" Indeed it wouldn't, so Greeley arranged a meeting of the swindler and his prey.

Gordon came right to the point with Gould and told him that his investors now had majority control of the stock and that he intended to remove him from the company unless he came to some sort of understanding about certain necessary changes. Jay Gould was aghast. He sputtered out a promise to implement new policies or tender his resignation if unable to do so. Gordon then demanded securities. After all, he had spent more than $1 million lining up investors and securing legal help. Gould hedged, but his vanity got the better of him and he promised Gordon a half-million dollars to cover expenses. "This pledge was not to be used by him, but was to be returned to me on carrying out my part of the agreement," Gould later explained.

With the stocks and securities in Gordon's hand, the "sting" was complete. He dumped the stock in Philadelphia, by which time Gould realized that he had been taken for $150,000. Gordon was arrested, but Cornelius Vanderbilt and other financiers who had been cheated in the Erie stock frauds paid for his defense counsel. Free on his own recognizance, Gordon realized that it was only a matter of time before the British authorities supplied the Americans the true facts of his life. He took a fast train to Fort

Garry, Manitoba, where he believed he would be safe. He had not counted on the persistence of Marshall and Sons, his first victims in Edinburgh, who had obtained a warrant for his arrest. Thomas Smith, the clerk of the firm, tried to serve the warrant but was rebuffed in Fort Garry by people who had come to regard their visitor as a shrewd investor and kind-hearted philanthropist. But in the end, Smith succeeded in getting Gordon to surrender. The night before he was scheduled to depart, a great farewell ball was given in his honor. At three that morning, Gordon shot himself to death in his room. See: **Gould, Jay.**

REF.: *CBA;* MacDougall, *Hoaxes;* Nash, *Hustlers and Con Men.*

Newgate Prison is set on fire during the bloody Gordon Riots of 1780.

Gordon Riots, 1780, Brit., riot. The man who led thousands of people to protest the granting of Roman Catholics full British rights let the march turn into a violent mob, although he himself converted to Judaism six years later. In 1778, Parliament passed the Relief Act, which cancelled the penalties suffered by Roman Catholics in Britain since 1699 under William III. Many Protestants, however, objected to the repeal, and they formed the Protestant Association under 28-year-old Lord George Gordon. On June 2, 1780, he led a gathering of 60,000 hymn-singing Protestants in a parade to the House of Commons to present a petition in favor of repeal. When they reached the Parliament buildings, anyone who was in the way was fair game—bishops, lords, secretaries. They imprisoned their own representatives in the House of Commons for hours. Mob rule took over and they swung swords and clubs, and carried torches, moving on towards whatever buildings someone suggested. A particular target of their destruction was the chapels of ambassadors from foreign Catholic countries.

The lord mayor of London and many of the aldermen were on the side of the Protestants and so did not move quickly to quell the riot. Newgate, Fleet, and King's Bench prisons were burned, as was the house of Sir John Fielding, who, with his half-brother Henry Fielding, founded the Bow Street Runners. The Old Bailey itself was burned, which forced police to release about three hundred prisoners awaiting trial. Any building that was known to be the home or business of a Catholic was burned, and after a while certainty was not even necessary. The mob tried to break into the Bank of England but was unsuccessful. Even hangman Ned Dennis, known to the public as Jack Ketch, was caught up in the rioting, helping to burn a shop, though he never could say what made him do it.

It was more than a week before enough military troops were brought into London from around England to stop the rioting. Acres of the city had been destroyed; the dead and injured were everywhere. Numerous rioters as well as people just caught up in the crowds were arrested and tried. Eventually twenty-one people were hanged, including two 14-year-old boys. Lord George Gordon was arrested and tried for treason. However, he was acquitted on the basis that he had had no intentions of doing anything against the government of England.

REF.: Armitage, *Bow Street Runners;* Bleackley, *Hangmen of England; CBA;* Godwin, *Murder U.S.A;* Reppetto, *The Blue Parade;* Thomson, *The Story of Scotland Yard.*

Goremykin, Ivan Longinovich, 1839-1917, Rus., assass. Minister of interior from 1895-99, and prime minister in 1906, and from 1914-16. He was arrested in 1917, for supporting the czar during the revolution, imprisoned at Caucasus, and killed by Bolsheviks. REF.: *CBA.*

Gorilla Murderer, The, See: **Nelson, Earle Leonard.**

Gorillas, See: **Gophers.**

Goring, Charles B., 1870-1919, Brit., penol.-criminol. A moderate practitioner of phrenology, Charles Goring spent twelve years in exhaustive research of British convicts, applying statistics and other data in the study of 3,000 inmates. He reported ninety-six traits among these criminals and compared statistics of these men against non-criminals. Goring then produced his major work, *The English Convict,* in 1913, which became a classic in its day. Moreover, Goring criticized the established works and theories of Cesare Lombroso, taking issue with Lombroso's theory of the "born criminal type."

It was Goring's belief that the Positivist and Correctionist schools of criminology of his day were wrong in believing that criminals were developed through hereditary genes and strict penal application was the only method in dealing with "criminal types." He advocated legislation that would moderate criminal behavior and said inherited tendencies toward crime could be blunted and altered through education. Moreover, Goring felt that imprisonment was no solution to recidivism. His studies showed that confinement did nothing to alter the course of professional criminals and, in fact, worked in a counter-productive manner, creating hardened criminals out of first-offenders who, he believed, should be fined and not jailed. See: **Lombroso, Cesare.** REF.: *CBA.*

Goring, George (Earl of Norwich), 1585-1663, Brit., treas. Arranged marriage of Prince Charles and Henrietta Maria of France. He fought for the army of King Charles I against Scotland, and was sentenced to death following the 1648 conditional surrender at Colchester. He was granted a reprieve when Charles II was briefly returned to power. REF.: *CBA.*

Görlitz (Countess of Darmstadt), d.1847, Ger., mur. vict. The flames of myth were fueled once more with the murder in 1847 of Countess Görlitz of Darmstadt. Her death by apparent asphyxiation and burn wounds ignited an investigation into the notion of "spontaneous combustion."

The then-current theory stated that the breath of a person who had drank a lot of alcohol could catch fire from an outside source, such as a candle flame, and that this fire would be fed by body fat. The court nearly accepted this excuse until one of the countess' servants confessed to the murder, thus solving the crime and advancing forensic pathology at the same time.

REF.: *CBA;* Thorwald, *The Century of the Detective.*

Göring, Hermann, See: **Goering, Hermann.**

Gorman, Sam, See: **Buffalo Bill House.**

Gorman, Sir William, Brit., jur. Admitted to the bar in 1921, and defended Margaret Allen and prosecuted Peter Griffiths in notable trials. He was appointed judge of the High Court of the Queen's Division in 1958, and presided over the murder trial of Adam Ogilvie. REF.: *CBA.*

Gorringe, Esther, b.1809, Case of, Brit., mur. Esther Gorringe, fifteen, seemed like a nice girl. In 1824, Mr. and Mrs. Sewell, who kept a grocer's shop in East Grinstead, England, trusted her for eighteen months with their two children. She appeared to be attached to both children, especially 10-month-old Martha Ann Sewell. Then the girl either dropped the baby into a copper boiler and allowed the child to drown or purposely threw her in and murdered her.

Nobody knows why Gorringe won acquittal of all involvement in the case. Esther testified that she had dropped Martha in the boiler while she was attempting to draw water from it. She called it an accident and said she just decided not to tell anyone about it, letting hundreds of worried family members and friends search the village for the missing baby. When questioned, Gorringe said, "I had half a mind to tell them where the child was, but then again I thought I wouldn't." She was acquitted at the next assizes and set free.

REF.: *CBA.;* Wilson, *Children Who Kill.*

Gorringe, Jack, prom. 1948, Brit., mur. Gorringe could have avoided a murder conviction if only he had kept his mouth shut. The 1948 murder conviction of Gorringe represents one the earliest examples of casts being made of teeth marks to be used successfully as courtroom evidence.

Newlyweds Jack Gorringe and Phyllis Gorringe were having a hard time adjusting to married life as their interests varied widely and they fought often. Their last fight began on Christmas Day 1947 with a disagreement on whether they would attend an upcoming dance and ended on New Year's Day 1948 with the young bride's murder. Because the two had decided to continue their fighting at a New Year's celebration and had been anything but discrete, Gorringe was immediately suspect. His alibi was weak and the detectives were clever.

Among other hideous marks of violence on the victim's body were severe bite marks on her right breast. With no other evidence, detectives made impressions, and from those, positive casts of Gorringe's teeth. Next, impressions were made of the dead woman's breast to determine the location and direction of bite marks, using the Moulage method of casting, considered then to be the best way to obtain an accurate model. Then the plaster impressions of the man's jaw were fastened into a dental tool known as an articulator, thus giving the two models the exact movement of the jaw when biting. A simulated bite with the plaster molds was made into the wax impression of the breast. This bite mark then was photographed and the negative placed over the actual bite injury for comparison. In this case, it was a perfect match. Every cusp mark of the simulated bite fitted every cusp mark of the injury.

In a short time the jury turned in its verdict of Guilty of murder. Gorringe went to prison for life and the models of teeth and breast were sent to the Gordon Museum at Guy's Hospital in England, where they will forever serve as a permanent illustration of progress made in police detective work.

REF.: *CBA; Cuthbert, Science and the Detection of Crime.*

Gorse Hall Murder, See: **Howard, Cornelius.**

Gorton, Samuel, 1592-1677, U.S., her. Founded a religious sect known as the Gortonians, who rebuffed established religious ceremonies, believing that heaven and hell were figments of the imagination and that Christ was partially human. In 1637, he brought his followers to the colony of Massachusetts, where he was tried for heresy and banished the following year. The Gortonians were rejected in other communities, until the Earl of Warwick allowed Gorton to settle in Rhode Island in 1648. He founded the town of Warwick and between 1649-66, he served a number of terms in the state legislature. REF.: *CBA.*

Görtz, Georg Heinrich von, 1668-1719, Swed., treas. Helped

Schleswig and Holstein maintain their independence from Denmark in 1713. He served as diplomat and chief financial adviser for Charles XII of Sweden in 1714, and negotiated finances and agreements concerning the Great Northern War. In 1718, he represented Sweden at the Aland congress. After Charles XII died, he was arrested by Frederick of Hess-Kassel, the future Frederick I, tried, convicted, and executed on charges of separating Charles from the Swedes. REF.: *CBA*.

Gosch, John David, 1970- , Case of, U.S., kid. Before dawn on Sept. 5, 1982, 12-year-old newspaper boy Johnny Gosch left his West Des Moines, Iowa, home to deliver the Sunday papers. When Johnny's parents, Noreen and John Gosch, were awakened at 7 a.m. by neighbors calling to say they had not yet received their papers, John Gosch immediately searched for his son. A short distance from the Gosch home, he found Johnny's wagon filled with papers. Some of the other newsboys told Gosch that they had seen a man approach Johnny, purportedly to ask for directions. When the stranger returned a second time, Johnny told his friends he thought the man's behavior odd and intended to go home. As Johnny turned toward home, one of the newsboys saw another man approach Johnny and follow him around the corner. The newsboys then reported hearing a car door slam. A child in a nearby house was awakened by the slamming door and looked out the window in time to see a blue car run through a stop sign and drive away.

The Gosches immediately notified police that they believed Johnny had been abducted. They gave police a description of the car and a partial license plate number. Despite the indications of kidnapping, the police regarded the boy as a probable runaway and did not aggressively investigate until seventy-two hours had passed. A detailed search of the area organized by neighbors and friends failed to produce any further evidence. Within the first week, the Gosches contacted the FBI, who indicated that they would probably not be involved in the investigation. Persisting in the search for Johnny with what they felt was inadequate assistance from the authorities, the Gosches hired an artist to sketch the man described to them by Johnny's fellow newsboys. They distributed the picture to coroner's offices, and bus, police, and gas stations around the country. They also contacted the newspapers and appeared on national television programs.

A month after Johnny's disappearance, they hired a private detective to follow up on the many leads their publicity generated. Although the detectives were unsuccessful in finding Johnny, the Gosches believe that on at least two or possibly three occasions, they have come close to finding their son. On Mar. 2, 1983, a boy fitting Johnny's description ran up to a woman on a Tulsa, Okla., street, identified himself as John David Gosch, and asked for help. Before the woman could respond, two men seized the boy and dragged him away. Unfortunately the woman failed to report the sighting until November of that year when she saw his photograph on a television program on missing children. In February 1984, Noreen Gosch received three phone calls from someone she believes to have been her son. The calls all came within twelve minutes and in them, the caller identified himself as Johnny Gosch. Mrs. Gosch said the caller sounded frightened and possibly drugged. He said he did not know where he was and was not all right. Police attempts to trace the call were unsuccessful. In February 1988, the Gosches received a letter sent from a city in the west in which the writer said he had been forced to do repulsive things, that his hair has been dyed, and that he would never be allowed to return home. The Gosches suspected the letter might be authentic because it was signed in the idiosyncratic manner in which Johnny had frequently signed notes to them before he disappeared.

In addition to the legitimate leads, the Gosches have received numerous false leads, occasionally from people intentionally harassing them or attempting to extort money. They have also received threats against their own lives relative to Johnny's disappearance. The Gosches' search for their son, although unsuccessful, has been responsible for significant changes in state laws—changes which now allow for investigations into potential kidnappings to begin immediately. The FBI is now also allowed to enter similar cases without delay. The Gosches' efforts and the publicity that their case has received was also in part responsible for the founding of the National Center for Missing and Exploited Children, a clearing house run in conjunction with the Justice Department that handles thousands of cases of missing children. REF.: *CBA*.

Goslett, Arthur Andrew Clement (AKA: **Captain Arthur Godfrey, Captain Goslett**), d.1920, Brit., big.-mur. Arthur Goslett was a man with two wives and two aliases. Calling himself "Captain" Goslett, he shared an apartment with his wife Evelyn Goslett, in Golders Green. He also shared a small cottage in Kew, with his wife Daisy. With her, he was known as Captain Arthur Godfrey. In fact, he had committed bigamy before, being convicted of it in Dover during WWI. He had also been convicted of diamond smuggling in West Africa, for which he served time in a German prison. In August 1919, Daisy became very ill while pregnant and had to go into a nursing home. When she returned to Kew, she found that the cottage had been returned to the owner that and Goslett had confessed to being a bigamist. However, he offered to let her and the new baby live with him and Evelyn in Golders Green as his brother's widow. Since he gave her no alternative, Daisy agreed, although she refused to let him sleep with her in his house.

When a woman who had known Daisy as Mrs. Godfrey heard her addressed as Mrs. Goslett, she went to Evelyn Goslett and told her about it. Evelyn demanded that they move to another part of London where people did not know the truth. But by then Goslett had another marriage in the works, with a wife living at Richmond, who became pregnant. On May 1, 1920, Goslett returned home about ten, and the servant saw him, most unusually, remove his shirt and jacket in the dining room and go to bed, not at all concerned about his wife not being there.

The next day, Evelyn Goslett's body was found in the river Brent at Hendon with four deep wounds on her head, though she had actually drowned. Blood was found on the river bank. She was identified through a shop bill, and Goslett was arrested within one day because the handbag she had had with her at Hendon was found in the house. "I am going to have the rope," he said, though he tried to place the blame for the murder on Daisy, saying that she had driven him to it. Superintendent Neil of Scotland Yard testified that there was no substance to Goslett's story. Goslett was tried and found Guilty. The last person to visit him before he was hanged on July 27, 1920, was the wife from Richmond, who forgave him.

REF.: *CBA*; Felstead, *Sir Richard Muir*; Logan, *Great Murder Mysteries*; Neil, *Manhunters of Scotland Yard*; Shew, *A Second Companion to Murder*.

Gosling, Harold L., 1853-84, U.S., west. lawman. Harold Gosling was born in Shelbyville, Tenn., and graduated from the Annapolis Naval Academy. He then took his law degree in Washington, D.C. He moved to Parsons, Kan., where he practiced law and later moved to Castroville, Texas, in Medina County where, in 1878, he established a newspaper, *The Quill*. A law-and-order man, Gosling was appointed U.S. marshal for the Western District of Texas in 1884. Gosling proved to be a courageous lawman, but he was shot to death by two train robbers he had captured and was taking to jail. One of the prisoners was later shot to death and the other was recaptured. Gosling was buried in San Antonio. REF.: *CBA*.

Gossage, Eben, c.1955- , U.S., forg.-theft-mur. Eben Gossage, twenty, and his 19-year-old sister, Amy Gossage, had the perfect life—a loving mother; their father, Howard Gossage, one of the country's greatest publicists; wealth and prestige; and each other. Then their parents divorced. In 1969, their father died of leukemia. Their mother became an alcoholic and died five years later. By 1975, all that the once-privileged Gossage kids had left were drug habits, shoddy educations, and a $50,000 inheritance to share. Within five months of his father's death, Eben Gossage had already exhausted his share of the estate. He forged checks in his mother's and grandmother's names for a total of $10,000, for which he served nine months in jail.

Eben started begging money from Amy, now living a loose and indolent life in San Francisco. She gave him what she could but it soon became apparent that the drug habits were much more than either could support. With heroin suppliers after him, Eben's insistence on money from his sister intensified until, on Feb.12, 1975, she expressed fear of her brother for the first time. She telephoned two friends to tell them she was frightened of Eben and asked what she should do. "Get out fast," one told her. "Like today."

In a confession two months later, Eben described how he and the sister he had loved so dearly fought bitterly about their inheritance. When she refused to give him any more of her money and blamed him for causing the family so much trouble, and he accused her of using cocaine and sleeping around, both lost control. Amy grabbed a hammer with one hand and a scissors with the other and threatened to stab Eben's eyes out. "All of a sudden I felt overpowered...I was scared bad." Eben grabbed the hammer and swung it against his sister's skull eight or ten times. She slid to the floor. He knew he had killed her. "Then, I got angry with her," he said. "I blamed her for what had happened. I started stabbing her with the scissors, cursing her. I don't know how many times I stabbed her. I was crying. I only stopped when I got exhausted." According to the court pathologist, Amy died from seventeen blows with a hammer before being stabbed forty-five times with scissors.

The court believed Eben had not deliberately killed his sister, and he was convicted of voluntary manslaughter, for which the maximum sentence is fifteen years in prison. Leaving the courtroom, Eben stared blankly ahead, saying, "Now I've lost everything. Everyone. My father, my mother, my sister. There's nobody left. I'm the last one...the last one."

REF.: *CBA*; Godwin, *Murder U.S.A.*

Gosse, Philip, b.1879, Brit., writer. Son of poet Sir Edmund William, he wrote *The Pirates' Who's Who* in 1924, *My Pirate Library* in 1926, *The History of Piracy* in 1932, as well as books on natural history and medicine. REF.: *CBA*.

Gosselin, Ambroisine, d.1849, Fr., mur. Ambroisine Gosselin and her lover killed her husband, who stood in the way of their happiness. She was tried and found Guilty. Sentenced to be guillotined, on Apr. 13, 1849, she was taken to the place of execution. While she drank coffee and ate cake, she was placed under the blade. When it descended, it stopped, stuck, and had to be freed and prepared again. She calmly awaited its repair and then positioned her head again.

REF.: *CBA*; Morain, *The Underworld of Paris*.

Gotarzes II, prom. 38-51 A.D., Parthia, mur. To become king, he slew his brother Artabanus III, and battled a third brother and a Roman-sponsored enemy. REF.: *CBA*.

Gotlieb, Matthias, prom. 1796, U.S., mur. A habitual drunkard, Matthias Gotlieb returned to his Newton, N.J., home to be greeted by his wife's scolding. Neighbors were used to this conduct, which had been going on for some years. One neighbor passed the Gotlieb home to see Gotlieb go to his porch where he stood unsteadily before a large whetstone, sharpening a long knife. Gotlieb then went back inside and promptly slit his wife's throat. Police were called and the drunkard meekly surrendered. He was hanged on Oct. 28, 1796.

REF.: *CBA*; Hunt, *A Sermon Preached at the Execution of Matthias Gotlieb*.

Goto Shojiro, 1838-97, Japan, rebel. Chief counsel to feudal lord of Tosa. In 1867, he headed the rebellion against shogunate, and protested the restoration of the emperor the following year. In 1881, he helped form the liberal Jiyuto party, the first political faction in Japan. REF.: *CBA*.

Gottfried, Gesina Margaretha, d.1828, Ger., mur. Gesina Gottfried of Bremen, Ger., chose to marry a good-looking alcoholic named Miltenberg. The pair had two children, but she

began a love affair with a man named Gottfried. She asked her mother to obtain some of the arsenic she used in killing mice, and added it to her husband's morning beer. Miltenberg died, but Gottfried's lover was slow in marrying her because he did not want her children. She poisoned their milk, and the children died.

Gesina's parents had never said no to her, but they objected to her marrying Gottfried so soon after her husband's death. Rather than relenting or delaying the marriage, she poisoned her parents. When Gottfried, probably suspecting that something was not right, still hedged on the subject of marriage, Gesina began to administer minute doses of arsenic to him, enough to keep him continually sick and weakening. She took such good care of him that he married her before dying. He left her everything in his will.

In 1825, a wheelwright named Rumf bought her house after foreclosure, and gave her a position as his housekeeper. One by one, Rumf's children died, as did his wife. In the spring of 1828, Rumf noticed a white powder on his food. When he observed it again a few days later, he took the food to the police for analysis. Arsenic was found, and the housekeeper was arrested.

When Gesina Gottfried was brought to trial, she appeared not as the plump, rosy-cheeked woman she had been, but as a worn, skeletal figure. She had regularly worn an increasing number of corsets to keep looking plump and appealing. She confessed to having killed at least thirty people and to have derived a sexual pleasure from the act. She was found Guilty and sentenced to be beheaded. See: **Blandy, Mary; Cotton, Mary Ann Robson Mowbray; DeMelker, Daisy Louisa; Jegado, Helene; LaFarge, Marie; Smith, Madeleine**.

REF.: *CBA*; Kingston, *Remarkable Rogues*; Nash, *Almanac of World Crime*; ____, *Look For the Woman*.

Gotti, Gene, 1947- , Case of, U.S., rack.-drugs. New York tried three times to successfully try Gene Gotti, 42-year-old younger brother of reputed Mafia godfather John "The Dapper Don" Gotti, on charges of running a multi-million dollar heroin ring. His eventual conviction on May 23, 1989, proved a coup for the FBI and prosecutors who had tried twice before to prove Gotti's involvement in leading a ring that smuggled hundreds of pounds of Southeast Asian heroin into New York in the early 1980s.

The Mafia sabotaged Gotti's first trial by its long-standing strategy of tampering with the jury. One jury member worried about his safety and two feared their identities were known. Gotti's second trial miscarried because one juror possessed cocaine and the eleven remaining jurors were deadlocked. In the third attempt one juror was dismissed after discussing the case at a Passover ceremony with his cousin, a government prosecutor. A second juror had to step down because he lived on the same block as the chief federal agent on the case. A replenished jury remained unable to reach a unanimous decision on Gotti and associate John Carneglia because one juror refused to convict. Later, the court learned that this juror, known only as "No. 9," was afraid he had been identified by the mob and dismissed him. The remaining eleven convicted both men. REF.: *CBA*.

Gotti, John, 1940- , U.S., org. crime. Reportedly the most powerful Mafia leader in New York at this writing, John Gotti favors expensive, tailor-made suits, limousines, and the finer New York restaurants. He heads the old Carlo Gambino Mafia family, which, by all accounts, controls all the important New York rackets. Gotti came up through the ranks of this family and was supported for his present top position by Aniello Dellacroce, an aging sub-boss of the Gambino family. In 1972, Manny Gambino, nephew to the all-powerful Carlo Gambino, was kidnapped and held for ransom. After the kidnappers received part of the $350,000 ransom they demanded, Manny Gambino was murdered and his corpse was later found in a New Jersey garbage dump. The enraged Gambino sent out his top enforcers to avenge his nephew's death. One of the kidnappers, James McBratney, was killed in a Staten Island bar by three of Gambino's men. One of these was Gotti who was sent to prison for seven years.

Upon his release, Gotti was rewarded for his loyalty and service by being named as one of the top bosses in the Gambino family. He was ruthless with underlings, according to police monitoring his movements, telling henchmen that if they refused to obey his orders, he would blow up their houses. He reportedly engineered the deaths of many of his rivals while climbing to the top of the Gambino family. On Dec. 2, 1985, Paul Castellano and Thomas Bilotti, both underbosses of the Gambino family, were shot to death as they emerged from a popular Manhattan steak house. Gotti took over the Gambino family a short time later. In the late 1980s, both state and federal authorities attempted to convict Gotti of several racketeering charges, but to the surprise of the press and the public alike, he has so far successfully been acquitted of all charges. Gotti remains the top mob man of New York at this writing.

REF.: *CBA;* Davis, *Mafia Kingfish;* Mustain, *Mob Star;* Zuckerman, *Vengeance Is Mine.*

Goucher, Allen (AKA: "Kid" Goucher, Roy Williams), prom. 1902, U.S., mur. On the night of Jan. 20, 1902, Goucher and his gang of hoodlums scoured San Francisco looking for trouble. That same night, police officer Eugene C. Robinson walked his beat looking for criminals. The chance meeting of the thugs and Robinson left the young lawman dead. Goucher and cronies Frank Woods, William Kaufman, William Kennedy, John Courtney and Henderson ran off, but on their tail was officer Charles Taylor. Taylor's arrest of Henderson proved to be all he needed. Henderson readily confessed to the crime and gave the names of his accomplices. One crook at a time, they were brought in.

Goucher made it from San Francisco to St. Paul, Minn., before being arrested on a burglary charge. He was put up in the Stillwater Penitentiary as "Roy Williams" the burglar, instead of in San Quentin Prison as Allen Goucher. But at the end of his term he was returned to San Francisco, and there he was sentenced to twenty-five years for his part in the Robinson murder. Goucher would have been hanged had it not been for influential family ties. His father, respected State senator Goucher, made a heartfelt plea to the jury that left his son alive and ungrateful and the rest of the courtroom in tears.

The other thugs were not quite as lucky. Woods was executed on Oct. 6, 1905, convicted of firing the fatal shot. Kaufman was sentenced to twenty-five years in San Quentin on Jan. 31, 1903. The charge against Kennedy was dropped because of insufficient evidence but the following year, arrested for burglary at Woodland, Yolo County, he was sentenced to forty-five years at Folsom Prison on Mar. 22, 1905.

REF.: *CBA;* Duke, *Celebrated Criminal Cases of America.*

Goudie, Thomas Patterson (AKA: John Style, Mr. Scott), b.1883, Brit., forg.-embez. Thomas Goudie, a trusted clerk at the Bank of Liverpool in 1900, paid for his bets on horse races by forging small checks on one account, that of a manufacturer named Robert William Hudson. When two touts at Newmarket named Thomas Kelly and William Stiles observed him losing week after week but increasing the size of his bets, they became friends with the 29-year-old Goudie and conned him into believing that Stiles was a bettor of great skill. Goudie gave them checks for his share of major bets, which grew and grew. He was not even aware that he was supposedly betting amounts that were higher than a bookmaker could accept.

Soon three other hoods began to notice Kelly and Stiles having money to throw around. They watched the two deal with Goudie and decided to get in on the action. An American named Mances, Dick Burge, a boxer, and Laurie Marks, a bookie, began to blackmail Goudie, and in one month in 1901, Goudie removed £91,000 from the millionaire Hudson's account. But on Nov. 20, another clerk discovered a discrepancy that Goudie had failed to take care of. Goudie, in a panic, fled the bank, and the police took over. Goudie was caught and quickly confessed the whole scheme, implicating the others. Mances, the American, disappeared and was never charged. Marks committed suicide before the trial. The other three were found Guilty. Goudie was

sentenced to ten years in prison but died after only three. Kelly and Stiles were sentenced to two years at hard labor.

REF.: Earl of Birkenhead, *Famous Trials of History; CBA;* Dilnot, *Celebrated Crimes;* Green, *Criminals;* Kingston, *A Gallery of Rogues.*

Gough, John, b.c.1820, Brit., mur. A boys' prank led to a man's death, which led to the death of two deaths—a waste of human life. On Feb. 16, 1835, four young Irish men from the poorest Birmingham slums were sharing a pint of ale. This minor breach of propriety led to a spurt of pickpocketing which spiraled out of the boys' control when the full-blown mugging of elderly William Painter became willful murder. William Dollman, William Knowles, Nathaniel Hedge, and 15-year-old John Gough jumped Painter, a 61-year-old tax collector, as he made his way home from work. They kicked and elbowed him and struck him violently on the jaw to steal one gold watch in a cracked enamel case. The boys then fled in one direction as a severely wounded Painter staggered off in another.

Days later the man died and the boys were charged with murder. Neither Dollman, Hedge, nor Gough put up a fight. Police had already nabbed the youngest suspect, Knowles, and offered him a pardon in exchange for a confession. In addition, Thomas Griffiths, who had been given the stolen watch to sell had turned in the prime evidence to police. The three main culprits were in the same helpless position Painter had been in just days earlier. Each was found Guilty of murder and sentenced to death. Gough wept bitterly, proclaiming, "I'm as innocent as a lamb." Far from innocent, but young just the same, Gough won a reprieve from death and got life in prison. Hedge and Dollman were hanged on July 4, 1835.

REF.: *CBA;* Wilson, *Children Who Kill.*

Gouin, Sir Lomer, 1861-1929, Can., jur. Prime minister and attorney general for the Province of Quebec from 1905-20. He was Canada's minister of justice from 1921-24, and belonged to the federal Parliament. REF.: *CBA.*

Gould, Jay (Jason Gould), c.1836-92, U.S., fraud. The shady financial manipulations of Jay Gould, the quintessential nineteenth-century robber baron, triggered "Black Friday" and the ensuing financial panic. Gould and his partner James Fisk were self-made men who lived in an era of overnight millionaires.

Gould was raised on his father's farm in Delaware County, N.Y. He later gave up the farm to go into partnership with his father in a hardware business. In 1857, Gould sensed the coming financial panic and sold his lumber and tanning business to buy controlling interest in the Rutland and Washington Railroad. He paid ten cents

Robber baron Jay Gould.

for every dollar share, and soon declared himself president, treasurer, and general manager of the company. Gould merged the line with the Rensoelaer and Saratoga Railroad and then sold his holdings at a 2,400 percent profit.

In New York Gould aligned himself with James Fisk, who and by the end of the Civil War was one of the most powerful figures in the investment world. Fisk sold his booming retail business to the Jordan Marsh Company of Boston, and then joined up with Daniel Drew, one of the principal officers of the Erie Railroad. Drew, like Fisk and Gould, made his fortune through hard work and guile. Drew's sole interest in life was the accumulation of wealth.

Gould, Fisk, and Drew formed an alliance against Cornelius Vanderbilt, known as the Commodore, who dreamed of monopolizing the railroad, coal, and steel industries. In 1867, Vanderbilt moved to acquire the Erie Railroad. He began buying up stock in large blocks, but the more he bought, the more Fisk ordered printed. The press in the company's basement, churned out as many stock shares as Vanderbilt wanted, and he lost $8 million. Vanderbilt reported the stock fraud to the government, and the a state supreme court ordered Fisk and Gould to return the money. Gould, the real mastermind behind the Erie War, escaped the court's jurisdiction by transferring his business to the New Jersey side of the Hudson River. With a $25,000 bounty on his head, Fisk ordered his army of hired thugs to move a twelve-pound cannon into place overlooking the river approach to their hotel headquarters. "The Commodore owns New York," Fisk thundered. "The Stock Exchange, the streets, the railroads, and most of the steamships there belong to him. As ambitious young men, there was no chance there for us to expand, and so we came here to grow up with the country."

Things were at a stalemate when Fisk sent Jay Gould to Albany with $500,000 in bribe money for the legislators. Fearful of arrest, Gould was rowed across the river under cover of darkness. Fisk was gambling that he could break Vanderbilt.

State senator William Marcy Tweed, later the "grand sachem" of Tammany Hall, played both ends against the middle. He and his cronies in the state house profited by the Erie Stock War, and in return for cash "contributions" passed a bill in September 1868 releasing Fisk, Gould, and Drew from any criminal liability. On Sept. 3, 1868, the triumphant young entrepreneurs met Vanderbilt in his New York hotel room. Peace was declared, and the Commodore was paid $4.5 million for his agreement to abandon his interest in the Erie line. "I've never been involved with such a bunch of gangsters before," Vanderbilt snarled. The location of the headquarters of the Erie Railroad in the ornate Pike's Grand Opera House shocked the staid New York financial community. While Fisk and Gould plotted strategy on the second floor, New Yorkers watched operettas and light comedy in the auditorium below. Fisk, calling himself the "Prince of the Erie," cavorted openly with his mistress Josie Mansfield, and posed for pictures in his military uniform. Gould, by contrast, was quiet and unassuming, but always scheming. In the next few years, the partners bought control of the Union Pacific, the Missouri Pacific, and the St. Louis and Northern railroads.

In June 1869, Gould and Fisk organized a combine to raise the price of gold. Control of the gold supply would have enabled them to control the national medium of exchange, and with it the economic destiny of the nation. With several other speculators they bought up $15 million worth of gold, but discovered that there was no change in the price. Hearing that the secretary of the treasury intended to sell a portion of the gold reserve (estimated at between $75 and $100 million), Gould tried to bribe government officials in hopes of influencing policy. Gould convinced Abel Corbin, brother-in-law of President Ulysses Grant, that his scheme would benefit the American farmer. Gould and his partners bought another $50 million in gold, and the price finally rose. But then Corbin, who had convinced the secretary of the treasury to suspend the sale of gold "for the good of the country," suddenly had a change of heart. He pulled out at the last moment, leaving Gould and Fisk exposed. Gould cancelled the scheme and ordered his agents to sell their gold immediately, thus setting in motion the Black Friday Panic of Sept. 24, 1869. The government revoked the previous order to suspend gold sales, and Jay Gould came out of the crisis virtually unscathed. He was driven out of the Erie Company in 1872, but bought the New York *World* later in the decade and was a major force in the railroad industry for years to come. Fisk was shot to death on Nov. 25, 1872, by Ned Stokes, Josie Mansfield's jealous lover. Gould died of tuberculosis twenty years later. See: **Drew, Daniel; Fisk, James, Jr.; Gordon-Gordon.**

REF.: Adams, *Chapters of Erie;* Bowers, *The Tragic Era;* Butterfield, *The American Past; CBA;* Churchill, *The Pictorial History of American Crime;* Clews, *Fifty Years in Wall Street;* Croffut, *The Vanderbilts and the Story of Their Fortune;* Duke, *Celebrated Criminal Cases of America;* Fuller, *Jubilee Jim: The Life of Colonel James Fisk, Jr.;* Hacker, *The United States*

Since 1865; Halstead, *Life of Jay Gould: How He Made His Fortune;* Hendrick, *The Age of Big Business;* Hunt, *A Dictionary of Rogues;* Jones, *The Life of James Fisk, Jr.;* Josephson, *The Robber Barons;* Klein, *The Life and Times of Jay Gould;* Lane, *Commodore Vanderbilt;* Lewis, *Nation-Famous New York Murders;* Marcuse, *This Was New York!;* Medbery, *Men and Mysteries of Wall Street;* Moody, *The Railroad Builders;* Morgan, *Prince of Crime;* Myers, *History of the Great American Fortunes;* Nash, *Bloodletters and Badmen;* ____, *Hustlers and Con Men;* ____, *Murder Among the Mighty;* Northrop, *The Life and Achievements of Jay Gould;* Peterson, *The Mob;* Poynter, *Forgotten Crimes;* Reppetto, *The Blue Parade;* Seitz, *The Dreadful Decade;* Smith, *Commodore Vanderbilt: An Epic of American Achievement;* Thompson and Raymond, *Gang Rule in New York;* Van Metre, *Economic History of the United States;* Warshow, *Jay Gould: The Story of a Fortune;* White, *The Book of Daniel Drew;* (FILM), *The Toast of New York,* 1937.

Gould, Richard, prom. 1840, Case of, Brit., rob.-mur. A young man in Islington who was out of work decided to solve his financial problems by robbing an old man who lived near by. On the evening that John Templeton had collected rents from his tenants, Gould broke into his house, bound his hands, blindfolded him, and then killed him. For this he got about £6. Templeton's cleaning woman found his body the next morning. The police did not have to search far because Gould's landlady came to them to report that her lodger had stayed out late and had plenty of money to spend the next day.

Unfortunately, a new, over-eager detective arrested Gould and sent him to trial without adequate preparation. The jury, unable to rid themselves of some doubt, acquitted him of the murder. The police decided to arrest Gould, at least for the robbery. In the process of arresting him, another detective got him to tell a story of the robbery that was patently false but contained enough truth for them to obtain the evidence they needed. Gould was found Guilty of robbery and sentenced to be transported for life.

REF.: *CBA;* Cobb, *The First Detectives.*

Gould, William, and **Lyons, William,** prom. 1908, U.S., rob. The sweet trill of canaries led to the apprehension of New York City's Scuttle Gang in 1908. A disreputable junk store in a rough part of town was an unlikely place to hear canaries singing a duet. Officers, knowing that a woman's apartment had recently been robbed of many valuables including two songbirds, investigated and obtained from the storekeeper a description of the man who brought in the birds. The description corresponded perfectly with that of a young, well-known crook. The officers even knew where the youth lived.

In no time, William Gould and his roommate William Lyons were questioned in connection with the apartment robbery and a string of other break-ins around the city. Gould and Lyons confessed and provided the names of four confederates, thus breaking a string of thirty burglaries in two months for which the so-called Scuttle Gang was responsible.

REF.: *CBA;* Livingston, *The Murdered and the Missing.*

Goulter, Sidney Bernard, 1903-28, Brit., mur. Sidney Bernard Goulter, twenty-four, frightened even his own mother, but when Constance Oliver, twenty-one, introduced the young man to her parents in 1927, she described him as "a delightful young man." Then her missing body turned up a few days later, brutally tortured, strangled, and burned.

Detectives were convinced that her burned clothing and scorched skin indicated an attempt by Oliver's assailant to burn the body. This strongly suggested the workings of an irrational mind, and Goulter was the obvious suspect. In December 1927, he stood trial for Oliver's death and after just one day of testimony and less than ten minutes of deliberation, the jury found him Guilty of murder. He was executed early in 1928.

REF.: Browne and Tullett, *The Scalpel of Scotland Yard; CBA;* Townsend, *Black Cap: Murder Will Out.*

Gounares, Demetrios (Gounaris), 1866-1922, Gr., assass. Prime minister from 1915-17, and from 1920-22. During the post-WWI revolution in Greece, he was court-martialed and executed. REF.: *CBA.*

Gourbin, Emile, prom. 1912, Fr., mur. Careless oversight led to the conviction of Emile Gourbin in 1912 for the first-degree murder of his sweetheart. Gourbin went to the trouble of prearranging an alibi, making plans to spend this particular night with friends in a country house playing cards. He set the clock ahead one-and-a-half hours so that at eleven-thirty his friends would go to bed thinking it was 1 a.m. and Gourbin could kill Marie Latelle at her parents' Lyon home several miles away. He planned to murder her by midnight, sneak back to the farmhouse as his friends slept, and use them as corroboration that he was with them at the time his beloved died.

But Gourbin forgot to change the clock back and thus set himself up for conviction of not just murder but the worse crime of premeditated murder. Further, he did not realize that as he strangled Latelle he gathered some pink powder she had dusted on her face and neck under his fingernails.

Detectives analyzed the powder, looked at the time, and Gourbin was found Guilty of first-degree murder.

REF.: *CBA; Dilnot, Great Detectives and Their Methods;* Thorwald, *Crime and Science.*

Gourgues, Dominique de, 1530-93, U.S., vigil. French soldier who exacted revenge for Spanish massacre of French Huguenot settlement at Fort Caroline, Fla., in 1565. He sailed three ships near the mouth of the St. John's River, allied himself with the Indians, and avenged the French victims by hanging their killers from the same trees on which the Huguenots had been hanged. REF.: *CBA.*

Gourier, Pere, prom. 1780s-90s, Fr., mur. Pere Gourier poisoned his victims not with arsenic, but with their own gluttony. In the last two decades of the eighteenth century, this wealthy Frenchman invited his chosen victims to his dinner table and indulged their appetites with rich, heavy foods. Gourier's preferred method was to secure a table at one of the fine Parisian restaurants of the day, such as Tortoni's, Café de Paris, Véjour, or Brébant. The mâitre d'hôtel knew Gourier well, and were anxious to serve him, as he spared no expense to satisfy his guests.

The seven to nine victims Gourier killed over ten years brought about their own demises. Eager to make the most out of the offer of free food, they ate until they dropped. This pattern continued until Gourier finally met his match in Ameline, the first assistant to the public executioner of Paris, Eugène Chavette. Ameline knew about Gourier's murderous dinners, and was anxious to expose him. He allowed himself to become the "victim," but was careful not to fall into the trap. After each sumptuous feast, Ameline would purge his system by taking castor oil and other laxatives. Gourier became obsessed with killing this difficult adversary. He spent a small fortune feeding Ameline the richest dishes to break down his resistance. Ameline showed no ill effects.

The end came at the Cadran bleu, one of the finest restaurants in Paris. After fourteen sections of sirloin beef, Gourier took sick. Unable to match Ameline slice for slice, he fell forward, dead. REF.: *CBA.*

Governor, Jimmy, d.1900, Aus., mur. Jimmy Governor was a mulatto whose flaming red hair and caucasian wife only aggravated a situation that in turn-of-the-century Australia was already bad enough. The couple's acquaintances added fuel to the flame with their jeers and insults aimed predominantly at Governor's wife, Ethel, until one day the sneers reduced the woman to tears and turned her husband into a homicidal maniac. Governor armed himself with a club and empty rifle and together with his aborigine friend, Jacky Underwood, who had armed himself with a club, headed for the house of Governor's boss John Mawbey, whose wife had made recent, unfortunate remarks. There they started killing. In the end, two Mawbey daughters, Helena Kerz, a school teacher staying with the family, and Mawbey's son Percy were dead. Elsie Clarke, a visiting cousin, was wounded.

Governor joined his brother Joe and left Underwood behind to be convicted and hanged. The brothers, with £1,000 on each of their heads, started killing again. Setting out to avenge the pressures of racism, they murdered Alexander McKay, an old farmer, a woman and her son, and 80-year-old Irishman Kerin Fitzpatrick. They outmaneuvered 200 police officers and 2,000 civilian vigilantes, but it was Herbert Byers, Kerz's fiancé, who caught up with the killers after a 200-mile chase. In October 1900, Governor was caught and hanged. His brother had been shot and killed by a settler. REF.: *CBA.*

Govind Singh, 1666-1708, India, assass. Last of ten Sikh apostles who developed military forces to fight the Muhammadans. He was known as *Singh,* "Lion," by his followers. Founded the *Khalsa,* "Pure" faction that battled the Moguls. He was killed by an Afghan in the Deccan. REF.: *CBA.*

Gow, John (John Smith), 1690-1725, Brit., rob.-pir.-mur. Because the father of John Gow's sweetheart would not permit the marriage until Gow, a sailor, was captain of his own ship, Gow, already thirty-five, did everything in his power to attain that rank—including piracy and murder.

With his goal in mind, Gow—under the alias John Smith—in 1724 accepted a tour as second mate and gunner aboard the English chartered *George Galley,* captained by Oliver Ferneau. Once aboard, Gow and another crew member concocted a scheme to wrest control of the ship from Ferneau. But Ferneau discovered it and ousted Gow's partner and two other men from the crew. Gow, however, remained on board, unsuspected. The *George Galley* set sail for Versailles on Aug. 1, and Gow contrived yet a second plan.

On the evening of Nov. 3, as Ferneau stood watch on deck, Gow, James Williams, Daniel McCawley, William Melvin, Peter Rawlisson, James Winter, and John Peterson crept into the berths of the ship's officers and murdered them as they slept. They then killed Ferneau, threw his and the other bodies overboard, imprisoned crew members who opposed them, and renamed the ship the *Revenge.* Gow had now attained his goal—his captainship.

For the next few months, Gow led his crew on a rampage across the high seas, plundering any vessel in their path of sails, ammunition, food, cannon, firearms, and alcohol. During Gow's two-month tenure as captain, the *Revenge* attacked more than seven ships and sank one.

On Dec. 28, after a successful raid on the French chartered *Lewis and Joseph,* Gow allowed a heavily laden merchant ship to pass unharmed because of its superior size and vast armaments. This decision, however, so enraged Gow's lieutenant, James Williams, that he pulled a gun on Gow in an attempt to take control of the *Revenge.* Although Williams was stopped and imprisoned, his mutinous act portended trouble to come. Nine days later, near the coast of Portugal, the *Revenge* plundered the *Triumvirate* and took its crew captive. Gow then repopulated the *Triumvirate* with his French prisoners and Williams, hoping that when the ship reached port, Williams would be hung for piracy. He then set sail for Carison, Scotland, his home and safe haven and the home of his beloved, whom he could finally marry.

Having moored the *Revenge,* Gow and his crew went ashore near Carison. Although Gow went directly to the home of his beloved and received from her father the long-sought-after approval to marry, it was beside the point now. Back on the ship, a prisoner had escaped and was on his way to the authorities. So the *Revenge* set sail, anchoring in nearby Calf Sound to abduct two women and murder their mother, and anchoring again at nearby Calf Point to plunder the nearest village.

Word of the pirates had reached Calf Point by the time of their arrival and they were captured while ashore. When Gow's crew did not return to the ship, he cut the anchor. The *Revenge* floated unchecked, only to run aground nearby. "We are all dead men!" Gow cried, realizing his imminent capture.

Extradited to England to stand trial, Gow and his crew were reunited with Williams, in British custody since his arrival on the *Triumvirate* in Lisbon. On May 25, 1725, the courts sentenced Gow and six of his crew to death for the murder of Ferneau and piracy on the high seas. On June 11, before an indignant crowd, all were executed in Wapping.

REF.: *CBA;* Culpin, *The Newgate Noose;* Gosse, *History of the Pirates.*

Gowdie, Isobel, prom. 1662, Scot., witchcraft. People living in Scotland in 1662 believed in witches. They found witches everywhere. Their preachers were witches; butchers who charged too much for meat were witches. If one's neighbor was too noisy, the neighbor was a witch. But Isobel Gowdier carried her belief to an extreme when she declared on Apr. 13, "I am a witch!"

Much of what people knew of witches they learned from Gowdie. She said she first became a witch in 1647 when she met the devil in an Auldearne church. Here she made a pact, denying Christian baptism and receiving the new name of Janet and the devil's mark on her shoulder. She accepted rebaptism in the blood the devil sucked from her and swore allegiance by placing one hand on her head and the other on the sole of her foot. The ceremony concluded with the devil, like a minister, reading from the pulpit.

Acting in her new capacity Gowdie said she would ride on straw, crying, "Horse and hattock, in the devil's name." From that vantage point she could shoot down any Christian who saw her and did not bless himself. Occasionally, she would turn herself into an animal by repeating a certain charm, or she might shoot elf arrows to injure or kill people.

Today psychiatrists can readily deduce that Gowdie was more insane than a witch. But in 1662 people knew her only as Witch Gowdie. Court records fail to tell her fate but if she was like all other witches of the time, she was certainly executed. REF.: *CBA.*

GPU, prom. 1920s, U.S.S.R., secret pol. The GPU was a name made up from the initials of the Russian words for the State Political Board. The GPU stemmed from the revolutionary secret police established by the Bolsheviks, which was known as the Cheka, 1919-22. It had sweeping powers of arrest and its members were more or less immune to regulations and controls. The GPU was no less feared than the Cheka, but its powers were diminished in that it was limited to political arrests, criminal arrests, and procedures controlled by local police. The techniques of torturing suspects, intimidating witnesses, and murdering those the Lenin and Stalin regimes wanted out of the way, were fully exercised by this dreaded organization. The GPU was later organized as the OGPU, which, in turn, gave way to the NKVD and the MVD. See: **MVD; NKVD; OGPU; Okhrana.**

REF.: Bornstein, *The Politics of Murder; CBA;* Dewar, *Assassins at Large;* Hurwood, *Society and the Assassins.*

Graber, Roland H., and **Aust, Hans Georg,** prom. 1969, U.S., fraud. Ask Graber and Aust about their summer vacation in 1969. They had big plans for trips to Mexico and Hawaii, but ended up in prison on a conviction for fraud instead.

Roland Graber, an unemployed cookie salesman, and Hans Aust, a self-employed pollster, left their homeland of West Germany for the U.S. where they thought they could become successful. America took them in but before long spit them both out.

What Graber and Aust decided to be were swindlers in the vacation business. At the beginning of 1969 they pooled their resources and placed a half-page ad in *TV Guide* on behalf of DeLuxe Vacationer Co., through which they offered 2,000 prizes to readers who answered four questions about their traveling preferences. The first prize would be a two-week, all-expenses-paid trip for two to Acapulco and the second a voyage to Hawaii.

The two men hired printers to make winners' certificates, but instead of making one of each, they made 28,000 for Mexico and 42,000 for Hawaii, leaning toward the believable when they included on the notice, "Tips and beverages not included," but slumped back again toward the far-fetched when they printed, "Note: According to regulations, a $25 registration deposit to secure your winner prize is required within ten days."

Graber and Aust failed to get the overwhelming response they had calculated. Seventy thousand winning certificates were ready to be mailed, but only 57,000 people answered the ad. Fewer than

that could believe what the Germans were trying to pull off. Why pay $25, or anything at all, for a free prize? And why, if there were only two winners, should the letter of notification be printed? Phones lit up all over the U.S. and Canada. The national headquarters of the Better Business Bureau heard from five hundred confused winners. Countless other calls were made to postal inspectors, police departments, district attorneys, chambers of commerce, newspapers, radio and television stations and, of course, *TV Guide.* The three most telltale calls, however, were made to postal inspector Charles J. Lerable. Each of the three callers announced proudly that he was one of two grand prize winners to win a trip to Hawaii.

Lerable and fellow inspector Maurice P. Jones took no time in tracking down vacation hosts Graber and Aust. When neither man could explain where the $22.8 million needed to send 57,000 people on free holidays was coming from, they were arrested.

On June 4, Aust and Graber were indicted on fifty-nine counts of mail fraud and one of fraud by wire. (While being questioned, the suspects answered a call from a "winner" who wanted to know how soon he could embark.) On June 30, the two swindlers pleaded guilty without a trial and on Aug. 11 they were sentenced.

Because they had been unable to post bail, each had already spent three months in prison. Graber was given an eighteen-month suspended sentence and promptly deported. Aust, the brains behind the scheme, was given a two-year jail sentence which he stretched out an additional three months by attempting to escape, before deportation. Ironically, the scheme that was supposed to bring in millions ended up costing Graber and Aust, in addition to the jail terms, $25,000, proving that for them crime did not pay.

REF.: *CBA;* Kahn, *Fraud.*

Grabowski, Klaus, c.1946-1981, Ger., mur. The mother of a 7-year-old murder victim shot and killed the accused man in front of judge and jury after he testified that he killed the girl only after she tried to blackmail him. Klaus Grabowski, thirty-four, had a long history of molesting young girls. His early offenses involved removing children's underclothes and tickling their genitals. When his infractions escalated to choking a girl until she passed out and then sending her home in tears, Grabowski was voluntarily castrated.

Even so, his interest in young females did not diminish, and a girlfriend of his would later testify that he had been taking hormone injections and was virile. On the morning of May 5, 1980, Marie Anne Bachmeier went to work, leaving her 7-year-old, Anna Bachmeier, at home to play. The girl ventured outside and never returned. Neighbors later testified that they had seen a man fitting Grabowski's description coaxing her into his house. He later confessed that he strangled Anna with her tights and buried her body at the east end of town. In his defense, however, he insisted he had no sexual feelings for the child and had only resorted to murder when she demanded money.

The first person to rise at the hearing the following day was mother Bachmeier. She stood up, crossed the courtroom and emptied a 5.6-mm Beretta pistol into Grabowski, killing him instantly.

A defense fund for Bachmeier reached thousands of pounds when details of her life became well-known. The daughter of a former Nazi SS officer, born in a refugee camp near Hanover, she was sexually assaulted at age nine by a man who gave her money and sweets. At sixteen, her parents disowned her for being pregnant. At eighteen, while pregnant again by a different man, she was raped. When Anna was born she swore never to give her up. The father, a local restaurant owner, persuaded her to marry his Pakistani chef so the man would not be deported.

The defense fund dried up, however, when women in prison with Bachmeier described her as arrogant and haughty and said she enjoyed playing the role of a sorrowing mother and that she had not genuinely cared for Anna. In March 1982, Bachmeier was sentenced to six years for manslaughter but was free on bail pending appeal.

REF.: *CBA;* Wilson, *Encyclopedia of Murder.*

Gracchus, Tiberius Sempronius, 163-133 B.C., and **Gracchus, Gaius Sempronius,** 153-121 B.C., Roman., assass. Brothers Tiberius and Gaius Gracchus came from an illustrious Roman family and they were wealthy but liberal young statesmen. They idealistically sponsored reform bills that would restore the small independent farming class in the new Republic, and restrict land purchases by the wealthy class, policies that angered the powerful elitists of the realm. Tiberius, a tribune, attempted re-election to his post, but was assassinated in a riot in 133 B.C., a mob action that was reportedly planned by powerful senators who wanted the Gracchus brothers out of the way. Tiberius and some of his supporters were attacked by a mob near the temple of Capitoline Jupiter. A number of senators and their hired killers then drew up their togas about their heads to hide their identities, Nasica in the lead, and pushed their way through the mob to club to death Tiberius and several of his supporters. The bodies were then dragged to the Tiber River and thrown into the waters.

Gaius Sepronius Gracchus emulated his brother and was marked for death by the same senators who had arranged the death of Tiberius. Gaius also attempted to effect reforms, but riots broke out in response to his public addresses. The riots were actually staged by Gaius' ene- mies in the senate, but the riots were then attributed to Gaius. He was branded an outlaw and chased through the streets of Rome and slain just after he crossed the Tiber.

Plutarch estimated that more than 3,000 persons were killed in the blood purge of Gracchus' followers. Gaius Gracchus' assassins were led by Opimius who served as consul for a year and was then given a mock trial for causing the death of Roman citizens without due process. He was

Tiberius Gracchus, assassinated in 133 B.C.

acquitted by the very men who sponsored his murderous actions. The assassinations of the Gracchus brothers were the first such political murders in the history of the young Roman republic.

REF.: Boren, *The Gracchi; CBA;* Earl, *Tiberius Gracchus: A Study in Politics;* Hurwood, *Society and the Assassins;* Johnson, *Famous Assassinations of History;* Lintott, *Violence in Republican Rome;* Plutarch, *Lives.*

Grace, Frank "Parky", c.1945- , U.S., (wrong. convict.) mur. They could give him his freedom but they can never return the eleven years Frank Grace spent in prison, convicted of a crime by a police frame-up. In 1974, Grace, a black, was found guilty by an all-white jury of the 1972 Boston murder of 19-year-old Providence, R.I., drug addict Marvin Morgan. Grace's conviction was based largely on testimony provided by Eric Baker and Jasper Lassiter, who said they saw Grace shoot Morgan. The named Grace's younger brother, Ross Grace, as an accomplice.

In 1983, information presented in an evidentiary hearing by the New England American Friends Service Committee showed that Grace, a former Black Panther and political activist, had been targeted by the New Bedford police as a troublemaker. He had been arrested more than twelve times but never convicted.

In 1984, eleven years after Grace's incarceration, Lassiter signed an affidavit saying Ross Grace alone had killed Morgan and that he saw Frank Grace for the first time at his trial. He admitted that police officers told him Frank would be sitting next to Ross in the courtroom and that he should testify that Frank fired the fatal shot. Ross Grace later confessed.

Finally, in 1985, Frank Grace was freed. REF.: *CBA.*

Grady, John, prom. 1866, U.S., rob. The convicted thieves knew what they had wanted to do, knock over the Adams Express Company train car they knew carried safes filled with currency. John Grady had observed the Adams messengers and determined that one was careless. When he was assigned to a run that carried a big haul on Saturday evening, Jan. 6, 1866, the crooks would wait until the safes were put on the train and three of them, covered by the noise of the train, would pry off the lock of the car with a crowbar and spike and hide in the train. The rest of the gang would wait crouched in bushes nearby.

The next step in their plan was to pull the signal cord and as soon as the train came to a stop they would push the car door open and hand the safes out to the gang waiting below. Unfortunately, the signal cord in the express car was encased in an iron tube and could not be touched. The men in the car were forced to pry open the safes, as planned, fill two suitcases with the loot, and then jump out at the set point. They then hid their money and unsuccessfully attempted to rent a buggy.

The men returned to retrieve the money but something happened they hadn't anticipated. New York City investigators were already on their trail. By talking to people along the train's route, they were able to track down Grady and an accomplice named Tristam. They raided the apartment Tristam hid out in and discovered $113,762 of the money still in Adams Express bags. Tristam had no other option but to confess. Misery loves company, so he implicated the other gang members, including Grady.

REF.: *CBA;* Horan, *The Pinkertons.*

Grady, John Francis, 1929- , U.S., jur. Chairman of criminal division of the U.S. Attorneys Office from 1956-61. He was nominated to the northern district court of Illinois by President Gerald R. Ford in 1975. REF.: *CBA.*

Grady Gang, prom. 1860s, U.S., org. crime. During the 1860s, John D. "Traveling Mike" Grady operated as a criminal fence in and around lower Broadway's Thieves' Exchange in New York City. Nightly, he would purchase up to $10,000 worth of contraband from the city's active criminals. But soon Grady organized his own gang, which included "Billy the Kid" Burke, who at age twenty-five had been arrested one hundred times. Other luminaries were Boston Pet Anderson, Hod Ennis, Eddie Pettengill, and Jake Rand. They realized their greatest score in March 1866, when they distracted wealthy financier Rufus L. Lord with an elaborate hoax and stole close to $2 million in cash and certificates from an opened vault. Most of the gang retired, but Traveling Mike continued his villainous ways. His rival fence, Marm Mandelbaum, had formed a gang of salaried thieves. Grady simply purchased the stolen goods from her staff at cut rate prices, and quickly eliminated her as a competitor.

REF.: Asbury, *The Gangs of New York; CBA.*

Graham, Adam, d.1747, Brit., mur. In 1747, Graham beat to death Christopher Holliday on Beck Moor in England. For this, he was executed at Carlisle and his body hanged in chains upon a twelve-yard-high gibbet, with 12,000 nails driven into it to prevent it from being cut down or carried away.

REF.: *CBA;* Laurence, *A History of Capital Punishment.*

Graham, Barbara (Barbara Elaine Wood), 1923-55, U.S., pros.-mur. Barbara Graham was born in 1923 in Oakland, Calif. When she was two, her mother, Hortense, was sent to a reformatory as a "wayward girl." As a result, Barbara was raised by neighbors and received only a superficial education. As a teenager, she was picked up for vagrancy and sent to the same reformatory where her mother had spent time. Barbara was released in 1939.

Graham enrolled in a business college to study for an office job. She also married and had a child. However, by 1941, she was divorced and traveled aimlessly around California for the next few years. Arrested twice in San Diego for vagrancy and "aggravated lewd and disorderly conduct," she served two months in jail before going to San Francisco, where she was arrested for prostitution in 1944. Also in San Francisco, she married a second time, but the marriage lasted only a few months. By 1946, Graham associated solely with criminals, many of whom had ties to organized crime.

For a time, Graham worked as a cocktail waitress in Chicago, but she moved back to San Francisco in 1947 to work as a call girl for the infamous madam, Sally Stanford. After an incident in which she perjured herself to defend small-time criminals Marck C. Monroe and Thomas M. Sittler, Graham tried again to straighten out her life. She became a nurses' aide in a hospital in Tonopah, Nev., in 1948, and married for the third time. She soon left her husband and moved to Seattle where, in 1951, she met and married Henry Graham. She stayed with Graham until 1953 and gave birth to her third child.

Henry Graham introduced Barbara to drugs and to a crook named Emmett Perkins. Graham left her husband and went to Los Angeles with Perkins, who introduced her to three other criminals, Baster Shorter, John L. True, and Jack Santos, members of a vicious robbers' gang.

On Mar. 9, 1953, Graham and the four men tried to enter the Burbank home of an elderly widow, Mrs. Monohan, who they believed had large amounts of expensive jewelry. Graham led the way and, when the elderly woman resisted, beat her with the butt end of her pistol. In the attack, the woman's skull was cracked and she died.

Condemned killer Barbara Graham.

Graham was arrested and brought to trial. Despite John True's testimony that she had committed the murder, Graham insisted that she was innocent. The prosecution finally planted in her cell a police officer posing as a mob figure, who offered to provide Graham with an alibi for $25,000. Graham accepted his terms and the prosecution made the deal public, forcing Graham to admit her guilt. She was convicted and sentenced to die in the gas chamber at San Quentin. After a number of appeals failed, Graham was executed at San Quentin on June 3, 1955.

REF.: *CBA;* Davis, and Hirschberg, *Assignment San Quentin;* deFord, *Murderers Sane and Mad;* Godwin, *Murder U.S.A.;* McComas, *The Graveside Companion;* Nash, *Bloodletters and Badmen;* ____, *Look For the Woman;* (FILM), *I Want to Live!,* 1958.

Graham, Dayton, prom. 1901, U.S., west. lawman. In 1901, Dayton Graham, a law officer from Bisbee, Ariz., became a sergeant in the Arizona Rangers. Within a few months, he was involved in a shoot-out with fugitive outlaw Bill Smith in the town of Douglas. Graham, accompanied by Tom Vaughn, a Douglas sheriff, was answering a complaint by a local merchant. Smith shot Graham in the chest and arm and wounded Vaughn in the neck. Graham appeared to be mortally wounded and his family gathered at his bedside, but he miraculously recovered and vowed to avenge his shooting. He began searching southern Arizona, and one day in 1902, found Smith at a card table in a saloon. This time Graham fired first, and Smith died from two shots to the stomach and one to the head. See: **Arizona Rangers.** REF.: *CBA.*

Graham, Eric Stanley George, d.1941, New Zealand, mur. Eric Graham tried repeatedly and unsuccessfully to breed pedigree Ayrshire cattle on his Koiterangi farm. Each time he failed, he grew increasingly angry and lost more money. He began arguing with neighbors, blaming them for his troubles. The neighbors finally lost their patience, when, on Oct. 7, 1941, Graham threatened one with his rifle. Police were called, and when they arrived Graham gunned down three and mortally wounded a fourth. Hearing this, two more men approached and Graham responded once again with his rifle, killing one of the men. He then ran off into the bush, later returning home to find Home Guardsmen there.

Upon returning to the scene of the crime, Graham killed two

guards and ran off. On Oct. 20, police finally found Graham in a remote farm building and fatally shot him. At the inquest for the six victims, the coroner commended the policeman who had shot Graham, stating he had "removed a great danger before there had been any further loss of life."

REF.: *CBA;* Goodwin, *Killers in Paradise;* Kelly, *The Gun in the Case.*

Graham, George E., prom. 1885, U.S., mur. George Graham had for some time been threatening to get rid of his wife Sarah so that when she disappeared on Sept. 30, 1885, the residents of Springfield, Mo., immediately suspected Graham of having murdered the woman. A large group of citizens went to Graham's farm. Graham calmly invited the mob to search the farm, which was his undoing. The well was inspected and the body of Sarah Graham was found at the bottom. Before Graham could stand trial, he was seized by a mob and lynched.

REF.: *CBA; The Graham Tragedy.*

Graham, Harrison (AKA: **Marty**), 1959- , U.S., mur. In 1987, "Marty" Graham, a 28-year-old self-employed handyman, was closest to Cookie Monster, a furry blue hand puppet. Graham and his best friend and confidant, Cookie Monster, strolled together through the North Philadelphia neighborhood where Graham lived in a $90-a-month apartment.

Although his best friend was a puppet, Graham did not lack girlfriends. However, the women he entertained in his apartment did find him and his surroundings odd. In particular, they questioned the odor coming from the back room behind a door which was nailed shut. When asked, Graham explained that the smell came from a bucket he had used as a toilet and kept in that room. If they knew what was best, he would add, they would not ask any more questions because the back room was "too much for them to handle." His visitors stopped asking questions, conceding that what they already knew of Graham and his relationship with Cookie Monster was enough.

In August 1987, Graham was evicted from his apartment after neighbors complained about the foul smell coming from his unit, and the woman living directly below found what looked like blood dripping down her wall. On Aug. 9 and 10, police found six human bodies decomposing in the back room, either stacked in a corner or covered by dirty mattresses and garbage. Part of a seventh body was found in a closet.

After police searched for him for a week, Graham turned himself in at his mother's urging. At first he told police that the bodies had been in the room when he rented it, but on Aug. 17, 1987, he confessed. He had strangled the women during intercourse, under the influence of drugs and alcohol.

Joel Moldovsky, Graham's court-appointed attorney, maintaining that the defendant was "incompetent, illiterate, and incoherent," recommended that he be confined to a mental-health care facility until he was fit to stand trial. A panel of psychiatrists disagreed, however, and a trial date was set for the spring of 1988. Graham and his attorney waived a jury trial, and on May 3, 1988, after a seven-week session, Judge Robert A. Latrone found Graham Guilty of seven counts of first-degree murder and sentenced him to one life sentence without the chance of parole and six death sentences—a lenient sentence, given that Graham could not be executed unless his life sentence was commuted.

Graham is now serving his life sentence for the murders of 30-year-old Robin DeShazor, 36-year-old Mary Mathis, 33-year-old Sandra Garvin, 22-year-old Barbara Mahoney, 26-year-old Valerie Jamison, 24-year-old Patricia Franklin, and 26-year-old Cynthia Brooks. REF.: *CBA.*

Graham, James (Fifth Earl of Montrose), 1612-1650, Scot., consp. Co-wrote 1638 covenant opposing episcopacy. In 1960, he was arrested for conspiring against Argyll when he commanded the Covenant forces at River Tyne. He was named First Marquis of Montrose at the start of the British Civil War in 1644, and appointed lieutenant general of the Scottish army. He built-up Irish and Scottish troops and won important battles between 1644-45, but eventually was defeated at Philiphaugh in 1645, by David Leslie. When he brought his troops to Orkney Islands in 1650, after a four-year exile, he was captured and hanged. REF.: *CBA*.

Graham, James, 1745-94, Brit., fraud. James Graham was a doctor in Philadelphia when he became acquainted with the new phenomenon of electricity. His treatment of any ills by immersing patients in a bath and subjecting them to mild electrical shock became the fashion, first in Philadelphia, then in London. In 1779, he expanded his business into The Temple of Health, which featured various ways to use electricity on the body, lectures by Graham, and demonstrations by 16-year-old Emma Lyons, who was called Vestina.

The following year he moved his quarters into a mansion in Adelphi Terrace called The Temple of Health and Hymen, at which Graham promised to cure nervous and sexual disorders. The main attraction at the Temple was the justly famed "Celestial Bed," a huge canopied couch that played music, gave off exotic scents, and tilted as required to guarantee conception—the main reason Graham was able to charge £50 for a night's use.

James Graham, notorious quack, holding a "health meeting" in London, 1779.

The following year Graham moved his Temple to Pall Mall, but its appeal was broken as it became less exclusive. In addition, the authorities began to view the place as more brothel than hospital. In 1783, he closed up shop and returned to his native Scotland. His mental instability led him to believe that permanent fasting was the only way to health. He died of starvation at age forty-nine. Vestina, however, eventually became Lady Emma Hamilton, mistress to Lord Nelson. REF.: *CBA*.

Graham, James, d.1814, U.S., mur. James Graham was traveling near Delhi, Del., on the night of July 14, 1813, with Hugh Cameron and Alexander M'Gillavrae. The three men were drinking as they ambled along and suddenly they began arguing. The bodies of Cameron and M'Gillavrae were found the next day. The two had been beaten to death and since Graham was known to have been with them, he was promptly arrested and charged with the murders. He was tried, found Guilty, and hanged. REF.: *CBA;* Clark, *Trial of James Graham*.

Graham, John (Graham of Claverhouse, First Viscount Dundee; AKA: Bloody Claverse, Bonny Dundee), 1648-89, Scot., law enfor. off. Jacobite and Scottish royalist who joined William of Orange's horse guards in 1672. He was commissioned by the Marquis of Montrose to battle the pro-Episcopal Covenanters from 1677-79, executing John Brown in Wigtown and defeating the Covenanters at Bothwell bridge in 1679. He was appointed sheriff of Wigtown in 1682, and major general in 1686. He commanded Scottish forces in 1688, as they moved to quell the revolution. He was killed in the battle in Killiecrankie. See:

Brown, John. REF.: *CBA*.

Graham, John, prom. 1800s, Brit., (wrong. convict.) mur. John Graham beat his daughter Susan mercilessly, as evident from the wails that could be heard from behind their farmhouse walls and from the deep brown scars that marked her young body. Neighbors in the English town of Cobham dreaded the day when Graham would kill the innocent child. Driven by their dread, it was they, not he, who committed murder.

Until the death of his wife Mary, Graham had been a good father and husband. After his loss he became vicious, seeming to resent his daughter's very existence. The police were sent to the troubled Graham home more than once to confront him for abusing his child, so when several days had passed and no one had seen Susan neighbors assumed the worst, that Graham had finally murdered her.

Once arrested, a pale and frightened Graham gave a different explanation, saying his daughter had run away the day before. With Graham in prison awaiting trial for murder, searchers turned his home inside out looking for a body or other evidence of foul play. They found nothing and Graham again claimed his innocence. A merciful judge granted him three months of freedom to find his daughter and prove his innocence.

Graham set off, but when he couldn't find Susan, he spent some of his borrowed time tracking down a Susan look-alike. In three months he returned with the girl, confident of acquittal. But one detail-oriented woman sitting under the witness box noticed that this "Susan Graham" lacked the scars of abuse the original had carried. She arose and declared, "She's no more Susan Graham than I am." The terrified girl then admitted being an impostor and Graham, still saying he was not guilty of murder, admitted he had bribed the girl into testifying. The judge and jury, convinced that the bribe meant "guilty," convicted Graham of murder and sentenced him to death. Graham was hanged and buried in a grave in the prison precincts.

Then a very much alive Susan Graham showed up. Mrs. Carter saw her first. Taking her by the wrist she brought the girl to the town inn, presented her to the shocked customers, and said, "They hanged an innocent man when they executed her father."
REF.: *CBA;* Ellis, *Black Fame*.

Graham, John Gilbert (Jack), 1932-57, U.S., embez.-forg.-bomb.-mur. John Gilbert Graham, called Jack by family and friends, was a clean-cut young man—tall, well-mannered, his hair cropped close to his head. A stranger might guess that he had played center for the local high school basketball team; his politeness and quiet voice suggested years as a Boy Scout. He would be the kid down the block selling cool drinks at a cardboard stand outside his house in the summer, the boy next door who shoveled the walk in winter, cut the grass in spring. But he was none of these things, as his neighbors in Denver, Colo., would slowly discover, along with the FBI. He was a killer, moreover a mass murderer who plotted not only the death of an overindulgent mother but would be responsible for the first in-flight plane bombing in U.S. history.

Mrs. Daisie King, Jack's mother, doted on her only son. She had led a roller-coaster life, marrying in and out of poverty three times. Her second marriage produced her only child, Jack, who was born in Denver in 1932. When Jack was five, his father, William Graham, died, and Daisie Graham was left without a dime, forced to place her son in an orphanage. In 1943, Daisie met and married a wealthy Colorado rancher, John Earl King, and she immediately recovered her son, bringing him to an upper-middle-class home where comfort and convenience replaced spartan discipline.

Yet the disparity of the two lifestyles young Jack had lived seemingly affected him little. He was bright, some said highly imaginative; he was an above-average student through his first year of high school. Then, at sixteen, he ran away to join the Coast Guard, lying about his age. Graham served only nine months, being AWOL for sixty-three days which caused his detention.

Officers learned that he was underage and dismissed him from the service. His mother took him back into her home and, when he said he did not want to complete school, nodded patient understanding.

Jack Graham went to work, taking odd jobs. To his neighbors he appeared the same easygoing boy, but close friends noticed that he would become restless when talking about his mother and then sink into brooding silence. Mrs. King urged her son to return to school so that he could qualify for a white-collar job. By 1951, Graham had accumulated enough night school credits to earn himself a job as a payroll clerk for a Denver manufacturer.

John Gilbert Graham, who murdered his mother and went to the gas chamber.

Graham's tastes were rich; he wanted fast, new cars and a handsome wardrobe. He insisted upon taking his girlfriends to better restaurants. He could afford little of this lifestyle on his $200-a-month salary, so Jack Graham did what had become a habit at home—he merely helped himself, in this case forging the name of his company's vice-president to checks he had stolen from his firm and cashing these to collect $4,200. He bought a fast convertible and drove away from Denver to see the sights. For several months, Graham went on a minor crime spree, but when he took up bootlegging in Texas, the Rangers and other lawmen closed in on him. Outside of Lubbock, police set up a roadblock on a tip that a young bootlegger would be taking a certain route, his car loaded with moonshine. Graham approached the barrier at high speed, ignoring police warnings to stop. When he drove through the roadblock, officers riddled his beautiful new convertible, which Graham crashed into a house. Miraculously he was uninjured when taken into custody.

After serving sixty days in the county jail, Graham was turned over to Denver officials who intended to prosecute him for forgery. But Daisie Graham King wouldn't hear of it. She couldn't bear to see Jack behind bars and begged authorities to be lenient toward her errant son, a good boy really, who had made

a mistake for which he was sorry. Mrs. King offered her son's former employer $2,500, saying that Jack would work off the balance of the stolen $4,200. Authorities agreed, placing the apprentice forger on probation. For a time, it seemed as if Mrs. King's unswerving belief in her son was vindicated. Graham did get a job and did make regular payments to the firm he had looted.

In 1953, Graham married Gloria Elson in Denver and settled down, working hard as a mechanic, righting his wrong. Like many another citizen, Jack Graham had his "brush with the law" and had been spared prison. It appeared that, like any other citizen having made one mistake, he was on his way to becoming a respected member of his community. His friends found him hardworking, conscientious, and a faithful husband. His relatives marvelled at the consideration and affection he showered upon his mother, especially after her third husband died in 1954.

Following King's death (he had been a successful rancher), a large sum of money was left to Mrs. Daisie Graham King. Thrice widowed, Mrs. King turned to her son for consolation and, to occupy her time, a business partnership. She invested $35,000 of her husband's money in a drive-in restaurant in West Denver; Jack became her partner, managing the restaurant. Graham labored to make the restaurant a success, and he continued working nights at a Hertz Drive-Ur-Self garage to further reduce the money owed against his forgery theft, until the balance remaining was no more than $106. He had learned his lesson, his mother was fond of saying; Jack was a good boy, a solid citizen.

Then, on Nov. 1, 1955, an ear-shattering event took place that would slowly strip away that upstanding image of John Gilbert Graham, penitent lawbreaker, hardworking married man, and dutiful son. At 7:03 p.m. on that day, United Airlines flight number 629, only eleven minutes from Denver's Stapleton Airport and en route to Portland, Ore., with forty-four passengers and crew members aboard, passed directly over a Colorado beet farm near Longmont. The farmer stood near his barn, looked up, and saw a terrific explosion that sent to earth the shattered remains of the silver plane, burning wreckage that littered his fields and sent him scampering for help when help was useless.

Within an hour, nearby citizens and National Guardsmen arrived to recover the mutilated bodies. These were taken to the National Guard Armory at Greeley, Colo. Responding to one of the worst air disasters in American aviation, the FBI routinely offered the aid of its Identification Division in an effort to help authorities pinpoint the identities of the victims. Two of the Bureau's fingerprint experts arrived in Greeley the following day. Of the forty-four aboard Flight 629, including one infant and five crew members, nine had already been identified by grieving relatives and friends; the FBI experts fingerprinted the remaining thirty-five bodies, or what was left of the bodies, and twenty-one of these were identified from prints which were in the Bureau's files. The reason why so many sets of prints were on file was explained by FBI officials: a Canadian couple had had their fingerprints taken in 1954 when applying for citizenship, another for personal identification, and many had been government workers during WWII, holding jobs requiring fingerprinting.

FBI experts also joined with investigators from United Airlines, the Douglas Aircraft Company, and the Civil Aeronautics Board to help in determining the cause of the crash. Mechanical failure and human error were high on the priority of probabilities; sabotage was an almost unthinkable possibility. At the same time, other investigators looked into the unthinkable by examining the backgrounds of every passenger and crew member. They were shocked to learn that a staggering $752,000 in flight insurance had been taken out by eighteen of the passengers, almost as if these travelers had had a collective premonition of disaster, making Flight 629 one of the most heavily insured flights in the history of commercial aviation up to that time. The policies were put through the checking mill.

Other experts collected the jagged pieces of the plane, from tail to nose, which, when falling from the fireball to earth had spread over a mile-and-a-half of cropland. The pieces were carefully moved to a Denver hangar and pieced together meticulously, until the ill-fated DC-6B's fuselage was completely reassembled except for a section near the tail from Number 4 Cargo Pit. Not a fragment remained of this section of the plane. The metal shell of the fuselage surrounding the area that had once been Number 4 Cargo Pit, engineers discovered, was bent outward in jagged pieces. This could only mean that a force more powerful than any crash had torn out that part of the plane. Moreover, bits of steel from the fuselage had been driven through the soles of some of the shoes worn by passengers sitting near the cargo section of the plane. Even the brass fittings of one suitcase had been driven through a stainless steel container known to have been in the hold. An explosion had occurred in the cargo hold and, since no gas lines or tanks were located near this section, experts concluded that *something* in the hold had exploded by accident, perhaps an illegal dynamite shipment or—and this was the last possibility any of the experts wanted to include—someone had deliberately sabotaged the plane, planting some sort of bomb on board.

The tragedy of Flight 629 was quickly known to many of those who had friends and relatives on board. One of them was John Gilbert Graham, whose mother, Mrs. Daisie Graham King, had been en route to Portland, then Seattle, and finally to Alaska, to visit her daughter. Graham and his wife Gloria, accompanied by their 2-year-old son, Allen, had driven Mrs. King to Stapleton Airport and walked her to the gate, kissing her goodbye. After Mrs. King boarded, the Grahams went to a nearby coffee shop to have a snack. Jack got sick, rushed to the rest room, and threw up. When he returned he told his wife: "It must be this airport food." As they were leaving the airport, they heard rumors that a plane had crashed. When they returned home, Jack turned on the radio to listen for news about the supposed air crash. Said his wife later: "We finally heard his mother's name on the radio and Jack just collapsed completely."

Graham appeared to be in shock for days after learning of his mother's death. Said one neighbor: "He was really broken up about it—they were very close." While Graham was recovering from the loss of his mother, FBI lab technicians were sifting through the smallest remains of the crash found in the sections of the plane and at the crash site. One technician finally emptied the contents of an envelope onto the desk of Roy Moore, assistant special agent in charge in the Denver FBI office, saying: "These fragments were found among the wreckage but they are the only pieces of debris that we have been unable to identify in any way with parts of the airplane or with known contents of the cargo." Before Agent Moore were five tiny pieces of sheet metal. The technician went on to say that the pieces of metal contained foreign deposits of white and dark-gray colors which consisted mainly of sodium carbonate and traces of nitrate and sulphur compounds. That added up to dynamite, and that meant a bomb had been placed in the luggage of one of the passengers on Flight 629; the cargo hold carried nothing that day but passengers' luggage.

The tedious job of checking every piece of luggage carried by the forty-four persons on board the flight began. The only person for whom no luggage, except tiny fragments, could be found was Mrs. Daisie King. Airport authorities then informed the FBI that Mrs. King had taken out $62,500 in flight insurance—very heavy for those days and far in excess of the amounts taken out by other passengers. The beneficiary was her son, Jack. Although Mrs. King's luggage had vanished in the explosion, the handbag she carried was found intact, and inside, tucked into a small purse, yellowed and folded into a wad, was a newspaper clipping which Mrs. King had been careful to keep with her. The clipping reported her son's forgery of stolen checks and his subsequent arrest. Why a mother so devoted to her son would carry about such an item, as one might carry about a keepsake, remains imponderable. Perhaps, some later theorized, she kept the clipping as a reminder of what her son was capable of doing, or,

it was also later said, she kept the clipping *to remind him* of his errant ways. No one ever knew for sure, but it was this very clipping—which Mrs. King may have wanted authorities to find should she ever meet with foul play—that led FBI agents to the door of Jack Gilbert Graham.

Before interviewing Graham, agents learned that he was not the penitent wrongdoer attempting to set things right. He and his mother had been arguing constantly about Jack's management of the drive-in restaurant, particularly about a strange fire from an even stranger gas explosion that had caused more than $1,200 in damages. The explosion had occurred only a few months before Flight 629 exploded in the clear skies of Colorado. Graham had tried to collect insurance on the restaurant after the fire but had failed. Insurance must have been much on Graham's mind, agents thought, when they discovered that on another recent occasion, the 23-year-old had apparently stalled his pick-up truck in front of a speeding railroad train to collect insurance. Then a neighbor told agents that Jack had boasted of his demolition work while serving in the Coast Guard.

On Nov. 10, 1955, agents went to the home of John Gilbert Graham. Jack was cordial, offering the agents coffee and telling them the story of his life, detailing his days in the orphanage, his mother's three marriages, even his forgery of stolen checks, being careful to point out that he had just about made complete restitution. He told them that his mother was going to Alaska to visit his half sister and hunt caribou. He added that she was carrying in her luggage a large amount of shotgun shells and other ammunition for hunting purposes. The agents nodded, already knowing that Mrs. King was an outdoorswoman, a woman who loved to fish and hunt.

Then one of the agents inquired: "Exactly what did she have in her luggage and did you help her pack it?"

"I can describe her luggage," replied Graham in an even voice, "but I can't tell you what was in it. Mother would never allow anyone to help her pack. She always insisted upon doing it herself."

Jack's wife, Gloria, stepped forward to support her husband's statements, saying that Mrs. King, who had recently been living with them, was always particular about her things. Jack excused himself, telling the agents he was going to make some more coffee. Gloria Graham then remembered a small item about Mrs. King's luggage: "Just before Mrs. King left for the airport Jack gave her a present, or, I presume he did."

Graham's mother, Mrs. Daisie King.

"A present?" asked one of the agents. "What kind of present?"

"Oh, I think it was a small set of tools, like drills and files. My mother-in-law used these things to make art gifts out of sea shells. Jack had talked of buying her a set for Christmas. On the day she was to leave, he came home with a package and took it to the basement where his mother was packing. I just assumed that this contained the tool set and that he gave it to her to take along."

When the agents left the house, they immediately interviewed Graham's next-door neighbors. One woman stated that she remembered the gift Jack had bought for his mother, that "he had wrapped it in Christmas paper and I was told that he put it in his mother's luggage before he left."

"What else were you told?" asked an agent.

"Nothing important...only someone told me later that Jack became suddenly ill only a short time after the plane had taken off, and was very pale. I remember also having been told that when the Grahams were informed of the crash, Jack remarked: 'That's it.' I guess he was too stunned to know what he was talking about. It was really a great blow to him...Why, the poor fellow has been unable to eat or sleep since. All he does is walk up and down the house."

On Nov. 16, agents called the Grahams and asked them to come to headquarters to identify, if possible, some fragments of luggage which might have belonged to Mrs. King. Both appeared on time and agreed that, yes, the pieces looked like parts from a small suitcase Mrs. King had taken with her. Agents then asked Graham to stay behind for some more routine questions, while sending his wife home.

The young man stretched out his six-foot-one-inch, 190-pound frame in an office chair and smilingly agreed to answer any questions. Agent Moore conducted the interrogation, beginning slowly, detailing all the facts the agents had gathered, then stating that Jack's wife had told them about the Christmas gift he had slipped into his mother's suitcase, a package approximately eighteen inches long, fourteen inches wide, and three inches deep, as described by Gloria Graham.

Graham's attitude was cool and cooperative. Calmly, and with a smile, he replied: "Oh, you've got your facts all mixed up. I had intended buying her a tool set but I couldn't find the right kind so I didn't buy any."

"But your wife told us you did and that you brought it home with you."

"She's wrong about that. I'd been talking a lot about the tools and I guess she just supposed I bought them. That's reasonable, isn't it?"

Moore did not respond but asked about Graham's conduct at the airport restaurant. "You did get sick, didn't you, Jack?"

"We had a snack to eat out there," he responded quickly, "but the food was miserable and it turned my stomach."

Then Moore took the hard line, saying: "I want you to know that you have certain rights. The door there is open. You can walk out any time you wish. There is a telephone. You can call your wife or an attorney if you wish. You don't have to tell us anything—and if you do, it can be used in a court of law. There will be no threats and no promises made while we talk with you." Moore stared at John Gilbert Graham for some moments, then said firmly to the smiling young man: "Jack, we have gone over what you told us. You blew up that plane to kill your mother, didn't you?"

"No, I didn't," Graham answered in a calm voice.

"Then you don't mind making any statements?"

"Of course I'll make a statement," Graham said. His voice was full of confidence. "Why shouldn't I? And I'll do a lot more. I'll take a lie detector test if you wish. What's more you have my permission to search my house, my car or anything else. I haven't done anything wrong."

To prove his claim, Graham signed a waiver giving the agents the right to search his home, eliminating a court-ordered search warrant. Agents went immediately to Graham's house. Within minutes one of them called to inform Moore that "Mrs. Graham says Jack told her not to tell about the Christmas present. She signed a statement." Moore immediately confronted Graham with his wife's contradiction of his statements.

Graham thought for a moment, then said: "Oh yeah, I remember now. I did get her that present." He related that he had bought an X-Acto tool set from "some guy" whose name he did not know, paying him $10 for it. Yes, he had slipped the present into his mother's luggage. It now came back to him, all of it, he said.

Agents busy searching the Graham home kept calling with more information. A small roll of copper wiring, a type used for detonating dynamite, had been found in a pocket of one of Graham's shirts. An hour later agents found the insurance policies his mother had signed at the airport, all of them making her son the beneficiary. These had been hidden in a cedar chest in Graham's bedroom. Then they found the shotgun shells and ammunition Mrs. King was supposed to have taken with her. Also left behind by Mrs. King were presents she intended to give to her daughter in Alaska.

Agent Moore outlined the discoveries to Graham, one by one, then summed up the evidence, mounting every minute, surrounding the suspect with his guilt. "Why didn't your mother take these things (the ammunition and gifts) with her?"

Graham grew solemn, then said: "I told her not to take them because her baggage was overweight."

Moore threw a report in front of Graham. "This is from our lab and it proves that the crash was caused by a dynamite explosion." The agent looked at his watch. It was past midnight. They had been at it for almost six hours.

Then Graham sat stiffly in his chair. "May I have a glass of water, please?" he said. He was given a glass of water, which he drank slowly with long gulps. He put down the glass and, in a hard voice, said: "Okay, where do you want me to start?"

"Wherever you want to," replied Moore.

"Well, it all started about six months ago. Mother was raising hell because the drive-in wasn't making any money." He then explained how he had caused the explosion that wrecked the kitchen of the restaurant.

"And what about the truck you left on the railroad tracks so that you could collect the insurance after the train had wrecked it?"

"I did that, too—for the insurance." Graham's confidence had vanished. He squirmed in the chair. Sweat welled up on his forehead and ran down his cheeks. When he wiped it away with his handkerchief, his hand visibly trembled.

Moore leaned close to Graham. "What about the plane crash? You did that, too, didn't you?"

Graham wet his lips and looked at the ceiling nervously.

"What about the plane crash, Jack?"

Graham drank some more water, spilling some on his shirtfront, but said nothing.

"Come on, Jack," Moore persisted. "The truth. You blew up that plane for your mother's insurance. We know it. Let's have the truth from you."

Graham's bloodless face greeted the question. Slowly, he nodded, as if unable to speak the words. He then asked for more water. This was brought to him and he drank slowly, then said: "I might as well tell you everything." With that, Jack Graham became calm and in a deliberate, seemingly indifferent tone, he told in exacting detail how he had made his bomb from twenty-five sticks of dynamite, two electric primer caps, a six-volt battery and a timer (the fragments of sheet metal found by the technicians were from the battery). He seemed proud to announce the fact that he had worked in an electric shop for more than a week to learn how to connect and activate the timer before buying the dynamite. Yes, he had taken the ammunition and the gifts for his half sister from the suitcase and replaced them with the bomb. After twenty minutes, Graham fell silent. A stenographer was then called into the office and he repeated the entire story, and then signed the confession.

John Gilbert Graham was arrested for sabotage and later turned over to Colorado authorities. The stores where he had purchased the dynamite and timer were checked and Graham was identified as the buyer. Graham's half sister arrived from Alaska and told how Jack had once grimly joked about the possibility of his mother's hunting ammunition exploding during one of her plane trips. She quoted him as saying: "Can't you just see those shotgun shells going off in the plane every which way? Can't you just imagine the pilots and the passengers and Mother jumping around?" She thought he was insane.

Graham was placed in the Denver jail to await trial. He refused to see his wife, to whom he had transferred all his assets, and told a guard: "You can send my mail to Canon City (Prison) until next month. After that, you can send it to hell."

Graham claimed that he was without funds on Dec. 9, 1955,

when being arraigned for murder. Three lawyers were assigned to defend him. He was then charged with murder in the first degree, but Graham, ignoring his confession, entered a plea of "innocent and innocent by reason of insanity before, during, and after the commission of the crime."

The State then sent Graham to the Colorado Psychopathic Hospital where four psychiatrists examined him. As a way of repudiating his confession, Graham told a weird, wholly unbelievable tale. He said to the doctors sitting before him: "While the FBI men were interviewing me in Denver, I saw a photograph on the wall and it fascinated me. It showed the capture of Nazi saboteurs on the coast of Florida during World War II and FBI men were digging up dynamite. Somehow, that gave me the idea of confessing that I'd used dynamite to blow up the plane but, really, I didn't do it."

Graham's ridiculous tale failed to convince the doctors that he was insane, and he was returned to jail to await trial. On Feb. 10, 1956, Graham was found by guards in his cell almost dead, after trying to strangle himself with a pair of socks. He was revived and made his confession all over again, almost word-for-word with the statement he had given the FBI. Night and day in his cell, he professed his deep sorrow for the murdering of his mother and forty-three other helpless human beings, but he would often recant his confession and turn brutally callous, telling guards that the people on Flight 629 were no more than strangers to him, saying the number of dead was unimportant, that "...it could have been a thousand. When their time comes there is nothing they can do about it."

Graham's trial took place on Apr. 16, 1956, at which time the confessed killer admitted signing his confession but said that the confession was not true. He chewed gum incessantly and shrugged indifference at the testimony of the eighty witnesses and 174 exhibits brought against him. Though he had bragged that he would take the witness stand and demolish the State's case, Graham never sat in the box. He was convicted of first-degree murder on May 5, 1956, by a jury of five women and seven men after they deliberated only seventy-two minutes.

The Colorado Supreme Court heard Graham's appeal on Aug. 8, upholding the decision of the lower court. Graham unexpectedly did take the stand this time, but only to inform one and all that his appeal had been made by his lawyers against his wishes. He was promptly sentenced to death. His lawyers went on appealing for many months, until the state supreme court ordered that the bomber's execution take place on Jan. 11, 1957.

On that Friday morning, Jack Gilbert Graham stepped coldly into the gas chamber at the Colorado Penitentiary where he would be pronounced dead within eight minutes after the lethal gas was let loose. Only a few moments before gingerly stepping into the death chamber, Graham turned to a few reporters standing nearby. One newsman who had incurred Graham's ire because of the criticism he had heaped on the bomber, asked the condemned man if he had any last words.

"Yeah," snapped Jack Graham, ending his life with a wisecrack: "I'd like you to sit on my lap as they close the door in there."

REF.: Block, *Fifteen Clues*; ____, *Science vs. Crime*; *CBA*; Fox, *Mass Murder*; Godwin, *Murder, U.S.A.*; Gribble, *Murders Most Strange*; Heppenstall, *The Sex War and Others*; Lester, *Crime of Passion*; Nash, *Almanac of World Crime*; ____, *Bloodletters and Badmen*; ____, *Murder, America*; Ottenberg, *The Federal Investigators*; Rowan, *Famous American Crimes*; Sparrow, *The Great Assassins*; Thorwald, *Crime and Science*; Whitehead, *The FBI Story*; Wilson, *Encyclopedia of Murder*.

Graham, Oaland (AKA: **Jackie**), prom. 1976, U.S., theft-pros.-mur. In 1976, Oaland Graham walked the streets of Seattle, Wash., calling himself "Jackie," wearing "falsies," a tight sweater, a bouffant wig, and skin-tight pink slacks. It was no surprise when Brad Lee Bass mistook him for a girl. The two made a $50 sexual agreement based on that faulty assumption. When Bass saw more clearly see the "date" he had just bought, a fight ensued. When Jackie's wig fell off he became enraged and fatally stabbed the man he had agreed to have sex with.

Graham appeared in court dressed in a tasteful pantsuit and insisted on being called "Ms." Oakland Graham was found Guilty of second-degree murder.
REF.: *CBA*; Godwin, *Murder U.S.A.*

Graham, Robert J., c.1938- , U.S., wh. slav. A Chicagoan received one-third the maximum sentence possible for organizing a white slavery ring wherein he kidnapped women, including minors, raped them, forced drugs on them, required them to work as prostitutes, and threatened to kill them and their families if they did not cooperate.

Assistant U.S. Attorney Thomas G. Dent, who prosecuted Robert J. Graham, thirty-eight, urged U.S. District Court Judge Frank J. McGarr to give Graham the maximum prison term of fifteen years because "this man is a definite threat to society." Several women testified to Graham's brutality, telling jurors he forced them to sniff cocaine before working as hookers because he wanted his "girls to have a good attitude when they are out with customers."

One 18-year-old victim from Whitewater, Wis., who became pregnant while working for Graham, said he took her to an abortion clinic and forced her to have an abortion, saying pregnancy was bad for business. Another woman, a 21-year-old University of Cincinnati college student, said Graham snared her into his racket by discussing her interest in architecture, offering her a modeling job in Chicago, taking her to dinner, and then raping her. She said he "threatened to blow my head off if I didn't do what he said."

It was this student who first alerted police to Graham's offenses. On July 29, 1973, she sneaked out of his apartment and notified the police. Graham was immediately arrested and on Mar. 7, 1974, sentenced to five years in prison. REF.: *CBA*.

Graham, William, See: **Brocius, Curly Bill.**

Graham, William Johnson, 1872-1937, U.S., jur. Illinois state's attorney from 1901-09, served in the state House of Representatives from 1915-16, and as a U.S. congressman from 1917-24. He was nominated to the Court of Customs and Patent Appeals by President Calvin Coolidge in 1924. REF.: *CBA*.

Graham Brothers, prom. 1870s, U.S., west. outl. The Graham brothers, Albert (also known as Charles Graves and Ace Carr), Charles, and Dollay, joined the Jesse Evans outlaw band which robbed its way through Texas and New Mexico. All of them were born and raised in Llano County, Texas, and they became rustlers at an early age, later joining Evans in robbing stores in Davis. Rangers cornered the gang and Dollay Graham was shot and killed. Albert and Charles Graham escaped to pillage west Texas. REF.: *CBA*.

Graham-Tewksbury Feud, 1887-88, U.S., mob. viol.-mur. The Graham-Tewksbury Feud was waged over range rights and the cattlemen's claims that sheep ruined the grazing lands for cattle-raising. It took place in the Pleasant Valley, Ariz., area near Globe, and began in 1887 when the Tewksbury clan started raising sheep on their ranch and the adjoining range. Cattleman John Graham and his men attacked the Tewksbury family and, in return, John D. Tewksbury and his three sons, Edwin, James and John, Jr., led raids against the Grahams. Several other families joined both factions. The Blevins family, led by Andy Blevins, were fierce allies of the Grahams and fought many gun battles with the Tewksburys, resulting in several deaths. Although the feud supposedly ended in 1888, hatred flared up between the quarelling parties for the next few years. The feud officially ended on Aug. 2, 1892, when John Graham, head of the Graham family, was shot and killed by Ed Tewksbury and ally John Rhodes. See: **Blevins, Andy; Tewksbury, Edward; Tewksbury, James.** REF.: *CBA*.

Grailly, Jean III (**Captal de Buch**), 1321-76, Fr., treas. Led a delegation to ask England's Edward III to appoint a royal ruler for conquered France in 1355. He was a skilled fighter whose notable battles include the 1356 drive against the French at Poitiers, attacks on French forces for Navarre, and campaigns for England against Spain from 1366-70. He was seized by the French

in 1371, and imprisoned for refusing to fight under Charles V.
REF.: *CBA*.

Grandier, Urbain, d.1634, Fr., witchcraft. No one was above
suspicion of witchcraft in the days when such sorcerers swept over
America and Europe, but especially not a lecherous French priest
who impregnated a young girl and used his gift for satirical wit
to offend the city's leading citizens.

Father Urbain Grandier was a handsome, dark-haired, and
silver-tongued man of the cloth who was appointed vicar in
Loudun, France in 1617. His eloquence and elegance won him
many friends, but his imprudence with pretty girls and impiety in
writing won him as many enemies. These adversaries, which
included the influential Richelieu, Bishop of Luçon, and Jean de
Laubardemont, finally got the better of him. When word spread
that several sisters of the Ursuline convent in Loudun were
possessed, the bishop and other enemies of Grandier pounced.
Soon the nuns were pointing possessed fingers at Grandier saying
it was he who bewitched them. De Laubardemont called for the
Father's arrest on Nov. 30, 1633.

As thorough and systemic a study possible concerning witches
and warlocks was made for Grandier's case. Testimony provided
by possessed sisters, results of examinations performed by doctors,
and exorcisms performed by divines indicated conclusively that
Father Grandier was a witch. A book he had written arguing
against priestly celibacy did not help his case. On Aug. 18, 1634,
Grandier was tied to a stake and burned alive for "injuries and
possessions practised upon the persons of several Ursuline nuns
of this town of Loudun as well as upon other seculars." His ashes
were scattered to the wind.

REF.: *CBA;* Robbins, *Encyclopedia of Witchcraft;* Summers, *The
Geography of Witchcraft;* Wilson, *Witches.*

Grannon, Riley, 1868-1908, U.S., gamb.-gunman. Riley
Grannon, a western entrepreneur, foresaw the future of Nevada.
In 1907, he purchased land in Rawhide intending to create a great
gambling center. He specialized in handicapping horse races, and
had won a much as $275,000 in a single afternoon. Grannon
sought to modernize gambling casinos, replacing dusty saloons
filled with card cheats and vigilante violence with an atmosphere
reflecting the tastes of a more sophisticated populace. He was
correct, but his timing was forty years premature. In April 1908,
Grannon died penniless, having squandered a fortune in pursuit
of his dream. REF.: *CBA*.

Grant, Garland (AKA: **Jesus Grant Gelbard**), 1950- , Cuba,
hijack. On Jan. 22, 1971, Garland, a member of the Black
Panthers organization, hijacked a Northwest Airlines Boeing 727
to Cuba. The flight, en route to Washington from Milwaukee, was
diverted to Cuba after Garland's demands to be flown to Algiers
were not met by airline officials who maintained that the plane
was unequipped to cross the Atlantic.

Six months after arriving in Havana, Garland was imprisoned
for picketing the Cuban Ministry of the Interior. No charges were
filed, but he served two-and-a-half years in jail. Upon his release,
he went to the Swiss Embassy, where he became involved in an
altercation while attempting to receive assistance to leave the
island country. This second arrest resulted in a three-year
sentence. He was released in March of 1974 and, at the time of
a 1977 interview, was living in a transient hotel with fifteen other
expatriate hijackers and was attempting to flee Havana for the
U.S.

"I just want to get back to the United States," said Garland,
who lost an eye in a beating administered by Cuban officials. "I'm
living like a dog in Cuba." REF.: *CBA*.

Grant, Jack (AKA: **Jack Jones, James Jones, James Grant**)
prom. 1937, Brit., burg. Welsh burglar Jack Grant met a man
in prison who was determined to invent a device that would cut
a four-inch hole in a safe. Grant, intrigued, opened a small
machine shop when he was released from prison early in 1937,
where his friend was successful in producing the tool. They
quickly pulled a number of small burglaries, and were at the shop
of a jewelry fence when they were spotted by a London detective,

who put the pair under surveillance. When they saw a fence going
into Grant's partner's house, they followed, just as the receiver
was handed a packet of jewels. Grant arrived, and all three were
arrested.

Determined to find the stolen jewels, the detectives kept a
twenty-four-hour watch on the house. Late at night on New
Year's Eve, they saw the partner's wife, who was home alone, go
into the garden and stay about ten minutes. Questioned about
dirt on her shoes, she said that she had been hunting for something she had lost. But at dawn they dug down into the soil and
found a metal box filled with stolen watches and jewelry. Grant
and his partner were tried and found Guilty. The partner, who
had done the driving on their expeditions, received a three-year
sentence, while Jack, the confirmed criminal, spent five years in
prison.

REF.: *CBA;* Greeno, *War on the Underworld.*

Grant, Jack, 1918- , U.S., attempt. mur. To save himself
from financial ruin, 32-year-old aircraft engineer Jack Grant
concealed a bomb aboard a United Airlines jet in order to blow
up the plane in flight and collect on insurance policies totalling
$55,000 for the deaths of his wife and their two children.

On Apr. 17, 1950, Betty Grant and her two children, 6-year-
old Marie and 5-year-old Bobby, arrived at Los Angeles International Airport to board United flight 258 en route to San Diego,
where they were traveling to celebrate Bobby's birthday. The
Grants checked their luggage at the ticket counter, including a bag
containing a homemade gasoline bomb set to explode at 2:30 p.m.
Before they boarded the flight, Grant purchased three life
insurance policies for his family, naming himself as beneficiary.
These policies, in addition to the airline's standard $10,000 per
person limit, would allow him to collect $55,000 once the plane
exploded over the Pacific Ocean.

As ramp workers were loading luggage into the DC-3's cargo
bay, the suitcase containing Grant's gasoline bomb crashed onto
the tarmac and caught fire. Grant watched through the windows
at the gate as ramp workers frantically extinguished the flames.
Realizing his plot had failed, he turned to his wife and said, "I'm
going to be arrested. I'm going to jail for sure." Shortly afterwards, police arrived at the gate and took him into custody.

Grant was brought to trial several months later after it was
revealed that he was on the verge of financial devastation, and
that for years he had been leading a secret double life. Police
investigators learned that Grant had recently consented to marry
American Airlines flight attendant Elizabeth Soumela upon the
death of his wife. Although he never told Soumela of his plans
to murder his family, he told her that his divorce was nearly
finalized. In addition, Grant had fathered a 3-year-old boy in New
York whose mother was currently suing him for unpaid child
support payments. He explained that blowing up the plane and
killing his family and others aboard seemed to be the most
sensible way of getting out of debt.

Grant was tried and convicted on Aug. 3, 1950, of the attempted murder of his wife and children and three other passengers aboard the flight. Although the DC-3 would have carried
the flight crew and thirteen passengers to their death, the jury
found Grant Guilty on only six counts of attempted murder. On
Sept. 18, Grant was sentenced to serve one to twenty years in a
California prison. REF.: *CBA*.

Grant, James, prom. 1869, Case of, U.S., mur. Henry Rives
Pollard, editor of a Richmond, Va., paper, published an account
of an elopement of a sister of James Grant in 1869. Incensed at
what he thought was a slur upon his sister, Grant hunted Pollard
on the streets of Richmond with a shotgun, shooting the editor
in the back and killing him. Grant was tried and acquitted by a
jury that upheld the strange "tradition of honor." Grant, as far
as the jury was concerned, was doing nothing more than upholding
the honor of southern womanhood.

REF.: *CBA;* Pollard, *Memoir of the Assassination of Henry Rives
Pollard.*

Grant, Robert Allen, 1905- , U.S., jur. Deputy prosecuting attorney of St. Joseph County, Ind., from 1935-36, served in the U.S. House of Representatives from 1938-48, and was nominated to the Northern District Court of Indiana by President Dwight D. Eisenhower in 1957. He was a member of the Committee to Implement the Criminal Justice Act from 1969-72. REF.: *CBA*.

Grant, Robert, See: **Sacco, Nicola.**

Grant, Thomas, 1905-   , Can., mur. Thomas Grant, a 45-year-old bus driver in Moose Jaw, Saskatchewan, killed his old friend Wenzel Wilhelm Hartel in a rural area of the province by first burning the man alive, then shooting him three times in the neck for good measure. No motive was ever determined.

Constable Art Zimmerman of the Royal Canadian Mounted Police was called into the investigation after two motorists discovered Hartel's partially nude body near a dirt road six miles south of Moose Jaw. Hartel had been shot and his body badly burned. Tire tracks matching those of Hartel's car led from the scene, and a partially full can of gasoline lay hidden behind a nearby fence.

At Hartel's funeral, Grant inadvertently exposed himself by suggesting to Zimmerman that he investigate Hartel's half-brother Eddie Miller, who Grant said had been quarreling with Hartel because Miller had recently broken off a relationship with his girlfriend, Lorraine Mitchell. This line of investigation led him directly back to Grant, who was taken into custody for questioning. After several days of incarceration and several futile attempts to secure an alibi, Grant admitted that he accidentally murdered Hartel and intentionally covered up the crime to protect himself.

Grant appeared before Justice Adrian Doiron in a King's Bench courtroom on Sept. 26, 1950, and was found Guilty of murder and sentenced to death. Grant immediately appealed the decision and his request was granted by the Saskatchewan Court of Appeals. A second jury once again found him Guilty, but only of manslaughter as the prosecution had failed to prove that he had premeditated the crime. Following the decision, Justice Harold F. Thomson sentenced Grant to nineteen years at a Canadian prison camp. REF.: *CBA*.

Grantham, Sir William, 1835-1911, Brit., jur. Member of Parliament in 1874 and 1886. He was appointed to the High Court of the King's Bench Division by Lord Halsbury in 1886, and presided over the murder trial of George Chapman. See: **Chapman, George.** REF.: *CBA*.

GRAPO (First of October Autonomous Revolutionary Group), prom. 1970s-   , Spain, terr. GRAPO, a radical leftist terrorist group, first took responsibility for killings after an incident in October 1975 when four police officers in Madrid, Spain, were slain. The organization started calling itself the First of October Autonomous Revolutionary Group after the murders. It is believed to be responsible for more than thirty murders since the 1975 incident, including four murders in 1981. On May 4, 1981, Brigadier General Andres Gonzalez de Suso, sixty-four, was shot dead one morning as he left his apartment in Madrid. A national police officer in the vicinity, Ignacio Garcia, jumped from his patrol car and was also fatally shot. Another officer was beaten with a pistol. One of the assassins was injured and captured. About the same time, two civil guards eating breakfast in a Barcelona bar, Justiniano Fernandez and Francisco Montenegro Jiminez, were shot in the backs of their heads by GRAPO members, according to police. REF.: *CBA*.

Gras, Jeanne Amenaide (AKA: Jeanne de la Cour, Baroness de la Cour), b.c.1837, and **Gaudry, Nathalis Mathieu,** prom. 1877, Fr., asslt. A promiscuous French woman in her forties, Jeanne Amenaide Gras, became the mistress of wealthy 20-year-old René de la Roche. Three years later, Gras was afraid of losing her lover, so she plotted to blind him. She told a male acquaintance, Nathalis Mathieu Gaudry, that she would marry him if he would attack the son of a man who had robbed her. On Jan. 13, 1877, Gras and her lover went to a masked ball at the opera in Paris. They left the ball at about 3 a.m., rode home, and alighted from the carriage. Approaching the house, Gras followed several feet behind her lover. Suddenly, Gaudry appeared and

threw sulfuric acid in de la Roche's eyes, blinding him.

Gras insisted on caring for de la Roche, and when authorities were informed of her actions they told de la Roche about her possible complicity in blinding him. The police also reportedly found letters that Gras wrote to a man, blackmailing him by telling him she had his child. Gras and Gaudry were arrested. Gras tried to commit suicide several times before the trial, which began on July 23, 1877. She was charged with using gifts and promises to persuade Gaudry to injure de la Roche and aiding Gaudry in committing the crime. They were both convicted. Gras was sentenced to fifteen years in prison with hard labor and Gaudry was given a ten-year sentence and stripped of a military medal. REF.: *CBA*; Williamson, *Annals of Crime*.

Grasso, Santo, 1935-73, Fr., rape-suic.-mur. Santo Grasso's rampage of terror began in Villennes, Fr. on Sept. 16, 1973, and ended the following morning five miles away in Ecqueville with five people dead.

Police were summoned to the residence of René and Nanette Maréchal when neighbors reported a quarrel followed by gunshots in their apartment. When they arrived, officers found the couple lying on the floor in a pool of blood. René Maréchal had died instantly after being shot in the head; his wife Nanette lay gasping for breath. In Nanette's dying breath, she identified their murderer as 38-year-old Santo Grasso, a Sicilian and tenant in the building. Grasso later told police that he had killed the couple because "they make too much noise" and kept him from sleeping. Grasso's apartment was vacant, but he was located when police received a second call reporting gunshots in the nearby suburb of Ecqueville.

Grasso had barricaded himself in the Ecqueville apartment of his former lover Monique Gaumer. In the apartment, Grasso held Gaumer and her 7-year-old son Jacques Gaumer hostage while he randomly shot at motorists and pedestrians from the apartment window. Armed with a virtual arsenal, Grasso held authorities at bay throughout the evening, repeatedly threatening to kill his two hostages if they attempted to take him by force.

At nine the next morning, Grasso brought the confrontation to a violent end; Grasso killed both hostages after raping the woman as her son watched. Hearing the gunshots, police stormed the apartment. But before he could be captured, Grasso pulled the trigger of his shotgun and blew off his own head. REF.: *CBA*; Dunning, *The Arbor House Treasury of True Crime*.

Graterford (Pa.) State Prison Escape, 1981, U.S., pris. esc. Four armed prison inmates tried to escape from the State Correctional Institution at Graterford, Pa., a maximum security prison, on Oct. 28, 1981. Triple murderer Joseph Bowen led Calvin Williams, Leroy Newsome, and Lawrence Ellison in an attempt to climb over a thirty-foot wall at about 6:30 p.m., but their efforts were halted after a watchtower guard fired a warning shot. When guards tried to arrest them, the four withdrew into the kitchen and took six prison employees and thirty-two inmates hostage. On Oct. 31, twenty-nine convicts were released by the captors. The three other inmate hostages, Otis Graham, Drake Hall, and Frank St. Clair, joined the captors. On Nov. 2, the remaining six hostages—three unarmed guards and three kitchen supervisors—were freed at about 6:30 p.m. and then the convicts surrendered. During the ordeal, the governor and Bowen's mother requested the service of Chuck Stone, a journalist who had helped negotiate other surrenders, and Stone agreed to help. During the talks, the prisoners requested a transfer, which was granted.

Officials filed charges against the original four culprits. Bowen, the leader, had been convicted of murdering a police officer and two prison wardens and was serving a life term. After the escape attempt, he was convicted on additional charges, including assault by a prisoner, terroristic threats, possession of a criminal weapon, kidnapping, and criminal conspiracy. Newsome, twenty-nine, had been imprisoned for shooting to death a 14-year-old boy in 1972 and was serving a life sentence. He was convicted on additional charges of assault by a prisoner, terroristic threats, kidnapping, and criminal conspiracy in connection with the attempted escape. Williams was serving a life prison sentence for murder, and was convicted after the escape on charges of assault by a prisoner, possession of a criminal weapon, kidnapping, and criminal conspiracy. Ellison, twenty-six, had been convicted of robbery and burglary and had been sentenced to eighteen to fifty-two years in prison. He was also convicted on a kidnapping charge. REF.: *CBA.*

Gratian (Flavius Gratianus), 359-383, Roman., emp., assass. Son of Valentinian I, he became emperor of the West in 375, and became emperor of the east after Valens' loss at Adrianople. With Theodosius, he fought against the Alamanni, Goths, and others from 379-81. He was murdered by rebel followers of Maximus at Lugdunum. REF.: *CBA.*

Graves, Thomas Thatcher, 1843-93, U.S., mur. Josephine Barnaby was the estranged wife of a successful clothing store owner in Providence, R.I. When her husband died, she inherited only $2,500 a year, while most of his estate went to his two daughters. On the advice of Dr. Thomas Thatcher Graves, who had treated her for occasional minor illnesses, Mrs. Barnaby contested the will. She also gave Graves power of attorney. When the will was reversed and Mrs. Barnaby inherited a large sum of money, Graves began to steal from her.

In order to keep the elderly Barnaby from discovering the fraud, Graves insisted that she take frequent, long voyages for her health. Eventually, Barnaby became suspicious of Graves and confronted him. Graves told her that she was incapable of handling her own affairs and threatened to place her in a nursing home. He even wrote his threats to her in a letter. On receiving the letter, Barnaby decided to return from her visit to California to rid herself of Dr. Graves.

On her way home from California, Barnaby stopped in Denver to visit her friend Mrs. Worrell. Waiting for her at Mrs. Worrell's home was a package containing a bottle of whiskey. A note on the bottle said: "Wish you a Happy New Year's. Please accept this fine old whiskey from your friend in the woods." The two women mixed drinks from the bottle, and although they noted that the liquor tasted "vile," drank them down. Both women became violently ill, and died six days later, on Apr. 19, 1891.

One of Mrs. Barnaby's daughters heard about the whiskey and ordered an autopsy, which revealed that her mother had died of poisoning. Dr. Graves was soon arrested. At his trial, the prosecution called as a surprise witness Joseph M. Breslyn, a young man who testified that he had met Graves at the Boston train station in November 1890. He said that Graves had approached him and, claiming to be unable to write, had convinced him to write the note which had accompanied the bottle of poisoned whiskey.

Graves was found Guilty and sentenced to die. While awaiting a new trial in April 1893, Graves committed suicide in his cell by taking a massive dose of poison.

REF.: Boswell and Thompson, *Practitioners of Murder;* Brownlee, *Dr. Graves: His Trial and His Suicide;* Boucher, *The Quality of Murder; CBA;* Conrad, *A Revolting Transaction;* Day, *Death in the Mail;* Fox, *Mass Murder;* Nash, *Almanac of World Crime;* ____, *Bloodletters and Badmen;* Pearson, *Five Murders.*

Gravina, Gian Vincenzo (Giovanni Vincenzo Gravina), 1664-1718, Italy, jur. Professor at Sapienza who wrote *Originum juris civilis* from 1708-13, and *Ragion poetica* in 1708. REF.: *CBA.*

Gray, Arthur, prom. 1721, Brit., attempt. rape-burg. Grizel Murray surprised Arthur Gray with her strength and fended off the would-be rapist/murderer, but many in the early-eighteenth-century British courtroom—the site of Gray's trial—dismissed Murray's heroism, preferring instead to blame her for the crime.

On the night of Oct. 14, 1721, Gray crept into Murray's room with a sword in one hand and a gun in the other. Murray screamed and then recognized Gray, a servant in the house she was visiting, and a man who had openly lusted after her.

Murray opened her mouth to cry out, but Gray threatened to kill her if she raised her voice. Gray approached. Murray stepped

back toward the bed, pleading with him to stop. Gray set down his sword. Now was his chance to pounce. But before he knew it, Murray had slammed him against the far wall, wrestled the gun from his grip, and had it pointed at him. Gray fled to his room, but was captured soon afterwards and confessed to the crime.

In December 1721, Gray's trial began with the retraction of his confession. He said that on the night in question he had heard a noise and had gone into Murray's room to protect her from a possible intruder. The jury did not believe him, however, and found him Guilty.

Then Gray's employer intervened. His clout with the judge resulted in a pardon for Gray, with the condition that he be deported. Many, however, never believed he had committed a crime in the first place. They blamed Murray as the cause of it all.

REF.: Bierstadt, *Curious Trials and Criminal Cases; CBA;* Mitchell, *The Newgate Calendar.*

Gray, Elijah, and **Gray, James**, prom. 1830, U.S., mur. On Jan. 2, 1830, Samuel Davis was murdered in upstate Le Roy, N.Y. Shortly after, James Gray and his father Elijah were arrested for the crime. In April 1830, in the Court of Oyer and Terminer of Genesee County, before Judge Gardiner, they were found Guilty and sentenced to die on Nov. 5 at noon. The sentence of Elijah Gray was later commuted to life imprisonment.

Samuel Davis had been suspected of running an illegal gambling house, and James Gray's son was his ward. On the morning of Jan. 2, Gray exchanged some ax handles he had carved for a knife. He began drinking, and during the course of the day had many conversations about Davis' illegal dealings and the care of Gray's son. It was known that Elijah Gray was about to complain formally about Davis' gambling den. The father and son, accompanied by Moses Herrick, entered Davis' saloon and were asked to leave by Davis and his son Isaac. James Gray pulled the knife, initially to cut a plug of tobacco, but then stabbed the elder Davis during a brief scuffle. Davis bled to death within minutes. Gray denied premeditation or participation by his father.

REF.: *CBA; The People Vs. Elijah Gray and James Gray.*

Gray, George, 1840-1925, U.S., jur. Attorney general of Delaware from 1879-85, and U.S. senator from 1885-89. He was nominated to the Third Circuit Court by President William McKinley in 1899, later founding the Society of International Peace, and serving as vice president of the organization. REF.: *CBA.*

Gray, Henry Judd, See: **Snyder, Ruth May.**

Gray, Horace, 1828-1902, U.S., jur. Court reporter for the Massachusetts Supreme Court from 1854-64, and directed the publication of a sixteen-volume set devoted to the court's decisions. In 1864, he became the youngest associate justice ever to serve on the Massachusetts Supreme Court, a post he held until 1873, when he became chief justice. He was nominated associate justice of the U.S. Supreme Court by President Chester A. Arthur, serving from 1881-1902. In the cases *Mayre v. Parsons* and *Poindexter v. Greenhow* in 1885, he unsuccessfully argued that it was unconstitutional to sue a state as a private citizen. He again dissented in *Bowman v. Chicago and North Western Railroad* in 1888, believing that states had the right to restrict the conveyance and importation of liquor. REF.: *CBA.*

Gray, Louis Patrick III, 1916-   , U.S., law enfor. off. On May 3, 1972, Louis Patrick Gray III was designated acting director of the FBI.

Born in St. Louis on July 18, 1916, Gray enrolled at Rice University in 1932, and in 1936 was appointed to the U.S. Naval Academy in Annapolis, Md., where he graduated in 1940 with a Bachelor of Science degree. Gray became a decorated war veteran, serving as a naval line officer, and commanded five different submarine combat patrols in the Pacific during WWII and three submarine patrols during the Korean War.

Gray began a career in law in 1949 when he received his Juris Doctor from George Washington University and began his practice in Washington, D.C. In 1958, he was admitted to the Connecticut

State Bar. He has practiced law before the U.S. Military Court of Appeals, the U.S. Court of Claims, the U.S. Court of Appeals for Washington, D.C., and the U.S. Supreme Court.

Gray held several high-level naval positions before his retirement from the navy, with the rank of captain, in 1960. His navy career included service as military assistant to the chairman of the Joint Chiefs of Staff and special assistant to the Secretary of Defense for Legal and Legislative Affairs.

In the of year his retirement from the navy, Gray joined the New London, Conn., law firm of Suisman, Shapiro, and Wool. He became a full partner in the firm of Suisman, Shapiro, Wool, Brennan, and Gray on Jan. 1, 1967. In 1969, Gray was appointed executive assistant to the Secretary of Health, Education, and Welfare, a position he held for a year before returning to private practice in 1970. Gray also served as a special consultant to President Richard Nixon's Cabinet Committee on Education, and was nominated by Nixon as assistant attorney general for the Civil Division of the Justice Department.

FBI Director L. Patrick Gray.

After his nomination as U.S. deputy attorney general in 1972, a Senate judiciary committee unanimously approved him for the position, but the nomination was withdrawn when he was named acting director of the FBI before the full Senate was able to hold a confirmation hearing.

REF.: *CBA*; Demaris, *The Director*; Ungar, *FBI*; Wicker, *Investigating the FBI*.

Gray, Roger, prom. 1600s, Brit., execut. Roger Gray was the public executioner at Exeter, England, in the 1600s, during which time he hanged several convicted criminals, including his own brother. Gray died in Topsham where he drowned while in a drunken stupor.

REF.: *CBA*; Laurence, *A History of Capital Punishment*.

Gray, Ronald Adrin, 1966- , U.S., rape-mur. An army specialist fourth class, 20-year-old Ronald Gray began his post as a cook at Fort Bragg, N.C., in the spring of 1986. Soon after, a wave of kidnappings, rapes, and murders hit usually bucolic Cumberland County, N.C.

In May 1986, on a rural foot trail in Fayetteville—home to the Fort Bragg army base—Teresa "Dusty" Utley was found badly beaten and shot in the head. Local residents believed that Utley, a known prostitute, had finally met her match, but opinions would change later that month.

On Apr. 29, 24-year-old Campbell University student Linda Jean Coats had been found dead in her mobile home in Fairlane Acres. She had been sexually assaulted, beaten, and shot in the head. Then 18-year-old Tammy Wilson was found in the woods behind Fairlane Acres. She, too, had been shot in the head. Local and military police were stumped and would remain so until the disappearance of a cab driver on Dec. 31, 1986.

Almost twelve hours after she had picked up a fare near a local convenience store, Kimberly Ruggles, a cab driver for Terminal Taxi, was found dead at Fort Bragg. She had been sexually assaulted and then murdered within 100 yards of her abandoned taxi. After Ruggles' murder, a Fayetteville woman told police of her recent abduction and rape by a Fort Bragg soldier. Her statement led to the arrest of Private Ronald Adrin Gray, a resident of Fairlane Acres mobile home park.

In April 1988, a military court handed Gray two death sentences for the rape and murder of Ruggles and Clay. He was also charged with three other kidnap-rapes and was a prime suspect in two other rape-murders. Having been dealt eight

consecutive life sentences from the Superior Court of Cumberland County, Gray at this writing awaits execution at the military prison in Fort Leavenworth, Kan. REF.: *CBA*.

Gray, Thomas, c.1663-1713, Brit., rob. The son of respected parents in Clerkenwell, early on an apprentice tailor, and later a restaurant owner, Thomas Gray could not from the beginning keep his hand out of the till, nor in the end settle into prison life. Both traits would be the death of him.

As his business began to fail and his debts began to mount, Gray returned to a livelihood of thievery that he had earlier learned in Short's Garden. His promotion to highwayman came in Beaconsfield when he robbed his first victim in a farmer's field. After robbing a peddler in Gloucestershire, however, Gray was confined to the Gloucestershire jail. He set it on fire and escaped, but three other prisoners died from smoke inhalation.

With practice, Gray became adept at ambushing coaches in the countryside, adventures that eventually led him to the Chelmsford jail. Vowing never to be caged like an animal again, however, Gray soon escaped with some fellow prisoners.

In 1713, with accomplices Edmund Eames and William Bigs, Gray committed a spree of robberies. Their reputations spread. No traveler felt safe while the trio was at large. The gang was finally captured, and all three were held on robbery charges at Newgate Prison. Gray and Eames received death sentences. On Wednesday, Mar. 10, 1713, the stone-faced Gray walked up the steps of the gallows at Tyburn to be hanged before an indignant crowd. Hanging next to him was his friend and criminal cohort Edmund Eames, who that day celebrated his thirty-second birthday.

REF.: *CBA*; Smith, *Highwaymen*.

Gray, William John, 1910- , Brit., mur. Sentenced to hang for the murder of his wife, William John Gray was saved from the noose because medical examiners determined that hanging would have put him in "extreme physical agony."

On Mar. 16, 1948, Gray was convicted of murdering his estranged wife Una Gray, while she and three friends walked down an Andover sidewalk. Gray shot Una and later turned the gun on himself, fracturing his jaw. He pleaded guilty to the crime and within five minutes was sentenced to death.

On Apr. 3, Gray was reprieved after medical examiners ruled that hanging would cause him too much pain. Their conclusion was based on the extent of his injuries, and they explained that if hung, the rope noose would not dislocate his neck and that he would either die of strangulation or he would be decapitated altogether as his injured jawbone was too weak to hold the rope around his neck, ensuring dislocation. They ruled that death by either of these methods would be inhumane and they could not condone his prescribed punishment.

REF.: *CBA*; Duff, *A New Handbook on Hanging*; Harrison, *Criminal Calendar*.

Gray, William McKinnon, prom. 1941, Brit., fraud-attempt. suic.-mur. Major William McKinnon Gray stationed at Chilcompton, Somerset, in 1941, drew £100 for his own use from the regimental accounts of which he was in charge. When he was changed to another command, he had no way to repay the money. He also wrote a bad check for £39 to cover his mess bill. On the day he was to leave, Apr. 10, he and his wife Amarylla Gray locked the door of the room they were in at the officers' mess. Apparently by agreement, he shot his wife in the head, killing her, and then shot himself, but failed to die. The bullet went through his skull without even knocking him unconscious.

The other officers found Major Gray about two hours later, rambling on about why he had done it. Gray was tried on a charge of murder after he came out of the hospital. Evidence was presented, to support an insanity defense, that Gray and his wife had previously planned a suicide pact in the event Germany won the war, but he was found Guilty on July 15, 1941, and sentenced to be executed. The death sentence was commuted, however, and Gray was sent to prison for life.

REF.: *CBA*; Hastings, *The Other Mr. Churchill*.

Gray, William Thomas, See: **Field, Jack Alfred.**

Great Bank of England Forgery, 1872-73, Brit., forg. By the time three U.S. con artists had determined to pool their resources to defraud European banks, each had already experienced limited success. The leader, 33-year-old George Bidwell, had been sentenced to two years imprisonment in July 1865 for defrauding grocers in Wheeling, W. Va., with his partner, a man using the name Dr. S. Bolivar. Bidwell escaped before completing his sentence. His brother, 25-year-old Austin Bidwell, had cashed £13,000 in stolen U.S. bonds in Europe in 1871, while Bostonian George MacDonnell had learned his criminal trade from the "Terror of Wall Street," master forger George Engel. However, none had undertaken a massive swindle until after their arrival in London in 1872.

The trio's modus operandi was relatively simple. They would visit a bank where one of them would obtain a letter of credit while the others stole the bank's letterhead. These letterheads were used to forge additional letters of introduction, which were then submitted to European banks. George Bidwell used this procedure at the London and Westminster Bank, calling himself Hooker—one of sixteen aliases he used during the endeavor. As Hooker, the elder Bidwell traveled to Bordeaux, Fr., and cashed a forged check for 50,000 francs. During the next two days he cashed forged checks for 62,000 francs in Marseilles, and 60,000 francs in Lyons. Following a relatively unsuccessful venture to a Brazilian bank, where the con still netted £10,000, the three embarked upon defrauding the Bank of England.

George Bidwell wired a fourth confederate, Edwin Noyes, in New York and he soon joined the swindle. Noyes acted as the group's delivery man, exchanging the notes obtained from forged checks for U.S. bonds, gold, and cash. Austin Bidwell, using the name of Frederick Albert Warren, met a society tailor named Edward Hamilton Green, whose introduction to the Bank of England provided the swindlers with an outstanding opportunity.

As Warren, Austin Bidwell deposited £1,200 and the con was underway. By November 1872, an additional £8,000, completely legitimate, was deposited. From Jan. 21 to Feb. 28, 1873, the foursome forged and cashed ninety-four bills of exchange, totalling £102,217. These funds were transferred to the Continental Bank, and exchanged for gold and £65,000 in U.S. bonds. On the last day of February 1873, the fraud was discovered. Until then, the forgers had been meticulous in preparing the forged documents. Because the Bank of England had no safeguards against fraudulent transactions used by the Bidwells, the fraud could only fail if the swindlers themselves made a mistake, as they did on Feb. 28, 1873.

The transaction of Feb. 28, 1873, failed to show a date of issue—a glaring error easily spotted by a bank clerk. Although the fraud was car-

George Bidwell, who masterminded the Great Bank of England Forgery.

ried out as usual, the bank contacted the alleged issuer of the worthless note, B.W. Blydenstein, for the missing date, and discovered that the bill had never been issued. The next day, Mar. 1, Noyes was arrested at the Continental Bank while making another deposit. His confederates fled when they heard the news, destroying all evidence of their illegal trade, except for the blotter upon which the forgeries had been drafted. MacDonnell escaped to New York where he was arrested as he disembarked from his transatlantic voyage. Austin Bidwell was apprehended in Havana, Cuba, and, like MacDonnell, returned to London. The last to be

captured was George Bidwell, who fled first to Ireland, and then to Edinburgh, Scot., after learning that a reward was offered in Ireland for his capture. A month later he too was returned to London after his arrest on Apr. 3, 1873.

During the trial, the judge actually wore a gun, fearing that friends of the defendants might attempt to free their comrades. The blotter, forgotten by the forgers, led to the conviction of all four men. Police were able to detect impressions left on the blotter which matched the gang's forgeries. Also used against the swindlers were the contents of a package, sent to Major George Matthews in New York. The package contained George Bidwell's jewelry and the ill-gotten U.S. bonds. George Bidwell had also boasted, in a letter to MacDonnell, of his dexterity in eluding capture, thus implicating the entire gang. Each of the four was sentenced to penal servitude for life.

The trial of the Bidwells, MacDonnell and Noyes at the Old Bailey, 1873.

George Bidwell, after an aborted suicide attempt and near starvation, was released from Dartmoor Prison on July 18, 1887, because of poor health. Bidwell returned to the U.S. where he wrote his autobiography, *Forging His Chains*. He also made a living touring the country, lecturing on the evils of crime. His younger brother was released in 1892. Together they traveled to Butte, Mont., in March 1899, where Austin Bidwell died on Mar. 7, and George Bidwell died on Mar. 25, lying in the same bed where his brother had died.

REF.: Bidwell, *Forging His Chains;* ____, *From Wall Street to Newgate;* CBA; Duke, *Celebrated Criminal Cases of America;* Griffiths, *Mysteries of the Police and Crime;* Hamilton, *Men of the Underworld;* Horan, *The Pinkertons;* Nicholls, *Crime Within the Square Mile;* Kingston, *Dramatic Days at the Old Bailey;* Rowan, *The Pinkertons;* Symons, *A Pictorial History of Crime.*

Great Coram Street Murder, See: **Boswell, Harriet.**

Great Gatsby, The, 1925, a novel by F. Scott Fitzgerald. This powerful work of fiction portrays as its central character, a noble bootlegger, Jay Gatsby, who has characteristics of the author's personality and the background of Fitzgerald's Long Island neighbor (at the time of the writing), Larry Fay, the dapper New York bootlegger who backed the 1920s speakeasy hostess, Texas Guinan, in her clubs. Fay was a clotheshorse, just as was Jay Gatsby and, through his bootlegging and racketeering, he managed to buy an expensive estate on Long Island where he gave sumptuous parties attended by the social elite, including Scott Fitzgerald and his wife Zelda. This lifestyle was captured wholly in Fitzgerald's brilliant novel. Three films, all with the same title as the novel, were made in 1926 (silent, with Warner Baxter as Gatsby), 1949 (with Alan Ladd essaying the tragic gangster in the best version of the lot), and 1974 (with an aesthetic Robert Redford anemically portraying Gatsby). See: **Fay, Larry.** REF.: *CBA.*

Great Gold Robbery, 1855, Brit., rob. The Great Gold Robbery of 1855 was engineered by Edward Agar, one of the most brilliant thieves of the nineteenth century. Agar, strikingly handsome with a thick head of black hair and heavy sideburns, was an ingenuous man whose clever abilities at forgery and robbery earned him a small fortune and, eventually, a long prison sentence. Early in life, the well-educated Agar pursued a business career but realized eventually that his station would not lead to a great fortune, his driving ambition in life. Through underworld contacts in London, Agar met James Townsend Saward, a successful barrister who was also a master forger and the underworld czar who organized London crime for more than two decades. Saward, considered the greatest forger of his day, was known as "Jim the Penman" to his cronies, and taught his techniques to the affable Agar.

In 1848, through Saward's underworld contacts, Agar met William Pierce, a lean man with a long, somber face, who worked for the South Eastern Railway in London as a ticket printer—a man of expensive taste and little money. Pierce was as venal as Agar but lacked Agar's intellect. Almost at once, Agar began to ask Pierce about the gold shipments that passed from London to Paris via the railroads. Pierce immediately realized that Agar was planning to rob one of these trains and excitedly told the forger all he knew about these gold shipments. Undoubtedly, Agar had developed a deep interest in these shipments after reading about the 1848 theft of £1,500 in gold sovereigns from a British train. The gold shipment, locked in a strongbox and under guard, was being transported from London to Bristol. Yet, when the box was delivered in Bristol it was discovered to have been broken open and the sovereigns were missing. Agar admired the theft—which was never solved—and said so.

Edward Agar, leader of the thieves who committed the Great Gold Robbery.

In long talks with Pierce, Agar learned how gold shipments were sent by train from London to Paris, and what rigid security measures were taken to protect the gold. The forger decided the risk was too great. He told Pierce that he would have to think of a method by which they could obtain the gold without use of force. He gave up the plan and traveled to the U.S. Some time in 1854, Agar returned to London. He looked up Pierce, and again began discussing the possibility of robbing the South Eastern Railway.

His plan was to bribe certain railway staff members to obtain copies of two keys to the safe containing the gold shipments on the night train from London to Folkestone. Agar had done his research well. He knew that gold from London goldsmiths was sent to railway officials in heavy wooden boxes bound with iron hoops. These boxes were weighed and sealed by South Eastern Railway officials and then put on board the night train to Folkestone in an iron safe in the express car. The safe could only be opened by *two* keys, one held in London, the other in Folkestone by railway security chiefs. The captain of the ship taking the shipment across the Channel to Boulogne had a set of keys, as did the bank officials receiving the shipment in Boulogne and in Paris. Once the shipments reached Boulogne, the boxes and their seals were again checked and then sent by train to the banks of Paris.

By the time Agar proposed this plan, Pierce had already been discharged from South Eastern Railway on suspicion of committing petty theft. Pierce, however, still knew key railway staff members and quickly contacted William George Tester, the station master at Margate. Tester was brought into the plot in

early summer of 1854. He was a vain dandy with a full head of thick hair. He primped before mirrors in public houses and prided himself on his trimmed beard. Tester wore a monocle and thought of himself as a man of destiny. He was given money by the well-off Agar and soon saw that his fortune lay in robbing a gold train. Through Tester, Agar, and Pierce secretly visited the railway offices in Folkestone at night where they studied the procedures of the arriving night trains and the transfer of gold shipments to the Channel steamers.

Agar hung about Folkestone, befriending railway workers in the local pubs. He came under the scrutiny of local policemen who warned railway men to stay away from him, saying that he was probably a clever pickpocket. Agar, learning of this, left for London immediately where Pierce had lined up another key railway employee, James

William George Tester, the railway official who worked with the thieves.

Burgess, one of the guards in the train car that carried the gold shipments. Burgess also joined the plot, believing that he would soon retire with his portion of the loot. Agar then went to work on the seemingly impossible job of obtaining the two separate keys to the train safe.

Tester involuntarily solved half of the problem. Without making the request, he was suddenly transferred from Margate Station to London and promoted to an executive position. Once in London, he saw an opportunity to obtain the first of the two keys. One of the safes used in the train shipments had to be sent to Chubb's for replacement, a chore which Tester handled personally. He made a wax impression of the single London key used for the replacement safe and gave this to Agar. To obtain the second key, the one held in Folkestone, Agar devised a clever scheme. In October 1854, he sent a shipment of £200 in gold from London to himself in Folkestone, using the alias C.E. Archer.

At the Folkestone station, Agar asked for his gold shipment. He watched carefully as the clerk retrieved the key to the safe, seeing that it was stored in a cupboard inside the station master's office. He then stayed in Folkestone, visiting the station often. Agar noticed that the night clerk regularly left the office unattended for a brief period each night. One night, with the clerk gone for only a few minutes, the bold Agar slipped into the office, retrieved the key to the safe and made a wax impression of it. He left the office undetected.

Returning to London, Agar and the others spent months perfecting the two keys made from the wax impressions, filing and shaping these. Next the thieves spent weeks cutting duplicate dies for resealing the bullion boxes. Then, with all in readiness, the

James Burgess, the railway guard who helped loot the train safes.

thieves waited for their opportunity. The train guard, Burgess, notified Agar that a large gold shipment, £14,000 in gold sovereigns, would be shipped from London to Folkestone on the night

London Bridge Station, where the gold began its trip to the European banks; it was here that Agar and Pierce boarded the gold train to rob its safes.

of May 15, 1855.

Agar and Pierce bought first class tickets on this train and arrived that night at London Bridge station. Pierce wore a wig and a false beard so that none of the railway workers he knew would recognize him. Agar and Pierce carried several satchels that were weighted with lead shot to the exact weight of the gold shipment, as given to them by station official Tester. Agar also carried the two keys to the safe, chisels, a mallet, dies for the resealing of the iron bands clamped about the gold boxes, sealing wax and tapers. A porter labored to carry the satchels onto the train and placed them in the baggage car where the gold safes were located. The guard on duty in the car that night was Burgess.

Agar and Pierce went to separate compartments and waited for the train to get up steam. As soon as the train pulled out of the station, Agar went to the gold car and Burgess let him inside. While Burgess acted as lookout, Agar went swiftly to work on the safes, opening them with his hand-made keys—which fit perfectly. Next he removed the iron bands clamped around the boxes and removed the gold, placing it in his satchels and replacing it with the lead from the satchels. The transfer completed, Agar nailed the iron clasps around the boxes and placed new seals on them.

When the train reached Redhill, Agar stepped off the train for a few minutes, with two satchels full of stolen gold sovereigns. He handed these to the waiting Tester. Then Agar got back on the train which rolled away toward Folkestone. Pierce next joined Agar and Burgess in the gold car where both men worked furiously to remove the many remaining gold boxes from the safes, replacing the sovereigns with the lead and then reclamping and sealing the boxes. When all the gold had been removed and was in the satchels stored next to the safes and the lead-filled gold boxes were locked in the safes, Agar and Pierce returned to their separate compartments and rested after their labors. When the train arrived in Folkestone, they simply got off the train and waited for the porter to carry their satchels from the gold car. The porter delivered several satchels to them and they then returned to London with the stolen gold. Meanwhile, the two

safes from the gold train were transferred, as usual, to a steamer, *Lord Warden,* which sailed for Boulogne. Once in Boulogne, the captain of the steamer opened the safes, and the boxes were weighed and the seals checked. They were pronounced secure and shipped on to Paris. The next day, bank officials opened the boxes and stepped back in shock to find nothing but worthless lead instead of the gold.

Authorities in Paris and London began a frantic investigation. Railroad employees in England and in France were interrogated. Scores of detectives investigated the theft but not a clue was found leading them to the thieves. The French indignantly insisted that the theft had been committed in England. The British police sternly claimed that the robbery had occurred in France. Six months went by and still authorities found no trace of the thieves or the gold. They were prepared to give up the hunt.

Agar and Burgess, removing the gold from sealed boxes.

The thieves gathered every day in Agar's large rented house at Cambridge Villas in Shepherd's Bush, London. They spent many hours melting down the gold sovereigns. Some of this they sold off and the rest they buried beneath the pantry floor. The four thieves split the profits equally and then went on their separate ways. Pierce retired, buying a house in Kilburn. Burgess remained a guard on the railroad. Tester banked his stolen loot and then improved his position mightily. The nervy Tester asked for and received a testimonial from the South Eastern Railway company. Their glowing recommendation aided him in obtaining an appointment as general manager of the Royal Swedish Railways.

Perhaps this robbery would never have been solved had it not been for the sexually wayward Agar. He had been living with his mistress, Fanny Kay, with whom he had a young son. Yet he began spending time and money on another woman, attempting to steal her affections from a thief named Humphreys. In revenge, Humphreys framed Agar on forgery charges. Agar was sentenced to transportation for life to Australia. Before Agar was sent to Australia, he arranged to have Pierce take £1,500 of his own money and about £3,500 from the gold robbery and give this to his mistress Fanny so that she and his son would have some security.

Pierce, however, reneged on his promise to turn over these sums to Fanny Kay. Moreover, he cruelly refused to pay the rent for Agar's mistress and son and they were thrown into the street, destitute, except for a few sovereigns. The mistress went to Newgate Prison to see Agar, but he had already been sent to a prison ship about to sail for Australia. Fanny, in despair, cried out her desperate plight to the warden of Newgate who realized that the money Agar had promised Fanny might be the loot from the gold robbery and ordered Agar back to Newgate. When Agar heard how Pierce had betrayed him, he took his revenge by informing on Pierce and the others, detailing the entire gold robbery to officials.

Pierce was arrested at his home in Kilburn and thousands of pounds were unearthed beneath the front step of his house. In the same month, November 1856, Burgess was also arrested. Tester was arrested a short time later when he returned from Sweden to meet with his family. All four men were placed on trial on Jan. 12, 1857, and, with Agar testifying against his fellow thieves, all were found Guilty of robbery. Tester and Burgess were sentenced to fourteen years transportation to a penal colony. Pierce, however, hired a crafty lawyer who found a flaw in the indictment against him, and he received only a two-year prison term. Agar was sent off to serve his life term.

Some justice existed for Fanny Kay and her son, however. Although all the recovered loot from the robbery was returned to the South Eastern Railway, Agar's own money, about £1,500, was set up in trust for Fanny and the boy. Thus ended England's great gold robbery. Its brilliant architect, Agar, died in an Australian penal colony many years later. Before he died, broken in spirit, a new prisoner arrived to tell him that he had become a legend in England's underworld. Replied Agar: "That means nothing, nothing at all!"

REF.: CBA; Dilnot, *Celebrated Crimes;* Kingston, *A Gallery of Rogues;* Nash, *Almanac of World Crime;* Nicholls, *Crime Within the Square Mile;* Stevens, *From Clue to Dock;* Symons, *A Pictorial History of Crime;* Twyman, *The Best Laid Schemes;* Whitbread, *The Railway Policeman.*

Great Mail Robbery, 1962, U.S., rob. A mail truck containing sixteen sacks of small, old bills totaling $1,551,277 was headed for Boston along deserted Route 3. Patrick R. Schena and William F. Barrett, the truck's occupants, had been making the usual daily stops at Cape Cod banks, picking up antiquated bills destined for the Federal Reserve Bank in Boston where they would be destroyed. Outside Plymouth, Mass., the truck made a turn in the road, and the driver brought it to a quick halt. The way was blocked by two cars parked in the road. A policeman wearing dark glasses, a cap pulled low over his face, walked to the mail truck. He carried a submachine gun.

Only minutes earlier, a man in an Oldsmobile following the mail truck, had blocked off the road south of this spot with traffic cones and an electric flasher mounted on a wooden horses. He also placed a detour sign in the road which instructed Boston-bound traffic to take the Clark Road cutoff. The driver of the Oldsmobile then leaped into his car and, driving ninety miles an

hour, caught up with and passed the mail truck, then drove ahead of it, around the bend. Here the driver met another car and both autos blocked the road before the mail truck came into view.

The man dressed in the policeman's uniform and carrying the submachine gun poked the lethal weapon in the driver's face and ordered Schena to turn over the keys to the back of the truck. Shena and Barrett turned over the keys and were forced to lie in the back among the mail sacks. Their hands and feet were bound and one of the thieves got behind the wheel and drove the truck slowly down the road. The truck stopped three times and the robber at the wheel tossed out some of the sacks containing the old currency at each stop to waiting confederates who drove off in separate cars. Schena and Barrett saw nothing at this point since they were face down on the floor of the truck. They heard the thieves address each other as "Tony," and "Buster."

On Route 128, the truck was brought to a halt and the driver, the man called "Tony," poked the mail employees with a gun and snarled: "Lie still or you're dead! Don't move for ten minutes!" A minute passed and Schena thought it safe to stand up in the rear of the truck. As he did so, the back door opened and "Tony," wearing a mask, shouted: "Lie down or I'll blow your head off! I mean it!"

Schena resumed his position on the floor of the truck. Five minutes or more went by and Schena tried again, this time cautiously working his way out of the truck, though he was still tied hand and foot. He saw a young man on a motor scooter, Ricardo G. Unda-Freire, a premedical student from Ecuador, driving toward him. "Robbed of millions of dollars!" Schena shouted to the youth. "Call the police!" Unda-Freire drove to a phone booth and called police but his thick accent caused the policeman on the other end of the line to suspect a hoax. Unda-Freire leaped on his scooter, raced to the Stoughton police station and repeated his breathless report, which was acted upon.

The thieves had vanished and left no clues by the time a massive manhunt was begun. No fingerprints were found; the robbers had all worn white gloves, according to the mail guards. The press seized upon this and labeled the thieves as members of the "White Glove Gang." It was apparent to investigators that this robbery had been engineered by someone inside the postal system since only certain postal employees would know that a contract with an armored car company had recently been cancelled and that postal trucks were temporarily moving the money. It proved impossible, however, to select likely suspects from hundreds of postal employees. Three suspects were later charged but these charges were dropped, the defendants being ably represented by the noted criminal lawyer, F. Lee Bailey. To this date, the Great Mail Robbery has never been solved nor has one dollar of the money been recovered. The methods employed by the thieves in this robbery were made public and may have inspired the robbery of the Royal Mail train a year later in England. See: **Bailey, F. Lee; Great Train Robbery, The.**

REF.: Bailey, *For the Defense;* CBA; Nash, *Almanac of World Crime;* (FICTION), Tidyman, *Big Bucks.*

Great Pearl Robbery, 1913, Brit., theft. Max Mayer's pearl necklace had taken years to "build up." It was a flawless masterpiece of sixty-one graduated oriental pearls valued at £150,000. Mayer, a dealer in precious stones, operated a shop in London's Hatton Garden. On July 16, 1913, his clerk received the midday mail containing a parcel Mayer had been waiting for: the pearl necklace sent by his agent in Paris, Henri Salamons. For months, Salamons had negotiated the sale of the pearls to a Frenchman, but the deal fell through and now the necklace was being returned to the owner.

Mayer ripped open the package and discovered that the necklace was not there. In its place were several lumps of sugar. Mayer immediately dispatched a wire to Salamons in Paris. "BOX ARRIVED BUT NO NECKLACE." Scotland Yard and the French Sûreté were brought into the investigation and a £10,000 reward was offered for the safe return of the necklace. In Paris, Inspector Puichard of the CID questioned a waiter who worked in a café near the post office about a "suspicious" man he had seen in his establishment the day of the robbery. The thief slipped six lumps of sugar into his pocket and decamped. Police in France and England still lacked a viable suspect. Nothing new turned up until August when Samuel Brandstater, an Antwerp jeweler, was approached by Leisir Gutwirth, a broker from North London. Gutwirth explained that he had a certain necklace and was putting it up for sale for a half-million francs.

Brandstater reportedly related the conversation to Inspector Ward of Scotland Yard, who told him to feign interest. The second meeting occurred at the Golden Cross Hotel where Gutwirth announced that the price had risen to a million French francs. Brandstater hedged. A meeting was proposed for the next day in Lyons. Plainclothes police from both sides of the English Channel observed the proceedings from inside the tea shop. Gutwirth soon was joined by two other men, Joseph Grizzard and James Lockett, both well-known to the police.

Lockett threw down a matchbox on the table. Grizzard opened it and peered at the three pearls lying on a bed of cotton. "There are more where they came from," Lockett said. "Just find me a buyer." Inspector Ward quickly realized that he was dealing with a highly organized criminal gang, experts in high-stakes international thievery. The next meeting took place at the First Avenue Hotel, where a fourth member of the gang was present. The thief, Simon Silverman, was an Austrian who attempted to inveigle Paris jeweler Max B. Spanier—who was helping police—into buying the pearls. The two

men parted on amicable terms and agreed to meet again the following Monday in the billiard room of the hotel. Although Spanier was shown a tin box containing fifty-eight of the pearls, he only bought two of them for 100,000 francs. "I cannot do business in dribs and drabs," Grizzard complained. "You must come to me with enough money on you to buy the lot. I am tired of these meetings. If we can't do business soon, then the whole thing is off."

James Lockett, one of those involved with the Great Pearl Robbery.

A final rendezvous was scheduled in the subway station outside the British Museum. Before the transaction could take place, Inspector Ward seized the crooks. Lockett, Grizzard, Gutwirth, and Silverman were arraigned on charges of theft, and placed on trial at Central Criminal Court. According to Prosecutor Muir, Silverman planned the theft at the Diamond Club, a restaurant in Hatton Garden. In Paris, Silverman, using a forged seal, intercepted the package before it could be delivered to Mayer's studio in London. He carefully removed the pearls and substituted the lumps of sugar. The four conspirators were each sentenced to up to seven years in prison. The pearls, which had been lost during the arrests, were found by a piano maker named Horne in a matchbox lying on the street. All but three of the pearls were in the box, which Horne turned over to police, keeping one for himself to sell for a "penny or a pint." REF.: *CBA*.

Great Salad Oil Swindle, See: **De Angelis, Anthony.**

Great Train Robbery, 1963, Brit., rob. On Aug. 8, 1963, fifteen men, some with criminal backgrounds, some with no records at all, stopped the Royal Mail train from Glasgow to London, near Cheddington Station, and committed the largest robbery in England up to that time, looting mail sacks of more than £2.5 million. This amazing crime caper, one which shocked the world with its suddenness and efficiency, had been in the planning a long while. The men involved, all known to each other and having had long associations, for the most part, in shady London deals, met more than a year before the train robbery at Cheddington.

To finance the train robbery, several of the leaders decided to commit another, similar theft.

On Nov. 27, 1962, three businessmen appeared in London's Heathrow Airport. They wore conservative pin-striped suits and bowler hats, and they carried walking canes or umbrellas. These men somehow got into a security area and then permitted five

Left, Bruce Reynolds, mastermind of the Great Train Robbery, and, right, henchman James E. White.

more men wearing balaclava helmets to enter the area. Security guards were overpowered and £62,500 in old bank notes, then en route to a London bank, were quickly taken. Of the eight men involved in the robbery, three were apprehended, but only one, Mickey Ball, was convicted, and then sentenced to five years imprisonment. As he was being led away, Ball sneered and said: "Well, at least you won't get me for the big job!" This remark confused police at the time, but they knew full well what Ball meant eight months later.

One of the elusive leaders of the train robbers, Charles Frederick Wilson, left, when apprehended following the robbery, and, right, in disguise after being recaptured following a prison escape.

The two men who were acquitted of the airport robbery, Charles Frederick Wilson and Gordon Goody, went on to participate in "the big job," the Cheddington train robbery. Using the loot from the airport robbery to finance the train heist, the thieves gathered in a large farmhouse in Leatherslade, Buckinghamshire, near Cheddington. Here, Bruce Reynolds, the mastermind of the robbery, outlined the details of the operation, running his men through their duties as would a drill sergeant. The methods and procedures employed by Reynolds and his top aides were decidedly military in nature.

When all was ready, this paramilitary band pinpointed Aug. 8, 1963, as the day for the robbery. From inside information, the leaders, Bruce Reynolds, Ronald Biggs, Buster Edwards, Charles Wilson, and others, knew that on that day the Royal Mail train would be carrying in its baggage car 120 bags stuffed with old, unmarked surplus bills. These notes were being sent from Scottish banks to their London offices for recycling or destruction, depending upon wear and tear. It was estimated that this regular shipment would contain between £2 million and £3 million, an enormous prize.

The mail train appeared on schedule a half-hour from its destination, Euston Station, and was stopped by a simple railroad procedure. The thieves merely blacked out the green "go" signal, and affixed a wire to a battery so that the red "stop" signal, would remain on. The engineer, seeing the red light, brought the train to a halt. Several men waiting alongside the tracks jumped into the engineer's cab and slugged the engineer. Others piled into the two mail cars immediately behind the engine, overpowered the guards, and then threw the sacks of money to others waiting outside. The sacks were hurriedly dumped into Land Rovers parked nearby. Then the engineer was forced to drive the train on to its destination as one of the masked robbers cavalierly waving to him and shouting "cheery-bye!"

The Leatherslade farmhouse where the robbery gang met before and after the train robbery and where the careless gang members left an abundance of clues for the police.

The bandits drove to the Leatherslade farmhouse and there divided the spoils, lesser members of the gang each given a small amount, "a drink" of the take, as one of the robbers later put it. The chief bandits received equal shares, £150,000 each. The entire amount came to a staggering £2,631,684, or about $7,000,000. After the split, the gang members, who had each made plans for individual getaways, went their separate ways. London police, when hearing the news, sent an army of investigators to the site of the robbery but they found no clues. The world's press heralded the robbery as the greatest theft of the century.

In five days, the police discovered the abandoned farmhouse in Leatherslade. Suspicious neighbors had seen a number of Land Rovers, and many men arriving at the building carrying sacks. Detectives found the place a mess. For all their careful planning, the thieves apparently panicked after the robbery and hurried their final arrangements. They left fingerprints everywhere and they had not taken the trouble to disguise the license plates of the Land Rovers, which were traced. England's greatest manhunt then began, and, one by one, the bandits were tracked down and arrested. They had brought further suspicion upon themselves by not remaining at their jobs, but by disappearing immediately after the robbery, going into hiding.

The small-timers were caught first and they cracked under interrogation, naming others. Most of the top men in the robbery ring were brought to trial a year after the robbery and, on Mar.

26, 1964, they received sentences that were considered harsh, even for their sensational crime. Thirty-year prison sentences were meted out to Reynolds, a car and antique dealer and the brains of the gang, Charles Wilson, a small-time bookie (who later escaped prison and was then recaptured), Thomas Wisbey, James Hussey, Robert Welch, Roy James, Douglas Goody, and Ronald

The Royal Mail train at Cheddington Station following the robbery.

Biggs. Roger Cordrey received twenty years, but this was later reduced to fifteen. William Boal, Brian Field, and Leonard Field (the Fields were not related) received twenty-four-year sentences each. The Fields appealed their sentences, as had Cordrey, and their prison terms were reduced to five years each. These punishments were considered severe in that there was only one injury involved in the robbery, that of the engineer who recovered.

Only £336,524 of the stolen money was recovered. It took several years to capture the leaders of the gang. James White, a cafe proprietor, was not arrested until 1966 and he drew an eighteen-year sentence. Buster Edwards was then tracked down and sent to prison for fifteen years. Bruce Reynolds, who had led the gang and escaped from prison, was finally recaptured in 1969 and sent back to prison for twenty-five years. Ronald Biggs also escaped from prison in 1965. He led authorities in an around-the-world chase through a dozen countries, until he landed in Brazil. He managed to fight off extradition and lived well with his wife and son on his ill-gotten money. Most of the missing money, officials concluded, had been spent by the gang members in their flight from police. They had paid enormous amounts to

The interior of one of the mail coaches which was looted by the train robbers.

underworld contacts for hiding places. In the end, the robbery got the thieves nothing more than long prison terms.

The most astounding tale connected with the Great Train Robbery emerged in the mid-1970s when informants stated that the real brains and financier behind this robbery was none other than the one-time Nazi super commando, Otto Skorzeny, who had fled to Spain after WWII and had there organized Odessa, a secret organization of former SS officers, one that had taken great sums of money out of Germany before the collapse of the Third Reich. Odessa financed the escapes and maintenance of wanted Nazi war criminals, and according to the story connected to England's great train robbery, financed enormous robberies to continually refill its coffers.

Some of the train robbers had reportedly met with Skorzeny or his representatives in Cologne, and it was Skorzeny who originally put up £80,000 to finance the first robbery at London Airport and helped to set up other details of the train robbery. One of his men was even in the Leatherslade farmhouse helping Reynolds and Biggs direct their men, according to one account. Skorzeny and his men went even further. Following the robbery, Skorzeny, who reportedly received £1 million of the stolen loot, arranged for his own men to smuggle Charles Wilson out of Winson Green prison. He also arranged for Buster Edwards to have his face altered through plastic surgery, and it was Otto Skorzeny who helped the elusive Ronald Biggs reach a safe haven in Brazil. Fantastic as this story might be, there is some evidence to make it credible. Skorzeny, however, was long dead by the time this tale was told.

REF.: *CBA;* Delano, *Slip-up;* Fewtrell, *The Train Robbers;* Fordham, *The Robbers' Tale;* Gosling, *The Great Train Robbery;* Hobsbawm, *Bandits;* Jackson, *Occupied With Crime;* Mackenzie, *Biggs: The World's Most Wanted Man;* Millen, *Specialist in Crime;* Read, *The Train Robbers;* Williams, *No Fixed Address;* (FILM), *The Great Train Robbery,* 1979.

Greco, Michele (AKA: **The Pope**), prom. 1970s-80s, Italy, org. crime-mur. In December 1987, following an extensive trial in Palermo that saw nineteen Mafia bosses and their henchmen sent to jail for life, former leader of the Sicilian Mafia Michele Greco was convicted for his involvement in thirty-two mob-related murders during the 1970s and 1980s.

The Palermo trial centered on the war between Sicilian crime families over control of worldwide heroin trade. Former boss Tommaso Buscetta, first to defy the Mafia code of silence, provided eyewitness testimony and was the state's key witness.

Greco, known in Mafia circles as "The Pope," and nineteen others were convicted primarily on Buscetta's testimony, which linked Greco to the 1982 assassination of Carlo Alberto Dalla Chiesa, leader of the nation's organized crime task force. In addition to Greco and the other crime bosses, the Palermo court found 100 defendants Guilty in absentia and acquitted 114 others for lack of evidence. REF.: *CBA.*

Green, Andrew Haswell, 1820-1903, U.S., mur. Began New York City law practice in 1844, and formed a partnership with attorney Samuel J. Tilden. He served on the Central Park Commission for thirteen years, and then as comptroller of New York from 1871-76. He worked to consolidate New York communities and was instrumental in consolidating part of the public library system. In 1903, he was killed by an insane man. REF.: *CBA.*

Green, Ann, d.1659, Case of, Brit., mur. The unmarried Ann Green, maid in the home of Sir Thomas Read in Duns Tew, Oxfordshire, miscarried in her fourth month of pregnancy as the result of the strenuous housework she was performing. She confessed to causing the infant's death and was hanged at Oxford Castle on Dec. 14, 1650.

Her body hung from the gallows and was beaten by castle guards for more than half an hour before it was cut down and the soldiers realized that she was still breathing. In an attempt to carry out the death sentence, soldiers stood on her chest and again beat her with their weapons. Afterwards, her body was taken for an autopsy, but the medical examiner again determined that she was alive. Under the doctor's care, she recovered. Many believed her triumph over death proof of her innocence, an intervention from God.

Prosecutors attempted to retry Green, but several high-ranking officials defeated their plans, and she was acquitted of the murder.

Fully recovered, Ann Green was released. She later married and bore three children before her death in 1659, nine years after her failed execution.

REF.: Atholl, *Shadow of the Gallows; CBA.*

Green, Anna Katharine, 1846-1935, U.S., writer. Specialized in fictional detective stories. Books authored: *The Leavenworth Case, The Sword of Damocles, The Millionaire Baby, The Step on the Stairs,* and others. REF.: *CBA.*

Green, Ben Charles, 1905-   , U.S., jur. Special counsel to the attorney general of Ohio from 1937-38, and was nominated to the northern district court of Ohio by President John F. Kennedy in 1962. REF.: *CBA.*

Green, Bill, prom. 1900s, U.S., embez.-arson. Bill Green, one of the most prominent men in Fairburn, Ga., was a Sunday school teacher, school board member, fraternal official, banker, and mayor of the town when he was arrested for robbing and burning the Fairburn Bank.

Mayor Green, who was working in the bank the day it was set on fire, was rescued from the burning building by citizens who had volunteered to put out the blaze. Once safe outside, Green told how two men brandishing guns stormed into the bank and robbed him at gunpoint. Green explained that the men then tied him in a back room, set the building on fire, and fled the scene. Police arrested Green two days later and charged him with setting the fire.

Investigators discovered that Mayor Green was having an affair with married Atlanta socialite Agnes Bradstreet. He gave her lavish gifts and settled her accounts at several of Atlanta's finest stores. Fairburn citizens were shocked when they learned that Bradstreet's gifts had been paid for with their deposits to the Fairburn Bank.

Green was convicted and served five years at a Georgia prison camp for embezzling and arson.

REF.: *CBA;* Cohen, *One Hundred True Crime Stories.*

Green, Clement Clay, prom. 1860s, Case of, U.S., mur. The owners of the Green and Howell's ferry, which spanned the Chattahoochee River outside of Atlanta, Ga., fought it out to the end with pistols in Dr. R.J. Massey's drugstore. Clement Clay Howell and Clement Clay Green had been boyhood playmates, both inheriting the lucrative ferry from their fathers. On Feb. 27, 1867, the two young men got into a hot argument over a southern belle and then began to throw punches. Green whipped out a pistol and fired several times at Howell. He missed his dodging target at close range. Howell attempted to reach a pistol on a counter but Green dove at him, clinched and then jammed his weapon to Howell's head, pulling the trigger and blowing away half his skull. With his lifelong friend dead at his feet, Green turned to Dr. Massey.

"What do I do now?" he asked.

"Wait here for the police," Massey replied, dry-voiced.

Green sat down in a chair and stared at Howell's corpse. The police led him away without a struggle. A mighty array of legal talent argued Green's "crime of passion," and he was found Not Guilty on a charge of murder. He went on to become a deputy sheriff for Fulton County and was buried next to his ferry. Howell was buried on a bluff on the other side of the river; the two graves faced each other into the next century. REF.: *CBA.*

Green, Cleo Joel, III, 1958-   , Case of, U.S., burg.-rape-mur. A man walked into the Clarksdale housing project in Louisville, Ky., sometime during the evening before or the early morning hours of July 3, 1983. He forced a door on the second floor and crept into the darkened apartment. Later that morning, Jimmy York found the mutilated corpse of his 76-year-old mother Ina Mae York lying in the bedroom. She had been decapitated and struck 200 times with a hatchet. She was the latest in a series of elderly Louisville residents attacked in the previous months.

By August 1983, police received more than thirty-two reports of attacks on elderly residents in the Shelby Park, Germantown, and Butchertown neighborhoods of the city. They linked York's attacker to the death of 80-year-old Marie Relkin, who died in

May 1983 after being robbed, beaten, and sodomized on two different occasions. Relkin died while hospitalized after the second assault.

On July 19, the killer struck again, less than two blocks from the site of Relkin's assault. Seventy-two-year-old Almira M. Watson was rushed to Humana Hospital after an unidentified attacker broke into her apartment and stabbed her several times in the neck before he ransacked her home.

At half past midnight on Aug. 13, double-amputee Rosetta M. Smith sat watching television. It was hot in the apartment, and she had opened the sliding glass door to her patio to catch a cool breeze through the screen. She noticed movement in the yard, where she saw a man climbing over the five-foot railing. He ran to the door and cut his way through the screen, freeing the lock. Once inside, he knocked Smith out of her chair, threw her on the bed, and removed her prosthetic legs, making it impossible for her to escape. Threatening her life, he ransacked the apartment searching for money. Finding none, he stripped off his clothing and attacked Smith. The 69-year-old woman successfully fought him off until he passed out on the floor an hour and a half later.

Unable to reach the telephone, Smith set off the building alarm system which alerted neighbors to call police. When they arrived, 26-year-old Cleo Joel Green III was still lying naked on the floor, where they roused him and took him into custody.

Charged with murdering York and assaulting Watson and Smith, Green was held in a mental hospital where he underwent psychological tests. At a hearing before Jefferson County Circuit Court Judge Richard Revel in August 1984, Green was found incompetent to stand trial. His attending doctors explained that Green believed he was possessed by a "Red Demon" who constantly tortured him. He maintained that the only way to relieve his agony was to sexually attack and murder his elderly victims so the demon could take over their bodies. Green was remanded into the custody of Central State Hospital for further psychiatric treatment.

REF.: CBA; Holmes, Serial Murder.

Green, Clovis Carl, 1943- , U.S., forg.-rape. Between 1972 and 1976, convicted rapist Clovis Carl Green filed more than 200 lawsuits in state and federal courts pleading for release or retrial.

Green, born in Hollis, Okla., in 1943, began his criminal career nineteen years later when he was sentenced to a Wyoming state prison on forgery charges. He was released in 1963 after serving two years, only to be sentenced to the Sandstone Federal Medical Center in Missouri in 1971.

At that facility, where he filed lawsuits in federal courts throughout the West, including those in Colorado, Kansas, Minnesota, and Oklahoma. Denying one such request, Kansas City Federal District Court Judge Elmo B. Hunter said that Green had "a continuing history of engaging in a gross abuse of the judicial process which is impeding the ability of the judiciary to carry out its proper function."

In 1975, Green began serving a ten-year sentence in a Missouri state penitentiary for rape. Green continued his appeals, filing an average of one every three days. Described as a "nuisance and a pest" by prison warden Donald W. Wyrick, Green filed habeas corpus writs, alleged that his civil rights had been violated, and questioned the evidence used to convict him of rape.

"Page after page of stuff each day—he must work sixteen hours a day," said Assistant Attorney General Philip M. Koppe. In 1976, the Missouri state's attorney filed for an injunction to halt Green's numerous appeals. REF.: CBA.

Green, Edward W., 1833-66, U.S., rob.-mur. The first bank robbery in the U.S. was carried out by a federal government employee, the postmaster of Malden, Mass., on Dec. 15, 1863. On that afternoon, Postmaster Edward Green, whose debts caused him to drink excessively, walked into the local bank. Finding only the banker's 17-year-old son, Frank Converse, present, Green suddenly realized how he could solve his problems and hurried home to get a gun. Back at the bank, he found young Converse still alone, so he shot him and then removed about $5,000 from the bank safe.

Green left town quickly, but did not go far and did not try to hide his new wealth. His free spending drew the attention of the police and, when arrested, he readily confessed. He was tried and found Guilty and executed on Feb. 27, 1866.

REF.: CBA; Cooper, Ten Thousand Public Enemies; The Life, Character and Career of Edward Green, Postmaster of Malden; Nash, Almanac of World Crime; ____, Bloodletters and Badmen.

Green, Everett D., b.c.1890, U.S., arson-mur. Facing eviction as the bank foreclosed on his boarding house, Everett D. Green decided to burn the building to the ground and kill himself in the process.

On the evening of May 26, 1953, Green wrote a suicide note and set fire to his Washington, D.C., apartment building. As the fire raged, Green lost his nerve and fled the building, leaving his only tenant, 83-year-old Bettie Brown, to choke to death on the thick smoke.

Green later claimed that a tall, bald, black man broke into the building and started the fire. But firefighters reported all the doors and windows were securely locked from the inside. Green was questioned and later charged with arson and first-degree.

A jury convicted him of the arson charge and of second-degree murder, for which he was sentenced to life in prison. He appealed the decision, and the second jury found him Guilty of first-degree murder and sentenced him to death. His lawyers immediately appealed the verdict, but the death penalty was affirmed.

On Dec. 16, 1957, the U.S. Supreme Court heard Green's case and reversed the original conviction, finding that Green had been subjected to double jeopardy. Having already completed his prison term for arson, Green was set free.

REF.: CBA; Nash, Bloodletters and Badmen; Seagle, Acquitted of Murder.

Green, George W. (AKA: Oliver Gavitt), d.1855, U.S., mur. George Green was a Chicago banker with a shady past. Green met another woman and decided to get rid of his wife, so he poisoned her with arsenic. But physicians examining the woman before her untimely death suspected foul play, and Green was charged with murder. At his trial, experts testified that arsenic was found in large doses in Mrs. Green's corpse, testimony that largely convicted Green of the murder. This was the first time that such forensic evidence was admitted in an Illinois murder case. Green was sentenced to death but cheated the executioner by hanging himself in his jail cell.

REF.: Andreas, History of Chicago; CBA; Life of the Chicago Banker, George W. Green.

Henry G. Green murdering Mary Wyatt.

Green, Henry G., 1823-45, U.S., mur. A recovered alcoholic, Henry Green regularly attended temperance lectures and at one of these fire-and-brimstone gatherings, he met 18-year-old Mary Ann Wyatt. The 22-year-old Green married the girl in Berlin, N.Y., but Green's mother opposed the wedding, telling her dominated son that his wife was not his equal and, therefore, not a fitting wife. The elder Mrs. Green nagged her son about his uneducated wife and criticized the girl at every opportunity. When Green's mother suggested he "get rid of that stupid girl," he took her advice literally. Green poisoned his wife with arsenic after being wed to her for only two weeks. The arsenic was detected and Green confessed to the murder. He was tried, convicted, and hanged at Troy, N.Y., on Sept. 10, 1845. The last thing Green read was a letter from his mother, in which she exonerated him.

REF.: *CBA; Confession of Henry Green; The Execution and Last Moments of Henry G. Green; Life and Confessions of Henry G. Green; Trial of Henry G. Green.*

Green, Joyce, d.1958, Brit., (unsolv.) mur. Six-year-old Stephen Green was the only witness to the murder of his mother in 1958. Her killer was never found, but police in Buckinghamshire, England, believe that someone in the town of Denham hid information that could have led to his capture.

On the morning of Aug. 25, 1958, Stephen and his mother, Joyce Green, were at home alone in their bungalow in Denham. About 10:45 a.m., a man in a blue suit walked into the house and attacked Green in her bedroom. Stephen watched as the tall, heavy-set man with a white face gagged his mother and strangled her to death. He fled from the house crying and told neighbors of the incident. When police arrived, they found Green lying on her bed, clothed only in her brassiere.

As weeks passed, authorities questioned residents of the town. But no one remembered seeing a man matching the boy's description of the killer. Investigators later learned that a Denham couple had spoken to the killer on the day of Green's death. But police were unable to locate the couple for questioning.

One year later, with the murderer still free, a spokesman for the Buckinghamshire police department said, "We are convinced that there are people in this village withholding vital clues."

REF.: *CBA; Furneaux, Famous Criminal Cases, vol. 6.*

Green, Leslie, c.1923-52, Brit., mur. Leslie Green was the chauffeur in the household of Cuthbert Wiltshaw, a pottery manufacturer. When Green was fired from his job, he left his wife, and unable to find work right away, decided to go back to the Wiltshaw's house to take their jewels. He arrived in the late afternoon, after the maids had left for the day, and only Mrs. Wiltshaw was home. He sneaked into the back door, picked up two small logs, and entered the kitchen. There he struck Alice Wiltshaw, who was cooking dinner, on the head with the logs. While Green went upstairs to get the jewels, Mrs. Wiltshaw recovered consciousness and went into the hallway to a telephone. Green saw her and beat her to death with a fireplace poker and a glass vase. On the way out he threw away his thin leather gloves because glass had torn through them and cut his finger. He also grabbed a raincoat out of the entryway to cover the bloodstains on his clothes. Green then went to a girlfriend and gave her an engagement ring from the stolen goods.

The former chauffeur, who had a record of theft as a teenager and was the only recent employee of the house who could not be readily found, was soon sought by the police, led by Divisional Detective Inspector Reginald Spooner. Green, seeing notices about the hunt for him in the newspapers, decided that he could bamboozle the police with a fake alibi and turned himself in. He claimed that he spent late afternoon of July 16 drinking at the Station Hotel in Stafford, fell asleep in the park across the road, woke and washed up at the hotel, then caught a train for Leeds, where his girlfriend lived. The police created intricate timetables of Green's movements and decided that there had been time to for him to have committed the crime. The raincoat turned up in a railway lost-and-found. The girlfriend, finding that her ring was stolen, turned it in. The last straw against Green was the pair of leather gloves found in the Wiltshaws' grounds. The hole in them exactly fit over the healed cut in Green's hand. Leslie Green was arrested and charged with murder. He was tried at the Staffordshire Assizes, found Guilty, and hanged on Dec. 23, 1952.

REF.: Andrews, *Intensive Inquiries;* Butler, *Murderers' England;*

CBA; Hoskins, *The Sound of Murder;* Millen, *Specialist in Crime;* Tullett, *Strictly Murder.*

Green, Rita (AKA: **Black Rita**), prom. 1900s, Brit., (unsolv.) mur. Known as Black Rita for her beautiful black hair, Rita Green lived her life in the violent London underworld. It is believed that one of her many male friends in the city's notorious gangs caused her death.

The 30-year-old Green was found dead in her apartment in London's Soho district. On the September evening that she died, neighbors and passerby rushed to her apartment after hearing gunshots from the building. They found Green's apartment door wide open, and her body lying on the floor. She had been shot three times in the back.

Investigators searched the area for clues and questioned residents. One woman told police that just before the shooting she saw Green talking to a man on the sidewalk outside her building. He carried what appeared to be a violin case. The neighbor assumed that their conversation was friendly, as the man accompanied Green into the building and apparently up to her apartment.

Suspecting one of Green's gangster friends, police searched the neighborhood nightspots for clues. They found that many of the gangsters believed Green was an informant because her late father had been a London police officer.

Following a futile investigation, police determined that Green's murderer was a foreigner hired by a gangster who believed she knew of his involvement in a recent crime. Two similar murders in the Soho area suggested a common thread.

Margaret Cook had been shot to death and Helen Freedman had been stabbed in Soho apartments around the time of the Green death. Like Green, the two women associated with criminals at local nightclubs, had access to sensitive information, and were killed by someone police believe was a stranger carrying a small bag or violin case. Although several similarities were found, all three deaths remain mysteries.

REF.: *CBA;* Firmin, *Murderers in Our Midst.*

Green, Robert, and **Berry, Henry**, and **Hill, Lawrence**, d.1679, Brit., (wrong. convict.) mur. The justice of the peace for Westminster, 56-year-old Sir Edmund Berry Godfrey, left his home on Oct. 12, 1678. His servants became worried when he did not return home that night. On Oct. 17, Godfrey's body was found lying face down in a ditch on the south side of Greenbury Hill, now Primrose Hill. He had been strangled and stabbed to death with his own sword. An examination revealed that he had not eaten for two days and since his shoes were clean, authorities reasoned he had been killed elsewhere. White wax, similar to that used by Roman Catholic priests, was found on his clothing, and he had not been robbed.

Popular opinion held that Godfrey, a staunch Protestant, had been murdered by Catholics. Dec. 21, 1678, a Catholic silversmith, Miles Prance was arrested for making fraudulent statements while a suspect in a religious conspiracy. After he was tortured, Prance implicated Robert Green, an employee of the queen's chapel, Henry Berry, a porter, and Lawrence Hill, a servant, as Godfrey's murderers. The three men were arrested, but prior to the trial, Prance withdrew his accusations. Several days later, Prance repeated the accusations. The three defendants were convicted and condemned. Hill and Green, who were Catholic, were hanged on Feb. 21, 1679, at Tyburn, and Berry, a Protestant, was hanged the next week. Later, Prance admitted again that his accusations were false, and on June 15, 1686, he pleaded guilty to a perjury charge. He was fined and directed to stand in the pillory and to be whipped during a journey from Newgate to Tyburn. Godfrey's murderers were never caught. REF.: *CBA.*

Green, Samuel, d.1822, U.S., burg.-rob.-theft-rape-mur. Samuel Green, as a boy in Meredith, N.H., was beaten for wrongdoings so often that he began venting his rage on anyone who was near. Green's family, giving up on him, sent him to a guardian named Mr. Dunne in Newhampton, who also was unable to control him. Green spent the final years of his youth working on ways to kill

Dunne, but his attempts failed until finally he left Dunne and went out on his own.

Green and a young man named Ash went to work for a counterfeiter, passing bad money throughout New England. The master criminal for whom they worked also taught Green to pick locks and burgle houses. Once when their burly mentor beat the two youths, they ambushed him later and left him naked in the cold night.

Green and Ash robbed a jewelry salesman, and Green smashed the man's head in with a club. Green soon switched from clubs to guns, using them freely whenever he wanted. He was often arrested, but either there was insufficient evidence to try him or his friend Ash helped him break out of jail. All of New England was beginning to fear the angry young man.

It was not a masterful crime that finally put Green behind bars, merely a $30 theft committed while drunk in Danvers, Mass. He was sentenced to prison for four years. The authorities, knowing of his propensity for escape, kept close watch on him. But even in prison he committed murder. Billy Williams, another prisoner, had informed on him at a previous **Thief and killer Samuel Green.** escape attempt, and Green, seeing Williams in prison with him, smashed his head and body with an iron bar. The raging Samuel Green, found Guilty of murder, was hanged on Apr. 25, 1822.

REF.: *An Account of the Execution of Samuel Green; CBA; Life of Samuel Green; CBA; Nash, Murder, America.*

Green, William S., 1920- , U.S., (wrong. convict.) mur. On the evening of Nov. 4, 1946, a night security guard on Philadelphia's south side was murdered as a friend watched from almost 100 yards away. Five months later, an innocent man was sentenced to life in prison for the murder.

While patrolling with a friend, security guard William Blount noticed that the back door of a neighborhood theater had been forced open. He went inside to investigate while his companion waited in the alley. Soon after, Blount came out of the building with another man. He had apparently thwarted a burglary attempt. The two men walked to a nearby police call box, and as Blount reached for the phone, his prisoner grabbed his gun and shot him dead. Two eyewitnesses who later told police that they had been standing less than forty feet from the shooting named William S. Green as the murderer. The 27-year-old Green was arrested and charged with first-degree murder.

Based on the testimony of James D. Hargett and another witness, Green was convicted of murder on Apr. 16, 1947. Defense Attorney Rose Kotzin produced many witnesses unable to identify Green as the killer, including the man who had accompanied Blount the night of the shooting. But Green was found Guilty and sentenced to life in prison. On appeal, the state supreme court upheld the decision.

Ten years later, Hargett voluntarily confessed to the district attorney that he had been paid for his testimony in the Green trial. The other "eyewitness" gave him $100 to finger Green because he wanted revenge against Green for beating him up after he had made unwelcome homosexual advances. When Green's attorney heard Hargett's confession, she petitioned the state to retry the case. The Pennsylvania Supreme Court ruled that the case was out of its jurisdiction, and that Green's only hope was a pardon from the governor.

On Apr. 18, 1957, after serving ten years in Eastern State Penitentiary and twice turning down chances for parole in order to clear his name, Green was pardoned by a Harrisburg Pardons Board. The following day, he walked from the prison arm in arm with attorney Kotzin and told reporters that he intended to spend the next two months relaxing.

"I'm going to keep practicing the saxophone and clarinet I learned inside there," Green said, "Maybe I'll take a stab at music for pay."

REF.: *CBA; Radin, The Innocents.*

Green, Winona, c.1920- , U.S., mur. The metal buckle off a shoe was found near a woman's footprint in the mud next to the bullet-ridden body of Robert Green, a railway employee in Arkansas. Detective Pitcock interviewed Green's son, LeRoy Green, and his wife, Winona, who lived some distance from the older Greens, at their own home. While there, he smelled something burning. Pitcock gave orders that all garbage from the Green home was to be collected. In it he found the remains of a pair of woman's shoes—only one had a buckle.

Going back to the Greens' home, he found that Winona Green and her mother-in-law, who had collected a large amount of life insurance on the death of her husband, had disappeared together. Pitcock started a search for the two and found only Winona, after she had cashed a large check, with her mother-in-law's signature forged. Under arrest, Winona tried to maintain her alibi, but eventually was forced to confess to killing Robert Green as well as his wife. After Green's death, Winona had loaned money to Mrs. Green, on condition that it be repaid out of the insurance money. Later, Mrs. Green refused to pay, holding some knowledge of the murder against Winona. Neither felt safe out of the other's sight, and so her mother-in-law willingly went along when Winona suggested that they go for a drive. Winona shot Mrs. Green in the head and buried her in deep woods, then went to cash the forged check. Pitcock arrested her when she returned to her husband. Tried and found Guilty, Winona Green was sentenced to life in prison.

REF.: *CBA; Whitelaw, Corpus Delicti.*

Greenacre, James, d.1837, and **Gale, Sarah,** prom. 1837, Brit., mur. James Greenacre, a London businessman secretly in need of money, had already lost three wives to illness when he became engaged to Hannah Brown, a 56-year-old widow rumored to be wealthy. On Christmas Eve 1836, two days before they were to be married, Greenacre brought her to his home. There he learned that the woman he thought would provide him some financial security owned only the few things she brought with her. Enraged, he attacked her, first knocking her eye out with a rolling pin and then killing her. At the trial he said that he just knocked her chair back, causing her to fall and accidentally strike her head on the fire guard, but there was evidence that he then cut Brown's throat.

Greenacre sawed the body into pieces and distributed them around London, carrying the wrapped head on an omnibus. A man on Edgware Road found the torso and arms, the legs were found in a marsh at Camberwell, and the head in the Regent's Canal at Stepney. Thousands viewed the head before the victim's brother identified her in March. The police soon learned of Brown's engagement to Greenacre. When they went to his house, they found him in bed with Sarah Gale, a woman he had lived with before his engagement. Greenacre soon confessed to the murder, though he exonerated Gale, who had cleaned up the blood in his house and accepted a pair of Brown's earrings. Greenacre and Gale were both tried. Gale was sentenced to seven years' transportation. Greenacre was sentenced to death and hanged before a huge crowd outside Newgate Prison on May 2, 1837.

REF.: Altick, *Victorian Studies in Scarlet;* Bleackley, *Hangmen of England;* Brock, *A Casebook of Crime; CBA;* Cobb, *The First Detectives;* Forster, *Studies in Black and Red;* Kingston, *A Gallery of Rogues;* _____, *Remarkable Rogues;* Logan, *Rope, Knife and Chair;* Pearce, *Unsolved Murder Mysteries;* Whitelaw, *Corpus Delicti.*

Greenbaum, Gus, 1894-1958, U.S., org. crime. As a young man, Gus Greenbaum aligned with Meyer Lansky on the Lower East Side of New York. He moved to Las Vegas after WWII, and with Morris Rosen and Moe Sedway, inherited the operation of the Flamingo Hotel after the murder of Bugsy Siegel. For the next decade, Greenbaum ran a number of casinos for the mob and oversaw bookmaking operations in Arizona. He ordered mob hits on Tony Broncato and Tony Tombino after the two robbed his hotel. He later became manager of the Riviera Hotel for the Chicago mob. In time, Greenbaum's excessive gambling, womanizing, and drug use got too expensive, and he began skimming money from the mob's profits. His bookkeeping methods were discovered, and in December 1958, Greenbaum and his wife were found dead, their throats cut, in their home in Phoenix. The "hit" was probably ordered by the Chicago mob, with the approval of Lansky, as a message to future clever bookkeepers. REF.: *CBA*.

Greenberg, Bertram, d.1971, U.S., rape-mur. Convicted rapist and former mental patient Bertram Greenberg was gunned down outside Gallup, N.M., after a bloody rampage across three states that left four dead and one injured. Greenberg found sexual pleasure only when he forced women to engage in the act.

It was Spring 1971 when a man walking through a city park in Los Angeles, Calif., noticed a couple who appeared to be making love in the nearby bushes. He changed his course, but returned when he heard a strange sound from the location. He saw the man jump into a Pontiac parked nearby. On the ground lay the body of 13-year-old Mary Louise Hill, who had been raped and strangled to death less than three hours earlier. The man realized that he had stumbled on her killer dumping the body in the park. Before the car sped away, he wrote down the license plate number and later notified authorities.

The automobile was registered to Bertram Greenberg, an L.A. resident who had been convicted of raping four women. He had been in and out of California prisons during the 1950s. An all-points-bulletin was issued for Greenberg, who was not seen again until Arizona state patrolman James Keeton pulled his car over.

A passing motorist called police when he saw Greenberg run from the Arizona patrolman's car with a gun in his hand. By the time officers found Keeton shot to death in the front seat of his patrol car, Greenberg had struck again, fatally injuring patrolman Don Beckstead with a bullet in the stomach after he too stopped Greenberg's Pontiac.

An hour later, Mr. and Mrs. James Brown, tourists traveling through New Mexico, stopped to help Greenberg when he flagged them down near Gallup. The couple agreed to give him a ride to a service station. After they had driven several miles, Greenberg pulled a gun on them, forced them to pull the car over, shot Mr. Brown dead, and raped and shot Mrs. Brown. Leaving her for dead, he fled in their Volkswagen.

Greenberg's final stand took place outside the town of Gallup, where officers had set up a roadblock. When the Volkswagen failed to stop, officers began an eight-mile chase that ended when Greenberg ran the car into a guard rail. When the car came to a stop, Greenberg slashed his wrists and stabbed himself three times with a two-and-a-half-inch pocketknife. Realizing his suicide attempt had failed, he jumped from the car and ran into the desert, where police fired at him several times before he fell to the ground.

"At least four bullets hit him," explained one policeman. "I know he had two bullets in the head, one beneath the left eye and one in the left shoulder...I'm convinced he wanted to die." REF.: *CBA*.

Greenberg, Sam, prom. 1920s-30s, and **Stein, Harry**, prom. 1920s, Case of, U.S., mur. In the early 1930s, a state commission was formed to investigate corruption that had spread within the New York City police department with the onset of prohibition. On Feb. 26, 1931, just before she was scheduled to testify before the commission, a wealthy New York madam was found dead in a Bronx park.

Vivian Gordon had been strangled to death, her body discarded on the side of a park road. Witnesses who had seen her earlier in the evening said she had been wearing a fur coat, a diamond ring, and an expensive wristwatch. Police found none of these items on the corpse, but refused to believe that robbery was the

motive. They believed someone was covering his tracks, since Gordon had a wealth of information on many of New York's law enforcers as well as criminals. For years, she had made it a practice to collect information about her customers in order to blackmail them later.

Police had many suspects, including Gordon's ex-husband, John Bischoff, who had, in 1923, set her up for arrest on prostitution charges in order to get custody of their daughter. Gordon had ended up serving time at the Bedford state prison, and her daughter Benita Gordon was placed in the care of a grandmother in New Jersey. Bischoff was later eliminated as a suspect in favor of Harry Stein, a man who had long been a friend and enforcer for Gordon, and his companions Sam Greenberg and Harry Schlitten. Before Gordon's murder, Stein had told Schlitten, "If I don't put a certain party away, a friend of mine is going to end up in jail." The friend he referred to was underworld attorney and Gordon's financial advisor and ex-lover John Radeloff. Police also learned that on the evening of Gordon's death, Stein had at-

Vivian Gordon, blackmailing New York madam who was murdered in 1931.

tempted to sell a fur coat, a diamond ring, and a wristwatch to a New York fence.

After his arrest, Schlitten turned state's evidence in return for immunity on murder charges. In court, he explained how Stein and Greenberg had strangled Gordon with a clothesline in the back seat of the car as he drove. Defense attorney Samuel Leibowitz portrayed Stein as a consummate liar, cheat, and career criminal. The jury surprisingly acquitted Stein and Greenberg.

After the trial, Gordon's 16-year-old daughter committed suicide, and in 1955, Stein was executed at New York's Sing Sing prison for his involvement in a robbery and murder.

REF.: *CBA; Nash, Open Files; Purvis, Great Unsolved Mysteries.*

Green Bicycle Murder Case, See: **Light, Ronald Vivian**.

Greene, Albert Gorton, 1802-68, U.S., jur. Justice of the municipal court in Providence, R.I., from 1858-67. REF.: *CBA*.

Greene, William, 1731-1809, U.S., jur. Son of Rhode Island Governor William Greene. He served as associate justice and chief justice of the Rhode Island Superior Court from 1776-77, and was elected to the first of two four-year terms as governor of Rhode Island in 1778. REF.: *CBA*.

Greenfield, Louis, prom. 1939, Case of, U.S., euth. Out of fear for the safety of his wife, and out of love for his handicapped child, Louis Greenfield killed his 16-year-old son.

Since his birth in 1922, Jerry Greenfield had been a burden to Louis and Anna Greenfield. Handicapped by Lawrence-Biedl disease, a congenital condition that attacks the central nervous system, Jerry fought a daily losing battle against the incurable disease. The boy grew too quickly for his age, becoming six feet tall and 170 pounds by the time he was sixteen. He was uncoordinated, unable to grasp things, and was never able to walk on his own.

Jerry required constant medical attention, which depleted the Greenfield's savings. When they chose to institutionalize the boy, he cried and became increasingly despondent. The couple lovingly cared for Jerry until the task overwhelmed them and, in the spring of 1939, Louis Greenfield decided to take Jerry's fate into his own hands.

One evening in May, he poured chloroform onto a rag and

smothered the boy. He then faced life in prison on charges of manslaughter.

Defended by famed lawyer Samuel Leibowitz, who accepted the case pro bono, Greenfield testified that he killed Jerry to put him out of his misery and to protect his wife. Greenfield explained that one of the child's doctors had told him there was a possibility that Jerry, who was the size of a man but had the mental capacity of a 2-year-old, might attack his mother.

On the stand, Greenfield explained, "It was against the law of man, but not the law of God...Because God urged me to kill him." Asked if he was sorry that Jerry was dead, Greenberg said, "For Jerry's sake, no. But for my sake, I am sorry. I miss him."

After only four hours of deliberation, the jury found Greenfield Not Guilty of manslaughter charges. REF.: *CBA*.

Green Hills Club, The, 1920s, U.S., gamb. Opened in 1928, The Green Hills Club, located just outside of Kansas City, Mo., was the brainstorm of local gambler and promoter Jake Feinberg, who felt that high-society patrons would flock to a tastefully decorated gambling operation in a lush, country club environment. He convinced the local political power, Tom Pendergast, and his crime boss, Johnny Lazia, that such an operation would net millions.

With enthusiastic support from Pendergast and Lazia, Feinberg opened this club with great fanfare, sending out invitations to those social lions who were already on the delivery lists of society bootleggers working for Lazia and his heavyset lieutenant, Solly Weissman. Thousands of high-class customers responded by sending dues in advance of the club's opening.

Located on one of the newest Missouri highways leading from Kansas City, The Green Hills Club offered every comfort and convenience to the hundreds of chauffeur-driven customers gliding through its doors each evening, including sumptuous meals prepared by French chefs, and the best imported champagnes and wines to be found in the U.S. Its gaming rooms, richly appointed and serviced by uniformed waiters serving free champagne (as was the custom in Monte Carlo, Feinberg pointed out to critical associates), offered all the gambling amenities. Here, the tuxedoed patron could waste tens of thousands at roulette, faro, and blackjack, and the stakes were unlimited to high rollers.

The local residents in Platte County, however, campaigned mightily against this lavish high-society gambling spa and enlisted the aid of Prohibition-minded clergymen who began pressuring the corrupt law-enforcement officers in the area to close down the club. The police, in turn, demanded that Feinberg and Lazia pay them more "protection" money, and when the nightly tallies of profits were learned by the local sheriff, the payoff demands became enormous. Lazia fumed at the thought of the very people on his payroll, the police, extorting his profits, and ordered the club closed down. It was not a total loss, however. He and Feinberg and others had pocketed several million dollars, and they made plans to establish an even more lucrative gambling enterprise, Cuban Gardens, that would continue to cater to the gaming pleasures of the rich. See: **Cuban Gardens**; **Lazia, John**; **Pendergast Machine**; **Weissman, William**.

REF.: *CBA*; Brown, *The Politics of Reform: Kansas City's Municipal Government, 1925-1950*; Redding, *Tom's Town*.

Greenleaf, Simon, 1783-1853, U.S., jur. Law professor at the Harvard University Law School from 1833-44. He authored the three-volume work, *A Treatise on the Law of Evidence*. REF.: *CBA*.

Greenlease Kidnapping Case, The, See: **Hall, Carl Austin**.

Greenlee, Charles, 1933- , and **Irvin, Walter Lee**, 1928-70, and **Shepherd, Samuel**, d.1951, U.S., (wrong. convict.) rape. In Groveland, Fla., in 1949, four young black men were arrested for raping a 17-year-old white divorcee. It wasn't until 1971, more than twenty years later, that their names were cleared.

Once the rape was reported, Lake County officials and Groveland volunteers organized a posse to track down Charles Greenlee, Walter Lee Irvin, Samuel Shepherd, and Ernest Thomas. Greenlee, Irwin, and Shepherd were quickly taken into custody while the search continued for Thomas. Once they cornered him, the angry mob shot him to death. The other three prisoners were arraigned and charged with rape.

Tensions in Groveland flared as the trial date neared. Mobs of angry whites rioted. They firebombed black homes and beat black residents. The National Guard restored order to the community. Defense attorneys felt selecting an impartial jury would be difficult, and they requested a change of venue. The request was denied and the three defendants appeared before a Lake County judge.

Greenlee, Irvin, and Shepherd were found Guilty by the all-white jury on circumstantial evidence. The prosecution's entire case was based on the fact that investigators had found an imprint of tire tracks at the scene of the crime that matched those made by Irvin's car. It is believed, but was never substantiated, that once Irvin and the others were arrested, Lake County Sheriff Willis McCall ordered a deputy to drive Irvin's automobile to the scene. Charles Greenlee, sixteen, was sentenced to life in prison, while Irvin and Shepherd were to be executed. Defense attorneys appealed the death sentences to the state supreme court where the decisions were reaffirmed.

Refusing to give up, the defense appealed to the U.S. Supreme Court, which ordered a new trial in April 1951. Irvin and Shepherd were fetched from prison for questioning. While transporting the two convicted men back to Lake County, Sheriff McCall shot Shepherd dead and critically wounded Irvin, maintaining that the men had attempted escape and that he used his weapon in self-defense. Irvin lived to testify, and told a coroner's jury that McCall was unprovoked and had intended to kill both men to stop them from testifying. The all-white coroner's jury sided with the sheriff and ruled that Shepherd's death was "justifiable." But the Supreme Court grand jury investigation awarded Irvin another date in court.

A change of venue was approved for the second trial and the proceedings were held in nearby Ocala, Fla. With a team of defense lawyers that included Thurgood Marshall, Irvin refused a plea bargain for a life sentence and was again convicted and sentenced to death. He was returned to Raiford State Penitentiary and the St. Petersburg *Times* began their own investigation of his case.

In 1953, following the election of LeRoy Collins as Florida governor, the *Times* revealed its findings and reported that "great doubt" existed that Irvin and the others were guilty. Sparked by the newspaper reports, letters and petitions demanding that Governor Collins pardon Irvin began arriving in Tallahassee. In 1955, Collins commuted Irvin's death sentence to life in prison, and Lake County Circuit Court Judge Truman G. Futch organized a grand jury to investigate Collins' activities. After the grand jury ruled Collins was within his legal rights to commute the sentence, Futch said the governor had shown himself "an innocent victim of the Communists by helping to save a Negro in the Groveland rape case from the electric chair."

In 1961, after serving eleven years of his life sentence, Charles Greenlee, then twenty-seven, was paroled. Walter Lee Irvin's freedom finally came when he was paroled in 1969. Irvin died of a heart attack the following year when he returned to Groveland for the first time since his sentence to attend the funeral of a friend. In 1971, Greenlee's parole was commuted and all four men were finally cleared of any wrongdoing in the Groveland incident. REF.: *CBA*.

Green Ones, The, prom. 1920s, U.S., org. crime. An all-Italian gang, The Green Ones operated in and about St. Louis, Mo., controlling all the rackets in vast sections of that city during the Prohibition era. A rival, non-Italian gang, The Cuckoos, openly warred throughout the mid-1920s with The Green Ones for control of the more lucrative territories in St. Louis, but were systematically eradicated. More than 100 gangsters on both sides of this seesaw battle were killed in a period of five years. See: **Cuckoos, The**.

REF.: *CBA*; Reid, *Mafia*.

Green River Killer, 1982-84, U.S., (unsolv.?) mur. The death toll stands at forty-one, though law enforcement officials in Washington, California, and Oregon estimate that as many as eighty-one people may have been killed the "Green River" killer between 1982 and 1984. For the most part, the madman preyed upon teen-age runaways and prostitutes, many of whom were last seen along Pacific Highway's Sea-Tac strip, Seattle's red-light district populated by pay-as-you-go motels and seamy bars.

The Green River Killer was well acquainted with the forests and streams of western Washington state. "The man we're looking for is a shade of gray," explained Lt. Dan Nolan of the King County Sheriff's Department. "He's very innocuous. He fits right in with the community." Experts who have followed this case since 1982 label the subject a sexual psychopath, whose problems became evident in youth. "Control is a big thing with him," theorized Pierce Brooks, police detective. "Serial killers are the biggest cowards in the criminal subculture. These victims are teenagers, some of them fifteen or sixteen years old. He's got to be physically stronger than his victims." The police are no closer today to identifying the killer than they were in 1982 when the killings began.

Sixteen-year-old Wendy Lee Coffield was the first victim. On July 15, 1982, two boys, bicycling across the Peck Bridge, twenty miles southeast of Seattle, found Coffield's body washed up against the pilings of the Green River, a brackish stream not far from the city airport. Two weeks later, Debra Bonner, twenty-three, was found lying dead on a sandbar in the same river. After that, the remains of other youthful victims turned up with gruesome regularity. Six of them were found in the thick underbrush on Star Lake Road southeast of Sea-Tac. Police attributed the slayings to the same person because the modus operandi seldom varied. The killer selected his victims from the red-light district, drove them to a secluded spot in the woods, and then strangled them.

In January 1984, the Green River Task Force drawn from the King County Sheriff's Department, the Seattle police, and other agencies, was expanded from five to thirty-six in an effort to track down the killer. In the next few years, $13 million was spent in the pursuit of the killer. The Task Force came under sharp editorial attack for its unsuccessful efforts. A $200,000 computer system with custom-designed software was installed to help wade through 20,000 leads. "Because he conceals his bodies because he doesn't want them found quickly, the means of death often isn't known even after autopsy," Nolan said, expressing the frustration of officers. The public was consoled by the fact that police found no new victims murdered after March 1984, suggesting that the killer might have gone into hiding or been arrested on another charge. Between 1982 and 1989 the police moved against five different suspects, but the lab tests failed to establish a positive link to the Green River murders.

In June 1985, officials in San Diego, Calif., established a Multiple Homicide Task Force patterned after the one in King County, Wash., when a rash of unsolved murders suggested that the Green River killer had moved south. The victims were young women connected to the prostitution and B-girl trade which flourished along the El Cajon Boulevard "strip." Logistic coordination between the police agencies of Seattle and San Diego was at first poor. By 1988, however, detectives from both cities closed ranks, and began monitoring reports submitted by the FBI's Violent Criminal Apprehension Program (VICAP) to establish possible links in the chain of unsolved murders.

The first real break in the Green River mystery came after the syndicated television program *Manhunt* was aired on Dec. 8, 1988. A caller from Portland, Ore., advised police to check on a third-year law student from Gonzaga University, William Jay Stevens II. During the two years that the killer terrorized the Pacific Northwest, Stevens was a fugitive from justice, having escaped a King County work release program in 1981 following conviction on a burglary charge. Stevens, thirty-eight, was arrested at his parents' home on Jan. 9, 1989. Police found photographs of nude women in his possession. According to acquaintances, Stevens

regularly paid money to prostitutes to pose for him. A collection of police badges, uniforms, and other items were confiscated at the residence. Law enforcement officials considered it possible that the Green River killer had a "cop fixation" and may have carried out his murders while in uniform. Stevens also expressed an admiration for Theodore Bundy, executed in Florida in 1989. According to a police affidavit, "Stevens talked frequently about serial killer Ted Bundy and appeared to be quite knowledgeable of Bundy's methods and victims."

During the time when the Green River killer was most active, Stevens frequently traveled from Portland to Seattle. Credit card receipts showed that he had dined at restaurants and patronized gas stations in Seattle within days of the disappearances. The body of one of the victims was found less than two miles from where he received a speeding ticket on rural Interstate 90. Stevens was ordered held without bond at the Spokane County Jail for violations of the federal weapons laws on Oct. 4, 1989. At present, investigators continue to probe the possible links Stevens may have had to the Green River murders. So far they have come up short. "If I knew anything about any of this, I would have told the task force long ago, but now I fear I have become the excuse for time and money they have spent," Stevens said. REF.: *CBA*.

Greenwood, David, b.c.1896, Brit., mur. David Greenwood, a 21-year-old employee of a London manufacturing firm, left work on a Saturday in February 1918 wearing an overcoat with a fake military badge fastened to it. When he returned to work on Monday, his co-workers noticed that the badge was missing. Over the weekend, 16-year-old Nellie Trew had been raped and murdered on Eltham Common. A fake military badge shaped like a tiger and a coat button made of bone with wire in it were found near the body. Pictures of the items appeared in the Sunday newspapers. A colleague questioned Greenwood about the objects, and persuaded him to go to the police. The detective interviewing him observed that Greenwood's overcoat had no buttons at all, and that the bottom one had clearly been torn off. Greenwood gave a variety of excuses as to why they were missing. He said he had used two of them to repair his lathe, which his boss said was impossible. Greenwood claimed to have sold the badge over the weekend.

Nellie Trew had gone to the library on Saturday evening and started home across the Common. Greenwood's mother's house was adjacent to the Common, and he had been there that evening. Greenwood was tried for murder on Apr. 26, 1918, and found Guilty. The jury recommended that he not be executed because he had suffered shell-shock as a soldier in WWI. He was sent to prison for life for what was called "the Button and Badge Murder," but sympathy for him grew. In response to petitions, authorities released him after fifteen years in prison.

REF.: Bresler, *Scales of Justice;* Brock, *A Casebook of Crime;* Browne and Tullett, *The Scalpel of Scotland Yard;* Carlin, *Reminiscences of an Ex-Detective; CBA;* Crew, *The Old Bailey;* Gribble, *Great Detective Exploits;* Humphreys, *A Book of Trials;* _____, *Seven Murderers;* Hyde, *United in Crime;* Kingston, *Dramatic Days at the Old Bailey;* Oswald, *Memoirs of a London County Coroner;* Shew, *A Companion to Murder;* Wilson, *Encyclopedia of Murder.*

Greenwood, Harold, c.1866-1929, Case of, Brit., mur. Solicitor Harold Greenwood settled in the village of Kidwelly, Carmarthenshire, Wales, in 1898. He was a brusque, outgoing man, but the local people found him rather unpleasant. They preferred his wife Mabel, who cared for their two children, Kenneth, ten, and Irene, twenty-one, at Rumsey House, a three-story mansion on the edge of the village. Despite Greenwood's modest reputation as a "ladies' man," few doubted that he and his wife were happy together. On June 15, 1919, Mrs. Greenwood became violently ill after eating lunch. She explained that a gooseberry tart had made her nauseous. Dr. Thomas Griffiths, the family doctor, gave her some medicine that contained bismuth.

What appeared to be a minor stomach disorder worsened through the night. Dr. Griffiths was again summoned to Mrs.

Greenwood's bedside, but there was little he could do and she died in great agony the next morning. The doctor certified that the cause of death was heart disease. In October 1919, rumors of foul play circulated through the village when Greenwood married 31-year-old Gladys Jones, the daughter of the publisher of the *Llanelly Mercury*. The police exhumed the body of the first Mrs. Greenwood in April of the following year and found in it a quarter grain of arsenic.

A murder indictment was returned against Greenwood, charging that he had put diluted weed killer in a bottle of burgundy served the afternoon of his wife's death. In November 1920, he went on trial at the Carmarthen Assizes. Sir Edward Marshall Hall defended Greenwood, and got him an acquittal by suggesting that Dr. Griffiths had accidentally put the arsenic in the bismuth. The quarter grain of arsenic was hardly enough to kill a human, Hall stated, but the

Accused wife-killer Harold Greenwood, 1920.

morphia in the medicine may have brought on death. When Irene Greenwood took the stand and said that she had drunk from the same bottle of burgundy as her mother, the prosecution's case collapsed. The jury acquitted Greenwood of murder, but suspicions lingered. Greenwood changed his name to Pilkington and moved to Herefordshire, where he died in poverty on Jan. 17, 1929.

REF.: Bowker, *Behind the Bar*; Browne and Tullett, *The Scalpel of Scotland Yard*; *CBA*; Duke, *Six Trials*; Glaister, *The Power of Poison*; Jacobs, *Aspects of Murder*; Lambton, *Thou Shalt Do No Murder*; Marjoribanks, *For the Defense, The Life of Sir Edward Marshall Hall*; McConnell, *The Detectives*; *Notable British Trials*; Rowland, *Murder Revisited*; Thompson, *Poison and Poisoners*; ____, *Poison Mysteries Unsolved*; Shew, *A Companion to Murder*; Warner-Hooke and Thomas, *Marshall Hall*; Willcox, *The Detective-Physician*; Wilson, *Encyclopedia of Murder*; (FICTION), Duke, *Bastard Verdict*; Huxley, *Mortal Coils* ("The Gioconda Smile").

Greenwood, John, d.1593, Brit., her. Clergyman who helped form an autonomous congregation at Nicholas Lane, credited along with Robert Brown for starting the Separatist church. He was arrested and hanged at Tyburn in 1593. REF.: *CBA*.

Greenwood, Vaughn Orrin (AKA: **Los Angeles Slasher, Skid Row Slasher**), 1944- , U.S., mur. For two months beginning in early December 1974, the bodies of Skid Row derelicts were found with their throats slit in alleys and doorways in Los Angeles. The murderer sought out alcoholic bums and slit their throats with a precision and regularity that amounted to a signature. The slayings were performed in a ritualistically: the murderer scattered salt around the corpses, removed the shoes, and pointed them at the victims' feet—details that police kept secret in order to prevent copycat murders. Seven bodies were found in Los Angeles, and in late January 1975, two more were found in transient hotels in Hollywood. The first eight victims were all between the ages of forty-two and sixty-seven, of small stature, and either lived alone or were homeless. Police developed a psychological profile of the killer as a sexually weak individual who killed in a psychotic or homosexual frenzy.

In the largest manhunt since the search for Charles Manson, police searched for a young, powerfully built white man with long blond hair, a composite description derived from dozens of interviews with Skid Row residents. On Feb. 3, 1975, however,

three days after the ninth victim was found, a black man, 31-year-old Vaughn Greenwood, was arrested for attacking two men with a hatchet in a Hollywood home. A month later, police announced that they expected to charge Greenwood in the "slasher" murders. On Mar. 18, Greenwood's attorney obtained a court-imposed gag order preventing police from discussing the case publicly.

Ten months later, on Jan. 23, 1976, Vaughn Greenwood was formally indicted for eleven murders, including the nine slasher slayings and two murders committed in 1964. On Dec. 29, 1976, Greenwood was convicted on nine counts of murder and one count of assault with intent to commit murder. A mistrial was declared on the two remaining murder charges. On Jan. 19, 1977, Judge Earl C. Broady, sentenced Greenwood to life imprisonment. REF.: *CBA*; Fox, *Mass Murder*; Holmes, *Serial Murder*.

Greer, Frederick Arthur (Lord **Fairfield**), 1863-1945, Brit., jur. Appointed by Lord Birkenhead to the King's Bench around 1919, appointed lord justice of appeal from 1927-38, and named Baron Fairfield of Caldy in Palatine County of Chester. One of the murder trials he presided over was that of Frederick Rothwell Holt. REF.: *CBA*.

Gregg, William, d.1708, Brit., treas. A well-educated English statesman of Scottish descent, William Gregg used the office of English Secretary Harley to inform enemies of the king on British activities.

Gregg began his political career as a secretary to the English ambassador to Sweden, serving the office well until he seduced a Swedish woman. For this, he lost his position and was expelled from the country.

Upon returning to London, Gregg was lured by Secretary Harley—a statesman responsible for communicating vital intelligence to Dutch allies in Holland and generating misinformation to France, then the enemy. Besides Gregg, Harley employed Valiere and Bara, two British intelligence agents who, posing as French spies, gathered information from France and supplied France with Harley's information. What Valiere and Bara did not know, however, was that Gregg often tempered with the "misinformation" they were carrying to France—instead they carried British intelligence designated for the Dutch, their allies.

After several British and Dutch defeats at the hands of the French, Harley's office came under fire. Opponents accused him of treason and suspected his spies of double-crossing England. Valiere and Bara were taken prisoner, and Harley resigned. A full-scale investigation was begun into the scandal, and everyone in Harley's office became suspect. When questioned about his knowledge of the affair, Gregg explained that anyone could have had access to classified documents. Harley took few precautions, often leaving manuscripts lying around the office.

After weeks of testimony, Gregg was charged with high treason for attempting to aid the enemies of England. Both houses of Parliament petitioned for his immediate execution, which was granted. Gregg made a full confession after the sentence was rendered. He also pleaded for forgiveness from the queen and for full exoneration for Harley, Valiere, and Bara, stating that they had unknowingly acted out the most vital roles in his treasonous play. On Apr. 28, 1708, William Gregg walked up to the gallows at Tyburn to be executed, a broken and ashamed man.

REF.: *CBA*; Mitchell, *The Newgate Calendar*.

Gregory V, c.1739-1825, Gr., treas. Patriarch of Constantinople from 1797-99, 1806-08, and 1819-21. He was killed by Turks, who hanged him on the doorway of his own church, for assisting the Greeks at the start of their war for independence. REF.: *CBA*.

Gregory VI (**Johannes Gratianus**), b.c.1048, Ger., consp. Second German pope in 1045, rivaled by Antipope Sylvester III. He was charged with purchasing his appointment as pontiff from Benedict IX, and was removed and banished after one year in office. REF.: *CBA*.

Gregory, Arthur John Peter Michael Maundy (AKA: **The Great Swindler**), 1877-1941, Brit., fraud. J. Maundy Gregory earned the sobriquet "The Great Swindler" through his highly accurate perception of what vanities people will pay for and precisely how much they will pay. Gregory was born poor, the son of a Hampshire clergyman. His father's occupation provided him a good education and some exposure to genteel society. After failing at a theatrical venture, Gregory discovered his life work—a con game in which he convinced people that he could get them a title. Gregory claimed to be able to arrange anything from a knighthood, for £10,000, to a peerage, for £100,000. He dressed and acted the part of an important gentleman and kept lavish offices on Parliament Street in Whitehall, between the Old Scotland Yard and the prime minister's home on Downing Street. No one actually knew who Gregory was, thanks in large part to his own efforts to obscure his identity. His manner and apparent wealth convinced many that he held a high position in the foreign office or the secret service.

Gregory's scam worked because he obtained the names of people actually being considered for a title. He then asked around to determine which of the candidates was particularly eager for such an honor. Often the candidates paid Gregory his fee, received the title, and never knew that they would have gotten it anyway. Gregory's reputation grew, and he enhanced it at every opportunity. Eventually, he drew suspicion. Victor Grayson, a socialist politician and former member of parliament, denounced Gregory. One evening in 1920, Grayson left a hotel bar in London after having a drink with friends and disappeared. Although nothing was ever proved, a number of people suspected that Gregory had arranged the disappearance. Gregory's name was also

High class con man J. Maundy Gregory.

mentioned in connection with the sudden and mysterious death of Mrs. Edith Rosse, who left him nearly £20,000. In 1925, perhaps in direct response to Gregory's activities, the Honours (Prevention of Abuses) Act, was passed.

In 1933, Gregory offered to arrange a knighthood for Edward Leake, a retired naval man. Leake agreed to Gregory's price, but really intended to turn him in. Leake alerted Scotland Yard to Gregory's offer, and in February 1934, Gregory was brought to court on charges of "Endeavouring to Procure the Grant of a Title or Honour Contrary to the Honours Act." Gregory wisely pleaded guilty and was fined £50 and sentenced to two months in prison. On his release, Gregory filed for bankruptcy and went to live in Paris. He failed to return for his bankruptcy hearing which showed that he had liabilities of £15,000. Gregory remained in France until the German occupation of June 1940, when he was arrested as an alien. He refused repatriation and died in a Paris hospital the following year.

REF.: Aldington, *Frauds;* Balfour, *Society Racket: A Critical Survey of Modern Social Life;* Blythe, *The Age of Illusion; CBA;* Cullen, *A Playful Panther: The Story of J. Maundy Gregory, Con Man;* Graves, *The Long Week-End;* King, *Strictly Personal;* Macmillan, *The Nonours Game;* Meyrick, *Secrets of the 43;* Mowat, *Britain Between the Wars;* Rose, *The World's Greatest Rip-offs;* Sparrow, *The Great Swindlers;* Symons, *J.F.A. Symons: His Life and Speculations;* Trewin, *Benson and the Bensonians.*

Gregory, Thomas Watt, 1861-1933, U.S., lawyer. Appointed special assistant to the U.S. attorney general in charge of prosecuting a northeastern railroad for violating the Sherman Antitrust Act, and served as U.S. attorney general from 1914-19. REF.: *CBA.*

Grellet, Stephen (Étienne de Grellet du Mobillier), 1773-1855, U.S., penal reform. Missionary minister who traveled throughout Europe and America, advocating upgrade of prison conditions. REF.: *CBA.*

Greig, Rodney, 1917-c.1938, U.S., mur. "For no reason at all, I raised the knife and let her have it. I don't know why, but I let her have it," said 21-year-old Rodney Greig to police, confessing to the murder of his girlfriend, Leona Vlught.

At 3 a.m. on the morning of Dec. 7, 1938, Greig pulled to a stop on a dirt road in the Oakland foothills and turned to his girlfriend. They talked and then wrestled with an object Vlught held in her hand. Then Greig got out of the car, walked around to the passenger side, and plunged a six-inch hunting knife into Vlught's breast.

Her heart ruptured instantly and she slumped against the dashboard. Greig reached into his pocket, lit a cigarette, and stood looking at the corpse for fifteen minutes before he rolled it from the car onto the ground and dragged the body twenty feet through the mud. Vlught's spike heels traced their path. Greig then stabbed the neck three more times and left Leona's body lying face up in the mud. Back behind the wheel of his Dodge, Greig made a U-turn and headed back to town and home to bed.

Twelve hours later, at Greig's parents' home in Berkeley, Oakland police arrested Greig and charged him with the murder of Leona Vlught, whose body was found by an airline employee searching for wild mushrooms. Once Vlught's body was found, police turned up only one substantial clue—tire tracks left by an automobile the night before. Analysis established that the treads were those of a late model Dodge that had made a U-turn at the site. Corroborating information from three of Vlught's friends then linked Vlught directly to Greig on the night of the murder.

Greig confessed, recounting to police the events that led up to the murder. He explained that Vlught had seemed depressed, and that she was talking about suicide. So he handed her a hunting knife he kept in the back seat of his car and dared her to end it all. Vlught jabbed the knife at him, playfully, he said, and then he took it from her. "I stabbed her just once, in the breast," he said, "and she folded up." Asked why he then stabbed her in the throat, he explained: "I just nicked her easy—three times—in the throat. She didn't bleed, so I know she was dead."

Greig was held in jail until he was convicted and executed. REF.: *CBA.*

Grenfell, T. Remington, and **Blodgett, Wilson A.,** prom. 1929, U.S., fraud. Even today, the competition between fruit sellers in New York City can be vigorous. With a stand on virtually every corner, a proprietor is always looking for ways to best a rival. This was no less true in 1929, when aggressive ambition dropped two immigrant brothers into what can only be considered the perfect swindle.

The elaborate scam began on Mar. 18, when a well-dressed man carrying an expensive briefcase stepped out of a chauffeur-driven limousine in midtown Manhattan and strolled up to the fruit stand of Nick Fortunato and his brother, Tony Fortunato. He presented his business card to the Italian immigrants announcing himself as T. Remington Grenfell, vice president of the Grand Central Holding Corporation. He informed the brothers that they were "the lucky ones." After a careful investigation of all of the major fruit sellers in Manhattan, they had been selected as the vendors most deserving of an irresistible offer.

At the very center of New York's vast Grand Central Station, there is an information booth. This booth was to be closed, Mr. Grenfell said, because so many travelers had been asking pointless questions of the attendants. On Apr. 1, the booth would be vacated and all questions would be answered, instead, at the train ticket windows. Grand Central Holding Corporation was offering the Fortunato brothers the opportunity to rent the information booth to run what would undoubtedly be the country's most successful fruit stand. And the Fortunatos could have all this for the meager rental fee, paid up front, of $100,000. This deal was so good that if after six months the stand was not making a minimum profit of $1,000 a week, the brothers could void the contract and receive $50,000 back.

Before the Fortunato brothers could reply, Grenfell produced from his briefcase blueprints for the magnificent stand, accompanied by pages of regulations stipulating precisely how the stand would need to be constructed to meet Grand Central Station's specifications. It was an elaborate presentation that must have thoroughly convinced the brothers of their good fortune. Certainly the rent was steep, but they had the money in savings, and by New York City's standards, the $8,300-a-month rent was a steal. With the stand operating twenty-four hours a day, the Fortunatos knew that before long they would make up what they had shelled out in overhead, assuring them a small fortune. Everything seemed to be in place—but they still wanted time to think it over. Grenfell regretfully explained that there was not enough time to think about it; if they were not able to accept this offer immediately, it would have to be extended to the second-best fruit vendor in Manhattan.

Seized by that unpleasant thought, the Fortunatos resolved to accept their destiny. They were whisked into Grenfell's limousine, taken to the Pan Am building, which connects to Grand Central Terminal, and brought to the offices of Grand Central Holding Corporation. There they met Wilson A. Blodgett, the president of the company, but not before they overheard a phone conversation in which Mr. Blodgett closed the same deal with another fruit seller. The president explained that there had been some confusion, and he had thought that the Fortunatos would not be able to present the $100,000 check to the company. The Fortunato brothers fervently assured him that this was not the case; they would have the check in the offices the next morning. Mr. Blodgett assured them that the deal was theirs.

A certified check was handed over to Blodgett and Grenfell early the next morning, the fine points of the deal were worked out, and the rental agreement was signed. The Fortunato brothers spent the next two weeks lining up carpenters and purchasing building materials and other necessities for their promising new business. On the morning of Apr. 1, the Fortunatos, their carpenters, and two truckloads of wood pulled up to Grand Central Station.

The entourage stood in the station and waited for 9:00 a.m., the time that the contract would take effect, and the men in the information booth would undoubtedly leave. But 9:00 came and went, and there was no indication from the railroad attendants that their duties were ending. Finally, with contract in hand, Tony walked up to the booth and asked them to vacate his booth. The attendants stared blankly and said they knew nothing of this arrangement. Tony became perturbed and began yelling at them. The police were notified, and the arduous task of straightening out the matter began.

Construction of the booth also began, for the carpenters were certain that the misunderstanding would be cleared up shortly. They had worked for an hour when word came from New York Central Railroad that there was no record of a company named the Grand Central Holding Corporation. The Fortunato brothers, still refusing to believe they had been duped, showed the authorities the deserted suite where the money had changed hands.

A check with the bank where the holding company kept its account revealed how crafty "Grenfell" and "Blodgett" (probably not their real names) had been. They led the bank to believe they were a brokerage firm and had persuaded the bank official to omit the formality of reference checks. Their deposit from the Fortunato ruse had sat in the account for a few days and then, so as not to arouse suspicion, small withdrawals between $10,000 and $20,000 were made every day until there was only $1,000 remaining. Grenfell and Blodgett then slipped out of the country and out of existence.

Great effort was made to try to locate the perpetrators, but all leads pointed to only one fact: the criminals had done an impeccable job of covering their tracks. Nick and Tony Fortunato would never recover their money. REF.: *CBA*.

Grenier, Jean, 1589-1610, Fr., witchcraft. In Europe and America during the fifteenth to seventeenth centuries, people were often executed for witchcraft on evidence that could, at best, be characterized as "flimsy." But the case of 14-year-old Jean Grenier was so farfetched that, as much as the boy pleaded his involvement with the occult, the courts would not hand him the ultimate sentence.

Young Grenier believed he had the ability to become a werewolf, and in 1603, tried to convince others in his village in southwestern France of that fact and that he was responsible for a number of murders. He explained, first to other children and later to the courts, that he had been introduced to the *Maitre de la Forêt,* a mysterious black man, who had given him a wolf pelt and ointment. With these materials, Jean claimed that he could transform himself into a flesh-eating animal.

His claims would probably have been given less credence had a number of children not been killed in the region during the previous few months. On May 29, a trial was held in which Jean repeated his story, and a number of girls testified against him. The case was passed to a higher court at Coutras, where it was revealed that Jean was a borderline idiot who had a reputation for storytelling. Instead of incarcerating Jean, authorities took his father and a neighbor into custody.

Because more and more children told tales of a wolf who had terrorized them, Jean was eventually sentenced to hang and his body burned.

At this point, the Parlement of Bordeaux decided to look into the case. The 14-year-old gave a detailed account of the children he had killed and devoured. In a rare display of wisdom, it asked that Jean be studied by doctors, who subsequently found him insane. The boy was sentenced to life imprisonment at the monastery of Franciscan Cordeliers, in Bordeaux. He died there seven years later. REF.: *CBA*.

Grenières, Deniselle, prom. 1459, Fr., witchcraft. In the last half of the fifteenth century, sixty-seven people were burned as witches in France alone. Papal Inquisitors launched Europe's first full-scale organized witch hunt in Arras, Fr., in 1459. They first arrested Deniselle Grenières, a weak-minded woman who confessed, under torture, and implicated five others. One of the five committed suicide, and the other four were burned alive, but not before they too identified others as witches. The inquisition snowballed until so many citizens of Arras were in prison for witchcraft that the town ceased functioning. Faced with this practical dilemma, two archbishops halted the investigations and released the prisoners. REF.: *CBA*.

Grenville, George (Baron Lansdowne), 1667-1735, Brit., rebel. Secretary of war in 1710, he was imprisoned for suspected Jacobitism from 1715-17. REF.: CBA.

Grenville, Richard (Richard Granville), 1600-58, Brit., embez. Grandson of British naval commander Sir Richard Grenville. In 1630, he was promoted from soldier to baronet. He defied orders to fight in the parliamentary army and joined King Charles I's forces in 1644. Two years later, he was exiled to Holland for insubordination and misappropriation of war funds. REF.: *CBA*.

Grese, Irma (AKA: The Beast of Belsen), 1923-45, Ger., war crimes. Irma Grese personified the inhuman depravity of the Nazi regime in the 1930s and 1940s. When she was ten, Adolf Hitler became chancellor of the German Reich. The public school system was forced to adopt Nazi teachings, and the Nazi philosophy of Aryan superiority. Irma Grese was one of thousands of youngsters compelled to study and espouse Nazi doctrine.

Against the wishes of her more pragmatic parents, Grese joined Nazi youth groups and became a loyal party member. In 1942 at the age of nineteen, she became a concentration camp supervisor in Ravensbruck. After being trained to run a camp and administer torture, Grese was sent to Auschwitz. Grese's father found her activities so repugnant that he beat her senseless during one of her visits home. Grese was unmoved by her father's disapproval and returned to the camp to supervise the female inmates in the compound.

Grese's day began promptly at seven. She dressed in the

dreaded S.S. uniform, complete with stiff-soled boots and carried a gun and bullwhip. Her usual floggings, pistol whippings, and physical torture were often accompanied by a more sinister mental torment. Irma Grese was particularly good at inflicting mental anguish. To one prisoner she would say, "you're lucky—you have another two weeks." Then she would have the person killed at once. Grese was accompanied on her rounds at Auschwitz by two baying Alsatian hounds trained to attack on command. She purposely kept these animals half-starved in order to make them even more vicious toward the prisoners. Grese often randomly picked a non-German speaking female Jewish prisoner and in a stern tone told the prisoner to fetch a tool which had been placed beyond the compound. As the prisoner pushed her way through the tangle of barbed wire, the sentry shouted a warning—which the prisoner could not understand—and then opened fire.

Nazi war criminal Irma Grese, who tortured and murdered helpless prisoners.

Shortly before the German surrender in 1945, Grese was transferred to the Belsen camp where she was arrested by the allied armies when they came to liberate it. During the trial of the war criminals, Grese faced her accusers stoically. "Himmler is responsible for all that has happened," she said. "But I suppose I have as much guilt as the others above me." The testimony of the survivors of the death camp was appalling. But the stories that were told confirmed that Grese was one of the Reich's most cold-blooded murderers. She was hanged on Dec. 13, 1945, in Hamelin, Ger.

REF.: *CBA;* Lustgarten, *The Business of Murder;* Nash, *Look For the Woman;* Playfair and Sington, *The Offenders;* Wilson, *Encyclopedia of Murder.*

Gresham, Walter Quintin, 1832-95, U.S., jur. Major general in 1865, from 1869-83, he served as U.S. district judge in Indiana, and was appointed U.S. postmaster general and U.S. secretary of the treasury in 1883 and 1884. He began work in 1884, as a U.S. circuit judge for the Seventh Judicial District, and from 1893-95, he was the U.S. secretary of state. REF.: *CBA.*

Gresheimer, Fred, prom. 1912, U.S., asslt. Showman Florenz Ziegfeld was rarely seen without a woman on his arm. When the woman was singer Lillian Lorraine, her estranged husband, wealthy playboy Fred Gresheimer, was not happy about it. In June 1912, Ziegfeld and Lorraine were dining at a New York restaurant when Gresheimer stormed in and began beating the 45-year-old Ziegfeld on the head with his cane. Gresheimer pulled Ziegfeld into an alley and thrashed him unmercifully.

Lorraine called the police. As they arrived, Gresheimer grabbed his wife, pulled her into his car, and drove her to his Long Island home, where he kept her captive for several days until the police came for him. He was convicted of assault and sentenced to five years in prison. REF.: *CBA.*

Gretzler, Douglas, c.1950-   , and **Steelman, William,** c.1945-   , U.S., mur. Douglas Gretzler, from the Bronx, N.Y., met Willie Steelman, a former mental patient and convict from the San Joaquin Valley in California, and the two became a team of mass murderers. They met in Denver, Colo., and traveled to Arizona where they randomly robbed homes and blithely killed anyone who got in their way. Arizona police attributed seven deaths to them, two of which were their partners in an alleged drug deal. The pair drove to just south of Sacramento, Calif., with Michael Adshade and Ken Unrein of Phoenix held captive in their van. There they killed and buried them by a small creek. They returned to Arizona where they offered two hitchhikers a ride, then killed them. In Tucson, they broke into the apartment of Michael and Patricia Sandberg, killed them, took their car,

and drove to the little farming community of Victor, Calif.

In the evening of Nov. 6, 1973, Walter and Joanne Parkin, who owned a successful grocery store in Victor, went bowling with their friends, Dick and Wanda Earl. They left their two children with teen-aged Debbie Earl, Dick, and Wanda's daughter, and the girl's brother, Rick and her boyfriend, Mark Lang. When the two couples returned, they were confronted by Gretzler and Steelman who were holding the children at gunpoint. One of the men took Parkin to his store and forced him to take $4,000 from the safe. They then returned to the Parkin's home, tied up all nine hostages and shot them one by one.

The next morning, Laura Carlson, a house guest who had returned late the night before and gone straight to bed, found the victims. First she saw the two children dead in their parents' bed. Then, she found the three older children and four adults all crammed into a bedroom closet. When the police arrived it was noticed that the ropes binding the victims were tied with unusual knots. A bulletin was put out and word was sent from Arizona that killers using similar knots there had been identified as Gretzler and Steelman. Photos of the two were immediately published in the newspapers. A hotel clerk in Sacramento recognized the pair as they were checking in and called the police. Gretzler was easily seized, but Stellman escaped and was not captured until a SWAT team had sent tear gas into the room where he had holed up.

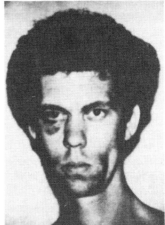

Left, Douglas Gretzler and, right, William Steelman, mass murderers.

Gretzler confessed to the killings and pleaded guilty. Steelman did not plead before the California judge, letting his grand jury testimony speak for him. They were both found Guilty of the nine murders in Victor. California had outlawed capital punishment, so the men were sentenced to life in prison, which would make them eligible for parole in seven years. California willingly sent the men to Arizona, where the death penalty was still in use. They were sentenced to death in the gas chamber for the killing of the Sandberg couple. It is believed that Gretzler and Steelman are responsible for at least eleven other murders for which they have yet to be tried, and as of this writing, they remain on Death Row.

REF.: *CBA;* Godwin, *Murder;* Nash, *Murder, America.*

Grey, Alice (AKA: **Alice Cavendish**), prom. 19th Cent., Brit., fraud. Some people are born with a remarkable talent, and express it through ventures such as art, altruism, or business. Alice Grey was endowed with beauty and an uncanny gift for deception, and she utilized both fully.

Grey decided at the age of nineteen that she had had enough of her drunken father's paltry existence. The first victim to contribute to her income was the London train station master, whom she convinced with tears in her eyes that her purse containing £8 and a return ticket to Dublin had been stolen. As he gave her passage and £1 from his own pocket, she assured him that her "affluent Irish family" would reimburse him upon her arrival in

Dublin. She was on her way to a prosperous career.

Her most successful of many ruses over the years exploited the rift between Protestantism and Catholicism. She would tell well-to-do Protestants that she had just run away from a wicked Catholic convent after trying to convert other nuns to Protestantism. Wealthy Catholics would hear a story about her cruel family who had just thrown her out because she had embraced Catholicism. Her flawless delivery combined with teary eyes and a wilting, humble demeanor guaranteed her plenty of spending money and jewelry, not to mention free room and board. When it became necessary to move on so that her story would not fall apart, she would first make a sweep of her hosts' homes and clean out all the jewelry and money she could find.

Her swindles forced her to keep moving around the United Kingdom to keep from stumbling across her old victims again. London, Limerick, Birmingham, Belfast, and Liverpool were just a few of the cities she visited. Her ploys varied, according to the situation. One of her favorites was to study someone—usually a child, since they were more susceptible to her accusations and the authorities' stern discipline—and then run to the police accusing that person of robbing her. She was so convincing that even if someone had an alibi clearing them of involvement in the crime, Alice's impassioned testimony would often result in conviction and she would receive "just compensation."

In one infamous instance, Robert Kennedy, a rich Limerick bachelor, fell in love with Grey, and was involved in an affair with her for some time. She later sued him for breach of promise of marriage. Although she had no proof—not even a love note to establish that he had a fondness for her—and although he insisted he had never indicated a desire to marry her, the jury ruled in her favor and the unfortunate man was forced to pay £500 plus her solicitor's fees.

When Grey was caught perjuring herself in court, she either received an exceptionally light sentence, or a sympathetic jury acquitted her. She remained virtually untouched by the law until she accused a man of a crime he had allegedly committed while he was fifty miles away. Upon dismissal of the case, Grey was arrested for perjury. Her reaction was a slew of expletives directed at the officials. Her behavior was so markedly out of character that the police placed her under scrutiny. An investigation uncovered her past and eventually a judge handed her a just sentence: four years in prison.

Alice Grey had over one hundred aliases. She brought twenty-nine innocent men to court for crimes they knew nothing about, nine of whom were convicted. Though she never did an honest day's work, she lived on an average of £50 a week. Alice Grey was one of the most proficient—and beautiful—swindlers in history.

REF.: *CBA*; Kingston, *A Gallery of Rogues*; Stevens, *Famous Crimes and Criminals*.

Grey, Arthur (Fourteenth Baron), 1536-93, Brit., mur. Eldest son of John de Grey, he ordered the 1580 massacre of 600 Italians and Spaniards at Smerwick. From 1580-82, he served as lord deputy of Ireland. He was on the panel of judges who prosecuted Mary, Queen of Scots, and wrote the report on Holinshed's defense of Guines. REF.: *CBA*.

Grey, Dora May, 1894-1912, Brit., (unsolv.) mur. The case moved from "intriguing" to "mystifying," and finally, "utterly confounding." Dora Grey's murder aggravated investigators because they could never discover so much as a motive for her death. She was found on a beach in Yarmouth, England, on the morning of July 15, 1912, apparently the victim of a strangling. Her shoes stood neatly a few feet from her, her stockings had been removed and tied around her neck. Underneath the stockings was a bootlace from one of her shoes. The police and doctors concluded that this had been the weapon used in the murder.

In some ways, Dora's life held as much mystery as her death. She was an illegitimate child, raised by a woman who had been paid less than three shillings a week by the natural mother. The mother eventually stopped paying altogether, but Dora's guardian continued to take care of her. The girl had always been described as quiet and reserved, though as she got older she assimilated her mother's penchant for keeping a great number of male friends.

Many confusing points in the murder investigation emerged. There was no sign of struggle. The sand around her had not been disturbed, and her hands were at her sides. There was no sand clinging to her feet, indicating that she had not moved from the spot where she was found after her shoes had been removed. This seemed to indicate that she was not killed on the beach but was brought there, most likely by automobile, since her body was found not far from a road.

Those who spent time investigating the case were bothered by another point. Twelve years prior to the discovery of Grey's body, another woman had been killed by her husband on the same Yarmouth beach. She had also died by strangulation with a bootlace, though there was evidence that, unlike Grey, she had struggled desperately for her life. It is possible that Grey's murderer had killed her by a discreet method—poison is the most likely candidate—then brought the body to the beach and prepared it to look like the murder from years past. This theory was never tested because the doctors who examined Grey's body, upon seeing the bootlace, concluded that strangulation was the cause of death, and never bothered to check for signs of poison.

The most perplexing dilemma investigators faced was establishing who Dora had been with on the evening she was murdered. She apparently had a great number of boyfriends, many of whom frequented the Yarmouth yacht station. At least four eyewitnesses testified to seeing her in different locations around the marina with a man on that Sunday, but descriptions of her escorts varied so radically that she must have spent time with several men that day. Only one of the men could be tracked down, but it was proven he was nowhere near the murder site that evening. Despite considerable effort, none of her other companions was ever located.

For weeks, police tried to shed more light on the mystery. They even placed two undercover men near the location where the body was found, in case the murderer returned to the scene. No useful clues were uncovered, however, and Dora Grey's murderer and their motive remain unknown.

REF.: Adam, *Murder By Persons Unknown*; Brock, *A Casebook of Crime*; *CBA*.

Grey, George, 1799-1882, Brit., jur. Grandson of First Earl Grey and nephew of Charles Grey. He was judge advocate general from 1839-41, and home secretary from 1846-52, 1855-58, and 1861-66. In 1848, he kept the Chartist reform movement under control, and in 1846, he was instrumental in the passage of the convict discipline bill which ended exile of prisoners and helped reform the British penal system. REF.: *CBA*.

Grey, Henry (Duke of Suffolk), d.1554, Brit., treas. Eldest son of Thomas Grey, who compelled his daughter, Lady Jane Grey, to marry the son of John Dudley to put her in line for the throne. He was pardoned for his role in trying to capture the throne with his daughter, but executed for helping Wyatt protest Mary Tudor's marriage to King Philip of Spain. REF.: *CBA*.

Grey, Lady Jane, 1537-1554, Brit., consp. Daughter of Duke Henry Grey, and a descendant of Henry VII. She was forced by her father to marry Lord Guildford Dudley to alter the line of succession. After the death of Edward VI, she was proclaimed queen in 1553, and imprisoned ten days later. She and Lord Dudley were beheaded after her father took part in Wyatt's Rebellion, the protest against Mary Tudor's wedding plans. REF.: *CBA*.

Grey, John de (Second Baron Grey de Wilton), 1268-1323, Brit., jur. Named lord ordainer in 1310, and appointed justice of North Wales in 1315. He was the father of conspirator William Grey. REF.: *CBA*.

Grey, Lord Leonard (Leonard Gray, AKA: Viscount Grane of Ireland), c.1490-1541, Brit., treas. Son of Thomas Grey, First Marquis of Dorset. During his tenure as lord deputy of Ireland from 1536-37, he was charged with indulging members of the Irish Geraldine family, denounced for treason, and eventually beheaded. REF.: *CBA*.

Greylord Judicial Investigation, 1977-89, U.S., brib.-polit. corr. The corruption in the Cook County Court system was deep and pervasive. For a fixed price, a minor traffic ticket or a serious charge of drunk driving could be dismissed by judges of the circuit courts. Corrupt defense lawyers slipped envelopes stuffed with $100 bills into the judges' robes or desk drawers. To systematize the payoffs, Judge Richard LeFevour, who headed the Chicago branch courts from 1980 until his conviction in July 1985, organized a "Hustler's Club" of lawyers who paid $2,000 a month directly to him and $500 to his cousin James LeFevour, a former Chicago policeman. In return for the payout, they agreed to assign cases to other judges who would "play ball." Those who collected the defendant's bond money as the payoff to keep quiet were transferred. "A judge didn't sit in a major courtroom for long unless I could see him," James LeFevour boasted.

The corruption involved at least eighty-four judges, lawyers, clerks, and Chicago policemen. On several occasions, Police Sergeant Cy Martin posed as Judge Raymond Sodini during the early morning "call" of vagrants and winos at Chicago's notorious Branch 26 court when the real judge was hung over or otherwise incapacitated. "He's always been a good guy," Martin said of Sodini, a friend from high school days. "And I was willing to help him because I didn't want him to be embarrassed by a courtroom full of bums and bozos and no judge to take care of them." Such was the level of judicial corruption in Cook County when the FBI began it's Operation Greylord Investigation in 1977.

U.S. Attorney Thomas Sullivan laid the groundwork for a massive probe into the court system in 1977, but it was the ambitious work of FBI agents Terrence Hake and David Ries that produced the evidence to convict fourteen judges and sixty-nine police officers and municipal employees.

Using sophisticated eavesdropping equipment, the two FBI men recorded snatches of conversations with lawyers and judges in the washrooms and corridors of Cook County courts. In the early months of Greylord — named after a racehorse, not bewigged British judges as is commonly believed — Hake posed as a corrupt lawyer seeking breaks for his clients. Later, as the investigation expanded, the agents bugged the private chambers of Judge Wayne Olson, who presided over narcotics court. Olson, a judge since 1962, told attorney Bruce Roth that he loved people who "take dough because you know exactly where they stand," referring to attorneys who solicited clients for bribe money to fix cases. Olson later boasted of making a "thousand a week." He was eventually sentenced to twelve years in prison, and assessed a $35,000 fine.

The first publicized reports of the Greylord Investigation were released to the press on Aug. 5, 1983, six years after Sullivan completed the preliminary work. Within weeks, dozens of lawyers and judges were pleading guilty to bribery and racketeering charges based on evidence taken from secret tape recordings. It was the testimony of James LeFevour, who appeared in the first seven Greylord trials, including his cousin Richard's, that sealed the fate of a dozen defendants. Judge LeFevour, fifty-six, became the highest-ranking jurist convicted when his verdict was handed down in July 1985.

Greylord resulted in two suicides. Despondent over his impending indictment on bribery charges, Judge Allen Rosin of the Cook County Circuit Court shot himself on June 22, 1987, at a health club. Rosin was named by James LeFevour as one of ten judges likely to accept bribes. Two years earlier, Chicago police officer Roger Murphy, fifty-three, had shot himself when the first of the Greylord indictments was handed down.

By early 1989, the scorecard of convictions listed fourteen judges, including: Richard LeFevour of the First Municipal District; Associate Judges John Murphy, Wayne Olson, Martin Hogan, John J. Devine, and Roger Seaman; and Circuit Judges John Reynolds, Frank Salerno, Raymond Sodini, James Oakey, Daniel Glecier, John McCollom, and John J. McDonnell.

Commenting on the lasting impact of the Greylord investigation, U.S. Attorney Anton Valukis pointed with pride to a cleaner, more efficient judicial system in Cook County. "Clearly there are no more blatantly corrupt courtrooms. People who might want to engage in this type of activity are much more circumspect." Thomas Sullivan offered a more ominous view of existing conditions. "It is naive to believe that all of the corrupt judges have been identified and rooted out," he said. "Most lawyers who practice here will not speak of this for publication, because they fear reprisals by the judges, but the existence of judicial corruption has been discussed among knowledgeable lawyers in Cook County for as long as I can recall." REF.: *CBA*.

Gribble, Kenneth, 1928- , Brit., mansl. The body of a young man was found near a ballast hole at Kempston, in Bedfordshire, England, on Aug. 15, 1944. Examination revealed that death was caused by numerous heavy blows to the head, and that the victim, a young male, had been dead for at least ten days.

Detective Chief Inspector Peter Beveridge and a few police officers scoured the location where the body had been found to find clues to the identity of the victim—and the identity of his murderer. The primary lead was a torn-up photograph of a girl. A police woman at the station identified her as someone she had often seen at a local dance hall. Police tracked down the girl, who identified the clothes of the deceased as belonging to her cousin, Robert Smith.

Smith had been working for a local firewood salesman, Mr. Gribble. The cousin said she had not seen Smith since Aug. 6 and assumed that he had found another job in the region for the time being. She recommended that the best person to ask about Smith's whereabouts was a close friend of his, and the son of his employer, Kenneth Gribble.

Kenneth, sixteen, was affable to Chief Inspector Beveridge. He said he, too, had last seen Smith on Aug. 6, in the afternoon, after giving Smith his week's pay. He said that he had never been to the ballast hole with Smith. Later, however, a friend of Gribble's told police that he had heard an unfriendly conversation between Smith and Gribble about Smith's wages and that there had been talk about a meeting at the ballast hole to settle their differences.

Gribble, when confronted with this information, admitted that there had been *plans* for a meeting, but it had never actually occurred: the boy had waited at the ballast hole for Smith, but Smith never showed up, so he eventually left.

By this time, the medical examiners had suggested that Chief Inspector Beveridge search the ballast hole area again, this time for a murder weapon. Doctors surmised from their examination that there had been a minimum of four blows, the third felling Smith, and at least one and possibly more blows delivered while the victim lay unconscious on the ground. A heavy tree bough was eventually uncovered, and analysis found blood and Smith's eyebrow hair on the stick. The same search of the ballast hole netted Smith's shoes and jacket.

Kenneth Gribble was questioned once again. He said he had been with a girl on that afternoon. Chief Inspector Beveridge dispensed with that story after a short interview with the girl, who had clearly not been with Gribble. But instead of challenging Gribble again, he ordered the boy put under secret observation.

Those observing him noted that Gribble talked about the murder a great deal. On Sept. 20, Chief Inspector Beveridge and a number of officers visited the Gribble home. Gribble continued to deny knowledge of the slaying, until at the urging of his father, he broke down and told his story.

He and Smith had met on Aug. 6 at the ballast hole and exchanged furious words. At some point, Smith had thrown a tree limb at Gribble, who then picked it up and struck Smith with it. Smith continued to attack Gribble, even after a second blow to the head. The third blow finally sent Smith to the ground, and Gribble hit him two more times. He tossed away the tree limb, tried in vain to revive Smith, and then hid the body in some bushes. He also hid Smith's shoes and jacket, removing a wallet from the jacket and destroying it later.

Gribble was tried for murder but, due to his story of self-defense and his young age, was found Guilty of manslaughter. He was sentenced and served a two-year prison term. **REF.:** *CBA; Lefebure, Evidence for the Crown; Simpson, Forty Years of Murder.*

Griboedov, Aleksandr Sergeevich (Aleksandr Sergeyevich Griboyedov), 1795-1829, Rus., assass. Russian minister of Teheran from 1828-29 who was murdered by an angry mob along with other members of the embassy staff. **REF.:** *CBA.*

Gridley, Jeremiah, 1702-67, U.S., lawyer. Attorney general of the Massachusetts Bay Providence known for defending the Writs of Assistance in 1761. **REF.:** *CBA.*

Griego, Francisco (AKA: Pancho), d.1875, U.S., west. gunman. Pancho Griego, a Colfax County, N.M., businessman and cowboy, was known for his mercurial temperament. On May 30, 1875, he encountered soldiers from the Sixth U.S. Cavalry at a hotel saloon in Cimarron, N.M. During an argument at a card table, Griego shot two soldiers to death, and killed another with a knife. Later that year, a gang led by Clay Allison lynched Cruz Vega, Griego's business associate. On Nov. 1, Griego found Allison in the same Cimarron hotel. The two men had a drink and as Griego was leaving, Allison shot him to death. See: **Allison, Clay.** **REF.:** *CBA; O'Neal, Encyclopedia of Western Gunfighters; Schoenberger, Gunfighters.*

Grier, Robert Cooper, 1794-1870, U.S., jur. Presiding district court judge in Allegheny, Pa., from 1833-46. He was nominated to the U.S. Supreme Court by President James K. Polk in 1846, and maintained his pro-Unionist leanings in several important cases. He agreed with the majority in the 1857 Dred Scott decision that invalidated the Missouri Compromise and prohibited slaves from suing others. **REF.:** *CBA.*

Grierson, Alan James, 1908-c.1936, Brit., fraud-rob.-mur. Alan Grierson was not a man to pass up an opportunity. The son of a Southampton, England, solicitor, he used his intellect in a life of crime. His surface display of culture and charm assisted him in a number of ruses early in his career, though he was not always successful. After doing time in prison, he moved to Australia in hopes of greater success. It wasn't long before he was arrested in Victoria for fraud and handed a year's sentence. When released, he returned again to England.

In Hammersmith, in 1935, he met a 20-year-old shop assistant who fell for his blue eyes, horn-rimmed spectacles, Roman nose, and noble deportment. She was so infatuated with Grierson that she failed to notice he was taking her for nearly everything she had. While helping to care for a family friend's flat during the owner's vacation, he helped himself to some of the lady's jewelry and pawned it. The young woman's mother was outraged when she discovered the missing finery, but Grierson apologized and promised better behavior in the future. Against her better judgment, the mother allowed him to return.

On June 15, Grierson told his girlfriend and her mother that he had a new job that required his driving a car down to the seaside town of Torquay, and asked if they would like to come along. They said they would and planned for the woman to meet Grierson at Marble Arch the next afternoon, after which they would pick up the mother and begin their trip.

This was Grierson's scheme to get the daughter out of the house, making it easier for him to steal another load of jewelry. She waited patiently the next day at Marble Arch for her love, but he never appeared. Dejected, she eventually took a bus to Shepherd's Bush, where she found the front door to her mother's house locked. At first she thought they were out, but after waiting another two hours, she finally had a neighbor force the door open—and found the place in shambles. The woman's mother was found in her bedroom in a pool of blood. She was rushed to the hospital, but died the next day of injuries caused by numerous blows to the head from a flatiron. The bloodstained weapon was found in the kitchen.

Investigators found Grierson's fingerprints throughout the house, but this was reasonable, since he had spent so much time there. There was a strong sense that Grierson was linked with the murder, but first they needed to find him. This, in itself, presented a formidable challenge because no one seemed to have a photograph of him. A woman came forward who knew Grierson and said she could sketch a nearly perfect likeness of him. She was also able to give valuable information as to his style of dress and places he frequented. Soon, a countrywide dragnet for Grierson was begun. The sketch of the wanted man was published and used for identification—making this the first time an artist's rendering was used to aid police in the identification of a criminal.

All the reports of Grierson "sightings" by amateur sleuths that poured in from all over England proved misleading. Finally, on June 30, a woman in Weybridge told a constable that there was a man staying at a friend's home who was the "downright image" of the man whose picture had appeared in the newspaper; in fact, he "might be a twin," she said. When the man was confronted, he told police that he knew a man named Grierson, "but I can assure you I'm not the man the police are looking for. I've seen the photograph, and, well, it's been obvious to myself it isn't of me." But the stranger couldn't give a clear account of where he had been during the past week. He was asked to go to the police station to confirm his identity.

Grierson hadn't been at the station long before he gave up his ploy. Suddenly he said, "Well, it's no use keeping it up any longer. I am the man. I'm sorry I lied to you." He told the police how he did not understand what had driven him to such cruel deeds, and that he was so disturbed by what he had done that he had considered suicide earlier that week.

On July 2, Grierson was charged with murder. Proving the charge, however, was an onerous challenge. To prove he had been at the scene of the crime, authorities needed to present an item he had stolen on that afternoon. At first the prosecution had been able to locate only jewelry pawned five days *before* the murder. Eventually, investigators found a silver cruet that the daughter had noticed missing the afternoon her mother had been killed. With that evidence, the court convicted Alan James Grierson of murder and sentenced him to death. **REF.:** Burt, *Commander Burt of Scotland Yard; CBA.*

Grierson, Isobel, d.1607, Scot., witchcraft. Isobel Grierson was put on trial at the Supreme Criminal Tribunal in Edinburgh, Scot., on Mar. 10, 1607. The court record shows six charges against her, all related to witchcraft. The first stated that she had appeared in the form of a cat and with a number of other cats, in the home of Adam Clark and his wife, whom she had harassed and frightened with excessive caterwauling.

She was also accused of using her witchcraft to kill William Burnet; cause Robert Peddan and his wife Margaret Donaldson to become gravely ill; and cause an alcoholic drink to turn "altogether rotten and black, thick like gutter dirt, with a filthy, pestilent odor ..." by walking past an open window where the ale was being brewed.

All of these charges, corroborated by witnesses, led to a final charge that Isobel was "a common sorcerer and a witch, and abuser of the people, by laying in and taking off of sickness and diseases, and using all devilish and ungodly means to win her living; and user of charms and other devilish practices." She was found Guilty of all charges, strangled to death, and burned at Castlehill, in Edinburgh. **REF.:** *CBA.*

Grieve, Elizabeth, b.1735, Brit., fraud. During the reign of King George III, a London woman named Elizabeth Grieve presented herself as a blood relative of Lord North, the Duke of Grafton, and Lady Fitz-Roy. For a price she assured anyone with the means to pay that she could dispense favors and jobs through her lofty connections. Several tradesmen seeking positions in the government doled out exorbitant sums for non-existent jobs. In 1774, Grieve was brought before the courts and found Guilty of fraud. She was transported to the American colonies, where she drifted into obscurity during the Revolution.

REF.: *CBA;* Nash, *Look For the Woman.*

Griffenfeld, Peder Schumacher (Count Griffenfeld), 1635-99, Den., polit. corr.-brib.-treas. Named secretary of King's chamber by Frederick III, promoted to high chancellor by Christian V in 1664, and wrote the Kongeloven of 1665, justifying absolutism. He attempted to keep peace with France and Sweden without informing the king, but was arrested in 1676, on the orders of Christian V, convicted of treason and sentenced to life imprisonment. REF.: *CBA.*

Griffin, Cyrus, 1748-1819, U.S., jur. Participated in the Continental Congresses of 1778-81 and 1787, and presided over the 1788 congress. He served as a judge for the district of Virginia from 1789-1810, and was nominated to the district court of Virginia by President George Washington in 1790. REF.: *CBA.*

Griffin, Henry, 1898-1923, Case of, Brit., mur. Tried for the murder of Ada Kerr in July 1923, Henry Griffin explained to the courts that he was not a killer, but a victim. He had been walking with the young woman in Whitton Woods, located near Twickenham, when he suddenly fainted. He awakened some time later in the woods with a wound on his throat. Ms. Kerr was nowhere to be seen. He covered the wound with handkerchiefs and went home.

Griffin's defense was that Ms. Kerr, who was found later in the same woods with her throat slit, had tried to kill him, and then committed suicide. His story, along with a doctor's testimony that the woman's wound could have been self-inflicted, caused enough doubt in the jury that they could not reach a final verdict. The trial was thrown out and Griffin was again tried a week later. Once again, the jury could not reach a verdict. Before Griffin could be tried a third time, he died of a heart attack in Brixton Prison.

REF.: *CBA;* Shew, *A Second Companion to Murder.*

Griffin, Jane, 1680-1720, Brit., mur. Jane Griffin of London had been arguing with her maid. As Griffin prepared dinner one evening in 1720, she needed some potatoes, which were kept in a locked cellar. She went upstairs to ask the maid for the key. The maid, still angry from their earlier confrontation, replied in anger, so Griffin drove the butcher knife she was holding into the maid's chest, killing her instantly. Griffin was tried and hanged for her moment of madness.

REF.: *CBA;* Nash, *Look For the Woman.*

Griffin, William, prom. 19th Cent., Case of, U.S., treas.-mur. A Confederate sympathizer during the U.S. Civil War, William Griffin clearly committed the murders for which he was acquitted in 1863. His exoneration stands as testimony to the extraordinary ability his counsel, William F. Howe, displayed, defending his first murder case and paving the way to an illustrious career.

While serving as first mate on a merchant ship during the Civil War, Griffin attempted to convince the captain of his ship to run the blockade in the South. A few days after the captain refused this bidding, he was found dead in his cabin. Foul play was not suspected, nor was there speculation when the man who replaced the first captain also died after refusing Griffin's orders. However, when the third master of the ship died, authorities took note of the connection between the three deaths and the first mate.

The body of the third dead captain was given a thorough autopsy. A lethal amount of copper sulphide was found in his stomach. Griffin was arrested and charged with three counts of murder. His guilt was so obvious that he asked to plead guilty to manslaughter, but the prosecution refused to plea bargain on grounds that Griffin was also guilty of treason. The prosecution's rejection of the guilty plea proved a fatal mistake.

Howe's defense of Griffin was stunning. He managed to turn around the prosecution's star witness' testimony to make it appear that the witness, a steward on the ship, may have committed the crimes. The trial ended with a hung jury, and a second trial was scheduled.

The second trial was very similar to the first, until the prosecution brought to the stand the three captains' widows. Aware that this was purely a sympathy ploy, Howe had Griffin's wife and daughter present during his summation. For a solid hour, he told the jury that the decision on which they were about to deliberate had the ability to "make that woman a widow—make that child an orphan...."

Henry Griffin, who had originally admitted his guilt for the three murders, was acquitted of any charge whatsoever.

REF.: *CBA;* Russell, *Best Murder Cases.*

Griffith, Elizabeth Ford, 1902-19, U.S., (unsolv.) mur. Seventeen-year-old Elizabeth Ford Griffith had led a very romantic life, considering her age. She had been engaged for some time to a physician in her hometown of Louisville, Ky., had broken the relationship off, and then became engaged to a soldier stationed at nearby Camp Zachary Taylor, just outside of Louisville. She was exceedingly attractive—and exceedingly emotional. It could have been this passion that drove her to commit suicide. Or, it could have been her ex-fiancé's same depth of feeling that caused him to commit murder. One must decide for oneself whether it was suicide or murder, because a Grand Jury could not.

Elizabeth was only fourteen when she met Dr. Christopher Schott, the 39-year-old doctor who would ask for her hand in marriage two years later. She worked as a stenographer and secretary in his office off and on for more than two years, even after she had broken the engagement. That is where her body was found by Dr. Schott on Christmas Eve, 1919. Dr. Schott deemed her death a suicide, but when Mrs. Griffith was informed of the tragedy, she insisted, "My little girl never took her own life!"

The coroner agreed with her. According to his study of Elizabeth's body and clothes, the gun had left "no powder burns either on her clothing or body, and from the range of the bullet it seems that it would have been almost impossible for the girl to have fired the shot herself." Captain William H. DeForester, assigned to investigate the case, studied the bullet's path as it traveled through her body, then lodged in the lower part of a dresser. He concluded that if someone else had fired the fatal shot while the girl was standing, he or she would have been standing in unlikely place: on top of the dresser. Whether Elizabeth or someone else fired the shot, she was most likely shot while in a kneeling position. The coroner also determined that the shot had been fired at 2:30 p.m.

As soon as Captain DeForester found out about Schott and Griffith's romantic history, the doctor was arrested and charged with the young woman's murder. A Grand Jury met to determine if enough evidence existed to convict him. Robert J. Hagen and Clem Huggins defended him.

Griffith and Schott's relationship became the centerpiece of the trial. She had apparently ended their engagement after a spat in which Dr. Schott's extreme possessiveness surfaced. In a letter written to her former love, she told him that she "will never marry a man who does not trust me.... Don't bother to think of me personally again, as I feel absolutely impersonal about you." In seeming contradiction, Griffith's note then asked Dr. Schott if she could still work for him, then closed with this strange adieu: "Every one wants to know who the good-looking man is on my dresser. Don't bust. It's you."

When asked whether he knew that Griffith was to be married to someone else in a week, Schott replied: "Absolutely—but I also knew that she was in love with me." He insisted that he had not pressed her again to marry him, but that his instincts told him that someday they would be together again and happy. He was convinced that Elizabeth felt likewise, though she had never "admitted" it to him.

As for the events of Dec. 24, Dr. Schott told the courts that he had spent the afternoon doing what he did every Christmas Eve: delivering gifts to each of his patients. Laurene Gardner, thirteen, corroborated his story, as she accompanied him when he delivered the gifts. Laurene, Elizabeth, and Dr. Schott had spent the morning wrapping gifts. At some point, Elizabeth picked up a manicure set and asked Dr. Schott who it was for; he teasingly replied that he was giving it to "another girl." This, according to both Laurene and the doctor, upset Elizabeth. Dr. Schott said he gave Elizabeth a ten-dollar bill as her gift, but she later returned it with a note saying, "If you don't think any more of me than *that,* you can take your present back."

The physician and the young girl left Elizabeth at the office about noon to deliver the first batch of presents. When they returned an hour later to pick up more gifts, Elizabeth was still upset about who was going to receive the manicure set. Continuing his teasing, Schott would not reveal that it was actually for an elderly patient. "I never dreamed she would take it so hard," he later said.

Dr. Schott and Laurene left on their second round and both their testimonies state that they did not return until 3:30 p.m. Ella Gerlach, a patient, was waiting outside the locked office. Dr. Schott called to Elizabeth and knocked on the door, which was locked from the inside, but there was no response. (Experiments with the office doors proved that they "could easily be latched from either side by means of a small instrument.") Dr. Schott, very jovial, and not showing any signs of nervousness or anger, jimmied the door open, walked in, and discovered Elizabeth's body. He called out that she had been poisoned, tried to revive her, and finally realized that she was dead.

There was testimony from several witnesses for the prosecution that strongly conflicted with the doctor's story. Katie May Griffith, Elizabeth's sister, said she had called the office twice that day: at 10 a.m., and again at 1:50 p.m. She claimed that Dr. Schott had answered the second time, and that it was clear from her sister's tone of voice that she and the doctor had been fighting. Katie also stated on the stand that "Dr. Schott had a hypnotic influence over my sister."

William J. Ryan testified that he had observed the doctor walking from his office to his automobile and that he was not accompanied by the 13-year-old. Another witness, Mrs. Ellis Rudolph, told the court that at 2:35 p.m., she was approached by Schott—once again, alone—who asked: "Did you hear a shot?" She went inside to inquire if anyone else had heard anything, and when she came back out, Schott had vanished.

On the other hand, the prosecution's testimony was challenged by the steadfastness of little Laurene Gardner's testimony. Under intense and incessant questioning and cross examination, she stated over and over that she had never been away from Dr. Schott for a moment between noon and 3:30 p.m. His story, as far as she was concerned, was the absolute truth. She addressed the conflicting testimony: "If Mr. Ryan saw the doctor in front of his office that afternoon, he was mistaken in the hour. And if Miss Griffith talked to a man over the telephone at the hour she said, it was not Dr. Schott, because he was not there."

Gardner's testimony, along with Schott's tear-filled statements, won his freedom: the grand jury decided there were not grounds for an indictment. In the years following, the Griffith family also forgave Schott, eventually allowing Elizabeth's body to be moved to the physician's own plot. Schott never married.

What really happened in Dr. Schott's office that Christmas Eve will never be known, but perhaps the words of Jennie Brands, a patient who called the office and spoke with Elizabeth several times throughout the afternoon, could explain the event. "It may sound strange," she said, "but as the day grew older the girl's voice grew sadder.... 'Have you received your Christmas gifts?' I asked her. 'Christmas means nothing to me,' she answered.... 'I am too sad to care.'" REF.: *CBA.*

Griffith, Griffith J. (AKA: **Colonel Griffith**), 1852-1919, U.S., attempt. mur. There was no question that Colonel Griffith was a most generous philanthropist. During his lifetime, he gave Los Angeles, Calif., two of its greatest landmarks: the 4,100-acre Griffith Park, complete with the copper-roofed Griffith Park Observatory; and the Greek Theater, still one of the most exceptional outdoor amphitheaters in the U.S. But there was a darker side to Griffith, as well, a side shaded by his substantial abuse of alcohol.

His chronic drinking caused Griffith to have delusions, the most prominent of which was that his wife, Christina Griffith, was trying to poison him. This hallucination grew, in part, out of Griffith's hatred for the Roman Catholic Church. Christina was involved in several community activities associated with the church and in his liquor-damaged mind, Griffith thought that after his wife killed him, the Catholic church would attempt to take the fortune he had built in real estate. In his mind, Griffith plotted ways to head off their intention.

Griffith's "counter-scheme" was carried out one summer day in 1903 while he and Christina were vacationing at the Arcadia Hotel in Santa Monica, Calif. In their suite, he handed his wife

Col. Griffith J. Griffith, whose delusions led to a murder scheme.

a prayer book, ordered her to kneel and pray, and took out a pistol. As she pleaded for mercy, he began to read a series of questions regarding her loyalty to him and her alleged plot to poison him. "Oh Papa, you know I have always been true to you!" she tearfully insisted. He placed the gun to his wife's temple, but as he pulled the trigger, she jerked her head away. The bullet destroyed her left eye.

Wounded and fearing for her life, Christina jumped out of the hotel room window and fell two stories onto a veranda, breaking her leg. She limped away and found help. When Griffith was located, he insisted that she had shot herself with his pistol.

The city of Los Angeles, acknowledging Griffith's high standing and valuable patronage, was prepared to ignore what they determined was simply a "domestic squabble," but Mrs. Griffith's family was bent on pressing charges. They hired a team of topnotch prosecutors, led by former California Governor Henry T. Gage. Griffith's counsel was the famous, highly successful defense attorney, Earl Rogers. Rogers was well-versed in an emerging field called "psychiatry," and his plan was to call for a defense of insanity due to alcohol abuse.

Early in the proceedings, Rogers created an uproar by demanding a continuance to give him time to effectively defend his client. He then suddenly withdrew the continuance on the first day of the trial. The prosecution was caught off guard—they had devoted all their time to gathering evidence to reject Rogers' continuance plea and had not further organized their strategy.

The jury eventually found Griffith Guilty of assault with intent to murder. He was sentenced to two years in prison and released on good behavior after serving one. He died in 1919. Although his defense probably eased Griffith's sentence, Rogers took the loss hard, and was rumored to have flirted with suicide for some time after the trial. He died, destitute and alone, in a Southern California rooming house in 1922. REF.: *CBA.*

Griffith, Sir Samuel Walker, 1845-1920, Aus., jur. First chief justice for Australia from 1903-19. REF.: *CBA.*

Griffith, Stiles H., and **Griffith, William,** prom. 1874, Case of, U.S., mur. Stiles and William Griffith, father and son, were visited in their Greenbush, N.Y., home by George Atchinson, son-in-law of Stiles Griffith. Atchinson was drunk when he arrived and he continued to drink heavily while attempting to convince the Griffiths to go with him on a business trip. The Griffiths refused, according to their later statements, but Atchinson insisted and then grew violent. He produced a knife and threw it at Stiles Griffith. Both father and son then leaped upon the burly Atchinson, who had grabbed another knife. In the struggle, Atchinson reportedly fell on his own knife and died. Both father and son were accused of murdering Atchinson and, after a sensational trial, beginning on Feb. 20, 1874, the Griffiths were acquitted.

REF.: *CBA;* Rodgers, *Opening Address of William Van Olinda.*

Griffiths, James, and **Brewer, Richard,** prom. 1862, Brit., forg. With ambitions of perfectly reproducing Bank of England bank-notes, copper plate printer James Griffiths of Birmingham spent years trying to create the special paper used for British bills. Even reducing real notes to pulp and manufacturing new paper from them did not work—and wasted a lot of money. So in 1862, Griffiths hired William Burnett to infiltrate the Portal paper works, which had the government contract. There, Burnett and his companion, 23-year-old Ellen Mills, befriended a young apprentice and pattern-maker, Richard Brewer. Brewer began to steal paper.

Back in London, just as the paper was reaching Griffiths, the apprentice decided to confess to authorities. Police walked in on Griffiths while he was printing one of the three denominations of notes he had plates for, and they set a trap for the others involved. Five men were found Guilty. Burnett was sentenced to twenty years, an engraver to four years, George Bruncher, who had distributed the counterfeit money, to twenty-five years, and Griffiths and Brewer to life in prison. REF.: *CBA.*

Griffiths, James, 1935-69, Scot., rob.-mur. As difficult as it was for the Scottish Regional Crime Squad to locate James Griffiths in connection with the murder of an elderly woman, it was virtually impossible for them to take him alive.

The crime for which he was sought stemmed from a robbery that he and an accomplice attempted on Abraham Ross, sixty-seven, and his wife, Rachel, seventy-two, at their home on Blackburn Place in Ayr, Scot. On July 5, 1969, the two men broke into the Ross' home, beat the couple, bound them, and then looted the house, taking £1,000 in money the Rosses had saved for their retirement. Rachel Ross died three days after the crime from the injuries she incurred.

It made sense to Scottish authorities that the robbers would attempt to hide in Glasgow, relying on their fellow criminals for cover. Authorities also thought that in a matter of time the criminals would run out of money and come out of hiding. They were right. On July 14, Griffiths' accomplice was apprehended and, under interrogation, revealed the name of the leader in the robbery-murder. It was clear that the apprehended man was more frightened of what Griffiths might do to him than of his possible punishment by the law.

Griffiths was living in an attic-sized flat in Glasgow under the name "Douglas." On a morning soon after his accomplice was caught, five plainclothes officers knocked on the door where they believed Griffiths was hiding. In response, bullets came roaring through the door, wounding a detective. The unarmed officers retreated to the street. Further gunfire was discharged from a window, felling two civilians in the street.

As armed police arrived on the scene, Griffiths used the ensuing confusion as cover for his escape from a back door. When his flight was impeded by crowds on a nearby street, he opened fire again. He then wounded a man getting into his car, and drove away.

The getaway ended in a crash. Griffiths ran from the automobile and into the Round Toll Bar, where he briefly held the entire clientele hostage. After wounding one customer and drinking a bottle of brandy, Griffiths commandeered a truck outside the bar and was on the run again.

Due to the alertness of a taxi driver who heard the description of Griffiths and his vehicle on police radio, the police were able to track the crazed man. The truck was found deserted, establish-

ing that Griffiths was once again on foot. Outside a building, he once again began to fire haphazardly. He shot into a playground, injuring a young woman and an 8-year-old boy.

Detective Chief Superintendent Malcolm Finlayson and Sergeant Ian Smith were first on the scene and began to close in on the building in which Griffiths was hiding. Finlayson, while standing at the entrance, caught sight of the heavily armed man in the lobby and realized he had only one chance to disable the killer. He aimed at Griffiths' shoulder and fired. Griffith collapsed to his knees.

Finlayson and Smith flung Griffiths' weapons out of the way and slapped handcuffs on him. Then suddenly he fell dead. The coroner revealed later that the bullet had entered Griffiths' shoulder, ricocheted inside his body and imbedded in his heart.

Miraculously, during the ninety minutes of shooting and mayhem, Griffiths had fatally wounded only one person: William Hughes, a patron at the besieged tavern. Eleven civilians and one police officer had been injured. Griffiths' accomplice in the Ross robbery-murder was later given a life sentence for his complicity in the crime.

REF.: Bloom, *Money of Their Own; CBA;* Gribble, *The Dead End Killers;* Nicholls, *Crime Within the Square Mile;* Stevens, *Famous Crimes and Criminals.*

Griffiths, Peter, 1926-48, Brit., rape-mur. The case of Peter Griffiths, a 22-year-old former Irish guardsman who abducted a child from a hospital and raped and killed her, prompted an intensive forensic investigation. Griffiths had earlier been a patient at the Queen's Park Hospital in Blackburn for two years. On May 14, 1948, he broke into the hospital and made his way to the children's ward, where he found 4-year-old June Anne Devaney sleeping on a cot. He carried the child out of the building to a hayfield on the hospital grounds, where he raped her and then killed her by beating her head against a wall.

Child killer Peter Griffiths.

By the time the child's body was discovered a few hours later, Griffiths was asleep on the couch in his parents' living room. The police found a large bottle next to the girl's hospital bed that Griffiths had apparently picked up to use as a weapon. The bottle had a full set of fingerprints and police set about trying to track the murderer with these prints. They suspected that the murderer was familiar with the layout of the hospital, and they identified and fingerprinted 642 people who had had lawful access to the children's ward during the previous two years. When these fingerprints did not produce a match, the police fingerprinted another 1,375 people who might have had access to the ward, but still could not find a match. The police then decided to fingerprint every man over the age of sixteen who had been in Blackburn, a town of 110,000, on the night of the murder. Although police eventually gathered 46,000 fingerprints, including prints from men who had since left town, the results were still negative. The police also circulated the fingerprints to every fingerprint bureau in the world, which meant that they had been compared to some nine million sets of prints.

The police next checked their list of Blackburn males against a list used in the issue of ration cards. This yielded a list of names that for some reason had not been included on the original list. Finally, on Aug. 12, an examiner came across the fingerprints of Peter Griffiths and made the match. When Griffiths was arrested, he made a full confession, and was further linked to the crime through fibers from his suit which were found on the girl's body and nightgown. Police suspected Griffiths of other assaults against children in the Lancashire area, including the murder of 11-year-old Quentin Smith. Griffiths was tried for the rape and murder

British police checking some of the more than 46,000 fingerprints examined in the Griffiths case.

of June Devaney at the Lancaster Assizes in October before Justice Oliver. The jury rejected his plea of insanity and found him Guilty. Griffiths was hanged at Walton Prison on Nov. 19, 1948.

REF.: Block, *Fifteen Clues;* ____, *Science vs. Crime;* Browne and Brock, *Fingerprints;* Butler, *Murderers' England; CBA;* Harrison, *Criminal Calendar;* Hatherill, *A Detective's Story;* Heppenstall, *The Sex War and Others;* Lucas, *The Child Killers;* Lustgarten, *The Story of Crime;* McGrady, *Crime Scientist;* McKnight, *The Murder Squad;* Millen, *Specialist in Crime; Notable British Trials;* Shew, *A Second Companion to Murder;* Thorwald, *Marks of Cain;* Wilson, *Encyclopedia of Murder.*

Griggs, John William, 1849-1927, U.S., jur. Governor of New Jersey from 1895-98, and U.S. attorney general from 1898-1901. He worked in the Hague as a judge on the Permanent Court of Arbitration from 1901-12. REF.: *CBA.*

Griggs, Ronald Geeves, b.1900, Case of, Aus., mur. Born and raised in Tasmania, Ronald Griggs decided in his early twenties that he wanted to be a Methodist minister. After graduating from Queen's College in Melbourne, Aus., with a Licentiate of Theology, he became the pastor of a Methodist congregation in Omeo.

Before starting his life as a clergyman, he married Ethel White, a young girl from Tasmania. They moved to their new home on the slopes of the Bowey Mountains in 1926 and began their new life together.

Griggs had lived in Omeo less than ten months before he started an illicit relationship with Lottie Condon, a 19-year-old girl from a nearby farm. His wife soon became aware of their behavior. She implored him to forget Lottie, but the minister had no intention of ending the affair. Provoked to her limits, Ethel Griggs returned to Tasmania with the couple's new baby in July 1927, vowing to come back to Omeo in six months to pick up her personal items. Griggs begged her to stay, but she did not give in.

Ethel returned on Dec. 31, 1927, and almost immediately became ill. Griggs and medical doctors attributed her illness to "heat and excitement," but she progressively worsened over the next few days and finally died on Jan. 3, 1928. The doctor who issued the death certificate indicated that her death was caused by complications rising from her return trip from Tasmania.

But the Omeo rumor mill, aware of the minister's affair and subsequent marital woes, was running a different version of the story. Finally, the minister himself instigated an inquiry so the gossip could be silenced. On Jan. 26, Ethel Griggs' body was

exhumed and another examination was made. Doctors found fifteen grains of arsenic in her body—reason to put Griggs on trial for murder. The trial began Mar. 7.

The prosecution tried to prove that Griggs had access to arsenic but Griggs maintained that he did not. He also denied ever receiving poison chemicals from the local druggist. No one denied that he had a motive, but actual proof that Griggs had given his wife arsenic could not be found. The jury finally gave up without a decision, and the judge ordered a second trial, which started on Apr. 17. This trial ran nearly identical to the first, except that the jury found Griggs Not Guilty. He was set free, but lost his Omeo parsonage.

REF.: Buchanan, *The Trial of Ronald Geeves Griggs; CBA;* Clegg, *Return Your Verdict.*

Grigoryants, Sergei I., c.1941- , U.S.S.R., rebel. A Soviet dissident, Sergei I. Grigoryants, spent five years in prison and labor camps during the late 1970s. After his release, the literary critic edited an underground dissident journal. In 1983, Grigoryants was arrested on charges of "anti-Soviet agitation and propaganda" and was sentenced to seven years in prison and three years in internal exile. Grigoryants, along with about 150 other political prisoners, was pardoned in early 1987 and he was released on Feb. 5, 1987, from Chistopol Prison at Kazan. That summer, he and other political dissidents established a new journal, *Glasnost,* the term used for the recent Soviet policy of increased government tolerance. The fledgling journal, which contained dissident news and commentary, was soon criticized by the government press and in October 1987, two assistants making copies in a library were arrested and their papers seized. On Oct. 30, 1987, police arrested Grigoryants at his home and held him in custody for three hours, but filed no charges.

The bimonthly publication had grown to become the largest and most influential of the new dissident literary works when it was halted in May 1988. On May 9, 1988, Grigoryants was arrested, charged with resisting arrest, and found Guilty. He was sentenced to a one-week jail term. When he was freed on May 16, he found that his printing equipment had been taken and his manuscripts and files were ruined. REF.: *CBA.*

Grillandus, Paulus, prom. 16th Cent., Rome, jur. Grillandus was a prominent judge in the city-state of Rome and most noted for his decisions and writings regarding witchcraft. His *Tractatus de Hereticis et Sortilegiis (Treatise on Heretics and Witches)* was one of the landmark works on witchcraft published during the sixteenth century. The work discusses a plethora of crimes associated with witchcraft, including possession, demonology, magic potions, and bodily transvection. All of these subjects are addressed in a learned, theological, and scientific manner, though even Grillandus admitted in the treatise that he had never caught a witch practicing black magic. REF.: *CBA.*

Grills, Caroline, b.c.1888, Aus., mur. In a case that could be considered a tribute to Joseph Kesselring's 1940s Broadway comedy, *Arsenic and Old Lace,* 65-year-old Caroline Grills was convicted of murdering four relatives and attempting to murder three others with rat poison.

Her motive for the murders was never fully explained, though the Crown Prosecutor, Mr. C. Rooney, Q.C., ventured that Mrs. Grills had killed Adelaide Mickelson, eight-seven, her stepmother, so that she could have the victim's cottage, and then continued poisoning her family because "she got a psychological lift and sense of power from watching the effect of poison."

For whatever reason, after Mrs. Mickelson died in 1947, Angelina Thomas, eight-four, a close friend of Mrs. Grill's husband, Richard, also died. Soon after, John Lundberg, a 60-year-old sailor and brother-in-law to Mrs. Grills, began losing his hair and finally died in October 1948. In February 1953, Mary Ann Mickelson, Mrs. Grill's sister-in-law, also died after a long period of illness and hair loss.

Detective-Sergeant Donald Fergusson was starting to notice that all these deaths were related — literally. He began to quietly investigate, though he had no idea who in the family might be responsible. It wasn't until John Downey, a cousin of Mrs. Grills, brought Sergeant Fergusson a cup of tea that he had a clear suspect in the deaths. Mr. Downey told the detective that he, his wife, and his mother-in-law had all started to show signs of having the afflictions their late relatives had had. Mrs. Grills had been making numerous visits to their house, and had often offered to make tea or other drinks. On two occasions, Mr. Downey had noticed the woman's hand come out of an apron pocket and hover over a cup that was about to be handed to his mother-in-law. On the second occasion, he took the cup away before his mother drank it and to the detective.

When the lab results on the liquid showed significant amounts of rat poison, Mrs. Grills was arrested for the attempted murder of John and Chrissie Downey, and Chrissie's mother, Eveline Lundberg, who eventually went blind from the poisoning. Soon after, the deaths of the other four relatives were also added to the charges.

The only thing in Mrs. Grills' favor at her trial was the fact that she had absolutely no motive to kill her relatives. The prosecutor, however, was able to place in the jury's collective mind the thought that there were sick people in this world "who poison for sport, for fun, for the kick of it, for the hell of it...." The jury found Caroline Grills Guilty, and in return for all of the lethal beverages and cakes she prepared for her kin, served her a life sentence.

REF.: *CBA;* Gurr and Cox, *Famous Australian Crimes.*

Grimes, Barbara, 1941-56, and **Grimes, Patricia,** c.1943-56, U.S., (unsolv.) mur. During the 1950s a series of baffling, unsolved child murders sorely tested the resources of the Chicago Police Department. In October 1955 three adolescent boys, Craig and Anton Schuessler, and their friend Robert Peterson were abducted and murdered by an unknown fiend. The horrific nature of the crime, and the fact that the police were unable to identify a suspect led to sharp criticism of Chief Timothy O'Connor and his detective force.

Patricia and Barbara Grimes, teenage murder victims in Chicago, 1956.

On Dec. 28, 1956, two South Side girls disappeared shortly after they had exited the Brighton Theatre, where Elvis Presley's movie, *Love Me Tender* was playing. Barbara Grimes, fifteen, and her sister Patricia, thirteen, were reported missing by their parents at around midnight. There was grave concern that the same murderer who had killed the Schuessler boys had abducted the Grimes sisters. The police thought that the girls might have attempted to emulate their leather-jacketed hero Elvis Presley, by running away from home. The singer was contacted in Memphis where he issued a statement to the press. "If you are good Presley

fans you will go home and ease your mother's worries." Barbara and Patricia were not the kind to rebel against parental authority. They were students in the Catholic parochial school system, and had shown no rebellious tendencies.

Newspaper columnist Ann Landers received a letter allegedly written by a young girl who was in the Brighton Theatre that day. It read:

"Betty asked me to go with her and her parents to visit her aunt. Later we decided to go to the movie. While looking for a seat Betty noticed Barbara and Pat Grimes sitting with some other kids. Outside the show we all got to talking and we exchanged phone numbers. When we got to the street where we turned off, we said good-by and we ran across the street.

Then Betty forgot something she had to tell Barbara and we ran back to the corner. A man about twenty-two or twenty-five was talking to them. He pushed Barbara into the back seat of a car and Pat in the front seat.

We got part of the license number as the car drove by us. The first four numbers were 2184. Betty thinks there were three or four numbers after that. We didn't think so much about it but it struck us as kind of funny. When we heard that they were missing we didn't know what to do."

The letter was not signed, raising suspicions that the killer might have written it. In January 1957, Police Sergeant Ernest Spiotto questioned a young man who had snipped off a lock of hair from a girl sitting in a movie house. The individual told of a troubling dream he had, in which two girls were found lying naked in a public park surrounded by trees and a tiny creek. The location that matched the description was only several miles away from the actual spot where the Grimes sisters were found on Jan., 22, 1957. Motorist Leonard Prescott was driving down German Church Road, a twisting two-lane highway in remote DuPage County when he spotted two "mannequins" lying in a ditch. Their frozen, lifeless bodies were piled on top of each other. The Grimes girls had at last been found, but the answers to the puzzle still eluded the police. A pathologist determined that the cause of death was due to exposure. There was little evidence of rape or sexual abuse.

The police interrogated the young man who had described the location where the bodies were found, but released him for lack of evidence. Who killed the Grimes girls, and the method they employed remains a mystery.

REF.: *CBA; Nash,* Open Files.

Grimes, Joseph, d.1874, Brit., (unsolv.) mur. Seventy-seven-year-old Joseph Grimes of Purton, England, possessed little but his life. That too, was taken from him by a cutting blow to the head in April 1874. His savings of £4 were untouched. Grimes' body was found by a little girl, but never his murderer.

REF.: Butler, *Murderers' England; CBA.*

Grimm, Baltazard, d.c.1882, Fr., mur. Grimm was convicted and guillotined for the murder of Cécile Renoux, a wealthy, elderly woman and a former prostitute, on Feb. 27, 1882. Before he was killed, he confessed to at least twenty similar murders. Grimm was one of a number of killers who made the acquaintance of rich women, many of them ex-prostitutes, and, after gaining their confidence, slit their throats.

REF.: *CBA;* Morain, *Underworld of Paris.*

Grimoald I (Duke of Benevento), b.671, Italy, rebel-assass. Stole the Lombard crown from the co-regents in 659. He triumphed over the invasion by the Byzantines, the revolt led by the Duke of Friuli, an attempted insurrection by his allies, and an assault by Hungary's Avar troops. REF.: *CBA.*

Grimoald III, d.c.806, Case of, Italy, prince, kid. Held prisoner by Charlemagne from 787-88, but was finally permitted to assume the Benevento's throne as a tool for the Franks. He regained his independence in 792, later triumphing militarily over the Byzantines and over the armies of Pepin in 792 and 800. REF.: *CBA.*

Grimwood, Eliza, d.1838, Brit., (unsolv.) mur. The "Waterloo Road mystery" of 1838 involved prostitute Eliza Grimwood and her bodyguard, lover, and cousin William Hubbard, who hid upstairs in Grimwood's house when she had business to conduct. On May 25, 1838, she was seen at the theater on the Strand with a bearded gentleman, and then in a cab, which took them to Waterloo Bridge. The next morning, Grimwood was found dead in her bed, stabbed in the throat and chest. The pillows held the impression of two heads.

Inspector Charles Field kept the case in the news as long as he could, with hopes that someone would come forward. One anonymous writer claimed that he had been with Grimwood that night, but left her with Hubbard. Hubbard was apprehended, but much to the public's dismay, soon released for lack of evidence. Grimwood's murder was never solved.

REF.: Altick, *Victorian Studies in Scarlet; CBA;* Cobb, *The First Detectives;* Logan, *Rope, Knife and Chair;* Pearce, *Unsolved Murder Mysteries.*

Grin (AKA: Louis de Rougemont), prom. 19th Cent., Brit., fraud. When the man who claimed to be a former chief of an Australian aboriginal cannibal tribe showed up on the doorstep of the British journal, *Wide World,* its editors were understandably skeptical. They brought in anthropologists and historians who carefully analyzed Louis de Rougemont's story. After extensive interviews and research, the experts came forward with their opinion: as incredible as it seemed, the man was authentic. Salivating at the thought of this unprecedented "scoop," the editors of *Wide World* ran an enormously successful series that depicted de Rougemont's life in the outback.

The hero told of being shipwrecked on a South Sea island where he was alone for two years, living off the land and riding 600-pound sea turtles. A family of aborigines washed up on shore, and together they constructed a makeshift boat and successfully sailed back to the family's homeland. Upon arrival, de Rougemont was welcomed into the tribe and allowed to marry Yamba, the mother of the shipwrecked family, who separated from her husband to make the marriage possible. De Rougemont eventually became chief and said he accepted their custom of eating their enemies' flesh, although he himself kept to his diet of kangaroo and fish.

De Rougemont's exploits were amazing but readily accepted—at least until he told of a bout with malaria, during which his wife ate their newborn child because, he reported she said, "I could not have nursed both of you, so I did what I considered best." He said he was healed of malaria when he slit open a buffalo and slept inside the carcass.

It was then that a rival newspaper, the *Daily Chronicle,* began an investigation into de Rougemont's past. They discovered that the alleged cannibal chieftain's real name was Grin, and that he was nothing more than a former butler who had done very thorough research at the British Museum library. The *Wide World's* editor retracted the tale, and Grin was reduced to panhandling the rest of his days in England. REF.: *CBA.*

Grinder, Martha, 1815-66, U.S., mur. In 1866, in Pittsburgh, Martha Grinder fed some arsenic to her neighbor, Mrs. Carothers, and then volunteered to nurse her. Each day she fed her more of the poison, fascinated by its effects, until Carothers died. Grinder confessed to the murder, adding, "Could I have had my own way, probably I should have done more." She was hanged on Jan. 19, 1866.

REF.: *CBA; The Grinder Poison Case; The Life and Confessions of Martha Grinder;* Nash, *Bloodletters and Badmen;* ____, *Look For the Woman.*

Gristy, Bill (AKA: Bill White), prom. 1856, U.S., west. outl. Bill Gristy, a California bandit and arsonist, joined Thomas Hodges in launching a crime wave in 1856. The pair had escaped from prison together after Gristy had been sentenced for murder. Forming a gang under Hodges' alias, Tom Bell, they robbed a wagon driver in early 1856. After a brief gunfight, Gristy made off with $300. On Aug. 11, near Marysville, Calif., the gang tried to rob a stagecoach, but were repelled by the driver, a messenger, a security man, and several passengers. A gang member and a passenger were killed, and several passengers were wounded. A posse was organized to apprehend the bandits. The following month, detectives Anderson and Harrison from Sacramento found Gristy and four others hiding near the Mountaineer House. The robbers tried to shoot their way to freedom. One of them named Walker was fatally wounded by Detective Harrison, while another bandit, Pete Ansara, was shot in the leg. Two others surrendered peacefully, but Gristy escaped. Detective Anderson apprehended him after a brief chase on horseback. Gristy was returned to prison, but was promised leniency for informing on Hodges. See: **Bell, Tom.**

REF.: *CBA;* Drago, *Outlaws on Horseback;* O'Neal, *Encyclopedia of Western Gunfighters.*

Grizzard, Joseph (AKA: Cammie, Cimi, Kemmy), d.1923, Brit., rob. Jewel thief and fence Joseph Grizzard was best known for his role in London's "Great Pearl Robbery" of 1913. London pearl and diamond merchant Max Mayer owned a necklace of sixty-one perfectly graduated and matched pearls that he hoped to sell for £150,000. A French agent tried but failed to sell it and returned it to Mayer by post in a carefully sealed box. When Mayer received the box on July 16, 1913, however, he opened it to find eleven cubes of sugar. Somewhere between Paris on the fifteenth and London on the sixteenth, the box had been opened and resealed with a slightly different wax and forged seal.

When police proved that the necklace could not have been stolen in France, en route, or in London, Lloyd's of London offered a reward of £10,000 for any information about the theft. Paris dealer Brandstatter, learning that a distant relative, Leisir Gutwirth was involved in the theft, introduced him to another cousin, Cohen Quadrastein, in hopes of locating the pearls. Gutwirth, thinking his cousins had a potential buyer, introduced them in London to Simon Silverman and Grizzard. The group met several times to negotiate, once appraising some pearls brought by a burglar named Lockett, but the necklace never appeared—even after Brandstatter and Quadrastein, who had been expected to produce a buyer, found a pearl dealer who pretended to play the role. Police watched and waited for the necklace to surface, but finally arrested Grizzard, Lockett, Silverman, and Gutwirth without it.

Two weeks later, an associate of the criminals took the pearls to police. He said he found a box that he thought contained wooden matches on a street in Highbury, but instead it contained the pearl necklace. He collected the reward, and the pearls appeared in court as evidence when the thieves and the fence went on trial. Testimony revealed that Silverman's office was next door to Mayer's and that the postman had "accidentally" left the package containing the necklace on Silverman's doorstep for five minutes before he retrieved it and delivered it to Mayer. All four men were found Guilty. Grizzard and Lockett were sentenced to seven years in prison, Silverman to five years, and Gutwirth to eighteen months at hard labor. Grizzard, known to have masterminded the Carlton House Terrace burglary of 1911, whiled away his sentence conferring with police, giving them inside information on various crimes. Released in 1920, he went to jail again in 1922 for conspiracy to obtain jewels by false pretenses, but died some months later of an illness.

REF.: *CBA;* Dilnot, *The Real Detective;* Humphreys, *Criminal Days;* ____, *A Book of Trials;* Nicholls, *Crime Within the Square Mile;* Thomson, *The Story of Scotland Yard;* Woodhall, *Secrets of Scotland Yard.*

Groake, Patrick, d.1930, Brit., (wrong. convict.) mur. In 1894, James and Patrick Groake, were tried for manslaughter, allegedly having kicked their mother to death. James Groake was acquitted, but Patrick, his older brother, was found Guilty and sentenced to twenty years in prison. Seven years later, James, on his deathbed, confessed that he had actually committed the murder. Patrick Groake was released, and lived another thirty years.

REF.: Brock, *A Casebook of Crime; CBA.*

Groce, Bunt, prom. 20th Cent., Case of, U.S., asslt.-mur. The son of a lumber company manager, Bunt Groce was never convicted of a number of violent crimes that he probably committed in North Carolina between 1916 and 1932. It is believed that he was acquitted because of his father's money and influence in the community, and because he was represented by a particularly crafty lawyer.

On Oct. 31, 1916, Groce and a man named Claxton Hill got into a drunken scrap during a Halloween party. When Claxton's sister, Louvenia Hill, attempted to break up the fight, she was hit by a bullet fired by Groce and intended for Claxton. She died later that evening. A jury inexplicably found Groce Not Guilty of murder.

A similar event happened on Oct. 10, 1922. This time the victim, Jes Crawley, was killed after a fight with Groce. Groce was again exonerated in January 1925. Groce's next meeting with the courts was in June 1932, for an assault with intent to murder Bryan Botts and David Hulse. Once again, he was found Not Guilty.

REF.: *CBA; Montell, Killings.*

Groesbeck, William Slocum, 1815-97, U.S., lawyer. Served as defense counsel at the impeachment trial of President Andrew Johnson. REF.: *CBA.*

Groesbeek, Maria, 1937-70, S. Afri., mur. Maria and Christiaan Buys married quickly and spent the next fifteen years quarrelling over Maria's inability to stop flirting with other men. In 1968, she met 20-year-old Gerhard Groesbeek. When Buys refused to divorce her so that she could marry young Gerhard, she began to feed him an arsenic-based ant poison. He was admitted to the hospital on Feb. 14, 1969, and died six weeks later. An autopsy showed the presence of arsenic, and Maria was arrested. She and Gerhard, now man and wife, were tried together. She said that she had poisoned Buys to make him sick enough to let her divorce him. Gerhard Groesbeek was acquitted, but Maria was found Guilty and hanged on Nov. 13, 1970.

REF.: *Bennett, This Was a Man; CBA; Nash, Look For the Woman.*

Grondkowski, Marian, and **Malinowski, Henry K.,** d.1946, Brit., mur. Marian Grondkowski and Henry K. Malinowski, two Poles involved in the London black market immediately after WWII, planned to rob Reuben Martirosoff (alias Russian Robert), an international criminal known to police all over Europe. Late on Oct. 31, 1945, Martirosoff met the pair at a subway station, then drove them to a pub, where they held a conference on their common business. When they left the pub, they found the car stalled. While Martirosoff sat at the wheel, the other two pushed until the engine turned over. And as they did, one of them suggested killing Russian Robert. One got into the front seat beside him. The other, in the back, shot him in the head. They pushed the body into the back seat, and took the cash he was carrying. They covered him with a blanket, then left the car in Notting Hill Gate.

The dead man was found early the next morning and quickly identified. Police noticed that Frank Everitt, a cab driver popularly called "the Duke," had been killed in a similar way two weeks before. Within a short time, the police learned that Martirosoff had received a phone call the previous evening from a Polish friend. From there, they soon determined that he had been friends with a Pole named Marian and a Polish naval officer. The Polish community identified the 33-year-old Grondkowski, and he was soon arrested. He was carrying a cigarette lighter and a wallet belonging to Russian Robert. He promptly blamed the 25-year-old Malinowski for the murder. Malinowski, when arrested, blamed Grondowski. They were both found Guilty and hanged. The police tried for a long time to link the two murderers to Everitt. Even as they were about to be hanged, an investigator subtly questioned them, hoping that they would confess at the last moment.

REF.: *CBA; Firmin, Murderers In Our Midst; Heppenstall, The Sex War and Others; Jackson, Occupied With Crime; Lefebure, Evidence for the Crown; Shew, A Companion to Murder; Simpson, Forty Years of Murder*

Groot, Huigh (AKA: **Hugo Grotius, Hugeianus de Groot**), 1583-1645, Neth., rebel. Attorney general for the province of Holland in 1607. He was given life imprisonment in 1618 by the order of Prince Maurice for actively supporting the Arminians, but escaped after three years by hiding in a trunk of books. Book authored: *De jure belli ac Pacis.* REF.: *CBA.*

Gross, Ernst William, d.1850, U.S., mur. Ernst Gross migrated from Germany and settled in Jeffersonville, Ind. He obtained a job working in a plant where John Peter Smith, a fellow worker, made fun of Gross, calling him a "greenhorn," and humiliating him by mocking Gross' thick accent. Smith was on his way home on the night of Nov. 1, 1849, when he was attacked and killed. His pockets were rifled as if someone had tried to rob him. Gross, whose dislike for Smith was well known, was arrested and charged with the murder. He was convicted after some of Smith's belongings were found in his residence and introduced into evidence at his trial. Gross was sentenced to death and hanged at New Albany, Ind., on Dec. 13, 1850.

REF.: *CBA; Meyer, Full Account of the Life, Adventures, and Execution of Ernst William Gross.*

Gross, Hans, 1847-1915, Aust., criminol. In the late nineteenth century Austrian-born Hans Gross emerged as one of the world's top criminologists. He was at the forefront of a scientific revolution that changed the usual ways police agencies investigated serious crime. Gross elevated criminal detection to a science, advancing his long-held theory that information received from witnesses and informants was no substitute for evidence uncovered through scientific and technical methods.

Gross was trained as a lawyer, but spent most of his professional career at the University of Prague, and the University of Graz where he taught criminology and penal law. In 1907 he published a landmark book titled *Criminal Investigation* which described his breakthrough experiments with colored liquids. Blood spots, he determined, were shaped differently they fell from a person in motion, as opposed to someone standing still. The pattern of the blood spots turned out to provide an accurate indication of the victim's movements, an invaluable aid to detective agencies within the big city police departments.

Gross introduced a previously unheard of level of sophistication into police work. He also greatly influenced novelist Arthur Conan Doyle who incorporated much of Gross' scientific research into the popular detective stories he wrote.

REF.: *CBA; Gross, Criminal Investigation; Scott, Concise Encyclopedia of Crime and Criminals.*

Gross, Harry, 1916- , U.S., gamb. Harry Gross ran a highly successful gambling business in Brooklyn, N.Y. When Gross was arrested and jailed in Brooklyn, N.Y., in September 1951, his business was pulling in more than $20 million a year. Gross eventually pleaded guilty to bookmaking, but in an effort to get a lighter sentence, he agreed to talk about the copious payoffs he had made to Brooklyn police, which enabled his business to thrive.

And talk he did: Standard bribes ranged anywhere from $2 a day for the average beat cop, to $6,500 a year for the police commissioner. In addition, officers were often given television sets, expensive clothes, or jewelry. The law reciprocated by looking the other way while Gross became one of the most successful bookies in New York. The astonished jury indicted twenty-one of Brooklyn's finest, and branded an additional fifty-six officers as "co-conspirators."

But Gross had a sudden change of heart at the hearings. When pressed to begin naming names, he suddenly walked off the witness stand and suggested, "Let's go to lunch." The prosecutor, District Attorney Miles McDonald, devastated by the silence of his key witness, withdrew all charges against the other officers. Judge Samuel Leibowitz sentenced Gross to a 1,800-day sentence and a $15,000 fine. It was believed by prosecutor McDonald that Gross had returned a favor and accepted $75,000 to keep his mouth shut about the graft.

REF.: *CBA; Hamilton, Men of the Underworld.*

Gross, Louis, prom. 20th Cent., U.S., (wrong. convict.) mur. Rabbi Joshua S. Sperka was as honest and benevolent a man as one would ever meet. Highly respected in Detroit where he lived, his word was considered wise and fair. So in 1945, when he took up the cause of Louis Gross, a man convicted of murder in a Detroit suburb thirteen years before, people took notice. Rabbi Sperka must have had ample reason to believe Gross' innocence to ask that the case be retried. The rabbi called on the Court of Last Resort, a group who took on the causes of those believed to have been wrongly convicted, and told them Gross' story.

Gross was a peddler in the largely Syrian community of Highland Park in 1932 when a man named Mortado Abraham was killed with a .38-caliber pistol. A highly questionable police investigation came to the conclusion that Gross had killed Abraham out of revenge for an unpaid bill. Gross' trial was, at the very least, a fiasco. Witnesses invariably contradicted each other, and "facts" about the case were found to be dubious. Still, the jury came back with a verdict of Guilty, and Louis Gross, protesting his innocence, was handed a mandatory life sentence.

The most amazing thing occurred next: as Gross worked to appeal the verdict, the court reporter discovered that his notes on that trial had been removed from his stenographer's notebook. Another court reporter for the pre-trial hearing found the same had happened to his books, and the prosecutor discovered that his private files had been looted and all information on the Gross case had been removed. A court decided, however, that without the information, the judge had no information to review and Gross' trial could not be reopened.

The case was closed despite Gross' continued pleas of innocence, and the peddler was eventually forgotten. When Gross told Rabbi Sperka the story, the rabbi took an immediate interest in the case. Through his pleading, the Court of Last Resort instigated a full-scale investigation in 1948. They found information indicating a major cover-up—Gross was most likely the "fall guy," intended to cover someone else's guilt.

Upon hearing of the apparent injustice, Gerald K. O'Brien, Detroit's prosecutor, announced he would conduct an investigation. When his efforts affirmed Gross' innocence, the prosecutor personally filed for a new trial. No sooner had the motion been accepted than O'Brien asked that the case be dismissed. This, too, was accepted and Gross was acquitted of any involvement in Abraham's murder. Louis Gross had spent sixteen years in prison.

REF.: *CBA; Gardner, The Court of Last Resort.*

Gross, Reginald R., 1961-   , U.S., mur. A former heavyweight boxer who once fought Mike Tyson was convicted on three murder charges in mid-1989. Reginald R. "Reggie" Gross, twenty-eight, was involved with a west Baltimore, Md., drug gang led by Warren Boardley. Gross admitted to the shooting of Andre J. Coxson on Sept. 12, 1986, as well as Zachary Roach, a narcotics dealer, and Rodney Young on Sept. 23, 1986, on Boardley's directive. Gross was paid between $2,000 and $3,000 for the murders. On June 5, 1989, Gross pleaded guilty and on July 27, 1989, he received three life sentences, two were consecutive and one was concurrent. Boardley, twenty-seven, had been sentenced to a forty-seven-year term a month earlier. REF.: *CBA.*

Gross, William, d.1823, U.S., mur. William Gross, a native of Philadelphia, patronized a whorehouse run by Kesiah Stow, a beautiful prostitute-madam. Gross fell in love with the brothel keeper but grew enraged every time his mistress serviced other men. He attempted to persuade Stow to abandon her profession but she refused. Some days later, Gross was seen taking a knife to a cutlery shop where he had a clerk sharpen the blade. That night

The execution of William Gross.

he waited for his mistress to return to her bawdy house. As she did so, Gross leaped from hiding and stabbed her to death with the butcher knife. One report had it that Stow had entered the house "glowing with excitement, fresh from a ballroom, with all her imperfections on her head." Gross was tried, convicted, and condemned. He was hanged in Philadelphia on Feb. 7, 1823.

REF.: *CBA; The Only True Confession, The Last Words and Dying Confession of William Gross; The True and Genuine Confession of William Gross.*

Grosscup, Peter Stenger, 1852-1921, U.S., jur. U.S. district judge for the northern district of Illinois from 1892-99, wherein he issued a court order preventing Eugene Debs and the American Railway Union from interfering with either the U.S. mail or interstate commerce. In 1899, he was appointed to the U.S. Circuit Court of Appeals, where he served for twelve years, six years as the presiding judge. Landmark cases include the Standard Oil of Indiana case, in which he reversed Judge Landis' decision to fine the company more than $29 million for accepting rebates. REF.: *CBA.*

Grossman, Israel G., c.1953-   , U.S., fraud. In July 1986, a pension lawyer working for a New York law firm unlawfully used inside information and tipped six friends and relatives about a lucrative investment. Israel G. Grossman was working for Kramer, Levine, Nessen, Kamin & Frankel when he learned from a colleague that Colt Industries, a firearms and automotive parts manufacturer, was planning to capitalize. Grossman, a Brooklyn resident, and the others purchased nearly $34,000 in Colt's stock options, gaining about $1.5 million in illegal profits. The unusually heavy trading was detected and investigated by the Securities and Exchange Commission (SEC). In September 1986, Grossman was fired from his company for reasons unrelated to the investigation. On Aug. 18, 1987, he was convicted on thirty-eight counts of securities and mail fraud in connection with the illegally used information. On Sept. 15, 1987, he was sentenced to a two-year prison term and fined $25,000. No criminal charges were brought against the investors, but the SEC did file civil suits against Grossman and his colleagues. REF.: *CBA.*

Grossmann, George, d.1921, Ger., can.-mur. The years between WWI and WWII in Germany were fraught with poverty and rates of inflation so high that a wheelbarrow of banknotes bought barely a loaf of bread. But meat, when it was available, sold well nonetheless. In 1921, tenants in a Berlin rooming house heard sounds of a struggle coming from one of the rooms, and upon investigation found George Grossmann with the body of a plump young woman. Grossman confessed to having picked up many a young woman, preferably plump, at Berlin's railroad station. Then he killed them, cut them into pleasing-looking cuts of meat, and sold them to the citizens of Berlin. Arrested and tried, Grossman was sentenced to death, but he killed himself in his cell before the execution.

REF.: *CBA; Wilson, Encyclopedia of Murder.*

Grotius, Hugo, 1583-1645, Neth., treas. Grotius was a legal scholar best known for his contribution of *Law of War and Peace* to the world of international law. The work, written mostly while he was imprisoned for religious treason, outlined his rules of International Law and became the backbone of a civilized code of conduct between nations.

In 1619, Grotius was serving as Pensionary of Rotterdam when he made public remarks to the effect that the Bible should not be taken literally, and that individuals should interpret its words in the way their highest principles might dictate. These statements resulted in his conviction and sentencing to a prison in Loevesteyn, Holland.

Grotius' punishment, however, was hardly cruel: he was confined to a fully furnished, two-room chamber, which his wife and two children were allowed to enter whenever they wanted. He was also allowed access to any books he wanted. This arrangement gave him ample opportunity to work on his own writings, and he was quite content. His wife, however, was not, and on Mar. 22, 1621, she arranged his escape by hiding him in a trunk which guards believed to be filled with legal tomes. The trunk was safely shipped without incident to a friend's house, and

Grotius' family followed closely behind.

Hugo Grotius died on Aug. 29, 1645, from an illness incurred after a ship he sailed in, bound for Lubeck, Germany, wrecked. REF.: *CBA*.

Grove, Sir William Robert, 1811-96, Brit., jur. Judge on the Court of Common Pleas in 1871, on the Queen's Bench in 1880, and privy counselor in 1887. REF.: *CBA*.

Groves, Wallace, and **Groves, George S.**, prom. 1930s, U.S., fraud. Wallace Groves was not yet out of Georgetown University before he was controlling a number of small loan companies in the Washington, D.C., area. In 1931, he sold those companies to raise capital for a chance on Wall Street, where he was just as successful, taking control of at least six securities trusts.

His private life was apparently as active as his public life, highlighted by his marriage to Monaei Lindley, a prominent film actress, and extravagant parties thrown for business associates. But this luxurious world collapsed when, in 1938, he and his brother, George S. Groves, were indicted by a Federal grand jury on fourteen counts of mail fraud and one count of conspiracy. The main charge stemmed from the purchase of 20,000 shares of General Investment Corp., one of his own corporation, for $87.50 a share, a transaction made immediately after he had sold the shares back to the same company for $102 per share, creating a profit of $290,000.

Wallace and George Groves were eventually convicted on Feb. 21, 1941. Wallace was sentenced to two years in prison, his brother eight months, and they were each fined $22,000. George Groves' verdict was overturned on Aug. 5, 1941, by the U.S. Circuit Court of Appeals. REF.: *CBA*.

Growden, Gerald, 1912- , U.S., (wrong. convict.) mur. Convicted of the murder of James B. Smith, a tobacco and candy salesman in 1929, 20-year-old Gerald Growden was freed after serving eight months of his sentence. His innocence was proven when Lawrence Hein and Harry Lancaster confessed to the murder and provided enough details to make it clear that Growden was not with them at the time of the murder.

Growden had originally been convicted on eyewitness testimony, and on the testimony of inmates who knew him when he was in prison before his trial and said he had bragged about the murder. He was freed on June 18, 1932, after having been convicted and sentenced the previous October. REF.: *CBA*.

Gruber, Emanuel Henry, and **Clark, Austin M.**, prom. 1860-63, U.S., count. Without breaking any laws, a Denver gold and banking firm coined its own gold pieces until it was bought out by Congress in 1863. The coins made by Clark, Gruber & Company looked similar to U.S. mint coins, but with the words "Pike's Peak" replacing "Liberty" on the Statue of Liberty side, and the company name in place of "United States of America." Emanuel Gruber and Austin Clark were trying to avoid the high cost of shipping gold dust to other minting facilities, and did not use any alloys in their coins, making them worth up to ten cents more than the coins provided by the government. The Congressional Ways and Means Committee investigated Gruber and Clark in 1862, concluding the men were not criminals, but were providing facilities for "fraud and villainy." The government bought the mint for $25,000 in April 1863, but did not use it for forty-three years, leading Gruber to conclude that the U.S. paid "to get rid of a dangerous competitor, who insisted on putting out a better, more valuable product."

REF.: Bloom, *Money of Their Own; CBA*.

Gruebert, Frederick, and **Agro, Salvatore**, and **Hirschorn, Stephen** (AKA: **Bertram Williams**), and **Leone, Louis Quentin**, and **Leone, Raymond**, and **Levine, Ave** (AKA: **Mal Reif, Morris Reif**), and **Witt, Herman**, prom. 1964, U.S., forg. Except for the unknown mastermind, thought to be from Buffalo, N.Y., every member of a check counterfeiting operation in Kings County, N.Y.—Frederick Gruebert, Salvatore Agro, Stephen Hirschorn, Louis Quentin Leone, Raymond Leone, Ave Levine, and Herman Witt—went to jail.

In 1964, either Louis of Raymond Leone contacted his neigh-

bor, Frederick Gruebert, comptroller for J.W. Mays, Inc., a department store in Brooklyn, to find out if he was willing to use his position in the interests of illegal profit. Gruebert said yes and passed along legitimate checks issued by Mays to pay large invoices. Before mailing them to the real payees, his cohorts had the checks photographed and the paper analyzed, and then had printing plates made from the photographs. Proper security paper was obtained by setting up a business that required security forms that featured a large, central blank area. The blank area was cut out of each form and used to print checks matching the real Mays checks.

Raymond Leone and Hirschorn set up seventeen actual companies and opened corresponding bank accounts. Then, each Saturday, the day Mays issued checks, they issued Mays checks to these companies and the checks were deposited. During succeeding days they withdrew the money, and sent it to a stock-brokerage account, taking cash at the end of the day. The cash was then turned over to the leaders of the operation, all nicely laundered, and often increased. This continued to the tune of nearly $1 million until one of the two J.W. Mays bank accounts being plundered was accidentally overdrawn. Raymond Leone walked into a staked-out bank to withdraw the previous Saturday's deposit and was arrested. The others were soon arrested too. All seven were found Guilty and sentenced to prison. REF.: *CBA*.

Grumbach, Wilhelm von, 1503-67, Ger., consp.-mur. Attempted to seize properties held by the Bishop of Würzburg, but the land was confiscated in 1553. In retaliation, he aided Franconia and ordered the assassination of the bishop in 1558, causing the "Grumbach feuds." Five years later, he finally seized Würzburg and the property. He was executed for trying to return John Frederick to power. REF.: *CBA*.

Grundy, Felix, 1777-1840, U.S., lawyer. U.S. congressman from 1811-14, U.S. senator from 1829-38 and 1839-40, and U.S. attorney general from 1838-39. REF.: *CBA*.

Grupen, Peter, prom. 1921, Case of, Ger., mur. A mysterious one-armed man appeared at Kleppelsdorf Castle, home of the widow Frau Eckert, Bertha Zahn, and Dorothea Rohrbeck, Eckert's young granddaughter. The man, Peter Grupen, posed as a distant relative of Eckert's husband, moved into the castle with his daughters, Ursula and Irma, and, to Zahn's dismay, quickly gained control over Frau Eckert. By the time he left, under arrest, two of the girls were dead.

When Zahn argued with Eckert that Grupen was an impostor interested in the family money, Eckert replied, "I can't really explain how I've changed. It is as though Peter has changed me, and I don't really like him. In fact, I fear him, but somehow I lack the will to resist any more." A detective later theorized that Grupen had hypnotized Eckert to gain her trust in financial matters, and increased his efforts after learning of Dorothea's considerable legacy.

In February 1921, Dorothea was found dead of a gunshot wound, with Ursula, shot twice, dying by her side. Grupen showed police a note in a child's handwriting which read, "Dear Grandmother, don't be angry with me for having taken father's pistol from the writing table. I wish to help you, and you will have no more trouble with Dorothea." Grupen explained that Ursula called Eckert grandmother, but had no answer as to how a young girl could accurately fire a heavy pistol that had not been used in more than four years, and, after injuring her friend, shoot herself twice. Police called the deaths accidental, but the detective continued to observe Grupen and his amazing influence over the women living in the castle. The detective concluded that Irma, who seemed to be living in a world of fantasy, and the others, had been hypnotized, and reopened the case. The investigation showed that Grupen had hypnotized many other women in the past, including one who tried to kill another he had hypnotized. His wife was also missing. Grupen was arrested and taken to Hirstberg Prison.

Prosecuting attorneys at the trial argued that Grupen had either hypnotized Ursula to make her kill her friend and herself, or had shot both girls and lied. He was found Guilty of both murders. The body of Grupen's wife was found in a Hamburg canal and he was charged with her murder as well. Grupen was attracting so much publicity that he was transferred to another prison, where he attempted to hang himself. He later faked an escape with the help of apparently hypnotized inmates, and the police and military launched a search throughout Germany. Grupen, however, was eventually discovered in the prison exercise yard, and sent back to solitary confinement, where he succeeded in hanging himself.

REF.: *CBA*; Gribble, *The Dead End Killers.*

Grzechowiak, Stephen, 1895-1930, and **Bogdanoff, Alexander**, 1895-1930, and **Rybarczyk, Max**, 1899-1930, U.S., mur. In the space of twenty minutes on the evening of July 17, 1930, three men were put to death in the electric chair at Sing Sing Prison in Ossining, N.Y. As the third man, Alexander Bogdanoff, entered the chamber, he asked to make a final statement. He turned to the witnesses and said: "Gentlemen, the state of New York has just killed two innocent men. I tried to save them but my word was no good."

Bogdanoff had asserted this for weeks. He had been convicted along with Stephen Grzechowiak and Max Rybarczyk of the murder of Ferdinand Fechter, a restaurant owner, during an armed robbery in Buffalo, N.Y. After receiving a death sentence, Bogdanoff accepted his own fate but vehemently denied that the two other men had anything to do with the crime. His accomplices, he maintained, were two Chicago gunmen who were still at large.

Saving Rybarczyk and Grzechowiak, who also asserted their innocence with the same fervor, from the electric chair should have been easy. All Bogdanoff had to do was give the names of the real gunmen. But he refused, asserting that the state would have to believe him when he said that the other two convicts were blameless.

Without those names, there was nothing the state could do. New York's governor gave all three men a two-week reprieve on July 3, perhaps hoping that Bogdanoff would disclose the names of the real killers, or that new evidence would come to light. When that time passed and nothing more was revealed, the three men went to their deaths. REF.: *CBA*.

Guadalajara-Mexico City Express Massacre, Mex., 1927. A band of revolutionaries, reportedly acting on the orders of the Mexican Episcopate, attacked a passenger train, killing more than fifty passengers and forty-eight military guards and wounding countless others on Jan. 8, 1927. The attack started when armed men stormed into the third-class cars, firing revolvers and stabbing passengers and train guards. No one in the first-class Pullman cars was injured, but all the men were robbed. The train was set on fire after unharmed passengers and guards fled, leaving many wounded to die in the flames. The killers broke open the train's safe, taking more than $200,000 in gold and silver coins and silver bars. Ten of the stolen bars were recovered by military officials led to the loot by Señor Villalobos, a former commander-in-chief of the Yurecuaro village police force, who was captured for his role in the massacre. Fifteenth Cavalry troops apprehended about twenty of the killers at the Quitupan ranch in the state of Jalisco, where most died in the ensuing gun battle. Eight of the bandits, after confessing to the robbery, were shot to death.

The rationale originally given for the attack was that the bandits believed General Ferreira, military commandant of the state of Jalisco, was on the train. According to news from offices controlled by President Plutarco Calles, the attack was ordered by the Mexican Episcopate. The Most Reverend José Mora y del Rio, Archbishop of Mexico, the Most Reverend Leopoldo Ruiz y Florez, Archbishop of Michoacan, and Bishops Ignazio Valdespino y Diaz of Aguascalientes, José Marie Echeverria of Saltillo, Januarius Anaya of Chiapas, and Salvador Uranga of Cuernavaca were put by government agents on a train to Laredo, Texas. Before leaving, the six denied that the Episcopate had any part in the rebellion, or that any priests participated in the January attack. Four months later, a group of Catholic extremists attacked

a Juarez-Mexico City military train near Salas. The 30-minute battle ended when the attackers discovered that they were not attacking a passenger train. Ten of the attackers died, according to an official report by General Amarillas. REF.: *CBA*.

Guadalupe Canyon Massacres, prom. 1881, U.S., west. gunfights. In July 1881, in the southwest border area of Guadalupe Canyon, members of the notorious Clanton Gang learned that a shipment of gold bullion was being moved by mule train through the Chiricahua Range. Twenty outlaws, including Curly Bill Brocius, Johnny Ringo, and Old Man Clanton himself, ambushed the nineteen Mexicans transporting the fortune, killed them, and escaped with over $75,000 in bullion. Two weeks later, the Mexicans avenged the massacre. As Old Man Clanton and five of his men were driving stolen cattle through the same mountain pass, they were ambushed from the same hidden positions they had used to their advantage. Clanton and all but one of his thieves were killed in the attack. Brocius, assuming leadership of the gang, led a second ambush against the Mexicans, killing six, and torturing another eight to death after they surrendered. See: **Brocius, Curly Bill; Clanton-McLowery Gang.** REF.: *CBA*.

Guadet, Marguerite Élie, 1758-1794, Fr., treas. Entered the Legislative Assembly in 1791, and participated in the National Convention in 1792. She led the moderate Republicans, or Girondists, in opposition to the Jacobins. She was beheaded in 1794. REF.: *CBA*.

Guardia, Francisco Ferrer, See: **Ferrer Guardia, Francisco.**

Guardian Angels, 1979- , U.S., crime prevention. The Guardian Angels, a controversial volunteer citizens patrol was founded in 1979 by 25-year-old Curtis Sliwa. Expelled from Brooklyn Preparatory School after he tried to change the dress code, Sliwa went on to establish the Rock Brigade, a neighborhood street cleanup organization, while working as assistant manager of a South Bronx McDonald's restaurant. In February 1979, Sliwa founded a thirteen-member subway patrol, the Magnificent 13, which became the nucleus of the Guardian Angels.

Sliwa, who is white, is the unsalaried president of the organization, whose members are primarily black or Hispanic and in their late teens or early twenties. The Guardian Angels are funded chiefly through donations, and no members are paid. The group has gained popular support, but has had difficulty winning sanction from official law enforcement agencies. Criticized for a lack of formal training, the group's members have been called vigilantes by New York City mayor Edward I. Koch. However, the members, who receive training in citizens' arrest laws, self-defense, and cardiopulmonary resuscitation, have been welcomed by others. In mid-1987, three women were murdered in Wisconsin Dells, Wis., and the Guardian Angels arrived to offer assistance, providing self-defense lessons and escort and house-sitting services. Although many women apparently appreciated the protection, Sliwa said some local men did not cooperate. "There was this Joe mountain-man type at the entrance to one road," said Sliwa, "He patted his .357 magnum and said, 'I got my Guardian Angel right here.'" The Guardian Angels have also been credited for rescuing a New York subway clerk who fell onto the train tracks, for training women in self-defense when a rapist was attacking in San Jose, Calif., and for offering to search for a child-killer in Atlanta. The Guardian Angels has more than 5,000 members and about sixty chapters in New York, Chicago, Los Angeles, San Francisco, San Diego, Atlanta, Houston, St. Louis, Seattle, Portland, Chattanooga, Yakima, and Indianapolis, as well as other cities in the U.S., Canada, France, and England. REF.: *CBA*.

Guardiola, Santos, d.1862, Hond., pres., assass. Led Honduran and Salvadoran troops against Nicaragua in 1844, and in 1855, led the revolt that ousted the president of Honduras. He served as president of Honduras from 1856 until his assassination in 1862. REF.: *CBA*.

Guatemotzin (Guatemoc, Cuauhtemoc), c.1495-1525, Mex., emp., assass. The last Aztec emperor, who succeeded his uncle, Montezuma II in 1520. He led the Aztec army in battles against

Spanish commander Hernando Cortes, directing the 1520 campaign in which the Spaniards were driven from Mexico City. He was seized and tortured by Cortes, but refused to tell where the Aztec treasures were located. Cortes executed him for treachery. REF.: *CBA*.

Guay, Albert, 1919-51, and **Pitre, Marguerite**, prom. 1949, and **Ruest, Genéreaux**, prom. 1949, Can., mur. On Sept. 9, 1949, Canadian Pacific Airlines Flight 108 from Quebec to Baie Comeau exploded in flight forty miles from Quebec. All twenty-three passengers and crew members were killed in the crash, which was initially considered an accident. But investigators found evidence of a dry battery cell and dynamite in the wreckage, indicating that a bomb had been planted on the plane.

Albert Guay, who engineered the blowing up of a Canadian airliner in 1949.

The cargo manifest listed a package being sent to a nonexistent address. Airport freight handlers recalled that a woman dressed in black had left the package. Ten days after the crash, a taxi driver came forward to say that he remembered driving a woman in black carrying a package to the airport on the day of the crash. He gave police an address that turned out to be that of Marguerite Pitre. When police arrived to question Pitre, however, they were informed that she was in the hospital recovering from a suicide attempt.

Pitre admitted taking the package to the airport, and told police that she had done so at the request of a friend and former lover, Albert Guay, a Quebec jeweler. She explained that it was all part of a plot to kill Guay's wife, Rita Morel Guay. Albert Guay had become involved with 19-year-old waitress Marie-Ange Robitaille and wanted to get rid of his wife so he could marry her. He got help from Pitre, who in turn convinced her brother, Genéreaux Ruest, to build the bomb. Guay asked his wife to go to Baie Comeau to pick up two suitcases of jewelry for him.

Guay, Pitre, and Ruest were arrested and charged with murder. All three were convicted and hanged.

REF.: *CBA*; Gribble, *When Killers Err;* Haines, *Bothersome Bodies;* Hynd, *Murder, Mayhem and Mystery;* Nash, *Almanac of World Crime;* Radin, *Headline Crimes of the Year;* Wilson, *Encyclopedia of Murder.*

Gubow, Lawrence, 1919-78, U.S., jur. Participated in the Michigan Bar Association committee to revise the Michigan Criminal Code in 1966, and was nominated to the district court of Michigan by President Lyndon B. Johnson in 1968. REF.: *CBA*.

Guenzel, Guel Sultan, 1956- , Turk., mur. In about 1968, an Adana, Turk., woman died of tuberculosis, leaving her husband and three daughters. Not long after the wife died, her husband, Kadir Karayigit, about thirty-seven, began sexually abusing his oldest daughter. He would give 13-year-old Guel Sultan strong, sweet wine after dinner, and after she passed out, he sexually assaulted her. When her two younger sisters also reached thirteen, the father treated them similarly. The oldest daughter's suspicion that she might not be a virgin was confirmed on her wedding night in June 1974. Six days later, on June 22, Guel Sultan Guenzel, eighteen, went to her father's restaurant at 3:30 p.m. She found him resting on a couch in his office and shot him once in the head and seven times in the groin. Then she wiped her fingerprints from the gun and tossed the weapon on the couch. A waiter, Omar Demir, found Karayigit and immediately ran out to the street, to call for help. Police first suspected Demir, but he was

released. One of the constables remembered that the eldest daughter was sitting inside the restaurant drinking wine after the murder. The young woman was questioned and she confessed, telling the story of abuse, which was confirmed by her two sisters. She was tried in September 1974 on a charge of premeditated murder. Guenzel was convicted and received a five-year suspended sentence. REF.: *CBA*.

Guérin, Eddie (AKA: **Eddy Edwards**), 1860-1940, Fr., rob.-pris. esc. Eddie Guérin was known throughout Europe and the U.S. as a clever but dangerous thief. He was also inaccurately credited with escaping from Devil's Island. Nevertheless, his exploits were recounted in book and newspaper form, making him an instant celebrity. Guérin was born in the U.S., and spent time in the old Harrison Street lockup in Chicago for various burglaries. However, he attained his real proficiency in crime while traveling on the continent.

In May 1889, for example, he was sentenced to ten years of penal servitude for stealing 247,000 francs from the Bank of France a year earlier. According to Guérin's version of the events, he spent the night of the burglary in a hotel on the Rue Vignon. Guérin's criminal associates revealed his whereabouts after learning that he had cheated them in the division of the loot. The Sûreté arrested Guérin, and the court shipped him to the prison at Riom where he remained until May 24, 1899. Deported to the U.S., Guérin found conditions there not to his liking and returned to France with his girlfriend "Chicago" May Churchill, also known as "Queen of the Criminals."

While in Paris in April 1901, Eddie planned his greatest caper: the robbery of the American Express office. Guérin, and two other men named Miller and MacManus gained entry to the building after it had closed. They bound and gagged the night watchman, and looted the safe of £40,000. At 5 a.m., when the job was completed the burglars disposed of their tools in the Seine and returned to their hotel to divide the money. May Churchill, who had been staying in England but longed to be at Eddie's side, provided the Sûreté with their first lead. Arrested in Paris, Churchill revealed that she had removed Guérin's luggage to England. In Berlin, a third member of the gang, Karl Leternee was circulating stolen traveler's checks in the city. His arrest led the police to Guérin, who was taken to the Court of Assizes of the Seine, June 14, 1902. There he received a life sentence and was sent to Devil's Island, in Guiana. For the next three years he languished on the "rock," a penal colony generally reserved for political prisoners and enemies of the state.

In May 1905 he was transferred to the St. Laurent penal camp on the edge of the Maroni River, in the same archipelago as the infamous Devil's Island. The wife of a prison guard who took pity on him provided Guérin with some money and the means to escape. With two other convicts, the emaciated Guérin set out for Dutch Guiana, 200 miles away. The two Spaniards plotted to kill Eddie along the way, but he was wise to their treachery and forced them to row the canoe at gunpoint. When they arrived on the Dutch Coast, Guérin decamped from the small boat and made his way into the forest where he was seized by local Indians. Once again he had to rely on his wits to escape to safety. He managed to do so, and it wasn't long before he made his way back to the streets of Chicago.

The city police, alerted to Guérin's presence by the Sûreté, were unable to locate and arrest him. Again, the wily thief chanced fate by sailing for England. He was arrested on Apr. 6, 1906 by two detectives and extradited back to France. Guérin spent his remaining years in and out of various European prisons. He died on Dec. 5, 1940 in a public institution in Bury, Lancashire, Eng. See: **Churchill, May Vivienne; Devil's Island**.

REF.: *CBA*; Fabian, *Fabian of the Yard;* Morain, *The Underworld of Paris.*

Guerin, Joseph, prom. 1971, U.S., mur. On Nov. 29, 1971, Albany, N.Y., police Sergeant Mike McNeil was fatally shot by a driver he had stopped because his license did not conform to his car's registration number. McNeil had frisked Joseph Guerin, who it was later discovered was wanted for grand larceny and robbery, but failed to find the pistol in his pocket. Guerin fled after the shooting, but a man and woman who were in his car stayed behind and gave police information that led to his arrest. He was convicted and sentenced to life in prison. REF.: *CBA*.

Guérini, Antoine (Antonio), d.1967, Fr., (unsolv.) mur. Antoine Guérini was the "godfather" of an extended underworld family in Marseilles, Fr. It was rumored in 1965 that the Guérinis were responsible for the murder of Robert Blémant, a mobster and former policeman. Two years later, on June 23, Antoine and his son Félix stopped for gas in a suburb of Marseilles. Two masked men on a motorcycle pulled alongside them and shot the father. No one was ever arrested for that murder.

As Guérini was being buried, a young Armenian named Claude Mandroyan and a friend broke into Guérini's widow's house and stole her jewels. The word went out from the Guérinis and no fence would touch the jewels. Mandroyan was told to deal with Barthélemy Guérini, Antoine's brother, for the gems' return . When the Guérinis called him, Mandroyan went to meet them and was murdered. Barthélemy (called Mémé) and Pascal Guérini were arrested for the killing, along with three other men. One man was acquitted, but Pascal and two others were sentenced to fifteen years in prison. Mémé, already an old man, got twenty years. REF.: *CBA*.

Guerrazzi, Francesco Domenico (Anselmo Gualandi), 1804-73, Italy, ban. Founded the journal *Indicatore Livornese* in 1829. He became premier of Tuscany in 1848, and soon became a triumvir and the dictator of the Republic of Florentine. He was imprisoned from 1849-53, after which he was banished to Corsica for eight years. He served in Parliament in 1862 and 1865. REF.: *CBA*.

Guerrero, Vicente, 1783-1831, Mex., pres., assass. Served under José Maria Morelos in the Mexican war of independence, and became a leader of the Mexican guerrillas. Guerrero was vice president of Mexico from 1824-28, and was selected for the presidency by the Congress in 1829. Six months later, his government was overthrown by Vice President Anastasio Bustamante. He was captured and shot. REF.: *CBA*.

Guesclin, Bertrand du, c.1320-80. Fr., duel. French soldier who fought under the Duke of Brittany, most notably at Vannes in 1342. He dueled Thomas Canterbury in 1356. REF.: *CBA*.

Guevara, Ernesto (AKA: Che Guevara), 1928-67, Bol., assass. Ernesto Guevara, known as Che, was born in Argentina in 1928, and took an early interest in politics under the influence of his mother, an active leftist. He trained as a doctor, and upon his graduation from medical school in 1953, left Argentina rather than serve in the army of right-wing dictator Juan Péron. He traveled in Latin America, assisting revolutionary movements in Bolivia, Peru, Ecuador, Panama, and Costa Rica. In 1954, he helped organize the futile resistance to the CIA's overthrow of Guatemala's elected reformer president, Jacobo Arbenz Guzmán. After hiding in the Argentine embassy, Guevara escaped to Mexico, where he met Cuban revolutionary leader Fidel Castro and joined his movement.

By 1958, Guevara was Castro's primary military commander, and he led forces that defeated Cuban president Fulgencio Batista and allowed Castro to take power of Cuba in 1959. Castro appointed Guevara to the revolution's highest economic post, and sent him around the world to negotiate commercial treaties for the new government. Guevara resisted Soviet efforts to turn Cuba into a satellite, preferring the model offered by Chinese communism. Guevara soon became a hero to revolutionaries around the world.

Guevara was second in command in Cuba until 1965, when he left to further other Latin American revolutions. His whereabouts for the next two years were kept secret, but in 1967 he turned up in Bolivia. He was disappointed there by the response of the Bolivian peasants, who looked upon him as an outsider. On Oct. 8, 1967, he and several other guerrillas, including several Cubans, were captured by the Bolivian army near Higueras. His captors killed him and displayed his body for reporters. Guevara was thirty-nine.

REF.: *CBA*; Paine, *The Assassins' World*; (FILM), *Che!*, 1969.

Gufler, Max, 1910- , Aust., mur. Max Gufler became a confidence man and "bluebeard" murderer after the police closed down the stand from which he had sold pornographic photos. Gufler was an illegitimate child who had moods of unpredictable violence after he was struck on the head with a stone at age nine. He drove an ambulance for the Wehrmacht in WWII and suffered a second head wound. After the war, he sold books for seven years. When he met Herta Jonn, the woman who became his mistress, he began working in her father's tobacco shop, extending the inventory to include pornography. Gufler's sales of pornographic photos led to prison terms for Gufler, his mistress, and her father. The tobacco stand was permanently closed.

Upon his release from prison, Gufler began his career as confidence artist and bluebeard. His method was to read matrimonial advertisements, write letters to lonely widows, and propose marriage. As a test of the woman's love, he would ask her to withdraw all her savings. On the way to the marriage ceremony, he drugged the victim, disposing of the body so that the death looked like suicide.

Gufler is suspected of eighteen murders, the earliest in 1946, but was convicted of only eight. He confessed to bludgeoning to death 50-year-old prostitute Émilie Meystrzik in her room in Vienna in 1952, and to giving an overdose of barbiturates to 45-year-old Josefine Kemmleitner, whose body was found in the Danube on June 3, 1958. Gufler also confessed to killing Maria Robas three months later, and 50-year-old Juliana Nass, found in the Danube on Oct. 15, 1958. Gufler was arrested following the Robas killing because he sent her father a letter eventually traced to Gufler saying he witnessed her death in a car accident. The police also found sufficient evidence to prosecute Gufler for murdering Augusta Lin-

Austrian bluebeard Max Gufler.

debner, Theresa Wesely, Juliana Emsenhuber, and Josephine Dangl, and suspected him of murdering ten other women. They also found intended victim Marlene Buchner in tears at the registry office. Gufler's arrest had prevented him from keeping their appointment. Gufler was sentenced to life imprisonment in May 1961.

REF.: *CBA*; Heppenstall, *The Sex War and Others*; Wilson, *Encyclopedia of Murder*.

Guifoyle Gang, prom. 1920s, U.S., org. crime. Located on the near Northwest side of Chicago, the Guifoyle Gang was led by Martin Guifoyle, a tough bootlegger and ally of Al Capone. This gang distributed liquor throughout the West Side and controlled beer and alcohol production through underground breweries and distilleries during the Prohibition era. Guifoyle was aided by Al Winge, a one-time Chicago policeman who had turned crook, and Matt Kolb, a politician with city hall connections. This gang was absorbed by the Capone-Nitti gang after the Volstead Act was repealed. See: **Capone, Alphonse.**

REF.: *CBA*; Kobler, *Capone*; Nash, *Bloodletters and Badmen*.

Guilford, Howard, c.1894-1934, U.S., (unsolv.) mur. Although newspaper publisher Howard Guilford fought a good battle against the gambling syndicates of Minneapolis and St. Paul, he was not strong enough to defeat the very men who exercised control over the local police and municipal judges.

Guilford waged a one-man war against organized crime through the vehicle of the press. In 1927 he founded *The Saturday Press,* and with the publication of the very first issue, became a target of the gangsters. On Sept. 21, 1927, while the editor was motoring through the city a car bore down on him from behind. Shots were fired at the vehicle, seriously wounding Guilford. While recovering from his wounds in the hospital, an assassin tried unsuccessfully to kill him.

Guilford had incurred their wrath by publishing an inflammatory article charging that gambling was wide open in Minneapolis. When the mobsters found out that the editor would not accept a bribe they targeted him for assassination. "Word has been passed that if we persisted in our exposé of conditions as they were in this city we would be bumped off," he wrote. "Just a moment boys, before you start something you won't be able to finish. The open season on editorial writers ended with the assassination of Editor Don Mellett of Canton, Ohio, by an imported gunman."

This was not the first time the crusading editor had defied the local powers. In 1913 he accused Police Chief Martin J. Flanagan of assaulting him. The St. Paul Police Board cleared the chief of any wrongdoing. A short time later Guilford was arrested for carrying a concealed weapon. In 1917 he was charged with libel and assessed a $100 fine for an article he ran attacking the reputation of a former probate judge and Wright County clerk. The Minneapolis police retaliated by suppressing his paper on the stands. A year later Guilford announced his intention to run for mayor of Minneapolis against Thomas Van Lear, whom he accused of protecting gambling and vice. Police Chief Lewis Harthill was singled out for criticism, but the voters rejected Guilford's reform platform and returned Van Lear to office.

His most famous fight was waged against Minnesota's famous "gag law." Guilford challenged the right of the police and the municipal authorities to suppress publication of *The Saturday Press.* The Minnesota Supreme Court twice ruled against Guilford, who enlisted the support of Colonel Robert Rutherford McCormick, the fiery publisher of the Chicago *Tribune* in his crusade against censorship. *Tribune* attorneys helped Guilford prepare his case which ended up before the U.S. Supreme Court. On June 1, 1931, the gag law was declared unconstitutional by the high court in a five-to-four decision.

It was an important victory for freedom of the press, but the gun toting thugs of the Minneapolis underworld ultimately prevailed. On Sept. 6, 1934, Howard Guilford was shot to death as he drove his automobile through the south side of Minneapolis. The Police were unable to locate a witness or identify the occupants of the other vehicle. The unsolved murder of Howard Guilford encouraged the syndicate bullies to do their worst against other journalists who dared to defy their rule. Walter Liggett, editor of the *Midwest American* was shot down on Dec. 8, 1935. A decade later Arthur Kasherman was mowed down by syndicate hit men. See: **Kasherman, Arthur; Liggett, Walter.** REF.: *CBA.*

Guillard, Pierre, prom. 1932, Fr., vandal. In August 1932, engineer Pierre Guillard entered the Louvre museum in Paris. Guillard approached *The Angelus,* an 1859 painting by Jean Francois Millet that depicts a peasant and his wife praying in the middle of a field. The visitor took out a jackknife and slashed, scratched, and stabbed the painting. A guard overpowered Guillard and the vandal, later found to be insane, was sent to jail. REF.: *CBA.*

Guillaume de Hauteville (Count of Apulia, AKA: Iron Arms), d.1046, Normandy, consp.-mur. Conquered southern Italy with his brothers Humphrey and Drogo, in alliance with Rainulf of Aversa. He earned his nickname by murdering a Muslim. In 1042, he was appointed count of Apulia. REF.: *CBA.*

Guillen, Jose, and Guillen, Antonio Arias, prom. 1974, U.S., mur. On June 16, 1974, Chicago police officer Robert J. Strugala was shot to death by two gunmen in Chicago's Rio Grande Lounge on West 26th Street. Strugala's partner, officer John A. Wasco sustained injuries to his right elbow, lower right side and right leg. The officers were stopped at a traffic light in their patrol car when they heard gunshots from inside the bar. They stormed inside only to face José Guillen, who had just fired four shots at the bartender with a .38-caliber automatic pistol. Guillen's cousin, Antonio Arias Guillen, sprayed about three dozen rounds from two pistols at the policemen. Wasco was hit, and fell back through the side door. Strugala, meanwhile, was reloading his pistol behind the bar when Antonio Guillen shot him from behind. José Guillen also shot the fallen officer. He was captured outside the bar by police officers Joseph Mucharski and Edward Kodatt, who had found their colleague's empty patrol car. For the murder of Strugala, Jose Guillen was sentenced to fifty to one hundred years at Stateville Correctional Center, and given concurrent terms of ten to thirty years for attempting to murder officer Wasco and the bartender. Antonio Guillen escaped to Mexico, according to police. REF.: *CBA.*

Guillotin, Joseph Ignace, 1738-1814, Fr., cap. pun. Deputy to States-General in 1789, who advocated capital punishment and proposed use of the beheading machine. The guillotine is named after him. REF.: *CBA.*

Guimares, Alberto Santos, See: **King, Dot.**

Guin, Junius Foy, Jr., 1924- , U.S., jur. He was nominated to the northern district court of Alabama by President Richard M. Nixon in 1973, and joined the faculty of Samford University as a lecturer in the Cumberland School of Law in 1974. REF.: CBA.

Guinness, Walter Edward (First Baron Moyne), 1880-1944, Ire., assass. Fought in the Boer war, and served as a major during WWI. He was a member of Parliament from 1907-31, the leader of the House of Lords from 1941-42, a deputy minister of state from 1942-44, among other federal posts. He was assassinated in Cairo in 1944. REF.: *CBA.*

Guise, François (François de Lorraine, AKA: The Scarred), 1519-63, Lorraine, assass. Son of Claude I, the second Duc de Guise. He was a French soldier who fought in Montmédy, Landrecies, and Boulogne between 1542-4, and then in 1552, in Metz, when it was attacked by Charles V. Catherine de Médicis forced him to resign after the death of Francis II in 1560. An insane Protestant, Jean de Poltrot, Seigneur de Méré, killed him in February of 1563. See: **Guise, Henri I de Lorraine; Henry III, King of France.** REF.: *CBA.*

Guise, Henri I de Lorraine (Third Duke of Guise, Henry of Guise; AKA: The Scarred), 1550-88, Fr., assass. The son of Francis of Lorraine, "le Grand Guise," young Henri Guise was only thirteen when his father died. He hated the French Huguenots, whom he blamed for his father's death. In 1572, Catherine de Médici solicited the help of the rich and powerful Guise family to get rid of Admiral Gaspard de Coligny, whose policies ran contrary to those of the Catholic monarch. On Aug. 24, during the bloody St. Bartholomew's Massacre against the Huguenots, Guise murdered Coligny—the Huguenot leader whom the duke held accountable for his father's death in 1563. However, he took no part in the massacre, and even sheltered Huguenots in his home. He emerged as the leader of the Catholic party in France and Catherine's "protector" against the intrigues of her scheming son François, duc d'Alençon.

In May 1574, Henry III acceded to the throne of France, and for a time the Catholic world was harmonious. Two years later the king made his peace with the Huguenot factions, alienating the Duke de Guise. For what he considered to be a betrayal of all French Catholics, the duke organized the Holy League of Nobles on May 5, 1576. Henry III checked the ambitions of the Guise family by placing himself at the head of the movement. Relations between the Guise family and the monarchy further deteriorated after the Peace of Poitiers was signed in September 1577, and the king elected to disband the Catholic associations. The Duke de Guise, now officially out of favor with the king, engaged in intrigue with the Spanish court, then headed by Philip II. During this time, the Holy League modified its position in light of the King Henry III's "heresy": Obedience would be given to the king only after the monarch had shown proof of his loyalty to the Catholic faith.

On May 12, 1588, later known as the "Day of the Barricades," the French rose up in popular insurrection against the king. The Duke de Guise, with the throne within his grasp, inexplicably quieted the mob, thereby permitting Henry III to escape to Chartres. On Aug. 4, Guise was appointed lieutenant general of the royal army after Henry gave in to the Holy League's demands.

The estates-general meeting at Blois warned the duke that the king was plotting new treachery. Henry III still wanted to appease the Huguenots. Heeding the concerns of the estates-general on his behalf, Guise nevertheless chose to remain in Blois. On Christmas Day 1588, the duke was summoned to the king's chamber during the sitting of the Royal Council. Henry's bodyguards seized the duke and stabbed him with swords and daggers. "I have crossed my Rubicon," the king sighed, as he looked down on the body of his fallen comrade. "May God have mercy on all our souls—and France." The next day the duke's brother, Louis II, the Cardinal de Guise, was murdered in similar fashion. The bodies were burned and the remains thrown into the Loire. See: **Coligny, Gaspard de; Henry III, King of France**.

REF.: *CBA*; Duhamel, *Henry of Guise*; Hurwood, *Society and the Assassin*; Lavisse, *Historie de France*; Soman, *The Massacre of St. Bartholomew*.

Guiteau, Charles Julius, See: **Garfield, James Abram**.

Guiteras, Antonio, 1907-35, Cuba, assass. Antonio Guiteras was born in Philadelphia, Pa., in 1907. Although he trained to be a pharmacist, Guiteras became involved in Cuban politics as a violent opponent of U.S. imperialism. After the Cuban revolution of 1933, Guiteras was made secretary of the army, navy, and interior in the new leftist government. But Guiteras fell from favor when Cuba's politics swung back to the right. Under the administration of President Carlos Mendieta and General Fulgencio Batista, Guiteras became an outlaw.

Batista accused Guiteras of a shooting, a kidnapping, and of engineering an unsuccessful general strike in March 1935. On May 8, 1935, Batista's soldiers caught up with Guiteras at Fort Morrillo, an old Spanish sea fort in the Matanzas Valley. While a number of his compatriots from a group called *Joven Cuba* covered him with machine gunfire, Guiteras tried to reach a yacht waiting in the harbor to take him to Mexico. Guiteras was killed by the soldiers' gunfire. The soldiers then arrested Guiteras' compatriots, who were tried at a court martial at San Severano military post in Matanzas in June. Xiomara O'Halloran, Conchita Valdivieso, and six other members of the group were acquitted of the charges against them. The remaining four members of the group received prison sentences ranging from eight to fourteen years. REF.: *CBA*.

Guittar, Lewis, prom. 1700, U.S., pir. Lewis Guittar commanded more than 150 men in capturing ships, prisoners, and cargo near Lynnhaven Bay, Fla., before being defeated by the crew of the *Shoreham*. On Apr. 20, 1700, Guittar's men, sailing on their ship, *La Paix*, seized the *Baltimore*, and then plundered and destroyed the sloop *George* two days later. The *Barbados Merchant*, a Liverpool vessel, was overwhelmed Apr. 23, and destroyed when its sixty-man crew refused to join the pirates. William Fletcher, the ship's captain, was beaten by the insulted pirates. The *Pennsylvania Merchant*, taken next near Cape Henry en route to Philadelphia, was burned after its thirty-one passengers and crewmen were robbed. The crew and passengers of the *Indian King*, assailed by the pirates on Apr. 28, were also robbed, and the ship sent back to Lynnhaven Bay. A Belfast vessel, the *Friendship*, was captured the same day, and the ship's captain, Hans Hammel shot to death by John Hoogling, *La Paix*'s pilot, who was considered by some of Guittar's men to be their real leader. The *Friendship*'s cargo, tobacco from Virginia, held little interest for the pirates, but they kept the boat, sending it back to Lynnhaven Bay. The *Nicholson*, just starting back to London, was overwhelmed by *La Paix* after a short gun battle, and its tobacco cargo dumped out, to be replaced by provisions from the *Indian King*. On Apr. 29, Guittar was finally confronted. The *Shoreham*, commanded by Captain Passenger, was determined to end the pirates' domination of the area. A gun battle ensued, and about fifty prisoners were locked in the hold below deck. The gunfight started at 7 a.m. and lasted more than nine hours, with Governor Nicholson encouraging the *Shoreham* crew with promises of gold rewards for defeating *La Paix*. The pirate ship was devastated, eventually running aground because the rudder was destroyed. Peter Heyman and three other *Shoreham* crewmen were killed, and at least twenty-six pirates were also killed, and some fourteen wounded, eight of whom eventually died. Guittar refused to surrender, however, threatening to blow up his ship and prisoners with his remaining thirty barrels of gunpowder unless his men were given quarter aboard the *Shoreham*. The pirates, 111 in all, were taken prisoner, and sent to England for trial. Lewis Guittar and twenty-three of his men were tried and convicted in London. They were all hanged on Nov. 23, 1700. Three of Guittar's men, Hoogling, François Delaunce, and Cornelius Franc jumped overboard before Guittar admitted defeat by the *Shoreham*, but were quickly apprehended and prosecuted at the Virginia General Court in May 1700. They were found Guilty, and ordered to be hanged near the area where their ship was confronted by the *Shoreham*, Princess Anne County. The three briefly escaped after sentencing, but were recaptured and put to death. About forty more of their colleagues were later found Guilty and executed in London. The pirate ship *La Paix*, was sold, as ordered by the admiralty court.

REF.: *CBA*; Rankin, *The Golden Age of Piracy*.

Gula, Demetrius, , and **Sacoda, Joseph S.**, 1912- , U.S., kid.-mur. In the first case to be tried under a new amendment of the New York State kidnapping law, Demetrius Gula and Joseph Sacoda were sentenced to die in the electric chair even though their kidnap and murder victim's body was never found.

Arthur Fried, the 32-year-old manager of a local office of the Colonial Sand and Gravel Company, was reported missing when he did not return home after an evening of drinks and the movies with family members. Hugo Fried, Arthur's brother, received ransom instructions by telephone telling him to go to a saloon. There he received another call instructing him to take an envelope from a shelf in the restroom, read the ransom note, and go immediately to the curb outside and burn the note and envelope. Hugo burned the envelope but saved the note; it demanded $200,000, or the kidnappers would kill Arthur.

Arthur Fried was abducted in early December 1937, after he left his wife and brother-in-law to pick up his car and follow them home from a movie theater. Once inside his car, he found that two men in another car had blocked his path. Threatening him at gunpoint, they demanded he drive with one of them while the other followed in the other car. This was witnessed by a group of high school students. The kidnappers took him to an apartment and held him there for four days. Fried was later shot in the head and his body thrown in the basement furnace of Ukrainian Hall, managed by Denis Gula, Demetrius Gula's father. Though his car was discovered shortly after the kidnapping, no trace was found of Fried's body.

FBI agents under J. Edgar Hoover obtained confessions from Demetrius Gula and Joseph A. Sacoda, though both later recanted their confessions at the trial. Gula, who confessed he helped dispose of the body after Sacoda shot Fried in the apartment, claimed FBI agents beat him for four days until he signed the confession. Sacoda protested that Gula pulled the trigger inside Ukrainian Hall and that his confession was obtained by a detective who threatened to kill him if he refused to sign a confession. At the trial, the judge denied objections that the confessions were obtained under duress.

On Jan. 27, 1939, after less than five hours of deliberation, Gula and Sacoda were found Guilty of kidnapping by a jury with no recommendation of mercy. On Jan. 30, Judge John J. Freschi sentenced them to die in the electric chair during the week of Mar. 6. REF.: *CBA*.

Gull, Sir **William Whithey**, 1816-1890, Brit., Ripper suspect.

Sir William Gull was the royal physician who attended Queen Victoria and other members of the royal household. It was later claimed that Dr. Gull had gone mad because of a stroke, and committed the atrocious slaughterhouse crimes attributed to Jack the Ripper in London in 1888. Another version has Gull assisting the real Ripper, the queen's grandson, Prince Albert Victor, the Duke of Clarence. Supposedly, the prince had contracted syphilis, then paresis of the brain, while patronizing West End whores and took his revenge by killing all the friends of the girl who gave him the dreaded disease. Still another version has Gull operating on Annie Crook, the commoner Prince Albert Victor secretly married who was later driven into prostitution. Gull did have a stroke just prior to the Ripper murders, but this so debilitated him that it would have been impossible for Gull to have committed the energetic Ripper killings. The claims of Gull's involvement with these murders are, at best, preposterous, although it is certain that the killer did have some medical knowledge, given his surgical butchering of the victims. See: **Jack the Ripper.** REF.: *CBA*.

Gump, Jean, and **Gump, Joseph**, 1927-   , U.S., consp. On Mar. 28, 1986, 60-year-old Jean Gump, Ken Rippetoe, and Larry Morlan, all Catholic peace activists, cut through a chain link fence surrounding Whiteman Air Force Base in Missouri, spray-painted the slogan "Disarm and Live" on a Minuteman II missile silo, splashed it with their own blood, and hammered electronic sensors into the tracks on which the silo covers travel. Arrested by armed troops half an hour later, the three activists later served as their own counsel during their trial in June 1986 held in Kansas City, Mo. Each was fined $424.48 and received a six-year prison sentence. Jean Gump refused to pay.

On Aug. 5, 1987, the forty-second anniversary of the nuclear destruction of Hiroshima, Joseph Gump, Jean's husband since 1949, and Gerald Ebner repeated Jean's act of civil disobedience. Like the other peace activists, Joseph defended himself in court and used a speech of Mahatma Gandhi as the model for his pre-sentencing speech. U.S. Attorney Robert Ulrich pushed for a more severe sentence than the one Jean Gump received the previous year, saying: "If we allowed every person to follow only the laws they determined would apply to them, anarchy would prevail."

For cutting through the fence and defacing government property, Joseph Gump and Ebner faced a maximum of fifteen years in prison and $500,000 in fines. They were sentenced on Dec. 11, 1987, to thirty months and forty months, respectively, in a federal prison.

While awaiting his sentence, Joseph Gump said, "We have done what we in conscience must do so we can live with our faith." A spirited and unrepentant Jean Gump proclaimed, "Disarmament is a must. I am willing to give up my life for the future of my children, grandchildren, and all humankind."

The Gumps have no intention of appealing their verdicts. They are the parents of twelve children, and the grandparents of four. REF.: *CBA*.

Gunderman, Stacey, prom. 1937, U.S., mur. On Sept. 12, 1936, 64-year-old Frank C. Monaghan was arrested for drunk driving. But before he could be taken to the Fayette County jail in Uniontown, Pa., he stabbed the arresting officer. The next day, Monaghan was dead; the coroner's report read, "Heart disease superinduced by acute alcoholism." But Monaghan's two sons were not satisfied. A second, more thorough autopsy detected a fractured jaw and nose, eleven broken ribs, and hemorrhages in the brain, throat, and internal organs. A three-day investigation led Pennsylvania Attorney General Charles J. Margiotti to conclude that Monagham had been savagely tortured in order to obtain a confession.

On Feb. 25, 1937, a jury found Stacey Gunderman, a burly, six-foot state trooper, Guilty of second-degree murder. He confessed to throwing Monaghan on a concrete floor and jumping on him, though he claimed to do this in self-defense when the old man attacked him. In his instructions to the jury, State Supreme Court Justice George W. Maxey condemned a third-degree verdict

and asked for the jury to return one of three verdicts: second-degree murder, voluntary manslaughter, or acquittal. "The practice of torturing prisoners or suspects in order to force them to confess crimes is a practice which belongs only in the barbaric ages of the world," stated Justice Maxey, who sentenced Gunderman to ten to twenty years in prison. But after only ten months in jail, the same justice paroled the former law officer, saying, "You have conducted yourself with candor, courage, and dignity. There is no malice in your make-up. I have complete confidence you will be a law-abiding citizen." REF.: *CBA*.

Gundimar II (Gondemar), d.532, Fr., king, assass. Son of Gundobad who assumed the throne of Burgundy after his brother Sigismund. His reign was distinguished by a victory over the Franks in 524, and a pact with the King of the Ostrogoths, Theodoric. He was ousted from power and killed by the sons of Clovis. REF.: *CBA*.

Gungunhana (Gungunyana), c.1850-96, Gaza, king. Reigned over the final autonomous Bantu kingdom. When the Portuguese conquered Gaza in 1895, he was banished to the Canary Islands. REF.: *CBA*.

Gunn, Raymond, d.1931, U.S., rape-mur.-lynch. Sixty National Guardsmen stood in the armory at Maryville, Mo., while a lynch mob burned alive Raymond Gunn, a black man accused of rape and murder.

In the schoolhouse outside the town of Maryville, Velma Colter, a 20-year-old schoolmarm, was raped and murdered in December 1930. Gunn confessed to the crime. But in January 1931, before he was tried, a mob followed by hundreds of on-lookers abducted Gunn, who was under the custody of Sheriff Havre English. The mob dragged him to the same schoolhouse where the rape occurred. Once there, they chained him to the rafters, poured gasoline over his body and the ceiling, and set the building on fire. Witnesses, reportedly numbering in the thousands, heard a wail of agony before the structure collapsed and the incinerated body fell to the desks below. This was the first lynching of 1931. REF.: *CBA*.

Gunness, Belle (AKA: **Bella Poulsdatter Sorensen Gunness, Belle Brynhilde Paulsetter Sorenson Gunness, Female Blue-beard**), 1859-1908?, U.S., arson-mur. A stonemason's daughter who was born near Lake Selbe, Trondheim, Nor., Belle migrated to the U.S. in 1883, following her sister to America. (Another report has it that Belle was born Belle Paulson in Christiana, Nor., and that her father was a traveling magician who taught Belle all sorts of magic and had her walk a tightrope as a child outside his tent to lure customers into his magic show.) She married Mads Albert Sorenson in 1884 in Chicago, a union that produced no children. Sorenson died in 1900, heavily insured, the cause of death listed as heart failure.

Belle immediately put in for the insurance money, $8,500, the day following her husband's funeral, a suspicious act, according to her in-laws. Sorenson's relatives claimed that Belle had poisoned her husband to collect the insurance money and an inquest was ordered, according to records. It is unclear, however, whether or not the inquest ever took place or whether Sorenson's body was exhumed to check for arsenic as his relatives had demanded. Belle used the insurance money to open a confectionery store at Grand Avenue and Elizabeth Street, but this store mysteriously burned down just after Belle had the place heavily insured. The insurance company at first resisted paying off, but they finally relented after the outspoken Belle threatened to take the matter into court and to the newspapers.

With her insurance money, Belle moved in 1902 to La Porte, Ind., where she purchased a large farm, six miles outside of town. She had, while married to Sorenson, adopted three children, all girls, Jennie, Myrtle and Lucy. Just after moving into a large farmhouse, Belle met a local man, Peter Gunness, a fellow Norwegian, and they were married a short time later. This union produced a son, Philip, in 1903. Gunness did not last long. He met with a "tragic accident," according to Belle's sobbing story, in 1904. While working in a shed on the farm, a meat chopper

Above left, Belle Gunness as a young woman; middle top, Belle and her three children; middle bottom, Jennie Olson, who disappeared with Belle and may have been the headless corpse the murderess left behind hoping pursuers and gravediggers would believe the body to be her own; right, the cover of a lurid pamphlet of 1908 which depicted Belle approaching one of her victims while he slept—she chloroformed her male suitors in their slumbers.

Left and center (police photos), Andrew Helgelien, one of Belle Gunness' last suitors, had a checkered past which his killer ignored after she learned that he possessed considerable property and a fat bank account; at far right, Asle Helgelien, Andrew's brother, who began investigating his brother's mysterious disappearance, and his snooping caused Belle to panic and quickly arrange her own horrible end, a faked death that included more grisly murder.

fell from a high shelf and struck Gunness square in the head, splitting his skull and killing him on the spot. Belle, still a great believer in insurance, had, of course, insured her husband Peter for just such an unforseen event. She collected another $4,000.

Local authorities refused to believe that Gunness, who ran the hog farm and butchering shop on the property, could be so clumsy. He was an experienced butcher and the local coroner reviewed the case and announced: "This was murder!" He convened a coroner's jury to look into the matter. Meanwhile, Jennie Olson, age fourteen, the oldest of Belle's adopted children, was overheard confessing to a classmate: "My momma killed my poppa. She hit him with a cleaver." Jennie was brought before the coroner's jury but denied having made this remark. While she testified, Belle sat nearby at a witness table, silently glowering at her adopted daughter. Then Belle took the stand and, weeping, told her tale. She managed to convince the coroner's jury that she was innocent of any wrongdoing and that she now bore the responsibility of raising her children without the help of a strong man. She was released and the matter was dropped.

In September 1906, Jennie Olson suddenly vanished. When neighbors inquired about her, Belle told them that she had sent Jennie to finishing school in Los Angeles. A short time later, Belle hired a somber little man with a drooping mustache, Ray Lamphere, to perform the chores on her farm. Next, in late 1906, she inserted the following advertisement in matrimonial columns of all the Chicago daily newspapers and those of other large midwestern cities:

Personal—comely widow who owns a large farm in one of the finest districts in La Porte County, Indiana, desires to make the acquaintance of a gentleman equally well provided, with view of joining fortunes. No replies by letter considered unless sender is willing to follow answer with personal visit. Triflers need not apply.

Several middle-aged men with comfortable bank accounts and property responded to Belle's lovelorn column ads. They traveled to Belle's La Porte farm, fat wallets in their pockets and deeds to their farms, all proving that they were men of substance and worthy of Belle's attentions. One of these was John Moo, who arrived from Elbow Lake, Wis. He was a husky man of fifty and brought along with him more than $1,000 to pay off Belle's mortgage, or so he told neighbors who were introduced to him by Belle as her cousin. He disappeared from Belle's farm within a week of his arrival. Next came George Anderson who, like Peter Gunness and John Moo, was a migrant from Norway. Anderson, from Tarkio, Mo., was also a farmer with ready cash and a lovesick heart.

Anderson, however, did not bring all his money with him. He was persuaded to make the long trip to see Belle in La Porte because her eloquent letters intrigued him. Once there, he realized that Belle, in her mid-forties and gone portly, was not the beauty he expected. Her face was hard, and she had a severe manner about her, but she made Anderson feel at home and provided good dinners for him while he occupied a guest room in her large farmhouse. One night at dinner Belle raised the issue of her mortgage. Anderson agreed that he would pay this off if they decided to wed. He was almost convinced to return to Takio and retrieve his money, then go back to Belle and eternal bliss. But late that night, Anderson awoke "all in a cold sweat," and he looked up to see Belle standing over him, peering down with a strange look in her eyes. She held a guttering candle in her hand and the expression on her face was so foreboding and sinister that Anderson let out a loud yell. Belle, without a word, ran from the room. Anderson jumped out of bed, dove into his clothes, and fled the dark farmhouse, running up the road and all the way into La Porte, peering over his shoulder down the moonlit road, expecting Belle to come chasing after him at any moment, wildly driving her carriage. Anderson reached the train station and waited for the next train to take him back to Missouri.

The suitors kept coming, but none, except for the apprehensive Anderson, ever left the Gunness farm. At this time, Belle began ordering huge trunks to be delivered to her home. Hack driver Clyde Sturgis delivered many such trunks to Belle from La Porte and later remarked how the heavyset woman would lift these enormous trunks "like boxes of marshmallows," tossing them onto her wide shoulders and carrying them into the house. She kept the shutters of her house closed day and night, and farmers traveling past her house at night saw Belle working in the hog pen area, digging. Her handyman, Lamphere, also spent a good deal of time digging in the hog pen and all about the house and barn.

Meanwhile, the suitors kept coming, all responding to Belle's enticing ads. Ole B. Budsburg, an elderly widower from Iolo, Wis., next appeared. He was last seen alive at the La Porte Savings Bank on Apr. 6, 1907, when he mortgaged his Wisconsin land there, signing over a deed and obtaining several thousand dollars in cash. His sons, Oscar and Mathew Budsburg, it seems, had no idea that their father had gone off to visit the widow Belle. They finally discovered his destination and wrote to Mrs. Gunness who promptly wrote back, saying she had never seen Mr. Budsburg.

Several other middle-aged men appeared and disappeared in brief visits to the Gunness farm throughout 1907. Then, in December 1907, Andrew Hegelein, a bachelor farmer from Aberdeen, S.D., wrote to Belle and was warmly received. The pair exchanged many letters, until Belle unleashed her most amorous masterpiece yet, a letter that overwhelmed the simple Hegelein, written in Belle's own careful handwriting and dated Jan. 13, 1908. (This letter was later found at the Hegelein farm in South Dakota.) It read:

To the Dearest Friend in the World: No woman in the world is happier than I am. I know that you are now to come to me and be my own. I can tell from your letters that you are the man I want. It does not take one long to tell when to like a person, and you I like better than anyone in the world, I know.

Think how we will enjoy each other's company. You, the sweetest man in the whole world. We will be all alone with each other. Can you conceive of anything nicer? I think of you constantly. When I hear your name mentioned, and this is when one of the dear children speaks of you, or I hear myself humming it with the words of an old love song, it is beautiful music to my ears.

My heart beats in wild rapture for you, My Andrew, I love you. Come prepared to stay forever.

That, of course, is exactly what the hapless Hegelein did. In response to her love-gushing letter, the farmer flew to her side in January 1908. He brought with him a check for $2,900, his savings, which he had drawn from his local bank. A few days after Hegelein arrived, he and Belle appeared at the Savings Bank in La Porte and deposited the check for cashing. Hegelein vanished a few days later but Belle appeared at the Savings Bank to make a $500 deposit and another deposit of $700 in the State Bank.

At this time, Belle started to have trouble with her hired hand, Ray Lamphere. The hired hand was deeply in love with Belle and was an apparent slave to her ambitions, performing any chore for her, no matter how gruesome. He became jealous of the many men who arrived to pitch woo at his employer and began making scenes. Belle fired him on Feb. 3, 1908, and then appeared at the La Porte courthouse and declared to authorities that Lamphere was not in his right mind and was a menace to the public. She somehow convinced local authorities to hold a sanity hearing and the grim little Lamphere was examined. He was pronounced sane and sent on his way. Belle was back a few days later to complain to the sheriff that Lamphere had arrived at her farm, despite the fact that she had fired him, and argued with her. She felt that he posed a threat to her family and had Lamphere arrested for trespassing.

Top left, the burned and smoking remains of the Gunness farmhouse outside La Porte, Ind., Apr. 29, 1908, a fire that the infamous Belle set herself; top right, Henry Gurholdt, another Gunness victim whose body was dug up in the pigpen of Belle's farm; bottom right, Ray Lamphere, Belle's ghoulish handyman who helped dig the many graves of her victims and went to prison for life; bottom left, the lonely roads near Belle's house choked with the curious and, middle left, searchers sifting the Gunness house ruins through sluices, looking for human remains.

The little handyman was persistent. He returned again and again to see Belle but she drove him away. Lamphere made thinly disguised threats about Belle and, on one occasion, said to farmer William Slater that "Hegelein won't bother me no more. We fixed him for keeps." Hegelein had long since disappeared from the precincts of La Porte, or so it was believed. His brother, Asle Hegelein, however, was disturbed when Andrew failed to return home and he wrote to Belle in Indiana, asking her about his brother's whereabouts.

Belle boldly wrote back, telling Asle Hegelein that his brother was not at her farm and probably went to Norway to visit relatives. Hegelein wrote back saying that he did not believe his brother would do that and, moreover, he believed that his brother was still in the La Porte area, the last place he was seen or heard from. Belle Gunness brazened it out, telling Hegelein that if he wanted to come to La Porte and look for his brother, she would help conduct a search for him, but she cautioned Hegelein that searching for missing persons was an expensive proposition, and if she was to be involved in such a manhunt, Asle Hegelein should be prepared to pay her well for her efforts.

Obviously worried about the turn of events, Belle went to a La Porte lawyer, M.E. Leliter, telling him that she feared for her life and that of her children. Ray Lamphere, she said, had threatened to kill her and burn her house down. She wanted to make out a will, in case Lamphere went through with his threats. Leliter complied, drawing up Belle's will. She left her entire estate to her children and then departed Leliter's offices. She went to one of the La Porte banks holding the mortgage for her property and paid this off. Oddly, she did not go to the police to tell them about Lamphere's life-threatening conduct. The reason for this, most later concluded, was that there had been no threats, but that Belle was merely setting the stage for her own arson.

Joe Maxon, who had been hired to replace Lamphere in February 1908, awoke on the night of April 28, 1908, smelling smoke in his room which was on the second floor of the Gunness house. He opened the hall door to a sheet of flames. Maxon screamed Belle's name and those of her children but got no response. He slammed the door and then, in his underwear, leaped from the second-story window of his room, barely surviving the fire that was closing in about him. He raced to town to get help, but by the time the old-fashioned hook and ladder arrived at the farm at early dawn, the farmhouse was a gutted heap of smoking ruins.

The floors had collapsed and four bodies were found in the cellar. The grand piano, Belle's pride and joy, was on top of the bodies. One of the bodies was that of a woman who could not be identified as Belle since she had no head. The head was never found. Nearby, after much searching, officials found Belle's false teeth. The pathetic little bodies of her children were found next to the corpse. Sheriff Albert H. Smutzer took one look at this carnage and immediately arrested Ray Lamphere who he knew had made threats about Belle. Lawyer Leliter came forward to recount his tale about Belle's will and how she feared Lamphere would kill her and her family, and burn her house down.

Lamphere did not help his cause much. At the moment Sheriff Smutzer confronted him and before a word was uttered by the lawman, Lamphere blurted: "Did Widow Gunness and the kids get out all right?" He was then told about the fire, but he denied having anything to do with it, claiming that he was not near the farm when the blaze occurred. A youth, John Solyem, was brought forward. He said that he had been watching the Gunness place (he gave no reasons for this) and that he saw Lamphere running down the road from the Gunness house just before the structure erupted in flames.

Lamphere snorted to the boy: "You wouldn't look me in the eye and say that!"

"Yes, I will," replied Solyem bravely. "You found me hiding behind the bushes and you told me you'd kill me if I didn't get out of there."

Lamphere was arrested and charged with murder and arson. Then scores of investigators, sheriff's deputies, coroner's men and many volunteers began to search the ruins for evidence. The body of the headless woman was of deep concern to La Porte residents. C. Christofferson, a neighboring farmer, took one look at the charred remains of this body and said that it was not the remains of Belle Gunness. So did another farmer, L. Nicholson, and so did Mrs. Austin Cutler, an old friend of Mrs. Gunness. More of Belle's old friends, Mrs. Nellie Olander and Mrs. Sigurd Olson, arrived from Chicago. They had known Mrs. Gunness for years. They examined the remains of the headless woman and said it was not that of Belle.

Doctors then measured the remains, and making allowances for the missing neck and head, stated that the corpse was that of a woman who stood five feet three inches tall and weighed no more than 150 pounds. Belle, according to her friends and neighbors, as well as the La Porte clothiers who made her dresses and other garments, swore that Belle was more than five feet eight inches tall and weighed between 180 and 200 pounds. Physicians then made detailed measurements of the body. These measurements were compared with those on file with several La Porte stores where Belle purchased her apparel. When the two sets of measurements were placed side by side, the authorities reeled back in shock:

	Victim (inches)	Mrs. Gunness (inches)
Biceps	9	17
Bust	36	46
Waist	26	37
Thigh	25	30
Hips	40	54
Calf	12½	14
Wrist	6	9

The headless woman could not have been Belle Gunness, even when the ravages of the fire on the body were taken into account. (The flesh was badly burned but intact.) Moreover, Dr. J. Meyers examined the internal organs of the dead woman. He reported that the woman died of strychnine poisoning. Asle Hegelein then arrived in La Porte and told Sheriff Smutzer that he believed that his brother had met with foul play at Mrs. Gunness' hands. Smutzer seemed disinterested in searching the blackened grounds of the Gunness farm once again, but Hegelein persisted. Then Joe Maxon came forward to tell the sheriff that Mrs. Gunness had had him bring loads of dirt by wheelbarrow to a large area surrounded by a high wire fence where the hogs were fed. Maxon stated that there were many deep depressions in the ground that had been covered by dirt. These filled-in holes, Belle had told Maxon, contained rubbish. She wanted the ground made level, so Maxon filled in the depressions.

Smutzer took a dozen men back to farm and began to dig. On May 3, 1908, the diggers unearthed the body of Jennie Olson. Then they found two more small bodies, that of unidentified children. Then the body of Andrew Hegelein was unearthed. As days progressed and the gruesome work continued, one body after another was discovered in Belle's hog pen: Ole B. Budsburg; Thomas Lindboe of Chicago, who had left Chicago and had gone to work as a hired man for Belle three years earlier; Henry Gurholdt of Scandinavia, Wis., who had gone to wed Belle a year earlier, taking $1,500 to her; Olaf Svenherud, from Chicago; John Moo (or Moe) of Elbow Lake, Wis.; Olaf Lindbloom from Iowa. There were many others who could not be identified. There were the remains of more than forty men and children buried in shallow graves throughout Belle's property.

Ray Lamphere was arrested and tried for murder and arson on May 22, 1908. He pleaded guilty to arson, but denied murdering Belle and her children. He was sentenced to twenty years in prison. The little handyman grew ill in prison and died of consumption on Dec. 30, 1909. On Jan. 14, 1910, the Rev. E.A. Schell came forward with a confession that Lamphere had made to him while the clergyman was comforting the dying man. In it, Lamphere revealed the true nature of Belle Gunness, a human monster who killed for profit and who survived her own reported death.

Lamphere had stated to the Rev. Schell and to a fellow convict, Harry Meyers, before his death, that he had not murdered anyone, but that he had helped Belle bury many of her victims. She had her lethal system down to precise procedures. When a victim arrived, Belle made him comfortable, charming him and cooking a large meal. She then drugged his coffee and when the man was in a stupor, she split his head with a meat chopper. Sometimes she would simply wait for the suitor to go to bed and then enter the bedroom by candlelight and chloroform her sleeping victim. A powerful woman, Belle would then carry the body to the basement, place it on a table, and dissect the body. She then bundled the remains and buried these in the hog pen and the grounds about the house. Belle had become an expert at dissection, thanks to instruction she had received from her second husband, the butcher Peter Gunness. To save time, she sometimes poisoned her victims' coffee with strychnine. She also varied her disposal methods, sometimes dumping the corpse into the hog-scalding vat and covering the remains with quicklime. Lamphere even stated that if Belle was overly tired after murdering one of her victims, she merely chopped up the remains and, in the middle of the night, stepped into her hog pen and fed the remains to the hogs.

The handyman also cleared up the question of the headless female corpse found in the smoking ruins of Belle's home. This woman had been lured from Chicago by Belle to serve her as a housekeeper only days before Belle decided to make her permanent escape from La Porte. Belle, according to Lamphere, had drugged the woman, then bashed in her head and decapitated the body, taking the head, which had weights tied to it, to a swamp where she threw it into deep water. Then she chloroformed her own children, smothered them to death, and dragged these bodies, along with the headless corpse, to the basement.

She dressed the female corpse in her old clothing, and removed her false teeth, placing these beside the headless corpse to assure it being identified as Belle Gunness. She then torched the house and fled. Lamphere had helped her, he admitted, but Belle had not left by the road where he waited for her after the fire began. She had betrayed him in the end by cutting across open fields and then disappearing into the woods. Lamphere said that Belle was a rich woman, that she had murdered forty-two men by his count, perhaps more, and had taken amounts from them ranging from $1,000 to $32,000. She had accumulated more than $250,000 through her lovelorn murder schemes over the years, a great fortune for those days. She had also left a small amount in one of her savings accounts, but local banks later admitted that Belle had withdrawn most of her funds shortly before the fire.

Belle Gunness was, for several decades, seen or sighted in throughout the U.S. Friends had spotted her on the streets of Chicago, San Francisco, New York, Los Angeles. As late as 1931, Belle was reported alive and living in a Mississippi town where she owned a great deal of property and lived the life of a grande dame. Sheriff Smutzer, for more than twenty years, received an average of two reports a month. She became part of U.S. criminal folklore, a female Bluebeard. A bit of doggerel later emerged which captured the character of the horrific Belle Gunness:

Belle Gunness lived in In-di-an;
She always, always had a man;
Ten, at least, went in her door—
And were never, never seen no more.

Now, all these men were Norska folk
Who came to Belle from Minn-e-sote;
They liked their coffee and their gin:
They got it—plus a mickey finn.

And now with cleaver poised so sure
Belle neatly cut their jug-u-lar
She put them in a bath of lime,
And left them there for quite some time.

There's red upon the Hoosier moon
For Belle was strong and full of doom;
And think of all them Norska men
Who'll never see St. Paul again.

REF.: Archer, *Killers in the Clear; CBA;* de la Torre, *The Truth About Belle Gunness;* Dilnot, *Rogue's March;* Duke, *Celebrated Criminals of America;* Gribble, *Such Women Are Deadly;* Gross, *Masterpieces of Murder;* Haines, *Bothersome Bodies;* Jackson, *The Portable Murder Book;* Logan, *Rope, Knife and Chair;* Nash, *Almanac of World Crime;* _____, *Bloodletters and Badmen;* _____, *Look for the Woman;* Scott, *The Concise Encyclopedia of Crime and Criminals;* Stevens, *Famous Crimes and Criminals;* Twyman, *The Best Laid Schemes;* Whitelaw, *Corpus Delicti;* Wilson, *Encyclopedia of Murder.*

Gunpowder Plot, 1605, Brit., treas. The poem beginning: "Please to remember the fifth of November/ The Gunpowder Treason and Plot," has been memorized by British children for almost 400 years. After King Henry VIII of England broke with the Roman Catholic church in 1535, English Catholics and Protestants were continually at odds. The government often publicized the discovery of Catholic "plots" against the Crown to keep the hatred of Catholics alive. Although this "politics by drama" was more prevalent before Catholic Mary, Queen of Scots died, it did not end with her execution, ordered by Queen Elizabeth in 1887. Mary's son, James VI of Scotland became King James I of England in 1603. He kept none of his promises about religious toleration, and encouraged Robert Cecil, his secretary of state, to invent excuses to persecute Catholics. Cecil undoubtedly played a major role in the development of the Gunpowder Plot.

In 1604, Guy Fawkes, a former soldier in Spain and a Catholic convert, was asked to help blow up the Houses of Parliament on Nov. 5, 1605, when James VI was scheduled to appear there. The major participants were Robert Catesby, Thomas Winter, and Thomas Percy, all prominent men. They rented a house next to Parliament and began to tunnel from the basement. In January, however, they rented a basement that was actually under Parliament. As November neared, Fawkes moved thirty-six barrels of gunpowder directly under the House of Lords. Historians later became certain that it was a government-run plot because gunpowder was strictly controlled.

On Oct. 26, Lord Monteagle, a Protestant, was given an anonymous letter indicating that Parliament was to be blown up on Nov. 5. He warned Robert Cecil, and when, on the assigned day, Guy Fawkes prepared to light the fuse to the gunpowder, he was arrested. He remained silent until torture forced him to name his cohorts. Fawkes and seven other men were hanged, beheaded, and quartered on Jan. 30 and 31, 1606. Each year, the Yeomen of the Guard heed the other two lines of the children's poem: "I see no reason why the Gunpowder Treason/Should ever be forgot." As the children of England celebrate Nov. 5, with fireworks and bonfires made of Guy Fawkes effigies, the Yeomen traditionally search the Houses of Parliament from top to bottom, looking for gunpowder.

REF.: *CBA;* Pearl, *The Dangerous Assassins;* Scott, *The Concise Encyclopedia of Crime and Criminals;* Williamson, *Historical Whodunits.*

Gunter, Thomas, prom. 1929, U.S., (wrong. convict.) mur. Based on the perjured testimony of his daughter and 7-year-old granddaughter, Thomas Gunter was convicted of murdering his sleeping son-in-law.

Marlin Drew, his wife Pearl, and their three children lived in the house of Pearl's parents, Mr. and Mrs. Thomas Gunter. During the summer of 1929, Pearl was pregnant and Marlin was unemployed. They argued continually over Marlin's drinking and womanizing, and Marlin claimed that he was not the father of the child. The Gunters supported their daughter.

In July 1929, Marlin Drew's body was found on his bed, shot through the chest. Although the investigators first called it a suicide, they later arrested Mr. Gunter on July 7. Dorthy Louise Drew, Gunter's granddaughter, told relatives that while she was sleeping in the same bed with her father, "granddad" shot "pop."

The trial was held on Aug. 16. Mrs. Gunter, a witness for the defense, claimed her husband was in a drunken stupor at the time of the killing—an assertion Mr. Gunter did not deny. But the jury found the defendant Guilty based on the convincing testimony of Dorthy Louise and the corroborating testimony of her mother. Judge Thomas E. Pegram sentenced Gunter to five years in prison.

After Pearl Drew recovered from the birth of her fourth child, she wrote to Governor Theodore Bilbo, confessing to the killing of her husband in the form of a variation on the famous folk ballad *A Jealous Lover in Lone Green Valley*. Claiming she always intended to confess to the murder of her husband after her pregnancy was over, she asked the governor to pardon her father, then sixty-three, as she had shot her husband in anger when he made insinuations about her unborn child.

On Nov. 19, Gunter's sentence was suspended for ninety days. Three months later the grand jury indicted Pearl Drew for murder and perjury, to which Mrs. Drew pleaded guilty. Judge Pegram suspended Drew's sentence while Governor Bilbo denied Gunter's application for a pardon. In a public statement, the governor said: "Somebody ought to be in the penitentiary all the time for the murder of a sleeping man. If Judge Pegram does not believe Mrs. Drew is guilty enough to serve her term, then the man convicted of the murder will have to serve his term. Husbands ought to have some protection."

Refusing to return to prison, Thomas Gunter fled Mississippi, as did his daughter Pearl. REF.: *CBA*.

Gurdjieff, George Ivan, prom. 1925-45, Fr., hoax. In the 1920s, George Gurdjieff, a Russian-born Greek occultist, opened The Institute for the Harmonious Development of Man near Paris. Begging for physical and emotional therapy, people came to him and did whatever he told them to do. His cures included chopping wood until exhaustion and dancing nonstop for hours. Short story writer Katherine Mansfield slept in a loft above the cows to breathe the air the cows exhaled. She had suffered from tuberculosis for years, and died a few weeks after Gurdjieff's treatment. The institute continued under Gurdjieff until after WWII.

REF.: *CBA; Nash, Zanies.*

Gurfein, Murray Irwin, 1907-79, U.S., jur. Employed by the U.S. prosecutor's office during the Nuremberg Trials, beginning in 1945. He was nominated to the Southern District Court of New York in 1971, and to the Second Circuit Court of New York in 1974 by President Richard M. Nixon. REF.: *CBA*.

Gurga, Jeffrey, 1947-   , U.S., mur. Attorney Jeffrey Gurga tried to commit the perfect murder. In his Chicago apartment, he sketched diagrams and made notes relating to his plans, and in the early hours of Aug. 9, 1982, he broke into a northwest Chicago apartment and stabbed 19-year-old Jeannine Pearson and fatally stabbed her mother, 39-year-old Kathleen Pearson. Gurga, who had worked as a McLean County prosecutor and a defense lawyer, was captured in the apartment where police later found his notes. During his trial, prosecutors argued that the 36-year-old, who was not acquainted with the women, had attempted to commit a perfect crime by murdering a person without getting caught. During his trial, Gurga, who in 1966 had spent four months in a mental institution, pleaded not guilty by reason of insanity. He was found Guilty, and on Aug. 24, 1983, Judge Thomas Maloney sentenced him to forty years in prison. The Illinois Appellate Court later decided that Gurga should have been found guilty but mentally ill and ordered Maloney to resentence the prisoner. The judge tacked mentally ill on to the ruling but resentenced the lawyer to forty years imprisonment on Oct. 9, 1987, saying, "the court finds no reason whatsoever to change the sentence." REF.: *CBA*.

Gurgel, Haroldo, 1931-53, Braz., (unsolv.) mur. Haroldo Gurgel was a 22-year-old reporter for *O Momento,* a newspaper of the provincial capital city of Goiânia, Brazil. In August 1953, Gurgel reported that the governor-appointed head of the Electric Energy Commission, Pedro Arantes, was rationing the electrical power of the state to suit his own ends. The headline read: "HE CAME AND PRODUCED LIGHT." Approaching Gurgel on the street shortly after the appearance of the story, Arantes slapped Gurgel on the face. But Arantes was not satisfied with this warning. The next morning as Gurgel was leaving his hotel, he was abducted by four armed men and taken to the city's central square where he was pistol-whipped until nearly unconscious and then shot twelve times as he attempted to crawl away. The gunmen wounded two men attempting to help him.

Protest within the state of Goiaz and throughout Brazil prompted Governor Pedro Ludovico Teixeira to dismiss Arantes from his position though Arantes had already fled. Further, police seemed unwilling to bring Arantes' henchmen to justice, and in one case, an officer was disciplined for insubordination after he had condemned the murder of Gurgel to his superior officer. Although Gurgel's murderers escaped justice, the people of Goiânia expressed their sentiments when, on a wall in the central square, the following words appeared written in Gurgel's blood: "HERE DIED A JOURNALIST DEFENDING FREEDOM OF THE PRESS." REF.: *CBA*.

Gurney, Joseph John, 1788-1847, Brit., penal reform. Quaker minister who traveled throughout Canada, the United States, and the West Indies from 1837-40, in a campaign to outlaw capital punishment, improve prison conditions, and free slaves. REF.: *CBA*.

Gürtner, Franz, 1881-1941, Ger., jur. Minister of justice under Adolf Hitler. In 1938, he co-authored anti-semitic decrees that stripped Jews of money and property. REF.: *CBA*.

Gustavus I (AKA: **Gustavus Eriksson, Gustavus Vasa**), 1496-1560, Case of, Swed., kid. Son of Erik Johansson and first of six Swedish kings named Gustavus. An enemy of Denmark's Christian II, he was held captive in Denmark from 1518-19, when he escaped and returned to the province of Dalarna. From 1521-23, after Christian II beheaded Gustavus' father, brother-in-law, and other Swedish nobles, Gustavus led a triumphant campaign against the Danes. He was named king of Sweden in 1523, and established the Vasa dynasty. REF.: *CBA*.

Gustavus III, 1746-92, Swed., king, assass. When Gustav assumed the throne of Sweden, his country was in near ruin, and long wars and a poorly organized economy had drained the government coffers and the spirit of the people. Gustav was appointed to his throne by a Diet (the Reichsrath), which was controlled by Swedish nobles who had no intention of strengthening the monarchy. Gustav was no monarch to be cowed. He was shrewd and diplomatic but also knew when to exercise his powers. His courage was equalled by his princely vanity, both in harmony with the attitude of Louis XIV, Gustav's idol, when Louis declared: "The state? I am the state!" At first his fearless, haughty posture won back all the power the monarchy had originally possessed, but in the end Gustav's imperious personality was to cost him his life.

A year after assuming an almost powerless throne, Gustav took pains to win the allegiance of the Royal Guard regiments, bestowing honors and money on favored troops. Moreover, his minions mounted a subtle campaign to demean the nobles who had established an oligarchy. In a bold move, Gustav visited the hostile Diet, took his seat, and listened for a few minutes as the nobles voiced insolence and near-outright insults in his direction. When Gustav heard one member talk loudly about arresting the king, the monarch rose, placed his hand on his sword hilt and then marched through the large hall, staring down all the nobles about him, as if to challenge them. None drew a sword, but looked away from Gustav as he strolled casually from the Diet. Once outside, the king mounted his waiting horse and rode at a fast gallop to the barracks of his Royal Guards, where he made an impassioned speech to his army commanders, telling them that the nobles were about to strip the king and the people of their rights. To a man his troops vowed to follow him anywhere. Gustav led them back to the Diet.

The building was surrounded by troops, and several thousand armed citizens joined these soldiers to demand the abdication of the Diet. The noblemen had no escape and no choice but to follow Gustav's will. The monarch soon set up a new constitution and regained his powers. Gustav instituted many reforms and established hospitals, orphanages, and poorhouses. He improved the highway systems and had canals channeled from the seacoast to the mineral mines, then the chief industry of Sweden. The currency was put on a sound basis, and for some years the country enjoyed prosperity and peace. But the growth was superficial, and Gustav was impatient to enjoy the fruits of a wealthy domain.

Gustav began to indulge his self-image of being another Louis XIV. He spent lavishly on his royal palace, gave grand balls, and spent more than existed in royal coffers. The king took on preposterous airs and designed extravagant costumes after flamboyant Spanish designs. When wearing these clothes Gustav drew snickers and sneers behind his back. Moreover, he wrote plays and poetry which consumed most of the time he would normally have given to the running of government. He spent a great deal of money on reorganizing the army, equipping it with the most modern artillery, and establishing a splendid supply system. Troop morale soared, and with it, Gustav's military ambitions. He saw himself as another Frederick the Great and, in 1788, decided to reclaim lands in Finland that had earlier been lost to Russia. He declared war on Russia, launching an expensive and protracted campaign with this giant, a war most of his generals knew Sweden could not win.

Gustavus III, king of Sweden, assassinated by nobles in 1792.

The army hierarchy had nothing to say about Gustav's ambitions, however, and the king himself took to the field to command his troops in Finland. After winning a few minor engagements, Gustav lolled about in the field, thinking of himself as another Alexander the Great. In Stockholm the still seething nobles issued a manifesto which denounced Gustav as having committed a criminal act by declaring war on Russia without first seeking the approval of the Diet. This act undermined Gustav's power as the field commanders refused to take orders from him and requested him to return to Stockholm. He began the long trip home but in the province of Dalecarlia, spoke eloquently to masses of citizens, rallying them to his cause. He managed to create a peasant army from the same province that had given power to Gustavus Vasa, his illustrious ancestor who had established the royal line. Gustav thus returned to Stockholm with strength intact.

He confronted the Diet and demanded full powers and recognition as the supreme sovereign of Sweden. The Diet grudgingly granted the powers and then Gustav dissolved this organization.

Gustav vexed and confounded his enemies, the noblemen. At one point he would appear to have bungled everything. In the next instant he would appear to take complete charge of any crisis, and emerged victorious. He was an obvious failure as a military strategist, having squandered time, money, and an army in the field in Finland. When he took command of the Swedish fleet to face an overwhelming Russian armada, the nobles rubbed their hands in glee, expecting their king to plunge into utter disaster. Gustav fought several huge naval battles where his courage and ingenious battle plans not only held off the superior Russian ships but, on July 9, 1790, at Swenskasund, utterly defeated the enemy fleet. Fighting personally from his flagship, Gustav managed to sail his fleet straight through the Russian vessels, burning or capturing fifty-nine Russian frigates, and capturing hundreds of guns. In the following August, Gustav signed a Peace Treaty with Russia which allowed Sweden access to the Baltic Sea, a large concession at a time when this avenue of commerce and travel had been permanently closed by the Russians.

Sweden's nobles were nevertheless as opposed to Gustav as ever and quickly let it be known that the king had all but bankrupted the country in waging his expensive war with Russia. Influencing some of these nobles was the French Revolution of 1789 in which the French monarchy had been toppled. Gustav was likened to the extravagant, careless Marie Antoinette, who would later meet the headsman for her treasury-looting ways. In fact, Gustav lamented the fall of the French monarchy so deeply that he proposed to unite with all the other European monarchs in sending an enormous royal army to France to crush the revolutionaries and restore the French king. He had already tried to free Louis XVI and Marie Antoinette from the clutches of the French terrorists. He had provided a Swedish coach and his own attendants in attempting to smuggle the royal family out of France. This plan had almost succeeded, but the carriage had been stopped at Varennes and the royal family taken back to Versailles to stand trial and subsequent execution.

To finance the international army he intended to raise to save the French king and queen, Gustav went to the Diet and ordered that body to appropriate huge sums of money. The nobles stalled and spread the word that the king was about to wage war—not against another sovereign but against the peoples' rights; he would appear in France as an oppressor, not a liberator. Under the guise of representing the people of Sweden who would certainly be next in line for Gustav's repressions, five nobles formed a conspiracy to assassinate the king. The group was led by Jacob John Anckarstrom, who had been one of the officers in Finland who had defied Gustav and refused to obey his field orders there. The others included the counts Ribbing, Horn, Pechlin, and Liliehorn.

At first the conspirators thought to abduct Gustav and force him to abdicate; they would name a successor to the throne who would restore the Diet and the nobles to power, and then become a titular monarch. But Gustav was too headstrong to bow to pressure, they concluded. It was easier and safer to kill him. Anckarstrom pointed out that the king was most vulnerable when attending the masked balls which he favored. Gustav loved to dress up in strange costumes and mingle with the guests, believing that he would never be recognized. Anckarstrom did try to kill the king at two of these celebrations but could not discover under which disguise the king was hiding, and so failed to murder the monarch. The last great masked ball of the season was to be held on Mar. 16, 1792, and Anckarstrom was sure Gustav would attend. He told the others he would ferret out the monarch and shoot him to death on the ballroom floor of the Grand Opera House. Thousands were expected to attend, as this was the event of the season in Stockholm. Anckarstrom would escape easily in the immense throng, he assured his fellow conspirators.

One conspirator, however, had second thoughts about murdering Gustav. At 10 p.m. on the night of the planned assassination, the king dined with Count Essen, his closest aide. He received a note written in French, explaining that four men would be on the ball room floor dressed in domino-patterned costumes and that they intended to kill him. This note was from Count Liliehorn, who stated that he was opposed to Gustav's suspension of the Diet and his depriving the nobles of power, but he could not tolerate the horrid act of regicide. Liliehorn begged the king in his note not to attend the ball. Gustav read the note carefully, then put it away without telling Essen its contents. When he appeared in his royal box at the ball Gustav boldly showed himself to the thousands below. He showed the note to Essen, who pleaded with Gustav not to go onto the dance floor.

Ever the adventurer, Gustav laughed and told Essen that when he attended the next ball he would wear a suit of armor. He would deceive his intended killers, Gustav told Essen, by changing into a costume of their own design, one so popular that dozens of men on the floor were wearing them, the black domino designed costume. He dressed in this costume and then went onto the floor with Essen, who nervously walked beside the king, begging with him to leave the ball. Swirling about Gustav were hundreds of men and women murmuring behind grotesque masks and outlandish costumes. Gustav took Essen's arm and said: "Now let's see if they will dare to attack me."

Gustav believed that his presence could not be detected but many in the crowd identified him, whispering, "There is the king!" Tiring of his arduous journey through the thick crowd, Gustav walked into a large sitting room. He was immediately surrounded by four men wearing black domino costumes like himself. He had walked right into the assassin's nest. One of the men, Count Horn, placed his hand upon the shoulder of the king, saying: "Good evening, my beautiful masquerader!" Horn had recognized Gustav in the few seconds when the king momentarily removed his mask; his statement was the signal to the other assassins that they finally had their man.

Anckarstrom came close to Gustav and stretched out his arm, which was wrapped with a cape, under which was hidden a gun. He fired the weapon once and the bullet smashed into Gustav's side. Then the conspirators, to create confusion and panic, began to shout: "Fire! Fire! Leave the hall!" The king fell backward into the arms of Essen, shouting: "Essen—quick, arrest the assassin! I am wounded!" The four conspirators dashed fled from the room with the hundreds racing toward the doors of the Opera House. Count Armfeld saw the king had been shot and ordered the hall doors closed, announcing to the masqueraders that there was no fire but that "a great crime has been committed."

Just as the doors to the Opera House were being closed, the assassins slipped outside. An officer held Anckarstrom's arm for a moment at the door and the killer, now unmasked, gave him a smirk, saying: "I hope you do not suspect me." The officer studied his face for a moment, then replied: "On the contrary. I am sure you are the assassin!" As the officer turned to call the guards, Anckarstrom pulled free of the officer's grasp and escaped. His flight was short-lived. Anckerstrom, along with all the other conspirators, was arrested the following morning.

Gustav remained in control. Though critically wounded, the king gave orders for the gates of Stockholm to be closed and the conspirators to be rounded up. He then delegated authority to several people who would continue operating the government. He let it be known that he had been shot by those being directed by the Jacobins of Paris, sworn enemies of the monarchy. It appeared the king would recover, such was his iron constitution, but, after twelve days, his condition suddenly worsened and he died on Thursday, Mar. 29, 1792.

Oddly, Gustav's long illness proved to be enlightening for him as well as his subjects. He had much time to reflect on his excesses and called many of his old enemies to him and made peace. His last days were filled with putting Sweden's government in order and he no longer displayed the arrogant attitude of the past. He even argued against executing the assassins. When told

that Anckarstrom had been condemned and the public was crying for his execution, Gustav said from his deathbed: "If Anckarstrom is to die, then let there be mercy at least for the others. One victim is enough." Shortly after Gustav III was buried, was executed and the other conspirators received prison terms.

REF.: *CBA; Johnson, Famous Assassinations of History; Paine, The Assassin's World.*

Gustloff, Wilhelm, d.1936, Switz., assass. Wilhelm Gustloff was a German citizen who lived in the resort town of Davos, Switz., and was the leading Nazi politician of that country. He had publicly stated his intention to make Switzerland into a vassal state of Adolf Hitler's Third Reich. On Feb. 4, 1936, David Frankfurter, a 27-year-old Jewish medical student from Yugoslavia, went to Gustloff's residence. He carried an automatic pistol in his pocket that he had purchased some weeks earlier, having resolved to kill Gustloff for the good of humanity.

Frankfurter's motives, he later stated, were altruistic: "I had no personal interest.... I am a Jew. I was impelled by idealistic motives...I had

Nazi leader Wilhelm Gustloff, assassinated in 1936.

grown extremely fond of Switzerland. It seemed to me disgusting that such a cur should soil the good things here...I am a medical student and he gave me the impression that he was a bacillus through whom a virulent pestilence might be introduced... It is the pestilence I aimed at, not the person."

The assassin had no trouble gaining access to Gustloff's residence. He was shown into a large parlor where a huge portrait of Adolf Hitler hung on the wall. He calmly waited for Gustloff to appear. When Gustloff walked into the room, Frankfurter withdrew

Assassin David Frankfurter, at his trial in Chur, Switzerland.

the automatic pistol, shot him dead, and then waited to be arrested. He was taken before a court of five judges in Chur, Switz., and judged Guilty on Dec. 14, 1936. He was given the maximum sentence allowed by law, a prison term of eighteen years.

REF.: *CBA; Hurwood, Society and the Assassin; Ludwig, The Davos Murder.*

Guterma, Alexander L., 1915-77, U.S., fraud. Alexander L. Guterma was born on Apr. 29, 1915, in Irkutsk, Russia. He illegally entered the United States via China in 1935. In 1951 he was president of the American Kenaf Corporation and gained public attention for selling $2 million of kenaf fibers, a jute substitute, to the Commodity Credit Corporation. In 1959, Guterma was found Guilty of stock fraud and served five years in prison.

In 1977, Guterma and five **Con man Alexander Guterma.**
members of his family were killed when their private plane crashed

in the Bronx. At one time, his multi-million dollar empire included holdings in the United Hotels Corporation, F.L. Jacobs Company, the Western Financial Corporation, McGrath Securities, and the United Dye and Chemical Company.

REF.: *CBA*; Nash, *Hustlers and Con Men*; Ottenberg, *The Federal Investigators*.

Guthrie, Charles John (Lord Guthrie) 1849-1920, Scot., jur. Presided over the controversial murder trial of Oscar Slater, after which he was criticized for misleading the jury. The conviction was later reprieved, and eventually rescinded, some eight years after his death. REF.: *CBA*.

Gutkind, Johann (AKA: The Human Fly), prom. 1920s, Ger., burg.-suic.-mur. During the flamboyance, glamour, and decadence of post-WWI Berlin, Johann Gutkind, known to the underworld as the Human Fly, nearly committed the perfect crime. Instead he was foiled by the Berlin Police Department's exhaustive Kriminal Archiv.

The 1920s were a period of exceedingly high crime for the city of Berlin. In an attempt to stem this rising torrent, Dr. Hans Schneickert created the Kriminal Archiv--an exhaustive library of criminals and crimes, as well as records of all persons living in and visiting Berlin. It was an exceedingly useful tool for law enforcement, and was also employed by Heinrich Himmler and the Gestapo, who later used the Archiv's list of known criminals for Gestapo recruitment.

One afternoon, the local police called in a headquarters commission of specialists to investigate the murder of the wealthy and reclusive diamond merchant, Herr Kernstoff, who was brutally slain with a blunt instrument during the burglary of his top-floor apartment. Police and specialists alike were puzzled by the lack of clues: no fingerprints or footprints, no weapon or sign of a forced entry, even the patterns of dust on the window sills were undisturbed. Yet the thoroughness with which the crime was committed made one thing certain: the murderer was practiced in violent crime. The blows that killed Kernstoff had nearly caved in his skull.

Using the modern criminology technique of *modus operandi*, Dr. Schneickert began researching the crime through his Kriminal Archiv, examining records from all parts of Germany. He was looking for a similar crime that had been committed and eventually found one: an unsolved case in Darmstadt where a burglar had entered a top-floor apartment in the tenant's absence, leaving no clues except for a few strands of hemp caught in the bricks of a chimney. Using this information, Schneickert investigated the chimney above Kernstoff's apartment. There, the investigators found pieces of hemp similar to those in the Darmstadt case. Using this information, Schneicker began looking for a suspect, a known criminal who had committed a similar crime. His research revealed the name Johann Gutkind, known to Berlin's criminal element as the Human Fly—an extremely agile burglar who had a decided preference for the apartments of the wealthy.

Probing further, Schneicker began asking tenants if any packages were delivered to the area at unusual times. This led to a caterer who claimed an employee had delivered linen and crockery to a party in the area around 2:30 a.m. Checking out the employee through the Archiv, Schneicker found his name cross-referenced as a friend of Gutkind.

The police followed Gutkind's friend who, after several days, led them to a house in a run-down neighborhood. Police raided the house after surrounding it and sealing off the district. Initially they discovered nothing, until they tore up a section of linoleum in a back room and discovered a trap door, bolted from the inside. Using crowbars, they pried open the door which revealed a damp, dark room below resembling a well. With the aid of a flashlight, the police found Gutkind lying on a coil of rope, shot through the side of his head with the gun he held in his hand.

REF.: *CBA*; Gribble, *Famous Manhunts*; Sanders, *Murder Behind the Bright Lights*.

Gutteridge Murder Case, The, See: **Browne, Frederick Guy.**

Guy, Ralph B., Jr., 1929-   , U.S., jur. Chief assistant to the U.S. attorney in Detroit, Mich., from 1969-70, and U.S. attorney from 1970-76. He became a charter member and vice president of the U.S. Attorney General's Advisory Committee in 1973, and was nominated to the Eastern District Court of Michigan by President Gerald R. Ford in 1975. REF.: *CBA*.

Guy, Thomas, prom. 1945, Aus., mur. The efforts of a forensic science laboratory in Brisbane, Aus., in 1936 led to the conviction of Thomas Guy for the murder of his wife, Bridget Guy. Working with doctors and biologists, the laboratory was able to establish the remains of Mrs. Guy in the ashes of a fire on their property. Search parties had discovered the fire site as well as horse-drawn wagon tracks from the Guy farm to the fire, and wool stuffing along the tracks which came from the cushion on the seat of Guy's wagon. The hoof and wagon prints matched those taken from Guy's horse and wagon. Using this evidence, the prosecution was able to convict Guy of his wife's murder.

REF.: *CBA*; Thorwald, *Crime and Science*.

Guylee, Edward Harold, prom. 1930s, Brit., fraud. Edward Harold Guylee, who lived in Surrey, England, was respected and esteemed by his neighbors. He operated Commerce, Industry and Finance, Ltd., a company which financed three outside brokerage houses that sold worthless securities to unwary individuals. Before being brought to trial for fraud, Guylee's company defrauded British citizens out of £120,000.

Guylee claimed that Maurice Singer, a man who was never discovered, had deceived him. The jury, unconvinced, found him Guilty, and he was sentenced to five years of hard labor.

Guylee returned to court as a witness for the prosecution in a case against a solicitor's managing clerk and another prosecutor, F.J. de Verteuil. Guylee claimed he gave both men bribe money before his trial "to grease the wheels of the High Court...." The defense claimed Guylee had fabricated the entire story. But the jury believed him and convicted the clerk and the prosecutor, sentencing them, like Guylee, to five years hard labor. REF.: *CBA*.

Guyon, Jeanne-Marie de la Motte (AKA: Madame Guyon du Chesnoy), 1648-1717, Fr., her. Imprisoned from 1695-1703, and was eventually banished to Blois for advocating quietism, a religion which holds that destruction of one's personal will and contemplation of divinity achieves spiritual peace. REF.: *CBA*.

Guyon, Melvin Bay (AKA: Tyrone Little), 1959-   , U.S., mur. In October 1978, officials issued a federal warrant for the arrest of Melvin Bay Guyon, who, with his brother Michael, was wanted on rape, kidnapping, and aggravated robbery charges. About 10:15 a.m. on Aug. 9, 1979, six FBI agents followed Preston Mathis to the apartment of his former girlfriend, Catherine Little, who lived in the Carver Park public housing project in Cleveland with her boyfriend, Guyon, and their two children. When Mathis knocked on the door, Guyon apparently told Little to let Mathis in and went into the bedroom with his son. One FBI agent entered, pushing Mathis and Little aside while 35-year-old Special Agent Johnnie L. Oliver, trailed by another agent, walked down a hallway, shouting that they were FBI officials. When Oliver entered the bedroom, Guyon fatally shot him in the chest with a pistol and then dove through a small window as the other agent fired at him. Oliver was the third FBI casualty on a day when an unprecedented three agents were shot to death.

A few hours after the shooting, Guyon was placed on the FBI's Ten Most Wanted list and the U.S. Justice Department offered a $10,000 reward for information leading to his capture. Five days later, the Cuyahoga County Police Chiefs Association offered an additional $10,000 reward and put the incident in its Silent Tip Observer Program. The search for Guyon became the most intensive and largest in Cleveland's history. Just after the shooting, 325 officials joined the hunt. Police received about 2,000 tips within a week after the shooting.

Meanwhile, Guyon escaped to Akron, Ohio, and then hitch-hiked to Youngstown, where police tracked him through a wiretap on a Cleveland home. On Aug. 16, agents spotted Guyon in a phone booth about 9:30 p.m. and tried to pin him in it with a car, but Guyon escaped. After tumbling down a twelve-foot bank, he ran to the home of Paul Flint. Bleeding, Guyon identified himself and said he was tired of running. Flint drove the fugitive to a hospital where Guyon turned himself over to a security guard. The guard notified Youngstown police who arrived at the hospital and arrested Guyon about 10:25 p.m. Guyon, pleading self-defense, was tried in Cleveland for murder. He said he had mistaken Oliver for a hit man hired by Mathis, Little's rejected boyfriend. On Nov. 1, 1979, he was found Guilty of first-degree murder and sentenced the same day to life imprisonment. Later, Guyon was convicted on a robbery charge, and on Dec. 1, 1979, he received a sentence of six to twenty-five years in prison. See: **Maloney, James.** REF.: *CBA.*

Guzik, Jake (AKA: Greasy Thumb), 1887-1956, U.S., org. crime. Born in Moscow in 1887, Jake "Greasy Thumb" Guzik was the financial genius of Al Capone's crime empire. They became allies after Guzik accidentally heard of a plan to assassinate the mob boss and informed Capone. Big Al was eternally grateful, and protected the diminutive Guzik, who was incapable of using a gun or otherwise defending himself. In May 1924, Guzik was assaulted by Joe Howard, a thug unaligned to a particular gang. Capone, hearing of Guzik's mistreatment, found Howard in a saloon on Chicago's South Wabash Avenue and killed him with a shot to the head at point-blank range.

Guzik was nicknamed Greasy Thumb for the amount of bribe money he paid to politicians and crooked policemen. He operated from a table at St. Hubert's Old English Grill and Chop House, receiving bagmen from local police precincts and city hall.

Jake "Greasy Thumb" Guzik, Capone's financial wizard.

In late April 1930, Guzik and Ralph Capone, brother of Al Capone, were convicted of tax evasion. The government proved that Guzik had earned over $1 million in three years, and had failed to report over $225,000. The feds continued to investigate the mob's taxes, eventually convicting Capone on a similar charge. In October 1930, in an effort to publicize their effort, Judge John H. Lyle issued warrants for the arrest of twenty-six Chicago mobsters, including Guzik, on the charge of vagrancy because they had no viable legal livelihood. The defense for Guzik angrily replied that he was a horse player, and since he lived within a block of the state's attorney, he must be an upstanding citizen. He was eventually sent to prison and quietly served five years.

Capone was no longer in power when Guzik returned, but Jake was given complete control of the mob's financial and legal affairs by subsequent bosses Frank Nitti, Paul Ricca, Tony Accardo, Sam Giancana, and Sam Battaglia. He continued greasing important palms until his death of a heart attack on Feb. 21, 1956, at his table at St. Hubert's restaurant. See: **Accardo, Anthony; Capone, Alphonse; Giancana, Sam; Nitti, Frank; Ricca, Paul.**

REF.: *CBA;* Cohen, *Mickey Cohen: In My Own Words;* Demaris, *Captive City;* ____, *The Last Mafioso;* Eisenberg and Landau, *Meyer Lansky;* Fried, *The Rise and Fall of the Jewish Gangster in America;* Gosch and Hammer, *The Last Testament of Lucky Luciano;* Kobler, *Capone;* Lait and Mortimer, *Chicago: Confidential;* Levine, *Anatomy of a Gangster;* McClellan, *Crime Without Punishment;* McPhaul, *Johnny Torrio;* Messick, *Lansky;* ____, *Secret File;* ____ and Goldblatt, *The Mobs and the Mafia;* Morgan, *Prince of Crime;* Peterson, *The Mob;* Reid, *The Grim Reapers;* Smith, *Syndicate City;* Spiering, *The Man Who Got Capone;* Wicker, *Investigating the FBI.*

Guzman, Rene Adolfo, and **Lopez, Leonardo Ramos**, 1937- , U.S., mur. Rene Adolfo Guzman was an elementary school dropout who came from a large family. In 1959 he was found Guilty of assault with intent to rob. By 1970, when he was released from the Texas State Penitentiary after serving a five-year burglary charge, Guzman was unemployed, uneducated, and addicted to heroin. Living near Dallas, Guzman began a career in burglary with his newly found partner, Leonardo Ramos Lopez.

In February 1971, the 33-year-old ex-convict and Lopez were caught by surprise in their house by three deputy sheriffs: Dallas County Deputies Samuel Garcia Infante and A.J. Robertson, and Ellis County Deputy Wendell Dover. The three deputies were working on a burglary in which witnesses had written down the license plate number of the escape car. The car was traced to Guzman's house and the deputies were sent to investigate. According to Dover, there was no hint of impending violence.

Before the deputies could enter the house, they were ambushed, disarmed, led into the house, and tied up. Two other Ellis County deputies, William Reese and A.D. McCurley, who were checking up on their fellow officers, were also disarmed and bound. At nightfall, the five were taken to the Trinity River Bottomlands, a dry river bed outside Dallas, in order to be killed execution-style. There, Infante and Reese attempted to attack Guzman, who opened fire on the officers. Infante, Reese, and Robertson were killed. Dover was shot twice, and McCurley escaped into the darkness. McCurley later identified Guzman and Lopez as the killers.

A large-scale manhunt ended with the capture of the two murderers on Feb. 20, in the apartment their girlfriends rented just a few days earlier. According to police, heroin dealers were questioned until one was found who knew where Guzman and Lopez were hiding. Police initially raided the wrong apartment, shooting and wounding an innocent man. After evacuating the entire complex, there was only one apartment still occupied. When officers broke down the door, Guzman immediately surrendered, dropping his weapon. Lopez, however, ran into the bathroom. When an officer followed him, Lopez pointed his gun and pulled the trigger, but the gun misfired.

Guzman and Lopez were arraigned on murder charges and denied bond. The two girlfriends, Angie Rojo Hernandez and Alice Rosales, were charged with harboring fugitives and being accomplices to murder. Of Rene Guzman, one relative said: "He's a mean man. He thinks he's Al Capone."

In late June 1971, Guzman and Lopez were brought to trial. After only one hour, the jury returned a verdict of Guilty. Guzman and his 24-year-old partner were sentenced to die in the electric chair. REF.: *CBA.*

Guzman y Pimental, Gaspar de (Conde-duque de Olivares), 1587-1645, Spain, polit. corr. Prime minister under Philip IV from 1621-43 who tried to unify all Spanish territory under one flag. His tenure was distinguished by futile attempts to reform the Spanish economy, the resumption of war with the Netherlands, and the start of a thirty-year war with France. He was dismissed and exiled at the Queen's request when a tax levy he had authorized touched off revolts in Catalonia and Portugal. REF.: *CBA.*

Gwin-McCorckle Duel, 1855, U.S., duel-attempt. mur. In 1855, Judge William M. Gwin and Joseph McCorckle decided to end a simmering feud by fighting a duel. A site was selected near the Presidio district outside San Francisco, and a messenger was engaged to relay the outcome to Gwin's wife. The first round was fired without injury and the news was rushed to Mrs. Gwin. After no one was hit with a second shot, the news was again duly reported. The third exchange produced the same report. After the fourth empty exchange, the exhausted messenger was invited to stay for dinner with Mrs. Gwin. When subsequent shots failed to produce a victim, the duel ended, and Judge Gwin went on to become the first Californian senator. REF.: *CBA.*

Gwinner, Else, d.1601, Ger., witchcraft. Accused of witchcraft by Rupprecht Silberrad, a member of a witch-hunting faction in the town council of Offenburg, Ger., Else Gwinner was brutally tortured on five occasions over a period of two months before she was burned on Dec. 21, 1601. Silberrad claimed she used witchcraft to cause the death of Silberrad's son. The accusation was motivated by Silberrad's wish to destroy George Laubbach, Gwinner's father and Silberrad's adversary on the town council. To obtain a confession, weights were attached to Gwinner's body, thumbscrews were applied and she was hanged by her wrists.

Gwinner never confessed, not even when the judges flogged her daughter, forcing her to lie about her mother. While the thumbscrews drew an admission of copulating with a devil, she later retracted the confession. At one point, the pain of the torture became so excruciating that cold water was thrown in her face to revive her. Less that two months after Gwinner's execution, the other town councilors arrested Silberrad. This late attempt at justice proved to be in vain, for Silberrad regained his position through the intervention of the Catholic Church and continued the witch-hunts. REF.: *CBA*.

Gwyer, Sir **Maurice Linford**, b.1878, Brit., jur. Solicitor to the treasury and procurator general from 1926-33. He was the first parliamentary counsel to the treasury from 1934-37, when he was appointed chief justice of India and president of the federal court. REF.: *CBA*.

Gwynne, Nell (**Nell Gwyn**), 1650-87, Brit., pros. Nell Gwynne, a prostitute, rose from servant girl to mistress of King Charles II. She was probably born in a brothel. Her mother either operated the brothel or sold fish in the streets. Her father was reportedly a captain, a yeoman, or a fruiterer. It is certain, however, that Nell was employed as a prostitute in the brothel of the famous Madame Ross. Later, she worked in the theater, rising from orange seller to actress through her careful selection of lovers. A popular comic actress, she was best known for her clever impersonations of men.

The celebrated Nell Gwynne, mistress of Charles II.

Gwynne was kept as the mistress of Lord Brockhurst in July 1667. Once among the nobility, Gwynne left the theater, though she returned briefly between her affairs with Brockhurst and Charles. King Charles II was notorious for his many mistresses. It was the Duke of Buckingham who brought Nell to the king's bed, a bed which she irregularly frequented until the king gave her a house. From that point on, Nell considered herself the king's mistress, maintaining that, though a prostitute, she was mistress to only one man. She eventually gave birth to two sons by Charles: James, who died while still a boy, and Charles, who became Earl of Buford and later Duke of St. Albans.

Nell died in 1687, soon after the death of Charles. Later in her life, she was the subject of songs, poetry, and stories, and considered "a symbol of Protestant womanhood" because she was the only Protestant mistress of Charles, who was secretly a Catholic. The common people loved her, as demonstrated when a mob nearly overturned her carriage, mistaking Nell for one of the Catholic mistresses. Allegedly, Nell poked her head outside the carriage and shouted "Pray, good people, be civil. I am the Protestant whore."

REF.: Bullough, *Illustrated History of Prostitution*; *CBA*; Henriques, *Prostitution*; (FILM), *Nell Gwyn*, 1986.

Gyges (**Gugu**), prom. c.680-648 B.C., Lydia, king, mur.-assass. Secured the throne by murdering King Candaules, and created the Mermanad dynasty. His reign was distinguished by warfare against the Greek Ionian cities, and threats by the Cimmerians, who eventually caused his death. REF.: *CBA*.

Gylippus, prom. 4th Cent. B.C., Sparta, embez. General who fought under Nicias and Demosthenes in victory over the Athenians. He later stole money consigned to him by Lysander and fled from Sparta. REF.: *CBA*.

H

Haakon VII (Prince Charles of Denmark), 1872-1957, king, Nor., exile. Became king of Norway in 1905, encouraged resistance to German occupation during WWII and was exiled to Britain from 1940-45. REF.: *CBA.*

Haarman, Fritz (AKA: Ogre of Hanover), 1879-1925, Ger., can.-mur. Fritz Haarman was born in Hanover, Ger., on Oct. 25, 1879. As a child he eschewed active games in favor of playing with dolls and dressing in his sisters' clothing. He spent some time as a teenager at a military school but was discharged when he showed signs of epilepsy. After a brief stint working in his father's cigar factory, Haarman was arrested for sexually assaulting small children and was sent to a mental institution. He escaped from the institution and joined the army but was eventually released as an undesirable.

German mass murderer and cannibal Fritz Haarman.

Back in Hanover, Haarman secured a position as a police informer, a job which gave him a small salary and a police badge. At the end of WWI large numbers of young boys poured into Hanover, hunting for work. They slept wherever they could, many camping out in the train station. It was here that Haarman found most of his victims. Beginning in 1918, Haarman, often with the help of his homosexual lover, Hans Grans, started the chain of rapes, cannibalism, and murder that earned him the title of the "Ogre of Hanover" or "Vampire of Hanover." Often using his police badge to intimidate the young men, he took them to his apartment in Hanover's Jewish ghetto where he sexually assaulted and then killed them, as he later testified at his trial, by biting their throats.

The house (arrow) where Fritz Haarman lived in Hanover.

Haarman's atrocities did not stop with the rapes and murders. When he had killed a victim, he took the body to an attic room where he butchered it. Any clothing or belongings of the victim were sold. Bones, skulls, and other unusable portions were thrown into the nearby river Leine. Haarman then transported the "edible" portions of the butchered flesh in buckets to the open market in Hanover where he sold it as horse meat to Hanover's starving citizens.

In May 1924, some boys fishing in the river found several human skulls and police investigated. The next month, a homeless boy who had been sleeping at the train station told police that Haarman had taken indecent liberties with him. As Haarman was being questioned, police searched his apartment and found incontrovertible evidence of his guilt. Haarman confessed to the murders and implicated his lover, Hans Grans, as his accomplice.

The skeletal remains dredged from the river and surrounding area accounted for twenty-seven victims. When asked how many boys he had killed, Haarman cavalierly responded, "It might have been thirty. It might have been forty. I don't remember." Estimates ranged as high as one hundred. Haarman and Grans were tried at the Hanover Assizes beginning on Dec. 4, 1924. While Grans remained quiet and withdrawn throughout the proceedings, Haarman smoked cigars, complained that too many women were in the courtroom, and acted bored. Of the twenty-seven murders with which he was charged, Haarman denied only three, in one case disdainfully claiming that one of the boys was not sufficiently attractive to have merited his interest. Haarman was finally convicted of the murders of twenty-four young men ranging in age from thirteen to twenty, and he was sentenced to death by decapitation. Grans was convicted also and sentenced to life imprisonment, a sentence later reduced to twelve years. Haarman was beheaded in Hanover Prison on Apr. 15, 1925.

REF.: Boar, *The World's Most Infamous Murders;* Bolitho, *Murder For Profit;* CBA; Dearden, *Queer People;* Dickson, *Murder By Numbers;* Douthwaite, *Mass Murder;* Godwin, *Murder U.S.A.;* Jackson, *The Portable Murder Book;* Kobler, *Some Like It Gory;* Lustgarten, *The Story of Crime;* Masters, *Perverse Crimes in History;* Nash, *Almanac of World Crime;* Rowland, *More Criminals' Files;* Wilson, *Encyclopedia of Murder.*

Habibullah Khan (Amir of Afghanistan), 1872-1919, Afg., king, assass. Son of Abd-er-Rahman Khan. Because of his friendly relations with the British in India, Habibullah was marked for death by a nationalist cabal and was assassinated in 1919. REF.: *CBA.*

Habron, William, b.1854, Brit., (wrong. convict.) mur. William Habron's and his two brothers, John and Frank, were local terrors at the Royal Oak pub in Manchester, Eng. Manchester police Constable Cock had repeated warned William in particular about his penchant for drunken brawls. When he had too much to drink, Habron was prone to violence and would engage anyone who crossed his path in a fight. After the final warning seemingly fell on deaf ears, Cock made good on his threat to bring Will Habron before the magistrate. "I promised you a sorry day if you ever ran afoul of me," Habron scowled in court.

On the evening of Aug. 1, 1876, Constable Cock was shot to death by a gunman lurking in the shadows as he made his rounds. With his dying breath, the policeman identified Habron as a possible assailant. Police Superintendent Bent pieced together a trail of circumstantial evidence that seemed to confirm Cock's accusation. A pair of muddy boots at Habron's home matched the tracks left behind at the scene of the murder. Two clerks in a small shop that sold weapons and ammunition identified Habron as the same man who had examined revolver cartridges the day before the murder. Their testimony, coupled with the ominous threat uttered by Habron in court, was enough to convict him of murder. On Nov. 28, 1876, the judge sentenced him to life in prison at Portland after the jury had attached a recommendation for leniency to its verdict.

William Habron served three years for a murder he never committed. The actual killer, Charles Peace, was a career criminal well known to the Crown as a violent and dangerous man. He had shot and killed Cock while committing one of his crimes. This was the story he told to police after being arrested on Oct. 10, 1878, near Blackheath for the murder of Albert Dyson. Peace went to the gallows on Feb. 25, 1879. William Habron was pardoned and given £500 compensation.

REF.: Borchard, *Convicting the Innocent;* Brock, *A Casebook of Crime;* Browne, *The Rise of Scotland Yard;* CBA; Kingston, *A Gallery of Rogues;* _____, *Law-Breakers;* Russell, *Best Murder Cases.*

Hácha, Emil, 1872-1945, Ger., war crimes. Second president of high court of Czechoslavakia from 1919-25, and first president from 1925-38. He was a judge on the Permanent Court of International Justice at The Hague, was Czechoslovakia's third president from 1938-39, and was made president of the German protectorate of Moravia and Bohemia from 1939-45. He was imprisoned for war crimes and died in jail waiting to be tried. REF.: *CBA.*

Hackman, Rev. James, d.1779, Brit., mur. Seized by an obsession he could not control, James Hackman successfully murdered the mistress of England's Lord Sandwich, whom he had loved from afar for almost a year.

Hackman, while serving in the army, met Lord Sandwich and his mistress of nineteen years, Miss Reay, at one of many dinners he was to have with the couple in Hunting-don, where he was stationed. For Hackman it was love at first sight with a woman al-most twice his age, a woman whose graciousness he mis-took for affection.

British murderer, Reverend James Hackman.

Just before Christmas in 1778, Hackman left the mili-tary to become a minister at the Wiverton Church in near-by Norfolk. It was then that his once harmless fantasies turned ominous. He began to follow Reay to public concerts arranged by Sandwich for her pleasure, and on the evening of Apr. 7, 1779, Hackman watched as Reay boarded Sandwich's coach to the theater.

Reverend Hackman shooting Miss Reay, then himself.

Hackman followed her to the show but left when he saw her in the arms of Sandwich. Returning later with two loaded guns, he waited outside until the end of the show and stalked the couple as they walked towards their waiting coach. As Reay stepped up into the coach, Hackman drew both guns. With one he shot Reay dead and with the other himself, but the one pointed towards his head misfired. Ammunition spent, he hit himself in the head with the butt of the gun. Eyewitness testimony and a letter that was to be delivered to Hackman's brother-in-law at his death con-firmed Hackman's premeditation. On Apr. 19, 1779, he was hanged at Tyburn.

REF.: Bleackley, *Hangmen of England; CBA;* Lawrence, *A History of Capital Punishment;* Melville, *Famous Duels and Assassinations;* Mitchell, *The Newgate Calendar;* Sparrow, *The Great Assassins;* Wilson, *Encyclopedia of Murder.*

Hackmeister, Ralph, prom. 1922, U.S., boot. During the early years of National Prohibition in the U.S., one of the toughest, most relentless foes of the rum-runners was Ralph Hackmeister, who knew every launch, inland waterway, and coastal rendezvous familiar to smugglers. In 1923 he resigned from the Custom's Patrol to make some quick money in the lucrative, but illegal business. He was arrested, but the charges were eventually dropped for lack of evidence.

REF.: *CBA;* Everest, *Rum Across the Border.*

Hadfield, James, 1771-c.1840, Brit., attempt. assass. Twice in the same day, assassins attempted to take the life of King George III of England. The errant bullets narrowly missed the monarch in each instance. The king, whose long reign was beset with various foreign and domestic calamities, showed resolute courage in the face of grave peril, thereby earning greater respect and admiration from his subjects.

On the morning of May 15, 1800, a stray bullet pierced the thigh of a man standing near the king in Hyde Park. George was reviewing the Grenadier Guards at the time of the shooting, but he dismissed it as nothing more than an accident. The Guards had been asked to fire a volley into the air for the benefit of the royal family.

That night the king, the Duke of York, the queen, and her daughters, Augusta, Amelia, Elizabeth, and Mary, attended a performance of *She Would and She Would Not* at the Drury Lane Theatre. Before the first act began, the king was greeted by a tumultuous standing ovation from the theater patrons. As the sovereign greeted his subjects, a disfigured, misshapen man arose from the second row of the pit. He aimed a pistol at the royal box and squeezed the trigger. His aim was bad; the bullet whizzed between the king and the Duke of York.

The man was hustled out of the auditorium and into an adjoining room where he was identified as James Hadfield, a former member of the Fifteenth Light Dragoons, commanded by the Duke of York in 1793. He was a loyal soldier and war hero who was badly wounded in combat, it was pointed out. Hadfield's face and neck had been badly severed by an enemy soldier's sabre. His life was saved on the operating table, but the nature of the head wounds brought on recurrent delusions and madness. Hadfield explained that he wanted to die, and had seized upon the notion of shooting the king as one sure way to accomplish these ends. "I did not mean to take away the life of the king," he said, "but I thought this attempt would answer my purpose as well."

Hadfield was indicted for high treason on June 26. He was defended by the eminent lawyer Thomas Erskine, who conducted a brilliant defense that earned his client an acquittal on the grounds of insanity. Defense witnesses said that the soldier had suffered severe delusion since his discharge, and was not respon-sible for his actions. The jury agreed. As a consequence of the Hadfield acquittal, a bill was rushed through Parliament which required future juries to determine whether the person was actually insane at the time the crime was committed.

REF.: *CBA;* Keeton, *Guilty But Insane.*

Hadfield, John (AKA: Alexander Hope), d.1803, Brit., fraud-forg.-big. John Hadfield was the son of a wealthy businessman in Cheshire, England, who hoped that John might prosper in the wool trade, but instead the boy went to the U.S. colonies in 1776 and married the niece of the Marquis of Granby. Hadfield then deserted her to return to London, where he amassed a sizeable debt. But his benefactor, the Duke of Rutland, paid off the debt. In 1792, Hadfield was thrown into debtor's prison for eight years. Posing as a fallen aristocrat, he wrote sentimental poetry which caught the eye of a wealthy widow, Mrs. Nation, who discharged Hadfield's debts and married him upon his release from prison in 1800. The unhappy marriage ended in 1802 when Hadfield took up with Mary Robinson, a 25-year-old waitress known as the "Beauty of Buttermere," who lived in Keswick in the Lake District.

Her parents hoped she might wed a gentleman and gain social status and a generous income.

Hadfield, using the name Colonel Alexander Hope, seemed just such a man. In October 1802, the couple married, but George Hardinge, senior justice of Brecon, knew Hadfield and exposed him. Three days after the wedding, Hadfield fled, leaving behind letters from Nation. A reward of £50 was put on Hadfield's head, and he was captured at Neath and tried at Carlisle in December 1802. He was charged with forging two bills of exchange and committing a fraud against the postal services. Complicating matters was the fact that Mary was pregnant with his child. Hadfield was condemned and hanged on Dec. 3, 1803. REF.: *CBA*.

Hadley, Charles B. (AKA: Charlie Start, John Bennett), prom. 1902, Case of, U.S., rape-mur. On Jan. 6, 1902, a classified ad was placed in the San Francisco *Chronicle* and *Examiner*. "Wanted— Young white girl to take care of baby; good home and wages." Answering the ad was 15-year-old Nora Fuller who was born in China, but was living on Fulton Street, San Francisco, in poverty.

With the blessing of her mother, Nora agreed to meet John Bennett on Jan. 11 at the Popular Restaurant. Shortly after she left for her interview, Mrs. Fuller received a call from her daughter saying that Bennett wanted her to begin immediately. The girl sounded agitated, but her mother just told her to come home and start the job the following Monday. That was the last anyone heard of Nora Fuller.

The owner of the Popular Restaurant explained that as usual Bennett entered the place and had ordered a porterhouse steak. Bennett told the waiter that a young girl was expected, and when she did not show up, he left the diner. The city newspapers gave heavy coverage to the disappearance of Nora Fuller, but no one had a clue as to her whereabouts.

Accused murderer Charles Hadley.

Finally, on Feb. 8, the police entered an abandoned house on Sutter Street. The two-story frame building had been rented to a C.B. Hawkins but after he missed his second rent payment the building inspector entered the premises to investigate. Nora Fuller was found dead in a virtually empty bedroom. She had been raped and strangled.

A business card bearing the name of M.A. Severbrinik was found near the body. Whoever this person was had departed for Peking, three hours before Nora first left her home to meet Bennett on Jan. 11. An acquaintance of Nora Fuller, Madge Graham, explained that Bennett was well known to her friend, and that the two of them had probably thought of a scheme of sorts to deceive her mother.

A $5,000 reward was posted but San Francisco police failed to turn up any possible suspects or motives. They then checked a missing person's report filed on Jan. 16 by a commercial business in the city. The missing man was Charles Hadley, who had run off with some company funds. The signatures of Hawkins, the man who rented the flat, and Hadley were compared. They were nearly identical.

It was learned that Hadley was also fond of porterhouse steaks. A girlfriend of his, Ollie Blasier, reported that she had discovered some blood-soiled clothing in his possession but had them burned. The police surmised that Hadley left town after reading about the disappearance of the Fuller girl in the newspapers.

A further investigation revealed that Hadley operated under the name of Charles Start in Chicago, and was known to be a man

of bad moral character. In 1889 the police chief of Minneapolis offered a $100 reward for the capture of Hadley on a charge of embezzlement. In 1900 he was implicated in a statutory rape case. The police were reasonably certain that they had identified the murderer of the young girl. However, Charles Hadley was never brought to justice. Many people believed that he committed suicide.
REF.: *CBA*; Duke, *Celebrated Criminal Cases of America*.

Hadley, Herbert Spencer, 1872-1927, U.S., lawyer. Attorney General of Missouri from 1905-09, notable for his prosecution of the Standard Oil Company case. He was governor of Missouri from 1909-13. REF.: *CBA*.

Hadrian, Emperor, See: **Apollodorus of Damascus**.

Haerm, Teet, 1954- , and **Thomas, Allgen Lars**, 1949- , Swed., mur. Beginning in 1984, a number of Swedish prostitutes were murdered and their bodies dissected. On July 19, 1984, the carefully dissected body of 28-year-old Catrine da Costa was found in a plastic garbage bag on a sports field used by the police department. The department's leading expert in forensic medicine, Dr. Teet Haerm, reconstructed the body and determined the identity through fingerprints. A week later, the body of another prostitute, 26-year-old Annika Mors, was found in a public park. Dr. Haerm determined that the victim was savagely murdered and then strangled, and that the same person committed both murders. On Aug. 1, the body of 27-year-old Kristine Cravache was found naked and strangled near Stockholm's red-light district. Lena Grans, Cats Falk, Lena Bofors, Lena Manson, and Lota Svenson subsequently disappeared and were assumed to have suffered the same fate. Police interviewed other prostitutes, who described a dark-haired boyish man who drove a white Volkswagen. One remembered the license plate number, which was traced and found to belong to Dr. Haerm.

Haerm was arrested as he was performing an autopsy, but he vigorously denied involvement. He was a widower whose wife, Ann-Catrine Haerm, was thought to have committed suicide on Jan. 7, 1982. But after his arrest, police found in Haerm's house pictures of Ann-Catrine with a cord around her neck. Haerm also had published articles in medical journals describing suicide by strangulation and methods of sexual psychopaths. Because of lack of evidence, Haerm was not indicted, but he was released from his medical position, after which time no other prostitute was attacked. In March 1985, the bodies of two of the previous victims, Lena Grans and Cats Falk, were found in a car submerged in the sea near Hamarby. And on Jan. 7, 1986, the body of 22-year-old Tazuga Toyonaga, a Japanese student, was found in Copenhagen, strangled and mutilated in similar fashion.

An interview with a four-year-old girl cracked the case. The social welfare department suspected that she had been sexually molested. The perpetrator was found to be her father, 38-year-old Dr. Allgen Lars Thomas, a colleague of Haerm. Thomas confessed to the molestation, saying that Haerm had been a witness. Then, he confessed to helping Haerm murder the prostitutes. He believed Haerm to be the head of a secret sect dedicated to the extermination of prostitutes, and to cannibalism and necrophilia. On Oct. 28, 1987, Haerm was arrested for the second time and charged with the murders of da Costa, Mors, Cravache, Grans, Falk, Svenson, Manson, Toyonaga, and his wife, Ann-Catrine. Thomas was charged with the rape and murder of Catrine da Costa, and incest with his daughter. Thomas pleaded guilty, while Haerm pleaded not guilty. On Sept. 16, 1988, both Haerm and Thomas were convicted and sentenced to life imprisonment. REF.: *CBA*.

Haga, Eric L., 1943- , U.S., mur. Five years after the Sheriff's Department of Kent, Wash., determined that there was not sufficient evidence to continue the investigation into the murder of Mrs. Judith Haga and her daughter Peri Lynn Haga, Prosecutor Christopher Bayley reopened the case and charged the woman's husband Eric L. Haga with first-degree murder on Aug. 30, 1971.

The case presented more than the usual amount of contradiction and innuendo, involving an unfaithful wife, a jealous husband,

and a mysterious prowler no one could identify. On the night of July 6, 1966, Haga's wife and daughter were strangled in their suburban home. The next morning, Haga awoke to find them both dead. It was alleged that a prowler had broken into the family's home in the middle of the night.

It was widely known that domestic relations between the Hagas had deteriorated ever since Judith began an extra-marital affair with Dennis Harman of Oregon. The case was reopened in 1971 after Mr. and Mrs. James Matuska of Bothell provided secret testimony to a grand jury concerning the murders. Matuska, who employed Haga as a race car driver, appeared for the prosecution when the case went to trial in December 1971. It was brought out during the trial that Haga doubted Peri Lynn was his daughter, and that he was driven to murder by revenge and desire. Mrs. Haga had a large insurance policy on herself and her daughter, the prosecution argued, which was to be used to finance the purchase of a new sports car. As to the identity of the killer, defense attorneys theorized that Harman, who had a record of mental illness, may have been the prowler who entered the Haga home that night. The argument did not sway the jury.

On Dec. 24, 1971, a Superior Court jury convicted Haga of first-degree murder. The jurors recommended against the death penalty, and Haga was instead sentenced to life in prison. REF.: *CBA*.

Hagan, Michael, 1964- , U.S., mur. Vowing to return to the streets with a vengeance, Los Angeles gang member Michael Hagan was sentenced to twenty-seven years to life in September 1987 for the rifle murder of 17-year-old Kellie Mosier, who was in the wrong place at the wrong time.

Claiming that he was high on the drug PCP at the time of the girl's death, Hagan promised that: "One day I'll be back on the streets, and I'm gonna be hard, hard, hard..."

Judge Robert Altman described the defendant as "one of the most remorseless and dangerous individuals" he had encountered during his career on the bench. REF.: *CBA*.

Hagerup, Georg Francis, 1853-1921, Nor., jur. Minister of justice in 1893, and member of the Hague Tribunal in 1903. REF.: *CBA*.

Haggart, David (AKA: **John Wilson, John Morrison, Barney M'Coul, John M'Colgan, Daniel O'Brien**), 1801-21, Brit.-Ire.-Scot., pris. esc.-rob.-mur. David Haggart began his criminal career when he was still a child by stealing a neighbor's bantam rooster. At sixteen, Haggart ran away from his home in Edinburgh, and became involved with Irish pickpocket Barney McGuire. Haggart learned quickly, and soon the two were picking pockets and occasionally breaking into houses. In Durham, England, they broke into a house and were caught, tried under false names, and condemned to die. While awaiting execution, they planned an escape with some other prisoners. Haggart escaped, but McGuire was left behind. Haggart went to Newcastle, England, then returned to free McGuire. On the way, he and his companion were attacked by two police officers, one of whom Haggart shot and killed. Haggart freed McGuire, and the two continued their illegal trade, until McGuire was recaptured. Haggart, using several false names, continued to steal, and was jailed on six occasions, but escaped four times. McGuire was eventually released and then recaptured again, to be sentenced to fourteen years' transportation. Haggart continued stealing for a time in Ireland, where he was captured again, just before his planned departure for France. While awaiting trial at Downpatrick Jail, Haggart was recognized by a Scottish policeman who knew of the murder charge and of Haggart's habit of escaping. Heavily loaded with irons, Haggart was taken to Dumfries, Scot., tried, and condemned to death. While awaiting execution, Haggart wrote his autobiography, *An Account of His Robberies, Burglaries, Murders, Trials, and Other Remarkable Adventures.* After Haggart's death by hanging in 1821, the proceeds from the book's sales were used to educate his siblings.

REF.: Birmingham, *Murder Most Foul; CBA*; Culpin, *The Newgate Noose*; Forster, *Studies in Black and Red*; Hunt, *A Dictionary of Rogues*.

Haggart, Robert Lee, 1951- , U.S., mur. Robert Haggart was a drifter. When he worked it was usually as a livestock auctioneer. At least this is what he was doing at the time he married Garnetta Post of Farwell, Mich., in February 1982. Haggart was an ex-convict who was wanted by the police for passing bad checks.

After less than six months of marriage, Garnetta realized she had made a mistake, and left her husband. She went to live in Florida, but returned to Michigan on Feb. 16 to finalize her divorce and to visit her parents and family members at their secluded frame house in Farwell, 150 miles north of Grand Rapids. It was to be a family reunion for George and Vaudrey Post, who were looking forward to seeing their grown children and grandchildren. Instead, it ended in wholesale slaughter.

Armed with a shotgun, the vengeful Haggart advanced on the Posts' home, which was tucked into the snow-covered backwoods. He shot and killed Garnetta, her parents George and Vaudrey, their other daughter, Helen Gaffney, and three of her children: Angela, ten, Tom, six, and Amy, four. A fourth child, one-year-old Mandy, narrowly escaped death only because her mother had thrown her body over her siblings when the shooting started. It was the first of two grisly Michigan mass murders in thirty days. A month later, five members of an Allendale family were found shot to death in their home. A deranged co-worker of one of the victims was charged in that shooting.

A seven-count murder warrant was issued for Haggart. He was arrested near Jasper, Tenn., on Feb. 18 after George Post's stolen automobile was recognized by a restaurant patron at a roadside diner not far from the Alabama state line. Extradition proceedings were filed with Tennessee authorities, and within a week the murderer was back in Michigan. Haggart was convicted of first-degree murder on Oct. 8, and sentenced to life in prison without parole two weeks later. REF.: *CBA*.

Hagger, Harold (AKA: **Sydney Sinclair**), prom. 1946, Brit., mur. On Halloween, 1946, the strangled corpse of a middle-aged woman was found in a clump of bushes on Labour-in-Vain Hill beside the A20 highway outside Wrotham, England. The dead woman was soon identified as Dagmar Petrzywalski, better known as Dagmar Peters, forty-eight, a spinster who traveled weekly to London to visit her brother. Peters' 80-year-old mother explained that her daughter would leave at 5 a.m. to hitchhike into the city, and always carried with her a briefcase and a yellow crocheted bag, a gift from her sister-in-law. Scotland Yard's Chief Inspector Robert Fabian, asked Peters' sister-in-law to crochet a duplicate, and then published its photograph in the newspapers. A 15-year-old farm boy, Peter Nash, recognized the bag as one he pulled from Clare Park Lake three days after Peters' body was found. Fabian learned from a local Girl Guide leader that objects tossed into the lake by the mill stream at East Malling floated to Clare Park Lake in a few hours, via an underground stream. Fabian visited the old mill, which had been turned into a cider factory, and tried the experiment with the crocheted purse.

Pieces of Peters' briefcase were found strewn for a mile along the highway. Fabian found at the cider works a pile of bricks delivered by truck on Oct. 31 by a Cambridge contractor. The driver, Sydney Sinclair, was questioned and soon admitted that his real name was Harold Hagger. An ex-convict with a record of sixteen convictions, including one for assaulting a woman, Hagger confessed that he had given Peters a ride. He claimed that she had tried to steal his wallet from a jacket pocket, they had struggled, and he had accidentally pulled her wool scarf too tight around her neck. Fabian abruptly asked Hagger, "Where was your jacket?" The accused said that it had been "hung on a peg inside the cab." When Hagger was tried at Maidstone Assizes, this ill-considered response (it was a bitterly cold morning when Peters left for London) helped convict him. Hagger was hanged for the murder.

REF.: Butler, *Murderers' England; CBA*; Fabian, *Fabian of the Yard*; Shew, *A Companion to Murder*; Simpson, *Forty Years of Murder*.

Haggerty, John, d.1847, U.S., mur. Haggerty was an Irish immigrant living in Lancaster, Pa. He was a notorious drunk and, during his alcoholic stupors, was deadly. He had killed one man in a drunken fit some years earlier before he took an ax to his neighbors, the Fordney family, slaying Melchoir Fordney, his wife, and their child. Haggerty was found coated with human gore while trying to guzzle more liquor. The defense counsel for Haggerty tried to prove that when his client drank he became insane and was therefore not responsible for his actions. Jurors were told how Haggerty had, some time earlier, killed his horse with a silver bullet because, after imbibing liquor, he came to believe the animal was evil and was plotting against him. It was evident that there were grounds for a reduction of the charges from first-degree murder to manslaughter, but Haggerty was nevertheless convicted of murder and hanged.

REF.: *CBA; Confession of John Haggerty; Report of the Trial and Conviction of John Haggerty.*

Haggerty, John F., prom. 1917, U.S., mur. Harry Lorenzo Chapin of Cleveland was a physician, poet, and a noted world explorer. His book of verse, *Twilight and Death,* in some ways foreshadowed his own untimely demise. What the poetry-reading public did not know was that Chapin was also a desperate cocaine addict, falling into debt with his supplier John Haggerty, former owner of a Cleveland drug store. In November 1917, Haggerty murdered Dr. Chapin in a room at the Colonial Hotel, off Public Square in downtown Cleveland. Impatient to receive the money that was due him from previous drug transactions, Haggerty tricked his client into meeting him at the hotel with the promise of receiving a new shipment of cocaine. Haggerty had sent the package of worthless junk from Chicago, and had claimed it at the express office.

The pusher and the junkie quarreled briefly; Chapin accused Haggerty of deceit. There was a brief struggle in which Chapin supposedly reached for his gun, according to the testimony later given by the accused murderer. Haggerty crashed a weight down on Dr. Chapin's head and fled the building. Cleveland detectives working closely with police officials in Chicago, traced Haggerty to Kansas City where he was arrested at the Washington Hotel. Extradited back to Ohio, Haggerty was indicted for first-degree murder at the Common Pleas Court on June 4, 1918. In a plea-bargaining arrangement Haggerty pleaded Guilty to a reduced charge of second-degree murder. Judge Manuel Levine sentenced him to life in prison in the Ohio Penitentiary. Eleven years later he was granted parole, but shortly after he was arrested in Illinois on a robbery charge. When Haggerty completed his sentence at the Joliet Penitentiary on Oct. 1, 1937, he was returned to Columbus to serve out his original term.

REF.: *CBA; Rodell, Cleveland Murders.*

Hahn, Anna Marie, 1906-38, U.S., mur. German-born Anna Marie Hahn moved to Cincinnati, Ohio, with her husband, Phillip Hahn, and their young son, Oscar, in 1929. With her rich contralto voice and her plump, blond good looks, Hahn delighted the elderly German men in the immigrant community and soon became an unofficial nurse, a self-described "angel of mercy." Many of those under her care died, but grateful relatives left her thousands of dollars from the estates anyway. Ernest Kohler died while under Hahn's care, in 1933, and left her a large house. Dr. Arthur Vos, the second-floor resident of that house, soon found several blank prescription forms missing from his offices and complained to the new owner who shrugged and suggested "maybe one of your patients took them." On June 1, 1937, Jacob Wagner became Hahn's patient. He died on June 2. Days later, George Opendorfer, seventy, died under Hahn's care. The fact that both men had died after acute stomach pains and vomiting was brought to Cincinnati police chief Patrick Hayes' attention. Hayes ordered an autopsy of Wagner's body, and discovered four types of poison in the corpse. Subsequent autopsies of Hahn's other patients, including a man named Palmer and George Gsellman, sixty-seven, revealed more evidence of arsenic and croton oil. Hahn denied killing anyone and asked Hayes, "Why pick on me, chief?" Hayes explained to her that the search of her home had turned

up "enough poison to kill half of Cincinnati."

At the trial, Hahn's history of theft, adultery, and forgery was brought out by her own defense lawyers, including Hiram Bolsinger, in an attempt to establish robbery, not murder, as her motive for her dealings with the old men. Dubbed "the beautiful blonde killer" by the press, Hahn was convicted and sentenced to die in the electric chair. The night before her execution, on Dec. 7, 1938, Hahn refused to see her husband or son, but threw a farewell party for the newsmen who had covered her trial, treating them to punch and cakes in her cell. None of these reporters came to her execution early the next morning. Hahn was the first woman to die in the electric chair in Ohio. She was thirty-two.

The poisoning nurse, Anna Marie Hahn.

REF.: *CBA; Nash, Look For the Woman.*

Haiat, Fred, prom. 1932, and **Haiat, Joe,** 1865-c.1931, and **Beale, Charles James,** b.1895, Brit., fraud-forg. John Albert Drinan was an eccentric old gentleman who lived to the age of eighty-three. He possessed considerable wealth, yet chose to carve out a miserly existence for himself in three locations: Nice, Mentone, and Cannes. Before he died on Jan. 6, 1931, in the south of France, Drinan had been victimized by two shrewd conmen, who wanted to prevent him from carrying through a plan to bequeath his fortune to the Poor Boxes of the Metropolitan Police Court. Concerned that the old man was no longer able to function properly, British vice consul Charles James Beale, who was assigned to Nice, personally took charge of Drinan in September 1930.

A mysterious Englishman, Fred Haiat, soon appeared before Drinan and presented himself as a member of the British consulate. He agreed to care for Drinan, and in return he got the old man to agree to transfer £600 from his bank account to one in the name of his father, Joe Haiat. In the presence of the vice consul, Drinan assigned 11,000 shares of the Canadian Pacific Railway, with a value of $25 each, to Haiat. It was a peculiar thing to do, given Drinan's well-known passion for economy and his determination to leave his money to charity. On Oct. 9, 1930, the first stock transfer forms were signed, which placed Joe Haiat, a man who had once served eighteen months in a Manchester prison for fraud, in control of 10,728 shares.

On Nov. 22, 1930, Joe Haiat requested that the bank sell the shares and reinvest part of the proceeds in various securities he had selected. Drinan's bank in New York became suspicious and asked for a verification of his signature before securing the deal. Haiat wrote back that the old man was in Italy and would not be coming back. The bank refused to expedite the matter, which prompted Joe Haiat to file suit in London. The investigators working on the case were satisfied that the signatures on the stock transfer forms were forgeries. A series of letters purportedly written by Drinan instructed his banks to send all correspondence to the British Consulate in Nice. Then, on November 17, the typewritten letters ceased. It was learned that Beale and Haiat were close friends who had engineered the fraud together. According to handwriting experts, the forged signatures belonged to Beale.

The vice consul was arrested in France and returned to England for passing forged stock transfers. Joe Haiat and his father fled the country. It was believed that Joe died in Egypt. Beale was sentenced to fifteen months at Wormwood Scrubs Prison. Drinan's estate, valued at £76,000, ended up in the Poor Boxes of London, where they were supposed to go all along.

REF.: *CBA*; Nicholls, *Crime Within the Square Mile.*

Haigh, John George (AKA: **The Acid-Bath Murderer, The Vampire Killer**), 1909-49, Brit., mur. In 1949, John George Haigh burst into the headlines of the British press as an inhuman monster who had been killing for profit for many years. Worse, according to his own statements, the mass murderer had dissolved his victims in acid after drinking their blood. Born in Stamford, Lincolnshire, England, on July 24, 1909, Haigh was raised with strict religious discipline. His parents were ardent members of the Plymouth Brethren, a severe religious sect for whom all manner of casual entertainment, movies, carnivals, musical shows, even the reading of magazines and newspapers, was sinful. A bright child, Haigh received a scholarship to the Wakefield Grammar School and then won another scholarship as a choirboy at Wakefield Cathedral. His life was governed by strict routines and he was allowed no freedom to enjoy the small entertainments shared by his peers.

Acid bath killer John George Haigh.

Haigh scratched for a living in his early twenties, usually working as a salesman. He was glib and somewhat flashy in his appearance, preferring loud ties and tight-fitting suits. He married Beatrice Hamer in 1934 but this marriage quickly collapsed after Haigh was arrested in November of that year for fraud. After serving a brief prison sentence, Haigh was released, and continued his illegal schemes, living hand to mouth through the 1930s and the war years. In 1937, Haigh was convicted of his second serious crime, attempting to obtain money by false pretenses and was given a four-year prison term. He was released in 1940. In 1943, Haigh managed to make enough money through his small-time schemes to take up residence at a highly reputable address, the Onslow Court Hotel in South Kensington where he occupied Room 404. The residents here were professional people and retired persons of some wealth. The other residents regarded Haigh as a congenial entrepreneurial businessman. However, he made few friends because he was a bit too gregarious and showy for the other residents' tastes.

In 1944, Haigh renewed his acquaintance with the McSwan family. In 1936, he had worked for W.D. McSwan as a secretary and chauffeur. The McSwans owned an arcade in an amusement center and had considerable means. At the time Haigh rented a small basement workroom at 79 Gloucester Road in Kensington where he devoted some time to his "inventions." He took the McSwan's one by one—first the son, Donald McSwan, on Sept. 9, 1944, then Mrs. and Mrs. W.D. McSwan the following year. When the McSwan couple expressed concern over their son's disappearance in 1944, Haigh was ready with a glib answer, explaining that their son had gone into hiding to avoid being drafted into the army, a not uncommon occurrence during the war. Haigh's murder system was simple; he invited the McSwan family members to see the place and there bludgeoned them to death. He destroyed their bodies by placing them in vats of acid and disposing of the remains by simply pouring the gooey residue onto the dirt surface of an open yard behind his workshop.

By forging McSwan's name on transfer deeds, Haigh was able to obtain the McSwan properties in Raynes Park, Wimbledon Park, and Beckenham, Kent, as well as £4,000 in cash. Endowed with considerable funds, Haigh tried to make a fortune through a betting system he had devised which he believed could predict regular winners at the dog track. When he lost, he turned again to murder for profit. This time his victims were Dr. Archibald Henderson and his wife Rosalie, well-to-do middle-aged retirees,

who, in August 1947, were advertising a house for sale. Haigh, though he had no money, answered the ad and began negotiating for the purchase of the Henderson house in Ladbroke Grove. He later explained that one of his business deals had fallen through, preventing him from purchasing the house immediately.

The amiable Hendersons struck up a friendship with the scheming Haigh. On Feb. 12, 1948, he drove Dr. Henderson to his workshop where he shot him in the head and disposed of the body by dumping it into a vat of sulfuric acid. He then returned to Mrs. Rosalie Henderson and told her that her husband had taken sick and needed her. She accompanied Haigh to his workshop where he killed and disposed of her body in the same manner. In both the McSwan and Henderson murders, Haigh duplicated his victims' handwriting and sent notes to their servants, relatives, and friends explaining that they had moved to Australia or some other distant place, mentioning that "Mr. Haigh" would settle their affairs. The profits from this double murder exceeded those in the McSwan killings. Haigh, through clever forgeries, sold off the Henderson house and car, and obtained more than £10,000 from their bank accounts. But, within a year, Haigh had gone through most of this money, losing heavily to an army of bookies.

Haigh as a choir boy.

By early 1949, Haigh was running out of money. He was overdrawn at the bank and the manager of the Onslow Court Hotel was pressing him for back rent. Desperate for money, Haigh was looking about for more victims when his needs were answered in the dining room of the Onslow Court Hotel. Sitting opposite Haigh in the hotel dining room was a wealthy, retired matron, Mrs. Henrietta Helen Olivia Robarts Durand-Deacon. The 69-year-old widow knew that Haigh was then in the business of leasing and renting expensive cars to rich patrons and believed that, as a salesman, he might be interested in promoting an idea she had about manufacturing plastic fingernails.

Haigh responded warmly to the idea and immediately suggested that Mrs. Durand-Deacon discuss the proposition further in his workshop. On Feb. 18, 1949, Mrs. Durand-Deacon accompanied Haigh to the Gloucester address. As soon as she entered the basement workshop, Haigh shot the woman in the back of the head, killing her instantly. He stripped her and then dumped her body into a 40-gallon vat of sulfuric acid. Haigh drained the vat through a basement sewer and then scraped the sludge from the vat and dumped this onto the dirt of the back yard. This was hard work and Haigh, according to his later statements, paused to go to the nearby Ye Olde Ancient Prior's Restaurant where he ate an egg on toast. He then returned to his workshop to "tidy up."

This killing produced little profit for the money-desperate Haigh. He sold Mrs. Durand-Deacon's Persian lamb coat and pawned her jewelry, obtaining only a few hundred pounds. He used this money to pay off his hotel bill and some other pressing expenses and then looked about for more victims. But Haigh had struck too close to home by killing the wealthy widow. To avoid being asked about the widow's disappearance, Haigh thought it clever that *he* make some inquiries about the missing woman. Haigh approached Mrs. Durand-Deacon's good friend, Mrs. Constance Lane, another retired lady living at Onslow Court, plying her with questions: "Do you know anything about Mrs. Durand-Deacon? Is she ill? Do you know where she is?"

Mrs. Lane shocked Haigh with her response: "Don't *you* know where she is? I understood from her that you wanted to take her to your factory."

Haigh said that he had not taken the widow with him to his factory, that he was not ready to show her his operation. "Well, I must do something about that," Mrs. Lane said.

The following morning, Haigh again asked Mrs. Lane if she had heard anything about Mrs. Durand-Deacon and she said that she had not, adding that she intended to report the matter to the police that day. In an attempt to avoid suspicion, Haigh then offered to go to the Chelsea Police Station and report the matter with her. But when Mrs. Lane and Haigh appeared in the police station, an officer recognized Haigh and had his background checked. His criminal record made the police suspicious and Haigh was brought in for questioning on Feb. 28, 1949. At first, he denied having had anything to do with the missing Mrs. Durand-Deacon but the police kept grilling him and finally Haigh blurted: "Mrs. Durand-Deacon no longer exists! I've destroyed her with acid...You can't prove murder without a body."

But Haigh was wrong. Police searching his workshop uncovered enough gruesome remains of Mrs. Durand-Deacon to make an identification. Though most of her remains had been reduced to hardened sludge that coated the back yard behind Haigh's workshop, forensic investigators unearthed twenty-eight pounds of body fat, false teeth which were identified as Mrs. Durand-Deacon's, a pelvis, an ankle, gallstones, and a red handbag found in the workshop beneath the acid vat. Haigh had been sloppy in his workshop, as well as in his room at Onslow Court. Here investigators found his diary in which he had kept abbreviated details of his previous murders. Some personal effects from the McSwan and Henderson families were also unearthed.

Haigh was charged with murdering Mrs. Durand-Deacon and placed on trial on July 18, 1949. Prior to this, while being held, Haigh had asked his jailors how hard it was to escape from Broadmoor, the prison where criminally insane persons were sent. Haigh then tried to convince everyone that he was insane. He stated that "in each case I had my glass of blood after I killed them." He then went on to describe in detail all sorts of ghoulish acts performed on his victims, before giving their bodies acid baths. The press, when learning of Haigh's statements, had a field day. No newspaper gave the story more sensational coverage than the London *Daily Mirror,* which, on Mar. 4, 1949, bleated to its fifteen million readers that "the Vampire killer will never strike again. He is safely behind bars, powerless to lure his victims to a hideous death." Above this front-page story, the tabloid emblazoned the headline: "Vampire—A Man Held."

The British courts were appalled at this coverage, so much so that the *Daily Mirror* was fined £10,000 and its editor, Silvester Bolam, was given a three-month jail term for contempt of court, the paper having been previously warned by Scotland Yard not to publish details of the case before Haigh's trial. Bolam, ironically, was placed in the same prison that held Haigh. The mass killer continued to feign insanity while in prison, purposely drinking his own urine in front of guards and performing other irrational acts to convince them that he was a lunatic.

Haigh was tried before Justice Travers Humphreys with Sir Henry Shawcross prosecuting. Sir David Maxwell defended, but he could do little more than plead his client insane. He brought Dr. Henry Yellowlees, a noted psychiatrist, to the stand to testify that he had examined Haigh and believed him to be a "paranoic," because of his early childhood and that he was "pretty certain" that Haigh drank the blood of his victims.

None of this impressed the jury. It took only fifteen minutes for the jury to render a verdict of Guilty. He was sentenced to death. While awaiting execution, Haigh penned his brief, nightmare-filled memoirs, recounting how all his boyhood pleasures had been suppressed by his father, a religious fanatic. His father, an electrician, had had an accident which caused him to bear a blue scar down the middle of his forehead. Haigh quoted his father as telling him when he was a boy: "I have sinned and Satan has

punished me. If you ever sin, Satan will mark you with a blue pencil likewise." For years, Haigh, as a child, nervously ran his fingers over his forehead, frantically looking into mirrors each morning to see if a blue scar had appeared while he had slept.

Haigh also related a recurring nightmare he had following a 1944 car accident when he was injured and blood ran down his forehead and into his mouth, the year in which he began his murders: "I saw before me a forest of crucifixes which gradually turned into trees. At first there appeared to be dew or rain dripping from the branches, but as I approached I realized it was blood...A man went to each tree catching the blood. When the cup was full he approached me. 'Drink,' he said, but I was unable to move."

Crowd outside Wandsworth Prison, waiting to read Haigh's death notice, Aug. 6, 1949.

These horrifying words were penned by a man who undoubtedly still thought he might be reprieved and sent to Broadmoor as criminally insane. Haigh was highly intelligent and able to contrive such lunatic images for his own ends, just as he very probably researched the methods he used in disposing of his victims' bodies, most likely reading about the exploits of George Sarret of France who used similar methods in 1925 to eliminate the bodies of his victims. Haigh's horror stories did him no good in the end. He was hanged at Wandsworth Prison on Aug. 6, 1949. See: **Sarret, George.**

REF.: Bailey, *The Fatal Chance;* Boar, *The World's Most Infamous Murders;* Brophy, *The Meaning of Murder;* Browne, *Sir Travers Humphreys;* Butler, *The Trial of John George Haigh;* Byrne, *John George Haigh: Acid Bath Killer; CBA;* Cuthbert, *Science and the Detection of Crime;* Dickson, *Murder By Numbers;* Fairlie, *The Reluctant Cop;* Firmin, *Murderers in Our Midst;* Gribble, *Famous Manhunts;* Harrison, *Criminal Calendar;* Heppenstall, *The Sex War and Others;* Hibbert, *The Roots of Evil;* Humphreys, *A Book of Trials;* Jackson, *John George Haigh;* _____ , *The Life and Cases of Mr. Justice Humphreys;* Knowles, *Court of Drama;* Labern, *Haigh: The Mind of the Murderer;* Lefebure, *Murder with a Difference: Studies of Haigh and Christie;* Lustgarten, *The Business of Murder;* Masters, *Perverse Crimes in History;* McCafferty, *Mac, I've Got a Murder;* Morland, *Hangman's Clutch;* Nash, *Almanac of World Crime;* _____ , *The Innovators;* Neustatter, *The Mind of the Murderer; Notable British Trials;* Phillips, *Murderer's Moon;* Robey, *The Jester and the Court;* Sanders, *Murder Behind the Bright Lights;* Scott, *The Concise Encyclopedia of Crime and Criminals;* _____ , *Scotland Yard;* Shew, *A Companion to Murder;* Simpson, *Forty Years of Murder;* Tullett, *Strictly Murder;* Webb, *Crime Is My Business;* Whitehead, *Journey Into Crime;* Wilson, *Encyclopedia of Murder.*

Haight, Edward, 1925-43, U.S., kid.-rape-mur. "No reason I can think of," said Edward Haight when asked why he raped and murdered 7-year-old Margaret Lynch and her 8-year-old sister,

Helen. Haight, however, did have a mission on Sept. 14, 1942—to find a victim, any victim, as he drove through the streets of Westchester County, N.Y., in his station wagon.

Haight began the morning of Sept. 14 by following Mrs. Elrich Davies in her car once she had dropped off her husband at the Stamford, Conn., train station. Haight ran her off the road and was about to demand that she come with him but was frightened off by her dog, a large boxer.

At 6 p.m., after a day of terrorizing women, Haight asked directions from 18-year-old Doris Ledwin, who was walking alone down a street in Bedford Hills, N.Y. She said she did not know how to get to New Castle and refused to get into his car, so Haight winked, smiled, cruised past her several times, and drove off. Just then seven-year-old Margaret and eight-year-old Helen Lynch were on their way home from a friend's house. They walked the route often and just as often met their father on his way home from work, so they were preoccupied with watching for his car when the station wagon pulled up beside them.

When Margaret and Helen were not home by 6:45 p.m., their father started searching, notifying authorities as soon as he heard that the girls had gotten into a strange car. After an all-night search conducted by police and federal agents and joined by the citizens of Bedford Village, N.Y., Margaret's body was found on the banks of Beaver Dam Brook. Badly beaten and mutilated, her legs tied together and her wrists severely bruised, Margaret had been conscious when Haight threw her from the bridge fifty feet upstream and had died only after fracturing her skull on a rock and drowning in the creek.

Early the next morning, Helen's body was found floating in Kensico Reservoir, south of Armonk. Like her sister, Helen had been sexually assaulted, beaten, and mutilated with a knife. Finding a stolen station wagon abandoned less than a mile from Haight's home in Stamford, Conn., Westchester County police apprehended the 17-year-old in connection with the gruesome slayings of the two children. Haight had earlier bragged to friends about engaging police in an auto chase the night before, and he immediately confessed to killing the two girls.

Throughout the trial, Haight, having pleaded insanity, sat giggling, snickering, and smirking at the prosecution as the evidence against him mounted. Only once did his attitude change—when the jury reached the verdict of Guilty. Presiding Judge Frank H. Coyne sentenced Haight to two death sentences, to be carried out in the electric chair at Sing Sing Prison. During the sentencing, however, Haight's father, who had served time at Sing Sing for burglary, stood outside the courtroom, unable to bear hearing the inevitable.

On July 8, 1943, Edward Haight, at seventeen, became the youngest person to die in New York State's electric chair. Haight was silent as he was strapped into the chair at 11:06 a.m.; four minutes later he was pronounced dead. REF.: *CBA*.

Haigler, Keith, and **Haigler, Kate**, d.1982, U.S., hijack-suic. Believing that the local television stations in and around Springfield, Mo., had slighted their "prophet" Emory Lamb, two religious fanatics commandeered a Continental Trailways Bus bound from Little Rock, Ark., to Wichita, Kan., on July 3, 1982.

Keith Haigler and his wife Kate Haigler ordered the driver of the bus to stop his vehicle on a bridge that spanned the Little Buffalo River. At gunpoint, the driver was told to notify the police of their demands, which included an interview with Jim Caldwell, news director at KYTV in Springfield. Unless the demands were met, one hostage would be killed every half-hour. Fourteen hostages sweated out the two-and-a-half-hour ordeal before a camera crew arrived on the scene.

The Haiglers criticized the media for not giving proper attention to their "messiah" Emory Lamb, known locally as Fou-Fou, meaning Fountain of Ubiquity. Two hours after the hostages were released, Kate shot her husband fatally in the face before turning the gun on herself rather than surrender to local authorities. REF.: *CBA*.

Haines, Charles, prom. 1896, U.S., asslt. John Johnson ran a gambling house in the old Custom House Levee of Chicago just before the turn of the century. Known as the "King of the Colored Gamblers" Johnson was a well-known sportsman in the black community. Charles Haines, an itinerant gambler and employee of one of the passenger railroad lines, considered him in somewhat different terms.

On Mar. 17, 1896, Haines returned to the gambling den to retrieve a pistol he had left behind. Believing that he had been cheated out of his winnings the night before in a rigged crap game, he shot the gambler-boss in the chest. When some black men outside the place saw what he had done, there were cries of "Hang him!"

Johnson did not die, however. Because of the efforts of Dr. Nicholas Senn, one of the esteemed physicians of his time, Johnson survived the attack. Haines, meanwhile was arraigned on May 18, 1896, on a charge of assault with intent to kill. He was convicted and sent to the penitentiary.
REF.: *CBA;* Wooldridge, *Hands Up.*

Haines, Ernest, prom. 1917, U.S., (wrong. convict.) mur. The case of Ernest Haines, a teenager of sub-normal intellect, became a rallying cry among the foes of capital punishment in the state of Pennsylvania. If WWI had not intervened, the death penalty would probably have been abolished.

Haines, along with his friend Henry Ward Mottern, sixteen, was convicted of the Aug. 2, 1916, murder of his father. There was no hard evidence linking Haines with his father's death, only the testimony of Mottern, who did not suffer the same defects of mind. Mottern's statements were later deemed reversible error by the state supreme court because he discussed a burglary allegedly planned months earlier.

Haines was granted a new trial that resulted in his acquittal. Mottern, who had pleaded guilty before, could not be granted a second trial under Pennsylvania law. Instead, the Board of Pardons commuted his sentence to life imprisonment on Jan. 1, 1918, after several earlier unsuccessful attempts. The publicity of this trial led to new demands to end capital punishment, but the issue soon died when war was declared.
REF.: Bye, *Capital Punishment in the U.S.; CBA.*

Haines, Thomas Harvey, b.1871, U.S., psychiatrist. Developed tests for the blind and examinations to evaluate criminal and mental deficiencies. REF.: *CBA*.

Haitian Death Squads, prom. 1988, Haiti, mur. A campaign of armed terror was waged on the island nation of Haiti in 1988, when Lieutenant General Henri Namphy, leader of the military junta, organized army death squads to halt the spread of democracy and free elections. According to U.S. Embassy personnel, Namphy reactivated the long dormant Tontons Macoute, a para-militaristic strike force employed by deposed ruler Eric Duvalier to stave off the impending national election. Successful in this endeavor, the Namphy government promised to run its own elections. REF.: *CBA*.

Hake, Edward, prom. c.1579, Brit., writer. Wrote *Newes out of Powles Churcheyarde,* a satirical publication addressing corruption of doctors, druggists, judges, and clergy. REF.: *CBA*.

Hakim, al- (**Abu Ali al-Mansur al-Hakim, AKA: The Mad Caliph**), c.985-1021, Egypt, polit. corr.-her. Caliph who reigned from c.996-1021, during which time he placed restrictions on non-Muslims, passed arbitrary laws, and destroyed Christian churches. He proclaimed that he was the incarnation of the Deity, and many missionaries of the new Druze sect considered him divine. REF.: *CBA*.

Halabja Massacre, 1988, Iraq, war crimes. Six fact-finding missions, sponsored by the United Nations, determined that Iraq was guilty between 1984 and 1988 of violating the 1925 Geneva Protocol which outlawed the use of chemical warfare between nations. A total of 105 countries had endorsed the agreement over the years, but in its ongoing war with Iran, the Iraqis frequently employed deadly nerve gasses, and cyanide to halt the advance of enemy troops.

In March 1988, the occupied village of Halabja in eastern Iraq was bombed by its own air force with chemical weapons, including mustard gas and cyanide. More than 4,000 civilians were killed or severely wounded. The devastation was widespread, and may have been prompted by the Iraqi government's desire to do something about the large and rebellious Kurdish population which had made Halabja a hotbed of political dissent. Iraq at first denied responsibility, but admitted in July 1988 to using "the silent killer" in its continuing war with Iran. REF.: *CBA*.

Halberstan, Dr. Michael, See: **Welch, Bernard Charles, Jr.**

Halbert, Henry, 1735-65, U.S., mur. After a long criminal career which began when he was a teenager, Henry Halbert, a native of Philadelphia, inexplicably attacked a boy, Jacob Woolman, and slit his throat in the plain sight of many witnesses. He gave no reason for this atrocious crime and was quickly condemned. On the day of his hanging in Philadelphia, Oct. 19, 1765, Halbert, encouraged by several preachers standing next to him on the scaffold, loudly announced to a large crowd that he had led a sinful life and was guilty of "drinking, whoring, cursing, swearing, breaking the Sabbath, and keeping all manner of debauched company." After these admissions, Halbert was promptly hanged.

REF.: *CBA; The Last Speech and Confession of Henry Halbert;* Nash, *Bloodletters and Badmen.*

Halbert, Sherrill, b.1901, U.S., jur. Chief deputy district attorney for Tulare County, Calif., from 1927-36, and deputy attorney general for California in 1942. In Stanislaus County, Calif., he served as chief deputy district attorney from 1944-49, and as district attorney in 1949. He was judge of the supreme court for the state of California from 1949-1954, and nominated to the eastern district court of California by President Dwight D. Eisenhower in 1954. REF.: *CBA*.

Hale, Kenneth B., 1920- , U.S., law enfor. off. Following his graduation from Michigan State University in 1941, Kenneth Hale joined the U.S. Secret Service where he served as a special agent until his retirement in June 1971. He was appointed chief of police of Indianapolis on Mar. 15, 1974, a position he held until Dec. 31, 1975, when he was succeeded by Eugene Gallagher. REF.: *CBA*.

Hale, Sir Matthew, 1609-76, Brit., witchcraft-jur. Chief Justice Matthew Hale presided over the trial of the Bury St. Edmunds witches in 1662, a landmark case that greatly influenced the judges who heard the evidence of witchcraft in Salem, Mass., nearly thirty years later. Sir Matthew's conduct in the Bury St. Edmunds case was prejudicial. A staunch believer in witchcraft, he admitted the hearsay testimony of 5- and 7-year-olds despite the clear evidence of fraud. Described as the "most profound lawyer of his time," Hale often directed juries based on his own prejudices.

So notorious was he during witchcraft cases, that his biographer, Bishop Gilbert Burnet, felt compelled to omit the details of the case from his book. See: **Bury St. Edmunds Witches.**

REF.: *CBA;* Hale, *Pleas of the Crown;* Robbins, *The Encyclopedia of Witchcraft and Demonology;* Summers, *The Geography of Witchcraft; A Trial of Witches at the Assizes of Bury St. Edmunds.*

Haley, Carl, d.1950, U.S., suic.-mur. On Aug. 3, 1950, Carl Haley shot and killed his wife in the Bear River Valley of Kentucky as she was on her way to vote in a local election. While horrified family members looked on, Haley turned the shotgun on himself. He had been hiding in a thicket of bushes waiting for his wife. The motive for the tragedy seemed to be tied to deteriorating domestic relations between the couple.

REF: *CBA;* Montell, *Killings.*

Haliburton, Thomas Chandler, 1796-1865, Can., jur. Judge of the Supreme Court of Nova Scotia from 1842-56, and member of Parliament in Britain from 1859-65. He wrote *The Old Judge, or Life in a Colony* in 1843. He also invented the newspaper serial character Sam Slick, who appeared in *The Clockmaker, or Sayings and Doings of Sam Slick* in 1837, 1838, and 1840, and *The Attaché, or Sam Slick in England* from 1843-44. REF.: *CBA*.

Halidé Edib Adivar, 1883-1964, Turk., treas. Backed Young Turks in 1909, and member of Nationalist party in 1919. She participated in the war with Greece as a supporter of Mustafa Kemal Atatürk, but was exiled from 1925-38 on the suspicion of working against him. She returned to Istanbul as a professor, and was a member of Parliament from 1950-54. REF.: *CBA*.

Halim Pasa, Said, 1863-1921, Turk., polit., assass. Served as grand vizier from 1913-16, and signed an alliance treaty with Germany in 1914. He served as senator from 1916-18, before being banished by the British to Malta, and subsequently assassinated. REF.: *CBA*.

Hall, Abraham Oakey, 1826-98, Case of, U.S., polit. corr. District Attorney of New York from 1855-58, and from 1862-68, and became a member of Tammany Hall in 1864. He was the mayor of New York from 1868-72 during the looting of the city by the Tweed Ring. He was tried for corruption, but was acquitted in 1872. REF.: *CBA*.

Hall, Andreas, d.1848, U.S., rob.-mur. A professional thief, Andreas Hall, a resident of Troy, N.Y., learned that an elderly couple, Noah and Amy Smith, kept considerable cash in their home. He invaded the Smith residence on the night of July 1, 1848. When the Smith couple awoke, Hall bashed their skulls with a club and then cut their throats. He ransacked the house and found $1,200 which he took with him when he fled. After police found the bodies, neighbors identified Hall as a man who had been making inquiries about the old couple, asking questions about the money they might have hoarded. Hall was apprehended and he quickly confessed. He was tried and hanged at Petersburgh, N.Y.

REF.: Baldwin, *Awful Disclosures!, The Life and Confession of Andreas Hall; CBA; Trial of Andreas Hall.*

Hall, Archibald (AKA: **Ray Fontaine**), 1924- , and **Kitto, Michael,** 1938- , Brit., fraud-rob.-mur. For most of his life, Archibald Hall concentrated on "trimming" the rich and wellborn of Britain through his easy, persuasive manner. Rather late in the game, the Glasgow-born jewel thief turned to murder before going to prison for the final time.

Hall was jailed for the first time in 1941 for theft. Two years later, he returned to prison on a charge of house-breaking. A psychiatrist concluded that he was mentally unstable and unfit for society. He was sent to an institution, but was soon back on the streets to resume his crimes.

In 1951, Hall secured the first of several jobs as a butler to wealthy Englishmen. In 1977, while employed by Lady Hudson, Hall committed his first murder. He shot David Wright, an ex-convict who was working on the grounds at the time. The corpse was hastily buried under a pile of stones, and remained undetected until Hall was implicated in the murders of his new employers, Walter Travers Scott-Elliott and his wife Dorothy.

The aging Scott-Elliott, a former member of Parliament, respected Hall and was pleased with his work. In December 1977, Hall rewarded his employer's confidence by conspiring with Michael Kitto and his former girlfriend Mary Coggle to rob the old gentleman. On the night of the Dec. 8, Hall and Kitto returned to Scott-Elliott's home where they smothered the old man's wife. The next day, they took Scott-Elliott to a lonely spot on the road near Glen-Affric, where Hall and his two confederates bludgeoned him to death. The elderly couple were buried in shallow graves. The gang members then quarreled over how to divide the loot.

Hall murdered Mary Coggle when she insisted on keeping the old lady's mink coat. Then he turned on his younger brother Donald, who had just joined the group after his release from prison, where he served time for sexual assault. The Hall brothers were never very close, and Archibald resented Donald's meddling in a crime in which he was not invited to participate. On Jan. 15, 1978, a hotel keeper at the Blenheim House in North Berwick became suspicious about two men who were traveling light. The police checked the license plate on their Ford Granada and found that it had been switched with another car.

Hall and Kitto were arrested in the hotel dining room as they finished their brandy. Eventually, the bodies of Donald Hall and

Mary Coggle were found and identified. Hall was sentenced to life in prison; Kitto received fifteen years. REF.: *CBA*.

Hall, Augustus Caesar, 1814-61, U.S., jur. Assistant U.S. marshal for Ohio in Washington, D.C., in 1839, and the prosecuting attorney of Union County, Ohio from 1840-42. He was a member of the U.S. House of Representatives from 1855-57, and was nominated to the northeast territorial court by President James Buchanan in 1857. He was also a delegate to the Northeast Constitutional Convention in 1860. REF.: *CBA*.

Hall, Ben, 1837-65, Aus., rob.-mur. The son of an Australian farmer, Ben Hall joined Frank Gardiner's gang of bushrangers in 1862. In his brief but exciting three-year career in crime, Hall was somewhat of a folk hero to many Australians who read about his exploits in the newspapers. In 1863 his gang took over the town of Canowindra, and opened the saloons and stores to the townspeople during a wild three-day spree. This Robin Hood of the Outback rarely turned his guns on innocent citizens, and would often leave his robbery victims with a small amount of cash so they could return home.

In a two-year period commencing in 1863, Hall robbed ten mail wagons and stole twenty-three racehorses. In 1865, the Hall gang turned to murder after they attacked the home of Henry Keightley, an assistant gold commissioner. Keightley shot and killed one of the gang members, which so enraged Hall that he declared a private war against all law enforcement officers. After the gang killed two policemen, the Australian government enacted the ancient Outlawry Act, a relic of medieval times, against the Hall gang.

The game ended for Hall on May 6, 1865, when his former sidekick, "Coobong" Mick Connolly, betrayed him to the police. Hall was ambushed and riddled with bullets near Billabong Creek. REF.: *CBA*.

Hall, Carl Austin, 1916-53, and **Heady, Bonnie Brown**, 1912-53, U.S., kid.-mur. The son of a wealthy St. Louis lawyer, Carl Austin Hall was a pampered son who never had to work for a living. His father died in 1946 and left Hall more than $200,000. Through wild drinking and drug addiction, Hall quickly squandered his fortune. To obtain more funds to feed his drug habit, Hall began to rob taxicabs. His clumsy robberies soon brought police to his door and he was given a five-year term in the Missouri State Prison. Hall served sixteen months and was released on Apr. 24, 1953. He immediately began planning the kidnapping and murder of a small child, the 6-year-old son of one of the wealthiest men in Kansas City, Mo., Robert Greenlease, a 71-year-old car dealer.

When Hall stepped from prison he was greeted by a woman who had never met him before, a plump, 41-year-old widow with a porcine appearance. She embraced Hall and kissed him passionately on the mouth, then introduced herself. She was Bonnie Brown Heady, who had been a gun moll in 1935 when she was married to bank robber Dan Heady who was imprisoned and then broke prison only to be shot down by a sheriff's posse while trying to reach his 23-year-old red-headed wife, Bonnie. When Mrs. Heady was told that her husband had been shot to death, she crinkled a crooked grin and said out of the side of her mouth: "That's too bad." Bonnie Heady was as addicted to criminal types as Carl Austin Hall was addicted to heroin. She had heard about Hall from ex-prisoners and became intrigued by the playboy crook. She took him to her home in St. Joseph, Mo.

Bonnie Heady was an alcoholic and drank most of her waking days. Hall either drank himself into stupors with her or mainlined heroin and was in a drugged state. When the couple were sober they worked out the details of the Greenlease kidnapping which Hall had been planning in prison. The idea of committing an atrocious crime excited the jaded Bonnie who listened to Hall's kidnapping and murder plan and then squealed: "Why, that's better than sex!" She readily agreed to take part in the atrocious crime. The night before the kidnapping, Hall and Heady, in a downpour, put on boots and took a shovel into Mrs. Heady's yard. There they dug out a small, shallow grave, one in which they intended to bury the body of the child they would kidnap the following day. After completing this ghoulish chore, the couple celebrated by getting drunk.

The next morning, Sept. 28, 1952, at 10:55, Bonnie Heady appeared at entrance of the French Institute of Notre Dame de Scion, an exclusive pre-grade school in Kansas City. She rang the front door bell which was answered by Sister Morand. She sobbingly told the nun that she was the sister of Bobby Greenlease's mother who had suffered a heart attack and was in St. Mary's Hospital. Mrs. Greenlease was calling for her son, Bonnie said, and she had come to fetch him.

Sister Morand asked Mrs. Heady to wait in the chapel and she returned with a small blonde-haired boy in a few minutes. Bonnie Heady was in a pew, on her knees. She got up and said to Sister Morand: "I have been praying for my sister's quick recovery. I am not a Catholic and I don't know whether or not God heard my prayers." This show of devotion further assured the nun that Bonnie Heady was who she said she was. Bobby Greenlease did not react to Mrs. Heady, and, even though she was a total stranger to him, he went along with her without a word of protest.

Mrs. Heady took the boy to the curb where she had a cab waiting. The cab took her and Bobby to Main and 40th streets where the woman got out, and holding the boy by the hand, walked across the street to a waiting 1947 Plymouth station wagon. The cab driver thought he recognized the driver, a balding man with drooping eyelids and a receding chin, who appeared to be half-asleep. Mrs. Heady and the little boy got into the station wagon and it drove away slowly, going toward Highway 169, south out of Kansas City.

About this time, Sister Morand realized her awful error. She called St. Mary's Hospital just after Bobby and the woman left the school, and learned to her horror that Mrs. Greenlease was not a patient. Then she called the Greenlease home and found Bobby's mother was well and at home. The nun told the story of how the woman had picked up Bobby. The Greenleases instantly realized their son had been kidnapped, and a ransom letter arriving the next morning proved it. The ransom note demanded that $600,000 be collected in ten- and twenty-dollar bills. The kidnappers ordered the Greenleases to place an ad in the Kansas City *Star* when the money was ready for delivery. The note assured the nervous parents that their child was "in good hands." Bobby Greenlease was by then dead. Carl Austin Hall had taken him for a ride with Heady and then dragged him out of his station wagon and fired three bullets into his head. Heady and Hall then wrapped the little body in a blanket and returned to her St. Joseph house where they buried the body on the night of the kidnapping.

When news of the kidnapping spread about the world, lawmen and the public alike were shocked. There had not been a major kidnapping in the U.S. since the racket-busting days of the 1930s, when the FBI had tracked down a number of vicious kidnappers. The Bureau, still hampered from acting immediately, could not enter the case for seven days under provisions in the 1932 Lindbergh Kidnapping Law. The law stated that after seven days, if the kidnap victim was not recovered, authorities could presume that the kidnappers had taken the victim across a state line and thus broken a federal law. The Bureau, despite inclinations of its agents to act promptly, waited. (Because of the tragic outcome of this case, the kidnapping law was later changed to allow federal agents to act immediately in any kidnapping.) The local police also waited at the insistence of the Greenleases, who still believed that no one would really harm an innocent little boy.

The kidnappers, however, dragged out negotiations for the ransom delivery for several weeks. Hall made more than a dozen calls to the Greenleases, ambiguously setting up arrangements for the delivery of the money and then altering the plans. He mailed sixteen ransom kidnap notes to the Greenleases, all contradictory and confusing. He was thinking with a liquor-clotted brain. He kept promising to delivery little Bobby "alive and well" in various parts of Kansas. At one point, the money was delivered, eighty-five pounds of it, stuffed into a duffel bag and thrown into high grass off a country lane. Hall arrived at the spot, but he was so drunk he could not find the duffel bag. He called the Greenleases and told them to retrieve the money and take it to a bridge near Junction 10E and Highway 40. This was done and Hall obtained the duffel bag. He called the Greenleases and again brutally lied, saying to a family friend: "You can tell his mother that she will see him in twenty-four hours. We will certainly be very glad to send him back."

The murdering kidnappers bought two large metal suitcases and dumped a total of about $300,000 into both, according to later statements. They reportedly buried these in an ash pit somewhere in south St. Louis. With about $300,000 the pair then fled to St. Louis where they got roaring drunk and spent lavishly, drawing attention to themselves. The pair then went to a cheap hotel room where Bonnie Heady passed out. As soon as she fell unconscious on the bed, Hall grabbed the suitcase, left $2,000 in his paramour's purse, and deserted her. He did not leave town, but merely went to the expensive Congress Hotel where he bought the favors of a young whore and then began to tip so lavishly that he drew the suspicions of hotel employees. One of these, alerted by the news coverage of the recent kidnapping in Kansas City and the enormous ransom paid—the largest ransom paid up to that time in U.S. history—called St. Louis police and reported that "a man is spending big money around the Congress Hotel and he doesn't look the part."

St. Louis Police lieutenant Louis Shoulders and patrolman Elmer Dolan went to investigate. They found Hall nurturing a terrible hangover in his room at the Congress Hotel. Inside his bags, according to Shoulders, the two officers found more than $250,000 and a .38-caliber snub-nosed revolver with three cartridges fired. Hall was taken in for questioning. Some hours later, police picked up Heady. Both were grilled until dawn. FBI agents went to Heady's home and here the body of Bobby Greenlease was found. They sadly informed the shocked parents. The callous killers then began to talk. Heady at first insisted that she did not know that she was part of a kidnapping. She said she thought Hall was the former husband of Mrs. Greenlease and that she was merely trying to help him obtain his son who had been kept from him. This story quickly evaporated when FBI men and local police confronted her with the real facts that proved she and Hall had been together since his prison release.

Hall and Heady then admitted the kidnapping, but loudly denied having killed the child. Hall place the blame on an ex-convict, Thomas John Marsh, a man he had known in prison. This, too, was another fabrication. Later, both suspects admitted killing the boy. They expressed regret to the parents, writing the Greenleases and begging for forgiveness. The two were tried on Nov. 16, 1953, and the jury quickly found them Guilty of kidnapping and murder on Nov. 19, 1953. The jury also recommended that both these callous killers be sent to the gas chamber. They were sentenced to death. Sneered Bonnie Heady: "I'd rather be dead than poor!" When the sentence was announced, the gallery in the courtroom exploded with thunderous applause. Said the elderly Robert Greenlease who had been sitting quietly in the courtroom throughout the trial: "It's too good for them, but it's the best the law provides."

Meanwhile, Hall no longer claimed that he buried half the ransom money. He insisted that all the $600,000 was in his hotel room when he was arrested, but only $250,000 was ever turned in by the two officers who arrested him. "That's a pack of lies," Lieutenant Shoulders said. Robert Greenlease said that he believed Hall was telling the truth about the money, saying: "With certain execution facing him, Hall has no reason to lie." The St. Louis Police also believed the condemned prisoner. Patrolman Dolan was suspended by the department, which announced that Shoulders would be charged with theft. The suitcases in Hall's room that contained the money, it was announced, were not delivered to police until an hour after Hall was booked. Shoulders was summoned before the St. Louis Board of Police Commissioners, but he was too ill to attend, a doctor stating that the lieuten-

ant was exhausted because of work and was in "too nervous a condition" to stand questioning.

The 55-year-old Shoulders, under great pressure, announced from his home that night: "The suitcases with the money were delivered to the police station at the same time as the prisoner. I can prove that the money I found in Hall's room was the same money I turned over to the FBI. Where that money is will come out at the right time, and when it does I know that Lou Shoulders will be in the clear." Shoulders later underwent a six-hour interrogation about the money. He then resigned from the St. Louis Police Department "to save the force further embarrassment," it was announced. Shoulders was not finished, however. He claimed that he was the victim of "character assassination."

Moreover, Shoulders said: "I got the kidnappers. I got the woman. I got the gun. I did not get the money." He wrote a letter of resignation which ended with: "After twenty-seven years as a police officer, to be castigated on the heels of performing my duty with the highest sense of responsibility is more than I can bear." Shoulders then packed his bags and flew to Hawaii to stay with his son, followed all the way to Honolulu by FBI agents who continued to keep an eye on him.

Hall and Heady, meanwhile, prepared to die. Heady would be the first woman executed in Missouri since 1834. She was permitted to visit her lover on the night of their execution and they dined together on their favorite meal, fried chicken. Heady sat outside of Hall's cell while he nervously gripped the bars. Bonnie Heady was clearly the strongest of the two, stroking his hands and patting his head, telling him that "everything is going to be all right." Hall had been terrified for days that he would be killed by inmates at the Missouri State Prison. Child killers, as the warden and guards knew, seldom survived in the general prison population. Fathers, brothers, sons, all with memories of children on the outside, hold these criminals in the greatest contempt and traditionally kill killers of women and, especially, children. For this reason, Hall was kept in a separate holding cell, away from the other prisoners.

The execution of these two killers attracted great attention. The warden of the prison originally announced that Hall and Heady would enter the gas chamber in bathing suits and the local newspapers had their artists draw Hall in swimming trunks and Heady in a two-piece swimming suit. This brought down the wrath of womens' groups who called this "unseemly and indecent." The warden changed his mind and ordered that Hall was to die wearing green denim slacks. Heady would wear a green denim dress. About a half hour before they were to die, the warden allowed the pair to be alone together in a cell, undisturbed and without supervision. When Hall stepped from the cell, lipstick was smeared on his mouth and neck.

Blindfolds were then placed on the condemned pair and they were led to the gas chamber. Heady's chief concern at the moment of her death was how she would appear before those witnessing her death. She had put her hair in curlers early that morning and spent several hours combing her hair and fixing her face. She was led trembling to a metal chair only inches from where Hall sat in the gas chamber. She turned her blindfolded face to the warden and said: "Thanks for everything. You've been very kind." Then she turned to her partner in cold-blooded murder and said to Hall: "Are you all right, honey?"

Hall replied in a dull, resigned voice: "Yes, Momma."

A U.S. marshal leaned close to Hall, still trying to determine the whereabouts of the missing $300,000, asking the killer: "Have you anything to tell me." Both Hall and Heady said nothing. The doors to the chamber were closed and witnesses could see through the glass of the chamber that Heady and Hall were talking quickly to each other, but none of their last words could be heard. The cyanide pellets were dropped in the small vats of sulfuric acid beneath the chairs in which the killers sat. Hall breathed deep, swallowed once, and died. Bonnie Brown Heady fought death to the last second, holding her breath until the fumes surrounded her and she had to take a breath, her last.

Above, Bobby Greenlease, Jr., the 6-year-old son of wealthy Robert Greenlease who owned a Cadillac dealership in Kansas City, Kan., who was kidnapped by Carl Austin Hall and his girlfriend Bonnie B. Heady on Sept. 28, 1953.

Below, police and officials digging behind the home of Bonnie Heady in St. Joseph, Mo., where they uncovered the body of Bobby Greenlease who had been shot to death by Hall and then wrapped in plastic; the killers had buried the little boy at night to avoid being seen by next-door neighbors.

Right, Bobby Greenlease only four days before he was kidnapped by Hall and Heady.

Middle right, Bonnie B. Heady and Carl Austin Hall, both hopeless alcoholics, blithely confessed to the kidnap-murder of Bobby Greenlease and indifferently faced their death sentences.

Bottom right, an artist's rendering of Hall and Heady as they sat side by side in their underwear, blindfolded, in Missouri's gas chamber, waiting for the lethal pellets to drop.

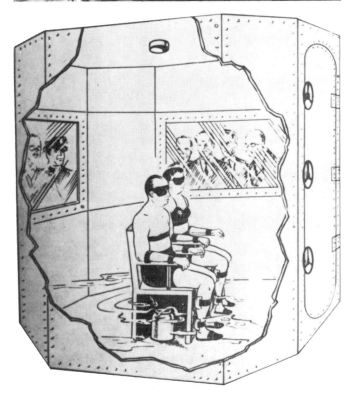

The story was still not over, however. The hunt for the money went on. Only a day after the execution of Hall and Heady, ex-patrolman Dolan was indicted for perjury by a federal grand jury, which declared he had given false evidence concerning the suitcases full of money found in Hall's hotel room. Then Shoulders was indicted and both men were placed on trial. After a prolonged court battle, both men were found Guilty of misappropriating the funds and perjuring themselves and sent to prison. Dolan was given a two-year sentence, Shoulders three years.

The Greenlease money never surfaced. Only a few of the marked bills appeared, some in Michigan, some in Mexico. Officers looked for it in Europe and South America, but no trace of it could be found. It was later concluded that the money had been sold at a cut-rate price, for about 25¢ on the dollar. In the hunt for this money, the press gave more coverage to its possible whereabouts than it rendered to the unsuspecting 6-year-old boy who paid for it with his unfulfilled, unlived life.

REF.: Alix, *Ransom Kidnapping in America; CBA;* Messick, *Kidnapping;* Nash, *Almanac of World Crime; _____, Look for the Woman; _____, Murder, America;* Playfair, *The Offenders;* Rowan, *Famous American Crimes;* Whitehead, *The FBI Story;* Wilson, *Encyclopedia of Murder.*

Hall, Charles Francis, 1820-71, Greenland, (unsolv.) mur. Charles Hall wanted nothing more out of life than to become the first man to discover the North Pole. He became obsessed with this goal after writing about the lost expedition of Sir John Franklin in the pages of the *Daily Penny Press,* published in Cincinnati. By 1870, Hall made several expeditions of his own, resulting in the discovery of Martin Frobisher's house on Kodlunarn Island, built nearly 300 years earlier. It was believed to have been the first permanent settlement of the Canadian Arctic by an Englishman.

With this impressive credential behind him, Congress authorized President Ulysses Grant to appoint Hall the leader of a polar expedition. With a team of research scientists on board, the 135-foot *Polaris* set sail from New London, Conn., on July 3, 1871. While relations between Hall and the German and Scandinavian crew were generally excellent, there existed personal and professional jealousy between Dr. Emil Bessels and the leader of the expedition.

By Aug. 30, the *Polaris* reached a shallow bay near the coast of Greenland, which Hall dubbed Thank God Harbor. With the approach of winter, it was decided to drop anchor and establish an observatory on land. After the first snows, Hall decided to set out and look for an overland route to the North Pole. Hall, the first mate, and two Eskimos left the campsite on Oct. 10, returning two weeks later satisfied with the results.

That night, Captain Hall complained of stomach cramps. In the next few days, his condition worsened until he slipped into delirium. The progression of his illness was assiduously reported in a private journal of George Tyson, the ship's navigator. On Nov. 3, Tyson recorded that Hall suspected treachery; someone, he charged, was trying to poison him. Suspicious of everyone, the captain refused medication. He died on Nov. 8, and was buried with honors above a thick layer of permafrost in a remote area of Greenland.

The mystery of whether Captain Hall had been poisoned or not intrigued future historians. In August 1968, the grave site was located by Professor Chauncey Loomis and a team of researchers from Dartmouth College. An autopsy on the remains was performed to determine if there was a presence of arsenic. Loomis concluded that Captain Hall was murdered. The arsenic content in the soil was high, but it was not distributed uniformly. The symptoms of arsenic poisoning that Hall had manifested before his death were not unlike that of similar cases. "In the strength of our analysis alone I would not be as certain as I am," he wrote, "if there had not been the symptoms." His findings were later published in a book titled *Weird and Tragic Shores: The Story of Charles Francis Hall, Explorer.* REF.: *CBA.*

Hall, Eddie and **Davis, Jim** (AKA: **Slim Jim**), and **Collins, Curly,** and **Dean, Dickie,** and **Murphy, Kid,** prom. 1887, U.S.,

fraud-asslt. Years before Captain Luke Colleran was appointed chief of detectives by Mayor Carter Harrison, he was assigned to the plain-clothes beat in Chicago's Loop.

On Dec. 2, 1887, Colleran was assaulted by five thieves and con-men who had attempted to swindle a produce farmer near the Randolph Street Haymarket. Just as Colleran prepared to pull the switch in the patrol box, which alerted the drivers of the "paddy wagon" to come and pick up prisoners, Curly Collins seized a piece of timber and struck the detective over the head. They tossed him over the side of a viaduct, and he bounced into a flat car. Colleran sustained severe injuries, but he survived this ordeal to earn various promotions, culminating in his appointment to head the detective department in 1897. The five gang members who attempted to kill him were sent to prison.

REF.: *CBA;* Wooldridge, *Hands Up.*

Hall, Edward Marshall, 1858-1927, Brit., jur. Defense lawyer who handled the murder cases of Jeannie Baxter, John Bennett, Madame Fahmy, Harold Greenwood, Frederick Rothwell Holt, Edward Lawrence, Frederick Henry Seddon, Alfonso Smith, Joseph Smith, and Lock Ah Tam. He and Sir Patrick Hastings prosecuted Jean Pierre Vaquier. He became a judge in 1898, and later served as a member of Parliament. REF.: *CBA.*

Hall, Edward Wheeler, See: Hall-Mills Case.

Hall, George Albert, 1906-54, Brit., mur. A little girl named Mary Hackett disappeared from her home in Halifax, Yorkshire, on Aug. 12, 1953. Scotland Yard was brought into the case when the local authorities had exhausted all their leads.

The girl's parents told officials that their daughter had gone to play just a few hundred feet from her home. Mary had simply vanished; but the detectives were reasonably certain that her murderer was in the immediate area. Across the road from the family home stood the Congregational church, with a maze of crypts and tunnels that had been constructed to protect the townspeople from air raids during WWII. The caretaker of the property, George Albert Hall, aroused the suspicion of Scotland Yard when he claimed to have heard voices emanating from the region of the crypt. After another day had passed, Hall explained that he had observed a stranger lurking on the grounds the day Mary Hackett disappeared.

Superintendent John Ball ordered a detail of police and firemen to dig out the church crypt. It was there, on Sept. 21, 1953, that Mary's body was found. She had been bludgeoned to death, and though Hall denied killing the girl, his testimony showed he knew that she had been battered before the police made this information public.

Hall was tried and found Guilty of murder. He was hanged at Leeds Prison in April 1954, protesting his innocence to the end.

REF.: *CBA;* Tullett, *Strictly Murder.*

Hall, Gordon Robert Castillo, 1962- , U.S., (wrong. convict.) mur. Gordon Hall, a 16-year-old Hispanic youth from Duarte, Calif., was accused of murdering Jessie Ortiz, twenty-seven, on Feb. 25, 1978, based on the eyewitness testimony of the victim's nephews, Victor Lara and Daniel Lara. Hall was sentenced to prison for life for a crime he did not commit.

At the urging of State Senator H.L. Richardson, the Los Angeles County Sheriff's office reopened the investigation. The two detectives who first worked on the case became convinced that Hall was innocent. Deputy District Attorney David Disco interviewed the two principle witnesses a second time. Under cross-examination, they said Hall was not the person they saw shoot their uncle.

On Dec. 17, 1981, the California Supreme Court overturned Hall's conviction. Murder charges were officially dismissed on Feb. 18, 1982, after Hall had spent nearly three years behind bars. REF.: *CBA.*

Hall, Jack (John), d.1707, Brit., rob. From his humble beginnings as a poor chimney sweep, Jack Hall became one of England's most notorious thieves. Hall began his career as a pickpocket and such was his skill that he once lifted a farmer's wallet and, a few hours later, replaced it in the unsuspecting man's pocket—minus most of the cash.

Despite his dexterity, Hall was often apprehended and suffered the usual punishments of the day—"ducking in the horse-pond" and repeated trips to Bridewell Prison. Graduating to shoplifting, Hall was convicted at the Old Bailey for stealing a pair of shoes and was "whipped at the cart's tail." No sooner was he free, however, than he took to housebreaking. In 1700, he was sentenced to hang for it, but was pardoned on condition that he sail for the American colonies. Hall boarded ship only to desert and return to England, taking up with his old accomplices and committing robberies.

One night, Hall, Stephen Bunce, and Dick Low broke into the house of Clare, the baker in the village of Hackney. After hog-tying Clare's journeyman and apprentice they threw them into the kneading trough. When the baker refused to say where he kept his money, Hall seized his 6-year-old granddaughter, swearing he would throw her into the oven if the old man did not produce the cash. "Damn me," Hall declared, "if (I) would not bake the child into a pie, and eat it, if the old rogue would not be civil." Clare quickly turned over his £80.

On Dec. 17, 1707, Hall, Low, and Bunce, were found Guilty of stealing "a considerable quantity of plate and other effects." All three were executed at Tyburn. See: **Bunce, Stephen; Low, Dick.**

REF.: *CBA;* Mitchell, *The Newgate Calendar;* Smith, *Highwaymen.*

Hall, James, d.1741, Brit., mur. Murdering and robbing his master of seven years seemed the perfect solution to James Hall's growing indebtedness, but Hall neglected to consider how he might reckon with his conscience in the aftermath.

An unremarkable, though educated, man from Wells in Somersetshire, Hall was destined for ordinariness. Not content with country life, however, he moved to London, married, had several children, divorced, then remarried and fathered another child. During this time he worked for and lived with gentleman John Penny in his chambers at Clement's Inn. Also during this time, Hall lived more and more beyond his means.

On June 7, 1741, Hall got drunk. He had to carry out his plan to murder and rob his master and thus get out of debt. When Penny came home at midnight, Hall helped him undress in the dining room and followed him into the bedroom. Then he struck him on the head with a large stick, over and over until he thought Penny was dead. Hall then stripped naked and with a small fruit knife cut Penny's throat. Before dumping the body in the outhouse, he collected five chamber pots of blood, which he poured down the sink.

Stealing thirty-six guineas from his master's pocket and writing desk, Hall, in his confusion, also took things of no use to him, like special delivery letters, and sealing wax. He spent the rest of the night trying to clean the blood-stained rooms and in the morning sent for the laundress to continue the work, telling her that Penny had had a nosebleed.

The next day, Hall wandered aimlessly. Some days later he went to Penny's nephew, Mr. Wooton, and asked for Penny, saying he feared some accident had occurred. When Wooton questioned him at length, however, Hall became agitated, which aroused Wooton's suspicions. Eventually, Wooton had Hall taken into custody on suspicion of murder. Hall at first maintained his innocence, but soon broke down and confessed.

The night before his execution he wrote to his wife, "I now heartily wish...that I was as innocent as you are, but freely own I am not." On Sept. 15, 1741, Hall was hanged at the end of Catherine Street, in the Strand.

REF.: Armitage, *Bow Street Runners; CBA;* Mitchell, *The Newgate Calendar;* Thomson, *The Story of Scotland Yard.*

Hall, James, 1793-1868, U.S., jur.-ct. mar. James Hall was court-martialed in 1817 and cashiered after getting into trouble with his superior officer. President James Monroe later cancelled his punishment and restored his rank. Hall went on to become an Illinois prosecuting attorney, noted for his vigorous efforts to rid a lawless nine-county region of its murderers, counterfeiters, and horse thieves. He later served as circuit judge. REF.: *CBA.*

Hall, James, 1954-   , U.S., (wrong. convict.) mur. James Hall claimed at the time of the murder, that he was in his dormitory room in Iowa City and had nothing to do with the strangulation death of nursing student Sarah Ann Ottens in March 1973.

Hall, a football star at the University of Iowa was eventually found Guilty of second degree murder and sentenced to a fifty-year term.

Appeals were brought to the U.S. Supreme Court, but the conviction was upheld and Hall went to jail. After serving nearly ten years for a crime he did not commit, a State District Court judge overturned Hall's original conviction in November 1983, declaring that he had not received a fair trial. The ruling resulted from the determined efforts of Hall's lawyer to secure the release of the previously withheld testimony from the County Attorney's office.

In May 1984, Judge L. Vern Robinson ruled that the grand jury indictment was not valid because of misconduct on the part of the prosecutor. The judge cited various racial slurs made against Hall, who was a black man. Evidence that implicated other suspects in the case had been withheld by Assistant Iowa Attorney General Garry D. Woodward who prosecuted the case, according to Robinson. On Sept. 1, 1984, a grand jury in Johnson County, Iowa, refused to return an indictment against Hall. After ten years in prison he was at last a free man. But as he pointed out, "Ten years of hell doesn't just go away." REF.: *CBA.*

Hall, James W., 1921-46, U.S., mur. "I guess I'll get the electric chair for this, but it don't matter. That would be better than life imprisonment," said James W. Hall, ruminating on his punishment for the murder of six people, five of them during a four-month period.

Not much mattered to the 24-year-old taxi driver from Enola, Ark., who laughed as he confessed to five of the murders, including that of his 19-year-old wife. When a detective asked if he had committed any other murders, Hall at first said no, but then, laughing again, said, "I killed a Negro woman in Salina, Kansas, when I was seventeen. That was seven years ago."

Described by his landlady in Little Rock as "a nice, clean boy who never smoked or drank or swore and who always paid his rent on time," Hall killed six people: Faye Clements Hall, his second wife; J.D. Newcomb, Jr., a state boiler inspector; Doyle Mulherin, a meat truck driver; E.C. Adams, a war plant worker; and an unidentified man and woman.

The son of a preacher farmer, Hall was drafted into the navy at nineteen, but discharged after six weeks for indifference. "I don't know what that means," Hall later complained to police once he had been apprehended. Pressed to explain himself, Hall spoke of the past, his ten brothers and sisters. "My early life was far from happy...My father was very strict," he said. Then, by way of explaining the murders, he tapped his head. "Something seemed to snap up here a long time ago," he said.

Hall found most of his victims while hitchhiking. The pattern was to thumb a lift, ride for a while, and then, after forcing the driver off the road, to shoot him or her in the face or the back of the head and take whatever they had. During the four months in which he committed five of the murders, Hall collected a grand total of less than $200, some cigarettes, electric clocks, watches, and a suitcase. "I always looked in the newspapers the next day to see who they were," he later said of his victims.

Hall's most brutal crime was the murder of his second wife. He decided to kill her because she was "wasting our money," he told detectives. "I took her out...near the Riverside golf course," he continued, "led her into a ravine on the riverbank and beat her to death with my hands. I must have hit her more than twenty times over the head." After demonstrating his technique on a police sergeant, Hall led police to the scene of the crime. There he identified his wife's skull. "There's the tooth that used to hurt me when I kissed her," he said.

Hall's mother-in-law, who called him "Red," said, "He...had a wonderful personality until you knew him and found the devil way back in him."

After a three-day trial, Hall was convicted of first-degree murder for killing his wife, a verdict that carried an automatic death penalty. On Jan. 4, 1946, Hall was executed. REF.: *CBA*.

Hall, James William, 1924-58, Aus., rob.-mur. James Hall was born in Launceston, Tasmania. At the age of eight he was committed to a state home for incorrigible children. He spent the next ten years there before joining the Civil Construction Corps at Darwin, Australia. His career from then on was a checkered one. In 1945 he was convicted of theft and was sentenced to twelve months in jail. Three years later Hall was examined by a psychiatrist after he had attacked another man in a fit of unprovoked anger. The doctor reported: "The acuteness of the condition had passed away when I saw him two or three days later, but I found him to be suffering from hysterical psychopathy. Psychopathy is a condition bordering on, but not reaching insanity except in exceptional cases."

In February 1952, Hall began to court a young woman named Avis Mary O'Toole. She came from a large family who lived on Lindsay Street in Launceston. Things progressed smoothly until O'Toole began to suspect her fiancé was involved in a £1,000 mail robbery. His obsessive jealousy finally convinced O'Toole to call off the engagement. When she gave him his ring back, Hall hit her in the face.

Hall vowed to kill himself in a long rambling letter dated May 26. Instead, he turned his rifle on the O'Toole family as they sat down to eat lunch on June 16, 1952. Demanding to see his girlfriend, he shot and killed Maude Eileen Cameron, the 23-year-old sister of O'Toole.

Hall sped away on his motorcycle in the direction of Galvin Street, where Avis was staying with her brother Ernest O'Toole, his wife Betty, and their children. "Where's Avis?" the crazed suitor asked. When he did not receive a satisfactory answer, Hall shot little Dennis O'Toole in the head. Betty Doreen O'Toole was killed in a similar manner.

While attempting to escape on his cycle, Hall careened off Hobart Road and crashed into a passing vehicle. He was presently identified at the Launceston General Hospital. Charged with first-degree murder, Hall went on trial Sept. 15, 1952, before Chief Justice, Sir John Morris. The jury, however, was discharged and a new trial date was established when Hall was declared physically unfit to stand trial. The case went to court the next month in front of Justice Marcus Gibson. A jury found him Guilty and the judge ordered the death sentence. An appeal was denied, but upon further consideration of the defendant's deteriorated mental condition, the sentence was commuted to life imprisonment on Dec. 12.

In prison Hall showed no visible signs of recovery. His state of mind was not good, and on Feb. 17, 1958, James Hall committed suicide in his cell.

REF.: *CBA*; Clegg, *Return Your Verdict*.

Hall, Jesse Lee (AKA: Red), 1849-1911, U.S., west. lawman. In 1871 Jesse Lee Hall retired from his job as a schoolteacher and became the city marshal of Sherman, Texas, rising within two years to deputy sheriff in nearby Denison. Hall was wounded during a gun battle in 1873, after agreeing to take part in a duel with an outlaw he was attempting to arrest. Two passersby fatally wounded the fugitive, saving Hall's life. In 1876, Hall left the local force to become a lieutenant with the Texas Rangers. He was immediately assigned to quell the notorious Taylor-Sutton Feud, and earned a reputation for fearlessness after he walked unarmed into a room filled with the feuding outlaws and arrested seven of them for murder. Hall was promoted to captain, and within two years had arrested more than 400 criminals. As captain of the Rangers, he patrolled the Mexican border and was present when the infamous Sam Bass was cornered and shot to death at Round Rock, Texas. In 1880, Hall married, retired from the Rangers, and became a cattle rancher. He befriended a young man named William Porter while Porter was recovering from a childhood illness. Later, Porter chronicled many of his ranch experiences

under the pen name of O. Henry.

In 1885, Hall became an Indian agent in Anadarko, Indian Territory. Two years later, he was suspected of accepting bribes and was fired, a charge he was exonerated of in 1889. Afterward, he held several law enforcement positions, including deputy sheriff of San Antonio. During the Spanish-American War, he organized several regiments of men to fight in the tropics because they were immune to yellow fever. In 1899, he joined the army and served in the Philippines. He returned to the U.S. and guarded gold mines in Mexico, and speculated in oil before he died in San Antonio on Mar. 17, 1911.

Lawman Jesse Lee Hall.

REF.: Bartholomew, *The Biographical Album of Western Gunfighters*; *CBA*; Gard, *Sam Bass*; McGiffin, *Ten Tall Texans*; Raymond, *Captain Lee Hall of Texas*; Webb, *Texas Rangers*.

Hall, Joseph, 1574-1656, Brit., consp. Bishop of Exeter from 1627-41, and Bishop of Norwich from 1641-47. He was impeached and put in prison in 1642, and later expelled from his mansion. REF.: *CBA*.

Hall, Katherine, and **Robinson, Margaret**, prom. 1602, Brit., scolding. At the Wakefield Sessions of 1602, Katherine Hall and Margaret Robinson were tried and convicted of scolding. Their nightly discords had so disturbed the peace and tranquility of the village, that they were ordered dunked in the pond. The sentence was carried out by John Mawde, the High Constable.

REF.: Andrews, *Old-Time Punishments*; *CBA*.

Hall, Leo (AKA: Stewart), 1902-c.35, U.S., mur. On a March day in 1934, a gruesome tragedy was uncovered at the Flieder cottage in Erland Point, Wash. The battered and bullet-riddled bodies of six people were found; Mr. and Mrs. Flieder, Mr. and Mrs. Chenovert, Mr. Jordan, and Bert Balcom. The motive was robbery, evidenced by the empty purses and wallets strewn about the house.

It took many months and a new county sheriff before headway was finally made on the case. In January 1935, Sheriff William Severyns assigned Chief Criminal Deputy O.K. Bodia to the case. Bodia had a tough assignment ahead, but he identified Leo Hall, who had been convicted of auto theft several years earlier, as a prime suspect. Loose barroom talk, and the desire for revenge on the part of one of his former associates who had lost his wife to Hall, further convinced Bodia that this was the man responsible for the tragedy.

Hall's wife told of her husband's desperate plan to rob the Flieders of their cash and valuables. Hall was arrested in Portland, Ore., when a complaint was filed with the local police about a man named Stewart who had professed interest in investing in a carburetor business. The individual registering the complaint had invented a carburetor and had discussed the possibility with Mr. Stewart, who had became threatening during the course of the interview. Escaping unhurt, the man tipped the police off about Hall, who was arrested shortly after.

On Dec. 9, 1935, Hall and his girlfriend went on trial. The woman who was a passive witness to the murders was acquitted. Hall was convicted and later hanged.

REF.: *CBA*; Cohen, *One Hundred True Crime Stories*.

Hall, Lucian, prom. 1843, U.S., mur. On Sept. 24, 1843, the body of Mrs. Bacon, who had been too ill to attend Sunday church services, was found on the floor of her home. The Bacon family was among the wealthiest in Westfield, Conn., and it was known that a large sum of money might be in the house. The murder weapon was a small cane, indicating that the intruder did not expect to encounter anyone. A former neighbor, Lucian Hall, was seen with blood on his clothing and a wound on his right hand. He had once been confined at the Connecticut State Prison for breaking and entering. Hall was arrested when he was unable to provide an alibi. He was hanged on June 20, 1844.

REF.: *Account of the Trial of Lucian Hall, Betheul Roberts and William H. Bell for murder, at the Middlesex Superior Court, Connecticut; CBA; A Minute and Correct Account of the Trial of Lucian Hall.*

Hall, Paul J., 1947- , U.S., child abuse-asslt. To hundreds of poor blacks residing on Chicago's South Side, the Reverend Paul Hall was a community leader and miracle worker who distributed food baskets and smoke alarms to the needy. Reverend Hall waged a relentless war against drug traffickers and gangs that corrupted and terrorized inner-city youth from a boy's club he founded adjacent to the Christ Universal Church on Ashland Avenue.

In the 1970s, Hall organized the Warriors Drum and Bugle Corps which performed for President Jimmy Carter at the White House in 1976. Three years later, he became a foster parent for the Department of Children and Family Services (DCFS). In the next ten years, twenty-one boys resided with him at his home on the South Side. Reverend Hall was praised as an effective, inspirational social worker, and his organization received $78,563 from the United Way in 1987 to further his community work.

On Jan. 19, 1988, a 15-year-old runaway was arrested at O'Hare Airport on a charge of loitering. He told Chicago Police that he had been living at Reverend Hall's home since Feb. 24, 1986, and had been sexually abused by the minister repeatedly over the course of nineteen months. The boy implicated the reverend in at least one other abuse case. The Illinois DCFS removed the five other boys in Hall's custody shortly after the investigation began. Hall denied the allegations, saying: "I can't preach one thing and live another."

On Apr. 11, 1988, State's Attorney Richard M. Daley announced a series of indictments charging Hall with sexual abuse and criminal assault. The boy's club, founded in 1960 when Hall was only fourteen, was closed. South Side residents circulated petitions attesting to his character, and a press conference was called by fifteen former residents of the home who expressed shock over the accusations leveled against Hall.

In May 1989, the South Side Reverend was convicted on seven counts of molesting a 15-year-old boy. The jury found the defendant Not Guilty on two specific counts of sexual abuse, allegedly committed on Dec. 19, 1987. In handing down a four-year prison sentence on July 6, Circuit Court Associate Judge Paul T. Foxgrover took note of the warm support and encouragement shown Hall by the members of the neighborhood. "I know the heart and spirit of that community when it truly loves an individual, but this does not overcome the crimes he has committed." REF.: *CBA.*

Hall, Peirson Mitchell, 1894-1979, U.S., jur. U.S. attorney from 1934-37, and nominated to the southern district court of California by President Franklin D. Roosevelt in 1942. REF.: *CBA.*

Hall, Robert Howell, 1921- , U.S., jur. Assistant attorney general for Georgia from 1953-61, and appellate judge for the Georgia Court of Appeals from 1961-74. He received the Harvard Law School Association Award in 1967. He was nominated to the northern district court of Georgia by President Jimmy Carter in 1979. REF.: *CBA.*

Hall, William, and **Dockery, John,** prom. 1892, U.S., mur. When the boundary commission surveyed and plotted out the state line separating Tennessee and North Carolina in 1819, they did not take into account the ingenious ways men would make use of the markings to avoid punishment of a crime. In order to evade local statutes against duelling, combatants would stand on each side of the boundary and fire at each other, thereby avoiding the prosecution of one state against two men.

By 1892, duelling was no longer in vogue. But an intriguing murder took place on July 11 in the Smoky Mountains of North Carolina near the Tennessee state line, which raised several legal questions and stirred up considerable debate about local jurisdiction.

The Halls, the Dockerys, and the Brysons were hill people related through marriage. They lived in Beaver Dam, a small settlement twenty miles outside of Murphy, N.C. William Hall and John Dockery were engaged in moonshining with Andy Bryson, a practice popularly known as "blockading." When the still they shared together mysteriously disappeared, Hall accused Bryson of stealing it.

Hall swore out a warrant for Bryson's arrest on a charge of carrying a concealed weapon. Dockery was deputized, and together with Hall set out to arrest Bryson. Near a dangerous rock cliff known as the Devil's Looking Glass, Hall shot Bryson dead.

The two men were charged with murder. At their trial, the question of whether Bryson stood in Tennessee or North Carolina at the time of the shooting became the real issue. The jury believed that all three men had their feet squarely planted on the North Carolina side, and in consideration of this they returned a Guilty verdict against the defendants on May 27, 1893. Eleven months later, on Apr. 24, 1894, the Supreme Court of North Carolina granted them a new trial on the grounds that murder had not in fact been committed within the state lines. Since Hall and Dockery were not actually in Tennessee at the time of the shooting they could not technically be fugitives, and by not being there in the first place they could not have fled.

Finally on Dec. 27, 1894, the Supreme Court of North Carolina handed down a second controversial decision which affirmed the doctrine that having never been fugitives, it was impossible to flee. Hall and Dockery were freed shortly after the Court handed down its decision on Dec. 27, 1894. Hall was brought to trial again in 1907 by the vengeful brother of the victim. He was acquitted again, but the rumors persisted that George Hall, a cousin of the defendant, had fixed it so there could be no other possible verdict than Not Guilty.

REF.: *CBA; Seagle, Acquitted of Murder.*

Hallaj, al- (Abu al-Mughith al-Husayn ibn Mansur al-Hallaj), c.858-922, Iraq, consp. Student of Sufi masters who tried to recruit others into the faith. He was imprisoned as a subversive from c.911-922, and shortly after his release was tortured and crucified in Baghdad. REF.: *CBA.*

Hallam, Robert, d.1732, Brit., mur. If Robert Hallam had followed his parents' advice and continued his maritime career, he might never have been executed for murder. A native of London, Hallam apprenticed to the captain of a trading vessel when he was in his youth. He was soon an able-bodied seaman with an excellent reputation and served on board several vessels as a mate.

Returning to his home port, Hallam married a woman who wanted him to give up the sea, so he acquired two small boats and made a successful living ferrying passengers on the Thames. Several children later, Hallam increased his holdings with the purchase of an alehouse. A perpetual scene of riot and confusion, however, it brought him nothing but misery and exacerbated his wife's alcoholism.

Hallam began to beat his wife—first for her drunkenness, later for her infidelity, and then retaliated with affairs of his own. One night, Hallam, drunk and enraged, locked his wife in the house. Then, when he went into another room for a cane, she locked him in. Breaking open the door, he threw her out the window headfirst. She died instantly of a broken back and a fractured skull.

Although the jury found him Guilty, Hallam protested to the end that his wife had thrown herself out the window before he entered the room. His unusual sentence was to be pelted to death by a rock-throwing mob. The execution was carried out at Tyburn in 1732.

REF.: *CBA; Mitchell, The Newgate Calendar; Scott, The Concise*

Encyclopedia of Crime and Criminals; Sutherland, *Ten Real Murder Mysteries Never Solved;* Wilson, *Encyclopedia of Murder.*

Hallett, Sir Hugh Imbert Perriam, b.1886, Brit., jur. Judge of Queen's Bench Division of High Court in 1939. He presided at the trials of George Russell and Jenkins, Geraghty, and Rolt. REF.: *CBA.*

Halliot, Henry, prom. 1868-70, U.S., fraud. After her rich, elderly husband died, Mrs. Willett was left a wealthy widow. While living at a Baltimore hotel, Willett befriended Jeanette Villiers, who introduced her to Henry Halliot, reputed son of a federal officer. Villiers came to live with Willett, who soon fell in love with Halliot, and agreed to marry him. Villiers became more than a confidant to Willett, and was soon advising her in her financial affairs. In 1869, Willett sold property for $40,000. Soon after, Halliot became suddenly ill, and the disconsolate Willett visited him often at his hotel. His health deteriorated, and Willett was finally summoned to his deathbed, where he miserably confessed that he was married to Villiers, who would soon have their child. He begged Willett to take care of them both after his death. The deceived woman consented, forgave her friend, and was not present when Halliot died. Within a month Willett gave $10,000 from her own estate to the expectant Villiers as a gift. Soon after the birth of a boy, Willett gave Villiers another $40,000. A week later, mother and child disappeared.

Willett's lawyer, against her protests, called in Baltimore detective Allan Pinkerton to investigate the matter. Pinkerton found Halliot living in comfort in St. Louis, along with a French "widow" and a young child under the name Hilliers. But Willett refused to press charges, even after she saw Halliot. Happy that he was alive, she refused to disrupt his happy little family. Willett, herself remarried, remained on good terms with the Halliots, and often saw them socially.

REF.: *CBA;* Gibson, *The Fine Art of Swindling.*

Hallman, Larry (AKA: **Jack Bumps**), and **Wilson, Eddie,** and **Peters, Warren,** prom. 1975, U.S., asslt.-rape-mur. In the seamy ghetto of Washington, D.C., despair, drugs and murder are often the culmination of urban poverty. On Oct. 22, 1975, a tragedy occurred on Delaware Avenue that was a grim reminder of criminal activity in the large cities.

On that day Curtis Arrington was stabbed in his apartment sixty-one times after he refused to reveal the whereabouts of his friend Slim, who was wanted by four young assailants who held him at knife point. When Arrington's girlfriend Lois Ann Davis appeared, she too was killed after pleading for her life. Afterward, the four men set the apartment ablaze and then went downstairs to wait for the firemen.

The men who committed these murders had lengthy criminal records. Larry Hallman had three assault and robbery convictions to his name and was living in a halfway house at the time of his arrest. Eddie Wilson and Warren Peters both pleaded guilty to 103 assorted charges ranging from kidnapping and rape, to armed robbery. Their favorite tactic was to commandeer a motorist in traffic, and then force the person to drive home where their possessions were looted.

Wilson and Peters each drew twenty-eight-year prison sentences from Superior Court Judge Nunzio who admitted that his judgment had been clouded by the spate of charges brought before him. He was largely ignorant of their roles in the double-slaying in the ghetto high-rise. Hallman was tried twice. He was sentenced to two consecutive twenty-year-to-life prison terms.

REF.: *CBA;* Godwin, *Murder U.S.A.*

Hall-Mills Case, 1922-26, (**Hall, Edward Wheeler,** 1882-1922, and **Mills, Eleanor Reinhardt,** 1888-1922), U.S., (unsolv.) mur. The secret affair between the Reverend Edward Wheeler Hall and Eleanor Reinhardt Mills, the petite, pretty woman who sang in his choir, brought these lovers to violent death, creating one of the U.S.'s greatest mysteries. The trials involving the Hall family that resulted from the double murder were some of the most lurid of the sensation-ridden 1920s. The press indulged itself in a glut of garish reporting, feeding on impossible characters they dubbed

"The Pig Woman," and "the Idiot." In the end, no one profited except the tabloid readers and the publishers.

It all began when an amorous couple, Raymond Schneider, twenty-two, and Pearl Bahmer, fifteen, strolled down a lover's lane three miles outside of New Brunswick, N.J., early on a Saturday morning, Sept. 16, 1922. The couple walked into a famous spooning area, De Russey's Lane, then into Phillips' Lane, named after the nearby Phillips farm. Schneider and Bahmer stopped dead in their tracks. Before them, under a crab apple tree, were the bodies of a man and woman. Both had been shot in the head. The man, the Reverend Hall, lay flat on his back, a wide Panama hat over his head. His own calling card was propped up against his foot, a grim joke of the killer. The woman, Mills, lay with her head cradled in Hall's arm.

Schneider and Bahmer ran for the police and soon the crab apple orchard was swarming with police and detectives. The balding, chubby, once-affable Hall had been shot only once. A .32-caliber bullet had been sent into the Episcopal minister's back. His death appeared to have been swift and almost merciful. Mrs. Mills, however, was another matter. Her killer had shot her three times in the middle of the forehead. The 34-year-old Mills had been the lead soprano in Hall's Church of St. John the Evangelist of New Brunswick. Her voice had thrilled the congregation as it lilted through one hymn after another. Someone, after shooting her to death, had undoubtedly remembered too often hearing that voice and had vindictively slashed Mills' throat from ear to ear. An autopsy, not fully described until four years later, showed that the killer had savagely cut off her tongue and then hacked out her vocal cords.

The murdered couple had obviously been caught in the middle of making love, or so police believed. Since both were married at the time, it was quickly thought that their cuckolded spouses could have been involved in the deaths. The manner in which the victims were neatly dressed also allowed some officials to speculate that they had not been killed when dressed, that they had been found naked, while making love, and killed. After murdering them, the killer or killers had dressed the victims, clothing Mills in her blue lawn dress with red polka dots, placing her blue velvet turban on her head, her black hose on her legs, and brown oxfords on her small feet. Reverend Hall was also neatly attired, wearing a gray worsted suit, white shirt with high stiff collar, white tie, black socks, and black shoes.

The killer had even been careful enough to button Reverend Hall's suitcoat and, when the Panama hat was removed, it was noted that the clergyman's glasses had been meticulously placed on the bridge of his nose. Mills' mutilated head was covered with a long scarf. The whole gruesome scene appeared to be a setting which had been set by a killer with a macabre sense of humor. He had mocked his victims, placing them together to signify their adulterous relationship. Scattered over the bodies and in the immediate area were dozens of love letters Mrs. Mills had written to the Reverend Hall over the years. By leaving these love notes, torrid by the day's standards, the killer further emphasized the illicit relationship between the murdered pair, as if to vindicate the killings. Later, these letters would be published widely in the nation's press. James Mills, husband of the slain choir singer, callously sold off his wife's missives, which gushed love for another man, at $500 a letter.

As police officers, detectives, and coroner's officials stomped about the murder site, newsmen as well as curious residents in the area, arrived and the site developed a carnival atmosphere. One of the reporters raced to a telephone and called Mrs. Francis Noel Stevens Hall, the pastor's wife, telling her that her husband had just been found dead, murdered, lying next to the body of his lead choir singer, Mrs. Mills. Was there anything between the couple, the naive newsman asked. Mrs. Hall did not reply, slamming down the receiver. Mrs. Hall was the richest woman in New Brunswick. She lived in the largest mansion in New Brunswick and was seven years older than her slain husband. Mrs. Hall was autocratic, arrogant, and utterly above gossip and scan-

Left, Rev. Edward Wheeler Hall, the Episcopal pastor of the Church of St. John the Evangelist of New Brunswick, N.J., a philandering cleric who was murdered in one of the most sensational cases of the 1920s.

Choir singer Mrs. Eleanor Mills, found murdered with Rev. Hall.

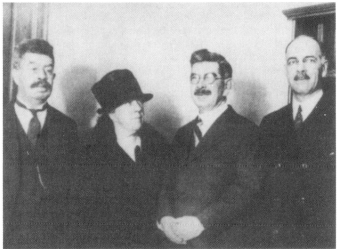

Willie Stevens, Mrs. Hall, Henry Stevens, Henry de la Bruyere.

Lonely De Russy's lane, where the dead lovers were found.

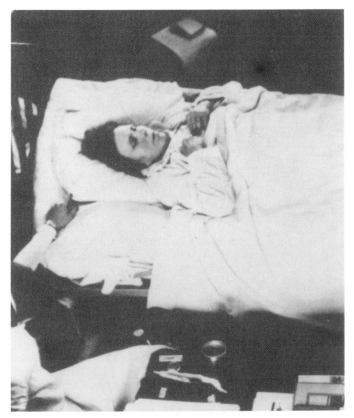

Ailing Jane Gibson testified from a hospital bed in court.

Charlotte Mills, the victim's daughter, wrote about the murder.

dal, or so she maintained all of her august life.

A half hour after the newsman's phone call, Mrs. Hall's wealthy cousin, Henry de la Bruyere Carpender, a leading member of New York's Stock Exchange, appeared at the murder site. With him was William E. Florence, New Jersey state senator, and the Hall family lawyer. Carpender ignored policemen at the site and went immediately to the body of his brother-in-law, kneeling for a moment at his side. He took the hand of the corpse briefly and said: "Well, old fellow, you never did this yourself." Carpender ignored the body of Mrs. Mills. Both he and Florence then departed without uttering a single word to the police, as if their visit were merely to verify Hall's death.

The authorities at the scene did not question Carpender because they were too busy heatedly arguing over the jurisdiction of the case. Azariah Beekman, prosecutor for Somerset County, pointed out that even though the bodies of the murdered couple were inside his county by 350 feet, they had been murdered in Middlesex County, which contained New Brunswick—the home of the deceased—and the case properly belonged with Middlesex officials. Middlesex authorities shouted back that it was a Somerset case since the corpses were found in that county, barely. Obviously no one wanted this case from the beginning.

Technically, this last position was correct and Beekman had to bow to the law. Somerset County assumed responsibility for the case and the bodies were sent to the morgue. After the bodies were removed, Somerset detective George Totten scooped up several .32-caliber cartridges, the same caliber bullets that had killed the murdered couple. In a few hours, the area was overrun with hundreds of spectators. Vendors appeared, hawking hot dogs, soda pop, and popcorn. Whatever clues might have been present were trampled into the dust. The first people police interviewed that day were James Mills and Francis Hall.

Mills, eleven years older than his slain wife, was the sexton and janitor of Hall's church. He was meek and a seemingly ineffectual man who openly admitted that his wife had been seeing Reverend Hall, but he insisted that their relationship was platonic. When pressed by reporters, Mills admitted that his attractive young wife had been leaving their house at all hours of the day and night for months. It was all innocent, he said. He pointed out that Reverend Hall had visited his home many times, staying for dinner.

Pressed for more details concerning Mrs. Mills' movements on the last night of her life, the mild-mannered Mills admitted that his wife had left their house at 7:30 p.m. on Thursday and that was the last time he had seen her alive. Before she left the house, Mills asked his wife where she was going. He quoted her taunting reply: "Why don't you follow me and find out?" He said he waited until midnight for his wife to return and then went to bed. He awoke at 2 a.m. and, finding his wife still not home, went to the church, which was empty. He returned home, went back to sleep, and by 9 the next morning, he was back at the church looking for Mrs. Mills.

Mills said he saw Mrs. Hall and told her his wife had not come home the previous night. He said that Mrs. Hall had stated that her husband, too, had not returned home. But there the spouses let the matter lay. They went about their business, saying nothing to anyone, including the police. When Mrs. Mills' body was found about thirty-six hours later, Mills was found in a New Brunswick drugstore, sipping a chocolate soda. The obvious unconcern of Mills and, especially of the very proper Mrs. Hall, as to the whereabouts of their spouses, brought suspicion on both.

Hall had married Francis Stevens in 1911. She was then thirty-six and wealthy. He was a struggling 29-year-old clergyman who, two years after his marriage to Francis, was appointed pastor of the well-endowed St. John the Evangelist church. Members of the wealthy Stevens family were the wealthiest supporters of this church. Francis Stevens was no prize. She was dowdy, over-weight, and had a decidedly unattractive face and a severe personality. New Brunswick residents who knew them believed Hall had married Francis Stevens for her money but the marriage

proved to be happy, at least on the surface. When Mrs. Hall finally consented to answer questions from police, she said that her husband had left their home at 7:30 p.m., giving the exact time as Mills had given when explaining his wife's departure. She said that the Reverend Hall had told her he had "some business to attend to."

Mrs. Hall said she had spent a "sleepless night" when realizing that her husband had not returned home, and the next morning, she had called the police, asking if there had been any "casualties" reported. This was an odd word but Mrs. Hall was not challenged; she was one of the most distinguished citizens in the community and authorities were cautious in interviewing her. Mrs. Hall also pointed out that police undoubtedly had a record of her call and that they had told her that no "casualties" had been reported.

Servants who worked in the Hall mansion emphatically stated that Mrs. Hall and her brother, Willie, who was thought to be rather dim-witted, had never left the house on Thursday night, the time of the murders. A watchman who patrolled the exclusive neighborhood, however, reported that a woman wearing a large gray coat entered the side door of the mansion at 2 a.m. on Friday, but he could not identify the woman as Mrs. Hall. Mrs. Hall then admitted that she had been the woman seen by the watchman, that she could not sleep, and had gone with her brother, Willie, to the church in search of her husband. She then added that she believed her husband had gone to give spiritual aid to some parishioner who "might have been taken ill." Mrs. Hall and her brother, said Mrs. Hall, then went to the Mills home, but when they saw no lights on, they returned home. It was apparent that Mrs. Hall had known for some time that her husband had been having an affair with the pert Mrs. Mills. In fact, the affair had been going on since early 1922. After eleven years of marriage, Mrs. Hall, at age forty-seven, was heavyset, gray-haired, and could have passed as her husband's matronly mother instead of his wife. Mrs. Mills, on the other hand, was young, vivacious, and attractive.

Willie Stevens, who appeared to be a big, oafish bachelor, and who was later ridiculed because of his ungainly appearance, at first insisted that he never left the Hall mansion, but under continued police questioning, admitted accompanying his sister to the church early Friday morning. Stevens was rather comical. His thick, uncombed hair stuck outward like a porcupine and his thick-lensed glasses made him appear myopic. He wore a walrus mustache over thick, sensuous lips, and his receding chin tucked itself into a bull neck.

Willie Stevens had been left a sizeable fortune, more than $150,000, but he was given only a $40-a-week allowance so that he would not "spend away his fortune." Stevens liked costumes and was made an honorary fireman. He spent a good deal of time at the New Brunswick Fire Department. He purchased expensive steaks with his allowance and took these to the department where he cooked them for the appreciative firemen, who treated him like a mascot. He was given a fireman's hat and Willie proudly wore this on strolls through the town's Hungarian quarter where extravagant costumes were the norm and Willie in his fireman's hat did not bring undue attention.

Henry Stevens, another brother who lived in Lavelette, N.J., and who was enormously wealthy, came under suspicion because his ability as a hunter and marksman was well known. It was pointed out that it would not take a sharpshooter to kill Hall and Mills since they were both shot at almost pointblank range. Henry Stevens was as arrogant and uncooperative with the police as his sister, conduct that made him appear that he was hiding something, but he produced an iron-clad alibi. He was at a waterfront party with a host of people when the murders occurred.

Several local suspects were picked up and questioned. Then police, seemingly helpless, promptly arrested the couple that had been unlucky enough to have found the bodies, Schneider and Bahmer. The youth was found to have recently left a wife of only two months. He was unemployed, an idler. Bahmer was por-trayed as a young vagrant. Both were arrested and charged with the murders but were held only briefly. Schneider, at this time, claimed that another youth, Clifford Hayes, had shot Hall and Mills, saying that Hayes thought he was killing Pearl Bahmer and her father. Hayes was arrested but discharged after proving to be innocent. Schneider later admitted lying under oath, giving no reason for implicating Hayes. He was convicted of perjury in a later trial and sent to prison for two years.

Then the strangest person in this strange cast of characters stepped forward, Mrs. Jane Gibson, also known as Mrs. Jane Easton. She was thrice divorced, owned a hog farm near the murder site, and became the chief witness against the Stevens family. The press immediately nicknamed Mrs. Gibson "The Pig Woman" because she owned a hog farm. Gibson came forward to state that she saw the killers, or heard them, on the night of the murders, Sept. 14, 1922. She had been riding her mule Jennie in search of poachers who had been stealing corn from a field, next to the Phillips farm. She said she heard men and women arguing in the nearby crab apple orchard, then shots. She mounted faithful Jennie and fled. This was not enough to indict the Stevens family members. On Nov. 27, 1922, a grand jury filed a "no bill" verdict, meaning no one had been indicted for the murders.

Mrs. Hall left for a year-long vacation in Italy. James Mills continued to ring the bells of the church and Mrs. Gibson returned to her hog farm. The case remained in limbo, the murders unsolved. Four years went by before New Brunswick police learned that Louise Geist, a maid in the Stevens mansion, had lied about Mrs. Stevens' whereabouts on the night of the murders. Geist had married a piano salesman, Arthur M. Riehl, who divorced his wife in 1926, charging that she was a liar, and stating that his wife had been paid $6,000 by the Stevens family to keep quiet about what she knew in connection with the Hall-Mills slayings.

This story was bannered in the New York *Mirror*. The paper's managing editor, Philip Payne, who had wrung every detail from the 1922 murders, urged New Jersey governor A. Harry Moore to reopen the case, based on Riehl's allegations. Payne persuaded Moore and others to charge the Stevens family by saying that he had employed a fingerprint expert who had found Henry Stevens' thumbprint on the calling card left at the murdered Reverend Hall's foot. On July 28, 1926, police marched into the Hall mansion and arrested an indignant Mrs. Hall in her nightgown, and sleepy-eyed Willie Stevens for murder. Henry Stevens was awakened at his residence and also charged with murder.

Mrs. Hall posted a $15,000 bond and was released, but she and her two brothers went on trial on Nov. 3, 1926, at Somerville, N.J. The courtroom in the small courthouse was packed with five hundred people, even though it was designed to hold no more than half that number. Scores of newsmen descended upon the town to write endless stories, real and imagined, about the case. Included among these headline-hunters was Charlotte Mills, the teenage flapper daughter of the slain Mrs. Mills. Her father appeared as a prosecution witness against the Stevens, but his memory was hazy and he offered little that would convict the family members. Again, Mrs. Gibson, the celebrated "Pig Woman," appeared for the prosecution. She had recently undergone a cancer operation and in a dramatic move, was brought into court on a hospital bed, moaning and groaning. She testified in this position, sometimes craning her head to stare at Mrs. Hall, who sat at the nearby defense table. Hall refused to even set her eyes on her accuser and she remained aloof during the entire proceedings.

Mrs. Gibson seemed to recall more details in 1926 than what she could remember in 1922 and it soon became apparent that she was playing to the crowd and enjoying her fame. Croaked Gibson: "I was peeking and peeking and peeking" into the crab apple orchard, and that she saw Mrs. Stevens, and her brothers Willie and Henry get out of a car near the crab apple tree. She said she heard a woman's voice, ostensibly Mrs. Hall's, shout: "Explain these letters!" She heard the Stevens' brothers arguing with the

Reverend Hall and then, she said, there was a struggle.

As she eked out her story, a nurse applied cold cream to Gibson's lips, so that she could continue to bravely unravel her murder tale. She said that there was more shouting and fighting and she became frightened and "I run for my mule." Gibson said she was fleeing from the scene when she heard "bang, bang, bang, three quick shots. Then I stumbled over a stump getting on the mule and I run for home." She went on to say that she had lost her moccasin and returned to the scene where she saw Mrs. Hall bending "over something."

Adding to the drama and confusion at that moment was Gibson's elderly mother, who sat behind her in the first row of the visitor's gallery, yelling loudly at her daughter's every utterance: "She's a liar! She's a liar! She's a liar!" The defense attorneys attacked Gibson's memory with a vengeance. They asked her if she could remember the names of her three ex-husbands. She could not. She could not remember when she had been married or when she was divorced from these men. How then, the defense pointed out to the jury, could Gibson remember anything about a murder case that was four years old? Gibson was then taken back to a Newark hospital but only after the ambulance stopped at her request to get her a pint of ice cream from a road vendor.

Mrs. Hall then went to the witness stand and was remarkably confident. She answered badgering questions from the prosecution with ease. Unruffled, she was dubbed the "Iron Widow" by the press. Willie Stevens also proved to be anything but "the Idiot," as the press had profiled him. He, like his sister, was cool and calm under fire and could not be moved from his original story regarding his actions and that of his sister's on the night of the murder. The jury was impressed enough to render a Not Guilty verdict on Dec. 3, 1926.

The Stevens family had not escaped unscathed, having to spend more than $200,000 in a trial that cost everyone twice that amount. Then the Stevens family sued the New York *Mirror* for $3 million. The case was settled out of court for an undisclosed amount. The editor, Phillip Payne, who had brought the 1926 court battle into existence, disappeared in a transcontinental flight in 1927, taking off in a monoplane piloted by Lloyd W. Bertaud in flight from Maine to Rome. The flamboyant editor and Bertaud vanished somewhere over the Atlantic. Payne was later profiled in the film *Five Star Final*, portrayed by Edward G. Robinson.

Mrs. Gibson died of cancer, still a celebrity on Feb. 7, 1930, in a Jersey City hospital. Mrs. Hall remained in New Brunswick for another twenty years, attending her husband's church and continuing her role as the grande dame of the community. Willie Stevens gave up his position as an honorary firemen in New Brunswick. He spent the remainder of his days with his sister behind the huge walls of the Stevens mansion. The murders of Reverend Hall and Mrs. Mills remained unsolved.

REF.: Bechhofer-Roberts, *Famous American Trials*; Busch, *They Escaped the Hangman*; CBA; Corder, *Murder My Love*; Gribble, *Strange Crimes of Passion*; Jones, *Unsolved*; Kunstler, *The Minister and the Choir Singer*; Morris, *Trial*; Nash, *Almanac of World Crime*; ____, *Open Files*; Pearson, *Instigation of the Devil*; Roberts, *Famous American Trials*; Scott, *The Concise Encyclopedia of Crime and Criminals*; Sutherland, *Ten Real Murder Mysteries Never Solved*; Wilson, *Encyclopedia of Murder*; Woollcott, *Long, Long, Ago*; (FICTION), Abbot, *About the Murder of the Clergyman's Mistress*; Connington, *The Twenty-one Clues*; Longstreet, *The Crime*.

Hall of the Bleeding Heart, 1845-58, U.S., gamb. The Hall of the Bleeding Heart, established in Washington, D.C., in 1845 by wealthy gambler Edward Pendleton, catered exclusively to government leaders and social bigwigs. The lavishly appointed gambling spa chiefly offered Faro but private rooms for poker, whist, brag, and short card games were available to the most distinguished residents. It was claimed that huge amounts of money were won at the Hall—as much as $50,000 in one sitting— but others, knowing the cleverly rigged Faro games Pendleton had installed, stated that the highest amount taken from the Hall in one sitting was no more than $1,200. The Hall was reportedly the most expensively decorated gambling den in the U.S., other than the Saratoga gambling resort later built and operated by America's super gambler Richard Canfield.

The Hall, which offered the finest in food and liquor to its patrons, had a $5 minimum bet and no high limit. Senators and representatives, especially from the West and South, squandered their congressional salaries in the Hall each week. Pendleton grew rich through his operation of the Hall of the Bleeding Heart; he was also accepted by Washington High Society, being a refined gentlemen who had the reputation of having a heart of his own. Numerous tales spread of Pendleton's kindness to heavy losers. After patrons lost almost everything at his Faro tables, Pendleton would loan them money to pay their bills, never expecting to be repaid.

Faro players at the Hall of the Bleeding Heart, 1850.

When Pendleton died in 1858, his social standing was such that President James Buchanan attended his funeral, and his pallbearers consisted of senators and congressman. The fixtures in the posh Hall were then auctioned off, but not before the ladies of Washington society, who had been excluded from this all-male gambling resort, were invited to visit the elegant Hall. Hundreds flocked to see the place where their husbands had flung fortunes at the Faro table. See: **Canfield, Richard Albert; Pendleton, Edward.**

REF.: Asbury, *Sucker's Progress*; CBA; Chafetz, *Play the Devil*; Gardiner, *Canfield*; Poore, *Perley's Reminiscences*; Wilson, *The Capital City and Its Part in the History of the Nation*.

Halloway, Ann, d.1705, Brit., rob. Ann Halloway was a notorious thief often compared to Nan Hereford, the highwaywoman who once set fire to Newgate. Halloway was hanged at Tyburn in 1705.

REF.: *CBA*; O'Donnell, *Should Women Hang?*

Halsbury, Hardinge Goulburn Giffard (Earl of Halsbury), 1880-1943, Brit., jur. Called to Bar in 1906, became earl in 1921, and judge in 1923. He prosecuted Price and Driscoll Rowlands. REF.: *CBA*.

Halsey, Jacob, d.1691, Brit., rob. "Lend me what thou hast without grumbling, for who cannot be in love...with this mild sort of taking from a man what he has, without an assault or violence." Thus did Jacobs Halsey, in Quaker idiom, relieve his fellow churchmen of their money and avenge himself of a practical joke.

Known to his contemporaries as "Mr. Yea and Nay" because of his piety, Halsey was an unlikely candidate for highwayman. Born to wealthy Quaker parents in Bedfordshire, he grew up to preach at Quaker meetings. A neighbor, however, thought little of Halsey's heavenly visions, and one night climbed up on Halsey's roof.

"Jacob, where are thou?" he asked.

Hearing the voice, Halsey arose naked and responded: "Here I am! What is thy will?"

The voice replied by calling Halsey "my beloved and chosen one," and telling him to break all the windows in the church. Doing just that, Halsey was jailed for three months in Bedford and fined £400.

Halsey made friends in jail and learned much about the craft of thieving. Upon his release, weary and ashamed and suffering the taunts of children, who mocked him in the streets for his glass-breaking folly, Halsey yearned to avenge himself on church people. Dressing differently, in the fashion of the day, yet preserving his Quaker speech, he took to the highways.

Apprehended in 1691 while attempting to rob the Right Honorable Earl of Westmorcland, Halsey was sent to Maidstone Jail and condemned to die. His long and sarcastic gallows speech ended with a regret: that "a man that is born of a woman has but a short time to stay upon her, and indeed my time is so short in this wicked world, that I shall never get upon another as long as I live."

REF.: *CBA*; Hibbert, *Highwaymen*; Smith, *Highwaymen*.

Halsey, John, 1670-1716, Brit., pir. John Halsey was a notorious South Seas pirate whose early nautical career was honest and above-board. Born in Boston, he went to sea as a youth. In 1693 he commanded the sloop *Adventure,* which was engaged in commercial trading between the coastal colonies of Massachusetts and Virginia.

The Royal Governor later commissioned him as a privateer, and in the service of the crown, Halsey plundered French shipping off the coast of Newfoundland. While commanding the brigantine *Charles* in August 1703, the craft was seized by the pirate John Quelch. The following June, the *Charles* was retaken, and Quelch and five crewmen were hanged. Halsey was given command of his ship.

In 1705, Captain Halsey turned pirate. He sailed to Madagascar where he was determined to claim only Moorish ships as his prize, but soon after Halsey began to prey on English shipping. He captured the *Rising Eagle,* and the *Essex,* which returned £50,000 of loot to the pirates. While laid up in Madagascar awaiting the completion of repairs on his vessel, Halsey was afflicted with a tropical fever. He died there, and was buried with great ceremony and honor in a watermelon garden. The grave had to be fenced for protection when wild hogs began uprooting the body.

REF.: Botting, *The Pirates; CBA;* Burney, *History of the Buccaneers of America;* Chatterton, *The Romance of Piracy;* Ellms, *The Pirates' Own Book;* Innes, *The Book of Pirates;* Kemp, *The Brethren of the Coast;* Maclay, *A History of American Privateers;* Mitchell, *Pirates;* Pringle, *Jolly Roger;* Williams, *Captains Outrageous;* Woodbury, *The Great Days of Piracy;* Wycherley, *Buccaneers of the Pacific.*

Halsey, Joseph, d.1759, Brit., mur. Although educated in the art of navigation, Joseph Halsey attained mastery as a sadist. When serving as the first mate on the *Amazon,* a ship en route from Jamaica to London in 1759, Halsey took command when Captain Gallop, fell ill only one week out of port. Besides Halsey and Gallop, the eight-member crew included four crewmen—John Father, John Edwards, Daniel Davidson, and Robert Green—and two galley boys—Thomas Symmes and William Mitchell.

No sooner did Captain Gallop fall ill than the ship sprang a leak. All hands had to pump to keep the vessel afloat, and Halsey missed no opportunity to abuse and beat the men fiercely in the name of forward progress. The men complained to the captain, charging Halsey with murder, but Gallop was powerless. "Halsey, we have but few men," he said, trying to reason with his first mate, "and, if you murder them, who will take care of the ship?"

Ignoring Gallop's pleas, Halsey continued his barbaric treatment. When Edwards and Davidson fell ill, he took it as an act of provocation and worked them harder, cutting their water rations and depriving them of shelter and sleep.

Edwards died first and was thrown overboard. Resolved to follow, Davidson lowered himself by rope into the sea to drown. When Halsey saw him rising on the surface of the water, however, he seized a rope to bring him back, declaring that "he should not escape him so." Davidson was then revived only to be beaten and tortured. When he was so weak that he could no longer stand, Halsey had him tied upright to beat him further. By morning, he was dead.

When the *Amazon* reached London, the crew reported the actions of their first mate. Halsey was taken into custody, charged with murder, tried, condemned, and hanged at Execution Dock on Mar. 14, 1759.

REF.: *CBA;* Mitchell, *The Newgate Calendar.*

Halsmann, Philipp, prom. 1929, Case of, Ger., mur. In the fall of 1928, a German college student named Philipp Halsmann went off on a mountain climbing expedition to the Zillertaler Alps with his father. Near the Olperer Massif, the father sustained a fatal fall. A blood-stained stone was thought to have been the murder weapon, but there was no hard evidence of the boy's guilt. Two trials were held in the early months of 1929. Halsmann was first convicted but later acquitted. The sensational nature of the trials resulted in the creation of a special laboratory for blood analysis at the Institute of Forensic Medicine at the University of Innsbruck.

REF.: *CBA;* Thorwald, *Crime and Science.*

Hamadi, Mohammad Ali, c.1964-   , Case of, Ger., skyjack.-mur. Mohammad Ali Hamadi, a Lebanese member of the fanatical Hezbullah terrorist group in sympathy with the Iranian fundamentalists, commandeered a TWA jetliner bound from Athens to Rome on June 14, 1985.

In return for the lives of 153 passengers, Hamadi and an accomplice demanded that Israel free 700 imprisoned Shiite Muslims. They ordered the pilot to fly the plane to Beirut, and then to Algiers, where forty passengers were freed. The next day the plane flew back to Beirut, where one of the terrorists shot and killed U.S. Navyman Robert Dean Stethem. On June 30, 1985, the last of the hostages were freed. Hamadi remained a fugitive until Jan. 15, 1987, when he was arrested at the Frankfurt Airport trying to smuggle bombs into West Germany. The U.S. State Department could not persuade the Bonn government to extradite Hamadi to the U.S. to stand trial. However, they secured a promise from the Germans that Hamadi would not be included in any prisoner exchange with any of the countries of the Middle East.

Charged with air piracy and murder, Mohammad Ali Hamadi went on trial in Frankfurt on July 5, 1988. During the ten-month trial, jurors heard testimony from flight attendant Hazel Hesp that the killer of seaman Stethem was Hassan Ezzeddine and not Hamadi. Ezzeddine, who was still at large when Hamadi was brought to trial, was identified as the leader of the hijackers and may have been involved in the 1983 bombing which killed 241 U.S. servicemen in Beirut.

Hamadi was found Guilty of murder and air piracy and sentenced to life imprisonment on May 17, 1989. Judge Heiner Mueckenberger noted that it was impossible to tell who fired the fatal shot, "But the defendant knowingly and willingly participated in Stethem's killing and actively took part in its preparation." REF.: *CBA.*

Hamaguchi Osachi (or Yuko), 1870-1931, Japan, prime minister, assass. Elected to the Japanese Diet in 1914, Hamaguchi consistently demonstrated a non-military approach to Japan's expansionist aims, urging economic trade agreements and appeasement with Western powers. After becoming prime minister in 1929, Hamaguchi attended the London Naval Conference and

gave ground to Western powers who accused Japan of violating international agreements by secretly building a super navy for purposes of aggression. Hamaguchi then instituted an economic austerity program which incensed Japan's militarists and incurred the displeasure of Emperor Hirohito, who secretly backed the militarists. Instead of allowing Japan's navy the 500 million yen (then $250 million), Hamaguchi slashed the budget almost in half. This promptly marked the prime minister for assassination by the militarists.

On Oct. 27, 1930, Sagoya Tomeo, a trained killer and a member of the secret Black Dragon Society, took a train to Tokyo and began to follow Hamaguchi about the city. The prime minister was told that he was being shadowed, and he contacted the home minister, Adachi Kenzo, who was in charge of the Tokyo police. Adachi, who was a member of the Black Dragon Society and was part of the assassination plot, did nothing but assign detectives to follow Sagoya about, not to arrest the professional killer but to make sure that he had freedom of movement.

The assassin, who spent time in Tokyo's most lavish brothels at the expense of the army which had hired him to murder the prime minister, was instructed that Hamaguchi was taking a train to visit the emperor, who was in the field on army maneuvers. Sagoya, given the exact time of Hamaguchi's departure, was at the train station on the morning of Nov. 14, 1930. Without interference from policemen or soldiers who were on hand, the assassin simply walked up to Hamaguchi and shoved a Mauser pistol into the prime minister's stomach, pulling the trigger several times and sending fatal bullets into Hamaguchi.

The stricken prime minister was taken to an office in the train station where two doctors examined him but did nothing to save his life. Hamaguchi was later removed to the infirmary of Tokyo Imperial University where he was X-rayed and given a transfusion after sections of his intestine were removed. Hamaguchi lingered in agony until Aug. 26, 1931, when he died. By then Hirohito had appointed a prime minister more readily disposed to his war aims.

Sagoya, apprehended immediately, was released a short time later on bond status. He was not imprisoned for three years, allowed to move about freely. He was treated more like a national hero than a ruthless murderer. On Nov. 6, 1933, Sagoya was found Guilty of assassinating Prime Minister Hamaguchi and was sentenced to death. Three months later, only hours before he was to be executed, Sagoya was set free on the personal orders of Emperor Hirohito. He lived out his life, richly supported by Japanese militarists until the end of WWII, and by wealthy supporters following the war. See: **Black Dragon Society; Toyama Mitsuru.**

REF.: Bergamini, *Japan's Imperial Conspiracy;* Byas, *Government by Assassination; CBA;* McNelly, *Politics and Government in Japan;* Morton, *Japan, Its History and Culture;* Mosley, *Hirohito: Emperor of Japan;* Scalapino, *Democracy and the Party Movement in Prewar Japan.*

Hambleton, John, d.1753, Brit., mur. Traveling on the King's Road to Chelsea on business, British soldier John Hambleton and his comrade Lattie robbed and murdered Mr. Crouch, the Earl of Harrington's cook. When Lattie and Hambleton demanded Crouch's money, the cook, unarmed, refused. So the soldiers fired their pistols at him. Crouch, however, wielding a pocketknife in self-defense, escaped their fire and wounded Lattie in the process. The soldiers then overpowered him, rifling his pockets for money and a watch. Slashing Crouch with his own pocket-knife, they pistol-whipped him about the head and left him to die.

Early the next morning some workers discovered Crouch still alive in the road. Alive enough to describe his assailants, he died nonetheless three days later. The murderers were soon captured, Lattie being easily identified by his recent wounds. Both were condemned, but Lattie died before he could be hanged. On Dec. 10, 1753, Hambleton was executed at Tyburn. His body was given to surgeons for dissection, then an illegal practice unless such examinations were performed on the corpses of executed felons who had forfeited their right to remain intact after death.

REF.: *CBA;* Mitchell, *The Newgate Calendar.*

Hamer, Frank, 1884-1955, U.S., law enfor. off. Frank Hamer spent more than forty years as a lawman, mostly with the Texas Rangers, but his fame has been distilled into the few moments that it took to kill Bonnie Parker and Clyde Barrow. Although famous as a result of this single confrontation, Hamer was involved in more than fifty gun battles, and was himself wounded twenty times. He killed between forty and one hundred criminals, during his career which spanned three generations.

The 22-year-old Hamer joined the Texas Rangers in 1906. The following year he was assigned to bring order to Doran, Texas, a town dominated by vice operator Haddon Slade, who had recently ordered the murder of the local sheriff. Slade planned to frame Hamer by killing him and using the lawman's gun to murder two others before returning the gun to the dead ranger's hand. But Hamer was faster and killed Slade with three bullets in the chest. The ranger became adept at apprehending bank robbers, almost relishing the ability to nab two or three at a time. He uncovered a ring of law enforcement officers who had become bounty hunters after a large reward was offered by the Texas Bankers Association. The bounty hunters were killing innocent men to obtain the $5000 reward. When the association failed to withdraw the reward offer, Hamer took the cause to the

Texas Ranger Frank Hamer, 1906. Twenty-seven years later Hamer led the posse that killed Clyde Barrow and Bonnie Parker.

newspaper and subsequently arrested the ring leaders. In 1934, disgusted with the political corruption of Texas governor "Ma" Ferguson, Hamer resigned from the Rangers. He worked briefly for a manufacturing plant as a security coordinator, but shortly after joined the Texas Highway Patrol.

Hamer was given the enormous assignment of apprehending Bonnie and Clyde. The two fugitives had blazed a bloody path through the southwest, killing several law officers in the process. On Feb. 10, 1934, Hamer began his search for Bonnie and Clyde. He followed the pair in a circle that started in Dallas, continued through Southern Missouri and Louisiana, before ending in Dallas. On May 23, 102 days after Hamer began his pursuit, he learned that the pair would be traveling on a rural back road. He and a group of officers lay in ambush, and killed the fugitives by firing hundreds of rounds of ammunition into their passing vehicle.

In 1935, Hamer returned to the Texas Rangers and served until his retirement at age sixty-five in 1949. He died six years later, on July 10, 1955, at his home in Austin, Texas. See: **Barrow, Clyde Champion**.

REF.: *CBA*; Edge, *Run the Cat Roads;* Hunter and Rose, *The Album of Gunfighters;* Louderback, *The Bad Ones;* Nash, *Bloodletters and Badmen;* Webb, *The Texas Rangers.*

Hamilton, Alexander, See: **Burr, Aaron**.

Hamilton, Alice, 1869-1970, U.S., toxicol. Director of Illinois survey of industrial poisons from 1909-10. She conducted investigations of occupational poisons for the U.S. Bureau of Labor from 1911-21. From 1919-35, she taught industrial medicine as an assistant professor at Harvard medical school. Books authored: *Industrial Poisons in the United States, Exploring the Dangerous Trades.* REF.: *CBA*.

Hamilton, Andrew, d.1741, U.S., lawyer. Defense counsel for John Peter Zenger, publisher of the New York *Weekly Journal.* He represented Zenger in a landmark seditious libel case that helped establish the free political press in America. REF.: *CBA.*

Hamilton, Claud (Lord Claud Hamilton, AKA: **Baron Paisley)**, c.1543-1622, Scot., consp. Forced to flee the country with brother, John Hamilton, in 1579, after they were charged with carrying out assassination plots for Mary, Queen of Scots that resulted in the death of two regents, Murray and Lennox. REF.: *CBA.*

Hamilton, Ian, prom. 1950, Case of, Brit., theft. The Stone of Destiny, seized by King Edward I of England from the Abbey of Scone in 1296 and transported to Westminster Abbey, was a symbol of Scottish nationalism. For centuries the 400-pound block of sandstone remained in Edward the Confessor's Chapel until Ian Hamilton, a patriotic young Scotsman, decided to snatch it back in December 1950.

He was imbued with a feeling of nationalism and a strong desire to restore a cherished historic treasure to its rightful location. To achieve these ends, Hamilton enlisted three confederates who shared his beliefs. They solicited funds from a Glasgow businessman and hatched a daring plan to remove the rock from the chapel during the height of the Christmas celebration, at a time when the English seemed most likely to let their guard down.

At 5 a.m. on Christmas Day, Hamilton left with the massive coronation stone from under the eyes of the local watchmen, and drove it to a secluded spot in Kent. After the New Year holiday passed, he returned to England once more to bring it back home. The plan was to hand it over to the Church of Scotland at the ruins of the Abbey of Arbroath. With a £1,000 reward posted by the English authorities, Hamilton brazenly placed his stone on the altar of the ancient church on Apr. 11, 1951.

It did not remain there long. The relic was brought back to Westminster Abbey where it remains. The government decided not to prosecute Hamilton or his three friends. REF.: *CBA.*

Hamilton, James (Second Earl of Arran, Duke of Chatelherault), c.1515-75, Scot., banish. Governor of Scotland in 1542. He was banished in 1566 for his opposition to the Darnley marriage. REF.: *CBA.*

Hamilton, James (Third Earl of Arran), 1530-1609, Scot., consp. Conspired with Lord James Stuart to try to seize Bothwell. REF.: *CBA.*

Hamilton, James, d.1818, U.S., mur. Hamilton was an enlisted soldier stationed at an army post outside of Albany, N.Y. He possessed a mean temperament, was insubordinate and refractory with his commanding officers, and quarreled often with his fellow soldiers. In July 1818, a black man tried to enlist at the post and Hamilton, who hated blacks, grabbed a bayonet and threatened to kill him, driving off the terrified recruit. Major Benjamin Birdsall, learning of this attack, upbraided Hamilton so severely that Hamilton exploded and, retrieving a rifle from his barracks, shot Birdsall to death. Hamilton was quickly tried in Albany, N.Y., and found Guilty. He was sentenced to be hanged. At his execution, on Nov. 6, 1818, the rope broke and Hamilton was taken to the scaffold a second time. Despite Hamilton's pleading that the rope breaking had been "an act of God" and that he was entitled to be set free, he was hanged a second time and officially pronounced dead minutes later.

REF.: *A Brief Account of the Life, Trial, Sentence, Last Words and Dying Speech of James Hamilton;* CBA; *Horrid Assassination: Sketches of the Life and a Narrative of the Trial of James Hamilton; The Last Dying Words, with a Particular Account of the Execution of James Hamilton; The Life and Dying Confession of James Hamilton; Sketches of the Life and a Narrative of the Trial of James Hamilton.*

Hamilton, James Douglas, See: **Hamilton-Mohun Duel**.

Hamilton, John, c.1511-71, Scot., consp. Helped Mary, Queen of Scots escape from Lochleven. He was archbishop of St. Andrews in 1546, and was hanged in pontifical garments for his supposed involvement in assassinating Murray, the regent. REF.: *CBA.*

Hamilton, John (Marquis of Hamilton), 1532-1604, Scot., consp. Son of James Hamilton, Second Earl of Arran. Loyal supporter of Mary, Queen of Scots along with brother, Claud Hamilton and relative John Hamilton, archbishop of St. Andrews, helped Mary escape from Lochleven and reinstalled her on the Scottish throne in 1568. He assisted with the assassination of Murray in 1570. REF.: *CBA.*

Hamilton, John, d.1716, Scot., mur. Related to the ducal family of Hamilton, John Hamilton's parents sent him to Glasgow to study law, but he abandoned law in favor of the military. At the same time he started gambling, confident his parents would cover his losses. They gave him an advance, but with a warning that their financing had limits.

With money in his pocket, Hamilton met his friends at a village inn near Glasgow. Drinking and gambling for days and nights on end, the friends, however, walked out on Hamilton while he was asleep, leaving him with a bill he could not pay. Hamilton and innkeeper Thomas Arkle quarrelled, and Arkle stripped the sheath from Hamilton's sword. Hamilton, however, did not notice the loss until he had left, but when he did he raced back to the inn clutching his sword. Arkle showered him with insults, so Hamilton stabbed him to death.

Arkle's blind daughter, present at the time, was able to rip off the hem of Hamilton's coat and grab hold of his sword before he escaped. Hamilton fled to Holland and stayed there for two years. When his parents died, he returned to Scotland and on the strength of the sword and coat he had left behind, was apprehended for the murder.

Although Hamilton pleaded intoxication and "extreme ill usage" from Arkle, he was found Guilty and beheaded on June 30, 1716. REF.: *CBA;* Kingston, *Law-Breakers;* Mitchell, *The Newgate Calendar.*

Hamilton, Jones S., prom. 1887, Case of, U.S., mur. Colonel Jones S. Hamilton was a powerful but corrupt Democratic leader in the Mississippi state legislature during the 1880s. He was an anti-prohibitionist at a time when temperance factions were gaining control of the legislature. The move toward a statewide ban on intoxicants was championed by Roderick Dhu Gambrell, the idealistic young editor of the Jackson *Sword & Shield,* the official organ of the prohibitionists.

Gambrell continued to publish editorials denouncing Hamilton and his associates who comprised the "State House ring" until one night someone burned down his print shop. Hamilton decided to publish a rival newspaper. But in a local referendum concerning saloon licensing, the temperance advocates won.

In the early spring of 1887, Hamilton took matters into his own hands after the *Sword & Shield* published a stinging article accusing him of official corruption, among other things. Hamilton and three of his cronies chased Gambrell through the town one night. They beat him and shot him at point blank range while City Marshal Carraway looked on.

Two trials were held. Hamilton and his hired accomplice Eubanks were found Guilty. Under appeal a second trial was granted with a change of venue to an adjoining county. On May 8, 1887, the senator walked out of the courthouse in Jackson a free man. It was alleged that Hamilton had bribed and intimidated the jurors.

A year later, Hamilton brought a libel suit against B.T. Hobbs, editor of the Brookhaven *Leader* for writing: "Hamilton the assassin was now at liberty and all good citizens who had any concern for their lives had better go in doors at night and bar the doors and windows." REF.: *CBA;* Kobler, *Ardent Spirits.*

Hamilton, Mary (AKA: Charles Hamilton, George Hamilton, William Hamilton), prom. 1746, Brit., big. Mary Hamilton was so good at impersonating a man that she was not found out until after she had wed her fourteenth wife.

Brought before the court in 1746 at Taunton in Somersetshire, Hamilton was indicted, but unofficially. There was no legal precedent nor law prohibiting marriage between women. Testifying against her "husband," Hamilton's fourteenth wife, Mary Price, swore that they had bedded and lived together as man and wife for more than three months, and that she did not suspect her spouse until female neighbors pointed out certain anatomical differences.

The verdict of the justices was complicated: "That the he, she, prisoner at the bar, is an uncommon cheat; and we, the Court, do sentence him or her, whichever she may be, to be imprisoned six months and to be whipped in the towns of Taunton, Glastonbury, Wells, and Shipton-Mallet." Hamilton was imprisoned and whipped accordingly in the winter of 1746. REF.: *CBA;* Gurr and Cox, *Famous Australian Crimes;* Mitchell, *The Newgate Calendar;* Nash, *Look For the Woman.*

Hamilton, Patrick, c.1504-28, Scot., her. Early supporter of the principles of the Reformation. He saw Martin Luther and Melanchthon (Philipp Schwarzert) at Wittenberg, and upon his return he was found Guilty of heresy and burned at St. Andrews. REF.: *CBA.*

Hamilton, Ray, 1912-35, U.S., rob.-mur. Ray Hamilton first met Clyde Barrow as a youthful mugger in Houston's Square Root Gang. He later served time with Barrow at a prison farm in Eastham, Texas, and was an occasional accomplice. During a brief but bloody career that began in 1932 when he was nineteen, Hamilton was involved in the armed robberies of more than two dozen enterprises, including seven banks. He was apprehended several times, but always managed to escape, including a prison break in 1934 when Barrow and Bonnie Parker helped him and fellow inmates Henry Methvin and Joe Palmer escape. He was apprehended, convicted of murder, but escaped from the death house in Huntsville, Texas. He was recaptured ten months later and executed on May 10, 1935. See: **Barrow, Clyde Champion.**
REF.: *CBA;* Edge, *Run the Cat Roads;* Gish, *American Bandits;* Louderback, *The Bad Ones;* Nash, *Bloodletters and Badmen.*

Hamilton, Thomas L., prom. 1952, U.S., consp.-asslt.-kid. On Jan. 18, 1951, in Columbus County, N.C., a mob of robed men broke down the door of 38-year-old Evergreen Flowers' home and severely beat her. They knocked her unconscious, bound and gagged her, and left her on a nearby road. This was only one of the many Ku Klux Klan raids that came to the attention of the Federal Bureau of Investigation (FBI). In February 1952, the FBI arrested eight Klansmen involved in thirteen attacks. Three of the victims were black and ten were white. As reasons for their attacks, the Klan cited everything from excessive drinking to nonpayment of debts. Three months later, on May 24, 1952, nine more Klansmen, including Imperial Wizard Thomas L. Hamilton, were arrested for flogging seven people. Hamilton, a 45-year-old grocer from Leesville, S.C., was held on $10,000 bond. On June 19, in Whiteville, N.C., Hamilton and twenty-three other Klansmen were indicted on thirty-eight counts of conspiracy, kidnapping and assault.

During his trial, on July 22, 1952, before Judge Clawson Williams of the Superior Court, Thomas Hamilton surprisingly pleaded guilty to flogging Mrs. Flowers. Twelve other Klansmen who had pleaded not guilty immediately changed their pleas to guilty or to no defense. By pleading guilty to two counts of conspiracy to assault, the Klansmen avoided the kidnapping charge, which was a felony. Horace Strickland, a former Columbus County deputy sheriff serving a prison sentence for a similar flogging case, corroborated Mrs. Flowers' testimony. On July 30, Hamilton was sentenced to four years in prison, while fifteen other Klansmen received sentences ranging from eighteen months to six years. Forty-seven others received suspended sentences and fines of up to $1,500.

On Oct. 22, 1952, a contrite Hamilton denounced the Klan. From a prison camp in Castle Hayne, N.C., Hamilton said, "I am through with the Ku Klux Klan and believe all my former associates will best serve themselves and society as a whole by taking a similar stand." REF.: *CBA.*

Hamilton-Mohun Duel, 1712, Brit., duel. James Douglas Hamilton and Charles Mohun, the Fourth Baron Mohun, duelled after a lengthy legal battle concerning Hamilton's land. Both men were killed in the duel. REF.: *CBA*.

Hamlin, Oliver D., Jr., 1892-1973, U.S., jur. Deputy district attorney of Alameda, Calif., from 1915-20, and judge on the superior court at Alameda from 1947-53. He was nominated by President Dwight D. Eisenhower to the northern district court of California in 1953, and to the ninth circuit court in 1958. REF.: *CBA*.

Hamm, William A., Jr., See: **Barker Brothers.**

Hammarskjoeid, Dag Hjalmer Agne Carl, 1905-61, Congo, assass. From 1953 until his untimely death on Sept. 18, 1961, Dag Hammarskjoeld served as secretary general of the United Nations. His term of office encompassed the early years of the Cold War, and at times this Swedish statesman found himself in the cross fire between east and west.

In 1960 a revolt in the Congo became a test of will between UN peace-keeping forces and Soviet-sponsored revolutionaries led by Patrice Lumumba, who sought to overthrow the last vestiges of Belgian colonial rule. The outcome of the struggle was never in doubt. The Belgians were willing to relinquish control of the region, but they were also more inclined to deal favorably with the west than Lumumba or the guerilla leader Moise Tshombe, who wanted to separate the Katanga province from the rest of the Congo. Hammarskjoeld wanted an orderly transition from Belgium to the moderate President Joseph Kasavubu, voted into office in 1960. The secretary general was denounced from both sides for his actions. The west believed he was timid in his employment of the peace-keeping troops. Soviet Premier Nikita Khushchev labeled him a "bloody-handed lackey of the colonial powers" after he sanctioned the use of Indian troops against Katangan rebels.

At the urging of the western powers, President Kasavubu arrested Lumumba in January 1961. With three of his supporters, Lumumba was turned over to the military forces of Katanga where he was murdered. The Soviet were infuriated by this development.

In September 1961 Hammarskjoeld agreed to fly to the Congo to meet with Tshombe in attempt to straighten out the tangled political situation in the new nation. On Sept. 18, he chartered a DC-6 in Leopoldville that had undergone an aerial attack just a day earlier. To throw off the press, pilot Per-Erik Hallonquist changed the flight plan at the last minute. The plane would land in Kasai province.

After about six hours of flying, the craft began its final approach from the southwest into Ndola. Suddenly there was a bright flash and an explosion. The plane, containing fourteen passengers and the UN secretary general, crashed deep in the forest. Searchers located the wreckage, but there was only one survivor, an American named Harry Jullian. Hammarskjoeld's body was found in the wreckage. An ace of spades was tucked into his jacket lapel and a revolver was found nearby.

It was determined that he had not died in the crash, nor had he been shot on the ground. The fuselage of the DC-6 was riddled with bullets and the hum of jet planes in the distance was reported by at least one eyewitness. Before Harry Jullian died of his wounds, he explained that Hammarskjoeld ordered the plane turned around shortly before the crash. No reason was given for his decision to abort the mission. A UN commission that investigated the matter could not say with certainty whether the crash was caused by sabotage or pilot error. See: **Lumumba, Patrice.** REF.: *CBA*.

Hammel, William Augustus, b.1865, U.S., law enfor. off. William Hammel served as sheriff of Los Angeles County from 1898 to 1904. He later became chief of police in Los Angeles, serving from Apr. 6, 1904, until Oct. 31, 1905. REF.: *CBA*.

Hammer, Armand, 1899-   , U.S., mansl.-corr. Armand Hammer was a founding member of the American Communist Party, and, at twenty-three, a millionaire who imported wheat into the Soviet Union while exporting furs and minerals for the Soviet government. In many ways, his life was a paradox. He was the scion of a large drug company fortune, but drew the ire of the press and U.S. State Department for his warm relationship with

the Soviets in the early 1920s. His economic ties to Russia endured through seven decades as Hammer branched out into oil, American-made pencils (which found their way into the Soviet school system), and Ford tractors.

While in college studying to be a pharmacist, Hammer developed a line of low-cost generic drugs. It was during this time, in 1919, that he was convicted of manslaughter for performing a fatal abortion. Hammer was sent to Sing Sing Prison, but was later pardoned. Years later he ran into trouble with the government again when it was revealed that he made an illegal campaign contribution to President Richard Nixon during his 1972 re-election campaign. For this he was sentenced to one year's probation and assessed a $3,000 fine. Hammer was again granted a pardon, this time by President George Bush in 1989. In 1987 his autobiography, *Hammer,* was published. REF.: *CBA*.

Hammerling, Peter, prom. 1896, U.S., asslt.-rob.-rape. Peter Hammerling's criminal record dates back to July 24, 1894, when he was convicted of assault, robbery, and rape in Chicago. He was released on July 24, 1895. But Hammerling, a compulsive rapist, did not stay out of trouble long. On Mar. 18, 1896, he assaulted Julia Allen on Chicago's South Side as she was returning home from the post office. He dragged Allen to her basement, raped her, and fled with three dollars. Assisted by women officials from the nearby YWCA, she gave an accurate physical description to Detective Clifton Wooldridge.

Inquiries placed Hammerling, who had been posing as a carpenter, in the vicinity. A week after Mrs. Allen was assaulted, Wooldridge arrested the rapist in an empty building where he was scheduled to work. However, the case eventually collapsed when Mrs. Allen broke down in court and was unable to provide hard evidence against her assailant. The prisoner's alibi was a good one, compelling the court to order his release.

Hammerling was arrested again on Oct. 22, 1900. This time however, a conviction on three rape charges was returned. He received an indeterminate prison sentence.

REF.: *CBA;* Wooldridge, *Hands Up.*

Hammersley, John Richard, and **Heath, Trevor Ernest,** and **Bellson, Samuel,** prom. 1956, Brit., brib.-corr. In 1956 two members of the Brighton Criminal Investigation Department (CID), and a local bookmaker were sentenced to prison in one of the biggest police corruption scandals to rock Great Britain in the twentieth century. The case involved the solicitation of bribes by police officers, a conspiracy to obstruct justice, and the violation of the closing ordinance in Brighton.

The accused police officers included Chief Constable Charles Field Williams Ridge, fifty-eight; Detective-Inspector John Hammersley, forty; and Detective-Sergeant Trevor Heath, thirty-six. A local gambling boss named Samuel Bellson, and the licensee of the saloon, Anthony Lyons, were also named in the indictment.

Bellson allegedly used his influence in police circles to have charges against Henry Leach of Brighton dropped in exchange for a £100 payment. It was further charged that Alan Roy Bennett, the proprietor of the Astor Club, was forced to pay £20 a week to Ridge in order to keep his place open after hours. The Astor Club had acquired an unsavory reputation as a hangout for known criminals and drunken brawlers. It was popularly known as the "Bucket of Blood." When a police raid was planned, Sergeant Heath routinely warned the owner not to open the club.

While the Astor Club enjoyed immunity from police raids, other establishments that did not participate in the graft were targeted for harassment. The gambler Bellson, it was charged, acted as the solicitor of bribes for Ridge.

Trevor Heath defended his record. He had in fact taken credit for the most arrests among all Brighton CID men. A "scorecard" of sorts was posted on the board, as officers competed with one another to rack up the highest number of arrests in a month. Justice Donovan would assail this dubious practice in his lengthy summation.

Constable Ridge produced a chart showing that during his eight years in office, the number of reportable crimes in Brighton had decreased from 2,183 to 1,674. He denied taking bribes to keep certain protected clubs open, arguing that licensing regulations were strictly upheld and gambling suppressed. Ridge was eventually cleared of all charges.

Hammersley and Heath were convicted and sentenced to five years' imprisonment, and Bellson to three when the case went before Justice Donovan at the Old Bailey in 1956.

REF.: *CBA;* Furneaux, *Famous Criminal Cases, vol. 5.*

Hammett, (Samuel) Dashiell, 1894-1961, U.S., detective writer. Born in Maryland, Dashiell Hammett's father was a hotel clerk who moved several times with his wife and three children. Hammett was raised in Philadelphia and Baltimore. Tall and lean at an early age, Hammett dropped out of school when he was fourteen and went on the bum. He was always fascinated with criminals and the underworld. In 1915, Hammett worked for a Baltimore brokerage firm but he had no head for figures and quit, taking a job with the Pinkerton Detective Agency in 1915. It was while he was with the Pinkertons that Hammett learned how to be a detective and also learned the rich background of criminal history he would later employ in his detective stories.

The man who taught Hammett as a detective was James Wright, the Pinkerton agent in charge of the Baltimore office. He was a wiry, tough detective with an idealistic code he drummed into his men, particularly Hammett, whom he especially liked. Wright's code was: never cheat the client, never break laws to achieve success, remain anonymous, and play a "straight game,"

The first appearance of Hammett's detective masterpiece, *The Maltese Falcon,* in *Black Mask* magazine.

below. The smugglers were a kind lot, rushing downstairs to drag the Pinkerton detective inside where they tended his bruises and stuck his injured foot into a pot of hot water.

all of the detective ethics later advocated by his greatest fictional detective, Sam Spade. Wright would serve as the role model in Hammett's "Continental Op" stories. Hammett's specialty was in surveillance; he was considered the best "shadow man" the Pinkerton Agency had in the South, the Baltimore office servicing all southern states.

One of those Hammett followed during WWI, a suspected German spy, was "a boring fat man," and it was this portly gentleman, with expensive tastes and a high lifestyle, that Hammett made into Casper Gutman, the scheming fat man plotter in *The Maltese Falcon.* Spade, of course, was Hammett himself, who, more or less, gave his great fictional detective his own first name. Hammett, of course, drew on other persons he dealt with in the criminal world, gunmen, pimps, gamblers, thieves of all stripes, to create his memorable characters.

Publicity photo of Dashiell Hammett, 1934.

During WWI, Hammett enlisted in the army but contracted tuberculosis, and was mustered out after serving eighteen months, without ever going to France to fight. He rejoined the Pinkertons, with a job in the agency's Northwest Territory. Always frail, Hammett became ill again and was hospitalized in Tacoma where he met an attractive nurse, Josephine Dolan, whom he married in 1921. In that year, Hammett joined the Pinkerton office in San Francisco where he experienced his wildest adventures. Again, he was a "shadow man" but he saw many reversals. On one occasion, Hammett, trailing smugglers, climbed onto the roof of a porch of a roadhouse to look into a second-story window. The roof suddenly gave way, sending Hammett crashing to the porch

On another occasion, Hammett tracked a man across half the country, searching for a ferris wheel the culprit had stolen from a circus. He worked with local police to get information but later said this was not always helpful. A southern sheriff once gave Hammett a detailed description of a man Hammett was seeking, including the position of several moles on the suspect's body, but omitted the fact that the suspect was missing an arm. Hammett's wife recounted an occasion when, in San Francisco, Hammett was shadowing a man, unaware that the suspect's confederate was shadowing Hammett. The second man came up from behind and hit Hammett on the head with a brick. He was knocked out and left with a permanent scar and a large bump on his head.

He could be tough. Hammett was escorting a prisoner to jail one freezing winter day, driving through the country which was deep with snow. He had been grilling the suspect throughout the trip but the man refused to admit any wrongdoing. The car broke down, or Hammett pretended that the car broke down, leaving the two men sitting in the unheated car. Hammett was dressed in heavy clothing to insulate himself against the freezing weather but the suspect was lightly clad in overalls and a shirt. According to Hammett the prisoner continued to "affirm his innocence...After shivering all night in the front seat his morale was low and I had no difficulty in getting a complete confession from him while walking to the nearest ranch the next morning."

Hammett also worked on the notorious Roscoe "Fatty" Arbuckle case where the silent film comedian had been accused of raping and causing the death of an attractive starlet, Virginia Rappe, during a wild party at the St. Francis Hotel in San Francisco. The nature of the detective's involvement was never made clear but most likely the Pinkertons were hired by the defense to find evidence to discredit the victim. Hammett reportedly spent a good deal of his own time looking for the instrument that Arbuckle had used on the dead girl, a search that was, in the end, futile.

Hammett testifying in 1952, before the House Un-American Activities Committee.

As a Pinkerton detective, Hammett scrupulously upheld the code of ethics he had learned from Jimmy Wright. On several occasions Hammett was offered bribes—often considerable amounts of money—to let fugitives go but he regularly refused these offers. He was offered a share of the huge spoils of a narcotics ring in San Diego to keep quiet about the activities of the group. Again he refused. Hammett was even offered $5,000 to kill a labor agitator but again shunned such vile ways of making a living. Hammett's code was summed up later in the words of his memorable character, Sam Spade, in *The Maltese Falcon,* when Spade is about to turn in Brigid O'Shaughnessy, a woman he loves but a murderess who has killed his partner:

> "Yes, angel," Spade tells his lover, "I'm going to send you over (to the police)...you're taking the fall...I won't play the sap for you...You killed Miles (Miles Archer, Spade's partner) and you're going over for it...Listen, this won't do any good. You'll never understand me but I'll try once and then give it up. When a man's partner is killed he's supposed to do something about it. It doesn't make any difference what you thought of him. He was your partner and you're supposed to do something about it. And it happens that we're in the detective business and when one in your organization gets killed, it's bad business to let the killer get away with it, bad all around, bad for every detective everywhere...I'll have some rotten nights after I've sent you over, but that will pass."

Hammett thought of himself as a good detective when working for the Pinkertons, later stating: "I was a pretty good sleuth but possibly overrated because of the plausibility with which I could explain away my failures, proving them inevitable and no fault of mine." All of what Hammett learned as a Pinkerton went into his precise, hard-hitting detective fiction which began appearing in such publications as *Black Mask* magazine in the mid-1920s. In 1929, Hammett published the novels, *Red Harvest* and *The Dain Curse.* In 1930, *The Maltese Falcon* appeared. Then, in 1931, *The Glass Key* came out, followed, in 1932, by *The Thin Man* with its memorable high society sleuths, Nick and Nora Charles. The wife in this and subsequent Thin Man stories was based upon writer Lillian Florence Hellman, with whom Hammett had a long and tempestuous affair, right up to the time of his death.

Hammett was a man of inner trouble but possessed steely nerves. When Hellman was berating him one night, he sat patiently through her abuse for quite some time, merely smoking cigarette after cigarette, refusing to respond to her tirade. Then, according to Hellman, Hammett took a burning cigarette and ground it out on his own cheek. Hellman expressed horror and shock at this action, asking Hammett why he had done such a terribly painful thing to himself. Replied Hammett: "To keep myself from doing it to you."

During the 1930s, with Hammett's literary star at its zenith, he went to work for the Hollywood Studios, earning as much as $8,000 a week while shaping his books and stories into screenplays. He became the darling of the Hollywood community of writers, which included Ben Hecht, Charles MacArthur, Dorothy Parker, and others. Hammett, a heavy drinker from youth, began to drink to excess and suffered terribly from alcoholic bouts which began to debilitate his energies. He earned enormous amounts of money at this time and Hollywood was later accused of spoiling Hammett's talents but Hammett spoiled his own ambitions.

During WWII, Hammett worked on the U.S. Army newspaper, *Stars and Stripes,* being stationed in Alaska at one point. Following the war, Hammett, who had long been associated with leftist causes, was accused of being a communist and incurred the wrath of the House UnAmerican Activities committee, drawing a prison sentence for contempt. Upon his release, Hammett continued to express his leftist beliefs and was something of a folk hero among his peers. He nevertheless ceased to be a functioning writer. His heyday of writing detective fiction—considered the best of its kind in the world, along with that of Raymond Chandler—was long over by the time Hammett died in 1961. See: **Arbuckle, Roscoe; Hecht, Ben; Pinkerton Detective Agency.**

REF.: *CBA;* Eames, *Sleuths, Inc.;* Falk, *Lillian Hellman;* Haycraft, *Murder for Pleasure;* Hellman, *An Unfinished Woman;* ____, *Pentimento;* ____, *Scoundrel Time;* Herron, *Dashiell Hammett Tour;* Hirsh, *The Dark Side of the Screen;* Johnson, *Dashiell Hammett, A Life;* Layman, *Shadow Man: The Life of Dashiell Hammett;* Madden, *Tough Guy Writers of the Thirties;* Marcus, *The Continental Op;* Margoles, *Which Way Did He Go?;* Moody, *Lillian Hellman, Playwright;* Morgan, *Prince of Crime;* Nolan, *Dashiell Hammett;* Ruehlmann, *Saint with a Gun;* Ruhm, *The Hard-Boiled Detective;* Steinbrunner and Penzler, *Encyclopedia of Mystery and Detection;* Tuska, *The Detective in Hollywood;* (FICTION), Gores, *Hammett;* (FILM), *The Maltese Falcon,* 1931; *Julia,* 1977.

Hammond, Amos, d.1854, U.S., (unsolv.) mur. Amos Hammond was shot to death in 1854 in Atlanta, Ga. His killer, never caught, was apparently not satisfied with the young man's demise. Hammond's body was placed at night on the tracks of the Macon and Western Railroad, where a freight train mangled it almost beyond recognition. REF.: *CBA.*

Hammond, Geoffrey, prom. 1969, Brit., mur. Considered a perfect student, Geoffrey Hammond of Wimbledon had won the Duke of Edinburgh's Award and had demonstrated life-saving techniques on British television. Together with his friends, Hammond selectively harassed homosexuals, on what the boys commonly referred to as "queer bashing" missions. The boys mostly confined their activities to the vicinity of the Queensmere subway, where they indulged in petty acts of vandalism. One night in 1969, Hammond and his gang pounced on 28-year-old clerk Michael de Gruchy. It was not known if de Gruchy was homosexual, but this did not matter to Hammond, who was eventually given a life sentence for the murder. Four other boys, ranging in age from fifteen to eighteen, were remanded over to the state. Hammond's father actually defended his son's actions, comparing him to the mountain climber who "scales a mountain just because it is there." REF.: *CBA.*

Hammond, John Hays, 1855-1936, S. Afri., rebel. Assisted Cecil Rhodes in developing South African resources and in instigating an insurrection in Transvaal to overthrow the South African Republic. He was arrested after the Jameson Raid, a raid into Transvaal in 1895, and sentenced to death. The sentence was reduced to 15 years in prison, but he was released after paying a $125,000 fine. REF.: *CBA*.

Hammond, Karl, 1963- , U.S., rape-mur. Karl Hammond "worries me the most," parole officer Joseph Ober-Hauser told FBI agents during their investigation of the rape and murder of Donna Lynn Vetter. Less than two years before, the 23-year-old honor student and Texas native was hired by the FBI as a legal secretary. Now they were looking for her murderer.

In January 1986, Donna Vetter moved into an apartment in San Antonio, Texas, only a short commute from the FBI offices where she worked. In August 1986, Vetter noticed that her door had been tampered with. She notified the security officer of the complex, who made a note to increase security patrols. One month later, on Sept. 4, security received a call from Donna's next-door neighbor, who noticed that the screen had been removed from Vetter's rear window. The guard investigated and found Vetter sprawled on the kitchen floor, dead. Neighbors had heard neither screams nor loud noises; nothing had been reported.

The FBI, routinely involved in cases whenever the victim of a crime is a bureau employee, developed a psychological profile of the killer and began to discover a pattern of similar rapes and near rapes in the vicinity. All of the victims had lived alone, and all had been raped at home at knife or gunpoint. From a list of fifteen suspects, parole officer Joseph Ober-Hauser pointed to 22-year-old Karl Hammond, paroled after serving less than four years of an eight-year sentence for burglary and rape.

On Sept. 15, 1986, eleven days after Vetter's slaying, police lifted fingerprints from the scene of another rape. They belonged to Hammond. Asked if he had raped the woman, Hammond said, "Yeah."

Hammond's attorney tried to raise an insanity defense. Hammond himself claimed he could not have murdered Donna Vetter because he was working the day she was killed. The jury, however, found him Guilty of murder and rape on Mar. 30, 1987. While waiting to be sentenced Hammond escaped and was on the streets for a day before he was recaptured. He was sentenced to die by chemical injection. A relative of Vetter's expressed regret that Hammond would not "feel what Donna felt," saying, "He ruined not only her future but her family's. She can never, ever be replaced."

By law, Hammond's death sentence will be automatically appealed to the state supreme court. Meanwhile, he resides on death row in the Texas Correctional Facility at Huntsville. REF.: *CBA*.

Hammond, Travis, prom. 1942, Case of, Brit., rape. On July 17, 1942, in London during WWII, a 16-year-old girl met an American soldier while drinking with a girlfriend after work. The following day, she went to the police claiming she had been raped by the soldier. Army private Travis P. Hammond was the first man tried by an army court-martial after a U.S.A. Visiting Forces Bill passed by Parliament removed the non-British members of the armed forces from local jurisdiction. On Aug. 10, 1942, the eleven-member court presided over by Colonel Milton M. Towner convened in London to hear the case. Hammond's fellow soldiers testified that he was guilty, and that he could not remember what had happened because he had been drinking. They further explained that Hammond admitted to the crime when confronted by his commanding officer, Major Lawrence Wogan. Other incriminating evidence included a handkerchief, belonging to the girl, found in Hammond's possession. In his defense, a civilian witness testified that they had not heard any screams, and the victim herself admitted during three hours of testimony that she had lent the soldier her handkerchief after the alleged rape. On Aug. 13, after four days of testimony, the tribunal found Hammond Not Guilty, a verdict which was applauded by the mostly British spectators. REF.: *CBA*.

Hammond, William Alexander, 1828-1900, U.S., corr. U.S. surgeon general who became a brigadier general in 1862. He was court-martialed and dismissed in 1864, but he was later reinstated by President Rutherford B. Hayes after a review of his case in 1878. REF.: *CBA*.

Hammons, Samuel, d.1968, U.S., (unsolv.) mur. Sam Hammons of Avon, Ohio, was an employee of the National Aeronautics and Space Administration (NASA). He was the father of five, and, by all appearances, a contented family man leading a quiet suburban existence.

On Feb. 24, 1968, he picked up a mysterious parcel at the Greyhound Bus Terminal in Cleveland. The package was postmarked Salt Lake City, via Chicago, and it bore his name. Hammons signed for it, then drove back to his residence in Avon. As he unwrapped the box in his kitchen, it exploded. Someone had sent Sam Hammons a bomb.

FBI bomb experts were dispatched to Cleveland to investigate. The bomb was a crudely fashioned device powered by a twelve-volt battery. There was no apparent motive for the murder until agents began digging into Hammons' movements during the previous six months. They learned that he had taken off four days the previous November to travel to Petaluma, Calif. His family had no knowledge of the trip, but airline records showed that he had booked a return flight. While in California, Hammons saw an old high school girlfriend from Central City. The murder of Hammons had been committed by the woman's jealous suitor, Albert Ricci.

Ricci employed the woman in his bank, and he feared that Hammons was about to interfere with his relationship. It was Ricci who sent the bomb to Cleveland on the bus. While returning from Salt Lake City, Ricci was involved in a fatal car accident which had all the earmarks of a suicide. Though no one was ever charged with the murder of Sam Hammons, the FBI was satisfied that Albert Ricci was the bomber.

REF.: *CBA*; Gribble, *The Deadly Professionals*.

Hamon, Clara Smith (Clara Smith), 1892- , Case of, U.S., mur. On Nov. 21, 1920, oil millionaire and Oklahoma Republican National Committeeman Jake L. Hamon shot himself while cleaning his gun at the Randol Hotel in Ardmore, Okla., or so it was reported in the press. Five days later one of the West's most prominent and powerful citizens was dead.

Two days after the shooting, Hamon's stenographer, Mrs. Clara Smith Hamon, disappeared. Described as "twenty-seven and pretty, wearing a fur coat and a number of diamond rings," she was accused of firing the shot that killed her employer of ten years.

An inexperienced schoolgirl when she met Jake Hamon, Clara Smith would three years later marry his nephew Frank Hamon, one year after that divorce him, and for nearly the next decade live with Jake Hamon as his mistress.

Under Hamon's tutelage, Smith became a woman of sophistication and wealth, Hamon's confidante and advisor in business and politics. Jake, moreover, never made a secret of their relationship. "I'll put you in the White House and make the whole world like it," he told her, speaking of his ambition to be president.

By the time Clara Smith Hamon—soon to become "Clara Smith," and then just "Clara" in the press—came home to Oklahoma, crossing over the border from Chihuahua, Mex., one month after Hamon's death, she was already a *cause célèbre*. Although Hamon's will left her one-fourth of his estate and he had named her the beneficiary of a $100,000 life insurance policy, public opinion was heavily in Clara's favor, largely, however, because of her diaries.

Printed on the front page of the *Daily Oklahoman,* the journal entries vacillated from the high life to the low. "I smiled at the big, black spider, then strolled into his net," she wrote in an early entry, claiming later that "happiness is everything, and it's not for sale." Calling Hamon, "the Colonel," she agonized that "the oil of his soul that fed the flame of desire for cruelty must exhaust itself and I was doomed to be its victim."

When Smith returned from Mexico to be tried, Hamon's wife, Georgea Hamon, surfaced. Depicted by the press as a tight-lipped, matronly "raven" dressed in widow's black, she was mercilessly compared to young Smith. At the trial, however,

Smith dressed down—gone were the platinum watch and diamonds, gifts from her dead lover. The newspapers called her "the Moth" and her Svengali-like lover, "the Flame."

Ex-police chief W.B. Nichols, testifying for the prosecution said Hamon told him Smith had shot him but made Nichols promise not to tell. Claiming that Hanon was so drunk when he arrived "that he kissed me," Doctor Hardy, attending physician at the sanitarium where Hanon died, explained that Hamon was suffering from cirrhosis of the liver and that his drunken state and weakened condition caused his death. Hardy also admitted to having treated Clara Smith at earlier dates for "permanent, serious trouble liable to cause death," and maintained that her fragile constitution "could not stand beating and cuffing."

Smith's story was that Hamon had come back to the hotel in a drunken frenzy and, after choking, beating, and kicking her, had smashed a rocking chair down on her arm, causing the revolver she had picked up in self-defense to go off.

On Mar. 17, 1921, the all-male jury, after thirty-nine minutes of deliberation, found Clara Smith Not Guilty of murdering her lover. Spectators in the courtroom climbed over chairs and railings to embrace and congratulate her. Smith shook hands with the jurors, and thanked them for acquitting her. "I knew you would—I never doubted you," she said. The foreman later told the press, "there never was any question about acquitting her from the start. We already had our minds made up."

Clara Smith went off to Hollywood to try her hand at acting and start a new life. While producing a film about the shooting of Jake Hamon, she met and married producer John W. Gormon. Three years later, however, she filed for divorce, charging cruelty and intoxication. REF.: *CBA*.

Hampden, John, 1594-1643, Brit., treas. Put in prison in 1627 because he refused to repay a loan. He was a member of the Short Parliament in 1640. The attorney general impeached him in 1642 for his opposition to the king's policies, but he evaded arrest. REF.: *CBA*.

Hampton, Mary Katheryn, 1942-   , U.S., (wrong. convict.) mur. At the age of seventeen, Mary Hampton left Sandy Hook, Ky., to live with her boyfriend Emmitt Monroe Spencer. Hampton lived with Spencer for eleven months, during which time she gave birth to an infant son.

In April 1960, Spencer was arrested and convicted of murdering a 36-year-old pipe-fitter in Key West, Fla. It was Hampton's testimony that helped send Spencer to Florida's Death Row. The killer concocted a story implicating Mary in two of his many murders. He told Louisiana authorities that she had participated in the murders of Benjamin Yount and Hermine Fiedler near Patterson on Dec. 31, 1959.

Mary Hampton was arrested back in Kentucky. She confessed on Apr. 11, 1961, after the police threatened her with the electric chair. The confession was accepted, and with it, the presumption of innocence was gone. There was no evidence linking her to the murders other than the faulty testimony of an unreliable witness. She was convicted on two counts of first-degree murder and sentenced to life in prison which she began serving at the Women's State Prison in San Gabriel, La., on Apr. 24, 1961.

Reporter Gene Miller of the Miami *Herald* began a one man rage in the pages of his newspaper to exonerate Mary Hampton. He spent three years investigating the case and interviewing witnesses before Hampton got a second chance in court. By that time, famed attorney F. Lee Bailey had become interested in the crusade and agreed to waive his fees and represent her. Bailey destroyed Spencer's testimony, which accused Mary of participating in forty-seven of forty-eight murders committed in a ten-year period.

Hampton's original conviction was upheld in court, but in a special hearing conducted in November 1966, her sentence was commuted by Louisiana Governor John McKeithen and the State Board of Pardons ordered her released. See: **Bailey, F. Lee**. REF.: *CBA*.

Hampton, Melvin, 1941-   , U.S., mur. The controversial

insanity plea came under sharp criticism in Cook County, Ill., when the Chicago Read Mental Health Center released murderer Melvin Hampton after determining that he was cured. Twenty months after his discharge on Oct. 24, 1974, Hampton strangled 59-year-old Ruth Thieben to death in her North Side Chicago apartment. The widow had taken pity on the homeless drifter and had provided him with food and lodging before he killed her on July 17, 1976. Police officials expressed amazement at Hampton's release after reviewing his lengthy criminal record.

He had been arrested thirty-seven times in California, Florida, Alabama, Georgia, and Illinois on charges of auto theft, theft of property, assault, and armed robbery. He was convicted only once for prowling. Melvin Hampton was first implicated in a murder in 1968. Three years later, he killed his 39-year-old girlfriend Martha Knight, but was ruled incompetent to stand trial on the grounds of insanity by Judge Louis Garippo. Hampton was sent to a mental health center in downstate Chester, Ill.

He was transferred to the Read Center on Aug. 28, 1974, where he remained until officials pronounced him cured. "The process is beginning to become like a revolving door," said Dr. Edward Kelleher of the County Circuit Court's Psychiatric Institute, echoing the concerns of court watchers. "Basically the law as it's written makes it impossible to keep a fellow like this confined."

Then, on July 27, 1976, Hampton was again found incompetent to stand trial. He was sent back to the Chester facility by Judge James Strunk of the Cook County Criminal Court. "Good Lord in heaven. It's appalling," commented Joseph DiLeonardi, he citywide homicide commander of the Chicago Police Department. "This is his third murder charge and he's beaten all three. That makes him a killer. It's the responsibility of the courts to review his record and put him away. I can see once maybe, but this is the third time. Let's lock him up and keep him there. If they (hospital officials) take into consideration his record, I don't see how they can let him go." REF.: *CBA*.

Hanau, Marthe, 1890-1935, Fr., fraud. The daughter of a Parisian industrialist, Marthe Hanau founded a financial news magazine, then used her influence and position to sell $4 million in worthless securities.

Born in 1890, Hanau married Lazare Bloch and founded a beauty cream firm with him, which collapsed when WWI decimated the work force. Although the marriage fell apart around the same time, Bloch and Hanau continued to work together. In 1919 Hanau bought a financial paper, *Gazette du Franc et des Nations*, and built it into a prosperous enterprise, with Bloch as the circulation and publicity manager. Using the paper to promote her own firms, which were vague operations with no products, she paid writers ten times the usual rate to promote her specious companies. To rival the established Agence Havas, the agency that had supplied financial news to the country's city pages, Hanau set up the Agence Interpresse, taking her news directly from Havas, or slanting it to suit her own purposes. Issuing short-term loans with an 8 percent interest, Hanau made profits as high as 40 percent.

By promising to accept the shares of other companies as securities, Hanau was given many investments which she quickly sold. She took options on good real estate and issued stock against them. Eventually, the banks became suspicious and realized Hanau's scheme. She managed to evade investigations by using her influential friends, including prominent government leaders, but Hanau's fraudulent schemes finally began to collapse when anxious investors tried to withdraw their funds.

Arrested along with Bloch and several assistants in December 1928, Hanau had assets of about 31 million francs and debts totalling 50 million francs. Jailed for swindling and bankruptcy, she waited for fifteen months in a St. Lazare prison, then went on a twenty-two day hunger strike to get her case into court, becoming a popular heroine in the process. Prohibited from forcibly feeding her in jail, police transferred Hanau to a hospital, where it took seven interns to feed her intravenously. Briefly left alone, the robust woman made a rope of sheets and escaped, leaving a note that said: "Disgusted by the violence to which I have been subjected I am leaving." She walked directly back to the St. Lazare jail, where she regained her health, then went on another hunger strike. She recovered in time for their trial in February 1931. Found Guilty, she was given a light sentence of two years in jail (most of which she had already served) and a fine of 3,000 francs.

Freed in December 1931, she started another paper, *Forces*, and was again arrested in April 1932 when the paper published her own police dossier, stolen from the Finance Minister's desk. Jailed again, Hanau was found dead in her cell of an overdose of sleeping pills on July 19, 1935. She had told her attorney the day before, "I shall always be mistress of my fate."

REF.: *CBA*; MacDougall, *Hoaxes*.

Hanberry, Jack, prom. 1981, U.S., Case of, theft. Jack Hanberry, an ordained Baptist minister, was also the warden at the Atlanta Federal Penitentiary.

On Sept. 27, 1981, Hanberry was arrested for allegedly stealing a hairbrush. A security guard testified that he had seen Hanberry put a brush in his pocket. Hanberry, who had served in prisons in Tallahassee, Fla., and Denver, Colo., was also named chaplain of the year by the 1971 convention of the American Correctional Association. He explained that he had purchased a brush at another store and discarded the receipt. While looking for another brush at the second store, he took the brush out of his pocket to compare them, then replaced the brush in his pocket. A jury deliberated for eight hours before acquitting Hanberry on Nov. 27, 1981. REF.: *CBA*.

Hancock, Edna, prom. 1944, Case of, U.S., perj. On July 1, 1944, an employee of the Brooklyn State Hospital found 30-year-old Edna Hancock, a nurses assistant, and Murray Goldman, having sex in an empty room in the women's dormitory at the hospital. Hancock accused Goldman of attempted rape and six months later, in January 1944, in the courtroom of Judge Samuel Leibowitz, Goldman was tried for the attack. The prosecution relied heavily on the testimony of Mrs. Hancock, who stated that she had never met Goldman and that she had screamed as he attacked her. Goldman stated that they had met six weeks earlier, had sexual relations seven times, and that during the alleged attack she had not screamed. The jury found Goldman Guilty, and sentenced him to ten years, but Judge Leibowitz set aside the conviction and ordered the district attorney to administer a lie detector test to Goldman. The test showed Goldman to be truthful and the judge released him. Edna Hancock was arrested and held at the Woman's House of Detention in Manhattan. On Feb. 18, 1944, a Kings County Grand Jury indicted Edna Hancock for perjury and fixed her bail at $25,000. However, on Mar. 3, 1944, in the Kings County courtroom of Judge Peter J. Brancato, the jury acquitted Mrs. Hancock. REF.: *CBA*.

Hancock, Joseph, b.1886, U.S., jur. Served as circuit judge of Jefferson County, Ky., from 1932-45, and sat on Kentucky parole board in 1964. He was nominated to the district court by President Harry S. Truman in 1948. REF.: *CBA*.

Hand, Dora, See: **Kennedy, James**.

Hand, Horace, 1893-1958, Brit., (unsolv.) mur. On July 11, 1958, Horace Hand, sixty-five, was battered to death on the cliffs near Newquay, Cornwall, England. Known as the "Policeman's Nightmare," around 40,000 people were interviewed in the officers' search for a young man who was seen running from the area shouting, "I'll fetch an ambulance." All witnesses in the vicinity were asked to identify their positions at 11:30 a.m. the day of the crime on an aerial photograph. Hand's body was found after an anonymous caller telephoned for an ambulance. His murderer was never found.

REF.: *CBA*; Furneaux, *Famous Criminal Cases, vol. 6*.

Hand, Learned (Billings Learned Hand), 1872-1961, U.S., jur. Served as U.S. district judge at Albany, N.Y. from 1909-24, and as judge of U.S. Court of Appeals, second circuit, from 1924-51. He heard special cases from 1951-61. The length of his tenure as a federal judge set a record. REF.: *CBA*.

Hands, Daniel, prom. 1875-79, Brit., Case of, perj. Daniel Hands started a hosiery factory in Leicester, England, in 1866, and faced bankruptcy after four mediocre years of business. A partial fire in the factory provided Hands with £4,000, which quickly disappeared to pay previous debts. With an urgent need for cash, Hands took on young Thomas Scampton as a partner; Scampton's father had offered to invest £500 as his part of the deal. While it did not thrive, the business survived another four years.

There was a running joke around Hands' offices that "nothing can save us except a fire." Hands carefully kept up with his insurance premiums, changing the machinery and stock value in 1875 from its 1871 estimate of £1,100 to £13,928. On Feb. 17, 1875, the hosiery company closed at its usual time, 8 p.m., and all the employees left. At 10:30, the building was in flames. Hands brought the news to Scampton early the next morning. The insurance company was suspicious about the fire and refused to pay.

Shortly afterwards, Hands went to the police, accusing Scampton of arson. The chief witness for the prosecution was Hands himself, supported by his brother, his son, and several employees.

Hands claimed that Scampton had let all the workers go home ten minutes early, and that he had put highly flammable yarn bundles in a cupboard under the stairs. As the accused, Scampton was not allowed to testify. Unfortunately for the young partner, his attorney was so confident that the charges were invented and would not hold up that he did not bother to present evidence for his client, and did not even call Scampton's father to testify. The jury found Scampton Guilty of arson, and he was given a sentence of twelve years at hard labor.

While Scampton served four years of his sentence, his father, friends, and wife, Georgiana Scampton searched for a way to prove his innocence. Finally, they raised funds and prepared the case, which opened at the Leicester Assizes in about 1879. The trial accused Hands of perjury, and the key witness was Scampton, who denied all the charges that had been brought against him. He explained that Hands had lied about his investment in the company, exaggerating the amount by about £2,800. Scampton's statements were corroborated by several other witnesses. He described how Hands had given him the initial news of the fire with no suggestion that it could have been anything but an accident; he had become disgruntled only after proposing two separate schemes, the first to defraud creditors, and the second to involve his partner's father-in-law as a creditor to collect more money. Scampton rejected them both. An innkeeper also testified that Hands had threatened to ruin Scampton.

Despite this evidence, Hands was found Not Guilty of perjury, perhaps because of Scampton's status as a convict, or because of the passage of time and the inaccuracy of memory after four years. The judge summed up by saying that the evidence against Hands was circumstantial. Scampton was returned to jail.

REF.: *CBA*; Cobb, *Trials and Errors*.

Hands of the Ripper, 1971, a British film directed by Peter Sasdy in which Angharad Rees, seeking psychiatric help, believes her father is Jack the Ripper (Brit., 1888) and is compelling her to commit atrocious murders. See: **Jack the Ripper**. REF.: *CBA*.

Handwriting Analysis, See: **Handwriting**, Supplements, Vol. IV.

Hänel, Gustav Friedrich, 1792-1878, Ger., jur. Studied the history of law and published *Corpus Legum ab Imperatoribus Romanis ante Justiniarum Latarum*. REF.: *CBA*.

Haneline, Scott Anthony, 1960- , U.S., Case of, mur. Sought in connection with a slaying, Scott Anthony Haneline is a reported narcotics user who should be considered armed and dangerous.

A blue-eyed blonde of about six-foot-one and medium build, Haneline has worked as a construction worker, a laborer and an electrician, and is said to be a loner who is extremely quiet. Wanted in connection with a killing in which the victim was shot several times in the head with both a pistol and a rifle, Haneline was last seen in Brunswick, Ga. He is not known to wear either a beard or a moustache. REF.: *CBA*.

Haney, Ebert Emory, 1879-1943, U.S., jur. Served as deputy district attorney for the fourth judicial district in Oregon from 1904-08, and as U.S. attorney for the U.S. Department of Justice, district of Oregon, from 1918-20. He was nominated to the ninth circuit court by President Franklin D. Roosevelt in 1935. REF.: *CBA*.

Han Fei (Han Fei-tzu), d.233 B.C., China, jur. A philosopher and disciple of Hsün Tzu and an expert in criminal law. He was put in prison because of a jealous rival official and committed suicide. REF.: *CBA*.

Han Fu-chü, 1890-1938, China, treas. General in Shantung province who switched alliance and supported the Nationalist government in 1929. He was the governor of Shantung from 1930-38, when war broke out with Japan. He betrayed China and was captured and shot by Chiang Kai-shek at Hankow. REF.: *CBA*.

Hangover Square, 1945, a film directed by John Brahm. This picture stars Laird Cregar featured in *The Lodger,* 1944 (also directed by Brahm), as Jack the Ripper (Brit., 1888). He plays a similar Ripper-type role in this film as a demented composer who wanders gas-lit London, murdering anyone who rejects his music, including Linda Darnell, a scheming dance hall singer who uses him to obtain his compositions and then rejects his affection. In turn, he not only murders the singer but puts her body into a public bonfire as Londoners celebrate Guy Fawkes Day. See: **Jack the Ripper**. REF.: *CBA*.

Hankins, Leonard, prom. 1933-53, U.S., (wrong. convict.) rob.-mur. The Third Northwestern Bank of Minneapolis was robbed by six bandits, one armed with a machine gun, on Dec. 16, 1932. Two policemen and a bystander were killed as the robbers escaped. Several days later, police followed a tip to look for the gang at a rooming house; Leonard Hankins was arrested when he walked into the house. At the trial, one witness swore Hankins was not the man stationed outside the bank, while several others noted a resemblance between the accused and the man whom they had seen at the crime. A co-defendant who pleaded guilty to the crime said he had never seen Hankins until some time after the robbery; several other members of the gang also denied knowing Hankins. Although a barber confirmed Hankins' alibi that he was getting a haircut at the time of the robbery, Hankins was found Guilty and sentenced to life in prison.

In 1935 the FBI arrested Jess Doyle, one of the wanted criminals, who confessed to his involvement with the robbery, masterminded by the infamous Barker-Karpis mob. He named all of his companions, saying that Hankins was not with them. The FBI notified the authorities in Minneapolis, Minn., but because the FBI would not release its files, Hankins was not released, remaining in jail for another thirteen years. His sister, Della Lowery, struggled to interest reporters, governors, attorney generals, and anyone she thought might help her brother. The attorney who had prosecuted Hankins apparently opposed any reopening of the case, not wanting exposure of procedural or prosecutorial mistakes.

Lowery finally managed to involve an Associated Press reporter and a Minneapolis detective who uncovered evidence, and Hankins was declared Not Guilty. It was not until 1951 that a pardons board ordered the wrongly convicted man freed in November, and it was another four years before the state legislature passed a bill granting him $300 monthly for life for his unjust imprisonment. In 1953, the man who had spent sixteen years in jail was given a "final unconditional release." Lowery was reimbursed by the state for $10,000 to cover her expenses in the long fight to free her brother. Hankins was never actually pardoned, only released.

REF.: *CBA*; Radin, *The Innocents*.

Hanks, Orlando Camillo (AKA: **Charley Jones, Deaf Charley**), 1863-1902, U.S., west. outl. O.C. Hanks was one of the most notorious train robbers in the West during the late nineteenth century, often aligning himself with Butch Cassidy's Hole-in-the-Wall gang. Despite his loss of hearing, Hanks was particularly adroit at covering an entire railroad car full of passengers, as associates stole their possessions. He was imprisoned at the Deer Lodge Penitentiary in 1892, receiving a ten-year sentence for robbing a Northern Pacific train at Big Timber, Mont. He rejoined Cassidy after his release on Apr. 30, 1901, accumulating a great deal of money from the successful robberies. He drifted to Texas to spend some of the funds, but attracted the attention of local lawman Pink Taylor, who shot him to death on Oct. 22, 1902. See: **Cassidy, Butch; Hole-in-the-Wall; Wild Bunch, The**. REF.: *CBA*.

O.C. Hanks, Wild Bunch member.

Hanlon, John (AKA: **Charles Hanlon**), prom. 1868, U.S., asslt.-mur. John Hanlon, a Philadelphia barber with a proclivity towards child molestation, coerced 10-year-old Jennie Vertis into his barber chair on the auspices of cutting her hair, and was interrupted by an intruder while attempting to fondle the child. On Sept. 6, 1868, 6-year-old Mary Mohrman, the youngest of five children, noticed Hanlon staring at her on a street corner. Claiming to be lost, Hanlon coerced the little girl to lead him to the city's Germantown section. He pulled her into an outhouse, molested her, and strangled her until she was unconscious. He moved the still-breathing body to the cellar of his house, where the next morning, upon discovering the little girl still alive, he beat her to death with a brick. Hanlon then removed the corpse from the cellar, and laid it at the edge of a nearby pond. On Sept. 8, 1868, the body was found, and the manhunt began. Hanlon was arrested on suspicion because of the previous incident with Jennie Vertis, but released. Six months later, he was arrested for drunkenness and disorderly conduct. Two weeks later, he was arrested on the same charges, and pledged not to drink again for five years. But, on Sept. 6, 1869, the anniversary of the murder of Mary Mohrman, Hanlon was arrested on the same drunk charge. In October 1869, two sisters, Annie Bowers and Clara Ritchie, were attacked in the village of Rising Sun, Pa., but were saved by the intervention of Oliver Ottinger, who subdued the attacker—John Hanlon. Hanlon was arrested but again released. The following month, Hanlon was arrested again, for attempting to attack a child outside of a church. He was convicted and sentenced to five years in prison.

During the course of his incarceration, Hanlon confessed the murder of Mary Mohrman to his cell mate, who told the police. On Oct. 31, 1870, at the Court of Oyer and Terminer, before Justice Ludlow and Justice Pierce, the murder trial began. On Nov. 17, Hanlon was found Guilty of first-degree murder, and on December 10, was sentenced to death. On Feb. 1, 1871, John Hanlon was hanged at the county prison in Philadelphia.

REF.: *CBA; Life, Trial, Confession and Conviction of John Hanlon for the Murder of Little Mary Mohrman, Containing Judge Ludlow's Charge to the Jury, and the Speeches of the Learned Counsel on Both Sides.*

Hannah, John, prom. 1856, Brit., mur. Jane Banham was the principal dancer of a small theatrical company that traveled around the West Riding towns near Leeds, England. Although married to another man, she lived for several years with John Hannah, a tailor, and their two children. Although Banham frequently worked on the road, the couple seemed to have a happy relationship until, for unknown reasons, she left Hannah around Christmas of 1855. She took the children with her to her father's house, rejecting Hannah's pleas for her return. When Hannah learned that Banham was performing at Armley, a district in western Leeds, he went to the Malt Hill Inn, again begging her to come back. When Banham refused, Hannah dragged her into a room and closed the door. Hearing cries, people rushed in to find him choking his lover. He then slit Banham's throat. His defense of manslaughter was rejected, and Hannah was hanged at York.

REF.: Butler, *Murderers' England; CBA.*

Hannington, James, 1847-85, S. Afri., assass. Went to South Africa as a missionary in 1882, became bishop of eastern equatorial Africa in 1884, and led an expedition to Lake Victoria in 1885. He was killed by natives. REF.: *CBA.*

Hannon, Charles, prom. 1910, U.S., wh. slav. Charles Hannon was arrested in late June 1910 by Detectives Hellyer and Maloney in Portland, Ore., for taking the money earned by a woman he had abducted from Iowa and forced to be a prostitute. Hannon pleaded guilty to a lesser offense, and was sentenced to three months on the Linnton rock pile, and fined $100, to be paid off or worked out at the rate of $2 a day.

REF.: *CBA;* Roe, *The Great War on White Slavery.*

Hanrahan, Edward V., c.1920- , U.S., Case of, consp. At 4:45 a.m. on Dec. 4, 1969, fourteen Chicago police officers raided a West Side apartment where members of the Black Panther Party were alleged to have stockpiled guns. A gun battle ensued in which at least 100 bullets were fired. Black Panther leaders, 21-year-old Fred Hampton and 22-year-old Mark Clark, were shot and killed. Four of the seven surviving members of the group were critically wounded and two police officers suffered minor injuries.

Immediately following the raid, accusations of an organized assassination were made against State's Attorney Edward V. Hanrahan, whose office planned and carried out the raid. Hanrahan denied the accusations, pointing out the abundance of weaponry recovered from the apartment and commending police for their "bravery, their remarkable self-restraint and their discipline in the face of this vicious Panther attack." The Black Panthers and other groups continued to call for an investigation into the raid. To quell the unrest, Hanrahan held a number of press conferences standing behind the officers who fired upon the Black Panthers.

Hanrahan told the press, "As soon as Sergeant Daniel Groth and Officer James Davis, who were leading our men, announced their office, occupants of the apartment attacked them with shotgun fire. The officers immediately took cover. The occupants continued firing at our policemen from several rooms within the apartment. Thereafter, three times Sergeant Groth ordered all his men to cease firing and told the occupants to come out with their hands up. Each time one of the occupants replied, 'Shoot it out,' and continued firing at the police officers." The state's attorney also showed photographs taken of the building which apparently showed bullet marks on the woodwork fired from inside in the direction of the raiding police officers. Chicago *Sun-Times* reporter Brian Boyer subsequently proved that these so-called bullet holes were nothing more than nail heads circled to bolster the state's case against the surviving Black Panthers. Upon further examination of the building, Boyer counted a total of 100 shots fired, ninety-nine of which had been fired in the direction of the Black Panthers.

On Jan. 30, 1970, less than two weeks after a special coroner's jury returned a verdict of justifiable homicide on the part of the police, the seven surviving Black Panthers were indicted by a Cook County grand jury on numerous charges, including attempted murder. All charges were dropped by Hanrahan on May 8, as the evidence against the raiding party continued to grow. A ballistics expert for the FBI established—and thus corroborated Boyer's finding—that all but one of the more than ninety shots had been fired by police.

Criminal Court Chief Judge Joseph A. Power ordered on June 27 that a special county grand jury with Barnabas F. Sears as special prosecutor, convene on Dec. 8 to officially investigate the raid. The grand jury was presented testimony and evidence which represented the false and misleading actions taken by Hanrahan and others following the police raid to justify their actions. On June 25, 1971, the grand jury returned a sealed indictment against Hanrahan and thirteen others for their part in the alleged cover-up of apparent police misconduct. Indicted members of the police raiding party included: Groth, Davis, Raymond Broderick, Edward Carmody, John Ciszewski, William Corbett, Joseph Gorman, and George Jones. Four other police officers not involved in the raid and Hanrahan's assistant, Richard Jalovec, were also indicted. Police Superintendent James B. Conlisk, Jr. was named as an unindicted co-conspirator.

After thirteen weeks of prosecution testimony in the conspiracy trial against Hanrahan, Jalovec, and the twelve officers, Circuit Court Judge Philip J. Romiti acquitted the defendants, stating that "the evidence is simply not sufficient to establish any conspiracy against any of the defendants." The defendants had been charged with wrongfully obtaining an indictment against the Black Panther members who survived the December 1969 raid. Coordinator of the Black Panthers' Illinois chapter, Bobby Rush, claimed the trial had been a political circus, and added that "the verdict of Judge Romiti, in effect, gives Hanrahan a license to kill blacks."

The seven Black Panther members who survived the raid and the families of Hampton and Clark filed a civil law suit seeking $47.7 million in damages from Hanrahan and twenty-seven others, claiming their civil rights had been violated. In December 1976 the case opened before U.S. District Judge Joseph Sam Perry. On Feb. 15, 1977, Hanrahan testified for the first time that the information his office had received about illegal weapons cached in the Black Panthers apartment had come from an FBI agent. This information, Hanrahan explained before Perry and the six-member jury, was used to obtain the search warrant for the raid. FBI agent Roy M. Mitchell, had previously testified in court to giving the state's attorney's office a detailed floor plan of the apartment, including the location of Hampton's bed. Mitchell's information came from paid FBI informant William M. O'Neal, Jr., who was Hampton's bodyguard and security chief for the Black Panthers. The prosecution attempted to establish that the FBI had used local law enforcement agencies to "neutralize" the Black Panthers. Before the trial's completion on June 20, 1977, Perry dismissed the charges against twenty-one of the defendants, including Hanrahan. The judge then directed the jury to acquit the remaining defendants of all charges after nearly eighteen months in court.

In 1979, the U.S. Court of Appeals in Chicago reinstated the civil charges against Hanrahan and twenty-three others and ordered a new trial. The U.S. Supreme Court, in June 1980, refused a motion by the defense to have the suit dismissed. The case opened once again in Chicago's U.S. District Court on Sept. 25, 1980, with the plaintiffs seeking an additional $24 million in damages, bringing the suit to $71.7 million. On Feb. 28, 1983, Judge John F. Grady approved the $1.85 million settlement in favor of the plaintiffs to be paid equally by the city, county, and federal governments. REF.: *CBA.*

Hanrahan, Gladys Margaret Irene, 1914-49, Brit., (unsolv.) mur. In October 1949, the body of Gladys Margaret Irene Hanrahan was found in Cumberland Green, Regent's Park, at about 10:20 p.m. Hanrahan, a reserved woman who did not, according to her family, have any male friends, had been strangled, and had a man's handkerchief embroidered with the letter "A" stuffed in her mouth. With no signs of struggle, and no screams heard by any passersby, the police had few clues. Hanrahan's money, about £5, was in her purse, and she wore a valuable ring, ruling out robbery as a motive. She had not been sexually assaulted. When Scotland Yard tracked down the owner of the handkerchief, he proved conclusively that it had been stolen or lost months earlier, and that he had been in a resort town seventy miles away when the murder occurred. Hanrahan occasionally walked through Regent's Park to visit relatives, but had not called on any of them the night she was slain. Leaving her home on the evening of the murder, she said she was going to the movies. Despite more than forty detectives called in to investigate, and even with Superintendent S. Burch, then deputy head of the fingerprint department, spending hours in an unsuccessful attempt to take a fingerprint from a small impression on Hanrahan's neck, no other clues were discovered.

An army officer and his wife contacted investigators to identify Hanrahan as the woman they had seen two nights in a row at a saloon in Regent's Park just prior to the murder. Police theorized that she had been murdered by someone who followed her through the park, or was killed at a secret meeting with a lover; or perhaps she was strangled somewhere else, then transported to the park. Although evidence indicated that Hanrahan's killer was someone she knew, the apparently motiveless and clueless crime was never solved.

REF.: *CBA;* Firmin, *Murderers In Our Midst.*

Hanratty, James (AKA: **James Ryan, The A-6 Killer**), 1937-62, Brit., (wrong. convict.?) rape-mur. Michael John Gregsten, a 36-year-old research physicist from London, was having an affair with his lab assistant, Valerie Storie. On the night of Aug. 22, 1961, the couple left a pub in Taplow, London, and parked in a deserted spot off the highway two miles from Deadman's Hill. A tap on the car window interrupted them, then a man stuck a gun in Gregsten's face and demanded the keys to the car. The gunman climbed into the back seat and spent the next two hours talking about his early life. He then forced Gregsten to buy him some cigarettes and food from a vending machine. Gregsten was ordered to drive the car back down the A-6 Highway near Deadman's Hill. When Gregsten made a sudden movement, the gunman shot him twice in the head. He then forced Storie into the back seat and raped her.

Convicted killer James Hanratty.

After dragging Gregsten's body out of the car, he asked her to show her how to operate the gear shift in Gregsten's car, he shot her in the spine, and drove away.

Miraculously, Storie survived seven gunshot wounds. She gave police a description of the killer, saying he had brown hair and brown eyes. London newspapers published a composite drawing the next day. Meanwhile, police found the car abandoned in Ilford and the murder weapon under a seat on a public bus. Authorities asked landlords to identify any suspicious people who might be "laying low" in their buildings, which turned up the first suspect: Peter Louis Alphon, the son of a Scotland Yard records clerk, who worked as a door-to-door almanac salesman. Alphon had been living at the Vienna Hotel where James Hanratty checked in the night before the murder. Hanratty, who went by the name James Ryan, had sustained brain damage during the London blitz and had a long record of petty crime.

Police found two spent cartridges in a sofa chair in Hanratty's room, and many believed Alphon planted them. The bullets were fired from the same weapon that killed Gregsten. On Sept. 7, a man matching Alphon's description attacked a Richmond woman. Police arrested Alphon, who could not account for his movements on the night of the murder, and put him in police lineup. Mrs. Dalal, the victim, identified Alphon as her assailant, but Storie picked Hanratty and the Vienna Hotel manager withdrew his earlier statements made to police about the movements of Alphon. Alphon was released, and the investigation centered on Hanratty, who had become a fugitive. On Oct. 11, he was arrested in a nightclub in Blackpool. Based on Storie's identification of Hanratty in a police lineup, the 25-year-old crook was charged with murder. But police questioned Storie's description. She first said the man who raped her had brown hair and brown eyes, but after picking Hanratty out of the lineup, she said the rapist had "saucer-like staring blue eyes." The original description fit Alphon,

the other fit Hanratty.

The case against Hanratty went before the jury of the Bedford Assizes in January 1962. It was to become the longest murder trial against one defendant in British legal history, lasting through twenty-one days of testimony. At issue was whether Storie had picked out the wrong man. Hanratty maintained throughout the trial that he had traveled to Liverpool by train at the time of the murder, and spent the day with three friends. Hanratty then changed his alibi, saying he had been in Rhyl. On Feb. 18, 1962, after nine and a half hours of deliberation, the jury returned a Guilty verdict. Hanratty was hanged on Apr. 4, 1962, but the issue of his guilt remained in doubt for some years. As early as May 1962, Alphon began to hint that he had been the killer. Despite his enigmatic notes to writer Jean Justice and a confession in May 1967 during an interview with journalist Paul Foot, no charges were brought against him.

REF.: Ambler, *The Ability to Kill;* Boar, *The World's Most Infamous Murders;* Brophy, *The Meaning of Murder;* Canning, *Fifty True Tales of Terror; CBA;* Foot, *Who Killed Hanratty?;* Franklin, *The Woman in the Case;* Furneaux, *Famous Criminal Cases, vol. 7;* Justice, *Murder vs. Murder;* Russell, *Deadman's Hill: Was Hanratty Guilty?;* Simpson, *Forty Years of Murder;* Wilson, *Encyclopedia of Modern Murder.*

Hanriot, Francois, 1759-94, Fr., rebel. Headed Paris national guard as commander in chief from 1793-94, and was important in Girondist overthrow in 1793. A follower of Robespierre, he was executed by guillotine with him. REF.: *CBA.*

Hansen, Arthur Emil, 1900- , U.S., mur. "I wanted to kill them both. I'm glad they're dead—they can't hurt anybody else. When I entered that courtroom and saw them whispering together to harass me further I could not stand it. When they started to whisper, that was the end." With these words, 38-year-old Arthur Hansen confessed to killing J. Irving Hancock and R.D. McLaughlin, the two lawyers who, by winning a series of judgements against him, cost him his property and life savings.

On June 22, 1938, at Hansen's final settlement hearing in Los Angeles Superior Court's Hall of Records, Hancock and McLaughlin sat, heads bent together, studying notes on the civil suit ruling they had recently won against Hansen, when Hansen, a farmer, entered the courtroom and sat down two rows behind the lawyers.

At one point Hansen thought he saw the attorneys look in his direction and smirk at him. Standing, he and pulled a pistol from the lining of his coat, and seconds later fired. Hancock slumped forward in his seat. McLaughlin stood and was met with a bullet in his head. Hansen emptied his gun, holstered it, and walked out the door.

"I regret nothing. I had nothing to lose," Hansen said in his confession to sheriff's deputies. Two and a half months after the shootings, a jury of six men and six women found him Guilty on two counts of manslaughter. He was sentenced to serve from two to twenty years in San Quentin Prison. REF.: *CBA.*

Hansen, Hans, and **St. Clair, Thomas**, prom. 1893, U.S., mur. Conspiring to kill their officers, seize the ship, and sell the cargo in Chile, three sailors succeeded in murdering the second mate but were then captured.

On Jan. 13, 1893, the ship *Hesper* was carrying valuable cargo from Newcastle when, on a stormy night, the captain's wife heard someone shriek, a dog bark, and then silence. Officers took arms and lanterns and investigated, unable to find second mate Maurice Fitzgerald, but they discovered blood on the deck and a hatchet covered with blood and human hair. Three sailors, who because of their sullen behavior were already under suspicion, were arrested and put in chains. Of the three, Thomas St. Clair, Hans Hansen, and Herman Sparf, only Sparf confessed, explaining that they had murdered Fitzgerald and thrown him overboard, attempting in the darkness to wash the blood off the deck, just before the officer appeared and overpowered them. Hansen and St. Clair were tried in the San Francisco federal court. They were found Guilty of murder and hanged at San Quentin Prison on Oct. 18, 1895.

REF.: *CBA;* Duke, *Celebrated Criminal Cases of America.*

Hanson, Alexander Contee, 1786-1819, U.S., rebel. Created *Federal Republican*, and ran anti-establishment articles from 1808-12. After a mob destroyed the premises where the newspaper was produced, he and his colleagues were arrested. The crowd then forced its way into the jail, killing one and injuring several others. He later served as a member of the U.S. House of Representatives from 1813-16, and as U.S. senator from 1816-19. REF.: *CBA*.

Hanson, Sir Richard Davies, 1805-76, Brit., jur. Jurist in London and later served as crown prosecutor in New Zealand from 1840-46. He was a founder of South Australia in 1846, contributed greatly to South Australia's constitution between 1851-56, and served as its chief justice from 1861-74. REF.: *CBA*.

Hanson, William P., 1949- , U.S., mur. A killer who apparently struck at random turned out to be a young man with a divided personality who believed he was avenging the rape of a former girlfriend. William P. Hanson confessed to his crimes, explaining, "I know at least four times I've tried to kill him."

On Oct. 16, 1973, Lorenzo Carniglia was gunned down by a slight blond man who ran up behind him on a San Francisco sidewalk, and shot him with a pistol he had concealed in a brown paper bag. A parking lot attendant watched the man flee, and another witness who had heard the shots looked out his window to see the assailant change shirts, get into a white van, and pull into traffic. Carniglia, who died later that day, was a middle-aged man with a slight limp. The killer became known to police and citizens as the Paper Bag Killer, because he concealed his weapon in a bag.

Detectives Frank Flazon and Jack Cleary investigated the murder, and culled a composite description of a white male, eighteen to twenty years old, with long, blond hair and a "baby face." Crime lab reports identified the murder weapon as a .22-caliber pistol. On Dec. 20, 1973, a man in an overcoat stood waiting for the free breakfast at the Life Line Mission at about 8:50 a.m. when a slight, young, blond man approached him. With a pump action shotgun partially hidden by a supermarket shopping bag, the youth fired on the heavy-set, middle-aged man, then sped off in a white Econoline van. Ara Kuznezow, the Paper Bag Killer's second victim, had, like Carniglia, been older and heavy-set, with an apparent limp.

Checking out vans, detectives Flazon and Cleary were contacted on Jan. 25 by a nervous young man who had information, but insisted on anonymity. Meeting with the caller, the detectives learned he was a friend of Hanson. Hanson had shown the youth several guns, and told him he was trying to kill a man who was raping young girls. Hanson explained to his friend that he had in fact killed the man several times, but he kept coming back. Tracking Hanson down to the Redco Delivery Service where he worked, Flazon and Cleary realized that he fit the description of the killer. At the records bureau, Hanson's name came up in connection with the February 1973 attempted knifing of a businessman. When the case was brought to trial, the businessman was traveling and was not present to testify, so charges were dropped. A similar case had occurred in December 1972 when a heavy-set, older man was stabbed at the Greyhound bus depot near Market Street; the man, who survived, had a limp.

On Jan. 26, 1974, Cleary and Falzon went to the upper-middle-class home where Hanson lived with his parents. Making no attempt to resist, Hanson directed them to the closet where they found the loaded shotgun that had killed Kuznezow. A new pistol, also loaded, was under Hanson's mattress; he had, he later explained, thrown the gun he had killed Carniglia with into San Francisco Bay. Clothing that linked him to both deaths was found in the closet.

Arrested and taken to the Hall of Justice, Hanson confessed. With murder indictments against him in both cases, he was transferred to county prison and held without bond. Attorney Patrick Hallinan told the court that Hanson had a longtime girlfriend who had been raped in late 1972, and believed he was somehow responsible for the occurrence, subsequently murdering in the twisted belief that he was killing her rapist. On May 16,

Judge Morton Convin found Hanson Not Guilty by reason of insanity. He was sent to the Atascadero State Hospital for the Criminally Insane.

REF.: *CBA*; Henderson, *The Super Sleuths*.

Han T'o-chou, d.1207, China, polit. corr. Minister under emperor Ning Tsung. He started a war to try to take back land in the north that had been captured by Juchen tribes. While attempting to sustain the war, which had become a catastrophe, his own people executed him and gave his head to the Juchen as a conciliatory gesture. REF.: *CBA*.

Han Yong-un (Manhae), 1879-1944, Korea, rebel. In 1919, helped draft anti-Japanese declaration of independence. He was imprisoned from 1919-22 for signing the document. REF.: *CBA*.

Hara Takashi (AKA: The Great Commoner), 1854-1921, Japan, prime minister, assass. Hara Takashi was a commoner who had been appointed prime minister of Japan in 1918 by Emperor Taisho, and he promptly began to undermine the power of the right-wing military. By 1921, Hara was loudly announcing that Japan would soon be a democracy. He had taken over much of the control of the army, and so alarmed were right-wing militarists that the army high command ordered the prime minister killed. Prince Konoye, who would become Japan's prime minister in 1937, was behind the assassination and later bragged to his friends that on the eve of the killing, a henchman working for the militarists, Iogi Yoshimitsu, had visited him and promised to carry out the assassination the next day.

On Nov. 4, 1921, Nakaoka Konichi, a right-wing railroad employee in the pay of the militarists, attacked Hara at the Tokyo Railroad Station, cutting open the prime minister's stomach. "The Great Commoner," as Hara was known, died immediately. Nakaoka was arrested and tried, but he had the nodding approval of the top Japanese generals and royal princes, including future emperor Hirohito. The assassin was given a twelve-year prison term. He was released from Sendai Penitentiary in 1934 welcomed as a hero by right-wing extremists, and given considerable funds to maintain a comfortable lifestyle that continued until his death many years later.

REF.: Bergamini, *Japan's Imperial Conspiracy*; *CBA*; McNelly, *Politics and Government in Japan*; Morton, *Japan, Its History and Culture*; Mosley, *Hirohito, Emperor of Japan*; Reischauer, *Japan: The Story of a Nation*; ____, *The United States and Japan*; Scalapino, *Democracy and the Party Movement in Prewar Japan*.

Harcourt, Simon, c.1661-1727, Brit., lawyer. Solicitor general from 1702-07, attorney general from 1707-18, and lord keeper of the seal in 1710. Served as lord chancellor from 1713-14, and became friends with many prominent literary figures such as Jonathan Swift, Alexander Pope, and John Gay. REF.: *CBA*.

Hardaker, Betty, 1915- , U.S., mur. "I didn't want her to endure what I had gone through," Betty Hardaker said by way of explaining why she had killed her 5-year-old daughter, Geraldine, a child her mother thought "too good to live."

On the afternoon of Feb. 19, 1940, Hardaker, twenty-five, of Montebello City, Calif., took Geraldine, her eldest and favorite child, for a walk in Montebello City Park. They rode the seesaw, looked at the fish, and then went to the rest room. "I hadn't decided on anything," she told Chief of Police Harry Bispham. "But suddenly I had a strange impulse to end it all...for both of us."

Hardaker then "raised Geraldine up real quick above me, and then pulled her down and hit her head as hard as I could on the washbowl so she wouldn't feel anything." After that, everything went black. Hardaker could not recall leaving the park but did find her way home, where she considered sticking her head in the stove. She decided against it, however, because "the others would be home soon."

Hardaker then put on a sweater and hitchhiked to a nearby Indian reservation, where she spent the night hiding in a shack. Picked up just after noon the next day, she said her name was "Betty Rice," and that she was married and had a small child.

Hardaker's estranged husband, 29-year-old Charles Hardaker,

told police that Betty had recently joined a cult that believed in human sacrifices. "She thinks God tells them to kill people."

"Betty started acting strange just a few months ago after she began attending this church," said Betty's mother, Etta Karnes, concurring with her son-in-law. Betty's father, Samuel Karnes, in turn revealed that his daughter had suffered a nervous breakdown three months earlier. And Hardaker herself told Palm Springs physician Dr. Russell Gray that her breakdown had been precipitated by the birth of her two youngest children, Charles, Jr., five months, and Dixie Ann, fifteen months.

Hardaker said, that during the last year she had thought often of killing herself by gassing and had once tried to throw herself in front of a truck. "I heard the voice of God every morning," she told Dr. Gray. "I can't understand what the voice tells me, but it wakes me up." Of her murdered child, Hardaker said, "I can't explain the reason for it. I didn't hate her. I loved her." Hardaker was judged insane. REF.: *CBA*.

Har Dayal, 1884-1939, India, rebel. Took part in anti-imperialist and anarchist activities trying to incite anti-British rebellions in India and Afghanistan. REF.: *CBA*.

Hardcastle Family, prom. 1900-20, U.S., boot. Between 1865 and 1935, 126 indictments were handed down in Tennessee against members of the Hardcastle Family, a clan of infamous bootleggers. Descended from pioneers, the Hardcastles set the tone for whiskey peddlers and for related violence in pre-Prohibition days. When the father of the family, Eagle Hardcastle, died around 1900, the family's whiskey business flourished. It was rumored that Bertha Hardcastle poisoned people she had grudges against by putting pellets in their moonshine, and that the Hardcastle family got people drunk, then robbed and killed them. The house, which was partly in Kentucky and partly in Tennessee, operated as a major still, serving customers in both states. Although selling whiskey was prohibited by state law, the Hardcastle's operation was legal due to a Federal government permit for making whiskey and selling corn liquor. In November 1914, Claxton Hardcastle, fifteen, one of Bertha's sons, got drunk and killed his friend, Lyn Faris, who worked at the home as a hired hand. After serving some time for the murder, Claxton lived in Chicago for a while before returning home, where he became a respected citizen, even becoming a deputy sheriff in the 1950s.

The whiskey mill flourished under the uneasily shared leadership of brothers Crane and Tault Hardcastle. Rivalry for control was intense, and Crane shot and wounded Tault in 1915. In good times, the Hardcastles still could not meet demand in the area, so they occasionally ordered from a licensed distillery and carried in the liquor secretly over dangerous mountain roads. In September 1916, the Hardcastles boasted they were "going through Jessetown or going to hell." The sheriff told them to bring along caskets. He and a posse ambushed Tault Hardcastle and several clan members as they came into Jessetown with the contraband. Killed in the attack was pregnant Fannie Hardcastle, and Schyler Dark, who continued shooting, propped up on his elbow with a bullet in his head, until he died. Among the wounded were Balm Hardcastle, Tault, and Chester Beary. The Hardcastles never recovered from this attack, and Tault moved to Peoria, Ill., with several other members of the family. Eventually, he fought with his son-in-law there, and died after being shot in the leg. According to his widow, he died of fright. "He'd been shot up during the ambush out yonder and lived through it and when he was shot in the leg he just died."

REF.: *CBA;* Montell, *Killings.*

Harden, Jacob S., d.1860, U.S., mur. Reverend Jacob Harden, pastor of the Methodist church in Mount Lebanon, N.J., married one of his parishioners after the girl's mother hounded and pestered him to do so. Harden poisoned his wife a short time later with arsenic and then babbled a confession, claiming he had fallen beneath the spell of a local fortune-teller who told him his wife would soon die in agony. Harden concluded that it would be kinder if he poisoned his spouse before she underwent a painful death from an ailment she had yet to contract! He was

tried, condemned, and hanged at Belvidere, N.J., on July 6, 1860.
REF.: *CBA; Life, Confession and Letters of Courtship of Jacob S. Harden.*

Hardenbrook, Dr. **John K.,** prom. 1849, Case of, U.S., mur. Dr. John K. Hardenbrook was the family physician of the Nott family of Rochester, N.Y. He had a secret affair with the alluring Mrs. Nott. When her husband, Thomas Nott, suddenly died in the prime of life, Hardenbrook was suspected of murdering Nott. Authorities proved that a short time before Nott's death, Hardenbrook had obtained considerable amounts of strychnine, and they believed he poisoned Nott. At his trial, Hardenbrook convinced a jury that he was innocent since the prosecution could not produce any poison taken from the remains. But the prosecution insisted that Dr. Hardenbrook had conveniently performed Nott's autopsy immediately after death and had washed out the stomach. Hardenbrook was acquitted and immediately left town with Mrs. Nott.

REF.: *CBA; The Trial of Dr. John K. Hardenbrook.*

Hardin, Andrew, 1956- , and **Payne, Clyde,** 1955- , U.S., mur. In the popular 1975 film *Cooley High,* about a high school near Chicago's Cabrini-Green housing project, the part of Robert, a street-tough, inner-city black man, was played by Norman Gibson. A year after the film's release, on Sept. 29, 1976, the 26-year-old Gibson was shot and killed near the same street corner where Hollywood talent agents had discovered him. Two men who jumped out of a car killed him with a shotgun blast to the middle of his back, followed by a shot to the head with a small-caliber handgun. Eyewitnesses were able to identify the attackers. The attack was in apparent retaliation for Gibson's assault of the sister of one of the attackers. Gibson had a long criminal record for robbery and narcotics, and had been released from the Cook County House of Corrections two days before his murder. The two assailants were subsequently arrested. On Jan. 31, 1978, before Judge R. Eugene Pincham, 22-year-old Andrew Hardin and 23-year-old Clyde Payne pleaded guilty to Gibson's murder and were each sentenced to between eighteen and ninety years in prison. REF.: *CBA*.

Hardin, John Wesley (AKA: **J.H. Swain**), 1853-95, U.S., west. outl.-gunman. The most feared gunman in Texas, killer of at least twenty-one men, was John Wesley Hardin. He was a quick draw artist, perhaps the fastest gun alive until he was shot in the back and died ignominiously, without a friend to mourn his passing. Before that shoddy fate embraced Hardin, he wrote his autobiography, a thrilling dime-novel affair which made up in imagination what it lacked in honesty. He claimed to have killed forty men—certainly the record for any gunman in the history of the Wild West.

Born in Bonham, Texas, on May 26, 1853, Hardin had the benefit of upstanding, hardworking parents. His background was anything but criminal, rooted in religion, nurtured by a God-fearing father who made a living as a hardworking Methodist circuit

Outlaw John Wesley Hardin.

preacher. Hardin's forefathers had illustrious positions in the history of Texas. One had fought at San Jacinto and another had signed the Texas Declaration of Independence in the fight against Santa Ana. Hardin's grandfather served with distinction in the Congress of the Texas Republic. Hardin County, Texas, was named after another of Hardin's relatives, Judge William B. Hardin. Somehow, Hardin's father believed that his son would follow in his footsteps and named him after the esteemed Methodist leader, John Wesley. None of this affected the conduct of John Wesley Hardin.

The Hardin family moved to southeastern Texas when Hardin was an infant. He grew up in these wilds, learning early the use of firearms as a hunter and was a marksman by the age of ten. He practiced by shooting at effigies of Abraham Lincoln, the most hated man in the South during the Civil War. He also demonstrated a killer instinct at an early age. When only eleven, Hardin got into a vicious knife fight with another boy. He stabbed the boy in the back and chest but the youth survived.

At age fifteen, in November 1868, Hardin visited his uncle who had a plantation near Moscow, Tex. He got into a wrestling match with one of his uncle's ex-slaves, a burly man named Mage and bested him. Mage told Hardin that he would kill him and when the boy was riding home, Mage stepped into the road with a large stick. When he stepped toward Hardin, the youth pulled an old Colt from his waistband and fired three shots into Mage's chest. The former slave died of his wounds two days later. Hardin fled, and went into hiding at a friend's farm in Sumpter, Texas.

He later wrote in his memoirs that he was being persecuted by Union soldiers who still occupied the territory for defending himself against a black man who "came at me with a big stick." He had run from the law of the Union military "not from justice but from the injustice and misrule of the people who had subjugated the South." Hardin heard that three Union soldiers were approaching the ranch where he was hiding and rode out to meet them, carrying a shotgun and a six-gun. He lay in wait in a creek bed and when the soldiers rode by jumped up and emptied the shotgun into two of them at close range, blowing them off their horses. The remaining soldier wheeled his horse about and began firing at the youth but Hardin drew his .44 and fired several shots, killing the third soldier. Ex-Confederate soldiers then arrived and buried the bodies of the three dead Union men while Hardin fled.

Hardin later claimed that when he was on the run in early 1869, he and his cousin, Simp Dixon, shot and killed two more Union soldiers who were chasing them. On Dec. 25, 1869, Hardin was playing cards in Towash, Texas. He won many hands and a town tough, Jim Bradley, a big loser, suddenly jerked forth a knife and threatened: "You win another hand and I cut out your liver, kid." Hardin was unarmed at the time and politely excused himself. He went to his room and strapped on two six-guns.

By then he had developed what was perhaps the fastest draw in the West, an unusual cross-draw. Hardin had sewn two holsters into a vest so that the butts of his two six-guns pointed inward across his chest. Hardin's draw was one sweeping movement where he crossed his arms, yanked forth the two six-guns and moved them in a lightning fast arch. This required one motion, a movement he practiced for hours a day, figuring that it was much faster than the traditional draw, where one reached to the side, drew a six-gun out of a hip holster and then leveled it to fire, a three-motion movement.

That night, Hardin stepped into the main street of Towash wearing his two guns. Down the street stood Jim Bradley, who also wore a gun and had been looking for Hardin. The tall youth with black hair and dark smoldering eyes resolutely walked toward Bradley who cursed him and then fired a shot in Hardin's direction, the bullet missing its mark. Hardin's hands flashed across his chest and his two six-guns were suddenly in his hands, both exploding at the same moment. The two bullets found their marks, one striking Bradley in the head, the second smashing into the gunman's chest. He crumpled to the street dead. This gunfight was witnessed by a dozen or more people who quickly spread the word that John Wesley Hardin was the fastest gun in the West, a reputation the boy upheld at every opportunity.

In January 1870, Hardin and a friend rode into Horn Hill, Texas, to see a local circus that had come to town. Several roustabouts from the circus got drunk that night and one of these big-shouldered men, half-drunk, spotted Hardin wearing his two guns. When he ridiculed Hardin, the youth told him to shut up. The circus man then slammed his huge fist into Hardin's face. Both men went for their guns but Hardin shot the man dead before he ever drew his six-gun. A few days later, Hardin arrived in Kosse, Texas, where he went into a cheap bar and met a saloon girl. While escorting her home, a man jumped Hardin from a dark alleyway, struggling to take his money. Hardin leaped backward and threw his money to the ground. The thief stooped to reach for the money and Hardin fired a single bullet into his head, killing him. He ran for his horse and raced out of town, a procedure that would become monotonous for the gunfighter.

Lawmen finally caught up with Hardin, arresting him for a killing he insisted he did not commit. Hardin and several other prisoners were being moved to Waco, Texas to stand trial. Only two guards rode with the prisoners who were shackled at the hands. On the second night of the trip, the group camped near Marshall, Texas. One of the guards rode off to a nearby ranch to obtain food for the horses. While he was gone, Hardin, using a six-gun smuggled to him in the Marshall Jail, shot and killed the other guard and fled on horseback. He later forced a blacksmith to cut away the shackles. Hardin claimed that three Union troopers then chased him across the Texas prairies for days, until his horse gave out and he ran on foot. The troopers tried to ride him down but, according to his own account, he turned and shot all three dead from their horses before they could get off a single shot.

Hardin next went to work as a cowboy for William C. Cohron, a trail boss, and while herding cattle in February 1871, in the company of his cousin, Emmanuel "Mannen" Clements, Hardin stopped at a Mexican camp in Gonzales County, Texas. Here he and Clements played cards with three Mexican vaqueros but a quarrel broke out and Hardin shot and wounded two of the Mexicans before riding off. Two months later, while rounding up strays in the Indian Territory, Hardin found an Indian trying to steal a cow and he shot and killed him with a single bullet. Then he and others hurriedly buried the Indian, fearing that if the body was found, his tribesmen would hunt down Hardin and the others.

Cattle rustlers were a problem and one of the worst of these was Juan Bideno. He gave up rustling briefly to join Cohron's trail herd as a cowboy but he was suspected of working in league with a band of rustlers who were waiting to steal Cohron's herd. Cohron accused Bideno of avoiding work and the Mexican threatened him. When the herd crossed the Cottonwood River in Kansas on July 5, 1871, Cohron accused Bideno of shirking his duties. Bideno went for his gun, shot Cohron dead, and then fled. Hardin, who was a close friend of Cohron's, heard the news when he was in Abilene, Kan., and, the next day, July 6, he organized a small posse to hunt down Bideno. Before leaving town that day, Hardin ran afoul of Charles Cougar, a tough gunman who threatened to kill him. Hardin pulled his gun and killed Cougar with a single shot, the bullet striking the gunslinger in the middle of the forehead from a distance of forty feet.

The next day, Hardin, with Hugh Anderson and Jim Rodgers at his side, rode into tiny Bluff City, Kan. They carried a warrant for the arrest of Juan Bideno, one issued to them by lawman John Cohron, who was a brother of the slain Billy Cohron. Hardin had learned that Bideno was in Bluff City and he located the rustler in a small cafe where he was eating dinner. While his friends surrounded the cafe, Hardin boldly entered the cafe and saw Bideno sitting at a table, a plateful of food before him. Hardin told Bideno that he carried a warrant for his arrest on the charge of murdering Cohron. He then ordered the Mexican to surrender.

Bideno smiled, dropped his knife and fork, and then leaned slowly back in his chair so that his holsters were clear. As he began to drop his hands to his holsters, Hardin whipped out his two six-guns in what was now a famous cross-draw and fired two bullets into Bideno's head, killing him. Another version of this shooting had Hardin challenging Bideno to a duel. Both men then reportedly mounted their horses and charged each other from opposite ends of the street, Bideno firing wildly as he rode madly toward Hardin. Hardin fired only one bullet, which took off the top of the Mexican's head.

In September 1871, two black Union soldiers, Green Parramore and John Lackey, were hunting Hardin for a previous killing. They stopped in Smiley, Texas, hearing that Hardin was in the vicinity. As they were eating crackers and cheese in the general store, a tall, dark-haired youth wearing two guns on his vest walked inside.

"I hear you two are looking for John Wesley Hardin. Do you know what he looks like?" the youth asked the soldiers.

"No, sure don't," said Parramore. "We have never seen him but we are looking for him and when we find him we'll arrest him."

"Well," said John Wesley Hardin, "you see him now!" With that, his hands a blur as they flashed across his chest, Hardin drew both guns and emptied them into both soldiers. Parramore fell, dead, but Lackey, wounded badly in the chest and mouth, ran from the store and survived.

It was in the year 1871, according to Hardin, that he backed down one of the great lawmen of the West, James Butler "Wild Bill" Hickok. According to Hardin's memoirs, he rode into Abilene, got drunk one night, and then stepped into the street. To liven up the town, Hardin began firing his gun into the air as he moved, wobbly-legged and half tipsy, down the street. He suddenly heard footsteps behind him and turned to see the six-foot-two-inch, long-haired Wild Bill glaring at him. Hickok, town marshal, told him in a low voice: "You can't hurrah (frighten or bully) me, I won't have it!"

"I haven't come to hurrah you," Hardin said, "but I'm going to stay in Abilene."

"I'll have your guns first," Hickok told him.

Hardin then offered his two six-guns to the famous marshal but as Hickok reached for them, his own hands extended far from his holsters, Hardin performed the famous "border roll" or "gun-spin." As Hardin later told it: "While he was reaching for them, I reversed them and whirled them over on him with the muzzles in his face, springing back at the same time. I told him to put his pistols up and he did."

Hickok historians take issue with Hardin's claim to this day, refusing to believe that the wily Wild Bill would ever fall for the "border roll," but it is a fact that Hardin did stay in Abilene and did not have another encounter with Hickok, a man Hardin openly admired. Hardin frequented the Bull's Head and Gambling House which was owned and run by Ben Thompson, one of the most feared gunmen in the West who hated Hickok for cowing him on several occasions.

Even Thompson was timid about confronting his nemesis, Wild Bill. He approached Hardin one night and told him that he would pay the gunman a considerable sum if he shot Hickok dead. Hardin was offended by this killer-for-hire offer, he later claimed, and told Thompson: "If Bill needs killing, why don't you do it yourself?" Thompson was disinclined to do so and dropped the matter. Hardin left Abilene abruptly a short time later after gunning down a saloon thug who announced that he hated all Texans and tried to crush his head with a pipe. Knowing Hickok would be looking for him, Hardin leaped on his horse and rode from the town.

In June 1872, Hardin arrived in Hemphill, Texas, with a herd of cattle for sale. A local policeman named Spites interrupted Hardin when he was quarreling about the sale of the cattle and warned him not to start any trouble. The officer had no idea who Hardin was but quickly learned that he was dealing with a lethal cowboy when, in a few seconds, a derringer appeared in Hardin's hand. Hardin fired a shot which wounded the lawman in the shoulder. At the same time someone shouted: "Watch out, that's Wes Hardin you got there!" Spites, clutching his shoulder and with a terrified look on his face, turned on his heel and ran down the street. Hardin hurriedly grabbed some cash for the sale of his cattle and then rode quickly out of town.

The gunman rode to Trinity City, Texas, in July 1872 to visit relatives. He and a cousin then got into a bowling contest which Hardin purposely lost. Phil Sublett, a local gunman who had been watching the match, then suggested he play Hardin for $5 a set. Hardin quickly beat Sublett six straight games and the gunmen realized that he had been suckered into the match. He began screaming that he had been swindled but Hardin drew his gun and forced Sublett to continue playing until he was out of money.

Hardin in his early twenties.

Then, while still holding the six-gun on his defeated foe, Hardin marched Sublett to a nearby saloon and bought him several drinks. Sublett then angrily left the bar, but returned a few minutes later with a shotgun, shooting both barrels in Hardin's direction. One load of buckshot caught the gunfighter in the side. Wounded, Hardin still managed to draw his six-guns and stagger into the street, chasing a fleeing Sublett. He shot his attacker in the back before he collapsed. Hardin's relatives picked him up and spirited him out of town to a hiding place, a deserted ranch house in Angelina County, Texas. In August 1872, while Hardin was recovering from his painful wounds, two policemen crept up on the ranch house, going to a window to see the gunfighter lying on a bed. They fired rifles at him through the window and wounded him in the thigh, but the hearty gunfighter rolled off the bed, grabbed a shotgun, and managed to get to the door where he began blasting them. The officers, both wounded, hobbled off and did not return.

Somehow, in the busy year of 1872, Hardin managed to meet and marry Jane Bowen. Their union produced two girls and a boy, but these children seldom saw their father, who was either on a cattle drive somewhere or was busy earning the reputation of the fastest gun in the West. Hardin did make an attempt at rehabilitation. Influenced by his young wife, Hardin rode into Gonzales, Texas, and surrendered his guns to Sheriff Richard Reagan, stating that he would face all charges against him and "wipe the slate clean."

As Hardin was being put into a cell in the local jail, a jittery guard, terrified of the now infamous gunfighter, nervously fingered his six-gun and accidentally sent a bullet into Hardin's leg. This was removed while Hardin languished in jail and authorities busied themselves with collecting all the charges against him. Hardin had second thoughts about his voluntary surrender, especially when he heard that he would be tried for several murders and he was expected to be found guilty and then hanged. Using a saw smuggled to him by a relative, Hardin cut through the bars of his cell's window and escaped. He went to DeWitt County where his relatives, the numerous members of the Taylor clan, were battling with the Sutton family.

The Sutton-Taylor feud had been raging since 1868 when Buck Taylor had been shot from ambush by William Sutton. The Taylors presented a formidable array of gunmen, more than 100 under the leadership of Pitkin, Creed, Josiah, William, and Rufus Taylor. Against them were more than 200 gunmen led by the Suttons. These included the ranch hands and gunslingers employed by cattle baron Joe Tumilson and the notorious brawler Abel Head "Shanghai" Pierce, who had, with his wild cowboys, terrorized the towns of Abilene, Dodge City, Wichita, and countless other cowtowns that served as railheads to which Pierce drove his massive Texas herds. Jack Helm, who was an official in the state police force, also backed the Suttons, who paid him handsomely to take their side in any dispute.

Hardin worked for the Clements family, headed by Mannen Clements, his cousin. They were allies and relatives of the Taylors. The Clements were headquartered in the little town of Cuero, Texas, and here Hardin entered a local saloon and encountered J.B. Morgan, one of Jack Helm's deputies and a stalwart Sutton man. Morgan shouted down the bar at Hardin that he was ugly, stupid, and a gunman who had earned his reputation by killing helpless drunks. Both men drew their guns at the same time. Hardin later reported that, "I pulled my pistol and fired, the ball striking him just above the left eye. He fell dead. I went to the stable, got my horse, and left town unmolested."

The Sutton-Taylor war raged on. In 1873, Jack Helm arrested two Taylor men and allowed his deputies to murder them. A few days later Pitkin Taylor was shot to death while he sat on the front porch of his ranch house. His son, Hardin's best friend, Jim Taylor, vowed that he would "wash my hands in old Bill Sutton's blood!" Hardin and Taylor were in Albuquerque, Texas, in July 1873, at a blacksmith's shop having their horses re-shod, when Jack Helm and six of his deputies rode past and spotted them. Helm and his men dismounted, hands on guns, and headed for the blacksmith's shack.

At the time, Helm no longer held any official position as a lawman, having been dismissed from the state police force for his ruthless treatment of prisoners. Helm was in the lead. He pulled forth a large knife as he walked, then ran toward Taylor, aiming this weapon at Taylor's chest. Hardin was holding a shotgun at the time and he leveled it at Helm, pulling both triggers and blasting Helm in the chest. Taylor then shot the writhing Helm in the head, killing him. Both Hardin and Taylor then turned their guns on the other deputies and drove them off with a barrage of flying lead.

After Jim Taylor fulfilled his vow by killing William Sutton in Indianola in 1874, the Sutton-Taylor feud ended and Hardin went to Comanche, Texas, to join his family. On May 26, 1874, the town of Comanche held horse races in honor of its native son, John Wesley Hardin, who was celebrating his twenty-first birthday. The local sheriff, John Karnes, was one of the few Texas sheriffs who held no warrants for Hardin's arrest. Karnes liked Hardin and played cards with the gunfighter often in one of Comanche's six roaring saloons. On that day, however, Comanche County Deputy Sheriff Charles Webb rode into town, intent upon arresting or gunning down Hardin. He made no show of doing so. In fact, he pretended he did not even know Hardin. Hardin, on the other hand, had been warned that Webb intended to arrest him. When Webb approached one of the saloons, Hardin was suddenly on the wooden sidewalk in front of him. The gunfighter spread his coat backward to reveal the jutting gunbutts in his vest holsters. "Have you any papers for my arrest?" Hardin asked Webb coolly.

"I don't know you," Webb lied. He had studied photographs of Hardin for weeks before going to Comanche.

"My name is John Wesley Hardin," the gunfighter said.

"Now I know you," Webb replied, "but I have no papers for your arrest."

Hardin nodded and then invited Webb to have a drink in the saloon. Webb agreed and Hardin turned his back, starting toward the saloon's swinging doors. At that moment one of Hardin's friends, Bud Dixon, shouted to Hardin: "Look out!"

In one movement of incredible speed, Hardin whirled about, cross-drawing his six-guns as he turned, and fired as he faced Webb, whose gun had just cleared the holster. Webb's bullet was fired after Hardin's guns roared. It struck Hardin in the side, but the gunfighter sent a bullet into the sheriff's head. As he fell, certainly dead or dying, a reflex movement caused Webb to get off another shot. Jim Taylor and Dixon, who were standing nearby, then shot Webb as he lay dying in the dust of the street. Webb was the fortieth man to be killed by John Wesley Hardin, according to the gunfighter's own careful count.

The Webb killing caused an uproar throughout Texas. Although Webb's actions had proved him to be shifty and double-dealing (understandably so since he was dealing with the worst killer in Texas history), the thousands of citizens of the state who held Webb in high regard demanded that Hardin be brought to justice. Hardin knew this shooting would be his downfall. He kissed his wife and children good-bye, and then, leading a string of fresh, fast horses behind him, fled eastward, planning to outrun any posse by regularly changing mounts. The posses pounded after him and, in their pursuit of Hardin, they caught up with many of his friends and relatives, those who had shielded and harbored him for years. A mob grabbed Hardin's older brother Joe, a completely innocent person, and lynched him. Lynch mobs hanged the Dixon brothers, Bud (also known as Bill) and Tom. Alex Barrickman and Ham Anderson, close friends of Hardin's, were then hunted down and shot to death. The state of Texas announced a dead-or-alive reward for Hardin and posted $4,000 for that purpose.

Powerful organizations sent scores of men to track down the gunfighter, including the Pinkerton Detective Agency and the Texas Rangers. Dozens of fast-draw gunfighters also searched for Hardin, hoping to shoot him down and gain a reputation as well as a reward for doing so. Posses numbering from ten to fifty heavily-armed men combed Texas for Hardin, and other lawmen kept vigil at his ranch in Comanche, expecting the gunfighter to return home. But John Wesley Hardin disappeared, as if swallowed by the vast Texas landscape itself. He was rumored to be robbing banks and trains in Florida, Georgia, Louisiana, and Alabama.

It was the Texas Rangers who finally tracked down the elusive gunfighter. For three years the Rangers searched for Hardin and finally learned that he would be boarding a train in Pensacola, Fla., on Aug. 23, 1877, with four gunmen, bound for his hideout in Alabama. Lt. John B. Armstrong of the Texas Rangers led a contingent of men to Pensacola and then boarded the train on which Hardin would be traveling. Armstrong limped to a seat with the aid of a cane; he was recovering from a recent injury. He sat down and looked across the aisle to see Hardin sitting alone in a seat, his head in the palm of his hand and his elbow resting on the window sill. Rangers piled on board the train car at either end. Then Armstrong got up and pulled his Peacemaker from its holster, pointing the seven-and-one-half-inch barrel at

Hardin's head.

The gunfighter turned slightly, saw the weapon and shouted: "Texas, by God!" He reached for his own weapons but his guns got tangled in his suspenders. Armstrong brought the Peacemaker down hard on the gunfighter's head, knocking him unconscious. Jim Mann, nineteen, one of Hardin's men, jumped from another seat and fired a shot that tore Armstrong's hat from his head. Armstrong fired a shot that hit Mann in the chest. For a few moments, the youth did a wild dance in the train car aisle, cursing the lawman, then dove through a window, landed on the station platform and staggered a few steps and fell dead at the feet of another ranger, James Duncan.

Put aboard a Texas-bound train, Hardin insisted that the rangers had made a mistake, that he was J.H. Swain, a businessman. He had been in Pensacola buying timber, he said. The gunfighter kept up this pretense until the wide Texas landscape came into view. He then admitted that he was the man they were looking for, John Wesley Hardin. He was taken to the sturdy jail in Austin, Texas, and held there to await trial for the murder of Sheriff Webb. He was in notorious company. Hardin's fellow prisoners at that time included the infamous Johnny Ringo who would later join the Clanton-McLowery rustling gang of Tombstone, Ariz., and go down before the guns of Wyatt Earp. Also on hand was Mannen Clements and Bill Taylor.

Hardin was placed on trial at Gonzales, Texas, and he chose to defend himself in court. Hardin surprised everyone with his eloquence and inspired oratory. "Gentlemen," the gunfighter told his jury, "I swear before God that I never shot a man except in self-defense. Sheriff Webb came to Comanche for the purpose of arresting me, and I knew it. I met him and I defied him to arrest me, but I did not threaten him...I knew it was in his mind to kill me, not arrest me. Everybody knows he was a dangerous man with a pistol." Hardin then looked about the courtroom, noting the scores of strange faces staring back at him. "I know I don't have any friends here but I don't blame them for being afraid to come out for me. My father was a good man and my brother, who was lynched, never harmed a man in his life."

Moving slowly about the courtroom, the tall, good-looking Hardin, dressed in a neat black suit, a starched white shirt and black string tie, appeared to be a preacher and his bearing was that of a man with authority and immense self-respect. It was later remarked that Hardin was, at that moment, mimicking the posture and presence of his own preacher-father whom he had studied as a child when the elder Hardin held his revival meetings. Certainly Hardin was out to save a soul that day—his own. The young man peered intently at the jury, saying: "People will call me a killer, but I swear to you gentlemen that I have shot only in defense of myself. And when Sheriff Webb drew his pistol, I had to draw mine. Anybody else would have done the same thing. Sheriff Webb had shot a lot of men. That's all, gentlemen." He walked slowly back to the defendant's table and sat down.

The jury retired and then shuffled back into the courtroom within an hour-and-a-half. It found Hardin Guilty of second-degree murder. The gunfighter's eloquence had saved his own life. He was sentenced to twenty-five years at hard labor. Guards escorted the gunman from the court and took him to the train depot en route to Rusk Prison in Huntsville, Texas. He served sixteen years of his prison term and spent most of his time behind bars studying law. When he emerged he told the press that he was completely reformed. He omitted the fact that during his first ten years of confinement he had created havoc by attempting many escapes and leading prison revolts. He had been whipped and starved and had spent months in solitary confinement before he stopped rebelling against the prison system. He became a model prisoner and settled down to the study of law in the last six years of his imprisonment.

Hardin was forty-one when he was released from prison. He had no place to go. His wife Jane had died about two years before he was set free and his children had grown up and gone off to make lives of their own. The gunfighter moved to El Paso

where he studied law and stayed out of trouble. Hardin proved to be a model citizen and was hailed in the El Paso *Times* as a living example of modern penal rehabilitation. Callie Lewis, an 18-year-old woman, met the gunfighter at a social gathering. She was impressed with the legend of John Wesley Hardin, and the two were wed, but on Hardin's wedding night, he reverted to his old ways and went to a saloon, got drunk, and picked a fight he did not win. He returned home, battered and bruised. Callie Lewis took one look at this bleeding hulk and packed her bags, leaving Hardin on their wedding night.

After taking to drink, Hardin caroused through the worst dives of El Paso and was often found in a drunken stupor in the gutter. He then took up with a married, overweight prostitute, Mrs. Martin McRose, whose husband was wanted for rustling. McRose, Tom Finnessey, Vic Queen, and others in the rustling band had been hiding in Mexico. When this gang crossed into the U.S., they were met by a large group of lawmen led by Ranger Jeff Milton and U.S. marshals George Scarborough and Frank McMahon. The outlaws were shot down to the last man, including McRose. When Hardin heard this, he drunkenly bragged in several El Paso saloons that he had paid the lawmen to kill McRose and the others so he could have McRose's wife to himself. Ranger Jeff Milton, one of the finest lawmen on the frontier, heard of Hardin's boasting and confronted him in a saloon, incensed at the thought that he could be paid to kill the husband of someone's paramour.

Milton accused Hardin of lying and then demanded the aging gunfighter apologize to him. Hardin told Milton that he was not carrying guns and that Milton knew it or he would not dare speak to him in such a way.

"You're lying," Milton said, "you're always armed. And you can go for your gun right now or tell all these men here and out loud that you lied."

Hardin shrugged, turned to his drunken friends, and said without hesitating: "Gentlemen, when I said that about Captain Milton, I lied."

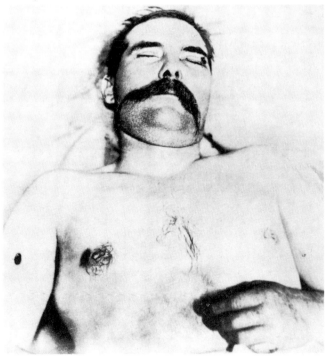

John Wesley Hardin, killer of forty men, by his own count, dead of gunshot wounds, 1895.

Days later, Mrs. McRose was thrown into the El Paso jail for drunk and disorderly conduct. Hardin berated the policemen in the case, John Selman, and his father, John Selman, Sr. He met the elder Selman on the street and cursed him, promising loudly that he would later kill both him and his son. He then spread the word through the saloons that the Selmans, especially the elder Selman, were marked for his guns. Apparently Hardin and the elder Selman had hated each other for years over a past but unstated grievance. "Old John had better go fixed at all times," Hardin kept repeating to his associates.

When the elder Selman heard this, he resolved to rid himself and El Paso of the lethal Hardin. He heard that Hardin was in the Acme Saloon on July 19, 1895, and he headed for this place. The gunfighter had been drinking all night, bragging about how he would "fix those damned Selmans." At 11 p.m., he was still at the bar, playing dice with a local businessman, H.S. Brown. He rolled the dice, watched the cubes bounce and stop on the bar, and then uttered his last words, saying to Brown: "Four sixes to beat!" He looked up a moment later to see in the mirror behind the bar the figure of old John Selman standing behind him. Before he could turn, Selman fired a bullet into the back of Hardin's head. The bullet took off the back of his head and emerged above the right eye. He toppled to the floor dead but Selman was taking no chances. He pumped two more bullets into the prone body, one slug going into the left arm, the other into the chest.

Selman insisted that Hardin had uttered a threat and had gone for his deadly guns in his vest holsters but none of the witnesses supported this claim. Selman was charged with murder and defended by Albert Fall, who was later the central figure in the Teapot Dome Scandal. Fall managed to persuade a jury that Hardin intended to kill Selman and that the old man had acted in self defense. He also maintained that the gunfighter had reached for his guns, causing Selman to defend himself. Selman was acquitted but no one, including the jury members at Selman's trial, believed that John Wesley Hardin had reached for his guns, or it would have been Hardin on trial for murder. See: **Armstrong, John Barclay; Bideno, Juan; Clements, Emmanuel, Jr.; Clements, Emmanuel, Sr.; Hickok, James Butler; Pierce, Abel Head; Ringo, John; Selman, John, Sr.; Sutton-Taylor Feud; Teapot Dome Scandal; Thompson, Ben.**

REF.: Allen, *The Real Book of the Texas Rangers*; American Guide Series, *Texas, A Guide to the Lone Star State*; Artrip, *Memoirs of Daniel Fore*; Asbury, *Sucker's Progress*; Bartholomew, *The Biographical Album of Western Gunfighters*; _____, *Kill or Be Killed*; _____, *Wyatt Earp, 1879-1882*; Black, *The End of the Long Horn Trail*; Boar, *The World's Most Infamous Murders*; Breakenridge, *Helldorado*; Breihan, *Great Lawmen of the West*; Brown, *Trail Driving Days*; Bruce, *Banister Was There*; Bush, *Gringo Doctor*; Bushick, *Glamorous Days*; CBA; Casey, *The Texas Border and Some Borderliners*; Clark, *Then Came the Railroads*; Connelley, *Wild Bill and His Era*; Cook, *Fifty Years on the Old Frontier*; Cunningham, *Famous in the West*; _____, *Triggernometry*; Debo, *The Cowman's Southwest*; Delony, *40 Years A Peace Officer*; Dils, *Horny Toad Man*; Douglas, *The Gentlemen in White Hats*; Drago, *Wild, Woolly & Wicked*; Durham, *The Negro Cowboys*; Dykstra, *The Cattle Towns*; Elman, *Fired in Anger*; Emmett, *Shanghai Pierce*; Erwin, *The Southwest of John H. Slaughter*; Faber, *Texans With Guns*; Farrow, *Troublesome Times in Texas*; Faulkner, *Roundup*; Fisher and Holmes, *Gold Rushes and Mining Camps*; Fitzpatrick, *This is New Mexico*; Foster-Harris, *The Look of the Old West*; Frantz, *The American Cowboy*; Gard, *The Chisholm Trail*; _____, *Frontier Justice*; Gaylord, *Handgunner's Guide*; George, *A Texas Prisoner*; Godwin, *Murder U.S.A.*; Greer, *Grand Prairie*; Grisham, *Tame the Wreckless Wind*; Haley, *George W. Littlefield, Texan*; _____, *Jeff Milton*; Hardin, *The Life of John Wesley Hardin*; Harkey, *Mean as Hell*; Havins, *Something About Brown*; Henderson, *100 Years in Montague County, Texas*; Hendricks, *The Bad Man of the West*; Hening, *George Curry*; Henry, *Conquering Our Great American Plains*; Holloway, *Texas Gun Lore*; Horan, *The Great American West*; _____ and Sann, *Pictorial History of the Wild West*; House, *City of Flaming Adventure*; _____, *Cowboy Columnist*; _____, *Old Field Fury*; _____, *Texas Treasure Chest*; Hunt, *Bluebonnets and Blood*; Hunter, *Peregrinations of a Pioneer Printer*; _____, *The Story of Lottie Deno*; _____ and Rose, *The Album of Gunfighters*; Huson, *Refugio*; Hutchinson, *Another Verdict for Oliver Lee*; _____ and Mullin, *Whiskey Jim and A Kid Named Billy*; Hyer, *The Land of Beginning Again*; Jennings, *A Texas Ranger*; Kelly, *The Sky was Their Roof*; King, *Ghost Towns of Texas*; King, *Mavericks*; Knight, *Wild Bill Hickok*; Lake, *Wyatt Earp*; Leftwich, *Tracks Along the Pecos*; Ludlum, *Great Shooting Stories*; McCarty, *The Enchanted West*; McGiffin, *Ten Tall Texans*; Mangan, *Bordertown*; Martin, *Border Boss*; Metz, *John Selman*; Middagh, *Frontier Newspaper, The El Paso Times*; Mills, *Forty Years at El Paso*; Monaghan, *The American West*; Morris, *Pictorial History of Victoria and Victoria County*; Myers, *The Last Chance*; Nash, *Bloodletters and Badmen*; Nordyke, *John Wesley Hardin*; _____, *The Truth About Texas*; North, *The Saga of the Cowboy*; O'Connor, *Wild Bill Hickok*; O'Neal, *They Die But Once*; Paine, *Texas Ben Thompson*; Parkhill, *The Wildest of the West*; Parsons, *The Capture of John Wesley Hardin*; Penfield, *Western Sheriffs and Marshals*; Phares, *Bible in Pocket, Gun in Hand*; _____, *Reverend Devil*; Plenn, *Texas Hellion*; _____ and LaRoche, *The Fastest Gun in Texas*; Poe, *Buckboard Days*; Polk, *Mason and Mason County*; Preece, *Lone Star Man*; Raine, *Famous Sheriffs and Western Outlaws*; _____, *Guns of the Frontier*; Rankin, *No. 6847, or The Horrors of Prison Life*; Rascoe, *Belle Starr*; Raymond, *Captain Lee Hall of Texas*; Redmond, *"Four Sixes to Beat"*; Rennert, *Western Outlaws*; Ripley, *They Died with Their Boots On*; Rosa, *The Gunfighter: Man or Myth?*; Russell, *Grandpa's Autobiography*; Sabin, *Wild Men of the Wild West*; Sandoz, *The Cattlemen*; Schaefer, *Heroes without Glory*; Scobee, *The Steer-Branded Murder*; Scott, *Such Outlaws as Jesse James*; Shipman, *Taming the Big Bend*; Shirley, *Toughest of Them All*; Siringo, *Lone Star Cowboy*; _____, *Riata and Spurs*; Small, *The Best of the True West*; Smith, *From the Memories of Men*; _____, *Frontier's Generation*; Smith, *Diamond Six*; Sonnichsen, *I'll Die Before I'll Run*; _____, *Outlaw*; _____, *Ten Texas Feuds*; Steckmesser, *The Western Hero in History and Legend*; Streeter, *The Kaw*; _____, *Prairie Trails and Cow Towns*; Sweet, *On a Mexican Mustang Through Texas*; Taylor, *Taylor's Thrilling Tales of Texas*; Thorp, *Story of the Southwestern Cowboy*; Waters, *A Gallery of Western Badmen*; Watson, *A Century of Gunmen*; Webb, *The Story of the Texas Rangers*; Wellman, *Trampling Herd*; Wendt, *Bet A Million!*; White, *The Autobiography of a Durable Sinner*; _____, *Lead and Likker*; _____, *Out of the Desert*; _____, *Texas, An Informal Biography*; _____, *Them Was the Days*; _____, *Trigger Fingers*; Williams, *Texas Trails*; Wilstach, *Wild Bill Hickok*; (FILM), *The Lawless Breed*, 1952.

Hardin, Rufus Howard, prom. 1959, U.S., forg. In early May 1959, a Florida clearinghouse discovered it had taken in four counterfeit U.S. Treasury notes. Within seven days, a trail of counterfeit checks were found in Mississippi, Texas, Louisiana, and Georgia, with operators forging checks for up to $100 in liquor stores, clothing shops, and supermarkets. By the middle of May, the U.S. Secret Service had issued warnings to store and bank owners.

On May 23, an alert store clerk in Louisiana spotted a forged check. A description of the passer provided to state police resulted in the arrest of the suspect, Arphy Justin Sonnier, two days later in Beaumont, Texas. With a previous narcotics conviction, Sonnier's record gave police further information and leads on his associates, including James Douglas Simmons and Carl Jay Schaaphok.

A woman named Jo Ann, a girlfriend of Sonnier's, was contacted by an undercover agent posing as a New York gangster visiting Louisiana. At a local bar, the agent met Jo Ann and bought eleven counterfeit checks for $275, then left to set up a larger trap. Through a telephone contact a buy was set up to take place in Washington, D.C., involving the delivery of $20,000 worth of counterfeit checks on July 8, 1959. Posing as buyers, two Secret Service agents waited to meet the counterfeiters, arresting Louis Emory Roger and Joseph Lovely Sonnier as they got off the plane from New Orleans. Moved to Alexandria, Va., for arraignment, Joseph Sonnier and Roger possessed 755 counterfeit checks, as well as counterfeit Social Security cards, Alabama driver's licenses, and military identification cards.

Under questioning, Joseph Sonnier and Roger admitted they had made several trips to Durango, Mex. Secret Service agents discovered the counterfeiting plant run by Ponciano Salas and his brother, and arrested the pair. Following the arrest of Jo Ann, agents were led to Rufus Howard Hardin, the mastermind of the operation. Previously charged, but not convicted, of murder, bank robbery, and a fraudulent timber swindle, Hardin was captured on Oct. 13, 1959, in Gulf Shores, Ala., and charged with manufacturing counterfeit checks. Fifteen other people, nine Americans and six Mexicans, were also arrested; all were convicted.

REF.: *CBA*; McGuire, *The Forgers.*

Harding, Sir John, prom. 1956, Gr., field marshal, attempt. assass. Had Field Marshall John Harding not insisted on fresh air as he slept, he might have lost his life in an assassination attempt in Cyprus in 1956.

The Nicosia active service unit of a right-wing Cypriote underground group, directing its activities against the British occupying forces, targeted Sir John for death because he had exiled Archbishop Makarios, the spiritual and political leader of the Cypriotes. Although Cypriote Colonel George Grivas was concerned that the bombs had not been perfected, the Nicosia unit proceeded with the assassination plan on Mar. 21, 1956. Harding's new valet, Neofytos Sofocleus, was instructed by leader Yacovos Patatsos to place the bomb under Harding's mattress. It would explode in twenty-four hours if kept at a constant temperature of sixty-seven degrees.

Sofocleus deposited the bomb and escaped. It did not explode, probably because Harding slept with the window open, or possibly because of a deficient fuse or lack of acid. It was discovered by another servant in the morning, long after Harding had departed, and was thrown into a pit in the garden, where it later exploded harmlessly. Harding was thought to be the target of another bomb that went off in the British Military Hospital on Jan. 5, 1956, just hours after his visit.

REF.: Bell, *Assassin; CBA.*

Harding, Warren G., See: **Teapot Dome Scandal.**

Hardy, Charles Leach, 1919- , U.S., jur. Served as assistant attorney general in Phoenix, Ariz., from 1956-59, and as judge of the superior court from 1966-80. He was nominated to the Arizona District Court by President Jimmy Carter in 1980. He was honored the same year by the Arizona Bar for helping prepare recommended Arizona criminal jury instructions. REF.: *CBA.*

Hardy, Francis, b.c.1949, Brit., mur. Francis Hardy, the 12-year-old son of a London taxi driver, was the youngest of three children in a family that lived in the suburbs. His parents were legally separated in 1958, but remained living together, partly to ensure Francis' welfare. Mrs. Hardy and her son were said to be close, but often quarreled because of the boy's violent temper.

In 1961 Francis' father was sent to the hospital and the boy was home alone with his 53-year-old mother. Asking her for some food, he then cooked some bacon to make a sandwich. According to Francis' testimony, when his mother threw the sandwich on the floor, he flung a carving knife at her. According to a pathologist, however, the woman had been stabbed. Of above average intelligence, Francis was permitted to plead not guilty to murder, but guilty to lesser manslaughter charges. The judge ordered a "fit person order," committing the boy to the care of Middlesex County.

REF.: *CBA*; Wilson, *Children Who Kill.*

Hardy, Vance, prom. 1924-50, U.S., (wrong. convict.) mur. Identified by a man who was coerced into perjured testimony, Vance Hardy was wrongly convicted of murder, and released only after his sister struggled for twenty-six years on his behalf.

On May 3, 1924, Louis Lambert of Detroit, Mich., who ran a soft drink business that was probably a front for a speakeasy, was leaving his bank when a Studebaker with three men inside pulled up to him. Shots rang out, Lambert staggered, and was pulled inside the car. Bruno Marcelt was in his kitchen when he looked out to see three men running away, then watched a dying Lambert fall out of the car. Rushing out, Marcelt heard Lambert whisper either that the "River Gang" or the "River Front Gang" got him.

Vance Hardy, a young man on the lookout for a fast dollar, was beginning to spend time in bad company. Police, angry at a gun-running scheme they could not break, hauled Hardy and another man into court and charged them with murder. Marcelt, brought in for extensive questioning, at first said he could not

identify the men he had seen fleeing. After coercion by police, as he would admit years later, he reluctantly identified Hardy as one of the men. Hardy's sister, Gladys Barrett, testified her brother had been with her, but he was convicted of first-degree murder and given a life sentence.

Insisting on his innocence, the bitter prisoner escaped from jail, was recaptured, and put in solitary confinement for ten years.

Barrett continued to champion her brother, eventually interesting crime writer Erle Stanley Gardner in the case. With Gardner's help, Marcelt repudiated his earlier statements, explaining that he had been forced into identifying Hardy. The charges were dropped at a new trial before Judge Joseph A. Gillis, and Hardy was finally released. The wrongly convicted man had spent twenty-six years in jail. See: **Gardner, Erle Stanley.**

REF.: *CBA*; Gardner, *The Court of Last Resort.*

Hardy, William, prom. 1806, Case of, U.S., mur. William Hardy seduced Elizabeth Valpy of Boston, promising that though he would not marry her, he would provide for any of their children. When Hardy's child was born in the home of Bridget Daley, wife of a condemned murderer Dominic Daley, Hardy took the infant, telling Valpy he was going to place the child with foster parents. The child's body was found strangled, a chain around its neck, near South Boston Bridge two weeks later. Hardy was charged with murder, convicted, and sentenced to death on Nov. 27, 1806. While awaiting execution, Hardy won a new trial on a technicality, and was acquitted at his second trial. See: **Daley, Dominic.**

REF.: *CBA; A Sketch of the Proceedings of William Hardy.*

Hare, Joseph Thompson, d.1818, U.S., rob. For many years the terror of the Natchez Trace was highwayman Joseph Hare. Born in Chester, Pa., Hare was raised in New York and went to sea at an early age. When his ship anchored in New Orleans, Hare went ashore and became obsessed with the venal city, especially the French Quarter and the impoverished districts where crime flourished. Joining the underworld, he soon had a gang of dedicated thieves who followed him into the Natchez Trace. Here the band preyed on stagecoaches and travelers moving along the Trace between Memphis, Tenn., and Natchez, Miss. Hare gleaned considerable profits from his robberies, and though known by name, he had never been identified, so he was able to return to New Orleans, his headquarters, where he lived in luxury. He dressed as a gentleman and was known as a man of "upstanding reputation."

In 1913, Hare was caught and sent to prison for five years, but upon his release he immediately went back to thieving. He and his men robbed the Baltimore night coach outside of Havre de Grace, Md., and took a strongbox containing more than $15,000 in gold, an enormous sum for that day. Hare was apprehended quickly since his identity was known and he was taken to Baltimore where he was quickly tried and condemned. The notorious highwayman ended his career on the gallows in the old Baltimore Jail yard on Sept. 10, 1818.

REF.: *CBA*; Coates, *The Outlaw Years;* Daniels, *The Devil's Backbone;* Howard, *The Life and Adventures of Joseph T. Hare;* Nash, *Bloodletters and Badmen;* Triplett, *History, Romance and Philosophy of Great American Crimes and Criminals.*

Hare, William, See: **Burke, William.**

Hargis-Cockerell Feud, prom. 1902-12, U.S., feud. The feuding spirit was fierce in the Kentucky region of Breathitt County; not since the Civil War had there been a release of the many feuds between families and political factions. The Hargis-Cockrell Feud lasted for ten years, dating back to 1869, when a political contest between the Republicans and Democrats for county offices resulted in men being thrown out of lawyers' offices at pistol point. Judge James Hargis was the Democratic candidate for county judge, and Tom Cockrell was the town marshal of Jackson, Ky.; his brother, James Cockrell, assisted him when he arrested Hargis for pulling a gun. Warrants for Hargis' arrest were issued by Police Judge T.P. Cardwell, whom Hargis refused to be tried by, as they had been bitter enemies for many years.

At a school election that year, J.B. Marcum, on the side of the Cockrells, faced off with Hargis, but no shots were fired and the fight was briefly patched up. Then, in July 1902, Tom Cockrell and Ben Hargis met in a saloon and fought with pistols; Hargis was killed. Later that same month, Jim Cockrell was shot and killed from a window on the second floor of the courthouse. On Nov. 9, 1902, Marcum sent a letter to the Lexington *Herald*, detailing how more than thirty people had been killed in Brethitt County in year.

The most renowned local man killed in the feud was James B. Marcum. For the previous year, Marcum had been considered a marked man and had spent more than two months as a prisoner in his own home. Venturing outside the courthouse in Jackson, Marcum was shot down at about 8:30 a.m. on May 4, 1903. After his murder, business in the town came to a standstill, with residents not daring to venture out after dark. On May 25, 1903, Curtis Jett and Tom White were indicted for the killing, and were tried together on June 12. Floyd Bird and Thomas Marcum prosecuted, and John B. O'Neal led the defense, which included seven other attorneys.

State militia troops were on hand to preserve order and protect the witnesses. With a divided jury, Judge Redwine ordered the case transferred to Harrison County, where it was tried on July 27, 1903, before Judge J.J. Osborne. The jury found both Jett and White Guilty, and they were sentenced to life in prison.

The feud continued with a case of patricide when Beach Hargis shot and killed his father, Judge James Hargis, with a gun he got from his father's store. The son was indicted for murder on Feb. 18, 1908, and found Guilty. Hargis was sentenced to life in prison.

The final murder in the Hargis-Cockrell Feud was that of Edward Callahan, a prominent mountain citizen who had been sheriff of Breathitt County, and was regarded as the leader of the Hargis faction. Along with Judge Hargis, he was indicted for murder five times, and tried in three different cities, on charges of killing James B. Marcum, Dr. B.D. Cox, Jim Cockrell, and others. Curtis Jett, Mose Feltner, John Smith, and John Abner all confessed to having participated in the killings, implicating Hargis and Callahan. Callahan was murdered on May 4, 1912, ambushed at 9 a.m. through the window of his store in Crockettsville. REF.: *CBA*.

Hargobind, 1595-1644, India, consp. Succeeded father, Guru Arjun in 1606 as Sikh Guru. He established a Sikh army. His influence was responsible for the military aspect of the Sikh religion. Emperor Jahangir of India had him imprisoned for twelve years. Later the Sikh army, under his direction, won four battles with the armies of Emperor Shah Jahan of India. REF.: *CBA*.

Hargraves, Dick, 1824-82, U.S., gamb.-mur. Born in England, Dick Hargraves immigrated to New Orleans as a 16-year-old, and after a short time as a bartender, became a renowned Mississippi riverboat gambler. Hargraves won a much as $30,000 from a single poker game and accumulated a fortune of $2 million. During his gambling career, he killed ten men who thought their losses to Hargraves were the result of his cheating.

Hargraves wore the finest clothes imported from England and France, and with his gambling ability, he attracted the attention of many women. He fought a duel with a banker over the affections of the man's wife, and was forced to shoot and kill the dead man's brother as well. Upon returning home, he was stabbed by the banker's wife, who then committed suicide. Hargraves recovered from the attack and retired to a more sedentary life, marrying a girl he had saved in a fire. He traveled to Cuba, and later became a Union officer in the Civil War. After the war, wealthy but suffering from tuberculosis, Hargraves moved to Denver where he lived until his death in 1882. REF.: *CBA*.

Harington, John (Baron Harington of Exton), d.1613, Brit., royal guardian. In 1603 James I was crowned and placed Princess Elizabeth under his guardianship. In 1605, he saved the princess from those behind the Gunpowder Plot. REF.: *CBA*.

Hariri, Hussein Ali Mohammed, 1966-   , Switz., skyjack. On July 24, 1987, Hussein Ali Mohammed Hariri hijacked an Air Afrique DC-10 airliner en route from Rome to Paris with 148 passengers and 15 crew members aboard. The plane had just departed Rome when Hariri, armed with a pistol and explosives wrapped around his waist, diverted the plane to Geneva, Switz., and demanded the release of his two Lebanese Shiite Moslem brothers, 22-year-old Mohammed Ali Hamadei and 28-year-old Abbas Ali Hamadei, who were being held in West Germany on terrorism charges. Hariri ordered the plane flown to Beirut or Saudi Arabia. When Swiss officials were slow to react, the gunman killed a passenger, 28-year-old Xavier Guillaume Beaulieu, a French wine merchant. A flight attendant then grabbed Hariri, who shot him in the stomach. While Swiss anti-terrorist officers stormed the front of the plane and apprehended the 21-year-old terrorist, passengers left the plane by emergency chutes at the rear entrance. On Feb. 24, 1989, after a three-day trial under heavy security in Lausanne, Hariri was sentenced to life imprisonment. REF.: *CBA*.

Harkey, Dee, 1866-1948, U.S., west. lawman. Dee Harkey was born in Texas in 1866 and became a lawman shortly after his sixteenth birthday. Orphaned at the age of three and raised by his older brother, Harkey witnessed a number of Indian raids as a child, and lost three brothers to gunfights before he was twenty-one. He eschewed an education, working on farms and on the range before becoming the teen-aged deputy of San Saba County, Texas, serving under his older brother Joe who was the elected sheriff. Two years later, in 1884, Harkey and another deputy arrested a man named Quinn in Richland Springs on the charge of stealing a mule. While the prisoner changed clothes at a hotel, Harkey and his partner were attacked by Quinn's wife and daughter. Harkey was slightly wounded in the abdomen by the girl.

In 1886, Harkey retired, married, and became a rancher in Bee County, Texas. Shortly afterward, he quarreled with neighbor George Young and during the argument, stabbed Young to death. Two years later, Harkey moved to Carlsbad, N.M., where he became a butcher, but continued to have trouble with his neighbors. He was involved in two shooting incidents with a customer named George High, impressing the citizenry enough with his skill with a gun to be named a deputy U.S. marshal. He served in that capacity until he retired from law enforcement for a second time in 1911. In 1895, in Phoenix, N.M., Harkey and Sheriff Cicero Stewart apprehended Tranquellano Estabo, a local gunman who was shooting up the town. In 1908, near Sacramento Sinks, Harkey led a posse of four lawmen in pursuit of Jim Nite, a member of the Dalton Gang who had escaped from a Texas jail. Nite and his accomplice, Dan Johnson, were found at daybreak and apprehended after a brief exchange of gunfire. Harkey later worked various jobs including town marshal and livestock inspector for a cattle raiser's association.

REF.: *CBA*; Hamilton, *Wagon Days on Red River*; Harkey, *Mean as Hell*; O'Neal, *Encyclopedia of Western Gunfighters*.

Harkins, William Hamilton, prom. 1900-30, U.S., forg. Born into a thrifty Scottish family in Washington state, William Hamilton Harkins desired a life of luxury. An intelligent man who graduated from college and became a licensed school teacher in 1893, Harkins married another teacher and they scrimped and saved $20,000 to buy a house. When their bank failed and they were left penniless, Harkins, maintaining that the bank had swindled them, vowed to take revenge and get his money back with interest. His wife left him, and Harkins embarked on a career of forgery that continued for the rest of his life.

Although he would be arrested some twelve or fifteen times by the mid 1920s, he repeatedly avoided conviction with the assistance of expensive lawyers. So convincing was Harkins that he submitted to many lie detector and truth serum tests and always passed. He even convinced judges and arresting officers that he was the victim of the crime, not the criminal.

Harkins was reported to have made around $1 million in bank hoaxes. Harkins himself estimated the figure at closer to $5 million. His brother, a preacher, used his influence to gain Harkin's release on a 1922 charge, promising to put him in psychotherapy, which Harkins refused, later explaining that he enjoyed hoaxing, and had no need of therapy.

Extradited to North Dakota in 1929, where he was charged with duping banks out of $100,000 and of posing as a physician, Harkins denied all charges. At the trial in 1928, his brother testified that Harkins had been with him at the time of the crimes. While this was technically true, Harkins had predated the fraudulent check. Despite this fact, he again was found Not Guilty. In 1930, when Harkins was sixty, he was captured again in Louisiana, convicted, and sent to prison for ten years. Disowned by his brother, the aging criminal said he had no regrets, having hurt no one, and having no enemies except the bankers who "are of no concern to me. After all, they bankrupted me once, and almost ruined me. An eye for an eye..." REF.: *CBA*.

Harlan, John Marshall, 1833-1911, U.S., jur. Served as judge of Franklin County, Ky., in 1858-59, and as attorney general of Kentucky from 1863-67. He was nominated in 1877 as an associate justice to the U.S. Supreme Court by President Rutherford B. Hayes, serving until his death. He often disagreed with the decisions of the other justices and was known as the "great dissenter." He strongly supported the constitutional rights of individuals, such as in *Hurtado v. California* in 1884, and in 1900 he opposed the majority in *Maxwell v. Dow*. Originally opposed to the Thirteenth and Fourteenth Amendments, he became a supporter of civil rights.
REF.: *CBA*; Navasky, *Kennedy Justice*.

Harlan, John Marshall, 1899-1971, U.S., jur. Grandson and namesake of Supreme Court Justice John Marshall Harlan. He worked as chief counsel to the New York State Crime Commission from 1951-53 to investigate ties between government and organized crime. He served as judge on the U.S. Court of Appeals for the Second Circuit between 1954-55, and he was nominated by President Dwight D. Eisenhower to the U.S. Supreme Court in 1954. Regarding criminal law, he disagreed with the majority decision in several instances, such as in *Mapp v. Ohio* in 1961, and *Ker v. California* in 1963. However, he voted with the majority when the Court ordered states to make free counsel available to indigent defendants. He also agreed in *In re Gault* with the 1967 Court ruling assuring certain constitutional procedures, such as the right to counsel for juveniles. He opposed the 1964 *Malloy v. Hogan* decision, and in 1966 dissented in the *Miranda v. Arizona* case. In most cases, he firmly supported decisions to prohibit racial segregation. He voted with the majority in *Brown v. Board of Education*, ruling that school segregation was unconstitutional. In general, he voted conservatively, advocating restraint on the part of the courts.
REF.: *CBA*; Navasky, *Kennedy Justice*.

Harlem Race Riot, 1935, U.S., mob vio. The nationwide despair caused by the U.S. depression in the 1930s was accented in Harlem, N.Y., by continued racial discrimination. The pent-up anger of the black community was released in 1935 when two events incited the brief Harlem Race Riot. In Harlem in early March 1935, a black man lost his eye during a beating by a New York City police officer. The man was then charged with assault on the officer, but was not indicted by a grand jury. On Mar. 19, a black teenager, 16-year-old Lino Rivera, was caught stealing a knife from the Kress Department store—a store well known for its discriminatory hiring practices. When police took the boy in for questioning, a crowd formed, fearing for the boy's safety following the earlier incident. Rumors spread through the crowd that officers had killed Rivera, and when a community group attempted to hold a public meeting on a nearby corner, police threatened to arrest the speakers for unlawful assemblage. A full-scale riot erupted. More than $2 million in property was destroyed as the mob looted more than 200 stores. More than 100 people were injured, and the police killed one black man. REF.: *CBA*.

Harley, Robert, See: **South Sea Bubble**. REF.: *CBA*.

Harley, Robert (Earl of Oxford), 1661-1724, Brit., polit. corr. Member of Parliament from 1689-1711, and through political ties with Marlborough became principle secretary of state. He tried to scheme against Marlborough and Godolphin by gaining influence with the queen, but he was forced out of office in 1708. He wrote to both the Hanoverians and the Jacobites and tried to negotiate peace separately from the Allies. Marlborough was dismissed, enabling him to carry the treaty of Utrecht in 1713. He lost the queen's favor and was ousted from office. He was imprisoned from 1715-17. REF.: *CBA*.

Harley Street Mystery, 1880, Brit., (unsolv.) mur. When James Spendlove worked as a butler at Mr. Henriques' house in Harley Street, he often mentioned an obnoxious smell emanating from the cellar. Drains had been cleared, and other attempts were made to clear it up. In June 1880, Spendlove and a footman, Kirkland, went to clean up the area and found in a cistern a sugar barrel containing the decomposing body of a middle-aged woman. The murderer had put chloride of lime over the body, mistakenly believing that this would help it decompose. Instead, the corpse was preserved. The victim had been killed by a stab wound to the chest, and medical experts set the death at about a year before discovery. Despite a £100 reward offered by police, and extensive questioning of servants, the murderer was never discovered. REF.: *CBA*.

Harlot's Progress, A (Splendeurs et Miseres de Courtisanes), 1838-47, novel by Honore de Balzac. Profiled in fiction is the redoubtable French criminal turned super detective Eugene Francois Vidocq, called "Vautrin" by Balzac, with elements of two French criminals of the day, Pierre Coignard and Anthelme Collet, fused into the Vautrin character. See: **Vidocq, Eugene Francois**. REF.: *CBA*.

Harlow, Bess, See: **Jenkins, Bess**.

Harmodius, See: **Hipparchus**.

Harmon, Alvin B., prom. 1935, U.S., fraud. Although scientific ways of detecting fraud have made literary fraud less prevalent, there was a plagiarism case as recently as June 1935. *Esquire* magazine printed a short story called "The Perlu," purportedly written by Alvin B. Harmon. Readers informed the magazine's editor that the story was a blatant paraphrase of "The Damned Thing," by Ambrose Bierce. Bierce's story was, in turn, suspected of being lifted from "The Horla" by Guy de Maupassant.
REF.: *CBA*; MacDougall, *Hoaxes*.

Harmon, Charles Preston, d.1931, U.S., rob. Texas born and bred, Charles Harmon was an habitual thief from early youth; he began robbing stores and banks in the 1920s, drawing two prison terms in Huntsville State Prison. Upon his release from Huntsville, after serving his second term, Harmon met and married a Texas girl, Paula Stevens, who had graduated finishing school, had married and divorced a steamship officer, and had become the comptroller of a Texas firm. She was enamored of Harmon's rough ways and the life of the bank robber excited her. She married Harmon and traveled with him on his various bank raids until Harmon was captured and sent to Leavenworth.

There Harmon's cell mate was Frank "Jelly" Nash, who had a long career as a bank robber dating back to the days of robbers on horseback, having been a member of the old Al Spencer gang. Nash later escaped Leavenworth and, when Harmon was released in 1930, he joined a gang made up of Nash, Thomas Holden, Francis Keating, and others. Harmon's wife met him upon his release, but when he learned that Paula Harmon had gone to Chicago and opened a whorehouse while he was in prison, Harmon's attitude toward his wife soured. They argued incessantly and Paula returned to Chicago to run her brothel. It was later claimed that she had taken up with Frank Nash while her husband was in prison and after Harmon was released and joined the Nash gang, he had been marked for death by Nash who wanted him out of the way so he could have Paula Harmon for himself.

Harmon participated in several bank robberies with Nash, Holden, and Keating. He joined these men to raid the Kraft State Bank in Menominee, Wis., in 1931. More than $100,000 was taken in this raid, but Charlie Harmon did not live to spend his share of the loot. His bullet-ridden body was found in a ditch not far from Menominee a few days after the raid. He had been killed by members of his own gang for reasons never explained, though Nash was considered to be the killer because of his relationship with Paula Harmon. See: **Holden, Thomas; Nash, Frank**.

REF.: *CBA*; Cooper, *Ten Thousand Public Enemies*; Gish, *American Bandits*; Hoover, *Persons in Hiding*; Louderback, *The Bad Ones*.

Harmon, Judson, 1846-1927, U.S., lawyer. Practiced law in Cincinnati, Ohio, and served as U.S. attorney general from 1895-97, and taught law at the University of Cincinnati in 1896. REF.: *CBA*.

Harmond, John H., prom. 1853, U.S., rob. In the summer of 1853, detective Allan Pinkerton noticed a man walking along Lake Street in Chicago. With no reason, merely a suspicion, Pinkerton followed him to a boarding house, the Waverley House, and saw that he registered as John H. Harmond of St. Louis. Watching the man's room until nightfall, Pinkerton returned early the next morning. Disguised in a shabby suit, the detective followed Harmond to the Michigan Central Railroad, watched him buy a ticket, and continued to trail him as he walked down to the lake. There he swiftly dug in the sand and pulled out a tray of jewelry, which he rapidly concealed. When Pinkerton followed him onto a day coach, Harmond realized he was being followed. The detective prevented the well-dressed thief from sliding out the window. Harmond noticed Pinkerton's uncouth costume and called out for assistance, pretending he was being accosted by a ruffian. The conductor was not taken in by the ruse and helped Pinkerton handcuff and subdue the thief.

Searching Harmond at the county jail, Pinkerton and warden Simon Doyle discovered a number of watches, rings, and pins, and more than $900 in cash. Returning to the Waverley House, Pinkerton informed the guests, almost all of whom Harmond had robbed, to go to the sheriff's office or the county jail. Harmond was indicted by a grand jury that same evening. The stolen tray of rings was returned to a Toledo, Ohio, jeweler named Isaacson. Harmond was tried, found Guilty, and sent to the Illinois penitentiary at Upper Alton for a nineteen-year term. See: **Pinkerton, Allan**.

REF.: *CBA*; Rowan, *The Pinkertons*.

Harms, John P. (AKA: **Carl Herman**), prom. 1896, U.S., theft. A stranger entered the San Francisco offices of Detective Hume of Wells, Fargo & Company on Feb. 7, 1896, with the story of "Carl the Tramp." According to the stranger, his friend Kohler, a blacksmith, had been good friends with Carl Herman who, until October 1894, had no money. Transformed after that date, Herman dressed in elegant clothing and fine jewels, and went to the race track, where he met May Vaughan. He lavished expensive gifts on her and her friends, eventually setting up an apartment for Vaughan. Traveling to Chicago, Herman sent Vaughan $1,000 to visit him. She received the cash, but did not go. Herman soon returned to San Francisco. According to the stranger, Herman could be found the next day, when he would be meeting Kohler for a morning appointment. Detectives White and Thatcher took Herman into custody and extracted a confession from him.

Herman explained that his real name was John P. Harms, and that he had slept in the bulrushes near Sacramento the night of the Davisville train robbery. The next morning Harms saw a spot that had been disturbed, dug up the hidden gold, and carried off $33,000 of the loot in his blankets. The detectives uncovered about $12,000 deposited in banks and notes by Harms, and returned it to Wells Fargo. Charged with grand larceny, Harms was convicted on May 31, 1896, and sentenced to a three-year term in Folsom Prison. He was released on Oct. 8, 1898.

REF.: *CBA*; Duke, *Celebrated Criminal Cases of America*.

Haro, Miguel Nassar, prom. 1988, Case of, U.S., theft.-pol. corr. In December 1988, Mexico City mayor Manuel Camacho Solis announced the appointment of Miguel Nassar Haro to director of the Mexico City police department's intelligence division, eliciting an outcry as soon as disreputable events in Haro's past were uncovered. Haro and other Mexican law enforcement agents, including the son of Mexico City police chief, Javier Garcia, were alleged to have been part of an auto theft gang responsible for stealing 600 luxury cars from southern California and smuggling them into Mexico. The gang was crippled when fourteen members were convicted and imprisoned in the U.S. Two defendants implicated Haro, who was indicted by U.S. Attorney William Kennedy. The Justice Department was opposed to the indictment because the CIA described Haro as one of its most important sources in Mexico and Central America. Haro was jailed briefly in San Diego, Calif., but released on $200,000 bond. He fled to Mexico and was never tried. Kennedy was subsequently fired as U.S. Attorney by President Ronald Reagan because the Justice Department said that "his improper comments about a pending criminal case were highly prejudicial to the interests of the United States." Haro was also alleged to have been a member of a secret police unit that had interrogated and tortured students in the 1960s. On Feb. 24, 1989, two months after the public disclosure, Haro resigned as director of intelligence. REF.: *CBA*.

Harold, Gille, c.1103-36, Nor., fraud. Born in Ireland, pretended to be son of King Magnus Barefoot of Norway. When King Sigurd I of Norway died in 1130, Harold was chosen successor and civil war broke out from 1134-35. He was killed by another man with a fraudulent claim to the crown. REF.: *CBA*.

Harpalus, c.355-323 B.C., Babylonia, governor, assass. Affiliated with Alexander the Great, he was put in charge of conquered Babylonia's royal treasure and government. He stole the treasure and escaped to Athens and then to the island of Crete, where he was assassinated. REF.: *CBA*.

Harpe, William Micajah (AKA: **Big**), and **Harpe, Wiley** (AKA: **Little**), prom. 1790s, U.S., west. outl. The Harpe Brothers were long remembered by the U.S. settlers who traveled west along the Wilderness Trail in the 1790s. William Micajah "Big" Harpe and his brother Wiley "Little" Harpe were born into a Tory family in North Carolina. When the British surrendered in 1781, the brothers fled west to escape persecution. In the lawless frontier, the Harpes quickly gained a reputation as a pair of cold-blooded killers. They often disemboweled their victims and threw the remains into the Barren River, weighted down with stones. A $300 reward was posted in the Tennessee territory, but the brothers moved on to Ohio, where they holed up in a remote fortress known as Cave-In-the-Rock. River pirates described the Harpes as "men turned into wild wolves."

The brothers murdered numerous settlers, one because he snored too loudly. In 1799, a posse trapped the Harpe brothers in the woods. Wiley escaped, but Micajah was shot off his horse. The posse members began to hack off his head while he still lived. Micajah cursed them and told them to get on with it. Later, they boiled his head and nailed the skull to a tree to deter potential desperadoes. Legend has it that Wiley was eaten by a pack of wolves sometime after 1800.

REF.: Botkin, *A Treasury of Mississippi River Folklore*; Carter, *Lower Mississippi*; *CBA*; Coates, *The Outlaw Years*; Daniels, *The Devil's Backbone*; Hall, *The Harpe's Head*; Hendricks, *The Bad Man of the West*; Holmes, *Serial Murder*; Horan and Sann, *Pictorial History of the Wild West*; Hough, *The Story of the Outlaw*; Humphreys, *The Lost Towns and Roads of America*; Marshall and Evans, *They Found It in Natchez*; Nash, *Bloodletters and Badmen*; Rothert, *The Outlaws of Cave-in-Rock*; Sabin, *Wild Men of the Wild West*; Smith, *Legends of the War of Independence and of the Earlier Settlements in the West*; Triplett, *History, Romance and Philosophy of Great American Crimes and Criminals*; Wellman, *Spawn of Evil*.

Harper, Calvin, prom. 1920s, U.S., mur. In a Midwestern city during Prohibition, August Greving gave a home brew party and angrily told one of his guests, Calvin Harper, to leave when the drunk man made overtures to Greving's wife. Threatening revenge as he left, Harper returned several hours later, rang the doorbell, and shot Greving dead when the host answered the door.

Eyewitnesses to the slaying included Greving's wife and two other female guests. Harper escaped, taking a train to a nearby town. Still inebriated, he let his gun fall to the floor of the train. It discharged, wounding a passenger.

When Harper was arrested at the next stop, police recognized him as Greving's murderer. In the long delay between the arrest and the trial, two of the eyewitnesses were killed in a car accident, and the other vanished. Because there were no ballistics services or medical examiners in the place where the slaying occurred, no autopsy was performed. The anxious prosecutor ordered the corpse exhumed, and was able to prove that the bullets in the body matched those in Harper's gun. The district attorney, concerned about getting a conviction, made a deal with Harper. Pleading guilty to second-degree murder, the killer was given a ten-year sentence.

REF.: *CBA;* Marten, *The Doctor Looks at Murder.*

Harper, Carey Judson, prom. 1917-44, U.S., fraud-tax. evas. Starting out his swindling career by running a restaurant in which the prices not only changed from day to day, but varied from customer to customer, Carey Judson Harper rapidly graduated to selling worthless stocks in Texas, Oklahoma, and Missouri.

Harper was a tall, well-dressed, good-looking man with a pleasing manner who easily gained people's confidence. In 1917, at the age of twenty-two, Harper opened an amusement club in El Paso and ran it for four years, undoubtedly skimming off the top of card games. In 1922, he moved to Ranger, Texas, and opened a restaurant which featured sliding prices. By the end of the year, Harper relocated to Fort Worth and began passing worthless checks. Harper repeatedly talked his way out of trouble, moving to Albuquerque, N.M., in 1926, and using his talents to organize the Panhandle Auto Finance Company, selling beautifully printed but worthless stock.

By 1927, Harper was in Amarillo with a quantity of useless securities, and a new firm, the West Texas Finance Company. He conned a wealthy, gullible physician into becoming the president of the fraudulent firm, and unloaded $100,000 of phony securities on the doctor's unsuspecting patients and friends. Taking a few thousand dollars of this money, Harper donated groceries and cash to needy families in Amarillo, making sure his charity was known. He then used his new-found respectability to unload another $100,000 in stocks. When it was time to pay dividends, the con man managed some intricate financial maneuvering and started a second stock issue in another fictitious company, the Southern Wheel Corporation.

Moving on to Coahoma, Texas, Harper bought controlling interest in a state bank, but was accused of swindling Amarillo out of nearly $350,000. Again talking his way out of trouble, the trickster was fined $500, and left for Oklahoma City. There, he continued his fraudulent schemes, convincing two prominent Oklahomans to become president and vice-president of his newest venture, a car wheel factory in Kentucky which existed only on paper. Harper bilked the locals and left for Kansas City, Mo., in 1928 to sell exclusive memberships to the Roosevelt Hunting Preserve organization. Visiting the Better Business Bureau, the audacious thief wrote them a check for $500, commending their good work. Pretending to receive calls from Franklin Delano Roosevelt, Harper continued to fleece prominent, wealthy citizens. In Wichita, Kan., selling stock in the Roosevelt Chain Hotel Corporation, Harper was indicted in 1929 for violation of the state's securities laws and was convicted. Released on a $10,000 bond, he fled to Los Angeles, traveling around the West Coast and selling attractive bonds for the National Carbonic Ice Company of Albuquerque. On Dec. 9, 1931, he was arrested by Intelligence Unit men in San Francisco as he attempted to buy a car, paying $6,000 in cash. Released from the Kansas State Prison in October 1935, he pleaded guilty to federal income tax fraud and went back to jail. On his release he traveled through Omaha and St. Louis, plying his trade, until he was indicted again for Securities Acts violations and mail fraud. Tried in 1943, he was convicted and sentenced to ten years in prison. Incredibly,

the inveterate huckster, from his disadvantaged position as an inmate at the county jail, attempted to sell interest in yet another endeavor to an Intelligence Unit agent, Kenneth L. Briggs, who was interviewing him about tax evasion.

REF.: *CBA;* Hynd, *The Giant Killers.*

Harper, Michael, prom. 1980, U.S., extor.-fraud-kid.-mur. Although missing since Jan. 29, 1980, George Mercer IV was not officially reported missing until Feb. 7, when the Savannah *Morning News* and the *Evening Press* reported his disappearance. From a prominent Savannah family, 22-year-old Mercer was known to have a lot of enthusiasm for schemes, but was thought by his friends to be gullible, and had been slow in school. After his disappearance, demands for ransom and complicated instructions were sent to his family. At one time, the ransom was left in a wooded area, but was never picked up.

FBI agents searching for Mercer also carried with them a picture of Michael Harper. A fast-talking man described as brilliant by some people, Harper had been sentenced in 1974 to a fourteen-month prison term for attempting to extort $4,500 from a former neighbor by threatening to murder the man and his family. Harper had also been arrested later in Augusta, Ga., where he was convicted of theft by deception, and put on probation.

A weekly Savannah newspaper, the *Georgia Gazette,* published a front page story on Feb. 11 revealing for the first time publicly that Mercer was presumed kidnapped, and that Harper was the primary suspect. The same day the story came out, Harper left Savannah, but hitched a ride with a van that was stopped for speeding and was back in jail within one day, held for violating probation.

By the end of April, police found Mercer's corpse buried in a shallow grave on the wooded college grounds of Armstrong State. He had been shot twice and was, according to a coroner's report, probably killed the first day he was missing. Charged with murder, Harper was brought to trial that winter. Pleading guilty to extortion, he maintained that Mercer was alive the last time he saw him. Telling a complicated story of how he and Mercer had tried, with two other men, to obtain funds to start a custom stereo business by buying $40,000 worth of marijuana to sell, Harper claimed the drugs had been stolen. The four partners then decided to extort money from Mercer's father, but the scheme fell apart. After four hours of deliberation, the jury found Mercer Guilty of first-degree murder. Sentenced to life imprisonment, Harper continued to maintain his innocence, offering condolences to the Mercer family and saying, "He was a friend of mine."

REF.: *CBA;* Trillin, *Killings.*

Harper, Richard, prom. 1830s, U.S., rob. Richard Harper, a nomadic alcoholic, drifted into Chicago in the early 1830s where he was arrested for robbery. In 1833, under the city's archaic vagrancy laws, Harper became the first white man to be sold at an auction in Chicago. He was purchased for twenty-five cents by George White, a black town crier, who led him away in chains. Harper purportedly escaped that night and was never seen again. REF.: *CBA.*

Harper, Robert N., prom. 1908, U.S., fraud. In the first court case to be tried under the 1906 Pure Food and Drugs Act, Robert N. Harper was accused of making "false and misleading" statements on his patent medicine Cuforhedake Brane-Fude, which many citizens were believed to read as being "good for a headache;" while the actual name was German for "brain food."

Harper, a trained pharmacist and prominent citizen, manufactured his Brane-Fude product in Washington, D.C. Harper had begun making headache remedies in 1888, using a coal tar derivative called acetanilid, said to bring down fever and deaden pain. By 1908, Harper had sold two million bottles of his product. After the institution of the Pure Food and Drugs Act, Harper went to the Bureau of Chemistry to determine how he should change his label, and was told he could not be given positive instructions, but must make his own decision about altering his label to conform. Harper adjusted his information to show that

Brane-Fude contained sixteen grains of acetanilid and thirty percent alcohol, leaving extant his claim that it contained "no poisonous ingredients of any kind." A controversy over acetanilid had recently been brought out when *Collier's* magazine published the names of twenty-two victims allegedly brought to death by acetanilid poisoning, and a well-known doctor presented a report on numerous cases of addiction and poisoning from the drug.

Harper was indicted in January 1908 and tried a month later. The sixteen-day debate was over definitions of terms, with Harper arguing in his own defense, insisting that through twenty years and two million bottles, he had heard of no harmful effects from his medicine. When the judge advised the jury to rule based on whether or not Harper's remedy could be considered brain food, and to consider how his labeling statements would affect the average citizen, the jury found Harper Guilty. Between the verdict and sentencing, President Theodore Roosevelt called the prosecuting attorney to the White House, instructing him "to make an example of this man." The manufacturer was charged the maximum penalty of $500, with another $200 on another count.

REF.: *CBA*; Young, *The Medical Messiahs.*

Harper's Ferry Raid, 1859, U.S., treas. The sleepy little town of Harper's Ferry, W. Va., became the site of one of the important events in U.S. history, precipitating the outbreak of the Civil War. Nestled in Jefferson County near the juncture of the Shenandoah and Potomac Rivers, Harper's Ferry was selected by President George Washington to become a federal arsenal because of its strategic location adjacent to the waterways. The land was purchased from the estate of Robert Harper in 1796. Harper was one of its original settlers, staking his claim in 1734. The town quickly became an important manufacturing center for rifles and ammunition.

Then, on Oct. 16-18, 1859, the fiery abolitionist John Brown led an abortive raid on the arsenal. Brown had been obsessed with the notion of freeing the slaves through an armed insurrection since 1849. He was active in the anti-slavery fight carried on in "Bleeding Kansas" in 1856-57, and went so far as to enlist the support of Boston, Mass., abolitionists who supported his plan to create a free Negro state with a $3,800 grant. In the summer of 1859 he rented a farm five miles from the federal arsenal, where he planned the ill-fated assault. With a regiment of sixteen whites and five free black men, he seized control of the armory on the night of Oct. 16. Ironically, the first person to be killed was a black man who worked as a baggage master at the railroad station. Alerted to the present danger, a compliment of local militia, as well as state and federal troops, descended on the besieged arsenal.

Brown and his supporters were overwhelmed after two days of intense fighting. Seventeen of the abolitionists, including Brown's son, were killed in the cross-fire before their leader was forced to surrender to Colonel Robert E. Lee. Brown was taken to the Charlestown jail and held there until treason charges could be filed. Despite seventeen affidavits from neighbors and friends who believed him to be insane, Brown was duly convicted and sentenced to die. On Dec. 2, 1859, John Brown became a martyr of the anti-slavery movement when he was hanged outside the jail. Harper's Ferry later became the site of an important Civil War battle fought on Sept. 13-15, 1862. Confederate armies under the command of General Thomas "Stonewall" Jackson captured the town and took 12,500 Union prisoners. See: **Brown, John.** REF.: *CBA*.

Harpur, Charles, prom. 1820s, Case of, Brit., mur. When Judith Morton was seventeen, she was the most sought-after young woman in Westmorland, Eng. In the early 1820s, three men, Charles Harpur, Robert Masters, and Richard Penson, were madly in love with her. Five years later, she married Masters, after Penson had become a lawyer in Liverpool, and Harpur had moved to the U.S. However, Harpur returned to Westmorland, and soon was fighting Masters for Morton's affections. A few days later, Masters was found dead in an open field, and an eyewitness, James Blundell, identified the murderer as Harpur, who was

promptly arrested. Morton sought the legal aid of Penson, and admitted to him in secrecy that she had killed Masters, and that if Harpur could be acquitted, she would take Penson as a lover. Agreeing to help her, Penson was able to discredit the testimony of Blundell by hiring a witness who implicated the eyewitness as the murderer. Harpur was immediately acquitted, and Blundell arrested. As Blundell attempted to mount his defense, Harpur and Judith Morton fled to the U.S. and married, leaving Penson to face the possible consequences of having a perjured witness. Morton sent Penson a letter, mocking him for being so gullible. Harpur was later killed in a midnight duel with William Harrison of Philadelphia, who eighteen days later became Morton's third husband. REF.: *CBA*.

Harran, Ian Noel, 1922- , Brit., child abuse. A schoolmaster accused of molesting several boys discharged his attorney so that he could give the summing-up speech to the jury, and was promptly found Guilty of all charges.

Ian Noel Harran, twenty-four, became a teacher in 1946 and served as assistant master at several private boarding schools for boys, despite his lack of academic credentials. Because of the scarcity of qualified men during the war years, it was easy for Harran to obtain posts.

Traveling on his bicycle, Harran went to the area west of Bournemouth, London, often finding his victims as they returned from Boy Scout meetings or church choir practice. He molested a number of children before he was finally arrested. Denying all charges, Harran indignantly counter charged the police with prosecuting him because he was a British Fascist. But the trial testimony from several victims, none of whom knew each other and who recognized both Harran and his bicycle, was irrefutable. Harran's defense attorney, J.T. Molony, had built a case for reasonable doubt, which Harran totally negated by insisting on making the speech to the jury himself, and withdrawing his retainer to do so. Harran gave a long speech, in which he told of a previous child abuse conviction in Wales, assuring the jury that this, too, was false and that he had been unjustly sentenced to three months in prison, explaining that the boy had made up the story out of spite.

The jury convicted Harran of all four charges. Sentenced to eight years of hard labor, the former schoolteacher cried as he was removed from the dock, shouting his innocence and repeating that he was being persecuted for his politics. Harran was later transferred to Broadmoor jail, from which he escaped, and was later arrested again in Ireland on child abuse charges and imprisoned.

REF.: *CBA*; Woodland, *Assize Pageant.*

Harrelson, Charles, prom. 1979, U.S., mur. On May 29, 1979, U.S. District Judge John Wood, about to preside over a drug conspiracy trial, was shot to death outside his home in San Antonio. A local drug kingpin, Jimmy Chagra, was about to appear before Wood—known as "Maximum John" for the severity of his drug case sentencing. Chagra, a former carpet salesmen, had been smuggling marijuana into the U.S. since the 1960s and had built a drug empire that stretched to both coasts. Local prosecutors and the FBI viewed the murder as an attack on the judicial system and spent three years and $11 million to conduct 30,000 interviews and collect over 500,000 bits of information in an attempt to apprehend the killer. Chagra's brother Joe told investigators that his brother had offered Charles Harrelson $250,000 to kill Wood. In 1983, Chagra was acquitted of murder and of conspiracy to commit murder. He did however, admit to another conspiracy and was sentenced to life imprisonment. To avert his sentence, he became a government witness, and is currently residing in prison under a new identity established by the Federal Witness Protection Program.

Joe Chagra, allowed to plea bargain, was sentenced to six years for his involvement in the conspiracy, but was paroled in March 1988. Charles Harrelson, although denying any involvement, was convicted of Wood's murder, and sentenced to two consecutive life sentences, as well as another five years for obstructing justice. Harrelson had previously served time for a 1968 murder-for-hire. His wife Jo Ann Starr Harrelson, accused of buying the murder weapon, was convicted of perjury and obstructing justice, and was sentenced to twenty-five years. Elizabeth Chagra, Jimmy's wife, was convicted of conspiracy, obstruction of justice, as well as tax fraud, and was sentenced to forty years. REF.: *CBA*.

Harries, Thomas Ronald Lewis, 1931-54, Brit., mur. John and Phoebe Harries owned a farm in Llanginning, Wales, and their 24-year-old nephew, Thomas Harries, lived with them. The Harries were last seen on Oct. 16, 1953, at a church service. Thomas Harries told Chief Constable T. Hubert Lewis of Carmarthenshire he had driven them to the Carmarthen railway station where they were to board a train to London for a "secret holiday." But it seemed uncharacteristic of 63-year-old John Harries and his wife to leave the farm in disarray and the animals unfed. Three weeks later, Lewis notified Scotland Yard.

Thomas Harries, British killer.

Chief Superintendent John Capstick soon learned from 15-year-old Brian Powell that Thomas Harries had made some peculiar remarks about his aunt and uncle. Summoned to help with the farm work, Powell heard Harries say, "They won't miss this one," as he slipped a paintbrush in his pocket. Capstick also noticed an uncooked piece of meat in the stove. Thomas Harries had recently cashed a check made out to his father on which £9 was overwritten to read £909.

Capstick strung reels of thread around the farm and every exit from it to the surrounding fields, believing that sooner or later Harries would visit the grave site where he had buried the bodies. On Nov. 16, police found the shallow graves of the victims, whose heads had been smashed in. "I am sorry to hear uncle and auntie are dead. I was their favorite," Harries said. Further investigation revealed that Harries had murdered the couple with a borrowed hammer. Harries was convicted on Mar. 16, 1954, and later hanged at Swansea Prison.

REF.: Capstick, *Given In Evidence*; CBA; Furneaux, *Famous Criminal Cases, vol. 2*; Hoskins, *The Sound of Murder*; Jacobs, *Aspects of Murder*; Rowland, *Criminal Files*; Webb, *Deadline for Crime*; Wilson, *Encyclopedia of Murder*.

Harriet, 1934, a novel by Elizabeth Jenkins. The systematic starvation of Harriet Staunton by her husband Louis, his mistress Alice Rhodes, and his brother and sister-in-law (Brit., 1877), is the basis of this work of fiction. See: **Staunton Family**. REF.: *CBA*.

Harrigan, Laurence, 1834-99, U.S., law enfor. off. Born in Ireland in 1834, Laurence Harrigan moved to Missouri in 1853 and became a shoemaker, joining the St. Louis police force in 1857. Sworn in as chief of the police force for the first time on June 1, 1874, he served for a year and a half, resigning in November 1875; he would resign and be reinstated three more times. Elected to the Missouri General Assembly in 1879, Harrigan served a two-year term, and was later selected by President Grover A. Cleveland for a federal appointment from 1886 to 1890.

Harrigan introduced to U.S. law enforcement the Bertillon Measurement System, a forerunner to fingerprinting in which criminal's fingers, skulls, arm lengths, and other body parts were measured as a means of identification, on the recommendation of Mathew Kiely, who would later succeed Harrigan as police chief. REF.: *CBA*.

Harriman, Joseph Wright, 1867-1949, U.S., embez. A respected socialite, bank president Joseph Wright Harriman was accused

and convicted of embezzling $1,713,000 and of misapplying $600,000 in assets.

In July 1932, Harriman was elected chairman of the Harriman National Bank & Trust Company in Manhattan. Harriman, a member of many exclusive clubs, was known as an old-fashioned traditionalist whose opinions were respected in Washington, D.C. In mid-March 1933, Deputy Marshall William Pinckley went to Harriman's exclusive Upper East Side apartment to arrest the banker on several counts of embezzlement and misappropriating funds.

Despite Harriman's doctors' claims that his physical condition was such that an arrest could kill him, Harriman was charged and brought to trial before Judge John C. Knox in June 1934. He was accused of misapplying millions of dollars from his recently defunct bank; tried along with him was his former vice president and aide, Albert Murray Austin. The prosecution contended that Harriman had, during 1929 to 1932, misapplied about $5 million, which bank officers had used to peg the price of the bank's national stock; $1,713,000 of this cash had been borrowed illegally from fourteen different depositors. Harriman's defense lawyers maintained that these unauthorized loans were "curious and stupid" mistakes that had been committed without Harriman's knowledge by his underlings, "like a college prank played upon a teacher." Harriman tried to shift the blame to his aide, Austin. In late June a jury found Harriman Guilty as charged, exonerating Austin on all counts. Harriman and his wife returned to the Doctor's Hospital where they had lived as patients since fall 1933, to await his sentencing. Three days after the court passed judgment, Harriman's private secretary of twenty-two years, Sarah A. Burke, fifty-five, killed herself by jumping out of a Manhattan skyscraper.

On June 28, 1934, Judge Knox imposed a four-and-a-half-year jail sentence on the 67-year-old Harriman, who served about two years of the term, and was then released on Aug. 27, 1936, from the Northeastern Federal Penitentiary. REF.: *CBA*.

Harrington, Jack (AKA: **Happy**), prom. 1850s, U.S., pros.-mansl. Owner of the Opera Comique, a bar-brothel on Jackson and Kearny Streets in San Francisco, Jack Harrington's operation competed with Bull Run Allen's notorious club, Hell's Kitchen. While Allen featured nearly nude dancers who also worked as prostitutes, the Opera Comique featured topless waitresses and belly dancers who wore strings of beads for skirts.

Lavish in his wardrobe, the drunken Harrington once walked into Danny O'Brien's, a nearby saloon, and got into a fight with a Virginia City, Nev., boxer named Billy Dwyer, whom he knifed and killed. Charged with murder, Harrington was purported to have spent $35,000 to get his charge reduced to manslaughter. He spent time in San Quentin for the conviction. Harrington's end came when he drunkenly began to wreck the sleazy Clover Club, a dive on Pacific Street, and Bart Freel, a habitual criminal and well-known pimp, murdered him with a small pocketknife. Freel was convicted and sent to prison for ten years.

REF.: *CBA*; Drago, *Notorious Ladies of the Frontier*.

Harrington, Michael, and **Rowland, Robert**, and **Kolbus, Donald**, and **Kolbus, Richard**, and **Bishop, Julius**, prom. 1988, U.S., pol. mal. In Fall 1988, more than twenty Chicago police officers were videotaped accepting bribes from morticians. The small amounts of cash were offered as a gratuity for delivering bodies to their funeral homes. In October, federal prosecutors offered the subpoenaed officers the choice of accepting a misdemeanor charge and quitting the force, but keeping their pensions intact, or facing indictment on felony charges. On Nov. 22, five funeral directors were also indicted.

On Feb. 13, 1989, U.S. District Court Judge Charles Norgle fined funeral director Michael Harrington $10,000 and put him on probation for one year. Earlier Robert Rowland was fined $5,000 and sentenced to one years' probation; Donald Kolbus and Richard Kolbus were each fined $2,500 and one years' probation; and Julius Bishop was fined $10,000, and sentenced to 300 hours of community service and five years' probation.

Thirty police officers pleaded guilty to accepting between $40 and $100 for each body delivered and were sentenced to two years probation and fined between $100 and $2,000 each. REF.: *CBA*.

Harrington, Orville, b.1878, U.S., burg. A mining engineer who was disgruntled by low pay and the earlier loss of a leg, Orville Harrington devised a clever method of robbing his employer, the U.S. Mint in Denver, Colo., in September 1919. At age eleven, Harrington was shot in the right leg, which so severely damaged the sciatic nerve that he required a series of operations over the years which saw, in succession, the loss of his toes, his foot, then his leg just below the knee. Throughout these painful years, however, he persisted in his studies and graduated from the Colorado School of Mines with an engineering degree. In 1903, he met and fell in love with his nurse, Lydia Melton, during one of his frequent visits to the hospital and the couple settled in Denver and Harrington went to work for the Colorado Fuel and Iron Company. In 1909, he went to work for the Denver Mint, working in the refinery where gold was melted down into solid bars. He left this routine job in 1916 to go to Cuba where he supervised a copper mining project. His leg, a constant source of aggravation, debilitated him. He was forced to leave Cuba to return to Denver and his former job at the Mint in September 1919.

Orville Harrington, who robbed the Denver Mint.

Though he had accumulated some savings and now owned ten lots of land at 1485 S. University Street, where he cultivated fruit trees and lived in a comfortable house with his wife and his 4-year-old daughter and 5-month-old son, Harrington was embittered. He had not advanced in life as he planned. The world had been cruel to him, he reasoned, depriving him of a leg that invariably cost him good jobs and a promising future. He had to stomp about on a wooden leg, hobbling his way through life. Harrington thought to get even by simply robbing the Denver Mint where he worked the evening shift from 3:45 p.m. to 11:45 p.m. It was his job, at $4 a day, to supervise the melting down of gold bullion which entered the mint in many forms, being refined to twelve-pound gold bars. Harrington sat right in the middle of the storage area which contained more than $5 million in gold.

On the night of Sept. 2, 1919, Harrington took one of the gold bars and slipped it into his hollow wooden leg. It was a perfect fit. When leaving work that night, he simply limped his way out of the mint with no one the wiser. Harrington's plan was to take out several hundred thousand dollars in gold and quietly resign his job some months later. He would then lease a mountain mine and melt down the gold, later claiming that it had come from his mine shaft. It was a simple, and, in the mind of Orville Harrington, a foolproof plan. Harrington went on stealing gold bars for more than three months, taking a bar about every three days. In January 1920, Thomas Annear, superintendent of the U.S. Mint, was given an inventory report that indicated a loss of many gold bars. Some employee was taking the gold, but security guards had no idea who the culprit might be. Annear called in Rowland K. Goddard, chief of the Secret Service in Denver.

The next day the fifteen refinery workers in the mint were placed under surveillance and, through a process of elimination, suspicion soon centered on Harrington. Other employees in the refinery reported that Harrington had been acting nervously; one worker stated that the engineer had placed a gold bar on his desk, then, looking about furtively, had replaced the bar on the nearby stacks, as if he realized he was being watched. Followed night and day in his movements, Secret Service agents saw Harrington go into one of his lots with a shovel on a February day and begin digging at the frozen earth. He produced a gold bar and buried it. On Feb. 4, 1920, Goddard followed Harrington home on a trolley car, and, when he got off near his home, the Secret Service chief identified himself to the engineer. Harrington, in the words of a writer for the Denver *Post*: "fairly crumpled. A grunt fell from his lips, as if from a man shot."

Harrington was taken back to the mint where he was accused of stealing gold. Still, the investigators were unsure of how the engineer was doing it. He aided them immediately by lifting his pants leg and unbuckling his wooden leg, pointing out a gold bar he had stolen that very night. He was taken home, handcuffed, and with tears running down his cheeks, led agents to a fake wall behind which were stacks of gold bars. As his shocked wife and small children watched, the engineer then hobbled out into the yard and directed agents to locations where more gold had been buried, fifty bars in all worth more than $80,000 at the time (one hundred times that amount today). The gold was returned to the mint and Harrington was jailed. On May 12, 1920, Harrington pled guilty before Judge Robert E. Lewis. The judge was astounded as he pointed to the huge pile of bullion before him, noting that it was "the greatest quantity of gold ever placed in evidence in court in the United States." Harrington was sentenced to ten years imprisonment and was sent to Leavenworth. He was paroled in 1924 and returned to Denver where he worked at odd jobs. He later deserted his small family for a construction project in Arizona and then disappeared altogether, reportedly dying in New York while living with his sister. Because of Harrington, security was tightened at the Denver Mint, but not before it was robbed in 1922 by mastermind bank caser Eddie Bentz, Harvey Bailey, and others. This was not the first time a clever employee had robbed a U.S. Mint. Henry S. Cochrane looted the Philadelphia Mint in 1893, employing a burglary technique as cunning as Harrington's, but one which produced the same results. Cochrane also went to prison. See: **Bailey, Harvey John; Bentz, Edward Wilhelm; Cochrane, Henry S.**

REF.: *CBA;* Flanagan, *Out West.*

Harris, Ann, prom. 1827, Brit., mur. Disposing of a would-be informer by murdering him, a gang of five were later turned in by the man they had tried to protect.

In the town of Market Drayton, Shropshire, England—also known then as Salop—a depraved gang of about fifty or sixty people engaged in stealing sheep and other livestock, pilfering potatoes, and robbing. Five of the most notorious gang members were Ann Harris, John Cox, Sr. and John Cox, Jr., Robert Cox, and James Pugh.

One of the mob, Ellson, was, in 1827, tried for stealing a sheep, with sometime gang member James Harrison giving evidence against him. Determined to revenge their cohort, the gang of five tried to procure arsenic to poison Harrison. When that failed, they contracted his death with Harris, who was Ellson's mother, and John Cox, Sr., contributing 50 shillings each to hire Cox's sons and James Pugh to kill the informant. Pugh and John Cox, Jr. eventually choked Harrison at his home, while Robert Cox dug a grave. Ellson, acquitted of the theft charge, was soon again arrested, this time for stealing fowls. Faced with possible transportation, Ellson turned in the five who had protected him. All were convicted and sentenced to death, with Harris and the elder Cox later reprieved to be transported out of the country instead.

REF.: Butler, *Murderers' England; CBA.*

Harris, Carlyle W., 1868-91, U.S., mur. In January 1891, 19-year-old Helen Potts, a student at the Comstock School in New York City, collapsed, complaining of numbness. A physician found her pupils symmetrically contracted and consequently suspected narcotic poisoning. A pill box inscribed "C.W.H. Student. One before retiring," was found near the bed. Potts' fellow students identified C.W.H. as Carlyle Harris, a medical student. Harris was called and admitted prescribing the pills, which when ordered from the pharmacist, had contained four and a half grains of quinine and one sixth grain of morphine.

Despite the doctors' efforts to revive her, Potts died. Several days after the burial, Potts' mother informed a New York publication called *The World* that Potts and Harris had married secretly the previous February. In the ensuing eleven months Potts became pregnant at least once. According to one account Harris performed an abortion on her while another says that the child was stillborn. Potts' mother claimed she had been pressuring Harris to make the marriage public and he had agreed to do so the very week her daughter died. The suspicion stirred up by Potts' death grew and her body was exhumed. An autopsy revealed that there was morphine and no quinine in the body. The police theorized that Harris had emptied one of the capsule and refilled it with morphine before giving the capsules to Potts.

Harris was indicted on murder charges by a grand jury on Mar. 30, 1891. His trial took place in New York in January 1892. The prosecutor, Francis L. Wellman argued that Harris, who had a reputation as a gambler and a womanizer, had substituted the morphine for the quinine in an attempt to kill his wife because he had grown tired of her and because he feared he would be disinherited if his family discovered he had married someone of lower social standing. He cited the autopsy results as proof that the morphine had caused Potts' death.

The defense, carried out in part by William Travers Jerome, argued that the autopsy results were inconclusive as to the cause of death. Harris himself never testified in his own defense. Contrary to expectations, Harris was convicted of first-degree murder and sentenced to die in the electric chair. He protested his innocence to the end, but was executed at Sing Sing on May 8, 1893. Harris' mother, Hope Ledyard, an author and lecturer, protested her son's innocence as well. When he was finally executed, she had his coffin labeled "Carlyle Harris Murdered May 8th, 1893." She later wrote a book about the case, *The Judicial Murder of Carlyle Harris.*

REF.: Boswell and Thompson, *The Carlyle Harris Case;* Carey, *Memoirs of a Murder Man; CBA;* Dunbar, *Murder in the Parlor;* Ellis, *Blackmailers and Co.;* Gribble, *They Had a Way With Women;* Gross, *Masterpieces of Murder;* Harris, *Articles, Speeches and Poems;* Nash, *Murder Among the Mighty;* Pearson, *Instigation of the Devil;* ____, *Murder at Smutty Nose;* Rodell, *New York Murders;* Smith, *Famous American Poison Mysteries;* Thorwald, *Century of the Detective;* ____, *Proof of Poison; The Trial of Carlyle W. Harris;* Wilson, *Encyclopedia of Murder.*

Harris, Charlotte, b.1819, Brit., mur. In 1848, Charlotte Harris was convicted of poisoning her husband after she discovered she was pregnant by another man. She rushed from her husband's funeral to marry her lover. Sentenced to death for the premeditated murder, Harris won a delay until she gave birth. In the interim, around 40,000 women petitioned Queen Victoria for a reprieve. The Society for the Abolition of Capital Punishment also pressured the Home Secretary. Popular opinion induced the queen to commute the sentence to life imprisonment. No pregnant woman was hanged again in Britain following this precedent.

REF.: *CBA;* Cooper, *Lesson of the Scaffold;* Nash, *Look For the Woman.*

Harris, Dennis, d.1866, U.S., rob.-mur. By the end of the U.S. Civil War, the uneducated blacks of Atlanta, Ga., their plantation work destroyed, were reduced to starvation. Many resorted to wholesale horse thievery to stay alive. Dennis Harris was typical of that chaotic era. He had been a field hand, and when the plantation where he lived was destroyed by Sherman in 1864, he, like thousands of other blacks, fled to Atlanta, which was burned down around him. He lived in a shanty with a dozen other ex-slaves and stole food to stay alive. On the night of Nov. 29, 1865, Harris, along with Henry Brown and another black named Bill, decided to rob the Lloyd Street office of the Georgia Railroad.

All three men had agreed that if James R. Crew, the station master who was known to carry large sums of money, resisted

them, he would be killed. The three blacks gained entrance to the railroad yard by entertaining the porters. Harris danced a jig for them. By the time they made their way to the station house, however, they found it locked and Crew gone. The three discovered that Crew had just left for home. They followed him, catching up with him in front of the home of William Solomon. Harris, carrying a crowbar, slipped up behind Crew and brought the bar down on the station master's head. Crew shouted out only two words: "Oh, me!" The thieves hurriedly went through his pockets and found only a key. They thought this was the key to the station house and returned there, but the key did not fit the lock. They fled. (The key was to the door of the Central Presbyterian Church, of which Crew was a deacon.) Two days later Crew died of a fractured skull.

A manhunt for Harris and the others ensued. Harris did not leave the city, thinking posses would be looking for him at all exits. He continued to roam Atlanta for almost a year, committing dozens of robberies. He was interrupted while breaking into one house and finally fled the city with bloodhounds on his trail. He was captured in 1866 outside of Irwinton and promptly hanged without benefit of trial.

Though certainly guilty of murder and robbery, Harris was but one of scores of blacks who were either lynched or burned at the stake after mob oratory pronounced them guilty. Many of these victims were innocent of the crimes for which they stood accused. REF.: *CBA.*

Harris, E.K., 1912-35, U.S., rape. In November 1934, Lillian Gibson, a 15-year-old girl who lived near Shelbyville, Tenn., ran to her school, her clothes torn, frantically screaming, "I'm gonna have a baby!" A posse of 300 men, led by Lillian's father, John Gibson, scoured the woods that night, and caught an illiterate 22-year-old black man, E.K. Harris. Accused of raping Lillian, Harris was taken to the Shelbyville jail. When a mob demanded he be released to them, Harris was taken away to Nashville. In late December, Harris' Shelbyville trial was scheduled to be heard in circuit court by Judge Coleman, who requested that Governor Hill McAllister provide militiamen to preserve order. Accompanied by the Tennessee National Guard, Harris was brought to the trial in a military truck. Hundreds marched on the courthouse as the proceedings commenced, charging twice as 110 guardsmen returned tear gas for rocks. On the third charge, militia officers fired, killing Pat Lawes, a man named Edwards, and two others, and wounding another twenty.

Judge Coleman declared a mistrial and Harris was returned to Nashville. The troops set up camp at the edge of Shelbyville, and the mob returned to the courthouse, setting four National Guard trucks and the 75-year-old courthouse on fire. By morning, the building was destroyed, along with all county records. At a mass meeting, Shelbyville businessmen formed a posse. Dr. Moody told reporters that he believed Lillian Gibson was not pregnant, nor had she been raped. Harris was later tried and convicted, and executed in Nashville on May 22, 1936. Warden A.W. Neely of the state penitentiary said Harris made a full confession just before his death. REF.: *CBA.*

Harris, Emil, 1839-1921, U.S., law enfor. off. An experienced detective, Emil Harris served as the second chief of police in Los Angeles, beginning in 1877. Succeeding Chief Jacob T. Jerkins, Harris had a long and distinguished career. A highlight of Harris' outstanding record as chief was his involvement in the arrest of bandit Tiburcio Vasquez. Harris died in 1921, at the age of eighty-two. REF.: *CBA.*

Harris, Frank, b.c.1898- , U.S., (wrong. convict.) mur. On Mar. 4, 1926, at 2 a.m., Frank Harris and Wilbert MacQueen were stopped by two Philadelphia policemen. When shots were fired, MacQueen was killed and Harris was wounded. Convicted of first-degree murder in a Quarter Sessions court in September 1926, the 28-year-old Harris was sentenced to life in prison.

Previous to his conviction, Harris had served two short terms for minor offenses. In 1946, a volunteer lawyer, Herbert L. Marris, visited the penitentiary to talk to prisoners who felt they were eligible for parole. He became convinced of Harris' innocence, and spent months finding evidence to prove that the bullet that killed MacQueen could not have come from Harris' gun. In 1947 Pennsylvania Governor James H. Duff commuted Harris' sentence. At the age of forty-nine, after twenty-one years in jail, the wrongly convicted man was released. REF.: *CBA*.

Harris, Jack, d.1884, U.S., gamb.-west. gunman. Jack Harris, born and raised in Texas, led an adventuresome life. At an early age he worked for the U.S. Army as a scout and Indian fighter. During the Civil War, Harris served in the Confederate cavalry, and following the war, he fought in Central American revolutions, losing a finger in Nicaragua. Returning to the U.S., Harris was one of the last great Buffalo hunters, providing meat and skins for the railroads moving west in the late 1870s. He then moved to San Antonio where he served briefly as a policeman, later becoming a gambler and winning several small fortunes. He and another gambler, Ernest Hart, formed a partnership and opened the Green Front Saloon, which had a full theater, the Vaudeville House, on the second floor. Harris' wealth grew, and he was well-liked in San Antonio. One of Harris' few enemies was Texas gunfighter Ben Thompson. The two men, who had earlier been friends, fell out in a poker game in 1880. Thompson nurtured a grudge ever after, believing Harris had cheated.

On July 11, 1882, Thompson rode into San Antonio drunk. He continued to drink and then stormed into the Green Front Saloon, demanding that Harris get a gun and meet him in the street. Harris, who entered the saloon after Thompson had left, got a gun and waited inside the saloon for his nemesis. Thompson appeared a short time later and saw Harris waiting with a shotgun behind some venetian blinds. Before Harris could fire, Thompson squeezed off a fatal round that smashed through the blinds and into Harris' right lung. The gambler fell to the floor and Thompson fired another round at him and left. Harris got to his feet, staggered upstairs to his apartment, and died there that night. Thompson, who was the city marshal of Austin,

Texas gambler and gunman Jack Harris.

Texas, at the time, resigned and turned himself over to the San Antonio sheriff. He pleaded self-defense in a quick trial and was acquitted. See: **Thompson, Ben**.

REF.: *CBA*; Horan, *The Authentic Wild West*; Hudson, *The Sunny Slopes of Long Ago*; Masterson, *Famous Gunfighters of the Western Frontier*; Miller and Snell, *Great Gunfighters of the Kansas Cowtowns*; Raymond, *Capt. Lee Hall*; Schoenberger, *The Gunfighters*; Streeter, *Ben Thompson, Man with a Gun*.

Harris, Jean Struven, 1923- , U.S., mur. Dr. Herman Tarnower, known as "Hi," grossed more than $11 million from his best-selling *Scarsdale Diet*, published in 1979. Tarnower met Jean Harris, a divorced mother of two, at a Manhattan dinner party in 1966. She had graduated *magna cum laude* from Smith College in 1945, and by 1972, was the headmistress of the exclusive Madeira School for girls in McLean, Va. Her students called her "Integrity Jean" because of her numerous lectures about self-control, commitment to excellence, and propriety.

Following their meeting at the home of Leslie Jacobson, Tarnower and Harris began their lengthy courtship. There was talk of marriage, but it never got past the discussion stage. Tarnower, fifty-eight at the time of his "engagement" to Harris in 1967, entertained a variety of women at his estate in Purchase, N.Y. One of them, Lynne Tryforos, a 38-year-old medical assistant, replaced Harris as the doctor's favorite. In 1977, Jean

Jean Struven Harris, rejected lover and killer; her victim, millionaire doctor Herman Tarnower.

Harris first became aware of Tarnower's philandering. On New Year's Day, Harris was with Tarnower at a Palm Beach resort when she saw a personal notice in the New York *Times* that read "Happy New Year, Hi T. Love Always, Lynne."

A long struggle followed between the two rivals for the doctor's affections. Harris and Tryforos cut up each other's clothes, and Harris accused Tryforos of placing obscene phone calls. It was clear that Tarnower favored the younger Tryforos, but he continued to rely on Harris to help him prepare his diet book. The situation soon became intolerable to Harris, who drove directly from McLean to the Tarnower estate on Mar. 10, 1980. In her purse was a .32-caliber handgun and the amphetamines she needed for courage. At eleven that night, after Tarnower's dinner guests had left, Harris drove up in her blue 1973 Chrysler. She climbed the darkened staircase, entered the doctor's bedroom, and fired four shots. Tarnower slumped over dead and Harris fled the grounds. Rushing to the window, the startled housekeeper saw Harris getting into her car.

Before Jean Harris could make her getaway, Scarsdale police intercepted her. "He wanted to live. I wanted to die," she told them. Harris' intention had been to persuade Tarnower to shoot her. A long, rambling letter describing her physical and mental subjugation to Tarnower corroborated her story and established

Dr. Tarnower's Scarsdale, N.Y., estate, the murder site.

a motive. Jean Harris was charged with second degree murder. Her trial, sensationalized in tabloids, began in the White Plains, N.Y., courtroom of Judge Russell R. Leggett in November 1980. On Feb. 4, 1981, the infamous "Scarsdale Letter," mailed from Virginia the day of the murder, was introduced into evidence. "Going through the hell of the past few years has been bearable only because you were still there and I could be with you," it read in part. The letter failed to sway the jury. On Feb. 24, they returned a verdict of Guilty. Harris was sentenced on Mar. 20 to life imprisonment at the Bedford Hills Correctional Facility. She remains an inmate there and is involved in prison reform. Her book about her prison experience, *They Always Call Us Ladies*, was published in 1988.

REF.: *CBA*; Nash, *Murder Among the Mighty*; Trilling, *Jean Harris*.

Harris, Leopold, 1894-   , Brit., consp.-fraud-arson. After Leopold Harris took charge of his father's respectable firm of fire assessors, Harris & Company, he became impatient with slow profits and began to set fires for pay. The first known case in the arson conspiracy was the fire at the Fabrique de Soieries Company in Manchester on Nov. 7, 1927; £29,000 in damages were paid, assessed by Harris. By 1932, evidence against Harris began to accumulate. Keeping agents on payroll and setting them up in business with highly combustible stocks to collect substantial insurance compensations, an error of judgment caused Harris to hire Harry Priest, a man who bragged at a London pub in May 1931, about the profitable operation. Boasting that it was simple to gain money by setting fires, the agent said there was little risk because "everybody is in it, assessors, fire brigades, salvage corps, accountants, everybody."

William Crocker began a two-year investigation, code-named "Willesden Junction," checking into the circumstances of twenty-nine fires. Harris was arrested in February 1933, to be tried along with fifteen others—including his brother David Harris and his brother-in-law, Harry Gould—on charges of arson, conspiracy, and fraud. A key witness for the prosecution, Camillo Capsoni, traded his testimony to have the charges against him dropped. Harris ultimately confessed, and was sentenced to a fourteen-year term. From his prison cell at Maidstone, Harris was said to have advised police on the investigation of other fire and insurance frauds until September 1935. He was released in 1940.

REF.: *CBA*; Jackson, *Occupied With Crime*; Scott, *The Concise Encyclopedia of Crime and Criminals*; Wild, *Crimes and Criminals*.

Harris, Mary, prom. 1865, Case of, U.S., mur. After Adonirum J. Burroughs promised to marry Mary Harris, she accompanied him to a brothel and had sex with him—her first time. Burroughs then withdrew his proposal, explaining to Harris that she was now "an immoral female." When she later learned that Burroughs had married someone else, Harris hunted him down in Washington, D.C., and shot him to death in a hall of the Treasury Building before several witnesses. In 1865, a Washington jury unanimously agreed that she was justified in her actions, and acquitted her of murder. Harris, holding a bouquet of flowers from the first lady, Mary Todd Lincoln, responded to the verdict by curtsying to the jury. See: **Lincoln, Abraham**.

REF.: *CBA*; Lambert, *When Justice Faltered*; Nash, *Almanac of World Crime*; *Official Report of the Trial of Mary Harris*.

Harris, Monty, prom. 1943, Brit., terr. A supporter of the Jewish terrorists fighting against British rule in Palestine in the 1940s, Monty Harris had a locksmith shop in Aldgate. Scotland Yard detectives suspected that Harris' store was a front for the manufacture of thermite incendiary bombs to be used in Palestine. They watched the store for several weeks, and once saw Harris run out in clouds of dense smoke, calling out, "No fire!" to prevent intrusion. The elusive Harris was finally captured when five special agents, dressed for tennis, surrounded him on a trolley as he headed for his arsenal. Arrested by Detective Superintendent Smith, Harris made no attempt to hide his support for the terrorists. Large quantities of supplies, including detonators, fuses, and aluminum powder, were found in the shop. Tried and convicted, Harris was sentenced to a seven-year jail term for possessing explosives without lawful object. Harris was released on July 24, 1950, and was alleged to have emigrated to Israel. REF.: *CBA*.

Harris, Nan (AKA: Sarah Davis, Sarah Thorn, Sarah Gothorn, Anne Harris), d.1705, Brit., rob. Nan Harris was born of poor but honest parents in the parish of St.-Giles-without-Cripplegate, but after being seduced by James Wadsworth (known to his companions as "Jemmy the Mouth"), took to a life of thieving.

When Wadsworth was convicted of felony and burglary and hanged at Tyburn at the age of twenty-four, he was to be the first of three lovers that Nan would lose to the gallows, two in less than three years. After "Jemmy" was executed Nan took up with William Pullman, (AKA: Norwich Will) who was hanged within the year, at twenty-six, for highway robbery.

Twice "widowed" Harris was not so busy grieving that she did not make time to learn the tricks of the trade, becoming an accomplished and imaginative thief. One day, dressed to the teeth and having hired both a hackney coach and a false "footman" for the occasion, Harris went to a silk merchant's shop in Ludgate and selected several bolts of expensive fabric. Explaining that the total, £200, was more than she had on her at the time she requested that the merchant go with her to her house where she would pay him in full. Putting the goods in her fine coach, the unsuspecting man accompanied Nan to a place that turned out to be the madhouse at Fulham, run by a Dr. Adams.

When they entered the place Harris announced to the doctor that she had brought the gentleman she had spoken to him about earlier that morning, and four burly men immediately grabbed the merchant to pin him down on the ground. When the merchant cried out, demanding his £200, the doctor declared that he was very bad off indeed and obviously raving mad, giving orders to shave his head at once. Graciously giving the doctor five guineas, Nan strictly admonished him to take the best care of her husband. When the frantic merchant objected that his wife was home in Ludgate Hill, and that Nan was a lying, thieving cheat, the doctor sadly realized that they would have to bleed him as well, and give him laxatives nightly, along with a strict diet of water and gruel for a week. While the merchant continued to protest his innocence and sanity Nan took off with her booty. She did, however, thoughtfully send a letter to let the man's wife know where he was, and he was released within four days.

An apparent affinity for doctors figured in another of Harris' exploits. With a friend, Charles Moor, in tow, Nan went to see a Dr. Case, student of physics and astrology. Presenting him with a urine sample, she declared that her poor husband, being very drunk the night before, had unfortunately fallen down some stairs. "The report of your great experience has brought me hither, humbly imploring your assistance." The flattered doctor carefully scrutinized the sample, then announced that her husband had bruised himself terribly falling down some stairs. Yes, said Nan, I know, but can you tell me how many? Not wanting to lose professional credibility, the doctor again "tested" the urine at even greater length before he told her that her husband had tumbled down half the stairs. Nan said, no, he fell down them all. The doctor, embarrassed by his inaccurate guess, defended himself by asking if this was all her husband's water. No, said Nan, only half. He angrily replied that had she brought all of the water he would have been able to make an accurate diagnosis. Excusing her ignorance Nan requested a prescription for her husband's speedy cure, and while the doctor was writing one out, she and Charles Moor came up behind him with a rope and half strangled him before taking off with a silver tankard and a cup.

Charles Moor, one of her many lovers, was executed for housebreaking, at Tyburn, becoming Nan's third companion to be hanged at that famous execution place. Moor, while waiting to die, wistfully told an official that, had he known how things were going to turn out, he would have hanged one or two people himself to see what it was like.

Harris had a clever trick for robbing goldsmiths. Taking a little ale, she would heat it till it became a thick syrup, then spread it on the palm of hand. This early version of "sticky fingers" netted her several gold rings and other light pieces of jewelry. Well-known to merchants on Ludgate Hill, Cheapside and Fleet Street, Harris was at last apprehended for stealing some calico. She had been so often burned in the face, a punishment for theft, that the hangman could find no room to mark her again. To evade sentence, she claimed to be pregnant, faking that condition by drinking quantities of fresh ale and stuffing her dress with a pillow.

A jury of matrons was called in, some of them probably friends of Harris, and Nan was granted a nine month extension. Not for want of trying, she did not manage to become pregnant in the allotted time, was called down on her former judgment and hanged at Tyburn, at the age of twenty, on a Friday the 13th, 1705.

REF.: *CBA*; Smith, *Highwaymen*.

Harris, Norman James, and **Forsyth, Francis**, and **Lutt, Terence**, and **Darby, Christopher**, prom. 1960, Brit., mur. In Hounslow, near London, four young men who had been drinking decided to rob whomever passed by. Alan Jee unluckily came along, and was attacked and held down so that Norman James Harris, twenty-three, could rifle his pockets. Francis Forsyth, eighteen, kicked Jee so viciously with his pointed shoes to "keep him quiet" that Jee later died as a result. Christopher Darby, twenty, was found Guilty of non-capital murder, while Harris, Forsyth, and Terence Lutt were found Guilty of capital murder. Because he was under eighteen, Lutt was not executed, but Harris was hanged at Pentonville Prison on Nov. 10, 1960, and Forsyth was executed at nearby Wandsworth Jail.

REF.: Brophy, *The Meaning of Murder*; *CBA*; Hibbert, *The Roots of Evil*.

Harris, Oren, b.1903, U.S., jur. Served as deputy prosecuting attorney of Union County, Ariz., from 1933-36, and as prosecuting attorney of the thirteenth judicial district of Arizona from 1937-40. He was a member of the U.S. House of Representatives from 1941-66. He was nominated to the eastern district and western district courts of Arizona by President Lyndon B. Johnson in 1965. REF.: *CBA*.

Harris, Phoebe, c.1756-86, Brit., count. A slight woman, 30-year-old Phoebe Harris had been condemned to hang for counterfeiting; she had come from a family of coiners. Led through the prison door just minutes after six men had been hanged, Harris was trembling so violently that she had to be carried by the sheriff's men. An eleven-foot post near the scaffold had been erected in the street, and the half-conscious woman was tied with the noose around her neck and her feet on a low stool. With her feet only twelve inches from the ground, Harris was slowly strangled. Two cart loads of embers were piled beneath her corpse and the body was incinerated.

REF.: Bleackley, *Hangmen of England*; *CBA*; Nash, *Look For the Woman*.

Harris, Pleasant, prom. 1923-28, U.S., mur. In New Orleans on May 20, 1923, just after midnight, a woman's screams were heard. Dashing toward the nearby police headquarters was Katherine Wilson, pursued by a man with a gun, who, overtaking the woman, beat her with the butt of his gun and then shot her. As scores of detectives and officers poured from headquarters, the killer vanished. The trail of blood followed by Captain Archie Rennyson, warden of the prison, and Detective Sergeant Joseph Hadley led to a boarding house, where they questioned Wilson's friend, Edith Wright. Wright told them she had met some friends of Wilson's, including Pleasant Harris, Wilson's sometime boyfriend. Harris had followed Wilson when she went downstairs to answer the doorbell and pursued her into the street, where he murdered her.

Tipped off about a fight in a bar the night prior to the killing, police learned that Harris had assaulted a friend of Wilson's. Superintendent of Police Thomas Healy tracked down Harris' brother's house; there he found a stained, pink silk shirt on a clothesline, and a matching collar flecked with blood. Further investigation showed that Harris was wanted in several other cities, including Detroit, Mich. In July 1926, more than three years after the crime, Detroit chief of detectives Fox tracked Harris through baggage checks to Atlantic City, N.J. Extradited to New Orleans, Harris was tried on May 27, 1927, before Judge J. Arthur Charbonnet; District Attorney Stanley and assistant J. Bernard Cooks prosecuted. The state's surprise witness, a woman who overheard Wilson and Harris fighting, testified that Harris had fired on Wilson another time before the murder. This, combined with the evidence of Cassius L. Clay, the city chemist, who proved that the silk shirt and collar were stained with human blood, convicted Harris after a four-day trial. Found Guilty of first-degree murder, Harris was sentenced by Judge Charbonnet to be hanged, but the sentence was later commuted by Governor Huey P. Long to a term of life in prison at Baton Rouge Penitentiary. See: **Long, Huey P.**

REF.: *CBA*; Cohen, *One Hundred True Crime Stories*.

Harris, Robert Alton, 1953- , U.S., mur. On the morning of July 5, 1978, two 16-year-old boys from Mira Mesa High School in San Diego, Calif., sat in their car in the parking lot of a fast food restaurant. As the youths, John Mayeski and Michael Baker, prepared to eat the hamburgers they had just bought, two brothers, Robert Alton Harris and Danny Harris, approached the car. Robert Harris showed the boys the 9-mm Luger he carried, told them he wanted their car for a bank robbery, and assured them that they would not be harmed. Harris then forced them to drive the car to a deserted area near the Miramar Reservoir.

Once at the reservoir, Harris had the boys get out of the car and shot both execution style. Robert and Danny Harris escaped with the stolen auto. Apparently unaffected by the slayings, Robert Harris consumed the half-eaten hamburgers the two boys had left in the car. Later that same day Robert Harris was arrested by San Diego police officer Steve Baker, who, at the time of the arrest, did not know that his son had been one of Harris' victims.

Harris was brought to trial in 1979. He took the witness stand twice during the trial and claimed that his brother, Danny, had killed the boys. Danny Harris testified later in the trial against his brother. Robert Harris was convicted of the murders and during the sentencing phase of the trial confessed to the killings and said he was sorry. He was sentenced to die in the gas chamber at San Quentin prison and has been on Death Row ever since. Harris and his lawyers have engaged in continual appeals since his conviction and sentencing. Four different execution dates have been set. Harris' attorneys have expressed concern that Harris' avenues for appeal are virtually exhausted and the most recent date for execution, Apr. 3, 1990, may in fact be the day Harris dies. REF.: *CBA*.

Harris, Thomas, prom. 1819, Brit., (wrong. convict.) mur. Hanged for a murder he did not commit, Thomas Harris was posthumously cleared when it came out that the chief witness for the prosecution had committed the crime.

Landlord of the Rising Sun Inn on the York-Newcastle Road, Harris was convicted and executed for murder in 1819. It was later established that the killer was a bartender at the inn. REF.: *CBA*.

Harris, Thomas Lake, 1823-1906, U.S., fraud. With a doctrine centering on the essentially bisexual nature of human beings, Thomas Lake Harris attracted a community of followers and divested them of their money.

At Mt. Cove, Va., Harris and two partners founded the utopian community called the Garden of Eden, encouraging members to turn over all their worldly goods "in trust for God." An imposing patriarchal figure, Harris effectively entranced and intimidated his disciples in part by throwing his voice, making it sound by turns booming and strong, then far away and ethereal. Breaking up with the partners over matters of policy, Harris relocated to form another society in Salem on Lake Erie in New York state. His teachings stated that human beings were not necessarily expected to achieve their bisexual nature until they gained it in Eternal Life, but they should seek it on earth all the same, with the goal of finding one's complementary other half in the arms of a mortal lover.

Setting an example for his flock, Harris' counterpart, Lily Queen worked with him to console and instruct the disciples—all of them attractive young women. Harris' most notable supporter was Laurence Oliphant, a diplomat whose wealthy bride turned over her money to the community; the couple were urged by Harris to avoid sexual relations. When Harris fell out of favor with the Oliphants, however, a lawsuit successfully returned Mrs. Oliphant's property and effectively demolished the Harris society. REF.: *CBA*; Hunt, *A Dictionary of Rogues*.

Harris, William, 1945- , and **Harris, Emily**, 1948- , U.S., kid. In February 1974, newspaper heiress Patricia Hearst was abducted from her Berkeley, Calif., apartment by members of the Symbionese Liberation Army (SLA), a newly formed radical terrorist group. During her eighteen months of captivity, Hearst was gradually transformed from a hostage victim into a willing and sympathetic participant in the gang's criminal endeavors. Her metamorphosis took place while in the care of William and Emily Harris, a couple who documented the indoctrination in a meticulously maintained diary. Within three months, Hearst renounced her parent's values, called them racists, and espoused the aims of the SLA. She participated in a bank robbery using her new moniker "Tania", and became an FBI target as a criminal instead of as a hostage. On Sept. 18, 1975, Hearst and Wendy Yoshimura were arrested by the FBI in a San Francisco apartment. William and Emily Harris had been arrested while standing on a San Francisco street corner an hour earlier.

On trial for the bank robbery, Hearst denounced her radical conversion, saying she complied in order to extract her freedom. The Harrises denied any coercion as well as the charges that she had been beaten, tortured, or raped. In August 1978, William and Emily Harris were found Guilty on the lesser charge of "simple kidnapping," rather than the more odious "kidnapping for ransom and with great bodily harm." See: **Hearst, Patricia Campbell**. REF.: *CBA*.

Harrison, Benjamin, 1888-1960, U.S., jur. Served as U.S. district attorney in Los Angeles, Calif., from 1937-40. He was nominated to the southern district court of California by President Franklin D. Roosevelt in 1940. REF.: *CBA*.

The home of Chicago mayor Carter Harrison on Oct. 28, 1893, a short time after Harrison was assassinated by Patrick Prendergast, inset.

Harrison, Carter Henry, Sr., 1825-93, U.S., mayor, polit. corr.-assass. Before Carter Harrison was elected mayor of Chicago in 1879, no political party enjoyed a clear edge in city government. Political power and patronage were distributed on the ward level, and Chicago mayors rarely served more than one term. Harrison and his son Carter, Jr., who became mayor in 1897, established the city's first political dynasty, forging a Democratic organization on spoils and a laissez-faire attitude toward vice and gambling.

Carter Harrison, Sr., was born near Lexington, Ky., and educated at Yale University. Claiming descent from Benjamin Harrison, a signer of the Declaration of Independence, and from President William Henry Harrison, Carter left his Kentucky plantation in 1855 to settle in Chicago where he prospered in the booming real estate market. In 1871, Harrison got his first taste

of elective office when he became a county commissioner on Joseph Medill's "Fire-proof" ticket. In 1874, Harrison was elected to the U.S. Congress, where he served two terms.

With the backing of the powerful downtown gambling syndicate headed by Mike McDonald, Harrison was easily elected mayor of Chicago in 1879. In return for the support, he forged a deal with McDonald, taking a percentage from criminal profits in return for guaranteed immunity. To further effect the immunity, Harrison replaced honest police chief Simon O'Donnell with a more submissive man, William J. McGarigle. In 1882, McGarigle was shifted to the post of Warden of Cook County Hospital, where he promptly awarded a $125,000 painting contract to McDonald. As a result, several aldermen were imprisoned and McGarigle was forced out of town, but Harrison and McDonald emerged unscathed.

Harrison's margin of victory grew in elections held in 1881 and 1883. He failed in a gubernatorial bid in 1884 but reclaimed the Chicago mayoralty a year later by a narrow margin. The 1886 Haymarket Riot and the damaging political repercussions convinced the mayor to step down, at least temporarily. Harrison did not stand for re-election in 1887, deciding instead to travel around the world a trip which formed the basis for two books: *A Race With the Sun* (1889), and *A Summer Outing and the Old Man's Story* (1891).

In 1893, Harrison was returned to office by acclamation to become Chicago's mayor during the Columbian Exposition. On Oct. 28, 1893, Harrison returned to his mansion on Ashland Boulevard after spending a full day at the fair. At 8 p.m., the doorbell rang and a young men presented himself to the maid, Mary Hansen. He said his name was Patrick Eugene Joseph Prendergast, and he had urgent business with the mayor. Instead of waiting in the foyer, Prendergast followed Hansen into the house. Harrison emerged from his room and spoke with the stranger for a few minutes. Hansen later recalled that the mayor's voice had risen. "I tell you I won't do it!" he said. Seconds later, three shots were fired and the mayor fell dead.

Prendergast, a 25-year-old Irish immigrant went to the Des Plaines Street police station and surrendered to Sergeant Frank McDonald. He explained that he had worked as a messenger for Western Union and as a distributor for two afternoon newspapers, the *Inter Ocean* and *Evening Post*, but had counted on Harrison for a political appointment, especially one such as city corporation counsel. Prendergast's legal training consisted of a quick reading of *Every Man His Own Lawyer*, a popular book of the day.

A grand jury returned a murder indictment against Prendergast on Oct. 30. "He deserved to be shot," Prendergast said of Harrison. "He did not keep his promise to me." Adjudged sane, Prendergast was found Guilty on Dec. 29. Sentenced to die on the gallows, the condemned man received an eleventh-hour stay of execution. A second trial was ordered, but Prendergast was again found Guilty and was hanged on July 13, 1894. See: **Haymarket Riot; McDonald, Mike**.

REF.: *CBA*; Duke, *Celebrated Criminal Cases of America*; Nash, *People to See*.

Harrison, Daniel Paul (Paul), b.1903- , U.S., mur. "I feel the overpowering urge to kill. I must conquer this impulse or it will drive me to take someone's life," wrote Daniel Paul Harrison in his diary. He could control the impulse only so long, however, before it began to control him. By the time he was apprehended, he had murdered five people, three of them friends.

Born in North Carolina to a genteel Southern family, Harrison spent the leisure hours of his childhood painting, writing poetry, making music, and reading Shakespeare. In his early twenties he moved to Chicago, found work as a clerk, and married. Life seemed to be on his side, but slowly he began to change. Observing himself with alarm, Harrison considered seeing a psychiatrist. "But I'm afraid to do so," he wrote in his diary, "for he may confine me to an institution."

One night, Harrison's wife, Marie, woke to find her husband leaning over her, a heavy clock in his hand. "I'm going to kill you!

Kill you!" he cried. Marie escaped and locked herself in the bathroom, and when she emerged thirty minutes later, Harrison was asleep. The next time she saw him, at her lawyer's office, he said he must have been having a nightmare and pleaded with her to return. Marie refused and soon filed for divorce.

Harrison remarried soon after, in an afternoon ceremony, but that very night his second wife, Margaret, walked out. Ostensibly having left for work that evening, Harrison returned to their rooming house at midnight to find his wife gone. (She had gone out for food.) "I'm going to kill her! Kill, kill, kill!" he shouted, brandishing a hammer at the landlady. Margaret returned to find Harrison gone. After listening to the landlady's alarming story, Margaret fled to her mother's and soon after filed for divorce.

Harrison was losing control. Fired from his clerking job, he found work as an auto mechanic but not for long. In December 1930, sent by his garage to repair a car that had broken down in a funeral procession, Harrison joined the mourners. Upon seeing the face of the deceased—a young woman—he felt an intense pleasure. So began his visits to wakes and the morgue. "Soon the satisfaction of looking at corpses probably will pass away and then I will kill! Oh, why was I born?" he wrote.

Fired from the garage and low on funds, Harrison moved into a dollar-a-week hotel on West Van Buren Street. One by one he sold off his mechanic's tools until only his hammer remained. Then one night he awoke from a dream of murder to find that he had smashed a fellow derelict in the head with his hammer.

On Mar. 1, 1931, Harrison met Joseph Hardy, a 26-year-old Kentucky mountaineer who was selling moonshine for twenty cents a pint to homeless men on West Madison Street. The two decided to go south together, and Hardy handed Harrison a revolver, "just in case." Hours later, in Elmwood Park, they forced Frank J. Murray and Norma Newby to drive them to the Elmwood Park Forest Preserve. There, in an isolated grove, Harrison, provoked when Newby called him "crazy," beat Newby to death with his gun and Murray into unconsciousness.

En route to Virginia, Hardy and Harrison robbed at least six businesses. One night, however, Hardy fled when he heard Harrison moan in his sleep of his need to kill. Harrison returned to Chicago and on Jan. 9, 1932, crushed the skull of his friend Charles Pagel, an itinerant laborer, with five hammer blows. Some days later he killed acquaintance Charles Tyrell with the same hammer.

On Jan. 23, Harrison visited Dr. James Shaffer, a 56-year-old dentist. Occupied by a crossword puzzle, Shaffer asked Harrison if he knew a five-letter word for "insane." "Crazy," murmured the dentist, answering his own question. Harrison killed him with the hammer. Then, on Jan. 31, Harrison visited acquaintance Gene Davis, twenty-two, at the garage where he worked. When Harrison asked Davis to loan him a car, Davis laughed and said, "You must be crazy." Harrison crushed his skull.

Finding a bottle of sleeping pills near Davis' body, police were able to track Harrison to his home. He confessed, and the next day was pronounced a homicidal maniac by two psychiatrists. On Feb. 25, 1932, Harrison entered the State Hospital for the Criminal Insane at Chester, Ill., where he would often request solitary confinement. "I feel it coming on," he explained to the guards. "If you leave me with the others, I'll have to kill."

On Feb. 12, 1938, Harrison and fellow inmate Peter Florek, escaped from the hospital, only to be recaptured several days later. Harrison often vowed to escape, once telling a guard: "I'm not mad. You're mad to think you can keep me in here. I'll get loose again some day and then I'll kill. Do you understand? Kill!" REF.: *CBA*.

Harrison, Henry, prom. 1692, Brit., mur. On Jan. 4, 1692, the strangled corpse of Dr. Andrew Clenche was found in a coach by the boy who had driven two men to Clenche's home, then left with three passengers and returned from an errand to find only one, a dead man. Clenche had lent about £120 to Mrs. Vanwicke, a close friend of Henry Harrison's. When Vanwicke did not make the payments on time, Clenche applied for an order to evict her,

beginning proceedings to take over the mortgage on her house, which was her collateral for the loan. Harrison was soon after overheard discussing the situation with Vanwicke, calling Clenche "a rogue," and declaring that he "deserves to have his throat cut."

About three weeks later, Harrison and another man hired a coach and rode to Dr. Clenche's house, asking him to come out and tend to a sick friend of theirs. The coachman was ordered to drive to the Leadenhall Market and, at about 11 p.m., was sent to buy poultry. On his return, the driver discovered Clenche's corpse, strangled with a handkerchief. Appearing as witnesses for his defense, two of Harrison's friends, Mr. Macaffee and his wife, swore that Harrison had been with them, drinking and playing cards at the time of the murder. But their characters were so dubious that their testimony did not sway the jury, which found Harrison Guilty. Harrison, who had been tried once before for murder but convicted of manslaughter, was sentenced to death, and died insisting on his innocence. Another man, John Cook, believed to be Dr. Clenche's other murderer, was tried and acquitted soon after Harrison's trial.

REF.: *CBA*; Parry, *Some Famous Medical Trials*.

Harrison, Hughey, and **Barlow, Neil**, and **Ahern, Bob**, prom. 1869, U.S., (attempt.) mur. James J. Brooks, a federal agent, was instrumental in breaking up the infamous "Whiskey Ring" bootlegging operation, which had cost the government millions of dollars. He was working in Port Richmond, Philadelphia, in the spring of 1869, arresting moonshiners and exposing their operations. The criminal underworld called a war council and agreed to take action, pledging $600 for "putting Brooks out of the way." The three who volunteered for the job were Bob Ahern, Neil Barlow, and Hughey Harrison. As Brooks continued to make arrests, he was trailed by the three criminals. On Sept. 6, 1869, they attacked. Barlow stayed in a yellow-wheeled carriage, waiting to make the escape, while Ahern shot Brooks, hitting him in the back; Harrison then went after the agent with a blackjack, beating the wounded man on the head.

As the trio sped off, Brooks gained consciousness long enough to observe the bright yellow wheels, and to see Harrison's distinctive eyes before the thug's mask slipped down. Between life and death for several weeks, Brooks eventually recovered and began to search for his assailants, looking in the business district for the carriage with yellow wheels. Spotting a taxi, he followed it to a ferry, then missed the boat and lost the trail, tracking it down a few days later to a liveryman who explained that he hired it out on a daily basis to Barlow. Finding Barlow through this connection, Brooks trailed him at length, finally arresting Harrison, whose eyes he recognized from the assault, as he posed as a salesman. Barlow was arrested the same afternoon, and both he and Harrison turned in Ahern. All three were tried, convicted, and sentenced to ten years in the Pennsylvania State Prison.

REF.: Barton, *True Exploits of Famous Detectives; CBA*.

Harrison, Thomas, 1606-60, Brit., her. Favored putting Charles I on trial. He was the king's escort from Hurst to London and he signed the king's death warrant. He assumed command while Cromwell was gone from Britain between 1650-51. From 1655-56 and from 1658-59 he was put in prison by Cromwell for his religious leanings towards the Anabaptists. At the beginning of the Restoration in 1600, he refused to leave the country or alter his position, and was executed. REF.: *CBA*.

Harrison, William, prom. 1660-62, Case of, Brit., fraud. In Chipping Camden, England, 70-year-old William Harrison disappeared after going out on Aug. 16, 1660, to collect some rents. When he did not return, his wife sent their son, Edward, and their servant, John Perry, to search for the elderly man. Finding no trace of him, the pair returned to Camden upon hearing that a poor woman had found a hat, comb, and collar. The items, belonging to the elder Harrison, proved to be bloody; the woman led them to where she had found them, but there was no sign of a body. The justice of the peace ordered Perry to be kept in custody while a further search was made.

About a week later, the judge again questioned the servant,

asking why he had confessed to several different people, saying that Harrison had been murdered by a tinker to one, by a neighbor to another, and telling a third that the corpse had been hidden in a bean silo. Perry then confessed, saying that Harrison had been killed by Perry's own mother and brother, claiming that they had long been after him to let them know when Harrison was going to collect rents, so they could rob and kill him. According to Perry, they robbed Harrison together, then Richard Perry had strangled the man while Joan Perry stood by. The three nefarious relatives had planned to take the body to a cesspool in the garden, but when John went to make sure there were no passersby, the body was spirited away. Perry said he had taken the hat, collar, and comb of his master and thrown them into the highway where they were later found. Joan and Richard Perry bitterly denied John's accusations, but he refused to change his story, further implicating his sibling by identifying as the murder weapon a piece of knotted, looped rope that fell from Richard's pocket.

The Perrys were tried in September at the Gloucester Assizes, charged with robbery and murder. Pleading guilty to robbery when the judge refused to try a murder case for lack of a body, they remained in jail for some time. John Perry eventually changed his story again, saying he had confessed previously in a fit of madness. Nonetheless, they were all found Guilty and hanged together on Broadway Hill. John Perry was left dangling in chains as additional punishment.

Two years later, William Harrison came back to Chipping Camden with a complicated and ludicrous tale of having been kidnapped, taken to the coast of Kent, carried away to Turkey and thrown in jail, then rescued by a Turkish man who wanted an Englishman with "some skill in physick" as a slave. After nearly two years as a slave, Harrison explained, he was released when his master died, and managed, penniless, to slowly work his way back to England via Portugal. The probability that Harrison had wanted to disappear, perhaps because he had embezzled funds, or knew too much about some business deals, so depressed his elderly wife, who had been in a deep state of melancholy since his disappearance, that she hanged herself not long after his return.

REF.: Butler, *Murderers' England;* Canning, *Fifty True Tales of Terror; CBA;* Kobler, *Some Like It Gory;* Williamson, *Historical Whodunits.*

British highwayman William Harrow caught poaching.

Harrow, William, d.1773, Brit., rob. Known as "the flying highwayman" for his athletic escapes on horseback, William Harrow gravitated to crime early in life.

Finally caught poaching game—Harrow was an avid cock-fighter—he threatened to murder the gamekeeper if he told. For these threats, however, Harrow was thrown into Hertford jail, but escaped before being tried. He then took to highway robbery, where he earned his nickname.

Posing as police looking for deserters, Harrow, Thomas Jones, and William Bosford broke into farmer Thomas Glasscock's home, tied up the farmer and his housekeeper, and rode off with a chest containing £300. After dividing up the money, Harrow and a female companion settled at an inn in Gloucestershire, where Harrow posed as a sailor who had won prize money. They lived there for two months until Harrow fought with another lodger. Soon after, a magistrate at Gloucester received a letter from Sir John Fielding ordering Harrow's arrest for robberies around St. Albans.

Harrow was traced to Wolverhampton, captured in bed with his companion, and jailed at Gloucester. From there, he was taken to Hertford, indicted for robbing Mr. Glasscock, and sentenced to die. On the night before his execution, he sawed off his leg irons but was unable to escape. Many came to see him hanged, along with the robber John Wright, on Mar. 28, 1773.

REF.: *CBA;* Mitchell, *The Newgate Calendar.*

Harrow School, prom. 1825, Brit., attempt. asslt. Boys at an upper-class British school became so abusive and threatening to one of their masters that he went to the Bow Street law enforcement offices to ask for protection, saying he feared for his life and that of his son.

On Mar. 2, 1825, Martin Jones, a master at the exclusive Harrow School, went before magistrate Minshull at the Bow Street offices to complain of excessive harassment. His roof, he explained, was tiled, and several boys from the school had repeatedly been breaking the tiles by throwing stones at them.

Toward the end of April, four or five were indulging in this popular sport once again when Jones' son told them to stop. The Harrow boys threatened to beat him up, bringing in another boy or so boys to back them up. The entire group, armed with sticks, then surrounded the house, swearing they would thrash both Jones and his son. Hiding his son in the workshop, Jones told the assailants that he was gone.

The next day, fifty Harrow School students returned, again armed with sticks; this time, however, the sticks were loaded with lead. Jones said his son was in London on an errand, and that he would report the mob to Headmaster Butler, if they did not leave. A day or two later, Jones' wife went to Butler to report the incidents and beg for protection. A student, Clarkes, was apparently punished as a result, and soon after, 150 boys carrying sticks descended on Jones' home. Running to the pub for safety, Jones was terrified as the students surrounded the pub, prevented from entering only by the forcefulness of the landlord. At this point, Butler, Evans, and another Harrow School master, ordered the gang to disperse, threatening immediate expulsion to anyone who did not leave. At about 5 p.m., thirty boys returned to Jones' house, breaking a window and trying to enter by tearing out the bars. One boy, Campbell, was armed with pistols.

Jones concluded his statement to Minshull by saying he was afraid for the lives of himself and his son. Ellis, a senior officer at Bow Street, was assigned to be Jones' bodyguard. Not long after this, Jones and Butler met privately and worked out an agreement, undoubtedly involving both a guarantee of future security and a financial compensation. When Jones was asked by Ellis if he wished the warrant to be put into action against any of his persecutors, the teacher said no.

REF.: Armitage, *Bow Street Runners; CBA.*

Harsent, Rose, See: **Gardiner, William.**

Harsh, George S., 1907-80, U.S., mur. In 1929, in Atlanta, George Harsh and Richard Gallory were sentenced to death by electrocution following their conviction for the murder of a drugstore clerk. The two men, both from wealthy, socially prominent families, were also accused of seven other crimes, including a second murder. Harsh's family sought to save his life and enlisted a dozen psychiatrists to explain his social inadequacies. Harsh and Gallory later had their sentences commuted to life imprisonment on a Georgia chain gang. In 1940, Harsh was paroled after saving a fellow prisoner's life by performing an appendectomy.

After his release, Harsh joined the Royal Canadian Air Force and was shot down by the Germans during WWII. Harsh was held in a Nazi prison camp and was instrumental in aiding more then 100 Allied prisoners escape, an effort which was documented in the film *The Great Escape*. After the war, Harsh began a crusade against capital punishment, recounting his moral redemption and experiences in an autobiography entitled *A Lonesome Road*. He brought attention to the fact that he had been saved only because he was a member of a wealthy and white class, and that a poor, underprivileged person might never have had the opportunity for redemption. Harsh lived in Toronto until his death on Jan. 25, 1980. REF.: *CBA*.

Harsnett, Samuel, 1561-1631, Brit., witchcraft. One of the rational voices that spoke out against witchcraft, calling it delusion and superstition, Samuel Harsnett rose in the ranks of the clergy to become Archbishop of York in 1628.

Educated at Cambridge, Harsnett was ordained as a priest and made a reputation for himself by 1584 by preaching against the Calvinist doctrine of predestination as an absolute, saying the idea was "monstrous." Returning to Cambridge for advanced theological studies, Harsnett was appointed chaplain to Bishop Bancroft in London, and used his position to investigate the exorcism practiced by John Darrell and the deceptions involved in the case of the Burton boy.

With these findings, he wrote an attack on fraud, called *Discovery of the Fraudulent Practices of John Darrel,* in 1599, later penning another discourse against exorcism, *A Declaration of Egregious Popish Impostures,* which would later be used as the source of the spirits in Edgar's speech in Shakespeare's *King Lear.* By 1603 the Church of England had prohibited ministers from casting out devils unless they had the special license of the bishop.

Harsnett was made master of Pembroke Hall, a post he held until 1616. In his final years, he bitterly watched the growth of Puritanism, a religion which stirred up and encouraged the persecution of witches in the mid-century. REF.: *CBA*.

Hart, Brooke, See: **Thurmond, Thomas Harold.**

Hart, Gene Leroy, 1944-79, Case of, U.S., mur. On June 13, 1977, three Girl Scouts, 8-year-old Lori Lee Farmer, 9-year-old Michele Guse, and 10-year-old Doris Denise Miller were beaten to death after being sexually assaulted near Pryor, Okla. Police suspected Gene Leroy Hart, a full-blooded Cherokee Indian who had escaped from the Mayes County jail four years earlier while serving a 140-year sentence for burglary, kidnapping, and rape. Hart was arrested ten months later, after being harbored by many who believed in his innocence.

Hart's controversial murder trial was the longest in Oklahoma's history. He was acquitted in March 1979 after his defense convinced the jury that the state's evidence had been in their possession up to three years before the murders, and adding that other Girl Scouts identified another man as the probable attacker. Friends of Hart had raised money for his defense by selling chili at support meetings. Their happiness was short-lived, because on June 4, 1979, while jogging in the prison yard, Hart died of a heart attack. While more than a thousand bereaved supporters paid homage to Hart, whose case had helped to further Indian rights, authorities claimed they had uncovered new evidence proving he murdered the three girls.

REF.: *CBA*; Wilkerson, *Some Cry for the Children.*

Hart, George, d.1812, U.S., mur. A native of New York City, George Hart was a penny-pinching drunkard who was forever accusing people of stealing money from him. In an alcoholic stupor, Hart awoke one morning to accuse his mistress, Mary Van Housen, of emptying his pockets. She explained that when he returned home the night before, his pockets had already been turned inside-out. Hart called her a liar, grabbed a piece of wood from the fireplace, and crushed his mistress' skull with it. He was found with the dead body, quickly condemned, and hanged on Jan. 3, 1812.

REF.: *CBA*; *Trial for Murder.*

Hart, Michael George, 1947-   , Brit., mur. A thorough and

painstaking investigation by Scotland Yard turned up a murderous bank robber, who was arrested within a year of his crime.

On Nov. 10, 1976, Michael George Hart walked into the Barclays Bank in Richmond, Surrey, England, on Upper Ham Road, and shoved a sawed-off shotgun at teller Angela Woolliscroft, twenty, ordering her to give him money and to hurry up. When Woolliscroft turned over £2,500 in notes of different denominations, the robber fired, hitting her in the chest and hand; she died on the way to the hospital.

Through the bank staff, Scotland Yard detectives James Sewell, Alan Wadsworth, and Bob Hancock put together a description of a slim man of about twenty-five, wearing large-framed sunglasses. When the killer fled, he had left behind a woman's yellow raincoat with two pieces of crumpled paper in the pocket, and an orange plastic bag that had once contained chemical fertilizer. The papers proved to be an entry to a wine-making contest, signed by "Grahame," and a shopping list. Grahame James Marshall heard this information on the radio and went to the police to identify his 1974 paper, explaining that the list was written by his sister. On Nov. 10, the sister had parked her car in a ramp space, and noticed that it was in a slightly different position when she returned. Her raincoat and sunglasses were also missing from the back seat; she did not bother to report it. Detectives pieced together the theory that the killer had parked his own car nearby, used Marshall's to commit the crime, then drove back to the ramp after the robbery, taking off with his original car.

When ballistics experts at the Scotland Yard laboratory determined that a twelve-gauge shotgun had been used in the slaying, they soon after received news from an informant that Hart had been observed transferring what appeared to be a shotgun from one car to another the day of the crime. Hart was interviewed, but, because he had a good alibi, and there was no evidence to connect him with the Barclays robbery, he was released, remaining just one of many suspects.

Twelve days after the killing, police answered a call about a car accident in Basingstoke; Hart had abandoned his car at the scene and fled. In the trunk of the auto police found a Hendal .22 automatic pistol and seventy-two rounds of ammunition. Police then went to Hart's home address, where they found a box containing cartridges that matched those found in Woolliscroft's corpse.

A self-employed builder before the slaying, Hart had worked at a gas station. On Jan. 20, 1977, he went to pick up some back wages from the Station Supreme Ltd. in Middlesex, and was arrested by officer Ronald Hines. Held for questioning, he unsuccessfully attempted to hang himself, then later confessed all, calling the death "an accident," and showing detectives where he had thrown the gun into the river. In the time following the murder, Hart had lived by burglary, fraud, theft, and receiving stolen property—sum thirty-nine offenses, often assisted by his chauffeur, Sharon Stacey. Stacey was sentenced at the Old Bailey to three years in prison for passing £777 in worthless checks while with Hart. Justice Melford Stevenson sentenced Hart to life in prison.

REF.: *CBA*; Tullett, *Strictly Murder.*

Hart, Nathan F., 1829-83, U.S., mur. In the small town of Tenants Harbor, east of Thomaston, Maine, a murder took place three days before Christmas 1877. Sarah Meservey, the wife of Captain Luther Meservey, who was away on a trip, was found bruised and strangled, a scarf knotted around her neck and her arms tied together with cod line. Meservey had not been seen since Dec. 22, and was thought to have gone to visit relatives in Thomaston. Her corpse was discovered in a spare bedroom in the Meservey home at the end of an isolated road. The room was disordered, with mirrors broken and furniture overturned, and Meservey's body was wrapped in a blanket. Bloodstains were found in other rooms, along with a peculiar, semi-literate note scribbled on brown paper. Dated "Monday Eveng 24," the note said: "i cam as A Womn She was out and i (waited) till she Come back, not for Mony but i kiled her." The murderer wanted to leave the impression that he had worn woman's clothing and that robbery was not the motive.

The sheriff's investigation turned up four primary suspects, some of whom were asked to submit handwriting samples, and even required to write, "I killed her," for comparison with the note. One of the investigators, Levi Hart, had visited the Meservey house. On Feb. 16, 1878, his wife received a letter similar to the note. It was postmarked Philadelphia, dated Feb. 10, 1878, and warned Mrs. Hart to "tell your husband to be careful," and that there was no use hunting for the murderer because "he will not be caught." By Mar. 8, a lifelong seafarer, Captain Nathan F. Hart, forty-nine, was arrested for the crime. Chemical analysis of Hart's clothes showed traces of human blood, and matches used in his house were the same as those found at the murder scene. A second anonymous letter came to Mrs. Mahala Sweetland of Tenants Harbour. It was a full, rambling confession from the killer, detailing his attempted seduction and consequent murder of Meservey.

Nathan F. Hart, killer of Sarah Meservey.

Hart was tried for murder before Chief Justice John Appleton at Rockland on Oct. 1, 1878. The trial lasted six days. Prosecuting attorneys were L.A. Emery and Lindley Murray Staples, with J.H. Montgomery and R.F. Dunton for the defense. Hart denied the killing, but was found Guilty as charged after the jury deliberated for an hour. Appleton sentenced Hart to life imprisonment at hard labor in the state penitentiary. The case was controversial, and some thought Hart was innocent. Alvin R. Dunton, a schoolteacher who had testified regarding Hart's handwriting, wrote *The True Story of the Hart-Meservey Trial,* published in 1882. Hart served only five years of his term before dying of jaundice in prison on Oct. 9, 1883.

REF.: *CBA;* Dunton, *The True Story of the Hart-Meservey Murder Trial;* Pearson, *Five Murders.*

Hart, Pearl (Pearl Taylor, AKA: Mrs. L.P. Keele), 1871-1925?, U.S., west. outl. Pearl Hart was the last Western bandit to rob a stagecoach and the only woman ever recorded as having committed that crime. Unlike Belle Starr or Cattle Kate Watson, Hart was not bred into Wild West crime. Born and raised in Lindsay, Ontario, Can., to a middle-class and respectable family, Pearl Taylor was one of several children. She was sent to a finishing school at an early age and, in 1888, at age seventeen, was seduced by a gambler, Frederick Hart. Pearl eloped with him but marriage to Hart proved to be one hardship after another. Hart was a small-time gambler and occasional bartender. Somehow he managed to scrape enough money together to take Pearl to Chicago to see the Columbian Exposition of 1893. There Hart became a barker for sideshows and Pearl worked odd jobs. She was thrilled at the Wild West shows and became enamored of the Old West, believing in all its legends and heroes.

Pearl left her ne'er-do-well husband abruptly and moved to Colorado where she gave birth to a son. She returned to her home in Lindsay briefly to leave the child in the care of her mother. She then went Phoenix, Ariz., where she quickly discovered that the Old West was no more and mostly likely never existed. To survive, she cooked in a lunch room and took in laundry. Her husband suddenly showed up in late 1895 and begged Pearl to return to him, promising that he would get a job. The couple was reunited, and Hart went to work as a bartender and hotel manager. For three years there was domestic peace and a second child, a girl, was born.

In 1898, Hart told Pearl that he was tired of supporting her and the child. During a fight, he knocked her unconscious and left, joining the army and going off to fight the Spanish in Cuba with Teddy Roosevelt's Rough Riders. Pearl took her second child to her home in Canada and then drifted back to the western mining camps. She worked in these hellholes as a cook until taking up with a carefree miner, Joe Boot. In 1899, Pearl received a letter from her brother telling her that her mother was ill and needed money for medical attention. Desperate, she talked to Boot about her dilemma. Boot suddenly had the idea to rob the Globe, Ariz., stage.

Boot said he knew all about the stagecoach that ran between Florence and Globe, Ariz.—that it always carried salesmen who had hundreds of dollars and that, since no one had robbed a stagecoach in years, it carried no shotgun rider, only an unarmed driver. This stage run was one of the last in the Arizona Territory, an antiquated form of transportation in 1899. By then the railroad reached into almost every town of the West. Pearl agreed to rob the stage with Boot, and the two rode to a watering hole where they knew the stagecoach would stop to rest the horses. Pearl was armed with an old .44 Colt. Boot carried a .45-caliber six-gun.

When the Globe stagecoach appeared, Pearl and Boot jumped in front of it, holding their guns on the driver. They ordered him to halt. Pearl was dressed as a man, wearing a man's gray flannel shirt, jeans, and boots. She had cut her hair short and had tucked the longer strands beneath a wide white sombrero. At first the driver thought she was a boy. Boot trained his weapon on the driver while Pearl ordered the passengers to step from the stage and line up.

After she took the driver's six-gun, Pearl held her gun on the passengers while collecting their money, about $450. Then, acting out the part of the Western badman, she peeled off three $1 bills from the stolen money and gave a bill to each of the three passengers, saying: "For grub and lodging." The passengers were then ordered to get back into the coach. Boot ordered the driver to whip the horses onward, and the stagecoach resumed its journey while Pearl and Boot mounted their horses and rode into the hills. The daring bandits had given little thought to their escape. They promptly got lost and, after wandering about in the wilds for several days, fell asleep next to a large campfire. Possemen roused them from their slumbers and put them under arrest.

Pearl Hart played her part as lady bandit to the hilt, telling the smiling lawmen that they would never have taken her alive if she had gotten to her gun. They agreed and then took her and Boot to jail. Pearl became an overnight celebrity as the last bandit to rob a stage. The fact that she was a woman made her even more of a curiosity, drawing crowds of admirers to the Globe jail to collect her autograph. She strutted behind the bars of her cell, playing the part of the outlaw. Some time later, with another prisoner, Ed Hogan, Pearl escaped. News of the manhunt for her spread through the newspapers of the East, further enhancing her fast-growing legend. When she was recaptured some days later, Pearl again played the part of the desperado.

Before her trial on charges of highway robbery, Pearl Hart made a flamboyant suicide attempt, one that was obviously intended to glean headlines, not insure death. While one of her guards stood in front of her cell, she suddenly cried out that she did not care to live any longer and threw a white powder into her mouth, then collapsed. A doctor was rushed to her cell and, after examining her, shook Pearl and shouted: "Stop pretending Pearl and get up!" As her eyes blinked open, the physician said: "No one ever killed themselves by swallowing talcum powder, Pearl."

Her trial took place in Florence, but Pearl insisted that no court had the right to place her on trial, loudly stating: "I shall not consent to be tried under a law in which my sex had no voice in making." Thus, Pearl Hart became one of the first champions for women's rights, giving interviews and urging her fellow females to revolt against the laws of the land until they were given the right to vote. Public sentiment was in favor of Pearl, who was tried separately from Boot. After listening to her lawyer plead that this was her first offense and that she had struggled all her life to obey the law, the jury retired and returned in fifteen minutes to acquit her.

Pearl Hart, last of the stagecoach robbers.

Judge Doan was furious and ordered another jury impaneled immediately to try Pearl on stealing the six-gun from the driver of the stage. Judge Doan warned the members of this second jury that they should not allow their natural sympathies for a woman to cloud their reason. The all-male jury listened to the case and found Pearl Guilty in ten minutes. Judge Doan then sentenced the lady bandit to five years imprisonment at the Territorial Prison at Yuma "to cure her of robbing stagecoaches." Joe Boot, in a separate trial, was convicted of highway robbery and sent to the same prison for thirty years. Reporters rode the train with Pearl to Yuma, filing colorful accounts which detailed her every move and utterance, including the fact that she smoked cigars during the trip and livened up the trip with her "salty conversation."

The warden at Yuma Prison had to prepare a special cell for Pearl, separating her from the all-male population. Within a few weeks, Pearl began to spread the gospel, giving fellow prisoners long lectures on their sinful ways and how crime does not pay. She continued this evangelistic campaign for a year-and-a-half until scores of Arizona citizens, hearing of her newly found religious

beliefs, petitioned for her release. She was set free after serving eighteen months, on Dec. 19, 1902, along with another female prisoner, Rosa Duran. Governor A.W. Brodie released these two women on the grounds that the state prison had no accommodations for women, but he was really bowing to public pressure to release Pearl Hart.

Pearl left for Kansas City where she joined her sister who had written a play about her and Pearl starred in this dime novel production which was titled *The Arizona Bandit*. The play closed after a short run and Pearl disappeared. She was arrested under the name of Mrs. L.P. Keele, in Kansas City two years later for buying stolen canned goods and given a brief jail term. Again Pearl disappeared and was not seen again until 1924 when she returned to Arizona and inspected the courthouse where she had been tried, smiling and telling an attendant that "nothing has changed." When the attendant asked who she was, she turned at the doorway and dramatically stated: "Pearl Hart, the lady bandit." She was thought to have died in 1925 in Kansas City while operating a cigar stand but other reports have it that she moved to the far West, perhaps San Francisco, where she lived until the mid-1950s.

REF.: Aikman, *Calamity Jane and the Lady Wildcats;* Argall, *Outlawry and Justice in Old Arizona;* Block, *Great Stagecoach Robbers of the West;* Brent, *The Hell Hole;* CBA; Chisholm, *Brewery Gulch;* Corle, *The Gila River of the Southwest;* Gardner, *The Old Wild West;* Harrison, *Hell Holes and Hangings;* Hayes, *Boots and Bullets;* Horan, *Desperate Women; ____, The Great American West; ____ and Sann, Pictorial History of the Wild West;* Hunter and Rose, *The Album of Gunfighters;* Liggett, *My Seventy-Five Years Along the Mexican Border;* Miller, *Arizona; ____, The Arizona Story;* Miller, *Shady Ladies of the West;* Nash, *Bloodletters and Badmen; ____, Look For the Woman;* Thorp, *Story of the Southwestern Cowboy;* Walters, *Tombstone's Yesterdays;* Way, *Frontier Arizona;* Wilson, *Treasure Express;* (FICTION), Busch, *Duel in the Sun;* (FILM), *Duel in the Sun,* 1946.

Harte, Robert Sheldon, d.1940, Mex., (unsolv.) mur. On May 24, 1940, a highly organized gang of heavily armed men attacked the miniature fortress in Coyoacan, Mexico, where Leon Trotsky, the last surviving representative of the Bolshevik Old Guard, lived in exile with his wife. The extreme efficiency and technical expertise of the maneuver made it obvious that the assassins were experienced in military actions, and had inside information about the layout of the fortress. Two men dressed in policemen's uniforms and another costumed to look like an army lieutenant approached the guard point without arousing suspicion, pulling guns when they were within striking distance, then disarming and tying up the guards. Storming the gates from within, the attackers rushed through, spraying the room where Trotsky and his wife lay sleeping with machine-gun fire; they bombed the library, destroying Trotsky's unfinished biography of Joseph Stalin. As the gang swiftly exited, Robert Sheldon Harte, one of Trotsky's bodyguards, went with them, either on his own or by force.

In June 1940, police from Mexico City drove to an isolated house near the village of Santa Rosa, looking for Harte. The empty rooms of this hideaway offered no clues, and police were about to leave when one officer noticed peculiar marks on a spot on the kitchen floor. A workman dug for hours, excavating the shallow grave in which lay the lime-covered corpse of Robert Harte. His killers were never found. See: **Stalin, Joseph; Trotsky, Leon.**

REF.: *CBA;* Dewar, *Assassins at Large.*

Hartigan, John Patrick, 1887-1968, U.S., jur. Served as assistant attorney general of Rhode Island from 1923-24, and as attorney general in 1933. He was nominated to the Rhode Island District Court by President Franklin D. Roosevelt in 1940, and to the first circuit court by President Harry S. Truman in 1951. REF.: *CBA.*

Hartley, John, and **Reeves, Thomas,** d.1722, Brit., rob. John Hartley and Thomas Reeves, robbed and battered a tailor and would have escaped punishment for their crime had a fiddler not intervened.

Because the tailor had only his clothes and two pence, Hartley and Reeves stripped him, bound him to a tree, and beat him. Rescued by some passersby, however, who took him to an alehouse, the tailor told his story and was overheard by a fiddler. The next day, in a pub, the fiddler saw two men trying to sell a coat. Recognizing the tailor's property, he offered to buy it and said he would be right back with the money. Returning instead with the tailor, he had Hartley and Reeves arrested. They were subsequently found Guilty and sentenced to die.

Highwaymen Hartley and Reeves robbing a traveler near Harrow.

While waiting to die, Reeves sang and swore while the other convicts prayed, insisting that he was as likely to go to Heaven from the gallows as he was from his bed. When asked by a guard if his wife had had any part in his robberies, Reeves said, "No, she is a worthy woman, whose first husband happened to be hanged. I married her, that she might not reproach me by a repetition of his virtues."

Hartley, in an attempt to save his life, had six young women dressed in white present a petition to the king at St. James that said if Hartley were released, the six women would cast lots and the winner would marry him. Unimpressed, the king said Hartley was more deserving of the gallows than of a wife. Reeves and Hartley were hanged at Tyburn on May 4, 1722.

REF.: *CBA; Mitchell, The Newgate Calendar.*

Hartley Mob, prom. 1870s, U.S., org. crime. The Hartley Mob, one of New York City's most vicious gangs, practiced murder and robbery in Lower Manhattan during the 1870s. The clever gang adroitly used funeral processions to further their criminal ways. Sometimes they would transport goods in the hearses and funeral carriages. And other times, they would use the procession as a cover against rival gangs. Once they over-whelmed their arch-rivals, the Five Points Gang, by swarming from the vehicles supposedly carrying grieving mourners. However, the gang was not as clever in seeking political or police protection, and within a few years most of the leaders were in prison and the gang disbanded.

REF.: Asbury, *The Gangs of New York; CBA;* Haskins, *Street Gangs.*

Hartshorne, Richard, 1888-1975, U.S., jur. Served as assistant U.S. attorney in New Jersey in 1925 and taught law at the New Jersey Law School from 1935-43. He was president of the Interstate Commission on Crime from 1935-43. He was nominated to the district court of New Jersey by President Harry S. Truman in 1951. REF.: *CBA.*

Hartson, Dorothy, prom. 1978, S. Afri., mur. On Aug. 13, 1978, Wilford Cahill, thirty-six, a strong, vital farmer in Cape Province, S. Afri., was discovered dead in his bed by his wife, Laura Cahill. When the family physician, Dr. Ian Barton,

examined the corpse, he told the widow he could not issue a death certificate until he had a second opinion. Dr. Peter Drysdale, the Cape Town coroner, confirmed Barton's suspicion that the rich farmer had been poisoned. Police discovered an empty beer bottle in the kitchen garbage that contained traces of strychnine. They also found a bundle of love letters in Laura Cahill's bedroom, and soon discovered through servants Buster Diggens, a 44-year-old mechanic on the farm, and Melanie N'Gomo, a 16-year-old maid, that Mrs. Cahill and the farm manager, Denis Hartson, had been carrying on an affair for almost a year. Hartson, who had come to the farm in May 1974, and married Dorothy Ekquist soon after, had been involved with his employer's wife since September 1977.

Both Cahill, the sole heir to her husband's estate, and Hartson were arrested and taken to Cape Town police headquarters for questioning. Both admitted to their liaison, and both denied killing Cahill. Suspicious that the couple could not maintain their stories independently, and unable to believe that they would have chosen such an obvious and detectable method, police questioned both N'Gomo and Diggens. Although he had been discharged twice before for violence against an employer, Diggens had an air-tight alibi. N'Gomo, who had accused Diggens of committing the crime, had thrown out the lethal beer bottle, but had not noticed anything unusual.

Laura Cahill and Denis Hartson were turned over to the prosecutors office and were about to be charged with murder and conspiracy to commit murder when, on Sept. 1, Dorothy Hartson went to Inspector Brian Harrison to tell him that she had killed Cahill, poisoning him, with the hope that his wife would be hanged for the murder, after she had discovered her husband's affair. "It didn't occur to me that Denis would be suspected," she explained, adding that she loved him even though he had cheated on her. In February 1979, Dorothy Hartson was tried and found Guilty, but given the relatively light sentence of twenty years in prison because of extenuating circumstances.

REF.: *CBA;* Dunning, *The Arbor House Treasury of True Crime.*

Hartung, Mary, prom. 1858-63, Case of, U.S., mur. After a jury deliberated for fifteen minutes, Mary Hartung was convicted of poisoning her husband and sentenced to be hanged, but was released from prison after just five years when the New York state legislature passed a bill that voided her sentence.

Emigrating from Germany after a revolution in her own country, Mary and her husband, Emil Hartung, quarrelled often. In their Albany, N.Y., home, a combination boarding house and beer saloon, they had two daughters, Rosy and Emma. Not long after Emma's birth, Mary took a boarder, William Rheimann, as her lover. In April 1858, Emil Hartung became ill with what he believed to be a bad cold, and went to the family physician, Dr. Joseph Levi. Emil's sickness grew steadily worse until, on Apr. 21, he died.

Mary Foell, the house servant, began to gossip to neighbors, telling how Mrs. Hartung had asked her to buy some arsenic for her, then later rescinded the order, saying she would get it herself. Charles A. Schindler, Emil Hartung's friend and sponsor, went to the widow on May 20 and confronted her with the rumor that she had poisoned her husband, saying he would have confidence in her if she would go with him to the district attorney's office and request an exhumation. Crying and pleading a headache, Mary agreed to go the next morning.

That night, she disappeared along with Rheimann, taking Emma with her. Four days later, police found Rheimann at an Albany tavern. He protested his innocence, and said Mary had told him she murdered her husband. They had gone together to Jersey City, N.J., and he had lost her in a crowd when they were together in Manhattan; he returned to their Jersey City lodgings to find she had checked out.

Police tracked Hartung to a Guttenburgh, N.Y., residence where she was working as a seamstress, returning her to Albany on July 11; she was arraigned on charges of murder on Sept. 21, and pleaded not guilty. The case opened on Jan. 31, 1859, in the

Court of Oyez and Terminer before the Honorable Ira Harris, a supreme court justice who would later become a U.S. senator. Hartung's boarder, Theodore Malder, had heard the deceased complain about a bitter taste in his coffee, and Mary Foell detailed her mistress' repeated attempts to obtain poison, explaining that Mary Hartung always added some phosphorous-smelling "seasoning" from a yellow pot when she cooked for her husband. Hartung was found Guilty after the jury deliberated for fifteen minutes. On Mar. 3, 1859, Judge Harris sentenced her to be hanged on Apr. 27, 1859, and she was taken to Maiden Lane Jail to await execution. Through a series of bills introduced in the New York legislature and the repeal of revised statutes, Hartung's sentence, though legal when pronounced, was declared unconstitutional following an act passed on Apr. 14, 1860. The act, contrived by Hartung's lawyers, William J. Hadley and A.J. Colvin, for the express purpose of freeing her, said that there was no longer any known sentence for those convicted of first-degree murder. Despite a plethora of newspaper editorials on the case, Hartung was released from prison just five years after she murdered her husband.

REF.: *CBA*; Seagle, *Acquitted of Murder*.

Hartwell, Alfred Stedman, 1836-1912, U.S., atty. gen.-jur. Member of the Massachusetts House of Representatives in 1867. He served as a justice of the supreme court of the kingdom of Hawaii in Honolulu from 1868-74, and as attorney general of Hawaii from 1874-8. He was nominated to the territorial court of Hawaii by President Theodore Roosevelt in 1904 and renominated in 1907. REF.: *CBA*.

Hartzell, Oscar Merril (The Baron), d.1943, U.S., fraud. Within months of the death of British privateer Sir Francis Drake on Jan. 28, 1596, Elizabethan con men were collecting money from "shareholders" convinced that part of an immense fortune left by Drake would be theirs. The con made its way to the U.S. around 1835. Even people with last names other than Drake were told that for a small contribution toward the legal fees necessary to straighten out the estate they, too, could share in this windfall.

Oscar Hartzell, whose Drake inheritance swindle netted him millions.

In 1919 two of Drake's con artists, Sudie Whiteaker and Milo F. Lewis, confronted a Madison County, Iowa, farm woman. Mrs. Hartzell listened to the pitch and decided to invest her life savings, $6,000 in cash. The con artists took her money, thanked her, and left, never to be heard from again. Their pitch, however, had been heard by Mrs. Hartzell's two sons, Oscar and Canfield. Oscar Hartzell's interest and innate criminal sensibilities were piqued by the scheme, and after researching Drake in the nearest library he tracked Whiteaker and Lewis to Des Moines where he confronted them with their swindle. The two admitted to having made $65,000 in Iowa in the previous two months. Oscar informed them that they had underestimated the scheme's potential and needed to make it legitimate by opening an office.

Within a week the three had formed a partnership they called the Sir Francis Drake Association. Initially they covered Iowa, Illinois, and Missouri, contacting only people with the last name of Drake. Eventually, however, they widened their market and accepted investments from virtually anyone. For two years Oscar and his partners covered these three states. Oscar understood the laws regarding mail fraud and studiously avoided ever personally having anything to do with the mails. Eventually he recruited a larger staff which included Harry Osborne, A.L. Cochran, C.A. Storla, C.C. Biddle, his brother Canfield, and Otto G. Yant. Yant was a former bank cashier and provided the Drake Association with lists of people with large bank accounts. The group's venture continued to thrive. In Quincy, Ill., they signed up every adult in the city with the full endorsement of the chamber of commerce.

In 1924, Oscar decided to travel to London. He told his investors this was to take charge of freeing the Drake estate from the bureaucracy of the British government. Once there, he lived as if he were Drake himself. His extravagant lifestyle was supported by weekly payments of $2,500 gathered and forwarded to him by his brother. During his sojourn abroad, Oscar tried to keep up his investors' interest and keep them contributing by alternately threatening to drop from the rolls and enticing them with estimates of the size of the estate ranging from $22 billion to $400 billion.

By 1927 many of the investors were getting nervous. In response, Hartzell stepped up the optimism in the telegrams he regularly sent home, claiming a settlement was almost within sight. Finally, however, word of the fraud reached postal authorities in the U.S. Their attempts to investigate the swindle were severely hampered by the fact that people who had invested everything they owned—in some case even taking out second mortgages on their homes to stay in Hartzell's good graces—refused to discuss it for fear of losing out. Iowa's attorney general publicly denounced the scheme and immediately received thousands of letters demanding his silence so the deal would not be ruined.

In January 1933 the U.S. State Department arranged to have Hartzell deported from England as an undesirable alien. On landing in New York he was arrested and taken to Iowa City to stand trial for postal fraud. The state presented an elaborately researched and documented case but Hartzell thought he would go free because he had never personally sent a letter pertaining to the Drake fraud or received one. He was, however, convicted for causing others to commit postal fraud and was sentenced to ten years in jail. His hold on his investors was so strong that even with his conviction many still believed in him. His bail and defense fund were provided by his loyal supporters. Hartzell encouraged their loyalty by alluding to a political conspiracy of enormous proportions that was behind his trial and conviction.

Hartzell finally entered Leavenworth in November 1933. When a group of his fellow con men who had continued to operate even after he had gone to prison were arrested, Hartzell was made to stand trial for a second round of postal fraud charges. He was convicted again and returned to Leavenworth to serve out his full sentence. In December 1936 prison officials ordered a psychiatric examination for Hartzell who had deteriorated mentally since his incarceration. He was adjudged incompetent and sent to the U.S. Medical Center in Springfield, Mo., where he died on Aug. 27, 1943. It was estimated that he had bilked 70,000 Midwesterners out of an estimated $1.4 million.

REF.: *CBA*; Gibson, *The Fine Art of Swindling*; Hynd, *Murder, Mayhem and Mystery*; Kahn, *Fraud*; MacDougall, *Hoaxes*; Nash, *Hustlers and Con Men*; Rose, *The World's Greatest Rip-offs*; Wade, *Great Hoaxes and Famous Imposters*.

Harvey, Alexander, II, 1923- , U.S., jur. Served as assistant attorney general of Maryland from 1955-57, and was nominated to the district court of Washington, D.C., by President Lyndon B. Johnson in 1966. He also served on the Committee on the Administration of the Criminal Law in 1975. REF.: *CBA*.

Harvey, Donald, b.c.1952, U.S., asslt.-mur. Donald Harvey worked at the Veterans Administration hospital in Cincinnati, Ohio, as a nurse's aide and autopsy technician for ten years. After he was caught trying to take home hospital books and was seen taking a loaded .38 handgun out of his locker, he was permitted to resign in 1985. He was also watched in the morgue after officials received reports of missing equipment and body parts, but no evidence was found to link Harvey to the disappearances.

Harvey, a native of Booneville, Ky., then worked for twelve years at the Drake Memorial Hospital. In March 1987 an autopsy on John Powell revealed the presence of cyanide, and the 35-year-old Harvey was arrested the same month. He allegedly confessed to murdering as many as fifty patients by poisoning their food or drink, or by putting toxins in their gastric tubes. He used a petroleum-based ether, arsenic, cyanide, or a hepatitis serum, or disconnected life support systems to kill his victims. In 1986, after an argument, Harvey had poisoned his roommate Carl Howeler, but then nursed him until he was well. Harvey's defense attorney said he worried that "people will consider him some kind of monster."

Originally, Harvey pleaded not guilty by reason of insanity, but after he was declared sane, he entered into a plea bargain with prosecutors. Their primary evidence was the Powell poisoning and Harvey's confession. Prosecutors agreed not to request the death sentence, and on Aug. 18, 1987, Harvey pleaded guilty to twenty-four counts of aggravated murder, four counts of attempted aggravated murder, and one count of felonious assault. He received three consecutive life terms in prison and was fined $270,000 plus court costs. REF.: *CBA*.

Harvey, James, prom. 1988, U.S., extort. Unemployed construction worker James Harvey decided to make some quick cash. The Jacksonville, Fla., man killed a mouse, shoved it into a can of beer made by the Adolph Coors Company, and then called the company's consumer complaint office. The firm offered him $1,500 compensation, but Harvey refused, asking for as much as $50,000. When Coors would not meet his new demands, Harvey went to Jacksonville television stations with his story. Coors then got a court order to inspect the can and the mouse. They found that the can had been sealed several months before, but the mouse had been dead only a week. Florida prosecutors charged Harvey with extortion and tampering with a consumer product. He was sentenced to eighteen months in a work-release program. Coors spent $750,000 for a Florida advertising campaign to reassure customers of their product's quality. REF.: *CBA*.

Harvey, Julian, c.1917-61, U.S., suic.-mur. A Green Bay, Wis., family chartered the sixty-foot yacht, *Bluebelle* for a week of cruising. On Nov. 8, 1961, the Duperrault family, including 41-year-old Dr. Arthur Duperrault, his 38-year-old wife, Jean, and their children, 14-year-old Brian, 7-year-old René, and 11-year-old Terry Jo, left Fort Lauderdale for the Bahamas. Five days later, on Nov. 12, the ship's Captain Julian Harvey apparently murdered his wife Mary Dene Harvey, who worked as crew and cook for the excursion, and the whole Duperrault family, except Terry Jo.

The next morning, the 44-year-old captain and the body of René were found. Harvey said the 7-year-old had drowned, and that the rest of the family and his wife had died in an unexpected tropical gale when a fire from the fuel tank destroyed the boat. But three days later Terry Jo was found floating at sea on a small cork raft. She was dehydrated and suffering from overexposure. When news of Terry Jo's survival reached Harvey during questioning, he excused himself from the room. The next morning, on Nov. 17, his body was found in a hotel, cut with a razor. He left a suicide note that said nothing about the tragedy on the chartered craft.

When Terry Jo recovered, she told detectives that she had been asleep when screams and feet tromping woke her. Investigating, she discovered the bloody bodies of her brother and mother. She asked Harvey what happened, and he pushed her back into the cabin. But the water rose around her bunk and she went up to the deck again. The last thing she saw was Harvey attempting to board a dinghy as the yacht sank.

Harvey was found to have scuttled two previous boats for insurance money. In 1946 he was involved in a suspect Florida accident in which his second wife, Joann, and his mother-in-law drowned after his car had gone off a bridge into a canal. He miraculously survived. Harvey was also being hounded by creditors at the time of the *Bluebelle* incident. He had taken out a $20,000 double-indemnity insurance policy on his wife two months before the *Bluebelle* cruise. REF.: *CBA*.

Harvey, Llewellin Garret Talmage, prom. 1854, Brit., mur. On May 17, 1854, 21-year-old Mary Richards was found savagely beaten in a field near Devonshire, England. She died on May 30. Before her death, she identified her attacker as Llewellin Garret Talmage Harvey, who was arrested on May 20. Harvey, recently transplanted from Oxford, had met a girl named Mary Allen, but she refused to accompany him when she noticed the handle of a hammer sticking out of his pocket. On May 17, he hid behind a hedge and attacked Mary Richards with a hammer as she walked by. He then dragged her to a field, sexually assaulted her, and left her. On July 28, 1854, in the courtroom of Justice Wightman at the Devon Assizes, Harvey was found Guilty and sentenced to death. The sentence was carried out on Aug. 4, 1854, when Harvey was hanged at noon before a large crowd.

REF.: Butler, *Murderers' England*; CBA.

Harvey, Margaret, d.1750, Brit., rob. A well-educated native of Dublin, Margaret Harvey married a nobleman's valet at sixteen. Soon, after her husband's six-month tour of duty in the navy, she became a victim. He returned possessed of unreasonable jealousy and began to beat her, so severely that she left him. But not for long. Her father, who believed Harvey's husband's claim that she had left him for no reason, sent her back—just in time to be beaten again and collect permanent scars on her arms and head.

Harvey was then taken in by a gentleman was willing to protect her. Her protector, however, soon grew tired of her and left her. So, Harvey decided to go back to her husband. She sailed for London, hearing that he had gone there, but after a long search took work as a maid on Marylebone Street.

Four months later, at a fireworks display celebrating the anniversary of peace with France, she met up with a group of women and sailors and with them drank the night away. Ashamed to return to work, she took a room and joined ranks with some prostitutes. After one excessive night of drinking she stole a gentleman's gold watch. Arrested that same night, she was taken to Newgate Prison the next day. Convicted of theft, she claimed to be pregnant and obtained a stay of execution. Nine months later, however, Harvey was sentenced to death, the eighteenth-century punishment for theft.

Intoxicated from brandy brought by friends, Harvey was hanged at Tyburn on July 6, 1750.

REF.: *CBA*; Mitchell, *The Newgate Calendar*; Nash, *Bloodletters and Badmen*.

Harvey, Sarah Jane, b.1895, Case of, Brit., mur. When 65-year-old Mrs. Sarah Jane Harvey went into the hospital for observation in April 1960, her son decided to redecorate her house in the seaside town of Rhyl on the North Wales coast. Opening an upstairs closet that his mother told him held the belongings of Mrs. Frances Knight, a former tenant, the son found an insect-infested room and a bundle on the floor. A human foot protruded from the bundle. Police found a preserved corpse, yellow-brown in color, which was hard as granite and totally immovable. The bizarre near-mummification had occurred by chance, when warm, dry air circulated up the stairs, preserving the body. Dr. E. Gerald Evans, pathologist, discovered a groove around the neck, indicating that Knight had been strangled with a stocking. The body had been in the closet from April 1940 to May 1960. Harvey had continued to draw the £2 weekly maintenance that Knight received from her husband, from whom she had separated in 1936.

In her murder trial at the 1960 Ruthin Assizes, prosecutors Sir Jocelyn Simon, Elwyn Jones, and Bertrand Richards tried to prove that Harvey murdered Knight for the maintenance money. The defense, with Andrew Rankin and Somerset Jones, contended that this could not be proved. After five days, the trial ended when medical evidence was found insufficient to prove murder. Justice Davies sentenced Harvey to fifteen months' imprisonment after she pleaded guilty to fraud for collecting more than £1,500 over twenty years.

REF.: Camps, *Camps On Crime*; CBA; Furneaux, *Famous Criminal Cases*, vol. 7.

Harvey-Bugg, William Benjamin, b.c.1931, Aus., mur. William Harvey-Bugg was raised primarily by his grandmother, and as a young boy was constantly in trouble with police. By the time he left school at age fifteen, he had been charged twice with theft and five times with burglary.

When Harvey-Bugg was seventeen, he decided to leave Sydney, Aus., to take a job as a farm hand in the Blue Mountains of New South Wales. On Sept. 26, 1948, his employer, 50-year-old James Lyon Walker Barton, and Barton's 45-year-old sister, Luie Loveday Walker Barton, drove to church, leaving the teenager to amuse himself. He practiced shooting a .22-gauge rifle and then read a crime paperback. When he heard the Bartons returning, he hid in the garage with the loaded gun, listening as Barton stopped the car to let his sister out. Barton drove into the garage, got out of the car, and the teenager shot him in the head. When the man dropped to the ground, Harvey-Bugg shot him in the head again. Then the youth shot at Barton's sister through the window of her upstairs bedroom. When she came out the front door, she saw the farm hand pointing the rifle at her. As she turned, he shot her twice in the back. After putting Barton's body in the grain shed and taking Luie Barton's body into the pantry, the young man stole about twenty-five war-savings certificates worth one pound face value each. He then packed and drove the Bartons' car to Sydney where he stayed with his friend, Charles Ivan le Gallien. He told le Gallien that he had killed his boss for the car, but le Gallien did not take him seriously.

Harvey-Bugg then traveled to Brisbane and checked into a Salvation Army hostel on Sept. 29. The next day he was arrested by New South Wales investigators and taken to Sydney for trial. About the same time, another murder was splashed across the newspapers. Charles Louis Havelock le Gallien had been killed by his son, Charles Ivan le Gallien.

At Harvey-Bugg's trial, his defense lawyer entered the first plea of insanity in Australia's history. The teenager was, however, found Guilty of murder and sentenced to life in prison.

REF.: *CBA; Gurr and Cox, Famous Australian Crimes.*

Harvey's Resort Hotel-Casino Bombing, 1980, U.S., bomb-extor. On Aug. 26, 1980, two men entered Harvey's casino in Stateline, Nev., wheeling in a metal box about four feet by two feet by two feet. They said they were delivering a photocopy machine, but actually the box contained a sophisticated homemade bomb made with about 1,000 pounds of explosives. A letter attached to the bomb demanded $3 million in exchange for directions on how to disable it. The note also told where to send the money. Harvey's officials tried to meet the extortion request, but the attempt to deliver the money failed. Specialists from the Nuclear Emergency Search Team were called in to assist in defusing the bomb, but it exploded on Aug. 27 while they tried to use a remote control mechanism to disarm it. It ripped a five-story hole in the casino and caused $18 million in damage. Harvey's was closed for reconstruction for eight months. No one was injured.

The crime and the culprit were uncannily similar to those in a then-unpublished play, *Getting Even,* by Jim Massey. In the play, several characters lose money at a casino and seek revenge by threatening to blow it up unless they are given $3 million in $100 bills. The real extortionists made the same demand. The ringleader, 59-year-old John W. Birges, Sr., lost $15,000 at the casino and also owed money to loan sharks. He built the bomb in his home in Clovis, Calif., and involved in his plot his companion, 47-year-old Ella Joan Williams, his sons, 20-year-old John W. Birges, Jr. and 19-year-old James W. Birges. He was also aided by two Fresno, Calif., residents Terry Lee Hall, twenty-five, and Willis Brown, fifty.

During the trial of the elder John Birges, his sons testified against him, saying that they and their mother, who committed suicide in 1975, had been mistreated. Their father was convicted on Oct. 22, 1982, on four counts of conspiracy to extort money and sentenced to two consecutive twenty-year prison terms. Terry Lee Hall and Willis Brown received seven-year sentences, and Ella Williams was freed after a mistrial. REF.: *CBA.*

Harwood, Jocelin, 1669-92, Brit., rob.-mur. Jocelin Hardwood came from a good family in Kent and was well educated. At thirteen he began to exhibit extreme misconduct in school and sometimes skip school altogether. By sixteen, after enduring severe punishments, he stole £60 from his father and ran away to London.

Harwood survived as a pickpocket for two or three years. But then he stole a horse, saddle, bridle, holsters, and pistols to set himself up as a highwayman. When he attacked two gentlemen at Blackheath they shot his horse from under him. But Harwood wounded them both. He soon became skillful at his new profession and over the next three or four years committed more than two hundred robberies, for a total take of about £5,000.

Then Harwood and two accomplices broke into a wealthy knight's house at Shropshire. After binding the servants, they found the knight and his lady in bed and bound their hands and feet. Harwood then found the knight's two young daughters in the next room. When the girls threatened to identify Harwood if he treated them harshly, he said "I'll prevent that then," and dismembered them with his sword. Swearing that they should not outlive their children, he then stabbed both parents through the heart. His frightened cohorts kept there distance during the slaughter. But later on the highway, they shot Harwood's horse from under him, bound him, and left him in the road with a piece of the knight's silver. When he was found, Harwood claimed that thieves had robbed him and in their haste, dropped the silver beside him. But his captors found large amounts of money in his pockets. They took him to the knight's house, where the servants identified him.

At Harwood's trial he spat in the faces of the judge and jury. He was sentenced to be hanged. Then, his corpse would be displayed in chains as a public spectacle and example. To the end of his life, Harwood swore, drank, and cursed the world. He was hanged in 1692, at the age of twenty-three.

REF.: *CBA; Smith, Highwaymen.*

Harwood, Levi, b.c. 1821, and **Jones, James,** b.c.1826, and **Harwood, Samuel,** b.c.1825, Brit., rob.-mur. On Sept. 27, 1850, Levi Harwood, James Jones, Samuel Harwood, and Hiram Smith gathered outside the Frimley parsonage between 10 p.m. and 11 p.m. Samuel Harwood stood guard outside while the others broke the scullery window, but he joined them for a feast. He later returned to his post while Smith, Levi Harwood, and Jones roamed the house, the latter two armed with pistols. Smith stole a gold watch and two other watches, as well as a bag of copper coins. Then the two armed men startled the sleeping Reverend G.E. Hollest and his wife. As Mrs. Hollest rose from the bed, Jones pushed her into a corner and threatened her. The pastor tried to grab a poker from the fireplace and, in a struggle with Levi Harwood, the burglar shot Reverend Hollest. The injured man got his own loaded gun and fired at the assailants as they ran from the house. Reverend Hollest died in the evening on Sept. 29.

Discovering that Levi Harwood, Jones, and Smith had not been home on the night of the crime, Inspector Hollington arrested the three at a pub. Samuel Harwood was arrested shortly afterward. Hiram Smith offered his confession and agreed to testify against the others. The trial was held on Mar. 31 and Apr. 1, 1851, and Levi Harwood and James Jones, the two armed men, were convicted. Samuel Harwood, the lookout, was acquitted. The two condemned men were sentenced to be hanged. Samuel Harwood was later arrested for a burglary in Sussex.

REF.: *CBA; Forster, Studies in Black and Red.*

Hasan al-Banna, 1906-49, Egypt, polit.-clergy, assass. Prominent political and religious figure who established the Muslim Brotherhood (al-Ikhwan al-Muslimun) in 1928 to promote Islam and Egyptian nationalism. The Egyptian government was involved in his assassination. REF.: *CBA.*

Hasan ibn-al-Sabbah, See: **Order of the Assassins.**

Haseltine, James (AKA: Shock Jem), c.1880s, Brit., fraud. James Haseltine was jailed on charges of defrauding the Tattersall company. His conviction was clinched by the efforts of George Ruthven, a police official who claimed he spent £3,000 of his own money to bring Haseltine to justice. Several years before the arrest, Haseltine had stolen Ruthven's wife and the police officer still held a grudge. Haseltine was sentenced to exile for seven years.

REF.: *CBA;* Dilnot, *Triumphs of Detection.*

Haskell, Flora Fanny, b.c.1874, Case of, Brit., mur. In November 1908, a Scotland Yard detective was sent to Salisbury where Flora Fanny Haskell, a 34-year-old widow, said she discovered her son dead the previous evening. She said when she went to investigate a sound, a man had dashed by her, and tossed a knife at her. She then found her son Edwin Richard Haskell, a 12-year-old boy with only one leg, lying in bed with his throat slit. The dead child was planning to buy a new cork leg and had saved £8, half of which was missing from a drawer that had been pried open. When Detective Dew arrived, the doctor had already cleaned the child's body and the house had been meticulously scoured, leaving no sign of blood. The murder weapon had been taken from the kitchen and had just been resharpened.

Flora Haskell was brought to trial, and accused of her son's murder, but a new trial was convened when the first ended in a hung jury. At the second trial, she was acquitted. Out of the case, Scotland Yard issued new procedures, insisting that crime scenes not be altered, nor a body moved, and that a police officer should stand guard over the site to ensure that it was not undisturbed.

REF.: Brock, *A Casebook of Crime; CBA;* Gribble, *Famous Judges and Their Trials;* Kingston, *Dramatic Days at the Old Bailey;* Nash, *Open Files;* Shew, *A Second Companion to Murder.*

Hassells, Samuel (AKA: **Bob Hays**), d.1869, U.S., west. outl. Born in Laporte, Iowa, Samuel Hassells went west at an early age and joined several gangs, committing many robberies. While living in Gonzales County, Texas, he reportedly was captured and drew a five-year prison sentence. He escaped four months before finishing this term in Huntsville, Texas. Hassells was identified as a member of a gang that robbed the post office in Separ, N.M., in October 1869. On Nov. 28, 1869, a large posse cornered the gang at the Diamond A ranch, about sixty miles south of Separ. A wild gun battle ensued and Hassells was killed.

REF.: Bartholomew, *The Biographical Album of Western Gunfighters; CBA.*

Hastie, William Henry, 1904-76, U.S., jur. Admitted to bar in District of Columbia in 1931 and served as district court judge in U.S. Virgin Islands from 1937-39. He was dean of the Howard University Law School from 1939-46, and governor of the Virgin Islands from 1946-9. He became the first black judge of the U.S. Circuit Court of Appeals, serving from 1949-71. REF.: *CBA.*

Hastings, James F., b.c.1926, U.S., fraud. In January 1976, after serving seven years as a U.S. Representative from New York James Hastings, resigned to take another post. In September 1976, he was indicted on charges of mail fraud and of making false statements to a government agency. On Dec. 17, 1976, the 50-year-old Hastings was convicted in Washington, D.C., of twenty counts of mail fraud and eight counts of submitting false statements to the House Finance Office. Hastings had received kickbacks from two men who were part-time employees paid from his Congressional budget. He was sentenced in early 1977 to twenty months to five years in prison. REF.: *CBA.*

Hastings, Jeffrey R., b.c.1951, and **Knowles, James H.,** b.c.1962., U.S., mansl. In August 1980, Captain Jeffrey Hastings and a deckhand, James Knowles, were piloting a 23-foot Llama Cat from Freeport, The Bahamas, to Florida. Also aboard were seventeen Haitian refugees who had paid about $500 each to be transported. The smugglers became alarmed when they saw a patrol car in West Palm Beach, Fla., cast a searchlight across the water. So the armed men pushed children into the water and forced the rest of the refugees into the ocean. Eleven of them swam to shore, but a mother and her five children drowned. The 29-year-old captain, of Hypluxo, Fla., and the 18-year-old deckhand, of Tarpon Bay, the Bahamas, were tried on first-degree murder charges in West Palm Beach, Fla. Both were convicted of manslaughter on Apr. 18, 1980. Hastings was sentenced to 180 years in prison and Knowles was sentenced to fifteen years in prison. REF.: *CBA.*

Hastings, John Simpson, 1898-1977, U.S., jur. Nominated to seventh circuit court by President Dwight D. Eisenhower in 1957. He published law review articles between 1965-70 concerning the Criminal Justice Act of 1964. REF.: *CBA.*

Hastings, Mary (Marie Sefholic), prom. 1896, U.S., Case of, pros. Mary Hastings operated some of the more successful brothels in Chicago in the late nineteenth century, but her unfortunate choices of suitors left her with little of her rewards, and mounting legal problems as well. Hastings, daughter of wealthy French parents, grew up in Paris in the 1870s, but yearned to see the world, especially Chicago. She arrived in San Francisco, where she fell in love and married. The marriage was turbulent, and after separating, divorcing and reuniting, the couple reached Chicago in 1888. Hastings arrived with $15,000 in gold and immediately built her first house of prostitution in the city's red light "levee" district. Hastings fell in love with a contractor, George Mullen, who was more interested in her property and schemed to get control of her lucrative ventures. In May 1891, he induced her to take a short trip, and upon returning on May 20, 1891, she was arrested on the charge of harboring young girls in a house of prostitution. She was released, but Mullen advised her go to Canada until things died down, and to turn over the real estate to him, so it could not be taken from her. She complied, but her lawyer, John C. King, saw through the scheme and refused to draw up papers. Mullen found another lawyer and the property was transferred. Hastings returned to Chicago a year later and demanded the property be returned, which Mullen refused to do. Mullen was able to hide the ownership through a series of aliases and Mary Hastings never recovered the property.

In Fall 1894, Hastings began a relationship with "Tom" Gaynor, a brutal man with political influence. Back in business, her houses were raided on an almost daily basis, and Gaynor was keeping most of the profits. When she demanded a fair share, Gaynor beat her and shot her in the leg. Upon recovery, she made a fateful trip to Ohio, in search of young girls for her houses. On Sept. 5, 1895, in Cleveland, Hastings met Lizzie Lehrman, Kittie Clair, Gertie Harris, and Florence Lapella. Hastings bought them drinks, then took them as prisoners on a train to Chicago, where they became prostitutes. On Sept. 18, she repeated the routine in Toledo, and brought May Casey, Ida Martin, Kittie McCarthy, Kittie Winzel, and Blanche Gordon to Chicago.

On Sept. 26, 1895, two of the girls escaped and went to the police. Detective Clifton R. Wooldridge immediately went to the house and arrested Mary Hastings, who was released later on a $2,100 bond signed by Gaynor. Wooldridge went before a grand jury with two of the girls and secured two indictments against Hastings. In each case she was free on $5,000 bond, again secured by Gaynor. On Oct. 14, the case was called, but Hastings was not present. Her attorney, George W. Crawford, asked for a ten-day continuance, but Wooldridge implored the judge to deny the application because it would perpetuate the cruel conditions which the girls were being kept under, while Hastings had forfeited her bond by not appearing. The judge agreed, the security was collected, and five of the girls were sent back to Toledo.

On Dec. 3, 1895, Hastings returned to Chicago and was found by Wooldridge and Detective Schubert drinking in Gaynor's saloon. After she was arrested, Gaynor stormed in and demanded to see the arrest warrant. Wooldridge refused, and when Gaynor attempted to draw a gun, he was apprehended by Wooldridge and subsequently charged with trying to aid a criminal to escape and interfering with an officer in the discharge of his duties. An attempt was made to discredit the detective when a number of witnesses testified under oath that there had not been a confrontation in Gaynor's saloon. Wooldridge was also mysteriously offered $4,000. In January 1896, the case against Hastings was called, but again she was not present. Under threat of forfeiture, she quickly appeared and the case was continued. This occurred innumerable times, until on May 13, 1897, the case was dropped because the witnesses had scattered. By that time, Gaynor had paid over $20,000 in forfeited bonds. In time Gaynor's cruelty became too much to bear, and Hastings moved to Toledo, leaving all of her Chicago possessions to him. REF.: *CBA*.

Hastings, Sir **Patrick**, 1880-1952, Brit., atty. gen. Served as member of Parliament from 1922-26. He also served as attorney general between 1923-24 for the government of Ramsay MacDonald. As attorney general he tried to prosecute John Ross Campbell, Communist editor of *Worker's Weekly*, but others forced the Prime Minister to withdraw the charge, and the situation caused the downfall of Mac-Donald government in 1924. He prosecuted Jean Pierre Vaquier, and was also known for his defense of Mrs. Elvira Barney, Ludomir Cienski, and John Williams.

Sir Patrick Hastings

REF.: *CBA*; Hastings, *The Autobiography of Sir Patrick Hastings*; Hyde, *Sir Patrick Hastings: His Life and Cases*; _____, *United in Crime*; Scott, *The Concise Encyclopedia of Crime and Criminals*.

Hastings, Warren, 1732-1818, Case of, Brit. brib.-polit. corr.-duel. Warren Hastings presided over India as Britain's first governor-general and was a representative of the East India Company. During his administration, he met with advisers on the Council of Five, one of whom was the vituperative Sir Philip Francis. Francis managed to sway three other members of the council, and together they antagonized the governor-general and ruined the reforms he had instituted. Additionally, when Hastings traveled to Bengal to eradicate corruption, he returned to find Council matters in disorder. Council members were also caught cheating the Indians. Furious, Hastings finally threw a glove angrily in front of Francis during a council meeting, challenging his antagonist to a duel. The two met a few days later at 6 a.m. in a Calcutta field. Francis did not get a clean shot, but Hastings shot his rival in the chest. Although Francis suffered a serious injury, he lived to destroy Hastings' career.

Francis returned to England where he spoke with politician Edmund Burke, berating Hastings and accusing the governor-general of corrupt behavior toward the natives of India. When Hastings retired in 1785 and went back to England, he faced the wrath of Burke. On Feb. 13, 1788, an impeachment trial opened in which Hastings was charged with corruption in his administration in India, accepting bribes, and misappropriating contracts. After great personal expense, Hastings was acquitted in 1795.

REF.: Earl of Birkenhead, *Famous Trials of History*; *CBA*.

Hatch, Carl Atwood, 1889-1963, U.S., jur. Served as New Mexico state district judge from 1923-29, U.S. senator from 1933-49, and as U.S. district judge for New Mexico from 1949-62. He was notable for his sponsorship in 1939 of the Hatch Act, or the Political Activity Act, which limited political activities of federal officials. REF.: *CBA*.

Hatcher, Charles Ray (AKA: **Richard Clark, Richard Lee Grady, Albert Price, Ron Springer, Dwayne Wilfong**), 1929-84, U.S. rob.-forg.-rape-mur. Charles Hatcher was born July 16, 1929, in Mound City, Mo., to an alcoholic ex-convict father and an unstable mother. Hatcher's father abused him and when he was six years old, he was present when his 8-year-old brother was accidentally electrocuted. Hatcher moved with his family to St. Joseph, Mo., in 1945, and was often in trouble with the authorities for automobile theft, burglary, and forgery. While in reform school and later in prison, Hatcher was a victim of homosexual rape. On May 18, 1959, Hatcher, then twenty-six, was released from prison. On June 26, Hatcher tried to kidnap 16-year-old Steven Pellham at knife-point as he delivered newspapers. Hatcher was arrested shortly after the attempted abduction while driving a stolen car. On Nov. 20, 1959, he was convicted of auto theft and intent to kill and was sentenced to five years in the Missouri State Penitentiary.

In the penitentiary, Hatcher became the primary suspect in the stabbing death of inmate Jerry Tharrington on July 2, 1961. Although he was never charged with the crime, prison officials kept Hatcher in solitary confinement for much of the rest of his prison term. Hatcher wrote a letter to prison officials, acknowledging that he needed psychiatric help. The officials in question viewed Hatcher's request as the work of a manipulative repeat offender and denied it. Hatcher was released from prison on Aug. 24, 1963, and on Aug. 30, was arrested for burglarizing a store in Maitland, Mo. Freed on bond, Hatcher, using the name of Dwayne Wilfong, was arrested for burglarizing a business in Iola, Kan. On Mar. 7, 1964, he escaped from the Allen County Jail in Iola. On May 28, Hatcher was sentenced to eighteen months in the Oklahoma State Penitentiary for car theft in Oklahoma City. On Sept. 20, 1965, he was sentenced to five years in the Missouri State Penitentiary for the burglary in Maitland. On Dec. 7, 1967, he was sentenced to the Kansas State Penitentiary for one to five years for car theft in Kansas City, Kan. He escaped from a prison farm on Aug. 21, 1969.

From all that is known of Hatcher's activities, a new chapter appears to have begun after this last escape. Years later, when Hatcher finally began to confess to his many assaults and murders, he explained his motivation to authorities: "I kill on impulse. It's an uncontrollable urge that builds and builds over a period of weeks until I have to kill. It doesn't matter if the victims are men, women, or children. Whoever is around is in trouble." The "uncontrollable urge" struck on Aug. 28, 1969. Hatcher abducted and murdered 12-year-old William Freeman in Antioch, Calif. The following evening, as Roger Galatoire was walking his dog in a deserted area in the hills outside San Francisco, he saw a man lying on the ground not far from the path. Assuming the man was drunk, Galatoire kept walking. As he returned, he saw that the man was sitting up and had with him a small naked boy who jumped up as Galatoire approached. The man grabbed the boy by the neck and threw him to the ground and began beating him. Galatoire ran to the nearest house and called police. Two policemen arrived and arrested the man, who later gave his name as Albert Price. He had raped and beaten the boy.

While being held for the assault, Hatcher made a superficial suicide attempt and began to affect behavior that he repeated during all subsequent detentions. He refused to talk to police or doctors, and when he did speak, his statements were irrational. His behavior suggested paranoid disorder. Once the authorities had correctly identified him, they gained access to Hatcher's criminal record. Even so, court-appointed psychiatrists found Hatcher insane. On Sept. 30, 1969, he was sent to the California State Hospital at Atascadero. After a period of treatment, Hatcher was found competent to stand trial, but psychiatrists again found him insane and returned him to the state hospital. This cycle was repeated four times before Hatcher escaped on June 2, 1972. One week later he was arrested for car theft in Sacramento under the alias Richard Grady. As before, Thatcher refused to speak to police and otherwise acted seriously disturbed. As Grady, he was returned to California State Hospital, where the staff identified him as Albert Price.

Hatcher's psychotic behavior caused hospital officials to request his transfer to the state prison hospital. He was transferred there in April, and in August was moved to San Quentin. Although Hatcher seemed driven to get caught and punished, he also appeared to fear confinement. Two days after arriving at San Quentin, still never having been formally tried or convicted in the assault of the boy in San Francisco, Hatcher wrote to the public defender and asked to stand trial. He was finally tried on Dec. 12, and five days later was found Guilty of lewd and lascivious conduct. In January 1973, a judge again committed Hatcher to the state hospital as a mentally disturbed sex offender. Late in March, Hatcher was caught trying to escape, after which hospital officials returned him to court for sentencing as untreatable and as a security and escape risk. In June 1973, Hatcher was finally put in maximum security at Folsom.

Hatcher was paroled on May 20, 1977, conditional on his taking an elaborate mix of anti-psychotic drugs and abstaining from alcohol, apparently a component in many of his crimes. Five days later, he violated parole. Although Hatcher committed numerous other crimes and was actually arrested at various times, authorities never caught up with him until he turned himself into the St. Joseph State Hospital under the name of Richard Clark on July 30, 1982. Richard Clark, who complained of voices in his head, had come almost directly from kidnapping, raping, and murdering 11-year-old Michelle Steele. He was found competent to stand trial and was indicted for first degree murder. While awaiting trial, Hatcher slipped a note to prison guards saying he wanted to talk to the FBI.

FBI agent Joe Holtslag came to talk to Hatcher, who would communicate only in writing. Hatcher hinted that he had other murders to confess to, but wanted the agent to guess the first murder he had in mind. To entice Holtslag into his bizarre game, Hatcher gave him information that led to the discovery of a body in Rock Island, Ill. It became clear that Hatcher had killed mentally retarded James Churchill, thirty-eight, who had disappeared in June 1981. Hatcher eventually admitted killing sixteen people, and Holtslag, who had served in the St. Joseph area for sixteen years, perceived where Hatcher had been leading him. Just over four years earlier, a 4-year-old St. Joseph boy, Eric Christgen, had been abducted from a play lot in a mall in downtown St. Joseph. His body was found the following day in a wooded area near the river, just a mile upstream from where Michelle Steele's body had been found. The boy had been sodomized and asphyxiated. Holtslag had participated in the FBI portion of the Christgen investigation, and knew that the man convicted of the murder, Melvin Lee Reynolds, was, despite his confession, an unlikely suspect.

It also became clear to Holtslag that Hatcher wanted to assure Reynolds' release from prison and to punish the St. Joseph authorities for botching the Christgen case. Finally, Holtslag came to understand that Hatcher was trying to assure that his complete confession would guarantee him the death sentence. After mailing Holtslag a written confession to the murder of Eric Christgen, Hatcher was indicted on capital murder charges.

After Eric Christgen was killed, the FBI predicted another attack by October or November. When authorities finally pieced together Hatcher's past, they discovered how accurate the FBI's prediction had been. On Sept. 4, Hatcher had been arrested in Omaha for a sexual attack on a 17-year-old boy. Between the autumn of 1978 and the spring of 1982, Hatcher was arrested for molesting a teenage boy, attempting to stab a 7-year-old boy, and fighting over payment for sex with a young man, all in Omaha. He was also arrested in Lincoln, Neb., for molesting a man, and in Des Moines for attempting to stab a man. In Bettendorf, Iowa, Hatcher was arrested for trying to abduct an 11-year-old boy from a mall. Hatcher was not jailed for any of these arrests. His ability to feign insanity assured him a stay in the local mental hospital and a speedy release. Also, authorities never sent Hatcher's fingerprints to the FBI, so his crimes were never linked. Hatcher was discharged from a mental health facility in Iowa on May 7, 1982. On July 27, he tried to abduct 19-year-old Stephanie Ritchie from the mall in St. Joseph. The next day, he tried to abduct 10-year-old Kerry Heiss from another shopping center. On July 29, he kidnapped, raped, and murdered 11-year-old Michelle Steele.

On Oct. 13, 1983, a judge in St. Joseph accepted Hatcher's guilty plea to the murder of Eric Christgen and sentenced Hatcher to life in prison. The next day, Melvin Reynolds was released from prison. Then, in 1984, more than two years after Michelle Steele's murder, Hatcher went to trial. On Sept. 21, he was found Guilty of capital murder. Although Hatcher took the stand and asked for the death penalty, the jury decided on life imprisonment. At various times Hatcher had complained of being driven to his crimes by voices in his head. Hatcher may have seen execution as a way of silencing them, but he had also expressed fear of reprisal in prison from another inmate on whom he had informed years before. On Dec. 7, 1984, Hatcher's body was found in his cell, hanging from an overhead pipe. Electrical cord was wrapped around his neck and his hands were tied behind his back with a shoe lace. Investigators determined that Hatcher had placed the cord around his neck, tied his hands in front of his body and then stepped through his tied hands before jumping off the toilet and strangling himself to death. See: **Reynolds, Melvin Lee.**

REF.: *CBA;* Ganey, *St. Joseph's Children.*

Hatchett, Joseph Woodrow, 1932- , U.S., jur. Served as chief assistant U.S. attorney in the Justice Department from 1966-70. He served as justice on the Florida Supreme Court from 1975-79, and was nominated to the fifth circuit court (later renamed the eleventh circuit court) by President James Earl Carter, Jr. in 1979. REF.: *CBA.*

Hatfield, Charles Sherrod, 1882-1950, U.S., jur. Served as prosecuting attorney of Wood County, Ohio, and was nominated to the court of customs appeals by President Warren G. Harding in 1923. The court is now called the Court of Customs and Patent Appeals. REF.: *CBA.*

Hatfield, John, 1769-1803, Brit., fraud. Born of poor parents in Cheshire, England, John Hatfield was gifted with a smooth manner of speech which he employed well through the years as a master swindler. He began as a line-draper and, in his travels, met a young woman distantly related to the ducal house of Rutland. Learning she had a small dowry, Hatfield married the young woman and the couple moved to London. The pair produced several children but when the dowry finally ran out, Hatfield deserted his wife and children and, under an assumed name, borrowed heavily, claiming he was in the employ of the wealthy Manners family. He was finally exposed as a swindler and sent to debtor's prison. His wife died in poverty and Hatfield contacted the Duke of Rutland, appealing to him in the name of his dead wife to aid him, saying that he now was the only surviving parent of starving children.

British swindler John Hatfield.

The duke secured Hatfield's release and when Rutland became Viceroy of Ireland, Hatfield followed him to Dublin, lodging in the best hotel and running up considerable bills, claiming to be in the duke's service. He was finally thrown into Marshalsea Prison in Dublin and smooth-talked his way into the best quarters, insisting that his arrest for bad debts was a mistake and that Rutland would soon have him released. Again Hatfield wrote to the duke, beseeching him to help him. The kind-hearted Rutland paid Hatfield's debts and had him released on the condition that Hatfield leave Ireland.

Hatfield went to Scarborough, England, where, after he operated several swindles, chiefly by posing as a wealthy gentleman and running up enormous bills, he was again exposed as a fraud and thrown into prison, serving almost nine years before he was released to a Devonshire woman named Nation who had visited Hatfield in prison and fallen under his oil-tongued spell. Hatfield married this gullible female, spending her money and then deserting her. He surfaced at the Queen's Hotel in Keswick, claiming to be Colonel Alexander Augustus Hope, claiming to be the brother of Lord Hopetoun. He seduced Mary Robinson, the attractive daughter of wealthy innkeepers. After cashing several forged checks, Hatfield ran off with Robinson, bigamously marrying her in Scotland.

After a short time, as was his custom, Hatfield deserted Robinson and appeared in Swansea where he called himself Tudor Henry and attempted to cash more forged checks for considerable sums. He was by then notorious and he was identified by wanted posters. Hatfield was arrested and tried at Carlisle where he was convicted and sentenced to death as a habitual criminal. The master swindler was hanged on Sept. 3, 1803.

REF.: *CBA; Griffiths, Mysteries of the Police and Crime.*

Hatfield, Paul Gerhart, 1928- , U.S., jur. Served as district judge for Montana from 1961-76, and as chief justice for Montana from 1977-78. He was a U.S. senator from 1978-79, and was nominated to the district court of Montana by President James Earl Carter, Jr. in 1979. REF.: *CBA.*

Hatfield, William, prom. 1908, Case of, U.S., mur. In late Summer 1908, a vicious multiple murder was committed in Santa Clara County, Calif. When a $2,220 reward was offered for the capture of a suspect named Dunham, a Sherman, Texas, woman turned in William Hatfield, positively identifying him as Dunham, with whom she said she was well acquainted. After his arrest, Hatfield gave a vague and unconvincing account of his activities the night the hatchet killings took place. Sheriff Langford of Santa Clara went to Texas and won the extradition of Hatfield to San Jose. When the suspect arrived in San Jose on Oct. 23, it was proven that he was not the killer, but it was legally necessary to charge him anyway. He was exonerated immediately after being charged. During Hatfield's incarceration, more than 20,000 people visited him.

REF.: *CBA; Duke, Celebrated Criminal Cases of America.*

Hatfield-McCoy Feud, prom. 1870s-1911, U.S., feud-mur. The infamous Hatfield-McCoy Feud lasted for more than thirty years in the rugged mountain region where the Tug Fork Stream separates Pike County, Ky., and the West Virginia border. The McCoys of Kentucky, and the Hatfields of West Virginia, had formed armed bands during the Civil War, supposedly to protect local citizens and property from invading Union or Confederate troops. Antagonism between the two clans exploded in the 1870s

A gathering of the Hatfield clan at the turn of the century.

when Randall McCoy accused Floyd Hatfield, later known as "Hog," of stealing two prize hogs. Stealing livestock, and particularly valued hogs, was a serious offense. A Kentucky judge once said that hogs seemed to be more valued than humans in that region. A trial took place in Raccoon Hollow, presided over by Anse Hatfield, also known as "Preacher" Hatfield. Both families attended fully armed. McCoy, whose plea to the jury was an impassioned indictment of all Hatfields as thieves and liars, lost

the case. Witness Bill Staton tried to attack the defendant in the courtroom.

Skirmishes and fist fights between the clans continued after the trial. The first of many murders occurred in 1865 when Anse Hatfield shot Harmon McCoy, but the real turning point was in 1880, when Staton saw Paris McCoy and Sam McCoy, fifteen, coming toward him in an isolated wood. Staton hid and fired, wounding Paris, who then fought him hand to hand. When Paris grew weak, Sam McCoy settled the struggle by shooting and killing Staton. The hidden corpse was discovered a few days later, and the McCoys were arrested and indicted for murder, but were quickly acquitted. Two years passed without fatalities. Then on Aug. 7, 1882, a drunken brawl resulted in the murder of Ellison Hatfield by Pharmer McCoy, who had been watching from the sidelines as Hatfield and Tolbert McCoy fought with knives. Pharmer and two other McCoys were captured, held as hostages, and slain when Ellison died the next day. From this point, the Hatfields and the McCoys engaged in full-scale warfare until 1896, when they had virtually wiped each other out. The feud was perceived as a matter of family honor, and stories and songs were written to commemorate it.

REF.: Ambler and Summers, *West Virginia: The Mountain State;* Campbell, *The Southern Highlander and His Homeland; CBA;* Crawford, *An American Vendetta;* Donnelly, *The Hatfield-McCoy Reader;* Ely, *The Big Sandy Valley: A History of the People and Country from the Earliest Settlement to the Present Time;* Hatfield, *The Hatfields;* Hatfield, *True Story of the Hatfield and McCoy Feud in the Hills of Kentucky and West Virginia;* Hurwood, *Society and the Assassin;* Johnson, *Famous Kentucky Tragedies and Trials;* Jones, *The Hatfields and the McCoys;* Kephart, *Our Southern Highlanders;* Lawson, *The Hatfield-McCoy Vendetta; or, Shadowing a Hard Crowd;* MacCorkle, *The Recollections of Fifty Years;* McCoy, *The McCoys: Their Story;* Mutzenberg, *Kentucky's Famous Feuds and Tragedies;* Reynolds, *History of the Feuds of the Mountain Parts of Eastern Kentucky;* Rice, *The Hatfields and The McCoys;* Stickles, *Simon Bolivar Buckner;* Tapp and Klotter, *Kentucky: Decades of Discord, 1865-1900;* Williams, *West Virginia and the Captains of Industry;* (FILM), *Roseanna McCoy,* 1949.

Hatry, Clarence, prom. 1927-30, Brit., fraud-forg. Beginning as an insurance salesman, Clarence Hatry advanced rapidly, and ran a group of British companies successfully for many years. But when he was forty, the group failed just as rapidly. In 1927 Hatry founded Austin Friars Trust to handle his financial interests, mainly in the jute and glass industries. In June 1929, Hatry and his partners met to discuss ways of retrieving around £1.5 million that had been lost. They decided to print £1.6 million in additional bearer certificates in the name of Corporation and General Securities as security against bank loans. Hatry later explained that he planned to redeem the duplicate stock when a pending merger was completed and the finances recovered. When the Stock Exchange realized there were too many script certificates around, they suspended trading in shares of Austin Friars. Friars was estimated to be about £15 million in debt. Hatry took his directors to meet with Sir Gilbert Garnsey, the Bank of England's investigator, and confessed. Panic ran through the London financial world as Hatry and his cohorts, Edmund Daniels, Mr. Tabor, and Mr. Dixon were arrested.

Tried in January 1930 before Justice Avory, Hatry was defended by attorney Norman Birkett, who soon advised him to withdraw his plea of not guilty as the evidence piled up against him. Hatry was sentenced to fourteen years in jail. Daniels was sentenced to seven years in jail, Dixon received five, and Tabor was given three. Avory, unimpressed by Hatry's claims that he intended to replace the money if a steel merger had come through, compared the promise to that of any clerk who robs the till hoping to back a winner at the races and replace the "loan."

REF.: Bowker, *Behind the Bar; CBA;* Lustgarten, *The Story of Crime;* Nicholls, *Crime Within the Square Mile.*

Hatto II, d.c.970, Ger., clergy, assass. Archbishop of Mainz in 968. According to legend, he burned down a barn filled with people who had stolen grain during a famine; he said their screams were similar to squeaking mice. His punishment was to be eaten alive by mice. He is said to have constructed the Mouse Tower on the Rhine River to try to get away from the mice. REF.: *CBA*.

Hatto, Moses, c.1830-c.1853, Brit., arson-mur. In 1853, Moses Hatto worked as a general servant and groom at the Burnham Abbey Farm, located about four miles from Windsor. His duties included helping the diligent 36-year-old housekeeper, Mary Ann Sturgeon, who continually berated and scolded him. In November 1853, Ralph Goodwin, the owner of the farm, left to spend the evening with friends. As was his custom, he was expected to return about midnight.

That evening, the housekeeper served Moses his dinner, but the portions were smaller than usual. When she brought him only half a glass of ale instead of his allotted full glass, he was infuriated. He struck the woman with a lard beater and after she fled upstairs to her bedroom, he beat her to death with a poker. Then he broke up a piece of wooden furniture and started a fire in the room. Goodwin returned to find the house ablaze and he alerted the groom and other farm hands.

Later, when police questioned Hatto, he denied any involvement. He was, however, put on trial and convicted of murder. After he was condemned, he admitted to the killing. He was hanged at Aylesbury.

REF.: *CBA*; Ellis, *Black Fame*; Whitelaw, *Corpus Delicti*.

Hauer, John, and **M'Manus, Charles**, prom. 1795-98, U.S., mur. After a long and costly courtship, John Hauer finally won the hand of Elizabeth Shitz, daughter of the richest man in Dauphin County, Pa. Hauer expected to inherit a sizable share of the Shitz wealth through his wife. But when Peter Shitz died in 1795, the patriarch left most of his money to his sons, Francis Shitz and Peter Shitz, Jr. The paltry $1,000 he left to his daughter was further reduced because she had drawn on her portion before her marriage.

Hauer became obsessed with the family money. He entered a claim against his father-in-law's estates, but his petition was denied. Hauer then went to his brothers-in-law and said that their father had appeared to him in a vision "from beyond the grave," and ordered them to share their inheritance with their sister. When the brothers laughed, Hauer warned them that their father would haunt them until they divided the property. Hauer broke into the Shitz attic one night and stomped around in heavy boots, rattling chains and mimicking his father-in-law's voice. When the brothers caught him in the attic, Hauer said the ghost of the father had called him there. The brothers threw him out of their house.

Hauer next planned to drive the heirs to suicide. He invited Peter Shitz, Jr., seventeen, to a drinking session, then tied up the very drunk young man with a rope, and bet him five gold pieces that he could not jump from a loft and survive a hanging from a high beam. Young Shitz leapt, saved only when the rope broke, leaving him with torn skin and a lifelong scar. For the next two years, Hauer brooded on ways to acquire the estate. He finally decided to have the brothers murdered. At Geiger's Inn in Heidelburg, Hauer met Irish immigrants Charles M'Manus, Patrick Donogan, Peter M'Donoghy, and Francis Cox, and offered them the job. On Dec. 28, 1797, a maid in the Shitz house heard noises and investigated to find men with pistols, their faces covered by handkerchiefs, crawling through the bedroom window. When a shot was fired, the maid and several other servants ran screaming from the house. The gunman ran to the kitchen, picked up an ax, and returned to clout the wounded Francis Shitz four times in the head with it, killing him. Peter Shitz, Jr. fought fiercely, and escaped by knocking down two of his assailants. The Irishmen were captured soon after the killing, and the murder weapon found to belong to M'Manus. All four Irishmen were indicted, along with Hauer, but only Hauer and M'Manus were found Guilty and sentenced to death. Hauer had been silent throughout the proceedings but, once in jail awaiting execution, he refused to eat, bathe, or wear clothing, and began to bite anyone who came close to him, seriously injuring a jailor. His attempt to prove insanity failed, and he was hanged on July 14,

1798, along with M'Manus.

REF.: *CBA*; Nash, *Murder, America*.

Hauk, A. Andrew, b.1912, U.S., jur. Served as judge on superior court of Los Angeles County, Calif., from 1964-66. He was nominated to the central district court of California by President Lyndon B. Johnson in 1966. REF.: *CBA*.

Haultain, Sir Frederick Gordon, 1857-1942, Can., jur. Held positions of premier, attorney general, and commissioner of education of Northwest Territories between 1891-1905. He served in the legislative assembly of Saskatchewan from 1905-12, and as chief justice of the supreme court of Saskatchewan from 1912-38. REF.: *CBA*.

Haun's Hill Massacre, prom. 1838, U.S., mur. The Haun's Hill Massacre was one of many crimes perpetrated against the Mormon's during their westward trek in the 1830s. On Oct. 30, 1838, over 200 townspeople, led by Nehemiah Comstock, attacked a Mormon encampment at Haun's Hill, Mo. Twenty people, including women and children, were killed and many more were wounded. One small boy crawled to a local blacksmith's shop and was shot in the head at point-blank range as he pleaded for his life. The corpses were gathered and disposed of in a well while the remainder of the camp was ransacked. Missouri Governor Lillburn W. Boggs encouraged these actions, stating that the Mormons should be exterminated for their religious beliefs. No one was ever prosecuted for the slaughter at Haun's Hill. REF.: *CBA*.

Haupt, Hans Max, b.c.1894, and **Haupt, Erna Emma**, and **Haupt, Herbert**, and **Froehling, Walter Otto**, and **Froehling, Lucille**, and **Wergin, Otto Richard**, and **Wergin, Kate Martha**, prom. 1940s, U.S., treas. In 1942, the U.S. was shocked to learn of the capture of eight German spies who had landed on their soil on June 13. The spies were tried secretly in the offices of the Department of Justice. On Aug. 8, 1942, the eight culprits were found Guilty and six were sentenced to be executed, including 23-year-old Herbert Haupt.

While the agents of the German Reich were standing trial, the FBI arrested friends and relatives of the condemned Herbert Haupt on charges of aiding, advising, and giving comfort to a spy. Haupt's parents, Hans and Erna Haupt, and his aunt and uncle, Walter and Lucille Froehling, were taken into custody. Otto and Kate Wergin, the parents of Wolfgang Wergin, a friend of the Haupts' son, were also arrested, and on Sept. 4, 1942, all were indicted.

During the trial, witnesses testified that Herbert Haupt had attended a spy school in April 1942 in Germany, and that the foreign agent had returned to the U.S. with the directive to destroy aluminum factories and railroads that served them. When Haupt reappeared at his parents' Chicago home on June 19, 1942, witnesses said the accused's relatives and friends were fully aware that the young man was a German spy. On Nov. 14, all were found guilty. Hans Haupt, Walter Froehling, and Otto Wergin received the death penalty, and their wives were each sentenced to twenty-five years in prison and a $10,000 fine.

The Court of Appeals struck down their convictions. All six were then separately indicted, again on treason charges, and Hans Haupt was the first to be retried. He was convicted a second time on June 8, 1944, sentenced to life in prison and fined $10,000. The prosecutors negotiated a plea bargain for the other five defendants. Walter Froehling and Otto Wergin pleaded guilty to misprision, and each received a five-year sentence. Erna Haupt was sentenced to denaturalization and confined in an internment camp for the remainder of the war, and Kate Wergin and Lucille Froelhing were freed.

REF.: Busch, *They Escaped the Hangman*; *CBA*.

Hauptfleisch, Petrus Stephanus François, c.1885-1926, S. Afri., arson-mur. Petrus Hauptfleisch served in WWI for four years before he returned in 1919 to Richmond, in Cape Province, with a wife and child. After losing his wife and child because of his drunken rages, Hauptfleisch lived with his 67-year-old widowed mother, Barbara Gertrude Hauptfleisch, in Richmond. He eventually took a job in a slaughterhouse and his drinking binges became more frequent. His mother discussed his temper with a neighbor and soon the town blacklisted him, preventing anyone from selling alcohol to him. Sober, his conduct improved and on Dec. 7, 1924, he was taken off the town's blacklist.

He stumbled home three days later, drunk and threatening to stone his mother to death. She was so frightened that she went to a neighbor's house and a constable was called. Hauptfleisch was jailed for the night to sober up, and two days later he was blacklisted again.

Hauptfleisch blamed his mother for cutting off his alcohol supply and on Jan. 13, 1925, he suffocated the old woman as she napped. Dragging her body to the kitchen, he poured gas on her and set her body on fire. Then he ran to a neighbor's house, yelling that his mother had died in a kitchen fire.

Hauptfleisch was arrested and tried for murder in September 1926. The residents of Richmond were so infuriated that the trial was moved to Cape Town. His mother was found to have been suffocated but no soot was found in her lungs, indicating that she did not die while cleaning a chimney with gas, as her son had claimed. He was convicted of murder, and on Dec. 23, 1926, he was hanged.

REF.: Bennett, *Famous South African Murders;* ____, *Too Late For Tears; CBA;* Morland, *Pattern of Murder.*

Hauptmann, Bruno Richard (AKA: Perlmeyer, Cemetery John), 1899-1936, U.S., kid.-mur. The crime for which Bruno Richard Hauptmann paid with his life was undoubtedly the most sensational in America's twentieth century, the kidnapping and murder of Charles A. Lindbergh, Jr. The victim was the 20-month-old son of America's greatest living hero, Charles Augustus Lindbergh, who, in 1927, flew across the Atlantic in an historic solo flight. For this startlingly heroic achievement, Lindbergh, a tall, clean-cut young man—an All-American youth by any standard—was honored and revered. Lindbergh was seen as a pathfinder, a pioneer, a man of singular honor and dedication who had risked his life in his small monoplane, *The Spirit of St. Louis,* for the future of aviation and the glory of the United States. He had married the beautiful and cultured Anne Morrow, from one of America's most prestigious families. The union produced a blond-haired, blue-eyed little boy, Charles Augustus Lindbergh, Jr.

The Lindberghs occupied a large two-story house outside Hopewell, N.J., in a district called Sourlands, where they lived an idyllic life. Sourlands was remote enough that the famous Lindberghs had some distance between themselves and the press which hounded them, chronicling their every move. Newspaper and magazine articles pinpointed the whereabouts of the spacious Lindbergh home, with photos to show its construction from the foundation up. The baby's room was on the second floor. On the cold, windswept night of Mar. 1, 1932, Mrs. Lindbergh entered the child's bedroom at about 9 p.m. She had been worried about the infant since he had recently caught a slight cold. He was sleeping soundly in his crib. Colonel Lindbergh was working at the time in his library when he heard a noise outside the house but attributed it to a broken shutter banging outside the window of the baby's room.

At a few minutes before 10 p.m., Betty Gow, the baby's 28-year-old English nurse, entered the nursery to find the child missing from his crib. She did not panic, thinking that Lindbergh might have taken the child from the room. She also knew, much to her chagrin, that the colonel was a practical joker. Some months earlier he had taken the baby from its crib and hidden it in a closet as a practical joke, one which only he had found amusing. Nurse Gow went downstairs and asked Lindbergh if he had again taken the child. He said no and a frantic search began. It was first thought that the baby might have somehow gotten out of the crib and crawled away. Everyone in the home, including Ollie and Elsie Whately, the Lindbergh butler and cook who had come from Scotland to work for the Lindberghs, joined in the desperate search.

Then Lindbergh found a note in an envelope on the window sill of the child's room. He did not open it, but shouted to Ollie Whately: "Don't let anyone touch it! Call the police and tell them that the baby has been taken!" He then grabbed a rifle and dashed outside into the darkness, hoping to track down the kidnapper whom he thought would be on foot somewhere on the Lindbergh estate. Hopewell chief of police Harry Wall arrived at the Lindbergh mansion first, but before he could begin a careful examination of the area, the estate was flooded with state police and officers from neighboring towns, all responding to a general alarm.

It was never determined exactly who had called in the additional police, but scores of troopers and patrolmen suddenly appeared and tramped through the mansion and about the grounds. A homemade ladder found next to the building at the window of the baby's room was so manhandled that any fingerprints the kidnapper might have left were obliterated. More than 500 sets of other fingerprints, mostly those of investigating officers, were taken from the ladder. The area around the house was muddy after a recent rain, but it was impossible to take any footprint casts since the state troopers had crisscrossed the area, trampling every clue underfoot. The ransom note was opened in the presence of the police. It was crudely written in ungrammatical English and read:

Have fifty thousand dollars ready, 25,000 in twenty-dollar bills 15,000 in ten-dollar bills, and 10,000 in five-dollar bills. In 4-5 days we will inform you where to deliver the money. We warn you for making anyding public or for notify the police. The child is in gut care. Indication for all letters are signature and three holes.

No clues were turned up by the police and no one was immediately found in the area who could testify to seeing anyone prowling about the Lindbergh place on the night of the kidnapping. Lindbergh realized that he had erred in having his butler immediately call the police. He preferred simply to pay off the kidnapper and retrieve his child with no police involvement. The only other approach, the most dangerous method, was to work closely with the police to develop a clever trap in which the child would be used as bait, the kidnapper caught, and the child returned unharmed. The procedure which they finally adopted fell somewhere in between. Unfortunately it proved ineffective and turned to disaster. Lindbergh soon realized that because each department had its own theories about the identities of the kidnappers and how best to handle them, the police were bumbling the procedures. In agony over the safety of his child, Lindbergh reached out to any and all who might be of help.

Meanwhile, the press blared the news of the kidnapping. It created the type of shock waves one might expect if a child had been abducted from the White House. Of course, the Lindberghs were American royalty of sorts, the colonel being the most famous and most respected citizen at the time. A number of strange characters became involved in the case. Society grande dame, Evalyn Walsh McLean, offered to pay $100,000, twice what the kidnappers were demanding, for the child's return. To that end, the naive heiress conferred with a bizarre hustler, Gaston Bullock Means, one-time agent for the Bureau of Investigation when that agency was under the command of William J. Burns during the corrupt Harding era.

Means had had a spectacular career of underhanded and illegal offenses. He had mulcted the federal government during WWI of considerable funds while pretending to spy on suspected German espionage agents. He had also functioned as a bagman for Jesse Smith and other Teapot Dome political chiefs, collecting huge sums of cash and delivering this money to cabinet ministers and federal officials of the Harding Administration. Means read of Mrs. McLean's humanitarian offer to pay off the kidnappers and immediately called and told her that, by virtue of his connections in the underworld, he was the perfect contact man.

Mrs. McLean gave Means several large cash payments for this purpose. When nothing happened over several months, she demanded results. Means suddenly appeared with a so-called underworld contact who informed the society matron that he was known as "The Fox" and represented the kidnap gang. More money was paid out. "The Fox" was later identified as a disbarred lawyer, Norman Whittaker, an associate of Means. Both Means and Whittaker were arrested and charged with fraud. They were convicted and given long prison terms. Such weird goings-on did nothing but confuse the desperate hunt for the Lindbergh child and caused one sensational claim after another to appear in print. Chicago crime czar Al Capone announced to the press that if the Lindbergh family would cooperate with *him,* he would have his men scour the country and return the baby within a week. Lindbergh did not respond to this offer.

John Hughes Curtis, another adventurer, called his socialite friends in Norfolk, Va., and put together an amateur detective club that made highly publicized searches for the baby. Curtis was given a great deal of attention by the press and the publicity went to his head. He began to hold daily press meetings and, for lack of anything better to tell reporters, he suddenly blurted that he had recently met with five persons, a woman and four Nordic sailors, who told him that they, indeed, were holding the baby and were waiting for the ransom. This story was wholly invented by Hughes who admitted the horrible fabrication when brought to the Lindbergh home and grilled by police captain John Lamb. Hughes was promptly escorted to the basement of the Lindbergh mansion where Lamb "beat the hell out of him," according to one reporter.

Lindbergh then began to receive more ransom demands by mail. There would be fourteen such notes sent to him. His greatest difficulty was in contacting the kidnapper. Moreover, his faith in the police was badly shattered, and he was constantly battling police efforts to locate the kidnapper. Two of the ransom notes had been sent from Brooklyn. New York police commissioner Edward Mulrooney learned that the two ransom notes were both posted from the same vicinity; he told Lindbergh that he planned to station men near these mailboxes, to identify anyone posting mail for the next week in an attempt to pinpoint the kidnapper. Lindbergh vetoed this plan, telling Mulrooney that such a tactic might alert the kidnappers who then might murder his child. Mulrooney backed off but, ironically, a third ransom note was received a few days later and from the same Brooklyn mailing area.

The kidnapper had thought out his series of ransom notes. To make sure that the Lindbergh family knew that his notes were genuine, all of the ransom notes bore the same symbol, three interlocking circles. No other notes were received from those pretending to be the kidnappers. Lindbergh then made another fateful decision. He brought an old family friend into the case, Dr. John F. Condon, asking the 70-year-old teacher to act as the go-between. Condon was to insert newspaper ads, as directed by the kidnapper, telling the kidnapper when the ransom money was ready. He was then to receive instructions on where to meet the kidnapper and deliver the ransom.

Condon was not a practical man. His role as arbiter of the child's fate caused him to see himself as the only lifeline between the child and his family. He imagined himself a Sherlock Holmes, an expert criminologist, as important to the case as the child or the Lindberghs. In his self-aggrandizing role, Condon helped to prolong the agony of the Lindbergh family, as well as confound police and confuse even the kidnapper. Condon enjoyed basking in the limelight of his appointed position and he play cloak-and-dagger games that gave him a sense of power. He devised his own code name, "Jafsie," which was the phonetic spelling of his initials, J.F.C. He used this name in his contact with the kidnapper. After Condon had responded to several ransom notes through advertisements in a Bronx, N.Y., paper, he met a tall man with a handkerchief covering his face in Woodlawn Cemetery in the Bronx on

the night of Mar. 12, 1932, eleven days after the kidnapping.

The man wore a suit, tie, heavy coat, and hat pulled low over his forehead. Only his deep-set eyes showed. He asked for the ransom money, but Condon told him that he could not bring the money until he had seen "the package," meaning the kidnapped Lindbergh baby. At that moment the man bolted, saying that there was a policeman inside the cemetery. Condon ran after him, catching up with him in a clump of bushes. In this murky area, the man finally said: "It is too dangerous. It might be twenty years. Or burn. Would I burn if the baby is dead?"

Alarmed at this statement, Condon asked about the child's condition and was told that the baby was fine. Then Condon embarked on a ridiculous harangue, telling the kidnapper that his mother would be ashamed of him and that he ought to leave the kidnapping gang. Condon offered him $1,000 to come with him and "get out of it." Instead of negotiating for the child's return, Condon attempted to reform the kidnapper! Condon listened to the man talk and, noting his accent, asked if he were German. The man quickly replied that he was "Scandinavian."

Then the kidnapper grumbled about not receiving the ransom which had not yet been assembled. He now demanded $70,000 instead of the original $50,000. Condon objected. The man began to leave, telling Condon that he should have brought the money. Condon then asked the man if he was connected to any friends of Betty Gow, the baby's nurse, and the man said no, that Gow was innocent of any crime. To convince Condon that he was dealing with the "right parties," the man showed the retired teacher the symbol of the three interlocking circles on a sheet of paper, the symbol carried on all the ransom notes. He told Condon that he would convince him further by sending the light blue sleeping suit, the child was wearing the night he was kidnapped.

The man reassured Condon that the baby was safe and that after the ransom was paid the following week the child would be returned. He claimed the child was on a boat some six hours away and that two women were caring for him. "You can put the baby's arms around Mrs. Lindbergh's neck," cooed the kidnapper. Condon was told to place an advertisement in next Sunday's edition of the Bronx *Home News,* an ad that would read: "Baby is alive and well. Money is ready." The man then shook hands with Condon and walked leisurely into the dark of the cemetery.

Later that night Condon described the man as having deep-set eyes, a small mouth, and high cheekbones. He also said that he was at least five-feet-ten-inches tall, was athletic and possessed a strong grip. Condon went on to describe the man's accent as decidedly German, pointing out that he pronounced the word "boat" as *boad,* the word "right" as *ride,* and the word "would" as *vould.* The kidnapper also pronounced the word "signature" as *singature.* The man had kept his hand inside his coat pocket, and Condon believed he had been armed. He spoke about others being involved in the kidnapping, which led Condon and the police to believe that they were dealing with a gang. A short time later, the baby's sleeping suit was sent to Lindbergh who was now convinced that he was dealing with the true kidnappers of his child. Also, Betty Gow found the baby's thumb guard on the gravel road leading to the Lindbergh mansion. This had apparently been dropped by the kidnapper as he ran from the Lindbergh house with the child in his arms.

Following instructions, Condon placed an ad in the Bronx *Home News* the following Sunday. More instructions soon arrived which led Condon back to another New York graveyard, St. Raymond's Cemetery, on the night of Apr. 2, 1932. Lindbergh, armed with a gun, accompanied Condon to this site. The ransom money, $50,000 in one package, and another $20,000 in a separate package, was in the car with Condon and Lindbergh. All of these bills were gold certificates and the serial numbers had been diligently recorded. Condon alighted from the car next to the cemetery and walked into the gloomy area, going down a path flanked by tombstones. No one was at the rendezvous point. He walked back toward the car and shouted to Lindbergh: "I guess

Anne and Charles A. Lindbergh.

Charles A. Lindbergh, Jr., kidnap victim.

The Lindbergh home in Hopewell, N.J., 1932.

The kidnap ladder next to the baby's bedroom.

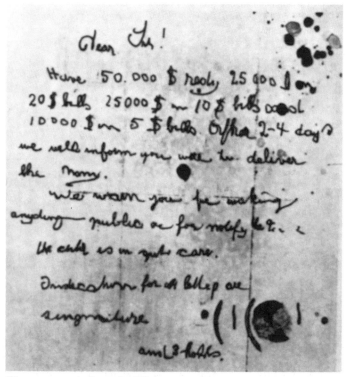

The ransom note from the kidnapper.

there's no one here! We better go back!"

At that moment a voice called: "Hey, Doctor!"

The figure of a man stood up behind a tombstone within the cemetery and waved Condon toward him. The man shouted loudly: "Hey, Doctor! Over here!" Lindbergh distinctly heard the man's voice, one that he would remember for the rest of his life.

Condon approached the kidnapper who said: "Did you got it, the money?"

"No, I didn't bring the money," Condon replied, walking toward the man. It is up in the car."

"Who is up there?" the kidnapper asked.

"Colonel Lindbergh."

"Is he armed?

"I don't know," Condon lied. Then he added: "No, he is not." Condon then began to bargain with the kidnapper, saying that $70,000 was too much money to be raised in a short amount of time, even for Lindbergh, and that "these are times of Depression. Why don't you be decent to him?" Condon said that he had brought $50,000.

The kidnapper, who had identified himself simply as "John" to Condon, shrugged and said: "Well, all right. I suppose if we can't get seventy, we get fifty."

Condon thought at that instant that John was acting alone, that there was no gang of kidnappers. How else could he make a decision to accept less of the ransom than what had been demanded? Condon returned to the car and proudly told the anxious Lindbergh that he had bargained with the kidnapper who was going to take only $50,000. Lindbergh handed him this money in a wrapped package, and Condon returned to the cemetery where he turned it over to the kidnapper. He then asked where the baby could be found. The kidnapper handed Condon an envelope, telling him that it contained instructions on how to locate the baby. The man calling himself John warned Condon that the envelope was not to be opened for six hours. Condon naively nodded as the man disappeared into the darkness of the cemetery.

Returning to the car, Condon handed the envelope to Lindbergh, telling him that they should do as instructed. The two then drove to a deserted house which Condon owned, one on Westchester Square, and there they sat, waiting. After a short while, Lindbergh opened the note. It was written in the same language as all the previous ransom notes and it read:

> the boy is Boad Nelly. it is a small Boad 28 feet long. two persons are on the Boad. the are in-nosent. you will find the Boad between Horse Neck Beach and Gay Head near Elizabeth Island.

Lindbergh and Condon were ecstatic. At last the child would be returned. The aviator immediately flew to the area which was in the Cape Cod district of Massachusetts. He searched every cove and bay but no one had ever heard of a boat named *Nelly*. A frantic search of the area ensued with Coast Guard cutters and even a Navy warship joining in. For days the waters around Elizabeth Island were scoured and scanned but the vessel was never found. This was because it never existed. It had been created in the mind of the kidnapper who knew that the Lindbergh child was already dead, that he had crushed the baby's skull on a rock only a few miles from the Lindbergh home after taking the baby from its crib on the night of the kidnapping and buried the small corpse in a shallow grave in some woods near the Lindbergh estate.

The search for the child went on through April and into May with no sign of the boy. The police by now felt that chances of finding the child were slim. The Lindbergh family continued to hope and pray that the little boy would still be found alive. All of that came to a tragic end on May 12, 1932, when two house movers pulled over to the side of a road near Mount Rose, a village only a few miles from the Lindbergh mansion. William Allen got out and went some fifty feet into the woods to relieve himself. In a small hollow, Allen saw what he first thought to be the remains of a dead animal, until, looking closer, he saw a baby's foot sticking up from the dirt. He bolted, running back to the truck to shout to his friend, Orville Wilson: "My God! There's a child, a dead child over there!"

Police were on the spot a few hours later. The Lindberghs were informed that their child had been dead, according to a local pathologist, since the night of the kidnapping. The bold kidnapper knew it, and still brazenly collected the ransom, risking the chance that the body had been found and that he himself would be arrested once he made his appearance to collect the money. No man but a supreme egotist would have been so bold, confident that the body would not be found and that his plans and moves were far superior to the gullible Lindberghs and their equally naive go-betweens, to believe that he could outwit the police and collect the ransom long before the body was discovered.

The Lindberghs were devastated. In their absolute grief, they remained silent. The public was in utter shock at the brutality of the crime as the details were graphically sketched in the nation's press. Hatred for the kidnapper-killer reached fever pitch and remained there for months. The Lindberghs, in their grief, left for Europe. Everything in the U.S. reminded them of their murdered child. They later sold the house in Hopewell, N.J. The hunt for the killer went on and on. He was now dubbed Cemetery John, after the rendezvous sites where Condon had met the kidnapper.

This crime had such impact that tough federal legislation was passed, and the Lindbergh Kidnapping Law went into effect, allowing the FBI to investigate these crimes, but restrictions for the Bureau remained. Agents were compelled to wait seven days after a kidnapping on the presumption that if the victim was not recovered in that period of time, the victim had been transported across a state line, thus making the crime a federal offense. That waiting period would be tested again and again, until agents were allowed to immediately act following the 1953 kidnapping of Robert Greenlease, Jr., which, because of the time delay, may have resulted in the boy's death.

Scores of suspects were picked up and relentlessly questioned. Even Betty Gow, the nurse, was suspect for a time. So was a maid in the Lindbergh home, English-born Violet Sharpe. She was picked up and questioned so many times that she was eventually driven to despair and committed suicide. A German-born gardener who worked for the Lindberghs also felt incredible police pressure and took his own life a short time later. The New Jersey State Police were criticized for their handling of the entire case, and years later, this force, while under the command of the aloof and authoritarian Colonel H. Norman Schwarzkopf, was blamed for pressuring the maid into taking her life—she drank poison rather than face another lengthy interrogation. Schwarzkopf was also criticized for mishandling the case, allowing his men to clumsily destroy clues and failing to follow up the slim leads that developed in the case.

Meanwhile, the ransom money began to appear only a few days after Cemetery John received the $50,000. The first bill, a $20 gold certificate, was deposited into the account of David Marcus at Manhattan's East River Savings Bank on Apr. 4, 1932. Marcus was tracked down, but he was proved innocent and he had no idea how he had come by the bill, the serial number of which matched one of the bills in the ransom payment. Hundreds of New York and New Jersey policemen continued to hunt for the kidnapper-killer.

In 1933, the gold certificates were called in and this left Cemetery John with an enormous amount of money that was dangerous to spend. The Treasury Department had issued a complete list of all the serial numbers of the bills passed to the killer and this list was sent to every bank and every business in the U.S. It became the civic duty of every person in the U.S., particularly in the New York-New Jersey area, to check any gold certificates against this list.

The ransom bills began to turn up with more regularity in 1933.

WANTED

INFORMATION AS TO THE WHEREABOUTS OF

CHAS. A. LINDBERGH, Jr.

OF HOPEWELL, N. J.

SON OF COL. CHAS. A. LINDBERGH

World-Famous Aviator

This child was kidnaped from his home in Hopewell, N. J., between 8 and 10 p. m. on Tuesday, March 1, 1932.

DESCRIPTION:

Age, 20 months
Weight, 27 to 30 lbs.
Height, 29 inches

Hair, blond, curly
Eyes, dark blue
Complexion, light

Deep dimple in center of chin
Dressed in one-piece coverall night suit

ADDRESS ALL COMMUNICATIONS TO
COL. H. N. SCHWARZKOPF, TRENTON, N. J., or
COL. CHAS. A. LINDBERGH, HOPEWELL, N. J.

ALL COMMUNICATIONS WILL BE TREATED IN CONFIDENCE

COL. H. NORMAN SCHWARZKOPF
Supt. New Jersey State Police, Trenton, N. J.

March 11, 1932

Top left, reward poster for the missing Lindbergh baby.
Top center, Bruno Richard Hauptmann, under arrest.
Top right, John F. Condon, the go-between during the kidnapping.
Center right, Hauptmann being booked for the kidnap-murder of the Lindbergh child.

Below left, the Hauptmann garage where police found most of the Lindbergh ransom money.
Below right, some of the ransom money hidden in a hollowed-out board found in the Hauptmann home.

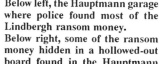
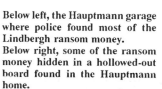

On May 1, 1933, someone calling himself J.J. Faulkner turned over $2,980 in gold certificates in compliance with the law that ordered these notes be exchanged for regular bills. All of the Faulkner bills were part of the Lindbergh ransom notes, but the federal reserve bank in New York that received these bills could not trace them back to Faulkner, although a Manhattan florist by that name was found and proven innocent. On Nov. 26, 1933, a New York movie ticket seller sold a ticket to a customer who paid with a $10 ransom note. The notes kept appearing throughout 1934. Then, on Sept. 15, 1934, an extraordinary event occurred. An alert, suspicious gas station manager, Walter Lyle, approached a 1931 blue Dodge sedan which had just pulled into his gas station, the Warner-Quinlan station at 127th Street and Lexington Avenue at the tip of upper Manhattan.

The driver ordered five gallons of gas. He got out of the car and stretched his long legs. He was a lean man with a prominent jaw, high cheekbones, and deep-set eyes. Lyle pumped the gas and then charged the driver 98¢. The driver gave him a $20 gold certificate. Lyle went into the station to get the change, but before he did so, he looked at the sheets sent by the U.S. Treasury Department that listed all the serial numbers of the Lindbergh ransom money. Lyle was an unusually conscientious citizen. He had read about the Lindbergh kidnapping and the bestial murder of the little boy. He religiously checked every gold certificate he received against the list. Lyle checked this gold certificate and then saw that it matched a number on the list, A73976634A. He then peered through the station window to note the license number on the car, 4U-13-41. Lyle wrote this number down on the gold certificate and then walked outside to hand the driver his $19.02 change.

"Don't see many of those gold certificates anymore," Lyle told the driver. The driver, speaking in what sounded like a German accent, agreed, adding that he had about 100 more at home. He then got into his car and slowly drove off. His gold certificate was deposited by Lyle, along with the rest of the station's receipts, at Manhattan's Corn Exchange Bank. Teller Miram Ozmec noticed the gold certificate with the license number on it and called authorities. New York and New Jersey state police, along with FBI agents, traced the license number. It belonged to 35-year-old Bruno Richard Hauptmann, a carpenter who lived at 1279 East 222nd Street in the Bronx. This was not far from the two cemeteries where the Lindbergh kidnapper, the man known as John, had met Dr. Condon. It was also close to the vicinity where many of the ransom notes had been mailed to the Lindbergh family.

Police moved in almost immediately. On Sept. 19, 1934, detectives waited until Hauptmann returned home and parked his car near the two-story house where he lived. Hauptmann, his wife Anna, and their infant son, Mannfried, occupied the second floor of the house, a five-room apartment with a living room, kitchen, two bedrooms, and bathroom. Officers approached Hauptmann as he sat behind the wheel of his car. Before he could utter a word, handcuffs were placed on his bony wrists. Detectives examined his large hands, noting that he had worked with them as a laborer. They were powerful hands, and the officers soon realized that Hauptmann closely matched the descriptions given of the kidnapper-killer, a man standing about five feet, ten inches, with deep-set eyes, high cheekbones, a small mouth, and a jutting jaw. He was lean and muscular. He had long legs, and when he walked, his stride was wide, a factor that later helped convict him of murder.

Officers hustled Hauptmann into his apartment and while his startled wife Anna stood with the baby in her arms, police stormed into each room, tearing the place apart in their search for the rest of the ransom money. They had already talked to the gas station manager, Walter Lyle, who had recalled his brief conversation with Hauptmann, telling officers about Hauptmann's remark that he had another 100 gold certificates at home. Officers did find $100 in gold pieces in a tin box. Hauptmann said that the gold pieces were what he was referring to in his talk with Lyle. The

officers went through Hauptmann's wallet and found another $20 ransom note.

Hauptmann said that he did not know where he had gotten the gold certificates. He said he had no more certificates than what the police had already found. While he was being questioned in his bedroom, Hauptmann kept furtively glancing out the window. One of the detectives noticed this and asked Hauptmann what he was looking at. The carpenter said he was looking at nothing in particular. The detective went to the window and saw a thin wire stretching from the window to the roof of a small garage behind the house. The car that Hauptmann parked there was a 1931 blue Dodge sedan that had been repainted from dark green to dark blue in 1932, shortly after the Lindbergh kidnapping.

"Is that where you have the money?" the detective asked Hauptmann.

The carpenter showed no emotion, saying in a monotone: "No. I have no money." He then explained that the wire was a homemade alarm system, that if someone opened the garage door during the night, lights would go on inside of the garage and frighten any burglar. The wire would also turn on a light inside the bedroom, alerting Hauptmann to the presence of intruders. Hauptmann was good at making homemade items, and the fact that he was a carpenter was not lost on the police, who knew that the ladder used in the Lindbergh kidnapping had been homemade. Hauptmann was arrested and then taken to police headquarters. There he was questioned by teams of police interrogators.

By then an inventory of the items of the Hauptmann household had been taken. Even though Hauptmann had been unemployed since the spring of 1932, he managed to pay $50 rent each month for his apartment, which contained a new console radio, purchased for $396. There was an expensive walnut bedroom set in his bedroom, recently purchased, and a costly ivory crib in which his baby son slept. He had recently purchased a $56 hunting rifle, a $109 canoe, which was stored in the garage, and paid $126 for a pair of powerful binoculars. Hauptmann sat passively as these purchases were read off to him. A detective returned from the Hauptmann house dangling a pair of new suede women's shoes, stating that the police had learned that Hauptmann had purchased these shoes only a few days earlier for his wife, using another ransom certificate. Also, Hauptmann had had plenty of money to take his wife on a luxury trip to Florida in 1933 and he also sent her home to Germany with first class accommodations for a family reunion in July 1932, three months after the Lindbergh ransom was paid. As an unemployed carpenter, Bruno Richard Hauptmann had been enjoying the good things of life with no financial worries.

Hauptmann coolly explained that he had made the money for all these items by playing the stock market. Then a detective approached Hauptmann and showed him a chisel, asking if he had ever seen it before. The carpenter said, no, he had not. He was shown the faded blue sleeping suit that the Lindbergh child had worn. He had never seen it before, said Hauptmann. The child's rust-stained thumb guard was shown to him. He had never seen that before either. For some time there was silence in the room.

Then a detective leaned close to the impassive Hauptmann and said with a firm voice: "Didn't you build a ladder and put it against the Lindbergh house, and didn't you go up that ladder and into that room and kidnap that child?"

For the first time, Hauptmann showed emotion. He trembled and tightly gripped the arms of the chair in which he sat. His piercing blue eyes widened and he shouted: "No!"

"And didn't you abandon that ladder and chisel and murder that child and strip the sleeping suit and thumb guard from its body?"

"No, I did not!," Hauptmann roared back.

The questioning went on, but Hauptmann was a strong-willed, steel-nerved suspect, one who would not yield under pressure and would not admit to anything dealing with the Lindbergh kidnapping. More discoveries, damning revelations, were made at the Hauptmann house, or, specifically, in the garage that so concerned

Bruno Richard Hauptmann, claiming innocence, is shown in his cell and in court; at right, his wife, Anna Hauptmann.

In court were, left and center, Charles and Anne Lindbergh, to watch, right, a smug and defiant Bruno Hauptmann.

Hauptmann repeatedly denied the kidnapping in court, saying another man gave him the ransom money to hold for safekeeping.

Bruno Richard Hauptmann. Behind a panel above Hauptmann's workbench, designed to conceal a hollow area, detectives, in the presence of Anna Hauptmann, found the cache of gold certificates from the Lindbergh kidnapping, each and every bill corresponding to the serial numbers on the Treasury list, a total of $18,860. Detectives also found maps Hauptmann had bought which pinpointed the area about the Lindbergh home and the Cape Cod area, the spot where Cemetery John had said the Lindbergh baby could be found on the mythical boat, *Nelly.* Also, found next to the hidden ransom money was a small Lilliput German automatic pistol, fully loaded.

Hauptmann said nothing about the maps, but he changed his story drastically regarding the ransom money hidden in his garage. He said he had been given this money by Isidore Fisch, a German national who had returned to Leipsig, Ger., and had died in early 1934. He said that Fisch had given him a box but did not tell him what it contained. He said that rain had caused damage to the box, which was stored in the garage and that he had opened this up to discover the money. Since Fisch owed him considerable sums, Hauptmann said, he merely took his share. All of this, of course, was another bold lie. Isidore Fisch was obviously a convenient dead scapegoat. Fisch had died in Leipsig, but he had left no money with Hauptmann.

The carpenter's brazen accusation of Fisch being the kidnapper was belied by Hauptmann's own actions. He was identified as having passed ransom gold certificates *six months* before he said Fisch had given him the money to hold for him. Also, Hauptmann's spending habits, when it came to the ransom notes, indicated that he had been exchanging tens and twenties for a number of years and had been living off this money, supporting his family with it, as early as spring of 1932, following the Lindbergh kidnapping.

Moreover, detectives quickly learned, Isidore Fisch, a small, mild-mannered businessman who bore no resemblance to Cemetery John (while Hauptmann fit the descriptions given by Dr. Condon) had no criminal background. Bruno Richard Hauptmann's case was an entirely different story. The carpenter was not only a convicted felon, but he had committed crimes in Germany that *employed the identical modus operandi used in the Lindbergh kidnapping.*

Investigators had quickly obtained Hauptmann's background. He had been born and raised in Kamenz, Ger., the youngest of three sons who had all fought in the WWI, Bruno being the only survivor. He had been a machine gunner and had been wounded and gassed. In 1918, when mustered out of the German army, Hauptmann, at nineteen, was penniless. He had had eight years of grade school and two years of trade school, where he had learned carpentry. Yet, there was little or no work for him in depression-torn Germany. In March 1919, Hauptmann, along with Fritz Petzold, a young friend who had served with him in the army, went to the nearby town of Bernbruch.

Here, Hauptmann scouted about and learned the location of the home of Mayor Schierach, determining exactly which second-story room was the mayor's bedroom. On a night when Hauptmann knew the mayor was out of town, he stole a ladder and, under cover of darkness, climbed the ladder to the mayor's bedroom. Hauptmann rifled the mayor's bureau drawers and took more than 100 marks and a silver watch. A few days later, the same pair again used a ladder to climb into the second-story bedroom of wealthy leather tanner Edward Scheumann and stole more money. Some days after this burglary, Hauptmann, using a ladder again, climbed into another bedroom and stole 200 marks and a gold watch.

While returning to Kamenz on foot, Hauptmann and Petzold saw two women pushing baby carriages filled with food, which, in impoverished Germany, was worth more than gold. Hauptmann produced a pistol and aimed it at the women, ordering them to turn the food over to him. They began to run, frantically pushing the carriages in front of them. Hauptmann shouted: "We'll shoot! We're radicals!" He shrewdly picked the word that would send

terror into anyone then living in Germany, *radicals,* since the country was overrun with radical revolutionaries who had a complete disregard for life. The women stopped and Hauptmann took the food.

The women begged Hauptmann to leave them something to eat. He refused and ordered them to "keep quiet or get a bullet." This was the kind of merciless act that Hauptmann would exhibit years later when planning to murder the Lindbergh child. Only the most ruthless, cold-blooded of killers could plan on kidnapping and *then* murdering the child while nervelessly continuing to negotiate and obtain the ransom for a child he knew to be dead. More importantly, all of Hauptmann's early burglaries were committed in the same fashion, *through the use of a ladder,* the same modus operandi he would employ in kidnapping the Lindbergh child.

Hauptmann and Petzold were captured at the end of March 1919, and Hauptmann, the leader, was convicted of burglary and sentenced to five years in prison. As soon as he was imprisoned, Hauptmann tried to solicit help from one of the revolutionary groups in Germany, writing to the Spartacists, pleading that they intercede for him, saying: "I have always been a faithful Spartacist." He received no reply. He was paroled four years later in March 1923. Hauptmann was arrested again a short time later for selling leather belting he had stolen from various shops in Kamenz. He was jailed, pending trial. A few days later, while being allowed exercise in an open yard, Hauptmann escaped, leaving his prison clothes in a neat bundle and with a note stating: "Best wishes to the police."

Within a few weeks, Hauptmann had made his way to the port of Hamburg and there he stowed away on the liner S.S. *George Washington.* He stayed in a hold for days, living off food and water he had brought with him, but he was discovered a few days before the ship landed in New York. Hauptmann was taken to Ellis Island for questioning. He gave the alias of Perlmeyer and was returned to Germany. He tried to stow away again on another ship the following month but was discovered before the ship left Hamburg. He was held on board while police were called. The desperate Hauptmann, knowing he would be exposed as a wanted fugitive, suddenly jumped off the ship, swam to the pier, and hid among the pilings, later escaping. This bruising experience did not deter Hauptmann.

He managed to smuggle himself aboard another liner, and wearing a disguise and carrying stolen identity papers, he landed in New York without being detained. Hauptmann had only a few pennies in his pocket, but he soon got work in a German community in the Bronx. He later met Anna Schoeffler, who had immigrated to the U.S. on Jan. 1, 1924, from Germany. They were married on Oct. 10, 1925. Hauptmann worked during these years as a dishwasher, dyer, and finally a carpenter, earning $50 a week. His wife also worked and they frugally saved every dime not spent on essentials. In the late 1920s, Hauptmann reportedly dabbled in the stock market, then plunged, using up much of his savings and that of his wife's. Still, the couple earned enough money for Hauptmann to buy a 1931 dark green Dodge sedan. This was the car that was repainted dark blue a short time after the Lindbergh kidnapping.

By 1931-32, the building boom collapsed and Hauptmann was out of work. He took odd jobs, but he could barely keep up with his bills. The Hauptmanns used up their savings, but in early April (only a few days after Cemetery John picked up the $50,000 ransom money from Dr. Condon in St. Raymond's Cemetery) Hauptmann announced to his wife that he had worked out a foolproof way to play the stock market that would bring in money regularly, large amounts of money. The uneducated Anna Hauptmann, a housewife who did not bother with "men's business," asked no questions. She was at first worried but was soon surprised to see her husband providing plenty of money. He sent his wife to Germany in July 1932 to visit with his mother in Kamenz and also hire a lawyer to settle with the police the old warrants still pending on him. The following year the statute of

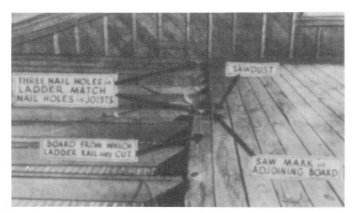

Boards in Hauptmann's attic which matched the kidnap ladder.

The kidnapper's ladder which matched the boards in Hauptmann's attic.

Wood expert Arthur Koehler matched the floorboard and ladder.

The army of reporters covering the Hauptmann trial.

Hauptmann, found Guilty, sentenced to the electric chair.

limitations on the old charges automatically called for their dismissal.

Now, with plenty of money, Hauptmann could return to Germany without fear of being arrested and imprisoned. He made plans to take his family to Germany in November 1934. These plans evaporated when he was arrested on Sept. 19, 1934, and charged with kidnapping and murdering the Lindbergh baby. After his arrest, Hauptmann was told he would be sent to New Jersey to stand trial for the kidnapping and killing of Charles Augustus Lindbergh, Jr. Hauptmann immediately retained lawyers to fight this extradition, a battle that waged for months until Hauptmann was ordered to stand trial in a New Jersey court. He was placed on trial on Jan. 2, 1935, in Flemington, N.J., appearing before 71-year-old Judge Thomas Whitaker Trenchard, one of the most distinguished jurists of his day, a judge who expressed himself with clear-mindedness and whose verdicts in murder trials had never been reversed.

Hauptmann was defended by Edward J. Reilly, a show-boating attorney who dressed like a tycoon, adorning himself with British-tailored suits, spats, and vests with silver piping. He believed in overwhelming juries with his own success and importance. Reilly had an amazing string of acquittals, but with Hauptmann, he was dealing with a truculent, arrogant client whose conduct in court alienated the bench and the jury. Prosecutor David Wilentz, thirty-nine, was wiry, aggressive, and indefatigable in presenting minute and involved detail in a concise manner. His approach was one of clarity, but he was also zealous in prosecuting Hauptmann, whom he rightly portrayed as a German "superman" with nerves of steel, one who mocked and smirked at attempts to convict him.

On the stand Hauptmann was defiant and aloof. He told his story about Isidore Fisch, saying Fisch had given him the ransom money to hold. When he related this tale, a sardonic smile played about Hauptmann's thin lips. Wilentz caught this look of contempt and turned on Hauptmann abruptly, saying: "This is funny to you, isn't it?"

"No, that is not true."

"You think you're a big shot, don't you," Wilentz said.

"No. Should I cry?" Hauptmann's face was a portrait of jutting granite.

"You think you are bigger than everybody, don't you?"

"No, but I know I am innocent."

"You wouldn't tell if they murdered you—"

"No!"

"Will power is everything with you."

"No, it is—I feel innocent—that keep me the power to stand up."

Wilentz portrayed Hauptmann as an inveterate liar, recounting how he had repeatedly lied about the gold certificates in his possession, and after the ransom money had been found in his garage, how he again lied, saying that Fisch had given him the money. Hauptmann, for the first time in many hours of testimony, exploded. His eyes narrowed as he leaned forward in the witness chair and thrust out a finger at Wilentz, waving it like a weapon at the prosecutor, shouting: "Stop that!"

A few minutes later, Wilentz stared back at Hauptmann, saying: "I see that you have stopped smiling. Things have become a little more serious."

Hauptmann's low voice answered: "I guess it isn't any place to smile here."

Wilentz then returned to Isidore Fisch, the man Hauptmann claimed had given him the Lindbergh ransom money to hold. The prosecutor described the life and career of Fisch, a mild-mannered businessman who was a friend of the Hauptmanns'. He pointed out that Fisch had died in spring of 1934 in Germany, and Hauptmann had said earlier that it was not until some time *after* Fisch's death that he examined the box he had been given by Fisch and found the money and then took sums he felt Fisch owed him. Wilentz then pointed out that Fisch had never given Hauptmann any money to hold, that he was a pauper and that if he had been

the kidnapper, he certainly would have taken the money with him to Germany, where he died in debt. In fact, Wilentz said, it was Hauptmann who was known as a man of means from his so-called stock deals, deals that Hauptmann failed to prove ever existed and it was Hauptmann who had loaned Fisch $5,500 of the ransom money. Hauptmann almost left the witness chair when he yelled his denial at this.

The prosecutor stood before Hauptmann, leaning close and saying: "Didn't you write to Mr. Fisch's family in Germany after his death, claiming that you have given Fisch $5,500 from your own private bank account?" Hauptmann again began to loudly deny when Wilentz produced the letter Hauptmann had written the Fisch family, reading the demands Hauptmann had made in the letter for the return of the $5,500.

"Well, I—" Hauptmann grumbled, squirming in the witness chair.

"My God," Wilentz said with a look of disgust, "don't you ever tell the truth?"

Handwriting experts took the stand to state that Hauptmann's handwriting and that of the writer of the ransom notes were one and the same. The defense put up its own handwriting experts but these experts were feeble in their claim that there were some "differences" in the handwriting. Copies of the ransom notes and Hauptmann's handwriting were blown up and shown to the jury, and even with the naked, untrained eye, most agreed, the writings were identical. Moreover, Hauptmann continued to mispronounce the very words that Cemetery John mispronounced in his conversations with Dr. Condon, *boad* for "boat," for instance.

Charles Lindbergh sat in the court throughout every day of the long trial. At one point, while sitting at the prosecution's table, he leaned forward and he was seen wearing a shoulder holster with a gun tucked into it. No one said a word about it. Lindbergh was called as a witness, and after hearing Hauptmann speak, said that the defendant's voice was the same he had heard calling after Dr. Condon on the night Cemetery John met with Condon at St. Raymond's Cemetery to receive the ransom money and turn over a message that led Lindbergh on a futile and agonizing search for his son, a child already murdered. Dr. Condon then appeared and identified Hauptmann as Cemetery John. The eccentric Condon had withheld his official identification of Hauptmann earlier when seeing him in a police line-up, preferring to make his grandstand identification in court where it would be more widely reported. These identifications damned Hauptmann as the man who received the ransom money, making sure of his conviction of extortion. But the next witnesses Wilentz paraded before the court were the ones who sent Bruno Richard Hauptmann to his death as convicted kidnapper and murderer.

The first of these was Cecelia Barr, a ticket agent who worked in the booth at Loew's Sheridan Square Theater, who positively identified Hauptmann as a man who gave her one of the gold certificates from the ransom money when he bought a ticket in November 1933, fully six months before Hauptmann said Fisch gave him the money to hold in a sealed box. John Perone, one of two taxi drivers who had delivered ransom notes to the Lindberghs, identified Hauptmann as the man who paid him to deliver the letter. Millard Whited, a student who lived close to the Lindbergh home outside of Hopewell then took the stand to state that he had seen Hauptmann twice walking about the woods near the Lindbergh home, studying it from a distance.

Then elderly Amandus Hochmuth took the stand. Hochmuth had a house right at the corner where the highway from Hopewell met the dirt road that led to the Lindbergh mansion. Hochmuth, eighty, stated that he spent a good deal of time sitting on his front porch and watching traffic, especially cars turning onto the dirt road where, because of the grade, the cars were forced to slow down or go into a ditch. He clearly stated that toward dusk on the day of the kidnapping, a Dodge sedan, dark green (the color of Hauptmann's car before he had it repainted dark blue) had turned onto the road and had stopped abruptly to avoid going into the ditch. The car had stalled. Hochmuth got up from his chair on the porch, he said, and walked out to the road. He was only a few feet from this car and saw the driver clearly. In the back seat of the car, Hochmuth said, was a wooden ladder that had several sections to it.

"Do you mind stepping down (from the witness chair) and showing us this man," Wilentz asked Hochmuth. The witness left the chair and slowly walked to the defendant's table. He unhesitatingly walked up to Bruno Richard Hauptmann. As all in the courtroom held their breath at this dramatic moment, Amandus Hochmuth reached out a steady hand and dropped it on Hauptmann's shoulder. "This is the man," he said in a resolute voice.

Hauptmann lost all composure, turning his head quickly to look at his wife who sat in the visitor's gallery. Shouted Hauptmann: *Der alter ist verrucht!"* ("The old man is crazy!")

Wilentz did not rest his case at this point, but brought forth the ladder used by the kidnapper and left at the side of the Lindbergh home after the child was taken on that cold and windy night of Mar. 1, 1932. Taking the stand was Arthur Koehler, the U.S. government's top wood expert who had been examining the kidnapper's ladder for more than two years. He knew every inch of that ladder, and he described it in detail, pointing out the various types of wood employed in the building of it. It was homemade, and built so that it telescoped one section into the other, so that it could, when its sections were joined, fit into the back seat of a car.

This ladder had much to say through the expert observations of Arthur Koehler. It had to have been made by someone who was an experienced carpenter. Koehler reported how an exact duplicate of this ladder had been made at his specifications. When the kidnapper's ladder was first inspected, Koehler stated, it was noted that the top rung of the ladder had broken under the kidnapper's weight as he went back down the ladder with the Lindbergh baby in his arms. (It could not have broken *before* the kidnapper entered the room since the space between the top rung and next rung was too widely separated to allow the kidnapper to then reach the room.) In the reconstruction of the ladder, the top rung was the exact same weight, length, and width as the original top rung. It was tested up to certain weights and broke at the weight of 210 pounds. The Lindbergh child had been weighed only a day before the baby's kidnapping and the child weighed exactly thirty pounds. This meant that the kidnapper weighed 180 pounds which was Bruno Richard Hauptmann's exact weight when he was arrested. Also, the space between each rung of the ladder had been built by the kidnapper to accommodate his own long step or stride, almost twice the distance between the rungs of a normal ladder. Hauptmann's long legs and his stride were measured against the spaces of these ladder rungs and fit his normal leg reach.

Moreover, the wood used in the kidnapper's ladder, identified Hauptmann as surely as if he had left a perfect set of fingerprints in the child's room. The ladder had been made from pieces of old wood, scavenged from a number of unknown sources. All of the wooden sections, except one, bore nail holes that contained rings of rust. These were obviously used pieces of wood that had been outside in the weather. One side section, however, bore square nail holes, uncommon for U.S. builders, but typical of European nails, and these holes were dry and without rust. This led Koehler to order a search of the Hauptmann house, especially the garage. He figured that, for this last side panel in the ladder, Hauptmann had cannibalized wood inside his house or garage. The attic of Hauptmann's house verified Koehler's suspicions. A piece of a floorboard in the attic had been cut lengthwise by Hauptmann and used to make the ladder. Koehler matched the grain, rings, and lines of the wood of the ladder section to the piece of board that remained in Hauptmann's attic. The match was perfect.

Against this overwhelming evidence, Reilly could present no effective witnesses. He gave an impassioned plea for his client's life, stating that *he* did not believe Hauptmann was guilty, but he reserved his final statements for Lindbergh, turning to the grim-faced aviator, saying: "May I say in closing that he has my profound respect. I feel sorry for him in his deep grief and I am quite sure that all of you agree with me that his lovely son is now within the gates of Heaven." Reilly had shown more concern for the victim than he had for his client, the steel-eyed Hauptmann.

Wilentz then addressed the jury with his closing argument on Feb. 12, 1935, and he showed no mercy in his attack on the defendant. Unlike the docile, almost indifferent summation by Reilly, Wilentz stepped forth like David about to slay Goliath, confident, demanding, and speaking, he believed, for every man, woman, and child in the U.S. He held up a Bible, which his opponent had earlier employed in his closing argument. "'Judge not lest ye be judged,' my adversary says. But he forgets the other Biblical admonition: 'And he that killeth any man shall surely be killed, shall surely be put to death." Wilentz went to the table holding exhibits of evidence and placed the Bible here, as if it, too, were part of the prosecution's evidence.

"For all these months, since October of 1934," Wilentz said while slowly pacing in front of the jury, "not during one moment has there been anything that has come to light, that has indicated anything but the guilt of Bruno Richard Hauptmann. Every avenue of evidence leads to the same door: Bruno Richard Hauptmann." Then Wilentz took a rather xenophobic view, one that gathered in the specter of sinister foreigners with super egos, the implication certainly conjuring the image of Nazi Germany's Adolf Hitler and the evil Nazi myth of the German Superman.

"What type of man would murder the child of Charles and Anne Lindbergh?" Wilentz asked the jury. "He wouldn't be an American. No American gangster ever sank to the level of killing babies. Ah, no! An American gangster that did want to participate in a kidnapping wouldn't pick out Colonel Lindbergh. There are many people much wealthier than the colonel. No, it had to be a fellow who had ice water, not blood, in his veins. It had to be a fellow who had a peculiar mental makeup, who thought he was bigger than Lindy—a fellow who, when the news of the crime came out, could look at the headlines screaming across the page, just as the headlines screamed when Lindy made his famous flight. It had to be an egomaniac who thought he was omnipotent."

Wilentz then described the character of Bruno Richard Hauptmann, slapping his hands together as exclamation points to his sentences. He pointed out that Hauptmann trusted no one and never told the truth to his wife, telling her that he was making money in the stock market without a shred of proof to support this claim to her or to the authorities after his arrest. Hauptmann was the kind of man, Wilentz pointed out, who held up at gunpoint women pushing baby carriages, as he had done in Germany, a man who would not talk, "even if you killed him. And let me tell you, men and women of the jury, the State of New Jersey and the Sate of New York, and the federal authorities have found an animal lower than the lowest form in the animal kingdom, Public Enemy Number One of this world—Bruno Richard Hauptmann!"

The prosecutor then slowly pointed out that Hauptmann had all along shouted that he was being framed. Who was framing him, Wilentz asked. Dr. Condon? Amandus Hochmuth? Arthur Koehler? For what purpose? There was none, there was only the truth. And if Hauptmann was as innocent of this terrible crime as he insisted he was, why then, Wilentz asked, did he fight so hard not to be extradited from New York to New Jersey? "When he heard that the State of New Jersey wanted him, did he say, 'I'll come right over?'"

Then Wilentz launched into a graphic description of the crime. He portrayed Hauptmann climbing up the ladder and entering the child's room through the window. As all eyes were focused upon Hauptmann, Wilentz went on: "I think a stranger could walk into a child's room, if the child were asleep, without the child awakening." He slammed his palms together loudly. "But let me tell you this! This fellow took no chances on the child awakening. He crushed that child right in the room, into insensibility. He smothered and choked that child right in that room. That child never cried, never gave any outcry, certainly not! The little voice was stilled right in that room. *He* wasn't interested in the child. Life meant nothing to him. That's the type of man we're dealing with.

"Public Enemy Number One of the world! That's what we're dealing with! You're not dealing with a fellow who doesn't know what he's doing. Take a look at him as he sits there! Look at him when he walks out of this room today—panther-like, gloating, feeling good!"

Hauptmann's face was red and his lips tightly closed as if he were fighting against making a loud outburst. He squirmed in his chair, using a handkerchief to wipe away perspiration. He had not shown the slightest appearance of uneasiness during the course of the long trial until this point. Now he moved in his chair, crossing and recrossing his legs.

Wilentz went on relentlessly: "Certainly he stilled that little child's breath right in that room! That child did not cry out when it was disturbed. Yanked from the crib—how? Not just taken up. The pins were still left in the bed sheets. (The nurse had pinned the baby's sleeping suit to the bed sheets to keep it from rolling over.) Yanked and its head hit up against the head-board—must have been hit. *He* couldn't do it any other way. Certainly it must have hit up against the board. Still no outcry. Why? Because there was no cry left in the child. Did he use the chisel to crush the skull at the time or knock it into insensibility? Is that a fair inference? What else was the chisel there for? To knock that child into insensibility right there in that room."

"And the note in the nursery. This fellow had planned this crime. He wasn't going to let any faker come in and take that money. He had something on the note so that Colonel Lindbergh could tell, if another one came, that it was from the right party. So he put his signature on it. You couldn't reproduce it. The blue circles, the red center and the holes—*b* in blue, for Bruno; *r* in red, for Richard; holes, *h* for Hauptmann." Then Wilentz pointed out another glaring error Hauptmann had made. He recalled for the jury his question to Hauptmann about the police asking him to duplicate the ransom notes and how he had asked Hauptmann on the witness stand if the police had asked him to write the word *singnature*. "They did," Hauptmann had replied.

"Why?" asked Wilentz of no one. "Because it was spelled that way in the ransom note and Hauptmann wanted to show that he didn't write it. So he swears that the police told him to spell it *singnature*." Again the slapping of the hands, like cymbals clashing. "Now, men and women of the jury, take those writings Hauptmann made in the police station. Go through every one of them and you won't find the word *signature* anywhere. He was never asked to write it, right or wrong! And still he swears on the witness stand that he was told by the police to misspell it!"

Wilentz closed down his attack, like a plane prop slowing its revolutions, saying solemnly: "There are some cases in which a recommendation for mercy might do—but not this one, not this one! Either this man is the filthiest and vilest snake that ever crept through the grass or he is entitled to an acquittal. And if you believe as we do, you have got to convict him. If you bring in a recommendation of mercy, a wishy-washy decision, that is your province, and once I sit down I will not say another word, so far as this jury and its verdict is concerned. But it seems to me that you will have the courage to find Richard Hauptmann guilty in the first degree."

As he sat down, Vincent Burns, an eccentric non-denominational religious leader, tried to interrupt the proceeding but he was led away before his comments could have created a mistrial. After long, precise instructions to the jury by Judge Trenchard, the jury retired. The next day, the four women and eight men of the jury found Hauptmann Guilty and recommended the death sentence. A number of appeals were filed on Hauptmann's behalf, but all were denied. While Hauptmann awaited execution in the New Jersey State Prison, he showed no emotion. He did not talk to other prisoners in the death house and ignored all those who walked to the execution chamber before him. John Favorito, a convicted murderer who had the cell next to Hauptmann's on Death Row, went to the electric chair on Oct. 15, 1935. He expected Hauptmann to say goodbye to him but when he passed Hauptmann's cell he saw the kidnapper-killer soundly sleeping and snoring.

Hauptmann's own turn to sit in the electric chair finally came on Apr. 3, 1936. He remained silent to the last. Bruno Richard Hauptmann, convicted baby-killer, walked wordlessly to the death chamber, sat down in the electric chair, and executioner Robert Elliott then sent the current into his body that killed him at 8:44 p.m. Anne and Charles Lindbergh were in London at the time. Their thoughts about the execution of their child's murderer were not recorded. Anna Hauptmann continued to believe that her husband was innocent, despite the overwhelming evidence against him. She lobbied for decades to have her husband's case re-opened, re-examined, to have him somehow proven to be anything other than what the world believed him to be, an inhuman beast who had slaughtered an innocent child. See: **Hall, Carl Austin.**

REF.: Alix, *Ransom Kidnapping in America;* Allen, *Only Yesterday;* ____, *Since Yesterday;* Block, *Science vs. Crime;* Boar and Blundell, *The World's Most Infamous Murders;* Brant, *The Story of the Lindbergh Kidnapping;* Busch, *Prisoners at the Bar; CBA;* Clutterbuck, *Kidnap and Ransom;* Condon, *Jafsie Tells All;* Davis, *The Hero: Charles A. Lindbergh and the American Dream;* Demaris, *The Director;* Elliott, *Agent of Death;* Furneaux, *Courtroom USA, vol. 1;* Gribble, *Hallmark of Horror;* Haring, *The Hand of Hauptmann;* Hibbert, *The Roots of Evil;* Horan, *The Desperate Years;* Hynd, *The Giant Killers;* ____, *Murder, Mayhem and Mystery;* Kobler, *Capone;* Lindbergh, *Hour of Gold, Hour of Lead;* Lustgarten, *The Story of Crime;* Marten, *The Doctor Looks at Murder;* Messick, *Kidnapping;* ____, *Secret File;* Moorehead, *Hostages to Fortune;* Morland, *Pattern of Murder;* Nash, *Almanac of World Crime;* ____, *Bloodletters and Badmen;* ____, *Citizen Hoover;* Ottenberg, *The Federal Investigators;* Powers, *Secrecy and Power;* Radin, *Twelve Against Crime;* Reppetto, *The Blue Parade;* Robinson, *Science Catches the Criminal;* Rowland, *More Criminal Files;* Sann, *The Lawless Decade;* Scaduto, *Scapegoat;* Scott, *The Concise Encyclopedia of Crime and Criminals;* Sheridan, *I Killed For the Law;* Shoenfeld, *The Crime and the Criminal—A Psychiatric Study of the Lindbergh Case;* Sparrow, *The Great Abductors;* Thompson and Raymond, *Gang Rule in New York;* Toledano, *J. Edgar Hoover;* Unger, *FBI;* Vitray, *The Great Lindbergh Hullabaloo: An Unorthodox Account;* Waller, *Kidnap: The Story of the Lindbergh Case;* Wendel, *The Lindbergh-Hauptmann Aftermath;* Whipple, *The Lindbergh Crime;* ____, *The Trial of Bruno Richard Hauptmann;* Whitehead, *The FBI Story;* Wicker, *Investigating the FBI;* Wilson, *Encyclopedia of Murder;* (FILM), *Miss Fane's Baby Is Stolen,* 1934.

Hauser, Frederick I. (AKA: **Red Hauser**), 1926-72, U.S., asslt.-mur. On Sept. 1, 1945, Frederick I. "Red" Hauser, nineteen, a sailor recently discharged after being wounded in the South Pacific, drove to the Johnson Restaurant in Monessen, Pa., and took Anna Elizabeth Dreyer, seventeen, a waitress at the restaurant, for a drive through several counties at 2 a.m. Hauser parked the car and began to make sexual advances. Dreyer's attempt to defend herself led to an intense and prolonged struggle which ended when Hauser beat her until she became unconscious.

According to Hauser's confession, he was unable to revive Dreyer so he dragged her back into his car, drove two miles, and abandoned her in some underbrush. Hauser said he then wrapped her belt tightly around her throat, and left her without knowing whether she was alive or dead. When Dreyer's nude body was discovered in a patch of poison ivy, Hauser claimed repeatedly that he did not assault her.

Police released Hauser when he convinced them that he had dropped off Dreyer about a hundred yards from her home at her request. Later police tried to find him for further questioning, but discovered that he had disappeared with Pete Prokopovech, seventeen, also of Monessen. Leonard Hobbs, a farmer who hired them, called police when he recognized Hauser's picture in a newspaper.

On Dec. 9, 1945, Hauser pleaded guilty to murder and was sentenced to life imprisonment by Judge W. Russell Carr. Seventeen years later, on Feb. 9, 1963, Hauser was paroled. He died on May 26, 1972, as a result of an accident at his place of employment. REF.: *CBA*.

Hauser, Joseph, prom. 1977, U.S., brib. The Securities and Exchange Commission filed a suit against Joseph Hauser, a Beverly Hills insurance company executive, alleging that he and others misappropriated $1.5 million in National American Life Insurance Company premiums paid for by the Teamsters Union Benefit Fund, for personal gain. In November 1976, Hauser was indicted on six counts of racketeering and bribery in connection with money paid to unions to induce them to purchase health insurance policies. He was tried and convicted on four counts of bribery, receiving a sentence of two-and-a-half years in prison and a fine of $40,000.

Two others were also indicted. Samuel S. Schwartz, a Los Angeles trustee of the local of the International Ladies' Garment Workers Union, and Darrel Shelton, a trustee of the welfare fund for a local of the Bridge, Structural and Ornamental Iron Workers, were charged with accepting bribes. Schwartz was acquitted, but Shelton was convicted on charges of filing a fraudulent tax return. He was sentenced to a six-month jail term and fined $5,000. REF.: *CBA*.

Hauser, Kasper, c.1812-33, Ger., (unsolv.) mur.? Kasper Hauser was found wandering about Nuremberg, Ger., in 1828 and was taken to the local police station. He appeared bewildered and could not recall who his parents were or anything about his background. Although he looked to be about sixteen years of age, he had the mentality of a three-year-old. His mannerisms were primitive and he could barely feed or dress himself. In his possession was a letter supposedly written by a laborer who had been looking after him since he was an infant. Enclosed within this letter was another allegedly written by his mother which gave his name and birth date and also stated that his father had been a cavalry officer.

Many believed that Hauser was actually the abandoned son of the Grand Duke Charles Louis of Baden, a rumor which received an official denial. Hauser was later placed in the care of educationist Georg Friedrich Daumer and then left with Lord Stanhope in 1932. On Dec. 17, 1833, Hauser was found dying of stab wounds. He stated before his death that the wounds had been inflicted by an unknown assailant. A similar incident had taken place prior to this in 1829, and Hauser claimed a stranger was responsible. Some believed the wounds may have been self-inflicted on both occasions. Hauser remains one of the great enigmas in German history. He became the subject of Jacob Wasserman's novel, *Casper Hauser*, published in 1909. REF.: *CBA*.

REF.: *CBA*; Poynter, *Forgotten Crimes*; Stevens, *From Clue to Dock*; (FILM), *Every Man For Himself and God Against All*, 1975.

Havana Conference, 1946, Cuba, org. crime. In December 1946, sensing a growing prosperity following WWII, the heads of the powerful American crime families met in Havana, Cuba, to settle their disputes and to plan the future. The meeting was called by Meyer Lansky and Charles "Lucky" Luciano, who had been exiled to Italy. The two sought to reassert Luciano's dominance over New York's Genovese and Costello families, who were beginning a territorial feud. Members attending the conference included Joe Adonis, Joe Bonanno, Frank Costello, Vito Genovese, Tommy Lucchese, Giuseppe Magliocco, Willie Moretti, Mike Miranda, and Augie Pisano from New York; Anthony Accardo, Charlie Fischetti and his brother Rocco Fischetti from Chicago; Carlos Marcello and Phil Kastel, from New Orleans; Steve Magaddino from Buffalo; and Santo Trafficante from Florida. Frank Sinatra also attended to act as window dressing to legitimize the conference.

The conference became a nightmare for Luciano. Genovese called for Luciano's retirement and complained about Albert Anastasia, the mob's most noted executioner, who seemed to have

become "kill crazy." He had been calling for the murder of Harry Anslinger, the director of the U.S. Bureau of Narcotics. While Luciano didn't advocate the mob's involvement in narcotics, he quickly realized that Anastasia might be a valuable ally against the increasingly hostile Genovese. The other crime chiefs, aware of the tremendous potential of drug trafficking, also opposed the aging Mafia chieftain. The third strike against Luciano was the Mafia "hit" ordered on Bugsy Siegel, his former partner. Siegel was suspected of skimming money the mob put up for the construction of the Flamingo Hotel in Las Vegas. A year later, Siegel was executed in the California home of his girlfriend, Virginia Hill.

After the conference, Luciano attempted to stay in Cuba, but the Cuban government forced him to return to Italy after Genovese reportedly tipped off the U.S. government about Luciano's whereabouts. Luciano was never able to return to the U.S., his New York empire disintegrated and the war he sought to prevent in Havana was fought in the boroughs of New York. REF.: *CBA*.

Haviland, John, 1792-1852, U.S., penal architect. John Haviland designed and built some of the first prisons in the U.S., during the 1830s: the Eastern State Penitentiary in Pennsylvania, the Western Penitentiary in Pittsburgh, and the New Jersey State Prison at Trenton. Western Penitentiary was constructed in the form of a V with the administration offices at the hub, whereas the Trenton Prison offered five wings stemming from administration offices which formed a half circle. Trenton, in that early day, came closest to the concepts of British penologist and reformer Jeremy Bentham who was first to design a prison in the form of a penopticon, later used in the 1921 contruction of Joliet State Prison in Illinois. In Haviland's Trenton design he included two-story wings, exercise yards detached from the cell blocks, and cell doors that opened into corridors. REF.: *CBA*.

Hawes, Nathaniel, 1701-21, Brit., rob. Nathaniel Hawes, was apprenticed to an upholsterer in London but robbed his master twice in less than two years. He was tried at the Old Bailey and sentenced to seven years of penal servitude in the British colonies. The sentence was not carried out, however, because Hawes turned in a man named Phillips who had bought from Hawes most of the goods that the young man had stolen from the master. Phillips received a sentence of fourteen years penal servitude, and Hawes was pardoned.

Hawes then joined a gang of robbers led by John James and Jonathan Wild. The gang fought over the division of some loot and Hawes, worried that James might incriminate him, informed on his leader. James was tried, convicted, and executed. Hawes, originally bound for Newgate, was sent to New Prison because several Newgate prisoners threatened to murder him for giving evidence against James. Hawes and another prisoner escaped and committed several more robberies together. After having split off on his own, Hawes tried to rob a gentleman who grabbed the gun from the robber's hand and forced him to surrender.

Hawes refused to enter a plea to his indictment because the jailers had seized the fine clothes in which he intended to be hanged. The judge cited him for contempt, and sentenced him to be pressed to death. Hawes was placed on his back with a 250-pound weight pressed against him, and after seven minutes, he begged to be taken back to court where he pleaded not guilty. However, the evidence against him was complete and Hawes was convicted and hanged at Tyburn on Dec. 22, 1721.

REF.: *CBA*; Mitchell, *The Newgate Calendar*.

Hawk, Ralph, prom. 1937, U.S., arson-mur. Ralph Hawk made plans to marry 20-year-old Catharine Gelwix on Jan. 1, 1937, but in the meantime found a new love in a nearby town. On Dec. 31, Hawk and Gelwix sat up late discussing their upcoming wedding. Then Hawk left, saying he might return. He later went back to the Gelwix house where he doused a sleeping Mrs. Gelwix and her daughter, 15-year-old Helen Louise, with kerosene. Setting them ablaze, he found his fiancée and struck her on the head with a flashlight. He then soaked her with kerosene and set her on fire. A couple sitting outside in a car saw the fire and the young man rushed into the house, pulling Catharine to safety.

Police had little to connect Hawk with the crime until they discovered that Mrs. Gelwix had written a letter to Hawk, accusing him of dating another girl. After questioning the girl, they arrested Hawk and he confessed to the crime. He was tried, convicted, and sentenced to death.

REF.: *CBA; Rice, Forty-five Murderers.*

Hawke, Sir **Edward Anthony,** b.1896, Brit., lawyer. Served as senior prosecuting counsel for the Crown from 1945-47, as common sergeant of the city of London, and as recorder. He prosecuted murder cases, including those of Arthur Robert Boyce, Neville Heath, and Donald Thomas. REF.: *CBA.*

Hawke, Sir **John Anthony,** 1869-1941, Brit., jur. Became a judge in 1913, and in 1923 became attorney general to the Prince of Wales. He served on the King's Bench Division of the High Court from 1928-41, and was also a member of Parliament. He presided over the murder trial of James Thomas Collins. REF.: *CBA.*

Hawkins, Dexter Arnold, 1825-86, U.S., lawyer. Reformer who condemned political corruption and helped oust the Tweed Ring, whose members swindled millions of dollars from New York City's treasury. REF.: *CBA.*

Hawkins, Edward W., d.1857, U.S., mur. Edward Hawkins, a resident of Estill County, Ky., made his living by theft and had reportedly killed four men. He was also a notorious forger, counterfeiter, and horse thief. In the spring of 1857, James M. Land and James Arvine caught Hawkins red-handed as he was rustling some of their horses. They placed him under guard and were taking him to the local sheriff when Hawkins broke free, grabbed a gun, and shot both men to death. This shooting was witnessed by a farmer who later led lawmen to Hawkins. The killer was convicted and hanged on May 29, 1857.

REF.: *CBA; The History and Confession of the Young Felon, Edward W. Hawkins.*

Hawkins, Sir **Henry (Baron Brampton),** 1816-1907, Brit., jur. Henry Hawkins was a well-known British lawyer and judge who handled the cases of several notorious criminals. He prosecuted Arthur Orton, the swindler who made a fraudulent claim to the Tichborne estates. He won a conviction, and Orton was sentenced to seven years in prison. In 1876, Hawkins was raised to the bench where his summing-up speeches during his twenty-two years as a judge were said to often be biased.

Hawkins presided at the trial of Charles Peace, who was then using the alias Ward, for shooting a policeman. Hawkins ordered him put in prison for life. The judge also heard the Louis Staunton murder case, in which Staunton and three others were convicted but later reprieved. Hawkins retired from his post in 1898.

REF.: *CBA; Scott, The Concise Encyclopedia of Crime and Criminals.*

Hawkins, Moll, c.1677-   , Brit., theft. Moll Hawkins spent three years apprenticing to a button-maker in Maiden Lane before she became a thief. One of her favorite tricks involved dressing in expensive clothing and arriving early in the morning at the home of a wealthy woman. Carrying an empty clothes box, she asked the servant if the woman was awake as she claimed to be delivering a specially ordered garment. When the servant went to give the message to his mistress, Hawkins filled her box with whatever she could. She once stole £50 worth of china from Lady Arabella Howard of Soho Square in this manner.

Hawkins, also a proficient pickpocket, was condemned on Mar. 3, 1703, for stealing goods from the shop of Mrs. Hobday in Paternoster Row. Using a popular ruse of the day, she won a nine-month reprieve by claiming to be pregnant. On Dec. 22, 1703, the 22-year-old Hawkins was executed at Tyburn.

REF.: *CBA; Smith, Highwaymen.*

Hawkins, Sir **Richard (Hawkyns),** c.1562-1622, Brit., pir. Son of magistrate Sir John Hawkins. He began a trip around the world in 1593, sailing around Cape Horn and up the west coast of South America. He pillaged Valparaiso and was caught in San Mateo Bay, Peru, in 1594. He was imprisoned in Spain from 1597-

1602, but was freed after a price was paid for his release. Later he served as vice admiral on a voyage against Algerian pirates, from 1620-21. REF.: *CBA.*

William Hawkins, with spiked club raised, leading a riot, 1768.

Hawkins, William, d.c.1768, Brit., riot. At the Old Bailey in July 1768, William Hawkins tried for assaulting and wounding two servants of the lord mayor of London, and for participating in a riot protesting the imprisonment of John Wilkes. A political reformer, Wilkes had attacked King George III in his paper *The North Briton.* He was expelled from the House of Commons in 1764 for seditious libel and outlawed for failing to stand trial. When he returning from exile on the continent in 1768, Wilkes was elected to Parliament, stood trial on the old charges, and was fined and imprisoned.

On May 9 a crowd had gathered outside the lord mayor's residence. They carried a wooden pole on which hung a boot and a petticoat, apparently political symbols. Mr. Way, a passerby, testified that he saw Hawkins beating Philip Pyle and Thomas Woodward, the lord mayor's servants, with a nail-studded stick. When the servants began to drag Hawkins into the Mansion House, the mob rescued him. Way collared him as he was escaping and, with the help of the servants, dragged him into the house. Hawkins was later found Guilty of rioting and sentenced to death.

REF.: *CBA; Mitchell, The Newgate Calendar.*

Hawkshurst Gang, See: **Kingsmill Gang.**

Hawley, Thomas Porter, 1830-1907, U.S., jur. Served as district attorney of Nevada County, Calif., from 1863-64, and as chief justice for the state of Nevada from 1872-90. He was nominated to the district court of Nevada by President Benjamin Harrison in 1890. REF.: *CBA.*

Hawthorne Inn, prom. 1920s, U.S., org. crime. A nondescript, two-story, brick and tile building at 4833 22nd Street in the Chicago suburb of Cicero, was the impregnable fortress of Al Capone during his 1920s crime empire. Every window was covered with bullet-proof shutters, while armed guards were stationed at each entrance. The second floor, known as Capone's Castle, was opulently furnished for the mobster's use. On Sept. 20, 1926, Capone was the target of rival mobster Hymie Weiss. Eleven automobiles carried Weiss' machine gun toting thugs as they sprayed the Hawthorne Inn with more than 1,000 rounds of ammunition, barely missing Capone, who was drinking a cup of coffee in the first-floor restaurant. Only Louis Barko, a Capone gangster, and an innocent woman seated in a car with her infant son, were wounded in the onslaught. The woman was shot in the forehead and nearly blinded, but Capone paid $5,000 in medical bills to save her sight. When reporters asked who had attacked, Capone told them to keep their eyes on the morgue, and three weeks later, Hymie Weiss was wheeled in.

Following Capone's demise, the Hawthorne Inn was renamed the Towne Hotel. Owned by Rossmar Realty, Inc., whose president was Chicago mobster Joseph Aiuppa, the hotel continued to be a syndicate meeting site. On May 23, 1964, Illinois State Police with an FBI warrant raided a dice game around the corner from the building and discovered a hidden passage leading to the basement of the Towne Hotel. Fifteen gamblers and gamekeepers were arrested as the game was broken up for the third time in less than a year. On Feb. 17, 1970, the Towne Hotel was completely destroyed by fire. At an inquisition about the building's ownership, Joseph Aiuppa pleaded the Fifth Amendment sixty times.

REF.: Asbury, *Gem of the Prairie; CBA;* Kobler, *Capone;* McPhaul, *Johnny Torrio;* Spiering, *The Man Who Got Capone.*

Hay, Donald Alexander, 1933- , Can., kid.-rape. When 12-year-old Abby Drover disappeared on her way to her Port Moody, Can., school on Mar. 10, 1976, a massive search and a reward offer turned up nothing. One of the searchers, 43-year-old Port Moody resident Donald Alexander Hay, a neighbor of the Drover family, looked avidly for the child, all the while holding her prisoner in a dank, cell-like room under his garage. The six-by-six-foot dungeon was soundproofed and littered with garbage, a filthy mattress, a toilet, and a sink. Hay had dragged the child into the prison, beat her savagely and repeatedly molested her. He then left her alone for weeks, with packaged foods to live on. Abby read her school books again and again by a single light, exercised, and prayed in her timeless confinement. On Sept. 6, 1976, police were called to the Hay residence to investigate a disturbance and found Hay climbing through a trap door behind an empty cupboard in his garage. Constable Paul Adams watched in shock as Drover, frail and emaciated, climbed from the shaft, ending her six months of torture.

A note from Abby Drover to Donald Hay was found in the dungeon. It said: "I know you think I am stupid and like you say everybody is entitled to their own thoughts but I do believe in God and I do believe in friends. And I just wish you would be my friend. I also know that I will get out of here so I'm not worried. God has helped me so far and He will help me to finish." On Feb. 3, 1977, Hay was convicted of kidnapping and sentenced to life imprisonment, with another eight years for statutory rape.

REF.: *CBA;* Nash, *Among the Missing.*

Hay, George, 1765-1830, U.S., jur. Representative to Virginia House of Delegates, and U.S. attorney for Virginia from 1803-1816. He was nominated to the district court of Virginia by President John Quincy Adams in 1825. REF.: *CBA.*

Hay, Gordon, b.c.1940- , Scot., mur. On Aug. 5, 1957, Gordon Hay met 15-year-old Linda Peacock at a fair in Scotland, and talked with her for less than a minute. The next night, at about 10:20, the 17-year-old struck Linda on the head and strangled her in a cemetery in Biggar, a town between Glasgow and Edinburgh. The graveyard was not far from Hays' boarding school. When detectives found her body the next day there was a bite mark on her right breast.

Hay was arrested after police investigations and forensic odontology linked him to the murder, the first murder suspect in Scotland to be identified by teeth marks. Hay was convicted of murder, but because he was a minor at the time of the crime, was sentenced to be held in custody.

REF.: *CBA;* Simpson, *Forty Years of Murder.*

Hay, Lucy (Countess of Carlisle), 1599-1660, Brit., treas. Beautiful, clever daughter of Henry Percy, the ninth earl of Northumberland. She revealed the king's plan to have the Five Members of the House of Commons arrested in 1642. She became affiliated with the Presbyterian party, and during the second Civil War she became an ardent supporter of royalty. After betraying secrets of both sides she was imprisoned in the Tower of London from 1649-50. REF.: *CBA.*

Haya de la Torre, Victor Raúl, 1895-1979, Peru, rebel. Exiled for inciting unrest against Augusto Leguia's government from 1923-31. He established the Alianza Popular Revolucionaria Americana, the Aprista movement, in 1924. Losing the presidential election, he was put in jail from 1931-33. He was a presidential candidate in 1962 until an army coup. A new election was held in 1963 and he lost to the army candidate, General Belaúnde. REF.: *CBA.*

Hayden, Herbert H., prom. 1879-80, Case of, U.S., mur. In 1879, the body of Mary Stannard, twenty-two, once a servant of Reverend Herbert H. Hayden, was found in one of Hayden's fields in Madison, Conn. Her throat was cut, her skull was fractured, and there was arsenic in her stomach. Stannard had spoken to several people about her recent pregnancy by Hayden, and explained that he was going to give her something to induce an abortion. She also said that she was planning to meet Hayden in the field to pick berries and discuss their future. Unable to account for himself during the time of the killing, Hayden was arrested after it was discovered that he had purchased an ounce of arsenic "to kill rats" the day of his former servant's death. One of his parishioners gave police an ounce of arsenic which he had found in the minister's barn. Hayden was held in jail for a year while a Yale professor went to England to analyze the arsenic in the barn and that from Stannard's stomach. At the three-month trial, a clairvoyant testified to the defendant's innocence, the first such incident in an American courtroom. A hung jury resulted in Hayden's release.

REF.: *CBA;* Denton, *Who Killed Mary Stannard?;* Hayden, *An Autobiography;* Nash, *Almanac of World Crime;* Pearson, *Instigation of the Devil; Poor Mary Stannard!, A Full and Thrilling Story of the Circumstances Connected with Her Murder;* Wilson, *Encyclopedia of Murder.*

Hayer, Talmadge, See: **Malcolm X.**

Murderess Catherine Hayes and accomplices Thomas Billings and Thomas Wood, decapitating John Hayes.

Hayes, Catherine (Catherine Hall), 1690-1726, Brit., mur. Born in Birmingham, England, young Catherine Hall left home at fifteen in 1705. Near the army officers' barracks in Great Ombersley, Worcestershire, soldiers paid her a few pieces of gold and she became the camp's mistress. For the next few years, she followed the army, until she met a wealthy Warwickshire farmer named Hayes. He hired her as a domestic against the wishes of his wife, who considered her a temptation to her son and other local boys.

John Hayes, the 21-year-old son, soon fell in love with Hall and in 1713, married her, to the great consternation of his parents. For six years, the couple lived on the family farm, but Catherine yearned for the city and in 1719 they moved to London where Hayes quickly became a successful coal merchant, moneylender, and pawnbroker. But Catherine's voracious appetite for luxuries led Hayes to cut off her allowance, and by 1725, the couple were resolute enemies. Catherine said it would be no more sin to kill her husband than to kill a mad dog.

A young tailor, Thomas Billings, appeared on the Hayes' doorstep one day looking for a place to stay. It was later rumored that Billings was Catherine's illegitimate son, but she carried on an affair with him. The situation was further complicated by the arrival of Thomas Wood, a merchant who became another lodger. Catherine began another affair with Wood, who happened to be a close friend of John Hayes, but soon was conspiring with Catherine to murder him.

The strangulation-burning execution of Catherine Hayes, 1726.

Catherine tempted Wood and Billings with the £1,500 inheritance she would get on Hayes' death. On Mar. 1, 1725, their plan to intoxicate Hayes and then kill him was put into effect. Billings and Wood bet a guinea that their host could not drink six pints of wine and stay sober, and John Hayes accepted the dare. However, after a few minutes the liquor took effect and Hayes collapsed on his bed. Billings crashed a hatchet down on Hayes' skull, but the wound was not fatal. Mrs. Springate, a tenant in the building, heard screams and went to investigate. She was assured that it was merely a "noisy guest." Meanwhile Billings and Wood had made a bloody mess of the murder, but finally succeeded in killing John Hayes. Catherine ordered the two men to cut off Hayes' head so it would be harder for authorities to identify the victim.

Wood and Billings let the head fall into oaken bucket and then threw both into the Thames, but they landed on an embankment and a watchman retrieved the head. Authorities impaled the head on a stake and paraded it around St. Margaret's Square so that it might be recognized. It became a great local curiosity as the frightened Wood went into hiding and Billings resumed his affair with Catherine.

Mr. Ashby, a business associate of John Hayes, identified the head, and Catherine and Billings were both arrested and charged with murder. Wood made his way back to London but was quickly apprehended and became the first to confess. He explained that John Hayes had been killed for being an "atheist and a free thinker." Later, the rest of Hayes' corpse was found at Marylebone. All three defendants were found Guilty and ordered executed. Wood, however, died in prison before the scheduled execution date of May 9, 1726. Billings was taken before Catherine and then hanged in chains.

Catherine was taken by cart to Tyburn, where the executioner, Richard Arnet, was to strangle her before being lighting the stake. But the plan went awry and Arnet released the rope just as the fire was lit. Catherine perished in the flames after enduring four hours agony.

REF.: Atholl, *Shadow of the Gallows;* Bleackley, *Hangmen of England; CBA;* de la Torre, *Villainy Detected;* Forster, *Studies in Black and Red;* Lambton, *Echoes of Causes Celebres;* Laurence, *A History of Capital Punishment;* Mitchell, *The Newgate Calendar;* Nash, *Look For the Woman;* O'Donnell, *Should Women Hang?;* Potter, *The Art of Hanging;* Whitelaw, *Corpus Delicti;* Wilson, *Encyclopedia of Murder*

Hayes, Charlotte, prom. 1700s, Brit., pros. Charlotte Hayes was a well-known madame, operating the Cloister, a brothel in London. Her elegant establishment catered to politicians, including members of Parliament. She retired with about £20,000.

REF.: *CBA;* Henriques, *Prostitution.*

Hayes, Daniel, and **Moriarty, Daniel,** prom. 1888, Ire., mur. Daniel Hayes and Daniel Moriarty were accused of fatally shooting Jerry Fitzmaurice, a farmer in Ireland. The two suspects were tried and convicted. Just before executioner James Berry hanged them in 1888, Hayes protested his innocence and Moriarty confessed that he had lied, implicating others to try to save himself.

REF.: Atholl, *The Reluctant Hangman; CBA.*

Hayes, Edward, prom. 1900s-30s, U.S., fraud. For about thirty years, Edward Hayes sold a drug called Marmola, which was purported to reduce weight caused by hypothyroidism. The drug was challenged by the Federal Drug Administration which won a cease and desist order in 1937, and federal agents seized the drug. Hayes died in 1939 before the decision was overturned in 1941. The Supreme Court, however, later reinstated the cease and desist order and the FDA continued to confiscate Marmola.

REF.: *CBA;* Young, *The Medical Messiahs.*

Hayes, Capt. **Henry** (AKA: **Bully**), prom. 1800s, Int'l., smug.-pir. In 1857, Captain Henry Hayes swam after and captured pirate Eli Boggs, who had jumped over the side of his ship near the coast of China. Hayes, a U.S. citizen, collected a $1,000 reward, and stole two of Boggs' chests that contained silver coins. He used this money to finance a group of bandits who robbed South Sea Island trading posts, ran guns, and abducted islanders to be sold as slaves.

In the 1870s, his Pacific operations were stopped by the British Navy and missionaries. While being held under arrest before being sent to Australia to be tried on charges of piracy, Hayes was freed by his pirate friend Ben Pease. Five years later, in Manila, Hayes was confined in jail, but freed after convincing a bishop that he was devoted to religion. He was later killed by a Scandinavian mate and tossed into the sea.

REF.: *CBA;* Mitchell, *Pirates.*

Hayes, Thomas Frank, b.c.1883, and **Leary, Daniel J.,** prom. 1930s, and **Kelly, Thomas P.,** prom. 1930s, U.S., consp. Thomas Hayes was elected mayor of Waterbury, Conn., in 1930. He immediately appointed Daniel Leary comptroller, and Thomas Kelley executive secretary, to assist him. In 1936, their activities were questioned by the *Republican* and the *American,* two Waterbury newspapers. The three were accused of taking city money, misrepresenting audits, paying exorbitant rates to certain contractors, and keeping disorderly records.

Accused of stealing more than $1 million from the city, they were indicted in 1938 on conspiracy charges. They were tried and all were found Guilty. Hayes, fifty-six years old, and Leary were each sentenced to ten to fifteen years in prison, and Kelly received seven to twelve years. REF.: *CBA*.

Haymarket, The, 1860s-1913, U.S., vice center. The Haymarket was the longest-running and most notorious gambling and vice den in New York and was known throughout the U.S. Any male visiting New York from the late 1860s to 1913, the year the place was closed, invariably heard about The Haymarket. Located on Sixth Avenue, just south of Thirtieth Street, this den was in the hub of the old Tenderloin District which was under the supervision of the venal police inspector, Alexander S. "Clubber" Williams. This area was also known as Satan's Circus and was the center of prostitution, gambling, drugs, and every known criminal pursuit.

The notorious Haymarket in 1879.

The Haymarket was a three-story structure painted a sickening sulphuric yellow, and above its main entrance hung a sign reading: "Haymarket—Grand Soiree Dansant." Inside, a large stage was surrounded on three sides with two levels of boxes, cubicles, and galleries where customers could watch the raucous, all-night show featuring can-can chorus lines and lacivious half-clad Eyptian dancers. Women were admitted free to The Haymarket but men were required to pay 25¢ each to gain entrance.

Prostitutes used the cubicles for assignation with customers, charging a few dollars for sexual pleasures. Most men patronizing these low whores invariably got drunk and were jackrolled for their wallets and valuables by the scores of thieves that infested the place, along with dozens of pickpockets. Although violence was kept to a minimum in The Haymarket, the place did have an occasional shooting or stabbing. Police overlooked the activities here since Inspector Williams and his men enjoyed a considerable percentage of the den's profits. By 1913, when reform swept New York, The Haymarket was finally closed.

REF.: Asbury, *The Gangs of New York; CBA*.

Haymarket Riot, 1886, U.S., mob vio.-mur. Chicago's Haymarket Riot of 1886 marked the bloodiest battle to date between labor and management, but it was really a confrontation between radical elements of the emerging labor movement and the Chicago police who had been labeled a tool of big business. At the center of this storm was the unions' struggle to establish an eight-hour work day. During the mid-1880s organized labor had scored great triumphs, the first of which was the organization of workers on Jay Gould's Southwestern Railroad System in 1885. Following this achievement, the membership of the Knights of Labor skyrocketed in one year from 100,000 to 700,000. In 1886 labor leaders turned their attention to establishing an eight-hour work day. Since the most radical elements of the labor movement were headquartered in Chicago, it became the hub of activity. The labor chiefs set May 1, 1886, as the date for a nationwide strike.

However, many of the most extreme radical groups were divided on what measures to take to assure success. The anarchists, under the direction of the dwarf-like Johann Most, advocated violence at all costs. Most insisted that the labor movement be of "a violent revolutionary character," and claimed further that "the wage struggle alone will not lead us to our goal." Dynamiting the property of the rich was advocated by such anarchist publications as *Alarm,* published by Albert Richard Parsons. According to *Alarm,* dynamite "will be your most powerful weapon, a weapon of the weak against the strong." Such revolutionary tactics were not lost on the authorities, particularly in Chicago, then a hotbed of anarchist activities.

The May 1, 1886, rallies across the nation saw between 200,000 and 300,000 workers gather in peaceful demonstrations and call for an eight-hour work day. The following night, anarchist George Engel, a leather-lunged rabble-rouser, addressed a large throng at the Bohemian Hall. He urged workers to blow up all police stations, slaughter the police and free all the prisoners so they could join union ranks to help battle the business tycoons. On May 3, 1886, violence erupted in Chicago at the McCormick Harvester Plant which had been struck by 50,000 workers. Anarchist August Spies was present and led a large number of members of the Lumber-shovers union in a clash with scab workers. As the picketing workers battled scab employees police charged into their midst, attacking the strikers. Officers fired pointblank into a line of strikers, killing one worker and injuring scores more. Labor leaders instantly responded by sending out thousands of flyers in English and German calling for a mass meeting at Haymarket Square the next night, at which time, the anarchists' circulars promised, labor leaders would "denounce the latest atrocious acts of the police."

About 3,000 workers began to fill up Haymarket Square on the night of May 4, 1886. There was much milling about and little organization. Mayor Carter Harrison, who owed much of his electoral support to labor, wanted to demonstrate that he was the working man's friend. He told Police Captain John "Clubber" Bonfield, to hold his 180 policemen in reserve, saying that he did not expect trouble, but if any violence erupted, he would call off the meeting. By 7:30 p.m. a few speakers addressed the crowd in docile terms and, believing nothing would happen, Mayor Harrison went home. However, on Jefferson Street, August Spies climbed onto a large wagon and shouted loudly to the jostling crowd: "Please come to order. This meeting is not called to incite any riot!" When Albert Richard Parsons next shouted: "To arms! To arms!" his meaning was ambiguous that the workers did not know whether Parsons wanted them to attack the authorities or merely arm themselves. Many in the crowd were already armed with pistols, knives, and clubs. One member of the crowd held a bomb which he had recently made.

At this point, a fire-eating, lanky man with a full white beard and long white hair mounted the wagon. He was an English-born teamster, Samuel Fielden, and he screamed at the crowd: "You have nothing more to do with the law!...Throttle it! Kill it! Stab it! Do everything you can to wound it!" Clustered about the wagon were the die-hard anarchists of the labor movement in Chicago and thus the most responsive to Fielden. As Fielden's harangue continued, members of the crowd began to shout back that action should be taken immediately, that certain men of authority and business should be shot or hanged.

As Bonfield and his solid ranks of police began to close in on the wagon, Fielden yelled to the officers: "We are peaceable!" At that moment—some later claimed the word "peaceable" was a signal—a round, cast iron, dynamite bomb was thrown over the heads of the workers, from the area of the wagon, landing directly in front of the advancing police ranks. The bomb exploded with an ear-splitting roar and cut down the police like a row of corn beneath a giant scythe. The crowd and the police were stunned and amazed. This was the first time dynamite had been used as a weapon in America and the shock of its terrible toll was visible on the faces of all present.

Police firing on the Haymarket rioters in Chicago, May 4, 1886, with many killed and wounded on both sides.

Samuel Fielden urging protest as the bomb explodes.

CPD Captain Michael J. Schaack, who wrote a book about the riot.

Four anarchists who caused the riot are hanged on Nov. 11, 1887.

Almost half of the police on hand were decimated: eight men fatally wounded and another sixty-seven officers seriously injured. The police regrouped within minutes and charged the workers, pistols blazing. The workers fled in all directions but many were cut down by the intense police fire. Long after the throng fled, the popping of guns could be heard echoing down the streets. Many workers were also killed and dozens were wounded; an exact toll of the deaths among the workers was never determined. The leading anarchists in the crowd escaped. The bomb-thrower was never identified. Police quickly arrested the chief anarchist labor leaders in the next few days and charged them with murder.

At a quick trial, presided over by Judge Joseph Easton Gary, eight of the anarchists were found Guilty of inciting to riot and murder. Five of these men were sentenced to death. These were August Spies, George Engel, Adolph Fischer, Louis Lingg, and Albert Richard Parsons. Samuel Fielden and Michael Schwab were given life sentences and Oscar Neebe was sentenced to fifteen years in prison. All of the condemned men, except Parsons, were German-born anarchists. Parsons was the only native American whose forefathers had fought in the Revolution. Parsons had been born in Montgomery, Ala., and, as a teenager, had fought in the Confederate Army during the Civil War. After working as a reporter in Galveston and Houston, Parsons, in 1873, had moved to Chicago where he became deeply involved in Socialist politics and where he formed the first printers' union. As time went on, he became more radical and later adopted anarchist views. According to many historians, Parsons and the others were singled out for persecution by Melville E. Stone, of the Chicago *Daily News,* who, in the words of one journalist, "railroaded" these men "to the gallows...because they were labor agitators and outspoken enemies of the capitalist system."

Before the execution date, one of the condemned men, Louis Lingg, committed suicide in his jail cell by exploding a dynamite cap in his mouth. The other four men mounted the gallows inside the Chicago jail on Nov. 11, 1887. The gallows had been built at the north end of the jail, as high as the second tier. More than 180 people, fifty of whom were newspaper reporters, filled makeshift pews beneath these high gallows. At 11:50 a.m., Spies, Fischer, Engel, and Parsons were paraded along the second floor tier, accompanied by a dozen heavily armed deputies. All the condemned men wore white shrouds that fell to their ankles. Beneath these shrouds, the prisoners' hands were manacled behind their backs. Once on the gallows, the four were placed under waiting nooses and their feet were tied together.

A guard moved behind all four men, dropping the nooses around their necks, and tightening them, fixing the knots under each doomed man's left ear. Fischer, who seemed to be the calmest of the group, smiled weakly when the guard affixed the rope around his neck, saying almost as if joking: "Don't draw it so tight. I can't breathe." All was in readiness. The guards left the platform and it appeared that the prisoners would not be allowed to say any last words. Spies suddenly boomed: "You may strangle this voice but my silence will be more terrible than speech!" Shouted Engel: "Long live anarchy!" Fischer repeated the same words, but in German: *"Hoch die Anarchie!"* Parsons then said: "Shall I be allowed to speak?" He looked at the impassive crowd before him and said: "Oh, men of America—" Sheriff Matson standing to the side said something to Parsons in a low voice. Parsons replied loudly: "Let me speak, Sheriff Matson!" He then turned to the crowd again and said: "Shall the voice of the people be heard—"

At that moment the executioner pulled a lever which released the entire platform upon which all four men stood and they shot downward together, Parson cut off in mid-sentence. None of the nooses had been fixed correctly, and all four men were allowed to slowly strangle to death. It was later claimed that this sloppiness on the hangman's part was deliberate. The authorities wished to cause the condemned men as much pain as possible, it was said, in retribution for the pain of the eight slain police officers. Fischer, a giant of a man, struggled violently in his

death throes, writhing wildly at the end of the rope. Four doctors stood next to the dangling men, checking their pulses and heartbeats. All died within eight minutes.

The remaining three anarchists languished in jail until Governor John Peter Altgeld, an idealistic reformer, pardoned Fielden, Schwab, and Neebe on June 26, 1893. This act caused a tornado of criticism that swept Altgeld from office in the following elections and virtually ruined his career. His actions had been dictated through conscience after he had reexamined the case and found that Judge Gary had committed flagrant improprieties and displayed great prejudice against the anarchists during the trial. But Altgeld's ruin was brought about by a public that was convinced for years afterward that unions and violent anarchy were synonymous. The Haymarket Riot did much to set back the struggling cause of labor in the U.S. Not until the turn of the century would millions of workers join the labor unions.

Until that time, the attitude toward unionism and workers was brutally summed up by Police Captain Bonfield, who, following the slaughter of his officers, thundered: "The trouble is that these strikers get their women and children mixed up with them, and we can't get at them. I would like to get three thousand of them in a crowd without their women and children and I will make short work of them!" See: **Altgeld, John Peter.**

REF.: *The Accused—The Accusers: The Speeches of the Eight Chicago Anarchists in Court;* Adamic, *Dynamite: The Story of Class Violence in America; Anarchy at an End;* Asbury, *Gem of the Prairie;* Barnard, *Eagle Forgotten: The Life of John Peter Altgeld;* Butterfield, *The American Past; CBA; The Celebrated Anarchists' Case;* Chaplin, *Rumor, Fear and the Madness of Crowds; The Chicago Anarchists and the Haymarket Massacre;* David, *The History of the Haymarket Affair;* Dedmon, *Fabulous Chicago;* Demaris, *America the Violent;* _____, *Brothers In Blood: The International Terrorist Network;* Duke, *Celebrated Criminal Cases of America;* Farr, *Chicago;* Flinn and Wilkie, *History of the Chicago Police;* Ginger, *Altgeld's America;* Harrison, *Stormy Years;* Heaps, *Riots, U.S.A.;* Hofstadter and Wallace, *American Violence;* Lait and Mortimer, *Chicago: Confidential;* Laquer, *Terrorism;* Lewis and Smith, *Chicago, A History of Its Reputation;* Lindberg, *Chicago Ragtime: Another Look at Chicago, 1880-1920;* Lum, *A Concise History of the Great Trial of the Chicago Anarchists in 1886;* McLean, *The Rise and Fall of Anarchy in America;* McPhaul, *Deadlines and Monkeyshines;* Mencken, *By the Neck;* Nash, *Almanac of World Crime;* _____, *People to See;* Reppetto, *The Blue Parade;* Schaack, *Anarchy and the Anarchists;* Spies and Parsons, *The Great Anarchist Trial;* Trumbull, *The Trial of the Judgment: A Review of the Anarchist Case;* (FICTION), Fast, *The American: A Middle Western Legend;* Norris, *The Bomb.*

Haynes, Dennis E., prom. 1850s, U.S., mur. Dennis E. Haynes, a lawyer in Atlanta, Ga., committed murder and, although sentenced to hang, was never executed. Haynes had purchased a house occupied by James Griggs and his family, but Griggs refused to vacate. On the evening of Apr. 29, 1854, Haynes and two friends stopped at the house and broke a lock on the well, attempting to get a drink.

Griggs heard the commotion and burst from the house, throwing rocks as he ran forward. Haynes' two companions fled, but the lawyer was steadfast. "Don't come another step," he ordered Griggs. But Griggs came on, cursing and pelting Haynes with rocks. The lawyer produced a shotgun and fired both barrels, killing Griggs.

A sympathetic jury recommended mercy for Haynes after finding him guilty of murder, but Judge Obadiah Warner ordered the young lawyer hanged on Dec. 22, 1854. Legal battles delayed the execution, and Haynes eventually managed to slip out of the noose after serving a few years in jail. REF.: *CBA.*

Haynes, Richard (AKA: **Racehorse**), 1923- , U.S., lawyer. Richard "Racehorse" Haynes is known as one of the most flamboyant defense lawyers in recent history. Known to command fees as high as $1 million, Haynes is also known to present almost anything as evidence in order to acquit his clients. He won an acquittal for one client even though the hairs of the dead woman, through nuclear activation, had been linked to his client. By convincing the jury that the high-tech process failed to meet the court's rigid standards for investigation, his client was exonerated. Haynes defended oilman T. Cullen Davis during his murder trial for the deaths of two family members and won an acquittal even though three eyewitnesses had positively identified Davis as the murderer. Haynes also won the case for a client who had already confessed to beating a woman to death.

Haynes attributes his high success rate to careful jury selection. He spends thousands of dollars for research, and often employs a psychologist during the selection process. He shrewdly maneuvers trials away from a hostile jurisdiction, such as the 1971 case where a black man was arrested and beaten to death by two white Houston police officers for stealing a car which was later proved he owned. Haynes secured a change of venue from Houston to the more conservative New Braunfels, Texas, where he won the case. Haynes is highly selective, choosing less than 15 percent of the cases offered him. But he will not shun a case which looks ominous, even when the client admits to committing the offense. REF.: *CBA*.

Haynes, Theodore Park, prom. 1898, U.S., mur. Theodore Haynes, an elderly tinsmith, argued with his neighbor, Alfred Hopkinson, on Mar. 23, 1898, about their property lines in San Francisco's Mission district. Haynes pulled a handgun during the dispute and shot at his neighbor, who then sought help from police officers. Two policeman went with Hopkinson to talk with Haynes, but when he threatened the officers with a gun, they left to inform their superior officer. Later, when Lieutenant William Burke arrived and walked toward Haynes' cabin, Haynes shot him twice in the groin. The wounded Burke fired two return shots, which missed, then crumpled to the ground. As Burke lay wounded, Haynes ran out, grabbed the officer's gun, and fired twice more into the wounded policeman. Burke was taken to the hospital where he soon died. Haynes was tried on Apr. 11, 1898. He was found Guilty and sentenced to life imprisonment at Folsom State Prison. Two officers, James Wilkinson and G. Marlowe, were accused of cowardice for retreating during the shooting of Officer Burke. They were tried, and on Oct. 7, 1898, they were discharged from the police force.

REF.: *CBA; Duke, Celebrated Criminal Cases of America.*

Haynsworth, Clement Furman, Jr., 1912- , U.S., jur. Nominated to the fourth circuit court by President Dwight D. Eisenhower in 1957. Also nominated to the U.S. Supreme Court by President Richard M. Nixon in 1969, but was not confirmed. REF.: *CBA*.

Hays, Arthur Garfield, 1881-1954, U.S., lawyer. Arthur Garfield Hays was known as an outspoken supporter of civil liberties, defending even those with whom he ideologically disagreed. Hays was born in Rochester, N.Y., and began practicing law in 1905 in New York City. He served as general counsel to the American Civil Liberties Union beginning in 1912. In that role, he was involved with the defense of Nicola Sacco and Bartolomeo Vanzetti in 1927, and helped Samuel Leibowitz represent defendants in the Scottsboro case in Alabama in 1932. He participated in ACLU cases for John Strachey, Tom Mooney, the Gastonia Communists, and Harry Bridges. In 1925, he helped Clarence Darrow defend John Thomas Scopes in the famous Tennessee anti-evolution trial.

Hays became well known when he participated in the Reichstag fire trial in 1933, in which he defended Georgy Dimitrov, a Bulgarian Communist. A Jew whose family had immigrated from Germany, Hays also supported the right of free speech of Nazis in the German-American Bund.

Hays was also known for his opposition to censorship of books. His works include *Let Freedom Ring*, 1928, and *Trial by Prejudice*, 1933, both on the topic of civil liberties. His *Democracy Works*, 1939, supported the American democratic system, and *City Lawyer*, 1942, was an autobiography. Hays died of a heart attack at the age of seventy-three. See: **Darrow, Clarence; Leibowitz, Samuel; Mooney, Tom; Reichstag Fire; Scottsboro Case.** REF.: *CBA*.

Hays, Bob, d.1896, U.S., west. outl. Bob Hays was one member of Black Jack Christian's outlaw gang which attempted to rob the International Bank of Nogales, Ariz., on Aug. 6, 1896. Hays and fellow bank robber Jess Williams were inside the bank when newspaperman Frank King accosted gang members stationed outside. When King began firing, Hays and Williams were forced to abandon their efforts and flee. Despite the failed attempt, the gang was pursued by an eight-man posse and was cornered at a hideout in San Simon Valley. In an exchange of gunfire, Hays was shot to death by lawman Fred Higgins.

REF.: *CBA;* O'Neal, *Encyclopedia of Western Gunfighters.*

Hays, Henry Francis, 1952- , and **Knowles, James Llewellyn** (AKA: **Tiger**), 1964- , U.S., mur. In 1981, a racially charged trial became the catalyst for a murder of an innocent teenager in Alabama. The trial, in which a black man was charged with the murder of a white Birmingham police officer, was originally scheduled to be held in Birmingham, but received a change of venue to Mobile at the last moment. Ku Klux Klan members in the town became incensed when jurors were unable to come to a decision, and a mistrial was declared on Mar. 30, 1981.

To retaliate, that evening two Klan members, 29-year-old Henry Francis Hays and 17-year-old James Llewellyn Knowles, went out searching for a black man to murder. They spotted 19-year-old Michael Donald, asked him for directions, and abducted him at gunpoint, forcing him into their car. The Klansmen drove to the next county where Donald attempted to flee his captors. Once recaptured, the two assailants beat him more than a hundred times with branches from a tree before slitting his throat. They put his body into their car and drove to a party at the house of Klansman Bennie Jack Hays. There, they hung Donald's body from a tree.

Hays and Knowles were tried for murder and on Dec. 10, 1983, a jury of one black and eleven whites found 29-year-old Hays Guilty and recommended life imprisonment. On Feb. 2, 1984, Circuit Judge Braxton Kittrell, Jr., increased the penalty, and sentenced the killer to be electrocuted. Knowles pleaded guilty to a federal civil rights charge, was convicted, and sentenced to life in prison.

Later, Michael Donald's mother, Beulah Mae Donald, and the National Association of Colored People sued the Ku Klux Klan. On Feb. 12, 1987, an all-white jury awarded them $7 million in damages. REF.: *CBA*.

Jacob Hays, the first high constable of New York City.

Hays, Jacob (AKA: **Old Hays**), 1772-1850, U.S., law enfor. off. Jacob Hays was a "terror to evil-doers" in old New York. Before the Metropolitan Police force was formally organized in the 1820s, Hays, armed only with his constable's staff, was the city's lone force against mob rule. Appointed High Constable in 1801, "Old Hays" and just six deputies kept the peace. His reputation spread worldwide as law enforcement agencies from around the country sought to emulate his success. In 1831, he singlehandedly solved the $200,000 robbery of the City Bank after allowing the only suspect in the case to go free. Hays shadowed the man to Philadelphia where the loot was quickly recovered. His powers of deductive reasoning and natural instincts about the habits of the common criminals intimidated the underworld in such a way that it was usually not necessary for him or his deputies to employ deadly force. Although he served for fifty years, Hays rarely carried a gun.

REF.: *CBA; Costello, Our Police Protectors; The National Cyclopaedia of American Biography; Reppetto, The Blue Parade; Scott, The Concise Encyclopedia of Crime and Criminals.*

Hays, John Coffey (Jack), 1817-83, U.S., west. law enfor. off. Born in Wilson County, Tenn., John Coffey Hays, who was later known as Jack Hays to his men in the Texas Rangers and the outlaws he doggedly hunted down, moved to San Antonio, Tex., in 1837, working as a frontier surveyor. He also developed a reputation as a gunman who would fight to uphold the law. When the Texas Rangers were formed in 1840, Hays was elected a major in this sterling organization. He led many posses in tracking down out-laws and thieves and more than once arrested deadly gunmen by simply walking up to them and knocking them senseless with the butt of his sixgun, a tactic successfully employed by Wyatt Earp. Hays is credited with introducing the Colt revolver to the Rangers.

John Coffey Hayes, a Texas Ranger who became the first sheriff of San Francisco.

Hays served the Texas Rangers for ten years and then moved to California where he became fabulously rich. He purchased a huge tract of land across the Bay from San Francisco, and this he later established as the city of Oakland. Hays became the first sheriff of San Francisco County (1850-53), and through him many police reforms were instituted. Hays, though a lawman all his life, had the distinction of never being wounded in a gunfight.

REF.: *CBA; Hunter and Rose, The Album of Gunfighters; Webb, The Texas Rangers.*

Hays, Wayne L., See: **Ray, Elizabeth.**

Hayward, George Frederick Walter, prom. 1927, Brit., rob.-mur. In 1927, an unemployed traveling salesman, George Hayward, was desperately indebted to his creditors, and he owed his former employers more than £70 in funds that he had collected from customers. Early in the morning of Oct. 11, 1927, he broke into the New Inn at Little Hayfield, Derbyshire, England. Attacking Amy Collinson, the wife of the licensee of the inn, with a lead pipe reinforced with wood, he pulled the woman across the sitting room and slit her throat with a knife. Then he took about £30 or £40 in silver and treasury notes. Hayward boarded a bus and went to New Mill, a town about three miles away, where he collected his unemployment check, and then he traveled to Manchester where he bought a money order for £4 to pay off a furniture bill. The next day police found the money in the chimney in his bedroom and Hayward was arrested. He was tried and found Guilty at Derby Assizes in February 1928, given the death penalty, and hanged.

REF.: *Butler, Murderers' England; CBA; Humphreys, Seven Murderers; Shew, A Second Companion to Murder.*

Hayward, Harry T., 1864-95, U.S., fraud-mur. The body of Catherine "Kitty" Ging, fiancée of Harry T. Hayward, was found on Dec. 13, 1894, on the shore of Lake Calhoun in Hennepin County, Minn. The distraught boyfriend, a swindler, swore he would find the killer, and spent a good deal of money in the search. But he himself had murdered Ging after convincing her to take out $10,000 in life insurance naming him as the beneficiary.

Before crushing her skull and shooting her in the back of the head, Hayward had attempted to hire Claus Blixt, a janitor who had collaborated with Hayward on other swindles, to do the job. When Blixt refused, Hayward went to his brother, lawyer Adry Hayward, who also refused and reported the conversation to another attorney. Harry Hayward's reputation for lying prevented

Minneapolis murderer Harry T. Hayward and his victim Kitty Ging.

the lawyer from taking action. Hayward's seven-week trial ended on Mar. 9, 1895, when he was found Guilty and sentenced to be hanged. His last wish was to have the rope and the gallows painted red, his favorite color. The sheriff complied partially. On Dec. 11, 1895, Hayward walked up the stairs of a fire-engine-red gallows. The rope, however, remained dull brown.

REF.: *CBA; Day, The Ging Murder and the Great Haywood Trial; The Ging Murder; Harry Haywood: Life, Crimes, Dying Confession and Execution of the Celebrated Minneapolis Criminal; Haywood's Confession; Nash, Bloodletters and Badmen; Wade, Harry T. Haywood's Life, Trial, Confession and Execution; ____, Lured to Death.*

Hayward, Samuel, 1800-1821, Brit., burg. Samuel Hayward was the son of a poor leather worker in Southwark, England, but had higher aspirations.

As an adolescent, Samuel Hayward worked as a tailor's apprentice, a waiter in a coffeehouse, a historian's assistant, and also as a traveling companion of a rich man. With his meager savings, Hayward disassociated himself from his family and acquaintances and began to move in London's aristocratic circles. He was unconditionally accepted and sought after as a mate for marriageable young women. Hayward could not continue his charade very long before his money ran out, so he tried to win money by gambling, even spending forged notes at the gambling tables. He then turned to pickpocketing and robbery and later joined a gang. To case a house in Somer's Town and learn where the valuables were located, Hayward began dating a woman who lived there. When the criminals broke into the house, Hayward was caught by a security man and charged with the crime. Another gang member, an artist named Mr. Elkins, was also arrested. The 21-year-old Hayward was tried, convicted, and hanged in 1821.

REF.: *CBA; Culpin, The Newgate Noose.*

Haywood, William Dudley (AKA: Big Bill), 1869-1928, Case of, U.S., mur. Frank R. Steunenberg, the good-natured editor of the Caldwell *Record,* a pro-labor Idaho newspaper, was elected governor of the state in 1896. He served his two-year term peacefully, and was elected for a second term in 1898. Steunenberg inherited the Western Federation of Miners' general strike, calling for a work stoppage in the rich Coeur d'Alene mining district. The warring strikers and strikebreakers resorted to hired thugs and Pinkerton guards, and mobs gathered as the situation worsened. When dynamite blew up the Sullivan and Bunker Hill mines, two men were killed and the mines were completely incapacitated. With no state militia available, Steunenberg asked

President William McKinley for federal troops. Hundreds of union miners and supporters were imprisoned in barbed-wire enclosures and held incommunicado for months. Hundreds more fled the state to escape. Steunenberg was branded an enemy of the Labor Party that put him in power. Denounced by every union organization in the West, he was kept under constant guard for the rest of his term as governor. Six years later, on Dec. 30, 1905, Steunenberg walked home from his work as president of the Caldwell bank, opened the wooden gate to his home and was blown to pieces by a bomb.

Tom Hogan, who had been staying at Caldwell hotels for five or six months posing as a sheep buyer, was arrested for the murder on Jan. 1, 1906. Better known as Harry Orchard, he denied any guilt, and was popularly believed to be a tool of the Western Federation of Miners. Public demand for the capture of Steunenberg's murderers ran high in Idaho and in Colorado, where the miner's federations were headquartered. Colorado had suffered through fifteen years of martial law, federal intervention, arrests and deportations. In June 1904, a bombing of the Independence, Colo., railroad depot killed fourteen non-union miners. Held in solitary confinement for ten days, Orchard spent the next thirty with James McParland, manager of the Pinkerton Detective Agency in Denver. On Feb. 19, 1906, Orchard was reported as having made a full confession which would be published a year later as his *Confessions and Autobiography*. He said that Charles H. Moyer and William Dudley Haywood, president and secretary-treasurer, respectively, of the Western Federation of Miners, had hired him. Orchard had been assisted by George Pettibone, a union member, and Jack Simpkins, an executive board member. Steve Adams worked with him in plotting and executing the assassination of Steunenberg and the bombing of the railroad depot, as well as many other crimes.

Left to right, Charles Moyer, "Big Bill" Haywood, and George Pettibone, union radicals, during their 1907 murder trial.

Arrested and held without legal counsel, Adams was put in a cell with Orchard. Alternately threatened with hanging and promised immunity, he soon confessed. The governor of Colorado was asked to extradite Haywood, Moyer, and Pettibone. The three were arrested on Feb. 17 and taken under armed guard to Idaho. Many questioned the legality of the extradition, but the state and the federal courts upheld the action. In December 1906, Clarence Darrow arrived from Chicago to head a defense team including Edmund Richardson, John Nugent, Edgar Wilson, and Fred Miller. Adams' case was rushed to trial in February 1907. The jury disagreed as to Adams' guilt or innocence, and Adams remained in prison. This was a victory for the three union men: Adams would not be a state witness. The public demanded the "big" trial. Haywood, a miner since the age of nine, had been a member of the Western Federation since 1896, and was a member of the Socialist Party as well. As an organizer for the Industrial Workers of the World, he openly advocated violence and revolution to secure labor rights. To many, Haywood was the epitome of lawlessness in union labor.

The trial began in Idaho, before Judge Fremont Wood, on May 9, 1907. Prosecutors were William E. Borah, James H. Hawley, Owen M. Van Duyn, and Charles Koelsche. Full accounts of Orchard's confession appeared for the first time in newspapers coast to coast. The press touted Orchard as a changed man who had found religion and renounced his criminal past. His confession detailed eighteen murders he claimed he had been hired to commit by Haywood, Moyer, and Pettibone. Pettibone, Orchard explained, was an amateur chemist who had instructed him in arson. Hawley's opening arguments for the state presented Orchard as a penitent man, and offered a fiery denunciation of the miners' organization and its leaders. Darrow, in fragile health at the time, responded by speaking for eleven hours without notes, destroying Orchard's credibility and defending Haywood and the union.

Speaking of Orchard, Darrow said, "He never did a courageous thing in his life, not one. If Orchard has religion now, I hope I may never get it." Darrow told the jury they could hang Haywood, but that the labor movement of the world would continue with others "who will risk their lives in that great cause which has demanded martyrs in every age of the world." Barely able to whisper by the end of his speech, Darrow concluded by defying anyone to convict another man on Orchard's testimony. On July 29, the jury retired for seven hours and returned to pronounce Haywood Not Guilty. The stunned crowd was silent.

At Adams' second trial, Darrow again carried the defense. Again the jury disagreed. Pettibone was brought to trial immediately following Adams' case. Darrow, now extremely ill, further Orchard's credibility. Darrow appeared in court the next day in a wheelchair, no longer able to proceed. He spent days in a Los Angeles hospital floating between life and death. When Pettibone too was found Not Guilty, the state decided to dismiss the case against Moyer. In 1917, Haywood was again arrested and tried along with other IWW (Industrial Workers of the World) agitators for sabotaging vital war industries. Sentenced to twenty years in jail, he was released on bail pending an appeal, and escaped to Russia where the Bolsheviks hailed him and later gave him a state funeral and burial at the Kremlin on May 18, 1928. See: **Darrow, Clarence; Orchard, Harry.**

REF.: Borah, *Haywood Trial;* Brissenden, *The I.W.W.;* Busch, *Prisoners at the Bar; CBA;* Chaplin, *Wobbly;* Commons, *History of Labor in the United States;* Crandall, *The Man from Kinsman;* Darrow, *The Story of My Life;* Foner, *History of the Labor Movement in the United States;* Grover, *Debaters and Dynamiters: The Story of the Haywood Trial;* Gunn, *Wisdom of Clarence Darrow;* Gurko, *Clarence Darrow;* Harrison, *Clarence Darrow;* Haywood, *Bill Haywood's Book;* Kurland, *Clarence Darrow;* McKenna, *Borah;* Mordell, *Clarence Darrow;* Orchard, *The Confession and Autobiography of Harry Orchard;* Paine, *The Assassins' World;* Powers, *Secrecy and Power;* Reppetto, *The Blue Parade;* Sayer, *Clarence Darrow: Public Advocate;* Stone, *Clarence Darrow for the Defense;* Tierney, *Darrow, A Biography;* Weinberg, *Attorney for the Damned;* ____, *Clarence Darrow, A Sentimental Rebel;* Whitehead, *Clarence Darrow—The Big Minority Man;* ____, *Clarence Darrow, Evangelist of Sane Thinking.*

Hazael, prom. 9th Cent. B.C., Syria, king, assass. Murdered Benhadad II and became king of Damascus in c.841 B.C. He became involved in combat with Israel, then oppressed and took over part of the country. REF.: *CBA.*

Hazel, Jessie, prom. 1870s, U.S., pros. In 1870, madame Mattie Silks established a brothel in Abilene, Kan. Jessie Hazel was one of ten prostitutes who worked in the exclusive house. Serving as town marshal at the time, Wild Bill Hickok favored the young Hazel. She had also attracted the attention of Phil Coe, co-owner of the Bull's Head Saloon. One afternoon, Hickok heard that Coe was with Hazel, and burst in on the two. The two men fought until they were forced apart by two other men. Hazel was later supported by Coe and lived in his cabin.

REF.: *CBA;* Drago, *Notorious Ladies of the Frontier.*

Hazen, William Babcock, 1830-87, U.S., ct. mar. Graduated from U.S. Military Academy at West Point in 1855, served in Civil War and became major general in 1864. In 1880, he was made chief signal officer in the U.S. Army, ranking as a brigadier general. He organized the Greely Arctic expedition in 1881. He was court-martialed in 1885 when he voiced disapproval after a relief expedition was detained by the secretary of war. REF.: *CBA*.

Head, William C., b.c.1885, U.S., embez. William Head, paymaster for a large subsidiary of Standard Oil, the Standard-Vacuum Transportation Corporation, stole as much as $600,000 in company funds. Head confessed to having embezzled the funds during a twenty-five year period by altering payroll records. He invested the money in cars and houses, and in two farms in Maine that produced mink and chickens.

After Head was indicted in November 1932, his supervisor, Edward M. Connaughton committed suicide at his New Jersey home. Connaughton had apparently not known of the misappropriation, but felt that Head's crimes had brought him disgrace. Head was tried and convicted of stealing between $500,000 and $600,000 during a seven-year period. He received a sentence of three to six years imprisonment in Sing Sing. REF.: *CBA*.

Headless Valley (AKA: Deadman's Valley), prom. 1904-45, Can., (unsolv.) mur. In a valley in northwest Canada in the Yukon and the Northwest Territories, stretching along the South Nahanni River, eleven people died between 1904 and 1945, earning the area the unofficial name, "Headless Valley." Gold prospectors were originally drawn to the valley in about 1898, and people began to die shortly thereafter. In 1904, Willie and Frank McLeod and a Scottish engineer went in, but never returned. The McLeods' headless skeletons were found by another brother, Charlie McLeod, three years later. In 1917, Martin Jorgensen disappeared; his headless remains were discovered in a burned cabin. Likewise, in 1926, Annie Laferte left to prospect in the area, but never returned, and in 1926, the skeleton of "Yukon" Fisher was found.

In 1929, three more men vanished, and in 1932 the charred body of Phil Powers was found in his burned cabin. Two more men who went into the valley in 1936, never returned, and, later, an unidentified body was discovered. In 1945, 41-year-old Ernest Savard did not come back after his second venture into the valley. His nearly decapitated body was found in his sleeping bag.

Indians in the area claimed the murders were committed by the evil spirits of "Mountain Men," beings similar, perhaps, to the legendary Sasquatch creature. No further explanation was found.

REF.: *CBA*; Miller, *Twenty Mortal Murders*.

Heads, Charles, 1947- , Case of, U.S., mur. Charles Heads joined the Marine Corps when he was nineteen years old, and fought in Vietnam for nine months before he suffered a gunshot wound and was transferred. Back in the U.S., Heads' wife left him and went, with their children, to live with her brother, Roy Lejay, in Louisiana. Heads went to Lejay's home intending to retrieve them. When Lejay refused to let him enter, Heads kicked in the door and fatally shot him.

At his trial in Shreveport, La., Heads' lawyer argued that his actions resulted from the combat stresses the 34-year-old veteran had suffered in Vietnam nearly ten years earlier. The lawyer contended that the former soldier had a flashback and, thinking that he was storming a Vietnamese hut, had used military survival techniques. Although this was the third case in Louisiana in which combat stress had been used as a defense, Heads was the first defendant to win an acquittal. On Oct. 10, 1981, he was found Not Guilty by reason of insanity. REF.: *CBA*.

Heady, Bonnie Brown, See: **Hall, Carl Austin**.

Healy, John, b.1886, Case of, Brit., mur. Elizabeth Ridgley, fifty-four, closed her general store in Hitchin, Herfordshire, England, on the evening of Jan. 25, 1919. Sometime after, she was attacked with a four-pound weight in the kitchen behind the store. Her Irish terrier was also struck on the head, and died.

Ridgley's body was found two days later, and John Healy, a 33-year-old laborer, was arrested as a suspect. He was reportedly seen in the vicinity of the store on the night of the murder, and a wound on his hand was similar to a dog bite. He was tried at Hertford, but because of the slim evidence, the jury acquitted him.

No other suspects were found.

REF.: Browne, *The Rise of Scotland Yard*; *CBA*; Shew, *A Second Companion to Murder*.

Healy, Maurice, 1887-1943, Brit., jur. Presided over several murder trials, including those of Frederick Nodder and Leslie George Stone. REF.: *CBA*.

Healy, William, 1881-1962, U.S., jur. Served as prosecuting attorney of Owyhee County, Idaho, from 1911-12. He was nominated to the ninth circuit court by President Franklin D. Roosevelt in 1937. REF.: *CBA*.

Hearn, Sarah Ann, prom. 1930-31, Case of, Brit., mur. Middle-aged widow Sarah Ann Hearn lived in Lewannick, Cornwall, with her invalid sister, Lydia Everhard, who died in July 1930. Hearn had nursed Everhard, who had a long history of gastric troubles and had been ill for several weeks before her death. Hearn's neighbors, William and Annie Thomas, visited her often and sometimes they went on picnics together. Hearn often prepared food for their trips. On Oct. 18, 1930, the Thomases drove Hearn to Bude, and shared her homemade salmon sandwiches while on the road. Annie Thomas became violently ill. At her request, Hearn stayed at the Thomas home and took care of her. Mrs. Thomas began to recover, but then took a turn for the worse. She died at Plymouth Hospital on Nov. 4. A post-mortem showed arsenic in her body, and a coroner's inquest later ruled that she had been poisoned. At the funeral, Mrs. Thomas' brother alluded to the salmon sandwiches, and Mr. Thomas mentioned to Hearn that inquiries were being made into his wife's death, suggesting to her that blame "would fall heavier on you than on me." The unnerved Hearn disappeared, leaving Thomas a note which said, "I am innocent, innocent, but she is dead and it was my sandwiches she ate." Her coat was later found near a cliff at Looe, suggesting suicide.

Hearn was found working as a housekeeper in Torquay in January 1931. The bodies of her sister and an aunt who had lived with them were exhumed, and both were found to contain arsenic. Brought to trial at the Bodmin Assizes in June 1931, Hearn was defended by Norman Birkett, assisted by Dingle Foot, with H. du Parq and Patrick Devlin for the Crown. The case was heard by Walter West, a Grimsby solicitor. Birkett contended that Thomas had become ill from food poisoning and had later been given arsenic, administered not by Hearn, but by someone else. Hearn testified that she had not killed anyone. Birkett contended that, had the sandwiches been laced with arsenic, they would have been blue. After the jury deliberated for fifty-four minutes, they found Hearn Not Guilty. The Crown offered no evidence against Hearn in any other murders.

REF.: Bardens, *Lord Justice Birkett*; Bowker, *Behind the Bar*; *CBA*; Duke, *Six Trials*; Hastings, *The Other Mr. Churchill*; O'Donnell, *Crimes That Made News*; Rowland, *Criminal Files*; Shew, *A Companion to Murder*; Smith, *Mostly Murder*; Thompson, *Poison Mysteries Unsolved*; ____, *Poisons and Poisoners*; Wild, *The Jury Retires*; Wilson, *Encyclopedia of Murder*.

Heart of the Midlothian, The, 1818, a novel by Sir Walter Scott. This enormous work is based almost wholly on two true crime incidents, the first being the Porteous Riots (Scot., 1736) which opens the novel, and the second being the strange story of Isobel Walker, condemned for infanticide, and her sister Helen's epic walk to London to plead for royal intercession on her sister's part. See: **Porteous, John**; **Walker, Helen and Isobel**. REF.: *CBA*.

Hearst, Patricia Campbell (Patty AKA: Tania), 1955- , U.S., rob. The Patty Hearst case was a drama replete with kidnapping, robbery, and revolution. On Feb. 4, 1974, a woman knocked on the door of the Berkeley, Calif., apartment shared by Patricia Campbell Hearst, 19-year-old heiress to the Hearst media fortune, and her fiancé, Stephen Weed. The woman asked Weed if she could use his phone, but he refused and closed the door in her face. A few seconds later two men broke the door down with rifles and attacked Weed whom they hit over the head with rifle butts. Bleeding and dazed, Weed stumbled from the apartment, calling for help. Patricia was then dragged outside to a nearby car and stuffed into the trunk. The attackers then drove off at high speed after firing several shots in the air, apparently to ward off anyone trying to save the girl or follow the kidnappers.

Although neighbors later told police that they heard Patricia screaming for help, some of the residents said they doubted the seriousness of the kidnapping because Hearst's screams seemed to be feeble or feigned. Eight blocks away from the Weed-Hearst apartment, the kidnappers stopped and transferred their hostage to a station wagon. They abandoned the other car which had been stolen a short time earlier, leaving its driver, Paul Benenson, bound and gagged on the floor of the car. He later told

Patricia Hearst with fiancé Stephen Weed.

police that he had no idea why he or his car had been taken.

The nation's press, especially the Hearst newspapers, gave great play to this story, and the nation waited for three days. There was considerable speculation as to the amount of money the kidnappers would demand for Hearst's return. The first of a series of ransom notes came as a shock. Hearst was in the hands of a revolutionary group which called itself the Symbionese Liberation Army, a small militant group of extreme left-wing activists led by a crackpot named Donald David DeFreeze. A convicted thief, terrorist, and a fugitive, the 30-year-old DeFreeze, a black, called himself "Cinque," after a rebellious slave of the nineteenth century. DeFreeze used a seven-headed cobra as the symbol of his homegrown SLA.

DeFreeze announced in the first note sent to authorities that Hearst was in "protective custody," and that any "civilian" who tried to interfere with the SLA in its war with "the fascist state" would be killed. DeFreeze had begun his organization while in prison, picking up his revolutionary ideas and rhetoric willy-nilly from other prisoners. DeFreeze was born in Cleveland to a family with eight children. He ran away at age fourteen and remained in trouble ever after, getting arrested several times for possessing guns and bombs. On one occasion when DeFreeze was arrested for running a red light on a bicycle, a bomb was found in the bicycle's basket. He was sent to prison for five years in California in 1969. After escaping in March 1973, he headquartered his SLA operations in Oakland.

The SLA attracted a weird bunch of white supporters as well as black. Most of the white women supporting the SLA were from upper middle-class families and had been educated by radical teachers at ultra-liberal schools in California. The SLA's first victim was Marcus Foster, the black school superintendent of Oakland. He was shot to death with cyanide-tipped bullets on Nov. 6, 1973, because he had endorsed a plan to photograph all Oakland students for identification purposes. To DeFreeze, this was a fascist move to identify any future adversaries of the government. In his typical gobbledygook logic he called it the "Internal Warfare Identification Computer."

On Jan. 10, 1974, two SLA men, Russell Little and Joseph Remiro, had been stopped by police in Concord, Calif. The two jumped out of their van and pulled guns. A battle ensued and Little was wounded and captured. Remiro escaped on foot but was apprehended four hours later, only a block from the secret headquarters of the SLA.

This building was burned some nights later but firemen managed to put out the blaze. Inside, police found a bomb factory, and great amounts of left-wing propaganda in the form of books, circulars and records. Many items left behind helped

police to identify several SLA members. Also found at this site was a small green notebook with a memo reading: "Patricia Campbell Hearst on the night of the full moon of January 7." Police took little notice of this note until Hearst was kidnapped the following month.

By then, DeFreeze sent a wild ransom demand, stating that if the millionaire publishing family wanted their daughter returned they would have to distribute $70 worth of food to each of the 5.9 million poor of California, an estimated cost of $400 million. To convince Randolph Hearst that the SLA meant what it said, DeFreeze enclosed a tape recording of his daughter. She sounded weary but assured her father that she was unharmed. She stated that "these people aren't just a bunch of nuts. They're perfectly willing to die for what they're doing."

Food parcels were quickly prepared and thousands of the elderly, homeless, and poverty-stricken received the food. In East Oakland, when a crowd of more than 5,000 persons rioted terrified clerks merely threw boxes of food from the trucks. Following the handout of more than $2 million in food, Hearst was accused of not doing enough, criticized on a tape by his own daughter, who reportedly was talking under threat of death. The food deliveries went on until Mar. 25. A short time later another tape was delivered to Radio Station KFTA.

Rioters in Oakland, Calif., during the Hearst food handout, part of the SLA ransom for Patty Hearst.

Patty Hearst recorded the following: "I have never been forced to say anything on tape. Nor have I been brainwashed, tortured, hypnotized or in any way confused." She went on to criticize her father as being stingy with the food giveaway and her mother for accepting a post with the University of California. Hearst went on to denounce her love for Weed, saying that she had "grown" and that she had an "unselfish love for my comrades" in the SLA. Patty Hearst had declared herself a revolutionary. She announced that she was to be known thereafter as Tania, after the woman who fought with Che Guevara in Bolivia. Mrs. Hearst refused to believe her daughter, who had been raised in a twenty-room mansion full of servants and had never had a worry in the world, had suddenly become a dangerous radical. Said Mrs. Hearst: "Only Patty in person can convince me that the terrible weary words came from her heart and were delivered of her own free will."

Such doubts were not shared by certain authorities, especially after Apr. 15 when five members of the SLA, four women and one man, entered the Hibernia Bank in San Francisco's Sunset District. They carried automatic weapons and quickly robbed the bank of $10,900. The bank's cameras were running at the time and recorded the identities of some of the robbers. Clearly visible, menacing bank customers and employees was Patricia Campbell Hearst. She used harsh language when ordering people about in the bank. DeFreeze, who was now calling himself "Field Marshal Cinque" was the lone man. Still, many doubted that Patty Hearst was capable of robbery. Attorney General William B. Saxbe refuted that argument, labeling her a "common criminal."

On May 17, 1974, William and Emily Harris, diehard SLA members, walked into Mel's Sporting Goods store in Inglewood and bought some items, but the owner caught them stuffing socks and other goods in their pockets and chased them outside. He was calling for help when Patty Hearst poked an automatic

Patricia Hearst, caught by bank camera during an SLA robbery in 1974.

weapon from a red-and-white van and opened fire, riddling the store with more than thirty rounds which, fortunately, injured no one. Under this covering fire, the Harris couple scampered across the street, jumped into the van, and escaped. Then Los Angeles police learned through a defecting SLA informer that the gang was holed up in a small stucco house located at 1466 E. 54th Street.

More than 400 officers, including FBI agents, surrounded the house. Scores of newspaper and TV reporters rushed to the site. When those inside were ordered to surrender, they let loose a terrible fusillade. The police returned fire and the battle raged

for hours, the police alone firing more than 5,000 rounds into the house. Finally, when tear gas canisters were fired through the windows, the house caught fire. Only one person, Nancy Ling Perry, who called herself Fahiza, burst through the door, firing at

Patricia "Tania" Hearst, posing with automatic weapon before the Cobra symbol of the SLA.

police. She was shot to pieces. The rest of the SLA members elected to die inside the burning house. When officers entered the smoldering rubble of the house they found the bodies of Camilla "Gabi" Hall, Angela "Gelisa" Atwood, William "Cujo" Wolfe, Patricia "Zoya" Soltysik, and the man behind all the madness, Donald De-Freeze.

Hearst and the Harrises were not present but the Harris couple was located on Sept. 19, 1975, and Hearst was taken a few days later. The Harris couple were convicted of robbery and sent to prison for twenty-five years. They were paroled in 1984. Hearst was convicted of robbing the Hibernia bank and was sent to prison for seven years. She served a year but was released

Donald DeFreeze, head of the murderous SLA.

on bail until an appeal was heard. When this was denied, Hearst was returned to prison, but President Jimmy Carter, exercising executive clemency, ordered Patty Hearst released in January 1979. She did not return to Weed but later married her bodyguard, Bernard Shaw. See: **Harris, William; Symbionese Liberation Army.**

REF.: Alexander, *Anyone's Daughter*; Baker, *Exclusive!: The Inside Story of Patricia Hearst and the SLA*; Boulton, *The Making of Tania Hearst*; CBA; Clutterbuck, *Kidnap and Ransom*; Cohen, *Mickey Cohen: In My Own Words*; Demaris, *Brothers In Blood: The International Terrorist Network*; Dobson and Payne, *Counterattack—The West's Battle Against the Terrorists;* ____ , *The Terrorists—Their Weapons, Leaders and Tactics;* Hacker, *Crusaders, Criminals, Crazies: Terror and Terrorism in Our Time;* Hearst, *Every Secret Thing;* ____ and Moscow, *Patty Hearst: Her Own Story;* Jimenez, *My Prisoner;* Laquer, *Terrorism;* McLellan and Avery, *The Voices of Laws;* Messick, *Kidnapping;* Moorehead, *Hostage to Fortune;* Nash, *Bloodletters and Badmen;* Schreiber, *The Ultimate Weapon—Terrorists and World Order;* Sloan, *Simulating Terrorism;* Unger, *FBI;* Wolfe, *Fallen Angels.*

Heath, John (or **Heith**), 1851-84, U.S., west. outl. John Heath was Texas born and raised, and at an early age became involved in criminal activities, including rustling and robbery. He reformed briefly and became a deputy sheriff in Cochise County, Texas, but resigned because of poor pay and went back to thieving. Heath later opened a dance hall and saloon in Clifton, Ariz., which became a hangout for many desperadoes and gunmen. Befriending William Delaney and Daniel Kelly, both notorious gunmen who had been credited with killing several men, Heath joined these men and others in a robbery of a Bisbee, Ariz., store on Dec. 8, 1883. In the course of this robbery, four people including a woman were killed before the robbers fled. This notorious raid was later known as the Bisbee Massacre, and the outlaws were tracked down one by one by determined lawmen.

The end of outlaw John Heath, lynched by a Tombstone mob in 1884.

Heath was arrested in his Clifton saloon on suspicion and taken to Bisbee, where he was convicted of second-degree murder in a quick trial on Feb. 21, 1884, after witnesses identified him as one of the killers in the store robbery. He was sentenced to life in prison but he served only one day of this term. Housed in the Tombstone jail, Heath was dragged from his cell by an incensed group of miners the day after his conviction and taken to a telephone pole where a rope was looped over a crossbeam and the other end around his neck. Heath claimed to be innocent of the crime for which he was convicted, but when he realized the determination of the miners to see justice done, he became philosophical in his last moments, saying: "I have faced death too many times to be disturbed when it actually comes." As the miners began to yank him skyward, Heath cried out: "Don't mutilate my body or shoot me full of holes!" He died seconds later as he dangled from the telephone pole. See: **Bisbee, Ariz., Massacre; Daniels, Benjamin F.; Delaney, William E.; Kelly, Daniel.**

REF.: Bakerich, *Gunsmoke;* Bartholomew, *The Biographical Album of Western Gunfighters;* ____ , *Western Hardcases;* Blythe, *A Pictorial Souvenir and Sketch of Tombstone, Ariz.;* Breihan, *Outlaws of the Old West;* Burgess, *Bisbee Not So Long Ago;* Burns, *Tombstone: An Iliad of the Southwest;* CBA; Chisholm, *Brewery Gulch;* Erwin, *The Southwest of John H. Slaughter;* Florin, *Boot Hill;* Ganzhorn, *I've Killed Men;* Gard, *Frontier Justice;* Hendricks, *The Bad Man of the West;* Holloway, *Texas Gun Lore;* Hughes, *South from Tombstone;* Hunter and Rose, *The Album of Gunfighters;* Ladd, *Eight Ropes to Eternity;* Lake, *Under Cover for Wells Fargo;* Lesure, *Adventures in Arizona;* McCool, *So Said the Coroner;* Martin, *Tombstone's Epitaph;* Miller, *Arizona: The Last Frontier;* ____ , *The Arizona Story;* Nunnelley, *Boothill Grave Yard;* Raine, *Famous Sheriffs and Western Outlaws;* ____ , *Guns of the Frontier;* Sonnichsen, *Billy King's Tombstone;* Walters, *Tombstone's Yesterdays.*

Heath, Neville George Clevely (AKA: **Lord Dudley, Group Commander Rupert Brooke, Lt. Col. Armstrong, Blyth, Denvers**), 1917-46, Brit., mur. On the night of June 20, 1946, Neville George Clevely Heath met Margery Gardner at the Panama Club in the South Kensington section of London. The rakish, handsome Heath was a recent veteran of the South African Air Force but was discharged in August 1945 for wearing military decorations he had not earned. Earlier in his career Heath joined the Royal Air Force, but was court-martialed in August 1937 for being absent without leave. Heath had been in trouble with the law before joining the military. In July 1938 he was sentenced to Borstal for housebreaking and stealing jewelry. But until he picked up Gardner, he had never murdered.

Gardner was separated from her husband, and lived a bohemian life, frequenting London pubs while earning her living as a part-time film extra. At the Panama Club she was known as "Ocelot Margie" for the imitation animal skin coat she often wore. Gardner and Heath left the Panama Club together. They took a taxi to the Pembridge Court Hotel in Notting Hill. The next morning the badly beaten corpse of Gardner was found in the hotel room. The body bore evidence of a sadistic sexual assault. Gardner had been tied to the bedpost and whipped. The police quickly identified Heath as the probable murder. Photographs of Heath were taken from his residence in Wimbledon, but the photos were withheld from the newspapers to avoid compromising the case against Heath. However, his name and description were released.

Heath then traveled down the south coast to the Sussex resort of Worthington. There he wined and dined Yvonne Symonds, a girl he had met at a public dance in Chelsea. Though she had known Heath for only a few hours, she found him fascinating. When she saw his name in the papers as a suspect in the Gardner murder, she confronted him, asking, "What sort of person could commit a brutal crime like that?" "A sex maniac, I suppose," Heath replied. He assured her that he planned to return to London to clear himself of the accusation, but instead proceeded to Bournemouth. He registered at the Tollard Royal Hotel using the name Captain Rupert Brooke, the British poet killed in Greece in WWI. Heath sent a letter to Police Superintendent Thomas Barratt disclaiming any responsibility for Gardner's murder. He did admit renting the room in which Gardner was found murdered. "She had met an acquaintance with whom she felt obliged to sleep," Heath went on to say. He said when he returned to the room later and found the body he realized he "was in an invidious position. I have the instrument with which Mrs. Gardner was beaten and am forwarding this to you today. You will find my fingerprints on it, but you should find others as well."

On July 3, Heath invited 21-year-old Doreen Marshall to tea. The young woman was recovering from influenza at the Norfolk Hotel, and appeared to be pale and distressed while in Heath's company. Two days later the hotel manager notified police of her disappearance. On July 8, a search party found the woman horribly mutilated and lying dead in a patch of rhododendron bushes in Branksome Chine. She had been slashed with a knife and a string of artificial pearls were found strewn about the body. They matched a single pearl found in Heath's pocket. Authorities also found in his pocket a cloakroom ticket, which led them to a suitcase in a locker, and the suitcase contained a riding whip.

Lady killer Neville Heath.

Heath was charged with murdering both women, but when the trial opened at the Old Bailey on Sept. 24, the court concerned itself only with the murder of Margery Gardner. Defense attorney J.D. Casswell attempted to show that his client was certifiably insane at the time the murders were committed. He called Dr. William Henry De Bargue Hubert to the stand. Hubert testified that Heath was "morally insane." But the jury was not satisfied that Heath was deranged when he murdered. A verdict of Guilty was returned, and the defendant was sentenced to death on Sept. 26. The sentence was carried out at Pentonville Prison on Oct. 26. Heath's last request was for a whisky. He said, "In the circumstances, you might make that a double!"

REF.: Adamson, *The Great Detective*; Bennett, *Why Did They Do It?*; Boar, *The World's Most Infamous Murders*; Brock, *A Casebook of Crime*; Butler, *Murderers' England*; Byrne, *Borstal Boy: The Uncensored Story of Neville Heath*; Casswell, *A Lance For Liberty*; CBA; Critchley, *The Trial of Neville George Clevely Heath*; Cuthbert, *Science and the Detective*; Firmin, *Murderers In Our Midst*; Harrison, *Criminal Calendar*; Heppenstall, *The Sex War and Others*; Hibbert, *The Roots of Evil*; Hill, *Portrait of a Sadist*; Hoskins, *The Sound of Murder*; Jacobs, *Pageant of Murder*; Lucas, *The Sex Killers*; Lustgarten, *The Business of Murder*; Morland, *Hangman's Clutch*; Nash, *Almanac of World Crime*; Neustatter, *The Mind of the Murderer*; *Notable British Trials*; Philipps, *Murderer's Moon*; Playfair and Sington, *The Offenders*; Scott, *The Concise Encyclopedia of Crime and Criminals*; Shew, *A Companion to Murder*; Simpson, *Forty Years of Murder*; Traini, *Murder for Sex*; Whitbread, *The Railway Policeman*; Wilson, *Encyclopedia of Murder*.

Heath, R. Lee, b.1881, U.S., law enfor. off. R. Lee Heath grew up in Mt. Pleasant, Pa., and later moved to California, where he joined the Los Angeles Police Department in 1904. When Heath was a young officer, the police department used police wagons drawn by horses to track down cattle rustlers and horse thieves. Heath won a promotion as captain of the Division of Records before he was appointed to chief of police, taking office on Aug. 1, 1924. During his tenure, he created a formal Police Training School with a three-month training program, instituted the Statistical Bureau, and oversaw the development of photo and chemical labs which were precursors to a Science Investigation Division.

Heath also established a Bureau of Public Relations, and when the Board of Park Commissioners allotted land for a shooting range, the police chief initiated monthly compulsory competence requirements. Heath retired from his post on Mar. 31, 1926. Having passed the California Bar in 1913, he began practicing law in Los Angeles. REF.: CBA.

Heathrow Airport Raid, 1948, Brit., burg. In a pub, a gang of thieves met a man employed as a cargo loader at London's Heathrow airport. After becoming friendly, they induced him to give them information about the airport that they needed to carry out their plan to rob the bonded warehouse, a building where valuables were stored. On the day of the robbery, they arranged to drug the tea in the canteen frequented by the crew of the British Overseas Airways Corporation who were in charge of the warehouse.

On July 29, 1948, the eight gang members drove to the airport in a covered van, arriving about 1 a.m., and expecting to find articles worth £500,000 as well as $1 million in bullion. Unaware that police had been tipped off about their scheme, seven of the men entered the building and located three B.O.A.C. employees who seemed drugged, presumably from the tampered tea. After tying up the officials, who were really policemen feigning grogginess, the crooks took their keys to the safe. As they attempted to open the safe, other police officers surrounded the gang. After a struggle, the men were arrested and taken to Harlington Police Station.

They were tried at the Central Criminal Court, convicted, and all eight were sentenced to between five and twelve years in prison. The airport loader who originally supplied the gang with information was bound over on his own recognizance of £10 for a period of two years.

REF.: CBA; Scott, *Scotland Yard*.

Heatter, Gabriel, 1890-1972, U.S., news reporter. Radio news broadcaster and New York City newspaper reporter, becoming well-known for his coverage of Bruno Hauptmann's 1935 trial for the kidnapping of the Lindbergh baby. REF.: CBA.

Hébert, Jacques René (AKA: **Père Duchesne**), 1755-94, Fr., rebel. Known for radical Republican newspapers, joined the Commune of Paris, and in 1793 proposed ousting the Girondists. In 1794, the Committee of Public Safety arrested him and in 1794 he and many of his supporters were executed by guillotine. REF.: CBA.

Hecht, Ben, 1894-1964, U.S., crime writer. Although Ben Hecht went on to become a celebrated novelist, short story writer, and playwright, as well as the highest paid and best writer of screenplays of his day, he first established himself in Chicago journalism as a top crime writer. Born in New York, Hecht moved with his family at an early age to rural Wisconsin, and he later migrated as a teenager to Chicago where he went to work for the Chicago *Journal* and later the Chicago *Daily News*. Hecht remained in Chicago until he was thirty, leaving for New York in 1924 to collaborate with Charles MacArthur on several hit plays. It was during his days as a reporter that Hecht distinguished himself as a journalist who specialized in crime. Much of this material would later find its way into his plays and film scripts, including *The Front Page*, which centers on a gallows watch by a group of hard-boiled reporters.

Chicago writer Ben Hecht, who covered crime when working for the old Chicago *Daily News*.

Hecht wrote about a bevy of homicidal crackpots from Chicago's streets in his feature stories for newspapers and later recounted their crimes in several of his books. Not the least of these was Carl Otto Wanderer, a WWI hero who cleverly arranged to have himself held up at gunpoint by a bum whom he then shot, while also shooting his pregnant wife, later blaming his wife's murder on the dead ragged stranger. It was Hecht and his friend MacArthur who discovered Wanderer was homosexual and feared his wife's giving birth. For arcane psychological motives which had something to do with escaping his responsibilities as a heterosexual, Wanderer had decided to murder his spouse.

Another celebrated case involved a convicted murderer whom

Hecht names as Frankie Piano in *Gaily Gaily*. His body was to be whisked away from the gallows by Hecht and MacArthur immediately after his execution and revived by a quack who claimed he had developed a "resurrection" fluid. The body was smuggled to the quack's laboratory, but several injections of the miracle fluid failed to revived the decidedly deceased Piano.

Fred Ludwig, who had confessed to killing and dissecting his paramour and secretly burying her body in a park, refused to reveal the whereabouts of the remains. Ludwig, a closet transvestite, according to Hecht's jailhouse discoveries, adamantly refused to tell authorities what he did with the remains until Hecht borrowed a female makeup kit and delivered this to the condemned man's cell. An hour before he was hanged, Ludwig smeared his face with powder, lined his eyes with mascara, and coated his cheeks with rouge and his lips with lipstick.

Happy at last, he admitted that he had ground up his girlfriend's body and made her into sausage. He then told Sheriff Peter Hoffman that the bones and other remains were buried "in Grant Park, behind the statue of General Logan. A wonderful man." Ludwig (Hecht calls him Dr. Hugo in another version of this story) was then hanged in all his painted glory. "Out of him," Hecht was to write, "hanging and turning in his death throes, there came a woman's high falsetto screech."

Hecht was hot on the heels of police officers who surrounded the Cottage Grove house of bandit Teddy Webb. When the policemen rushed the house after a gun battle, one officer dropped dead of a heart attack. Police Chief Scheuttler entered the house, saw the dead cop, and, to save the department embarrassment, fired a bullet into the policeman's armpit so that it would appear that he died in the line of duty.

Undoubtedly, the most spectacular murder case Hecht covered as a reporter occurred before his very eyes in a Chicago courtroom. A towering giant named Manow had been found Guilty of murder and was brought before the court to be sentenced. When the judge ordered the cretinous immigrant to be hanged, Manow suddenly produced a long knife which he had secreted on his person. He shouted: "Hang me, will you!" With that, Manow reached across the dais and drove the knife to the hilt into the judge's chest. The gallery in which the reporters sat, including Hecht, was petrified, along with the rest of the stunned courtroom. The judge fell forward on the bench, gasping out his last moments of life. None of the tough-minded reporters in the court could move, so paralyzed were they with the horrible scene before them.

Then Hecht noticed, out of the corner of his eye, a young reporter from the *Inter-Ocean,* who was furiously writing, the only newsman with enough presence of mind to capture the story. He shouted for a copy boy, one of many who were then present in courtrooms. The boy ran to the gallery, scooped up the report and was about to dash out of the courtroom to his newspaper with the scoop. Said Hecht later: "None of us in the courtroom had moved. We were all paralyzed by the attack. Yet here was this guy from the *Inter-Ocean* who had nerves of steel, who had never paused in doing his job. I had to find out what he had written." Hecht ran after the copy boy, catching him by the arm and grabbing the long yellow page of copy paper the *Inter-Ocean* reporter had given him. The page contained, in a jittery handwriting, the following repetitive report: "The judge has been stabbed, the judge has been stabbed, the judge has been stabbed, the judge has been stabbed, the judge has been stabbed..."

REF.: Casey, *Such Interesting People; CBA;* Featherling, *The Five Lives of Ben Hecht;* Hecht, *Charlie;* _____, *A Child of the Century;* Gaily, *Gaily;* McPhaul, *Deadlines and Monkeyshines;* Morgan, *Prince of Crime;* Nash, *Bloodletters and Badmen;* _____, *The Innovators;* _____, *People to See;* Robbins, *Front Page Marriage.*

Heddon, 1922, a play by E.H.W. Meyerstein. This drama is based on the Frederick Seddon murder case (Brit., 1912). See: **Seddon, Frederick Henry**. REF.: *CBA.*

Hedgepeth, Marion, d.1910, U.S., rob. Marion Hedgepeth could supposedly outdraw and shoot a man whose pistol had already cleared the holster. Dressed all in black, Hedgepeth wore

a large wing collar, a diamond stickpin in his cravat, and a derby hat. He ran away from Cooper County, Mo., when he was fifteen and traveled west to Colorado and Wyoming to become a cowboy. By 1890 he had turned to crime, heading an outlaw gang that included himself, Albert "Bertie" Sly, James "Illinois Jimmy" Francis, and Charles F. "Dink" Burke, known collectively as the "Hedgepeth Four." On Nov. 4, 1890, the thieves held up their first passenger train, robbing the Missouri Pacific near Omaha, Neb., of $1,000. Eight days later, the band assaulted the Chicago, Milwaukee & St. Paul line, dynamited the express car, and got away with $5,000. Miraculously, the guard survived the explosion.

Several weeks later, Hedgepeth's gang robbed a train near Glendale, Mo., of $50,000 without firing a shot. They traveled to St. Louis, buried their weapons in a shed, and hid out. A little girl playing in the shed dug up the weapons and found the envelopes from the Glendale theft. Authorities tracked Hedgepeth to his room and captured him with his mistress. Under heavy guard, he awaited trial. The dressy bandit was deluged with flowers from female admirers during his sensational trial in 1892. While awaiting judgment in St. Louis, Hedgepeth met Chicagoan H.H. Holmes, whose real name was Herman Webster Mudgett. Mudgett would soon be infamous himself for the slaughter of more than two hundred women in his own personal horror chamber of a house, later dubbed

Robber Marion Hedgepeth.

the "Murder Palace." Holmes, arrested for fraud, asked Hedgepeth for the name of a lawyer who could get him released, which Hedgepeth, for a fee, supplied. Holmes was released, but Hedgepeth, who later revealed Holmes' murders to authorities, was sentenced to twelve years at the Jefferson City Prison. Released near the end of his term, Hedgepeth went to Omaha, Neb., and was soon caught breaking into a company safe.

Returned to jail for another two years, Hedgepeth reappeared in the West in 1908, living off small-time robberies with a new gang of thieves. On Jan. 1, 1910, he went behind the bar of a Chicago saloon, armed with a six-gun, and filled his pockets from the till. A passing policeman saw him, drew his pistol, and demanded Hedgepeth's surrender. Weak and thin from tuberculosis contracted in jail, Hedgepeth coughed, then yelled, "Never!" Both men shot simultaneously, the policeman's bullet mortally wounding Hedgepeth, who fired all his ammunition into the sawdust as he died on his knees. See: **Mudgett, Herman Webster.**

REF.: Asbury, *Gem of the Prairie; CBA;* Duke, *Celebrated Criminal Cases of America;* Nash, *Bloodletters and Badmen.*

Hedley, Ronald (AKA: Silver), 1918- , and **Jenkins, Thomas James**, 1919- , Brit., burg.-mur. On Dec. 8, 1944, four thieves driving a stolen car stopped in front of a jewelry store in London around noon. One of the gang broke the steel window guard with an ax, and two others grabbed jewelry worth close to £4,000. As they jumped back into the getaway car driven by the leader, 26-year-old Ronald Hedley, a pedestrian tried to stop the burglars. Captain Ralph Binney, a 56-year-old retired naval officer, stepped in front of the car, extending his arms. Hedley hit the man with the car and drove over him, then backed over him and speeded away. Binney, entangled by his clothing became trapped beneath the vehicle and was dragged for more than a mile. He died soon after.

Hedley and 25-year-old Jenkins were arrested, and tried at the Old Bailey in March 1945. Hedley was found Guilty of murder and given the death penalty, which was later reprieved, and he went to prison. After serving nine years, he was freed in 1954. Jenkins was convicted of manslaughter and sentenced to eight years in prison.

REF.: *CBA;* Fabian, *Fabian of the Yard;* Lefebure, *Evidence For the Crown;* Shew, *A Second Companion to Murder;* Simpson, *Forty Years of Murder.*

Hee, Park Chung, See: **Park Chung Hee.**

Heeber, Dr. Allen, prom. 1911, U.S., wh. slav.-mur. In 1911, Dr. Allen Heeber purportedly ran a missionary training school for girls in the Ozark Mountains in Oklahoma. His "House of Deuteronomy" was actually used to collect girls to be sold into white slavery. They were delivered by James Garrett, who, posing as an assistant pastor, collected $250 plus expenses for each girl. The demise of the ring came when the body of one of the girls, Josie Byers, was found in the mountains with a bullet in her head. An autopsy placed her death close to Sept. 15. Heeber later said he had loved Josie and wanted to marry her, but that the jealous matron, Cora Wentworth, had, instead, ordered him to shoot her. When Wentworth was near death in a sanitarium, she told police that Josie had fallen in love with Heeber and threatened to reveal his scheme if he did not marry her.

Sheriff Ben Totten of Ottowa County, Okla., began investigating the supposed missionary training school and located one of Heeber's girls, Dolly Slade, in St. Louis. Other girls were soon rescued in police raids in the city. Dolly Slade and another victim, Ina Lackey, agreed to testify, but by that time the white slavers had abandoned their Ozark headquarters. Heeber was later arrested in Los Angeles, and Garrett was apprehended soon after. When Garrett offered an unshakable alibi for the night of Josie's murder, Heeber confessed to the killing. Back in his cell, the ringleader ingested a poison and was dead an hour later.

REF.: *CBA;* Rice, *Forty-five Murderers.*

Hefeld, Paul, and **Meyer, Jacob** (AKA: **Jacob Lepidus**), prom. 1909, Brit., theft-suic.-mur. Russian revolutionaries Paul Hefeld and Jacob Meyer surfaced in Paris where, along with Jacob's brother, Peter Meyer, they tried to assassinate French President Armand Fallières in 1907. Jacob Meyer reputedly built bombs that were smuggled to Russia. One of those bombs was to end the French president's life, but it exploded prematurely in Peter Meyer's pocket. Hefeldt and Meyer escaped to England and on Jan. 24, 1909, they struck again. A clerk at a rubber factory in Tottenham, 17-year-old Arthur Keyworth, returned to the plant with his week's salary of £80, that he had just received from the bank. As he entered the factory, the two armed Russians grabbed his money and ran. They were pursued for nearly two-and-a-half hours, running on foot, holding up a streetcar, commandeering a milkman's cart and the cart of a fruit and vegetable dealer. During the chase, they shot and killed Police Constable William Frederick Tyler and 15-year-old Ralph John Joscelyn.

The two were pursued by a policeman and a mob of people. At Tottenham Marshes, the exhausted Hefeldt shot himself in the head. He died nineteen days later. Meyer climbed over a barbed-wire fence and hid in the house of a coal worker, Charles Rolston. Police stormed the house and fired through an upstairs bedroom door. When they finally burst into the room, Meyer was found with gunshot wounds in his head. He died soon after with a grin on his face.

REF.: *CBA;* Macnaghten, *Days of My Years;* Nicholls, *Crime Within the Square Mile;* Shew, *A Companion to Murder.*

Heffley, Michael W., 1948-88, U.S., (unsolv.) mur. On Nov. 19, 1988, Michael Heffley, forty, and his 32-year-old wife, Jamie, went rafting in southwestern Texas with their guide, Jim Burr. They had gone about two miles of their planned twelve-mile journey down the Rio Grande when four snipers on the Mexican side of the river opened fire on them. The 36-year-old guide, wounded in his right thigh, steered the raft near the bank and then continued down the river under more gunfire. When the three reached land again, Jamie Heffley was hit trying to get out of the raft; as her husband attempted to help her, he was fatally shot

in the back. Jamie and Burr concealed themselves in bushes, and under the cover of darkness Burr left to seek help. A rancher saw him the next morning near Texas Highway 170. Burr and Jamie Heffley both survived. Investigators found twelve shell casings in an area near the Mexican shore accessible only by boat or helicopter and known to for marijuana production. REF.: *CBA.*

Hefner, Cecil, prom. 1920, U.S., (wrong. convict.) mur. In December 1920, in North Carolina, Cecil Hefner was found Guilty of second-degree murder in the death of Glenn Lippard and was sentenced to fifteen years in prison. On Apr. 4, 1921, Hefner was pardoned by Governor Cameron Morrison after the prosecutor, Solicitor Huffman, with the concurrence of Judge Thomas J. Shaw, proved in a post-trial investigation that Hefner was not present when Lippard was murdered. REF.: *CBA.*

Heiberg, Peter Andreas, 1758-1841, Den., consp. Exiled in 1799 after writing satirical, anti-government material, he then went to Paris where he served in the department of foreign affairs. REF.: *CBA.*

Heideman, Frank, d.1912, U.S., rape-mur. On Nov. 9, 1910, Frank Heideman attacked 9-year-old Marie Smith. The child was on her way home from school, walking along a lonely road in Asbury Park, N.J. The florist struck Marie on the head with a hammer, then strangled and raped her. The child's body was found in nearby woods.

Although police had little evidence, they suspected the German-born Heideman and trailed him to New York. There, Karl Neimiester, a German-speaking agent who worked for the police befriended Heideman. After Neimiester staged a phony killing, he pretended to make plans to return to Germany because he was afraid that Heideman would inform the police. Heideman said that he, too, had murdered, and confessed to slaying the New Jersey girl. Heideman was arrested, convicted, and sentenced to death. He was electrocuted in May 1912.

REF.: Block, *The Wizard of Berkeley;* CBA; Nash, *Almanac of World Crime;* Scott, *The Concise Encyclopedia of Crime and Criminals.*

Heidnik, Gary M., 1943- , U.S., rape-mur. Gary Heidnik told his father he was going to be a millionaire and went away, at his own request, to a military academy when he was sixteen. He returned to his home town, a Cleveland, Ohio, suburb, for his senior year, but dropped out after only a month and left town. A month later, Heidnik enlisted in the army.

Heidnik's army experience was unusual. He was sent to Germany after four months of basic training, and served only seven months there, though overseas assignments are seldom for less than a year. On his return he was sent to a military hospital and treated for psychiatric problems for three months. In January 1963, Heidnik was discharged with a rare "100 percent disabled" status, entitling him to lifetime maximum disability benefits.

In February 1964 Heidnik enrolled in a practical nursing program in Philadelphia. Ten months later he graduated as a licensed practical nurse with a satisfactory record and no disciplinary problems. Within three years he bought a house in Philadelphia's University City. Heidnik's brother Terry was also living in Philadelphia and, in 1971, the two established themselves as ministers in their newly-formed United Church of the Ministers of God. The congregation consisted of eight other members, all mentally retarded. According to Robert Rogers, a tenant in his building, Heidnik began to talk about a coming "race war." In the Fall of 1976 Heidnik shut off the utilities in his building and barricaded himself in the basement with a supply of food, a rifle, and a pistol, apparently expecting and hoping that his tenants would complain. When Rogers crawled through a basement window to confront the landlord, Heidnik shot him in the cheek. Charges of aggravated assault were dismissed, and Heidnik sold the house and moved.

By May 1978 Heidnik was living with a woman who was apparently retarded. Heidnik went with her to visit her mentally retarded sister at an institution. He pretended to take the woman out for a ride, but took her to his house and kept her in a storage area until she was found by authorities two weeks later. Heidnik was charged with rape, kidnapping, deviant sexual intercourse, interference with the custody of a committed person, recklessly endangering another person, and unlawful restraint. When tried by Judge Mirarchi, Heidnik testified that he suffered from schizophrenia and was taking three different drugs for the condition. He was sentenced to three to seven years in prison and served four years and four months, shuttled back and forth between prison and psychiatric hospitals.

On his release, he lived in a trailer for a year, then bought a home in a poor, mostly black neighborhood on Philadelphia's southwest side. A clever investor, Heidnik accumulated half a million dollars and cruised the neighborhood in a Cadillac or a Rolls Royce, seducing women. He also began to build a torture chamber in his basement. After a two-year correspondence with Betty Disto, a Filipino woman, he flew her to Philadelphia and married her in October 1985. Disto left Heidnik three months later, saying he had raped and assaulted her and forced her to watch him have sex with other women. In November of 1987, mentally retarded young black women began to disappear from the neighborhood. Missing were Josefina Rivera, twenty-six; Sandra Lindsay, twenty-four; Lisa Thomas, nineteen; Deborah Johnson Dudley, twenty-three; Jacqueline Askins, eighteen; and Agnes Adams, twenty-four.

On Mar. 25, 1987, Rivera escaped from Heidnik's car after she persuaded him to let her go lure another woman to his house. At 4 a.m., police broke into Heidnik's house and found Thomas, Askins, and Adams chained to pipes in the basement. The body of Dudley was found the next day at the Wharton State Forest in Camden County, N.J. where Heidnik had dumped it. Dudley had been electrocuted when Heidnik ran electrical wires into a water-filled pit in the basement. Lindsay had died after being hanged by an arm from a pipe for several days. Parts of Lindsay's body were found in a freezer. Other remains were discovered in pots on the stove. Surviving victims were dehydrated and suffering from malnutrition. Heidnik had fed them dog food and dog biscuits, as well as remains from Lindsay's body. They had been severely beaten and had had screwdrivers driven into their ears.

On July 12, 1988, a jury convicted Heidnik of first-degree murder, kidnapping, and rape, rejecting the defense's claim that he was insane. After deliberating for two hours, the jury ordered that Heidnik should die in the electric chair. REF.: *CBA.*

Heilbron, Rose (Mrs. Nathaniel Burnstein), 1914- , Brit., jur. In 1949 became one of Great Britain's first women judges. She served as defense counsel for George Kelly. REF.: *CBA.*

Hein, Piet (Pieter Heyn), 1577-1629, Neth., pir. Affluent merchant captain who became a director of the Dutch West Indies Company in 1621. In 1624, he was a vice admiral of a fleet of Dutch ships. He was credited with the capture of twenty-two Portuguese ships in 1627. His seizure of Spanish ships loaded with great treasure helped support the Dutch war efforts against Spain. He died in a fight with Dunkirk pirates. REF.: *CBA.*

Heinrich, Edward Oscar, 1881-1953, U.S., criminol. Edward Heinrich was a brilliant investigator and a pioneer in using scientific analysis in crime detection. Born in Clintonville, Wis., he became knowledgeable in geology, chemistry, botany, handwriting analysis, and ballistics. In July 1919, he founded a laboratory in San Francisco, Calif., dedicated solely to crime detection, the first of its kind in the nation. "Crime analysis is an orderly procedure," he argued. "It's precise and it follows always the same questions that I ask myself: precisely what happened, when, where, why, and who did it."

During WWI, Heinrich's testimony helped convict Chandra Kanta Chakravarty, an Indian scholar recruited by German consul Franz Bopp. Chakravarty instigated a revolution in his homeland to divert British troops to India from Europe. Heinrich's demonstration that no two typewriters had the same typeface was crucial to the prosecution's case against Chandra. In 1923 Heinrich helped Southern Pacific Railroad track three men who had attempted to hold up train No. 13, and killed four railway employees. A pair of overalls and a Colt revolver with the serial

numbers sawed off were all investigators had to go on. Heinrich noticed some fir pitch stain in the material. "These overalls were worn by a left-handed lumberjack who has worked around fir trees in the Pacific Northwest," he deduced. A second set of serial numbers concealed within the revolver's chamber, were easily identified. Three brothers, Roy, Hugh, and Ray D'Autremont, who worked as lumberjacks in Oregon, were arrested and convicted.

Edward Heinrich did much to revolutionize criminal investigating procedures. "I base all of my conclusions on science, and science you know, is never wrong," he liked to say. See: **D'Autremont Brothers; Schwartz, Charles Henry.**

Criminologist Edward Oscar Heinrich, who solved many murder cases.

REF.: Block, *The Wizard of Berkeley;* CBA; Nash, *Bloodletters and Badmen;* ____, *Citizen Hoover;* Scott, *Concise Encyclopedia of Crime and Criminals.*

Heirens, William George (AKA: George Murman), 1929- , U.S., burg.-kid.-mur. Raised in the upper middle-class environment of Lincolnwood, a Chicago suburb, William Heirens had more advantages than most. He was sexually frustrated as a child, his puritanical mother warning him that "all sex is dirty" and "if you touch anyone, you get a disease." The boy grew up harboring sexual fantasies. He secretly obtained female clothing and would don this apparel when alone. Heirens began a scrapbook when turning into his teens, one into which he pasted the pictures of Nazi leaders Adolf Hitler, Paul Josef Goebbels, and Heinrich Himmler.

In 1942, at the age of thirteen, just before graduating from eighth grade at Chicago's St. Mary's of the Lake parochial school, Heirens was arrested for carrying a concealed weapon. Investigating officers went to his home and there found several weapons hidden behind a refrigerator. Atop the roof of the boy's home, more automatic weapons and ammunition were found. Heirens admitted that he had committed eleven burglaries and set fire to six houses in only a few months prior to his arrest. Heirens' mother and father were dumbfounded. His father, George Heirens, a reputable steel company employee, had no explanation for his son's conduct and his mother could only say that she had given her son everything he wanted. The couple (who later changed their name to avoid the stigma their son would heap upon it) promised to keep their boy out of trouble if the courts would allow them to send Heirens to a private correctional institution in Indiana. Heirens himself showed remorse and promised to reform. The court allowed probation to the Indiana school.

After a year in the Gibault correctional institution, in Terre Haute, Ind., Heirens was allowed to transfer to St. Bede's Academy in Peru, Ill. He showed himself to be a brilliant student and when he graduated from this high school he entered the University of Chicago, skipping the freshman term and entering as a sophomore. Although he proved himself to be a model student, Heirens had not reformed at all. He had continued his burglaries, becoming a skillful thief. While attending the University of Chicago, Heirens burglarized apartments in the posh North Side of Chicago. He later explained that burglaries gave him sexual gratification. "If I got a thrill, I didn't take anything." The very fact that he could enter someone else's apartment and invade their private living space was often enough to satisfy Heirens' offbeat cravings.

The burglaries turned to murder when the occupants of the

William Heirens, burglar-killer.

Above, 6-year-old Suzanne Degnan, kidnapped and horribly murdered by Heirens.

Left, Heirens under arrest, caught in the act of burglary.

Right, Heirens during his trial; he insisted he was innocent and that a mysterious friend did the killings.

for heavens sake catch me before I kill more I cannot control myself

The note Heirens wrote to police.

Heirens beginning his life sentence.

Heirens (at left) applying for appeal.

apartments either discovered Heirens prowling around in the darkness or resisted his attempt to rob them. All the murder victims were females. The first was Mrs. Josephine Alice Ross, an attractive 43-year-old widow who lived on North Kenmore Avenue. Her body was found on June 3, 1945. In a later statement, Heirens admitted that Mrs. Ross caught him burglarizing her apartment early that morning. He stabbed her repeatedly in the face and neck, severing her jugular vein. She bled to death, but Heirens did not immediately flee. For inexplicable reasons, he remained in the apartment for almost two hours. He washed his victim's wounds and then placed bandages on all the wounds.

The gaping wound in Mrs. Ross' neck so upset Heirens that he obtained a red evening gown and wrapped this around her neck to cover the brutal slash. He then walked about the apartment, going slowly from room to room, reaching a sexual climax, he later said. He then took $12 from Mrs. Ross' purse and left. As he was departing, Heirens brushed past Jacqueline Miller, Mrs. Ross' daughter, who was just then returning from work. The next attack came on Oct. 1, 1945. Veronica Hudzinski, nineteen, was at her desk in her apartment on North Winthrop Avenue when she heard a tapping at her window. As she went to draw the shade, two bullets ploughed through the glass, one wounding the woman in her shoulder. Police found a revolver outside the woman's window but it bore no fingerprints.

On Oct. 5, 1945, Evelyn Peterson, a former army nurse, awoke to noises in her apartment on Drexel Avenue, which was in the University of Chicago district. Just as she began to get out of bed, a heavy metal bar slammed against her head, knocking Peterson unconscious. She revived to find herself bound by a lamp cord. Freeing her arms, she discovered that $150 had been taken from her purse. She was later taken to a hospital where it was learned that her skull had been fractured. Police again were frustrated in not finding any clues at the Peterson apartment, except for a partial thumbprint. The intruder had taken pains to wipe away his prints.

The so-called "lipstick murder" occurred next. On Dec. 10, 1945, Frances Brown, thirty-three, an ex-Wave living in a stylish sixth-floor apartment at the Pine Crest Hotel on Pine Grove Avenue, came out of her bathroom to find Heirens ransacking her apartment. He had entered through a window facing a fire escape. She began to scream and Heirens, drawing a revolver, fired two shots at her almost point-blank. Brown was killed instantly but Heirens did not flee. He ran to the kitchen, grabbed a butcher knife and plunged this several times into the already dead woman, leaving the knife jutting from one wound. The blood bothered Heirens, he later claimed, and he dragged the corpse into the bathroom where he washed the wounds, leaving the body draped over the bathtub. Heirens then rifled the woman's purse and prepared to leave. Impulsively, he grabbed a lipstick and wrote on the wall:

> For heavens
> sake catch me
> Before I kill more
> I cannot control myself

Again, Heirens had attempted to wipe away all his fingerprints but he overlooked one, a bloody print of his right index finger which police discovered on the jamb of the dressing room door between the bathroom and the living room. This print and the thumbprint taken from the scene of the Ross slaying, still produced no identification. Detective Chief Storms realized that he was dealing with a pathological killer who would continue to slay as a matter of compulsion. He told his men: "He's killed twice and will keep on killing until we catch him. We're working against time."

On the night of Jan. 7, 1946, 6-year-old Suzanne Degnan was awakened in her room in a North Side apartment. An upstairs neighbor, Ethel Hargrove, later told police she had heard a noise outside and then the child's voice, clearly saying: "I don't want to

get up. I'm sleepy." Heirens had built a ladder to climb into the Degnan apartment in a kidnapping scheme that he had obviously prepared long in advance. He gagged and bound the child and then carried her down the ladder. A note he left was found some hours later. It read:

> Get $20,000 Ready & Waite for Word. Do Not Notify FBI or Police. Bills in 5's and 10's. BURN THIS FOR HER SAFETY (This last sentence appeared on the opposite side of the note.)

The kidnapper had no intention of ever freeing the child. Heirens took the girl to a basement nearby and murdered her, then dissected her body. Wrapping the dismembered pieces of the body in the child's bedclothes, Heirens walked about the streets early that morning, dropping the remains of Suzanne Degnan in one sewer after another, forcing these gruesome remains through the gratings. Heirens was seen at about 1 a.m. as he moved along the streets, pausing at sewers, first by an ex-soldier, then a janitor in the neighborhood. Heirens was carrying a large shopping bag. No ransom was ever paid because Heirens failed to send instructions about delivering the money. He might have become too frightened to carry out his plan. He had also become careless. While kidnapping the Degnan child, Heirens had left his fingerprints everywhere in her room. The remains of Suzanne Degnan were then found, piece by piece.

Though the Chicago police had searched its own files and sent copies of the prints taken at the Degnan apartment to the FBI, no identity was turned up. Then, on June 25, 1946, Richard Russell Thomas, a house painter and nurse living in Phoenix, Ariz., confessed to murdering the Degnan girl, giving authorities a great deal of details about the kidnapping and murder. Chicago detectives flew to Phoenix, but after interviewing Thomas they realized that his claim was false. Thomas was about to be convicted on a morals charge in Phoenix and to avoid this he decided to confess to the Degnan murder. He believed that he would be taken to Chicago, charged with the crime, and then prove himself innocent, avoiding the Phoenix conviction.

A day after Thomas made his phony claim, the janitor of the Wayne Manor Apartments on Chicago's north side, called police, saying that there was a prowler in the building. Police detectives Tiffin P. Constant and William Owens responded to the call. When they arrived the officers were told that the prowler was armed and on a back porch of the apartment building. Constant ran to the rear of the building and looked up. Seven feet away, a young man was leaning over a railing, aiming a revolver at him. He fired twice but the gun misfired both times. Constant fired three shots at the young man, Heirens, all of which missed. He ran up the stairs after the youth.

Heirens threw his gun at Constant but missed. He then dove downward on top of the officer, knocking the gun out of the detective's hand. He fought to get the officer's gun, wildly flaying at Constant. The detective later described Heirens' face as having "a maniacal look...He was throwing his teeth around and grimacing. The expression on his mouth kept changing." An off-duty policeman, Abner Cunningham, who lived in the area and had run to the scene barefooted, raced up the stairs to see Constant and a youth with thick black hair and whose eyes "gleamed like a panther's." Both men were struggling for the possession of the gun, the older, blond-haired man on top the other.

Cunningham had grabbed some small flower pots to use as weapons as he ran up the stairs of the porch. He stood there above the two struggling men, then asked Constant: "Is this the right man?"

"That's him," Constant gasped, trying to hold down Heirens' arms.

With that Cunningham crashed the flower pots down on Heirens' head. Heirens threw up his hands, then rolled over and lay still.

"That's enough," Constant told Cunningham.

Heirens was brought to police headquarters where he gave an address on Touhy Avenue in Lincolnwood where his mother, father, and a younger brother resided. He had a room at Gates Hall on the University of Chicago campus. Captain Michael Ahern of the Rogers Park Police Station remembered Heirens as the teenage burglar he had booked in 1942. He was now seventeen, five feet ten inches, and muscular. At Gates Hall, police found pistols, ammunition, jewelry, and $1,800 in war bonds. Many of the items found there had been taken from the Ross and Brown apartments and police now realized that they had the pathological burglar they had been seeking for almost a year. Heirens' fingerprints were taken and compared with those found in the Degnan home. They matched.

Charged with murder, Heirens blamed someone else for all his crimes, a man named George Murman. He even possessed letters from Murman, but these, like the ransom note he had written to the Degnan family, were proved to have been written by himself. The lipstick message on the wall of the Brown apartment was also identified as having been written by the youthful burglar. Heirens had invented Murman (*Murder*man) as an alter ego, someone who lived only in his own mind, someone other than himself who would be responsible for all the horrible crimes William George Heirens had committed. Heirens knew all about the burglaries and killings. But George Murman had done all these terrible things, not him.

Heirens was quickly convicted and sentenced to three consecutive life terms, never to be paroled. His age was a mitigating factor against his being electrocuted. Heirens resides in the Illinois State Prison at this writing. He still files regular appeals to be paroled but each time the parole board has denied his requests. He also still believes that George Murman is alive somewhere. "To me he is very real," Heirens was quoted as saying some years ago. "He exists. You can accept George as being me, but, well—it's hard to explain. A couple of times I had talks with him. I suppose I was really talking to myself. I wrote lots of notes to him which I kept." At that time, Heirens failed to state at that time that George Murman also wrote to him and these letters were written by the same person, the same killer, William George Heirens.

REF.: Alix, *Ransom Kidnapping in America; CBA;* DeFord, *Murderers Sane and Mad;* Freeman, *Before I Kill More;* Halper, *The Chicago Crime Book;* Nash, *Almanac of World Crime;* _____, *Bloodletters and Badmen;* Radin, *Crimes of Passion;* Scott, *The Concise Encyclopedia of Crime and Criminals;* Wilson, *Encyclopedia of Murder.*

Heith, John, See: **Heath, John.**

Heitler, Michael (AKA: **Mike "de Pike"**), d.1931, U.S., org. crime. Prostitution thrived in Chicago during the late nineteenth and the twentieth centuries catering to all levels of clientele from the opulence of the Everleigh Club to the more pedestrian House of All Nations. For those seeking bargain basement prices, Mike "de Pike" Heitler operated a brothel on West Madison Street dispensing favors at fifty cents apiece. Heitler ran the operation like a retail check-out line, sitting at a cash register and collecting the money as the girls became available. Heitler's girls were given a brass check for each client, which they later redeemed for half the price De Pike charged the clients. If

Chicago brothel operator Mike "de Pike" Heitler.

customers stayed too long in the cramped cubicle, an ugly employee suitably called Charlie "Monkey Face" Genker would peer through the transom, preventing further activity. Heitler

operated independently for years, bribing police officials while enduring an occasional arrest for white slavery.

Heitler's autonomy began to deteriorate in the 1920s when crime became organized through the efforts of Johnny Torrio, followed by Al Capone. Forced to align with Capone, Heitler became a reluctant employee, and when Harry Guzik began to dominate Capone's prostitution operation, Heitler began informing about the mob's criminal activities. He told Judge John H. Lyle about the gangsters torturous methods of enforcement carried out in a club named the Four Deuces. However, after Heitler wrote a letter to the State's Attorney detailing Capone's prostitution operation, the letter mysteriously appeared on Capone's desk. Capone summoned Heitler to his headquarters at the Lexington Hotel, and summarily fired him. Heitler angrily continued his correspondence with law enforcement officials. In one letter, he implicated Capone in the murder of Chicago *Tribune* reporter Jake Lingle, and again the letter found its way to Capone's desk. On Apr. 30, 1931, Heitler's charred remains were found in the ashes of a fire-ravaged house in the Chicago suburbs. See: **Capone, Alphonse.**

REF.: Asbury, *Gem of the Prairie; CBA;* Kobler, *Capone;* Lait and Mortimer, *Chicago: Confidential;* Landesco, *Organized Crime in Chicago;* Reppetto, *The Blue Parade;* Smith, *Syndicate City.*

Helas, Robert William (AKA: **Mark Langtry**), prom. 1950s, Brit., pros. When Robert Helas met his soon-to-be wife, Joyce Langtry, at a political meeting, he got the impression that she ran a modeling business. In truth, she ran a call-girl service. In July 1953, police raided her agency, and she was tried and convicted. By that time, Helas had opened his own London escort service. Operating legitimately at first, his business grew to include up to 1,000 escorts, some of whom offered to provide their clients with sexual services. Like his wife, Helas eventually was arrested, tried, and convicted at the Old Bailey. In March 1955, he received a sentence of eighteen months in prison.

REF.: *CBA;* Furneaux, *Famous Criminal Cases,* vol. 2.

Held, Leo A., 1928-67, Case of, U.S., mur.-suic. In 1967, Leo Held lived in Loganton, a small community in central Pennsylvania. The 39-year-old Held seemed to be a reasonable, responsible citizen. He was married, had four children, one of whom attended college. He was a Boy Scout leader, a member of the school board, a church member, and a volunteer fireman. For nineteen years, he had been employed as a lab technician at the Hammermill Paper Company in Loch Haven, Pa., about seventeen miles from his home.

One day, in a small skirmish with a neighbor, 71-year-old Ella Knisely, Held quarreled about a branch that had fallen on the ground. He became very angry and hit the woman with the bough. She took him to court, charging him with assault and battery, but the charge was dismissed by the judge.

Then Held's calm exterior shattered. He waited for his 36-year-old wife, Alta, to leave for her secretarial job, and for three of their children to go to school. Leaving his lunch on the kitchen table, Held armed himself with two handguns, a Smith & Wesson .38 and a .45 automatic. He got into his station wagon and drove to the paper mill where he was expected at 8 a.m. Inside the mill, Held opened fire. He killed five people, including Superintendent Donald V. Walden, supervisors Richard Davenport and Carmen H. Edwards, and lab technicians Elmer E. Weaver and Allen R. Barrett. Held injured Manager Woodrow Stultz, Superintendent James Allen, lab technician Richard Carter, and machine operator David Overdorf. Most of his targets were supervisors and people who had received promotions when he had not.

After the bloodbath, Held drove to Loch Haven airport where he fired a gun four times at switchboard operator Geraldine Ramm, hitting her twice. Ramm had been a member of Held's car pool and had refused to ride with him three months earlier because she thought he drove recklessly.

Back in his car, Held drove to his children's school, where all of the children had been locked inside for safety. Held proceeded back to his own neighborhood and broke into the home of Floyd

Quiggle. While Quiggle and his wife slept, Held fatally shot Quiggle, wounded his wife, and raided Quiggle's gun collection. He had complained to the Quiggles not long before that smoke from their burning leaves irritated him. Held then went across the street to his own house where police officers found him. As police fire wounded him in the thigh, shoulder, and wrist, he yelled, "Come and get me. I'm not of taking any more of their bull." As he lay dying, Held reportedly told a nurse, "I had one more to go." REF.: *CBA*.

Heldenberg, Raymonde, 1916-   , and **Heldenberg, Isoline**, 1943-   , and **Heldenberg, Martine**, 1954-   , Fr., mur. Robert Heldenberg, a 56-year-old Parisian trumpet player who drank heavily and chased women, frequently beat his 53-year-old wife, Raymonde. In early 1966, Raymonde Heldenberg sought and obtained a legal separation, which allowed cohabitation until the end of September. On Sept. 26, 1966, Raymonde and her two daughters, 26-year-old Isoline and 15-year-old Martine, murdered Robert Heldenberg by giving him barbiturates and strangling him with a scarf. They overturned furniture and gave bruises to one another to support a defense of justifiable homicide. After three years, on Sept. 23, 1969, Raymonde Heldenberg was found Guilty of the murder of her husband and sentenced to five years in prison. The two daughters received suspended sentences.

REF.: *CBA*; Heppenstall, *The Sex War and Others*.

Heldt, Henning, and **Hubbard, Mary Sue**, and **Willardson, Gregory**, and **Snider, Duke**, and **Weigand, Richard**, and **Hermann, Mitchell**, and **Raymond, Cindy**, and **Wolfe, Gerald Bennett**, and **Thomas, Sharon**, prom. 1978-79, U.S., theft-consp. L. Ron Hubbard established the Church of Scientology in 1954, and its membership in the U.S. soon grew to about three million. The church eventually went to great lengths to protect its interests, including infiltrating government offices and stealing government documents. Their activities were first noticed by a guard who saw two people often copying documents late at night, apparently U.S. attorney's files concerning Scientology suits against various government organizations. One of the thieves, Michael Meisner, came forward, and based on his information, 150 FBI agents entered the Scientology headquarters in Los Angeles and Washington on July 8, 1977, in a twenty-four hour raid. They seized wiretapping equipment, a blackjack, handguns, ammunition, and lock picks. Investigators also found evidence that the church had placed spies in the Justice Department, bugged a meeting of the Internal Revenue Service, and stolen information from the Justice Department, the U.S. Attorney's office, and the IRS.

Nine church members, eight of them from California, were indicted in 1978 and on Oct. 26, 1979, eight were convicted on criminal conspiracy charges in connection with breaking into government offices and stealing documents, positioning spies in government offices, and obstructing justice. Mary Sue Hubbard, the founder's wife, received a sentence of five years in prison and a fine of $10,000. Deputy Guardian Henning Held, leader of the church's U.S. operations, Duke Snider, Gregory Willardson, and Richard Weigand were all sentenced to four years in prison and fined $10,000 each. Three other members, Mitchell Hermann, Cindy Raymond, and Gerald Bennett Wolfe, were given sentences of four to five years in prison and fined $10,000. The ninth defendant, Sharon Thomas, was convicted on a theft charge. She was sentenced to six months in jail, five years' probation, and fined $1,000. REF.: *CBA*.

Helfgott, Marvin, prom. 1974, U.S., gun control. In 1974, Marvin Helfgott, a West Los Angeles pharmacist, founded the Coalition for Handgun Control. He and his family were bombarded with hate mail, including one letter addressed to "Filthy Cur Dog," and another signed "Adolf Hitler." His pharmacy was peppered with BB gun shot, he and his family received numerous abusive phone calls, their windows were smashed, and handbills calling for a boycott of his business were sent throughout his neighborhood. The Helfgotts eventually joined the National Gun Control Center, based in Washington, D.C.

REF.: *CBA*; Godwin, *Murder U.S.A.*

Heliogabalus (Elagabalus, Varius Avitus Bassianus, AKA: Marcus Aurelius Antoninus), 204-222, Roman., emp., assass. Pronounced emperor in 218 and defeated Macrinus in Syria. He became a morally corrupt spendthrift and put many senators to death. Roman imperial bodyguards assassinated him. REF.: *CBA*.

Hell, Said the Duchess, 1934, a novel by Michael Arlen. Instead of Jack the Ripper in this work of fiction it is Jane the Ripper. See: **Jack the Ripper**. REF.: *CBA*.

Heller, Isaac (AKA: Isaac Young), d.1836, U.S., mur. Isaac Heller, a farmer living outside of Liberty, Iowa, was emotionally unbalanced and had demonstrated erratic behavior long before he slaughtered his wife and three small children with an ax. Nevertheless, he was convicted and condemned to death, being executed on Apr. 29, 1836.

REF.: *CBA*; *The Life and Confession of Isaac Heller*.

Hell Fire Club, prom. 1750s-60s, Brit., secret soc. The Twelfth-Century ruins of the Medmenham Abbey became headquarters for an exclusive private club committed to proving the existence of Satan and his demon helpers. The Hell Fire Club was conceived by Sir Francis Dashwood, a dandy said to have "fornicated" his way across Europe while completing a Grand Tour in 1729. His insatiable interest in the occult prompted him to lease the crumbling abbey in 1752, turning it into a playground of perversion for jaded friends like Thomas Potter, son of the Archbishop of Canterbury; George Bubb Dodington, member of the British Cabinet during the reign of George III; Charles Churchill, poet; John Wilkes; the Earl of Bute, who later became prime minister; and Paul Whitehead, the club steward.

The club was divided into two sects known as the Superior (Dashwood and his twelve "apostles"), and the Inferior (whoever else he cared to admit). Outfitted in ornamental costumes, Dashwood and his friends would gather in darkness for sexual orgies with demimondes clad in nuns' garb. The ceiling of the old abbey was covered with pornographic illustrations which established the mood for the black masses held to conjure up the devil. On one occasion, John Wilkes concealed the club mascot, a small baboon, in a large trunk. He covered the animal's face with a devil's mask and in the darkness Dashwood and his apostles were convinced that the frightened creature was the devil's imp.

Wilkes, who edited the newspaper *North Briton,* was opposed to Dashwood and his gang on political and ethical grounds. Hell Fire Club members curried the king's favor and gained powerful government positions though they were corrupt and rapacious. In issue number forty-five of his newspaper, Wilkes exposed the gang, which ultimately led to the dismissal of Dodington and Dashwood from their government posts. In retaliation Dashwood exposed the hypocrisy of Wilkes. Wilkes survived the scandal, however, and eventually became Lord Mayor of London. See: **Dashwood**, Sir Francis. REF.: *CBA*.

Hellier, Thomas, d.1678, U.S., theft-mur. A slave on a Virginia plantation, Thomas Hellier, a white man, was sentenced to bondage for several thefts. His master sold him to another farmer, Cutbeard Williamson, who owned the Hard Labor estate. Hellier waited until the Williamson family was sleeping, then entered the mansion. With an ax he murdered Williamson, his wife, and their maid. Hanged on Aug. 5, 1678, at Westover, Va., Hellier's corpse was tied in chains to a tall tree overlooking the James River. The body remained on the tree for several years, left as a warning to other rebellious servants.

REF.: *CBA*; Nash, *Bloodletters and Badmen; The Vain Prodigal Life and Tragical Penitent Death of Thomas Hellier*.

Hell's Angels, prom. 1960s-70s, U.S., org. crime. The Hell's Angels motorcycle gang began sometime in the late 1940s or early 1950s, and periodically swelled to popularity. In the 1940s, the Angels membership picked up after ex-G.I.'s returned from WWII. A small percentage of them, unable to adjust to civilian life, took to the road on motorcycles, living an outlaw existence and comparing themselves to modern-day Texas Rangers or other famous western bandits and desperados like Billy the Kid. The

Hell's Angels was officially founded in Fontana, Calif., in 1950, and soon romanticized in the 1953 film *The Wild One,* starring Marlon Brando and Lee Marvin as cleaned-up Angels who took over a small town. In the 1950s, after the Korean War, Hell's Angels' popularity again picked up, as it did in the 1960s in conjunction with the war in Vietnam. A violent, sexist, and often murderous or suicidal group, the Hell's Angels proudly wore the symbol of a winged skull wearing a motorcycle helmet, and sported Nazi insignia like swastikas and iron crosses. In addition to the American chapters, which were concentrated on the Pacific Coast, the Angels had footholds in England and especially in Australia, where the wide open spaces agreed with their lifestyle.

Many Angels chapters, with names like "Devil's Disciples" and "Satan's Sinners," were loosely organized along military lines, with sergeants-at-arms, lieutenants, and presidents of each group. The majority of Angels members had criminal records, often for petty theft. In the 1970s, they moved in on the drug scene. Rape was one of the most commonly alleged crimes against Angels. In their society, women were often tattooed as "property of" their "master" of the month, or commonly shared and routinely subjected to gang rape or forced orgies.

The Angels were particularly prominent in California, and one of the most highly publicized incidents in their history happened at a Rolling Stones concert in Oakland. The Angels had been hired, for $500 worth of beer, to act as security guards at the free concert. They had performed a similar function many times before at rock festivals and concerts with routine incidents of violence and beatings. At the 1969 Altamont Rock Music Concert, with 300,000 people in attendance, Hell's Angel Allan Passaro, twenty-two, of San Jose, stabbed 18-year-old Meredith Hunter five times near the stage where the Rolling Stones were performing. The incident was filmed by a crew shooting the documentary film *Gimme Shelter,* and was played several times for Oakland jurors at the trial. The poor-quality film, which was not shown publicly in San Francisco for several years after the incident, showed Passaro striking Hunter as he tried to grab a revolver out of the youth's hand. Passaro, who claimed self-defense, was found Not Guilty on Jan. 15, 1971.

In 1973, two former British Hell's Angels were convicted of the April 1973 murder of 16-year-old Clive Olive in Shoreham Harbour, in southern England. Olive, who had been hanging around with the "Mad Dogs of Sussex" chapter of the group, had become enraged when other Angels raped his 16-year-old girlfriend. His body was later found tied and weighted at the bottom of a river.

In the 1970s in California, many Hell's Angels boasted that they were bigger than the law, and stories of suspected murders, drug pushing, extortion, and gang rapes abounded. In 1975, the federal government launched an intensive two-year probe which resulted in a forty-five page indictment and a June 13, 1979, raid by police officers on several Angels hangouts. Among the thirty-two gang members indicted on charges ranging from racketeering and murder to blackmail, drug trafficking, and mail fraud were Oakland chapter president Ralph Hubert "Sonny" Barger, forty-one, and his wife, Sharon Barger, twenty-nine. The trial, one of the largest felony cases in U.S. history, began in a San Francisco Federal Court in October 1979 with Federal Judge Samuel Conti hearing the case of the group sometimes referred to as the "Motorized Mafia." In the complicated early legal maneuvering by more than 300 defense attorneys for the Angels Conti roared, "I'd like to get this case over with in my lifetime." U.S. District Attorney Robert Donero charged in his opening statements that the motorcycle gang garnered most of its income from drug trafficking, and that the Angels' by-laws required every member to become a drug pusher, with murder and terrorism routinely used to keep control over the market. Donero said the Angels had massive arsenals of hand grenades and machine guns. Defense attorneys Richard Mazer and Alan Caplan contended that the Angels were the victims of unconstitutional federal harassment, with Caplan explaining, "The Hell's Angels is a social

organization devoted to the advancement of motorcycles."

On July 2, 1980, the eight-month, multimillion-dollar trial ended in a hung jury. After seventeen days of deliberation, it had been unable to reach a verdict on major counts against eighteen of the defendants. The remaining twelve defendants, including Barger, were found Not Guilty on the charge of racketeering. One hundred and ninety-four witnesses had appeared in the six months of prosecution testimony. Narcotics officers and Angel-turned-informant Thomas Bryant drew a picture of sadism, violence, massive drug deals, rapes, beatings, and murders. Only one defendant, Manuel Rubio, forty-three, was convicted—on one count of racketeering. A second trial, which began on Oct. 3, 1981, ended on Feb. 25, 1982, the case when racketeering charges against the remaining eleven defendants were dropped. Federal Judge William Orrick declared a mistrial when the jury announced it was deadlocked. Orrick asked assistant U.S. District Attorney Robert Mueller what the government's intentions were, and Mueller responded, "There will be no retrial in this case." On Apr. 14, 1983, narcotics and firearms convictions of five Hells Angels were overturned in the U.S. 9th District Court of Appeals, which cited no probable cause for a search warrant in the June 13, 1979, raids.

One of the final chapters in the dissipation of the outlaw gang occurred on Aug. 27, 1983, when four Hells Angels pleaded guilty in a San Diego federal court to charges of conspiracy stemming from the Angels' 1977 "war" with the Mongols biker gang over a dispute about common wording on their jackets. Two Mongols were machine-gunned to death and several others wounded because the Mongols dared to wear the word "California" on the bottom line of their leather jacket insignia. Pleading guilty to conspiracy in exchange for the dismissal of other felony racketeering and weapons counts were Thomas "Crunch" Renzulli, thirty-five, Larry Gaskins, thirty-nine, David Harbridge, thirty-six, and Guy Castiglione, thirty-two. U.S. District Judge Judith N. Keep sentenced the defendants to the maximum six years in federal prison, with credit for time already served on other charges.

Books about the Hells' Angels include *Hell's Angels, The Strange and Terrible Saga of the Outlaw Motorcycle Gang,* journalist Hunter S. Thompson's 1966 account of his year on the road with the gang, and *A Wayward Angel,* by George Wethern, the former vice president of the Oakland Chapter of the gang.

REF.: *CBA;* Haskins, *Street Gangs;* Kirby and Renner, *Mafia Enforcer;* Reuter, *Disorganized Crime;* (FILM), *Hell's Angels on Wheels,* 1967; *Angels From Hell,* 1968; *Hell's Angels '69,* 1969; *The Losers,* 1970; *The Danger Zone,* 1987.

Hell's Kitchen Gang, prom. 1860s-70s, U.S., org. crime. Hell's Kitchen, a large neighborhood west of the Manhattan intersection of Eighth Avenue and 34th Street, was rife with crime before the Civil War. Dominated by the Hell's Kitchen Gang, led by Dutch Heinrichs, gang members mugged pedestrians and extorted money from storekeepers for twenty years. In 1870, they merged with the Tenth Avenue Gang, led by Ike Marsh, and turned their focus from the streets to the more lucrative practice of raiding the Hudson River Railroad yards near 30th Street. The gang prospered until the railroad began offering its detectives a bounty for each gang member apprehended. Heinrichs was eventually arrested and was sent to prison for five years. While the strength of the gang waned, the unfortunate Hell's Kitchen neighborhood remained prey to gang activity for the next fifty years.

REF.: Asbury, *The Gangs of New York; CBA;* Haskins, *Street Gangs.*

Helm, Boone, 1823-64, U.S., west. outl.-can. At an early age, Boone Helm was considered a fierce criminal. While in his teens he stabbed to death a man named Littleburg in his native Log Branch, Mo., before fleeing west. In the 1850s, Helm roamed through California, prospecting for gold but, often enough, robbing miners. In 1858, he reportedly shot a miner in California before leaving for Oregon where he became a mountain man. One account has Helm starving in the mountains and slaying a pioneer family, then eating their remains. Helm then moved to Utah and hired his gun to the highest bidder, taking part in the

Mountain Meadows Massacre. Helm was later described as "a low, coarse, cruel, animal ruffian," and he became one of the most feared outlaws of his day.

Helm joined Henry Plummer's outlaw gang, robbing and killing through Idaho and Montana. He shot and killed a man in Florence, Idaho, and was jailed, but he bribed the jailer and was allowed to escape. He used many aliases while hiding out in the Montana mining camps, aware of several warrants issued for his arrest. He rejoined the Plummer gang but vigilantes put an end to these outlaws on Jan. 13 (or Jan. 14, according to another account), and was hanged, along with Jack "Three-Fingered Jack" Gallagher, Hayes Lyons, George "Clubfoot" Lane, and Frank Parrish in Virginia City, Mont.

These five men were placed on boxes with ropes around their necks, the ropes tied to a crossbeam of an unfinished log building at Van Buren and Wallace streets. Helm treated his miserable fate as if it were a gruesome joke. He was slightly drunk at the time and laughingly asked Gallagher for his handsome coat, telling his fellow outlaw: "Jack, give me that coat. You never gave me anything." Gallagher was hanged first and Helm shouted up to his dangling body: "Kick away, old fellow! I'll be in hell with you in a minute!" He then announced his loyalty to the Confederacy by shouting to the vigilantes: "Every man for his principles! Hurrah for Jeff Davis! Let her rip!" A vigilante kicked the box out from beneath Helm and he was dead minutes later. See: **Gallagher, Jack; Plummer, Henry.**

REF.: Barrows, *The United States of Yesterday and Tomorrow;* Barsness, *Gold Camps;* Bartholomew, *The Biographical Album of Western Gunfighters;* ____, *Henry Plummer, Montana Outlaw;* Birney, *Vigilantes;* Blankenship, *And There Were Men;* Breihan, *Badmen of Frontier Days;* ____, *Outlaws of the Old West;* Briggs, *Frontiers of the Northwest;* Bruffey, *Eighty-one Years in the West;* Carson, *Doc Middleton; CBA;* Dimsdale, *The Vigilantes of Montana;* Drumheller, *Uncle Dan;* Drury, *An Editor on the Comstock Lode;* Fisher and Holmes, *Gold Rushes and Mining Camps;* Florin, *Boot Hill;* Fogarty, *The Story of Montana;* Fultz, *Famous Northwest Manhunts and Murder Mysteries;* Gard, *Frontier Justice;* Gardner, *The Old Wild West;* Glasscock, *The War of the Copper Kings;* Hamilton, *From Wilderness to Statehood;* Hawley, *History of Idaho;* Hendricks, *The Bad Man of the West;* Holloway, *Texas Gun Lore;* Hough, *The Story of the Outlaw;* Howard, *Northwest Trail Blazers;* Kane, *100 Years Ago with the Law and the Outlaw;* Kelly, *The Outlaw Trail;* Kennedy, *Cowboys and Cattlemen;* Langford, *Vigilante Days and Ways;* Lavender, *Land of Giants;* Lucia, *Tough Men, Tough Country;* Mencken, *By the Neck;* Raine, *Guns of the Frontier;* Sabin, *Wild Men of the Wild West;* Salisbury, *Here Rolled the Covered Wagons;* Sanders, *A History of Montana;* ____, *X Beidler, Vigilante;* Splawn, *Ka-Mi-Akin: The Last Hero of the Yakimas;* Stout, *Montana;* Warner, *Montana Territory;* Wilson, *Out of the West;* Winther, *The Great Northwest;* Wolle, *The Bonanza Trail;* ____, *Montana Pay Dirt.*

The killing of Jack Helm by John Wesley Hardin, 1873.

Helm, Jack, d.1873, U.S., west. lawman. Jack Helm, a Texas cowboy, served in the confederate army during the Civil War, once killing a black man for merely whistling a Yankee song. Returning to Texas, he became involved in the bloody Sutton-Taylor feud, and became the unofficial leader of 200 Sutton regulators. In San Patricio County in July 1869, Helm and C.S. Bell murdered Taylor men John Choate and his nephew Crockett Choate. On Aug. 23, Helm and Bell killed Hays Taylor and wounded his brother Doboy during an ambush at the Taylor ranch. That month, Helm was appointed captain of the Texas State Police. In 1873, Helm was ordered to arrest Taylor relatives, William and Henry Kelly. Helm and his posse, consisting of Sutton supporters, apprehended the pair in DeWitt County and murdered them in a spate of vigilante justice. Following a public outcry, Texas governor E.J. Davis fired Helm from the state police, but he continued as sheriff of DeWitt County. The infamous outlaw and Taylor relative, John Wesley Hardin, encountered Helm several times, once killing his deputy, and another time shooting two Sutton supporters after an intended truce meeting. In July 1873, while in Albuquerque, Texas, Helm spotted Hardin and Jim Taylor in a blacksmith's shop. As he approached, Hardin turned and killed him with a shotgun blast. See: **Hardin, John Wesley.**

REF.: Bartholomew, *Kill or Be Killed;* Casey, *The Texas Border and Some Borderliners; CBA;* Cunningham, *Famous in the West;* Dobie, *Cow People;* Farrow, *Troublesome Times in Texas;* Gard, *Frontier Justice;* Hardin, *The Life of John Wesley Hardin;* Hendricks, *The Bad Man of the West;* Holloway, *Texas Gun Lore;* Horan and Sann, *Pictorial History of the Wild West;* Judson, *Montana;* Koller, *The American Gun;* McCarty, *The Enchanted West;* Nunn, *Texas Under the Carpetbaggers;* Ovitt, *Golden Treasure;* Pace, *Golden Gulch;* Penfield, *Western Sheriffs and Marshals;* Plenn and LaRoche, *The Fastest Gun in Texas;* Raine, *Forty-five Caliber Law;* Rennert, *Western Outlaws;* Ripley, *They Died With Their Boots On;* Siringo, *Riata and Spurs;* Sonnichsen, *I'll Die Before I Run;* Sutton, *Sutton-Taylor Feud;* Webb, *Handbook of Texas;* White, *Lead and Likker;* ____, *Trigger Fingers.*

Helvering, Guy Tresillian, 1878-1946, U.S., jur. Served as prosecuting attorney of Marshall County, Kan. from 1907-11, as a member of the U.S. House of Representatives from 1912-18, and as commissioner of internal revenue for the U.S. Government from 1933-1943. He was nominated to the district court of Kansas by President Franklin D. Roosevelt in 1943. REF.: *CBA.*

Helvidius Priscus, d.c. 75 A.D., Roman., rebel. Executed for his insistence on freedom of speech and his belief that the Senate should have rank equal to the emperor. His ideas greatly angered the Vespasians. Served as a Senator under Nero and as a praetor in 70 A.D. REF.: *CBA.*

Hembyze, Jan van (Imbize), 1513-84, Neth., treas. Executed for treason because of a plot to turn Ghent over to the Spanish. He became mayor of Ghent after leading an effort to overthrow the Ghent Catholic government in 1577. Tried to completely suppress Catholicism from 1578-79, but Prince William I of Orange disagreed with his stand against Catholics and attacked Ghent in 1579. He escaped and in 1583 returned to Ghent and was elected mayor. REF.: *CBA.*

Hemmerde, Edward George, 1871-1948, Brit., lawyer. Became judge in 1908. He also served as a member of Parliament from 1906-10, 1912-18, and from 1922-24. He was involved in the murder trials of George Fratson, John Starchfield, and William Herbert Wallace. REF.: *CBA.*

Hemming, Richard, prom. 1806, Case of, Brit., mur. The residents of Oddingley parish, Worcestershire, England, detested their rector, Reverend George Parker. He owned more land than anyone in the area, and his credit terms were harsh. Eventually, six men decided to have the rector murdered, so they asked Richard Hemming, a carpenter from Droitwich, to do the job. On June 24, 1806, the hired killer allegedly got a gun from Captain Evans and shot Parker to death in his garden. Then Hemming apparently went to a barn on Netherwood Farm, the home of conspirator Thomas Clewes, to collect his £50. However, either because he blackmailed the men or because they feared he would blackmail them in the future, the plotters killed Hemming and buried him in the barn.

Twenty-four years later, another owner of Netherwood Farm decided to renovate the property, and workers discovered a skeleton in the barn. Hemming's widow identified the remains by his shoes, teeth, and a carpenter's measure. Clewes, the former owner of the farm, was arrested and he confessed, incriminating the other two living conspirators, John Barnett and George Bankes. William Barnett, Captain Evans, and John Marshall had all died. The penniless Clewes was charged with murder and the other two, now prominent citizens, were charged as accessories. They were all acquitted.

REF.: *CBA; Kingston, Dramatic Days at the Old Bailey; Wilson, Encyclopedia of Murder.*

Henderson, Charles, prom. 1921, U.S., senator, attempt. assass. The day after Nevada senator Charles Henderson left office in 1921, he was shot by August Glock, a Reno, Nev., lawyer. Glock's desire to kill Henderson stemmed from the senator's refusal in the 1890s to represent Glock during court proceedings involving a land dispute. Henderson recuperated from his wound.

REF.: *CBA; Paine, The Assassins' World.*

Henderson, Clem (Clemmie), 1947-88, U.S., mur. The shooting rampage that Clem Henderson began on Sept. 22, 1988, might have lasted a good deal longer than it did, and cost many more lives than the five who died, if not for two Chicago police officers who happened to be on hand. Although both officers were shot by Henderson, 38-year-old patrolman Gregory Jaglowski shot the gunman to death with his last bullet, as he lay at the side of his dead partner.

Almost three years before the shooting, on Oct. 6, 1985, Henderson was alleged to have been shot in the head by youthful attackers; an incident believed to have led to the murder spree. No police record of the shooting was on file however, and the autopsy of Henderson revealed no evidence of the earlier shooting—though the Cook County Hospital did have a record of Henderson shooting himself in the head. Henderson also had been arrested twelve times between 1973 and 1984, spending more than six years in jail and one-and-a-half years on probation for mostly battery and disorderly conduct charges.

The 1988 shooting began at the Comet Auto Parts store on Chicago's Near West Side. In the store, Henderson fired his .38-caliber revolver three times, killing the store's 41-year-old owner John Van Dyke, and 27-year-old manager Robert J. Quinn, and missing 24-year-old employee Christopher Ferguson, who pretended he was shot as Henderson left the building. Outside the store Henderson wounded city street and sanitation worker Chestnut Ladose, with a gunshot to his hand, and then ran toward the Moses Montefiore Public School—a school for problem youths in need of discipline—where he shot 34-year-old school custodian Arthur Baker in the chest. Baker staggered to the principal's office and gasped, "Please call the police," before he fell to the floor and died. The police, however, were already on the premises, answering a call about a student who had pushed a teacher. By the time Jaglowski and his 40-year-old partner, Irma Ruiz, arrived, the student had fled, but on their way out they encountered the killer.

Jaglowski reached the front entrance ahead of Ruiz, and a bullet barely missed his face before he dove to the ground where Henderson shot him in the leg. Henderson left Jaglowski lying on the sidewalk and ran into the school where he shot Ruiz in the chest. The mother of four became only the second female officer in Chicago to be killed in the line of duty. (Dorelle C. Brandon was accidentally killed by her partner on Jan. 25, 1984, as the two struggled with a suspect for control of her service revolver.) While Henderson was reloading his gun down a corridor, Jaglowski went to Ruiz's aid, and was calling for help on her radio when Henderson returned. During an exchange of gunfire, Jaglowski was shot in the other leg before he fatally shot Henderson. For his heroics, Jaglowski received the Blue Star Award on Sept. 28, 1988, for being wounded while in the line of duty. Jaglowski was also promoted to detective by Police Superintendent LeRoy Martin, in lieu of a $500 check presented to the department by an appreciative citizen. Officers are not allowed to accept monetary gifts for performing their duty. Jaglowski did not see himself as a hero, but claimed that Ruiz was the true hero. REF.: *CBA.*

Henderson, Demetrius, 1967- , and **Croft, Curtis**, 1968- , and **Campbell, Kevin**, 1967- , and **Woodard, Alonzo**, 1967- , U.S., kid.-rape-mur. On July 12, 1986, 15-year-old Kimberly Boyd was abducted by four teenagers after a party at the home of 18-year-old Curtis Croft in Chicago. Nineteen-year-old Demetrius Henderson, Kevin Campbell, and Alonzo Woodard, along with Croft, repeatedly raped the South Shore High School sophomore, then under the direction of Henderson blindfolded her and placed her in the trunk of a car. Fearing the girl would tell of the rape, though she allegedly promised not to, Henderson and Croft drove her to an alley and killed her. The two youths stabbed Boyd several times, before running her over with the car. When this did not kill her, they stabbed her again, and then drove over her a second and third time. Boyd was stabbed a total of thirty-seven times.

In Cook County Criminal Court, Assistant State's Attorneys Rick Beuke and Randy Rueckert read the jury Henderson's chilling fifteen-page confession of how the victim refused to die. Defense attorney, James Linn, maintained that police officers forced the confession and backed up the statement by producing Henderson's mother, grandmother, and cousin, who testified that Henderson was home during the murder. The jury was not convinced and, on May 13, 1987, found Henderson Guilty of murder, aggravated sexual assault, and aggravated kidnapping. Judge Richard Neville found Croft Guilty of the same offenses, but found Campbell and Woodard Guilty only of the rape as evidence was produced to show the two did not take part in the murder. At the sentencing hearing, Linn maintained that Henderson had been perversely influenced by his past and his family—statements which quieted Henderson's laughter and changed his grin to a blank stare. Linn told how Henderson's father had been shot to death before the defendant was one year old, how his grandfather had been convicted of murder, and how his mother flaunted her sexual promiscuity to her son, who was further taunted by her latest lover. Neville did not find the past a mitigating factor and sentenced Henderson to death on June 18, 1987. The judge also sentenced Croft to life in prison without possibility of parole—as he was too young for the death penalty—and Campbell and Woodard to twenty-eight years in prison. REF.: *CBA.*

Henderson, George, prom. 1920, Brit., forg. A cable was sent in February 1920 from Capetown, S. Afri., informing the Union Castle Mail Steamship Company in London: "Steward Henderson buried at sea. Death from natural causes." The message was signed by the ship's purser, and relayed to Mrs. Henderson, who moved out of her home and went into mourning. Her despair did not last long; midway through March, the *S.S. Goorka* arrived in London with Henderson on board. Not long after his mysterious return from the sea, Henderson demanded that his company pay him £100 for the expense and trouble which arose from the false report of his death. Scotland Yard was asked to investigate the matter, and a comparison of Henderson's handwriting with the cablegram form proved conclusively that Henderson had forged announcement of his death. He claimed his innocence, but was found Guilty at the Old Bailey and imprisoned for forgery.

REF.: *CBA; Drago, Notorious Ladies of the Frontier; Nicholls, Crime Within the Square Mile.*

Henderson, Henry Perry, 1843-1909, U.S., jur. Served as prosecuting attorney of Ingham County, Mich., from 1874-76, as a representative to the Michigan state legislature, and as mayor of Mason, Mich. He was nominated to the territorial court of Utah by President Grover Cleveland in 1886. REF.: *CBA.*

Henderson, William Finley, 1839-90, U.S., jur. Nominated to the territorial court of New Mexico by President Grover Cleveland in 1885. REF.: *CBA.*

Hendricks, David, 1954- , U.S., mur. Between the hours of 8:30 p.m. on Nov. 8, 1983, and 2 a.m. the following morning, 30-year-old Susan Hendricks and her three children, aged five to nine, were stabbed and bludgeoned to death with an ax and butcher knife in their Bloomington, Ill., home. Her husband,

David Hendricks, claimed that he had left on a business trip to Wisconsin at 11 p.m. on the night of the killings. Evidence later showed that Hendricks had left much later.

The prosecution case sought to demonstrate that Hendricks had changed from a member of a fundamentalist religious organization, called the Plymouth Brethren, into a man who craved extramarital affairs. He was accused of committing the brutal murders because his wife and children stood in the way of his social life, which had changed considerably since 1980 when he shaved his mustache, got a new hairstyle, and began to dress more fashionably. Aside from the change in his appearance and character, prosecutors noted that the murder weapons belonged to Hendricks, no forced entry into the home was used, and the alleged business trip was probably a poorly planned alibi.

After a ten-week trial, Hendricks was found Guilty in 1984 following a change of venue to Rockford, Ill., where Judge Richard Baner refused to invoke the death penalty because he was not without a reasonable doubt that Hendricks was guilty. Instead, he sentenced Hendricks to four consecutive terms of life in prison.

Hendricks appealed his conviction to the Illinois Supreme Court which upheld the jury's decision on Dec. 21, 1988. Justice William Clark, who wrote the dissenting opinion for the court, argued that the prosecution's case was based solely on the defendant's character, and that a man's past did not point to a motive and thus was no basis for conviction of murder. In writing the majority opinion, Justice Joseph Cunningham agreed with Clark, but in the case of Hendricks he felt that "the relationship between the two key aspects of the motive theory is not tenuous but convincing." REF.: *CBA*.

Hendrickson, John, Jr., 1833-53, U.S., mur. Newlyweds John Hendrickson, Jr. and Maria Hendrickson were unhappy in their marriage. They lived with seven members of Hendrickson's family in Bethlehem, N.Y. In an atmosphere of constant bickering and fights—caused, according to the husband's relatives, by the strong-willed 19-year-old bride—Hendrickson gave his wife a fatal dose of aconite poison. It was the first known use of such poison in the U.S. Although the family tried to conceal the killing, Hendrickson was convicted and hanged on Mar. 6, 1853.

REF.: Barnes, *Trial of John Hendrickson, Jr.*; *CBA*; Cohen, *One Hundred True Crime Stories*; Nash, *Bloodletters and Badmen*; Swinburne, *Poisoning by Aconite*.

Heney, Francis Joseph, 1859-1937, U.S., lawyer. Prosecuted Portland, Ore., fraud cases involving land in 1903, and responsible for indicting many, including U.S. attorney John H. Hall. As San Francisco deputy district attorney, he handled the prosecution for cases in which Mayor Eugene Schmitz and political boss Abe Ruef were convicted. REF.: *CBA*.

Henlein, Konrad, 1898-1945, Ger., war crimes. On May 10, 1945, 47-year-old Konrad Henlein, who plotted against Czechoslovakia in WWI, aiding Hitler's attempt to occupy the country, surrendered to the U.S. Army's First Infantry Division. Already sentenced to death by Czech patriots for selling them into Nazi bondage, Henlein denied involvement, claiming he was in constant disagreement with Heinrich Himmler, head of the SS and the Gestapo. He avoided answering questions by saying he was "only a little man" bound to carry out orders without question. The next day, Henlein committed suicide by slashing his wrist with a razor blade he had concealed in a cigarette case. REF.: *CBA*.

Henley, Elmer Wayne, See: **Corll, Dean Allen**.

Hennessey, David C., d.1890, U.S., (unsolv.) mur. On May 6, 1890, an ongoing rivalry between factions of Italians in New Orleans over who would control the piers resulted in a gun battle which left several people dead and wounded, including innocent pedestrians. Chief of Police David C. Hennessey arrested several people, and said he would testify "to expose the secrets of the Mafia society" in forthcoming trials. Neither threats nor bribes deterred Hennessey from his campaign to "break the Mafia in New Orleans." He arrested scores of men during the summer and fall of 1890. On Oct. 15, as Hennessey walked home in the rain, five men fired on him with pistols and shotguns. Captain Bill O'Con-

nor of the New Orleans police force said his dying friend had whispered to him that the assailants were "dagos." Nineteen Italians were arrested almost immediately and scheduled for trial, but no one was ever convicted. Italians had been lynched in other areas of the country, and hostility against them was rampant in New Orleans following Hennessey's murder. Among those arrested in New Orleans were Joe Macia, head of the Macia Steamship Line; Rocco Gerace, a wealthy Italian businessman; and Charles Matranco, a prosperous citizen better known as "Millionaire Charlie."

The nineteen suspects came to trial on Feb. 16, 1891, before Judge Baker in the Old New Orleans Courthouse. William Pinkerton, head of the famous detective agency, had been a friend of Hennessey's, and had worked with several of his operatives to prepare testimony for the trial. But some witnesses disappeared and others clammed up, responding to threats or bribes. On Mar. 12 the jury returned a Not Guilty verdict. On Mar. 14, after a mass meeting at Clay Square, an angry mob of about 12,000 stormed the Parish Prison, where the defendants were being held. The crowd murdered eleven Italians, including three previously acquitted, three whose court cases had ended in mistrials, and five who had never been tried. Another eight prisoners escaped by hiding under mattresses or in closets. Slain were Joseph Macheca, Manuel Pollize, Antonio Scaffidi, Antonio Bagnetto, Frank Romero, Vincent Caruso, Charles Trahina, Pietro Monsterio, Rocco Geraoci, Lorenzo Comitz, and Antonio Marchesi. The anti-Italian prejudice was so strong in the U.S. at that time that more than half of the country's major newspapers approved of the slaughter. New Orleans mayor Shakespeare, asked if he regretted the killings, said, "No, sir. I am an American citizen and I am not afraid of the devil. These men deserved killing and they were punished by peaceable and law-abiding citizens."

For several days after the incident, Italians held protest meetings throughout the country. On Apr. 3, a New Orleans grand jury indicted two of the jurors in the Hennessey case on charges of accepting bribes. Private detective Dominick O'Malley, Thomas McCrystal, and four others were indicted for trying to bribe jurors. Confessing, McCrystal implicated O'Malley. But his testimony could not be corroborated and O'Malley was dismissed. McCrystal pleaded guilty. None of the people who took part in slaying the eleven prisoners was ever charged. The Italian ambassador, Baron Fava, visited the White House and the State Department to lodge official protests and demand punishment of the mob leaders. Secretary of State James G. Blaine angrily proclaimed his indifference to the situation when Fava pressed for retribution. Antagonism on both sides increased until there was fear of an international incident. On Dec. 19, 1891, President Benjamin Harrison denounced the affair in a message to Congress. The incident set off by Hennessey's murder was finally closed after Secretary Blaine announced a $25,000 indemnity award by the U.S. government to be distributed among the families of the slain men. See: **Black Hand; Mafia; Pinkerton, William.**

REF.: *CBA*; Davis, *Mafia Kingfish*; Duke, *Celebrated Criminal Cases of America*; Fox, *Mass Murder*; Gambino, *Vendetta*; Horan, *The Pinkertons*; Nash, *Bloodletters and Badmen*; Peterson, *The Mob*; Reppetto, *The Blue Parade*; Servadio, *Mafioso*.

Hennessy, Thomas, prom. 1893, U.S., mur. On June 16, 1893, Michael O'Brien was shot to death on a Chicago street corner. An accomplice to the crime, Fred Harris, told police that Thomas Hennessy had pulled the trigger. Harris stated that Hennessy was angry with O'Brien for not equally dividing the profits of an earlier hold up. In his confession, Harris claimed that Hennessy had asked him to kill O'Brien, but upon his refusal, had shot the man twice himself. Detective Clifton R. Wooldridge obtained witnesses to corroborate Harris' statement, but convicting the elusive killer was not as easy.

Hennessy was captured in St. Louis, Mo. Another Chicago police officer was sent to retrieve the fugitive, and on his return took over the case. At Hennessy's arraignment, the new officer failed to appear, and an enraged Inspector Kipley ordered Wooldridge to quickly round up witnesses for the trial the following day. Wooldridge managed to find five witnesses, and Hennessy was convicted on Dec. 2, 1893. Judge Philip Stein sentenced the killer to twenty-five years in prison.

REF.: *CBA*; Wooldridge, *Hands Up*

Henning, Edward J., 1868-1937, U.S., jur. Served as assistant U.S. attorney of the eastern district of Wisconsin from 1901-10, and as U.S. attorney for the same district between 1910-11. He was also assistant U.S. secretary of labor from 1911-25, and received his Doctor of Laws degree from Columbia University in 1925. He was nominated to the southern district court of California by President Calvin Coolidge in 1925. REF.: *CBA*.

Hennis, Timothy Baily, 1958- , Case of, U.S., rape-mur. Responding to concerned calls from neighbors, a Cumberland County deputy went to investigate the Summer Hill, N.C., home of the Eastburn family. There, he found the nude body of Kathryn Eastburn lying next to the body of her 3-year-old daughter, Erin, in the master bedroom. Five-year-old Kara was found in the next bedroom; all three had had their throats slashed. A third child, 18-month-old Jana, was found unharmed.

According to Julie Czerniak, a 15-year-old babysitter for the family, Mrs. Eastburn had been receiving strange phone calls from a man; her husband, Gary Eastburn, an Air Force captain, had begun eight weeks of military training at the Maxwell Air Force Base in Montgomery.

An investigation led to the arrest of Timothy Baily Hennis, a 28-year-old career army sergeant. When the Eastburn family had recently learned of their transfer to Great Britain, Mrs. Eastburn had placed an ad to find a home for the family dog. Responding to the ad, Hennis went to the Eastburn home on May 7. Investigators believe he murdered Kathryn and her children two or three days later. One witness, Patrick Cone said he saw Hennis leave the Eastburn house early on May 10. Another witness said she saw Hennis in his car across the street from the house, and a third witness saw him near Methodist College in Fayetteville, where bank records showed that someone withdrew money using Captain Eastburn's bank card on May 11. Hennis was sentenced to life in prison for the rape of Mrs. Eastburn, and sentenced to death for the three murders. After his sentencing, Hennis made this remark to Judge E. Lynn Johnson: "The only thing I can say, your honor, is that I am not as guilty as I have always been."

The State Supreme Court granted him a retrial on the grounds that the prosecution exhibited an unnecessary number of prejudicial photographs of the crime scene. He was acquitted at the second trial. REF.: *CBA*.

Henrietta Anne, 1644-70, Brit., (unsolv.) mur. Daughter of King Charles I and wife of Philippe, Duc d'Orléans, becoming the Duchesse d'Orléans. Popular with Louis XIV, she became his representative to Charles II. She may have been poisoned at her husband's command. REF.: *CBA*.

Henriot, Michel, 1910-45, Fr., mur. Silver fox breeder Michel Henriot of Kerbennec, Fr., needed money to raise his foxes, and to remedy this predicament, he decided to marry—with his eye on the dowry a wife would bring him. The 24-year-old bachelor met Georgette Deglave, nineteen, through a matrimonial journal, and the two were married on Oct. 10, 1933; Deglave brought 160,000 francs with her. That amount proved insufficient for his needs, so Henriot set about to insure the life of his new bride.

Deglave was an unhealthy girl, having sustained a head injury early in life which left her partially paralyzed, and she did not enjoy physical or sexual contact. In addition to Henriot's ugly appearance, he had sadistic tendencies—it was well known in Brittany that he would shoot animals just to watch them die, rather than kill them outright—to which he soon subjected Deglave. Before the wedding, her family did not heed her reservations about marrying Henriot, but her younger sister retained all the letters Deglave wrote telling of the horrors her husband perpetrated.

While the two lived at the isolated home on the dunes of Kerbennec, Henriot arranged for he and his wife to be insured. The policy he finally settled on would bring him 800,000 francs in the event of Deglave's death due to "accidents, murder and cyclones." The policy, Henriot later noted, also covered his untimely death; a clause which proved highly unnecessary.

On May 8, Deglave refused her husband's sexual advances. Enraged by her refusal, Henriot grabbed a fireplace poker and beat her over the head. She managed to free herself and staggered up the stairs to the telephone where she called for help. She had contacted the operator when five shots from Henriot's Lebel 5.55mm gun interrupted the call. Deglave fell dead with wounds to her head and chest, and the operator, not understanding the importance of the gunshots and screams he heard, disconnected the line. Blood stains indicated that Henriot then dragged his wife's body into the bedroom, before running out to inform his neighbors of the mysterious intruder who had shot her. Understandably, they saw no stranger enter or leave the home.

Before making a statement to the police, amid tears and spells of faintness, Henriot instructed someone to contact his insurance company in Paris. At first the police did not suspect the husband—mainly because his father was the local prosecutor—but Henriot was soon the suspect when police learned that an intruder would not likely know how to use Henriot's foreign shotgun with its complicated mechanism. The discovery of Deglave's incriminating diary, along with the letters to her sister, heaped suspicion on Henriot. The last entry, five days before the killing, noted, "Michel told me he would kill me." Henriot confessed and stated that "the argument began over a sexual matter...but there was also the desire in me to see blood flowing." He later added, "I wanted the pleasure of shooting something new." Henriot was found Guilty but insane at his trial in Vannes.

REF.: *CBA*; Heppenstall, *Bluebeard and After*; Kershaw, *Murder in France*; Wilson, *Encyclopedia of Murder*.

Henry (Duke of Swabia, AKA: Henry VII), 1211-42, Ger., consp. Reigned as German king from 1220-35. Conspired against bishops and princes, was forced out of power, and was confined in Sicily until his death. REF.: *CBA*.

Henry I de Lorraine, See: **Guise, Henry I de Lorraine**.

Henry II, See: **Becket, Thomas**.

Henry II de Lusignan, 1271-1324, Mid. East, rebel. Succeeded Charles of Anjou as king of Jerusalem, reigning from 1285-1324. His rule was ineffectual and he lost his power in 1291. His brother Amalric forced him to be exiled to Cilicia, a country of southeast Asia Minor. He was returned to power by the barons. REF.: *CBA*.

Henry III, 1551-89, Fr., king, assass. In the sixteenth century, almost constant warfare and political upheaval between the Huguenots and the Roman Catholics plagued France. In February 1563, Francois de Lorraine, the second Duc de Guise, was assassinated by Huguenot fanatic Jean de Poltrot. Thereafter the powerful Catholic De Guise family held a grudge against Gaspard de Coligny, an advisor to King Charles IX, whom the family suspected of arranging the duke's murder. In 1572 Henri de Guise, Francois' son and now the second Duc de Guise, was recruited by King Charles' mother, Catherine de Medici, to assassinate de Coligny whom she feared would cause Charles to unwittingly strengthen the Protestant faction in Europe. An unsuccessful attempt against de Coligny resulted in Charles consenting to a wholesale massacre of the French Protestant population.

The St. Bartholomew's Day Massacre purged the countryside of hundreds of Protestant sympathizers and consolidated the regency of young King Charles IX. The rule of the Catholic king and his ruthless mother, Catherine de Medici, was short-lived, however. Charles suffered greatly under the strain and died at age twenty-four in 1574. Summoned from Poland, where, with his mother's help, he had been elected king, Henry III (1574-89) returned to France to attempt a reconciliation between the two bitterly divided religious groups. In his younger years, Henry had been a close friend of the Protestant leader Henry of Navarre. "Both sides must make concessions," the new king declared, "in the interest of unification. France is more important than any self-interest." But standing in the way of peaceful coexistence was ambitious Henry de Guise, leader of the Catholic League and the instigator of the St. Bartholomew's Day Massacre. As the last male member of the House of Valois, Henry stood in a precarious position. If he were to be pushed aside and de Guise emerged triumphant, every Protestant in France might be exterminated..."like dogs," the Duke said. To protect himself and ensure that moderation prevailed, Henry named Henry of Navarre his successor in the event of his death. The king believed it was a shrewd move and a good hedge against any notions de Guise might have of killing him.

Pressure began to build. The Catholic League denounced the king and finally, in 1587, bowing to the demands of de Guise, Henry ordered a military expedition against the Protestant leader to force him to renounce "heresy." The campaign was a disaster, with the armies of Henry III routed at the Battle of Coutras.

The assassination of Henry III of France.

After an armistice was signed, Henry returned to Paris to face de Guise one last time, but this final plea for peace was rejected by the leader of the Catholic League. Realizing the futility of further pleading, the king signalled to his bodyguards to attack de Guise, who was killed instantly. "May God have mercy on all our souls—and France," the king said.

The Catholic League then opened a drive against Paris. Driven from the city, Henry joined Henry of Navarre who placed his troops at the king's disposal. On Aug. 1, 1589, a Dominican monk named Friar Jacques Clement sought an audience with the King outside the gates of Paris. "I beseech you," he said to Henry. "Renounce the heretics and swear your allegiance to the League." As the king motioned for the monk to leave, the man suddenly brandished a long knife and stabbed the king. The friar was cut down by the king's guards, but Henry III lay dead. See: **Henry IV.**

REF.: Bell, *Assassin; CBA;* Hurwood, *Society and the Assassin;* Melville, *Famous Duels and Assassinations;* Nash, *Almanac of World Crime;* Pearl, *The Dangerous Assassins.*

Henry IV, 1050-1106, Ger., her. Reigned as king of Germany and emperor of Holy Roman Empire from 1056-1106, although his rule was marked by political turmoil. Excommunicated in 1076 after quarrels with Pope Gregory VII over the issue of lay investiture, he was absolved in 1077 and then excommunicated again in 1080. In 1084 he was removed from power by Pope Gregory, but in the same year he was pronounced emperor by Clement III, an antipope. From 1093-1105, he faced his sons' resistance and in 1105, his youngest son pushed him out of power and had him put in prison. REF.: *CBA.*

Henry IV (Henry of Navarre), 1553-1610, Fr., king, assass. Like his predecessor, King Henry III, the new French monarch also was assassinated. In 1589, Henry of Navarre (1589-1610) witnessed the murder of Henry III who had attempted to reconcile conflict between the Catholic and the Huguenot factions. In 1594 the war of the Holy League came to an end when Henry IV agreed to the Catholics' demand that he renounce Protestantism for their pledge to recognize the legitimacy of his rule. However, he made little effort to convert Protestants to the Catholic faith and usually favored the Huguenots in all major political disputes. Numerous attempts were made on the life of Henry IV. The twentieth attempt succeeded.

Henry IV of Navarre.

Believing that the king was about to initiate a war against the Pope, a 31-year-old barrister from Angoulême named François Ravaillac stabbed the king as he rode in his private carriage on the Croix-du-Tiroir. The assassination, carried out in daylight on the afternoon of May 14, 1610, was witnessed by hundreds of onlookers on the crowded promenade. Ravaillac, dumbfounded by his own actions, was seized and taken to the Hôtel de Retz for questioning. French authorities believed he was part of a wider conspiracy, perhaps led by the Jesuits or the warring Hapsburgs. In actuality, Ravaillac acted out of religious fanaticism.

Francois Ravaillac assassinating Henry IV of Navarre on a Paris street, 1610.

After nearly two weeks of round-the-clock interrogation, the assassin was declared Guilty by the Paris Parlement and sentenced to a ghastly death. Placed on a rack, the screws were turned until his joints broke. Near the Notre Dame Cathedral he stood on the scaffold while the king's men tore out pieces of his skin with red-hot pincers. The arm used to commit the murder was plunged into a vat of burning sulfur. The torture went on for nearly an hour until a team of four horses pulled in opposite directions tore his body apart. Afterward, the assassin's home was destroyed, all his private belongings confiscated, and his parents were forced to flee the country.

REF.: Bell, *Assassin; CBA;* Johnson, *Famous Assassinations of History;* Nash, *Almanac of World Crime.*

Henry VII (Henry Tudor), 1457-1509, Brit., mur. The presumed murders of the young princes, Edward V and his younger brother Richard, are often blamed on Richard III, who was slain on the battlefield by the Earl of Richmond, later Henry VII. But many historians believe that Henry ordered the executions of the royal children, probably in July 1486. One of Henry's first acts after attaining power was to order that the act proclaiming the illegitimacy of Edward IV's children be removed from the books and burned, with every copy of it being returned to him under penalty of imprisonment. Both Stillington and John of Gloucester, illegitimate royal children, were imprisoned and either murdered or left to die. The Earl of Warwick was also arrested, held in the Tower, and eventually killed. Fabyan, a London alderman, kept a diary, noting on July 16, 1486, that it was common knowledge that the young princes had been slain in the Tower, supposedly by executioner James Tyrrel, who was forced to murder the children at the king's command. In a ploy to get rid of young Warwick, already imprisoned in the Tower, the king arranged for two agents to provoke Warwick and young Perkin Warbeck to try to escape, then had them both executed for the attempt.

REF.: *CBA;* Williamson, *Historical Whodunits;* (FILM), *Richard III,* 1956.

Henry, Sir Edward Richard, 1859-1931, Brit., law enfor. off.-criminol. Although Sir Edward Richard Henry served as London's Commissioner from 1903 to 1918, he was best known for his work in developing the fingerprint classification system used by Scotland Yard and the Indian Civil Service.

Henry, along with Sir Francis Galton and Sir William Herschel, invented the Henry fingerprint system, which replaced the Bertillon method of anthropometry. Henry's system categorized the fingerprints of all known criminals, suspects, and those lifted from crime scenes. He introduced the method in India where he served as Inspector-General of the Bengal police since 1891. By 1900, the procedure was fully operational in India—replacing the Bertillon method completely in 1914

Sir Edward Henry

and was adopted by Scotland Yard in 1901. Henry was named Assistant Commissioner of the Metropolitan Police force in 1901, and served until 1903 when he became commissioner. He was presented with the Grand Cross Order of Dannebrog, the Order of St. Sava, and the Order of Villa Vicosa. See: **Faulds, Henry; Galton, Francis; Herschel, William John.**

REF.: *CBA;* Rhodes, *The Tracks of Crime;* Scott, *The Concise Encyclopedia of Crime and Criminals.*

Henry, Emile, 1872-94, Fr., bomb.-(attempt.) mur.-mur. Emile Henry was a remarkably intelligent youth, earning a Bachelor of Science degree at the age of sixteen, but after attending anarchist meetings where his brother, Fortuné Henry spoke, Henry turned his mind toward murder. He studied the intricate design of bombs and worked with a watchmaker where he learned to manufacture the mechanisms he could use to detonate his explosives. With the conclusion of a miners' strike, which favored the company, Henry decided to put his knowledge to use in avenging the strikers' cause.

On Nov. 8, 1892, Henry placed his first explosive at the door of the Paris office of the Carmaux mines. The bomb, consisting of twenty cartridges of dynamite with a detonator of fulminate of mercury, was designed to explode upon being turned upside down or shaken. A porter discovered the device and instructed an office boy to place it in the street. The boy, along with police Sergeant Formorin and Detective Reaux, carried the device to the Rue des Bons Enfants police station. Once inside the building, the bomb exploded killing the three men, police secretary M. Pousset, and Inspector Grouteau. A sixth officer died later.

Suspicion fell on Henry because the bomb had been wrapped with numerous *Temps* newspapers. The papers had articles of anarchist meetings attended by Henry, but no further evidence against the bomber. Henry left Paris, possibly committing more bombings under the direction of another anarchist named Ortiz, but returned in early 1894 to start anew.

Henry's next target was the bourgeoisie. On Feb. 12, 1894, Henry went, bomb in hand, to the Café Terminus and after having a few drinks, and waiting for the crowd to increase, lit the fuse of the explosive he held between his knees. As he exited, he tossed the bomb into the restaurant. The explosion killed two people and injured seventeen. A waiter attempted to stop Henry at the door, but he slipped past. Then he shot M. Etienne, and a hairdresser's assistant who attempted to stop him. He also shot police officer Poisson, who had pulled out his sword to apprehend him, but was unable to escape the grasp of two more policemen.

He was tried on Apr. 28, 1894, with the prosecution conducted by M. Bulot. Henry freely confessed to both bombings, and to his disappointment that more were not killed—an admitted failure on his construction of the bomb—as well as to his inability to kill Poisson. The jury found him Guilty, at which Henry jumped up proudly and saluted the court. He was guillotined on May 21, 1894.

REF.: *CBA;* Irving, *Studies of French Criminals;* Williams, *Heyday For Assassins.*

Henry, Leroy, prom. 1944, Brit., rape. U.S. Army corporal Leroy Henry was charged with the rape of a Bath, England, woman, whom he claimed he had paid in return for sex. According to the woman, the soldier stopped at her home and when he asked directions to Bristol, she consented to point him in the right direction. As the two walked down the road, she claimed he threw her over a wall and raped her at knifepoint. Henry denied her statement and testified that he had paid the woman £1 twice before for sexual favors. A court-martial trial was conducted before seven white officers and one black. The defendant was black.

At Henry's court martial, a police surgeon testified that the woman showed no signs of resisting the alleged attack. Henry claimed that his confession was obtained only after he was deprived of food for twenty-four hours. The officers apparently did not believe Henry's story, and ignored the physical evidence; he was found Guilty and sentenced to death in June 1944. As a result of this verdict, the English press, and the public in general, created a tremendous uproar over the obvious prejudicial proceedings. So great was the commotion that Allied commander General Dwight D. Eisenhower set aside the death penalty, though he refused to set aside the conviction, on June 17, 1944. Henry returned to duty on June 22. REF.: *CBA.*

Henry, O., See: **Porter, William Sydney.**

Henry, Patrick, 1736-99, U.S., rebel. Famous for words "Give me liberty, or give me death," declared during provincial convention in 1775 to urge that American colonies be placed in a state of defense. He was born in Hanover County, Va., and practiced law in Virginia. A member of that colony's legislature in 1765, he vehemently opposed the Stamp Act and proposed measures against it. He became the head of a radical Virginia group beginning in 1765. Together he, Thomas Jefferson, and Richard Henry Lee started the Intercolonial Committee of Correspondence in 1773. As a member of the Virginia Constitutional Ratification Convention in 1788, he did not favor ratification. His influence was a major cause for the adoption of the U.S. Constitution's first ten amendments. In 1799, he gained a seat in the Virginia legislature, but died before he began serving his term. REF.: *CBA.*

Henry, Toni Jo (AKA: Annie Beatrice McQuiston, Annie Beatrice Henry), 1916-42, U.S., mur. Toni Jo Henry had spent the better part of her life in and out of trouble. This reformed drug addict became a prostitute in her early teens; was arrested six times between seventeen and twenty-one; once for beating a man with a bottle and snipping his ears.

Claude D. "Cowboy" Henry was a customer of his wife-to-be

in the Fall of 1939; they married in November. Claude Henry had been convicted of killing a former San Antonio, Texas, police officer after a barroom fight, and was out on bail awaiting a retrial when the two met and married. On Jan. 27, 1940, a second jury in Hondo, Texas—after a change of venue was ordered—found him Guilty and he was sentenced to fifty years in prison. Within two weeks, Toni Henry decided to break her husband out of prison with the help of Harold Finnon "Arkansas" Burks, also known as Lloyd Adams, a former prisoner held at the same prison in Huntsville. She paid two youths to steal sixteen guns, mostly .32-caliber and .38-caliber revolvers, and ammunition from a Beaumont, Texas, hardware store. Henry and Burks then hitch-hiked along a Louisiana highway looking for a fast getaway car.

Unfortunately for Joseph Calloway, he picked up the rain-drenched hitchhikers en route to Jennings from Houston. After passing through Lake Charles, La., Henry pulled a gun on Calloway, and then Burks drove the car toward the Gulf of Mexico. Burks pulled the car over and Henry forced Calloway to walk a short distance from the car. Out of Burks' view, she told Calloway to strip and say his prayers. He did as he was told, and Henry shot him directly between the eyes with her .32-caliber revolver. She grabbed his clothes so her husband could change out of his prison gray's after his escape, and returned to the car. At that point, Burks became scared of his partner and soon ditched her in Camden. He was later arrested in Warren, Ark., and Henry turned herself in.

The police did not at first believe Henry's story of murder when she surrendered to authorities in her hometown of Shreveport, La. Nor did the story seem plausible as the search, led by Henry herself, failed to turn up a dead body. The "haystack," where the body was supposed to be hidden, proved to be a rice-chaff stack, and when police finally believed her story, she remembered she still carried the man's wallet and license.

Henry became quite unruly after the body was found, attacking newspaper photographers, and refusing to identify Burks until convinced to do so by her husband. She then retracted her confession and blamed Burks for the killing, but her detailed account of the murder scene proved to be too knowledgeable for the innocent man. Burks, in his turn, claimed he never intended to break her husband out of jail.

Defense lawyers for Mrs. Henry managed to have separate trials for the murderers. Each was found Guilty and sentenced to die in the electric chair. Henry appealed the conviction, but a second jury also found her Guilty. She again appealed, and a third jury convicted her on Jan. 24, 1942. This conviction was upheld by the Louisiana State Supreme Court. With the governor, Sam H. Jones, stating no pardon would be granted, her death was scheduled for Nov. 28, 1942. With this in mind, Mrs. Henry admitted she alone killed Calloway, but Burks was executed anyway in March 1943.

Announcement of Henry's impending execution prompted her husband to escape from a prison farm on Nov. 22, with the hope of freeing her. Rumors spread throughout the area that he planned to kidnap or kill the judges, John T. Hood at the first trial, and Mark Pickrel of the last two, and security around the men as well as the prison holding Henry was extremely tight. Claude Henry made it as far as Beaumont before a number of heavily armed officers apprehended the escaped convict in a hotel. Husband and wife were not allowed to see each other, but a long-distance phone call was granted and the condemned woman told her husband to give up crime.

REF.: *CBA;* Radin, *Crimes of Passion.*

Henry, William (Duke of Cumberland), b.c.1745, Brit., adult. Although William Henry, the Duke of Cumberland, professed that he was not guilty of sleeping with Lady Grosvenor, she was caught trying to flee from his bedroom at an inn where the two had met on Dec. 21, 1769.

At the duke's trial for adultery in March 1770, letters and testimony from witnesses indicated that Henry and Grosvenor had been sexually involved for some time. Suspicious of this fact,

Richard, Lord Grosvenor, employed John Stephens, an adjutant with the Cheshire militia, to follow his wife on her journey to London. Stephens learned that the two lovers were sharing a room at the White Hart Inn, and after being assured that whispers inside the room were Henry and the Lady, he had servants break the door open. It took the servants four tries before the door burst open, revealing Henry lying in bed, and Grosvenor lying on the floor after falling while running to her adjoining room. As a result, the court decided in the favor of Lord Grosvenor and ordered Henry to pay him £10,000 in damages. The Grosvenor marriage also came to an end with the conclusion of the proceedings.

REF.: Bierstadt, *Curious Trials and Criminal Cases; CBA.*

Henry of Cornwall (Henry of Almaine), 1235-71, Brit., nobleman, assass. Son of Richard of Cornwall who was slain by the sons of de Montfort. REF.: *CBA.*

Henry of Lausanne (Henry of Bruys, Henry of Cluny, Henry of Toulouse, Henry the Deacon), prom. 1100s, Fr., her. Heretic put in prison for teaching Petrobrusian concepts. REF.: *CBA.*

Henry Street Gang, prom. 1890s, U.S., org. crime. Chicago's most violent street gang at the end of the nineteenth century was the Henry Street Gang, led by Chris Merry. A huge man given to streaks of pathological violence, Merry and his marauders terrified merchants on Chicago's Southwest side. The gangsters would take what they wished from street peddlers, and would kick in locked doors and steal more at gunpoint. Merry was a notoriously vicious fighter. During physical combat, Merry used any weapon he could find, employing as well his teeth, feet, and fists. Merry's criminal career ended when he murdered his invalid wife by kicking her to death. The violence perpetrated by the Henry Street Gang ended when Merry was hanged.

REF.: Asbury, *Gem of the Prairie; CBA.*

Hensey, Florence, b.c.1714, Brit., treas. In 1756, England joined Prussia in fighting Austria, France, Saxony, and later Russia, in the Seven Years War. At the insistence of a prying and overly suspicious postman, Dr. Florence Hensey was arrested and tried in June 1758 for sending treasonous letters to France.

Hensey was accused of spying on his country and sending tactical information to the French government, which allegedly paid him twenty-five guineas per quarter for his services. Evidence obtained against Hensey was in the form of twenty-nine letters confiscated by the post office, which stopped delivering his mail abroad when postman James Newman grew suspicious. Newman came to suspect Hensey because the doctor was a Roman Catholic, which the mail carrier testified was reason enough for him to look upon a person as "an inveterate enemy to my king." Once opened, authorities discovered they contained military information, although defense counsel later argued that the information was, at the time of writing, already obsolete.

Hensey's trial for high treason was held at Westminster Hall before a full court of judges. The prosecution was conducted by Attorney General Pratt, Solicitor General Charles Yorke, Mr. Gould, Sir Richard Lloyd, Mr. Norton, Mr. Perrot, and Serjeant Poole, while Hensey was defended by Mr. Howard and Mr. Morton. As the only evidence against Hensey was the letters, witnesses for the prosecution were called to identify the writing as Hensey's. These witnesses however, were almost comical. One had only seen Hensey write—and then only in the dark—but had not seen the doctor's actual written characters. The other handwriting witness, Mendez da Costa, who admitted he was no expert, but was familiar with the doctor's writing, declared that the letters were written by Hensey. His decision was made without even a comparison to a letter known to be in Hensey's hand. Hensey's attorney argued that since the letters were not delivered, he had not committed treason. Prosecutors dismissed this tactic, explaining that the intent to commit treason was still present. The jury agreed with the prosecution, and after deliberating for one half hour they found Hensey Guilty. He was sentenced to death, but eventually set free after several respites.

REF.: *CBA;* Parry, *Some Famous Medical Trials.*

Henson, Nicholas, 1958- , Brit., mansl. A schoolyard fight in 1972 between two 14-year-old boys led to the death of one when Nicholas Henson pulled a knife from his pocket and stabbed Samuel Tuke in the heart.

Samuel died in the hospital a short time later. The boys who had tried to break up the fight during recess, eventually found Nicholas, who had escaped through a hole in the playground fence. He claimed the killing was an accident, and at his trial, four months later at Old Bailey, defense counsel demonstrated how Nicholas, a shy boy who was often bullied at school, and had meant no harm. The prosecutor accepted the boy's plea of Guilty to manslaughter, for which the judge placed Nicholas under a care order, stipulating that until the age of eighteen Nicholas was to remain in a community home, and then be supervised for an unspecified time.

REF.: *CBA; Wilson, Children Who Kill.*

Henson, Tom, prom. 1943-44, U.S., mur. On June 6, 1943, the bodies of Milt and Clyde Clayton were found on Lookout Mountain, near Gadsden, Ala. Their throats had been cut and their pockets emptied, indicating a possible robbery. Milt's car was discovered abandoned two-and-one-half miles from the bodies. The front seat was soaked with blood—apparently the site of the murder. A complaint to the police earlier that morning by Tom Henson provided the first lead in the case. Henson notified Gadsden's Chief of Detectives, Fay Boman, that the night before a man named Jed Johnson had forced him at gunpoint to jump off Noccalula Falls. Henson claimed that Johnson had threatened to kill him after he had beaten up a friend of Johnson's, Harry Paxton, and that Milt had intervened on his behalf. According to Henson, Johnson decided not to kill him, but still ordered him to jump over the falls. Henson claimed that before he jumped, he heard Johnson threaten the Claytons. It was true that Henson had beaten up Paxton, but the rest of his story was false.

Police questioned Johnson, and though he knew of Henson and Clyde, he claimed he did not even know who Milt was. His alibi of drunkenness the night before was corroborated by the operator of a bootleg joint. Johnson was even wearing the same clothes he wore the previous evening, which should have been blood-stained if he had killed the Claytons. Boman decided to question Henson once again. The chief realized that Henson knew too much and was probably lying. He believed that Henson had dressed like Johnson—accounting for witnesses who saw a man wearing similar clothes—and killed the Claytons for the $800 that Milt was reported to have been carrying. Boman's hunch was correct; after cleverly bluffing, Henson confessed. Two trials were needed before the jury was convinced of Henson's Guilt, and on Feb. 17, 1944, he was sentenced to life in prison at the Alabama State Penitentiary.

REF.: *CBA; Rice, Forty-five Murderers.*

Henszlein, Klein, d.1573, Ger., pir. In the sixteenth century, notorious pirate Klein Henszlein sailed the North Sea, until in 1573 a fleet from Hamburg, Ger., managed to capture him along with thirty-three of his men. The pirates were paraded through Hamburg and then beheaded by an executioner so proficient at his work that it was claimed he hacked off all their heads with a sword in just forty-five minutes. Each head was then placed upon a stake for all to see.

REF.: *Botting, The Pirates; CBA.*

Henwood, Frank Harold, 1879-1929, U.S., mur. On May 24, 1911, a dispute between 31-year-old Frank Harold Henwood and 32-year-old Sylvester Louis "Tony" Von Phul over the affections of Isabelle Patterson Springer ended in the shooting death of Von Phul and an innocent bystander, who died one week later.

In the spring of 1911, Von Phul, a St. Louis wine salesman, had come to Denver, where Mrs. Springer and her wealthy banker husband John W. Springer lived. He soon became involved in an intimate relationship with Mrs. Springer, as letters the two wrote one another clearly showed. The wine salesman returned to St. Louis, and in his absence, Henwood arrived in April and replaced him as Mrs. Springer's lover. On May 18, the two were

observed in compromising situations at the Springer's ranch by the maid, the housekeeper, Cora Carpenter, and the chauffeur, Thomas Lepper. Mrs. Springer told Henwood of some letters Von Phul was threatening to reveal to her husband, unless she continued as his mistress. On May 23, Von Phul returned to Denver, and Henwood met him at the Brown Palace Hotel, where Springer rented a suite for his wife. The two agreed to discuss matters that evening.

Before their arranged encounter, Henwood caught Von Phul meeting with Mrs. Springer and her mother at a department store. An argument ensued in which the two men agreed to settle later at the hotel. Once inside the hotel room, Von Phul locked the door, and after Henwood pleaded with him to return the letters in question, he slapped him and then struck him over the head with a wooden shoe rack. Von Phul then threatened Henwood with a gun, that he carried in his hip pocket and ordered him to leave. Von Phul returned to Mrs. Springer's suite and warned her to stay away from Henwood. He mutilated her photographs of the man, and later mailed them to his rival.

Meanwhile, Henwood notified Police Chief Armstrong of the fight, but Armstrong could do nothing unless Henwood filed a complaint, which he refused to do. That night Von Phul exchanged his hotel room for one next door to Mrs. Springer's, during the change his gun was placed in the hotel safe, where it remained for the fatal confrontation the following night.

On the morning of May 24, Von Phul again warned Mrs. Springer not to go near Henwood. She in turn, warned Henwood, who after purchasing a .38-caliber revolver tried to persuade her to speak to Armstrong. Springer refused. Later that night in the hotel bar, Von Phul walked up to Henwood and stuck his finger in Henwood's glass of wine and made a comment that caused an angry reply from Henwood. Von Phul then punched Henwood in the face, knocking him to the floor. Henwood drew his gun and fired all six shots. The first bullet hit Von Phul in the shoulder, the second in the wrist, and the third in the groin. Henwood's remaining shots were fired at random, one struck J.W. Atkins and two hit G.E. Copeland; both men were shot in the leg. Henwood surrendered to police in the lobby. Von Phul was taken to the hospital by taxi—refusing an ambulance. He died the next morning without revealing the reason for the fight. On May 31, District Attorney Willis Elliot officially charged Henwood with murder and repeated the charge on June 2, the day after Copeland died from gangrene. Mrs. Springer, meanwhile had fled Denver, but returned to the city on June 12, the day Henwood's trial for the murder of Copeland began.

For Henwood to be found Guilty of murdering Copeland, the prosecutor would have to prove he murdered Von Phul first, but for reasons unknown the case before Judge Greely W. Whitford was for the murder of Copeland. John T. Bottom represented Henwood, but to no avail, especially after Mrs. Springer testified that Henwood was an "unwanted meddler" in the affair. The jury found him Guilty of second-degree murder on June 28, 1911. Before sentencing, Bottom informed the judge and prosecutor that if the Von Phul case was tried and his client found Not Guilty, he would demand Henwood's release with a writ of habeas corpus. The Von Phul charge was not pressed. On July 26, Bottom called for a new trial, complaining of Judge Whitford's charge to the jury—he had informed them that "there is no manslaughter in this case"—and of collusion on the part of the district attorney. Henwood then made a statement in which he harangued Whitford for holding prejudicial proceedings and of cavorting with the prosecution. Whitford sentenced him to life imprisonment. The Colorado Supreme Court agreed to look into the matter, allowing Henwood to remain in the city jail under a writ of supersedeas. Because of Whitford's charge to the jury, a new trial was granted and began on May 28. In February, Bottom was granted a dismissal of the Von Phul murder charge, but was unable to have the Copeland murder charge dismissed. Judge Charles C. Butler presided over the retrial, allowing testimony from the first trial to be read, since Carpenter, Lepper, and Mrs. Springer no longer lived in Denver. On June 17, Bottom introduced Springer on Henwood's behalf. Henwood thought he would be acquitted after Springer said only good things about Henwood. The jury felt otherwise and found Henwood Guilty of first-degree murder. He was sentenced to death, and after numerous appeals by Bottom were denied, the lawyer finally convinced Governor Elias M. Ammons to commute the sentence to life in prison on Oct. 16, 1914, a week before his scheduled execution. Ten years later Henwood was paroled, but was returned to prison after a waitress filed a complaint against him.

REF.: *CBA;* Rodell, *Denver Murders.*

Henzi, Samuel (Samuel Hentzi), 1701-49, Switz., consp. Banished from 1744-48 after petitioning the Council of Bern to revise the constitution. He was caught conspiring to abolish the constitution and was executed. REF.: *CBA.*

Hepburn, James (Earl of Bothwell), c.1536-78, Brit., pir. The life of James Hepburn is inextricably involved with that of Mary, Queen of Scots, whom he kidnapped and married. He later went insane when forced to leave her. Born around 1536, Hepburn was the son of the third Earl of Bothwell. In September 1556, he inherited his father's estates and titles, including that of lord high admiral of Scotland. In 1562, he was imprisoned for conspiring to kidnap Queen Mary, but escaped to France. Four years later, Mary took refuge with him. In 1567, he was accused of plotting the murder of her husband, Lord Darnly, but was acquitted of the charge. On Apr. 24, 1567, he kidnapped Mary, and three weeks later, on May 15, he became her third husband, and was named Duke of Orkney and Shetland. However, other nobles, enraged by the marriage, forced him to flee to Orkney and then to Shetland, and later to Norway. He pursued a career as a pirate until he went insane and was captured by the king of Denmark. Hepburn died during his imprisonment at the castle of Malmo in Sweden in 1578. REF.: *CBA.*

Hepper, William Sanchez de Pina, 1891-1954, Brit., rape-mur. When 11-year-old Margaret Rose Louise Spevick broke her arm, it was recommended that she recover at the flat of 62-year-old William Sanchez de Pina Hepper, in Hove, England, near Brighton. Hepper's estranged wife was a good friend of Margaret's mother. Hepper informed Mrs. Spevick that her daughter would be well taken care of by the flat's resident nurse, and that her stay would give him a chance to paint a portrait of the girl.

On Feb. 2, 1954, Margaret left for Hove. Two days later she was seen at Brighton Hospital with an elderly man, and on Feb. 6 her mother decided to visit. Margaret did not meet her mother at the railroad station as arranged, and when Mrs. Spevick went to the flat owned by Hepper, there was no answer. Inside, Spevick found her daughter lying on a divan. She had been raped and strangled to death. An unfinished portrait rested on a nearby easel. Hepper, who had a dying brother in Spain, was arrested in Irun, Spain, at the Pension España, three days later. After extradition to Britain, Hepper was charged with murder of Margaret on Mar. 24 at the Hove Magistrate's Court. At his trial at the Lewes Assizes on July 19, 1954, before Justice Jones, Hepper was represented by Queen's Counsel Derek Curtis-Bennett, who argued that Hepper was insane, producing seven doctors to testify on the defendant's behalf. Hepper, who suffered head injuries in a car accident that led to amnesia, spent three hours on the witness stand, telling of his dreams, hallucinations, memory loss, and sexual impotence. He also collapsed at one point. The prosecution, however, displayed letters in which Hepper wrote of attacking his wife in his flat, from which prosecutor R.F. Levy, Q.C., surmised that Hepper possibly thought he was hurting his wife and not Margaret. Hepper was found Guilty and hanged on Aug. 11, 1954, at Wandsworth Prison.

REF.: Butler, *Murderers' England; CBA;* Gribble, *Famous Judges and Their Trials;* Knowles, *Court of Drama;* Lucas, *The Child Killers;* Wilson, *Encyclopedia of Murder.*

Heraclian (Count of Africa), d.413, Roman., assass. Murdered Stilicho in 408 on orders from Emperor Honorius. In 413, as a count of Africa, he rebelled against Rome. Officials of the emperor assassinated him at Carthage. REF.: *CBA.*

Herault de Sechelles, Marie Jean, 1759-94, Fr., consp. Served as counsel to Parliament of Paris in 1785, and served on Legislative Assembly in 1791. He commanded the arrest of Girondins and helped draft a new constitution in 1793. He was charged with plotting with Hébertists and was executed by guillotine in Paris in 1794. REF.: *CBA.*

Herbert, Edward, c.1591-1657, Brit., polit. corr. Served as attorney general in 1641. He introduced impeachment proceedings on orders of Charles I against six members of Parliament for undermining basic laws. Later, he was himself impeached by the House of Commons. REF.: *CBA.*

Herbert, Sir Edward (Earl of Portland), c.1648-98, Brit., jur. Served as chief justice for both the King's Bench in 1685 and for the common pleas in 1687. REF.: *CBA.*

Herbert, Philemon T., prom. 1856, Case of, U.S., mur. A U.S. congressman from California, Philemon T. Herbert was a demanding and short-tempered man who was used to having his own way. This was demonstrated with lethal consequences one day in 1856. At the time, Herbert was dining at the Willard Hotel in Washington, D.C. He demanded that the waiter servicing his table take his order and "be damned quick about it." When his food failed to arrive, Herbert began to shout at Thomas Keating, a wealthy resident who was dining at the next table and who seemed to have no trouble being served. Herbert yelled at Keating to have the waiter serving Keating come to his table to make sure his order was delivered. Keating shouted back: "You have one servant waiting on you and that's enough!" With that, Herbert drew a gun and shot Keating dead. The congressman was convicted but won an appeal on an error in the first trial. He was acquitted in the second trial, even though claims of jury-tampering had been made.

REF.: *An Argument in the Case of the United States versus Philemon T. Herbert; CBA.*

Herbert, William (Earl of Pembroke), d.1469, Brit., jur. Fought in War of the Roses, and served as chief justice of South Wales in 1461, and of North Wales in 1467. Beheaded by the northern Lancastrians. REF.: *CBA.*

Herbert, William (Baron Powis), 1573-1656, Brit., consp. Leader of Catholic aristocracy in England. He was arrested and put in prison on suspicion of conspiring in the Popish Plot. REF.: *CBA.*

Herbert, William (Marquis of Powis, Earl of Pembroke), 1580-1630, Brit., consp. Literary patron and chancellor of Oxford, imprisoned in 1601 as aftermath of affair with Mary Fitton, the maid of honor in Queen Elizabeth's court. REF.: *CBA.*

Herd, Alexander T., prom. 1940s, U.S., fraud. Alexander T. Herd had already been arrested six times, with no convictions, when the New York City district attorney's office was tipped off to another fraud the swindler was working. During 1943, Herd finagled $9,100 from a 72-year-old woman who believed that Herd was cultivating bountiful crops and grazing a huge herd of cattle. In reality, Herd had never tilled the soil, and owned only 150 of an alleged 6,000 head of cattle. Herd had also charged her for taxes, which he never paid, and made a hefty profit on the forty acres he purchased at $2 an acre by reselling them at $800 an acre. The con artist would continually ask the woman, who kept fairly detailed records of the transactions, for more money in an effort to pay for his living expenses in Washington, D.C., where he lobbied congressmen to help with a lawsuit against the U.S. government, which Herd claimed owed him money for a purchase of ships during WWII. Investigator Thomas Fay eventually gathered enough information. Herd was indicted by a grand jury on sixteen counts of grand larceny. He was returned to New York, where he pleaded guilty, but he avoided sentencing for almost three years because of alleged health problems. Fay proved the health problems were phony, and Herd was sentenced to one year in prison at Riker's Island, which he began serving on July 2, 1946.

REF.: *CBA;* Danforth, *The D.A.'s Man.*

Heredia y Campuzano, José Maria de, 1803-39, Cuba, rebel. Poet banished from Cuba as rebel in 1823, later settling in Mexico. REF.: *CBA.*

Hereford, Anne (AKA: Nan Hereford), 1662-90, Brit., arson-rob. Anne Hereford was seventeen when her parents died. She went to London to work as a maid, but after six months, having grown tired of her poor but honest life, took to robbery for her livelihood.

Dressing in expensive clothes and renting elegant rooms on King Street in Westminster, Hereford employed an elderly woman as an assistant to help her with her schemes. Hearing about a prosperous druggist who was known for his greed, Hereford sent her grandmotherly accomplice on errands to his store. The assistant became friendly with the druggist, eventually telling him that she once worked for the niece of a rich Londoner. Explaining that the niece would come into a dowry of £2,000 at her marriage, but that she had a very strict uncle who kept a tight rein on her, the old woman provoked the druggist's interest. She gave him the name of a man in London who had a niece slated to inherit money when she married. The druggist checked out the facts and found them to be accurate. Extremely eager to meet the young woman, he promised the assistant a share of the profit if they married. The old woman pretended indifference to all but the happiness of her former "charge."

The old woman brought Hereford, posing as the niece, to meet the druggist, who began to court her. He asked the older woman to help him win his suit, offering her £100 pounds for her help. The old woman accepted, and soon after he proposed marriage to Hereford.

To stall the marriage, Hereford told the druggist that she was worried he would treat her with the same miserliness she was experiencing from her uncle. As a token of his love and good faith, the anxious druggist gave Hereford 250 guineas. Hereford married him immediately and left a few days later, telling him to pick her up at her uncle's house where they could claim her dowry. In fact, she and the old woman moved to a rooming house on the other side of town. The druggist came to pick up his bride and her money, prepared for a struggle with his new wife's stingy uncle. When the wealthy Londoner denied any knowledge of his niece's marriage, the druggist demanded to see his bride and realized that he had been cheated. He was unable to find his lying "wife" and her accomplice.

Hereford later teamed up with an actor; to support him she became a shoplifter. To further supplement their income, the actor resorted to highway robbery but was caught on his first attempt, sent to Newgate, and hanged. After six years and nearly £4,000 stolen in London and Westminster, Hereford was caught stealing a bolt of muslin. She was sent to Newgate and sentenced to hang.

Hereford attempted to escape by setting the prison on fire; for this she was kept then in chains and handcuffs until her execution on Dec. 22, 1690, at the age of twenty-eight. Her body was given to surgeons for experimentation. At that time, it was illegal for doctors to examine the internal organs of the human body unless the body had once belonged to an executed felon.
REF.: *CBA;* O'Donnell, *Should Women Hang?;* Smith, *Highwaymen.*

Hereward (Hereward the Wake), d.c.1071, Brit., rebel. Legendary outlaw who escaped from William the Conquerer's forces after leading a revolt against him in 1070. REF.: *CBA.*

Herlands, William Bernard, 1905-69, U.S., jur. Served as assistant U.S. attorney of the southern district of New York, N.Y., from 1931-34, as commissioner of investigation for New York City from 1938-44, and as justice of the domestic relations court of New York City in 1940. He was nominated to the bench of the southern district court of New York by President Dwight D. Eisenhower in 1955, and served until 1969. REF.: *CBA.*

Hermann, Marie (AKA: The Duchess), b.c.1850, Brit., pros.-mansl. As a young lawyer, Edward Marshall Hall had to contend with what seemed insurmountable odds in handling his first cause célèbre. The evidence against the defendant, 43-year-old pros-titute Marie Hermann, was bleak. She had been charged with murder after the brutally beaten body of Henry Stephens, Sr., seventy-one, was found in a trunk she owned. Hermann admitted killing the man on Mar. 15, 1894, but only in self-defense after he attacked her. A 15-year-old neighbor believed she heard the man scream "murder" twice before dying, while another neighbor claimed that she had not helped Hermann conceal the body as the defendant professed. Unfortunately for Hall, Hermann had also become quite wealthy after the alleged murder; prior to meeting Stephens, she was penniless. Not only did Hall have to overcome overwhelming evidence against Hermann, and newspaper headlines that prejudged the case, but he also had to contend with the Crown's best prosecutors, Charles Mathews and Archibald Bodkin.

At the trial before Justice Wills in the Old Bailey, Hall earned his reputation as a great lawyer. Hall reconstructed the scene of the killing for the court, and demonstrated that the crime was not murder. He persuaded Henry Stephens, Jr. to admit that his father probably had no money at the time he was killed, and that the man was prone to violence, thus supporting Hermann's story that Stephens had sought sexual favors for free and on her refusal had attacked her. In cross-examining the medical experts, Hall demonstrated that Hermann probably acted out of self-defense and did not strike Stephens from behind as the prosecution claimed. Dr. Taylor testified that the marks on the throat of the defendant—twelve bruises, according to Dr. Walker of the prison—could not have been made by Stephens after he was struck and, therefore, he was the aggressor. Testimony by Dr. Lloyd and Mr. Pepper only contradicted one another, and gave credit to Hall's synopsis of the attack. Hall held that Hermann had been attacked as she said, and in desperation had struck her attacker with the fireplace poker as he lay on top of her, accounting for the blows to the back of the head. The lawyer had young Louise Hutchins confess that she could not be sure she had heard Stephens cry "murder" during the argument she overheard.

Although Hall never coaxed Mrs. Bricknell to confess to helping Hermann place the corpse in the trunk, the trunk had been noticed by the prying Mrs. Hutchins, who contacted police after Hermann had moved out of the apartment building, and led to the discovery by Sergeant Kane. In his three-hour closing statement to the jury, Hall dared them to bring back a Guilty verdict, and added in reference to Hermann, who had become a prostitute to feed her children, "Look at her. God never gave her a chance—won't you?"

Hall's plea to the jury paid off, especially after Wills, who did not previously agree with Hall, summed up in Hermann's favor. After deliberating for fifteen minutes, the jury returned a verdict of Not Guilty of murder, but Guilty of manslaughter. Hermann was sentenced to six years of penal servitude.
REF.: *CBA;* Marjoribanks, *For the Defense, The Life of Sir Edward Marshall Hall;* Sparrow, *Vintage Victorian Murder.*

Hermenegild (Ermenegild), d.585, Spain, rebel. Son of Leovigild, king of the Visgoths in Spain, he married Ingunthis, a princess of Catholic faith. Having converted from the beliefs of his father, he rebelled unsuccessfully against him, was put in prison, and later slain. REF.: *CBA.*

Hermione Boys, The, prom. 1797-1806, Brit., mur. Captain Hugh Pigot became commander of *H.M.S. Hermione,* a British frigate stationed in the Caribbean Sea, in 1797. His ruthless command was to be cut short, however, by the mutiny his actions occasioned.

While patrolling the Mona Passage between Puerto Rico and the Dominican Republic with another frigate on Sept. 20, 1797, the *Hermione* came across an enemy ship and gave chase, but a sudden storm prevented pursuit. Pigot ordered his men to reef the topsails, threatening that the last man down would be flogged. In their haste to complete the job, three sailors fell to their deaths. The unsympathetic captain had the corpses tossed overboard, and had ten sailors flogged the next morning. Coupled with the almost daily floggings ordered by Pigot, this incident was the last straw. About twenty-five men planned to mutiny that night.

Early on Sept. 22, before sunrise, the soldier guarding the captain's cabin was knocked unconscious, and the mutineers burst in on Pigot. They attacked him with swords and bayonets and threw him overboard. Three more officers were given similar treatment, including Lieutenant Archibald Douglas, whom the crew particularly hated. Douglas was spotted hiding from the mob by his servant, 14-year-old James Allen, and repeatedly stabbed and hacked with pikes and hatchets. He was eventually dragged by the heels up a ladder to the deck, and given one last blow to the head with a hatchet before he was tossed into the sea. Allen was later accused of taking part in the killing, joyfully striking his master with a hatchet. Later that morning, six more officers were taken from their prison in the gunroom and thrown over the side. James Hayes, Dr. Samon's 14-year-old servant, made sure the ship's surgeon was among the last to die, taunting the doctor, and later boasting of his death. The remainder of the 180-man crew who did not participate in the mutiny made no protest, but complied with the mutineers.

On Sept. 27, 1797, the *Hermione* docked in the Spanish port of La Guaira, Venez. The ship was turned over to the Spaniards along with ten men, including officer Edward Southcott, who were held as prisoners of war until their exchange in March 1798 for Spaniards held by the British. Eight years later, when the last of the mutiny trials was conducted, only thirty-three other crew members had been accounted for. Seven of these men were found Not Guilty or turned King's evidence, and twenty-six were sentenced to death, of whom twenty-three were hanged, two were pardoned, and one was transported despite pleas by Sir Hyde Parker to execute all but the ten prisoners of war. Among the crew members tried, five were mere boys.

The two sailors pardoned by the king were 15-year-olds James Barnett and William Johnson. Barnett claimed at his court martial on July 23, 1799, that he was not a party to the mutiny, partly substantiated by his refusal to join the *Hermione* crew leaving La Guaira. His story was further corroborated by Pigot's cook, John Holford Sr., who, along with his 12-year-old son, John Holford, Jr., had been acquitted of all charges. The court nevertheless found Barnett Guilty and sentenced him to death, though with a recommendation for mercy. King George III's pardon arrived four months later. Johnson was tried aboard the *H.M.S. Gloucester* on July 2, 1801, and though found Not Guilty of murder, thanks to testimony from Southcott, was convicted and sentenced to death for helping the mutineers. Like Barnett, he was not executed.

Allen, Douglas' servant, was captured on a ship in the Caribbean and sent to Portsmouth, England, in 1800. At his court martial, Southcott, Sergeant Plaice, and Moncrieff, the cook testified against the youth. He denied their statements, but was found Guilty and hanged from the yardarm of the *Gloucester* on Aug. 7, 1800. Another who maintained his innocence was Hayes, who before his sentencing remarked that he deserved punishment, but for other crimes. Hayes, the surgeon's servant, was captured in October 1806, and his trial proved to be the last. Southcott again testified against the defendant and Hayes was found Guilty and hanged in Plymouth, England, on Oct. 11, 1806.

REF.: *CBA*; Wilson, *Children Who Kill*.

Hermippus (AKA: **The One-Eyed**), d.c.430 B.C., Gr., lawyer. Responsible for prosecution of Aspasia for impiety and immorality. Aspasia was the wife of Pericles, a political rival. REF.: *CBA*.

Hermle, Raymond, 1956- , U.S., mur. Convicted of beating one man to death, Raymond Hermle was accused of attacking another man just three days after his release on bond pending an appeal of the verdict.

On July 30, 1975, 32-year-old Donald Baker was beaten to death with a tire iron in the kitchen of his Chicago home. Hermle was convicted of the crime and sentenced by circuit court Judge Louis A. Wexler to fifteen to forty-five years in prison. The judge allowed his release on a $100,000 bond on Apr. 18, 1977, while the conviction was under appeal. Hermle was arrested after 19-year-old Mauro Jasso filed a complaint that the convicted

killer had attacked him Apr. 21 over a $5 debt. Jasso claimed that Hermle hit him while holding a metal pipe in his fist. Wexler revoked Hermle's bond. REF.: *CBA*.

Hermocrates, d.c.407 B.C., Si., assass. General and politician in Syracuse, eventually banished from the city. When he tried to take over the city in 409 B.C., he was murdered. REF.: *CBA*.

Hernández, Francisco Javier Ovando, d.1988, Mex., assass. The hotly contested Mexican presidential elections in 1988 reached a boiling point with the assassination of political strategist Francisco Javier Ovando Hernández just four days before voting took place.

Since 1929, the Institutional Revolutionary Party (PRI) had ruled Mexico, garnering at least seventy percent of the vote in every election. But the 1988 election threatened to topple this dynasty. Opposition came from the rightist National Action Party led by Manuel Clouthier, and even stronger contention from a coalition of four leftist parties led by Cuauhtémoc Cárdenas. Cárdenas, fifty-four, had once served as a governor for the PRI but was expelled in the fall of 1987 when he opposed the party's candidate selection process. His campaign against PRI candidate Carlos Salinas de Gortari was conducted from a donated van, which he rode throughout the country, gaining enormous popularity.

Hernández, who worked for Cárdenas, was in his car with his private secretary, Román Gil Heraldez, when both men were shot to death in Mexico City. Cárdenas condemned the assassinations, holding President Miguel de la Madrid Hurtado responsible. The police claimed that Hernández was probably murdered by enemies he made as attorney general for the state of Michoacán. But many Mexicans remain skeptical of this explanation. REF.: *CBA*.

Hernández, Javier Barba, See: **Barba Hernández, Javier**.

Hernandez, Joe Frank, prom. 1985, U.S., rape. For several months in 1984, a 15-year-old girl was kept a virtual prisoner after her mother sold her to 70-year-old Joe Frank Hernandez. Hernandez forced her to have sex with him and others until she escaped in February 1985. She contacted police and, later that year, Hernandez was convicted of sexual assault and sentenced to eight years in prison. However, in June 1988, his conviction was overturned in the Fourteenth Court of Appeals in Houston, which ruled that defense attorneys for Hernandez should have been allowed to introduce evidence of the teenager's sexual history, which included several sexual liaisons with boys her own age. A quirk in Texas law allows dismissal of sexual assault charges based on evidence of promiscuity as long as the complainant is fourteen, fifteen, or sixteen years of age, but not older or younger. Opponents of the decision speculated that the ruling would make some teenage girls "fair game" for rape by older men. Houston district attorney Linda West appealed the ruling. REF.: *CBA*.

Hernandez, Jose Conrado, 1849-1932, U.S., jur. Judge under Spanish administration of Puerto Rico. He was nominated to the Supreme Court of Puerto Rico by President William McKinley in 1900, and to the same court by President William H. Taft in 1909. He received a Doctor of Laws degree from the University of Puerto Rico in 1916. REF.: *CBA*.

Hernandez, Peter J., 1921- , U.S., mur. On July 20, 1946, 24-year-old Angelina Loya was found severely beaten in a vacant lot. She had just left a dance at the Avodon Ballroom in Los Angeles.

Though Loya had gone to the dance with three friends, she told Hortense Ortega that Peter J. Hernandez would escort her home. A passerby soon found the dying Loya, her skull fractured at the base, her body badly beaten and disemboweled with a sharp knife. Loya died a few minutes later at the Georgia Street Receiving Hospital. Police searched the home of Hernandez, a 25-year-old butcher, on the advice of Ortega and found a blood-stained tie soaking in cleansing solution. Hernandez surrendered that night and more blood stains were discovered on his hands and body. He was arrested and charged with the murder of Loya. Hernandez denied the accusation, claiming that the blood was a result of Loya's constantly falling down from having drunk too much. A coroner's jury named Hernandez as the murderer on July 25, 1946. He later admitted he was the killer, pleaded Guilty, and was sentenced to life in prison. REF.: *CBA*.

Hernández Girón, Francisco, 1510-54, Spain, rebel. Fought against Gonzalo Pizarro in Peru from 1545-48 as member of royalist army. He led a rebellion against royalist forces in 1553 and won in 1554. Later he was captured and beheaded. REF.: *CBA*.

Herndon, Angelo, 1913- , U.S., rebel. During the summer of 1932, 19-year-old Angelo Herndon traveled from Cincinnati to Atlanta to participate in a hunger march for the unemployed. There he was arrested for proffering Communist literature and held for eleven days without a formal charge. The State of Georgia finally resurrected an ancient statute stating that anybody trying to induce others to join in combined resistance to lawful authority would receive the death penalty.

Herndon's trial began in December 1932 in the Atlanta courtroom of Judge Lee B. Wyatt. Defense attorney Benjamin Jefferson Davis, Jr. stated that the area lynching of more than 3,200 blacks represented a greater threat to lawful authority than the sole pamphleteer, but the prosecution adamantly pursued the death penalty. The jury found Herndon Guilty after deliberating for two hours, and he was sentenced to eighteen-to-twenty years on a Georgia chain-gang.

Released pending appeal on a $7,000 bond posted by the International Labor Defense, Herndon became a passionate defender of Communist causes. The Georgia Supreme Court affirmed his sentence but the case was appealed to the U.S. Supreme Court, which sent it back to Georgia because of an improper presentation. The conviction was affirmed again, but in late April 1937, the U.S. high court set aside the sentence in a 5-4 decision. Justice Owen Roberts read the majority opinion which said Georgia's timeworn statute was a violation of the guarantees of liberty contained in the 14th Amendment. REF.: *CBA*.

Herndon, William Henry, 1818-91, U.S., lawyer. Born in Greensburg, Ky., he was Abraham Lincoln's legal partner beginning in 1844. Book authored: *Herndon's Lincoln: the True Story of a Great Life*. See: **Hertz, Emanuel**. REF.: *CBA*.

Herrera, Manuel Ibarra, See: **Ibarra Herrera, Manuel**.

Herrera Family (AKA: The Company), prom. 1960s-80s, Mex.-U.S., drugs-org. crime. Jaime Herrera Nevares, one of eight brothers and sisters from the small mountain village of Los Herreras, Durango, Mex., got into the heroin business at the end of WWII, and by the 1960s was the largest supplier of heroin to Chicago and the Midwest; the Chicago-based Herreras alone, grossing $60 million a year by 1978. The Herrera clan now numbers 2,000 blood relatives and at least 3,000 "associates."

Herrera Nevares worked as a state judicial police officer in Durango for ten years, beginning in 1966. By the 1980s he owned a 10,000-acre ranch, two hotels, the most expensive home in the region, and several restaurants and bars. His important political ties give him virtual immunity from prosecution. "Don Jaime," as Herrera Nevares is known, bestows gifts on the community and invests heavily in many legitimate business enterprises, and in turn is supported by the peasants, mostly his relatives, who work the opium fields of the Sierra Madre Occidental. Herrera Nevares spent six months in prison—after turning himself in on Oct. 10, 1978—when two of his confederates were caught with thirteen pounds of heroin, but he was released when the two men changed their stories.

The Herrera "pipeline" runs from Ciudad Juárez across the Rio Grande through El Paso, Texas, and into Chicago. Heroin is carried in spare tires, gas tanks and even drive shafts. By 1977, the Herreras controlled Chicago's entire heroin supply. Arrests and seizures of drugs and equipment occurred more often in Chicago than in Mexico., but investigators did not score a breakthrough until July 23, 1986, when, as a part of a federal investigation called "Operation Durango," they convicted two family members, Juan Manuel Herrera Medina and his brother Rodolfo, of drug trafficking. In July 1985, authorities learned that the Herreras were closely associated with the Puerto Rican Zambrana Family, headed by Jesus Zambrana and based in Gary, Ind. After a two-year investigation, FBI and DEA agents arrested 130 people, confiscated $1.5 million in cash, 1,000 pounds of marijuana, forty pounds of cocaine, twenty pounds of heroin, and forty-seven properties in a raid on Herrera's Gary headquarters, called "the Ranch."

A year after the arrests, a number of leaders in the Herrera ring were convicted on drug charges. On Feb. 5, 1987, Ruben Herrera was sentenced to twelve years in prison for running operations in the absence of his brother, Jesus Herrera Diaz. His nephew Manuel was sentenced to three and a half years in prison. Baltazar Lopez received fifteen years in prison for answering phone calls at the Ranch, and his assistant, Gilberto Martinez, received six years. Adela Herrera, the wife of Herrera Diaz, was placed on probation for warning her husband that investigators were after him. Herrera Diaz, forty-five, pleaded guilty to racketeering and operating a continuing criminal endeavor, and was sentenced on May 8, 1987, to twenty-five years in prison. But these arrests did little to disrupt operations in Durango. By the mid-1980s, the Herrera family's income was estimated at $200 million a year, much of it from the manufacture of cocaine, a lucrative joint venture with the Colombian cartel.

REF.: *CBA*; Shannon, *Desperados*.

Herrin, Richard, prom. 1978, U.S., mansl. After a two-year relationship, Bonnie Garland broke up with her boyfriend, Richard Herrin. Herrin, however, was not ready to let go of his first love. Rather than part with her, he bludgeoned her to death with a claw hammer while she slept in her Scarsdale, N.Y., home during the summer of 1978.

The couple met while attending Yale University, and it was the community at Yale, especially the Catholic clergy, who came to Herrin's defense. His supporters raised $30,000 on his behalf, enough to hire a top lawyer from Manhattan. Just thirty-five days after murdering Garland, Herrin was out on bail and in the company of priests in Albany, N.Y.

After a long and bitter trial, Herrin, who pleaded insanity, was found Not Guilty of murder, but Guilty of manslaughter. The Garlands were infuriated with the outcome, as were Herrin's supporters when he received a sentence of a minimum of eight and one-third years in prison. An outraged Joan Garland, Bonnie's mother, remarked, "If you have a $30,000 defense fund, a Yale connection, and a clergy connection, you are entitled to one free hammer murder..."

REF.: *CBA*; Gaylin, *The Killing of Bonnie Garland*.

Herrin Massacre, 1922, U.S., mob vio. Tensions between union and non-union coal miners were escalating in early 1922. The soft-coal workers went on strike on Apr. 1, but the United Mine Workers (UMW) union allowed a strip mine in Herrin, Ill., owned by William Lester, to continue operations with the provision that the coal would not be immediately transported. As Lester's supply grew to 60,000 tons, he broke his promise, fired his union miners, and attempted to ship the coal using non-union scabs. The tension culminated on June 21, 1922, when the union men looted local hardware stores for guns, emboldened by a sheriff who refused to apprehend them. During the night, 5,000 miners surrounded Lester's mine, and at dawn began firing at the scab workers. The workers surrendered on a promise of safety. The miners took them in groups to a field outside Herrin and ordered them to run for their lives. The scabs did run, but twenty-one were killed, and many more wounded, as they fled under the barrage of machine gun fire. Many women and children reportedly took part in the massacre. While many arrests were made for the murders, all defendants were acquitted after a five-month trial. REF.: *CBA*.

Herring, Robert, 1870-1930, U.S., rob.-mur. As a teenager in Texas, Robert Herring stole a herd of horses with two accomplices. But when they sold the horses in New Mexico, Herring grabbed the money and fled on the fastest horse. In 1894, he formed a gang with outlaw Joe Baker and two others named Six Toes and Buck, and pulled a number of robberies, including one which netted $35,000 in gold. Again, Herring absconded with the loot, but Baker pursued him in what became known as the "Herring Hunt." Baker trailed Herring as far as Montana, but there returned to crime, and was shot to death while stealing horses. Six Toes was arrested for a minor offense, and shot to death while trying to escape from jail. Five years later, in 1899, Herring encountered Buck, the last gang member, in Dallas. After a vehement argument, the two drew pistols and Herring killed Buck and two innocent bystanders. Herring was convicted of murder and sentenced to thirty-five years. Five years before his scheduled release, Herring died, never having revealed the location of the hidden fortune in gold. REF.: *CBA*.

Herriot, Edouard, 1872-1957, Fr., rebel. Held prisoner by Nazis from 1942-45 after France fell. He was the mayor of Lyons, and held the position of senator from 1912-19. Starting in 1919, he headed the Radical party. He was the French premier and foreign minister from 1924-25, and became premier again in 1932. From 1947-54 he was president of the National Assembly. REF.: *CBA*.

Herschel, Sir William John, prom.1880s, Brit., jur.-criminol. William John Herschel was a British civil servant working in India who first began to experiment with fingerprinting in 1858, having Indian merchants sign their contracts with him by imprinting their palm and fingerprints to documents as a form of security. In 1860, while working as a magistrate in India for the East India Company, Herschel devoted a great deal of time to fingerprinting, using it as a method of checking the identities of Indian workers who all looked alike to him and who had been cheating the government by sending relatives and friends to collect salaries repeatedly in the same name. Herschel first collected all the fingerprints of the workers; when they arrived to receive their pay, they had to "sign" for this money by pressing inked fingers to receipts.

By 1874 Herschel had come to realize that fingerprints did not change over the years and were ineradicable. In that year, Herschel wrote to the Inspector General of India, presenting him with his findings and urging him to use fingerprinting as an identification system, stating such an I.D. system would offer "the means of verifying the identity of every man in jail." The Inspector General, however, rejected the idea and Herschel did not pursue it. In 1880, he read an article by Henry

Sir William Herschel, first to discover fingerprints as an I.D. system.

Faulds in the publication *Nature* in which Faulds claimed to have discovered fingerprinting as an identification system for criminals.

Herschel wrote a letter to the publication, claiming that *he*, not Faulds, had invented an identification system using fingerprints *before* Faulds, and thus began a controversy that lasted several decades. In the end, Herschel was credited with making the first practical use of fingerprinting, but it was Faulds who received credit for first establishing the fact that fingerprints were ineradicable and thus an almost foolproof way in which to establish identities. See: **Faulds, Henry; Galton, Francis; Henry, Edward.**

REF.: Browne and Brock, *Fingerprints*; *CBA*; Cummins and Midlo, *Fingerprints, Palms and Soles*; Herschel, *The Origin of Fingerprinting*; Moenssens, *Fingerprint Techniques*; Scott, *Concise Encyclopedia of Crime and Criminals.*

Hersey, George Canning, prom. 1860, U.S., mur. In January 1860, widower George Hersey was engaged to Mary Tirrell, but she died suddenly. She was not, however, the last of Hersey's intimates to die.

With the death of his fiancée, Hersey was invited by her parents to live in their house. The offer was made more attractive by the presence of 25-year-old Betsy Frances Tirrell, the oldest surviving daughter. Hersey and Tirrell were soon intimate, and Hersey remained in the Tirrell home in South Weymouth, Mass. Unknown to her family, Tirrell was pregnant with Hersey's child. To remedy this scandalous situation, Hersey purchased some strychnine in Boston on the pretense of needing to kill a dog. On May 3, 1860, Hersey convinced Tirrell to take a spoonful of jam laced with strychnine, telling her that the medicine would abort the pregnancy. That night, after suffering the painful convulsions associated with the poison, Tirrell died. Her parents, suspicious of the coincidental deaths surrounding Hersey, demanded an autopsy.

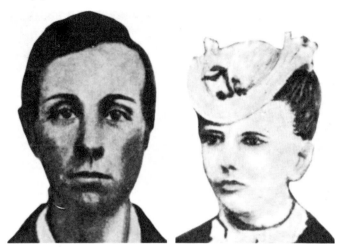

George Hersey and one of his victims, Betsy Frances Tirrell.

Dr. Charles S. Tower performed the autopsy in the presence of Hersey, who asked to be present despite having earlier protested the operation because it would mutilate Tirrell's body. Dr. Tower found that she had been three months pregnant and that her death was due to strychnine. Hersey was quickly arrested and tried for her murder. The spoon with traces of strychnine was found in Tirrell's bedroom fireplace. At his trial on May 28, 1861, defense lawyers argued that Tirrell had committed suicide because of the unwanted pregnancy. This theory did not convince jurors, who had already heard testimony from a Boston doctor who said that Hersey had asked him to perform an abortion for a friend, and when he refused, asked the doctor for strychnine, which he again refused. Hersey was found Guilty and sentenced to death by hanging. After the verdict he confessed to the murder, but maintained his innocence on the death of Mary Tirrell.

REF.: *CBA*; Pearson, *Instigation of the Devil*; Rodell, *Boston Murders*; Yerrington, *Report of the Case of George C. Hersey.*

Hertz Corporation, 1978-86, U.S., fraud. A U.S. government probe revealed in January 1988 that the Hertz Corporation, the largest automobile rental agency in the U.S., had defrauded 110,000 customers and insurance companies of at least $13.7 million in faulty accident claims and overpriced repairs. Hertz pleaded Guilty to the charges on Aug. 4, 1988.

In the plea bargain made in the U.S. district court in Brooklyn, N.Y., Hertz agreed to pay a fine of $6.85 million and to make full restitution to the persons the company victimized from Jan. 1, 1978, to the summer of 1985. Hertz admitted that it had paid wholesale prices for repairs to damaged cars, but charged retail prices without notifying the customers or insurers. The corporation also prepared phony repair appraisals and charged for work that was never performed. Hertz fired twenty employees, including the manager of accident control. As part of the agreement, Hertz deposited $13.7 million (and will deposit more if necessary) in a special fund to be handled by a court-appointed administrator for distribution of the restitution. The company was also required to publish notification of the fund and how to apply for payment, and to personally notify as many victims as possible. In a separate case, Hertz agreed to repay $2 million to 10,000 other customers and insurers defrauded from June 1, 1985, to May 31, 1986, after the first case's time limit. The civil suit was filed in forty-one states. REF.: *CBA*.

Hertzog, James Barry Munnik, 1866-1942, S.Afri., lawyer. Served as Boer general in Boer War from 1899-1902, and opposed peace with British. He served as Orange River Colony's attorney general and minister of education from 1907-10, and he was South Africa's minister of justice from 1910-12. Continuing to urge that ties with Britain be cut, in 1924 he became South Africa's prime minister, serving until he was coerced into leaving office in 1939. REF.: *CBA*.

Herwegh, Georg, 1817-75, Ger., rebel. Went to Switzerland in 1839 to avoid military duty. After writing poems calling for revolution, he went back to Germany in 1842. After he ridiculed the German king, Frederick William IV, he was forced to flee Germany a second time. In 1848 he returned to Germany and headed a revolt in Baden. The revolution eventually forced the king to issue a constitution. From 1848-66 he lived in exile in Switzerland and France. REF.: *CBA*.

Hesilrige, Sir Arthur (or **Haselrig**), d.1661, Brit., consp. Impeached in 1642 by Charles I as one of the Five Members of Parliament. He was placed in charge of a reserve army by Oliver Cromwell, but later opposed Cromwell's government. He conspired against Cromwell's son Richard in 1658, and was imprisoned in the Tower of London until his death. REF.: *CBA*.

Heslin, Peter, d.1927, U.S., rob.-mur. Patrolman Charles Reilly spotted Peter Heslin holding up a group of men on a New York City street corner in the spring of 1926. Gunshots were exchanged between police officer and bandit. Heslin was wounded in the leg, and Reilly was killed. Heslin hobbled off to a friend's apartment, but left a clear trail for police officers, and he was soon taken into custody. Police took him to a back room, stripped him to his underwear and placed him on a table. Though it was evident that Heslin was guilty and little or no questioning was necessary, police tortured him for several hours. Officers took turns striking his wound with a leather strap, or rubbing dirt or cigarette ash into his leg. Others ground out cigars and cigarettes on his genitals, or threw ice-cold water in his face when he asked for a drink. Heslin survived the brutality to stand trial, where he was found Guilty and sentenced to death. He was electrocuted in July 1927. REF.: *CBA*.

Hess, Rudolf (Walther Richard Rudolf Hess), 1894-1987, Ger., war crimes. Rudolf Hess came from upper middle-class society. He was born and raised in Egypt where his father, a German merchant, had a lucrative business. Hess, at age fourteen, was sent to the Rhineland in Germany to continue his education. He served with bravery in the same regiment with Adolf Hitler, but he did not know the "Bohemian Corporal" at the time. Hess was wounded twice and then became a flyer, ending the war as a decorated pilot. Following the war, Hess became a student of economics at the University of Munich, but he spent most of his time distributing anti-Semitic literature in beer halls.

Nazi leader Rudolf Hess, 1940.

When the Communists briefly took over Munich in 1919, Hess fought in the street against the leftists and was wounded in the leg. In 1920, he heard Hitler speak at a meeting of the German Workers' Party and he was forever after Hitler's slavish associate. He participated in the Beer Hall Putsch in 1923 and later joined Hitler at Landsburg Prison, where he helped him write *Mein Kampf*. Hess rose in the hierarchy of the Nazi Party and when Hitler became chancellor of Germany in 1933, Hess became deputy fuehrer, but he lacked the power exercised by such Nazi chiefs as Hermann Goering, Heinrich Himmler, and Paul Joseph Goebbels.

In 1941, just as Hitler embarked on his war with Russia, opening a second front, Hess inexplicably flew to England, attempting to convince the British government to end the war. He parachuted into rural England and demanded to be taken to British authorities. He gave an alias and wore a Luftwaffe officer's uniform. When he was identified, Hess demanded to see Winston Churchill, but the prime minister refused. Hess was locked up for the duration of the war and he was later tried at Nuremberg, where he was found Guilty of helping to create WWII. Hess was sentenced to life imprisonment and, long after all other German prisoners had been released from Spandau Prison, he remained the lone captive, guarded by members of the U.S., British, French, and Russian army.

Hitler thought Hess mad at the time of his flight to England and he seldom, if ever again, mentioned Hess' name. Hess died in Spandau Prison in 1987. According to later unsubstantiated claims, Hess was murdered in England just after landing and an imposter took his place and spent the rest of his life in Spandau. See: **Goebbels, Paul Joseph; Goering, Hermann; Himmler, Heinrich; Hitler, Adolf.**

REF.: Bird, *The Loneliest Man in the World; CBA*; Douglas-Hamilton, *Motives for a Mission: The Story Behind Hess' Flight to Britain*; Fest, *Hitler*; Goebbels, *The Goebbels Diaries*; Heiden, *Der Fuehrer*; Hess, *Prisoner of Peace*; Hess, *Reden*; Hutton, *Hess: The Man and His Mission*; Jarman, *The Rise and Fall of Nazi Germany*; Manvell and Fraenkel, *Hess*; Orlow, *The History of the Nazi Party*; Payne, *The Life and Death of Adolf Hitler*; Rees, *The Case of Rudolf Hess*; Thomas, *The Murder of Rudolf Hess*.

Hessberger, George L., 1947- , Case of, U.S., mur. Chicago lawyer George L. Hessberger suffered from manic depression. When he decided to kill himself in the summer of 1974, he did not want anyone to stop him, especially his wife, Marie Hessberger. To prevent her from turning off the gas range, which he intended to use to kill himself, Hessberger strangled her and slit her throat with a butcher knife. He then surrendered to police instead of carrying out his plan.

Hessberger was placed under psychiatric care, and eventually found Not Guilty by reason of insanity. On Jan. 30, 1975, he was committed to the custody of the Illinois Department of Health. Within three months he was pronounced fit to leave and discharged. He resurfaced in the news when he asked the Illinois Supreme Court to allow him to practice law again. The court concluded that his becoming a lawyer would pose no more threat to society than his holding another job. Since his release, Hessberger has required daily medication to prevent a recurrence of the depression that led to the killing. He was hospitalized twice in 1977 after failing to take his medication. The supreme court's decision on June 9, 1983, stipulated that Hessberger, who had since remarried, must first work as a lawyer's assistant for one year, after which time a medical examination would be conducted to determine his fitness. REF.: *CBA*.

Hetenyi, George Paul, c.1909- , U.S., mur. The body of 25-year-old Jean G.R. Gareis Hetenyi was found in the Genesee River near West Brighton, N.Y., on Apr. 23, 1949. Her death resulted from two .25-caliber bullets that lodged in her torso after entering her body at each shoulder and following a downward path. Two days later, after more than 600 people had paraded through the morgue, fingerprints taken during a job application were matched to those of the victim, an Amherst, N.Y., mother of two. Suspicion fell upon her husband, the Reverend Paul George Hetenyi, who had not yet reported his wife missing. He first refused to identify the body, but finally consented. Prior to returning to Rochester with Sheriff Albert W. Skinner to view his wife's corpse, Hetenyi was taken to breakfast where he remarked, "I prefer to pay for my breakfast. I only will let you pay for my funeral."

Though at first held only as a material witness, Hetenyi was officially charged with murder on Apr. 27. Police discovered that a slug found in the Hetenyi car matched the slugs found in Mrs. Hetenyi's body. The car also displayed signs of a careless attempt to remove blood stains from the upholstery, and blood-stained rags were found behind the driver's seat. It was also determined that the woman's death had occurred in Monroe County, where the trial would be held, and not in Erie or Genesee county as earlier believed. Witnesses noted that the Hetenyis fought constantly since their marriage on Aug. 16, 1945. William B. Gareis claimed that Hetenyi had threatened his daughter's life. The defense argued that Hetenyi was insane. He had displayed fits of rage, including breaking a window with his hand, before being charged with the murder. But on June 4, 1949, he was found fit to stand trial.

A jury deliberated for seven hours before finding Hetenyi Guilty of second-degree murder on Dec. 16, eleven days after the trial began. One month later, Monroe County Judge Daniel J. O'Mara sentenced the Hungarian-born pastor to fifty years in prison. Defense counsel George J. Skivington, who argued that no motive had been proved, successfully appealed the decision, which was reversed on July 13, 1950. The success was short-lived, however, for a second jury took six hours on May 12, 1951, to find Hetenyi Guilty of first-degree murder. Judge James P. O'Connor sentenced him to death in the electric chair on May 29. This verdict was also appealed, and, as before, a new trial was granted. Hetenyi was found Guilty for a third time on Mar. 6, 1953, again for second-degree murder. He was sentenced to forty years in prison on Mar. 30. He remained imprisoned until his parole on June 6, 1966. REF.: *CBA*.

Heth, Joice, prom. 1836, U.S., hoax. One of circus impresario P.T. Barnum's most famous exhibits was Joice Heth, a black woman purported to be 161 years old and to have nursed the infant George Washington. Writer Richard Adams Locke wrote the news report of Heth's autopsy, at which he had been present, as an exposé. A day later, on Feb. 27, 1836, an exposé of Locke's exposé appeared in the New York *Herald*. The piece was either by, or inspired by, James Gordon Bennett, and alleged that the deceased was actually a woman known as "Aunt Nelly," from Harlem, and that Heth was still on exhibit in Connecticut. The *Herald* story was written from information supplied by Barnum's assistant, Levi Lyman, and proved to be further misinformation. Bennett chastised Lyman for misleading him, and Lyman then gave Bennett background material for articles which were published in the *Herald* on the Joice Heth hoax. Lyman's version of the tangled myth was that Barnum had found the elderly black woman on a Kentucky plantation, had all her teeth extracted, coached her on the Washington's story, and exhibited her in Louisville, Cincinnati, Pittsburgh, and Philadelphia at, respectively, 110, 121, 141, and 161 years old. Barnum later wrote in his autobiography that Lyman's tale was just another lie.

REF.: *CBA*; MacDougall, *Hoaxes.*

Hetherington, Joseph, d.1856, U.S., mur. A dispute over money Joseph Hetherington claimed was owed him by Dr. Andrew Randall ended with the shooting death of Randall in his San Francisco, Calif., office. He was shot on July 24, 1856, and died two days later. Hetherington was arrested by Captain of Detectives I.W. Lees, but never went to trial.

The day Hetherington was arrested, a group of vigilantes known as the Vigilance Committee ambushed Lees and took his prisoner because they did not want to see Hetherington acquitted. On Aug. 1, 1853, Dr. John Baldwin had been shot to death during a quarrel over property. Hetherington was tried for the murder and found Not Guilty. Rather than allow a similar outcome, the Vigilance Committee held their own trial and found Hetherington and Philander Brace—who allegedly shot and killed deputy police officer Joseph P. West on June 3, 1856—Guilty, and hanged them on July 29, 1856. They were the last men hanged by the Vigilance Committee, who held their final parade through San Francisco on Aug. 18, and were greeted by the crowds who lined the streets.

REF.: *CBA*; Duke, *Celebrated Criminal Cases of America.*

Hetzer, Ludwig (or **Häzer** or **Haetzer**), d.1529, Switz., her. Ludwig Hetzer and Johannes Denk made the first translation of Old Testament Hebrew prophets into German. Hetzer was the Swiss head of the radical Protestant Anabaptists and of other organizations who called for radical changes in religion. He was put in prison in 1528 for heresy and beheaded in 1529. REF.: *CBA*.

Hewart, Gordon (Baron Hewart), 1870-1943, Brit., jur. Served as king's counsel beginning in 1912, as solicitor general from 1916-19, and as the attorney general from 1919-22. He became the lord chief justice of Britain in 1922, holding the position until 1940. He prosecuted Frederick Rothwell Holt and Lieutenant-Colonel Rutherford, and also presided over the murder trial of Leslie Stone. REF.: *CBA*.

Hewett, Jack, c.1906- , Brit., mur. Sarah Ann Blake, the 55-year-old widow who owned the Crown and Anchor Inn between Pangbourne and Henley, England, was found dead on the morning of Mar. 4, 1922, the victim of a brutal attack the previous night. More than sixty bruises and wounds covered her body, according to pathologist Sir Bernard Spilsbury, who conducted the autopsy. Blake's skull had been fractured four times, and it was apparent that many of the blows and stab wounds had been inflicted after the fatal four-inch-long gash to the back of the neck. No weapon was found on the premises, though there was evidence of a violent struggle, and blood-stained beer mugs indicated that the murderer might have been a guest. The last guest to see the woman alive was 15-year-old Jack Hewett, but no one suspected the boy, who was eager to help police.

On Mar. 14, the knife that killed Blake was found in a hedge thirty-three yards from the inn. Three days later Robert Alfred Shepperd, who had just been released from jail for a petty offense, confessed to the crime, but it was proved he could not have committed the murder. It was not until almost a month later that a photo of the knife was recognized by Joseph Haynes, foreman of the Paddocks Farm where Jack Hewett worked. Haynes identified the knife as Hewett's. Jack was questioned on Apr. 4, 1922, by local Police Superintendent Wastie, Scotland Yard Chief Inspector Helden, and Detective Sergeant Ryan. He confessed to the murder and signed the statement. Following his arrest, Jack stated, "I wish I had never seen the pictures. They are the cause of all this." Two days later he made a second confession to Caversham police constable Buswell, identifying his beer mug from a picture of the crime scene. Jack's trial took place on June 2 and 3 before Justice Shearman at the Oxford assizes.

At his trial Jack recanted his confessions, claiming that he had not known what he was signing. The evidence against the youth, however, was overwhelming. The murder weapon had been identified as his and he was placed at the scene of the crime. Two officers had observed him searching through the hedge where the knife was later found. No one had seen him outside the grocery store during the time of the murder, when Jack claimed he was there. Grocer Samuel Smith did not remember seeing Jack at all that night. Human blood stains were found on the jacket he wore that day. Jack asserted his innocence, stating he had sold the knife long ago, though to whom he could not remember. The only evidence in his favor was that the iron bar used to bludgeon Blake was never found, nor was the mysterious bicyclist witnesses claimed to have seen on Mar. 2. The jury found Jack Guilty, but spared him the hangman's noose. He was sentenced to be detained indefinitely.

REF.: Browne and Tullett, *The Scalpel of Scotland Yard;* Butler, *Murderers' England; CBA;* Shew, *A Second Companion to Murder;* Wilson, *Children Who Kill.*

Hewitt, Marvin (AKA: **Julius Ashkin, Clifford Berry, George Hewitt, Kenneth Yates**), 1922- , U.S., hoax. At the age of ten Marvin Hewitt displayed a talent for advanced mathematics. He did not, however, have an interest in other studies and dropped out of high school at seventeen. Six years later, without any subsequent schooling, Hewitt was appointed a senior preparatory teacher for a military academy.

Hewitt informed his new employers that he had graduated from Temple University. He left that position in the spring and landed another job under false pretenses, this time using a name from *Who's Who* to become an aerodynamicist at an aircraft factory. That summer, he took the name of Julius Ashkin, who had graduated from Columbia University and would soon begin teaching at Rochester University. The Philadelphia College of Pharmacy and Science hired Hewitt as a physics teacher and paid him $1,750 a year. Hewitt dazzled his students, performing complicated calculus in his head. But he wanted more and believed Ashkin, at least his Ashkin, deserved better pay. He added to his dossier the Christie Engineering Company as a reference. Naturally, when the Bemidji State Teachers College in Minnesota contacted Christie, better known as Hewitt, the company had nothing but good things to say, and Hewitt was hired at $4,000 a year. The affluent 'professor' married, and his wife, Estelle Hewitt, had no problem with the arrangement, even having mail addressed to Mrs. Hewitt sent to a post office box. But a problem arose with the school's president, who had attended Columbia University.

Though Hewitt avoided the president and conversations about 'their' alma mater, he knew it was time to move on. He applied at St. Louis University, and though so nervous about being caught that he declined an interview, Hewitt was given a position teaching nuclear physics, statistical mechanics, and tensor analysis to graduate students for $4,500 a year. Another scare came in Spring 1948 when the real Julius Ashkin published an article in the *Physical Review*. Hewitt stalled, telling the school that he had written the article at Rochester University to explain the designation under the author's name. Meanwhile, he applied to the University of Utah at Salt Lake City, where he was appointed head of the physics department, made a full professor, and paid $5,800 a year. Hewitt had now surpassed the real Ashkin, who, using the same qualifications—qualifications which the real scholar had earned—was still an assistant professor at Rochester. The real Ashkin, however, had caught up with Hewitt. A letter from Ashkin arrived in Utah asking Hewitt to quit the hoax. Before Hewitt could leave Utah, a colleague of Ashkin's notified the school, which immediately fired Hewitt but offered him a fellowship to earn the degree he sought. Hewitt declined and moved home to Philadelphia.

After a year and a half of obscurity, Hewitt renewed the hoax. In Spring 1950, he received an appointment to the Arkansas University college of engineering as George Hewitt, who ostensibly held a doctor of science degree from Johns Hopkins University and had worked for RCA communications. But when his previous employment was mentioned to an RCA official who was recruiting at the university, Hewitt fled. He next became Clifford Berry, Ph.D., from Iowa State and landed a job at New York State Maritime College. After a failed attempt to enter the technical industry, he became Kenneth Yates, Ph.D., from Ohio State University and went to work at the University of New Hampshire in January 1953. Hewitt was exposed once again after a suspicious student learned that the real Kenneth Yates worked for an oil company in Chicago. When newspapers heard of Hewitt's remarkable career as a professor, they spread story across the country, and brought his academic career to a quick end. REF.: *CBA*.

Heydrich, Reinhard Tristan Eugen (AKA: Der Henker; the Hangman), 1904-42, Nazi official, assass. Reinhard Heydrich was Adolf Hitler's epitome of the Aryan superman in the Nazi Third Reich. He was tall, lanky, blue-eyed, and blonde-haired. His nose was thin, long, and pointed, as was his chin. Everything about the man seemed pointed, like the tip of a spear. Heydrich joined the German Navy but he was cashiered by Admiral Erich Raeder for not wedding the daughter of a shipbuilder whom he had seduced. Heydrich immediately went to Heinrich Himmler, and ingratiated himself with the future chief of the S.S. and Gestapo.

He longed to be reinstated to the rank of an officer and Himmler was his passport to this post, as well as to incredible power.

Heydrich was born on Mar. 7, 1904, in Halle on the Saale, the son of an opera singer and an actress. He joined the Frei Korps upon high school graduation. This was a militant organization of the right wing, which employed the school's cadets. Heydrich went to Kiel as a naval cadet in 1922. He served on the training cruiser *Berlin* in July 1923 and there met the skipper of the ship, Captain Wilhelm Carnaris, who later became head of Navy Intelligence and whom Heydrich called "the cleverest brute of them all." In 1926, Heydrich was promoted to sub-lieutenant and attended Naval Signal School. He excelled as a navigator and a mathematician. He played the violin with expertise and would often weep openly while playing long pieces, typical of a man whose personality was split between the sentimental and the cruel. After serving on the flagship *Schleswig-Holstein,* Heydrich was promoted to lieutenant in 1928. He had few friends, being aloof and arrogant. The rank and file feared and disliked him for his harsh mannerisms and habit of blurting commands.

Heydrich's style was typical of the Prussian officer, even though he had no such background. His manner was without cordialities or courtesies. He gave an order with a guttural bark and expected total obedience from underlings. In 1930, Heydrich dallied with the daughter of a director of I.G. Farben, the industrial conglomerate that would, like Krupp, produce war materials for Hitler's armies. When the girl asked Heydrich to marry her after he had made her pregnant, he replied that he could never wed a woman who had given herself to him before proper nuptials. When her father protested to his friend, Admiral Raeder, Heydrich was brought before a court martial. His overbearing manner, haughty poses, and outright defiance of his Navy commanders, caused him to be cashiered in April 1931. Officially, Heydrich was dismissed "for impropriety."

A short time later Heydrich married Lina Mathilde von Osten, a tall blonde woman who idolized Heinrich Himmler. It was Heydrich's wife who convinced the apolitical Navy officer to attach his future to the Nazi Party. Through contacts in the SA, the Brown Shirts, Lina arranged for Heydrich to meet Himmler on June 14, 1931. Himmler at the time was looking for a competent counter-espionage officer to head his Security Service. After a twenty-minute interview with Heydrich, the diminutive Himmler approved him for the post. A short time before this, Heydrich had had the presence of mind to join the Nazi Party. He was later named as head of the S.D. (Sicherheitsdienst), a secret police inside the secret police. Heydrich and his men spied on Nazi Party members, checking their loyalty to the party and to Hitler. As such, Heydrich became one of the most dreaded men in the party and later in Germany.

Heydrich, in the words of a fellow SD agent, was "a born intelligence officer...a living card index, a brain that held all the threads that wove them all together." He devoted himself fully to his chores. His only hobby was fencing, at which he became a master, and competed so adeptly that he found few who would accept a challenge from him. It was Heydrich who organized the S.D., then the S.S. and its Gestapo into an internal secret state police force, answerable to no one except Himmler. To his face, Heydrich was servile to Himmler but behind his back he showed nothing but contempt for his superior, calling him "weak and without courage." It was the *authority and power* of the S.S. that intrigued and captivated Heydrich. He loved power above all.

Throughout the 1930s, Heydrich's star rose with that of Himmler, until, in 1941, he was the second-most powerful man in the S.S.-Gestapo. It had been Heydrich who developed the concentration camp extermination systems to implement Hitler's plan of ridding the Reich of Jews and political opponents, as well as others the Nazis found undesirable. This "final solution" was systematic genocide, a mass murder that began in the late 1930s. Others such as Adolf Eichmann worked out the logistics of transportation and methods of murder, but it was Heydrich who outlined the general procedures and set in motion the awful

Heydrich, fourth from left, with Himmler, second from left, 1941.

Heydrich's open touring car, ripped to pieces by a bomb.

Reinhard Heydrich with his wife in Prague, 1942.

Traitor Karel Curda, arrow, identifies bodies of parachutists.

Four of the brave Czech parachutists who assassinated Heydrich, left to right, Josef Gabcik, Jan Kubis, Josef Valcik, Adolf Opalka.

slaughter. As the creator of such, Heydrich was termed "Hitler's Hangman" and "The Blonde Beast."

In September 1941, while secretly plotting to oust Himmler from his position, Heydrich engineered a new post for himself, Acting Protector of Bohemia and Moravia. This included most of what was left of Czechoslovakia, which had fallen to the Nazis three years earlier. Heydrich moved into the Hradcany Castle in Prague, the ancient seat of the Bohemian kings, and ruled Czechoslovakia with an iron hand. Within a few weeks of his arrival, Heydrich ordered hundreds of suspected political opponents executed without trial, with thousands more sent to concentration camps. The walls of Prague buildings were plastered and re-plastered with lists of those who had been arrested and shipped off to concentration camps to their deaths.

Heydrich, Hitler, and Himmler were convinced, had Jewish blood in him, and it was this nagging fact that drove Heydrich to vindicate himself in their eyes by ruthlessly oppressing the Jews. According to his own Jewish biographer, however, along with most traceable documents, Heydrich had no Jewish ancestors. He ordered the wholesale slaughter of the Jews as an expedient to Nazi philosophy but he himself was not a philosopher and hated any discussions of ideologies. Heydrich was a methodical bureaucrat who enjoyed exercising his life-and-death power over the helpless Czech people.

The Free Czech Government, in exile in London and headed by President Eduard Benes, realized that many collaborators made it appear that the Czechs as a nation had gone over to the Nazi camp. It was necessary to change this image, as well as rid Czechoslovakia of the murderous beast Heydrich. To that end, a group of Czech parachutists were dropped into the country in early 1942. There were eight specially trained Czech guerrillas: Jan Kubis, Josef Gabcik, Adolf Opalka, Jan Hruby, Josef Bublik, Josef Valcik, Jorslav Svarc, and Karel Curda. Heydrich was targeted for assassination by these men who, once inside Czechoslovakia, donned civilian clothes and boldly traced the Protector's moves. This was more difficult than expected since Heydrich carefully avoided routines and purposely took different routes each day from his villa outside of Prague to his offices in the Hradcany Castle.

Several assassination attempts were planned and then called off. On May 23, 1942, Josef Novotny, a watchmaker, was called to Heydrich's offices to repair an antique clock. He was a member of the underground, and while he was repairing the clock, he quickly looked over documents on Heydrich's desk. He found the Reichprotector's complete schedule for May 27, 1945, the day Heydrich was to leave Prague for Germany. Novotny crumpled the piece of paper and threw it into a waste can, which was later emptied by a Czech housekeeper. The schedule was retrieved and the parachutists made plans to assassinate Heydrich on May 27. Gabcik, Kubish, and Valcik were to position themselves along the route Heydrich was driven in his limousine to his offices. At a bend in the road where the car would be forced to slow down, Grabcik would step from the curb and empty his sten gun into Heydrich and his driver, Lieutenant Klein.

Backing up Gabcik was Kubish, who carried a bomb. If Gabcik failed to kill Heydrich, Kubish would demolish the car with his bomb. On the sunny, mild morning of May 27, 1945, Heydrich left his villa at 10 a.m. He had dallied that morning to play with his three children. His wife was expecting another child soon. Heydrich's car proceeded along an open road for some time. Another car preceded it, keeping slightly in front of it. This car was driven by another underground worker, Rela Fefek. When both cars approached the bend in the road, Valcik took out a mirror which he used to signal Gabcik and Kubish, to let them know that Heydrich's car was approaching. At the bend, Fefek slowed the underground's car almost to a halt, which caused Klein, at the wheel of Heydrich's car, to stop abruptly.

Gabcik was at the curb, a sten gun hidden beneath a raincoat. He threw away the raincoat and aimed the sten gun at Heydrich. He squeezed the trigger but nothing happened. The gun had jammed. Heydrich and the driver, Klein, were at first paralyzed at the sight of the would-be assassin, but they regained their composure and both drew pistols. Heydrich stood in the open car and aimed the pistol at the helpless Gabcik who frantically worked the Sten gun without success. At that moment, Kubish ran forward and took a bomb from his briefcase. He hurled this into the air in a high arch. The bomb landed at the rear of the car and went off immediately. Both Gabcik and Kubish, showered with shrapnel, ran across the street to escape.

When the bomb exploded the rear portion of the Mercedes, Heydrich received a piece of shrapnel in the back. He stood for a moment and then collapsed onto the seat of the car. Klein was also seriously injured. Pedestrians walked past the car and two stricken men as if they did not exist. Heydrich called out for help but no one came to his assistance. A trolley car packed with people went around the car, its passengers looking down approvingly on the bloody scene. Finally, a woman, a collaborator, commandeered a van and Heydrich was placed inside of this and driven to the Bulkova Hospital. It was first thought that he would survive his wound, which had missed the spine, kidneys, and major arteries. But infection set in and Heydrich was dead of septicemia on June 4, 1942.

By then the S.S. and the Gestapo, as well as regular German troops, were swarming through Prague and neighboring villages in search of the parachutists. One of their number had deserted these patriots. Karel Curda had gone to the S.S. offices and claimed a reward for telling the Nazis that his fellow parachutists, seven of them, were hiding in a basement crypt of the Church of St. Cyril and St. Methodius.

Hundreds of troops surrounded the church where a battle broke out. After a prolonged gunfight in which the Nazis used automatic fire, bombs, and gas to try to force the parachutists to surrender, the freedom fighters either died at their posts or committed suicide rather than give up to the Germans. The fate of these heroes was repeated in ghastly numbers over the next few weeks as Hitler and Himmler, seeking vengeance for the death of their arch executioner, order wholesale reprisals. On the day of Heydrich's death, 152 Jews were summarily executed in Berlin. Himmler announced that the assassination of the Reichprotector had been a Jewish plot and used this ploy to order the murder of thousands of more Jews in concentration camps all over German-occupied territories and within Germany.

On June 9, 1942, Captain Max Rostock led ten truckloads of German Security Police into the small town of Lidice, which was near Prague. All the males sixteen and over in this community were rounded up and placed in barns and other buildings on the farm owned by Mayor Horak. All 172 were taken out the next day in groups and shot in the open fields. All 195 women were shipped to concentration camps, and half were executed. The orphaned children of these victims were sent to German homes to be raised as "good Germans." No trace of these children was ever found. When the men had been killed and the women and children removed, the town was burned to the ground, the remains dynamited, and bulldozers then leveled the area so that no trace of Lidice existed. Heydrich, though given a pomp-filled funeral in Berlin, was not mourned by his fellow Nazis. He was feared even among the high-ranking Nazis who had used him for their own ends, including the sadistic mass murderer Heinrich Himmler and his lunatic chief, Hitler. Sepp Dietrich, a Panzer general and ardent Nazi, spoke for his peers when he said, after hearing of Heydrich's death: "The hog has finally gone to the butcher!" See: **Himmler, Heinrich; Hitler, Adolf; Lidice Massacre.**

REF.: Aronson, *Heydrich und die Anfänge des SD und der Gestapo;* Bartz, *Downfall of the German Secret Service;* Bell, *Assassin!;* Bullock, *Hitler; CBA;* Crankshaw, *The Gestapo: Instrument of Tyranny;* Eisenbach, *Operation Reinhard;* Fest, *Hitler;* Frischauer, *Himmler;* Goebbels, *The Goebbels Diaries;* Heiden, *Der Fuehrer;* Höhne, *The Order of the Death's Head: The Story of Hitler's SS;* Ivanov, *Target: Heydrich;* Jarman, *The Rise and Fall of Nazi Germany;* Manvell and Fraenkel, *Himmler;* Masur, *En Jud taler med Himmler;* Nash, *Almanac of World Crime;* Orlow, *The*

History of the Nazi Party; Payne, *The Life and Death of Adolf Hitler;* Reitlinger, *The Final Solution;* ____, *The S.S.: Alibi of a Nation;* Shirer, *The Rise and Fall of the Third Reich;* Speer, *Infiltration;* ____, *Inside the Third Reich;* Vogt, *The Burden of Guilt;* Wighton, *Heydrich;* Wulf, *Heinrich Himmler;* (FILM), *Hangmen Also Die,* 1943; *Hitler's Madman* (AKA: *Hitler's Hangman*), 1943; *Operation Daybreak,* 1976.

Heymann, Robert L., c.1920-   , U.S., fraud. With his father Walter M. Heymann as vice chairman of the bank and himself as senior vice president, no one suspected Robert L. Heymann of defrauding the First National Bank of Chicago. A federal grand jury did, however, and an investigation was begun in 1974, with an indictment handed down on Feb. 3, 1977, charging Heymann with fifteen counts of fraud, including the alleged misapplication of $248,000 in bank funds.

Heymann pleaded not guilty on Feb. 16 before Federal District Judge Joel M. Flaum. The charges against Heymann were broken down into six counts of mail fraud, eight counts of misapplication of funds—for writing false entries in bank records—and one count of submitting a false financial statement to American National Bank to renew an unsecured loan of $37,500. Prosecutors claimed that Heymann had failed to disclose to First National that he was a consultant for Hardwicke, Inc. Hardwicke had secured a $30 million loan from the bank with the approval of Heymann, who received $1,000 to $2,000 a month from Hardwicke over two and a half years. The indictment also claimed that Heymann had approved $300,000 in loans to the Kenosha Full Fashioned Mills investment company in Kenosha, Wis., of which $248,000 was returned to Heymann. In January 1978 Heymann pleaded guilty to two of the charges, admitting that he had helped Hardwicke get the loan. But he said he arranged for only $110,000 to be funneled back to him from Kenosha Full Fashioned Mills. Under the plea agreement worked out among defense lawyers George Cotsirilos and William J. Martin and Assistant U.S. Attorney Robert W. Tarun, the prosecution did not recommend prison time for Heymann. Federal District Court Judge John P. Crowley sentenced Heymann to four years of probation on Mar. 9, 1978. REF.: *CBA.*

Heys, Arthur, b.c.1907, Brit., rape-mur. On the night of Nov. 8, 1944, Winifred Evans, a 27-year-old radio operator in the British air force, went to a dance at an American camp near Beccles, Suffolk, where she was stationed. Returning late with her friend, Corporal Margaret Johns, Evans left to do a late night shift of duty. A few minutes later, just after midnight, Johns went into the washroom and found airman Arthur Heys, thirty-seven, who claimed he had lost his way trying to return to his own camp. Johns gave him directions, and Heys left down the same road Evans had taken. The next morning Evans' body was found in a ditch. She had been raped and suffocated, jumped on with such force that her liver had burst.

At the next pay parade, police asked Johns to identify the man she had seen in the bathroom and she picked out Heys. Although Heys said he was back in his quarters by 12:30 a.m., his barracks mates said it was closer to 1 a.m. or 1:30 a.m. The next morning, he had missed breakfast because he took a long time cleaning his clothes. Pathologist Dr. Eric Biddle discovered bloodstains on Heys' jacket, and found mud and dust on his pants, as well as rabbit hairs that matched those found on the dead woman's clothing. While he was being held in Norwich Prison to await trial, Heys smuggled out an "anonymous" letter to the commanding officer of his squadron, claiming that "an airman" (Heys) had been wrongly accused. The letter, received on Jan. 9, 1945, gave several details that only the killer could have known. Fingerprint and handwriting expert Superintendent Cherrill identified the handwriting as Heys'. The trial was held at the Bury St. Edmunds Assizes in January 1945 before Justice Macnaghten, with John Flowers for the prosecution and F.T. Alpe for the defense. Flowers pointed out that the letter writer had described Evans telling him about a drunken RAF airman, a detail that no one but Heys could have known. Heys was convicted and hanged for the murder.

REF.: Butler, *Murderers' England; CBA;* Cherrill, *Cherrill of the Yard;*

Greeno, *War on the Underworld;* Jacobs, *Aspects of Murder;* Lefebure, *Evidence For the Crown;* Shew, *A Second Companion to Murder;* Simpson, *Forty Years of Murder;* Wilson, *Encyclopedia of Murder.*

Hibner, Esther, d.1829, Brit., mur. Esther Hibner and her daughter apprenticed young Frances Colpitts from the St. Martin's Workhouse in London. The Hibners gave Colpitts only a slice of bread and a cup of milk a day, and to diminish her hunger she stole scraps of meat from the dog. Her death was attributed to a lack of food, and her corpse revealed sores suffered from constant floggings. Both women were tried at the Old Bailey. The elder Hibner was found Guilty on Apr. 11, 1829, while her daughter was acquitted. Two days later, executioner William Calcraft was called upon to perform his first hanging. Hibner, however, had no intention of meeting her doom quietly. During her incarceration police had used a straitjacket to control the ferocious woman, but she still managed to cut her throat in a failed suicide attempt. Hibner, dressed in only a black skirt and nightgown, was dragged and carried to the scaffold by two officers. Her arrival was greeted enthusiastically, and the hisses from the crowd did not cease until Calcraft released the drop.

REF.: Bleackley, *Hangmen of England; CBA;* Laurence, *A History of Capital Punishment;* Potter, *The Art of Hanging;* Poynter, *Forgotten Crimes.*

Hickey, John Joseph, b.1911, U.S., jur. Served as prosecuting attorney of Carbon County, Wyo., from 1938-46, as U.S. attorney in Cheyenne, Wyo., in 1949, and as governor of Wyoming from 1959-61. He was nominated to the tenth circuit court by President Lyndon B. Johnson in 1966. REF.: *CBA.*

Hickman, Sophia, d.1903, Brit., suic. In Summer 1903, Dr. Sophia Hickman disappeared while on duty at the Royal Free Hospital in London. No one saw her leave the hospital, and for two months police could find no trace of the missing woman. Author W.T. Stead once again called on the clairvoyant he had employed to discover the body of a missing stockbroker. In this case she did not have any luck, nor did other such attempts. Finally, Hickman was discovered, or at least what remained of her mutilated and partially decomposed body.

Two boys found Hickman's corpse while gathering chestnuts in a densely wooded area of Richmond Park. At first police believed the doctor had been murdered, but medical experts argued that the mutilations may have been the result of rats. Morphia was found in her organs, and the equipment for injecting a fatal dose found near the body suggested suicide. An objection to this version of Hickman's death was raised by the disappearance of her purse and the money within—at least £3. Investigators wondered why her purse was missing if she had killed herself. They were also puzzled by the surgical knife found next to the corpse. The owner of the knife was never identified. Based on evidence provided by medical experts, the jury for the inquest of Hickman's death returned a verdict of "suicide while of unsound mind."

Hickman's family and others were outraged at the decision. A colleague claimed that Hickman would never have killed herself, and that the wounds were not the result of rats or other rodents. Others added that the morphia did not prove that Hickman had injected the drug herself, and that the disappearance of her purse was a sure sign of foul play. Investigators and others who took up the public debate argued that the purse may have been pilfered by a transient who did not bother to report the body after finding his prize. Those in favor of the suicide verdict also pointed to the fact that no sign of struggle was apparent where the body was found, remarkable considering the size and strength of the doctor. This point was refuted on the grounds that her body was likely placed there long after her death, since it was unlikely that such a popular and crowded place as Richmond Park could have concealed the body for more than two months. The jury's verdict, however, stood and Hickman's death was recorded as suicide. REF.: *CBA.*

Hickman, William Edward (AKA: **The Fox**), 1907-28, U.S., rob.-kid.-mur. A brilliant but mentally twisted individual, William Hickman decided that the only way he could pay the $1,500 he

Above, left to right, Marian Parker, Mrs. Parker, Marjorie Parker; the Parker family was wealthy and the twin sisters lived an idyllic life.

Left, Marian Parker, age twelve, kidnap and murder victim.

Right, the Hickman family, poor and uneducated, Mrs. Hickman, her errant son William Edward, her daughter Mary and (rear), a family friend.

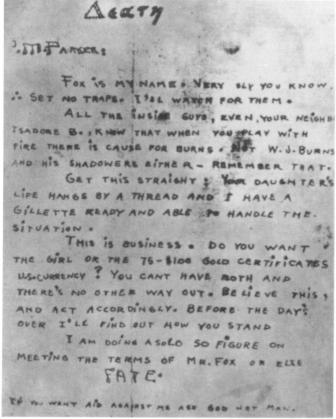

The cryptic ransom note sent by Hickman, signed "The Fox."

Hickman, smug and under arrest.

Hickman reading trial transcript.

Hickman just before execution.

needed for college tuition was to kidnap the daughter of wealthy Los Angeles banker Perry Parker. He knew Parker adored his 12-year-old twin daughters, Marian and Marjorie, because he had briefly held a menial job at the Los Angeles First National Trust and Savings, where Parker worked.

On the afternoon of Dec. 15, 1927, Hickman drove to Mt. Vernon Junior High School in Arlington, a suburb west of Los Angeles. Hickman told the school principal that Parker had been injured in an auto accident and that he had been sent to take Marian home. There was nothing unusual about such a request, and the well-dressed, articulate Hickman inspired confidence among the school administrators. The school officials released Marian from her classes and the two drove away. It was the last anyone would see of her alive. An hour later a telegram arrived at Parker's office from Pasadena which read: "Do positively nothing till you receive special delivery letter. Marian Parker. George Fox." A telegram from Alhambra arrived a few hours later. It read "Marian secure. Interference with my plans dangerous. Marian Parker. George Fox."

The next day a special delivery letter written in a script style and followed with a Greek triangle, representing delta or death, arrived at the Parker home. The kidnapper demanded seventy-five $20 gold certificates, or $1,500 in currency, as the price of Marian's safe return. The ransom note read: "Failure to comply with these requests means no one will ever see the girl again. Except the Angels in Heaven." Two more letters, one written by Marian pleading for her release, were received on Dec. 17. The second letter from the kidnapper was signed the "Fox" and contained an unexplained change in the ransom demand. It read:

Fox is my name. Very sly you know. No traps. I'll watch for them. All you inside guys even your neighbor the B., know that when you play with fire there is cause for burs. NOT W.J. Burns and his shadows either. Remember that. Get this straight. Your daughter's life hangs by a thread and I have a Gillette ready and able to handle the situation. This is business. Do you want the girl or seventy-five $100 gold certificates, U.S. currency? You can't have both and there's no other way out. Believe this and act accordingly. Before the day's over I'll find out how you stand. I'm doing a solo so figure on meeting the terms of Mr. Fox or else FATE.

Parker was instructed to drive alone with the money to the corner of 10th and Gramercy and wait. The police laid a trap, which Hickman sensed and refused to show himself. A second note from Marian arrived the next day begging her father not to bring the police with him. Hickman added an ominous postscript. "Today is the last day. I mean Saturday, Dec. 17, 1927. You are insane to ignore my terms with death fast on its way. I cut the time to two days and only once more will I phone you. I will be two billion times as cautious, as clever, as deadly from now on." However, Hickman decided at this point to kill the child. He strangled her with a dish towel and severed her arms and legs. Deciding that he could still extort the money from Parker, he telephoned and arranged a second drop by phone. This time Parker complied with carefully worded instructions and met Hickman in a secluded spot outside Los Angeles. The father demanded to see his daughter. Hickman pulled back a blanket covering Marian's body, revealing only her face. "Don't follow me and be careful," Hickman said. "I'll drive up there and put her out and you can get her." Parker handed over the money and waited as Hickman drove down the street, finally placing the body curbside before fleeing. Parker rushed to his daughter's side. He pulled back the blanket only to recoil in horror. The madman had combed her hair, powdered her face, and tied her eyelids open with pieces of black thread. Within hours, news of the tragedy leaked out to the newspapers and radio. Frightened parents locked their children inside their homes as the police went to work.

One of the most intensive manhunts in California state history began. There was only one tangible clue found at the drop site for the police to work with, a blood-stained towel monogrammed "Bellevue Arms Apartments." That night detectives went to the Bellevue Arms and found Hickman in his apartment. Although they also found guns, a blood-stained floor, and rolls of cash in the apartment, they left the building without arresting him. Years later, the theory came out that the Los Angeles detectives had known all along that Hickman was their man, but it was a Sunday and the First National Bank, the politicians, and the county board did not have enough time to set a reward for the capture of the felon. Acting under orders from Chief James Edgar "Two Gun" Davis, they planned to wait until Monday to arrest Hickman in the hope of collecting a sizable reward. Taking advantage of the opportunity to escape, the murderer fled the city and headed toward Seattle. Hickman arrived there on December 22. He stole a green Hudson automobile and drove back to Arlington, Ore., a distance of eighty-six miles west of Pendleton.

After his picture had appeared in the local papers, Hickman was picked up by local police in Echo, Ore., after a high-speed car chase along the Columbia River. "I am the Lone Wolf," Hickman boasted as he was being led away. "Do you think I'll be as famous as Leopold and Loeb?" Extradited back to Los Angeles, Hickman was tried for murder in the courtroom of Judge Carlos Hardy, who reserved ringside seats for his close friends and local politicians. Hardy was an intimate of Aimee Semple McPherson, the famous evangelist of the 1920s whose celebrated "disappearance" created a national uproar. Hickman's insanity plea was rejected. He was found Guilty and ordered to hang at San Quentin Prison. On Feb. 4, 1928, before a standing-room-only crowd of 400, the noose was fastened around his neck. On the first attempt, the rope snapped, and Hickman had to go through the gruesome ordeal a second time.

REF.: Alix, *Ransom Kidnapping in America;* Cantillon, *In Defense of the Fox;* CBA; Goodman, *Posts-Mortem: The Correspondence of Murder;* Kobler, *Some Like It Gory;* McComas, *The Graveside Companion;* MacKaye, *Dramatic Crimes of 1927;* Messick, *Kidnapping;* Nash, *Bloodletters and Badmen;* Robinson, *Science Catches the Criminal;* Wolf, *Fallen Angels;* (DRAMA), Shipman, *Trapped;*

Hickock, Richard Eugene, 1932-65, and **Smith, Perry,** 1929-65, U.S., mur. Richard Hickock and Perry Smith were habitual criminals, professional burglars, and thieves. Neither man was mentally sound, according to reports. Hickock had suffered headaches since a car crash in 1950 and Smith was diagnosed a paranoid long before both men became infamous for their slaughter of the Clutter family. While serving time in the Kansas State Penitentiary at Lansing, Hickock learned from his cellmate, Floyd Wells, of a wealthy farmer in Holcomb, Kan., Herbert W. Clutter. Wells, who used to work for Clutter, told Hickock that the farmer often kept as much as $10,000 in a safe in his home.

Upon his release, Hickock teamed up with Smith. Both men planned to rob the Clutter family and then retire to South America where they would while away their lives diving for treasure from a boat they would buy from the spoils of the Clutter robbery. The two thieves entered the home of the Clutter family on the night of Nov. 15, 1959. Both men held their victims at bay with guns and knives, deciding what to do with them. They tied them up and then systematically searched the house. Failing to find anything other than about $50, Hickock and Smith turned in a rage upon the helpless Clutter family, which included Herbert Clutter, forty-eight; Bonnie Clutter, forty-five; daughter Nancy, sixteen; and son Kenyon, fifteen. They stabbed and shot the four members of the family and then fled the Holcomb, Kan., farmhouse.

Wells, who was still an inmate of the Kansas State Prison, heard the news of the Clutter deaths on the radio in his cell and he asked to see the warden, telling him about Hickock's talk with him earlier concerning the Clutters. Detective Al Dewey then led an exhaustive hunt for Hickock and Smith, finally running both men down in Las Vegas, N.M., where they were arrested. The murderous thieves immediately turned on each other. Hickock told authorities that "Perry Smith killed the Clutters. I couldn't stop him. He killed them all!"

Smith denied killing anyone. Then he said of Herbert Clutter: "He was a nice gentleman. I thought so right up to the time I cut his throat." He later said he killed only the wife, Bonnie Clutter, and that Hickock murdered the rest. Smith added, as if to make himself appear noble, that Hickock insisted upon raping the 16-year-old daughter Nancy but he had kept Hickock from sexually abusing the girl. Only Herbert Clutter was knifed, his throat cut from ear to ear and his body then thrown into the basement of the house. The others were murdered as they sat tied to chairs, Hickock and Smith taking turns blowing off their heads with a shotgun.

Richard Hickock and Perry Smith, killers of the Clutter family.

Both Hickock and Smith were tried in March 1960 in Kansas City. The prosecutor in the case aggressively pilloried the two men, aptly describing them as inhuman beasts and reminding the jury that "chicken-hearted jurors" before them had allowed ruthless murderers to go free. The jury found Hickock and Smith Guilty on four counts of murder and both men were sentenced to death. Appeals were denied and each man, quaking and screaming for mercy, were half-dragged to the gallows inside the Kansas State Prison at Lansing on Apr. 14, 1965, and promptly hanged.

REF.: Capote, *In Cold Blood; CBA;* Nash, *Bloodletters and Badmen;* Wilson, *Encyclopedia of Murder;* (FILM), *In Cold Blood,* 1967.

Hickok, James Butler (AKA: **Wild Bill**), 1837-76, U.S., west. lawman. Born on May 27, 1837, in Homer, Ill. (later Troy Grove), Hickok was the fourth of six children. His father, William Alonzo Hickok, was a farmer and operator of a general store which was also used as part of the underground railroad where runaway slaves were hidden and smuggled to "safe" farms. As a boy, Hickok helped guide slaves to freedom. Big for his age, Hickok had a wild brawl with Charlie Hudson, a fellow teamster, in 1855. The teenage Hickok so badly beat Hudson that he thought he had killed him. He fled with his brother Lorenzo, going to St. Louis and then to Kansas, which was then torn between pro-slavery and anti-slavery forces. Hickok joined the ranks of Jim Lane, leader of the anti-slavery men, known as Redlegs. Learning that their mother, Polly Butler Hickok, was ill, Lorenzo returned home, but Hickok stayed on, becoming the town constable of Monticello in Johnson County.

There was little or no work for Hickok, except to lock up an occasional drunk. He busied himself by homesteading and then took a job as a stagecoach driver, following the Santa Fe Trail. In 1860, he became a freighter for Russell, Majors & Waddell.

One day at Raton Pass, a ravenous bear jumped Hickok and badly mauled him before Hickok killed the beast with two guns and a knife. He recuperated from severe wounds in Kansas City. The freight line then assigned Hickok to handle their Rock Creek Station in Nebraska. It was during this period that Hickok befriended the hunter and cavalry scout William Frederick Cody, the celebrated Buffalo Bill. They became fast friends and Hickok often visited the Cody home in Leavenworth, Kan.

At Rock Creek, Hickok worked as a stock tender. Also at the station was its manager, Horace Wellman, his common-law wife, and Doc Brink, a stable hand. Living nearby was rancher David McCanles, who had financial difficulties with the Russell freight line. Moreover, Hickok took to visiting McCanles' mistress, Sarah Shull. McCanles insulted Hickok on several occasions, calling him "Duck Bill" because of the shape of his nose and mouth, and a hermaphrodite.

On July 12, 1861, McCanles, enraged at Hickok's seeing his mistress once again, went to the Rock Creek Station, standing outside the cabin and calling for Hickok to come outside. Hickok refused and McCanles went to a side door. It is unclear whether or not he pulled his six-gun. "Come out and fight fair!" McCanles shouted. Hickok did not step outside. Then McCanles shouted that he would go inside the cabin and drag Hickok outside. "There'll be one less s.o.b. if you try that," Hickok shouted back. McCanles then entered the side door of the cabin and Hickok shot him through the heart. McCanles' 12-year-old son, Monroe, ran into the cabin to hold his dying father.

Meanwhile, McCanles' cousin, James Woods, and James Gordon, a ranch hand who worked for McCanles, came toward the cabin. Hickok shot Woods twice and sent a bullet into Gordon. Both men fled but Wellman appeared with a hoe and ran after Woods, knocking him down and hacking him to death. Doc Brink raced after Gordon and killed him with a shotgun blast. These killings were later much in debate and it was claimed that McCanles was unarmed when he threatened Hickok. One report had it that Hickok shot McCanles from ambush, standing behind a curtain and firing through it.

Following this incident, Hickok, in October 1861, hired out as Union freighter, working in Sedalia, Mo. He later worked as a spy for Union general Samuel R. Curtis. He was also credited in 1862 as having fought as a sharpshooter at the battle of Pea Ridge, Ark. It was during the Civil War that Hickok earned his sobriquet, Wild Bill. One report has it that he was given this name to distinguish him from his younger brother, Lorenzo, who was called Tame Bill. Hickok became Wild Bill. Another story has it that Hickok stopped a lynch mob from hanging a youth and a woman shouted: "Good for you, Wild Bill!" The name stuck and would follow Hickok to the grave and beyond into legend.

By the summer of 1865, Hickok and other scouts had been mustered out of the Union Army. Hickok was then in Springfield, Mo. He was well known in the streets, always armed with two revolvers. With him was his friend Davis Tutt, who also wore two six-guns. Both men reportedly courted the same woman, one Susanna Moore, and this led to a break in their friendship. Hickok and Tutt next met in the Lyon House, a Springfield saloon and gambling hall, on the night of July 20, 1865. Hickok beat Tutt at cards and Tutt threw down his cards, snarling that Hickok owed him $40 for a horse trade. Hickok paid him. Then Tutt recalled another old debt, one for $30. Hickok said no, it was only $25 he owed Tutt and he said he would settle that matter later. Tutt grabbed Hickok's valued Waltham watch from the gaming table, telling him he would wear it the next day on market square. Hickok told Tutt that if he tried that, he would pay with his life.

The gunfight was set for 6 a.m., and half the town was up to witness the duel between Hickok and Tutt. Both men appeared on opposite sides of the square and slowly advanced toward each other. When they were separated by about seventy-five yards, Hickok yelled: "Don't come any closer, Dave!" Tutt kept moving toward Hickok. He pulled his six-gun and fired a shot that went wild. Hickok then drew his gun with his right hand and steadied

Left to right, "Wild Bill" in 1867, gunman Samuel Strawhim, killed by Hickok in 1869, and gunman David McCanles, killed in 1861 by Hickok.

Left, "Wild Bill" turns on hostile crowd after shooting Dave Tutt, 1865, and, right, feeding his horse in a Deadwood saloon, 1875.

Left, an artist's sketches of Hickock-McCanles fight at Red Creek, and, right, "Wild Bill" sitting down to his last poker hand in Deadwood.

it with his left, slowly squeezing off a round that smashed into Tutt's heart, killing him instantly. Hickok promptly turned himself into Union authorities and was charged with murder, a charge later reduced to manslaughter. He was tried on Aug. 5-6, 1865, and was found Not Guilty.

The verdict upset many people in Springfield, especially those who had been friendly to Tutt. Yet Hickok remained in Springfield, where he later campaigned for the post of town marshal. Out of five candidates, Hickok ran second. Wild Bill then left for the West and for the next four years served as a scout for the U.S. Cavalry. He was a scout for General George Armstrong Custer and the famed Seventh Cavalry. He left the service in 1869, taking various jobs in Colorado Territory. There, in July 1869, Hickok got drunk and was involved in a shooting scrape. He shot no one but received three minor wounds.

Hickok then went to Hays City, Kan., where, in the summer of 1869, he was elected sheriff. On Aug. 22, 1869, a local tough, Bill Mulvey (or Melvin, or Mulrey) started to shoot up the town. Hickok confronted the drunken ex-cavalryman, ordering him to surrender his guns and submit to arrest. Mulvey, who was with a number of equally drunken friends, shouted that he would never be arrested. He fumbled for his six-gun and Hickok shot him once. Mulvey was taken to a doctor's office where he died the next morning. Hays City was a wild town in those days, a freight and cattle center, and it attracted some of the worst gunmen of the day. One of these was a brutish teamster named Samuel Strawhim who arrived with a half dozen teamsters on Sept. 27, 1869. He and his friends stormed into John Bitters' Beer Saloon that night and began to wreck the place.

A few minutes later Hickok, accompanied by Deputy Peter Lanihan, arrived at the saloon and ordered Strawhim to surrender his guns. Strawhim laughed and drew his guns. Wild Bill drew both his 1851 Navy Colts, blasting Strawhim to death. A coroner's jury later stated that the Strawhim shooting was justifiable homicide. Aside from cattlemen, teamsters, and gamblers, Hickok also contended with numerous drunken cavalrymen from nearby Fort Hays. On July 17, 1870, Hickok was in a saloon when seven intoxicated troopers jumped him and held him down. One of them held a six-gun to Wild Bill's ear and pulled the trigger but the gun misfired. Wild Bill managed to regain his feet and he pulled his pistols, shooting Private Jerry Lanihan through the wrist and knee and another trooper, John Kile, who was hit in the stomach. The rest of the troopers backed off as Hickok retreated from the saloon. Lanihan survived but Kile died the next day.

Hickok's reputation as a fearless lawman was now firmly established and the authorities of Abilene, Kan., one of the roughest cattle towns on the frontier, sent for him. He became marshal of Abilene on Apr. 15, 1871. Abilene was then experiencing a boom in Texas cattle but the cowboys who drove the great herds to the railhead in Abilene were fast draw artists, not the least of whom was John Wesley Hardin. Hickok confronted Hardin one night while the Texan was shooting up the town. He ordered Hardin to turn over his two six-guns but, according to Hardin, the gunman pulled his guns out of two holsters sewn to his vest, drawing cross-armed, handing the guns' butts first to Hickok. When the marshal reached for the guns, Hardin twirled the guns about in a "border roll" and got the drop on the lawman before leaving town. This story, of course, was all Hardin's and is unsupported elsewhere.

Another story has it that Ben Thompson, then one of the most feared gunmen on the frontier, had had several run-ins with Hickok and that the lawman had pistol-whipped Thompson, disgracing him in front of his friends and employees in a saloon Thompson was then running in Abilene. Thompson, who invariably would face any man with his guns, could not work up his courage to meet Wild Bill in a showdown. Hickok may have been the slower gun but his accuracy was deadly. He was probably the greatest marksman in the west with his Navy Colts, firing with unerring aim whenever he was forced into a gunfight. Thompson

reportedly asked young John Wesley Hardin to kill Hickok, offering to pay Hardin several thousand dollars to do the job. To Hardin's credit, he told Thompson that Hickok was an honorable man and if Thompson wanted the lawman dead he had better shoot him himself, if he could. Thompson dropped the matter.

One story that was not apocryphal is Hickok's meeting with the deadly gunman and gambler, Phil Coe, who had confronted the marshal on several previous occasions. On Oct. 5, 1871, Coe led about fifty Texans into town. Hickok warned Coe and the others to behave themselves, but at 9 that night a shot was fired outside the Alamo Saloon and Hickok went to investigate. When he arrived, he saw a dozen Texans, including Coe, with guns in their hands. Coe admitted that he had fired the shot, claiming that he fired at a wild dog. Hickok drew his guns, saying as he did so that Coe had to surrender his six-guns. Coe fired twice at Hickok at a distance of about fifteen feet. Both shots whizzed through Wild Bill's coat. Hickok fired once, his bullet smashing into Coe's stomach. The gunman crumpled to the ground. Hickok said: "I have fired too low."

At that moment, Mike Williams, a friend of Hickok's, thought to help the marshal. He broke through the crowd and crossed in front of Hickok who thought he was a member of the Texas group trying to shoot him. Wild Bill fired off two shots, killing Williams on the spot. Coe was carried away and he lingered in agony for three days before dying. Hickok was depressed at having accidentally shot Williams. He paid for the man's funeral and was said never to have fired another shot at any man.

For several years, Hickok participated in several wild west shows sponsored by his good friend Buffalo Bill Cody, although he was a reluctant showman, according to most reports, drinking heavily and grousing about having to "play act" to earn a living. By 1876, Hickok was in Deadwood, Dakota Territory, where he spent much of his time drinking and gambling. He knew Calamity Jane in those days but only as a friend. He was never this tomboy's lover, as Calamity Jane later claimed. Hickok had earned many enemies up to that time, after his several years as a lawman. One of those who hated him was a small, cross-eyed little man, Jack McCall, a common laborer who was also known as Bill Sutherland. On Aug. 1, 1876, McCall had lost $110, all the money he possessed, to Hickok in a card game. Even though Hickok had loaned McCall money to have breakfast, McCall swore revenge.

The following day, Hickok was sitting in Saloon Number 10, playing poker with William Rodney Massie, a one-time riverboat captain, Charlie Rich, and Carl Mann, who was part-owner of the saloon. Wild Bill was apparently uneasy since his chair faced two open doors to the saloon. On several occasions, Hickok asked Rich, whose chair was against a wall, to exchange seats with him. Rich laughed and refused each time, saying that he did not want to get shot in the back. At about 4 p.m., McCall entered Saloon Number 10. He ordered a drink at the bar. He slowly walked up behind Hickok and then pulled an old six-gun, firing once into Wild Bill's back. The great gunman toppled sideways in his chair, falling to the floor dead. He clutched his poker hand, aces and eights, which was forever after known as "The Dead Man's Hand." The other poker players at first did not realize what had happened until they saw McCall standing with the smoking gun in his hand. Bartender Anson Tipple jumped over the bar and tried to grab McCall who unsuccessfully tried to fire his weapon at Tipple. McCall dashed out the side door of the saloon while several persons ran about the streets of Deadwood, shouting: "Wild Bill has been shot! Wild Bill is dead!" The bullet that killed Hickok passed through his body and lodged in Massie's wrist. The gambler never had it removed and it was still embedded in Massie's wrist when he died in 1910.

McCall was later found hiding in a nearby barber shop. He was arrested and charged with murder. Some claimed that McCall had been given $200 by Hickok's enemies to kill Wild Bill, although this claim was never corroborated. Meanwhile, Wild Bill was buried the next day with great ceremony. A huge throng was

Left to right, "Wild Bill" Hickok, the deadly gunslinging lawman in 1863, 1871, and 1874.

Left to right, "Wild Bill" with "Texas Jack" Omohundro and William F. "Buffalo Bill" Cody.

"Wild Bill" in buckskins, 1869.

present for the services. McCall was tried on Aug. 3, 1876, the day of Wild Bill's funeral. He was tried before Judge W.L. Kuykendall. He was prosecuted by Colonel George May and he was defended by Judge Miller. McCall insisted that he was blinded with rage since Hickok had killed his brother years earlier in Kansas. This, of course, was a lie, but the jury believed McCall and he was acquitted.

McCall, fearing that Wild Bill's friends would seek him out and kill him, fled first to Cheyenne and then to Laramie City. Here he was again arrested for killing Hickok. It was ruled that the Deadwood trial was illegal and McCall was again tried on Dec. 4-6, 1876, in Yankton, Dakota Territory. He was found Guilty of murdering Wild Bill and, on Jan. 3, 1877, he was sentenced to death. He appealed this sentence but President U.S. Grant refused to intervene. McCall went to the gallows on Mar.1, 1877. He stood quaking on the scaffold, trembling and begging for someone to save him. The rope was placed around his neck and just before he fell through the trap to his death, McCall cried out: "Oh, God!" The body went into an unmarked grave. Hickok's body was later removed to Mount Moriah, where an elegant marker was later built. It is visited yearly by thousands of travelers who still seek the legend of Wild Bill. See: **Calamity Jane; Hardin, John Wesley; Thompson, Ben.**

REF.: Adams, *Album of American History, Vol. II*; Allen, *Adventures with Indians and Game*; American Guide Series, *Kansas, A Guide to the Sunflower State*; ____, *Nebraska, A Guide to the Cornhusker State*; ____, *A South Dakota Guide*; Andreas, *History of the State of Nebraska*; Asbury, *Sucker's Progress*; Atherton, *The Cattle Kings*; Atkinson, *Adventures of Oklahoma Bill*; Barber, *The Longest Rope*; Ballou, *Early Klickitat Valley Days*; Barkley, *History of Travis County and Austin*; Beals, *Buffalo Bill*; Bechdolt, *When the West Was Young*; Beebe, *The American West*; ____, *U.S. West, The Saga of Wells Fargo*; Benedict, *The Roundup*; Bennett, *Old Deadwood Days*; Bliss, *The Life of Hon. William F. Cody*; Bloss, *Pony Express*; Bloyd, *Jefferson County History*; Botkin, *A Treasury of American Folklore*; ____, *A Treasury of Western Folklore*; Bracke, *Wheat Country*; Breihan, *Great Gunfighters of the West*; Brininstool, *Fighting Red Cloud's Warriors*; Brown, *The Black Hills Trails*; Bryan, *An Illinois Gold Hunter*; Buel, *Heroes of the Plains*; ____, *Life and Marvelous Adventures of Wild Bill*; Buffum, *On Two Frontiers*; Burk, *Life and Aventures of Calamity Jane*; Burke, *Buffalo Bill*; Burt, *American Murder Ballads*; Carter, *The Old Sergeant's Story*; Casey, *The Black Hills and Their Incredible Characters*; ____, *The Texas Border and Some Borderliners*; Cattermole, *Famous Frontiersmen*; CBA; Chafetz, *Play the Devil*; Chapel, *Guns of the Old West*; ____, *Levi's Gallery of Western Guns and Gun-fighters*; Chapman, *The Pony Express*; Chilton, *The Book of the West*; Chrisman, *Lost Trails of the Cimarron*; Clairmonte, *Calamity Jane Was Her Name*; Clarke, *The Autobiography of Frank Tarbeaux*; Cody, *Memoirs of Buffalo Bill*; Conn, *Cowboys and Colonels*; Connelley, *Wild Bill and His Era*; Cooper, *High Country*; Coursey, *Beautiful Black Hills*; ____, *Wild Bill*; Crawford, *Rekindling Campfires*; Croft-Cook, *Buffalo Bill*; Cunningham, *Famous in the West*; ____, *Triggernometry*; Cushman, *The Great North Trail*; Dalton, *Beyond the Law*; ____, *Under the Black Flag*; Dawson, *Pioneer Tales of the Oregon Trail and Jefferson County*; Day, *Big Country*; Dobie, *Southwestern Lore*; Donoho, *Circle Dot*; Douglas, *The Gentlemen in White Hats*; Drago, *Great American Cattle Trails*; ____, *Notorious Ladies of the Frontier*; ____, *Wild, Woolly & Wicked*; Driggs, *Western America*; Durham, *The Negro Cowboys*; Dykstra, *The Cattle Towns*; Edwards, *Early Days in Abilene*; Eisele, *The Real Wild Bill Hickok*; Elman, *Fired in Anger*; Emmett, *Shanghai Pierce*; Faulkner, *Roundup*; Fellows, *The Way to the Big Show*; Fielder, *Wild Bill and Deadwood*; Fisher and Holmes, *Gold Rushes and Mining Camps*; Flannery, *John Hunton's Diary*; Foote, *Letters from Buffalo Bill*; Franks, *Seventy Years in Texas*; Frantz, *The American Cowboy*; French, *Wild Jim*; Gann, *Tread of the Longhorns*; Gard, *The Chisholm Trail*; ____, *Frontier Justice*; ____, *The Great Buffalo Hunt*; ____, *Sam Bass*; Gardner, *The Old Wild West*; Garst and Garst, *Wild Bill Hickok*; Gaylord, *Handgunner's Guide*; Gilfillan, *A Goat's Eye View of the Black Hills*; Godwin, *Murder U.S.A.*; Grant, *The Cowboy Encyclopedia*; Graves, *The Life and Letters of Rev. Father John Shoemaker*; Greever, *The Bonanza West*; Gregory, *True Wild West Stories*; Haley, *George W. Littlefield*; Hall-Quest, *Wyatt Earp*; Hardin,

The Life of John Wesley Hardin; Hardy, *Wild Bill Hickok*; Harris, *My Reminiscences as A Cowboy*; Hart, *Old Forts of the Southwest*; ____, *My Life East and West*; Haskell, *City of the Future*; Hebard, *The Pathbreakers from Rivers to Ocean*; Hendricks, *The Bad Man of the West*; Henry, *Conquering Our Great American Plains*; Hill, *Historic Hays*; ____, *Rome, the Predecessor of Hays*; Hobbs, *Glamorland*; Holbrook, *Little Annie Oakley & Other Rugged People*; ____, *Wild Bill Hickok Tames the West*; Hollon, *The Southwest, Old and New*; Holloway, *Texas Gun Lore*; Hooker, *The Prairie Schooner*; Horan, *Desperate Women*; ____, *The Great American West*; ____ and Sann, *Pictorial History of the Wild West*; Hough, *The Story of the Outlaw*; House, *City of Flaming Adventure*; Howard, *Doc Howard's Memoirs*; Howe, *Timberleg of the Diamond Tail*; Hoyt, *A Frontier Doctor*; Hudson, *Andy Adams*; Hueston, *Calamity Jane of the Deadwood Gulch*; Hughes, *Pioneer Years in the Black Hills*; Hunt, *The Long Trail from Texas*; Hunter and Rose, *The Album of Gunfighters*; Hutchens, *One Man's Montana*; Hutchinson, *The Life & Personal Writings of Eugene Manlove Rhodes*; ____, *A Notebook of the Old West*; Ingraham, *Wild Bill, The Pistol Dead Shot*; Isely and Richards, *Four Centuries in Kansas*; Jackson, *Anybody's Gold*; Jameson, *Heroes by the Dozen*; ____, *Miracle of the Chisholm Trail*; Jennewein, *Calamity Jane of the Western Trails*; ____ and Boorman, *Dakota Panorama*; Johnson, *Famous Lawmen of the Old West*; Johnston, *Famous Scouts*; ____, *The Last Roundup*; ____, *My Home on the Range*; Jones, *The Story of Rice County*; Kane, *One Hundred Years Ago with the Law and the Outlaw*; Karolevitz, *Newspapering in the Old West*; Kelsey, *History of Our Wild West*; Kemp and Dykes, *Cow Dust and Saddle Leather*; Kennedy, *Cowboys and Cattlemen*; Knight, *Wild Bill Hickok*; Knowles, *Gentlemen, Scholars and Scoundrels*; Koller, *The Fireside Book of Guns*; ____, *The American Gun*; Kuykendall, *Frontier Days*; Lake, *Wyatt Earp*; Lamar, *Dakota Territory*; Lathrop, *Tales of Western Kansas*; Lavender, *The American Heritage History of the Great West*; Leedy, *Golden Days in the Black Hills*; Lemley, *The Old West*; Leonard and Goodman, *Buffalo Bill*; Lewis, *Between Sun and Sod*; Logan, *Buckskin and Satin*; Lucia, *Klondike Kate*; Lyon, *The Wild, Wild West*; McCarty, *Adobe Walls Bride*; ____, *Some Experiences of Boss Neff*; McCarty, *The Gunfighters*; McClintock, *Pioneer Days in the Black Hills*; McGillycuddy, *McGillycuddy, Agent*; Macguire, *The Black Hills of Dakota*; ____, *The Coming Empire*; McKennon, *Iron Men*; McMurray, *Westbound*; Marsh, *Recollections*; Marshall, *Swinging Doors*; Masterson, *The Tenderfoot's Turn*; Mayfield, *The Backbone of Nebraska*; Metz, *John Selman*; Michelson, *Mankillers at Close Range*; Miller, *Bill Tilghman*; Miller, *Kansas Frontier Police Officers*; ____, *Some Widely Publicized Western Police Officers*; ____ and Snell, *Why the West Was Wild*; Milner, *California Joe*; Monaghan, *The Great Rascal*; ____, *The Legend of Tom Horn*; ____, *The Book of the American West*; Montague, *Wild Bill*; Mumey, *Calamity Jane*; ____, *Hoofs to Wings*; Myers, *Doc Holliday*; Nash, *Bloodletters and Badmen*; Ned, *Buffalo Bill*; Neider, *The Great West*; Nelson, *Land of the Dakotahs*; North, *The Saga of the Cowboy*; O'Connor, *Wild Bill Hickok*; Orman, *A Room for the Night*; Otero, *My Life on the Frontier*; Paine, *Texas Ben Thompson*; Parker, *Odd People I Have Met*; Parker, *Gold in the Black Hills*; Parkhill, *The Wildest of the West*; Parrish, *The Great Plains*; Peattie, *The Black Hills*; Pence, *The Ghost Towns of Wyoming*; Penfield, *Western Sheriffs and Marshals*; Peterson, *Through the Black Hills and Bad Lands of South Dakota*; Plenn and LaRoche, *The Fastest Gun in Texas*; Preece, *Lone Star Man*; Preston, *Wild Bill*; Price, *Black Hills*; ____, *Ghost Towns of Golconda*; ____, *Saga of the Hills*; Pride, *The History of Fort Riley*; Quiett, *Pay Dirt*; Raine, *Famous Sheriffs and Western Outlaws*; ____, *Forty-Five Caliber Law*; ____, *Guns of the Frontier*; Rath, *Early Ford County*; Ray, *Buffalo Bill*; ____, *Famous American Scouts*; Rennert, *Western Outlaws*; Rhoades, *Recollections of Dakota Territory*; Riegel, *America Moves West*; Ripley, *They Died with Their Boots On*; Rister, *Outlaws and Vigilantes*; Robertson, *Soapy Smith, King of the Frontier Con Men*; Robinson, *Doane Robinson's Encyclopedia of South Dakota*; Roenigk, *Pioneer History of Kansas*; Romer, *Makers of History*; Root and Connelley, *The Overland Stage to California*; Rosa, *Alias Jack McCall*; ____, *The Gunfighter: Man or Myth?*; ____, *They Called Him Wild Bill*; ____, *The West of Wild Bill Hickok*; Rosen, *Pa-ha-sa-pah, or, The Black Hills of South Dakota*; Russell, *The Lives and Legends of Buffalo Bill*; Ryan, *Me and the Black Hills*; Sabin, *Wild Men of the Wild West*; Sandoz, *The Buffalo Hunters*; ____, *The Cattlemen*; ____, *Love Song of the Plains*; Scott, *Such Outlaws as Jesse James*; Scott, *The Black

Hills Story; Schoenberger, *The Gunfighters;* Sell and Weybright, *Buffalo Bill and the Wild West;* Senn, *Wild Bill Hickok, Prince of Pistoleers;* Shackleford, *Buffalo Bill Cody;* ____, *Gunfighters of the Old West;* Sherlock, *Black Powder Snapshots;* Shirley, *Pawnee Bill;* ____, *Touhest of Them All;* Simpson, *Llano Estacado, or, The Plains of West Texas;* Sims, *Gun-Toters I Have Known;* Siringo, *Riata and Spurs;* Small, *Autobiography of a Pioneer;* Small, *The Best of True West;* Smith, *The Story of the Pony Express;* Snell, *Painted Ladies of the Cowtown Frontier;* Sollis, *Calamity Jane;* Spring, *Colorado Charley, Wild Bill's Pard;* Stanley, *Jim Courtright;* Stanley, *My Early Travels and Adventures in America;* Steckmesser, *The Western Hero in History and Legend;* Steele, *Forty Years in Canada;* Sterling, *Famous Western Outlaw-Sheriff Battles;* Strauss, *Levi's Roundup of Western Sheriffs;* Streeter, *Ben Thompson: Man with a Gun;* ____, *The Kaw: Heart of a Nation;* ____, *Prairie Trails and Cow Towns;* Sutley, *The Last Frontier;* Sutton, *Hands Up!;* Tallent, *The Black Hills;* Thorp, *Spirit Gun of the West;* Tilden, *Following the Frontier;* Tilghman, *Marshal of the Last Frontier;* Trenholm, *Footprints on the Frontier;* Triplett, *Conquering the Wilderness;* Verckler, *Cowtown-Abilene;* Visscher, *Buffalo Bill's Own Story;* Vivian, *Wanderings in a Western Land;* Waldo, *Dakota;* Walsh, *The Making of Buffalo Bill;* Walton, *Life and Adventures of Ben Thompson;* Waters, *A Gallery of Western Badmen;* Watson, *A Century of Gunmen;* Webb, *Buffalo Land;* Wellman, *The Trampling Herd;* Wetmore, *Last of the Great Scouts;* Wheeler, *Buffalo Days;* ____, *The Frontier Trail;* Whisenand, *This is Nebraska;* White, *Bat Masterson;* White, *Trigger Fingers;* Whittemore, *One-Way Ticket to Kansas;* Williams, *The Black Hills;* Williams, *Buffalo Bill;* Wilson, *Out of the West;* Wilstach, *Wild Bill Hickok;* Winget, *Anecdotes of Buffalo Bill;* Yost, *The Call of the Range;* Young, *Hard Knocks;* (FILM), *Wild Bill Hickok,* 1923 (silent); *Aces and Eights,* 1936; *The Plainsman,* 1936; *The Plainsman,* 1937; *Frontier Scout,* 1937; *Across the Sierras,* 1941; *Badlands of Dakota,* 1941; *North From Lone Star,* 1941; *Wild Bill Hickok Rides,* 1942; *Dallas,* 1950; *Calamity Jane,* 1953; *Pony Express,* 1953; *I Killed Wild Bill Hickok,* 1956; *The Raiders,* 1964; *The Plainsman,* 1966; *Little Big Man,* 1970; *The White Buffalo,* 1977; *The Legend of the Lone Ranger,* 1981.

Hicks, Albert E. (AKA: William Johnson), 1819-60, U.S., pir.-mur. On the misty morning of Mar. 17, 1860, the sloop *A.E. Johnson* was found aimlessly drifting in the lower bay by the schooner *Telegraph.* Crew members of the *Telegraph* boarded the sloop and found no one on board. They did discover, however, blood spattered on the ceiling, floor, table, and bunks in the ship's interior. Furniture was scattered and broken. Heel marks that seemed to be from a heavy body trailed from the cabin to a railing. The railing itself was coated with dark splotches of blood. Next to this spot, on the deck, were four neatly severed human fingers and a thumb.

Mass murderer Albert Hicks.

After the tug *Ceres* towed the derelict *A.E. Johnson* to the Fulton Market slip, authorities released the story of the deserted vessel and its gory clues. The crew had obviously been killed and dumped overboard, but by whom? John Burke, who owned a boarding house on Cedar Street, and one of his boarders, Andrew Kelly, thought they had the answer. With fresh newspapers relating the strange story of the blood-soaked ship curled in their hands, these two men entered the police station commanded by Captain Weed and gushed out an accusation.

"Hicksey is your killer," one of them said. "Twenty-four hours before that ship was discovered, he was back in the house."

"He had a lot of money," the other put in, "but when we asked how he came by it, he talked of other things. Yes, Hicksey is your man."

Albert E. Hicks, Hicksey to a rare few, had lived with his wife and child in Burke's boarding house and had inexplicably come into a large sum of money. Knowing his background, his acquaintances did little guessing as to how. A thief, pirate, and killer-for-hire, the large, middle-aged Hicks was a lone wolf who sometimes, if the pay was promising, would join with one gang or another in raids for loot, but he owed no one his allegiance. This brutish but somewhat intelligent thug would fight with various gangs, sometimes on the side of the Daybreak Boys. On other occasions, he would stand with the Dead Rabbits. The highest bidder owned his knife hand.

Police had a long file on Hicks, one that told them he had run away from his home in Rhode Island where his father had been a tenant farmer. As a teenager, he stole some money and was imprisoned. Hicks escaped twice and was recaptured and put into solitary confinement. Upon his release, Hicks, by then a broad-shouldered, towering man, hardened by long years of prison, signed on board a merchant ship and traveled around the Horn. He led a violent mutiny, which was suppressed. Hicks was flogged, tossed into the hold, and turned over to authorities when the ship sailed back to port. Again, he was sent to prison. Released, Hicks pursued many criminal activities, mostly theft, while disguised as a peddler. Pickings were slim, so he again signed on board a ship, the ill-fated *E.A. Johnson,* using the alias, William Johnson.

Captain Weed selected his best patrolman, a man named Nevins, and ordered him to track Hicks down and bring him in. Through tips, Nevins trailed the gangster to Providence and, with the aid of a local police squad, arrested him in a rooming house. (Nevins later stated that he found Hicks asleep in his room and that the sleeping suspect emitted "buckets of sweat." Hicks and his wife and child were returned to New York. The thug was locked up in the Tombs, his hands manacled and his feet chained to a large stone block in the center of a cell. A police officer entered his cell shortly after Hicks had been chained, and held up a gold watch.

"Hicks," the officer said, "this was found in your room at Burke's place."

The thug stared at the watch which swung from a chain gripped in the officer's large hand. He said nothing.

"This watch belonged to the skipper of the *A. E. Johnson,* Captain Burr." He next held out a daguerreotype of an attractive young woman. "This portrait was given to one of the two Watts boys, Oliver, by his sweetheart. This was also in your room."

"I don't know what those things were doing in my room," Hicks growled. "I never saw those things a'fore."

"You shipped on that sloop under the name of William Johnson. You then killed Captain Burr and Oliver and Smith Watts."

"My name ain't Johnson and I never been to sea on that ship."

"Oh yes you have, Hicks. And you're going to swing for it."

Hicks clenched his hands into fists and violently rattled his manacles, and with short kicks jangled his chains. He spat and cursed at the officer. He then remained silent. The questioning was brief. Officials knew Hicks' background and his reputation as being tight-lipped. They also concluded that he was violently insane. Hicks' brother, who had murdered several persons in recent years, had also been considered a lunatic and had been scheduled to die on the gallows, but had escaped and completely disappeared.

Circumstantial evidence was weighty in the Hicks trial held on May 18, 1860 in the U.S. Circuit Court before Judge Smalley. The pirate was found guilty of slaying the entire crew of the *A. E. Johnson.* Sentenced to die, Hicks suddenly decided to not only confess to this multiple killing but offer in a small-book form his biography, the proceeds of which were to keep his family "all snug." Mrs. Hicks, however, made it appear to prison warders that she had no intention of being "snug" from her husband's murder profits. When she first visited her husband in the Tombs, she held up her small child to the bars and screamed: "Look at your offspring, you rascal, and think what you have brought on us! If I could reach you, I'd tear your bloody heart out!"

"Why, my dear," Hicks replied in a quiet, soothing voice, "I've done nothing. It will be all out in a day or two." The murderer talked many times again with his wife, jailors hopelessly straining to hear their conversations. It was felt that Hicks had told his wife where the loot from his many killings and robberies was hidden and that she eventually recovered this large amount of money.

The published confession was only a smoke screen to make it appear to authorities that Mrs. Hicks' newfound riches came by way of royalty payments for his book. These payments were paltry at best, but authorities did not learn this until much later, when Hicks had been executed and his wife moved on with her child to live out a life of relative ease. It was the last act of a scheming criminal who turned his own hanging into a plot to protect his ill-gotten fortunes. And it worked.

No doubt a reader of the more lurid press of the day, Hicksey belched out a sensational tale of brutal killings, robberies, and licentiousness that encompassed several decades in New York's underworld. When speaking of the crime that had condemned him, Hicks insisted that he had been shanghaied. He had been drinking, he said, in one of the low dives along Cherry Street on the night of Mar. 14. The owner was apparently one of those

Interior of the sloop *E.A. Johnson.*

exceptional Iagos who feared not the wrath of the terrible Hicks and slipped just enough laudanum in the thug's ale to knock him out (too much of this drug was fatal, as the death of Daniel Payne in the Mary Rogers case well proved). Unconscious, Hicks was carted to the *A. E. Johnson,* where Captain Burr threw him into the cabin. When he came to, Hicksey was told to "get to work" and in a few hours found himself at the helm.

"I was steering," he told his publisher, "and Captain Burr and one of the Watts boys were asleep in the cabin. The other Watts was on lookout at the bows. Suddenly, the devil took possession of me and I determined to murder the captain and crew that very night."

Lashing the wheel to maintain course, Hicks grabbed a capstan bar and, on his hands and knees, crawled slowly toward the bow. Oliver Watts turned slightly when he noticed Hicks' shadow, but the hoodlum was quicker, leaping up and forward, crashing the bar down on the boy's head. Watts managed one scream before the blow sent him toppling to the deck. The noise had awakened the other brother, Smith, and he came running up from the cabin. Hicks was waiting for him with an ax, and as Watts emerged on deck, the killer took a full swipe at him. "It was like chopping a small tree. His whole head came off. The rest of him took a few steps, spouting blood like a fountain. Then it sagged down as the head rolled along the deck."

Peering into the dark cabin, Hicks leaned on the ax. He was looking for the heavyset Captain Burr. The thug took a step into the dark room and knocked over a chair. Burr awakened to see Hicks standing over him, his arms over his head, and the ax already descending. The captain moved slightly and the blow missed his head by inches, the ax thudding through the pillow and part of the wooden headrest of the bed. Rolling onto the floor, Burr took a moment to come to his senses. Hicks yanked his ax out of the wood and turned, rushing toward Burr, who also sprang

forward from a crouch. Clasping the murderer's legs and driving forward, the captain was able to topple Hicks backward, but the thug obstinately clung to the ax.

Burr managed to crawl on top of the gangster and get his hands around Hicks' throat, but the killer worked his way into a roll and shoved the captain against the hot stove, stunning him. Hicks then jumped up, brought the ax down in one slashing chop, and drove it deep into Burr's skull. "The blow took away half of Burr's head...half of his eye was on the blade, a piece of his nose, some beard."

Tired from his grisly labors, Hicks went up on deck for some air. His chores were not completed, however, for Oliver Watts, whom he had attacked first, had only been knocked unconscious and was just then staggering to his feet. Hicks rushed over to him and hit him with the blunt end of his ax. He then lifted Watts to his shoulders and carried him to the rail. Again, the youth recovered and, just as Hicks was letting him over the side, Watts reached out and tenaciously clung to the rail. The gangster swore at him as he tried to pry the boy's fingers loose. Hicks then grabbed the ax and brought it down on one hand, cutting off Oliver Watts' four fingers and thumb, which plopped to the deck. The youth slipped down into the water and disappeared.

Such slaughter was work enough to tire any hearty man. Hicks paused to drink several tankards of ale which he took from the captain's stores. It tasted strange, and while pouring himself a fourth drink, he finally noticed in the dim light that the tankard was coated with blood, human gore that had dripped from his own hands. He threw the tankard overboard and then tossed the bodies of Smith Watts and Captain Burr in after it. He almost forgot the decapitated head of Smith Watts and had some difficulty locating it. This, too, he hurled into the water. Rifling the lockers of the captain and crew, Hicks took all the valuables on board the sloop, including Burr's watch and the picture Oliver Watts kept over his bunk.

It was almost dawn when Hicks made out the coastline of Staten Island. He steered for it in the fog and when he neared land, he lowered the small lifeboat and rowed for shore, setting an open-sea course for the *A. E. Johnson.* The tides, however, caused the sloop to drift in the wrong direction, and the *Telegraph* spotted it before it disappeared. By then, Hicks had reached land and gone home where he made the mistake of paying his rent and several other bills the moment he walked into Burke's boarding house. He ostentatiously withdrew the money from Burr's sea bag. The suspicious Burke and another roomer, Kelly, later went to police when the mystery of the *A. E. Johnson* was publicized.

Death by hanging was to be meted out to Hicks on July 13, 1860. It was a Friday. "That date and day have never held good for me," Hicks complained to the dozens of curious spectators who came to gape at him through the bars of his cell, the horribly vivid details of his crimes gouged into their imaginations by his widely published memoirs. Among the many notables visiting Hicks was the irrepressible P.T. Barnum, who was always on the lookout for curiosities with which to enliven his museum. Barnum wanted a death mask and the condemned man's clothing to display in his building, but he was wary of dickering with the money-grubbing Hicks. Instead, he bartered with Warden Charles Sutton.

Showman and jailor haggled in the corridor outside of Hicks' cell, while the killer silently glared at them. For $25 cash, Sutton agreed to turn over Hicks' clothing to Barnum, a death mask to be thrown in for free. When Hicks protested, Barnum promised to send him two boxes "of the finest cigars." They were delivered some hours later, and Hicks happily puffed on these until the time he met his doom. The killer was less enchanted with the suit of clothes Barnum sent to replace Hicks' "murder suit."

"This suit I got in exchange for my own," Hicks complained to Sutton, "is shoddy." Oddly, with no thought to the waiting rope, he added bitterly: "It won't last." (Barnum later had a sinister-looking wax effigy made of the mass murderer, which was exhibited at his museum for decades and was catalogued thusly:

"No. 74. Life-Size Model of Albert E. Hicks, the murderer of the crew of the oyster-smack. *E.A. Johnson,* on or about March 18, 1860, attired in the very clothes worn by him when he butchered his victims with an ax. Note dark stains on jacket. The face was modelled from a plaster cast made by P.T. Barnum, of the Greatest Show on Earth, a fortnight before Hicks was hanged. Acknowledged to be a wonderful likeness of the infamous pirate.")

Sutton, hearing that the hanging was to be an enormous, gala event, decided that his star Tombs boarder should be more presentable and prevailed upon officials to provide better clothing. The day before Hicks was to hang, he was given a suit of blue cottonade with gilt buttons and needlework anchors. It pleased Hicks enormously. "I look like an admiral," he beamed.

At 5:30 p.m. on Thursday, July 12, Mrs. Hicks was shown into her husband's cell. He was free of his chains and wearing his new suit. He shook her hand briskly and then kissed her twice, murmuring each time, "Goodbye, goodbye." The woman showed no emotion whatever and only a faint smile played about the killer's lips when she departed.

True or not, Hicks manifested a spiritual change during the last hours of his life and prayed with Father Duranquet until midnight when he told the priest he was tired. He flopped onto his bunk and was soon sound asleep. Guards had to shake him awake at 3 a.m. He then renewed his prayers, pronouncing his words loudly, as if he wanted his jailors to overhear his devotions. A large breakfast was brought to Hicks and not only did he devour the eggs, bacon, and bread, washing it down with several cups of tea, but asked for more. Another meal was brought, and he finished it. He then methodically washed his face and hands, put on a clean shirt and his new sailor's suit. He brushed the dust from his shoes with a rag, saying with a grin: "Hicksey should look his best this day. My, my, won't New York be proud!"

Hicks was still preening himself when the jailors opened his cell door at 6 a.m. It was time, they told him. He stepped into the corridor and signaled to a janitor who mopped out the cells: "Take what you find in there," he told the man and then quizzically looked at his jailors.

"How do you feel, Hicks?" a guard named Clackner asked.

"I feel very well," the killer responded.

Another guard reminded Hicks that Barnum wanted the empty cigar boxes, which he would also place on display with other Hicks memorabilia. Hicks jammed the last cigar into his mouth and pointed to his cell. "Under the bed...That man overlooks nothing."

Suddenly, Hicks leaned forward and firmly grasped the lapel of Officer Dugan. Looking the guard straight in the eyes, the murderer gritted: "I am the worst man who ever lived!"

Dugan gently removed Hicks' hand.

"You don't seem to think I mean what I say, Dugan."

"Yes," Dugan replied solemnly, "I believe you would not say what was not true when so near your end."

Then, they walked down to the main corridor. Awaiting them was a large group of officials headed, ironically enough, by U.S. marshal, Isaiah Rynders. Captain Rynders had for some twenty years been the political boss of the Sixth ward, and a Tammany stalwart and mentor and financial backer to dozens of New York's super criminals. Unknown to all but two present on the day of the execution, Rynders had employed Hicks on several occasions. The hooligan had handled the more unsavory jobs in the dark doings of Isaiah Rynders.

Hicks smiled when he saw Rynders, but before he could speak, the calculating politician and U.S. marshal, wearing a long, clanking sword especially for the affair, stepped forward and unraveled a long scroll, stating in stentorian tones: "Albert E. Hicks, it is now my painful duty to read to you in the presence of these officers of the law, the warrant of execution which I have received from the President of the United States." The killer was still smiling at his sometimes employer as Rynders read the document, ending with: "This is my authority for now carrying out the sentence of the law. The prisoner will prepare to depart."

Rynders, Sheriff Kelly, Father Duranquet, and Hicks then left the Tombs and got into a carriage. Several other carriages carrying dozens of guards formed the procession to the foot of Canal Street. On the way, Rynders devilishly stared at Hicks, who returned his gaze. The marshal inquired: "And what do you think the future holds for you, Mr. Hicks?"

Hicks squinted at his one-time employer, who showed no trace of apprehension that his former thug for hire would reveal their dealings. The killer mouthed his words carefully: "That is a matter I would rather leave to Father Duranquet."

A huge throng was gathered on Canal Street next to the dock. Frantic members of this curious mob pushed past guards, and, to get a better glimpse of Hicks, smashed the carriage windows and tore away the curtains. The killer gave them his most derisive smile. Rynders and his guards shoved their way through the crowd, their prisoner in tow, and boarded the already jammed *Red Jacket,* a ship chartered by U.S. authorities to take the execution party to Bedloe's Island, where Hicks was to be hanged in full view of the harbor. The killer was taken to the ladies' cabin and there held court, conversing calmly with many reputable and famous people who wished to talk with "the worst man in the world." Hicks seemed to enjoy it all, smiling at his visitors and acting for all the world like he was merely on a pleasant outing.

Excursion boats clogging New York Harbor at the hanging of Albert Hicks.

Once on Bedloe's Island, the killer was led to a scaffold, which was promptly surrounded by 200 marines. These troops formed a hollow square around the gallows. The harbor was full of tooting vessels, hundreds of spectators lining the rails, all of whom had paid large sums to ships' captains for the privilege of witnessing the execution. Huge ships like the *Harriet Lane* and the *Great Eastern* joined the procession of bobbing vessels. The multiple decks of the *Lockwood* and the *Chicopee,* giant sidewheelers, were crammed with people. As an act of either grim irony or strange vengeance, the *A. E. Johnson,* on whose decks the blood of Hicks's victims had been spilled, had been ordered drawn up close to the island. It had been freshly painted, and Hicks was placed on the scaffold so that he could not help but see the vessel.

More than 10,000 shouting persons coated the small island and the floating ships nearby. It was an unreal scene of civilized bedlam. A reporter for the New York *Times* stood near the scaffold, which had been purposely erected on a knoll to afford a good view of the execution. The newsman took in the cacophonous spectacle, and scribbled: "Steamboats, barges, oyster sloops, yachts and rowboats swarmed everywhere in view of the gallows. Large steamers such as carry hundreds of people away on pleasure excursions were there, so laden with a living freight of curious people, that it seemed almost a wonder that they did not sink. There were barges there with awnings spread, under which those who were thirsty imbibed lager beer. There were rowboats with ladies—no, females of some sort—in them, shielding their complexions from the sun with their parasols, while from beneath the fringe and the tassels they viewed the dying agonies of the choking murderer." The ships were decked out with colored bunt-ing, and colored flags snapped in the wind. The incessant crowd roared: "Down in front!...Get out of the way!"

On the scaffold, Hicks turned to Rynders and was heard to utter: "This is your show, isn't it, Marshal Rynders?" The remark was thought insignificant at the time, but it was later pointed out that Rynders reaped a fortune from the circus; he had issued tickets for the execution and those thousands in attendance had unwittingly purchased these from his private agents. His own man, Hicks, would perform one last service up to the moment of his death, once again filling his former employer's pockets.

The executioner, George Isaacs, came forward and placed the rope around Hicksey's neck. "Mr. Isaacs," Hicks said sternly, "hang me quick—make haste!" Isaacs stalled for more time after getting a signal from Rynders, who obviously wanted the event to drag out for the edification of the spectators.

The roar of the crowd to "Stand away in front!" became deafening, and the troops, fearing a riot, moved to one side of the square so that the view from the water was better. Hicks had had enough. He jerked his head violently in the direction of Rynders, and the marshal, displaying his only signs of nervousness—perhaps thinking his one-time bully boy was about to reveal their sinister relationship—hurriedly motioned Isaacs to get on with his work.

At the drop of an arm, Isaacs cut the rope and Hicks was hanged. A thunderous din of approval went up from the throng at that moment, and cheers went on unabated for six minutes. Then, a hush fell over the crowd as Doctors Woodward and Guilmette approached the body. They determined that Hicks' third cervical vertebra had been broken almost at once when the rope had jerked him upward. They then examined his heart. A repeated shout rippled through the crowd on land and above those gathered on the tightly packed ships: "They found pulsations! He still lives!" And then thousands began to chant in mass hysteria: "Hang him some more...hang him some more...the body was left to hang another twenty-eight minutes, allowing those visitors who had brought their lunch to eat in a leisurely fashion. At 11:45 a.m., Hicksey's corpse was taken down and placed in a wooden box, which was carried to the tug, *Only Son*. The tug moved off to the dock of the customs house while boat whistles whined and horns blared, signaling the end of the "grand" celebration.

Mrs. Hicks waited for her husband's body in vain. Rynders had purposely misinformed her as to the eventual whereabouts of the corpse. She sat alone on the wrong dock for hours while officials quickly buried her husband in Calvary Cemetery without her knowledge. In a few days, the body of the mass killer and terror of New York disappeared altogether. Ghouls, it appeared, had dug up the corpse and made away with it. In reality, Isaiah Rynders had turned yet another profit on his dutifully silent protégé, Albert E. Hicks. Rynders had sold Hicksey's body to medical students for dissection. See: **Rynders, Isaiah**.

REF.: Asbury, *The Gangs of New York; CBA;* Duke, *Celebrated Criminal Cases of America;* Kobler, *Some Like It Gory; The Life, Trial, Confession and Execution of Albert Hicks, The Pirate and Murderer; The Life, Trial, Confession and Execution of Albert W. Hicks;* Logan, *Masters of Crime;* Nash, *Almanac of World Crime;* Pearson, *Instigation of the Devil;* Sutton, *The New York Tombs, Its Secrets and Mysteries;* Van Every, *Sins of New York.*

Hicks, Edward L., prom. 1921-24, U.S., (wrong. convict.) theft. As a switchman for the Terminal Railroad Association of St. Louis, Edward L. Hicks was walking across the railroad yard when he was met by Railroad Detective Fitzgerald, who arrested Hicks for stealing a package of shirts. At the trial in May 1921, at the Federal Eastern District Court of Missouri, the question rested on the testimony of Fitzgerald and Hicks. The jury believed Fitzgerald, and on May 9, Judge C.B. Faris sentenced an innocent man to two years of imprisonment at the federal penitentiary in Leavenworth, Kan., for possessing stolen items from an interstate freight shipment.

During the trial, and earlier at the grand jury proceedings, Fitzgerald testified that he had noticed the stolen merchandise on a freight car and waited for the criminal to return for the loot.

He claimed that Hicks picked up the package and that he then arrested Hicks. Hicks denied the accusation. He said his foreman had ordered him to cross the yard, where he ran into Fitzgerald. Apparently he and Fitzgerald had argued earlier and Fitzgerald had threatened to get even. According to Hicks, Fitzgerald forced him at gunpoint to pick up the package of shirts, and when he had done so, the detective arrested him. The court granted Hicks the right to file a writ of error on May 13, 1921, but the Circuit Court of Appeals dismissed the writ on Mar. 8, 1924.

Meanwhile, Fitzgerald boasted to attorney Wayne Ely of his success in getting even with Hicks. Ely notified the Department of Justice in Washington and an investigation was begun. Judge Faris and U.S. Attorney Allen Curry notified the Department of Justice of their belief that Hicks was innocent. The two suggested a pardon for Hicks, and the investigating agent for the Justice Department agreed. President Calvin Coolidge granted the wrongly convicted man a full and unconditional pardon on Aug. 11, 1924. REF.: *CBA.*

Hicks, Larry, 1958-   , U.S., (wrong. convict.) mur. After trying to help two female neighbors move furniture from one apartment to another in Gary, Ind., Larry Hicks left in disgust because more drinking than moving was taking place. The next morning, police discovered that two of the movers had been brutally beaten and stabbed to death. A trail of blood from the snow-covered alley led to an apartment where two women were cleaning up blood stains and Bernard Scates, covered in blood, was sleeping. The women said Hicks and Scates had fought and killed the other two helpers. Scates also blamed Hicks for killing the two men; he later admitted his guilt.

A few days after the arrest of Scates and Hicks, Scates was found dead in his jail cell, allegedly the victim of a suicide. Before he died though, he admitted that Hicks did not murder anyone. Nevertheless, Hicks was placed on trial in August 1978 for the February murders, with the only substantial evidence against him being the testimony provided by Scates' girlfriend—the other woman removed by the prosecution as a hostile witness. The trial lasted only a day and a half before Hicks was found Guilty and sentenced to death. During that time, court-appointed defense lawyer Robert Vegter apparently failed to properly defend Hicks. Transcripts reveal that none of the girlfriend's claims were challenged, witnesses were not called on Hicks' behalf, Hicks' blood-stained clothing was not produced, and the fact that the county coroner stated death occurred after 6 a.m. the next day—not late the night before, as alleged—was not raised by the defense counsel. Hicks also did not testify, though Vegter argued this was the defendant's decision and not his. But when Vegter had failed to appeal the sentence, which the attorney must do for the 'automatic appeal' of a death penalty, Hicks asked attorney Nile Stanton, who was visiting another prisoner at the Indiana State Prison on May 15, 1979—two weeks before Hicks' scheduled execution—to look into his case.

Stanton agreed to help, and a stay of execution was granted after the prison warden contacted Hicks' attorney. The death row prisoner assented to Stanton's request to take two polygraph tests, which were conducted by state expert John O. Danberry, and substantiated by national expert Leonard Harrleson. Hicks passed each test, and then Stanton contacted the Playboy Foundation and arranged for the magazine to help with Hicks' defense. The foundation provided $3,000, which was used to pay private investigator Martin Bell to dig up evidence. Bell found a number of holes in the prosecution's case as well as the police story. The knife held was not the murder weapon, no physical evidence linked Hicks to the murders, no effort was made to check Hicks' story, others at the apartment that night were not questioned, and one of the victims was not stabbed in the back as the prosecution had contended. Gary police Lieutenant William Allen, who had since died, had said that the case was poorly conducted by the detective bureau he headed. With this information, and the probability that Hicks, who had a low IQ, was unable to understand the trial proceedings clearly enough to contribute to his defense, Stanton convinced Lake County Superior Court Judge James C. Kimbrough, who had sentenced Hicks, to order a retrial in March 1980. Prosecutor Jack Crawford refused to dismiss the charges and the second trial began in November 1980.

The trial lasted almost two weeks and the jury deliberated for six hours before returning a verdict of Not Guilty. Because not all evidence and testimony was allowed, the jury's decision was not unanimous, but Hicks was pronounced a free man on Nov. 20. REF.: *CBA*.

Hicks, Lucy, prom. 1945, U.S., pros. Lucy Hicks was no ordinary madame. When Hicks left Kentucky and arrived in Oxnard, Calif., around 1910, she quickly became well known and liked by the community's wealthier families for her cooking. So well-liked, that when arrested, after opening a whorehouse, Hicks was immediately bailed out by affluent banker Charles Donlon, who had a dinner party that night and desired the best cook in town. Hicks' prosperity grew as Oxnard grew. The one house the prostitutes worked in became an entire block of houses, and though Hicks ran them, the town's rich did not mind—or believed that the madame personally engaged in the business. Further, the town still requested that Hicks prepare meals and help their daughters dress. As men went off to WWII, Hicks threw lavish going-away parties, and was even asked by the local paper for a quote after the death of U.S. President Franklin D. Roosevelt. By the end of the war, Hicks was wealthy enough to have purchased $50,000 in war bonds, but not wealthy enough to prevent Dr. Hilary R. Mangan from examining the madame and her prostitutes.

Mangan performed the exams after the U.S. Navy traced a case of venereal disease to Hick's operation in October 1945. Hicks strongly protested the inspection, especially since she had only been the proprietor and not a prostitute. Nevertheless, Mangan insisted and discovered what no one in more than thirty years had detected. Hicks was no ordinary madame. Hicks was a man. REF.: *CBA*.

Hicks, Lutien Roy, 1921- , Sing., mansl. In an attempt to cover up the accidental death of his wife on Sept. 18, 1959, Sergeant Lutien Roy Hicks started a fire in his Singapore home. This 'accident' to conceal an accident only fueled suspicions that he had murdered Helga Hicks.

Unfortunately for the British officer, the fire did not consume his wife's body. Medical experts determined that Mrs. Hicks had not died of carbon monoxide poisoning, as the victim of smoke inhalation would have, but had died prior to the fire. Confronted with this information, Hicks admitted that he had accidentally killed his wife and set the fire because he believed no one would believe his story.

His story, just as he had felt, was at first not believed. Hicks claimed that his wife had been sick on Sept. 16, apparently from a self-induced abortion. Two days later she had diarrhea, and as Hicks helped her up, Mrs. Hicks fell screaming. She fell again, striking her head. At that point, Hicks thought the neighbors might think he was beating his wife, so he grabbed her throat to stop her screams. Mrs. Hicks fell again into the bathtub with the water running. When the servant the Hicks employed, Ow Chin, arrived, Hicks told her to leave. He sent her on an errand so that he could tend to his wife, whose swollen head, Hicks felt, would make Chin believe he had beaten her. On returning to the bathroom Hicks realized that his wife was dead, and was convinced that he had drowned her accidentally. The sergeant was further convinced that no one would believe his story, and feared that if he was accused of murder he would lose his son. As a result of these fears, Hicks decided to burn the body of his dead wife. He purchased paraffin, placing it around the bedroom where Mrs. Hicks had lain since her death that morning. Hicks then started the fire and left, but the flames failed to destroy damning medical evidence and proof that the fire was intentional, thus leading to Hicks' confession.

In March 1960, Hicks was tried for murder in a military court. The court martial consisted of Major-General J.A.R. Robertson,

Brigadier D. Welsh, Colonel J.S. Douglas, Lieutenant-Colonels P. Mears and H.G. Brayne, and Majors D.J. Joyce and R.G. Harvey. Judge Advocate for the proceeding was W. St. John Tayleur; with the prosecution conducted by Colonel John Cumberlage and Major D.A. Boyle; and the defense provided by David Marshall and P. Cumaraswamy. Aside from the medical evidence and paraffin found in the apartment, testimony was provided by Chin, who claimed the Hicks were a happy and loving couple; neighbors, who heard a man shout "be quiet" during the screaming; and the defendant, who provided his story of the incident. Hicks' explanation that his wife drowned was disproved by medical examinations which revealed a plum-colored bruise on Mrs. Hicks' throat. The bruise led experts to conclude that the woman died from damage inflicted to the thyroid gland. Marshall proposed to the court that the defendant had not committed murder, but had accidentally killed his wife when he attempted to quiet her. Cumberlage accepted Hicks' plea of manslaughter, which the court also accepted; the sergeant was found Guilty, and sentenced to eighteen months in prison and a reduction in rank.

REF.: *CBA*; Furneaux, *Famous Criminal Cases, vol. 6.*

Hicks, Mary, and **Hicks, Elizabeth,** prom. 1716, Brit., witchcraft. In England, people often practiced fraudulent "magic" to manipulate their gullible neighbors into giving them donations and gifts in order to protect themselves from harm. Mary Hicks, one of these primitive "sorceresses," told authorities she and her 11-year-old daughter, Elizabeth Hicks, had made a pact with the devil. She was questioned after her neighbors began to vomit pins. Hicks and her child were hanged at Huntington on July 28, 1716.

REF.: *CBA*; Hibbert, *The Roots of Evil*; Nash, *Look For the Woman.*

Hicks, Xenophen, 1872-1952, U.S., jur. Nominated to the eastern district and middle district courts of Tennessee by President Warren G. Harding in 1923, and to the sixth circuit court by President Calvin Coolidge in 1928. REF.: *CBA*.

Hicswa, Joseph, prom. 1946, U.S., mur. Private First-Class Joseph Hicswa was found Guilty of murder for the killing of two Japanese civilians during a drunken fight. For the crime the U.S. Army sentenced Hicswa to death, but in May 1946, President Harry S. Truman used his power as chief executive to reduce the sentence to thirty years at hard labor. The president's decision was based on the advocate general's review of the case, which claimed there was no premeditation, Hicswa was mentally incapacitated at the time, and the death penalty was excessive punishment. Truman's decision also overturned what would have been a case involving the first serviceman executed for killing or raping a German or Japanese citizen. REF.: *CBA*.

Hidalgo y Costilla, Miguel, 1753-1811, Mex., rebel. Priest who wanted better conditions for Mexican natives. His efforts led to the start of the war for Mexican independence, which began in 1810. He was later shot and killed. REF.: *CBA*.

Hiempsal I, d.c.117 B.C., Numidia, king, assass. Ruler of ancient Numidia in North Africa. Assassinated by Jugurtha. REF.: *CBA*.

Higdon, Lloyd, prom. 1963-67, and **Brumit, Lucille,** 1938- , U.S., rape-mur. As a rapist, Lloyd Higdon did not act alone. Nor did he commit murder on his own. Each time he was accompanied by a woman in the crimes against teen-aged girls.

On July 4, 1963, Higdon and his wife brought a neighbor's 14-year-old daughter to their home in Ypsilanti, Mich. Higdon ordered the girl to remove her clothes, saying otherwise she would be sold into white slavery. The girl did as she was told, and Higdon raped her. The girl told her parents of the incident, and Higdon spent two years in prison for statutory rape.

Upon his release, Higdon teamed up with 28-year-old Lucille Brumit, following the same crime pattern as with his wife. His victim this time was 13-year-old Roxanne Sandbrook. Sandbrook, however, did not believe the threat of white slavery, so Higdon strangled her and then raped the dead girl. Because he did not change his modus operandi, police soon caught up with Higdon, and in his confession he implicated Brumit. Each was found Guilty and sentenced to life in prison. REF.: *CBA*.

Higginbotham, Aloyisus Leon, Jr., 1928- , U.S., jur. Served as assistant district attorney of Philadelphia County from 1953-54, as special deputy attorney general of the Commonwealth of Pennsylvania from 1956–62, and as special hearing officer for the U.S. Department of Justice from 1960-62. He was nominated to the eastern district court of Pennsylvania by President Lyndon B. Johnson in 1964, and to the third circuit court by President Jimmy Carter in 1977. He was a member of the Commission of Reform of Federal Criminal Laws and of the Commission on Correctional Facilities and Services. REF.: *CBA*.

Higginbotham, Patrick Errol, 1938- , U.S., jur. Nominated to the northern district court of Texas by President Gerald R. Ford in 1975. Special prosecutor in the case of *U.S. v. Jake Jacobsen,* he also published various works concerning antitrust law. REF.: *CBA*.

Higginbottom, Henry James, b.c.1884, Brit., mur. Henry James Higginbottom had been unemployed for some time when he returned from drinking to his Islington, England, home on the evening of Apr. 23, 1910. He asked his sister-in-law, who lived in the house, if could see his three small children alone in his room. In his room Higginbottom took a razor and slit open the throats of his children, nearly severing their heads. He killed 3-year-old Albert James Higginbottom, 2-year-old Mary Louisa Higginbottom, and 4-month-old Harry Higginbottom. Higginbottom did not resist arrest, and at his trial he was found Guilty but insane and sentenced to spend his life at the Broadmoor Criminal Lunatic Asylum.
REF.: *CBA*; Neil, *Man-Hunters of Scotland Yard*.

Higgins, Fred R., prom. 1890s, U.S., west. lawman. In the 1890s, Fred Higgins was a deputy U.S. marshal in the Arizona Territory. In the San Simon Valley in 1896, Higgins and seven other lawmen formed a posse to pursue Black Jack Christian, Bob Hays, and two other bandits. The lawmen found the fugitives' lair and set up an ambush. When the outlaws appeared, a furious gunfight broke out. Hays fired three shots at Higgins, who was sprayed with splinters of rock, but not hit. Higgins returned the fire and killed Hays with two shots. The other criminals escaped. The following year, on Apr. 28, Higgins and three others, while still in pursuit of the remaining three bandits, tracked them to a cave near Clifton, Ariz. Again while attempting an ambush, they mortally wounded Black Jack Christian, but the other two bandits escaped. A few years later, Higgins moved to New Mexico and became the sheriff of Chaves County.
REF.: *CBA*; Haley, *Jeff Milton*; Harkey, *Mean as Hell*; Keleher, *Violence in Lincoln County*; O'Neal, *Encyclopedia of Western Gunfighters*.

Higgins, James W., prom. 1939, Case of, U.S., consp.-gamb. In Fall 1939, in Buffalo, N.Y., former police commissioner James Higgins, former-Democratic county chairman Frank Carr, two police lieutenants, and three others were acquitted of conspiring to protect gamblers. However, in December 1939, they were strongly suspected of conspiring to influence the jurors in the previous trial. The jurors announced the acquittal before the testimony had ended, and when an eighth defendant pleaded guilty to the same charges, state supreme court justice Albert Conway demanded an explanation. Subsequently four jurors were fined $250 each for accepting bribes and jailed for thirty days. Later it was revealed that a "fixer" had been on the same hotel floor as the sequestered jury. One of the ten deputy sheriffs guarding the jury heard rumors, but did not act on them. During the sequester, one juror, 29-year-old Angeline Muscarella, had a sexual relationship with Deputy Sheriff Alfred Warner. The outraged judge fined Warner $500 and sent him to jail for sixty days. Sheriff William Pollack fired Warner, two women assigned to guard Muscarella, and the deputy who did nothing about the fixing. REF.: *CBA*.

Higgins, John Calhoun Pinckney (AKA: Pink), 1848-1914, U.S., west. gunman. Pink Higgins, born in Georgia in 1848, moved to Texas in 1857 and settled with his family on a ranch in Lampasas County. As a young man, he became a fervent member of the Ku Klux Klan, and owned a saloon and butcher shop. Higgins was wounded twice during Indian battles, and in the 1870s became a central figure in a feud with the notorious Horrell clan. The two families had been friendly, even combining their cattle on common range land, but in 1873, the Horrell brothers killed one of Higgins' relatives and two other law officers. Higgins retaliated by killing two Horrell cowboys, Zeke Terrell in 1874 and Ike Lantier a year later. The feud escalated on Jan. 22, 1877, when Higgins killed the unarmed Merritt Horrell in a Lampasas saloon. Two months later, Higgins was among a group which ambushed Sam and Mart Horrell, but both men survived. The hostility continued on June 14, 1877, when Higgins and three others fought seven Horrells for several hours on the streets of Lampasas, leaving Frank Mitchell, Higgins' brother-in-law, dead. Citizens finally convinced the two factions to ride out of town in opposite directions, but the following month the feud continued after Higgins, with a full complement of men, invaded the Horrell ranch. They contained the Horrells in the ranch buildings, but after a two-day siege, the Higgins forces ran out of ammunition and were forced to retreat. The Texas Rangers, making dire threats to both families, forced the two factions to sign a peace treaty.

Higgins stayed out of trouble until 1884, when he shot a man to death at the border town of Ciudad Acuna, Mex., after the man had reneged on the sale of 125 horses. Higgins escaped by swimming back across the Rio Grande after nightfall. In the early 1900s, Higgins became embroiled in a feud with a Texan named Bill Standifer. On Oct. 4, 1903, in Kent County, Texas, they drew rifles on each other. Standifer's shot struck Higgins' horse, but the return was on the mark, and Standifer was dead from a bullet wound to the heart. Higgins died of a heart attack at age sixty-six in 1914.
REF.: *CBA*; Douglas, *Famous Texas Feuds*; Gillett, *Six Years With the Texas Rangers*; Laine, *Campfire Stories*; O'Neal, *Encyclopedia of Western Gunfighters*; Raine, *Guns of the Frontier*; Sinise, *Pink Higgins*; Sonnichsen, *I'll Die Before I'll Run*; Webb, *Texas Rangers*.

Higgins, Otto, b.c.1893, U.S., pol. mal. Otto Higgins was believed to have been a lawyer that hated Kansas City's Democratic political machine boss Thomas J. Pendergast as much as Pendergast, who controlled the city's vice, hated him. Unfortunately for the city of Kansas City, Mo., this relationship did not hold true after Higgins was appointed director of police by Henry F. McElroy on Apr. 15, 1934.

The appointment of Higgins immediately followed the resignation of Eugene C. Reppert, who was criticized for the lackluster effort put forward in the investigation of the June 17, 1933, killings at Union Station. A group of gangsters, including Charles "Pretty Boy" Floyd and Verne Miller, shot and killed three police officers and a federal agent in an attempt to release prisoner Frank Nash, who was en route to a federal penitentiary. Nash was also killed.

Higgins handled the post with an even greater eye toward corruption. He continually held meetings in his office with Charles Carrollo, the man who replaced John Lazia after Lazia was gunned down July 10, 1934, as Pendergast's lieutenant on the city's North Side. Higgins' connection to the underworld was so apparent that in his first year-and-a-half, vice operations began to thrive as never before. Higgins himself was far wealthier than his $5,000 a year salary the city provided; wealthy enough to build a home at Lake Lotowana, where several police officers were employed. The director of police's involvement with vice became clear to federal investigators when Pendergast was indicted for tax evasion on Apr. 7, 1939. Higgins resigned exactly five years after taking office on April 15. Investigation of Higgins revealed that his first four years in office had brought him an alleged $100,000 in graft. To stave his inevitable conviction, Higgins hastily provided the government with amended income tax returns for 1934, 1936, 1937, and 1938, and a late return for 1935. However, he was found Guilty, along with Carrollo and Pendergast for tax evasion. Higgins was imprisoned at the U.S. penitentiary in Leavenworth, Kan.

REF.: *CBA;* Hynd, *The Giant Killers.*

Higgins, Patrick, d.c.1913, Scot., mur. The murder of 6-year-old William Higgins and his 4-year-old brother John Higgins in October 1911 went undetected for twenty months, until their bodies, tied together with rope, and tossed into a quarry filled with water in Winchburgh, Scot., surfaced in June 1913. Although the corpses were greatly decomposed, identification was still possible and their father, Patrick Higgins, was soon arrested. The single parent was found Guilty of the killings, and despite a recommendation for mercy from the jury, he was executed at Edinburgh.

REF.: *CBA;* Shew, *A Second Companion to Murder.*

Higgins, Vannie, 1897-1932, U.S., org. crime. Vannie Higgins was a product of Brooklyn, N.Y. He had grown up in the streets of the Bay Ridge section, learning the trade of pickpocket and petty thief while in his early teens. By the mid-twenties, Higgins had assembled a fierce gang of sluggers and killers. He controlled all bootlegging operations in Bay Ridge and by 1927, had branched out into other areas of Brooklyn. He aligned himself with Manhattan bootlegger "Big Bill" Dwyer and provided him with a rum-running service that brought in the best Canadian liquor for Dwyer's high society customers. Higgins later became an associate of Jack "Legs" Diamond, Vincent Coll, and Anthony Carfano, also known as Little Augie Pisano, when his bootlegging operations and other rackets moved into

New York gangster Vannie Higgins, shot to death in 1932.

Manhattan. This action brought Higgins and his allies into battle with Dutch Schultz and others.

In 1928, Higgins, though a gang boss, was directly involved in several shootings. He liked to brag that "I don't let my boys take no risks I don't take." A gang battle broke out in Brooklyn's Owl's Head Cafe at Sixty-ninth Street and Third Avenue, which involved Higgins and his mob and a rival gang. Police arrived and began firing in all directions. Patrolman Daniel Maloney was shot and killed by crossfire from other policeman. Higgins was seen fleeing from the scene with his ace gunman "Bad Bill" Bailey. Some weeks later Brooklyn bootlegger Samuel Orlando was found shot to death, and Higgins and two of his gunmen, including Bailey, were arrested. They had been identified as the rival gangsters who had killed Orlando in order to gain control of his bootlegging territory, but by the time the case came up for trial, the witnesses against Higgins had vanished.

A few months later, Higgins and Bailey were shot at by a carload of gangsters firing submachine guns, but both men, driving in another car, escaped unharmed. Bailey, it turned out, lived a charmed life. He was reportedly involved in dozens of gun battles and knife fights and never received a gunshot wound or was cut by a blade. He survived the Roaring Twenties and died in bed of pneumonia in the late 1930s. Higgins, on the other hand, had his share of gang battle scars. In 1931, he and some of his men invaded the Blossom Heath Inn on West Fifty-seventh Street in Manhattan. Higgins had words with the proprietor, Frank McManus, brother of gambler George "Hump" McManus, one of the last persons to see the murdered crime boss Arnold Rothstein alive in 1928. (He was later suspected of being Rothstein's murderer.)

Frank McManus ordered Higgins and his men to leave his cafe. When they proved reluctant to do so without getting a order for a truckload of beer and liquor, a fight broke out in which Higgins received several knife wounds. He was taken to Polyclinic

Hospital but, in the tradition of the underworld, he refused to name his attacker. Later that year, Higgins and Bailey were suspected of killing one of Higgins' own men, Robert Benson, whom they believed had secretly joined the ranks of the detested Dutch Schultz and was feeding the Dutchman information about Higgins' organization and liquor shipments. Both Higgins and Bailey were arrested for this murder but were later released for lack of evidence.

Higgins owned several planes along with his fleet of fast speedboats, which he used for his liquor smuggling. He was also a pilot who flew his planes for business and pleasure. One day he flew to Baltimore on business. As he was leaving a speakeasy a gunfight broke out between rival gangsters. Higgins was not part of these warring factions and decided to flee. As he was running away, a local cop, answering an alarm, thought Higgins was one of the local gangsters and shot him in the leg, a slight wound which Higgins laughed off as he recuperated in a hospital.

A flashy dresser, Higgins was a show-boating gangster, who liked to appear in public and pose for news photographers. He wore imported suits made in England and was driven about in limousines. He was seldom without bodyguards. Higgins was utterly reckless when it came to gang battles, and his offices and home were heavily stocked with automatic weapons. When Higgins obtained a shipment of grenades from a federal arsenal, he and Jack "Legs" Diamond employed these explosives to blow up several speakeasies owned and operated by Dutch Shultz in their prolonged war with the Dutchman.

Higgins was also well-connected with New York politicians and bigwigs. This was clearly demonstrated when he flew one of his planes to Comstock, N.Y., to visit an old friend, Joseph H. Wilson, warden of the Comstock Prison. Wilson had ordered a meadow near the prison cleared by convict labor so that his friend Vannie could land his plane there. Higgins dined with Wilson in warden's residence inside the prison. Governor Franklin D. Roosevelt heard that Warden Wilson had entertained the notorious Higgins at his prison, and he upbraided Wilson for consorting with a ruthless gangster. Wilson tartly informed Roosevelt that he had known Higgins since boyhood and he would entertain whomever he pleased.

The end for Vannie Higgins came on the night of June 18, 1932. He was leaving the Knights of Columbus clubhouse in Prospect Park, accompanied by his wife, mother-in-law, and daughter Jean, who had just performed in a dancing recital. As the Higgins family stepped to the street, submachine gun fire from a car moving slowly past the clubhouse splattered the building and sidewalk. Jean Higgins was nicked in the ear and dove, screaming, into her father's car. Mrs. Higgins and her mother, screaming, started to run back into the clubhouse. Higgins, instead of taking cover, drew his gun and darted after the carload of gangsters, firing at them as they returned a hail of bullets.

"Vannie, come back!" screamed Mrs. Higgins. "You'll get killed!"

"No!" Higgins shouted back to his wife, running and firing at the men in the car, "I'm gonna kill *them*!" A burst from a submachine gun finally knocked the volatile gangster to the ground. He was mortally wounded and was rushed to the Methodist Episcopal Hospital. Here police vainly tried to learn from the dying gangster the identities of those who had shot him. Witnesses had already identified one of the machine gunners in the car as Bo Weinberg, Dutch Schultz's top gunman. But Higgins kept the code of the underworld to the end.

He suddenly bolted to a sitting position and screamed at police detectives: "The rats! They tried to wipe out my family!" He looked about wildly, as if expecting gunmen to burst through the door of the hospital room at any moment. Then he fell back on a pillow, dead. See: **Carfano, Anthony; Coll, Vincent; Diamond, Jack; Dwyer, William; Schultz, Dutch.**

REF.: *CBA;* Levine, *Anatomy of a Gangster;* Nash, *Bloodletters and Badmen;* Peterson, *The Mob;* Raymond and Thompson, *Gang Rule in New York.*

Higgins, William R., c.1945-89, Lebanon, kid.-mur. U.S. Lieutenant Colonel William R. Higgins was the leader of a seventy-six member United Nations observer group in southern Lebanon when he was captured by members of the pro-Iranian Shiite Moslem sect, Hezbullah, on Feb. 17, 1988. He was abducted while on his way from Tyre to Naqoura, headquarters of the 5,800-member U.N. Interim Force. The actual abduction, though well planned, was fraught with bad luck. The brown Volvo Higgins was forced into became stuck in the mud, and its exhaust system was broken by the bulldozer used to free it. A white Peugeot was then employed, but it collided with a truck carrying oranges. This car was replaced by a red Mercedes, which made good the abduction. During this misadventure, four other brown Volvos were deployed throughout the area to mislead investigators.

The captors, a unit of Hezbullah known as the Oppressed on Earth, claimed that Higgins was a CIA spy—which the U.S. denied—and sentenced him to death. Although it was never learned exactly where Higgins was held or if he was alive for more than a year, the Israeli kidnapping of Moslem spiritual leader Sheik Abdul-Karim Obeid in July 1989 prompted Higgins' kidnappers to follow through on their death threat. The terrorists released a videotape after Obeid's abduction which portrayed Higgins, or a man similar in appearance, hanging from a makeshift gallows. The FBI later determined that the man who was hanged was Higgins, although the CIA felt that he was murdered before July 31. Obeid, whose capture was acknowledged as the catalyst, informed his captors that Higgins was alive prior to his own kidnapping. REF.: *CBA*.

High Sierra, 1940, a novel by W.R. Burnett, also a motion picture of the same name (1941), with Humphrey Bogart, who bore a striking resemblance to John Dillinger (U.S., 1933-34), in the role of the aging, hunted gangster. This work, although the locale is primarily set in California, is based upon the life and spectacular criminal career of Dillinger. See: **Dillinger, John Herbert.** REF.: *CBA*.

Hightower, Rudy, 1925- , U.S., theft-burg.-mur. In the early morning of Halloween 1968, Dan Cannon was shot to death outside his College Park, Ga., apartment. Cannon was obviously surprised by the murderer, who sped off in a dark blue 1966 Mustang, leading police detective Garon Glover to surmise that the killer knew Cannon or at least his habits. The lieutenant ruled out robbery, as no money was stolen, and learned that Cannon had dated a divorced woman, Ruth Williams, which might lead a jealous ex-husband to commit murder. Glover correctly identified the motive, but the murderer was another man.

Later that day, Oct. 31, Glover discovered that Williams' former husband was not the suspect, but that the estranged husband of Peggy Hightower might be. Cannon had left his beauty salon partnership with Williams and met Mrs. Hightower at Horne's Restaurant in Chamblee, where he was assistant manager and she was a waitress. The two began dating in August, and the divorce between Mrs. Hightower and her 43-year-old husband, Rudy Hightower, was to be final on Nov. 27. Hightower, who had been convicted of auto theft, burglary, and once sentenced to eighteen months in a federal prison for post office burglary, was violently jealous. Mrs. Hightower feared the jealousy that her husband possessed, and therefore kept her relationship with Cannon a secret. On Oct. 22, Hightower found out. On that day, the two men almost fought when Hightower arrived at his wife's home and Cannon was there. Nine days later, Hightower shot Cannon with the small-caliber pistol his wife noted was missing from her home. She also noted that her husband had borrowed her Mustang on the night of the murder.

Hightower eluded police for ten days before a high-speed chase ended with his capture. After striking several cars and breaking through three roadblocks, Hightower ran the Mustang into a bakery truck. He then locked the doors and refused to surrender even after police shot a bullet through the windshield. The killer finally gave up when police shot him in the shoulder as he reached for his glove compartment.

At his trial, Hightower almost got away with the murder when Atlanta businessman C.S. Reid testified that the defendant was with him when the shooting took place. His testimony was soon disbelieved by the jury when it was shown that Reid was Hightower's brother-in-law. Hightower was found Guilty and sentenced to life in prison. REF.: *CBA*.

Hightower, William A., b.1877, U.S., mur. William Hightower committed the crime considered most odious to hardened criminals who otherwise have no qualms about murder: He killed a priest. Born in Texas, Hightower left home to seek his fortune in the West. He worked in dozens of roadside restaurants learning the culinary arts. In time he became an accomplished baker, specializing in pastries. In 1910, he married a Fresno, Calif., girl, but since she was the daughter of a religious fundamentalist, and Hightower enjoyed drinking and carrying on, they soon separated. He also worked as a cook and fancied himself a genius inventor. During WWI, he claimed to have invented a new machine gun, but before anyone could test its effectiveness the plans were "stolen." "I was going to have it patented and give it to the government when the models got into the hands of German sympathizers," he said.

Hightower eventually settled in Bakersfield, Calif., where he opened a bakery, but it failed in the years following the war. He took to the road, trying desperately to peddle another one of his inventions: a candied fruit substitute. There were no takers. By 1921, Hightower was cooking for a section gang on the Southern Pacific line outside Salt Lake City, Utah. He soon quit and drove to San Francisco, where he concocted a perfect money-raising scheme after noticing in the paper that 15,000 members of the Knights of Columbus, a Roman Catholic organization, were to arrive in the city for their thirty-ninth annual convention. In a moment of maniacal inspiration, the failed chef concocted a scheme that he thought would make him a fortune.

Hightower appeared on the doorstep of the Holy Angels Church in Colma on the night of Aug. 2, 1921. The housekeeper, Marie Wendel, opened the door and found an oddly dressed man shielding his face from view, who spoke in a foreign accent, saying, "I would like to see the Father. He is very needed. My friend is dying. We want the Father at once." The housekeeper summoned Father Patrick E. Heslin from his study. Hightower told him that his friend was seriously injured in an auto accident and had requested last rights. Father Heslin left the house with Hightower, the housekeeper watching them drive off into a fog-shrouded night. When the Father did not return, she contacted Archbishop Edward J. Hanna who deemed it prudent to wait a few hours before calling police. Later, the archbishop was sent a ransom note demanding $6,500. The hastily scrawled note was given to Carl Eisenshimmel and Chauncey McGovern, two experts in the field of graphanology. They could only state the obvious: the author of this note was a "deranged person...a demented person."

The story was leaked to the press and within hours the city—including the thousands of delegates of the Knights of Columbus Convention—was in an uproar. Police conducted an exhaustive search through the city and its environs, but after eight days still found no sign of Father Heslin. Armed vigilantes combed the city streets, the surrounding hills, and the isolated beaches, to no avail. A second ransom note arrived, but did not specify where the drop was to be made. What was particularly unusual was the kidnapper's demand for $6,500—rather than an even sum. "Fate made me do this," is all it said. Handwriting experts Carl Eisenshimel and Chauncy McGovern characterized the note as having been written by a "goof" or a "deranged person." On Aug. 10, the "goof" appeared before the archbishop. He was wearing a Palm Beach suit and he carried in his hand a Panama "boater," typical mid-summer wear for the era.

Hightower explained that he could help the police find the missing priest. "A man who fried flapjacks all the time is watching over him," he said. A reporter for the San Francisco *Examiner*

Father Patrick E. Heslin

William A. Hightower

Helsin's body unearthed; Hightower at lower left.

The priest's body is taken from the beach.

With body, at right, Chief O'Brien and Hightower.

A handwriting expert testifying at Hightower's trial.

San Quentin inmate William Hightower in old age.

standing nearby reasoned that the stranger referred to an Albers Milling Company billboard which featured a miner cooking flapjacks over an open fire. The billboard overlooked Salada Beach, a lonely strip of coastal highway running out of San Francisco.

Two women named Dolly Mason and Doris Shirley, both prostitutes, had tipped Hightower off about a cache of bootleg liquor buried under the sand, he told the archbishop. While digging for the Scotch he hoped to sell on the open market, Hightower had unearthed a black scarf which he figured belonged to the priest. "I left the scarf as a marker on the beach. Father Heslin, poor soul, is probably at the other end of it," Hightower said.

Accompanied by Police Chief O'Brien, a squad of detectives, and several reporters from the *Examiner* who sensed a scoop in the making, Hightower led them to a deserted strip of Salada Beach. The curious young man babbled incessantly about his nomadic life, and the jobs he took while on the road. There was the time he inadvertently shot the hat off a garrulous Texas Ranger, for example. "I sneaked over the county line and kept on going that night boys," he drawled. "Strange way for a man to lose his job, don't you think?"

In the swirling fog it was difficult for the search party to gain its bearings. Hightower, who was satisfied that he would collect a fat reward for uncovering the body, jubilantly called to the detectives. "Over here, boys. Just this way!" he called. Constable Silvio Landini warned him to be careful with his digging. He might strike the face and obliterate valuable evidence. "Don't worry I'm digging at the feet!" Hightower said.

"Didn't you say you didn't know if there was a body down there or not?" the chief asked.

"That's what I said." He kept digging.

Father Heslin's body was quickly removed from the sand. A blow in the back of the head had crushed his skull and two gunshots had been fired into the body. Doris Shirley was located, and she admitted to spending one night with Hightower. Dolly Mason turned out to be Hightower's invention. On Aug. 13, a local pawnbroker told police that Hightower had recently pawned a .45-caliber pistol—the same one used to kill Father Heslin. Inside Hightower's hotel room police found the typewriter used to prepare the ransom note. Hightower was indicted for murder and convicted after a short trial. "That a poor priest going to assist a man in the throes of death could meet foul play seems so incredible that the archbishop hopes that in the clearing up of the death of Father Heslin some excuse may be found that will save the name of San Francisco," exclaimed Archbishop Hanna, trying to make some sense of the whole thing. To reporters, the convicted killer added his own snide observation: "Ish ka bible!"

Hightower was sentenced to life in prison, despite the crusading efforts of the San Francisco *Examiner,* which called for the death penalty. At San Quentin he was assigned to work as the prison chef. Here he became an accomplished cook who won praise for his skill and dexterity in preparing cakes and pastries. Warden Duffy praised his efforts. "He made a candy out of fruit which was so delicious that Gladys (his wife) asked him for the recipe. Neither she nor anyone else could duplicate it even after he wrote it out for her." An otherwise reclusive individual, the prisoner published a newsletter titled *Observations from A. Hightower,* a collection of nonsensical prose he truly believed would one day rival that of H.L. Mencken for literary genius. Enamored with himself, Hightower demanded of publisher William Randolph Hearst that he be given editorial space in the pages of the *Examiner* so that he could publish a column. It was only fair, Hightower believed in his own convoluted way of thinking, since the newspaper had sent him to prison in the first place. In 1960, the priest-killer sent a message to Warden Duffy which read: (Hightower who) was supposed to be very ignorant (when sent to prison) is now such a wizard of words that he has surpassed all other men in writing punch lines." It was exactly the same kind of writing style used in the ransom notes, though Hightower never mentioned Father Heslin by name during his entire period of incarceration.

REF.: Block, *Science Vs. Crime;* _____, *The Wizard of Berkeley; CBA;* Nash, *Murder, America;* Rodell, *San Francisco Murders.*

Hijacking, See: **Supplements, Vol. IV.**

Hiker Slayings, prom. 1980, U.S., (unsolv.) mur. Near the beautiful Point Reyes National Seashore, about thirty miles from San Francisco, a vicious killer murdered several hitchhikers. Two women from the Sierra Club, Diana O'Connell, twenty-two, and Shauna May, twenty-three, were separated from their companion while hiking. Their nude bodies were found lying across each other in a wooded area the day after Thanksgiving 1980. Both had been shot through the head. Searching the area, police found a teenaged couple who had been missing for several weeks. Each of them had also been shot in the head. Fifteen months before these killings, three other women had been killed in the same way. From descriptions by a witness who saw a man fleeing the scene of one of the murders, police produced a composite sketch of a "clean-cut white man in his late twenties or early thirties, of medium build with medium-length hair," wearing hiking clothes and carrying a knapsack. The patterns of the slayings indicated a probable ritual, in which the victims had been forced into submissive postures before they were killed. Sheriff Al Howenstein described the murderer as a sadist who perpetrated "mental torture in which the victim pleads not to be murdered." R. William Mathis, a criminal psychologist, said that the killer "gets his maximum excitement by mentally terrifying his victims." At the time of this writing the killer is still at large.

REF.: *CBA;* Nash, *Open Files.*

Hilaire, Marcel, 1906-   , Fr., mur. Hard-working Marcel Hilaire put in long hours at the mill he owned and ran in the Loire Valley, in the small town of Mer, Fr. He thought that a man working this hard deserved a little pleasure, and he found his in a tryst with Christiane Page, the 20-year-old daughter of one of Hilaire's investors. Odette Hilaire, Marcel's wife, hoped that his interest in the woman half his age would eventually wane.

Hilaire's relationship with Page had started in January 1948, and had never been very discreet. She worked as his secretary in his new business—importing and selling agricultural machinery. This business required frequent trips to Paris, and Page always accompanied Hilaire. As time passed, she began pressuring him to get an apartment in Paris. In December 1948, he finally relented, though he was not happy about how much it cost to keep his mistress.

Soon after Page moved into her new home in Sceaux, the couple began to have frequent and often brutal fights. Hilaire was apparently having second thoughts about sacrificing a prosperous career to support both a family and an affair. He tried to break off the relationship, but Page would not let him go. She claimed she wanted to become a nun and got all the way to the gate of the Convent of Salbris before losing her nerve and begging Hilaire to take her back.

He did, but only until another plan could be formulated. That plan was carried out on Feb. 20, 1949, when Hilaire and the foreman of his Mer mill, Roland Petit, picked Page up for a drink at the airport in Orly. They stopped off at Saint-Ay, where they picked up another friend, Robert Bouguereau. With Hilaire driving, the four were riding along the busy highway when Hilaire suddenly killed the headlights, claiming there was something wrong with the car. When they pulled over, Page got out to stretch. Hilaire walked up behind her and shot her twice in the back of the head.

With the help of Petit and Bouguereau, Hilaire dumped the body in the well on the Hilaire property in Mer. The killer promptly terminated his lease on the home in Sceaux, and returned to his wife and three daughters. Two weeks later, when a rotten smell was wafting up from the well, Hilaire ordered Bouguereau and Petit to fill the well with sand. Mrs. Hilaire, relieved that her husband had reappeared, asked no questions.

The police asked questions, but not for almost ten months.

The landlord of Page's Sceaux apartment was suspicious of her disappearance, and of Hilaire's story that she had run off after a fight. Pressed by police, Hilaire lost his confidence and his story became shaky. Eventually, he admitted to the killing.

A confession might seem enough to convict a man of premeditated murder, which in France is known as *assassination*. But Marcel Hilaire hired the most able defense attorney in France, René Floriot, who managed to convince the jury that the murderer made too many mistakes to have planned it. Killing Page on a busy highway in front of two witnesses proved that Hilaire had acted on the spur of the moment, Floriot argued.

The argument worked, and Hilaire was found Guilty of murder, not *assassination*. He was sentenced to life in prison, but eventually had his sentence reduced due to good behavior and because, while serving as chief accountant for the Melun penitentiary, he devised an accounting system that was to be accepted by the entire French penal system. Roland Petit was found Guilty of complicity and sentenced to two years. Robert Bouguereau was found Guilty of illegally receiving and disposing of a human body, and was given a two-year suspended sentence.

REF.: *CBA;* Goodman, *Crimes of Passion;* Heppenstall, *The Sex War and Others.*

Hilbery, Sir Malcolm, b.1883, Brit., jur. Became judge in 1928 and served as judge of the Queen's Bench Division of the High Court beginning in 1935. Presided over several murder trials, including those of James Camb and Donald George Thomas. REF.: *CBA.*

Hildegard, Evelyn (Katie Prado, AKA: Diamond-tooth Lil), 1882-1957, U.S., wh. slav. Born in Vienna, Katie Prado immigrated to the U.S. when she was a child, growing up what Youngstown, Ohio, natives called a "bohunk," a child of Bohemian and Hungarian descent. When she was only fourteen, she married 19-year-old Percy Hildegard and moved to Chicago, where she fell in love with the stage. It was the beginning of a long career as a saloon and dance hall singer/yodeler. She was best known for her version of the song "Meet Me in St. Louis, Louie."

Throughout the early 1900s, she led a promiscuous life, divorcing and marrying a number of men and traveling around the U.S. to perform.

Bordello keeper Evelyn Hildegard, also known as "Diamond Tooth Lil."

She eventually took the name Evelyn Hildegard, though she had long since separated from Percy. A later affair with "Diamondfield" Jack Davis probably was the inspiration for the diamond she had set in one of her front teeth, thus earning her the nickname "Diamond-tooth Lil."

She had heard about a major silver strike in Idaho in 1909, so she rounded up four women from Reno, Nev., and they set their sights on Silver City, where business apparently boomed.

Diamond-tooth Lil and her traveling bordello followed the silver and gold craze wherever there was work, until she finally settled in Boise and ran a discreet "rooming house," catering to many in-state and out-of-state politicians.

The madame worked the rest of her days unhindered by the Boise police, since her establishment was deemed to be so "respectable." She moved to California in the 1950s, and died there in 1957.

REF.: *CBA;* Drago, *Notorious Ladies of the Frontier.*

Hileman, Doyle, 1939-71, U.S., suic.-mur. In 1971, Doyle Hileman approached his step-daughter Diane Linn McConnell, sixteen, on a Des Moines, Iowa, street, and attempted to pull her into his car. When she broke free and ran, Hileman took a .22-caliber pistol and fired twice into her back. He walked up to her and fired once more into her stomach, then returned to his car and drove away.

Diane died in an ambulance on the way to the hospital. The police later found Hileman's car in a bean field near Des Moines, with a hose hooked to the exhaust pipe and leading into the car. Hileman's body was in the back seat. It was revealed through the step-father's diaries that he had been in love with his step-daughter and had attempted in the past to seduce her, but she had spurned his advances. REF.: *CBA.*

Hill, Clarence, 1911-   , U.S., rape-mur. Known as the "Spooner Slayer" because all of his victims were couples parked in lovers' lane, Clarence Hill was also referred to as the "Moon Mad Killer." His pattern was to wait a day or two after an autumn full moon, then commit double murders of couples romancing in or around Duck Island, Trenton, N.J.'s most popular trysting spot. When his shotgun blasted for the last time, Hill had killed six people and attempted murder at least two additional times.

On Nov. 7, 1938, 15-year-old Mary Mytovich and her 22-year-old married lover, Vincenzo "Jim" Tonzello, were parked in the secluded woods around Duck Island when they were surprised by a black man who demanded money. When Tonzello resisted, the man shot him in the neck, then raped Mytovich. When she ran away, the assailant shot her in the neck. A couple passing by several hours later heard the wounded woman's cries and she was taken to the hospital. Before her death, thirty-six hours later, Mytovich managed to describe the gunman as five-feet, seven-inches, tall, wearing a suede jacket and cap. She also told police that he had used a "big gun." A special force put on the case turned up no other clues.

On Sept. 28, 1939 there was another full moon. Two days later Katherine Werner, thirty-seven, and Frank J. Kasper, twenty-eight, who were having an extramarital affair, were found dead. They had been killed by double shotgun blasts on Sept. 30. Kasper, slumped in the back seat of his car, had been murdered by a shotgun fired from close range into his neck and head. Werner had apparently been ordered out of the car; her body was found buried under a pile of garbage about 100 feet away. She had buckshot wounds in her breast, her right arm was blown off, and her skull was crushed by a heavy slab of concrete.

After the Werner-Kasper murders, local and state police patrolled the Duck Island area regularly, warning couples not to loiter in the lonely, secluded spot. On Sept. 16, the anniversary of the murder of the second couple, police patrols were out in full force.

Howard Wilson, nineteen, was in his car with a female friend on Bath Road, Bristol, not far from Duck Island, on the night of Nov. 2, 1940, when a shotgun blast nearly tore off his arm. On his way to the hospital he dropped off his unharmed companion, and collapsed when he reached Harriman Hospital. On Nov. 15 there was a full moon; the following night there was a third double-murder in Cyprus Lane, a few miles from Duck Island. Dead from shotgun blasts were Carolina Moriconi, twenty-seven, and her next door neighbor, Louis Joseph Kovacs, thirty-five. The couple had been killed while embracing, fired upon at close range. Kovacs' chest was shattered and Moriconi's arm torn off; eight slugs had pierced her heart and lungs. All shots were fired at such close range that there were powder marks and burns on both bodies. Police still had no clues; police from Pennsylvania entered the investigation, suspecting that the killer was the same man who had attacked a young couple parked in an isolated spot across the road from Duck Island, a few weeks earlier. The young man leaped at the assailant, seizing the gun. Both barrels fired, tearing off the man's arm. The attacker had fled.

The next year went by without incident but, on Mar. 7, 1942, John Testa, an army private, was seated in his car with a woman friend when a shotgun fired through his window. Testa's arm had to be amputated. The woman escaped, but not before the killer clubbed her over the head with his gun. Left behind was a small section of wood from the barrel of a shotgun; the numerals on the piece led to the arrest of Clarence Hill.

A private in the army, Hill was arrested at a camp at Moultrie-ville near Charlotte, S.C., in mid-December 1943. He was later transferred to Fort Dix. Hill at first denied guilt. But by the end of January 1944, the 33-year-old Hamilton County resident confessed to all six murders. Married and the father of two small children, Hill re-enacted the crimes when police took him to the scenes of the murders.

On Dec. 29, 1944, Hill was found Guilty of the first-degree murder of Mary Mytovich. He was sentenced on Jan. 12, 1945, to life in prison, and was released by the New Jersey Department of Corrections in 1973. REF.: *CBA*.

Hill, David Bennett, 1843-1910, U.S., lawyer. Assisted Samuel Tilden in uncovering the Tweed Ring in 1871. He practiced law in Elmira, N.Y., served as New York's governor from 1885-91, and as a U.S. senator from 1892-97. REF.: *CBA*.

Hill, Delmas Carl, b.1906, U.S., jur. Served as U.S. attorney in Kansas from 1934-36. He was nominated to the district court of Kansas by President Harry S. Truman in 1950. REF.: *CBA*.

Hill, Gregory, 1954-   , U.S., burg.-rob.-pris. esc. While awaiting trial for a series of high-rise robberies, Gregory Hill led five other inmates of Cook County jail in Chicago, Ill., in an escape on Mar. 23, 1984. Hill managed to elude police for seven days—longer than Ray Greer, Reginald Mahaffey, Jerry Mahaffey, Brian Daniels, and Aryules Bivens, who were all recaptured within five days. But he feared that the heavy publicity describing him as a dangerous man would lead to his being shot on sight, so he surrendered on Mar. 30 to Russ Ewing, a Chicago television reporter who often negotiated with criminals for their surrender.

Hill, described by his family as harmless, insisted that he "never ever hurt anyone and never wanted to hurt anyone.... I love people." He said he committed a number of robberies and burglaries in high-rise apartments to support his drug habit, and never fired the gun he wielded during some of those crimes. In July 1984, he was convicted of eleven counts in connection with the robberies, and was sentenced to fifty years in prison in September. In October, he pled guilty to six more holdups and received an additional thirty-year sentence, to run concurrently with his earlier conviction. REF.: *CBA*.

Hill, Harold, 1916-42, Brit., mur. On Nov. 22, 1941, the bodies of Doreen Joyce Hearne, eight, and Kathleen Trendle, six, were found in Rough Wood, a small copse near Buckinghamshire, England. The girls had been strangled and stabbed. Found at the scene was a khaki kerchief with a military laundry mark. Fingerprints were also taken off Doreen's gas-mask container.

Interviews with the victims' schoolmates revealed that the girls had asked for a ride from the driver of a truck with military markings. Two boys gave a thorough description of the truck, which was traced to the 86th Field Regiment of the British Army. The kerchief proved to be from the Royal Artillery branch, and belonged to a gunner named Harold Hill.

Hill was driving the truck on Nov. 20, and had made an unauthorized trip of fourteen miles. Bloodstains were found on a tarpaulin in the truck, and his fingerprints matched those on the gas-mask container. Hill was arraigned on murder charges in January 1942 and was found Guilty. He was hanged in April 1942.

REF.: Browne and Tullett, *The Scalpel of Scotland Yard; CBA; Gerber, Criminals Investigation and Interrogation;* Hatherill, *A Detective's Story;* Tullett, *Strictly Murder.*

Hill, Harry, prom. 1880s., U.S., vice. Harry Hill operated a notorious dive called Harry Hill's Concert Saloon on West Houston Street, just east of Broadway. The saloon occupied two sprawling frame buildings and had two stories and two front entrances, one for ladies, admitted free, the other for men, who were charged 20¢ each admission. Inside was a rough-and-tumble dance hall made of crudely fitted floorboards. Here pickpockets, thieves, and burglars met to plan their next capers, while scores of prostitutes plied unsuspecting tourists with liquor waiting for them to fall into alcoholic stupors so they could rob them.

Hill was present every night, reciting his own crude poetry and working as a bouncer. He had been a fighter in his day and welcomed any pugilist to his establishment. John L. Sullivan fought his first New York match in Hill's place, beating Steve Taylor in two and a half minutes on the night of Mar. 31, 1881. He then promptly drank Hill and everyone else "under the table." Though there were a number of knife fights and a few shootings in Hill's place, no police officer ever stepped inside of the saloon. Hill had warned that any policeman to do so would "get a broken jaw for his pains."

Harry Hill's concert saloon, 1883.

As Hill's place grew in fame, its owner reformed somewhat, restricting the number of tourists who could be jackrolled each night in his place. Hill would sit like some potentate at a table on a high box, watching the festivities and wild dances. Prostitutes would approach him and point out a sucker they wished to drug with laudanum, and Hill would decide whether or not the customer was "safe enough" to mug and rob. Harry Hill's place was finally closed at the turn of the century through the efforts of reformers like Anthony Comstock.

REF.: Asbury, *The Gangs of New York; CBA.*

Hill, James (AKA: **John the Painter**), d.1777, Brit., arson-treas. James Hill was so enthusiastic about the American Revolution that he volunteered his services as an arsonist, coming up with an original plan to destroy English dockyards and fortifications. Hill earned the nickname John the Painter when he worked as a journeyman in Titchfield.

Born in Scotland, Hill travelled at an early age to America, where he spent most of his life. When the American rebellion against England broke out, Hill was such an ardent supporter of the cause that he planned to set fire to British dockyards and shipping areas, and then went to American diplomat Silas Dean with his scheme. Dean supplied Hill with money, a French passport, and a letter of recommendation to a merchant in London. Hill also claimed to have been rewarded with a commission in the American Army after his acts of arson.

On Sept. 7, 1776, a fire burned down a storage building on Portsmouth dock. Arson was suspected when, on Jan. 5, 1777, workers in a nearby rope factory found a tin can resembling a tea canister, and a wooden box containing a variety of highly flammable materials. Hill, who had been seen on site in the past several months, was suspected and, after newspapers advertised a reward of £50 for his arrest, was picked up at Odiham. On Feb. 17, Hill was questioned by John Baldwin, a painter, at Sir John Fielding's offices in Bow Street. Hill admitted that he had looked over dockyards and naval buildings throughout England, noting the number of ships in the British Navy, gathering extensive information on the weight and type of their cargos, and the number of men in their crews. He had then gone to Dean with his findings; the diplomat gave the self-styled informer £300 and letters of recommendation to merchants in Portsmouth. (When he later feared he might be found out, Hill destroyed the letters.)

Hill had a specially-designed tin canister made and, on Sept. 6, 1776, went to a hemp factory on the docks. Placing a candle in a wooden box, he put the canister over it, then sprinkled turpentine on the hemp and went to the nearby rope factory. There he splashed turpentine on the rope, threw matches and flammable materials about, then returned home. The matches were cut into various sizes so that they would burn for twenty-four hours, giving Hill time to escape. He had rented rooms in two other houses, intending to set them both on fire, believing that the fire department would be too busy to give all its attention to the fire at the dock. On Sept. 7, he went again to the hemp factory planning to set it on fire, but some of the matches he had left there were wet and would not light. This plan thwarted, Hill went to the rope house and set fire to it instead. He was unable to return to his lodgings, and grew increasingly anxious because he had left behind a pistol and the French passport with his real name.

Arsonist James Hill setting fire to a rope house in Portsmouth, England.

Proceeding to London, Hill met up with a contact there, but the man was skeptical about Hill's identity since he did not have his passport, and the letters of recommendation from Dean, that he had destroyed earlier. Hill wrote to the man as soon as he was on the road again, informing him that he was on his way to Bristol where the "handy works he meant to perform there would soon be known to the public." Once in Bristol he set fire to several houses, with damages amounting to £15,000. Hill also set several oil barrels on the wharf on fire, but they did not burn.

During his trial at Winchester Castle on Mar. 6, 1777, Hill claimed that Baldwin had lied about Hill's confession, that it was easy for witnesses to corroborate these lies, and that the newspapers and public opinion were already prejudiced against him. The jury delivered a nearly instant verdict of Guilty and Hill was hanged at Portsmouth on Mar. 10, 1777. His body was hanged in chains on Blockhouse Point for several years.

REF.: *CBA;* Mitchell, *The Newgate Calendar.*

Hill, James Douglas, 1959-   , U.S., mur. Eight years after he murdered a 12-year-old girl, James Douglas Hill was in plea negotiations to reduce his death sentence to a twenty-five-year prison term.

Hill, a mildly retarded 29-year-old, was convicted and sentenced to death for the 1980 murder of Rosa Lee Parker. The girl's partially clad body was found in a water-filled ditch on Tampa, Florida's Eastern Side, an area referred to by residents as "The Pits." The key witness, Daniel Munson, testified that on the night Parker was killed, Hill told him that he had thrown the girl in the water to make sure she was dead. Police later wired Munson, and the subsequent recording of another conversation between Munson and Hill was the deciding evidence in the trial. Hill was

on death row for more than five years until Florida state rulings re-opened the case for a possible reduction of sentence.

The Florida Supreme Court ruled that Hill's trial judge should have held a hearing to determine whether the defendant, who had an IQ of between sixty-six and seventy-nine, was competent to stand trial. Although Hill was found competent, another judge ruled that Munson's taped conversation was illegally obtained by police and could not be used as evidence in a new trial.

Hill could no longer be convicted of first-degree murder, and could not be returned to death row or given a life sentence. Assistant State's Attorney Stephen Crawford complained that he could no longer find witnesses. Hill's lawyer, Sarasota defense attorney Dan Danheisser, asked for a conviction of second-degree murder for a maximum sentence of twenty-five years. At this writing, Hill remains in prison pending further legal action.
REF.: *CBA.*

Hill, Joe (Joel Emmanuel Hägglund, Joseph Hillstrom), 1879-1915, U.S., mur. Joe Hill, best known for his songs and poems created in the infant days of the American labor movement, was convicted and executed for murdering an one-time Salt Lake City policeman and his son in revenge for previous oppressions against striking workers. Hill became a martyr to the union movement but he was unmistakably a killer who deserved his grim fate. Born on Oct. 7, 1879, in Gävle, Swed., as Joel Emmanuel Hägglund, Hill was one of nine children. His father, Olaf, was a railroad conductor who was killed in a railway accident in 1886, leaving 8-year-old Joe to go to work to help support the family. He went to sea, sending most of his earnings back to his mother. When she died in 1902, and his brothers and sisters were grown to adulthood, Hill immigrated to the U.S. and immediately became involved in the labor movement. He was unschooled, rough-mannered, and believed that the way to labor reform was through violence. After spending a year in New York City, Hill moved to Chicago where he worked as a machinist, but was fired from his job when he tried to organize the workers of his plant.

To avoid the traditional blacklisting, Hill then changed his name to Hillstrom but he was known far and wide as Joe Hill, the name under which he wrote stirring union songs, such as the memorable "Casey Jones, The Union Scab." His most popular work was entitled "The Preacher and the Slave," which contained a line that later became a permanent part of American idiom: "You'll get pie in the sky when you die." Hill's rhymes and lyrics were packed with irony, expressing hopeless resignation for a doomed American work force that would never rise to the good things of life until capitalism was completely destroyed—a paradoxical credo in that if such a thing were to happen, there would be no jobs at all. Of course, Hill was really advocating early-day communism, or primitive Marxism, without providing a constructive course for workers to follow.

In 1910, Hill joined the Industrial Workers of the World (the IWW), or the Wobblies as they were popularly known, a radical union sect that was headed by such bombastic personalities as William D. "Big Bill" Haywood, who was, along with others, later tried for union violence, destruction and murder. His chief executioner, Harry Orchard, was sent to jail for terrorist bombings that took the lives of workers, government figures—just about anyone who got in the way of the IWW. From Chicago, Hill went to Los Angeles where he worked with IWW radicals who later blew up the Los Angeles *Times* building, killing many non-union workers, a crime for which the McNamara Brothers were later convicted, despite a vigorous defense of their case by Clarence Darrow. Hill may well have helped plan the *Times* explosion in 1910 but was never charged.

In 1913, Hill left Los Angeles, intending to return to Chicago to organize machinists, but he stopped in Salt Lake City and took a job there as a miner. He grew ill and was fired after having been absent from his job for two weeks. Penniless, Hill moved to Murray, Utah, and stayed with the Eselius Brothers, IWW organizers. The IWW in Salt Lake City was a hotbed of union terrorists who busied themselves with the blowing up of mines and the killing of all those who opposed their movement. IWW organizers were issued guns and bombs, along with lists of those to be executed. One of these was John Morrison, a prosperous storeowner in Salt Lake City. Morrison had been a police officer who had helped to break many strikes, had uncovered many IWW plots to bomb mines in the Salt Lake City area, had made countless arrests, and had survived shootouts with union thugs, killing and wounding a number of Wobblies. He left the Salt Lake City police force and established a store in the city but lived in constant apprehension of retaliation from the fierce IWW goons. Twice he had survived attempts on his life. He and his two sons, Arling and Merlin, kept revolvers behind the counters of their store and never went anywhere without their weapons.

On the night of Jan. 10, 1914, Hill and another Wobbly thug, Otto Applequist, left Murray for an unknown destination. About two hours later, at approximately 10 p.m., two men wearing masks and brandishing pistols barged into Morrison's grocery store just as Morrison and his sons were closing the place. One of the men shouted: "We've got you now!" The intruders opened fire just as Morrison and his boys went for their revolvers. Within minutes Morrison and his son Arling were dead and the killers had fled. Inside the store, filled with gunsmoke, Merlin Morrison rose from the floor to find Arling's revolver, which his brother had apparently used to fire off a single shot.

Murderer Joe Hill, who became a legend in the U.S. labor movement.

At 11:30 p.m., Joe Hill appeared at the home of Dr. Frank M. McHugh, showing him a gunshot wound and saying: "Doctor, I've been shot. I got into a stew with a friend of mine who thought I had insulted his wife." He would not give the name of the "friend." Dr. McHugh noted that the bullet had passed through Hill's body, grazing the left lung, but that the patient would easily recover. He dressed and bandaged the wound and Hill returned to the home of the Eselius Brothers to recuperate. When McHugh heard of the Morrison killings, he notified police about Hill's wound. Police arrived at the Eselius house in Murray and ordered Hill to come with them. He reached quickly for something on a table and an officer fired a shot at him, shattering his hand. The object Hill was reaching for, it was later proved, turned out to be a handkerchief. Four other suspects had been arrested and charged with the Morrison murder, but they were released when Hill was brought in. Applequist, the man who had accompanied Hill on the night of the killing, was never seen again.

Hill's reputation as an IWW terrorist convicted him out of hand, and his whereabouts on the night of the murder, his mysterious bullet wound and his earlier statements about "getting even" with Morrison all stood in evidence against him. When tried, Hill proved to be a recalcitrant client. He argued with his attorneys and then fired them. Other defenders were appointed by the court but had little success in getting their client to cooperate. Hill adamantly refused to reveal how he had been wounded. The circumstantial evidence against Hill appeared overwhelming to the court and Hill was convicted and sentenced to die on July 18, 1914. Big Bill Haywood, head of the IWW, then organized a massive campaign to save Hill's life, and he was profiled as a sacrificial lamb to be slaughtered on the altar of capitalism. The campaign to save Hill caused several appeals and stays of execution. Many notable citizens sent pleas for clemency

to Utah authorities and these included Helen Keller, President Woodrow Wilson, and Swedish Foreign Minister W.A. F. Ekengren. In the end, Hill's execution was firmly fixed and he accepted his fate, sending a wire to Haywood: "Don't waste any time mourning—organize!"

The state of Utah offered condemned prisoners (and still does today) a selection of one of two methods of execution; they could elect to be hanged or shot. Joe Hill chose a firing squad, saying: "I'll take shooting. I'm used to that. I have been shot a few times in the past, and I guess I can stand it again." But Hill thought to cheat the firing squad. At 5 a.m. on the day he was scheduled to die, Nov. 19, 1915, Hill broke a broom and used the jagged handle to tear apart his blankets in his cell, using the strips to tie the cell door together. He then barricaded himself behind his mattress. Wardens broke into the cell a half hour later and it took several guards to subdue the violently struggling Hill who was dragged outside to the courtyard and strapped to a wooden chair. "Well," said Hill, "I'm through. You can't blame a man for fighting for his life." A paper target was pinned over his heart and he stared at a canvas twenty feet away. Five holes had been cut in the canvas and rifle barrels projected through them. As is the custom, one of the marksmen in the execution squad had a blank in his rifle. None of the squad would know who had the blank so that all would aim to kill and none would know who had done the actual killing. A warden then shouted: "Ready...aim..." Hill himself then shouted: "Fire! Go on and fire!" The five rifles barked and jumped behind the canvas and three bullets ploughed into the heart of Joe Hill, instantly killing him. From that moment on he became a martyr to the cause of unionism and, as late as the radical 1960s, a coffeehouse hero where his songs were wailed by folk singers who had, for the most part, never heard of the IWW, Wobblies, Big Bill Haywood, or, specifically, John and Arling Morrison, who were murdered in cold blood and for whom no poignant, rabble-rousing tunes had ever been written. See: **Darrow, Clarence**; **Haywood, William D.**; **McNamara Brothers**; **Orchard, Harry**.

REF.: *CBA;* Chaplin, *Wobbly;* Commons, *History of Labor in the United States;* Flanagan, *Out West;* Haywood, *Bill Haywood's Book;* Powers, *Secrecy and Power;* Reppetto, *The Blue Parade;* Smith, *Joe Hill;* (FILM), *Joe Hill,* 1971.

Hill, John, d.1972, U.S., (unsolv.) mur. John Hill married into money. In 1958, this up-and-coming young plastic surgeon exchanged vows with Joan Robinson, the 26-year-old adopted daughter of Texas oil millionaire Ash Robinson. Hill prospered in his new setting. Life with Joan was an endless series of gala parties, social extravaganzas, and horse shows. Unfortunately for Hill he did not share his wife's equestrian interests, but rather leaned more toward the arts, especially music.

In the 1960s, Hill tired of the arrangement and began consorting with other women. Joan Robinson increasingly concentrated on her horses. Other than their son, the couple had little in common. On Mar. 17, 1969, Joan fell sick. Two days later her husband took her to Sharpstown General Hospital, a facility he partly owned. Joan died the next morning from a "mysterious infection" later believed to be hepatitis. Hospital officials neglected to inform the medical examiner's office, normally a common procedure. By the time they were alerted to the circumstances of her death, the body already was embalmed. An autopsy performed by medical examiner Dr. Joseph Jachimczyk proved inconclusive but Ash Robinson charged his son-in-law with criminal neglect in the death of his daughter. Three months later Hill married his girlfriend Ann Kurth.

Ash Robinson intensified his accusations against Hill, prompting the doctor to file a $5 million libel suit against his former father-in-law. In August 1969, Dr. Jachimczyk performed another autopsy. He found the brain had been previously removed and doubt was raised about the authenticity of the one supplied by medical officials. Dr. Milton Helpern concluded that "death was the result of an acute inflammatory disease" of undetermined origin. In April 1970 Hill was indicted for "murder by omission," meaning he had failed to provide his wife with proper medical treatment at the time of her illness.

By this time Hill was faring no better with Ann Kurth than he had with his first wife. On June 29, with his wife as passenger, the doctor drove his car into the side of a guardrail and later, in a confused mental state, confessed to poisoning Joan. Fearing for her life and those of her children, Kurth separated from Hill in November 1970. On the witness stand she testified that her husband had brought home poisoned pastries and had been growing deadly bacteria in three Petri dishes in the bathroom. When she expressed the opinion that Hill tried to kill her in the car accident, the judge declared a mistrial. Following his divorce from Kurth in March 1971, Hill married a third time. In September 1972, six weeks before the second trial was scheduled to begin a masked gunman invaded the surgeon's home.

Hill's new wife, Connie Hill, escaped from the house just before her husband was shot dead by the home invader. The Houston police identified a hit man named Vandiver as the assassin, who was killed while resisting arrest and could provide little in the way of evidence. Suspecting that Ash Robinson had hired the gunman through a Galveston brothel keeper, the police gave him a lie-detector test which absolved him of any guilt. The murder of John Hill went into the books as unsolved.

Months later, Ann Kurth told police she believed John Hill was still alive and harassing her with phone calls in the middle of the night. "I don't know if he's out there. I don't know if somebody else is harassing me," she said. "But I do know different people from different walks of life claim to see him." Kurth believes that a plastic surgeon created a look-alike who took Hill's place the night of the home invasion. Thomas Thompson, author of *Blood and Money*, dismissed this as nonsense. "If John Hill is alive," Thompson said. "He's living with John Kennedy and Elvis Presley in a small town in Mexico called Dementia."

REF.: *CBA; Purvis, Great Unsolved Mysteries; Thompson, Blood and Money; Wilson, Encyclopedia of Modern Murder.*

Hill, Matthew Davenport, 1792-1872, Brit., penol. Well-known penologist. He wanted to reform treatment methods for offenders who had been released for good behavior. He thought offenders who could not be rehabilitated should serve a life term with no possibility of probation. He wrote *Suggestions for the Repression of Crime* in 1857 and his recommendations were included in the Penal Servitude Acts of 1853 and 1864. As a judge, he served in Birmingham from 1839-65. REF.: *CBA.*

Hill, Mildred, b.1881, U.S., fraud. Mildred Hill operated a matrimonial scam out of her Washington, D.C., home for several years in the early 1940s, recruiting her most attractive daughter—one of ten children she sired—to pose as a prospective bride for lonely bachelors. A photograph of the girl was circulated along with a love letter written by Hill promising marriage. After bilking the victim out of as much money as she could, Hill would tell the man that her daughter had suddenly eloped with a stranger, a car salesman typically, and there was little to be done. In 1945 the postal authorities caught up with the swindler. Hill was sentenced to five years in prison for using the postal system for fraudulent purposes.

Con woman Mildred Hill.

REF.: *CBA; Nash, Look For the Woman.*

Hill, Miriam, 1911-   , Case of, Brit., mur. The Chepstow district of England was saturated with rumors when young Dennis Albert Hill, nineteen, married Miriam Kingsmaur, forty-nine, on Apr. 2, 1960. When Hill quit his job, saying that he wanted to help take care of his wife's two children, the gossip increased: the new Mrs. Hill must have been blind not to see that her money was what Dennis had fallen in love with.

In this case, the rumors turned out to be true. After only six weeks of marriage, dreadful arguments about money had started between the newlyweds. Hill reportedly beat his wife often and without warning. He blew up at the smallest disagreement, was known to go on rampages, and then suddenly be perfectly calm again. Finally, on June 6, Hill was charged with disturbing the peace. He moved out of the house, but did not stop harassing Miriam. She was terrified enough to sleep with a loaded shotgun.

On June 13, the police received a phone call from Mrs. Hill, who asked them to come at once. By the time they arrived, Dennis Hill lay dead from a gunshot wound. Mrs. Hill explained that when he entered the home she had grabbed her shotgun and asked him to leave. When he kept advancing, she warned him to stop or she would shoot. He took another step forward, and she shot him. She said later she had no idea that the shotgun could kill a person.

Charged with murder, Miriam Hill was tried at Staffordshire Assizes on July 26-27, 1960. A.B. King-Hamilton, Mrs. Hill's defense counsel, was successful in proving that his client had probable reason to believe that her life was in danger. The fact that she had warned Hill and had waited until she was cornered in the kitchen helped convince the jury this was a case of self-defense. She was found Not Guilty of murder and manslaughter, thus clearing her of any responsibility in Hill's death.

REF.: *CBA; Furneaux, Famous Criminal Cases, vol. 7.*

Hill, Robert Andrews, 1811-1900, U.S., jur. Served as attorney general of Wayne County Circuit in Tennessee. He was nominated to the district court of Mississippi by President Andrew Johnson in 1866. REF.: *CBA.*

Hill, Rufus, d.1808, U.S., mur. A native of Chenango County, N.Y., Rufus Hill was a bully who had so brutalized his first family, his wife and children left him. He again married, but treated his second family the same as his first. He beat to death one of his children from this second marriage and then demanded his wife cook him dinner. He was tried, condemned, and hanged in June 1808.

REF.: *CBA; The Trial of Rufus Hill.*

Hill, Thomas C., d.1859, U.S., mansl. Some of the early homicides in Atlanta, Ga., appear ridiculous in the light of today's calculating killers. Such a one was the slaying of Benjamin Stowers, a 50-year-old farmer who sauntered into Thomas C. Hill's general store to play a practical joke.

Hill was a heavy drinker and had a habit of sleeping off the previous night's binge the following afternoon in his store. Knowing this, Stowers entered the store on July 16, 1841. He approached the snoring Hill. He put his hand against the sleeping Hill's head and slapped this hand with the other, making a loud noise which startled Hill awake. Guffawing, Stowers began to walk out of the store. Hill, enraged, picked up an iron weight and hurled it after Stowers. It struck the farmer on the head (Hill was forever hurling objects at people who interrupted his sleep and became an expert marksman). The blow knocked Stowers to the floor and, despite efforts to revive him by a crowd of customers, he died in five minutes.

Charged with manslaughter, Hill was sent to the Milledgeville Penitentiary to serve several years. Upon his release, he married Lucinda Ivy, daughter of an Atlanta pioneer, Hardy Ivy, and went on to become one of the most successful merchants in the city before his death in 1859. REF.: *CBA.*

Hill, Tom (AKA: Tom Chelson), d.1878, U.S., west. outl. Tom Hill became acquainted with crime in the early 1870s as a cattle rustler in New Mexico with a gang led by Jesse Evans. After an October 1877 raid on the ranches of Dick Brewer and John Tunstall in Lincoln County, Hill, Evans, Frank Baker, and a man named Davis were apprehended by a fifteen-man posse after a two-day chase. All four surrendered after a furious exchange of gunfire and were taken to the jail in Lincoln, N.M.

Two weeks later, thirty-two members of the Evans gang raided the jail and freed the four prisoners. In January 1878, the gang tried to rustle a herd of horses in Grant County, but Hill and Evans were wounded in the struggle.

A month later, on Feb. 18, 1878, as sides were being taken in the impending Lincoln County War, a posse which included Hill confronted John Tunstall on his ranch. Finding Tunstall alone and on foot, Hill shot Tunstall to death. On Mar. 13, 1878, Hill and Evans tried to rob the camp of a sheepherder at Alamo Springs, N.M. They surprised a camp guard, but after looting a wagon, and preparing to steal the livestock, they were involved in a gun battle as they tried to leave. The thieves wounded the guard, but he crawled to camp and shot the two bandits at point-blank range, killing Hill and wounding Evans' wrist.

REF.: Bartholomew, *Jesse Evans*; ____, *Western Hardcases*; Bechdolt, *Tales of the Old Timers*; Brent, *The Complete and Factual Life of Billy the Kid*; Burns, *The Saga of Billy the Kid*; *CBA*; Collison, *Life in the Saddle*; Cunningham, *Triggernometry*; Fulton, *Maurice Garland Fulton's History of the Lincoln County War*; Hendricks, *The Bad Man of the West*; Holloway, *Texas Gun Lore*; Horan, *The Great American West*; Horn, *New Mexico's Troubled Years*; Hough, *The Story of the Outlaw*; Keleher, *Violence in Lincoln County*; Moore, *The West*; Mullin, *A Chronology of the Lincoln County War*; Nolan, *The Life and Death of John Henry Tunstall*; Raht, *The Romance of Davis Mountains and the Big Bend Country*; Wellman, *The Trampling Herd*.

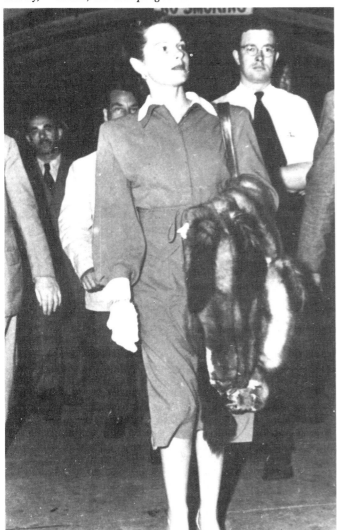

Mob woman Virginia hill, paramour of the ill-fated Bugsy Siegel.

Hill, Virginia, 1916-66, U.S., org. crime-drugs. She was a mob moll and bag woman for the national crime syndicate, a woman who was the "kiss of death" to those who fell under her spell.

Most of all, Virginia Hill was Bugsy Siegel's girlfriend and the subject of endless speculation by a generation of gossip columnists from New York to Hollywood. She lived a riotous life, and was big news in the 1940s—quite an achievement for a girl born and raised in the backwoods of Alabama.

The Hill family—there were twelve of them in all counting parents Mack and Margaret—lived in Lipscomb, but eventually

Virginia Hill testifying before the Kefauver Committee in 1951.

moved to nearby Bessemer. Mack Hill's prospects were none too good. An alcoholic, he was a poor provider for his children and Margaret rebelled and finally moved out. She went to work leaving her nine younger children in the care of Virginia who had loftier ambitions. At seventeen, Virginia struck out for Chicago to work on the Midway of the 1933 World's Fair, the Century of Progress. She accepted a job as a waitress and might have otherwise been doomed to a life of obscurity if not for the intervention of Joseph Epstein, an ungainly little mobster who functioned as Jake Guzik's lieutenant in the racing wire racket.

Epstein made up for whatever he lacked in appearance with a thick bankroll. The balding, myopic gangster met Virginia in a cheap restaurant in Chicago's Loop one night and fell in love with her. Recognizing that an opportunity stared her in the face, Hill befriended Epstein and soon was functioning as his party hostess and love interest. She got to know all the important U.S. mobsters: Frank Nitti, Rocco Fischetti, Tony Accardo, Frank Costello, Charles "Lucky" Luciano, and Joe Adonis, fondly known as "Joey A." With Epstein paying the bills, Virginia traveled across the country to rendezvous with her new-found friends. In time she became the mistress of Adonis. The mob recognized her for what she was: a street-smart woman who was nobody's fool. Virginia Hill became the courier for the syndicate, shuttling thousands of dollars from one mobster to the next. In between her missions to Mexico—where she paved the way for drug-smuggling routes—she became the toast of café society, with columnists taking notice of the lavish parties she threw at various syndicate-owned nightclubs in Manhattan. The liquor flowed till dawn, as Virginia tangoed and rhumbaed her way into the national limelight.

Her romance with Siegel though, brought her the most attention. She met the gangster in the early 1940s, at a time when she was helping the mobsters plan their incursion into Mexico. Provided with letters of introduction to top Mexican politicians, Hill crossed the border to "conduct business." When she returned to California she took up with Siegel, a man of small stature who envisioned a kingdom of dice and cards in Las Vegas, Nev.—all of it legal. Owner of the multi-million dollar Flamingo Club, Siegel's dream began to turn to ashes by 1945. Back East the Chicago and New York mobs which had invested heavily in the enterprise became uneasy with the poor return on their dollars. They called in their loans but Siegel offered them only dirty words. Luciano, Costello, and Adonis suspected Siegel was skimming the profits off the top and using Virginia to convey the money to Swiss bank accounts.

Sensing that these were dangerous times for the both of them,

Hill advised Siegel to cut his losses and sell the Flamingo. When he refused, she fled Las Vegas, leaving her boyfriend to contemplate his future in her lush Beverly Hills mansion.

On June 10, 1947, Virginia broke off the relationship and headed to Paris. Ten days later snipers pumped Siegel full of lead as he sat in the living room of the mansion. Amidst speculation that Virginia helped the New York mobs engineer Siegel's murder, she returned to the states defiant. "His name wasn't Bugsy Siegel," she said. "It was Ben. Ben Siegel! And he was no gangster—what do you know? Why, that man loved poetry! There was a poem both of us kept—." She looked in her purse but could not find it. "Aw, you jerks wouldn't understand anyway!"

Summoned before the Kefauver Rackets Committee in 1951, Hill coyly told investigators that her income was derived from "gifts" her boyfriends showered on her. When pressed for additional details by Senator Charles Tobey, she told about her sexual prowess, which made for scintillating reading. The IRS however, was not amused. After determining that she had spent $500,000 without paying a dime in taxes, the government began to move in. Hill thwarted the investigation by marrying a Sun Valley ski instructor, Hans Hauser, and moving to Europe. The IRS, however, auctioned off her house and remaining private property to help pay for back taxes. Hill remained in exile for the last fifteen years of her life, receiving $250,000 in cash from the dutiful Epstein who had never forgotten her.

But Virginia Hill did not find what she was looking for, let alone happiness, in the capitals of Europe. She separated from her husband and died on the ski slopes of Salzburg, Austria, in March 1966 after ingesting a heavy dose of sleeping pills. It was a suicide despite allegations that the mob had her assassinated to prevent her from publishing a tell-all memoir of her adventures back in the U.S. At the time she was being supported by her 15-year-old son Peter who was working as a waiter. See: **Epstein, Joseph; Siegel, Benjamin "Bugsy"**.

REF.: Carpozi, *Bugsy*; *CBA*; Cohen, *Mickey Cohen: In My Own Words*; Eisenberg and Landau, *Meyer Lansky*; Fried, *The Rise and Fall of the Jewish Gangster in America*; Gage, *Mafia, U.S.A.*; ____, *The Mafia is not an Equal Opportunity Employer*; Gosch and Hammer, *The Last Testament of Lucky Luciano*; Jennings, *We Only Kill Each Other*; Katz, *Uncle Frank*; Lait and Mortimer, *Chicago: Confidential*; Messick, *Lansky*; ____, *Secret File*; ____ and Goldblatt, *The Mobs and the Mafia*; Ottenberg, *The Federal Investigators*; Peterson, *The Mob*; Reid, *The Grim Reapers*; Servadio, *Mafioso*; Smith, *Syndicate City*.

Hill, William, d.1826, U.S., pir.-mur. William Hill was part of a group of black slaves being transported on the schooner *Decatur* from Baltimore to be sold in New Orleans. Hill and three other slaves were freed from their chains and ordered to wash mud from the ship's anchor while the vessel was off the Carolina coast. Hill and his fellow slaves seized the opportunity to attack the captain, Walter R. Gallaway, throwing him and the mate overboard and taking control of the ship. Untrained in seamanship, Hill and the other slaves allowed one white sailor to survive, ordering him to sail to the islands of the West Indies, but the sailor beached the schooner and the slaves were captured. Hill was the only one of the piratical slaves identified as the killer of Captain Gallaway. He was quickly tried and hanged on Ellis Island in New York.

REF.: *CBA; Trial and Confession of William Hill*.

Hill, William (Billy), prom. 20th Cent., Brit., org. crime. William Hill's criminal instincts could be described as genetic—his whole family led lives of crime. With a pickpocketing brother, a shoplifting sister, and a safecracking brother-in-law, it is no wonder that Billy found his way into the London world of crime at a young age.

He spent much time in prison, where he probably did more to refine his unlawful techniques than to reform them. In 1931, after serving a nine-month sentence, he formed the Camden Town Gang and taught them their violent methods of crime, including their signature vertical-slash style of wielding a knife. Hill was in and out of jail all through the 1930s and early 1940s for various crimes committed with his gang.

In 1947, he pooled the forces of the Camden Town Gang, the Elephant Mob, and other assorted London criminals to overthrow the reign of the Black Gang, the most notorious organized criminals in the city up to that time. His rule continued into the mid-1950s, and included the Great Mailbag Robbery, the most lucrative robbery of its time, netting his gang £287,000.

Around 1954, Billy Hill left England for Tangiers, where he penned his memoirs, *Boss of Britain's Underworld* (1955). The new celebrity flew off the handle, however, when Jack ("Spot") Comer, the gangster who had replaced Hill upon his retirement, had his own biography published three months later. Comer became a marked man: he was attacked twice, once in September 1955, and once in May 1956, by friends of Hill. Frankie Fraser and Robert Warren received seven-year jail terms for their involvement in the second assault. Hill, hoping to get revenge on Comer one last time, also had one of his men slashed in an attempt to frame Comer, but the ruse fell through when one of Hill's men became a police informant. Hill later retired permanently. REF.: *CBA*.

Hill, William Henry, 1767-1809, U.S., jur. Served as U.S. attorney, as North Carolina state senator, and as U.S. congressman from 1799-1803. He was nominated to the district court of North Carolina by President John Quincy Adams in 1801. REF.: *CBA*.

Hillside Strangler, The, See: **Bianchi, Kenneth**.

Hilton, Paul Emanuel, d.1927, U.S., mur. Henry Groh, known to his fans as "Heinie," spent the best years of his baseball career playing third base for the New York Giants. He retired after the 1927 season with a batting average of .292, almost 1,300 games at third base, and one assist in the apprehension of a murderer.

Paul Hilton was stubborn: if he could not play third base for the prison baseball team, he simply would not play. He always stood or sat near third base when watching a game. And, in the words of a friend, Hilton held Heinie Groh in high esteem. "He thinks Heinie oughta be President of the United States," the man told investigators. It would be the clue they needed to catch Hilton.

In February and March 1926, a total of four Queens, N.Y., policemen had been shot in the line of duty. All of them had been shot after approaching a man in a light overcoat, gray cap, and scarlet muffler. Upon being questioned, the man would go to his inside overcoat pocket, presumably to reveal some identification. Instead, his hand would come out holding a pistol. Four officers had been shot in the side of the neck. Detective Arthur Kenny had died.

One of the survivors, Detective George McCarthy, had managed to get a good look at his assailant before being shot, and was able to pick out Hilton's photo. Once detectives James A. Pyke and William Jackson knew that Hilton was their prime suspect, they began to compile information on him. From prison guards they learned of Hilton's penchant for baseball. They hung out in a bar that they knew Hilton used to frequent and talked baseball, until eventually someone mentioned Hilton and his love for the New York Giants, especially their third baseman.

By this time it was April, and the Giants' home opener was imminent. Pyke and Jackson had a hunch that if Hilton's baseball hero was playing in that game, he could probably be found sitting in a seat on the third-base side of the Polo Grounds. The detectives' suspicion paid off: Heinie Groh was slated to start at third base that day. They positioned themselves outside the entrance to the park that was nearest third base and waited. It was not long before Paul Hilton strolled into their trap. He attempted to pull a gun on the detectives, but they disarmed him and he was placed under arrest. Hilton was charged with first-degree murder. He was eventually convicted and executed in the electric chair on Feb. 17, 1927.

REF.: Carey, *Memoirs of a Murder Man*; *CBA*.

Himmler, Heinrich, 1900-45, Ger., mur.-war crimes. Next to his chief, Adolf Hitler, no other man in Germany's Third Reich held as much awesome and terrible power as did Heinrich Himmler. He was the most feared Nazi, and rightly so for he made a business of terrorism, torture, and mass murder. As head of the SS and the Gestapo, Himmler ruled the concentration camps of Nazi Germany, ordering mass exterminations of Jews, Christians, political opponents, and those the Nazis labeled social misfits—more than 11 million persons by some counts, making him the ultimate mass murderer of all time. Himmler was born on Oct. 7, 1900, in Bavaria. His father was a professor and his mother a hard-working housewife. The family lived comfortably and Himmler as a child lacked little.

Himmler was an average student, concentrating on agricultural studies in high school and later at the University of Munich. Although he served in the German Army during WWI, he apparently saw no action and spent most of his time training to be a machine gunner and, later, an officer. He never became an officer, although he claimed, years later, that he led men in battle on the Western Front. Following the war, Himmler took a degree in agronomy and worked on a poultry farm but his poor health forced him to quit.

Heinrich Himmler, Nazi chief of the dreaded SS.

In 1922, Himmler formed liaisons with militarists who had established right-wing organizations working against Communists and other left-wing groups. He met Captain Ernst Roehm, who was a regular army officer and who was established with the newly born Nazi party and its nominal leader, Adolf Hitler. Himmler was introduced to Hitler through Roehm and was captivated by his dynamic speaking style and his ardent and fanatical dream of a new Germany. The Nazi hatred for Jews also appealed to Himmler who, by then, had developed into a rabid anti-Semite. He joined the Nazi party in August 1923 and was part of the Munich Beer Hall Putsch in November of that year. On Nov. 9, 1923, Himmler, carrying an old Imperial German flag, marched with Roehm in the takeover of the War Ministry in Munich. At the time, Himmler felt that Roehm, not Hitler, was the man who would lead the Nazis to power. The diminutive Himmler, at the time, was also an ardent monarchist and longed for the return of the deposed Kaiser Wilhelm.

When the Putsch failed and Hitler and Roehm were imprisoned, Himmler was left without leaders or a party. He then attached himself to Gregor Strasser, another leading Nazi, helping him build up the party in 1924 throughout Bavaria and making hundreds of anti-Semitic speeches. He also rabble-roused against the Communists, democracy, and liberals. Because of his efforts, many Nazi deputies were swept into office in the following elections. In 1925, he became Strasser's secretary, receiving a salary of 120 marks a month.

Himmler moved with Strasser to Berlin to develop the Nazi party; there he slowly came under the mesmerizing influence of Adolf Hitler. He then became a toady and philosophical lackey to Hitler, calling him "the greatest brain that ever lived!" Roehm was still enormously influential in the party, particularly since he headed the Brownshirt (SA) goon legions who backed up Hitler's terror campaign against Jews and liberals. Himmler, through Roehm, became head of the intelligence unit of the SA, and rose slowly in stature and power as he assembled dossiers on all the leading Nazi opponents, as well as secret files on Nazi leaders Hitler later desired to purge, including Roehm and Strasser.

In 1926, Himmler met Margarete "Marja" Boden, daughter of a wealthy landowner. She was statuesque, blue-eyed, and blonde, Himmler's concept of a German goddess. He married her on July 3, 1928. Marja Himmler was as supportive of the Nazi party as was her scheming, calculating husband, and she rejoiced

in his appointment by Hitler, on Jan. 6, 1929, as head of the SS, the Nazi secret police force. Himmler grew a Hitler-like mustache and proved to be a fanatical policeman, a picky, methodical, unimaginative man who would wield incredible power.

Himmler worked slowly behind the scenes, aligning himself in the early 1930s with Hitler's closest associates, Hermann Goering and Paul Josef Goebbels. He slowly established the SS as a unit independent of Roehm's massive SA. When Hitler became chancellor of Germany in 1933, he broadened Himmler's powers, making him head of the secret police, the Gestapo, which had formerly been under the command of Goering. In 1934, when Hitler ordered the purge of the SA, it was Himmler, along with Goering and Goebbels, who drew up the list of persons to be assassinated, and it was Himmler's top SS troops who carried out the executions.

As Hitler's high executioner, Himmler had political opponents kidnapped and murdered. He organized a concentration camp system to which hundreds of thousands of Jews and "enemies of the Reich" were sent in the 1930s, millions as Nazi Germany swallowed up one country after another during WWII. Himmler was not above attending to Hitler's personal problems. Though no proof was ever forthcoming, it was strongly rumored that Himmler personally shot and killed Hitler's niece and lover, Geli Rebaul, in 1931 when the attractive girl tried to leave Hitler to pursue a singing career in Vienna. Himmler showed no emotion or guilt for his chief role in exterminating the Jews. He reveled in the fact that his aides, Reinhard Heydrich, Ernst Kaltenbrunner, and Adolf Eichmann, were able to develop mass extermination methods which saw the wholesale murder of men, women, and children through shooting and later gassing. He paraded through concentration camps regularly to view the hapless creatures awaiting Himmler's orders that would send them to their deaths. To Himmler these poor wretches were "lice...vermin...slave scum" to be eliminated from the face of the earth.

The fearsome Himmler was not physically imposing. Short and nondescript looking, with his hair cropped close to the skull, Himmler wore pince-nez eyeglasses and spoke in a high falsetto voice. He was an enigma to his fellow Nazis and members of the German Army Corps. General Friedrich Hossbach later said of him: "This man, Hitler's evil spirit, cold, calculating and ambitious, was undoubtedly the most purposeful and most unscrupulous figure in the Third Reich." General Heinz Guderian thought of Himmler as "a man from another planet." Swiss diplomat Carl Burckhardt aptly portrayed Himmler thusly: "What made him sinister was his capacity to concentrate upon little things, his pettifogging, conscientiousness and inhuman methodology; he had a touch of the robot." Nazi philosopher Alfred Rosenberg, later hanged, remembered: "I was never able to look Heinrich Himmler straight in the eye. His eyes were always hooded, blinking behind his pince-nez."

The blueprints that outlined the systematic extermination of the Jews were drawn up by Himmler's ice-blooded aides, Heydrich and Kaltenbrunner, but it was Himmler who modified and improved these plans. It was Himmler who doggedly sought to increase the numbers of those murdered each day in such concentration camps as Dachau, Auschwitz, and Buchenwald. It was Himmler who constantly urged army commanders to ferret out Jews and others in conquered territories to be rounded up and sent back to his SS troops for ultimate imprisonment. It was Himmler, as Germany began to lose the war, who stepped up extermination to the point where he insisted army troops execute Jews, Poles, Catholics, and others in the field.

So vile were Himmler's tactics that he took to ordering the mutilation of countless human beings under the guise of "medical experiments"; women and men were sterilized, children were frozen and burned to test tolerances, lethal injections were made into other children to see how long it took them to die, gas was administered to prisoners to see how long it would take them to choke to death. Killer doctors such as Karl Gebhardt, hanged as a war criminal on June 2, 1948, and Fritz Fischer, later sent to prison for life, experimented on innumerable concentration camp prisoners, killing thousands in their ruthless, barbaric experiments which were fully endorsed by Himmler—in fact, ordered by him.

As the Third Reich fell apart in 1945 under the juggernaut of the Allied armies, Hitler, in desperation, turned to his policeman, Himmler, placing him in command of fast-disintegrating German armies on the Eastern front. But these troops simply melted away under the onslaught of the Russian armies. Himmler proved inept at regrouping these forces, giving the same kind of ridiculous, fatalistic orders as did Hitler: Victory or Death. As the Nazi armies collapsed, Himmler fled to Ploen and tried to negotiate a separate peace with the Allies. He failed at this, too. Hitler, learning of Himmler's defection, denounced him and named Admiral Karl Doenitz as his successor. As Germany was overrun by U.S., Russian, British, and French troops, Himmler went into hiding.

He shaved off his mustache and threw away his pince-nez, placing a patch over his eye so that he looked like a dwarfish pirate. He stripped the insignias from his uniform and pretended to be a simple policeman. Himmler had seen to the condemnation of one Heinrich Hitzinger, but he kept this victim's papers and now passed himself off as Hitzinger. He was captured at Bremervörde by the British

Left, Himmler and, right, his ruthless executioner, Reinhard Heydrich.

but was not recognized and was detained in a prison camp. Following three days of imprisonment, Himmler asked to see the commandant. He was brought before Captain Tom Selvester, an intelligence officer. Suddenly Himmler tore off the eye patch and put on glasses. He announced in a weak voice: "Heinrich Himmler."

Selvester asked Himmler to sign his name to verify his identity, but Himmler, confused, thought he was being asked for his autograph. He signed the paper, then resumed his old dictatorial ways by ordering Selvester to destroy the paper after he had examined it. Selvester told him through an interpreter that *he* would decide what would be destroyed and what would not. Selvester found a vial of poison on Himmler but he suspected that the former Reich minister might have another vial hidden somewhere in his mouth. This had been the case with other recently captured Nazis.

To make sure this was not the case, Selvester ordered some thick bread, cheese, and tea. He watched Himmler eat normally and concluded that nothing was hidden in his mouth. Himmler's clothes had been taken from him and he wore prison garb. Selvester offered him a British private's uniform but Himmler refused, thinking that he would be photographed in the enemy's uniform and thus be ridiculed and disgraced. A doctor, Captain J.L. Wells, later had Himmler undress, and the naked little man was completely searched for hidden poison capsules. The physician then ordered Himmler to open his mouth. He placed two fingers inside after seeing a small black knob sticking out between a gap of teeth on Himmler's lower jaw. As the doctor struggled for the object, Himmler turned his head away and ground his teeth together.

"He's done it!" shouted Wells. The doctor and a sergeant leaped on Himmler, knocking him down to the floor and turning him onto his stomach so that he could not swallow the contents of the vial secreted in his mouth. Wells grabbed Himmler's throat, trying to force him to spit out the contents. A stomach pump and emetics were used but it was futile. Himmler had managed to

swallow cyanide and died within fifteen seconds. The disgusted British officials threw a blanket onto the mass killer and left him lying on the floor of the cell. Two days later, Himmler's body was wrapped in a blanket, then camouflage netting. It was taken to a fresh grave near Lüneberg and dumped into it. The grave was unmarked and the plot was quickly covered up and forgotten. See: **Eichmann, Adolf; Goebbels, Paul Josef; Goering, Hermann; Heydrich, Reinhard; Hitler, Adolf; Kaltenbrunner, Ernst; Roehm, Ernst.**

REF.: Aronson, *Heydrich und die Anfänge des SD und der Gestapo*; Bartz, *Downfall of the German Secret Service*; Best, *Die Deutsche Polizei*; Biss, *Die Stop der Endlösung: Kampf gegen Himmler und Eichmann in Budapest*; Buchheim, *SS und Polizei*; Bullock, *Hitler*; *CBA*; Crankshaw, *The Gestapo*; Delarue, *History of the Gestapo*; Demaris, *The Director*; Fest, *Hitler*; Frischauer, *Himmler*; Georg, *Die wirtschaftlichen Unternehmungen der SS*; Goebbels, *The Goebbels Diaries*; Guderian, *Panzer Leader*; Heiden, *Der Fuehrer*; Hilberg, *The Destruction of the European Jews*; Himmler, *Die Schutzstaffel als antibolschewistische Kampf-organisation*; Hirsch, *SS Gestern, heute und...*; Höhne, *The Order of the Death's Head*; Jarman, *The Rise and Fall of Nazi Germany*; Kaplan, *Scroll of Agony*; Kogon, *The Theory and Practice of Hell*; Levin, *The Holocaust*; Manvell and Fraenkel, *Himmler*; Masur, *En Jud taler med Himmler*; Nash, *Almanac of World Crime*; Neusüss-Hunkel, *Die SS*; Orlaw, *The History of the Nazi Party*; Payne, *The Life and Death of Adolf Hitler*; Reitlinger, *The Final Solution*; _____, *The S.S.: Alibi of a Nation*; Shirer, *The Rise and Fall of the Third Reich*; Speer, *Infiltration*; _____, *Inside the Third Reich*; Suhl, *They Fought Back*; Vogt, *The Burden of Guilt*; Wighton, *Heydrich*; Wulf, *Heinrich Himmler*; Zipfel, *Gestapo und Sicherheitsdienst*; (FILM), *The Strange Death of Adolf Hitler*, 1943; *The Magic Face*, 1951.

Hinckley, John W., Jr., See: **Reagan, Ronald.**

Hind, James, 1618-52, Brit., rob.-mur. His loyalties to the Crown led Captain James Hind, a bold and celebrated highwayman, to perpetrate the majority of his robberies against Republicans, members of the party he loathed.

Hind, the son of a saddle maker, was born in Chipping Norton in Oxfordshire. At the age of fifteen, he was sent to apprentice with a butcher in his hometown. Tiring of his surroundings and his employer, who was a churlish, angry man, Hind got £3 from his doting mother and left for London before he had served his two years. Getting drunk one night, he was arrested by the local patrols and sent to the Poultry Compter, a local jail. There he met Thomas Allen, a notorious highwayman; when the two were set free they became partners. During an early robbery, the fledgling Hind took £15 from a gentleman and his servant while the experienced Allen stood at a distance, ready to step in if his assistance was needed. Hind gave the gentleman back twenty shillings of the stolen money so that he could cover the expenses of his journey, and Allen was apparently pleased at his new comrade's refinement.

On another occasion, Hind met Hugh Peters on the road to Enfield Chase. Peters, a clergyman who would later be executed as an accomplice in the assassination of King Charles I, was already known as an outspoken preacher. When Hind demanded that Peters "stand and deliver," the minister began quoting lines of scripture, exhorting him not to steal, especially not from the poor. The educated Hind traded Bible verses with the parson, telling him not to "despise a thief," and further berating him for his part in the murder of the king, "whom your cursed Republican party unjustly murdered before his own palace." Ending with a threat to "send you out of the world in a moment," Hind got thirty pieces of gold from Peters, and stripped him of his coat as well. When Peters preached against the sin of theft the following Sunday, quoting the Bible verse, "I have put off my coat, how shall I put it on?" a wit in the congregation cried out: "Sir, I can't tell, unless Captain Hind was here."

Once robbing a coach filled with women, Hind hauled in £3,000 in gold, the dowry of one of the travelers who was going to be married; the nuptials were canceled when she arrived at her destination without the funds. Hind lost his robber companion when the ambitious pair went after Oliver Cromwell, Lord Protector of England. Outnumbered by seven men, Hind barely escaped, forced to leave behind Allen who was captured and later hanged.

Out of his respect for the royal family, who were now all in exile, Hind looked for Republicans to rob. Sergeant Bradshaw, well known for his anti-royalist sentiments, was one of his victims. Robbing him of more than forty shillings in silver, Hind told Bradshaw it was not enough, swearing that he would shoot him through the heart if he did not come up with more. Bradshaw came up with a considerably larger purse, and Hind rewarded his victim with a lengthy speech about the value of gold and the villainy of the Republicans, ending his diatribe by shooting all six horses out from under the Sergeant's coach.

Hind's career of highway robbery lasted about nine years, until an acquaintance turned him in; he had been living above a barbershop near St. Dunstan's Church in Fleet Street under the alias of Brown. He was brought before the Speaker of the House of Commons to be questioned, then taken to Newgate prison in leg chains and kept under tight guard. On Dec. 12, 1651, Hind was tried at the Sessions House in Old Bailey, where nothing could be proved conclusively against him. He was then taken from Newgate to Reading Jail in Berkshire on Mar. 1, 1652, where he was arraigned before Judge Warberton for killing George Sympson in the village of Knole.

Hind was found Guilty of murder but was nearly released when a Royal Decree was issued the day after his conviction, pardoning all condemned men except those guilty of crimes against the state. But by an order of council, he was removed to Worcester Jail where a Bill of High Treason was issued against him. Hind was hanged, drawn, and quartered on Sept. 24, 1652, at the age of thirty-four. His head was set on the Bridge Gate over the River Severn; the other parts of his body were taken to other gates around the city and left to decompose. Hind's head was taken down after a week and buried.

REF.: *CBA*; Pringle, *Stand and Deliver*; Smith, *Highwaymen*.

Hindenburg Disaster, 1937, Ger., bomb. In 1937, the *Hindenburg* was the world's largest airship and the pride of Germany, a symbol of national prestige. A technological marvel, it was more than 800 feet long, stabilized by a tailfin as high as a ten-story building. As luxurious as an elegant hotel, the *Hindenburg* could travel six days and 10,000 miles without refueling, sailing along at 80 mph. Its enormous bulk was held together by ten miles of girders. Used to advertise the Nazi regime, the airship had floated over major cities in Germany blaring Adolf Hitler's name over loudspeakers and dropping Nazi propaganda leaflets. In the spring of 1937, SS-Sturmbannführer Karl Hufschmidt called a top secret emergency meeting at his Berlin office to tell Luftwaffe intelligence officers Colonel Fritz Erdmann, Major Franz Witt, and First-Lieutenant Klaus Hinkelbein that he had been informed of a plot to sabotage the *Hindenburg*. The officers rode the ship disguised as regular passengers to locate tactical landmarks, military installations, and factories as the airship sailed over Britain and France. Hufschmidt told them that the main suspect was an American acrobat and comedian, Joseph Spah, who had toured Germany for years and was believed to be involved with political undesirables.

German airships had carried nearly a million passengers without incident, due in part to their stringent safety precautions. On the morning of May 2, 1937, a three-hour search of the *Hindenburg* turned up nothing. At the flight point, where passengers boarded, authorities conducted an intensive security check, confiscating cigarette lighters, matches, and even a toy that gave off sparks. Spah was checked thoroughly, and watched carefully as he fed his dog, at his insistence, back in the freight compartment. The Germans kept him under surveillance throughout the *Hindenburg's* flight from Frankfurt to New Jersey. Meanwhile, in the rear of the airship, a homemade bomb was sewn into the canvas at the base of one of the giant gas cells, awaiting a touch to set it off. On May 6, at dawn, the airship was eight hours behind schedule, and about 350 miles from

Boston, Mass. Scheduled to land at the Lakenhurst, N.J., airfield at 6 a.m., the *Hindenburg* approached the field at 4 p.m. only to run into a fierce storm, which forced it to delay landing. Minutes before 6 p.m., someone cut into the canvas and set the detonator's clock for two hours. The incendiary device was built so that when the phosphorus burned away the canvas, the hydrogen and the incoming oxygen would unite and explode. Radio clearance for the *Hindenburg* was sent from the Lakenhurst station at 6:12, but not until 6:44 did the ship alter its course toward the airfield.

On the ground, over 200 men were setting up for the docking, maneuvering a 75-foot mast into position. At 7:21, the *Hindenburg* dropped its streamer-like landing lines, only thirty-nine minutes before the bomb was timed to detonate. The gas cell where the bomb was tucked away collapsed like a punctured lung and a wave of orange flame lit up the inside of the cell, growing brighter as the explosion ripped through the entire ship. Broadcaster Herb Morrison of Radio WLS in Chicago was on hand to describe the landing. His recording, which careens from excited admiration of the *Hindenburg* to a horrified, gasping description of the blast, is a famous moment in radio history. At 7:25, a 400-foot ball of flaming hydrogen rolled over the airship. Within thirty-four seconds after the big explosion, the blackened frame of the *Hindenburg* settled to the ground. Twenty-two of the crew were killed, and thirteen passengers died in the flames. Joseph Spah escaped by performing an acrobatic fall. Ernst Lehmann, captain of the *Hindenburg*, and Colonel Erdmann were among the dead.

At the court hearing, the Americans and Germans agreed not to mention the possibility of sabotage, to avert dangerous and, for the Germans, embarrassing implications. General Hermann Goering, chief of the Luftwaffe, did not want to bring to light anything that could cast a negative light on the Third Reich. According to Goering, the disaster "was an act of God." The official explanation was that the *Hindenburg* had been brought down by the phenomenon of St. Elmo's fire, an unusual atmospheric electrical discharge. Detective George McCartney of the New York police department's bomb squad pieced the bomb together. According to a later study of the case by Michael Mooney in his book *The Hindenburg*, the bomb had been placed by Eric Spehl, one of the crew members. Spehl became so disenchanted with the Nazis after aiding a Gestapo torture victim, that he decided to alert the world to their atrocities by destroying the most notable symbol of the Reich. He had intended the bomb to explode after the passengers had disembarked. Spehl was one of those killed in the Hindenburg Disaster. See: **Goering, Hermann; Hitler, Adolf.**

REF.: *CBA;* Mooney, *The Hindenburg;* (FILM), *The Hindenburg,* 1975.

Hindley, Myra, See: **Moors Murders.**

Hindman, George W., d.1878, U.S., west. lawman-gunman. In 1875, George Hindman moved a herd of cattle to New Mexico from his native Texas, and decided to stay and work on a ranch in Lincoln. But Bill Humphreys, part owner of the herd, became angry with Hindman's desertion, and after an argument, both men drew their guns. Hindman's shot grazed Humphreys' head, knocking him unconscious, while Hindman was wounded by a shard of metal when a bullet hit his gun. Hindman escaped and became a ranch hand for Robert Casey. Hindman encountered a more stalwart foe when he wrestled a grizzly bear who refused to die after being shot. The bear mauled Hindman, permanently crippling his arm and hand. In 1877, Hindman was appointed deputy sheriff to William Brady, and the following February was part of a posse which instigated the Lincoln County War with the fatal shooting of John Tunstall. On Apr. 1, 1878, Hindman was accompanying Sheriff Brady to the Lincoln courthouse when they were ambushed by an outlaw gang which included Billy the Kid, Henry Brown, Jim French, John Middleton, and Fred Wait. Brady died instantly, and Hindman shortly thereafter.

REF.: Bartholomew, *Jesse Evans;* _____, *Western Hardcases;* Bechdolt, *Tales of the Old Timers;* Breihan, *Bad Men of Frontier Days;* Brent, *The Complete and Factual Life of Billy the Kid;* Casey, *The Texas Border and*

Some Borderliners; CBA; Charles, *More Tales of the Tularosa;* Coe, *Frontier Fighter;* Cunningham, *Famous in the West;* ____, *Triggernometry;* Cushman, *The Great North Trail;* Durham, *The Negro Cowboys;* Ealy, *Water in A Thirsty Land;* Fable, *Billy the Kid;* Fulton, *Roswell in Early Days;* Garrett, *The Authentic Life of Billy the Kid;* Hamlin, *The True Story of Billy the Kid;* Hendron, *The Story of Billy the Kid;* Hening, *George Curry;* Holloway, *Texas Gun Lore;* Horan and Sann, *Pictorial History of the Wild West;* Hough, *The Story of the Outlaw;* Keleher, *Violence in Lincoln County;* King, *Pioneer Western Empire Builders;* Klasner, *My Girlhood Among Outlaws;* Lamar, *The Far Southwest;* Leckie, *The Buffalo Soldiers;* Lovell, *A Personalized History of Otero County;* Moore, *The West;* Nolan, *The Life and Death of John Henry Tunstall;* Nye, *Pistols for Hire;* O'Connor, *Pat Garrett;* Otero, *The Real Billy the Kid;* Rennert, *Western Outlaws;* Shinkle, *Reminiscences of Roswell Pioneers;* Shirley, *Toughest of Them All;* Shumard, *The Ballad and History of Billy the Kid;* Steckmesser, *The Western Hero in History and Legend;* Thorp, *Story of the Southwestern Cowboy;* Wallis, *Cattle Kings of the Staked Plains;* Wellman, *The Trampling Herd;* White, *Lead and Likker;* ____, *Trigger Fingers.*

Hinds, Alfie, 1917- , Brit.-Ire., smug.-rob.-pris. esc. Alfie Hinds was convicted in 1953 of leading a gang of robbers in a London department-store robbery that netted the criminals £30,000. He maintained his innocence, and vowed that he would clear himself of all charges. But fighting those charges from Nottingham Prison proved to be a difficult task, so he planned an escape to Ireland, where he felt sure an Irish court would find him innocent of the crime. He successfully broke out in 1956.

His first act as a free man was to explain publicly, via letters to newspapers, why he had escaped. He also demanded a new trial, but England did not relent. He moved to Dublin, and had not been there long when he was arrested and brought back to Pentonville, where there was still no interest in reopening his case. Hinds tried to prove that not only did he have nothing to do with the robbery, but he had also been unlawfully deported from Ireland.

It was two more years before Hinds escaped again. He had spent that time studying law with devotion, looking for ways to appeal his case. But this escape, though initially successful, was not to be long-lasting. Hinds, his brother, and a friend were apprehended at the Bristol airport a few hours after his breakout.

He escaped again in 1958. This time he made it to Dublin again, where he set up shop as a car dealer. In 1960, he was arrested for smuggling cars and was sentenced to six months in prison, after which he was once again returned to England to finish his twelve-year sentence.

His last attempt to clear his name came in 1962, when he sued ex-Chief Superintendent Herbert Sparks for libel. Sparks had written a series of articles about the department-store robbery, implying that Hinds was guilty. Although Hinds had already been convicted, he managed to push his suit through and was awarded £1,700 in damages. The libel case did the trick: the day after it ended, Home Secretary Henry Brooke ordered Hinds' release. Hinds finally gained his freedom, but was never able to get the robbery conviction removed from his record. REF.: *CBA.*

Hindu Conspiracy, prom. 1916-17, U.S., consp. At the start of WWI, a Hindu Conspiracy in the U.S. was working toward an international insurrection of Indian people against British rule in India. The German consul general in San Francisco, Franz Bopp, played a major role in the scheme, supporting the uprising financially and politically. In a secret meeting in San Francisco, a team of investigators planned to expose the intrigue. Included were American officials from Washington, federal undercover agents, and British consular officers. Correspondence regarding the conspiracy had been gathered, and agent Edward Oscar Heinrich volunteered to master several complicated Indian dialects in order to translate it. Heinrich discovered that the plot was instigated about five years before the war began and financed by Germany. Har Dyal, a famous Hindu philosopher, had traveled from Switzerland to Germany to organize the Berlin Committee, the central authority for the scheme.

The Pacific Coast of the U.S. was a major focus of the plot,

with plans underway for recruiting Indians in the western states and sending them to India armed and trained in terrorist tactics. Taraknath Das was in charge of the West Coast operation. Detective William A. Mundell, called in by the British consul, organized a group of undercover agents who worked for months infiltrating ranches, lumber camps, and road crews where recruiting was taking place. Around 8,000 men had already been recruited. A woman operative got information from a German baron who was a society figure in San Francisco, and traced the operations of Lieutenant Wilhelm von Brincken and of Ram Chandra and other Hindu leaders who met with von Brincken at his Nob Hill apartment. The primary propaganda newspaper, *Ghadr,* had passed from Har Dyal to Ram Chandra's editorship. Analysis of chemicals in inks, handwriting samples, and typewriter styles proved that a Dr. Chakravarty in New York was transmitting orders from Count Johann-Heinrich von Bernstorff, German ambassador to the U.S., to German and Indian leaders in San Francisco. With all the evidence in place, Heinrich, Mundell, and the others turned over their information to U.S. district attorney John W. Preston, who presented it to a grand jury.

Thirty-two persons were charged with conspiracy to violate American neutrality. Among them were Bopp, von Brincken, Eckhart von Schack, the vice-consul in San Francisco, Chakravarty, Ram Chandra, Ram Singh, and Tarknath Das. With Heinrich as the key witness for the prosecution, the trial opened on Nov. 22, 1917, in the U.S. district court of Judge William C. Van Fleet. Of the thirty-two defendants, only one minor figure was acquitted. On Apr. 30, 1918, Judge Van Fleet sentenced Bopp and his aide, von Schack, to two years each in the federal prison on McNeil Island and fines of $10,000 each. Von Brincken was given a two-year sentence and Das was given twenty-two months. Chakravarty was sentenced to a short term in the county jail and the other Indians were also given short jail terms. Two of the defendants were never sentenced. The day before closing arguments, Ram Singh leaped up in court and shot Ram Chandra from point-blank range with a revolver, killing him. U.S. marshall James B. Holohan fired at Ran Singh, who fell forward dead. The two defendants had allegedly been arguing over money just before the shootings.

REF.: Block, *The Wizard of Berkeley; CBA.*

Hines, James J., 1877-1957, U.S., polit. corr.-org. crime. Jimmy Hines of New York, a third-generation politician, who followed in the steps of his grandfather, a Tammany Hall captain under Boss William Tweed, and his father, who served Richard Croker loyally for years. Hines was the last of a dying breed of politicians who controlled the police, the courts, and organized crime factions. A favor-giver, he learned his lessons at his father's knee.

In the 1890s, Hines' father owned a business shoeing horses on the Upper West Side of Manhattan. His contract with the city put food on the table and brought Jimmy into contact with the rough-and-tumble elements of the Tammany Hall political ma-

Tammany boss James J. Hines, who sponsored gangsters and crime.

chine. By the time he was twenty-one young Hines was running the family business and looking out for the interests of his ten brothers and sisters. When a reform administration came in, as it often did when levels of corruption became intolerable, times were hard for the family. In 1902 Republican Mayor Seth Low cancelled the Hines contract and for a few years Jimmy had to live by his wits.

In 1907, he was elected alderman from the Eleventh Assembly District. Six years later he became chief clerk of the board of alderman at a salary of $5,000 a year. From there he never looked back. After a hitch in the armed forces he returned to New York to defeat Abraham Kaplan for leadership of his district. A year later Hines scored a major political coup by running for borough president against the wishes of Boss Charles Murphy, Tammany grand sachem. Though Hines lost, he had sent word that he, and not Murphy, was the coming power in the volatile world of New York politics. With the onset of Prohibition, Hines improved on his earnings. A frequent visitor to the racetracks and betting parlors, Jimmy Hines provided exclusive "services" to the Sun & Surf Club at Atlantic Beach, L.I., and the New Hampshire Breeders. From 1929 to 1935 he never bothered to file an income tax return but lived comfortably nevertheless. The government soon became suspicious.

Jimmy Hines entering Sing Sing Prison to serve four years behind bars.

Hines' legal problems dated to 1928 when the district attorney accused him of accepting $7,500 from two convicted numbers runners. For allowing backroom gambling to go on at the Monongahela Club in Harlem, Hines was paid $500 a month. It was further charged that the political boss was keeping company with a bevy of organized crime figures including Charles "Lucky" Luciano and bootlegger Owney Madden. Hines and Luciano vacationed together at the winter resort in Hot Springs, Ark. Hines realized that the times were changing. No longer able to control the rackets, the Irish political boss was forced to make compromises with the Italian and Jewish gangsters who had come to dominate the action in New York.

In the 1930s, Hines supplied the political clout for Arthur "Dutch Schultz" Flegenheimer, Harlem numbers boss, at a salary estimated to be between $500 and $1,000 a week. The racket was worth $20 million a year to the crime syndicates. "Hines...could and did have cops transferred when they bothered the numbers," explained J. Richard "Dixie" Davis, a syndicate lawyer. When Schultz was assassinated in 1935 Jimmy Hines transferred his allegiance to the Lucky Luciano-Frank Costello combine. The arrangement continued until District Attorney Thomas Edmund Dewey launched a frontal assault against the top New York mobsters. Unlike his predecessor, William C. Dodge, whom Hines once described as "stupid, respectable, and my man," Dewey

refused to be bought off or intimidated. On May 25, 1938, Hines was charged with being a "co-conspirator and part of the Dutch Schultz mob." Dewey's first attempt to send the boss to prison ended in a mistrial when the state's star witness, numbers racketeer George Weinberg, committed suicide. The case collapsed but Dewey brought Hines back to trial in 1939 with better results. On Feb. 25, 1939, jury foreman Leonard T. Hobert returned a verdict of Guilty on each of thirteen counts against Hines.

In passing sentence Judge Charles Nott Jr. criticized the defendant for using his office to further the aims of criminals. "Instead of using his political power and influence for the well-being of the city and for the promotion of law-and-order and good government, he used his position for the promotion of the interests of this crowd of criminals." Jimmy Hines exhausted his appeals and was sent to Sing Sing in 1940, where he toiled in the prison greenhouse for the next four years. On Sept. 12, 1944, the parole board granted him his freedom on the condition that he refrain from engaging in political activity of any kind. See: **Davis, J. Richard; Dewey, Thomas; Luciano, Charles; Schultz, Dutch.**

REF.: *CBA*; Danforth, *The D.A.'s Man*; Eisenberg and Landau, *Meyer Lansky*; Fried, *The Rise and Fall of the Jewish Gangster in America*; Gosch and Hammer, *The Last Testament of Lucky Luciano*; Katz, *Uncle Frank*; Lait and Mortimer, *Chicago: Confidential*; Levine, *Anatomy of a Gangster*; Messick, *Lansky*; _____, *Secret File*; _____ and Goldblatt, *The Mobs and the Mafia*; Peterson, *The Mob*; Reid, *The Grim Reapers*; Reppetto, *The Blue Parade*; Sann, *Kill the Dutchman*; Thompson and Raymond, *Gang Rule in New York*.

Hines, Walker Downer, 1870-1934, U.S., lawyer. Began practicing law in New York in 1921. REF.: *CBA*.

Hinkman, William, 1908-28, U.S., kid.-mur. Twelve-year-old Marian Parker was abducted on her way home from school in Los Angeles, Calif., in December 1927. Her parents received a telegram the next day instructing them to deliver $1,500 in exchange for their daughter's safety. After a botched first drop-off attempt, Mr. Parker handed the money to a man in a car. Marian was apparently asleep in the seat next to the driver, who said he would drop the girl off further up the road. When Mr. Parker reached his daughter and uncovered her body, he found she had been strangled to death and her legs amputated.

The brutality of the crime prompted an intense search by police and civilians. A description that appeared in the newspapers prompted a number of men who resembled the suspect to be apprehended, and sometimes injured by angry civilians. After certain individuals had been stopped for questioning several times, the police finally had to issue identity cards to the innocent men who resembled the killer.

The public rejoiced when authorities arrested William Hinkman on Dec. 22. Hinkman, nineteen, had formerly worked at the bank where Mr. Parker served as an official. The police who had collared the man were lauded as celebrities. Hinkman earned a distinction of his own: he was the first man in the U.S. to be put to death for a crime resulting from a ransom kidnapping.

REF.: *CBA*; Moorehead, *Hostages to Fortune*.

Hinks, Reginald Ivor, c.1900-34, Brit., mur. A petty thief and fast talker, Reginald Ivor Hinks was a vacuum cleaner salesman in Bath, England, when he met Constance Anne Pullen, a divorced woman with one child who lived with her 85-year-old, senile father, James Pullen. Interested in her inheritance of about £2,000, Hinks courted Pullen, and married her in March 1933. He soon got rid of Mr. Pullen's full-time male nurse, and put the old man on a strict diet in the hope of further enfeebling him. With £900 of his father-in-law's money, Hinks moved the family from their large house to a smaller one in Bath. When Hinks tried to use more of the money, Pullen's lawyer stopped him. Despite his anger, Hinks could not get at the cash. He began to take the elderly Pullen on long walks, hoping to exhaust him, and even sent him out by himself. When no fortuitous accidents occurred, Hinks took matters into his own hands. On Dec. 1, 1933, he called the Bath fire department to report that he had found Pullen dead in the kitchen with his head in the gas oven. Voluble as always,

Hinks explained that he had found his father-in-law, turned off the gas, and tried to revive him before summoning the police, the fire department, and a doctor. He helpfully explained, "If you find a bruise on the back of his head, that happened when I pulled him out of the gas oven." It was proved that the bruise had been caused before death. Tried before Justice George Branson at the Old Bailey, Hicks was convicted, and hanged on May 4, 1934.

REF.: Butler, *Murderers' England*; *CBA*; Jesse, *Comments on Cain*; O'Donnell, *Crimes That Made News*; Rowland, *Criminal Files*; Shew, *A Second Companion to Murder*; Wilde, *Crimes and Cases of 1934*.

Hinojosa, Pedro de, 1489-1553, Spain., gov., assass. Helped Gonzalo Pizarro take over Peru. He and Pizarro again joined forces in a 1545 uprising. As a fleet commander, he next conquered Nombre de Diós and Panama before his entire fleet defected with him to the royal side in 1546. He was then made governor and commander of the army of Charcas. Conspirators killed him. REF.: *CBA*.

Hinshaw, W.E., prom. 1895, U.S., mur. The Reverend W.E. Hinshaw and his wife, Thurza, settled in Bellville, Ind., in 1892. In their late twenties, they were popular in the community. Three years later, early in the morning of Jan. 10, 1895, neighbors heard shots and found the Hinshaws on the ground outside their home. The reverend was wounded superficially, while Thurza Hinshaw lay fatally wounded by a shot in the head. Hinshaw said that burglars entered the house, shot his wife, and attacked him, and that, following a desperate fight, they stole $80 and his revolver. But police found no signs of a struggle, nor any tracks in the fresh snow. The following day, Hinshaw's wallet, bloody trousers, and razor were found near his barn. His revolver, which proved to be the murder weapon, was discovered near the coal house. Hinshaw was arrested for murdering his wife. At the federal court in Indianapolis, the jury found W.E. Hinshaw Guilty of first-degree murder and sentenced him to life imprisonment.

REF.: *The Bellville Tragedy*; *CBA*.

Hinton, Edward, 1673-94, Brit., rob. Edward Hinton was only nine years old when he stole thirty shillings from his sister's closet and ran away from home with it. After several days he was found and brought home; soon after, he robbed his father's office of a large sum and ran away a second time.

Hinton's father, a man of good standing, tried to give his son a good education at St. Paul's School, but, as young Hinton continued to steal and persistently gravitated toward companions of bad character, his father bought him a post as an officer on a ship. Edward Hinton sailed to the Straits and, for the only time in his life, behaved honorably as an officer for a brief period. When the ship returned to England, however, he left his post and took up with a gang of thieves, quickly becoming involved in his first major robbery when he helped break into Admiral Carter's country house.

Hinton continued on to London and began his work in earnest. With several cohorts he robbed Lady Dartmouth's house in Blackheath, taking a large quantity of silver, which they sold to a refiner near Cripplegate. Upon seeing news of the robbery in the papers, Hinton complained bitterly to the refiner that they had been cheated; the man had told them that one of the cups they sold to him was silver gilt, and the paper listed it as gold. "To see the roguery of this world!" exclaimed Hinton, "There's no trusting anybody!" Hinton was caught, tried, and condemned for the robbery, but released because of his age and the influence of friends.

The youthful thief continued to pick pockets, break into houses, and rob on the highway until he was again arrested, this time for the robbery of Sir John Friend's house in Hackney. He received the death sentence a second time and was again reprieved, being sent instead to Barbados with a shipload of other convicts. On the way there, Hinton organized an escape, and the criminals jumped ship at the Isle of Wight. Hinton left his cohorts and traveled alone, begging along the way, until he reached London, where he gathered up his former gang and was nicknamed by them "Captain" in honor of his leadership abilities.

Meeting a Dutch colonel on the road, Hinton robbed him of his horse, his arms, and his cloak, and spent a short period robbing while wearing the man's clothes and marks of rank. For several months Hinton and his gang continued to pilfer, until they were pursued during an attack on the Southampton coach on Hounslow Heath, and several were captured. Not one to rest idle, the Captain got involved with a group of housebreakers including a man named Butler and two brothers, Joseph Dewster and H. Dewster. With this new crew, Hinton helped rob the house of the Dewsters' grandmother, an elderly Frenchwoman in Spitalfields. They bound and gagged the woman, tied her to a chair, and stole a large sum of cash. After they left, the woman fell over in the chair and was suffocated by the gag in her mouth. Before the old woman's burial, one of her grandchildren began to tremble with fear while being fitted for gloves, giving himself away as one of the murderers. Charged with the crime, the young man confessed. He and his brother, as well as Butler, were found Guilty and hanged in chains.

For a third time, Hinton got away undetected but was later arrested for other robberies. The clever thief fooled the jury with an elaborate and completely false story. His intricate ruse involved the testimony of five witnesses, two claiming to be old school friends, another saying he was the youth's landlord, a fourth pretending to be the innkeeper where the two friends had supper the day of the robbery, and a fifth saying that he was the boatman who had ferried them to and from the restaurant. After being acquitted, Hinton was again arrested for highway robbery in Surrey and Hertfordshire, accused by a member of his own gang. Although his fellow thief later retracted his statements, swearing that Hinton was not involved in the robbery, the man who was robbed identified Hinton as the person who forced him off his horse and took his watch. The jury found him Guilty; he received the death sentence the next morning, and was hanged that afternoon. He was twenty-one years old.

So committed had Hinton been to thieving that, when an acquaintance upbraided him for his criminal bent, Hinton declared that even if he had had an independent income, he enjoyed robbing so much that he would have done it just the same.

REF.: *CBA*; Smith, *Highwaymen*.

Hipparchus, d.514 B.C., Gr., assass. Hipparchus was the son of Peisistratus and brother of Hippias, a tyrannical ruler of Greece. He fell in love with a man named Harmodius and made several passes that were rejected. Harmodius and his lover, Aristogiton, conceived a plot intended to kill two birds with one stone: by killing Hippias, they would cause the Greeks to demand liberation from his despotic rule, and his brother would no longer be in favor with the government and thus would be shunned. The plan was finalized after Hipparchus, angry with Harmodius' denial, publicly insulted Harmodius' sister.

The assassination was to be carried out at the festival of Panathenaea, a time when the citizens were allowed to carry arms. The plan was believed to have been ruined, however,

The Greek lovers Harmodius and Aristogiton, who assassinated Hipparchus in 514 B.C.

when one of the co-conspirators was suspected of betraying Harmodius and Aristogiton. The two upset lovers saw Hipparchus, the man they felt was responsible for their problems, and killed him on the spot. Harmodius was slain when help arrived. Aristogiton escaped into the crowd but was later captured, tortured into implicating many collaborators who did not exist, and was finally killed by Hippias himself.

Although Hipparchus was not directly responsible for the harsh rule of his brother, his association with Hippias was enough to have him branded as a tyrant himself; thus, Harmodius and Aristogiton were immortalized in Greek history as courageous men who conquered an oppressor.
REF.: Bell, *Assassin!; CBA;* Hyams, *Killing No Murder;* Ross, *The Works of Aristotle; Thucydides.*

Hippasus of Metapontum, prom. 6th Cent. B.C., Gr., consp. Philospher who studied Pythagoras' teachings. Supposedly, he disclosed a mathematics secret of the Pythagorean brotherhood and was drowned. REF.: *CBA.*

Hiranuma, Kiichiro, b.1867, Japan, jur. Served as minister of justice from 1911-12, and as president of supreme court from 1921-38. From 1939-40 he held the position of premier. In 1940 he was the minister of home affairs. He was also an imperial advisor. REF.: *CBA.*

Hirasawa Sadamichi (AKA: Dr. Shigeru Matsui, Dr. Jiro Yamaguchi) 1891-1987, Japan, rob.-mur. In what was probably the most controversial murder case in post-WWII Japan, an elaborate bank robbery resulted in the deaths of twelve people, and divided the country over whether the man convicted of the crime was truly guilty. On Jan. 26, 1948, as a branch of Tokyo's Teikoku Bank was closing for the day, an official-looking, middle-aged man wearing a white smock and an arm band emblazoned with the word "Sanitation" stepped into the last unlocked door and made his way to the bank manager's office. Introducing himself as Dr. Jiro Yamaguchi, and presenting his calling card, he told the manager that he had come from General Douglas MacArthur's headquarters with instructions to administer medicine to the bank's employees to help prevent the spread of a dysentery epidemic. The bank manager, aware that the Americans occupying Japan at that time were enthusiastic about health codes, believed the doctor and gathered his employees.

The doctor instructed everyone to hold out their teacups, into which he poured a liquid. He told them to drink it quickly, and repeated his orders with a second liquid. Almost immediately, the employees began to choke, and then to reel over in agonizing pain as the doctor calmly watched. He left the bank quickly and quietly after collecting over 180,000 yen (roughly equivalent to $600).

Twelve of the fifteen bank workers died of potassium cyanide poisoning. The first weeks of a search for the culprit proved fruitless, though detectives learned of two other attempts at this type of robbery/mass murder. The first time, a doctor had administered a weaker solution of "medicine," and the employees had taken ill but were not incapacitated. The second time, a manager had found the imposter's story suspicious and he fled. It was believed that the same man had attempted all three crimes.

The investigation was based almost entirely on a composite sketch of the killer and a calling card found at the scene of the crime. Calling cards are usually exchanged in Japan when two strangers meet, and the card that the charlatan had presented led detectives to the doorstep of Hirasawa Sadamichi, a 57-year-old artist living in Otaru. A number of additional clues resulted in Hirasawa's arrest, among them his unexplained knowledge of chemicals, especially potassium cyanide; deposits made to his and his wife's accounts totaling over 100,000 yen a few days after the robbery, which Hirasawa could not satisfactorily account for; confirmation by handwriting analysts that his writing matched an endorsement of a check stolen from the Teikoku Bank; and a leather bag that was seen on the murderer.

In 1949, Hirasawa was found Guilty of murder and sentenced to death, though many were convinced of his innocence. Only two of forty witnesses had identified Hirasawa, and even they later admitted they were not positive. The artist adamantly refuted the charges, explaining that the confession he had given had been coerced. On appeal, the sentence was confirmed in 1955. However, so much controversy surrounded the case that Japan's justice ministers refused to approve the order of execution.

Hirasawa spent thirty-two years in prison—the longest time in criminal justice history that any death row prisoner has spent in prison without being executed or acquitted. On May 10, 1987, he died of pneumonia in a medical detention center in Hachioji.
REF.: *CBA;* Henderson, *The Super Sleuths;* Whitehead, *Journey Into Crime.*

Hirohito, Emperor, See: **Tojo Hideki**.

Hisayuki, Machii, See: **Machii Hisayuki**.

Hiss, Alger, 1904-   , U.S., perj. In 1948 a high-ranking State Department employee, Alger Hiss, was accused of supplying the Russians with highly classified documents. The charges were brought to light by a young California Congressman, Richard Nixon, who tied his political fortunes to the then prevailing anti-Communist mood of the nation. Historians have disagreed about whether Hiss was a Russian spy or the scapegoat of ambitious politicians.

Hiss was a 1926 graduate of Johns Hopkins University, where he was Phi Beta Kappa. After graduating from Harvard Law School in 1929, he clerked for Supreme Court Justice Oliver Wendell Holmes. In 1933 he joined the Department of Agriculture and ended up in the State Department by the end of WWII. In 1945 Hiss accompanied President Franklin Roosevelt to the Yalta Conference where he served as a policy advisor. He was named temporary secretary general of the United Nations at the San Francisco Conference, and elected president of the Carnegie Endowment for International Peace in 1946.

In 1948 Hiss' career was shattered by revelations that he had been an active member in the Communist Party before WWII. The accusations were voiced by journalist Whittaker Chambers, former

Alger Hiss, who had been accused of treason in 1948.

editor of the *Daily Worker* and an avowed Communist from 1925 until 1938. In August 1948 Chambers appeared before Nixon and other members of the House Committee on Un-American Activities to denounce Hiss as a communist. By this time Chambers had abandoned the party on philosophical grounds. "When Chambers decided to break with the Communists," explained Thomas Murphy, prosecutor, "he had to go into hiding and sleep with a gun beside him." In 1939 Chambers went to work for *Time* Magazine, becoming a senior editor. He tearfully resigned in 1948, citing a "moral dilemma." "When *Time* hired me in 1939, its editors knew that I was an ex-Communist; they did not know that espionage was involved." He said, "I cannot share this indispensable ordeal with anyone."

Hiss denied the charges and sued Chambers for slander. On Dec. 6, 1948, the House committee published sworn testimony taken from Chambers that Hiss was supplying the Russians with secret information. The drop point was a pumpkin patch on Chambers' 390-acre farm in northern Maryland and the journalist had retrieved the microfilmed documents from Hiss in a hollowed-out pumpkin on the grounds. Defense Attorney Claude Cross accused Chambers of receiving typed copies of State Department memoranda from Henry Julian Wadleigh, a former employee of the Trade Agreements Division, and not Hiss.

A federal grand jury summoned both men to appear and provide testimony, which resulted in a two-count federal indictment against Hiss on Dec. 15, charging perjury. Hiss was accused of lying to the grand jury when he denied he had given Chambers the documents in question. He had further stated that he had nothing to do with Chambers since Jan. 1, 1937, and knew him only as "George Crosley," a freelance writer who solicited his help during the preparation of a series of articles about the Nye Committee hearings in 1934. He was, in Hiss' words, "a man I knew in 1933 and 1934...a sort of deadbeat who purported to be a cross between Jim Tully and Jack London." Defense attorneys were more direct. They produced a psychiatrist and psychologist who testified that Chambers was psychopathic. Hiss accused the government of wiretapping his telephone between Dec. 13, 1945, and Sept. 13, 1947. The information gleaned from private phone calls between family members was turned over to Chambers, according to Hiss' version of events. Chambers then went on the witness stand and claimed that he had been an intimate friend of Hiss for years, ticking off his former associate's favorite hobbies, among them tennis and ornithology.

Hiss pleaded not guilty to perjury charges. Prosecutor Murphy attempted to show that he had in fact provided documents to Chambers up to 1938, which were carefully typed on a Woodstock machine by Hiss' wife, Priscilla Hiss. The existence of the typewriter and the documents made it exceedingly difficult for Hiss and his attorneys to disprove Chambers' charges. He feebly argued that Chambers had stolen typing samples from his desk and had somehow constructed a machine capable of typing correspondence in precisely the same manner.

The first of two trials ended in a hung jury in 1949. In January 1950, Hiss was found Guilty and sentenced to prison for five years by Federal Judge Henry Goddard. In March 1951 the Supreme Court refused to review the case, and Hiss went to jail.

He served three years at the Lewisburg, Pa., federal penitentiary before being released in December 1954. As the years passed Hiss continued to maintain his innocence. In 1980 he filed a 250-page legal brief in the Federal District Court in Manhattan attempting to overturn his 1950 conviction. Chambers' performance was a deliberate frame, Hiss charged, but he was still at a loss to explain why the ex-Communist felt compelled to single him out for persecution.

REF.: Busch, *Guilty or Not Guilty; CBA;* Demaris, *The Director;* Nash, *Citizen Hoover;* Scott, *The Concise Encyclopedia of Crime and Criminals;* Toledano, *J. Edgar Hoover;* Unger, *FBI;* Whitehead, *The FBI Story.*

Histiaeus, d.494 B.C., Gr., assass. Ruled ancient city of Miletus in Asia Minor under Persian king Darius I. He suppressed an uprising in Ionia, an area of Asia Minor. Harpagus caught him in 494 B.C., and Artaphernes crucified him at Sardis. REF.: *CBA.*

Hitchcock, Alfred Joseph, 1899-1980, Brit., film director. The master of crime and suspense films was born in London on Aug. 13, 1899. Alfred Hitchcock's father, a severe disciplinarian, took his little son, at about age six, to the local police station and had him locked up in a cell. He said nothing to the terrified child and left him alone there for about an hour. When Hitchcock's father returned and the boy was released, the elder Hitchcock told him that now he knew "what to expect" if he ever committed a crime or got into serious trouble. This traumatic experience left an indelible mark on Hitchcock, one which may have caused his lifelong fascination with crime and criminals. He himself was forever after terrified of policemen and jails. When he moved to the U.S. in the late 1930s after establishing himself as the foremost suspense director in England, he refused to drive a car. He later explained to the author that to do so meant to risk being stopped by a policeman and, perhaps, being locked up in a jail cell, a prospect he found horrifying.

Policemen in Hitchcock's films were usually shown as otherworld humans, remote and somewhat sinister, a lurking authority

which could, at any moment, pounce upon the innocent as well as the guilty. The motorcycle policeman in *Psycho* who stops Janet Leigh on the road after she has just embezzled a fortune from her boss, looms large and menacing, wearing dark glasses to shield his identity which is all uniform, all authority. The Scotland Yard inspector in *Dial "M" for Murder* is cagey and apparently unsympathetic to the female victim. The police in *North By Northwest* are stupid and uncaring, doggedly tracking the hero like bloodhounds. The police detective in *Rear Window* is a friend of the hero but sneers at his fears and murder theories; he is patronizing, indifferent to real danger. In *The Wrong Man* the police are coldly oppressive as they go about collecting information that will convict an innocent man. The police in *Saboteur* always seem to side, and ruthlessly so, with the villains as they blindly pursue another innocent man. Only in *Notorious* and *Shadow of a Doubt* do detectives or federal agents appear sympathetic and only because they are tied to the love interest of the film which has nothing to do with their duties, which they unswervingly uphold.

Alfred Hitchcock with author Jay Robert Nash, 1970.

The concept of the police in Alfred Hitchcock's mind and their overall portraits in his films were those designed to almost equal the terror of the real villains, a perception undoubtedly stemming from the time of Hitchcock's childhood lockup. Criminals, on the other hand, were shadowy figures for the most part, all evil and without compassion, those who thrived on murder and other repulsive crimes. Hitchcock himself was fascinated with the criminal mind. He studied the careers of many real-life criminals such as the British Acid-Bath Killer, John George Haigh, and mass murderer Charles Manson and his lunatic "family." The director, day by day, examined the trial in progress of Haigh and took special note of a report where Haigh asked jailers: "What's it like at Broadmoor?" The question regarded the prison for the criminally insane, one where Haigh hoped to be sent as an insane killer, rather than to the gallows which was his eventual destination.

Many of Hitchcock's films were based on real murderers, the first being *The Lodger,* a silent film released in 1927. This film was based upon Jack the Ripper, a mass killer for whom Hitchcock held a lifelong fascination. His favorite film, *Shadow of a Doubt,* is based upon woman-killer Earle Leonard Nelson, with a touch of Henri Desire Landru thrown in. *Rope* is based upon the wealthy thrill-killers Nathan Leopold and Richard Loeb, who murdered Bobby Franks in Chicago in hopes of committing "the perfect crime." The eerie *Psycho* is wholly taken from the life of cannibal-murderer Ed Gein of Wisconsin, and *The Wrong Man* took its entire plot from the real-life story of Emmanuel Balestrero, a bass player in New York's Stork Club who was accused of armed robbery and was almost convicted until his real-life doppelganger was found.

Though he never dealt directly with criminals, Hitchcock had personal problems with some of his more offbeat actors while making his films. Peter Lorre proved to be the most bizarre. Lorre, at the time he made *Secret Agent* with Hitchcock, was addicted to morphine and was often in a stupor, or he would hide inside the soundstage and Hitchcock would have to send people to find him. On one occasion, Hitchcock was about to shoot a scene which called for Lorre's appearance, but there was no Lorre to be found, although it was known the strange little actor was *somewhere* inside the soundstage. Finally, Hitchcock and his crew heard Lorre cackling high above them. Looking up, they saw Lorre clinging to a crossbeam above them, his head rolling about. Hitchcock calmly said to him: "Come down now, Mr. Lorre. It's your scene. That's a good fellow." Lorre eased himself down to the set and then proceeded to give a masterful performance which later he could not recall.

Hitchcock himself had many fears, and it was rightfully assumed by his friends and biographers that he frightened himself with his own filmic pursuits. He was not the wry and aloof filmic connoisseur of crime the world thought him to be. He made sure each night that the doors and windows of his home were locked and all precautions against dark intruders had been taken before retiring to his nightmares. The author at one time asked Hitchcock if he ever thought, *after* he had locked himself and family in for the night, that he may have locked himself *in with* a criminal. "That's too horrifying to contemplate," he responded.

In 1970, the author asked Hitchcock, "If you were to be murdered, which of the diabolic plans shown in any of your movies would you select?"

"To be murdered?" he gasped. Then, through squinting eyes that reflected a devilish warming to the subject, Alfred Hitchcock replied: "I think a nice overdose of arsenic would be as good as any, providing it wasn't too painful. You know, if you had a gun pointed at you, you would be inclined to say, 'Be careful, that thing might go off.' And it does! Always reminded me of the man being led to the gallows. He marches up the steps, walks over to the trap door, and jumps up and down on it. Then he turns to the hangman and says: 'I say, is this thing safe?'"

REF.: Armes, *A Critical History of the British Cinema*; Balcon, *Michael Balcon Presents*; Bankhead, *Tallulah: My Autobiography*; Bergman, *Ingrid Bergman: My Story*; Betts, *The Film Business*; Bogdanovich, *The Cinema of Alfred Hitchcock*; Brian, *Tallulah, Darling*; CBA; Eisner, *The Haunted Screen*; Feathering, *The Five Lives of Ben Hecht*; Gardiner and Walker, *Raymond Chandler Speaking*; Hecht, *A Child of the Century*; Higham, *Marlene: The Life of Marlene Dietrich*; Highsmith, *Strangers on a Train*; Korda, *Charmed Lives*; LaValley, *Focus on Hitchcock*; MacShane, *The Life of Raymond Chandler*; Nash, *The Innovators*; _____, *The Motion Picture Guide*; Rank, *The Double*; Samuels, *Encountering Directors*; Spoto, *The Dark Side of Genius*; Taylor, *Hitch: The Life and Times of Alfred Hitchcock*; Truffault, *Hitchcock*; Viertel, *The Kindness of Strangers*; (FILM, Directed by Hitchcock), *Downhill*, 1927 (Brit., Silent); *Easy Virtue*, 1927 (Brit., Silent); *The Lodger*, 1927 (Brit., Silent); *The Mountain Eagle*, 1927 (Brit., Silent); *The Pleasure Garden*, 1927 (Brit., Silent); *The Ring*, 1927 (Brit., Silent); *Champagne*, 1928 (Brit., Silent); *The Farmer's Wife*, 1928 (Brit., Silent); *The Manxman*, 1928 (Brit., Silent); *Blackmail*, 1929 (Brit.); *Juno and the Paycock*, 1930 (Brit.); *Murder!*, 1930 (Brit.); *Number Seventeen*, 1931 (Brit.); *The Skin Game*, 1931 (Brit.); *Rich and Strange*, 1932 (Brit.); *Waltzes from Vienna*, 1933 (Brit.); *The Man Who Knew Too Much*, 1934 (Brit.); *The 39 Steps*, 1935 (Brit.); *Sabotage*, 1936 (Brit.); *Secret Agent*, 1936 (Brit.); *The Lady Vanishes*, 1938 (Brit.); *Young and Innocent*, 1938 (Brit.); *Jamaica Inn*, 1939 (Brit.); *Foreign Correspondent*, 1940; *Rebecca*, 1940; *Mr. and Mrs. Smith*, 1941; *Suspicion*, 1941; *Saboteur*, 1942; *Shadow of a Doubt*, 1943; *Lifeboat*, 1944; *Spellbound*, 1945; *Notorious*, 1946; *The Paradine Case*, 1947; *Rope*, 1948; *Under Capricorn*, 1949; *Stage Fright*, 1950; *Strangers on a Train*, 1951; *I Confess*, 1953; *Dial "M" for Murder*, 1954; *Rear Window*, 1954; *To Catch a Thief*, 1955; *The Trouble with Harry*, 1955; *The Man Who Knew Too Much*, 1956; *The Wrong Man*, 1956; *Vertigo*, 1958; *North by Northwest*, 1959; *Psycho*, 1960; *The Birds*, 1963; *Marnie*, 1964; *Torn Curtain*, 1966; *Topaz*, 1969; *Frenzy* 1972; *Family Plot*, 1976.

Hitchcock, Alpheus, d.1807, U.S., mur. Alpheus Hitchcock, a native of Sullivan, N.Y., took a mistress and then decided to murder his wife, Belinda, slipping arsenic into her coffee. Examining doctors found traces of arsenic and Hitchcock was confronted with murder charges. He casually admitted his guilt, saying: "I thought I could live more agreeably with some other woman than my wife." He was tried on July 3, 1807, convicted, and sent to the gallows a month later.
REF.: *CBA*; Richards, *The Trial of Alpheus Hitchcock*.

Hitchcock, Ethan Allen, 1835-1909, U.S., law enfor. off. Served as U.S. secretary of interior from 1898-1907. Discovering fraud in public land administration, he subsequently ousted or prosecuted many dishonest officials. REF.: *CBA*.

Hitchcock, Samuel, 1755-1813, U.S., jur. Served as attorney general of Vermont from 1790-93, and as a representative in the Vermont state legislature between 1789-93. He was nominated to the district court of Vermont by President George Washington in 1793. REF.: *CBA*.

Hite, Robert Woodson (AKA: **Wood**), 1848-81, U.S., west. outl. Wood Hite was a Kentucky cousin of Jesse James. After serving in the Confederate Army during the Civil War, Hite joined his illustrious relative's gang in 1870. After the gang's disastrous 1876 holdup attempt in Northfield, Minn., and a few train robberies in Kentucky, he returned to his father's home disenchanted. In 1881, Hite shot a black man to death after a brief argument. However, he bribed a jail guard with a $100 bill and escaped to the Missouri home of Bob Ford. While there, he began feuding with Dick Liddell, another fugitive, over the affections of Martha Bolton, Ford's widowed sister. The feud culminated one day in January 1882 when the two exchanged gunshots one morning. Hite was wounded in the right arm and Liddell was hit in the leg. While Hite writhed on the floor, Ford murdered him in cold blood. See: **James, Jesse**.

REF.: Breihan, *The Complete and Authentic Life of Jesse James*; _____, *The Day Jesse James was Killed*; CBA; Crittenden, *The Crittenden Memoirs*; Dacus, *Life and Adventures of Frank and Jesse James*; Donald, *Outlaws of the Border*; Drago, *Outlaws on Horseback*; Hoole, *The James Boys Rode South*; Horan, *Desperate Men*; _____ and Sann, *Pictorial History of the Wild West*; Love, *The Rise and Fall of Jesse James*; Miller, *The Trial of Frank James*; Settle, *Jesse James was His Name*; Wellman, *A Dynasty of Western Outlaws*.

Hitler, Adolf, 1889-1945, Ger., mur.-war crimes-attempt. assass. The most sinister person to emerge in the twentieth century was the German dictator Adolf Hitler, a shrewd and cunning politician. A raving maniac with a mercurial personality, Hitler's insatiable bloodlust and love of conquest caused the destruction of countries and the deaths of twenty-five million people. Like many tyrants before him, Hitler began as a little man with a loud voice and a great lie. His cause was a cancer of the mind, one evil cell feeding upon the next, a cause of race hatred, xenophobia, and a utterly false concept of German superiority that led a whole nation into self-destruction and international disgrace. Ironically, this arrogant racist, was not a German, but an Austrian, born on Apr. 20, 1889, in a small inn, Gasthof zum Pommer in Braunau am Inn, a small town near the Bavarian border.

His father, Alois Hitler, born illegitimately in 1837, was a minor Austrian customs official. After two marriages, Alois Hitler married Klara Poelzl, a woman twenty-three years his junior, on Jan. 7, 1885. Hitler was the third child of five produced in this marriage. Two brothers and a sister died in infancy and a sister, Paula, was born in 1894; she lived to see her brother rule Europe and die in shame. As a child, Hitler attended five different grade schools; his restless father kept moving from one village to the next, buying and selling small businesses and farms. During this period, Hitler, who had been raised a Catholic, attended a school operated by Benedictine friars at Lambach, where he sang in the choir and thought of becoming a priest.

The Hitler family finally settled in Leonding, near Linz, where Adolf's father paid for him to attend high school so that he too could become a civil servant. Hitler rebelled at the thought of sitting at a desk for the rest of his life, sorting and filing papers.

He told his father repeatedly that he had no intention of becoming a civil servant and shocked him when he stated that he would become an artist. The severe and dominating Alois Hitler would have none of that. Painters were loafers and no-accounts. He often tore up his son's primitive drawings and destroyed his paints and brushes whenever he found them hidden about the house.

Hitler rebelled against his father and against his teachers. His grades were so poor that he had to transfer to a state school at Steyr where he did little better, and left before graduating. He blamed the teachers and the academy for his personal failure, later branding them "mad" unthinking elitists who suppressed any expression of individuality. Hitler held the academy and intellectuals in contempt, calling them "congenital idiots" and "tyrants" who had "no sympathy with youth," an attitude he held until the day of his death. One of these "congenital idiots," according to Hitler's evaluation, Professor Eduard Huemer, later testified on Hitler's behalf when he was tried for leading his abortive Munich Beer Hall Putsch in 1923. Professor Huemer recalled that "Hitler was certainly gifted, although only for particular subjects, but he lacked self-control and, to say the least, he was considered argumentative, autocratic, opinionated and bad-tempered, and unable to submit to school discipline. Nor was he industrious; otherwise he would have achieved much better results, gifted as he was."

On Jan. 3, 1903, Hitler's father died suddenly of a lung hemorrhage. Following his father's death, Adolf was doted upon by his mother and barely managed to pass his course at school. As he approached sixteen, Hitler developed a lung illness which caused him to drop out of school. He was so overjoyed at the prospect of escaping the discipline of school that he got drunk and was found near Steyr by a passing milkmaid who picked him up and helped him home. He was so ill from this bout with liquor that he vowed never again to drink spirits. He kept his word, and he also became a devout vegetarian and abstained from tobacco. For the next three years, despite the fact that his widowed mother had to struggle to make a living, Hitler refused to work, claiming illness. He loafed about, tolerated by a loving and indulgent mother, and spent most of his days wandering through the countryside, reading romance novels. He attended the opera as much as he could, especially when the works of Richard Wagner, his idol, were being performed. The brooding, bombastic Wagnerian music held a deep attraction for Hitler and he befriended the Wagner family long after he became supreme ruler of Germany.

Between the ages of sixteen and nineteen, Hitler traveled about Austria and Bavaria acting as if he were an anointed prophet. He harangued total strangers in the street if the mood came on him, spewing forth the most sophomoric philosophies, mostly espousing his racial hatreds and promoting the idea of a strong military establishment to keep law and order. Much of the racial anger Hitler felt had to do with his own peasant heritage. He later tried to disguise that heritage, claiming that his father was a military man, an esteemed member of the Austrian border police when, in truth, he was simply a customs officer.

Thin, pale, and sickly, Hitler wandered through the streets of Linz like a ghost. He fell in love with a blonde-haired beauty named Stephanie but never approached her, preferring to love her from afar and, no doubt, not wishing to risk rejection. There was nothing carefree in this gaunt youth. He was silent even when with his few friends like August Kubizik. When anyone disagreed with him, Hitler flew into an hysterical tantrum, screaming to the point of near collapse.

It was also during this period that Hitler attempted to enter the Vienna Academy of Fine Arts. He visited the city at the age of seventeen and was enthralled by this cosmopolitan capital still alive in the genteel traditions of the old and crumbling Habsburg empire. In October 1907, Hitler took the entrance examination to the Academy but the 18-year-old would-be painter was rudely shocked when he was told he had no aptitude for art and was rejected. This was one of the most devastating blows Hitler received in his youth and he made Vienna and Austria pay for this rejection with a vengeance three decades later when he humiliated its government and sent his stormtrooping soldiers through Vienna's streets after a trumped-up *Anschluss* which bloodlessly annexed this empire to Germany.

Teachers at the Academy told Hitler that he showed promise at architecture but because he had not finished high school, he could not expect to be accepted in the Vienna School of Architecture. Another blow occurred on Dec. 21, 1908, when Hitler's overworked mother died. He suddenly found himself hounded by relatives who had helped to finance his wandering life and who complained loudly about having nothing to show for it. The young man was not a student, did not work and had no prospects for a promising future. Hitler, emotionally wrecked by his mother's death, drifted into the backwaters of lower-class Vienna society at nineteen and, from 1909 to 1913, he lived a hand-to-mouth existence just above the gutter level. While his clothes went to rags, Hitler wandered about cafes trying to sell sketches he had drawn of Viennese buildings, sterile and unimaginative drawings which never impressed people. There were few purchasers and Hitler found himself each day standing in long queues, waiting to be fed by charity kitchens, a humiliation that he never overcame.

With no vices to support, Hitler just managed to survive. Living all about him were a great number of Jews. During these fateful years Hitler developed his intense hatred for the Jews. He occupied his time by immersing himself in the writings of Georg Ritter von Schoenerer, the leader of Pan Germans, who came from Hitler's own Austrian district near the German border. It was von Schoenerer who advocated unification of Austria and Germany to form a superpower that would eventually control Europe, an obsession of Hitler's that would later lead to WWII.

Vienna, with a population of more than two million at the time, was home to 200,000 Jews. Hitler saw them everywhere, relegating them to the status of foreigners. "Wherever I went," Hitler later wrote, "I began to see Jews, and the more I saw, the more sharply they became distinguished in my eyes from the rest of humanity... Later, I often grew sick to the stomach from the smell of these caftan-wearers." His hatred for Jews went to the marrow of his being: "Was there any form of filth or profligacy, particularly in cultural life, without at least one Jew involved in it? If you cut even cautiously into such an abscess, you found, like a maggot in a rotting body, often dazzled by the sudden light—a kike!" White slavers operated widely in Vienna, and prostitution was rampant. All this, in his warped and twisted views, Hitler blamed on the Jews: "I recognized the Jew as the cold-hearted, shameless and calculating director of this revolting vice traffic in the scum of the big city, a cold shudder ran down my back."

In this way, Hitler began to develop his lifelong habit of blaming the Jews for all the world's vices and miseries. They were the perfect scapegoats in his prosaic mind, a helpless, homeless people. It was also at this time that Hitler discovered and embraced an obscure, crackpot French philosopher, Count Joseph Arthur de Gobineau, author of a four-volume work, *Essai sur l'Inégalité des Races Humaines,* in which he contended that "the racial question dominates all the other problems of history." Gobineau, who had been a French diplomat living in Germany, actually drew up a chart of sorts in which he listed the nationalities and races in the order of their declining importance. Those on the bottom of the list were decidedly "inferior." This became the hub of Hitler's racial theories, along with those stemming from an English philosopher, Houston Stewart Chamberlain, later a mentor of Hitler, who advocated the bigoted ideas of Gobineau and more. It was remained for Hitler to put the theories of these strange racists into his Nazi manifesto, *Mein Kampf* (My Struggle) and later into horrible practice through Heinrich Himmler's dreaded SS and Gestapo.

Hitler lived as a vagrant in Vienna until May 1913, when he learned that he would be drafted into the army, and fled. He went to Germany, the country of his heart and soul, settling in Munich. It was here, while standing in the square in front of the

Adolf Hitler as an infant.

Hitler's mother, Klara Poelzl.

Hitler's father, Alois.

Hitler at sixteen.

Leaders of the Beer Hall Putsch, 1923, Hitler fourth from right, Ludendorff in center.

Corporal Adolf Hitler.

Hitler in a Vienna crowd, inset, as war is announced, 1914.

Adolf Hitler, December 1924, after being released from Landsberg Prison.

Feldherrnhall in Munich, on Aug. 2, 1914, that Hitler wildly cheered the announcement that Germany and Austria-Hungary were at war with the Allies. An amazing photo, found years later by one of Hitler's biographers, shows Hitler standing in the crowd, an ecstatic look on his face at news that would otherwise sadden any normal man. He enlisted in the 16th Bavarian Reserve Infantry Regiment and was one of the first to see action in October 1914, at the first battle of Ypres. It was here that Hitler's regiment was all but wiped out, only 600 out of 3,500 surviving as the British turned back the German drive toward the Channel.

For most men WWI was hell, but Hitler never complained of the filth and privation, incurring the wrath of his fellow soldiers. In Hitler's perception, the war was the fulfillment of Germany's destiny, one which decreed the conquest of Europe. The records indicate that Hitler was a brave soldier, wounded twice. He was hit in the leg on Oct. 7, 1916, at the battle of the Somme and was hospitalized. He returned to his regiment where he was promoted to corporal and participated in the battle of Arras and the third battle of Ypres. On Oct. 13, 1918, Hitler was gassed in the last German offensive of the war. At the time he was a dispatch runner and he later stated: "I stumbled back with burning eyes, taking with me my last report of the war. A few hours later, my eyes had turned into glowing coals; it had grown dark around me."

Twice decorated for bravery, given the Iron Cross first and second class, Hitler's courage on the battlefield is not specified in records. Later, his Nazi biographers claimed he had captured fifteen enemy soldiers single-handed, but there is no evidence to support this. Hitler would later claim great comradeship with his fellow soldiers during WWI, but this certainly was not the case. He was not well-liked, thought of as a monarchist fanatic and a war-lover. When his peers complained about the rigors of war and the "big shots" who had sent them into the trenches, Hitler remained silent. Toward the end of the war, when it was apparent to all that Germany was losing, Hitler burst forth with tirades about how Germany was being betrayed into the hands of the enemy by "invisible foes" such as the Jews and Marxists.

When the Germans sued for peace, Hitler, like many other diehard militarists, reacted by claiming that Germany had been "stabbed in the back" by politicians, not its army and military leaders. This, of course, was not the case, since the German High Command had capitulated. Yet, it was this lie that Hitler and his cronies repeated to the German voters years later—one which a desperate, Depression-torn people came to believe and acted upon by making Adolf Hitler their supreme ruler. When Hitler returned to Munich after the Armistice in November 1918, he found the city in chaos, under the control of a Marxist regime which had defected from the hastily constituted new Weimar Republic. A soviet republic was declared under the direction of Kurt Eisner, a Jewish writer who had overthrown the Bavarian government by simply leading a few hundred socialists and communists to the government buildings and taking over in a bloodless coup. Eisner himself was later assassinated by Count Anton Arco-Valley, a member of the right-wing military cabal. The Weimar Republic quickly put down Eisner's revolution with regular troops. The Reichswehr, the standing army, had been drastically reduced by the terms of the Versailles Treaty, but its generals connived to establish right-wing order by secretly financing tens of thousands of veterans in free corps (Freikorps) units which fought the communists and socialists throughout Germany.

It was a time of upheaval and uncertainty, time when Hitler, overflowing with his radical right-wing views and racial hatreds, was most appealing to those like him. The government in Munich, after the social democrats were thrown out of office, was headed by Gustav von Kahr, who had the backing of the Reichswehr. During this chaotic time, Hitler roamed about Munich, attending many political meetings of the far right, finally adopting a right-wing group calling itself the German Workers party which was headed by Anton Drexler, a locksmith. It was this party's aim to rid Germany of all Marxists and communist trade unions.

Hitler became Drexler's minion, performing all sorts of errands for Drexler who dreamed of establishing a strong country-wide association of workers which would be nationalist in philosophy.

At one of the party meetings, Hitler met Ernst Roehm, an army captain with a distinguished military history. His face, with small piggish eyes, was scarred with the ravages of war and he was a flagrant homosexual, as was the case with most of the early-day storm-troopers he recruited who would form the brown-shirted SA. Yet, Roehm was a war hero and an expert organizer. Hitler immediately recognized Roehm's organizing abilities and befriended him, using him for his own ends as he quickly worked to take over the German Workers party. Another member of this embryonic political group, Dietrich Eckart, became Hitler's mentor, and helped shape him into a political entity. Eckart was an alcoholic playwright and a morphine addict. He had been confined in a lunatic asylum in Vienna during WWI and it was here that he wrote his rabidly racist plays, using the inmates to enact these weird dramas.

Eckart, following WWI, went to Munich and here became a local celebrity, drinking and speaking in beer halls. He joined the German Workers party and, from the moment he heard Hitler speak, realized that he had a certain force which could captivate audiences. Eckart, who was fifty-eight at the time, took Hitler aside and tutored him in the use of the German language, writing his speeches and introducing him to others who shared their common hatred for Jews, foreigners and communists. Eckart introduced Hitler to wealthy people who paid for Hitler's living expenses and contributed to the party. It was through Eckart that Hitler met Rudolf Hess and Alfred Rosenberg, who was to become the so-called "philosopher" of the Nazi party.

Hitler was made propaganda chief of the tiny party in 1920 and immediately organized a huge rally at Munich's enormous beer hall, the Hofbräuhaus, which caused party leaders to label him insane. The event, occurring on Feb. 24, 1920, was a smokescreen where Hitler put up as the main speaker a right-wing homeopathic physician, Dr. Johannes Dingfelder. A huge crowd attended and Dr. Dingfelder's rambling, almost incoherent speech drew no applause whatsoever. Then Hitler, who had not be scheduled to speak, suddenly appeared at the rostrum. He ranted for four hours, exhausting himself and his listeners, outlining twenty-five points of the party. His crude, non-stop hortatory attack, filled with raw emotion but little common sense, captivated the crowd and Hitler became, at that moment, the nominal leader of the party, whose name was changed on Apr. 1, 1920, to the National Socialist German Workers' party, or the Nazi party for short.

The points Hitler made during his first significant public address would make up Hitler's lifelong political and military program. He insisted that all Germans be unified in a greater Germany. He demanded that Jews be denied any political office in Germany and their citizenship be revoked. All Jews who had entered Germany after the outbreak of WWI, Hitler stated, would be banished from Germany. A "sound middle class" was to be supported and maintained. All traitors to Germany were to be executed and these, Hitler implied, would be any and all who had a hand in surrendering Germany into the hands of the Allies at the end of WWI.

The symbol Hitler chose to represent his party and thought was an ancient one, the hakenkreuz, the hooked cross, known as the swastika. This emblem had been used by right-wing groups such as the free corps Ehrhardt Brigade, which had entered Munich to crush Eisner's short-lived communist revolution in Bavaria and Hitler undoubtedly saw the swastika painted on the helmets of these troops. The swastika, later to become the symbol of evil under Hitler's oppressive regime, dated back to the time of Troy and ancient China, its origins and original meaning unknown. It was nevertheless a distinctive symbol and Hitler adopted it for exclusive use by the Nazi party. He ordered flags, armbands, stationery, posters, circulars, flyers, and medals to be adorned with the swastika. He created a flag of red, white and black, the colors of the old monarchist flag, with the swastika in the middle of a white circle.

To the flag, Hitler added ornamentation, which he took from the banners of the Roman legions, employing an eagle squatting atop a metal swastika affixed to a metal rectangle which bore the initials NSDAP. There was almost a mystical aspect to the symbol of the swastika and Hitler employed it as such, saying that it represented all the ancient codes of historic Germany. The dispossessed, the impoverished, the criminal, the social outcasts of the day, seized upon this ambiguous symbol and crackpot political party to represent their own distorted views of politics and humanity. The ranks of the Nazi party began to swell. Political fanatics and social malcontents such as Paul Joseph Goebbels, Heinrich Himmler, and Hermann Goering joined the party later, becoming obedient henchmen to Hitler. They operated effectively as propaganda experts and organizational leaders who galvanized the warrior Germans under Hitler's banner.

By 1923, the Nazis in Bavaria had grown to great strength, their numbers were swelled by thousands of ex-soldiers and they won the support of middle-class shopkeepers and landowners who felt threatened by the many left-wing parties and groups that attempted to seize control of the government. Unrest was universal and the Germany economy was almost at a standstill. The French occupied the vast industrial district of Germany, the Ruhr, cutting off any real growth in heavy industry. Moreover, inflation was rampant. Each day the mark devalued to the point where hundreds of thousands of marks would buy only a loaf of bread.

The poorly organized, shakily supported Weimar Republic could do little except print more worthless money. It was in this atmosphere of despair and desperation that Hitler rose to immense power. Since he represented the political aims of the army, he was secretly funded by the Reichswehr. Moreover, high ranking militarists such as General Erich von Ludendorff openly sided with Hitler in his drive to suppress the spread of socialism and communism.

The province of Bavaria was at the center of the turmoil. Gustav von Kahr refused to carry out orders from Berlin and threatened to form an independent Bavarian state. He also refused to suppress Hitler's newspaper, *Voelkischer Beobachter*. He ordered the local military units to swear allegiance only to Bavaria. It appeared as if Bavaria would secede from the Republic. It was at this moment that Adolf Hitler chose to attempt a *putsch,* a takeover of the Bavarian government. His brown-shirted storm troopers, the SA, was made up of thousands of brutal thugs who demanded action and SA leaders advised Hitler to act politically before the storm troopers ran amuck. Then Kahr made Hitler's revolution easier by announcing that he planned to speak on Nov. 8, 1923, at a huge beer hall, the Buergerbräukeller on the southeastern outskirts of Munich, to outline his plans for a new Bavaria. On that night at 8:45 p.m., after Kahr had just finished a long-winded speech to several thousand beer-drinking supporters, scores of storm troopers surrounded the beer hall and Hitler marched inside, a military retinue surrounding him.

Outside the beer hall, storm troopers set up machine gun posts. Inside the hall, Hitler went to the front of the hall and leaped upon a table. He fired a pistol into the air to get immediate attention. Kahr stood motionless at the dais while Hitler then made his way toward the podium. A major thought to stop him but backed away when Hitler pointed the pistol at him. Kahr, who appeared "pale and confused" at this point, stepped back nervously from the podium and Hitler stepped forward, saying: "The National Revolution has begun! This building is occupied by 600 heavily armed men. No one may leave the hall. Unless there is immediate quiet I shall have a machine gun posted in the gallery. The Bavarian and Reich governments have been removed and a provisional national government has been formed. The army and the police are marching on the city under the swastika banner!"

Hitler then ordered Kahr and General Otto von Lossow and Munich police chief, Colonel Hans von Seisser, into a back room to discuss the transference of power, ushering them off the speaker's platform with the point of his pistol and with the help of other armed storm troopers. The crowd grew sullen but Hermann Goering, his corpulent body bursting through his tight fitting brown shirt uniform, a swastika arm band on his sleeve, stomped up to the rostrum and announced in a booming voice: "There is nothing to fear. You've no cause to grumble. You've got your beer!"

Inside a back room, the future dictator of Germany nervously paced the floor and flourished his pistol like any street thug. "No one leaves this room alive without my permission," he snarled. Hitler than told Kahr and the others that they would be well taken care of in his new government, that they would all receive high-ranking posts in the government he was forming with General Ludendorff. The name of this elderly war hero impressed Kahr and the others but they refused to talk to Hitler, remaining silent while he went on with his harangue about his new government. Meanwhile, Ludendorff, who knew nothing of the Nazi movement but was in sympathy with all right-wing organizations, was roused from his home by storm troopers and brought to the beer hall.

Hitler, before Ludendorff's arrival, became melodramatic in the back room, telling Kahr: "I have four shots in my pistol! Three for my collaborators, if they abandon me." He meant, obviously, the three men in the back room with him. "The last bullet for myself! If I am not victorious by tomorrow afternoon, I shall be a dead man!" He then ordered the three men to stay in the back room while he raced back to the podium, addressing the crowd once more. He then boldly lied, stating that Kahr and the others had joined him in establishing a new government. "I propose that the direction of policy be taken over by me!" He then played his trump card: "Ludendorff will take over the leadership of the German National Army. Tomorrow will find either a national government in Germany or us dead!"

Believing that Kahr and the others had, indeed, vowed allegiance to Hitler, the crowd began to cheer. Then Ludendorff, surprised at being taken to this beer hall, appeared and marched to thunderous applause to the podium where Hitler bowed and welcomed him. Ludendorff said only a few words to Hitler, unheard by the crowd and these were words of anger at being used in such a fashion. But he was now compromised and he accepted the accolades of the crowd. Kahr and the others were brought out of the back room and they quickly made short speeches, saying they would be loyal to the new regime. Hitler was then told that storm troopers and regular soldiers were clashing at nearby barracks and he left the beer hall. Ludendorff, who had been in retirement, suddenly took control of things and began addressing the crowd.

Kahr, Lossow, and Seisser then managed to slip out of the beer hall. Only hours later Kahr and the others repudiated their sworn allegiance to the new regime. Kahr issued a proclamation which was posted on walls throughout Munich. It read: "The declarations extorted from myself, General von Lossow and Colonel von Seisser at the point of a revolver are null and void." Kahr then ordered Hitler and his gang arrested but this was easier said then done. Hitler and his men had already taken over key government buildings and storm troopers were everywhere in Munich's streets declaring a new government. Ernst Roehm and several hundred storm troopers had taken over the War Ministry Building. Outside a barbed wire barricade had been thrown up around the building and near the entrance Heinrich Himmler stood with storm troopers. Himmler held the flag of the deposed monarchy. Regular troops and police massed to clear them away. Hitler, desperate, was faced with a bloody revolution, fighting the very forces he hoped to enlist in his cause. Ludendorff, now fully committed to this comic opera coup, told Hitler that they would march together to the center of the city, that no policemen, who were mostly ex-soldiers, or regular army troops would fire on him. These men, Ludendorff was sure, would join him in seizing the government.

The march began in the gardens of the beer hall at 11 a.m. the following morning, Nov. 9, 1923. Hitler and Ludendorff were in the lead, with 3,000 storm troopers following close behind. A detachment of police blocked their way at a nearby bridge, but Goering ran forward and told the police commander that if they were not allowed to pass unmolested, several hostages at the rear of the column would be shot. There were no hostages, but Goering knew how to employ the Big Lie as well as Hitler. The marchers were permitted to cross the bridge. They headed straight for the War Ministry where Roehm's men were surrounded by regular troops poised to attack.

The marchers, to get to the War Ministry, decided to march down a street so narrow it was more like an alley, the Residenzstrasse. At the end of this street, their way was blocked by a large contingent of police, more than 100 men armed with carbines. The police ordered the marchers to halt, but Ludendorff and Hitler kept moving forward. Suddenly a hailstorm of bullets filled the air as firing broke out on each side. Sixteen Nazis were shot and killed and scores more wounded, including Goering, who was hit in the leg. Hitler had thrown himself to the pavement as soon as the firing commenced, as did all the rest of the Nazis. The only man who remained standing, proud and erect, marching forward unscathed, was General Erich Ludendorff. He was permitted to pass through the police ranks, but he went alone, not a single Nazi following him.

The Nazi revolution had been stopped, for the time being. Hitler immediately stood up and was ushered to a waiting car that roared away, taking the Nazi leader to a hideout in the country. The once-brazen revolutionary had left his men dying and bleeding in the street, abandoning them. Police arrested Hitler two days later, charging him with the attempted violent overthrow of the government. Hitler appeared, at first, to be in disgrace. His party was abolished and his followers were on the run. All of the leaders of the putsch had been arrested, including all the top Nazis. Only Rudolf Hess and Hermann Goering managed to escape.

Tried for treason on Feb. 26, 1924, Hitler shrugged off the idea of being condemned. The trial of the conspirators was a wide open forum for Hitler who knew that the world's press would cover the proceedings. He also knew that a lenient sentence awaited him. Franz Guertner, the Bavarian minister of justice, had secretly been an ardent supporter of Hitler's and had contributed substantial funds to the Nazi party. Guertner had already spoken with the presiding judges on Hitler's behalf and he assured the Nazi leader that the court would be his showroom. Hitler, arrogant and brimming with confidence, dominated the proceedings. He interrupted witnesses at will and addressed the court whenever he pleased and without warnings or restrictions from the judges.

He boldly admitted that "we wanted to destroy the state. I alone bear the responsibility. But I am not a criminal because of that. If today I stand here as a revolutionary, it is as a revolutionary against the revolution. There is no such thing as treason against the traitors of 1918." His was the same old litany about Germany being "stabbed in the back" by foreigners and leftists. His was the cause of crushing evil Marxism and holding the government in check against chaos. His was *the* righteous cause and Kahr and the others, he said, were as culpable and responsible for what happened as were the Nazis. Had they not discussed the same aims as the Nazis for months? Had they not endorsed the putsch, only to go back on their word. Hitler mocked and ridiculed Kahr, Lossow, and Seisser when they testified against him, making *them* appear to be the traitors.

For hours Hitler spoke, his voice rising to shrieks and then descending to guttural phrases. He paced about, flailing his arms, grimacing, and staring, all his movements exaggerated and spellbinding. He was either a genius or a madman, many of the world's reporters said when viewing this spectacular performance. Hitler seemed like a man possessed as he finally turned to the judges, whom he knew had been cowed by Minister of Justice Guertner, and from whom he expected a minimum sentence.

Armed with this secret, the shrewd Hitler spat defiance at them for the sake of establishing an heroic public image. Thundered the Nazi: "For it is not you, gentlemen, who pass judgment on us. That judgment is spoken by the eternal court of history. You may pronounce us guilty a thousand times over, but the goddess of the eternal court of history will smile and tear to tatters the brief of the state prosecutor and the sentence of this court. For she will acquit us."

Only Ludendorff, however was acquitted. Hitler was given a five-year sentence, instead of the life imprisonment mandatory by law for all convicted of treason. But, of course, he knew this would be his fate and that he certainly would never serve all of this prison time. The time he did serve in Landsberg, the old fortress-prison, was comfortable. He was welcomed and treated as if he were a visiting dignitary. Hitler was given an apartment with sleeping quarters, parlor, and study. His meals were catered and paid for by the Nazi party, whose membership swelled under the influence of Hitler's ostensible martyrdom.

Rudolf Hess turned himself in and received a prison sentence so that he could be near his beloved Fuehrer, becoming Hitler's secretary. It was to Hess that Hitler dictated his book, *Mein Kampf* (My Struggle). Into it he dumped all of his race hatred, describing in detail the horrors of Jewish controlled banks and businesses that had helped wreck the German economy and thus brought about the nation's defeat in WWI. That was part of the Big Lie. He ranted through the pages of *Mein Kampf* about all other European nationalities, putting them on a sliding scale downward from the Aryan race, the German people, which included Germans and Austrians. He sought to establish a powerful, reunified Germany, Hitler claimed in his book, one where a strong army would keep order and an even stronger dictatorship would eliminate communism and all the leftist-liberals that had so long corrupted the morals and mentality of the German people. Adolf Hitler, according to Adolf Hitler, was the only man to be that unconquerable dictator.

After serving less than a year, Hitler was released from Landsberg five days before Christmas, 1924. He immediately began rebuilding the banned Nazi party. It had been secretly recruiting thousands to its swastika banners and had been built up by stalwart Nazis Gregor Strasser, Julius Streicher, Goebbels, Roehm, Himmler, Goering, Rosenberg, and others. But membership and support fell when Germany began to recover from its terrible depression. Jobs reappeared in 1925 and industry began to be reestablished in the private sector. Hitler busied himself with organizing the Nazis into a tough, cohesive organization that took root, small at first, all over Germany. His was no longer a Bavarian movement but a national German movement.

There were few women in Hitler's life, although he bragged that he was inundated by female suitors. "At this period," he later recalled, "I knew a lot of women. Several of them became attached to me. Why, then, didn't I marry?" The reason he later gave was that he did not want to leave a wife behind if he should be arrested and imprisoned, or shot down while leading his Brownshirt legions to glory. Most of this was nonsense and the one woman Hitler loved wanted nothing to do with him. This was Geli Rebaul, Hitler's attractive niece. Angela Rebaul, Hitler's widowed half-sister from an earlier marriage of his father's, became Hitler's housekeeper in 1928, maintaining the villa Hitler rented in the mountains above Berchtesgaden. Accompanying Angela Rebaul were her two grown daughters, Geli and Friedl. Geli was a blonde beauty of twenty.

In 1929, when the Nazi party began once more to receive considerable funds from the military, the junker class and the industrialists, Hitler rented a luxurious nine-room apartment on the Prinz Regentenstrasse in Munich and installed his niece there. She was his mistress, but he pretended that he was merely taking care of Geli, furthering her career in music. She was a light opera singer and had a fair voice, but Hitler had no intention of advancing the girl's career. He forbade her to appear in public unless with him and she was held a virtual prisoner in the Munich

Hitler, standing, at a Nazi Party meeting, 1925.

A cartoon depicting Hitler selling *Mein Kampf* in beer halls.

Hitler with bulletproof vest beneath his shirt, 1925.

Hitler delivering one of his diatribes, 1928.

Women in Hitler's life, left, Geli Rebaul, right, Eva Braun.

Hitler, standing, flanked by Frick and Strasser, 1932.

apartment. Some of the more prim and proper Nazi leaders insisted that Hitler either marry Geli or send her on her way. He became furious at such suggestions, threatening dire consequences to the next man who dared to mention his niece's name.

Hitler was deeply in love with his niece, but Geli Rebaul did not return that love. They began to argue, Hitler believing that his niece had had an affair with one of his former bodyguards, Emil Maurice. Geli, it was claimed, was jealous of Hitler because he fawned over other women. She threatened to leave him and Hitler became furious. Geli insisted that she go to Vienna where she would continue her voice studies, but Hitler absolutely refused to allow her to go. For weeks the couple battled over this matter. On Sept. 17, 1931, Hitler left to attend party meetings in Hamburg. As he reached the street, Geli shouted from a window to him: "Then you won't let me go to Vienna?"

"No!" Hitler screamed back at her and got into a car that sped away. The next morning, the 23-year-old Geli Rebaul was found dead in her room of Hitler's apartment. A coroner labeled her death suicide, but there persisted a strong rumor that she had been killed by Himmler, either on Hitler's orders or without them and for the good of the Nazi party since the woman had caused Hitler emotional strife and put him in a confused state of mind.

According to a pathologist's report, Geli Rebaul was killed by a bullet that entered her left shoulder and entered the heart, hardly an angle that would be conducive to a self-inflicted wound. Moreover, nothing in Geli Rebaul's conduct on the morning of her death indicated dejection or the kind of deep depression that might have put her into the mood to commit suicide. In fact, she told neighbors only a few hours before her body was found that she planned to visit her mother in Hitler's mountaintop retreat. She began to write a letter to a friend, one that was never finished. Following Geli's death, it was her mother who told a friend that she believed Heinrich Himmler had taken it upon himself to murder the girl, but this was never substantiated. There were ugly rumors about Hitler's inability to make love, driving Geli Rebaul to her death but this, too, was never supported.

Hitler was devastated by Geli Rebaul's death, or he appeared to be, mourning her passing for weeks. Gregor Strasser said he stayed with Hitler for several days following Geli's death for fear that Hitler would take his own life. In early 1932, Hitler took up with Eva Braun, the mistress who was to stay with him until the moment of his death, joining him in suicide in 1945 in the Berlin bunker. Born in Munich on Feb. 7, 1912, Eva Braun was a plumpish blonde with little education. She worked as a secretary for Hitler's official photographer, Heinrich Hoffmann and Hitler met her in 1929 in Hoffmann's studio, apparently never to forget her. Unlike Geli Rebaul, Eva Braun was no headstrong young woman with personal ambitions. She worshipped Hitler and became his servile woman. He treated her cruelly over the years and Braun filled many diaries complaining about how he ignored her or mistreated her. Yet she remained loyal to Hitler.

By 1932, Hitler and the Nazi party were a power to be reckoned with in Germany. Within three years, as a great depression swept the world, Germany was once again in desperate economic straits. Thousands were homeless and tens of thousands were unemployed. The ranks of the Brown shirts were once again swelled by malcontents and unemployed soldiers. Hitler's star rose once more and through the misery of the German people, desperate for a strong leader, his party scored a large victory at the polls in 1933. The aging General Paul von Hindenburg Germany's military leader during WWI, headed a badly managed government that tottered on the brink of disaster. Hitler, backed by the army and all of Germany's wealthy industrialists, now had huge funds at his disposal. Hitler played his usual game. Since the Nazi delegates to the Reichstag, Germany's parliament, did not have control, Hitler sought through his usual devious means to wrest power from the ailing Hindenburg.

He called the general's son, Oskar von Hindenburg and Otto von Meissner, secretary of state, to the Berlin home of Nazi politician Joachim von Ribbentrop, a one-time champagne salesman and later Hitler's crafty minister of foreign affairs. Here Hitler threatened both Hindenburg and Meissner that if he was not named chancellor of Germany, terrible fates would befall both. When these threats did not work, Hitler tried appeasement and then generously offered to reward both men if they arranged his appointment. Oskar von Hindenburg then agreed to sell out his country. He would persuade his father to name a new government under Hitler as chancellor. On Jan. 30, 1933, the Hitler cabinet was formed and tens of thousands of Nazi storm troopers paraded through the streets of Germany by torchlight to celebrate. A dark age then descended upon Germany.

Hitler consolidated his power with the vast resources of the government. He decreed all Communists banned and his Brownshirt thugs broke up the meetings of Social Democrats and other opposing political parties. On the night of Feb. 27, 1933, the Reichstag suddenly burst into flames. Goering announced that this had been the work of the Communists, and to his good luck, a half-wit Dutch Communist, Marinus van der Lubbe, was found wandering through the gutted ruins of the building with incendiary materials. Goering's own storm troopers had set the fire but the Nazis now had a convenient Communist scapegoat to prove that the Communists had set the Reichstag ablaze. Van der Lubbe was quickly tried and condemned and the Communists were declared enemies of the state. They were hunted down like wild animals and imprisoned or killed.

With the general elections approaching on March 5, 1933, Propaganda Minister Paul Joseph Goebbels used the radio and the national press to overwhelm the German public with Nazi propaganda, but voters still refused to give the Nazis the majority. Hitler's party won only 44 percent of the electoral vote and still did not control the Reichstag. The Social Democrats were simply shouted down in parliament meetings. Moreover, Hitler decreed that no party except the Nazi party was legal in Germany. He outlawed all political opposition. On Mar. 23, under the bogus threat of a revolution from the left by Communists, Hitler ordered the Reichstag to turn over to him all constitutional powers to save Germany from destruction. He thus became dictator over 33 million people.

When President Hindenburg died on Aug. 4, 1934, the last hope for a free Germany disappeared. Three hours after Hindenburg's death, Hitler's minions in the Reichstag announced that the post of president had been abolished and that Hitler was now Reich chancellor and fuehrer, dictator for life. The Nazi victory, won by deceit, fraud, and murder, was now complete. The nightmare in Germany began. Brownshirts burned millions of books written by liberal intellectuals. Tens of thousands of intellectuals were rounded up and thrown into Himmler's newly created concentration camps. All opposing politicians joined them. The strongest force at this time that could have eliminated Hitler, the Reichswehr, did nothing. The regular army had backed Hitler for a decade, secretly supplying him, as did the industrialists, with enormous amounts of money, believing that once this "Bohemian Corporal" was in office, he would become their pawn.

Ernst Roehm and his massive brown-shirted storm troopers, however, formed Hitler's private army, tens of thousands of armed men who went about the streets as common street thugs, terrorizing anyone who disagreed with their ruthless policies. They painted the Star of David on shops owned by Jews and stood outside these stores screaming at anyone who dared to enter. They stopped Jews in the street and made them kneel and wash the cobblestones. If they caught any German women fraternizing with Jews they hung signs from their necks stating "I am a swine" or "I have tainted my German blood by sleeping with Jewish pigs." Catholics and other religious organizations were singled out for persecution. Churches were burned, and priests and clergymen were attacked and beaten senseless in front of their parishioners. Their sinister presence was everywhere. The German Army took alarm at the power of the SA and the high command met with Hitler, telling him that he would have their full cooperation in the future if he eliminated this huge paramilitary force. This would mean the execution of Ernst Roehm and his thugs, the very men who had enforced Hitler's edicts for a decade, who had bullied Hitler year by year into power. The fuehrer did not hesitate. He ordered the SA purged. He, Goering, Goebbels, Himmler, and others prepared death lists in preparation for what later became known as the Night of the Long Knives, June 30, 1934. Hitler flew to a retreat at Wiessee, a lakeside resort near Munich. Roehm and the Brown Shirts were ordered to "go on leave" by Hitler and Roehm undoubtedly expected something. Before he departed for a "convention" of top-ranking SA members, he issued a statement that was nothing more than a veiled threat at the high command of the regular army, stating that when the SA was reinstated by his beloved Hitler, the enemies of the SA "would receive their answer."

Hitler, accompanied by a heavily armed escort of Himmler's SS, stormed into the inn where Roehm and other SA leaders were sleeping. Hitler was appalled at seeing most of these leaders sleeping with other men, the leadership of the SA being mostly homosexual. He called these loyal Nazis "repugnant beasts" and ordered them shot. Roehm was taken to a nearby prison and given a pistol, told that he should take his own life. Shocked and puzzled, Roehm asked to see Hitler, questioning why he was being eliminated. This was denied and when Roehm failed to take his own life, two SS men entered his cell and shot him to death. Hundreds of SA leaders across the country were rounded up and shot down by machine guns without trial. Roehm's top deputy in Berlin, Karl Ernst, was about to go on his honeymoon and could not believe that he was being executed, right up to the time he was placed in front of a firing squad. He died giving the Nazi salute and shouting "Heil Hitler!"

The dictator used this night of mass murder to also eliminate all his old enemies. General Kurt von Schleicher, who had been Germany's last chancellor before Hitler and had strenuously opposed Hitler's cabinet, also died that night. He opened the door of his villa outside of Berlin and was shot to death by SS men. His wife of only eighteen months ran forward and she too was shot down and killed. Gregor Strasser, one of the leading members of the early Nazi party who had fallen out with Hitler, was also shot and killed that night. Catholic Action leader Erich Klausener was shot to death in his office and his staff shipped to a concentration camp. Gustav von Kahr, who had betrayed Hitler during the Munich Beer Hall Putsch, was taken to a forest near Dachau by Nazi thugs and hacked to death with pickaxes.

Father Bernhard Stempfle, a renegade Catholic priest who had joined Hitler early and helped edit *Mein Kampf,* was taken to a forest near Harlaching in Bavaria. Nazi goons broke his neck and then fired three bullets into his heart. Stemplfe's offense to Hitler had been his wagging tongue. It was Stempfle who, it was reported, had told intimates that Geli Rebaul had taken her life because of Hitler's sexual inadequacies. The slaughter was seemingly indiscriminate. Willi Schmid, a music critic for a Munich newspaper, was dragged from his home and murdered, his body returned to his family four days later in a sealed coffin. His was a case of mistaken identity. Himmler's SS assassins had mistaken Schmid for Willi Schmidt, an SA leader who had been marked for extermination.

Hitler announced some days later that seventy-seven "enemies of the state" who had been planning an overthrow of the government had been executed. Another lie. More than 1,000 people, mostly old enemies of Hitler's had been murdered. The SA was disbanded and Hitler now received the wholehearted endorsement of the regular army, although its top commander, General Werner von Blomberg, head of the Wehrmacht, the German High Command, had given Hitler little more than lip service since his takeover of the government. As Hitler removed the old guard politicians from office and replaced them with servile, obedient Nazis, he also planned to unseat the aristocratic members of the Wehrmacht, replacing these old guard commanders with his own slavish yes-men, such as generals Wilhelm Keitel and Alfred Jodl.

Blomberg's downfall, and that of the Wehrmacht's was centered upon an attractive blonde, Erna Gruhn. This statuesque, bosomy woman entered the Wehrmacht headquarters to become Blomberg's secretary and he soon became enamored of her. It was later rumored that Gruhn was planted in Blomberg's office to develop the subsequent scandal that brought Blomberg to disgrace and undermined the authority of the Wehrmacht over Hitler. The widowed Blomberg fell so deeply in love with Erna Gruhn that he thought to marry her. He first went to Hermann Goering to seek his advice and Goering reportedly advised him to go ahead, after having checked the woman's background and approving of her. Erna Gruhn was a commoner and Blomberg a member of the German aristocracy. The general believed that Hitler might not approve of a wedding between the head of the general staff and a woman with an obscure background. Hitler, however, did approve of the marriage.

A short time after the couple wed, Hitler's Gestapo suddenly unearthed Erna Gruhn's shocking background. She had grown up in a Berlin brothel run by her mother. She had been arrested many times as a common prostitute and had been convicted of posing for pornographic photographs and appearing in pornographic movies. The resulting scandal caused Hitler to demand Blomberg's resignation. The aristocratic officer resigned after Hitler promised that when the storm blew over he would restore Blomberg to his position. This never happened. Blomberg was ignored thereafter and his services were rejected at the outbreak of WWII. He remained with his wife, living in Wiessee until the end of the war, dying in a Nuremberg prison cell in 1946. Next Hitler managed to oust Colone General Freiherr Werner von Fritsch, who took Blomberg's place. After that, the dictator removed one aristocratic general after another until his own generals, who blindly followed his edicts, were in charge of the Wehrmacht.

At that stage, Hitler's plans for conquest began to take shape. He forged alliances with Benito Mussolini's fascist Italy and Emperor Hirohito's conquest-bent Japan, forming the Axis. Then Hitler began to expand by bullying western leaders. He retook the Saar, the Ruhr, the Rhineland, all the territories Germany had lost under the terms of the Versailles Treaty. Through his Nazi fifth columnists, he arranged for the assassination of Austrian dictator Engelbert Dollfuss in 1934, but he did not manage to annex Austria until 1938. Hitler, in that year, demanded the return of German Sudetenland, which was then part of Czechoslovakia. Inside that country, fifth columnists under the command of Nazi Konrad Henlein lobbied to have portions of the country turned over to Germany.

This crisis brought British prime minister Neville Chamberlain to Munich to confer with Hitler. England had signed a strong mutually protective treaty with Czechoslovakia. Hitler promised that if the Sudetenland were returned to Germany, his demands for more territories would cease. He signed an agreement to this effect and Chamberlain, a flagrant appeaser, returned to England waving this useless document and naively telling the English public that he had brought them "peace in our time." Hitler then proceeded to ignore his agreement and he quickly gobbled up the rest of Czechoslovakia. Next was Poland. Following the signing of a non-aggression pact with Soviet Russia that would safeguard against Russian confrontation in Poland, Hitler ordered his armies to cross the Polish border on Sept. 1, 1939. This act caused the western allies to declare war on Germany. Hitler declared war on France and England and launched his blitzkreig against Poland, bombing its cities ruthlessly from the air and smashing its antiquated armies with lightning panzer divisions.

The war would rage on for six long, terrible years. For the first three years, Hitler's legions were triumphant, swallowing almost all of Europe, except valiant England. Hitler then brought the terror of the SS and the Gestapo to these occupied countries. Jews were tracked down in France, Austria, Belgium, Holland, Denmark, Czechoslovakia, Rumania, Hungary, and Poland, millions of them being sent to scores of concentration camps where they were shot to death, gassed, or killed by medieval medical "experiments." For years, inside Germany, groups of men secretly met to form an underground network that worked against Hitler but not until the closing days of the war, in 1944, with Germany losing on all fronts, was any action taken. At that time, it was decided by a small group of German military and civic leaders that Adolf Hitler had to be assassinated to save Germany from utter ruination.

With the Normandy invasion of the Allies on June 6, 1944, coupled with massive attacks by the Russian armies along the Eastern Front, Hitler's Third Reich began to crumble. Germany could no longer count on its allies. Italy had all but collapsed and its satellite fascist states had been overrun. There had been for years, inside Germany, small groups of conspirators who had been planning to overthrow Hitler's totalitarian regime, but they all proved ineffective. Only the military possessed enough authority and strength to eliminate Hitler and his gang of thugs. But here there was also indecision and endless debate about how to achieve this end. Hitler himself had publicly announced to his generals as early as Aug. 22, 1939, on the eve of the invasion of Poland, that he could be assassinated "by a criminal or an idiot," at any time. On May 2, 1942, he stated that "there can never be absolute security against fanatics and idealists...If some fanatic wishes to shoot me or kill me with a bomb, I am no safer sitting down than standing up." A fanatic himself, Hitler knew well what a dedicated assassin could achieve.

German civilians had been plotting to get rid of Hitler long before the outbreak of WWII, the most important group of these underground activists was led by Dr. Carl Goerdeler, the former mayor of Leipzig, and one-time minister in Hitler's 1937 cabinet, now retired. Joining Goerdeler was religious leader Dietrich Bonhoeffer and Ulrich von Hassell. Goerdeler slowly enlisted the aid of many liberal-thinking civilians, but he knew that to overthrow Hitler, the military must take an active part. He recruited many of the top ranking German generals for this purpose, including generals Ludwig Beck, Henning von Tresckow, Erich Hoepner, Eduard Wagner, Friedrich Olbricht, Heinrich von Stuelpnagel, Field-Marshal Guenther von Kluge, Field-Marshal Erwin von Witzleben, and Germany's greatest hero, Field-Marshal Erwin Eugen Rommel, the celebrated "Desert Fox" who had electrified the world with his brilliant victories in north Africa during the early years of the war. Also included in the conspiracy was a bevy of junior officers, including Major Fabian von Schlabrendorff, Colonel Cäsar von Hofacker, and Count Claus Schenk von Stauffenberg, the most ardent of the group and the most daring.

The generals plotted incessantly but seemed to get nowhere. Not until Rommel became an active conspirator did any real plans begin to formulate. Rommel had seen Hitler slowly turn into an irrational and hysterical creature, wholly irresponsible in his mad direction of the war, moving imaginary armies about on maps, ordering his generals into suicide attacks and squandering tens of thousands of soldiers on capricious tactics. When Hitler failed to listen to Rommel's warning that Germany was facing utter annihilation at the hands of the Allies, and that a truce should be sought, he threw his lot in with the conspirators, informing an aide that "the people in Berlin can count on me."

It was agreed that the best place to assassinate the elusive Hitler—he changed his daily schedules without notice so his whereabouts were always uncertain—would be at the Wolf's Lair, his military retreat in Rastenburg, East Prussia, which he regularly visited to direct the war against the Russians. Stauffenberg was selected at the man to do the job, plant a bomb in Hitler's conference building in East Prussia and blow the dictator and his closest aides to pieces. As chief of staff of the Home Army, Stauffenberg had access to Hitler and made frequent reports to him on the status of the civilian soldiers who had been called into army reserves. On July 20, 1944, Stauffenberg arrived in Rastenberg from Berlin to attend a staff conference where Hitler would be present. The dedicated colonel, who had lost an arm and the sight in one eye during the war, carried a briefcase in which a time bomb was carefully concealed.

Since it was a hot day, the conference was held above ground and not in the underground bunker which was the usual meeting place. This was one of the those accidental events that conspired to save Hitler's life. Had the bomb exploded underground, Hitler and his retinue would all certainly have been killed. The building in which the conference was held was a squat, one-story structure. The windows were opened to let in fresh air. Hitler and his officers gathered about a large table supported by solid wooden blocks. Stauffenberg made his brief report to Hitler, placing the briefcase at Hitler's feet, next to one of the large wooden blocks. Stauffenberg then excused himself and stepped outside the conference building, moving away some distance to await the explosion. Meanwhile, in another quirk of fate, Hitler moved around the large conference table to examine war maps of the Eastern front. As he did so, the bomb went off. It was 12:42 p.m. A terrific explosion tore through the one-room building, blowing out windows and belching flame and smoke. Debris and most of the roof shot skyward. Bodies were hurled like rag dolls through the windows and doors. Stauffenberg stood about 200 yards away with General Erich Fellgeibel, one of those involved in the plot and head of communications for the Rastenberg retreat. Stauffenberg believed that no one could have survived the blast and told Fellgeibel to wire to the other conspirators in Berlin that Hitler was dead.

This was the signal to General Beck and others to occupy all the key government buildings in Berlin, especially the national radio station. Meanwhile, Stauffenberg went directly to the airport and flew back to Berlin. Inside the scorched and blown out building, several bodies were strewn about, a stenographer named Berger had been blown through a window and Colonel Heinz Brandt had been blown through the roof. General Rudolf Schmundt, Hitler's adjutant, was dying of wounds as was General F. Kortner. Generals Alfred Jodl, Karl Bodenschatz, and Adolf Heusinger received a severe wounds. Miraculously, Hitler survived. Only minutes after Stauffenberg left to report him dead, the Fuhrer emerged from the building, staggering over debris and bodies. His trousers were torn and his legs had been burned. He clutched his right arm which was bruised and momentarily paralyzed; he would let this arm hang slack for the rest of his days, or tuck his hand in his pocket. A falling beam had struck Hitler's back cutting him but breaking no bones.

Both of Hitler's eardrums had been punctured. He was a grim, comic figure as he stepped from the smoking ruins. His hair had been singed and smoke curled up from his hair and clothes. His face was blackened and his eyes rolled in his head. General Wilhelm Keitel, who had also amazingly escaped injury, caught up with Hitler and supported him to a rest area. From later statements, it was determined that had Hitler stayed in his position at the table where Stauffenberg had left the bomb in the briefcase, he certainly would have been killed. But only minutes after Stauffenberg departed, Col. Brandt moved the briefcase to the other side of the heavy wooden table support and Hitler moved down the table away from it to inspect his maps. It was Brandt who took the full impact of the explosion.

Heinrich Himmler, who was in another building at the time, rushed forward with a group of SS men to inspect the building. He took a look at the deep hole in the floor of the ruined building and immediately concluded that someone had planted a bomb beneath the building. He ordered a team of special detectives to fly from Berlin to investigate. Stauffenberg was not yet suspected. While in the air and heading toward Berlin, Stauffenberg expected that the generals there, after having receiving his coded message that Hitler had been killed, would have seized all the important government buildings, arrested Goering, Goebbels and other top Hitler henchmen and declared a new government. Nothing of the kind had occurred.

General Olbricht had taken over the War Ministry building but the radio station was still in the hands of the master propagandist, Goebbels, who was desperately trying to contact Rastenberg.

Hitler as chancellor, with Hindenburg, 1933.

Hitler dining with mistress Eva Braun.

Hitler and Eva Braun at Berchtesgaden.

Left to right, Hitler, Goering, Goebbels, reviewing troops.

A Nazi parade honoring Hitler at Nuremberg.

Benito Mussolini and Adolf Hitler.

Communications had been shut down between the Wolf's Lair and Berlin, thanks to conspirator Fellgeibel. Most of the high-ranking generals involved in the plot vacillated or did so little that they were wholly ineffective. Field Marshal Witzleben arrived at military headquarters to discover that troops loyal to the conspiracy had not been called out and most of the key buildings and posts in Berlin were still controlled by fanatical Nazis devoted to Hitler. He stormed out of Wehrmacht headquarters and went back to his country estate where he was arrested the next day.

It was two hours before the shaken Nazis in Rastenberg began to suspect Stauffenberg as the assassin. A sergeant reported to Himmler that Stauffenberg had hastily departed the Wolf's Lair with an aide, heading toward the airport just before the explosion. Someone then recalled seeing Stauffenberg place his briefcase next to Hitler beneath the table where the bomb went off. Himmler ordered Stauffenberg arrested when he landed in Berlin but the message was delayed because Fellgeibel had shut down the communications center on the excuse that he did not want the world to know that an attempt on Hitler's life had been made. He stalled as long as possible before opening up the line to Berlin.

Meanwhile, Hitler was preoccupied with having to greet his fellow dictator, Benito Mussolini, who was arriving at Rastenberg at 4 p.m. by train on a state visit. The Italian dictator himself had little support left in his native country. He had been imprisoned by his own black-shirted fascists and had only recently been rescued by crack German commandoes under the direction of Otto Skorzeny. Hitler managed to regain his composure and greet Mussolini at the small train station. He then escorted the shocked Italian dictator to the ruins of the conference building, showing him with almost maniacal pride how he had managed to escape death only hours earlier.

The two dictators who had been responsible for the deaths of untold millions, stood in the still smoking ruins of the building and vowed eternal support for each other. Hitler, slightly hysterical, launched into one of his self-aggrandizing tirades as Mussolini stared and listened. Hitler told him: "I was standing here by this table. The bomb went off just in front of my feet...It is obvious that nothing is going to happen to me. Undoubtedly, it is my fate to continue on my way and bring my task to completion...What happened here today is the climax! Having now escaped death...I am now more than ever convinced that the great cause which I serve will be brought through its present perils and that everything can be brought to a good end."

Mussolini nodded, then replied: "Our position is bad, one might almost say desperate, but what has happened here today gives me new courage. After this miracle, it is inconceivable that our cause should meet with misfortune." The two ruthless dictators stood there congratulating each other on being alive and able to pursue their plans for world domination, world destruction, if need be. With that, the two deluded men retired to a comfortable rest house with other ranking Nazis and sat down to tea, a tea party as mad as any occurring in Alice's strange wonderland. Communications were then reestablished with Berlin and it was reported that the assassin had not acted alone, that there was a widespread coup attempt in process in the heart of Berlin. The traumatic reaction to the bombing and the possible putsch going on in Berlin then burst forth from the top Nazis, who began screaming accusations at each other.

Hitler sat in stony silence, and Mussolini's face reddened with embarrassment at the shouts and antics of the top Nazis. Admiral Karl Doenitz, who had just arrived from Berlin after hearing the news of the assassination attempt, stormed after Goering, head of the Luftwaffe, accusing Goering of not doing enough to curb the traitors in the army. Goering shrieked that it was all the fault of the Foreign Office, and he lashed out at Foreign Minister Ribbentrop. The arrogant Ribbentrop accused Goering of mismanaging the air force and not providing enough protection for Germany against the air armadas that were bombing their homeland. Goering lifted his heavy Field-Marshal's baton and held it menacingly over Ribbentrop's head, shrieking: "You dirty

little champagne salesman! Shut your damned mouth! I am still the Foreign Minister," Ribbentrop shot back, "and my name is *von* Ribbentrop!"

Heinrich Himmler reminded everyone present that this attempt against the life of his beloved Fuehrer was not dissimilar to that attempted by Ernst Roehm and his SA ten years earlier. So deluded were these Nazi leaders by their own lies, that they had come to accept as reality a coup on the part of Roehm and his brown shirts when it was Hitler himself who manufactured the Roehm coup in order to purge the SA. Hitler at this moment, who had been sucking on pills fed to him by his toady physician, Dr. Theodor Morell, suddenly jumped out of his seat, causing the startled Mussolini to spill the contents of his tea cup.

Froth dripped from Hitler's quivering lips and his eyes rolled and darted. "What happened to Roehm and his followers is nothing compared to what will happen to the traitors who made the attempt on my life today! I'll put their wives and children into concentration camps and show them no mercy!" As Hitler raved on, SS servants in white jackets went on serving tea to all present, undisturbed by Hitler's shrieks. This was to be expected, this was the Fuehrer's usual conduct. Benito Mussolini sat back, stunned into silence. He later stated to an aide before his own assassination that the scene at Rastenberg was terrifying: "The place was like an asylum and the lunatics were everywhere. They were in charge."

Meanwhile, the plot to kill Hitler and wrest control of the government from the Nazis, Operation Valkyrie, as the conspirators had labelled it, had utterly collapsed. General Olbricht had not ordered his troops out of their barracks to take over key Berlin installations as he had promised. He was waiting for confirmation of Hitler's death. General Friedrich Fromm, head of the Home Guard, managed to get a phone call through to the Wolf's Lair from Berlin. Fromm was a pivotal player in the coup. If he went along with the conspirators, there was a chance that they might succeed. Fromm was surprised to get General Keitel on the line. Keitel assured Fromm that all was "as usual" in Rastenberg.

"I have just received a report that the Fuehrer has been assassinated," Fromm said.

"That's all nonsense," replied Keitel, trying to appear calm. "It is true that there has been an attempt, but fortunately, it has failed. The Fuehrer is alive and only slightly injured. Where, by the way, is your Chief of Staff, Colonel Count Stauffenberg?"

"Stauffenberg has not yet returned to us," replied Fromm. He hung up the phone, now knowing that the coup was a disaster.

At that moment, the elder statesmen among the plotting generals, General Ludwig Beck, arrived at the War Ministry, wearing a plain dark blue suit. He was ready to take over the reigns of government but there was nothing to take over. A few minutes later Stauffenberg, out of breath, arrived at the War Ministry. Olbricht told him and Beck that Fromm had just talked to Keitel at the Wolf's Lair and that Hitler was still alive. It mattered not, Stauffenberg said. They must go ahead with the coup. Beck agreed. In occupied Paris, General Stuelpnagel had made more headway. His troops had locked up more than 1,200 SS and Gestapo members and the coup was well underway.

General Fromm, an expert fence-sitter who had tentatively agreed to cooperate with the plotters, now feared that Hitler was, indeed, alive, and that his interests would best be served by deserting the conspirators. Into his office barged General Olbricht, Colonel Stauffenberg and Colonel Mertz. Stauffenberg tried to persuade Fromm, as chief of the Home Guard, to go ahead with the coup. Fromm cut him off, booming: "Count Stauffenberg, the attempt has failed. You must shoot yourself at once!"

"I refuse," Stauffenberg said coolly.

Fromm then ordered all three men to place themselves under arrest.

Olbricht retorted: "You deceive yourself. It is we who are now going to arrest you."

A scuffle took place in which the fat, red-faced Fromm was subdued and locked up in an office. Stauffenberg then went to his own office while others cut the phone lines in the building. Gestapo agents then arrived and tried to arrest Stauffenberg but he disarmed them and locked them up in a closet. Nazi generals dedicated to Hitler arrived at the War Ministry and when they refused to cooperate with the conspirators, they, too, were locked up. A cordon of troops loyal to the conspirators was thrown around the War Ministry but this was the only building in Berlin that the rebels controlled.

Meanwhile, Paul Joseph Goebbels had been busy. He had surrounded the national broadcasting building with loyal Nazi troops and he constantly aired the news that Hitler had not been killed and would go on the air to confirm this shortly. SS Colonel Otto Skorzeny, the tough commando who had rescued Mussolini, heard of the coup and, about 9 p.m., persuaded the local tank commanders to remain loyal to Hitler. He then rounded up several SS units and loyal Nazi officers slipped into the War Ministry. There they freed Gen. Fromm and placed Hoepner, Olbricht, Beck, Mertz, and Stauffenberg under arrest. Stauffenberg broke away and dashed out into a corridor and down the stairs, bullets flying after him. He was wounded in his one good arm and taken back to the office where Fromm had taken command. The conspirators were quickly rounded up and Fromm was released. He paced in front of them, brandishing a pistol and telling them that they must all commit suicide for the good of the army before Hitler ordered them arrested and brought them to trial and national shame, which would also bring disgrace upon the army. He ordered the conspirators to turn over their weapons.

Elderly General Beck held onto his weapon and said to Fromm: "You wouldn't make that demand of me, your old commanding officer." He held his pistol at his side. "I will draw the consequences from this unhappy situation myself."

"Well keep it pointed at yourself," Fromm told Beck.

"At this moment it is the old days that I recall," Beck said.

"We don't want to hear that stuff now. I ask you to stop talking and do something."

Beck sat down and put the pistol to his head and pulled the trigger but he only succeeded in inflicting a superficial wound to his head. As blood dripped from his temple, he slumped in his chair. "Help the old gentlemen," Fromm told two Nazi officers but Beck asked to keep his weapon, saying he wished to try to commit suicide once more. Fromm nodded agreement. He then told Olbricht, Hoepner, Mertz, the wounded Stauffenberg and Lt. Werner von Haeften, who had been part of the conspiracy, that they had all been found guilty of treason in a special court martial and would be shot. Those that wished could take a few minutes to write letters to their wives.

Olbricht, Hoepner, Mertz and Haeften quickly wrote notes. Fromm, of course, had held this split-second courts martial and issued his summary death sentences for his own protection. If these men were dead, they could not implicate him in the conspiracy which he had vaguely considered. Fromm then ordered Olbricht, Stauffenberg, Mertz and Haeften to follow the SS guards to the courtyard. He asked Gen. Hoepner to follow him. The four condemned men were taken to the courtyard and just before dawn, were lined up against a wall. The firing squad nervously rushed the execution since air raid sirens began to wail and Allied planes were expected momentarily; they had begun to bomb Berlin with terrifying regularity. The guards shouted for the prisoners to stand up and face them. Stauffenberg shouted: "Long live our sacred Germany!" The four conspirators were then shot to death.

Fromm, meanwhile, had escorted Gen. Hoepner, and old friend, to another room overlooking the courtyard, saying to him: "Well, Hoepner, this business really hurts me. We used to be good friends and comrades, you know. You've got yourself mixed up in this thing and must take the consequences. Do you want to go the same way as Beck? Otherwise I will have to arrest you now."

"I do not feel so guilty and believe I can justify my actions," Hoepner told Fromm.

"I understand that," Fromm said and then ordered Hoepner taken to the Moabit Prison and placed in a cell to await trial for treason. Fromm then went back to the office where Beck had failed in his second attempt to take his own life. Fromm shook his head disgustedly and said to two officers: "Help the old gentleman." The officer standing next to Gen. Beck refused to execute Beck. An SS sergeant then seized Beck who was bleeding from two head wounds, and dragged him into a small room where he shot and killed the general with a bullet sent into the back of his neck.

In the early hours of July 21, 1944, Goebbels had set up a special radio hookup between Rastenberg and Berlin so that Hitler's voice could be heard throughout Germany, to let everyone know that Hitler was alive. Hitler's guttural voice crackled over the airwaves: "German racial comrades! I do not know how many times an assassination attempt against me has been planned and carried out. If I speak to you today, I do so for two reasons: First, so that you hear my voice and know that I myself am uninjured and well; secondly, so that you may also learn the details about a crime that has not its like in German history.

"A very small clique of ambitious, wicked and stupidly criminal officers forged a plot to eliminate me and along with me virtually the entire staff of the German leadership of the armed forces. The bomb that was planted by Colonel Count von Stauffenberg burst two meters to the right of me. It very seriously injured a number of associates dear to me. One of them has died. I myself am completely uninjured except for some very small scrapes, bruises and burns. I regard it as a confirmation of my assignment from Providence to continue to pursue my life's goal as I have done hitherto...

"The group represented by these usurpers is ridiculously small. It has nothing to do with the German armed forces, and above all, with the German army. It is a very small coterie of criminal elements which is now being mercilessly extirpated...We will settle accounts the way we National Socialists are accustomed to settle them."

Hitler could in no way indicate that the conspiracy had been broad and deep throughout the high command of the army which would have spread dissension throughout an already demoralized German public. Those of the conspirators who were still at large heard Hitler's words and began to either commit suicide or flee. Baron General Henning von Tresckow, Chief of Staff for Army Group Center in Russia, one of Germany's most able and liberal officers, bid farewell to his adjutant, Major Fabian von Schlabrendorff, saying: "Everyone will now turn upon us and cover us with abuse. But my conviction remains unshaken. We have done the right thing. Hitler is not only the archenemy of Germany. He is the archenemy of the world. In a few hours, I shall stand before God, answering for my actions and for my omissions. I think I shall be able to uphold with a clear conscience all that I have done in the fight against Hitler." On the morning of July 21, 1944, Tresckow drove to the center of the fighting on the Russian front, crawled into no-man's-land and pulled the pin on a grenade which blew off his head.

Within hours, thousands of suspects were rounded up, along with their families and thrown into concentration camps or prisons. They were railroaded in a kangaroo court presided over by the rabid Nazi, Judge Roland Freisler. Dozens of officers, guilty and innocent, were strung up with piano wire to pipes in bombed out buildings, questioned, tortured, and then strangled to death. The Nazi vengeance was, as Hitler promised, merciless. The trials commencing on July 20, 1944, before Freisler were travesties of justice—show trials in which the conspirators were ridiculed, mocked and dishonored before receiving automatic death sentences. Field Marshal Witzleben was brought before Friesler in shabby clothes. His false teeth had been taken away and he had trouble keeping his trousers up since he had been denied suspenders or belt. "You dirty old man," Friesler mocked Witzleben, "why do you keep fiddling with your trousers?"

The same shabby treatment was given to General Hoepner, General Hemuth Stieff, and Count Peter Yorck von Wartenburg, a cousin to the heroic Stauffenberg. In the West, the revolt collapsed because Field Marshal Guenther von Kluge believed that since Hitler had not been killed it was futile to continue the revolt. He ordered the SS men who had been arrested in Paris freed and then announced to General Stuelpnagel, his Chief of Staff, and Colonel Hofacker, Stauffenberg's cousin, that "the attempt has failed. Everything is over." Kluge advised Stuelpnagel to flee. He did, driving toward Berlin and then attempting to kill himself. He shot himself in the head but only succeeded in blinding himself. He was later carried on a stretcher before Freisler's court and was abused for several hours before being condemned and then strangled to death. Kluge himself would not escape the wrath of Hitler. He was later replaced as commander in Paris by Field Marshal Walther Model and ordered to report to Berlin. Kluge wrote an apologetic letter to Hitler, then drove leisurely toward Berlin with no intention of ever arriving. Near Metz, on Aug. 18, 1944, he had his aides spread out a picnic for him next to a quiet stream. He ate a catered meal in silence while sitting on the grass and then took poison.

Carl Goerdeler, who was to have been appointed Chancellor of Germany, was in hiding three days before the attempt on Hitler's life. He had learned that the Gestapo had issued a warrant for his arrest. He was not located until Aug. 12. Starved and exhausted, Goerdeler had hidden in the dense forests of East Prussia. He finally went to an inn in Konradswalde and was identified by an old family friend, Helene Schwaerzel, who turned him in. Goerdeler was tried before Freisler, condemned and sentenced to death. His execution, scheduled for Sept. 8, 1944, was delayed by Himmler who intended to use Goerdeler toward the close of the war as an exchange for his own life. Goerdeler nevertheless was hanged on Feb. 2, 1945, after Hitler learned he was still alive.

General Fromm, who thought he had redeemed himself in Hitler's eyes by suppressing the coup, was arrested and tried before Freisler in February 1945, charged with "cowardice." He was shot by a firing squad on Mar. 19, 1945. The list of those tried and executed included scores of leading military officers and civilians. These included Count Friedrich Werner von Schulenburg, Ulrich von Hassell, Count Fritz von Schulenburg, General Fellgeibel and General Fritz Lindemann, Pastor Dietrich Bonhoeffer, Colonel Georg Hansen, and Count Berthold von Stauffenberg, brother of the ringleader of the coup. Even Admiral Wilhelm Carnaris, head of the German Secret Service, was arrested and charged with being involved with the coup attempt, although it is not known if he was an active participant. Carnaris was dragged naked from a concentration camp cell and hanged on Apr. 9, 1945, before a large crowd of laughing SS men.

Colonel Fabian von Schlabrendorff was not arrested until much later and he escaped execution as miraculously as Hitler did the bomb explosion on July 20, 1944. Led into Freisler's People's Court on Feb. 3, 1945, Schlabrendorff was just about to be tried when a sudden air raid occurred and bombs rained down upon the courthouse. Freisler was killed by a beam which crushed his head and most of the documents concerning the conspirators. Schlabrendorff escaped, surviving the war to chronicle the story of the abortive coup to kill Adolf Hitler. The most significant casualty of the bloody reprisals brought about by Hitler was none other than Field Marshal Erwin Rommel, commander of the Normandy area. Though he had committed himself to the coup, Rommel had been severely wounded on July 17, 1944, when his staff car was strafed by Allied war planes as it moved from the Normandy front to Rommel's headquarters. He was thus removed from the core of the coup and without his strong leadership, the top generals became indecisive, assuring failure.

Rommel, after a long hospitalization, was given sick leave and remained at his home in Herrlingen near Ulm. He had suffered two skull fractures, an injury to his left eye and his face was pockmarked with shrapnel wounds. As he recuperated, Rommel watched as the coup leaders were rounded up, tried and executed. General Hans Speidel, his chief of staff, who had been deeply involved in the conspiracy and who had recruited Rommel for the coup, so far had not been suspected. He visited Rommel on Sept. 7, 1944, telling him of the reprisals and grim executions Himmler's SS had meted out to thousands of those suspected of being conspirators. Rommel knew Hitler well by this time, saying to Speidel: "That pathological liar has now gone completely mad. He is venting his sadism on the conspirators of July 20, and this won't be the end of it!"

His words were prophetic when it came to his own fate. Speidel was arrested on Sept. 8, 1944, after visiting Rommel. He was imprisoned and tortured but said nothing. His SS captors were uncertain as to his involvement in the conspiracy. Colonel Hofacker had not involved Speidel in the conspiracy, even though he had been arrested months earlier and had been continually tortured and drugged. However, after being tortured repeatedly one day, Hofacker did blurt out Rommel's participation, quoting the Field Marshal's statement: "Tell the people in Berlin they can count on me." Rommel was a marked man, but Hitler could not, as he had done with other high-ranking officers, drag this greatest of German heroes before Roland Freisler's kangaroo court. The maniacal dictator had already stated that no important military commanders had been involved with the conspiracy. To arrest and conduct a public trial of Rommel would be to admit that the coup attempt went to the heart of the Wehrmacht.

Instead, on Oct. 14, 1944, Hitler had Rommel's home surrounded by a heavily armed contingent of SS troops. At noon of that day, two of Hitler's stooge generals, General Wilhelm Bergdorf and General Ernst Maisel, arrived to meet with Rommel. The three men went into Rommel's study. There Bergdorf told Rommel that they had the confession of Hofacker and others implicating him in the July 20, 1944, plot to kill Hitler and that he had two options. He could face Freisler in open court or he could commit suicide. Bergdorf had brought cyanide along for that purpose and dropped this into Rommel's hand. The SS general also told Rommel candidly that if he chose to stand trial, the security and safety of Rommel's wife and son could not be guaranteed. In short, Hitler would not kill Rommel's family if he chose to commit suicide. His death would be attributed to his wounds, Bergdorf told Rommel.

Rommel nodded and was given time to say goodbye to his wife, Lucie, and his son, Manfred. After spending a short time in a bedroom with his wife, Rommel emerged and took his son Manfred aside, telling him: "I have just had to tell your mother that I shall be dead in a quarter of an hour...Hitler is charging me with high treason. In view of my services in Africa I am to have the chance of dying by poison. The two generals have brought it with them. It's fatal in three seconds. If I accept, none of the usual steps will be taken against my family...I am to be given a state funeral. It's all been prepared to the last detail. In a quarter of an hour you will receive a call from the hospital in Ulm to say that I've had a brain seizure on the way to a conference."

With that, Rommel, courageous to the end, sacrificing his life for the lives of his family, dressed in his full Field Marshal's uniform, embraced his wife and family and drove off with Bergdorf and Maisel. He was dead in fifteen minutes. His death was announced over the radio and through the nation's press, all controlled by Goebbels, as a tragic loss. Germany's great hero was given a state funeral and Field Marshal Gerd von Rundstedt, long critical of Hitler and the ranking German military commander, officiated at Rommel's funeral. His brief statement was, in hindsight, both ironic and sarcastic, aimed at Hitler himself. Said von Rundstedt: "His heart belonged to the Fuehrer."

More than 7,000 persons, according to highest counts, paid with their lives for the attempt on Hitler's life. It was a great toll and a useless one in that Hitler himself would do what the conspirators failed to do, on Apr. 30, 1945. As the Russians closed in on the Fuehrer's bunker near the Reich Chancellory, advance units only a few blocks away, Hitler, cowering in his underground bunker,

The ruins at Wolf's lair, 1944.

Fabian von Schlabrendorff

Henning von Tresckow

Erwin Rommel

Guenther von Kluge

Ulrich von Hassell

Heinrich von Steulpnagel

Claus Schenk von Stauffenberg

Cäsar von Hofacker

Hitler's last photo alive, with boy soldiers, 1945.

Freidrich Olbricht

Ludwig Beck

Hitler in 1939 and, dead, Apr. 30, 1945.

raved at his generals and politicians for betraying his great goals. He blamed the German people for failing him and told his most devout followers, Goebbels, who would kill his children and commit suicide with his wife, and his slavish secretary, Martin Bormann, that Germany deserved to be annihilated, deserved to be in ruins, as was most of Europe.

All had failed him. He then went into a small bedroom with the utterly devoted Eva Braun, whom he had married only hours earlier, and shot himself in the mouth while Braun swallowed poison. Their bodies were then taken out of the bunker and placed in shallow grave where they were drenched with kerosene and burned. Both bodies were later discovered by Russian troops and Hitler's remains were positively identified through a comparison of remains and dental records. The world's worst mass murderer had finally come to the end desired by millions, living and dead. See: **Bormann, Martin; Dollfuss, Engelbert; Eichmann, Adolf; Ernst, Karl; Frank, Hans; Frick, Wilhelm; Goebbels, Paul Joseph, Goering, Hermann; Hess, Rudolf; Heydrich, Reinhard; Himmler, Heinrich; Jodl, Alfred; Kaltenbrunner, Ernst; Keitel, Wilhelm; Mussolini, Benito; Reichstag Fire; Ribbentrop, Joachim; Roehm, Ernst; Rosenberg, Alfred; Sauckel, Fritz; Streicher, Julius.**

REF.: Adler-Rudel, *Ost Juden in Deutschland;* Baur, *Hitler's Pilot;* Becker, *Hitler's Children—The Story of the Baader-Meinhof Terrorist Gang;* Bell, *Assassin;* Bennecke, *Hitler und die SA;* Bezymensky, *The Death of Adolf Hitler;* Bishop, *Executions;* Boldt, *In the Shelter with Hitler;* Bormann, *The Bormann Letters;* Bracher, *Die Deutsche Diktatur;* Brook-Shepherd, *The Anschluss;* Bullock, *Hitler: A Study in Tyranny;* Calic, *Secret Conversations with Hitler;* Carrell, *Hitler Moves East;* ____, *Scorched Earth; CBA;* Ciano, *The Ciano Diaries, 1939-1943;* Clark, *Barbarosa;* Clark, *The Fall of the German Republic;* Clutterbuck, *Guerrillas and Terrorists;* Crankshaw, *Gestapo;* Daim, *Der Mann, der Hitler die Ideen Gag;* Davidson, *The Making of Adolf Hitler;* Deakin, *The Brutal Friendship;* ____, *The Six Hundred Days of Mussolini;* Demaris, *Brothers in Blood: The International Terrorist Network;* ____, *The Director;* Diels, *Lucifer Ante Portas;* Dollinger, *The Decline and Fall of Nazi Germany and Imperial Japan;* Engel, *Heeresadjutant bei Hitler, 1938-1943;* Fest, *Hitler;* Gilbert, *Hitler Directs His War;* Goebbels, *The Goebbels Diaries;* Görlitz, *Hindenburg;* Hacker, *Crusaders, Criminals, Crazies: Terror and Terrorism in Our Time;* Hanfstaengl, *Unheard Witness;* Hanser, *Putsch, How Hitler Made a Revolution;* Hassell, *The Von Hassell Diaries, 1938-1944;* Heiber, *Hitlers Lagebesprechungen;* Heiden, *Der Fuehrer;* ____, *A History of National Socialism;* Heinz, *Germany's Hitler;* Henderson and Morris, *War in Our Time;* Hitler, *Hitler's Secret Book;* ____, *Mein Kampf;* Hitler, *My Brother-in-Law, Adolf;* Höhne, *The Order of the Death's Head;* Hurwood, *Society and the Assassin;* Hyams, *Killing No Murder;* Irving, *Hitler's War;* ____, *On the Trail of the Fox;* Jarman, *The Rise and Fall of Nazi Germany;* Jenks, *Vienna and the Young Hitler;* Jetzinger, *Hitlers Jugend;* Jukes, *Stalingrad, The Turning Point;* Keegan, *Barbarosa;* Keitel, *The Memoirs of Wilhelm Keitel;* Kogon, *The Theory and Practice of Hell;* Kubizek, *Young Hitler;* Kuby, *The Russians and Berlin, 1945;* Laquer, *Terrorism;* Lewin, *Rommel as Military Commander;* Liddell, *The German Generals Talk;* ____, *History of the Second World War;* Ludecke, *I Knew Hitler;* McGovern, *Martin Bormann;* McRandle, *The Track of the Wolf;* Majdalany, *The Fall of Fortress Europe;* Manvell, *The Conspirators, 20th July 1944;* ____ and Fraenkel, *Goebbels;* ____, *Hermann Göring;* ____, *Himmler;* ____, *The Men Who Tried to Kill Hitler;* ____, *SS and Gestapo: Rule by Terror;* Martienssen, *Hitler and His Admirals;* Maser, *Adolf Hitler;* ____, *Hitlers Mein Kampf;* ____, *Hitlers Briefe und Notizen;* Mend, *Adolf Hitler im Felde;* Mendelssohn, *The Nuremberg Documents;* Mosley, *On Borrowed Time;* O'Ballance, *Language of Violence—The Blood Politics of Terrorism;* Olden, *Hitler;* Orlow, *The History of the Nazi Party;* Paine, *The Assassins' World;* Payne, *The Life and Death of Adolf Hitler;* Pearl, *The Dangerous Assassins;* Picker, *Hitlers Tischgespräche im Führerhauptquartier, 1941-42;* Rabitsch, *Aus Adolf Hitlers Jugendzeit;* Rauschning, *Hitler Speaks;* Rechtenwald, *Woran hat Hitler gelitten?;* Reed, *Nemesis: The Story of Otto Strasser and the Black Front;* Reich, *Aus Adolf Hitlers Heimat Land;* Remak, *The Nazi Years;* Roberts, *The House That Hitler Built;* Röhrs, *Hitler, L'Autodestruction d'une Personnalité;* Rommel, *The Rommel Papers;* Ryan, *The Last Battle;* Salomon, *Fragebogen;* Santoro, *Hitler Germany as Seen by a Foreigner;* Schellenberg, *The Labyrinth;* Schlabrendorff, *The Secret War Against Hitler;* Schmidt, *Hitler's Interpreter;* Schoenbaum, *Hitler's Social Revolution;* Schramm, *Hitler: The Man and the Military Leader;* Screiber, *The Ultimate Weapon—Terrorists and World Order;* Schuman, *The Nazi Dictatorship;* Schuschnigg, *Austrian Requiem;* Semmler, *Goebbels: The Man Next to Hitler;* Senger, *Neither Fear Nor Hope;* Shirer, *Berlin Diary;* ____, *End of a Berlin Diary;* ____, *The Rise and Fall of the Third Reich;* Smith, *Adolf Hitler: His Family, Childhood and Youth;* Speer, *Infiltration;* ____, *Inside the Third Reich;* ____, *Spandau;* Strasser, *Hitler and I;* Strawson, *Hitler as Military Commander;* Taylor, *Sword and Swastika: Generals and Nazis in the Third Reich;* Thyssen, *I Paid Hitler;* Tobias, *The Reichstag Fire;* Toledano, *J. Edgar Hoover;* Toller, *I Was a German;* Tolstoy, *The Night of the Long Knives;* Trevor-Roper, *Blitzkrieg to Defeat: Hitler War Directives, 1939-45;* ____, *The Last Days of Hitler;* Viereck, *Metapolics: The Roots of the Nazi Mind;* Vogt, *The Burden of Guilt;* Vrba and Bestic, *I Cannot Forgive;* Warlimont, *Inside Hitler's Headquarters;* Watt, *The Kings Depart;* Welles, *The Time of Decision;* Wheaton, *The Nazi Revolution, 1933-35;* Wheeler-Bennett, *The Nemesis of Power: The German Army in Politics, 1918-1945;* Wilmot, *The Struggle for Europe;* Wiskemann, *The Rome-Berlin Axis;* Wykes, *Hitler;* ____, *Nuremberg Rallies;* Zeller, *The Flame of Freedom: The German Struggle Against Hitler;* Ziemke, *Battle for Berlin: End of the Third Reich;* Zoller, *Hitler Privat;* (FILM), *The Great Dictator,* 1940; *Mein Kampf,* 1940; *Man Hunt,* 1941; *The Devil with Hitler,* 1942; *Hitler—Dead or Alive,* 1942; *Star Spangled Rhythm,* 1942; *To Be or Not To Be,* 1942; *The Strange Death of Adolf Hitler,* 1943; *That Nazty Nuisance,* 1943; *The Hitler Gang,* 1944; *The Miracle of Morgan's Creek,* 1944; *The Desert Fox,* 1951; *The Magic Face,* 1951; *The Last Ten Days,* 1956; *The Story of Mankind,* 1957; *The Two-Headed Spy,* 1959; *Hitler,* 1962; *They Saved Hitler's Brain,* 1964; *Don't Call Me a Con Man,* 1966; *Is Paris Burning?,* 1966; *Which Way to the Front?,* 1970; *Hitler, The Last Ten Days,* 1973; *Massacre in Rome,* 1973; *Our Hitler, A Film From Germany,* 1980.

Hitler Diary Hoax, 1983, Ger., hoax. In April 1983, the German news magazine *Stern* made public a secret they had been keeping for three years: it claimed to possess sixty notebooks filled with the personal secrets of Adolf Hitler, penned in the cramped handwriting of the Nazi leader from 1932 until a few weeks before his death in 1945. Without examination, many WWII historians immediately declared the diaries, which *Stern* called "the journalistic scoop of the post WWII period," a forgery. But editors at *Stern* claimed that three handwriting experts had found the handwriting to be Hitler's. In addition, Hugh Trevor-Roper, a prominent British authority on Germany during WWII, proclaimed the documents authentic, and even went so far as to say that the books "will significantly alter historical judgments on Hitler's strategic thinking, exercise of power, and personality."

What apparently needed alteration, however, was the historian's claim, and on Apr. 25, only two days after his first substantiation was printed, he back-pedaled, saying that the editors' account of how the journals had ended up in their hands was open to suspicion. *Stern* stood by its story that the books had been recovered from a fiery plane crash in Boernersdorf, Germany (now East Germany), in April 1945, just a few days before Hitler committed suicide in his bunker. The Nazi officer who found the books concealed them in a hayloft in Boernersdorf, where they stayed until 1981. It was then that Gerd Heidemann, a reporter for *Stern,* supposedly tracked down the diaries through an East German military officer, purchased them, and had them smuggled to Switzerland, where they were studied by the magazine's experts.

On May 6, West Germany's Interior Ministry concluded through their own investigation that the alleged diaries were an elaborate, expensive hoax. Tests showed that the paper, binding, and binder's glue contained chemicals that were not in existence until at least ten years after Hitler's death. Also, residents of Boernersdorf who had witnessed the plane crash in 1945 insisted that even if there had been diaries on the plane, nothing could have withstood the heat of the explosion. Even without this evidence, the forgers made mistakes in the content of the diaries: they had used as part of their source material information published in the early 1960s that had since been found by historians to be incorrect.

Stern was forced to admit their mistake, and London's *Sunday Times,* which had already made a downpayment of $200,000 to publish excerpts, demanded their money back. The day after the government's findings were published, two editors-in-chief on the magazine's staff resigned. Heidemann, the reporter responsible for uncovering the diaries, was fired and accused of embezzling some of the $3.75 million the magazine paid to purchase the diaries. The exact source of the fraudulent diaries has never been found, although the prevalent theory is that they were forged in a government-sponsored workshop in Potsdam, East Germany. REF.: *CBA.*

Hitz, William, 1872-1935, U.S., jur. Served as special attorney for the U.S. Department of Justice from 1914-16. He was nominated to the supreme court of Washington, D.C., (now the District Court of Washington, D.C.) by President Woodrow Wilson in 1916, and to the Washington, D.C. Circuit Court by President Herbert Hoover in 1931. REF.: *CBA.*

Hlinka, Andrej, 1864-1938, Czech., rebel. Founded and became head of Slovakian political party advocating an independent Slovakia. He opposed a union with Bohemia, then part of Austria-Hungary, and at the post-WWI peace conference in 1919 he demanded a direct vote by the Slovakian people. Arrested and jailed, he was elected to the legislature in 1920 and later freed. REF.: *CBA.*

Hoar, Ebenezer Rockwood, 1816-95, U.S., jur. Member of Massachusetts state senate as Whig in 1846, and opposed to slavery. He served as judge on the Massachusetts Court of Common Appeals in 1849, as associate justice of the supreme judicial court of Massachusetts in 1859, and as U.S. attorney general from 1869-70 during the Grant administration. He was nominated to the U.S. Supreme Court by President Ulysses S. Grant in 1869, but was denied confirmation. He also served in the U.S. House of Representatives from 1873-75. REF.: *CBA.*

Hobbes, Thomas, 1588-1679, Brit., consp. Philosopher exiled because of his political ideas. Went to France in 1641 and returned to Britain in 1652. REF.: *CBA.*

Hobbs, William, and **Agnew, John,** and **Rose, Vincent,** prom. 20th Cent., U.S., attempt. burg.-mur. William Hobbs, John Agnew, and Vincent Rose were wiling away an evening drinking in Hamilton, Ohio, when they decided that they wanted to "make some easy money." They attempted to break into a restaurant but were surprised by Patrolman Arthur Sponsel. The police officer called for them to freeze, but Rose broke into a run. As Sponsel shot at Rose to stop him, Hobbs shot the officer with a .32-caliber pistol.

Police eventually tracked down Hobbs and insinuated that Rose had confessed, when in fact he had not. Hobbs then gave his own confession. He was convicted of first-degree murder, the jury making no recommendation for mercy, and was sentenced to death. Agnew pleaded not guilty, but was also convicted and sentenced to life in prison. Vincent Rose was convicted of second-degree murder and sentenced to life with a chance of a pardon. REF.: *CBA.*

Hobbs, William Cooper, prom. 1919-1938, Brit., embez.-consp.-blk.-forg.-fraud. The son of a barge owner, William Cooper Hobbs held a variety of jobs in city offices before he was hired by Mr. Dodds' money lending firm. Domineering and clever, Hobbs had a penchant for litigation, and was soon so successful that he became Dodds' employer. Later, Hobbs worked for a solicitor's firm, Appleton & Company, and became involved in a blackmail scheme. At the Victory Ball on Nov. 11, 1919, at the Albert Hall, Sir Hari Singh, twenty-four, future Maharajah of Kashmir, met and fell in love with Mrs. Florence Maud Robinson, thirty-two. Their meeting, an apparent accident, had actually been engineered by a con man friend of Mrs. Robinson, Montague Noel Newton, with the assistance of Captain Charles Arthur, Singh's aide-de-campe. The two planned to blackmail Singh. Newton, pretending to be the incensed husband, burst into the Paris hotel room occupied by Singh and Robinson. Through Arthur, the blackmailers demanded the staggering sum of £300,000, to be paid

in two checks. Newton then returned to England to inform the real Charles Robinson that his wife was in Paris with an Indian. He suggested that Robinson divorce her and recommended Appleton & Company for the proceedings, particularly William Cooper Hobbs of that company.

Robinson began the divorce suit and was amazed to find his wife at Appleton's offices a month later when he called for a progress report. Hobbs offered the irate husband £25,000 on behalf of Singh to drop the divorce suit, but Robinson refused, tossing the money on his wife's lap. Hobbs had actually taken Singh's first check for £150,000 and used it to open an account in Robinson's name, from which the £25,000 was drawn. Appleton & Company took £4,000 for costs, and gave Mrs. Robinson £21,000. She later claimed that Newton immediately appropriated £10,000 of this and knocked her across the room. Hobbs, Newton, and Arthur planned to go to Paris and divide the remaining

British swindler William Cooper Hobbs.

£120,000. Singh stopped payment on the second check, which was not dated or endorsed. When Arthur lost his share of the money, he returned to England to tell Robinson that Singh had paid £150,000, not £25,000, to get him to drop the divorce action. Robinson sued the Midland Bank to claim the other £125,000, but the bank won the case. Hobbs was arrested and tried at the Old Bailey before Mr. Justice Avory, defended by Sir Henry Curtis-Bennet and St. John Hutchinson, with Newton appearing against him as a witness. Hobbs was found Guilty of participating in the conspiracy and was sentenced to two years of hard labor.

On Oct. 12, 1934, Willy Clarkson, a well-known theatrical costumer, died. Clarkson was said to be an arsonist who had made many false insurance claims, assisted by Hobbs, his lifelong friend and cohort. Clarkson's will, dated Jan. 22, 1927, did not dispose of his estate which, because he was illegitimate, would go to the Crown. Hobbs, one of the executors, discovered another will a few days after Clarkson's death, this one dated June 24, 1929. The new will came from the Chancery Lane office of solicitor Edmond O'Connor, and named Hobbs as legatee, with O'Connor as the sole surviving witness. Through careful analysis of the evidence, including an erased signature, the will was proved to be forged. Hobbs and O'Connor were tried together at the Old Bailey in March 1938 before Judge Gerald Dodson. On Mar. 29, both men were found Guilty; Hobbs was sentenced to five years in prison and ordered to pay up to £500 in court costs, and O'Connor was given seven years' penal servitude.

REF.: *CBA;* Hyde, *United in Crime.*

Hobday, Stanley Eric, d.1933, Brit., rob.-mur. In the pre-dawn hours on a Sunday in August 1933, a woman was awakened by the sound of glass crashing on a lower floor in her home. She sent her husband down to check on the disturbance, heard a rustling, then a groan, and called out for her husband to come back. He did and fell into her arms. Charles William Fox died from the bowie knife stuck in his back.

Stanley Hobday had committed the murder after breaking into the house to steal fourteen shillings. As Mrs. Fox screamed for help, Hobday left the home, walked down the street, and broke into a butcher shop, where he ate and shaved before leaving. Police identified Hobday by a fingerprint left on a milk bottle at the butcher shop. They sent out a description of the suspect on the radio—the first time in history the radio was used to apprehend a criminal. Walter Bowman, a farmer, recognized Hobday and alerted police. Hobday swore to his innocence, explaining that the suitcase containing the knife had been stolen before the murder had been committed. But the prosecution disproved his alibi. He was found Guilty and sentenced to death. His execution came in December 1933, at Winson Green Prison, Birmingham, England. Fourteen shillings was the take. REF.: *CBA*.

Hoch, Johann Otto (John Schmidt, AKA: Jacob Huff, Martin Dotz, Henry Bartels), 1862-1906, U.S., theft-mur. Johann Hoch was bald and sported a handlebar mustache. He was a bigamist, who, in the 1890s, passed on six rules for success with women in an article appearing in the Chicago *Sun* in 1906, shortly before he was hanged for murder. "The average man can fool the average woman if he will only let her have her own way at the start," was one of them.

Hoch was born in Horweiler, Ger. In 1887, he left his wife, Christine Ramb, and their three children. After arriving in Wheeling, W.Va., in 1895 under the name Jacob Huff, he opened a saloon in a German area and began to look for monied widows and divorcees to marry. In April he married Caroline Hoch (Johann adopted the last names of his wives) in a small ceremony. Reverend Hermann C.A. Haas, who performed the nuptials, recalled seeing Hoch give his wife some white powder, which he thought to be a poison. The woman died in agony a few days later and was buried with great haste. Hoch sold the house, withdrew his wife's savings, and cashed a $2,500 life insurance policy. After apparently pretending to commit suicide, he was not seen in Wheeling again.

In 1898, Inspector George Shippy of the Chicago Police Department investigated Hoch for cheating a furniture dealer. Not knowing that this man was responsible for perhaps a dozen murders from coast to coast, Shippy was surprised to receive a letter from Reverend Haas who saw a newspaper photograph of the bigamist in a Chicago journal. Hoch, who was using the name of Martin Dotz, admitted his identity when confronted by Shippy. Hoch was convicted of swindling and sent to the Cook County Jail for a year, but authorities did not have evidence substantial enough to charge him with murder.

Reverend Haas theorized that Hoch had feigned suicide by leaving personal belongings on the banks of the Ohio

Wife-killer Johann Otto Hoch.

River, and had waded out to a moored boat and sailed away to his freedom. Shippy investigated Hoch's progress after he was released from jail. From New York to San Francisco he found reports of dozens of abandoned women who had been murdered for their money, perhaps fifty of them, Shippy surmised. He contacted the police in Wheeling and asked them to exhume the remains of Caroline Hoch to be tested for arsenic poisoning. Local officials discovered that the vital organs had been removed, leaving no tell-tale clues. He made one mistake, however. Hoch lingered too long in Chicago.

On Dec. 5, 1904, he married Marie Walcker and then poisoned her shortly after their marriage. Before she died, Hoch hugged his sister-in-law, Amelia. "I cannot be alone in the world. Marry me when she goes," he pleaded. "The dead are for the dead," he told the shocked woman. "The living are for the living." Days after Marie died, Amelia married Hoch and turned $750 over to him. Then he vanished. Inspector Shippy then had Walcker's body exhumed and he mailed the suspect's photograph to newspapers nationwide. The photo was recognized by Katherine Kimmerle in New York, who had taken Hoch in as a new boarder. He had proposed to her twenty minutes after renting the lodging. He was immediately arrested and returned to Chicago.

Hoch was convicted of murdering Marie Walcker and was hanged on Feb. 23, 1906, still maintaining his innocence.

REF.: Boar, *The World's Most Infamous Murders*; Duke, *Celebrated Criminal Cases of America*; Kobler, *Some Like It Gory*; Logan, *Rope, Knife and Chair*; Nash, *Almanac of World Crime*; ____, *Murder, America*.

Hochberg, Alan, 1941- , U.S., polit. corr. Bronx assemblyman Alan Hochberg insisted he was a victim of unusual circumstances when he was convicted of three counts of corruption and fraud in connection with his political position. He said that what he did was no different than President Gerald Ford's offering Ronald Reagan a position in his cabinet. Hochberg had approached Charles Rosen, a prominent Bronx politician and the man most likely to oppose Hochberg in the next primary election, and offered Rosen a paid position on the assemblyman's staff with the assurance that when Hochberg moved on to another position, he would support Rosen in his bid for the assembly post. Rosen, in collaboration with special prosecutor Charles Hynes, recorded his meetings with Hochberg, during which they discussed the arrangement. Hochberg was charged with corrupt use of his government position, fraudulently affecting a primary election result, making unlawful fees and payments, and second-degree grand larceny. Ironically, the assemblyman was serving as chairman of the State Assembly Ethics Committee at the time.

On Dec. 15, 1976, a state supreme court jury in Albany, N.Y., found Hochberg Guilty of three of the four charges; he was acquitted of grand larceny. On Jan. 27, 1977, he was sentenced to one year in jail. Due to a New York State law requirement, he was also disbarred after twenty years as a lawyer. REF.: *CBA*.

Hocker, Thomas Henry, prom. 1845, Brit., mur. On Feb. 21, 1845, at around 7 p.m. the body of music teacher James Delarue was found in a field near Hampstead, England. His face and head had been battered in with a stick, and by repeated kicks. At the nearby Swiss Cottage pub, a cry of "Murder!" was shouted out and heard by two men near the pub. One fellow outside the bar stood completely still for about ten minutes after he heard the news, then walked over to Constable Baldock, who stood near the body, and asked him what was going on. They chatted for some time, and the questioner, later revealed to be Thomas Henry Hocker, twenty-two, also reached over to check the pulse of the victim. That evening Hocker visited a friend, Jane Philps, to show off his new watch and ring. He explained buttons missing from his clothes, bloodstains on his shirt front, and a missing shirt cuff by saying he had fallen and had also had a fight with a friend. He later told his brother he had redeemed the watch from a pawn shop with money borrowed from an older woman friend. Hocker talked with his family about the murder of his close friend Delarue, never mentioning his talk with Officer Baldock. In Delarue's pocket was found a love letter from "Caroline," scolding him for his unfaithfulness to her and asking him to meet her at their usual place. The letter was addressed to "James Cooper," a nickname Hocker had often used for Delarue, and was written in blue ink.

Detective Inspector Shackell questioned Hocker about the watch, which Hocker first said he had redeemed from a pawnbroker, then said he had received as a gift from Delarue. His alibis did not hold up, and the bloodstains and disheveled state of his clothing indicated Hocker was the killer. While he was being held in Marylebone station, Hocker admitted to constable James Euston that he had been at Swiss Cottage, claiming that as his alibi. Brought to trial at the Central Criminal Court before Justice Coleridge and Justice Coltman, Hocker read a long and involved statement, declaring that he and Delarue had been rivals over an unnamed "genteel young lady" and that, when he discovered his rival lying dead, he felt responsible and had "sought out a slaughterhouse in Hampstead and there disfigured his clothes in a pool of blood." But, in addition to the other evidence, the ink and paper from the "Caroline" letter matched that found in Hocker's room. The jury took ten minutes to find him Guilty and he was sentenced to death for his crime. His execution took place Apr. 28, 1845. REF.: *CBA*.

Hodapp, Jacob Frederick, d.1866, U.S., mur. A German immigrant, Jacob Hodapp lodged on a farm outside of Norristown, Pa., along with other immigrants from his native land. When Hodapp discovered that 19-year-old Julius Wochele possessed $40 in gold, Hodapp beat him to death and took the money. He was caught in flight a short time later and he quickly confessed to the crime. Hodapp was tried at Norristown on Nov. 15, 1866, and convicted. He was hanged a short time later.
REF.: *CBA; Dittmann, The Murder on Dr. Tiedeman's Farm.*

Hoddenbach, Keith, prom. 1980s, U.S., mur. Keith Hoddenbach, a gang member in the Humboldt Park neighborhood of Chicago, Ill., set out to kill a rival gang member on Dec. 11, 1984. He stepped into Max's Red Hots, a local hot-dog stand, and opened fire with a pump shotgun on some teenagers playing video games. Santos Martinez, fifteen, died of wounds to his chest, and three other adolescents were injured.
Daniel Murray, Hoddenbach's defense lawyer, attempted to show in court that the murderer's actions grew out of his being raised by an abusive, alcoholic father. The defense was unsuccessful, however, and Judge Roger Kiley, Jr., stating that "society has to be protected from you," sentenced Hoddenbach to 110 years in prison. REF.: *CBA.*

Hodge, Orville Enoch, 1905- , U.S., polit. corr. During his tenure as Illinois state auditor, Orville Hodge was considered one of the top contenders for the governor's seat in 1960. When Hodge was running to retain his seat in 1956, however, the Chicago *Daily News* ran stories—a series that eventually won a Pulitzer Prize—that uncovered an embezzlement scam in which Hodge had taken almost $1 million out of state funds.
Hodge's office manager, Edward Epping, would bring a load of checks to Chicago's Southmoor Bank and, through a special arrangement with Ed Hintz, the bank president, the checks would be cashed and some of the money put aside for Hodge to pick up later. "I just don't know why I did it," Hodge told Illinois Governor William Stratton upon resigning from his position. "I didn't need the money."
On Aug. 20, 1956, Hodge was sentenced to twelve to fifteen years at Menard State Prison. He was released after serving six-and-a-half years and returned to his home town of Granite City, Ill., to start a real estate business with his family. REF.: *CBA.*

Hodge, Walter Hartman, 1896-1975, U.S., jur. Served as prosecuting attorney of Skagit County, Wash., from 1921-24, as assistant U.S. attorney for the U.S. Department of Justice in Cordova, Ark., in 1926, and as a justice of the supreme court of Arkansas from 1959-60. He was nominated to the district court of Arkansas by President Dwight D. Eisenhower in 1960. REF.: *CBA.*

Hodges, Thomas, See: **Bell, Tom.**

Hodges, W.O., 1909-54, U.S., law enfor. off. Most people would have chosen to end their career in law enforcement after suffering a debilitating injury in the line of duty. But that would have been difficult for W.O. Hodges: he was wounded only seven days after beginning his term as sheriff of Denton County, Texas. The new sheriff was blinded when he was shot in the face by a crazed gunman. But instead of looking for another line of work, he acclimated himself to his new way of life and continued to serve his term. His work changed from that of public figure to behind-the-scenes director of six deputies, taking care of the sheriff's office, and fine-tuning his detective skills to become an ace interrogator. Denton County was convinced that Sheriff Hodges had overcome his setback: they elected him to office for two more terms.
For a long time Sheriff Hodges hoped there would be a way to restore his sight, but he finally resigned himself to the permanence of his condition and obtained a seeing-eye dog. The dog was walking him to work one particularly foggy morning in December 1954 when a car struck both the sheriff and his dog and killed them. The courageous sheriff, a hero to his constituents, was honored with one of the largest funerals in Denton County's history. REF.: *CBA.*

Hodzic, Shefka, c.1950- , Yugo., kid.-mur. In a village as steeped in tradition as Jusic, Yugoslavia, a woman who cannot bear children is a woman shunned by her community. Such was the fate of Shefka Hodzic. Her best friend, Alija Hasanovic, was only twenty-two and was one week away from giving birth to her second child. Shefka, embarrassed that she could not become pregnant, declared that she too was pregnant, carefully placing rags under her clothes and convincing everyone that she would soon give birth to her first child.
The two women went for a walk in the woods on Jan. 28, 1970. When Shefka judged that they were safely deep in the woods, she took a nine-millimeter pistol and shot the expectant mother in the back of the head. She then performed a crude Caesarian cut in the mother's womb and removed the baby. Alija's body was found by her brother, Emin Ibrahimovic. Vowing revenge, he walked thirty miles to Tuzla, the closest town with police, and an investigation immediately began.
For a long time the detectives were stumped, mostly because they had been working under the assumption that Alija had been alone that morning. When they discovered she had been with Shefka, they went to the friend's home and found her nursing her newborn baby boy. But the baby seemed upset—there did not seem to be any milk in the new mother's breast. An examination was ordered to confirm whether or not Shefka had given birth. When it was discovered that she had not, she admitted to murdering her best friend and stealing the baby. "I had no choice," she cried. "Don't you understand? The shame! The shame!" The jury, to a certain extent, sympathized with her predicament: they ordered her to serve eight years in prison, an unusually light sentence considering the brutality of the crime. REF.: *CBA.*

Hoel, Halvor Nielsen, 1766-1852, Nor., rebel. Representative of peasant concerns. He wanted to install direct royal rule and to eliminate the parliament, which was controlled by urban interests. In 1815 he was not allowed to have a parliament seat. That same year he incited riots at the coronation of Charles XIV, was arrested and imprisoned, but was later granted a pardon by the king. REF.: *CBA.*

Hoeppel, John Henry, and **Hoeppel, Charles J.** (AKA: **Charles Alexander**), prom. 1930s, U.S., polit. corr. Congressman John H. Hoeppel swore that the only reason he had appointed star high school athlete James W. Ives to West Point Academy was because some army officer friends wanted a good football player on the Army team. But the congressman had made an arrangement with another congressman: he would appoint Ives if the other man would appoint his son, Charles Hoeppel. A monkey wrench was thrown into the plan, however, when the star athlete "resigned" from the prestigious military academy after discovering that he had received an illegal appointment.
Ives had been approached by a man who called himself Charles Alexander in May 1934 and was told that he could secure his appointment from Congressman Hoeppel if he signed a promissory note for $1,000. When asked in court who Charles Alexander was, Ives pointed to the congressman's son. The elder Hoeppel swore he knew nothing about the transaction. A jury did not believe him and convicted the father and son of conspiracy to solicit a bribe. Hoeppel was the first congressman in almost a decade to be convicted of a felony.
In January 1936 they were sentenced to a term of four to twelve months in prison, but failed to show up the following October to begin serving their sentences. Authorities located them in Richmond, Va., and incarcerated them. On Apr. 3, 1937, John Hoeppel was pardoned by the District of Columbia Parole Board, but his son was left in prison to serve out the remainder of his sentence. REF.: *CBA.*

Hoess, Rudolf Francis Ferdinand, 1900-47, Pol., war crimes. Proud of having built the first three gas chambers at the Nazi death camp in Auschwitz, Rudolf Hoess proclaimed at his 1947 trial before the Warsaw Supreme Court in Poland: "Why, I could have done twice as much." He was referring to his responsibility for two million deaths at the concentration camp. Hoess was captured in April 1946 in his hiding place at Lüneberg, Ger., and was one of the few high-level Nazis who openly admitted to all of his atrocities.

At his sentencing held a year later, Hoess was asked how it felt to have been responsible for four million deaths. His flat response was, "It was only two million." Explaining that the murders "resulted from orders which I received," he told of building the gas chambers that held a capacity of 2,000, among other abominations. Hoess was hanged in Apr. 15, 1947, on the same gallows used for many of his own victims.

Nazi concentration camp commander Rudolf Hoess.

REF.: Bullock, *Hitler;* CBA; Crankshaw, *Gestapo;* Delarue, *History of the Gestapo;* Gilbert, *Nuremberg Diary;* Hilberg, *The Destruction of the European Jews;* Levin, *The Holocaust;* Manvell and Fraenkel, *Himmler;* Shirer, *The Rise and Fall of the Third Reich;* Smith, *Reaching Judgment at Nuremberg;* Suhl, *They Fought Back;* West, *On Trial at Nuremberg;* Wilson, *Encyclopedia of Murder.*

Hofer, Andreas, 1767-1810, Tyrol, rebel. Led a successful revolt against Bavarian government ruling Tyrol in 1809. Afterward, he lost to Bavarian and French forces and went into hiding, but was betrayed and shot. REF.: *CBA.*

Hoff, Max (AKA: Boo Boo), prom. 1920s, U.S., org. crime. Max Hoff had a criminal background in Philadelphia that went back to the turn of the century. Hoff, a large, powerful man with organizational talents, merged his gang with others, rather than battle his opponents. By the advent of Prohibition in 1920, Hoff was the undisputed crime boss of Philadelphia and he reaped millions by streamlining bootlegging operations. He also organized local gambling under his cartel's domination and then added organized prostitution to his rackets. Hoff was one of the most enthusiastic supporters of the 1929 Atlantic City crime conference, the first in the nation. He threw his support to Al Capone when Capone proposed that his friend, Moses Annenberg, set up the national wire service for all syndicate-controlled gambling operations. See: **Annenberg, Moses; Atlantic City Conference; Capone, Alphonse.**

REF.: Asbury, *The Chicago Underworld;* Eisenberg, Dan, and Landau, *Meyer Lansky;* Fried, *The Rise and Fall of the Jewish Gangster in America;* Gosch and Hammer, *The Last Testament of Lucky Luciano;* Katz, *Uncle Frank;* Kobler, *Capone;* Levine, *Anatomy of a Gangster;* Peterson, *The Mob;* Smith, *Syndicate City;* Spiering, *The Man Who Got Capone.*

Hoffa, James Riddle (Jimmy), 1913-75, U.S., org. crime-brib.-(unsolv.) mur. James Riddle Hoffa was one of the most dynamic and corrupt union leaders in the U.S., his powerful Teamsters union having long been linked to organized crime by federal investigators. A tough, ruthless bully, Hoffa was the power behind union leader David Beck, president of the International Brotherhood of Teamsters union, with its 1.5 million members and unlimited millions at its disposal. Hoffa's dealings with members of organized crime were well known, but he managed to evade prosecution for racketeering until Robert F. Kennedy made him a special target.

Kennedy's relentless campaign to convict Hoffa began when Kennedy was chief counsel for the Senate Select Committee on Improper Activities in the Labor or Management Field, which was headed up by Senator John McClellan. He continued to wage an all-out battle to convict Hoffa when he became attorney general under his brother, President John F. Kennedy. In 1962, Hoffa was finally brought to trial through Kennedy's exhaustive investigation for extorting money from a firm employing Teamsters, but the trial resulted in a hung jury. When Kennedy was

able to prove that Hoffa had tried to bribe one of the jurors in the case, the union leader was convicted of bribery and given an eight-year prison sentence. Hoffa was then convicted of misappropriating $1.7 million in union funds in 1964 and given an additional sentence. He battled through many appeals to stay out of prison but finally went behind bars in 1967, serving almost five years.

President Richard Nixon pardoned Hoffa in 1971 on the proviso that he stay out of union activities for ten years. This, of course, Hoffa did not do. Immediately upon his release, Hoffa began to attempt to regain control of the Teamsters. Organized crime figures, however, feared his comeback would mean they would lose the control of this most lucrative of unions. According to the later statements of Charles Allen, a mob executioner, Hoffa approached him in 1975, ostensibly employing Allen to murder Teamsters president Frank Fitzsimmons and his organized crime boss sponsor, Anthony "Tony Pro" Provenzano.

Allen, who had served time with Hoffa and was his bodyguard while in prison, later told authorities that when Hoffa was released from prison, he was told by Fitzsimmons that he could not, as earlier agreed, again take over the Teamsters union. At that time, according to Allen, Hoffa told Allen to kill Fitzsimmons and New Jersey trucking czar and underworld boss, Anthony Provenzano, the strong arm behind Fitzsimmons. Hoffa also confided these intentions to his adopted son, Charles "Chuckie" O'Brien, according to Allen, and O'Brien "went over to Tony's side." This treachery was explained by Allen as resulting from Hoffa's refusal to allow O'Brien to run for a powerful union post.

James Hoffa testifying before a Senate subcommittee, 1961.

An attempt was made upon the life of Fitzsimmons' son Richard. The younger Fitzsimmons' car was blown up in a parking lot, but Fitzsimmons escaped when he went back to retrieve a jacket left in a restaurant. This act, attributed to Hoffa goons, caused Fitzsimmons and Provenzano to take action. Instead of Fitzsimmons and Provenzano being killed, it was Hoffa who became the marked man. On July 30, 1975, Hoffa was lured from his home in a Detroit suburb to a so-called union meeting at the Manchus Red Fox restaurant. He arrived at 2 p.m. and called his wife a half hour later to tell her that the men he was to meet had not yet arrived. This was the last anyone ever heard of James Riddle Hoffa. He was seen driving away from the restaurant with several men about 2:45 p.m. and was never seen again.

The murder of Hoffa was attributed to Salvatore Briguglio, a Provenzano man, who, with others, reportedly took the union boss to a syndicate hideout and garroted Hoffa to death. His body was then taken to a meat-grinding plant and was, according to Allen, "ground up in little pieces, shipped to Florida and thrown into a swamp." Other versions of Hoffa's demise still continue to flourish. One has it that he was poured into concrete and became part of a cornerstone of any number of skyscrapers in New York, New Jersey, or Michigan. Another account reports his body being stuffed into a fifty-five-gallon drum, which was also packed with wet concrete, and then taken out to sea and dumped in the Gulf waters.

No one to this day knows for certain the exact fate of Jimmy Hoffa. Briguglio was reportedly ready to pinpoint to the FBI the whereabouts of the union leader's remains in 1978, but he was shot to death a short time later outside a New York City restaurant. Fitzsimmons never mentioned Hoffa's name to the day he died of cancer. Provenzano, while later serving time in a California prison, through a representative, contacted the author, saying that Tony Pro wanted to "tell all he knew" about Hoffa's end if the author would write a book about Provenzano. This proposition was declined. See: **Beck, David; Teamsters, The.**

REF.: Brill, *The Teamsters; CBA;* Cressey, *Theft of the Nation;* Davis, *Mafia Kingfish;* Demaris, *Captive City;* ____, *The Director;* ____, *The Last Mafioso;* Eisenberg and Landau, *Meyer Lansky;* Fried, *The Rise and Fall of the Jewish Gangster in America;* Gage, *Mafia, U.S.A.;* James, *Hoffa and the Teamsters;* McClellan, *Crime Without Punishment;* Messick, *Lansky;* ____, *Secret File;* ____, *Syndicate in the Sun;* ____ and Goldblatt, *The Mobs and the Mafia;* Moldea, *The Hoffa Wars;* Morgan, *Prince of Crime;* Navasky, *Kennedy Justice;* Peterson, *The Mob;* Powers, *Secrecy and Power;* Reid, *The Grim Reapers;* Sheridan, *The Rise and Fall of Jimmy Hoffa;* Sullivan, *The Bureau: My Thirty Years in Hoover's FBI;* Toledano, *J. Edgar Hoover;* Velie, *Desperate Bargain: Why Jimmy Hoffa Had to Die;* Wicker, *Investigating the FBI;* Zuckerman, *Vengeance Is Mine.*

Hoffman, Abbie (AKA: **Barry Freed**), 1936-89, U.S., drugs-suic. Abbie Hoffman, a leader of the 1960s protest movement and co-leader of the Youth International Party or Yippies, was one of the Chicago Seven tried for conspiracy in 1971 for disrupting the 1968 Democratic National Convention. The trial ended in an acquittal of the conspiracy charges, and an appellate court later acquitted them of lesser charges. In August 1973, Hoffman was charged with selling cocaine to an undercover agent. Rather than face the charge, he went underground. He remained a fugitive for almost seven years, disguising himself by growing a beard, having facial surgery, straightening his hair, and altering his walk and his speech patterns. He lived in upstate New York as "Barry Freed" and became an avid environmentalist, even testifying before a Congressional committee.

On Sept. 4, 1980, sensing a favorable political climate, Hoffman surrendered to authorities in New York. He was released without bail and later held briefly in the Brooklyn House of Detention. In April 1981, Hoffman was given a three-year sentence for the drug charge, but was allowed to serve the time by performing community service. He spent the next six years integrating his environmental concerns with the public persona of "Abbie." He emerged briefly in 1988 during a retrospective of the convention twenty years before. But mostly he led a private life around his home in Good Hope, Pa., where he became increasingly troubled by personal and public events. Hoffman, the eternal teenager, was now gray and paunchy, and described by friends as manic-depressive. On Apr. 12, 1989, Hoffman was found dead in his Pennsylvania home. Six days later, a coroner ruled his death a suicide caused by a mixture of phenobarbital and alcohol. REF.: *CBA.*

Hoffman, Etta, prom. 20th Cent., U.S.-Belg., smug. Etta Hoffman was apprehended at a customs station in the U.S. when she arrived from Brussels, Belg. The customs officer, Joseph Koehler, could not give any real reason why he felt suspicious about her except that something seemed strange. Then he finally put his finger on it: Hoffman was abnormally tall. Her thick-soled shoes were found to be hollow, filled with diamonds. More contraband gems were found in a false bottom in her suitcase.

Hoffman said a stranger who called on her at her apartment in Belgium promised to pay her $100 for smuggling the diamonds into the U.S. But upon opening the envelope handed to her as she stepped on the plane, she discovered that she had received only $80. She was found Guilty of transporting illegal goods and sentenced to eighteen months in prison. REF.: *CBA.*

Hoffman, Harold Giles, 1896-1954, U.S., embez. Harold Hoffman served as a mayor, assemblyman, congressman, and governor in his native New Jersey. He also embezzled over $300,000. Hoffman began embezzling as a bank official in South Amboy and used some of the stolen money for subsequent campaigns. Using his various political offices to gain access to public funds, Hoffman was able to cover the trail of misappropria-tion. The stealing went undetected. Hoffman was elected governor in 1935 and could have become a Republican candidate for national office had he not ruined his own political career by trying to reopen the investigation of the Lindbergh baby killer, Bruno Richard Hauptmann. Hoffman was never elected to public office again, but was rewarded with the patronage job of director of unemployment compensation, where he continued to disguise his financial maneuvers. However, by the early 1950s, authorities became suspicious of Hoffman's finances, and in 1954 Governor Robert B. Meyner suspended him pending an investigation. Irregularities over the renting of state offices and the purchase of supplies were found, as well as an investment scheme which returned favored friends close to $2 million on an investment of less than $100,000. Two months later, while awaiting prosecution, Hoffman died of a massive heart attack in a New York hotel room before officials learned the full extent of his crimes. REF.: *CBA.*

Hoffman, Harry L., prom. 1920s, Case of, U.S., mur. Trying to protect himself from a lynching, Harry Hoffman almost signed his own death warrant. When the police announced they were looking for a man who wore horn-rimmed glasses and a brown hat, and owned a .25-caliber gun, Hoffman figured he would be a leading suspect in the 1924 murder of Mary A. Bauer in Staten Island, N.Y. He had read a lot about the lynching of Leo Frank, a Jewish manufacturer, by an angry gentile mob, and did not want to end up the same way. So he mailed his pistol to his brother. This action became the backbone of the prosecution's case against the Staten Island movie projectionist.

The people of New York demanded that someone be punished, and Hoffman was convicted of first-degree murder. But a new trial was ordered after it was found that the wording of the original indictment was faulty. At his second trial, Hoffman's lawyer suddenly collapsed on the courtroom floor with a heart attack; a mistrial was called. The third trial ended differently but just as unsuccessfully: the jury was hung. Finally, five years after the crime had been committed, a ballistics test entered as evidence during the fourth trial showed that the bullets recovered from Mary Bauer had not been fired from Hoffman's gun.

Hoffman was acquitted and released in 1929, though he had little to come home to. The state, for all the trouble it had caused him, claimed to owe him nothing but the six cents it confiscated from Hoffman when he went to jail. His car, which was im-pounded as evidence, was never returned to him. His daughter had been placed in an orphanage after his wife left him for another man; she returned to him when her lover suddenly left her. Ironically, Hoffman's attorney asserted when his client was freed that the Hoffmans were "going to begin life afresh, right where they left off five years ago." REF.: *CBA.*

Hoffman, Jerome D., 1933- , U.S.-Brit., fraud. During a nineteen-month period, Jerry Hoffman ran one of the most ambitious and lucrative investment scams ever attempted. Half of his success was built on his remarkable ability to sell anybody anything; the other half was sheer luck that no one took a closer look at the truth about the Real Estate Fund of America (REFA), his offshore property fund.

The major trick that Hoffman used to get investors' money in REFA was to fill his board of directors with influential names. Among them were Reginald Maudling, the deputy leader of England's Conservative party, and Robert F. Wagner, mayor of

New York City for many years. Hoffman would fill the sales literature and brochures with the names of major investors who had never heard of REFA and with color photographs of property REFA did not own. Hoffman promised that property purchased through REFA would be built on and improved, but no building ever occurred. This was just one of the hundreds of guarantees that Hoffman would make repeatedly, with no intention of giving his investors a penny. Investors were told that they could demand their money back at any time, but Hoffman made the redemption process as complicated as possible, and hardly ever delivered.

Hoffman's profits snowballed, allowing him to launch further lucrative and fraudulent ventures, such as the Fund of the Seven Seas (FOSS), an investment plan in which Hoffman promised to "have one of the largest shipping fleets in the world." Of course, his promotional material included photos of ships that were not his, and names of banks that had not invested. Some of his funds, such as FOSS, fell apart, but REFA kept on producing money—and nothing else. Finally, in June 1969, when the London *Sunday Times* published the fact that Hoffman had been barred from selling anything in the U.S. more than a year before, Reginald Maudling was forced to resign from his post as president of REFA. But he wrote a letter asserting that REFA was still "a good and sound investment." Hoffman used this letter and exploited Maudling's name to continue pulling in investors from all over South America.

With their money, he continued to "gear"—borrow on money that is sometimes not even 20 percent paid off. He used this tactic to push his loans-to-assets ratio up to 12:1.

By December 1970, as unpaid bills mounted, employees jumped ship, and investors demanded their money back, Hoffman shut down REFA and slipped underground. By that time, he was wanted in the U.S. on thirty-two counts of mail fraud. He entered the U.S. again in January 1972, to "face his responsibilities." Actually, he had a new scheme: Homesteads Mount Canaan. He had purchased 190 acres in Israel with money he did not have, and was planning on marketing it to American Jews. Unfortunately for Hoffman, he was convicted of mail fraud and sent to jail for two years. He was paroled after ten months and quietly slipped out of sight.

Before Hoffman shut down the Real Estate Fund of America, it had built up more than $50 million in debts. Directors who did not get out early enough were stuck, since the laws governing the corporation forbade a director to leave without nominating a substitute. In the end, Wagner, New York lawyer John Lang, and Holmes Brown, the last president of REFA, settled out of court with their own money. The 1,200 investors pulled into the scam, spread out over twenty-nine countries, collectively recovered 10 percent of the almost $8 million they invested. REF.: *CBA.*

Hoffman, John Thompson, 1828-88, U.S., lawyer. Practiced law in New York City beginning in 1849. He became a member of the Tammany Society in 1859, was elected mayor of New York in 1865 and 1867, and as the governor of New York in 1868 and 1870. The Tweed Ring flourished while he was in office and even though he was never indicted, his political career was ruined after Tweed was convicted. REF.: *CBA.*

Hoffman, Julius Jennings, b.1895, U.S., jur. Served as judge of the superior court of Cook County, Ill., from 1947-53. He was nominated to the northern district court of Illinois by President Dwight D. Eisenhower in 1953. He edited the *American Journal of Criminal Law and Criminology.* REF.: *CBA.*

Hoffman, Peter, prom. 1920s, U.S., law enfor. off. Peter Hoffman was a political hack who became sheriff of Cook County. He was perhaps one of the most corrupt lawmen in Chicago during the 1920s. Prisoners having money to bribe him could enjoy pleasures in the county jail, including liquor and even women who were brought into the sheriff's private offices for assignations with favored prisoners. When more important Chicago gangsters such as Frankie Lake and Terry Druggan were sent to serve time in Hoffman's jail in 1924, Hoffman's pockets were lined with $20,000. The money was delivered by Morris

Eller, political front-man for the Druggan-Lake gang, who told Sheriff Hoffman to "treat the boys right." Druggan and Lake spent little time in their so-called cells, private rooms with their own baths. They were let out during the day to tend to their bootlegging empires and returned at night to sleep at the jail. When this arrangement was discovered by the press, Hoffman was brought to trial. He was fined $2,500 and sentenced to thirty days, which he spent behind the bars of his own jail. Hoffman had been portrayed as Sheriff Peter Hartman in the play *The Front Page,* by Ben Hecht and Charles MacArthur.

REF.: Asbury, *The Chicago Underworld; CBA.*

Hoffman, Victor Ernest, 1946- , Can., mur. At 5 a.m. on Aug. 15, 1967, Victor Ernest Hoffman went for a drive to stave off his urge to kill. But at a farm just outside Spiritwood, Saskatchewan, he could no longer resist.

By 3 p.m., an inquest was being held at the farm of James Hodgson Peterson and his wife, Evelyn May Peterson. A neighbor had found both of them dead of gunshot wounds. Seven of their eight children, ranging in age from one to seventeen years old, were also dead. The uninjured survivor was three-year-old Phyllis Peterson. Except for James Peterson, who had been shot several times in the stomach, all of the victims had been shot once in the head with a .22-caliber rifle bullet. The only evidence was five shotgun shells and three bloody footprints.

Three days later, a tip from a farmer led police to the Hoffman home, and Victor Hoffman was questioned about the night of the murder. Hoffman, who had earlier been convicted of breaking and entering three times and was under medication for a psychiatric disorder, said that he had been home the night of Aug. 14. He said he had a .22-caliber rifle and a pair of rubber boots, and wouldn't mind having the police examine them. Subsequent examination proved that Hoffman's Browning rifle was the gun used in the murders and that his boots matched the footprints found at the Peterson home. On Aug. 19, Hoffman was arrested for the murder of James Hodgson Peterson.

Hoffman confessed soon after he was arrested. "I don't know what made me do it," he said. He explained that he had tried to collect all the cartridges after the shooting and thought he had them all. He planned to change the firing pin and the rifling on the gun so that no one could identify it as the weapon. The devil had led him to do this, he said.

Hoffman, according to doctors, was a schizophrenic, and had been off his medication for about a week. According to his family, he had been acting strangely the past few weeks, shooting his gun at the sky and saying he was shooting at the devil. He often talked gibberish and was withdrawn. At Hoffman's trial in January 1968, a jury found him Not Guilty by reason of insanity, and he was committed to the Correctional Institute at Prince Albert, Saskatchewan. REF.: *CBA.*

Hoffman, Walter Edward, 1907- , U.S., jur. Taught at William and Mary Law School in Virginia from 1933-42. He was nominated to the eastern district court of Virginia by President Dwight D. Eisenhower in 1954. REF.: *CBA.*

Hoffner, Anna, and **Greil, Hans,** prom. 1938, Ger., rob.-mur. When the body of Wilhelm Hayn was found stabbed seventeen times and shot twice in the basement below his shop, the town of Dortmund, Ger., had no idea who would want to kill this friendly shoemaker. But the police soon had a motive: Hayn's cobbler shop was a front for the more lucrative and illegal business of fencing stolen goods. It was suspected that one of his underground clients had been disappointed with his services. There was little evidence, however, and the myriad of fingerprints found at the scene of the crime were unidentifiable. The long strands of auburn hair found there were of little help; whoever had murdered the shoemaker did not have a prior police record.

A lead eventually came with the arrival in town of a young gang, all men except for their leader, a red-headed woman. When an officer noticed a woman with auburn hair acting nervous in front of a cinema, he watched her closely. She eventually went into the theater alone but came out with another man. The police followed the two back to her apartment. When the young man left alone with a briefcase, he was approached. He ran, dropping the case. Inside the case were some stolen gold plates.

The apartment belonged to Anna Hoffner, the apparent leader of the gang. Some days later, a drunken man creating a disturbance was arrested and linked with the gang. He eventually confessed that Hoffner had killed Hayn with another gang member, Hans Greil. This caused quite a disturbance: Greil happened to be the son of the police chief of Dortmund. Hoffner and Greil were charged and found Guilty of murder. The two were too young to be executed, but they were sentenced to lengthy prison terms. The police chief, although he had no direct connection with the crime, was forced to resign. REF.: *CBA*.

Hoffner, Louis, 1913- , U.S., (wrong. convict.) mur. Convicted of the murder of bartender Peter Trifon, killed during a New York City holdup on Aug. 8, 1940, Louis Hoffner knew that a death sentence meant an automatic appeal. "I am not guilty," he told his sentencing judge, "and I have the right to have the higher court review this case." The judge refused to "play with Hoffner's life." He sentenced him to life in prison.

That may have been the end of the story, except that in 1947, a law school professor mentioned the case to newspaper reporter Edward Mowery as an example of a miscarriage of justice. Hoffner had been indicted, the professor told Mowery, on the flimsy identification of one witness, after two other witnesses had said Hoffner clearly was not the murderer. Mowery spent years putting together witnesses' accounts that corroborated Hoffner's alibi. He presented this new information to the prosecutor's office.

In November 1952, after almost twelve years, Hoffner's conviction was thrown out and he was released. Almost three years later, court of claims judge Fred A. Young, finding that the district attorney's office had withheld information and falsely imprisoned Hoffner, awarded him $112,291, stating that "any (financial) reward is bound to be a mere token" of redress for the wrongs done to Hoffner, "but it should compensate as well as the medium allows."

REF.: *CBA*; Radin, *The Innocents*.

Hofman, Mark W., 1955- , U.S., forg.-mur. A self-described "eighth generation Mormon," Mark Hofman was a native of Salt Lake City, Utah. He was fascinated with Joseph Smith, the founder of the Church of The Latter-Day Saints, describing him as a man who understood how to "create history." Hofman's father insisted on absolute adherence to the Mormon doctrine. Apparently, Hofman became disillusioned with his religion as a teenager, and, unable to express his doubts, channelled them into an elaborate plan.

By his mid-twenties, Hofman was a celebrated and respected member of the Mormon community. He had sold scores of historical documents, earning more than $2 million for his "discoveries." The early documents justified the church's position, and were sold to the Mormon church as well as to collectors. But then Hofman began to "find" papers that cast serious doubt on the origins and truth of the church's history. They included the infamous "White Salamander Letter" which linked church founder Joseph Smith with early nineteenth century folk magic, including such superstitious practices as digging for money, spell casting, and divining the future with "seer stones." The letter said that a spirit in the form of a white salamander, not an angel, had told Smith to found the church. Hofman sold the letter in 1984 to Steven F. Christensen, a Mormon bishop, for $40,000. Another forgery suggested that Joseph Smith's sacred *Book of Mormon* was really a fictional story about American Indians. Concerned Mormon officials bought Hofman's papers at exorbitant prices and hid them in church vaults to keep them from critics and curious historians.

Hofman began to deal in other historical materials, including a document supposedly prepared by seventeenth century members of the Massachusetts Bay Colony. The Library of Congress confirmed the paper's authenticity through the Federal Bureau of Investigation, and planned to buy it. But it later decided it could not afford the $1 million price.

Hofman came increasingly under suspicion. He bounced checks, and was unable to deliver a forged "McLellin Collection" that he had promised the church. A Mormon leader had already arranged a $185,000 bank loan to make the purchase.

Facing angry investors and obligations he could not possibly meet, Hofman looked to murder as a way out. He planted pipe bombs that killed Steven Christensen, thirty-one, his associate in the document trade, and Kathleen Sheets, fifty, the wife of James Gary Sheets, Christensen's business partner. Christensen had recently been hired as a consultant in a deal Hofman was working on and would have known Hofman's articles were counterfeit. Both murders occurred on Oct. 15, 1985. On Oct. 16 Hofman himself was badly injured when a third bomb exploded in his car in downtown Salt Lake City, just minutes away from the Mormon Temple. Although Hofman later claimed that he had tried to kill himself, authorities believe the third explosive was meant for another Mormon document collector.

Hofman was initially charged with first-degree murder, which, in Salt Lake City, carries a mandatory death penalty. A plea bargain reduced the charges to two counts of second-degree murder, though Hofman's father encouraged Hofman to accept death according to the Mormon doctrine of "blood atonement." On Jan. 23, 1987, Hofman pleaded guilty to two counts of second-degree murder and multiple counts of fraud in the forgery of historical documents. He was sentenced to five years to life in prison. In September 1988 he overdosed on an antidepressant drug and was found comatose by his cell mate at Utah State Prison, but survived.

There are several books about Hofman's exploits, a film is in development, and a four-hour miniseries, *The Mormon Murders*, was cancelled indefinitely for "script rewrites and revisions," possibly due to the influence of the Church of the Latter-Day Saints. REF.: *CBA*.

Hofmann, Kuno, 1931- , Ger., burg.-can.-necro.-mur. Between April 1971 and May 1972, sections of northern West Germany were besieged by a series of sick crimes. Corpses were removed from their resting places and defiled in various ways—decapitated, mutilated, or partially eaten. There were also instances of attempted sexual intercourse. Finally, on May 6, 1972, in the village of Lindelburg, when a teenage couple was shot dead in their car, a witness saw a man with a leather hat and glasses dash away on a red motorbike. There was evidence that the murderer had drunk some of the dead young woman's blood and had been examining her genitals before he fled. He became the prime suspect.

On May 10, a transport company worker told authorities that the man they wanted was quitting his job at the company, and that they had better apprehend him quickly. The police drove quickly to the company and arrested Kuno Hofmann, forty-one. Hofmann and his brother had been brutally beaten by a sadistic father as they grew up, beatings that had left Hofman a dwarfish deaf-mute with an IQ of seventy. Hofmann, who had served nine years for theft, confessed to all the crimes against the corpses and several others as well. In addition to killing the teenagers, he had shot and wounded mortuary attendant George Warmuth, who discovered him kissing a corpse. Doctors explained that he could not separate reality from the fantasy crimes he committed in his head.

Searching Hofmann's house, which he shared with his brother and sister, police found books on satanism and witchcraft. Hofmann had garnered from these books the idea that he could be strong and handsome if he performed rituals on dead bodies. When that had not worked, he had switched to live victims, killing the two teenagers. He was never brought to trial, but was committed for life to an institution for the criminally insane. REF.: *CBA*.

Hofmann, Melchior (Melchoir Hoffmann), c.1495-1544, Fr., her. German who became a Lutheran lay minister and traveled to several countries. Frederick I of Denmark made him a preacher at Kiel, but he was opposed to Martin Luther's view of Eucharist and so he was banished from Denmark. Later he became an Anabaptist. He won many followers after establishing a doctrine that said the world would end. In 1533 he was arrested in Strasbourg, Fr., and imprisoned for life. REF.: *CBA*.

Hofrichter, Adolph (AKA: **Dr. Haller**), b.1879, Aust., mur. On Nov. 18, 1909, Captain Richard Mader of Austria's High Command received a package containing "potency pills" and a letter describing their wonderful effects. He eagerly ripped open the pill packet, according to an aide, and was dead by the time the aide returned thirty minutes later. Dr. Stuckart, chief of the criminal investigation department of Vienna, soon learned that eleven other officers received the same packages but had not taken the enclosed wonder drugs. The pills were analyzed, and identified as potassium cyanide. Austrian Emperor Franz Josef I, concerned that a conspiracy was afloat to dismantle his army, assigned Colonel Freiherr von Kutschera and Captain-Auditor Kunz to investigate. They searched for someone within their ranks who could benefit from the deaths of General Staff officers. Kunz discovered that all of the package recipients graduated from the Military Academy in 1905. A search of records revealed that 1905 graduate Lieutenant Adolph Hofrichter, had been rejected for a permanent General Staff post after a temporary, unsuccessful appointment to the staff. His handwriting matched that on the letters sent with the packages.

On Nov. 27, Hofrichter, now serving with the 14th Infantry Regiment in Linz, was arrested. Two cardboard boxes identical to the packages, a mimeograph machine, and capsules were found in his home. As an amateur photographer, he had access to potassium cyanide. The War Ministry issued a statement that they suspected Hofrichter "with a probability bordering on certainty." He was taken to the military prison in Vienna, where he was held for seven months before his court-martial began. Hofrichter was denied visitors after trying to escape and attempting to smuggle a letter to his wife requesting atropine or hyoscyamine with which to kill himself. Lieutenant Hofrichter signed a confession after his wife was arrested for being an accessory to murder. He retracted the confession three days later, after the charge against his wife was dropped.

Hofrichter was tried before a military tribunal on June 8, 1910. As he was not allowed to have his own attorney, Captain Kunz served as prosecutor and defense lawyer in the case. Trying to give more impact to circumstantial evidence, Kunz explained that one of the letters was addressed with a misspelling—an identical misspelling occurred on a list of army officers in the Linz garrison that Hofrichter had apparently copied. The capsules found at Hofrichter's home, however, were dog medicine, Kunz said in Hofrichter's defense.

Hofrichter's case was particularly damaged by witnesses who verified rumors that the officer had committed crimes under the alias Dr. Haller. One young woman stated that Hofrichter, using his Haller identity, tried to assault her when she answered an advertisement for a babysitter. The cases for and against Hofrichter were presented in one day, and on June 9, the lieutenant was ordered dishonorably discharged and sentenced to twenty years at Mollersdorf jail. REF.: *CBA*.

Hogan, Barbara Ann, c.1952- , S. Afri., treas. The first person in South Africa to be convicted of treason without being suspected of violent activity, Barbara Ann Hogan was sentenced to ten years imprisonment for high treason. Hogan, a white anthropologist, denied any criminal wrong-doing in her October 1982 trial, but admitted she was a member of the African National Congress (ANC), banned since 1961. Membership in a banned organization is a violation of South African law. Lawyers against Hogan argued in court that in 1977 she joined the ANC in Swaziland and made five trips to nearby Botswana to receive secret codes and be given secret directives. She admitted writing reports regarding labor matters that were smuggled to exiled ANC leaders and to organizing consumer boycotts to help striking black trade unions. Rand Supreme Court Judge H.P. Van Dyk found Hogan guilty of

organizing unemployed people to fight apartheid and of working with black labor groups. In August 1982, two security policemen were acquitted of assaulting Hogan during interrogation. A doctor at their trial testified that he found bruises on Hogan that she could not have inflicted on herself. REF.: *CBA*.

Hogan, Danny (AKA: **Dapper Danny**), d.1928, U.S., smug. During Prohibition, "Dapper" Danny Hogan was the "Smiling Peacemaker" of the St. Paul., Minn., underworld. He was so active that police acknowledged him as a positive influence in keeping crooks out of town. On Dec. 4, 1928, Hogan was fatally injured when a bomb exploded as he started his car. Before he died, he said he did not have an enemy in the world. Scores of volunteers, including prominent businessmen, donated blood in a futile attempt to save his life. Police attributed the attack to a gambling feud or a fight over bootlegging territory. One suspect was George Musey, who banished Hogan from bootlegging on the Gulf Coast. Musey himself was murdered in Galveston, Texas. REF.: *CBA*.

Hogan, Frank, prom. 1940s-50s, U.S., crim. law. Frank Hogan was one of the more aggressive district attorneys for New York City, who was responsible for exposing the myriad swindles enacted by corporate stock con man Lowell McAfee Birrell in the late 1950s. Hogan also was instrumental in working with Navy intelligence during WWII, in setting up what was later termed the Luciano Project. Charles "Lucky" Luciano, who had been one of New York's top crime bosses, was serving time on vice convictions. Hogan and others convinced Luciano to aid the Navy by using his contacts in Sicily to help in the invasion of that island in 1943. It was Luciano's report-

New York district attorney Frank Hogan.

ed cooperation in this matter that assured his release from prison following the war, on the proviso that he be deported to his native Italy. See: **Birrell, Lowell McAfee; Luciano, Charles**.

REF.: *CBA*; Cressey, *Theft of the Nation*; Demaris, *Captive City*; ____, *The Director*; Fried, *The Rise and Fall of the Jewish Gangster in America*; Gage, *Mafia, U.S.A.*; -----, *The Mafia is not an Equal Opportunity Employer*; Gosch and Hammer, *The Last Testament of Lucky Luciano*; Katz, *Uncle Frank*; McClellan, *Crime and Punishment*; McPhaul, *Johnny Torrio*; Martin, *Revolt in the Mafia*; Messick, *Lansky*; Messick and Goldblatt, *The Mobs and the Mafia*; Nash, *Hustlers and Con Men*; Navasky, *Kennedy Justice*; Peterson, *The Mob*; Reid, *The Grim Reapers*; Reuter, *Disorganized Crime*; Sann, *Kill the Dutchman!*; Servadio, *Mafioso*; Wicker, *Investigating the FBI*.

Hogan, Michael J., prom. 1930s, U.S., polit. corr. After serving two years in Congress as a Republican, U.S. Representative Michael J. Hogan returned to Brooklyn, N.Y., where he opened a private office and peddled his political influence. Hogan was charged with accepting $725 from two men wanting city plumbers' licenses in 1934. In April 1935, as a confidential clerk to the Collector of the Port of New York, he was charged with taking $300 from three Italians in exchange for illegal citizenship papers. Convicted in a federal court six months later, Hogan was fined $100, and sentenced to 366 days in prison. REF.: *CBA*.

Hogg, Douglas McGarel (Viscount Hailsham), 1872-1950, Brit., atty. gen. Practiced law in 1902 and became an attorney general for the Prince of Wales in 1920. He was a member of Parliament from 1922-28, served as attorney general from 1922-38, and from 1931-35 served as the secretary of war. REF.: *CBA*.

Hogg, Mary Anne, b.1838, Brit., (unsolv.) mur. Two wealthy spinster sisters, 68-year-old Mary Anne Hogg and 62-year-old Caroline Gwinnell Hogg, lived together in Camberley, England. On the afternoon of June 11, 1906, Caroline appeared covered with blood at a neighbor's house. Mary Anne lay dead on the floor of their home. Both had been struck repeatedly with a cloth-covered hammer and had their throats slit with a knife. At an inquest a month later, Caroline stated that on the day of the attack she encountered in the stairwell of the home a man dressed as a bricklayer, whose face was camouflaged by a light-colored string net. While Caroline attempted to give him money, Mary Anne staggered in from the garden covered in blood. The man then attacked Caroline. A pathologist said that the attacks were similar and the wounds caused by great force, ending any speculation that they were self-inflicted. The police mounted a full investigation, but the murderer was never apprehended. REF.: *CBA*.

Hohenau, Walter (Frederick Jonas), prom. 1927, U.S., fraud. Born in Germany, Walter Hohenau was involved with con games from an early age. He served two prison terms in Germany for swindles, one at age fourteen, before he migrated to the U.S. In 1927, Hohenau appeared in Houston, Texas, and established himself as an inventor with substantial European credentials (all false). He spent months promoting his secret new energy formula, giving interviews, and conducting tours of his impressive-looking factory where several dozen fellow scientists seemed to be hard at work. After establishing important business contacts, Hohenau gave an enormous banquet in one of Houston's largest hotels for scores of Houston's leading businessmen.

In the middle of the sumptuous fete, Hohenau unveiled his new invention, one which towered above the guests and shimmered with lights that flashed and glimmered. Gadgets on the machine whirred and twirled and bells rang. The noises emanating from this incredible machine were positively alien to this world, or so some guests claimed. A powerful electric engine hidden in the contraption generated part of the noise and this was supplemented by an ammeter, a voltmeter, and a score of strange devices that were later determined to be door buzzers.

Hohenau then told his guests that his machine could split oxygen atoms which, in turn, would produce powerful hydrogen gas. "The world will never be without power again!" shouted Hohenau to his applauding audience. "It will cost practically nothing to provide fuel purely from water, all achieved by my marvelous hydroatomizer!" As he talked, Hohenau flicked a switch back and forth which shot bursts of hydrogen flames from a hidden hydrogen tank. Hohenau then produced small amounts of "fuel" from his contraption, and gave these samples to investors interested in his Hydro Production Company. The samples were very much like refined gasoline, which was successfully tested on autos and speedboats. Investors rushed to give Hohenau more than $100,000. The inventor then closed shop, paid off his factory workers, small time con men, and left Houston.

Hohenau next appeared in Mexico, where he employed a similar ruse to swindle President Putarco Calles out of a substantial but unspecified sum of money. The colossal fraud brazenly sold variations of his useless hydroatomizer to German president Paul von Hindenburg and many other world leaders. He was finally exposed and thrown into a German jail from which he escaped during WWII when Allied bombs blew the walls of his cell away. He reportedly returned to the U.S. and lived out his life under an alias.

REF.: *CBA*; Nash, *Hustlers and Con Men*.

Hohensee, Adolphus, 1911- , U.S., fraud. Adolphus Hohensee irritated both the Food and Drug Administration (FDA) and the American Medical Association (AMA) for decades with his success at passing himself off as a nutritionist. Before trying his hand at food fraud, Hohensee had defrauded victims in a real estate scam in Galveston, Texas, where they would pay him to help sell their property. After being caught eagerly taking client's money but making little effort to sell their property, Hohensee was arrested. He pleaded guilty to charges of mail fraud and was sentenced to a one-month jail term and five years' probation. Hohensee then began a sightseeing venture in Washington, D.C., that included ownership of several gas stations and 140 taxis. Also less than

legitimate, the operation was closed and Hohensee was arrested several times for bouncing checks and other misdemeanors. Later, four assault charges were brought against him, but he was never prosecuted.

Early in the 1940s, Hohensee started lecturing on nutrition, misrepresenting himself as a medical doctor. From 1943-46, Hohensee collected three dubious medical degrees including an honorary degree of Doctor of Medicine from the Kansas City University of Physicians and Surgeons, an uncredited institution that closed the next year. He traveled throughout the West, charging lecture fees and selling products such as tar shampoo, soybean lecithin, and herbal laxatives under the Adolphus Brand label. Hohensee would also sell self-help pamphlets to his nutrition classes, with titles such as *Your Personality Glands* and *Better Eyes without Glasses*.

At the start of his career, Hohensee was charged with a crime in nearly every town he lectured, paying from $50 to $200 fines for selling drugs without a license, and, in San Francisco, paying a $300 fee for posing as a physician. Hohensee's war with the FDA began in December 1943, when the department seized a large shipment of the con man's pamphlets and nutritional products on grounds that both were deceptive. The goods were destroyed after Hohensee made no effort to reclaim them. The loss was slight to Hohensee because he could earn approximately $45,000 in one lecture series.

Criminal charges were finally brought against him, charging Hohensee with mislabeling his products. He was found Guilty of misbranding in Phoenix, Ariz., in February 1948, and fined $1,800. The conviction did not stop Hohensee from attracting large audiences, however, and the law only stopped him from selling his wares at lectures. Showing his typical adroitness, Hohensee arranged for his products to be sold at health stores in cities where he was lecturing. He even extended the Adolphus Brand product line to expensive gadgets, such as a $195 tenderizer he said was necessary to prepare his special, healthful recipes.

FDA agents continued to attend his lectures, carefully recording his words and methods. Hohensee frequently disparaged national brand foods; he would, for example, wad a ball out of a loaf of bread and drop it to the floor to demonstrate that it was made from flour robbed of vitamins and minerals. He would then pitch his own "all natural" products, such as El Rancho Adolphus apple juice, named for Hohensee's Scranton farm, to which he charged admission. Hohensee could not be stopped by petty fines in various cities, so the Federal Trade Commission eventually ordered him to stop making false claims in his advertising. He was again taken to court by the FDA in Scranton in November 1954, charged with mislabeling his products by failing to explain what illnesses they supposedly cured. He was found Guilty, and sentenced to one year and a day in prison. The FDA and the AMA eventually issued educational programs to protect audiences from people like Hohensee, but criminal prosecution did little to change the opinions of an adoring public. REF.: *CBA*.

Holbrook, Ernest, Jr., 1963- , U.S., (wrong. convict.) rape-mur. On Oct. 29, 1981, 12-year-old Tina Harmon was last seen in a grocery store in Creston, Ohio. Her body was found on Nov. 3, dead from strangulation and bearing evidence of sexual molestation. Within three months, Ernest Holbrook, Jr., a part-time worker on a potato farm, and Herman Ray Rucker were arrested for the rape and murder. On June 9, 1982, Rucker was convicted and sentenced to life in prison, and two months later, Holbrook received the same sentence. They were convicted largely on the testimony of Holbrook's cousin, Curtis Maynard, and his girlfriend, Susan Sigler, who both stated that Rucker had admitted killing the girl after she resisted his sexual advances. However, Holbrook had been at a wedding at the time of the abduction, and there was no physical evidence linking the two convicted men to the crime. Also, after they were taken into custody, two similar child murders occurred.

The prosecution's two witnesses had lied repeatedly. Sigler, who had been married four times, stated on another marriage application in July 1982 that she had been married only once before. Shortly after, she was convicted of filing a false rape charge. Meanwhile, Maynard was found to be mentally retarded, with a previous record of felony convictions. After he was arrested again for theft, he recanted the testimony which had convicted Rucker and Holbrook. Rucker was granted a new trial, and was acquitted in June 1983, while Holbrook remained in detention.

On July 17, 1982, 11-year-old Krista Lea Harrison was abducted near her home in Marshallville, Ohio. Her body was found a short time later, in a garage on a nearby rural road. Police found carpet fibers which were identical to those found at the site of the Harmon murder, and traced them to a van owned by Robert A. Buell, a former employee of the city of Akron. Buell was convicted of the murders, and on Apr. 11, 1984, was sentenced to die in the electric chair. On May 4, 1984, all charges against Holbrook were dropped and he was released from the Lima, Ohio, Correctional Facility. REF.: *CBA*.

Holden, Alan, prom. 1967, U.S., miss. per. On July 3, 1967, Dr. Alan Holden, co-chief of the psychiatric prison ward at Bellevue Hospital in New York City, was seen for the last time. His disappearance from his home office on Park Avenue coincided with a series of violent crimes at Bellevue, including the rapes of nurses, the shooting of a doctor, the stabbing of another doctor, as well as assorted burglaries and robberies. Holden's disappearance may have been intentional. His safe-deposit box was empty, and his passport was missing. However, a number of his paychecks were uncashed, and the near-sighted doctor's glasses were found in his apartment. He may have been kidnapped by a psychotic patient, but no ransom was ever demanded. A woman patient with alleged Mafia connections was suspected, but nothing was proven. In June 1983, Holden's colleague, Dr. Martin Lubin, suggested that the missing doctor may have been murdered, as he received many threats at Bellevue. REF.: *CBA*.

Holden, Frank, 1883-1914, U.S., smug. A native of Ohio, Frank Holden was raised in an upper middle-class family and, upon graduation from high school, moved to New York City, looking for adventure. He fell in with a white slave gang and for a while became a runner and then a pimp, but he found this criminal pursuit unsavory. With his earnings, Holden traveled to the West Coast in 1909, and, through his underworld contacts, joined a gang of smugglers in San Francisco. He soon became the head of this gang and established a regular ferry system from Vancouver to San Francisco, smuggling Chinese into the U.S. Holden became rich within five years and purchased a large home and considerable real estate. He married and his wife bore him a son.

By day, Holden appeared to be a law-abiding real estate broker, but at night, he met with his gang of smugglers and continued his operations. On July 9, 1914, while aboard a fast boat running along the California shoreline, Holden encountered an armed Coast Guard vessel. He and his men tried to outrun the boat, firing at it as they attempted to turn out to sea with their cargo of Chinese. A shell from the Coast Guard ship struck Holden's vessel below the waterline. Before the federal craft could come to the rescue, his boat sank and all on board except one perished. The surviving gang member revealed Holden's story to police. REF.: *CBA*.

Holden, James Stuart, b.1914, U.S., jur. Served as prosecuting officer of Bennington County, Vt., from 1947-48, as chief superior justice of Vermont from 1949-56, as associate justice of Vermont from 1956-63, and as chief justice of Vermont from 1963-72. He was nominated to the district court of Vermont by President Richard M. Nixon in 1971. REF.: *CBA*.

Holden, Thomas, and **Keating, Francis (The Evergreen Bandits)**, prom. 1920s-30s, U.S., rob. Thomas Holden and his close friend Francis Keating were products of the Midwest, having grown up together in Illinois. They both held legitimate jobs when in their twenties, usually as cab drivers. They tired of their work and low pay and decided, after considerable conversation about

Jesse James and other bandits of the Old West, to rob a train. They studied the schedules and mail shipments containing federal reserve money, obtaining this information from Charles S. Wharton, former U.S. Congressman and state's attorney.

Holden, Keating, Charles "Limpy Charlie" Cleaver, and three other men planted a bomb beneath the tracks of the Grand Trunk Railway in a remote spot of Evergreen Park, Ill., and exploded it on the night of Feb. 25, 1928, bringing the mail train to a halt. The bandits broke into the mail car and quickly carried out mail sacks containing more than $133,000 in cash and securities. Cleaver was later picked up and questioned. He admitted Wharton's role in the robbery. Much of the loot was found hidden in Wharton's Chicago home. Holden and Keating, also turned in by Cleaver, were arrested; the other three bandits were never apprehended. Wharton received a two-year sentence but Cleaver, Holden, and Keating were each given twenty-five-year sentences in the federal penitentiary at Leavenworth.

Through George Barnes (later known as George "Machine Gun" Kelly), a prisoner who worked in the identification office of the penitentiary, Holden and Keating, on Feb. 28, 1930, obtained fake passports that allowed them to simply walk out of the prison. They immediately went on a bank-robbing spree with various gangs, including that of Charles Harmon, Frank Nash, Harvey Bailey, and the Barker Brothers. Both Holden and Keating were golf enthusiasts and they joined Harvey Bailey on July 8, 1932, to play the links at the Old Mission Golf Course in Kansas City, Mo. Only hours before these three gangsters arrived at the gold course, all smartly attired in golfing knickers and cleated spectator shoes, they fenced bonds worth thousands of dollars which had been taken from their robbery of the Fort Scott, Kan., bank on June 17, 1932. (Freddie Barker, Alvin Karpis, Larry DeVol, and Bernard "Red" Phillips had been with the three on the Fort Scott raid.)

Just as the gangster trio began to play, FBI agent Raymond Caffrey, who knew the robbers' penchant for golf and had spotted Keating days earlier at the course, stepped forth with other agents and arrested Bailey, Holden, and Keating. Holden protested, telling Caffrey that they were "just three innocent guys trying to play a round of golf."

"Cut that," Caffrey said, as local police trained guns on the trio. "The jig is up, Tommy. You boys will be back in Leavenworth by tomorrow morning." Caffrey was correct. He helped escort Holden and Keating to Leavenworth the next day. Caffrey

1930s bank robber Tommy Holden.

would lose his life the following year in the Kansas City Massacre.

At the time of their arrest, Lillian Holden, thirty, and Marjorie Keating, twenty-six, were sitting in a car, watching their husbands on the golf course. When they saw them manacled by policemen, they ran forward. Caffrey allowed Holden and Keating to sign over their golf clubs and other possessions (except cash) to their wives. Bailey was also arrested, giving the alias of John Brown, but he was later identified as a wanted bank robber and was tried and sent to prison. He escaped several times and was later implicated in the kidnapping of Charles F. Urschel, a crime of which he was innocent, one that had really been committed by George "Machine Gun" Kelly, his wife Kathryn Kelly, and Albert Bates.

Holden and Keating spent several years in Leavenworth and were later transferred to Alcatraz. Both men were released decades later. Keating retired to Florida and was never again involved in crime. Holden, returning to his wife in Chicago, became an alcoholic; in a drunken rage, he killed his wife and mother-in-law and then fled to the state of Washington, where he was apprehended. He was returned to Illinois, convicted of second-degree murder, and sent to the Joliet State Prison, where he died of a heart attack. See: **Bailey, Harvey John; Barker Brothers; Cleaver, Charles; Harmon, Charles Preston; Kansas City Massacre; Karpis, Alvin; Kelly, George; Nash, Frank.**

REF.: *CBA;* Cooper, *Ten Thousand Public Enemies;* Edge, *Run the Cat Roads;* Gish, *American Bandits;* Karpis, *The Alvin Karpis Story;* ____, *On the Rock;* Louderback, *The Bad Ones;* Nash, *Bloodletters and Badmen;* Wellman, *A Dynasty of Western Outlaws.*

Holden, William, 1770-1817, and **Ashcroft, James, Sr.,** 1764-1817, and **Ashcroft, David,** 1769-1817, and **Ashcroft, James, Jr.,** 1785-1817, Brit., rob.-mur. Thomas Littlewood of Pendleton arrived home one evening in 1817 to find his wife, 75-year-old Mrs. Marsden, and boarder, 20-year-old Hannah Partington, dead in the kitchen. They had been beaten and mutilated with a fire poker and meat cleaver. Money, along with some articles of clothing, was missing from the house. Four men who were seen near the house on the day of the murders were later observed at both the Black Horse and the Horseshoe pubs, showing off bank notes and quantities of gold. William Holden, James Ashcroft, Sr., David Ashcroft, and James Ashcroft, Jr., were arrested for robbery and murder, along with John Robinson, who was seen whispering with the others, before the murders, at the Crown and Anchor Inn. After brief deliberations, four of the men were found Guilty; Robinson was acquitted. On Sept. 8, 1817, the convicted killers were hanged. REF.: *CBA.*

Holder, Cale James, b.1912, U.S., jur. Served part-time as deputy felony prosecutor of the nineteenth judicial circuit of Indiana from 1941-2, and in 1946. He was nominated to the district court of Indiana by President Dwight D. Eisenhower in 1954. REF.: *CBA.*

Holder, Luther, prom. 1942, Case of, U.S., pol. mal.-lynch. On Oct. 16, 1942, an armed mob broke into the Laurel, Miss., jail, seizing Howard Wash, a black man convicted only hours earlier of murdering his white employer, Clint Welborn. The mob hanged Wash at Welborn's Bridge, with no interference from police officials, including Deputy Sheriff Luther Holder, who apparently saw the killers take Wash. Demands by Mississippi Governor Paul B. Johnson, outraged by the third Mississippi lynching in a month, and apparently inspired by a scathing editorial in the Jones County *Leader-Call,* led to federal indictments against Holder, Barney Jones, Allen Pryor, William Oscar Johnson, and Nathaniel T. Shotts. The Holder case was the third time that federal charges were brought against southern lynchers; the two earlier cases ended in acquittals. Tried before Federal Judge Sidney C. Mize, Holder, Jones, and Pryor were found Not Guilty. Charges against Johnson and Shotts were dropped because of a lack of evidence. REF.: *CBA.*

Hole-in-the-Wall, prom. 1890s-1900s, U.S., west. outl. hideout. The Hole-in-the-Wall was a seemingly impenetrable hideout used by Butch Cassidy and members of the Wild Bunch during the heyday of this last of the Old West's super bandit gangs. This hideout, which no one has been able to pinpoint to this day, was somewhere in the deep mountain ravines and gorges near the meeting place of the Colorado, Utah, and Wyoming state lines. It was reportedly discovered by George "Big Nose" Curry, one of the elder statesmen of the Wild Bunch, and it was home for more than twenty years to the likes of Butch Cassidy, the Sundance Kid (Harry Longbaugh), Kid Curry (Harvey Logan), O.C. Hanks, Ben Kilpatrick, William "News" Carver, Harry Tracy, Elza Lay, and dozens of other desperadoes. When these outlaws were all either imprisoned or killed, use of Hole-in-the-Wall ceased. The exact location of this legendary hideout is still a mystery. REF.: *CBA.*

Hole-In-The-Wall Saloon, prom. 1850s-70s, U.S., vice. The Hole-in-the-Wall Saloon at the corner of Dover and Water streets in Lower Manhattan remained a haven for thieves, muggers, and other criminals for twenty years beginning in the early 1850s. The owner, One-Armed Charley Monell, employed two bouncers, Kate Flannery and a six-foot English woman named Gallus Mag.

Gallus Mag, who earned her nickname by wearing galluses to keep her skirt up, carried a pistol on her belt and a blackjack on her wrist, and while employing both weapons would grab a troublemaker's ear with her teeth and drag them out the door. If any resistance was offered, she severed the ear completely and placed in a trophy jar behind the bar. In 1855, two lowlifes named Slobbery Jim and Patsy the Barber fought a duel over twelve cents, the profits from an earlier mugging, the victim of which had drowned after being placed unconscious on a seawall near Battery Park. The duel lasted thirty minutes, and ended when Slobbery Jim slashed the Barber's throat and kicked him to death. Eventually, complaints about the Hole-In-The-Wall got too numerous to ignore. In early 1871, seven murders were reported there within two months, with an unknown number going unreported. Later that year, police closed the saloon, ending twenty years of bloody criminal activity.

REF.: *CBA;* Thrasher, *The Gang.*

Holland, Anne (AKA: **Anne Andrews, Anne Charlton, Anne Edwards, Anne Goddard, Anne Jackson**), d.1705, Brit., rob. One of Anne Holland's favorite ploys was to get herself hired as a servant so she could steal from her employers. In one case, her mistress had just left home when the master attempted to seduce Holland. She insisted that he remove his stiff boots first. She helped him off with the first one, began to remove the second, then grabbed a two quart silver tankard and went downstairs, supposedly to bring up some beer. Holland disappeared with the silver, leaving her employer in a highly compromising position, unable to get his boot off or on. On another occasion Holland stayed up all night making dresses of her mistress' fine sheets, and left the next morning wearing several layers of clothes.

Holland apparently accepted several suitors. She married a Mr. French, but he was appalled when his wife delivered a baby girl only six months after the marriage. French turned Holland out of his home and moved to Ireland, where he soon died. Left to provide for herself, Holland became an adept pickpocket. She then married James Wilson, a celebrated highwayman who was hanged at Maidstone in Kent soon after the wedding.

The resourceful Holland soon became involved with Tristram Savage, whom she met in Newgate Jail. Savage had been jailed for distributing "The Black List," a political tract against the Tory government. With her new lover, Holland went to visit an astrologer, Dr. Trotter in Moorfields, to have her horoscope done. Trotter, believing he had two female clients (Savage was dressed in women's clothes), cast Holland's fate according to the stars, telling her she would soon have a rich husband. The couple gagged and tied Trotter, stole twenty guineas, a gold watch, a silver tobacco box, and two rings.

In 1705, Holland was again arrested for stealing. Taken to Tyburn, she remained unrepentant at the gallows, cursing the hard heart of the judge, the strictness of the laws, and the hangman before she died. REF.: *CBA.*

Holland, Henry Edmund, 1868-1933, N. Zea., consp.-sedition. Born in Australia where he worked as labor leader between 1892-1912. In 1912 he went to New Zealand and edited the *Maoriland Worker* from 1913-18. From 1913-14 he was put in prison for sedition and for agitating others to revolt against the government. Later he founded the Labour party, and served as its head from 1919-33. REF.: *CBA.*

Holland, James Buchanan, 1857-1914, U.S., jur. Served as district attorney of Montgomery County, Pa., from 1893-96, and as district attorney for the U.S. Department of Justice from 1900-04. He was nominated to the eastern district court of Pennsylvania by President Theodore Roosevelt in 1904. REF.: *CBA.*

Holland, John (Duke of Exeter, Earl of Huntingdon), c.1352-1400, Brit., consp. Helped Richard II fight Glouscester and Arundel in 1397. Later he was accused of conspiracy against Henry IV and was executed. REF.: *CBA.*

Holland, Kenneth Raymond, 1920- , Case of, U.S., mur. Kenneth Raymond Holland, a former Norfolk Co., Va., police officer, was convicted and later acquitted of murdering Charles

Everett Utt on June 17, 1948. Utt, who had known Holland for five years, was found bludgeoned to death in his car. Holland was convicted of the murder and sentenced to twenty years' imprisonment in November 1949. The conviction was overturned for lack of sufficient evidence, and Holland was retried several months later.

Holland was originally linked to the crime by a photograph of the dead man's wife, Mary Lee Utt, which he kept in his apartment. Officers who questioned Holland about the photo noticed bloodstained clothes in the man's laundry room. Holland told them that he had been in a fight with a neighbor, Vaden Tomblin, in which he had broken Tomblin's nose. The fight led to a lawsuit filed by Tomblin; evidence was presented by defense attorneys at both of Holland's trials. Mary Lee Utt testified that she had given Holland her photograph and had dated the defendant, with her husband's consent, while he was serving in the Navy. Nell Duke, one of Utt's neighbors, testified that she had seen Holland driving Utt's car the night before the murder, but under questioning revealed that she had never seen the defendant at close range before the trial. After less than one hour of deliberation, a jury acquitted Holland on Apr. 14, 1950. REF.: *CBA*.

Holland, Tom, prom. 1954, Case of, U.S., mur. In May 1954, frenzied prospectors filled the hills around quiet Kanab, Utah, searching for uranium, which had been found there three months earlier. Leroy Albert Wilson, a burly 62-year-old brawler who was excommunicated by the Mormon church for defending polygamy, prospected with a partner, 49-year-old Tom Holland. Wilson was found dead on a sandy flat with six .45-caliber bullet holes in his head and back. Holland was arrested, but had a plausible alibi which was backed up by witnesses at his trial. The jury found Holland Not Guilty, and Wilson's murderer was never found. REF.: *CBA*.

Holle, Edward, prom. 1938, U.S., mur. On Apr. 17, 1938, the body of 23-year-old Sophie Kujat was discovered in the Passaic River by two men working a small skiff near the derricks and oil tanks of Newark, N.J. The corpse had been submerged for one week with forty-foot-long automobile chains that weighed more than sixty pounds. A medical examination by Essex County coroner Harrison Martland determined that Kujat was dead before her killer dumped her body in the river. Police detectives learned that she had once been engaged to Edward Holle, who had married another woman ten months earlier, and that she had been seen with Holle on the night she disappeared. Officers apprehended Holle in East Orange, N.J., and took him into custody for questioning.

For two days, Holle insisted he was innocent. Visiting an oil refinery near where the body had been found, detectives discovered that chains used on the company's trucks were identical to those in which Kujat's dead body had been wrapped. In addition, a set of chains were missing from the storehouse. A night watchman said he had seen Holle on the docks several weeks earlier, and that Holle had borrowed a hand truck from him. Accompanying police to headquarters, the watchman was brought into the room where Sergeant of Detectives Luke Conlon, and officers John Staats, John Haller, and Thomas Bolan were questioning Holle. Taking one look at the watchman, Holle turned pale, cursed, shook his fist, and then confessed. He explained that he had been trying to break off his relationship with Kujat after he married, and had been having an argument with her when he choked her. Not knowing if she was dead or merely unconscious, he strangled her with a clothesline, stuffed her body in the trunk of his car, drove to the garage, and wrapped her in chains before borrowing the truck and discarding her in the river. The day after his confession, Holle reenacted the killing in front of a police camera, marking the first time film had been used to present a case before a New Jersey jury. Arraigned on May 16 before Police Judge Klein, Holle was tried for murder and sentenced in July to a twenty-year to life term. REF.: *CBA*.

Holles, Denzil (Baron Holles), 1599-1680, Brit., polit. corr. He and another member of the House of Commons held down the speaker in his chair when, at the king's command, he attempted to close a 1629 meeting. He was put in prison and received a hefty fine, although the Long Parliament later compensated him. In 1642 he was impeached as one of the Five Members, and was impeached again in 1647 by the Parliamentary army. He left the country for France, but eventually returned to Britain. REF.: *CBA*.

Hollest, George Edward, prom. 1850, Brit., (unsolv.) mur. In 1850 a rash of burglaries and robberies plagued the villages of Eversely, Hampshire, and Frimley. The 54-year-old curate of the Frimley parish, Reverend George Hollest, was shot by thieves who broke into his bedroom at 3 a.m. Hollest, who was considered a strong, active man, struggled with his assailants and was killed. Novelist and Eversely rector Charles Kingsley, bolted and barred his rectory doors in response to his contemporary's murder. Kingsley also took to sleeping with loaded pistols beside him. REF.: *CBA*.

Holliday, Bertram Redvers, prom. 1949, Case of, Brit., fenc.-burg.-suic. The Scotland Yards Flying Squad worked with local police to solve a series of burglaries in Surrey in November 1947, and watched local criminals closely. The first break in the case occurred in February 1949, when Buckinghamshire Chief Inspector Tomlin was called to look into the theft of some cheese from the Dumb Bell Hotel in Taplow. Two men had come into the hotel bar and ordered drinks. As the bartender watched, one of the men hid the cheese under his coat. Tomlin questioned the suspect, Bertram Redvers Holliday, who denied any knowledge of the incident. Tomlin conveyed his suspicions to Superintendent Lee, who remembered Holliday from twenty-four years earlier, when he had been an active burglar. Officers kept Holliday under supervision for three months, during which time he moved to London where they learned that he did not merely receive stolen goods, but with an accomplice, also committed burglaries.

On Dec. 13, Holliday and a man named Oades, also known as Poofy Len, drove in Oades' car to Chelsea bank, where Holliday picked up a parcel. Police stopped the pair, and during a search, found valuable jewelry which Holliday claimed as his own. When officers searched the bank, they found a deed box and a suitcase that contained silver plates and cutlery. Holliday's wife claimed the cutlery, but had no knowledge of the silver. A search of his home uncovered an array of valuable items.

Holliday was charged with unlawful possession of the jewelry and was brought before a West London magistrate and released on a £2,000 bail. Moments later, one of the silver cups was verified as stolen in a 1946 burglary, and Holliday's wife was arrested and charged with receiving stolen property. On Dec. 21, Holliday was found dead, shot through the head at a Virginia Water hotel in Staines. Police estimated that Holliday committed burglaries in and around Surrey, Berkshire, and Buckinghamshire from 1932-49. Mrs. Holliday was tried and found Not Guilty of receiving stolen goods. The court believed that she had been under the influence of her husband. REF.: *CBA*.

Holliday, John (AKA: John Simpson), d.1700, Brit., rob. In his career as a soldier, John Holliday found ample opportunity to steal, including among his victims the king he served under and a church that had given him sanctuary.

Holliday, a soldier in King William III's army, was discharged after the peace of Ryswick, following England's war with France. Holliday, along with several confederates, formed a gang in London with Holliday, using the name of Simpson, as their leader. They plied their trade as highwaymen and housebreakers. In 1700, Holliday was arrested and charged with burglarizing the home of Elizabeth Gawden, where he stole two feather beds along with other goods; he pleaded Guilty and was sentenced to hang.

While awaiting execution, Holliday made a complete confession to a long list of crimes. During the war, when he was a soldier in Flanders, he often robbed the tents of the officers. On one occasion, when the army was stationed at Mons and King William himself was in command, Holliday was one of the soldiers chosen to guard the royal tent. When the King, accompanied by the Earl, soon-to-be Duke of Marlborough, and Lord Cutts went out to review the troops, Holliday went into his tent and stole £1,000. When the theft was finally discovered several days later, Holliday was not under suspicion.

Holliday confessed that he had committed more robberies than he could remember, both in Flanders and in England. He recalled that the gates of the city of Ghent had once been shut twice in ten days to prevent his escape. When he was at last captured in that city his arms, legs, neck, and back were secured in irons; he was carried through the streets in that condition to be publicly shamed.

With two companions, Holliday frequently robbed early-morning churchgoers, and repeatedly broke into churches in Brussels, Mechlin, and Antwerp to steal silver from the altars. Also indicted and condemned for murdering a companion during his military career, Holliday was sentenced to die in full view of the army, which was called out to view the execution. Escaping during the night, he found refuge in the church of St. Peter in Ghent. The priests there took up Holliday's case with Prince Eugene; together, the priests and the prince interceded with King William, and were able to obtain a full pardon for Holliday, who rejoined the army. A few days after being pardoned, Holliday broke into the church where he had been sheltered, robbing it of £1,200; it was easy work since he knew the church's layout so well. He was captured and taken into custody but as he had quickly disposed of all the evidence, he was again released.

For stealing two feather beds from Elizabeth Gawden, Holliday was hanged at Tyburn in 1700. REF.: *CBA*.

Holliday, John Henry (AKA: **Doc**), 1852-87, U.S., west. gunman. John Holliday was, on occasions, either a self-appointed lawman or an outlaw and gunman for hire. Born in Griffin, Ga., Holliday was raised as a polite scion of a rich southern family. He studied dentistry while in his twenties and practiced the profession whenever in need of funds. About 1872, this slender man with florid manners contracted tuberculosis and traveled west to seek a dry climate.

From 1873 to the late 1870s, Holliday demonstrated an apparently innate skill with firearms. His aim was deadly. Unlike most of the western gunslingers of his day, Holliday was never impatient to pull his six-guns. He drew his weapons with dedicated calm, and while his opponent was

The deadly gunfighter John H. "Doc" Holliday.

firing wildly at him, this little, beady-eyed killer, would carefully level his Colt and nervelessly fire, invariably inflicting a mortal wound upon his enemy.

Holliday's reputation in the West as a deadly gunslinger was earned in the boom towns of Dallas, Cheyenne, Denver, Pueblo, Leadville, Dodge City, Tucson, and Tombstone. It was during the early 1870s that Holliday befriended a man to whom he gave his undying loyalty, Wyatt Earp, the legendary lawman whose cool-headedness and gritty dedication Holliday sought to emulate. The deadly dentist undoubtedly studied Earp's mannerisms when Earp faced dozens of bad men in the saloons and gambling halls of Ellsworth, Wichita, Dodge City, and especially, in Tombstone, Ariz., where both men, along with Earp's two stoic brothers, Virgil and Morgan, shot it out with the fierce Clanton-McLowery band in the historic gunfight at O.K. Corral.

Holliday's fearful reputation as a gunman was established more by rumor than reality. The actual record of his gunfights reveal a limited number of smoking pistol showdowns. The earliest verifiable gunfight in which Holliday participated was in Dallas,

Texas, on Jan. 1, 1875. He was gambling in a saloon owned by a man named Austin. An argument over a card hand caused Holliday and Austin to fire single bullets at each other. Neither was injured and both parties decided to settle their differences without further gunplay.

Saloons, dance halls, and bordellos formed the social world of Doc Holliday. An inveterate gambler, Holliday often served as the "in-house" cardsharp. Suckers were invited to try their luck with Holliday and he invariably won, sharing his winnings with the saloon owner who financed his play. Though a small man, Doc was wiry and strong, and he often doubled in a saloon as the resident gunman and bouncer so he not only fleeced patrons with alacrity and dexterity, but he quickly cowed their indignation at being euchred.

By 1879, Holliday was earning goodly sums as a part-owner of a saloon in Las Vegas, N.M. His partner and financial backer was one-time lawman for Dodge City, John Joshua Webb. On July 19, 1879, Webb and Holliday were seated at a card table in the saloon when Mike Gordon, a bully boy and former army scout, began an argument at the bar, ordering one of the saloon women, who had been his mistress and who had lately rejected him, to quit her job and leave town with him. The woman rejected Gordon's offer and he stormed from the saloon, standing in the street and shouting obscenities at Holliday. Gordon then drew his gun and began firing bullets into the front of the building and this drew Holliday forth. Doc stepped outside and a bullet from Gordon's pistol whizzed past him. He drew his gun slowly, then fired a single shot which sent Gordon crashing into the dirt. The wound was fatal and Gordon died the following day, cursing Holliday with his last breath.

In June 1880, Holliday entered a Las Vegas saloon and quickly got into an argument with bartender Charley White, a man Doc had run out of Dodge City some months earlier. Both men pulled guns, and as usual, Holliday's aim was better. White collapsed behind the bar, Doc assuming he was dead. Holliday left him there and was surprised to learn the next day that White had survived, having received only a slight wound.

Much has been written about the strange friendship Holliday developed with Wyatt Earp. Earp presented the image of the incorruptible lawman but he was seen regularly with Holliday in the Kansas cow towns where he kept the peace. Holliday, on the other hand, was considered by most upstanding citizens as a decided lowlife. Stories abound with pithy details that describe how Earp saved Holliday from a lynch mob but the location is sketchy, or how the lawman actually financed Holliday's gambling operations, taking a sly share of the profits. That Holliday looked up to Earp there is no doubt; he openly admired Earp's nervy and decisive behavior with bad men. As their legends began to grow from cow town to cow town, Holliday was more than content to be known as Earp's "back-up" man, an unofficial peace officer who made it his responsibility to see that Earp was not shot in the back. Earp, in turn, paid oblique homage to little Doc, spreading the gunman's reputation with surly strangers who came to town so they would quickly realize that to face Earp with guns was also to face Holliday.

Doc Holliday was a man who truly had but one friend, Wyatt Earp. The gunman wanted it that way, seeking the company of only those who played cards with him or drank with him at the bar. He was closed-mouthed and mean-minded, quick to see an insult where none was intended and even quicker to prompt gunplay, which, as he knew, would seldom come to reality because of his terrible reputation, earned or not. Countless times, he would force an issue with a bar patron or a green cowboy so that he could have the pleasure of seeing his victim cringe and beg off. Night after saloon-struck night, Holliday would go through this tireless routine of challenge, taking grim pleasure in seeing the other man back away, a weak smile on his face that edged up the huge handlebar mustache adorning a heavy upper lip. In this regard, Holliday was typical of most western gunmen, thriving each night on such petty triumphs and feeding a dime novel vanity that insisted he go to bed victorious.

Only one woman was known to have won Holliday's guarded affections, an ungainly prostitute, Big-Nosed Kate Fisher (real name Katherine Elder) who left Davenport, Iowa, as a young girl and traveled west to seek her fortune, landing in a Kansas bordello where Holliday allegedly met her. She was a large woman who stood inches above Doc and was loud, crass, and drunk most of the time. Yet, Holliday, for many years, was inexplicably drawn to her, showing her the kind of attention usually reserved for respectable ladies. One unsupported story had it that Holliday and Big-Nosed Kate were actually married in St. Louis in the late 1870s.

Big-Nosed Kate followed the little gambler around from town to town, and she was present in Tombstone in 1881 when Holliday backed the Earp brothers in their famous fight with the Clanton-McLowery group at O.K. Corral. Fisher and Holliday were a twosome in Tombstone until Spring 1881. The Wells Fargo Stage was held up by a band of outlaws and the driver, Bud Philpot, was shot and killed by the bandits, who were driven off by shotgun guard Bob Paul.

Holliday was accused of leading the bandits by his then-sworn enemies, the Clanton brothers whom Big-Nosed Kate had befriended after Doc had thrown her out of his rooms following a drunken argument. Fisher, seething with anger at Holliday, and undoubtedly nursing a severe hangover, made out a deposition that stated Holliday had bragged to her about holding up a stage. Holliday was politely asked by the local sheriff, John Behan, to answer the deposition. The gunman walked to the jail and flatly denied the charge, pointing out that the bandits failed to get the money in the stage's strongbox. "If I had pulled that job," Holliday told Behan, "I'd have gotten the eighty thousand!" With that, Holliday strolled out of the jail and back to the Oriental Saloon to resume his card game. He was never indicted, especially since his good friend Wyatt Earp was presently U.S. deputy marshal and exonerated Doc from all responsibility concerning the robbery, later bringing in his own suspects.

Holliday, however, was incensed by the accusation and he told Kate Fisher that she was never to speak to him again. When he heard that Mike Joyce, a Tombstone bar owner who had taken Fisher in, was also repeating her story about the stage robbery, Holliday rushed into Joyce's saloon. Both men drew weapons and Doc shot the pistol out of Joyce's hand, sending a bullet through the palm, a feat that enhanced Holliday's reputation as an expert marksman which he was not; it was a lucky shot Holliday quietly admitted later.

The gunman's real anger was aimed at the Clanton-McLowery clan for both stealing Kate Fisher and accusing him of the stage holdup. He sought out Ike Clanton on Oct. 26, 1881, and cursed him loudly in one of Tombstone's saloons. Clanton, by nature a cowardly creature who created arguments without the nerve to settle them with guns, pleaded to be spared and was later pistol-whipped in the street by Wyatt Earp. This caused the Clanton and McLowery brothers to send out a challenge to the Earps the next day to meet them in a showdown at the O.K. Corral.

With the Earps, walking toward the corral the next day, was Holliday, Wyatt's ever-loyal friend. During that famous gun battle, Holliday produced a shotgun (some said from beneath his long coat) and shot Tom McLowery to death with it after having been slightly wounded in the side by Frank McLowery. Seeing Ike Clanton fleeing from scene, Holliday pulled out his pistol and fired after the catalyst of the battle, but Doc's shots failed to find their mark.

The feud raged on for another year, with Morgan Earp being murdered in Tombstone on Mar. 18, 1882. Holliday joined Wyatt Earp and others in a posse that went after one of Morgan Earp's killers, Frank Stilwell. They found the gunman in the Tucson train station on Oct. 20 and Stilwell, drawing his pistol, was killed by thirty bullets, some from the gun held in Holliday's hand. Another member of the murder band who had shot Morgan Earp from ambush, Florentino Cruz, was tracked down by Earp,

Holliday, and others and killed outside of Tombstone on Mar. 22.

Tombstone was the last of the roaring cow towns where Holliday held court. When Wyatt Earp packed away his family and guns and headed for California, Holliday decided to stay behind in the West he knew, one of saloons, dirt streets, and gunplay. He was part of a dwindling society of gunmen who were compelled to ride into the backwater towns as law and order came to the West.

By the time Holliday arrived in Leadville in 1884 his health was failing; he had been forced to retreat several times to crude sanitoriums in the high mountains to fill his wheezing lungs with thin air. The tuberculosis afflicting him caused him to go into painful coughing fits that sometimes went on for days. Moreover, Holliday's luck ran out at the card tables. Broke, he began to borrow money and seldom repaid it. Bill Allen, a Leadville bartender, became irate at Holliday when the gunman was late in paying back five dollars.

Allen was not impressed with Holliday's reputation. As far as the bartender was concerned, Doc Holliday was a has-been. He nagged Doc about the $5 debt and bragged to his friends that if Holliday did not repay the loan soon he would "lick the tar out of him." When he next encountered Holliday, Allen demanded his money and insulted Holliday, but the gunman merely waved him away and walked into a saloon. Allen rushed after him, charging him at the bar, fists raised. Holliday stared for a moment, then drew his gun. Allen was a big man who outweighed Doc by seventy pounds and the gunman had no intention of fighting him. Holliday fired one shot into Allen's upraised arm which sent the bartender running outside where he was taken to a doctor. He survived and wrote off the debt, but Holliday was arrested and charged with attempted murder. He was tried but acquitted. This was Doc Holliday's last recorded gunfight.

In late 1887, Holliday was an emaciated wreck and went to his favorite health spa in Glenwood Springs, Colo., to "take another cure." But he found no cure and certainly no peace of mind. His nights were haunted by terrible dreams of blood and death and he kept next to his bed a fully-loaded shotgun, a Bowie knife, and his nickel-plated six-gun, ready to battle the phantoms of his sleep. In his waking hours he gulped down great quantities of whiskey. On the morning of his death, Nov. 8, 1887, Doc Holliday asked a nurse to pour him one more drink and begged that his boots be put on his bare feet. By the time the boots were found in a closet, Holliday had coughed himself to death. See: **Earp, Wyatt; O.K. Corral, Gunfight at.**

REF.: American Guide Series, *Arizona, A State Guide;* Asbury, *Sucker's Progress;* Axford, *Around Western Campfires;* Bakarich, *Gun-Smoke;* Bartholomew, *The Biographical Album of Western Gunfighters;* ____, *Western Hard-Cases;* ____, *Wyatt Earp, 1848-1880;* ____, *Wyatt Earp, 1879-1882;* Bechdolt, *When the West was Young;* Beebe, *The American West;* Bishop, *Old Mexico and Her Lost Provinces;* Boyer, *An Illustrated Life of Doc Holliday;* ____, *Suppressed Murder of Wyatt Earp;* Breckenridge, *Helldorado;* Breihan, *Great Gunfighters of the West;* ____, *Great Lawmen of the West;* Brent, *Great Western Heroes;* Bristow, *Tales of Old Fort Gibson;* Brophy, *Arizona Sketch Book;* Brown and Schmitt, *Trail Driving Days;* Burgess, *Bisbee Not So Long Ago;* Burns, *Tombstone, An Iliad of the Southwest;* Callon, *Las Vegas, New Mexico, The Town that Wouldn't Gamble;* CBA; Chapel, *Guns of the Old West;* Chilton, *The Book of the West;* Chisholm, *Brewery Gulch;* Chrisman, *Lost Trails of the Cimarron;* Clum, *It All Happened in Tombstone;* Clum, *Apache Agent;* Cunningham, *Triggernometry, A Gallery of Gunfighters;* Cushman, *The Great North Trail;* DeArment, *Bat Masterson;* Drago, *Great American Cattle Trails;* ____, *Wild, Woolly and Wicked;* Dunlop, *Doctors of the American Frontier;* Durham, *The Negro Cowboys;* Erwin, *The Southwest of John H. Slaughter;* Faulk, *Dodge City, The Most Western Town of All;* Florin, *Ghost Town Album;* Franke, *They Plowed Up Hell in Old Cochise;* Frantz, *The American Cowboy;* Ganzhorn, *I've Killed Men;* Gard, *Frontier Justice;* Gardner, *The Old Wild West;* Gaylord, *Handgunner's Guide;* Gregory, *True Wild West Stories;* Hall-Quest, *Wyatt Earp, Marshal of the Old West;* Hamlin, *Hamlin's Tombstone Picture Gallery;* Hart, *Old Forts of the Southwest;* Henricks, *The Bad Man of the West;* Hertzog, *A Directory*

of New Mexico Desperadoes; Hogan, *The Life and Death of Johnny Ringo;*
Holloway, *Texas Gun Lore;* Hopper, *Famous Texas Landmarks;* Horan,
Across the Cimarron; ____, *The Great American West;* ____ and Sann,
Pictorial History of the Wild West; Hughes, *South From Tombstone;* Hunter,
The Story of Lottie Deno; ____ and Rose, *The Album of Gunfighters;*
Jaastad, *Man of the West;* Jahns, *The Frontier World of Doc Holliday;*
Johnson, *Famous Lawmen of the Old West;* King, *Mavericks;* ____,
Wranglin' the Past; Knight, *Wild Bill Hickok;* Koller, *The Fireside Book of
Guns;* ____, *The American Gun;* Lake, *Undercover for Wells Fargo;* Lake,
Wyatt Earp, Frontier Marshal; ____, *He Carried a Six-shooter;* Lieberson,
The Columbia Records Legacy Collection; McCarty, *Some Experiences of
Boss Neff;* McCarty, *The Gunfighters;* McClintock, *Arizona Prehistoric;*
McCool, *So Said the Coroner;* Marshall, *Swinging Doors;* Martin, *The
Earps of Tombstone;* ____, *Silver, Sex and Six Guns;* ____, *Tombstone's
Epitaph;* Masterson, *Famous Gunfighters of the Western Frontier;* Metz,
John Selman, Texas Gunfighter; Miller, *Bill Tilghman;* Miller, *Arizona, The
Last Frontier;* ____, *The Arizona Story;* Miller, Langsdorf and Richmond,
Kansas, A Pictorial History; Myers, *Doc Holliday;* ____, *The Last Chance;*
Nash, *Bloodletters and Badmen;* Nordyke, *John Wesley Hardin, Texas
Gunman;* North, *The Saga of the Cowboy;* O'Connor, *Bat Masterson;*
Olsson, *Welcome to Tombstone;* Oman, *A Room for the Night;* O'Neal,
Encyclopedia of Western Gunfighters; Otero, *My Life on the Frontier;*
Parsons, *The Private Journal of George Whitwell Parsons;* Patch, *Reminis-
cences of Fort Huachuca;* Penfield, *Western Sheriffs and Marshals;* Preece,
Lone Star Man; Raine, *Famous Sheriffs and Western Outlaws;* ____, *Guns
of the Frontier;* Rickards, *Buckskin Frank Leslie;* ____, *Mysterious Dave
Mathers;* Ringgold, *Frontier Days in the Southwest;* Rosa, *The Gunfighter,
Man or Myth?;* ____ and May, *Gun Law;* ____, *They Called Him Wild
Bill;* Sandoz, *The Buffalo Hunters;* Santee, *Lost Pony Tracks;* Sloan, *History
of Arizona;* Small, *The Best of True West;* Stanley, *Dave Rudabaugh, Border
Ruffian;* Sterling, *Famous Western Outlaw-Sheriff Battles;* Tilghman,
Marshal of the Last Frontier; Upshur, *As I Recall Them;* Urquhart, *Roll
Call;* Vestal, *Queen of Cowtowns, Dodge City;* Wallace, *Gunnison County;*
Walters, *Tombstone's Yesterdays;* Ward, *Bits of Silver;* Waters, *A Gallery
of Western Badmen;* Waters, *The Story of Mrs. Virgil Earp;* Way, *The
Tombstone Story;* Wellman, *Glory, God and Gold;* ____, *The Trampling
Herd;* White, *Bat Masterson;* White, *My Texas 'Tis of Thee;* Wilson, *Out
of the West;* Wister, *Owen Wister Out West;* (FILM), *Law and Order,* 1932;
Frontier Marshal, 1934; *Frontier Marshal,* 1939; *Tombstone—The Town Too
Tough to Die,* 1942; *My Darling Clementine,* 1946; *Law and Order,* 1953;
Masterson of Kansas, 1954; *Gunfight at the O.K. Corral,* 1957; *Hour of the
Gun,* 1967; *Doc,* 1971.

The hanging of W.H. Hollings.

Hollings, W.H., d.1814, Brit., mur. W.H. Hollings, an otherwise
unremarkable former tax man, was so infatuated by a young
woman left in his care that he killed her, unable to tolerate her
rejection.

As a British tax officer, Hollings became friendly with Mr.
Pitcher, a colleague who, on his deathbed, asked Hollings to look
after his young daughter and his wife. The 21-year-old daughter,
Elizabeth, lived with Mr. Cartwright in Lower Grosvenor Street,
where she worked as a servant. Hollings, a married man of fifty
whose wife did not live with him, began to visit the young woman
and became obsessed with the idea of capturing her as a lover.
Elizabeth rejected him and, on July 4, 1814, he came again to see
her, asking the butler to send her outside to see him. She did,
and a few minutes later the butler heard a shot. Running out, he
found Hollings holding the woman; she was shot through the
heart.

Hollings made no attempt to escape. He held a second pistol;
the first was shattered by the force of the blast. A small glass
bottle of arsenic and water lay on the steps, the explosion of the
pistol having knocked it out of his hands. When the patrol came
to arrest him Hollings said, "Don't seize me; I shall not attempt
to go away." He asked if Elizabeth was dead, wondering if he
could be allowed to kiss "her cold lips."

At the station, he explained that he had killed Elizabeth
because she had rejected his advances. Hollings was violently ill
throughout the night, having drunk enough of the arsenic and
water to poison, but not kill, himself.

On Sept. 16, he was charged with murder and tried at the Old
Bailey. Although several witnesses were called in an attempt to
prove that Hollings was insane, since he had been discharged from
tax service for strange conduct, the court found his actions entirely
premeditated and he was found Guilty. Hollings told the court
that he had been tried and convicted fairly, and hoped that his fate
would be a warning to all against the danger of violent passions.

Addressing the crowd that came to see him hanged on Sept.
19, 1814, Hollings wept as he told them: "Here, you see, I stand,
a victim to passion and barbarity: my crime is great; and I
acknowledge the justice of my sentence." His body was sent to
St. Bartholomew's Hospital for dissection, in keeping with the law
that proclaimed that only executed felons could be used for
medical studies.

REF.: *CBA; Newgate Calendar.*

Hollins, Jess, d.1950, U.S., (wrong. convict.?) rape. In 1931,
in Sapulpa, Okla., a black man, Jess Hollins, was accused of
raping a white woman. Frightened by rumors of lynching and
unaided by an attorney after his arrest, Hollins pleaded guilty.
Tried by an all-white jury, he was convicted in less than an hour,
and was sentenced to die.

Just three days before the scheduled execution, the National
Association for the Advancement of Colored People, (NAACP),
appealed the case on the grounds that no blacks had ever served
on juries in Okmulgee County, Okla., where Hollins' trial was
held. At a second trial in 1934, again before an all-white jury.
Hollins was convicted and condemned to die. Upon appeal, the
conviction was upheld. Thirty hours before his second scheduled
execution, the U.S. Supreme Court granted a stay, overturning the
conviction because of the absence of blacks on the jury.

A third all-white jury trial took place in 1936, with only the
testimony of the alleged victim as evidence. Defense attorneys
maintained that the witness had voluntarily engaged in sexual
intercourse with Hollins, crying rape only when they were caught
in the act. Hollins, however, was convicted again, and sentenced
to life in prison.

A newspaper editor covering the case reported that a number
of whites privately told him that the prosecution's case was
unbelievable. Having almost lost his life twice, Hollins would not
risk another trial. He died in prison in 1950. REF.: *CBA.*

Hollins, Lawrence Henry, d.1931, S. Afri., suic. In May 1931,
a South African named Mallalieu notified police that he had found
his closest friend, Lawrence Henry Hollins, dead in their shared
hotel room; the victim of an apparent suicide. Hollins had a bullet
hole in his head and an Astra pistol in his hand. Suffering from
a venereal disease, he showed friends and acquaintances telegrams
from England which said his mother had been hit by a taxi and
had died. The telegrams later turned out to be frauds. Hollins

had been showing them to people either to elicit sympathy, or to provide an excuse for the self-destruction he was planning.

Police believed that Hollins had been murdered by someone who knew about the extensive suicide note he left to Mallalieu, in which he apologized for the inconvenience of his suicide, and asked his companion to take care of his affairs, also advising him against marrying too soon. The day after Hollins' death, Mallalieu gave police a cartridge case, explaining it must have ricochetted into a shoe. One theory suspected Mallalieu as the killer. When Hollins' body was exhumed several months after his death, a wound was alleged to have been found on the side of his head, supporting the idea that he had been knocked unconscious, and then slain. REF.: *CBA*.

Hollis, David Lee, c.1960-   , U.S., mur. On Feb. 27, 1982, police in Hammond, Ind., found the bodies of 18-year-old Debbie Hollis, 18-year-old Kim Mezei, and Mezei's 2-year-old son, Craig Mezei, stabbed to death with a butcher knife in an apartment complex. The following day, 21-year-old David Lee Hollis, the estranged husband of Debbie, was arrested in neighboring Griffith, Ind., after he broke into the apartment of his friends William Davidson and Donald White and held them hostage with a 12-gauge shotgun. He bound the men with electrical cord, but when Hollis fell asleep they escaped. Police using tear gas stormed the apartment, but found it empty. They searched the complex and eventually found Hollis hiding in a clothes dryer.

On Oct. 13, 1982, in the Lake County Criminal Court of Judge James Clements, Hollis surprised even his own defense attorney by pleading Guilty to the murders. On Nov. 12, 1982, Hollis was sentenced to die in the electric chair. He remains on Death Row. REF.: *CBA*.

Hollister, Cassius M. (AKA: **Cash**), 1845-84, U.S., west. lawman. Cash Hollister moved to Caldwell, Kan., from his native Cleveland as a 31-year-old in 1877. Two years later, he was elected mayor after the sudden death of the incumbent. He exhibited a tempestuous temperament, frequently got involved in fights, and was fined for assaulting a man named Frank Hunt. In 1880, Hollister chose not to run for reelection, but three years later was appointed a deputy U.S. marshal. On Apr. 11, 1883, he became embroiled in a shootout near Hunnewell, Kan., while trying to arrest a family of horse thieves. One brother was killed and another wounded before the remaining Ross family members surrendered. On Nov. 21, 1883, Hollister and Ben Wheeler tried to arrest Chet Van Meter, who was accused of beating his family and threatening others. Van Meter fired at the lawmen as they approached, but was killed by five shots in the chest. A year later, on Nov. 20, 1884, Hollister attempted his final arrest. Bob Cross, the son of a minister, was accused of adultery after he abandoned his wife for the daughter of a local farmer. Hollister and three other lawmen went to the Cross farm in Hunnewell, Kan. Cross' wife and sister denied he was there, but as the posse searched the house, two shots fatally wounded Hollister.

REF.: *CBA*; Miller and Snell, *Great Gunfighters of the Kansas Cowtowns*; O'Neal, *Encyclopedia of Western Gunfighters*.

Holloway, Jerome, See: **Smith, Byron**.

Holloway, John, and **Haggerty, Owen**, d. 1807, Brit., mur. John Cole Steele, a lavender water merchant, left London on Nov. 5, 1802, to visit his lavender plantation at Bedfont. When he did not return, his family became worried and notified the police. Steele's body was found in a ditch near Feltham at Hounslow Heath. He had been bludgeoned to death and dragged some distance after a struggle near the main road. Four years later, a criminal named Hanfield was waiting at Portsmouth to be deported in the next convict ship when he confessed to the murder. Hanfield said he had joined John Holloway and Owen Haggerty in their plot to rob Steele. The three drank together for several hours, then hid in some trees near the highway. Hanfield said Holloway attacked and killed Steele. Hanfield also said he left the other two to dispose of the body, and did not share in the profits because he had not shared in the killing.

The confession of a condemned convict was insufficient, and it was popularly believed that the Bow Street Runners, the British police force at that time, manufactured corroboration in order to convict the accused. A constable who had hidden himself at the Worship Street Station swore that he heard Holloway and Haggerty discussing drinking together before the murder. With this flimsy "corroboration," Holloway and Haggerty were convicted. Both declared their innocence, even as they were walking to the gallows. The execution took place on Feb. 23, 1807, in front of the Newgate Jail. Also on the gallows was Elizabeth Godfrey, a prostitute convicted of murdering Richard Prince, a client, by stabbing him to death with a pocketknife. Partly because Holloway and Haggerty were popularly believed to be innocent, a huge crowd of more than 40,000 people had gathered. By 8 a.m., the crowd was so dense directly in front of the scaffold that people were struggling to get out. While Godfrey shuddered uncontrollably, Holloway and Haggerty again proclaimed their innocence. As people surged forward to hear better, others were trampled underfoot, and cries of "Murder!" were heard as people were crushed or suffocated. The frantic mob apparently unnerved hangman William Brunskill, who did an inept job of hanging Godfrey. She was still kicking and struggling a half-hour after she had been dropped. Over forty people were killed in the crowd, many of them women and children. But public hangings in Britain were not abolished until sixty years later, in 1868. See: **Brunskill, William; Godfrey, Elizabeth**. REF.: *CBA*.

Holloway, John William (AKA: **William Goldsmith**), 1806-31, Brit., mur. John William Holloway had developed into a local Don Juan by the time he was nineteen. In 1826, he met Celia Bashford at the racetrack. When she became pregnant by him, he reluctantly married her. They had a second child together and, in 1830, Holloway left her, changed his name to William Goldsmith, and worked in the blockade service. Visiting Rye, he became involved with Ann Kennett and married her bigamously. He traveled around with his new wife, working odd jobs, including counterfeiting coins and forgery. When he drifted back to Brighton in 1831, Bashford tracked him down and forced him to make support payments of two shillings a week. Holloway, twenty-six at the time, sent the money via Kennett, who was apparently terrified of her violent husband. After an explosive fight on July 14, 1831, between Holloway and Bashford, he lured her into an alley known locally as Donkey's Row and killed her, cutting up the corpse and burying some of it in Preston Village in the Lover's Walk area, and throwing the rest into a cesspool near the tenement where he lived with Kennett. Within a month of the slaying, both packages came to light. At the Lover's Walk site, Holloway apparently left part of Bashford's red dress sticking out of the ground. Both Kennett and Holloway were charged with the murder. Kennett was soon acquitted, and Holloway made a full confession, confirming Kennett's innocence. Holloway was hanged at Lewes on Dec. 16, 1831.

A man who had suffered all his life from an unsightly cyst on his neck asked the hangman, Calcraft, to allow him to come on the scaffold to try out the old superstition that rubbing a boil with the hand of a hanged man would cure it. As soon as Holloway's body went limp, Calcraft complied, much to the revulsion of the crowd, which started hissing. Local sheriffs quickly halted the procedure, and Calcraft almost lost his job for complying with the request. REF.: *CBA*.

Holloway, Joseph, and **Harman, Mary Ann**, and **Robinson, Herbert**, prom. 1904, Brit., forg. During the latter half of 1904, a flurry of forged £5 Bank of England notes were discovered in circulation. The case was assigned to Inspector Ottoway, who was assisted by Officer Arthur Collyer and Detective Charles Atkins. Police had been informed that a man named Paquin, sometimes known as Pearce, had recently arrived in London and was known to be involved in counterfeit currency. On Dec. 22, 1904, Officer Collyer disguised himself as a sailor and traveled to the East End to infiltrate the counterfeiter's gang. There, he met Herbert Robinson, who responded to his request to purchase fraudulent currency by giving him a counterfeit banknote. After several drinks, Robinson introduced the undercover officer to his boss, Joseph Holloway, and a woman named Mary Ann Harman who was presented as Holloway's wife.

Collyer traced the bill back to Paquin and to a West End pawnbroker. After meeting Robinson a second time, Collyer was given two Bank of Engraving notes. Known as "lills," these notes were legal currency often carried and used by con men. Following a series of deals, Collyer was invited to Holloway's home, where he watched him make the forgeries which gave police enough evidence to raid the home and arrest Holloway and Harman on Dec. 30, 1904. Robinson was arrested later that morning at a Holborn bar.

The three men were tried before Justice Darling at the Old Bailey on Feb. 9, 1905, with Charles Matthews and Attorney Lesse prosecuting for the Crown, and J.D.A. Johnston, Huntley Jenkins, and Dr. Counsel for the defense. Although Counsel attempted to show that Collyer had gotten Robinson drunk, and that his client mistakenly believed they were discussing the "lills" the whole time, both Robinson and Holloway, were found Guilty. They were each sentenced to five years of penal servitude. Harman was acquitted for lack of evidence. REF.: *CBA*.

Holloway, William, d.1712, Brit., rob.-mur. Raised to be a farmer, William Holloway chose instead to make a living robbing and killing. Born at Newcastle-under-Lyne, in Staffordshire, he left for London to pursue a career as a thief. An inventive and clever man, Holloway once went to a knight's house dressed as a laundryman, went upstairs, and came back with two or three footman's uniforms. When stopped at the door by the knight's coachman, who asked him where he was going with the outfits, Holloway replied that because Parliament would be in session the following week, the master of the house had ordered him to clean the uniforms. "Here then," said the coachman, "take my coat and scour it well." Holloway took off with a larger haul than he expected, and the coachman was teased by local boys for a long time after with the slogan: "Here, take my cloak, too." In another instance, when several coaches were stopped in Fleet Street, Holloway distracted a gentleman while a cohort removed his coach seat; when the gentleman turned to see what was happening, Holloway ran off with the other one.

One day Holloway found a Mr. Emes, owner of the Punch House in Hemlock Court, in his coach. Emes was very drunk and asleep at the reins. After taking a watch and two guineas from the man's pocket, Holloway pulled the pinwheel out of the axles of the cab, tied the man's legs together, started the horse, and watched the coach leave. Holloway watched as the drunken man held the coach together as he slowly limped home. Later, Holloway became a highwayman, robbing a farmer on the road between Farringdon and Abingdon in Berkshire. He saw that the man was paid £10 at a nearby inn, and demanded the cash. The farmer pulled out a sword to defend himself, but Holloway shot his horse out from under him and got away with the money.

In another instance, he met a man who had just been robbed on a dangerous road. Holloway's unsuspecting victim warned him against the highwayman and, as they traveled along together, told the thief that he had put his gold in the rolls of his stockings in case he was stopped again. Holloway took the man's eighty guineas.

Arrested for robbing a house on Hounslow Heath, Holloway was sent to Newgate and condemned, but reprieved by a general royal decree. Too impatient to await his release, he escaped, and soon after went to the Sessions House at the Old Bailey where court was being held. Several angry jailors recognized him and threatened to lock him up again. A fight broke out and Holloway shot to death one of the irate jailors. Along with an accessory, Mrs. Housden, Holloway was condemned a second time.

He and his companion were hanged at the end of Giltspur Street in September 1712; his body was later hanged in chains at a place, oddly, called Holloway on one side of Islington. Just before he was executed, Holloway said that he never had any hard feelings against the jailor whom he had shot, and that he had not

known what he was doing because he was so drunk. REF.: *CBA*.

Holloway, William Judson, Jr., 1923- , U.S., jur. Served as attorney in the general litigation section, claims division, of the U.S. Department of Justice from 1951-52. He was nominated to the tenth circuit court by President Lyndon B. Johnson in 1968. REF.: *CBA*.

Hollyday, William, 1667-97, Brit., rob. Born in St. Giles in the Fields, England, of very poor parents, William Hollyday was orphaned when he was very young. Forced to fend for himself, he entered the regiment of the so-called Blackguards—the scullions, horse-boys, and other menial servants who followed the army. Even with no formal education, Hollyday was so notably intelligent and clever that he was soon recognized by his peers and superiors. In a mock trial of the Viscount Stafford, a traitor who had been denounced for plotting to murder King Charles II, Hollyday was chosen to play the part of the Lord High Steward. The boy who played the part of the Viscount was hanged, and cut down the next morning by a groom who found him swinging from the rafters in a stable.

Hollyday was soon chosen to be the captain of the regiment of Blackguards, instituting guidelines for his raggedy young crew. The new rules included an edict barring the boys from wearing shirts. Whatever money the troops earned cleaning boots or shoes was to be immediately gambled away. If any of them could read or write, they were to forget both, because their captain would not have any under him who were more learned than himself. Any contributions of shoes or stockings were to be converted into money to gamble with. Blackguards were not to "clear themselves of vermin by killing them or eating them." They were to pick pockets without bungling, swear whenever possible, and lie as much as they could. A final, and oddly traditional, law required all boys to report to work at 9 a.m., unless sick, to receive orders for the day.

Hollyday served as the Blackguards leader until he was twenty years old; he then decided he had outgrown the appointment, gave up his post, and took up a career as a highwayman. After ten years in this nefarious trade, he was arrested, tried, and sentenced to die. He was executed, along with John Shorter and Will Jones, at Tyburn on Dec. 22, 1697, at age thirty. REF.: *CBA*.

Holman, George, prom. 1944, U.S., arson. In Oakland and San Francisco, Calif., between Mar. 25 and Mar. 28, 1944, pyromaniac George Holman set eleven fires, mostly in poor tenement and hotel districts. Twenty-two people died in the fires. Identified by a janitor who saw him running from a burning building with a can of kerosene in his arms, Holman was convicted and sent to San Quentin Prison to serve twenty-two consecutive life sentences for murder and arson. REF.: *CBA*.

Holman, Jesse Lynch, 1784-1842, U.S., jur. Judge of state supreme court of Indiana Territory from 1816-1830. He was nominated to the district court of Indiana by President Andrew Jackson in 1835. REF.: *CBA*.

Holman, Libby (Elizabeth Lloyd Holzman), 1904-71, Case of, U.S., mur. Libby Holman was one of a handful of celebrated white torch singers in the 1920s who will be forever remembered for singing one song. With Helen Morgan it was "My Bill," with Fannie Brice it was "My Man," and with Libby Holman it was "Moanin' Low." She was identified with other songs, of course, including "Body and Soul," which she introduced; "Can't We Be Friends;" and "Something to Remember You By," from the 1930 musical *Three's a Crowd*. It was in this show that Holman selected a member of the band to sing to, the same band member each night, a man wearing a sailor suit and standing with his back to the audience. This was Fred MacMurray in his first Broadway appearance. This star of the stage would become involved in the sensational 1932 murder of her then-husband, Zachary Smith Reynolds, tobacco tycoon and, from all reports, cuckolded spouse.

Libby Holman was born Elizabeth Lloyd Holzman in Cincinnati, Ohio, on May 23, 1904. Her father, Alfred Holzman, was a successful stock broker, her mother, Rachel (Workum) was an attractive school teacher. The couple produced three children,

Marion, Elizabeth (Libby), and Alfred, Jr. A year after Libby was born her father and his brother, Ross Holzman, declared bankruptcy. Holzman and Company had speculated too broadly in the volatile cotton market and had overextended themselves. More than $1 million was lost by investors, according to one report, this being the biggest financial disaster to date in Cincinnati. Then it was learned that Ross Holzman had ostensibly gone to Louisville, Ky., to raise more funds. He was never seen again. Gone with Holzman was $150,000 in bonds he had borrowed from a Kentucky utilities firm, along with $7,000 he had embezzled from the distinguished Cincinnati Club while a member.

Alfred Holzman was left in disgrace and poverty. His brother Ross never again surfaced, but it was believed that he went to Honduras, a country he had often talked about. The Holzman family sank into debt and both parents took menial jobs to survive. Libby was raised with the rumors of her family's former wealth, and from childhood, all she thought about was becoming a millionaire. She fantasized about her thieving uncle Ross Holzman, referring to him as Uncle Honduras, believing that one night he would appear and shower the family with money. But it was Holman's marriage to a troubled young tobacco heir that would bring such a fortune.

To rid himself of some of the taint his financial failure and his brother's thefts had heaped upon his name, Alfred Holzman, in 1918, petitioned the courts to have the family name changed to Holman. This was granted and Libby later stated that the name change delighted her. With her stage and singing ambitions, Holman was a better name, she felt, with which to forge a show business career. Libby Holman graduated high school in 1920, still wearing the hand-me-down dresses of her older sister, Marion. She entered the University of Cincinnati to study drama and graduated in 1924. Then she was off to New York to make a name for herself on Broadway. She haunted the casting offices and stood for hours in line to try out for parts but without success. Then she got her big break, the part of a streetwalker in a play called *The Fool*.

In 1925, after taking several bit parts in Broadway plays, Libby Holman, more because of her shapely legs than her voice, was given a part in the *Garrick Gaieties* written by Richard Rodgers and Lorenz Hart. She sang a sensuous opening number, "Ladies of the Box Office," and was suddenly the darling of the theater crowd. Her success boomed after that until she had become a top star in 1929. In that year, playboy Zachary Smith Reynolds, heir to the $40 million Reynolds tobacco fortune, went to see *The Little Show*. He sat in the first row wearing riding boats and jodhpurs and became enthralled by the singer on stage, Libby Holman, whose deep voice chanted out "Moanin' Low." She was twenty-five at the time, he eighteen. Reynolds pursued her with flowers, candy, jewelry. She ignored him.

Reynolds was used to having his way. He and his older brother Richard, who had been raised by servants as maharajahs after their parents died early in life, spent their money along Broadway recklessly, courting statuesque chorus girls and giving lavish parties. Dick Reynolds, a heavy drinker, went to England in 1929 and got drunk before recklessly killing a pedestrian with his sports car and spending several months in jail. Zachary, called Smith by his friends and relatives, idolized his older brother, who busily corrupted him with the thought of Broadway and its fleshpots. Reynolds, from the first moment he saw Libby Holman, swore she would be his and Holman yielded under his constant demands to see her. They dated throughout 1931. Reynolds bought Holman a pistol, telling her that kidnappers were everywhere and that it would be a good idea if she had a weapon. He taught her how to shoot, giving her a .32-caliber Mauser automatic.

Meanwhile, the Depression deepened. Libby Holman's career soared. She made $2,500 a week in her Broadway shows. She bought a smart town house and an even snappier sports car. Reynolds, meanwhile, devoted himself to aviation and planned several long-distance flights, an adventuresome hobby that captured Holman's imagination. Finally, the Depression reached Broadway and Holman's fortunes began to dip. More and more she eyed the comfort and security the Reynolds millions might bring her. Reynolds took her for a flight over the Reynolds' ancestral estate in Winston-Salem, N.C. She gasped when she learned that the thousand acres over which they were flying all belonged to Reynolds. Moreover, Reynolda, the palatial mansion she entered, staggered her. This was real wealth, she concluded. Holman finally consented to marry Reynolds, who quickly obtained a divorce from his estranged wife, Anne Cannon, on Nov. 16, 1931. He and Libby Holman were wed that day. After traveling around the world for months, the couple settled in Reynolda and, in the early summer of 1932, gave one lavish party after another.

The parties were non-stop affairs with catered meals, flowing liquor, and champagne. There were motorboat rides at night and car races during the day. The party never stopped. A visiting reporter from the New York *News* attended a week-long festivity at Reynolda and returned to his paper to write: "Whirligig: Speed: Faster: Crazier: Champagne cocktails...Corn liquor straight...Pour it on...Step on the gas...Shoot the works...Speed: Gin, rye, bourbon, sex. Dizzy dames. Dizzy house parties. A thousand-acre estate. Private golf course. Tennis courts. Swimming pool. Lake. Moonlight dips. Dances. Joyrides. Airplanes. Yachts. High powered car. Speed. Chasing a new thrill today. Tiring of it tomorrow. Nowhere to go but places. Nothing to do but things. Speed, with youth at the throttle. Millions to spend...and bored stiff. Life's blah. The world's a phoney. The whirligig spins on."

Holman was always the center of the party, singing her Broadway hit tunes over and over again to a captive audience. Theater people like Clifton Webb and Tallulah Bankhead visited the estate. So did Blanche Yurka, Peggy Fears, and Beatrice Lillie. This crowd, according to Jim Baggs, a friend of Reynolds, was "little more than a convention of homosexuals." Holman had, in fact, cultivated homosexual friendships throughout her theater career. It was later claimed that Libby Holman really had no interest in men but was in love with a number of women and that her marriage to Reynolds quickly fell apart when he learned the truth about her sexual inclinations. He became moody and withdrawn during the summer of 1932. His best friend, Albert "Ab" Walker, seemed to spend more time with Libby than did her husband. Walker was the son of a successful Winston-Salem realtor who had been a high school football hero. Short and well-built, Walker was outgoing while Reynolds was introverted. Walker was gregarious while Reynolds was tight-lipped.

Reynolds felt that his wife was avoiding him and accused her of evading him. Holman denied it. On July 5, 1932, another party was given at Reynolda with the guests leaving around midnight. Actress Blanche Yurka retired to her room at that time. Ab Walker, who was staying at the mansion, sat around drinking with Holman and Reynolds. Tipsy by then, Holman went outside, and Walker and Reynolds went to search for her. Holman was found wandering around in her nightgown and both young men took her back to the mansion. What happened next is in doubt. One story has it that Holman and Reynolds went into Walker's bedroom and Walker followed them. A fight broke out and Reynolds was suddenly killed by a bullet. Another has it that Holman and Reynolds retired at about 12:30 p.m., but an hour later, Yurka was aroused by the sound of shrieks and yelling from their room. Holman suddenly appeared on the balcony above the living room, her gown coated with blood, and announced to Walker, who was cleaning up: "Smith, Smith shot himself!"

Walker, who was wearing only swimming trunks, raced up the stairs and found Reynolds sprawled on a bed on a sleeping porch outside the master bedroom he shared with Libby. Blood seeped from a bullet hole in his head. Yurka, Walker, and Libby carried his limp form to a car and rushed to the Baptist Hospital. Here, the unconscious Reynolds was taken to an operating room while two doctors examined him. There was little that could be done other than to wait for the tycoon to die. Despite orders to leave the operating room, Ab Walker remained at his friend's side. Dr.

Libby Holman, torch singer with bee-stung lips, 1928.

Clifton Webb, Libby, and Fred Allen in *Three's A Crowd*.

Zachary Smith Reynolds and his best friend Ab Walker.

Libby with son Topper.

Reynolda, the palatial estate of the Reynolds family.

Libby, son, and Ralph Holmes.

Libby Holman, 1966.

Alexander Cox later stated that he got the idea that Walker was waiting to see if his friend Reynolds would talk.

Holman was finally taken to a hospital room where her blood-soaked negligee was replaced with hospital garments. Ab Walker walked into the room, asking head nurse Ruby Jenkins to leave, saying that he had to talk to Holman alone. As she was leaving, Jenkins heard Walker tell the torch singer: "Don't talk, don't say anything. Don't say anything to anybody!" Some minutes later Jenkins heard a noise and entered the room without knocking. She found Walker on the floor with Holman on top of him. Libby nervously explained that she had fallen out of bed and had dragged Walker with her. She then announced that she was pregnant with the child of the 20-year-old man dying in a room downstairs.

On July 6 at 5:25 a.m., Zachary Smith Reynolds died in his hospital bed. That morning, Reynolda was swarming with policemen and sheriff's deputies under the command of 34-year-old Transou Scott, who had been sheriff of Forsyth County for two years. The weapon used in Reynolds' death, a .32-caliber Mauser, the same kind Reynolds had given Holman a year earlier, was found on the sleeping porch, a few feet from the bed where Reynolds had been found. Police also found a pair of Holman's sleeping pajamas in Ab Walker's room, which was some distance from her room and that of her husband's. Walker, by that time, had gone home to bed. Later that day he told his father that he had had nothing to do with Reynolds' death. He saw a friend, Bob Critz, later that day and explained what happened but Critz said that he felt Walker was holding something back. "Well," Walker sighed, "there is something I'm going to take to my grave."

When Walker was later questioned by Sheriff Scott, he proved to be uncooperative and truculent, saying as little as possible. Blanche Yurka, still a guest at Reynolda, went riding with C.G. Hill that night, discussing the Reynolds death with him. Hill later went to Sheriff Scott and said that the actress had told him that no one who was in the mansion on the night of the shooting would ever reveal what had happened. When confronted with this statement, Yurka angrily denied ever having said such a thing.

A strange coroner's inquest was held on July 8, 1932, at Reynolda, in the very bedroom Holman and Reynolds had shared. The coroner's jury jammed itself into this room and questioned Walker, Yurka, and Holman. Walker was asked if he knew "if Mrs. Reynolds was a Jewess?" He said that he had not. He was then asked if he ever heard Reynolds express opinions about Jews and Walker replied that he had not. This line of questioning was peculiar and it seemed to stem from Libby Holman, that she had somehow talked to officials, saying that her husband had recently learned that she was Jewish and this put him in a suicidal mood. It was claimed that Reynolds had always had a suicide complex. A scrap of writing he had scribbled at age sixteen, where Reynolds stated his unhappiness at being turned down by a girl, was offered up to prove this complex. "Goodbye forever," Reynolds had written, "goodbye cruel world." This, of course, was nothing more than the lovesick moanings of a teenager who, through his words, may have meant that he was running away, not committing suicide. But the effect of this kind of testimony caused Coroner W.N. Dalton to quickly close the hearing, stating that Reynolds had met death by suicide.

Sheriff Scott would have none of this. He and local officials reopened the case. Coroner Dalton suddenly changed his mind and ordered another inquest. This time Holman said that Reynolds had killed himself because he was sexually inadequate, an absurd claim in that she had already admitted that she was pregnant with Reynolds' child. The dead tycoon was also the father of a 2-year-old child through his marriage to Anne Cannon. The second coroner's inquest ended with the a verdict that Reynolds died "from a bullet wound inflicted by a person or persons unknown." Still, Forsyth County authorities were not satisfied. Neither was Richard Reynolds, the dead man's older brother. He arrived in Winston-Salem on Aug. 24, 1932, and immediately told the press: "In view of all the facts available at this time, I believe my brother's death was murder. If it is, I want to see justice done. I do not think Smith was of a temperament that would allow him to commit suicide." W.N. "Will" Reynolds, uncle to Zachary Smith and Richard Reynolds, and chairman of the board of the R.J. Reynolds Company, echoed his nephew's beliefs, not accepting for a minute the fact that Zachary Smith Reynolds committed suicide.

Libby Holman was then charged with murdering her husband, Zachary Smith Reynolds, and Ab Walker was named as an accessory. The charge was later reduced to second-degree murder. Reynolds' body was exhumed and re-examined. The powder burns evident on his face, and the path of the death bullet indicated to experts that the victim had not committed suicide but had been shot to death by someone other than himself. Released on bond and joined by her father and mother, Holman gave an interview to her friend, Ward Moorehouse, of the New York *Sun*. She sat before the newsman knitting a pink sleeping suit for her unborn child. Gushed Holman: "It's knowing that I am going to give birth to the child of the man I loved that affords me my only gleam of happiness, that gives me any desire to live at all. The fact that within four long months I will have a child, *his* child, makes me strong enough to fight for a complete and absolute vindication.

"I didn't shoot Smith Reynolds. God in heaven knows that. The Reynolds family know it in their hearts. I loved Smith as I never loved anyone before or will ever love again. The fullest and richest hours of my life were spent with that dear boy. I loved him tenderly, dearly and completely and to him I meant everything, everything. When I realized he was gone...I didn't want to live...my life was over...And now I want to go through with the trial. I want no strings left, no doubts left in people's minds as to my innocence. I don't want only an acquittal, I want a complete apology."

She got neither. Libby's trial was scheduled for Nov. 21, 1932, but, on Oct. 18, solicitor Carlisle Higgins received a startling letter from W.N. Reynolds, head of the Reynolds family, in which Reynolds asked that the case against Libby Holman and Ab Walker be dropped. This was done and Libby Holman was no longer charged with murder. She was neither exonerated nor convicted, but many would form their own opinion about her guilt in the years to come. Libby Holman herself was unsure of what happened that fateful night, saying to a friend later: "I was so drunk that night I don't know whether I shot him or not."

Holman's child, a boy she named Christopher, not Smith, as she had vowed, was born two months later. She had to battle in the courts for a number of years before approximately $6.5 million was awarded her son. The singer married Ralph Holmes, another aviator, in 1941. Holmes, the son of Broadway actor Taylor Holmes and brother of screen actor Phillips Holmes, was then serving with the Royal Air Force. The couple separated in 1945 and a few months later Holmes was found dead from an overdose of sleeping pills. Libby Holman continued to appear in public occasionally, singing the old torch songs that had made her famous. Her son grew to be a tall, strapping fellow who was killed in 1950 while climbing a mountain in California. Holman became even more reclusive, but, in the early 1960s, she did make a rare singing appearance on Broadway. During one of these appearances, Tallulah Bankhead, Holman's on-and-off friend for decades, was appearing in another play nearby. One day the outspoken Tallulah asked her co-star Patsy Kelly to invite Holman to join them for a tea break.

"Is Libby working again?" asked Kelly.

"Yes, darling," replied Tallulah. "She's between murders."

In her last years, though wealthy, Libby Holman suffered repeated attacks of depression. She was at the time married to artist Louis Shanker and lived in a luxurious home in Stamford, Conn. She took large doses of lithium, but nothing helped to cure her deep fits of depression. On the evening of June 18, 1970, the 67-year-old Libby Holman was found by servants in her garage on the front seat of her Rolls Royce wearing only a bikini bottom.

She was in a stupor. Rushed to a nearby hospital, she died without speaking a few hours later.

REF.: Bradshaw, *Dreams That Money Can Buy: The Tragic Life of Libby Holman; CBA;* Horan, *The Desperate Years;* Katz, *Uncle Frank;* Lamparski, *Whatever Became Of...?;* Machlin, *Libby;* Nash, *Open Files;* Tanner, *All the Things We Were;* Walker, *The Night Club Era;* Yurka, *Bohemian Girl;* (FICTION), Wilder, *Written on the Wind;* (FILM), *Reckless,* 1935; *Written on the Wind,* 1956.

Holmes, Alexander William, b.1812, U.S., mur. In April 1841, during a North Atlantic crossing from Liverpool to Philadelphia, the *William Brown,* a passenger ship captained by George L. Harris, hit an iceberg and sank. Sixty people made it into two lifeboats, but a disproportionate number clamored into the second boat after the captain and eight crew members left in the first. Thirty-one people, mostly children, perished as the ship sank. The second lifeboat, captained by First Mate Francis Rhodes, filled with eleven people more than its capacity, began to list and take on water. Finnish born seaman Alexander Holmes and another crew member began tossing passengers overboard. Within a short time, ten men were flung to their death, lightening the fragile craft by almost 2000 pounds. The following morning, in calmer seas, two male passengers were found hiding under women's skirts. When the water became turbulent again, these two were also jettisoned. Later in the day, the survivors were rescued by a ship bound for Le Havre. The rescue set off a public debate over the conduct of the crew.

The New York *Courier* and the Philadelphia *Public Ledger* railed against the barbarous behavior of the sailors, and in Philadelphia, U.S. Attorney William Meredith issued indictments for murder against Francis Rhodes and Alexander Holmes. Rhodes disappeared, probably with George Harris, the captain of the *William Brown,* leaving Holmes to stand trial alone. The prosecution, using the testimony of three women survivors, scolded Holmes for not including any crew members among his victims, and for not using a more equitable system of selection, such as drawing lots. Holmes' defense, led by noted attorney David Paul Brown, stated that any solution under the trying circumstances was bound to draw criticism, and that the solution, however horrible, did produce eighteen survivors.

After eight days of hearings, the case went to the jury. They reached no decision after deliberating for sixteen hours. After another ten hours, they found Holmes Guilty, but with a recommendation for mercy. The Philadelphia *Public Ledger,* which had earlier been one of Holmes' more vociferous critics, now urged a presidential pardon. Holmes was sentenced to six months in prison and fined $20. After serving the sentence, he returned to sea. The case set a landmark precedent, after which a sailor was required to place a greater value on the lives of others than on his own. REF.: *CBA.*

Holmes, H.H., See: **Mudgett, Herman Webster.**

Holmes, Jimmy Jack, and **Allison, William Stafford,** and **Cook, John Clarence,** and **Gordon, Herman Hy,** and **Powers, Otto,** and **Habib, Jacob,** prom. 1968-70, U.S., fraud-theft. Jimmy Jack Holmes and William Stafford robbed post offices from August, Ga., to Indianapolis, Ind., during a two year period from Feb. 8, 1968, to Mar. 8, 1970. This well-traveled pair and their accomplices were responsible for forty-five attempted burglaries in nine states. Their thirty-three successful efforts brought in over $1.3 million in cash and stamps.

Holmes and Stafford's main fences, operating out of Miami, Fla., were John Clarence Cook and Herman Hy Gordon. They paid close to 40 percent of the face value of the stamps, and were said to be well connected with organized crime. Cook's criminal record dated back to 1948, and included many charges but few convictions, no doubt because of his association with the mob. In one illustrative instance, a key witness against him in a murder case disappeared before the trial.

In 1969, Allison and Holmes switched fences, transferring their business to Otto Powers, a stamp and coin collector in Tampa, who paid 60 percent of the face value of the stamps.

Known as "cullers," the postal bandits dealt primarily in postage dues, precanceled, and other difficult to dispose of items. Trailed by the Postal Inspection Service to New York, Powers vanished on Jan. 15, 1970. On Mar. 8, an Indianapolis post office was burglarized, and Holmes and Allison were arrested soon after as they went to meet with Powers. While waiting to be tried, Holmes traded the name of a New York stamp dealer in a bid for leniency; Jacob Habib was arrested on Sept. 1 in his Nassau Street store in Manhattan, with several batches of stolen stamps. Pleading guilty to one count of mail fraud, he was sentenced to prison for one year and one day. Holmes and Allison received five years each, and Powers was sentenced to eighteen months in prison. REF.: *CBA.*

Holmes, John, and **Williams, Peter,** prom. 1870s, Brit., rob. In London in the late 1800s, it was common for "resurrection men," or grave robbers, to practice their ghoulish trade. The shroud or other burying garments were stripped from bodies as they were dragged through the streets at night, destined to be marketed to anatomy teachers or surgeons for illegal autopsies. One well-known anatomy teacher, Mr. Hunter, had a surgical laboratory behind his London house on Windmill Street. So many corpses were brought to service his popular student lectures that Hunter dug a well behind his house to dispose of them. An alkali was added to hasten their decay. In March 1776, a monthly publication reported finding more than twenty bodies in a shed on Tottenham Court Road.

John Holmes, a grave digger at St. George's in Bloomsbury, along with Peter Williams and Esther Donaldson, stole the corpse of Jane Sainsbury, who had died on Oct. 9, 1777. But they were caught before they were able to get away with the body. Holmes and Williams were convicted at Middlesex Court in December 1777. Donaldson was acquitted and released. In addition to a six-month prison sentence, Holmes and Williams were publicly whipped in the streets, along a half-mile route from the end of Kingsgate Street, Holborn, to Dyot Street, St. Giles. Crowds of approving spectators gathered to watch. REF.: *CBA.*

Holmes, John, and **Thurmond, Thomas H.,** prom. 1933, U.S., kid.-mur. The 22-year-old son of one of San Jose's wealthiest department store owners was kidnapped in mid-November 1931. Brook Hart was abducted by two men and driven to the San Mateo bridge across San Francisco Bay. There, they got out of the car with Hart and smashed his skull from behind with a brick. They then bound him with baling wire, stole his wallet, and dropped his body into the bay. Three hours later, a call was made to the Hart home in San Jose. Brook's sister was told by the caller that her brother was being held hostage and that a $40,000 ransom must be paid. Two letters and a printed card were later received, assuring the family that Hart was unharmed and "being treated as well as possible." For six days the family waited. On Nov. 20 when another call was received, police intercepted it and traced it to a garage near the San Jose City Hall. There, they arrested Thomas H. Thurmond. John Holmes, an unemployed oil worker, was arrested at a nearby hotel. The killers gave a full confession, explaining that they had slain Hart because they "...didn't want to bother lugging him around the countryside." To prevent mob violence, Holmes and Thurmond were held in a San Francisco jail, but when Hart's body was found, angry citizens began to gather outside the jail in the park across the street. Asked if he would order the militia to protect the criminals, Governor James Rolph, Jr. said, "What! Call out the troops to protect those two guys?"

Late one November evening, the mob which numbered about 6,000 rushed the jail. Undeterred by tear gas, the mob knocked the sheriff unconscious and dragged Holmes and Thurmond out of their cells and hanged the murderers from two trees in the park.

When he heard about the lynchings, Governor Rolph said, "This is the best lesson California has ever given the country. We show the country that the State is not going to tolerate kidnapping. If anyone is arrested for the good job, I'll pardon them all."

Of the hundreds present, the only person who objected to the governor's statement was Reverend John Haynes Holmes, who called it "the crowning disgrace of the whole ghastly history of lynching in America."

The day after the hangings, 18-year-old Anthony Catalbi, who claimed to be the leader and organizer of the mob, said he recruited most of the gang from speakeasies, and explained "...that is why so many of the mob were drunk." REF.: *CBA*.

Holmes, Leonard, prom. 1944, Brit., mur. In October 1944, after returning home to New Ollerton, Nottinghamshire, England, at the end of WWII, Leonard Holmes suspected that his wife, Peggy Agnes Holmes, had been unfaithful to him. After coming home from an evening of drinking in a local pub, the couple began to fight. Peggy Holmes responded to her husband's accusations by saying, "If it will ease your mind, I have been untrue to you." Holmes hit her in the head with a hammer and then strangled her. Tried for murder before Justice Charles in February 1945 at the Nottingham Assizes, Holmes was found Guilty and sentenced to death.

Holmes appealed to the Court of Criminal Appeals claiming the trial judge did not offer the jury the option to consider a verdict of manslaughter rather than murder. Justice Wrottsley explained in the appeal judgement that a person who has been absent and returns, suspecting that his wife has been unfaithful, may not use lethal weapons on his spouse, and may not "...claim to have suffered such provocation as would reduce the crime from murder to manslaughter." Previous to this judgment, the discovery of a wife or husband in the act of adultery had long been held to be adequate provocation to justify a manslaughter verdict. Holmes was executed on May 28, 1945. REF.: *CBA*.

Holmes, Nathaniel, 1815-1901, U.S., jur. Practiced law in St. Louis, Mo., and served on the Missouri Supreme Court from 1865-68. REF.: *CBA*.

Holmes, Oliver Wendell, Jr., 1841-1935, U.S., jur. Justice Oliver Wendell Holmes sat on the bench of the U.S. Supreme Court from 1902 until 1932. When he retired, he was two months shy of his ninety-first birthday. No other justice before or since has served on the high court at such an advanced age. And no other justice has had as profound an impact on the American judicial system as the "Great Dissenter" from New England. Holmes believed that the making of laws was up to the legislative branch of government and not the courts. Freedom of speech was an inherent right guaranteed by the Constitution, limited only by what he called a "clear and present danger," which he outlined in the case of *Schenk vs. the U.S.* in 1919. "The most stringent protection of free speech would not protect a man in falsely shouting fire in a theatre and causing a panic," he once said. It was a philosophy that guided him through his entire judicial career.

Justice Holmes was descended from the Puritan poet Anne Bradstreet. His father, Oliver Wendell Holmes, Sr., was both a physician and writer whose work frequently appeared in the pages of the *Atlantic Monthly*. Holmes was educated in private schools before being sent on to Harvard College, where he graduated in 1861. At the onset of the Civil War, he enlisted as a private in the Fourth Battalion of Infantry on the Union side. Holmes was later commissioned a lieutenant in the Massachusetts Regiment of Volunteers, and was wounded three times, at Chancellorsville, Antietam, and Ball's Bluff. "I trust I did my duty as a soldier respectably," he said years later, "but I was not born for it and did nothing remarkable in that way."

Holmes entered Harvard Law School in the Autumn of 1864 against the advice of his father who believed there was nothing to be gained by becoming an attorney. The novelist William James recalled that there was no love lost between the father and son during these difficult years. Following the successful completion of his studies in 1866, the young lawyer traveled abroad. In 1867, Holmes was admitted to the bar and for the next fifteen years was employed by a private firm, taking time out to edit the *American Law Review*. He also delivered lectures to students at

the Harvard Law School and the prestigious Lowell Institute in Boston. The lectures Holmes gave in 1880-81 formed the basis of his well-received book *The Common Law*. A year later he was appointed a full Professor of Law at Harvard. In December 1882, Holmes was appointed to sit on the bench of the Supreme Judicial Court of Massachusetts, a position he held continuously for the next twenty years. His progressive social views frequently ruffled the feathers of Boston's conservatives, a trait that endeared him to the liberal wing of the Republican Party. On Aug. 5, 1899, he was named Chief Justice of Massachusetts, and served in this capacity until, in December 1902, President Theodore Roosevelt called upon him to fill a vacancy on the high court created by the resignation of Justice Horace Gray.

Holmes was a strict constructionist whose reputation was built around his many dissenting views, delivered with a mixture of Yankee pragmatism, cold "Puritan passion," and undeniable eloquence. "The provisions of the Constitution are not mathematical formulas having their essence in their form," he wrote in the case of *Gompers vs. the United States*, "they are organic living institutions transplanted from English soil. Their significance is vital not formal; it is to be gathered not simply by taking the words and a dictionary, but by considering their origin and the line of their growth."

Even after undergoing major surgery in 1922, Justice Holmes continued to serve for another decade, during which time he submitted some of his most forceful opinions. Finally, he sent his resignation to President Franklin Roosevelt on Jan. 12, 1932, because as he explained, it was time "to bow to the inevitable." He died on Mar. 6, 1935. In his eulogy, President Roosevelt cited Holmes long and impressive record on the court. "For him law was an instrument of just relations between man and man."

REF.: Bent, *Justice Oliver Wendell Holmes*; Biddle, *Mr. Justice Holmes*; Bowen, *Yankee from Olympus*; CBA; Frankfurter, *Mr. Justice Holmes*; ____, *Mr. Justice Holmes and the Supreme Court*; Howe, *Justice Oliver Wendell Holmes*; Konefky, *The Legacy of Holmes and Brandeis*; Lerner, *The Mind and Faith of Mr. Justice Holmes*.

Right, Sherlock Holmes, with Dr. Watson, as drawn by Sidney Paget of *The Strand* magazine.

Holmes, Sherlock, fictional detective created by writer Arthur Conan Doyle. The greatest detective in the annals of fiction is undoubtedly the indefatigable Sherlock Holmes, a British sleuth of amazing physical talents and superhuman intellectual abilities. His nemesis, Professor James Moriarty, whom Holmes calls "The Napoleon of crime," is undoubtedly based upon the American criminal mastermind, Adam Worth, but with elements of British master thief Jonathan Wild incorporated into his character. Holmes himself, or many of his sleuthing characteristics and eccentricities, conform to the personality of Professor Joseph Bell, who was Doyle's intellectual idol and teacher when the author attended Edinburgh University. Bell had startling powers of observation, and his deductive reasoning so impressed Doyle that Bell became the role model for the great Holmes. See: **Doyle, Arthur Conan; Wild, Jonathan; Worth, Adam**. REF.: *CBA*.

Holmes, William, and **Rosewaine, Edward**, and **Warrington, Thomas**, d.1818, U.S., pir.-mur. William Holmes was a member of the crew of the schooner *Buenos Ayres*. He, along with Edward Rosewaine and Thomas Warrington, served on board the ship, which was a pirate vessel. The crew was mostly Spanish but was commanded by an American, Captain Jacobs. On July 7, 1818, Holmes, assisted by Rosewaine and Warrington, threw Jacobs overboard, along with his mate, and put the Spanish crewmen on shore at the Cape Verde Islands. The pirates then sailed the ship to Scituate, Mass., where they were apprehended attempting to sell the ship. Though the vessel flew under the Argentine flag, the murder of Jacobs caused Holmes, Rosewaine, and Warrington to be charged with murder. All three men were found Guilty and hanged in Boston.
REF.: *CBA; Execution of the Pirates; The Pirates; The Trial of William Holmes, Thomas Warrington and Edward Rosewaine.*

Holmyard, William John, prom. 1929, Brit., mur. A young musician who was charged with killing his 72-year-old grandfather, was the first person in English history to be defended by a woman barrister, Venetia Stephenson.

On Dec. 7, 1928, the elder William Holmyard, namesake of his grandson, was found with his face streaming with blood, clutching the railings outside his home on Tachbrook Street, Pimlico. He died of shock three days later, the result of injuries including a fractured skull.

William John Holmyard was charged with the murder. He explained in court that he had gone to see his grandfather to ask for help in finding a job. Once there, the older man called him a "spendthrift" and "a rat," and then picked up a chair and threatened him with it. Holmyard said that he had struck out at his grandfather with fire tongs, but he kept advancing. The youth struck him again, then ran, unaware that he had inflicted serious harm. Pleading self-defense, defense attorney Venetia Stephenson maintained: "Youth has as much right to protect itself as old age," The jury did not agree and found Holmyard Guilty of murder. He was hanged. REF.: *CBA*.

Holroyd, Susannah, prom. 1816, Brit., mur. In 1816, Susannah Holroyd lived in Ashton-under-Lyne, England, with her husband Michael, their three children, and a lodger Anne Newton, who had an infant child. Susannah was allegedly having an affair with another man, and some questioned the legitimacy of her children. On Apr. 15, 1816, Michael Holroyd became ill, and his wife gave him a bowl of gruel. He became progressively worse and died three days later. Six hours after he died, the couple's 8-year-old son also died. The following day, Apr. 19, 1816, the infant son of the lodger became the third fatality.

A month before the deaths, Susannah Holroyd had told Anne Newton that she had had her fortune read and that within six weeks, three people would die in her household, even predicting the three eventual victims. Police discovered that Holroyd had purchased arsenic from a local chemist. An autopsy revealed the presence of arsenic in the victims' stomachs. Susannah Holroyd was arrested and charged with petty treason for attempting to take the life of her husband and with murder for administering the poison. She made a full confession of her husband's murder, but said her son died because her husband gave him a taste of the gruel. She said the death of the lodger's son was of natural causes. There existed further concern that Holroyd had poisoned other children.

On Sept. 17, 1816, Holroyd was found Guilty by a jury and sentenced to death. The following week, at the Lancaster Assizes, Susannah Holroyd was hanged, her body dissected and buried behind the prison wall. REF.: *CBA*.

Holschuh, John David, 1926-   , U.S., jur. Nominated to the southern district court of Ohio by President Jimmy Carter in 1980. REF.: *CBA*.

Holsinger, Maurice Paul, prom. 1940s-50s, U.S., fraud. A professional swindler from an early age, Maurice Paul Holsinger preyed upon the lovelorn. He placed ads in lonely hearts columns in East Coast newspapers, claiming to be any number of rich, handsome men. He would send photos of attractive men to lonely, wealthy women, stating that he could put them in touch with these bachelors for a small service fee. Enormous amounts of money poured into his Washington, D.C., offices—about $2,000 each day. Of course, Holsinger never responded to any female once she had sent her "Cupid's Fee." Holsinger, a crafty fellow, moved his offices regularly, knowing complaints from customers would put postal investigators on his trial.

Captured con man Maurice Paul Holsinger.

By the time Washington detectives got a line on Holsinger, he had left town, settling in Philadelphia, where he started his lovelorn racket all over again. He made $12,000 in about ten days and then, with postal inspectors hot on his trail, closed up shop. Holsinger moved west, bilking thousands of lonely ladies, and moving almost each week to stay ahead of pursuing officers. They finally caught up with him at the Des Moines, Iowa, airport.

One of the detectives stared at a strange-looking middle-aged woman about to board an airplane, who walked with the stride of a longshoreman and had beard stubble on a prominent jaw. He approached the woman, who resisted him, screaming: "You brute!" The detective reached forward and grabbed the woman's hair, and a wig of curly black hair fell into his hands. The bald Holsinger was taken into custody and his matrimonial scam came to an end. He was convicted of using the mails to defraud and given a long prison term.
REF.: *CBA;* Nash, *Hustlers and Con Men.*

Holt, Alice, prom. 1863, Brit., mur. Alice Holt was a British murderess, convicted of slaying her mother. She was hanged in 1863 at Chester. REF.: *CBA*.

Holt, Emory, prom. 1949, U.S., suic.-mur. When Emory Holt married Norma Bew in 1943, they seemed an odd match. He liked classical music and chess and she had a penchant for good times and flirting. An engineer officer in the Merchant Marines, Holt returned from a tour of duty to find his wife acting strangely. With methodical, professional care he recorded her actions in his log, noting her drunkenness, her smeared lipstick, and meticulously keeping nautical-time for his facts. He hired a private detective who confirmed his suspicion that she had taken a lover. Holt wrote a note to his mother in North Carolina, which said: "I expect to be dead in a few hours...All my love." He then left, carrying a gun, to find Norma Holt at her lover's apartment. It was a March night in 1949 when Mrs. Elsie Thomas in Hollywood, Calif., received a phone call from her daughter, Norma, who pleaded, "Emory is going to kill us. Please talk him out of this awful thing."

Thomas begged her son-in-law "Please be a good boy," and heard him respond, "It's too late, Mama, it's too late." She passed out as she heard shots and screams from the Manhattan apartment of David Whittaker, and telephoned the New York police when she recovered. Manhattan officers discovered Holt's body sprawled over a chair, with his 9-mm. Luger still clutched in his hand. The corpses of his wife and her lover were on the couch. REF.: *CBA*.

Holt, Frederick Rothwell (AKA: Eric), d.1920, Brit., mur. Frederick Holt was drafted into the British army at the onset of WWI. In 1918, after suffering amnesia and depression, Holt was discharged. He returned home to Lancashire where he met Harriet Elsie "Kitty" Breaks, an attractive woman whose marriage had fallen apart. For the next eighteen months they lived together.

On the morning of Dec. 24, 1919, the body of Kitty Breaks was discovered partially buried in the St. Anne's sand hills close to Blackpool. She had been shot with three bullets. A revolver and a set of footprints matching Holt's were discovered and he was arrested and charged with murder.

The trial was conducted at the Manchester Assizes in February 1920, where defense counsel Marshall Hall attempted to show that his client carried out the crime as a result of uncontrollable passion while in a state of shell shock and mental illness. Holt had been badly jarred by the Festubert bombing. The jurors and even the judge wept when love letters written by Holt to Breaks were read aloud in court. But the appeal to sentiment was squelched by Sir Gordon Hewart who accused Holt of murdering for profit. Holt had taken out a £5,000 insurance policy on Breaks' life and was also named in Breaks' will. The jury found the defendant Guilty of murder. The Home Secretary ruled that Holt was sane, thereby paving the way for his execution, which took place at Strangeways Prison on Apr. 13, 1920. REF.: *CBA*.

Holt, George Chandler, 1843-1931, U.S., jur. Lectured at Cornell and Columbia Law Schools. He was nominated to the southern district court of New York by President Theodore Roosevelt in 1903. REF.: *CBA*.

Holt, Sir John, 1642-1710, Brit., witchcraft. A lawyer who was the son of a lawyer, Sir John Holt, was a staunch proponent of civil rights, and arguably the most influential judge in the history of witchcraft, being personally responsible for a large number of acquittals. Holt was known for his fairness and impartiality in insisting that the due rights of defendants be enforced.

In the regime of William of Orange, Holt was made chief justice. In this capacity, he directed jury after jury to render acquittals in witchcraft cases. The opinions in his cases, which were widely distributed, influenced lower courts and helped to bring an end to the senseless persecutions that occurred under the name of witchcraft.

In one case, Holt went so far as to have an allegedly possessed youth examined for six months. The accusation was based on noises made by the boy, as well as a series of other impostures. When it was discovered that his possession was based on pins hidden in his trousers, Holt took the unusual action of having the boy's employers, who had accused him of witchcraft, brought into court. Responsible for dismissing at least eleven cases of witchcraft, Holt, along with the shock of the Salem trials influencing English opinion, helped to end the nightmare instituted by prosecutors Matthew Hopkins and former Chief Justice Matthew Hale. With the influence of Sir John Holt, mass trials and executions for witchcraft came to an end. (The last execution in England was in 1684; Scotland continued the practice until 1722.) See: **Hopkins, Matthew.**

REF.: *CBA*; Holt, *Modern Cases*; Robbins, *The Encyclopedia of Witchcraft and Demonology*; Summers, *The Geography of Witchcraft*.

Holt, Joseph, 1807-94, U.S., jur., Practiced law in Kentucky. He served as U.S. secretary of war in 1861 and as judge advocate general for the U.S. Army from 1862-75. While in the latter post, he handled the prosecution of those accused of conspiring to kill President Abraham Lincoln. He was said to have suppressed

evidence, and when the military commission suggested clemency for Mrs. Surratt, keeper of the boarding house where the conspirators met, he did not advise President Andrew Johnson. Surrat was hanged. REF.: *CBA*.

Holt, Sam, d.1899, U.S., lynch. (vict.). The most horrendous mob execution in nineteenth-century Georgia occurred at Newnan, a short distance from Atlanta. Sam Holt, a black, was the lynch victim. Holt was the accused killer of farmer Alfred Cranford. Holt had crept up behind Cranford, the story went, and sunk an ax into his head while the farmer sat with his family eating his evening meal. Holt then knocked the Cranford child senseless and, worse to all southern minds, hurled Mrs. Cranford to the floor and raped her in a pool of her own husband's blood. On Apr. 23, 1899, more than 2,000 persons from Newnan, Palmetto, and Griffin assembled in front of the Newnan jail. Sheriff Brown took one look at the rope-carrying mob shouting for Holt's head, and turned the prisoner over. The mob dragged Holt to the town square.

Racing his buggy through the crowd, W.Y. Atkinson, a former governor of Georgia, stood up and yelled to the crowd: "My fellow citizens and friends! I beseech you to let this affair go no further! You are hurrying this Negro on to death without an identification. Mrs. Cranford, whom he is said to have assaulted and whose husband he is said to have killed, is sick in bed and unable to be here to say whether this is her assailant. Let this Negro be returned to jail. The law will take its course, and I promise you it will do so quickly and effectually. Do not stain the honor of the state with a crime such as you are about to perform!" Judge A.D. Freeman of Newnan also stood up and appealed to the mob, but leaders in the crowd began to slap and punch Holt viciously, shouting: "Burn him! Think of his crime!"

Word spread throughout the mob that a fast train from Atlanta carrying 1,000 people would soon arrive. The lynch-bent mob thought this to be a trainload of militia and, in a panic to finish the public execution without interference, dragged Holt a mile out of town. While hundreds of spectators urged on the ringleaders, the black was tied to a pine tree in a clearing just off the main road. His clothes were torn from him. A woman produced a heavy chain and ran crazily around the tree, wrapping the chain so tightly about Holt's body that it tore his flesh in spots. A dozen men brandished knives and waved them in Holt's face. He said nothing at first.

Atkinson had not given up trying to save Holt's life. He once again appeared in the midst of the yelling throng and screamed: "Some of you are known to me and when this affair is finally settled in the courts, you may depend upon it that I will testify against you!"

One of the members of the mob drew a pistol and aimed it at Atkinson's head. Others grabbed his arm and took the pistol away. "We ain't gonna kill no white man today," a leader said to the would-be assassin. There was some debate over killing Holt, many averring to Atkinsons' remarks about Holt not being properly identified. Then Mrs. Cranford's mother appeared from the crowd and, stepping resolutely forward, pointed her finger at Holt. "That's the man," she was reported as having said.

A half-dozen knives suddenly flashed and Holt's naked body was slashed. A man who proudly announced that he was from a northern state (Pennsylvania) poured a tin of kerosene over the black. A mound of branches and twigs beneath him was lighted, and the flames danced upward. The blood flowing from the knives' wounds actually began to sizzle and for the first time the stoic Sam Holt verbalized his pain, shouting: "Oh, my God! Oh, Jesus!"

"Who paid you to do these horrible things?" one of the leaders asked the burning Holt. The victim nodded, as if he were ready to tell. Quickly, the mob freed him from the sapling and pulled him from the fire. "Who?" they demanded.

"Lige Strickland gimme $20 to do the deed," Holt gasped.

"That's what we wanted to know."

Holt was taken back to the sapling and strapped once more

over the raging fire. Before the flames again shot upward, scores of knife-wielding citizens darted forward. One man sliced off an ear and held it out for the agonized black to see. The other ear was cut off and also held up. The end of his nose was hacked off and shoved into his mouth. One by one, his fingers were cut off and these were put into his pockets as keepsakes of the momentous occasion. An elderly woman arched over the fire and grabbed Holt's genitals, cutting them away with a butcher's knife and then tossing them into the air as one would a coin for the cheering edification of the blood-lusting crowd.

The *Springfield* (Mass.) *Republican* later wrote how Sam Holt "pleaded pitifully for his life while the mutilation was going on, but stood the ordeal of fire with surprising fortitude. Before the body was cool, it was cut to pieces, the bones were crushed into small bits, and even the tree upon which the wretch met his fate was torn up and disposed of as souvenirs. The Negro's heart was cut into several pieces, as was also his liver. Those unable to obtain the ghastly relics direct paid their more fortunate possessors extravagant sums for them. Small pieces of bones went for 25 cents, and a bit of the liver crisply cooked sold for 10 cents. As soon as the Negro was seen to be dead there was a tremendous struggle among the crowd, which had witnessed his tragic end, to secure the souvenirs. A rush was made for the stake, and those near the body were forced against it and had to fight for their freedom. Knives were quickly produced and soon the body was dismembered."

Lige Strickland, the black preacher in Palmetto who had been named by Holt as the instigator of the murder and rape of the Cranfords, was the mob's next target. He was hanged in Palmetto from a persimmon tree the next day. The preacher staunchly insisted his innocence. He was pulled up and let down three times to give him time to confess. Finally, he was yanked off the ground and slowly strangled to death as his ears and one finger were cut off.

Found pinned to his carved-up chest was a bloody piece of paper. On one side it read: "We must protect our ladies." (The tree against which Holt was burned carried a placard reading: "We must protect our Southern women.") The other side of the paper read: "Beware all darkies. You will be treated the same way." REF.: *CBA*.

Holt, Thomas J., Jr., 1956- , U.S., rape-kid.-mur. In June 1979, Thomas J. Holt, Jr., of Kenosha, Wis., followed 18-year-old Alice D. Alzner from Dad's Place disco near Kenosha to her home in Lake Forest, Ill., where he forced her into his car. Holt then drove Alzner to Wisconsin, where he raped, assaulted, and strangled the young woman, burying her body in a rose garden across the alley from his home. Holt was linked to the crime by a Lake Forest police officer, who had written down the license number of Holt's car, parked near Alzner's home, the night she disappeared.

Lake County Circuit Court Judge John L. Hughes presided over Holt's trial, in which his wife, Cindy Holt, testified against her husband, stating that he returned to their Kenosha home on the night of the murder at 4:30 a.m., sweaty and unkempt. Holt's sister, Shirley, testified that her brother had been interested in Alzner since he first saw her at Dad's Place a week before the killing. Holt was convicted of murder, rape, and aggravated kidnapping on Nov. 1, 1979, and, one month later, sentenced to die in the electric chair. The Illinois Supreme Court overturned Holt's murder conviction on June 18, 1982, because Alzner was killed in Wisconsin. His 30-year sentence for kidnapping remained intact, and Holt was tried before a Kenosha jury. He was found Guilty of murder, rape, and theft from a corpse on Nov. 5, 1983. Circuit Court Judge Robert V. Baker sentenced the killer to life for the murder conviction, ten years for sexual assault, and three years for theft. The sentences were to run concurrently with the Illinois kidnapping sentence. REF.: *CBA*.

Holtzendorff, Franz von, 1829-89, Ger., jur. Expert on international and criminal law. REF.: *CBA*.

Holtzoff, Alexander, 1886-1969, U.S., jur. Worked for U.S.

attorney general as special assistant from 1924-45, and as executive assistant in 1945. He was nominated to the district court of Washington, D.C., by President Harry S. Truman in 1945. In addition, he was a member of the commission on revision of the Naval court-martial system. REF.: *CBA*.

Holy Child Orphanage Case, 1951, China, mur. Five French-Canadian Catholic nuns were charged with murder following the deaths of 2,116 infants brought to the Holy Infant Orphanage in Canton for medical treatment. Arrested on Mar. 19, 1951, Antoinette Couvrette, Germaine Gravel, Elizabeth Lemire, Germaine Tanguay, and Imelda Lapierre worked at the orphanage, where abandoned babies were brought. Of all the infants brought to the orphanage from October 1950 to February 1951, 135 survived. The nuns were also charged with mistreating, enslaving, and illegally selling the babies that lived. On Dec. 2, 1951, the women were formally tried at Sun Yat-sen Memorial Hall, which was packed with more than 6,000 people, many bearing signs and shouting for revenge. Listeners to the Canton radio station broadcasting the two-hour session could hear Chief Justice Wen Szehsien warn the crowd not to "beat the nuns" or swarm too closely by the platform on which they were placed. The five were paraded and spat upon after the hearing. Couvrette and Gravel were sentenced to five years imprisonment each, and the others were ordered deported from the country. Father Thomas J. Bauer and Sister St. Joseph, Mother Superior of the Order of the Immaculate Conception from where the nuns originated, said the five had committed no crimes, and that little could be done for the infants, who were dying when they were brought to the orphanage. REF.: *CBA*.

Holzaptel, Floyd Albert, See: Peel, Joseph Alexander.

Holzhay, Reimund (AKA: **Black Bart**), b.1866, U.S., rob. A German immigrant, Reimund Holzhay moved to Shawano, Wis., in 1882 and later took to robbing trains and stagecoaches in northern Wisconsin and Michigan. He was nicknamed Black Bart but never attained the infamy of the more celebrated Black Bart of California. Holzhay operated alone and was one of the most daring outlaws of his day. He was apprehended on Aug. 31, 1889, just after having committed a robbery, and he was sent to the Wisconsin state prison for life. He attempted to escape in 1890 but was stopped after the warden shot off Holzhay's finger.

REF.: Bartholomew, *A Biographical Album of Western Gunfighters; CBA*.

Holzheimer, William Andrew, b.1870, U.S., jur. Nominated to the territorial court of Arkansas by President Woodrow Wilson in 1917. REF.: *CBA*.

Home, Daniel Dunglas, 1833-86, Brit., fraud. A famous medium at a time when spiritualism was the rage, especially in Europe, Daniel Dunglas Home had a long and successful career contacting the spirits for a number of clients, most of them wealthy, and many of them women.

Born in Scotland near Edinburgh, Daniel Home was nine years old when he went with a maiden aunt to Norwich, Conn. A pampered and sickly child, Home turned to poetry, playing piano, and singing sentimental ballads, and soon was a favorite, entertaining middle-aged women. By his teens, Home claimed he was the illegitimate son of an Earl, and began to perform sessions in which "spirits" would move or rap on tables at seances. Specializing in table turning, spirit rapping, and "spirit-hands," in which physical contact was supposedly established between the ethereal and the temporal world, Home's fame grew. With his successes, he moved to Europe, performing for royalty in Prussia, France, Bavaria, and Russia.

Home most often performed in darkened rooms in the homes of his friends. The poet, Elizabeth Barrett Browning, was an ardent believer in his talents, and her husband, Robert Browning who thought Home a fraud, parodied his performances in a long poem called "Mr. Sludge, the Medium." Although Home did not charge for his sessions, he accepted frequent and extravagant gifts from his rich followers, and lived luxuriously throughout his adult life, supported particularly by wealthy older women. In his book,

Light and Shadows of Spiritualism, Home warned against frauds and charlatans, which he considered all other spiritualists to be. He continued to perform successfully until his death in 1886. REF.: *CBA.*

Home, George, prom. 1611, Brit., (unsolv.) mur. A Scottish noble, George Home, Earl of Dunbar, was said to have been poisoned by Secretary Cecil, who gave him what he claimed were "tablets of Sugar...for expelling the cold." The doctor who conducted the post mortem, Martin Souqir, was said to have tested the poison by putting his finger on the corpses' heart and "touching it with his tongue." This was, apparently, a common clinical test for poison in those times; unfortunately, the doctor died of the test a few days later. REF.: *CBA.*

Home, George K., b.1879, U.S., law enfor. off. Raised in Los Angeles, George K. Homes joined the city's police force when he was twenty-five, serving as a patrolman for two-and-a-half-years, after which he took a leave of absence to work as an oil driller in Tampico, Mexico. Returning to L.A., Home served as an acting detective for several months and was then made a detective. In 1913, he was promoted to detective sergeant, and was named inspector of police at headquarters a few months later. In January 1915 he became the first deputy chief of the department, and rose to the rank of detective lieutenant within a year. Appointed chief of detectives on May 1, 1917, he served in that post until July 1919 when he was appointed Chief of Police by M.P. Snyder. Home continued as police chief until he retired to become part of the National Credit Men's Association. REF.: *CBA.*

Home, Henry, 1696-1782, Scot., jur. Served as lord of the justiciary from 1763-82. REF.: *CBA.*

Homecoming, 1935, a novella by Miriam Allen deFord. This work took its story and characters from the lynching of kidnapping killers Thomas Thurmond and John Maurice Holmes (U.S., 1933). The Thurmond-Holmes tale also served as the role model for Fritz Lang's film, *Fury.* See: **Thurmond, Thomas Harold.**

Home Counties Riots, prom. early 19th cent., Brit., mob vio. With England in a state of uproar, the Home Counties Riots involved almost nightly acts of incendiarism. Agricultural machines, like threshing machinery, were destroyed in Norfolk, and effigies of political leaders Carlisle, the Duke of Wellington, and Sir Robert Peel burned. Public opinion about the liability of police was sharply divided. An attempt was made to murder Superintendent Thomas, who was stabbed, but saved by the folds of cloth in his waistcoat. A few nights later at Milwall, a constable on duty was seized by four sailors and dropped into the Thames River; he fell into the mud and cut his cheek. The men escaped. REF.: *CBA.*

Home-Stake Case, prom. 1977, U.S., fraud. On Feb. 2, 1977, the U.S. Justice Department dismissed charges against the last of thirteen defendants in a fraud-conspiracy case, the Home-Stake Case. The main defendant, Kent M. Klineman, a tax lawyer and tax shelter salesman in New York City, had been accused with twelve others of conspiring to bilk investors in a tax-sheltered oil-drilling venture out of millions of dollars.

The cumbersome prosecution began when the defendants were first indicted in December 1974 in Los Angeles. For complicated reasons, twelve of the defendants were reindicted in February in L.A., and seven of that number, including Klineman, were indicted yet again in Tulsa, Okla., where the Home-Stake Production Company was based, in February 1976. Five of the accused pleaded guilty or no contest to reduced charges, while three were acquitted. Klineman was the fifth and final defendant against whom charges were dropped. A Manhattan U.S. attorney explained that, "...the evidence against Mr. Klineman isn't sufficient to justify the expenditure of the resources necessary to try the case, since it appears that the prosecution would be successful." REF.: *CBA.*

Homestead (Pa.) Strike, 1892, U.S., riot-treas. A long debate over the behavior and responsibility of the Pinkerton Detective Agency began in 1892, several years after founder Allan Pinkerton's death. The Carnegie Iron and Steel Company of Homestead,

Pa., brought in 300 Pinkerton agents to deal with a worker's strike. A serious wage dispute had resulted in a deadlock between management and members of the Amalgamated Association of Iron and Steel Workers. On June 20, two days before the expiration of the current wage contract and while negotiations were still in progress, Carnegie's president, Henry C. Frick, contracted with Robert Pinkerton in New York City for 300 armed guards at the rate of $5 each per day. The union workers organized for battle, cutting holes in the board fence the company had erected around the plant.

The Pinkerton guards were to travel by boat to Ashtabula, Ohio, to Homestead, about eight miles east of Pittsburgh, by July 6. Allegheny County Sheriff McLeary opposed the hiring of the Pinkerton agents, but made no effort to strengthen his own force. By July 1, the union declared a strike, took charge of the fenced-in works, and determined not to admit strikebreakers. On July 5, they permitted sheriff's deputies to enter the grounds and see that no damage had occurred. On July 6, the Pinkerton men arrived on two barges accompanied by two small steam tugs. At 4 a.m., a steamer used by the strikers to patrol the river gave the whistle alarm, which was rapidly picked up by every engine in town controlled by the workers. Strikers and their families streamed down to the river banks. No damage had been done in Homestead until that time. As the barges neared the shore, gunfire erupted on both sides. No one would later admit firing the first shot. Several people were wounded or killed. The Pinkerton guards retreated behind the barges. Gunfire resumed later that morning, and was heaviest when sixty Pinkertons tried to land and were driven off. The agent in command, Captain Hinde, was wounded twice. The strikers poured oil on the water and lit it, but a strong breeze blew it away from the Pinkertons' barges. Presidents then tried to aim a natural gas pipe at one of the barges. A cannonball fired into one of the crowds of workers decapitated a striker. A Pinkerton agent jumped ship and drowned. In the afternoon, the barges raised white flags but were answered with dynamite charges. At 5 p.m., Homestead leader Hugh O'Donnell grabbed an American flag and pleaded mercy for the men on the barges. The agents were allowed to leave the barges after laying down their arm. The raging mob destroyed the barges and the Carnegie pump house. Although he had promised to protect the Pinkerton agents, O'Donnell was unable to do so. One agent had his eye poked out with an umbrella, and others were blinded by sand thrown in their faces. One of the Pinkertons stepped out to address the crowd. He said he had no understanding of the situation, that he had been told he would be dealing with foreigners, and that he would not have come had he known what was happening in Homestead. The crowd cheered him and allowed him to leave.

When medical assistance finally came, the tally was 145 wounded, with twenty-one hit by bullets in the fighting and the others seriously hurt on the way to the makeshift jail. Eleven workers and nine agents had been killed. O'Donnell and thirty-two Homestead residents were arrested and charged with treason, though no federal officers had been on the scene. The defendants were tried in October 1892, and all were acquitted. At the July 23 congressional hearing, both William and Robert Pinkerton appeared. They admitted that their agents had been armed, but denied that the barges had been sheathed with metal inside. The Pinkerton company finally admitted that they had sent an undisciplined force under false pretenses to a town on the brink of an uprising.

REF.: Adamic, *The Story of Class Violence in America; CBA;* Demaris, *America the Violent;* Dulles, *Labor in America;* Foner, *History of the Labor Movement in the United States;* Hofstadter and Wallace, *American Violence;* Wolfe, *Lockout: The Story of the Homestead Strike;* Yellin, *American Labor Struggles.*

Homma Masaharu (or Honma), 1887-1946, Japan, war crimes. Homma Masaharu was the commanding officer who directed the invasion of the Philippines in 1941-42, which resulted in many atrocities. Most notable was the infamous Bataan Death March, in which U.S. and Filipino prisoners of war were marched hundreds of miles, barefooted, to distant prison camps by barbaric Japanese troops who beat, bayoneted, and shot them without mercy and in total violation of all codes of war. This inhuman treatment of prisoners, which included the continuing barbaric treatment of inmates in Japanese concentration camps, was attributed to Homma.

During his trial in 1946, conducted by a U.S. military tribunal in Manila, Homma claimed innocence, stating that he had given no written orders for such an atrocity nor did he have knowledge of the atrocities committed by his disobedient or unruly troops. This, of course, was a bold-faced lie on Homma's part in that the Death March continued for a week. Witnesses came forward to uphold the fact that Homma and his top officers had given verbal orders for the Death March and that the ragged columns of tragic prisoners, who staggered northward, passed almost right in front of Homma's headquarters.

War criminal Homma.

The Japanese general was convicted of these and other war crimes and sentenced to death by firing squad. He appealed the sentence to the U.S. Supreme Court, which denied the appeal. Homma appealed to General Douglas MacArthur, who refused to interfere in the decision of the court. In a desperate attempt to save his life, Homma sent a last-minute appeal to President Harry Truman, asking that the execution be commuted to life imprisonment. President Truman refused to take action. Homma was marched before a firing squad on Apr. 3, 1946, and executed. See: **Bataan Death March; Yamashita Tomoyuki.**

REF.: Bergamini, *Japan's Imperial Conspiracy; CBA;* Kenworthy, *The Tiger of Malaya: The Inside Story of the Japanese Atrocities;* Kerr, *Surrender & Survival: The Experience of American POWs in the Pacific, 1941-1945;* Knox, *Death March: The Survivors of Bataan;* Manchester, *American Caesar;* Morris, *Corregidor: The End of the Line;* Rutherford, *Fall of the Philippines;* Toland, *The Rising Sun.*

Honduran Death Squads, prom. 1980s, Hond., kid.-tort.-mur. On July 29, 1988, the Inter-American Court of Human Rights blamed the Honduran government for the mysterious disappearance of a Honduran citizen abducted in 1981 by Honduran Death Squads.

The court, the first international tribunal convened to judge a case regarding the violation of civil liberties, was recognized as a legitimate judicial organization by Honduran President José Azcona Hoyo, but not by many other member nations of the organization of American States (O.A.S.). The court ordered Azcona's government to pay damages to the family of Angel Manfredo Velásquez Rodriguez, and blamed his abduction on the Honduran Death Squads formed by General Gustavo Alvarez Martinez in the early 1980s. Martinez's Death Squads are a group of government soldiers responsible for silencing civilians for speaking out against the ruling military regime. Between 1981 and 1984, more than 150 people described as a threat to the country's national security were abducted by the group.

"Manfredo Velásquez was a victim of this practice, and was kidnapped, presumably tortured, executed, and buried secretly by agents of the Honduran armed forces," said the court in the first direct verdict against the government of any O.A.S. member. REF.: *CBA.*

Honeymoon Gang, prom. 1850s, U.S., org. crime. The Honeymoon Gang terrorized citizens on New York City's East Side in the early 1850s, stationing thugs on each corner of the intersection of 29th Street and Madison Avenue to prey upon well-dressed pedestrians. Late in the evening, the gang members would meet at a nearby saloon to divide the spoils. In late 1853, George W. Walling was appointed police captain of the neighborhood, and quickly instituted measures to improve public safety. He organized a Strong Arm Squad consisting of six burly plainclothes officers armed with billy clubs. They regularly beat and arrested every Honeymooner sighted in the area, and within two weeks, scattered the gang to other wards.

REF.: Asbury, *The Gangs of New York; CBA.*

Hongisto, Richard, 1937- , U.S., cont./ct. The sheriff of San Francisco County, Calif., Richard Hongisto, was jailed for contempt of court in 1977 when he refused to deliver eviction notices to tenants living in a residential hotel in San Francisco's Chinatown neighborhood. At the time of his arrest, he became the first California sheriff ever to be sent to jail.

In May of 1977, Sheriff Hongisto declined to evict seventy poor, elderly Filipino residents from a transient Chinatown hotel at the request of the building's owner, a Taiwanese corporation that sought to demolish the building in order to construct a new development in the profitable, high-rent district. Hongisto, who had a great number of followers from the city's liberal population for his support of blacks, gays, and various minority causes, maintained that the evictions would have sparked a riot, which his department would have been unable to handle. Hongisto estimated a revolt by more than 10,000 Chinatown residents in which his deputies would have been outnumbered 100 to one.

Superior Court Judge John E. Benson disagreed with Hongisto's handling of the situation and fined him $500 and sentenced him to five days in jail for contempt of court. Hongisto's attorneys appealed the decision to the California Supreme Court, but were denied a hearing. Upon learning of the high court's decision, Hongisto voluntarily walked into the San Mateo, Calif., jail to serve his sentence. REF.: *CBA.*

Honka, Fritz (AKA: **Fiete Honka**), 1936- , Ger., asslt.-necro.-mur. While battling a fire at an apartment building in Hamburg, Germany's St. Pauli district on the morning of June 17, 1975, fire fighters uncovered the secret of the missing women of the Golden Glove. In the attic apartment, where the building's caretaker lived, they found the charred remains of dismembered human bodies and a plastic bag filled with the decayed and liquified body parts of four elderly prostitutes who had disappeared from a seedy neighborhood bar over the last four years.

The Golden Glove was a St. Pauli district saloon frequented by many of the neighborhood's prostitutes and its customers. Beginning in 1971, prostitutes began disappearing from the bar; all of whom were elderly, shorter than five foot, five inches, and toothless. No one seemed to notice their disappearance until the decapitated head of 42-year-old Gertraude Braeuer was discovered by two children playing in a vacant lot three blocks from the bar. Upon investigation, the Hamburg police department found all of the remaining pieces of the woman's body, except her torso, which was rotting in the storage area hidden in the walls of Fritz Honka's upstairs apartment.

Honka was the caretaker of a neighborhood apartment building where he worked in exchange for a rent-free attic apartment. Honka, an alcoholic, spent many evenings at the Golden Glove. After a heavy bout of drinking, Honka would return home drunk, oblivious to the stench that had begun to circulate through the building. Although unaware himself, two of his live-in lovers had noticed, and many of the building's tenants complained. Some moved out, including Honka's former girlfriends.

When fire fighters burst into his apartment in 1975, they ripped through the walls in an attempt to extinguish remaining embers. They were shocked when they tore the wooden panels from the walls. Hidden within was Braeuer's torso, and the mutilated bodies of 54-year-old Anna Beuschel, 57-year-old Frieda Roblick, and 52-year-old Ruth Schult.

After police took Honka into custody, he confessed to the

crimes and explained that he had strangled the women only after they had refused to comply to his demands to perform oral sex. He later disposed of the corpses by cutting them up with a knife and a handsaw in the kitchen sink, and hiding the remains in the attic. When the stench from the decaying bodies, which were hidden in the walls, became too overpowering he would bathe the room in deodorant spray. Police also learned that at least on two occasions, Honka had sexual intercourse with the corpses.

Honka, who had previously been charged with assaulting two other St. Pauli women, was found Guilty and sentenced to life in prison.

REF.: *CBA*; Dunning, *The Arbor House Treasury of True Crime*.

Hood, Linda, 1952- , U.S., child abuse-mur. Linda Hood, a 34-year-old Palatine, Ill., woman who attempted to murder her child on July 23, 1986, finally succeeded less than three weeks after authorities and medical professionals ignored the warnings of family members who pleaded that 2-year-old Michelle Hood be protected.

On Aug. 6, 1986, Hood strangled Michelle with a bathrobe sash and held the child under water in the bathtub until she stopped breathing. Afterward she dried and dressed the body before laying the dead girl on her bed and calling her husband home from work. Hood told her husband, "Come and see what I've done," as she led him into their daughter's bedroom where the body was on display.

Hood was taken into custody and charged with murder. On Jan. 21, 1988, she was found Guilty but mentally ill. During her trial, Illinois Assistant State's Attorney Sander Klapman explained how Hood had "practiced" strangling the baby two weeks earlier in an incident that sparked family members to plead with the woman's psychiatrists to hospitalize her for treatment.

In March 1988, Hood was sentenced to thirty years in prison where she was to be treated by psychiatrists. Hood left the courtroom crying, "I just want to go someplace where I can get some help." REF.: *CBA*.

Hood, Vera, 1913-24, Brit., (unsolv.) mur. The body of 11-year-old Vera Hood was found four days after she disappeared after walking home alone from a music lesson. Her body was found hidden under bushes near her home in Chichester, England. Hood had been strangled, and while unconscious, she was sexually molested. No one has ever been charged with the murder.

REF.: *CBA*; Nicholls, *Crime Within the Square Mile*.

Hoodoo War, See: **Mason County War**.

Hooe, William F., d.1826, U.S., mur. A gambler down on his luck, William Hooe lured William Simpson, a wealthy land owner, to a lonely spot near Centreville, Va., on the promise of delivering slaves that could be bought cheaply. Hooe killed Simpson and took the money he had brought along to purchase the slaves. He was later caught with some of Simpson's personal affects and was arrested and charged with the murder. Hooe was convicted and hanged on June 30, 1826, near the Fairfax County Courthouse.

REF.: *CBA*; *The Interesting Trial of William F. Hooe*.

Hooijaijers, Frans, prom. 1971, Neth., mur. A former monk, Frans Hooijaijers murdered patients in the nursing home where he worked by giving them overdoses of insulin. Although he was convicted of only five murders, prosecutors estimate that Hooijaijers may have killed as many as 259 patients. He was sentenced to thirteen years in prison.

REF.: *CBA*; Nash, *Almanac of World Crime*.

Hooker, Cameron, 1953- , U.S., kid.-sod.-rape-tort.-mur. Cameron Hooker, a 24-year-old lumber mill worker, displayed few outward signs of sociopathic behavior, but he was fascinated by bondage and humiliation. He had an extensive collection of magazines depicting such practices, and subjected his wife, Janice Hooker, to the humiliation of being hung naked from a tree and photographed. She had married Hooker as a 16-year-old in 1975 after feigning pregnancy, and then became his accomplice.

On May 19, 1977, 20-year-old Colleen Stan was hitchhiking on Interstate 5 near Red Bluff, Calif., when a young couple with a baby in a small sedan picked her up. For the next seven years,

Cameron Hooker and his wife Janice would keep her in captivity. At the couple's small home in Red Bluff, Colleen was handcuffed and fitted with a "head box," a wooden contraption which encircled her head. She was stripped and hung by leather straps from a basement ceiling beam, and methodically tortured and raped. After a few days she was placed in a flat box slightly larger than a casket where she was kept for up to twenty-three hours a day for most of the next seven years.

Colleen Stan lived in the box in the basement, without light, ventilation, or toilet facilities. She could not sit, and could barely turn sideways. When let out for an hour a day, she was sexually abused. After three months, she was allowed to wash her hair, but was nearly drowned in the tub. Janice Hooker left in the summer of 1977, but told no one of her husband's activities, and she soon returned. The couple set Stan to work at macrame and sold her wares at local flea markets.

In January 1978, Hooker designed a "Slave Contract" issued by a fictitious organization known as "The Company," and forced Stan to sign it. He warned her of constant surveillance, and immediate retaliation for disobeying orders. She was then allowed the freedom to baby-sit for the Hookers, to appear outside, and occasionally to accompany Hooker into town on errands. She was given a Company registration card, and the single letter "K" became her new name. The Hookers moved to a small trailer in a rural wooded area, and Stan lived in a slightly different box beneath the Hookers' waterbed. On Sept. 4, 1978, as Stan lay in captivity, Hooker delivered the couple's second child directly above her.

When Stan's brainwashing was complete, Janice Hooker took a job at a convenience store and left Stan alone at home with the children. On Mar. 20, 1981, Stan was allowed to visit her family for the first time in almost four years. She divulged nothing of her plight, and returned to another three years in the box under the bed. She began digging a dungeon with Hooker outside of the house so he could practice his sadism away from his growing children. By January 1984, Stan was out of the box and sleeping in the living room. In May, she was allowed to look for a job to bolster the household income and became a motel maid. She also began attending church services with Janice Hooker. By the summer of 1984, Hooker was sleeping regularly with his "slave wife" and talking about kidnapping more slaves. But Janice Hooker had enough and confessed to a clergyman, Pastor Dabney, who in turn informed Detective Al Shamblin.

On Nov. 9, 1984, Janice Hooker was granted immunity from prosecution and implicated Cameron Hooker in the 1976 murder-abduction of Marie Elizabeth Spannhake, but could not locate the grave. Three days later, Shamblin found Colleen Stan visiting her parents and heard her story. On Nov. 18, 1984, Cameron Hooker was arrested and arraigned on two dozen charges, including kidnapping, rape, and sodomy, and held in Red Bluff under a $500,000 bond.

His trial began on Sept. 24, 1985, in Redwood City at the San Mateo County Courthouse with Judge Clarence Knight presiding. The prosecution, led by Christine McGuire, sought to prove that Colleen had been brainwashed and so could not free herself while without constraint in public. Kidnapping was also difficult to prove as the statute of limitations ran out three years after the crime. The defense, led by Rolland Papendick, argued that Stan was a willing participant in the practice of bondage, and that she was free to come and go as she pleased. Janice Hooker testified against her husband and produced photographs showing her and Stan in bondage. On Oct. 31, 1985, Cameron Hooker was found Guilty on ten felony counts, and on Nov. 22, 1985, he was sentenced to 104 years in Folsom Penitentiary. REF.: *CBA*.

Hook Gang, prom. 1860s-70s, U.S., org. crime. The Hook Gang was a group of thieves and river pirates centered in New York's Corlears' Hook section between the late 1860s and 1870s. They were an unpredictable lot, led at various times by James Coffee, Terry Le Strange, Suds Merrick, and Tommy Shay. They would commit any crime, including stealing the boat from an eight man rowing crew. They would brazenly cordon off a street, and would loot a building or ship at their leisure. One member, Slipsey Ward, attempted singlehandedly to rob a ship manned by a crew of six. He was overcome after killing three crewmen, and sentenced to Auburn Prison. Another, named Wallace, was arrested when he attempted to rob three men in a rowboat who turned out to be police detectives. In 1876, the New York Police organized a Steamboat Squad and brought to an end most of the river piracy. REF.: *CBA*.

Hooley, Ernest Terah, 1859-1947, Brit., fraud. An enterprising swindler, Ernest Terah Hooley was the son of a Nottingham, England, lacemaker. He set himself up as a stockbroker, and developed a fraud that involved acquiring control of established companies, juggling the accounts, and then issuing outlines and prospectuses in order to float public companies at many times their actual value.

Hooley purchased the Dunlop Tyre Company after securing an option on it, then bought his own company for £3 million and refloated it for £5 million. Earning an early reputation in the 1890s, Hooley was the subject of a popular song sung to the tune of *The Man Who Broke The Bank At Monte Carlo*. He lived in the Midlands, making millions and consorting with royalty and other celebrities. In 1896 Hooley moved to London and after he presented a set of gold plate to St. Paul's Cathedral, it was rumored that he was going to be given a title. Shortly afterwards Hooley went bankrupt, in complicated proceedings that dragged on for years. His debts totalled more than £1.5 million. Hooley admitted bribing his way into a nomination for Parliament, and offering £50,000 to be made a baronet. Part of his success lay in his technique of cultivating friendships with famous people and then trading on their names to get others to invest.

In May 1904, Hooley and his partner, H.J. Lawson were charged with fraud in connection with a London cologne company. Lawson was convicted of issuing false statements, but Hooley was acquitted and continued to make money under suspicious circumstances for another eight years. In 1912, he was arrested for inducing a young man, George Leech Tweedale, into invest £21,500 of his £27,500 inheritance. Hooley wept in the Central Criminal Court in February 1912 as he listed the many country mansions he had been forced to sell. Judge Phillimore decided to punish him only for defrauding the man of £2,000, and gave him a lenient one-year sentence. Hooley was again tried at the Old Bailey in 1922, and this time sentenced to three years' penal servitude for his conspiracy in the case of the Jubilee Cotton Mills. Following his release in 1924, Hooley was frequently in court, as litigant or defendant. He continued in business until his death at the age of eighty-eight.

Swindler Ernest Hooley.

REF.: Bowker, *Behind the Bar*; Browne, *Rise of Scotland Yard*; *CBA*; Humphreys, *A Book of Trials*; Scott, *The Concise Encyclopedia of Crime and Criminals*; Thomson, *The Story of Scotland Yard*.

Hoolhouse, Robert, 1917-38, Brit., mur. Margaret Jane Dobson and her husband had a farm at High Grange near Wolviston, England. A dispute with a tenant laborer in 1933 resulted in the Dobsons' evicting the family, the Hoolhouses, who moved to a village four miles away. Five years later, on Jan. 18, 1938, Margaret Dobson's body was found on a farm track. The 67-year-old woman had been stabbed and sexually assaulted. Among those questioned was Robert Hoolhouse, twenty-one, the son of the family ousted from their home. Within thirty-six hours, Hoolhouse was arrested on considerable circumstantial evidence. He had a motive to kill Dobson, he approximately matched the description of a man seen near the farm, and there were scratches

on his face as well as blood and hair on his clothes. At his trial at Leeds Assizes in March 1938, his defense declared that the prosecution had no case, but did not offer any evidence. Although the prosecutors acknowledged that a footprint near the body was not that of Hoolhouse, and an acquittal was expected, the jury found the accused Guilty. An appeal was dismissed, and a 14,000-signature petition for a reprieve was rejected. Hoolhouse was hanged on May 26, 1938, at the Durham Jail.

REF.: *CBA*; Furneaux, *Robert Hoolhouse*.

Hooper, Harney E., Jr., prom. 1977, U.S., extor. On Feb. 17, 1977, a federal judge in New Orleans, La., found Harney E. Hooper, Jr., former president of the St. Charles County, La., police jury, Guilty of extorting funds from local businessmen. Hooper was the fifth member of the seven-member county organization to be convicted on charges of receiving kickbacks from architects, engineers, and other businessmen developing property in the county's industrial riverfront region.

Based on the testimony of Leonard J. LeDoux, Frank J. Pizzolato, Stephen J. DiBeneditto, and Roosevelt A. Dufrene, four men previously convicted on charges of extortion, Hooper was fined $10,000 and sentenced to two years in jail. LeDoux, DiBeneditto, and Dufrene all previously received two-year sentences, while Pizzolato had cooperated with prosecutors and received only fifteen months. REF.: *CBA*.

Hooper, John, d.1555, Brit., her. Became a Protestant and in 1539 left Britain to avoid persecution. He went back to Britain and became the bishop of Gloucester in 1550, and the bishop of Worcester in 1552. Queen Mary stripped him of his position and he was executed by being burned at the stake for heresy. REF.: *CBA*.

Hooper, John, prom. 1700s, Brit., execut. John Hooper began serving as a public hangman at Newgate Prison when he was appointed on Aug. 15, 1728. Known as the Laughing Hangman, Hooper cheered and jeered criminals sentenced to execution as they rode to the gallows, causing the attending crowd to erupt in hilarity.

Hooper's most sensational hanging was that of 25-year-old Sarah Malcolm on Mar. 7, 1733. At the time, Malcolm was England's most infamous female murderer—she single-handedly strangled and slashed three of her servants.

It is not known exactly when or why Hooper retired as public executioner, but by 1735 he had been replaced by John Thrift. REF.: *CBA*.

Hooper, Murray, 1946- , **Collins, Roger Lee** (AKA: **Cochise**), 1948- , and **Bracy, William**, 1942- , U.S., org. crime-mur. On Nov. 13, 1980, three Chicago narcotics dealers were found murdered in their automobile parked under an overpass, just two blocks away from Chicago Central Police Headquarters. The gangland-style murders were suspected to be the work of a Chicago street gang known as the Royal Family. Shortly after the bodies of 35-year-old Frederick Lacey, 28-year-old Richard Holliman, and 41-year-old R.C. Pettigrew were found in the abandoned vehicle, three members of the gang were taken into custody. Murray Hooper, Roger Lee Collins, and William Bracy were charged in the triple homicide. It was learned that the three victims owed the Royal Family money for a recent drug deal; when they failed to pay, they were executed.

In 1981, the three defendants appeared before Criminal Court Judge Thomas A. Maloney. Described by Assistant State's Attorneys Gregg Owen and Michael Goggin as a "cunning, calculated hit man," the jury found Hooper and the two other defendants Guilty. They were later sentenced to death. See: **Royal Family**. REF.: *CBA*.

Hooton, Dr. Earnest A., 1887-1954, U.S., criminol. Dr. Earnest A. Hooton was a highly touted Harvard anthropologist who, in the 1930s, conducted a study that linked criminal behavior with an individuals' physical attributes, and demonstrated the biological inferiority of criminals.

In 1926, Hooton began a ten-state study of more than 17,000 criminals in an attempt to link their offenses to their physical attributes. Hooton believed that anatomical differences were a determining factor in those prone to criminal behavior, and even those likely to commit a particular type of crime.

In establishing his theories, he examined different racial types, and categorized persons in subgroups of individuals displaying similar physical characteristics. Hooton established nine characteristic types and directly correlated their anatomical design with specific types of crimes. His study defined "Old Americans" as those persons born in the U.S. to white parents, and described this group as persons who are of less than average height and weight; have shorter, broad faces; narrow jaws; sloping shoulders; and longer, thinner necks. Features of "Old Americans" often display signs of retarded development or the retention of primitive features. "Pure Nordics," described as having long heads, ash or golden blonde hair, and blue eyes, were more likely to commit offenses of forgery and fraud, whereas Hooton's "Dinarics," persons with round heads, mixed skin pigmentation, and narrow noses, led the list in sex offenses. Hooton also dispelled several myths commonly held by white Americans. He found that "Old Americans," white immigrants, and the children of white immigrants committed the majority of the country's rapes, and that blacks committed more burglaries but fewer rapes than once believed.

Hooton published his first volume, *The Native White Criminal of Native White Parentage,* of his three-volume series, *The American Criminal,* in 1939. During the same year, he authored a condensed layman's version entitled *Crime and the Man.* On May 3, 1954, Hooton died of a heart attack at the age of sixty-six. REF.: *CBA.*

Hoover, J(ohn). Edgar, 1895-1972, U.S., law enfor. off. No other U.S. law enforcement official in the twentieth century wielded as much power and exercised as much influence with presidents and Congress as did J. Edgar Hoover, whose name is now synonymous with the FBI. He was not, in the strict sense, a complete lawman but was an effective administrator, a masterful propagandist, and a dogged, unflinching bureaucrat whose pettiness and prejudices often led him dangerously close to dismissal if not censure. Under Hoover's long tenure as director of the FBI, the Bureau's once tainted image was transformed into that of an impeccable and incorruptible organization that, as far as the American public was concerned, "always got its man." Under Hoover's direction, the Bureau achieved spectacular results in the apprehension of notorious criminals, subversives and espionage agents. It also made spectacular errors, often compounded by Hoover's testy, superior attitudes, which it unfailingly refused to acknowledge. Largely on Hoover's initiative, the Bureau became a world leader in the fields of fingerprint identification and forensic sciences.

Always a very private person, Hoover was born in Washington, D.C., to Dickerson and Ann (Scheitlin) Hoover on Jan. 1, 1895. He was the youngest of three children. His father, like his father before him, was a dedicated civil servant. At Brent Public School he remained aloof from the neighborhood gangs. He was studious and serious and made few friends. While attending Washington's Central High, Hoover, who was raised to read the Bible daily, considered entering the ministry. He was devoutly religious and regularly attended church and Sunday school, habits that did not change when he entered George Washington University in 1913, where he defrayed his expenses by working as a clerk in the Library of Congress.

Hoover's college years were unspectacular. He did not participate in sports, although he enjoyed all games. In high school he attempted to play football, but a drop-kicked football flattened his nose. He proved to be an excellent debater, and graduated with honors in 1916 with a law degree, obtaining his master's in 1917. That year, he took a job as a legal clerk in the Department of Justice at an annual salary of $990. He remained with this department for the next fifty-five years. He went on living at home with his parents. When war came in 1917, Hoover remained in the U.S. but was part of an army reserve company.

Later, he would attain the rank of major in the army reserve and always delighted at being addressed with that rank. During the war, Hoover was appointed to the staff of John Lord O'Brien, special assistant in charge of war work under Attorney General Thomas W. Gregory.

At the time, hundreds of thousands of self-appointed vigilantes were running about making citizen's arrests of any "suspicious" looking or sounding foreigners. Anyone with a foreign accent was subject to impromptu arrest and beatings. This situation became so flagrant that O'Brien was put in charge of sorting out the innocent immigrants from legitimate suspects. Hoover headed the Enemy Alien Registration section of O'Brien's office. He and his small staff diligently processed tons of paperwork dealing with aliens, and Hoover's tireless efforts resulted in a number of "credits" being added to his impressive dossier. He had helped to pinpoint a goodly number of suspected spies and draft dodgers.

His career progressed rapidly after two anarchists planted a bomb on the front doorstep of the new U.S. attorney general, A. Mitchell Palmer, on June 2, 1919. At 11:15 that night, the two would-be assassins ignited a homemade bomb in front of Palmer's residence. It went off with a deafening roar and tore the front of Palmer's house to pieces. It blew out the windows of half the neighborhood and also blew up the two anarchists. A bloody piece from one of their bodies landed on the front stoop of the house directly across the street from Palmer's, where Franklin Delano Roosevelt, then secretary of the navy, lived. A ring of anarchists, targeting senators, congressmen, judges, and business tycoons, had sent out or planted thirty-eight bombs. Only one man, a servant of Senator Tom Hardwick of Georgia, was injured.

The resulting "Red Menace" scare caused panic among federal officials, including Attorney General Palmer who selected the 24-year-old Hoover, with his background in alien registration, to head the department's General Intelligence Division. Hoover was ordered by Palmer to examine subversive movements and then determine how suspected saboteurs and anarchists could best be prosecuted. Hoover threw himself into this work with savage dedication, reading all he could on the theories of Karl Marx, Freidrich Engels, Vladimir Lenin, and Leon Trotsky, giving himself a crash course in world political theory. He emerged, weeks later, with the belief that he was a leading authority of the radical left. He had also acquired a lifelong fear of the "Red Menace."

Palmer, meanwhile, ordered wholesale arrests of anyone suspected of being a Marxist, Communist, anarchist, or socialist. Hundreds were rounded up and jailed pending trial. Hoover was placed in charge of preparing the legal briefs that charged Emma Goldman and Alexander Berkman with treason and subversive activities. Both were convicted and ordered deported to Russia, a signal victory for Hoover. Goldman and Berkman, along with 245 others, were put aboard the ancient steamer *Buford,* dubbed "the Soviet Ark" by the press, on Dec. 2, 1919. Hoover was photographed as he escorted several of the deportees to the gangplank. Many Washington dignitaries were on hand for this event which they celebrated like a national holiday. A U.S congressman on the dock looked up to see a grim-faced Emma Goldman at the railing of the ship and shouted: "Merry Christmas, Emma!" She sneered and then thumbed her nose at him.

William J. Flynn, chief of the Division of Investigation as the FBI was then called, was on hand to bid farewell to the anarchists. The volatile Alexander Berkman shook his fist at the Washington bigwigs lined up on the dock, yelling: "We'll come back and when we do, we'll get you bastards!" Flynn told Berkman to calm down, and then handed the anarchist a cigar and suggested that he enjoy the voyage. Eight days after the *Buford* sailed, Hoover submitted his report on the Communist conspiracy to overthrow the U.S. government to Palmer. After reading Hoover's briefs, Palmer ordered another series of raids. This time his agents rounded up members of the Communist Party of America and the Communist Labor Party.

These "Red Raids" began on Jan. 2, 1920. More than 2,500

Young lawyer Hoover, 1924.

Cadet J. Edgar Hoover.

Hoover as Gang-Buster, on the FBI firing range, 1935.

Left, star G-Man Melvin Purvis and Hoover, 1934.

Typical G-Man hype, 1936.

Hoover at height of power.

were arrested in wild break-in arrests where agents, many without warrants, smashed down doors and indiscriminately arrested aliens. Often, identities were not properly checked so that many innocent persons were illegally placed in custody. Of this number, 446 persons were later deported, but the display of raw power and illegal arrests alarmed the press and Congress alike. Palmer was severely criticized and he bombastically defended himself and his agents. Hoover, nondescript and working inside the labyrinthine bureaucracy of Washington, D.C., the man responsible for inspiring the raids, went unnoticed. He went on compiling dossiers as his GID agents assiduously scoured the countryside for Reds.

Hoover's work was nevertheless considered beneficial, so much so that he was selected to help establish procedures at the badly-run Bureau of Investigation as the FBI was then called. He was transferred to the Bureau on Aug. 22, 1921, and given a $4,000-a-year salary. He arrived bearing a new name. Up to this point, Hoover was known as John Edgar Hoover but when he learned that another Washington resident had the same name, he shortened his name to J. Edgar Hoover. The main reason for this name change (not officially changed in court) was that the other John Edgar Hoover was known as a spendthrift, a man who owed considerable money to creditors. J. Edgar Hoover paid his bills on time, all the time, and was horrified at the prospect that another man's bad credit might injure his own through a confusion of names.

J. Edgar Hoover was a very particular young man. He lived for his work and seldom left his home, except for an occasional dinner at a sedate restaurant. He had the ambition of a bureaucrat, one who inches himself forward into the hierarchy without becoming noticed too fast, without stepping into the limelight. He operated best in the shadow of other men at this time but worked toward his own ends. Hoover thought very little of the director of the Bureau at that time, William J. Burns, who had been a brilliant private detective but who ran the Bureau haphazardly and did not keep a strict watch on his agents, many of whom were rather slippery types with shady connections and larceny in their hearts. The worst offender was an agent named Gaston Bullock Means, who reported to no one in particular at the Bureau. It was understood that Means was really an operative for the shadowy Jesse Smith, a crony of the then-U.S. Attorney General Harry Daugherty.

Smith, who had an unmarked office in the Department of Justice, was a go-between for the most corrupt members of the venal administration of President Warren G. Harding and business tycoons like Harry Sinclair, who were busy misappropriating oil-rich government lands in return for huge bribes to such people as Albert B. Fall, secretary of the interior. It was Means' job to arrange secret meetings between these huckstering crooks, along with providing women and the best illegal liquor that graft could buy, for the edification of his corrupt bosses. The garrulous Means took to stopping by Hoover's office, flashing a big bankroll and telling him that he could obtain women or illegal liquor for him at any time, as he did for Washington bigwigs. Hoover found the man repugnant, particularly his lascivious comments about women.

Women in Hoover's life were either good, like his self-sacrificing mother, or bad. He had no girlfriend and never would have one. Hoover's idealized concept of women did not allow for the presence of women in his industrious life. One early day critic later stated: "No women are among his intimates, for Hoover—and he would have every G-Man be likewise—is a woman-hater. This may be due to his cardinal creed as a crime fighter, the traditional French directive: *Cherchez la femme*." ("Look for the Woman") Hoover's view of any female consorting with criminals was constant throughout his life: these were "dirty, filthy, diseased women," who deserved no better treatment than their male counterparts.

Hoover gave special consideration only to his mother. When his only sister, Lillian, later became an invalid, Hoover ignored

her and contributed nothing to her upkeep, possibly because he disapproved of her marriage to a man named Robinette. His nephew, Fred Robinette, an FBI agent, had to go into debt to keep his mother alive. Hoover, when moving to the Bureau, was heard to complain about the number of prostitutes allowed to ply their trade in Washington and when Agent Means began visiting his office and offering up women to him, Hoover exploded. He ordered Means never to bother him again and then filed a complaint against Means with his boss, William J. Burns, telling the director that Means was amoral and an opportunist.

The corrupt Harding administration came apart in 1923 when the Teapot Dome Scandal broke, and it was revealed that Harding's closest cabinet members had sold off government lands, embezzled government funds, and had otherwise looted the land. The inept Burns was pressured into resigning from the Bureau and agents like Gaston Means were given the boot. President Harding had died and Means took advantage of the president's death by writing a book claiming that Mrs. Harding had poisoned him! When Calvin Coolidge took over the office of president upon Harding's death, he fired Harry Daugherty and appointed the reputable New York lawyer Harlan Fiske Stone to replace him as U.S. attorney general. Stone then looked about for a man to replace Burns. Stone mentioned his search to Secretary of Commerce Herbert Hoover. Hoover, in turn, mentioned the quest for a new Bureau chief to one of his aides, Larry Richey, one of Hoover's few close friends at the time.

Richey suggested that young J. Edgar Hoover, his good friend, would be a good candidate for the job. Stone interviewed Hoover, who was straightforward in his answers to the attorney general. Hoover later stated that he would take over the job only if he had a free hand to weed out the deadwood at the Bureau and if his policies were enforced. He would hire only agents who were trained lawyers and accountants, he said, and had clean records. There would be neither patronage nor politically appointed positions in the Bureau, except for his own. He would establish strict regulations and codes, and any agent who did not live by them would be dismissed. Liking what he heard, Stone officially appointed the 29-year-old Hoover chief of the Bureau of Investigation on May 10, 1924.

Hoover's first seven years at the Bureau were effective organizing the agency into a cohesive unit. His emphasis at that time was the establishment of a mammoth but efficient fingerprinting division which would eventually grow to enormous proportions, with the fingerprints of a third of the adult U.S. population on file at the Bureau. The Bureau opened up a training academy, which taught its lawyers and accountants the martial arts and the best of police procedures, although no agent was then allowed to carry firearms or make an arrest unless accompanied by local law enforcement officials.

Hoover established a superb ballistics division, and a forensics division. He also expanded the field offices so that the Bureau was represented with specially trained agents in almost every major city. The Bureau was still in its infancy but was growing steadily in power and in prestige. Gone were the corrupt agents and the political cronies. In their place were well-educated young men dedicated to fighting crime. Most of the cases handled by the Bureau during this time were those of an auditing nature, but as the Bureau's responsibilities enlarged, so did its activities against such organizations as the Ku Klux Klan.

At the dawn of the 1930s, a rash of bank robberies and kidnappings erupted and Hoover was suddenly confronted with a hitherto unseen criminal, the ruthless gangster employing the submachine gun with its wasp-like firepower. He labeled these reckless criminals "public enemies." These included the infamous Barker Brothers and their notorious mother, Ma Barker, Charles Arthur "Pretty Boy" Floyd, George "Machine Gun" Kelly, Alvin "Creepy" Karpis, George "Baby Face" Nelson, and the man who was to become Hoover's nemesis, John Herbert Dillinger. The gangsters of that day, whom Hoover's FBI combated were throwbacks to the days of the western outlaws, farm boys for the most part, as had been Jesse James and the Younger Brothers in the nineteenth century. The modern bank robber, however, used the Thompson submachine gun instead of the six-gun and escaped in a souped-up auto instead of on horseback.

Much was said later of Hoover's inability to deal with the city gangsters and their crime czars such as Al Capone, Dutch Schultz, and Charles "Lucky" Luciano, but the Bureau's lack of activity in this quarter had to do with its inability to make arrests or even investigate the city-wide crime organizations due to its jurisdiction. Bank robbers and kidnappers such as the Barkers, Floyds and Dillingers, however, were a different matter. These outlaws escaped across state borders and committed other offenses that violated federal statutes, thus falling into the Bureau's area of responsibility. These were elusive criminals in that they were protected by a network of friends, relatives, and associates in the criminal organizations of big cities. These outlaws fled from town to town, from Kansas City, Mo., to St. Paul, Minn., to Chicago to Hot Spring, Ark., all "safe" havens where they were shielded by corrupt police departments and crooked politicians who were themselves in the employ of the city crime bosses.

Moreover, these daring and flamboyant bank robbers flourished during the Depression, when banks had little credibility among the homeless and the dispossessed who had lost homes and businesses to foreclosure. These outlaws became folk heroes of sorts, representing, in truth or not, a good deal of the American population that had been callously uprooted by an uncaring, seemingly cruel economic system. When farm boys like Dillinger or Floyd robbed a bank, it seemed poetic justice to some. As the fame of these robbers spread, Hoover counteracted their influence by enlisting the media on his side. He asked for and got the full cooperation of Hollywood. Film producers began to portray the Bureau and its agents as intrepid and fearless lawmen, the last line of defense against brutal kidnappers and bank-robbing killers. Hoover assigned agents to oversee film productions such as *G-Men* and *You Can't Get Away with It*. It became standard policy in Hollywood to clear any crime production dealing with federal cases after 1935 with Hoover.

Hoover concentrated on image and invented the "G-Man" out of whole cloth, spreading the story many years after the fact, that George "Machine Gun" Kelly had begged agents who cornered him in a Memphis, Tenn., flophouse in 1933 not to kill him, shouting: "Don't shoot, G-Man! Don't shoot G-Man!" This, of course, was untrue. Kelly said no such thing, but it made for good reading and it boosted the image of Hoover's hard-pressed agents to the invincible. His agents did prove to be courageous and death-defying, especially after an unarmed FBI agent, Raymond Caffrey, was shot to death in cold blood, along with other lawmen, in the Kansas City Massacre of 1933. This slaying enabled Hoover to successfully lobby to have agents armed by law, following which his men were trained in the use of all types of firearms, including submachine guns. Hoover himself became proficient in firing a submachine gun and was photographed firing a Thompson on the FBI shooting range.

Other agents died at the hands of the 1930s gangsters, including H. Carter Baum, killed by George "Baby Face" Nelson (Lester Gillis) near Manitowish Waters, Wis., in 1934. Nelson also killed Herman Hollis and one of Hoover's favorite special agents, Samuel Cowley, in a submachine gun duel in late 1934. One agent, Melvin Purvis, became so popular with the press that his limelight outshone Hoover's which caused the director considerable anxiety. Purvis was the agent in charge of the Chicago office when the pursuit of John Dillinger became the focal point of all FBI activities in that area. Hoover had developed a fixation about Dillinger and had named him Public Enemy Number One in 1934, although Dillinger had broken only one federal law at the time, that of driving a stolen car across a state line.

The publicity-hungry Purvis reaped enormous benefit from his supervision of the Dillinger manhunt and the shooting outside the Biograph Theater in Chicago on July 22, 1934, in which Purvis claimed to have killed Dillinger. In October of that year, it was

Purvis, Herman Hollis, and other FBI agents who ran down Pretty Boy Floyd near East Liverpool, Ohio, and killed him (or executed him, according to one eyewitness). These spectacular cases caused Purvis to be held in higher esteem than Hoover himself by the press and certain members of Congress, a situation Hoover found unbearable. He began to apply pressure to Purvis, hounding him to conform to all kinds of bureaucratic procedures. He also ordered Purvis to refrain from giving interviews and bridled the agent's natural inclination to seek publicity where his name would be prominently mentioned and Hoover's not at all. Purvis, resenting the muzzle, resigned his post in 1935.

Hoover himself came under severe criticism in the 1930s. As his power consolidated and his agency began to receive sweeping authority in handling federal cases, some Washington politicians became alarmed, believing Hoover was amassing too much power. One particularly vehement critic, Senator Kenneth D. McKellar, in 1934, accused Hoover of using "trigger-happy" agents to apprehend criminals. He accused Hoover's agents of recklessly shooting up Little Bohemia Lodge in an attempt to capture John Dillinger on the night of April 22, 1934, pointing out that Melvin Purvis led a contingent against the front of the lodge and shot three men, killing one, who had just emerged from the building and had gotten into a car. These three innocent men were CCC workers. McKellar went on to blame Hoover for all kinds of misuse of power and remained his most severe critic throughout the 1930s.

It was McKellar who challenged Hoover's ability to perform as a real lawman, stating that the director had never made a personal arrest. Hoover exploded at what he considered to be an affront to his courage. He informed his field offices that as soon as Alvin Karpis, the then-Public Enemy Number One, was located, he was to be notified. He, J. Edgar Hoover, would make the arrest. In 1936, Karpis was trailed to New Orleans and Hoover flew to that city. He waited on a quiet street with a dozen FBI agents and when Karpis appeared, two FBI agents collared him. Hoover then stepped from a doorway and made the formal arrest. Newsreel photographers and press photographers had been alerted and were on hand to photograph Hoover leading Karpis into FBI headquarters in New Orleans, the bank and train robber led by a belt which had been taken from the pants of one of Hoover's men because the arresting agents had forgotten to bring along handcuffs.

By then Hoover had become an astute politician. He courted the favor of powerful politicians who backed his programs and lobbied for vital increases in the FBI annual budget. He was so firmly entrenched as director of the FBI, the only person with any real identity, that all thought of replacing him vanished. He protected that identity with a vengeance. After Purvis left the Bureau, there was only one G-Man, J. Edgar Hoover. Thereafter only Hoover issued statements to the press regarding FBI cases and activities. He proved to be as theatrical as Purvis had been. On one occasion he invited reporters into his spacious Washington office for an interview and was interrupted, according to his own design, by several calls in which he grabbed the phone and issued terse orders to have unnamed desperadoes cornered and captured: "You say you have identified the fingerprints. Latent? Good. Where is he? Move in on him right now! Call me back when you have him under arrest!"

Hoover by the late 1930s projected the G-Man in the personage of J. Edgar Hoover. He was photographed and filmed on all matters related to the Bureau. Hoover had by then affected snap-brim hats, and conservative suits, stylishly tailored so that they were pinched slightly at the waist. His shoes were always polished to a high gloss. His shirts were white and his ties were never loud. This became the code dress of all agents. No other agent for the next thirty-some years, received any publicity of note. Clyde Tolson, who had joined the Bureau in 1928 and had become Hoover's friend and most intimate confidante, remained at Hoover's side until his death. Tolson went everywhere Hoover went, following respectively behind the director by a few steps.

The pair took their vacations together and exchanged gifts on Christmas. Both were bachelors and their constant companionship later led critics to claim that this was a homosexual relationship, a claim that was never proved.

If anything, Hoover was asexual, channeling his sex drive into his work, working tirelessly at the Bureau, although his enormous glass-top desk was always clean and clear of paperwork. Hoover followed a daily checklist in which he contacted one department after another, so that he appeared to be everywhere in his supervisory role. He insisted on documentation of all FBI activities and compelled all departments and field offices to file daily reports of all activities occurring, a policy that created enormous paperwork which had to be filed and stored for easy access. His staff grew and so did the Bureau so that by the early 1940s, thousands were on the FBI payroll.

So assiduously did Hoover apply his reporting system that agents worked with incredible angst to provide their daily reports. The Bureau's field offices, having nothing to really report on a given day, with cases stalled and stagnated in court procedures, relied (and still do to some extent) on local newspapers to provide them with material for their daily reports. Many agents busied themselves with rewriting crime articles appearing in the daily newspapers of their cities and sending this on to Washington as part of their ongoing investigative activities. Files in the field offices bulged with newspaper clippings that far exceeded the actual reports of investigative work done each day.

Fantastic stories were later told about Hoover and his penchant for these daily reports. The director designed a form which specified the margins on each page of each report. One energetic agent, the story goes, packed his reports with so much copy that it spilled over onto the margins which Hoover noticed. He made a notation on one of these reports which read: "Watch the borders!" So literal were his commands taken, the tale goes on, that the field office receiving this edited report back from Hoover misinterpreted the director's command and sent agents flying to the Canadian and Mexican borders to watch for spies, smugglers, and aliens. This, of course is a canard, but it emphasizes the awesome power Hoover wielded while in office.

By the advent of WWII, Hoover became the spy-hunter. His agents had considerable success in tracking down and apprehending Nazi and Japanese spies for which Hoover took full credit. Again, Hoover relied on Hollywood to build up his reputation and that of the FBI in this area. Films such as *The House on 92nd Street* did much to cement the idea that the FBI was invincible against the machinations of the most clever Nazi spy rings. Following WWII, the Cold War presented Hoover with his old bugbear, The Red Menace. The Director warned the world that the real and present danger were the Communists in his lengthy, legitimate attack on Communist subversion, *Masters of Deceit,* a best-seller (in which the reader could discover gems of information concerning Communists such as being able to tell Reds when driving on the road; they were the ones who kept making repeated left turns). Like all Hoover's books, this work had been ghosted by others in the Bureau, as had been his earlier works, such as *Persons in Hiding.* Hoover maintained close relationships with certain Bureau-approved authors over the years, writers whose books about the Bureau, chiefly Hoover, were completely praiseworthy and without criticism. In the 1930s, Hoover relied on the flamboyant Courtney Riley Cooper, a newspaperman, to write the glories of the FBI, while pumping up Hoover's image. Cooper produced heady prose in which the Bureau always triumphed, always got its man, taking the historic image of Scotland Yard and transposing it to the Bureau in such works as *Ten Thousand Public Enemies, Designs in Scarlet,* and *Here's to Crime.* In later years, Don Whitehead, with his paean of Bureau praise, *The FBI Story,* became Hoover's "appointed" author.

Hoover had, from the administration of Franklin D. Roosevelt, who relied heavily on the director to run his own shop, reported only to the president. Several U.S. attorney generals simply allowed him compete autonomy, not wishing to experience confrontations with the bullheaded Hoover. Not until the election of John F. Kennedy as president was Hoover's authority challenged, nor was he required until that time to answer to the office of the attorney general. All that changed when President Kennedy appointed his brother Robert Kennedy attorney general in 1961. Robert Kennedy, through his brother's urging, began to make life uncomfortable, then unbearable for Hoover.

Kennedy insisted that Hoover address civil rights violations in the Deep South and that he also create an aggressive campaign against organized crime. The director bristled at receiving directives, especially when ordered to increase the number of blacks on the staff of the FBI. Hoover insisted that there were blacks in the Bureau but these proved to be his chauffeur, his office servant, and a few clerks. Hoover grudgingly obeyed, ordering his field offices to quickly add black agents to their staffs. This was done so rapidly that absurd situations developed. In the Chicago office, a black janitor was transformed overnight into an FBI agent, although he functioned as little more than a chauffeur. In the South, the Bureau through conscientious agents, made some headway in protecting blacks attempting to break the racial barriers. But Hoover's antipathy toward blacks was well-known and no active widespread FBI campaign to aid oppressed blacks was inaugurated.

Hoover's hatred for civil rights activist Martin Luther King was also well-known. He believed King to be a profligate and a Communist stooge. To discredit King, Hoover had the phones of the civil rights leader bugged and he had King followed, keeping dossiers on his extra-marital sexual relations, or so it was later reported. He also maintained files on his boss, Robert Kennedy and on President Kennedy himself, gathering information on Kennedy's own affairs with actress Marilyn Monroe, mob woman Judith Exner, and Washington socialite Mrs. Mary Myers. By this time, much of Hoover's power rested in the files he had his agents put together on Washington politicians. No important politician in Washington during the 1960s was unaware of such surveillance and all feared it. This was the way in which Hoover maintained his authority and position, and exercised his power and influence, a subtle form of blackmail. If anyone dared to oppose him, he risked Hoover's wrath in the form of scandalous material that might be leaked to the press.

Hoover's dislike for the Kennedys turned quickly into hatred and he was in daily combat with Robert Kennedy whom he felt was out to humiliate him. Kennedy, a rather capricious person, learned that Hoover took long naps in his office during the afternoon and he often crept into Hoover's inner sanctum, without announcing himself to Hoover's secretary, and sit before Hoover as the director lay sprawled on a leather couch snoring and oblivious to his superior's presence.

Kennedy kept pressuring Hoover to mount an attack against organized crime in the U.S., but the director resisted this move for quite some time, arguing that there was no such thing as a crime cartel or crime syndicate in America. This, of course, was patently absurd in that Hoover himself had provided the McClellan Committee and the Kefauver Committee before it with comprehensive dossiers on leading crime syndicate bosses. Hoover himself, in 1939, through his good friend, columnist Walter Winchell, had personally taken custody of Louis "Lepke" Buchalter in New York. Buchalter was then a fugitive who arranged to turn himself into Hoover to face a federal charge of racketeering, and thus avoid New York prosecution for murder.

Hoover knew full well that Buchalter was one of the members of the board of directors of the national crime syndicate which had been established as early as 1929 when Al Capone had called all the top crime bosses together at the first crime cartel enclave in Atlantic City. Of course, there was much criticism to be avoided by Hoover through his denial of the existence of organized crime. If it did exist, then why, over the past three decades, had not the Bureau identified its leaders and rooted it out for prosecution and extermination? To do so would admit failure and Hoover and his Bureau never failed. It remained for Robert Kennedy to take the

The director aims a camera at his aide, Clyde Tolson, associate director of the FBI, in a moment of levity during the Hollywood production of *You Can't Get Away With It,* an FBI-endorsed propaganda film.

Hoover (center, hands up in mock surrender) at play, a New Year's Eve party at the Stork Club in New York City, his favorite haunt, where a booth was kept reserved for him at all times by pal Sherman Billingsley.

FBI director J. Edgar Hoover being decorated by President Dwight D. Eisenhower; Hoover was left to pursue his own investigative ambitions during the Eisenhower administration, a period when he consolidated his power.

Hoover flanked by President John F. Kennedy and U.S. Attorney General Robert Kennedy, two men the director disliked, if not hated, for telling him how to do his job and urging him to attack organized crime, which Hoover said did not exist.

The director and his good friend of twenty years, President Lyndon Johnson, who pressured Hoover to enforce civil rights legislation; Johnson thrived on bed-time reading made up of Hoover's FBI reports about the indiscretions of Washington politicians.

Hoover with President Richard Nixon, two men much alike, furtive, with a preference for shadows and secrecy; Hoover balked at Nixon's insistence that the Bureau use illegal surveillance techniques against Nixon's political enemies.

initiative here, bringing dozens of crime syndicate cases to prosecution with Hoover reluctantly providing criminal histories for such cases.

After President Kennedy was assassinated in Dallas on Nov. 22, 1963, Hoover came under severe criticism in that the Bureau had not taken the proper precautions to ferret out would-be assassins like Lee Harvey Oswald. The protection of the president in Dallas, of course, as it was with all presidents, fell to the Secret Service, but it was the more public Bureau that took the full brunt of criticism for this assassination. Hoover, it was recorded, took sadistic delight in informing Robert Kennedy and the Kennedy family that the president had been shot and killed in Dallas, delivering this message in a terse, unemotional, and wholly unsympathetic phone call.

With the passing of the Kennedys and the assumption of power by the vice president, Lyndon B. Johnson, Hoover's position was strengthened. President Johnson, preoccupied with the Viet Nam War, allowed Hoover to go his own way, despite Johnson's public displays of support for civil rights workers. Johnson was a power broker himself and used Hoover as a political weapon against his critics. He also delighted in reading dossiers Hoover sent to him each day, reports on the sexually activities of Washington politicians. Johnson took these scandal-dripping reports to bed with him each night and fell asleep reading them. When Hoover failed to make a delivery of these reports one day, Johnson called him and complained, saying that he could not go to sleep without reading his reports.

Hoover's relationship with President Nixon was even closer than the one he had enjoyed with Johnson. Nixon believed Hoover to be a paragon of crime fighters, one beyond reproach and allowed the director to stay in office long past the mandatory retirement age. When Nixon became president, he jokingly reminded Hoover that, in 1937, when he graduated from Duke University, he had applied for a job with the FBI as an agent but had been turned down by Hoover himself. Hoover did not recall the rejection, but Hoover's arbitrary hiring and firing of agents for decades was a matter of personal whim and bias. He once fired an agent for wearing a tie he considered too loud, another for marrying a foreign woman, another, a war hero who had had massive plastic surgery performed on his face, because he was too ugly.

The director, at the end of his life, had altered little in his routine and had increased only his prejudices. He had few pleasures beyond the immense power he wielded. He seldom went anywhere between his modest Washington home and the Bureau offices. When in New York, he went to the Stork Club, where a table was always held in reserve for him and Clyde Tolson. Here he would sip a few mild drinks (Jack Daniels) with his few friends, club owner Sherman Billingsley, and columnist Walter Winchell, who kept Hoover's name prominent in the news and who had been made an "honorary" FBI agent by Hoover. Hoover continued to collect antiques to the end of his days, read sanitary mystery stories and, religiously, *The Reader's Digest*. Until he grew infirm and too old to move easily about, Hoover regularly attended boxing matches, sitting ringside, and he attended the race track, always making two-dollar bets.

During work days, Hoover and Tolson always lunched together, with Hoover ordering the same thing with monotonous regularity: grapefruit and cottage cheese. In his office and home bathrooms, Hoover, extremely germ-conscious in his old age, had installed ultra-violet lights to assure sanitation. If the lights went out, Hoover would not use the facilities until they were replaced. Hoover's use of lights, or more specifically a night-light, became the source of heated controversy in his last years, so much so that Thomas Bishop, an assistant FBI director, publicly announced: "The rumors that Hoover sleeps with a night-light are just not true!" This ill-advised public announcement resulted in a flood of T-shirts emblazoned with the words: "J. Edgar Hoover sleeps with a night-light!"

The one achievement in his twilight years that edified J. Edgar

Hoover most was his appointment as a 33rd Degree Mason in a local Washington Lodge. He had connived, cajoled, and lobbied for this Masonic position for thirty years and he delighted in telling one and all that he had now reached the pinnacle of this fraternal order. He had also reached the zenith of bureaucratic power in the federal government. In 1972, at the age of seventy-seven, Hoover could boast of having survived more than fifty years of government service. As he grew increasingly infirm, Hoover still maintained a full schedule, leaving his home at 8:30 a.m., working a full day, and then returning home. He often dined with Clyde Tolson in Tolson's home before returning to his own residence and retiring. This was his routine on the night of May 1, 1972.

The next morning, his housekeeper arrived and prepared his breakfast, one which never varied: toast, soft-boiled eggs, and coffee. Hoover did not appear for breakfast, nor was he downstairs when his chauffeur arrived to drive him to Bureau headquarters. The housekeeper, Annie Fields, went to the director's bedroom, knocked, and then entered to find Hoover sprawled on the floor, still in his pajamas. He was dead of a heart attack. L. Patrick Gray was appointed acting director of the FBI after it was decided that Clyde Tolson was too ill to assume the post. President Nixon decreed a state funeral which was handled by the army and offered up to the public like a military operation. The body lay in state in the Rotunda on May 4, 1972, and was visited by considerable crowds, mostly Washington politicians who were still in awe of the small, shriveled body resting, finally, in its coffin. See: **Atlantic City Conference; Barker Brothers; Buchalter, Louis; Burns, William John; Capone, Alphonse; Dillinger, John Herbert; Federal Bureau of Investigation; Floyd, Charles Arthur; Kansas City Massacre; Karpis, Alvin; Kelly, George; Kennedy, John F.; Kennedy, Robert; Means, Gaston Bullock; Nelson, George; Palmer, A. Mitchell; Purvis, Melvin; Stone, Harlan Fiske; Teapot Dome Scandal.**

REF.: Alexander, *The Pizza Connection*; Ambrose, *Eisenhower, The President*; Ayer, *Yankee G-Man*; Bell, *The Radical Right*; Bergman, *We're in the Money*; Biddle, *In Brief Authority*; Blumenthal, *Last Days of the Sicilians*; Bonanno, *A Man of Honor*; Bontecou, *The Federal Loyalty Security Program*; Buitrago and Immerman, *Are You Now or Have You Ever Been in the FBI Files: How to Secure and Interpret Your FBI Files*; Burns, *Roosevelt: The Lion and the Fox*; Caesar, *Incredible Detective*; Campbell, *The Luciano Project*; Caute, *The Great Fear*; CBA; Coben, *A. Mitchell Palmer*; Cochran, *FBI Man, A Personal History*; Cohen, *Mickey Cohen: In My Own Words*; Collins, *The FBI in Peace and War*; Cook, *The FBI Nobody Knows*; Cooney, *The American Pope*; Cooper, *Designs in Scarlet*; ____, *Here's to Crime*; ____, *Ten Thousand Public Enemies*; Cowan, *State Secrets*; Crawford, *Thunder on the Right*; Cressey, *Theft of the Nation*; Cummings and McFarland, *Federal Justice*; Davis, *Mafia Kingfish*; Dean, *Blind Ambition*; Demaris, *Captive City*; ____, *The Director*; ____, *The Last Mafioso*; Donner, *The Age of Surveillance*; Donovan, *Conflict and Crisis*; ____, *Tumultuous Years*; Downes, *The Scarlet Thread*; Draper, *The Roots of American Communism*; Dubofsky and Theoharis, *Imperial Democracy*; Dumenil, *Freemasonry and American Culture*; Edelman, *The Symbolic Uses of Politics*; Edge, *Run the Cat Roads*; Ehrlichman, *Witness to Power*; Eisenberg and Landau, *Meyer Lansky*; Eisenhower, *Mandate for Change*; ____, *The White House Years*; Elliff, *Crime, Dissent and the Attorney General*; ____, *The Reform of FBI Intelligence Operations*; Falk, *Love, Anarchy and Emma Goldman*; Felt, *The FBI Pyramid*; Floherty, *Inside the F.B.I.*; Freedman, *Roosevelt and Frankfurter*; Fried, *The Rise and Fall of the Jewish Gangster in America*; Gage, *Mafia, U.S.A.*; Gitlow, *The Whole of Their Lives*; Garrow, *The FBI and Martin Luther King, Jr.*; Godwin, *Murder U.S.A.*; Goldman, *Living My Life*; Goldstein, *Political Repression in Modern America*; Goodman, *The Committee*; Gosch and Hammer, *The Last Testament of Lucky Luciano*; Goulart, *Line Up, Tough Guys*; Green, *Washington*; Guthman, *We Band of Brothers*; Halperin, *The Lawless State*; Harris, *Justice*; Hechler, *Working with Truman*; Hibbert, *The Roots of Evil*; Higham, *Strangers in the Land*; Hook, *Heresy, Yes—Conspiracy, No*; Hoover, *J. Edgar Hoover on Communism*; ____, *J. Edgar Hoover Speaks*; ____, *Masters of Deceit*; ____, *Persons in Hiding*; _____, *A Study of Communism*; Howe and Coser, *The*

American Communist Party; Huie, *Three Lives for Mississippi;* Hurt, *Reasonable Doubt;* Hyde, *The Atom Bomb Spies;* Ickes, *The Secret Diaries;* Irons, *Justice at War;* Jaffe, *Crusade Against Radicalism;* Jensen, *The Price of Vigilance;* ____, *Military Surveillance of Civilians in America;* Johnson, *The Vantage Point;* Katz, *Uncle Frank;* Kayser, *Bricks Without Straw;* Kearns, *Lyndon Johnson and the American Dream;* Kelly, *The American Constitution;* Kempton, *Part of Our Time;* Kimball, *The File;* Kleindienst, *Justice;* Kobler, *Capone;* Kutler, *The American Institution;* Lait and Mortimer, *Chicago: Confidential;* Lasch, *The Agony of the American Left;* Latham, *The Communist Controversy in Washington;* Lindemann, *The Red Years;* Lisio, *The President and Protest;* Lowenthal, *The Federal Bureau of Investigation;* McClellan, *Crime Without Punishment;* MacDonald, *Television and the Red Menace;* Maas, *The Valachi Papers;* Martin, *Hollywood's Movie Commandments;* Martin, *Revolt in the Mafia;* Mason, *Harlan Fiske Stone;* Masterman, *The Double Cross System;* Meel, *The Ohio Gang;* Messick, *Lansky;* ____, *Secret File;* ____ and Goldblatt, *The Mobs and the Mafia;* Mitchell, *1919: Red Mirage;* Morgan, *FDR;* Morgan, *Prince of Crime;* Murray, *Red Scare;* Nash, *Bloodletters and Badmen;* ____, *Citizen Hoover: A Critical Study of the Life and Times of J. Edgar Hoover and His FBI;* ____, *A Dillinger Dossier;* ____, *Hustlers and Con Men;* ____, *Zanies;* Navasky, *Kennedy Justice;* ____, *Law Enforcement;* ____, *Naming Names;* Nelson and Ostrow, *The FBI and the Berrigans;* Nixon, *The Memoirs of Richard Nixon;* O'Neill, *Coming Apart;* O'Reilly, *Hoover and the Un-Americans;* Ollestad, *Inside the FBI;* Oshinsky, *A Conspiracy So Immense;* Ottenberg, *The Federal Investigators;* Overstreet, *The FBI in Our Open Society;* Parmet, *Eisenhower and the American Crusades;* ____, *Jack: The Struggles of John F. Kennedy;* ____, *JFK: The Presidency of John F. Kennedy;* Perkis, *Cointelpro: The FBI's Secret War on Political Freedom;* Perrett, *Days of Sadness, Years of Triumph;* ____, *Dream of Greatness;* ____, *America in the Twenties;* Peterson, *The Mob;* Philbrick, *I Led Three Lives;* Pileggi, *Wiseguy;* Powers, *The Man Who Kept the Secrets;* ____, *Secrecy and Power;* Preston, *Aliens and Dissenters;* Purvis, *American Agent;* Radosh and Milton, *The Rosenberg File;* Rather and Gates, *The Palace Guard;* Reppetto, *The Blue Parade;* Russell, *The Shadow of Blooming Grove;* Sann, *Kill the Dutchman;* Schlesinger, *The Imperial Presidency;* ____, *Robert Kennedy and His Times;* ____, *A Thousand Days;* ____, *The Vital Center;* Schott, *No Left Turns;* Scott, *The Concise Encyclopedia of Crime and Criminals;* Seldes, *Witch Hunt;* Sherwood, *Roosevelt and Hopkins;* Shannon, *Desperados;* Shils, *The Torment of Secrecy;* Smith, *The Shadow Warriors;* Smith, *Syndicate City;* Smith, *An Uncommon Man;* Spiering, *The Man Who Got Capone;* Spolansky, *The Communist Trail in America;* Steinberg, *The Great "Red" Menace;* Stone, *The Haunted Fifties;* ____, *The Truman Era;* Stripling, *The Red Plot Against America;* Sullivan, *The Bureau: My Thirty Years In Hoover's FBI;* Summers, *Goddess: The Secret Lives of Marilyn Monroe;* Swisher, *Homer Cummings, Selected Papers;* Szulc, *The Illusion of Peace;* Theoharis, *The Truman Presidency;* ____, *Beyond the Hiss Case;* Toledano, *J. Edgar Hoover: The Man And His Time;* Trohan, *Political Animals;* Tully, *The FBI's Most Famous Cases;* Truman, *Memoirs;* Tully, *Inside the FBI;* Turner, *Hoover's FBI: The Men and the Myth;* Unger, *FBI;* Villano: *Brick Agent: Inside the Mafia for the FBI;* Watters and Gillers, *Investigating the FBI;* Weinstein, *Perjury;* Wellman, *A Dynasty of Western Outlaws;* Weyl, *The Battle Against Disloyalty;* White, *Breach of Faith;* Whitehead, *The FBI Story;* ____, *Attack on Terror;* Whitney, *Reds in America;* Wicker, *Investigating the FBI;* Wilson, *The Investigators: Managing FBI and Narcotics Agents;* Wolfe, *The Seamy Side of Democracy;* Woodward, *The Strange Case of Jim Crowe;* Wright, *Whose FBI?;* Zuckerman, *Vengeance Is Mine;* (FILM), *Walk East on Beacon*, 1952; *The Private Files of J. Edgar Hoover*, 1978.

Hoover, Tuck, d.1894, U.S., west. gunman. Tuck Hoover, was a rancher near Alleyton, in South Texas. In 1878, while with Dallas Stoudenmire and others, Hoover encountered another group of men led by two brothers named Sparks. The two groups had a violent argument over the ownership of a herd of cattle, and in the ensuing gun battle the Hoover faction killed Benton Duke and his son and wounded one of the Sparks brothers. Around 1894, Hoover began arguing with a man named Burtshell, the owner of an Alleyton saloon. During the following gun battle, Hoover shot Burtshell to death. Hoover was arrested, but was released on bond only to lose his final gunfight in Alleyton to a young rowdy named Jim Coleman.

REF.: *CBA;* Metz, *Dallas Stoudenmire, El Paso Marshal;* O'Neal, *Encyclopedia of Western Gunfighters;* Sonnichsen, *I'll Die Before I'll Run.*

Hope, Edgar, 1960- , U.S., mur. Chicago police officers Robert Mantia and James E. Doyle were patrolling on the city's South Side on the evening of Feb. 5, 1982. Mantia, a fourteen-year veteran of the force, was training the rookie Doyle when 22-year-old Charles Harris flagged them down. Harris told the officers that he had seen a man who had recently robbed him riding the 79th Street Chicago Transit Authority (CTA) bus. The officers stopped and boarded the bus.

As Officer Doyle was removing the suspect from the bus, the man reached under his coat, pulled out two handguns, and shot Doyle to death. He fled the vehicle firing wildly and injured two passengers, 17-year-old Cynthia Houston and 23-year-old Kevin Page, before Officer Mantia brought him down with one of seven bullets he fired into the dark.

At police headquarters, the gunman was identified as 22-year-old Edgar Hope, an ex-convict paroled in June 1981 after serving a two-and-a-half-year sentence for armed robbery. Police found two revolvers in his possession, one of which was registered to off-duty sheriff's policeman Lloyd Wickliffe, who had been murdered during an attempted burglary at a South Side McDonald's on January 11. Wickliffe had been working at the fast food chain as a security guard when two men entered the restaurant and opened fire, killing him and wounding his partner, Alvin Thompson.

Hope was charged with the murder of Officer Doyle and the attempted murder of his partner Mantia, and in a police lineup, Thompson identified him as one of the two men involved in the January shooting. Shortly after Hope's arrest, police apprehended his partner in the restaurant shooting, Alton L. Logan, and both were charged with murder.

Hope's trial for the murder of Doyle began on Oct. 20, 1982. Hope was found Guilty, and presiding Judge James M. Bailey sentenced him to be executed in the electric chair.

Already sentenced to death for the CTA murder, Hope and Logan were found Guilty on Feb. 16, 1983, of the shooting death of Lloyd Wickliffe, and for the attempted murder of his partner. REF.: *CBA.*

Hope, James (Jimmy), 1836-1905, U.S., rob. On June 27, 1881, following a bank robbing career during which he and fellow gang members stole more than $3.8 million from U.S. banks, three-time prison escapee, James Hope, was behind bars in San Francisco. Hope and an accomplice, Dave Cummings, were arrested entering San Francisco's Sather Bank after police received a tip from the bank's janitor that he believed a burglary was in progress.

Hope had established himself as a preeminent safecracker after he and several accomplices pulled off two jobs in New York City. The two

Bank burglar Jimmy Hope.

jobs set records for the largest hauls in the city up to that time. In the fall of 1868, Hope, Ned Lyons, and Mark Shinburn opened a carpet store in the basement of the Ocean National Bank building. The store served as a front so they could drill their way into the upstairs bank, and on June 27, 1869, steal $1.2 million in securities and cash.

Hope was jailed on Nov. 28, 1870, for his part in a robbery of Smith's Bank in Perry, N.Y., after a year-long spree of robbing small institutions. He and three other prisoners escaped from Auburn prison less than three years later, and on Nov. 7, 1873, they robbed the First National Bank in Wilmington, Del. All four burglars were returned to jail less than one month later after receiving forty lashes with a whip and sentences of ten years each. Within a year, they had escaped again.

In 1878, Hope was back at work in New York City. Hope, once again with Shinburn and Lyons, stole nearly $2.8 million from the Manhattan Savings Bank. Depositors, shocked by the robbery, rushed to withdraw their money from what they perceived as unsafe banking institutions throughout New York City. The rush sparked by the burglary nearly caused the financial collapse of the city's banking industry. Following a nationwide manhunt, authorities captured Hope and nine others believed to be involved in the burglary. Several of the suspects, including Manhattan Bank security guard Patrick Shevlin and police officer John Nugent, were granted immunity for their testimony against Hope, who was once more sentenced to ten years at Auburn; he soon escaped a third time.

Hope was sentenced to seven years in a California prison on Oct. 15, 1881, after police detectives hiding inside the Sather Bank apprehended him as he crawled through a hole in the bank's ceiling above the vault. A janitor had noticed the hole the previous evening and notified police, who waited inside for the burglars after the bank closed.

After serving his full term, Hope was transferred to New York's Auburn prison where he was to finish his unexpired terms.

REF.: Asbury, *The Gangs of New York;* Byrnes, *Professional Criminals of America; CBA;* Duke, *Celebrated Criminal Cases of America;* Farley, *Criminals of America;* Robinson, *Science Catches the Criminal.*

Hopkins, Matthew, d. 1647, Brit., witchcraft. Matthew Hopkins was a not very successful lawyer who moved to the village of Manningtree in Essex, England, when he was unable to make a living in Ipswich. In March 1644, he decided there were witches in the area, meeting near his house, and denounced an elderly woman named Elizabeth Clarke. After several days of sleep deprivation, Clarke confessed to suckling familiars, including a spaniel, a rabbit, a greyhound, and a polecat.

Within a short time, thirty-two women were arrested. Four of them died in jail and twenty-eight were tried in a special court at Chelmsford. Hopkins testified in court that he had seen Clarke's familiar, and his eager assistants corroborated his claims. Nineteen women were hanged. With four assistants to help him ferret out witches, Hopkins traveled through Essex, paid for his efforts as the first real witch finder, instigating countless trials. Hopkins is believed to have been responsible for the deaths of several hundred people, mostly women, in one year. With John Stearne as his "witch pricker," and using a wide variety of tortures, Hopkins sent more witches to the gallows in fourteen months than all other previous English witch hunters combined.

One of Hopkins' early methods was "swimming," which consisted of tying up a witch and throwing her, or occasionally him, into water to see if they drowned. If they did not, they were witches and would be condemned. If they did, they were saved because they were innocent, but still dead. This clever technique was stopped in August 1645. But other less blatant tortures, like starvation, forcing the accused to sit for prolonged periods cross-legged on a stool, sleep deprivation, and forced continuous walking until the feet blistered or bled, were effective in extracting hundreds of confessions, most of them from elderly women. Hopkins found wealth and fame by going through Suffolk and Norfolk finding witches everywhere. In April 1646, clergyman John Gaule, attacked Hopkins from his pulpit. When Hopkins threatened him, Gaule published his *Select Cases of Conscience,* in which he exposed Hopkins' torture techniques. Despite an effort to respond in the pamphlet *Discovery of Witches,* in which Hopkins tried to couch his excesses in a cloak of legality and

sanctity, Hopkins' career quickly ended as public opinion turned against him.

REF.: *CBA;* Hunt, *A Dictionary of Rogues;* Robbins, *Encyclopedia of Witchcraft;* Whitelaw, *Corpus Delicti;* Wilson, *Witches.*

Hopkins, Richard Joseph, 1873-1943, U.S., jur. Served as judge of the supreme court in Kansas from 1923-30. He was nominated to the district court of Kansas by President Herbert Hoover in 1929. REF.: *CBA.*

Hopkins, William Seeley, d.1889, U.S., mur. William Hopkins, a resident of Philipsburg, Pa., was a henpecked husband and he was regularly demeaned and humiliated by his mother-in-law, in whose house he lived. Hopkins objected to the men his wife brought home and the fact that he was treated like a servant in his mother-in-law's house, ordered to wait on these gentlemen callers. He was ordered to keep his mouth shut and do as he was told. Hopkins reacted to this unbearable treatment by shooting both his wife and mother-in-law to death on Sept. 21, 1889. He then turned the weapon on himself, but only succeeded in slightly wounding himself. He was convicted of murder and hanged at Bellefont, Pa., on Feb. 20, 1890.

REF.: *CBA; History of the Crime and a True Confession of William Seeley Hopkins.*

Hopkinson, Joseph, 1770-1842, U.S., jur. Practiced law in Philadelphia, Pa., served in the U.S. House of Representatives, and from 1828-42 was a judge on the U.S. district court for the eastern district of Pennsylvania. REF.: *CBA.*

Hopson, Howard Colwell, 1882-1949, U.S., fraud. In 1941, Howard Colwell Hopson, utilities magnate extraordinaire, was convicted of defrauding $20 million in assets from the Associated Gas and Electric System, a holding company of several other utilities. After an eight-week trial, Hopson was found Guilty of seventeen counts of mail fraud and sentenced to seventeen five-year terms to run concurrently. Tried with Hopson as accomplices were two of his lawyers, Charles M. Travis and Garrett A. Brownback. Both were acquitted of all charges.

Prosecuting attorney Hugh A. Fulton claimed that Hopson had committed the largest fraud of his time, and revealed three of his schemes to line his own pockets with assets from Associated Gas. Fulton claimed that Hopson, planning a future swindle, bought out General Gas and Electric with an overly large sum of money from his own company. He alleged that Hopson stole money from the employees of the Utility Employees Securities Company which, since 1931, was required to invest ten percent of its wages in the company. Fulton explained that Hopson earned $95,000 from illegal stock maneuvering on the sale of the National Public Utilities Corporation. Hopson died on Dec. 22, 1949, in the Brooklea Sanitarium after a five-year bout with an illness. REF.: *CBA.*

Hopwood, Edward, 1867-1912, Brit., mur. Edward Hopwood fell in love when he saw actress Florence Dudley perform in a play at London's Tivoli Theater. His fatal love led to murder less than four months later.

Dudley, whose real name was Florence Alice Bernadette Silles, was murdered in a taxi on Sept. 28, 1912. In the back of the car, Hopwood shot her to death and then turned the gun on himself. Distraught that Dudley had broken off their relationship after discovering that he was married and was wanted by police for passing bad checks, Hopwood developed this scheme to murder the woman and kill himself. Although she was dead, his suicide attempt had failed. He succeeded in injuring himself, but was nursed back to health to stand trial at the Old Bailey.

The three-day trial ended after the jury deliberated only twelve minutes and returned with a conviction for Hopwood, who had maintained that he intended only to kill himself and not Dudley. Justice Avory, in what was believed to be his first murder trial, sentenced Hopwood to death. He was hanged in December 1912.

REF.: *CBA;* Felstead, *Sir Richard Muir;* Lang, *Mr. Justice Avory;* Nicholls, *Crime Within the Square Mile;* Shew, *A Companion to Murder.*

Hora, Nicolae (Horea, Horia), 1730-85, Rom., rebel. Led peasant revolt in 1784. He was caught, given a short, predictable trial, and executed. REF.: *CBA.*

Hormizd III, d.459, Persia, king, assass. Served as king of Persia from 457-459 until he was overthrown and killed by his brother, Firuz. REF.: *CBA.*

Hormizd IV, d.590, Persia, king, assass. King of Persia from 578-590, he continued his father Khosrow I's war against the Turks and the Byzantine Empire. He was ousted and slain in a rebellion led by General Bahram Chubin. REF.: *CBA.*

Horn, Adam (AKA: **Andrew Hellman**), d.1843, U.S., mur. Adam Horn, who had a long criminal history, tired of his wife Malinda and strangled her while she slept. He next chopped up her body and buried the remains in the orchard of their Baltimore, Md., home. Horn carelessly left some of the body parts in plain sight and when these were discovered he was arrested. He confessed to not only murdering his wife but another person. He was hanged after a quick trial.

REF.: *CBA; The Confession of Adam Horn; The Life of Andrew Hellman, Alias Adam Horn.*

Horn, Philip de Montmorency (**Hoorn, Hornes, Count of Horn**), 1518-68, Fr., treas. Served as admiral for fleet of ships from Flanders. He, Edgmont, and William, Prince of Orange disapproved of some of Spain's policies, including the Inquisition. After the Duke of Alva gained control, he and Edgmont were arrested in 1567. He was beheaded for treason at Brussels. REF.: *CBA.*

Horn, Tom (AKA: **James Hicks**), 1860-1903, U.S., west. lawman-outl.-mur. Tom Horn was a legendary western scout, Pinkerton detective, and range detective. When his luck ran out, he hired his gun to the highest bidder for murder and for this, he went to the gallows. Born in Memphis, Mo., on Nov. 21, 1860, Horn was raised on a farm. As a youth he liked the outdoors, but hated school and was often truant. His father, a strict disciplinarian, took the boy aside when he was fourteen and gave him such a severe whipping that Horn ran away from home, going west. He worked on the railroad, drove wagons for a freight company, and later became a stagecoach driver.

Horn was a scout for the army at age sixteen and was involved in many campaigns for more than a decade. In

Tom Horn at the time he worked as a cavalry scout.

1885, Horn replaced the celebrated Al Sieber as chief of scouts in the Southwest and he was involved in the historic Geronimo campaign in 1886. It was the intrepid Horn who, as chief of scouts, tracked Geronimo and his band to his hideout in the Sierra Gordo outside of Sonora, Mex. He rode into the Indian camp alone and negotiated Geronimo's surrender. Geronimo, with Horn guiding him and his tribe, crossed the border, officially surrendering, and ending the last great Indian war in America.

After quitting his post as chief of scouts, Horn wandered through the gold fields and then became a ranch hand. He proved himself to be a great cowboy, entering the rodeo at Globe, Ariz., in 1888 and winning the world's championship in steer roping. Horn joined the Pinkerton Detective Agency in 1890 and used his gun with lethal effectiveness. He worked out of the agency's Denver offices, chasing bank robbers and train thieves throughout Colorado and Wyoming. He was fearless (some said mad) and would face any outlaw or gunman. On one occasion, Horn rode into the outlaw hideout known as Hole-in-the-Wall and single-handedly captured the notorious Peg-Leg Watson (alias McCoy) who had recently robbed a mail train with others. Horn tracked Watson to a high mountain cabin and called out to him, telling the outlaw that he was coming for him.

Watson stepped from the cabin with two six-guns in his hands. He watched, open-mouthed, as Horn walked resolutely toward him across an open field, his Winchester carried limply at his side. Watson never fired a shot and Horn took him to jail without a struggle, telling admiring deputies that Watson "didn't give me too much trouble." This feat was heralded across the West and Horn became a living legend. Yet working for the Pinkertons bothered Horn. He had reportedly killed seventeen men as an agent. Hunting down men very much like himself upset the lawman, however, and he quit, saying: "I have no stomach for it anymore." Yet Horn had enough stomach to hire out as a gunman in 1892 to the Wyoming Cattle Growers' Association.

It was Horn's job to recruit gunmen for the association and he put together a formidable army which later attacked and slaughtered homesteaders in the bloody Johnson County War, although there is no indication that Horn participated in this one-sided battle. In 1894, Horn was working as a horse breaker for the Swan Land and Cattle Company. His real duties were to track down and kill rustlers and hector settlers homesteading on the range. He demanded and got $600 for each rustler he shot and killed. Horn proved to be a methodical manhunter and ruthless killer.

He would spend several days tracking a rustler, learning the man's habits and observing him as the rustler

Horn at the time he turned killer in the 1890s.

made camp each night. Finally, using a high-powered, long-distance Buffalo gun, Horn would lay a careful ambush and kill his man with a single, well-aimed bullet. Horn was no longer the stand-up gunman who faced his adversaries in a fair fight. He killed from hiding and he killed often. Rustlers, more than a dozen, were found shot to death on the range. Beneath each man's head was a large rock. This was Horn's trademark. "Killing men is my business," he announced one night in a saloon when questioned about his activities. Tom Horn's legend changed to that of a fearsome murderer, one who killed with the law behind him and one who apparently enjoyed taking lives. The residents of Cheyenne came to know and fear him as a blood-stained slayer.

When the Spanish-American War broke out in 1898, Horn left the West and joined the cavalry. He served with distinction in Cuba but saw little action, being in charge of Teddy Roosevelt's pack trains. Following the war, Horn returned to Wyoming and went to work for wealthy cattle baron, John Coble. He was once again a hunter of rustlers and his tactics had changed little since he began this bloody business a decade earlier. Typical of Horn's ambush techniques was the manner in which he killed rustler Matt Rash. He tracked Rash to his cabin near Cold Springs Mountain in Routt County, Colo., pretending to be a prospector named James Hicks. Rash invited him to dinner and Horn joined him on the evening of July 8, 1900. Following the meal, Horn excused himself and went outside. He hid behind a tree, and as his host stepped outside, Horn pumped three bullets into him. Horn then rode to Denver to set up an alibi. Rash lived long enough to try to write the name of his killer with his own blood, but wrote the alias Horn had given him and Horn was therefore not immediately identified.

A black cowboy, Isom Dart, who, with a gang of five other black cowboys, had been rustling cows, was found at his Routt County hideout by Horn on Oct. 3, 1900. Horn hid behind a large rock and, after Dart and his companions had their breakfast and left their cabin to inspect the cattle pens that held their rustled cattle, Horn fired two shots from a .30-.30 rifle. Both bullets struck Dart's head, shattering his skull and killing him instantly. His five companions raced back to the cabin and cowered there while Horn mounted his horse and rode away.

Horn's last killing was his undoing. He had perfected the art of long-distance murder, using powerful weapons that could bring down a target at a distance of hundreds of yards. On the morning of July 18, 1901, on the Powder River Road near Cheyenne, Wyo., Horn lay in wait for rancher Kels P. Nickell, who had been marked for death by competing ranchers. He had only seen Nickell once from a distance, so Horn did not recognize Willie Nickell, the rancher's tall 14-year-old son, who appeared that morning, driving his father's wagon out of the ranch yard. Willie wore his father's coat and hat and when he got down from the wagon to open a gate, Horn fired a shot that struck the boy. Willie Nickell staggered to his feet and tried to get back to the wagon but Horn fired another shot, striking him in the back of the head and killing him.

Though this killing was immediately attributed to Horn because of its method, no real proof could link him to the murder. Joc Lefors, one of the great lawmen of the West, resolved to uncover the truth and bring Horn to justice. He rode to Denver and there got Horn drunk in a small saloon. While using a crude listening device, Lefors' deputies hid in a back room while Horn talked about the Nickell killing, describing it in such detail that his words amounted to a confession. Lefors arrested Horn for the killing and returned him to Cheyenne where he was later tried and condemned to death. The wealthy cattleman, Coble, along with Glendolene Kimmel, a schoolteacher whose father was also a cattle baron and who was Horn's sweetheart, attempted to obtain a commutation for Horn, but public resentment against the hired killer was so intense that none was forthcoming.

Horn, realizing that he would soon face the hangman, broke out of the Cheyenne Jail with another prisoner, Jim McCloud. They leaped on Deputy Sheriff Richard Proctor, struggling for his gun in a hallway of the jail. Proctor squeezed off four shots, wounding McCloud, before he was overpowered. McCloud ran outside and leaped on the only available horse, riding wildly out of town. Horn fled on foot, followed by O.M. Eldrich, a citizen. Eldrich fired several shots at Horn, one of these grazing his head. As he struggled to work the jammed gun he had taken from Proctor, Eldrich and other residents charged up to Horn and knocked him to the ground. They began beating him with sticks and clubs until Proctor arrived and stopped them. Horn was restrained and returned to his cell, and McCloud was also recaptured and taken back to the Cheyenne Jail.

Horn resigned himself to his death, spending his last

Tom Horn awaiting execution; he was hanged with the rope he is shown making.

months writing his memoirs and weaving a rope that was later used to hang him. The hired killer mounted the gallows in Cheyenne on Nov. 20, 1903. His sweetheart, Kimmel, and his employer John Coble stood by as witnesses. Tom Horn looked down at them and then turned to the executioner, telling him to "hurry it up. I got nothing more to say." He was promptly hanged.

REF.: Allen, *Men of Daring;* American Guide Series, *The Oregon Trail;* Bartlett, *History of Wyoming;* Botkin, *A Treasury of Western Folklore;* Brown, *Trial Driving Days;* Burns, *Wyoming Pioneer Ranches;* Burroughs, *Where the Old West Stayed Young;* Burt, *Powder River; CBA;* Chapel, *Guns of the Old West;* Chatterton, *Yesterday's Wyoming;* Clay, *My Life on the Range;* ____, *The Tragedy of Squaw Mountain;* Clover, *On Special Assignment;* Coe, *Juggling a Rope;* Coolidge, *Fighting Men of the West;* Cunningham, *Triggernometry;* Dunham, *Our Strip of Land;* Durham, *The Negro Cowboys;* Erwin, *The Southwest of John H. Slaughter;* Faulk, *The Geronimo Campaign;* Forrest, *Arizona's Dark and Bloody Ground;* Fowler, *Timber Line;* Gann, *Tread of the Longhorns;* Ganzhorn, *I've Killed Men;* Gard, *Frontier Justice;* Gardner, *The Old Wild West;* Hendricks, *The Bad Man of the West;* Holloway, *Texas Gun Lore;* Horan, *The Authentic Wild West;* ____, *Desperate Men;* ____, *Pictorial History of the Wild West;* Horn, *Life of Tom Horn;* Howard, *This is the West;* Hudson, *Andy Adams;* Hunter and Rose, *The Album of Gunfighters;* Hutchinson, *The Life and Personal Writings of Eugene Manlove Rhodes;* Kelly, *The Outlaw Trail;* King, *Mavericks;* Krakel, *The Saga of Tom Horn;* Kuykendall, *Ghost Riders of the Mogollon;* Larson, *History of Wyoming;* Leckenby, *The Tread of the Pioneers;* Leckie, *The Buffalo Soldiers;* Lefors, *Wyoming Peace Officer;* Look, *Unforgettable Characters of Western Colorado;* Mazzulla, *Outlaw Album;* Mercer, *The Banditti of the Plains;* Monaghan, *The Legend of Tom Horn;* Nash, *Bloodletters and Badmen;* Paine, *Tom Horn: Man of the West;* Penfield, *Western Sheriffs and Marshals;* Penrose, *The Johnson County War;* ____, *The Rustler Business;* Raine, *Famous Sheriffs and Western Outlaws;* Rockwell, *The Sunset Slope;* ____, *Memoirs of a Lawman;* Rollinson, *Hoofprints of a Cowboy and U.S. Ranger;* Sandoz, *The Cattlemen from the Rio Grande Across the Marias;* Shirley, *Toughest of Them All;* Siringo, *Riata and Spurs;* ____, *Two Evil Isms;* Speer, *Western Trails;* Spring, *William Chapin Deming;* Thrapp, *Al Sieber, Chief of Scouts;* Tittsworth, *Outskirt Episodes;* Trenholm, *Footprints on the Frontier;* ____ and Carley, *Wyoming Pageant;* Walker, *Stories of Early Days in Wyoming;* Waller, *Last of the Great Western Train Robbers;* Way, *Frontier Arizona;* ____, *Sgt. Fred Platten's Ten Years on the Trail of the Redskins;* Wellman, *A Dynasty of Western Outlaws;* Wyman, *Nothing But Prairie and Sky;* (FILM), *Tom Horn,* 1980.

Horne, Brian, 1930- , Brit., mansl. Fifteen-year-old Brian Horne was convicted of manslaughter in March 1945 after two women burned to death in a fire he started at a Manchester, England, factory where he was employed. Horne caused £158,000 damage and was sentenced to three years in prison.

REF.: Brock, *A Casebook of Crime; CBA.*

Horne, Carlton (AKA: Squirrel), 1955- , U.S., rob.-bat.-rape-attempt. mur. On May 11, 1982, while on parole from a conviction for slashing the throat of a 53-year-old woman, 27-year-old Carlton Horne broke into a Chicago home, raped the two women inside, and set them on fire while three children slept in the bedroom. Horne forced his way into the West Side apartment after following one of the women home from a convenience store. Once inside, he beat them both with a hammer and raped them repeatedly. Before leaving, he wrapped the two women in blankets, doused them in lighter fluid, and set them ablaze. Neither of the women died, but one lost all of her toes from severe burns.

One of the women was acquainted with her attacker and told police where he could be found. Police found Horne in the alley behind his house, hiding in a garbage dumpster with electrical equipment stolen from the apartment. Less than one year later, Horne appeared in court before Criminal Court Judge Kenneth L. Gillis, who sentenced him to serve 120 years in prison. REF.: *CBA.*

Horne, William Andrew, 1685-1759, Brit., mur. In 1759, William Andrew Horne, seventy-four, was sentenced to die for murdering his three-day-old son. The child, however, whose mother was Horne's sister, had been dead for thirty-five years.

Wealthy and dissipated, given to seducing his servant or his sister, Horne insisted, one night in February 1724, three days after the birth of his son, that his brother Charles go for a ride with him. Placing his son in a bag, Horne and his brother rode five miles to Annesley in Nottinghamshire, taking turns holding the bag. When they arrived Horne asked Charles if the child was still living. Told that he was, Horne laid him behind a haystack and covered him with hay.

Thirty-five years later, Horne would claim that he had meant to leave the child with Mr. Chaworth of Annesley, but had been frightened away by barking dogs. He had placed the child under a haystack, he continued, hoping that servants would find him the next morning.

Soon after the murder, the Horne brothers quarrelled, and Charles confessed the crime to his father. His father, however, made him promise to keep the infant's death a secret. This Charles did, until 1747. After the death of his father at 102 years of age, Charles confessed to a magistrate, who advised him to keep quiet to protect his family's reputation. Some years later, Charles, in ill health, confessed yet again to Mr. White of Ripley, admitting that he could not die in peace without revealing his secret.

Murderer William Horne, discovered hiding in a chest by constables.

William Horne, meanwhile, spent his time making enemies. During a tavern argument over hunting laws, a Mr. Roe called Horne an "incestuous old dog." Horne sued for libel and won, but the angry litigant started investigating rumors he had heard about Horne's past and had him brought in for questioning. Worried that his brother would betray him, Horne offered friendship to Charles if he would deny all. Charles refused, but did agree to leave town if Horne would give him £5. Horne refused and was arrested soon after the magistrates talked to his brother.

"It is a sad thing to hang me," Horne said when police apprehended him, "for my brother Charles is as bad as myself and he cannot hang me without hanging himself." The jury, however, thought otherwise. Jailed at Nottingham, Horne was found Guilty and sentenced to death. At the end he told a clergyman that he forgave all his enemies, even his brother Charles, but added that if "God Almighty should ask him how his brother behaved, he would not give him a good character." On Dec. 11, 1759, William Horne was executed at Nottingham, at the age of seventy-four.

REF.: Atholl, *Shadow of the Gallows;* Butler, *Murderers' England; CBA;* Culpin, *The Newgate Noose;* Mitchell, *The Newgate Calendar;* Smith-Hughes, *Eight Studies in Justice.*

Horner, Joe, See: **Canton, Frank M.**

Horner, Nicholas, 1687-1719, Brit., rob. Nicholas Horner was a parson's son who became a thief at an early age. Seven years exile in India did not deter him from his crimes, however, and he was executed for his many robberies when he was thirty-two.

An attorney's clerk in Lyon's Inn, Holywell Street, when he fell in with bad company and began to gamble, drink, and philander, Horner took to the highways to support his habits. His first robbery on the road, however, was thwarted; he was apprehended, sent to Winchester Jail, and condemned to death. Through the influence of his wealthy father the sentence was commuted to a pardon, on condition that he leave England for seven years. Unable to reduce the sentence any further, Horner's father sent his son to Madura in the East Indies.

After seven years Horner returned to England to find that his parents had died. Quickly squandering his £500 inheritance, he again took to the highway. Although he had a penchant for lecturing his victims, Horner himself was once outwitted when a wealthy woman acted the part of a madwoman so well that Horner left her coach in disgust before finding her money and goods. The story of this encounter was published in the *Weekly Journal,* or *British Gazetteer,*" on Dec. 27, 1718. Horner was so incensed that he threatened to cut his own throat, yet when another potential victim tried the same scam he was ready. "I was once bit this way by one of your sex, do you think I must always be so?" he said.

Horner was arrested for attempting to rob several gentleman on the road from Exeter to London. He was sent to Southgate Jail and hanged on Apr. 3, 1719.

REF.: *CBA;* Pringle, *Stand and Deliver;* Smith, *Highwaymen.*

Hornig, Frank, d.c.1887, Aus., rob.-mur. In October 1886, German gold prospector Frank Hornig was arrested and charged with the robbery and murder of a fellow prospector after a shepherd discovered Anthony Johnson's body in a shallow grave in the Australian outback.

Jock McAlister stumbled on the grave the morning after he heard the tinkling of a horse's bridle coming from a nearby ditch, close to where he had set up camp for the evening with his flock. Upon finding the body, wrapped in a blanket, McAlister notified authorities who accompanied him to the site and exhumed the body. They learned that the dead man was a gold prospector, who often traveled the region with Hornig. From tracks leading up to the campsite, they determined that two men had ridden to the site the night before, but that only one had left.

Following a manhunt led by a native Australian tracker, the mounted police apprehended Hornig for questioning. As they prepared to return their prisoner to the nearest jail, one of the police horses bolted, and the opossum rug that Johnson had been buried in fell to the ground. Upon seeing the rug, Hornig attempted suicide, later confessed, and was found Guilty of robbery and murder. Hornig was quickly executed.

REF.: *CBA;* Wren, *Masterstrokes of Crime Detection.*

Hornigold, Benjamin, prom. 1700s, Brit., pir. Captain Benjamin Hornigold stood at the helm of several ships flying the black and white colors of the Jolly Roger until his retirement, when the king of England granted him and many other pirates amnesty.

Up until 1718, Hornigold was one of the most infamous high-seas pirates. Under his command, the *Mary* and the *Ranger* plundered the waters of the Caribbean and Atlantic oceans preying on both French and Spanish ships, but primarily attacking the galleons transporting gold stolen by conquistadors exploring the New World. Hornigold vowed never to attack an English ship, a comfort to the king of England.

In 1718, the king made an offer of freedom to Hornigold and all pirates who committed crimes before Jan. 5, 1718. He offered amnesty to all those who renounced their activities by Sept. 5, 1718, in return for service to the crown. Some joined the military in the war with Spain, others, like Hornigold, were pressed into service as captors of remaining pirates who stole English booty. It is believed that Hornigold and his crew continued their piratical attacks only when they were assured of not bringing down on themselves the wrath of the king. Hornigold died at sea.

REF.: *CBA;* Rankin, *The Golden Age of Piracy.*

Hornung, Ernest William, 1866-1921, Brit., writer. Wrote fiction and created the character Raffles, the gentleman burglar. Books authored: *The Amateur Cracksman, Stingaree, Mr. Justice Raffles, The Crime Doctor.* REF.: *CBA.*

Horowitz, Harry, See: **Becker, Charles.**

Horrell-Higgins Feud, prom. 1870s, U.S., mob vio. The six Horrell brothers, Ben, John, Mart, Merritt, Sam, and Tom, returned from the Civil War to rustle cattle and cause mayhem in Texas and New Mexico in the 1870s. John Horrell became the first casualty when he was shot to death in Las Cruces, N.M., but the other five built a ranch near Lampasas, Texas, and with neighbor John Calhoun Pinckney Higgins participated in a joint cattle drive in 1872. But Higgins feuded with Tom Horrell, and began a five-year battle which became known as the Horrell-Higgins Feud.

On Mar. 19, 1873, members of the Texas State Police led by Captain Tom Williams tried to arrest Horrell ranch hand Clint Barkley at the Matador Saloon in Lampasas. During a shoot-out, Williams was killed and Mart and Tom Horrell were wounded. Mart was later arrested. A few days later, the remaining Horrells battered their way into a Georgetown, Texas, jail and freed their brother. They all traveled to Lincoln County, N.M. On Dec. 1, 1873, Ben Horrell got drunk and became embroiled in a gunfight in Lincoln. Ben was killed, as were his companions Jack Gylam and Dave Warner, as well as lawman Juan Martinez. Ben suffered a final indignity by losing a gold ring to a thief who chopped off his finger. The four remaining brothers avenged his death on Dec. 20 when they invaded a Mexican wedding party and killed four guests and wounded two. The Horrells returned to Lampasas and the feud with Higgins continued.

On Jan. 22, 1877, again in the Matador Saloon, Merritt Horrell was shot to death by Higgins after being accused of tampering with a herd. Two months later, on Mar. 26, Tom and Mart Horrell were ambushed by members of the Higgins gang as they were on their way to court in Lampasas. Tom was wounded, but both escaped. In June, the Horrells counterattacked, killing a Higgins ranch hand and wounding another in an ambush at dawn. On June 14, the feud escalated into a three-hour public gunfight on the streets of Lampasas. Higgins lost Frank Mitchell, his brother-in-law, and Bill Wren before the townspeople convinced the two factions to take the feud elsewhere. The following month, Higgins and fourteen gunmen invaded the Horrell ranch and kept their rivals under siege. Two Horrell ranch hands were wounded during the two-day siege, which ended when the Higgins party ran short of ammunition. The Horrells retaliated again on July 25, 1877, when they ambushed Carson Graham, a Higgins employee. Mart, Sam, and Tom Horrell were all arrested by a Texas Ranger party led by Major John B. Jones. Exasperated, Jones brought both factions together and a peace treaty was signed. However, in 1878, after being suspected of robbing and murdering a Bosque County merchant, Mart and Tom Horrell were lynched in their jail cell as they awaited trial. Samuel Horrell, the last brother, left Texas in 1880 to live a peaceful life in New Mexico with his two daughters. See: **Higgins, John Calhoun Pinckney.**

REF.: Askins, *Texans, Guns & History;* Bartholomew, *Kill or Be Killed;* CBA; Coe, *Frontier Fighter;* Douglas, *Famous Texas Feuds;* Elzner, *Lamplights on Lampasas County;* Fulton, *Lincoln County War;* Gard, *Frontier Justice;* Gillett, *Six Years with the Texas Rangers;* Haley, *Jeff Milton;* Keleher, *Violence in Lincoln County;* Monaghan, *The Book of the American West;* Raine, *Guns of the Frontier;* Roberts, *Rangers and Sovereignty;* Sinise, *Pink Higgins;* Sonnichsen, *I'll Die Before I'll Run;* Walker, *Home to Texas;* Webb, *Texas Rangers.*

Horridge, Thomas Gordon, 1857-1938, Brit., jur. Became a judge in 1901, and served as a judge of the King's Bench Division of the High Court from 1910-37. He presided over the murder trials of Ronald Light and Mrs. Pace. REF.: *CBA.*

Horry, George Cecil (AKA: George Arthur Turner, Charles Anderson), 1907- , N. Zea., forg.-mur. In August 1951, George Cecil Horry was convicted of murder for the death of a woman whose body was never found. Mary Eileen Spargo was last seen in Auckland, N. Zea., on July 12, 1942, while she honeymooned in Titirangi with her new husband, George Arthur Turner, a British Secret Service agent. Turner and Spargo were married the previous day—the day after Spargo had sold her house for £676 in preparation for a move to Europe with her new husband.

Later that day, Horry drove his fiancee, Eunice Mercel Geale, to her parents' home in the Auckland suburb of Mt. Eden. When the couple arrived, Geale's parents noticed that Horry had two

suitcases and a hat box in his car. It appeared that he was either planning, or had just returned from, a trip, but neither questioned the items. Horry and Geale were married on Dec. 12.

The week after the wedding, George Turner appeared at the home of his in-laws, Mr. and Mrs. William Spargo. Turner, visibly upset, explained that their daughter had been killed after a German U-boat sunk the cruise liner *Empress of India* as they sailed to England. The Spargos were shattered. They believed their son-in-law until several months later, when they learned that no ship named the *Empress of India* had sailed since WWI. Mr. Spargo then went to police with this information, and took with him a letter mysteriously delivered to him several months before while Turner and his daughter were honeymooning.

Police detectives, with assistance from the Auckland post office, captured the man who had been passing himself off as George Arthur Turner. In reality, Turner was George Cecil Horry, a man who during a 19-year span received forty-seven separate convictions. Horry was immediately suspected in the disappearance of his wife, whom he said he married at her request as she had been involved with a married man and wanted to move with him to the U.S. Even though his story was weak, police were unable to link him to her death until nine years later, when legal limitations on missing persons had expired and Spargo was legally pronounced dead. Police immediately arrived at his home and took him into custody on murder charges.

Horry's trial began on Aug. 5, 1951. Based on testimony from the dead woman's friends and relatives, letters Horry mailed to Spargo's parents during their "honeymoon," the jury found him Guilty and sentenced him to prison. The most damaging evidence came when Horry's wife asked why police were arresting him.

With police officers at the door, she asked, "What's the matter?"

"It's that Turner business," answered Horry.

"Why? Has she turned up?"

"That's impossible. She couldn't have."

The body of Mary Elaine Spargo Jones has never been found.

REF.: *CBA;* Reynolds, *Murder 'Round the Clock.*

Horsey, Dr., and **Joseph, Charles,** and **Spalding, John,** prom. 1514, Case of, Brit., mur. In December 1514, Dr. Horsey, the Bishop of London's chancellor, was acquitted of the murder of convicted heretic Richard Hunne, who was found hanging in his prison cell at Lollards Tower.

In court, Charles Joseph, a warder at the jail, confessed that he, Horsey, and John Spalding entered Hunne's cell and murdered him on Horsey's orders. Joseph explained to the court that Horsey hung the body from the bars to make Hunne's death seem a suicide. But, owing to the influence of the Bishop of London, Horsey and the other two defendants were acquitted of all charges. Horsey immediately left London for Exeter, where he remained until his death.

REF.: *CBA;* Postgate, *Murder, Piracy and Treason.*

Horsford, Walter, d.1898, Brit., mur. Walter Horsford of Spaldwick was hanged at the Cambridge gallows for poisoning his mistress. She had asked him for a drug that would abort her pregnancy—her fourth, and the second by Horsford. Annie Holmes had been having an affair Horsford for several years when in December 1897 she learned that she was again pregnant. She believed the child to be her lover's and not her husband's. When she asked him for some medication to end her pregnancy, Horsford purchased several packets of strychnine and told her to take it in some water before bedtime. On the evening of Jan. 7 she died in her home after suffering violent convulsions. In her bedroom, relatives found several packets of strychnine and a note from Horsford explaining how to use the "medication." Horsford was tried at Huntingdon Assizes and executed on June 28, 1898.

REF.: Brock, *A Casebook of Crime;* Butler, *Murderers' England;* CBA; Laurence, *A History of Capital Punishment.*

Horsley, Albert, See: **Orchard, Harry.**

Horton, Floyd, b.1896, and **Johnston, Anna,** prom. 1936, U.S., mur. Lovers Floyd Horton and Anna Johnston were sentenced to life in prison for poisoning Horton's wife Elta, who died on their farm near Bedford, Iowa, on Feb. 15, 1936.

Horton and Johnston had been involved in an affair for some time before they plotted to kill Elta Horton with strychnine. On the evening of Feb. 14, Horton administered the fatal dose to his wife. Johnston had purchased the poison several weeks before, telling the local pharmacist it was to kill rats in her basement.

An autopsy of Elta Horton's body revealed strychnine poisoning. Floyd Horton and Anna Johnston were charged with murder. Prosecutors coerced a confession from Johnston by convincing her that Horton had turned state's evidence against her. She provided investigators with a full confession, and she and Horton were convicted of first-degree murder. Horton was sentenced to life in the state prison in Fort Madison, Iowa, and Johnston served her life sentence at the State Women's Reformatory.

REF.: *CBA; Cohen, One Hundred True Crime Stories.*

Horton, Kenneth, 1923- , Brit., mur. In March 1939, 16-year-old Kenneth Horton murdered his employer, who had threatened to fire him from his job as a clerk at a London paper mill. Horton had worked at the mill for two months, but was warned in February that he faced termination if his performance did not improve.

On Mar. 2, Horton's employer worked late. That evening, Horton beat him over the head more than thirty-four times with a ruler, hammer, and chisel, fracturing his skull twenty-two times. The man's disfigured body was found by the building's janitor later in the evening.

Horton was apprehended two days later at a hotel in a seaside resort. Upon being taken into custody, he confessed to the murder and explained that he had also stolen money from the man. Horton was tried at the Old Bailey, where he was convicted and sentenced to spend an indeterminate time in prison.

REF.: *CBA; Wilson, Children Who Kill.*

Horton, William Robert (AKA: **Willie**), 1951- , U.S., rob.-rape-mur. On Oct. 26, 1974, William Robert Horton robbed a Lawrence, Mass., gas station and killed the station's 17-year-old attendant Joseph Fournier by stabbing him nineteen times. Horton stole more than $100 from the cash register, but left $57 in Fournier's pocket. On Nov. 8, the 23-year-old Horton and two other men, 37-year-old Roosevelt Pickett and 30-year-old Alvin L. Wideman, were arrested in their Lawrence homes in connection with the robbery and murder. Horton, eventually convicted of the murder, was sentenced to life and incarcerated in the Northeast Correctional Center.

Horton remained behind bars for twelve years until he escaped in 1987. He was one of the Massachusetts convicts approved for the state's prison furlough program, which allowed inmates short leaves and temporarily eased overcrowding in prison. Though Governor Michael Dukakis did not enact the program, he supported it, believing furloughs an integral part of the state's prison program. In June, Horton failed to return to prison following his scheduled furlough period, and Massachusetts law enforcement authorities began a statewide search for him. Ten months later, officers shot Horton as he fled the Oxon Hill, Md., home of Mr. and Mrs. Clifford Barnes. Horton had forced his way into the home, tied Barnes up, and raped his wife as the man watched.

At the time of this attack, Governor Dukakis was running for president in the 1988 election. As the race continued, nationwide polls showed Dukakis, the Democratic nominee, gaining on incumbent Vice-President George Bush. In an attempt to sway public opinion, the Bush campaign launched an extremely successful negative advertising blitz designed to portray Dukakis as a "liberal" who was "soft on crime." In their most effective television spot, they used the Willie Horton case to illustrate how Dukakis dealt with criminals in his own state. Advertisements included appeals from the victimized Barnes couple, who were shown pleading with voters to elect Bush. The ads also accused the Massachusetts penal system of having an open-door policy for convicted criminals. Although the ads were repeatedly denounced

for exploiting racial prejudice (Horton was black and Mrs. Barnes white), they were probably the single most important issue in the campaign that won Bush the presidency.

After his capture in 1988, Horton was convicted of the Barnes attack and sentenced to double life plus eighty-five years. He is currently serving his sentences in the Maryland Penitentiary. Governor Dukakis has since signed legislation prohibiting furloughs for inmates convicted of murder. REF.: *CBA.*

Horwood, Sir William Thomas Francis, 1868-1943, Brit., law enfor. off. Sir William Horwood held several high-ranking military positions, and was Chief of Police on the London and North Eastern Railway from 1911-14. Horwood was first appointed to Scotland Yard as assistant commissioner in 1918. In 1920 he became Commissioner of the Metropolitan Police, a position he held until 1928. REF.: *CBA.*

Hosein, Arthur (AKA: **King Hosein**), c.1936- , and **Hosein, Nizamodeen** (AKA: **Nizam**), c.1948- , Brit., blk.-kid.-mur. Brothers Arthur and Nizamodeen Hosein were poor immigrants from Trinidad who settled in England. Arthur, a tailor, arrived in September 1955, hoping to make £1 million. In 1967, he and his German-born wife, Else, bought Rooks Farm, ten acres outside the village of Stocking Pelham. Nizamodeen arrived in May 1969 on a visit with his papers marked for a January 1970 expiration date.

On Oct. 3, 1969, kidnapping for ransom apparently occurred to the Hosein brothers as they watched David Frost interview Australian media tycoon Rupert Murdoch on television. Murdoch lived in London with his wife Anna. Arthur, thirty-four, and Nizamodeen, twenty-two, decided to seize Anna Mur-

Kidnap victim Muriel McKay.

doch and hold her for £1 million ransom.

Slowly the plan took shape. They identified the Murdochs' Rolls-Royce and followed the car home. What they did not know was that the Murdochs were in Australia on vacation and had entrusted the car to Alick McKay, deputy chairman of the *News of the World*. McKay lived on Arthur Road in Wimbledon. In

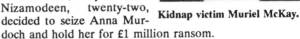

The McKay home in Wimbledon.

the midst of the preparation for the kidnapping, Arthur's wife, who was not a conspirator, left to spend Christmas in Germany.

On Dec. 29, 1969, the Hoseins mistakenly grabbed 56-year-old Muriel Frieda McKay, the wife of the deputy chairman. She was taken to Rooks Farm and blindfolded while the Hoseins made contact with the family. A letter postmarked from the north of London contained a written message from the kidnappers and an urgent plea from Mrs. McKay: "Please do something to get me home. I am blindfolded and cold. Please cooperate for I cannot keep going. I think of you constantly and the family and friends. What have I done to deserve this treatment?" The kidnappers called the family in the next few weeks and demanded £1 million. Arthur Hosein called his two-man abduction team "Mafia Group 3," or M-3. Nothing more was heard from them in the first two weeks of 1970. The calls resumed on Jan. 14, as the police futilely checked all available records, but there was little evidence and nothing prior was known about the M-3 group.

A letter dated Jan. 26 warned that Mrs. McKay would be executed if the money was not paid. During the first attempt to collect the ransom, the Hoseins had seen police in the area and the rendezvous was aborted. A second unsuccessful attempt was made on Feb. 6 at Bishop's Stortford in Essex. The Hosein brothers circled the area in their Volvo, but they thought police were in the area, so they drove off without retrieving the money. This time, though, the police observed the car and checked the license plates. The detectives went immediately to Rooks Farm, but there was no trace of Muriel McKay. Incriminating items were found, and the brothers were found and arrested, but refused to say anything about the location of Muriel McKay. It was presumed that the woman had been executed, and her remains cut up and fed to the livestock at Rooks Farm. A neighbor testified that she had heard a gunshot on or about New Year's Day. The pigs had been sold or butchered by then, however, making forensic investigation all but impossible.

Left, Arthur Hosein, and his brother Nizamodeen, kidnappers and murderers.

The Hoseins were convicted of blackmail, kidnapping, and murder at the Old Bailey. Justice Sebag Shaw sentenced them both to life imprisonment for murder, tacking on an additional twenty-five years for Arthur and fifteen for Nizamodeen. In passing sentence Shaw noted, "The kidnapping and detention of Mrs. McKay was cold-blooded and abominable," and the punishment must be sanguine so that law-abiding citizens will be safe in their homes."

REF.: Borrell, *Crime in Britain Today;* Butler, *Murderers' England; CBA;* Cooper, *Shall We Ever Know?;* Deeley and Walker, *Murder in the Fourth Estate;* Heppenstall, *The Sex War and Others;* Lucas, *The Murder of Muriel McKay;* Lustgarten, *The Story of Crime;* O'Flaherty, *Have You Seen This Woman?;* Wilson, *Encyclopedia of Modern Murder.*

Hoshen, 1750-99, China, embez.-suic. Served in several high-ranking government positions under Emperor Ch'ien Lung. While heading efforts to suppress the White Lotus Society rebellion, he embezzled enormous amounts from the treasury while soldiers pillaged the citizens. When the emperor died, he was pushed out of office and compelled to commit suicide. REF.: *CBA.*

Hoshi, Iba, See: **Iba Hoshi.**

Hosius (Osius), d.358, Spain., her. Bishop of Cordova in the early 300s and attended Council of Necaea in 325 with other

bishops. In 355 he would not condemn Athanasius, so the Emperor Constantius II banished him from Spain. Later he was pressured into signing a document approving of Arianism, but still resisted condemning Athanasius, though he was reinstated as a bishop. REF.: *CBA.*

Hotel Pierre, See: **Comfort, Robert.**

Hotsy Totsy Club, prom. 1920s-30s, U.S., org. crime. During Prohibition, the Hotsy Totsy Club was a notorious speakeasy located on the second floor of a building on Broadway between 54th and 55th streets in New York City. Though owned by Hymie Cohen, the club served as a headquarters for mobster Jack "Legs" Diamond, who occasionally killed his enemies in a back room. One night in 1929, Diamond and top aid Charley Entratta began feuding with another thug named Red Cassidy. While Cohen told the band to play louder, Diamond shot Cassidy to death, while Entratta killed an innocent bystander named Simon Walker. The mobsters fled, and shortly thereafter, eyewitnesses began to disappear, including the club bartender, assorted customers, employees, and Hymie Cohen himself. Diamond and Entratta later surrendered to the police, but were released due to lack of evidence.

REF.: *CBA;* Fried, *The Rise and Fall of the Jewish Gangster in America;* Haskins, *Street Gangs;* Katz, *Uncle Frank;* Logan, *Against the Evidence;* Peterson, *The Mob;* Thompson and Raymond, *Gang Rule in New York.*

Houchard, Jean Nicolas, 1738-93, Fr., rebel. Served as soldier in French Revolution. In 1792 he was made general of a brigade, and made general of a division in 1793. At a battle at Hondschoote in 1793 he defeated the British, but did not use their loss to his benefit. His forces lost at Courtrai shortly after, and he was arrested and guillotined. REF.: *CBA.*

Houck, Charles Weston, 1933- , U.S., jur. Nominated to the district court of South Carolina by President Jimmy Carter in 1979. REF.: *CBA.*

Hough, Benson W., 1875-1935, U.S., jur. Served as justice of the Ohio Supreme Court from 1919-23, and as district attorney of the southern district of Ohio between 1924-25. He was nominated to the southern district court of Ohio by President Warren G. Harding in 1925. REF.: *CBA.*

Houghton, Charles, d.1929, Brit., mur. Elinor Drinkwater Woodhouse and her sister Martha Gordon Woodhouse lived on their 300-acre estate near Hereford, England. On Sept. 6, 1929, they notified Charles Houghton that he was to be released as their butler because his alcoholism was beginning to affect his work. They gave him a twenty-four-hour notice and two months' wages. The next morning, after serving the two women breakfast, he shot them dead. He was apprehended in his room where he had attempted suicide by cutting his throat with a razor.

Houghton was charged with murder and tried at Hereford Assizes. In his defense, his attorneys cited a history of epileptic seizures that often resulted in uncontrollable actions. The judge failed to see their case, and sentenced Houghton to be executed. He was hanged on Dec. 6, 1929.

REF.: Butler, *Murderers' England; CBA;* Shew, *A Companion to Murder.*

Houghton, Hugh, prom. 1700s, Brit., rob. Unemployed ex-serviceman Hugh Houghton was convicted for robbing the Bristol mail coach as it traveled near Knightsbridge, England. At the time, many believed him innocent.

Houghton lived in a London boarding house where he owed a substantial amount of overdue rent. His landlord became suspicious one morning when Houghton paid his debt in full. When investigators traced the money back to the Bristol mail coach that had been robbed several days earlier, they arrested Houghton and charged him with the crime.

The prosecution secured a conviction with only circumstantial evidence. At the time of his arrest, Houghton had money in his possession that was traceable to the robbery. He explained that he had found it in a wallet in Covent Garden on the night of the robbery. In addition, a witness testified that Houghton had asked him to act as an accomplice in several robberies. Houghton denied the witnesses testimony explaining that the witness was unreliable as the two men had recently argued. Nevertheless, the judge sentenced Houghton to be executed. Houghton refused to confess, and before reaching the gallows, hanged himself in his jail cell.

REF.: *CBA*; Pringle, *Stand and Deliver*.

Houghton, Joab, 1813-76, U.S., jur. Served as chief justice of the supreme court of the provisional government of New Mexico from 1846-51, and as U.S. attorney in New Mexico in 1861. He was nominated to the territorial court of New Mexico by President Andrew Johnson in 1865. REF.: *CBA*.

Houghton, Thomas, d.1697, Brit., forg. Before he turned to forgery, Thomas Houghton had a career as a mountebank, a combination quack doctor and fortune teller, working small country towns and villages. He would set up a stage, and give a high-flown speech, setting himself up as a seer. At Sherbourne, in Dorsetshire, Houghton told his audience: "Let those who have need of my counsel in their affairs repair unto me one by one, to my lodgings at the Red Lion Inn."

One of those who came to Houghton was a farmer with a pregnant daughter. He explained that he had four servants, and suspected that one of them was the father. He asked Houghton how he could prove the paternity. His daughter could not identify her seducer, who had come to her in the dark. Houghton told the farmer to leave the daughter's door unlocked and gave him a "magical" ointment of lamp black and oil with which the daughter was to mark her lover when he came again. The daughter did so, but also asked the man his identity. When she realized it was her father's shepherd, whom she cared for, she informed him of the plot. He borrowed the ointment and marked all three of the other servants as well. When the perplexed farmer returned, Houghton told him that the servant with oily black fingers was the father. The farmer identified the shepherd as the seducer, and at first wanted to arrest him. But he finally consented to his daughter's marriage to the shepherd, and sang the praises of the "mind reader" Houghton.

Houghton was working as a candlemaker at St. Margaret's Westminster when, with his partner Francis Salisbury, he forged and sold a counterfeit sixpenny stamp used on vellum, paper, and parchment. Houghton was indicted at the Sessions House of the Old Bailey in October 1697. He and Salisbury were accused of stamping five hundred sheets of paper with the forged stamp and selling them. Houghton claimed that he took the paper in payment of a debt, but the pair were found Guilty and sentenced to death. Houghton paid careful attention to the prayers and instructions given to him at the scaffold to prepare his soul for the future when he was hanged on Nov. 3, 1697, along with Salisbury.

REF.: *CBA*; Smith, *Highwaymen*

Hounds, prom. 1840s, U.S., org. crime. The San Francisco Society of Regulators, more commonly known as the Hounds, were organized during the Gold Rush of 1849 to prevent foreigners from accumulating wealth. The Hounds roamed the gold fields beating and stabbing those they considered undesirable, mostly people of Spanish descent. The violence was endorsed by local law enforcement and political figures. But the Hounds expanded their terrorism to San Francisco where they preyed on white pedestrians and shop owners, pillaged restaurants and saloons, and set businesses on fire. Most of the Hounds were veterans of the Mexican War, and in Summer 1849, they donned their uniforms and violently wiped out a Mexican shanty town. Finally, a band of 230 volunteer deputies were organized to capture the Hounds. Twenty gang members were arrested, including Sam Roberts, purportedly one of the leaders. Roberts and a man named Saunders received ten years at hard labor, but the gang's political benefactors interceded and the sentences were never served. The gang was never again a social force. REF.: *CBA*.

Houndsditch Murders, prom. 1910, Case of, Brit., rob.-mur. On Dec. 16, 1910, suspicious sounds were heard after hours coming from the back of a jewelry store in Houndsditch. A neighbor reported the noises to a constable, who investigated and, wary of the man who answered the door, called in assistance. Around 11 p.m., two police officers and three sergeants arrived on the scene. Sergeant Bentley entered the house next to the jewelers and, as he was looking around, several men rushed down the back stairs, shooting as they ran. Bentley was fatally wounded and the other four officers, Sergeants Tucker and Bryant and Constables Woodhams and Choate, all unarmed, were also shot down. The two who survived were disabled for life. Choate died with twelve bullet holes in his body. The massacre was unprecedented in the history of the British police. At least fourteen people were involved in the robbery attempt and the murders, including three women. Calling themselves anarchists, they were either Letts or Russians associated with the Italian anarchist Malatesta. About six had been in the house, including Nina Vassileva and Joe Levi, and Peter Piatkow (alias Peter Schtern, or "Peter the Painter"). Police offered a reward of £500. The gang lived in the Whitechapel neighborhood, an ethnically mixed slum area outside London's city limits. The day after the murders, a man alleged to be part of the gang, George Gardstein, was found dead, with a loaded gun and ammunition under his pillow. Other arrests were made, but the gang members remained at large.

On Jan. 2, 1911, Inspector Wensley received a call from Superintendent Ottoway, who had learned from an informer that two of the wanted men, Fritz Svaars and Joseph Marx, (alias Joseph Vogel), were at a house in Sidney Street, Whitechapel, and were expected to move to a new hideout soon. After dark, a large group of armed, plainclothes policemen came in vans to Sidney Street and surrounded the house. No one came out. The informer changed his story, and officers came back the next night, when the procedure was repeated. Ottoway and Wensley, deciding to take action, brought 100 uniformed policemen to Sidney Square at 2:30 a.m. on Jan. 3. The neighbors were evacuated from their houses under protest, and the entire area was cordoned off by police. A heavy rain and sleet began to fall. At 7:30 a.m., six shots rang out from inside the house. Sergeant Leeson of the Metropolitan Police was wounded. Twenty Scotland Yard troops and a horse artillery battery from the St. John's Wood Barracks were called within the hour. Home Secretary Churchill, Superintendent Quinn of the Special Branch, and Melville Macnaghten, head of the Central Intelligence Division, arrived. The conflict continued for several hours, with six casualties. After 1 p.m., the house was on fire. The two charred bodies brought from the ruins were those of Marx and Svaars. Five firemen were injured when part of the gutted building collapsed.

Eight of the remaining gang members were eventually captured, but lack of evidence led to the release of four of them. Three more were acquitted after a trial at the Old Bailey, and the conviction of Nina Vassileva for conspiracy was dropped in the criminal appeal court. Malatesta, the alleged leader, was later deported on unrelated charges. Three of the original fourteen were believed to have escaped overseas. The one most remembered was Peter Piatkow, or Peter the Painter, who painted scenery for anarchist dramas and probably played a very minor part in the conspiracy. Because police obtained a photo of him, his face was displayed on wanted posters all over the city.

REF.: Browne, *The Rise of Scotland Yard; CBA*; Cobb, *Murdered On Duty*; Dilnot, *Rogues' March*; Thompson, *The Story of Scotland Yard*; Wensley, *Forty Years of Scotland Yard*.

Housden, Jane, d.1712, Brit., consp.-mur. Convicted of the crime of "coining" (a form of counterfeiting), Jane Housden, an experienced offender in her mid-thirties, was brought before the judge at the Old Bailey to receive her sentence. Her former lover, William Johnson, entered the courtroom seconds before she was placed in the dock. Johnson pushed aside the guards to whisper a few words of encouragement to Jane. "You must wait until the hearing is finished before you can speak to the woman," declared the turnkey Spurling. Johnson, who refused to let court procedures get in the way, withdrew a pistol from his vest and shot Spurling through the heart.

The other guards seized Johnson and Housden who had shouted encouragement from the dock. They were charged with murder, convicted, and sentenced to die on the gallows. The sentence was carried out on Sept. 19, 1712. The murderers shouted curses at the crowd before being hanged. Afterward Johnson was hanged in chains between Highgate and Islington.

REF.: *CBA;* Mitchell, *The Newgate Calendar;* Nash, *Look for the Woman.*

Housden, Nina, 1916-   , U.S., mur. Nina Housden imagined that her husband, Charles, a bus driver, was engaged in an endless string of affairs. The couple lived in a modest apartment in Highland Park, Mich., a suburb of Detroit. Despite his protests to the contrary, Charles Housden was unable to convince his wife of his fidelity. When he visited the local bowling alley, Nina would there and embarrass him in front of his friends. Finally Charles had enough. He filed for divorce and moved out. But on Dec. 18, 1947, Mrs. Housden phoned her husband and told him to come over just one more time. That night she plied him with a generous amount of liquor. Charles accepted his wife's hospitality and promptly passed out.

Seeing her chance, Nina wrapped a clothesline around his neck and strangled him. She rolled back the carpets, got a meat cleaver, and mutilated his body. Afterward she wrapped the body parts in Christmas paper and piled them into the back seat of her car. The next day she left Michigan for her family home in Kentucky where she planned to bury the remains. In Toledo, Ohio, Nina encountered car problems. She left the vehicle with a local car mechanic who told her that it would take at least two days to the correct the problem. "It's okay, I'll live in the front seat until you're done. I'm low on cash and can't afford a motel," she replied.

The mechanic went along with the arrangement and permitted the woman to sleep in the garage. On the second day he noticed a powerful odor wafting from the back of the car. Nina explained that this was venison intended for her family. Later that night the mechanic decided to have a look for himself. He found the remains of a human leg protruding from the package. Nina Housden was extradited to Michigan, judged sane by the courts, and tried for murder. She was found Guilty and sentenced to life in prison.

REF.: *CBA;* Nash, *Look For the Woman;* Wilson, *Encyclopedia of Modern Murder.*

House, James Arthur, prom. 1920s-30s, U.S., fraud. The president of Guardian Trust Bank of Cleveland, Ohio, James Arthur House, was fined $10,400 and sentenced to six years in prison for using money from the bank's pension fund to boost bank stock during a slowing market. House, who had once advised the Federal Reserve Board, was convicted on Oct. 6, 1934, by a Cleveland U.S. District Court on twenty-six charges of misapplication of funds and ten charges of false entry to cover up his fraud. Guardian Trust later declared bankruptcy.

Immediately after Judge Samuel H. West pronounced his sentence, House was freed on $10,000 bail, and attorney William H. Boyd vowed to appeal the decision. In 1935, the U.S. Circuit Court of Appeals and the U.S. Supreme Court upheld the lower court's decision, and on Oct. 29, House began serving twenty-six concurrent three-year sentences, one for each count of misapplication of funds, and ten additional concurrent three-year sentences for covering up his actions. On Sept. 3, 1943, several months after his release from jail, House, once one of the richest men in Cleveland, officially filed for bankruptcy in U.S. District Court. At the time, his liabilities were $2,118,394, and his assets to pay them totaled $468. REF.: *CBA.*

House in Queen Anne Street, The, 1920, a novel by William Darling Lyell. The celebrated Madeleine Smith case (Scot., 1857) forms the basis of this fictional work, although the author takes pains to introduce characters and situations far afield of the actual poisoner. See: **Smith, Madeleine.** REF.: *CBA.*

House Of All Nations, prom. 1890s-1900s, U.S., pros. An 1890s house of prostitution, the House of All Nations was an economically priced alternative to the more opulent brothels in Chicago's Levee district. The Armour Avenue house was known to offer various services at different prices, but it was learned that the same women worked both the two-dollar and the five-dollar entrances, offering identical services. The House of All Nations thrived for two decades until it was closed in a general vice crackdown prior to WWI.

REF.: Asbury, *The Chicago Underworld; CBA.*

House of Rest for Weary Boatman, prom. 1800-40s, U.S., pros.-gamb. One of the worst sinkholes in the Swamp, the notorious vice district of early New Orleans, the House of Rest for Weary Boatmen was a thieves' paradise. Scores of innocent travelers and citizens were waylaid in this wicked den, robbed, most often killed, and their bodies left to rot inside the foul-smelling rooms of this brothel-hotel or simply dumped in the nearby alleyways. The skimpy New Orleans Police Department ignored the countless murders occurring in the House of Rest and seldom, if ever, penetrated the dark byways of the Swamp. One report had it that an early-day New Orleans police official was asked to seek a young man from a good family who was suspected of having been kidnapped, taken to the House of Rest, and murdered for his money and clothes. The official frowned and reportedly replied: "Go in there? The Swamp? That place, the House of Rest? My God, man—we'll all be killed!"

The House of Rest was, even to the evil denizens of the Swamp, known as the most notorious gambling dive in the district, and only the most stupid or naive boatmen swaggered through its doors to test its faro or roulette tables, games which were rigged so that no one ever won. If, by accident, a lucky boatman did win a few dollars, he was immediately accused of cheating by the proprietors and quickly stabbed or bludgeoned to death by hoodlums who were employed for that purpose. The slain body of the boatman was then allowed to remain on the floor for several days as an example to those who aspired to win at the tables. See: **Swamp, The.**

REF.: Asbury, *The French Quarter;* Castellanos, *New Orleans As It Was; CBA; History of New Orleans Police Department* (Anon.).

Housman, Dr. Nathan S., d.1952, U.S., perj. Long believed to be an integral part of San Francisco's underworld, Dr. Nathan Housman was suspected in many of the city's most notorious crimes, possibly even gang-related murders. Housman was a successful physician from a prominent San Francisco family. He was considered something of a playboy in society circles. He first came under suspicion in 1931 when police believed he offered medical treatment to wounded gangsters and provided drugs for the city's elite. Once, in a taped conversation, he was overheard planning murder with then Public Defender Frank Egan. On the tape, Egan told Housman that he had devised a scheme to kill Jessie Scott Hughes, an elderly woman whose incessant telephone calls were driving Egan crazy. Police warned Hughes and watched her home for several weeks to no avail. Months later, in April 1931, Hughes was found dead on a city street, her body battered by an apparent hit-and-run driver. Shortly thereafter, ex-convict Verne Doran confessed that he and Albert Tinin murdered on orders from Egan and Houseman. No concrete evidence linked Houseman to the plot, but Egan was found Guilty and sentenced to life in prison. He was paroled on Oct. 1, 1957, for good behavior.

Police again thought they had nailed Housman when one of his patients, elderly Alma Black, was found dead in 1939. A coroner's inquest found that for three years the doctor had prescribed strong narcotics for the woman's illness. Authorities ordered him to present all of Black's prescription records. He told them he kept no such records—a misdemeanor in California—and police again believed they had caught him. But during his trial, Housman shocked investigators by providing the prescription records. He was quickly acquitted. Police later enlisted the help of a special investigator who tested the ink of Houseman's records and discovered that, although they spanned a three-year period, Houseman had written all of the prescriptions on the same day.

A grand jury investigation into the case resulted in charges of perjury, preparing false evidence, and providing false evidence to the court while under oath. A jury convicted Housman who, with his attorneys, appealed the decision for the next two years. In 1941, the U.S. Supreme Court upheld the lower court's ruling and Housman began serving his sentence at California's San Quentin Penitentiary on Nov. 9. On Dec. 18, 1942, after serving only thirteen months in jail, Housman was paroled and later pardoned by California Governor Culbert Olson.

REF.: Block, *The Wizard of Berkeley*; *CBA*.

Houston, Temple L., 1860-1905, U.S., crim. law. Temple Houston practiced law with a singular style during the late nineteenth century in the West. The son of Sam Houston, he was known as much for his appearance as for his oratory, with his shoulder-length hair, white sombrero, and rattlesnake ties. Houston often practiced outrageous methods of defense. Defending a gunman at trial, he drew and fired a gun loaded with blanks at a jury. As the jury scattered and mingled with spectators, Houston declared them no longer sequestered and after a second trial, won freedom for his client. Houston once killed an opposing lawyer after a trial and successfully won his own acquittal by pleading self-defense. Adept with a pistol, Houston often

Criminal lawyer Temple Houston.

led posses in search of fugitives, and once bested Bat Masterson in a shooting contest. This unique lawyer died of a stroke at age forty-five while visiting Woodward, Okla.

REF.: Anderson, *History of New Mexico*; Beebe, *The American West*; Campbell, *Oklahoma*; *CBA*; Dobie, *Cow People*; Haley, *Charles Goodnight*; Hopper, *Famous Texas Landmarks*; Hunter and Rose, *The Album of Gunfighters*; Jennings, *Beaten Back*; Laune, *Sand in Your Eye*; McKennon, *Iron Men*; Osborn, *Let Freedom Ring*; Shirley, *Sixgun and Silver Star*; ____, *Toughest of Them All*; Timmons, *Twilight on the Range*; Tolbert, *An Informal History of Texas*; Wallis, *Cattle Kings of the Staked Plains*; Wellman, *A Dynasty of Western Outlaws*.

Houston, Tom, d.1893, U.S., west. lawman. Tom Houston was a law officer in the Oklahoma Territory during the early 1890s. On Nov. 29, 1892, in Orlando, Okla., Houston, accompanied by Chris Madsen and Heck Thomas, tried to apprehend bank robber Ol Yantis. They cornered him at his sister's farm, and after a brief exchange, Houston killed him. On Sept. 1, 1893, Houston and a large posse traveled to Ingalls, Okla., in search of the Doolin Gang. After a ferocious gun battle, the gang escaped, with the exception of Arkansas Tom Jones. Before he was arrested, Jones killed three lawmen, Dick Speed, Lafe Shadley, and Houston.

REF.: *CBA*; Croy, *Trigger Marshal*; Drago, *Outlaws on Horseback*; O'Neal, *Encyclopedia of Western Gunfighters*.

Howard, Catherine, c.1520-42, Brit., adult. Fifth wife of Henry VIII of England, after his divorce from Anne of Cleves. She was convicted of adultery and beheaded after confessing to prenuptial unchastity. REF.: *CBA*.

Howard, Baron **Charles (Earl of Nottingham),** 1536-1624, Brit., jur. Served as ambassador to France in 1559 and as lord chamberlain from 1574-85. At the trial of Mary, Queen of Scots in 1586, he served as commissioner. REF.: *CBA*.

Howard, Cornelius (The Gorse Hall Murder), prom. 1909, Case of, Brit. mur. The killing of prominent mill owner George Henry Storrs, of Cheshire, England, on Nov. 1, 1909, was one of the most celebrated murders of the Edwardian era. On the night of the murder, Storrs was playing solitaire in the dining room of his large mansion, Gorse Hall. His wife and niece, Marion Lindley, were seated nearby, sewing. Mary Evans, the family cook, came up from the cellar at about 9:30 p.m. and saw a man hiding behind the kitchen door. The man pointed a revolver at her and growled from the shadows: "If you make a single sound, I'll shoot you!" Mary Evans dashed for the dining room, shouting that there was an intruder in the house.

The armed man was right on her heels. When the man saw Storrs, he jumped on him, trying to club the mill owner with his revolver. Storrs, however, was more than a match for the intruder. The mill owner was a tall, well-built man of forty-nine and in top physical condition. As the women screamed, Storrs battered him into submission. The intruder, a blond-haired young man with a thin mustache, held up his hands and begged: "Please don't strike me again." He handed Mrs. Storrs the revolver and stood trembling before the towering Storrs, who backed him into a corner.

"Go upstairs and ring the alarm bell," Storrs told his wife. Mrs. Storrs hurriedly went upstairs where she rang the alarm to summon the police. Then she shoved the revolver beneath a carpet. None of the other women were present in the house. Marion Lindley, Mary Evans, and Ellen Cooper, a maid, had all fled the house when the fight began and were frantically searching for a constable. Meanwhile, Storrs made the mistake of turning his back on the intruder while looking out a window. As he did so, the young man pulled a long knife from his pocket and plunged it into Storrs' back several times.

Storrs, though mortally wounded, grabbed the man and dragged him down a hallway where he shoved him into a pantry, locked the door, and then collapsed on the floor. A constable burst through the front door of the mansion, with Marion Lindley, Mary Evans, and Ellen Cooper behind him. He rushed down the hall to find Storrs dying, a large pool of blood spreading from his body. There was a crash of glass when the constable opened the pantry door, and he discovered that the intruder had smashed the pantry window with a wash basin and fled.

The wounded Storrs was conscious for another twenty minutes. He told the constable repeatedly that he had no idea who the attacker had been. He then died in his wife's arms. His death stunned the countryside where he was well-known, liked, and respected, and had no known enemies. A wide dragnet was organized and hundreds of young, blond-haired men were picked up and questioned, but none were held. On Nov. 17, 1909, Cornelius Howard, a 31-year-old butcher and Storrs' distant cousin, was arrested and charged with murder. When arrested, Howard was found with a pair of blood-stained socks in his pocket, and his coat and pants were bloodstained. He was also carrying a sharp knife. Howard, a resident of Huddersfield, denied any guilt, saying that he had been cut by falling glass as he entered his boarding house. He changed his story later, admitting that he had been cut when committing a burglary in Stalybridge. Then Howard was identified by Marion Lindley, the cook, and the maid as the man who had invaded the Storrs' household. Mrs. Storrs found it difficult to identify Howard and moved close to him, stared him in the face, and finally told police officers: "I *think* he is the man. He knows."

Howard was placed on trial, but he had an unshakable alibi. He was able to prove that he was playing dominoes in the Ring O' Bells Public House in Huddersfield at the exact time of the murder. Many of the pub's customers came forward to support Howard's claim. He was found Not Guilty and released. A second man, Mark Wilde, was then charged and tried as the killer. Wilde, who had served in the army, had been brought to trial purely on the testimony of other army veterans who had served with him.

These ex-soldiers identified the revolver left by the intruder as having been Wilde's, but this was never proven. The women from Gorse Hall all identified Wilde as the killer, but since they had positively identified Howard, their second identification was less credible. Moreover, Wilde proved that the blood found on *his* clothes by police when he was arrested had resulted from a fistfight he had in Staleybridge on the very night of the murder, a fight witnessed by several people who testified for Wilde at his trial. He, too, was acquitted and released. The Storrs murder at Gorse Hall remained unsolved and is still one of the most puzzling mysteries in the history of homicide in England.

REF.: Adam, *Murder by Persons Unknown*; Bresler, *Scales of Justice*; Brock, *A Casebook of Crime*; *CBA*; Duke, *Six Trials*; Ellis, *Blackmailers and Co.*; Logan, *Guilty or Not Guilty?*; Mitchell, *The Scientific Detective and the Expert Witness*; Nash, *Open Files*; Pearce, *Unsolved Murder Mysteries*; Shew, *A Second Companion to Murder*; Shore, *Crime and Its Detection*; Symons, *A Reasonable Doubt*; Villiers, *Riddles of Crime*.

Howard, David, prom. 1863, U.S., mur. In October 1863, gold prospector Lloyd Magruder left Lewiston in the Idaho Territory for a camp in the Bitterroot Mountains to pick up a shipment of gold. He was accompanied by three guards, David Howard, Chris Lowery, and James Romaine, as well as two prospectors, four muleteers, and a man named Bill Page. One night the guards murdered everyone except Page, whom they needed to escort them through the treacherous mountain passes. Bad weather forced them to retreat to Lewiston, where they encountered Hill Beachy. A few nights earlier, Beachy had a dream that Magruder had been murdered, and became suspicious when his guards returned without him. A dream was no grounds for prosecution, and the three guards left Lewiston peacefully.

A few days later, Magruder's possessions and dead pack animals were found in the mountains. Beachy got himself deputized and tracked Page and the three fugitives to the Washington Territory and Oregon with warrants for their arrest. He finally apprehended them in California and brought them back to Idaho to stand trial. He convinced Page to testify against the other three, and the guards were convicted of the murders of the Magruder party. On Mar. 4, 1864, a crowd of more than 10,000 people turned out to witness the hangings of the three men. REF.: *CBA*.

Howard, Eleanor, b.1784, Case of, Brit., big. When her father refused to let her marry, Eleanor Howard eloped with Mr. Whitford. The two were married on Nov. 25, 1801, by David Sang, a tobacconist at Gretna Green. Whitford paid him £5 for his services, and Eleanor gave him two shillings for the marriage certificate. Her father eventually forgave her and set Whitford up in the drapery business. The business failed, and in 1805 the couple returned to London, where Whitford found a job in a linen warehouse. In poverty, the Whitfords took in a 60-year-old boarder named Robert Jacques James.

Shortly after James arrived in the Whitford household, Eleanor left a note telling her husband that she was leaving him. Eleanor said she would reclaim her own name, and that she was convinced they had never been legally married. She soon married the elderly James and was arrested a few months later for bigamy. In acquitting her of the charge, the judge said he would not receive the law of Scotland from a tobacconist. REF.: *CBA*.

Howard, Elizabeth (Countess of Beauregard, AKA: Elizabeth Ann Haryett), c.1822-65, Brit., pros. Elizabeth Howard was a British prostitute in her mid-20s who captured the attention of Louis Napoleon, who lived in exile in England from 1846 to 1848. When the French Revolution broke out in 1848, Howard gave the exiled Napoleon money so he could return to France. After he became Napoleon III, his status prevented him from continuing his acquaintance with Howard. However, as a sign of his fondness, he gave her about $1 million, a chateau, and made her Countess of Beauregard. She died at age forty-three and was interred in England as Elizabeth Ann Haryett. REF.: *CBA*.

Howard, Frances, 1593-1632, Brit., mur. Lady Frances Howard was at the center of one of England's most famous Royalist intrigues of the Seventeenth Century. Jealousy, passion, and greed were at the heart of the matter, and in the end one of the court's most learned men paid with his life.

Frances Howard was only fifteen when she was introduced to Robert Carr, the homosexual lover of King James I. By currying the favor of the king, Carr had become the second-most powerful figure in the land. His sexual favors were rewarded with a peerage. James, a bloated and petulant monarch, had made his dandy the Viscount Rochester.

Carr had made the acquaintance of Sir Thomas Overbury, a knight of high intellectual capacities but slavish devotion to those considered favorites of the King. It was Overbury who introduced Carr to Frances Howard, the daughter of the Earl of Suffolk. The 15-year-old charmer turned the head of Viscount Carr, who temporarily forgot about his royal obligations to woo her. Carr, who was unable to read or write, engaged Overbury to write his love letters. At first Overbury was a willing participant to the intrigue and eager to please Carr. When Frances Howard's husband, the 14-year-old Earl of Essex, returned from his travels, Overbury condemned the relationship as immoral.

Lady Frances Howard, murderess.

Angered more with Overbury than the hopeless state she found herself in, Howard enlisted Anne Turner, a reputed witch and alchemist, to help her prepare the poison she was going to use against Overbury. Meanwhile, Carr inveigled the King to imprison Overbury in the Tower of London on the thinnest pretense. The guards who stood watch over Sir Thomas were replaced with men sympathetic to the scheming Carr and his mistress.

Mrs. Turner secured her poison from a physician named James Franklin. Tarts and various candied jellies were laced with rose algar, sublimate of mercury, arsenic, and diamond powder, before being fed to Overbury by Sir Gervase Helwys and his assistant Richard Weston. There was enough poison in the delicacies to kill twenty people. Not surprisingly, Overbury died on Sept. 15, 1613. Three days later, Frances' marriage to the Earl of Essex was annulled and King James bestowed on Carr the title of Earl of Somerset. Carr married Frances in a great ceremony, and soon they became the favorites of the court, commanding enormous power and prestige.

Their crime might have been covered up if not for the deathbed confession of Paul de Lobel, an apothecary's assistant who had participated in the poisoning plot. De Lobel named the conspirators, and on Oct. 23, 1615, Richard Weston was hanged at Tyburn. He was followed in death on Nov. 9 by Mrs. Turner. Sir Gervase Helwys and James Franklin marched to the gallows on Nov. 20, and Dec. 9, respectively. A great public outcry led to the arrest and conviction of Carr and his wife on May 24, 1616. Lady Somerset was prosecuted by Sir Frances Bacon who treated her, at the king's behest, with only the greatest of respect.

Both were convicted and ordered to hang, but through King James' intervention Carr and his wife were spared the death penalty. The king no doubt feared that he might also be named as a co-conspirator by the vengeful Carr, so he was anxious to make amends. Though they escaped the gallows, it can be said that Carr and Lady Somerset endured a fate perhaps worse than death. They retired to their country estate where they soon grew tired of each other. The rancor Lady Somerset felt for her husband was such that she did not speak to him for five years. She died in 1632 from a painful uterine disorder.

REF.: *CBA*; Nash, *Look For the Woman*; Williamson, *Historical Whodunits*; Wilson, *Encyclopedia of Murder*.

Howard, George, Jr., and **Howard, George, Sr.**, prom. 1960s-

70s, U.S., mur. George Howard, Jr., thirty-two, got three small diamonds, some loose change and life in prison for murdering Sara Robin. Howard's father, George Howard, Sr., sixty-three, was imprisoned for standing by while his son committed the grisly act.

When a hunter on his way home happened upon the body of 63-year-old Robin leaning against a tree, her murder was already half solved. Father and son did nothing to cover their tracks. Detectives traced initials from the woman's wedding ring to the nearby town of Olean, N.Y., found her address and spoke with her neighbors. They said the Howards did odd jobs for Robin. Police asked the Howards to come to the morgue for questioning. Authorities made the body look as mutilated as possible by shining bright lights up underneath it. The interrogation went on until the younger Howard grew weary. In frustration, he finally shrieked, "I done it. And I'd just as soon burn for it. I'm sick." Howard then explained that he had tuberculosis and would die soon anyway. He had killed Robin, he said, because she constantly pestered him to marry her. Howard was given life in prison and his father, who watched him commit the murder, received twenty-five to thirty years. REF.: *CBA.*

Howard, George William Frederick, 1802-64, Brit., law enfor. off. Founded juvenile reformatory. He served as a member of parliament in 1826, as chancellor of the duchy of Lancaster from 1850-52, and as viceroy of Ireland from 1855-58 and from 1859-64. REF.: *CBA.*

Howard, Henry (Earl of Surrey), c.1517-47, Brit., treas. Wounded while a marshal in 1544, and succeeded by Lord Hertford. Hertford and his supporters had him and his father condemned on treason charges. REF.: *CBA.*

Howard, Henry (Earl of Northampton), 1540-1614, Brit., treas. Queen Elizabeth I was wary of his relationship with Mary, Queen of Scots. After he published material in 1583 that criticized judicial astrology, he was put in prison on charges of treason. He later created the edict against duelling that was issued by James I. REF.: *CBA.*

Howard, John, 1726-90, Brit., pris. reform. In 1773, 47-year-old John Howard was appointed high sheriff of Bedfordshire, England. He took the largely ceremonial position more seriously than his predecessors, and was appalled at conditions in British prisons. Prisoners starved among open sewers and rodents, and corrupt prison guards extorted them for the smallest favors. The conditions were extensively depicted in British art of the era, but any attempt at reform met with indifference.

In 1777, after four years of witnessing the degradation, Howard published *The State of Prisons in England and*

Penal reformer John Howard.

Wales, which, in graphic detail, assessed the status of prisons and described necessary reforms. The suggestions included classifying the prisoners according to their offenses, employing and training them for useful labor, hiring more honest prison guards, improving sanitary conditions and prison clothing, and creating individual cells where each prisoner could sleep alone. The notion that the prisoners should work together during the day and be alone at night met the approval of influential lawyers Sir William Eden and Sir William Blackstone and led to the Penitentiary Houses Act of 1779. In his later years, Howard toured Europe, and died in Russia on Jan. 20, 1790. The Howard League for Penal Reform, founded in 1921, carries on his name and his work.

REF.: *CBA; Howard, John Howard, Prison Reformer; _____, The State of the Prisons; Nicholls, Crime Within the Square Mile; Scott, The Concise Encyclopedia of Crime and Criminals.*

Howard, John, prom. 1869-70, U.S., (unsolv.) mur. Alabama planters John Brantley and John Howard lived near each other, hated each other and walked around armed against each other. So in the spring of 1869, when Howard was found shot dead in a swamp virtually in Brantley's backyard, Brantley was the number one suspect.

Regardless of how guilty he looked, Brantley was released on a technicality and immediately fled to Mississippi, where he lived for over a year without anyone suspecting he was a fugitive. Someone was keeping an eye on Brantley, however. On Dec. 4, 1870, while Brantley waited at the Shuqualak Railway Station for his wife's train to arrive, someone on the platform took aim at him and fired one deadly shot. Brantley died instantly. REF.: *CBA.*

Howard, John C., prom. 1948, U.S., rape. In 1948, in an apparent breakthrough in racial equality, an Alabama jury of white men found another white man Guilty of raping a black woman. Prosecuting attorney Winston Huddleston told the jury to approach the case "just like you would if a Negro was charged with raping a white woman...and show the Negro that he can get justice in court."

John C. Howard, thirty, was found Guilty of rape and sentenced to forty-five years in prison, though almost all blacks convicted of raping Alabama white women had been sentenced to death. REF.: *CBA.*

Howard, Joseph, prom. 1864, U.S., forg. During the Civil War, Joseph Howard of the Brooklyn *Eagle* forged President Abraham Lincoln's signature on a proclamation calling for four thousand recruits between the ages of eighteen and forty-five and announcing a day of fasting and prayer.

Two leading New York City newspapers, the *World* and the *Journal of Commerce,* printed the proclamation, which reached their news offices at 3 a.m. on May 18, 1864. The announcement arrived too late for careful editing but in time for printing. Other papers received the same story but were suspicious and decided not to run it.

Howard was arrested and imprisoned at Fort Lafayette. Despite the fact that the two papers immediately printed retractions, military guards were stationed in their offices and publication was suspended for four days.

Opposition papers viewed these suspensions as evidence that Lincoln did not respect free speech. Secretary of War Stanton was charged with persecuting the *World* because the paper opposed Lincoln's policies. REF.: *CBA.*

Howard, Joseph Clemens, 1922-   , U.S., jur. Served as probation officer for the supreme bench of Baltimore City, Md., from 1958-60, as assistant state's attorney of the chief trial section from 1964-67, and as associate judge of the supreme bench from 1968-79. He was nominated to the district court of Maryland by President Jimmy Carter in 1979. REF.: *CBA.*

Howard, Leonard (AKA: Edward Thomas), d.1877, U.S., mur. An habitual criminal, Leonard Howard was sent to Auburn prison to serve another long sentence. He remarked that such a life was a "living hell" and he intended to end it, not by suicide, but by forcing the authorities to execute him. To that end, Howard brutally selected a random victim, Richard Sheffield, and murdered him in front of several guards. Howard got his wish; he was convicted of murder and executed.

REF.: *CBA; Life of Leonard Howard.*

Howard, Margaret, prom. 1849, U.S., mur. Margaret and John Howard eloped on Apr. 18, 1841. They moved to Cincinnati, and on Mar. 19, 1842, had their first child. Howard made his living as a gambler, and often beat and berated his wife. Despite the poor prospects of this marriage, a second child was born on Sept. 25, 1843. Howard's erratic behavior continued. He chased his wife with a knife, hit her with a chair, threw dishes and food from the table, fired a pistol through a window, drank to excess, and left his wife and children in an unheated room on a frigid night. In the spring of 1844, Margaret asked her sister to live with them, hoping her husband's behavior would improve. But the sister had little patience for his temper, and soon left. On Sept. 19, 1844, after three and a half years of turbulence, Margaret

Howard deserted her husband and went to Cleveland to live with her sister. But she returned to him a few months later.

During the holiday season, she found her husband with multiple stab wounds, which he later told people she inflicted. Margaret now had to flee, and was reduced to begging for food and shelter.

Margaret Howard, beaten by her drunken husband.

For three years she led this transient life, until Feb. 2, 1849, while in Cincinnati, she killed her husband's mistress, Mary Ellen Smith, by slitting her throat with a knife. At her trial before Judge Brough on Apr. 30, 1849, Margaret Howard was found Not Guilty by reason of insanity at the time of the crime. However, she was ruled still insane and committed to jail in Hamilton County.

REF.: *CBA; Trial of Mrs. Margaret Howard, for the Murder of Miss Mary Ellen Smith, Her Husband's Paramour, in Cincinnati, on the Second of February Last.*

Howard, Mendell, prom. 1900s, Brit., forg. It took two years, but Scotland Yard Investigator Fred Jarvis finally stopped the forgeries of bonds and notes that had been plaguing France, Germany, Spain, and other countries. Jarvis was directed to Mendell Howard by a nosy old lady from Eaton Square. She didn't know why her neighbor seemed strange, it was just her gut feeling. For months Jarvis observed the man but learned only that he liked to take pictures. Background interviews revealed that Howard fancied himself an inventor and was even respected in the U.S. for his ingenuity. Jarvis witnessed a meeting between Howard and colorful criminal "Big Frank," known throughout Europe for his forgery conspiracies. Jarvis put a group of Scotland Yard detectives on Howard's trail. When the notorious Johnnie Carr, organizer and financier of criminal enterprises, called on him, Jarvis arrested Howard.

Howard was tried at the Old Bailey and sentenced to fifteen years in prison. Through his trial, authorities were able to implicate his associates, and in two years, stopped Carr's operations as well. REF.: *CBA.*

Howard, Philip (Earl of Arundel), 1557-95, Brit., consp. Suspected of making plans with Francis Throckmorton and others in 1583 that favored Mary, Queen of Scots. He and his wife became Roman Catholics in 1584. After trying to flee from Britain, he was put in prison until his death. REF.: *CBA.*

Howard, Sumner, 1835-90, U.S., jur. Served as prosecuting attorney of Genesee County, Mich., from 1858-61 and from 1865-71. He was U.S. district attorney of Utah from 1876-77, and a member of the Michigan House of Representatives in 1883. He was nominated to the territorial court of Arizona by President Chester A. Arthur in 1884. REF.: *CBA.*

Howard, Thomas, I (Duke of Norfold, Earl of Surrey), 1443-1524, Brit., consp. Caught at Bosworth Field in 1485 and ordered by Henry VII} to be put in the Tower of London, where he was imprisoned for three years. Later, his civil rights were reinstated. REF.: *CBA.*

Howard, Thomas, II (Duke of Norfolk, Earl of Surrey), 1473-1554, Brit., treas. Roman Catholic lord steward presiding at trial of Anne Boleyn, his niece. In 1540 he arrested Thomas Cromwell.

When his niece Catherine Howard, also married to Henry VIII, was executed for adultery, his influence with the court slipped. During the rule of Edward VI, he was put in prison for treason because he was condemned as being an accomplice of his treasonous son, Henry Howard. He was freed in 1553 when Mary became queen. REF.: *CBA.*

Howard, Thomas, III, 1536-72, Brit., consp. Plotted to marry Mary, Queen of Scots and was put in prison from 1569-70. He conspired with Philip of Spain for Spain to attack Britain to release Mary. When the plan did not succeed, he was beheaded. REF.: *CBA.*

Howard, Lord Thomas (Earl of Suffolk, Baron Howard de Walden), 1561-1626, Brit., embez. Served as vice-admiral over ships that went to Cádiz harbor to capture Spanish ships. He held positions as lord chamberlain from 1603-14, and as lord high treasurer in 1619. He and his wife were put in prison in 1619 for embezzlement. They were freed after ten days and regained favor. REF.: *CBA.*

Howard, Wilse, and **Turner, Robert E. Lee**, prom. 1882, U.S., feud. A disagreement during an 1882 poker game led to an eight-year feud, which left several people dead and disrupted the daily life of Harlan County, Ky. In April 1882, Wilse Howard won money in a poker game. Robert E. Lee Turner forced him to return his winnings at gunpoint. Three days later, Howard killed Turner in an ambush, and the feud began with virtually everyone in the county aligned with one side or the other. For eight years, the factions sniped at each other in the Kentucky hills. The Turners, led by county judge Lewis, called out the militia when Wilse Howard threatened to raid the town. The group attacked the Howards at dawn, killing four people, wounding seven, and chasing the remaining Howards from the county.

REF.: *CBA; Life and Trial for Murder of Wilson Howard.*

Howarth, Kenneth (AKA: Crock of Gold Man), and **Chambers, Wayne**, prom. 1970s, Brit., fraud. In the 1970s, swindlers Kenneth Howarth and Wayne Chambers preyed on Americans and Britons looking for a sure-fire, get-rich-quick scheme. For the right price, these wheelers and dealers offered investors the "Pot of Gold" at the end of the rainbow.

Howarth, once described as a "most agreeable con-man," and Wayne Chambers, contrarily described as a rough Oklahoman mining engineer, founded and operated E.J. Austin International. The phony California company promised unheard-of payoffs on investments in their mining operations, made possible by their new-fangled excavating technique. Chambers, the company's engineering expert, explained it like this: "You put a certain chemical in the first tank and the copper comes out. Then you put another chemical in the second tank and the silver comes out. I mix local dirt with the liquor...You just can't analyze it—it's like Coca-Cola."

And people invested in it. If it had been up to investment manager Henry Gorrell-Barnes, of England's well-known merchant bankers Morgan Grenfell, the bank would have sunk £1 million into the scheme. Gorrell-Barnes flew to Los Angeles where he spent the weekend with friends. He was whisked out to the mining site on Monday and flew back to London the same day. He reported seeing a crushing machine working with concentrates coming out of it. He said it was all very confusing but that Morgan Grenfell should invest. Fortunately, they didn't, and their follow-up inquiries were instrumental in exposing the bogus business.

Investigators and security guards swarmed the mining site. They ascertained that the rock Barnes saw had been trucked in, and that there was no output of metals. In fact, the only semi-precious metals to be found were the samples of copper powder put in canning jars to show investors.

In November 1970, Howarth was arrested in New York and charged with conspiring to possess $40,000 worth of stolen securities and with making false statements to the U.S. Immigration & Naturalization Service. He was deported to London. Not coincidentally, sitting next to him on the plane were two British inspectors. Investigations against Howarth ensued, resulting in 1975 in thirteen charges of fraud. He was accused of attempting to obtain £6.5 million worth of shares from his company, and of dishonestly obtaining a £30,000 loan from his stockbroker. On May 15, 1975, Howarth was found Guilty on eleven of the thirteen counts and sentenced to five years in prison. Chambers escaped prosecution. REF.: *CBA.*

Howdeshell, Roy, prom. 1950s, U.S., rape-mur. Authorities had no trouble tracking down 80-year-old Alice Imlay's murderer. Roy Howdeshell was the only suspect they ever had, but for the wrong reason.

Forensic pathologist Dr. Larson gleaned many clues from the mutilated body of the elderly Imlay. She had been raped, beaten, and stabbed numerous times with a knife. In addition, her assailant had bitten both of her breasts, leaving his "dental signature" on the body. There was also a bloody heel print on the floor. The print was distinctive, small and narrow, and appeared to have been made by a motorcycle boot. When Larson and his assistant learned that the man next door rode a motorcycle, he was the first person they saw.

Howdeshell, eighteen, did not own the boots they were looking for, but he did blurt out a heinous confession. Blood of Imlay's type was found on a small button on one of Howdeshell's shirts, under his fingernails, in the hair on his head, and under the foreskin of his penis. He was convicted and sentenced to life imprisonment.

REF.: *CBA;* McCallum, *Crime Doctor.*

Howe, Allan, 1927- , U.S., morals. On June 12, 1976, U.S. Representative Allan Howe, Democrat of Utah, was arrested for offering police decoys Margaret Hamblin and Kathleen Taylor $20 for a sex act. Howe denied any guilt, saying it was a case of entrapment. On July 23, 1976, in the U.S. District Court of Judge Raymond Uno, Howe was convicted of sex solicitation, sentenced to thirty days in jail, and fined $150. The case was automatically appealed, and Howe assured his constituency he would win. He vowed to continue his re-election campaign. On Aug. 25, 1976, before District Court Judge Bryant B. Croft, Howe was again found Guilty, given a thirty-day suspended sentence and ordered to pay court costs. On the same day, Howe's temporary campaign manager, 24-year-old Timothy Charles Allen, was arrested for selling marijuana to an undercover agent.

REF.: Bullough, *An Illustrated History of Prostitution; CBA.*

Howe, Michael (AKA: Black Mike), d.1818, Brit.-Aus., rob. After deserting the British Navy, Michael Howe became a highwayman in his native Yorkshire. In 1811, he robbed a miller, for which he was sent to Van Dieman's Land in Australia. Upon his arrival, he escaped. He was recaptured and escaped again. In 1813, "Black Mike" Howe joined a gang of thirty other wanted criminals and became their leader, calling himself "The Admiral" and the "Governor of the Ranges," and cutting off his deceased predecessor's head to keep it out of enemies' hands. He led his boys through pillage and plunder, meticulously recording each adventure in his kangaroo skin diary in kangaroo blood.

By 1817, however, Black Mike's gang had turned against him and on Oct. 21 of the following year, he was ambushed and beaten to death with musket butts. His severed head was displayed in Hobart for the satisfaction of the townspeople. REF.: *CBA.*

Howe, Samuel Gridley, 1801-76, U.S., penal reform. Sought elimination of debtors prisons. He served as the chief of the Perkins Institution for the Blind from 1832-76, was interested in care for the mentally retarded, and also supported the abolition of slavery. REF.: *CBA.*

Howe, William F., 1828-1902, and **Hummel, Abraham H.,** 1851-1926, U.S., crim. law. The most successful and the most corrupt criminal lawyers of the 19th century U.S. were William F. Howe and Abraham H. Hummel. These two colorful characters who practiced in New York from 1869 to 1906 thought nothing of bribing witnesses, jurors, and judges, as well as presenting false testimony and fake evidence. They went to any lengths to free a client, making them the most sought-after defense attorneys of

their day. They made enormous amounts of money and became quite wealthy. They also became so notorious that judges grew red-faced and apprehensive whenever these two conniving and calculating lawyers would appear in their courts. Howe, a towering, heavyset man with a thick mustache, tried the cases with elan. At one moment he was bellowing bombast and the next he was weeping sorrowfully for his client's widowed mother or destitute little family. Hummel was the legal brains behind the firm, a diminutive and wiry man who spent every waking moment looking for loopholes in the law.

Born in England, Howe apparently had been a doctor at one time. He had reportedly practiced medicine in London and had been jailed for performing an illegal abortion on a woman who died under his knife. In 1860, at the age of thirty-two, Howe appeared in New York, and after studying law for three years, opened a legal practice on Center Street. Sometime in the 1860s, Howe hired little Abe Hummel to assist him in researching his growing number of criminal cases. The crafty little law clerk was so adept that Howe quickly promoted Hummel to a full partnership. Typical of a Howe-Hummel defense was the case of a notorious arsonist. This man, who hired out as a professional arsonist to those wishing to burn their businesses for insurance money or other purposes, was caught red-handed while attempting to set fire to a livery stable. Hummel suggested to Howe that they plead the man guilty of attempted arson, which they did. The judge, in a bench trial, accepted the plea, then realized that there was no penalty for *attempted* arson, as Hummel had learned, and was compelled to let the man go. This tactic caused the state legislature to hurriedly pass laws covering such acts.

So dedicated in his research was Abe Hummel that he seized upon a lapse in time specified by new laws that dictated the method of execution for condemned killers. At that time, in 1888, New York had abandoned hanging, replacing it with the electric chair. "Handsome Harry" Carlton, a Howe & Hummel client, had been convicted of murder and was about to be sentenced to death, but the sentencing occurred during a month not covered by either hanging, which had been specifically abolished a week earlier, or electrocution, which was to begin the following month. Since neither execution method was in force, Howe argued that the judge could not sentence his client to death. This proved to be so, but prosecutors took the case to the state Supreme Court, and there Howe's claim was overruled and his client subsequently executed.

This particular case caused a statewide uproar, one that established Howe and Hummel as *the* criminal lawyers in New York City. Their offices were ever after jammed with clients begging for defense and foisting money upon the shrewd lawyers. Howe and Hummel then wrote a book about crime in the big city. It was no more than a criminal's guide to successful operation and became a best-seller that made them famous in the underworld. Their clients at the time included the most notorious criminals in New York, including the infamous lady fence, Fredericka "Marm" Mandelbaum and gangster Paul Kelly, head of the notorious Five Points Gang. Howe and Hummel managed to win Not Guilty pleas for more than 70 percent of their clients, although, according to one legal expert of the time, "ninety percent of their clients were guilty." A survey showed that Howe and Hummel, in one month, were representing twenty-three out of the twenty-five persons held on a charge of murder in the New York Tombs. In 1884, seventy-three brothel operators were arrested in a police sweep in one week. All named Howe and Hummel as their attorneys.

A good deal of these Not Guilty verdicts were won through the acting talents of William Howe, who could turn a jury of hardened men into a sobbing and empathetic group within minutes. Theater producer David Belasco once watched Howe in action in court and later stated: "I could make that man into a Broadway star overnight!" Howe and Hummel turned their clients into actors too. Often as not, they would arrive with a client bound up in bandages, his face and hands covered with thick gauze. His client had recently suffered incredible burns or lacerations, Howe would claim, that caused him insufferable agony. As Howe talked, and on cue as rehearsed, the client would writhe in agony at the defense table, moaning and appearing to be at the point of collapse. On other occasions, the lawyers used the "berserk act," in which their client pretended to be insane and appeared to be a helpless idiot not responsible for his actions. The client rolled his eyes, and his tongue lolled loosely out of his mouth while his head seemed to come unhinged from his neck, flopping about from one shoulder to the other. Such impersonations drew great sympathy from juries and invariably resulted in Not Guilty verdicts.

A caricature of criminal lawyers William F. Howe with partner Abe Hummel on his knee.

The hard-living Howe died in 1902 after a final bout with liquor. Abe Hummel attempted to carry on alone, but he proved less effective than his highly dramatic partner had been. Moreover, he was caught bribing a juror in a divorce case in 1905 and was sent to prison for two years and disbarred. Hummel, upon his release, retired to England where he lived in comfort. He died in 1926 in London, where he was regarded as an expert on British law. See: **Kelly, Paul; Mandelbaum, Fredericka.**

REF.: Asbury, *The Gangs of New York; CBA;* Howe and Hummel, *In Danger, or, Life in New York, A True History of the Great City's Wiles and Temptations;* Rovere, *Howe and Hummel, Criminal Lawyers;* Scott, *The Concise Encyclopedia of Crime and Criminals;* Train, *True Stories of Crime;* (FICTION), Train, *The Confessions of Artemus Quibble.*

Howell, David, 1747-1824, U.S., jur. Served as justice of the peace for Providence, R.I., in 1779, and as justice of the common pleas court in Providence in 1780. He was a delegate to the Continental Congress in Philadelphia, Pa., from 1782-85. He also served as associate justice of the Rhode Island Supreme Court from 1786-87, and as district attorney of Rhode Island. He was nominated to the district court of Rhode Island by President James Madison in 1812. REF.: *CBA.*

Howell, Everett, prom. 1928, U.S., (wrong. convict.) rob. On Jan. 25, 1930, Everett Howell left the County Court in Golden, Ill., a free man after spending sixteen months in jail trying to clear his name.

Albertus Janssen, cashier of the Exchange State Bank of Golden was robbed of $4,305, in the early morning on Aug. 20, 1928. He and customer James Garrison were forced at gunpoint to retreat to the bank's vault. Later, the two men would testify conclusively that Howell was the man with whom they had dealt. Henry J. Gerdes, Samuel R. Woerman and Frank F. Winkle, who had sold gasoline to a man driving a car similar to the getaway car, provided descriptions of the driver. Based on these, Howell was arrested in Peoria, Ill. Earlier, police had tracked down Farmer Barnhill by piecing together scraps of paper found along the path of the get-away car.

On Sept. 20, 1928, just one month after the crime, Barnhill and Howell were indicted. They denied knowing each other, and Howell provided an alibi corroborated by disinterested witnesses. But the jury, apparently believing the witnesses from Golden over those from Farmington and Canton, returned a verdict of Guilty against Barnhill and Howell. Each was sentenced to the state penitentiary for terms of from one year to life.

Then, for the first time in a year, tides turned in favor of Howell. Before he had a chance to appeal, Barnhill made a full confession to the crime and said Howell had nothing to do with it. He instead named Gilbert Ammerman and Peter McDonald as the ones who had joined him in the robbery. They eventually confessed, pleaded guilty and accepted their punishment.

On Jan. 25, 1930, Judge Wolfe ordered a new trial. The state's attorney dropped the case, and freed Howell. He and Ammerman bore only a slight resemblance to each other, yet five people, including the principal victim, were positive that Howell was guilty. REF.: *CBA.*

Howell, Frank, prom. 1929, U.S., (wrong. convict.), rob. Circumstantial evidence and unfortunate physical likenesses implicated Frank and Norma Howell in a West Virginia filling station hold-up in 1929, and would have meant as many as fifteen years in prison for Frank Howell had it not been for a last-minute confession by the true culprits, Irene Crawford Schroeder and Walter Glenn Dague, two notorious convicts awaiting execution for murder.

Howell spent fourteen months in prison for a crime he did not commit. Surprisingly, his wife was acquitted, though she was tried on the same charge and with the same testimony.

During his trial, prosecutors made several arguments against Howell. First, they pointed out that Norma had expressed concern that police would think she and her husband were the guilty couple because they fit the physical description. C.W. Edgell, the Howells' landlord, reported that they were usually late in paying rent, but on Sept. 7, two days after the robbery, Norma Howell paid him $10. Jack Cotts, owner of the gas station, swore to the jury that Howell was the guilty man. "I couldn't be mistaken," he said.

Howell testified that on the day of the crime he had helped George Coburn move, which Coburn corroborated. That evening, Howell and his wife were at home when, at 9 p.m., their three children returned from the movies. The children corroborated the story.

The jury turned in a verdict of Guilty and Howell was sentenced to fifteen years in prison. He was saved by the confession on Jan. 5, 1931, of two murderers awaiting execution. There was a remarkable likeness between the two couples, but that did not explain the discrepancy in evidence presented at the trial. On Jan. 14, 1931, Governor Conley granted Howell a full pardon, and the state of West Virginia paid him $1,000 in compensation. REF.: *CBA.*

Howell, James, c.1594-1666, Brit., consp. Author who sided with Royalists in the Civil War. He was imprisoned for his politics from 1643-51. REF.: *CBA.*

Howell, William Thompson, 1810-70, U.S., jur. Served as prosecuting attorney of Hillsdale County, Mich., from 1840-43, as acting probate judge of Hillsdale County from 1855-54, as prosecuting attorney of Mescota County, Mich., from 1859-61, and as a member of the Michigan House of Representatives from 1861-63. He was nominated to the territorial court of Arizona by President Abraham Lincoln in 1863. REF.: *CBA*.

Howitt, Alfred William, 1830-1908, Aus., law enfor. off. Traveled to Australia in 1852, exploring the central region of the country in 1859 and studying the aborigines. He served as the police magistrate of Gippsland from 1862-89. REF.: *CBA*.

Howry, Charles Bowen, 1844-1928, U.S., jur. Served as representative to Mississippi's state legislature from 1880-84. He was U.S. district attorney of the northern district of Mississippi from 1885-89, and was assistant attorney general of the U.S. Department of Justice from 1893-97. He was nominated to the court of claims by President Grover Cleveland in 1897. REF.: *CBA*.

Hoxsey, Harry M., prom. 1950s-60s, U.S., fraud. Harry M. Hoxsey sold his family's home remedy for cancer to desperate, unsuspecting people. In 1936, he opened his first cancer "clinic," the Hoxide Institute, in Taylorsville, Ill. It quickly became a success, financially if not medically. He attracted fearful thousands, promising them effective cancer cures supposedly not yet known to the mainstream medical community. Hoxsey either paid people off or bullied them into substantiating his claims. But his enterprise was never without its challengers. The American Medical Association and the U.S. Food and Drug Administration watched Hoxsey, warning the federal government, state governments and patients that he was a fraud. An AMA analysis of Hoxsey's special cancer-fighting paste revealed that the key ingredient was arsenic. But people were slow to learn.

Hoxsey was convicted in several states of practicing medicine without a license, for which he was fined a nominal fee and told to move on. While despairing cancer patients died, influential leaders, including congressmen and fundamentalist ministers, rallied behind Hoxsey and his miracle cure. Frustrated physicians cried out their warnings but were hardly heard over the cheers.

For a while, Hoxsey was safe at his clinic in Dallas, Tex., where he was granted an honorary Doctor of Naturopathy degree, became a licensed naturopath, and avoided conviction. Hoxsey actually won two judgments in libel suits against Morris Fishbein and the *Journal of American Medicine*. A federal judge refused the government an injunction to stop the interstate distribution of Hoxsey's tonics.

The FDA refused to give up its battle against Hoxsey. In 1950, the government tried to stop Hoxsey from shipping his medicines across state lines. To this end, the FDA testified that all of Hoxsey's claimed cures fell into one of three categories: either the patients had never had cancer, or they had been cured of cancer by traditional surgical or radiation treatment before seeing Hoxsey, or they had had cancer and either still had it or had died. Through an appeal, the government finally won an injunction against Hoxsey, but rather than forbid his shipments, it merely required that the medicine carry labels describing the controversy over its use.

The FDA persevered in its struggle for more rigid restraints on Hoxsey, while he allied with other foes of the FDA and AMA and accused these groups of conspiring to stifle medical freedom. In April 1956, the FDA issued a warning calling Hoxsey's methods "worthless" and "imminently dangerous to rely on...in neglect of competent and rational treatment." They prepared a "Public Beware!" poster and displayed it in 46,000 post offices. In the end, the government sought an injunction to stop Hoxsey's Portage, Penn., clinic from operating in interstate commerce, effectively causing the collapse of that operation. The federal government does not have the power to stop a state clinic from treating cancer patients, but in response to the federal injunctions and the FDA campaign, a Texas court in 1957 revoked the licenses of Hoxsey's doctors and granted a permanent injunction to prevent his practice

of medicine in Texas. By 1960, Hoxsey's influence was virtually wiped out.

Although Hoxsey fought hard to hide the incriminating fact, his father, the source of the wonder cure, had himself died of cancer in 1919. Hoxsey's mother died of cancer two years later. REF.: *CBA; Young, The Medical Messiahs*.

Hoyos, Carlos Mauro, c.1939-1988, Col., atty. gen., assass. Carlos Mauro Hoyos, forty-nine, Colombia's attorney general, was assassinated on Monday, Feb. 1, 1988, on his way to work, where he struggled bitterly against a growing drug trafficking problem in his country.

It was not difficult for assassins to track Hoyos. Each Friday, the attorney general went for the weekend to Medellin, his hometown and home of the world's biggest cocaine distribution ring, the Medellin cartel. Hoyos was on his way to the airport with his driver and bodyguard on Monday morning when two cars forced his Mercedes off the road. Armed gunmen opened fire, killing the driver and the bodyguard instantly and seriously wounding Hoyos. The Colombian executive was whisked away, and hours later his body was found fourteen miles outside Medellin, where an unidentified caller had said it would be. The caller, who said he was speaking for "The Extraditables," said Hoyos was guilty of betraying the country and claimed "the war will continue."

Hoyos had become a target of drug traffickers involved in the Medellin cartel when he decided to investigate the mysterious release from prison of cartel kingpin Jorge Luis Ochoa Vásquez. At the time of Hoyos' assassination, the Colombian syndicate, which cropped up in the late 1970s, had come to supply four-fifths of the cocaine sold in the U.S. Medellin developed into a trading site for the drug world, where orders would be placed and filled through a network of suppliers in Colombia, Bolivia, and Peru.

Hoyos' murder forced Colombian president Virgilio Barco into tougher action against drug dealers. Following the brutal slayings, Barco announced a "national crusade" against terrorism and organized crime. He issued executive orders broadening the legal definition of terrorism and stiffening the penalties for engaging in it, and established 5,000 new judicial posts to handle the anticipated influx of new cases. REF.: *CBA*.

Hoyt, George, See: **Earp, Wyatt**.

Hoyt, John Philo, 1841-1926, U.S., jur. Served as prosecuting attorney of Tuscola, Mich., from 1868-72, as representative in Michigan's House of Representatives from 1873-76, and as justice of the Washington Supreme Court from 1889-97. He taught at the University of Washington in Seattle from 1902-07 as a professor of law. He was nominated to the territorial court of Washington by President Rutherford B. Hayes in 1879. REF.: *CBA*.

Hsiang Yü, 233-202 B.C., China, rebel.-suic. Headed the Ch'u revolt against the Ch'in dynasty. His forces took over the capital and murdered the emperor in 206. He tried to establish himself as the king over feudal kingdoms, but he lost to Liu Pang and committed suicide. REF.: *CBA*.

Hsiao Yen (Wu Ti), 464-549, China, emp., rebel.-assass. Established himself emperor of the Liang dynasty in 502 after overthrowing the Southern Chi'i dynasty. His rule was the longest of all the southern rulers and he was instrumental in instituting Buddhism in southern China. In 549 he was caught by a barbarian general and was starved to death in a monastery. REF.: *CBA*.

Hsiu-Cheng, Li, See: **Li Hsiu-Cheng**.

Hsüan-chi Yü, prom. 800, China, mur. Hsüan-chi Yü was a talented young woman who became a prostitute in ninth-century China. Although prostitution was not illegal, she broke the law by not registering her business with the government. Still, it was not until the once-lovely and popular Hsüan-chi grew old and fell out of favor that she was convicted, probably falsely, of beating to death a maidservant in the brothel she ran. She was executed. REF.: *Bullough, An Illustrated History of Prostitution; CBA*.

Hsü Ta, 1329-83, China, rebel. General who joined with Hung-wu rebels in 1353. In 1368 he assisted in establishing the Ming dynasty after heading a revolt against the Mongol dynasty and taking control of Peking. REF.: *CBA.*

Huáscar, Prince, c.1495-1533, Peru, assass. Incan prince conquered in 1532 and assassinated by Atahualpa, his half-brother. REF.: *CBA.*

Hubbard, C.R. (AKA: **J.J. McDonald, C.H. Greer**), prom. 1921, U.S., theft. From 1918 until late summer 1921, C.R. Hubbard spent his days charming people out of their precious jewels. By the time he was arrested, he estimated his take at over $1 million worth in diamonds from dupes in Illinois, Utah, Colorado, Nebraska, Nevada, and California. Hubbard was detained from 1921 to 1927, first in the Nevada State Prison and, upon his parole, in the Salt Lake penitentiary in Utah.

Hubbard posed as a workman to get into wealthy people's homes. Victims of his robberies, never suspecting the kindly electrician/plumber, described the offender variously as a man over six feet tall, a dwarf, a tow-headed or red-headed skinny person, or a massive black man. Meanwhile, people were innocently and ignorantly letting Hubbard in to fix pipes that weren't broken.

Police finally caught up with Hubbard in Reno, Nev., where he had recently robbed five mansions, passing himself off as an electrician from the Truckee River Light and Power Company. One detective's call to that enterprise revealed that no electrician had been sent out, and regardless of how unwilling people were to believe that that self-effacing, fine young serviceman was the culprit, the evidence was there. Reno detectives learned that a man fitting Hubbard's description was staying at the Riverside Hotel, and was scheduled to meet a diamond customer that night coming off the Southern Pacific. Police were there to meet Hubbard and arrest him.

On Aug. 23, 1921, Hubbard was sentenced to two to fourteen years in the Nevada prison. On Apr. 6, 1923, he was paroled. Officers from Utah met him at the gate, returning him to the Salt Lake penitentiary for a four-year term for parole violations. On June 15, 1927, Hubbard was finally freed. A week later, reports came from Burlingame, Calif., that a man posing as an inspector for a telephone company had looted several homes. REF.: *CBA.*

Hubbard, Fred D., prom. 1969-71, U.S., embez. Chicago politician Fred D. Hubbard was elected to the City Council as an independent black reformer in 1969, and was an outspoken critic of the Daley machine. Besides serving as alderman of the Second Ward, Hubbard held a $25,000-a-year job as the head of the Chicago Plan, a federal program to search out jobs in construction for Chicago minorities. Hubbard disappeared in May 1971, and $110,000 from the federal program vanished with him. The FBI searched for fifteen months, and finally found Hubbard in a poker parlor in Gardena, Calif., penniless after having gambled away everything. Hubbard was convicted and sentenced to two years in jail for embezzlement. While in jail, he wrote a thick manuscript detailing, according to him, how a politician had robbed organized crime to help the poor. Reporters who walked him to the bus station listened as he explained, "I don't think anyone will buy it," then gave him the $9.65 for a bus ticket back to Chicago. As of this writing, Hubbard works as a cab driver in Chicago.

REF.: *CBA;* Nash, *Among the Missing.*

Huber, Charles, prom. 1894, U.S., rob. In 1894, managers of Siegel, Cooper & Co. in Chicago, the largest department store in the world, noticed that someone had been stealing birds from them. A boy alerted a store clerk after seeing a man reach in a cage and pull out a mockingbird. When Detective Clifton R. Wooldridge came on the scene, Charles Huber had both hands in his pockets. Wooldridge asked him what he was hiding, and as Huber replied, "Nothing," the bird began singing, *Going to Leave My Happy Home.* Huber confessed to stealing other birds and selling them. He was sent to the House of Correction.

REF.: *CBA;* Wooldridge, *Hands Up.*

Huber, Max (Hans), 1874-1960, Switz., jur. Taught in Zürich

from 1902-21. He served as judge of the Permanent Court of International Justice from 1921-30, and as its president from 1925-28. REF.: *CBA.*

Huber, Seba Cormany, 1871-1944, U.S., jur. Served as prosecuting attorney of Tama County, Iowa, and as U.S. attorney of Hawaii from 1916-22. He was nominated to the district court of Hawaii territory by President Franklin D. Roosevelt in 1934. REF.: *CBA.*

Huberty, James Oliver, c.1943-83, U.S., mur. On July 18, 1984, James Oliver Huberty of San Diego, Calif., told his wife he was "going hunting for humans." Despondent over a recent job loss, the 41-year-old Huberty took a rifle, shotgun, pistol and hundreds of rounds of ammunition to a local McDonald's restaurant and started shooting. By the time the SWAT team arrived and shot Hubert, twenty-one people, mostly children, lay dead beside him. Nineteen others were wounded in California's largest single mass shooting to date.

REF.: *CBA;* Fox, *Mass Murder.*

Hubmaier, Balthasar, 1485-1528, Aust., her. German who preached at Regensburg, located in western Germany, in 1516. In 1521 he traveled to Switzerland and became head of the Anabaptists. He was arrested in Zürich in 1525 and forced to disavow his faith. Later he began preaching the Anabaptist faith again and was burned at the stake in Vienna. REF.: *CBA.*

Hudson, Frederick (AKA: **Mr. Nodder**), prom. 1937, Brit., mur. In 1935, Mr. and Mrs. Tinsley took Frederick Hudson into their Newark, England, home to perform odd jobs around the house. Two years later, Hudson kidnapped and strangled the couple's 10-year-old daughter Mona.

Mona knew Hudson only as "Uncle Fred" for the three weeks that he worked for the Tinsleys. He then abruptly went to Retford, where he introduced himself around as Mr. Nodder. Two years later, 10-year-old Mona disappeared. She was last seen on Jan. 5, 1937, when she left school at 4 p.m. Nodder was seen in the vicinity of the school. Later, a bus driver noticed Nodder and the girl on his bus and saw them get off at Retford. Later that day, a woman saw the child standing at the back door of Nodder's cottage. When Mona failed to return home or to school the next day, Nodder was the first person police wanted to see. He claimed that he met Mona that day and at her request put her on the bus at Retford with instructions to visit a friend in Sheffield. Mona was never seen alive again. Nodder was found Guilty of "decoying" and "enticing" the child away by fraud. But, as it turned out, Nodder got off easy with a sentence of seven years' penal servitude. Two months later, the girl's body was found in the River Idle, near Bawtry, Nottinghamshire, thirty miles from her home.

At his murder trial, Nodder failed miserably in his cross examination, leaving no doubt in the jury's mind that he had murdered the girl. He was hanged.

REF.: Bowker, *Behind the Bar; CBA.*

Hudson, Jeffery, 1619-82, Brit., consp. Dwarf who was captured twice by pirates. In 1649 he was put in prison because he was thought to have been involved with the Popish plot. REF.: *CBA.*

Hudson, Manley Ottmer, b.1886, U.S., jur. Taught international law at Harvard in 1923 and from 1927-38 was director of research in international law at Harvard Law School. In 1919, he attended the Paris Peace Conference, and served as a member of the legal section of the Secretariat of the League of Nations from 1919-23. He served as a judge of the Permanent Court of International Justice in 1936. REF.: *CBA.*

Hudson Dusters, N.Y., 1890s-1910s, U.S., org. crime. Organized in the late 1890s by such fierce New York gangsters as Circular Jack, Kid Yorke, and Goo Goo Knox, the Hudson Dusters took their name from their first headquarters, a second-floor two-room apartment on Hudson Street. There the prized possession of the gang was a battered piano upon which Knox crudely banged out popular songs of the day. Knox was a Gopher gang veteran but he had fled the provinces of the Gophers after unsuccessfully trying to unseat Marty Brennan and others in a power play to control the gang. In an uncustomary move, the Gophers took no revenge on Knox and, in fact, became allies of the Hudson Dusters throughout the life of both gangs.

The territory controlled by the Hudson Dusters encompassed the West Side of Manhattan below Thirteenth Street and east to Broadway, their border at this point crowded the territory controlled by the empire-building Paul Kelly. The Dusters began small, but after winning pitched battles with the Boodle Gang and the Potashes, ineffective Gay Nineties gangs, the Dusters were soon masters of their province, although they were constantly besieged by small but fierce gangs, the Fashion Plates, the Pearl Buttons, and most lethal of the lot, the Marginals. The battles fought between these gangs and the Dusters were always over the lucrative Hudson River dock area which was rich in loot and plunder. But the Dusters invariably won by sheer numbers since they could muster at least 200 gangsters for these showdowns and could count on a few more hundred thugs aiding them from the Gophers camp, as long as the Dusters paid the Gophers a tribute of one fourth of all the loot taken monthly from the barges and ships.

As the Dusters grew in size and importance, members such as "Red" Farrell, Mike Costello, "Rubber" Shaw, Rickey Harrison, and "Honey" Stewart became specialists at rigging elections through repeater votes and intimidation at the polls, thus earning the political protection of their governmental sponsors. The Hudson Duster ranks had many colorful characters, not the least of whom was an enterprising Fagin called Ding Dong. This thug took great care to train the young boys of the district in crime and he rewarded them with a considerable share of the stolen goods. Ding Dong's technique was simple. He stood on a corner with a half-dozen of his young apprentice thieves, and when spotting a passing express wagon, gave a loud whistle. The boys jumped on board the moving wagon while Ding Dong ran behind it. The boys then began to toss packages from the wagon to the panting thug racing behind them with open arms. When police arrived, the boys harassed officers and led them away from the fleeing Ding Dong.

Newsmen frequenting the popular pubs of Greenwich Village constantly came in contact with the Dusters who controlled the territory and as a result, the Hudson Dusters received more publicity than any other gang of the period. Journalists did not write about the gang's proclivity for drugs, however. Most of the leaders of the Dusters were cocaine addicts and the rank and file members also used drugs. Following their cocaine parties, the Dusters prowled the boundaries of their domain, and, in this drugged state, they were lethal, to be avoided at all costs by rival gangs.

Police gave the Dusters a wide berth, although the Strong Armed Squad occasionally raided the Dusters headquarters and threw the furniture, especially Knox's beaten up piano, into the street, more as a way to humiliate the gangsters than to impede their rackets. The Dusters, to keep one step away from the police, regularly moved their headquarters. Their last official residence was on Bethune Street. The Dusters taxed goods of all merchants in their area and few complained to authorities. Woe to the merchant who refused a request for "supplies." One such was a saloon keeper who failed to deliver a half dozen kegs of beer for a Dusters' party. About forty Dusters marched into the saloon the next day and demolished the place, smashing the mirrors, glasses, and liquor bottles.

The saloon keeper had a dear friend in policeman Dennis Sullivan of the Charles Street Station. He was a towering, broad-shouldered patrolman who openly vowed that he would smash the Hudson Dusters and he went looking for gang leaders. Sullivan alone cornered Red Farrell and ten of his men in a pool hall and tied them together with a rope and dragged them to the station on vagrancy charges. So incensed were the Dusters that they planned to equally humiliate Sullivan. The Dusters coerced a merchant into calling Sullivan to make a complaint against a Duster gangster. When Sullivan came on the run, twenty thugs

jumped on him, knocked him down, and beat him into unconsciousness, stripping him of his uniform. To disgrace the officer, the gangsters ripped away his shield and threw it down a sewer. They pocketed his gun and broke his nightstick, leaving it in pieces on sidewalk. Before they left the bloodied Sullivan, five thugs rolled him over and jumped on his back, breaking his ribs and then kicked him repeatedly in the face so that his features were hideously scarred permanently.

Sullivan's life was narrowly saved by a police flying squad arriving some minutes later. The officer was hurried to a hospital where he was slowly nursed back to health. Sullivan, hospitalized for a month, was made painfully aware of his humiliation by none other than "One-Lung Curran", one of the leaders of the Gophers gang. The Gophers greatly appreciated the Dusters' mistreatment and abuse of officer Sullivan. Gopher leader Curran himself, then a patient in the tuberculosis ward of Bellevue Hospital (where he would later die when his only good lung gave out), was inspired to write a bit of doggerel to commemorate the attack. Curran, who was thought of as the poet of gangsterdom, wrote the following:

> Says Dinny, "Here's me only chance
>   To gain meself a name;
> I'll clean up the Hudson Dusters,
>   And reach the hall of fame."
> He lost his stick and cannon,
>   And his shield they took away,
> It was then that he remembered
>   Every dog has got his day.

The Dusters reveled in Curran's sneering ditty and had the work (along with several other verses) printed on thousands of sheets. The copies were distributed to every barber shop and saloon in their territory and copies were sent to the Charles Street Station and were scattered throughout the hospital where Sullivan was recuperating. In the streets, hordes of novice hoodlums led by Ding Dong, paraded up and down the byways chanting the verse to their own made-up song. But it was Sullivan who lived to have the last laugh on this thug fraternity that disintegrated shortly before WWI. By then, most of its leaders died of drug overdoses or had been sent to Sing Sing. At that time Tanner Smith, leader of the Marginals, which had grown considerably over the years, eliminated the Hudson Dusters from the streets of their own territory. After subduing the Pearl Buttons, Smith's Marginals dominated the area for the next decade. See: **Gophers; Kelly, Paul.**

REF.: Asbury, *The Gangs of New York; CBA;* Fried, *The Rise and Fall of the Jewish Gangster in America;* Haskins, *Street Gangs Yesterday and Today;* Lait and Mortimer, *Chicago: Confidential;* Levine, *Anatomy of a Gangster;* Lewis, *The Apaches of New York;* Peterson, *The Mob;* Reppetto, *The Blue Parade;* Servadio, *Mafioso;* Thompson and Raymond, *Gang Rule in New York;* Thrasher, *The Gang.*

Hudspeth, Harry Lee, 1935-   , U.S., jur. Served as trial attorney for U.S. Department of Justice in Washington, D.C., from 1959-62, as assistant U.S. attorney in San Antonio, Texas from 1962-65, and in El Paso, Texas from 1965-69. He was the U.S. magistrate of the district of Texas from 1977-79, and was nominated to the western district court of Texas by President Jimmy Carter in 1979. REF.: *CBA.*

Huebler, Anton, 1837-1925, U.S., law enfor. off. Anton Huebler, twenty-two, left his native Ruchheim in Bavaria and served the U.S. as captain of volunteers during the Civil War. Later, he became a loyal member of the police force in St. Louis, Mo. Holding the office of chief of police from May 4, 1886, to May 20, 1890, Huebler was first chief to have a thirty-year career unbroken by exits and demotions. He received a disability retirement in 1894, at age fifty-seven, and died on Mar. 26, 1925, at eighty-eight. REF.: *CBA.*

Hufnagel, Thomas E., 1903-1979, U.S., suic.-mur. Thomas E. Hufnagel, the 76-year-old custodian of a four-unit house in San

Francisco, was fussy about its appearance. He had warned tenant Joel Blackman, a young lawyer from Madison, Wis., not to park his car on the sidewalk in front of the house, but Blackman ignored the elderly man. Hufnagel's wife Isabel also ignored Hufnagel when he began drinking heavily and told her he would kill Blackman, her, and himself.

On Friday, Jan. 19, 1979, Hufnagel shot Blackman and his 28-year-old companion, Mimi Rosenblatt, with a .38-caliber revolver and a 12-gauge shotgun. The two were seriously injured in what would turn into Hufnagel's six-and-a-half-hour siege against his tenants. Another tenant, Catherine Henry, forty-five, was shot as she stood in the hallway and Mark Johnson, who left his twenty-fourth birthday party to help Blackman, was shot and killed. Blackman and the two women were rushed to San Francisco General Hospital.

Hufnagel went on to exchange fire with police officers before barricading himself in his apartment. After waiting five hours and emptying six tear gas canisters, police entered the apartment to find that Hufnagel had killed himself. Hufnagel's wife escaped unharmed. REF.: *CBA*.

Hufstedler, Shirley Ann Mount, 1925- , U.S., jur. Served as special legal consultant to California between 1960-61, as judge of Los Angeles County Superior Court from 1961-66, and as justice of California Court of Appeals from 1966-68. She was nominated to the ninth circuit court by President Lyndon B. Johnson in 1968. Also honored as Los Angeles *Times* Woman of the Year in 1968. REF.: *CBA*.

Hughes, Charles Evans, 1862-1948, U.S., jur. Associate Justice and Chief Justice of U.S. Supreme Court. He served as governor of New York from 1907-10, ran for president in 1916, but lost to Wilson. From 1921-30 he served as the U.S. secretary of state and also served as a member of the Hague Tribunal. He was a judge on the Permanent Court of International Justice from 1928-30. In 1910, he was nominated as associate justice of U.S. Supreme Court by President William H. Taft, serving from 1910-16. In 1930, he was nominated by President Herbert Hoover to the U.S. Supreme Court, serving as chief justice from 1930-41. He at first supported Roosevelt's New Deal legislation. However, from 1935-36, the Court reversed its policy toward the legislation, as in 1935, in *Schechter Poultry Corp. v. United States*.

REF.: *CBA;* Hendel, *Charles Evans Hughes and the Supreme Court;* Pusey, *Charles Evans Hughes;* Reppetto, *The Blue Parade.*

Hughes, Daniel, 1698-1714, Brit., rob. When executed for robbery with his confederate Kit Moore, Daniel Hughes was only sixteen. Born in Gravesend, Kent County, in 1698, Hughes was raised to go to sea. Instead, he took to thieving. With his cohort Moore, Hughes drank, gambled, and committed more than fifty robberies in London and Westminster and the Borough of Southwark. The crime for which they were hanged, however, was the night burglary of the house of Thomas Wright, in which they made off with a pair of silver candlesticks, eight teaspoons, a lamp, and a teapot.

While riding in the cart toward Tyburn to be executed, Hughes and Moore pulled off their shoes and threw them into the crowd. "Our parents often said we should die on a fish-day with our shoes on," they said. "But though the former part of their prediction is true, yet will we make them all liars in the latter part of it." They were hanged at Tyburn on Mar. 10, 1714.

REF.: *CBA;* Smith, *Highwaymen.*

Hughes, Hector, b.1887, Brit., lawyer. Helped found Irish Socialist party in 1918, and began serving as a member of Parliament in 1945. He was the defense counsel for Reginald Sidney Buckfield and George Silverosa. REF.: *CBA*.

Hughes, Howard, See: **Irving, Clifford.**

Hughes, John Reynolds (AKA: Border Boss), 1857-1946, U.S., west. lawman. John Hughes was born in Illinois, but moved to Texas at age fourteen. A year later he was shot in the right arm during a battle with Choctaw Indians. Hughes ranched until 1886, when he sold out, unable to fight the cattle rustlers. He had recently killed four rustlers and wounded another two after trailing

them for a week through northwestern Texas. In July 1887, Hughes and Texas Ranger Ira Aten trailed Judd Roberts, an escaped murderer, to the Texas Panhandle. Six shots killed Roberts as he tried to escape the lawmen.

Hughes became a Texas Ranger the following month, and by 1889, attained the rank of corporal and had made a reputation for his border patrol along the Rio Grande. Later that year, Hughes was doing undercover work in a Shafter, Texas, silver mine after some of the ore was reported missing. Hughes discovered that a crooked foreman placed the silver on burro trains bound for the Mexican border. Setting a trap at the mine entrance with rangers Lon Oden and Ernest St. Leon, Hughes fought an hour-long gun battle. The Rangers finally killed three of the thieves and apprehended and arrested the

Texas Ranger John R. Hughes.

foreman. On Christmas Day, near Vance, Texas, Hughes and a ranger posse killed Will and Alvin Odle, two brothers who were violently resisting arrest for cattle rustling.

In 1893, while arresting Desidario Duran in the San Antonio Colony, the rangers killed Florencio Carrasco, who was trying to free his friend. In March 1896, Hughes and his rangers arrested notorious bandit Miguel de la Torre when they surprised him on a street in Bajitas, Texas, and tied him on an extra horse. Later that year, on Sept. 28, Hughes and his men trailed three cattle rustlers to Nogalitos Pass. The fugitives fired at the posse, and during the ensuing gunfight the lawmen killed two of them, brothers Art and Jubel Friar, while Ease Bixler, the third man, escaped. Hughes retired from the Rangers in 1915, and committed suicide in 1946 at age eighty-nine.

REF.: Bartholomew, *The Biographical Album of Western Gunfighters; CBA;* Hughes, *The Killing of Bass Outlaw;* Martin, *Border Boss;* O'Neal, *Encyclopedia of Western Gunfighters;* Webb, *Texas Rangers.*

Hughes, John W., 1833-66, U.S., mur. On Aug. 9, 1865, in Bedford, Ohio, 17-year-old Tamzen Parsons was shot and killed by her lover, 32-year-old John W. Hughes. They were married the previous December in Pittsburgh, but Hughes was found to be already married and was imprisoned for bigamy. In November 1865, Hughes was convicted of the murder of Tamzen Parsons and sentenced to death. In jail, he attempted suicide by swallowing morphine, but failed. He lived until his hanging on Feb. 9, 1866.

REF.: *CBA; The Life and Trial of Dr. John Hughes, for the Murder of Miss Tamzen Parsons; With a Sketch of His Life, As Related By Himself.*

Hughes, Mrs., and **Peach, Phillip,** and **Wellings, Edward,** and **Willing, Maud,** prom. 1905, Brit., forg. British check forgers Mrs. Hughes, Phillip Peach, Edward Wellings and Maud Willing schemed in 1905 to obtain signatures of well-to-do persons so that they could be copied on dummy checks, but did not pull in much money. When one was caught, all were essentially caught. As a result of Wellings' big mouth and false friendship, all four forgers ended up owing years of penal servitude.

Hughes, a clergyman's widow, made her way by writing letters begging for money. When she received a check, she could use the signature she procured to forge an even bigger check.

Hughes worked with Wellings, Willing, and as would be known later, Peach. Hughes provided Wellings and Willing with a bishop's check for £150, which they forged with his signature.

Authorities easily apprehended the three. Wellings and Willing pleaded guilty and received sentences of seven years of penal servitude and five years of penal servitude, respectively. Hughes, who pleaded not guilty, was given three years.

Peach was soon tracked down when an anonymous letter addressed to New Scotland Yard arrived describing the forging business. Wellings ascertained that his past accomplice, Peach, had written the letter and told authorities of Peach's role in his forgeries. Peach was brought in for passing a £900 check forged with Colonel Gascoigne's name. Police would have caught it sooner if the Colonel hadn't died immediately after the bank note passed. Peach sentenced to seven years' penal servitude. REF.: *CBA*.

Hughes, Richard, 1677-1709, Brit., rob. The son of a gentleman farmer born in Bettus, Denbigshire, in North Wales, Richard Hughes tried his hand at thievery on his first trip into London. He stole a pair of fireplace tongs at Pershore in Worchestershire, was caught, and sent to Worcester Jail. Found Guilty of only petty larceny, however, Hughes was fined ten pence and set free.

In keeping with this inauspicious beginning, Hughes was never a successful criminal. His general ineptitude especially showed itself at Billingsgate when he encountered the actor and comedian Joe Haynes at an inn. Having wrapped piles of dust into neat parcels, Haynes and a companion were explaining that the dust was a miraculous medicinal powder that not only healed burns but could prevent them. The actor demonstrated by rubbing powder onto his friend's leg. The man then plunged his leg into a pot of boiling water and lifted it out unscathed. Duped by the fact that the man's leg was made of wood, the patrons at the inn, Hughes included, bought out the powder at 12 pence a package. Soon after, on a bet, Hughes demonstrated the powder and almost lost his leg. It was nine months before he was able to walk again.

Apprehended for breaking into the home of George Clark at Twickenham, Hughes was sent to Newgate, and condemned to die. En route to his execution, Hughes' wife, who had been following the cart her husband was riding in, came over to Hughes and whispered in his ear: "Who must find the rope that's to hang you, we or the sheriff?" When her husband said it was the sheriff's responsibility, she sighed and said she had already spent two pence to buy one. "Well, well, perhaps it mayn't be lost, for it may serve a second husband," her husband replied. Hughes was hanged at Tyburn on June 24, 1709, at thirty years of age.
REF.: *CBA*; Smith, *Highwaymen*.

Hughes, Susan Piasecny, prom. 1977, and **Piasecny, Henry**, d.1977, U.S., mur. The Piasecny family of Manchester, N.H., had a troubled history of violence and emotional problems, culminating in the murders of two family members. Hank Piasecny returned from WWII to open a small grocery store in Manchester. Fifteen years later, with an attractive wife and two children, he was proprietor of a thriving sporting goods store. But Hank drank a great deal and was ferociously jealous. His wife Doris, a Manchester secretary, pushed him to buy material possessions. Police were called repeatedly to quell threats of domestic violence, until 1963, when Doris Piasecny was granted a divorce.

In December 1963, Doris and John Betley, a Manchester architect, were alone in her house following a Christmas party, when Hank Piasecny emerged from a hiding place and stabbed both of them to death with a kitchen knife. Hank was found drunk a short time later at his store after having smashed his truck on a highway guardrail. During his arraignment, Hank was examined by a Boston psychiatrist who determined him to be legally insane. The state committed him to the New Hampshire hospital at Concord. Two years later, Piasecny's lawyer, claiming Hank was no longer a threat to himself or others, petitioned for his release. On Aug. 6, 1966, Piasecny was released and went to work in a Manchester boat store. But as he sought to return to a peaceful existence, his relationship with his daughter Susan deteriorated.

Susan Piasecny was a talented and intelligent girl who had recurring emotional problems before and after her mother's brutal murder. At age fourteen, she falsely claimed to have been abducted while returning from a babysitting job. Two years later, she was hospitalized, temporarily unable to speak. After her mother's death she spent several weeks in a Massachusetts mental hospital. She finished college, married, and in 1967, entered medical school at the University of Vermont. Shortly afterward,

her marriage broke up, and one day she was found unconscious on the side of a road, having been beaten or tossed from a car. She claimed that her former husband had ordered her beating, but police were suspicious, given her emotional past. In 1970, she entered the same New Hampshire hospital where her father had been incarcerated, and remained there for three years. After her release, she married a fellow patient, Edward Hughes, but the union ended quickly when Hughes slit his throat with a razor blade and died in the presence of his wife. Susan began working various jobs in nursing homes and had petty legal problems from passing bad checks. Finally she moved in with her father.

In June 1977, Hank and Susan had a violent argument and Hank said he never wanted to see her again. In late August, Susan pleaded no contest to two charges of forgery. The following week she phoned police asking them to check up on her father because he had sounded so distraught. They found him dead, half his head blown off, from an apparent shotgun blast. It seemed to be suicide. However, his daughter suspected murder because the body was found ten feet from the pool of blood, and an autopsy revealed the presence of a second bullet, a .22-caliber slug, in Hank's chest. A month later, Susan confessed to the murder, saying she had shot him in the chest with the handgun stolen from a cousin, and then in the head with his own shotgun. Susan Hughes became the second family member to be found Not Guilty by reason of insanity and was again sent to the New Hampshire Hospital "for life until or unless earlier discharged, released or transferred by due process of the law." .
REF.: *CBA*; Trillin, *Killings*.

Hughes, William Morris, 1864-1952, Aus., atty. gen. Born in Wales and emigrated to Australia in 1884. He was a member of the New South Wales legislature from 1894-1901, and of the federal Parliament from 1901-52. He served as attorney general from 1908-09, 1910-13, 1914-21, and from 1939-41, and was Australia's prime minister from 1915-23. REF.: *CBA*.

Hugon, Daniel, c.1936- , Fr., mur. The trial of Daniel Hugon, later found Guilty of murdering an elderly French prostitute in 1965, represented one of the earliest cases where a person's abnormal genetic makeup was considered in determining a verdict.

Hugon, described as tall, myopic, moon-faced, and balding, possessed a chromosome structure of XYY, instead of the normal male XY. Court physician Lejeune suggested this may have accounted for diminished responsibility on the part of the accused, but did not directly cause the murder. Hugon was sentenced to seven years in prison. REF.: *CBA*.

Hugues, Clovis, 1851-1907, Fr., consp. Politician who helped in Marseilles communist efforts in 1871 and was put in prison from 1871-75. REF.: *CBA*.

Hugues, Theobald Charles Laure, See: **de Praslin, Duke**.

Huie, J. Robert, and **Kermit C. Edwards**, and **John Ike Griffith**, and **Bob Moore, Jr.**, and **Frank O. Whitten, Jr.**, prom. 1961-70, U.S., fraud. Beginning in 1945 Alabama quickly gained a reputation as a divorce mill. A provision in the state code allowed for quick divorces without requiring applicants to reside in Alabama, so long as the court gained jurisdiction over both parties. The process was so fast that nonresidents could apply through an Alabama lawyer and receive a divorce the same day. Then on Oct. 31, 1961, Alabama's Supreme Court decreed that lawyers who knowingly represented a couple in divorce proceedings where one or both were nonresidents would be disbarred.

Lawyers Robert J. Huie, Kermit C. Edwards, and John Ike Griffith, whose practices rested exclusively in out-of-state divorces, continued business as usual. Huie and Edwards enlisted the help of Judge Bob Moore, Jr., while Griffith partnered with Judge Frank O. Whitten, Jr.. The group of five made more than $2.5 million through some 5,000 very questionable divorces. While the divorce papers the attorneys sent to the couples via the U.S. Postal Service were complete with Moore's or Whitten's signature, court seal, and seal of the Register in Chancery, they were, according to federal judges, "as worthless as a blank sheet of paper" as they were never seen by a judge or officially filed.

In March 1967, Huie was disbarred but Edwards simply began signing all the divorce documents and the practice continued without hindrance. Edwards was later disbarred but allowed to practice general law after he agreed never to represent divorce cases. Griffith was disbarred and found Guilty of practicing law without a license in 1970. Judge Moore was charged with granting nonresident divorces in 1964, but it was decided the rules made by the bar association for the conduct of lawyers did not apply to judges. Regardless of the charges brought against them, all continued their lucrative divorce racket.

Finally, through the combined efforts of U.S. postal inspectors and the American Bar Association, the five accomplices' offices were raided and they were brought to justice. The result of two jury trials—one for the Huie-Edwards-Moore team, the other for Griffith-Whitten—found all five men Guilty. Sentences consisted of a minimum of three years in prison and fines of $10,000 each. REF.: *CBA; Kahn, Fraud.*

Hulen, Rubey Mosley, 1894-1956, U.S., jur. Served as prosecuting attorney of Boone County, Mo., from 1920-24. She was nominated to the eastern district court of Missouri by President Franklin D. Roosevelt in 1943. REF.: *CBA.*

Hull, Fred, prom. 1935, U.S., mur. When a man convicted of second-degree murder appealed his case, he was convicted of first-degree murder and sentenced to die in the electric chair.

On an anonymous phone tip, police raided a garage and found the body of Samuel Drukman stuffed in a canvas bag in the trunk of a car. Fred Hull and Meyer and Harry Luckman were in the garage as well--their hands covered with blood. Drukman was the brother-in-law of Meyer Luckman, Harry was Meyer's nephew, and Hull, an ex-convict employee.

Initially, the grand jury failed to indict the three for murder but, amidst charges of bribes, corruption, and racketeering, a special investigation was ordered by New York governor Herbert Lehman, that brought the murderers to trial. On Feb. 20, 1936, the three were convicted of second-degree murder and sentenced to twenty years to life in prison. Because Hull's lawyer, Joseph A. Solorei, was not present for the first day of the trial, Hull decided to appeal, hoping to be acquitted. However, this gamble did not pay off as a jury convicted Hull of first-degree murder in August 1937 and sentenced him to die by electrocution. REF.: *CBA.*

Hull, George, 1821-1902, U.S., hoax. In an attempt to prove that giants once roamed the earth, cigar salesman George Hull commissioned an artist to sculpt a fake one for him. In the Chicago workshop of Edward Burghardt the twelve-foot, four-inch tall "Cardiff Giant" was born.

George Hull conceived of the idea while visiting his sister in Ackerly, Iowa, in 1866. An atheist, Hull spent much of his time arguing evolution to religious skeptics while experimenting with gasses and stone to produce gold. He went to great lengths to defend his point of view against those who sought to discredit him. In Ackerly one day he engaged the local minister—Reverend Turk—in a furious debate over the existence of a race of giants. Hull argued that such creatures had flourished, and to prove his point he solicited the aid of a friend, H.B. Martin, to "create" the monster.

Two years later Hull sunk $2,600 toward the purchase of a seven-ton block of gypsum. The slab was crated to Chicago where the artist Burghardt fashioned a figure in the likeness of Hull. To give the image the appearance of life Hull pounded the statue with a board of darning needles. When he was finished the giant had its own flesh pores. After dousing the statue in sulfuric acid, Hull's creation was shipped off to Cardiff, N.Y., where it was buried on the farm of William C. Newell, a relative. There it moldered in the ground for twenty years until workmen discovered it on Oct. 16, 1889.

The "Cardiff Giant," as it was dubbed in the press, astounded the world. It was stood up and placed on display in Syracuse, N.Y., where eager crowds paid a nominal admission fee for the privilege of viewing the curiosity of the century. O.C. Marsh, a

paleontologist at Yale University, examined the statue and declared it to be "of very recent origin and a decided humbug." And so ended Hull's colossal hoax, though his creation lived on. P.T. Barnum tried to buy the giant (which Hull had already sold for $30,000), but was rebuffed. It toured about the country, continuing to attract and delight crowds until it was purchased by the Farmer's Market in Cooperstown, N.Y., in 1948 where the object remains on permanent display.

REF.: *CBA;* MacDougall, *Hoaxes;* Nash, *Zanies;* Wade, *Great Hoaxes and Famous Imposters.*

Hull, William, 1753-1825, U.S., rebel.-ct. mar. Served in American Revolution as officer and from 1805-12 was governor of the Michigan Territory. He was made a brigadier general in 1812 and later that year surrendered to the British. He was court-martialed for neglect of duty and cowardice, and was sentenced to be shot, but was reprieved because he fought in the Revolutionary War. REF.: *CBA.*

Hulme, Juliet Marion, 1939-   , and **Reiper, Pauline Yvonne,** 1938-   , N. Zea., mur. So that they could remain together, a teenage girl and her best friend killed her mother. Juliet Hulme and Pauline Reiper were very close, writing novels together, sending letters to each other, bathing together, sleeping often in the same bed, and talking with each other about sex. Pauline's mother, Honora Mary Reiper, forty-five, grew anxious about their relationship and at one point voiced her concerns to Juliet's father. When Juliet's father decided to move from Christchurch, N. Zea., to South Africa and take Juliet with him, the two girls decided they were "...sticking to one thing. We sink or swim together." Pauline decided she would move to South Africa with her friend, but when her mother would not allow it, the two girls plotted to kill her.

On June 22, 1954, while the girls and Mrs. Reiper walked along a path in a park, Pauline and her mother began to argue. Pauline swung a brick stuffed inside a stocking at her mother, hitting her repeatedly, and then Juliet took the brick and continued to hit her. Their clothes were stained with blood. After pulverizing Mrs. Reiper, the two girls ran to a tea house, hysterical, and gasped, "Please help us. Mummy's been hurt. She's hurt, covered with blood." They claimed Mary had slipped on a board, fell, and bumped her head on a brick while her head "kept bumping and banging."

The pathologist's examination revealing forty-five distinct injuries proved the girls were lying. Arrested, Pauline confessed and took the blame for the murder stating that Juliet had been walking ahead and witnessed nothing. But when Pauline was caught trying to burn a note saying she was "taking the blame for everything," Juliet confessed to the murder as well.

At their trial they pleaded not guilty by reason of insanity, a plea impossible to maintain when Pauline claimed, "I knew it was wrong to murder and I knew at the time I was murdering somebody. You would have to be an absolute moron not to know murder was against the law." The jury found the two girls Guilty of murder and sentenced them to prison until the queen chose to release them. They were released four years later, in 1958.

REF.: *CBA;* Wilson, *Children Who Kill.*

Hulme, William Edward, prom. 1935, Brit., libel. The chief executive and founder of the Disabled Soldiers' and Sailors' Agencies and Supplies, William Edward Hulme, brought a libel suit against the periodical *John Bull* for an article it ran headed "War-Maimed Exploited for Profit." The article made critical and libelous statements to the effect that Hulme's company was not genuine and that it exploited and swindled veterans by using them to sell wastepaper baskets and typewriter ribbons. Nothing could have been further from the truth.

Several years before the *John Bull* article, Hulme, an ex-army officer, and four other unemployed army personnel organized the business with the sole purpose of giving out-of-work veterans a job. To this end they were successful and the business expanded to five cities. Before the case went to court several bitter disputes arose between Hulme and *John Bull.* Yet once in court the defendants did not even cross-examine Hulme and agreed to the £5,000 judgment. Upon settlement, Lord Chief Justice Hewart said, "If ever I have seen a good Samaritan, it is Mr. Hulme."

REF.: Bowker, *Behind the Bar; CBA.*

Hulten, Karl Gustav, 1923-45, and **Jones, Elizabeth Maud** (AKA: **Georgie Grayson**), 1926- , Brit., mur. Born in Stockholm, Swed., Karl Hulten was taken to the U.S. as an infant and raised as an American citizen by his parents. He worked as a clerk and a mechanic shortly before his induction into the U.S. Army in 1943. Hulten was assigned to the 501st Parachute Infantry Regiment and stationed outside of London at the time he deserted his outfit in September 1944.

On Oct. 3, Hulten met a "party girl" named Elizabeth Jones, who was employed as a strip-tease dancer in a local night club. In the next few days the fast-living Jones dared him to "do something dangerous," like steal a U.S. Army vehicle from the base. According to her version of the events, Hulten passed himself off as a Chicago gangster who controlled a mob in London. The thrill-seeking couple went out for a walk the night of Oct. 7. As they made their way along the Hammersmith Road, they spotted a car driving slowly toward them. Hulten stepped into the shadow, while Jones flagged down the car. The driver of the vehicle, George Edward Heath, thirty-four, was not a licensed taxi driver but was operating the car as such in defiance of local statutes.

Killers Karl Hulten and Elizabeth Jones.

Hulten and Jones got in and directed the driver to proceed to Great West Road. According to Jones' sworn testimony, Hulten fired two shots into Heath. Afterward, the woman rifled through the pockets to remove whatever valuables she could find. The body was dumped alongside the road. Hulten was arrested two days later in a house outside Fulham Palace Road, and soon he was dubbed the "Cleft Chin Murderer" by the press for the hollow in his chin. Jones was captured later that day after casually remarking to a war reserve policeman that "if you had seen someone do what I have seen done you wouldn't be able to sleep at night." The remark was reported to Inspector Tansill at the Hammersmith Police Station, culminating in her arrest.

The U.S. Government agreed to waive its rights under the terms of the Visiting Forces Acts. Hulten was tried at the Old Bailey on Jan. 16, 1945. Both were found Guilty, but the jury recommended mercy in the case of Jones. Hulten was hanged on Mar. 8. Elizabeth Jones served nine years of her sentence before being released in May 1954.

REF.: Brophy, *The Meaning of Murder;* Casswell, *A Lance For Liberty; CBA;* Hastings, *The Other Mr. Churchill;* Lustgarten, *Edgar, The Murder and the Trial;* Nash, *Look For the Woman; Old Bailey Trials;* Shew, *A Companion to Murder;* Webb, *Crime Is My Business;* Wilson, *Encyclopedia of Murder*

Humbert I (Umbert I), 1844-1900, Italy, king, assass. Humbert I, Duke of Savoy, was the son of Victor Emmanuel II, and at the beginning of his reign, was known as an Italian patriot. As the Duke of Savoy, he had supported his father in the wars to unify Italy. When he assumed the throne (1878-1900), Humbert tried to close old wounds between the many Italian political and regional factions. To strengthen Italy's position in Europe, as well as to change its image as a weak nation, Humbert brought his country into the Triple Alliance with Germany and Austria-Hungary in 1882. In the early 1890s, Humbert, like Mussolini after him, sought to subdue and conquer Ethiopia, which Italy had long considered its own territory in North Africa. But this military campaign proved costly and ineffective, ending in disaster in 1896 with Humbert's armies defeated at Adowa. The military defeat was all the more humiliating because the Ethiopian forces were poorly equipped and lacked modern weapons, yet they were patriotically inspired and overwhelmed a superior Italian force.

Social unrest, stemming from radical leftist parties, caused Humbert to impose martial law in 1898. He went further, stating that he was an unchallengeable monarch, an autocrat who demanded complete subservience from his subjects. Humbert forced his generals and admirals to swear allegiance to him, not to Italy. Humbert had replaced the premier and other important ministers with these military yes-men and had, for all practical purposes, suspended the Republic and all democratic political activities. He was considered a tyrant even by moderates and no amount of pleading on the part of officials could persuade Humbert to relax his decrees. Anarchists in Italy and in the U.S. marked him for death. A group of Italian anarchists who had migrated to the U.S. and were employed as silk weavers in Paterson, N.J., held regular meetings in early 1900, discussing how to assassinate Humbert. They finally chose lots and the task fell to Gaetano Bresci, who sailed for Italy with only one object in mind, to murder Humbert I.

The Italian king was not unfamiliar with assassins. During the year of his coronation, on Nov. 17, 1878, he almost met his death at the hands of a lone would-be assassin. At the time, Humbert, his wife Margherita, his little son, his father Victor Emmanuel II, and the prime minister, Benedetto Cairoli, were entering Naples on the king's first triumphant tour of Italy. The Naples reception was a costly affair. Gold and silver gifts had been purchased for the queen and half the city had been decorated. The carpet from the king's private train car to his carriage, stretching thirty-some feet, had been hand-painted by Giovanni Morelli, one of Italy's great artists of the day. To pay for this lavish reception, every person in Naples had been taxed the equivalent of one penny. One man, Giovanni Passanante, an unemployed cook, felt the reception for the king was exorbitant and he resolved to murder Humbert.

When Humbert's carriage slowly turned into the Palazzo Carrera Grande, which was packed with cheering throngs, the royal family suddenly noticed a pale-faced young man running alongside the carriage. Mounted guards rode before and after the carriage and those behind could not, because of the pressing crowds, ride forward to shield the carriage from Passanante. His right hand was covered with a red cloth and when he leaped upon the running board of the open carriage, he threw away this cloth to reveal a long knife. (Leon Czolgosz, when murdering President William McKinley in 1901, employed the same technique, hiding his revolver beneath a handkerchief wrapped about a hand, which appeared injured.) As Passanante raised his knife to strike Humbert, the queen screamed to Prime Minister Cairoli to "save his highness!"

The brave Cairoli quickly leaned forward, shielding the king with his own body so that Passanante's knife plunged into the Prime Minister's thigh, a deep wound that was not life-threatening. Queen Margherita pushed her son, Prince Victor Emmanuel, to the floor, while Humbert repeatedly hit Passanante over the head with his sword, still in its scabbard. The queen slapped the assassin's face and pummeled him with the bouquet of flowers she had been given by the mayor at the train station. (Interestingly, Queen Amélie of Portugal also hit her husband's assassin with a bouquet of flowers when King Carlos was murdered in an open carriage in 1908. The assassin also killed her son.)

Passanante, hit by both the king and queen, lost his balance on the running board and fell backward into the arms of several policemen. He was dragged away and thrown into prison. He was later tried for treason and attempted assassination. The reason Passanante gave for trying to kill Humbert was that he thought the king was a spendthrift. "From what I have read," Passanante said, "I gather that kings spend too much." His defense counsel attempted to prove him insane, but Passanante refused to plead insanity. A jury promptly convicted him and he was executed. That day, King Humbert drove to the palace on the Palazzo Reale, where a few nights later he was the guest of honor at a huge formal dinner. His seemingly indifferent, almost amused attitude toward the attempted assassination was summed up when he told the dinner guests: "Let us be seated and let us not keep the cooks waiting; you have seen, ladies and gentlemen, what they are capable of."

Twenty-two years later, King Humbert was faced with a more determined assassin. Bresci, after sailing from Paterson, N.J., studied Humbert's routines and schedules. His would be no random attack, as was Passanante's in 1878. He would determine exactly where the king would be at a certain hour and then strike when he was assured of success. Humbert, an anathema to democracy, had imposed even more restrictions in response to increasing demands for an open government and a free press, and especially after bloody demonstrations broke out in the summer of 1900. He declared martial law in several cities and his royal police made sweeping arrests of suspected anarchists.

Bresci learned that Humbert would be attending a gymnastic event in Monza where he would be handing out prizes. On the day of the sports show, Bresci bought a ticket to the games and sat in the crowd, close to where the king would stand when giving awards to the winners. Humbert gave the awards, but he received such a tepid reception that he decided to return to the palace immediately. As he turned to go, Bresci stood on a grandstand seat, pulled forth a revolver and shot Humbert at close range, killing the king on the spot. Bresci was quickly subdued and thrown in jail. When the anarchist group in Paterson, N.J., heard the news of Humbert's assassination they celebrated by spending their hard-earned blue-collar money on champagne, toasting Bresci's feat.

In Italy, the Republicans applauded the assassin's act, although officials and politicians publicly condemned the deed. Bresci, meanwhile, was not tried nor did he ever face execution. He was thrown into a solitary cell, a dungeon-like room crawling with rats and without light. He shortly went mad, or so it was said, and hanged himself. It was later stated that warders simply hanged him by his own belt from a beam in his cell. Gaetano Bresci was officially listed as a suicide and the case was closed. Weeks later, Leon Czolgosz, an anarchist in the U.S., read of Bresci's assassination of Humbert I and immediately resolved to kill the U.S. president, William McKinley. See: **McKinley, William**.

REF.: Bell, *Assassin!*; *CBA*; Demaris, *Brothers In Blood: The International Terrorist Network*; Dorman, *Secret Service*; Hyams, *Killing No Murder*; Nash, *Almanac of World Crime*; _____, *Jay Robert Nash's Crime Chronology*.

Humbert, Thérèse Daurignac, and **Humbert, Frédéric**, prom. 1902, Fr., fraud. While traveling on the Ceinture Railway one day, Thérèse Humbert, the daughter of a peasant family from Toulouse, Fr., claimed to have met the man who changed her life: American industrialist Robert Henry Crawford.

Hearing moans in the next compartment, Humbert rushed to the aid of a violently ill man—Crawford. She comforted him and remained at his side until the train reached Paris. Shortly after this gallant act, Humbert, herself the daughter-in-law of France's minister of justice, announced that the grateful Crawford had made her the sole heir of his vast fortune. Then a second will turned up, in which Humbert was to share the estate with two nephews, Henry and Robert Crawford, and her own sister Maria. Under the terms of the latter will, the three legatees were obligated to pay $40,000 a year to Thérèse in interest payments.

According to published accounts an agreement was struck between the principal heirs in which the major securities comprising the inheritance were to be locked in a safe at the Humbert residence until a final decision could be reached about the division of the assets. The minister of justice, Thérèse's father-in-law, declared that her inheritance was legitimate. Meanwhile, the leading French banks expressed their willingness to advance her large sums of money, with the understanding it would be repaid once the safe was opened. In a twenty-year period Madame Humbert succeeded in humbugging the moneylenders and entrepreneurs who forked over between $6 million and $9 million to her. All believed that someday they would reap a tidy sum. To divert suspicion, Humbert appears to have initiated a series of civil suits against herself which were supposed to be the work of the disgruntled Crawford nephews.

Each of these cases went before the civil magistrates, with neither side gaining a favorable decision. The two nephews involved in the fraudulent litigation were her two brothers, Emile and Romaine. The attending publicity of the mysterious safe, the countless lawsuits, and the fueled speculation prompted journalists from *Le Matin* to launch an investigation. Nervous creditors demanded an accounting, so the French courts ordered that the safe be opened in 1902. Inside, the astonished officials found an empty jewel box, $1,000 in negotiable bonds, and some worthless brass buttons. The public had been hoodwinked. Thérèse and her husband Frédéric went to jail, as did the "nephews." This followed at least a dozen reported suicides in France by ruined investors. In 1906 Thérèse emerged from prison still maintaining her innocence. She explained that Henry Crawford had appeared to her in court and made a sign that she should keep quiet. "I decided to suffer even imprisonment rather than speak out," she said.

REF.: *CBA*; MacDougall, *Hoaxes*; Nash, *Hustlers and Con Men*; Stevens, *Famous Crimes and Criminals*; Wade, *Great Hoaxes and Famous Imposters*.

Humboldt Park Riot, 1977, U.S., mob. vio. On June, 4, 1977, a dispute between the rival Latino street gangs in Chicago turned into a riot in Humboldt Park on the city's Northwest side. Police officers Thomas Walton and Robinson Urbane attempted to break up a fight between the Spanish Cobras and the Latin Kings when they were fired upon by 26-year-old Julio Osorio. Osorio missed the officers, but when they fired back, they fatally shot Osorio and a bystander, 25-year-old Raphael Cruz. A growing crowd pelted the officers with rocks and set three police vehicles afire. An extra-alarm fire broke out in a nearby apartment building, but fire fighters were told initially to ignore the blaze. The crowd spilled out into the neighboring commercial area, looting and burning businesses. The park was loaded with people in the sweltering heat after an all-day celebration of Puerto Rican Day. By midnight, 150 people were arrested and eighty-five more injured; twenty five policemen and two firemen were treated for injuries at local hospitals.

At noon the following day, the looting and rock throwing started again. Following an afternoon standoff, the riot erupted full-scale at nightfall with a rock throwing incident between the mob and the police. Eighteen people were injured including thirteen police officers. One hundred officers dressed in riot garb quelled the disturbance, allowing city maintenance crews to clean up the debris. Neighborhood taverns were closed as a further precaution. Many called for an end to the annual Puerto Rican Day parade, which seemed to instigate violence every year. Community leaders blamed unemployment, inadequate housing, and police harassment as the cause of the violence.

The families of Osorio and Cruz filed a $48 million civil rights lawsuit against Thomas Walton and other police officers and city officials for the shooting deaths that began the riot. On Oct. 9, 1981, the case was declared a mistrial when U.S. District Judge Prentice Marshall was forced to undergo open-heart surgery. On May 4, 1984, the case was settled out of court when the city agreed to divide $625,000 between the two families. Chicago mayor Harold Washington decried the use of excess force by the police department, a sentiment echoed by police superintendent Fred Rice. REF.: *CBA*.

Hume, Brian Donald, c.1919-   , Brit., rob.-mur. Murderer Brian Hume of England had not counted on the ocean currents washing his bloody parcels ashore, but in the end the swift flowing tides revealed the diabolical nature of his crimes.

Hume was a former RAF pilot turned gangster. He frequented the shady hotels and bistros of London's West End where his boyish charm won him many female admirers. His business associate, Stanley Setty, a 46-year-old car dealer born in Baghdad, was both black marketer and fence, and in 1949 entered an arrangement whereby he would procure stolen cars which Hume later would sell.

Hume and his partner had a falling out which resulted in the Oct. 5, 1949 murder of Setty. Believing that the only way to ensure that he did not get caught was to dispose of the body properly, Hume rented a private plane from the United Services Flying Club at Elstree. Over the next two days, Hume flew his craft over the English Channel and dropped three large bundles out the side door. Returning to the airfield, Hume thought

Murderer Brian Hume.

he had committed the perfect crime. But the tides had washed one of the parcels to the Essex flats at Tillingham where it was recovered by a farm laborer named Sidney Tiffen. Inside, he found the severed limbs of a man. An autopsy was conducted, and through old criminal records it was learned that the deceased was Stanley Setty, who had been born Sulman Seti. Fingerprints on record with Scotland Yard confirmed the identity of the victim. From the manager of the Flying Club, detectives were able to trace the murder of Setty to the civilian pilot Hume.

Arrested on Oct. 27, Hume stoically denied complicity in the crime. After further questioning he admitted that three underworld figures, identified only as Greeny, Mac, and "The Boy," had hired him to dispose of three hot properties—believed to be printing plates used to manufacture forged gasoline coupons. These men were never found and Hume was bound over for trial at the Old Bailey on Jan. 18, 1950. However, the jury failed to arrive at a verdict.

Justice Lewis ordered that another jury be sworn in and then directed the jury members to return a verdict of Not Guilty on the murder charge. Hume pleaded guilty to the lesser charge of being an accessory, and was sentenced to twelve years at Dartmoor prison. He served only eight years, and was back on the streets Feb. 1, 1958. In May, he disparaged the British judicial system by brazenly confessing to the *Sunday Pictorial* newspaper that he had killed Setty in his London apartment in 1949, knowing full well that he could not be tried again for the same crime. Mac, Greeny, and "The Boy" were all literary inventions designed to cover the murder, he said.

Just as this story made front page news for the second time, Hume was already planning a new caper: the robbery of the Midland Bank in Boston Manor Road. On Aug. 2, 1958, he shot and wounded a cashier at the bank and then made off with £1,500. He hit this bank a second time on Nov. 12, seriously wounding a branch manager, and tucked the money away in Zurich, Switz., but was arrested there on Jan. 30, 1959, after holding up the Gewerbe Bank. While attempting to escape Hume shot and killed a taxi driver named Arthur Maag. Since there was no capital

punishment in Switzerland, Hume was spared the death penalty but he did his utmost to feign insanity. Said Chief Investigator Hans Stotz, "I think he is a very good actor." Brian Hume was tried at Winterthur, found Guilty, and sentenced to prison for life.

REF.: Archer, *Killers in the Clear*; Beveridge, *Inside the CID*; Boar, *The World's Most Infamous Murders*; *CBA*; *Celebrated Trials*; Cuthbert, *Science and the Detection of Crime*; Furneaux, *Famous Criminal Case, vol. 6*; Haines, *Bothersome Bodies*; Harrison, *Criminal Calendar*; Heppenstall, *The Sex War and Others*; Hibbert, *The Roots of Evil*; Hoskins, *The Sound of Murder*; Hynd, *An International Casebook of Crime*; ____, *Sleuths, Slayers and Swindlers*; Jackson, *Francis Camps*; Reynolds, *Murder 'Round the World*; Scott, *Scotland Yard*; Shew, *A Second Companion to Murder*; Thorwald, *The Century of the Detective*; ____, *Dead Men Tell Tales*; Totterdell, *Country Copper*; Webb, *Crime Is My Business*; West, *A Train of Powder*; Williams, *Hume, Portrait of a Double Murderer*; Wilson, *Encyclopedia of Murder*.

Hume, Fergus, 1859-1932, Brit., lawyer-writer. Wrote detective books. He originally practiced law in New Zealand, moving to Britain in 1888. Books authored: *Mystery of a Hansom Cab, The Bishop's Secret, Jonah's Luck, The Other Person*, and *The Caravan Mystery*. REF.: *CBA*.

Hume, Sir Patrick (Baron Polwarth, Earl of Marchmont), 1641-1724, Scot., consp. Went on Argylle's expedition in 1684. He was outlawed in 1685 after participating in the Rye House Plot, later escaping to Utrecht. REF.: *CBA*.

Hummel, Abraham H., See: **Howe, William F.**

Humphrey (Duke of Gloucester, Earl of Pembroke), 1391-1447, Brit., consp. Tried to have his uncle, Henry Beaufort, removed from his position of cardinal in 1432. He disagreed with Beaufort's peace policy toward the French, and in 1445 urged that the truce with France be violated. He was thought to be plotting to kill the king, and he died while he was being detained. REF.: *CBA*.

Humphrey, Geneva M., b.1899, U.S., mur. Mrs. Geneva Humphrey, forty-seven, suspected her husband of having an affair. On the night of Dec. 7, 1945, after drinking at a local bar in Little Falls, N.J., she chased 43-year-old Hugh Edward Humphrey with her car into an alley and smashed him between a cellar door and the car bumper.

At her trial, Humphrey consistently denied premeditated murder and claimed she could not see her husband as the windshield was steamed over and the wipers did not work. She further denied saying, after running him over, "Well, I got that so and so." On Jan. 30, 1946, Humphrey was convicted by a jury of men and women of manslaughter and sentenced by Judge Joseph A. Delaney to eight to ten years in New Jersey State Prison, the state's maximum sentence for manslaughter. REF.: *CBA*.

Humphrey, J. Otis, 1850-1918, U.S., jur. Served as U.S. attorney of southern district of Illinois from 1897-1901. He was nominated to the southern district court of Illinois by President William McKinley in 1901. REF.: *CBA*.

Humphreys, Murray Llewellyn (AKA: The Camel), 1899-1965, U.S., org. crime. Murray "The Camel" Humphreys feuded with Al Capone over control of the Chicago mob and lived to tell about it. The only Welshman in the Mafia, Humphreys used money rather than guns to control of rackets. Known as "the Camel" because he wore camel hair coats, Humphreys worked closely with Capone to forge a strong alliance with political, business and labor leaders. He was implicated but not convicted in the December 1931 kidnapping of union president Robert G. Fitchie. In 1933, Humphreys framed Ca-

Chicago gangster Murray Humphreys.

pone's opponent Roger Touhy for the apparent kidnapping of John "Jake the Barber" Factor, who was awaiting extradition to England to stand trail for stock swindling.

Factor, vital to the prosecution of Touhy, was allowed to stay, and eventually moved to Las Vegas. Touhy was sentenced to twenty-five years, and was shot to death a month after his release in 1959. Humphreys was strongly suspected in the mob hit. Six months later Humphreys bought shares in an insurance company, which he redeemed eight months later, for a profit of $42,000. When the original seller turned out to be none other than Jake the Barber, the IRS became very interested. The profit was clearly a payment for the 1933 kidnapping, and the Camel was forced to pay taxes on it. In 1965, he pulled a revolver on FBI agents as they were arresting him for lying to a grand jury. The behavior worried other mobsters, and within hours, Humphreys was dead, apparently of a heart attack. However, it is possible that he was killed by air injected with a hypodermic needle, as a slight wound was found near his right ear. See: **Capone, Alphonse; Factor, John; Touhy, Roger.**

REF.: *CBA;* Davis, *Mafia Kingfish;* Demaris, *Captive City;* Fried, *The Rise and Fall of the Jewish Gangster in America;* Gage, *The Mafia is not an Equal Opportunity Employer;* Kobler, *Capone;* Lait and Mortimer, *Chicago: Confidential;* McClellan, *Crime Without Punishment;* Messick, *Secret File;* ____ and Goldblatt, *The Mobs and the Mafia;* Morgan, *Prince of Crime;* Nash, *Citizen Hoover;* Peterson, *The Mob;* Smith, *Syndicate City.*

Humphreys, Sir Travers, 1867-1956, Brit., jur. Served as counsel to the Crown at Middlesex Sessions and North London Sessions beginning in 1905. He was made junior counsel to the Crown at Old Bailey in 1908, senior treasury counsel in 1916, and chief senior treasury counsel in 1924. He then served on the King's Bench Division of the High Court from 1928-51. He was counsel in the trials of Hawley Harvey Crippen, Lieutenant Douglas Malcolm, and George Joseph Smith. He presided over the trials of Mrs. Elvira Barney, Wallace Benton, Ernest Brown, Edward Royal Chaplin, Ludomir Cienski, John George Haigh, Chung Yo Miao, Theodosios Petrou, and others.

REF.: *CBA;* Hyde, *United in Crime.*

Humphreys, Travers Christmas, b.1901, Brit., lawyer. Son of Travers Humphreys. He became a Treasury counsel in 1934, senior prosecuting counsel to the Crown in 1950, and senior prosecuting counsel to the Crown in 1959. He was involved in the trials of Wallace Benton, George Brain, Edward Royal Chaplin, Sidney George Paul, John Robinson, Henry Sidney, and Leslie George Stone. He led the Crown's prosecution of Brian Donald Hume. REF.: *CBA.*

Humphreys, West Hughes, 1806-82, U.S., jur.-rebel. Served in Tennessee House of Representatives from 1835-38. He was later Tennessee attorney general, and reporter of cases for the Tennessee Supreme Court from 1839-51. In 1853 he was nominated by President Franklin Pierce to serve as the U.S. district judge of Tennessee. Nine years later he was appointed as district judge for the Confederacy, later to be impeached by the U.S. House of Representatives, with Senate conviction in 1862. He was the only official to be so treated during the Civil War. REF.: *CBA.*

Humphries, John R., prom. 1850s, U.S., mur. John R. Humphries of Atlanta, Ga., was told that an enemy, Elisha Tiller, was looking for him, intending to put a bullet into him. Both men met in James Kile's grocery in January 1853.

Humphries stood a few paces off, while Tiller looked at some leather bridles. "I heard you were going to kill me on sight," Humphries stated.

Tiller went on examining the bridles. "No, that's not true. I have nothing against you."

"Look over this way," Humphries asked.

Tiller looked over to see Humphries raise a double-barrel shotgun. He fired one barrel directly into Tiller.

The murder was described in the down-home writing style of the *Tri-Weekly Times and Sentinel:* "Tiller was killed so dead as not even to kick after he fell. Humphries burst the cap of the other barrel at Kile, the grocer, but the gun missed fire."

Humphries, the son of Charner Humphries who had begun the first saloon in Atlanta, the Whitehall Tavern, was oddly never brought to trial. Like the landed Birds, who managed to buy Elijah Bird's freedom after he had committed a murder, the Humphries family had influence. See: **Bird, Elijah; Costley, Cann.** REF.: *CBA.*

Humud, Mohammed, d.c.1955, Zanzibar, mur. Although a British colony until 1963, Zanzibar was dominated by an Arab elite. In 1955, the British decided to allot legislative seats on a racial basis, in an attempt to usurp Arab power. Racial tensions between Africans and Arabs led to violence when in November 1955, an unidentified Arab stabbed retired police inspector Ahmed el-Mugheiry as he walked down the street. Seriously wounded and hospitalized, he was attacked again, fatally, by Mohammed Humud. Humud was convicted and sentenced to death, but received a reprieve when the sultan commuted his sentence. REF.: *CBA.*

Hungate, William Leonard, 1922- , U.S., jur. Served as prosecuting attorney of Lincoln County, Mo., from 1951-56, as deputy attorney general of Missouri from 1958-60, and as special assistant attorney general of Missouri from 1961-64. He was nominated to the eastern district court of Missouri by President Jimmy Carter in 1978. REF.: *CBA.*

Hungerford, Lady Alys, prom. 1523, Brit., mur. In order to marry a nobleman, a servant girl had her husband killed. Then after her nobleman husband died, Lady Alys Hungerford was convicted of murder and hanged.

Alys married John Cotell when she was young. She was called beautiful and it appears that she consorted with several men on the side including William Inges and William Mathewe, two villagers she kept under her influence. While born poor, she had ambitions. When she gained employment at Farleigh Castle in Wiltshire, the lord of the house, Sir Edward Hungerford, grew fond of her and they had an affair. Soon after Alys' arrival, Lady Jane Hungerford died of unknown causes. Then on July 10, 1518, Mathewe and Inges entered Farleigh Castle, throttled Cotell, and stuffed his body into the castle's furnace. Cotell's sudden disappearance did not arouse much suspicion as Sir Edward married Alys shortly after.

For five years Alys lived as Lady Hungerford and spent most of her time in London. Sir Edward made out his will in December 1521 with Alys to receive all his possessions. He died five weeks later. In the summer of the same year, Alys and cohorts Mathewe and Inges were arrested for complicity in the murder of Alys's first husband. The trial was postponed in Ilchester and King Henry VIII ordered the case brought to him where the three were found Guilty. While Lady Alys and Mathewe were hanged, there is no record of Inges' execution.

REF.: *CBA;* O'Donnell, *Should Women Hang?*

Hung Jenkan (Hung Jin), 1822-64, China, rebel. Escaped to Hong Kong during the Taiping Rebellion in 1850. Western missionaries taught him, and in 1859 he went to Nanking, the rebel capital, to teach Protestant Christianity. His cousin, Hsiu-chüan, made him a prime minister. He tried to institute Western administrative policies and encourage building hospitals, telegraphs, banks, and railroads. Other leaders disagreed with his policies and he was demoted and executed after Nanking was captured by government soldiers. REF.: *CBA.*

Hung Yai, prom. 650 B.C., China, pros. History remembers Hung Yai as the first madam of a prostitution house when, in the mid-seventh century, B.C., prostitution was licensed in China through the efforts of statesman Kuang Chung. This is the first known occurrence of licensed prostitution.

REF.: *CBA;* Nash, *Almanac of World Crime.*

Hunt, Dora, 1864-1923, Fr., (unsolv.) mur. On Nov. 23, 1923, Dora Hunt, a 59-year-old Englishwoman living on the Riviera, was bludgeoned to death in her Hotel St. Georges bedroom near Cannes, Fr. Her body, discovered three to four hours after the murder, lay on the blood-spattered bed. The likely motive for the murder was robbery as Hunt was known to own expensive jewelry.

The Cannes police followed several hunches and promising clues without success. They discovered that a villa across the way from Hunt's room had been slept in the night of the murder while the owners were away—the bedding was changed and the intruder left behind two bottles of an unrecognizable perfume. Police speculated that Hunt went out dancing with a professional dancer—a gigolo in those days—who later entered her room, took the little jewelry she had not locked in the hotel vault, and, for some unknown reason, killed her. The wallet of the dead woman was discovered two days after the murder but did not reveal any clues. Scotland Yard was called in to assist in the investigation, but not even its involvement brought the police any closer to the killer.

Then, ten years after the murder, an anonymous letter confessing to the crime was received by the Cannes police. In part it read:

> I hid under the bed and waited there...to steal
> Mrs. Hunt's jewelry. A chambermaid came in at
> 9 p.m....Mrs. Hunt woke up. I hit her on the
> head with my revolver, and as I did so the revolver
> went off and a bullet went into the mattress.

The letter apparently was from the murderer as a maid did enter Hunt's room around 9 p.m., and a bullet was discovered in the mattress. No further leads developed in this case until February 1936, when French police informed Hunt's eldest son that a professional dancer attempted to sell some of his mother's jewelry at a state pawnshop. Even with this substantial development, no arrests were made and the case remained unsolved.

REF.: *CBA*; Greenwall, *They Were Murdered In France*.

Hunt, Henry, 1773-1835, Case of, Brit., asslt. Henry Hunt, a political activist who advocated universal suffrage and voting by ballot, was known as an agitator in London and was frequently arrested for his violent temper as well as his insistence on governmental reforms.

In 1818, when Mr. Downing, a newspaperman with the *Observer*, made critical remarks about him in the paper, Hunt called him a government spy. Indignant, Downing threatened to horsewhip Hunt when he next saw him. Downing fulfilled his promise and whipped Hunt while Hunt responded by striking Downing several times with his cane.

Arrested, they were brought before magistrate Mr. Birney at Bow Street who dismissed them when neither pressed charges. The two men appeared before Birney a few weeks later when Downing filed charges after Hunt lightly struck him in the face and knocked off his glasses.

Apparently, quick tempers ran in the family, as recorded in later proceedings at Bow Street. Henry Hunt's son, Thomas Hunt, at age twenty-two nearly choked another young man who had accused him of putting sawdust in his hat. This case was also dismissed as witnesses claimed Hunt was sufficiently provoked.

REF.: Armitage, *Bow Street Runners*; *CBA*.

Hunt, J. Frank, d.1880, U.S., west. lawman. In 1880, J. Frank Hunt was the deputy marshal of Caldwell, Kan., a frontier boomtown. On June 19, 1880, George Flatt, a drunken former lawman was shot to death as he neared a Caldwell restaurant. A man identified as Hunt was seen fleeing the murder scene. Flatt's death was avenged on Oct. 11, 1880, when an unidentified gunman fatally wounded Hunt as he sat near a window at the Red Light saloon and dance hall.

REF.: *CBA*; Drago, *Wild, Woolly and Wicked*; Miller and Snell, *Great Gunfighters of the Kansas Cowtowns*; O'Neal, *Encyclopedia of Western Gunfighters*.

Hunt, Joe, 1960-   , U.S., mur. Joe Hunt, wealthy and supposedly charismatic, was the founder and leader of an investment group called BBC Consolidated, commonly referred to as the "Billionaire Boys Club." Its membership consisted of friends from Harvard Business School whose sole purpose was to make a fortune. Ronald G. Levin, a 42-year-old journalist and con artist,

set up an account with BBC that supposedly contained $5 million. Through their efforts BBC turned the initial investment into $13 million; however, in actuality the initial $5 million never existed. While Hunt and his cohorts thought they had earned $8 million, in fact no money had been made.

Hunt learned of Levin's trick and retaliated. According to Dean Karny, a BBC member granted immunity for his testimony, Hunt and the BBC security officer Jim Pittman, confronted Levin in his Beverly Hills, Calif., duplex on June 6, 1984. Hunt forced Levin to write a check for $1.5 million (which bounced), then bound and gagged Levin, killed his dog, shot Levin in the face with a shotgun, and dumped his body in Soledad Canyon. The body was never found. Later, Hunt bragged to his BBC brothers of committing the perfect crime and warned them not to tell anyone or they would be dealt with "severely."

Police charged Hunt with the murder of Levin after obtaining seven sheets of paper from Levin's duplex containing Hunt's fingerprints and handwriting. On the pages were lists, the top page headed "At Levin's TO DO," delineating such tasks as "close blinds, scan for tape recorder, tape mouth, handcuff, put gloves on, explain situation, kill dog."

At the trial, Brooke Roberts, Hunt's close friend, testified she and Hunt were elsewhere at the time of the murder. Defense attorney Arthur Barens claimed that Levin vanished to escape creditors and is, in fact, alive, having pulled off the ultimate con. To support this theory, the defense produced two witnesses who claimed they saw Levin near Tucson, Ariz., in a car with another man. The prosecutor, Fred Wapner, son of *The People's Court* judge, claimed that Hunt killed Levin for "profit and revenge" and produced the pages of lists as well as a Billionaire Boys Club member, Dean Karny, who testified to the details of the murder.

The jury found the prosection's case more convincing and, on Apr. 22, 1987, found Joe Hunt Guilty of first-degree murder. Though Hunt was eligible for the death penalty, Judge Laurence J. Rittenband of the California Superior Court sentenced him to life in prison without the possibility of parole.

When convicted of the crime, Hunt told reporters, "It's just astonishing...I think it's a tragedy because Ron Levin's alive."
REF.: *CBA*.

Hunt, Leamon R., 1928-84, Italy, assass. Shortly before 7 p.m. in Rome on Feb. 15, 1984, Leamon R. Hunt, American diplomat, was gunned down while his armored limousine stopped at a red light. The only witness was the chauffeur who claimed two olive-skinned men jumped out of a car behind the limousine, opened fire with automatic weapons, and then fled on foot.

A man with a Roman accent claiming to represent the group responsible for the assassination said, "The Imperialist forces must leave Lebanon. Italy must leave NATO." Experts speculated it was the Fighting Communist Party or another group connected to the Red Brigades who killed Hunt. Hunt was the director-general of the multinational peacekeeping force that patrolled the Sinai peninsula, monitoring the Israeli-Egyptian peace treaty made at Camp David. Hunt, a 56-year-old civilian, served more than thirty-two years in the U.S. foreign service and was the first American diplomat killed by terrorists in Italy. He is survived by his wife, the former Joyce Conneally. REF.: *CBA*.

Hunt, Richard (AKA: Zwing), 1858-82, U.S., rob.-mur. Born in Washington County, Texas, Richard Hunt, called Zwing by his friends, went to work as a cowboy and log-hauler at an early age. He worked on and off for several ranchers about Tombstone, Ariz., including the Clanton-McLowery gang of cattle rustlers. He then branched out on his own, rustling cattle with Billy Boucher, also known as "Billy the Kid" Grounds. Hunt and Boucher became notorious for stealing Mexican cattle, running these herds across the border into Arizona, and selling the cattle at bargain-basement prices. Hunt and Boucher then turned to robbery and held up several ranchers. They wore masks so their identities were never confirmed. On Mar. 25, 1882, M.C. Peel, the chief engineer for the Tombstone Mining and Milling Company, was held up by two robbers who shot and killed him.

Tombstone deputy sheriff William Breakenridge discovered one of the robbers' hats at the scene of the crime and identified this as belonging to Hunt. Moreover, boot prints and horses' hoof prints which were traced to Hunt and Boucher convinced Breakenridge that these two men were indeed Peel's killers. He tracked them down to the Stockton ranch where the two outlaws shot it out with the posse. Boucher was killed and Hunt was wounded. He was taken back to the Tombstone jail but he was removed by unnamed men on the night of Apr. 27, 1882, and reportedly lynched.

On June 10, the Tombstone *Epitaph* reported that Hunt "was a child of circumstance and a creature of excitement. Generous to a fault, rash to the extremity of foolishness, and as brave as an Arabian fire-worshipper, Zwing would do to go tiger hunting with, but he is dead." See: **Breakenridge, William Milton.**

REF.: Bakarich, *Gun Smoke;* _____ and Bennett, *There's Treasure in Our Hills;* Bartholomew, *A Biographical Album of Western Gunfighters;* _____, *Western Hardcases;* Bechdolt, *When the West was Young;* Breakenridge, *Helldorado;* Burns, *Tombstone: An Iliad of the Southwest;* Casey, *The Texas Border and Some Borderliners; CBA;* Cunningham, *Triggernometry;* Dobie, *Coronado's Children;* Hill, *Then and Now;* Holloway, *Texas Gun Lore;* McCool, *So Said the Coroner;* Martin, *Tombstone's Epitaph;* Penfield, *Dig Here!;* Raine, *Famous Sheriffs and Western Outlaws;* Walters, *Tombstone's Yesterdays;* Wellman, *The Trampling Herd.*

Hunt, Sam (AKA: **Golf Bag**), d.1956, U.S., org. crime. Sam Hunt became known as "Golf Bag" in 1927, when he and "Machine Gun" Jack McGurn were discovered with a still-warm machine gun in a golf bag filled with clubs at the scene of a recent murder. As the two mobsters innocently told police they were playing a round of golf, the corpse mysteriously disappeared, leaving only a pool of blood on the grass. Hunt had a long career as one of Al Capone's toughest enforcers, with more than twenty murders attributed to him. He died of a heart ailment in 1956.

REF.: *CBA;* Kobler, *Capone;* Lait and Mortimer, *Chicago: Confidential;* McClellan, *Crime Without Punishment;* Morgan, *Prince of Crime;* Peterson, *The Mob;* Smith, *Syndicate City;* Spiering, *The Man Who Got Capone.*

Hunt, Virnell, 1955- , U.S., rape-mur. Virnell Hunt, twenty-five, was the janitor for the Madison, Wis., apartment complex where Jeanne Broomell and her husband Ron Broomell lived. On Jan. 20, 1970, Hunt, using his janitor keys, entered the Broomell apartment, grabbed Jeanne from behind, pistol-whipped her, dragged her unconscious to the bedroom, and raped her. When she regained consciousness, Hunt, knowing she would recognize him, shot her in the chest with a .22-caliber pistol.

Police followed the few clues Virnell left behind, such as a piece of cloth with paint on it used as a gag. Eventually they linked him to the murder through a jacket he wore the day of the rape-murder that held some of Jeanne's hair. Virnell's brother then turned over a .22-caliber pistol which ballistic tests proved fired the bullet found in Broomell's lung. Virnell Hunt confessed to the rape-murder when confronted with the evidence, was found Guilty at his trial, and sentenced to life in prison. REF.: *CBA.*

Hunt, Ward, 1810-86, U.S., jur. Associate justice of U.S. Supreme Court. An abolitionist, he split with the Democratic party over the slavery issue and helped found the Republican party in New York in 1855. He was elected judge of the state court of appeals in 1865, and was chief judge of the court from 1868-69. He was nominated by President Ulysses S. Grant in 1872 to the U.S. Supreme Court, serving from 1873-82. He was not a major influence on the Court, suffering a heart attack after six years and retiring three years later. REF.: *CBA.*

Hunt, William Henry, 1823-84, U.S., jur. Practiced law in New Orleans. He was appointed attorney general of Louisiana in 1876. He was named an associate judge of the U.S. Court of Claims by President Rutherford B. Hayes in 1878. He also served as the U.S. secretary of the navy from 1881-82, and as U.S. minister to Russia from 1882-84. REF.: *CBA.*

Hunt, William Henry, 1857-1949, U.S., jur. Served as district attorney of Choteau County, Mont., from 1884-86, as associate justice of the Montana Supreme Court at Helena from 1887-94, as secretary of state of Puerto Rico from 1900-1901, and as governor of the Territory of Puerto Rico from 1901-04. He was nominated to the District Court of Montana by President Theodore Roosevelt in 1904. REF.: *CBA.*

Hunted Down, 1859, a novel by Charles Dickens. This work of fiction is based upon the life and bad times of Thomas Griffiths Wainewright, a noted literary light and habitual poisoner (Brit.-Fr., 1830s). Dickens calls him Julius Slinkton in this novel. See: **Wainewright, Thomas Griffiths.** REF.: *CBA.*

Hunter, Benjamin F., d.1878, U.S., mur. After losing $7,000 in a music publishing firm owned by John M. Armstrong, Benjamin F. Hunter devised a scheme to recoup his loss. He insured Armstrong for $25,000 and then, with the aid of Tom Graham, hired as a henchman, lured Armstrong to Camden, N.J., promising to provide the publisher with more investors. Once Armstrong entered a room rented by Hunter for the bogus investors' meeting, Hunter crashed an ax down on Armstrong's head. Hunter left Armstrong for dead, along with the ax which he had marked with another man's initials, hoping in this way to fix blame for the murder on another.

Armstrong, however, survived the vicious attack and was returned home where his head was bandaged. Before he was able to talk to authorities, Hunter visited Armstrong and, while alone with the stricken man, ripped off Armstrong's bandages and pounded his old wounds so that Armstrong died a short time later. Graham, however, after not receiving his pay from Hunter, as promised, confessed to his part in the crime. Hunter was convicted and sentenced to death while Graham received a light prison sentence. Hunter was hanged "by hand," in that the executioner had to chop a rope at the side of a small gallows to release a weight. When the weight shot down, it yanked up the rope affixed about Hunter's neck, jerking him upward to death.

The hanging of Benjamin Hunter.

REF.: *CBA; Hunter-Armstrong Tragedy.*

Hunter, David, 1802-86, U.S., law enfor. off. West Point graduate who became a major general in the Civil War. He served as president of the military commission responsible for trying the conspirators in the Lincoln assassination. REF.: *CBA.*

Hunter, Edward, d.1864, U.S., mur. After twenty-five years of marriage, Edward and Elizabeth Hunter, residents of New York City, could no longer stand the sight of each other and decided to separate. They divided their property, but the night before the couple was to go their separate ways, Hunter decided that his wife was entitled to none of their belongings. He beat her to death and was found with blood-smeared clothes a short time later. He was convicted and hanged.

REF.: *CBA;* Clinton, *Speech of Henry L. Clinton, Esq. to the Jury Upon the Part of the Defence on the Trial of Edward Hunter.*

Hunter, Thomas, d.1700, Brit., mur. A chaplain well on his way to becoming an ordained minister, Thomas Hunter, born in Fife County in Scotland, and educated at the University of St. Andrew, followed clerical tradition by becoming a live-in tutor for a wealthy man's children while working towards his ordination. A prominent merchant and an alderman of Edinburgh, Mr. Gordon brought Hunter into his home to tutor his daughter and two sons. For the next two years Hunter served the family well, but then became involved with Mrs. Gordon's personal attendant. The couple, however, was one day discovered by the children. The next day, the servant was dismissed, but Hunter was allowed to stay, after he had apologized, and promised not to repeat the lapse.

Clergyman Thomas Hunter killing the Gordon boys.

Hunter plotted retribution. One evening the Gordons were invited to dinner in Edinburgh and took only their daughter. Hunter took his ritual walk in the fields with the two boys, and at one point sat down, pretending to rest in the grass while the boys caught butterflies and picked flowers. Hunter then called the boys over to him, reproached them for telling their parents what they had seen, and said he was going to kill them. The boys tried to flee, but he caught them and cut their throats. A man walking by on the road witnessed the murders, and Hunter was captured on the bank of the river where he had gone to drown himself. Brought to trial, he pleaded guilty, and said that his only regret was that he had not been able to kill the daughter as well.

According to the Scottish law of the times, Hunter was condemned to be executed at the spot where he had murdered the children—a special gallows was built for the hanging. His right hand was to be cut off at the wrist prior to the execution, and afterwards his body was to be hanged in chains between Edinburgh and Leith, with the knife he had used to commit the murders stuck through his hand.

"There is no God—I do not believe there is any; or, if there is, I hold him in defiance," Hunter said on his last day—Aug. 22, 1700. REF.: *CBA.*

Hunter, William, 1865-1957, Brit., jur. Became a judge in 1905, and member of Parliament in 1910. He served as solicitor-general for Scotland in 1910, and as judge of the court of session in Scotland in 1911. In 1919, he was sent to India to preside over an inquiry into the Amritsar shootings that hampered relations between Britain and India. REF.: *CBA.*

Hunt-Gant Gang, prom. 1920s-30s, U.S., rob. The most dangerous gang of robbers in Florida and adjoining states for almost two decades was the Hunt-Gant Gang, led by Riley and Hugh Gant and Alva Dewey Hunt. The Gants and Hunt were brothers-in-law and they began operations about 1920, stealing autos and changing the serial numbers, then creating fake titles and reselling the cars. These men soon took to robbing post offices throughout the South, along with rural stores and small banks. Hunt was born on Nov. 23, 1898, in Bushnell, Fla. He was first arrested on Feb. 19, 1924, charged with auto theft. He was later sent to the federal penitentiary in Atlanta for a year and a day, being released on Feb. 5, 1931. His erstwhile partner in crime, Hugh Gant, was born in Tampa, Fla., on Jan. 2, 1900. He

was arrested for auto theft on Nov. 4, 1927, but he escaped.

When Alva Hunt was released from Atlanta, he rejoined the Gants and they immediately began to rob banks. Riley Gant was killed in August 1933 while attempting to rob a store at Penny Farms, Fla. Hugh Gant was caught next, on Sept. 6, 1933, following a post office robbery, but he escaped and rejoined Hunt. On Feb. 28, 1935, Hunt and Gant robbed the State Bank of Haines, Fla., of $4,000. On May 17, 1935, Hunt and Gant robbed the State Bank at Bowling Green, Fla. In August 1935, the two men robbed the bank at Mulberry, Fla. On Jan. 14, 1936, Hunt, Gant, and two others robbed the Dixie County State Bank at Cross City, Fla., stealing about $5,000. The gang raided the Columbia Bank at Ybor City, Fla., on March 3, 1936, taking $30,459, their largest haul to that time. On June 2, 1936, Hunt, Gant, and others struck the Farmers and Merchants Bank at Foley, Ala., taking more than $7,000.

Of the two, Alva Hunt was the most outgoing, a man who loved tailored clothes and fine restaurants. He also had an insatiable appetite for female companionship. Gant often warned Hunt that a woman would be his downfall. Hunt and Gant were later caught when one of the many women Hunt was seeing turned the gang members into police. Both men were given life sentences.

REF.: *CBA;* Gish, *American Bandits.*

Huntington Library Fakes, U.S., forg. Founded in 1919, the famous Huntington Library in San Marino, Calif., is the home of fifty-four of fifty-five forged first editions of almost every English writer of the Victorian period. These forgeries, which fooled their American buyers who paid an enormous sum for them, include: Elizabeth Barrett Browning's *Sonnets from the Portuguese,* Kipling, Stevenson, Dickens, and Tennyson. Huntington holds these editions in high value, as they are among the greatest forgeries in the history of literature.

REF.: *CBA;* MacDougall, *Hoaxes.*

Hunton, Joseph, prom. 1829, Brit., forg. Joseph Hunton, once a very wealthy Quaker, turned to forgery later in life but was caught and sentenced to die by the Privy Council's notorious "hanging judges."

Common sentiment ran that the sentence was too severe for the crime, but the judges refused a pardon. Hunton was hanged on Dec. 8, 1829, by one of England's more famous—albeit less skilled—hangman, James Foxen. Foxen used an unusually long rope to hang Hunton as he was a small man and did not weigh much. Unlike many hanged by Foxen, Hunton died instantly.

REF.: Bleackley, *Hangmen of England; CBA.*

Hunyadi, Lásziló (Ladislas Hunyady or **Huniades),** 1433-57, Hung., mur. Fought in battles along with father, János, but was accused by enemies of his family of killing him in 1456. Without a trial, he was condemned and beheaded. REF.: *CBA.*

Hurd, Roosevelt Carlos, Sr., 1902- , Case of, U.S., mur. Roosevelt Carlos Hurd, Sr., the leader of a lynch mob, was tried along with thirty taxi drivers for murder and conspiracy to commit murder in Greenville, S.C.

On Feb. 15, 1947, a taxi driver named Thomas Watson Brown picked up Willie Earle, a 24-year-old black man who asked to be taken to his mother's home. The taxi never got there and Earle walked home. Brown was discovered near his taxi just a few miles from where he picked up Earle, bleeding from deep knife wounds and taken to a hospital were his condition did not improve. The apparent motive for the assault was robbery. Earle, recently released from serving time in a penitentiary on an assault charge, was quickly arrested and jailed.

The following evening, the Pickens County jailer, J. Ed Gilstrap, called the sheriff to say that he had been forced to give Willie Earle to a mob of about fifty men who arrived in taxis, a mob organized by Hurd. The jailer had released Earle to the mob when they simply asked, saying, "I guess you boys know what you're doing..." The jailer requested only that they not use profanity as his wife might overhear them. The mob took Earle to a side road between Greenville and Pickens, beat him senseless, stabbed him repeatedly, and then shot him in the head. They left his body on the side of the road, his brain tissue splattered in the surrounding bushes.

When local authorities did not act, Attorney General Tom C. Clark called in the FBI. While an obvious lynching, the FBI brought in indictments against thirty-one men for conspiring to murder, accessories before and after the fact of murder, and murder. At the trial on Feb. 17, 1947, the defendants were—not surprisingly—acquitted of all charges by an all-white jury of their peers. Only one juror appeared ashamed. And when Judge James Robert Martin, Jr. read the verdict, his face flushed and he left the courtroom without thanking the jury.

REF.: *CBA; West, A Train of Powder.*

Hurkos, Peter (Pieter Van der Hurk), 1911-88, Neth., crime psychic. Some claim a gift of prophecy but can deliver little in the way of proof. Others, like Peter Hurkos, have demonstrated psychic abilities and have used their gifts to help police solve baffling crimes.

Hurkos was born in Dordrecht, Neth., in 1911. Born blind, he did not gain his sight for six months. He later earned his living as a sailor but gave up the sea to become a house painter like his father. On July 10, 1941, while painting a four-story building in The Hague, Hurkos tumbled off a scaffold and suffered a concussion. When he awoke in the Zuidwal Hospital he stared up at the nurse as an image flashed before him. "Be careful. I see you on a train," he said. "You may lose a suitcase that belongs to a friend of yours." It so happened that the woman did leave a friend's suitcase on the dining car of the train that same day. From then on Hurkos claimed he could foretell the future and recite a person's history by examining a personal belonging.

After WWII, he gave private readings for a number of women in The Hague and solved a rash of arson fires in Arnhem and Mijegen, Neth. His fame and popularity quickly spread, but it was not until 1950 that he involved himself in police detection on an international level. On Christmas Day of that year a group of Scottish students removed the Stone of Scone, a sacred artifact dating to 1296, from London's Westminster Abbey.

Hurkos, invited by Scotland Yard to lend his talents to the investigation, examined the Coronation Chair where the stone rested and was able to formulate a distinct impression. "I see it in the remains of an old church," he said. "It has gone north of the border to Scotland. It was taken by students. It will be found within a month." Four weeks later the stone was found in the ruins of Arbroath Abbey. The English denied they had solicited his help.

Hurkos spent the next five years assisting the French Sûreté in Paris. He traveled to the U.S. for the first time in 1957, and a year later was asked by the Miami police to help them locate and identify the person who killed a local cabdriver. Hurkos told them the assailant was a man called "Smitty" who was "tall and thin, who walks like a sailor," adding that the suspect had also killed a navy commander in Key Largo, Fla. A month later Charles Smith, a merchant seaman, was arrested in New Orleans and charged with murder. He was subsequently imprisoned for life for the crimes.

Between June 1962 and January 1964, thirteen women of varying ages were assaulted and killed in Boston. The local police were stymied in their efforts to track down this serial killer, known as the "Boston Strangler." Hurkos was brought to a hotel suite in the city and shown photographs of the murdered women. He demonstrated for the police the positioning of the victims. "That woman," he said. "Like this!" The psychic closely examined items of clothing belonging to the victims, and a letter written by one of the purported suspects. The murderer he said, was a middle-aged man with effeminate characteristics, and connected to the shoe trade in some way. The Boston police already had such a man in custody, a door-to-door salesman who specialized in nurses' shoes. Hurkos left town satisfied that the killer had been found. "My work here is finished," he said. "The strangler will not strike again." But it was Albert DeSalvo, and not the shoe salesman

Hurkos identified, who was eventually charged with the murder. DeSalvo was a small-time burglar who confessed to the crimes. But there were many, Hurkos included, who believed the police fingered the wrong man.

In the 1960s, the Dutch psychic counseled such Hollywood celebrities as Marlon Brando, Tony Bennett, and Tony Curtis, who played the role of DeSalvo in the movie version of the *Boston Strangler.* In 1969 Hurkos was drawn into the Tate-LaBianca murder investigation, and the slayings of eight young women near the campus of the University of Michigan. "I see pictures in my mind like a television screen," Peter Hurkos explained. "When I touch something, I can then tell what I see." He died in Los Angeles on June 4, 1988, from heart failure. See: Collins, John Norman (The Ypsilanti Ripper); DeSalvo, Albert Henry. REF.: *CBA.*

Hurley, William J., d.1909, U.S., brib. Arrested and acquitted for accepting a bribe while a juror, William J. Hurley was arrested again Jan. 28, 1895, for attempting to bribe a juryman serving on a perjury trial. He pleaded guilty, saying he had received $500 for hanging the first jury and was promised $5,000 for hanging the second. Hurley was found Guilty on Mar. 29, 1895, and sentenced to five years in prison. During his trial, he attempted suicide twice.

REF.: *CBA; Duke, Celebrated Criminal Cases of America.*

Hurst, Sir Cecil James Barrington, 1870-1963, Brit., jur. Judge of the permanent court of international justice at the Hague from 1929-46, and president of the court from 1934-36. REF.: *CBA.*

Hurtado de Mendoza, Diego, 1503-75, Spain, exile. Spanish diplomat who served as governor of Siena in 1547 and as imperial representative in Rome in 1549. After being exiled to Granada, he authored *Guerra de Granda,* a description of the Morisco revolt. REF.: *CBA.*

Husbands, Hermon, 1724-95, U.S., rebel. Led rebels in Maryland and headed the 1794 Whiskey Insurrection in Pennsylvania. He was tried and condemned to be executed but was subsequently pardoned. REF.: *CBA.*

Huss, John (Johannes Hus von Husinetz, Jan Hus, Hus), c.1369-1415, Bohemia, her. Religious reformer of Bohemia who began preaching after studying Wycliffe but was excommunicated in 1410. There was a papal censure issued against him in 1412. Protected by King Wenceslaus and Emperor Sigismund, he went to the Council of Constance in 1414. He was tried for heresy, condemned, and burned at the stake. His execution incited a furor that resulted in the Hussite War, which lasted from 1419-34. REF.: *CBA.*

Hussein (ibn Talal), 1935-   , Jor., King, 1953-   , (attempt.) assass. At age seventeen, Hussein was proclaimed king of Jordan after his father Talal was forced to step down because of mental illness. The young monarch continued his father's cautious pro-western policy that brought economic prosperity to his nation because of continuing financial aid from the West.

In the late 1950s, Gamal Abdel Nasser, the volatile ruler of Egypt, began pressuring Hussein to sever his ties with the West and align himself with the Palestinians who were fighting to re-establish autonomy in the region now known as Israel. Nasser encouraged Palestinian refugees and militant factions within Jordan to assassinate Hussein to bring the region more into line with prevailing Arab philosophies. On six occasions, hired assassins tried and failed to kill the king, often through diabolical means. One morning Hussein opened his medicine chest to apply some nosedrops. As he tilted his head back, a single drop fell into the basin. The king watched with amazement and horror as a deadly acid burned a hole through the enamel and on to the floor.

In 1967 the Israelis smashed Jordan during the Six-Day War, claiming the West Bank, an area that has remained in dispute ever since. Hussein suffered further political embarrassments when the Palestinian Liberation Organization (PLO) established guerrilla bases deep in the heart of Jordan to carry out covert raids against Israel. In September 1970 Hussein's army attempted to expel the

PLO following a series of devastating battles in the capital city of Amman several months earlier. The PLO was driven out a year later, but the Black September Movement, named after the bloody fighting inside Jordan gave new meaning to international terrorism. Since that time King Hussein has pursued a cautious policy of reconciliation with the Arab world while maintaining close ties to the U.S. and Great Britain. See: **Arafat, Yasir; Black September; Palestine Liberation Organization.**

REF.: Bell, *Assassin;* CBA; Paine, *The Assassins' World.*

Hussein Avni Pasha, 1819-76, Turk., consp.-rebel.-assass. Fought in Montenegro from 1859-60 and in Crete from 1867-69. He served as the minister of war from 1869-71 and in 1875, as grand vizier in 1874, and as governor of Smyrna in 1875. He headed the plan in 1876 in which Murad V ousted Abdul-Aziz and was assassinated shortly thereafter. REF.: *CBA.*

Hussey, Charles, d.1818, Brit., mur. When Mr. Bird was noticed missing from his usual seat in church on Feb. 8, 1818, neighbors broke into his house and found he and his housekeeper murdered and the house robbed.

After weeks of investigation, suspicion fell on Charles Hussey, a penniless man observed loitering in front of Bird's house and who roomed in the boarding house directly behind Bird's residence. Brought in and questioned by the police, he was quickly turned loose as there were no grounds on which to hold him. On his release, Hussey immediately fled the vicinity and was captured and arrested in Deddington, a seaport, and returned to London to stand trial. Found Guilty on July 31, 1818, he was hanged the following morning.

REF.: Armitage, *Bow Street Runners;* CBA; Logan, *Masters of Crime.*

Hussmann, Karl, 1908- , Case of, Ger., mur. In the early morning of Mar. 23, 1928, Helmuth Daube, a 19-year-old student, was killed in front of his parent's home in Gladbeck, Ger. Seven people heard his screams but none investigated. Daube had died by the time a doctor arrived on the scene to find his throat slashed and his genitals cut off.

Police learned that Daube had attended a fraternity party with two friends, Karl Labs and Karl Hussmann, a 20-year-old student from another town. Though Inspector Klingelhöller had already made up his mind that Daube committed suicide, his suspicions were aroused when he questioned Hussmann, the last person with Daube. He noticed Hussmann's shoes were wet and bloodstained. Also, Hussmann seemed vague about the time he left Daube and arrived home. Klingelhöller asked for Hussmann's shoes for further examination, thinking Hussmann had witnessed Daube's suicide. But when Klingelhöller learned Daube had been emasculated with several cuts of a knife, his suspicion turned more acutely toward Hussmann.

Hussmann was arrested and jailed when the blood on his shoes proved to be Daube's blood. Police examined the coat and trousers Hussmann wore the night of the murder and found them bloodstained, but lab tests revealed this blood was Hussmann's. Confronted with this information, Hussmann said he cut his finger, but the cut was not substantial and was already long healed. More evidence accumulated against Hussmann—the discovery of a knife he hid in a garden after the police searched there, the revelation of a sadistic homosexual relationship between Hussmann and a reluctant Daube, and the blood on Hussmann's shoes which laboratory tests proved was type A human blood and not cat or frog blood as Hussmann had claimed.

Klingelhöller hypothesized that when Daube broke their relationship off, Hussmann slit his throat from behind. The struggle left Hussmann with a bloody nose and Daube's blood on his shoes. Hussmann's homosexuality was confirmed when police discovered love letters sent by Hussmann to another inmate while in jail.

The two-week trial began on Oct. 16, 1928, in Essen. While the jury was unconvinced of Hussmann's innocence, it was unwilling to convict on purely scientific evidence. Hussmann was acquitted.

REF.: CBA; Thorwald, *Crime and Science.*

Hutcheson, Charles Sterling, 1894-1969, U.S., jur. Served as U.S. district attorney of the eastern district of Virginia from 1933-44. He was nominated to the eastern district court of Virginia by President Franklin D. Roosevelt in 1944. REF.: *CBA.*

Hutchings, Harvey, 1678-1704, Brit., rob. Apprenticed to a silversmith in Shrewsbury at fourteen, Harvey Hutchings was soon dismissed for stealing from his employer and was sent to Shrewsbury Jail, where he heard of London's notable robberies and criminals. Upon his release he made his way to London in search of Mr. Constantine. Finding him at Snottynose Hill's Dog Tavern in Newgate Street, Hutchings explained that he wanted to study with him to learn the trade. Giving the boy six pence and a few glasses of wine, Constantine agreed to take him on as a pupil if he proved himself diligent.

The next night Constantine took Hutchings to an alehouse in Cheapside. Months before, Constantine had stolen a silver drinking pitcher from the premises, and having returned since then in disguise, knew of other silver there. If Hutchings could get out with another silver tankard, Constantine told the boy, he would take him on as an apprentice. Just before they entered the alehouse, the boy asked Constantine if he was a good runner. Constantine said he was and then went inside and asked for a room. Hutchings, following as his servant, then asked at the desk if a tankard had been stolen recently, and pointed to Constantine as the thief. Constantine ran out, the proprietor in pursuit, and Hutchings grabbed a silver tankard off the bar.

After three years with Constantine, Hutchings lived well and profitably for some nine years as a thief in and around London and Westminster. Apprehended for robbing a house at Duke's Place of some £400 in money and silver, he was hanged at Tyburn in 1704, at the age of twenty-six.

REF.: *CBA;* Smith, *Highwaymen.*

Hutchins, Harry Burns, 1847-1930, U.S., lawyer. After practicing law from 1876-84, became law professor at the University of Michigan from 1884-87. He served as the dean of the law school at Cornell University from 1887-95, and of the University of Michigan from 1895-1910. He became the president of the University of Michigan in 1910, holding the position until 1920. REF.: *CBA.*

Hutchins, Robert Maynard, 1899-1977, U.S., lawyer. Served as dean of Yale Law School from 1927-29. He was the president of the University of Chicago from 1929-45, and chancellor from 1945-51. REF.: *CBA.*

Hutchinson, Amy, d.1750, Brit., mur. Born on the Isle of Ely, Amy Hutchinson, at sixteen, fell in love. Her lover, however, despite having promised to marry her, decided to go to London saying he would marry her when he returned. In revenge, she married John Hutchinson, even though she had never liked him.

A few days after her wedding, Hutchinson renewed her relationship with her lover, and the two plotted to kill the unwanted spouse. Spiking her husband's ale with arsenic, Hutchinson watched him drink and then offered to shop for dinner. By dinner time he was dead.

After the funeral, Hutchinson's lover indiscreetly renewed his visits, and the widow was immediately taken into custody. Tried, convicted, and sentenced to die, she left a letter of warning with her clergyman: "That they [other young women] should never leave the person they are engaged to in a pet, nor wed another, to whom they are indifferent, in spite; for, if they come together without affection, the smallest matter will separate them." Amy Hutchinson was strangled and burned at Ely on Nov. 7, 1750. REF.: *CBA.*

Hutchinson, Anne (Anne Marbury), 1591-1643, U.S., sland.-her. Born in Britain, married William Hutchinson and in 1634 came to Boston, Mass. She preached that a person could be saved by knowledge of God's grace and love, and that salvation did not depend on adherence to church or government rules. She was tried, convicted in 1637, and banished from the Massachusetts Bay Colony for slandering ministers. Indians murdered her and her family in 1643.

REF.: *CBA*; Mitchell, *The Newgate Calendar*; Nash, *Look For the Woman*.

Hutchinson, Francis, d.1739, Brit., witchcraft. Before Francis Hutchinson became bishop of Down and Connor in 1721, he wrote his landmark *Historical Essay Concerning Witchcraft*, the work largely responsible for the "death" of witchcraft trials. In it, he refuted witchcraft as a dying superstition in which no intelligent person would believe. Having witnessed witchcraft trials on a grand scale, including the notorious trials at St. James' at Bury St. Edmunds in 1662 where he had recently been made vicar, Hutchinson pointed out the obvious political and monetary motivations of past witchcraft trials and the indefensibility of accusations made by "possessed" persons.

In *Historical Essay* he wrote, "...for if any wicked person affirms, or any crackbrained girl imagines, or any lying spirit makes her believe, that she sees any old woman, or other person pursuing her in visions, the defenders of the vulgar witchcraft tack an imaginary, unproved compact to the deposition, and hang the accused parties for things that they were doing when they were, perhaps, asleep upon their beds, or saying their prayers, or, perhaps, in the accuser's own possession with double irons upon them." REF.: *CBA*.

Hutchinson, John, 1615-64, Brit., regicide. Governor of Nottingham and member of Parliament. He signed the death warrant of Charles I and was imprisoned after the Restoration.

REF.: *CBA*; Roughead, *Reprobates Reviewed*; Shew, *A Companion to Murder*; Thompson, *Poison Mysteries Unsolved*.

Hutchinson, St. John, 1884-1942, Brit., lawyer. Practiced law after 1909 on the Southeastern Circuit, and became a judge in 1935. He served as defense counsel for Frederick Field and Alfred Arthur Kopsch. REF.: *CBA*.

Hutchinson, Thomas, 1711-80, U.S., rebel. Administrator in colonial America whose strict attempts to enforce Stamp Act and other British policies indirectly hastened the American Revolution. He served in the Massachusetts legislature from 1737-49, and as a member of the governor's council from 1749-66. A mob tore down his house in 1765 because of his support of the Stamp Act. He ruled as the royal governor of Massachusetts from 1771-74. He found that his actions only fanned rebellion, and in 1774 he was forced into permanent exile in Britain. REF.: *CBA*.

Hutchison, Harvey Macleary, b.1878, U.S., jur. Served as special justice department prosecutor for Puerto Rico from 1904-11, as judge of the district of Guayama from 1911-12, and as judge of the district of Mayaguez from 1913-14. He was nominated to the supreme court of Puerto Rico by President Woodrow Wilson in 1914. REF.: *CBA*.

Hutchison, John James, 1887-1911, Brit., suic.-mur. John James Hutchison, a chemist's assistant who speculated heavily in stocks, found himself in financial trouble and decided to poison his father and collect on a life insurance policy worth £4,000.

On Feb. 3, 1911, Mr. and Mrs. Charles Hutchison gave a dinner party. John and his fiancée were in attendance as well as seventeen other guests. After dinner, John served coffee, which three guests declined. Within minutes those who drank the coffee were writhing in agony as John had put arsenic in it. Charles Hutchison and the local grocer died from the poisoning, while the others were taken to a hospital where they made slow, painful recoveries.

John quietly left town but a warrant was issued for his arrest. On Feb. 20, he was found by Sergeant Burley in a boarding house on the island of Guernsey. But before the sergeant could get him out of the house, Hutchison swallowed a vial of prussic acid and died before a doctor could be summoned. REF.: *CBA*.

Hutten, Philipp von, c.1511-1546, Venez., assass. Conquered Venezuela along with a group sent by the Augsburg family of Welser. He began serving as the captain general in 1540 but left to explore the interior of the South American country. When he returned to the coastal capital in 1546, he found a Spanish governor in power, who ordered his execution. REF.: *CBA*.

Hutton, Peregrine, d.1820, U.S., rob.-mur. A thief since childhood, Peregrine Hutton graduated to highway robbery in his twenties. He and his novice partner, Morris N.B. Hull, twice attempted to rob the Baltimore mail stage but were driven off when the driver fired several shots at them. A determined pair, Hutton and Hull planned to attack the stagecoach some days later. Hutton got Hull to promise him that he would help kill the driver if they thought the driver recognized them. They did stop the stage and Hutton killed the driver, believing that he had been recognized. Taking the small amount of money carried in a strongbox, the careless robbers overlooked a passenger hiding on the floor of the stagecoach, one who knew Hutton and later went to authorities to identify him. Hutton and Hull were quickly apprehended, tried, and convicted. Both men were hanged in Baltimore on July 14, 1820.

REF.: *CBA*; Hutton, *The Life and Confession of Peregrine Hutton*; Nash, *Bloodletters and Badmen*; *A True and Correct Account of the Confession of Peregrine Hutton*.

Huynh Phu So (Huyen, AKA: **Dao Khung, Mad Monk, Phat Song**), 1919-47, Viet., her. Wandering Buddhist preacher who developed new religion called Phat Giao Hoa Hao. The religion emphasized an ascetic, simple form of worship based on Confucianism, Buddhism, animism, and sorcery. Although he gained a following as a faith healer and prophet, he was persecuted and exiled by the French. He was imprisoned by the Japanese during WWII and ultimately executed by the communist Viet Minh. REF.: *CBA*.

Hwan, Chun Kyung, 1943- , S. Kor., brib.-embez. As head of a rural development organization subsidized by the government, Chun Kyung Hwan embezzled close to $10 million dollars in private and public funds before he was discovered. The 45-year-old Hwan, the younger brother of Chun Doo Hwan, a former president of South Korea, was sentenced to seven years in prison in September 1988 for embezzlement and accepting bribes. REF.: *CBA*.

Hyde, Dr. **Bennett Clarke**, b.1869, U.S., mur. Dr. Bennett Clarke Hyde was an opportunistic physician who reportedly tried to wipe out an entire family through systematic poisoning. At age forty, the tall, good-looking Hyde was married to the niece of Thomas Swope, the richest man in Kansas City, Mo. Hyde was the medical adviser to the Swope family and lived in Swope's huge mansion. Swope, in 1909, was eighty-two and in ill health. He appointed James Hunton, an old family friend, as executor of his will and estate. Hyde realized that to control the Swope millions he would have to position himself in Hunton's role. When Hunton fell ill in September 1909, Hyde treated him, or, more specifically, mistreated him by using an ancient cure-all of doctors.

Dr. Bennett Clarke Hyde, who tried to kill off the Swope family.

He bled Hunton to "purify" his blood. In truth, Hyde simply bled the old man to death and then attributed the cause of his death to apoplexy, signing Hunton's death certificate himself.

Swope was so overwhelmed by the death of his good friend that he himself grew ill and Dr. Hyde tended to him. A nurse attending to Swope later reported that Dr. Hyde took her aside one day and said to her: "Now that Hunton is dead, Mr. Swope will require a new administrator for his estate. I think it would be a good idea if you suggested to Mr. Swope that I take over those duties." The nurse refused, telling Hyde that it was not her place to make such suggestions. Hyde then went into Swope's bedroom and gave him a number of pills. In a few minutes, Swope's pallor turned a marked blue and his skin was cold to the touch, according to the nurse.

"I wish I hadn't taken those pills!" Swope cried out to the nurse.

Hyde told the nurse to leave the millionaire's room, ordering her to boil some water. When she returned with the water about ten minutes later, she saw Hyde covering Swope's face with a bed sheet. "He's gone, poor soul," the doctor told her.

"What? Already?" The nurse checked Swope's pulse. There was none. He was dead and the nurse found it hard to believe that the patient could have died in such a short amount of time, especially from the symptoms he had manifested.

"At that age, they can go quickly," Dr. Hyde told her. He then added that the cause of death was apoplexy, which had also claimed Hunton. Swope's millions were then distributed to several nephews and nieces. Mrs. Frances Hyde received more than $250,000, of which her husband immediately took control. Though that was a great fortune for the day, Dr. Hyde meant to obtain the rest of the money. Four of the five nephews and nieces were quickly stricken by what their doctor diagnosed as attacks of typhoid. Christian Swope, one of the nephews, died in November 1909, while being tended by Hyde in the old Swope mansion, but the others recovered. Hyde reported the death as a result of typhoid. The family nurse went to Frances Hyde and told her: "People are being murdered in this house."

Mrs. Frances Hyde, who believed her husband innocent of murdering her relatives.

Instead becoming suspicious, the devoted spouse angrily fired the nurse and then reported the nurse's statements to the family lawyer, which brought suspicion upon Hyde himself. The lawyer cautioned Mrs. Hyde to employ another doctor to tend to the still-living nieces and nephews. Another doctor was brought in and he consulted with a bacteriologist, who reported that there were no typhoid germs in the family's water supply system. Hyde no longer tended to the sick Swope relatives and they improved greatly.

While under suspicion, Hyde began taking long walks at night and was followed on one of these nocturnal sojourns. He was seen taking something from his pocket, which he crushed into a mound of snow. The object, a capsule, was retrieved by the person following the doctor; it proved to contain grains of potassium cyanide, a deadly poison. Family members went to the police and a full-scale investigation ensued. The bodies of Hunton and Swope were exhumed and were found to contain strychnine and cyanide. Hyde had cleverly poisoned both men with the two poisons, knowing that each poison would disguise the symptoms of the other. The physician was charged with murdering Swope and Hunton on Feb. 9, 1910. The resulting trial made headlines coast to coast. Shocked readers learned how Hyde intended to murder off the entire Swope family to gain the family millions. Only Frances Hyde believed her husband innocent and she put up the money to cover the $100,000 bond to free her husband until the conclusion of his trial.

A pharmacist testified that Hyde had purchased both strychnine and cyanide from him. At the time, said the pharmacist, Hyde said he needed these deadly poisons to get rid of wild dogs who had been "howling near my house and causing me no end of sleepless nights." Then Dr. L. Stewart, a bacteriologist, testified that Hyde had come to him, stating that he intended to take up the study of bacteriology and, for that purpose, he needed typhoid germs. Stewart gave these cultures to Hyde but, a short time later,

he grew nervous about releasing such dangerous germs to Hyde and went to Hyde's home, asking that the cultures be returned. Hyde told him that, unfortunately, he had dropped the glass slides containing these cultures and that he had thrown them out for fear of contamination. This was only a few days before Christian Swope died of typhoid.

Such damning testimony brought a verdict of Guilty after a month-long trial. Dr. Hyde was given a life term but, before leaving for prison, the physician turned to reporters and used his greatest weapon, his wife, who was convinced of his innocence. "This case is not closed," Hyde told members of the press with a smug smile. "My wife Frances will not forsake me. She knows that this is a plot by certain members of the Swope family to get rid of me. They have hated me from the start—thought of me as an interloper. Yes, Frances will know what to do."

Frances Swope Hyde remained loyal to her murderous husband, as he knew she would. She hired the most expensive and talented lawyers available and they bombarded the courts with every known appeal. Mrs. Hyde went so far as to hire a publicist who spread the news that the Swope family had formed a conspiracy to defame her husband. By that time, Mrs. Hyde had denounced her entire family and had vowed her undying loyalty to her imprisoned husband. Mrs. Hyde's lawyers found some technical errors in her husband's trial and convinced the Supreme Court of Kansas to order a new trial in 1911. At the end of this trial, one juror grew ill and the proceedings were declared a mistrial. This juror's ailments were never disclosed and it was claimed that he was bribed to feign sickness. A third trial ended in a hung jury. It was again claimed that Mrs. Hyde's money was used to bribe several members of this jury to bring about a hung jury.

Hyde was sent to trial a fourth time in 1917, and this trial, like the two before it, had been the systematic plan of Hyde's clever lawyers. As soon as this trial commenced they moved to have their client released, pointing out a rule of law that stated that their client had gone to trial three times and, according to existing laws, could not be tried a fourth time. Dr. Bennett Clarke Hyde was released and went to live with his wife. He no longer practiced medicine. Almost a decade later, Mrs. Hyde separated from her husband. She had complained to him one day of a stomachache and he told her that he would prepare a special medicine for her. At that juncture, Mrs. Hyde thought it was time she left her husband, preferring the treatment of another doctor and, apparently, the preservation of her own life.

REF.: Archer, *Killers in the Clear; CBA;* Duke, *Celebrated Criminal Cases of America;* Furneaux, *The Medical Murderer;* Nash, *Almanac of World Crime;* ____, *Murder Among the Mighty;* Smith, *Famous American Poison Mysteries;* Stevens, *From Clue to Dock.*

Hyde, Charles Cheney, 1873-1952, U.S., jur. Taught international law from 1907-25 at Northwestern University and at Columbia University from 1925-45. He served as a solicitor for the U.S. department of state from 1923-25, and as a member of the Permanent Court of Arbitration at the Hague from 1951-52. REF.: *CBA.*

Hyde, Edward (Earl of Clarendon), 1609-74, Brit., mur. Chief advisor to King Charles and Charles II, and lord chancellor for Charles II in 1658. He was influential in restoring a national monarchy. As lord chancellor in 1660, he controlled many governmental departments, but fell from favor with the sale of Dunkirk and the start of the Dutch War. He was dismissed in 1667 and fled to France under the threat of impeachment by the House of Lords. He was killed by an irate English seaman. REF.: *CBA.*

Hyde, Fanny, prom. 1872, Case of, U.S., mur. The supervisor in a hair net factory in New York City, Fanny Hyde shot and killed George W. Watson, the owner, in 1872. Her brother, an employee at the factory, discovered his sister standing over Watson holding a smoking gun and said to her, "Fanny, I told you not to do this." At the trial, Hyde tearfully told how Watson had seduced her. The jury released her, ruling that violation of a woman's chastity was sufficient cause for murder.

REF.: *CBA;* Nash, *Almanac of World Crime.*

Hyde, Henry (Earl of Clarendon, Viscount Cornbury), 1638-1709, Brit., consp. Served as viceroy of Ireland from 1685-87. He disapproved of William and Mary's ascension to the throne, and wa put in prison from 1690-91. REF.: *CBA.*

Hyde, Sir Nicholas, d.1631, Brit., jur. Defended the Duke of Buckingham when he faced impeachment by the House of Commons in 1626. He served on the King's Bench from 1627-31, and condemned parliamentarians Sir John Eliot, Baron Holles, and Benjamin Valentine for conspiracy in 1629. REF.: *CBA.*

Hyde de Neuville, Jean-Guillaume, 1776-1857, Fr., rebel. Carried out orders for Louis XVI at start of French Revolution. He was involved in the royalist revolt in 1796 at Berry and tried to convince Napoleon to reinstate the Bourbon monarchy. He was the only person to vote against the Duc de Bordeaux from succeeding to the throne in 1830. REF.: *CBA.*

Hyde Park Riots, 1866, Brit., mob vio. In July 1866, rioters retaliated when a ban was placed on meetings in Hyde Park. Mobs tore down the park railings and threw stones at police. The violence grew so intense that for the first time in a London riot, military troops were called in to assist police.

REF.: *CBA;* Thomson, *The Story of Scotland Yard.*

Hyderabad Massacre, 1988, Pak., mur. Tensions in Pakistan between the Mohajirs and Sindhis had existed since the Mohajirs migrated to the region of Sind after India's partition in 1947. Mohajirs had taken government posts and many of the good jobs and demanded that their language be the official language of Sind. The Sindhi felt threatened and began to react.

In July 1988, Sindhi terrorists attempted to assassinate the Mohajir mayor of Hyderabad. In October 1988, violence again erupted in Hyderabad as local Sindhi massacred no fewer than 160 Mohajirs, opening fire in movie theaters, on congested street markets, on a wedding party, and at bus stops. Then, 100 miles away in Karachi, one of Pakistan's largest cities, Mohajirs retaliated, gunning down about fifty people in a Sindhi neighborhood. Pakistani troops quickly suppressed the violence but did not extinguish the hatred and fear between these two groups. REF.: *CBA.*

Hyun Hee, Kim, See: **Kim Hyun Hee.**

Hynes, James (AKA: Harry Goodman), d.1943, Brit., burg.-asslt. A one time cohort of such New York crime bosses as Jack "Legs" Diamond and Little Augie, the Brooklyn mobster James Hynes chose to leave the country when the gang wars grew suddenly fierce in the early 1930s. He and Henry Kleinz traveled to London where they figured they were less likely to be shot.

Once there they put together a small gang and targeted a Newcastle-on-Tyne jewelry shop. The two gangsters were forced to commit the crime unarmed as every London thief refused to go on a "job" with anyone carrying a gun. The burglary was foiled by two unarmed police and all the gang members were eventually arrested. Hynes and Kleinz received five years in prison. While in prison, Hynes decided he would only conduct business "Chicago style." They were released in 1937 and extradited.

Hynes and Kleinz returned to London via France and quickly choose the target for their next crime, the famous jewels of Millicent Hesketh-Wright. On the night of Nov. 9, 1937, three masked men waving revolvers and making threats entered Hesketh-Wright's home, bound and gagged her and her housekeeper, and coerced the safe keys from her after threatening to open the safe with an electric drill. They emptied the safe of £20,000 in jewelry, a quantity of French currency, and £100 in English currency, and left with the threat, "Don't make a noise for thirty minutes."

Chief Inspector Arthur "Nat" Thorp was assigned to the case and learned that the leader of the group was short, pudgy, and had icy green eyes. With only this information, Thorp began investigating. For all his strong-arm tactics, Hynes was a stupid crook. Thorpe discovered the shop where Hynes bought the electric drill and the shopkeeper remembered Hynes' green eyes and that Hynes said he enjoyed Turkish baths because he hated London's cold weather. Following this lead, Thorp found some patrons at a Turkish bath who remembered an American who bragged about his days with "Legs" Diamond.

Hynes was arrested in a Turkish bath when Thorpe identified him by bullet scars on his stomach. The money and the jewelry were quickly recovered by a careful canvas of recently opened safe-deposit boxes. Hynes' girlfriend unwittingly led police to the box and received nine months in prison after pleading guilty as an accessory. Hynes received twelve years and died in prison on Apr. 13, 1943.

REF.: *CBA;* Fabian, *Fabian of the Yard.*

Hypatia, d.415, Gr., assass. Hypatia was an intelligent, respected, and famous philosopher-mathematician who lived in Alexandria, Gr., in the early fifth century. She had many admirers, including Orestes, the governor of Alexandria, who frequently consulted with her on matters of state. Others such as Archbishop Cyril, later canonized St. Cyril, saw her as a threat to his power over the affairs of Alexandria and to the flowering of the early Christian Church. Cyril planned and carried out her assassination.

In March 415, as Hypatia sat in her carriage in front of her home, a mob of monks and women led by a fanatical priest known as Peter the Reader, pulled her from her carriage, ripped her clothes off, and dragged her to the Caesarium (a church). Inside the sanctuary, the Christians slashed her with pottery shards and tore her apart. Alexandria was shocked and angered by the senseless brutality, and prominent Christian leaders loudly denounced the assassination.

REF.: *CBA;* Johnson, *Famous Assassinations of History.*

Hyperbolus, d.411 B.C., Gr., assass. Politician who became the leader of the democratic party in 422 after Cleon. He was assassinated by the oligarchy on Samos, a Greek island. REF.: *CBA.*

Hyperides (Hypereides), d.322 B.C., Gr., assass. Orator and statesman who favored Demosthenes' anti-Macedonian policy. He encouraged the Lamian War, and when Athens lost at Cranon, he was condemned to death. He escaped to Aegina, but he was captured and executed. REF.: *CBA.*

I

Ianniello, Matthew (AKA: Matty the Horse), 1920-   , U.S., org. crime. A captain in the Genovese crime family, Matthew Ianniello reigned over the seamy side of New York City for years. His connection to massage parlors, peep shows, topless bars, homosexual and transvestite bars, and discos—many in the Times Square area—was longstanding. Though targeted in many federal and state investigations, Ianniello managed to elude the law time after time.

Nicknamed "Matty the Horse" because of his muscular five-foot-ten, 220-pound frame, Ianniello was charged with criminal contempt after refusing to cooperate with a Manhattan grand jury investigating police corruption in 1971. He received a one-year suspended sentence and was fined $1,500. Ianniello's domain was also said to include several well-known restaurants, including the Peppermint Lounge and Umberto's Clam Bar (where Joey Gallo was slain in 1972). Though involved in a garbage collection service, the mob boss was never listed as the owner of any businesses, but made his money by skimming profits from establishments under his control.

In 1985, Ianniello was arrested in Florida on charges of racketeering and participating in organized crime and returned to New York to stand trial. His December 1985 trial ended with the Mafia chieftain being judged Guilty of skimming $2 million from businesses he controlled. In February, he was sentenced to six years in prison and many of the businesses were confiscated by the federal government.

Two months later, "Matty the Horse" was indicted along with five other reputed gang members on charges of controlling the refuse collection for Consolidated Edison Co. Ianniello and his co-defendants were charged with using fraudulent means to retain the lucrative Edison contract ($60,000 per month) and discourage other companies from bidding for the work. He was also charged with concealing his involvement in Consolidated Carting. In a jury trial, Ianniello and the other defendants were acquitted of all charges. Two days after the acquittal, federal prosecutors announced another indictment against the Mafia lord, this time on charges of construction bid-rigging, labor racketeering, gambling, extortion, and conspiracy to commit murder.

The May 1986 charges stemmed from the alleged takeover of an Edgewater, N.J., gravel company in 1984 by Ianniello and eight associates. At the conclusion of the thirteen-month trial in October 1988, Ianniello was sentenced to thirteen years in prison and fined $505,000. The prosecutors maintained that the men had rigged bids for a number of projects, including the construction of the Jacob K. Javits Convention Center a project that cost more than $30 million. REF.: *CBA*.

Ibarra Herrera, Manuel, prom. 1982-85, Mex., law enfor. off. Mexican president Miguel de la Madrid appointed Mexico City attorney Manuel Ibarra Herrera director of the Mexican Federal Judicial Police (MFJP) in 1982. His task was to transform the corrupt law enforcement agency into an effective crime fighting organization. The U.S. DEA considered Ibarra Herrera best of a "new breed" of Mexican officials impervious to the corrupting influences of the drug cartel. He appointed his cousin, Miguel Aldana Ibarra, head of the Mexico City office of Interpol, giving him access to sensitive documents pertaining to the anti-drug war. Aldana Ibarra appeared at the scene of major drug raids—posing for newspaper photographers—as a part of "Operation Pacifico," but the raids never captured any leaders. The DEA suspected someone within Operation Pacifico of warning the cartel about impending raids, and voiced these concerns to Ibarra Herrera following the abduction of DEA agent Enrique Camarena on Feb. 7, 1985.

Ibarra Herrera allegedly allowed Honduran gangster Juan Matta Ballesteros to slip through his hands during a DEA raid on Feb. 16, 1985. On Feb. 14, the DEA had found Matta Ballesteros in the posh Colonia de Valle section of Mexico City, and told Ibarra Herrera, who they presumed would arrest him.

Nothing happened the next day, and on the night of Feb. 16, Ibarra Herrera's deputy was goaded into action by Francis "Bud" Mullen, administrator of the DEA. Moments before the Federales were to storm the building, Ibarra Herrera inexplicably delayed the raid, and Matta Ballesteros and three others escaped. Ibarra Herrera later explained that he believed Matta Ballesteros was being provided protection by the Federal Security Directorate (DFS) and that he did not want to risk a shootout between two law enforcement agencies. On Apr. 17, 1985, when the DEA discovered a tape recording of agent Camarena's final hours, Ibarra Herrera and Mexican attorney general Sergio Garcia Ramirez denied knowledge of such information. Ibarra Herrera was subsequently removed from office. See: **Camarena, Enrique; Mullen, Francis M., Jr.**

REF.: *CBA*; Shannon, *Desperados*.

Ibn al-Abbar (Abu Abd Allah Muhammad al-Ouda), 1199-1260, Tun., her. Muslim historian and theologian who served as secretary to the Muslim governor. After Christians captured Valencia in 1238, went to Tunisia where he studied Islamic poets of Spain and wrote satirical works. He was executed, possibly for a poem that satirized al-Mustansir, ruler of Tunisia. REF.: *CBA*.

Ibn al-Jawzi (Abd ar-Rahman ibn Ali ibn Muhammad Abu al-Farash ibn al-Jawzi), 1126-1200, India, her. Muslim theologian and preacher who favored orthodox Islam, and became the head of several Baghdad religious colleges. He began a movement to persecute non-orthodox Muslims, especially Shiites and Sufis. In 1194, he fell from favor and was banished from Baghdad, although he was later permitted to return. REF.: *CBA*.

Ibn-Hanbal (abu-Abdullah Ahmad ibn-Hanbal), 780-855, Arabia, her. Founded Muslim sect of Hanbalites. Caliphs were displeased by his conservatism and in 842, they put him in prison. Caliph al-Mutawakkil released him in 846. Hanbalites worship him as a saint. REF.: *CBA*.

ibn Jabr, Rahmah, 1756-1826, Int'l., pir. Leading Arab, black, and Baluchi pirate crews, Rahmah ibn Jabr operated from a base at Katif in the early 1800s. He reputedly plundered along the Persian Gulf. In 1826, Rahmah, seventy years old and blind, saw his last battle. Armed with one ship, the *Ghatrusha*, Rahmah faced the fleet of a Khalifah foe of Bahrein, Sheikh Suleiman. After the *Ghatrusha* was battered, Rahmah threw a lighted object into the powder magazine, killing himself, Suleiman's son, Ahmed, and many other Khalifahs. REF.: *CBA*.

Ibn Khallikan (Shams ad-Din Abu al-Abbas Ahmad ibn Muhammad ibn Khallikan), 1211-82, Syria, jur. Served as Muslim chief judge of Damascus from 1261-71, and from 1278-82. He is well-known for a classic Arabic biographical dictionary, *Wafayat al-ayan wa-anba abna azzaman*. REF.: *CBA*.

Ibn Shaddad (Abu al-Mahsin Yusuf ibn Rafi ibn Shaddad Baha ad-Din), 1145-1234, Syria, jur. Joined service of Saladin in 1187. He served as judge of the army, of Jerusalem, and of Aleppo, a city of northern Syria. REF.: *CBA*.

Ibn-Tamas, Beverly Ann, 1943-   , Case of, U.S., mur. She was defending herself when she shot and killed her husband, Beverly Ann Ibn-Tamas told a Washington, D.C., courtroom in Fall 1976. The prosecution contended that Ibn-Tamas shot her husband, a neurosurgeon, in the head at close range as he pleaded for his life. After three days of deliberation, a jury convicted Ibn-Tamas of murder. In April 1977, Superior Court Judge Bruce S. Mencher overturned the verdict because a juror had looked in a dictionary, during the deliberation process, for formal definitions of the words "reasonable" and "fact." In handing down his recommendation for a new trial, Mencher said there was an inherent danger in dictionary consultation.

In turning to the dictionary, Elizabeth Sadoff said she just wanted to help a stalemated jury resolve the murder case by defining the terms. Mencher ruled that Sadoff's reading and recitation of the definition of "fact" had prejudiced the jury. "If I had it to do over again, I'd do the same thing," Sadoff said. "I fail to see the wrong in what I did. I wanted to believe the jury system works when I was called for duty. I have some doubts now." REF.: *CBA*.

Ibn Taymiyah (Taqi ad-Din Abu al-Abbas Ahmad ibn Abd as-Salam ibn Abd Allah ibn Muhammad ibn Taymiyah), 1263-1328, Syria, her.-rebel. Muslim theologian who openly criticized religious philosophy and politics and was put in prison several times for his views. He led the resistance movement when the Mongols occupied Damascus from 1299-1308, and he was in prison and under surveillance in Alexandria and Cairo from 1306-13. He died while confined. REF.: *CBA*.

Ibrahim Lodi, d.1526, Afg., king, assass. Member of Lodi dynasty who ruled Delhi. Baber, a Mongol invader, conquered and murdered him. REF.: *CBA*.

Icardi, Aldo Lorenzo, 1921- , Case of, Italy, mur. Major William V. Holohan led a three-man undercover operation into northern Italy in 1944. U.S. soldiers Holohan, Sergeant Carl G. LoDolce, twenty-two, and Lieutenant Aldo L. Icardi, twenty-three, were dropped behind German lines to aid the underground war effort against the Nazis. In the hills northwest of Milan the three established radio contact with Secret Service forces and arranged for equipment and arms to be dropped into the area. During the first airdrop, the guns and ammunition fell into the hands of Italy's Communist party. The Communists and the area's non-Communists were vying for post-war control of the region and arms were precious to each cause. Holohan wanted the airlifted goods to go to the area's non-Communist faction and ordered a halt to the drops until he could ensure that the weapons got into the right hands. Icardi said politics were getting in the way of the mission, which was to gather military information and arm the Italians against Germany.

Icardi managed to convince LoDolce and the group's two Italian aides, Giuseppe Manini and Gualtiero Tozzini, that the mission would run more smoothly with the major out of the picture. On Dec. 6, 1944, Holohan, forty, was given minestrone soup laced with cyanide. When he retired to his room complaining of a stomachache, LoDolce followed him upstairs and shot his commanding officer. The four men dumped Holohan's body into Lake Orta and reported that he had been killed in a Nazi attack. The quartet proceeded to funnel arms and equipment to the Communist party.

While Joseph R. Holahan (A mix-up in school records caused the variation in name spellings) was reluctant to accept the story of his brother's death, he wanted to find his body and return it to the U.S. for a proper burial. In 1949, an Italian officer stationed near Lake Orta started inquiring about Holohan. Lieutenant Elio Albieri talked to the Italians who had assisted the U.S. undercover operation and one year later Tozzini confessed to participating in the crime and Manini confirmed the story. In June 1950, Albieri dredged up Holohan's body from the bottom of the lake. The U.S. Army's Criminal Investigation Division reopened the case and interrogated LoDolce. After first denying any involvement in the murder, LoDolce confessed to shooting Holohan. Icardi maintained he was innocent.

The fact that two Americans had been honorably discharged and the murder was committed in a foreign country tied the hands of the U.S. government. The Italian courts found both men guilty of murder *in absentia*. In 1955, Icardi was indicted on charges of perjury. But in his 1956 appeal, attorney Edward Bennett Williams persuaded the judge that the subcommittee hearing, at which the perjured testimony was reportedly given, had gone beyond its limits in questioning Icardi. In the eleven years following Holohan's death, the U.S. government spent some $300,000 in attempting to convict Icardi. REF.: *CBA*.

Ida the Goose War, prom. 1900s, U.S., org. crime. In the early 1900s, many battles were fought on the streets of New York City over the affections of a beautiful woman named Ida the Goose. Ida was usually mistress to leaders of the Gopher gang from Hell's Kitchen, one of the city's most powerful gangs following the imprisonment of rival gang leader Monk Eastman.

However, a splinter group of the Eastman Gang, The Trickers, led by Chick Tricker, began to encroach upon Gopher territory, and when Tricker gangster Irish Tom Riley, lured Ida away from the Gophers, a full-scale war ensued.

The following weeks were filled with several fistfights and stabbings although none caused any fatalities. Eventually the Gophers seemed to lose interest, and Ida continued her life with Riley. But, one evening in October 1909, four members of the Gophers walked into a saloon occupied by six members of the Trickers, including Riley, who was accompanied by Ida the Goose. Suddenly, the Gophers drew guns and shot five Trickers, leaving only Riley unhurt, cowering under Ida's skirt. Nothing happened until Ida raised her skirt and told her lover to come out and take it like a man, whereupon he was killed by the four gunmen as he crawled across the floor. Ida the Goose followed the gunmen back to her original haunts with the Gophers in Hell's Kitchen. REF.: *CBA*.

Ide, Henry Clay, 1844-1921, U.S., jur. Served as chief justice of Samoa from 1893-97. He was also a member of the Philippine Commission from 1900-04, the Philippine governor general in 1906, and the U.S. minister to Spain from 1909-13. REF.: *CBA*.

Iggulden, George William, prom. 1923, Brit., mur. "Lonely bachelor desires marriage with homely person (spinster or widow)," read the advertisement that George William Iggulden placed in a London newspaper. Ethel Eliza Howard, a divorcee with two children, responded to the ad. Within a short time, Iggulden, a portrait painter, had proposed marriage to Howard. On Nov. 15, 1923, as the couple rode in a taxi, Iggulden reached into his pocket and pulled out a razor. After slashing Howard's throat, he told the driver to take him to the nearest police station.

While admitting he was responsible for the murder of his fiancée, Iggulden said he did it because Howard was always talking about suicide, and he wanted to end her pain and suffering. Judged fit to stand trial, Iggulden was found Guilty of murder. Despite the jury's recommendation for mercy, the judge sentenced Iggulden to death. His penalty was later reduced and the convicted murderer was removed to the Broadmoor Criminal Lunatic Asylum.

REF.: *CBA*; O'Donnell, *The Trials of Mr. Justice Avory*; Shew, *A Second Companion to Murder*.

Iglesias, José Maria, 1823-91, Mex., jur. President of the supreme court of Mexico in 1873. When Lerdo de Tejada was ousted, he served as president of Mexico until Diaz was installed in power. REF.: *CBA*.

Igoe, Michael Lambert, 1885-1967, U.S., jur. Served as U.S. Attorney of the northern district of Illinois from 1915-17, as a member of the U.S. House of Representatives in 1935, and again as U.S. Attorney for the northern district of Illinois from 1935-38. He was nominated to the northern district court of Illinois by President Franklin D. Roosevelt in 1938. REF.: *CBA*.

Igor, c.877-945, Rus., prince, extor.-assass. Led campaigns that failed, one in Transcaucasia from 913-14, and others in 941 and 944 against Byzantium. He was murdered when he tried to force payment from Drevlyane Slavs. REF.: *CBA*.

I Ho Chuan, See: **Boxers, The**.

Illingworth, Monty, prom. 1932-42, U.S., mur. On a summer morning in 1939, two fishermen hooked an inanimate object in Crescent Lake, Wash. As they pulled the heavy bundle to the surface they discovered what looked like a foot projecting out from the blanket wrapped around the object. The two men were not sure whether it was the body of a woman or a mannequin. There was no odor, the facial area was obscured, and the whole bundle weighed less than fifty pounds.

In examining the fishermen's catch authorities determined that it was the body of woman in her early thirties, the body remarkably well-preserved underneath the covering. In fact it had turned almost entirely to soap due to process called saponification. The victim became known as the "Lady of the Lake."

Not until 1942 did police positively identify the body as that of Hallie Illingworth, a waitress from nearby Port Angeles. During the investigation, evidence surfaced that Illingworth's jealous husband often beat her. Through exhaustive research the city coroner from Olympia, Dr. Charles P. Larson, estimated 1932 as the year of death, the same year in which Monty Illingworth had told friends and neighbors that his 36-year-old wife had run off to Alaska with a sailor. Now remarried and living in California, Monty was extradited to Washington and charged with murdering his wife. With little evidence to support his story of desertion, Illingworth was found Guilty of murder in the second degree and sentenced to life imprisonment.

REF.: *CBA;* McCallum, *Crime Doctor.*

Ily, Nicole, 1932- , Fr., mur. A web of childhood fantasies involving secret agents, hidden fortunes, and dangerous underworld figures spun by 16-year-old Nicole Ily of Paris, encouraged two of her classmates to shoot and kill Alain Guyader, the son of a French writer and public official in December 1948. The senseless killing took the French police more than two years to solve. Eventually two schoolboys, Claude Panconi and Bernard Petit, were convicted of the killing and received ten-year and three-year prison sentences, respectively. Petit, the son of a police inspector in Paris, had stolen his father's shotgun to protect the "honor" of Nicole, who was sent to prison for three years.

REF.: *CBA;* Nash, *Look For the Woman.*

Imbert, Sir **Peter Michael,** 1933- , Brit., law enfor. off. At the age of twenty, Peter Michael Imbert joined London's Metropolitan Police force, transferring to the CID in 1956. Serving in the special branch, Imbert was involved from 1971 to 1976 with investigations of terrorist activities in Britain as well as Northern Ireland. From May 1973 to January 1976, he served as deputy operational head of the police anti-terrorist squad, and was one of two police negotiators during London's Balcombe Street Siege in December 1975. Promoted to Detective Chief Superintendent in 1976, he continued his study of subversive factions, traveling to Vienna after the OPEC building siege and twice to Holland to investigate attacks by the Moluccan terrorists.

An acknowledged expert on terrorist activities, Imbert has lectured throughout the world. He was awarded the Queen's Police Medal in 1980 and served as deputy chief constable in the Surrey Constabulary and deputy constable of Thames Valley Police prior to being named deputy commissioner of the Metropolitan Police on Feb. 1, 1985, and commissioner on Aug. 1, 1987. In June 1988, Imbert was knighted in the Queen's Birthday Honors list. REF.: *CBA.*

Imbler, Paul Kern, 1917- , U.S., (wrong. convict.) mur. "I have no bitterness or hatred after what I went through," Paul Kern Imbler said after serving ten years in prison for a murder he did not commit. "But I'm disillusioned and disgusted. I'm not an isolated case. There are others."

In January 1961, Imbler, a poverty-stricken ex-felon with two failed marriages behind him, robbed a gas station. As Imbler and his partner sped away from the Pomona, Calif., site, the getaway car overturned, killing the driver, Leonard Lingo. Imbler escaped, but turned himself in to police the next day.

On Jan. 17, 1961, Imbler pleaded guilty to charges of second-degree robbery and was sentenced to prison. Before he could begin serving his robbery sentence, he was charged, convicted, and sentenced to death for the Jan. 4 slaying of Morris Hasson, co-owner of the Purity Market in Los Angeles. A number of witnesses identified Lingo as an accomplice and said Imbler shot Hasson. Just a week before he was scheduled to die, Imbler was granted a stay of execution. Due to the diligence of Dr. LeMoyne Snyder, evidence surfaced that many of the witnesses who testified at Imbler's murder trial had perjured themselves and that the prosecution had acted improperly in conducting their case.

The Supreme Court of California reviewed the case in 1963 and ruled there was no reason for a new trial. Imbler's execution was reset for Mar. 10, 1964. The U.S. Supreme Court initially declined to review the case but after learning that Imbler had been denied access to a lawyer through much of the appeal process the justices agreed to hear only the penalty phase of the case. The

convicted murderer's sentence was then reduced to life imprisonment.

Evidence of deceptive practices on the part of the prosecution finally resulted in Imbler being granted a new trial on Apr. 23, 1969. Judge Warren J. Ferguson of the Ninth Circuit U.S. District Court overturned Imbler's murder conviction because he said the prosecutors had influenced the witnesses and a number of the witnesses had committed perjury. Imbler's $2.7 million lawsuit against the state was disallowed by the U.S. Supreme Court on the basis of prosecutorial immunity.

REF.: *CBA;* Wolfe, *Pileup on Death Row.*

Imbrie, Robert W., prom. 1924, Per., assass.? Melin Seymour and Major Robert W. Imbrie, the U.S. vice consul, stopped at a fountain in Tehran to take pictures in July 1924. Little did they know that picture-taking was considered sacrilegious by Persians who had gathered around the city's sacred fountain to discuss their dreaded religious enemies, the Bahaists. As the two Americans innocently snapped a few pictures, the Persians accused the men of being Bahaists and dragged them from their carriage. The angry mob cut, kicked, and beat Imbrie and Seymour. Several hours later, Imbrie died from his injuries. Persian police arrested hundreds of people in connection with the murder but U.S. citizens wanted to know why they had done little to prevent the violence.

A number of articles speculated that Imbrie had been killed as part of a British plot to stir up bad blood between the U.S. and Persia. In October, Private Morteza was executed for the murder of Imbric and the Persian government gave Imbrie's widow $60,000. One month later, two other suspects came to trial for the murder of Imbrie, but their death sentences were not carried out. For the protection of citizens abroad, U.S. Secretary of State Charles Evans Hughes insisted the two prisoners be put to death, and the Persian officials complied by killing them. REF.: *CBA.*

Impastato, Nicolo, 1900- , U.S., drugs-org. crime. A "made member" of the Sicilian Mafia, Nicolo Impastato was deported to Italy by the Mexican government in 1955 as an undesirable after his conviction for violation of U.S. narcotics laws. Before the U.S. could take steps against him, Impastato fled across the Mexican border, where he was promptly arrested when his plan to establish an international drug trade was revealed. Prior to this, Impastato was well known to the crime families of New York, Kansas City, New Orleans, and Florida. His top associates included Carlos Marcello, James Balistrere, and Anthony "Ducks" Corallo. REF.: *CBA.*

Impey, Sir **Elijah,** 1732-1809, Brit., jur. Presided as chief justice of Bengal, India from 1774-89. He served as a member of Parliament from 1790-96. REF.: *CBA.*

Imredy, Béla, 1891-1946, Ger., war crimes. Served as premier of Hungary from 1938-39. He favored anti-Semitic, pro-German, right-wing ideology and while premier oversaw the passage of laws limiting the activities of Jews. In 1939, when his Jewish ancestry was revealed, he was forced to resign. He maintained close ties with the Nazis during WWII, using his position as Hungary's minister of economy to aid the German war effort. After the war, Imredy's association with the Nazis led to his trial and execution as a war criminal. REF.: *CBA.*

Inagawa Kakuji, prom. 1945- , Japan, org. crime. Inagawa Kakuji came to the attention of the post-WWII American occupation forces in 1950 when the U.S. consul general based in Yokohama sent a cable to Washington, D.C., advising his superiors of the threats posed by this powerful gangster. The cable warned, "The activities of this gang ranged from blackmail and intimidation, in connection with the collection of 'protection' money, to control and direction of bands of thieves which were regularly placed aboard foreign merchant ships calling at Yokohama and Shimizu in the guise of cleaning crews."

During the war, Inagawa organized a small street gang in Yokohama to harass and intimidate the Koreans and Chinese who controlled the city's black market. Over the years the organization gained tremendous stature within the Japanese underworld. The Kakusei-kai gang, as it came to be known, was nearly equal to that of Tsuruoka Masajiro, then the reigning "godfather" of Yokohama and Inagawa's criminal mentor during the early years. By the 1960s Inagawa's influence had spread from Yokohama to Tokyo and the northern island of Hokkaido. His major source of revenue came from the lucrative casino gambling rackets, which he singlehandedly controlled. The Tokyo Metropolitan police reported that the gangster had taken in $175,000 in fees from just one card game in 1965. Continued police harassment, however, compelled Inagawa to seek legitimacy through political channels. In 1963 he changed the name of the gang to Kinsei-kai and petitioned the authorities to grant it political status. In its fight against the Communists, the Japanese government frequently overlooked the misdeeds of the yakuza, whose sympathies were tied to the political right.

Inagawa pushed for an alliance with the other yakuza gangs against the common enemy. He reminded his rivals that "We gamblers cannot walk in broad daylight. But if we unite and become a wall to stop com-munism we can be of service to the nation. If anything happens, we would like to stake our lives for the good of the country." The dream of unification did not come to pass until Oct. 24, 1972, for during the intervening years Inagawa had been incar-cerated in Japan's Fukushima Prison. When freed in Janu-ary 1969 he discovered that his once-powerful gang had been decimated by internal mutinies, defections, and police arrests. Meanwhile, the

Japanese gangster Inagawa Kakuji.

Yamaguchi-gumi gang had supplanted the Kinsei-kai as the most formidable yakuza on the island nation. Under the aegis of Kodama, an alliance was forged with the Yamaguchi gang. The powerful criminal combine now controlled all but four prefectures in Japan. Virtually every yakuza gang in the nation was under the thumb of the Yamaguchi-Inagawa brotherhood.

By the late 1970s, Inagawa's syndicate had branched out into drug dealing, loan sharking, and other forms of vice. The police estimated that the illegal enterprises were fronted by 879 legiti-mate businesses in 1979 including construction firms, restaurants, and entertainment companies whose combined yearly income was almost $200 million. The syndicate is run much like a large corporate conglomerate with twelve "bosses" representing 119 gangs on a board of directors. Inagawa oversees his criminal empire from a lavish hotel suite in downtown Tokyo. He enjoys close contact with the Tokyo police, and is on intimate terms with the movers and shakers of business, commerce, and entertainment. Every third and fourth Monday the aging gangster sponsors a golf tournament in the Kanagawa Prefecture where professional athletes and show people share in his hospitality. In 1984 a feature film about Inagawa was released in Japan that was an equivalent of the *Godfather*. It was called *Shura no Mure* (A Band of Daredevils). The elder statesman of the Japanese underworld is reflective about the future of the yakuza. "In the future," he said, "there'll be one mob. Like my organization, the bigger firms will take over. You can see the move towards a more corporate structure." See: **Kimura Tokutaru; Kishi Nobusuke; Kodama Yoshio; Machii Hisayuki; Nakasone Yasuhiro; Jirocho Shimizu no; Ogawa Kaoru; Osano Kenji; Sasakawa Ryoichi; Taoka Kazuo; Yakuza.**

REF.: *CBA;* Kaplan and Dubro, *Yakuza.*

Indian Territory, 1834-96, U.S., crime district. The Indian Territory, also called The Cherokee Strip for the Indians that occupied it, was a strip of land in what is now Oklahoma, a state

which remained without statehood for sixty-two years. This area, with the town of Ingalls at its hub, was also referred to as Bad Man's Territory because it was a known sanctuary for many notorious outlaws who mistakenly believed that no U.S. law enforcement officer had jurisdiction there. As a territory, the Indian Territory fell under the jurisdiction of the Western District of Arkansas at Fort Smith, where federal judge Isaac Parker presided. Parker, known as the "Hanging Judge," supervised a small army of U.S marshals who made regular sweeps each month through the rough terrain of the Indian Territory in search of wanted desperadoes.

Prior to the Civil War, the Territory was indeed utterly lawless. Because no court existed in the Territory no extradition could be legally made from it to an existing state where a fugitive was wanted on felony charges. From about 1870 to 1896, when it became part of the Oklahoma Territory, even the U.S. marshals were cautious when riding through the Indian Territory and seldom rode into Ingalls to confront the outlaws who gathered there. On Sept. 1, 1893, however, this did actually happen; Bill Doolin's gang was trapped by a small army of lawmen, resulting in a wild gun battle in which several men died.

The Indian Territory was, for the most part, inhabited by prostitutes, cattle and horse thieves, whiskey peddlers, escaped convicts, and many outlaw gangs. The more notorious outlaws who rode in and out of the Indian Territory included the Dalton Brothers, the Doolin Gang, Belle Starr, Jim Reed, Ned Christie, the Buck Gang, Crawford Goldsby (better known as Cherokee Bill), Jim French, the Cook Gang, and the last of the old-time outlaws, Henry Starr and Al Spencer. By the time Oklahoma became a state in 1907, the Indian Territory and the hordes of outlaws that had once called it home had long disappeared. See: **Buck Gang; Christie, Ned; Cook, William Tuttle; Dalton Brothers; Doolin, William M.; French, Jim; Goldsby, Crawford; Parker, Judge Isaac; Spencer, Al; Starr, Belle; Starr, Henry.**

REF.: Barnard, *A Rider of the Cherokee Strip;* Bearss and Gibson, *Fort Smith: Little Gibraltar on the Arkansas; CBA;* Croy, *He Hanged Them High;* Dalton, *Beyond the Law;* ____, *When the Daltons Rode;* Emery, *Court of the Damned;* Gish, *American Bandits;* Graves, *Oklahoma Outlaws;* Hanes, *Bill Doolin, Outlaw;* Jones, *The Experiences of a Deputy U.S. Marshal of the Indian Territory;* Lamb, *Tragedies of the Osage Hills;* Linzee, *Development of Oklahoma Territory;* Miller, *Bill Tilghman, Marshal of the Last Frontier;* Nix, *Oklahombres;* Penfield, *Western Sheriffs and Marshals;* Rainey, *The Cherokee Strip;* Ray, *The Dalton Brothers and Their Oklahoma Cave;* Shirley, *Belle Starr and Her Times;* ____, *Henry Starr: Last of the Real Badmen;* ____, *Law West of Fort Smith;* Ward, *The Dalton Gang;* Wellman, *A Dynasty of Western Outlaws.*

Infelice, Ernest (AKA: Rocco, Rocky), 1922-   , U.S., org. crime. Over a period of seven days, used-car dealer Steve Hospodar lost more than $11,000 illegally betting on basketball games. It was money Hospodar did not have for the crime syndicate figures from Chicago's West Side who began threatening him in January 1981 when he was unable to pay. In fear for his life, Hospodar disclosed his actions to the FBI, who in turn wired him for sound and sent him out to meet with the men demanding he make good on his gambling debt.

Not until three years later, in January 1984, were extortion charges handed down against reputed West Side Mafia chieftain Ernest Infelice, a convicted heroin dealer, and five co-defendants, Joseph Grieco, Lewis Marino, Charles Cesario, John Manzella, and Salvatore Delaurentis, all reputed Mafia figures. In February, all six were acquitted of terrorizing Hospodar in order to force payment of a gambling debt.

A state probe into a national stolen auto-parts ring once again focused attention on Infelice in July 1988. State investigators impounded a 1987 Mercedes-Benz that Infelice had purchased from a firm under investigation as part of a suspected theft ring. Officials said they could find no evidence to support Infelice's claim that he had purchased the used car for $27,000 from Master Auto Inc. After six days, investigators returned the vehicle to Infelice after determining that the Mercedes did not contain any stolen parts. In September, the 66-year-old former Mafia enforcer joined in a $60 million federal civil rights suit against the Illinois secretary of state's office. Master Auto, Inc., owners Charles and Joanne Bellavia and Master Auto employee Michael Simon charged the state with denying them business licenses. Infelice maintained he was hospitalized with chest pains as the result of rough treatment by two of the investigators who had seized his car.

When reputed mob hit man Gerald Scarpelli was found dead in a shower stall at Chicago's Metropolitan Correctional Center in May 1989, the prison released handwritten confessions in which Scarpelli implicated Infelice, along with other crime syndicate figures, in a number of robberies, payoffs, and murders. See: **Maltese, Frank.** REF.: *CBA.*

Ingalls, James Monroe, 1837-1927, U.S., ballistics. Army officer who established department of ballistics at U.S. Army artillery school at Ft. Monroe, Va., in 1882. REF.: *CBA.*

Ingeborg (Ingeburge or **Ingelburge)**, c.1176-c.1237, Fr., impris. In 1193, married Phillip Augustus, who was not fond of her. He tried to arrange a separation, but Popes Innocent III and Celestine III did not approve. She was put in prison until 1213 when her rights were reinstated. REF.: *CBA.*

Ingely, James Myers, prom. 1985-87, Case of, Brit., sex abuse. In January 1987, London newspaper headlines screamed of the alleged molestation of a 6-year-old British girl by an American clergyman, the husband of a diplomat. At that time in December 1985, officials sought to charge James Myers Ingely with "gross indecency," a crime punishable by five years in prison, but the Americans had exercised their diplomatic immunity to remove Ingely from Britain.

The British were outraged that the incident had taken so long to come to light and that the Americans were uncooperative in the judicial process. British and U.S. officials issued statements saying that rape was not involved in the incident. In February 1987, an attempt to extradite Ingely was dropped. David Mellor, home office minister of state, said there was not enough evidence to prosecute him. REF.: *CBA.*

Ingenito, Ernest, 1924- , U.S., mur. Ernie Ingenito was a violent youth from the time his parents separated in 1937. Mrs. Ingenito found it impossible to control him during his childhood, and by the time he was fifteen he was known to police in Gloucester County, Pa., as an incorrigible thug. Before another year had passed, Ingenito was serving a term in the Pennsylvania State Reformatory, convicted of attempted burglary. After his release, he returned to his mother's home. Her death in 1941 created an emotional scar the young man found difficult to overcome.

Ernie Ingenito, who murdered his family in 1950.

Ingenito married at seventeen, but his angry tirades were too much for his young bride and she left him while she was pregnant. He then enlisted in the army where his habit of sleeping late did not endear him to his sergeant or the officers on the base. In 1943, during an argument, he beat up a sergeant and an officer. Imprisoned in a stockade for two years, he was dishonorably discharged in 1946. The next year he met Theresa Mazzoli, a dark-haired Italian beauty whose parents owned and operated a prosperous truck farm in Gloucester County, and though Theresa's mother objected loudly to the couple's relationship, they soon married.

The impoverished young couple went to live with the Mazzolis in their home and from the start there was trouble. Pearl Mazzoli, the mother, did not care for her son-in-law and daily made a point of expressing her disapproval of him. At first Mike Mazzoli, the father, took Ernie's side. But when he learned that Ingenito had cheated on his daughter, he immediately evicted Ingenito from the home.

Ingenito moved to a residence a short distance away, to be near his two sons. When Theresa refused him visitation rights, Ernie consulted a lawyer, Fred Gravino, of Woodbury, N.J., who told Ernie to get a court order to see his children. Ernie rejected the advice because it would take too long, he said. A second lawyer told him the same thing. Agitated, Ingenito selected two pistols and a carbine rifle from his extensive weapons collection and, on Nov. 17, 1950, banged on the Mazzoli's front door armed with his guns.

Theresa fled. When Mike Mazzoli appeared, Ernie leveled a German-made Luger and fired two times, then stepped into the house and fired on his estranged wife, wounding her. Next, he went after Pearl Mazzoli but was unable to locate her in the house for she had run screaming to the home of Armando and Theresa Pioppi who lived down the block. "It's Ernie!" she cried, running upstairs to hide in a bedroom closet. "He's shooting everybody!"

Before Gino Pioppi, Pearl's brother, could summon police, Ernie burst through the door with his guns blazing. He fired on Mrs. Pioppi and Gino's wife Marion, killing them. Ernie fired repeatedly at Pearl Mazzoli and then fired on his 9-year-old daughter before exiting the Pioppi home.

As he left, Gino's brother John grabbed a knife lying on the kitchen table and chased the gun-toting madman across the lawn until Ernie turned and fired, killing Pioppi instantly. Ingenito next drove to the home of Frank Mazzoli in Minatola, N.J. Screaming a torrent of curses he shot Hilda and Frank Mizzoli and then tried to escape.

The killing spree had begun at 9 p.m., and ended shortly after midnight when a patrol car flagged Ingenito down. As the police officers approached, Ernie tried to kill himself with the jagged edges of a tin can but failed. Speaking from her hospital bed, Theresa told a reporter: "I wish they would hang Ernie." In January 1951, Ingenito was tried for the murder of his mother-in-law. His severe psychological problems led to a sentence of life imprisonment at the New Jersey Hospital for the Insane, in Trenton. In 1956 he was brought to trial for four additional murders committed that same night, and received a sentence of life for each killing.

REF.: *CBA*; Nash, *Almanac of World Crime;* _____, *Bloodletters and Badmen;* Steiger, *The Mass Murderer.*

Ingersoll, Charles Anthony, 1798-1860, U.S., jur. Served as probate judge for New Haven, Conn., from 1829-53, and as state attorney for Connecticut from 1849-53. He was nominated by President Franklin Pierce as judge of the district court of Connecticut in 1853. REF.: *CBA.*

Ingersoll, John E., 1929- , U.S., law enfor. off. After serving with the U.S. Army counterintelligence corps during the Korean war, John E. Ingersoll joined the Oakland Police Department in 1957. After only four years on the force he was placed in charge of planning and research for the department. For five years, he served as director of field services for the International Association of Chiefs of Police before taking charge of the police force in Charlotte, N.C., in 1966. In 1968, Ingersoll was appointed director of the Bureau of Narcotics and Dangerous Drugs. On Jan. 12, 1970, the University of California-Berkeley graduate was appointed by President Richard M. Nixon to the U.S. commission on Narcotic Drugs of the Economic Social Council of the United Nations.

In addition to his work in law enforcement, Ingersoll contributed a number of professional papers to the field and also taught at Oakland City College and the University of California. In 1968, for his work in human relations, Ingersoll was awarded a Silver Medallion by the National Conference of Christians and

Jews. REF.: *CBA*.

Ingersoll, Robert Green, 1833-99, U.S., lawyer. Joined Union army in Civil War and later served as attorney general of Illinois from 1867-69. REF.: *CBA*.

Ingersoll, Sarah, b.1840, Case of, U.S., mur. On the same day he was supposed to be photographed with his brothers in Sparta, Wis., Daniel Ingersoll became seriously ill. Ingersoll vomited for ten minutes straight, after which his health rapidly deteriorated. The offer of food and drink or the slightest noise would send Ingersoll's body into uncontrollable spasms. Three doctors saw him during the next three days and agreed that he suffered from spinal meningitis or tetanus. They plied Ingersoll with every cure imaginable, including soda water, bromide, chloroform, opium, ether, croton oil, asafetida, and mustard. Ingersoll died in March 1873, only four days after becoming ill.

After a member of the community told officials that Sarah Ingersoll had twice purchased strychnine from a local drug store, authorities ordered an autopsy done on the body. Only by poisoning a cat with strychnine were the medical examiners able to conclude that the deceased had also been poisoned. Sarah was then ordered to stand trial for murdering her husband, a charge to which she pleaded not guilty.

During the thirteen-day trial in Fall 1874, it was revealed that Mrs. Ingersoll had taken out an insurance policy on her husband's life. Other witnesses testified that the Ingersolls had marital difficulties. The defense counsel argued that Ingersoll had died of natural causes and that the doctors should be held responsible for improperly diagnosing the illness. Mrs. Ingersoll's attorneys, John Turner and Colonel William F. Vilas, went so far as to suggest that the examiners, in performing the post-mortem on Ingersoll's stomach, may have placed the organ in strychnine. The jury found Sarah Ingersoll Not Guilty of murdering her husband. A popular nineteenth century Wisconsin novelist Ella A. Giles published *Out from the Shadows,* a thinly veiled version of the Ingersoll case, in 1875.

REF.: *CBA*; Derleth, *Wisconsin Murders*.

Ingledue, Richard, c.1940- , U.S., asslt. A 15-year-old Anoka, Minn., high school sophomore, Richard Ingledue was assigned to write a book report in January 1955. Instead, he wrote, "This book does not have a title but is a story of a boy who was fed up of living...It's what he will do that will shock you." Ingledue then described a boy's attack on his parents, ending with, "This story is not fiction although it sounds fantastic it happened in my family." Apparently, Ingledue was irritated by his parents' refusal to let him use the family car. The night after Ingledue wrote the essay, the teenager armed himself with a shotgun and went into his parents' bedroom where he fired the gun twice, wounding them. Then, taking the family car, he drove eighty miles before he decided to surrender to police. The Ingledues recovered, but the mother still bore scars on her legs. The teenager was sent to a reformatory in Sauk Centre, Minn., for several months, and after he returned home, the family moved to Phoenix, Ariz. REF.: *CBA*.

Inglis, James, prom. 1932, Case of, Scot., theft. In the early 1930s Scottish courts were working to clarify laws regarding fingerprinting of defendants who had been charged but not tried. On Dec. 14, 1932, James Inglis, accused of theft, was on trial in the Glasgow High Court before Lord Hunter and a jury. Inglis' prints had been taken with his consent in a waiting room at the Central Police Office. But his defense attorney, Robert MacInnes, argued that "the actions of the police were illegal, proceeding as they did without obtaining a warrant as provided by regulations," and that the prints should be disallowed in court because they had been taken at a time when Inglis was not "confined in prison." A 1904 regulation stated that no member of the police force could take the prints of a defendant in prison except by the order of a warrant signed by the Procurator-Fiscal or a police officer at or above the rank of superintendent, or by an order from the Secretary of Scotland. Any of these warrants was also to be approved by either a justice of the peace or a sheriff.

Ruling on MacInnes' argument, Lord Hunter said that the issue was very important, explaining, "The rules of criminal evidence are hard and fast, and are always insisted upon in criminal trials." Hunter agreed with MacInnes that Inglis had not been "committed to prison at the time," and instructed the jury to return a verdict of Not Guilty so that the case was withdrawn.

REF.: *CBA*; Cherrill, *Cherrill of the Yard*.

Ingram, Mack, 1907- , Case of, U.S., asslt. In June 1951, North Carolina farmer Mack Ingram needed to borrow a wagon to harvest his hay crop. The 44-year-old black man walked to the house of a white neighbor, Aubrey Boswell, and mistakenly followed one of the Boswell children across a field before realizing it was not the father. In the afternoon, Ingram was arrested and charged with assault with intent to rape.

Willa Jean Boswell told authorities that Ingram had chased her for an extended time and kept watching her. The 17-year-old girl told police that the closest Ingram came to her was twenty-five feet, but he would not stop looking at her. Ingram, the father of nine children, said he mistook the girl for her father because she was wearing dungarees and a hat. Prosecutor W. Banks Horton wanted Ingram to stand trial. Recorder Ralph Vernon, having duties comparable to a justice of the peace, deemed Ingram Guilty of "assault on a female" and sentenced him to two years of hard labor. A North Carolina law stated that assault can occur without physical contact.

The National Association for the Advancement of Colored People took up the issue, helping Ingram appeal his case. In November 1951, a mistrial was ordered when a mixed jury could not reach a verdict. One year later, an all-white jury in Yanceyville upheld the assault ruling despite agreeing that the farmer never came within fifty feet of the girl. In March 1953, the state supreme court reversed the lower court decision. REF.: *CBA*.

Inkpaduta, prom. 1857, U.S., kid.-rape.-mur. In March 1857, a former Sioux Indian chief, Inkpaduta, and a dozen Indians were hunting near Spirit Lake on the Iowa-Minnesota border. Inkpaduta had been ostracized from the tribe for killing Chief Tasagi. As the Indians hunted for food, a dog belonging to one of the local white settlers bit an Indian who then killed the dog in retaliation. In front of a mob of settlers, the Indian was subsequently beaten by the owner of the dog.

To avenge the attack, the Indians raided a nearby settlement and killed all but four women. They looted the town and made the women carry the stolen property. Two of the women became so weak on the Indians' journey that they were killed. Mrs. Marble and Miss Gardner were released after a ransom was paid. Later the same month, members of the Indian pack allegedly massacred seventeen people in Springfield, Minn. The snow was so deep that soldiers were unable to track the Indians that winter.

REF.: *CBA*; Duke, *Celebrated Criminal Cases of America*.

In Muffled Night, 1933, a novel by D. Erskine Muir. The strange murder case of Jessie McClachlan (Scot., 1862) is the basis of this work of fiction. See: **McClachlan, Jessie**.

Innes, John, d.1794, Brit., forg. Convicted and sentenced to death for forgery, John Innes admitted his guilt as he stood before the gallows. Innes said his "abominable extortion and wickedness" warranted death, and warned those in attendance not to sin.

REF.: Atholl, *Shadow of the Gallows*; *CBA*.

Inoue Junnosuke, See: **Inukai Tsuyoshi**.

Inquisition, The, 13th-19th Cent., Int'l., tort.-mur. For several centuries, mass torture and execution were national policy in Imperial Spain, the Netherlands, and other parts of the former Roman Empire, including Spanish colonies in the Western hemisphere. The terror was used mainly to extort funds from the wealthy classes and the civil aristocracy, and provide thousands of women as mistresses for the ruling class. From the thirteenth into the nineteenth century, The Inquisition operated by the Roman Catholic Church and the Spanish monarchy used public and private torture and execution with the alleged aim of eradicating heresy. Victims were questioned about their supposed heresy, and if they refused to confess, they were quickly burned at the stake. All their possessions, including any comely women in their households, were forfeited to the state. The remaining family members were cast out into the street to become virtual slaves. If the victim confessed, he was tortured a second time to find out what he was trying to hide in the first place. In the third round of torture, the victim named other heretics to keep the whole process operating.

Pope Sixtus IV ordered church clerics, with the Dominican Fathers as the field troops, to persecute infidels and heretics, mostly Jews and Muhammadans. When Tomas de Torquemada, confessor to Queen Isabella, was appointed Inquisitor-General, the Inquisition got solidly underway. Torquemada went after Jews because they had money. The Inquisition, conceived as a massive effort to cancel debts, and used the *auto-da-fé* (mass execution of convicted heretics) in the most protracted spree of state-sponsored homicide in human history.

Those who fled Spain were executed in effigy and thus forfeited all their possessions, and condemned their relatives as well. Officials took attractive women for sexual service, and threw the old or unattractive into the countryside to starve. Most of the women abducted were repeatedly raped and then murdered, often crushed to death with stones. Many of those who survived went insane. Male relatives of those who fled were driven to stealing to survive. Sons of exiles were killed immediately by the state. Those who stayed behind and endured torture often lost only a part of their fortunes, leaving some legacy behind for their bereaved families. In Torquemada's time, at public burnings in town squares, as many as several hundred victims, most already weakened by torture, were burned alive at ceremonies, attendance at which was mandatory at pain of treason. More than 10,000 people were burned alive in Torquemada's reign, with another 100,000 imprisoned or exile for life. About 235,000 Jews, terrified for their lives and families, converted to Christianity at the beginning of the seventeenth century. The friars who specialized in torture, known as "familiars," conducted continuous executions of the already tortured to clear the dungeons for more. *Braseros,* or burning places, were built in all major cities, and *secretos,* the secret prisons and torture chambers, were built in the fortresses, castles and monasteries where the tribunals sat.

The Inquisitors held absolute power. At mass burnings, a section was cordoned off where as many as 500 black-robed familiars, close to the dying victims and in full view of the spectators, watched the flames in silence, usually producing a new crop of informants after the executions. A class of spies called "delators" collected commissions for reporting assets that the tortured had managed to conceal. After murdering the prisoner and reporting the death as an accident, the familiar would tell a delator where to find the property, and the delator got a percentage of the take. Delators were in a precarious position, as they would be able to report the familiars, and so they were often tortured themselves. The familiar often had their tongues removed prior to executing them along with other victims.

By the middle of the sixteenth century, the Spanish clergy and royalty found that the Inquisition, with the thousands of persons needed to keep its records, the cost of executioners, the upkeep of castles and monasteries, was losing money. The Inquisitors turned to the Netherlands, then newly under Spanish rule, as a source of revenue and victims. Heretics were plentiful there, thanks to the growing Protestant movement in Northern Europe. In 1555, Madrid gave orders to rack and kill a great number of heretics quickly to inspire the surviving citizens of that country to turn over their money and goods. According to a Valenciennes citizen in *A Short History of the Inquisition,* "Men and women were broken on the wheel, racked, dragged at horses' tails; their sight was extinguished, their tongues torn out by the roots, their hands and feet burned, and executed in every slow and agonizing way that malicious inventiveness could devise." A massive emigration from the Netherlands took place until it was forbidden, with death

pronounced as the sentence on any wagoners or shipmasters who tried to help people leave. The Duke of Alba was sent from Spain with 10,000 men, accompanied by 2,000 non-heretical prostitutes so that the workers would not be swayed by female heretics' allure. Mass carnage was committed to crush the growing revolt against the clergy. On the "Day of Infamy," Feb. 16, 1568, The Inquisition condemned all of the Netherlands' inhabitants to death as heretics, ordering the execution of three million people. About eight hundred victims were hanged or burned in the first week, causing the people to revolt.

The Duke of Alba, returning to Spain, boasted that he had ordered 28,000 executions, with tens of thousands more dying as every city and town was systematically terrorized. Male heretics were tied in pairs and drowned, and female victims were raped and then killed. It would be eighty years before the Inquisition's hold on the Netherlands was finally loosed and the reformed faith was sanctioned on a large scale. REF.: *CBA.*

Inskip, Thomas Walker Hobart (Viscount Caldecote), 1876-1947, Brit., atty. gen.-jur. Worked for Admiralty in intelligence and law divisions from 1915-18. He served as solicitor general from 1922-28, and from 1931-32, and as attorney general from 1928-29, and from 1932-36. He presided as lord chief justice from 1940-46. REF.: *CBA.*

Insull, Samuel, 1859-1938, Case of, U.S., embez.-fraud. The high rollers of high finance of the 1920s, from Harry Sinclair to Ivar Kreuger, were wheeler-dealers who dared any adventure for gain and flirted with arrest and imprisonment for the power that money could bring them. Many a tycoon saw the inside of a prison cell while others, insulated with their fortunes against such indignities, blithely ignored the law and skipped from country to country, like Robert Vesco, to avoid prosecution.

The first financial powerhouse to employ this evasive action, albeit a forlorn procedure in his case, was Samuel Insull, whose Horatio Alger image exploded in scandal when his utilities empire collapsed during the Depression, leaving tens of thousands of investors with useless stocks. Insull, born in London, boasted no aristocratic background. In fact, he came from a dirt-poor family whose economic

Samuel Insull, being interviewed while a fugitive on board the steamer *Exilona.*

position was so dire that Insull was compelled to quit school and go to work at age fourteen as an office boy, taking home $1.25 a week.

Insull later became a clerk for Thomas A. Edison's representative in London and so impressed the boss with his diligence that he was recommended as an assistant to Edison himself. The great inventor hired Insull, sight unseen, and Samuel, at age twenty-one in 1881, immigrated to the United States where he became the inventor's personal secretary, setting up Edison's various companies.

Sent to Chicago to manage the vast utility firm there, Insull proved himself such a company wizard that he became president of the Chicago Edison firm in 1902. Five years later the empire builder had amalgamated all the power and light firms in the area into the enormous Commonwealth Edison Company.

The position Insull held already assured him of a vast fortune, yet he was obsessed with gathering every utility in the Midwest under his spreading umbrella, and by the end of the 1920s, the light and power czar was president of eleven companies, the director of eighty-five other firms, and was the board chairman of sixty-five additional companies. More than 75,000 employees worked for Insull, and his empire encompassed the Midwest, reaching down the Mississippi Valley and into New England.

When the stock market crashed in 1929, Insull, like many other self-centered tycoons, made the mistake of thinking he was bigger than any panic and hurled his $100 million personal fortune into the abyss in a desperate gamble, to keep up the level of his own stocks. After going through his own money, Insull borrowed heavily from friends and family and managed to salvage most of his firms. Just when he thought he had saved the day, however, he was challenged in a head-to-head power play by Cyrus Eaton, a multimillionaire from Cleveland.

With reckless abandon for his own shaky fortune, Eaton attempted to purchase the controlling stock interest in all of the Insull companies, most of which had huge blocks of stock available at depressed values. When Insull discovered what Eaton was doing, he dove into the open market in an incredible battle to buy up enough of his own stock to keep control—an effort that used up another $60 million, depleting Insull's coffers and gutting many of his firms.

Depleted of capital, the magnate could not withstand another financial crisis. As the Insull firms began to collapse in the summer of 1932 under the onslaught of the grinding Depression, investors in those firms were wiped out. Losses to stockholders soared to more than $750 million and Samuel Insull, one-time titan of American utilities, was nearly penniless. Disgraced and humiliated, the ex-tycoon sailed for Paris, where he intended to retire. But the loss of his fortune was not his only problem. Within months, tens of thousands of irate investors sued Insull. His creditors also brought suit in the millions. More serious were charges against him for embezzlement and mail fraud. It was claimed that he had looted the funds of his companies illegally in his wild stock battle with Eaton.

Extradition of the broken czar was laboriously arranged between France and the U.S., but before Insull could be returned to the U.S., the 72-year-old man, ill and harassed, hurriedly collected the money from his $21,000-a-year pensions (from three of his surviving companies) and fled to Greece, where he was given a year's sanctuary. Upon arriving in Athens, Insull went into seclusion, while every U.S. correspondent throughout the Continent hunted him for interviews. Cornelius Vanderbilt, Jr., then a correspondent for *Liberty* magazine, received a tip which gave him Insull's address in Athens, and he flew to that city, amazed to discover that Insull was staying at a maternity home. Vanderbilt found Insull, formally dressed in a morning coat, sitting in a courtyard, and reading an article that described his flight in an English newspaper published in Rome.

Vanderbilt introduced himself as a *Liberty* correspondent and asked that the old man tell him the story of his life. Insull, taking off his pince-nez, betrayed his desperation for cash by immediately inquiring: "Do you people intend to pay me, or am I to give you my story free?" He went on to ask for $100,000, and when Vanderbilt stated that his magazine would be disinclined to remit such a staggering amount (for those days), the old man shook his white-haired head and stroked his white mustache. He then began dickering with Vanderbilt, who said that *Liberty* might pay as much as $20,000 for the full story. Insull replied he would think about it; that he would get back to Vanderbilt. He never did.

U.S. demands for Insull's extradition forced the Greek government to close in on the ex-tycoon in 1934. Using almost his last dime, Insull chartered a leaking steamer and sailed aimlessly about the Mediterranean for almost two weeks. Running out of provisions, the tramp ship made port in Istanbul, where Turkish authorities immediately seized the old man and sent him back to face trial with his brother, Martin Insull, who was already under arrest.

Insull's arrival in New York on the *Exilona* was a sensation. The press flocked to the dock in the hundreds. Still photographers and newsreel cameramen mobbed the old man as he

resolutely marched down the gangplank where his son, Samuel Insull, Jr., managed to wedge through the crowd and slip a piece of paper into his father's hand. Reporters punched and shoved one another to get close to the old man, shouting and screaming questions at him. Many of them *ordered* Insull to answer their queries, treating him as if he were already a convicted felon, the embezzler several Chicago indictments claimed him to be. Incensed, Samuel Insull suddenly regained his old firebrand personality for the moment. He whipped off his hat to show his snow-white hair and jutted his jaw, shouting back at reporters: "Keep quiet! There is plenty of time for taking pictures, but this is my mug and I have a proprietary interest in it."

The old man then looked briefly down at the piece of paper his son had handed him, a statement he had never seen until that moment. Trusting his son's judgment, Insull announced: "I have a statement for the gentlemen of the press...I have erred, but my greatest error was in underestimating the effect of the financial panic on American securities and particularly on the companies I was working so hard to build. I worked with all my energies to save those companies. I made mistakes, but they were honest mistakes. They were errors in judgment, but not dishonest manipulations." The old man then reminded the press that "...you only know the charges of the prosecution. Not one word has been argued in even feeble defense of me, and it must be obvious that there is also my side of the story. When it is told in court, my judgment may be discredited, but certainly my honesty will be vindicated."

Insull awaiting trial for fraud in Chicago.

Insull had read this written speech without error and without pause, but upon finishing, he turned to his son and asked in a low voice: "Where in the hell did that statement come from?" His son told him that a brilliant publicist the firm had hired, Steve Hannagan, had written it. Hannagan, Insull was informed, would continue to direct the old man's public posture. Minutes later, federal agents seized Insull and he was led to a waiting car and taken to New Jersey (to prevent New York authorities from claiming the old man for charges pending there, it was later alleged). In New Jersey, Insull was put aboard a westbound train to Chicago.

Publicist Hannagan advised Insull once the old man arrived in Chicago, insisting that he not pay the $200,000 bail demanded—which his family and friends could have easily raised—but instead spend time in the Cook County Jail. Insull meekly agreed to follow the publicity plan to earn sympathy from the public. He was photographed while being booked as a common felon. Photographers delighted in taking his picture as he stood, small and ancient, in his cell, no longer the decisive tycoon. After a few days of subjecting Insull to these indignities, Hannagan decided that the old man had gleaned enough pity. The bail, then reduced, was paid, and the old man moved into a $4-a-day room at the less-than-posh Seneca Hotel, although he could just as easily have moved into his son's Gold Coast apartment. Again, this was Hannagan's plan to glean more sympathy for Insull.

The Chicago press flooded readers with Insull's plight, describing how he had sold off his $9 million Hawthorn estate for a mere $780,000 while trying to shore up sagging stocks; he was portrayed as a heroic U.S. businessman risking his own fortune to save the stock of his "little man" investors. Chicagoans were also reminded that it was Insull who had built the Civic Opera House building.

All of this, of course, stemmed from the fertile brain of publicity wizard Hannagan, who made sure that Insull was followed about Chicago while awaiting trial, shown entering movie theaters like any common man and pictured giving up his seat to a woman on a streetcar. He was even photographed smelling flowers he bought from a street vendor, ostensibly spending his last dollar.

The public attitude toward Insull began to radically change. The "man in the street," even those who had lost their life savings in his stock purchases, began to express sympathy for the "hounded" old man. But there were others, hundreds, who sent anonymous letters to authorities and to the Insull family, threatening to shoot, stab, or bomb the Insulls out of existence. With that, the old man was guarded twenty-four hours a day by dozens of hired men. He moved to better quarters and traveled to and from court in a bullet-proof limousine.

On Oct. 2, 1934, Insull went on trial before federal judge James H. Wilkerson for using the mail to defraud in the sale of stock of the Corporation Securities Company of Chicago. His lawyer, Floyd Thompson, a one-time judge, shrewdly placed his client on the stand immediately and asked him to tell his rags-to-riches story and of his close relationship with Thomas Edison, who was an American institution. The saga so enthralled Judge Wilkerson that by the time prosecutor Dwight H. Green objected, the judge overruled him. Day after day, Insull continued his charismatic tale, winning the judge and jury. On Nov. 24, 1934, he was acquitted. But who got the money? Answered Thompson: "Old Man Depression." The spendthrift era of the 1920s was blamed for the loss of countless millions, not Samuel Insull.

Immediate accusations were made that the jury had been bribed. The press at large felt that the old man had glibly talked himself out of a conviction. Columnist Franklin P. Adams write: "The public is a masochist at heart, and not only likes to be cheated, but has admiration for those who deceive and defraud it." The *Nation* was even more adamant in its belief that Insull was guilty as charged, stating that the acquittal "illustrates once more the difficulty of sending a rich man to jail, no matter how flagrant his crime." Two more trials awaited Insull. He faced charges of embezzlement, along with his brother, Martin, on Mar. 12, 1935, and on June 11, 1935, with his son, charges of illegally transferring funds before declaring bankruptcy in one of their companies.

The scattered debris of the Insull paper empire was so vast, so complicated, that the government could find no concrete evidence that Insull or his brother and a son had indeed embezzled or hid funds. Hundreds of his minions had handled the actual transference of money into stock purchases in a web of accounting so intricate that the best government experts were nonplussed to figure out the system. The same held true for the mail fraud charges, and finally the old man, by then a wreck, was set free. He sailed back to Paris to live out his days and, on July 16, 1938, at seventy-nine, died in a Paris subway of a heart attack. He left an estate of less than $1,000 to his wife Gladys, an 1890s actress, and more than $14 million in personal debts. At the moment of Samuel Insull's death, he was wearing monogrammed underwear and had 85¢ in his pockets.

REF.: Alexander, *Panic! The Day the Money Stopped*; Allen, *The Big Change*; Allen, *Since Yesterday*; Armstrong, *The Book of the Stock Exchange*; Asbury, *Gem of the Prairie*; Baker, *Back to Back*; Braithwaite, *The Hungry Thirties*; Broadfoot, *Ten Lost Years, 1929-1939*; Busch, *Guilty or Not Guilty*; Butterfield, *The American Past*; CBA; Chandler, *America's Greatest Depression*; Dedmon, *Fabulous Chicago*; Ellis, *A Nation in Torment, The Great American Depression, 1929-1939*; Farr, *Chicago*; Feis, *1933: Characters in Crisis*; Fisher, *The Stock Market Crash—and After*; Galbraith, *The Great Crash*; Horan, *The Desperate Years*; Lewis and Smith, *Chicago, The History of Its Reputation*; McDonald, *Insull*; Mayer, *Wall Street, The Inside Story of American Finance*; Mayer and Wade, *Chicago, Growth of a Metropolis*; Muggeridge, *The Thirties*; Nash, *People to See*; Patterson, *The Great Boom and Panic*; Ramsay, *Pyramids of Power, The Story of Roosevelt, Insull and the Utility Wars*; Rees, *The Great Slump*; Robbins, *The Great Depression*; Rogers, *I Remember Distinctly*; Sann, *The Lawless Decade*; Shannon, *The Great Depression*; Tanner, *All the Things We Were*; Thomas, Morgan, and Witts, *The Day the Bubble Burst*; Tugwell, *The Brains Trust*; Wee, *The Great Depression, Revisited*.

International Pearl Necklace Theft, prom. 1916, Fr.-Brit., theft. When Max Mayer of London opened a specially-delivered package from France in September 1916, he expected to find a £100,000 pearl necklace. Instead Mayer found sugar and pieces of a French newspaper. With only this evidence to begin the case, police deduced the crime had been committed in Britain and began sifting through the names of known jewel thieves. A French detective posing as a go-between for a cartel of jewelers finally made connections with one of the men who had stolen the pearls.

Scotland Yard waited until the thieves were all together before arresting four suspects who refused to disclose the whereabouts of the necklace. The search for the necklace continued until one morning when a piano tuner turned up at a London police station with the pearls. The necklace had apparently been discarded by the wife or girlfriend of one of the robbers, and the man picked it up thinking it was a set of fake pearls. The robbers were convicted and sentenced to prison.

REF.: CBA; Kingston, *Dramatic Days at Old Bailey*.

Interpol (International Criminal Police Organization), 1914- , Int'l., law enfor. agency. Contrary to popular belief, Interpol is not a law enforcement agency making its own arrests, but rather is a data-collecting and information-dispensing agency to which almost all national law enforcement agencies belong. At the request of Prince Albert I of the Principality of Monaco, dozens of high-ranking police officials, jurists, and magistrates from almost every European country met in Monaco in 1914, just prior to WWI, to establish a cooperative organization that would universally share information in identifying and tracking international criminals. International criminals were defined as those who operated illegally from country to country, such as white slavers, drug traffickers, swindlers with firms in several countries, or fugitives who had committed a crime in one country and had fled to another. With the coming of WWI, the idea for such an international police organization was shelved.

In 1923, Johann Schober, president of Police of Vienna, convened another meeting to establish the organization that came to be known as Interpol. The group consisted of 130 delegates representing twenty countries, and it decided to form the International Criminal Police Commission (ICPC) which was to be headquartered in Vienna. These headquarters were abandoned when the Nazis annexed Austria in 1938; the organization ceased to function at that time, except as an arm of the Gestapo and SS. Nazi SS chief Reinhard Heydrich became head of Interpol during the war, but he subverted the original aims of the organization and used it as a tool to persecute innocent persons.

Unfortunately, the laboriously produced files and indexes listing criminal history fell into the hands of the Nazis and much of this information was lost by the time Interpol was reconstructed following WWII. F.E. Louwage, inspector general of the Belgium police, convened the next meeting of Interpol in Brussels in 1946, and nineteen member nations agreed to elect a president, a secretary-general, and an executive committee for Interpol. Headquarters were established in Paris and Louwage became the first president of the organization.

In 1956, another meeting in Vienna produced a charter which legalized all of Interpol's activities. Membership had grown to fifty-five countries and the name of the organization was officially changed to the International Criminal Police Organization. A general assembly of all members was organized and would meet every year. The president would be elected to a four-year post, and two vice presidents would be elected to three-year terms. The secretary-general would hold his position for five years. An executive committee of nine members, including the president and one vice president, was also established to oversee procedures. Interpol established a constitution that called for mutual assistance from all member countries in providing information that would identify and track all international criminals. The constitution prohibited any interference with Interpol activities from political, religious, or military groups.

The most vital activity of Interpol is the sharing of information between all member countries. The police force for each member country is responsible for funneling data on criminals to Interpol, including fingerprints, voice prints, and photographs. Hundreds of thousands of criminal history files and fingerprints have been collected and computerized, making Interpol the great clearinghouse of data on active criminals. Identification of criminals to member countries often results in the speedy apprehension of these wanted fugitives, and arrests, though made locally by police in each country, are processed through Interpol for extradition from one country to another.

A powerful telecommunications and radio system, working from a sophisticated communications center in Paris, allows Interpol operators to maintain round-the-clock contact with all police department members. Interpol's identification systems, fully computerized today, offer "memory bubbles" which can store staggering amounts of information on a single disk, as much as 700,000 full files. Several million files, offering fingerprints and photos, along with the world's largest cross-reference files on aliases and monikers, reside at Interpol's Paris headquarters. Of the more than 100 countries that are active members of Interpol, England, through New Scotland Yard, France, and Germany, are its leading exponents.

The U.S. resigned from Interpol in 1950 over a matter dealing with Communists. This was largely the doing of J. Edgar Hoover, then director of the FBI. It was Hoover's contention that Interpol could not be trusted with "sensitive" data stored in FBI repositories, but Hoover really objected to sharing information. The U.S. later reinstated its membership. Interpol has been criticized by members of the U.S. Congress as being dominated by political elements opposed to the U.S., even though Interpol's constitution prohibits political influence of its operations. Critics also dislike the idea of sending information on U.S. citizens to Interpol that may not be directly related to known criminals. Others claim Interpol infringes upon the civil rights of citizens the world over, though no substantial evidence has ever proven this. Interpol, in recent years, has been particularly effective in tracking international drug smugglers and traffickers, which has aided in worldwide arrests of kingpin criminals. See: **Federal Bureau of Investigation; Heydrich, Reinhard; Hoover, J. Edgar; New Scotland Yard; Scotland Yard.**

REF.: Alexander, *The Pizza Connection; CBA;* Demaris, *Brothers in Blood: The International Terrorist Network;* Dobson and Payne, *Counterattack—The West's Battle Against the Terrorists;* Fooner, *A Guide to Interpol;* Gage, *Mafia, U.S.A.;* Garrison, *The Secret World of Interpol;* Lee, *Interpol;* Nash, *Hustlers and Conmen; Schreiber, The Ultimate Weapon—Terrorists and World Order;* Scott, *The Concise Encyclopedia of Crime and Criminals;* Shannon, *Desperadoes;* Unger, *FBI;* Whitehead, *Journey into Crime;* (FILM), *The Narco Men,* 1986.

Inukai Tsuyoshi (Ki), 1855-1932, prime minister, Japan, assass. A liberal politician, Inukai Tsuyoshi began his career as a journalist, working as a correspondent for *Hochi Shimbun* during the Satsuma rebellion of 1877. He later became that publication's editor, a position he held until 1890 when he entered politics and became a member of the first House of Representatives of the Imperial Diet, Japan's parliamentary government. Inukai became minister of education in 1898, and he proved to be an ardent foe of military expansionism. In 1922, Inukai formed his own party, Kakushin Karabu (Reformation party), a liberally bent, small organization that continued to oppose Japan's militarists. In 1924, to gain political strength, Inukai merged his party with the Rikken Seiyukai party, which immediately appointed him its leader. Under the banner of the Rikken Seiyukai, Inukai gained considerable stature and was made prime minister in 1931.

The diminutive and feisty Inukai openly opposed the Japanese army's ruthless goals of conquest in Manchuria and consistently devised methods to impede Japanese incursion there, such as

drastically curtailing budgets for the army. This won him the enmity of the militarists, who marked him for assassination. Nine air force and navy cadets, who had been indoctrinated for months on the evil ways of Inukai's administration, were told that the prime minister was secretly negotiating with Chiang Kai-shek of China to give back territory won by the blood of Japanese troops, stood ready to murder Inukai. They called their cabal the Blood Brotherhood. Emperor Hirohito, as usual, played a waiting game. According to reliable reports, he approved of the assassination of his prime minister, but he wanted the assassins to appear as though they were acting on their own and in the interests of patriotic nationalism.

Other members of the Blood Brotherhood had been active. This group, financed by Japan's top militarists, was also sponsored by the insidious and criminal Black Dragon Society headed by the cunning Toyama Mitsuru, crime boss of Japan for thirty years. Inoue Nisho, one of Toyama's henchman, a burly, strapping friar who could have passed for a sumo wrestler, enlisted eleven young military officers and assigned them to assassinate various Japanese politicians and businessmen who had opposed the militarists and Hirohito and their plans for conquest.

Inoue recruited 22-year-old Konuma Tadashi, a carpenter's apprentice who was a member of the Blood Brotherhood and had been trained in assassination techniques. Inoue gave Konuma a Browning automatic pistol and a handful of bullets and ordered him to murder Japan's former finance minister, Inoue Junnosuke (no relation to the friar). The 66-year-old Inoue

Japan's Prime Minister Inukai, assassinated in 1932.

had been reluctant to finance the militarists when in office and his assassination would make him an example. On Feb. 9, 1932, Konuma, after receiving instructions from Friar Inoue, waited for former finance minister Inoue to appear at a political rally in Tokyo. After Inoue stepped from a car to address a sidewalk crowd, Konuma shot him three times in the back, killing him instantly.

While Konuma allowed himself to be arrested by friendly police, Friar Inoue moved into a house owned by Black Dragon leader Toyama Mitsuru, and planned the next assassination. His target was Baron Dan Takuma, a long-time U.S. supporter. In 1871, at the age of thirteen, Dan Takuma had been sent to the U.S. as part of the first student exchange program and having spent seven years there, considered it his second country. He was openly friendly to U.S. citizens and his Tokyo home was always open to traveling U.S. students. As director of Japan's largest business cartel, Baron Dan was also opposed to Japanese military expansion and denied the militarists considerable funds to further their aggressions abroad. He, like Finance Minister Inoue, was marked for death by the Blood Brotherhood. Friar Inoue summoned another assassin, Hisanuma Goro, gave him a Browning automatic pistol and bullets, and told him to kill Baron Dan Takuma. After obtaining Baron Dan's daily schedule, Hisanuma stationed himself outside the Mitsui Bank Building on Mar. 5, 1932. When the baron's car arrived, the assassin tried to open the door, but found it locked. Before the baron's chauffeur could drive to safety, Hisanuma fired through the window, one bullet killing Baron Dan immediately.

Some weeks later, Hirohito's representative, Lieutenant General Segawa Akitomo met with the cadets at an inn outside Tokyo and briefed them on their task. He gave them directions to the prime minister's residence and told them how they must enter the building and where to locate Inukai. He then got them drunk and lectured them on their patriotic duty. The cadets then held a murder council and elected leaders. One of them noted that Hollywood movie actor Charlie Chaplin was arriving in Tokyo on Saturday, May 14, 1932, the day before the planned assassination. The cadet proposed they kill the comedian along with Inukai when the prime minister entertained Chaplin on the night of May 14 to bring international attention to their cause.

This plan was seriously considered until another cadet pointed out that police, already alerted to a death threat to Chaplin—a fake threat to slacken security for Inukai—would go all out to protect the comedian on Saturday night. Therefore, most of the force would be resting and off-guard the following day, which had been set aside for the prime minister's murder. The vote was taken to allow Charlie Chaplin to live. Inukai would be killed in his residence on Sunday.

The five army cadets and four navy fliers, ranging in age from twenty-four to twenty-eight, then left by train for Tokyo. Upon arriving, the men rode in two taxis to the Yasukuni Shrine, a Shinto temple where they prayed to their heroes—the 126,363 men who had sacrificed their lives for the military glory of Japan and the emperor. As they left, one bought charms and gave them to his associates, telling them that the curios would protect them from police bullets. They piled back into two cabs and drove to Inukai's residence, which was near the emperor's estate. The prime minister's residence had been modeled after Frank Lloyd Wright's Imperial Hotel and featured a foyer that was almost as large as a hotel lobby, with horizontal wood and stone slabs built in tiers.

At the same time, two other groups of young officers had gathered at strategic points in the city and were moving toward their destinations. The nine young men at Inukai's residence marched into the lobby and asked a policeman to direct them to the prime minister's living quarters. The policeman began chatting about the weather instead, and as he did so, a plainclothes officer who had been sitting nearby, got up from his chair and bolted for the main entrance. One of the cadets shot and wounded him. The uniformed officer was stunned into silence. He refused to utter another word and the nine cadets then ran into the building, dashing through corridors and hallways, breaking into rooms. They found several servants, but none would tell them the whereabouts of Inukai's living quarters.

Then the cadets heard a noise behind a second-floor door, which they easily broke down. They shot the lone police bodyguard to death and rushed into Inukai's private quarters. They found the

Friar Inoue, who gave the assassins their targets in 1932.

little prime minister sitting calmly at a table smoking a cigarette and wearing a thin kimono. Navy cadet Mikami walked quickly to the 76-year-old Inukai, put a revolver to his head, and pulled the trigger several times. Nothing happened. Mikami had forgotten to load the weapon. The prime minister shook his head and stroked his white goateed chin. Mikami accused Inukai of sending secret letters to Chinese warlords and generally betraying Japan.

"Now wait," Inukai said. The five-foot-tall prime minister stood up and began walking toward his desk, motioning the cadets to follow him and discuss matters reasonably. "You will under-

stand if you talk with me for a while. Let's go over here to my workroom."

Mikami later stated to police: "I decided that it would be only a warrior's mercy to listen to what he had to say in his last testament." The cadets followed the prime minister into his office, leaving behind Inukai's terrified daughter-in-law, who stood holding an infant in her arms. Cadet Mikami loaded his revolver.

Prime Minister Inukai standing in the very spot where he was shot a few days later by Japanese officers.

"I didn't have any personal grudge against him," Mikami added in court testimony, "but I had a tragic feeling. I tried to convince myself that we were straws in the wind of revolution. And so nothing changed my will to kill."

As the cadets entered the prime minister's office, Inukai, still using a calm voice, said: "Not too hasty, not too hasty." Then he looked down at the boots the cadets were wearing and said: "What about your shoes? Why don't you take them off?" The prime minister seemed more concerned with preserving Japanese etiquette than protecting his life.

One of the cadets shouted: "Worry about that later! You know why we are here! Do you have anything to say before you die?"

Then Lieutenant Yamagishi Masayoshi yelled: "No use talking! Fire!" Several shots were fired, and Mikami fired almost point blank at Inukai's head, sending a bullet into the prime minister's right temple. Inukai collapsed onto a table and Mikami ordered the cadets out of the room. Mikami later stated that he did not like being rushed in his assassination; he had wanted to tell Inukai "wish you a peaceful slumber" before he shot him, but there was no time for formalities.

After the cadets ran outside and back to their taxicabs, the prime minister's family members rushed to his side, and to their surprise, found him still alive. The bullet fired into his temple had slashed his forehead and become embedded in the bridge of his nose. Another bullet had pierced his left nostril, entering his mouth and exiting through his right cheek. He was lucid and talking, saying to his doctor, who had been on the premises: "Call them back. I want to talk to them." More doctors were called. Bandages were applied to Inukai's wounds and since he evidenced no shock, the physicians concluded that his wounds were not critical. The tough little prime minister then called a cabinet meeting, which was held at his bedside an hour later. He learned that the execution squad had jumped into cabs and that they had ordered the drivers to speed past the nearby Metropolitan Police Headquarters, where they fired their weapons wildly into the air. They did the same thing at the Bank of Japan. They then drove to the offices of the Secret Police in Kojimachi and surrendered to officers sympathetic to the militarists. A second group of conspirators had thrown grenades at a few government buildings and had also turned themselves into the Secret Police. The third group of plotters had bombed the empty headquarters of Inukai's Rikken Seiyukai party, but injured no one before they, too, surrendered to the Secret Police. The military coup was ended.

Inukai dismissed his cabinet at about 8 p.m. and then began to bleed heavily. More doctors arrived and gave him a small transfusion, mixing the blood of Inukai's son with a "solution." In a few minutes the prime minister collapsed into a coma. Yet he continued to cling to life, and in the Imperial Palace, Hirohito was told that the prime minister was not yet dead. The emperor sent his personal physician to "attend" to the stricken Inukai.

Meanwhile, other young officers approached their superiors, demanding that these older generals who had been behind the coup give orders that would cause a general uprising among the military. The generals refused since they did not have the blessing of the war minister, and especially since young Emperor Hirohito was vacillating. Hirohito was unable to decide whether to unleash his fanatical young officers to establish a military dictatorship that he would secretly control but would make him appear hostage to their control. This is exactly what Hirohito planned to do, but not at this time. He would find conditions more favorable in 1936 after his war machine had been properly equipped and strengthened.

Prime Minister Inukai hung on. At 9:30 p.m. he spat up blood. A physician gave him a tablet and Inukai said: "I feel much better now." He then fell back into a coma and was seized by convulsions. At 11:20 p.m. the emperor was told that Inukai was dead, but this proved untrue. Now that the prime minister's death officially had been recorded, it was imperative that he, indeed, die. More doctors attended Inukai, and finally, after being injected with what was probably a lethal substance, Inukai died at 2:36 a.m., May 16, 1932. Not until he was convinced that his political foe was dead did Hirohito retire to his royal bed chamber and go to sleep.

A few days later the elderly Admiral Saito Makoto was appointed interim prime minister, chosen because he would do as he was told by the militarists acting on Hirohito's behalf. When Saito proved truculent, he was executed in the so-called military uprising of 1936. Fifty-four persons, mostly young officers, were arrested and brought to trial in what western correspondents described as "leisurely justice." None was sentenced to death and only six leaders of the death squad, including those who had assassinated the prime minister, were sent to prison. These men were released in 1939 and 1940, in time to resume their military careers and help invade the Philippines and the islands of the South Pacific.

REF.: Bergamini, *Japan's Imperial Conspiracy*; Bornstein, *The Politics of Murder*; Byas, *Government by Assassination*; CBA; Hurwood, *Society and the Assassin*; McNelly, *Politics and Government in Japan*; Morton, *Japan: Its History and Culture*; Mosley, *Hirohito: Emperor of Japan*; Paine, *The Assassins' World*; Reischauer, *Japan: The Story of a Nation*; Scalapino, *Democracy and the Party Movement in Prewar Japan*; Toland, *The Rising Sun*.

Invincibles, prom. 1882, Ire., secret crim. soc. The Fenians were a secret Irish revolutionary brotherhood formed in 1858 in New York to free Ireland from English rule. In 1882, in Phoenix Park, Dublin, the Invincibles, a group of ex-Fenian terrorists, killed Lord Frederick Cavendish and Thomas Burke, the chief secretary and undersecretary, respectively, of Ireland. At the time, the English Liberal Party was planning to introduce several reform measures in Ireland. It seemed that independence would come by political means, so the Invincibles' action was embarrassing to the Irish cause. After efforts in Parliament to pass Irish home rule bills failed, the revolutionaries again became active. In an attempt to stem the influx of English culture, they revived Gaelic, the Irish national language. The revolutionary movement culminated in the formation of the *Sinn Fein* party in 1905. As in several other nineteenth-century movements, revival of traditional culture inspired renewed revolutionary activity. See: **Cavendish**, Lord **Frederick Charles.**

REF.: *CBA*; Lacquer, *Terrorism*; MacKenzie, *Secret Societies*; Pollard, *The Secret Societies of Ireland*.

Ippolito, Joseph, 1943- , Case of, U.S., mur. When former aldermanic candidate and Chicago policeman Joseph Ippolito was implicated in a murder-for-hire scheme in 1982, a bizarre tale of obsessive love unfolded in the Chicago courtroom of Judge James M. Bailey.

Prosecutors said that soon after Hanover Park grandmother Kathryn Specht began babysitting for Ralph and Mary Gordon, the woman became unnaturally attached to the Gordon's 4-year-old daughter, Annie. Specht, who believed the child resembled her dead grandson, plotted to obtain custody of the girl, the prosecution said. Evidence was introduced that Specht had forged Ralph Gordon's signature on a document granting her guardianship of Annie and making her the beneficiary of a $20,000 insurance policy on Mr. Gordon's life. Mary Gordon testified that Specht said she had friends who could kill Ralph.

In the fall of 1980, the windows of Mr. Gordon's car were shattered by bullets. In November, he began to receive calls from a man who identified himself as a police officer. The "policeman" wanted to talk with Gordon about a number of outstanding traffic tickets. The 28-year-old printer knew he was innocent and got a gun before he was supposed to meet with the "cop" on Nov. 25. The next morning, Gordon's body was discovered in his car on the 4600 block of West Berteau. The engine was still idling when police found Gordon with bullet wounds in his forehead and cheek. Gordon's "bribe" money and gun were still in his pocket.

On Jan. 29, 1981, Ippolito was arrested and charged with murder after police discovered he had made a number of phone calls to Specht on the day of Gordon's murder. In July, Specht was also indicted on murder charges. During the May 1982 trial, Judge Bailey acquitted Specht and Ippolito of all charges, saying that without a witness, a confession, or a murder weapon, the state had failed to prove its case. REF.: *CBA*.

Ipswich Witchcraft Case, prom. 1878, Case of, U.S., witchcraft. During the early days of Christian Science, a number of followers debated the teachings of Mary Baker Eddy, the religion's founder. The misconceptions of the new religion moved Lucretia Brown, on advice from her "healer," Dorcas Rawson, to file a lawsuit against Daniel Spofford, a fellow student of Christian Science, in Ipswich, Conn. The suit charged Spofford with controlling Brown's life to the point where she was suffering great pain in both her body and her mind. Brown said she feared she would never be able to escape from Spofford's mesmerizing powers.

While Eddy opposed filing the suit, she did appear in court with Brown, only to see the case dismissed on the grounds that the court was unable to control Spofford's mind. Claiming ignorance of the legal system, Mrs. Eddy later tried to disassociate herself from what became known as the "Ipswich Witchcraft Case."

REF.: *CBA*; Robbins, *The Encyclopedia of Witchcraft and Demonology*; Wilbur, *The Life of Mary Baker Eddy*.

Iredell, James, 1751-99, U.S., jur. As attorney general of North Carolina from 1779-81, he collected and revised all the state laws to create a new code. He was nominated as associate justice of the U.S. Supreme Court by President George Washington in 1790 and served from 1790-99. While serving on the Court, he asserted the independence of the court in cases such as *Calder v. Bull* in 1798, in which he stated that courts had the power to declare legislation unconstitutional if it contradicted the Constitution. REF.: *CBA*.

Ireland, William Henry, 1777-1835, Brit., forg. At eighteen, William Ireland forged documents he claimed were the work of William Shakespeare. He impudently announced to the literary world, that he had discovered a lost play by the great Elizabethan bard titled *Vortigem and Rowena*. Richard Sheridan eagerly produced the play at the Drury Lane Theatre. Having succeeded in deceiving the theater-going public and the British critics, Ireland wrote a second play, *Henry II,* which was accepted without question by the experts.

Literary forger William Henry Ireland.

The opportunistic young playwright and forger even claimed that his ancestors had inherited a portion of Shakespeare's estate upon his death. The learned George Chalmers and Sir James Bland Burgess examined the forgeries in Samuel Ireland's book shop and called them authentic. Only Edmund Malone and John Kemble expressed any skepticism about the "discoveries." Malone in particular assailed Ireland in print for perpetrating a colossal fraud on the public. Not until 1805 did the truth come out, when Ireland admitted that the whole thing had been a hoax, a confession he recanted in 1832. Later James Boswell would call them "Ireland's sin."

REF.: *CBA*; Hunt, *A Dictionary of Rogues*; MacDougall, *Hoaxes*; Nash, *Zanies*.

Irene, 752-803, Roman., consp. In 769 she married Leo IV, who died in 780. She became regent, ruling while her son was a minor, from 780-90, and reinstated image worship in the eastern church. Her son Constantine VI became ruler in 790 and she was given the title empress. She plotted to overthrow her son from 792-97, and in 797 she had him arrested, put in prison, and later killed. She held power from 797-802, then was ousted and exiled to the island of Lesbos. REF.: *CBA*.

Irey, Elmer Lincoln, 1888-1948, U.S., law enfor. off. Born in Kansas City, Mo., Elmer Lincoln Irey moved to Washington, D.C., as a child, when his father became an employee in the government printing office. After working as a stenographer in the Post Office Department, Irey's law enforcement career began as a clerk in the office of the Chief Postal Inspector. Twelve years later, Irey transferred to the Bureau of Internal Revenue, where he helped form an intelligence unit to investigate tax fraud. The U.S. income tax law was relatively new and Irey was charged with its enforcement, serving in an office that made background checks on applicants for Treasury jobs and investigating tax officials and income tax violators.

Top treasury agent Elmer Irey.

Throughout his illustrious career, Irey was involved in many celebrated tax cases, including those of gangster Al Capone, Louisiana governor Huey Long, and

publisher Moses Annenberg. Irey also was credited with the capture of Bruno Richard Hauptman because he alone insisted the serial numbers on the bills used for the kidnapped Lindbergh baby's ransom be recorded. Irey's IRS unit, which came to be known as the T-Men, with the "T" standing for Treasury, was credited with nabbing more than 15,000 tax cheats over the course of his twenty-seven years in the IRS. The department maintained a conviction rate of more than 90 percent and Irey and his 200-man force saved the U.S. government hundreds of millions of dollars with their work.

In 1942, Irey was appointed coordinator of the Treasury's enforcement agencies and guided the department's law enforcement efforts for four years. In ill health, Irey resigned from his post in 1946 and died two years later at the age of sixty. See: **Annenberg, Moses; Capone, Alphonse; Long, Huey.**

REF.: *CBA;* Demaris, *The Director;* Fried, *The Rise and Fall of the Jewish Gangster;* Lowenthal, *The Federal Bureau of Investigation;* Smith, *Syndicate City;* McPhaul, *Johnny Torrio;* Messick, *Lansky;* ____, *Secret File;* ____, *Syndicate In the Sun;* ____ and Goldblatt, *The Mobs and the Mafia;* Ottenberg, *The Federal Investigators;* Peterson, *The Mob;* Reppetto, *The Blue Parade;* Sann, *Kill the Dutchman;* Spiering, *The Man Who Got Capone;* Thompson and Raymond, *Gang Rule In New York;* Tully, *Treasury Agent.*

Irigoyen, Hipólito, 1852-1933, Arg., attempt. assass. Termed a "Radical Autocrat," two-time Argentine President Hipólito Irigoyen lived in a small apartment above a tobacco shop in Buenos Aires and donated his salary to charity. One December morning in 1930, as Irigoyen's chauffeur and bodyguards waited for the president, a man ran out into the street and began shooting at the president's car. Irigoyen's chauffeur maneuvered the car to safety. Within seconds, the president's security staff had dropped Gualterio Marinelli with a barrage of bullets. Two police officials were wounded in the attack. Marinelli, an Italian dental mechanic, was a known anarchist who worked just a few doors from Irigoyen's apartment. Neighbors were at a loss to explain his motivation for the assassination attempt. REF.: *CBA*.

Irish Republican Army (IRA), prom. 1919- , Ire., secret crim. soc. The paramilitary Irish Republican Army was organized in January 1919, following the dissolution of the Irish Volunteers Group, which had employed violence in order to achieve political independence from Britain, since 1913. The IRA is the militant wing of Sinn Féin, the Irish nationalist party which seeks to promote the cause of independence through legitimate political channels. The historic enmity of the Irish against the British dates to the Middle Ages. Wolfe Tone's Rebellion of 1798, the Irish Rebellion of 1848, and the rise of the Fenian Movement in the mid-Nineteenth Century spawned the IRA and its various splinter groups which have gained notoriety in the modern era.

During the 1919-21 civil war the IRA carried out military raids against English installations, forcing a negotiated settlement. Ireland was partitioned into a Free State with dominion status within the empire. A number of IRA members opposed this on principle, resulting in a split within the ranks. The "Irregulars" organized armed resistance groups against the Irish Free State, resulting in another civil war in 1922-23. Although the defeated Irregulars were driven underground, the outlawed IRA remained a viable presence, recruiting and drilling new members in terrorist tactics.

In 1939 the resurgent IRA launched a series of bombings in England thought to have been inspired by Nazi agents eager to exploit the domestic turmoil in Britain. During WWII, five top leaders of the underground movement were executed. In December 1948 the Irish Free State withdrew from the British Commonwealth and was re-organized as a republic. The IRA formulated a new campaign, one aimed at unifying Protestant Northern Ireland, still part of the United Kingdom, with the Republic of Ireland to the south. The 1950s and early 1960s were generally quiet times in Ireland. The Catholics in the North remained peaceful and seemed unwilling to endorse the aims of the radical IRA. All this changed by the late 1960s when the Catholic minority in Ulster expressed outrage against the discriminatory actions of the Protestants who sought to exclude them from direct participation in the elective process.

A campaign of violence and terror aimed at the Ulster Protestants and the British government was commenced by the IRA. Yet within the organization itself, there was sharp disagreement about how far the agitation should go. At a Sinn Féin conference in December 1969 an accord was reached dividing the IRA into "official" and "provisional" wings. The official branch committed itself to a permanent political union of Catholics and Protestants under the socialist banner of a newly created Irish Republic. The more radical "Provos," composed primarily of younger Ulster Catholics, committed themselves to terrorist activities to force British troops to withdraw from Northern Ireland.

In 1972, law and order in Northern Ireland all but collapsed after the largely Protestant parliament at Stormont was abolished by order of the London government. These actions further complicated a tense situation, resulting in the formation of Protestant secret societies, among them the Ulster Volunteer Force, the Red Hand Commandos, and the Ulster Defense Association, composed primarily of working class men from the ghettos of Belfast. The once peaceful city became the battleground of an ugly, protracted guerrilla war.

The Provos, viewed as the "defenders" of the Catholic faith despite internecine warfare with the official IRA, stepped up their attacks killing and wounding many civilians and British government and military personnel. On "Black Friday," in July 1972, twenty-two bombs were exploded in downtown Belfast, killing nine people and wounding 130. In the next few years the IRA targeted prominent British officials for assassination. Among the casualties were Ambassador Christopher Ewart-Biggs, killed in a bomb blast on July 21, 1976, as he drove from his residence outside Dublin to the embassy in Merrion Square. On Aug. 27, 1979, British war hero and First Earl Louis Mountbatten was assassinated as he fished off the coast of Donegal Bay. Their murders, and a wave of terrorist bombings at home and abroad, were the work of the Provos.

On May 12, 1981, 27-year-old Bobby Sands died in Belfast's notorious Maze Prison after refusing to eat for sixty-six days. Sands, who had been elected to fill a vacancy in Parliament, was serving a 14-year sentence for possession of firearms. A week later a second inmate of the prison, Francis Hughes, passed away following a fifty-nine day hunger strike. Their deaths protested the long-standing British policy of treating IRA prisoners as common criminals rather than political detainees.

Commenting on the massive demonstrations that followed Sand's death, British Prime Minister Margaret Thatcher, herself the target of a botched 1984 IRA assassination attempt, said: "There can be no compromise with murder and terrorism."

REF.: Bell, *Assassin;* Bennett, *The Black and Tans;* Borrell, *Crime in Britain Today;* Burt, *Commander Burt of Scotland Yard;* Carty, *Ireland;* CBA; Clutterbuck, *Guerrillas and Terrorists;* Coogan, *Ireland Since the Rising;* Curtayne, *The Irish Story;* Demaris, *Brothers in Blood: The International Terrorist Network;* Desmond, *The Drama of Sinn Fein;* Dobson and Payne, *Counterattack—The West's Battle Against the Terrorists;* _____, *The Terrorists—Their Weapons, Leaders and Tactics;* Edwards, *Patrick Pearse: The Triumph of Failure;* Figgis, *A Chronicle of Jails;* Hacker, *Crusaders, Criminals, Crazies: Terror and Terrorism in Our Time;* Henry, *The Evolution of Sinn Fein;* Hyde, *United in Crime;* Inglis, *The Story of Ireland;* Irish Times, *Eamon de Valera;* Lacquer, *Terrorism;* Landreth, *Dear Dark Head;* Liston, *Terrorism;* Macardle, *The Irish Republic;* MacKenzie, *Secret Societies;* MacManus, *The Story of the Irish Race;* McClellan and Avery, *The Voices of Guns;* O'Ballance, *Language of Violence—The Blood Politics of Terrorism;* _____, *Terror in Ireland: The Heritage of Hate;* O'Hergarty, *A History of Ireland Under the Union;* O'Sullivan, *The Free State and Its Senate;* _____, *The Victory of Sinn Fein;* Paine, *The Assassins' World;* Pollard, *The Secret Societies of Ireland;* Roper, *Prison Letters of Constance Markievicz;* Schreiber, *The Ultimate Weapon—Terrorists and World Order;* Scott, *The Concise Encyclopedia of Crime and Criminals;* Shannon, *The American Irish: A Political and Social Portrait;*

Shew, *A Second Companion to Murder;* Steffan, *The Long Fellow: The Story of the Great Patriot, Eamon de Valera;* Thompson, *The Imagination of an Insurrection: Dublin, Easter, 1916;* Trevelyan, *History of England;* Van Voris, *Constance de Markievicz: In the Cause of Ireland.*

IRS Scandal, prom. 1951, U.S., cor. In May 1948, Delaware Senator John Williams launched an investigation into the activities of the Internal Revenue Service. Three years later, Chicago lawyer Abraham Teitelbaum testified in front of a House subcommittee that two ex-convicts, Frank Nathan and Burt K. Naster, told him he could avoid trouble with the U.S. government over unpaid taxes if he would pay the men $500,000. Teitelbaum, whose most famous client was Al Capone, balked but named several influence-peddlers in Washington. As the investigation unfolded, it revealed an intricate web of scandal. In 1951 alone the IRS dismissed 113 employers and officers.

The investigation revealed influence peddling in which IRS agents, for cash or gifts of property, would overlook a tax case or reduce the penalty owed the government. Implicated was U.S. Attorney General J. Howard McGrath and Theron Lamar Caudle, who had been fired from his post as head of the Justice Department's tax division the previous month, and the bureau's chief counsel, Charles Oliphant. The name of Henry Grunewald, a Washington deal-maker, was mentioned prominently throughout the hearings. He received commissions for matching those in trouble over taxes with IRS employees, officials charged. Williams also called for an investigation into Joseph D. Nunan, Jr., the commissioner of Internal Revenue from 1944 to 1947. A tax judgment for an Indianapolis brewery had been reduced from $636,000 to $4,500 and the reduction had been approved by Caudle and Oliphant.

In 1952, former tax collector and friend of President Harry S. Truman, James P. Finnegan, was sentenced to two years in prison and fined $10,000 for abusing the privileges of his office. Grunewald was sentenced to ninety days in jail and fined $1,000 for refusing to answer questions from Congress. In 1954, Nunan was brought to trial and found Guilty of income tax evasion. The former commissioner was sentenced to five years in prison and fined $15,000 for defrauding the government out of more than $100,000 in tax revenue. One year later, Grunewald was on trial again for conspiracy to fix a tax case, found Guilty, and sentenced to a five-year prison term and fined $10,000. Daniel A. Bolich, a former assistant commissioner of the IRS, received the same sentence for his part in the Grunewald tax fix.

In 1957, Caudle received a two-year prison sentence and was fined $2,500 for his role in the tax fraud conspiracy. In 1959, Bolich's conviction was overturned. Grunewald died before his case could be heard again. Former Truman aide Matthew J. Connelly, convicted on charges of conspiring to violate the internal revenue laws and defraud the federal government, served six months in prison before he was pardoned by President John F. Kennedy in 1962. REF.: *CBA.*

Irvin, Leslie 1924-83, U.S., mur. On Apr. 8, 1955, police in Henderson, Ky., arrested 30-year-old construction worker Leslie Irvin for burglary. Irvin had been paroled a year earlier, after serving nine years on the same charge. During the interrogation, the suspect confessed not only to some thirty burglaries, but also to six cold-blooded murders recently committed in the Kentucky-Indiana area

On Mar. 28, 1955, Goebel Duncan, his son, Raymond Duncan, and his daughter-in-law, Elizabeth Duncan, were found bound and shot to death in Evansville, Ind. Irvin also confessed to wounding Goebel Duncan's wife, Mamie Duncan, and to shooting Elizabeth Duncan as her 2-year-old daughter looked on. He admitted to killing 36-year old Mary Holland, an Evansville liquor store owner on Dec. 2, 1954; 32-year-old Wesley Kerr, Evansville gas station owner on Dec. 23; and 47-year-old Wilhelmina Sailor, a Mount Vernon, Ind., housewife on Mar. 21, 1955. During his previous incarceration, Irvin was placed in solitary confinement seven times, and earlier was dishonorably discharged from the army.

Irvin was found Guilty of the homicides and, in December

1955, was sentenced to death. On Jan. 18, 1956, Irvin escaped from prison in Princeton, Ind. He stated he would return if granted a new trial, but a Circuit Court judge denied the request. He was apprehended and his sentence was commuted to life imprisonment at the Indiana State Prison in Michigan City. He died at age fifty-nine on Nov. 9, 1983. REF.: *CBA*.

Irvin, Walter Lee, 1929- , U.S., rape. On July 16, 1949, a 19-year-old white woman, Norma Padgett, was raped by four black men on her farm near Groveland, Fla. Walter Lee Irvin, Samuel Shepherd, and Charles Greenlee were arrested after being apprehended by a posse. The fourth man, Ernest Thomas, was shot to death during the chase. Irvin, Shepherd, and Greenlee were found Guilty in Tavares, Fla., Circuit Court by Judge Truman G. Futch. Irvin and Shepherd were sentenced to die in the electric chair, while Greenlee was given a life sentence.

Lawyers for the NAACP appealed to the U.S. Supreme Court, and, in a decision noting that the black men had been convicted by an all-white jury, the verdict was overturned and a new trial ordered for Irvin and Shepherd. As the two were being driven back to Tavares by Lake County Sheriff Willis McCall and his deputy James Yates, the police car seemingly had a flat tire. According to McCall, a prisoner smashed his head with a flashlight and attempted to take his revolver, at which time the lawmen shot each prisoner three times, killing Shepherd. However, Irvin contended that the shooting was done in cold blood after they were ordered from the car to change the tire. A local coroner declared the shooting was done in self-defense, and on Nov. 14, 1952, McCall and Yates were exonerated of any wrongdoing by a federal grand jury in Jacksonville.

In his second trial before Judge Futch, Irvin was defended by future Supreme Court Justice Thurgood Marshall who accused the state of making false plaster casts of footprints near the scene of the rape, and produced a witness who stated that Mrs. Padgett had not mentioned the rape shortly after the alleged crime. On Feb. 14, 1952, another all-white jury found Irvin Guilty and the original death sentence was upheld. The execution was slated for Nov. 7, 1954, but the day before, Irvin received a stay of execution from the Supreme Court after a frantic appeal by the NAACP. A further appeal was denied on Jan. 10, 1955, but later that year, on Dec. 15, Irvin's sentence was commuted to life imprisonment by the Florida Pardon Board. REF.: *CBA*.

Swindlers Clifford and Edith Irving.

Irving, Clifford, 1930- , U.S., fraud. Clifford Irving, a hustling writer with a three-book contract with McGraw-Hill Publishers of New York, picked up a copy of *Newsweek* in December 1970 and in an article came across the signatures of Howard Hughes and of Hughes' aides, Chester David and Bill Gay. Knowing Hughes was a fanatical recluse who had not made a public

appearance in years, Irving decided to fake an "authorized" biography. He spent considerable time developing phony correspondence between himself and Hughes, duplicating Hughes' handwriting from the samples appearing in *Newsweek*. In one of the fake letters, Hughes agreed to "tell all" to Irving in the only authorized version of his fabulous and secretive life.

Irving presented the idea to his publishers, McGraw-Hill, offering the fake correspondence to authenticate his relationship with Hughes. McGraw-Hill hesitated, especially when Irving demanded a $750,000 advance for the priceless biography. Editors wanted to know how the relatively unknown Irving had met one of the world's most elusive men. Irving was evasive, hiding behind the commonly accepted notions that Hughes was eccentric, occasionally befriended strangers, and lived and operated in near complete secrecy. In the end, McGraw-Hill seized the opportunity to publish a book they believed would make millions.

Irving went to work faking the biography, piecing together Hughes' life from various other books written by those who had known the recluse. Some time earlier he had been asked to work on a book about Hughes by a friend, Stanley Myers, who had assembled considerable research from the investigations of James Phelan, a newsman, and Noah Dietrich, once a top executive for Hughes. Myers sent this research to the unscrupulous Irving who copied and then returned it, saying he was not interested. He then used the insider research for his own faked book on Hughes.

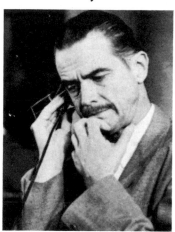

The reclusive billionaire Howard Hughes, who came out of hiding to expose the literary fraud of Clifford Irving.

When McGraw-Hill announced the book's publication in December 1971, spokesmen for Rosemont Enterprises, Inc., a Hughes firm, loudly denounced the book. Rosemont had been established by Hughes to prevent anyone from ever using his name. McGraw-Hill confronted Irving, who brazenly shrugged off the Rosemont statements, saying that Hughes was so secretive that he had undoubtedly failed to inform his own people that he had authorized the Irving biography. Then Irving told McGraw-Hill that Hughes, despite the fact that he was a billionaire, wanted more money. He persuaded McGraw-Hill to write a check for $275,000 in the name of H.R. Hughes, and another for $25,000 made out to himself.

Even though many began to publicly state that the Irving book was a fake, McGraw-Hill was convinced of its genuineness and advanced another $325,000 to Irving, mostly in checks made out to H.R. Hughes. These checks were deposited in a Swiss numbered bank account with Credit Suisse by Irving's collusive wife, Edith, under the name Helga Rosencrantz Hughes. More denials from Hughes' executives were made, but Irving continued to insist that Hughes was paranoid and would not tell anyone of his private arrangements with him. Irving was convinced that not even the most outrageous claims could prompt Hughes into making a public appearance to quash the swindle. In this he completely miscalculated.

Hughes did come forth, in January 1972, holding a phone interview with several newsmen who had known him well over the years and convinced them that he had never met Irving or had dealings with him. Still, Irving stuck to his story, insisting that he would soon reveal his inside contact to Howard Hughes. Meanwhile, his wife busied herself with flying to Switzerland and withdrawing all the money from the H.R. Hughes bank account. In March 1972, a reporter from *Time* magazine, thinking Irving was getting his information from John Meier, a Hughes executive, called Irving and left a message on his answering machine. "We know all about Meier," the reporter stated, testing the waters. Irving thought the reporter meant Stanley Meyer, the man from whom he had stolen his research, and admitted his swindle.

Both Irving and his wife Edith were brought to trial and convicted of fraud. Edith Irving was tried in Switzerland and received a two-year sentence, of which she served fourteen months. Irving received a two-and-a-half-year sentence and was released after seventeen months. When he emerged he wrote a book about the Hughes swindle for which he received a much smaller advance than the one he had conned from McGraw-Hill. His marriage had gone to pieces and his credibility as an author was utterly destroyed. Irving, who at first was thought clever by more venal readers, has since been aptly labeled a thief and a liar.

REF.: *CBA; Kahn, Fraud; Rose, The World's Greatest Rip-offs; Wade, Great Hoaxes and Famous Imposters.*

Irving, John, d.1883, U.S., org. crime. John Irving headed the Dutch Mob which operated near New York's Bowery area during the 1870s. Irving began his career as a juvenile sneak-thief and pickpocket and, until 1877, ran a school for pickpockets, with more than 300 thieves on his payroll. That year, the newly appointed NYPD Captain Anthony Allaire, adopted tough techniques to eliminate pickpockets. Squads of police officers invaded Irving's domain, especially along Houston and Fifth streets, and ignoring proper arrest procedures and warrants, simply clubbed anyone who looked like a thief.

Irving abandoned his Fagin-like pickpocket operations and became an independent bank burglar. In 1883, Irving and his friend and fellow burglar, Billy Porter, entered Shang Draper's notorious Sixth Avenue saloon where they met John "Johnny the Mick" Walsh, a rival gangster who had previously threatened to kill Irving. Both men drew pistols and began shooting. When Walsh shot Irving in the chest and killed him, Billy Porter shot Walsh dead. From behind the bar, Shang Draper then shot Porter who survived his wound.

REF.: *Asbury, The Gangs of New York; CBA; Nash, Bloodletters and Badmen.*

Irwin, Estelle Mae, 1923- , U.S., rob. Estelle Irwin ran away from her Topeka, Kan., home in 1937 and joined Bennie Dickson, an accomplished bank robber who had served seven years of a ten-year sentence for holding up the State Bank of Stotesbury, Mo. Estelle, a novice in crime, married Dickson in Los Angeles and then returned with him to his home in Lake Benton, Minn. There in the seclusion of the North Woods, he taught his young wife how to shoot and handle the wheel of a getaway car—indispensable skills for an accomplished bank robber.

On Aug. 25, 1938, with her "education" complete, Estelle and Dickson drove to Elkton, S.D., to rob the Corn Exchange Bank. Since the vault of the bank operated on a time-safety device, they held the employees at bay until 3 p.m. when the doors sprung open. Estelle scooped up $2,174.64 and ordered the hostages into the vault where they remained while the couple escaped.

Having succeeded their first time out, the couple continued on to Topeka where they outfitted themselves with new clothes and a new car. Their next target was the Northwest Security National Bank of Brookings, S.D., on Oct. 31, 1938. Again they were told that the vault was controlled by an automatic timer, set to go off in two hours. Undaunted, the Dicksons trained their guns on the employees and sat down to wait.

Meanwhile the tellers were permitted to go about their business. "I'm going to cut all the wires in this joint, so nobody can call for help," Dickson drawled. "But my partner is Annie Oakley's little sister. She can hit the narrow end of a pin at a hundred yards and loves to do it. So keep your feet on the ground—the ground they're on now!" The vault opened on time and Estelle Mae retrieved $17,529.99 in cash and $29,640.50 in securities. The desperados fled unmolested with two bank officials forced to ride on the running board.

With the FBI now on their tail, Estelle and Bennie drove to

Detroit to spend a portion of their loot. They zigzagged back through the Midwest for an impromptu visit with Estelle's parents in Topeka. Bennie, however, made the mistake of returning to a garage he had used during the Brookings robbery. He was fingered by the FBI and cornered with his wife in a nearby tourist camp. Estelle escaped on foot, but her husband was wounded in the gun battle. Dickson continued on to Clinton, Iowa, where he switched cars with a passing motorist. He then doubled back to Topeka to pick up his wife where they switched cars a second time.

They did not know that an all-points bulletin for their arrest had been issued. In Michigan they were recognized on a rural road. With the police in pursuit Estelle, now a crack shot, poked a rifle out of the back window and began firing on the squad car. She blew out the tire of the police car, sending it into a ditch. The Dicksons switched cars again outside South Bend, Ind., and headed east to Hammond where they rented a private garage, hid their stolen car, and bought a beat-up Ford. They decided to take a southerly route, ending up in St. Louis. There, on Apr. 6, 1939, FBI agents laid a trap for the bank robbers in a local hamburger stand. When Dickson refused to surrender he was shot.

Estelle sped away in the car. She made it as far as Kansas City where she was forced to surrender to FBI agents on Apr. 7, 1939. She was convicted of robbing the South Dakota bank, for which she received a ten-year prison sentence.

REF.: *CBA; Nash, Look For the Woman.*

Irwin, James, d.1930, U.S., lynch.-mur. In Ocilla, Ga., in 1930, James Irwin, a black man, was tried and convicted of murder. Irwin was dragged from his jail cell at night by a raging mob and shackled to a tree, tortured, soaked with gasoline and set on fire, and used as a target for pistol practice.

REF.: *CBA; Hurwood, Society and the Assassin.*

Irwin, Robert (AKA: **Fenelon Arroyo Seco Irwin**), prom. 1937, U.S., mur. Robert Irwin was born in Los Angeles during a religious convention, a portent of things to come; the notion of original sin plagued him for much of his adult life. While still a child, Irwin was abandoned by his father, and as a result, became increasingly withdrawn and attached to his mother, a woman obsessed with religion. At an early age he developed an interest in art, particularly soap sculpting. In 1930, Irwin drifted to New York, where he began consulting psychiatrists. At one point he requested someone to castrate him to conserve his sexual energy for "higher purposes." In October 1932, he severely injured himself in an attempt at self-emasculation and was placed in an asylum.

Religious delusions and increasing paranoia drove Irwin to commit one of New York's most heinous murders of the 1930s. In June 1934, he rented a room from a family of Hungarian immigrants named Gedeon in midtown Manhattan. Joseph Gedeon, an upholsterer, his wife Mary and their two grown daughters, Ethel and Veronica, shared living quarters. Ethel Gedeon was a pragmatic woman who did not share her sister Veronica's "wild" compulsions—Veronica worked as an artist's model and dreamed of being a movie star.

Irwin had known Ethel for some time and was secretly in love with her. When Ethel married and left home, Veronica showed an interest in Irwin. When he rebuffed her attempt at seduction, she spread rumors that he was homosexual. Meanwhile, domestic relations between the elder Gedeon and his wife deteriorated after frequent quarrels about Veronica's promiscuous lifestyle, and Joseph Gedeon moved out of the house.

Irwin had left the Gedeon's home and had begun studies at a theological seminary. However, he fought with a fellow student, and was expelled from the institution. In despair, he vowed to end his life, but only after he had taken care of Ethel. On Mar. 27, 1937, the day before Easter, Irwin went to the Gedeon home. He entered the apartment but Ethel was not there. After strangling Mrs. Gedeon, and stabbing to death lodger Frank Byrnes, Irwin waited in Veronica's room. When she returned from a date some time later, he strangled her. The three bodies were found the next day, but the police were stymied. There were no fingerprints, and the motive did not appear to be robbery or sex. Joseph Gedeon was taken into custody and grilled about the triple murder which became a sensation.

The first break in the case came a few days later when a suitcase was found in Grand Central Station. Among its contents were a pair of trousers from the Rockland State Hospital—Irwin's last known address. A check of the serial number printed on the pants established his identity. After learning that Irwin was a sculptor by trade, things began to add up. A sculptor's tool had been used to kill Byrnes; strong, powerful hands had strangled the two women—a sculptor's hands.

Irwin fled to Chicago where he contacted the *Herald & Examiner*, offering to sell his story to the newspapar. The Hearst paper ran a blazing front page extra on June 25 and the sculptor seemed to enjoy his moment in the limelight, laughing and joking with reporters at the Morrison Hotel. By prior arrangement, Irwin surrendered to the Cook County sheriff and was extradited to New York where he was arraigned on murder charges. Famed defense attorney Samuel Leibowitz represented him when the case went to trial in November 1938. Leibowitz maintained his record of never losing a client to the electric chair by securing for Irwin a sentence of 139 years in prison.

REF.: *CBA;* Hynd, *Murder, Mayhem and Mystery;* Scott, *The Concise Encyclopedia of Crime and Criminals.*

Irwin, Warren Lee, prom. 1951, U.S., kid.-rape-suic. Just as Lawrence Gilbert finished proposing to his 17-year-old girlfriend Carolyn Jane Barker, the couple's attention turned to an armed man standing outside their car. Warren Lee Irwin waved his pistol and ordered the couple to drive him to Virginia because the FBI was chasing him. As the trio left the Washington, D.C., area, the car broke down. On a deserted dirt road, Irwin ordered Barker to tape Gilbert's hands together. He then raped the girl. Following the attack, Irwin released the young man and bought the couple drinks at a nearby gas station.

Irwin and Barker then boarded a bus bound for Washington, where they checked into a hotel and Irwin raped her repeatedly throughout the evening. With police in pursuit, Irwin and Barker drove to Pennsylvania, where the kidnapper stole money and a car from his aunt and uncle. Near Flemington, N.J., two state troopers finally tracked down the stolen vehicle and an 80-mile-per-hour chase ended when Irwin drove into a ditch. While Barker escaped, Irwin vanished into the roadside brush. A massive manhunt ended the following morning when a plane sighted Irwin, who had shot himself in the head. REF.: *CBA.*

Isaac, Bernard (AKA: **Bernard Isaac Robert, D.S. Windell, Davitt Stanley Windell**), and **King, Francis Reginald**, prom. 1908, Brit., fraud-forg. On a September day in 1908, a man calling himself D.S. Windell got into a cab at Victoria Station and traveled to thirteen branches of the London and South Western Bank, writing a check for £290 at each. D.S. Windell was actually Bernard Isaac who would later be charged and sentenced as Bernard Isaac Robert. At the time of his check writing spree, D.S. Windell (a clever play on the words "the swindle"), was twenty-three years old. Originally from Rotterdam, Isaac was the grandson of a revered rabbi and had grown up as a precocious child. Coming to England at twenty with a tentative grasp of English, he lived by his wits and taught himself typing and shorthand, and worked as a translator, an envelope addresser, secretary to a journalist, and a strolling guitar player.

In early September, Isaac met Francis Reginald King, thirty, a like-minded vegetarian with socialist leanings who worked as the second cashier at the Clapham branch of the London South Western Bank. On Sept. 23, Isaac, armed with the daily password and transfer balance slips sent ahead by King in the name of "D. Stanley Windell," identified himself to managers at each bank, gave a sample of his signature, and wrote out a check for £290, taking £90 in gold sovereigns. Before the fourteenth bank on his tour, Isaac became suspicious of the cab driver and told him to drive to "Head Office in Lothbury." Isaac walked straight through the bank and escaped out the back, bilking even the driver of his

fare. Realizing the heist was an inside job, police investigated about 1,300 bank clerks. After months of work, the printed advice note forms, from a slightly flawed batch, were traced to three branches. King came under suspicion when his handwriting proved to match notes on the forged slips, and he was charged and arrested. Shortly after, Isaac was arrested in Madrid, almost seven months after the bank thefts. He had given away most of the money and had committed the crime, he said, for the fun and excitement of it. Tried in June 1909 at the Old Bailey before Sir Archibald Bodkin and Travers Humphrey, Isaac and King were found Guilty. King, as the initial perpetrator, was sentenced to seven years of penal servitude, while Isaac was given eighteen months of hard labor. At least £600 of Isaac's share of the money was never recovered. REF.: *CBA.*

Isaacs, Godfrey, prom. 1912, Brit., libel. With the invention of the wireless at the beginning of the twentieth century, Guglielmo Marconi revolutionized the communication industry. Used mainly for ship-to-ship or ship-to-shore communication in the early 1900s, Marconi sought to expand his business on land, and in 1910 his company applied to the British government for a license to erect a number of wireless stations throughout the country.

So that he could devote more time to his scientific research, Marconi hired Godfrey Isaacs as managing director and marketing manager of his product. Isaacs represented the company during negotiations with the government which began in December 1911. Four months later a deal was finalized in which the British government would build and the company would outfit six stations for around £60,000 apiece. The Marconi Wireless Telegraph Co., Ltd., would receive ten percent of all royalties for a twenty-eight year period in exchange for all present and future patents.

In journals such as *Eye Witness* and *New Witness,* editor Cecil Chesterton said the proposed deal unnecessarily favored the Marconi Co. The company's stock jumped as investors speculated about the signing of a government contract, but Chesterton urged the House to vote down the contract proposal. While the onset of WWI delayed ratification of the deal, Chesterton's attacks continued. He began to attack the Jews and their influence in British politics. The scope of Chesterton's protest was so widespread that Isaacs was consistently harassed. Ultimately, Isaacs sued Chesterton for libel. The trial lasted for ten days in the summer of 1913 and Chesterton was convicted on five of six counts of libel. Because he honestly believed what he had written to be the truth, the judge released Chesterton after the writer paid a fine. See: **Isaacs, Sir Rufus.**

REF.: *CBA;* Earl of Birkenhead, *Famous Trials of History.*

Isaacs, Sir Isaac Alfred, b.1855, Aus., jur. Held positions in Australian government, including attorney general from 1905-06, justice of the high court from 1906-30, and chief justice from 1930-31. He also served as governor general of Australia from 1931-36. REF.: *CBA.*

Isaacs, Sir Rufus Daniel, 1860-1935, and **Lloyd George, David**, 1863-1945, Case of, Brit., polit. corr. Colorful and charismatic, Rufus Daniel Isaacs had a diverse and distinguished career in law and the government. Isaacs served as a lawyer, a judge, a member of Parliament, Viceroy of India, cabinet minister, and Lord chief justice. In March 1913, while serving as minister of legal affairs, Isaacs and David Lloyd George, the chancellor of the exchequer (and future prime minister of England), appeared before the House of Commons on char-

Judge Rufus Daniel Isaacs.

ges they had used their positions to gain personal wealth. The committee was investigating specific charges that the two men had invested in Marconi Wireless Telegraph Co. stock (Isaac's brother Godfrey was the managing director of the Marconi Co.) and then pushed through a governmental agreement with the company, causing stock prices to soar and the government employees to profit by it. Isaacs and Lloyd George admitted they were involved with a group of investors who purchased U.S., and not British, shares of stock in the company. A move to oust the government officials was defeated. See: Isaacs, Godfrey. REF.: *CBA*.

Ishbosheth (Ishbaal, Eshbaal), prom. 11th Cent. B.C., Isr., king, assass. Last member of Saul family to rule. He commanded the army and became involved in a war with Judah. He was slain by soldiers. REF.: *CBA*.

Ishii, Maj. Shiro, prom. 1930s-40s, Japan, war crimes. In 1937, the Japanese built the first germ warfare facility in the world at Pingfan, a village about forty miles south of Harbin, Manchuria. Major Shiro Ishii, a surgeon, was placed in command of the operation, called Unit 731, and its staff of 3,000 soldiers, nurses, and scientists. The staff produced and injected subjects with germs causing smallpox, typhus, salmonella, gas gangrene, typhoid, cholera, tick encephalitis, tetanus, plague, anthrax, tuberculosis, and cholera. Most of the subjects were Russian, Chinese, and Korean prisoners of war, but some of the subjects may have been British, U.S., and Australian war prisoners. The staff also performed various experiments on human subjects, such as placing them under X-ray exposure until they died, and setting off gas grenade bombs next to subjects who were restrained. After the Japanese surrendered in August 1945, numerous staff members took cyanide pills, the complex was burned down, and the human subjects were slain. At first, Ishii denied during interrogation that humans had been used in experiments, but in a cable sent to Washington, D.C., on May 6, 1947, Ishii offered to tell details of the germ warfare operation if he and his co-workers were granted immunity from prosecution. The U.S. agreed to the bargain and later, the Japanese government verified the existence of the project. REF.: *CBA*.

Islamic Tendencies Movement (AKA: MTI), prom. 1980s, Tun., terr. When Habib Bourguiba assumed power in Tunisia in 1956, he outlawed polygamy and closed down the religious courts that had administered justice for years. Bourguiba initiated a mosque-building program in the country and backed the Islamic fundamentalist party. In attempting to build a society in which Muslim clerics played no political role, Bourguiba alienated many citizens, and as a result the leftist Islamic Tendencies Movement flourished. Throughout the country, Bourguiba sought to eliminate opposition from the outlawed MTI group. In 1987, seven death sentences (five in absentia) were rendered on charges of sedition, defaming Bourguiba, and membership in an illegal organization. REF.: *CBA*.

Ismael, Muley, prom. 1000, Alg.-Mor., extort.-kid.-slavery. Prison for profit was Muley Ismaei's claim to fame in Northern Africa. He ruled over the penal system in Morocco, extorting money from the families of the prisoners and trying to force them to convert to the Muslim religion. For those who conformed, or turned "Turk," life was often easier. The converts would often assume mercenary status on Moroccan ships and sometimes marry their owner's daughters. For many of the 2,000 or so prisoners, who were poor or who refused to convert, Ismael made their existence miserable. The men worked in the quarries or as galley slaves on ships and ate little more than bread covered with vinegar. Suicide was rampant and Ismael like to bury the dead inside walls or watch wild animals pick apart their bodies. REF.: *CBA*; Moorehead, *Hostages to Fortune*.

Ison, Hobart, b.1899, U.S., asslt.-mansl. Hugh O'Connor, a Canadian filmmaker produced the highly acclaimed Labyrinth show at Montreal's Expo 67. Based on his work in Canada, American producer Francis Thompson hired him to work on a documentary for an upcoming Hemisfair in San Antonio. O'Connor and his four-man crew were in eastern Kentucky in September 1967, shooting footage of the impoverished mining country around the town of Jeremiah, where the ramshackle houses and unkempt appearance of the natives had intrigued the filmmakers. After a few hours of filming, a woman drove her car up to where the crew was working and told them the owner of the land was angry and on his way to see them.

In minutes, 69-year-old Hobart Ison waved his pistol around and ordered the film crew off his land. The five men moved quickly toward their cars with their equipment. Ison fired twice. The shots ripped into the woods but hastened the crew's departure. As O'Connor carried a large battery toward the car, he turned to tell the enraged land owner that they were leaving. Ison fired another shot that hit O'Connor in the chest. The Canadian was dead in minutes.

Ison was arrested and charged with murder but the prosecutors had the trial moved to Harlan because they did not believe they would be able to assemble an impartial jury around Jeremiah. A great deal of sentiment for Ison existed in the mountains of Eastern Kentucky. Ison's first trial resulted in a hung jury in May 1968. Eleven people deemed the old man guilty, but a lone holdout forced a retrial. A defense psychiatrist termed Ison a paranoid schizophrenic and prosecutor Daniel Boone Smith blamed the woman, Judy Breeding, who had told Ison about the filmmakers. Smith said he would like to be prosecuting the woman instead of Ison because her mouth had triggered the incident. A March 1969 retrial saw Ison plead guilty to voluntary manslaughter and receive a ten-year prison sentence.

REF.: *CBA*; Trillin, *Killings*.

Actor Arthur Kennedy, second from right, portraying Harold Israel in the film *Boomerang*.

Israel, Harold F., prom. 1924, Case of, U.S., mur. Israel was a young itinerant laborer who was picked up by frantic police shortly after a priest, Father Hubert Dahme, had been killed at 7:40 p.m. on Feb. 4, 1924, as he stood on Main Street in Bridgeport, Conn., while taking his evening constitutional. The 56-year-old priest stopped momentarily to look across the street to the front of the Lyric Theater where enthusiastic theater-goers were lining up to see the resplendent Ethel Barrymore appear in *The Laughing Lady*. Father Dahme, the much-liked pastor of St. Joseph's Roman Catholic Church, took a few steps to the corner, paused to light his pipe and suddenly a figure stood behind him, raising a revolver and firing a bullet into his brain, killing him instantly. The killer, wearing a long overcoat with the collar turned up and a cap pulled low over his face to apparently hide his identity, fled up the street while dozens of shocked citizens stared after him.

Eight days later, on Feb. 11, 1924, South Norwalk, Conn., detective John R. Reynolds eyed a young man who seemed to be walking about in a daze. He identified himself as Harold F. Israel, a native of Bridgeport, and told Reynolds that he was penniless, hungry, and had no place to sleep. The plainclothes cop, in sympathy, took Israel to the station house to get him a hot meal and give him a warm cell as an overnight vagrant. But, as was the routine, the youth was searched and a rather ancient, Spanish-make, .32-caliber revolver was found in Israel's pocket. Officers looked the young man over with gathering suspicions.

They were well aware of the ruthless murder of Father Dahme by this time and began to grill Israel, who told them he was trying to get to his sister's home in Connerton, Pa. Bridgeport police were contacted and their vague description of the killer seemed to match the vagrant. Israel was taken to Bridgeport police headquarters where he was grilled endlessly without sleep and very little food and water. Detectives in Bridgeport were sure that they had gotten the priest-killer and had already entered the old revolver taken from Israel as Exhibit B in a case that they later felt, despite its surprising outcome, an open-and-shut file. Several passersby who had seen the young man in the shabby overcoat shoot the priest on Main Street came forward and, with goading from officers, halfheartedly identified the young man as the murderer. Moreover, Israel, groggy from sleepless nights, confessed to the killing. He was quickly placed on trial and a speedy conviction was expected from the energetic state's attorney, Homer Cummings, a rising political star.

Cummings, however, was an exacting and conscientious prosecutor who after examining the evidence against Israel, decided to re-investigate. He learned the questionable conditions under which police had extracted the confession from Israel. He discovered that Israel made his so-called confession to one police officer, Captain John H. Regan, head of Bridgeport's detective division. After interviewing Regan, Cummings realized that the detective suggested to Israel that he killed Father Dahme, and the youth, thoroughly exhausted after two days of grilling, blurted: "There ain't no use of my denying it any further or any longer. You got the gun, you got the cartridge, you have the one who knows me there. What is the use of me denying it any further?" A police stenographer took down a confession from Israel which appeared "coached" to Cummings.

The murder weapon was another matter that troubled Cummings. It had been found on Israel when he was picked up—an old, rusty weapon which actually belonged to Israel's roommate, Charles Cihal. Both Israel and Cihal had served in the army together in the Canal Zone and when discharged in the summer of 1923, decided to room together. The young man sometimes took the revolver to the woods and did some practice shooting. The "cartridge" from this gun, which Israel supposedly referred to in his confession, was the cartridge found in Israel's Bridgeport room, and this was used by a local ballistics expert to match it against the bullet extracted from the victim's brain. Yet Cummings learned that, according to Israel's landlady, the youths often left empty cartridges in their room after they had used the revolver for practice shooting.

The ballistics report on this weapon was probably the most damning to Israel's case, other than his so-called confession. One of the most distinguished experts in that field, Captain Charles J. Van Amburgh, had positively identified the bullet taken from the priest's brain as having been fired by the weapon found in Israel's overcoat pocket. Van Amburgh, one of the top engineers for the ballistics division of the Remington Arms Company, had taught weaponry to U.S. troops during WWI as an ordnance expert and marksman. He was considered to be one of the best ballistics experts available and had, for years, testified in important criminal cases as to identifying murder weapons through ballistics analysis, and this included the sensational 1921 Sacco-Vanzetti case. Van Amburgh insisted that the bullet that killed Father Dahme was fired by the .32-caliber revolver found on Harold Israel.

Cummings delved into the procedures employed by Van Amburgh in his comparison with the murder bullet and the revolver, now marked Exhibit B. Six additional ballistics experts were brought in to examine the revolver, and Cummings himself asked Van Amburgh to walk him through the expert's own examination of the weapon and the murder bullet. Van Amburgh demonstrated a less-than-exacting procedure, pointing out that he merely compared photographs of the murder bullet and several bullets fired from the gun taken from Israel. He had slit the photograph of the murder bullet, separated the photo, and then inserted the blowup of a photo of a bullet fired from the Israel weapon. For some minutes he moved both photos around so that "all the markings coincide," as he informed Cummings. But the expert was really manipulating both photographs so that only certain markings seemed to match up. Cummings ordered Van Amburgh to "lift up the flap (of the photo) and see what is under it." When this was done, the markings did not match. Further, Cummings had his own experts from the New York Police Department, the Winchester Operating Arms Company, and Van Amburgh's own firm, Remington, carefully examine the weapon, test fire it, and compare its spent bullets with the murder bullet. The universal report to him from these experts was that "there is no evidence that the mortal bullet came out of the Israel revolver," and that the murder bullet had been fired from "some other unknown weapon." So much for Exhibit B.

Israel's so-called confession nagged at Cummings so he sent several doctors to interview the young man. The accused was still in an exhausted state when the physicians examined him and reported later to Cummings that Israel had been asked if he had killed the priest, and he admitted and denied the act in almost the same sentence. Cummings took note that after these examinations, when Israel was no longer under tremendous nervous stress, he denied ever having killed the priest and never deviated again from that denial. Moreover, the suspect's competency was in great doubt. Examining psychiatrists concluded that the suspect "was a person of low mentality, of the moron type, quiet and docile in demeanor, totally lacking in any characteristics of brutality or viciousness, of very weak will, and peculiarly subject to the influence of suggestion."

Retracing the grilling of the police, Cummings realized that investigators walked the suspect through the crime, drove him along the murder and escape route of the killer, narrating the action of the killer and suggesting that he, Israel, had enacted the murder. It was in *response* to these pointed suggestions that Israel supposedly blurted his confession, an admission that was nowhere in the documented evidence as having been his own idea. In other words, Harold Israel did not *volunteer* his guilt; he merely agreed with the police officers who detailed the crime step by step and pinned it on him. As Cummings would later point out to the court: "All the admissions of an incriminating character were admissions with reference to facts already known to the police prior to the examination of the accused and presumably related to the accused during the period of his examination."

There was one other significant factor in this case which kept Cummings up endless nights. Harold F. Israel had no motive for killing Father Hubert Dahme. He did not know the priest, nor was there any record that the two men ever exchanged words, let alone glances. When he was being grilled by police in his sleepless state, the accused groggily nodded that he had shot "the man," never referring to the victim as a priest or a clergyman. This "admission" was in light of the statement by Israel that he was unaware of what his supposed victim looked like and that he was wearing a Roman collar when killed. It was assumed by police, according to Cummings' investigation, that Israel, for no apparent reason, merely walked up behind Father Dahme, picking him out as a random victim, and shot a nameless stranger to death. Of course, it was an easier task for detectives to arrest a drifter with a gun in his pocket than sift through other suspects who might have had a reason to kill the clergyman. Oddly, none of the priest's parishioners were interviewed to determine if Father Dahme had any enemies who hated him enough to kill him.

Then there was the dubious question concerning the so-called eyewitnesses who identified Israel in a lineup as the young man they had seen shoot the priest and then flee up the street and into the darkness. One by one, Cummings painstakingly examined these witnesses. The killer had been wearing a cap and a long overcoat, most of the witnesses agreed (Israel had been wearing a long overcoat when arrested). Edward Flood had first reported seeing the fleeing man run up the street past him but never mentioned his wearing a cap. When Cummings read the same person's testimony at a later inquest, he noticed that by then Flood had added that the killer had been wearing a cap, a description easily available from newspapers after the killing and before the inquest. Ralph Esposito, a delivery boy who had been standing on Main Street some twenty feet from where the priest was killed, said the killer wore a gray cap. Cummings noted that Israel's cap was green. Esposito also said that he had gotten a good look at the murder weapon and told the coroner that it was "one of those black pistols that do not shine." Cummings went back to the so-called murder weapon, Israel's .32-caliber revolver, and noted that it was nickel-plated and would have certainly glowed somewhat in the light from the street lamp near which the priest stood when killed.

Esposito's other remarks describing the killer's escape and his manner of running perplexed the coroner at the inquest. Said Esposito: "When I see the man run, he run like a Jewish man." This stumped the Fairfield County coroner, John G. Phelan, who replied: "I never heard of that before. What kind of a run is that?" Esposito shrugged, as if he had described a commonplace and identifiable gait, stating: "Did you ever see a Jewish man walk from one side to the other?" Said Phelan: "A kind of a side-wheel movement?" To that Esposito said "yes," and added: "I didn't see the man clear in the face." Margaret Morrill, a social worker, said she saw the killer run up the street but could not positively identify him, only his manner of running, "a rather long stride." She thought the murderer was tall. Railroad station ticket agent James H. McKiernan described the killer as a "little fellow" and said he saw only a portion of the killer's face. Frederick Morris, a carpenter, had been closest to the priest, and the killer, and he had identified Israel in a lineup as the murderer. Yet later, Morris, Cummings took special note, was asked to state at the inquest whether he still felt Israel was the killer. "His side face did look familiar to me the night I was called to identify him, but I couldn't swear to the man because it just didn't look like him at that time." There were others, many of them who had picked Israel out of the lineup as the killer after he had been arrested. Later, Hilda Baer, a German immigrant, was unsure. Nellie Trefton, a waitress who first said Israel walked past the window of the restaurant where she worked only seconds before Father Dahme was killed, was now unsure. Teenager Alfred Berry was positive about Israel, later unsure. One by one, the witnesses fell.

Cummings had destroyed his very own case, systematically picking apart what had first amounted to an "open-and-shut" conviction of an illiterate, confused, and utterly accessible suspect, a conviction that would have won for him accolades, not to mention an avalanche of votes, from an anxious and enraged public. Yet he chose to exonerate a man he came to believe innocent, which won for him an heroic image of a prosecutor who sought justice before personal aggrandizement. Dramatically, he demonstrated how anyone could stand wrongly accused when he selected several persons in an open courtroom and asked them into his office where they were identified as looking very much like the murderer of Father Dahme. Said Cummings later: "It shows how easy it is for similarities in appearance, and especially similarity in clothes, to be made the basis for a mistaken identity."

Going before Judge L.P. Waldon Marvin in the Criminal Superior Court on May 27, 1924, Cummings presented the findings of his independent investigation, one which had consumed more than three months, and requested Marvin to dismiss charges against the defendant. He stated: "In view of what I have said about every element of the case, I do not think that any doubt of Israel's innocence can remain in the mind of a candid person. Therefore, if Your Honor approves, as I trust you will, of my conclusion in this matter, I shall enter a nolle (refusal to prosecute) in the case of State vs. Harold Israel."

Israel went free and quickly moved to Pennsylvania where he later married and raised two children, working honestly as a miner and becoming a regular churchgoer. Cummings kept in touch with Israel as late as 1938, sending him gifts of money from time to time. He later recalled: "I went out on a limb for him and

I wanted to make sure he never got in trouble again." Cummings later rose to great prominence as U.S. Attorney General (1933-39) during the first two terms of President Franklin D. Roosevelt. He later admitted that he had no logical reason to question the Israel case when it was first put before him. "The case against the accused seemed overwhelming. Upon its face, at least, it seemed like a well-nigh perfect case...In fact, it seemed like an *annihilating* case. There did not seem a vestige of reason for suspecting for a moment that the accused was innocent."

Yet everything was too perfect for the prosecution, too convenient. Cummings looked over the evidence and then, for no other reason than an intuitive urge, which he later admitted, decided to challenge that evidence. He concluded; "There were sufficient circumstances of an unusual character involved to make it highly important that every fact should be scrutinized with the utmost care and in the most impartial manner. It goes without saying that it is just as important for a state's attorney to use the great powers of his office to protect the innocent as it is to convict the guilty." See: **Cummings, Homer; Dahme,** Father Hubert.

REF.: *CBA; Cooper, Ten Thousand Public Enemies; Kunstler, The Case for Courage; Nash, Almanac of World Crime; Swisher, Homer Cummings; ____, Selected Papers;* (FILM), *Boomerang,* 1947.

Iszard, Henry, prom. 1959, U.S., rape. In the month of September 1959 fifteen women were assaulted in New York City. The assailant would enter office buildings along Madison Avenue at the end of the work day and find a woman working in an isolated area. Producing a gun, he would force the women into an empty nearby office and rape them. Using descriptions given by the victims, police assembled a composite sketch of the attacker, and from the sketch patrolman Eugene O'Neil identified the man as Henry Iszard.

Police went to the Bronx apartment house where Iszard lived but found only his wife and infant son. While questioning Mrs. Iszard, a sixteenth rape was reported to police. When Iszard returned home that night, police arrested him and charged him with rape after most of the victims identified Iszard as their attacker. The rapist was sentenced to a minimum of sixty years in prison. REF.: *CBA.*

Italian Dave Gang, prom. 1840s-60s, U.S., org. crime. A New York criminal named Italian Dave ran a veritable boarding school for pickpockets in the city's Paradise Square for over twenty years, beginning in the 1840s. Dave always had about forty boys between the ages of nine and fifteen ready to be employed in his pickpocket army. He conducted daily classes in everything from the fine art of procuring a wallet or purse, to the selection of a potential victim. Dave oversaw the operation after his students graduated to the streets, collected the money they stole, and kept most of it for himself. A student who failed an assignment was made to dress in a police uniform and battered with a billy club. Long after his troops had abandoned him because of his penurious ways, such graduates as Jimmy Dunnigan, Jack Mahaney, and Blind Mahoney continued to prey upon the public with lessons well learned at Italian Dave's. REF.: *CBA.*

Iturbide, Agustin de (Augustin I), 1783-1824, Mex., emperor, assass. Fought in Spanish army against Guerrero in 1820, but helped Guerrero later to establish the Plan of Iguala in 1821. After Mexico was guaranteed independence from Spain with the Treaty of Córdoba in 1821, he became chief of the provisional government. He ruled as emperor from 1822-23, but his despotic reign resulted in revolt. He relinquished power, and lived in exile in Europe. After returning to Mexico in 1824, he was captured and shot. REF.: *CBA.*

Ivan IV Vasilyevich (AKA: Ivan the Terrible), 1530-84, Rus., czar, 1533-84, rape-mur. The murderous reign of Ivan IV of Russia was marked by unspeakable horror and mass genocide. From 1560, the year his wife died, until 1580 when he dealt a fatal blow to his son, Ivan the Terrible showed little regard for human life.

The future ruler of Russia was the son of Vasily III, the Grand Duke of Muscovy, who died when the boy was three. Ivan was raised by the powerful and wealthy boyars, noblemen he soon came to despise. His tutors instilled in him a casual disregard for human life, a quality he displayed at the age of fourteen when he ordered one of the boyars thrown to the dogs. On Jan. 16, 1547, Ivan proclaimed himself czar, the first Russian ruler to use this title formally. He then ordered the provincial governors to help him select a wife by sending to Moscow the most attractive women in Russia. Two thousand young women answered the call. Finally, Ivan selected Anastasia Romanovna Zakharin-Koshkin, whose descendants formed the Romanov Dynasty.

The first few years of his reign were characterized by many notable reforms. In 1547 the Great Fire of Moscow leveled much of the city, a calamity the superstitious Ivan interpreted as a sign from God. Two years later he convened the first national assembly, or "Zemsky Sobor," to denounce the sins of the past. The last of the boyars were deposed and the merchant class rose to prominence for the first time. In 1560, following a series of impressive military victories at Kazan and Astrakhan, Ivan's wife and his son Dimitri died. Their passing marked a change in the czar's conduct toward his people. In 1569 he sent his troops to ransack Novgorod, the second wealthiest city in the czardom after receiving erroneous information from one of his advisors, a man of infamous character named Peter.

Ivan the Terrible.

Five hundred monks were taken prisoner, and a 100-mile trail of pillage and desecration was left behind by the rampaging troops. The troops entered the city on Jan. 8, 1570, to punish those who had conspired against the czar. Hundreds of people were doused in cauldrons of boiling oil. Thousands more were gored by red-hot irons. Ivan took possession of the archbishops' residence and turned it into the site of a depraved orgy. "Such scenes of horror, iniquity, and inhumanity had not been seen in the world since the destruction of Jerusalem," reported one eye witness. By the time the carnage was at an end, some 35,000 of the 400,000 inhabitants had been massacred. Not one rooftop remained on the farm buildings and residences of Novgorod.

High priests of the church who displeased the czar were singled out for assassination. On Mar. 22, 1568, Ivan entered the cathedral in Moscow expecting to receive the sacraments. Instead, the Metropolitan denounced him as a bestial tyrant with blood on his hands. For daring to speak out, the priest was imprisoned at Tver for life. A year later a member of Ivan's entourage strangled the holy man.

The bloodletting came to an end in 1580 when he struck and killed his eldest son Ivan, whom he deeply loved. The tragedy was a devastating blow for the czar. He withdrew behind the walls of a monastery where he was known now as the monk Jonah. He died on Mar. 18, 1584.

REF.: Almedingen, *The Romanovs*; Bakrushin, *History of Moscow*; Baynes and Moss, *Byzantium*; Bazilievich, *External Policy of the Russian Centralized State in the Second Half of the 15th Century*; Boar, *the World's Most Infamous Murders*; Bond, *Russia at the Close of the 16th Century*; CBA; Eckhardt, *Ivan the Terrible*; Fennell, *The Correspondence Between A.M. Kurbsky and Tsar Ivan IV*; ____, *Ivan the Great of Moscow*; Grey, *Ivan the Terrible*; Hurwood, *Society and the Assassin*; Johnson, *Famous Assassinations in History*; Karamzin, *History of the Russian State*; Klyuchevsky, *Course of Russian History*; Korotkov, *Ivan the Terrible, His Military Activity*; Likhachev and Lur'ye, *Letters of Ivan the Terrible*; Miliukov, *History of Russia*; Pember, *Ivan the Terrible*; Platonov, *Ivan the Terrible*; Riasanovsky, *A History of Russia*; Solovyev, *History of Russia From Earliest Times*; Staden, *Concerning the Moscow of Ivan the Terrible*; Tikhomirov, *Russia in the 16th Century*; Ustryalov, *The Statement of Prince Kurbsky*; Vernadsky, *A History of Russia*; ____, *Kievan Russia*; ____, *The Mongols and Russia*; ____, *Russia at the Dawn of the Modern Age*; Waliszewski, *Ivan the Terrible*; Willan, *The Early History of the Muscovy Company, 1553-1603*; Wipper, *Ivan Grozny*; Zabelin, *The Domestic Life of the Tsars and the Tsaritsas*; ____, *History of the City of Moscow*; (FILM), *Ivan the Terrible*, 1947.

Ivan VI Antonovich, 1740-64, Rus., czar, assass. The infant czar of Russia, whose miserable existence was terminated by the assassin Vasily Mirovich, was the son of Prince Antony Ulrich of Brunswick and the princess Anna Leopoldovna of Mecklenburg. On Oct.17, 1740, following the death of Empress Anne, Ivan VI was declared emperor and Ernest Johann Biron, the duke of Courland, was named his regent. Biron was overthrown scarcely a month later on Nov. 8, with the regency reverting to the infant's mother, Anna.

A political coup took place on Dec. 6, 1741, which brought Elizabeth Petrovna to the throne. Ivan and his family were imprisoned in the fortress of Dünamünde where they remained until 1744. That year, 4-year-old Ivan was permanently separated from his family and imprisoned at Kholmogory where he remained in isolation for the next twelve years.

In 1756 he was secretly moved to the fortress of Schlüsselburg and closely watched by his jailers. There were few outside the royal family who even knew the identity of the young man. When Peter III came to power, rumors grew that Ivan might be released, but the new emperor, unable to consolidate his power, was quickly deposed. A letter sent by Prince Churmtyev instructed the jailers at Schlüsselburg to maintain a strict guard over the "nameless one." Ivan was chained to the wall and kept in isolation, a policy maintained by Catherine II (Catherine the Great) when she came to power in 1762. Nearly twenty years had passed since the young monarch had seen the light of day. The long years of solitary confinement had taken their toll, for Ivan was considered mentally unbalanced.

On July 5, 1764, Ivan VI was assassinated by Vasily Mirovich, a lieutenant of the guard who was eager to curry the favor of Empress Catherine. Believing that Catherine was grateful to him, Mirovich made no attempt to defend himself in court. He was officially charged with attempting to abduct Ivan with the intention of restoring him to the throne of Russia. The court sentenced him to death, but to the last minute he maintained a stoic posture, believing that a reprieve would soon be sent from the palace. When he realized that he had been duped, Mirovich unsuccessfully tried to escape from his executioners. He was beheaded moments later. See: **Catherine II.**

REF.: *CBA*; Hurwood, *Society and the Assassin*; Johnson, *Famous Assassinations of History*; Melville, *Famous Duels and Assassinations*.

Ivanovich, Dmitri, 1581-91, Rus., czar, assass. Ivan Vasilyevich, perhaps better known as Ivan the Terrible, the first formally proclaimed czar of Russia, was survived by two sons when he died in 1584, 27-year-old Feodore Ivanovich and 3-year-old Dmitri Ivanovich. Feodore, something of a weakling, married the sister of the ambitious Boris Godunov, who controlled his feeble brother-in-law and aspired to the throne. In 1591, at Uglitch, a small town on the Volga River, Dmitri Ivanovich, then ten, lived in exile with his mother and his court. His affairs were overseen by Michael Biatagoffski, an agent of Godunov, who spread rumors that Dmitri was a cruel tyrant.

On May 15, 1591, an assailant attacked Dmitri in the courtyard of his mansion and cut his throat. The boy died almost instantly. His mother accused Biatagoffski and the boy's governess of the murder—later the governess' son was killed. When Czar Feodore died in 1598, the clergy asked Godunov to become czar and he accepted. After 1601, rumors surfaced that Dmitri was alive and well and would claim the czardom.

In 1603, a young man serving a Polish prince fell ill, and told a Catholic priest that he was Dmitri, presenting a jeweled cross as proof of his identity. The young man was presented to the king of Poland. Godunov, citing hundreds of impostors in Russia during the seventeenth and eighteenth centuries, issued a proclamation that Dmitri was dead, and that the pretender was a monk, Gregory Otrepieff. In 1604, the claimant brought together an army of several different nationalities and invaded Russia. In 1605, when Godunov died, the son who was supposed to succeed him was immediately denied. By June, the pretender entered Moscow and was proclaimed czar. He quickly neglected important Russian customs and surrounded himself with Polish favorites, including his bride, Marina. Vasili Shuiski, a member of the commission which investigated Dmitri's death, denounced the claimant, saying he had seen Dmitri slain. He was condemned to death for this pronouncement, but then was pardoned by the new czar Vasili and a group of followers who stormed the Kremlin Palace, and murdered the pretender in May 1606.

Still more rumors that Dmitri was alive surfaced. A Polish Jew, Michael Moltchanoff, claimed the role of czar. In 1608, at the Volkhoff battle, when the claimant's forces defeated Czar Vasili, Marina, acknowledged the new claimant as her supposedly dead husband. Jealous enemies murdered Moltchanoff at Kaluga in 1610. Another Dmitri appeared in 1611, and yet another in 1612; the first was captured by Vasili's soldiers, who took him to Moscow and strangled him, and the cossacks executed the second, thus bringing an end to the false claims. REF.: *CBA*.

Ivers, Alice (AKA: **Poker Alice**), 1851-1930, U.S., gamb. Born in Sudbury, Devonshire, Eng., on Feb. 17, 1851, Alice Ivers migrated with her family to the U.S., settling in Virginia first, then moving to Fort Mead, Colo., where her father was a school teacher. Alice grew up admiring the cardsharps and high-hatted gamblers that traveled the cow towns and she learned their card-playing wiles. While in her teens, Ivers went to Deadwood, S.D., where she became a dealer, specializing in poker and soon earning the sobriquet "Poker Alice." She smoked thick, black cigars, and during the 1870s and 1880s, became a well-known and successful gambler in all the famous cowtowns, from Deadwood to Tombstone, Ariz.

Poker Alice Ivers, lady gambler.

Poker Alice would not tolerate a cheat and was never challenged by other gamblers. She was known to carry several guns, one in her purse and one in a pocket of her dress. On occasion, she would practice her marksmanship by shooting knobs off the frames of pictures hanging in bars to warn gambler gunmen that she was capable of defending herself. Wild Bill Hickok reportedly asked Poker Alice to sit in with him and others during a poker game in Saloon No. 10 in Deadwood on the day he was shot by Jack McCall; she declined, saying that she had agreed to play with another group down the street in Mann's Saloon.

When hearing that Wild Bill had been shot in the back, she rushed to Saloon No. 10 and saw Hickok sprawled dead on the floor and McCall fleeing out the back door. "Poor Wild Bill," she said of Hickok as she peered down on his corpse, "he was sitting where I would have been if I had played with him." She later claimed that she had refused to play with Wild Bill on that fateful day because she "had a queer feeling that all would not be right that day."

Alice Ivers later married Frank Tubbs, a gambler who did not possess half her playing talents and one who took to drink early in their marriage. Poker Alice was forever getting her husband out of trouble. Tubbs was knifed one night by a disgruntled player, and Poker Alice stormed into the bar and shot the man in the stomach at thirty feet (he recovered). She and Tubbs moved on to Silver City, Nev., where she broke the bank in the biggest saloon, winning an estimated $150,000, a great fortune for those days. She and Tubbs then bought a huge Colorado ranch which Poker Alice later lost. Following her husband's death, Poker Alice moved to Rapid City, S.D., where she ran a small poker club. She died there, a grand old lady of western lore, on Feb. 27, 1930. See: **Hickok, James Butler; McCall, Jack.**

REF.: Bartholomew, *The Biographical Album of Western Gunfighters; CBA*.

Ives, George, d.1863, U.S., mur. With the discovery of gold in the Montana territory in 1861, the area found itself deluged with not only prospectors but also thieves who made their living by preying on the hard work of the miners. The country was wild and unsettled. There were few laws and even fewer people to enforce them. The thieves, who became known as "road agents," operated on horseback, ambushing miners thought to be carrying gold from their diggings.

When George Ives shot and killed Nicholas Tbalt after he had robbed the man of two mules, a group of citizens organized a posse and tracked down Ives. In front of a jury which consisted of twenty-four miners, Ives was judged Guilty and his hanging ordered. Much to the dismay of Ives, the hanging took place only minutes after he was convicted. The incident touched off a wave of vigilante justice in the gold-crazed country.

REF.: *CBA*; Mencken, *By the Neck*.

Ivory, Henry, and **Perry, William**, and **Stirling, Amos**, prom. 1900, U.S., mur. When police discovered the brutalized body of Professor Roy Wilson White on a side street near Powelton Avenue Station in Philadelphia, the University of Pennsylvania community was shocked. The popular law professor had distinguished himself with students and colleagues and had yet to turn thirty. White had been beaten over the head with an iron bar and robbed of some of his possessions. Within an hour of the May 19, 1900, murder, Ralph Hartman, a messenger at the train station, reported to police he had seen two black men near the murder scene at around 10 p.m. and had even engaged in a brief conversation with one of them.

From Hartman's description, police rounded up 135 suspects, narrowed down to sixteen. In a lineup Henry Ivory was identified by Hartman as the man with whom he had spoken. The suspect admitted conversing with the messenger at the train station but denied knowledge of the crime. After intense questioning he confessed to being party to the murder but swore he did not kill the victim. The police traced White's stolen watch to William Perry, and a city employee, John Leary, helped identify a third suspect in the murder. When police apprehended Amos Stirling in New Jersey, the man's clothes were covered with blood. Stirling said his nose had been bleeding and that he was innocent of any crime. A few weeks later Ivory finally told police the complete story. He said Stirling had pounded the victim with the iron bar and then they had robbed the professor. All three men were tried and convicted on murder charges. Ivory, Perry, and Stirling were then hanged.

REF.: Barton, *True Exploits of Famous Detectives; CBA*.

IWW Riot, 1928, U.S., mob vio.-mur. In January 1928, the International Workers of the World (IWW) struck against Colorado mine owners. The mine workers, also known as "Wobblies," wanted better working conditions and more money from the owners. The longer the strike went on, the weaker the miners' organization became. With the arrival of the State Industrial Commission in Walsenburg, the workers had hopes of resolving their dispute, but those hopes were dashed when the state police sharpshooting squad accompanied the SIC, ordered by Walsenburg Mayor John J. Pritchard. "Bolshevism shall not prosper in Walsenburg as long as I am mayor," Pritchard said.

Following a meeting in the IWW hall the miners decided to

go to the courthouse where the commission was meeting. As the men marched along Main Street they were accompanied by police who attempted to divert them. Without warning, a mine worker stepped from the crowd and shot a policeman. As the gunman bolted from the crowd he was shot and killed by police, who then turned their attention to the rest of the "Wobblies." In the IWW hall police killed another man and wounded one miner.

A coroner's jury later called the shooting by Colorado State Police unprovoked. The IWW sued the police officers and Mayor Pritchard for $100,500. Emil Rozansky, a leader of the "Wobblies," was fined $400 for his part in the melee. REF.: *CBA*.

J

Jablonski, Kazimiriz, 1958- , U.S., burg.-mur. First arrested in 1974, at the age of sixteen, Kazimiriz Jablonski was sentenced to three to nine years in prison on a burglary charge when he was nineteen. After serving three years, Jablonski was paroled in 1980 only to find himself back in court on another burglary charge. He was again sentenced to three years in prison. Jablonski was serving his time at the Joliet, Ill., Community Correctional Center, a work-release facility, when he was granted a pass for the Labor Day weekend in 1981.

On Sept. 5, the first evening of his three-day pass, Jablonski reunited with friends in Chicago's Kilbourn Park. A gang fight broke out as taunts and jeers turned to flying fists and broken bottles. When more dangerous weapons were produced, many of the youths fled the scene. Jablonski and Boguslaw Dabrowski chased Steven Beverly, a rival gang member, up an embankment onto nearby railroad tracks. When the 17-year-old tripped and fell, Jablonski and Dabrowski jumped on him.

As they kicked and punched him, Beverly pulled a knife. Jablonski wrestled the knife from Beverly and stabbed him as Dabrowski held him down. Jablonski was arrested when he returned to the correctional facility. Less than one week later, he and Dabrowski were charged with murder and armed robbery. In December 1982, Dabrowski was convicted of aggravated battery and found Not Guilty on murder charges. In January 1983, Judge Fred Suria reduced Jablonski's murder charge to voluntary manslaughter and sentenced him to ten years in prison. REF.: *CBA.*

Jaccoud, Pierre, prom. 1958, Switz., mansl. A senior lawyer in Geneva., Switzerland, Pierre Jaccoud was the leader of the Geneva Radical party and head of the Bar association. He was accused of the murder of Charles Zumbach, a 68-year-old agricultural machinery dealer. On the evening of May 1, 1958, at 10:58, Geneva police were called to Plan-les-Ouates, at the foot of the French Alps, by a neighbor of the Zumbachs. Charles Zumbach had been shot and stabbed to death and his wife, Marie Zumbach, was wounded. Coming home from a meeting, she had heard shots and cries for help from the room of her son, André Zumbach. On opening the door, she saw a stranger with a gun, who shot her in the shoulder as she backed away. He then fled on a bicycle. In addition to the efforts of the Geneva Sûreté, the investigation was aided by Charles Knecht, chief of police, P. Moriaud, the examining magistrate, and Charles Cornu, the 70-year-old prosecutor-general of Geneva. Zumbach had been murdered with a .25-caliber pistol. There was no sign of forced entry and nothing had been stolen, although the killer had made a shambles of the house searching for something. Police found a dark coat button across the street from the house.

Swiss lawyer Pierre Jaccoud.

André Zumbach, music director at a local radio station, admitted having been involved briefly with Linda Baud, thirty-five, a secretary at the station. Baud was also the longtime mistress of Pierre Jaccoud, but had been trying recently to break up with him. André had received threatening anonymous phone calls, and two letters from "Simone B." telling him of Baud's "loose morals" and enclosing nude photographs of her. Jaccoud met André once, late in 1957, to ask if he intended to marry Baud. André told him he did not, but the lawyer was not satisfied with his response. Although apparently unwilling to risk the damage to his family and his career by revealing his affair, Jaccoud would not let his mistress leave him. He went to the Zumbach home hoping to recover the anonymous letters he had sent to the son. On May 19, 1958, police questioned Jaccoud for the first time. He explained that the split between himself and Baud had begun a year and a half ago, and that he could not understand how he might be a suspect in the killing. His original alibi did not hold up. Baud told police Jaccoud had threatened her in the past year and threatened suicide with a small gun, which would match the murder weapon. Then Jaccoud returned from a trip with his brown hair dyed blond. Evidence, including blood stains on Jaccoud's clothing, began to pile up and, by Nov. 2, 1959, Jaccoud was charged with the crime.

The trial began on Jan. 18, 1960, in the Geneva Law Courts before Judge Barde. The press showed intense interest in the case due to Jaccoud's status, and because several United Nations secretaries and officials were questioned. The case rested on circumstantial evidence and a parade of witnesses testified, bringing no new information to light. Defended by famed attorney René Floriot and a team of lawyers, including Raymond Nicolet, Jaccoud was convicted of manslaughter on Feb. 4 and was given a seven-year sentence, which was later reduced to three years.

REF.: *CBA;* Heppenstall, *The Sex War and Others;* Thorwald, *Crime and Science;* Wilson, *Encyclopedia of Murder.*

Jacks, George H., and **Willows, William,** prom. 1898, U.S., rob.-mur. On the morning of Feb. 26, 1898, 70-year-old Andrew Fergus McGee left his Chicago home for what he thought was a routine sales call for the Charles Creamery Company. But the two men he met at 2030 Indiana Avenue bashed in his skull and he died a few hours later.

Two days after the murder, Chicago police arrested George H. Jacks for trying to hold up a drug store less than a block from the site where McGee had been murdered. One of the officers also found an iron pipe that Jacks discarded as he fled the scene. Police learned that Jacks had been at a local resort when McGee called on its proprietor, and that Jacks had pawned McGee's watch. William Willows was identified as an accomplice in the murder. Eventually, Jacks confessed to killing McGee. He said that he and Willows set up the salesman because he was known to carry large amounts of money.

During the investigation, it was revealed that Jacks had been police chief of Muskegon, Mich., but lost his job when neighbors tried to extinguish a fire at his house, and discovered their stolen property inside. Jacks was tried and convicted of murder and hanged. Willows was sentenced to fourteen years in prison.

REF.: Barton, *True Exploits of Famous Detectives; CBA.*

Jackson, Andrew, 1767-1845, U.S., attempt. assass. Andrew Jackson, the seventh president of the U.S., was the first president to be fired on by an assassin. His assailant, Richard Lawrence, a sometime house painter with a record of violent outbursts, had previously been arrested twice, once for threatening his landlady and once for attacking his sister. On both occasions he was found mentally incompetent and freed. Lawrence became increasingly disturbed and began to think he was King Richard III of England and that huge sums of money were held in trust for him in the Bank of the United States. Apparently, this fantasy brought President Jackson into Lawrence's sights. Jackson opposed the Bank of the United States, a policy that Lawrence believed was the cause of his money problems. On one occasion he actually had an audience with Jackson during which he demanded his "due share" of the bank's funds. Another time he cornered Vice President Martin Van Buren on the Capitol steps and demanded money from him. Both dismissed him as harmless.

For his assassination attempt, Lawrence bought a pistol to match one he already owned and practiced shooting both until he was satisfied with his aim. On Jan. 30, 1835, Lawrence planted himself in the back of the Capitol rotunda, where the funeral of Representative Warren Davis was being held. When the funeral procession began to file out of the Capitol, the 68-year-old Jackson took his place just behind the pallbearers. As they reached the building's entrance, Lawrence leaped from behind a pillar, pulled out one of the pistols, and fired. Though the gun made a loud noise and many people thought the president had been hit, it actually had misfired. Lawrence then discarded the first pistol and switched the second pistol from his left to his right hand for another shot. Jackson, his cane raised, turned on him. Lawrence fired again. This pistol also misfired and Lawrence was seized and taken away, leaving Jackson shaken but unharmed.

Later, the guns and the ammunition were checked and found in first-class order. Lawrence was tried on a charge of assault with intent to kill (in 1835 an assault on the president's life was considered a misdemeanor) and

President Andrew Jackson, who survived an assassination attempt in 1835.

was found Not Guilty by reason of insanity. He was sent to an insane asylum for the rest of his life. See: **Jackson-Dickinson Duel.**

REF.: *CBA*; Hurwood, *Society and the Assassin*; James, *The Life of Andrew Jackson, Portrait of A President*; Johnson, *Famous Kentucky Tragedies and Trials*; Lester, *Crime of Passion*; Paine, *The Assassins' World*; Parton, *The Life of Andrew Jackson*; Pearl, *The Dangerous Assassins*; Schlesinger, *The Age of Jackson*; Van Deusen, *The Jacksonian Era, 1828-1848*; Ward, *Andrew Jackson, Symbol for an Age*; (FILM), *The Gorgeous Hussy*, 1936; *Man of Conquest*, 1939; *The President's Lady*, 1953.

Jackson, Arthur R., 1936- , U.S., attempt. mur. After her appearance in the critically acclaimed film *Raging Bull*, Theresa Gilda Saldana's career was on the rise. Her mother in Brooklyn gave Theresa's Los Angeles address and telephone number to a man claiming to work for director Martin Scorsese. On March 15, 1982, only days after the phone call, Saldana was stabbed repeatedly by illegal Scottish immigrant, Arthur R. Jackson outside her apartment in West Hollywood.

If not for the intervention of delivery truck driver Jeff Fenn, the 27-year-old actress would have died. Fenn grabbed Jackson from behind, knocked the knife from his hand and pinned him to the street. Saldana, stabbed in the chest and hand more than ten times, required four hours of surgery, twenty-six pints of blood, and more than 100 stitches, but survived. After several weeks in the hospital and additional surgery, she was released.

Jackson was charged with attempted murder, and police discovered a diary in which the attacker mentioned Saldana's name more than fifty times. At his 1982 trial, Jackson was sentenced to twelve years in prison for stabbing Saldana. While imprisoned, Jackson said he was also responsible for a murder during a robbery in London. Saldana went on to play herself in a made-for-television movie based on the incident, and to organize a group called Victims for Victims.

But the nightmare was far from over for Saldana. While in prison, Jackson continued to send her letters in which he threatened to kill her so they could be reunited in heaven. It was his "divine mission" to murder her, Jackson wrote to Saldana. In 1989, Jackson became eligible for parole after serving seven years in prison. His June 15 parole date was postponed when the California Board of Prison Terms sentenced him to an additional 270 days in prison for taking part in a prison uprising, in which Jackson broke windows and refused to cooperate with officials. Attorneys for Saldana, who was pregnant at the time of Jackson's initial parole hearing, have said they will file charges against

Jackson for threatening her. REF.: *CBA*.

Jackson, Calvin, 1948- , U.S., rape-mur. A Manhattan police detective admitted that "depersonalization" and a "lack of interest" on the part of the homicide squad was partly to blame for the murder of nine elderly women at the seedy Park Plaza Hotel between April 1973 and September 1974. Even after the first victims had been found dead in their shabby, ill-equipped apartments, "no immediate police action was taken on any of them." The shoddy detective work and casual disregard for the lives of these elderly women led to a general shakeup in the New York City Police Department's Fourth Homicide Zone. Lieutenant James Gallagher, who failed to consider that the murders might have been the work of one man, was transferred to internal affairs. The long overdue re-organization had unfortunately come at the expense of at least nine lives.

The Park Plaza was located on West 77th Street in Manhattan. Despite the rather elegant name, most of its elderly residents lived barely above the poverty level in tiny, cramped rooms. The corridors were poorly lit and many residents dead bolted their doors at night to keep out muggers, thieves, and rapists. The eleven-story hotel was a seedbed of crime on the West Side. Beginning on Apr. 10, 1973, when 39-year-old Theresa Jordan was found suffocated in her apartment, the Park Plaza took on an even more sinister character. A homicidal maniac was loose in the building, but the police were hard pressed to provide answers to the anxious residents.

The killer struck again on July 19. Kate Lewisohn, sixty-five, was strangled to death and her skull crushed by the unknown assailant. For the next few months no more bodies were found, until on Apr. 24, 1974, 60-year-old Mabel Hartmeyer was found dead in her room. The Medical Examiner's Office attributed her death to "occlusive coronary arteriosclerosis." Although the police accepted this verdict without question, it was subsequently shown that the woman had been strangled and raped. Four days later 79-year-old Yetta Vishnefsky, a retired sewing machine operator, was stabbed to death with a butcher knife. She had been bound, gagged, and raped before she was murdered. A television set, some jewelry,

Mass killer Calvin Jackson.

and a few items of clothing had been stolen. Following the Vishnefsky murder the body count rose steadily. Forty-seven-year-old Winifred Miller, an accomplished pianist and singer, was the victim on June 8; followed by Blanche Vincent, seventy-one, on June 19; Martha Carpenter, sixty-nine on July 1; and 64-year-old sculptor Eleanor Platt, on Aug. 30. At first the medical examiner ruled out homicide in the cases of Vincent and Platt. Their deaths were blamed on chronic alcoholism and heart failure. Detectives from the Fourth Homicide Zone classified their files as "pending," an acknowledgment that murder could not be ruled out entirely.

On the morning of Sept. 12, 1974, the police received a frantic call from Dorothy May, the maid of Mrs. Pauline Spanierman, a 59-year-old widow living in an apartment building adjoining the Plaza. She said that her employer had been murdered. The medical examiner affixed the time of death at shortly after 3 a.m. It was the first time the killer had selected a victim outside the residential hotel. Police detectives questioned the residents of Spanierman's building and learned that a suspicious-looking man had crawled down a fire escape clutching a small TV set under his arm. Later that afternoon police detectives arrested 26-year-old Calvin Jackson at the intersection of 77th Street and Columbus

Avenue and charged him with murder and possession of stolen property. Jackson was a former inmate at the Elmira, N.Y., State Correctional Facility, with a long record of robbery and drug convictions. He had been living at the Park Plaza Hotel since 1972 and had been arrested on Nov. 7, 1973, for pilfering a television and stereo set from one of his neighbors—a crime for which he plea-bargained his way to a thirty-day sentence rather than the fifteen years it normally carried. Jackson returned to the Plaza where he earned his living working as a porter.

Born in Buffalo, Jackson's career up to the time he moved into the Park Plaza with his girlfriend Valerie Coleman was a road map of crime. He had drifted aimlessly from one flophouse to another, committing petty robberies and dealing drugs. He was described by Coleman as a soft-spoken, "caring" individual. "Jack was the kind of person if you needed something and he had it, he'd give it to you," she said. Jackson was taken to the Manhattan Criminal Court for arraignment the day after his arrest. Under direct questioning from Assistant District Attorney Kenneth D. Klein and a battery of detectives, Jackson confessed in hushed tones to killing Spanierman and the other elderly women. He was kept under close watch at the Manhattan House of Detention for Men to prevent a suicide attempt.

On Nov. 3, 1974, State Supreme Court justice Joseph A. Martinis ruled that Jackson was mentally competent to stand trial, against the vociferous objections of defense attorneys Donald Tucker and Robert Blossner. "If Calvin Jackson is not legally insane, who is legally insane? He raped women, some in their seventies and eighties. He raped some of them after death. Is this a legally sane man?" Tucker wanted to know. "He went to the refrigerator in nearly every apartment. He prepared a meal and ate it as he watched the body. Sometimes he stayed for an hour. Is this a legally sane man?" The jury agreed with the judge, returning a verdict of Guilty against Jackson on nine counts of murder on May 25, 1976. Jackson's five-hour taped confession that had been played inside the jury room was a major factor in their decision. Justice Aloysius J. Melia of the State Supreme Court sentenced the defendant to two life terms for each victim. Jackson will not be eligible for parole until the year 2030.

REF.: *CBA*; Fox, *Mass Murder*; Godwin, *Murder U.S.A.*; Nash, *Murder, America*.

Jackson, Charles, prom. 1893, U.S., rob. Chicago police met Frank Drake on the evening of Jan. 20, 1893, as he entered a State Street pawnshop with two new overcoats. When Drake had trouble explaining how he acquired the garments he was arrested. At the police station, a store owner identified his merchandise by the private labels and Drake told police that four other men had given him the coats to pawn for them. Henry Jackson, Frank Smith (alias Leper), Charles Jackson, and Henry Johnson (alias Kerley) were arrested and charged with robbery. During the trial in April, the other three defendants accused Charles Jackson of stealing the goods and he was sentenced to two years in prison. Johnson, Smith, and Henry Jackson were all released.

REF.: *CBA*; Wooldridge, *Hands Up*.

Jackson, Cobb, prom. 1897, U.S., rape. Thirteen-year-old Fannie Gray came to Chicago in June 1897 to find work. Discouraged, she sat on a curb at 35th Street and Michigan Avenue and cried. Mary Anderson saw the girl and told her she would find a place to sleep, and might find a job at Fannie Wright's at 3507 N. Dearborn St. Anderson asked Cobb Jackson to see that Gray made it there.

Instead, Jackson took Gray on a tour of nearby saloons and then forced her up to his room in the Diamond Hotel. Jackson raped Gray and then fell asleep around 2 a.m. While he slept, Gray, dressed only in nightclothes, forced open the third-story window and escaped the hotel. She told her story to police, who arrested Jackson and charged him with rape. On June 2, 1897, he was found Guilty and sentenced to ten years in prison.

REF.: *CBA*; Wooldridge, *Hands Up*.

Jackson, Ed, 1873-1954, Case of, U.S., consp.-brib. Nearly five years after he allegedly bribed the former governor of Indiana,

Ed Jackson was brought to trial on conspiracy charges. At the time of his 1928 trial, Jackson was himself governor of Indiana and his predecessor, Warren T. McCray, had just been released from federal prison after serving time on a charge of using the U.S. mails to defraud. After two grand jury panels had failed to return indictments against Jackson, the governor surrendered to sheriff's police in Indianapolis in September 1927 and pleaded not guilty to conspiracy charges.

Prosecuting attorney William H. Remy set out to prove that Jackson had offered McCray, who had recently been indicted, $10,000 to appoint a friend to the position of Marion County prosecutor. In return for the appointment, which Jackson hoped would secure him the gubernatorial nomination, Remy said Jackson also promised McCray that he would not be convicted for his crimes. When McCray refused the offer, Jackson and David C. Stephenson, the Grand Dragon of Indiana's Ku Klux Klan, allegedly threatened McCray again. While the case against Jackson seemed to be open and shut, Indiana prosecutors learned that the state's statute of limitations in crimes of bribery is limited to two years. The state could not prove Jackson had tried to conceal the crime, and the governor was exonerated. See: **Stephenson, David C.** REF.: *CBA*.

Jackson, Eddie, 1873-1932, U.S., rob. Eddie Jackson survived more than 2,000 arrests during a forty-year career as a Chicago pickpocket, which began at the tender age of fourteen. Stylistically, Jackson favored the more dramatic confrontation of jostling his victim, called "kissing-the-sucker", although he was equally adept at extracting a wallet without making any contact with its owner. Using up to four accomplices, Jackson earned as much as $1,500 a week around the turn of the century. He retained a lawyer, Black Horton, to whom he reported hourly. If Horton failed to hear from Jackson, he went immediately to the local police station and bailed him out. After an arrest, Jackson usually bought his way out by returning some of the stolen cash. Though he was arrested over 2,000 times, Jackson was convicted only twice, serving just over a year in prison. Eventually, Jackson's dexterity abandoned him, and he died penniless in 1932. REF.: *CBA*.

Jackson, Edmond D., 1944- , U.S., (wrong. convict.) mur. In 1978, Edmond D. Jackson spent Christmas with his family for the first time since he was imprisoned eight years earlier for a crime he did not commit. In 1970, Jackson was convicted of murdering bartender Harold Dixon in a Queens, N.Y., holdup and sentenced to two concurrent terms of twenty years to life in prison.

Attorney Helen Bodian doggedly fought to have Jackson's conviction overturned and, in 1978, Federal District Court Judge Vincent L. Broderick dismissed the former mechanic's murder conviction. The judge ruled that the defendant had been convicted solely on the testimony of four people who could not possibly have seen the gunman for more than a few seconds. The U.S. Circuit Court of Appeals upheld the ruling and criticized officials in Queens. They said the evidence against Jackson was circumstantial at best, and that police had ignored another suspect. REF.: *CBA*.

Jackson, Edward Franklin, Jr., 1944- , U.S., rape. From 1977 to 1982, William Bernard Jackson served time at Ohio's maximum security prison in Lucasville. In those five years, Edward Franklin Jackson, Jr. was building up a practice as an internist and was named to the board of directors at St. Anthony's Hospital in Columbus. On Sept. 22, 1982, the unrelated Jacksons crossed paths for the first time. William Jackson had just been released from prison, where he was serving fourteen to fifty years on two rape convictions. Edward Jackson was being indicted on thirty-six counts of rape, forty-six counts of aggravated burglary, four counts of attempted rape, five counts of gross sexual imposition, and two kidnapping charges. Two of the rapes Edward Jackson was charged with in 1982 were the crimes that William Jackson was convicted of in 1977.

On Sept. 5, police arrested Dr. Edward Jackson on charges of attempted burglary. While the residents of the apartment in question did not report anything missing, they did find a ski mask and three pieces of rope with knots tied at each end that had been left behind by the prowler. The rope matched that used by the "Grandview Rapist," for whom Columbus police had been searching for seven years in connection with about 100 rapes in the city. A search of Dr. Jackson's black Mercedes turned up a change of clothes, a piece of rope and a list with the names of approximately sixty-five women, many of them rape victims. The community was shocked when indictments were handed down against the prominent physician.

During the trial, which began in August 1983, Edward Jackson's attorney John Bowen acknowledged that his client had committed many crimes, but described him as a sick man and pleaded him innocent by reason of insanity. The twenty-one-day trial resulted in Jackson's conviction of twenty-one rapes and twenty-nine aggravated burglaries, as well as several additional charges. Before his sentencing, Dr. Jackson told the court he had overcome the angel of death in his professional career, but succumbed to its influence in the struggle against rape fantasies and bondage. William Jackson, who bore a remarkable resemblance to the doctor, said he felt no animosity toward the two victims who picked him out of a lineup. But the apology from the state wasn't enough. "They took away part of my life, part of my youth," he said. "I spent five years down there and all they said was 'We're sorry'... And they can never make up those five years." REF.: CBA.

Jackson, Edwin Aubrey, and **Watkins, Phillip Benjamin,** prom. 1949, Brit., police corr.-rob. When an old lady from Catford, England, died in 1949, the police were entrusted with her house. Property was soon reported missing, however, and was discovered contained in the residence of Sergeant Phillip Benjamin Watkins, who was arrested along with two other officers and charged with robbery and receiving stolen property. On trial at the Old Bailey in July 1949, Edwin Aubrey Jackson and another constable admitted their guilt and testified against their superior officer.

Watkins maintained his innocence despite testimony that he encouraged the constables to loot the widow's house. The sergeant said some of the property was his and that he had received the rest from Jackson. The contradictory testimony resulted in Watkins being found Guilty of receiving stolen goods, but Not Guilty of stealing. He was sentenced to seven years in prison. Jackson was sentenced to five years in prison for his part in the crime.

REF.: CBA; Harrison, Criminal Calendar.

Jackson, Francis (AKA: **Dixie**), and **Williams, John** (AKA: **The Matchet**), and **White, John** (AKA: **Fowler**), and **Slader, Mr.,** and **Parkhurst, Walter,** prom. 1664-74, Brit. theft-mur. Well-known among seventeenth century highwaymen, Francis Jackson's everlasting fame came from a book published the year he died. Jackson's Recantation; or, the Life & Death of the Notorious High-way-man now Hanging in Chains at Hampstead, delivered to a Friend, a little before the Execution was a definitive examination of the highwayman's trade by one who knew it well. Jackson's book provided a look at how a highwayman operated and gave tips on how to avoid becoming a victim. Interspersed with Jackson's prose was commentary from Samuel Smith, the Newgate prison chaplain who attended Jackson as he awaited execution.

While in Newgate, Jackson also wrote a shorter work, The Confession of the Four Highway-men, as it was Written by One of them, and Allowed by the Rest the 14th of this Instant April (being the Day before their Appointed Execution). An effort to set the record straight, the book detailed Jackson and his cohorts' last attempted robbery, on the road between Staines and Hounslow in 1674. After the robbery, Jackson, John Williams, John White, Walter Parkhurst, and Mr. Slader were confronted by an angry mob of armed Englishmen. Wounded and exhausted, the five criminals did, however, escape from Hounslow and that evening reached Heath, only to be met by the town's forewarned citizenry that evening. Despite a valiant fight in which Slader and at least one townsman were killed, Jackson and his gang were arrested and

charged with robbery; Jackson alone was charged with murder. The men were convicted and executed within a month of their capture. Jackson, who wrote in his confessional that any highwayman who had £500 could be saved from hanging, violated one of his own rules—he committed murder.

REF.: CBA; Hibbert, Highwaymen.

Jackson, Frank (AKA: **Blockey**), b.1856, U.S., west. outl. Born in Texas in 1856, Frank Jackson was trained to be a tinsmith after being orphaned as a youth. His interest in his trade quickly waned, and by the time he turned twenty he was working as a cowboy in Denton, Texas, on the Murphy ranch, notorious for harboring the outlaw Sam Bass. Jackson started his life as an outlaw by murdering Henry Goodall, a black man accused of stealing horses. The two fought over a stolen horse, and settled when Goodall gave Jackson a mount. They rode off together, but as they stopped to water the horses, Jackson shot Goodall and cut his throat.

Jackson next joined Bass for a two-year career of robbing trains and banks. On Apr. 10, 1878, the gang lost a number of members during a retreat from an aborted train robbery in Mesquite, Texas. Two months later, on June 13, the gang narrowly escaped an ambush near Salt Creek, Texas, losing only Arkansas Johnson. By July the gang had dwindled to four. In Round Rock, Texas, on July 19, 1878, the gang was surprised by lawmen who had been tipped off by Jim Murphy, a remaining gang member. In a store next to the bank, the gang killed Deputy Ellis Grimes and wounded his accomplice, Morris Moore. As they left the store, outlaw Seaborn Barnes was shot to death and Bass was critically wounded. Bass escaped with Jackson's help, but was found bleeding to death the following day. He died without revealing Jackson's destination, and the final member of the Bass gang was never found. If, in his final moments, Bass revealed the location of the loot he acquired over a lifetime of crime, Jackson may have retired as a prosperous man. See: **Bass, Sam.**

REF.: Bartholomew, The Biographical Album of Western Gunfighters; Bates, History and Reminiscences of Denton County; Blacker, The Old West in Fact; Breihan, Badmen of Frontier Days; ____, Outlaws of the Old West; Brent, Great Western Heroes; Casey, The Texas Border and Some Border-liners; Castleman, Sam Bass; CBA; Chapel, Guns of the Old West; Chilton, The Book of the West; Coblentz, Villains and Vigilantes; Cowling, Geography of Denton County; Cunningham, Triggernometry; Fallwell, The Texas Rangers; Fletcher, Up the Trail in '79; Gard, Sam Bass; Grisham, Tame the Reckless Wind; Hendricks, The Bad Man of the West; Hill, The End of the Cattle Trail; Hogg, Authentic History of Sam Bass; Holloway, Texas Gun Lore; Horan, and Sann, Pictorial History of the Wild West; Hullah, The Train Robber's Career; Hutchinson, The Life & Personal Writings of Eugene Manlove Rhodes; McGiffin, Ten Tall Texans; Martin, A Sketch of Sam Bass; Myers, The Last Chance; Penfield, Dig Here!; Preece, Lone Star Man; Raine, Guns of the Frontier; Raymond, Captain Lee Hall of Texas; Richardson, Adventuring with a Purpose; Siringo, Riata and Spurs; Stanley, Socorro; Steen, The Texas News; Sterling, Famous Western Outlaw-Sheriff Battles; Sterling, Trails and Trials of a Texas Ranger; Thorp, Story of the Southwestern Cowboy; Walters, Tombstone's Yesterdays; White, Trigger Fingers.

Jackson, Harold (AKA: **Doc**), prom. 1926, Case of, U.S., lynch-mur. For more than two months, Harold "Doc" Jackson sat in jail in Gulfport, Miss. He was suspected in the Feb. 18, 1926, slayings of federal entomologists William M. Mingee and John A. McLe-more. A grand jury convicted Jesse Favre of murder, but failed to return an indictment against Jackson, who was then moved to Poplarville, Miss., seat of Pearl River County, where he was wanted for the 1924 murder of Emaline Pearson.

On Apr. 23, nearly 100 men stormed the jailhouse where Jackson was being held. Using acetylene torches, they burned their way into the cellblock. With no help from the police, Jackson, clad only in a nightshirt, stood paralyzed before the angry mob who had begun to melt the lock on his cell door. With handkerchiefs over their faces, the men tied a rope around Jackson's neck and would not allow him to dress. They drove Jackson to a bridge near Picayune, where the entomologists had been murdered, and forced him to jump off the bridge with the rope around his neck. REF.: *CBA*.

Jackson, Howell Edmunds, 1832-95, U.S., jur. U.S. Supreme Court justice. A Tennessee lawyer who originally opposed secession, he joined the Confederate army after Tennessee broke from the Union. After the Civil War, he returned to his private law practice, was named to western Tennessee's Court of Arbitration in 1877, and was elected to the state house of representatives three years later. In 1881, he was elected to the U.S. Senate as a compromise candidate. In 1886, he resigned his seat after President Grover Cleveland urged him to fill a vacancy on the sixth federal circuit court. He served in the federal court until 1891, when he was nominated to be the first presiding judge of the U.S. Court of Appeals in Cincinnati. In 1893, shortly after the death of associate justice Lucius Lamar, he was appointed to the Supreme Court by President Benjamin Harrison. He contracted a severe case of tuberculosis after one year on the court. One of his contributions was in *Pollock v. Farmers' Loan and Trust Company* in 1895, regarding the right of Congress to levy federal income taxes. REF.: *CBA*.

Jackson, Humpty, d.1914, U.S., org. crime. Crime broker Humpty Jackson always carried three guns. What was more surprising, he also always carried a volume of a literary classic, sometimes in the original Greek or Latin.

Jackson dispensed criminal assignments from a graveyard in lower Manhattan, sending his charges to commit crimes from mugging to warehouse looting while seated on a tombstone. He gave more than fifty gangsters their start, including Spanish Louie, Nigger Ruhl, the Grabber, and the Lobster Kid. Occasionally he indulged his violent temper, and committed an act of mayhem himself. Jackson was arrested and convicted more than twenty times during his criminal life, the final time in 1909, for ordering an execution. In 1914, he died in the midst of his twenty-year sentence, presumably with a book in his hand.

REF.: Asbury, *The Gangs of New York*; *CBA*; Nash, *Bloodletters and Badmen*.

Jackson, Rev. Jesse, prom. 1988, U.S., assass. plot. In 1984, during his first campaign for the White House, Jesse Jackson received a number of death threats. So it was not without trepidation nor warnings from his family that he ran again in 1988. Surrounded by Secret Service agents throughout the primaries, Jackson, during the New York primary, accused New York Mayor Edward Koch of fostering a climate of hatred that resulted in further death threats.

In Washington, Mo., some fifty miles west of St. Louis, Londell and Tammy Williams were struggling to support their three young children. Londell, a handyman, was on probation for a gun charge, while his wife was on probation for possession of marijuana. Acting on a tip that Londell Williams had bragged of belonging to a white supremacist organization and that he was going to kill Jackson, Franklin County Sheriff Robert Bruns put the Williamses under surveillance. An informant then tape-recorded Londell admitting to membership in the Neo-Nazi group, the Covenant, the Sword and the Arm of the Lord (CSA). A search of the Williams' house turned up an illegal automatic AR-15 rifle and a telescopic sight.

The Williamses were arrested and charged with threatening the candidate, two counts of threatening a government informant, and possession of an illegal weapon. On the campaign trail, Jackson called the Missouri couple "dream busters." In August, Londell Williams pleaded guilty to threatening the presidential candidate and possessing an unregistered weapon. The charges of threatening the informant were dropped in a plea-bargaining agreement. The 30-year-old Williams said Jackson was "trying to make a fool out of us white people." Londell was sentenced to two years in prison and fined $100. In November, Tammy Williams was given a twenty-month prison sentence for her part in the threat on Jesse Jackson's life. REF.: *CBA*.

Jackson, John, prom. 1537, Scot., execut. The first appointed hangman in Scotland, John Jackson served the city of Edinburgh for a salary of roughly 12 shillings a year. Appointed before the City of London employed such a public servant, Jackson was provided with a house to live in and outfitted with an unofficial uniform. Between stints of public service, he also earned money by scavenging and cleaning the streets.

REF.: Atholl, *Shadow of the Gallows*; *CBA*.

Jackson, John (AKA: **Firth**), prom. 1930s, Brit., pris. esc.-mur. For one month, John Jackson was England's most-wanted criminal. Sentenced to six months in prison for stealing from a job site, the plumber was serving time in Manchester's Strangeways Prison when he was asked to repair a pipe on the staff side of the jail. Not content to wait until his parole date, Jackson struck a prison guard over the head with a hammer. He escaped by climbing out on the roof and jumping to the street below, then hid until dark and stole a suit of clothes to cover up his prison uniform.

The police followed many leads, but they failed to pick up the trail of the escaped convict. Only after Jackson tried to steal ox tongue from a grocer in Bradford, did police apprehend him, booking him, however, as a disheveled man named Firth on theft charges. Had Jackson not been carrying the dead prison guard's knife, he may never have been correctly identified. He was tried, convicted of murder, and executed.

REF.: *CBA*; Kingston, *A Gallery of Rogues*.

Jackson, John Jay, Jr., 1824-1907, U.S., jur. Served as prosecuting attorney for Wirt County, Va., in 1848, and as attorney for the Commonwealth of Virginia from 1848-50. He served in the state house of delegates from 1851-55, and was appointed to the western district court of Virginia by President Abraham Lincoln in 1861. REF.: *CBA*.

Jackson, Joseph, 1949-   , U.S., mur. After sentencing convicted murderer Joseph Jackson to twenty to forty years in prison, Judge John F. Hechinger was disturbed by the smile on the defendant's face. Jackson stopped grinning long enough, however, to ask the judge if he wouldn't mind performing another ceremony. Linda McBride had come to the sentencing with an Illinois marriage license. With a deputy sheriff as best man, an assistant public defender as matron of honor, and three of the bride's children as witnesses, McBride married Jackson, who had just been convicted of murdering her stepfather, Abram O'Neil. Hechinger allowed the newlyweds a few minutes of privacy before Jackson was taken to prison in August 1975. REF.: *CBA*.

Jackson, Louie (AKA: **Louise, Louisa Gomersal, Louie Calvert**), b.1897, Brit., mur. When Arthur "Arty" Calvert hired Louie Jackson as housekeeper for his Hunslet, England, home in 1925, he knew only that she was a widow with two small children. As the weeks went by, the watchman grew intimate with Jackson. Soon she informed Calvert she was pregnant with his child and they were married. With the baby due soon, Louie told her husband that she was going to stay with her sister until the baby was born. Three weeks later she returned with a baby girl. A suitcase arrived at the house, which Louie Calvert said contained baby clothes. Later that day, the police came to the house and arrested her.

Louie was better known to English officials as Louisa Gomersal, a thief and prostitute, and now she was wanted on charges of murder. Gomersal had lied to Calvert about the pregnancy and left to find a baby. She took a room in a boarding house run by Lily Waterhouse, and found a 17-year-old girl willing to give up her baby. While she waited for the baby to be born, Gomersal stole from Waterhouse. The 40-year-old spiritualist, who had already confronted the hot-tempered Louisa, went to the police with her complaint. Waterhouse was found dead the next day. A letter in the rooming house led authorities to Calvert's home. Police found cutlery in the bag which supposedly contained baby clothes. Gomersal was found Guilty of murder and her plea of pregnancy was disregarded. Before her execution, Louie Calvert admitted also killing John Frobisher and dumping his body in a canal in 1922.

REF.: Butler, *Murderers' England*; *CBA*.

Jackson, Mary Jane (AKA: **Bricktop**), b.1836, U.S., pros.-mur. Born in New Orleans, Mary Jane Jackson became a prostitute at the age of fourteen. Known as Bricktop because of her red hair, she was feared throughout the city. Her blood lust and physical prowess made her notorious as the toughest woman the French Quarter had ever known. When her former lover, a Poydras Street bartender, evicted her, Jackson dashed into his bar and beat him so viciously that he lost an ear and part of his nose. She then went to work at Archie Murphy's Gallatin Street Dance-House. Around 1856, she beat a man to death with a huge club, and later murdered a seven-footer named Long Charley with a custom-designed knife that had two five-inch blades on either side of a silver grip. With this knife, Jackson "could slash, cut, and stab in any direction without changing the position of her hand." After losing the business of intimidated customers, Murphy turned Jackson out of his bordello.

Jackson opened her own house on Dauphine Street, adding to her staff three women almost as violent as herself—Delia Swift, a lethal prostitute better known as Bridget Fury; America Williams, a six-foot amazon who enjoyed cracking skulls; and Ellen Collins, another tough fighter. After Jackson, Swift was the most feared female in the quarter, with a reputation that followed her from her days as a 12-year-old prostitute in Cincinnati, Ohio. In 1858, Swift followed a customer who refused to pay to the Poydras Street Market where she buried an ax in his skull before hundreds of witnesses. Swift was sent to prison for life for the killing. On Nov. 7, 1859, Jackson, Collins, and Williams were drinking at a beer garden on Rampart and St. Peter streets when Laurent Fleury, sitting at a nearby table, foolishly criticized their manners. When Jackson swore at him, Fleury reached over and slapped her. Within seconds, all three women attacked him. When restaurant owner Joe Seidensahl tried to defend Fleury, Jackson slashed him repeatedly with her custom-made knife. A man tried to drive off the enraged women by firing a shot at them from an upstairs window and was hit with a hail of bricks and rocks. Collins escaped over a fence, but Jackson and Williams were wrestled to the ground by two dozen policemen.

Seidensahl recovered, but Fleury died from his wounds. While in jail awaiting trial, Jackson met prison turnkey John Miller, a 29-year-old thug who had served time for murder. He bribed officials to make him a guard after his release so he could collect bribes from inmates in exchange for favors. Jackson's lawyer slipped the coroner some money and suggested that Fleury had succumbed to heart trouble. The coroner made an ambiguous decision on cause of death, and Jackson and Williams were released. Miller quit his job, and Jackson moved into his shack in Freetown and spent two years fighting brutally with him. They would sometimes knock each other unconscious, later making love with comparable ferocity in front of the broken-down cabin and local residents. In October 1861, Jackson cut Miller up with her personalized double blade, and went back to New Orleans. After he recovered, Miller begged Jackson to return to him. When she did, on Dec. 5, 1861, he attacked her with a bullwhip, yelling, "You're getting too fresh, whore! You need a good thrashing to cure your evil ways!" Wrestling the whip away in seconds, Jackson began beating Miller with it. He swung at her head with a ball and chain attached to the stump of his left arm, but she ducked and pulled him toward her. He tried to cut her throat, but she bit his hand and got the knife, which she drove into him five times, killing him.

Arrested and imprisoned for Miller's murder, Jackson was described in the *Daily Crescent* as "remarkable for bestial habits and ferocious manners." She was convicted and sent to prison, but was released by Union general George F. Shepley after the fall of New Orleans in 1862. To show his contempt for the South, Shepley freed all felons from Southern jails. Jackson fled New Orleans and was never heard from again.

REF.: *CBA*; Nash, *Look For the Woman*.

Jackson, R.E., prom. 1962, and **Jackson, Clemmie**, 1943- , U.S., mur. At sixty-one years of age, Samuel L. Resnick suffered from incurable cancer, heart trouble, and diabetes. The jeweler from Albany, N.Y., had retired to Phoenix, Ariz., and now he wanted to die there. He scanned the job-wanted ads in the newspapers each day for someone to end his pain. At least five men turned Resnick down when he asked them to kill him. Resnick finally contacted Clemmie Jackson, a Texas farmhand who had arrived in Arizona with dreams of owning a car wash.

Jackson first refused to have any part of the murder plot, but when Resnick promised the 19-year-old enough money to open his own business, Jackson agreed. Jackson recruited his brother, R.E. Jackson, and three other youths to help. Resnick promised the young men cash and jewelry and drove with four of them into the desert just north of Phoenix. By this time, Clemmie Jackson had backed out. When the youths tried to strangle Resnick to death, the rope broke. Resnick then assisted the amateur murderers in completing their task. The killers ended up with $3,000 worth of jewelry, but no cash. Three days later the body was discovered and the youths had left so many clues that they were quickly apprehended. The four conspirators were all tried, convicted and sentenced to life imprisonment. Clemmie Jackson was acquitted.

REF.: *CBA*; Wyden, *The Hired Killers*.

Jackson, Robert Houghwout, 1892-1954, U.S., atty. gen.-jur. Launched political career working in Franklin D. Roosevelt's first successful bid for the presidency. He was appointed by President Roosevelt as general counsel for the Bureau of Internal Revenue in 1934, and successfully prosecuted the heavily-publicized $750,000 income tax suit against Andrew W. Mellon, a former secretary of the treasury. He joined the newly-created Securities and Exchange Commission as special counsel in 1935, held office as assistant attorney general from 1936-38, and later headed the anti-trust division of the Department of Justice. He served as solicitor general from 1938-39, and was named to the Roosevelt cabinet as attorney general in 1940, a post he held until 1941, when he was appointed to the Supreme Court. He had a conservative reputation on the Court. He was appointed to the International Military Tribunal by President Harry S. Truman in 1945, and served as the chief U.S. prosecuting attorney at the first Nuremberg trial, and received the Medal of Merit from President Truman in 1946. Returning to the Court as an associate justice, he continued to vote conservatively.

REF.: *CBA*; Lowenthal, *The FBI*; Nash, *Citizen Hoover*; Toledano, *J. Edgar Hoover*; Wicker, *Investigating the FBI*.

Jackson, Scott, and **Walling, Alonzo M.**, d.1897, U.S., mur. At 8 a.m. on Feb. 1, 1896, John Hewling, a young boy going through the woods near Fort Thomas, Ky., came upon the awful sight of a headless female body. He dashed to the house of a nearby farmer who called police. The decapitated corpse was removed to Newport, Ky., where it was examined. No identification could be immediately made which was obviously the purpose of those who had beheaded the victim. The body was dressed only in undergarments but it was determined that the corpse was that of a young woman in her early twenties. A careful search of the area where the body had been found was made and detectives turned up a single female glove which bore the manufacturer, Lewis & Hayes of Greencastle, Ind. Investigators learned that this glove had been sold to a Pearl Bryan of Greencastle. Her father, A.S. Bryan, a wealthy Greencastle farmer, was notified and he traveled to Newport where he identified his child from birthmarks. Bryan had no idea why anyone would want to murder his daughter, who had left home to visit friends in Indianapolis on Jan. 26, 1896.

Further investigation revealed that Pearl Bryan had not gone to Indianapolis on that date but to Cincinnati where she met a young dental student, Scott Jackson, whom she had been secretly seeing. She became pregnant and, fearing exposure, Jackson promised to arrange an abortion. Jackson was arrested in Cincinnati on Feb. 5, 1896, along with his fellow student and roommate, Alonzo M. Walling. After some routine questioning, Walling was released but Jackson was held on a murder charge.

The youth admitted that he had met Pearl Bryan in Greencastle in the summer of 1895, while visiting his mother and that the two had fallen in love. He insisted that another young man in Greencastle, Will Wood, had had an affair with Pearl before he had met her and that she was pregnant with Wood's child, not his. Wood was then arrested but he convinced authorities that Jackson had made the woman pregnant and that Jackson and Walling were responsible for her murder, a claim he would later uphold in court when testifying against Jackson.

A waiter working in a Cincinnati saloon came forward and told police that he had seen Jackson and Walling in the saloon on the night of Jan. 31, 1896, accompanied by a young woman whom he identified as Pearl Bryan, after looking at a family photo. The waiter said he overheard Jackson telling Walling: "I would like to have a woman's head to dissect." Walling was again arrested and charged with murder along with Jackson. Both young men quickly began to accuse the other of the killing. Walling stated that Jackson had murdered his sweetheart by promising her that he and Walling would perform an abortion on her. Instead, he injected her with prussic acid or cocaine, he was not sure which. Jackson insisted that it was Walling who had agreed to perform the operation, panicked at the last minute, and then injected Pearl with a lethal dose of morphine. The corpse was examined and cocaine was found. Both men accused the other of cutting off the woman's head after she had died from the injection. Blood-coated trousers Walling had worn were found hidden in his room and Jackson's bloody coat was fished out of a Cincinnati sewer where Walling said he had thrown it.

A coroner's jury in Jackson County, Ky., where the body was found, sifted the evidence and concluded that Pearl Bryan had been taken to Jackson's room in Cincinnati and was there given a lethal dose of morphine either by Jackson or Walling. She was unconscious but alive when one or the other man, or both, then cut off her head. This occurred at the burial site of the headless corpse which was in Kentucky and had jurisdiction of the case. The two men were tried in Newport, Ky. There, on Apr. 22, 1896, Jackson was tried separately. Several persons testified against him, including Will Wood, who had quoted incriminating letters he had received from Jackson. George H. Jackson (no relation to the accused), a carriage driver, then testified that on the night of Jan. 31, 1896, Walling paid him $5 to take him, a man, and a woman to a remote spot around Fort Thomas, Ky. Walling sat with him on the driver's seat and Jackson and Pearl Bryan sat inside the enclosed carriage.

Artist's drawing of Jackson and Walling leading Pearl Bryan to her death.

When the driver heard strange noises coming from within the carriage, he got frightened and tried to jump from the driver's seat and flee but Walling stopped him, putting a revolver to his head and saying: "You drive that horse or I'll make an end of you very quickly." Jackson continued to drive the carriage as instructed by Walling, who told the driver as they neared the burial site: "If we get into any trouble, we have friends on the outside who would follow you up and kill you." Jackson said that Walling ordered him to halt on a lonely road near a thicket and that he and his friend were going to take a woman through the thicket to a house of a friend and leave her there and then would return. Walling again threatened Jackson that if he did not wait for them, he would be sought out and murdered. "The man in the surrey got out first and helped the woman," Jackson testified. "She leaned on him heavily and as she walked, she dragged her feet. It was too dark for me to see anything." He went on to say that Walling got down from the driver's seat and helped Jackson support the woman, who seemed to be half-conscious and wore a thick black veil over her face. After some minutes, Jackson reported: "I heard a very queer noise, something like scuffling in the leaves, along with a noise that I cannot describe, that I think was made by a woman. It sounded like a woman's cry in distress." He said he then leaped from the carriage and ran off down the road. He did not arrive at his Cincinnati home until eight hours later.

Scott Jackson was convicted of murdering Pearl Bryan. Walling asked for a change of venue and was tried in an adjoining county but the legal move made no difference. He, too, was convicted. Both men were sentenced to death. They filed many appeals but the Kentucky Supreme Court turned them down. On the day of execution, Mar. 20, 1897, Jackson reportedly made a full confession in which he stated that Walling was innocent of murdering Pearl Bryan. When he was told that this confession would not secure any clemency for him, he retracted his statement, saying that he was innocent and that Walling had committed the murder. Both men mounted the scaffold in Newport, where they stood glaring at each other. As the rope was placed about Jackson's neck, he said: "I am not guilty of the crime for which I am now supposed to pay the penalty of the law." Another rope went around Walling's neck and he was asked if he had any last words. "Nothing to say," Walling snapped, "only you are about to take the life of an innocent man! I call upon God to be my witness." According to a later report: "With this falsehood upon their lips, the two hardened wretches shot through the double trap and met death by slow strangulation." Pearl Bryan's head was never found.

REF.: *CBA; The Mysterious Murder of Pearl Bryan; Pearl Bryan or A Fatal Ending;* Pinkerton, *Murder in All Ages;* Poock, *Headless, Yet Identified.*

Jackson, Sergeant H., 1953- , U.S., (wrong. convict.) mur. When Sergeant H. Jackson was on trial for the murder of a San Diego gas station attendant in February 1974, he swore he was in church when Robert Hoke was killed. Hoke's wife identified a wallet found on Jackson when he was arrested as her husband's. After first claiming he received the wallet from relatives, Jackson admitted that two friends had taken it in a burglary. He also denied that he had confessed to a prosecution witness. Jackson was found Guilty and taken to a medium security prison in Tracy, Calif.

Seven months later, Charles R. Blunt confessed to the murder and named Andrew Donelly as his accomplice. The charges against Jackson were dismissed and he was freed in October. A jury award of $280,000 for false imprisonment was overturned by a judge who said Jackson was eligible for compensation only for the time he was under warrantless arrest. As it turned out Jackson had been apprehended originally without a warrant. The city of San Diego paid Jackson $17,000. REF.: *CBA.*

Jackson, Terry (Silas Trim Bissell), 1942- , U.S., asslt.-bomb. In 1979, Judith Emily Bissell was convicted of conspiring to damage federal property during a 1970 anti-war protest at the University of Washington. Eight years later, in 1987, Silas Trim Bissell was arrested in Eugene, Ore., and charged with the same crime. Bissell and his wife, who separated in the mid-1970s, had been members of the Weathermen, a radical organization opposed to U.S. involvement in Vietnam. They went underground in 1970 after being charged with trying to blow up an ROTC building on the Seattle campus. The bomb never exploded.

While underground, Silas Bissell changed his name to Terry Jackson and earned a master's degree in physical therapy. When Jackson was arrested on Jan. 20, 1987, he was working as a physical therapist. Jackson pleaded guilty to a federal charge of possessing an unregistered destruction device after the government dropped a conspiracy charge. On June 26, Bissell, of the Bissell carpet cleaning family, was sentenced to two years in prison. The defendant and his attorneys argued that he should be treated leniently based on his recent peaceful behavior. U.S. District Court Judge Walter McGovern rejected the argument. REF.: *CBA*.

Jackson, Theresa, 1946-   , U.S., forg.-child abuse. Tina Mancini was just seventeen when she put a gun in her mouth and ended her life in March 1986. Nineteen months later, Mancini's mother, Theresa Jackson, was on trial for forgery, child abuse, and procuring a sexual performance by a child. Three months before Mancini committed suicide, Jackson forged the signature of the girl's father, a notary public, on her birth certificate. Jackson then found a job for her daughter as a topless dancer in the Ft. Lauderdale, Fla., area and lived off Tina's earnings.

The state charged that Mancini's being forced to dance nude caused her depression and resulted in suicide. "Taking your daughter to a naked bar and watching her dance is not a proper thing for a mother to do—or acceptable," said Broward Circuit Court Judge Arthur Franza before sentencing Jackson, in January 1988, to a year in jail on the forgery charge, two years of community control, and three years' probation. REF.: *CBA*.

Jackson, Thomas Henry, prom. 1929, Case of, Brit., mur. Thomas Henry Jackson and his wife Kate Jackson lived in Kenilworth, Lymesand, The Mumbles, near Swansea, England. On Feb. 4, 1929, Mrs. Jackson returned from the movies with her neighbor, Mrs. Dimick, around 10 p.m. Dimick was not yet inside her house when she heard loud screams coming from the Jackson cottage. She ran over to find Mrs. Jackson bleeding profusely from head wounds, unconscious in her husband's arms. She died two days later in the hospital, never having regained consciousness. Jackson said he had been sleeping and was awakened by his wife's cries. Detectives found a tire wrench under a cushion in the bungalow. Although it was proved that this was not the murder weapon, Jackson was accused and stood trial the following July at the Glamorgan Assizes at Swansea before Justice Wright, with Trevor Hunt for the prosecution and Jenkin Jines for the defense.

At the trial, it came out that Mrs. Jackson had been a part-time prostitute, specializing in married men who could be blackmailed. One of her victims, who had embezzled more than £20,000 to pay her, spent five years in jail for his crime. She received several anonymous, threatening letters, including one that read:

Dear Madame,

We are still watching and waiting. The pleasure is ours. When you don't expect us we will drop on you, and when we have finished with you your own mother won't know you. You foul thing. Call yourself a woman, do you? You are a disgrace to the name. How many more men have you blackmailed until they have to pinch money to shut you up?

Although the prosecutors contended that Jackson had written the letters to divert suspicion from himself, the allegation was never proved. After an hour of deliberation, the jury returned to acquit Jackson.
REF.: Adam, *Murder Most Mysterious; CBA*; Nash, *Open Files*; Shew, *A Second Companion to Murder*.

Jackson, William, b.c.1737-95, Brit., treas. Edited the daily *Public Ledger*, a radical London newspaper. He moved to France to support the revolution. After seeking the aid of the United Irishmen Society in backing a French invasion of England in 1794, he was arrested and convicted of treason, and committed suicide.
REF.: *CBA*; Mitchell, *The Newgate Calendar*.

Jackson-Dickinson Duel, 1806, U.S., duel-mur. Before Andrew Jackson became a commander at the Battle of New Orleans or the seventh president of the U.S., he fought a personal battle with Charles Dickinson, a Tennessee lawyer, who had insulted Jackson's wife, Rachel. Jackson challenged Dickinson to a duel, and Dickinson immediately accepted.

At the agreed-upon site outside of Nashville, lots were drawn. Dickinson won the first shot and Jackson was to be allowed to give the word to fire. The two men faced each other at a distance of twenty-four feet, and, after being asked if they were ready, Jackson's second, a man named Overton, gave the order to fire. Dickinson, one of the best shots in Tennessee, fired and hit Jackson near the heart, but the future politician remained standing and prepared to return the shot. Jackson's bullet hit Dickinson in the hip and travelled through the body to the opposite side. Bleeding profusely, Dickinson collapsed.

While walking away from the site with Overton, Jackson confided that he had indeed been struck, but he didn't want to give Dickinson the satisfaction that his aim had been accurate. Dickinson's internal bleeding could not be stopped, and he died the same evening in a nearby house. Dickinson's bullet had lodged near two of Jackson's ribs, but had done no internal damage and Jackson carried the bullet in his chest for the rest of his life, because it was too close to his heart to remove. See: **Jackson, Andrew**. REF.: *CBA*.

Jack the Dropper, See: **Kaplan, Nathan**.

Jack the Ripper, prom. 1888, Brit., mur. No other killer in British history rivaled that of the gruesome, mocking, utterly superior Jack the Ripper, a multiple murderer whose arrogance and boldness defied the entire police department of London and held in terror a great city for as long as he cared to roam its streets and slay at will. He was a murderous braggart who gave himself his own grim name, publicly signing "Jack the Ripper" in notes and letters to the authorities to taunt them. His ability to kill whenever an evil whim urged and the inability of the police to apprehend him indelibly stamped his black fame in the minds of all, from the street urchins of the East End to Queen Victoria fretting over his identity in her palace. From the notorious reputation the Ripper has gleaned in more than a century, one might assume that he slaughtered dozens or more helpless victims. The truth, according to most authorities past and present, is that Jack the Ripper killed five women within a ten-week period, from Aug. 31 to Nov. 9, 1888. Other killings before and after that were also attributed to bloody Jack but they differed, some radically so, in style and method and were most likely the dark deeds of others.

Some diehard Ripperologists insist that this mass murderer slew as many as nine or more female victims, from April 1888 to February 1891, and perhaps beyond. But the five *definitive* Ripper slayings were unmistakably his handiwork. All five women had their throats slashed, were disemboweled and mutilated; the killer paid obsessive attention to the destruction of female organs. Not only did he dare the police to find and arrest him, he proved his identity by proudly sending human remains to authorities. In one instance, he actually foretold a "double event," one in which he would murder two women on the same night, a haughty prediction which came all too true. The Metropolitan Police of London seemed inept and powerless to stop the fiend from his appointed murderous rounds. They had never before had to contend with such a monster who killed purely for the sadistic pleasure of killing.

Pressured by the Crown, the press, and the public, the police, under the direction of Sir Charles Warren, frantically exhausted their forces in futile searches and wild speculations unconnected to the slim facts unearthed. The East End of London, where the murders occurred, was infested with thousands of criminals and prostitutes. There were sixty-two brothels in this area in the year 1888, and 233 lodging houses catered to whores. Inside these dirty little rooms, heated by small charcoal-burning stoves and lighted by a single candle, thousands of assignations occurred each night. There was no way in which the police could monitor these one-night stands and check each prostitute's customers. It was clear from the start that the Ripper had chosen one sort of person to murder, whores, but these hapless, diseased creatures, ranging in age from their late teens to their seventies, outnumbered on-duty police fifty to one.

Most of those prostitutes plying their trade in the East End were middle-aged, alcoholic females. They had no education for the most part and invariably were infected with myriad venereal diseases. One such was Emma Elizabeth Smith, forty-five, who, on the night of Apr. 3, 1888, was fatally assaulted while returning to her single small room at 18 George Street, Spitafields. Earlier, Smith had been seen soliciting a well-dressed gentleman who wore a dark suit and sported a white scarf. A constable saw Smith staggering toward the door of her lodging house. She collapsed in his arms, babbling about being attacked earlier by four men on Osborn Street. She thought one of these assailants had been a teenager but was not sure. The men had beaten her about the face and had slashed off her ear. Worse, these attackers had brutally inserted a foreign object in her vagina and broken it off. Emma Smith died of peritonitis a few hours later.

The next killing often attributed to the Ripper, and more in keeping with his grisly *modus operandi,* was that of Martha Tabram (or Turner), another middle-aged prostitute. Stabbed no fewer than thirty-nine times, she was discovered dead at 3 a.m. on Aug. 7, 1888, at George Yard Landing, later Gunthorpe Street, in Whitechapel. The killer had paid particular attention to Tabram's female organs and parts, as most of the fatal wounds were administered in these areas.

Police were baffled at these first two attacks. Both occurring in the early morning hours, these killings involved women who had been seen only a few hours before they were found dying or dead. In neither instance was anyone seen running from the area, and neither victim had called out or given an alarm that would have been heard in the densely populated districts. It was assumed that Smith and Tabram had solicited men who pretended to buy their sexual favors and, when they turned their backs to prepare for a street assignation, who had slashed them to death and quietly left the area.

Mary Ann "Polly" Nichols, age forty-two, was the next victim, the first of the Ripper victims, according to dedicated Ripperologists. She was an alcoholic harridan who was known for her barroom brawls. A tough and uncompromising harlot, Nichols could have put up a ferocious fight for her life but she was apparently given no chance to do so by her killer. Her body was found on Buck's Row by a patrolling constable at 3:15 a.m. on Aug. 31, 1888. The Ripper had slashed her throat twice, two incisions about an inch apart so deep that the blade had cut to the vertebrae. The victim was almost decapitated.

When the body was taken to the Old Montague Street Workhouse morgue, further inspection revealed deep slashes on Nichols' abdomen and in the area of the vagina, but no organs had actually been removed. It was later speculated that the Ripper had had no time to perform this grisly chore since he was probably interrupted by the approaching footsteps of the constable and fled. However, five front teeth of the victim were missing. It was not reported if these teeth had been removed by the killer or lost when the victim was still alive. Again, the victim had not cried out, even though she was apparently standing beneath the open window of a bedroom where another woman was sleeping.

The depth and width of the wounds, especially around the neck, caused examining doctors to believe that the killer had employed a blade from six to eight inches long. Since the incisions had been made cleanly and appropriately across the jugular vein to assure death, the examiners also speculated that the killer possessed some medical experience or knowledge of post-mortem operations. Nichols had been married but had left her husband, William Nichols, who was brought to the morgue to identify the mutilated remains of his estranged spouse. At first reluctant to look upon the corpse and bitterly complaining that his wife had left a good home to turn to prostitution more than three years ago, Nichols said that he did not wish to look upon her again. He did, however, view the remains and then he sobbed, while staring at the corpse and saying: "I forgive you for everything, now that I see you like this!"

After three prostitutes had been murdered, police concluded that if these victims had the same killer, he had no motive for

murdering them except for an abiding hatred for whores. Detectives fanned out through the East End, searching for any man who had mistreated prostitutes. The name "Leather Apron" kept recurring in their investigations. "Leather Apron" turned out to be a bootmaker named John Pizer who had manhandled and pushed about prostitutes when he was drinking in the lowlife pubs of Whitechapel. Pizer, who earned his sobriquet from a leather apron he wore when repairing boots, occupied his cramped workshop-lodgings, and many small, sharp knives were found on the premises. Pizer told police that the knives were essential to his bootmaking trade, and he demonstrated their uses. Moreover, his family swore that he was at home when all three of the previous murders had occurred. He was interrogated at length and then released.

While the police had been looking for Leather Apron, constables picked up a strange-acting character named William Piggott, who bore a close resemblance to Pizer. This man had been drinking heavily in a Gravesend pub and had begun to talk to himself and chant incoherently, alarming the proprietor who called police. His clothes and one hand were bloodstained and, after considerable questioning, Piggot told detectives that he had gone to aid of a woman who had been having some sort of fit. As he steadied her, he said, she grabbed his hand and bit it so hard that she pierced the flesh, causing blood to flow. The story sounded fabricated, and Piggott was held for further questioning. He was placed in a cell but the minute he was behind bars, he began to howl like a dog and bang his head against the walls and bars of the cell. Doctors were called and quickly pronounced Piggott insane. He was removed to a lunatic asylum.

The press by this time was screaming alarm about a berserk killer, an unnamed fiend who lurked in the shadowy lanes and narrow streets of the East End, murdering women at random while police seemed powerless to stop him. The slaying of Nichols was the third murder that could realistically be attributed to the Ripper. At that time, the newspapers had taken notice of the first two murders, that of Smith and Tabram, and had coupled these killings to the Nichols slaying, attributing all three killings to the same man. Irrespective of the hindsight Ripperologists of a century later that insisted Nichols was the first true Ripper victim, the press of the day considered her the *third* victim and part of a one-person murder spree. All three women, Smith, Tabram and Nichols, were whores, and all three were middle-aged and down on their luck. All three were abroad in the early morning hours, and all three were found on lonely, narrow lanes with no one about.

What continued to perplex the police was the fact that not a single person had seen these women in anyone's company near the time of death and, even more puzzling, none of the victims had cried out. However, the Metropolitan Police of London did not, at that time, have investigative branches that specialized in types of crime, including prostitution. Had a vice squad as such existed at the time, police would have known *why* none of the victims before and after this time gave no call of alarm. No police officer ever came forward to describe the methods of the street whores in relationship to the murder method of Jack the Ripper. The victims simply had no idea that they were about to be killed and never saw the long, sharp knife that Jack the Ripper wielded when he so clinically cut their throats. The practice of street whores in London at the time was to solicit customers and go to an out-of-the-way corner or back lot or alleyway to have a quick assignation. Invariably, the whore turned her back on the customer and flipped up her skirts, allowing entry from behind. Standing unseen behind the victim, Jack withdrew his knife from the black surgical bag he carried, came close to the woman bending over in front of him, then reached forward, bringing the knife over the shoulder of his victim and with one or two slashes across her neck, cut her throat from behind. Pulling the knife toward him while pushing the weight of the victim away from him, the killer unleashed great force against the blade, almost severing the necks of his victims. Moreover, by killing in this manner, the

GHASTLY
MURDER
IN THE EAST-END.
DREADFUL MUTILATION OF A WOMAN.
Capture : Leather Apron

Ripper victims, left, Annie Chapman, middle, Elizabeth Stride, and, right, a broadside of the day announcing the fiend's handywork.

Ripper victims, left, Mary Kelly, and, right, a policeman discovering the body of Mary Ann Nichols.

A typical Ripper suspect, left, as envisioned by artists of the day, and, right, the image of the murderer stalking London in 1888.

Ripper avoided being spattered with blood. The blood shot out from the front of the victim, in the opposite direction of Jack, who was behind the victim. In this way, he avoided soaking his clothes with blood. Without being covered with blood, Jack was able to return home without drawing suspicion upon himself.

As the killings continued, the residents of the East End, especially Whitechapel, the hub of the killing area, panicked. No one talked of anything but the deranged cutthroat who roamed their streets, murdering at will. Police were openly jeered and derided as they made their rounds. When would the monster strike again? Terrified residents had not long to wait. Eight nights after the slaying of Nichols, on Sept. 8, 1888, the Ripper struck again. Annie Chapman, a 47-year-old prostitute, drunk and bragging through the pubs of Whitechapel that she would know how to deal with the killer if he came her way, staggered down Dorset Street in the early morning hours. She asked for a room at a cheap boarding house but, not having enough money, she was turned away.

Chapman lurched down the street and turned into narrow Hanbury Street. Here she was seen by a woman to stop and talk to a stranger who was later described as about 40-years-old, wearing dark clothes, with a dark complexion which marked him as a foreigner. He was described as a "gentleman." Chapman was seen to talk to this man in a friendly manner at 5:30 a.m. The "gentleman," according to the witness, a park keeper's wife, wore a duck-billed deerstalker hat later associated with Sherlock Holmes. The stranger was heard to say to Chapman: "Will you?" Chapman was heard to reply: "Yes." The two went down the street arm-in-arm.

A half hour later, Annie Chapman's chopped up corpse was found in a small yard behind 29 Hanbury Street. Chapman had been nearly decapitated and her head was held by a strand of flesh and some bone to her torso by a scarf she had been wearing when last seen alive. Chapman was found lying on her back with her legs drawn up, her left arm resting on her left breast. Her body has been savagely mutilated. A doctor who examined the corpse at the scene of the crime tersely reported: "...small intestines and flap of the abdomen lying on the right side above right shoulder attached by a cord with the rest of the intestines inside the body, two flaps of skin from the lower part of the abdomen lying in a large quantity of blood above the left shoulder; throat cut deeply from left and back in jagged manner right around the throat." In addition, two front teeth were missing from Chapman's mouth. Even more gruesome was the fact that the murderer had removed the victim's kidney and ovaries from the body and taken them with him.

A piece of leather was too conveniently left under a nearby tap. Police reasoned that the killer believed that authorities were still seeking Leather Apron, although Pizer was found and cleared two days after Chapman's murder. This seemed to be a calculated move on the part of the murderer to pin the blame for the crimes on the suspect Leather Apron. The killer also left another false clue, a piece of a blood-soaked envelope with the crest of the Sussex Regiment upon it. The murderer was undoubtedly a newspaper reader who kept the clips reporting all the murders.

It had been reported that several hours before her death Martha Tabram had been seen by witnesses in the company of a soldier. Her wounds were later described as possibly having been inflicted by a soldier's knife or bayonet. It was well known that witnesses who had seen the soldier with Tabram had scrutinized a whole company of soldiers from the Tower who were paraded before them. Not one was identified. Obviously, the Ripper planted the torn piece of envelope to cause police to believe that a soldier still might be the culprit. Detectives, however, believed this clue was too obvious and ignored the idea of searching for a military man.

Twenty days after the slaying of Annie Chapman, the killer identified himself for the first time as Jack the Ripper by mailing a letter to the Central News Agency on Sept. 28, 1888. Dated three days earlier, it read:

Dear Boss,

I keep on hearing that the police have caught me but they won't fix me just yet. I have laughed when they look so clever and talk about being on the right track. That joke is about Leather Apron gave me real fits. (This was undoubtedly a reference to the false clue the Ripper left behind after the Chapman killing.) I am down on whores and I shan't quit ripping them until I do get buckled. Grand work the last job was. I gave the lady no time to squeal. (Another reference to Chapman, the killer was taunting police with his knowledge that he murdered the woman only a short distance from a boarding house where seventeen people were sleeping in rooms with open windows.) How can they catch me now. I love my work and want to start again. You will soon hear of me with my funny little games. I saved some of the proper red stuff (blood from Chapman who had been drained of blood) in a ginger beer bottle over the last job to write with but it went thick like glue and I can't use it. Red ink is fit enough I hope *ha ha*. The next job I do I shall clip the lady's ears off and send to the police officers just for jolly wouldn't you. Keep this letter back till I do a bit more work, then give it out straight. My knife is nice and sharp and I want to get to work right away if I get a chance. Good luck.

Yours truly, Jack the Ripper

Don't mind me giving the trade name. Wasn't good enough to post this before I got all the red ink off my hands, curse it.

The postscript to this letter refers to physicians who examined the wounds made on the bodies of the Ripper's victims and stated the possibility of the killer being an unhinged doctor or a demented medical student, given the knowledge of the human anatomy and the surgical skill employed in making incisions and removing internal organs. A second letter arrived at the Central News Agency on Sept. 30, 1888, the day of the fourth murder (or second, depending upon at which point you begin counting), a murder which Jack brazenly predicted in this missive:

I was not codding dear old Boss when I gave you the tip. You'll hear about saucy Jack's work tomorrow. Double event this time. Number one squealed a bit. Couldn't finish straight off. Had not time to get ears for police. Thanks for keeping last letter back till I got to work again.

Jack the Ripper

After Jack attacked and murdered two more women in the predawn hours of Sept. 30, 1888, the so-called "double event," he immediately sat down and wrote to the Central News Agency, boasting of the killings, couching these murders as preplanned killings. The first of these victims was Elizabeth "Long Liz" Stride, a 45-year-old Swedish prostitute. Her real name was Elizabeth Gustaafsdotter, and she was also known on police blotters as Annie Fitzgerald. At 1 a.m., Louis Deimschutz, a delivery man, drove his horse-drawn cart into the back yard of the International Working Men's Education Club on Berner Street, near Commercial Road. Clattering noisily over the cobblestones, he suddenly brought his cart to an abrupt halt when he saw a body stretched before him.

Deimschutz jumped from the cart and ran to the body of Long Liz Stride. It was warm to his touch and there was a great pool of blood, more than two quarts according to later estimates, welling about the corpse. The victim's throat had been slashed, a long, deep incision, but the Ripper had apparently been interrupted by the delivery man and had fled at the sound of his approaching cart. (He had said in his recent missive: "Couldn't finish straight off.")

At the time Jack was attacking Stride, another harlot, 43-year-old Catherine Eddowes, had been released from the Bishopsgate Police Station, where she had been placed behind bars some hours earlier for creating a drunken disturbance. Police were later criticized for turning this woman out at the very time of night when they knew the Ripper was most actively seeking prostitutes to murder. A constable stood at the entrance to the station and saw Eddowes emerge. She turned to him and said: "Night, old cock." She then walked toward Mitre Square, Houndsditch, and painful death.

At about 1:30 a.m., Eddowes met the man known as Jack the Ripper and undoubtedly agreed to sexually service him, going off toward Mitre Square with the fiend. Within fifteen minutes, Jack had slit her throat, viciously slashed her face, even nicking her eyelids with his slashing knife, then cut at her ears, which were left attached. ("Had not time to get ears for police," the maniac had written.) He had disemboweled Eddowes, slicing through the abdomen and removing the left kidney and entrails. The intestines, as had been the case with Annie Chapman, had been strangely thrown over the shoulder. A constable turned into tiny Mitre Square and in the corner of this area thought he saw a pile of rags. He turned his light upon the heap of clothing to find the bloody remains of Catherine Eddowes.

These two killings sent the whole of London into a panic. Police Commissioner Warren sputtered apologies and promises before a disturbed Queen Victoria, who demanded action. She wanted the monster caught no matter the cost and time to the police. Warren told her that everything possible was being done to find and arrest this fiend. He stated that he had special bloodhounds out in the streets and that he was considering newly designed rubber-soled shoes for his policemen. Warren explained to the queen that the hob-nailed boots then worn clattered loudly on cobblestones and could be heard for some distance, undoubtedly warning the Ripper of an approaching constable. The new rubber-soled shoes would allow policemen to approach in almost total silence. The queen merely clucked her disgust with such inane, straw-clutching proposals.

Meanwhile, George Lusk, a volatile resident of Whitechapel, had formed the Whitechapel Vigilance Committee, and he loudly proclaimed that if the police could not catch the Ripper then he and his bully boys, now hunting Jack in the streets in armed groups, would locate the killer and lynch him from the nearest lamppost. Lusk had been warned by police not to take matters into his own hands, but Lusk and his pub-crawling supporters sneered at the authorities, labeling them do-nothings. On Oct. 16, 1888, Lusk received a small package and a note reading:

From Hell

Mr. Lusk:

   Sir I send you half the Kidne I took from one woman prasarved it for you tother piece I fried and ate it was very nise I may send you the bloody knif that took it out if you only wate a whil longer signed Catch me when you can Mishter Lusk

Inside the small package, Lusk found a human kidney and this was matched to the remains of Catherine Eddowes. This message and grisly package proved to be one of the genuine missives sent by Jack the Ripper. By this time, there were scores of pranksters and disturbed London residents inundating the police with messages and letters claiming to be from the notorious Jack. The letter Lusk received was obviously disguised in ungrammatical text to convince authorities that Jack was an unschooled Irishman, particularly after the way he phonetically spelled the word "preserved" as "prasarved," giving the word a spelling in keeping with its pronunciation with a thick Irish accent.

None of this aided the police. Patrols were doubled, then tripled, and street prostitutes and inmates of bordellos were warned repeatedly to keep off the streets at night, but this was tantamount to telling these near destitute creatures to stop living.

Police headquarters and Scotland Yard saw a steady stream of pickets before their entrances, all demanding action. Buckingham Palace was swamped with petitions signed by thousands of citizens from all over London. These petitions were directed at Queen Victoria and asked her to bring this horror to an end. The queen was, of course, as powerless as the police. She spent many nervous hours deliberating over the matter. Victoria came to believe that the killer had to be a foreigner, a seaman visiting the fair city of London. It was inconceivable to her that the monster could be an Englishman. No native son, she was convinced, possessed the brutality, the bestial inclinations, to perform the kind of slaughterhouse acts committed by Jack the Ripper. He had to be an alien from foreign shores.

Victoria wrote to her home secretary: "Have the cattle boats and passenger boats been examined? Has an investigation been made as to the number of single men occupying rooms to themselves? The murderer's clothes must be saturated with blood and kept somewhere." Queen Victoria was aware of the woefully ineffectiveness of her policemen. Following the murder of Mary Kelly, supposedly the last of the Ripper's victims, Victoria wrote on Nov. 11, 1888, to Lord Salisbury, her prime minister: "All these courts must be lit and our detectives improved. They are not what they should be."

Jack the Ripper had become a national calamity. This was never more clearly illustrated than by the fact that Lord Salisbury actually convened a cabinet meeting specifically designed to deal with him. Yet little came of the meeting. Sir Charles Warren could only shake his head, stating once more that he had taken extraordinary measures to track down the Ripper, that he had set bloodhounds on the killer's trail. He failed to mention that the two bloodhounds employed for this purpose, Barnaby and Burgho, had been trained to follow what the police thought might be the scent of the killer, taken from the piece of leather and other scraps left at the scenes of the killings. Warren did not mention to Lord Salisbury that he himself had pretended to be Jack, having the bloodhounds following *his* scent to see if they could perform their duties and how he had run so far ahead of the dogs that he had lost them. The dogs themselves then broke loose, ran away, and had to be hunted down by other dogs and police. The use of the bloodhounds was an utter failure and was later lampooned in the press.

Warren was the worst sort of man to be in charge of this impossible case. He was an old-fashioned bureaucrat, one without imagination who followed traditional police methods that were obviously obsolete in dealing with a killer who murdered without apparent motive, selecting victims at random. Warren's concept of catching this lunatic was simply to throw more men into the dark, labyrinthine streets of Whitechapel and surrounding areas, but these dragnets were also useless. Four, sometimes six constables together clumped along noisily through the fog-bound alleyways, their approach so obvious that they might as well have been preceded by brass bands bleating bugles and thumping drums. The furtive and slinking Jack could easily avoid these large patrols. And who were they looking for, really? An obscure man wearing dark clothes, a "gentleman," a man wearing the commonly worn deerstalker hat? How would they know their man unless they actually caught Jack in the act, leaning over his victim, slicing away.

Warren also did not tell Lord Salisbury that he had wiped out clues as to the possible identity of the Ripper. Following the double killing of Stride and Eddowes, a constable had found a scrap of cloth soaked with blood, a piece of fabric torn from Eddowes' dress and apparently used to wipe off Jack's bloody knife. This bit of apron was found on Goulston Street near Mitre Square, and when the constable turned to a nearby wall and flashed his light upon it, he saw a message written there. It read:

> The juwes are not the
> men that will be blamed
> for nothing.

The wall writing had been done only a few hours after the Eddowes killing, according to authorities. Sir Charles Warren was called to the spot, he looked at the writing, and then quickly ordered the words wiped off the wall. It was obvious to him, or so he said, that the Ripper was attempting to place the responsibility for the killings on a Jew or a Jewish group of killers. Warren's apologists later claimed that the commissioner had acted in the best interest of the community—by wiping out this racial slur, he prevented anti-Semitic outbursts. There were tens of thousands of Jewish immigrants then living in London, with more arriving each day from the continent. Dislike for Jews was widespread. Yet Warren, in his zeal to keep the peace, had violated a cardinal rule of police work. He had destroyed evidence, important information that begged for analysis. By wiping away the Ripper's words, he made it impossible to have experts analyze the handwriting.

Warren had been motivated to destroy this wall note for another reason, some later argued. He was a high-ranking member of the Masons, the secret fraternal association, and he immediately recognized the peculiar spelling of the word "Juwes," instead of "Jews." This spelling was the ancient way of spelling the word in old Masonic rites. Warren feared that the true link to be made to this wall writing would be to the Masons. Moreover, the disemboweling of the victims, particularly in the instances where the entrails had been thrown over the right shoulder, was reportedly in keeping with ancient Masonic rites of sacrifice. It would be claimed, many years after, that Jack was a representative of a high-positioned radical Masonic group that had conspired to rid London of its plague of prostitutes.

On Nov. 9, 1888, Mary Jane Kelly, another prostitute, was murdered by Jack the Ripper. This was the most gruesome killing of all. Mary Jane Kelly, also known as Mary Ann Kelly or Mary Jeannette Kelly, was unlike all the previous victims. She was only twenty-four and was attractive and intelligent. She was in the prime of life and made a good living at her unsavory trade. Kelly had lived with a fish peddler until the couple quarreled and he moved out. She then turned to full-time prostitution, although she had practiced the trade on and off, even when living with other men. She maintained her own small lodgings, a first-floor room with a separate entrance at 13 Miller's Court near Dorset Street. Behind on her rent, Mary Kelly began to solicit men with regularity on Nov. 7, 1888. Two nights later, on Nov. 9, at 2 a.m., Mary Kelly approached a man she knew and tried to borrow six pence. He refused and, a few moments later, the man saw Kelly standing in the street talking to "a well-dressed gentleman."

Between 3:30 a.m. and 4 a.m., Elizabeth Praten, who lived in a room above Kelly's, heard Kelly cry out: "Oh, murder!" Praten was half asleep and thought she was having a dream. She went back to sleep. Such cries in that crime-infested area were commonplace and did not necessarily mean that someone was being murdered but that there was a domestic battle, a drunken brawl, at worst, a robbery taking place. At 10:45 a.m., rent collector Thomas Bowyer knocked on Kelly's door. Getting no response, he peered through the first-floor window and gasped in horror. Next to the bed close to the window, Bowyer saw two mounds of flesh, carved as if by a butcher, and on the bed, the gutted body of Mary Jane Kelly. There was a huge pool of blood beneath the bed. Bowyer ran for the owner who returned with him, looked into the window, and *then* summoned the police.

Police arrived and blocked off the small street, posting guards at the door to Kelly's small room. No officers entered the premises while detectives waited for Sir Charles Warren. The police commissioner had given strict orders that, in the event of another Ripper killing, he was to be summoned immediately and no officer was to do anything until his arrival. This day, however, was Lord Mayor's Day, and there were festivities and parades only a few blocks from the murder scene. News of the Kelly slaying was captured in headlines within a few hours, and newsboys by the dozens raced through the streets shouting: "Murder, horrible murder!" The Ripper had chosen this particular day, it

was later claimed, to upstage the lord mayor of London, such was Jack's bloated ego.

Warren could not be found, and finally other officers ordered Kelly's door broken down. A half dozen officers took turns battering the door with their shoulders and when it finally gave way, these burly men rushed inside, only to stagger outside again to retch from the awful carnage they had seen. There was very little left of Mary Kelly to examine. The Ripper had apparently spent more than an hour mutilating the corpse after murdering the woman by slitting her throat. This was the first murder he had committed indoors and he had taken his time in cutting up his victim, enjoying an orgy of bloodletting. It was Jack's most vile and disgusting crime. Even the doctors who arrived to make their official report found themselves queasy at the sight of the devastated remains of Mary Kelly. The report, published in its entirety the next day in *The Illustrated Police News,* read:

> The throat had been cut right across with a knife, nearly severing the head from the body. The abdomen had been partially ripped open, and both the breasts had been cut from the body. The left arm, like the head, hung to the body by the skin only. The nose had been cut off and the forehead skinned, and the thighs, down to the feet, stripped of the flesh. The abdomen had been slashed with a knife across downwards, and the liver and entrails wrenched away. The entrails and other portions of the frame were missing, but the liver, etc., were placed between the feet of this poor victim. The flesh from the thighs and legs, together with the breasts and nose, had been placed by the murderer on the table, and one of the hands of the dead woman had been pushed into her stomach.

This savage killing established a new hallmark in the history of British murder. Nothing like it had ever been seen or reported. The mutilation of Mary Kelly had been ferocious. The madman had indulged himself in the most bestial acts, taking his time as he sliced and cut away the remains. So much blood had been produced that Jack had to wipe it away with rags, which he burned in the small stove as he worked. These charred remains were later found in the grate. He had also burned a hat and portions of other clothes that may have been his own blood-soaked garments. Mary Kelly's daily clothes were found neatly folded on a nearby chair so it was assumed that she had entered the room with Jack, disrobed in front of him, and then went conveniently to the bed where, instead of making love, he reached out with his lethal knife. It may have been that the Ripper, coated with blood, had burned his own clothes and left by the window, where traces of blood were found, wearing only a long cloak and his boots.

When Police Commissioner Warren heard the news of the ghastly murder in Miller's Court, he only shook his head. He resigned his post a short time later, admitting his utter failure to capture the fiend. The killing of Mary Kelly, in the staunch opinion of most Ripperologists, was the last murder committed by Jack the Ripper, but there were at least two, perhaps three more murders occurring after this time, that could be attributed to Jack. They fit his *modus operandi* to some degree. Elizabeth Jackson's headless corpse was found floating in the Thames in June 1889. She was later identified from scars and was a known prostitute operating in the Chelsea area. On the night of July 17-18, 1889, Alice McKenzie, a prostitute working in Whitechapel, was found with her throat cut from ear to ear and her sex organs cut out. The last murder of any similarity close to the time of Jack's known killings was that of Frances Coles, a street whore commonly known as "Carroty Nell" because of her red hair. She was found on Feb. 13, 1891, in Swallow Gardens, Whitechapel, with her throat slashed and mutilations on her abdomen.

In the course of the last murder, Constable Ernest Thompson, out for the first time on night patrol, turned into Swallow Gardens and saw a man bending over Frances Coles. He stood up and fled, running at great speed and soon disappeared. Thompson

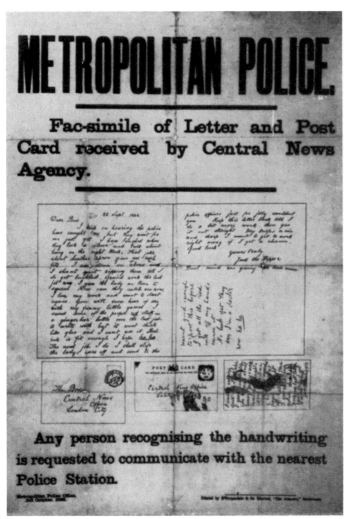

Police poster which reproduced a letter sent by the Ripper to authorities; tens of thousands of copies of this poster were distributed through the East End of London in hopes of identifying the killer's handwriting.

Various signatures purported to be that of Jack the Ripper, one of which was believed valid.

Dr. William Withey Gull, the Queen's physician and later a suspect, although too disabled to be the Ripper.

Sir Charles Warren, head of the Metropolitan Police, ineffective against the Ripper's random slayings.

Suspect James K. Stephen, mad, homosexual poet, rake and rapscallion, and friend of the Duke of Clarence.

Suspect Montague J. Druitt, a favorite candidate of the police; the Ripper killings stopped after his suicide by drowning in the Thames.

Suspect Thomas Neill Cream, poisoner of prostitutes, whose last words before falling through the trap were: "I am Jack—".

Suspect George Chapman, lady-killer, who worked as a barber's surgeon in Whitechapel during the Ripper murders. He was hanged twelve years later.

Suspect Prince Albert Victor, the Duke of Clarence, a Ripper taking revenge, according to some, for contracting lethal syphilis from a Whitechapel whore.

rushed to the side of the Coles who was still alive. She remained unconscious for a few hours, but doctors were unable to save her or to revive her so she gave no information about her killer. This may have been the only occasion where the Ripper was seen by a police officer, but Thompson's description of the man was vague at best since he did not get a good look at the man who was quite a distance from him when Thompson entered Swallow Gardens.

There were descriptions of Jack the Ripper, many of them, provided by witnesses who came forward to state that they had seen men with the women who were killed by the maniac. Jack was described as being short and stout, standing only five feet, five inches. He was also described as tall, five feet, ten inches, and slender. He was described as wearing the clothes of a gentleman, or those worn by the upper class: tailored suits, a deerstalker hat, a dark slouch hat, a derby, an Inverness cloak or a long dark coat, and, in many instances, carrying a small black bag, the type that doctor's or surgeons used. It was speculated that inside that bag Jack carried the tools of his horrific trade, his sharp knives, perhaps scalpels and other medical instruments. Jack was described by many as a "foreigner," a man who had a dark complexion and dark hair. It was not by happenstance that Jack, observed by others while talking to his victims-to-be, stood purposely in a way as to shield his face, either turning his back to others or standing in the shadows, the brim of his hat pulled low over his forehead in order to hide his face.

One of those who gave the most detailed description of the Ripper, if he was the Ripper, was George Hutchinson, who knew Mary Jane Kelly. He told police that he had seen Kelly only an hour before her murder, at 2 a.m. Hutchinson said that Kelly picked up a man while walking to her lodgings, a slender man who stood about five feet, six inches, with a pale face and a dark, thin mustache turned up at the ends. He was well-dressed and Hutchinson made a point of saying that the man looked "Jewish" to him, and that he would estimate his age at thirty-five. He wore a long, dark, well-tailored coat that hung loosely on him. Beneath the overcoat, he wore a dark-colored jacket and a light-colored waistcoat. A gleaming gold chain crossed the waistcoat from pocket to pocket. He also wore dark trousers with white-buttoned gaiters, a white shirt, a black tie, and an expensive horseshoe pin affixed to the tie. It was this description that would be fixed in the minds of all who thought about Jack the Ripper for decades to come, a dashing and handsome young man, wealthy, polite, a gentleman whose good looks and fine manner lured women into the arms of a homicidal maniac.

This man, Hutchinson observed, was standing on Thrawl Street and, as Kelly passed him, he gently tapped her on the shoulder. She stopped, smiled, and began talking to him. "All right," she was heard to say to the man.

"You will be all right for what I have told you," the man said in a low, smooth voice.

"All right, my dear," Kelly told the dark man. She put her arm around his shoulder and began to lead him toward her lodgings. "Come along. You will be comfortable."

The couple strolled past Hutchinson who followed them to Kelly's first-floor lodgings. They went inside and Hutchinson saw a candle being lit through the window. He stood some distance away from the small one-room flat, curious, he told police later, about such an aristocratic-looking customer. He wanted to see how long this man would stay with Kelly. Hutchinson left, he said, after about half an hour, which would make the time about 2:30 a.m. It was a short time after this, according to police estimates, that Jack the Ripper withdrew his knife and began to carve up Mary Kelly.

A few hours after police had arrived at the gory scene of Mary Kelly's blood-spattered room, a man who matched Hutchinson's description stopped before a Mrs. Paumier, who sold roasted chestnuts. He was a gentleman wearing a long dark coat, a black silk hat, and a thin black mustache turned up at the ends. He gripped a small black bag. "Have you heard that there has been another murder?" asked this man of Mrs. Paumier.

"I have," replied the chestnut vendor.

"I know more of it than you do," the handsome stranger said through a strange grin. He then walked away. Mrs. Paumier told police that this very same man had stopped three women, all prostitutes, on the night of Mary Kelly's murder, offering them money to go with him. All three women, for various reasons, refused. The third woman asked the man: "What's in that bag you're carrying?"

The well-dressed stranger began walking away, but said in a low, menacing voice: "Something the ladies don't like." When reports of the shiny black bag carried by the man thought to be the Ripper were published, these kind of bags, popular with doctors and professional people, suddenly went out of style. No one dared to carry this kind of bag lest he be suspected of being the worst murderer London had ever seen.

How, everyone asked, did the Ripper manage to leave Whitechapel and other murder areas? Police were everywhere in the streets after the bodies were discovered, covering all major exits of the district. One theory had it that Jack never left the district after committing murder. He simply went to one of thousands of small boarding houses and rented a cheap room for the night. At dawn, he washed, dressed, and casually left the area. Yet the identity of the Ripper has continued to plague police, psychiatrists, amateur sleuths, and crime historians. The police did have suspects, 176 of them, but none were charged with the killings. Theories abound to this day and many suspects were offered as likely candidates for the gory role of Jack the Ripper. None of these individuals were ever established as the real mass murderer. Some had criminal records, some were mad, some were entirely innocent, but their station in life and previous indiscretions caused sensation-seeking writers to brand them guilty. One of the most impossible of the suspects was a mad Russian physician, Dr. Alexander Pedachenko. He was reportedly sent to England by the Ochrana, the Czarist secret police, to embarrass British detectives. It was also claimed in another version of the Pedachenko tale that this madman had murdered several women in a fashion similar to that of the Ripper but, because of his high social position, was sent to England, where he continued his slaughtering ways. He was also known as Michael Ostrog, Mikhail Ostrong, Vassily Knoovalov, and Andrey Luiskovo. Pedachenko worked at a clinic in London's East End and reportedly treated Martha Tabram, Mary Nicholls, Annie Chapman, and Mary Kelly.

Pedachenko was reported to be the Ripper in a manuscript found in the basement of Gregory Rasputin after the Mad Monk's assassination in 1916. The manuscript, written in French, was examined by William Le Queux, a journalist, and his tale was later supported by mystery writers Sapper and E. Philips Oppenheim. But others have pointed out that Rasputin did not have a basement in his house, neither wrote nor read French, and was not the least interested in criminals. Dr. Thomas Dutton, a friend of Chief Inspector Frederick Abberline, believed that Pedachenko was the best suspect in the Ripper case, according to one report, but his reasons were never made public.

Sometime in late 1888, Pedachenko supposedly left London, returned to Russia, and lived in St. Petersburg (now Leningrad), where he killed a woman and was sent to a lunatic asylum for life. Sir Basil Thompson, head of Scotland Yard's Criminal Investigation Department, was convinced to his dying days that Pedachenko was Jack the Ripper.

Another medical man, Dr. Stanley by name, reportedly contracted syphilis from Mary Kelly and went in search of her, killing off her friends and associates before tracking her down and cutting her body to pieces in his blind vengeance. Dr. Stanley supposedly died in Buenos Aires in 1929, from the ravages of Kelly's disease, after confessing his grim crimes to a student. Very little exists to even prove that a Dr. Stanley existed, and, according to the precise records of the General Medical Council of Great Britain, no Dr. Stanley practiced in London in 1888-89.

A man named V. Kosminski was also a suspect. He was described as "a vice-ridden Polish Jew" and lived in Whitechapel, where he was known to have abused prostitutes whom he threatened to "slice up some day." Kosminski was arrested in March 1889 for attacking several people and he was quickly judged to have homicidal tendencies. He, like Pedachenko, was sent to an asylum, where he later died. Thomas Cutbush was arrested on Mar. 5, 1891, a month after the murder of Coles, who was possibly the last Ripper victim. He had been stabbing women in the buttocks. Cutbush was also determined to be insane and he was shipped off to an asylum. A painter and close friend of Oscar Wilde named Frank Miles was, many years later, also claimed by some to be the notorious Ripper.

Even a newspaper writer of the gaslight era, one Roslyn D'Onston, was, decades later, named as the Ripper. A failed physician, who was also an alcoholic and drug addict as well as a friend of black magic advocate Aleister Crowley, D'Onston, it was said, actually killed the whores of Whitechapel in order to write about them for London's newspapers. He became a suspect when he included in his detailed reports information that only the Ripper would have known. Yet D'Onston was never charged and, if he was ever picked up by the police and questioned, records of this detention have been lost.

A resident who boarded at 27 Sun Street in Finsbury Square, G. Wentworth Bell Smith, became another strong suspect, at least as far as the killings of Nichols, Chapman, Stride, Eddowes, and Kelly were concerned. Smith, a solicitor of a trust society in Toronto, Can., was the role model for Marie Belloc-Lowndes' *The Lodger*, her imaginative profile of Jack. Smith was forever complaining to his landlord, E. Callaghan, about the whores in the streets and how these strumpets had the audacity to enter churches. "They should all be drowned," Smith once told Callaghan.

Smith was a nocturnal prowler who left Callaghan's house late at night, wearing rubber-soled shoes and a long dark coat. He said that he was an insomniac and would often return just before the dawn with early-edition newspapers beneath his arm. On occasions, Smith left Callaghan's boarding house with a small black shiny bag. When Smith was in his room, he paced the floor constantly, his loud treading heard by Callaghan who lived below. Smith was a paranoid and expected trouble at any moment. He kept three loaded revolvers in his bureau and would stand in front of it whenever anyone was in his room with him, ready to reach for these weapons at any moment. Smith left Callaghan's house in early 1889 and was never seen again.

Various nondescript and anonymous suspects were dredged up with considerable effort to identify the elusive Jack. One preposterous claim was that the killer was a Jewish *shochet*, the slaughtering butcher who killed animals according to Talmudic law. This theory is rooted in the fact that there was a large Jewish population in Whitechapel at the time of the murders and therefore many such workers and abattoirs who performed the ritualistic butchering for Jewish meat shops. These slaughterers possessed the sharp knives and the ability used in the attacks on the murdered women, but they lacked motive. Other than technique, there was little credence in this theory.

Frederick Bailey Deeming was another suspect, a mass murderer who had killed his wife and children in England and then, in 1891, fled to Australia, where he murdered another wife and was about to kill a third woman when apprehended. Deeming, who was executed on May 23, 1892, claimed while awaiting the hangman that he was Jack the Ripper. But this was mere boasting and an attempt to prolong his own life by being sent back to England, where he hoped to be tried for the Ripper killings and then prove himself innocent, possibly evading the gallows. Deeming, nevertheless, according to his documented movements, could not have been at the scenes of the murders committed by Jack. Another mass killer, Dr. Thomas Neill Cream, who had murdered several people in the U.S. and who poisoned London prostitutes in 1891-92, went to the scaffold on Nov. 15, 1892. He was heard to say by the executioner, only a moment before he dropped through the trap: "I am Jack—" The rope cut off the final

words "the Ripper." It was this last act of vanity and a final taunt to the police that caused Cream to be considered a prime suspect in the Ripper killings.

Cream, however, according to prison records in Illinois, was sent to Joliet State Prison on Nov. 1, 1881, and was not released until July 31, 1891, long after the Ripper murders had been committed. Moreover, Cream's method of murder differed widely from that of Jack. He was a sly killer, poisoning all his victims, and his timid personality would never have permitted him to perform the slaughter that Jack so much enjoyed. Being a sickly weakling, Cream lacked psychological and physical strength, whereas Jack the Ripper was obviously in top physical condition, judging from his ability to run from the police and move with such lightning speed when murdering his victims.

One of the most popular suspects, the favorite among police officials, was Montague John Druitt, a handsome young man who came from a well-to-do family. He had graduated Oxford and probably studied medicine for about a year, which would explain his ability to murder with surgical precision if, indeed, he was the mass killer. Druitt was left little money upon the death of his father and he became a barrister, but his practice failed. Next, Druitt took a job as a schoolteacher in Blackheath. He was dismissed in 1888 for getting "into trouble." Druitt, apparently a homosexual, had taken liberties with a young boy, according to one account, and had been summarily fired. Druitt's mother, by this time, had been institutionalized, and it was later learned that there was a streak of insanity running through Druitt's family.

Following Druitt's dismissal from his teaching job, he moved to Whitechapel and wandered its streets day and night, living hand-to-mouth. Reports of his exact whereabouts during the Ripper killings were vague at best. Some said he was present in Whitechapel at the time, while others claimed that he had already been sent to an asylum. Druitt was despondent but not violent. He had no criminal background and had never committed an act of violence. Druitt was released from an asylum toward the end of 1888 and wrote a note to himself, which was later found by his brother. It read: "Since Friday I felt I was going to be like mother and the best thing for me was to die." He disappeared on Dec. 3, 1888. A month later constables fished his badly decomposed body out of the Thames River. Druitt had loaded his pockets with rocks and had drowned himself. The reason why Druitt remained the favorite suspect for police was that he committed suicide shortly after the murder of Mary Kelly, who was considered the last authentic Ripper victim. But this was merely a convenience for the police, whose officials, to quiet apprehension, concluded publicly that the Ripper killings ended after Kelly's death. Yet, as stated earlier, there were several similar deaths as late as 1891. Druitt became a suspect only by reason of the time of his death. As such, he was no suspect at all.

George Chapman was one of the most promising suspects. A Polish immigrant, Chapman's real name was Severin Antoniovich Klosowski. He had worked in a hospital in Prague before emigrating to England. He worked as a barber's surgeon in Whitechapel during the time of the Ripper killings, and possessed sharp knives with which he removed warts and moles, as well as practicing minor bloodletting to "clean the blood," a primitive medical technique that even by the 1880s had fallen into disfavor. Chapman went on to murder three women, all common-law wives or mistresses, from 1897 to 1902, but his method of murder was poison, not throat-slitting. Chapman was hanged on Apr. 7, 1903.

After Chapman's arrest, Chief Inspector Abberline, who had been in charge of the investigations into the Ripper killings, went to Inspector Godley and told him: "You've got Jack the Ripper at last!" He never explained this remark but it was later thought that Chapman had been on Abberline's suspect list in 1888 when he was desperately and fruitlessly searching for the evasive Jack. It was later speculated that though Chapman murdered those women close to him with poison, he could have very well have employed the more gruesome method of slitting the throats and disemboweling whores with whom he was not associated. He may have believed that poison would not be as readily identified and that by killing those close to him with this method he could evade detection. This remained speculation. Chapman never confessed to any of his killings.

Another latter-day suspect was the unnamed secretary of William Booth, founder of the Salvation Army. According to Booth, his secretary stated a few days before the slaying of Frances Coles in 1891: "Carroty Nell will be the next to go." The secretary disappeared after Frances "Carroty Nell" Coles was slain on Feb. 13, 1891. Thomas Sadler, an alcoholic railroad worker, was later claimed to be Coles' killer. He had been arrested as a strong suspect in the killing of Alice MacKenzie in 1889 but, because of lack of evidence, he was never charged with this killing or that of Coles, whom he also knew.

There were those, including the redoubtable creator of Sherlock Holmes, Arthur Conan Doyle, who believed that a woman, a midwife, was the real Jack the Ripper, "Jill the Ripper," according to some. This theory holds that "Jill" was a midwife who had been sent to prison for performing illegal abortions. Upon her release, this powerful, unhinged woman haunted the streets of Whitechapel, taking her vengeance out on prostitutes—careful to dissect her victims with some surgical skill, which midwives then possessed, and especially mutilate the sex organs of her victims in a throwback to her previous profession.

Where Doyle looked for suspects in low places, others saw the Ripper as a member of the professional class, the idle rich, or even royalty. One account insists that Dr. William Gull, physician to Queen Victoria, was the Ripper. Spiritualist William Lees, who had performed seances for the queen, envisioned several Ripper murders and was so terrified that he fled to the continent. He returned after these murders and, when getting off a bus, saw a man he intuitively felt was the killer. He followed this man to Gull's mansion and then confronted the man, who turned out to be Gull himself. The physician admitted that he was having blackouts, according to Lees, since suffering a stroke in 1887. Gull did visit a surgery in Whitechapel but he was never known to have roamed the crime-ridden area at night, as some later claimed. Further, Gull's stroke had left him partially paralyzed and there was no way in which this invalid could have committed the energetic acts of Jack the Ripper.

Next, the wealthy poet and ne'er-do-well James Kenneth Stephen was named as a strong suspect. He was eccentric and obsessed with violence, which permeated his writing. It was said that Stephen's eccentricities merely cloaked pure madness and that, as a homosexual suitor who was rejected by no less a person than Prince Albert Victor, Duke of Clarence, heir to the British crown, Stephen went berserk and took his rage out on the whores of Whitechapel, an area where Stephen and Prince Albert had reportedly visited an exclusive homosexual club.

Such a club did exist, and many distinguished British men did meet here for homosexual assignations, but none were ever arrested. This place was rarely raided, and authorities notified the proprietors far in advance so that their elegant clients could depart ahead of the police and save embarrassment all around. It was claimed that Stephen wrote the Ripper letters, affixing his own thumbprint to one of them, and purposely misspelled certain words and omitted simple punctuation to convince police that the killer was unschooled. Stephen's handwriting and that of the Ripper's were compared. A few similarities were not enough to identify Stephen as the Ripper.

It was also claimed that Stephen wrote the letters and even sent the kidney from the disemboweled Catherine Eddowes, but he was merely covering up for his dear friend, the real Jack the Ripper, who was none other than the Duke of Clarence himself. The eldest son of future king Edward VII was suffering from syphilis, it was claimed, which he had contracted through a Whitechapel whore, a disease that caused advanced paresis of the brain and the prince's premature death in 1892. Prince Eddy, as the Duke was nicknamed, had sought out Whitechapel whores to murder as he slowly went insane, taking his vengeance out on these poor creatures. Most of this wild theory stems from the research of Dr. Thomas Stowell, who, in 1970, examined the papers of Dr. William Gull and said that Gull's own unpublished records supported this story. Stowell's research was destroyed by his family after his death and Gull's records have yet to be examined by anyone else.

The absurd theory expands on Prince Eddy being the culprit and the London police authorities knowing about it and using it to blackmail Queen Victoria into political sanctions for certain inept ministers. In return, they kept Prince Eddy's identity as the Ripper a secret. This is the most preposterous theory of the lot. Though autocratic and rather cold, Queen Victoria was a principled person who, history and her personal conduct has shown, would never have shielded even one of her own family had they been guilty. Examining the records showing the whereabouts of the Duke of Clarence during the Ripper slayings proves that he could not have committed these crimes. In several instances he was out of the country at the time of the murders.

None of the above suspects really fit into the horrific mold created by the Ripper. He was not, in the opinion of the author, a vicious homosexual seeking vengeance on low-class prostitutes. Why, if this were the case, would he select only common prostitutes to murder? He was not a demented doctor or an unhinged prince. He was not one of many poisoners who later went to the hangman. He was a young man, full of ideals, one who had once been married to a woman who had turned to prostitution, who had deserted him and her family. This was the common thread connecting all the victims. All nine women had been married one way or another and had left their husbands and their families, turning to prostitution. They had betrayed the concept of the family, then the most sacred of institutions. It should be remembered that Mary Kelly was three months pregnant when horribly murdered and butchered.

All of the prostitutes murdered from 1888 to 1891 went regularly to small clinics in the East End and their records and examinations were on file, a regular murder list for the medical man who examined them all, the man who eventually hunted all of them down, the man whose own wife had deserted him for the streets, selling her favors to other men, betraying family and motherhood. The police, the medical experts, and the historians following in their footsteps decades later looked only, and continue to look, into Whitechapel as an area *into which* the killer went in search of victims and bloodletting. They look still for a maniac of bizarre nature, a diseased homosexual, a foreigner with odd political motives tied to mass murder, one poisoner or another from a later era. None stood within Whitechapel and looked out as would an incensed husband deserted by a woman who cuckolded him with strangers she did not know nor love. He was there all the while, this enigmatic Jack. He worked there. He lived there. He murdered there, this young intern at a clinic where the names and addresses of his victims were in files at his fingertips. He did not, after each murder, flee the area, but returned to the clinic where the blood on his clothes and hands counted for nothing more than the badge of his profession.

Of course this intern would have blood on his clothes and his hands. It was part of his job, operating on the countless patients that came to his clinic with ugly lesions and festering sores. And with a knife he was an expert, preserving the living, and, on those dark nights in the streets, bringing death to those already dead in his own distorted mind. He would outlive the era of his dark fame but not the haunting self-image which lurked inside his own shadow. He crossed into the twentieth century unmolested. Comfortable and distinguished in his profession, he looked back like any other upon the gaslight era of Jack the Ripper and, like any other, beheld this mass killer as a dark barbaric stranger from another time. See: **Abberline, Frederick George; Chapman, George; Cream, Dr. Thomas Neill; Deeming, Frederick Bayley; Doyle, Sir Arthur Conan; Gull, Sir William Whithey; Warren, Charles.**

REF.: Adam, *The Trial of George Chapman;* Alan, *Great Unsolved Crimes;* Alexander, *Royal Murder;* Ambler, *The Ability to Kill;* Anderson, *Criminals and Crime;* _____, *The Lighter Side of My Official Life;* _____, *The Police Encyclopedia;* Archer, *Ghost Detectives;* Barker, *The Fatal Caress;* Barnard, *The Harlot Killer;* Barnett, *Canon Barnett;* Baverstock, *Footsteps Through London's Past;* Beattie, *The Yorkshire Ripper;* Beaumont, *The Fifty Most Amazing Crimes;* Bell, *Jack the Ripper;* Bell, *Virginia Woolf;* Bermant, *Point of Arrival;* Besant, *East London;* Binney, *Crime and Abnormality;* Birmingham, *Murder Most Foul;* Bloch, *Sexual Life in England;* Blundell, *The World's Greatest Mysteries;* Boar, *The World's Most Infamous Murders;* Booth, *Life and Labor of the People of London;* Borchard, *Convicting the Innocent;* Brewer, *The Curse Upon Mitre Square;* Bridges, *The Tragedy at Road Hill House;* Brock, *A Casebook of Crime;* Brookes, *Murder in Fact and Fiction;* Brophy, *The Meaning of Murder;* Browne, *The Rise of Scotland Yard;* Buckle, *The Letters of Queen Victoria;* Butler, *Murderers' London;* Camps, *Camps on Crime;* _____, *The Investigation of Murder;* Cargill, *Scenes of Murder;* Cathcart, *Lord Snowdon;* CBA; *Chambers' Encyclopaedia* (*Jack the Ripper* by Leonard Gribble); Chester, *The Cleveland Street Affair;* Clark-Kennedy, *The London;* Cobb, *Critical Years at the Yard;* Crow, *The Victorian Woman;* Crowley, *The Confessions of Aleister Crowley;* Cullen, *Autumn of Terror;* Davis, *Jack the Ripper;* Deacon, *A History of the British Secret Service;* _____, *A History of the Russian Secret Service;* Dew, *I Caught Crippen;* Dilnot, *Scotland Yard;* Douglas, *Will the Real Jack the Ripper;* Doughtwaite, *Mass Murder;* Downie, *Murder in London;* Dunbar, *Blood in the Parlor;* DuRose, *Murder Was My Business;* Dyos, *The Victorian City;* East, *'Neath the Mask;* Ehrlich, *London on the Thames; Encyclopaedia Americana* (*Jack the Ripper* by Dorothy Gardiner); Farson, *The Hamlyn Book of Horror;* _____, *Jack the Ripper;* Fishman, *East End Jewish Radicals;* _____, *The Streets of East London;* Ford, *Return to Yesterday;* Fox, *A History of the Whitechapel Murders;* Franklin, *The World's Worst Murderers;* George, *Lloyd George;* Godwin, *Peter Kurten;* Goodman, *Bloody Versicles;* Gribble, *Famous Manhunts;* Griffiths, *Mysteries of the Police;* Haines, *Crime Flashback;* Halstead, *Doctor in the Nineties;* Harrison, *The Dark Angel;* Harrison, *Clarence;* _____, *The World of Sherlock Holmes;* Hayne, *Jack the Ripper;* Hibbert, *The Roots of Evil;* Higham, *The Adventures of Conan Doyle;* Hill, *The New Earth;* Hodge, *The Black Maria;* Honeycombe, *The Murders in the Black Museum;* Hyde, *Carson;* Hynd, *Murder Unlimited;* _____, *Sleuths, Slayers and Swindlers;* Jackson, *Francis Camps;* Jesse, *Murder and Its Motives;* Jones, *The Ripper File;* Jones, *Outcast London;* Jones, *Unsolved;* Kingston, *The Bench and the Dock;* Knight, *The Brotherhood;* _____, *Jack the Ripper;* Lacassagne, *Vacher L'Eventreur et les Crimes Sadiques;* Leeson, *Lost London;* LeQueux, *Things I Know About Kings;* Logan, *Masters of Crime;* London, *The People of the Abyss;* Longford, *Queen Victoria;* Lowndes, *Diaries and Letters;* Lustgarten, *The Story of Crime;* McCormick, *The Identity of Jack the Ripper;* MacDonald, *Le Criminel Type;* _____, *Criminology;* MacNaghten, *Days of My Years;* Madison, *Great Unsolved Cases;* Magnus, *King Edward the Seventh;* Marjoribanks, *The Life of Lord Carson;* _____, *For the Defense: The Life of Sir Edward Marshall Hall;* Masters, *Sex Crimes in History;* Matters, *The Mystery of Jack the Ripper;* May, *Tiger Woman;* Menard, *Certain Connections of Affinities with Jack the Ripper;* Moore, *Famous Lives;* Moore-Anderson, *Sir Robert Anderson;* Moylan, *Scotland Yard;* Muusmann, *Hvem var Jack the Ripper?;* Nash, *Almanac of World Crime;* _____, *Open Files;* Neil, *The World's Greatest Mysteries;* Neil, *Manhunters of Scotland Yard;* Newton, *Crime and the Drama;* Nicholson, *The Yorkshire Ripper;* Oddie, *Inquest;* Odell, *Jack the Ripper;* O'Donnell, *Confessions of A Ghost Hunter;* _____, *Great Thames Mysteries;* _____, *Haunted Britain;* Owen, *Tempestuous Journey;* Pearsall, *The Worm and the Bud;* Pearson, *Age of Consent;* Pearson, *More Studies in Murder;* Pimlott, *Toynbee Hall;* Platnick, *Great Mysteries of History;* Prothero, *The History of the Criminal Investigation Department at Scotland Yard;* Pulling, *Mr. Punch and the Police;* Richardson, *From the City to Fleet Street;* Rumbelow, *The Complete Jack the Ripper;* Scott, *The Concise Encyclopedia of Crime and Criminals;* Shaw, *Collected Letters;* Shew, *A Companion to Murder;* Sims, *The Mysteries of Modern London;* Sitwell, *Noble Essences of Courteous Revelations;* Sitwell, *A Free House;* Smith, *From Constable to Commissioner;* Snyder, *A Treasury of Great Reporting;* Sparrow, *Crimes of Passion;* Spiering, *Prince Jack;* Springfield, *Some Piquant People;* Stephen, *The Life of Sir James Fitzjames Stephen;* Stewart, *Jack the Ripper;* Symonds, *The Great Beast;* Symons, *Crime and Detection;* _____, *The Criminal Classes;* Thomson, *The Story of Scotland Yard;* Thorwald, *The Century of the Detective;* _____, *The Marks of Cain;* Volta, *The Vampire;* Von Hentig, *The Criminal and His Victim;* Wagner, *The Monster of Dusseldorf;* Walbrook, *Murders and Murder Trials;* Wensley, *Forty Years of Scotland Yard;* Whitelaw, *Corpus Delicti;* Whitmore, *Victorian and Edwardian Crime and Punishment;* Whittington-Egan, *A Casebook on Jack the Ripper;* Williams, *The Hidden World of Scotland Yard;* Williams, *Round London;* Williams, *The Life of General Sir Charles Warren;* Wilson, *A Casebook of Murder;* _____, *A Criminal History of Mankind;* _____, *Encyclopedia of Murder;* _____, *Order of Assassins;* _____, *Rasputin and the Fall of the Romanovs;* Winslow, *Recollections of Forty Years;* Woodhall, *Crime and the Supernatural;* _____, *Jack the Ripper;* Yallop, *Deliver Us from Evil;* (DRAMA), Barnes, *The Ruling Class;* Greer, *Ripper;* Pember, *Jack the Ripper, A Musical Play;* Reade, *The Stranger;* Vachell, *The Lodger* (based on the Lowndes novel); (FICTION), Alexander, *Terror on Broadway;* Alexander, *Time After Time;* Allen, *Whitechapel Murder;* Arlen, *Hell! Said the Duchess, A Bed-Time Story;* Barry, *The Michaelmas Girls;* Beeding, *Death Walks in Eastrepps;* Brewer, *The Curse Upon Mitre Square;* Brooke, *Man Made Angry;* Brown, *The Screaming Mimi;* Burroughs, *Nova Express;* Capon, *The Seventh Passenger;* Cashman, *The Gentleman from Chicago;* Chaplin, *By Flower and Dean Street and The Love Apple;* Chetwynd-Hayes, *The Unbidden* (story, "The Gatecrasher"); Desmond, *Death Let Loose;* _____, *A Scream in the Night;* Dibdin, *The Last Sherlock Holmes Story;* Erskine, *Give Up the Ghost;* Farmer, *A Feast Unknown;* _____, *Lord of the Trees;* Gardner, *The Return of Moriarty;* Gordon, *The Private Life of Jack the Ripper;* Hamilton, *Hangover Square;* Lovesey, *Swing, Swing Together;* Lowndes, *The Lodger;* Lustgarten, *One More Unfortunate;* MacDonald, *Mystery of the Dead Police;* Marsh, *Singing in the Shrouds;* Morland, *Death for Sale;* Oliver, *The Whitechapel Mystery;* Pinkerton, *The Whitechapel Murders;* Queen, *A Study in Terror;* Reppetto, *The Blue Parade;* Russell, *Unholy Trinity;* Shew, *Hands of the Ripper;* Skene, *The Ripper Returns;* Sladek, *Black Aura;* Stevens, *By Reason of Insanity;* Veheyne, *Horror;* Walsh, *The Mycroft Memoranda;* Wilson, *Ritual in the Dark;* Zola, *La Bete Humaine;* (FILM), *Waxworks* (alt. title, Ger., *The Three Waxworks*), s., 1924; *The Lodger,* s., 1926; *Pandora's Box,* s., 1929; *The Phantom Fiend,* 1935; *The Lodger,* 1944; *Hangover Square,* 1945; *Lured,* 1947; *Room to Let,* 1949; *The Man in the Attic,* 1953; *Jack the Ripper,* 1959; *A Study in Terror,* 1966; *The Monster of London City,* 1967; *Hands of the Ripper,* 1971; *Dr. Jekyll and Sister Hyde,* 1972; *Lulu,* 1978; *Murder By Decree,* 1979; *Time After Time,* 1979.

Jack The Stripper, prom. 1964-65, Brit., (unsolv.) mur. In a chilling emulation of Jack The Ripper, a psychopathic killer in London began murdering prostitutes in early 1964, strangling his victims and then stripping them. The first victim was Hannah Tailford. On Feb. 2, her nude body was found floating in the Thames. Within the next year and a half, five more women, all prostitutes, were found either strangled or suffocated, their corpses tossed in the Thames or left along isolated roads. The killer eluded intensive police investigation. Several of the victims had their front teeth knocked out. Irene Lockwood, discovered on Apr. 8, had been strangled, as had Birdie O'Hara. Margaret McGowan, a prostitute who

Police composite sketch of Jack the Stripper.

had testified in the infamous Profumo sex scandal, was found in a pile of garbage on Nov. 25, 1964. All of the women disappeared between 11 p.m. and 1 a.m., so it was supposed that the murderer worked a night shift. Scotland Yard chief superintendent John Du Rose, acting on the discovery that four of the six bodies were flecked with spray paint, launched a search of all garages and small factories in the western section of London. When the murders stopped in late 1965, Du Rose searched through records of suicides, jailings, and accidental deaths since the killing. A night security guard had killed himself, leaving a suicide note saying, "I am unable to stand the strain any longer." Although no definitive evidence against him was established, it was conveniently assumed that he had been Jack The Stripper. The file on the cases, however, remains open. See: **Jack The Ripper; Profumo Scandal.**

REF.: *CBA;* DuRose, *Murder Was My Business;* McConnell, *Found Naked and Dead;* Nash, *Open Files;* Purvis, *Great Unsolved Mysteries;* Wilson, *Encyclopedia of Modern Murder.*

Jacobi, Frank C., Jr., 1958-   , Case of, U.S., mur. Based on psychological testing, Illinois Criminal Court Judge Frank J. Wilson ruled that Frank C. Jacobi, Jr. was Not Guilty of murdering his mother and father. Marion and Frank Jacobi, Sr. were stabbed to death in their Western Springs home in 1975. The judge said the 17-year-old boy did not understand the criminal nature of his actions and placed Jacobi in the custody of the Illinois Department of Mental Health. REF.: *CBA.*

Jacobs, Elmer P., prom. 1928, U.S., (wrong. convict.) rob. In August 1928 in Los Angeles, someone stole four cabs in five days and robbed each of their drivers. Police arrested Elmer P. Jacobs for stealing a car and included him in a lineup of suspects in the cab thefts. All four taxi drivers identified Jacobs as their assailant. Even though he had pleaded guilty to grand larceny and been sentenced to prison, Jacobs was forced to appear before Judge Emmett H. Wilson on Oct. 30, 1928.

The drivers appeared in court and positively identified Jacobs as the robber. Jacobs tried to establish alibis, but he was found Guilty on four counts of robbery. One month later he was sentenced to from fifteen years to life in prison. During the same week, police arrested four men who confessed to robbing the taxi drivers and stealing their cabs. After police verified their stories, Jacobs was freed and all charges against him were dropped in December. REF.: *CBA.*

Jacobs, Jack, 1932-   , and **Foreman, Leslie,** 1935-   , and **Yiorgalli, Dinos,** 1944-   , and **Trowell, Nicholas,** 1956-   , Brit., kid. When kidnappers abducted 18-year-old Cypriot Alio Kaloghirou from her sister's London home, they left a ransom note warning relatives not to contact police. With little hesitation, the victim's brother-in-law Loucas Neocleous called Scotland Yard on Nov. 6, 1975. The kidnappers demanded a £60,000 ransom, an unattainable sum for the girl's family. After a number of phone calls, the demand had been reduced to £17,000 in used notes. The kidnappers assumed the police were not involved in the case, but authorities were working behind the scenes to set up a drop site for the ransom money. Scotland Yard officials asked members of the media not to report the incident because it would endanger the girl's life.

For nine days, Kaloghirou was kept in a tiny room in a multi-family dwelling. Whenever her captors left her alone, they bound and gagged her, but for the most part treated her civilly. On the tenth day the kidnappers arranged for the ransom money, wrapped in a plastic bag, to be left near Bounds Green railroad station. They released Kaloghirou near the drop site. After police found the girl, the nearly 100 detectives working the case took less than five hours to arrest five suspects. Jack Jacobs, Leslie Foreman, Takis Cosmas, Dinos Yiorgalli, and Nicholas Trowell were charged with kidnapping. Foreman, Yiorgalli, Trowell, and Jacobs received sentences ranging from eight to twelve years in prison, while Cosmas was acquitted. REF.: *CBA.*

Jacobs, John J., prom. 1900, U.S., fraud. When Chicago police officers burst into the offices of John J. Jacobs, they confiscated phony stock certificates with a face value of nearly $70,000. The manager of the Montana Mining and Investment Company, Jacobs was operating what resembled a lottery according to police. The company had distributed literature, claiming that for less than $2, a person could buy into the company and then be eligible for extravagant loans without having to furnish collateral. The catch was that only those patrons whose certificate numbers appeared

monthly were eligible to borrow the money. Based on documents which they found and irate customers whom they heard from, officials surmised there were very few "eligible" customers on the company's list.

Jacobs was charged with promoting a lottery scheme, conducting a lottery and selling lottery tickets. The lottery scam was being perpetrated across the country. The issuing agent would actually lend some money every once in awhile or pay a friend to spread the word that he had received a collateral-free loan in an effort to drum up new business.

REF.: *CBA;* Wooldridge, *Hands Up.*

Jacobs, Robert (AKA: **Michael Knowles**), b.c. 1940, and **Porter, Ian**, prom. 1970, Brit., fraud. With the cost of auto insurance in England increasing in the late 1960s, Michael Knowles started the Irish-American Insurance Company, which offered rates as much as one-third lower than those of the major British Insurance Association firms. With an insurance broker from Tunbridge Wells named Ian Porter as the "point man," the company took in more than £1 million in premiums during its first year. Knowles began to acquire other insurance firms, and offered brokers outrageous commissions of 20 percent. His companies insured as many as 750,000 motorists in the early 1970s.

Behind the success of the cut-rate insurance companies was a skimming operation that deposited premiums in Knowles' pockets. Soon the companies were out of money to pay claims. Many of the motorists, judged "bad risks," jumped from one discount firm to another, only to see them all fold. Fourteen insurance companies and numerous brokerages were involved in the fraud. Nearly £40 million in premiums had been collected, and much of it was never recovered. Many of the nation's drivers found themselves with useless insurance policies after paying premiums to sometimes as many as six companies.

The police arrested Knowles, and he was later sentenced to eight years in prison. Porter was acquitted. Authorities believed that Knowles had distributed his illegal profits in companies around the world, but were unable to prove the charge.

REF.: Borrell, *Crime in Britain; CBA.*

Jacobs, William M., 1862-1934, **Kendig, William L.**, d.c.1928, **Bredell, Baldwin S.**, 1878-1956, **Taylor, Arthur**, b.c.1875, **Downey, Samuel B.**, prom. 1899, **Ingham, Ellery P.**, prom. 1899. **Newitt, Harvey K.**, prom. 1899, U.S., arson.-count.-fraud. During the 1890s, Lancaster, Pa., was home to many of the leading cigar-makers in the U.S. William M. Jacobs and William L. Kendig were cigar manufacturers headed in opposite directions. For Jacobs, business was booming. Two suspicious fires at his fully-insured factories had brought him to Lancaster, where he bought a huge six-story building and employed many people at his Postal Cigar Company. Kendig had won a recent court ruling forcing insurance companies to compensate him for a fire that had gutted his factory, but in 1893 he declared bankruptcy. He and Jacobs then masterminded a credit swindle that netted the pair a couple thousand dollars.

Not content with small gains, Jacobs and Kendig enlisted the aid of two Philadelphia printers in a counterfeit scam. Baldwin S. Bredell and Arthur Taylor were young and talented and wanted to open their own printing shop. In exchange for counterfeiting federal tax seals (to be used on boxes of cigars), Jacobs set the pair up in their own printing shop. For a few thousand dollars, Kendig enlisted the aid of local Internal Revenue collector Samuel B. Downey. In one year, Jacobs increased his cigar production to 45 million and paid $82,000 for internal revenue stamps instead of the $162,000 he should have paid.

Jacobs' next idea was to manufacture $10 million in $100 bills. When investigators discovered several phony $100 bills in Philadelphia in 1897 they recalled some $26 million worth of silver certificates. Bredell and Taylor had spent some samples of their work on a southern vacation. Police traced the bills to the printers through a trail of extravagant spending. While under twenty-four-hour surveillance, Bredell and Taylor led investigators to Jacobs and Kendig, who in turn led agents to Ellery P. Ingham and Harvey K. Newitt. After Kendig got wind of the investigation, he tried to bribe Ingham, a former U.S. attorney in Philadelphia, and Newitt, his law partner.

After more than two years of amassing evidence, officials moved against the counterfeiting ring in April 1899. Police arrested eight men, including Kendig henchman James Burns, and charged them with involvement in the counterfeiting scheme. Jacobs, Kendig, Burns, Downey, Taylor, and Bredell all pleaded guilty and U.S. Attorney James M. Beck opted to use the six men in his trial against Ingham, his predecessor, and Newitt. In October 1899, Newitt and Ingham were pronounced Guilty and sentenced to thirty months in prison. Jacobs and Kendig each received twelve-year prison sentences and were fined $5,000. Downey, for asking for and accepting bribes, was sentenced to two years in prison and fined $400. Kendig and Jacobs were each sentenced to twelve years in prison and fined $5,000. Burns was sentenced to eight years in prison. Downey received a two-year prison term and fined $400. Taylor and Bredell received seven-year sentences. In July 1905, President Theodore Roosevelt pardoned Kendig and Jacobs.

REF.: Bloom, *Money of Their Own; CBA.*

Jacobson, Howard (AKA: **Buddy**), 1930-89, U.S., mur. At the age of seventeen, Melanie Cain arrived in New York in 1972 with dreams of becoming an actress. Within months, the Naperville, Ill., native signed with one of New York's top modeling agencies and began a relationship with her landlord, Howard "Buddy" Jacobson. Formerly one of the country's top trainers of thorough-bred race horses, following a dispute with the New York Racing Association Jacobson was forced to turn to real estate, a field in which he became successful. When Cain was fired from Eileen Ford's modeling agency, she and Jacobson started their own agency. Christened My Fair Lady after Cain's favorite musical, the agency prospered with Melanie as its star attraction.

Jacobson, who had told Cain he was twenty-nine, was really forty-two. The two men he introduced as his brothers were really the divorced man's sons. For nearly five years, Cain tolerated rumors that her boyfriend slept with a number of women at the agency. In 1978, Cain met handsome young restaurateur Jack Tupper while jogging, and within weeks she left Jacobson and moved in with her new boyfriend, who also lived in Jacobson's building.

Jacobson harassed Cain and Tupper with phone calls and noise. He turned off the hot water in their apartment and offered the 34-year-old Tupper and some of his friends $100,000 if Cain would return to him. On the morning of Aug. 6, 1978, Cain left the apartment building at 155 E. 84th St. to sign the lease for a new apartment, so she and Tupper could escape their tormentor.

When Cain returned early that afternoon, Tupper was not home and she went to Jacobson's apartment. No one answered the door and Cain returned to her apartment to wait for Jack. Upon hearing noise in the hallway, she peeked out to see Jacobson and one of his sons tearing up the rug in the hallway. After the men left, Cain stepped out in the hall and discovered reddish, moist stains on the padding which had been covered by white paint. She also found a tuft of hair, a smeared palm print on the elevator, and other spots in the hall that had been freshly painted. Cain returned to Jacobson's apartment and asked him where Tupper was, but he said he hadn't seen him all morning. Cain called police.

The next day, Estella Carattini identified a car belonging to Jacobson. She said that Jacobson and one of his employees, Salvatore Prainito, dragged a crate from the trunk of the 1974 Cadillac into a vacant lot, set fire to the crate and then fled the scene. When police found Jack Tupper's body, it was barely identifiable. He had been beaten, stabbed repeatedly, and then set afire. Police arrested Jacobson and charged him with murder. In a 1980 trial, Jacobson was found Guilty of second-degree murder. But only three days before he was scheduled to receive his prison sentence, he escaped from jail on May 31 by calling in a debt. An old friend, Anthony DeRosa, posing as a lawyer,

brought a razor and a change of clothes into the Brooklyn House of Detention and Jacobson walked out minus his bushy moustache. Jacobson's latest girlfriend, Audrey Barrett, was waiting in the parking lot and the two fled the state. The court sentenced Jacobson in absentia to twenty-five years in prison.

On June 29, Barrett surrendered to authorities and was charged with criminal facilitation, first-degree escape, and possession of legal stationery. Ten days later, in the Los Angeles suburb of Manhattan Beach, local police arrested Jacobson. He was on a restaurant pay-phone calling the district attorney's office in Brooklyn to make arrangements to turn himself in. Jacobson died of cancer in Buffalo, N.Y., in May 1989. REF.: *CBA.*

Jacobson, Jacob, prom. 1909, U.S., wh. slav. On July 19, 1909, Jacob Jacobson was charged with persuading a woman to enter a whorehouse to practice prostitution. Jacobson was also charged with procuring another female. By the end of July 1909, a jury had been chosen and Jacobson was tried, convicted, and sentenced to two months in prison and fined $600. The conviction was upheld upon appeal. REF.: *CBA.*

Jacobus, d.1178, Italy, jur. Widely admired expert in Roman law. One of the Four Doctors of Bologna, along with Bulgarus, Hugo, and Martinus. REF.: *CBA.*

Jacoby, Henry Julius (AKA: **Harry**), 1904-22, Brit., mur. Henry Jacoby, eighteen, who worked at Spencer's Hotel on Portman Street, London, had planned for weeks to rob one of the wealthy guests at the hotel. His opportunity came on the night of Mar. 14, 1922, when he crept into the room of Lady Alice White, believing that the 60-year old dowager was not in. In precarious health since the previous December, she was asleep in her room.

Alice White, the widow of Sir Edward White, a former London County Council chairman, was startled by Jacoby's invasion, and he struck her with a hammer. The elderly woman died the next morning. Jacoby was arrested and charged with murder a few days later. He casually re-

Lady killer Henry Jacoby.

marked to a police officer, "Isn't it funny how much strength a man's got?" referring to the brutal blow he had given White.

The trial began at the Old Bailey on Apr. 28, 1922. Jacoby said he had "heard voices" and had gone to the guests' rooms to investigate. Room Number 14, White's, stood open. "I thought I heard murmurings inside," Jacoby said, "I rushed in and seeing a form, lashed out. I did not know it was Lady White." Jacoby was found Guilty of murder, but the jury recommended mercy, given his age. The plea was rejected by the home secretary and Jacoby was hanged at Pentonville Prison on June 5 over a storm of protest. Ronald True, a member of a titled family, had recently murdered a London prostitute, but had been reprieved on the grounds of insanity.

REF.: Browne and Tullett, *The Scalpel of Scotland Yard; CBA;* Cornish, *Cornish of the "Yard";* Hoskins, *They Almost Escaped;* Neil, *Manhunters of Scotland Yard;* Oswald, *Memoirs of a London County Coroner;* Pollock, *Mr. Justice McCardie;* Rowland, *Unfit to Plead?;* Shew, *A Second Companion to Murder;* Tullett, *Strictly Murder;* Wensley, *Forty Years of Scotland Yard;* Wilson, *Encyclopedia of Murder;* (FILM), *Night Must Fall,* 1937; *Night Must Fall,* 1964.

Jacquier, Nicholas, b.c.1402, Fr., jur. One of the most famous medieval inquisitors, Nicholas Jacquier was operating in northern France in 1452 when he wrote *Tractatus de Calcatione Demonum.* Through his writing and research, Jacquier helped establish witchcraft as a form of heresy. He determined that witchcraft was demonic because the witches knowingly renounced both the Catholic Church and God. In 1458, Jacquier wrote *Flagellum Haereticorum Fascinariorum (A Flail Against the Heresy of Witchcraft)*. He presided over inquisitions at Tournay in 1465, Bohemia in 1466, and at Lille from 1468-72. REF.: *CBA*.

Jagado, Hélène, See: **Jegado, Hélène.**

Jagusch, August, prom. 1951, U.S., mur. August Jagusch's father stabbed the 12-year-old in the arm with a bread knife when the youngster refused to eat unpeeled potatoes. Jagusch ran away from home after the incident, but upon his capture by the police his father suggested he should be locked up. For sixteen months, Jagusch endured a series of sexual liaisons at Children's Village in Dobbs Ferry, N.Y. He was assaulted by male counselors, and slept with female teachers and fellow inmates, all before turning fifteen.

Upon his release from the children's home, Jagusch continued to be sexually promiscuous. Although he later married and had a daughter, the relationship ended in divorce. In June 1951, Jagusch strangled to death a young Staten Island prostitute named Mildred Fogarty. His ex-wife turned Jagusch in to the police when he contacted her after the murder. He told police that Fogarty had enraged him during a sex act and that he went berserk and strangled the woman. Jagusch was found Guilty of second-degree murder and sentenced to twenty years in prison. He was released on Aug. 23, 1967, after serving sixteen and a half years in Auburn State Prison. REF.: *CBA*.

Jahnke, Richard J., 1967- , U.S., mur. The beatings began at age two for Richard J. Jahnke. His father, Richard C. Jahnke, also beat young Richard's sister, Deborah Jahnke, and his mother, Maria Jahnke. The IRS agent and his family lived in Cheyenne, Wyo. He collected guns, had few friends and rarely socialized with neighbors or co-workers. After years of unreported abuse, 16-year-old Richard confided in Major Robert Vegvary, his ROTC instructor at Central High School. In May 1982, Vegvary accompanied Jahnke to the sheriff's office to file a complaint. A perfunctory visit to the Jahnke household a few weeks later only enraged the father.

Richard C. Jahnke told his son that he would never forgive him for going to the authorities. On Nov. 16, Richard fought with his mother over cleaning the basement. Later, as the parents left to celebrate their twentieth anniversary, Jahnke told his son he did not want to see him there when he returned.

During the hour-and-a-half the couple were gone, Richard and his sister loaded a number of guns and placed them around the house. Deborah was stationed in the living room with a rifle, and her brother hid in the garage with a shotgun. The parents' car pulled in the driveway, and the elder Jahnke turned off the engine and got out of the car. As he approached the garage door entrance to the house, two shotgun blasts hit the 38-year-old man. The younger Jahnke fired four more times into his father who lay on the garage floor. Richard C. Jahnke died within minutes from chest wounds. His son was arrested and charged with murder.

In February 1983, a jury deliberated seven hours before declaring Jahnke Guilty of voluntary manslaughter in the death of his father. He was also found Not Guilty on one count of conspiracy. Although his murder conviction was upheld by the Wyoming Supreme Court, Jahnke's five- to fifteen-year sentence was reduced to three years by Governor Ed Herschler. REF.: *CBA*.

Jalal-ad-Din Mingburnu (Jelalad-Din), d.1231, Khwarazm, shah, assass. Unsuccessfully fought the armies of Genghis Khan, eventually losing on the banks of the Indus in about 1220 and was forced to flee to India. He managed to partially reinstate the khanate, but was defeated and murdered by Mongols. REF.: *CBA*.

Jalal ud-Din (Jalal-ud-Din Firuz Khalji), d.1296, India, ruler, assass. Sultan of Delhi in 1290 who went on to become ruler of the Khalja dynasty until his assassination by his son-in-law Ala-ud-Din, who then succeeded him in the throne. REF. *CBA*.

James I, 1394-1437, Scot., king, assass. King Robert III of Scotland sent his 12-year-old son, the future King James I, to France for his safety. Eighteen years later, in 1423, after spending time in England, James assumed control of Scotland. He arrested and executed many of the nobles who had kept him from the throne and run the country in his absence. He banished Sir Robert Graham for his part in the uprising.

On Feb. 20, 1437, an old woman who had warned the king of danger appeared at the castle door. James told servants to send her away, but before she left, the old woman prophesied that she would not see the face of the king again. That evening, as the king and queen prepared for bed, they heard the woman shout from outside the castle that Graham had returned. As they turned to lock the doors they found that the keys had been stolen and the bolts removed. Castle guards battled the intruders. A serving woman, Catherine Douglas, pointed out that the monastery vaults were beneath the floor where James stood.

The king pried up the floorboards and hid himself before Graham and his men burst into the room. The men searched the castle when they found the king had vanished. James tried to climb back into the room as the intruders searched for him elsewhere, but the women could not lift him through the hole in the floor. Graham's men returned and the women were unable to replace the floorboard in time. Two men with torches dropped into the hole armed with knives. As the king fought to hold them off, Graham slipped into the vault. While the king knelt on his two assailants, Graham ran him through with a sword. REF.: *CBA*.

James I, 1566-1625, Brit., witchcraft. An absolute autocrat, King James practiced cruelty and bigotry throughout his long reign (1603-25), asserting the divine right of kings. James alienated almost everyone in his kingdom, the Presbyterians by embracing episcopacy, and the Catholics by reducing the power of their nobles, which prompted the Gunpowder Plot of 1605. He was obsessed with witchcraft, ordering wholesale purges throughout England where hapless citizens were summarily accused, tried, and executed for witchcraft, particularly under James' bizarre Statute of 1604, which profiled and proscribed witches small and large.

This Stuart King of England was a fanatic about witchcraft from the moment he ascended the throne in 1603. It was the lunatic legacy of James I that the Puritans in America unhappily inherited. According to one historian, James I "was the performing idiot of the Seventeenth century. His face was hideous, his form misshapen, and his mind distorted. From his father, Lord Darnley, he inherited the sullen brutality of a murderer. From his mother, Mary, Queen of Scots, came the vain cunning of a trickster, who, for his own pleasure, would sacrifice a kingdom."

James thought the Devil and many covens of witches conspired against him when a storm sank half his grand fleet, which was returning from Denmark to England with his child-bride Anne, Princess of Denmark. He sat down and wrote a book on demonology, and established myriad methods of detection and punishment of witches, the agents on earth of Satan. Those who were reluctant to admit that they were witches were tortured into confession. James ordered his prisoners' ears and tongues cut out, fingers sliced off, and eyes gouged until they admitted being witches. He personally attended many of these inhuman tortures and delighted in watching women who had been stripped naked walk over hot coals until they fell unconscious from pain.

One of James' favorite tortures was his own, warped concoction. He ordered the big toes and the thumbs of an accused witch tied together. The woman (rarely was the subject for conversion a man) was next thrown into a huge vat of water. If the accused sank, there was no doubt about her innocence (or death). If the accused floated, she was a witch and was immediately burned at the stake.

King James was positive that mostly women were selected to be instruments of the Devil, because: "That sex is frailer than man is, and it is easier to entrap them in the snares of the Devil, as was proved to be true by the serpent deceiving Eve in the Garden. Many of them are lean and deformed, shadowy and melancholic in their faces, to the horror of all who see them. They are scolds and devilish in their characters, and go about begging from house to house for a pot full of meal. They promise anything you want, and lie whenever it is convenient..."

Any, James insisted, who came into contact with a witch should, without reservation, also be suspected of being a witch. This included family members related directly to known witches. James added: "Who sups with the Devil has need of a large spoon. Witches can raise a storm and tempest in the air, or upon sea or land. They cannot weep in any event over three tears; if they do, they are crocodile tears. God decreed that the water should refuse to receive a witch into its bosom, so that accused should be thrown into the water. If they are witches, they will float on the surface, but if they be innocent they will sink."

Countless hundreds were imprisoned and executed under the witchcraft terror conducted by James I, a hypocritical ogre who whimsically sent scores to their deaths because of his own fears and paranoia, while all the while a bevy of lickspittle scholars put together a new version of the Bible, named in his honor as the King James Bible (1611).

REF.: *CBA;* Hughes, *Witchcraft;* James I, *Demonology;* Kittredge, *Studies in History of Religions;* Notestein, *A History of Witchcraft in England;* Robbins, *The Encyclopedia of Witchcraft and Demonology;* Seth, *Witches and Their Craft;* Summers, *The Geography of Witchcraft;* Wilson, *Witches.*

James II, 1430-60, Scot., king, attempt. assass. Son of assassinated Scottish king James I. He took strict command of the government in 1449, and executed his guardian, Sir Alexander Livingstone, the following year for removing the queen mother from the joint guardianship they had shared. Like his father he created enemies by seeking to limit the powers of the feudal lords. He defended himself against one notable assassination plot in 1452 by fatally stabbing the Eighth Earl of Douglas. He removed the civil rights of the Ninth Earl of Douglas, and confiscated the property of both the Ninth Earl and that of the Earl of Mornay. He was killed by an accidental cannon blast during a siege of Roxburgh Castle. REF.: *CBA.*

James V, 1512-42, Scot., king, impris. Son of Scottish King James IV and Margaret, a daughter of British king Henry VII. He was jailed in 1525 along with other nobles by the Earl of Angus, Archibald Douglas, and held prisoner for three years. He assumed power upon his release, making the protection of commoners from nobles a top priority. He waged war on England, but was defeated in 1542 at Solway Moss. He died three weeks later, and was succeeded by the future Mary, Queen of Scots, his week-old daughter. REF.: *CBA.*

James, Saint (AKA: **the Just**), d.c.62 A.D., Jerusalem, consp. Early Christian leader and, according to St. Paul, an apostle of Jesus Christ not among the original twelve. He is interpreted variously as being Jesus' brother, step-brother, or cousin, based on a biblical passage describing him as "the Lord's brother." He was executed on the order of Ananus, a high priest. REF.: *CBA.*

James, Albert T., Sr., prom. 1981, U.S., asslt.-attempt. mur. Chicago police officers Elmer Atkinson, Keith Sullivan, and Richard Lionhood were traveling down South Indiana Avenue in their unmarked squad car on the afternoon of Aug. 30, 1981. A motorist began following them closely and honking his horn. The policemen stopped at the corner of 90th Place and South Indiana Avenue and the car pulled up behind them. As Atkinson stepped out to investigate, the driver of the car, Albert T. James, Sr., pointed a derringer at the officer and fired twice.

The wounded Atkinson answered with one shot before his partners jumped out of the car and fired on James, killing him. James' son Albert, who was in the car with his father, told police that his father knew he was following a police car. He also told authorities that his father had been in an inexplicable rage all day. REF.: *CBA.*

James, Alexander Franklin, See: **James, Jesse Woodson.**
James, Francis, prom. 1934, Brit., mansl. Francis James, an unemployed seaman from Jamaica, had a strange hold over Beryl Smith. He turned the 24-year-old Smith out into the London streets to support him. Under the threat of violence, she obeyed James until one day she found the courage to leave. For days, James stalked her and finally caught up with her in a cafe on West India Dock Road.

As Smith left the cafe, James jumped her and started slashing her with a razor. Another prostitute, Jean Thompson, tried to help Smith. James turned on Thompson momentarily, and when police arrived, he fled. The Jamaican used the razor on his own throat, but the cut was only superficial and he was arrested. Smith survived the brutal attack, but Thompson died in the hospital while undergoing minor surgery. James was charged with Thompson's murder and the attempted murder of Smith. In court, James' attorney, Mr. Peregrine, argued that a local rather than a general anaesthetic would have prevented Thompson's death. The charge against James was reduced to manslaughter and he was sentenced to five years in prison. Smith died two years later as a result of injuries sustained in the attack, but a one-year statute of limitations prevented authorities from retrying James.

REF.: Burt, *Commander Burt of Scotland Yard; CBA.*

James, Henry (Baron of Hereford), 1828-1911, Brit., jur. Served as member of Parliament from 1869-85 and from 1886-95, and became a peer in 1895. He also served as attorney general in 1873 and from 1880-85, and as the chancellor of the duchy of Lancaster in 1895. REF.: *CBA.*

James, Jesse Woodson (AKA: **Dingus, Thomas Howard**), 1847-82, U.S., rob.-mur. Born on his father's farm near Kearney, Clay County, Mo., on Sept. 5, 1847, Jesse Woodson James would become America's most famous bandit, rivaling in lore and legend that of England's Robin Hood. Millions of words would be written about this handsome, dashing, and utterly ruthless bank and train robber. To many of his peers, he appeared a folklore hero who took vengeance in their name upon an industrial society that was grinding the old agrarian lifestyle to ashes. To others, he and his band represented the last vestiges of the Old South and its lost cause of secession.

A good deal of truth was in the tale that Jesse James the bandit was created by oppressive troops of the Union Army, and worse, operatives working for the then widely disliked Pinkerton Detective Agency. Detectives of this agency killed innocent members of the James family and thus unified the rural communities of Missouri in protecting and nurturing this greatest of outlaws. Beyond the myriad propaganda and countless myths about this western legend, lived a farm boy who became a professional thief and a cold-blooded killer. He was at large for sixteen years. He committed dozens of daring robberies and killed at least a half dozen or more men. He died at the age of thirty-four.

Jesse James was raised with little formal education. His father, Robert James, was a Baptist preacher and his mother, Zerelda Cole Mimms, was a hard-working, strong-willed farm woman. Jesse's older brother, Frank (Alexander Franklin James, 1843-1915), a taciturn, withdrawn, and Bible-reading youth later followed his younger, more aggressive brother into banditry. It was because of the notorious and celebrated exploits of the James Brothers, the Younger Brothers who rode with them, and the Dalton Brothers who came later, the state of Missouri, their home state, became known as "The Mother of Bandits." The James and Younger boys were products of what was then known as the Middle Border, the wild and still unsettled states of Missouri and Kansas.

The parents of the James boys were hardy pioneers. Robert James married Zerelda Cole Mimms when she was seventeen. The couple moved from Kentucky to western Missouri where James became the pastor of a small Baptist Church outside of Kearney, Mo. He and his wife, with the help of neighbors, built a log cabin in the wilderness and began to carve out a farm. On Jan. 10, 1843, the couple's first child, Alexander Franklin James, was born. Jesse was born four-and-a-half years later. Robert James, though a cleric, was consumed by the gold fever, and in

1850, when Jesse was only three, left his family and went to California to seek his fortune, telling his wife that he would send for her as soon as he struck it rich. He slaved in the gold fields and found nothing but an early death from pneumonia.

A short time later, Zerelda James married a man named Simms, but their marriage dissolved within a few months. She was a woman of strong opinions who fiercely guarded her sons from criticism, one of the contributing factors in the breakup of her second marriage. In 1855, she married a third time, to Dr. Reuben Samuels. The physician was well-to-do, docile, and allowed his wife to make important family decisions. When it came to the boys, Mrs. Samuels made all the decisions. A third child, Archie Samuels, was born. He was retarded and was kept close to home, his older brothers doting upon him.

The James brothers stayed on the farm begun by their father, and through Dr. Samuels' acquisition of adjoining property, the James holdings grew. The family bought some slaves to work the land, and Frank and Jesse also farmed through their teenage years. When the Civil War broke out, the James brothers sided with the Confederacy. First Frank, then Jesse, rode off to fight with Confederate guerrillas under the command of William Clarke Quantrill. Quantrill later fought as William "Bloody Bill" Anderson and was part of the guerilla band that attacked and sacked Lawrence, Kan. In 1863, Union soldiers swooped down on the farm and looted the place, setting fires to crops and driving the slaves off the property. When the teenage Jesse attempted to stop the soldiers, he was beaten almost to death.

When he recovered, 17-year-old Jesse rode off to join his brother Frank and Cole Younger, who were fighting Union troops and raiding Union towns with Quantrill. Jesse was by then an expert horseman and crack shot with pistols and rifles. He was part of Anderson's contingent when it raided and burned Centralia, Kan., in 1864, helping to shoot down seventy-five Union prisoners in what later became known as the Centralia Massacre. A large Union force pursued Anderson's detachment, but the Confederates turned about and ferociously attacked the Union troops, routing them and slaying dozens. Jesse James was seen riding pell-mell into the Union ranks, the reins of his horse held by his teeth, firing two pistols. He shot down six northern soldiers and was credited with killing three of them.

That night, Jesse James sat at a campfire, taking no part in the discussion about the day's battle. He spent his time cleaning his pistol. Suddenly, the gun's hair trigger went back and a bullet took off the tip of James' left middle finger. He stared momentarily at the bloody finger, then said as he wrapped a kerchief about it: "Well, if that ain't the dingus-dangest thing!" His fellow guerrillas laughed with him and nicknamed him "Dingus" James. The James boys grew to such prominence that the Samuels were singled out for persecution by Union troops, who raided the farm and compelled the Samuels family to move to Nebraska. Following the end of the war, the James brothers returned to a ruined and vacant farm. As guerrillas that were not part of regular Confederate armed forces, they were still considered outlaws and rewards were posted for them dead or alive.

In early 1865, when a general amnesty was offered guerrillas, Jesse James led a small band toward Lexington, Mo., intending to surrender. The group included his brother, Frank James, and Cole Younger. A company of Union troops ignored the amnesty, and waiting in ambush, opened fire on the Confederate guerrillas. Jesse, in the lead, was shot off his horse, a bullet puncturing his lung. As the guerrillas fled, James crawled to nearby underbrush. Two Union soldiers pursued him, but he shot and killed one of their horses and they thought better of trying to capture James, who escaped. He was found by a friendly farmer the next day in a creek bed, trying to tend to his severe gunshot wound. The farmer bandaged James' wound and then helped him travel to Nebraska, where his mother and stepfather nursed him back to health.

James, believing he would not recover, begged his mother to take him back to Missouri, saying: "I don't want to die in a northern state." She and her husband put him in a wagon and rode slowly to Harlem, Mo., taking Jesse to a boarding house owned by Mrs. Samuels' brother, John Mimms. There, Jesse met young Zerelda Mimms, his cousin, who had been named after his mother. She nursed him back to health and the two fell in love. Zee, as she was called, was too young to marry, but the two promised to wed in the future. Nine years later they took their vows. When Jesse was almost well, his mother and stepfather took him back to the family farm near Kearney. He worked sporadically with Frank in the fields, although he had relapses with his wounded lung and was often bedridden. Both he and Frank, when in the fields, wore guns on their hips, and kept saddled horses nearby in the event Union troops acting as occupying forces in Missouri after the war swooped down to arrest or even shoot them, such was the bitterness that survived the war.

The war had changed much in the national character of the U.S. and it had also changed the perspective of the farm boys who fought in it. The James boys had tasted battle and blood, adventure, and danger. They had survived the worst carnage ever seen in the country, and either out of boredom or an ambition that went beyond the dull chores of their farm, they, like many others in that turbulent era, buckled gun belts, mounted horses, and rode into small towns to rob banks. The rationale the raiders later said was "we were driven to it." They blamed Yankee bankers and railroad magnates for impossible farm mortgages and threatening foreclosure in underhanded land-grabbing schemes. And to some small degree it was true.

The first bank robbery attributed to the James Brothers occurred on Feb. 13, 1866. Ten men rode into Liberty, Mo. While eight waited outside with the horses, two went into the Clay County Savings Bank. One of these men was later identified as Frank James. The other was Cole Younger, the oldest and most daring of the Younger Brothers (this included three out of thirteen children who later took up robbery, Coleman, James, and Robert).

One of the robbers, allegedly Frank James, approached father and son cashiers Greenup and William Bird, and said: "If you make any noise, you will be shot." He then demanded all the money behind the teller's cage and in the vault be stuffed into a wheat sack. Both men held pistols aimed at the Birds. The robbers emerged from the bank without incident a few minutes later. Inside the wheat sack was more than $60,000 ($15,000 in gold and $45,000 in non-negotiable securities).

The men outside joined the two coming from the bank and the ten rode slowly out of town. Then George "Jolly" Wymore, en route to classes at William Jewell College, paused in the town square and stared at one of the riders as if he knew him. The rider slowed his horse, rode a few feet away from Wymore, then wheeled in his saddle, drawing his pistol and firing three shots into the startled Wymore, who collapsed and died on the spot. Apparently, the rider realized that Wymore had recognized him. As Wymore fell, the entire gang drew weapons and began firing wildly into the air as they spurred their horses down the street and out of town. A posse was quickly formed, but it lost the bandits, who had crossed the Missouri River on a ferry and disappeared in a raging snowstorm.

The Liberty raid was the first daylight bank robbery in the U.S. by an organized band of robbers. (The first U.S. bank robbery was committed by lone postal employee Edward W. Green, who held up a bank in Malden, Mass., on Dec. 15, 1863.) Whether or not Jesse James was present at the Liberty bank robbery was debated by several western historians. Some claimed he was at home nursing his old lung wound. Others insist that Jesse was outside the bank with the other riders, waiting for his brother Frank and Cole Younger to emerge. However, Jesse was certainly a member of the same gang that robbed the Alexander Mitchell Bank in Lexington, Mo., on Oct. 30, 1866.

A tall young man who stood a little under six feet entered the bank while another young man stood outside the front entrance. The first young man went to a teller's cage and held out a $50 bill to cashier J.L. Thomas. "Can you change this for me?" he asked.

The original James-Samuel cabin in Clay County, Mo.

Jesse, left, and Frank James in their twenties.

Zerelda James Samuels

Jesse James as a teenager.

Frank James at twenty.

Jesse when he rode with Bill Anderson.

Frank James during the Civil War.

Frank James, 1867.

"No," the suspicious Thomas said, remembering the Liberty bank had just been robbed and that a man first asked to change a large bill.

The young man then drew a gun and leveled it at Thomas. Three other men entered the bank and also drew guns, training these on the bank employees. The tall young man said: "You've got one $100,000 in this bank. Unless you turn it over to me, you'll be killed."

"That's not true," Thomas said, denying the bank had that much money.

"Let's have the key to the vault," the tall young man demanded.

"I don't have it," Thomas told him.

The bandits went through Thomas' pockets and found nothing. They then stuffed $2,011 into a wheat sack and left cursing. Actually, the vault held considerably more cash. The tall young man was identified as Jesse James and this was the first time the bandit was linked to robbery.

On Mar. 2, 1867, the James-Younger gang rode into Savanna, Mo., and went into the local bank. They aimed guns at bank president, Judge John McClain, who refused to turn over the vault keys. One bandit stepped forward and shot McClain in the chest. The bandits ran from the bank and rode quickly from the town. McClain survived. On May 22, 1867, it was a different story. The James-Younger gang decided to adopt guerrilla tactics when raiding the Hughes and Wasson Bank of Richmond, Mo. They rode into town shooting their weapons and whooping like drunken cowboys. Pedestrians ran in all directions while six men—Jesse and Frank James, Cole, Jim, and Bob Younger, and James White—broke down the locked front door of the bank. The bandits stuffed $4,000 into a wheat sack and then raced to the street.

Citizens grabbed their guns and began firing on the bandits as they mounted their horses and attempted to flee. Mayor John B. Shaw tried to rally residents as he ran to the bank with a pistol in his hand. The bandits fired many shots at him and Shaw fell to the street dead, seven bullets in him. Impetuously, the bandits decided to attack the jail instead of fleeing, having heard that several ex-guerrillas were being held there. They tried to batter down the jail's front door. Frank Griffin, the 15-year-old son of the jailer, ran behind a tree with a rifle and began shooting at the bandits. They rode past him and riddled his body, killing him. His father, B.G. Griffin, then raced forward, but a bandit caught him and fired a bullet into his head, leaving him dead beside his son.

The gang then rode quickly out of town, but a large posse caught up with them at sundown. A pitched battle ensued and the bandits escaped under the cover of darkness. Several were tracked down. The first was Payne Jones. A young girl guided a posse to the Jones farm and Jones came running out of his farmhouse with two guns blazing. He shot down the girl and killed a posse member. Jones was captured but later killed in a gun battle. Next, Richard Burns was tracked to his farmhouse near Richmond. Vigilantes took him to a large tree, and with torches flickering, quickly tried and convicted him of the Richmond robbery and murders. He was then hanged. Andy Maguire and Tom Little, identified as Richmond raiders, were apprehended and lynched.

The James brothers were also identified and several vigilante groups assembled. Before the vigilantes rode to the James farm, "alibi cards" were sent to the vigilante leaders. The cards bore signed statements from Frank and Jesse James saying they had no part in the Richmond bank raid, and incredibly, their word was accepted. If the James brothers said they were innocent, then that was the end of the matter, such was their reputation in western Missouri. Nowhere in Clay or Ray counties would a Missourian betray these men. Anyone who continued to insist that they had robbed the bank risked being shot and killed while traveling lonely roads. Merchants who labeled the boys thieves and murderers risked boycotts and being put out of business. This fierce loyalty to the ex-guerrillas lasted until the day Jesse Woodson James was

executed by two traitorous men.

The James-Younger gang continued robbing banks despite the threat of Union soldiers, lawmen, and vigilantes. There were always farmers, men who had fought in the Civil War on the southern side, who were willing to ride with them on a raid or two to get enough money to pay off a mortgage or support a family. The James and Younger brothers were the professionals and kept most of the loot. After Richmond they were careful to select banks some distance from their homes and made only a few raids each year, then returning to their farms to resume peaceful, law-abiding ways. In these early years they robbed with leisure, but later they became desperate, infamous and much-wanted. So they sought the "big strike," a robbery that would yield a great sum and allow them to permanently retire, to resettle in California or to flee to Mexico or even South America.

Jesse and Frank James and Cole and Jim Younger, along with four other men, rode far afield on Mar. 21, 1868, arriving in Russellville, Ky. Actually, Frank James had been in the area for some days, scouting the Southern Bank of Kentucky. He had used the alias Frank Colburn, pretending to be a cattle buyer from Louisville. He entered the bank and approached the managers, Nimrod Long and George Norton. He asked Long to cash a $100 bill, but Long became suspicious. Frank James pointed to a tall, blue-eyed man standing in the door of the bank. "I've got to pay off one of my hired hands," he said.

Long looked over the bill carefully and then said: "This bill is counterfeit, Mr. Colburn."

Frank James laughed, took the bill back and tucked it into his vest pocket, saying: "I reckon it is." He then drew his pistol and aimed it at Long. "But this isn't, Mr. Long. Open the vault."

The young man in the doorway was also holding a pistol and aiming it at him. Long turned and then dashed for the rear door of the bank, but Jesse fired a single shot that grazed the banker's scalp and sent him unconscious to the floor. Then Jesse ran to him and hit Long on the head repeatedly with his gun butt. Long, a burly man, rolled over and grabbed the bandit's hands. Frank James stood next to the struggling men, shouting for Jesse to "finish him!" He aimed his pistol at the banker but could not fire for fear of hitting his brother.

Suddenly, Long found enough strength to throw off Jesse and jump up. He ran to the door and outside into an alley. Jesse and Frank fired at him, but the two bullets merely struck the door frame. Once outside, Long raced down the alley, yelling: "They're robbing my bank! They're robbing my bank!" Citizens misunderstood Long's message and thought his bank was on fire. Several raced about the streets grabbing water buckets. Meanwhile, Frank and Jesse James dragged two sacks full of gold from the bank, about $14,000, and put the heavy sacks on the saddles of the gang's horses. An old man, half blind, wandered into the middle of the street. Cole Younger rode up to him, saying: "Old man, we're having a little serenade here, and there's danger of you getting hurt. Just get behind my horse here and you'll be out of the way." Younger moved his horse gently next to the old man so that he edged him out of the road. The bandits then formed a single line and raced out of the town hollering and firing their weapons as if in a cavalry charge. A fifty-man posse gave pursuit but lost the experienced riders in the wilderness.

The Pinkerton Detective Agency was hired by an association of bankers and began its long crusade to capture the James-Younger band. Their detectives interviewed George Hite, a neighbor of the James Brothers, but he insisted he knew nothing of the Russellville raid and that the James Brothers were innocent. He was lying. His own sons often rode with Jesse and Frank James and it was George Hite, upon Jesse's assassination, who explained how the gang met in barns and in kitchens of farmhouses to plan their robberies. They would scout a town and determine whether or not the local bank held a substantial amount of cash. They might send someone from the gang to make deposits, who, as a depositor, would ask questions about security and whether or not the bank was solvent and thus learn from the

The First National Bank at Northfield.

Some of Northfield's citizens who fought the James gang.

Jesse James in 1876.

Cole Younger

Clell Miller, dead.

Jim Younger

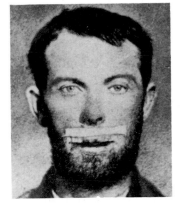

Bill Chadwell, dead.

Frank James in 1876.

REWARD!
- DEAD OR ALIVE -

$5,000.$⁰⁰ will be paid for the capture of the men who robbed the bank at
NORTHFIELD, MINN.

They are believed to be **Jesse James** and his Band, or the Youngers.

All officers are warned to use precaution in making arrest. These are the most desperate men in America.

Take no chances! Shoot to kill!!

J. H. McDonald.

Reward poster for the James boys.

Bob Younger

Charlie Pitts, dead.

bankers the amount of money usually kept on hand.

In these days, the gang operated democratically, its members selecting a target bank and then voting whether to rob it. Jesse James was not then the leader of the gang, although he was considered by its members as the most daring and the one most likely to kill anyone who interfered in a robbery. Not until the gang's disastrous raid on Northfield, Minn., in 1876 did Jesse become the overall leader, and by then his authority rested upon his widespread reputation which he enjoyed and used to advance his own image among his fellow outlaws. He was also by then a deadly killer, who even threatened to shoot his own brother Frank for disagreeing with him.

Frank James was almost as much an enigma as his younger brother Jesse. Well-read, Frank liked to quote the Bible and Shakespeare, but his fellow bandits thought him sanctimonious, hypocritical, and overly cautious to the point of annoyance. He vexed the impetuous Younger brothers, especially the good-natured Cole Younger. But Frank James was no mere toady to Jesse. He was resolute and a deadly marksman, as feared a gunman as his younger brother. It was Cole Younger, however, who was the most experienced horseman and gunman, and it was Cole who lent balance and authority to the gang. Jesse and Frank James showed their murderous natures on Dec. 7, 1869, when they rode into Gallatin, Mo., going into the Davies County Savings Bank.

Frank James offered a $100 bill to cashier John W. Sheets, asking him to change it. Sheets began walking to his desk. Sheets had been a Union officer during the Civil War and the brothers apparently held a deep hatred for him. It was later claimed that it had been Sheets who had commanded the Union troops who had fired on Jesse and wounded him when he had attempted to surrender in 1865. Jesse James, without warning, suddenly shot and killed Sheets as he stood next to his desk. Jesse fired twice, hitting Sheets in the head and chest. Frank James then ran behind the counter and gathered up about $500, which he threw into a wheat sack. William McDowell, a clerk, ran toward the front entrance of the bank and Frank shot him in the arm. The wounded clerk staggered to the street and shouted an alarm. The bandit brothers raced to their horses. Frank mounted but Jesse's foot caught in the stirrup of his expensive horse and the animal bolted, dragging the outlaw almost forty feet down the middle of the street. Frank turned back, stopped Jesse's horse, allowing the younger James to jump on Frank's horse. They rode from town with bullets smacking at their single horse's hoofs. They later stole another horse and finished their escape.

The horse the bandits left behind was identified as having belonged to Jesse James, but he reported that his horse had been stolen just before the Gallatin robbery. Jesse had earlier established another identity for himself after robbing the Gallatin bank. As he and Frank left town, they stopped a Methodist minister named Helm, and Jesse told the pastor that he was "Bill Anderson's brother. I just killed S.P. Cox who works back there in the bank at Gallatin. He killed my brother in the war and I got him at last!" Jesse had purposely lied about himself and his victim, wrongly identifying Sheets, to cover his murder. But this ruse did not work. A large posse headed for the James farm on Dec. 15, 1869, and when they arrived, Jesse and Frank James, mounted two fast horses and raced from the barn. The posse pursued them, with Deputy Sheriff John Thomason in the lead. Thomason dismounted and trained his rifle on the two fleeing James boys, but his horse bolted and spoiled his shot. Thomason's horse then caught up with the James brothers and Jesse shot the animal dead. The boys escaped.

Somehow, the James boys managed to convince local authorities that they were not the bandits responsible for the bloody Gallatin holdup, even though most citizens were certain they were. For almost two years, the James gang remained inactive. Then, on June 3, 1871, Jesse and Frank James, Cole, Jim and Bob (or John) Younger, Jim Cummins, Charlie Pitts (alias Samuel Wells), and Ed Miller took a leisurely ride to the sleepy little hamlet of Corydon, Iowa. Jesse and Frank James and Cole Younger entered the Ocobock Brothers Bank and found only one clerk. The other bandits waited outside the bank and noticed the streets were empty. Frank asked the clerk where everyone had gone and the clerk explained that Henry Clay Dean, a celebrated Methodist preacher, was giving a lecture at the local church, and the entire town had turned out to hear him.

"All the better," Jesse said, drawing his pistol and aiming it at the clerk. Within a few minutes the bandits had cleaned out the bank, taking with them more than $45,000 in gold and bills. The bandits rode slowly out of town, but when they came to the church where the townspeople had gathered, Jesse smiled and told his men to wait. He got off his horse and went into the church, standing in the middle of the aisle at the back of the church, where he loudly announced: "Folks, you should know that some riders were just down to the bank and tied up the cashier. All the drawers are cleaned out. You folks best get down there in a hurry!" He then began to laugh loudly and, while the congregation stared in awe at the tall young man with piercing blue eyes, he slowly turned and walked back to his horse. He and his men rode out of town slowly, all laughing uproariously.

Finally, one man in the church shouted: "For God's sake! It's the James gang! They've just robbed the bank!" After finding the cashier bound, the citizens of Corydon hastily formed a posse and rode after the bandits, but the gang outdistanced them and they lost all trace of the thieves by the time they reached Clay County, Mo. The gang did not wait long to plan and execute its next raid, this time riding to Columbia, Ky., on Apr. 29, 1872. Jesse and Frank James entered the bank. Outside waiting with the horses were Clell Miller and Cole Younger. Jesse demanded the key to the safe but cashier R.A.C. Martin balked and Jesse shot him three times, killing him. Frank James casually stepped over Martin's body and cleaned out the cash drawers, taking only $600. The gang rode quickly out of town. A huge posse seeking vengeance for the Martin slaying rode after the bandits, but the James gang, old hands at evasion by then, doubled back on their own trail twice, circled Columbia, and then rode on to Missouri, completely confusing the pursuing lawmen.

On May 23, 1872, Jesse James, Cole and Bob Younger, Clell Miller and Bill Chadwell (alias Bill Stiles) rode into Ste. Genevieve, Mo., entering the local bank where cashier O.D. Harris recognized the bandits. He quickly complied with their demands and filled a grain sack with more than $4,000 in gold and bills, and the gang left town at a gallop. No posse pursued the robbers. By then, it seemed inevitable that every town in Missouri would receive a visit from the James-Younger gang and most local lawmen became apathetic in their efforts to catch the thieves, knowing that the bandits were protected by almost everyone in Clay and Ray counties. A short distance outside of Ste. Genevieve, Jesse dismounted to readjust the gold sack hanging from his saddle and, at that moment, his skittish horse ran off into a field.

A farmer appeared on the road and Jesse asked him to go after the animal. He refused but quickly changed his mind when the other members of the gang aimed six-guns at him. The farmer chased the horse across the field and returned him to Jesse. He grinned at the outlaw chief with a toothless smile and then asked with a thick accent: "I catch der horse. Vot do I get for dot, yah?"

Jesse mounted the animal and replied: "Your life, Dutchy. Vot you tink, yah?" He rode off laughing. By then Jesse James was very much aware of his growing reputation and he enjoyed his notoriety. He even played up to his self-image of the unbeatable bad man, a daring bandit with a sense of humor and intelligence to outwit any country bumpkin posse. He demonstrated his belief in his fame on Sept. 26, 1872, when he, Frank James, and Cole Younger rode to the fairgrounds outside of Kansas City, Mo. At the main gate, Jesse dismounted and went to the cashier. He smiled at Ben Wallace, the cashier, and then said in a pleasant voice: "What if I was to say that I was Jesse James and I told you to hand out that tin box of money? What would you say?"

"I'd say I'd see you in hell first," snapped Wallace.

"Well, that's just who I am and you'd better hand it out pretty damned quick or—" He aimed a pistol at Wallace. The cashier handed over the money in the tin box, $978. Stuffing this in the traditional sack, Jesse mounted his horse. The feisty Wallace ran from the cashier's box and grabbed the stirrup on Jesse's horse, holding on to it. "It's the James gang!" he shouted, but few in the crowd heard him. Jesse turned the horse away from Wallace, drawing his pistol and firing a shot that went wild and struck a girl in the leg. The three men then galloped into some nearby woods and vanished. En route home, Jesse cursed the bad luck. Frank James said nothing. He had scouted the fair and had reported that as much as $10,000 was kept on hand with the cashier. He had been right, but shortly before the bandits arrived to rob the cashier, thousands of dollars had been taken from the strongbox and sent to a local bank for safekeeping.

The paltry sum taken at Kansas City caused the bandits to believe that robbery simply was not worth the effort anymore. Even banks were unreliable in having large sums of cash on hand. Trains, however, always carried large amounts of gold, silver, and currency. They knew well that the first train robbery had been committed by the ill-fated Reno Brothers of Indiana, but they felt themselves superior to the Hoosier bandits and believed they would have no trouble in successfully looting trains. So the gang rode to Adair, Iowa, in mid-July 1873. Frank James had taken several trains west, as far as Omaha, Neb., riding the Chicago, Rock Island, and Pacific Express (while reading *Pilgrim's Progress*). He reported to the rest of the gang that when the Express reached Adair on July 21, 1873, it would be carrying more than $100,000 in gold, destined for eastern banks.

Gang members arrived outside Adair on that day and removed a section of track. These included Jesse and Frank James, Cole and Jim Younger, Clell Miller, Bob Moore, and Commanche Tony. As the Express came around a bend, its engineer, John Rafferty, saw the break and reversed the engine. It was too late. The engine raced into the open track and crashed onto its side, crushing Rafferty to death. Jesse and his men rode from a nearby wood and went to the baggage car, pointing guns at the clerks who opened the safe to give them not $100,000 but only $2,000 in federal reserve notes. The gold that was supposed to have been on board had been rescheduled that morning and had gone through Adair four hours earlier on a fast Express. The bandits rode back to Missouri discouraged. They decided to go back to farming and for six months, the James-Younger gang was inactive.

Before attacking their next train, the James-Younger gang committed a vintage holdup. On Jan. 15, 1874, the bandits rode south to Arkansas and, outside of Malvern, held up the Concord Stagecoach, one of their few such robberies. Cole Younger, who was the experienced hand and practical hub of the gang, proved during this robbery that he, too, had his moments of caprice. After the gang stopped the stage, driver and passengers were ordered to step down and line up before the gang as guns were trained on them. More than $4,000 in gold, bills, and jewels were taken from the well-to-do passengers. When Cole Younger took a gold watch from a man who protested in a strong southern accent, the bandit paused. "Are you a southerner?" he asked, a rather ridiculous question since there were few northerners traveling in Arkansas at that time.

"Yes, suh," replied the gentleman traveler.

"Were you in the Confederate Army?"

"I had that distinction, suh."

"State your rank, regiment, and commanding officer," Younger demanded.

When the passenger gave Younger this information, he was startled to see Younger hand him back his watch. "We are all Confederate soldiers," Younger said with some pride, enjoying his magnanimity. "We don't rob southerners, especially Confederate soldiers." He pointed his finger at the rest of the passengers and said in a solemn voice: "But Yankees and detectives are not exempt."

In fifteen days, the gang had ridden back to Missouri, and on Jan. 31, 1874, entered the small flag station at Gadshill, Mo., a depot along the line of the Iron Mountain Railroad. The bandits, which included Jesse and Frank James, Cole, Jim, and Bob Younger, Jim Cummins, Clell and Ed Miller, Sam Hildebrand, Arthur McCory, and Jim Reed, flagged down the Little Rock Express. As the train came to a stop, the bandits jumped into the baggage car and quickly opened the safe, shooting off its locks. They took from it more than $22,000 in gold and bills. Some of the bandits went through the cars, robbing the passengers. Jesse James then mounted his horse and rode up to the engineer's cabin where Cole Younger held the engineer under his gun. "Give her a toot, Cole!" Jesse shouted to him. Cole Younger grabbed the whistle cord and yanked on it. As the whistle shrieked, Younger laughed like a small boy with a new toy.

Before the gang departed, Jesse threw a stick to the engineer. Around it was wrapped a piece of paper. James told the engineer: "Give this to the newspapers. We like to do things in style." The scrap of paper contained Jesse's own press release of the robbery which he had written only a few hours before the train had been stopped. It read:

THE MOST DARING TRAIN ROBBERY ON RECORD!

The southbound train of the Iron Mountain Railroad was stopped here this evening by five (there were ten bandits) heavily armed men and robbed of _____ dollars. The robbers arrived at the station a few minutes before the arrival of the train and arrested the agent and put him under guard and then threw the train on the switch. The robbers were all large men, all being slightly under six feet. After robbing the train they started in a southerly direction. They were all mounted on handsome horses.

PS: They are a hell of an excitement in this part of the country.

After the Gadshill raid the robberies stopped, and it seemed as if the James-Younger gang had been swallowed by the earth. There was no trace of any of the bandits for almost a year. With the spoils from the robbery, Jesse decided to finally wed Zeralda Mimms, his cousin. They had met often in wooded retreats and lonely cabins in the wilderness. Now Zee Mimms insisted that they either marry or never see each other again. Jesse and Zee went to Kansas City and were married. They then traveled to Galveston, Texas, where a reporter for the St. Louis *Dispatch* interviewed Jesse before he and Zee boarded a steamer headed for Vera Cruz where they planned to honeymoon. Jesse candidly told the reporter: "On the 23rd of April, 1874, I was married to Miss Zee Mimms, of Kansas City, and at the house of a friend there.

"About fifty of our mutual friends were present on the occasion and quite a noted Methodist minister (Reverend William James, Jesse's uncle) performed the ceremonies. We had been engaged for nine years and through good and evil report, and not withstanding the lies that had been told upon me and the crimes laid at my door, her devotion to me has never wavered for a moment. You can say that both of us married for love, and that there cannot be any sort of doubt about our marriage being a happy one." Jesse and Zee James, however, did not take ship for Vera Cruz but traveled back to Missouri and settled on a small farm near Kearney, living in a log cabin. Jesse James was by then dedicated to a way of crime and had no thought to retire or reform. His wife's attitude about his criminal ways was never learned, but Wood Hite, a family friend, later stated that "she looked the other way...out of love." Hite went on to say that Jesse James was a devoted husband and loved his wife very much. The couple produced two children, Jesse, Jr., and Mary James. The outlaw spent a great deal of time with his children, playing with them whenever he was home. The couple continued to travel, living in Texas, then Tennessee, and even in the heart of Kansas City.

Frank James would also marry two years later, eloping with 17-year-old Annie Ralston, a union that would produce a son, Robert, in 1878. While Jesse was settling down to a farming life, the Pinkerton Detective Agency increased its efforts to arrest and try the James boys for their past crimes. Detectives roamed in pairs and in groups through western Missouri, seeking the James brothers and their allies, the Youngers. The detective agency had been waging a private war with the James-Younger clan for sometime. On Mar. 16, 1874, Jim and John Younger were riding through the woods near Osceola, Mo. Two Pinkerton detectives, Louis J. Lull and E.B. Daniels, who had been trailing them, suddenly found themselves faced by the two Youngers. The detectives claimed they were cattle buyers but Jim Younger correctly guessed them to be Pinkertons. The detectives and the Youngers both went for their guns at the same time and Lull and Daniels were killed. So was John Younger. A month later Jesse James, Clell Miller, and James Latche, killed another Pinkerton agent, John W. Whicher. From that day on, the Pinkertons hounded the James-Young gang.

The Pinkertons watched the Samuels farm on and off, believing that Jesse and Frank would pay their mother a visit. Detectives learned, on Jan. 26, 1875, that the boys would arrive at the Samuels farm after sundown. They stationed men near the farmhouse and then shouted for Jesse and Frank to come outside. A light in the window went out and then a bomb of some sort was thrown through the window by one of the Pinkerton men. It exploded with a deafening roar. The bomb blew off Mrs. Samuel's arm and a fragment of the bomb tore through the side of Archie Peyton Samuel, the 8-year-old half-brother of Jesse and Frank. The child died within an hour in great pain and agony.

No other act than this "inexcusable and cowardly deed," as the press termed it, could have earned more sympathy for the James boys. The newspapers vilified the Pinkertons, who were universally hated, and labeled them child-killers and inhuman monsters who attacked defenseless women. Even though Allan Pinkerton repeatedly denied that any of his men had thrown a bomb into the Samuels' home, his agency fell into disgrace. Jesse was so incensed at the killing of his little half-brother and the mutilation of his mother that he spent long hours planning the execution of Allan Pinkerton. According to Wood Hite, he actually took a train to Chicago and spent hours waiting for Pinkerton to show up at his headquarters there, planning to shoot the detective on sight. He did see Pinkerton but did not shoot him on a crowded Chicago street. He later told Hite: "I had a dozen chances to kill him when he didn't know it. I wanted to give him a fair chance but the opportunity never came."

For some time after this, Jesse and Frank James fell out. Frank had apparently tried to convince his younger brother to retire, that bank and train robbing were getting too dangerous. Jesse, on the other hand, called Frank a coward, especially since he refused to try to track down Allan Pinkerton and take vengeance on him for the death of this half-brother. Frank refused to associate with Jesse or the rest of the gang for some time. He remained on a farm, reading and writing letters to Missouri newspapers, attempting to vindicate himself and stating that he was not responsible for the robberies attributed to him. He went on to say that he and his brother Jesse "were not good friends (at the time of Kansas City fairgrounds robbery) and have not been for several years."

By early 1875, the brothers were reunited and led the Youngers to Texas where, on May 12, they robbed the San Antonio stage of $3,000. Cole Younger reportedly had to be persuaded to join the band. He was busy romancing Belle Starr, the daughter of Collins County rancher John Shirley. Cole Younger then had the notion to quit banditry. He told Jesse and Frank James that he was thinking of settling in Dallas, where he had a job offer as a census taker. Jesse talked him out of this idea and Younger followed the James boys back to Missouri where an important train robbery was planned.

Through a bribed railroad clerk, the gang learned that the United Express Company would be shipping more than $100,000 on the Missouri Pacific Railroad. On July 7, 1875, Jesse and Frank James, Cole, Jim and Bob Younger, Clell Miller, Charlie Pitts, and Bill Chadwell were waiting for the train as it slowed to cross an old railroad bridge east of Otterville, Mo. The gang trained pistols on the engineer who brought the engine to a halt. The bandits then approached the Adams Express car and entered it, ordering guard John Bushnell to open the safe. "It can't be done," Bushnell nervously told Jesse. "I don't have the keys to it. It's locked all the way through and the keys are at the other end of the run."

"Get an ax," Jesse told Bob Younger who took a fire ax from the wall of the baggage car and began chopping away at the safe. It was useless. All Younger succeeded in doing was making a few dents in the heavy iron safe. Then Cole Younger demanded the ax. A tall, powerful man, Younger repeatedly swung his 200 pounds against the safe for ten minutes, finally making a small hole in the top of the safe. Jesse reached through the hole and pulled up a leather pouch from which the bandits took more than $75,000. They stuffed the money into a grain sack and then tossed it to Frank James and the others waiting outside. Jesse, Cole, and Bob Younger then climbed on their horses, but before riding off, Jesse told Bushnell: "If you see any of the Pinkertons, tell 'em to come and get us."

This strike, the gang's largest to date, convinced Jesse and the others that with the proper information they could commit robberies that would bring them quick fortunes and enough money to retire. Bill Chadwell, a native of Minnesota, was sent to scout the large First National Bank in Northfield, Minn., reputedly one of the wealthiest banks in the Midwest. Though far afield from their regular haunts, the Northfield bank promised as much as $200,000 in cash and gold, perhaps more. The gang members were further lured to rob this bank because its two principal stockholders were Ben Butler and W.A. Ames, who had been Union officials in the Civil War and were still much hated for the oppressive measures they employed when occupying southern cities. Butler, the general in charge of conquered New Orleans, had issued an order which allowed his soldiers to treat women there as common streetwalkers. Ames was considered the worst carpetbagger to ever plague the South. Both men had enriched themselves through the spoils of war and the misfortune of the devastated southerners.

In August 1876, the James-Younger band began its ride north, moving slowly and with great confidence. They had never experienced any serious setbacks and their members had remained unharmed in ten years of robbery. The bandits were all mounted on the finest horses available and looked prosperous. All wore new suits, shiny black boots, and long linen dusters like those worn by cattle buyers. They carried new carbines and heavy Colt pistols on their hips. Jesse wore two more Colts in shoulder holsters.

The eight men rode into Northfield, Minn., on Sept. 7, 1876. To the bandits, Northfield looked like any other town they had raided, with a main street and small stores nestled next to the bank. Yet Northfield was unlike any town the gang had ever visited. Its residents were industrious pioneers who placed great value on thrift and an even greater value on the law. Minnesota was not Missouri, where roving bands of outlaws were commonplace. The state was relatively free of such bandits and the natives of Northfield were fiercely protective of their town and the savings in their bank. And, as they proved with lethal dedication, they would battle anyone who tried to take what they had earned by the sweat of their brows.

At 2 a.m., Jesse, Charlie Pitts, and Bob Younger entered the First National Bank while Cole Younger and Clell Miller waited outside the bank, holding the horses. At the end of the street Frank James, Bill Chadwell, and Jim Younger sat on their horses, guarding the exit of the town, ready to protect the gang when it fled Northfield. Trouble began almost immediately. J.A. Allen,

Jesse James, 1881.

PROCLAMATION
$5,000.00
REWARD
FOR EACH of SEVEN ROBBERS of THE TRAIN at
WINSTON, MO., JULY 15, 1881, and THE MURDER of
CONDUCTER WESTFALL
$ 5,000.00
ADDITIONAL for ARREST or CAPTURE
DEAD OR ALIVE
OF JESSE OR FRANK JAMES
THIS NOTICE TAKES the PLACE of ALL PREVIOUS
REWARD NOTICES.
CONTACT SHERIFF, DAVIESS COUNTY, MISSOURI
IMMEDIATELY
T. T. CRITTENDEN, GOVERNOR
STATE OF MISSOURI
JULY 26, 1881

Reward poster, 1881.

Bob Ford holding the gun he used to kill Jesse James.

Jesse's home in St. Joseph, Mo., where he was killed.

Charlie Ford, a suicide.

Jesse James, dead, 1882.

Jesse's children, Mary and Jesse James, Jr.

Jesse's wife, Zee James.

a hardware store owner, spotted the men outside the bank and walked over to investigate. Clell Miller grabbed his arm and said: "Keep your goddamned mouth shut!" Allen broke free of Miller's grip and began to run down the street, shouting: "Get your guns, boys! They're robbing the bank!" Henry Wheeler, a university student home on vacation, saw Allen and took up the alarm. He, too, began to shout: "Robbery! Robbery! Robbery! They're all at the bank!" Cole Younger and Miller quickly mounted their horses and they were joined by Frank James, Jim Younger and Chadwell. The five outlaws began racing up and down the street, shouting to the startled residents: "Get in! Get in!" This technique had worked many times in Missouri where gun-shy natives raced for cover. But the citizens of Northfield did just the opposite. Dozens of men, young and old, grabbed pistols, rifles, and shotguns and ran to the street or took positions in windows, behind doors, and at the corners of buildings.

Inside the bank, Jesse James held his pistol on acting bank cashier Joseph Lee Heywood, telling him: "Don't holler! There's forty men outside the bank." Heywood nodded as Jesse added in a menacing voice: "Open the goddamned safe before I blow your head off!" "I can't do that," Heywood said, "there's a time lock on it." Pitts ran forward with a knife and cut the cashier's throat slightly. He and Bob Younger both stuck their pistols into Heywood's stomach. The cashier kept insisting that the safe was on a time lock. None of the bandits bothered to check the safe. Heywood was lying. The safe was unlocked and had no time lock. Then a clerk, A.E. Bunker, ran into a back room. Pitts fired a shot at him but missed. Bob Younger went through the cash drawers and found only a small amount of money. Firing could be heard in the street and Pitts went to the front entrance of the bank. He turned to Jesse and shouted: "The game's up! Pull out or they'll be killing our men!"

Bob Younger and Jesse James followed Pitts out the front door, but one of them—it was never determined which—turned and shot Heywood in the head. He fell dead to the bank floor. The scene that greeted Jesse as he stepped into the street was as bloody as any battle he had experienced in the Civil War. Clell Miller was riding crazily about, his face blasted to pulp and gushing blood. Elias Stacy, a resident, had rushed him moments earlier and let loose a shotgun blast that caught Miller full in the face. He was unrecognizable. His flesh hung in shreds from his jaw and his shirt front was soaked with blood. He moaned and screamed wildly, firing his six-gun indiscriminately. One of Miller's wild shots struck and killed Nicholas Gustavson, a terrified immigrant who was trying to reach the cover of a building.

A bullet smacked into Cole Younger's shoulder. Then A.B. Manning fired a shot that struck Bill Chadwell square in the heart. The outlaw stood straight up in his saddle for a moment then toppled to earth, dead. Wheeler, the university student, had gotten a gun and repeatedly shot the already wounded Clell Miller until he also fell from his horse dead. Bob Younger raced forward on his horse, firing at Manning, and Wheeler fired a shot at him, wounding him in the hand. Younger switched his weapon to the other hand and fired back at Wheeler.

By that time the citizens had blocked both ends of the street and dozens of men were firing at the outlaws who rode up and down the street through a murderous cross fire, looking desperately for an escape route. A bullet struck Charlie Pitts, then Jim Younger, then Cole Younger. The gang was being shot to pieces. "It's no use, men!" Jesse shouted to the others. "Let's go! Let's go!" Bob Younger, who had been shot from his horse, managed to climb up behind his brother Cole and what was left of the gang rode wildly down the street through heavy fire. Scores of citizens who did not have weapons threw rocks at them.

Some miles outside Northfield, the gang rested for a few minutes. Jesse looked at Bob Younger's wounds and then told his cousin Cole Younger that Bob was too seriously wounded to continue. He suggested that either Bob be left behind or "we put him out of his misery." Reaching for his six-gun, Cole Younger, who had taken Jesse's orders for years, glared at Jesse and told

him that he would not leave his brother behind. "Maybe it's best we split up," he said. Jesse and Frank, the only bandits in the gang not wounded, nodded and then rode off in one direction.

The Younger brothers and Pitts headed in another direction. The Youngers were slowed by their wounds and left a clear trail for pursuing lawmen to follow. Fourteen days later they were trapped in a swamp outside of Madelia, Minn. More than fifty men surrounded them and a full-scale battle ensued. An hour later, Sheriff Glispen shouted to the outlaws who were behind a large fallen tree: "Do you men surrender?" As the lawmen waited for an answer, they reloaded their weapons and prepared for further battle. Then the silence was pierced by a voice from behind the large tree. "I surrender!" Bob Younger, bleeding from five wounds, stood up unsteadily and waved the possemen forward. "They're all down, except me." The lawmen came forward cautiously, guns at the ready. They found Cole Younger wounded seven times and Jim Younger wounded five times. Both were still alive. Charlie Pitts lay flat on the ground, his six-guns and rifle empty of bullets. There were five bullet wounds in his chest. He was dead.

The Younger Brothers were taken into custody, and as they rode in an open cart through the small Minnesota towns, en route to medical attention, citizens came out by the thousands to see them, curious about these strange men from Missouri who had traveled hundreds of miles to risk their lives. All three brothers were tried and sentenced to life imprisonment. As they entered the state penitentiary at Stillwater, Minn., Cole Younger was asked why he and his brothers had turned to crime. "We were victims of circumstances," he explained, not half believing his own oft-repeated words. "We were drove to it, sir."

The Northfield raid made national headlines and Jesse and Frank James became the most sought-after outlaws in the U.S. But they were nowhere to be found. Hundreds of possemen scoured Minnesota, Wisconsin, and Iowa for them as the brothers moved slowly south. They traveled on foot, stole horses, and then abandoned them. They slept in abandoned farm buildings during the day and moved only at night. They ate raw vegetables and hid from sight, believing that all were their enemies. It took them three weeks to reach Missouri and by then they looked like scarecrows, their clothes in rags. Both Jesse and Frank realized that they were too notorious now to remain in Missouri. The murders they had committed in Northfield had branded them cold-blooded killers. Even many of their former supporters in Missouri found it hard to excuse their actions. Hiding in a covered wagon, Jesse and Frank were driven to Tennessee. Both purchased small farms outside of Nashville and lived there in obscurity for three years with no thought of returning to the outlaw trail.

Jesse, however, ran low on money and organized a new gang in Fall 1879 that included his brother Frank, Bill Ryan, Dick Liddell, Ed Miller, Tucker Basham, and Wood Hite. On Oct. 7, 1879, the gang held up the Alton Express near Glendale, Mo., and took more than $35,000 from the baggage car safe. The outlaws were inactive for almost a year and a half before they robbed a stage in Muscle Shoals, Ala., of only $1,400. On July 10, 1881, Jesse led the same men to Riverton, Iowa, where they held up the Sexton Bank, looting it of $5,000. Five days later, they stopped the Chicago, Rock Island, and Pacific train at Winston, Mo. When Frank McMillan tried to interfere with the robbery, Jesse shot him dead. The train engineer, William Westfall (or Westphal), refused to do as Jesse ordered and the bandit chief shot him dead in the engine cabin. The outlaws got only $600 from this bloody robbery which caused Missouri governor Thomas T. Crittenden to offer a $10,000 reward for the capture and conviction of Frank and Jesse James.

This amount of money was staggering for the day. In earlier times, this kind of reward would not have tempted any member of the James gang. The Younger brothers, cousins to the James boys, were blood kin and absolutely loyal. Other earlier members were fellow veterans of the guerrilla battles of the Civil War and were tied to the James and Younger brothers through old associ-

Left, crowds running to the James house following the outlaw's murder.

Right, Frank James in 1882.

 THE DAILY GRAPHIC

AN ILLUSTRATED EVENING NEWSPAPER

39 & 41 PARK PLACE

VOL. XXVIII.   All the News   Four Editions Daily   NEW YORK, TUESDAY, APRIL 11, 1882. $12 Per Year in Advance   Single Copies, Five Cents.   No. 2814

Cartoon showing how Jesse James was glorified for children.

Jim Cummins

Jesse James, Jr., 1900.

ations and loyalties. But the new members Jesse had recruited for the band had little or no allegiance to them. This included Robert and Charles Ford, two young men who had learned of the reward and planned to murder Jesse.

Bob Ford, the younger of the Ford Brothers was not a regular member of the gang. He spent time around gang members, clamoring to ride with the bandits, but was mostly used to run errands, a fact which caused him to become resentful and embittered. Charlie Ford rode with Jesse and Frank James, however, on Aug. 7, 1881, in a strange robbery that occurred near Blue Cut, outside Glendale, Mo., near the site where the gang had stopped a train two years earlier. The gang, consisting of Jesse and Frank James, Charles Ford, Wood and Clarence Hite, and Dick Liddell, stopped the train by piling large timbers across the track.

Engineer Jack Foote brought the train to a halt and the bandits used a pickax to chop their way into the locked express car. They hammered open the safe but were disappointed at the small amount of money in the safe. The outlaws then walked through the train, robbing the passengers. Jesse, wearing a thick, black beard, and the only bandit without a mask, made no effort to disguise himself. In fact, he reveled in his notoriety. He had taken to collecting the dime novels that Eastern presses had churned out about his exploits. "I'm Jesse James," he said to several stunned passengers and then he boldly introduced other members of the gang. The bandits rode off grumbling about the meager loot, less than $1,500. This was Jesse James' last robbery.

Following this robbery, Frank rode back to his farm near Nashville. Jesse, accompanied by the Ford Brothers, rode to Missouri to visit his mother. The three men slept in the Samuels barn. Jesse kept his pistols at the ready, believing that the Pinkertons might arrive at any moment. When he fell asleep, the Ford Brothers began discussing how to kill the man they followed. They had been planning to murder Jesse for months but were cautious and fearful of this deadliest of outlaws. Robert Ford was already in contact with Governor Crittenden, promising him that he would kill Jesse James in the near future. After having breakfast at his mother's home for the last time, Jesse, still accompanied by the Ford Brothers, rode to St. Joseph, Mo., where he was living under the name of Thomas Howard with his wife and two children. The family occupied a small but comfortable house atop a hill and in this quiet community, Jesse went on planning robberies. He sent the Ford boys out to scout several banks he was thinking of robbing.

The second James gang began to disintegrate quickly. Ed Miller was found dead, his body shot to pieces and dumped on a rural Missouri road. Jim Cummins later claimed that Jesse had murdered Miller after learning that Miller planned to turn himself in and inform on the rest of the gang. Wood Hite was then killed by Dick Liddell and Bob Ford over a split of the loot from the second Glendale train robbery at Blue Cut. Liddell, thinking that the Ford brothers intended to murder him, surrendered and confessed all he knew. His statements led to the arrest of Clarence Hite, who was tried and convicted of robbery and sent to prison for twenty-five years.

Only four active members of the James gang were now at large: Jesse, Frank, and the Ford brothers. Still, Jesse was undaunted and planned another robbery, summoning the Fords to his St. Joseph home on the morning of Apr. 3, 1881. Zee James made breakfast for the three men and the two small James children were sent out to play in the back yard. Following the meal, Jesse and the Fords went into the small parlor to further plan the robbery of the Platte County bank. When Jesse glanced at a newspaper containing Dick Liddell's confession, Charlie Ford, according to his later statements, was suddenly gripped by fear that Jesse would learn of the Fords' secret meeting with Governor Crittenden. Bob Ford also became nervous, and later stated at James' inquest: "I knew then that I had placed my head in the lion's mouth. How could I safely remove it?"

James put the newspaper aside, stood up, walked to the window and looked outside to see his children playing. He then turned and spotted a picture that was hanging crooked on the wall. According to the Fords, he then removed two gun belts, one about his hips, another around his shoulders. Each belt contained two big Colts, four guns in all. James looped the gun belts around a chair. Why he took the belts off was never known. The Fords may have told this story to make their target all the more dangerous. Some claimed that Jesse wore no guns in the house at any time, at least not *four* weapons, especially in the company of men he trusted. Given his belief in his invulnerability, it is most likely that James was never armed that morning.

The outlaw chief stood upon a small stool to reach the picture on the wall. As he adjusted the picture, Jesse exposed his back to the Fords. Robert pulled his pistol and aimed it squarely at the bandit's back. His hand shook so that the had to steady it with the other. At a distance of about four feet, he fired several times. James turned slightly to give his assassin a fierce look and then fell lifeless to the floor. Zee James rushed in from the kitchen, and kneeling at her husband's side, cradled his head in her arms, sobbing. Robert Ford sputtered that his gun went off by accident.

The Fords raced from the house. As Bob Ford ran down the hill toward the telegraph station he yelled loudly to anyone who would listen: "I killed him! I killed Jesse James! I killed him! I killed him! I killed Jesse James!" Only a few minutes later, he wired Governor Crittenden that the most wanted man in the U.S. was dead, that he, Bob Ford, had killed the infamous Jesse James. He immediately demanded his reward. The Ford Brothers were later charged with murder, but Crittenden, keeping his word, had the charges dropped and the reward money sent to the Fords.

The news of the bandit's murder was bannered in almost every newspaper in the U.S., from New York to California, from Maine to Texas. "Jesse by Jehovah!" read the front page headline in the St. Joseph *Gazette*. "Goodbye, Jesse!" read the Kansas City *Journal*. The newspapers and the dime novelists who had churned out endless copy on the outlaw for sixteen years lamented his passing, if only for commercial reasons. Almost immediately, the legend and lore of Jesse James began to be embellished so that within a few months, he was known as a hero. The ruthless killer and thief, the real Jesse James, was somehow forgotten and in his place sprang up a sterling, enviable Robin Hood.

The heavily bearded body of the outlaw was officially identified by his wife and by Mrs. Zee Samuels, his mother. The old woman appeared the next day at an inquest where the Ford Brothers and Dick Liddell testified. When Mrs. Samuels took the stand, she wept and said: "I live in Clay County and I am the mother of Jesse James...My poor boy...I have seen the body since my arrival and I have recognized it as that of my son Jesse...The lady by my side is my daughter-in-law and the children hers...He was a kind husband and son." Then she fixed her eyes on the Fords and Dick Liddell. She held up the stump of her arm and shook an empty sleeve in their direction, shouting: "Traitors!" The Fords and Liddell were hurried out of the courtroom by officers. Their lives were thought to be in great jeopardy, and Frank James would appear at any moment, leading a large band of men, with the single thought of killing the Fords.

Mrs. Samuels took Zee Mimms and her children back with her to the Clay County farm and with them the body of her son, which had been placed in a $500 coffin, an expensive casket for that day. The outlaw was buried on the Samuels farm and a white marble headstone was placed over the grave. It read:

Jesse W. James
Died April 3, 1882
Aged 34 years, 6 months, 28 days
Murdered by a traitor and a coward
Whose name is not worthy to
appear here.

On Oct. 5, 1882, five months after his brother's murder, Alexander Franklin James, last of the outlaw band, surrendered to Governor Crittenden. The 39-year-old bandit marched into the governor's office and took off his gun belt, placing it before Crittenden and saying: "Governor Crittenden, I want to hand over to you that which no living man except myself has been permitted to touch since 1861." The governor promised James protection and a fair trial. James was a celebrated prisoner and reporters flocked to interview him. One asked: "Why did you surrender? No one knew where you were hiding."

"What of that," James replied. "I was tired of an outlaw's life. I have been hunted for twenty-one years. I have literally lived in the saddle. I have never known a day of perfect peace. It was one long, anxious, inexorable, eternal vigil. When I slept it was literally in the midst of an arsenal. If I heard dogs bark more fiercely than usual, or the hooves of horses in a greater volume than usual, I stood to my arms. Have you an idea of what a man must endure who leads such a life? No, you cannot. No one can unless he lives it for himself."

Universal sympathy for Frank James and the James family was exhibited. The cowardly way the Ford brothers had killed Jesse almost assured Frank James an acquittal. After a number of long trials, that is exactly what he received. He returned to the Samuel farm and took up peaceful pursuits, working as a horse trainer and a racetrack starter. After the turn of the century, he appeared in a small Wild West show with his friend Cole Younger, who, by then, had been released from prison. Frank James died in a small bedroom of the Samuels farmhouse on Feb. 18, 1915.

Cole and Jim Younger were not released from the penitentiary at Stillwater, Minn., until July 10, 1901. Bob Younger had died in prison of pneumonia on Sept. 16, 1889. Jim Younger fell in love with a young woman in St. Paul, but she rejected him when he asked her to marry him. Younger went to his hotel room and shot himself to death. Cole Younger returned to Lee's Summit, Mo., where he lived a quiet life. He became a farmer and later appeared at local fairs, sometimes with Frank James. As the two bandits aged, they gave lectures to Sunday school classes and at ladies tea parties, thundering their condemnation of the outlaw life. The tall and muscular Cole Younger was the last of the outlaw band to die, suffering a heart attack on Mar. 21, 1916.

The Ford brothers, following Jesse's death, enjoyed some brief notoriety but were mostly shunned as "vile cowards." Charlie Ford was consumed by fear that Frank James or some of Jesse's other relatives would hunt him down and kill him. He was plagued by nightmares and became an insomniac. He finally committed suicide. Bob Ford moved west, traveling from town to town, opening up several saloons with the reward money he had received. He was finally shot to death in Creede, Colo., a decade after he became the most infamous "traitor" in the U.S. by shooting Jesse James in the back. Ford's shooting of Jesse James was challenged by J. Frank Dalton, who appeared in the late 1940s to claim that he was Jesse James and that the man shot in 1882 in St. Joseph, Mo., was an imposter. But it was generally agreed that Dalton was the impersonator and that the man buried in James' grave was indeed Jesse.

From the moment Jesse Woodson James was put into his grave, his life became a great fiction and he was lionized as a hearty pioneer, a brave son of the Middle Border, an embodiment of the spirit of adventuresome America. Fabulous tales were told of his kindliness and generosity. One abiding canard involved a widow woman who had given the James boys breakfast as they fled from a bank robbery. She informed her guests that she was about to lose her farm, that she did not have the money to pay the mortgage. Jesse reportedly gave her the money and then hid as the land owner appeared and collected this sum from the woman, signing back the deed to the farm to her. Jesse then rode after the landlord and held him up, recouping his loan to the widow woman. Jesse was kind to children and chivalrous to women. Journalists of the day took pains to point out that he never robbed a woman in a bank, in a stagecoach, or on a train. They omitted the many murders he was known to have committed.

Most of these tales had no foundation, but generations of small boys were thrilled by these stories and Jesse James became their tarnished idol, much to the chagrin of lawmen and parents. A decade later, the Dalton Brothers tried to emulate the James boys and were destroyed at Coffeyville, Kan. In the next century, the likes of John Dillinger and Charles Arthur "Pretty Boy" Floyd, who both admired Jesse James in their youth, not only followed his career closely, but copied his bank robbing techniques. The bandit's myth deepened so that it became part of the core of the American character or psyche, one of dash and quick action, one of fearless adventure. A song created by an amateur composer came into existence almost overnight following the bandit's death and did much to perpetuate the legend of this strange and mysterious man whom no few called friend and whom no one really knew. This melodramatic ballad captured the myth if not the reality of Jesse Woodson James:

Jesse James was a lad who killed many a man.
He robbed the Glendale train.
He stole from the rich and he gave to the poor,
He'd a hand and a heart and a brain.

(Chorus)
Jesse had a wife to mourn for his life,
Two children, they were brave,
But that dirty little coward that shot Mister Howard
Has laid poor Jesse in his grave.

It was Robert Ford, that dirty little coward,
I wonder how does he feel,
For he ate of Jesse's bread and he slept in Jesse's bed,
Then he laid Jesse James in his grave.

Jesse was a man, a friend to the poor.
He'd never seen a man suffer pain,
And with his brother Frank, he robbed the Gallatin bank
And stopped the Glendale train.

It was on a Wednesday night, the moon was shining bright.
He stopped the Glendale train.
And the people all did say for many miles away,
It was robbed by Frank and Jesse James.

It was on a Saturday night, Jesse was at home,
Talking to his family brave.
Robert Ford came along like a thief in the night,
And laid Jesse James in his grave.

The people held their breath
    when they heard of Jesse's death
And wondered how he ever came to die.
It was one of the gang called little Robert Ford,
Who shot Jesse James on the sly.

Jesse went to his rest with his hand on his breast,
The devil will be upon his knee.
He was born one day in the County of Shea
And he came from a solitary race.

This song was made by Billy Garshade,
As soon as the news did arrive,
He said there was no man with the law in his hand
Could take Jesse James when alive.

See: **Anderson, William; Dalton Brothers; Dalton, J. Frank; Dillinger, John Herbert; Floyd, Charles Arthur; Ford, Robert; Green, Henry G.; Quantrill, William Clarke; Reno Brothers; Starr, Belle; Younger Brothers.**
REF.: Allsopp, *Folklore of Romantic Arkansas;* Altrocchi, *Traces of Folklore and Furrow;* Alvarez, *The James Boys in Missouri;* American Guide Series, *Missouri, A Guide to the "Show Me" State;* Appler, *The*

Guerrillas of the West or The Life, Character and Daring Exploits of the Younger Brothers; ____, *The Younger Brothers;* Ardmore, *The James and Younger Brothers in Missouri;* Argall, *The Truth About Jesse James;* Arthur, *Bushwhacker;* Atkinson, *The Adventures of Oklahoma Bill;* Ballenger, *Around Tahlequah Council Fires;* Barclay, *The Liberal Republican Movement in Missouri, 1865-1871;* Barker, *Missouri Lawyer;* Beaumont, *G.H. Beaumont's Railroad Stories;* Beebe, *The American West;* ____, *Hear the Train Blow;* Belden, *Ballads and Songs Collected by the Missouri Folklore Society;* Benet, *Golden Fleece;* Black, *You Can't Win;* Boar, *The World's Most Infamous Murders;* Botkin, *A Treasury of American Folklore;* ____, *A Treasury of Southern Folklore;* ____, *A Treasury of Western Folklore;* ____, *A Treasury of Railroad Folklore;* Bradley, *The Outlaws of the Border or The Lives of Frank and Jesse James;* Bragin, *Dime Novels, Bibliography, 1860-1928;* Breihan, *The Complete and Authentic Life of Jesse James;* ____, *The Day Jesse James Was Killed;* ____, *The Outlaw Brothers, The True Story of Missouri's Younger Brothers;* ____, *Quantrill and His Civil War Guerrillas;* Briggs, *Arizona and New Mexico, 1882;* Bronaugh, *The Youngers' Fight for Freedom;* Brownlee, *Gray Ghosts of the Confederacy;* Buel, *The Border Outlaws;* ____, *Jesse and Frank James;* Burnham, *Taking Chances;* Burt, *American Murder Ballads;* Byers, *With Fire and Sword;* Callison, *Bill Jones of Paradise Valley, Oklahoma;* Callon, *Las Vegas, New Mexico;* Case, *History of Kansas City, Mo.;* Casey, *The Texas Border and Some Borderliners;* Castel, *A Frontier State at War, 1861-1865;* ____, *William Clarke Quantrill: His Life and Times;* CBA; Chapel, *Guns of the Old West;* Chilton, *The Book of the West;* Chrisman, *Lost Trails of the Cimarron;* Clark, *Then Came the Railroads;* Clarke, *The Autobiography of Frank Tarbeaux;* Clemens, *Life on the Mississippi;* Cochran, *Bonnie Belmont;* Conard, *Encyclopedia of the History of Missouri;* Connelley, *Quantrill and the Border Wars;* Corbin, *Why News is News;* Crabb, *Empire on the Platte;* Cressey, *Theft of the Nation;* Crittenden, *The Crittenden Memoirs;* Croy, *Corn Country;* ____, *He Hanged Them High;* ____, *Jesse James Was My Neighbor;* ____, *Last of the Great Outlaws: The Story of Cole Younger;* Cummins, *Jim Cummins' Book;* Dacus, *Life and Adventures of Frank and Jesse James;* ____, *Illustrated Lives of Frank and Jesse James and the Younger Brothers;* Daggett, *The Outlaw Brothers, Frank and Jesse James;* Dalton, *Beyond the Law;* Dalton, *The Life of Father Bernard Donnelly;* Dalton, *Under the Black Flag;* Darby, *"Show Me" Missouri;* Davidson, *Down Through the Years;* Davis, *The West from a Car Window;* DeBarth, *The Life and Adventures of Frank Grouard;* Debo, *The Cowman's Southwest;* Demaris, *The Director;* DeMilt, *Story of an Old Town;* DeWolf, *Pawnee Bill;* Dibble, *Strenuous Americans;* Doctor, *Shotguns on Sunday;* Donald, *Outlaws of the Border;* Doughitt, *Romance and Dim Trails;* Drago, *Great American Cattle Trails;* ____, *Outlaws on Horseback;* Draper, *Old Grubstake Days in Joplin;* Duke, *Celebrated Criminal Cases in America;* Dunlop, *Doctors of the American Frontier;* Earle, *History of Clay County and Northwest Texas;* Edwards, *John N. Edwards;* Edwards, *Noted Guerrillas;* Elman, *Fired in Anger;* Evans, *Adventures of the Great Crime-Busters;* Every, *Sins of New York;* Fellows and Freeman, *This Way to the Big Show;* Finger, *The Distant Prize;* ____, *Foot-Loose in the West;* Fisher and Holmes, *Gold Rushes and Mining Camps;* Fishwick, *American Heroes, Myth and Reality;* Foster-Harris, *The Look of the Old West;* Gard, *The Chisholm Trail;* ____, *Frontier Justice;* Gardner, *The Old Wild West;* Garwood, *Crossroads of America;* Gaylord, *Handgunner's Guide;* Ginty, *Missouri Legend;* Gish, *American Bandits;* Goodwin, *Nat Goodwin's Book;* Gordon, *Jesse James and His Band of Notorious Outlaws;* Greene, *America Goes to Press;* Gregory, *True Wild West Stories;* Haley, *Jeff Milton;* Hall, *The Two Lives of Baby Doe;* Harlow, *Old Waybills;* ____, *"Weep No More My Lady";* Harrington, *Hanging Judge;* Haskell, *City of the Future;* Hawes, *Frank and Jesse James;* Hayes, *Iron Road to Empire;* Heckman, *Steamboating Sixty-five Years on Missouri's Waters;* Henderson, *Keys to Crookdom;* Henderson, *100 Years in Montague County, Texas;* Hendricks, *The Bad Man of the West;* Henry, *Conquering Our Great American Plains;* Hertzog, *A Directory of New Mexico Desperadoes;* Hicks, *Adventures of a Tramp Printer;* Hicks, *Belle Starr and Her Pearl;* Hill, *The End of the Cattle Trail;* Holbrook, *Let Them Live;* ____, *The Story of American Railroads;* Holcomb, *History of Marion County, Mo.;* Holloway, *Texas Gun Lore;* Hoole, *The James Boys Rode South;* Horan, *Desperate Men;* ____, *Desperate Women;* ____, *The Great American West;* ____, and Sann, *Pictorial History of the Wild West;* ____, *The Pinkertons;* Hough, *The Story of the Outlaw;* House, *City of Flaming Adventure;* Hoyt,

A Frontier Doctor; Hubbard, *Railroad Avenue;* Humphrey, *Following the Prairie Frontier;* Hunter and Rose, *The Album of Gunfighters;* Huntington, *Robber and Hero;* Hurd, *Boggsville;* Hutchinson, *The Life & Personal Writings of Eugene Manlove Rhodes;* Jahns, *The Frontier World of Doc Holliday;* James, *Frank James and His Brother Jesse;* James, *James Boys;* James, *Jesse James and the Lost Cause;* James, *Jesse James, My Father;* Jameson, *Heroes by the Dozen;* Johnson, *History of Cooper County, Missouri;* Johnson, *Wagon Yard;* Jones, *The Hatfields and the McCoys;* Jordin, *Memories;* Kane, *100 Years Ago with the Law and the Outlaw;* Keleher, *Violence in Lincoln County;* Kelley, *Jesse James;* ____, *The Outlaw Trail;* Kelly, *The Sky was Their Roof;* Kemp, *Cow Dust and Saddle Leather;* Kennedy, *Jesse James' Mysterious Warning;* ____, *Jesse James Wild Leap;* King, *Ghost Towns of Texas;* Koller, *The American Gun;* Lait and Mortimer, *Chicago: Confidential;* Lawson, *Jesse James at Long Branch;* Lemon, *The Northfield Tragedy;* Leopard and McCammon, *History of Davies and Gentry Counties, Missouri;* Lewis and Smith, *Oscar Wilde Discovers America;* Lillie, *Life Story of Pawnee Bill;* Lord, *Frontier Dust;* Love, *The Life and Adventures of Nat Love;* Love, *The Rise and Fall of Jesse James;* Lyon, *The Wild, Wild West;* Marshall, *Santa Fe;* McAfee, *College Pioneering;* McCarty, *The Enchanted West;* McCarty, *The Gunfighters;* McCready, *Railroads in the Days of Steam;* McDougal, *Recollections;* McKennon, *Iron Men;* McRill, *And Satan Came Also;* Metz, *John Selman;* Michelson, *Mankillers at Close Range;* Miller, *Shady Ladies of the West;* Mitchell, *Daring Exploits of Jesse James;* Mitchell, *Linn County, Kansas;* Mitchell, *Lost Mines of the Great Southwest;* Monaghan, *The Legend of Tom Horn;* ____, *The Book of the American West;* Morse, *Cavalcade of Rails;* Munsell, *Flying Sparks;* Murbarger, *Sovereigns of the Sage;* Musick, *Stories of Missouri;* Myers, *Doc Holliday;* Nash, *Almanac of World Crime;* ____, *Bloodletters and Badmen;* Nesbit, *An American Family;* Nordyke, *John Wesley Hardin;* O'Neal, *They Die But Once;* Otero, *My Life on the Frontier;* Parkhill, *The Wildest of the West;* Paxton, *Annals of Platte County, Missouri;* Phares, *Bible in Pocket, Gun in Hand;* ____, *Reverend Devil;* Plenn, *Saddle in the Sky;* Preece, *The Dalton Gang;* Quinn, *Fools of Fortune;* Raine, *Guns of the Frontier;* Rainey, *No Man's Land;* Rascoe, *Belle Starr;* Ray, *The Border Outlaws, Frank and Jesse James;* ____, *The James Boys;* ____, *The James Boys and Bob Ford;* ____, *Jesse James' Daring Raid;* Ray, *Legends of the Red River Valley;* Rayburn, *The Eureka Springs Story;* ____, *Ozark County;* Raynor, *Old Timers Talk in Southwestern New Mexico;* Rea, *Boone County and Its People;* Rennert, *Western Outlaws;* Reppetto, *The Blue Parade;* Riegel, *America Moves West;* Roberts, *Famous American Trials;* Robertson, *Famous Bandits;* Roe, *The James Boys;* Roe, *Our Police;* Rogers, *The Lusty Texans of Dallas;* Rosa, *The Gunfighter: Man or Myth?;* ____, *They Called Him Wild Bill;* Russell, *Behind These Ozark Hills;* Russell, *The Lives and Legends of Buffalo Bill;* Rutledge, *A Few Stirring Events in the Life of Col. Dick Rutledge;* Samuels, *The Magnificent Rube: The Life and Gaudy Times of Tex Rickard;* Sanders, *The Sumner County Story;* Schlesinger, *The Rise of the City;* Schrantz, *Jasper County, Missouri;* Scott, *Belle Starr in Velvet;* Scott, *Some Memories of a Soldier;* Scott, *Such Outlaws as Jesse James;* Seeley, *Pioneer Days in the Arkansas Valley in Southern Colorado;* Settle, *Jesse James Was His Name;* Shackleford, *Gunfighters of the Old West;* Shackleton, *Handbook of Frontier Days of Southwest Kansas;* Shaner, *The Story of Joplin;* Shirley, *Henry Starr;* ____, *Law West of Fort Smith;* ____, *Outlaw Queen;* ____, *Sixgun and Silver Star;* ____, *Buckskin Joe;* Shoemaker, *Missouri, Day by Day;* Simpson, *Llano Estacado, or The Plains of West Texas;* Small, *Autobiography of a Pioneer;* Small, *The Best of True West;* Smith, *A Comprehensive History of Minnehaha County;* Smith, *From the Memories of Men;* Sonney, *The American Outlaw;* Sonnichsen, *I'll Die Before I'll Run;* ____, *Outlaw Bill Mitchell;* Stambaugh, *A History of Collins County, Texas;* Steckmesser, *The Western Hero in History and Legend;* Sterling, *Famous Western Outlaw-Sheriff Battles;* Stewart, *The History of the Bench and Bar in Missouri;* Sutley, *The Last Frontier;* Sutton, *Hands Up!;* Thorndike, *Lives and Exploits of the Daring Frank and Jesse James;* Tibbles, *Buckskin and Blanket Days;* Triplett, *History, Romance and Philosophy of Great American Crimes and Criminals;* ____, *The Life, Times and Treacherous Death of Jesse James;* Tyler, *Whatever Goes Up;* Vestal, *The Missouri;* Vivian, *Down the Avenue of Ninety Years;* Walker, *Jesse James;* Waller, *Last of the Great Western Train Robbers;* Ward, *My Grandpa Went West;* Ward, *The James Boys of Old Missouri;* ____, *Jesse James' Dash for Fortune;* ____, *The Younger Brothers;* Warman, *Frontier Stories;* Waters, *A Gallery of Western*

Badmen; Watson, *A Century of Gunmen;* Wellman, *A Dynasty of Western Outlaws;* White, *Bat Masterson;* White, *The Autobiography of a Durable Sinner;* ____, *Lead and Likker;* Williams, *Missouri, Mother of the West;* Williard, *The Trans-Mississippi West;* Wilson, *Treasure Express;* Winget, *Anecdotes of Buffalo Bill;* Winn, *The Macadam Trail;* Winther, *The Transportation Frontier;* Woodson, *History of Clay County, Missouri; Younger Brothers of the Great West;* (FILM), *Days of Jesse James,* 1939; *Jesse James,* 1939; *The Return of Frank James,* 1940; *Bad Men of Missouri,* 1941; *Jesse James at Bay,* 1941; *Jesse James, Jr.,* 1942; *The Remarkable Andrew,* 1942; *Badman's Territory,* 1946; *Fighting Man of the Plains,* 1949; *I Shot Jesse James,* 1949; *The Great Missouri Raid,* 1950; *The Return of Jesse James,* 1950; *Best of the Badmen,* 1951; *The Great Jesse James Raid,* 1953; *Kansas Raiders,* 1953; *Jesse James versus the Daltons,* 1954; *Jesse James' Women,* 1954; *The True Story of Jesse James,* 1956; *Hell's Crossroads,* 1957; *The True Story of Jesse James,* 1957; *Fighting Man of the Plains,* 1959; *Young Jesse James,* 1960; *The Outlaws Is Coming,* 1965; *Jesse James Meets Frankenstein's Daughter,* 1966; *The Great Northfield, Minnesota Raid,* 1972; *The Long Riders,* 1980; *Last Days of Frank and Jesse James,* 1989.

James, John, prom. 1700, U.S., pir. At the end of the seventeenth century, the coasts of Virginia, Maryland, and the Carolinas were swarming with pirates, making it almost impossible to enter the seaports. One infamous pirate captain of the period, a sadistic Welshman named John James, loved to terrify prisoners by identifying himself as Captain Kidd. James' ship, which he had stolen from South Carolina businessman William Rhett, was alternately called the *Alexander* or the *Providence Galley.* Among James' conquests were the *Maryland Merchant* and the *Roanoke Merchant.*

REF.: *CBA,* Rankin, *The Golden Age of Piracy.*

James, Lydia Ruth, d.1948, and **Skewes, Jeanne R.,** 1915-48, Indo-China, (unsolv.) mur. Lydia Ruth James and Jeanne R. Skewes, career U.S. government employees, worked for the State Department in Saigon, French Indo-China (Vietnam), in 1948.

French Indo-China was in turmoil. Anti-French guerrillas were trying to liberate the country after a century of French rule. Security perimeters had been established around the capital city of Saigon. On the evening of Mar. 6, 1948, James and Skewes traveled outside this zone of security.

French soldiers found the bullet-riddled bodies of James and Skewes and the charred remains of the jeep the next day on a deserted road three miles outside Saigon. Despite a State Department investigation, the murders were never solved. Skewes, director of the U.S. information service in Indo-China, and James, a secretary at the U.S. consulate, were ambushed at about 7 p.m. by gunmen hiding in a rice field near the hamlet of Tom Sonnhutt. James and Skewes were traveling toward the Saigon Airport. REF.: *CBA.*

James, Robert (Raymond Lisemba), d.1942, U.S., mur. Born Raymond Lisemba in rural Alabama in 1895, Robert James had done the back-breaking work of a cotton baler until he inherited $2,000 from each of two uncles who had named him beneficiary of their insurance policies. Receiving such a windfall without expending any effort made a lasting impression on the young man. He took his inheritance and traveled to Birmingham, Ala., where he attended a barbers' college and changed his name to James. It was also in Birmingham, in 1921, that he met and married Maud Duncan. This first marriage ended when James' wife could no longer tolerate his requirements of her for sadomasochistic sex. In the divorce suit, Duncan claimed that James frequently stuck hot curling irons under her nails.

James reportedly had also fathered several illegitimate children during his time in Birmingham and decided it would be healthier to move on. He then moved to Emporia, Kan., where he opened a small barber shop and married again. He suddenly left Emporia and his wife when the father of a girl he had gotten pregnant threatened his life. Only weeks after arriving in Fargo, N.D., his next stop, he opened another barber shop and married for a third time to Winona Wallace. The newlyweds' honeymoon trip to Colorado's Pike's Peak was marred when Winona was seriously injured in a car accident. When she recovered sufficiently to be released, James took her to a remote cabin in Canada. A few days after their arrival, James appeared at the police station to report that his wife, dizzy from the accident, had drowned in the bathtub. Shortly after the funeral, James collected $14,000 in life insurance—a policy he had taken out on her life a day before the wedding.

In Alabama, in 1934, James met a local girl, Helen Smith. The two were marred and moved to Los Angeles. Helen Smith later told authorities that James was sexually impotent unless she whipped him. This fourth wife became suspicious when he told her he wanted her to have a medical examination for a life insurance policy. She refused saying that "people who have it (insurance) always die of something strange." James resented her obstinacy and the two were soon divorced. Next, James took out a $10,000 life insurance policy on a nephew, Cornelius Wright, then a sailor stationed at San Diego. Wright had a long history of being accident-prone—he had been hit several times by cars; some scaffolding had once collapsed on him; he had been knocked unconscious at a baseball game. James, playing the magnanimous uncle, loaned him his car to use while on leave and told him to go off and have a good time. Three days later, Wright drove the car off a cliff near Santa Rosa and died. Only later did the mechanic who towed the wrecked car away tell police that something was wrong with the steering wheel.

With the money he collected on his nephew's death, James opened a posh barber shop in Los Angeles and he began an affair with his manicurist, 25-year-old Mary Bush. When Bush became pregnant and insisted that James marry her, he did so. Not long after their marriage, however, James again took out another insurance policy. Then he persuaded one of his employees to find a couple of poisonous snakes, explaining that he had a friend whose wife was bothering him and he wanted the snakes to "take care of her." In July 1935, the employee, Charlie Hope, went to "Snake Joe" Houtenbrink, a reptile collector, and procured two Crotalus Atrox rattlers. James then brought Hope in on his plot to kill his wife and promised him part of the insurance money.

After working out the details, James took Hope home with him for dinner one evening, introducing him as a doctor. After Hope had been in their home for a brief period, he told the pregnant Mrs. James that she didn't look well and probably should not go through with her pregnancy. The naive woman agreed to let this "eminent physician" perform an abortion on her that very night. In lieu of anesthetic, James encouraged her to drink whiskey until she passed out. Once she was incoherent, he brought the snakes into the house in a specially designed box constructed so that he could insert her leg into it without letting the snakes escape. He left her for several hours with her leg in the box, and she was bitten repeatedly. She did not die, however. When she revived and complained of terrible pain in her leg, James assured her it was nothing important. The leg, however, swelled to twice its normal size and became increasingly painful. Early in the morning, James suggested to her that she take a bath to soothe the pain. He ran the water into the bathtub for her and stood by to help her into the tub. As she got into the tub, James pushed her down, pulling her legs up high enough that her head was submerged and held her in this fashion until she drowned.

After dressing her, he and Hope carried her body to the yard, where they placed it face down in a small lily pond in such a way as to make it appear that she had become dizzy and collapsed, and accidentally drowned. After going over the alibi with Hope, James went on to work. He worked through the day as though nothing at all was wrong, and that evening returned home with two friends whom he had invited to dinner, ostensibly after clearing the impromptu dinner party with his wife. As planned, the three "discovered" his wife's body in the pond. The death was classified as accidental.

Three months later, however, a Los Angeles captain of detectives, Jack Southard, saw a report that James had been arrested for mashing and thought it peculiar that a man so recently

Robert James under arrest.

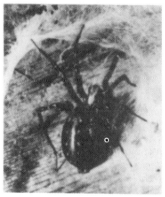

Left, Mrs. Mary James, murder victim; center, Charles Hope (left) and Robert James (center) at the pool where Mrs. James drowned; right, a black widow that failed.

Hope tries the rattlesnake box in court.

The rattlesnake that would not murder.

Robert James on the witness stand; he was executed.

widowed should be apprehended for such a crime. Southard learned from neighbors that a green Buick sedan had been seen outside the James home and that Charles Hope had been phoning James constantly. Southard also discovered that Hoped owned a green Buick sedan, so he searched Hope's apartment. There he found a receipt for two rattlesnakes. Southard collected enough evidence against Charlie Hope to arrest him on suspicion of murder. Once arrested, Hope confessed, implicating James. James was arrested in May 1936 and after a quick trial, was sentenced to death. Hope received a life sentence. James remained in the Los Angeles County Jail for the next four years while appealing his case. In 1940, he was finally moved to San Quentin. As it became evident that commutation of his sentence was unlikely, James fought to die in the gas chamber instead of by hanging because the law changing the manner of execution was enacted after his sentencing. On May 1, 1942, Robert James was hanged at San Quentin, the last man to be hanged in California.

REF.: *CBA; Nash, Murder, America; Rodell, Los Angeles Murders; Wilson, Encyclopedia of Murder.*

James, Thomas Lemuel, 1831-1916, U.S., law enfor. off. Served as U.S. postmaster general from 1881-82. He assisted the attorney general in halting the Star Route frauds. REF.: *CBA.*

Jameson, James, d.1807, and **M'Gowan, James**, d.1806, U.S., rob.-mur. Earning his living by stealing in Harrisburg, Pa., James Jameson worked with a partner, James M'Gowan. On Aug. 28, 1806, the team robbed Jacob Eshelman from Hummelstown, Pa. When Eshelman tried to resist the robbers, they beat him to death with tree branches. They were caught carrying Eshelman's life savings of $500, convicted, and sentenced to death. On Dec. 29, 1806, M'Gowan was hanged. Jameson escaped the Dauphin County Jail only to be recaptured a few days later, hiding under his mother's bed in Reading, Pa. Jameson was hanged in Harrisburg on Jan. 10, 1807.

REF.: *CBA; The Lives and Confessions of James M'Gowan & James Jameson; Nash, Bloodletters and Badmen; A Report on the Trial of James Jameson.*

Jameson, Sir Leander Starr, 1853-1917, S. Afri., rebel. Born in Edinburgh, Scot., he befriended future Cape Colony prime minister Cecil Rhodes, and assisted his negotiations with the natives. In 1891, he explored and became administrator of the Mashonaland, adding Matabele territory two years later. In 1895, he headed the Jameson Raid, the famed attempt to cross the Transvaal to Johannesburg and help the Uitlanders overthrow the Boer government of Transvaal. After his defeat in 1896, British officials tried and briefly imprisoned him in England. In 1900, he returned to South Africa and joined the Cape legislature. REF.: *CBA.*

Jameson, William James, b.1898, U.S., jur. Appointed to the district court of Montana by President Dwight D. Eisenhower in 1957. He presided over the American Bar Association from 1953-54, and received the American Bar Association's Gold Medal in 1973. REF.: *CBA.*

Janus, Christopher G., 1911- , U.S., fraud. In 1973, Christopher G. Janus, an investment banker, claimed that the Chinese government had hired him to find the bones of the 500,000-year-old Peking Man. The curator of the Peking Natural History Museum had the bone fragments of some forty prehistoric humans packed in two footlockers. The footlockers had not been seen since WWII. Janus told potential investors that the Canadian Broadcasting Corporation was going to make a documentary film about the search, and that a gross income of $10 million to $25 million could be expected from the film. Otto Preminger would also be involved in the film, Janus said. The allure for investors, Janus confided, was not only the involvement in a historic undertaking, but the potential for a large tax shelter.

Janus, in his search for Peking Man, raised $520,000 in loans from nine banks and $120,000 from at least twelve private investors. In 1974, he reported to the federal government that the partnership formed in the film making deal lost $136,000. One year later, Janus listed losses at $302,000. Investors wrote off these reported losses on their tax returns. In February 1981, almost eight years after he had begun his alleged search for the prehistoric man, Janus was indicted on thirty-seven counts of mail fraud, bank fraud, and tax fraud. The government charged Janus had misrepresented himself in obtaining loans and then used investors' money for personal gain. In exchange for a guilty plea on two counts of bank fraud, the government dropped the remaining thirty-five counts. In July 1981, U.S. District Judge Prentice H. Marshall sentenced the 70-year-old Janus to four years of probation and ordered him to perform 1,000 hours of community service. REF.: *CBA.*

Jaramillo, Anibal, 1955- , U.S., (wrong. convict.) mur. After his arrest at Miami International Airport in 1981 for grand theft, Anibal Jaramillo, twenty-seven, was linked to the December 1980 slayings of two Colombian men. Jaramillo's fingerprints were found on several items at the Miami townhouse where Gilberto Caicedo and Candelario Castellanos were bound and gagged, then machine gunned to death. During his trial in April 1981, Jaramillo said he had been at the house the night before the murders helping Caicedo's nephew clean out the garage, but that he had nothing to do with the killings. Although authorities could not determine when Jaramillo left the prints, a jury found him Guilty on two counts of first-degree murder. The one man who might have cleared him, Edison Caicedo, disappeared before the trial. Although the jury recommended life imprisonment, Dade County circuit judge Ellen Morphonios-Gable sentenced Jaramillo to die.

In July 1982, the Florida Supreme Court overturned the death sentence, arguing that the suspect's fingerprints at the scene were insufficient to convict him. The ruling marked the first time a man had been removed from death row since the reinstitution of the death penalty in 1972. REF.: *CBA.*

Jarmain, Peter Joseph, prom. 1945, Brit., mur. In 1945, Peter Joseph Jarmain, armed with a revolver, held up the cashier of the Red Arrow Garage at Thornton Heath, Surrey. When the cashier, Ivy Phillips, refused to hand over the money, Jarmain shot the woman dead. He was arrested, tried, convicted of murder, and sentenced to death. REF.: *CBA.*

Jarman, George B., 1780-1828, U.S., mur. George B. Jarman, the only son of a religious father, was born on June 30, 1780. He became a practicing physician in New York but left the profession to become take a position as a schoolmaster. In his later years, Jarman became a drunkard. In April 1828, Jarman got drunk at a tavern near New Brunswick, N.J. When insulted by a companion, he produced a knife and stabbed the man twice. He then wheeled around and stabbed a man named Titus in the heart. The first man survived, but Titus died instantly. Jarman was so intoxicated that he could not remember anything about the stabbings. He was tried and convicted of murder in June 1828 and hanged in New Brunswick on Aug. 8.

REF.: *CBA; The Life and Confession of George B. Jarman.*

Jarnac-Châteigneraie Duel, 1547, Fr., duel-mur. Compte Guy Chabot de Jarnac and Compte de la Châteigneraie were bitter rivals. They asked King Francis I for permission to fight a duel, but he had refused to allow it. Jarnac accused Châteigneraie of spreading a rumor that Jarnac was sleeping with his mother-in-law. When he insisted his rival retract the statement, Châteigneraie refused, saying Jarnac had confessed the sin to him on several occasions. When Francis I died in 1547, Henry II reluctantly gave permission for the men to fight.

The combatants took the oath required of them. Jarnac, as the injured party, asked Châteigneraie to furnish over thirty sets of arms from which to choose the duelling weapon. Jarnac chose swords. The men began the duel clad in demi-armor that reached only to the knees. They battled on equal terms for several minutes. In an unorthodox move, Jarnac suddenly cut Châteigneraie on his unprotected hamstring. Before he could react, Châteigneraie felt Jarnac's blade across his other hamstring and fell to the ground.

Jarnac stood above his helpless opponent and proclaimed that he would spare Châteigneraie's life if he would renounce his accusations. When Châteigneraie refused, Jarnac turned to the king and asked for forgiveness were he to kill his rival. Henry II didn't answer and Jarnac once again begged Châteigneraie to restore honor to his tarnished name. Instead of giving in, Châteigneraie took a swipe at Jarnac from his prone position. The king finally answered Jarnac's plea to spare his victim, but it was too late. Châteigneraie died from loss of blood. Following his trusted advisor's death, King Henry II forbade duelling. The cut that Jarnac used became known as *le coup de Jarnac*.

REF.: *CBA; Melville, Famous Duels and Assassinations*.

Jarrell, Sanford, prom. 1924, U.S., hoax. On Aug. 13, 1924, the New York *Herald Tribune* received a report that alcohol was being sold from a large ship that was located between West Hampton and Bay Shore. A cub reporter, Sanford Jarrell, was sent to investigate. During the next two days that Jarrell was out on the assignment, he contacted the city editor, confirming the reports. His article appeared on Aug. 16, 1924, under the headline: "NEW YORKERS DRINK SUMPTUOUSLY ON 17,000-TON FLOATING CAFE AT ANCHOR FIFTEEN MILES OFF FIRE ISLAND." Jarrell described the vessel's chorus girls and the rich clientele dancing and drinking on board. When Jarrell returned to collect follow-up information on Aug. 18 and 19, his accounts were not as detailed. Newspaper officials became skeptical and ordered a separate investigation. Finally, Jarrell confessed that the story was a fraud. The newspaper printed a retraction on Aug. 23. REF.: *CBA*.

Jascalevich, Mario E., 1927-   , Case of, U.S., mur. More than ten patients died following "minor" elective surgery at Riverdell Hospital in Oradell, N.J., in 1965 and 1966. Officials began an investigation when they discovered eighteen vials of curare in the hospital locker of Chief Surgeon Mario E. Jascalevich. Most of the vials were empty. The doctor told Bergen County officials he was using the powerful muscle relaxant in experiments on dying dogs at Seton Hall Medical School in Jersey City. Authorities interviewed the hospital staff and patients, but the grand jury returned no indictment and the case against Jascalevich was dropped.

In 1975, the New York *Times,* acting on an anonymous letter, assigned reporter Myron Farber to investigate allegations that Jascalevich was responsible for as many as thirty deaths. On the basis of Farber's findings, the paper published a two-part series on a suspected serial murderer,

Dr. Mario E. Jascalevich, tried for murder in 1978.

calling him "Dr. X." Bergen County officials exhumed the bodies of five Riverdell patients who died while Jascalevich was the hospital's head surgeon. In May 1976, Jascalevich was charged with murdering five patients after traces of curare were found in the exhumed bodies.

The case came to trial in 1978. It was Sybil Moses' first big case as a prosecutor. Flamboyant veteran attorney Ray Brown defended Jascalevich. Brown wanted to see Farber's notes, he told Judge William Arnold, but the reporter refused to relinquish them and was sent to jail. Federal Judge Frederick Lacey accused him of a conflict of interest when it was revealed that Farber had received a $75,000 advance from Doubleday to write a book about the Jascalevich case. Brown maintained the notes would show his

client was being framed, and that other doctors were responsible for the deaths and were now trying to blame Jascalevich.

Brown shifted the focus of the case from murder to the first amendment. Expert witnesses claimed that curare wasn't stable enough to be found in a body ten years after death. Farber spent forty days in jail before turning over a copy of his book manuscript to Judge Arnold, who fined the New York *Times* $285,000 for their part in the incident. In the jury trial, Jascalevich was acquitted of all charges. The doctor moved to Argentina in 1981 and Farber's book, *Somebody is Lying: The Story of Dr. X,* was published in 1982. REF.: *CBA*.

Jaureguy, Jean, See: **William of Orange**.

Jaurès, Jean Léon, 1859-1914, Fr., assass. French politician Jean Léon Jaurès, a deputy from Tarn, retired to teach and write philosophical essays. He later became interested in socialism, and led the Socialist party in France from 1904. With Aristide Briand, Jaurès founded and edited *L'Humanité* and fought militaristic legislation prior to the outbreak of WWI. Jaurès' most famous book was *The New Army,* which dealt with the question of extending military service in anticipation of the upcoming war.

On July 27, 1914, about 10,000 anti-war protestors demonstrated in the streets of Paris. On July 28, in Brussels, Belg., Jaurès made patriotic speeches to a crowd of around 8,000 at the Royal Circle, and called for peace. Raoul Villain, who had once had fantasies of killing Germany's Kaiser Wilhelm II, transferred his obsession to Jaurès. Villain left his home at Reims

Jean Jaurès, assassinated in 1914.

after arguing with his father and brother over what he considered their inadequate patriotism. He took a train to Paris on July 29, and loitered around Jaurès' house with a 6.35mm pistol in his pocket. The next morning he bought a .32-caliber Smith & Wesson.

On July 31, while Jaurès spent most of the day at the Chamber of Deputies, Villain removed all identifying labels from his clothes and went to Notre Dame Cathedral to light a candle. He then walked to Jaurès' office in the Rue Montmartre. At around 9:45 p.m., as Jaurès finished his dessert at a cafe where he had dined with colleagues, two shots rang out. One pierced his skull, and Jaurès died about five minutes later. A passing policeman saw Villain back away from the window from which the shots had been fired and arrested him. Indicted in October, Villain said he had acted out of duty and expressed no regret. His trial was scheduled for Dec. 20, but was then postponed indefinitely. Villain was kept at the Santé Prison for two years, then transferred to Fresnes. On Mar. 4, 1919, he was taken to the Conciergerie, and tried at the Law Courts on the Ile de la Cité on Mar. 24, nearly five years after Jaurès' murder. Several witnesses had died, and others, like the policeman who arrested Villain and a priest who had watched Villain practice at a shooting range, were inexplicably not called upon. A series of tributes to Jaurès took up several days, and included speeches by a former minister of war, a Nobel Peace Prize winner, and several leftist leaders. Defending attorneys were Zevaès and Henri Géraud, with Paul-Boncour for the prosecution. Géraud spoke eloquently of Villain's "impossible chastity, your patriotic dream," and asked for an acquittal.

The twelve elderly bourgeois jurors—the youngest was fifty-three—deliberated for half an hour before acquitting Villain, judging that he was neither guilty of willful murder, nor of premeditating his act. As a final irony, Jaurès' widow was ordered to pay the court costs. Villain, however, did not escape the ghostly vengeance of his victim. In 1936, Villain was living in Majorca, a supporter of the Falange, the fascist organization led by Francisco Franco, later dictator of Spain. Republican gunmen swept through Villain's residence and caught him as he was about to flee. He was executed on the spot and the Socialist martyr Jaurès was avenged.

REF.: *CBA*; Goldberg, *The Life of Jean Juarès*; Heppenstall, *Bluebeard and After*; Tuchman, *The Guns of August*; ____, *The Proud Tower*; Wright, *Insiders and Outliers: The Individual in History*.

Jay, John, 1745-1829, U.S., jur. First chief justice of the U.S. Supreme Court. He started his political career as secretary of the royal boundary commission in 1773, developing his diplomatic skills in negotiations concerning a New York-New Jersey border dispute. He was a member of the first Continental Congress and president of the second Continental Congress in 1778. He helped write New York's first state constitution in 1777, and instituted the new laws as the first chief justice of the state supreme court from 1777-78. He was the U.S. minister to Spain in 1779, during the peak of confrontation with Great Britain, and was successful in obtaining limited financial backing for the Revolutionary War effort. His next assignment was to assist Benjamin Franklin and John Adams on the Paris commission from 1782-3, negotiating the Treaty of Paris which formally ended the war. He served as secretary of foreign affairs from 1784-89. He published his views on foreign affairs in five essays appearing in *The Federalist* from 1787-88. He was appointed chief justice of the Supreme Court by the new president in 1789. As the first chief justice, he had a major role in shaping the Court's jurisdiction, and asserted the Court's authority to condemn unconstitutional acts by Congress. In 1794, he negotiated the pact later known as Jay's Treaty, resolving lingering difficulties with Great Britain. He resigned his court seat to become governor of New York, serving from 1795-1801. REF.: *CBA*.

Jaybird-Woodpecker War, 1889, U.S., west. range war. The Jaybird-Woodpecker War occurred in Fort Bend County, Texas, and involved two large cattle ranches and dozens of cowboys. Several gun battles between these two factions resulted in a half dozen deaths. Lawman Ira Aten is credited with bringing this feud to an end. See: **Aten, Ira**. REF.: *CBA*.

Jayne, Silas, 1908- , U.S., mur. The Jayne brothers of Illinois were self-made millionaires who bred pure-blood horses for high stakes, including each others' lives. The Jayne feud is one of the most bizarre on record, one that began with sinister sibling threats and ended in bombings, arson, and murder. Silas and George Jayne were the oldest and youngest sons of a Barrington, Ill., farmer, with twelve other children spread between them. Silas was born in 1908, his kid brother George in 1924, there being sixteen years difference in their ages. Yet it was the younger, George Jayne, who first made his mark in horse shows, selling, training, and riding thoroughbreds, an occupation that made him a millionaire. By the 1950s, Silas was assisting his brother, and the profits from their horse breeding, training, and riding at exclusive horse shows allowed both brothers to establish stables in the wealthy suburban communities just west of Chicago.

At first, the brothers worked together, displaying a brand of violence that marked the Jaynes as dangerous characters. Silas and another Jayne brother, Frank, once cornered a rider who was winning a horse show, and pinioned his arms while George Jayne, then still in his teens, beat the rider mercilessly. This kind of conduct was, however, more aptly displayed by Silas, who liked to brag that he served a year in Joliet State Prison for killing a man. "Yeah, I stabbed a guy," he was once quoted as saying, "I can still see the blood coming out of his chest." This dark claim, however, proved to be a lie, although Jayne did serve a short term in the Illinois State Reformatory for rape when he was seventeen.

The first indication that there was strife between George and Silas came when Silas began to rant against the rules set up by the American Horse Shows Association, rules he "did not believe in," according to Marion Jayne, George's wife. Next, Silas grew angry with George when Silas reportedly proposed to bomb the homes and farms of competitors and George refused to participate. Open warfare erupted between the brothers during the 1961 Oak Brook (Ill.) Horse Show. Rider Cherie Rude had been fired by Silas but had been hired for the show by George and won a hotly contested competition in the jumping class. Silas screamed a protest that Rude had missed a fence, but the committee voted in favor of Rude and George. Silas, stunned, let his brother know exactly how he felt at the next show when George's horse beat Silas' entry.

Silas walked up to George Jayne, his wife, and a groom, and said: "You son-of-a-bitch, I'll kill you!" Death threats became Silas' regular salutation to his brother George for the next three years. On one occasion, when Silas bumped into his brother at the International Amphitheater, he reportedly snarled: "I'll get you, one way or another." In 1965, when George's horse was again besting Silas' entry, Silas drove his car up a loading ramp, narrowly missing his brother who was standing at the top. "You'll never make it home!" he told George. At the swanky Lake Forest show in the same year, Silas told George: "You're as good as dead."

Most thought these to be idle threats; Silas Jayne was a hothead, always had been, and he liked to talk tough. Yet, on June 14, 1965, the sibling rivalry blossomed into murder. Cherie Rude, the 22-year-old horsewoman who had won so many championships for George Jayne and who had bested Silas' riders, went on an errand for George. She stepped into his Cadillac, and the minute she turned the ignition switch, the car blew up, killing her instantly.

George Jayne accused his brother of the murder, stating that the bomb had been meant for him. Silas was indicted in 1966, but all charges were dropped when prosecution witnesses refused to testify.

The blood feud between the millionaire horsemen flared up again when George sold a much-touted Canadian horse named Happy Landings to wealthy horseman Patrick Butler. George stated that the payment of $18,000 had to be in cash, explaining that the owner for whom he was acting had tax problems. Butler paid the $18,000, but later learned from Silas, who took every opportunity by then to thwart his brother's business, that Happy Landings was older than he had been represented and that an operation had been performed on one of the horse's hooves. The horse proved to be a loser, winning only one major championship, and Silas' claims, including the fact that the original price for the horse was only $8,000, proved to be correct.

With passions at white heat, family members desperately arranged a meeting between the two brothers in 1967. At that time, Silas and George agreed "to help each other," in Silas' words, but Silas ended the conference with a lecture about George's doping of horses. He looked upon his younger brother as the culprit, and when shaking his hand, he said: "If you'll just straighten out and fly right, we will...forget about all this. I can help you and you can help me."

Unexpected "help" came the following year when dynamite was thrown at George's expensive Inverness, Ill., home. The feud was on again, or perhaps it was never off. George later revealed that as early as 1962, assassins hired by Silas had been firing rounds into his home and pot-shooting at him as he drove home.

In 1969, it was Silas' turn. Frank Michelle, Sr., a former policeman, was hired as a bodyguard by George Jayne. Michelle planted an electronic beeper in Silas' car so that George would always know when his brother was in the vicinity. Michelle's son, Frank, twenty-eight, a man with a criminal record, suddenly appeared at Silas' Elgin home one night in January 1969, firing through the door. Silas, who was watching TV at the time, jumped up and grabbed two loaded pistols conveniently at hand, returning fire, sending bullets whistling through his front window and door at the fleeing Michelle, who was hit repeatedly and dropped dead only a few feet from Silas' front door.

Police arriving a short time later found a scrap of paper in Michelle's pocket with George Jayne's telephone number on it and also directions on how to reach Silas' Elgin, Ill., farm. To Silas it was a simple "hit" engineered by his brother George. It was later stated by George Jayne's wife, Marion, that Michelle had gone to Silas' home with his wife and child, an unlikely procedure for a hit man. Yet Silas was not charged with the killing. Self-defense was ruled and Silas proclaimed the shoot-out "a great victory," adding: I'm going to stay right here and wait for the next one."

The close misses ended on Oct. 28, 1970. That night, the George Jaynes celebrated the birthday of George, Jr., who had just turned sixteen. The family had eaten dinner and George, his wife Marion, and his daughter Linda and her husband had retired to the family den to play bridge. Just as George began shuffling the cards, a shot from a 30-06 rifle smashed through the den window which looked down upon the group. The single bullet plowed into George Jayne's chest and killed him instantly.

The murder remained unsolved for almost seven months. Then agents of the Illinois Bureau of Investigation received an anonymous phone call which fingered Mel Adams, thirty-nine, of suburban Posen, as being directly involved in the death of George Jayne. It was soon learned that Adams was close to one Edward Nefeld, chief of detectives for Markham, a notorious suburban town where police corruption had long been a hallmark. Detectives of the IBI soon learned that Nefeld was in the horse business and was a friend of Silas Jayne. Both men were pulled in for questioning and both revealed that Silas had offered them a contract on his brother's life.

Adams, who had the reputation of a local roughneck in Posen and who had served time in Leavenworth for credit card forgery, met Nefeld in 1969 and was told by the detective that his friend, Silas Jayne, had offered an expensive contract on his brother, George. Adams asked for more details, and Nefeld introduced him to Joseph LaPlaca, a 48-year-old handyman employed by Silas Jayne. LaPlaca offered Adams $10,000 for the hit but warned that there would be no money in advance since a previously hired killer had failed to perform a similar contract after taking "up-front" payments.

A meeting between Adams and Silas Jayne was then set up. The two met in Jayne's car, which was parked along a lonely road, and for an hour the conspirators calmly discussed how to murder George Jayne. Silas at first suggested that Adams machine-gun George as he was driving home or, if that was inconvenient, according to Adams, waylay George, stuff him in a car trunk, and deliver him to Silas at his Elgin farm where George would be buried alive. Adams rejected these proposals, telling Silas he would develop his own murder plans.

While working as a meat processor at the Chicago Stock Yards, Mel Adams took time out to follow the horse shows around the country, thinking to kill George Jayne in some deserted spot. Adams stalked his prey at a San Antonio horse show, but Jayne stayed in crowds. Then Adams saw a chance to kill George at the New Orleans fairgrounds where he was attending a horse show. George walked out to a lonely parking lot and Adams followed, a .38-caliber pistol in his pocket. He had decided to shoot Jayne on the spot, to "blow out his brains," but lost his nerve. "I didn't have the courage or whatever it takes," Adams was later quoted.

Back in Chicago, Adams began complaining to LaPlaca that the $10,000 fee for the killing was not enough. LaPlaca came back to him, stating: "Si likes you. We'll go to $20,000." Still, the would-be hit man balked, telling LaPlaca that another man was needed in the killing and that the fee had to be increased to $30,000. After consulting with Jayne, LaPlaca agreed to the price, and Adams hired Julius Barnes, a fellow stockyards worker, to help him murder George Jayne.

Barnes listened to the half-baked murder plans and then suggested that a high-powered rifle would work best. To that end, Adams' girlfriend purchased a 30-06 Savage rifle, and this was used in target practice at Silas Jayne's farm. Then, Adams and

Barnes went in search of their prey. Finally, they drove boldly onto the grounds of George Jayne's home and ranch on the night of Oct. 28, and, while Adams stayed by the car, Barnes went to the window overlooking the family recreation room, saw Jayne playing cards, and fired the round that killed him. An IBI agent later stated that he heard Barnes saying to adams: "Yeah, I got him good. I got him dead center."

Adams, LaPlaca, Barnes, Nefeld, and, finally, while he insisted that he was innocent, and does to this day, Silas Jayne, were subsequently arrested and charged with murder. Adams was given immunity for turning state's evidence, and Nefeld, in April 1972, pleaded guilty to conspiring to murder and was given three to ten years in prison.

Barnes, LaPlaca, and Silas Jayne were held without bond from May 23, 1971 to May 25, 1973, while they were tried and subsequently convicted of the murder of George Jayne. Despite a spirited defense by the flamboyant F. Lee Bailey, Silas Jayne was given a six to twenty-year prison term for conspiracy to commit murder. In addition to the testimony of Adams, the evidence against Jayne was strong. The bullet taken from his brother's body matched slugs dug out of trees on Silas' Elgin estate and, moreover, Silas' thumbprint was found on one of the payoff bills in the $30,000 paid out for the murder.

LaPlaca received the same sentence as his employer, and Barnes, the actual killer, was sent to prison for twenty-five to thirty-five years. Mrs. Marion Jayne, George's widow, stepped from the courtroom after the sentencing to tell reporters: "Now, maybe, George can rest in peace. I think the law should be changed, however. It's not enough for conspiracy to commit murder."

Even while serving his sentence, however, Silas Jayne became the subject of more criminal charges. In 1978, he was named a suspect in the burning of two Wisconsin stables where scores of horses perished, prosecutors stating that two years earlier, Jayne, from his prison cell, had ordered the stables of rivals burned. The charges were not proved, and Jayne, after serving only seven years of his term, was paroled on May 24, 1979.

The volatile horseman emerged from prison to face a $1 million judgment Marion Jayne had gotten against him for the murder of her husband. He claimed that his fortune was gone. He had spent enormous funds on his defense and had sold his sprawling Northwest Stables in Morton Grove. His horse farm outside of Elgin, Jayne pointed out, was in his wife's name.

Alive at this writing and still holding a hand in the flashy world of exclusive horse shows, Silas Jayne insists that he had nothing to do with his brother's death. The facts have proved otherwise. The Jayne feud, which ended in murder, was one of the more remarkable escapades of the wealthy, where playing the country squire for thoroughbreds, blue ribbons, and millions of dollars, as well as murder, proved to be a rich man's game. REF.: *CBA*.

Jeanneret, Marie, d.1884, Switz., mur. Swiss nurse Marie Jeanneret was a young woman when she poisoned her first victim, her friend Berthet, in 1866. A sadist by nature, Jeanneret murdered for pleasure. Her favorite poison was belladonna, also known as deadly nightshade, which she used to murder the entire Juvet family. Dr. Binet, who suspected the nurse but could not prove anything against her, once warned a patient, "Don't have anything to do with her. All her patients die." When Dr. Rapin expressed his suspicions to the authorities, they arrested Jeanneret. The corpses of her previous clients were exhumed and examined, and traces of many types of poisons were found, including atropine, a belladonna derivative; morphine; and the poisonous mineral, antimony. Although convicted of killing seven people, Jeanneret swayed the jury in her favor and was given a sentence of twenty years in prison.

REF.: *CBA*; Morain, *The Underworld of Paris*; Nash, *Look For the Woman*.

Jeffcott-Hennis Duel, 1833, Brit., duel-mur. Sir John Jeffcott, a judge of Sierra Leone, became angered in May 1833 when he thought that Dr. Peter Hennis had slandered him. On May 10,

1833, he challenged Hennis to a duel. Although Hennis affirmed the conversation, he said that he did not mean the words the way Jeffcott interpreted them. Jeffcott then called the doctor a "calumniating scoundrel." The two men met at a place near Exeter and Jeffcot shot and fatally injured Hennis. On July 26, Jeffcott was charged with murder at the Exeter Assizes, and Charles Melford, George Anthony Halstead, and Robert Holland, who were present during the duel, were charged as accessories to murder. Jeffcott fled the country, but the other three were tried and acquitted.

REF.: *CBA; Melville, Famous Duels and Assassinations.*

Jefferds, Charles, prom. 1860, U.S., mur. A successful immigrant from England, John M. Walton owned a distillery in Manhattan and was worth more than $100,000. He was in the process of divorcing his wife, and had been threatened by her son, Charles Jefferds. On the night of June 30, 1860, Walton left the Eighteenth Street distillery with his friends Terrance Dolan, John W. Matthews, and Richard Pascal at around 11:15 p.m. Jefferds watched from the shadows with a loaded pistol in his pocket. When Matthews stepped into a Third Avenue drugstore, Jefferds stepped up to Walton, placed the gun against his head and fired one shot. Walton collapsed into the arms of Pascal. As the killer disappeared into the shadows, Matthews emerged from the drugstore, saw what had happened and ran after him. At Sixteenth Street, the killer turned, carefully took aim, and murdered Matthews with a single shot to the heart. The killer ran on until he leaped over an iron fence at 37 East Sixteenth Street and hid under a porch for several minutes as police searched for him. Jefferds believed he had not been seen, but there were several witnesses, including Mary Davis, a cook, a butcher named Hessel, and Pascal.

Jefferds' friend, William Bett, convinced him to turn himself in. Held in the Tombs, Jefferds talked with A. Oakey Hall, a politically ambitious lawyer hired by Jefferds' mother. Hall was confident that District Attorney Nelson J. Waterbury had no case against Jefferds, counting on inside information that a recent New York capital punishment law did not provide for a method of execution. Waterbury produced two indictments against Jefferds, one for the first-degree murder of his stepfather and the other for the second-degree murder of Matthews. Waterbury also stalled the trial, expecting the legislature to correct its error in the July 1861 session. Although the Assembly conditionally reinstated the death penalty, it again did not specify the means of execution. Hall, who wanted and eventually got Waterbury's office, demanded that Jefferds be tried. Waterbury uncomfortably presented his case, with witnesses less sure of their identifications a year after the killings. Hall called no witnesses for the defense and had his junior partner address the jury, implying that the case was obviously trumped up. The jury fell for it, and acquitted Jefferds of Walton's murder. Hall moved that the charges against Jefferds for Matthews' killing be dismissed as well, and Waterbury reluctantly agreed. The killer was free in an hour.

The humiliated Waterbury vowed revenge and hired William Moore, a small-time Broadway actor and sometime gambler, to pose as an undercover agent, become friendly with Jefferds, and try to get him to confess to the slayings. With an interest in his dead brother's estate, William Walton gave Moore several hundred dollars as well. With the November elections for district attorney coming up, Waterbury was anxious to get the confession before Hall was elected to replace him in office. On Nov. 14, 1861, Moore and Jefferds, both very drunk, toured the bars in the Bowery, and ended up at Walton's saloon. Jefferds threw a coin to Walton, and belligerently told him, "I am Charles Jefferds who shot your brother, and I will shoot you as quick, for you are the man who kept me in prison a whole year!" The next morning, Fourth Precinct officer George H. Webb arrested Jefferds for the murder of Matthews. Jefferds, as he was being taken away, begged Moore, "Go see Oakey Hall. He'll know what to do." Hall, however, wanted nothing more to do with the case, having already obtained the publicity he needed. Although the courts had cleared

Jefferds of the murder of his stepfather and so could not try him again, he had not been specifically exonerated in Matthews' death. He was now tried for first-degree murder in that killing. Judge John T. Hoffman presided, as he had over Jefferds' earlier trial. Eyewitnesses Davis, Hessel, and Pascal again testified, and a surprise witness, gun store clerk Robert Shultery, said he had sold the murder weapon to Jefferds. Walton, Moore, and a police captain who had been in civilian clothes at Walton's tavern all told how Jefferds had drunkenly admitted his guilt. After an hour of deliberation, the jury returned a verdict of Guilty. Jefferds was sentenced to die on Feb. 20, 1863. But, because the means of execution was still undefined legally and had not been specified by the court, the condemned man spent years in jail. He repeatedly filed petitions from Sing Sing, and was eventually killed in a fight with another prisoner. Hall, who became prominent in Boss Tweed's corrupt Tammany Hall, was later tried for embezzlement. See: **Tweed, William Marcy.**

REF.: *CBA; Nash, Murder, America; Rodell, New York Murders; Trial of Charles M. Jefferds for Murder, at New York, December, 1861.*

Jefferies, Christopher, b.1778, Brit., mur. In 1793, after suffering innumerable abuses, 10-year-old William Sellard died from injuries sustained at the hands of his two partners with whom he operated a boat on the Oxford Canal. Sellard's partners, William Harrison, twelve, and Christopher Jefferies, fifteen, regularly tortured the younger boy. They once tied him to the boat's rudder and sailed through the canal. A coroner's jury charged the two youths with murder and they were jailed. While Harrison was acquitted of all charges, Jefferies was found Guilty of the reduced charge of manslaughter and received a prison sentence of one year in solitary confinement. He was also fined one shilling.

REF.: *CBA; Wilson, Children Who Kill.*

Jefferson, Eddie, 1918-79, U.S., (unsolv.) mur. Jazzman Eddie Jefferson, a pioneer of vocal techniques, was named best jazz singer of 1975 by *Downbeat* magazine. A native of Pittsburgh, Jefferson's best known work was a 1953 version of saxophonist James Moody's "I'm in the Mood for Love."

After finishing a gig at Baker's Keyboard Lounge in Detroit in May 1979, Jefferson was shot to death leaving the club. Jefferson had just finished a set with saxophonist Richie Cole when a car squealed to a halt outside the popular Detroit jazz club and someone in it fired a shotgun. The fatal blast hit Jefferson in the chest. REF.: *CBA.*

Jefferson, Leroy, 1919- , U.S., drugs. One of the most powerful drug traffickers in America, according to U.S. Senate crime probes, Leroy Jefferson controlled all illegal drug trafficking along the Pacific Coast; his headquarters was in Los Angeles. He had a virtual monopoly on heroin traffic and controlled hundreds of professional black drug pushers who worked through the black population in California, Oregon, and Washington. Jefferson, who originally began by organizing vast prostitution rings, moved into the drug trade in the 1950s, after establishing important contacts in Mexico. He became so successful as an independent source of illegal drugs that syndicate members actually battled over who would be able to use him as their main conduit for heroin.

REF.: *CBA; Nash, Bloodletters and Badmen.*

Jeffery, Henry Edward, and **Terroni, Anthony,** and **Walker, John,** prom. 1961, Brit., theft. Acting on a tip that a heist was being planned, officers from the English Flying Squad tailed Henry Edward Jeffery and Anthony Terroni. Jeffery had just been released from prison after serving a six-year sentence for office-breaking. The two men were seen in their van outside Matthew Hall and Co., a building contractor. The following week, on a day when paychecks were scheduled to be sent from the company to employees across the country, officers stationed themselves throughout the area.

Officers tailed a postal van to the Hall Co., where the driver picked up the checks. Not far from the pickup sight, the van in which Jeffery and Terroni were riding pulled in front of the mail van. The officers rammed the thieves' van and tried to arrest

Jeffery as well as five other masked men hidden in the back of the van. After a brief scuffle, all six bandits escaped, with Terroni driving another car.

Two suspects were arrested the day of the attempted hold-up, but it was five weeks before police located the ringleaders. Jeffery and Terroni, along with John Walker, were arrested, tried and convicted of attempted theft. The men were sentenced to a total of forty-six years in prison. REF.: *CBA*; Jackson, *Occupied with Crime.*

Jeffrey, Lord Francis, 1773-1850, Scot., jur. Helped establish *Edinburgh Review* in 1802, and was its editor from 1803-29. He served as judge in the court of session from 1834-50. REF.: *CBA.*

Jeffreys-Moore Duel, 1806, Brit., duel. As the public's taste for duelling grew in the early 1800s, British police were seeking ways to end the bloodshed. After receiving a tip about a scheduled duel, three British policemen staked out a field near Chalk Farm at 6 a.m. in August 1806. As they arrived, the duelers' seconds had moved out of range, and Francis Jeffreys and Thomas Moore were ready to settle their differences. A policeman named Carpmeal tried to stop them, but as he walked into the open field, one of the duelists raised his pistol, aiming for the officer. Carpmeal was saved by fellow officer Crocker who knocked the gun out of the man's hand. Jeffreys and Moore were arrested and each posted a £400 bond. Each of the seconds also was required to post a £200 bond. Examining the duelling pistols, police discovered that Jeffreys' gun was not loaded, and that Moore's contained a wad of paper. REF.: Armitage, *Bow Street Runners*; *CBA.*

Jeffreys, George (Baron Jeffreys of Wem, AKA: **Bloody**), 1648-89, Brit., jur. At the age of twenty-three, George Jeffreys was elected Common Sergeant after only three years of practicing law. After aligning himself with the Duke of York, the graduate of Trinity College, Cambridge, was appointed Recorder of London in 1679. He also served as counsel for the state in prosecuting conspirators in the Popish Plot.

Judge George Jeffreys, who was almost lynched because of his harsh sentences.

Jeffreys gained a reputation for his hard drinking and quick temper. He was once forced to kneel before the Speaker of the House of Commons and receive a public reprimand for misconduct. The shameful scolding did little to keep Jeffreys from abusing people in court and trying to win the favor of nobility.

Jeffreys assisted King Charles II in his fight to gain power from Parliament, and was rewarded with the position of Lord Chief Justice. At the age of thirty-five, he was one of the youngest

chief justices in British history. Two years later, when the Duke of York became James II, Jeffreys was moved into the House of Lords as Baron Jeffreys of Wem. Following the government's suppression of a rebellion by the Protestant Duke of Monmouth, Jeffreys was one of five judges to try the rebels. In what became known as the "Bloody Assize," the judges conducted trials in six cities in which more than 1,300 people either pleaded guilty or were found Guilty. The number of executions was estimated to be as high as 320, while another 800 prisoners were deported. Jeffreys' contemptible conduct with prisoners and fellow judges throughout the proceedings inspired the nickname Bloody Jeffreys.

When he returned to London, Jeffreys was rewarded with the title of Lord Chancellor and served until James II was toppled from power by William of Orange. The judge tried to flee the country disguised as a seaman, but was identified by patrons in a Wapping pub. Jeffreys was saved from a lynch mob by two policemen, who arrested him and locked him in the Tower of London. In ill health at the time of his arrest, Jeffreys died at the age of forty-one in April 1689 before he could be brought to trial. REF.: *CBA*; Scott, *The Concise Encyclopedia of Crime and Criminals.*

Jeffries, Elizabeth, d.1752, Brit., mur. At about age eighteen, Elizabeth Jeffries took a position as overseer of her uncle's estate in Walthamstow. The uncle, also named Jeffries, worked the girl mercilessly, but she stayed because Jeffries had promised to leave the estate to her when he died. Whenever he became dissatisfied with her work, however, the old man threatened to disinherit her. After a number of such erratic shifts of mind, Elizabeth hired John Swann, a servant in the household, to murder the uncle. On July 3, 1751, Swann, who was to receive £100 for the murder, shot Jeffries while Elizabeth put the family silver in a bag and hid it. She then ran to a neighbor's house and told them that highwaymen had forced their way into the Jeffries' home and robbed them. The authorities believed her until Swann began talking about the crime while drunk. Arrested, he implicated Elizabeth. The two were tried at Chelmsford on Mar. 11, 1752. Elizabeth wrote out a detailed confession and was condemned along with Swann. Both were hanged in Epping Forest on Mar. 28, 1752. Swann's body was left to rot on a gibbet erected on a well-travelled road as a warning to other potential murderers. REF.: *CBA*; Nash, *Look for the Woman*; Mitchell, *The Newgate Calendar II*; O'Donnell, *Should Women Hang?*

Jeffries, Mary, prom. 1885, Brit., pros. An infamous nineteenth century madam, Mary Jeffries is often credited with transforming prostitution into a progressive business. After a lengthy career as a prostitute and a procuress, Jeffries established her own brothel with the backing of several wealthy clients. Determined to move the profession into the 1900s, Jeffries' establishment offered such novelties as a flogging house.

Backed by powerful and politically connected patrons, Jeffries managed to remain on friendly terms with the police. She was, however, brought to trial in 1885 on charges of keeping a disorderly house. Jeremiah Minahan, an ex-policeman, sought to prove that officials had taken bribes to overlook crimes committed by Jeffries. In a farcical trial, Jeffries pleaded guilty to a breach of the peace and was fined £200. After paying the fine and posting a security bond, Jeffries returned to her business. REF.: Bullough, *Illustrated History*; *CBA.*

Jeffs, Amelia, c.1874-90, Brit., (unsolv.) mur. In West Ham, England, in the late 1880s, a dozen or more children and teen-agers, mostly girls, vanished. The final disappearances occurred in January 1890, when three girls, at three separate times, vanished. A woman had been seen talking to each of the girls prior to their disappearance. The body of just one, Amelia Jeffs, fifteen, was found. She had been raped and strangled after a desperate struggle to survive, indicated by caked blood and flesh found under her fingernails. REF.: *CBA*; Nash, *Among the Missing.*

Jeffs, Doreen, d.1965, Brit., mur. In November 1960, in Eastborne, England, Doreen Jeffs killed her baby daughter and then fabricated a kidnapping. When the corpse was found, Jeffs' story was challenged and she soon confessed and pleaded guilty to murder. Her defense attorney successfully presented a case for duress based on the fact that the child, Linda Jeffs, was a month premature. Contending that Jeffs was "a woman who committed an offense while under the stress of childbirth," the lawyer got Jeffs sent to a mental institution. She was later put on probation. Jeffs attempted suicide by taking gas, but was interrupted. Over four years later, in January 1965, she neatly folded her clothes by a cliff overlooking the English Channel near Beachy Head and dove into the ocean. Her body surfaced near the shore several days later.

REF.: *CBA;* Gribble, *The Dead End Killers;* Nash, *Look For the Woman.*

Jeffs, Frederick Walter, 1919-57, Brit., (unsolv.) mur. In April 1957, the body of 37-year-old Frederick Walter Jeffs, a shopkeeper, was found in a wooded area outside of Birmingham, England. He had been bludgeoned to death by a heavy instrument. Jeffs was separated from his wife and was last seen talking to an attractive woman in his store who was heard saying "see you later." The police tried to find a male customer accompanying the woman, but nobody was ever apprehended for the murder.

REF.: *CBA;* Furneaux, *Famous Criminal Cases, vol. 5.*

Mass murderer Hélène Jegado, preparing another lethal meal.

Jegado, Hélène (Jagado), d.1851, Fr., theft-mur. An illiterate peasant, Hélène Jegado became a cook in her late thirties, and eventually rose to fame as one of France's foremost mass poisoners. Usually working for clergymen, Jegado was easily offended and expressed her displeasure by adding arsenic to her culinary creations. A thrill killer, she enjoyed seeing her victims dying in agony. One of her meals destroyed a family of seven, including her own sister. Not long after this incident, Jegado remarked, "Wherever I go, people die." She retired to a convent to become the cook there, but left after several of the sisters became ill.

Jegado moved to Rennes, France, in 1849 to cook for university professor Théophile Bidard, who was also a surgeon. When Rosalie Sarrazin, another servant in the household, was poisoned in July 1851, Bidard called the police. When officers arrived, Jegado, who had not been accused, loudly protested, "I am innocent!" Investigations uncovered at least twenty-three deaths caused by Jegado's cooking between 1833 and 1841. It was estimated that she may have been responsible for as many as sixty murders. Tried in Rennes in December 1851, she was found Guilty and was executed on the guillotine.

REF.: Brock, *A Casebook of Crime; CBA;* Glaister, *The Power of Poison;* Griffiths, *Mysteries of Police and Crime;* Heppenstall, *French Crime*

in the Romantic Age; Morain, *The Underworld of Paris;* Nash, *Almanac of World Crime;* ____, *Look For the Woman;* Thompson, *Poisons and Poisoners;* Williamson, *Annals of Crime;* Wraxall, *Criminal Celebrities.*

Jehoiachin (Joachin), c.615-560 B.C., Judah, impris. Successor to Jehoiakim whose brief reign ended when he was held prisoner and taken to Babylon by Nebuchadnezzar. He was released after thirty-seven years by Evil-Merodach, who seized the throne of Babylon. REF.: *CBA.*

Jehoram (Joram), d.c.843 B.C., Israel, king, assass. Younger son of Ahab. Put down several revolts but was killed by Jehu, who took control of the kingdom. REF.: *CBA.*

Jelf, Arthur Richard, 1837-1917, Brit., jur. Appointed to serve on the King's Bench of the High Court in 1901. He presided over the murder trial of Edward Lawrence and served as a judge until 1910. REF.: *CBA.*

Jelke, Minot F. (AKA: Mickey), 1930- , U.S., pros. For Minot F. Jelke it was not enough that he stood to inherit close to $3 million when he turned thirty. The heir to the oleomargarine fortune was a high-profile Manhattan playboy in his late teens. With a generous allowance, Jelke cruised New York's nightspots in his powder-blue Cadillac. In 1948, Jelke met Pat Ward, formerly Sandra Wisotsky, and the couple began a relationship that lasted many years. In 1953, Jelke was indicted by a jury on charges of coercing Ward into a life of prostitution and of attempting to do the same with former hat-check girl Marguerite Cordova.

For the first two weeks of the trial, which began in February 1953, newsmen were barred by Manhattan General Sessions Judge Francis L. Valente, who feared extensive press coverage would focus on the sensationalism of the trial. Valente found Jelke Guilty and sentenced him to three to six years in prison. While he was free on $50,000 bail, Jelke's conviction was overturned in a 1954 appellate court ruling. The upper court said that Valente's ban of the news media had prevented Jelke from receiving a fair trial.

In April 1955, Ward was asked to retell her story of being abused by Jelke. Ward told the courtroom that, despite promises of marriage, her lover asked her to help him by becoming a prostitute. Jelke introduced many of his wealthy friends to Ward, who charged up to $100 a date. Jelke then took most of her earnings, Ward said, and loaned her to a madam when he was out of town. Four other prostitutes testified against Jelke, and ex-convict Richard Short told the court that the defendant had helped secure customers for his wife, prostitute Pat Thompson. During the ten-day second trial before Judge Valente, Ward refused to answer questions about whether she was still working as a call girl, and defense attorney George Washington Herz called her a "Fifth Amendment prostitute with crocodile tears." Prosecutor Anthony Liebler proclaimed Jelke "a male madam." On Mar. 31, 1955, Jelke was found Guilty of compulsory prostitution and was later sentenced to two to three years in prison.

REF.: *CBA;* Hibbert, *The Roots of Evil;* Nash, *Hustlers and Con Men.*

Jem (Djem, Zizim, Cem), 1459-95, Turk., consp.-rebel. Younger son of sultan Mohammed II. He made a futile attempt to usurp his brother, Bajazet II, in 1481. He led a revolt by the nobles in Anatolia, but was eventually defeated after years of battle. He lived in exile in Rhodes and Rome. REF.: *CBA.*

Jenkin, William Thomas Francis, 1934- , Brit., mur. On Apr. 13, 1959, the body of 12-year-old Janice Anne Holmes was found in Binbrook, Lincolnshire, England. Four days later, a 24-year-old truck driver, William Thomas Francis Jenkin, of Hall Farm Estate, was arrested for the murder. The prosecution charged that Jenkin lured the little girl into the woods, where he assaulted and strangled her. He denied the charge, and his wife claimed that he had spent the evening searching for the missing child. The first trial ended with a hung jury, but at the retrial on July 16, 1959, Jenkin was found Guilty of the murder and sentenced to life imprisonment.

REF.: *CBA;* Furneaux, *Famous Criminal Cases, vol. 6.*

Jenkins, Allison, 1960- , U.S., mur. For Chicago police

officers Jay Brunkella and Fred Hattenberger, Sept. 22, 1986, was a routine day in the war on drugs. The officers, part of an eight-man unit assigned to patrol the neighborhoods north of Howard Street, near Evanston, were staked out on the third floor of an aging elementary school. The officers observed small-time dope peddlers in operation, and radioed the license plate numbers of buyers to an arrest car waiting a few blocks away. Allison Jenkins was a familiar face to Brunkella. The 28-year-old native of Belize had been arrested on a number of minor charges, most recently for selling cocaine to an undercover police officer. When the policemen observed what they thought was a drug transaction, they left the building to arrest Jenkins.

During the attempted arrest of the pusher, Hattenberg's gun discharged and hit Brunkella in the chest. There were no ambulances immediately available to transport Brunkella to the hospital, so his fellow officers placed him in the back of the squad car. After eleven days in intensive care, Brunkella died on Oct. 4, 1986. Jenkins, who had originally been charged with selling marijuana and aggravated battery was now charged with the murder of a police officer. In January 1987, a jury convicted Jenkins of delivering a controlled substance, and Criminal Court Judge Joseph Urso sentenced him to six years in prison.

Urso also presided over Jenkins' murder trial, which began in September. The defendant's lawyer, Craig Katz, argued that his client was framed by a trigger-happy cop who had taken unnecessary risks with his weapon. The prosecution contended that Jenkins, on parole, had tried to flee from the officers. State's Attorney Dennis Dernbach argued that Jenkins and Hattenberger struggled, and that the defendant caused the policeman's gun to fire. A jury found Jenkins Guilty of murder, but within days one juror called the judge and said that she had been pressured into rendering a Guilty verdict. Katz then petitioned the court to set aside the jury's verdict because he had new evidence in the case.

Police officer James Crooks then testified that he had seen Hattenberger use unnecessary force on one occasion. It was also revealed that Hattenberger had once before wounded a fellow officer in the line of duty. On Nov. 13, 1988, Urso denied the motion for a new trial. Jenkins was sentenced to twenty years in prison for murder. REF: *CBA*.

Jenkins, Carrie Lee (AKA: **The Dust Cloth Bandit**), 1941- , U.S., burg. During a two-year period, Carrie Lee Jenkins of Miami, Fla., stole jewelry and household goods estimated to be worth $400,000. At her trial for the burglary of a home in Beverly Hills, Calif., testimony revealed that Jenkins gained access to households in cities across the U.S. by answering ads for housekeepers, and, once left alone by her new employers, packed what she could carry, and returned home to Florida that same day.

Police credited Jenkins' arrest and successful prosecution to the investigation and testimony of the Organized Crime Bureau of the Dade County Public Safety Department and to the efforts of a private citizen known as Mrs. Columbo. Columbo, a New York resident who requested her name to be withheld and who was subsequently nicknamed by a Los Angeles area victim of a "rob-and-run" housekeeper, was burglarized in 1978 in a crime like the one for which Jenkins was finally arrested. Frustrated with the local police's failure to apprehend the felonious housekeeper, Columbo began an intensive investigation of her own, evidence from which eventually led to Jenkins' arrest and conviction on twenty counts of grand theft and burglary in the Santa Monica Superior Court. Jenkins was sentenced in 1980 to nine years in prison. REF.: *CBA*.

Jenkins, Charles Henry (AKA: **King of Borstal**), See: **Geraghty, Christopher James**.

Jenkins, David, 1952- , U.S., drugs-fraud. In 1972 David Jenkins was a member of Great Britain's Olympic silver-medal-winning 400-meter relay team. Fifteen years later, on Nov. 6, 1987, the British Olympian faced U.S. District Judge J. Lawrence Irving and pleaded guilty to four counts of smuggling steroids into the U.S. from Mexico. Although Jenkins faced up to sixteen years in prison and a $1 million fine for charges that included defraud-

ing the U.S., holding counterfeit steroids for sale, introducing misbranded steroids into interstate commerce, and receiving anabolic steroids subject to seizure, he was actually sentenced on Dec. 12, 1988, to seven years in federal prison, five years probation, and fined $75,000.

Although Judge Irving referred to the case as "one of the worst tragedies" he had seen in his tenure on the bench, and intended by way of the sentence to send a message to the athletic community that "illegal trafficking of steroids in the United States will not be tolerated," Irving was scheduled on June 9, 1989, to formally consider Jenkins' release after he had served only six months of his sentence. The proposed release was delayed, however, when prosecutor Phillip Halpern, an assistant U.S. attorney, persuaded a court clerk to remove a letter from Judge Irving's courthouse mailbox. By intercepting the judge's mail—in this instance a letter from a U.S. Customs Service official who opposed reducing Jenkins' prison term—Halpern said he was trying to prevent an illegal direct communication between an agency head and a judge. Jenkins, a U.S. resident, was to remain in Boron Federal Prison in the Mojave Desert until Judge Irving rendered a decision. REF.: *CBA*.

Jenkins, E.B. d.1890, Brit., mur. In a killing in which few details are known, E.B. Jenkins murdered a young woman named Emily Joy on Jan. 7, 1889, in a studio on Brighton Road in Godalming. Jenkins was hanged for the murder at Wandsworth in March 1890. Emily Joy was buried at Farncombe and her grave was marked by a tombstone donated by a Guilford townsman named Patrick. REF.: *CBA*.

Jenkins, Ferguson, 1943- , Can., drugs. Former Chicago Cubs and Texas Rangers pitcher Ferguson Jenkins, winner of more than 200 major league baseball games, joined the ranks of major sports figures implicated in possession of illegal drugs when he was arrested Aug. 25, 1980, in Toronto and charged with possession of four grams of cocaine, two ounces of marijuana and two grams of hashish. Although Jenkins was found Guilty of cocaine possession on Dec. 18, 1980 (the other charges were dropped during the court proceedings), Judge Jerry Young of Ontario Provincial Court exercised a judicial prerogative frequently employed in Canada in cases involving first offenders and erased the verdict after a brief deliberation, giving the 37-year-old pitcher a complete discharge.

The judge told Jenkins, a native of Ontario, in explaining his decision, "You seem to be a person who has conducted himself in exemplary fashion in the community and in the country, building up an account. This is the time to draw on that account." Jenkins was removed from the Rangers' active roster in September by order of baseball commissioner Bowie Kuhn because he refused to answer questions about the arrest. But Jenkins was restored when a grievance filed by his lawyers and the Major League Baseball Players Association was upheld. REF.: *CBA*.

Jenkins, Harry, 1957- , U.S., rob.-asslt.&bat.-attempt. mur. On May 10, 1976, 19-year-old Harry Jenkins, of Chicago's West Side, shot a neighbor, 58-year-old Nicholas Comito, while trying to rob him. Jenkins shot Comito, a retired machinist, once in the side and once in the face while Comito was mowing the yard around his home on West Chicago Avenue. The second shot permanently blinded Comito in both eyes.

Although Comito could not identify Jenkins during the trial, he could describe him. Jenkins' conviction on Oct. 20, 1976, on charges of attempted armed robbery, aggravated battery, and attempted murder was also made possible by the testimony of 15-year-old Elvin Webster, an accomplice to the crime. Charged with the same offenses as Jenkins, Webster received only one month in custody and two years probation—a trade-off for pleading guilty in Juvenile Court and agreeing to testify against Jenkins.

During the trial, Comito testified that Jenkins shot him when he refused to turn over his wallet. "I shot him," Jenkins admitted in his confession to Oak Park police. "He wouldn't go down, so I shot him again." Jenkins' family and attorney Sheldon Grauer contended, however, that Jenkins was beaten when arrested and forced to confess under duress. Grauer also objected to the lack of blacks on the jury; Jenkins was black, Comito white.

Police denied having beaten Jenkins, and on Nov. 10, 1976, he was sentenced to 100-200 years in prison. Under Illinois law, Jenkins would become eligible for parole after serving eleven years and three months of his sentence. REF.: *CBA*.

Jenkins, James Gilbert, 1834-64, U.S., rob.-mur. James Jenkins was a professional criminal having a long history of highway robberies and murders. It was reported that he had killed eight white men and ten Indians throughout Missouri, Texas, Iowa, and California. While living in Napa City, Calif., Jenkins became acquainted with Patrick O'Brien in order to establish a sexual liaison with O'Brien's wife. Mrs. O'Brien, a lusty, attractive woman with a strong will, goaded Jenkins into murdering her husband, or so he later said, although Jenkins' willingness to murder needed no encouragement.

Jenkins got drunk, marched into O'Brien's home, and shot him, but he was caught almost immediately and quickly confessed. Mrs. O'Brien denied having anything to do with the murder and was released. Jenkins was convicted and sentenced to death. Before he was hanged, Jenkins lamented his sloppy habits and the fact that he had gotten drunk, believing that if he had been meticulous in his killing of O'Brien, he never would have been caught. His last words on the scaffold were: "That whiskey that I drank the morning before I shot O'Brien was what caused me to do it when I did, and in so careless a manner."

Killer and robber James Gilbert Jenkins.

REF.: Bartholomew, *The Biographical Album of Western Gunfighters*; *CBA*; Guinn, *A History of California*; Kirsch and Murphy, *West of the West*; Wood, *Life and Confessions of James Gilbert Jenkins*.

Jenkins, James Graham, 1834-1921, U.S., jur. Attorney for city of Milwaukee from 1863-67, and appointed to the eastern district court of Wisconsin by President Grover Cleveland in 1888. He was later named by Cleveland to the seventh circuit court in 1893. In addition, he held office as dean of the law school at Marquette University from 1908-13. REF.: *CBA*.

Jenkins, John, d.1851, U.S., theft. The Vigilance Committee was a group of citizens who banded together in Long Wharf, Calif., in June 1851 to combat the lawlessness of the west. Their first act after establishing a constitution was the trial and hanging of John Jenkins. On June 10, 1851, Jenkins broke into a store in Long Wharf and stole the safe. When he was spotted carrying a large sack on his back, the alarm was sounded and he was chased. When Jenkins got into a boat and headed out into the bay, a dozen boats pursued him. Just before he was captured, he threw a bag into the water. It was recovered and found to contain the stolen safe. The Vigilance Committee took Jenkins to their rooms on Battery Street near Pine Street and rang the bell of the Monumental Engine Company at around 10 p.m. to call the committee together.

About eighty members were admitted after giving the secret password. Crowds of people waited outside for the results. The committee examined the evidence for two hours and at midnight, rang the California Engine House bell, indicating that Jenkins had been condemned to death by hanging. Just before 1 a.m., S. Brannan came out to announce the decision to the crowd. The execution would take place in an hour at the plaza. He then asked if the people approved of the action, and was greeted by many shouts of "Aye, Aye," with only a few cries of "No." A clergyman gave last rites to the condemned man. Just before 2

a.m., the committee emerged with the prisoner and walked to the plaza. A suggestion that Jenkins be hanged from the flagstaff was angrily overruled, and the rope was thrown over a beam projecting from an adobe building. About twenty people grabbed the end of the rope, and dragged Jenkins along the ground until they raised him over the beam and held him there until he was dead.

REF.: *CBA*; Duke, *Celebrated Criminal Cases of America*.

Jenkins, John James, 1843-1911, U.S., jur. Circuit court clerk in Wisconsin from 1867-70. He served as county judge in Chippewa County, Wis., from 1872-76, and as U.S. Attorney from 1876-80. In addition, he served in the U.S. House of Representatives from 1895-1909. He was appointed to the court of the Puerto Rican territory by President William H. Taft in 1910. REF.: *CBA*.

Jenkins, Lawrence Hugh, 1858-1928., India, jur. Served on Bombay's high court of judicature from 1899-1908. He was a member of the Council of India from 1908-09, and served as chief justice of the high court located in Bengal from 1909-15. REF.: *CBA*.

Jenkins, Lonnie, 1902- , U.S., (wrong. convict.) mur. On Oct. 15, 1931, Lonnie Jenkins, a 29-year-old Detroit street car conductor, notified police of his wife Edith's suicide. He said he found his wife lying on her back on the floor in a pool of blood. She had been shot through the head and the automatic pistol still lay on her chest. A suicide note was nearby. Because Mrs. Jenkins had attempted to kill herself only a few weeks earlier, a coroner deemed her death a suicide.

The detectives found Jenkins' description of the body's position unusual. In their experience, suicides by shooting almost always fell forward. They persisted in their investigation despite the jury's finding. They questioned a woman named Betty, a former neighbor of the Jenkins, who for a time had lived with the couple and helped Mrs. Jenkins with cleaning and the care of her daughter Helen. Betty told the police that she wrote the suicide note at Mr. Jenkins' urging, that she and Jenkins had been involved in a love affair, and that Jenkins had promised to marry her. On the strength of this statement and other circumstantial evidence, Jenkins was arrested and charged with the murder of his wife. Though Jenkins maintained his innocence throughout the trial, the jury found him Guilty of first-degree murder and sentenced him to life in prison.

Jenkins' defense attorney, Allen W. Kent, concentrated on the way the body would fall in a suicide of this type. In a freak accident, Kent shot himself in the head while attempting to demonstrate his theory to the deputy chief of detectives. Jenkins' daughter took up the fight in his behalf after Kent's death. On Dec. 23, 1940, Jenkins was granted a new trial in which the defense presented ballistics evidence that the position of Mrs. Jenkins' body was not unusual for a suicide. The defense also presented certification from FBI handwriting experts that the suicide note had indeed been written by Mrs. Jenkins. And, finally, Betty recanted her earlier testimony. On the strength of the new evidence, Lonnie Jenkins' conviction was overturned and he was freed after spending nine years in prison. REF.: *CBA*.

Jenkins, Thomas, 1920- , Brit., rob.-mur. A gang called the Elephant Boys figured prominently in the resurgence of youth gang crime in London after WWII. On Dec. 8, 1944, Thomas Jenkins, a 24-year-old welder, and 26-year-old Ronald Hedley, both members of the Elephant Boys, drove up to a jeweler's shop on a busy London street. Hedley stayed at the wheel while Jenkins smashed the jewelers' window and grabbed items worth £3,795. As the two sped away, retired naval captain Ralph Douglas Binney placed himself in the path of the car. Hedley did not hesitate. Not only did he run Binney down, but on seeing that the road ahead was blocked, he backed up and ran over him again. This time, however, Binney's clothing got caught on the bottom of the car and he was dragged, screaming for help, over a mile before being thrown free. He died within hours.

Jenkins and Hedley were identified and arrested soon thereafter. They were both tried for robbery and murder, but because

Hedley drove the car, only he was sentenced to death (and later hanged), while Jenkins received the comparatively light sentence of eight years in prison.

Soon after his release, Jenkins tried to rob a clerk transporting money from a bank to a factory. But police had been alerted in advance and foiled the attempt. Jenkins and his accomplices, Robert Sanders and John Cracknell, were apprehended after a chase. On Mar. 30, 1953, Jenkins was found Guilty and sentenced to five years in prison.

REF.: *CBA;* Lefebure, *Evidence for the Crown;* Scott, *Scotland Yard;* Simpson, *Forty Years of Murder.*

Jenks, Edward, 1861-1939, Brit., lawyer. Director of the Law Society's legal studies from 1903-24 and a professor based in London. REF.: *CBA.*

Jennings, Alphonso J. (Al), 1863-1961, U.S., west. outl. One of the more comic characters of the Old West, Al Jennings, was raised with his brothers Edward, Frank, and John at Kiowa Creek, Okla., near the town of Woodward. The Jennings boys, sons of Judge J.D.F. Jennings, were a fun-loving lot who dreamed of becoming bandits. In the mid-1890s, while working as cowboys they met some outlaws who later became members of the Bill Doolin gang. Al and Frank Jennings decided to become outlaws. They started off by obtaining fake U.S. marshal's badges and using them to collect "tolls" from gullible trail herders moving their cattle through the Oklahoma Territory.

Train robber Al Jennings.

Ed and John Jennings had followed their father's lead and became lawyers. The Jennings boys practiced in their father's court but they proved to be unorthodox and hot-headed. On Oct. 8, 1895, both brothers acted as defense for some young cowboys accused of stealing some barrels of beer. Acting for the prosecution was the flamboyant Temple Houston, son of Texas' greatest hero Sam Houston. Temple Houston, who was later the role model for Yancy Cravat in Edna Ferber's *Cimarron,* was an excellent lawyer; he was also deadly with a gun and took insults from no man. When the Jennings brothers began to shout at him in court, Houston accused both of them of being "grossly ignorant of the law."

Ed Jennings slammed his hand down hard on a table and then shouted at Houston: "You're a damned liar!" Both he and his brother drew their guns just as Temple Houston's six-gun cleared its holster. Before a shooting battle erupted, the opponents were restrained. That night, Judge Jennings reproached his sons, telling them that their uncontrollable tempers had embarrassed him. He warned them to curb their emotions if they intended to practice law. Some hours later Ed and John Jennings entered the Cabinet Saloon in Woodward and went to the bar. They saw Temple Houston playing cards in a nearby room and took their guns from their holsters, carrying them at their sides. They entered the gambling room and Houston stood up. "Ed, I want to see you a minute," Houston said to Jennings, motioning for Jennings to accompany him out a back door.

Ed Jennings was apparently drunk. He shouted at Houston: "See me here and now, you s.o.b.!" Both men drew their guns, as did John Jennings. Houston fired six shots at both Jennings brothers. John was hit in the arm. Ed was struck in the head by a stray bullet from his brother's gun. When two more of Houston's bullets struck Ed Jennings he fell dead onto the barroom floor. John Jennings staggered out of the bar with half his arm in shreds. Though John had accidentally fired the shot that killed

his brother, Houston was charged with murder. He was acquitted on grounds of self-defense.

Al Jennings told his father when they buried Ed that he intended to kill Houston but Judge Jennings shook his head, saying: "Do you want to heap another tragedy on this one?" Jennings, rebuked by his father, saddled his horse and, with his brother Frank, rode into southern Oklahoma where he was joined by several members of the Doolin gang. They planned to rob trains. On the night of Aug. 16, 1897, Al and Frank Jennings, with Little Dick West and Morris and Pat O'Malley, stopped a southbound Santa Fe train at Edmond but were unable to shoot or blast the safe open.

A few nights later Al Jennings tried to flag down another train by standing directly in the center of the tracks, holding a lantern and frantically waving a red flag. The engineer, however, kept his hand on the throttle and the train roared forward. Jennings, screaming for the engineer to halt, finally leaped out of the way at the last moment. The train raced on into the night as Jennings and the rest of the outlaws stood cursing in the darkness. A few days later Jennings and his brother Frank rode alongside a fast-moving Santa Fe train, near Bond Switch, firing their six-guns in the air as a signal to the engineer to stop. The engineer merely waved a friendly hello and kept going. The Jennings brothers, their horses exhausted, fell behind and then came to a panting stop as they watched their prey chug from sight.

These miserable failures were capped by a disastrous raid on a southbound Rock Island passenger train at 11 a.m. on Oct. 1, 1897. Al and Frank Jennings, Little Dick West and the O'Malley brothers found the train stopped at a water station eight miles south of Minco. They boarded the baggage car but again could not open the safe. "I've been waiting for that," Al Jennings said and he produced several sticks of dynamite. He tied these together, stuck a long fuse into one stick, lit it, and placed it alongside the safe. The baggage car clerk and the outlaws leaped from the train car and ran some distance from it, waiting.

Al Jennings in Hollywood, 1940.

"How much dynamite did you use, Al?" Frank asked his brother.

"You got to use a lot of dynamite to dent a big safe like that," Al Jennings answered knowingly.

A few seconds later, the entire car blew up, sending a shower of wooden and iron splinters in all directions. There was no safe, let alone money, to be found. The frustrated gang members then went through the passenger coaches and robbed everyone down to their last dollar. They also took diamond stickpins, women's jewelry, even a new pair of boots from a traveling salesman. The gang fled into the Indian nation where, on Oct. 29, 1897, they robbed the till of the Crozier and Nutter Store in the town of Cushing in Payne County. The robbery netted the thieves a mere $15. This was the last straw for Little Dick West and the O'Malleys. They rode in one direction, the Jennings brothers in another.

Little Dick West disappeared and would not be found until Apr. 7, 1898, when he was tracked down by Sheriff Frank Rinehart and other lawmen at the Harmon Arnett ranch southwest of Guthrie where he was working. At first Little Dick gave an alias, claiming he was merely a hired hand. Sheriff Rinehart told him to "cut the act" and arrested him under his real name. West broke away, pulled a six-gun and began firing at the lawmen who then shot him dead. The O'Malley brothers were captured earlier. This left only the inept Al and Frank Jennings at large. Marshal James F. "Bud" Ledbetter of Muskogee, Okla., one of the toughest lawmen in the West, then received a tip that the Jennings brothers would be hiding in a covered wagon moving through the Indian Nation. He tracked down the wagon and ordered Al and Frank Jennings to come out from some blankets under which they had been hiding.

The boys meekly surrendered and Ledbetter captured them without firing a shot. He threw them a rope and ordered them to tie each other up. Thus hog-tied, Ledbetter threw them over the backs of horses and led them ignominiously to town. This was the end of the Al Jennings gang, an outlaw band that never really got started and one that earned its members less than $200 each. Frank Jennings and the O'Malleys were given five-year terms in Leavenworth. Their leader and mastermind of the most absurd train robbery attempts on record, Al Jennings, was sent to the federal prison at Columbus, Ohio to serve a life term. Here Jennings met the writer William Sydney Porter, who wrote under the pseudonym of O. Henry. Jennings filled Porter's ears with mythical stories about himself which the writer later used in some of his best stories.

Al Jennings was freed within five years. His brother Frank had been set free earlier and returned to the family homestead in Oklahoma. Al, however, refused to settle down and headed for California. He settled in Hollywood where he became a fixture, an "adviser" on motion pictures about the West. He told wild tales of his outlaw years, almost all of his claims being complete fabrications. Sheriff Jim Herron of Oklahoma later stated: "Old Al Jennings was around California for years, stuffing dudes with nonsense and telling them wild yarns about himself in the early days." Jennings convinced many a film producer that he was an expert on western banditry and he earned a considerable living as a consultant. He even wrote two books about his imagined life and his story was made into a motion picture. Although none of his claims were true, Jennings came to believe he was not only one of the most celebrated bad men of the West but he also had been a peer and friend of Jesse James.

When the ancient imposter, J. Frank Dalton, appeared in 1948 to claim that he was Jesse James, it was Al Jennings who rushed to his side. Jennings took one look at the old man and shouted with glee: "It's him! It's Jesse!" It made no difference to Al Jennings that he had never met the notorious Jesse James. Jennings babbled on about his fabulous exploits until his death in 1961, believing himself to be one of the great outlaws of the Old West. See: **Dalton, J. Frank; Doolin, William M.; Houston, Temple L.; Porter, William Sydney; West, Richard.**

REF.: Bartholomew, *The Biographical Album of Western Outlaws;* Beebe and Clegg, *The American West;* Block, *Great Train Robberies of the West;* Botkin, *A Treasury of Western Folklore;* Breihan, *Great Lawmen of the West;* Bristow, *Tales of Old Fort Gibson;* Byrne, *Tale of the Elk;* Campbell, *Oklahoma; CBA;* Chrisman, *Fifty Years on the Owl Hoot Trail;* Clark, *Then Came the Railroads;* Crosthwait, *The Last Stitch;* Croy, *Trigger Marshal;* Davis and Maurice, *The Calif of Bagdad;* Douglas, *Territory Tales;* Drago, *Outlaws on Horseback;* Foreman, *A History of Oklahoma;* French, *A Gallery of Old Rogues;* ____, *Gray Shadows;* Gish, *American Bandits;* Glasscock, *Then Came Oil;* Graves, *Oklahoma Outlaws;* Hamilton, *Men of the Underworld;* Harlow, *The Most Picturesque Personality in Oklahoma, Al Jennings;* Henderson, *100 Years in Montague County, Texas;* Hendricks, *The Bad Man of the West;* Hollon, *The Southwest;* Holloway, *Texas Gun Lore;* Horan, *The Great American West;* ____, and Sann, *Pictorial History of the Wild West;* Howe, *Timberleg of the Diamond Tail;* Hunter and Rose, *The Album of Gunfighters;* Hutchinson, *The Life & Personal Writings of Eugene Manlove Rhodes;* James, *They Had Their Hour;* Jennings, *Beating Back;* ____, *Number 30664 by Number 31539;* ____, *Through the Shadows;* Johnson, *Wagon Yard;* Jones, *The Experiences of a U.S. Deputy Marshal of the Indian Territory;* Langford, *Alias O. Henry;* Laune, *Sand in Your Eye;* Long, *O. Henry: The Man and His Work;* McCarty, *The Enchanted West;* McKennon, *Iron Men;* McPherren, *Empire Builders;* McRill, *And Satan Came Also;* Millar, *Hail to Yesterday;* Miller, *Bill Tilghman;* Miller, *Pioneering North Texas;* Mootz, *The Blazing Frontier;* Nash, *Bloodletters and Badmen;* Newsom, *The Life and Practice of the Wild and Modern Indian;* Nix, *Oklahombres;* Osborn, *Let Freedom Ring;* Phares,

Bible in Pocket, Gun in Hand; Poe, *Buckboard Days;* Ray, *Famous American Scouts;* Raymond, *Captain Lee Hall of Texas;* Rosa, *The Gunfighter, Man or Myth?;* Shirley, *Sixgun and Silver Star;* ____, *Toughest of Them All;* Smith, *O. Henry;* Stansbery, *The Passing of the 3D Ranch;* Sutton, *Hands Up!;* Tilghman, *Marshal of the Last Frontier;* ____, *Outlaw Days;* Watson, *A Century of Gunman;* Wellman, *A Dynasty of Western Outlaws;* (FILM), *Al Jennings of Oklahoma,* 1951.

Jennings, Augustus Otis, d.1852, U.S., mur. A resident of St. Joseph, Mo., Augustus Jennings had dealings with Edward H. Willard, a notorious deadbeat. When Willard failed to repay a loan, Jennings rounded up three of Willard's unpaid creditors and proposed teaching their debtor a lessor. With Jennings leading, the four men abducted Jennings and took him to a remote spot outside of St. Joseph. Here they each took turns whipping Willard; Jennings administered the most severe beating. Willard died of the whipping and Jennings was charged with murder. Jennings explained at his trial that he and the others only intended to teach Willard a lesson and had no intention of killing him. Jennings was nevertheless convicted and later hanged.

REF.: *CBA; Confession of Augustus Otis Jennings.*

Jennings, George Augustine (AKA: **E.W. Watts, Frank Oswald Charteries, Bishop of Coventry, Bishop of the Falkland Islands, Bishop of Bradford, Rev. John Knox, Gen. A.C. Critchley, Sir Piers Mostyn**), b.1890, Brit., forg.-fraud. In one of his earliest frauds, George Augustine Jennings, along with Austin Henry Dockney, executed a swindle involving advertising orders for a foreign trade directory. The two netted about £20,000, but they were caught, tried and convicted of fraud and sentenced to a year in prison. Between 1920 and 1933, Jennings was involved in numerous swindles. One of his boldest moves was to stand as a National Liberal Candidate for Parliament with his comrade, Dockney, as one of his Election Agents. He won 6,444 votes, an impressive showing for a convicted criminal.

In 1930 and 1931, Jennings used the aliases "Bishop of Coventry," "Bishop of the Falkland Islands," "Bishop of Bradford," and "Rev. John Knox" to solicit £50 donations for "noble" causes such as the thwarting of the "white slave traffic." Jennings was arrested, convicted of fraud and related crimes on numerous occasions, and received sentences ranging from three to five years.

REF.: *CBA;* Nicholls, *Crime Within the Square Mile.*

Jennings, Glenn, prom. 1928, Case of, U.S., asslt.-mansl. In an instance of overly zealous enforcement of Prohibition, two Niagara Falls, N.Y., coast guardsmen, Glenn Jennings and Frank Beck, shot Jacob Hanson as he drove home in the early morning hours of May 28, 1928. Jennings and Beck signalled Hanson to stop his car but, as they were not in uniform, Hanson sped up. Jennings and Beck took this as evidence that he was smuggling liquor, opened fire on the car and hit Hanson in the eye.

Hanson was not carrying liquor in his car. The coast guardsmen were initially indicted by the Niagara County grand jury for second-degree assault, but when Hanson died four months later, Jennings and Beck were reindicted for second-degree manslaughter. They were tried and acquitted in federal court.

REF.: *CBA;* Kobler, *Ardent Spirits.*

Jennings, Henry, prom. 1718, Bahamas, pir. Henry Jennings, captain of the pirate ship *Bathsheba,* plundered the Bahamas, burning houses and raping women. Hoping the pirates would turn themselves in, the local government offered to pardon any pirates for crimes committed before Jan. 5, 1718, if the offenders would come forward before Sept. 5, 1718. Jennings accepted the offer, and he was forgiven for all the murders committed and was allowed to keep his accumulated loot.

REF.: *CBA;* Rankin, *The Golden Age of Piracy.*

Jennings, James Brandon (AKA: **Kid Carter**), b.1880, U.S., mur. On New Year's Day 1913, James Brandon Jennings, better known to his boxing fans as "Kid Carter," shot and killed Bill MacPherson after a fight began in Garrity and Prendergast's Saloon in Boston's South End. Although there were many witnesses to the crime, no one was able to give a reason for the slaying. Jennings was taken into custody immediately and tried for the murder beginning on Mar. 24, 1913. On Mar. 28, the jury returned a verdict of Guilty of murder in the second degree. On Apr. 18, 1913, just after his sentencing to life in prison, Jennings blurted out to a crowded courtroom that he had also murdered his girlfriend, Mildred Donovan, as well as "many others." No further legal action was taken against "Kid Carter," although he was found unfit to serve time in the state penitentiary and was committed instead to the Bridgewater State Hospital for the criminally insane.

REF.: *CBA;* Rodell, *Boston Murders.*

Jennings, Jasper, prom. 1905-06, U.S., (wrong. convict.) mur. On Sept. 7, 1905, Jasper Jennings and his sister Dora Jennings were accused of killing their father, Newton M. Jennings. In January 1906, Jasper was tried separately, convicted of first- degree murder and sentenced to be hanged. But in November of that year, the Oregon Supreme Court reversed the conviction due to improper testimony by a prosecution witness. At a new trial, the charges against Jasper Jennings were dismissed because Dora Jennings had told others that she committed the crime. REF.: *CBA.*

Jennings, John, prom. 1798, Brit., (wrong. convict.) rob. While working at the Bell Inn, a roadside tavern, John Jennings was accused of the armed robbery of a traveller. The victim's marked coins were found in Jennings' possession, leading to his speedy trial and execution. A year later, however, it was discovered that the real robber was Brunnell, the owner of the Bell Inn. Apparently, Brunnell had planted the marked coins on the sleeping Jennings when he learned from the victim that the coins had been marked. Only when Brunnell was sentenced to death for another crime did he confess that he had framed Jennings to protect himself.

REF.: *CBA;* Stevens, *From Clue to Dock.*

Jennings, Napoleon Augustus, 1856-1919, U.S., west. lawman. Born and raised in Philadelphia, Napoleon Jennings ventured to Texas as an 18-year-old and lived a life filled with adventure for the next ten years, before returning to the East. He worked initially as a farmhand, later becoming a Cavalry clerk and a surveyor's aid. In 1876, Jennings became a Texas Ranger under the direction of L.H. McNelly and John B. Armstrong. He was immediately thrust into the Sutton-Taylor feud, fought along the Mexican border, and was with Lee Hall when the rangers ended the disturbance.

On Oct. 1, 1876, Jennings was involved in the raid of an outlaw camp near Carrizo, Texas, which resulted in the death of two of the ten fugitives. One bandit named McAlister was arrested after being wounded by Jennings. Four days later, Jennings and two other Rangers were involved in a case of mistaken identities when a group of men firing upon Jennings' party turned out to be a reinforcement contingent of Rangers. Jennings retired from the Rangers after two years, moving further west to work as a cowboy, stage drive and gold prospector. In 1884, his thirst for adventure sated, Jennings returned East to write for newspapers and magazines until his death in 1919. REF.: *CBA.*

Jenny Newstead, 1932, a novel by Marie Belloc Lowndes. Much of this story is taken from the murderous operations of George Joseph Smith (Brit. 1912-15). See: **Smith, George Joseph.**

Jensen, Thomas Peter, prom. 1934, Case of, U.S., mur. In 1913, John Holmberg, Frank Adams, and Marie Schmidt were seen for the last time near Fairbanks, Alaska. The following year, the bones of Holmberg were found on a sandbar in the lower Kuyouyok River. Natives found the body of Schmidt further down the river, but it was swept away by high tide before they could retrieve it. Adam's body was never found. Police sought Thomas Johnson, known as "Blueberry Tom," for the murders, but could not find him. Twenty years later, in Brooklyn, N.Y., a Danish seaman, Thomas Peter Jensen, was arrested for the murders. In the courtroom of Magistrate Malbin, Jensen was identified as "Blueberry Tom" by Frank Ely Allen. However, it was a case of mistaken identity and Jensen was released July 10, 1934, by Martin C. Epstein, the U.S. commissioner in Brooklyn. REF.: *CBA.*

Jeppesen, Louise, 1910-34, U.S., (unsolv.) mur. Louise Jeppesen, twenty-four, attended a party at the William Taylor Hotel in San Francisco on the evening of Saturday, May 12, 1934. On Sunday, her body was found in a dimly lit pedestrian passageway in Golden Gate Park. She had been beaten, assaulted, and strangled with her own belt.

Two days after the murder, police arrested Millard Hickman, fifty-three, and charged him with killing Jeppesen. They learned that the party she attended Saturday was at Hickman's hotel apartment. Detective Captain Charles Dullea said Hickman and the woman scuffled at the hotel shortly before the slaying, and they had visited the park on their first meeting a week prior to the murder. Hickman told police that his bruised kneecap and a scratch on his left arm were probably the result of the evening's merriment.

Hickman admitted to being with Jeppesen, but said he put her out of his apartment at 3 a.m and never saw her again. He told police she was intoxicated, and that he asked her to leave when she mistook his attempts to make her more comfortable as sexual advances. The police maintained that Hickman and Jeppesen had argued in the elevator and that his car had been removed from the garage between the hours of 3 and 4 a.m. Following a sensational trial, Hickman was acquitted on July 24, 1934. REF.: *CBA.*

Jermyn, Edmund Beson, 1867-1934, U.S., rack. On Apr. 12, 1930, Edmund Beson Jermyn, a member of one of the wealthiest families in Scranton, Pa., and a two-term mayor of that city from 1914 to 1918 and from 1926 to 1930, was convicted of conspiracy to set up a slot machine monopoly that reportedly netted $35,000 a year. Convicted along with Jermyn was Harry J. Friend, whom Jermyn had appointed during his second term to the post of Civil Service Commissioner. The testimony of three others accused of conspiracy indicated that during his tenure as mayor, Jermyn had received monies in a scheme requiring slot machine owners to pay up to four dollars a day for protection of the machines.

Jermyn was sentenced to serve one year in the county jail but because of bad health was paroled after serving fifty-eight days and paying a fine of $10,000. Jermyn died on Nov. 14, 1934, in Scranton. REF.: *CBA.*

Jernegan, Prescott Ford, and **Charles E. Fisher,** prom. 1897, U.S., hoax. In 1897, Baptist minister Prescott Ford Jernegan of Middletown, Conn., promoted the idea that gold could be extracted from seawater. With his partner, Charles E. Fisher, he displayed an apparatus which apparently collected by means of a mercury-covered device. The machine was lowered into the ocean and brought up coated with gold. To sell the gold extractor, the Electrolytic Marine Salts Company was formed in Portland, Maine, capitalized at $10 million and selling stock at $1.00 per share. Construction soon began on a larger plant and the company sold hundreds of thousands of dollars in stock. When the plant was finished, the current was switched on to start the process. After a full day of operation, no gold appeared in the accumulators. The stockholders called for Jernegan and discovered that he had fled to France with $100,000 of company funds. It turned out that Fisher, a con man, had a primitive diving suit. At the demonstration, he had groped about underwater, salting the zinc-lined boxes with enough gold to make the process look viable. During the testing period, Fisher used the proceeds from the sale of stock to buy gold to plant in the accumulators. The theory that Jernegan was an innocent party in the hoax was supported by the fact that he voluntarily sent back $80,000 to repay the corporation's debts. But he could not be extradited from France. Jernegan later returned to the U.S. and lived the rest of his life quietly.

REF.: *CBA;* Moore, *Wolves, Widows and Orphans;* Nash, *Hustlers and Con Men.*

Jerome, William Travers, 1859-1934, U.S., lawyer. Born to wealth in New York, William Jerome studied law and proved to be a brilliant student. He entered politics as a reformer and vigorously attacked the corrupt Tammany Hall regime. When he was elected district attorney of New York County on a reform Fusion ticket in 1900, he vowed to clean up the venal New York Police Department. Once in office, he launched a campaign to clean up Manhattan's gaudy vice district, the Tenderloin. He personally led raids against the posh gambling houses owned by super gambler Richard Canfield, and he purged the police department of its most corrupt officers.

Jerome was elected for a second term, and he continued his illustrious career by prosecuting Harry K. Thaw, mad millionaire killer of architect Stanford White. Thaw had slain White over the affections of his showgirl wife, Evelyn Nesbit. Jerome was involved in many sensational trials, including the murder trial of showgirl Nan Patterson, and Albert T. Patrick, murderer of millionaire William Rice. As district attorney, Jerome also prosecuted Abraham Hummel, a one-time partner of William Howe of Howe and Hummel, the celebrated and crooked criminal lawyers. Jerome easily could have reached the governorship of New York, but his refusal to cooperate with the crooked

Crusading New York district attorney William Travers Jerome.

leaders of Tammany Hall prevented his ascent to a higher office. See: **Canfield, Richard Albert; Howe, William F.; Patterson, Nan; Tenderloin, The; Thaw, Harry Kendall.**

REF.: Amory, *Who Killed Society?;* Asbury, *The Gangs of New York;* Baldwin, *Stanford White;* Barrett, *Joseph Pulitzer and His World;* Cassity, *The Quality of Murder;* CBA; Churchill, *Park Row;* Collins, *Glamorous Sinners;* Gardiner, *Canfield;* Leslie, *The Remarkable Mr. Jerome;* Levy, *The Nan Patterson Case;* Lord, *The Good Years;* Mackenzie, *The Trial of Harry K. Thaw;* Myers, *The History of Tammany Hall;* O'Connor, *Courtroom Warrior: The Combative Career of William Travers Jerome;* Rovere, *Howe and Hummel;* Stoddard, *Master of Manhattan;* Train, *From the District Attorney's Office;* Werner, *Tammany Hall.*

Jerome of Prague, c.1365-1416, Bohemia, her. Preached religious views of Jan Hus and John Wycliffe, his professor at Oxford. Joined Hus at Prague in 1407, where they openly criticized papal practices and the church in general. In 1412, he and Hus denounced the extravagances of antipope John XXIII. He was condemned for heresy at the Council of Constance and was burned at the stake in 1416. REF.: *CBA.*

Jesse, Frederick William Maximilian, b.1897, Brit., mur. Frederick William Maximilian Jesse strangled and dismembered his aunt, Mabel Jennings Edmunds on July 21, 1923. A week later when Jesse confessed, police found Mrs. Edmunds' legs on the table on the top floor, and her trunk on the bed wrapped and tied with rope. According to Jesse, he and his aunt quarrelled and when he went to his room to get away from her, she followed and continued to hit him and throw a liquid on him. By Jesse's account the next thing he remembered was finding his hands around his dead aunt's neck. He told police that he had intended to dispose of the body but became afraid. Jesse was tried at the Old Bailey in September 1923. He was found Guilty, sentenced, and, on Nov. 1, hanged.

REF.: *CBA;* Shew, *A Second Companion to Murder.*

Jessup, Charles (AKA: C.E. Jessup, Jack Charles Jessup), 1916- , U.S., fraud. Border radio, with its immensely powerful transmitters broadcasting into the U.S. and Canada from just over the U.S.-Mexico border (safely outside the jurisdiction of the Federal Communications Commission) provided an irresistibly attractive opportunity for many a con man. In the 1940s and 1950s, advertisements for everything from live baby chicks to guaranteed cures for sexual impotence were aired. Charles Jessup,

one of America's foremost charlatans, used these uncensored radio broadcasts, along with direct mail solicitations and revival meetings, to amass his $10 million fortune.

Jessup professed to be an ordained minister and liberally used the title "Reverend," though he had no ministerial credentials. As a boy of fourteen, he had had an affiliation with a small Fundamentalist sect in Mississippi, but it had never ordained him. He was actually dropped from its membership when he was nineteen for questionable moral behavior.

Jessup was born in 1916 to an itinerant Mississippi River valley preacher known as Brother Jessup. Perhaps from this genetic connection and early training, Jessup developed a style of preaching (and soliciting) that provided him with willing victims throughout his career.

Whether over the airwaves, in person, or through the mail, the majority of Jessup's victims were women. In exchange for their donations and, in some cases, tithes, Jessup offered them inspirational messages, "prayer insurance" (for a substantial enough premium Jessup would single out the policy holder by name in his daily prayers), and individual "prayer records" (messages from Jessup to God on behalf of the concerned party). Jessup's other cons included a faith healing hospital and fasting-and-praying expeditions to the Holy Land.

Jessup's troubles began with investigations into complaints of fraud being perpetrated against American citizens by the users of Mexican broadcasting facilities. In 1961, the Federal Communications Commission, the Department of Justice, and the Post Office Department joined forces to investigate these complaints. By 1964 they had compiled sufficient evidence to indict and arrest Jessup. Freed on bond, Jessup claimed he was being persecuted and resumed his evangelistic activities with renewed vigor. A trial date was finally set for Jan. 22, 1968. When his former wife, Rose Jessup, and former assistant Murphy Maddux, Jr. agreed to give voluntary statements to the prosecution detailing the inner workings of many of Jessup's schemes, Jessup pleaded *nolo contendere.* Nine months later, Jessup was sentenced to one year in federal prison; he was also given five years' probation and a fine of $2,000. The sentencing judge summed up Jessup's career by saying, "Instead of praying for the multitude, he preyed on the multitude." Jessup served only nine months of his sentence.

REF.: *CBA;* Kahn, *Fraud.*

Jett, Curtis, b.c.1876, U.S., mur. During the early 1900s, Breathitt County, Ky., was the site of a feud involving several families, including the Cockrills, Hargises, and Callahans. Within two years, thirty-seven people were killed.

One of the casualties of the feud was James B. Marcum, a lawyer, politician, trustee of Jackson, Ky., and trustee of the Kentucky State College. Marcum had been warned that he was a target, and planned to move. However, when he discovered that his rivals wanted to buy his property, he changed his mind. On May 4, 1903, Marcum went to the Jackson Court House and, after finishing his business, stepped out of the building. Just outside the front door of the court house, a friend, a deputy sheriff, began talking with Marcum when he was shot from inside the court house. The deputy sheriff apparently knew the killer, Curtis Jett, who then approached Marcum and shot him again in the head. Numerous bystanders also saw Jett, who had a long criminal record, enter the court house before the shooting and leave afterward.

At first no one came forward and no suspects were arrested. However, the public was angered and requested help from the governor. Finally, a posse apprehended Jett at his mother's house in Madison County. He was tried at Jackson, but subsequently the case was sent to Harrison County where he was convicted and sentenced to life. Jett was also convicted of murdering James Cockrill. He was sentenced to hang, but the sentence was later commuted to another term of life in prison. He proved himself a model prisoner and was eventually granted a pardon to enroll in college where he studied ministry. After graduation he became an evangelist. REF.: *CBA.*

Jette, Sir Louis Amable, 1836-1920, Can., jur. Served on superior court at Quebec from 1878-98. He was Quebec's lieutenant governor from 1898-1908 and chief justice on the Court of King's Bench from 1909-11. REF.: *CBA*.

Jewell, Stephen, prom. 1968, Brit., mur. For murdering crime figure Tony Maffia, British coal merchant Stephen Jewell was sentenced to life in prison at the Old Bailey on Nov. 19, 1968. A majority of jurors found him Guilty shortly after majority verdicts became admissable in British courts.

REF.: *CBA*; Heppenstall, *The Sex War and Others*.

Jewett, Ellen (or **Helen, Dorcas Doyen**), See: **Robinson, Richard P.**

Jimmy Curly Gang, prom. 1910s, U.S., org. crime. Of all the gangs in New York, from 1910 to the beginning of WWI, one of the most feared was the Jimmy Curly Gang, which operated along 59th Street. This was a gang of about twenty or more gunmen who specialized in extortion, kidnapping, and murder-for-hire. It was led by vicious hoodlum Jimmy "Gold Mine" Carrigio. The Gas House Gang, under the leadership of Tommy Lynch, battled the Jimmy Curly Gang in 1914, shooting up 59th Street for hours. Following the battle, a half-dozen gangsters were sent to the hospital with wounds and Lynch was sent to the morgue, reportedly killed by Carrigio. Following the war, Jimmy Carrigio was imprisoned and his gang disbanded.

REF.: *CBA*; Nash, *Bloodletters and Badmen*.

Jim the Penman (AKA: **Saward, James Townsend**), 1799, and **Anderson, James**, b.1821, Brit., forg. James Townsend Saward was called to the Bar of the Inner Temple in 1840. The elegant and gracious barrister maintained a thriving practice in London for the next seventeen years. But Saward also trafficked in stolen goods and was a criminal forger of the highest rank. Years later, Saward was known as Jim the Penman, for his remarkable skills. Not until 1857 did anyone connect him to the spate of forgeries in London over the past twenty years.

Deciding that it was much too risky to hand a forged check to a bank cashier, Saward hit upon the idea of securing blank and cancelled checks through burglars and pickpockets. He studied and duplicated the signatures, then sent his confederates to the bank to cash the checks. Since they were drawn in relatively small amounts, the tellers were never unduly suspicious. By the time the forgery was detected, the identity of the Penman was all but impossible to trace.

In 1856, his cunning got the best of him. Saward recruited three accomplices to help him swindle a branch of Barclay's Bank in London. Ex-convict William Salt Hardwicke, an old friend, had just returned to the city from an Australian penal colony. The other two were Henry Atwell and James Anderson. Saward instructed Hardwicke to deposit £250 in Barclay's Bank under the name of Whitney. The money was to be transferred to a bank in Yarmouth to establish Saward's financial credibility before he arrived from London. When Hardwicke tried to claim the money in Yarmouth on Aug. 18, he used the name "Ralph," which the bank naturally refused to recognize. The Penman told Hardwicke to reassure the bank but by then the authorities were on the gang's trail. Hardwicke and Atwell were both arrested. The police found a letter from Saward in Hardwicke's possession, and Atwell proved to be a cooperative witness. After hearing of this setback, the Penman went into hiding, but was eventually arrested by the City Police on Oxford Street.

Saward and Anderson were tried at the Old Bailey on Mar. 5, 1857. They pleaded not guilty, but the testimony of Atwell and Hardwicke convicted them. On Mar. 6, Saward and Anderson were sentenced to transportation for life. See: **Atwell, Henry**. REF.: *CBA*.

Jirocho Shimizu no (**Jirocho of Shimizu**), 1820-93, Japan, org. crime. Jirocho Shimizu no was a real-life Robin Hood of Japan. His story is familiar to generations of Japanese schoolchildren. Each year thousands of people visit his grave, paying homage to the one they remember as a champion of the rights of the people, albeit through less than honest ways.

Jirocho was the third son of a tailor, born in what is now modern-day Yokohama. At an early age, Jirocho's father put him up for adoption, trying to evade a local superstition that held that babies born on New Year's day grew up to be geniuses or criminals. The elder Shimizu apparently feared the worst. When his adoptive father died, Jirocho inherited the family's rice planting business, but soon fell in with a group of gamblers who plied their trade up and down the Tokaido Highway. He decided to separate from his wife and family. He lived by his wits for three years as a vagabond, a fighter, and, most importantly, a mediator.

Returning to his home village, Jirocho decided to organize the local gamblers into a "bakuto" (gambling) gang. Contemporary estimates placed the total membership of the Jirocho gang at 600. His influence stretched from Fuji River to Tokyo and on toward Kyoto. Jirocho's armed band of ne'er-do-wells often fought pitched battles with the highway robbers and gamblers who preyed upon the peasants. Jirocho aligned himself with the imperial forces who sought to expel the Tokugawa shogunate from Japan. In return his past crimes were forgiven, once his objective was accomplished. Jirocho became a highly-admired elder in his village of Shimizu. He began an English school, paved the way for sorely-needed agrarian reforms in the prefecture, and even started a penitentiary. Jirocho died in 1893. At the foot of Mount Fuji, a Shinto shrine was erected by the grateful farmers whose lands he had once reclaimed. See: **Inagawa Kakuji; Kimura Tokutaro; Kishi Nobusuke; Kodama Yoshio; Machii Hisayuki; Naksone Yasuhiro; Ogawa Kaoru; Osano Kenji; Sasakawa Ryoichi; Taoka Kazuo; Toyama Mitsuru; Yakuza.**

REF.: *CBA*; Kaplan and Dubro, *Yakuza*.

Joan (AKA: **Joanna**), prom. 872-82, Italy, hoax. Posing as a male monk, Joan allegedly ascended to the papacy under the name of John VIII. Breaking another of the church's rigid canons, she also allegedly gave birth to a baby girl while riding in a papal procession.

Although Catholic laymen question her existence, Joan appears in *Lives of the Popes*, by the fifteenth-century historian Platima. In 1886, her story was retold in Greek by Emmanuel Royidis and in 1954 translated into English by Lawrence Durrell. Fact or fiction, the story of Pope Joan has survived for a thousand years. REF.: *CBA*.

Joanna I, c.1326-82, Naples, queen, mur.-assass. A scheming murderess, Queen Joanna (1343-82) arranged for the death of her husband, Prince Andrew of Hungary. She was driven from the throne by Andrew's brother, Louis I of Hungary, but was restored in 1352. Joanna was deposed by Pope Urban VI. She was captured by Charles III of Hungary while attempting to regain her throne and was assassinated. REF.: *CBA*.

Joanna II, 1371-1435, Naples, mur. As ruthless as her predecessor's, Joanna II's reign (1414-35) was marked by ceaseless wars and several murders which she planned and which were carried out by her palace assassins. Joanna was married three times. She exiled her second husband and had her third husband murdered. Joanna was controlled by the wealthy Sforza family, the financial and military power behind her throne, which kept Italy in chaos for a generation. REF.: *CBA*.

Joan of Arc, 1412-31, Fr., her. Compelled by the voices of St. Michael, Ste. Catherine, and Ste. Margaret, Joan of Arc, the "Maid of Orleans," had a mission to free France from the English. While Henry VI of England sat on the French throne—in 1422 the infant king, with the aid and support of France's Philip of Burgundy, was proclaimed King of France—Joan sought out the dauphin, Charles VII, the rightful heir.

Convinced of her mission, Charles VII rewarded her with the command of a five-thousand-man army. On Apr. 29, 1429, Joan invaded Orleans and on May 8 recaptured the city from the English. In September, she was wounded while trying to capture Paris, and in December she and her family were ennobled with the surname of du Lis. Her nobility was short lived, however; on May 23, 1430, she was captured during the siege of Compiegne.

Pierre Cauchon, the bishop of Beauvais and friend of the English, claimed jurisdiction for the trial. Rather than trying Joan in a civil trial for crimes of war, Cauchon wanted her tried in a church tribunal for heresy because of the voices she claimed to have heard.

The trial revolved around her claims that she had acted on these divine voices, that she wore men's clothing, and that she refused to accept the authority of the Church. During sixteen inquisition sessions, Joan was asked questions such as, "Did the Saints speak in English or French?" and "Does God hate the English?", and on Mar. 27, 1431, she was brought to formal trial before thirty-seven clerical judges at Rouen Cathedral.

Before the court, Joan admitted that she had disobeyed the "voices" in trying to escape from prison and in urging the attack on Paris. Had she disobeyed revelations from God? the court wondered. Indeed, had she obeyed the Devil? Finding that "She sets herself up as an authority, a doctor, a master," the tribunal charged her with heresy.

On Apr. 18, 1431, the inquisitors pleaded with Joan to recant her testimony, but she refused. With her execution imminent, she made a last-minute appeal to the Pope, but then disavowed her earlier testimony with a signed confession, admitting that "I have previously sinned, in falsely pretending to have had revelations from God and his angels." She was sentenced to life imprisonment.

Forced again before a tribunal, Joan retracted her confession, insisting that her revelations were divine. On May 30 she was excommunicated and ordered executed by the bailiff of Rouen. Placed high on a pyre, she was crowned with a miter that read "Relapsed, heretic, apostate, idolater," and slowly burned before a crowd.

On June 16,1456, her conviction was annulled, and over four hundred years later, "to advertise the intimate union between patriotism and the Catholic faith," interest in Joan of Arc was revived. Canonized and beatified in the early twentieth century, she is now celebrated in an annual festival in France on May 30th.

REF.: *CBA*; Furneaux, *True Mysteries*; (FILM), *Joan of Arc*, 1948; *Joan at the Stake*, 1954; *The Story of Mankind*, 1957; *The Legend of Billie Jean*.

Joan of Navarre (Joanna), 1370-1437, Brit., witchcraft. Married John V, the Duke of Brittany, in 1386, with whom she had eight children. After her husband's death in 1399, she married England's King Henry IV, and maintained a friendship with her stepson when he succeeded his father. During a period of anti-French sentiment in Britain from 1419-22, she was imprisoned for witchcraft. REF.: *CBA*.

Joasmis, prom. 19th Cent., Int'l., pir. The Joasmis, a tribe that lived along the Persian Gulf, looted and pillaged as far to the east as Bombay. In about 1804, the Joasmis reportedly took some British officers and civilians prisoner, transporting them back to their capital, Ras-al-Khaima. In 1809, the city was razed by an attack by the military of India. In 1816, the Joasmis started another period of looting along the Red Sea, but they were finally overcome in 1819 by a navy fleet that included some ships of the East India Company and some from the sultan of Muscat.

REF.: *CBA*; Mitchell, *Pirates*.

Jobin, Marie, prom. 1920, Fr., mur. In 1920, Gaston and Marie Jobin were married and living in Paris. Marie consorted with other men and Gaston led a life of petty thievery.

On Mar. 23, 1920, Gaston Jobin was seen for the last time. Marie claimed that he had fled to Spain to avoid military conscription. On Apr. 8, 1920, however, a man's torso, minus head and limbs, was dragged from the Seine. Then, eighteen months later, a postal official examining a stack of undeliverable mail discovered an underlined paragraph about the body's discovery in a letter addressed to Paul Jobin, Gaston's brother. The letter had been sent by their sister in Switzerland, who was convinced that their brother was murdered.

The police again visited Marie Jobin, who was living in a Toul hotel with a man named Burger. Although Marie repeated her original story, she asked her lawyer a curious question: Legally,

when would she be free to marry again? This from a woman who claimed her husband was alive and well. Mr. Warrain, the interrogator, kept at them until the two confessed to having murdered Gaston Jobin on Mar. 23, 1920. Burger was sentenced to death, and Marie Jobin to hard labor for life. She died a few years later.

REF.: *CBA*; Jacobs, *Pageant of Murder*.

Jocker, Harry, and **Frazier, Jessie**, prom. 1910, U.S., wh. slav. Hilda ran into Harry Jocker one day and fell for the oldest line in the book. "I can get you a good job in a chorus line," Harry said. "I wouldn't take a job cleaning houses if I could get a better position and better pay," added his friend Jessie Frazier.

Jocker sold Hilda to Madam Nellie, a brothel operator on Chicago's West Side. The madam tried to keep her in the background because she looked so young, but detectives Bowler and Cullett, on a tip, discovered her and brought her to the police station, where she implicated Jocker and Frazier.

On Dec. 29, 1910, Judge Isadore Himes at the Des Plaines Street court, sentenced Jocker to six months in prison for pandering and fined him $500. Found to be contributing to child delinquency, Frazier was fined $100.

REF.: *CBA*; Roe, *Great War*.

Jodl, Alfred, d.1946, Ger., war crimes. Colonel General Alfred Jodl was Adolf Hitler's chief of the General Staff during the Nazi reign in WWII. He personally prepared a plan for the bombing and invasion of Prague on Oct. 1, 1938, leading to the expansion of the war. Jodl unabashedly admired Hitler, often comparing him to Napoleon. But, when the end came, Jodl was one of the first officers to be tried by the International Military Tribunal at Nuremberg. On Oct. 1, 1946, Jodl and twelve other Nazi's were sentenced to die by hanging within fifteen days. His wife pleaded with General Eisenhower to intercede on his behalf, but to no avail. Jodl spent his last days hiding his head under the blankets while cowering in his prison cell. On Oct. 16, 1946, Jodl was hanged with nine other war criminals, for the atroci-

Alfred Jodl, German war criminal.

ties committed during the Nazi regime.

Jodl was the eighth man to hang and he entered the execution chamber nervously, constantly wetting his lips. He mounted the scaffold slowly and when he stood upon the trap door, the rope was placed about his neck and he was asked if he had any last words. He nodded and said: "My greetings to you, my Germany." He had nothing else to say. A minute later he shot through the trap; six minutes later he was pronounced dead.

REF.: *CBA*; Davidson, *The Making of Adolf Hitler*; Fest, *Hitler*; Heiden, *Der Fuehrer*; Shirer, *The Rise and Fall of the Third Reich*; Snyder and Morris, *A Treasury of Great Reporting*.

Joe Bananas, See: **Bonanno, Joseph**.

Joe the Greaser Gang, prom. 1910s, U.S., org. crime. Before WWI, many labor slugging gangs flourished in New York's East Side. These gangs were hired by management to disrupt pickets and strikes and by labor to create work stoppage and sabotage assembly lines. None of the gangs worked exclusively for either group and took jobs as they came. These included gangs led by Benjamin "Dopey Benny" Fein, Jack Sirocco, and Joseph "Joe the Greaser" Rosenzweig. Numbering at least one hundred labor sluggers, the Joe the Greaser Gang was aptly named.

This gang used brass knuckles and lead pipes to wage profitable wars, and it was considered the worst labor mob in the city. Its members enjoyed breaking arms and legs and did not hesitate to murder. Rosenzweig, like Fein, Sirocco, and others, enjoyed immunity from police interference through their political connections, chiefly Tammany Hall politicians for whom they worked and to whom they paid considerable percentages of their profits. These labor gangs seldom battled each other, but in early 1913, William Lustig and one-time Rosenzweig slugger Philip "Pinchy" Paul formed labor gangs of their own and began competing with Fein and Rosenzweig. This brought about an open pitched battle between Paul's gang and Joe the Greaser's gang. They met at Grand and Forsyth streets in late 1913 and fought each other with pistols and knives for more than an hour. More than 200 gangsters participated in this battle, but miraculously, no one was killed, although dozens were seriously injured and hospitalized.

Rosenzweig learned that Al Jewbach, one of Pinchy Paul's lieutenants, had urged Paul to openly attack Rosenzweig and kill him. Joe the Greaser sent his top killer, Benjamin "Nigger Benny" Snyder (or Schneider), to kill Jewbach but Snyder only succeeded in cutting up Jewbach in a knife fight. Jewbach then stated that he would go to the police and inform on the top labor sluggers. Rosenzweig and five other men found Jewbach at home recuperating. They pulled him out of bed and Joe the Greaser, using a long, sharp blade, sliced away part of Jewbach's tongue and threw this gory trophy out a window, shouting at the screaming Jewbach: "Let that learn you not to talk so much!"

Next, Rosenzweig, with Snyder, Hyman "Little Hymie" Bernstein, Jacob "Tough Jake" Heiseman, and others tracked down Pinchy Paul and shot him to death. Snyder was seen at the murder site and was arrested. He quickly confessed, but put the blame for the Paul killing on Rosenzweig, saying that Joe the Greaser had come to him in May 1914 and said: "We've got to do away with this guy because he's always in my way. He goes around and knocks me. He's knocking me with the Furrier's Union, and he's trying to get the furriers away from me." Snyder told his boss at the time: "I always took your orders. You're supposed to be smarter than I am. Anything you say, I will do."

When Rosenzweig was arrested for the Paul murder, he began to confess, stating that he did not kill Pinchy Paul, but others did the deed. He also claimed that he was present in a recent gun battle between his gang and that of Jack Sirocco, in one in which an innocent man, Frederick Straus, had been "accidentally" shot to death near Segal's Cafe on Second Avenue. Rosenzweig rattled off a roster of his own best killers, saying that the following were really responsible for the deaths of Paul and Straus: Isidore "Jew Murphy" Cohen, Waxey Gordon (real name Irving Wexler), Abraham "Little Abie" Beckerman, Julius "Little Yutch" Eisenberg, David "Battleship Dave" Sanders, Harry "Shorty" Gordon, Morris "The Mock" Kaplan, August "Augie the Wop" DelGrasio, and Joseph "Brownie" Brown. These gangsters were rounded up but only Cohen and Gordon were tried and, after a protracted court battle, both were acquitted for lack of evidence.

Rosenzweig and Snyder were tried for the Paul killing and both were convicted. Snyder, who actually pulled the trigger, was given a twenty-year sentence. Joe the Greaser Rosenzweig received a ten-year sentence and was shipped off to Sing Sing in December 1915. He was released some years later to find his gang disbanded. He went to Waxey Gordon, who was by the 1920s one of the top bootleggers in Manhattan. Gordon loaned him enough money to leave town, telling his former boss that he had not forgotten the fact that Rosenzweig had turned him in for the Straus shooting.

"You used to be my boss," the magnanimous Gordon supposedly said to Joe the Greaser, "so I won't kill you now. I'm gonna give you enough scratch to take a powder. But if me or any of my boys ever see you in New York again, you're gonna be pushing up lilacs in a cemetery and you'll go into a box with pennies on your eyelids!" Rosenzweig quickly left town and was not heard of again. See: **Fein, Benjamin; Gordon, Waxey; Sirocco, Jack.**

REF.: Allsop, *The Bootleggers*; Asbury, *The Gangs of New York*; *CBA*; Fried, *The Rise and Fall of the Jewish Gangster in America*; Nash, *Bloodletters and Badmen*; Thompson and Raymond, *Gang Rule in New York*.

Jogues, Isaac, 1607-46, U.S., (unsolv.) mur. French Jesuit missionary who explored with Indians strait in Great Lakes he named Sault de Ste. Marie. In 1642, he was captured and tortured by the Iroquois, who mutilated his hands. He was saved from further attacks by the Dutch, who brought him to New Amsterdam, now New York City. He was later murdered at an area now known as Aurlesville, N.Y. He was sainted in 1930. REF.: *CBA*.

John (AKA: **John the Fearless, Jean sans Peur**), 1371-1419, Brit., regent, assass. Became regent of France in 1392, after Charles VI went insane. Although absolved of the crime, his sponsorship of the murder of Louis, Duc d' Orléans in 1407 provoked the civil war from 1411-12. His attempts to reconcile with the future Charles VII resulted in his being murdered. REF.: *CBA*.

John II (AKA: **John of Avesnes**), c.1247-1304, Neth., consp. Son of John of Avesnes, and served as count of Holland and Zeeland from 1299-1304, and of Hainaut from 1257-1304. He became count after the death of the son of Count Floris of Holland, who was assassinated after John II had convinced him to switch his allegiance from England to France. REF.: *CBA*.

John II, 1397-1479, Spain, mur. Son of Ferdinand I and king of Aragon. In 1420, he married Blanche, heiress to Navarre, and married Juana Henriquez in 1447. He arranged the 1461 death of Charles of Viana, his son and heir, and survived revolt in Catalonia from 1462-72. REF.: *CBA*.

John III (Duke of Finland), 1537-92, Swed., consp. Dethroned brother King Eric XIV in 1569 with help of brother Charles, later known as Charles IX. He converted to Roman Catholicism from Protestantism in 1578, but failed to convert the entire country. REF.: *CBA*.

John XIV (Pietro Canepanova), d.c.984, Italy, assass. Served as Bishop of Pavia prior to being elected pope at the suggestion of Otto II. He was jailed and slain by a faction which backed antipope Boniface VII. REF.: *CBA*.

John bar Qursos (AKA: **John of Tella**), 483-538, Syria, her. Bishop of Tella who opposed council denouncing monophysitism as heretical. He was persecuted and murdered by members of the orthodoxy who took violent opposition to his religious views. REF.: *CBA*.

John Frederick (Johann Friedrich, AKA: the Magnanimous), 1503-54, Ger., consp.-impris. Son of John the Constant, elector of Saxony, and served as elector of Saxony from 1532-47. He was named one of the heads of the League of Schmalkalden and from 1546-47 battled his cousin Maurice, from the Albertine line. He was imprisoned at Mühlberg by Charles V following his defeat. He was released by Maurice in 1552, but never regained political office. REF.: *CBA*.

John Hyrcanus II, d.30 B.C, Judaea, king, assass. Son of Alexander Jannaeus and Salome Alexandra and became high priest in 72 B.C. He became ruler after Salome, but was ousted by his brother Aristobulus after only three months. He regained the priesthood through an appeal to Pompey, the Roman general, but was rendered impotent by Mark Anthony in 42 B.C. Two years later, his ears were cut off as punishment for attacking the Parthians. He was in exile in Babylon from 40-36 B.C., and was put to death by Herod. REF.: *CBA*.

John of Lancaster (Duke of Bedford), 1389-1435, Brit., mur. Third son of England's King Henry IV, he permitted the execution of Joan of Arc at the stake in 1431. REF.: *CBA*.

John of Leiden (Jan Beuckelszoon or Bockelson or Johann Buckhold), 1509-36, Neth., her. Led Anabaptists in Münster, where he proclaimed himself king of Zion in 1534. After a brief reign marked by ostentation and brutality, he was jailed by the bishop of Münster and executed. REF.: *CBA*.

John of Nepomuk (Johannes Wölfin, AKA: Pomuk), b.c.1345, Bohemia, assass. Patron saint of Czechoslavakians. He served as the archbishop's vicar general in 1390, and defended him against King Wenceslaus IV. He was tortured and drowned in the Vltava River upon orders from Wenceslaus. He became a saint in 1729, by the order of Pope Benedict XIII. REF.: *CBA*.

John of Wesel (AKA: **Johannes Ruchrath** or **Ruchrad**), d.c.1481, Ger., her. Religious reformer who wrote *Disputatio adversus Indulgentias,* not published until 1757. Despite recanting his religious beliefs, he was condemned in 1479 to live the rest of his life in a monastery. REF.: *CBA.*

John Paul II, 1920-   , Italy, pope, attempt. assass. On May 13, 1981, Mehmet Ali Agca, a 23-year-old Turkish terrorist, shot Pope John Paul II twice while the Pope was being driven into St. Peter's Square in Vatican City. Dropping his weapon, Agca was immediately arrested by Italian police.

The premeditated act was thought to be rooted in a centuries-old religious struggle between Turkey's Catholic minority and Muslim majority. The pontiff's 1979 trip to Turkey was seen as an attempt to unite the Roman Catholic Church and the Eastern Orthodox Church and so threaten Islamic dominance. During this visit, moerover, Agca had written to a Turkish newspaper, threatening to kill the pope.

As Agca's movements during the previous year were uncovered, however, speculation arose about a conspiracy. Trips to Italy, Switzerland, and West Germany, and a terrorist school near Tripoli, Libya, were discovered, as well as possible links between Italian terrorist Maurizo Folini, Libya, and the KGB.

On July 22, 1981, Agca was sentenced to life in prison , and on Sept. 24, 1981, an Italian court determined that a conspiracy had been involved. Agca was not a religious zealot, but a well-trained terrorist for an extreme right-wing Turkish organization. In May of 1982, he partially confessed to Italian authorities and in December revealed his escape plans, which implicated the KGB and the Bulgarian Secret Service.

On June 9, 1984, prosecutor Antonio Albano delivered a report that accused the Bulgarian Secret Service of complicity in a conspiracy to assassinate the pope. Their alleged motive was to quell the Polish labor movement. Conspiracy indictments were handed down on Oct. 25, 1984, against three Bulgarians and four Turks, but the defendants were acquitted on Mar. 25, 1984.

The pope was attacked a second time on the eve of the anniversary of the first attack. On May 12, 1982, Father Juan Fernandez Krohn, a dissident conservative priest, lunged at him with a knife in Fatima, Port. On May 3, 1983, Krohn was sentenced to six and one-half years in prison for attempted murder and deportation upon completion of his sentence.
REF.: *CBA;* Dobson and Payne, *Counterattack—The West's Battle Against the Terrorists.*

Johnson, Andrew, 1808-75, Case of, U.S., impeach. Andrew Johnson became U.S. president on Apr. 15, 1865, following the assassination of Abraham Lincoln. The well-meaning but poorly educated Johnson was forced to preside over the reconstruction of the nation in the wake of the Civil War. He faced the problem of how to govern the still-rebellious South, an issue that pitted hardline Republicans against moderates. Born in Tennessee, where he once owned slaves, Johnson was selected by Lincoln to run on the Republican ticket in 1864. Although Johnson was a Democrat, Lincoln hoped to win the favor of the border states in the coming election. The unforseen consequences of this strategy bitterly divided the nation.

President Andrew Johnson in 1868 at the time of his impeachment trial.

In May 1865, Johnson antagonized radical Republicans by granting amnesty to a number of former secessionists. At the same time, a Republican countermove to disenfranchise white Southern voters who traditionally voted Democratic was thwarted, thus checking their ambition to build a political coalition of "carpetbaggers" and black voters. Johnson did little to assuage Republican anxieties that the Democrats would regain power in the Congress.

He tried and failed to build a third party sympathetic to his own interests in 1866. His Republican critics in the House and Senate called him a traitor and a drunkard, and tried to undermine his constitutional powers by passing an act in March 1867 which placed the command of the army's major generals under Ulysses Grant. The Tenure of Office Act, passed that same month, prevented Johnson from removing any officeholder, including those in his own cabinet, without Senate approval. After accusing two Republican congressmen of conspiring to murder Lincoln, Johnson removed Edwin Stanton, secretary of war and a leading hardliner against the South. In the ensuing years, Stanton would be rumored to be a possible suspect in Lincoln's killing, a charge never proven.

The climax of three years of political sniping between the chief executive and his opponents occurred on Feb. 24, 1868, when Congress voted to impeach Johnson by a 126-47 vote, the first such action in U.S. history. The indictment against him drew attention to his handling of the Stanton affair and for bringing "disgrace, ridicule, contempt and reproach (to) the Congress of the United States," meaning that he had declared its legislation invalid. On Mar. 23, Johnson denied the allegations, saying he

Opening of President Johnson's impeachment trial.

had expressed honest dissent. To the charge that he had acted illegally in the handling of the Stanton dismissal, the president pointed out that his executive powers gave him that right. A "jury" of fifty-four senators, however, had to confirm the congressional decision, and the prosecution opened its case on Mar. 30, led by the fiery Benjamin Butler of Massachusetts. The case against Johnson, as presented to Congress, was repeated, though it was clear to most impartial sources that the charges were politically motivated and lacked substance. The "jury's" vote on whether to remove him from office took place on May 26, 1868, and resulted in a 35-19 margin in favor of removal, one vote short of a two-thirds majority required to trigger the action. It was clear that a few Republican congressmen had voted their conscience. Six months later, Johnson lost his renomination bid to the Republican candidate, General Grant. The results of the election were surprisingly close, and Johnson might have won had former Confederate soldiers been permitted to vote. See: **Lincoln, Abraham.**

REF.: Bacon, *Life of Andrew Johnson;* Butterfield, *The American Past; CBA;* Cowan, *Andrew Johnson;* Hall, *Andrew Johnson;* Hunt, *Impeachment Trial of Andrew Johnson;* Jones, *Andrew Johnson;* Kennedy, *Profiles in Courage;* Lomask, *Andrew Johnson: President on Trial;* McKitrick, *Andrew Johnson and Reconstruction;* Ross, *History of the Impeachment of Andrew Johnson;* Savage, *Life of Andrew Johnson;* Seward, *Andrew Johnson;* Stryker, *Andrew Johnson: A Study in Courage;* Thomas, *The First President Johnson;* Winston, *Andrew Johnson, Plebian and Patriot;*

(FILM), *Tennessee Johnson*, 1942.

Johnson, Carl (AKA: **Ed Shapiro**), 1928-82, U.S., embez. Carl Johnson, a confessed embezzler and man of many identities was killed along with four FBI agents in a plane crash near Cincinnati on Dec. 16, 1982, in the midst of unraveling the complications he had caused during the last seven years.

In 1975, Johnson embezzled $650,000 from the National Bank of Albany Park on Chicago's Northwest Side. Abandoning his wife and parents, Johnson emerged as Ed Shapiro in both Cincinnati and San Diego. He spent money at a rate of $3,000 a month, but without an identity he couldn't make investments, and became increasingly unhappy. Finally, in November 1982, he revealed his identity to the Rev. Sharron Stroud, who helped him surrender to authorities in Chicago.

He was leading the agents to $50,000 stashed in Cincinnati when the plane crashed, killing all six people aboard. Although that money was never recovered, another $30,000 was found in a San Diego bank one month later. REF.: *CBA*.

Johnson, Charles S., 1854-1906, U.S., jur. Held office in Nebraska House of Representatives from 1883-85, as prosecuting attorney for Nuckolls County, Neb., from 1885-89, and as U.S. district attorney from 1889-94. He was appointed to the court of the Alaska Territory by President William McKinley in 1897. REF.: *CBA*.

Johnson, Christopher, and **Stockdale, John**, prom. 1753, Brit., mur. After Christopher Johnson and John Stockdale were executed in July 1753, a debate arose about whether the corpses should be dissected or hung in chains. With the bodies already in Surgeons Hall, instructions were issued that they should instead be hung in chains. Once they were in chains, however, the Earl of Leicester received an anonymous letter containing a threat to blow his brains out and set fire to his house if he did not unchain John Stockdale. The furor eventually subsided. Johnson and Stockdale remained in chains.

REF.: *CBA;* Turner, *The Inhumanists*.

Johnson, Claude F., b.1889, U.S., law enfor. off. On Sept. 7, 1910, after only three months on the Indianapolis police force, 21-year-old recruit Claude Johnson was charged with "conduct unbecoming an officer." Exonerated on that charge, he rose during the next ten years to the rank of captain. In January 1922, however, he was demoted to detective sergeant, in 1924 again promoted to lieutenant, and on Jan 4, 1926, he was appointed chief of police.

He was chief for only eight months. On Sept. 1, 1927, after an extended leave of absence, Johnson was demoted to captain of detectives. In December 1927, he was further demoted to dectective sergeant. And on Aug. 26, 1931, completing his "bell curve," he was demoted to his original position, patrolman, second grade. REF.: *CBA*.

Johnson, Courtland C., d.1854, U.S., mur. Courtland C. Johnson was a hard-working resident of Middleton, Pa., who was married to a voluptuous, flirtatious woman. Johnson suspected that his wife was carrying on an affair with a friend, Nathaniel Colyer. He pretended to go on a business trip but returned some hours later to find his wife and Colyer in the garden behind his house. Both Mrs. Johnson and Colyer were at that moment caught *in flagrante delicto*. Brandishing a pair of pistols, Johnson chased the naked, screaming couple about the garden and through the house, firing wildly. He finally managed to shoot them both. He was tried for the double murder and convicted, despite his defense of "the unwritten rule." Johnson was hanged at Harrisburg, Pa., on Aug. 25, 1854.

REF.: *A Brief Account of the Life, Christian Experience and Execution of Courtland C. Johnson; CBA*.

Johnson, Edward Earl, 1961-87, U.S., mur. On June 2, 1979, Marshal J.T. Trest of Walnut Grove, Miss., was murdered while investigating a burglary report. Edward Johnson, despite his protestations of innocence, was convicted of the murder. He was denied a stay of execution and executed in Mississippi's gas chamber on May 20, 1987. REF.: *CBA*.

Johnson, Edwin (AKA: **Robert Anderson**), prom. 1880, Can., count. Edward Johnson was one of the most prominent counterfeiters of the late nineteenth century, whose avariciousness led to his downfall. The brilliance of his reproductions actually helped to apprehend him, as only one more man was considered capable of his engraving.

In the spring of 1880, Canada was flooded with over $1 million in counterfeit bills. They may have gone undetected, had there not been a similar incident in the United States in 1875. The signatures were so perfect that the real signer could not detect the forgery. Only two men were judged capable of this perfection, John Hill and Ed Johnson. When suspicions of Hill were eliminated, the focus shifted to Johnson.

A detective named John Murray was assigned to the case. He found a trail that criss-crossed northeastern U.S. during the American counterfeiting episode, but then abruptly ended. Murray guessed that the counterfeiters had returned to Canada and went to Toronto. Amazingly, within minutes of his arrival, he spotted Ed's son Johnnie Johnson in a saloon. He tailed the suspect, and after a five day vigil, Edwin Johnson walked across his path.

Johnson was just running errands. But every time he paid for something, he used a counterfeit bill, which was quickly retrieved by Murray. Finally, Johnson was confronted and charged with counterfeiting. Initially, Johnson denied the charge but later tried to bribe Murray to forget the whole thing. Wearying of the interrogation, Johnson finally capitulated. The plates, wrapped in oilcloth and sealed in beeswax, were hidden in a forest. He implicated his children, saying that they had been trained since childhood.

Johnson's trial began on Oct. 28, 1880, at the York Assizes in Toronto, before Judge Galt. He refused to offer any defense, even naming the arresting detective Murray to be his attorney. He pleaded Guilty to seven indictments, but only received a suspended sentence.

His children were less fortunate. His sons, Tom, Charlie, Johnnie and David Henry were convicted in Kingston, Ont., and received various sentences, up to ten years. Even their mother Mrs. Johnson was arraigned and charged with the distribution of counterfeit bills. Edwin Johnson died in the 1890's. Even detective Murray admitted that "crime lost a genius." REF.: *CBA*.

Johnson, Ellsworth (AKA: **Bumpy**), 1906-68, U.S., org. crime. Bumpy Johnson was an intermediary between the black street gangs of Harlem and the organized crime families of New York. A black man, Johnson became a millionaire by cooperating with the white syndicate, often getting the contract to quell a disturbance caused by another black. He was imprisoned three times for dealing in narcotics, and became a self-educated man, studying history and philosophy while serving his sentences. Johnson also wrote several poems, many of which were published during the civil rights movement. In 1968, about to go to trial facing a fourth conviction, the Johnson died of a heart attack. REF.: *CBA*.

Johnson, Enoch (AKA: **Nucky**), b.1883, U.S., polit. corr.-fraud-tax evas. Nucky Johnson was the corrupt political boss of Atlantic City, N.J., for nearly thirty years, until he was brought down by a massive federal effort that included five years of undercover surveillance.

In 1908, Johnson became sheriff of Atlantic County. He quickly became known as a man who could dispense graft and political favors in the courtroom. He aligned himself with Republican boss Louis Kuehnle, who ran the city's gambling and prostitution. In 1914 an investigation, led by Governor Woodrow Wilson, netted Kuehnle on charges he illegally received county contracts. Johnson inherited Kuehnle's clout and was elected County Treasurer in 1914. In 1916, he became Clerk of the State Supreme Court.

For the next fifteen years, Nucky was at the pinnacle of his political power. He not only oversaw the vice in Atlantic City, but also controlled Republican politics for the entire state. While he was paid a yearly salary of only $6,000, he spent $1,500 a week, dropped $100 tips, and had a lavish apartment on Central Park South in New York City. The Internal Revenue Service became suspicious as early as 1928, but Johnson's machine was so well oiled that no one would testify against him.

In November 1936, special agents William E. Frank and Edward A. Hill infiltrated Atlantic City's casinos, horse-racing betting rooms, numbers headquarters, and houses of prostitution to determine if and how Johnson was profiting from their operation. For the next three years, hundreds of people admitted their own involvement in the rackets, but no one would implicate Nucky.

The initial trials began in May 1939. For the first time in his political career, Johnson was unable to control the verdicts. His hold over his constituency dissipated, and gradually his underworld army turned against him. He was convicted in July 1941, and sentenced to ten years in prison and fined $20,000.

REF.: *CBA;* Fried, *The Rise and Fall of the Jewish Gangster in America;* Gosch and Hammer, *The Last Testament of Lucky Luciano;* Hynd, *The Giant Killers;* Katz, *Uncle Frank;* Kobler, *Capone;* Lait and Motimer, *Chicago: Confidential;* Messick, *Lansky;* ____, *Secret File;* ____ and Goldblatt, *The Mobs and the Mafia;* Peterson, *The Mob;* Reppetto, *The Blue Parade.*

Johnson, Frank Minis, Jr., 1918- , U.S., jur. U.S. Justice Department attorney in Birmingham, Ala., from 1953-55. Appointed to the middle district court of Alabama by President Dwight D. Eisenhower in 1955. A former Republican, he was appointed to the fifth circuit court (designated the eleventh circuit court since 1981) as an independent by President Jimmy Carter in 1979. REF.: *CBA.*

Johnson, George, d.1882, U.S., lynch. vict. In October 1882, George Johnson attempted to rob a stagecoach near Tombstone, Ariz. A shot was fired and a passenger named Kellogg died. Johnson's horse reared at the shot, unseating him, and he ran from the scene. The wife of the dead man was dispatched to bring the sheriff, and the driver set off to apprehend Johnson. The driver caught him after a short chase and took him into town. But before the sheriff returned, a lynch mob hanged him from a nearby tree. However, when it was learned that the passenger had died of a heart attack and not of a gunshot wound, the repentant citizens of Tombstone raised $800 to ease the grief of the now-widowed Mrs. Johnson. An acknowledgement of the misdeed was etched on Johnson's tombstone, stating that he was "Hanged By Mistake."

REF.: *CBA;* Dilnot, *Triumphs of Detection.*

Johnson, George E.Q., 1874-1949, U.S., jur. U.S. attorney in Illinois from 1927-32, and appointed to the northern district court of Illinois by President Herbert Hoover in 1932. REF.: *CBA.*

Johnson, Henry (AKA: Kerley), prom. 1893, Brit., rob. Only six months before murdering his mistress, Miranda Whitesides, in October 1893, Henry Johnson had been involved in a violent struggle with Detective Clifton R. Wooldridge, who attempted to arrest him on robbery charges.

Johnson was accused along with three others of the robbery of $500 worth of garments from a clothing store. On Apr. 13, 1893, he was arraigned, but was later discharged despite his struggle with Wooldridge. He fled, and was never arrested for the murder of Ms. Whitesides.

REF.: *CBA;* Wooldridge, *Hands Up.*

Johnson, Hiram Warren, 1866-1945, U.S., lawyer. Practiced law in Sacramento, Calif., and San Francisco, and successfully prosecuted Abe Ruef for corruption in 1908, replacing attorney Francis Heney. He served as California governor from 1911-17, ran unsuccessfully for vice-president with Theodore Roosevelt on the 1912 "Bull Moose" ticket, and was elected to the U.S. Senate in 1917, where he served until 1945. REF.: *CBA.*

Johnson, Jack (AKA: Turkey Creek), prom. 1870s, U.S., west. lawman-gunman. Jack "Turkey Creek" Johnson roamed the high plains to the Arizona Territory from the mid 1870s until the early 1880s. Originally a gold miner in Deadwood, Dakota Territory,

he moved to Arizona after killing his two partners in a gunfight. Following a quarrel in the Deadwood saloon in late 1876, the three retired to a local cemetery where Johnson killed the two men. He paid for their burials, although dynamite had to be used to make a hole in the frozen ground.

In Arizona, he became a temporary deputy marshall to Wyatt Earp, and aided in the apprehension of stage robbers. On Mar. 20, 1882, two days after the murder of Morgan Earp, Johnson joined a posse which included Wyatt and Warren Earp, Doc Holliday, and Sherman McMasters, in pursuit of Frank Stilwell, the presumed murderer. The posse cornered Stilwell near Tucson and shot him to death. Two days later, while in pursuit of other murder suspects, Johnson and others encountered Florentino Cruz in a wood camp near Tombstone. Cruz was thought to have confessed to a murder before he was killed in the hail of a bullets. Johnson and Sherman McMasters later drifted into Utah and northern Texas.

REF.: *CBA;* Jahns, *The Frontier World of Doc Holliday;* Lake, *Wyatt Earp;* Myers, *Doc Holliday.*

Johnson, Jack, prom. 1912, U.S., wh. slav. Jack Johnson became heavyweight boxing champion of the world on Dec. 26, 1908, by knocking out Tommy Burns in Sydney, Aus. He proved to be a colorful, brawling and raucous champion. He was hated—mostly because he was black—as much as he was loved. He lost his crown on Apr. 5, 1915 in Havana, Cuba, to the towering white champion, Jess Willard. The reason Johnson fought Willard in Havana was because he was then a wanted fugitive in the U.S. In 1912, Johnson went to a Chicago brothel and fell in love with a white woman. He persuaded her to leave the bordello and become his mistress. He took her across a state line and thus violated the Mann Act, which had gone into law in 1910, to combat the then flagrant white slavery operators who were importing thousands of girls from different states and Europe to stock their whorehouses.

Johnson was brought to trial and convicted of white slavery. He was released on bond while his lawyers filed appeals. Then, disguising himself as a baseball player for a minor league Negro team, he fled to Canada and remained a fugitive for seven years. Johnson roamed the

Jack Johnson, U.S. heavyweight boxing champion, convicted of white slavery.

world, defending his title in other lands. After he was defeated he went on fighting for small prize money. Even though the white woman married Johnson, it made no difference in his conviction. Finally, weary of running and hiding, Johnson returned to the U.S. and surrendered to federal marshals. He served his sentence of one year. When he stepped out of prison he found himself all but forgotten. REF.: *CBA.*

Johnson, James, 1780-1811, U.S., mur. James Johnson was born on Feb. 1, 1780, in Long Island, N.Y. On Oct. 23, 1810, he hosted a party at his home in New York City. Johnson became angry when one guest, Lewis Robinson, was unable to pay the fee Johnson asked for entrance to the party. Later in the evening when Robinson insulted Johnson's wife, the two men fought. Johnson, intoxicated, picked up a knife from a nearby table and fatally stabbed Robinson. Johnson was tried for first-degree murder and found Guilty. The jury determined that he had killed Robinson without reasonable provocation and sentenced him to death. He was hanged on Jan. 25, 1811.

REF.: *CBA; A Correct Journal of the Conduct of the Two Unfortunate Prisoners, Sinclair and Johnson, from the Time of Their Conviction Until Their Execution, With a Biographical Sketch of Their Lives, As Delivered By Themselves, the Day Previous to Which They Were to Be Executed.*

Johnson, Jerome, 1946-71, U.S., mur. Jerome Johnson shot and wounded New York mob boss Joe Colombo, Sr., on June 28, 1971, during an Italian-American Unity Day rally in New York City. Within seconds, Johnson was killed by an unknown gunman.

Johnson seemed an unlikely assailant. Black, illiterate, and a drifter, he was far removed from the highly powerful Mafia. The New York mob wars had escalated during the late 1960s and the annual Unity Day was designed to alleviate these hostilities. Joseph Gallo, recently released from prison and suspected as the mastermind behind the killing, went into seclusion.

It was never determined why Johnson obtained a phony photographers' credential to get near Joe Colombo. The name and motive of Johnson's killer also remain a mystery. REF.: *CBA.*

Johnson, John, d.1824, U.S., rob.-mur. In New York City in 1824, John Johnson murdered his roommate, James Murray, in his sleep with a hatchet and stole his pouch of money. Johnson wrapped the corpse in a blanket and carried it toward the harbor to dispose of it, but dropped it and ran when a passing policeman called out to him. When Murray's body could not be identified, police displayed the corpse for days at City Hall Park until someone at last recognized him. Johnson was quickly arrested, tried, found guilty and sentenced to death. On Apr. 2, 1824, 50,000 spectators came to the heart of New York City to watch Johnson hang at Thirteenth Street and Second Avenue.

REF.: *CBA; Complete Account of the Horrid Murder of James Murray!; Johnson, Trial and Sentence of John Johnson; The Life and Confession of John Johnson; Narrative of the Murder of James Murray; Nash, Bloodletters and Badmen; Stanford, A True Account of the Confession of John Johnson; The Trial and Confession of John Johnson; Trial of John Johnson.*

Johnson, John (AKA: **Liver-Eating Johnson, Crow-Killer**), prom. 1880s, U.S., west. lawman-can. Moving from Missouri to Montana in 1870, John Johnson became a mountain man who trapped deer, bear, and buffalo and was considered the greatest hunter of his day. He maintained a cabin near Rock Creek, near Red Lodge, Mont., which William "Buffalo Bill" Cody used as a camp for his buffalo hunting expeditions. Johnson reportedly maintained a private war with the Crow Indians, who murdered his Indian wife and child. He killed dozens of tribe members over ten years. One Easterner who hired Johnson to take him into the hills to hunt bear witnessed Johnson creep up on an Crow camp and attack it single-handedly, wounding several Indians and killing two. He then casually butchered the two corpses and ate their livers, thus earning the sobriquet "Liver-Eating Johnson."

John "Liver-Eating" Johnson in old age.

A large man who stood more than six feet tall and weighed 200 pounds, Johnson was a keen-eyed hunter and agile runner. He was also an expert knife-thrower, and he served for some years as an Indian scout for the U.S. Cavalry under General Nelson Miles. In 1880, he was appointed sheriff of Coulson, Mont., a rough-and-tumble town of mountain men and miners. He carried a rifle around town, never a six-gun. He always settled disputes with his fists and he later proudly stated that he never had to shoot a man to keep the peace. Offered princely sums to appear in Cody's Wild West shows, Johnson refused to travel to the East,

stating that "civilization will kill you faster than God's great outdoors." Johnson maintained law and order for several years in Coulson before moving into the high mountains and disappearing.

REF.: Bartholomew, *The Biographical Album of Western Gunfighters; CBA;* Nash, *Bloodletters and Badmen;* Tate, *Pickway, A True Narrative;* (FICTION), Fisher, *Mountain Man;* Thorp and Bunker, *Crow Killer;* (FILM), *Jeremiah Johnson,* 1972.

Johnson, John A., prom. 1911, U.S., (wrong. convict.) mur. John Johnson was coerced into a confession of murder before an angry crowd. A former mental patient, he served more than ten years for a crime he did not commit.

On Sept. 6, 1911, 7-year-old Annie Lemberger disappeared from her bed. Four days later she was found dead in a nearby lake. There was a small wound behind her left ear, but no water in her lungs, proving she did not drown. After pursuing a number of disconnected leads, the police arrested Johnson.

After initially pleading not guilty, Johnson confessed to the murder in a detailed testimony on Sept. 25. He demanded to be taken immediately to prison, but from his cell he again stated his innocence.

Ten years later, on Sept. 27, 1921, in hearings conducted by Rufus B. Smith, Johnson stated that he had been frightened into a confession by Detective Edward L. Boyer. Aware that Johnson was mentally deficient, and that he had witnessed a lynching, Boyer warned him to stay away from the windows, as the angry crowd was out to get him.

As the hearing was about to end, Mae Soronson identified Martin Lemberger, the little girl's father, as the real killer. On Jan. 5, 1922, Lemberger was convicted of second-degree murder, but because of a ten-year statute of limitations, Judge Hoppman was forced to release him. On Feb. 17, 1922, Governor Blaine commuted John Johnson's sentence.

REF.: Borchard, *Convicting the Innocent; CBA;* Derleth, *Wisconsin Murders.*

Johnson, Johnny, 1919-53, U.S., rob.-mur. Johnny Johnson had befriended Los Angeles *Mirror* editor Sid Hughes after being paroled from Alcatraz. Hughes helped him obtain a driver's license so he could work as a truck driver. Hughes lost track of him when Johnson became a suspect in the strangulation death of Richard Fagner.

Two months later, in October 1953, Johnson called Hughes. Hughes tipped off the FBI, who traced the call to a theater in Baltimore. Surrounded by FBI agents, Johnson pulled a gun, killing agent John Brady Murphy and wounding another, before dying in a torrent of bullets. REF.: *CBA.*

Johnson, John R., 1941- , U.S., drugs. John R. Johnson, a twice-convicted burglar and member of Paul "Peanuts" Panczko's Chicago gang was arrested along with Robert Pullia on July 7, 1987, and charged with trafficking cocaine. He disappeared Jan. 12, 1988, the day his trial was to begin. The disappearance was not considered voluntary, as he had recently posted $10,000 and his home as bond collateral. Pullia had previously pleaded guilty, and was sentenced to ten years.

After his arrest, Johnson was further identified as a thief who took part in a $2 million Florida jewelry heist in 1962, along with Panczko and Anthony Legato. Panczko admitted to the theft, and it was with his cooperation that Johnson was arrested with three kilograms of cocaine in 1987. Legato was found slain in a car trunk in Chicago in 1981. REF.: *CBA.*

Johnson, Laura, prom. 1895, U.S., rob.-asslt. Laura Johnson was a well-known Chicago thief who lured John Dayton into an opium den and robbed him of $950 in 1895. She was arrested by Detective Clifton Wooldridge, but had only half the money in her possession. Another man, Jerry Carmichael, was reputed to have the remaining amount. During an attempted search, Carmichael attacked Wooldridge, but the detective found none of the money. Carmichael was fined for vagrancy and sent to a workhouse.

On Apr. 9, 1895, Johnson was arraigned before Justice Bradwell and the case was presented to a grand jury. When the grand jury failed to act quickly, the victim, Dayton, was called away from the city and was unable to testify. Johnson was freed, but continued to cause trouble.

She stabbed Irene Moore over a quarrel of affections for Carmichael. Moore's arm was nearly severed and she almost died of blood poisoning. Johnson was arraigned and charged on Aug. 25, 1896, with assault to do bodily harm. She was sentenced to six months in the House of Correction by Judge Baker. REF.: Asbury, *Gem of the Prairie; CBA;* Wooldridge, *Hands Up.*

Johnson, Mary, d.1648, U.S., witchcraft-mur. Laws forbidding witchcraft and Satanism were first defined and established in the New World at Plymouth, Mass., in 1636. The first execution of a self-declared witch occurred in Boston in 1648. In that year, a hapless creature named Mary Johnson, following a long trial in which she was bullied, jeered, harassed, cajoled, and threatened, admitted to being a witch and having had "familiarity with the Devil." Mary Johnson confessed to almost anything of which she stood accused by her badgering, Puritan judges. Yes, she murdered a child, she told the magistrates. Yes, she had intercourse not only with scores of men but with demons, lots of them. Yes, the Devil came to her whenever she was in need of him.

Mephistopheles, however, failed to appear to save Mary Johnson, witch, when she was taken to Boston Common and hanged until dead. Hanging, not burning as in the Old World, was the prescribed treatment for witches. The European belief rampant among the peasantry, that witches returned from the grave as vampires to suck the blood from their executioners and victims, did not take hold in the colonies. Hanging would do. REF.: *CBA;* Demos, *Entertaining Satan;* Mather, *Magnalia Christi Americana II.*

Johnson, Mary, prom. 1912, Case of, Brit., (wrong. convict.) mur. threat. Mary Johnson was a shopowner in Earlswood, England, and her husband was a traveling salesman. In October 1912, Mrs. Johnson was accused of sending letters, threatening her neighbors, Mr. and Mrs. Woodman, with murder. Since March the Woodmans had received the letters almost daily. The letters had been delivered in various ways, including one wrapped around a rock that had been flung in the direction of Mrs. Woodman. Mrs. Johnson denied these acts, but was sentenced to six months' imprisonment.

She was released in Mar. 1913, but within six months, was again accused of sending threatening letters to the Woodmans, as well as other neighbors. She was convicted, and this time sentenced to twelve months' hard labor. Released in June 1914, the letters started again. This time a jury found her Not Guilty. The police began to suspect Mrs. Woodman.

Without her knowledge, Mrs. Woodman's stationery was secretly marked. Predictably, the threats recurred using this paper. Eliza Ellen Woodman was sentenced to eighteen months of hard labor. Mrs. Johnson received £500 in compensation, but her business had collapsed during her two imprisonments. REF.: *CBA;* Cobb, *Trials and Errors.*

Johnson, Milton, 1950- , and **Lego, Donald,** 1933- , U.S., mur. In the summer of 1983, five multiple murders in Will County, Ill., resulted in seventeen deaths. A small, citizen-financed crime fighting organization, Crime Stoppers of Will County, helped apprehend two suspects, Milton Johnson and Donald Lego. Lego was convicted in the stabbing and bludgeoning murder of an 82-year-old widow, the last of the seventeen victims, on Mar, 16, 1984. On the same day, Johnson pleaded not guilty to charges of the murder of an 18-year-old man and the rape of his 17-year-old female companion. In August, he was convicted of the attacks and when given the choice of being sentenced by Judge Michael Orenic, or by the jury, he opted for the judge. On Sept. 19, 1984, Judge Orenic, who was on record as opposing the death penalty, sentenced Milton Johnson to die by lethal injection. On Jan. 28, 1986, Johnson was convicted of four more deaths in the same murder spree. REF.: *CBA.*

Johnson, Mushmouth (John V. Johnson), d.1907, U.S., gamb. "Mushmouth" Johnson a cigar-chomping native of St. Louis who never placed a bet, became one of Chicago's most successful gamblers by controlling the black rackets in Chicago for twenty years beginning in the 1880s. After working as a waiter at the Palmer House, he was hired by Andy Scott to work as a floorman at a South Clark Street gambling den. Johnson's proficiency earned him a partial interest in the establishment which he sold in 1890 to open his own gambling hall and saloon a few blocks away.

With Bill Lewis and Tom McGinnis, Johnson, although a black man, opened the Frontenac Club, which operated for an exclusively white clientele. The clubs flourished until a general vice crackdown in 1907 closed most of Chicago's illegal establishments. Johnson earned more than $250,000 in his career, but claimed he paid more than $100,000 in fines, and large sums went for the police protection which allowed him to operate. Shortly before his death in 1907, he claimed to have only $15,000. REF.: *CBA.*

Johnson, Nicholas de Clare, See: **Brook, John.**

Johnson, Noble Jacob, 1887-1968, U.S., jur. Deputy prosecuting attorney for forty-third judicial circuit court of Indiana from 1917-18, and prosecuting attorney for the same court from 1921-24. He served as a U.S. congressman from 1925-31 and from 1939-48. A Republican, he was nominated to the court of customs and patent appeals by Democratic President Harry S. Truman in 1948. REF.: *CBA.*

Johnson, Peggy, prom. 1987, Case of, U.S., mur. William G. Johnson of Columbia, S.C., was killed while sleepwalking. His wife, Peggy, tried to wrest away a gun he was carrying, but it fired at point-blank range. The man, who worked at a mental retardation clinic, had a history of nightmares and sleep-walking. After testimony before Deputy Coroner Wayne Siebert Peggy Johnson was absolved of any wrongdoing. REF.: *CBA.*

Johnson, Ray, c.1927- , U.S., burg. Ray Johnson decided to "go straight" in 1968 after a lifetime devoted to crime. He became a consultant for crime prevention and produced a home-protection video. He also became the subject of a TV movie, *Dangerous Company,* starring Beau Bridges.

Johnson stole his first car at age nine, and was convicted of auto theft at sixteen. He was then remanded to the Sonoma State Home. He escaped twice, returning after the second time, to release other prisoners. He was sterilized after his recapture in 1943. During the next twenty-five years he did time in San Quentin, Chino, Soledad, and Folsom prisons. In 1958 he escaped from Folsom, was quickly recaptured, and spent the next four years and nine months in solitary confinement. He was paroled in 1968 and began using his criminal mind for crime prevention. REF.: *CBA.*

Johnson, Reverdy, 1796-1876, U.S., jur. Served as U.S. senator from 1845-49 and from 1863-68. He was appointed attorney general in 1849 by President Zachary Taylor, but his involvement with the secretary of war William Crawford in the Galphin suit caused him to resign in 1850. He defended Dred Scott, the slave who attempted to sue for his freedom in the 1857 landmark Supreme Court case. A supporter of President Abraham Lincoln, he served in the U.S. Senate during the Civil War. He served as U.S. minister to Great Britain from 1868-69. REF.: *CBA.*

Johnson, Richard, d.1696, Brit., attempt. esc. In 1696, Richard Johnson, sentenced to be hanged at Shrewsbury in England, obtained a promise from the under-sheriff that his body would not be stripped but would be placed in the coffin fully dressed. Under a double shirt and a periwig, Johnson had tied ropes around his body which were connected to hooks at his neck. He had also arranged for medical attention after his "execution." When he had been hanging for a half hour and still showed signs of life, a man sent up to examine him discovered the supporting device. Johnson was taken down, stripped of his protection, and "hanged in an effectual manner." REF.: Atholl, *Shadow of the Gallows; CBA;* Nash, *Almanac of World Crime;* ____, *Bloodletters and Badmen.*

Johnson, Richard, d.1829, U.S., mur. Richard Johnson's mistress, Mrs. Ursula Newman, gave birth to a child, but refused to marry Johnson. She laughed when he demanded that Newman give the infant his name. Johnson grabbed a pistol and fired buckshot into his lover on Nov. 20, 1828, killing her instantly. Nine slugs were removed from her corpse. Johnson considered suicide, but abandoned the idea. According to one report,

Richard Johnson shooting his mistress, Mrs. Ursula Newman, in 1828.

Johnson only imagined that he had fathered Newman's child, and had had this same bizarre fantasy about other women with children. Tried in New York City, Johnson confessed to the slaying and was hanged on May 7, 1829, on Blackwell's Island.

REF.: *A Brief Summary of Some of the Principal Incidents Relative to the Life of Ursula Newman and the Intercourse Subsisting Between Her and Richard Johnson; CBA; A Correct Copy of the Trial & Conviction of Richard Johnson; Execution of Richard Johnson;* Nash, *Bloodletters and Badmen;* Sparhawk, *Report of the Trial of Richard Johnson; Trial, Conviction and Sentence of Richard Johnson; Trial of Richard Johnson.*

Johnson, Richard, prom. 1860s-70s, U.S., west. outl. Richard Johnson, called Dick, was a Texas cowboy who sided with the Lee faction in the bloody Lee-Peacock Feud that raged through Grayson County, Texas, during the 1860s. Johnson was a half brother of the Dixon Brothers, Simp, Bob, and Charles, who all fought with Bob Lee against the forces of Lewis Peacock. Bob Lee, leader of the Lee faction, was killed in June 1869 and Johnson moved to west Texas to raise cattle. When Charles Dixon was killed by the Peacocks in 1871, Johnson returned to Grayson County to hunt down and kill Lewis Peacock, leader of the Peacock clan. Accompanied by Joe Parker, Johnson went to Peacock's ranch and climbed into a tree in the middle of the night, perching there with

Western gunman Richard Johnson.

a rifle. At dawn on July 1, 1871, Lewis Peacock emerged from his ranch house and stood on the front porch. Johnson fired a bullet into Lewis Peacock's heart, killing him on the spot. He then fled and was never apprehended for this murder. The Lee-Peacock Feud came to an abrupt end. See: **Lee-Peacock Feud; Peacock, Lewis.**

REF.: Bartholomew, *The Biographical Album of Western Gunfighters; CBA;* O'Neal, *Encyclopedia of Western Gunfighters;* Sonnichsen, *I'll Die Before I'll Run.*

Johnson, Robert, 1924- , U.S., mur. Robert Johnson, of Wilmington, N.C., clubbed four of his children to death within twenty-four hours of his wife's abandoning the family in September

1971. A fifth child survived the brutal beatings. His wife Bonnie Louise Johnson had recently threatened to leave him, saying that she felt trapped in her marriage and that she had too many children to care for.

Before clubbing his children, Johnson had contacted a Wilmington television station, hoping to broadcast an appeal for his wife's return. Two hours later, he contacted police and led them to the murder site. He was charged with the murders of the four children and the attempted murder of one daughter, the only survivor. He was sent to Cherry Hospital in Goldsboro, N.C., for a sixty-day mental observation period, and later to prison at Southport, N.C.

Johnson had a troubled past. He received a dishonorable discharge during WWII, after serving time for desertion. He also had a civilian record for forgery and the interstate transportation of a stolen airplane. But he had stayed clear of trouble for twelve years until September 1971. REF.: *CBA.*

Johnson, Robert L., and **Jones, Calvin S.,** and **Kirkland, Haywood T.,** and **Bowman, John H.,** and **Knight, Arthur B.,** and **Chatham, Linwood,** prom. 1969, U.S., rob. Shortly after 6 a.m. on Dec. 23, 1969, several men robbed a postal service vehicle in Washington, D.C., and made off with $381,000. Only $62,000 was ever recovered, but five men were apprehended for the crime.

A fingerprint of Calvin Jones was found in a van that was used in the getaway. He and Robert Johnson had been involved in the Black Panther movement and professed the money had been used to buy Christmas presents for black children. More likely, however, the money was used for a romp through California and Hawaii, as well as for cocaine, two rifles and a revolver. Johnson tended bar in Washington at a Panther hangout, the African Hut, where a one-time postal employee, Haywood Kirkland, had a proprietary interest. Soon after, a bank teller became suspicious, when a man named Linwood Chatham asked for a cashier's check in return for a wad of scuffed fifty and hundred dollar bills. Further investigation added the names of John Bowman and Arthur Knight. All six were charged with armed robbery.

In June 1970, a seventh man Kyle H. Price, tried to buy a Ford Thunderbird using hundred-dollar bills, and deposited $47,000 in a bank. He was arrested at his mother's house. Despite the seven apprehensions, $315,000 of the stolen money has yet to accounted for.

REF.: *CBA;* Kahn, *Fraud.*

Johnson, Sam D., 1920- , U.S., jur. District attorney of Hillsboro, Texas, from 1955-59. He served as a Texas district judge from 1959-65, as appellate judge in the fourteenth court of civil appeals in Houston, Texas, from 1967-73, and as an associate justice on the Texas Superior Court from 1973-79. He was appointed to the fifth circuit court in Texas by President Jimmy Carter in 1979. REF.: *CBA.*

Johnson, Terry Lee, 1949- , U.S., mur. Johnson, an ex-Marine from rural Alabama, turned to a life of crime after being released from the service. Dealing in narcotics replaced the occupations of carpet installing, landscaping, logging, welding, and construction work. Through his Marine experience, Johnson was adept at living in the wilderness and with handling a wide array of firearms. He was charged and convicted of the murder of an unarmed farmer.

Johnson subsequently escaped from prison and was last seen in Alabama, carrying a high-powered rifle. At this time he is still a fugitive. REF.: *CBA.*

Johnson, Thomas, 1732-1819, U.S., jur. Began political career as delegate to Maryland Provincial Assembly in 1762. He fiercely opposed the Stamp Act and was selected to be a delegate to the Annapolis Convention of 1774, and represented Maryland in the first Continental Congress from 1775-76. In 1776, he helped write Maryland's first constitution, and was elected the state's first governor in 1777. In 1788, he participated in the state convention for ratification of the new U.S. Constitution. He served as chief judge of Maryland's general court from 1790-91, and was appointed associate justice of the U.S. Supreme Court by President

George Washington in 1791. He helped plan the new federal capital and rejected a nomination to be secretary of state under President Washington in 1795. REF.: *CBA*.

Johnson, Thomas, 1772-1839, Brit., smug. Thomas Johnson was a nineteenth-century smuggler who alternated between prison sentences and being decorated for valor. In 1798 he was convicted of smuggling, bribed a warden to escape, and was pardoned by the British government because of service during the Napoleonic wars. Soon he was jailed for debts and smuggling, but escaped by throwing himself over the prison wall.

Returning to sea, he was next captured by the French, trying to smuggle gold coins. Napoleon offered him freedom if he would pilot an invasion against the English, but he refused and escaped. In 1809, he swam ashore with explosives that destroyed a Dutch garrison, and was awarded with a life pension. He was then given a job with the revenue service, apprehending other smugglers, at which he proved ineffective.

Johnson received a second offer from Napoleon after the Emperor was exiled on St. Helena. The captain was to earn £40,000 by securing the Emperor's release. Napoleon died just as Captain Johnson was coming to get him.
REF.: *CBA;* Hunt, *Dictionary of Rogues;* Kobler, *Ardent Spirits.*

Johnson, Thomas, prom. 1971-73, Case of, U.S., mur. Thomas Johnson of the Bronx was arrested for the stabbing death of a construction worker in Dec. 1971. The conviction did not occur until July 1973, fifteen months later. This delay subsequently brought about his release from prison on a legal technicality.

In 1974, Congress passed the Speedy Trial Act, which required that the accused be tried within ninety days. However, no more money was appropriated for the additional personnel that were needed for compliance. Therefore, hundreds of felons had their sentences thrown out of court. Johnson, the beneficiary of this congressional action, was released from prison in 1975.
REF.: *CBA;* Godwin, *Murder U.S.A.*

Johnson, Vateness, 1951- , and **Johnson, Frank,** c.1947- , U.S., mur. Vateness Johnson and her husband, Frank Johnson, were convicted of the Mar. 12, 1985, murder of 5-year-old Judy Moses, who was in their foster care. The child, along with her three-year-old sister, were put in the Johnson's care after the Illinois Department of Children and Family Services deemed their real father incapable of properly caring for them. The children were repeatedly beaten and on the last day of her life, 5-year-old Judy was tied to a chair in the Johnson's unheated garage.

In 1985, Vateness Johnson was convicted and sentenced to sixty years in prison while her husband was sentenced to twenty-two years. The Illinois Court of Appeals ordered a new trial, saying that the couple should have been tried separately. Frank Johnson denied the actual beatings, and was allowed to plea-bargain a lesser sentence of involuntary manslaughter. His sentence was reduced to eight years. On Nov. 24, 1988, a Will County, Ill., jury was shown pictures of the brutally-beaten children, listened to a medical examiner's report, and upheld the earlier conviction of Vateness Johnson. REF.: *CBA*.

Johnson, Watterson, and **Leigh, John,** and **Kassow, Raymond,** and **Ingle, Carl,** prom. 1970, U.S., rob.-mur. Four women were killed during a robbery that netted only $275 at a suburban Cincinnati bank in 1970. The Cabinet-Supreme Savings and Loan, in Delhi Hills, Ohio, had been under surveillance for days, as suspicious characters had continually made small deposits and withdrawals. A nationwide search ensued for the murderers, and four days later, two men, Watterson Johnson and John Leigh, were apprehended while sleeping in their car near Gallup, N.M. Earlier, two others, Raymond Kassow and Carl Ingle, were arrested in their homes near the scene of the robbery.

Johnson, Leigh, and Kassow were given separate murder trials and each was sentenced to the electric chair. Ingle was released because of lack of evidence. REF.: *CBA*.

Johnson, Will H., prom. 1946-56, U.S., fraud. Rumors of Adolf Hitler's survival and escape to unknown points were rampant just after WWII. Will H. Johnson, a semiliterate miner in Middles-

boro, Ky., began a scheme impersonating Hitler through the mails. The correspondence was inane and ridiculous, with bizarre stories of Hitler's plans for invisible boats, space ships, and underground ammunition centers. According to the letters, Hitler had escaped the bunker and hidden with several of his staff members in Kentucky, where they were making plans to take over the U.S.

Johnson's market consisted of right-wing semi-fascists throughout the U.S. and Canada. Many of his customers were of German descent. His most durable client was a German-American ex-soldier in Bristol, Va. In rambling letters, which he would sign "Adolf Hitler," "Eva Hitler", and "Chief of Staff," Johnson kept his Bristol sucker asking for more. Although he often referred to himself as the "Furrier," the error was not noticed by his satisfied customer, who forked over about $4,000 in a ten-year period. Johnson once wrote as Hitler to say he had been forced to call off an important meeting because he was without shoes, requesting, "Please send size 11." The Furrier's needs were met by his Bristol friend. Unfortunately for Johnson, the Bristol client dropped dead in August 1956. Among his effects were found Western Union payments and cancelled money orders to Hitler. Postal inspectors tracked down the "chief of staff", finding Johnson living with his family in a dilapidated shack.
REF.: *CBA;* Nash, *Hustlers and Con Men.*

William Johnson, encouraged by Jane Housden, shooting jailer Spurling.

Johnson, William, and **Housden, Jane,** d.1712, Brit., rob.-burg.-mur. A native of Northamptonshire, England, William Johnson sailed to the island of Gibraltar after a string of business failures. Working as a surgeon's mate in a garrison, he saved enough money to return home, but when that ran out, he turned to robbery.

A conviction and subsequent pardon for robbery failing to deter him, Johnson joined up with Jane Housden, a convicted forger. The day she was to be tried for coining at the Old Bailey, Johnson asked to speak with her. When Mr. Spurling, the jailer, denied Johnson's request, Johnson shot him in full view of a packed courtroom.

The judges immediately dropped Jane Housden's coining charge and swiftly convicted both her and Johnson of Spurling's murder. Both Housden and Johnson denied their crime until the last moments of their lives and showed little remorse for their actions. They were hanged on Sept. 19, 1712, and Johnson's body was then hung in chains near Holloway, between Islington and Highgate.
REF.: Bloom, *Money of Their Own;* *CBA;* Mitchell, *The Newgate Calendar.*

Johnson, William, 1771-1834, U.S., jur. Began career in government as representative in South Carolina's legislature from

1794-98. He served as speaker of the state House of Representatives in 1798, after which he was one of three judges appointed to the court of common pleas, the highest state court, where he served from 1799-1804. He was nominated as associate justice on the U.S. Supreme Court by President Thomas Jefferson in 1804. He distinguished himself in court as a fiery competitor of Chief Justice John Marshall. He remained on the Court until his death. REF.: *CBA*.

Johnson, William Eugene (AKA: **Pussyfoot Johnson**), 1862-1945, U.S., law. enfor. off.   Chief special officer in U.S. Indian Service from 1908-11, where he gained his nickname for tracking criminals in the Indian Territory. An avid supporter of temperance who frequently lectured on the topic, he worked as managing editor of publications for the Anti-Saloon League from 1912-16, and as publicity director for the group from 1916-18. REF.: *CBA*.

Johnson, William H., d.1878, U.S., west. lawman-gunman. Following the Civil War, Confederate Captain William Johnson moved west to New Mexico, married the daughter of prominent rancher and fellow southerner Henry Beckwith, and became co-owner of a cattle ranch. In 1876 he was drawn into the infamous Lincoln County War, he and his partner Wallace Olinger aligning themselves with the Riley-Dolan faction. In the midst of the feud he was made a deputy to Sheriff William Brady. On Apr. 22, 1877, at Seven Rivers, Johnson successfully defended his father-in-laws ranch from a cattle raid led by John Chisum, who was convinced that Beckwith was stealing his herd.

A year later, on Apr. 30, 1878, Johnson joined a posse seeking to apprehend outlaws Frank Coe, Frank McNab, and Ab Sanders. The posse caught up with the band when they stopped to water their horses near Lincoln, N.M. The posse shot McNab and Sanders to death and arrested Coe. Johnson returned to ranching, but his relationship with his father-in-law became uncomfortable. On Aug. 16, 1878, after arguing at Beckwith's ranch, the old man fatally shot Johnson in the neck and chest with a double-barreled shotgun. Johnson's partner, Olinger, returned the fire, hitting Beckwith in the face, but the old man survived.

REF.: *CBA;* Fulton, *Lincoln County War;* Keleher, *Violence in Lincoln County;* Klasner, *My Girlhood Among Outlaws.*

Johnson, William Samuel, 1727-1819, U.S., jur. Served in Congress of Confederation from 1784-87. He acted as a delegate to the 1787 Constitutional Convention, and signed the Constitution. He served as a judge on the supreme court of Connecticut from 1772-74. Later, he held a U.S. senate seat from 1789-91 while working from 1787-1800 as the first president of Columbia College. REF.: *CBA*.

Johnson, W. Lee, prom. 1951, U.S., jur. Prison made a powerful impression on Judge W. Lee Johnson when he was initially exposed to it as a young attorney. He thought that a brief visit would be just the right tonic to keep a young offender from leading a life of crime. As a judge, he put his theory to the test.

Jim Kimbrell pleaded guilty to robbing a man at gunpoint. Judge Johnson sentenced him to five years, but said he would consider probation after the youth was exposed to life behind bars for twenty-four hours. Kimbrell ate with the other inmates and was even given a courtesy examination of the electric chair. The judge gave him probation the following day. REF.: *CBA*.

Johnson County War, 1892, U.S., west. feud. In 1892, the owners of the largest ranches in Johnson County, Wyo., declared war on the smaller ranchers and local homesteaders in the guise of driving out cattle rustlers. The big ranchers hired "range detectives" to kill a few alleged rustlers, hoping with these killings to scare off smaller ranchers who were vying for the land.

The barons then attempted to influence the state legislature and the press. They ordered the lynching of a prostitute named Cattle Kate, accusing her of accepting their stolen beef as payment for her services. The press believed and accented their stories of her depravities.

Within the Wyoming Stock Growers' Association, a secret "hit" list was prepared and forty-six regulators led by Colonel Frank Wolcott and Frank H. Canton, himself wanted for murder, were sent to the ranges to carry out the executions. They killed ranchers Nate Champion and Nick Ray, but other small ranchers organized a resistance army of 200 men who chased the regulators to Buffalo, Wyo., where they were arrested and saved by the U.S. Cavalry. The Cavalry leader refused to surrender them to Red Angus, the sheriff of Cheyenne, known to be sympathetic to the homesteaders. Although none of the regulators were prosecuted, the Johnson County War ended without further extermination of the small ranchers by the cattle barons.

REF.: Aikman, *The Taming of the Frontier;* American Guide Series, *Wyoming, A Guide to Its History, Highways, and People;* Atherton, *The Cattle Kings;* Barber, *The Longest Rope;* Bard, *Horse Wrangler;* Bartlett, *History of Wyoming;* Beals, *American Earth;* Branch, *Westward;* Brown, *The Plainsmen of the Yellowstone;* _____, *Before Barbed Wire;* Bruce, *Banister Was There;* Burns, *Wyoming Pioneer Ranches;* Burt, *The Diary of A Dude Wrangler;* _____, *Powder River;* Burt, *American Murder Ballads;* Canton, *Frontier Trails; CBA;* Chaffin, *Sons of the West;* Chapel, *Guns of the Old West;* Clay, *My Life on the Range;* Clover, *On Special Assignment;* Cushman, *The Great North Trail;* Dale, *Cow County;* David, *Malcolm Campbell, Sheriff;* Dick, *The Sod-House Frontier;* Douglas, *The Cattle Rustlers of Wyoming;* Durham, *The Negro Cowboys;* Flannery, *John Hunton's Diary;* Frantz, *The American Cowboy;* Frink, *Cow Country Cavalcade;* _____, and Jackson and Spring, *When Grass Was King;* Gage, *The Johnson County War is a Pack of Lies;* Gard, *Frontier Justice;* Garst, *The Story of Wyoming;* _____, *When the West Was Young;* Guernsey, *Wyoming Cowboy Days;* Howard, *This is the West;* Hudson, *Andy Adams;* Hultz, *Range Beef Production;* Larson, *History of Wyoming;* Lavender, *The Big Divide;* LeFors, *Wyoming Peace Officer;* Lindsay, *Big Horn Basin;* Linford, *Wyoming, Frontier State;* Linn, *James Keeley, Newspaperman;* McCallum, *The Wire That Fenced the West;* McPherren, *Trail's End;* Mercer, *The Banditti of the Plains;* Mokler, *History of Natrona County;* Monaghan, *The Book of the American West;* Osgood, *The Day of the Cattlemen;* Paine, *Tom Horn;* Peattie, *The Inverted Mountain;* Penrose, *The Johnson County War;* _____, *The Rustler Business;* Price, *Memories of Old Montana;* Price, *A Summer in the Rockies;* Raine, *Guns of the Frontier;* Rennert, *The Cowboy;* Rollins, *The Cowboy;* Sandoz, *The Cattleman;* Small, *The Best of True West;* Smith, *The War on Powder River;* Smythe, *The Conquest of Arid America;* Swallow, *The Wild Bunch;* Trenholm, *Footprints on the Frontier;* Walker, *Stories of Early Days in Wyoming;* Wellman, *The Trampling Herd;* West, *Rocky Mountain Cities;* Winn, *The Macadam Trail;* Wyman, *Nothing But Prairie and Sky;* (FILM), *Heaven's Gate,* 1980.

Johnston, Bruce, Sr., 1939- , and **Johnston, David**, 1948- , and **Johnston, Norman**, 1951- , U.S., mur.   In two separate trials in eastern Pennsylvania in 1978, the Johnston brothers were convicted of murdering six people, including a family member, and of attempting to kill one other person.

Two generations of the Johnston clan formed a theft ring that was accused of stealing well over $1 million in cars, jewelry, and farm equipment. When family member Bruce Johnston, Jr. suspected his father of having raped his friend Robin Miller, however, he went to authorities, unaware that his betrayal would result in five murders.

On July 17, 1977, Bruce Johnston, Sr. murdered Gary Wayne Crouch, thirty-one. Then on Aug. 16, 1978, David and Norman Johnston murdered James Johnston, eighteen, Bruce Jr.'s half-brother, Wayne Sampson, eighteen, and Duane Lincoln, seventeen, near Chadds Ford, Pa. On Aug. 20, Wayne's brother, James Sampson, twenty-four, became the fourth victim. And on Aug. 30, Bruce Jr. and his fiancée Robin Miller, fifteen, were ambushed; Miller died.

On Mar. 18, 1980, in Edensberg, Pa., David and Norman Johnston were convicted of four murders and were each sentenced to four life sentences. On Nov. 15, 1980, in the West Chester courtroom of Judge Leonard Sugarman, Bruce Johnston, Sr., after testimony by 126 witnesses, including his son, was found Guilty of all six murders and sentenced to life in prison.

REF.: *CBA;* Fox, *Mass Murder.*

Johnston, Douglas Harold, 1907- , Brit., lawyer. Served as Scotland's solicitor-general from 1947-48, and was elected to the

House of Commons as a member of the Labor Party. He headed the prosecution in the second trial of Patrick Carraher. REF.: *CBA*.

Johnston, Duncan, prom. 1938, U.S., mur. Duncan Johnston was a prominent local jeweler and the former mayor of Twin Falls, Idaho. When a bloody body was found in a parked car on May 24, 1938, Johnston identified it as a missing business associate. A number of people, including Johnston, stated that they had given the dead man large sums of money, yet his pockets contained only $45. He also was reputed to have had in his possession $15,000 worth of jewels.

Police Chief Howard Gillette had police plant a wiretap next to Johnston's jewelry store. To their amazement, the bag of jewels was found in a crevice near the intended tap site. Now it was simply a matter of waiting to see who retrieved the bag. The next morning the door opened and Duncan Johnston went for the gems. On Dec. 11, 1938, he was found Guilty of first-degree murder and sentenced to life in prison by District Judge James W. Porter.

REF.: *CBA*; Cohen, *One Hundred True Crime Stories*.

Johnston, Erin Elizabeth, 1970-88, China, (unsolv.) mur. At the age of eighteen, Erin Elizabeth Johnston joined her parents, Allen and Mary Pindt, on the faculty of Northeast University of Technology in Shenyang, China. The morning of Jan. 23, 1988, a friend found Elizabeth Johnston's body in the campus apartment she shared with her parents. Shenyang police said they were investigating a "possible murder," but no suspects were arrested. REF.: *CBA*.

Johnston, James A., 1874-1954, U.S., warden. James Johnston was the warden of three of the most notorious prisons in the U.S. In 1911, he was appointed warden at Folsom prison. Two years later, he assumed the same position at San Quentin. He remained there until 1925, when he left for a career in banking. In 1934 he was appointed to head a new prison built over a military installation on Alcatraz island in San Francisco Bay.

The Rock was the prison of last resort. The code was punishment, not reformation. Only prisoners judged to be too tough for other prisons were sent there. Guests included Al Capone and "Machine Gun" Kelly. Johnston remained at the fortress until 1948. Twice he was exposed to violence. In 1937 he was

Warden James A. Johnston of Alcatraz.

slugged from behind while walking through the prison dining room. In 1946, a guard was killed during an attempted prison break. After reaching the mandatory retirement age for wardens, he served as assistant director of the U.S. Bureau of Prisons, and later as a member of the Federal Pardon and Parole Board. See: **Alcatraz**.

REF.: *CBA*; DeNevi, *Alcatraz '46*; Heaney, *Inside the Walls of Alacatraz*; Johnston, *Alcatraz Island Prison*; Karpis, *On the Rock*.

Johnston, Sir John, and **Campbell, James**, and **Montgomery, Archibald**, prom. 1690, Brit., kid. Mary Wharton, a 13-year-old heiress, was a favorite of King William III. She was abducted on Nov. 4, 1690, by John Johnston, James Campbell, and Archibald Montgomery allegedly because Campbell intended to marry her. The king offered a reward for their capture, but Campbell escaped to Scotland. Johnston was betrayed by his landlord for £50.

Mary Wharton later wrote to an aunt that she had not been taken by force, and that she had married Campbell willingly. However, the marriage was annulled by an Act of Parliament on Dec. 20, and three days later Johnston was executed. Later, it

became apparent that the girl's guardian, Colonel Bierly, had forbidden Mary to wed outside the clan, as she was heir to £50,000. She later married Bierly, who was a commander for King William III.

REF.: *CBA*; Sparrow, *The Great Abductors*.

Johnston-Noad, Edward, prom. 1950s, Brit., fraud. As a young man, Edward Johnston-Noad inherited £100,000, allowing him to host lavish parties, and making him popular with fashionable women. He was also a swindler, known as the Count.

During an acute shortage of London housing, the Count offered two flats for sale. He then took deposits from seventy people for the property and even sold the furniture to several different people. When his victims becamse wise to his scheme, he fled to Paris, finding a job with the British Embassy.

Scotland Yard suspected that he might have fled to the continent and dispatched his picture to Interpol. Detective Roger Ravard happened to be carrying the picture in his wallet when his wife, who worked for the British Embassy, recognized her fellow employee's photo. The Count was arrested and sentenced to four months for possessing false papers. Extradition took a year, but when he was returned to court at the Old Bailey, he was sentenced to ten years for fraud. REF.: *CBA*.

Johnstown, Pa., Flood, 1889, U.S., loot. In the aftermath of one of the worst disasters in U.S. history, the darker side of human nature revealed itself. In the 1889 Johnstown Flood, over 2,000 people died when a 100-foot-high earthen dam broke, flooding the valley surrounding Johnstown, Pa. The bodies of some victims were not found until fifteen years later. As the waters subsided, dozens of looters descended upon the town, pillaging businessess and stripping valuables from the bodies of the flood victims. Rescue workers were forced to become vigilante law enforcers, sometimes killing the looters on the spot. When citizens found one man with a ring still on a severed finger, they promptly drowned him. A man masquerading as an undertaker was also caught stealing a valuable ring from a victim's finger. Dozens more were arrested as an overburdened police force was distracted from their frantic rescue attempts. REF.: *CBA*.

Joiner, Charles Wycliffe, 1916- , U.S., jur. Law professor and acting dean at University of Michigan from 1947-68, and professor of law and dean of the law school at Wayne State University from 1967-72. He was appointed to the eastern district court of Michigan by President Richard M. Nixon in 1972. REF.: *CBA*.

Joliet Penitentiary in Illinois.

Joliet State Penitentiary, U.S., 19th Cent.- , prison. The Joliet State Penitentiary in northern Illinois is one of the largest penal institutions in the U.S. and is actually two prisons. Joliet is the site of the old prison that was remodeled in the 1930s and Stateville, built in 1921, is located about five miles from the Joliet prison and is part of the same system. Together, the facilities house about 5,000 prisoners and have incorporated the idea of "penopticon," a design featuring circular cell blocks in which all cells, built in many tiers, can be monitored from a single guard center at the hub of each cell block. This was the visionary architectural concept of British penologist and reformer Jeremy Bentham. This penitentiary system has proven one of the most difficult from which to escape and inmate riots are infrequent due to the cell block design, which allows for tight controls by guards. One of the most spectacular escapes from this prison was committed by Chicago bootlegger Roger Touhy, gangster Basil "The Owl" Banghart, and others in 1942. See: **Bentham, Jeremy; Touhy, Roger.**

REF.: *CBA;* Erickson, *Warden Ragen of Joliet;* Ragen and Finston, *Inside the World's Toughest Prison.*

Jon, Gee, d.1924, U.S., mur. After he was found Guilty of murder and sentenced to death, Gee Jon was held in the Carson City, (Nev.) Courthouse and became the center of a controversy. In an effort to clean up Nevada's image as a comparatively lawless frontier state, Governor Emmet Boyle signed a new capital punishment bill from the state legislature in 1921. There had been debate over whether to abolish the death penalty entirely or to substitute some improved form of execution. The bill rejected electrocution, and instead mandated introducing a lethal gas into the convict's cell while he slept. When it proved too complicated for the public executioner to introduce lethal gas into an ordinary cell, Jon was temporarily saved from execution. When the Nevada Supreme Court declared the gas execution bill valid and ordered the sentence to be carried out, an improvised structure was constructed and made air tight. On Feb. 8, 1924, Jon died from inhaling cyanide gas.

REF.: Bishop, *Executions; CBA.*

Jones, Adam, d.1837, U.S., rob.-mur. Adam Jones was born in England and after immigrating to Canada, moved to Louisville, Ky. He had been a robber in Canada and he continued his criminal pursuits in Kentucky. He visited the shop of William S. Thomas, a moneylender, in July 1837, and tried to rob Thomas. The moneylender fought and Jones hit him on the head with a club, crushing his skull and killing him. Grabbing some gold coins, Jones fled but was quickly apprehended after he began to spend his stolen money. Jones claimed that he had not intended to murder Thomas, only to rob him. The jury ignored the weak defense, convicted Jones of murder, and he was hanged a short time later.

REF.: *CBA; Confession of Adam Jones.*

Jones, Arthur Albert, prom. 1960, Brit., kid.-rape-mur. Brenda Nash's mother waved goodbye to her daughter the night of Oct. 28, 1960. The 12-year-old was on her way to a Girl Guide meeting at a local church near her home in Heston, Middlesex, England. When she failed to return home that night, 200 officers and fifty bloodhounds began searching for her. The area had been troubled in recent weeks by a rapist who had assaulted another girl a month earlier. The victim had escaped. But Brenda Nash was found dead by three boys playing near the village of Yateley in Hampshire on Dec. 11. The strangled girl was found lying in a field of tall grass, wearing her scout uniform.

The investigation was helped by the statements of Lesley Carruthers, who told West Hampstead police that her coworker, Christine Eldridge, had said an uncle of her's matched the description of the suspect. The uncle, Arthur Albert Jones, was taken in for questioning on Dec. 28. Jones explained that on Sept. 9, the date of the first Heston rape, and on Oct. 28 when Brenda Nash disappeared, he had been visiting his sister-in-law in Beckenham. The police learned that by prior arrangement with Jones and his wife, she had given a false alibi. Jones later said that on the two nights in question he had driven to London's West End looking for prostitutes. One other piece of evidence linked Jones to the September rape against the first Girl Guide. The assailant was seen driving away in a black Vauxhall automobile. A check showed that Jones was driving such a car at the time.

On Mar. 7, 1961, the rape case went before a jury at the Old Bailey. A Guilty verdict was returned and Jones was sentenced to fourteen years in the Wandsworth prison. While serving his sentence, he met an inmate named Roberts. Jones told Roberts he had murdered Brenda Nash, but said he had never been formally charged with the crime. Hearing of this, the director of public prosecutions ordered that Jones be paraded before the original witnesses for identification. Based on their statements, murder charges were filed against Jones. His second trial began at the Old Bailey on June 12, 1961. It took the jury only seven minutes of deliberation to return a verdict of Guilty. Justice Eric Leopold Sachs handed down a sentence of life imprisonment.

REF.: *CBA;* Furneaux, *Famous Criminal Cases, vol. 7;* Jackson, *Occupied With Crime;* Jones, *My Own Case;* Lucas, *The Child Killers;* Simpson, *Forty Years of Murder.*

Jones, Bennie, 1955-   , U.S., rape. Bennie Jones, a security guard from Harvey, Ill., worked at a wire factory on Chicago's West Side. While on duty one day in February 1976, he attacked a 13-year-old girl, raped her, and slashed her throat. She lay in a pool of blood for sixteen hours before being discovered, but she survived. Jones was questioned the day after the attack, denied any knowledge of the crime, and was released. However, the victim identified his picture from her hospital bed, and he was arrested at his mother's house.

Jones was tried in May the following year, before Circuit Court Judge Robert J. Collins. On June 1, 1977, he was found Guilty of rape, attempted murder, and taking indecent liberties with a child, and received concurrent sentences of fifty to a hundred years on each charge. REF.: *CBA.*

Jones, Brant, d.1931, U.S., boot.-mur. A recent college graduate, Brant Jones was unemployed when the Depression set in and searched for new opportunities. In early 1931, Jones organized a small gang of other unemployed college graduates into a bootlegging ring. They obtained weapons and practiced shooting on a farm outside Atlanta, Ga. When they felt they were accomplished gunmen, the gang embarked on a series of hijacking raids, stealing trucks from local Atlanta bootleggers, chiefly those of a local gangster, Vito Ravelli. The college bootleggers, as the gang came to be known, peddled this liquor to local college campuses and to high society homes, earning considerable sums of money. Ravelli, however, learned Jones' identity and, on Aug. 4, 1931, reportedly sent three gunmen to Jones' apartment where the college gangster was seized and taken for the traditional underworld ride. He was never seen again and his gang quickly disbanded. It is presumed that Jones was killed in a remote area and his body secretly buried on a farm outside Atlanta. REF.: *CBA.*

Jones, Catherine, prom. 1720s, Case of, Brit., big. While her husband of six years was away at sea, Catherine Jones married Constantine Boone in the same Mint, Southwark, house where she married her husband, John Rowland. Upon Rowland's return in 1719, she was arrested for bigamy. Indicted Sept. 5, 1719, Catherine said the marriage to Boone was illegal because he was a known hermaphrodite. Boone convinced the jury that the female sex in him was dominant, thus negating his marriage to Catherine Jones and absolving her of bigamy.

REF.: *CBA;* Mitchell, *The Newgate Calendar.*

Jones, Charles, 1875-1954, U.S., suic.- mur. In 1900, Charles Jones worked as a valet to eccentric 84-year-old millionaire William Marsh Rice in New York City. Rice's death, allegedly from an overdose of baked bananas, was only slightly more bizarre than the aftermath. While the household seemed to be in order, the finances and the will of the Rice estate had been left in disarray by lawyer Albert T. Patrick. Rice had intended to bequeath most of his money to found a school in Texas. Patrick and Jones had better plans for the money, methodically bilking the old man during the previous year. Each time Rice issued a check, the two accomplices would destroy it, forge another for that amount, and deposit it in their own account. When a Texas firm complained of not receiving a promised loan of $250,000, the scheme was threatened with exposure. Jones killed Rice with chloroform, after feeding him nine baked bananas.

The Wall Street firm of S.M. Swenson & Sons discovered similarities between the bank accounts of the two perpetrators and those of the deceased. When handwriting experts compared the signatures, Jones and Patrick were arrested for forgery. In jail, Jones attempted suicide by cutting his throat, but failed. Patrick was convicted of murder, served ten years, and was pardoned by New York Governor John Dix. Jones was released when he turned state's evidence against Patrick. But in 1954, when he was seventy-nine, his second suicide attempt was successful. Meanwhile, Rice's fortune, estimated at $10 million, became the foundation of Rice University in Houston. REF.: *CBA*.

Jones, Charles E., prom. 1857, U.S., rob.-mur. Isaac Jackson, a Jewish peddler, was attacked and murdered by Charles E. Jones outside Springfield, Mass., on Dec. 7, 1857. Jones was found a short time later spending Jackson's money and carrying his victim's personal effects. He was quickly tried and condemned but it was clear that Jones, who laughed and sang through his trial, was mentally unhinged. His sentence was commuted to life imprisonment in a lunatic asylum.

REF.: *CBA; The Life and Confessions of Charles E. Jones*.

Jones, Charles F., See: **Patrick, Albert T.**

Jones, Cornelius, 1796-1817, U.S., mur. Cornelius Jones, a 21-year-old youth living with his mother and stepfather in Dyberry, Pa., had planned to kill his stepfather for sometime. He hated Isaac Roswell for marrying his mother after the premature death of his father, and he tried to poison Roswell several times. He slipped opium, then copperas, then precipitate into his stepfather's coffee, gruel, and cider, but none of it worked. Finally, Jones purchased some arsenic and dosed Roswell's cider with it. When Roswell died in agony, physicians became suspicious and found a record of Jones' purchase of the arsenic. The youth broke down when confronted and admitted the murder. He was tried and executed at Bethany, Pa., on Nov. 15, 1817.

REF.: *CBA; A Short Narrative of the Life and Execution of Cornelius Jones*.

Jones, Elizabeth Marina (AKA: Georgina Grayson), See: **Hulten, Karl Gustav.**

Jones, Frank, 1856-93, U.S., west. lawman. Frank Jones became a Texas Ranger at seventeen and quickly proved himself as a lawman. A year later, Jones killed two Mexican horse thieves and arrested another when they ambushed him. In 1880, Jones shot an outlaw and arrested two others, while searching for Scott Cooley, who sparked the 1875 Mason County War. Jones also killed a couple of rustlers in separate barroom incidents, including the notorious Tex Murietta.

Texas Ranger Frank Jones.

In October 1891, Jones and a seven-man posse chased four train robbers in Crockett County, Texas. During a shootout at Howard's Well the posse wounded three of the bandits, while the fourth, John Flint, committed suicide as he was about to be nabbed after an eight mile chase. Jones' last gunfight occurred on June 29, 1893, when he attempted to arrest a Mexican cattle thief, Jesús Maria Olguin and his son, Severio. He and his Ranger posse trailed them across the border to the settlement of Tres Jacales, Mex., where they fired at the two men, wounding them. As the lawmen attempted to enter a building where the two men were hiding, Jones was shot to death by the bandits inside. The Olguins were never prosecuted because the incident occurred on the Mexican side of the Rio Grande. See: **Aten, Ira.**

REF.: Bartholomew, *The Biographical Album of Western Gunfighters; CBA;* Hunter and Rose, *The Album of Gunfighters;* Martin, *Border Boss;* Webb, *The Texas Rangers.*

Jones, Genene, 1951- , U.S., mur. In September 1982, a 15-month-old baby girl mysteriously died in Kerrville, Texas, after a routine examination by a local pediatrician. A powerful muscle relaxer, Anectine, which had not been prescribed, was later found to be the cause of death. Six other children at the clinic had suffered similar attacks in a six-week period, with nurse Genene Jones always nearby. Aiding healthy babies did not offer a great enough challenge, so Jones created "life-and-death" situations. She became euphoric when administering CPR and other life-saving techniques to her victims.

A subsequent investigation in San Antonio uncovered more horrors. When Jones worked the night shift at a local hospital, more than twelve inexplicable deaths had occurred, earning her the name of the "Death Nurse." On Feb. 15, 1984, she was convicted of murder and sentenced to ninety-nine years in prison.

REF.: *CBA;* Fox, *Mass Murder.*

Jones, George, 1811-91, U.S., journalist. A founder of the New York *Times* in 1851, he participated in the campaign against the Tweed Ring in 1871. REF.: *CBA.*

Jones, Harllel, 1940- , U.S., (wrong. convict.) mur. Harllel Jones, of Cleveland, Ohio, was convicted of second-degree murder for the Aug. 7, 1970, shooting death of John H. Smith, and was sentenced to life in prison. A member of the black nationalist organization Afro Set, he was accused of ordering the random shooting in retaliation for the death of a fellow member. His lawyers appealed when they found that the prosecution had withheld evidence.

Jones was implicated by a co-defendant and admitted triggerman who turned FBI informant to avoid first-degree murder charges. In 1977, after Jones had spent five years in prison, Victor Harvey and two other witnesses testified that Jones did not pull the trigger. Jones was released by U.S. District Court Judge Frank J. Battisti pending a new trial. The original prosecutor, John T. Corrigan, vowed to retry the case, but his efforts failed when key witnesses could not be located. Corrigan was forced to recommend dismissal of the case on Oct. 18, 1978, and Jones remained free. REF.: *CBA.*

Jones, Harold, 1906- , Brit., rape-mur. On Feb. 4, 1921, 9-year-old Freda Burnell disappeared in Abertilly, England. She had visited a local seed merchant and did not return. The following day, her body was found near the shop with evidence of strangulation and attempted rape. When her handkerchief was found in a shed adjacent to the seed shop, a 15-year-old employee, Harold Jones, was arrested. He was tried at the Maidstone Assizes and acquitted on June 23.

Weeks after his acquittal, on July 18, 1921, another girl, Florence Irene Little, disappeared. This time the body was found in the attic of the Jones' house. At his trial in November 1921, at the Monmouth Assizes, Jones confessed to both murders. However, because he was not yet sixteen, he was ineligible for the death penalty. He was sentenced to be detained during His Majesty's Pleasure.

REF.: Brock, *A Casebook of Crime;* Calvert, *Capital Punishment in the Twentieth Century; CBA;* Firmin, *Murderers in Our Midst;* Shew, *A Second Companion to Murder;* Wilson, *Children Who Kill.*

Jones, James McHall, 1823-51, U.S., jur. U.S. district attorney from 1850-51. He was appointed to the southern district court of California by President Millard Fillmore in 1850. REF.: *CBA.*

Jones, James Warren (Jim), 1931-78, Guyana, tort.-suic.-mur. Boyhood friends of the Reverend James Jones would recall the times when he held mock funeral services for dead animals in the Indiana town of Lynn, whose cottage industry was casketmaking. "Some of the neighbors would have cats missing and we always thought he was using them for sacrifices," recalled Tootie Morton. Jones, whose father was a drunken Klansman unable to hold a job, became obsessed with religion. At fourteen, the Bible-toting boy delivered his first sermon. In 1949, Jones married Marceline Baldwin, his high school sweetheart.

After dropping out of Indiana University, the couple moved to Indianapolis where they started a Methodist Mission, but the church fathers found his religious pretensions objectionable. He was expelled in 1954 and then raised money by importing monkeys and selling them for $29 each. Jones accumulated $50,000, which was used to purchase a rundown synagogue in a black neighborhood of Indianapolis. During this time he and his wife adopted eight Korean and black children.

The mayor of Indianapolis, impressed with Jones' community work in the impoverished neighborhoods of the city, appointed him director of the Human Rights Commission. But when Jones found Indianapolis too provincial in its racial attitudes, he moved to Belo Horizonte, Braz., after reading that this was the safest spot in the world to survive a nuclear holocaust. The family later relocated to Rio de Janeiro where Jones taught in an American school. Hearing that the People's Temple in Indianapolis, which he had founded in 1957, was in the midst of a leadership crisis, Jones returned home. In 1964, he affiliated his group with the Disciples of Christ and was ordained a minister.

The psychopathic religious fanatic James Warren Jones.

Influenced by the Reverend Ross Case, and half-believing that the world was about to end, Jones led a migration of 100 followers from Indiana to Redwood Valley, in Mendocino County, Calif. The minister purchased a synagogue in the deteriorating Fillmore district of San Francisco. He provided a day-care center and food kitchens for the black inner-city residents, who accounted for 80 percent of the congregation of the People's Temple and won the enthusiastic support of politicians. Governor Jerry Brown was a visitor to the People's Temple. Mayor George Moscone appointed Jones to serve on the city's housing authority as a reward for his political support in the 1975 election. After hearing of the Jonestown horror, Moscone would say, "I proceeded to vomit and cry."

Money began to roll in. Jim Jones purchased Greyhound buses and began traveling around the country accompanied by bodyguards and press aides. At the same time he preached sexual abstinence to his congregation, he surrounded himself with female followers. In 1974, he purchased 27,000 acres of rain forest in Guyana on the northern coast of South America, which he hoped to turn into a socialist utopia for himself and his followers. Despite warm endorsements from top Democratic leaders like Henry "Scoop" Jackson, Walter Mondale, and Jimmy Carter, whom Jones supported for president in 1976, he became obsessed with the notion of mass suicide as a way of escaping governmental persecution, a fascination with suicide dating to 1953 when Ethel and Julius Rosenberg were executed in the U.S. as spies. By 1976, Jones was indoctrinating his followers in the concept of a "White Night," a mass suicide ritual that was being "rehearsed" at his People's Temple.

The first clue the public had about Jones' hidden agenda and the secret cult activities occurred at an anti-suicide rally held at the Golden Gate Bridge on Memorial Day 1977. Speaking before hundreds of spectators, Jones called for the construction of an anti-suicide barrier to be constructed on the bridge. Dr. Richard Seiden, professor of behavioral science at the University of California, later recalled how the direction of Jones' speech changed. His condemnation of suicide became almost a blanket endorsement for it. "He saw himself as the victim, persecuted and attacked, and from there proceeded to the concept of suicide as an appropriate response. We were not aware of the nuances and implications," Dr. Seiden said.

Membership in the People's Temple swelled to nearly 20,000, and his services became increasingly bizarre. He claimed to have the power of faith healing, and would draw out the "cancer" from the sufferer during ceremonies—the cancer actually a bloody chicken gizzard. No longer content to be the reincarnation of Jesus, Jones began calling himself God. With the help of local authorities in Guyana and private contributions from his followers, he began clearing large sections of jungle in 1977. That year, the religious colony of Jonestown was founded and about 1,000 members made their exodus from San Francisco to the jungle retreat.

Jones enforced his will through physical and mental coercion. The San Francisco *Examiner* reported in August 1977 that members were publicly flogged for minor infractions like smoking and falling asleep during religious sermons. Electrodes were attached to children who were ordered to smile at the mention of the leader's name. These reports began filtering back to California congressman Leo Ryan, fifty-three, who pressured the U.S. State Department to investigate. A delegation from the U.S. embassy in Georgetown interviewed seventy-five members of the cult, but none indicated a desire to leave. Ryan was not convinced. His friend, Robert Houston of the Associated Press, had lost a son to the cult. The young man had been murdered in San Francisco after attempting to quit the People's Temple. Ryan embarked on a fact-finding mission on Nov. 14, 1978, accompanied by eight journalists and several relatives of Jonestown cultists.

They were greeted by the congenial Jones, who led a guided tour through the compound, proudly showing off the spacious library, hospital, and living quarters. That night Congressman Ryan and his party were entertained at the pavilion. Even Ryan was impressed. He arose from his chair and said, "From what I have seen, there are a lot of people here who think this is the best thing that has happened in their whole lives." Jones led the thunderous applause.

The bodies of Jones' deluded parishioners in Guyana, after being forced into mass suicide, 1978.

The next day NBC reporter Don Harris asked Jones about his military arsenal and if it were true that the compound was under heavy guard. Jones exploded in rage. "A bold-faced lie!" he screamed. One of the cultists slipped a note to Ryan which read "Four of us want to leave." There were other similar requests. While Ryan spoke with Jones about moving these people out, a cultist named Don Sly attacked him with a knife but was subdued by attorney Charles Garry. Ryan and his entourage departed for the airfield at Port Kaituma and an awaiting Cessna. As they deliberated about the best way to squeeze the extra passengers into the tiny craft, a flatbed truck rumbled by. Three armed men standing in the trailer suddenly opened fire. From inside the plane, Larry Layton produced a gun and began shooting. The crossfire left five persons dead—Congressman Ryan, photographer Greg Robinson, NBC cameraman Bob Brown, Don Harris, and one of the departing cultists, Patricia Park.

While Ryan and his entourage were being fired upon, Jones was preparing to order his followers carry out "revolutionary suicide" at the compound. The brainwashed followers, who had rehearsed this scenario dozens of times, were herded into the main pavilion where they received purple Kool-Aid laced with cyanide. Mothers gave cyanide voluntarily to their children. Infants received the substance with a syringe squirting it into their mouths. Next came the older children who received it in paper cups, and finally the adults who accepted the poison as a loudspeaker intoned, "We're going to meet again in another place!" Those who refused to accept this fate were prodded by heavily armed guards. Within five minutes, most of the 913 victims were dead. Not since the Japanese citizens of Saipan hurled themselves from the rocky cliffs of the island in WWII had the world witnessed anything like this.

Jones, like Adolph Hitler years earlier, killed himself with a bullet to the head. No eyewitnesses survived. Investigators found rows of bodies, most of them lying face down. The U.S. Air Force sent planes to retrieve the remains of the victims while experts in human behavior and sociology grappled with larger issues. "Most members have little or no sense of inner value," theorized Stefan Pasternack, associate clinical professor of psychiatry at Georgetown University. "In joining (Jones) they regress and relax their personal judgments to the point that they are supplanted by the group's often primitive feelings. With a sick leader these primitive feelings are intensified and get worse."

One person went to trial for complicity in the Jonestown Massacre. Thirty-five-year old ex-Quaker Layton, a member of Jones' death squad, was charged with injuring U.S. diplomat Richard Dwyer and conspiracy to kill Congressman Ryan. The jury in the San Francisco courtroom was unable to agree on a verdict. The courtroom was packed with relatives of the victims when, on Sept. 23, 1981, a mistrial was declared by Judge Robert Peckham.

REF.: *CBA*; Fox, *Mass Murder*; Kearns and Wead, *People's Temple, People's Tomb*; Kilduff and Javers, *The Suicide Cult*; Krause, *Guyana Massacre*; Lane, *The Strongest Poison*; Reston, *Our Fathers Who Art in Hell*; Wilson, *Encyclopedia of Modern Murder*; Wooden, *The Children of Jonestown*; Yee, *In My Father's House*; (FILM), *Guyana, Cult of the Damned*, 1980; *Doomed to Die*, 1985; *Inferno in Diretta*, 1985.

Jones, Jeremiah, 1913- , Brit., mur. As a youngster, Jeremiah Jones, the son of a London chambermaid, had a violent and unpredictable nature. At only six years old, he was a truant, a delinquent, and a thief. In June 1920, at age seven, he was playing with two younger boys when one refused to give him a toy. He pushed the child into a canal, stoned him, and stepped on his fingers until he drowned. When accused, he testified that the boy had fallen, and the death was ruled accidental.

He soon began to have wild outbursts. When interviewed by child psychiatrist Cyril Burt, Jones admitted to the murder. The other boy agreed, saying that he had remained silent because Jones threatened him. Jones was sent to a series of homes, where his temper remained violent and he developed an intense fear of water. At age nine, he began to show signs of stability. It is unknown what happened to him in his adult life.

REF.: *CBA*; Wilson, *Children Who Kill*.

Jones, John, prom. 1842, Brit., mur. John Jones was tried and convicted of murdering his girlfriend and was scheduled to die by public execution in 1842 in Nottingham, England. However, there was a great debate surrounding the practice of this public display. The Society for the Abolition of Capital Punishment argued passionately before a Royal Commission about the futility of execution and its pervasive danger.

By the time his execution day arrived, Jones was lauded as an exemplary prisoner, praised by the local chaplain, and fawned over by the Nottingham ladies. But despite all the fanfare, Jones was executed publicly.

REF.: *CBA*; Cooper, *Lesson of the Scaffold*; Mitchell, *The Newgate Calendar*.

Jones, John, d.1879, U.S., west. outl. Born in Iowa, John Jones moved to New Mexico in 1866, and became embroiled in the Lincoln County War a decade later. The Jones family drifted to several different ranch sites, selling at one time to the infamous Horrell brothers, who were fleeing justice in Texas. In 1878, Jones became a cattle rustler with the Murphy-Dolan Gang. During a gunfight, he killed Bob Riley and avoided prosecution in the unruly Lincoln County.

On July 15, 1878, at the climactic battle of the bloody war, Jones and forty others attacked the store owned by Alexander McSween, the leader of the opposing group. After setting the store on fire, Jones and his men systematically slaughtered McSween, Harvey Morris, Vincent Romero, and Francisco Zamora as they fled the burning building. Tom O'Folliard and Hijino Salazar were also shot, but survived. On Aug. 26, 1879, at Seven Rivers, N.M., Jones shot John Beckwith to death following an argument over the ownership of cattle. Jones was pursued by lawmen Bob Olinger and Milo Pierce, who caught up with him a month later in Lincoln County. Jones angrily demanded a settlement to the rumors that he had killed Beckwith, cocking his rifle and firing a shot toward Olinger. The lawman responded with three shots which fatally wounded John Jones. See: **Lincoln County War.**

REF.: Ball, *Ma'am Jones of the Pecos*; *CBA*; Fulton, *Lincoln County War*; Hunt, *Tragic Days of Billy the Kid*; Keleher, *Violence in Lincoln County*; Klasner, *My Girlhood Among Outlaws*.

Jones, John B., 1834-81, U.S., west. lawman. Born in South Carolina on Dec. 22, 1834, John B. Jones was four when his family resettled in Travis County, Texas. Jones attended Baylor College and Zion College in Winnsboro, S.C. After serving in the Confederate Army in the Civil War, Jones was elected to the Texas legislature in 1868. He was then commissioned a major in the Frontier Battalion of the Texas Rangers and he became one of the leading law enforcement administrators in Texas, commanding six companies of Rangers and sending them across thousands of miles to battle outlaws and Indians. He often accompanied his men in various sweeps when dozens of desperate fugitives were captured. Jones was

John B. Jones, Texas Ranger.

involved with a number of gun battles with outlaw bands and he was responsible for bringing the bloody Horrell-Higgins Feud to an end. Jones died in Austin, Texas, on June 19, 1881. See: **Horrell-Higgins Feud.**

REF.: Bartholomew, *The Biographical Album of Western Gunfighters*; *CBA*; Webb, *The Texas Rangers*.

Jones, John Gale, See: **Burdett, Sir Francis.**
Jones, Mary, See: **Diver, Jenny.**
Jones, Mary, prom. 1771, Brit., theft. Mary Jones, a happily married woman with two children, lived on Red Lion Street in

Whitechapel, England. Her life was disrupted in 1771 when a gang seized her husband and forced him off to sea. The 19-year-old woman was left penniless, with two starving children. Their clothes were reduced to rags. Her desperation led her to steal four pieces of muslin, valued at slightly over £5, from a draper's shop in Ludgate.

Larceny of all sorts had been rampant throughout the country-side. Two hundred persons had been tried during the last Sessions, so sterner punishments were recommended. Jones was brought before two judges and a jury at the Old Bailey, on the charge of stealing. She was sentenced to death by hanging. When the realization of her sentence set in, she cursed the court with such intensity that she had to be dragged from the dock. A judge later said she might have been spared but for the outburst.

A petition drive was mounted to spare her life but the effort proved futile. On Oct. 16, 1771, Jones was led from Newgate Prison to the gallows in Tyburn. In her final moments she cradled one of her children before a silent crowd. The child was then taken from her arms, and she was hanged.

REF.: Bleackley, *Hangmen of England*; *CBA*; O'Donnell, *Should Women Hang?*; Potter, *The Art of Hanging*.

Jones, Mary, 1884-1947, U.S., kid. Austrian-born Mary Jones became the primary suspect in the kidnapping on Mar. 29, 1925, of 3-year-old Raimondc von Maluski because of her known hat-red of the victim's family. Also, Jones was observed riding around the New York City neighborhood where the family lived several days before the child was abducted. Jones' husband, Harold Jones had worked with von Maluski in maintaining the building where the von Maluskis lived. Mary Jones' antipathy for von Maluski dated to when she turned her husband in for a parole violation and she subsequently visited the von Maluski residence to collect his belongings. After this visit, von Maluski accused her of stealing a diamond stickpin and $10 in cash.

Angered by the accusations, Jones tried to hire three hoodlums from the Bowery to kill him for $100. Police hypothesized that when the men refused, Mary Jones decided to take her revenge by kidnapping the child and taking him to a secluded area, where she killed him and buried his body. Though during her trial she allegedly confided to another inmate that the von Maluski child "was dead and that's the end of it" she never acknowledged her guilt in court. Regardless, she was found Guilty and sentenced to twenty-five to forty years in Auburn Prison. Raimonde von Maluski was never found.

REF.: *CBA*; Nash, *Look For the Woman*.

Jones, Michael, and **Lovett, George**, d.1834, U.S., mur. A nomadic thief, Michael Jones had an uncontrollable temper. He and fellow thief George Lovett got into an argument with John Tandy in Louisville, Ky. When Tandy ordered the pair to leave his premises, Jones went outside, picked up a large rock, and attacked Tandy with it as Lovett held the victim down. Jones crushed Tandy's head and then he and Lovett looted the Tandy house. They were later apprehended and freely admitted the crime. After a speedy trial, both were hanged in Louisville on Aug. 1, 1834. Jones, before he was hanged, donated his body to medical research, leaving his corpse to a Dr. Donne because of "an amiable feeling to Mr. Charles Donne," the physician's brother and one of Jones' drinking companions.

REF.: *CBA*; *The Last Dying Confessions and Remains of Michael Jones*.

Jones, Moll, 1666-91, Brit., rob. When Moll Jones' husband spent the couple into poverty, she was reduced to picking pockets. She was arrested twice for theft and had her hand burned on both occasions. But she exacted revenge on the second man who had her arrested, Constable Smith.

A rogue she hired to pose as a servant of Smith's "late" uncle convinced Smith that the uncle had left him a fortune. Smith and the impostor traveled in luxury to the allegedly deceased uncle's hometown, where the rogue abandoned him. The constable, who had bragged of his impending wealth, returned empty-handed and became the laughing stock of the neighborhood. Moll Jones'

revenge was short-lived, however. Disguised as the Duchess of Norfolk, she was caught stealing a piece of satin. Moll Jones was hanged at Tyburn on Dec. 18, 1691.

REF.: *CBA*; Smith, *Highwaymen*.

Jones, Nathaniel Raphael, 1926- , U.S., jur. Assistant U.S. attorney from 1961-67, and general counsel of the National Association for the Advancement of Colored People from 1969-79. He was appointed to the sixth circuit court by President Jimmy Carter in 1979. REF.: *CBA*.

Jones, Noel, 1900- , U.S., law enfor. off. Noel Jones served the Indianapolis Police Department well for nearly forty years. He entered the force as a probationary patrolman in October 1928, and retired in early 1967, after having served as Chief of Police for three years. He had risen through the ranks from First Grade Patrolman to Sergeant, and to the rank of Lieutenant in 1945. At this rank, he received four commendations in the late 1940s for outstanding police work.

In September 1946, he arrested two robbery suspects. In January 1947, he arrested three soldiers who had burglarized City Market, and in November, apprehended the suspects on charges of kidnapping and rape. In 1949, he was commended for gathering information that led to the arrests of a gang of holdup men. Jones rose to thc rank of Captain in 1952 and a year later to Inspector of Detectives where he remained until Jan. 7, 1964, when he was named Chief of Police. REF.: *CBA*.

Jones, Peter, prom. 1950s, U.S., rob.-mur. In the late 1950s the body of an expensively dressed man was found in a gutter near Elysian Park, Calif. The victim had been shot once behind the left ear and bore no identification except a book of matches from a hotel. At the hotel, the dead man was identified as a Colombian importer. Investigators traced his movements to cab driver Peter Jones, thrity-three, who admitted driving the victim to several night clubs. When Jones' responses under questioning became inaccurate and contradictory, officers suggested a lie detector test and Jones agreed. The polygraph unit used at that time in Los Angeles was the Stoetling Deceptograph, which measured physiological changes in the body, based on the assump-tion that these changes occur when a person lies. An ancient Chinese version of the lie detector test had suspects chew a handful of raw rice, which was then collected. If the rice remained dry, it was thought that fear of discovery had obstructed the flow of saliva. Lie detectors, which are still not accepted in court as definitive evidence, are subject to human interpretation and show a margin of error of up to twenty percent. In Jones' case, the polygraph indicated that the suspect had given false answers twice, and that his alibi was false as well. Detectives searched Jones' house and found the murder weapon and $140 stolen from the victim's wallet. Jones confessed and was sentenced to life imprisonment.

REF.: *CBA*; McGrady, *Crime Scientists*.

Jones, Reginal, d.1982, U.S., mur. A sniper in River Rouge, Mich., killed two people and wounded four on July, 18, 1982. The gunman, Reginal Jones, was killed by police when they returned fire. He had begun shooting randomly with a 30-caliber rife from the porch of his second-story apartment. He killed Desiree Burton, a 15-year-old girl, and Mabel Arrington, an elderly woman who was sitting on her porch. Four others, including a River Rouge policeman, were wounded. REF.: *CBA*.

Jones, Rex Harvey, prom. 1950s, Brit., mur. Rex Harvey Jones, a miner in the Rhondda Valley of rural Wales, was a man of exemplary character. But after drinking seven pints of beer with his 20-year-old girlfriend, he strangled her. He then called the police and led them to her body. During his trial, the judge told the jury, "You have to steel your hearts against good charac-ter and steel your hearts in order to see that justice is done." Despite this admonishment, the jury made a strong recommenda-tion for mercy. But the judge was adamant, and Jones was hanged.

REF.: *CBA*; Hibbert, *The Roots of Evil*.

Jones, Roger Lee, 1945- , U.S., child abuse-rape-fugitive. Roger Jones, a former car salesman, was accused of child molestation following the sexual assault of three children. He endeared himself to neighborhood kids and gradually enticed them to higher levels of sexual contact. He then videotaped the scenes.

Jones was known to frequent adult bookstores and topless bars. To avoid arrest, he altered his appearance and changed automobiles often. He was last seen in Tampa, Fla., and is still at large. REF.: *CBA*.

Jones, Samuel Milton (AKA: Golden Rule Jones), 1846-1904, U.S., crim. just. A scrupulously ethical industrialist who served as mayor of Toledo, Ohio, from 1897-1904. He spearheaded campaigns against political corruption and fraud. REF.: *CBA*.

Jones, Thomas, d.1824, U.S., mut.-mur. Captain Samuel Brown of the brig, *Holkar*, sailed from New York in 1818 with an all-black crew, heading for the West Indies. After picking up cargo, the ship was returning to New York, but near Curacao one of the black seaman, Thomas Jones, led a mutiny. Captain Brown, his white mate, and a white passenger were killed with knives, harpoons, and a crowbar. Their bodies were tossed overboard. The ship then sailed to Santo Domingo where the cargo was sold and the ship scuttled. One of the crewmen was later convicted of another crime six years after the disappearance of the *Holkar*. To avoid a death sentence, he told the governor of New York he would solve the riddle of the missing *Holkar*, but only if he were given a pardon. The pardon was issued and the crewman testified that Jones led the mutiny. Jones, who had returned to New York, was quickly apprehended and convicted. He was hanged on June 11, 1824, in a public execution before thousands of spectators.

REF.: *CBA; Life, Trial, and Confession of Thomas Jones*.

Jones, Tom, c.1672-1702, Brit., rape-mur. Tom Jones stole £80 and a horse from his parents shortly before his twenty-second birthday. Thereafter, he made his way as a highwayman, robbing whomever crossed his path.

Jones found one such victim, Mr. Storey, relieving himself in the woods. After initially refusing to surrender his money, Storey said, "Truly, I'm brimful, therefore take care what you do sir, for if you stir me but ever so little, I shall run all over." "Don't tell me," Jones replied, "of your being brimful of liquor, are you brimful of money, for 'tis money I want." No sooner had Tom Jones uttered these words than Storey urinated in his face. Ever the professional, Mr. Jones cleaned himself off and robbed Storey of £6. On Apr. 25, 1702, Jones was hanged at Launceston for robbing and raping a farmer's wife in Cornwall.

REF.: Brock, *A Casebook of Crime; CBA;* Mitchell, *The Newgate Calendar;* Smith, *Highwaymen*.

Jones, Wesley Livsey, 1863-1932, U.S., lawyer. Held office as U.S. congressman from 1899-1909, and as U.S. senator from 1909-32. He wrote the Jones Act of 1929, which called for more severe penalties for violators of the Volstead Act. REF.: *CBA*.

Jones, Will (AKA: Will Goodwin), 1667-93, Brit., rob. Will Jones was a spoiled young man who once shot a school master through a keyhole. Before he turned twenty, Jones inherited a large estate from his grandfather and married.

Jones soon became bored and turned to whoring. One night, during a drunken quarrel, Jones stabbed a man to death. He became a highwayman to maintain his extravagant lifestyle. Ultimately, Jones was arrested for robbery and committed to Newgate. At the age of twenty-six, on July 26, 1693, Jones was hanged at Tyburn.

REF.: *CBA;* Smith, *Highwaymen*.

Jones, William (AKA: Canada Bill), d.1877, U.S., fraud. One of the great gambling legends of the old Mississippi riverboats, William "Canada Bill" Jones' specialty was cheating suckers with three card monte. Born in England, Jones migrated with his family to Canada and became an accomplished card cheat at an early age, studying the techniques of a con man Dick Cady. For years, Jones traveled across Canada, fleecing suckers with three card monte, losing only when he wished to convince gullible players that they could win. He employed the bent card routine in being able to pick the correct card. (Three card monte was a game where three cards, two aces and a queen, were dealt face

down. The sucker would then be told to point to the queen in order to win the bet. It appeared easy, and they were permitted to win several hands before Jones so dazzled and confused the suckers that he invariably won the escalating stakes.)

By 1850, Canada Bill Jones was known throughout Canada, and with his game played out, he moved south and began to ply his tricky trade on the Mississippi riverboats. He met another talented sharper, George Devol, and formed a partnership with him, occasionally using other card cheats to back his crooked play. Jones' favorite ruse was to pretend to be a country bumpkin who attempted to outwit his patrons but who acted in such a bumbling, idiotic manner that the sucker was easily convinced that *he* could take advantage of Jones. As a card sharp, few could rival the dexterity and delivery of Canada Bill but as an actor, he had no equal in the world of cheating.

Canada Bill Jones, confidence man, 1875.

George Devol described him thusly: "Imagine a medium-sized, chicken-headed, tow-haired sort of a man, with mild blue eyes, and a mouth nearly from ear to ear, who walked with a shuffling, half-apologetic sort of a gait, and who, when his countenance was in repose, resembled an idiot. His clothes were always several sizes too large, and his face was as smooth as a woman's and never had a hair on it.

"Canada Bill was a slick one. He had a squeaking, boyish voice, and awkward gawky manners, and a way of asking fool questions and putting on a good-natured sort of a grin, that led everybody to believe that he was the rankest kind of sucker—the greenest sort of a jake. Woe to the man who picked him up, though. Canada was, under all his hypocritical appearance, a regular card shark, and could turn monte with the best of them."

Jones and Devol suckered thousands of riverboat gamblers and passengers through the 1850s, but following the Civil War the river trade diminished and the sky-high gamblers and plungers vanished. Canada Bill was not without flaws. He was himself an inveterate gambler, one who insatiably sought action, no matter the risk. This was never better demonstrated than on the occasion when Devol found Jones in a Natchez gambling den, playing faro.

Devol walked up to his partner and said in a startled voice: "Bill, you here! What's the matter with you? Of all people—you know this faro game is fixed, it's always been fixed! You can't win!"

"I know, I know," replied Canada Bill, as he delivered the classic gambler's lament, "but it's the only game in town."

Canada Bill dressed as a country bumpkin.

The partnership between Jones and Devol dissolved when Canada Bill discovered that Devol was trying to swindle him out of his share of their mutually pooled funds. Taking his enormous earnings, Jones left for Kansas City and there he teamed up with another sharper named Dutch Charley. The pair roped a group of wealthy Kansas City bankers into an investment swindle and realized more than $200,000 before the city big shots learned they had been suckered. By then Canada Bill was long gone from the city, relocating in Omaha. He then took to riding the trains between Omaha and Kansas City, fleecing anyone foolish enough to play three card monte with him. For fifteen years he rode the rails, gleaning a fortune.

Officials of the Union Pacific heard of this one-man confidence plague and they ordered train detectives to eject anyone playing three card monte on their trains. Canada Bill was incensed when he heard this edict and he wrote to the president of the line, complaining how unfair the new rule was. He then offered to pay the Union Pacific $10,000 a year, plus an annual percentage of his take, if he were allowed to have an exclusive franchise of playing three card monte on its trains. Moreover, he promised that he would only swindle wealthy passengers and Methodist ministers. The railroad authorities declined Canada Bill's offer, generous though it was.

Canada Bill fleecing suckers in three-card monte on a Mississippi riverboat.

Railroad officials had posters of Canada Bill plastered on the walls of its trains. Every conductor and railroad detective knew him and looked for him. Though he disguised himself, Jones was repeatedly recognized and thrown off the Union Pacific cars. He finally quit the railroads in 1874 and moved to Chicago where, with gamblers Charles Starr and Jimmy Porter, Jones established four huge gambling dens in the Levee or the Red Light District (Chicago's First Ward). Within six months, Jones had taken in more than $150,000 but he lost almost every dime in crooked casino games and he moved on to Cleveland. Here he was known and shunned, too infamous to convince anyone that he was anyone other than the celebrated Canada Bill. In 1877, Jones appeared in Reading, Pa., where he grew ill. He was taken to the Charity Hospital where he died broke in 1877.

Dozens of gamblers, including Devol, attended Canada Bill's funeral. One sharper bet $100 that "Bill is not in the box," but no one took this jesting wager to heart. Another stepped up and delivered the gambler's eulogy:

> O, when I die, just bury me
> In a box-back coat and hat
> Put a $20 gold piece on my watch chain
> To let the Lord know I'm standing pat.

See: **Devol, George.**

REF.: Asbury, *Sucker's Progress*; Bushick, *Glamorous Days*; *CBA*; Chafetz, *Play the Devil*; Devol, *Forty Years a Gambler on the Mississippi*; Hamilton, *Men of the Underworld*; Nash, *Bloodletters and Badmen*; _____, *Hustlers and Con Men*; Pinkerton, *Criminal Reminiscences*; Robertson, *Soapy Smith, King of the Frontier Con Men*; Stanton, *When the Wildwood Was in Flower*.

Jones, William Blakely, 1907-79, U.S., jur. Special assistant to Montana's attorney general from 1935-37, and attorney for Department of Justice from 1937-43. He was appointed to the district court of Washington, D.C., by President John F. Kennedy in 1962. REF.: *CBA*.

Jones, Willie, 1952-77, U.S., Case of, suic.-mur. Shortly after noon, on Apr. 14, 1977, four people were killed by gunfire, in a home on South Colfax Avenue in Chicago. The shootings ended the turbulent marriage of Willie and Rena Radcliff Jones. Twice, Willie Jones had threatened to kill the couple's three young children. He was stopped short of throwing one child in frigid Lake Michigan, and once threw a plugged-in TV set into their bath water. On Apr. 14, during another domestic feud, Willie fired twelve shots, the last one killing himself. Also killed were, Rena Radcliff Jones; Anthony Radcliff, her brother; and Larry Williams, her teenaged nephew.

Other family members descended on the house and fought with police. George Williams, Larry's brother, was arrested and charged with battery when he punched a female police officer in the face. Two more officers were treated at a local hospital and released. REF.: *CBA*.

Jones, Willie Lee, b.1952, U.S., kid.-mur. In 1977, Willie Lee Jones was charged with the abduction and murder of three men in Prince George's County, Md. Judge Jacob Levin's sentences were harsh. Jones was sentenced to three terms of life imprisonment on three counts of first-degree murder, one hundred and twenty years' imprisonment on four counts of kidnapping, and an additional sixty years on four counts of using a handgun in connection with the murders.

REF.: *CBA*; Godwin, *Murder U.S.A.*

Jones Brothers, d.1900, U.S., west. outl. John and Jim Jones were raised in Dallas County, Mo., and both young men, originally farmers, became outlaws in 1892. They moved to Texas where they reportedly killed the sheriff of Hamilton County. The Jones Brothers then fled to Colorado, where they robbed stagecoaches and small banks. The brothers robbed a Union Pacific train near Hugo, Colo., on Aug. 11, 1900, taking a small amount of money from the baggage car. A large posse pursued the Jones Brothers for hundreds of miles and finally cornered them in a small ranch house. The lawmen and outlaws exchanged fire for several days until officers set fire to the building. Jim Jones, rather than surrender, shot himself inside the burning building. His brother,

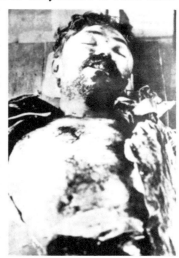

Outlaw John Jones, dead, 1900.

John, leaped through the front door, two six-guns blazing. He was riddled by rifle fire and fell dead.

REF.: Bartholomew, *The Biographical Album of Western Gunfighters*; *CBA*; Hunter and Rose, *The Album of Gunfighters*.

Jonestown Massacre, See: **Jones, James Warren.**

Joniaux, Marie Thérèse, b.1844, Belg., mur. Marie Joniaux's father, General Jules Ablay, was a cavalry officer and aid-de-camp to King Leopold II. Her mother ruled Brussels' high society. When Marie entered the Belgian Court in 1864, her beauty and grace were already legendary. But the family was poor. They accrued a mountain of debts. When confronted for payment, Marie threw an impressive twelve-course banquet, and offered the creditors a deal. If they would extend a little more credit, she would find a proper suitor, marry him, and repay all debts with interest in six months. She did find a man, Frederick Faber, and married him. But Faber didn't have a cent. Astonishingly, the couple avoided debts and lived in great style until 1884, when Faber died of heart disease.

Again, Marie set out to find a rich husband, and again she found a poor one: Henry Joniaux. The couple's debts exceeded 200,000 francs, so they fled to Antwerp. The merchants there were not as tolerant and, now past fifty and a little plump, Marie could not charm them. In despair she sought her sister's comfort. But she didn't tell her sister she had a 70,000 franc insurance policy on her life. Her sister turned up dead one morning, and after a suitable showing of grief, Marie Joniaux turned up at the door of the Gresham Insurance Company. With check in hand, she set her sights on a wealthy uncle, Jacques Vandenkerchove.

Hoping to be included in the rich man's will, she hired a blue-ribbon chef to prepare a magnificent meal. But Jacques died of cerebral congestion the night after the extravagant meal and naturally Marie was not included in his will. As the debts piled even higher, she turned to her brother, Alfred Ablay, the family scamp, and insured his life for 100,000 francs. When he died of cerebral hemorrhage a week later, the Gresham Insurance Company was suspicious. They refused to pay the policy, and medical examiners were ordered to exhume the three bodies.

On Apr. 18, 1894, detectives visited Marie Joniaux, and returned almost daily for nine months. Small amounts of morphine and atropine were found in the house, but she had excuses and the undertakers were sure the three victims had died of natural causes. But the authorities cited Marie's lifetime of financial problems, and the coincidental nature of the three deaths created doubt. When a judge warned that anyone could be her next victim, a jury quickly convicted her and sentenced her to death. A final intervention by Leopold II spared her, but she was sentenced to life imprisonment.

REF.: *CBA;* Kobler, *Some Like it Gory;* Williamson, *Annals of Crime;* Wyndham, *Crime on the Continent.*

Jordan, Chester, d.1912, U.S., mur. Chester Jordan and his wife Honora Jordan were actors in Boston in 1908. One day in September, he bought a pair of shears, a hacksaw, and a knife. A few days later, he was seen around town carrying a trunk that was unusually heavy for its size. A hackman reported this to police officers Irving Peabody and Michael Crowley. Two officers went to the Jordan home to investigate. Jordan showed the men the trunk, which held a few light articles of clothing. However, it also emitted a powerful stench, and when asked what was at the bottom, Jordan confessed that it was the torso of his wife. He had struck and pushed her down a flight of stairs. After she died he dissected her, and tried to burn her head and legs. He was arraigned on murder charges on Sept. 3, 1908.

With the help of his brother-in-law, famous stock-market plunger Jesse Livermore, Jordan raised money for his defense. The trial began Apr. 20, 1909, in the Superior Court of Middlesex County in East Cambridge, before Justices William B. Stevens and Charles U. Bell. The prosecution paraded witnesses, including police officers, medical experts, neighbors, a cab driver, and Jordan's landlady. Particularly gruesome was the exhibition of the late Mrs. Jordan's skull, tongue, and larynx, all carefully preserved in formaldehyde. The defense countered that Jordan was not mentally fit due to suffering from cerebro-spinal syphilis during early manhood. His family agreed, adding their versions of various emotional traumas. The jury was not dissuaded and handed down a Guilty verdict on May 4, 1909.

However, four days later, the jury foreman, Willis A. White, was committed to an insane asylum. The defense appealed the conviction, but the motion was rejected by Justices Stevens and Bell, A further appeal to the Massachusetts Supreme Court was also rejected. On Mar. 12, 1911, with appeal attempts exhausted, Jordan was sentenced to death by execution. The appeal was taken to the U.S. Supreme Court, where it was denied on May 27, 1912. On Sept. 24, 1912, Jordan was electrocuted in Massachusetts.

REF.: *CBA;* Rodell, *Boston Murders.*

Jordan, Clayton, 1970- , U.S., mur. On Jan. 9, 1988, Taneka Jones, an 11-year-old girl, was sexually molested and murdered in her home in unincorporated Du Page County, Ill. Her mother found her in a basement storage room the following afternoon. A 10-year-old upstairs neighbor provided testimony which implicated three men: Clayton Jordan, John Kines, and Saul Berry. Jordan was prosecuted in Du Page County Circuit Court before Judge John Bowman.

Jordan had been sentenced earlier to five years on battery charges and was free on bail. He was convicted of the murder and assault of Taneka Jones, and sentenced to eighty years for murder, and to concurrent terms of thirty years for aggravated criminal sexual assault, five years for intimidation of a witness, and five years for concealment of a homicide. He was ordered to serve out the earlier battery sentence before beginning the murder sentence. Berry received a 70-year sentence and Kines fifty years. REF.: *CBA.*

Jordan, Frank M., 1935- , U.S., law enfor. off. Frank Jordan entered the San Francisco Police Department as a 22-year-old recruit, and rose through the ranks to become Chief of Police.

During his police work, Jordan attained a degree in Government from the University of San Francisco, and a Lifetime Teaching Credential in Police Science at the California Community College. He was twice named Police Officer of the Year, first by the Optimists Club in 1981, and later by the San Francisco Chamber of Commerce in 1984. He worked in the California Crime Prevention Officers Association, the California Crime Resistance Task

San Francisco police chief Frank M. Jordan.

Force, and the Widows and Orphans Aid Association. From 1977 until 1980, Jordan was a guest speaker at the FBI National Academy in Virginia. REF.: *CBA.*

Jordan, Gilbert Paul, 1932- , Can., mansl. On Oct. 12, 1987, Vancouver, Can., police found 27-year-old Vanessa Lee Buckner dead in her hotel room. Before her death, she had consumed an enormous amount of liquor. Her blood alcohol reading was .91—more than eleven times the amount necessary to be deemed legally drunk. At first, the death was ruled accidental, but on Nov. 26, Gilbert Paul Jordan, the man who reported finding the body, was charged with murder.

During opening remarks on Oct. 5, 1988, Prosecuting Attorney Sandra Watson sought to prove that eight other women had died under similar circumstances after being with Jordan. Witnesses testified that Buckner rarely drank, and Watson produced evidence of at least four other murders, including two in Jordan's barbershop. Beginning in 1984, one survivor stated that Jordan tried to empty a bottle down her throat, but she escaped. On Oct. 16, Watson introduced Jordan's diary as evidence. Jordan, realizing that the five women had died while in his company, admitted buying the liquor to get them drunk. After sexual intercourse, he asked them to leave. Jordan conceded that his actions were aberrant, but he claimed that each death came as a surprise. Jordan was found Guilty of manslaughter in the death of Buckner, and was sentenced to fifteen years. REF.: *CBA.*

Jordan, Theodore, prom. 1932, U.S., (wrong. convict.) mur. In 1932, Theodore Jordan was convicted of the murder of F.T. Swift in Klamath Falls, Ore., and sentenced to hang. There was evidence that Jordan's confession had been coerced during a beating following his arrest. Following a public outcry, his sentence was reduced to life imprisonment. He served twenty-two years and was paroled in 1954.

In 1964, Jordan was arrested for shoplifting in Portland. He left the state in violation of his parole, and was sentenced to three years to be served concurrently with the original life sentence, which was again in effect. He appealed the original murder sentence, and it was reversed in 1964. However, he remained Guilty of shoplifting. REF.: *CBA*.

Jordan, Thomas, 1860-1909, U.S., mur. Anton Nolting was a well-educated and popular patrol sergeant when he reported for duty on Jan. 8, 1909, in San Francisco. Shortly after 1 a.m., he heard a shot, and ran to see a soldier with a drawn pistol forcing two other soldiers down the street. When Nolting confronted them, the two hostages were able to flee, leaving the officer to grapple with the assailant. A shot was fired, wounding the officer, and three more were fired, killing him as he lay on the ground. The assailant, Thomas Jordan, was quickly apprehended.

Jordan testified that he was a member of the Coastal Artillery stationed at Fort Baker, but that his mind was a complete blank regarding the shooting of Sergeant Nolting. Hiram Johnson was hired as special prosecutor, and on Mar. 12, 1909, Jordan was found Guilty of murder and sentenced to life imprisonment.

REF.: *CBA; Duke, Celebrated Criminal Cases of America.*

Jordan, Vernon, Jr., 1935- , U.S., attempt. assass. Vernon Jordan, Jr., president of the National Urban League, was shot and wounded in a hotel parking lot in Fort Wayne, Ind., on May 29, 1980. Jordan had recently been the guest speaker at a League banquet. Initial suspects included local Ku Klux Klan members, as well as a 36-year-old divorcee, Martha Coleman, who was accompanying Jordan. Yet, no charges were filed.

The FBI began mounting evidence against Joseph Paul Franklin, an avowed racist, who had recently been convicted of the slaying of two black men in Salt Lake City. Through handwriting analyses and interviews, they determined that Franklin had been in Fort Wayne for a week before the shooting and for at least a day afterward. He had also boasted to a cellmate in Salt Lake City that he had shot a political figure in Fort Wayne.

On June 2, 1982, Franklin was indicted on the charge of shooting Jordan, and returned to Federal District Court in South Bend, Ind. On Aug. 18, 1982, a jury acquitted Franklin, and the government stopped any further investigations into the shootings. Franklin was returned to the federal prison in Marion, Ill., to continue serving his earlier sentences. REF.: *CBA*.

Jordano, Frank, 1900- , Case of, U.S., mur. On May 24, 1918, Mr. and Mrs. Maggio were found with their throats slit in the apartment behind their New Orleans store. A safe had been opened, but money was found on the floor, leading police to suspect that the apparent robbery was a decoy. The case resembled a series of 1911 ax murders, in which the victims were all Italian grocers and their wives. The Mafia and the Black Hand had been suspected. On June 28, 1918, a second couple was attacked. Louis Besumer survived, but his companion, Harriet Lowe, died five weeks later. Curiously, Besumer was the first non-Italian to be attacked. Before she died, Mrs. Lowe testified that Besumer had struck her, and that he was a German agent. He was arrested on Aug. 5, and that night the axman struck again. A pregnant woman was attacked in her bed, but survived. On Aug. 10, two children awakened to find a man attacking their uncle. Their screams scared him away, but the man died two days later.

On Mar. 10, 1919, 2-year-old Mary Cortimiglia became the next victim. The girl's parents accused Italian grocer Iolando Jordano and his son Frank, who lived across the street. On Apr. 30, Louis Besumer stood trial for the attack on Mrs. Lowe. He was acquitted because the Secret Service had no evidence of treasonous activities. As the city guarded itself for future attacks, the New Orleans *Times-Picayune* received an ominous letter, purportedly from the attacker. He was not a human, the letter said, but a spirit, impossible to catch because he was invisible. Further, he would strike next the following Tuesday at exactly 12:15. In macabre fashion, a series of "Axeman" parties celebrated the event. But nothing happened.

Frank and Iorlando Jordano went on trial for the murder of Mary Cortimiglia on May 21, 1919, in the courtroom of Judge John H. Fleury. After five days of testimony and forty minutes of deliberation, the jury found the Jordanos Guilty. Frank Jordano was sentenced to be hanged, while his father Iolando

received life imprisonment. However, the axman went to work again on Aug. 10, when another Italian grocer was attacked. On Sept. 2, a New Orleans druggist used a revolver to shoot through a door someone was trying to break open. No one was there after he fired. On Sept. 3, a 19-year-old woman was knocked unconscious and a bloody ax was found near her window. The woman survived. These murders seemed to clear the Jordanos.

On Dec. 7, 1920, Rosie Cortimiglia, the little girl's mother, confessed to a newspaper reporter that she had lied on the witness stand. She was taken to Frank Jordano's jail cell, where she threw herself to the floor, kissed his feet, and avowed his innocence. The Jordanos were soon released.

On Dec. 2, 1920, a New Orleans man, Joseph Mumfre, was murdered in Los Angeles by the widow of the axman's latest victim. Mrs. Mike Pepitone recognized the man as her husband's murderer. Mumfre had been released from prison shortly before the initial attacks in 1911. Coincidentally, he had gone back to prison and was released shortly before the first attack in 1918. And while he was in jail for burglary between August 1918 and March 1919, there had been no attacks. Mrs. Pepitone was tried in Los Angeles and pleaded guilty, but to a justifiable homicide. She was sentenced to ten years, and was paroled after three.

REF.: *CBA; Tallant, Ready to Hang.*

Jorgensdatter, Siri, b.1717, Case of, Swed., witchcraft. In 1730, 13-year-old Siri Jorgensdatter told friends of the myth of the Blakulla. A previous recitation of the story in 1669 brought hundreds to trial for witchcraft. Many had been condemned and executed. Siri's version of the tale was almost impossibly accurate. Further, she said she heard the story from her grandmother, who had claimed to be a witch. A Swedish magistrate sent for the girl, suspecting her of witchcraft. However, she was never tried, as the bishop and the governor dismissed all charges. REF.: *CBA*.

Jorgensen, Jorgen, 1779-c.1845, Ice., rob. Jorgen Jorgensen was an adventurer, who, with a small armed force in June 1809, seized Iceland and announced himself ruler. He pillaged the small communities, but his band of thieves were overpowered by a naval force under the command of British officers who landed in Iceland in August 1809. Jorgensen was taken to England in chains. He was found guilty of robbery and sent to the penal colony in Botany Bay, Aus., where he reportedly died in 1845. REF.: *CBA*.

Josaphat Kuncewicz (Jan Kuncewicz), 1580-1623, Pol., bishop, assass. Priest who worked to unify the Roman and Lutheran Orthodox churches. He became the archbishop of Polosk in 1617 and was murdered by unification foes six years later. REF.: *CBA*.

Joubert, John J., 1963- , U.S., mur. A native of Portland, Maine, John J. Joubert joined the Air Force after flunking out of Norwich University in Vermont. Stationed at Offutt Air Force Base near Omaha, Neb., the 21-year-old Joubert was fascinated by detective magazines and their glossy reenactments of sex and violence. In 1983, the fantasy world of Joubert exploded.

Danny Jo Eberle, thirteen, was abducted Sept. 18, 1983, on his way to school. His bound body was found three days later south of Bellevue, Neb. He had been stabbed repeatedly. Three months later, on Dec. 5, the brutalized body of Christopher Walden, twelve, was found northwest of Papillion, Neb. The autopsy reported that Joubert had

Murderer John Joubert.

first tried to strangle the boy and then stabbed him five times. While there was no evidence of sexual assault, both boys were forced to strip down to their underwear before being killed. On Jan. 11, 1984, Joubert was arrested for the murders of Eberle and Walden.

During his trial, psychiatric evidence showed that Joubert had been fantasizing about bizarre acts with women and young boys since he was six years old. Police found twenty-four detective magazines in his room, and Joubert admitted to having sexual fantasies about the captives depicted in them. On July 3, 1984, Joubert confessed to the murders of Danny Jo Eberle and Christopher Walden.

Three months later, a three-judge panel sentenced him to death. The parents of both victims had implored the court to give Joubert the death sentence, while Beverly A. Joubert had asked that her son be spared so that he might help other prisoners. John J. Joubert awaits execution at the Nebraska State Penitentiary in Lincoln. REF.: *CBA*.

Joubert, Petrus Jacobus (AKA: **Piet**), 1831-1900, S. Afri., lawyer. Elected to Volksraad in 1860. He was South Africa's attorney general in 1870 and acting president in 1875. REF.: *CBA*.

Jourdemayne, Margerie (AKA: **The Witch of Rye**), prom. 1441, Brit., witchcraft. In 1441, Margerie Jourdemayne, Roger Bolingbroke, Thomas Southwell, and Eleanor Cobham were accused of trying to kill the king with sorcery. On July 23, 1441, they gathered in a churchyard at Paul's Cross, with effigies of demons and of the king. The notorious Jourdemayne had been known as the Witch of Rye since 1430, when she was imprisoned at Windsor Castle for sorcery. Released in 1432, she disappeared for the next eight years. Jourdemayne was found Guilty as a traitor and a relapsed heretic and was burned at the stake. REF.: *CBA*.

Jovanovic, Slobodan, 1869-1958, Yug., exile. Professor in Belgrade from 1897-1939. Regarded as an expert on constitutional law, he served as prime minister of the exiled Yugoslav government in London from 1942-43, and as presiding officer of the Yugoslav National Committee in exile, starting in 1946. REF.: *CBA*.

Jovellanos, Gaspar Melchor de (**Jove-Llanos**), 1744-1811, Spain, jur.-writer. Served on king's court in Madrid as chief justice in 1778, and as minister of justice in 1797. He was exiled to Gijón because of a rivalry with prime minister Godoy. He also wrote works on government and reform, as well as plays and verse. REF.: *CBA*.

Jovinian, prom. 1380s, Italy, her. Denounced for his religious beliefs and banished by the councils of Milan and Rome in 1390. REF.: *CBA*.

Jowitt, Sir William Allen, b.1885, Brit., lawyer. Member of Parliament, attorney general from 1929-32, and solicitor general from 1940-42. Director of British reconstruction plans after WWII. REF.: *CBA*.

Joyce, John (AKA: **John Davis**), 1783-1808, and **Matthias, Peter**, 1781-1808, U.S., mur. Two former slaves, John Joyce, twenty-four, and Peter Matthias, twenty-six, murdered a Philadelphia shopkeeper, Sara Cross, on Dec. 18, 1807. As the two men were strangling the shopkeeper with a piece of rope, 14-year-old Anne Messinger entered the store to buy a piece of candy. Despite the fact that she had witnessed the crime, Davis and Matthias did not harm her. They did, however, make her hold a candle for light while they burglarized the shop of money and valuables. As the two men fled, Messinger began screaming. The culprits were caught the following day and identified by Messinger. In February 1808, the two men were tried and convicted of murder. The following month they were hanged.

REF.: *CBA; Confession of John Joyce, alias Davis, Who Was Executed on Monday, the 14th of March, 1808 for the Murder of Mrs. Sarah Cross.*

Joyce, William, d.1696, Brit., burg. William Joyce left home at the age of twenty and on his first day in London was relieved of the twenty-five guineas his father had given him. After being duped a few more times, William himself turned hustler and highwayman. He was barely successful as a robber, and moved to Bristol where he married a woman with a large dowry.

Joyce posed as a linen-draper and said he was due a large inheritance from his father. Thus established in the community, he was able to rent a large house next door to a goldsmith. On his first night in the house, Joyce and several accomplices broke through the wall to the goldsmith's shop and emptied the place. Joyce and two others were arrested that same night and hanged in July 1696. They said they would have killed the goldsmith's wife and children had they known they would be captured so soon.

REF.: *CBA*; Smith, *Highwaymen*.

Joyce, William (AKA: **Lord Haw-Haw, Fritz Hansen**), 1906-46, Brit., treas. William Joyce was born in Brooklyn, N.Y., on Apr. 24, 1906, the son of a wealthy man, Michael Joyce, and was raised in England. He was an excellent student at London University and entered politics at an early age. He was decidedly right wing and anything fascist in nature appealed to him. In 1932, with the rise of Hitler in Germany, Joyce joined the British Union of Fascists which was led by Sir Oswald Mosley. He graduated with honors from London University but instead of entering British politics as his friends urged him to do, Joyce threw himself completely into the activities of Mosley's fascist group. He became Mosley's propaganda chief and later a deputy leader of the party.

After Mosley and Joyce argued, Joyce formed his own fascist party, the British Nationalist Socialist League. He embraced the brutal philosophy of Adolf Hitler and became an ardent supporter of the Nazis. Dressed casually and handling himself with an easy air, Joyce attracted unsophisticated followers who were mesmerized by his dynamic speaking abilities. He had a mellifluous distinctive voice that captivated listeners and many remarked that he should have chosen a career in radio. When war with Germany appeared imminent, Joyce suddenly disbanded his organization, collected his savings, and sold his property. He had been warned that Scotland Yard might arrest him at any moment as a supporter of Nazi Germany under

Traitor William Joyce broadcasting for the Nazis, 1942.

the Emergency Powers Act. Mosley had been arrested under this act and had been briefly imprisoned. In August 1939 Joyce renewed his British passport and then left with his wife Margaret for Germany.

Once in Berlin, Joyce sought out a friend, Christian Bauer, who worked in the German Propaganda Ministry, and asked if Bauer could obtain a job for him. Bauer tried but failed. Joyce, being British, was suspect and, just before war was declared, Bauer warned Joyce that if he did not return to England, he and his wife would probably be sent to a concentration camp as enemy aliens. Joyce tried to book passage back to England on the next ship but he was stymied by his own actions. He had converted all his British money into German marks when arriving in Germany. Now, according to German regulations, he could not spend marks to arrange foreign travel and he could not convert his marks back to British currency.

Joyce, who spoke and wrote German fluently, obtained a job as a translator, then as broadcaster. His distinctive voice was beamed throughout western Europe by Nazi radio stations controlled by Propaganda Minister Paul Joseph Goebbels. He found a large listening audience in England, speaking in what sounded like a parody of the upper-class. Joyce spouted Nazi propaganda and worked hard to demoralize the British public in its life-and-death struggle with the Nazis, particularly after France collapsed and England stood alone against Germany, being bombed day and night by Hermann Goering's Luftwaffe. Joyce was encouraged by Goebbels to make it appear that the Nazis had a widespread espionage organization in England and Joyce complied enthusiastically. He talked about trivial, almost incidental things, streets in small British hamlets that needed repair, suggesting troop movements in large trucks had broken down the pavement.

Dubbed Lord Haw-Haw, Joyce became an institution of Goebbels' propaganda machine and the Nazi leader made sure that Joyce and his wife lived in comfort. He received about $75 a week and a rent-free luxury apartment. Hitler himself bestowed upon Joyce the German War Merit Cross, first class. When the war came to a close, Goebbels personally arranged for Joyce and his wife to be sent to Denmark where he hoped to get passage to the U.S. A British officer, however, saw the Joyce couple walking across a field and Joyce made the mistake of saying "good morning" to the officer in a crisp and familiar accent. The officer walked up to the man and said: "You wouldn't be William Joyce by any chance?" Joyce, whose own voice had betrayed him, produced forged passports that claimed he was a Fritz Hansen but he was arrested as a wanted man by the British and shipped back to London to be tried for treason.

Joyce was charged with committing treason under the Treason Act of 1351. He claimed that he could not be so tried since his father was an American citizen and he was born in New York and was also a citizen of the U.S. Moreover, he said that he had taken German citizenship and renounced any citizenship in England but he had no way of proving this. British authorities countered that since he had obtained a British passport, he was therefore protected by the British government, and, as such, owed his first allegiance to that government. When he made anti-British broadcasts, he was actually committing treason against the government to which he outwardly claimed citizenship, even though he had been born elsewhere. It was a novel and contentious charge with which many took issue. But Joyce was nevertheless charged and stood trial before Justice Sir Frederick Tucker at the Old Bailey on Sept. 17, 1945.

Attorney General Sir Hartley Shawcross prosecuted and Joyce was defended by Gerald Slade, Derek Curtis-Bennett, and James Burge. The defense argued hotly that jurisdiction was lacking but the prosecution made great headway at proving that Joyce had, indeed, openly stated that he was a British citizen when obtaining his British passport before going to Germany. Of course, as the leading propagandist whose voice was beamed from Germany daily during the war, he was also a repugnant personality, particularly to the upper-class British whom his voice and manner of speaking mocked and mimicked. He was a living symbol of the evil Nazi regime and he had been placed on trial for that fact, as well as the technical charges brought against him that made up the overall charge of treason.

Joyce was convicted and sentenced to death but he assumed all along that he would be reprieved, that his sentence was symbolic. It was not. He was executed at Wandsworth Prison on Jan. 3, 1946. The 39-year-old Joyce showed great dignity and courage in the last moments of his life, playing chess until midnight with a guard. He rose at 6 a.m. and, without shaving or eating breakfast, went to the scaffold without a word, stony conduct that impressed the hangman, Albert Pierrepoint. See: **Goebbels, Paul Joseph.**

REF.: Burt, *Commander Burt of Scotland Yard; CBA;* Forester, *Fatal Fascination;* Scott, *The Concise Encyclopedia of Crime and Criminals.*

Juanita, 1828-1851, U.S., mur. Juanita, a 23-year-old Mexican woman who lived in a mining camp near Downieville, Calif., was a reformed prostitute, having found true love with a Mexican miner. On July 4, 1851, a former customer, Jack Cannon, unaware of her recent reformation, sought to procure her services for a bag of gold dust. She refused him but he smashed his way into her cabin, where after a brief fight, she stabbed him to death. Juanita, her clothing covered in Cannon's blood, was dragged to a local saloon to face the justice of a vigilante trial.

The primary "trial" argument seemed to be whose rope would be used in the hanging. A traveling attorney hastily appointed to defend Juanita was tossed out of the saloon when he attempted to plead self-defense. The camp doctor, C.D. Aiken testified that Juanita was pregnant, but was quickly overruled by three medical "experts" and given twenty-four hours to leave town. Juanita was found Guilty and given one hour to prepare for her hanging. No priest was allowed to visit, as the horde made her last hour even more intolerable by cursing her and pelting her cabin with rocks.

Juanita was brought to a bridge spanning the Yuba stream, a noose was placed around her neck, and she was made to walk a six-foot plank extending over the water. As she cursed the crowd in Spanish, the plank was kicked away, and Juanita became the first woman to be hanged in California, following a "trial" verdict. REF.: *CBA.*

Jud, Charles, b.1834, Fr., mur. Victor Poinsot, president of the Fourth Chamber of the Imperial Court of Paris, was found dead in a train compartment on Dec. 6, 1860. After searching railway records of ticket purchases, a man named Matricon was suspected. The motive was apparently robbery, resembling another railway attack three months earlier. Charles Jud had been arrested for the earlier attack on Nov. 28, but had escaped by overpowering two prison guards. When police searched Matricon's hotel room in Troyes, they found handcuffs taken during Jud's escape. The search was futile and on Oct. 15, 1861, Jud was tried in absentia, found Guilty, and sentenced to death. Now, they only had to find him.

On Nov. 24, 1861, a man thought to be Jud was arrested in Montelimar and sent to Paris, but he was soon released. A rumor surfaced that Poinsot had been murdered for trying to penetrate Prussian state secrets. Jud was alleged to have fled to Switzerland, but extradition attempts proved futile. Although Jud officially received the death sentence, he was never found.

REF.: *CBA;* Williams, *Manners and Murders in the World of Louis-Napoleon.*

Judd, John Waltus, b.1839, U.S., jur. Appointed to the court of Utah Territory by President Grover Cleveland in 1888. He served as U.S. district attorney from 1893-98, and was a law professor at Vanderbilt University. REF.: *CBA.*

One of the trunks containing one of Winnie Ruth Judd's victims.

Judd, Winnie Ruth (Winnie Ruth McKinnell), 1906- , U.S., mur. Born and raised in a well-to-do Illinois family, Winnie Ruth Judd moved to California to study nursing and there met and married an elderly, wealthy physician, Dr. William J. Judd. She contracted tuberculosis and was sent to the desert community of Phoenix where it was hoped the dry air would cure her condition.

In 1931, Judd moved in with two of her best friends, Agnes Ann LeRoi, thirty, and Helwig Samuelson, twenty-three. The three women shared a trim bungalow and all went well for some months. But then Judd, according to later statements, began to harbor deep resentment toward LeRoi and Samuelson whom, she claimed, were stealing her male friends.

Judd was then twenty-five, had a curvaceous figure, copper hair, and large blue eyes. She confronted her two friends on the night of Oct. 16, 1931, and asked them why they were interfering with her love life. Both women laughed at her, she later claimed. With that, Judd pulled a small revolver and shot both women dead. She crammed their bodies into a trunk and booked a reservation on the Golden State Limited, intending to return to California. For some strange reason, she intended to take the bodies of her friends with her. A train porter arrived at the bungalow and told Judd that the trunk was too heavy to be shipped as personal luggage. Winnie told him that it contained important medical books belonging to her husband. The porter suggested that she rearrange the books into two

Winnie Ruth Judd with bandaged hand during her murder trial.

trunks, and she agreed. She had the porter take the large trunk to an apartment she had rented and there she removed Samuelson's body, and sawed it into pieces so that it would fit into a smaller trunk and a suitcase. She then shipped these three pieces of baggage to Los Angeles and climbed aboard the Golden State Limited.

Once she arrived in Los Angeles, Judd took a taxi to the University of Southern California, going to the political science building to see her 26-year-old brother, Burton J. McKinnell. When he arrived, Winnie implored McKinnell to accompany her to Union Station to retrieve her trunks. "You must help me get them right away!" she told him. "We must take them to the beach and throw them into the ocean!" She was frantic and her hand was bandaged. (Judd had fired a bullet into her own hand at the time of the LeRoi and Samuelson killings so that she could later claim she had been shot by LeRoi and had killed the two women in self-defense.) McKinnell, so as not to agitate his sister further, agreed to help her. They went to Union Station and, at the baggage counter, claimed the two trunks and large suitcase. Baggage clerk Andrew Anderson, however, suspected that Judd and her brother, who had no idea that his sister was a murderer, were meat smugglers. Hunters had recently shot deer illegally in Arizona and had been secretly shipping venison to Los Angeles in trunks.

One of the trunks smelled like a dead animal, Anderson believed, and the other trunk was seeping a dark, gluey substance. He told Judd and her brother that he had to inspect the baggage she was claiming before he could turn it over to her. Judd quickly answered that only her husband had the keys to the baggage and she would have to get them first. She turned on her heel and walked quickly away, her puzzled brother following. Anderson trailed the pair to the parking lot and there spotted the couple getting into a car. He wrote down the license plate and then called the police. Two detectives arrived at the station and broke open one of the trunks. They stepped back in shock. Some spectators standing nearby became ill at the sight of Samuelson's dismembered corpse. A woman fainted.

Police traced the license number Anderson had written down

to McKinnell, who was then meeting with Dr. Judd. He told detectives that his sister had told him as they drove away from Union Station that there were "two bodies in those trunks and the less you know about it, the better off you are." She had borrowed a few dollars from him and then gotten out of his car at Sixth and Broadway in downtown Los Angeles, disappearing into a crowd. A police dragnet for Winnie Ruth Judd ensued but she was nowhere to be found. Judd was, at the time, hiding in an unused building on the grounds of the La Vina Sanitarium in Altadena where she had once been a TB patient. She remained in the empty building for three days, sneaking into the sanitarium's kitchen at night to steal food. Meanwhile, her hand, which bore a gunshot wound, became infected. After three days, Judd picked up a newspaper and read an ad which her husband had placed, in which he begged her to surrender herself.

Winnie contacted her husband, who took her to a clinic where her hand was treated. Police then arrived to arrest her. She was extradited by the state of Arizona and tried for the murders of LeRoi and Samuelson. Winnie at first claimed that she had killed her two friends in self-defense. She held up her hand and said that Samuelson had shot her in the hand and that she had struggled with her, grabbing the gun and shooting first Samuelson, then LeRoi when the other woman also attacked her. The jury, believing that Judd had shot herself in the hand to support her claim of self-defense, convicted her and sentenced her to death. While awaiting execution, prison doctors became convinced that Judd was insane and a mental hearing was held. Winnie's mother and other relatives stepped forward to state that the McKinnell family had, for generations, been afflicted by insanity.

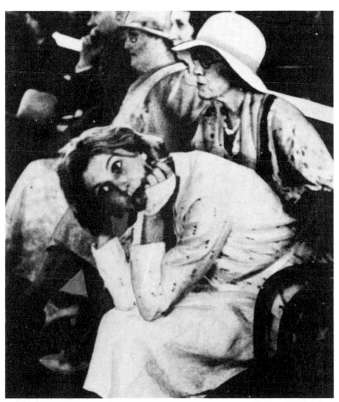

Winnie Ruth Judd at her sanity hearing.

Winnie made a great show of being deranged. She pulled at her hair, constantly ripped away at her clothes, mumbled to herself and, at one point, leaped up and pointed to the jury and shouted: "They're all gangsters!" She later called her husband to her side and said, loud enough for the courtroom to hear: "Let me throw myself out that window!" Guards finally had to be called in to remove Winnie, who had become hysterical. It was agreed that she was hopelessly insane. Her death sentence was commuted to a life sentence in the Arizona State Mental Asylum.

She escaped many times. Once she made a "sleeping dummy" of herself and fled into the wilderness, walking many miles before she was picked up by a motorist who returned her to the institution. "When she looked at you with those great big eyes brimming with tears you would believe anything she told you."

In 1952, Judd escaped again but was recaptured. She was brought before a committee looking into conditions in mental hospitals. Before she could testify, guards found a passkey hidden in her hair and a razor secreted under her tongue. She escaped again in 1962 and managed to reach Concord, Calif. There she became a live-in housekeeper for John and Ethel Blemer, earning additional money as a baby-sitter for neighbors. She was recognized on a street in 1969 and arrested. She managed to fight extradition back to Arizona for some time, defended by Melvin Belli, but the governor of California, Ronald Reagan, returned Judd to Arizona.

On Dec. 22, 1971, the Arizona Parole Board commuted Judd's life sentence to time served and she was released on the provision that she live out her life in California. She returned to the Blemer home to resume housekeeping duties. Ethel Blemer died in 1983 and Winnie sued for a goodly portion of the Blemer estate, claiming that the Blemers, since her 1971 parole, had kept her a virtual "indentured servant," and that she had been "thrown out" of the Blemer home after Ethel's death by other Blemer relatives. She was eventually awarded a $225,000 settlement, plus $1,250 a month for life. See: **Belli, Melvin**.

REF.: *CBA*; Dobkins and Hendricks, *Winnie Ruth Judd: The Trunk Murders*; Haines, *Bothersome Bodies*; Nash, *Bloodletters and Badmen*; ____, *Look for the Woman*; Radin, *Crimes of Passion*; Rodell, *Los Angeles Murders*; Wolf, *Fallen Angels*.

Judgment Day, 1934, a play by Elmer Rice. The Reichstag Fire (Ger., 1933) is the basis of this drama. Since Rice took his basic information from the headlines of the day, he does not fully detail how the Nazis, in an attempt to unite Germany against a common enemy, set the parliament building in Berlin on fire so as to blame the Communists for an insidious piece of arson that went unexplained until after WWII. See: **Reichstag Fire**. REF.: *CBA*.

Judson, Edward Zane Carroll, See: **Buntline, Ned**.

Judy, Steven T., 1957-81, U.S., asslt.-rape-mur. On Apr. 28, 1979, two men looking for mushrooms discovered the naked body of 21-year-old Terry Chasteen in White Lick Creek, Ind. Down-stream were the bodies of her three children, Misty Ann, five, Stephen Michael, four, and Mark Lewis, two. Chasteen had been raped and strangled, and the children drowned in the creek. A red and silver pickup truck had been seen in the area at 8 a.m. on the day of the murder. The owner of the truck, Steven T. Judy, twenty-two, a bricklayer, was arrested at the home of his foster parents, Mary and Bob Carr, in Indianapolis. In court, Judy confessed to murdering Chasteen and her three children. He pulled up beside her on Interstate 465 and indicated that there was something

Mass murderer Steven Judy, executed in 1981.

wrong with her car. When she pulled over, he opened up the hood and surreptitiously disabled the engine, then offered to drive Chasteen and her children to a filling station. In the truck, he turned to Chasteen and said, "I guess you know what's going to happen now?" and then took them to White Lick Creek, where he gagged, tied, raped, and murdered Chasteen before drowning her screaming children.

Steven Judy grew up in a violent, abusive household where his father viciously and repeatedly beat his mother, once slaughtering the family dog in his rage. At ten, Judy was arrested for the first time for knocking down and molesting a woman. At twelve, he was charged with burglary, and when he was thirteen he followed an Indianapolis woman from her car to her home, then knocked on her door and said he wanted to sell her Boy Scout raffle tickets. Once inside, he raped her at knifepoint, stabbing her forty-one times before the knife broke. Judy went to the kitchen to get another knife, and returned to find the woman holding a hatchet to defend herself. He took the hatchet from her, buried it in her skull and then cut off her thumb. Miraculously, after brain surgery, the woman survived and testified against Judy in court. Sent to a mental home from which he was released after nine months, Judy spent eight of the eleven years since his first rape – he would later confess to thriteen – in mental institutions or jails. His foster parents, the Carrs, met Judy when he was in the mental hospital, where he became friendly with Mrs. Carr's half-brother, who was also an inmate. Judy lived with the Carrs and their three children between jail and hospital stays. According to Mrs. Carr, their family "never really saw the other side of him, the dangerous side of him." Judy was free on bond, awaiting trial on charges of robbing a grocery store in Indianapolis, when he murdered Chasteen and her children. Bob Carr said, "He described the murders to me once. He said it was like a dream, like he stood back and watched it. "

In the Morgan County Superior Court in Martinsville, Ind., on Feb. 25, 1980, the unrepentant Judy told Special Judge Jeffrey Boles, "I honestly want you to give me the death penalty because one day I may get out. I think I showed that about a week ago." Judy had been caught breaking out of his cell on Feb. 16. He boasted to jurors that he had committed thirteen rapes, 200 home burglaries and fifty armed robberies. When he was convicted of murder, Judy told the judge and jury, "You'd better vote for the death penalty or it might be one of you or your family next." He was sentenced to die in the electric chair, and initially agreed to an appeal but soon changed his mind and told his lawyer to stop the process. His execution at the Michigan City, Ind., jail, on Mar. 9, 1981, was slightly delayed, explained Bob Carr, because Judy asked to have pictures taken of his newly shaved head, prepared for the electrodes. "He was proud of his bald appearance," said Carr. Judy's final words were, "I don't hold no grudges. It was my doing. I'm sorry it happened."

REF.: *CBA*; Fox, *Mass Murder*; Wilson, *Encyclopedia of Modern Murder*.

Juenemann, Charlotte, 1911-35, Ger., mur. Charlotte Juenemann kept her three children locked in a basement room until they died in 1935. The woman, whose husband was in an insane asylum, had been given welfare money but refused to apply it to the children. Instead, she became enamored with a musician and spent the money on nightlife. At the time of her arrest, she was pregnant.

On Mar. 30, 1935, Juenemann was sentenced to death by beheading. Nazi Germany's new justice also determined that her unborn baby would be a debit to the race. The sentence was carried out on Aug. 27, 1935, at Plotzenee prison. REF.: *CBA*.

Jukes Family, prom. 1700s-1870s, U.S., org. crime. The Jukes Family was a loosely traced clan that lived in New York state for seven generations beginning in the mid-1700s. In an 1870s study, *The Jukes, A Study in Crime, Pauperism, Disease and Heredity*, Richard L. Dugdale declared that the clan consisted of 540 blood relatives and another 169 related by marriage or cohabitation. Of these, 140 were known criminals, and another 300 were wards of the state in various capacities. The clan was known to be involved in murder, rape, prostitution, theft and other sundry crimes. The origins were traced to a Dutch saloon keeper who fathered two sons, who in turn married two illegitimate sisters. Twentieth-century historians are somewhat skeptical about Dugdale's findings, convinced that he thought any unidentified criminal to be a member of the Jukes clan, and that every Jukes was supposedly a criminal. However, Dugdale's research was bolstered in 1916 when Arthur H. Estabrook stated that the Jukes family had continued to produce more criminals following the study in the 1870s. REF.: *CBA*.

Julia, 39 B.C.-14 A.D., Roman., morals. Daughter of Emperor Augustus Caesar. Married several times, she was banished by her father for depravity. REF.: *CBA*.

Julia, d.28 A.D. Roman., morals. Granddaughter of Augustus Caesar who married Lucius Aemilius Paulus, by whom she had Aemilia, the future first wife of Emperor Claudius. Like her mother, Julia, she was banished by her grandfather (in 9 A.D.) for moral corruption. REF.: *CBA*.

Julia Mamaea, d.235, Roman., polit. corr.-assass. Daughter of Julia Maesa, aunt of Roman emperor Elagabalus and mother of Alexander Severus, she sought to control government. She dominated the 232 exploration of Persia, was held responsible for its failure, and was killed by soldiers along with Alexander. REF.: *CBA*.

Julian, Anthony, 1902- , U.S., jur. Faculty member at Boston College from 1934-37, and served in Massachusetts legislature from 1937-38. He earned the Bronze Star medal in 1945 for meritorious service in WWII. He was appointed to the district court of Massachusetts by President Dwight D. Eisenhower in 1959. REF.: *CBA*.

Julian of Eclanum, 380-c.455, Italy, her. Unseated and banished in 421 for opposing Pope St. Zosimus' *Epistola tractoria* expelling Pelagius from the church. Julian, named Bishop of Eclanum about 417, advocated Pelagius' teachings that man has a free will and that the doctrine of original sin is false. REF.: *CBA*.

Julian of Goathland, prom. 9th Cent., Brit., mur. The legend of the Gytrash of Goathland, or Padfoot of Goathland, and its demise by Spinning Gytha was a result of a cruel murder committed by Julian of Goathland.

Julian was a fierce Danish conqueror of the Saxons in England, a man that both enemies and followers feared. He settled in the Vale of the Mirk Esk, which extends from present-day Pickering to Grosmont, where he built a castle. He believed in the Danish god Odin and his son Thor, and to insure the strength of his fortress he sought to appease them by sacrificing a young maiden. The sacrifice was accomplished by entombing a beautiful young girl within the walls of the building. Julian chose the daughter of the local miller, 14-year-old Gytha of the Mill. Earlier, Gytha had rebuked Julian's advances. The miller, Gurth, was himself ordered to help build the wall around his daughter, who was buried along with a jug of water, a loaf of bread, and her spinning wheel so that she might not "be idle," according to Julian. Alfred the Great. The Saxon king, could do nothing to prevent this barbarous act. Gytha is believed to have died four days after the final bricks were set in place, as that was the last time her screams were heard. Over the next three years, legend has it that Julian was haunted by a dream each April, the month in which Gytha died, where he heard screams and saw a ghostlike figure spinning thread above his body, causing paralysis wherever she spun.

People said that after Julian died, his spirit roamed the region in the form of a large dog or goat, called the Gytrash, or the Padfoot, and would kill whomever crossed his path alone, especially young women. A legend that ran concurrently was that of Spinning Gytha, whose spirit would scream every April. To rid themselves of these apparitions, the villagers held a phony funeral, and as the story goes, the Gytrash visited the grave that night looking for plunder, and Spinning Gytha sealed it inside, ending its reign of terror and her own torment. REF.: *CBA*.

Julian Street, prom. 1870s, U.S., vice dist. Prostitution and gambling were rampant in the gold mining town of Cripple Creek, Colo., in the 1870s. Furthermore, the city elders were proud of their reputation, entreating traveling passengers with signs promising the favors of the brothels and bistros on Myers Avenue. Julian Street, a journalist, wrote a scathing article for *Colliers*

magazine, exposing the behavior in Cripple Creek to the entire nation. The unrepentant city officials changed the name of Myers Avenue to Julian Street, making the thought of the vice district synonymous with the man who most ardently opposed it. REF.: *CBA*.

July, Jim, See: **Starr, Belle.**

Jumpertz, Henry, 1833-c.1859, U.S., mur. Born in Bonn, Ger., Henry Jumpertz was the eldest son of Ferdinand and Albertina Jumpertz, a devout Roman Catholic couple. When he was nine he dissected a live dog "to see how long it would live under the knife." He enrolled at the Medical College of Bonn, and he worked in the dissecting room as a physician's assistant. His professors commented favorably on his work. In 1854, Jumpertz left school to accompany his brother Franz to the U.S. There were unconfirmed rumors about a scandal the young medical student was involved in, but Jumpertz was resolved to put his past behind him as he proceeded to Chicago.

At the time that Jumpertz arrived in the Midwest, a German couple, Frederick and Sophie Werner, lived on Dearborn Street on the North Side. The husband worked as a barber at the Young America Hotel, owned by two businessmen named Hulme and White. Frederick made life miserable for his wife. In 1855, he traveled to Europe and returned with a live-in housekeeper, Adolphina Drautman, who became his mistress. Tiring of the arrangement, Sophie Elten Werner deserted her husband to move in with Henry Jumpertz. Meanwhile, Frederick Werner was arrested for stealing silver plate from his employers. Adolphina Drautman then left him at his wife's mercy. Sophie urged the courts to be lenient. The original larceny suit was dropped and upon securing his freedom Werner fled to Rochester, N.Y., leaving $300 to his wife.

Sophie, who had never secured a divorce, continued to live with Jumpertz, who worked as a journeyman for the firm of Frazza and Rabolla. In the spring of 1857, she became pregnant with his child. Not willing to face the scandal of an illegitimate child, Jumpertz took Werner to Milwaukee where they settled into a small house on Market Street. In May, he went to work for A.W. Goetz, a former Chicago acquaintance. When asked about his intentions regarding Sophie Werner, a "hard-working, saving woman," Jumpertz said he could not marry her. She was simply too old, according to the testimony later provided by Goetz.

The baby was stillborn and in December, Jumpertz broke off his relationship with Werner and returned to Chicago to resume his former position with Frazza and Rabolla. A series of letters passed between them over the next few months. Werner reaffirmed her love for Jumpertz, who remained adamant in his decision not to marry her. Finally on Mar. 3, Sophie Werner took the train to Chicago. She stepped off the train heavily veiled as per Jumpertz' instructions. A drayman took her belongings to his small apartment near the Clark Street bridge. After that Sophie Werner was never seen alive again.

A month later, New York City newspapers reported the discovery of a barrel outside a railroad depot at Canal and Washington streets with the disemboweled remains of a woman preserved in a solution of chloride of lime. It was learned that an identical barrel had been shipped from the Michigan Central Freight Depot in Chicago on Mar. 16 by a dark-haired man with whiskers. City marshal Jacob Rehm and private detective Cyrus Parker Bradley, sifting through available evidence, determined that Jumpertz best matched the description, and he was arrested on May 7.

Jumpertz admitted he had sent the barrel to New York but denied killing Sophie. She already was dead, he explained. She had hanged herself with a cotton rope, leaving behind a suicide note saying that she "could not live" and that she wished to be reunited with Frederick Werner. Jumpertz decided not to report the suicide but put his dissection skills to use. He had cut up the corpse, first burying the liver and intestines before sending the parcel to New York.

Jumpertz was indicted for murder. The state contended that

the defendant poisoned Werner with laudanum and then attempted to hide his crime. The trial began on Jan. 26, 1859, in Cook County Circuit Court. On Feb. 10, the jury returned a verdict of Guilty after considerable debate. Jumpertz was sentenced to hang. The verdict was sustained under appeal and the execution date was set for May 6, 1859. Resigned to his fate, Jumpertz was housed in the city's Bridewell jail. His ultimate fate remains a mystery, however, because newspapers of the time do not mention his execution.

REF.: *"The Barrel Mystery"; or the Career, Tragedy and Trial of Henry Jumpertz Tried and Convicted . . . for the Murder of Sophie Elten Werner, his Mistress, at Chicago, March 6, 1858; CBA.*

June, Clarence, and **Davis, Mildred**, prom. 1939, U.S., illegal cohabitation. Farmer Clarence June had a wife, ten children, a cow, and a one-room house. Factory worker George Davis had a wife and four children. One day, June traded his wife, seven of his ten children, and his cow in return for Davis' wife and four children.

The merriment lasted a scant three months before the two couples were arrested in Lapeer County, Mich., and charged with illegal cohabitation. Judge Louis Crampton sentenced Clarence June and Mildred Davis to six months in jail. George Davis and Edith June were given only a year's probation. REF.: *CBA.*

June 2nd Movement, prom. 1967, Ger., kid.-terr.-mur. The June 2nd Movement was created in memory of Benno Ohnesorg, a student who was killed by police while protesting against the Shah of Iran's visit to Germany in 1967. The group was not taken seriously until the President of the West German Supreme Court, Gunter von Drenkmann, was shot in the face at his front door by four young men carrying flowers. The Movement took credit, stating that it was revenge for the deaths of two students. Holger Meins died in prison after a fifty-six-day hunger strike. The radical movement sought revolutionary change to heal "the late capitalist performance society of the Federal Republic."

The Movement's most dramatic act occurred in February 1975, when it kidnapped West Berlin lawyer Peter Lorenz. The leader of the opposition in the City Parliament Lorenz was running for reelection on the Christian Democrat ticket. The Movement's demands included: annulment of the sentences of students who rioted after Holger Meins' death, no police searches for the kidnappers, and the freeing of six jailed Red Army Faction (RAF) prisoners. The kidnapping was turned into a television spectacular, and German President Helmut Schmidt acquiesced to the demands. On Mar. 3, five prisoners were released. The elections had already taken place, making Lorenz the first politician to win an election while in captivity. The June 2nd Movement, buoyed by the success of the kidnapping, sought next to kidnap the pope. However, they thought better of it when it was learned that there would be no asylum for the kidnappers in the Arab world.

REF.: *CBA;* Dobson and Payne, *The Terrorists—Their Weapons, Leaders and Tactics;* Moorehead, *Hostage to Fortune.*

Jung, Lem, and **Gop, Chew Tin**, prom. 1897, Case of, U.S., mur. Chinese living in San Francisco at the turn of the century were organized into secret societies called tongs, which resembled criminal gangs. For years the most powerful tong was the Sum Yop Tong, which was led by Fung Jing Toy or Little Pete. The Sum Yop Tong became so powerful that a dozen lesser Tongs banded together and offered a $3,000 reward for killing Little Pete, who slept in a barred and locked room, wore a hat with armor plating, and a coat of chain mail. All professional efforts failed.

Lem Jung and Chew Tin Gop had no criminal records and no experience with firearms. However, they belonged to the Suey Sing Tong, which had been humiliated by the Sum Yops. Because they were not known for gang activity, Jung and Gop were able to approach Little Pete in a barber shop. As Little Pete leaned over a wash basin, the two men fired five shots underneath his vest, into his unprotected spine. The two men escaped, collected their reward, and returned to China.

REF.: Brophy, *The Meaning of Murder; CBA.*

Junius, Johannes, c.1573-1628, Ger., witchcraft. On June 28, 1628, Johannes Junius was examined, without torture, on the charge of witchcraft. He claimed to be wholly innocent, to have never renounced God and knew nothing of witchcraft. On June 30, thumb screws were applied, but he still did not confess, or cry out in pain. Then came leg vices, but still no confession or pain. He was stripped and found to have a bluish mark on his right side, that when pricked, did not draw blood. Yet, when confronted without torture on July 5, he confessed.

He was accused of participating in a witch gathering and was heard to have said, "I renounce God in Heaven and his host, and will henceforth recognize the Devil as my God." It was alleged that his paramour had taken him to sabbats, and that when he wished to be transported, a black dog would appear at his side. He would mount it, and the dog would raise itself in the Devil's name and fly off. He confessed on July 7 that two months earlier, on a day following an execution, he was at a witch dance at the Black Cross when Beelzebub had come to ridicule and taunt them. Junius was ordered to kill his son and two daughters. A week before his arrest he had been met by the Devil in the form of a goat, he said, and told that he would soon be imprisoned. On Aug. 6, 1628, he ratified his confession, stating that he would stake his life on it. He was found Guilty and burned at the stake. REF.: *CBA.*

Junqueiro, Abilio Manuel Guerra, 1850-1923, Port., treas. Opposed Braganzas and was prosecuted for high treason in 1907. REF.: *CBA.*

Juricic, James, 1932-   , U.S., rape. On Apr. 4, 1970, in Chicago's western suburbs, a 15-year-old girl was ordered at gunpoint into a car. She was driven into a garage, blindfolded, and raped. In another case, two girls were kidnapped at once, the kidnapper telling the second girl that she was his fifty-sixth victim. The police knew the make of the car and the first five digits of the license plate, and because he never drove his victims very far, they were able to limit their search.

In May 1970, traffic officers noticed the suspected car and arrested James Juricic of Western Springs, Ill., a research worker at Boeing. He was identified by victims and sentenced to life in prison. REF.: *CBA.*

Justinian I (Flavius Petrus Sabbatius Justinianus, AKA: the Great), 483-565, Roman., emp.-jur. Nephew of Roman Emperor Justin I, named his co-emperor in 527, the year of Justin's death. He appointed Tribonian as his chief legal minister, placed him in charge of recording Roman law for posterity, and named him as one of the ten commissioners who gathered imperial statutes for the *Codex Constitionum,* from 528-29. He oversaw the production of *Digests,* or *Pandects,* in 533, a collection of writings by Roman jurists, *Institutest,* in 533, a textbook, a revision of the *Codex,* in 534, and *Novellac,* from 534-65, recording the new laws. These works comprise the *Corpus Juris Civilis,* the basis of modern law in most of continental Europe. REF.: *CBA.*

Justinian II (AKA: Rhinotmetus, With-the-nose-cut-off), Roman., c.669-711, consp.-assass. Ruler of Eastern Roman Empire who reigned from 685-95 and from 705-11. He was defeated by the Bulgarians in 689, and by the Arabs in Armenia in 692. His persecution of the Manichaeans created religious upheaval and he was defeated in 695 by his own general, Leontius, who hacked off his nose. Four years later, he was exiled by Leontius to Cherson in the Crimea. He returned as head of the Bulgarian army and conquered Constantinople in 705. With the murder of Leontius the same year, he gained a measure of revenge, but was betrayed, captured and killed by Philippicus, who proclaimed himself emperor. REF.: *CBA.*